American Casebook Series

Hornbook Series and Basic Legal Texts

Nutshell Series

of

WEST PUBLISHING COMPANY

St. Paul, Minnesota 55102

ACCOUNTING

Fiflis and Kripke's Cases on Accounting for Business Lawyers, 687 pages, 1971.

ADMINISTRATIVE LAW

Davis' Basic Text on Administrative Law 3rd Ed., 617 pages, 1972.

Davis' Cases, Text and Problems on Administrative Law, 5th Ed., 650 pages, 1973.

Gellhorn's Administrative Law in a Nutshell, 336 pages, 1972.

ADMIRALTY

Healy and Currie's Cases on Admiralty, 872 pages, 1965.

AGENCY

Seavey and Hall's Cases on Agency, 431 pages, 1956.

Seavey's Text on Agency, 329 pages, 1964.

See Agency-Partnership.

AGENCY PARTNERSHIP

Henn's Cases on Agency, Partnership and Other Unincorporated Business Enterprises, 396 pages, 1972.

Seavey, Reuschlein & Hall's Cases on Agency and Partnership, 599 pages, 1962.

Steffen's Cases on Agency and Partnership, 3rd Ed., 733 pages, 1969.

ANTITRUST LAW

Oppenheim's Cases on Robinson-Patman Act, Pamphlet, 295 pages, 1967.

Oppenheim and Weston's Cases on Antitrust, 3rd Ed., 952 pages, 1968.

Oppenheim and Weston's Supplement, 1972.

BANKRUPTCY

MacLachlan's Text on Bankruptcy, 500 pages, 1956.

See Creditors' Rights.

Selected Commercial Statutes, 988 pages, 1973.

BILLS AND NOTES

Aigler and Steinheimer's Cases on Bills and Notes, 670 pages, 1962.

Britton's Text on Bills and Notes, 2nd Ed., 794 pages, 1961.

See Commercial Transactions.

See Negotiable Instruments.

BUSINESS ORGANIZATIONS

See Agency-Partnership.

See Corporations.

CIVIL PROCEDURE

See Pleading and Procedure.

CLINICAL TEACHING

Freeman and Weihofen's Cases on Clinical Law Training—Interviewing and Counseling, 506 pages, 1972.

COMMERCIAL PAPER

See Bills and Notes.

See Commercial Transactions.

See Negotiable Instruments.

COMMERCIAL TRANSACTIONS

Speidel, Summers and White's Teaching Materials on Commercial Transactions, 1144 pages, 1969.

Murray and White's Problem Teaching Materials on Commercial Transactions, 292 pages, 1973.

White and Summers Text on the Uniform Commercial Code, 1054 pages, 1972.

Selected Commercial Statutes, 988 pages, 1973

See Negotiable Instruments.

See Sales.

COMMON LAW PLEADING

Koffler and Reppy's Text on Common Law Pleading, 663 pages, 1969.
McBaine's Cases, Introduction to Civil Procedure, 399 pages, 1950.
Shipman's Text on Common Law Pleading, 3rd Ed., 644 pages, 1923.

COMMUNITY PROPERTY

Burby's Cases on Community Property, 4th Ed., 342 pages, 1955.
Huie's Texas Cases on Marital Property Rights, 681 pages, 1966.
Verrall and Sammis' Cases on California Community Property, 2nd Ed., 398 pages, 1971.

CONFLICT OF LAWS

Cramton and Currie's Cases—Comments—Questions on Conflicts, 915 pages, 1968.
Ehrenzweig's Text on Conflicts, 824 pages, 1962.
Ehrenzweig's Conflicts in a Nutshell, 2nd Ed., 392 pages, 1970.
Ehrenzweig and Louisell's Jurisdiction in a Nutshell, 3rd Ed., 291 pages, 1973.
Goodrich's Text on Conflict of Laws, 4th Ed., 483 pages, 1964.
Scoles and Weintraub's Cases on Conflict of Laws, 2nd Ed., 966 pages 1972.

CONSTITUTIONAL LAW

Lockhart, Kamisar and Choper's Cases — Comments — Questions on Constitutional Law, 3rd Ed., 1,487 pages, 1970.
Lockhart, Kamisar and Choper's Cases on The American Constitution, 3rd Ed., 1099 pages, 1970.
Lockhart, Kamisar and Choper's Annual Supplement.
See Constitutional Rights and Liberties.

CONSTITUTIONAL RIGHTS & LIBERTIES

Lockhart, Kamisar and Choper's Cases on Constitutional Rights and Liberties, 3rd Ed., 1118 pages, 1970.
Lockhart, Kamisar and Choper's Annual Supplement.

CONSUMER CREDIT

Kripke's Cases on Consumer Credit, 454 pages, 1970.
Schrag's Cases on Consumer Credit, 2nd Ed., Pamphlet reprint from Cooper, et al. Law and Poverty, 2nd Ed., 199 pages, 1973.

CONTRACTS

Calamari & Perillo's Text on Contracts, 621 pages, 1970.
Corbin's Cases on Contracts, 3rd Ed., 1381 pages, 1947. 1953 Supplement, 36 pages.
Corbin's Text on Contracts, Student Edition, 1224 pages, 1952.
Freedman's Cases on Contracts, 658 pages, 1973.
Fuller and Eisenberg's Cases on Contracts, 1043 pages, 1972.
Jackson's Cases on Contract Law in a Modern Society, 1404 pages, 1973.
Simpson's Cases on Contracts, 592 pages, 1956.
Simpson's Text on Contracts, 2nd Ed., 510 pages, 1965.
White and Summer's Text on the Uniform Commercial Code, 1054 pages, 1972.

COPYRIGHT

Nimmer's Cases on Copyright and Other Aspects of Law Pertaining to Literary, Musical and Artistic Works, 828 pages, 1971.
Nimmer's 1972 Supplement.

CORPORATIONS

Henn's Text on Corporations, 2nd Ed., 956 pages, 1970.
Stevens and Henn's Statutes, Cases on Corporations and Other Business Enterprises, 1448 pages, 1965.
Stevens and Henn's Practice Projects Supplement, 81 pages, 1965.

CORRECTIONS

Krantz' Cases on the Law of Corrections and Prisoners' Rights, 1130 pages, 1973.

CREDIT TRANSACTIONS

Maxwell & Riesenfeld's California Cases on Security Transactions, 371 pages, 1957.
Maxwell & Riesenfeld's Supplement, 68 pages, 1963.

CREDITORS' RIGHTS

Epstein's Teaching Materials on Debtor-Creditor Relations, 525 pages, 1973.
Epstein's Debtor-Creditor Relations in a Nutshell, 309 pages, 1973.
Riesenfeld's Cases on Creditors' Remedies and Debtors' Protection, 669 pages, 1967.
Riesenfeld's Case and Statutory Supplement, 1972.

CRIMINAL LAW

Dix and Sharlot's Cases on Criminal Law, 1360 pages, 1973.

LaFave and Scott's Text on Criminal Law, 763 pages, 1972.

Miller's Text on Criminal Law, 649 pages, 1934.

Stumberg's Texas Cases on Criminal Law, 505 pages, 1954.

Stumberg and Maloney's Texas Cases Supplement, 117 pages, 1965.

CRIMINAL PROCEDURE

Hall, Kamisar, LaFave and Israel's Cases on Modern Criminal Procedure, 3rd Ed., 1456 pages, 1969.

Hall, Kamisar, LaFave and Israel's Cases on Basic Criminal Procedure, 3rd Ed., 617 pages, 1969.

Hall, Kamisar, LaFave, and Israel's Annual Criminal Procedure Supplement.

Israels and LaFave's Constitutional Criminal Procedure in a Nutshell, 423 pages, 1971.

Federal Rules of Civil-Appellate-Criminal Procedure, Law School Edition, 296 pages, 1973.

DAMAGES

Crane's Cases on Damages, 3rd Ed., 337 pages, 1955.

McCormick's Text on Damages, 811 pages, 1935.

See Remedies.

DECEDENTS ESTATES

See Wills, Intestate Succession, Trusts, Gifts and Future Interests.

DICTIONARIES

Black's, one volume.

Bouvier's, two volumes.

DOMESTIC RELATIONS

Clark's Cases on Domestic Relations, 870 pages, 1965.

Clark's Text on Domestic Relations, 754 pages, 1968.

Paulsen's Cases on Family Law and Poverty, 2nd Ed., Pamphlet reprint from Cooper, et al. Law and Poverty, 2nd Ed., 200 pages, 1973.

See Juvenile Courts.

EQUITY

Cook's Cases on Equity, 4th Ed., 1192 pp., 1948.

McClintock's Text on Equity, 2nd Ed., 643 pages, 1948.

Van Hecke, Leavell and Nelson's Cases on Equitable Remedies and Restitution, 2nd Ed., 717 pages, 1973.

See Remedies.

EVIDENCE

Broun and Meisenholder's Problems in Evidence, 130 pages, 1973.

Cleary and Strong's Cases on Evidence, 967 pages, 1969.

McCormick, Elliott & Sutton's Cases on Evidence, 4th Ed., 1088 pages, 1971.

McCormick, Cleary, et al., Text on Evidence, 2nd Ed., 938 pages, 1972.

Rothstein's Evidence in a Nutshell, 406 pages, 1970.

FEDERAL ESTATE AND GIFT TAXATION

See Taxation.

FEDERAL INCOME TAXATION

See Taxation.

FEDERAL JURISDICTION AND PROCEDURE

Currie's Cases on Federal Courts, 823 pages, 1968.

Currie's Supplement, 1973.

Ehrenzweig and Louisell's Jurisdiction in a Nutshell, 3rd Ed., 291 pages, 1973.

Forrester, Currier and Moye's Cases on Federal Jurisdiction and Procedure, 2nd Ed., 933 pages, 1970.

Forrester, Currier and Moye's Supplement, 1973.

Wright's Text on Federal Courts, 2nd Ed., 745 pages, 1970.

Wright's Supplement, 1972.

FUTURE INTERESTS

Gulliver's Cases on Future Interests, 624 pages, 1959.

Powell's Cases on Future Interests, 3rd Ed., 1961.

Simes Text on Future Interests, 2nd Ed., 355 pages, 1966.

See Wills, Intestate Succession, Trusts, Gifts and Future Interests.

GRATUITOUS TRANSFERS

See Wills, Intestate Succession, Trusts, Gifts and Future Interests.

HOUSING AND URBAN DEVELOPMENT

Berger's Cases on Housing, 2nd Ed., Pamphlet reprint from Cooper, et al. Law and Poverty, 2nd Ed., 254 pages, 1973.

Krasnowiecki's Cases on Housing and Urban Development, 697 pages, 1969.

Krasnowiecki's Statutory Supplement 1969.

See Land Use.

INSURANCE

Keeton's Cases on Basic Insurance Law, 655 pages, 1960.

Keeton's Basic Text on Insurance Law, 712 pages, 1971.

Keeton's Case Supplement to Keeton's Basic Text, 398 pages, 1971.

Keeton's Programmed Problems in Insurance Law, 243 pages, 1972.

Keeton & Keeton's Compensation Systems, Pamphlet Reprint from Keeton & Keeton's Cases on Torts, 85 pages, 1971.

Vance's Text on Insurance, 3rd Ed., 1290 pages, 1951.

INTERNATIONAL LAW

Friedmann, Lissitzyn and Pugh's Cases on International Law, 1,205 pages, 1969.

Friedmann, Lissitzyn and Pugh's Supplement, 1972.

INTRODUCTION TO LAW

Fryer and Orentlicher's Cases on Legal Method and Legal System, 1,043 pages, 1967.

Kempin's Historical Introduction to Anglo-American Law in a Nutshell, 2nd Ed., 280 pages, 1973.

Kimball's Historical Introduction to Legal System, 610 pages, 1966.

Kinyon's Introduction to Law Study and Law Examinations in a Nutshell, 389 pages, 1971.

Smith's Cases on Development of Legal Institutions, 757 pages, 1965.

See Legal Method.

JURISPRUDENCE

Christie's Text and Readings on Jurisprudence—The Philosophy of Law, 1056 pages, 1973.

JUVENILE JUSTICE

Fox's Cases on Modern Juvenile Justice, 1012 pages, 1972.

Fox's The Law of Juvenile Courts in a Nutshell, 286 pages, 1971.

LABOR LAW

Oberer and Hanslowe's Cases on Labor Law, 1091 pages, 1972.

Oberer and Hanslowe's Statutory Supplement, 1972.

Sovern's Cases on Racial Discrimination in Employment, 2nd Ed., Pamphlet reprint from Cooper et al. Law and Poverty, 2nd Ed., 167 pages, 1973.

LAND USE

Beuscher and Wright's Cases on Land Use, 788 pages, 1969.

Hagman's Cases on Public Planning and Control of Urban and Land Development, 1208 pages, 1973.

Hagman's Text on Urban Planning and Land Development Control Law, 559 pages, 1971

LEGAL BIBLIOGRAPHY

Cohen's Legal Research in a Nutshell, 2nd Ed., 259 pages, 1971.

How To Find The Law, with Special Chapters on Legal Writing, 6th Ed., 313 pages, 1965.

How To Find The Law Student Problem Book.

Rombauer's Legal Problem Solving, 2nd Ed., 212 pages, 1973.

Rombauer's Problem Supplement.

LEGAL ETHICS

Mellinkoff's Text on The Conscience of a Lawyer, 304 pages, 1973.

Pirsig's Cases on Professional Responsibility, 2nd Ed., 447 pages, 1970.

LEGAL HISTORY

Kempin's Historical Introduction to Anglo-American Law in a Nutshell, 2nd Ed., 280 pages, 1973.

Kimball's Historical Introduction to Legal System, 610 pages, 1966.

Radin's Text on Anglo-American Legal History, 612 pages, 1936.

Smith's Cases on Development of Legal Institutions, 757 pages, 1965.

LEGAL INTERVIEWING AND COUNSELING

See Clinical Teaching.

LEGAL METHOD—LEGAL SYSTEM

Fryer and Orentlicher's Cases on Legal Method and Legal System, 1043 pages, 1966.

See Introduction to Law.

LEGAL PROCESS

See Legal Method.

LEGAL PROFESSION

See Legal Ethics.

LEGAL WRITING STYLE

Weihofen's Text on Legal Writing Style, 323 pages, 1961.
See Legal Bibliography.

LEGISLATION

Nutting, Elliott and Dickerson's Cases on Legislation, 4th Ed., 631 pages, 1969.

LOCAL GOVERNMENT LAW

Michelman and Sandalow's Cases on Government in Urban Areas, 1216 pages, 1970.
Michelman and Sandalow's 1972 Supplement.
Stason and Kauper's Cases on Municipal Corporations, 3rd Ed., 692 pages, 1959.
See Land Use.

MASS COMMUNICATION LAW

Gillmor and Barron's Cases on Mass Communication Law, 853 pages, 1969.
Gillmor and Barron's 1971 Supplement.

MORTGAGES

Osborne's Cases on Secured Transactions, 559 pages, 1967.
Osborne's Text on Mortgages, 2nd Ed., 805 pages, 1970.
See Sales.
See Secured Transactions.

MUNICIPAL CORPORATIONS

See Local Government Law.

NATURAL RESOURCES

Trelease, Bloomenthal and Geraud's Cases on Natural Resources, 1131 pages, 1965.

NEGOTIABLE INSTRUMENTS

Nordstrom and Clovis' Problems on Commercial Paper, 458 pages, 1972.
See Commercial Transactions.

OFFICE PRACTICE

A.B.A. Lawyer's Handbook, 557 pages, 1962.
See Clinical Teaching.

OIL AND GAS

Hemingway's Text on Oil and Gas, 486 pages, 1971.
Huie, Woodward and Smith's Cases on Oil and Gas, 2nd Ed., 955 pages, 1972.
See Natural Resources.

PARTNERSHIP

Crane and Bromberg's Text on Partnership, 695 pages, 1968.
See Agency-Partnership.

PATENTS

Choate's Cases on Patents, 1060 pages, 1973.

PERSONAL PROPERTY

Aigler, Smith and Tefft's Cases on Property, 2 Vols., 1339 pages, 1960.
Bigelow's Cases on Personal Property, 3rd Ed., 507 pages, 1942.
Fryer's Readings on Personal Property, 3rd Ed., 1184 pages, 1938.

PLEADING AND PROCEDURE

Brown, Karlen, Meisenholder, Stevens, and Vestal's Cases on Procedure Before Trial, 784 pages, 1968.
Cleary's Cases on Pleading, 2d Ed., 434 pages, 1958.
Cound, Friedenthal and Miller's Cases on Civil Procedure, 1075 pages, 1968.
Cound, Friedenthal and Miller's Cases on Pleading, Discovery and Joinder, 643 pages, 1968.
Cound, Friedenthal and Miller's Civil Procedure Supplement, 1972.
Ehrenzweig and Louisell's Jurisdiction in a Nutshell, 3rd Ed., 291 pages, 1973.
Elliott & Karlen's Cases on Pleading, 441 pages, 1961.
Hodges, Jones and Elliott's Cases on Texas Trial and Appellate Procedure, 623 pages, 1965.
Hodges, Jones, Elliott and Thode's Cases on Texas Judicial Process Prior to Trial, 935 pages, 1966.
Karlen and Joiner's Cases on Trials and Appeals, 536 pages, 1971.
Karlen's Procedure Before Trial in a Nutshell, 258 pages, 1972.
McBaine's Cases on Introduction to Civil Procedure, 399 pages, 1950.
Federal Rules of Civil-Appellate-Criminal Procedure, Law School Edition, 296 pages, 1973.

LAW SCHOOL PUBLICATIONS — Continued

POVERTY LAW

Cooper, Dodyk, Berger, Paulsen, Schrag and Sovern's Cases on Law and Poverty, 2nd Ed., 1208 pages, 1973.

Cooper and Dodyk's Cases on Income Maintenance, 2nd Ed., Pamphlet reprint from Cooper, et al. Law and Poverty, 2nd Ed., 450 pages, 1973.

LaFrance, Schroeder, Bennett and Boyd's Text on Law and the Poor, 558 pages, 1973.

REAL PROPERTY

Aigler, Smith & Tefft's Cases on Property, 2 Vols., 1339 pages, 1960.

Berger's Cases on Housing, 2nd Ed. Pamphlet reprint from Cooper, et al. Law and Poverty, 2nd Ed., 254 pages, 1973.

Browder, Cunningham & Julin's Cases on Basic Property Law, 2d Ed., 1397 pages, 1973.

Burby's Text on Real Property, 3rd Ed., 490 pages, 1965.

Moynihan's Introduction to Real Property, 254 pages, 1962.

Phipps' Titles in a Nutshell—The Calculus of Interests, 277 pages, 1968.

Smith and Boyer's Survey of the Law of Property, 2nd Ed., 510 pages, 1971.

See Housing and Urban Development.

REMEDIES

Cribbet's Cases on Judicial Remedies, 762 pages, 1954.

Dobb's Text, on Remedies, 1067 pages, 1973.

Van Hecke, Leavell and Nelson's Cases on Equitable Remedies and Restitution, 2nd Ed., 717 pages, 1973.

Wright's Cases on Remedies, 498 pages, 1955.

York and Bauman's Cases on Remedies, 2nd Ed., 1381 pages, 1973.

See Equity.

RESTITUTION

See Equity.
See Remedies.

REVIEW MATERIALS

Ballantine's Problems.
Burby's Law Refreshers.
Smith Reviews.

SALES

Nordstrom's Text on Sales, 600 pages, 1970.

Nordstrom and Lattin's Problems on Sales and Secured Transactions, 809 pages, 1968.

See Commercial Transactions.

SECURED TRANSACTIONS

Henson's Text on Secured Transactions, 364 pages, 1973.

See Commercial Transactions.

See Sales.

SURETYSHIP AND GUARANTY

Osborne's Cases on Suretyship, 221 pages, 1966.

Simpson's Cases on Suretyship, 538 pages, 1942.

TAXATION

Chommie's Text on Federal Income Taxation, 2nd Ed., about 1000 pages, 1973.

Chommie's Review of Federal Income Taxation, about 90 pages, 1973.

Hellerstein's Cases on State and Local Taxation, 3rd Ed., 741 pages, 1969.

Kragen & McNulty's Cases on Federal Income Taxation, 1,182 pages, 1970.

Lowndes & Kramer's Text on Federal Estate and Gift Taxes, 2nd Ed., 951 pages, 1962.

McNulty's Federal Estate and Gift Taxation in a Nutshell, about 335 pages, 1973.

McNulty's Federal Income Taxation in a Nutshell, 322 pages, 1972.

Rice's Problems in Federal Estate & Gift Taxation, 2nd Ed., 496 pages, 1972.

Rice's Problems in Federal Income Taxation, 2nd Ed., 589 pages, 1971.

Selected Provisions of the Internal Revenue Code, Treasury Regulations and Related Authorities, about 1000 pages, 1973.

TORTS

Green, Pedrick, Rahl, Thode, Hawkins and Smith's Cases on Torts, 1311 pages, 1968.

Green, Pedrick, Rahl, Thode, Hawkins and Smith's Cases on Injuries to Relations, 466 pages, 1968.

Keeton and Keeton's Cases on Torts, 1193 pages, 1971.

Prosser's Text on Torts, 4th Ed., 1208 pages, 1971.

TRADE REGULATION

See Anti-Trust Law.
See Unfair Trade Practices.

TRIAL AND APPELLATE PRACTICE

See Pleading and Procedure.

TRUSTS

Bogert's Text on Trusts, 5th Ed., about 650 pages, 1973.

Powell's Cases on Trusts and Wills, 639 pages, 1960.

See Wills, Intestate Succession, Trusts, Gifts and Future Interests.

UNFAIR TRADE PRACTICES

Oppenheim's Cases on Unfair Trade Practices, 783 pages, 1965.

Oppenheim and Weston's Supplement.

Oppenheim's Robinson-Patman Act Pamphlet, 295 pages, 1967.

WATER LAW

Trelease's Cases on Water Law, 364 pages, 1967.

WILLS

Atkinson's Text on Wills, 2nd Ed., 975 pages, 1953.

Mennell's Cases on California Decedents' Estates, 566 pages, 1973.

Turrentine's Cases on Wills, 2nd Ed., 483 pages, 1962.

See Wills, Intestate Succession, Trusts, Gifts and Future Interests.

WILLS, INTESTATE SUCCESSION, TRUSTS, GIFTS AND FUTURE INTERESTS

Gulliver, Clark, Lusky and Murphy's Cases on Gratuitous Transfers: Wills, Intestate Succession, Trusts, Gifts and Future Interests, 1017 pages, 1967.

WORKMEN'S COMPENSATION

Malone and Plant's Cases on Workmen's Compensation, 622 pages, 1963.

HANDBOOK

OF THE

LAW OF CORPORATIONS

AND

OTHER BUSINESS ENTERPRISES

By

HARRY G. HENN

Edward Cornell Professor of Law

The Cornell Law School

SECOND EDITION

HORNBOOK SERIES

ST. PAUL, MINN.
WEST PUBLISHING CO.
1970

Henn Corporations 2d Ed. HB
3rd Reprint—1973

To My Mother

PREFACE TO THE SECOND EDITION

The reception of the first edition of this *Handbook of the Law of Corporations and Other Business Enterprises* by the legal profession—bench, practising bar, law teachers, and especially those for whom the work was originally written, law students, who after all are the future members of all branches of the profession—has been most gratifying.

Like the first edition, this second edition follows the trilevel approach: (1) the overview in the bold-face summaries at the beginning of each of the 389 sections; (2) the adequate coverage for law students in the 834 pages of text; and (3) the guides to further information and research in the some 5,250 footnotes.

For some law teachers, a hornbook probably spoils their classroom fun, but for most, a hornbook should permit more intensive classroom treatment of the more important subjects, with the hornbook serving to supplement coverage of other perhaps less interesting aspects.

Since 1961, many developments have occurred in the area of corporations and related subjects, necessitating a general updating and the inclusion of a few new sections and the omission of some obsolete material. To facilitate the finding of the appropriate section in this second edition by a reader having a reference to the first edition, a conversion table has been included as Appendix B immediately preceding the Table of Cases Cited.

Among the more significant developments during the past decade have been (1) the emergence of increasingly-strict federal corporation law, based primarily on federal securities legislation, which federal case law development began in the late 1940's but burgeoned in the 1960's—as compared to state corporate law revisions in some half of the states during the past decade of expanding permissiveness—patterned after the highly-touted Delaware revision of 1967–69 (doubling Delaware's annual incorporations) with its band-wagon effect on other states—a throwback to the 1875–1900 period of intensive interstate incorporation competition; (2) the some 25 corporate statutory revisions, including the 1969 Model Business Corporation Act revision —many of them—in a period of much unrest—encouraging corporate irresponsibility; and (3) the Federal Tax Reform Act of 1969, with its complicated transitional rules, superimposing some 255 pages of legislation on the already 1012-page Internal Revenue Code of 1954, with its 1,117 pages of amendments prior to 1969.

Even the Model Business Corporation Act, which has provided the pattern for corporate statutory revision in some 32 states and the District of Columbia, and which was drafted initially "as a modern statute that preserves in proper balance the interests of the state and the rights and interests of corporations, shareholders and management"—with recognition that the Act "may not appeal to a state that is soliciting corporate business"—has become increasingly permissive, epecially in the 1969 revision, some of the more sensitive provisions of which were drafted by the Committee on Corporate Laws of the American Bar Association in collaboration with the revisers drafting the Delaware General Corporation Law of 1967 and its 1968 and 1969 amendments. Discussion of the Model Act can be deceptive if one is not aware of the various versions, and optional and alternative sections, adopted over the years by different so-called "Model Act jurisdictions".

The 1969 Model Act revision changed the numbering of the sections, which had remained uniform in the pre-1969 versions and which are used in this second edition. A conversion table listing the changes in numbering of the sections appears as Appendix A immediately following section 389.

The period of the preparation of this second edition was saddened by the passing of my first law school Dean, later colleague, long-time mentor, and close friend, Robert Sproule Stevens (1889–1969).

Principal acknowledgment for this second edition is due my dedicated and indefatigable secretary, Mrs. Mary D. Mignano, whose contributions throughout were beyond expectation; to Frank J. Franzino, Jr., of the Cornell Law School Class of 1970, for his research assistance; to Dean W. Ray Forrester, for his constant encouragement; to the Cornell Law Library staff, under Professor Harry Bitner, Law Librarian, and especially Miss Lorraine A. Kulpa and Mrs. Betty Prior Reese, for their unfaltering assistance in legal research; not to mention the Law Library's magnificent facilities for research and scholarship; to my colleagues, Professors Robert S. Pasley, Ian R. Macneil, David L. Ratner and John Skidmore Brown, for reviewing portions of the text; and to my now more than 1,500 former students for their stimulation.

The Preface to the first edition began with a quotation from Blackstone's *Commentaries*. This Preface to the second edition might well end with Blackstone's epitaph:

> "Who rescu'd law from pedant phrase,
> Who clear'd the student's clouded eyes,
> And led him through the legal maze."

HARRY G. HENN

Ithaca, New York
March 1, 1970

PREFACE TO THE FIRST EDITION

"FOR the truth is, that the present publication is as much the effect of necessity, as it is of choice. The notes which were taken by his hearers, have by some of them (too partial in his favour) been thought worth revising and transcribing; and these transcripts have been frequently lent to others. Hence copies have been multiplied, in their nature imperfect, if not erroneous; some of which have fallen into mercenary hands, and become the object of clandestine sale. Having therefore so much reason to apprehend a surreptitious impression, he chose rather to submit his own errors to the world, than to seem answerable for those of other men. . . ."

By odd coincidence, the writer of this quoted passage began lecturing on the law in 1753, exactly two centuries before I was invited to teach the course in "Business Associations" at The Cornell Law School.

When I started teaching, after ten years of corporate practice with a large metropolitan law firm, I found no single volume which adequately covered the materials which I thought the students should have. Stevens on Corporations was excellent. Its orderly arrangement, pervasive scholarship, sound logic, emphasis on fundamentals, concern for high ethics, and revelation of the law as it should be, make it a corporation law classic. However, it does not purport to cover the rules respecting partnerships and other noncorporate forms of business enterprises, red-flag the major tax aspects, outline bankruptcy and corporate reorganization so far as relevant to business enterprises, or summarize relevant securities regulation, antitrust aspects, and stock exchange requirements; nor was its orientation primarily from the point of view of actual practice.

I attempted to cover the missing material by supplementary reading assignments and by lecture. In 1957, a few enterprising students prepared and mimeographed a 207-page summary of the basic course. Good as it was, the summary left much to be desired, and, as a result, I began the preparation of this handbook.

My principal reason for preparing this handbook, however, was more fundamental. In teaching, I soon found that a problem method can be very profitably employed in a course in partnership and corporation law. Under Dean Stevens' leadership at Cornell, problem methodology had been established in upper-class seminars known as "problem courses", and the satisfactory completion of at least one problem course was a prerequisite to graduation. However, integration of the problem method in the large casebook courses had not progressed beyond the experimental stage. Use of a problem method requires that the students enjoy ready access to information useful in the solution of the problems. This handbook was prepared primarily to supply that need.

PREFACE TO THE FIRST EDITION

Since this handbook was written to prepare law students for corporate and related practice, it should, to the extent that it has achieved that purpose, be a helpful handbook for practitioners.

The above-quoted 18th century lecturer devoted 19 pages, out of a total of 1884 pages on the law, to "corporations". In the final chapter of his first book entitled "The Rights of Persons", he discussed corporations. Practically nothing was said about business corporations; his citations of authority were sparse, fewer in his entire four-volume work than in some of the following chapters. The author was English, and his peroration concerning the corporation was: "But our laws have considerably refined and improved upon the invention [of the corporation in Roman law], according to the usual genius of the English nation".

Few knowledgeable 20th century Englishmen would hesitate to admit that American corporation law is today incomparably richer and more highly developed than its English parent was then or is now. Fifty-one jurisdictions—excluding the federal government and Puerto Rico—compared to one, and Fletcher's some twenty volumes of Cyclopedia on the Law of Private Corporations, compared to Blackstone's 19 pages, are convincing evidence.

Acknowledgment is due Dean Emeritus Robert S. Stevens and my other faculty colleagues for their helpful suggestions and assistance; Dean Gray Thoron for encouragement; Professor Lewis W. Morse, Law Librarian, and the staff of the Cornell Law Library for their cooperation—in Professor Morse's case, far beyond the call of duty; Philip J. Loree, Robert S. Banks, Paul C. Szasz, Sanford B. D. Wood, Jr., Lyell G. Galbraith and Richard H. Senn, for research assistance; James F. Spoerri, of the Illinois Bar, director of the American Bar Foundation project to annotate the Model Business Corporation Act, for the experience of working with him on the project for six months during my Sabbatical leave; Morton S. Wolf, of the Illinois Bar, for many valuable comments; the New York State Joint Legislative Committee to Study Revision of Corporation Laws for insights gained as a consultant in connection with the drafting of the proposed New York Business Corporation Law; Kathryn Trapp, Judith K. Hodge, Dawn Cottle, Ruth Roberts, Elda Franceschina, Sharon C. DeGroff, and David C. Brown, for typing and helping to compile the manuscript; and my 702 students who have helped me to learn the subject during the past eight years.

HARRY G. HENN

Ithaca, New York
April, 1961

XIV

SUMMARY OF CONTENTS

SUMMARY OF CONTENTS

SUMMARY OF CONTENTS

TABLE OF CONTENTS

CHAPTER 1. INTRODUCTION

A. SUBJECT MATTER

CHAPTER 2. SELECTION OF FORM OF BUSINESS ENTERPRISE

A. FORMS AND FACTORS IN SELECTION

B. INDIVIDUAL (OR SOLE) PROPRIETORSHIP

C. GENERAL PARTNERSHIP

TABLE OF CONTENTS

D. LIMITED PARTNERSHIP

E. FORMS RELATED TO PARTNERSHIP

F. STATUTORY PARTNERSHIP ASSOCIATION

G. JOINT (AD)VENTURE

H. JOINT-STOCK COMPANY (OR ASSOCIATION)

I. BUSINESS (OR MASSACHUSETTS) TRUST

TABLE OF CONTENTS

CHAPTER 3. NATURE OF CORPORATENESS OR CORPORATE PERSONALITY

A. INTRODUCTION

B. CORPORATION AS "PERSON"

C. CORPORATION AS "DOMICILIARY"

D. CORPORATION AS "RESIDENT"

E. CORPORATION AS "CITIZEN"

F. CORPORATION AS "NATIONAL"

G. CORPORATION AS "STATE"

TABLE OF CONTENTS

CHAPTER 4. SELECTION OF JURISDICTION OF INCORPORATION

CHAPTER 5. PREINCORPORATION PROBLEMS

A. PROMOTERS

B. DUTIES AND LIABILITIES OF PROMOTERS

C. PREINCORPORATION AGREEMENTS

CHAPTER 6. INCORPORATION, ADMISSION, AND DOMESTICATION

A. INTRODUCTION

TABLE OF CONTENTS

B. ARTICLES (OR CERTIFICATE) OF INCORPORATION

C. DRAFTING BYLAWS

D. FORM(S) OF SHARE CERTIFICATES

E. ORGANIZATION MEETING(S)

F. ADMISSION AND DOMESTICATION PROCEDURES

CHAPTER 7. RECOGNITION OR DISREGARD OF CORPORATENESS

A. INTRODUCTION

B. DEFECTIVE INCORPORATION

C. DISREGARD OF CORPORATENESS

TABLE OF CONTENTS

TABLE OF CONTENTS

J. RECORD OWNERSHIP OF SECURITIES

CHAPTER 9. CORPORATE MANAGEMENT STRUCTURE

A. INTRODUCTION

B. PURPOSES (OR OBJECTS) AND POWERS

C. INCORPORATOR(S)

D. SHAREHOLDER(S)

E. DIRECTOR(S)

TABLE OF CONTENTS

CHAPTER 10. SPECIAL PROBLEMS OF CLOSE CORPORATIONS

A. INTRODUCTION

B. INCORPORATION

C. FINANCIAL STRUCTURE

D. MANAGEMENT STRUCTURE

E. SHARE TRANSFER RESTRICTIONS

F. DRAFTING TECHNIQUES

TABLE OF CONTENTS

CHAPTER 11. SPECIAL PROBLEMS OF LARGER CORPORATIONS

A. INTRODUCTION

TABLE OF CONTENTS

C. DIVIDEND PREFERENCES AND OTHER RIGHTS

D. SHAREHOLDERS' "RIGHTS" TO DIVIDENDS

E. SHARE DISTRIBUTIONS

F. MISCELLANEOUS DIVIDEND AND RELATED PROBLEMS

G. REDEMPTION OR PURCHASE BY CORPORATION OF OWN SHARES

H. DIVIDEND AND REDEMPTION TAX ASPECTS

CHAPTER 13. EXTRAORDINARY CORPORATE MATTERS

CHAPTER 14. CORPORATE LITIGATION (INCLUDING DERIVATIVE ACTIONS)

A. GENERAL PROCEDURAL PROBLEMS

TABLE OF CONTENTS

TABLE OF CONTENTS

†

HANDBOOK

OF THE

LAW OF CORPORATIONS

AND

OTHER BUSINESS ENTERPRISES

CHAPTER 1

INTRODUCTION

A. SUBJECT MATTER

A. SUBJECT MATTER

SCOPE OF SUBJECT MATTER

1. This handbook discusses the law of corporations and other forms of business enterprise, with primary emphasis on the law of business corporations. The business corporation is a key institution in contemporary society and in the American free enterprise profit system. The law of business corporations is largely based on state statutes, of which Delaware, New York, and the jurisdictions follow-

1

ing the Model Business Corporation Act of the American Bar Association are the most significant. In recent years, a growing body of federal corporation law has emerged.

"Corporations and Other Business Enterprises" is a rather broad title for the subjects which receive major treatment in this handbook. It has a more general connotation than "Business Associations" or than the even more limited name "Business Corporations". The term "Business Associations" excludes one frequently encountered form of business organization which is not an association—the individual or sole proprietorship with its substantial tie-in with agency law. The term "Business Corporations" excludes all unincorporated business organizations, thereby excluding not only the individual proprietorship, but the very prevalent forms of partnership, and the relatively rare joint-stock association and business trust. In contrast with both "Business Associations" and "Business Corporations", the term "Corporations and Other Business Enterprises" comprehends all the relevant forms of business enterprise.

From the point of view of emphasis, "Business Corporations" is the more accurate term for much of what follows, since the dominant focus is on the incorporated business enterprise. While treatment of the unincorporated forms of business enterprise is mainly by way of comparison with the corporation, it is intended to provide both a reasonably integrated description of such forms (involving some introduction to the more important applicable principles of partnership law) and a sound basis for selecting and tailoring the form most suitable to the business involved.

Some 11,479,000 business enterprises have been estimated to exist in the United States, of which 1,469,000 are corporations, 923,000 are partnerships, and 9,087,000 are individual proprietorships.[1] Only some 72,000 busi-

ness enterprises employ 100 or more employees; more than one-half employ fewer than four persons; in two-fifths, the concern consists of the boss himself. While far fewer in number than unincorporated forms of business enterprise, business corporations are the dominant form.

In any event, reference to nonbusiness enterprises will be only incidental. Despite some similarity of origin and legal principles, the very common nonbusiness association, whether noncorporate or corporate, such as governmental (public, municipal), educational, charitable, religious, or social corporations, is beyond the scope of business enterprises.[2]

The key subject, then, will be the business corporation, with its infinite variations. The business corporation [3] is a type of a cor-

___

1. Statistical Abstract of the United States 1969, 472, 475 (U.S. Dep't of Commerce).

2. See, e. g., H. Ford, Unincorporated, Non-Profit Associations, Their Property and Their Liability (1959); Developments in the Law—"Judicial Control of Actions of Private Associations", 76 Harv.L. Rev. 983 (1963).

3. Even in statutes entitled "Business Corporation" Act or Law, the term "business corporation" is often not defined. E. g., ABA–ALI Model Bus.Corp. Act § 2; McKinney's N.Y.Bus.Corp.Law, § 102. Such definitions as have been attempted usually provide that a business corporation is a corporation subject to the Business Corporation Act or Law. For a more precise definition, see the abortive Restatement of Business Associations 9 (Tentative Draft No. 1, Apr. 10, 1928): *"Definitive Section.* In the Restatement of this Subject the term 'corporation for profit' means that two or more persons are associated under a statute in a common business enterprise, and that with respect to this common business enterprise

   a. they have adopted a common (corporate) name;

   b. they can sue and be sued and hold and convey property only in this common name;

   c. the individual primary responsibility of each for obligations arising from the common business enterprise is limited to his interest in the property of the Association;

   d. the individual secondary responsibility of each for obligations arising from the common business enterprise is generally limited to his unpaid subscription to the property of such enterprise, or to a fixed maximum amount in excess thereof;

   e. the common business enterprise of the persons associated therein (usually called 'shareholders') is managed by persons (usually called 'directors') whom the 'shareholders,' or

poration formed to collect a fund of capital and to dedicate such fund to a more or less definite commercial purpose for profit. Most jurisdictions distinguish between the business corporation and the nonprofit corporation, often having a separate act for each,[4] the statutes for profit corporations of-

> a class of 'shareholders,' elect at intervals, although the 'shareholders' may have some control of the management;
>
> *f.* their rights and obligations are divided into units called 'shares' and such units are transferable; the transference of all the 'shares' to one person does not terminate the foregoing legal incidents."

4. E. g., ABA–ALI Model Bus.Corp.Act §§ 2(a), (b), 3 (1966) (applicable to all corporations for profit except those with banking or insurance purposes); ABA–ALI Model Non-Profit Corp.Act § 2(a), (b), (c) (1964) (applicable to "non-profit corporation", i. e., "a corporation no part of the income of which is distributable to its members, directors or officers"). Corporations may be organized under the Model Non-Profit Corporation Act "for any lawful purpose or purposes, including, without being limited to, any one or more of the following purposes: charitable; benevolent; eleemosynary; educational; civic; patriotic; political; religious; social; fraternal; literary; cultural; athletic; scientific; agricultural; horticultural; animal husbandry; and professional, commercial, industrial or trade association; but labor unions, cooperative organizations, and organizations subject to any of the provisions of the insurance laws of this State may not be organized under this Act." Id. § 4. See Note, "Nonprofit Corporations—Definition", 17 Vand.L. Rev. 336 (1963). For purposes of federal income taxation, an organization may be exempt as an "exempt organization" if it is organized and operated exclusively for one or more of the following purposes: (a) religious, (b) charitable, (c) scientific, (d) testing for public safety, (e) literary, (f) educational, or (g) prevention of cruelty to children or animals. Treas.Reg. § 1.501(d) (1) (1967). Symposium: "Non-Profit Organizations' Problems", 14 Clev.-Mar.L.Rev. 203 (1965); Lesher, "The Non-Profit Corporation—A Neglected Stepchild Comes of Age", 22 Bus.Law. 951 (1967); Bromberg, "Non-Profit Corporations: Organizational Problems and Tax Exemptions", 17 Baylor L.Rev. 125 (1965); Webster, "Effect of Business Activities on Exempt Organizations", 43 Taxes 777 (1965). See also Symposium: "Foundations, Charities and the Law: The Interaction of External Controls and Internal Policies", 13 U.C.L.A.L.Rev. 933–1099 (1966); M. Fremont-Smith, Foundations and Government: State and Federal Law and Supervision (1965); Folk, "Regulation of Charitable Foundations—The Patman and Treasury Reports", 20 Bus.Law. 1015 (1965); Riecker, "Foundations and the Patman Committee Report", 63 Mich.L.Rev. 95 (1964). The Model Non-Profit Corporation Act, first published in 1952 and revised in 1957 and 1964, has been used as the basis

ten being entitled "Business Corporation" or "Stock Corporation" Acts or Laws.

Other jurisdictions, however, have "General Corporation" Acts or Laws, under which provision is often made for incorporation of nonprofit as well as profit corporations.[5] Nearly all jurisdictions leave the public or municipal corporation to be governed by entirely separate statutory provisions. In New York, because of its somewhat unique over-all statutory setup, all corporations have been divided into three basic types: (a) public corporations, (b) stock corporations, and (c) nonstock corporations. Stock corporations were defined as corporations having shares of stock and authorized by law to distribute dividends to the holders thereof. Stock corporations, in turn, had a sevenfold subclassification: business corporations, corporations subject to the banking law and corporations subject to the insurance law (collectively called "moneyed corporations"), railroad corporations, transportation corporations, stock cooperative corporations, and stock corporations chartered by the regents of the university.[6]

for nonprofit corporation statutes in Wisconsin (1953), Alabama (1955), North Carolina (1956), Virginia (1956), Texas (1959), Nebraska (1959), North Dakota (1959), Oregon (1959), and District of Columbia (1962). Illinois, Missouri, and Ohio have statutes which are similar to it in substantial respects. It is under consideration in other jurisdictions where nonprofit corporation statutes exist in almost endless variety. It prohibits a nonprofit corporation from issuing shares or paying dividends. Id. § 26. ALI-ABA Joint Committee on Continuing Legal Education, Handbook D, The Model Nonprofit Corporation Act (With Official Forms and Optional and Alternative Sections (ALI rev. 1964)); Haller, "Model Non-Profit Corporation Act", 9 Baylor L.Rev. 309 (1957). See also H. Oleck, Non-Profit Corporations, Organizations, and Associations: Origin, Management and Dissolution (2d ed. 1965); R. Boyer, Nonprofit Corporation Statutes: A Critique and Proposal (1957). See also W. Carroll & I. Rosenblatt, California Nonprofit Corporations (California Continuing Education of the Bar 1969).

5. Del.Gen.Corp.Law, § 101(b) (1967) (". . . to conduct or promote any lawful business or purposes, except as may otherwise be provided by the constitution or other law of this State.").

6. McKinney's N.Y.Gen.Corp.Law, §§ 2, 3(5)–(10). See section 14 infra. Anglo-American jurisdictions

References herein to such other important classes of corporations as municipal corporations, religious corporations, membership, and other nonprofit corporations will do little more than point out their existence and their place in the overall statutory scheme.[7]

Finally, any treatment of the law of business enterprises, to have meaning, must recognize the social and economic implications of such enterprises. Because of its size, power, and impact, the modern business corporation is a key institution in contemporary society and in the American free enterprise profit system—somewhat analogous to the feudal system of old. It is part of the so-called military—industrial—academic—labor union—congressional complex.

In 1966, corporate assets exceeded one and three-fourths trillion dollars ($1,845,-000,000,000); corporate revenue approximated $1,306,000,000,000 annually; American shareholders in 1970 numbered more than 26,500,000, excluding indirect ownership by another 100,000,000 persons through banks, insurance companies, pension funds, and investment companies. The 500 largest American corporations embrace nearly two-thirds of all nonagricultural economic activity, and employ one in every seven American workers. Altogether, corporations employ three-fourths of the nation's labor force and wield considerable power, explicit and implicit, over other institutions as well.[8] Like

distinguish between public or municipal corporations, on the one hand, and private corporations, on the other. The standard definitive up-to-date encyclopedia on American corporation law, for example, is entitled Fletcher's Cyclopedia of the Law of Private Corporations, hereinafter cited W. Fletcher, Private Corporations. The private corporation should not be confused with the English private company. The public corporation or municipal corporation, should not be confused with the English public company. See section 259, nn. 17–20 infra. Nor with the public service corporation or public utility; nor with the so-called "quasi-public corporation" or publicly-held corporation. See Chapter 11 Special Problems of Larger Corporations, infra.

7. See section 14 infra.

8. The dominant role of the corporation is not a recent phenomenon. See Field, J., in Paul v. Virgin-

all such institutions, the corporate system is in a state of flux, reasonably orderly to be sure but pronounced and inevitable. The past 35 years have witnessed a substantial growth not only in the size, power, and impact of business corporations but also of government regulation, especially at the federal level, of court-developed concepts of fiduciary duties owed by the managers and those in control, of mounting tax consequences, and of different, if not always more enlightened, attitudes on the part of corporate entrepreneurs.[9]

ia, 75 U.S. (8 Wall.) 168 at 181–182, 19 L.Ed. 357 at 360 (1868): "At the present day corporations are multiplied to an almost indefinite extent. There is scarcely a business pursued requiring the expenditure of large capital, or the union of large numbers, that is not carried on by corporations. It is not too much to say that the wealth and business of the country are to a great extent controlled by them." See also "American Business Abroad—The New Industrial Revolution", 52 Saturday Review, No. 47, 31 (Nov. 22, 1969).

9. A. Berle, Power Without Property: A New Development in American Political Economy 38–58 (1959). See also A. Berle, The American Economic Republic (1963); A. Berle, The 20th Century Capitalist Revolution (1954); Temporary National Economic Committee (T.N.E.C.) Hearings and Monographs (1938–1944). A. Berle & G. Means, The Modern Corporation and Private Property (1933).

See A. Jay, Management and Machiavelli—An Inquiry into the Politics of Corporate Life (1968); J. Galbraith, The New Industrial State (1967); Northwood Institute, Corporate Policy and Ethics (1967); R. Eells, The Corporation and the Arts (1967); D. Votaw, Modern Corporations (1965); L. Hodges, The Business Conscience (1963); R. Manley & S. Manley, The Age of the Manager (1963); W. Moore, The Conduct of the Corporation (1962); R. Spurrier, Ethics and Business (1963); R. Eells, The Government of Corporations (1962); G. Means, The Corporate Revolution in America: Economic Realty vs. Economic Theory (1962); V. Packard, The Pyramid Climbers (1962); W. Warner, The Corporation in the Emergent American Society (1962); B. Levy, Corporation Lawyer: Saint or Sinner? (1961); R. Eells, The Meaning of Modern Business: An Introduction to the Philosophy of a Large Corporate Enterprise (1960); D. Forbush, Management's Relationships with Its Publics (1960); E. Mason, The Corporation in Modern Society (1960); J. Livingston, The American Stockholder (1958); A. Berle, Economic Power and the Free Society (1957); H. Maurer, Great Enterprise Growth and Behavior of the Big Corporation (1956); C. Mills, The Power Elite (1956); T. Quinn, Giant Corporations: Challenge to Freedom (1956); H. Holbrook, The Age of Moguls (1954); J. Galbraith, American Capitalism: The Concept of Countervailing Power (1952); J.

In 1968, some 100 large corporations undertook to cooperate with the federal government to provide jobs for some 500,000 hard core unemployed by 1971. Under the program designated Job Opportunities in Business Sector ("JOBS") program, the corporations would provide on-the-job training with the government financing extra expenses for transportation, education, medical services, etc. Coordinating the program was a 65-man National Alliance of Business Men headed by an executive board of 15 top business leaders. Meanwhile, many corporations were recruiting employees in ghetto areas.[10]

Burnham, Managerial Revolution (1941); T. Arnold, Folklore of Capitalism (1937); P. Drucker, Concept of the Corporation (1936); W. Ripley, Main Street and Wall Street (1927); T. Veblen, Absentee Ownership and Business Enterprise in Recent Times— The Case of America (1923); L. Brandeis, Other People's Money (1914); Berle, "Corporate Decision-Making and Social Control", 24 Bus.Law. 149 (1968); Taylor, "The Corporation and the Law", 24 Bus.Law. 159 (1968); Gullander, "The Future Direction of the Modern Corporation", 24 Bus.Law. 165 (1968); Manne, "Our Two Corporation Systems: Law and Economics", 53 Va.L.Rev. 259 (1967); Vagts, "Reforming the 'Modern' Corporation: Perspective From the German", 80 Harv.L.Rev. 23 (1966); Berle, "Property, Production and Revolution", 65 Colum.L.Rev. 1 (1965); Ruder, "Public Obligations of Private Corporations", 114 U.Pa.L.Rev. 209 (1965); Harbrecht, "The Modern Corporation Revisited", 64 Colum.L.Rev. 1410 (1964); Israels, "Are Corporate Powers Still Held in Trust?", 64 Colum.L.Rev. 1446 (1964); Weiner, "The Berle-Dodd Dialogue on the Concept of the Corporation", 64 Colum.L.Rev. 1458 (1964); Berle, "Modern Functions of the Corporate System", 62 Colum.L.Rev. 433 (1962); Manne, "The 'Higher Criticism' of the Modern Corporation", 62 Colum.L.Rev. 399 (1962); Manne, "Current Views on the 'Modern Corporation'", 38 U.Det.L.J. 559 (1961). See also D. Finn, The Corporate Oligarch (1969).

See also E. Smigel, The Wall Street Lawyer: Professional Organization Man? (1964); Bibliography: "The Corporate Legal Department", 19 Record of N.Y.C.B.A. 204 (1964).

10. Demaree, "Business Picks Up the Urban Challenge", 79 Fortune, No. 4, 103 (Apr.1969); Albrook, "Business Wrestles with Its Social Conscience", 78 Fortune, No. 2, 89 (Aug.1968); Comment, "Community Development Corporations: A New Approach to the Poverty Problem", 82 Harv.L.Rev. 644 (1969). See also T. Cross, Black Capitalism: Strategy for Business in the Ghetto (1969); ABA National Institute: "Business in the Ghetto", 25 Bus.Law. 1 (Special Issue, Sept. 1969); Goodpaster, "An Introduction to the Community Development Corporation", 46 J.Urban Law 603 (1969); Comment, "From Private Enterprise to Public Entity: The Role of

The American law of business enterprises, in the sense of the legal principles controlling the formation and ordinary operations of most business enterprises, has traditionally been almost entirely state law, with substantial statutory bases. Federal law, except for federal bankruptcy and reorganization, historically took the form of superimposed regulations to protect the public interest (mainly on the basis of federal power over interstate commerce) and tax structure. In recent years, however, a growing body of federal corporation law has emerged. While some attempt has been made herein to red-flag the more important regulatory aspects of federal law, more detailed treatment of such aspects are left to presentations on antitrust and trade regulation, securities regulation, labor law, etc., and of taxes to full-blown presentations thereof.

Agency law is largely court-developed, and sufficiently similar in the different jurisdictions to have warranted a Restatement (1933) and the Restatement (Second) of Agency (1958). Partnership law, too, had its basis in decisional law and is codified, at least to some extent, in the widely-adopted Uniform Partnership Act (1914). Limited partnerships were created by statute; they are now governed in most jurisdictions by the Uniform Limited Partnership Act (1916). Despite the growing body of federal corporation law, corporation law still remains largely state law and substantially statutory, with considerable variation from state to state.

Most applicable are the corporation statutes [11] of Delaware, New York, and the jurisdictions following the Model Business Cor-

the Community Development Corporation", 57 Geo. L.J. 959 (1969).

11. Restatement (Second) of Conflict of Laws ch. 12, Agency and Partnerships ch. 13, Business Corporations (Proposed Official Draft Pt. III, Apr. 22, 1969). Reese & Kaufman, "The Law Governing Corporate Affairs: Choice of Law and the Impact of Full Faith and Credit", 58 Colum.L.Rev. 1118 (1958). See section 98 infra.

poration Act of the American Bar Association. Of the 600 largest industrial, merchandising and utility corporations, with assets totaling $316,936,132,000, more than a third are incorporated in Delaware, followed by New York (one-seventh), New Jersey (one-ninth), followed by Pennsylvania, Ohio, Illinois, California, Maryland, Indiana, Virginia, Maine, Michigan, Massachusetts, Missouri, and Florida.[12] Of the 1,278 corporations listed on the New York Stock Exchange, 452 or more than one-third were incorporated in Delaware, followed by New York (158), New Jersey (79), Pennsylvania (71), Ohio (69), California (49), Illinois (40), Maryland (39), Michigan (37), Massachusetts (28), Virginia (26), Maine (22); other states account for 69 listings; foreign countries for 29.[13] In number of business

12. "The Fortune Directory of the 500 Largest U.S. Industrial Corporations . . .", 79 Fortune, No. 6, 166–202 (May 15, 1969).

13. E. Folk, The Red Book Digest of the New Delaware Corporation Law—1967 (Corporation Service Company, 45th ed. 1968).

incorporations annually, New York leads with approximately 17 percent, followed by California with approximately seven percent, Delaware is sixth in number with some four and one-half percent.[14]

Besides rather systematic treatment of the corporation law of Delaware, New York, and the Model Act jurisdictions, attention herein is also given to the more unusual statutory and decisional rules in other jurisdictions.

Jurisdictions adhering to some version of the Model Business Corporation Act, prepared by the Committee on Corporate Laws of the American Bar Association, include Wisconsin, Oregon, District of Columbia, Texas, Virginia, North Dakota, Alaska, Colorado, Iowa, Wyoming, Utah, Mississippi, Nebraska, South Dakota, Washington, New Mexico, Montana, Georgia, and Rhode Island; similar to the Model Act in some respects

14. New business incorporations by states during 1969:

*New York	41,720		Oklahoma	2,795
California	22,723		**Alabama	2,721
Florida	18,274		***Oregon	2,628
***Texas	13,584		***Iowa	2,571
**New Jersey	13,168		***Mississippi	2,328
*Delaware	12,228		**Arkansas	2,293
Ohio	12,061		**South Carolina	2,286
*Pennsylvania	9,688		Kansas	2,111
Michigan	9,586		***Utah	1,857
**Illinois	8,717		***District of Columbia	1,577
*Massachusetts	7,349		***Nebraska	1,489
Missouri	5,727		**Rhode Island	1,471
***Georgia	5,629		Hawaii	1,221
**Maryland	5,619		West Virginia	1,063
*North Carolina	4,935		New Hampshire	972
Louisiana	4,659		***New Mexico	960
***Virginia	4,650		Maine	941
Minnesota	4,312		Idaho	848
**Indiana	4,293		***South Dakota	837
***Wisconsin	4,245		***Alaska	690
***Colorado	4,068		Vermont	680
***Washington	4,020		***Montana	598
*Connecticut	3,938		***Wyoming	471
*Tennessee	3,933		***North Dakota	422
Nevada	3,232			
Arizona	3,181		TOTAL	274,267
Kentucky	2,898			

*** Indicates jurisdiction adhering to Model Business Corporation Act, with more or less minor variations.
** Indicates jurisdiction with many provisions similar to Model Act.
* Indicates jurisdiction with some provisions similar to Model Act.
Business Economics, Monthly New Incorporations, Y–12, No. 1 (Dun & Bradstreet, Inc., Feb. 21, 1970).

are the more recent statutes in other states.[15]

Mention is also made of the more relevant provisions of the Uniform Commercial Code,[16] and other germane uniform acts.[17]

To illustrate securities exchange requirements are references to the rules, policies, practices, and procedures of the New York Stock Exchange.[18]

TREATMENT OF SUBJECT MATTER

2. This handbook, after an introduction to the subject of corporations and other forms of

15. The Model Business Corporation Act was first drafted on the basis of the Illinois Business Corporation Act of 1933, which was extensively followed in Pennsylvania in 1933 and Missouri in 1943; first published in 1946; and revised in 1950, 1953, 1955, 1957, 1959, 1962, 1964, 1966, and 1969 (with alternative and optional provisions). Garrett, "History, Purpose and Summary of the Model Business Corporation Act", 6 Bus.Law. 1 (Nov.1950); Garrett, "Model Business Corporation Act", 4 Baylor L.Rev. 412 (1952); Campbell, "The Model Business Corporation Act", 11 Bus.Law. 98 (July, 1956). The Model Act is intended to serve as a drafting guide and not a uniform act. It should not be confused with the old Uniform Business Corporation Act, sponsored by the National Conference of Commissioners on Uniform State Laws in 1928, adopted by Idaho, Kentucky, Louisiana, and Washington, renamed the "Model Business Corporation Act" in 1943, and completely withdrawn by the Conference in 1958. 9 U.L.A. 49 (1951).

16. U.L.A. (2 vols. 1962) (adopted in all states except Louisiana and in the District of Columbia and the Virgin Islands). Article 8, entitled "Investment Securities", deals with the problems of negotiability, transfer, and registration of transfer of the classes of instruments it affects. It applies to corporate bonds previously under the Uniform Negotiable Instruments Act, and replaces the Uniform Stock Transfer Act with respect to share certificates, bearer shares, and bearer warrants, other statutes on the negotiability of securities, and, in many jurisdictions, the Uniform Fiduciaries Act and the Uniform Act for Simplification of Fiduciary Security Transfers. Israels, "Investment Securities as Negotiable Paper—Article 8 of the Uniform Commercial Code", 13 Bus.Law. 676 (1958). See sections 155, 176–178 infra.

17. E. g., Uniform Fiduciaries Act, Uniform Fraudulent Conveyance Act, Uniform Principal and Income Act, Uniform Gifts to Minors Act, Uniform Securities Act, Uniform Act for Simplification of Fiduciary Security Transfers, Uniform Disposition of Unclaimed Property Act, Uniform Division of Income for Tax Purposes Act.

18. N.Y.S.E. Company Manual; see section 316 infra.

business enterprise in Chapter 1, treats the subject in as chronological manner as possible: Selection of form of business enterprise; Nature of corporateness or corporate personality; Selection of jurisdiction of incorporation; Preincorporation problems; Incorporation, admission, and domestication; Recognition (in case of defective incorporation) or disregard of corporateness; Corporate financial structure; Corporate management structure; Special problems of close corporations; Special problems of larger corporations, especially those whose securities are publicly-held; Dividends and other distributions; Extraordinary corporate matters; Corporate litigation, including derivative actions; Corporate liquidation, arrangement, and reorganization.

Chapter 1 constitutes a brief introduction, ending with a summary of the laws affecting business enterprises, federal and state, and substatutory intracorporate provisions.

Thereafter the treatment is as chronological as the subject matter permits.

Chapter 2 explores the problem of selecting the most suitable form of enterprise for the business involved from among the available forms—individual proprietorship, types of partnership and forms related thereto, joint venture, joint-stock association, business trust, corporation, and professional corporation or association—and the permissible variations possible within each form, outlining the more relevant considerations—theoretical and functional, nontax and tax—in the process. Suitable introduction to the law of partnership is included.

Chapter 3 is more theoretical in approach, attempting to define the nature of corporateness or corporate personality by first summarizing the theories and traditional attributes of corporateness and then applying such theories to problems involving the status of the corporation in the legal system as a person, domiciliary, resident, citizen, national, or the state.

Chapter 4 reverts from the theoretical approach to the functional approach, discussing the practical considerations involved in selecting the jurisdiction of incorporation.

Chapter 5 treats preincorporation problems. It begins by defining promoters and their duties inter se to the corporation, and to third parties. Then it discusses the various difficulties involved in preincorporation "agreements", including preincorporation subscriptions, resulting from the rule that a nonexistent corporation cannot be a party to a contract or even the recipient of an offer.

Chapter 6 takes up incorporation procedures. The various steps in the incorporation process are listed, followed by summaries of the factors involved in drafting the articles of incorporation, bylaws, and share certificates, and holding organization meetings. Admission and domestication procedures of a foreign corporation qualifying to do business in a jurisdiction other than its jurisdiction of incorporation are also outlined.

Chapter 7 discusses the recognition or disregard of corporateness from two opposite poles: (1) When the courts recognize the attributes of corporateness in the case of defective incorporation, and (2) When they disregard corporateness ("pierce the corporate veil"; "disregard the corporate fiction") in the case of technically-correct incorporation.

Chapter 8 explores the corporate financial structure—debt securities and shares. After the various types of debt securities are outlined, the nature of shares is explored, followed by analysis of the distinctions between par value shares and shares without par value, the creation of classes of shares, voting rights, dividend rights, liquidation rights, preemptive rights, and redemption, conversion, and other features. Share subscriptions, share options, and shareholders' liabilities for payment for shares are included. The special financial problems of close corporations and of larger corporations, and systematic treatment of dividends and other distributions, are left to later chapters.

Chapter 9 charts the corporate management structure, and the respective management functions of the incorporators, shareholders, board of directors, and officers and other corporate agents. The statutes, judicially-recognized fiduciary duties, frequently-encountered substatutory provisions, and corporate practice are analyzed. Compensation for management and incidentally other corporate personnel is also discussed. The special managerial and control problems of close corporations and of larger corporations are reserved for more systematic treatment in Chapters 10 and 11, respectively.

Chapter 10 concentrates on the special problems of close corporations stemming from the fact that the same statutes and often the same "statutory norms" control the corporate leviathan and the one-man corporation and "incorporated partnership". From the point of view of incorporation, financial structure, management structure, "shareholder" agreements, share transfer restrictions, arbitration, and dissolution, permissible ways of combining in the corporate form various advantages of the partnership and of the corporation are suggested.

Chapter 11 highlights the special problems of larger corporations, especially those whose securities are offered to the public and may be traded publicly, either on a securities exchange or "over-the-counter", or whose activities might engender antitrust or trade regulation problems. Emphasis here is on the various federal statutes administered by the Securities and Exchange Commission, state "blue sky" laws, federal and state antitrust and trade regulation, and securities exchange requirements.

Chapter 12 is on dividends and other distributions. It sets the stage by reviewing applicable accounting principles and practices and then compares the various rules defining the funds legally available for dividends and other distributions and their application, and by analogy, the rules applicable to a corporation's redeeming or purchasing its own shares. The various possible dividend rights of shareholders are contrasted. Some special distribution problems, including tax aspects, are also raised.

Chapter 13 takes up various extraordinary corporate actions and transactions which are usually beyond the managerial functions of the board of directors and require shareholder approval: sale of assets not in the regular course of business, amendments of the articles of incorporation (including reclassification), merger, consolidation, and dissolution. The approach is fourfold, treating (a) the extent to which the transaction is authorized by law; (b) the required intracorporate procedures; (c) the equitable limitations involved; and (d) appraisal and other remedies of dissenting shareholders.

Chapter 14 summarizes the subject of corporate litigation, including derivative actions, distinguishing them from direct actions by shareholders and discussing their several unique and sometimes paradoxical features.

Chapter 15 witnesses the end of corporate existence by liquidation, outside of and in bankruptcy, and the possibilities of rehabilitation of corporations in financial difficulties by means of corporate arrangements or reorganization under the Federal Bankruptcy Act.

STATUTORY AND NONSTATUTORY MATERIALS

3. While statutes, primarily the Uniform Partnership Act, the Uniform Limited Partnership Act, and the applicable corporation statutes, are the backbone of business associations law, certain large and important areas remain almost exclusively the subject of case law development. Included are the permissible variations in the setup of close corporations in many jurisdictions, and practically the entire concept of fiduciary duties.

The backbone of business associations law are the statutes, primarily the Uniform Partnership Act,[1] the Uniform Limited Part-

nership Act,[2] and the applicable corporation statutes.[3] Up-to-date versions of the corporation statutes are readily available in Delaware Corporation Law Annotated,[4] New York Laws Affecting Business Corporations,[5] Model Business Corporation Act,[6] pamphlet copies of corporation statutes of each jurisdiction,[7] and, of course, the complete statutory compilations of the respective jurisdictions. The six-volume looseleaf Prentice-Hall Corporation service includes four volumes of annotated, up-to-date, corporate statutes of all 50 states and the District of Columbia. Recent revisions have

2. 6 U.L.A. 559 (1969), adopted in 43 states, District of Columbia, and Virgin Islands.

3. Every American jurisdiction has a general incorporation statute, usually entitled "General Corporation", "Business Corporation" or "Stock Corporation" Act or Law. The corporation statutes themselves are found in the Prentice-Hall Corporation Service and in the Corporation Manual, published annually by the United States Corporation Company; digests are found in CCH Corporation Law Guide and Martindale-Hubbell Law Directory.

4. Published biennially by Corporation Trust Company; see also E. Folk, The Red Book Digest of the New Delaware Corporation Law—1967 (Corporation Service Company, 45th ed. 1968).

5. Published annually by United States Corporation Company.

6. ALI–ABA Joint Committee on Continuing Legal Education, The Model Business Corporation Act, Revised 1969 (1969). See also Official Forms for use under the Model Business Corporation Act, Revised 1969, 1969 Addendum and Conversion Table (ALI 1970). The Model Act itself, without comments, appears in the Martindale-Hubbell Law Directory. The American Bar Foundation in 1960 completed a $175,000 project, supported by the contributions of corporations and law firms, to annotate the Model Act. Each of the some 160 annotations contains (1) the text of the Model Act provision; (2) descriptions of comparable and other statutory or constitutional provisions in the 50 states, the District of Columbia, and Puerto Rico; (3) digests of selected cases; (4) comment; (5) practically exhaustive bibliographical references; and (6) citations to relevant constitutional and statutory provisions. Model Business Corporation Act Annotated (3 vols. 1960, Supp.1962, 1964, 1966). Seward, "The Project of the American Bar Foundation to Annotate the Model Business Corporation Act and the Model Non-Profit Corporation Act", 11 Bus.Law. 4 (Apr.1956). A second edition is scheduled for 1971 publication.

1. 6 U.L.A. 1 (1969), adopted in 40 states, District of Columbia, Virgin Islands, and Guam.

7. Often obtainable without charge from corporation service companies.

improved the organization and draftsmanship of many of the statutes.

When new Business Corporation Acts were passed in Iowa, Minnesota, and the District of Columbia, the old acts were not repealed and remain applicable to many corporations, which may elect to come under the new acts. In Iowa, new corporations may be formed under the old or new act.[8] In Indiana, the old act was repealed, but existing corporations continued to be governed by it, absent an election by them to come under the new act.[9]

The statutes, basic as they are, tell only part of the story. Even in areas where the statutory coverage seems reasonably complete, judicial decisions are constantly interpreting statutory language. More importantly, certain large and significant areas have remained almost untouched by most legislatures, leaving the law in such areas to be developed by the courts as the cases happened to arise. As a result, a substantial body of case law has arisen, fairly comprehensive on many points but rather spotty on others, and in many instances not readily discoverable in the annotated statutory compilations. Typical of the matters largely delineated by cases are the extent to which a partnership may be formed with attributes different from those set forth in the partnership statute, when corporateness will be recognized in the case of defective incorporation and denied in the case of technically-correct incorporation, the permissible variations in the setup of close corporations in many jurisdictions, and practically the entire concept of fiduciary duties in their expanding ramifications under federal and state law. The more important court opinions are referred to in the text or footnotes, with special attention to case law developments since World War II.[10]

Apart from the statutes and case law, administrative rulings and regulations, including opinions of the state attorneys general, are part of the "law" of business enterprises. Relevant also might be nongovernmental rules and regulations, such as those of securities exchanges.

A Restatement of the Law of Business Associations, sponsored by the American Law Institute, was abandoned in 1932 after 24 preliminary drafts and three tentative drafts of three chapters had been prepared.

8. Iowa Bus.Corp.Act § 142 (1959); Minn.Bus.Corp. Act § 301.60 (1933); D.C.Bus.Corp.Act § 141 (1954).

9. Ind.Gen.Corp.Act § 25–245 (1929).

10. References to law review notes on the various cases are listed along with the cases in the Table of Cases Cited (Keyed to Commentary in Legal Periodicals), infra. For comprehensive bibliographies, see Association of American Law Schools, Law Books Recommended for Libraries, No. 8, Business Enterprises (1968); Henn & Feeney, "Recent Publications on Corporations and Other Business Enterprises", 5 Corp.Prac.Comm. 101, 122–150 (Aug.1963), reprinted as Special Report, "Bibliography of Corporation Texts, Publications and Other Materials", The Corporation Law and Tax Report.

B. HISTORICAL BACKGROUND

HISTORICAL BACKGROUND— IN GENERAL

4. In early recorded history, certain fundamental corporate concepts were well-developed. While the law of corporations and other forms of business enterprise is constantly in a state of flux, certain basic concepts occur and recur.

A brief survey of the historical background of business enterprises [1] is not only of cultural value. It reveals that when groups were formed because of the gregarious nature of man, the legal system had to deal with them, that some fundamental corporate concepts were well-developed even in early recorded history, that the legal solutions to social problems are as varied as the ingenuity of man, and that while the law is constantly changing in form and content, certain basic concepts occur and recur.

ANCIENT AND ROMAN LAW

5. Corporate personality, recognized to some extent as early as the Code of Hammurabi, was a concept of ancient and Roman law, which came to regard it as existing by concession of the state.

In antiquity, groups existed for various purposes and received more or less jural recognition. References to societies, for example, are found in the Code of Hammurabi (c. 2083 B.C.).

In Roman law, the republic (*"Populus Romanus"*, *"Senatus populusque Romanus"*— *"S.P.Q.R."*, *"Res publica"*) was the "original" corporation. During the early republic, groups gradually developed spontaneously: the religious *sodalitas*, the *universitas*, the

collegium (formed for diverse objects by three or more persons [1]), the governmental *municipium*, and the *societas* (a form of non-commercial as well as commercial partnership).

During the Roman Empire, the concept was fostered that corporate groups could be formed only by imperial fiat, thus assuring greater governmental control. The underlying theory was that a legal group could come into existence only by the creative touch of sovereign power. Such concept is a phenomenon common to several legal systems. The two principal offshoots of Roman law are canon law and, although the codes have broken with the past, modern civil law.

CANON LAW

6. Canon law distinguished between the "corporation sole" (composed of a single person, usually the incumbent of some ecclesiastical office) and the "corporation aggregate" (composed of several persons), and probably developed the "fiction theory"—that a corporation is an artificial legal person.

Canon law, the first offshoot of Roman law, had to deal with ecclesiastical property-holding clerics and groups, distinguishing between the "corporation sole" (composed of one person, say, the incumbent of a bishopric or other ecclesiastical office) [1] and the "corporation aggregate" (composed of several persons). By tradition, the principal theoretical contribution of canon law to corporation law was by Pope Innocent IV in the early 13th century who is said to have developed the concept of the corporation as a

---

[§ 4]

1. See Mason, "Corporation", in 3 Int'l Encyc. Soc. Sci. 396–403 (1968); Berle & Means, "Corporation", in 4 Encyc. Soc.Sci. 414–423 (1931); Burns, "Partnership", in 12 id. 3–6 (1934); Llewellyn, "Agency", in 1 id. 483–485 (1930); Williston, "A History of The Law of Business Corporations Before 1800", 2 Harv. L.Rev. 105 (1888), reprinted in revised form in 3 Select Essays in Anglo-American Legal History 195 (1909).

[§ 5]

1. M. Radin, The Legislation of the Greeks and Romans on Corporations (1909). Blackstone refers to the Roman maxim: "tres faciunt collegium". 1 Blackstone, Commentaries *457. For traditional requirement of three incorporators, see sections 131, 185 infra.

[§ 6]

1. Corporations sole are relatively rare in the United States and are not to be confused with the one-man corporation. See sections 258, 260 infra.

"persona ficta" or artificial person to be created and controlled by papal authority—analogous to the Roman imperial approach.[2] The logical application of this "fiction theory" was the legal separation of the artificial person from the natural persons composing it, and the nonimputation to the corporation of intent, *mens rea*, or any essentially human attribute, in effect making the corporation incapable of committing the torts and crimes requiring such elements.

LAW MERCHANT

7. **Agency, partnership, and corporation law developed as part of the law merchant, which was selectively absorbed into the English common law during the 18th century, but which survived as "commercial law" in the commercial codes in civil law countries.**

Even in ancient times, the needs of commerce resulted in the recognition of the usages of merchants and traders as law, often by courts composed of the merchants themselves. Over the centuries developed a body of law, known as the law merchant (*"Lex Mercatoria"*) and transcending local law, which imported uniformity and stability into commercial transactions before the rise of national courts. The early substantive law of agency, partnership, and corporations was part of the development.

On the European continent, the law merchant, often administered by separate courts, survived as a reasonably intact body of law (known as "commercial law") until the 19th century codifications which continued to preserve its integrity by the enactment of separate commercial codes, in addition to the basic civil codes.[1]

In England, the administration of the law merchant, originally by separate courts,[2]

was gradually taken over on a case-to-case basis by the common-law courts. This selective absorption of the law merchant into the common law was accelerated by Chief Justice Holt at the beginning of the 18th century and practically completed by Lord Mansfield in the latter part of the same century. Rejected in the process was the law merchant's entity theory of partnership; preserved was the concept that partnership should be limited to active cooperation in business.

Even modern legislation, such as the Uniform Partnership Act,[3] the Uniform Limited Partnership Act,[4] and the Uniform Commercial Code,[5] provides that as to matters not covered or unless displaced by the legislation, the law merchant shall govern or supplement the provisions thereof.

CIVIL LAW

8. **Modern civil law recognizes as separate entities commercial partnerships (general, limited, limited with shares) and corporations, which developed as variations of the commercial association according to the principles of contract and agency rather than by sovereign grant; has integrated regulatory features into the incorporation process; and does not have the complications of the law-equity distinction of the common-law system.**

Civil law, with its national codifications of the 19th and 20th centuries, as exemplified by the modern French, Swiss, and German Codes, is the dominant legal system of continental Europe. While these codifications vary, they have, as a result of the unifying influence of Roman law, many common features, both in concepts and in terminology.[1] Civil law has spread to many parts of the

---

[§ 6]

2. Cf. Rooney, "Maitland and the Corporate Revolution", 26 N.Y.U.L.Rev. 24, 32, 37–38 (1951).

[§ 7]

1. Thayer, "Comparative Law and the Law Merchant", 6 Brooklyn L.Rev. 139 (1936).

2. E. g., courts of piepowder, borough courts, courts of the staple. The Court of Admiralty made sever-

al unsuccessful attempts to administer the law merchant.

3. Uniform Partnership Act § 5.

4. Uniform Limited Partnership Act § 29.

5. Uniform Commercial Code § 1–103.

[§ 8]

1. R. Schlesinger, Comparative Law: Cases-Text-Materials 168–189 (2d ed. 1959).

world, including Latin America,[2] Quebec, Scotland, South Africa, and Louisiana.[3]

As one would expect from the discussion of Roman law and canon law, the corporation is a separate entity in the civil law. So also to a considerable extent are the various forms of partnership. Since the law merchant survived on the continent as a rather intact body of principles until the 19th century civil law codifications, as compared to England where it was selectively absorbed into the common law prior to 1800, commercial law remains a distinguishable body of law applicable to commercial partnerships (general, limited, limited with shares) and corporations, which developed as variations of the commercial association[4] according to the principles of contract and agency and not by sovereign grant.

As abuses developed from freedom of contract, corporate reform movements led to substantial restrictions on corporate financing and publicity requirements,[5] which were built into the incorporation process rather than superimposed as regulation, as in the United States, where federalism complicates the matter.

Civil law, of course, does not have the law-equity distinction which is unique to the common-law world, and does not have some of the peculiar remedies for the enforcement of fiduciary duties which have been developed by English and American chancery or equity courts.[6]

The civil code provisions of the western European countries are tending to become more uniform.[7]

COMMON LAW

9. Early common law recognized the corporation sole, ecclesiastical, eleemosynary and charitable corporations, municipal corporations, and domestic trade corporations, such as the medieval guilds, markets, and fairs. Perpetual existence and, in the case of the latter, monopoly privileges, were the distinguishing features. The early 17th century witnessed the development of the "concession theory", with corporateness treated as a concession of the state and therefore justifying increased state regulation and taxation. The common law limited the "entity theory" to corporations, applying the "aggregate theory" to partnerships.

Under early common law, as developed in England, the monarch was regarded as a corporation sole, as were bishops, every parson *quatenus* parson, etc. Well developed by the 14th century were ecclesiastical corporations, eleemosynary or charitable corporations (hospitals, colleges), and early types of so-called "temporal" corporations, primarily municipal (boroughs, counties, hundreds, townships). The 16th century, with urban society replacing the manor of the feudal system, wider trade, and the evolution of the

2. Eder, "Company Law in Latin America", 27 Notre Dame Law. 1, 223 (1951–52); Gladstone, "Theory and Operation of Partnerships under the Latin American Codes", 16 Tul.L.Rev. 27 (1951).

3. For a selective bibliography of civil law references to business enterprises, see R. Schlesinger, Comparative Law: Cases-Text-Materials 551–555 (2d ed. 1959).

4. Hence the various types of civil law associations are usually called societies (e. g., "sociétés" in French, "Gesellschaften" in German), qualified by appropriate phrases to indicate their type, e. g., société en nom collectif, offene Handelsgesellschaft (partnership); société en commandite simple, Kommanditgesellschaft (limited partnership); société en commandite par actions, Kommanditgesellschaft auf Aktien (limited partnership in which interests of the limited partners are represented by shares); société par actions, société anonyme (S.A.), Aktiengesellschaft (A.G.) (stock corporation); société à responsabilité limitée (Sarl), Gesellschaft mit beschränkter Haftung (GmbH) (close corporation). Germany also has the "GmbH & Co.", a special form of Kommanditgesellschaft (limited partnership) in which a GmbH is the general partner and manager.

5. R. Schlesinger, Comparative Law: Cases-Text-Materials 420–422 (2d ed. 1959).

6. R. Schlesinger, Comparative Law: Cases-Text-Materials 266–275, 409–411, 447–449 (2d ed. 1959).

7. Kohler, "The New Limited Liability Company Law of France", 24 Bus.Law. 435 (1969); Ault, "Harmonization of Company Law in the European Economic Community", 20 Hastings L.J. 77 (1968); Kohler, "The New Corporation Laws in Germany (1966) and France (1967) and the Trend Towards a Uniform Corporation Law for the Common Market", 43 Tul.L.Rev. 58 (1968).

law merchant, witnessed the development of corporations engaged in domestic trade, such as the medieval guilds, markets, and fairs.[1] These often held charters or patents,[2] enjoyed monopoly privileges and displayed occasional pageantry; their members traded on their own, and hence limited liability was immaterial. In short, the distinguishing feature was perpetual existence, often accompanied by monopoly or special privilege, and not corporate personality in the modern sense.

During the reign of the Tudors and of James I, whatever spontaneity existed in group formation tended to disappear with the reemergence of the old Roman and papal fiat theory that a corporation could only be created by proper authority—royal assent as manifested by charter or special act of Parliament[3] (except for well-established corporations like an officer or the City of London which did not fit the theory and were sanctioned as corporations by virtue of office or by prescription)—thereby justifying increased governmental control and taxation. Even Lord Coke subscribed to and advanced such views. This theory, which came to be known as the "concession theory" because corporateness is treated as a concession from the state, differs from the "fiction theory" only in emphasis, and is the cause of some strange modern consequences.

The common law never accepted the entity theory for partnerships as did the law merchant and civil law, but instead applied the aggregate theory to the partnership and limited the entity theory to the corporation.[4]

The first edition of Sir William Blackstone's *Commentaries* provides an excellent summary of English "company law" as of 1765. His treatment of corporations, constituting about one percent of the *Commentaries*, is part of his discussion of the law of "persons". Here, again, the emphasis is on corporations as "artificial persons", created by the sovereign with "perpetual succession". Mention is made of the trinitarian idea of three persons composing a corporation. Lack of mention of limited liability and business corporations (except for passing reference to trading companies) is noteworthy.[5]

Limited liability developed as a sort of afterthought. Since the corporation was a separate legal person, the corporate assets were protected against the claims of creditors of a shareholder. Limited liability of the shareholder with respect to claims of creditors of the corporation was illusory because the corporation usually (expressly and possibly impliedly) had the power to make leviations (or calls) on its shareholders for money to pay its liabilities and its creditors could derivatively assert such corporate power directly against the shareholders by a process resembling subrogation. By legal ingenuity, the corporation's power to make levies on its shareholders was expressly excluded or limited—thus achieving limited liability.

PROTOTYPES OF BUSINESS CORPORATIONS

10. In the 16th and 17th centuries, the great overseas trading companies and joint-stock companies developed in England. These

1. C. Gross, The Gild Merchant (1890); Calvert, "Some Speculation About the Law of Business Association in the Early Common Law", 9 Am.J. Legal Hist. 1 (1965); Lubasz, "The Corporate Borough in the Common Law of the Late Year-Book Period", 80 L.Q.Rev. 228 (1964).

2. Select Charters of Trading Companies, 1530–1707, 28 Selden Society (1913).

3. Incorporation was deemed part of the royal prerogative. Incorporation by special act of Parliament did not become the more common practice until the latter part of the 18th century.

4. Wang, "The Corporate Entity Concept (or Fiction Theory) in the Year Book Period", 58 L.Q.Rev. 498 (1942), 59 L.Q.Rev. 72 (1943).

5. 1 Blackstone, Commentaries *455–473.

became the prototypes for the modern business corporation.

The two closest common-law prototypes of the modern business corporation developed in the late 16th and 17th centuries: the great overseas trading companies and the joint-stock companies.[1]

Overseas Trading Companies

The overseas trading companies were chartered, and therefore known as "regulated companies", to engage in exploration, foreign trading (somewhat akin to the guild in domestic trade) and colonization, with governmental powers and trading privileges. Their precursors were the mercantile houses of the Italian and Hanseatic Leagues. Consistent with the prevailing mercantile system, they were regarded as arms of the state.

Trading at first was on one's "own bottom" or on the members' own individual accounts, but developed into trading on joint account or "joint stock". Initially the investment was for a single venture, but this was eventually replaced by more permanent investment, beginning with the example of the Dutch East India Company in 1602. The British East India Company, formed in 1600, began to issue shares on a several-voyage or several-year basis in the 1610's and on a permanent basis in the 1650's. It abolished private trading in 1692.

Many of these companies are well-known to students of history:

Russia Company (1554) (with Russian trading privileges from Czar Ivan the Terrible; an early example of recognition of a foreign corporation; first on joint stock basis)

British East India Company (1600), which acquired great power in India and prospered until 1833. Its full name was "The Governors and Companies of Merchants of London trading into the East Indies".

Virginia Company (1609) ("The Treasurer and Company of Adventurers and Planters of the City of London, for the First Colony of Virginia"), which founded the Virginia colony (and incidentally granted privileges to the Pilgrims who, however, landed elsewhere).

Massachusetts Bay Company (1629) ("The Governor and Company of the Massachusetts Bay in New England"), which founded the Massachusetts Bay colony.

Hudson's Bay Company (incorporated May 2, 1670) ("The Governor and Company of Adventurers of England Trading into Hudson's Bay")—today known as "The Bay"—Canada's third largest retailer.[2]

South Sea Company (1711) ("Governor and Company of the merchants of Great Britain, trading to the South Sea and other parts of America and for Encouragement of the Fishing")—which stimulated the company promotion and speculation mania known as the "South Sea Bubble".

The quaint names reveal the haziness of the then prevalent corporate concepts and emphasize their political tie-in. In formal setup and nomenclature not only did they resemble governmental subdivisions; in fact, some of them were. Such similarity led

---

1. W. Scott, The Constitution and Finance of English, Scottish and Irish Joint-Stock Companies to 1720 (1910–1912); Hein, "The British Business Company: Its Origins and Its Control", 15 U.Toronto L.J. 134 (1963); Holdsworth, "English Corporation Law in the 16th and the 17th Centuries", 31 Yale L.J. 382 (1922).

2. 80 Time, No. 25, 73 (Dec. 21, 1962). See also Phillips v. The Governor & Co. of Adventurers of England Trading into Hudson's Bay, 79 F.2d 971 (9th Cir. 1935); The Governor & Co. of Adventurers of England Trading into Hudson's Bay v. Hudson Bay Fur Co., 33 F.2d 801 (D.Minn.1928) (both decisions enjoining use of plaintiff's name).

Blackstone to call the corporation "this little republic".[3]

Bank of England

In 1694, the Bank of England was granted a royal charter.[4]

Joint-Stock Companies

The joint-stock companies were more informally created, either without charter or with an obsolete charter acquired from a defunct company, by contract among the members, and were unregulated by the state.

DEVELOPMENT OF ENGLISH COMPANY LAW

11. In England, the Bubble Act of 1720, for the 105 years during which it was in effect until its repeal in 1825, arrested the development of English corporations (or "companies"), and accounts for the substantial differences between the subsequent development of English company law and American corporation law. England, since 1908, has given separate statutory recognition to the close corporation (or "private company").

English company law ("company" being for most purposes the English equivalent of "corporation") can be divided into three historical periods: (a) Before the Bubble Act of 1720, (b) Between the Bubble Act of 1720 and its repeal in 1825, and (c) After the repeal of the Bubble Act in 1825.[1]

Before Bubble Act of 1720

The principal developments during this period have been traced above.[2] However, inspired by the very influential South Sea Company, the Bubble Act was enacted in 1720.[3] Poorly drafted, it was intended to eliminate the unchartered joint-stock companies, by barring them from opening their books for public subscription, presuming to act as if they were corporate bodies, pretending to make stock transferable, and pretending to act under obsolete charters. The Act and the threat of proceedings under it provided such an immediate shock to credit that it burst the "South Sea Bubble", as the then rampant speculative mania was called, causing one of the worst financial panics in history with resulting business failures throughout the country.[4]

While Bubble Act was in Effect, 1720–1825

The Bubble Act had a paradoxical effect, stimulating the very type of enterprise it was supposed to suppress. So distrustful were people of the incorporated company that charters were issued sparingly and only for such business as banking, fire and marine insurance, canal, and water enterprises. Even Adam Smith in his celebrated *Wealth of Nations* (1776) questioned whether the corporation would or should have a larger role.[5]

Meanwhile, with the chartered company so circumscribed, joint-stock companies continued to be formed by contracts (deeds of settlement) drafted to avoid the ambiguous proscriptions of the Bubble Act. The role of the lawyers became more pronounced and a sort of specialized corporate bar came into its infancy, becoming increasingly daring and imaginative as time passed without any invocation of the Bubble Act. While technically without limited liability, unincorporat-

[§ 10]
3. 1 Blackstone, Commentaries *456.

4. As of March 1, 1946, it was nationalized, its shares being transferred to the Treasury Solicitor.

[§ 11]
1. L. Gower, The Principles of Modern Company Law 21–58 (2d ed. 1957).

2. See sections 9, 10 supra.

3. Bubble Companies, etc., Act 1825, 6 Geo. 4, c. 91.

4. Ventures of the various companies included fishing for a wreck off the Irish coast; making salt water fresh; making oil from sunflower seeds; importing jackasses from Spain; "for carrying on an undertaking of great importance, but nobody to know what it is." J. Carswell, The South Sea Bubble (1960); V. Cowles, The Great Swindle: The Story of the South Sea Bubble (1960); L. Melville, The South Sea Bubble (1921); G. Erleigh, The South Sea Bubble (1933); 1 W. Scott, Joint Stock Companies to 1720, chs. XXI, XXII (1909).

5. A. Smith, Wealth of Nations 317 et seq. (Nicholson ed. 1887).

ed associations procedurally were difficult to sue and their members were sometimes difficult to identify; hence immunity in fact was often enjoyed.[6]

Such was the arrested state of English company law in 1776 when the United States declared its independence from England—a fact which largely accounts for the substantial differences between the subsequent development of English company law and American corporation law.[7]

Not until the early 19th century was the Bubble Act again invoked and then before Lord Ellenborough who refused to apply it but warned of its future enforcement. All told, nine cases under the Bubble Act were commenced. Meanwhile the pressures created by the Napoleonic Wars, the development of the railroads, and the onset of the Industrial Revolution combined to call for its repeal, which occurred in 1825.

After Repeal of Bubble Act in 1825

With the repeal of the Bubble Act in 1825, no other company legislation was immediately forthcoming until the Trading Companies Act of 1835, the more comprehensive Joint Stock Companies Act 1844 (sponsored by Gladstone as President of the Board of Trade), and Companies Clauses Consolidated Act 1845. The Limited Liability Act[8] was enacted in 1855, to be followed by a series of Companies Act revisions down to the Companies Act 1948,[9] as amended by the Companies Act 1967.[10] Meanwhile, the Partner-

ship Act 1890,[11] Limited Partnerships Act 1907,[12] and Companies (Consolidation) Act 1908[13] (recognizing the close corporation or "private company")[14] were enacted.

English incorporated companies are of four basic types: (a) registered—formed under the Companies Act, (b) statutory—formed by private bill, (c) chartered—by the Crown, and (d) "cost book companies". Of the some 10 varieties of registered companies, the three most important are the unlimited company, the company limited by guarantee, and the company limited by shares. The company limited by shares may be a "public company" or a "private company".[15]

DEVELOPMENT OF AMERICAN CORPORATION LAW

12. Historically, American corporation law can be divided into seven periods: (a) Incorporation by special legislative act; (b) General incorporation; (c) Competition among the states for the business of incorporation; (d) Superimposed federal regulatory legislation; (e) State statutory and decisional reform; (f) Emergence of federal corporation law; and (g) Increased competition among the states for the business of incorporation.

The history of American corporation law can be divided into seven periods: (a) incor-

6. A. DuBois, The English Business Company after the Bubble Act 1720–1800 (1938).

7. Gower, "Some Contrasts Between British and American Corporation Law", 69 Harv.L.Rev. 1369 (1956); Gower, "Corporation Law in England and America", 11 Bus.Law. 39 (Nov. 1955).

8. Under which registered companies—see text accompanying note 15 infra—could obtain limited liability. Limited Liability Act 1855, 19 & 20 Vict., c. 47 (requiring, inter alia, that "Limited" be added to company's name).

9. Companies Act 1948, 11 & 12 Geo. 6, c. 38.

10. Companies Act 1967, 15 & 16 Eliz. 2, c. 81.

11. Partnership Act 1890, 53 & 54 Vict., c. 39.

12. Limited Partnerships Act 1907, 7 Edw. 7, c. 24. The advantages of the private company account for the rareness of limited partnerships in England.

13. Companies (Consolidation) Act 1908, 8 Edw. 7, c. 69.

14. English private companies must have at least two but not more than 50 members (exclusive of employees and ex-employees), must have made no public offering of their securities, and must have share transfer restrictions. See section 259 infra.

15. S. Magnus & M. Estrin, Companies—Law and Practice (4th ed. 1968); S. Magnus & M. Estrin, The Companies Act, 1967 (1967); H. Farrar, Elements of Company Law (9th ed. 1967); Pennington, "Companies Act, 1967", 111 Sol.J. 707, 727 (1967). For an excellent text dealing with the Companies Act of 1948, see L. Gower, The Principles of Modern Company Law 39–58 (2d ed. 1957). See also P. Rowland, United Kingdom Corporation Tax (1965).

poration by special legislative act, (b) general incorporation, (c) competition among the states for the business of incorporation, (d) superimposed federal regulatory legislation,[1] (e) state statutory and decisional reform, (f) emergence of federal corporation law, and (g) increased competition among the states for the business of incorporation.

Special Incorporation

During the American colonial period, some of the English trading companies and a handful of native business corporations carried on business here.[2]

While the Bubble Act was extended to the "plantations", including the American colonies, in 1741, it never had any appreciable effect here. English company law was in a suspended state in 1776 under the Bubble Act; Adam Smith's pronounced views against incorporated business and Blackstone's very brief commentaries on corporations,[3] of course, circulated widely here. Only after the Revolutionary War did any real need and desire for incorporation arise.

Between the Declaration of Independence and United States Constitution, about 20 more business corporations were formed in the several states.

Under the Articles of Confederation, the federal government, with only expressly-delegated powers, had no power to incorporate.[4]

At the constitutional convention in 1787, Madison twice proposed a federal incorporation provision but the proposal was defeated. The federal government [5] enjoys no express incorporation power but has implied power to incorporate when "necessary and proper" to such express powers as the fiscal, war, interstate commerce, territorial, and seat of government (District of Columbia) powers.[6] As a result, practically all American business corporations are organized under state law.

In the decade following the Constitution, some 200 more business corporations were incorporated in the United States under special acts of state legislatures.[7] Fears of crown and monopoly made this a jealously-guarded legislative function.[8] Corruption and bribery of the state legislators, coupled with the impact of the Industrial Revolution, called for a change.

tered in Pennsylvania, its home state, and in several other states. When Pennsylvania repealed its charter in 1785, the bank secured a new charter in Delaware and again in Pennsylvania in 1787. 2 J. Davis, Essays in the Earlier History of American Corporations (1917).

5. Canada also has a federal system but under the British North American Act of 1867 the dominion government enjoys reserved powers. Corporations doing business within one province must be formed under its laws but otherwise may be formed under dominion law or the law of one of the provinces. In most other federal systems, e. g., Brazil, German Federal Republic, Mexico, corporations are formed only under federal law.

6. See, e. g., McCulloch v. Maryland, 17 U.S. (4 Wheat.) 316, 4 L.Ed. 579 (1819).

7. 2 J. Davis, Essays in the Earlier History of American Corporations 8, especially 26 (1917) (18th century charters to business corporations, classified by purposes and years); S. Livermore, Early American Land Companies; Their Influence on Corporate Development (1939).

8. Governor William Livingston of New Jersey attempted to grant a charter in 1778, whereupon the state legislature passed a resolution that the power of granting patents of incorporation, under the constitution, vested solely in the legislature, to which the governor acquiesced. 2 J. Davis, Essays in the Earlier History of American Corporations 9 (1917).

1. R. Stevens, Handbook on the Law of Private Corporations 5–10 (2d ed. 1949).

2. See generally E. Dodd, American Business Corporations Until 1860 (1954), reviewed in 40 Cornell L. Q. 631 (1955); 2 J. Davis, Essays in the Earlier History of American Corporations (1917) (four water companies, two wharf companies, two trading societies, one mutual fire insurance society); Baldwin, "American Business Corporations before 1789", in 1 Annual Rep't of American Historical Ass'n 253–274 (1902).

3. See section 9 supra.

4. Congress under the Articles of Confederation in 1781 purported to grant a charter to the Bank of North America. However, the bank was also char-

General Incorporation

North Carolina in 1795,[9] Massachusetts in 1799,[10] New York in 1811,[11] and Connecticut in 1837,[12] led the way by enacting general incorporation statutes, under whose provisions persons could form corporations without special legislative favor. The privilege at first was circumscribed with limitations and requirements as to permissible purposes, maximum authorized capital, minimum paid-in capital, par value, trust fund theory, limited duration, residence of incorporators and directors, maximum indebtedness, powers, etc.[13]

Beginning near the end of the 19th century, all American jurisdictions except Connecticut, Massachusetts, New Hampshire and, of course, the District of Columbia, ratified constitutional provisions prohibiting special incorporation and requiring incorporation under general law. Some exclude certain classes of corporations, such as charitable, educational, penal, and reformatory, from the prohibition; others make a general exception when "the objects of the corporation cannot be attained under general laws".[14]

Interstate Incorporation Competition

So long as business corporations remained local, each state was in full control of the situation. Then came the interstate railroads and increase in interstate commerce. In Paul v. Virginia,[15] the United States Supreme Court held that a state could exclude a foreign corporation from engaging in intrastate commerce within the state or could attach reasonable conditions to the permission given such corporation to carry on such business. The corollary of this holding was that a state had no power to exclude a foreign corporation from doing interstate business.

Now interstate enterprises could shop for the most favorable state of incorporation, and some of the smaller states began to "liberalize" or "modernize" their corporation laws in "charter-mongering" competition or, stated more euphemistically, "to meet the needs of modern business." [16] New Jersey became the first "mother of corporations" in 1875. Maine too was an early forerunner;

---

9. Limited to the formation of corporations for the purpose of cutting canals.

10. Limited to the formation of aqueduct corporations. The Massachusetts Manufacturing Corporations Act of 1809 provided for regulations applicable to all manufacturing corporations formed thereafter by special charters. E. Dodd, American Business Corporations Until 1860, 228 (1954).

11. N.Y. Laws 1811, ch. 67. Five or more persons could incorporate to manufacture textiles, glass, metals and paint by filing a certificate of incorporation setting forth the corporate name, its location, objects, capitalization, number of shares, and the names and addresses of its first board of directors. Capital was limited to $100,000; corporate duration was limited to 20 years; shareholders were subject to additional liability for the benefit of creditors if assets on dissolution were insufficient to discharge liabilities.

12. Formation of corporations for "any lawful purpose". Not until 1866 did New York enact a similar provision.

13. See notes 9–11 supra; see also Brandeis, J., dissenting in Louis K. Liggett Co. v. Lee, 288 U.S. 517, 548–564, 53 S.Ct. 481, 490–496, 77 L.Ed. 929, 944–953, 85 A.L.R. 699, 714–723 (1933) (history of early incorporation statutes).

14. E. g., N.Y.Const. art. X, § 1. Instances of special incorporation thereunder include the General Electric Co. in 1892 to prevent its migration to New Jersey, whose general incorporation statute was more favorable, and the College Retirement Equities Fund (variable annuity company) in 1952.

15. 75 U.S. (8 Wall.) 168, 19 L.Ed. 357 (1868).

16. Relaxation involved the acceptance of property or services in addition to cash as consideration for shares, abolition of maximum capitalization and indebtedness, broadening of permissible purposes and powers, including power to acquire shares in other corporations, denial of preemptive rights, authorization of nonvoting shares and shares without par value, and broad authorization for charter amendments. To prevent the new District of Columbia statute from competing with Delaware, the United States senators from Delaware insisted that the statute require that District of Columbia corporations conduct their principal business in the District. Such requirement has been held inapplicable to District of Columbia corporations incorporated under the prior District incorporation statute. Murphy v. Washington American League Baseball Club, Inc., 167 F.Supp. 215 (D.D.C.1958), aff'd 105 U.S.App.D.C. 378, 267 F.2d 655 (1959), cert. denied 361 U.S. 837, 80 S.Ct. 89, 4 L.Ed.2d 77 (1959).

Delaware followed in 1899 by adopting a statute based on the New Jersey statute and has been second to none ever since—a policy advanced in the 1967–1969 revisions of the Delaware General Corporation Law. New York, to prevent corporate migration across the Hudson River to New Jersey, gave General Electric special legislative incorporation in 1892, and later liberalized its general incorporation statutes. Governor Woodrow Wilson took New Jersey out of the competition by his antitrust measures known as the "Seven Sisters Acts" in 1913.

One means urged to correct these abuses was a Uniform Business Corporation Act, recommended after many years of study by the National Conference of Commissioners on Uniform State Laws in 1928. Adopted by only a few states, it served as source material for important revisions in California (1929–33), Illinois (1933), Michigan (1931), Minnesota (1933), and Pennsylvania (1933). From 1943 until it was withdrawn in 1958, it was called the "Model Business Corporation Act"—not to be confused with the model statute of the same name drafted by the corporate laws committee of the American Bar Association.

Corporations increasingly amassed power within and without their jurisdiction of incorporation. With theoretical perpetual existence they often tended to become autonomous self-perpetuating oligarchies.

Superimposed Federal Regulatory Legislation

From time to time more federal control over the formation of corporations has been urged in the form of either a federal incorporation statute [17] or an interstate compact for uniform corporate legislation supplemented by a federal licensing act. [18]

Federal intervention instead has mainly taken the form of superimposed regulatory legislation, antitrust and trade regulation, labor laws, and securities regulation, as well as corporate reorganization and taxing statutes.

State Statutory and Decisional Reform

Following World War II, a rather widespread movement for corporate legislative revision developed in many jurisdictions, [19] gathering momentum in the 1950's–1960's which witnessed general revisions becoming effective in Wisconsin (1951), Oregon (1953), Florida (1953), District of Columbia (1954), [20] Texas (1955), [21] North Carolina

---

17. In 1943, the American Bar Association Committee on Business Corporations drafted a suggested Federal Corporation Act in case there should be a serious demand for such legislation.

18. Stevens, "Uniform Corporation Laws through Interstate Compacts and Federal Legislation", 34 Mich.L.Rev. 1063 (1936).

19. The avowed conception behind these revisions has been simplification and modernization consistent with sound regulatory and protective policy, but the implementation has varied widely and sometimes paradoxically. Sowards & Mofsky, "Factors Affecting the Development of Corporation Law", 23 U. Miami L.Rev. 476 (1969); Folk, "Corporation Statutes: 1959–1966", 1966 Duke L.J. 875; Latty, "Why Are Business Corporation Laws Largely 'Enabling'?", 50 Cornell L.Q. 599 (1965); Symposium: "The New Look in Corporation Law", 23 Law & Contemp. Prob. 175 (1958); Emerson & Latcham, "Law and the Future: Corporation Law", 51 Nw.U. L.Rev. 196 (1956); Luce, "Trends in Modern Corporation Legislation", 50 Mich.L.Rev. 1291 (1952); see also Rutledge, "Significant Trends in Modern Incorporation Statutes", 3 U.Pitt.L.Rev. 273 (1937), 22 Wash.U.L.Q. 305 (1937). Most of the new corporation statutes repeal the old law and apply both to preexisting and to new corporations; others provide for a transitional period, during which existing corporations may elect to come thereunder and at the end of which the old law is repealed and existing corporations automatically become subject to the new law, but require new corporations from the start to be formed under the new law. Iowa is unique in allowing new corporations to be formed under either the new or the old law; existing domestic corporations may elect to come under the new law. Iowa Bus.Corp.Act § 142 (1959).

20. See Philipson, "District of Columbia Business Corporation Act Amendments of 1963", 30 D.C.B. Ass'n J. 508 (1963).

21. Carrington, "The Texas Business Corporation Act As Enacted and Ten Years Later", 43 Texas L.

(1955), Virginia (1956),[22] Puerto Rico (1956), North Dakota (1957), Alaska (1957), Colorado (1958), Alabama (1959), Iowa (1959), Connecticut (1959),[23] Wyoming (1961),[24] Utah (1962),[25] Mississippi (1963), Alaska (1963), New York (1963), Nebraska (1963),[26] South Carolina (1964),[27] South Dakota (1965),[28] Massachusetts (1965),[29] Missouri (1965),[30] Pennsylvania (1966), Arkansas (1966),[31] Washington (1967),[32] Maryland (1967), Delaware (1967), Indiana (1967),[33] New Mexico (1968), Montana (1968), Louisiana (1969),[33a] New Jersey (1969), Georgia (1969),[34] Tennessee (1969),[34a] Connecticut (1969), Massachusetts (1969), and Rhode Island (1970).[34b]

Such legislation has not only reorganized and simplified the corporation statutes, but, at least until 1967, had also attempted to balance more fairly the interests of shareholders, management, and employees and the public interest.

Meanwhile, case law has been enhancing business morality by increased recognition of the fiduciary duties of directors, officers, and controlling shareholders.[35]

Among the most significant corporate statutory revisions were the 1947 revisions of the California Corporations Code with its regulatory features built into both the General Corporation Law and the Corporate Securities Law;[36] the 1955 North Carolina revision of the Business Corporation Act with

Rev. 609 (1965); Comment, "The First Five Years Under the Texas Business Corporation Act", 12 Baylor L.Rev. 401 (1960).

22. Gibson & Freeman, "A Decade of the Model Business Corporation Act in Virginia", 53 Va.L. Rev. 1396 (1967).

23. Cross, "Stock Corporation Act—A Review of the First Five Years", 40 Conn.B.J. 564 (1966); Cooper, "New Connecticut Corporation Laws", 34 Conn.B.J. 225 (1960).

24. Rudolph, "New Wyoming Business Corporation Act", 15 Wyo.L.J. 185 (1961).

25. Note, "The Transition to the Model Business Corporation Act in Utah", 9 Utah L.Rev. 689 (1965).

26. Symposium: "Nebraska State Bar Association Institute on Corporation Law, The Nebraska Business Corporation Act", 43 Neb.L.Rev. 296 (1963); Comment, "Nebraska Corporation Law in Light of the American Bar Association's Model Business Corporation Act", 39 Neb.L.Rev. 575 (1960).

27. Symposium of South Carolina Corporation Law, 15 S.C.L.Rev. 275 (1963); Folk, "The Model Act and South Carolina Corporation Law Revision", 18 Bus.Law. 351 (1963).

28. See Clark, "South Dakota's General Incorporation Law—Need for Revision", 9 S.D.L.Rev. 72 (1964).

29. Casey "The New Business Corporation Law", 50 Mass.L.Q. 201 (1965); Hosmer, "New Business Corporation Law", in 1964 Annual Survey of Massachusetts Law 3; Note, "Massachusetts Corporate Provisions", 6 B.C.Ind. & Com.L.Rev. 226 (1965).

30. See Erbacker, "A Current Look at the Corporate Law Field in Missouri", 31 U.Kan.City L.Rev. 278 (1963).

31. Symposium: "Arkansas Business Corporation Act", 21 Ark.L.Rev. 455 (1968); "Institute on Arkansas Corporation Law", 17 id. 347 (1964).

32. Kummert, "The Financial Provisions of the New Washington Business Corporation Act", 41 Wash.L. Rev. 207 (1966); Comment, "The Model Business Corporation Act—An Appropriate Starting Place", 38 Wash.L.Rev. 538 (1963).

33. Deer & Burus, "The 1967 Amendments to the Indiana General Corporation Act", 43 Ind.L.J. 14 (1967).

33a. Miller, "The 1968 Business Corporation Law of Louisiana", 29 La.L.Rev. 435 (1969).

34. Hodgson, "Proposed for Georgia—A Business Corporation Act", 4 Ga.St.B.J. 193 (1967); O'Neal, "Georgia's Urgent Need for a Modern Corporation Statute", 3 Ga.St.B.J. 265 (1967); Cohn & Leavell, "Georgia's Corporation Law: Is It Adequate?", 2 Ga.St.B.J. 153 (1965).

34a. "The New Tennessee General Corporation Act: A Symposium", 36 Tenn.L.Rev. 324 (1969); "New Corporation Laws: Georgia and Tennessee", 25 Corp.J. 411 (1969).

34b. "Rhode Island's New Corporation Law", 26 Corp.J. 55 (1969–70).

35. See sections 235–241 infra.

36. Buhler, "1947 California Corporation Code, and Other Corporation Legislation", 35 Calif.L.Rev. 423 (1947); Sterling, "Modernizing California Corporation's Laws", 12 Wis.L.Rev. 453 (1937). See G. Sterling & D. Pearce, Ballantine and Sterling California Corporation Laws (4th ed. 1962) (2 vols. loose-leaf); Advising California Business Enterprises (1958); N. Schlei, State Regulation of Corporate Financial Practices: The California Experience (1962).

its statutory treatment of many new aspects, regulatory provisions, and express accommodation to the special problems of close corporations;[37] and the 1957–1968 New York revisions of the corporation laws, resulting in the replacement, so far as business corporations are concerned, of the General Corporation Law and Stock Corporation Law by the new Business Corporation Law.[38]

Since 1967, some of the corporate law revisions have become increasingly "permissive".[39]

Considerable credit for the revisions has been due the example of the Model Business Corporation Act, as evidenced by the fact

that most of the revisions have substantially followed one or more versions of that Act in whole or part.[40]

Emergence of Federal Corporation Law

The federal regulatory legislation superimposed on state corporate laws in the 1930's has resulted in a growing body of federal corporation law, starting some 20 years ago and burgeoning in recent years.

Federal court determination of litigation involving corporate disputes is nothing new.

---

37. Folk, "Revisiting the North Carolina Corporation Law: The Robinson Treatise Reviewed and the Statute Reconsidered", 43 N.C.L.Rev. 768 (1965); Latty, "Close Corporations and the North Carolina Business Corporation Act", 34 N.C.L.Rev. 432 (1956); Powers, "Drafting a Corporation Code for North Carolina", 10 Ark.L.Rev. 37 (1955–56); Latty, "Pseudo-Foreign Corporations", 65 Yale L.J. 137 (1955); Latty, Powers & Breckenridge, "Proposed North Carolina Business Corporation Act", 33 N.C. L.Rev. 26 (1954). See R. Robinson, North Carolina Corporation Law and Practice with Forms (1964).

38. Hornstein, Appendix 1, "Analysis of Business Corporation Law", and Henn, Appendix 3, "Informational Summary", in 2 N.Y.Bus.Corp.Law 441–585 (McKinney 1963); C. Israels, Corporate Practice (PLI 2d ed. 1969); I. Kantrowitz & S. Slutsky, White on New York Corporations (13th ed. 1963–); Andrews, "The New York Business Corporation Law", 27 Albany L.Rev. 202 (1963), 28 id. 45 (1964); Latty, "The New Business Corporation Law of New York", 1962 J.Bus.L. 406; Lesher, "Introduction to Symposium on New York Business Corporation Law", 11 Buffalo L.Rev. 429 (1962); Henn, "The Philosophies of the New York Business Corporation Law of 1961", 11 id. 439; de Capriles, "New York Business Corporation Law: Article 5—Corporate Finance", 11 id. 461; Stevens, "Close Corporations and the New York Business Corporation Law of 1961", 11 id. 481; Hoffman, "The Status of Shareholders and Directors Under New York's Business Corporation Law: A Comparative View", 11 id. 496; Latty, "Some General Observations on the New Business Corporation Law of New York", 11 id. 591; Stevens, "New York Business Corporation Law of 1961", 47 Cornell L.Q. 141 (1962); Hoffman, "New Horizons for the Close Corporation in New York under Its New Business Corporation Law", 28 Brooklyn L.Rev. 1 (1961); de Capriles & McAniff, "The Financial Provisions of the New (1961) New York Business Corporation Law", 36 N.Y.U.L.Rev. 1239 (1961). See also Interim Reports to 1957–1969 Sessions of New York State Legislature.

39. See notes 51, 52 infra.

40. The Model Business Corporation Act is "enabling", "permissive", and "liberal", as distinguished from "regulatory" and "paternalistic". See Preface to 1953 Revision of Model Business Corporation Act:

> The Act has been prepared as an enabling statute under which a corporation may be organized and continue to exist, controlling its internal affairs and determining its relation with the state of its creation while its existence continues. It is not, and is not intended to be, a statute regulating its business or external affairs. Regulation as such is regarded as the province of other statutes.

See Folk, "The Model Act and the South Carolina Corporation Law Revision", 18 Bus.Law. 351 (1963); Katz, "The Philosophy of Midcentury Corporation Statutes", 23 Law & Contemp.Prob. 177 (1958); Jennings, "The Role of the States in Corporate Regulation and Investor Protection", 23 id. 193; Emerson, "Vital Weaknesses in the New Virginia Stock Corporation Law and the Model Act", 42 Va.L.Rev. 489 (1956); Harris, "The Model Business Corporation Act—Invitation to Irresponsibility?", 50 Nw.U.L. Rev. 1 (1955); Comment, "The Model Business Corporations Act—'An Appropriate Starting Place' ", 38 Wash.L.Rev. 538 (1963). See Model Business Corporation Act Annotated (3 vols. 1960, Supp.1962, 1964, 1966), described in section 3, n. 6 supra. The earlier versions of the Model Business Corporation Act "discarded many of the liberal provisions found in states that have been bidding for corporate business." (Preface to 1950 Revision). The principal draftsmen were members of the Chicago Bar and the initial draft reflected the Illinois Business Corporation Act which in turn benefited from the Uniform Business Corporation Act. Subsequently, as the corporate laws committee increased its representation of eastern lawyers, optional, and alternative sections were added. Indicative of the changing attitudes was the active cooperation of the committee with the Delaware revisers and the joint drafting of a section entitled "Indemnification of Officers, Directors, Employees and Agents; Insurance"—Del.Gen.Corp.Law § 145 (1967); ABA–ALI Model Bus.Corp.Act § 4A. This section has been called "America's most advanced provision for indemnification of officers and directors." E. Folk, The Red Book Digest of the New Delaware Corporation Law—1967, iv (Corporation Service Company, 45th ed. 1968).

Where federal jurisdiction existed, such as diversity-of-citizenship or occasional federal question or pendent jurisdiction, federal courts have long decided such cases.

Relevant in federal court cases involving federal or nonfederal matters were the Federal Judicial Code and any applicable federal procedural or equity rules.[41] Federal substantive law applied to federal matters. Even in diversity-of-citizenship cases, as to nonfederal matters, in the absence of controlling state statute, substantive federal "common law" was applied.[42]

Reversal came in 1938, with the concurrence of two events: (a) The United States Supreme Court holding in Erie R. R. v. Tompkins [43] that a federal court in a diversity-of-citizenship case must apply the substantive law of the forum; and (b) The Court's promulgation of the Federal Rules of Civil Procedure. Henceforth the federal courts were to follow the Federal Rules as to "procedural" matters and in diversity-of-citizenship cases, the state law of the forum as to "substantive" matters.[44]

Then, beginning 1947,[45] violations of various federal statutes, were held to afford implied private rights of action in favor of persons harmed by such violations. The earlier cases arose under Rule 10b–5, promulgated by the Securities and Exchange Commission in 1942 under the Federal Securities Exchange Act, 1934, prohibiting fraud in con-

nection with the purchase or sale of any security using interstate commerce, the mails, or a national securities exchange.[46]

Later cases included violations of the S.E.C. Proxy Rules, offering full federal relief against extraordinary and other corporate matters where shareholder or other approval therefor was secured by proxy solicitations in violation of the S.E.C. Proxy Rules.[47]

The 1964 amendments of the Federal Securities Exchange Act doubled the number of corporations subject to the S.E.C. registration, disclosure, and reporting requirements; the S.E.C. Proxy Rules; and insider trading restrictions.

Implied private rights of action have also been recognized under the Federal Investment Company Act, 1940.[48]

For violations under the post-1933 federal securities regulation statutes, and S.E.C. rules and regulations thereunder, the federal courts have exclusive jurisdiction.

Thus entry to the federal courts under such statutes is possible under the Federal Judicial Code because the case is one "arising under . . . the laws of the United States," regardless of diversity-of-citizen-

---

41. E.g., Hawes v. Oakland, 104 U.S. 450, 26 L.Ed. 827 (1882).

42. Swift v. Tyson, 41 U.S. (16 Pet.) 1, 10 L.Ed. 865 (1842).

43. 304 U.S. 64, 58 S.Ct. 817, 82 L.Ed. 1188, 114 A.L. R. 1487 (1938).

44. See Guaranty Trust Co. of New York v. York, 326 U.S. 99, 65 S.Ct. 1464, 89 L.Ed. 2079, 160 A.L. R. 1231 (1945), reh. denied 326 U.S. 806, 66 S.Ct. 7, 90 L.Ed. 491 (1945) (application of "outcome determinative test" deeming "substantive" rule which would substantially determine outcome of litigation).

45. Kardon v. Nat'l Gypsum Co., 73 F.Supp. 798 (E. D.Pa.1947), supplemented 83 F.Supp. 613 (E.D.Pa. 1947).

46. Fleischer, " 'Federal Corporation Law': An Assessment", 78 Harv.L.Rev. 1146 (1965); Friendly, "In Praise of Erie—and of the New Federal Common Law", 19 Record of N.Y.C.B.A. 64 (1964); Panel Discussion: "The Emergence of 'Federal Corporation Law' and Federal Control of Inside Information", 34 U.Mo.Kan. City L.Rev. 228 (1966); Painter, "Inside Information: Growing Pains for the Development of Federal Corporation Law under Rule 10b–5", 65 Colum.L.Rev. 1361 (1965); Note, "Securities Regulation—Rule 10b–5—A Federal Corporations Law?", 43 N.C.L.Rev. 637 (1965).

47. J. I. Case Co. v. Borak, 377 U.S. 426, 84 S.Ct. 1555, 12 L.Ed.2d 423 (1964) (action by shareholder); Studebaker Corp. v. Allied Products Corp., 256 F. Supp. 173 (W.D.Mich.1966) (action by corporation).

48. Compare Brown v. Bullock, 294 F.2d 415 (2d Cir. 1961), with Brouk v. Managed Funds, Inc., 286 F.2d 901 (8th Cir. 1961), cert. granted 366 U.S. 958, 81 S. Ct. 1921, 6 L.Ed.2d 1252 (1961), judgment vacated and case remanded with directions to dismiss 369 U.S. 424, 82 S.Ct. 878, 8 L.Ed.2d 6 (1962); Eisenberg & Lehr, "An Aspect of the Emerging 'Federal Corporation Law': Directorial Responsibility Under the Investment Company Act of 1940", 20 Rutgers L.Rev. 181 (1966).

ship. Not only do the Federal Rules govern the procedural aspects,[49] but as to such violations of federal law, federal substantive law applies. Federal provisions for service of process, which often also incorporate by reference state-law service-of-process provisions, facilitate securing in personam jurisdiction over the defendants, sometimes by nationwide service. Broad federal venue provisions offer a wide choice of forums, including more sophisticated federal district courts and courts of appeals.

Concerning such aspects as statutes of limitations, burden of proof, and contemporaneous-share-ownership, demand on board of directors and shareholders, security for expenses, and settlement in shareholder derivative actions, state law requirements are inapplicable.

Finally, the probably stricter federal standards for the conduct of corporate directors, officers, and other personnel often result in liabilities which would not be imposed under state law.

Under pendent jurisdiction, the original federal jurisdiction based on a federal claim extends to any substantial nonfederal claim sufficiently related to the federal claim, and survives dismissal on the merits of the federal claim. While the Federal Judicial Code and Federal Rules of Civil Procedure apply, quaere as to the application of other federal laws.[50]

49. Hanna v. Plumer, 380 U.S. 460, 85 S.Ct. 1136, 14 L.Ed.2d 8 (1965) (Federal Rules of Civil Procedure deemed prima facie "procedural" and, if covering situation, applicable even in diversity-of-citizenship cases even though determining outcome); Siegel, "The Federal Rules in Diversity Cases: *Erie* Implemented, Not Retarded", 54 A.B.A.J. 172 (1968); Zabin, "The Federal Rules in Diversity Cases: *Erie* in Retreat", 53 A.B.A.J. 266 (1967).

50. Shakman, "The New Pendent Jurisdiction of the Federal Courts", 20 Stan.L.Rev. 262 (1968); Lowenfels, "Pendent Jurisdiction and the Federal Securities Acts", 67 Colum.L.Rev. 474 (1967); Comment, "The Expanding Scope of Federal Pendent Jurisdiction", 34 Tenn.L.Rev. 413 (1966); Annot., 5 A.L.R.3d 1040 (1966).

Increased Interstate Incorporation Competition

Delaware, in 1967, revised its General Corporation Law of 1935. The new law, while using the old law as a framework and preserving much of its traditional language, is far more "permissive" in practically every respect than the corporation statute of any other jurisdiction.[51] Besides making Dela-

51. General Corporation Law of Delaware, Preface (The Corporation Trust Company) (1967). ("The State of Delaware has a long history as the domicile of nationally known corporations, and has traditionally provided a favorable climate for corporations. The official attitude of the Legislature and administrative officers of Delaware has consistently been one of sympathetic understanding of the problems of the corporate organization. New developments in the corporation law field have been quickly adopted to keep the law modern, and the existing law has been constantly improved and clarified upon the advice and with the cooperation of the Delaware Bar.

. . . Unlike many states which have discarded their old laws and substituted completely new ones in their place, the Delaware legislators have used the existing law as a framework upon which to build the new. Many new and modern concepts have been adopted; certain provisions have been revised to reflect court decisions and modern corporate practice; outmoded provisions have been revised or repealed; obscure provisions have been clarified and complex ones simplified. The result is a corporation law adapted to the needs of the day, a law which retains the well settled principles of corporate flexibility and freedom which have always been the chief characteristics and attractions of the Delaware Corporation Law."); E. Folk, The Red Book Digest of the New Delaware Corporation Law—1967, 1 (Corporation Service Company, 45th ed. 1968).

"The new Delaware General Corporation Law, signed by the Governor on July 3, 1967 and taking effect at once, represents a major revision of the classic statute under which thousands of corporations have organized and operated for years. This recasting of the Delaware law is unique among statutory revisions in this country. On the one hand, the new law retains much of the traditional language of the Delaware statute. In this way, the great body of judicial decisions interpreting the statute remains in full effect. Thus, the new Delaware law preserves the certainty and predictability which traditionally have been among its major features. On the other hand, by including many of the newest ideas in corporation statutes, the Delaware law has been modernized and can now deal effectively with today's corporation problems. The Delaware law is therefore a unique blend both of the certainty and predictability resulting from its continuity of language, and of the flexibility associated with its new provisions. Today—even more than in the past—

ware even more attractive as a state of incorporation for larger corporations, the new law includes a subchapter available to close corporations.

New Jersey, the "mother of corporations" before Delaware, disturbed by the migration of some of its important corporations to Delaware, revised its corporate statute in 1968

to make it more attractive to corporate management. In 1967–1969, the Model Act underwent revisions to make it more "permissive".[52]   Not to be outdone, the Delaware bar in 1969 approved further amendments to the Delaware General Corporation Law of 1967, which were promptly enacted by the Delaware legislature.[53]

C. LAWS AND PROVISIONS AFFECTING BUSINESS ENTERPRISES

FEDERAL LAWS AFFECTING BUSINESS ENTERPRISES

13. **Business enterprises are usually formed under state law, but federal laws also increasingly apply to them. Relevant are the United States Constitution (with no express but with implied incorporation powers), federal laws made in pursuance thereof, treaties made under the authority of the United States, and various federal statutes and administrative regulations enacted pursuant to the federal taxation and other fiscal powers, powers over interstate commerce and the mails, and bankruptcy powers, including corporate reorganization powers.**

Although most business enterprises are formed under state law, federal laws also increasingly apply to them.

The United States Constitution contains several provisions which affect business enterprises. Under the aggregate theory, the

members of an association, as distinguished from the association as an entity, are usually the foci of attention for purposes of the various constitutional provisions. However, under the entity theory, the corporation as such sometimes enjoys constitutional status. This will be discussed more fully in the treatment of the nature of corporateness or corporate personality and the problems of assigning the corporation an appropriate position in the legal system.[1]   The more relevant federal constitutional provisions include:

(a) Requirement that direct taxes be apportioned among the several states according to population;[2]

(b) Powers of Congress to tax, pay debts, and borrow money; to regulate interstate and foreign commerce; to establish uniform laws on the subject of bankruptcies throughout the United States; to establish post offices, etc.; to declare war, etc.; to exercise exclusive jurisdiction over the District of Columbia and all places purchased

the practicing attorney from every state will find that the Delaware corporation statute affords his clients the very best which American corporation law can offer."); S. Arsht & W. Stapleton, Analysis of the New Delaware Corporation Law (Prentice-Hall, Inc. (1967); Arsht & Stapleton, "Delaware's New General Corporation Law: Substantive Changes", 23 Bus.Law. 75 (1967); Comment, "Vestiges of Shareholder Rights under the New Delaware Corporation Law", 57 Geo.L.J. 599 (1969). Actively collaborating with the Delaware revisers were the corporate law committees of the American Bar Association and of the Association of the Bar of the City of New York. Enactment of some of the Delaware provisions by other states has not only been urged but effected. See Canby, "Delaware's New Corporation Law", 39 Penn.B.A.Q. 380 (1968); Comment, "Law for Sale: A Study of the Delaware Corporation Law of 1967", 117 U.Pa.L. Rev. 861 (1969).

52. Scott, "Changes in the Model Business Corporation Act", 24 Bus.Law. 291 (1968).

53. E. Folk, Amendments to the Delaware General Corporation Law (Effective July 15, 1969) and Technical Amendment Act (Effective January 2, 1968) (Corporation Service Company 1969); Arsht & Stapleton, "Delaware General Corporation Law: 1969", 25 Bus.Law. 287 (1969).

1. See sections 80–91 infra.

2. U.S.Const. art. I, § 2, cl. 3. See notes 4, 22 infra.

for the erection of needful buildings; and to make all laws necessary and proper for carrying into execution the foregoing powers; [3]

(c) Prohibition against any direct tax unless apportioned; [4]

(d) Prohibition against tax or duty laid on articles exported from any state;[5]

(e) Prohibition against state impairment of the obligation of contracts;[6]

(f) Prohibition against state, without consent of Congress, laying any imposts or duties on imports or exports, except what may be absolutely necessary for executing its inspection laws; [7]

(g) Prohibition against state without consent of Congress, laying any duty of tonnage or entering into any agreement or compact with another state;[8]

(h) Federal judicial power over all cases arising under Constitution, laws of United States, treaties, controversies to which United States is party; controversies between two or more states; controversies between state and citizens of another state; and controversies between citizens of different states;[9]

(i) Requirement that each state give full faith and credit to the public acts, records, and judicial proceedings of every other state; [10]

(j) Rights of citizens of each state to all privileges and immunities of citizens in the several states;[11]

(k) Power of Congress to legislate respecting federal territory or other property; [12]

(l) Supremacy of United States Constitution, federal laws made in pursuance thereof, and treaties made under the authority of the United States;[13]

(m) Prohibition against federal violation of the right of the people to be secure against unreasonable searches and seizures; [14]

(n) Prohibition against self-incrimination and against federal deprivation of any person of life, liberty, or property, without due process of law;[15]

(o) Preservation of right of trial by jury in suits at common law where value in controversy exceeds $20;[16]

3. U.S.Const. art. I, § 8, cl. 1, 2, 3, 4, 7, 11–14, 17, 18.

4. U.S.Const. art. I, § 9, cl. 4. See note 22 infra.

5. U.S.Const. art. I, § 9, cl. 5.

6. U.S.Const. art. I, § 10, cl. 1. See section 340 infra.

7. U.S.Const. art. I, § 10, cl. 2.

8. U.S.Const. art. I, § 10, cl. 3. See section 12 supra.

9. U.S.Const. art. III, § 2, cl. 1. See sections 88, 353 infra.

10. U.S.Const. art. IV, § 1.

11. U.S.Const. art. IV, § 2. See section 89 infra.

12. U.S.Const. art. IV, § 3, cl. 2.

13. U.S.Const. art. VI, cl. 2. See Treaties in Force (U.S. Dep't of State 1960); R. Wilson, United States Commercial Treaties and International Law (1960); H. Hawkins, Rights of Businessmen Abroad under Trade Agreements and Commercial Treaties (1960); Comment, "Corporations Formed Pursuant to Treaty", 76 Harv.L.Rev. 1431 (1963).

14. U.S.Const. amend. IV.

15. U.S.Const. amend. V; George Campbell Painting Corp. v. Reid, 392 U.S. 286, 88 S.Ct. 1978, 20 L.Ed. 2d 1094 (1968), aff'g 20 N.Y.2d 370, 283 N.Y.S.2d 31, 229 N.E.2d 602 (1967); Wilson v. United States, 221 U.S. 361, 31 S.Ct. 538, 55 L.Ed. 771 (1911); Heligman v. United States, 407 F.2d 448 (8th Cir.1969); Wild v. Brewer, 329 F.2d 924 (9th Cir.1964), cert. denied 379 U.S. 914, 85 S.Ct. 262, 13 L.Ed.2d 185 (1964) (denying privilege against self-incrimination to corporation and corporate personnel with respect to corporate records, even of close corporation).

16. U.S.Const. amend. VII; Ross v. Bernhard, —— U.S. ——, 90 S.Ct. 733, —— L.Ed.2d —— (1970), rev'g 403 F.2d 909 (2d Cir. 1968); DePinto v. Provident Security Life Ins. Co., 323 F.2d 826 (9th Cir. 1963), cert. denied 376 U.S. 950, 84 S.Ct. 965, 11 L.Ed.2d 969 (1964) (holding shareholders in federal court derivative action are guaranteed jury trial on issues triable by jury if corporation were suing directly). See section 358, n. 21 infra. See also Duncan v. Louisiana, 391 U.S. 145, 88 S.Ct. 1444, 20 L.Ed.2d 491 (1968); Bloom v. Illinois, 391 U.S. 194, 88 S.Ct. 1477,

(p) Reserved state powers;[17]

(q) Dependency of state citizenship on residence;[18]

(r) Prohibition against state abridgement of privileges and immunities of citizens of the United States;[19]

(s) Prohibition against state deprivation of any person of life, liberty, or property, without due process of law;[20]

(t) Prohibition against state denial to any person within its jurisdiction of the equal protection of the laws,[21]

(u) Power of Congress to lay and collect taxes on incomes, from whatever source derived, without apportionment.[22]

At the federal level, there is no general legislation dealing with the formation of business associations. The federal government enjoys no express power to do so and its implied powers, especially over interstate commerce, have been exercised only to a limited extent.[23]

Federal laws mainly involve exercise of federal powers over interstate commerce and the mails, taxation, bankruptcy, and procurement.[24] Typical are the federal laws dealing with antitrust and trade regulation,[25] labor, securities regulation,[26] small business financing,[27] taxation, and corporate bankruptcy, arrangement, and reorganization.[28] Under such laws, administrative agencies

---

20 L.Ed.2d 522 (1968) (holding that 14th amendment guarantees right of jury trial in criminal cases which, if tried in federal court, would come within 6th amendment guarantee).

17. U.S.Const. amend. X.

18. U.S.Const. amend. XIV, § 1. See sections 82–87 infra.

19. Ibid. See section 89 infra.

20. Ibid. Note, "Constitutional Law—Freedom of Speech and the Corporation", 4 Vill.L.Rev. 377 (1959). Quaere, whether action by powerful corporations should be equated with state action. See Marsh v. Alabama, 326 U.S. 501, 66 S.Ct. 276, 90 L. Ed. 265 (1946) (corporation running company town treated as state); A. Miller, Private Governments and the Constitution (1959); Berle, "Legal Problems of Economic Power", 60 Colum.L.Rev. 4 (1960). See also Lewis, "The Meaning of State Action", 60 Colum.L.Rev. 1083 (1960).

21. U.S.Const. amend. XIV, § 1. See Boman v. Birmingham Transit Co., 280 F.2d 531 (5th Cir.1960) (segregated seating by bus company held state action). See also WHYY, Inc. v. Borough of Glassboro, 393 U.S. 117, 89 S.Ct. 286, 21 L.Ed.2d 242 (1968) rev'g 50 N.J.2d 6, 231 A.2d 608 (1967), Gorum v. Oklahoma Liquefied Petroleum Gas Board, 235 F.Supp. 406 (W.D.Okl.1964), appeal dismissed, sub nom. Ozark Butane Co. v. Oklahoma Liquefied Petroleum Gas Bd., 380 U.S. 928, 85 S.Ct. 932, 13 L. Ed.2d 817 (1965) (alleged denial of equal protection of laws to foreign corporations). Quaere, as to denial of equal protection of laws to domestic corporations when corporate statute regulatory features are not applicable to foreign corporations doing business in state.

22. U.S.Const. amend. XVI.

23. For list of corporations chartered by special act of Congress, see S.Rep.No. 30, 80th Cong., 1st Sess. 4–13 (1947). Under the Federal Small Business Investment Act of 1958, 15 U.S.C.A. §§ 661–688, the Small Business Administration is authorized to issue federal charters to small business investment companies (SBIC's) until June 30, 1961 if they cannot be chartered under state law. See Small Business Investment Companies, Law—Regulations—Explanation (1959); McCallum, "Small Business Investment Act of 1958—Its First Year of Operation", 45 Va.L.Rev. 1039 (1959). The attorneys general of a few states have ruled that SBIC's cannot be formed under their corporation statutes.

24. J. Paul, United States Government Contracts and Subcontracts (ALI 1964); Weidenbaum, "Effects of Government Contracting on Private Enterprise", 35 Geo.Wash.L.Rev. 378 (1966); Roberts, "Small Business Policy in the Government Procurement Process", 15 J.Pub.L. 30 (1966); Beach, "Role of the General Accounting Office in the Regulation of Industry", 21 Bus.Law. 235 (1965); Hannah, "Regulation of Industry Through Government Contracts: Have We Reached the Point of Diminishing Returns", 21 id. 247 (1965); Ignatius, "Government Involvement in Management Decisions", 21 id. 255 (1965); Keller, "The Role of the General Accounting Office", 21 id. 259 (1965); Hannah, "Government by Procurement", 18 id. 997 (1963).

25. See sections 309–314 infra.

26. See sections 294–304 infra.

27. See Federal Small Business Investment Act of 1958, discussed in note 23 supra. Over an insolvent state-incorporated SBIC, exclusive federal court jurisdiction has been asserted. United States v. Norwood Capital Corp., 273 F.Supp. 236 (D.S.C.1967). Quaere, as to solvent state-incorporated SBIC's.

28. See sections 383–388 infra.

have often been established with rule-making authority.

Furthermore, litigation in the federal courts involving corporations, whether based on federal-question (including pendent jurisdiction) or diversity-of-citizenship jurisdiction, is subject to the Federal Judicial Code and Federal Rules of Civil Procedure.

Thus, the modern corporation lawyer must give increased attention to the expanding federal law applicable to state-created corporations.

Federal taxation takes many forms, but the individual and general corporation income taxes in most cases have the greatest impact. There are special taxes on regulated investment companies, life insurance companies, exempt corporations, personal holding companies, corporations improperly accumulating surplus; also social security taxes, not to mention a host of excise, import, occupational, and miscellaneous taxes.[29] Tax aspects will be no more than red-flagged herein.

Federal regulatory legislation is of four principal types:

(a) Certain interstate industries or areas of interstate concern are singled out for regulation: interstate carriers (Interstate Commerce Commission), utilities (Federal Power Commission), telegraph, telephone, radio, and television (Federal Communications Commission), aviation (Civil Aeronautics Board, Federal Aviation Agency).[30]

(b) Under the fiscal powers are regulated national banks and member banks of the Federal Reserve System (Comptroller of the Currency and Federal Reserve Board), federal savings and loan associations, federal

credit unions, etc.[31] Banking corporations are beyond the scope of this handbook.

(c) Interstate competition and fair trade practices are policed:

Sherman Act (control of monopoly and contracts and conspiracies in restraint of trade); [32]

Clayton Act (control of monopoly and restraint of trade through Federal Trade Commission as well as courts; prohibition of specific practices: price discrimination, exclusive dealing, acquisition of shares or assets of competitor, interlocking directorate); [33]

Federal Trade Commission Act (control of unfair or deceptive acts or practices through Federal Trade Commission); [34]

Robinson-Patman Act (control of price discrimination); [35]

Miller-Tydings Act (McGuire amendment) (resale-price maintenance—"fair trading"); [36]

Wheeler-Lea Act (false advertising).[37]

Such legislation will be only briefly outlined herein.

(d) The interstate distribution and trading of securities are regulated:

Securities Act, 1933 (primary distribution of securities); [38]

Securities Exchange Act, 1934 (secondary distribution of securities, take-over bids, proxies, insider trading, national

---

29. Int.Rev.Code of 1954, 26 U.S.C.A. §§ 1–8023.

30. 49 U.S.C.A. §§ 1–1022; 16 U.S.C.A. §§ 791a–825r; 47 U.S.C.A. §§ 151–609; 49 U.S.C.A. §§ 1301–1542; Wellington, "Labor and the Federal System", 26 U. Chi.L.Rev. 542 (1959).

31. 12 U.S.C.A. §§ 21–214c, 221–522, 1461–1468, 1751–1772.

32. 15 U.S.C.A. §§ 1–7. See section 310 infra.

33. 15 U.S.C.A. §§ 12–27. See section 312 infra.

34. 15 U.S.C.A. §§ 41 et seq. See section 311 infra.

35. 15 U.S.C.A. §§ 15–21a. See section 313 infra.

36. 15 U.S.C.A. § 1. See section 314 infra.

37. 15 U.S.C.A. §§ 41–58. See section 314 infra.

38. 15 U.S.C.A. §§ 77a–77aa. See section 295 infra.

securities exchanges, brokers, dealers) ; [39]

Public Utility Holding Company Act, 1935 (interstate gas and electric holding company systems) ; [40]

Trust Indenture Act, 1939 (trust indentures securing debt securities; independent active trustee) ; [41]

Investment Companies Act, 1940 (investment companies, including "mutual funds") ; [42]

Investment Advisers Act, 1940 (investment advisers).[43]

Some treatment of the more important aspects of securities regulation is included herein (especially in Chapter 11 on the special problems of public-issue corporations), but more complete coverage is left to presentations on corporate finance.

Federal bankruptcy and corporate rehabilitation or reorganization, under the Federal Bankruptcy Act,[44] involve straight or ordinary (liquidation) bankruptcy under Chapters I to VII of the Act, arrangements (not affecting secured debt or shares) under Chapter XI, and reorganizations affecting secured debt or shares, or public-issue corporations, under Chapter X (Chandler Act of 1938, as amended—successor to § 77B and equity receivership). These aspects will be discussed herein briefly in Chapter 15. Fuller treatment will be left to presentations on creditors' rights, bankruptcy, and corporate reorganization.

STATE LAWS AFFECTING BUSINESS ENTERPRISES

14. At the state level are various state constitutional provisions applicable to corporations and other forms of business enterprise, state statutes governing partnerships, limited partnerships, and other unincorporated forms of business enterprise, corporate statutes, regulatory statutes such as "blue sky" laws and antitrust and trade regulation provisions, and state taxing laws. The state statutory provisions range from a relatively simple arrangement to a complex of statutes.

State constitutions are obviously paramount to state statutes. Many state constitutions contain considerable detailed provisions on many things within the province of the state government, including business associations. Thus, most state constitutions reserve the power to amend or repeal corporation statutes or charters [1] (to avoid the Dartmouth College case doctrine) ;[2] all states except Connecticut, Massachusetts, and New Hampshire constitutionally prohibit special incorporation and require incorporation under general laws, with exceptions; [3] some constitutions prohibit corporations from engaging in any activities other than those authorized by their charters;[4] Wyoming until 1960 barred a corporation from being formed for more than a single purpose; [5] the Missouri and Oklahoma con-

---

39. 15 U.S.C.A. §§ 78–78jj. See sections 296–298 infra.

40. 15 U.S.C.A. §§ 79–79z–6. See section 299 infra.

41. 15 U.S.C.A. §§ 77aaa–77bbbb. See sections 156, 300 infra.

42. 15 U.S.C.A. §§ 80a–1 through 80a–52. See section 301 infra.

43. 15 U.S.C.A. §§ 80b–1 through 80b–21. See section 302 infra.

44. 11 U.S.C.A. §§ 1–1103.

---

1. Such constitutional reservations are found in all states except Alaska, Connecticut, Illinois, Minnesota, Missouri, New Hampshire, Oregon, Rhode Island, and West Virginia, all of which have statutory reservations. Many jurisdictions have parallel reservations in both their constitutions and their statutes. E.g., Del.Const. art. IX, § 2; Del.Gen. Corp.Law § 394 (1967); N.Y.Const. art. X, § 1; McKinney's N.Y.Gen.Corp. Law, § 5; McKinney's N.Y.Bus.Corp. Law, § 110; Corporation Manual No. 1 (1969 ed.). See Index Digest of State Constitutions 112–128 (2d ed. 1959).

2. Trustees of Dartmouth College v. Woodward, 17 U.S. (4 Wheat.) 518, 4 L.Ed. 629 (1819). See section 340 infra.

3. Corporation Manual No. 1 (1969 ed.). See section 12 supra.

4. Corporation Manual No. 39 (1969 ed.).

5. Wyo.Const. art. X, § 6 (amendment effective Dec. 2, 1960).

stitutions restrict ownership by corporations of rural real estate not necessary and proper for their business purposes; [6] some constitutions prohibit a corporation from issuing shares except for money paid, labor done, or property actually acquired by the corporation,[7] with the additional provision in some states that all fictitious increase of shares or indebtedness shall be void;[8] approximately one-third of the states have constitutional provisions making cumulative voting for directors mandatory;[9] ten states constitutionally provide that all corporations (sometimes broadly defining the term to include unincorporated enterprises with corporate characteristics) shall have the right to sue and shall be subject to suit in all courts in like cases as natural persons; [10] two state constitutions limit the duration of business corporations; [11] several states constitutionally prohibit monopolies;[12] Delaware constitutionally provides that shares in a Delaware corporation when owned by persons or corporations without the state shall not be subject to taxation by any existing or future law; [13] some state constitutions provide that a shareholder shall not be individually liable otherwise than for the unpaid shares owned by him.[14]

At the state level are the basic laws governing the formation of business associations. For partnerships, there are the partnership statutes, in most jurisdictions the Uniform Partnership Act and Uniform Limited Partnership Act.[15] A few jurisdictions also have statutory or limited partnership

6. Mo.Const. art. XI, § 5; Okl.Const. art. XXII, § 2. Compare McCaleb v. Shantz, 318 S.W.2d 199 (Mo. 1958) and State ex rel. Reidy v. International Paper Co., 342 P.2d 565 (Okl.1959), with Simler v. Wilson, 210 F.2d 99 (10th Cir. 1954), cert. denied 347 U.S. 954, 74 S.Ct. 681, 98 L.Ed. 1099 (1954), reh. denied 347 U.S. 973, 74 S.Ct. 786, 98 L.Ed. 1113 (1954). See also Le Force v. Bullard, 454 P.2d 297 (Okl.1969) (formation of corporation for purpose of farming, with power to hold such real estate as is necessary to accomplish purpose, held not prohibited by state constitution or statutes).

7. E.g., Del.Const. art. IX, § 3; Colo.Const. art. 15, § 9; Haselbush v. Alsco of Colorado, Inc., 161 Colo. 138, 421 P.2d 113 (1966).

8. E.g., Okl.Const. art. IX, § 39; Pa.Const. art. XVI, § 7. Compare Evans v. Ideal Brick & Brikcrete Mfg. Co., 287 P.2d 454 (Okl.1955), with McCandless v. Furlaud, 296 U.S. 140, 56 S.Ct. 41, 80 L.Ed. 121 (1935), reh. denied 296 U.S. 664, 56 S.Ct. 304, 80 L. Ed. 473 (1936).

9. Arizona, Idaho, Illinois, Kentucky, Mississippi, Missouri, Montana, Nebraska, North Dakota, Pennsylvania, South Carolina, South Dakota, and West Virginia. Corporation Manual No. 30 (1969 ed.). The constitutional cumulative voting provision has sometimes been construed as violated by staggered boards of directors (Wolfson v. Avery, 6 Ill.2d 78, 126 N.E.2d 701 (1955); Mo.Op.Att'y Gen.No. 238, Aug. 24, 1964. Contra, Janney v. Philadelphia Transp. Co., 387 Pa. 282, 128 A.2d 76 (1956)) or by nonvoting shares (People ex rel. Watseka Tel. Co. v. Emmerson, 302 Ill. 300, 134 N.E. 707, 21 A.L.R. 636 (1922). Contra, State ex rel. Frank v. Swanger, 190 Mo. 561, 89 S.W. 872 (1905); Mont.Op.Att'y Gen. 328, Aug. 31, 1938)). See Note, "Non-Voting Shares —The Code and the Constitution", 16 S.C.L.Rev. 657 (1964). See Hanks v. Borelli, 2 Ariz.App. 589, 411 P.2d 27 (1966).

10. Alabama, California, Kansas, Minnesota, Montana, Nebraska, Nevada, New York, North Carolina, and Washington. See also Corporation Manual No. 39 (1969 ed.). See Oliner v. Mid-Town Promoters, Inc., 2 N.Y.2d 63, 156 N.Y.S.2d 833, 138 N.E.2d 217 (1956) (holding N.Y.Const. art. X, § 4 not violated by statutory requirement that corporation may appear in action only by attorney duly licensed to practice in the state).

11. Okl.Const. art. II, § 32 (may not be perpetual); Miss.Const. art. 7, § 178 (99 years).

12. E.g., Ala.Const. art. IV, § 103; Ariz.Const. art. XIV, § 15.

13. Del.Const. art. IX, § 6; see also N.Y.Const. art. XVI, § 3.

14. E.g., Ala.Const. art. XII, § 236; Or.Const. art. XI, § 3. Of historical interest is Cal.Const., art. XII, § 3 which provided:

"Each stockholder of a corporation, or joint-stock association, shall be individually and personally liable for such proportion of all its debts and liabilities contracted or incurred, during the time he was a stockholder, as the amount of stock or shares owned by him bears to the whole of the subscribed capital stock, or shares of the corporation or association. . . . [Const. of 1849, art. IV, § 36, revised 1879]."

This was amended in 1908 to except any exposition company organized to promote and carry on any international exposition or world's fair within California, and in 1928 to broaden such exception and to except any California corporation using "Limited" or "Ltd." at the end of its corporate name. The section was completely repealed on November 4, 1930.

15. See sections 19, 28 infra.

association statutes.[16] The formation of joint-stock associations [17] and business trusts has to some extent been formalized by statute.[18] For corporations, each state, the District of Columbia, and Puerto Rico has its own statute or statutes enabling incorporation and dealing not only with domestic corporations but also with foreign corporations doing business within the jurisdiction. References to the more important differences among such statutes are found in Chapter 4.

Besides the basic laws are numerous state regulatory measures under the state police power, including regulation of securities issues under the "blue sky" laws, the full application of which has been expressly preserved by the Federal Securities Act of 1933,[19] and antitrust and trade regulation provisions.[20]

State taxing provisions are also profuse.[21]

The New York statutory system affecting corporations, for many years, has been considerably more comprehensive and complicated than most, with (a) a three-tier structure of statutory provisions applicable to public corporations; (b) two-tier structures applicable to special nonstock corporations (excepting corporations subject to the Not-For-Profit Corporation Law after September 1, 1970) and to six kinds of specialized stock corporations [22]—corporations subject to the Insurance Law; and, as of September 1, 1970, a not-for-profit corporation statute applicable to nonstock corporations other than corporations subject to the Education Law, the Religious Corporations Law, and the Benevolent Orders Law, railroad corporations, transportation corporations, stock (as well as nonstock) cooperative corporations, business development corporations, and stock educational corporations, and (c) one corporate statute for business corporations; another statute

---

16. See section 41 infra.

17. See section 50 infra.

18. See section 58 infra.

19. See generally L. Loss & E. Cowett, Blue Sky Law (1958). See also sections 305–308 infra.

20. See section 315 infra.

21. More than three-fourths of the states, the District of Columbia, and several cities impose income taxes on corporations. State and Local Taxes on Business (Tax Institute of America 1965); State Tax Handbook (Commerce Clearing House, Inc. 1965); 1968 Guidebook to New York Taxes (Commerce Clearing House, Inc.); H. Steutzer, Massachusetts Taxation of Corporations (6th ed. 1965); R. Schoen, Connecticut Taxation of Corporations

(2d ed. 1965); D. Rosenbluth, Pennsylvania Business Taxes (ALI 1959); Nourse, "State and Local Taxes Affecting California Business", in Advising California Business Enterprises 99–119 (1958). New York, for example, has a personal income tax, corporate franchise tax, unincorporated business tax, gross receipts tax on public utilities, estate tax, unemployment insurance tax, share transfer tax, motor fuel tax, sales tax, alcoholic beverage tax, cigarette tax, parimutuel tax, racing admissions tax, truck mileage tax, bank taxes, mortgage tax, not to mention local property and possibly local sales and income taxes, etc.

22. Stock corporations were defined as corporations having shares of stock and authorized by law to distribute dividends to holders thereof. McKinney's N.Y.Gen.Corp.Law, § 3(5); see note 27 infra.

applicable to corporations under the banking
law. At the apex, of course, is the United

States and New York State Constitutions and
any superior federal laws or treaties:

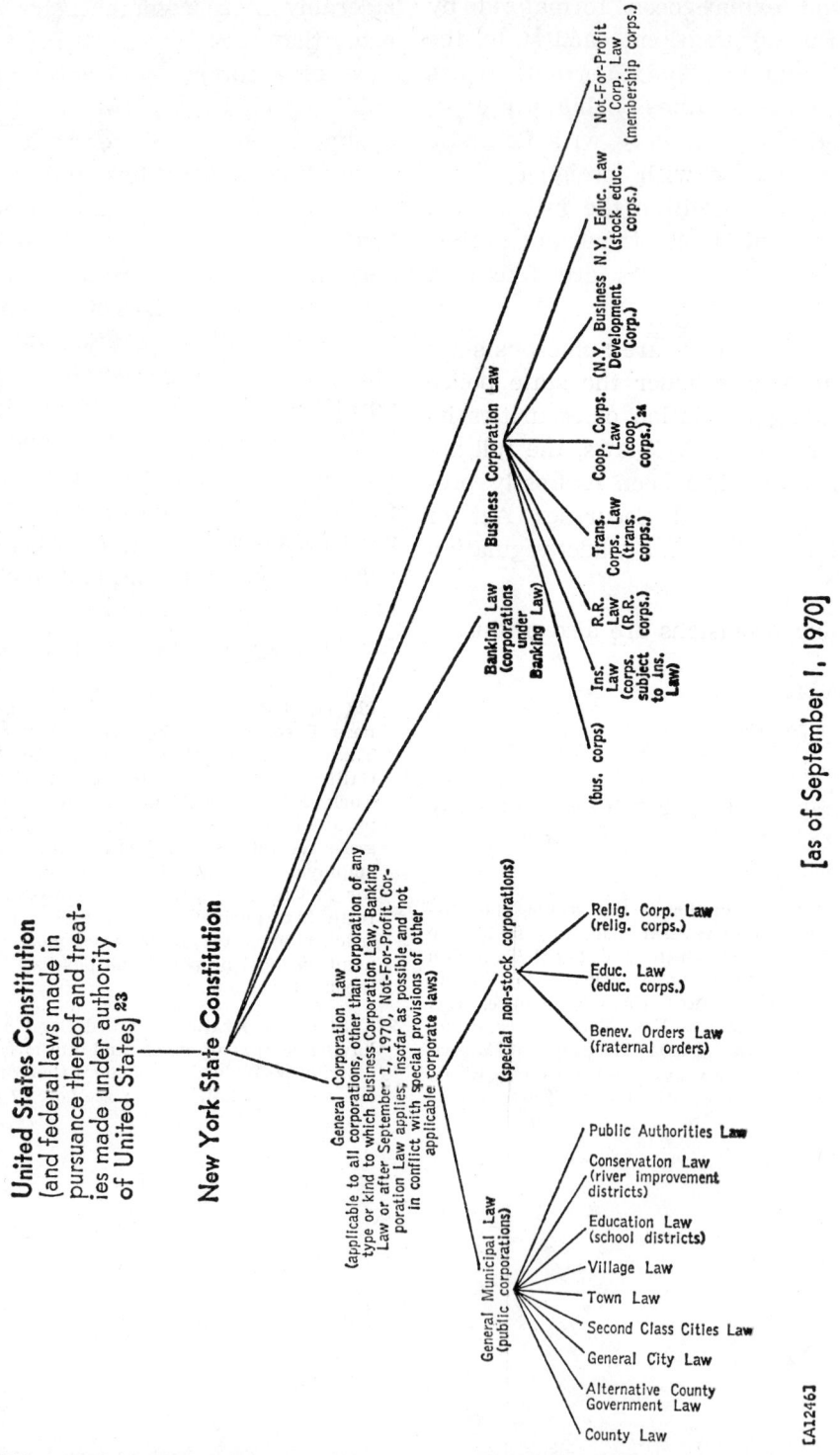

23. See Franklin Nat'l Bank of Franklin Square v.
New York, 347 U.S. 373, 74 S.Ct. 550, 98 L.Ed. 767
(1954); Note, 55 Colum.L.Rev. 1234 (1955).

24. Cooperative corporations (whether stock or nonstock) are subject to the Cooperative Corporations
Law and the Business Corporation Law. Mc-

Thus, business corporations incorporated or doing business in New York, since September 1, 1963, have been subject to a single corporate statute—the New York Business Corporation Law.[25] From 1924 to 1963, business corporations were formed under the Stock Corporation Law,[26] and were subject

also to the General Corporation Law;[27] prior to 1924, business corporations were governed by a statute known as the Business Corporations Law.

Many other New York statutes also substantially affect corporations and other business enterprises.

SUBSTATUTORY INTRACORPORATE PROVISIONS

15. **Below the constitutions and applicable statutes and administrative regulations is a substatutory intracorporate hierarchy of provisions, in the form of articles of incorporation, bylaws, shareholder resolutions, board of directors resolutions, shareholder agreements, indentures, loan agreements, employment contracts, voting trusts, proxies, and share certificate legends.**

Below the federal and state constitutions and applicable statutes and administrative regulations is a substatutory intracorporate hierarchy of provisions, in the form of articles of incorporation, bylaws, shareholder resolutions, and board of directors resolu-

---

Kinney's N.Y. Co-op. Corp. Law, §§ 5, 10. See Whitebook, "The Cooperative Apartment", 9 Prac. Law. 25 (Apr.1963); Hershman, "The How and Why of Real Estate Co-operatives", Isaacs, "History and Development of the Co-operative Apartment", Bernstein, "Formation of a Co-operative Apartment Venture", McLaughlin, "The Co-operative Apartment Corporation", Bachner, "Tax Problems of the Co-operative Apartment", Morris, "Middle-Income Co-operative Apartments", 5 Prac.Law. 59 et seq. (Nov.1959). See also Comment, "Community Apartment: Condominium or Stock Cooperative", 50 Calif.L.Rev. 299 (1962).

25. Also subject to the Business Corporation Law are corporations under the Insurance Law, railroad corporations, transportation corporations, cooperative corporations (whether stock or nonstock), business development corporations, and stock educational corporations, which are subject respectively also to the Insurance Law, the Railroad Law, the Transportation Corporations Law, the Cooperative Corporations Law, the Banking Law, and the Education Law. If any provision of the Business Corporation Law conflicts with any provision of the Insurance Law (§ 7(a)), the Railroad Law (§ 6(a)), the Transportation Corporations Law (§ 4(a)), the Cooperative Corporations Law (§ 5(a)), or Article V–A of the Banking Law (§ 210(2)) (N.Y. Business Development Corp.), the respective latter provision shall prevail; absent conflict, the provisions of both shall apply. Corporations under the Banking Law, except for business development corporations, are subject only to the Banking Law and not to the Business Corporation Law. Educational corporations are usually formed under and subject to the Education Law. With the consent of the Commissioner of Education, an educational corporation may be formed under the Business Corporation Law or pursuant to the Membership Corporations Law. McKinney's N.Y.Educ.Law, § 216. The former would be subject to the Education Law and the Business Corporation Law; the latter to the Education Law, the Membership Corporations Law, and the General Corporation Law before September 1, 1970, and thereafter to the Education Law and the Not-For-Profit Corporation Law.

26. The Stock Corporation Law was repealed, effective September 1, 1966. As of September 1, 1963, it ceased to apply to business corporations, but remained in effect for the more specialized stock corporations until the more specialized corporate statutes respectively applicable to them could be made

independent of the Stock Corporation Law and General Corporation Law and either correlated with the Business Corporation Law (as of June 1, 1964 for the Transportation Corporations Law; as of September 1, 1964, for the Insurance Law and Railroad Law; as of September 1, 1966 for the Cooperative Corporations Law) or made self-sufficient (as of September 1, 1964 for the Banking Law).

27. As of September 1, 1963, the General Corporation Law ceased to apply to business corporations; as of June 1, 1964 to transportation corporations; as of September 1, 1964 to corporations subject to the Insurance Law or Banking Law or to railroad corporations; as of September 1, 1966 to cooperative corporations; and as of September 1, 1970 to corporations subject to the Not-For-Profit Corporation Law. The General Corporation Law, while no longer applicable to any stock corporations, remains in effect for public corporations and for special nonstock corporations other than cooperative corporations and after September 1, 1970, other than corporations subject to the Not-For-Profit Corporation Law. A self-sufficient Not-For-Profit Corporation Law becomes effective September 1, 1970.

tions (omitting for the time being share-holder agreements, indentures, loan agree-ments, employment contracts, voting trusts, proxies, and share certificate legends):

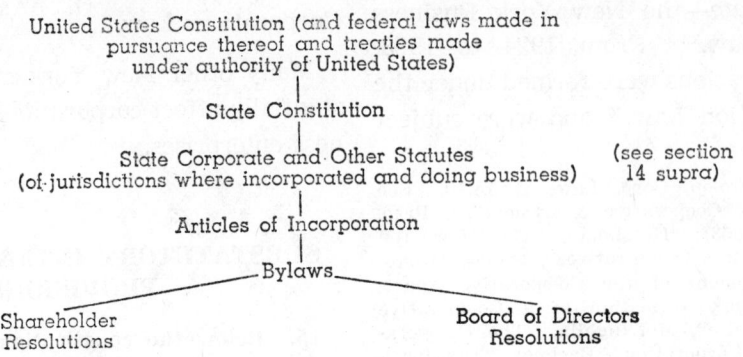

It need hardly be pointed out that in the event of conflict, the higher authority prevails, e. g., constitution over statute,[1] constitution over articles of incorporation,[2] constitution over bylaws,[3] statute over articles of incorporation,[4] statute over bylaws,[5] and articles of incorporation over bylaws.[6]

Within the framework of articles of incorporation, bylaws, and shareholder and board of directors resolutions, financial and management functions might also be subject to shareholder agreements, indentures, loan agreements, employment contracts, voting trusts, and proxies. Various provisions, in order to be binding, especially on persons without actual knowledge thereof, should be noted by legends on share certificates.

1. E.g., Wolfson v. Avery, 6 Ill.2d 78, 126 N.E.2d 701 (1955).

2. E.g., State ex rel. Carter v. Harris, 273 Ala. 374, 141 So.2d 175 (1961); People ex rel. Watseka Tel. Co. v. Emmerson, 302 Ill. 300, 134 N.E. 707, 21 A.L. R. 636 (1922).

3. E.g., Sensabaugh v. Polson Plywood Co., 135 Mont. 562, 342 P.2d 1064 (1959). Quaere, as to enforcea-bility of invalid bylaw as shareholder agreement. See sections 267, 275 infra.

4. E.g., People ex rel. Barney v. Whalen, 119 App. Div. 749, 104 N.Y.S. 555 (3d Dep't 1907), aff'd mem., 189 N.Y. 560, 82 N.E. 1131 (1907).

5. E.g., Matter of William Faehndrich, Inc. 2 N.Y.2d 468, 161 N.Y.S.2d 99, 141 N.E.2d 597 (1957).

6. E.g., Lasker v. Moreida, 38 Misc.2d 348, 238 N.Y. S.2d 16 (Sup.Ct.1963); Matter of Rogers Imports,

Inc., 202 Misc. 761, 116 N.Y.S.2d 106 (Sup.Ct.1952). However, where a statute authorizes the bylaws to change the number of directors, such a bylaw change is effective despite the fact that the articles of incorporation provide for a fixed number of directors. Rockford Life Ins. Co. v. Production Press, Inc., 15 Ill.App.2d 50, 145 N.E.2d 276 (1957); Gow v. Consolidated Coppermines Corp., 19 Del.Ch. 172, 165 A. 136 (Ch.1933). Implied amendment of bylaws is possible by corporate action similar to that required for bylaw amendment. Magnus v. Magnus Organ Corp., 71 N.J.Super. 363, 177 A.2d 55 (1962).

CHAPTER 2

SELECTION OF FORM OF BUSINESS ENTERPRISE

A. FORMS AND FACTORS IN SELECTION

A. FORMS AND FACTORS IN SELECTION

AVAILABLE FORMS OF BUSINESS ENTERPRISE

16. The selection of the form of business enterprise most advantageous for a particular business requires consideration of many factors, nontax and tax. From the nontax viewpoint, there are seven principal forms of business enterprise: (a) Individual proprietorship; (b) General partnership; (c) Limited partnership; (d) Joint-stock association; (e) Business trust; (f) Corporation; and (g) Professional corporation or association. From the federal income tax viewpoint, there are four forms: (a) Individual; (b) Partnership; (c) Corporation (including "association") not making election under Subchapter S; and (d) Corporation (including "association") making election under Subchapter S. Within each form, there is a range of permissible variations.

The selection of the most advantageous form of enterprise for a particular business involves the weighing of many considerations: nontax and tax.

Generally speaking from the nontax viewpoint, there are seven principal forms; federal income taxwise, only four forms:

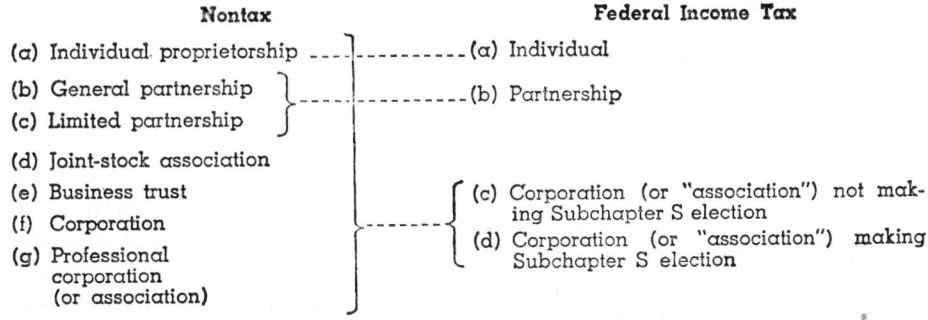

Nontax	Federal Income Tax
(a) Individual proprietorship	(a) Individual
(b) General partnership	(b) Partnership
(c) Limited partnership	
(d) Joint-stock association	
(e) Business trust	(c) Corporation (or "association") not making Subchapter S election
(f) Corporation	(d) Corporation (or "association") making Subchapter S election
(g) Professional corporation (or association)	

Of the seven (nontax) forms, the first five are unincorporated and traditionally involve the aggregate theory in contrast to the entity theory applicable to the corporation. However, recent years have witnessed increasing reliance on an entity approach to the unincorporated forms of business association for some purposes.[1]

Inhering in the corporation as a separate entity are certain traditional attributes: (a) power to take, hold, and convey property in the group name; (b) power to sue and to be sued in the group name; (c) centralization of management; (d) ready transferability of interests; (e) perpetual succession; and (f) limited liability. All of them do not exist to the same extent in all corporations, and some of them can be substantially varied when desired. Furthermore, some of them exist or can be secured in the unincorporated forms.

In short, each form can be more or less molded to the individual situation. Therefore, a sophisticated selection must take into consideration not only the traditional attributes, but the permissible variations of each form.[2] This selection process, furthermore,

---

1. McBratney, "Corporate Aspects of Non-Corporate Entities", 14 Bus.Law. 728 (1959). For a work dedicated to the thesis that it is improper to apply the entity theory and to give corporate advantages in the absence of incorporation under legislative authority, see E. Warren, Corporate Advantages Without Incorporation (1929). In the case of modern small businesses, the trend is to achieve the internal characteristics of the partnership and avoidance of double taxation (e. g., Subchapter S election), without loss of the limited liability and fringe tax benefits of the corporation. For an article demonstrating again that corporateness and limited liability are not necessarily logically coterminous and calling for a more flexible legislative extension of limited liability to other business modes, specifically a new form of business enterprise to be known as a "partnership corporation", see Kessler, "With Limited Liability For All: Why Not a Partnership Corporation?", 36 Fordham L.Rev. 235 (1967) (with appended preliminary draft of "Partnership Corporation Act").

2. See R. Kessler, New York Close Corporations ch. 3 (1968); Institute on Continuing Education of the Illinois Bar, Organizing and Advising Illinois Businesses (Illinois Practice Handbook No. 6, 1968); C. Rohrlich, Organizing Corporate and Other Business Enterprises 73–265 (4th ed. 1967); R. Knapp & M. Semmel, Forms of Business Organization and the Federal Tax Laws (PLI rev. 1966); L. Sarner & G. Shinehouse, Organizational Problems of Small Business (ALI rev. 1961); 1 G. Hornstein, Corporation Law and Practice § 32 (Checklist: Whether to Incorporate—Non-Tax Factors), § 49 (Checklist: Whether to Incorporate—Federal Tax Factors Only); § 65 (Form: Memorandum to Client Recommending the Corporate Form) (1959); Kramer & Orr, "Selecting the Form of Entity", in Advising California Business Enterprises 87–98 (1958); Clink, "To Incorporate or Not to Incorporate", 48 Mich.St.B.J. 19 (Feb.1969); Maer & Francis, "Whether to Incorporate", 22 Bus.Law. 571 (1967); Cavitch, "Recent Developments Affecting the Choice of a Business Organization", 17 W.Res.L. Rev. 669 (1966); Kramer & Ziegler, "Choice of Form for the Family Owned Business", 16 Hastings L.J. 509 (1965); Townsend, "Selecting the Appropriate Business Unit—Kansas and Missouri", 4 Kan. L.Rev. 487 (1956); Comment, "Business Associa-

cannot be done in the abstract but only by reference to the normal incidents and permissible variations recognized by the laws of the jurisdictions in which business is to be transacted.

As indicated above, the federal income tax law distinguishes between individuals, partnerships, corporations (including "associations") not making Subchapter S election, and corporations (including "associations") making Subchapter S election.

Subchapter R of the Code permitting an individual proprietorship or all the members of a partnership, under prescribed circumstances, to elect to report and be taxed, to a certain extent as a corporation, was repealed, effective January 1, 1969.

The Code defines "partnership" to include "a syndicate, group, pool, joint venture, or other unincorporated organization, through or by means of which any business, financial operation, or venture is carried on, and which is not, within the meaning of [such law] a trust [meaning a trust other than a business trust] or estate or a corporation . . . ." [3]

The Code also defines "corporation" to include "associations, joint-stock companies, and insurance companies." [4] The Regulations [5] enumerate six characteristics of corporations: (a) associates; (b) an objective to carry on business and divide the gains therefrom; (c) continuity of life; (d) centralization of management; (e) liability of corporate debts limited to corporate property, and (f) free transferability of interests. Other factors might be significant. If the corporate characteristics are such that the organization more nearly resembles a corporation than a partnership or trust, it will be treated as an association or corporation. The regulations in effect preclude a general partnership subject to a statute corresponding to the Uniform Partnership Act, and make it very difficult for a limited partnership subject to a statute corresponding to the Limited Partnership Act, from being treated as an association or corporation. Under earlier regulations, the term "association" included any organization which, like a corporation, continued notwithstanding that its members or participants changed, and the affairs of which, like corporate affairs, were conducted by an individual or group acting in a representative capacity. The term "association" was defined to include a voluntary association, a joint-stock association, a business trust, a statutory partnership association, and any other type of organization (by whatever name known) which was not, within the meaning of the Code, a trust or estate or partnership. [6]

Since 1958, the federal income tax situation has been further complicated by the Technical Amendments Act of 1958 [7] and the Small Business Tax Revision Act of 1958. [8]

Under the Technical Amendments Act, a "small business corporation", as defined in

---

tions—Registered Partnership, Partnership or the Corporation—Selection of the Suitable Form in Pennsylvania", 2 Vill.L.Rev. 285 (1957); Garrett & Garrett, "Choosing the Form of Business Enterprise", 1954 Ill.L.F. 359. See also "Business Organizations: A Symposium", 27 Tenn.L.Rev. 143 (1960).

3. Int.Rev.Code of 1954, 26 U.S.C.A. § 7701(a) (2). If an organization has corporate characteristics—see note 4 infra—it might be an association, taxable as a corporation. Treas.Reg. § 301.7701-2 (1960). Depending upon its character in such respects, a limited partnership is classified for the purposes of the Code as an ordinary partnership or as an association taxable as a corporation. For want of such characteristics, a limited partnership is to be considered as an ordinary partnership, notwithstanding other characteristics conferred upon it by local law.

4. Int.Rev.Code of 1954, 26 U.S.C.A. § 7701(a) (3). See § 17, n. 2 infra.

5. Treas.Reg. § 301.7701-2 (1960).

6. Former Treas.Reg. 118, § 39.3797-2 (1953). If the conduct of the affairs of a corporation continues after the termination of its existence, it probably becomes an "association".

7. Int.Rev.Code of 1954, Subchapter S—Election of Certain Small Business Corporations as to Taxable Status §§ 1371–1377, 26 U.S.C.A. §§ 1371–1377.

8. Int.Rev.Code of 1954, 26 U.S.C.A. § 1244.

Subchapter S,[9] may elect not to be taxed on its net income as a separate entity but to have its income, net long-term capital gains to a limited extent, and net operating losses, passed through and taxed to its shareholders.[10]

Under the Small Business Tax Revision Act, losses on "small business stock", as defined in Section 1244 ("section 1244 stock")[11] are treated more favorably than

most losses on debts (assuming no Subchapter S election).[12]

FACTORS IN SELECTION

17. **Factors in selection of the most advantageous form of business enterprise are (a) Formalities of organization; (b) Capital and credit requirements; (c) Management and control; (d) Profits and losses; (e) Extent of liability; (f) Transferability of interest; (g) Continuity of existence; and (h) Tax, especially federal income tax, considerations. For most businesses, a full choice of the several forms is available. However, there are some legal and practical limitations. Whether there should be a single form or a combination of forms might also be a question. As conditions or the laws, especially the taxing laws, change, a switch to another form might be desirable.**

Various factors may be relevant in the selection of the most appropriate form. The powers to take, hold, and convey property, and to sue and to be sued, do not vary among the various forms today as significantly as they did prior to certain innovations modernizing the status of the unincorporated forms in such respects.[1] In any

9. A "small business corporation" is defined, for purposes of Subchapter S, as a domestic corporation which (a) has no more than 10 shareholders, (b) has no shareholder who is not an "individual" or an "estate", (c) has no nonresident alien shareholder, (d) has no more than one class of shares, and (e) is not a member of an affiliated group for consolidated return purposes. To be eligible for election, such a corporation may not derive more than 20 percent of its gross receipts from royalties, rents, dividends, interest, annuities, and sales or exchanges of shares or securities, or more than 80 percent of its gross receipts from sources outside the United States. A partnership shareholder renders the corporation ineligible; a husband and wife owning shares jointly or as community property are counted only as one shareholder. Large businesses might qualify since there are no limitations on worth of the corporation, number of its employees, or scope of its business. Unincorporated "associations" otherwise eligible may elect under Subchapter S. See sections 76, 262 infra.

10. The definition of "small business corporation" for purposes of Subchapter S differs from the definition of the same term for purposes of Section 1244. See note 11 infra. Int.Rev.Code of 1954, 26 U.S.C.A. § 1372. See Price, "The Small Business Tax Revision of 1958", 14 Bus.Law. 329, 334–350 (1959).

11. "Section 1244 stock" is defined as common shares of a domestic corporation if (a) such corporation adopted a plan after June 30, 1958 to offer such shares within two years after the adoption of said plan, (b) such corporation at the time of the adoption of said plan was a "small business corporation" (see infra) (its status at time of issue or loss is immaterial), (c) at the time of the adoption of said plan, no portion of a prior offering was outstanding, (d) such shares were issued by such corporation, pursuant to said plan, for money or other property (other than shares and securities), and (e) for the five taxable years of the corporation ended before the loss (or lesser period of the corporation's existence) less than 50 percent of its gross receipts was from investment sources, such as interest, dividends, rents, and shares and security gains; but this rule does not apply if deductions (excluding those for operating loss, partially tax-free interest, and dividends received) exceed gross income. A "small business corporation" is defined for purposes of Section 1244 as a corporation (a) which has not

more than $1,000,000 equity capital (assets, taken at basis for gain, less liabilities *except debt to shareholders*), and (b) whose capital paid in after June 30, 1958 (as capital or paid-in surplus) does not exceed $500,000—in either case counting the amount of shares which can be offered under the plan. Int.Rev.Code of 1954, 26 U.S.C.A. § 1244(c). The definition of "small business corporation" for purposes of Section 1244 differs from the definition of the same term for purposes of Subchapter S. See note 9 supra. See sections 76, 262 infra.

12. "Section 1244 stock" losses are fully deductible as business losses up to $25,000 ($50,000 on a joint return) per year; as capital losses to the extent of any excess. Int.Rev.Code of 1954, 26 U.S.C.A. § 1244(a), (b).

1. E.g., Uniform Partnership Act § 8(3); McKinney's N.Y.Part.Law, § 12(3) (partnership property in partnership name); McKinney's N.Y.Gen.Ass'ns Law, § 6 (joint-stock association's property in president's name); McKinney's N.Y. CPLR, § 1025 (partnership litigation in partnership name); McKinney's N.Y. Gen.Ass'ns Law, §§ 12, 13 (litigation involving association in president's or treasurer's name). Under the Federal Rules of Civil Procedure, the capacity of any litigant other than an individual or corporation to sue and be sued is governed by the law of the forum, except that a partnership or unincorpo-

event, they are rarely important factors in selection. Differences with respect to the other traditional attributes, however, can be of substantial importance, and for purposes of discussion can be compared under the following headings:

- (a) Formalities of organization
- (b) Capital and credit requirements
- (c) Management and control
- (d) Profits and losses
- (e) Extent of liability
- (f) Transferability of interest
- (g) Continuity of existence

To these can be added an eighth—tax considerations—which in many situations may be the controlling factor.

Many taxes, federal and state, apply without distinction as to the form of business enterprise; the impact of other taxes depends upon the classification of the enterprise for the purpose of the particular tax involved. A tax statute may classify an unincorporated business as a corporation,[2] may impose an unincorporated business tax designed to equalize the tax treatment of incorporated and unincorporated business enterprises,[3] may permit an unincorporated enterprise to elect to report and be taxed, to some extent, as a corporation,[4] or may permit a corpora-

tion to elect to be taxed, to some extent, as a partnership.

Of all the various taxes, the federal income tax looms largest. Its current rates range from 14 to 70 percent for individuals and from 22 to 48 percent for corporations. Corporations, absent Subchapter S election, suffer from "double taxation"—income taxed once to the corporation when earned and again to the shareholders when received in the form of dividends—but have some counterbalancing tax advantages. Subchapter S election, when available, avoids taxation at the corporate level, and hence double taxation, and at the same time retains some tax "fringe benefit" advantages.[6]

Generally-speaking, if all earnings are to be distributed, a partnership is usually preferable to a corporation, absent Subchapter S election. Formation of a corporation, even when an existing business of any form is transferred to it, can, if the parties wish, usually be tax-free; however, a transfer from a corporation to a partnership or individual proprietorship has immediate tax consequences. If earnings are retained by a corporation, subject to some limitations, personal income tax can be avoided altogether. Current social security and medicare tax rates are 4.8 percent (with periodic increas-

rated association without such capacity under such law may sue or be sued in its common name where a federal substantive right is involved in the litigation. Fed.R.Civ.P. 17(b).

2. E.g., Int.Rev.Code of 1954, 26 U.S.C.A. § 7701(a)(2)—see section 16, n. 3 supra; McKinney's N.Y. Tax Law, § 208 ("corporation" defined to include joint-stock association and business trust for purposes of franchise tax—5½ percent of net income allocated within New York).

3. E.g., McKinney's N.Y.Tax Law, § 701 (4 percent of net income of unincorporated business from activities carried on in New York). Murphy, "The Unincorporated Business Tax", 29 N.Y.St.B.Bull. 359 (1957).

4. E.g., Int.Rev.Code of 1954, Subchapter R—Election of Certain Partnerships and Proprietorships as to Taxable Status, 26 U.S.C.A. § 1361 (repealed, effective Jan. 1, 1969).

5. Int.Rev.Code of 1954, Subchapter S—Election of Certain Small Business Corporations as to Taxable Status, 26 U.S.C.A. §§ 1371–1377. See section 16, n. 7 supra, and sections 76, 262 infra. Some states have followed the federal pattern in this respect.

6. See section 76 infra. See also U.S.Int.Rev.Serv., Tax Guide for Small Business—Individuals, Corporations, Partnerships—Income, Excise, and Employment Taxes (1968 ed. 1967); B. Bittker & J. Eustice, Federal Income Taxation of Corporations and Shareholders (2d ed. 1966); Matties, "The Advantages and Disadvantages of a Corporation", 31 N.Y. St.B.Bull. 380 (1959); H. Shockey & H. Sweeney, Tax Effects of Operating as a Corporation or Partnership (1957); Strecker, "When Will the Corporate Form Save Taxes?", 18 Vand.L.Rev. 1695 (1965); Bromberg, "Tax Influences on the Law of Business Associations", 16 Baylor L.Rev. 327 (1964). A growing number of states base their income tax on federal tax legislation.

es up to 5.9 percent) by employer and the same percent by employee on the first $7,-800 of annual compensation, whereas a self-employer including partner, pays a "self-employment" tax of 6.9 percent (with periodic increases up to 7.9 percent).

For most businesses, a full choice of the several forms is available, but there are some exceptions. Corporations, except for "professional corporations" or "associations",[7] may be barred from practicing law [8] or other so-called learned professions such as medicine, dentistry, physiotherapy, osteopathy, nursing, optometry, podiatry, chiropody, veterinary medicine, architecture, or engineering; [9] conversely, na-

tional banks or members of the Federal Reserve System or other specified businesses under state laws must be incorporated.[10] Sometimes as a practical matter, there is only one sound choice.[11] Community or other practices might also suggest a particular form.[12]

The most appropriate form or combination of forms of business enterprise for a particular business can be selected only after full appreciation of all of the facts involved. Initially one must consider:

(a) Nature of the business;

(b) Number of participants; their respective functions, responsibilities, contributions, salaries, sharing of profits

7. See section 77 infra.

8. E.g., McKinney's N.Y.Jud.Law, § 495. See also Comment, "Unauthorized Practice of Law by Title Companies", 7 N.Y.L.F. 191 (1961); Note, "The Corporation and the Practice of Law", 21 U.Miami L. Rev. 889 (1967); Note, "Estate Planning by Corporate Fiduciary as an Unauthorized Practice of Law", 26 Md.L.Rev. 192 (1966); Note, "The Legal Profession—Unauthorized Practice of Law—Formation of Corporations", 17 Mercer L.Rev. 322 (1965); Note, "Unauthorized Practice of Law—Corporation and Layman Enjoined from Preparing Estate Plans Embodying Legal Analysis either as Separate Service or as Incident to Selling Insurance", 9 Vill.L. Rev. 353 (1964). Annot., 73 A.L.R. 1327 (1931), 105 A.L.R. 1364 (1936), 157 A.L.R. 282 (1945), 69 A.L.R. 2d 404 (1960).

9. John B. Waldbillig, Inc. v. Gottfried, 16 N.Y.2d 773, 262 N.Y.S.2d 498, 209 N.E.2d 818 (1965) (engineering); People v. Sterling Optical Co., 11 N.Y.2d 970, 229 N.Y.S.2d 419, 183 N.E.2d 698 (1962) (optometry); Matter of McNeely v. DeSapio, 6 A.D.2d 976, 176 N.Y.S.2d 457 (3d Dep't 1958), aff'd mem., 6 N.Y. 2d 727, 185 N.Y.S.2d 812, 158 N.E.2d 506 (1959) (hospital); Potomac Engineers, Inc. v. Walser, 96 U.S. App.D.C. 64, 223 F.2d 356 (1955) (engineering); State ex rel. Harris v. Myers, 128 Ohio St. 366, 191 N.E. 99 (1934) (optometry). Compare People by Kerner v. United Medical Service, Inc., 362 Ill. 442, 200 N.E. 157 (1936), with State Electro-Medical Institute v. State, 74 Neb. 40, 103 N.W. 1078 (1905) (medicine). See also Willcox, "Hospitals and the Corporate Practice of Medicine", 45 Cornell L.Q. 432 (1960). A New Jersey statute barring corporations from practicing "mortuary science" was found to violate the state constitution. Trinka Services, Inc. v. State Board of Mortuary Science, 40 N.J.Super. 238, 122 A.2d 668 (1956); Busse & Borgmann Co. v. Upchurch, 60 Ohio App. 349, 21 N.E.2d 349 (1938); Note, "The Corporate Practice of Architecture", 11 W.Res.L.Rev. 616 (1960); Stitt, "Corporate Practice of Engineering", 14 Bus.Law. 969

(1959); Jones, "Professional Corporation", 27 Fordham L.Rev. 353 (1958); Annot., 103 A.L.R. 1240 (1936), 165 A.L.R. 1098 (1946), 56 A.L.R.2d 726 (1957). See also O'Keefe, "North Dakota Anti-Corporate Farming Act: A Dissenting Opinion", 41 N. D.L.Rev. 333 (1965); McElroy, "North Dakota's Anti-Corporate Farming Act", 36 N.D.L.Rev. 96 (1960); Note, "An Analysis of House Bill 782: The Latest Attempt to Repeal North Dakota's Ban on Corporation Farming", 44 N.D.L.Rev. 255 (1968).

10. 12 U.S.C.A. §§ 21, 24, 321.

11. E.g., federal income tax advantages of engaging in foreign trade as corporation rather than individual resident citizen. Kaczmarek, "Tax Saving Incentives to Foreign Trade", 47 Geo.L.J. 88 (1958); see Seghers, "The Western Hemisphere Trade Corporation—What It is and How to Use It to Advantage", 42 Taxes 582 (1964); Raskind, "The Western Hemisphere Trade Corporation: A Functional Perspective", 16 Vand.L.Rev. 1 (1962); Hannon, "Choice of Business Organization for Latin American Operations", 34 Tul.L.Rev. 733 (1960); Crawford, "Western Hemisphere Trade Corporations", 47 Calif.L.Rev. 621 (1959); Wender, "Use of Tax Haven Corporations and Western Hemisphere Trade Corporations", U.So.Cal. 1959 Tax Inst. 253; Flynn, "Western Hemisphere Trade Corporations: Quo Vadis?", 12 Tax L.Rev. 413 (1957); Note, "Western Hemisphere Trade Corporations Reconsidered", 9 Wm. & Mary L.Rev. 205 (1967). See also Hochberg, "Foreign Investors Tax Act: its impact on personal holding companies", 27 J. Taxation 118 (1967); Jenks, "Export Trade Corporation: Orphan of the Storm", 67 Colum.L.Rev. 1187 (1967); Mihaly, "New Federal Tax Status of Foreign Corporations", 42 L.A.B.Bull. 341, 416 (1967).

12. E.g., use of limited partnership by Broadway production "angels". See Taubman, "Motion Picture Co-Production Deals and Theatrical Business Organization", 11 Tax L.Rev. 113, 303 (1956).

and losses; their marital status and
ages;

(c) Other possible financing; credit considerations;

(d) Probable earnings of the business (amount and nature) and income of participants from the business and from other sources; probable extent of retention of earnings in the business;

(e) Financial risks; practical importance of limited liability;

(f) Desirability of transferability of interest;

(g) Proposed name and/or trademark.

Whether a single form of business enterprise, or a combination of forms, should be selected, sometimes presents an additional question, requiring careful consideration of tax and other aspects. Among the possible advantages of multiple forms are separating sales from manufacturing and increasing efficiency; limiting the liabilities to each enterprise; dividing income at lower tax rates between the several enterprises; effectuating estate planning; creating entities which will permit the eventual sale at capital gain; increasing the combined borrowing capacity of the resulting companies; creating a separate entity to handle a competitive line; incorporating a separate entity in a different locality to avoid prejudice against absentee ownership; transferring certain of the activities to another state whose laws favor a domestic corporation. Contrariwise, combination of two or more businesses might provide a diversification to provide a hedge against economic changes, advantage of new management, reduction of administrative costs, combined power of advertising and marketing, savings of duplicate reports, bookkeeping systems, qualifications in for-

eign states, and use of consolidated tax returns, which enables the losses of one venture to be offset against the profits of another.[13] Combinations, of course, might raise antitrust problems.

Sometimes different forms recommend themselves at different stages of the business —depending upon changes in the business, personnel, and legal developments. Taxing statutes are especially susceptible to change.[14] While the initial selection need not be irrevocable, change of form can cause embarrassment. Considerable care, therefore, should be exercised in selecting the form or forms most appropriate under the particular circumstances, and in setting up the enterprise as advantageously as possible in the light of all possible contingencies.

13. Silver, "Choosing the Best Form of Doing Business in Canada—The Tax and Non-tax Aspects", 27 J. Taxation 246 (1967); Harper, "Forms of Business Organization for Doing Business in Latin America", 71 Com.L.J. 355 (1966); Spier, "Analysis of Legal Forms of Business Organization in Western Germany and the United States", 3 Am.Bus.L.J. 287 (1966); Wardenburg, "Business Reasons for Dividing Businesses", 37 Taxes 149 (1959); Culbertson, "Choosing the Number of Business Enterprises", 1954 Ill.L.F. 386; Conard, "Forming a Subsidiary in the European Common Market", 59 Mich.L. Rev. 1 (1960); Symposium: "The Formation and Operation of Foreign Subsidiaries and Branches, Including the Extent to Which Foreign Subsidiaries Are Entitled to Special Treatment under the Law of Their Incorporation or under International Law", 16 Bus.Law. 402 (1961).

14. E.g., Tax Reform Act of 1969, H.R. 13270, 91st Cong., 2d Sess. (1969); Bailey, "Basic Tax Reform", 54 A.B.A.J. 127 (1968); Dodyk, "Tax Simplification: The Long Amendment and the Mills Proposal", N.Y. U. 25th Inst. on Fed.Tax. 1443 (1967); Keogh, "A Sound Tax Policy and a Sound Economy", N.Y.U. 25th Inst. on Fed.Tax. 1381 (1967); Tax Revision Compendium (U.S. Gov't Printing Office 1959); Cary, "Reflections upon the American Law Institute Tax Project and the Internal Revenue Code: A Plea for a Moratorium and Reappraisal", 60 Colum.L. Rev. 259 (1960); "Revolution in Tax Laws Coming?", 47 U.S. News & World Rep. No. 24, 54–58 (Dec. 14, 1959).

B. INDIVIDUAL (OR SOLE) PROPRIETORSHIP

INDIVIDUAL PROPRIETORSHIP

18. The individual or sole proprietorship is the oldest, simplest, and most prevalent form of business enterprise. It can be organized informally, is subject to minimal regulation, and involves few problems of management and control. The individual proprietor retains all profits and bears all losses. However, the individual proprietorship ends on the proprietor's death or retirement; the business is rather freely transferable. Ordinarily, the individual proprietorship is taxed as an individual.

The individual proprietorship or sole proprietorship—the two terms being interchangeable—is the oldest, simplest, and most prevalent form of business enterprise.[1] Rules of contract, torts, property, and agency law loom large in its legal character.[2]

"A man may carry on his business as sole proprietor. Such assistance as he needs in the way of services he may procure by hiring others, with whom he enters into the relation of master and servant, or principal and agent. If he needs more capital than he owns he may borrow from others, creating the relation of debtor and creditor. If he needs more real estate or tangible personal property than he owns he may rent from others, creating the relation of landlord and tenant, or bailor and bailee. The entrepreneur who utilizes the services of others is bound to pay wages or salaries. He must pay rent to the landlord or bailor, and interest to whoever lends him money. If there are losses he must bear them alone, to the extent of his resources. If there are profits he does not have to share them, unless he has agreed to compensate his employees, landlord or money lender with a share of profits in lieu of fixed wages, rent or interest." [3]

In short, the individual proprietor is the "boss"; he personally employs others—his employees or agents. The business contracts—those made by him personally or by his agents within their actual or apparent authority or, when made beyond the agency power, ratified by him—are his contracts. As to torts, he is responsible directly for those he personally commits and vicariously (respondeat superior) for those committed by his employees within the scope of their employment. His personal liability, therefore, is unlimited, subject to possible protection by contractual stipulation or insurance. To the extent that most of his personal assets might already be invested in the business, limited personal liability would not add much benefit as a practical matter. Credit can be had for the business to the extent of not only the business assets but also the proprietor's personal assets.

Not a form of business *association*, it can become one, thereby ceasing to be an individual proprietorship, by being incorporated (possibly as a one-man corporation) and/or by admitting others to the business (e. g., partnership).

There are no formalities involved in the organization of an individual proprietorship, and no expense beyond the capital needs of the enterprise need be incurred. These factors make this form of doing business espe-

1. C. Rohrlich, Organizing Corporate and Other Business Enterprises 76–81 (4th ed. 1967); Lyons, "How to Plan for a Sole Proprietorship", 17 J.Am. Soc'y of C.L.U. 257 (1963). Of an estimated 11,-479,000 business enterprises in the United States, some 9,087,000 were listed as individual proprietorships. Statistical Abstract of the United States 1969, 472 (U.S. Dep't of Commerce).

2. See W. Seavey, Handbook of the Law of Agency (1964); R. Powell, The Law of Agency (2d ed. 1961); M. Ferson, Principles of Agency (1954); P. Mechem, Outlines of the Law of Agency (4th ed. 1952); A. Rotwein, Law of Agency (3d ed. 1949); W. Seavey, Studies in Agency (1949); Restatement, Second, Agency (1958) (3 vols.); "Note on Agency Law, in R. Stevens and H. Henn, Statutes, Cases, and Materials on the Law of Corporations and Other Business Enterprises 75–83 (1965).

3. J. Crane, Handbook on the Law of Partnership and Other Unincorporated Associations 2 (2d ed. 1952).

cially suitable to small one-man enterprises. There is little restriction on his doing business in other jurisdictions, although such activity might make him amenable to process there.[4]

Of course, if the proprietor is entering a licensed trade, he must obtain such license —just as he would if he were to operate his business under any other form.[5] If he desires to conduct his business under an assumed name (e. g., John Doe d/b/a "College Shop"), statutes in many jurisdictions require that a certificate to that effect be filed in a public office.[6] Some jurisdictions prohibit the use of the words "& Co." or the like when no actual partner is represented thereby.[7] Obviously, use of the name may not be such as would constitute unfair competition, trademark infringement, or invasion of right of privacy.

The obtaining of credit by the individual proprietor is limited by his own solvency. On the other hand, he is not bothered by problems of management and control. Since there is a single owner, there are no problems of relations with co-owners and therefore no contract between the owners—often a difficult drafting task in the partnership and small corporation. The relation of master and servant or principal and agent or employer and employee exists between him and anyone else associated with the enterprise.[8] He retains all the profits of the business and likewise must bear all the losses, and he remains fully liable for any business debts although the business is dissolved.[9]

There is generally no continuity of existence because on the death of the proprietor, his proprietorship obviously ends. However, some continuity may be obtained by a proper testamentary disposition. Thus, a proprietor may vest authority in his executor to continue the business so that his legatee may receive a going concern—thereby technically starting a new individual proprietorship.[10] To the extent that the business did not depend as a practical matter upon the personal efforts of the sole owner, the business might thereafter be carried on by another. Continuity is also obtained in some jurisdictions by means of special statutes applicable to decedents' businesses in general or to certain types of businesses.[11]

4. Henry L. Doherty & Co. v. Goodman, 294 U.S. 623, 55 S.Ct. 553, 79 L.Ed. 1097 (1935) (Iowa statute); McKinney's N.Y.CPLR, § 302.

5. A great and growing complex of licensing regulations surround many occupations. Some of them are self-encouraged to discourage competition and attain "professional" status. More than 1,200 licensing statutes are in effect in the United States.

6. New York statutes provide that any person who conducts business "under any name or designation other than his real name" must file in the county clerk's office in each county in which such business is being conducted a certificate containing his business name and address along with his own name and address. McKinney's N.Y.Gen.Bus.Law, § 130; [1946] N.Y.L.Rev'n Comm'n Rep. 1946 Legis.Doc.No. 65(G) 197–226; [1947] N.Y.L.Rev'n Comm'n Rep. 1947 Legis.Doc.No. 65(C) 53–72; [1948] N.Y.L.Rev'n Comm'n Rep. 1948 Legis.Doc.No. 65(A) 25–37. Noncompliance might bar the proprietor from maintaining or defending actions. Chaikin v. Skolnick, 201 So.2d 588 (Fla.Dist.Ct.App.1967); McClintock, "Fictitious Business Name Legislation—Modernizing California's Pioneer Statute", 19 Hastings L.J. 1349 (1968).

7. E.g., McKinney's N.Y.Gen.Bus.Law, § 132; Or.Op. Att'y Gen. No. 5865, Sept. 28, 1964; Nev.Op. Att'y Gen. No. 244, Aug. 20, 1961.

8. Blake, "Employee Agreements Not to Compete", 73 Harv.L.Rev. 625 (1960).

9. A transferee who pays full value for an individual proprietor's business is not liable to former employees of the individual proprietor for wages where the transferee is not aware thereof and has not agreed to assume the debts. Pringle v. Hunsicker, 154 Cal.App.2d 789, 316 P.2d 742 (1957).

10. Scheifly, "The Sale of the Family Business and Estate Planning Implications", 46 Taxes 85 (1968); Polasky, "Planning for the Disposition of a Substantial Interest in a Closely Held Business", 44 Iowa L.Rev. 83 (1958); Jardine, "Estate Planning for Proprietorship and Partnership Interests", 6 Utah L.Rev. 169 (1958); Comment, "Continuation of a Decedent's Unincorporated Business in Pennsylvania", 104 U.Pa.L.Rev. 679 (1956); Annot., 83 A.L. R.2d 1406 (1962).

11. See, e.g., McKinney's N.Y. SCPA, § 2108, permitting fiduciary to petition for continuation of business of which decedent was sole owner; also McKinney's N.Y. Alcoholic Bev. Control Law, § 122, giving the executor or administrator of a licensed

The interest of an individual proprietor in his business is freely transferable with a few possible exceptions: dower or curtesy rights, if they still exist,[12] the restrictions contained in the bulk transfers law, and fraudulent conveyance law. Generally the bulk transfers law prevents the defeat of the interests of business creditors by the sale of a going concern.[13] Insofar as tax considerations are concerned, the individual proprietorship or proprietor is like any other person and treated accordingly.[14] His business income and other income, business losses and other losses, etc., are treated together. On the total taxable income, the owner pays his tax at the current individual rate: 14 percent on the first $500, with some 25 graduations, up to 70 percent on $100,000 or more, subject to a 50 percent maximum on earned income.

On the other hand, the individual proprietor is not subject to double federal taxation as are the shareholders and their corporations absent Subchapter S election.[15] At the state level, however, his business might be subject to an unincorporated business income tax.[16]

Capital gains possibilities exist upon the sale of the business, with gains on inventory being taxed as ordinary income. The basis of any capital assets acquired from the deceased owner would be the fair market value of the property either at the date of the decedent's death or as of the alternative valuation date for federal estate tax purposes, thus permitting a stepped-up basis without income tax consequences.

For tax purposes, the sale of an individual proprietorship is the sale of the individual assets comprising the business, with gain or loss figured according to the classification of each asset.[17]

Although the individual proprietor is not treated as an employee of the business (as are those employed by him) for purposes of deductions for employee benefit plans and the like given to corporations, tax advantages of qualified retirement plans have been made available to self-employed persons. Since 1968, full deduction can be taken on contributions to retirement plans up to a maximum of $2,500, or 10 percent of gross annual "earned income", whichever is less. Those who devote full time to their businesses will be able to take 100 percent of their net profits as "earned income." [18]

retailer of alcoholic beverages the power to continue the deceased's business.

12. Abolished in New York, effective September 1, 1930. McKinney's N.Y. Real Prop. Law, §§ 189–190.

13. E.g., Uniform Commercial Code §§ 6–101 et seq. See W. Hawkland, Sales and Bulk Sales (ALI rev. 1958); Annot., 85 A.L.R.2d 1211 (1962).

14. W. Vernon, L. Vernon & J. Nolan, Federal Income Taxation of Individuals (ALI rev. 1967). Prior to 1969, under Subchapter R of the Internal Revenue Code, an individual proprietorship with certain kinds of income was able to elect to be taxed, to some extent, as a corporation. See section 17, n. 4 supra.

15. Willis, "Subchapter S: A Lure to Incorporate Proprietorships and Partnerships", 6 U.C.L.A.L.Rev. 505 (1959).

16. E.g., McKinney's N.Y. Tax Law, §§ 701 et seq.

17. For federal tax purposes, the assets are classifiable as (a) capital, (b) noncapital, and (c) section 1231; the contract of sale should break down the assets and assign a reasonable value to the various classes, including any agreement not to compete and assignment of goodwill. The allocation to a covenant not to compete is usually ordinary income to the seller and an amortizable expense to the buyer; the allocation to goodwill, a nondepreciable capital asset, affords capital gain treatment to the seller but is not subject to depreciation deduction by the buyer. In the absence of fraud, duress, undue influence or some other such factor as between the parties would justify an alteration of the agreement, buyers and sellers must accept the tax consequences of their own allocation. Comm'r v. Danielson, 378 F.2d 771 (3d Cir.1967), cert. denied 389 U.S. 858, 88 S.Ct. 94, 19 L.Ed.2d 123 (1967). See S. Hagendorf, Tax Guide for Buying and Selling a Business (1967).

18. Self-Employed Individuals Tax Retirement Act of 1962 (popularly referred to as "Keogh Act" or "H.R. 10"), as amended in 1966 and 1968, Int.Rev. Code of 1954, 26 U.S.C.A. §§ 401–405. See H.R. 10— For You and Now (PLI 1968); Fross, "The Wonderland of H.R. 10 Distributions", 55 A.B.A.J. 785 (1969); Pincus, "Retirement Planning for the Self-Employed: A Review of Possible Techniques", N.Y. U. 26th Inst. on Fed.Tax. 1079 (1968); Kern, "The New Look of H.R. 10", 54 A.B.A.J. 311 (1968); Taylor, "Retirement Plans for Self-Employed—A

On the whole, it may be said that as important as tax considerations are, the choice between incorporating and operating as an individual proprietorship generally hinges upon the choice between limited liability with greater government regulation and full liability (possibly limited by contractual provisions or covered by insurance) with a high degree of freedom and secrecy of operation.

C. GENERAL PARTNERSHIP

GENERAL PARTNERSHIP—IN GENERAL

19. Partnerships are more numerous than business corporations, and range from two to many partners and from small to large businesses. A partnership is an association of two or more persons to carry on as co-owners a business for profit. Partnerships are either general partnerships or limited partnerships. A general partnership is a partnership of two or more partners, all of whom are general partners. A general partnership can be formed with little formality. Recognized at common law, a general partnership is governed very often by statute, in most jurisdictions, the Uniform Partnership Act. By agreement, relations among the partners can be varied substantially from the statutory pattern. Generally, a partnership is not regarded as a separate entity, but there are exceptions.

Partnership law is, in large part, a body of distinct law, not merely the application to given facts of principles of the general law of contracts, torts, property, and agency. Partnership involves the creation of a peculiar type of relationship between two or more persons, which involves rights and duties and regulates the conduct of these persons. The sources of this law are in the common law, civil law, equity, and the law merchant.

Partnership law has a double aspect, involving as it does (a) the application of agency law, and (b) the delineation of the characteristics of a particular form of business enterprise, from which several other forms of business enterprise evolved.

Look At H.R. 10 As Amended", 34 Tenn.L.Rev. 632 (1967); Snyder & Weckstein, "Quasi-Corporations, Quasi-Employees, and Quasi-Tax Relief for Professional Persons", 48 Cornell L.Q. 613 (1963).

Numerically, there are more partnerships than business corporations,[1] ranging in size from two partners to over a hundred partners,[2] and from the smallest to very large businesses.[3]

"A partnership is an association of two or more persons to carry on as co-owners a business for profit." [4]

Where the following five elements are present:

(a) Association;

(b) Of two or more persons (with legal capacity to be partners);

(c) Carrying on a business (more than single venture;[5] business purpose);

(d) As co-owners;

(e) For profit—

a partnership exists. Rules for determining the existence of a partnership have been codified by statute.[6]

1. Of an estimated 11,479,000 business enterprises in the United States, 923,000 were listed as partnerships, as compared with 1,469,000 corporations. Statistical Abstract of the United States 1969, 472 (U.S. Dep't of Commerce).

2. A British partnership, other than of accountants, solicitors, and stockholders, may not have more than 20 members. Solicitors may, but barristers may not, practice in partnership. Of practicing American attorneys, some one-third practice as partners in law partnerships.

3. For many years, Gimbel Bros. and F. W. Woolworth Co. were partnerships.

4. Uniform Partnership Act § 6.

5. For discussion of joint venture, see section 49 infra.

6. Uniform Partnership Act § 7. The receipt by a person of a share of the profits of a business is prima facie evidence that he is a partner in the

Partnerships are of two basic types: the general partnership, derived through the law merchant from the continental *sociétés*, and the limited partnership, derived from the *commenda* or *société en commandite*. A general partnership consists of two or more partners, all of whom are general partners with full status (unlimited personal liability; managerial control), and may be formed with little or no statutory formality. A limited partnership consists of one or more general partners and one or more limited partners (limited liability; little managerial control), and, being a statutory creation, may be formed only by compliance with statutory requirements.

The general partnership will be discussed in this section and sections 20–27; the limited partnership in sections 28–36. Except as qualified in the latter sections, the discussion of the general partnership in this section and sections 20–27 applies to the limited partnership as well.[7]

The general partnership was recognized, at common law, but much of the law is codified in the Uniform Partnership Act, which has been adopted in some four-fifths of American jurisdictions.[8] Some jurisdictions have no statute but rely on the common law.[9] Such law, whether codified or not, defines the sterotype partnership, but permits, considerable variation in the partnership setup.[10]

business, but no such inference shall be drawn if such profits were received in payment of a debt, wages, rent, annuity to a widow or representative of a deceased partner, interest on a loan, consideration for the sale of the goodwill of a business or other property by installments or otherwise. Comment, "Partnership: Tests Used in Determining Its Existence", 35 Tul.L.Rev. 448 (1961); Note, "Partnerships—Profit Sharing by Lender", 40 N.C.L.Rev. 355 (1962). Cf. Cox v. Hickman, 8 H.L.Cas. 268, 11 Eng.Rep. 431 (1860); Nelson v. Seaboard Surety Co., 269 F.2d 882 (8th Cir.1959). Joint tenancy, tenancy in common, tenancy by the entireties, joint property, common property, or part ownership does not of itself establish a partnership, whether such co-owners do or do not share any profits realized from the use of the property. Annot., 131 A.L.R. 508 (1941), 150 A.L.R. 1003 (1944). In general, any one with full contractual capacity may become a partner. The partnership contracts of infants and of insane persons may be voidable, but their investment in the business remains liable for partnership debts. Where married women have full contractual capacity, they may become partners. Amsler, "The Status of Married Women in Texas Business Association", 43 Texas L.Rev. 669 (1965). For validity of partnership agreements between husband and wife, see Annot., 20 A.L.R. 1304 (1922), 38 A.L.R. 1264 (1925), 157 A.L.R. 652 (1945). Public policy forbids the nationals of countries at war with each other to be copartners. At one time, it was the general rule that corporations could not become partners, on corporation law grounds that it was ultra vires their corporate powers or would divest their board of directors of management of corporate affairs, but this rule has been modified where statutes empower corporations to be partners or possibly where the articles of incorporation so provide. ABA-ALI Model Bus. Corp. Act § 4(g). Armstrong, "Can Corporations Be Partners?", 20 Bus. Law. 899 (1965). See text accompanying section 183, nn. 38–44 infra. A partnership may be a partner in another firm. A. Bromberg, Crane and Bromberg on Partnership § 6 (1968). See Reiman, "Trust Participation in a Partnership", 2 Hastings L.J. 24 (1951). See also State v. Atlantic City, 23 N.J. 337, 129 A.2d 293 (1957) (4–3) (holding city and state to be in partnership with respect to certain federal funds). On necessity and manner of pleading denial of partnership in action by third person against partners, see Annot., 68 A.L.R.2d 545 (1959).

7. See Uniform Partnership Act § 6(2) (Act to apply to limited partnerships except insofar as statutes relating thereto are inconsistent).

8. 6 U.L.A. 1 (1969); approved 1914; adopted (with some local variations) in Alaska, Arizona, Arkansas, California, Colorado, Connecticut, Delaware, Idaho, Illinois, Indiana, Kentucky, Maryland, Massachusetts, Michigan, Minnesota, Missouri, Montana, Nebraska, Nevada, New Jersey, New Mexico, New York, North Carolina, North Dakota, Ohio, Oklahoma, Oregon, Pennsylvania, Rhode Island, South Carolina, South Dakota, Tennessee, Texas, Utah, Vermont, Virginia, Washington, West Virginia, Wisconsin, Wyoming, District of Columbia, Virgin Islands, and Guam.

9. Common-law rules prevail to a greater or lesser extent in Alabama, Florida, Iowa, Kansas, Maine, and New Hampshire.

10. See generally A. Bromberg, Crane and Bromberg on Partnership (1968); C. Rohrlich, Organizing Corporate and Other Business Enterprises 98–110, 212–265 (4th ed. 1967); "Note on Partnership Law", in R. Stevens & H. Henn, Statutes, Cases, and Materials on the Law of Corporations and Other Business Enterprises 84–95 (1965); S. Rowley, Rowley on Partnership (2d ed. 1960); J. Barrett & E. Seago, Partners and Partnerships: Law and Taxation (1956); Mersky, "The Literature of Partnership Law", 16 Vand.L.Rev. 389 (1963); Hirsh, "Medical Partnerships", 13 DePaul L.Rev. 28 (1963); Bromberg, "Texas Uniform Partnership Act—The Enacted Version", 15 Sw.L.J. 386 (1961); N. Krausz & F. Mann, Partnerships in the Farm Business (U. Ill. Extension Circular 786, 1958); Ham, "Kentucky

In this respect, the partnership is more flexible than the corporation. Unless one is aware of the permissible variations and ways of effectuating them, the full potentiality of the partnership is not realized. Awareness of such matters promotes a more sophisticated comparison of the relative advantages and disadvantages of the partnership and, if the partnership is selected, a more ingenious partnership setup tailored to the needs of the situation.

Generally, a partnership is not recognized as an entity apart from its members even under the Uniform Partnership Act.[11] There are, however, certain exceptions. A partnership may, of course, do business with or without a distinctive firm name or even under an assumed name providing that it complies with any filing requirements which may exist in a particular jurisdiction in which it is doing business.[12]

The common law adopted a strict view and accorded no recognition to the partnership as an entity for purposes of ownership of real property, contract, suit, etc. Under the Uniform Partnership Act, however, a partnership may acquire, hold, and convey even real property in the partnership name,[13] and a partner may contract with his partnership,[14] but not engage in *law* suits with it.[15] In addition the procedural rules of many states recognize the partnership entity for the purpose of actions by and against the firm.[16]

Foreign partnerships may be amenable to process on a basis similar to that of foreign corporations,[17] or, by rare statute, required

Adopts the Uniform Partnership Act", 43 Ky.L.J. 5 (1954); Comment, "Farm Partnership: Ownership and Use of Real Property", 47 Iowa L.Rev. 689 (1962).

11. The early drafts by James Barr Ames & William Draper Lewis of the Uniform Partnership Act were based on the entity theory but were rejected by the Commissioners on Uniform State Laws. The Act was redrawn on the aggregate theory "with the modification that the partners be treated as owners of partnership property holding by a special tenancy which should be called tenancy in partnership." This accounts for the several vestiges of the entity approach in the Act. Jensen, "Is a partnership under the Uniform Partnership Act an Aggregate or an Entity?", 16 Vand.L.Rev. 377 (1963); Ballantine, "Adoption of Uniform Partnership Act in California", 17 Calif.L.Rev. 623 (1929); Note, "The Partnership as a Legal Entity", 41 Colum.L.Rev. 698 (1941). A partnership in Louisiana, under the civil law, is a civil person. Birmingham Fire Ins. Co. v. Adolph, 379 F.2d 948 (5th Cir.1967); Trappey v. Lumbermen's Mut. Cas. Co., 229 La. 632, 86 So.2d 515 (1956); O'Neal, "An Appraisal of the Louisiana Law of Partnership", 9 La.L.Rev. 307, 450 (1949). The Louisiana Civil Code has been held to define a partnership as "a synallagmatic and commutative contract." State ex rel. Waterman v. J. S. Waterman & Co., 178 La. 340, 351, 151 So. 422, 426 (1933).

12. See section 20, n. 5 infra. In selecting a name, unfair competition, invasion of privacy, etc., should be avoided. The names of persons not interested in the firm may not be used except where a partnership name is continued, with appropriate filing, after the withdrawal of a name partner, as permitted

by statute. E.g., McKinney's N.Y. Part. Law. §§ 80–91.

13. Uniform Partnership Act §§ 8, 10.

14. 1 Restatement of Contracts § 17 (1932).

15. Arnold v. Arnold, 90 N.Y. 580 (1882); cf. Cole v. Reynolds, 18 N.Y. 74 (1858); Annot., 21 A.L.R. 21 (1922), 58 A.L.R. 621 (1929), 168 A.L.R. 1088 (1947). To this traditional rule there were some exceptions: where the subject of the litigation is separate and distinct from partnership affairs; where the action is to enforce a partner's right to participate in management; and where the partnership has been dissolved in violation of the partnership agreement. The rule itself seems to be breaking down. See Smith v. Hensley, 354 S.W.2d 744 (Ky.1961) (holding that one of eight partners could maintain action against all partners, including himself by name, to recover damages for value of truck owned individually by him and allegedly destroyed by negligence of employees of partnership); Annot., 98 A.L.R.2d 345 (1964). For discussion of recent development of partnership derivative actions, see section 28, n. 10 infra.

16. In New York, for example, an action may be brought by or against a partnership in the names of all the partners or in the partnership name by serving one or more of the general partners. If less than all the general partners are served, any judgment obtained will be enforceable against the partnership property and the individual property of those partners served. McKinney's N.Y. CPLR, §§ 1501, 1502, 5201(b); 11 N.Y. Judicial Council, 1945 Legis.Doc. No. 15(c) 221–240. Cf. Ingersoll Corp. v. Rogers, 217 La. 79, 46 So.2d 45 (1950).

17. Intercontinental Leasing, Inc. v. Anderson, 410 F.2d 303 (10th Cir. 1969); Lewis Mfg. Co. v. Superior Court in and for Los Angeles County, 140 Cal. App.2d 245, 295 P.2d 145 (1956); McKinney's N.Y. CPLR, § 302(a) (1). See section 28, nn. 7, 8 infra.

to qualify to do business and to designate a registered agent for service of process.[18]

Under the Federal Rules of Civil Procedure, actions may be brought by and against the partnership in the firm name except in diversity cases wherein the applicable state rule will be followed.[19] Diversity of citizenship is determined by looking to the citizenship of each partner and not by considering the partnership as an entity.[20]

The Federal Bankruptcy Act accords some recognition to the partnership as an entity, defining "person" as including a partnership [21] and providing that "a partnership, including a limited partnership . . . may be adjudged a bankrupt either separately or jointly with one or more of its partners." [22]

Although no federal income tax is assessed upon the profits of a partnership as the income of a business organization, the Internal Revenue Code does recognize a partnership as an entity for certain purposes. Thus, a partnership is required to file an information return.[23] Prior to 1969, under Subchapter R, a partnership meeting certain requirements, could have elected to be treated to some extent as a corporation.[24] If a partnership is set up in such a manner that it has sufficient corporate attributes of a corporation, it may in fact be treated as an "association" and taxed as a corporation.[25]

Finally, a partnership may be recognized as an entity in special situations where justice or public policy may demand that it be treated as a single person.[26] A partnership continuing in business cannot collect on a claim arising after the old partnership was dissolved.[27] A partnership becoming a member of another partnership may be treated as a single person with respect to the second partnership.[28] An Iowa criminal statute

---

18. See section 20, nn. 7, 8 infra.

19. Fed.R.Civ.P. 17(b). Leh v. General Petroleum Corp., 165 F.Supp. 933 (S.D.Cal.1958).

20. Comment, "Diversity of Citizenship for Unincorporated Associations", 75 Yale L.J. 138 (1965). See ALI Study of the Division of Jurisdiction between State and Federal Courts 10 (1969) (proposal that, for purposes of diversity-of-citizenship jurisdiction, partnership or other unincorporated associations capable of suing or being sued in its common name in forum be deemed citizen of state or foreign nation where it has its principal place of business).

21. 11 U.S.C.A. § 1(23).

22. 11 U.S.C.A. § 23(a). But cf. id. § 1(19); Francis v. McNeal, 228 U.S. 695, 33 S.Ct. 701, 57 L.Ed. 1029 (1913) (partnership not insolvent unless all general partners insolvent). See Rifkind, "Dilemma of Partnership Bankruptcy Administration under Present Section 5 of the Bankruptcy Act", 33 Ref.J. 108 (1959). An amendment of § 1(19), proposed by the National Bankruptcy Conference, would add the clause: "and if such 'person' is a partnership then exclusive also of the property of the partner or partners." Kennedy, "A New Deal for Partnership Bankruptcy", 60 Colum.L.Rev. 610, 656 (1960); MacLachlan, "Partnership Bankruptcy", 65 Com.L. J. 253 (1960). For exemption problems, see Phillips v. C. Paloma & Sons, 270 F.2d 791 (1959); Annot., 4 A.L.R. 300 (1919).

23. Int.Rev.Code of 1954, 26 U.S.C.A. §§ 701, 6031.

24. Int.Rev.Code of 1954, 26 U.S.C.A. § 1361 (repealed, effective Jan. 1, 1969). See section 17, n. 4 supra.

25. Treas.Reg. § 301.7701–2 (1960); Morrissey v. Comm'r, 296 U.S. 344, 56 S.Ct. 289, 80 L.Ed. 263 (1935). See section 16, nn. 4–6 supra. Concerning Subchapter S election see sections 76, 262 infra.

26. United States v. A & P Trucking Co., 358 U.S. 121, 79 S.Ct. 203, 3 L.Ed.2d 165 (1958) (5–4) (partnership indictable as person under 18 U.S.C.A. § 835); United States v. Silverstein, 237 F.Supp. 446 (S.D.N.Y.1965), aff'd per curiam 344 F.2d 1016 (2d Cir.1965), cert. denied 382 U.S. 828, 86 S.Ct. 65, 15 L.Ed.2d 73 (1965) (denial of privilege against self-incrimination to general partner holding subpoenaed records of large limited partnerships, by analogy to corporate officer re corporate records); Eule v. Eule Motor Sales, 62 N.J.Super. 250, 162 A.2d 601 (App.Div.1960), rev'd 34 N.J. 537, 170 A.2d 241 (1961) (wife allowed to maintain action against husband's partnership for personal injuries sustained through husband's negligence occurring within course of partnership business notwithstanding common-law doctrine of interspousal immunity); Keegan v. Keegan, 194 Minn. 261, 260 N.W. 318 (1935) (widow-partner held entitled to workmen's compensation award against her partnership for death of her husband, employee of partnership).

27. Ardolino v. Ierna, 225 App.Div. 439, 233 N.Y.S. 477 (3d Dep't 1929).

28. See Baker v. Bd. of Ed. of Central School Dist. No. 2 of Towns of Bath, Steuben County, 309 N.Y. 551, 132 N.E.2d 837 (1956) (holding that where individual and two-man partnership united in contract with third party containing arbitration clause, indi-

prohibiting the lending of bank funds to certain persons was held not to bar the lending of funds to a partnership in which one of such persons was a partner.[29]

GENERAL PARTNERSHIP—FORMALITIES OF ORGANIZATION

20. A general partnership may arise informally, although the sound practice is to define the relationships among the partners in written articles of partnership or partnership agreement. Usually there are no organization fees or taxes. Statutes sometimes provide for the public filing of the partnership name.

A general partnership, being a voluntary, personal relationship, may arise informally, the agreement being express or implied. Although no formal (or even express) agreement is necessary, it is customary (and sounder practice) to define the rights and duties of the partners inter se (as distinguished from their relationship with third parties) in a written instrument known as "articles of partnership" or "partnership agreement" which usually deals with partnership name, names of partners, date of agreement, purposes of partnership, location of business, duration, investment of each partner (realty, personalty, cash, choses in action, services), any loans to partnership of assets or cash, partners' sharing of profits and losses, any remuneration for services, management and voting powers, arbitration or other provision for deadlock or disagreement, voluntary or compulsory retirement, purchase or sale of deceased or retiring partner's interest with method for determining value, possible cross-insurance, respective duties of partners, books of account, accounting periods, banking arrangements, authority to sign partnership checks, make

loans, hire and discharge employees, fix their salaries and wages, etc.[1]

In the absence of provisions in the agreement to the contrary (as to which there is considerable latitude), such rights follow a prescribed pattern. Therefore, whenever the partners desire to change any of the normal incidents of the partnership relation, a written instrument is desirable. The Uniform Partnership Act permits the partners to vary their rights and duties in their agreement,[2] but the partner claiming that there has been a deviation from the statutory pattern might be faced with difficulties of proof if there is no writing.[3] A written agreement is also highly desirable for tax reasons. While the formation of a partnership is not within the statute of frauds, various ancillary transactions involved in the creation may fall within the statute. These include: the transfer to the partnership of an interest in real property; the contract to form a partnership to endure for more than one year; the assignment by one partner of his interest in the partnership to another

1. J. Mulder, M. Volz & A. Berger, Drafting of Partnership Agreements (ALI 5th ed. 1967); "General Partnership Agreement" in R. Stevens & H. Henn, Statutes, Cases and Materials on the Law of Corporations and Other Business Enterprises 75–98 (1965); 1 J. Rabkin & M. Johnson, Current Legal Forms, with Tax Analysis 33–308 (1963); A. Willis, Handbook of Partnership Taxation 500 et seq. (1957); P. Carrington & W. Sutherland, Articles of Partnership for Law Firms (ABA 1962); Cantor, "Pitfalls in the Formation of Law Partnerships", 49 A.B.A.J. 155 (1963); Wren, "Planning Problems of Partners and Partnerships", 1963 U.Ill.L.F. 400; Cleveland, "Comments on Louisiana Law Partnership Agreements", 7 La.B.J. 175 (1959); Jones, "The Law of Partnership Agreement", 29 N.Y.St.B.Bull. 126 (1957); Foote, "Form of Partnership Agreement for Professional Men", 11 Bus.Law. 136 (July 1956); Heyler, "Drafting Problems of Partnership Agreements", 40 Calif.L.Rev. 67 (1952); Worcester, "The Drafting of Partnership Agreements", 63 Harv.L. Rev. 985 (1950). See Walzer, "Formation of General and Limited Partnerships," and Levin, "Formation of Professional or Personal Service Partnerships", in Advising California Business Enterprises, 179–262, 263–280 (1958).

2. Uniform Partnership Act § 18.

vidual member of resulting partnership could, as agent thereof demand arbitration without consent of partnership partner). Quaere, whether one of three equal partners could compel arbitration.

29. State v. Haesemeyer, 248 Iowa 154, 79 N.W.2d 755 (1956).

3. See, e.g., Jacobson v. Wikholm, 29 Cal.2d 24, 172 P.2d 878 (1946).

(the sale of a chose in action); but the assumption by an incoming partner of past partnership obligations is a promise directly to the debtors, and thus not within the statute (even if made directly to the creditors it is said to be in consideration for the consent to the novation and the same result follows).[4]

There are generally no organization fees or taxes.

Statutes sometimes provide for filing of partnership names under "assumed name", "fictitious name", or "registration of trade name" statutes.[5]

In choosing a firm name, the partnership is subject to the general law of unfair competition, trademark infringement, and right of privacy. In addition, a partnership is often expressly precluded from using the name of one not interested in the firm.[6]

New Hampshire, in 1965,[7] enacted a statute requiring qualification of foreign partnerships doing business in the state and their maintenance of a registered office and registered agent in the state.[8]

GENERAL PARTNERSHIP—CAPITAL AND CREDIT REQUIREMENTS

21. A partnership requires no minimum capital. Partners usually contribute cash, property, or personal services to the partnership. A partner may loan money or property to the partnership. Provision for interest on contributions might also be made. The partnership agreement should deal with these matters and withdrawal of capital.

The uniform acts do not require that a certain amount of capital be amassed by a partnership prior to the commencement of business. Normally, the partners contribute cash, property, or personal services to the firm, but a partnership interest may be received by way of gift.

The general partnership is in the same situation as the individual proprietor with regard to the question of the availability of credit. That is, the amount of credit available is limited by the value of the partners' personal resources as collateral; partnership interests are ordinarily not pledgeable for loans or credit; the partnership does not ordinarily issue bonds or debentures.

A partner may loan money or property to the partnership instead of giving it outright as a capital contribution. Unlike the capital contribution (assuming no provision in the partnership agreement to the contrary), interest may be collected by the partner on money or property loaned to the partnership. Money or property not given outright is not partnership property even as to creditors of the firm. A partnership may borrow money, seek additional contributions from the members, or attract additional capital by the admission of additional partners, thereby

4. A. Bromberg, Crane and Bromberg on Partnership 502 (1968).

5. McKinney's N.Y.Gen.Bus.Law, § 130, providing that a partnership must file in the office of the county clerk in every county in which it does business, a certificate setting forth the designation under which and the address within the county at which such business is conducted, the full names of all the partners with their addresses and the age of any who may be infants. The certificate must be executed and acknowledged by all the partners. The section does not apply to law partnerships. Neither does it apply to partnerships which have filed a certificate of continued use of a firm name. McKinney's N.Y.Part.Law, § 81 (no corresponding section in Uniform Act). Nor does it apply to limited partnerships, which must satisfy other filing requirements. Uniform Limited Partnership Act §§ 2, 24; McKinney's N.Y.Part.Law, §§ 91, 113; [1939] N.Y.L.Rev'n Comm'n Rep. 1939 Legis.Doc. No. 65(D) 75–99; [1946] N.Y.L.Rev'n Comm'n Rep. 1946 Legis.Doc. No. 65(G) 197–226; [1947] N.Y.L.Rev'n Comm'n Rep. 1947 Legis.Doc. No. 65(C) 53–72; [1948] N.Y.L.Rev'n Comm'n Rep. 1948 Legis.Doc. No. 65(A) 25–37.

6. See, e.g., McKinney's N.Y.Part.Law, § 82 (no corresponding section in Uniform Act).

7. N.H.Rev.Stat.Ann. ch. 305–A (Supp.1965).

8. Sanctions for noncompliance include disability to sue in any of the courts of the state, restraint from further prosecution of business in the state, and a fine of not more than $500. Note, "Qualification of Foreign Partnerships", 52 Cornell L.Q. 157 (1966).

technically becoming a new partnership, or by the admission of a limited partner, thereby becoming—assuming compliance with the statutory requirements—a limited partnership.[1]

The question of the capitalization of a particular partnership presents a problem in draftsmanship. In the first place, the draftsman must be sure that any property contributed to the partnership is adequately described in the partnership agreement. If a special asset is contributed—a seat on a securities exchange, for example—there should be a provision as to how the asset will be treated on dissolution or upon retirement of the contributing partner. It is also essential in such case that the agreement contain a provision prohibiting the partnership—or the contributing partner if the asset is merely leased to the partnership—from selling or otherwise disposing of such property during the duration of the partnership. Presumably, such a provision prohibiting the transfer of partnership property would not be void as a direct restraint on alienation.

Where the sole contribution of one of the partners is to be in the form of services, it may be desirable to provide that he will be entitled to cash from his share of the earnings only up to a certain amount, the remainder to be withheld by the partnership as his capital contribution until he has contributed an amount equal to that of the other partners.

On the other hand, if capital is scarce at the time the firm is organized, it might be wise to provide that only a certain percentage of the profits be distributed each year to each partner. The amount withheld may be placed in a reserve account for withdrawal later if it is not needed. Since the partners are usually taxed on partnership income at the time it is earned rather than at the time of distribution, the setting up of a reserve

account can have no adverse tax consequences.

If the partners plan to start their business on a small scale and to expand at a later date, the partnership agreement may provide that an additional capital contribution will be required at a later date or at such time as the managing partners may require it. If capital contributions in advance are to be permitted, the agreement should so state with a provision for interest if it is to be payable. If the agreement is silent, a partner is entitled to reasonable interest on capital advances from the date of the advancement to the date when the contribution is due.

Provisions for interest are useful devices for achieving an equitable distribution of partnership profits.[2] This is especially true where equal partners make disproportionate capital contributions. By providing that interest at a set rate will be paid on all capital contributions, the partnership agreement will assure the partner who makes a large capital contribution of obtaining a fair return on his investment as compared with the investment of the other partners. It should be borne in mind when setting the interest rate that the partner receiving the payment is being charged with his pro rata share of the payment, since the amount of interest charges are deducted from partnership profits in determining net distributable income. Thus, a partner with a one-third interest in a partnership who receives $75 in interest payments from the partnership actually receives $75 more than any of the other partners; however, $25 of such $75 was deducted from his share of the partnership income.

The partnership agreement should have some provision for the withdrawal of capital. If the agreement is silent, there is no right of withdrawal prior to the end of the partnership term without the consent of all the partners. Obviously, the withdrawal of cap-

---

1. See section 29 infra.

2. Annot., 66 A.L.R. 3 (1930).

ital can be a serious matter for the partnership and should be provided for even if no deviation from the statutory pattern is intended. Provisions for the withdrawal of capital, however, are generally effectual only between the partners. A general partner cannot avoid his liability to creditors of the firm merely by withdrawing his capital.

GENERAL PARTNERSHIP—MANAGEMENT AND CONTROL

22. Absent agreement to the contrary, general partners have equal voice in the management and control of the partnership. Ordinary matters require majority vote; extraordinary matters require unanimous approval, as does amendment of the partnership agreement. Under the general mutual agency among partners, the act of every partner within the apparent scope of partnership business binds the partnership unless the third party knows of lack of the partner's authority to do the particular act. Among partners there is a fiduciary relationship.

Unless otherwise agreed, all general partners have an equal voice in the management and control of the partnership.[1] In a large firm, however, management of partnership affairs is generally vested in a managing partner or managing committee, but the managing partner or partners cannot be vested with authority to the extent that one or more general partners will have no voice whatsoever in the management of partnership affairs.

The general and ordinary business of the partnership is conducted by majority vote. Presumably, majority in number rather than majority in interest controls, but it would be wise to clarify this point in the partnership agreement. In extraordinary matters, a unanimous vote may be required. No act in contravention of the partnership agreement may be done without the consent of all partners.[2] An amendment of the partner-

ship agreement, under contract law principles, also would require unanimity.[3]

One of the characteristic features of a partnership is the general mutual agency which exists between all of the partners. That is, the act of every partner within the apparent scope of partnership business binds the partnership unless the person with whom a partner is dealing has knowledge of the fact that said partner has no authority to do the particular act.[4]

According to the aggregate theory of partnership, each partner is both a principal and an agent of the other partners in transacting partnership business since he binds both himself and his copartners. According to the entity theory, every partner is the agent of the partnership for the purpose of its business, and he exercises that agency subject to the control of the partnership.

The agency power includes certain usual powers, such as the power to execute instruments (including sealed and negotiable instruments), to borrow money, to transfer and purchase property, and to hire and fire employees to the extent that such transactions are reasonable and proper for the partnership business.

Unless authorized by the other partners, a partner has no authority to do the following acts, and all persons dealing with the partner are charged with knowledge of his lack of authority to:[5]

(a) Assign partnership property in trust for creditors or on the assignee's promise to pay the debts of the partnership;

(b) Dispose of the goodwill of the business;

(c) Do any other act which would make it impossible to carry on the ordinary business of the partnership;

---

1. Uniform Partnership Act § 18(e).

2. Uniform Partnership Act § 18(h).

3. Natusch v. Irving, 2 Coop.t. Cott. 358, 47 Eng.Rep. 1196 (Ch.1824).

4. Uniform Partnership Act § 9(1), (2).

5. Uniform Partnership Act § 9(3).

(d) Confess a judgment; or

(e) Submit a partnership claim or liability to arbitration or reference.

The partnership is liable for the wrongful acts and omissions of any of the partners acting in the ordinary course of business to the same extent as such wrongdoing partner.[6] It must also account for any breaches of trust committed by a partner while apparently acting within the scope of his authority.[7]

The general agency among partners extends to admissions and representations made by a partner concerning partnership affairs. Admissions and representations made by a partner within the scope of his authority are binding upon the partnership unless the person to whom the admission or representation was made knew that in fact the particular partner had no authority to act in the particular matter.[8] Similarly, a partnership is chargeable with the knowledge of or notice to a partner with respect to any matter relating to partnership affairs.[9]

Coincident with the general agency in the conduct of partnership affairs is the fiduciary relationship among partners. Since one partner may bind all of his fellow partners by his acts, it is natural to expect that there would be a corresponding duty to act in good faith. Thus, a partner must account to his firm for any secret profits that he may obtain, and the partnership will have a claim superior to an ordinary creditor if it can trace any property or money wrongfully withheld by a partner.[10]

In view of this fiduciary relationship, it may be desirable to state in the partnership agreement the amount of time each partner will be expected to devote to partnership affairs, and the permissible scope of outside activity for those partners devoting less than full time to the firm. If the agreement is silent, a partner cannot undertake any activity which in any way competes with the business of the firm.

Partners are also required to render on demand full information of all things affecting the partnership to any partner or legal representative of any partner.[11] Furthermore, any partner has a right to a formal accounting of partnership affairs if he is wrongfully excluded from the partnership business; if any partner is making a profit in violation of his fiduciary duties to the partnership; if the agreement so provides; or in any other circumstances that would make it equitable.[12]

All partners shall at all times have access to and may inspect or copy any partnership books.[13]

GENERAL PARTNERSHIP—PROFITS AND LOSSES

23. Absent agreement to the contrary, profits are shared equally by the partners regardless of differences in the amounts of their capital contributions, and losses are shared in the same proportion as profits. Different arrangements can be made in the partnership agreement. Provisions for sharing of losses are effective only among the partners, and do not affect the partners' liability to partnership creditors. The partnership agreement might also

---

6.   Uniform Partnership Act § 13.

7.   Uniform Partnership Act § 14.

8.   Uniform Partnership Act § 11.

9.   Uniform Partnership Act § 12.

10.   Uniform Partnership Act § 21. See Note, "Fiduciary Duties of Partners", 48 Iowa L.Rev. 902 (1963).

11.   Uniform Partnership Act § 20.

12.   Uniform Partnership Act § 22. If no account is rendered voluntarily a court may decree an accounting, though usually such a step is taken only as an incident to a dissolution. If a dispute arises concerning the obligations arising from transactions between a partner and the partnership concerning the business of the partnership, the usual remedy is an accounting, usually incident to dissolution (since the partnership can not function if partnership obligations must be settled in court). A. Bromberg, Crane and Bromberg on Partnership § 72 (1968). But see section 19, n. 15 supra.

13.   Uniform Partnership Act § 19.

provide for salary or interest payments to the partners.

While the sharing of profits and losses from the business may not be an important consideration in choosing one form of business organization over another, the method of distributing income does present a problem in draftsmanship if a partnership is being organized.

If there is no provision in the partnership agreement relating to the distribution of profits and losses, profits are shared equally by the partners regardless of differences in the amounts of their capital contributions, and losses are shared in the same proportion as profits.[1]

As a practical matter, a partnership agreement is rarely silent on the question of the sharing of profits and losses. How they ought to be shared in a given partnership must be determined on the basis of the particular facts at hand.

It should be noted that the provisions as to the sharing of losses are effective only inter se and can have no effect on the liability of a partner to partnership creditors.

In actual practice almost any desired distribution can be obtained by payment of salaries, interest on advances and capital, and various profit distributions. Profits often can be withdrawn currently under so-called drawing accounts.

Partners generally have no right to salaries at common law or under applicable statutes, except that a surviving partner is entitled to a salary while winding up partnership affairs.[2] If a salary is provided for in the partnership agreement,[3] it is treated as an expense of the firm in determining net distributable income. In effect, then, a partner pays part of his own salary from his share of the partnership income.

Interest may be collected by a partner from his firm only with respect to payments or advances in aid of the partnership beyond the amount of capital which he agreed to contribute, and capital contributions not repaid to him at the time set for repayment.[4] Like salary, interest payments are considered an expense of the firm. Payments of interest on capital contributions may be provided for in the partnership agreement, and, as suggested above, such payments may provide a means of achieving a fairer return where the capital contributions of the partnership are disproportionate.

GENERAL PARTNERSHIP—EXTENT OF LIABILITY

24. General partners are subject to unlimited liability to partnership claimants. Such liability is joint and several for tort or breach of trust, and joint for all other partnership obligations. In some jurisdictions, such joint liability can be enforced by suing the partnership and one or more partners, and enforcing the resulting judgment against the partnership assets and the individual assets of the partners served. Under the doctrine of marshaling of assets, when applicable, partnership creditors must first proceed against partnership assets before proceeding against the partners individually. Rights of contribution exist among partners. A creditor of an individual partner may proceed against the latter's property other than the latter's interest in the partnership. Such creditor also may subject his debtor's interest in the partnership to a charging order, but he cannot attach specific partnership property. Absent assumption, an incoming partner is not personally liable for existing partnership debts. A retiring partner remains personally liable, absent release or novation, for partnership debts incurred while he was a partner, is liable for new debts to persons who had extended credit to the partnership in the past and had no knowledge or notice of his retirement, and is liable for new debts to persons who had not extended credit in the past but had known of the partnership and had no knowledge or notice of such retirement, absent publication of notice of such retirement.

1. Uniform Partnership Act § 18(a).

2. Uniform Partnership Act § 18(f); Annot., 81 A.L. R.2d 445 (1962).

3. Annot., 66 A.L.R.2d 1023 (1959).

4. Uniform Partnership Act § 18(c), (d).

A traditional attribute of doing business under the partnership form is the full liability of each partner in his personal capacity. Even in a limited partnership there must be at least one general partner with full personal liability.

The general partners are jointly and severally liable for the damages caused by any tort or breach of trust committed by a partner within the scope of partnership business. They are jointly liable for all other partnership obligations.[1] Under joint debtor acts such joint liability may be enforced by suing them in all of their names or in the partnership name and serving one or more, in which case the resulting judgment would be enforceable against the partnership assets and the individual assets of the partners who were served.[2]

Under the doctrine of marshaling of assets, when applicable, firm creditors must proceed against the assets of the firm before seeking satisfaction of their claims out of the individual property of the general partners.

If a partner makes any payment or incurs a personal liability in the ordinary and proper course of partnership business, the partnership is obligated to indemnify him for the payment so made or the liability so incurred.[3] Thus, if a judgment on a firm obligation is satisfied out of the personal property of one partner, he may seek contribution against his fellow partners, at least where the judgment was not based upon a wrong committed by the paying partner.[4]

Confusion as to the rights of partners with respect to contribution can and should be avoided by means of a provision in the partnership agreement. Generally, it would seem desirable to provide that tort liability will be considered as an expense of doing business and that therefore the partners will share the burdens of such liability along with other expenses. Of course, an exception should be made for willful and malicious torts and breaches of trust. Contribution among partners is not permitted until after a final accounting and settlement of partnership affairs.[5] The partners may wish to provide in their agreement that the right to contribution will arise immediately upon the payment of the partnership debt.

A creditor of an individual partner may seek satisfaction of his claim out of the individual's property other than the debtor's interest in the partnership. Such creditor also may subject his debtor's interest in the partnership to a charging order, but he cannot attach specific partnership property.[6] A creditor who obtains a charging order may ask for dissolution of the partnership, but the remaining partners may redeem the interest so charged and thereby avoid dissolution.

An incoming partner, newly joining an established partnership, is liable personally on only those obligations incurred after he joined unless he assumed voluntarily the liability of a retiring partner, but his share in the partnership property can be used to satisfy both old and new obligations.[7]

1. Uniform Partnership Act § 15; Annot., 175 A.L.R. 1310 (1948). Where the liability is joint, the release of one partner releases all, and a judgment against some releases all partners within the jurisdiction of the court. A release of, or judgment against, one or more of joint and several obligors releases the joint obligation of all, but generally not their several obligation. A. Bromberg, Crane and Bromberg on Partnership 338 (1968). But see note 2 infra.

2. See McKinney's N.Y. CPLR §§ 1501, 5201(c) (3). For any sum remaining unpaid upon such judgment, a subsequent action may be maintained against any partner not served in the original action; such partner in the subsequent action may raise any defenses or counterclaims that he might have raised in the original action if the summons had been served on him. Id. § 1502.

3. Uniform Partnership Act § 18(b).

4. See Uniform Partnership Act § 18(b); Restatement of Restitution §§ 88, 102, comment (f) (1937); Kiffer v. Bienstock, 128 Misc. 451, 218 N.Y.S. 526 (N.Y.C.Mun.Ct.1926).

5. Goff v. Bergerman, 97 Colo. 363, 50 P.2d 59 (1935).

6. Uniform Partnership Act § 28.

7. Uniform Partnership Act § 17; Annot., 45 A.L.R. 1240 (1926).

A retiring (withdrawing) partner, absent release or novation, remains personally liable for partnership obligations incurred while he was a partner.[8] As for debts incurred after withdrawal, the retiring partner is liable to those persons who had extended credit to the partnership in the past and who had no knowledge or notice of the retirement, and he is also liable to new creditors, who had known of the partnership, and those who had dealt in the past with the partnership on a cash basis, but who had no knowledge or notice of such retirement, if notice of retirement had not been published in a newspaper of general circulation where the partnership business was regularly carried on.[9] It is customary for the continuing partners to indemnify the retiring partner against further liability on firm obligations.[10] The necessity of such complicated arrangements is a disadvantage of the partnership.

8. Uniform Partnership Act § 36(3); Faricy v. J. S. Brown Mercantile Co., 87 Colo. 427, 288 P. 639 (1930).

9. Uniform Partnership Act § 35. Comment, "Partnerships—Continued Liability of a Retiring Partner Receiving Payments", 20 Sw.L.J. 151 (1966). Partners who incorporate the partnership business, to achieve limited liability for the corporate business, should give actual notice to creditors of the former partnership and advertise the fact of its dissolution. Gay Harris & Son v. E. H. Schlather & Sons, 423 S.W.2d 467 (Tex.Civ.App.1968); Central Islip Plumbing Supply, Inc. v. John Capparelli Plumbing Co., 151 N.Y.L.J. No. 84, 20 (Sup.Ct.1964). Cf. Warren Co. v. Neel, 284 F.Supp. 203 (W.D.Ark.1968). See Lyon v. Johnson, 21 Conn. 1 (1859). A possible exception to a retiring partner's liability to new creditors of the firm may arise where such partner was unknown to the creditor and was so unknown and passive in partnership affairs that the business reputation of the partnership could not be said to have been in any degree due to such "dormant" partner's connection with it.

10. See White v. Brown, 110 U.S.App.D.C. 232, 292 F.2d 725 (1961). See also Uniform Partnership Act § 18(b): "The partnership must indemnify every partner in respect of payments made and personal liabilities incurred by him in the ordinary and proper conduct of its business, or for the preservation of its business or property."

GENERAL PARTNERSHIP—TRANSFERABILITY OF INTEREST

25. The doctrine of delectus personae applicable to partnerships precludes the admission of any new partner without the consent of all the partners. Partners have three types of property rights: (a) Rights in specific partnership property, held in tenancy in partnership; (b) Interest in the partnership (share of profits and surplus); and (c) Right to participate in management. Only the partner's respective interest in the partnership is assignable by him.

A partner's rights are generally not transferable. Under the doctrine of delectus personae or delectus personarum, a person cannot be made a partner without the consent of all the partners.[1]

Partners have three types of property rights: [2]

(a) Rights in specific partnership property (tenancy in partnership: co-ownership, nonassignable except by all partners, attachable by partnership creditors but not attachable by creditors of individual partner, right of survivorship, free from rights of spouse); [3]

(b) Interest in the partnership (share of profits and surplus: assignable, subject to charging order by creditors of individual partner);

(c) Right to participate in management (nonassignable, nonattachable).

A partner's rights in specific partnership property are not assignable unless all the partners assign their rights.[4] On the other

1. Uniform Partnership Act § 18(g).

2. Uniform Partnership Act § 24.

3. "All property originally brought into the partnership stock or subsequently acquired, by purchase or otherwise, on account of the partnership is partnership property. Unless the contrary intention appears, property acquired with partnership funds is partnership property." Uniform Partnership Act § 8(1), (2). Property can be held in the name of the partnership. Id. § 8(4).

4. Uniform Partnership Act § 25(2) (b); Annot., 39 A.L.R.2d 1365 (1955).

hand, the interest in the partnership of a particular partner may be assigned, but the assignee cannot take part in the management of partnership affairs. The assignee may, however, receive his assignor's share of the profits and of the partnership assets on dissolution,[5] and may obtain dissolution by court decree at the end of the partnership term or at any time if the partnership was one at will at the time he acquired his interest.[6]

On the death of a general partner, his estate does not become a partner in the firm unless it is expressly so provided in the partnership agreement.[7]

---

5.   Uniform Partnership Act § 27.

6. Uniform Partnership Act, § 32(2). The rights of a creditor of an individual partner to partnership property are roughly the same as those of an assignee. Id. § 28(2).

7. "On the death of a partner his right in specific partnership property vests in the surviving partner or partners, except where the deceased was the last surviving partner, when the right in such property vests in his legal representative. Such surviving partner . . . has no right to possess the partnership property for any but a partnership purpose. A partner's right in specific partnership property is not subject to dower, curtesy, or allowance to widows, heirs, or next of kin." Uniform Partnership Act § 25(d), (e). Since the decease of a general partner operates to dissolve the partnership, the estate will receive its share at the conclusion of the winding-up period, unless the interest of the deceased partner is purchased for the purpose of continuing the business. Under the statute the entire interest of a partner passes as personalty, but under the common law, the legal title to the partner's share of partnership real estate passed to his devisees or heirs (including incidents such as dower and curtesy rights) though a temporary "equitable conversion" enabled the surviving partners to sell the real estate. See Uniform Partnership Act § 26. ("A partner's interest in the partnership is his share of the profits and surplus, and the same is personal property"); Matter of Havemeyer, 17 N.Y.2d 216, 270 N.Y.S.2d 197, 217 N.E.2d 26 (1966); (deceased partner's interest in domestic partnership owning out-of-state real property held intangible personal property under Uniform Partnership Act out-and-out equitable conversion under tenancy-in-partnership (as distinguished from common-law in-and-out equitable conversion under tenancy-in-common) and hence subject to New York estate tax even though out-of-state estate tax had been paid on such real property); Comment, "Characterization of Partnership Property Upon the Death of One of the Partners", 16 U. Miami L.Rev. 92 (1961); Annot., 80 A.L.R.2d 1107 (1961).

GENERAL PARTNERSHIP—CONTINUITY OF EXISTENCE

26. **The partnership is technically dissolved whenever any general partner ceases to be such. Dissolution occurs at the end of the specified term of the partnership's existence, upon the death, bankruptcy, withdrawal, or expulsion of any general partner, by court order, etc. Absent provision to the contrary, dissolution is followed by winding up and termination of the partnership. In winding up, the assets of the general partnership are distributable according to the following priority: (a) Claims of creditors who are not partners; (b) General partners' claims other than those for capital and profits; (c) General partners' claims in respect to capital; and (d) General partners' claims in respect to profits.**

When any general partner ceases to be a member of the firm, there is a technical dissolution of the partnership. Thus, as in the case of the individual proprietorship, a theoretical perpetual life does not characterize the partnership form of business enterprise. Nonetheless, some continuity of existence may be provided for in the partnership agreement.

The term of existence for a partnership may be set forth in the partnership agreement, and it is highly desirable that some term be adopted. Providing for a definite term is also useful as a means for discouraging partners from withdrawing from the firm prematurely. A partner cannot be forced to remain with his firm against his will; however, withdrawal before the time set for dissolution can be made unattractive. For one thing, he might not be able to withdraw his capital contribution before the end of the partnership term if his withdrawal from the firm is wrongful.

Dissolution will occur at the end of the term specified. It will also occur as a matter of course upon the death, bankruptcy, withdrawal, or expulsion of any general partner. Upon the commencement of war between the countries of two or more of the partners, or upon any event which makes it unlawful for the partnership business to be continued, the partnership will be dissolved regardless of the wishes of the partners. Finally, a partnership may be dissolved by court order. Generally, such an order will issue if it has become inequitable to carry on the partnership from the viewpoint of any partner (small profits are not grounds for the issuance of a court decree), or if the petitioner for the order is the purchaser of a partner's interest and the partnership term has ended.[1]

Dissolution does not terminate the partnership. The firm continues in existence until the winding up of its affairs is completed. The dissolution does, however, terminate the fiduciary relationship between partners so that a partner may, for example, immediately begin a competing line of business.[2] On the other hand, the partners retain authority to act for the partnership in so far as it is necessary to wind up its affairs; in this narrow area, the fiduciary duties of a partner remain.[3]

Unlike the complete informality of the creation of a partnership, the process of winding up is rather carefully defined by statute. The winding up of partnership affairs normally requires a liquidation of partnership assets and an accounting, with attendant expenses. It is therefore desirable to provide in advance that in so far as possible each partner will receive back his contributions in kind. This is especially true in the case of a contribution of a special asset. In addition, when a contribution is received back in kind, no loss or gain is realized by

the partner for income tax purposes until he disposes of the property.[4]

Provisions for continuing partnership business even after certain events which technically work a dissolution of the firm are desirable in that they save the partnership from the expense of liquidation. A provision setting forth the term of the partnership existence has some effect in this direction since the Uniform Partnership Act states that when a partner wrongfully withdraws from the firm prior to the date set for dissolution, the remaining partners shall have the right to continue the business by posting a bond to secure the payment of the withdrawing partner's interest at the end of the term.[5]

Another method of obtaining continuity of existence is to provide for the purchase of the interest of any partner who does not wish to continue in business when the end of the partnership term is reached.

One approach often adopted is to provide that on the death of a partner, his executor or administrator will become a partner of the firm for a limited time. Coupled with this is an option in the surviving partners to purchase the decedent's interest.[6] If the

1. Uniform Partnership Act §§ 31, 32; Bromberg, "Partnership Dissolution—Causes, Consequences, and Cures", 43 Texas L.Rev. 631 (1965); Annot., 75 A.L.R.2d 1036 (1961).

2. Comment, "Partnership—Covenant Not to Compete—Right to Enjoy after Technical Dissolution", 46 Iowa L.Rev. 927 (1961).

3. Uniform Partnership Act § 33; Annot., 60 A.L.R. 2d 826 (1958).

4. Comment, "Dissolving and Distributing the Assets of a Solvent Iowa Partnership", 12 Drake L.Rev. 131 (1963).

5. Uniform Partnership Act § 38. See generally Schwartz, "Partnership Dissolution Agreements", and Ackerman, "Corporate and Partnership Buy and Sell Agreements", in Advising California Business Enterprises 313–337, 909–951 (1958); Polasky, "Planning for the Disposition of a Substantial Interest in a Closely Held Business—Planned Disposition of a Partnership Interest", 45 Iowa L.Rev. 46 (1959). On liability of corporation acquiring partnership business for partnership debts, compare Zanone Co. v. Standard Oil Co., 322 S.W.2d 710 (Ky.1959), with St. Clair Lime Co. v. Ada Lime Co., 196 Okl. 29, 162 P.2d 547 (1945). See also Lazarus v. Manufacturers Cas. Ins. Co., 105 U.S.App. D.C. 357, 267 F.2d 634 (1959); Jackson v. Hunt, Hill & Betts, 8 A.D.2d 414, 187 N.Y.S.2d 168 (1st Dep't 1959), rev'd, 7 N.Y.2d 180, 196 N.Y.S.2d 647, 78 A.L.R. 2d 272 (1959); Annot., 173 A.L.R. 444 (1948), 2 A.L. R.2d 1084 (1948), 65 A.L.R.2d 502 (1959).

6. Gabay v. Rosenberg, 23 N.Y.2d 747, 296 N.Y.S.2d 795, 244 N.E.2d 267 (1968) (specific performance of option to surviving partner to purchase partnership

agreement is silent on these matters, the executor cannot become a partner and the surviving partners would have to negotiate with the executor for the sale of the interest.[7] The main problem in this area is the question of the valuation of the deceased partner's interest.[8] This problem is especially acute where each partner contributed only personal services to the firm. In any case, cross-purchase insurance plans may be desirable.[9]

When there is a winding up of partnership affairs, the general partnership assets must be distributed according to the following priority: [10]

(a) Claims of creditors who are not partners;

(b) General partners' claims other than those for capital and profits;

(c) General partners' claims in respect to capital;

(d) General partners' claims in respect to profits.

When a partnership is in the process of winding up and a court has both partnership property and individual property of the individual partners to distribute, "partnership creditors shall have priority on partnership property and separate creditors on individual property."[11]

In bankruptcy, under the so-called "jingle rule" for marshaling of assets, firm creditors are entitled to priority in the distribution of firm assets and personal creditors of individual partners have prior claims against the respective individual assets.[12]

GENERAL PARTNERSHIP—TAX CONSIDERATIONS

27. A partnership ordinarily is not a taxpaying unit but as a conduit for tax purposes must file an information return. In the unlikely event that a partnership has sufficient corporate characteristics of an "association" for federal income tax purposes, it is taxable as a corporation, and, if otherwise eligible, may elect under Subchapter S. Partners are generally not considered employees for employee tax advantages. Family partnerships offer possibilities of spreading income among persons in lower tax brackets. Tax-planning can achieve various results, especially with respect to capital contributions and the sale or liquidation of a partnership interest. State statutes sometimes impose an unincorporated business income tax on partnerships.

As previously indicated,[1] a partnership is one of the four forms of business enterprise for federal income tax purposes. The part-

interest of deceased partner for $100). See also Matter of Hillowitz, 22 N.Y.2d 107, 291 N.Y.S.2d 325, 238 N.E.2d 723 (1968) (upholding partnership agreement provision transferring partnership interest to wife on death upheld as third-party beneficiary contract and not testamentary disposition); Note, "Partnership: Continuation of the Business Upon the Death of a Partner", 20 Okl.L.Rev. 456 (1967).

7. Comment, "Right of a Surviving Partner to Purchase a Deceased Partner's Interest under the Uniform Partnership Act", 62 Mich.L.Rev. 106 (1963).

8. Jardine, "Estate Planning for Proprietorship and Partnership Interests", 6 Utah L.Rev. 169 (1958); Note, "Valuation of Assets on Death of Partner", 53 Mich.L.Rev. 972 (1955); Annot., 47 A.L.R.2d 1425 (1956).

9. See A. Guild, D. Davis & D. Hoxie, Business-Partnership Purchase Agreements (1962); Annot., 83 A. L.R.2d 1347 (1962).

10. Uniform Partnership Act § 40. Cf. Uniform Limited Partnership Act § 33, discussed in text accompanying section 35, n. 3 infra.

11. Uniform Partnership Act § 40(h).

12. See Brannan, "The Separate Estates of Non-Bankrupt Partners in the Bankruptcy of a Partner Under the Bankruptcy Act of 1898", 20 Harv.L.Rev. 589, 592 (1907) ("firm estate to firm creditors, separate estate to separate creditors, anything left over from either goes to the other"). The "jingle rule" is criticized in J. MacLachlan, Handbook of the Law of Bankruptcy 424 (1956), as affording an undue preference to a partner's creditor prejudicial to creditors of the partnership. An amendment proposed by the National Bankruptcy Conference would provide: "The creditors of the partnership may file and prove their claims against the estate of a general partner by or against whom a proceeding under this Act has been filed in the same manner and to the same extent as all other creditors of such general partner, and the court may permit proof of the claim of the partnership estate against the individual estates, and vice versa."

1. See section 16 supra.

nership provisions are found in Subchapter K of the income tax subtitle of the Internal Revenue Code of 1954.[2] A partnership ordinarily is not a tax paying entity, but as a conduit for tax purposes must file an information return.[3]

Prior to 1969, a partnership, under prescribed circumstances, was able to elect to report and to be taxed, to a certain extent, as a corporation.[4]

In rare instances, a partnership may be treated as an "association" and taxable as a corporation despite the wishes of its partners if it has too many of the characteristics of a corporation. It becomes important in drafting a partnership agreement with an eye to gaining certain advantages of the corporation to consider the tax effect of the provisions adopted.[5]

Assuming that a "partnership" within the meaning of the Code does exist, under the aggregate approach, all partnership income

2. Int.Rev.Code of 1954, 26 U.S.C.A. §§ 701–771; Treas.Reg. §§ 1.701–1—1.771–1 (1956); 118 § 39.-3797–4 (1953); A. Aronsohn, Partnerships and Income Taxes (PLI rev. 1966); A. Willis, Handbook of Partnership Taxation (1957); J. Barrett & E. Seago, Partners and Partnerships: Law and Taxation (1956); P. Little, Federal Income Taxation of Partnerships (1952, 1957 Supp.); H. Shockey & H. Sweeney, Tax Effects of Operating as a Corporation or Partnership (1957); D. McDonald, D. Dohan & P. Phillips, Federal Income Taxation of Partners and Partnerships (ALI 1957). See also R. Ash, Tax Problems Encountered in the General Practice of Law 19–22 (ABA 1960); McKee, "Income Tax Aspects of Partnerships", in Advising California Business Enterprises 281–311 (1958); Benjamin, "Problems in Transition from Sole Proprietorship or Partnership to Corporation", N.Y.U. 26th Inst. on Fed.Tax. 791 (1968); Nassau, "Tax Considerations in Writing a Partnership Agreement: Suggested Clauses", N.Y.U. 26th Inst. on Fed.Tax. 125 (1968); Dixon, et al., "Partnerships and Subchapter S: A Comparison of Tax Advantages: A Panel Discussion", N.Y.U. 25th Inst. on Fed.Tax. 151 (1967); Westfall, "Corporate Analogues in Partnership Taxation", 80 Harv.L.Rev. 765 (1967); Corneel, "Using Partnerships to Solve Close Corporation Problems", N.Y.U.22d Inst. on Fed.Tax. 629 (1964); McKee, "Primer on the Federal Income Taxation of Partnerships", 5 Prac.Law. 24 (May 1959); Sullivan, "Conflicts between State Partnership Laws and the Internal Revenue Code", 15 Tax.L.Rev. 105 (1959); Willis, "Subchapter S: A Lure to Incorporate Proprietorships and Partnerships", 6 U.C.L.A.L.Rev. 505 (1959); McDonald, "Income Taxation of Partnerships—A Critique", 44 Va.L.Rev. 903 (1958); Willis, "Drafting Partnership Agreements: The General Lawyer's Responsibility for Income Tax Consequences under the Internal Revenue Code of 1954", 9 Wyo. L.J. 106 (1955); Ashby & Rabb, "The Drafting of Partnership Agreements under the 1954 Internal Revenue Code", 31 Ind.L.J. 45 (1955), 10 Bus.Law. 29 (Apr. 1955).

3. Int.Rev.Code of 1954, 26 U.S.C.A. §§ 701, 6031. The taxable years of a partnership and of all of its principal partners must coincide absent establishment of a business purpose for different taxable years. Int.Rev.Code of 1954, 26 U.S.C.A. § 706; Horn, "Taxable Years of Partners and Partnership", N.Y.U. 19th Inst. on Fed.Tax. 297 (1961).

4. Int.Rev.Code of 1954, 26 U.S.C.A. Subchapter R, Election of Certain Partnerships and Proprietor-

ships as to Taxable Status § 1361 (1964) (repealed, effective Jan. 1, 1969). Such election did not make the partners "employees" for purposes of various fringe benefits. See section 17, n. 4 supra.

5. A general partnership, subject to a statute corresponding to the Uniform Partnership Act, could not, under the present regulations—see section 16, nn. 4–6 supra—sufficient corporate characteristics. Of the six major corporate characteristics, two—(a) associates and (b) an objective to carry on business and divide the gains therefrom—are common to both partnerships and corporations and therefore are not considered. Of the remaining four major corporate characteristics, three—(c) continuity of life, (d) centralization of management, and (e) limited liability—are lacking in a general partnership under the Uniform Partnership Act. So also would be the sixth major corporate characteristic—(f) free transferability of interest—unless each partner had power, without the consent of other members, to substitute another person for himself as partner. Thus, the tally is 4 to 0, or possibly 3 to 1, against "association" status. In the some 10 jurisdictions with partnership statutes other than the Uniform Partnership Act or without any such statute, a general partnership conceivably might attain more corporate characteristics.

To achieve federal corporate tax status, with tax favored benefits denied the self-employed (see note 10 infra), partnerships, especially in the professions which may not incorporate, have tried to insert various provisions to achieve characterization as an "association". United States v. Kintner, 216 F.2d 418 (9th Cir.1954); Galt v. United States, 175 F. Supp. 360 (N.D.Tex.1959); Stutsman, "How to Organize Professional Men for Corporate Tax Status under Kintner", 11 J.Taxation 336 (1959); Comment, "Clarification of 'Association' for Corporate Tax Purposes: The Proposed Kintner Regulations", 34 St. John's L.Rev. 372 (1960); Comment, "Tax and Other Legal Aspects of the Practice of Medicine", 13 Vand.L.Rev. 744 (1960); Hewitt, "Associations Taxable as Corporations", 47 A.B.A.J. 215 (1961). An "association", if otherwise eligible, may elect under Subchapter S. Treas.Reg. § 1.1371–1(b) (1959). See section 76, nn. 9–12 infra. State "professional corporation" or "association" statutes are discussed in section 77 infra.

is treated as personal income of the members, whether distributed or not; the accumulation of earnings is immaterial. The individual rates (14 to 70 percent) apply.

Each partner, for his individual income tax purposes, adds his distributive share of the partnership short-term and long-term capital gains and losses, other gains and losses, charitable contributions, dividends, taxes, and other items of income, gain, loss, deduction, and credit, whether distributed to him or not—their character being retained [6] —to his respective individual items. A partner's distributive share is usually determined by the partnership agreement.

Business losses may be offset against business and individual income not only currently but with a three-year carry back and a five-year carry forward.

Any excess of capital losses over capital gains may be offset against income, up to the lesser of one-half of long-term capital loss over net short-term capital gains, etc., or $1,000 ordinary income, for the current and succeeding years.[7] The individual charitable contribution limitation (20/30 percent of net income) applies to the partner's personal contributions and his share of partnership contributions.[8]

Depreciation, depletion, or gain or loss with respect to contributed property is usually allocated among the partners in the same manner as if such property had been purchased by the partnership. However, the partnership agreement may provide that such items may be shared among the partners so as to take account of the variations between the basis of the property to the

partnership and its fair market value at the time of contribution.[9]

Partners are not generally considered employees but since 1962, as self-employed persons, have been extended more fully the fringe-benefit tax privileges reserved to employees by the Code.[10]

Family partnerships present a special problem. These partnerships are often formed with the hope of spreading the income of a business among the members of a family in lower tax brackets. The Code recognizes a person as a partner "if he owns a capital interest in a partnership in which capital is a material income-producing factor, whether or not such interest was derived by purchase or gift from any other person." If some of the partners contribute in no way to the business, their partnership status may be denied recognition for federal income tax purposes and the entire profits will be considered the income of the active members of the partnership. Therefore, family partnerships should be carefully set up. A written partnership agreement fully complying with local law, and deeds of gifts clearly expressing donative intent (with appropriate gift tax returns filed) should be employed. Children should be given complete control over their interests (if infants, by resort to independent trustees or custodians under gifts-to-minors statutes). Provision should be made for reasonable compensation for services and distribution of profits in exact proportion to the partners' respective capital interests.[11] Although the split-income feature of the Code (since 1948) ob-

6. Int.Rev.Code of 1954, 26 U.S.C.A. §§ 702, 703. See Wolfman, "Level for Determining Character of Partnership Income—'Entity' v. 'Conduit' Principle in Partnership Taxation", N.Y.U. 19th Inst. on Fed.Tax. 287 (1961).

7. Int.Rev.Code of 1954, 26 U.S.C.A. §§ 1211(b), 1212(b).

8. Int.Rev.Code of 1954, 26 U.S.C.A. § 170(b).

9. Int.Rev.Code of 1954, 26 U.S.C.A. § 704; Buschmann, "Reallocation of Taxable Income of Partners", 50 A.B.A.J. 996 (1964).

10. See section 18, n. 18 supra. See also Bravenec, "Partnership Taxation Rules and Keogh Plans", 56 A.B.A.J. 88 (1970).

11. Int.Rev.Code of 1954, 26 U.S.C.A. § 704(e); Treas.Reg. § 1.704(e) (1956); C. Rohrlich, Organizing Corporate and Other Business Enterprises 98–104 (4th ed. 1967); Rothenberg, "Minors in Family Partnership Since 1954", 46 Taxes 17 (1968).

viates this tax-avoidance (or evasion) device to divide income between spouses, the device might prove advantageous when children are taken into the business. A family sub-partnership is another possible device.

Contributions to Capital

Gain or loss is not recognized to the partnership or to any of its partners where property is transferred to the partnership in exchange for an interest in the partnership.[12] In such a case, the partner's basis for the property carries over as the partnership's basis,[13] and such basis governs the partner's basis for his interest in the partnership.[14]

If any of the property contributed has a basis different than its fair market value, considerable difficulties arise. If the partnership agreement is silent on this matter, depreciation, depletion, and gain or loss with respect to the property contributed, as previously mentioned, is allocated among the partners as if the property had been purchased by the partnership. One result is that if a partner contributes an asset having a tax basis in excess of its fair market value, he is sharing with his partners a tax advantage which he previously possessed by himself, i.e., an abnormally large depreciation allowance. Conversely, the partner who contributes property with a basis below its fair market value, is burdening the partnership with property for which it cannot obtain an adequate depreciation allowance.

The Code gives to the partners a right to include in their agreement a provision for the manner in which depreciation, depletion and gain or loss with respect to contributed property shall "be shared among the partners so as to take account of the variation between the basis of the property to the partnership and its fair market value at the time of contribution." [15] The drafting of such a proviso for inclusion in the partnership agreement is a task of no mean proportions.[16]

If a contribution to a partnership is in the form of the use to certain property, the contributing partner retaining title, none of the above difficulties is encountered. This method of setting up a partnership has, at least, simplicity as an advantage. However, the contributing partner must report as ordinary income the rents received from such an arrangement.

Another method of avoiding the complex problems with respect to the basis of partnership property is to have the partner sell his property to the partnership. In such case, the partnership receives a basis equal to the price it paid for the property and the selling partner must report a capital gain or loss. However, certain Code provisions militate against such method; [17] furthermore, the partner might not desire to sell because of possible adverse tax effects on himself.

Other difficulties arise where the contribution of a partner is in the form of personal services. The Internal Revenue Service has taken the position that the provision that no gain or loss shall be recognized in the case of a contribution of property to a partnership,[18] does not apply where a partner receives a capital interest in return for his personal services. As to such a partner, the capital interest received constitutes ordinary income. The partners who contribute money or property are correspondingly entitled to deduction.[19] This raises some difficult questions with respect to when the tax

12. Int.Rev.Code of 1954, 26 U.S.C.A. § 721.

13. Int.Rev.Code of 1954, 26 U.S.C.A. § 723.

14. Int.Rev.Code of 1954, 26 U.S.C.A. § 722.

15. Int.Rev.Code of 1954, 26 U.S.C.A. § 704(c)(2).

16. For a discussion of possible contractual arrangements, see Jackson, Johnson, Surrey, Tenen & Warren, "The Internal Revenue Code of 1954: Partnerships", 54 Colum.L.Rev. 1183, 1203–1210 (1954).

17. Int.Rev.Code of 1954, 26 U.S.C.A. § 707.

18. Int.Rev.Code of 1954, 26 U.S.C.A. § 721.

19. Treas.Reg. § 1.721–1(b)(1) (1956).

event occurs and how much is to be taxed or deducted.[20]

Sale or Liquidation of Partnership Interest

A partner's interest in his firm is normally considered a capital asset, and the gain or loss on the sale thereof is a capital gain or loss. In the case of liquidation, if property is distributed in kind, no gain or loss is recognized until the property is disposed of by the partner; otherwise, the gain or loss to the partner will be a capital one.

The general rule above stated is subject to two exceptions. These exceptions arise when the partnership assets include at the time of the sale or liquidation:

"Unrealized receivables" (basically, contractual rights to payment for goods or services);[21] and

(b) "Substantially appreciated inventory" (inventory items whose fair market value exceeds 120 percent of their basis and 10 percent of the fair market value of all partnership property other than money).[22]

On the disposition of a partnership interest, the amount received in exchange for the partner's interest in "unrealized receivables" and "substantially appreciated inventory" may be taxed as ordinary income to the recipient.

In view of the difference in the tax treatment of unrealized receivables and substantially appreciated inventory, a partner selling his interest in the firm will want as small a portion of the purchase price as possible to be allocated to these items. The Regulations permit such an allocation between buyer and seller if there is an arm's

length bargain.[23] However, the buyer will want a greater part of the purchase price allocated to such receivables and inventory since if he has a high basis therein, he may obtain the benefit of an ordinary loss or, at least, a smaller amount of ordinary income. As a result of the countervailing interest between buyer and seller, the hope of obtaining a tax advantage by means of a beneficial provision in the sales agreement relating to the allocation of the purchase price, is rarely realized.

The treatment of a "sale" of a partnership interest differs from the treatment accorded "payments to a retiring partner or a deceased partner's successor in interest"[24] and "distributions in liquidation".[25] As to the former, the law may be summarized as follows:

(a) Payments made for "unrealized receivables" are taxed as ordinary income to the recipient and may be taken as a tax deduction by the remaining partners;

(b) Payments made for goodwill are taxed as ordinary income to the recipient and are deductible by the remaining partners unless the partnership agreement provides for such payments;

(c) Payments measured by income of the partnership, except to the extent that they represent payments for an inter-

---

20. See D. McDonald, D. Dohan & P. Phillips, Federal Income Taxation of Partners and Partnerships 34–41 (ALI 1957).

21. Int.Rev.Code of 1954, 26 U.S.C.A. § 751(c).

22. Int.Rev.Code of 1954, 26 U.S.C.A. § 751(d).

23. Treas.Reg. § 1.751–1(a)(2) (1956); S. Hagendorf, Tax Guide for Buying and Selling a Business (1967); Lyons, "Partnerships: Valuation of Good Will and Covenant not to Compete; How to Distinguish between Them", 16 J. Taxation 228 (1962); Note, "Tax Aspects of Good Will and Covenants Not to Compete in the Transfer of Partnership Interests", 16 U.Fla.L.Rev. 440 (1963).

24. Int.Rev.Code of 1954, 26 U.S.C.A. § 736. See Peril, "Tax Aspects of Partner's Withdrawal from a Partnership", 64 Dick.L.Rev. 191 (1960); Bougher, "Tax Problems on Termination of a Partnership", 48 Ill.B.J. 92 (Oct.1959); Bromberg, "Taxable Income without Gain on the Sale of Deceased Partner's Interest: Code, Common Law, and Community Property", 13 Sw.L.J. 343 (1959).

25. Int.Rev.Code of 1954, 26 U.S.C.A. § 732.

est in partnership property, are taxed as ordinary income to the recipient and are deductible by the remaining partners.

On the basis of the above three points, it is readily apparent that tax considerations dictate the form the agreement will take in respect to the purchase of the interest of a retiring or deceased partner. It must be decided upon the organization of a firm whether the surviving partners are to receive the tax benefits or bear the burdens in buying out the interest of a retiring or deceased partner.

A distribution in liquidation is in some respects similar to a sale of a partnership interest. There are, however, substantial differences as well. The most singular difference arises from the fact that there may be distributions of property in kind, as to which no gain or loss is recognized until the property is disposed of by the distributee partner.[26]

State Unincorporated Business Income Taxes

State statutes sometimes impose an unincorporated business tax on partnerships.[27]

D. LIMITED PARTNERSHIP

LIMITED PARTNERSHIP—IN GENERAL

28. **A limited partnership is a partnership formed by two or more persons under a limited partnership statute—the Uniform Limited Partnership Act in some seven-eighths of American jurisdictions—having as members one or more general partners and one or more limited partners. In many respects, the principles applicable to general partnerships apply to limited partnerships, which are sometimes called special partnerships.**

A limited partnership is "a partnership formed by two or more persons" under a limited partnership statute, "having as members one or more general partners and one

or more limited partners."[1] It should not be confused with the statutory partnership association, sometimes known as the limited partnership association.[2] The limited partnership is sometimes called a special partnership, limited partners then being called

---

26. Int.Rev.Code of 1954, 26 U.S.C.A. § 731; Swihart, "Tax Problems Raised By Liquidations of Partnership Interests", 44 Texas L.Rev. 1209 (1966).

27. McKinney's N.Y. Tax Law, §§ 701–723; Young v. Bragalini, 3 N.Y.2d 602, 170 N.Y.S.2d 805, 148 N.E. 2d 143 (1958) (holding that New York partnership which had to establish other business entities in foreign jurisdictions in order to do business there was precluded from benefits of allocation of income under law as such partnership was deemed not to be doing business in such other jurisdictions). See also Matter of Havemeyer, 17 N.Y.2d 216, 270 N.Y. S.2d 197, 217 N.E.2d 26 (1966) (deceased New York partner's interest in New York partnership's Connecticut real property which, under Connecticut law, remained interest in real property held not excludable from New York gross estate as interest in foreign real property since partner's interest in partnership under New York Partnership Law, was, by equitable conversion, intangible personal property).

1. Uniform Limited Partnership Act § 1, 6 U.L.A. 559 et seq. (1969). See A. Bromberg, Crane and Bromberg on Partnership § 26 (1968); C. Rohrlich, Organizing Corporate and Other Business Enterprises 111–115 (4th ed. 1967); Freshman, "Current Developments in Regulation of Limited Partnerships by the Division of Corporations", 43 L.A.B.Bull. 249 (1968); Kessler, "With Limited Liability for All: Why Not a Partnership Corporation?", 36 Fordham L.Rev. 235 (1967); Hurd & Mayer, "Ohio Limited Partnerships—Business Use and Effect", 27 Ohio St.L.J. 373 (1966); Bicknell, "Advantage of a Limited Partnership", 116 New L.J. 237 (1965); Taubman, "Limited Partnerships", 3 Corp.Prac. Comm. 15 (Feb. 1962); Painter, "Reaching, Assets of the Limited Partner: A New Avenue of Attack?", 14 Hastings L.J. 62 (1962); Basye, "A Survey of the Limited Partnership Form of Business Organization," 42 Ore.L.Rev. 34 (1962); Roberts & Alpert, "New Regulations Provide Workable Rules for Real Estate Limited Partnerships", 14 J. Taxation 230 (1961); Nadler, "Limited Partnership under the Uniform Limited Partnership Act", 65 Com.L.J. 71 (1960); Chel, "The Limited Partnership", 2 U.C.L. A.L.Rev. 105 (1954); Crane, "Twenty Years of the Uniform Limited Partnership Act", 2 U.Pitt.L.Rev. 129 (1936); Crane, "Are Limited Partnerships Necessary?", 17 Minn.L.Rev. 351 (1933); Note, "Limited Partnerships in Kansas: The New Act", 7 Washburn L.J. 335 (1968).

2. See section 41 infra.

special partners. In Louisiana, its equivalent is the partnership *in commendam*.[3]

Unknown at common law, the limited partnership was derived from the *commenda* or *société en commandite* of continental Europe to permit a person to invest and share in the profits of a partnership business and yet limit has liability to his investment. It was first recognized in the United States by a New York statute of 1822.[4] It is now recognized by statute in all American jurisdictions.[5] Some seven-eighths of the states, the District of Columbia, and the Virgin Islands have adopted the Uniform Limited Partnership Act.[6]

The Uniform Partnership Act applies to limited partnerships except insofar as the Uniform Limited Partnership Act is inconsistent therewith.[7]

In a limited partnership, the status of the one or more general partners is substantially the same as that of the two or more general partners in a general partnership. However, the limited partner's status differs from that of the general partner in four significant respects: (a) the liability of each limited partner is limited to his agreed-upon contribu-

tion; (b) the limited partner should not participate in the control of the business; (c) the limited partner may contribute money or other property, but not services; and (d) upon liquidation, each limited partner has priority over the general partner or partners in net assets.

Only the features which distinguish the limited partnership from the general partnership, and the status of limited partners, will be discussed in this section and sections 29–36. Except as qualified herein, the discussion of the general partnership in sections 19–27 applies to the limited partnership.

The limited partnership has been held to come within the definition of "corporation" under the Federal Bankruptcy Act and has been treated as a corporation for some other purposes.[8]

At least one case has recognized that the limited partnership is a "creature of statute" and a separate entity for purposes of pleading, holding that in a suit by a limited partnership against a nonpartner, the defendant may not counterclaim against the partners for liabilities unrelated to partnership affairs.[9]

In recent years, especially in New York, limited partners have been allowed to sue to

---

3. Comment, "Partnership in Commendam—Louisiana's Limited Partnership", 35 Tul.L.Rev. 815 (1961). Wyoming uses the term "special partnership".

4. N.Y.Laws 1822, ch. 244. The New York version of the Uniform Limited Partnership Act is found in McKinney's N.Y.Part.Law, §§ 90–119.

5. And in England since 1907. Because of the advantages of the English "private company" (see section 259 infra), English limited partnerships are rare.

6. Approved 1916; adopted with some local variations in Alaska, Arizona, Arkansas, California, Colorado, Connecticut, Florida, Georgia, Hawaii, Idaho, Illinois, Indiana, Iowa, Kansas, Maryland, Massachusetts, Michigan, Minnesota, Mississippi, Missouri, Montana, Nebraska, Nevada, New Hampshire, New Jersey, New Mexico, New York, North Carolina, North Dakota, Ohio, Oklahoma, Pennsylvania, Rhode Island, South Carolina, South Dakota, Tennessee, Texas, Utah, Vermont, Virginia, Washington, West Virginia, Wisconsin, District of Columbia, and Virgin Islands.

7. Uniform Partnership Act § 6(2).

8. 11 U.S.C.A. § 1(8); Ira Haupt & Co. v. Klebanow (Klebanow v. Chase Manhattan Bank), 343 F.2d 726 (2d Cir. 1965) (disqualifying limited partners as "members" of "corporation" from voting for trustee under 11 U.S.C.A. § 72(a). See United States v. Silverstein, 314 F.2d 789 (2d Cir. 1963), cert. denied 374 U.S. 807, 93 S.Ct. 1696, 10 L.Ed.2d 1031 (1963) (holding that general partner's personal privilege against self-incrimination did not extend to books and records in his possession of several limited partnerships having aggregate capital in excess of $5,-000,000 and having from 25 to 147 limited partners each, by analogizing general partners in such large limited partnerships to officers of corporations who enjoyed no such privilege). See also notes 9, 10, infra, and section 36, nn. 1, 2 infra.

9. Ruzicka v. Rager, 305 N.Y. 191, 111 N.E.2d 878, 39 A.L.R.2d 288 (1953). Prashker contended the same reasoning should apply to general partnerships. L. Prashker, New York Practice 374, n. 12 (4th ed. 1959).

enforce claims of the limited partnership—in the nature of derivative actions—when the general partners are unable or improperly refuse to assert such claims.[10]

LIMITED PARTNERSHIP—FORMALITIES OF ORGANIZATION

29. A limited partnership may only be created in accordance with the formalities prescribed by statute, including the filing and possibly the publication of a limited partnership certificate. Often there is also a limited partnership agreement, governing the relations among the members, which is not filed or published. Ordinarily, the name of a limited partner should not be included in the name of the limited partnership. A limited partnership intending to do business in another jurisdiction should first assure itself of its status there.

A limited partnership may only be created in accordance with the formalities pre-

scribed by statute. These include the filing [1] of a sworn certificate stating the character of the business, the name of the partnership, the names of all general and limited partners, the contribution to be made by each limited partner, and various other items of relevant information.[2] Besides the certificate there frequently is a limited partnership agreement (which is not filed or published) governing the relations among the members, especially when departure from the normal incidents is desired.[3]

A limited partnership is formed if there has been substantial compliance in good faith with the filing requirements.[4]

A trustee may be a limited partner; [5] so also possibly may a corporation with such

10. Riviera Congress Associates v. Yassky, 18 N.Y.2d 540, 277 N.Y.S.2d 386, 223 N.E.2d 876 (1966); Lichtyger v. Franchard Corp., 18 N.Y.2d 528, 277 N.Y.S. 2d 377, 223 N.E.2d 869 (1966); Klebanow v. New York Produce Exchange, 344 F.2d 294 (2d Cir.1965). But see Millard v. Newmark & Co., 24 A.D.2d 333, 266 N.Y.S.2d 254 (1st Dep't 1966) (holding, 3 to 2, that limited partners had no standing to maintain derivative action against general partners for alleged wrongs against partnership); Note, "Standing of Limited Partners to Sue Derivatively", 65 Colum.L.Rev. 1463 (1965). Legislation was enacted in 1968 in New York (1) to codify the right of a limited partner to bring a derivative action and establish certain procedures and requirements in connection with the action; (2) to make it clear that participation in a derivative action does not subject a limited partner to liability as a general partner; and (3) to establish a general partner's right to indemnification for expenses incurred in defending a derivation action against him. McKinney's N.Y.Part.Law §§ 96, 115–a, 115–b, 115–c; see also id. § 115 contributor, unless general partner, not proper party to proceeding by or against partnership except where object is to enforce limited partner's right against or liability to partnership or in case of limited partners' derivative action brought in right of limited partnership to procure judgment in its favor); [1967] N.Y.L.Rev'n Comm'n Rep. 1967 Legis.Doc.No. 65(B). See sections 361, 362, 364, 372, 374, 377, 380 infra. Limited partners have not been allowed to sue where their partnership's trustee-in-bankruptcy was suing the same defendants on the same claims. Sloan v. Clark, 18 N.Y.2d 570, 277 N.Y.S.2d 411, 223 N.E.2d 893 (1966).

1. Filing and publication in New York. McKinney's N.Y.Part.Law, § 91(1) (b) (publication not required by Uniform Act).

2. Uniform Limited Partnership Act §§ 1–2. For liability for false statements in certificate, see Uniform Limited Partnership Act § 6. Verification is required by Uniform Limited Partnership Act § 2(1) (a). New York permits either acknowledgment or verification. McKinney's N.Y.Part.Law, § 91(1) (a). For form of certificate of formation of limited partnership under Uniform Limited Partnership Act and comments, see J. Mulder, M. Volz & A. Berger, Drafting of Partnership Agreements 40–43, 117–119 (ALI 5th ed. 1967). In drafting the limited partnership certificate, two practices have developed: (a) Include only the required items and have a separate limited partnership agreement; (b) Make it so complete as to serve also as the limited partnership agreement. The former method avoids public filing (and publication) of confidential information and minimizes filing (and publication) fees.

3. J. Mulder, M. Volz & A. Berger, Drafting of Partnership Agreements (ALI 5th ed. 1967); "Limited Partnership Agreement", in R. Stevens & H. Henn, Statutes, Cases, and Materials on the Law of Corporations and Other Business Enterprises 107–110 (1965); 1 J. Rabkin & M. Johnson, Current Legal Forms, with Tax Analysis 459–590 (1963); A Willis, Handbook of Partnership Taxation 500–566 (1957).

4. Uniform Limited Partnership Act § 2(2); with filing and publication requirements in New York. McKinney's N.Y.Part.Law, § 91(2). Failure to file under Uniform Limited Partnership Act has been held not to prevent recognition of a limited partnership in litigation involving only dispute between parties to limited partnership agreement. Hoefer v. Hall, 75 N.M. 751, 411 P.2d 230 (1965).

5. See A. Bromberg, Crane and Bromberg on Partnership 50 (1968); Rieman, "Trust Participation in a Partnership", 2 Hastings L.J. 24 (1951).

power under statute or possibly its articles of incorporation.[6]

In choosing a firm name,[7] the name of a limited partner should not be included. If his surname is included (unless it is also the surname of a general partner or the business was carried on under a name containing his surname prior to his becoming a limited partner), the limited partner is liable as a general partner to partnership creditors who extend credit to the partnership without actual knowledge that he is not a general partner.[8]

A limited partnership intending to do business in another jurisdiction should first ascertain whether or not it will enjoy such status there.

LIMITED PARTNERSHIP—CAPITAL AND CREDIT REQUIREMENTS

30.   Admission of a limited partner is a means of attracting capital to the limited partnership. The immunity of the limited partner from unlimited liability is dependent upon his not taking part in the control of the business. A limited partner may contribute cash or other property but not services; his contribution must be fully described in the filed limited partnership certificate. Absent provision to the contrary, a limited partner may demand the return of his capital on six months' notice.

---

6.   See section 19, n. 6 supra; Port Arthur Trust Co. v. Muldrow, 155 Tex. 612, 291 S.W.2d 312, 60 A.L. R.2d 913 (1956). See also Burman, "The Limited Partnership: Taxes and Limited Liability", 25 N.Y. County Law. Ass'n B. Bull. 72 (1967); Laundry, "The GmbH & Co. Kommanditgesellschaft: German Partnership Vehicle for Joint Ventures", 23 Bus. Law. 213 (1967).

7.   A limited partnership is excepted from the name-filing requirements of the New York statute, McKinney's N.Y.Gen.Bus.Law, § 130(7), since it must file and publish similar data to exist as a limited partnership. See notes 1, 2, 4 supra. See J. C. Wattenbarger & Sons v. Sanders, 191 Cal.App.2d 857, 13 Cal.Rptr. 92 (1961) (creditor action against limited partner upheld where limited partnership certificate duly filed but filed and published fictitious name certificate failed to indicate his limited partner status).

8.   Uniform Limited Partnership Act § 5.

Admission of a limited partner is a means of attracting additional capital to the partnership. However, a partnership is not an ideal risk for an investor even if he is offered limited liability because there is some question as to how much of a voice he may take in partnership affairs in order to protect his investment without subjecting himself to the liability of a general partner. The Uniform Limited Partnership Act provides that a limited partner is not liable to the firm's creditors unless "he takes part in the control of the business."[1] It is not clear what constitutes taking part in the control of the partnership, so that the limited partner is often afraid to act. As a practical matter the investor must have great personal faith in the general partners before he will be willing to advance capital to the partnership.

The respective contributions of the limited partners, which may be cash or other property but not services,[2] must be fully described in the filed certificate.[3] In the case of a limited partner, the withdrawal rights are spelled out by the Uniform Limited Partnership Act.[4] If no time is set in the partnership agreement for the return of capital or for the dissolution of the partnership, a limited partner can demand the return of his capital on six months' notice.[5]

LIMITED PARTNERSHIP—MANAGEMENT AND CONTROL

31.   A limited partner loses his limited liability if he takes part in the control of the business. Any act in contravention of the filed limited partnership certificate requires the written consent of the limited partners.

---

1.   Uniform Limited Partnership Act § 7—see note 2 infra.

2.   Uniform Limited Partnership Act § 4.

3.   Uniform Limited Partnership Act § 2(1).

4.   Uniform Limited Partnership Act § 16.

5.   Uniform Limited Partnership Act § 16(2) (c).

As indicated, a limited partner may not take an active part in the control of partnership business; if he takes on any managerial functions, he may lose his limited liability. Nonetheless, a limited partner does have the right to inspect partnership books, to be informed fully of all things affecting the partnership, and to have a formal account of partnership affairs whenever circumstances render it just and reasonable.[1]

Any act in contravention of the filed partnership certificate requires the written consent of the limited partners.[2] The Uniform Limited Partnership Act sets forth seven situations in which general partners may not act without the consent of the limited partners.[3] Nor may the general partners "do any act which would make it impossible to carry on the ordinary business of the partnership."[4]

LIMITED PARTNERSHIP—PROFITS AND LOSSES

32. Each limited partner's share of profits must be set forth in the filed limited partnership certificate. Absent provision to the contrary, losses, up to the limit of the limited partner's liability, are shared in the same proportion.

Each limited partner's share of profits must be set forth in the filed certificate.[1] Losses, up to the limit of such partner's liability, would in the absence of provisions to the contrary be shared in the same proportion.

LIMITED PARTNERSHIP—EXTENT OF LIABILITY

33. The liability of the limited partner is limited to the amount of his capital contribu-

tion, provided he does not take part in the control of the business or his surname does not improperly appear as part of the name of the limited partnership. A limited partner might be liable for misrepresentations in the filed limited partnership certificate, and is liable for any unpaid contributions. Erroneous belief by a person that he is a limited partner does not necessarily subject him to the liability of a general partner.

Limited liability of the limited partner or partners in a limited partnership is, of course, the normal feature. In every limited partnership, as indicated above, there must be at least one general partner with full personal liability.[1] He might possibly be judgment proof.

A limited partner is not liable to the creditors of the partnership beyond the amount of his capital contribution, unless "he takes part in the control of the business,"[2] or that his surname does not improperly appear as part of the firm name.[3] If a partner is both a general and a limited partner, he has the liability of a general partner to creditors of the partnership.[4]

A limited partner might be liable for misrepresentations in the filed certificate,[5] and would be liable for any unpaid contributions.[6] He would, notwithstanding any pro-

[§ 33]

1. Uniform Limited Partnership Act § 1.

2. Uniform Limited Partnership Act § 7; Plasteel Products Corp. v. Helman, 271 F.2d 354 (1st Cir. 1959); Grainger v. Antoyan, 48 Cal.2d 805, 313 P.2d 848 (1957); Note, "Business Associations—Uniform Limited Partnership Act—Activities Making a Limited Partner Liable as a General Partner", 56 Mich.L.Rev. 285 (1957); Note, "Participation in Management by Limited Partner", 26 Wash.L.Rev. 222 (1951). See section 30, n. 1 supra. California, since 1963, has expressly permitted limited partners to have the right to elect or remove general partners and to terminate the partnership agreement without thereby becoming subject to personal liability.

3. Uniform Limited Partnership Act § 5.

4. Uniform Limited Partnership Act § 12.

5. Uniform Limited Partnership Act § 6; Annot., 34 A.L.R.2d 1454 (1954).

6. Uniform Limited Partnership Act § 17.

[§ 31]
1. Uniform Limited Partnership Act § 10.

2. Uniform Limited Partnership Act § 9(1) (a).

3. Uniform Limited Partnership Act § 9.

4. Uniform Limited Partnership Act § 9(1) (b).

[§ 32]
1. Uniform Limited Partnership Act §§ 2(1) (a) (ix), 10(2).

vision in the partnership agreement to the contrary, remain liable to creditors to the extent of his contribution if he withdraws his capital at a time when the liabilities of the firm exceed its assets.[7]

If a person contributes to the capital of a business erroneously believing that he has become a limited partner in a limited partnership, he is not liable as a general partner to creditors of the firm [8] if he renounces his interest in the profits of the business immediately upon ascertaining his true status. This provision of the statute permits a limited partner to take advantage of the de facto existence of a firm formed without substantial compliance with the statutory formalities.[9]

LIMITED PARTNERSHIP—TRANSFERABILITY OF INTEREST

34. The limited partner's interest in capital and profits is assignable, but the assignee is not substituted as a limited partner absent the consent of the other partners or a provision to such effect in the limited partnership agreement.

The principle of delectus personae also applies to limited partners. While the limited partner's interest in capital and profits is assignable, the assignee is not substituted as a limited partner in the absence of consent of the other partners or a provision to such effect in the limited partnership agreement.[1]

The executor or administrator of a limited partner is given all the rights of a limited partner for the purpose of settling his estate.[2]

A limited partner who withdraws from the firm will not generally retain any liability to creditors of the firm. He will, however, remain liable to the extent of his capital contribution if his withdrawal does not satisfy the requirements of the Uniform Limited Partnership Act.[3]

LIMITED PARTNERSHIP—CONTINUITY OF EXISTENCE

35. Withdrawal of a limited partner does not necessarily work a dissolution of the limited partnership. Absent provision to the contrary, a limited partner may withdraw his capital on six months' notice. In winding up, the assets of the limited partnership are distributable according to the following priority: (a) Claims of creditors who are not general partners; (b) Limited partners' claims for profits and income; (c) Limited partners' claims in respect to their capital contributions; (d) General partners' claims other than for capital and profits; (e) General partners' claims in respect to profits; and (f) General partners' claims in respect to capital.

The withdrawal of a limited partner does not necessarily work a dissolution of the firm. Again the limited partnership agreement controls, but generally a limited partner is not essential to the operation of a business, providing, of course, that other capital may be obtained. However, the withdrawal of such a partner will necessitate an amendment of the limited partnership certificate.[1] If no set term is provided, limited partners may withdraw their capital at any time on six months' notice.[2] However,

7. Uniform Limited Partnership Act § 16(1) (a).

8. Uniform Limited Partnership Act § 11; Note, "Section 11—Uniform Limited Partnership Act—A Renunciation Subsequent to a Six Month Delay is not Timely", 32 Mo.L.Rev. 386 (1967); Annot., 18 A.L.R.2d 1360 (1951).

9. Cf. Uniform Limited Partnership Act § 2(2). For the older view, see Tournade v. Methfessel, 3 Hun 144 (N.Y.Gen.T. 1st Dep't 1874).

[§ 34]
1. Uniform Limited Partnership Act § 19(4); Note, "Sale of Limited Partnership Interests", 14 Hastings

L.J. 176 (1962). The offer and sale of limited partnership interests can be subject to federal and state statutes regulating securities.

2. Uniform Limited Partnership Act § 21.

3. Uniform Limited Partnership Act § 16.

[§ 35]
1. Uniform Limited Partnership Act § 24.

2. Uniform Limited Partnership Act § 16. See McKinney's N.Y.Part.Law § 96 (commencement of **or**

the same result may be achieved by setting forth a time for the return of the limited partner's contribution.

When there is a winding up of a limited partnership, its assets must be distributed according to the following priority: [3]

(a) Claims of creditors (including any creditor claims of limited partner) who are not general partners;

(b) Limited partners' claims for profits and income;

(c) Limited partners' claims in respect to the capital of their contributions;

(d) General partners' claims other than those for capital and profits;

(e) General partners' claims in respect to profits;

(f) General partners' claims in respect to capital.

Limited partners may share equally, or the limited partnership agreement may provide for different classes of priority.[4] If the agreement is silent, they are entitled only to payments in cash, regardless of the nature of their contribution to the partnership.[5]

LIMITED PARTNERSHIP—TAX CONSIDERATIONS

36. For tax purposes, the limited partnership and general partnership usually are similarly treated. For federal tax purposes, a lim-

ited partnership is somewhat more likely to have the characteristics of an "association" and hence to be taxable as a corporation, and, as such, if otherwise eligible, may elect under Subchapter S.

The same tax considerations which apply to the general partnership generally apply to the limited partnership. The term "partnership" is defined in some statutes to mean a general partnership or a limited partnership.

For federal tax purposes, a limited partnership is even somewhat more likely than a general partnership to fall within the definition of "association" and be treated as a corporation.[1] A limited partnership organized under the provisions of the Uniform Limited Partnership Act is usually treated as a partnership but, if it has sufficient corporate characteristics, could be treated as an "association" or corporation.[2]

[§ 36]

1. Treas.Reg. § 301.7701–2 (1960). Bernstein, "Limited Partnerships—Their Use in Real Estate Syndications", 46 Taxes 549 (1968); Driscoll, "Association Problems in Joint Venture and Limited Partnerships", N.Y.U. 17th Inst. on Fed.Tax. 1067 (1959); Taubman, "Theatrical Limited Partnerships", 37 Taxes 979 (1959); Comment, "A Tax Comparison of the Limited Partnership and the Subchapter S Corporation", 43 Minn.L.Rev. 964 (1959).

2. See section 16, nn. 4–6 supra. Of the six major corporate characteristics, two of them—(a) associates and (b) an objective to carry on business and divide the gain therefrom—are common to both the corporation and the limited partnership and are not considered in determining whether or not corporate characteristics predominate. A limited partnership subject to a statute corresponding to the Uniform Limited Partnership Act lacks (c) continuity of life. Such a limited partnership generally does not have (d) centralized management unless substantially all the interests therein are owned by the limited partners. If no general partner in a limited partnership has substantial assets (other than his interest in the partnership), (e) limited liability exists. If members owning substantially all of the interests in a limited partnership have the power, without the consent of other members, to substitute for themselves in the same firm a person who is not a member of the firm, (f) free transferability of interests exists. An "association", if otherwise eligible, may elect under Subchapter S. Treas.Reg. § 1.–1371–1(b) (1959). See section 76, nn. 9–12 infra.

other participation by limited partner in limited partners' derivative action brought in right of limited partnership to procure judgment in its favor not to be deemed to be taking part in control of business within meaning of section).

3. Uniform Limited Partnership Act § 23. Cf. Uniform Partnership Act § 40, discussed in text accompanying section 26, n. 10 supra.

4. Uniform Limited Partnership Act § 14.

5. Uniform Limited Partnership Act § 16(3)

E. FORMS RELATED TO PARTNERSHIP

FORMS RELATED TO PARTNERSHIP
—IMPLIED PARTNERSHIP

37. An implied partnership arises by operation of law which results in the application of the principles of partnership law to the relations between the associates and third parties but not among the associates themselves. Examples are partnership by estoppel, defective limited partnership, defectively-organized corporation not within de facto doctrine or corporation-by-estoppel principles, unqualified foreign corporation in a few jurisdictions, and the business trust in the few jurisdictions which do not recognize such a form and elsewhere if the beneficiaries have excessive control.

An implied partnership arises by operation of law and is not strictly a form of business organization freely chosen by the entreprenuer. Implied partnerships are best considered herein that they are subject to the principles of partnership law with respect to the relationship of partners to third parties. However, the members of an implied partnership are not generally treated as partners in so far as their rights and duties inter se are concerned.

Partnership by Estoppel

A person may be treated as a partner of a going firm or of an individual where the traditional elements of estoppel arise. Such person is called an ostensible partner. Thus, for example, when a person represents himself or consents to be represented as a partner of a firm, he is liable as a partner to any persons who, on the strength of such representation, have given credit to such firm. As to the true members of the firm, if they consented to the representations they are liable to the third parties for the acts of the partner by estoppel to the same extent as if the person acting were a true partner.[1]

Defective Limited Partnership

A limited partner may become a general partner of his firm by operation of law for noncompliance with the limited partnership statute as to either the organization or the operation of the firm.[2]

If the firm is defectively-organized,[3] a limited partner will be liable as a general partner unless he renounces his interest in the profit of the business immediately upon discovering his true status.[4]

A limited partner will also lose his limited liability if he takes an active part in partnership business or if he permits the improper use of his surname in the firm name.[5]

quiring that extension of credit be solely in reliance on credit of ostensible partner), with Brown & Bigelow v. Roy, 71 Ohio L.Abs. 438, 132 N.E.2d 755 (Ohio App.1955). See also Anfenson v. Banks, 180 Iowa 1066, 163 N.W. 608 (1917). Cf. Rowland v. Canuso, 329 Pa. 72, 196 A. 823 (1938). A. Bromberg, Crane and Bromberg on Partnership § 36 (1968); Painter, "Partnership by Estoppel", 16 Vand.L.Rev. 327 (1963); Comment, "Partnership by Estoppel", 13 Drake L.Rev. 87 (1963); Note, "Partnerships—Partnership by Estoppel—Proof of Reliance by Creditor Dealing with Persons in Belief of Partnership", 56 Mich.L.Rev. 139 (1957). A corporation using a name not indicating corporateness, especially one formed by incorporating a partnership, might be treated as a partnership by estoppel where a third party with which it deals has neither knowledge nor notice of such incorporation. See Hobbs v. Triangle Supply Co., 378 S.W.2d 726 (Tex. Civ.App.1964); Central Islip Plumbing Supply, Inc., v. John Capparelli Plumbing Co., 151 N.Y.L.J., No. 84, 20 (Sup.Ct.1964): ". . . The partnership liability continues as to all persons who have had actual dealings with the firm until they have been given actual notice of the firm's dissolution . . .."

Herring v. Mishawaka Rubber & Woolen Mfg. Co., 192 Ark. 1055, 95 S.W.2d 1141 (1936); Look v. Watson, 117 Me. 476, 104 A. 850 (1918); Ingle System Co. v. Norris & Hall, 132 Tenn. 472, 178 S.W. 1113, 5 A.L.R. 1578 (1915).

2. A. Bromberg, Crane and Bromberg on Partnership § 32 (1968).

3. By failure to file and/or publish as required. See section 29, nn. 1, 2, 4 supra.

4. Uniform Limited Partnership Act § 11.

5. See section 33 supra.

1. Uniform Partnership Act § 16. J. & J. Builders Supply v. Caffin, 248 Cal.App.2d 299, 56 Cal.Rptr. 365 (1967). Compare Wisconsin Telephone Co. v. Lehmann, 274 Wis. 331, 80 N.W.2d 267 (1957) (re-

Defectively-Organized Corporation

If a corporation is defectively-organized and there is not a sufficient compliance with the corporation statutes to constitute the organization a de facto corporation and there is no basis for estoppel,[6] the members of the firm may be subjected to the full liability of general partners in their relations with third parties.[7]

Unqualified Foreign Corporation

When a corporation incorporated in one jurisdiction does business within another jurisdiction, it must be admitted or qualified by acquiring a certificate of authority to do business in the latter jurisdiction.[8] If a corporation fails to secure the required authority, the penalty imposed by some jurisdictions is to impose some personal liability on the directors, officers, or agents of the corporation.[9]

Business Trust

In the few jurisdictions which do not recognize the business trust, the beneficiaries will be treated as partners. They suffer the same fate in most jurisdictions when they have excessive control.[10]

**FORMS RELATED TO PARTNERSHIP—
MINING PARTNERSHIP**

38. **The mining partnership, recognized by judicial decision in several mining jurisdictions, is distinguished from the ordinary partnership by the absence of any general mutual agency and the principle of delectus personae.**

The somewhat unique mining partnership has been recognized by judicial decision in several jurisdictions, including California, Colorado, Kansas, Kentucky, Michigan, Missouri, Montana, Oklahoma, Texas, Utah, West Virginia, and Wyoming.[1] As its name suggests, it may be set up for the development of mining property by the co-owners thereof.

Involved are (a) Joint ownership of mineral interests; (b) Sharing of profits; (c) Actual joint exploration; (d) Community of interests; and (e) Mutual agency in lease management and exploration.[2]

The material distinctions between the mining partnership and the general partnership are that the mining partnership involves neither any general mutual agency nor the principle of delectus personae. The death of a partner of the transfer of an interest by a partner does not dissolve the partnership; instead the devisee, heir, or purchaser of the partner's interest, even without the consent of the copartners, becomes a partner.[3]

**FORMS RELATED TO PARTNERSHIP—
SUB-PARTNERSHIP**

39. **A sub-partnership is not a partnership but the relation between a partner and a nonpartner for the sharing of the partner's share of partnership profits and losses.**

Properly speaking, the sub-partnership is not a partnership relation but a term used to describe the relation between a partner and a nonpartner, between whom there is an agreement for the sharing of the partner's

---

6. See sections 140, 141 infra.

7. A. Bromberg, Crane and Bromberg on Partnership § 30 (1968); see section 145 infra.

8. See sections 96, 100 infra.

9. Idaho Bus.Corp.Act § 30-508 (1929); Mass.Gen. Corp.Law c. 181, § 5 (1962); Va.Stock Corp.Act § 13.1–119 (1957).

10. See section 64 infra.

1. See generally 2 H. Williams & C. Meyers, Oil and Gas Law §§ 435–435.2 (1959); A. Bromberg, Crane and Bromberg on Partnership § 27 (1968); W. Summer, The Law of Oil and Gas ch. 24 (Perm. ed. 1938); McKay, "Joint Ventures and Mining Partnerships", 7 Kan.L.Rev. 22 (1958); Jones, "Mining Partnerships in Texas", 12 Texas L.Rev. 410 (1934); Gray, "Mining Partnerships", 3 Wis.L.Rev. 13 (1924); Note, 17 Okl.L.Rev. 342 (1964); Annot., 24 A.L.R.2d 1359 (1952).

2. Kiesling, "Mining Partnerships", 12 Baylor L.Rev. 103 (1960).

3. Id. at 105–106.

share of the partnership profits and losses. It may be made into a possible form of risk evasion if the (moneyed) sub-partner promises only to pay the (impecunious) partner his share of any losses he may sustain (not enforceable by third parties, except by a trustee-in-bankruptcy) rather than promising to pay his share of the losses to the partnership (enforceable by third party beneficiaries).[1]

FORMS RELATED TO PARTNERSHIP—REGISTERED PARTNERSHIP

40. The registered partnership, once recognized by statute in Pennsylvania, permitted all the partners to limit their liability to their subscribed capital. Various statutory requirements had to be observed, including public filing and publication, addition of word "Registered" to partnership name, and use of term "Limited Liability" in commercial dealings. The statute has been partially repealed.

Pennsylvania by statute recognized a form of partnership, known as a "registered partnership", which could have perpetual duration and in which all the partners could limit their liability to the amount of capital they subscribed. Statutory prerequisites were the filing and publication of prescribed articles of partnership. The word "Registered" had to be added to the name of the partnership; and the words "Limited Liability" had to be added to the names of the partners on any signs, stationery, bills, etc.

Dissolution did not result from the transfer of interest or the death of a partner, and the principle of delectus personae could have been eliminated.

The statutory provisions for registered partnerships were repealed in 1966 but continued in effect until January 1, 1971, insofar as they related to registered partnerships existing on January 1, 1966, which were neither accepted nor reorganized under the Uniform Limited Partnership Act.[1]

F. STATUTORY PARTNERSHIP ASSOCIATION

STATUTORY PARTNERSHIP ASSOCIATION—IN GENERAL

41. The statutory partnership association created by statute in Michigan, New Jersey and Ohio, has some attributes more closely resembling those of the corporation than the partnership.

The statutory partnership association—sometimes called limited partnership association or partnership association—has been created by statute in Michigan,[1] New Jersey,[2] and Ohio.[3] Pennsylvania in 1966 repealed its partnership associations provisions except as to associations solely of professional persons not authorized by law to practice their profession as a corporation.[4] Such partnership association has more of the attributes of a corporation than does the general or limited partnership, and yet is recognizable as a form related to partnerships.[5]

2. N.J.Stat.Ann. §§ 42:3–1 to 42:3–30 (1940, Supp. 1969).

3. Ohio Rev.Code Ann. §§ 1783.01 to 1783.12 (Page 1964) (3–25 members).

4. See Pa.Stat.Ann. tit. 59, §§ 341–461 (Supp.1969), tit. 15, §§ 12701–12710 (Purdon 1967); Comment, "Business Associations—Registered Partnership, Partnership Association or the Corporation—Selection of the Suitable Form in Pennsylvania", 2 Vill. L.Rev. 385 (1957).

5. A. Bromberg, Crane and Bromberg on Partnership § 26A (1968); Schwartz, "Limited Partnership Asso-

[§ 39]
1. A Bromberg, Crane and Bromberg on Partnership § 28 (1968); Burnett v. Snyder, 81 N.Y. 550 (1880).

[§ 40]
1. Pa.Stat.Ann. tit. 59, §§ 241–321 (Purdon 1964, Supp.1969). See Comment, "Business Associations —Registered Partnership, Partnership Association or the Corporation—Selection of the Suitable Form in Pennsylvania", 2 Vill.L.Rev. 385 (1957).

[§ 41]
1. Mich.Stat.Ann. §§ 20.91 to 20.107 (1964).

Generally, the entity rather than the aggregate approach is taken in determining the status of the partnership association.[6]

STATUTORY PARTNERSHIP ASSOCIA- TION—FORMALITIES OF ORGANIZATION

42. The statutory partnership association is required to make a public filing of specified information. The statutes require the use of the word "limited" as the last word of its name. Treatment of the statutory partnership association in the large number of jurisdictions which do not recognize such form is doubtful.

At least three, and in Ohio [1] no more than 25 persons may form a partnership association. The partnership association is much like a limited partnership under the Uniform Limited Partnership Act in that it must prepare and file in a public office a statement setting forth all of the data concerning the association which would be of interest to creditors (e. g., names and addresses of all members, capitalization, etc.).

The name of a partnership association may include the name of one or more of its members. In this respect, it differs from a

ciation—An Alternative to the Corporation for the Small Business with 'Control' Problems?" 20 Rutgers L.Rev. 29 (1965). Jones & Laughlin Steel Co. was a partnership association until 1922. A more modern example is Producers Oil Co., Ltd. (some 600 members).

6. Property is held and litigation carried on in the name of the partnership association. Carle v. Carle Tool & Engineering Co., 36 N.J.Super. 36, 114 A.2d 738 (1955); Hill-Davis Co. v. Atwell, 215 Cal. 444, 10 P.2d 463 (1932); Whitney Realty Co. v. Deland, 228 Mich. 96, 199 N.W. 669 (1924). Partnership associations are within the Federal Bankruptcy Act definition of "corporation", 11 U.S.C.A. § 1(8). Cf. Great Southern Fireproof Hotel Co. v. Jones, 177 U.S. 449, 20 S.Ct. 690, 44 L.Ed. 842 (1900) (partnership association held to have no citizenship apart from its members for purposes of federal diversity jurisdiction—see section 88 infra), 193 U.S. 532, 24 S.Ct. 576, 48 L.Ed. 778 (1904) (amended complaint showing diverse citizenship between all members of plaintiff partnership association and defendant upheld). See ALI Study of the Division of Jurisdiction between State and Federal Courts 10 (1969).

1. Ohio Rev.Code Ann. § 1783.01 (Page 1964).

limited partnership. However, it is required to use the word "limited" as the last word of its name,[2] and the failure to do so might make the members, or at least those who participate in the omission individually liable.

If the partnership association is to do business in another jurisdiction, it may be required to obtain a certificate of authority just as a corporation is generally required to do before commencing business in a jurisdiction other than that of its incorporation; [3] it may be treated as a general partnership outside of its jurisdiction of formation, especially in the large number of jurisdictions which do not recognize such form of business enterprise.[4]

STATUTORY PARTNERSHIP ASSOCIA- TION—CAPITAL AND CREDIT REQUIREMENTS

43. The statutory partnership association has the attraction to investors of recognizing their limited liability notwithstanding their active participation in the business.

Credit can be obtained by a partnership association, because of its limited liability, only to the extent that the partnership association itself is solvent. There are no general partners whose personal solvency increases the credit standing of the firm. On the other hand, a partnership association is more attractive for investment purposes than is a limited partnership. The member of a partnership association is not relegated to as passive a role in management as is the limited partner, and yet he still enjoys limited liability. Therefore, it would appear that the partnership association has advantages similar to those of a corporation in so far as attracting additional capital to the firm is concerned.

2. See N.J.Stat.Ann. § 42:3–3 (1940).

3. See sections 100, 136, 137 infra.

4. See Edwards v. Warren Linoline & Gasoline Works, Ltd., 168 Mass. 564, 47 N.E. 502 (1897).

The statutes vary as to the requirement that a certain amount of capital be amassed before the partnership association can be formed.

STATUTORY PARTNERSHIP ASSOCIATION—MANAGEMENT AND CONTROL

44. The statutory partnership association has an elected board of managers to manage the business. It might also adopt bylaws for the regulation of its affairs.

The corporate attribute of centralized management in an elected board characterizes the partnership association. The same result may be achieved in an ordinary partnership by the insertion of a proper provision in the partnership agreement; however, in the case of a partnership association, the election of a board of managers is mandatory,[1] and there is no implied general mutual agency as in the case of a partnership. Prompt recording of debts and liabilities is required at risk of liability of the individual members for debts and liabilities contracted during such failure. To be binding on the partnership association, debts and liabilities exceeding $500 might have to be reduced to writing and signed by at least two managers. In addition, a partnership association may adopt bylaws or rules for the regulation of its affairs.[2] Thus, with respect to management and control, the partnership association is more like the corporation than the partnership. It should be noted, however, that the partnership association may not have the same freedom to place restrictions on the control of the majority as exists in the case of the corporation.[3]

[§ 44]
1. N.J.Stat.Ann. § 42:3–4 (1940) (3 to 5 managers).

2. Mich.Stat.Ann. § 20.95 (1964).

3. See section 71 infra.

STATUTORY PARTNERSHIP ASSOCIATION—PROFITS AND LOSSES; EXTENT OF LIABILITY

45. In the statutory partnership association, profits are shared according to the members' respective interests. Their liability is limited to the amount of their subscribed capital.

Profits, to the extent distributed, are shared proportionately according to the members' respective interests. Their liability is limited to the extent of their capital investment, assuming statutory compliance, including proper use of the word "limited" and recording of debts and liabilities, except possibly for labor performed for the partnership association.[1] As in the case of a limited partner whose capital contributions or a corporate shareholder whose shares are not fully paid, a member of a partnership association will be liable to creditors of the firm to the extent that he has not fully paid in his capital contribution.

STATUTORY PARTNERSHIP ASSOCIATION—TRANSFERABILITY OF INTEREST

46. In the statutory partnership association, interests are transferable, but a transferee may not participate in the business unless elected a member by vote of the members.

Generally, there is free transferability of an interest in a partnership association. However, the transferee usually may not participate in the firm's business—delectus personae principle—unless he is elected a member by vote of the members.[1] Under the partnership association statutes, however, the interests apparently may be made inalienable by a proper bylaw provision.

[§ 45]
1. Mich.Stat.Ann. § 20.92 (1964).

[§ 46]
1. N.J.Stat.Ann. § 42:3–11 (Supp.1969).

STATUTORY PARTNERSHIP ASSOCIATION—CONTINUITY OF EXISTENCE

47. **The statutory partnership association exists only for the statutory period, not more than 20 years, with possible renewal. It can be dissolved by majority vote of its members. Upon dissolution, its existence continues for the purpose of winding up.**

The main distinction between a partnership association and a corporation is that the theoretical existence of the latter is usually perpetual (although it may have a limited duration) while the former can exist only for its stated duration. The maximum statutory duration for a partnership association is 20 years with possible renewal.[1]

A partnership association may be dissolved at the end of its fixed term, but it cannot be dissolved prior to that time except by the majority vote of its members.[2] Thus, an association of this nature is not so easily dissolved as is a partnership and yet it may be less difficult to cause its dissolution than it would be to cause the dissolution of a corporation.[3]

The dissolution of a partnership association does not terminate its existence, but it continues for the purpose of winding up its affairs.[4]

STATUTORY PARTNERSHIP ASSOCIATION—TAX CONSIDERATIONS

48. **The statutory partnership association is an "association" and taxable as a corporation for federal income tax purposes. If otherwise eligible, it may elect under Subchapter S.**

A partnership association, having by virtue of the statutory provisions under which it is organized, the characteristics essential to an "association" within the meaning of the Internal Revenue Code,[1] is taxable as a corporation for federal income tax purposes.

G. JOINT (AD)VENTURE

49. **The joint venture or adventure differs from other business undertakings by two or more persons in that it is usually formed to carry out a particular venture, dissolving upon the completion thereof. No formality is usually required. Principles of partnership law are somewhat applicable, although there is sometimes said to be no general mutual agency. The parties to a joint venture are in a fiduciary relationship. Liability is unlimited. Absent characteristics of an "association", a joint venture is usually taxable as a partnership.**

A joint venture (or joint adventure, coadventure, syndicate, group, pool, joint enterprise, joint undertaking, joint speculation)[1] differs from other business undertakings by two or more persons in that it is usually

[§ 47]

1. N.J.Stat.Ann. § 42:3–2 (1940).

2. N.J.Stat.Ann. § 42:3–14 (1940).

3. See sections 280, 348 infra.

4. See Leventhal v. Atlantic Rainbow Painting Co., 68 N.J.Super. 406, 172 A.2d 710 (1961) (holding partnership association which continued business after expiration of its duration to be general partnership and not partnership association de jure, de facto, or by estoppel).

[§ 48]

1. Treas.Reg. § 301.7701–2 (1960). An "association", if otherwise eligible, may elect under Subchapter S. Treas.Reg. § 1.1371–1(b) (1959). See section 76, nn. 9–12 infra.

[§ 49]

1. A. Bromberg, Crane and Bromberg on Partnership § 35 (1968); C. Rohrlich, Organizing Corporate and Other Business Enterprises 115–123 (4th ed. 1967); J. Taubman, The Joint Venture and Tax Classification (1957); Jaeger, "Joint Ventures: Recent Developments", 4 Washburn L.J. 9 (1964); Jaeger, "Partnership or Joint Venture?", 37 Notre Dame Law. 138 (1961); Jaeger, "Joint Ventures: Origin, Nature and Development", 9 Am.U.L.Rev. 1 (1960); Jaeger, "Joint Ventures: Membership, Types and Termination", 9 Am.U.L.Rev. 111 (1960); McKay, "Joint Ventures and Mining Partnerships", 7 Kan. L.Rev. 22 (1958); Nichols, "Joint Ventures", 36 Va. L.Rev. 425 (1950); Mechem, "The Law of Joint Adventures", 15 Minn.L.Rev. 644 (1931); Comment, "Joint Adventure—The Sharing of Losses Dilemma", 18 U.Miami L.Rev. 429 (1963); Comment, "The Joint Venture: Problem Child of Partnership", 38 Calif.L.Rev. 860 (1950).

formed, not to carry on a business as in the case of a partnership, but to carry out a particular venture—a sort of "temporary partnership"—dissolving upon the completion thereof.[2]

There is some difficulty in determining when the legal relationship of joint venture exists, with authorities disagreeing as to the essential elements. Most would agree on the following:

    (a) Agreement (express or inferred);

    (b) Joint interest (contribution);

    (c) Sharing profits (and usually losses— unlimited liability);

    (d) Mutual right to control.

Others would add fiduciary relationship and right to an accounting, but these are usually treated as consequences rather than prerequisites. Sharing of losses and mutual right to control are not alway emphasized in the cases.[3]

The joint venture is not as much of an entity as is a partnership.[4] Although property may be owned jointly, there is usually no group name.

No formality is usually required. The agreement may be oral, subject to applicable requirements of contract law that an agreement, if in writing, be sufficiently definite and complete, and of the statute of frauds,[5] and the parole evidence rule.

Generally, joint ventures are governed by some of the principles of partnership law,[6] with some differences resulting from the more limited extent of the business undertaken by the joint venture. The authority of an adventurer to bind the others is more limited, and there is sometimes said to be no general mutual agency.[7]

The parties to a joint venture are in a fiduciary relationship, owing fiduciary duties to each other.[8] The parties, of course, are

---

2. If no duration is specified, the venture presumably lasts until the completion of the particular undertaking; otherwise it may be terminated at will. Harrington v. Sorelle, 313 F.2d 10 (10th Cir. 1963). Compare definition of partnership, section 19, n. 6 supra.

3. Colonial Refrigerated Transportation, Inc. v. Mitchell, 403 F.2d 541 (5th Cir. 1968); Pinkowski v. Coglay, 347 F.2d 411 (7th Cir. 1965), cert. denied 386 U.S. 1036, 87 S.Ct. 1473, 18 L.Ed.2d 599 (1967); Safway Rental & Sales Co. v. Albina Engine & Machine Works, Inc. v. Safway Rental & Sales Co., 343 F.2d 129 (10th Cir. 1965), 305 F.2d 77 (10th Cir. 1962); Cross v. Pasley, 270 F.2d 88 (8th Cir. 1959), cert. denied 362 U.S. 902, 80 S.Ct. 608, 4 L.Ed.2d 554 (1960); United States v. Standard Oil Co. of California, 155 F.Supp. 121 (S.D.N.Y.1957), aff'd 270 F.2d 50 (2d Cir. 1959); Taubman, "What Constitutes a Joint Venture", 41 Cornell L.Q. 640 (1956). But see Book Review, 33 N.Y.U.L.Rev. 108 (1958). Annot., 48 A.L.R. 1055 (1927), 63 A.L.R. 909 (1929), 138 A.L.R. 968 (1942).

4. Fallone v. Misericordia Hospital, 23 A.D.2d 222, 259 N.Y.S.2d 947 (1st Dep't 1965), aff'd 17 N.Y.2d 648, 269 N.Y.S.2d 431, 216 N.E.2d 594 (1966) (joint venture held employer for purposes of workmen's compensation law); Note, "Jurisdiction and Venue of Joint Venture in Diversity of Citizenship Suit", 47 Iowa L.Rev. 745 (1962).

5. For forms of joint venture agreements, see 1 J. Rabkin & M. Johnson, Current Legal Forms, with Tax Analysis 591–724 (1963); Note, "Joint Venture Corporations: Drafting the Corporate Papers", 78 Harv.L.Rev. 393 (1964); see Note, "Trust—Joint Adventure—Statute of frauds: Constructive Trust", 32 U.Cin.L.Rev. 127 (1963); Note, "Business Associations: Necessity of Writing for Joint Venture to Purchase and Exploit Real Property", 45 Calif.L. Rev. 373 (1957).

6. See Friedman v. Gettner, 7 N.Y.2d 764, 194 N.Y.S. 2d 35, 163 N.E.2d 141 (1959) (holding that creditor of joint venture, like partnership creditor, could not maintain action against estate of deceased member on joint contractual obligation of enterprise without showing inability to collect from surviving members or out of assets of enterprise); Gordon, "Buying Out the Deceased Co-Adventurer: the Use of Insurance", N.Y.U. 19th Inst. on Fed.Tax. 673 (1961).

7. Matanuska Valley Bank v. Arnold, 15 Alas. 557, 223 F.2d 778 (1955). See also Friedman v. Wilson Freight Forwarding Co., 181 F.Supp. 327 (W.D.Pa. 1960); Stone v. Guthrie, 14 Ill.App.2d 137, 144 N.E. 2d 165 (1957). Compare the distinction between a general agent and a special agent in agency law. 1 Restatement, Second, Agency § 3 (1958).

8. Himoff Industries Corp. v. Srybnik, 19 N.Y.2d 273, 279 N.Y.S.2d 31, 225 N.E.2d 756 (1967); Omohundro v. Matthews, 161 Tex. 367, 341 S.W.2d 401 (1960); Martinson v. Andrews, 219 Or. 233, 347 P.2d 53 (1959); R. C. Gluck & Co. v. Tankel, 24 Misc.2d 841, 199 N.Y.S.2d 12 (Sup.Ct.1960); Meinhard v. Salmon, 249 N.Y. 458, 464, 164 N.E. 545, 546, 62 A.L.R. 1, 4– 5 (1928): "Joint adventurers, like copartners, owe to one another, while the enterprise continues, the duty of the finest loyalty. Many forms of conduct

also bound by the terms of their joint venture agreement.[9]

Assuming authority and absent contractual stipulations with third parties to the contrary, liability is unlimited.

A joint venture is usually taxed as a partnership, absent the corporate characteristics of an "association".[10]

Even in jurisdictions where a corporation may not be a partner, it usually has power to be a party to a joint venture, at least when within the corporate purposes.[11]

Promoters of a corporation prior to incorporation usually comprise a joint venture.[12]

In such a situation, incorporation may terminate the joint venture, on the principle that, although a corporation may enter a joint venture, it may not be formed to carry out a joint venture, with the individual associates being treated as joint venturers among themselves and as shareholders of a corporation with respect to others.[13]

Underwriting groups sometimes take on some of the aspects of joint ventures.[14]

A rather modern device is the formation of joint ventures by two or more business enterprises, corporate or otherwise, especially in the oil, chemical, electronic, and atomic power fields.[15] The resulting enterprise— although loosely called a joint venture— might be incorporated. In such a case the resulting enterprise is a corporation, governed by corporation law, although called a "joint venture corporation".

Joint ventures to engage in business abroad are becoming increasingly frequent, although with corporate venturers in contrast to the gentlemen adventurers of the

permissible in a workaday world for those acting at arm's length, are forbidden to those bound by fiduciary ties. A trustee is held to something stricter than the morals of the market place. Not honesty alone but the punctilio of an honor the most sensitive, is then the standard of behavior. As to this there has developed a tradition that is unbending and inveterate. Uncompromising rigidity has been the attitude of courts of equity when petitioned to undermine the rule of undivided loyalty by the 'disintegrating erosion' of particular exceptions. . . . Only thus has the level of conduct for fiduciaries been kept at a level higher than that trodden by the crowd. It will not consciously be lowered by any judgment of this court." Annot., 10 A.L.R. 193 (1921), 62 A.L.R. 13 (1929).

9. Alpert v. Hein, 16 Misc.2d 862, 173 N.Y.S.2d 387 (Sup.Ct.1958).

10. Treas.Reg. 301.7701-2 (1960); United States v. Stierwalt, 287 F.2d 855 (10th Cir. 1961); Winger, "Joint Ventures with Corporate Participants (Including Questions on Characterization as an 'Association')", N.Y.U. 22d Inst. on Fed.Tax. 611 (1964); Driscoll, "Association Problem in Joint Ventures and Limited Partnerships", N.Y.U. 17th Inst. on Fed.Tax. 1067 (1959). See sections 16, nn. 4–6 supra. If an "association" and otherwise eligible, it may elect under Subchapter S. Treas.Reg. § 1.-1371-1(b) (1959). See section 76, nn. 9–12 infra.

11. See Pigg v. Bridges, 352 S.W.2d 28 (Mo.Sup.Ct. 1961); Weisman v. Awnair Corp. of America, 3 N.Y.2d 444, 165 N.Y.S.2d 745, 144 N.E.2d 415 (1957); United States Fidelity & Guaranty Co. v. Dawson Produce Co., 200 Okl. 540, 197 P.2d 978 (1948); Nolan v. J. & M. Doyle Co., 338 Pa. 398, 13 A.2d 59 (1940); Excelsior Motor Mfg. & Supply Co. v. Sound Equipment, Inc., 73 F.2d 725 (7th Cir. 1934), cert. denied 294 U.S. 706, 55 S.Ct. 352, 79 L.Ed. 1241 (1935). The purposes of the venture may have to be within the corporate purposes. See ABA–ALI Model Bus.Corp.Act § 4(g).

12. Macklem v. Marine Park Homes, Inc., 17 Misc.2d 439, 191 N.Y.S.2d 374 (Sup.Ct.1955), aff'd 8 A.D.2d

824, 191 N.Y.S.2d 545 (2d Dep't 1959); see section 103 infra.

13. Weisman v. Awnair Corp. of America, 3 N.Y.2d 444, 165 N.Y.S.2d 745, 144 N.E.2d 415 (1957); Tow v. Moore, 24 A.D.2d 648, 262 N.Y.S.2d 134 (2d Dep't 1965); Manacher v. Central Coal Co., 284 App.Div. 380, 131 N.Y.S.2d 671 (1st Dep't 1954), aff'd mem., 308 N.Y. 784, 125 N.E.2d 431 (1955); Mills v. Mills, 70 Ohio L.Abs. 111, 127 N.E.2d 222 (Ct.App.1952). But see Arditi v. Dubitzky, 354 F.2d 483 (2d Cir. 1965); DeBoy v. Harris, 207 Md. 212, 113 A.2d 903 (1955); Dambach, "Survival of Joint Adventure Agreements After Incorporation", 3 U.C.L.A.L.Rev. 94 (1955); Comment, "Corporation—Survival of Joint Adventure Agreements", 7 Washburn L.J. 110 (1967).

14. Although usually with only several liability under the underwriting agreement. See section 292 infra.

15. Adkins, Gilpatric & Abraham, "Corporate Joint Ventures in Operation", 14 Bus.Law. 285 (1959); Berle, "Developments in the Pattern of Corporate Joint Enterprise", 14 Bus.Law. 309 (1959); Broden & Scanlan, "The Legal Status of Joint Venture Corporations", 11 Vand.L.Rev. 673 (1958); Brady, "Many Tax Advantages Found in Joint Venture of Corporate Partners: How It Works", 9 J. Taxation 258 (1958); Note, "'Team Ventures': Air Technology Corp. v. General Electric Co.", 17 Hastings L.J. 842 (1966).

17th century. Such practice is in contrast with the older practice of their forming wholly-owned subsidiaries to do business abroad. Some 40 percent of foreign business during the past 10 years has been carried on in such form—often with the foreign venturer owning a 50 percent—sometimes greater—interest in the consortium.[16]

The impact of the antitrust laws on joint ventures is still in the formative stage.[17]

H. JOINT–STOCK COMPANY (OR ASSOCIATION)

JOINT–STOCK COMPANY— IN GENERAL

50. The joint-stock company or association derives its name from its "joint stock", or capital of its members pooled in a common fund rather than each member's trading on his own account. Today it is usually an unincorporated business enterprise with ownership interests represented by shares of stock. Recognized at common law, it has been subjected to some statutory regulation and treated as an entity for certain purposes.

The joint-stock company or association developed early in English company law, the term being used to distinguish companies which operated on a joint account and with a "joint stock" (in trade) of their members from companies (now obsolete) each member of whom traded on his separate account with his own stock in trade. Many of them were incorporated by royal charter, often to achieve some monopoly in trade or governmental power over some foreign area. While the Bubble Act was in effect (1720–1825), numerous unincorporated joint-stock companies were formed by "articles of association" and/or by "deeds of settlement", and based on principles of contract, agency, and trust law.[1]

In American jurisdictions, the joint-stock company is generally an unincorporated business enterprise with ownership interests represented by shares of stock. These companies, no longer a very prevalent form,[2] were recognized at common law, but they are now subject to some statutory regulation.

16. W. Friedmann & G. Kalmanoff, Joint International Business Ventures (1961); Gordon, "Joint Business Ventures in the Central American Common Market", 21 Vand.L.Rev. 315 (1968); Ross, "The Foreign Joint Venture Corporation: Some Legal and Business Considerations", 45 Denver L.J. 4 (1968); Meek & Feltham, "Foreign Sales, Distribution, Licensing and Joint Venture Agreements", 17 DePaul L.Rev. 46 (1967); Laundry, "The GmbH & Co. Kommanditgesellschaft: German Partnership Vehicle for Joint Ventures", 23 Bus.Law. 213 (1967); Bradshaw, "Joint Ventures in Japan", 38 Wash.L.Rev. 58 (1963); Weiser, "Antitrust Aspects of the Joint Venture in the European Economic Community", 111 U.Pa.L.Rev. 421 (1963); Taubman, "Venturesome Joint Venture: Observations on 'Joint International Business Ventures'", 7 Antitrust Bull. 629 (1963); Raymond, "Tax Aspects of Joint Ventures and Oil Operations in Latin America", 4 Inst. Private Investments 63 (1962); Comment, "International Joint Venture Corporations: Drafting of Control Arrangements", 1963 Duke L.J. 516.

17. See United States v. Penn-Olin Chemical Co., 389 U.S. 308, 88 S.Ct. 502, 19 L.Ed.2d 545 (1967) (4–4), aff'g 246 F.Supp. 917 (D.Del.1965), 378 U.S. 158, 84 S.Ct. 1710, 12 L.Ed.2d 775 (1964); McLendon, "Restraint of New Enterprise Joint Ventures as a Matter of Unreasonable Probability", 23 Sw.L.J. 299 (1969); Pitofsky, "Joint Ventures under the Antitrust Laws: Some Reflections on the Significance of Penn-Olin", 82 Harv.L.Rev. 1007 (1969); Mead, "Competitive Significance of Joint Ventures", 12 Antitrust Bull. 819 (1967); Handler, "Emerging Antitrust Issues: Reciprocity, Diversification and Joint Ventures", 49 Va.L.Rev. 433 (1963); Weiser, "Antitrust Aspects of the Joint Venture in the European Economic Community", 111 U.Pa.L.Rev. 421 (1963).

1. See sections 9, 10 supra.

2. A. Bromberg, Crane and Bromberg on Partnership § 34 (1968); C. Rohrlich, Organizing Corporate and Other Business Enterprises 183–193 (4th ed. 1967). In years past, they were a popular form for express companies, used to minimize taxation and regulation. As an aftermath of the so-called "Great Salad-Oil Scandal", the American Express Company, a New York joint-stock association formed in 1868, was incorporated in 1965 in New York under McKinney's N.Y.Gen.Ass'ns Law, § 7–a, enacted in 1964. Claims for missing soybean and cottonseed oils totaling $135,000,000 were made against American Express Warehousing, Ltd., a corporation with a net worth of $100,000 engaged in the field-warehousing business which, having issued warehouse receipts for the oil, was liable for loss of the oil. The latter's shares were owned by American Ex-

Several state constitutions include within the definition of "corporation" joint-stock associations having corporate characteristics.[3]

New York has rather extensive statutory provisions relating to "joint-stock associations". The New York General Associations Law defines a joint-stock association in terms of unincorporated enterprises (other than business trusts) having "written articles of association and capital stock divided into shares."[4]

At common law, the joint-stock company was not recognized as a legal entity. Under statutory law, there has been some change in this respect. It may hold and convey real property in New York in the name of its president.[5] Actions may be brought by or against the association by naming and joining all the members where the liability is joint or against one or more of the members where the liability is several or joint and several (as at common law), or by statute or decisional law in many jurisdictions, in the name of the association,[6] or by statute in states like New York in the name of the president or treasurer.[7] In New York, a judgment obtained against an association in

press Company, a joint-stock association with a net worth of approximately $80,000,000, with some 24,000 shareholders, of whom some 1,600 were New York residents. The claims against the subsidiary corporation were also asserted against the parent joint-stock association on the theory that the separate entity of the subsidiary should be disregarded. To the extent that such claims against the joint-stock association might be sustained in excess of its net assets, its shareholders would be held personally liable to the claimants. See Faltermayer, "The Future of American Express", 69 Fortune, No. 4, 158 (Apr.1964). The American Express Company previously had acknowledged a degree of "moral responsibility" for the debts of its subsidiary, then under Chapter XI of the Federal Bankruptcy Act. Settlements with the subsidiary's creditors were eventually negotiated. See N. Miller, The Great Salad Oil Swindle (1965).

3. See Ala.Const. art. XII, § 240; Ariz.Const. art. XIV, § 1; Cal.Const. art. XII, § 4; Kan.Const. art. XII, § 6; Mich.Const. art. XII, § 2; Minn.Const. art. X, § 1; Mont.Const. art. XV, § 18; N.Y.Const. art. X, § 4; N.C.Const. art. VIII, § 3; Utah Const. art. XII, § 4; Wash.Const. art. XII, § 5.

4. McKinney's N.Y.Gen.Ass'ns Law, § 2(1). See also reference in McKinney's N.Y.Gen.Ass'ns Law, § 10 to "joint-stock association, consisting of seven or more persons". The New York General Associations Law consists of four articles. Article 1 (§ 2) defines "joint-stock association", "business trust", and *for purposes of Article 4*, "association". Article 2 deals only with joint-stock associations. In contrast, Article 3 deals with litigation by or against "unincorporated associations" an undefined term which, at least under § 13, includes "Any partnership, or other company of persons, which has a president or treasurer". Article 4 deals with designation of and service on the secretary of state as process agent for every "association" doing business within the state.

5. McKinney's N.Y.Gen.Ass'ns Law, § 6. Cf. McKinney's N.Y. EPTL, § 3–1.3(b) (devise or bequest to unincorporated association lacking capacity to take such property valid only if association incorporates within three years after probate of will); [1951] N.Y.L.Rev'n Comm'n Rep.1951 Legis.Doc.No. 65(J) 325–499; [1952] N.Y.L.Rev'n Comm'n Rep. 1952 Legis.Doc.No. 65(F) 147–161.

6. Fed.R.Civ.P. 17(b) (capacity to sue governed by law of forum, except that partnership or unincorporated association without such capacity may sue or be sued in its common name where federal substantive right involved in litigation). United Mine Workers of America v. Coronado Coal Co., 259 U.S. 344, 42 S.Ct. 570, 66 L.Ed. 975, 27 A.L.R. 762 (1922). Concerning service of process on joint-stock companies, see Annot., 79 A.L.R. 305 (1932). See note 11 infra.

7. McKinney's N.Y.Gen.Ass'ns Law, §§ 12, 13 (applicable to "unincorporated associations" generally, and not only joint-stock associations and business trusts, § 2(4); included expressly for purposes of actions against such associations are partnerships or other companies of persons which have a president or treasurer. § 12). Actions by or against all members are expressly recognized. § 17. An action in the association name is not allowed in New York. International Union, etc. v. Aircooled Motors, Inc., 284 App.Div. 835, 132 N.Y.S.2d 411 (4th Dep't 1954) (labor union). Cf. N.Y.Const. art. X, § 4 (defining "corporations" for purposes thereof to include all associations and joint-stock companies having any of the powers or privileges of corporations not possessed by individuals or partnerships, and providing that all corporations shall have the right to sue and shall be subject to be sued in all courts in like cases as natural persons). Except for enforcing association claims against its members, actions in the name of the president or treasurer are limited to situations where the claim involved is by or against all the members. Martin v. Curran, 303 N.Y. 276, 101 N.E.2d 683 (1951). See Sturges, "Unincorporated Associations as Parties to Actions", 33 Yale L.J. 383 (1924). See also Gross v. Cross, 145 N.Y.L.J. No. 7, 14 (Sup.Ct.1961) (foreign unincorporated association not doing business in New York held suable by service in New York on president or treasurer); cf. section 97 infra.

such an action must first be satisfied out of the association's assets. The property of the members is not subject to execution to satisfy such a judgment, but a new action must be brought against them for the damages uncollected under such judgment.[8]

A joint-stock company is assimilated to the corporation under the Federal Bankruptcy Act,[9] and for various other purposes.[10]

A joint-stock company is probably not a citizen, apart from its members, for purposes of federal diversity-of-citizenship jurisdiction [11] or the privileges-and-immuni-

ties-of-citizens clause of the federal constitution; in any event, reasonable police power restrictions may be imposed on its right to do business in a jurisdiction other than that in which it was formed.[12]

JOINT–STOCK COMPANY—FORMALITIES OF ORGANIZATION

51. The joint-stock company can be created with little formality in most jurisdictions, although some now require public filings. Articles of association are a common feature, but these usually are not required to be filed.

The formation of a joint-stock company at common law involved no formalities in the sense of public filings, but has since been slightly formalized by statute. Thus, in New York, a written certificate must be prepared, stating the name and date of the organization of the association, the number of its shareholders, the names and residences of its officers, and its principal place of business. Such certificate must be filed within 60 days after its formation, *and* in each January thereafter, with *both* the secretary of state and the clerk of the county in which the principal business is carried on.[1]

In addition, every joint-stock association transacting business in New York must file a certificate with the department of state setting forth certain data and designating the secretary of state as agent for service of process against the association.[2] Noncompliance bars the association from suing in New York on a contract made by it in New York prior to the filing of the certificate.[3]

8. McKinney's N.Y.Gen.Ass'ns Law, §§ 15, 16. With damages enhanced by the costs of the first action and tolling of the statute of limitations in the interim. §§ 16, 17. These provisions requiring first resort to the association's assets apply where the action is in the name of the president or treasurer, but not where all the members are joined in the action. So also does the provision for non-abatement by death or legal incapacity of a member. § 14. If the officer named ceases to be such, the action may continue in the name of his successor. § 14. The officer, of course, is not personally bound by actions against him in his representative capacity. § 15. The judgment against the association is not res judicata and the individual liability of the members must be proven in the subsequent action as if the first action had not been brought. Lubliner v. Reinlib, 184 Misc. 472, 50 N.Y.S.2d 786 (Sup.Ct. 1944). Cf. actions in partnership name under McKinney's N.Y. CPLR § 5201(b), where property of any partner served in initially subject to execution.

9. 11 U.S.C.A. § 1(8).

10. But see sections 79–87 infra.

11. United Steelworkers of America v. R. H. Bouligny, Inc., 382 U.S. 145, 86 S.Ct. 272, 15 L.Ed.2d 217 (1965) (unincorporated labor union). Compare Mason v. American Express Co., 334 F.2d 392 (2d Cir. 1964), with Brocki v. American Express Co., 279 F. 2d 785 (6th Cir. 1960), cert. denied 364 U.S. 871, 81 S.Ct. 113, 5 L.Ed.2d 92 (1960). See Comment, "Citizenship of Unincorporated Associations For Diversity Purposes", 50 Va.L.Rev. 1135 (1964); Note, "Federal Procedure: Diversity Jurisdiction: Unincorporated Associations: United Steelworkers of America v. R. H. Bouligny, Inc., 382 U.S. 145 (1965)", 51 Cornell L.Q. 827 (1966). The American Law Institute has approved a proposal that, for purposes of federal diversity-of-citizenship jurisdiction, an unincorporated association capable of suing or being sued in its common name in the state in which an action is brought shall be deemed a citizen of the state or foreign country where it has its principal place of business. ALI Study of the Division of Jurisdiction between State and Federal Courts 10 (1969).

12. See Brown v. Farmer & Ochs Co., 209 F.2d 703 (6th Cir. 1954) (New York joint-stock association barred from suing on contract in Michigan under Michigan statute which barred suits by unqualified foreign corporations and broad Michigan constitutional definition of "corporation" to include joint-stock association).

1. McKinney's N.Y.Gen.Ass'ns Law, § 4.

2. McKinney's N.Y.Gen.Ass'ns Law, §§ 18, 19. The same provisions apply to joint-stock associations and business trusts. §§ 1(4), 18(1). See section 59, n. 4 infra.

3. McKinney's N.Y.Gen.Ass'ns Law, § 18(4).

Articles of association are also usually prepared but there is generally no requirement for the filing thereof. There is considerable leeway in drafting the articles.[4]

JOINT–STOCK COMPANY—CAPITAL AND CREDIT REQUIREMENTS

52. The joint-stock company requires no minimum capital. Shareholders are personally liable for association obligations.

The joint-stock company, like all other unincorporated associations, is not required to have a minimum paid-in capital before it begins business.

As to the obtaining of credit, the joint-stock company stands in a moderately strong position. Shareholders of the company are personally liable for the debts of the company.[1] The company may also issue debt securities. Both shares and debt securities which come within the definition of "security" under Article 8 of the Uniform Commercial Code[2] are negotiable.[3] The drafts, checks, certificates of deposit, and notes of a joint-stock company, if in proper form, may be negotiable even though they provide that they are payable only out of the assets of the company.[4]

[§ 51]

4. For form of articles of association of a joint-stock association, see 2 S. Eager, Bender's Forms for the Consolidated Laws of New York, Form 521, 401–406 (1952); R. Stevens & H. Henn, Statutes, Cases, and Materials on the Law of Corporations and Other Business Enterprises 133–134 (1965).

[§ 52]

1. See section 50, nn. 7, 8 supra.

2. Uniform Commercial Code § 8–102.

3. Uniform Commercial Code § 8–105. See Hibbs v. Brown, 190 N.Y. 167, 82 N.E. 1108 (1907) (promise otherwise unconditional not made conditional under former Uniform Negotiable Instruments Law by limiting payment to assets of association issuing bonds).

4. Uniform Commercial Code § 3–105(1) (h) (and Comment 7). Article 3 of the Code applies to "commercial paper", meaning drafts, checks, certificates of deposit, and notes, but not "investment securities". The latter are treated in article 8; see nn. 2, 3 supra.

JOINT–STOCK COMPANY—MANAGEMENT AND CONTROL

53. The joint-stock company is usually managed by a board of directors and by officers, to whom management functions are delegated by the shareholders. The shareholders are the principals; the directors, officers, employees, agents and subagents are their agents or subagents.

The management of a joint-stock company is usually delegated by the shareholders to a board of directors (sometimes called board of trustees or board of managers) and officers, who are usually appointed by such board. Under the New York statute, the articles of association *may* prescribe the number of its directors, not less than three, to have the *sole* management of its affairs.[1] This is in contrast to the New York Business Corporation Law provision requiring that, subject to three permissible provisions in the articles of incorporation, the business of a corporation *shall* be managed by its board of directors.[2] It also differs from the partnership principle of joint management by all of the general partners. While some centralized management may be obtained in the case of a partnership, a general partner may never be deprived of his voice in partnership affairs to the extent that company members may.

Another major distinction between partnerships and joint-stock companies is the absence of any general agency among the members of a company. The only agency which exists is between the directors/officers/employees (agent/subagents) and the shareholders (principals). Therefore, the relationship among shareholders is not the same as in the case of the partnership or corporation.

The management structure of a particular joint-stock company may be varied considerably in the articles of association. The New York General Associations Law provides

[§ 53]

1. McKinney's N.Y.Gen.Ass'ns Law, § 3(2).

2. McKinney's N.Y.Bus.Corp.Law, § 701.

that the articles may contain "any provision for management of its affairs not inconsistent with law." [3] Conceivably, then, a joint-stock association may copy the partnership scheme of management (i. e., with all shareholders having joint control over the affairs of the association), or that of the corporation (i. e., management in a centralized board with shareholders' control, apart from electing the board of directors, limited to extraordinary matters.) Even *sole* management of a joint-stock association may be conferred on the board of directors.[4] It would seem that under the New York General Associations Law, a joint-stock association could be set up along lines similar to that of a close corporation.[5]

JOINT–STOCK COMPANY—PROFITS AND LOSSES; EXTENT OF LIABILITY

54. In the joint-stock company, profits are shared in proportion to the interests of the respective shareholders. The same is true of losses, but only among the shareholders. As to creditors, the liability of the shareholders is unlimited for the authorized acts of their agents—the directors, officers, employees, etc., of the company. Modern statutes have made the joint-stock company more easily suable and the shareholders' liability secondary. Shareholders' personal liability might be avoided by contractual stipulation and minimized by insurance.

Profits are shared in proportion to the interests of the respective shareholders, in accordance with any provision in the articles. As among the shareholders, but not so far as creditors are concerned, losses too would be proportionately shared.

The fact that a joint-stock company, like a partnership, is not generally recognized as a jural person or entity, is the theoretical cause of the main disadvantage of doing business as such company: personal unlimited liability of the shareholders for the debts of the company.[1] Since such an association is not a legal entity for most purposes, those who have claims against the company are considered to have claims against the members thereof, who are bound as principals for the *authorized* acts of their agents—the directors/officers/employees of the company. Modern statutes, on the one hand, have made companies more easily suable,[2] and, on the other, have made the members' liability, for judgments in cases brought under the relaxed procedure, secondary in the sense that execution against the company's assets must first be returned unsatisfied.[3]

Because there is no general agency among the members of a joint-stock company, the risk of personal liability is not as great here as it is in the case of partnerships since only the directors/officers/employees are agents and their authority is not presumptively general and may be circumscribed. Thus, it is possible to limit the contractual liabilities of the shareholders by contractual stipulation and/or proper provision in the articles of association. As to the former, parties are bound by their express contract; with respect to the latter, where the articles are filed in a public office, any third party dealing with the directors/officers/employees of the association might be chargeable with knowledge of the limitations of their authority under general principles of agency. In like manner, a third party dealing with a shareholder who is not a director/officer/employee cannot recover on any claim arising

[§ 53]

3. McKinney's N.Y.Gen.Ass'ns Law, § 3(3).

4. McKinney's N.Y.Gen.Ass'ns Law, § 3(2).

5. McKinney's N.Y.Gen.Ass'ns Law, §§ 3(3), 7 (amendment of articles). See Chapter 10 infra. See Note, "Joint Stock Company and the Problems of the Close Corporation", 50 Iowa L.Rev. 118 (1964).

[§ 54]

1. Flint v. Culbertson, 319 S.W.2d 690 (Tex.Civ.App. 1958) (defense of coverture to such liability).

2. See section 50, nn. 6, 7 supra.

3. See section 50, n. 8 supra. Also the equitable doctrine of marshaling of assets might apply.

from those dealings as against the company or other shareholders thereof (absent estoppel, ratification, etc.).

Tort liability cannot, of course, be limited by contractual stipulation or by any provision in the articles. The shareholders, as principals, are liable jointly and severally for torts under the agency rule of respondeat superior, but might be able to cover their risks by insurance.[4]

The law of agency also governs the liability of the directors/officers/employees of a company, who function as agents of the shareholders. They may recover from the shareholders any expense properly incurred in the course of business, but they are primarily liable for their own negligence and must indemnify the shareholders for any loss resulting therefrom.[5]

JOINT–STOCK COMPANY—TRANSFERABILITY OF INTEREST

55. In the joint-stock company, the share interests are generally freely transferable.

An interest in a joint-stock company is represented by shares which are generally freely transferable. Thus, while a joint-stock company resembles the partnership with respect to unlimited liability, it is not governed by the partnership principle of delectus personae.

However, restrictions on the transfer of shares presumably may be adopted here as in the case of corporations.[1]

---

4. Crane, "Liability of Unincorporated Association for Tortious Injury to a Member", 16 Vand.L.Rev. 319 (1963).

5. Restatement of Restitution §§ 76, 86, 96 (1937). But see 2 Restatement, Second, Agency §§ 438 et seq. (1958) (indemnification of agents).

[§ 55]

1. See sections 281, 282 infra.

JOINT–STOCK COMPANY—CONTINUITY OF EXISTENCE

56. The joint-stock company may have perpetual existence. Dissolution occurs at the end of any term specified in the articles of association or as otherwise provided therein or as provided by any applicable statute.

Unlike any of the forms of business enterprise considered up to this point, the joint-stock company theoretically may have perpetual existence—like the corporation—as the result of the inherent transferability of its interests and lack of statutory restriction with respect to duration.

A joint-stock company is not easily dissolved. In the language of the New York statute:[1]

"A joint-stock association shall not be dissolved except in pursuance of its articles of association, or by consent of all its stockholders, or by judgment of a court for fraud in its management, or for good cause shown."

The articles may provide that the death of a shareholder or the transfer of his shares will not work a dissolution of the firm,[2] and may not set forth any specific time for expiration, thereby obtaining an indefinite existence. However, if any event or time is specified for the expiration of the association, absent provision to the contrary in the articles, the event may be changed or the time extended upon the vote or written consent of two-thirds of the shareholders.[3]

[§ 56]

1. McKinney's N.Y.Gen.Ass'ns Law, § 5.

2. McKinney's N.Y.Gen.Ass'ns Law, § 3(1).

3. McKinney's N.Y.Gen.Ass'ns Law, § 7.

JOINT–STOCK COMPANY—TAX CONSIDERATIONS

57. The joint-stock company is often treated as a corporation for federal and state tax purposes. If otherwise eligible, it may elect under Subchapter S.

Often the joint-stock company is treated as a corporation for tax purposes by defining the term "corporation" as including such a company. This is the approach of the federal income tax provisions,[1] and also of some state franchise tax provisions.[2]

I. BUSINESS (OR MASSACHUSETTS) TRUST

BUSINESS TRUST—IN GENERAL

58. The business or Massachusetts trust is an unincorporated business association established by a declaration or deed of trust, and governed to a great extent by the law of trusts. Legal title is in the trustees, who hold and manage the property for the benefit of the members, who are beneficiaries of the trust with equitable interests, usually represented by transferable certificates. For some purposes, the business trust is treated as an entity.

The business trust (otherwise known as "Massachusetts trust" or common-law trust or voluntary or business association founded under a deed or declaration of trust) is an unincorporated business association set up by a declaration of trust.[1] It resembles somewhat the English joint-stock company established by deed of settlement to trustees.

The business trust was developed in Massachusetts from 1910 to 1925 to achieve limited liability and to avoid restrictions then existing there on a corporation's acquiring

and developing real estate,[2] by adoption of the trust device developed in the English chancery courts in the 16th century. As such, it perpetuated a tradition in the exercise of equitable ingenuity: (a) by the invention of the use as early as the 11th century; (b) then, by the development of the trust after the enactment of the Statute of Uses in 1535; and (c) by the creation of the business trust a half century ago [3]—a tradition carried on by (d) the modern investment trusts,[4] and (e) the real estate investment trusts ("REIT") [5].

[§ 57]

1. Treas.Reg. § 301.7701–1 (1960). See Burk-Waggoner Oil Ass'n v. Hopkins, 269 U.S. 110, 46 S.Ct. 48, 70 L.Ed. 183 (1925). An "association", if otherwise eligible, may elect under Subchapter S. Treas.Reg. § 1.1371–1(b) (1959). See section 76, nn. 9–12 infra.

2. E. g., McKinney's N.Y.Tax Law, § 208(1). Since the joint-stock association is subject to the franchise tax, it is excluded from the definition of "unincorporated business" for purposes of the unincorporated business income tax. McKinney's N.Y.Tax Law, § 703.

[§ 58]

1. "Business trust" is defined by McKinney's N.Y. Gen.Ass'ns Law, § 2(2) as "any association operating a business under a written instrument or declaration of trust, the beneficial interest under which is divided into shares represented by certificates." See A. Bromberg, Crane and Bromberg on Partnership § 33 (1968); C. Rohrlich, Organizing Corporate

and Other Business Enterprises 193–212 (4th ed. 1967); Comment, "The Massachusetts Trust", 31 Tenn.L.Rev. 471 (1964); Brown, "Common Law Trusts as Business Enterprises", 3 Ind.L.J. 595 (1928); Cook, "The Mysterious Massachusetts Trusts", 9 A.B.A.J. 763 (1923); Thulin, "A Survey of the Business Trust", 16 Ill.L.Rev. 370 (1922); Aaron, "The Massachusetts Trust as Distinguished from Partnership", 12 Ill.L.Rev. 482 (1918); Comment, "The Business Trust as an Organization for Practicing Law", 39 Ind.L.J. 329 (1964); Annot., 156 A.L.R. 22–231 (1945). A business trust should not be confused with an ordinary trust or a voting trust. For discussion of latter, see section 197 infra.

2. This restriction on Massachusetts incorporation was eliminated in 1912. But see Mass.Ann.Laws ch. 156, § 7 (1959) (limiting duration of real estate corporations to 50 years).

3. G. Thompson, Business Trusts as Substitutes for Business Corporations (1920); Wrightington, "Voluntary Associations in Massachusetts", 21 Yale L.J. 311 (1912). An important current example is New England Gas and Electric Association, formed in 1926.

4. See section 301 infra.

5. Kelley, "Real Estate Investment Trusts after Seven Years", 23 Bus.Law. 1001 (1968); Buck, "Real Estate Investment Trusts", 32 Tenn.L.Rev. 583 (1965); Lynn, "Real Estate Investment Trusts: Problems and Prospects", 31 Fordham L.Rev. 73 (1963); Symposium: "Real Estate Investment

To a great extent, the law of trusts governs the conduct of business in this form. The property is held and managed by trustees (who have legal title thereto) for the benefit of the members (who are beneficiaries with equitable interests in such property). At least some of the members or beneficiaries are often the settlors of the trust and usually hold transferable certificates evidencing their interests in the business.

As one would expect, the approach to the business trust has combined aggregate and entity theories. Property, of course, is held and conveyed in the name of the trustees, and actions must be brought by and against the trustees in their own names. However, some jurisdictions permit the maintaining of actions in the name of the trustee serving as president or treasurer (if the duties of the trustees have been so divided).[6]

The Federal Bankruptcy Act defines "corporation" to include "any business conducted by a trustee or trustees wherein beneficial interest or ownership is evidenced by certificate or other written instrument."[7] The business trust has been held to be sufficient-ly like a corporation to be denied protection under the privileges-and-immunities-of-citizens clause of the United States Constitution and to justify a state's treating it as a foreign corporation.[8]

BUSINESS TRUST—FORMALITIES OF ORGANIZATION

59. The business trust is formed by a written declaration of trust setting forth the terms of the trust, powers and duties of the trustees, and interests of the beneficiaries. Some statutes require public filing or otherwise regulate the business trust. The issuance of transferable certificates to the beneficiaries is often involved. Not all jurisdictions recognize the business trust, in which case it might be treated as a partnership where the rights of third parties are involved.

A business trust is formed by a written declaration of trust setting forth the terms of the trust, powers and duties of the trustees, and interests of the beneficiaries.[1] More recent statutes have imposed greater regulation, including filing requirements.[2] For such purposes, some states assimilate the business trust to a corporation.[3] Others,

Trusts", 48 Va.L.Rev. 1007 (1962); Godfrey & Bernstein, "The Real Estate Investment Trust: Past, Present and Future", 1962 Wis.L.Rev. 637; Rubin, "Limitations on the Management and Operation of Real Estate Investment Trusts: Powers of the Trustee, Permissible Service to Tenants", N.Y.U. 20th Inst. on Fed.Tax. 671 (1962); Schlitt, "Real Estate Investment Trusts: Title Company Viewpoint: Requirements", id., 689; Dockser, "Real Estate Investment Trusts: An Old Business Form Revitalized", 17 U.Miami L.Rev. 115 (1962); Shafran, "Limited Liability of Shareholders in Real Estate Investment Trusts and the Conflict of Laws", 50 Calif.L.Rev. 696 (1962); Roberts & Shapiro, "Real Estate Investment Trusts", N.Y.U. 19th Inst. on Fed.Tax. 1047 (1961); Report, "Real Estate Investment Trusts", 16 Bus.Law. 900 (1961). See section 67, n. 1 infra.

6. McKinney's N.Y.Gen.Ass'ns Law, §§ 12, 13 (defining "unincorporated association" as including "any partnership, or other company of persons, which has a president or treasurer" for purposes of litigation *against* an unincorporated association). But see McKinney's N.Y.Gen.Ass'ns Law § 2(2), (4); Fed.R.Civ.P. 17(b).

7. 11 U.S.C.A. § 1(8).

8. Hemphill v. Orloff, 277 U.S. 537, 48 S.Ct. 577, 72 L.Ed. 978 (1928).

1. See composite form, and complete form, with annotations and checklist, in Annot., "Massachusetts or Business Trusts", 156 A.L.R. 25, 65–71 (1945); "Agreement and Declaration of Trust", in R. Stevens & H. Henn, Statutes, Cases, and Materials on the Law of Corporations and Other Business Enterprises 145–149 (1965); 1 J. Rabkin & M. Johnson, Current Legal Forms, with Tax Analysis 725–832 (1963).

2. E. g., Massachusetts, New York, Oklahoma, Washington, Wisconsin. See Gose, "Washington Legislation–1959: Corporation Law: The Massachusetts Trust Act of 1959", 34 Wash.L.Rev. 305 (1959).

3. Hemphill v. Orloff, 277 U.S. 537, 48 S.Ct. 577, 72 L.Ed. 978 (1928) (upholding Michigan court's construction of foreign corporation qualification statute as applicable to business trust as not violating privileges-and-immunities-of-citizens, due process, and commerce clauses of United States Constitution); Harris v. United States Mexico Oil Co., 110 Kan. 532, 204 P. 754 (1922), appeal dismissed 260 U.S. 694, 43 S.Ct. 11, 67 L.Ed. 467 (1922). See also Reilly v. Clyne, 27 Ariz. 432, 234 P. 35, 40 A.L.R. 1005 (1925); Weber Engine Co. v. Alter, 120 Kan. 557, 245 P. 143, 46 A.L.R. 158 (1926); State ex rel.

like New York, have special provisions requiring every association (defining such term to mean a business trust or joint-stock association) doing business within the state to file a certificate in the department of state setting forth prescribed information and designating the secretary of state as agent for service of process on such association. Any association which fails to file may not maintain any action in the state upon any contract made by it in the state prior to the filing of the certificate.[4]

One other formality to be met in the formation of a business trust is the preparation and issuance of transferable beneficiary certificates. In this, the business trust is similar to the joint-stock company and the corporation.

The question of whether a valid and enforceable trust has been created is mainly one of the law of trusts. However, the law of each jurisdiction in which it is intended to conduct business must be consulted since some courts reason that a business association must be a general partnership, a limited partnership, or a corporation—with limited liability conferred by statute only on the latter two. By such reasoning, a business trust, since it is neither formed under the limited partnership statute nor incorporated under the corporate statute, must be treated as a partnership where the rights of third parties are involved.[5]

Colvin v. Paine, 137 Wash. 566, 243 P. 2, 247 P. 476, 46 A.L.R. 165 (1926).

4. McKinney's N.Y.Gen.Ass'ns Law, §§ 18–19. Prior to the enactment of these sections, the New York foreign corporation qualification requirements were construed as not intended to apply to business trusts. Burgoyne v. James, 156 Misc. 859, 282 N.Y. S. 18 (Sup.Ct.1935), aff'd mem., 246 App.Div. 605, 284 N.Y.S. 977 (1st Dep't 1935). Accord, Spotswood v. Morris, 12 Idaho 360, 85 P. 1094 (1906). See [1937] N.Y.L. Rev'n Comm'n Rep. 1937 Legis.Doc.No. 65(I) 249–342; [1938] N.Y.L. Rev'n Comm'n Rep. 1938 Legis.Doc.No. 65(H) 89–94.

5. See section 64, n. 2 infra.

BUSINESS TRUST—CAPITAL AND CREDIT REQUIREMENTS

60. The business trust is unattractive to some investors because of their lack of familiarity with such form and their lack of control over the affairs of the business.

As in every other form of unincorporated association, the business trust needs no more capital than that required to carry on the business.

The business trust is in a weak position in so far as obtaining credit or new capital is concerned. A business trust is an unattractive investment in that it is not a very familiar form of business to most people,[1] and there can be little or no control in the certificate holders (beneficiaries) over the affairs of the trust. The amount of credit obtainable is limited by the solvency of the trust since the beneficiaries usually are not personally liable. Although the trustees may be personally liable, they are likely to insist upon a stipulation against personal liability when contracting with others in behalf of the trust.

Obligations issued by a business trust, even when payable only out of trust assets, can be negotiable under the Uniform Commercial Code.[2]

All told, however, the business trust is not the most desirable form of business organization for the enterprise which anticipates a need for additional capital in the future.

BUSINESS TRUST—MANAGEMENT AND CONTROL

61. In the business trust, management and control is generally vested in the trustees. Participation by the beneficiaries in management and control in many jurisdictions destroys their limited liability which might other-

1. But see Hauser v. Catlett, 197 Okl. 668, 173 P.2d 728 (1946) (business trust with both preferred and common certificates).

2. See section 52, nn. 3, 4 supra.

wise exist. The trustees are subject to the usual fiduciary duties between trustees and beneficiaries.

The management and control of a business trust is generally vested in the trustees, who may or may not constitute a self-perpetuating body. In some jurisdictions the exclusive control of the trustees is essential to the enjoyment of limited liability by the beneficiaries; in most jurisdictions, considerable sacrifice of control on the part of beneficiaries is required to insulate them against personal liability.

In an absence of provision to the contrary, the trustees must act unanimously, at least as to discretionary matters. Trust property is held jointly in the name of the trustees, and each trustee is subjected to the usual fiduciary duties between trustee and cestui que trust.

The centralized control found in a business trust involves substantially greater separation of beneficial ownership and control than that involved in other forms of business association. Even the corporation, with its management vested in a board of directors, has its directors elected by shareholders and reserves extraordinary matters for shareholder action.[1] However, beneficiaries in some jurisdictions may be given more control by the trust instrument, either directly or by confining the powers of the trustees— subjecting the beneficiaries to unlimited liability if they are given excessive control.

BUSINESS TRUST—PROFITS AND LOSSES

62. In the business trust, profits and losses are shared proportionately to the beneficiaries' interests. Usually the beneficiaries enjoy limited liability.

[§ 61]

1. See Kroese v. New York Stock Exchange, 227 F. Supp. 519 (S.D.N.Y.1964) (dismissing action by certificate holder to order Exchange to require business trust to hold regular meetings of certificate holders—only four such meetings had been called during prior 20 years).

Profits are shared proportionately to the beneficiaries' respective interests in the trust. Liability for losses is limited to the beneficiaries' respective contributions in most jurisdictions by setting up a valid trust relationship. That beneficiaries are always subject to unlimited liability (absent contractual stipulation) is the minority rule.

BUSINESS TRUST—EXTENT OF LIABILITY OF TRUSTEES

63. In the business trust, the trustees are usually personally liable to third parties, absent contractual stipulation to the contrary. If so liable, the trustees may seek indemnification from the trust estate and possibly from the beneficiaries.

A trustee may be personally liable to third parties for all trust obligations unless he exempts himself from liability by contract; an express contractual provision negating his personal liability is the safest method.[1] The names in which the trustee signs contracts in behalf of the trust may be important. If the signature clearly indicates that the trustee is acting only in his representative capacity, he may thereby avoid personal liability. The use of the word "trustee" after his name is insufficient to limit his liability,[2] but the phrase "as trustee but not individually" might suffice.

If the trustee is held personally liable on an obligation properly incurred in his representative capacity, he may, of course, indem-

[§ 63]

1. The more cautious practice is to sign "[name of trust] by [name of trustee], Trustee, officially and not personally". Pennsylvania Co. for Assurance on Lives & Granting Annuities v. Wallace, 346 Pa. 532, 31 A.2d 71, 156 A.L.R. 1 (1943) (where declaration of trust, recorded as part of title to real property, stipulated that neither trustees nor beneficiaries were to be personally liable but that all persons dealing with the trustees should look only to the property of the trust for payment); Commercial Cas. Ins. Co. v. North, 320 Ill.App. 221, 50 N.E. 2d 434 (1943) (third party who had examined declaration of trust, containing exemption from personal liability, held bound by implied contract to look solely to trust assets).

2. Annot., 138 A.L.R. 155 (1942).

nify himself out of the trust estate and possibly from the beneficiaries. A question arises as to the rights of trust creditors where the trustee has successfully stipulated against personal liabilities. Most states permit an action against the trust in the names of the trustees; Massachusetts permits an attachment of trust property in an action at law to the same extent that the property of a corporation may be attached.[3]

BUSINESS TRUST—EXTENT OF LIABILITY OF BENEFICIARIES

64. In the business trust, the beneficiaries usually enjoy limited liability, although a minority of jurisdictions subject them to the liability of partners. Many jurisdictions impose personal liability on the beneficiaries when they exercise sufficient control—sometimes called "ultimate control"—over trust affairs to make the trustees their agents, on principles of joint venture or partnership. To the extent that the trustees can seek indemnification from the beneficiaries, creditors might be able to enforce the same for their own benefit.

The beneficiaries of a business trust generally have no personal liability for the trust obligations incurred by the trustees.[1] Such result is based on trust law principles. Full liability is imposed upon the beneficiaries in a minority of jurisdictions which refuse to recognize limited liability except as specifically conferred by statute.[2] Most jurisdic-

tions impose personal liability on the beneficiaries when they exercise sufficient control —sometimes called "ultimate control"—over trust affairs to make the trustees their agents. New York appears to take a strict view in this area and the slightest control exercised by the beneficiaries may cause the court to consider the organization as a partnership or joint venture rather than a business trust.[3] The New York test was stated as one of ownership and control. For a trust to exist, the trustees must be self-perpetuating and the members' rights must be limited to receiving dividends and sharing in the final distribution when the business is wound up.

To the extent that the trustees can seek indemnification of any liability from the beneficiaries, creditors might be able to enforce such rights for their benefit against the beneficiaries if the trustees fail to pay and the trust estate is insufficient.

BUSINESS TRUST—TRANSFERABILITY OF INTEREST

65. In the business trust, the certificates representing the beneficial interests are usually freely transferable.

brand, "Liability of Trustees, Property and Shareholders of a Massachusetts Trust", 2 Texas L.Rev. 139 (1924); Hildebrand, "Massachusetts Trust—A Sequel", 4 Texas L.Rev. 57 (1925).

3. See Brown v. Bedell, 263 N.Y. 177, 188 N.E. 641 (1934), reargument denied 264 N.Y. 453, 191 N.E. 510 (1934), motion denied 264 N.Y. 513, 191 N.E. 541 (1934); cf. Goldwater v. Oltman, 210 Cal. 408, 292 P. 264, 71 A.L.R. 871 (1930). See generally Magruder, "The Position of Shareholders in Business Trusts", 23 Colum.L.Rev. 423, 443 (1923) ("Where a business is thus conducted under a declaration of trust, with the management exclusively vested in trustees, neither the power in the shareholders, (1) to fill vacancies among the trustees, nor (2) to elect trustees at stated intervals, nor (3) to remove trustees, nor (4) to alter or amend the declaration of trust, nor (5) to terminate the trust, nor (6) any combination of these powers, should be held to turn the trust into a partnership contrary to the intent of the parties."); Judah, "Possible Partnership Liability under the Business Trust", 17 Ill.L.Rev. 77 (1922); Stevens "Limited Liability in Business Trusts", 7 Cornell L.Q. 116 (1922).

[§ 63]
3. Mass.Ann.Laws ch. 182, § 6 (1955). See Comment, "Remedies of Creditors Against the Trust Estate or Capital Used in the Business", 27 Calif.L.Rev. 432 (1939).

[§ 64]
1. E. g., Crehan v. Megargel, 234 N.Y. 67, 79, 136 N.E. 296, 300 (1922); Williams v. Inhabitants of Milton, 215 Mass. 1, 102 N.E. 355 (1913).

2. See e. g., McClaren v. Dawes Electric Sign & Mfg. Co., 86 Ind.App. 196, 156 N.E. 584 (1927); Weber Engine Co. v. Alter, 120 Kan. 557, 245 P. 143, 46 A.L.R. 158 (1926); Thompson v. Schmitt, 115 Tex. 53, 274 S.W. 554 (1925); Reilly v. Clyne, 27 Ariz. 432, 234 P. 35, 40 A.L.R. 1005 (1925); Willey v. W. J. Hoggson Corp., 90 Fla. 343, 106 So. 408 (1925); State v. Hinkle, 126 Wash. 581, 219 P. 41 (1923); Jones, "Business Trusts in Florida—Liability of Shareholders", 14 U.Fla.L.Rev. 1 (1961); Hilde-

The certificates held by the beneficiaries of a business trust are freely transferable, and consequently the partnership characteristic of delectus personae does not characterize this type of association. Restrictions on transfer, assuming that they could be validly adopted, would generally be of no value since the beneficiaries usually have little control over business affairs.

BUSINESS TRUST—CONTINUITY OF EXISTENCE

66. In the business trust, the duration may depend upon the rule against perpetuities and allied rules of trust law, including those applicable to the termination of trusts.

Business trusts have the advantage of a long duration if properly drafted. Since there is usually no statutory limit on the term of a business trust, the question of duration turns upon the application of the rule against perpetuities and allied rules of trust law.

Since legal title is vested in the trustees and equitable title in the beneficiaries, there is no question of remoteness of vesting. In like manner, the trustees are generally given the power to convey trust property and the interests of the beneficiaries usually are freely transferable so that no suspension of the power of alienation occurs.

Accumulations of income from the trust beyond the permissible period of the rule against perpetuities should be avoided.

While it is not clear that the rule limiting certain trusts to the permissible period would apply to business trusts, the draftsman would do well to include a provision limiting the duration of the trust to the permissible period. The permissible period of the rule against perpetuities, while not a duration as great as that theoretically available to corporations, is sufficient to satisfy most business requirements.[1]

[§ 66]

1. Yourman v. Meyer, 154 N.Y.L.J. No. 117, 13 (Sup. Ct.1965), citing Whiteside, "Restrictions on the Du-

Dissolution of a business trust is governed by the law applicable generally to trusts.[2]

In considering the business trust as a form for conducting a business, it may be well to bear in mind the law of the particular state with regard to spendthrift provisions and the effect of merger of legal and equitable titles in one or more persons. As to the latter, the general rule is that the trust will continue although all the beneficiaries are trustees so long as there is more than one person involved.

BUSINESS TRUST—TAX CONSIDERATIONS

67. The business trust is often treated as a corporation for federal and state tax purposes. If otherwise eligible, it may elect under Subchapter S.

Business trusts are classified as "associations" and hence taxable as corporations under the federal income tax law.[1]

Several states treat business trusts as corporations for purposes of their income or franchise taxes.[2]

ration of Business Trusts", 9 Cornell L.Q. 422 (1924).

2. State Trust Co. v. Hall, 311 Mass. 299, 41 N.E.2d 30 (1942) (dissolution by beneficiary not possible in partnership manner even though control reserved by beneficiaries might be sufficient to make them personally liable as partners).

[§ 67]

1. Treas.Reg. § 301.7701–1 (1960). For such purposes, business trusts (as "associations") are clearly distinguished from the ordinary "trust". Id. § 39.-3797–3 (1953). See Morrissey v. Comm'r, 296 U.S. 344, 56 S.Ct. 289, 80 L.Ed. 263 (1935); Comm'r v. Gibbs-Preyer Trusts, 117 F.2d 619 (6th Cir. 1941). An "association" if otherwise eligible, may elect under Subchapter S. Treas.Reg. § 1.1371–1(b) (1959). See section 76, nn. 9–12 infra.

A troublesome problem under the Internal Revenue Code is distinguishing an ordinary "trust" (taxable under the trust sales of Subchapter J) from an organization technically cast in the trust form having the corporate characteristics of an "association" and therefore taxable as a corporation. Generally speaking, an arrangement will be treated as a "trust" under the Code "if it can be shown that the purpose of the arrangement is to vest in trustees

2. See note 2 on page 92.

J. BUSINESS (OR STOCK) CORPORATION

BUSINESS CORPORATION— IN GENERAL

68. The corporation, in terms of business and capital, is the most important form of business enterprise. Innumerable variations are possible in setting up the corporation. For most purposes, the corporation is treated as an entity. It is subject to greater governmental regulation, formalities, and publicity than other forms of business enterprise.

Of the several forms of business enterprise, the corporation, in terms of business and capital, is by far the most important.[1] Corporations range in size from one shareholder (one-man corporation) to more than 3,150,000 shareholders (American Telephone & Telegraph Co.); from the smallest businesses to the multibillion dollar giants, the largest being American Telephone & Telegraph Co. with some $40 billion assets, paying more than $1.66 billion in federal taxes and more than $1.2 billion in state and local taxes, and having a net income after taxes of over $2 billion.

Basically statutory in form, corporations are far from monolithic structures. Innumerable variations are possible in setting up the corporation,[2] so long as permissible methods and applicable limitations are observed.

Since the remaining chapters will be devoted to corporation law, this section will be limited to a discussion of the more important features of the corporation by way of contrast with the various features of the several unincorporated forms of business enterprise explored in the preceding sections.[3]

The term "incorporate" literally means to form into a body. A now obsolete meaning of "corporation" is the state of being incorporated. By definition, then, a corporation, is an entity, and is so regarded for most legal purposes. Under abnormal or very limited circumstances, the corporate entity will be disregarded,[4] but such an approach constitutes a relatively minor exception to the general rule.

Many consequences logically follow from the entity theory of corporateness. The corporation as such is subject to bankruptcy, reorganization, and arrangement proceedings under the Federal Bankruptcy Act.[5] For the purposes of various taxes, it is usually treated as an entity.

[§ 67]

responsibility for the protection and conservation of property for beneficiaries who cannot share in the discharge of this responsibility and, therefore, are not associates in a joint enterprise for the conduct of business for profit." Treas.Reg. § 301.7701–4(a) (1960). Regulated investment companies (which may be common trust funds) and real estate investment companies (defined to include unincorporated trusts meeting certain requirements) are subject to federal income tax treatment under Subchapter M, under which the company is taxed only on undistributed income while the members report the distributed income as ordinary income or capital gain as the case may be. Int.Rev.Code of 1954, 26 U.S.C.A. Subchapter M—Regulated Investment Companies and Real Estate Investment Trusts §§ 851–855, 856–858. MacDonald, "Real Estate Investment Trusts Under the Internal Revenue Code of 1954: Proposals for Revision", 32 Geo.Wash.L.Rev. 808 (1964); Roeder, "Requirements for Qualifications of Real Estate Investment Trusts", N.Y.U. 20th Inst. on Fed.Tax. 631 (1062); Sexton, "Taxation of the Real Estate Investment Trust and Its Certificate Holders", id. 647. See also section 58, n. 5 supra.

2. E. g., California, Idaho, Michigan, Minnesota, New York, Oklahoma, Oregon, Utah, Wisconsin. In New York, business trusts are treated as corporations for purposes of the franchise tax and hence are not subject to the unincorporated business income tax. McKinney's N.Y.Tax Law, §§ 208(1), 703.

[§ 68]

1. Of an estimated 11,479,000 business enterprises in the United States, only 1,469,000 were listed as corporations. Statistical Abstract of the United States 1969, 472 et seq. (U.S. Dep't of Commerce). The great importance of corporations in the American economy and society has already been noted. See section 1 supra.

2. See Chapters 6, 8, 9, 10 infra.

3. See sections 16–67 supra.

4. See sections 146–153 infra.

5. 11 U.S.C.A. §§ 1(8), 22, 526, 706(3). See sections 152, 383–388 infra.

The corporation is subject to greater governmental regulation and control than other forms of business enterprise in its formation, operation, and dissolution. More formalities must be observed; more reports prepared and filed; more publicity suffered. On the other hand, borrowing by corporations is often free from the restrictions of the usury laws.[6] While corporations are protected as persons under the due process and equal-protection-of-the-laws clauses of the United States Constitution,[7] they do not enjoy the protection of the privileges-and-immunities-of-citizens clause.[8] When doing business or conducting transactions in other jurisdictions, corporations traditionally are subject to greater amenability to process, regulation, taxation, and formal requirements than unincorporated businesses, especially the individual proprietorship or partnership.[9]

The corporation has a corporate name [10] and usually a corporate seal.[11] It enjoys many of the powers of natural persons.[12] For most purposes, it is a person separate and apart from the persons who compose it.

Generally, the corporation may take, hold, and convey property in the corporate name.[13] Contracts are made in the corporate name.[14] The corporation may sue and be sued in the corporate name.[15] For purposes of federal diversity-of-citizenship jurisdiction, the corporation is deemed a citizen of its state of incorporation and of its principal place of business, and the citizenships of its shareholders are immaterial.[16]

BUSINESS CORPORATION—FORMALITIES OF ORGANIZATION

69. **The expense and formality of organization and operation of a corporation, including initial and annual fees and taxes, drafting of incorporation documents, notices, minutes, reports, and public filing requirements, militate against the corporate form for smaller businesses which want to operate freely and informally.**

Incorporation involves greater expense and formality than the formation of any other form of business enterprise. Typical are organization taxes, filing fees, franchise taxes, etc.,[1] the drafting of preincorporation agreements,[2] articles of incorporation,[3] bylaws,[4] the minutes of organization meetings of incorporators and board of directors,[5]

---

6. E. g., McKinney's N.Y. Gen.Obl.Law, § 5–521. A "corporation" (including associations and joint-stock companies having any of the powers and privileges of corporations not possessed by individuals or partnerships) may not, with one exception applicable to a corporation whose principal asset is a one or two family dwelling, interpose the defense of usury in any action. See section 150 infra.

7. See section 80 infra.

8. See section 89 infra.

9. See sections 96–101 infra.

10. ABA–ALI Model Bus.Corp.Act §§ 4(a), 7. See section 119 infra.

11. ABA–ALI Model Bus.Corp.Act § 4(c). See sections 135, 228 infra.

12. ABA–ALI Model Bus.Corp.Act § 4. See sections 122, 182–183 infra.

13. ABA–ALI Model Bus.Corp.Act § 4(d), (e); McKinney's N.Y. Bus.Corp.Law, § 202(a) (4). In New York, a testamentary disposition of property may be made to any person having capacity to acquire and hold such property. McKinney's N.Y. EPTL, § 3–1.3(a).

14. ABA–ALI Model Bus.Corp.Act § 4(h). Proper corporate signature is "XYZ CORP. by John Doe, President" (or other duly authorized officer). When the seal is affixed, it is sometimes attested by the secretary or similar officer. The corporate form of acknowledgment may require a reference to the affixing of the corporate seal, or if the corporation has no seal, a statement to such effect in lieu of such reference. E. g., McKinney's N.Y. Real Prop.Law § 309.

15. ABA–ALI Model Bus.Corp.Act § 4(b); McKinney's N.Y. Bus.Corp.Law, § 202(a) (2). See section 352 infra.

16. See sections 88, 353 infra.

1. ABA–ALI Model Bus. Corp. Act §§ 120–127. See sections 76, 99, 158 infra.

2. See sections 107–115, 260, 284 infra.

3. See sections 118–132, 285 infra.

4. See sections 133, 286 infra.

5. See section 135 infra.

shareholder agreements,[6] share certificates with possible legends,[7] holding of formal meetings,[8] filings in one or more public offices,[9] not to mention additional complications when securities are to be offered publicly [10] or traded on a securities exchange.[11] During corporate existence, there are continuing requirements of notices,[12] meetings,[13] minutes, reports,[14] filings, other formalities.[15] Formalities and expense are compounded when the corporation does business in other jurisdictions.[16] All of this militates against the corporate form for smaller businesses which want to operate freely and informally.

BUSINESS CORPORATION—CAPITAL AND CREDIT REQUIREMENTS

70. **The corporation is often subject to statutory minimum authorized, subscribed, or paid-in capital requirements. The corporation can attract capital by a wide variety of debt and equity securities to fit almost every conceivable need. Shares, absent restrictions to the contrary, are freely transferable.**

Unlike the other forms of business enterprise, the corporation may be subject to statutory minimum capital requirements. Such requirements may specify minimum authorized, subscribed, or paid-in capital; compliance may be a condition precedent to incorporation or to doing business or a condition subsequent.[1] In jurisdictions with such requirements, personal service enterprises might find it more convenient to defer incorporation pending the accumulation of sufficient business capital.

In terms of availability of credit, the corporation is in a strong position. Funds may be enlisted not only by the issue of equity interests to the public but also by loans and the issue of debt securities. Combined equity and debt financing offers several possible advantages.[2] For no other form of business enterprise is there such a wide variety of types of securities—in almost limitless permutations and combinations—to fit almost every conceivable need. This is one of the principal advantages of the corporation. Debt securities, if in proper form or duly assigned, may be negotiable, despite the fact that payment is limited to corporate assets.[3] Shares, absent restrictions to the contrary,[4] are freely transferable, often in a readily available market, and rarely subject the shareholder to personal liability; they also may be readily pledged as collateral for loans. The corporation lends itself to easy expansion by capitalization of earnings or issue of additional securities.

6. See sections 198, 213, 267, 275, 287 infra.

7. See sections 134, 290 infra.

8. See section 135 infra.

9. See section 132 infra.

10. See sections 292 et seq. infra.

11. See sections 293 et seq. infra.

12. See sections 191, 209 infra.

13. Ibid.

14. ABA–ALI Model Bus. Corp. Act §§ 118, 119. See, e. g., section 199 infra.

15. See Chapter 13 infra.

16. See sections 96–101, 136–137 infra.

1. ABA–ALI Model Bus. Corp. Act § 51 ($1,000). A decreasing number of American jurisdictions require payment of some capital before commencing business, some specifying minimum amounts ranging from $300 to $1,000 and others requiring that the amount stated in the articles of incorporation be paid in or subscribed before commencing business. Other formalities, such as filing of affidavit of payment, might be required. New Jersey, until 1968, required that at least $2,000 capital be authorized, at least $1,000 be subscribed by the incorporators, and at least $1,000 be paid in; Delaware and New York have no mandatory minimum paid-in capital requirement; the Model Act in 1969 abolished its requirement.

2. See sections 155–164 infra.

3. The Uniform Commercial Code, article 8, entitled "Investment Securities", governs debt securities and shares. Article 3 ("Commercial Paper") deals with drafts (bills of exchange), checks, certificates of deposit, and notes.

4. Transfer restrictions may be desirable in close corporations. See sections 281, 282 infra.

BUSINESS CORPORATION—MANAGEMENT AND CONTROL

71. The corporation is managed by its board of directors, which is elected by the shareholders. Otherwise, the shareholders' management functions are usually limited to approval of extraordinary matters. Neither the directors nor the officers are agents of the shareholders; their principal duties are to the corporation, but they owe certain fiduciary duties to shareholders. Shareholders are neither agents of the corporation or of each other nor owners of the corporation's assets. Only in limited situations, are shareholders subject to fiduciary duties among themselves.

Management of a corporation is vested in its board of directors, who determine policy matters and appoint (and remove) officers to execute such policy and administer corporate affairs. The board must usually have at least three members, all of whom are subject to certain responsibilities. Directors usually may act only as a board, voting per capita in contrast to shareholder voting usually in proportion to interest. The principal functions of the shareholders are to elect (and, under certain circumstances, remove) directors, and to approve extraordinary corporate actions and transactions.[1]

The control of the shareholders, while circumscribed in theory, and usually more so in practice, is more significant than the control exercisable by a limited partner or a beneficiary of a business trust. On the other hand, the shareholder as such does not have the managerial power of a general partner.

While neither corporate directors nor corporate officers are agents of shareholders, they do owe the shareholders certain fiduciary duties.[2] Not only these duties but also those duties owed directly to the corporation may, with some limitations, be enforced by the shareholders.[3] Furthermore, the shareholders are not agents of the corporation or of each other, nor owners of the corporation's assets. In like manner, they generally owe no duty to the corporation or each other, with some exceptions.[4] In contrast are the mutual agency and fiduciary relationship among partners.

BUSINESS CORPORATION—PROFITS AND LOSSES

72. In the corporation, profits are shared proportionately to share ownership, subject to any dividend preferences and other rights when there is more than a single class of shares outstanding. Holders of shares which are full-paid and nonassessable are generally not personally responsible for corporate losses, although losses reduce their proportionate equity in the corporation. Upon dissolution, shareholders participate proportionately to their share ownership, subject to any liquidation preferences and other rights.

Profits are shared by the shareholders to the extent that they are distributed by way of dividends. Sharing is proportionate to share ownership, subject to complications of any dividend preferences and other rights when there is more than a single class of shares outstanding.

Holders of shares which are fully paid and nonassessable are generally not personally responsible for corporate losses. Such losses do reduce their equity and may affect their dividends and the price realizable upon the sale of the shares. Otherwise, the incidence

---

1. Centralization of management is one of the six major corporate characteristics—really four, since (a) associates and (b) an objective to carry on a business and divide the profits therefrom are common to both corporations and all unincorporated business associations—for determining whether an unincorporated enterprise is an "association" taxable as a corporation for federal income tax purposes. For management functions of board of directors, see sections 203 et seq. infra; of officers, see sections 219 et seq. infra; of shareholders, see sections 186 et seq. infra and Chapter 13 infra. In the large corporation, the corporate structure is often modified to retain control in management (see sections 180–230 infra), whereas in the close corporation, protection for the minority interests, possibly in the form of a veto against "freeze-out", is often the purpose of special provisions (see sections 263–280, 283–290 infra).

2. See sections 239–241, 276 infra.

3. See Chapter 14 infra.

4. See sections 240, 268 infra.

of corporate losses is realized upon liquidation and distribution of net assets among shareholders, either proportionately to share ownership, or according to any liquidation preferences and other rights.

BUSINESS CORPORATION—EXTENT OF LIABILITY

73. In the corporation, the shareholders' liability is usually limited to their respective capital contributions, although in a few jurisdictions, unlimited or double liability corporations, are still possible. In a very few jurisdictions, shareholders are personally liable for unpaid wages of the corporation's wage earners. Where shareholders guarantee corporate obligations, they are personally liable under such guaranty. Directors, officers, and other corporate personnel, acting in their representative capacities, are not personally liable on corporate contracts or for torts unless they participate in the tort; they might be indemnified by the corporation for reasonable litigation expenses incurred by them as such. No other form of business enterprise assures such a degree of limited liability without greater sacrifice of control.

Limited liability is probably the most attractive feature of the corporation, although it has come to be recognized primarily during the past century.[1] Generally, the shareholder's liability for corporate obligations is limited to what he has invested in the corporation.[2] However, where corporate formalities are not duly observed, or where the corporation is undercapitalized, or where other special circumstances exist, a court might disregard the corporate entity as an insulator or nonconductor of liability.[3]

In a few jurisdictions, unlimited liability corporations are still possible.[4] Double liability, in some states triple or unlimited liability, once the common feature of bank stock, has been largely eliminated by state constitutions, statutes, charter revision, and other procedures.[5] In a decreasing number of states, shareholders are personally liable for unpaid wages of the corporation's wage earners.[6] Of course, if shareholders guarantee corporate obligations, they would be personally liable under such guaranty.

Directors, officers, and other corporate personnel, acting in their representative capacities, are not personally liable on corporate contracts or for torts unless they participate in the tort.[7]

Directors, officers, and other corporate personnel might be indemnified by the corporation for reasonable litigation expenses incurred by them as such, or in a growing

1. Blackstone did not mention limited liability in discussing corporate attributes. In England, limited liability was recognized by statute in 1855, but "unlimited" companies may still be incorporated there. See note 4 infra. See also W. Hohfeld, "Nature of Stockholders' Individual Liability for Corporation Debts", 9 Colum.L.Rev. 283 (1909), "The Individual Liability of Stockholders and the Conflict of Laws", 9 Colum.L.Rev. 492 (1909), 10 Colum.L.Rev. 283, 520 (1910), in Fundamental Legal Conceptions as Applied in Judicial Reasoning and Other Legal Essays 194, 229, 260, 303 (1923).

2. Where the full subscription has not been paid or where the shares are "watered", there generally is liability for an amount equal to the amount unpaid on the shares. For general discussion of limited liability, see Note, "Limited Liability in Commercial Enterprises", 57 Colum.L.Rev. 84 (1957). See sections 146–148, 202 infra.

3. See sections 146–148 infra.

4. E. g., England ("unlimited" companies), Delaware. L. Gower, The Principles of Modern Company Law 67 (2d ed. 1957); Del.Gen.Corp.Law § 102(b) (6) (1967). Until 1923, such corporations could be formed in New York. Until 1928, all shareholders of corporations in California were, with minor exceptions, subject to unlimited liability on a proportionate basis. See former Cal.Const. art. 12, § 3 (repealed, effective Nov. 4, 1930).

5. 48 Stat. 189 (1933), 49 Stat. 708 (1935), 67 Stat. 27 (1953), 12 U.S.C.A. § 64a; McKinney's N.Y. Bank. Law, §§ 113–b, 305–a, 322–a. In half of the states, such additional liability was not abolished; the law merely permitted banks to take action to make such liability inapplicable to their shareholders. Fewer than 100 banks have failed to take action. The Federal Deposit Insurance Corporation may waive such liability to the extent that it is subrogated to depositors' rights. 12 U.S.C.A. § 182(g). See Vincens, "On the Demise of Double Liability of Bank Shareholders", 12 Bus.Law. 275 (1957). Shareholders' double liability still exists in joint-stock land banks. 12 U.S.C.A. § 812.

6. See section 202 infra.

7. See sections 218, 230 infra.

number of jurisdictions insured against such risks.[8]

No other generally recognized form of business enterprise assures such a degree of limited liability without greater sacrifice of control.

BUSINESS CORPORATION—TRANSFER-ABILITY OF INTEREST

74. In the corporation, the interests of the shareholders are usually evidenced by share certificates. Absent reasonable restrictions on transfer, usually important in permitting the close corporation to remain close, share certificates are usually freely transferable. Recordation on the corporate books is usually prerequisite to the corporation's recognition of the shareholder's status. Share transfers are governed by the Uniform Commercial Code, in nearly all jurisdictions, and also possibly by bylaws. Transferability facilitates family and estate planning.

The interests of shareholders in a corporation are usually evidenced by share certificates. Traditionally, these are freely transferable, with some aspects of negotiability, although recordation of the transfer on the corporate books is usually prerequisite to recognition by the corporation of the transferee's rights. The validity and effect of transfer are governed by the Uniform Commercial Code in nearly all jurisdictions, and possibly also by bylaws.

Reasonable restrictions on share transfers may be imposed, thereby injecting into the corporation the partnership principle of delectus personae.[1] Such restrictions may be important to preserve the close nature of the membership, along with the combined corporate advantage of limited liability.

The ready transferability of corporate shares facilitates family and estate planning with respect to a closely-held business.[2]

---

8. See sections 379, 380 infra.

[§ 74]

1. See sections 281–282 infra.

2. Polasky, "Planning for the Disposition of a Substantial Interest in a Closely Held Business—The

BUSINESS CORPORATION—CONTINU-ITY OF EXISTENCE

75. The corporation is the only form of business enterprise which theoretically may have perpetual existence in most jurisdictions, a prime practical advantage. Some jurisdictions limit corporate duration, and practically all jurisdictions permit the formation of corporations with less than perpetual duration. Difficulty of premature dissolution can cause embarrassment, especially in the deadlocked close corporation.

The corporation is the only form of business enterprise which theoretically may have perpetual existence in most jurisdictions.[1] Perpetual existence historically was considered one of the principal ad advantages of incorporation,[2] and is a prime practical advantage today. While corporations usually may be formed with a stated duration which is less than perpetual,[3] most are formed for perpetual duration when possible.[4] Thus, the possible embarrassment of premature termination is avoided. Con-

---

Corporation: Stock-Purchase Agreements and Redemption of Shares", 46 Iowa L.Rev. 516 (1961).

[§ 75]

1. ABA–ALI Model Bus.Corp.Act § 4(a). The constitutions of Louisiana, Oklahoma, and Mississippi limit corporate duration. See section 14, n. 11 supra. Statutes in Arizona, Georgia, Kansas, Montana, New Mexico, and Oklahoma, limit corporate duration to periods ranging from 25 to 100 years, with possible renewals in some jurisdictions. See section 120 infra.

2. Blackstone referred to "perpetual succession" as "the very end" of incorporation. 1 Blackstone, Commentaries *463. Continuity of life uninterrupted by changes in membership is one of the six major corporate characteristics considered in determining whether an unincorporated enterprise is an "association" taxable as a corporation for federal income tax purposes. In effect, it is one of four relevant corporate characteristics since two of the six —(a) associates and (b) an objective to carry on business and divide the gains therefrom—are not considered because they are common to both corporations and unincorporated business associations.

3. California provides for perpetual existence of all business corporations. Cal.Gen.Corp.Law, § 308 (1947).

4. In jurisdictions with awkward dissolution provisions and convenient provisions for renewal or extension of corporate existence, corporations of limited existence are sometimes formed.

versely, the difficulty of dissolution when the corporation is deadlocked[5] or when holders of less than the requisite number of shares are willing to effect dissolution[6] could prove a disadvantage, especially in the close corporation.

BUSINESS CORPORATION—TAX CONSIDERATIONS

76. The corporation is regarded as a separately taxable entity for most federal and state tax purposes. "Double taxation", with corporate tax and surtax on its income and individual tax on shareholders on their dividends, to the extent of dividend distributions of corporate earnings and profits among shareholders, is the most significant possible tax disadvantage of the corporation. Apart from dividend relief provisions and consolidated return provisions in the case of affiliated corporations, Subchapter S election is the most important method of avoiding double taxation by eliminating the tax at the corporate level. Minimization of double taxation can be achieved by maximizing corporate deductions for reasonable salaries, interest, rent and royalties, and contributions to pension and profit sharing plans and other employee fringe benefits. The corporation also offers advantages in transmuting ordinary income to capital gain, especially on the sale of corporate shares or possibly corporate assets. The corporation's potential liability under the federal accumulated earnings tax or under the federal personal holding company tax applicable to close corporations can be a serious tax risk. An individual proprietorship or a partnership often can be converted tax-free into a corporation, although a taxable transfer is sometimes more desirable. Various other federal, state, and local taxes often provide a greater burden on the corporation than on other forms of business enterprise.

Many tax statutes distinguish the "corporation", as that term happens to be defined for such purpose, from business enterprises which are not included within such statutory definition. While there may be problems as to whether or not a particular unincorporat-

ed business falls within such definition.[1] such definitional problems ordinarily do not exist where the enterprise is actually incorporated under the corporation statutes. Of all the taxes, the impact of the federal income tax is most significant.[2] In the light of the probable earnings of the business and of the individuals involved, under present and prospective rates, tax considerations can be evaluated.

Despite protestations from the taxing authorities that tax results should only follow business results, there is little question that

1. See section 16, nn. 4–6 supra.

2. B. Bittker & J. Eustice, Federal Income Taxation of Corporations and Shareholders (2d ed. 1966); Tax Management Portfolios (BNA); Prentice-Hall 1970 Federal Tax Course ¶¶ 3100 et seq.; D. Kahn, Basic Corporate Taxation (ICLE 1970); R. Molloy, Federal Income Taxation of Corporations (ALI rev. 1966); C. Rohrlich, Organizing Corporate and Other Business Enterprises 217–265 (4th ed. 1967); R. McDonald, Corporations and Corporate Distributions (PLI 1962, Supp.1966); R. Ash, Tax Problems Encountered in the General Practice of Law 22–32 (ABA 1960); Sharp, "Tax Considerations in Organizing a Corporation", 53 A.B.A.J. 1159 (1967); Maer & Francis, Checklist: "Whether to Incorporate", 22 Bus.Law. 571 (1967); Emry, "Tax and Estate Planning Consequences of Farm Incorporation", 2 U. San Francisco L.Rev. 14 (1967); Sneed & Will, "Family Corporation Uses in Estate Planning", 20 Okl.L.Rev. 243 (1967); Strecker, "When Will the Corporate Form Save Taxes?", 18 Vand.L.Rev. 1695 (1965); Hare, "Public Policy Aspects of Farm Incorporation", 20 Bus.Law. 933 (1965); Hall, "Agricultural Corporations: Their Utility and Legality", 17 Okl.L.Rev. (1964); Cavanaugh, "Agricultural Corporations and the Homestead Laws", 18 Bus. Law. 453 (1963); Panel Discussion: "Agricultural Corporations", 17 Bus.Law. 221 (1961); Symposium: "Family Farm Corporations", 1960 Wis.L.Rev. 555; Matties, "The Advantages and Disadvantages of a Corporation", 31 N.Y.St.B.Bull. 380 (1959); Fager, "A Primer on the Federal Income Taxation of Corporations", 4 Prac.Law. 13 (May 1958); Weiss, "Organizing the New Corporation; Some Tax Considerations", 42 Marq.L.Rev. 202 (1958); Shoemaker, "Incorporation of Family Agricultural Businesses", 30 Rocky Mt.L.Rev. 401 (1958), 36 Taxes 515 (1958); Pennell, "Tax Planning at the Time of Incorporation", 35 Taxes 927 (1957); Kirby, "Accelerated Depreciation and the Treasury Regulations", 54 Nw. U.L.Rev. 434 (1959); Greenfield, "Corporate Benefits in Using the Sale-Leaseback Device", 37 Taxes 1017 (1959); Barron, "LIFO Cost or Market—Sound Accounting Principle or Tax Device?", 12 Nat'l Tax J. 367 (1959). See also Rendall, "The Impact of Canadian Income Tax Law on Domestic Subsidiaries of U.S. Corporations—B.C. and A.D.", 17 Buffalo L.Rev. 135 (1967).

5. See section 280 infra.

6. See section 348 infra.

the "silent partner" seated at every conference table where choice and form of business enterprise is discussed is, or ought to be, the Commissioner of Internal Revenue.[3]

Federal Income Tax

Under the federal income tax law, the corporation, as has been seen, is treated as a separate taxable entity. Corporate rates have only a two-step graduation: 22 percent normal tax on first $25,000 of taxable corporate income; 48 percent (22 percent normal tax and 26 percent surtax) on taxable corporate income in excess of $25,000.[4] In contrast, individual rates undergo some 25 graduations, ranging from 14 percent on the first $500 of taxable income to 70 percent of taxable income over $100,000.[5]

The most significant possible tax disadvantage of the corporation, absent Subchapter S election, is "double taxation": payment by the corporation of tax on its income at the corporate rates, and by the shareholder of tax on his dividends at the individual rate applicable to him on the basis of his total income from all sources.[6] In the case of

parent-subsidiary, etc., corporations, there could be triple, etc., taxation.

Some relief against "double taxation" has been afforded since 1954 by the provisions (a) for a dividends-received exclusion of the first $100 ($200 for spouses filing joint return) in dividends of certain domestic corporations from gross income of the recipient;[7] (b) for limiting the tax on dividends received by a corporation from most domestic corporations by an 85 percent dividends received deduction;[8] and (c) for consolidated returns by affiliated corporations.[9]

returns, treatment of regulated investment companies as a conduit for federal income tax purposes. In England, dividends, until 1965, were excluded from individual standard income tax, but not surtax; after 1965, England followed the American example. Canada has proposed an "integrated" income tax, designed as a comprehensive tax on all income. For avoidance of double taxation in regulated investment companies as well as in real estate investment trusts, see Int.Rev.Code of 1954, 26 U.S. C.A. §§ 851–858.

7. Int.Rev.Code of 1954, 26 U.S.C.A. § 116; Treas. Reg. § 1.116 (1956).

8. Int.Rev.Code of 1954, 26 U.S.C.A. §§ 243 et seq.; Treas.Reg. §§ 1.243 et seq. (1956) (thus reducing the corporation's tax on such dividend income to a 7.2 percent maximum).

9. Int.Rev.Code of 1954, 26 U.S.C.A. §§ 1501–1504. When two or more corporations file a consolidated return, only one surtax exemption may be claimed. The additional surtax of two percent on consolidated taxable income was repealed in 1964. Int.Rev. Code of 1954, 26 U.S.C.A. § 913. See J. Crestol, New Consolidated Return Rules (1968); F. Peel, Consolidated Tax Returns: A Treatise on the Law of Consolidated Federal Income Tax Returns (1959); B. Bittker & J. Eustice, Federal Income Taxation of Corporations and Shareholders §§ 13.40–13.43 (2d ed. 1966); Crumbley, "Double-Barreled Attack on Consolidated Returns: Unfair?", 46 Taxes 38 (1968); Dunn, "The New Consolidated Return Regulations May Preempt the Field in Determining the Allowance of Operating Losses", 23 Tax L.Rev. 185 (1968); Comment, "The New Consolidated Return Regulations: An Analysis", 116 U.Pa.L.Rev. 131 (1967); Dale, "Consolidated Return Regs Introduce New Concepts For Taxing Intercompany Profits", 24 J. Taxation 6 (1966); Peel, "Losses on Consolidated Returns: A Checklist of Special Rules", N.Y.U. 22d Inst. on Fed.Tax. 271 (1964); Dale, "Flaws and Pitfalls in New Consolidated Returns Regulations", 20 J. Taxation 66 (1964); Hackney, "Financial Accounting for Parents and Subsidiaries—A New Approach to Consolidated Statements", 25 U.Pitt.L. Rev. 9 (1963); Dale, "Recent Developments in Consolidated Returns", N.Y.U. 20th Inst. on Fed.Tax.

3. Sharp, "Tax Considerations in Organizing a Corporation", 53 A.B.A.J. 1159 (1967).

4. During the first year, the surtax can be avoided by ending the first taxable year when corporate taxable income reaches $25,000, since the corporation can select its own taxable year. Int.Rev.Code of 1954, 26 U.S.C.A. §§ 441, 443. As to possible tax savings by resorting to multiple corporations and allowances of the $25,000 surtax exemption for each corporation, see note 27 infra.

5. For single persons not qualifying as head of household or surviving spouse, and, although at less favorable graduated rates, for married persons filing separate returns. The rates are more favorable for married persons filing jointly or a single person qualifying as a surviving spouse, and for heads of households.

6. A statistical study concludes that such double taxation results in overtaxation at the bottom of the shareholder income scale and undertaxation at the top. D. Holland, The Income-Tax Burden on Stockholders (1958). See also Symposium on Business Taxation, Wayne State University, 1964, Effects of Corporation Income Tax (1964); Goode, "Who Bears the Corporation Income Tax?", 32 U.Chi.L. Rev. 410 (1965). Double taxation is not an inevitable consequence of the entity theory, as witness Subchapter S election, provisions for consolidated

Substantial relief against "double taxation" was afforded to eligible "small business corporations" [10] by the Technical Amendments Act of 1958,[11] which added Subchapter S to the Internal Revenue Code of 1954. Under Subchapter S, a "small business corporation" may elect not to be taxed at the corporate level, but to have its income, whether distributed or not, passed through and taxed pro rata to its shareholders as ordinary income. All shareholders must consent to the election.[12] Corporations making such election are known as "Subchapter S corporations" or "tax-option corporations". Election can be terminated by unanimous shareholder revocation and is terminated by the loss of eligibility of the corporation as a "small business corporation". Other tax advantages include pass-through of net operating losses, of corporate net long-term capital gain as such, and nonapplication of the accumulated earnings tax. The redemption of shares by an electing corporation is not expressly treated in Subchapter S but might have different tax consequences than would otherwise be the case. The tax advantages of corporate pension and profit sharing plans and other employee fringe

benefits are not lost by Subchapter S election, but the limitations of the Self-Employed Individuals Retirement Act now apply.[13]

The corporation enjoys several possible tax advantages, some of which in effect permit minimization of "double taxation".

In the first place, the corporation as an entity is entitled to deductions for certain expenditures even when made to persons who are also shareholders: (a) reasonable salaries; [14] (b) interest (so long as too-"thin incorporation" is avoided); [15] (c) rents and royalties; [16] and (d) contributions to pension and profit-sharing plans and other employee fringe benefits.[17] Corporate charitable con-

---

491 (1962); Swift, "The Consolidated Return", 36 Taxes 583 (1958); Alliegro v. Pan American Bank, 136 So.2d 656 (Fla.Dist.Ct.App.1962), cert. denied 149 So.2d 45 (Fla.1963); Case v. New York Cent. R. R., 15 N.Y.2d 150, 256 N.Y.S.2d 607, 204 N.E.2d 643 (1965).

10. For definition of "small business corporation" for purposes of Subchapter S, see section 16, n. 9 supra.

11. Int.Rev.Code of 1954, Subchapter S—Election of Certain Small Business Corporations as to Taxable Status, 26 U.S.C.A. §§ 1371–1377; Treas.Reg. § 1.1371 (1959). An increasing number of states, including New York, follow federal income tax law in many respects, including Subchapter S treatment.

12. Unanimous shareholder consent may avoid the issue of unconstitutionality implicit in Eisner v. Macomber, 252 U.S. 189, 40 S.Ct. 189, 64 L.Ed. 521, 9 A.L.R. 1570 (1920). Election must be made during the first month of the taxable year or the month prior thereto. If an election has been terminated, Internal Revenue Service consent is required for re-election within five years. There can be no carry over to a nonelection year; nor of a pre-election year corporate loss to shareholders in election year.

13. R. Anthoine, Corporate Tax Election to Pass Income and Loss to Shareholders (PLI 1959). See section 262 infra. Treatment of Subchapter S corporation pension plans is now similar to self-employed retirement plans—see text accompanying section 18, n. 18 supra, and section 77, nn. 7–9 infra.

14. Int.Rev.Code of 1954, 26 U.S.C.A. § 162(a) (1); see also id. § 267. See sections 243 et seq. infra.

15. For possible advantages and disadvantages of "thin incorporation", see section 166 infra. Interest minimizes double taxation in corporations not making a Subchapter S election. The Tax Reform Act of 1969 limits the amount of interest deductible on "corporation acquisition indebtedness" to acquire shares or two-thirds of all the operating assets (excluding cash) of another corporation. Loss on shares, other than "section 1244 stock", or on a non-business bad debt is subject to capital loss restrictions, whereas a business bad debt is deductible in full. Under the Small Business Tax Revision Act of 1958, Int.Rev.Code of 1954, 26 U.S.C.A. § 1244, losses on "section 1244 stock" (for definition, see section 16, n. 11 supra) are treated as ordinary losses ($25,-000/$50,000 on joint return limitation; balance as capital loss). See section 262 infra. Losses on worthless shares (except "section 1244 stock"), securities, and loans are usually deductible as capital losses.

16. Greenfield, "Corporate Benefits in Using the Sale-Leaseback Device", 37 Taxes 1017 (1959).

17. Besides the advantage of possible corporate deduction, the directors, officers, and employees, notwithstanding that they might be shareholders, enjoy certain tax privileges (benefit not treated as income or deferred as income) available under the Code with respect to share option, share bonus, share purchase, deferred compensation, pension and profit-sharing, group and other insurance, death benefit, medical payment, wage continuation plans and other fringe benefits. See sections 246–254 infra.

tributions may be deducted up to five percent of taxable income (with five-year carry over provision),[18] without affecting the shareholders' individual charitable contribution deduction of 20/30 percent. Maximizing deductions for salary and interest payments, etc., to persons who are also shareholders obviously minimizes double taxation.

Under the entity approach, corporate losses may not be offset against individual income, but may be carried back for the preceding three years and carried forward for the succeeding five years, and applied against any corporate profits realized during such years.[19] Any ultimate loss to the shareholder would be a capital loss and not a business loss, except for "section 1244 stock".

In the case of a corporation, absent Subchapter S election, shareholders pay individual income tax generally only upon the profits distributed to them. Therefore distribution may be deferred or leveled out over the years. Furthermore, income and deductions lose their character upon distribution through the corporate strainer to the shareholder. For example, distribution of funds which were tax-exempt interest or capital gains to the corporation may be taxed as ordinary income to the shareholders; conversely, shareholders selling their shares or having it redeemed might be able to enjoy the more favorable capital gains treatment [20]

for increments resulting from corporate retention of ordinary income. Transmuting ordinary income to capital gain, when possible, offers obvious advantage in many situations.

Offsetting these possible advantages is the accumulated earnings tax imposed on corporations in addition to the other federal corporate income taxes. The penalty rates are 27½ percent of the first $100,000 of accumulated taxable income, and 38½ percent of such income in excess of $100,000. Accumulations to meet the "reasonable needs" of the business do not constitute such income. In addition, there is a $100,000 lump-sum credit for most corporations.[21]

For top bracket individuals, retention of earnings and payment of the accumulated earnings tax might be preferable to distribution of dividends, so long as the application of the personal holding company tax is avoided.

The personal holding company tax [22] generally applies when two requirements are met: (a) Stock ownership requirement—at least 50 percent of the shares are owned by not more than five persons (after applying attribution rules), and (b) Adjusted ordinary gross income requirement—at least 60 percent of the adjusted ordinary gross income

18. Int.Rev.Code of 1954, 26 U.S.C.A. § 170(c).

19. Int.Rev.Code of 1954, 26 U.S.C.A. § 172; Browne, "Traffic in Tax Loss Corporations", 2 Boston B.J. 27 (Oct.1958); Comment, "Net Operating Loss Carryovers and Corporate Adjustments: Retaining an Advantageous Tax History under Libson Shops and Sections 269, 381, and 382", 69 Yale L.J. 1201 (1960).

20. Long-term (more than six months) capital gains for individuals are subject to a maximum 29.5 to 32.5 percent tax and for corporations are subject to a 28 to 30 percent tax. The alternative 50 percent deduction method is available only to taxpayers other than corporations. Int.Rev.Code of 1954, 26 U.S.C.A. § 1202. Corporate capital losses may be offset only against corporate capital gains with five-year carry forward. Int.Rev.Code of 1954, 26 U.S.C.A. § 1211. An individual may offset his capital losses against not only his capital gains but also against the lesser of one-half of

the excess of long-term capital loss over net short-term capital gains, etc., or $1,000 ordinary income per year with unlimited carry forward. Such limitations do not exist in the case of business losses. Surrey, "Definitional Problems in Capital Gains Taxation", 69 Harv.L.Rev. 985 (1956). Transfer by gift or death could avoid income or capital gains tax. The donor's basis would carry over to the donee; the basis of property acquired from a decedent is the fair market value at the date of death or alternative valuation date for estate tax purposes, thus permitting possible stepped-up basis without income tax. Int.Rev.Code of 1954, 26 U.S. C.A. §§ 1014, 1015.

21. Int.Rev.Code of 1954, 26 U.S.C.A. §§ 531–537; R. Holzman, The Tax on Accumulated Earnings (1956); R. Kilcullen, Taxing the Improper Accumulation of Corporate Surplus (PLI rev. 1956). Resort to multiple corporations might, prior to 1975, result in credits for each corporation. But see note 27 infra. See section 339 infra.

22. Int.Rev.Code of 1954, 26 U.S.C.A. § 542.

(i. e., gross receipts less cost of goods sold, subject to certain adjustments) is "personal holding company income" (income from investments, personal service contracts, etc.). Such a corporation is liable for such tax, in addition to the regular corporate normal tax and surtax, at the confiscatory rate of 70 percent on the "undistributed personal holding company income" (undistributed ordinary taxable income after certain adjustments and deductions). Such a corporation is not subject to the accumulated earnings tax. Closely-held non-investment corporations with some income from investments, personal service contracts, etc., can become subject to the tax if other operations result in a loss or insufficient income; hence corporations with fewer than 10 shareholders are potential personal holding companies.

While a sale of corporate shares or of corporate assets [23] ordinarily results in capital gain treatment, the so-called "collapsible corporation" provision can result in ordinary income tax treatment.[24]

Under the Code, organizational expenditures can be amortized over a 60-month period.[25] An individual proprietorship or partnership may often be converted tax-free into a corporation.[26]

Since 1964, payments of estimated corporate income taxes have been accelerated under a plan which will have all corporations on a current payment basis by 1972.

Furthermore, the prospect of possible future excess profits taxes applicable only to corporations must be considered. During the two world wars and the Korean war, a tax was levied on "excess profits income" (30 percent tax after allowance of a $25,000 credit).

How much of the business to incorporate is also a problem. For example, tax advantages might result from retaining assets to be rented to the corporation, from a cash basis individual's retaining unpaid liabilities, from retaining assets to be sold in the near future (especially "§ 1231 assets"), or from retaining assets to avoid bunching of income.

Until 1975, there is the possibility of multiple corporations, each with its own $25,000 surtax exemption and $100,000 accumulated earnings tax credit; however, affiliated corporations are allowed only one surtax exemption for the group or alternatively required to pay an additional six percent tax on the first $25,000 of their income.[27]

Of course, as financial operations and tax laws change,[28] the form of business enterprise might be altered to take advantage of such change. However, some things can be safely done initially which would cause tax embarrassment if introduced at a later time.

---

23. See Slawson, "Taxing as Ordinary Income the Appreciation of Publicly Held Stock", 76 Yale L.J. 623 (1967). See also sections 341, 381 infra.

24. Int.Rev.Code of 1954, 26 U.S.C.A. § 341. See section 381, n. 27 infra.

25. Int.Rev.Code of 1954, 26 U.S.C.A. § 248; B. Bittker & J. Eustice, Federal Income Taxation of Corporations and Shareholders § 2.26 (2d ed. 1966).

26. Int.Rev.Code of 1954, 26 U.S.C.A. §§ 351, 731. To be tax-free, the transfer of property must be to a new corporation solely in exchange for its shares or securities (but not cash or short-term notes, "boot", which would render the transfer taxable) if immediately after the transfer the transferors are in control of at least 80 percent of the voting shares and 80 percent of the shares of each other class. The corporation takes over the tax basis of the transferred property in the hands of the transferors. However, it might be more desirable to make the transfer taxable, for recognition of any loss, or even when there is gain to achieve a stepped-up basis for depreciation or future sale. This can be achieved by not meeting the requirements for a

tax-free transfer. Paul & Kalish, "Transition from Partnership to Corporation", N.Y.U. 18th Inst. on Fed.Tax. 639 (1960).

27. B. Bittker & J. Eustice, Federal Income Taxation of Corporations and Shareholders §§ 13.30–13.33 (2d ed. 1966).

28. Gifford, "Changing a Partnership into a Corporation—Some Considerations Affecting the Time When Incorporation May Benefit the Owners of a Growing Business", 16 Vand.L.Rev. 351 (1963). With the pendulum swings of tax law, some enterprises have switched their forms five times during the last 20 years. See 1 G. Hornstein, Corporation Law and Practice 35 (1959).

Other Taxes

Various other federal, state, and local taxes usually provide a greater burden on the corporation than on other forms of business enterprise. Such taxes as organization and capital taxes,[29] original issue taxes,[30] taxes on transfers of shares and other corporate securities,[31] franchise taxes,[32] and corporate income taxes,[33] apply only to corporations and forms of business enterprise assimilated to them for such purposes. Even when a tax is imposed on "unincorporated business" to try to equalize the tax treatment of the "corporation" and the "unincorporated business" the rate on the former might exceed the rate on the latter.[34]

K. PROFESSIONAL CORPORATION (OR ASSOCIATION)

PROFESSIONAL CORPORATION (OR ASSOCIATION)

77. Professional persons, traditionally unable to practice in corporate form, were, as self-employed persons, denied the retirement tax advantages available to corporate employees. Nearly all of the states enacted professional corporation or association statutes, but the Internal Revenue Service, until 1969, resisted corporate tax treatment of such organizations. Meanwhile, the Federal Self-Employed Individuals Tax Retirement Act (Smathers-Keogh Act, H.R. 10) has liberalized the benefits for the self-employed, but are less generous than corporate benefits.

Corporations traditionally have been barred from practicing law and other so-called learned professions by judicial decisions, often supplemented by statute.[1]

Although fringe tax benefits for many years have been enjoyed by corporations and their employees (including shareholder-employees),[2] self-employed persons (individual proprietors and members of partnerships) were denied such benefits, since, under the aggregate theory, no employer-employee relationship existed. Barred from incorporating, ingenious professional persons attempted to practice under unincorporated arrangements having sufficient corporate characteristics to qualify as an "association" treated as a corporation for federal income tax purposes.[3]

Meanwhile, professional associations lobbied for the enactment of (a) federal legislation conferring on self-employed persons—individual proprietors and partners—the tax fringe benefits allowed employees;[4] (b) state statutes for incorporating professional

29. E. g., McKinney's N.Y. Tax Law, § 180. See section 158 infra.

30. Imposed only by Florida and South Carolina. See section 158 infra.

31. Imposed only by Florida and New York (McKinney's N.Y. Tax Law, §§ 270 to 281–a). See section 177 infra.

32. E. g., McKinney's N.Y. Tax Law, §§ 183 to 219–qq.

33. Approximately four-fifths of the states impose direct income taxes on corporations; some states have a "privilege tax" based on net income. See sections 81, 99 infra. See also section 14, n. 21 supra.

34. E. g., McKinney's N.Y. Tax Law, § 219–a (4½ percent franchise tax on net income of "business corporations"); §§ 701–723 (approximately 4 percent tax on net income of "unincorporated businesses").

1. See section 17, n. 9 supra.

2. Int.Rev.Code of 1954, 26 U.S.C.A. §§ 79, 101, 104–105, 119, 274, 401–404, 421–424—see sections 246–254 infra.

3. In United States v. Kintner, 216 F.2d 418 (9th Cir.1954), the court found that a Montana group of physicians operating a clinic had more corporate than partnership characteristics and was an "association", not a partnership, even though under Montana law a corporation could not engage in the practice of medicine, so that the physicians were "employees", not partners, for purposes of Int.Rev. Code of 1939, § 165 (Int.Rev.Code of 1954, 26 U.S.C. A. § 401), and their pension trust therefore qualified as a "plan of an employer for the exclusive benefit of his employees". Accord, Foreman v. United States, 232 F.Supp. 134 (S.D.Fla.1964); Galt v. United States, 175 F.Supp. 360 (N.D.Tex.1959); Bittker, "Professional Associations and Federal Income Taxation: Some Questions and Comments", 17 Tax L.Rev. 1 (1961).

4. Rapp, "The Quest for Tax Equality for Private Pension Plans: A Short History of the Jenkins-Keogh Bill", 14 Tax L.Rev. 55 (1958).

corporations or associations;[5] and (c) federal legislation to make professional corporations and associations "corporations" for federal income tax purposes.[6]

In 1962, after 10 years in the congressional hopper, the Federal Self-Employed Individuals Tax Retirement Act (Smathers-Keogh Act, H.R.10)[7] was passed by Congress. Benefits thereunder for self-employed persons, however, were not as favorable as the liberal benefits available to corporate employees.[8] The benefits were made more generous in 1966,[9] effective in 1968, but are less than corporate benefits.[10]

Meanwhile, beginning in 1961, some three-fourths of the states enacted statutes for the incorporation of professional corporations or formation of professional associations.

Professional Corporation (or Association) Statutes

Upsetting long-established traditional and statutory taboos, state legislatures, beginning in 1961, enacted special corporate statutes enabling professional persons to form corporations or associations.[11]

The statutes varied widely in their coverage of professions. Some applied to all professions licensed to practice in the state; others to one or more specified professions —accountants, architects, attorneys, chiropractors, dentists, engineers, naturopaths, nurses, optometrists, osteopaths, pharmacists, physicians, podiatrists, surgeons, surveyors, veterinarians. A few states enacted two or more statutes to apply to different professions. Most of the statutes were rather brief, being superimposed on business corporation statutes and providing that the business corporation act should apply to professional corporations to the extent that it is not inconsistent with the professional corporation statute.

The statutes usually require that share ownership be limited to duly-licensed professional persons[12] and retain personal liability

5. Wormser, "A Plea for Professional Incorporation Laws", 46 A.B.A.J. 755 (1960).

6. For action of American Bar Association House of Delegates on resolution proposed by Committee on Professional Corporations, see 51 A.B.A.J. 402 (1965).

7. Int.Rev.Code of 1954, 26 U.S.C.A. §§ 401–404; Becker, "Self-Employed Retirement Plans and H.R. 10", 49 A.B.A.J. 39 (1963); Lipoff, "Self-Employed Individuals Tax Retirement Act of 1962: H.R. 10", 49 A.B.A.J. 103 (1963).

8. An individual proprietor or a more-than-10-percent partner was considered an owner-employee subject to certain limitations. Annual contributions were limited to $2,500 or 10 percent of "earned income", whichever was less. Where capital was a material income-producing factor, "earned income" was limited to 30 percent of net earnings. Only one-half of the amounts contributed for the self-employed were deductible. Lump-sum distributions to the self-employed were subject to ordinary income tax (with averaging provision), rather than capital gains, treatment. Becker, "Self-Employed Retirement Plans and H.R. 10", 49 A.B.A.J. 39 (1963); Grayck, "Tax Qualified Retirement Plans for Professional Practitioners: A Comparison of the Self-Employed Individuals Tax Retirement Act of 1962 and the Professional Association", 63 Colum.L.Rev. 415 (1963).

9. Effective January 1, 1968, full deduction on contributions to retirement plans up to $2,500 or 10 percent of gross annual income, whichever was less, became allowable. The 30 percent provision in the definition of "earned income"—see note 8 supra— was eliminated. Taylor, "Retirement Plans for Self-Employed—A Look at H.R. 10 As Amended", 34 Tenn.L.Rev. 632 (1967); Note, "Is H.R. 10, As Amended and Properly Implemented, Still 'A Lion Who Merely Squeaks?'", 43 Notre Dame Law. 521 (1968). Corporate deductions, in contrast, might approximate 20 percent of gross income without any $2,500 ceiling.

10. Quaere, whether collective investment funds set up as investment media for retirement funds will

be investment companies subject to the Federal Investment Company Act, 1940—see section 301 infra— or the interests therein securities subject to the Federal Securities Act, 1933—see section 295 infra.

11. For texts of statutes, see 2 CCH Pension Plan Guide ¶¶ 9000 et seq.; Frost, "Some Comments as to Professional Corporation Statutes", 4 Ariz.L.Rev. 169 (1963); Buchmann & Bearden, "The Professional Service Corporation: A New Business Entity", 16 U.Miami L.Rev. 1 (1961); Annot., 4 A.L.R.3d 383 (1965). See Hall, Gissel & Blackshear, "Professional Incorporation in Texas", 48 Texas L.Rev. 84 (1969).

12. See Street v. Sugarman, 202 So.2d 749 (Fla.1967) (shares in Florida professional corporation held not immune from judgment creditor seizure, subjecting corporation to dissolution for shareholding by ineligible person).

of professional persons for their acts and the professional acts performed under their supervision.[13]

State governmental licensing authorities having jurisdiction over one or more professions and national professional associations redrafted or reconstrued their regulations or codes of ethics to permit incorporation at least where the practitioner's personal liability to his client was retained.[14]

Internal Revenue Code and Regulations

In 1960, the Internal Revenue Service adopted the so-called "Kintner" regulations.[15] They set forth six major corporate characteristics, of which four—continuity of life, centralization of management, limited liability, and free transferability of interests—determined whether an organization was to be taxed as an association (or corporation) or as a partnership. For association status, more than two of such four corporate characteristics had to exist. The regulations, in effect, ruled out association status for any organization subject to a statute similar to the Uniform Partnership Act. Continuity of life

could not be achieved because any change in membership caused technical dissolution. The general mutual agency was inconsistent with centralization of management. The personal liability of each general partner ruled out limited liability. Free transferability of interest could not exist because only the interests in the profits and surplus, and not the rights in specific partnership property or the right to participate in management, were assignable.[16]

Proposed revised regulations were published in late 1963 and adopted in 1965.[17] Where local law or rules pertaining to professional practice made sharing of profits dependent upon an employment relationship, continuity of life and free transferability of interests were ruled lacking. Where a member retained the traditional professional autonomy with respect to professional decisions, centralization of management was ruled not to exist. The net effect was to deny corporate status to all professional service organizations, even when formally incorporated under state law.

Litigation resulted in the 1965 regulations uniformly being held invalid as inconsistent with the Internal Revenue Code and the judicial construction thereof and constituting the exercise of a non-delegable legislative function.[18]

13. Bittker, "Professional Service Organizations: A Critique of the Literature", 23 Tax L.Rev. 429 (1968); Jones, "Formation of California Professional Corporations", 44 L.A.B.Bull. 59 (Dec.1968); Jacobs, "Florida's Professional Service Corporation Act", 42 Fla.B.J. 149 (1968); Morrison, "The New Missouri Professional Corporation Act", 18 Bus. Law. 1154 (1963); Horsley, "The Virginia Professional Association Act: Relief for the Underprivileged?", 48 Va.L.Rev. 777 (1962); Kahn, "The Wisconsin Service Corporation Law of 1961", 1962 Wis.L.Rev. 65; Comment, "Professional Service Organizations: A Comment", 24 Tax L.Rev. 291 (1969); Comment, "Professional Service Organizations: A Reply", 24 Tax L.Rev. 300 (1969); Comment, "Wisconsin Professional Service Corporations under the New 'Kintner' Regulations", 49 Marq.L. Rev. 564 (1966); Comment, "The Illinois Professional Act", 57 Nw.L.Rev. 334 (1962). Prior to 1970, professional incorporation bills had been introduced in the New York Legislature but had not passed.

14. ABA Advisory Opinion No. 303 (Ruling on Professional Corporations), 34 N.Y.St.B.J. 217 (1962). See Greenwood, "Ethical Problems Raised by the Association and Incorporation of Lawyers" (ABF Research Memorandum Series No. 28, 1961).

15. Treas.Reg. § 301.7701–1, 1–2 (1960). See note 3 supra.

16. Overbeck, "Current Status of Professional Associations and Professional Corporations", 23 Bus. Law. 1203 (1968).

17. Treas.Reg. § 301.7701–2(h) (1965); Bittker, "Professional Service Organizations: A Critique of the Literature", 23 Tax L.Rev. 429 (1968); Maier & Carter, "Is the Commissioner's Authority Exceeded in the Proposed Regulations for Professional Firms?", 48 Marq.L.Rev. 361 (1964–1965); Hart, "Legislation by the I.R.S. and the Proposed Amendments to the Kintner Regulations", 20 Bus.Law. 235 (1964).

18. O'Neill v. United States, 410 F.2d 888 (6th Cir. 1969), aff'g 281 F.Supp. 359 (N.D.Ohio 1968) (holding regulations, which in effect established more stringent standards of corporate tax treatment for professional service organizations than for all other kinds of organizations, invalid for lack of factual or legal characteristics justifying different tax treatment, and that professional association—

In 1969, the Internal Revenue Service conceded that professional corporations or associations would, generally, be treated as corporations for tax purposes, and that its regulations would be modified accordingly.[19]

changed in form from partnership for nontax business purposes—was classifiable as corporation for federal income tax purposes); United States v. Empey, 406 F.2d 157 (10th Cir.1969), aff'g 272 F.Supp. 851 (D.Colo.1967) (construing Code definition of "partnership" to include only "unincorporated" organizations; holding regulations inconsistent with Code and judicial construction thereof; and concluding that, even under regulations, professional corporation more nearly resembled corporation than partnership); Smith v. United States, 301 F.Supp. 1016 (S.D.Fla.1969); First Nat'l Bank & Trust Co. of Tulsa v. United States, 23 Am.Fed.Tax R.2d 69-903 (N.D.Okl.1969); Wallace v. United States, 294 F.Supp. 1225 (D.Ark.1968); Cochran v. United States, 299 F.Supp. 1113 (D.Ariz.1969); Holder v. United States, 289 F.Supp. 160 (N.D.Ga.1968) (holding regulations invalid on grounds that they were not supported by Code, judicial precedent, or sound tax policy; change from partnership to professional association had nontax business purposes—centralization of management, limited liability; and professional association met all characteristics necessary for taxation as corporation); Kurzner v. United States, 413 F.2d 97 (5th Cir. 1969), aff'g 286 F.Supp. 839 (S.D.Fla.1968) (hold-

Obviously, a professional corporation or association will not be treated as a corporation if it does not function as the owner and employer.[20]

ing regulations invalid because they discriminated against professional service organizations by imposing more stringent standards for achieving corporate tax status than they do on other types of service organizations and by contradicting Code section which excludes incorporated organization from being classified as partnership, and holding that professional corporation had all characteristics of corporation under existing case law); Fowler v. United States, 24 Am.Fed.Tax R.2d 69-533F (N.D. Ohio 1969); Williams v. United States, 300 F. Supp. 928 (D.Minn.1969); Ahola v. United States, 300 F.Supp. 1055 (D.Minn.1969); Van Epps v. United States, 301 F.Supp. 257 (D.Ariz.1969); Mendelsohn v. United States, 24 Am.Fed.Tax R.2d 69-54F1 (D.Ark.1969); "Federal Taxation of Professional Corporations", 26 Corp.J. 51 (1969-70); Comment, "Another Round in Corporate Tax Treatment for Professionals", 68 Colum.L.Rev. 358 (1968).

19. T.I.R. No. 1019, Aug. 8, 1969.

20. Roubik v. Comm'r, 53 T.C. No. 36 (1969) (income of medical professional service corporation which merely served as record-keeping conduit held taxable to physicians as partners rather than to corporation or ground corporation did not carry on business and earn income).

CHAPTER 3

NATURE OF CORPORATENESS OR CORPORATE PERSONALITY

A. INTRODUCTION

A. INTRODUCTION

THEORIES OF CORPORATENESS OR CORPORATE PERSONALITY

78. The corporation, regardless of legal theories, has group interests distinguishable from the individual interests of its individual members. Under the "fiction" or "entity" theory, the corporation is regarded as a fictitious, artificial, legal person or entity. Under the "fiat", "concession", or "franchise" theory, the corporation is said to derive its being by concession from the state. Under the "realist" theory, corporate personality is the legal recognition of group interests which as a practical matter already exist. The "enterprise" theory stresses the underlying enterprise. The "symbol" theory deems the corporation as a symbol for the aggregate of the associates in their group personalities. As the late Dean Robert S. Stevens suggested, persons associated together in a business enterprise have legal personalities different from their legal personalities in their other jural relations. Regardless of legal theory, the group and non-group relations of the associates must be distinguished, and the corporation must be assimilated into a legal system whose norm is the individual per-

son. The "contract" theory treats incorporation as involving contracts among the members, between the members and the corporation, and between the members or the corporation and the state. Even in the same jurisdiction, different corporations may have different corporate personalities; in jurisdictions other than that of its incorporation, even the same corporation often has a somewhat different corporate personality.

A corporate body, literally, is a body of bodies; technically, an artificial person composed of natural persons; and, regardless of choice of legal theory,[1] from the point of view of legal relationships, has group interests more or less distinguishable from the individual interests of its individual members.

The traditional corporate theory goes back to Roman and canon law, law merchant, and early common law: that a corporation is a fictitious, artificial, legal person or juristic entity (*"persona ficta"*) created by proper authority.[2] This has come to be known as the "fiction theory" or "entity theory"[3] and was not extended by the common law to unincorporated business associations, as to which the underlying concept was the "aggregate theory".

When the emphasis is on the creation of the corporation by grant from the sovereign, or state, the theory is sometimes called the "fiat theory", "concession theory", or "franchise theory".[4] Such emphasis often results in rather strict construction of corporation statutes by the courts which insist that the corporate form adhere rather strictly to the statutory norms.

The "realist theory" tends to view the corporation as a group whose group activities are such as to require separate legal recognition, with many of the attributes of a natural person; the "enterprise theory" stresses the underlying enterprise; the "symbol theory" regards the corporation as the symbol for the aggregate of group jural relations of the persons composing the enterprise.[5]

Under most of these theories, incorporation is deemed to result in a new legal entity which, being distinct from *its* members, owns the corporate property and owes the corporate debts, is the creditor to sue or the debtor to be sued, has perpetual existence, and can act only through its duly constituted organs, primarily *its* board of directors.[6]

The late Dean Robert S. Stevens has suggested that persons associated together in a business enterprise have legal personalities different from their legal personalities in their other jural relations, and that the law authorizing incorporation permits the incorporated associates to limit *their* liabilities, to own *their* property in a common name, to sue and be sued in such name, to transfer *their* interests without the necessity of a dis-

1. See F. Hallis, Corporate Personality: A Study in Jurisprudence (1930); W. Hohfeld, Fundamental Legal Conceptions 228, 274, 303 (1923); E. Freund, Legal Nature of a Corporation (1896); Radin, "The Endless Problem of Corporate Personality", 32 Colum.L.Rev. 643 (1932); Dewey, "The Historic Background of Corporate Legal Personality", 35 Yale L. J. 655, 665 (1926); Vinogradoff, "Juridical Persons", 24 Colum.L.Rev. 594, 600 (1924); Laski, "The Early History of the Corporation in England", 30 Harv.L.Rev. 561, 575 (1917); Machen, "Corporate Personality", 24 Harv.L.Rev. 253, 347 (1911). Cardozo, Ch. J., in Petrogradsky Mejdunarodny Kommerchesky Bank v. Nat'l City Bank, 253 N.Y. 23, 170 N.E. 479 (1930), reargument denied 254 N.Y. 563, 173 N.E. 867 (1931), cert. denied 282 U.S. 878, 51 S.Ct. 82, 75 L.Ed. 775 (1931). See also Kitagawa, "Some Reflections on the Corporate Theory—Including a Japanese Perspective", 1960 Duke L.J. 535.

2. See sections 5–9 supra.

3. Timberg, "Corporate Fiction, Logical, Social and International Implications", 46 Colum.L.Rev. 533 (1946).

4. The term "franchise" has at least two meanings: the "primary franchise" or corporate charter or right to be a corporation, and the "secondary franchise" or power to do various acts, especially those of a quasi-public nature. See Industrial Bank of Wyandotte v. Reichert, 251 Mich. 396, 232 N.W. 235 (1930); People v. North River Sugar Refining Co., 121 N.Y. 582, 24 N.E. 834 (1890).

5. 1 G. Hornstein, Corporation Law and Practice § 12 (1959).

6. R. Stevens, Handbook on the Law of Private Corporations § 1 (2d ed. 1949).

solution and accounting, and to have the business managed by the board of directors as *their* representatives.[7]

Under both the traditional "it" approach and Dean Stevens's "they" approach, it is still necessary to distinguish between the group and the non-group relations of the members. The law deals with legal persons, whether the focus be on the corporation as an artificial legal person or on the corporate personality of the natural legal persons who compose it. The problem remains because the law's norm is so much the individual person and the group must be fitted into individualistically-conceived legal patterns.[8]

Not inconsistent with the foregoing theories is the "contract theory" whereby incorporation is deemed to involve contracts among the members, between the members and the corporation, and between the members or the corporation and the state.[9]

All of these theories have been, and continue to be, significant in the development of the law of business associations. From the point of view of defining the respective attributes of the different forms of business association, as has been seen,[10] the choice between entity theory and aggregate theory is often controlling.

Of all the views, the concrete import is "that a corporation is more nearly a method than a thing."[11]

To a greater or lesser extent, each corporation formed in a particular jurisdiction may be somewhat unique, and may have a different corporate personality than other corporations. When it engages in business in other jurisdictions, its corporate personality there often differs from its corporate personality in its jurisdiction of incorporation.[12]

And in a world of increasing imagery, corporations, too, are projecting their images.[13]

TRADITIONAL CORPORATE ATTRIBUTES

79. **Modern corporate attributes—all consistent with the concept of the corporation as a separate entity—traditionally include (a) Power to take, hold, and convey property in the corporate name; (b) Power to sue and to be sued in the corporate name; (c) Centralization of management in the board of directors; (d) Ready transferability of interests; (e) Perpetual succession; and (f) Limited liability. Such attributes are not necessarily found in all corporations, and some of them now inhere or can be achieved in unincorporated forms of business enterprise.**

Blackstone, who had substantial impact on American law in its formative period, referred to the corporation as "but one person in law, a person that never dies: in like manner as the river Thames is still the same river, though the parts which compose it are changing every instant", and listed five at-

7. R. Stevens, Handbook on the Law of Private Corporations 4–5 (2d ed. 1949). See Wedderburn, "Corporate Personality and Social Policy—The Problem of the Quasi-Corporation", 28 Modern L.Rev. 62 (1965); Note, "Corporate Personality—A Functional Approach", 23 U.Pitt.L.Rev. 172 (1961).

8. Rutledge, J., in United States v. Scophony Corp., 333 U.S. 795, 803, 68 S.Ct. 855, 859, 92 L.Ed. 1091, 1098 (1948).

9. Trustees of Dartmouth College v. Woodward, 17 U.S. (4 Wheat.) 518, 4 L.Ed. 629 (1819) (contract with state, protected against state impairment of the obligation of contract by U.S.Const. art. I, § 10, cl. 1). See section 340 infra.

10. See section 16 supra.

11. Bijur, J., in Farmers' Loan & Trust Co. v. Pierson, 130 Misc. 110, 119, 222 N.Y.S. 532, 543 (Sup.Ct. 1927).

12. See Restatement, Second, of Conflict of Laws ch. 13 (Proposed Official Draft, Pt. III, Apr. 22, 1969); Reese & Kaufman, "Law Governing Corporate Affairs: Choice of Law and the Impact of Full Faith and Credit", 58 Colum.L.Rev. 1118 (1958); Annot., 18 A.L.R. 130 (1922), 126 A.L.R. 1503 (1940). See sections 96–101, 352–357 infra.

13. L. Golden, Only By Public Consent: American Corporations Search for Favorable Opinion (1968). Corporations sometimes commission publication of their histories. See Dempsey, "How to Succeed on Company Time", 47 Saturday Review, No. 29, 28 (July 18, 1964); 47 Saturday Review, No. 28, 56 (July 11, 1964). Many corporations publish house organs. See Sullivan, "The Corporate Publication —All in the Family", 50 Saturday Review, No. 32, 62 (Aug. 12, 1967). As to pictorial corporate symbolism, see "The Graphic Art of Corporate Image", 76 Fortune, No. 1, 127 (July 1967).

tributes or powers "inseparably incident to every corporation, at least to every corporation aggregate": [1]

(a) To have "perpetual succession . . . the very end" of its incorporation;

(b) To sue and be sued, grant and receive in the corporate name, and do (subject to limitations of corporate capacity) all other acts as natural persons may;

(c) To purchase lands, and hold them, for the benefit of the members and their successors;

(d) To have a common seal, through which the corporation acts and speaks, the seal evidencing joint assent of the whole;

(e) To make bylaws, which are internally binding, unless contrary to law.

Blackstone's list is more of historical importance than of practical value. He does not even mention the principal aspect of the modern corporation—limited liability.[2]

For federal income tax purposes, six major corporate characteristics are considered in distinguishing a corporation from other organizations: [3]

(a) Associates;

(b) An objective to carry on business and divide the profits therefrom;

(c) Continuity of life;

(d) Centralization of management;

(e) Limited liability; and

(f) Free transferability of interests.

A practical, modern listing of corporate attributes would include:

(a) Power to contract and to take, hold, and convey property in the corporate name; [4]

(b) Power to sue and to be sued in the corporate name; [5]

(c) Centralization of management in the board of directors; [6]

(d) Ready transferability of shares; [7]

(e) Perpetual succession; [8]

(f) Limited liability.[9]

---

1. 1 Blackstone, Commentaries *456, *463–466. A similar earlier summary is found in Sutton's Hospital, 10 Coke 23a, 30b, 77 Eng.Rep. 960, 970 (K.B. 1612). Blackstone's list was cited in St. Lawrence University v. Trustees of Theological School of St. Lawrence University, 20 N.Y.2d 317, 282 N.Y.S.2d 431, 229 N.E.2d 431 (1967) (holding that board of trustees of theological school, having sufficient corporate attributes by legislation, was a separate corporation rather than a department of the university).

2. Limited liability and incorporation have been tending to become synonymous only during the past 100 years. In England, Crown charters were construed as creating limited liability; registered companies, except when "unlimited", have enjoyed limited liability only since 1855. See section 11 supra. Early American corporations variously had limited liability, double liability, or unlimited liability. Until 1928, the shareholders of California corporations did not enjoy limited liability. Calif. Const. art. XII, § 3. In Arizona, limited liability must be stated in the articles of incorporation. Ariz. Gen.Corp.Law § 10–122(9) (1956); Delaware permits unlimited liability corporations. When corporations can make assessments or leviations for additional funds from their members, creditors might be able to enforce such corporate right. Under several modern corporation statutes, a seal is no longer mandatory. ABA–ALI Model Bus. Corp.Act § 4(c); Collins v. Tracy Grill & Bar Corp., 144 Pa.Super. 440,

19 A.2d 617 (1941). Quaere, whether bylaws are necessary in all jurisdictions.

3. Treas.Reg. § 301.7701–2 (1960). Since two of the characteristics—(a) associates and (b) an objective to carry on business and divide the profits therefrom—are common to both unincorporated business associations and corporations, the presence or absence of the other four is controlling.

4. See section 68, n. 13 supra.

5. But see section 352 infra.

6. Centralization of management is one of the six major corporate characteristics considered in determining whether a business enterprise is an "association" for federal income tax purposes. See note 3 supra. But see sections 271–277 infra.

7. Free transferability of interests is another of the six major corporate characteristics for the federal income tax definition of "association". See note 3 supra. But see sections 281, 282 infra.

8. But see section 120 infra. Continuity of life is another of the six major corporate characteristics of "association" for federal income tax purposes. See note 3 supra.

9. But see note 2 supra. See section 202 infra. Limited liability is another of the six major corpo-

All of these attributes are consistent with the concept of a corporation as a separate entity but all are not necessarily found in all corporations; in some situations, certain of them are not even desired, and ingenuity is sometimes required to achieve valid varia- tions in such respect.[10] Conversely, some of them now inhere or can be achieved in unincorporated forms of business enterprise [11]— thus demonstrating that different consequences do not inevitably follow from the entity theory or the aggregate theory.

B. CORPORATION AS "PERSON"

CORPORATION AS "PERSON"

80. The corporation is usually regarded as a "person" unless the subject matter or context of constitutional, statutory, or other provisions limits their application to natural persons. The problem is one of construction. Under the United States Constitution, the corporation is protected against unreasonable searches and seizures, deprivation of liberty or property without due process of law, and denial of the equal protection of the laws. Recognizing the corporation as a person does not solve the problems of its domicile, residence, citizenship, nationality, etc., and the extent to which such characteristics of its members will be attributed to it for various legal purposes.

The law—constitutional, statutory, and decisional—basically deals with persons. As a rule of thumb, "person" is a generic term including both natural and artificial persons unless the subject matter or context limits the term to natural persons.[1] The term person might even include unincorporated groups.[2] The problem is one of interpretation.

Thus, under the United States Constitution, a corporation enjoys the right of the "people" to be secure against unreasonable searches and seizures.[3] The corporation does not enjoy the privilege afforded a person against self-incrimination,[4] but does enjoy the right of a person not to be deprived of . . . liberty or property without due process of law,[5] and the right of a person

---

rate characteristics of an "association" for federal income tax purposes. See note 3 supra.

10. See Chapter 10 infra.

11. See sections 18–67 supra.

1. But see Stone, J., in In re Clarke's Will, 204 Minn., 574, 578, 284 N.W. 876, 878 (1939): "A corporation is not a person, but has a legal and real individuality. Neither is it artificial, save as it is a generation of law rather than nature. It is in simple fact a legal unit—a very real one—endowed by its creator with many of the rights and attributes of persons. It is so much *sui generis* that to attempt to define it, rather than to describe or enumerate its peculiar features, in terms of the law of persons, tends to obstruct rather than facilitate comprehension. Much worse is it to fictionize in decision concerning a thing about which there is no trace of the fictitious."

2. See, e. g., 1 U.S.C.A. § 1 (defining "person" to include "corporations, companies, associations, firms, partnerships, societies, and joint-stock companies, as well as individuals"); Uniform Commercial Code § 1–201(30) (defining "person" as including individual or organization), § 1–201(28) (defining "organization" as including "a corporation, government or governmental subdivision or agency, business trust, estate, trust, partnership or association, two or more persons having a joint or common interest, or any other legal or commercial entity"); McKinney's N.Y.Gen.Const.Law, § 22 ("words of the masculine gender include . . . the neuter, and may refer to a corporation . . . or other body . . . of persons"), § 37 ("person" defined as including corporation or joint-stock association).

3. U.S.Const. amend. IV; Oklahoma Press Pub. Co. v. Walling, 327 U.S. 186, 208–209, 66 S.Ct. 494, 505, 90 L.Ed. 614, 629, 166 A.L.R. 531 (1946).

4. U.S.Const., amend. V; Wild v. Brewer, 329 F.2d 924 (9th Cir. 1964), cert. denied 379 U.S. 914, 85 S. Ct. 262, 13 L.Ed.2d 185 (1964).

5. U.S.Const. amend. V; Sinking-Fund Cases, 99 U. S. 700, 718–719, 25 L.Ed. 504, 504–505 (1878); amend. XIV; Grosjean v. American Press Co., 297 U.S. 233, 244, 56 S.Ct. 444, 446, 80 L.Ed. 660, 665 (1936) (liberty); Munn v. Illinois, 94 U.S. 113, 24 L. Ed. 77 (1877); Minneapolis & St. L. Ry. v. Beckwith, 129 U.S. 26, 9 S.Ct. 207, 32 L.Ed. 585 (1889) (property). But see dissenting opinion of Black, J., in Connecticut General Life Ins. Co. v. Johnson, 303 U.S. 77, 85, 58 S.Ct. 436, 440, 82 L.Ed. 673, 680 (1938).

within a state not to be denied the equal protection of the laws.[6]

The corporation has been held to be a "client" entitled to invoke the attorney-client privilege.[7]

While a corporation may sue for defamation,[8] and, a fortiori, for trade disparagement,[9] it usually has no right of privacy.[10]

Despite constitutional and statutory provisions to the effect that corporations shall have the right to sue and shall be subject to being sued in all courts in like cases as natural persons,[11] a corporation cannot appear, at least in a court of record, unless represented by a licensed attorney.[12]

Issues of a similar nature are constantly arising.[13]

6.   U.S.Const. amend. XIV; Munn v. Illinois, 94 U.S. 113, 24 L.Ed. 77 (1877); Santa Clara County v. Southern Pacific R. R., 118 U.S. 394, 6 S.Ct. 1132, 30 L.Ed. 118 (1886). But see dissenting opinion of Douglas, J., (Black, J., concurring) in Wheeling Steel Corp. v. Glander, 337 U.S. 562, 576, 69 S.Ct. 1291, 1299, 93 L.Ed. 1544, 1553 (1949). See Green, "Corporations as Persons, Citizens, and Possessors of Liberty", 94 U.Pa.L.Rev. 202 (1946).

7.   Radiant Burners, Inc. v. American Gas Ass'n, 320 F.2d 314, 98 A.L.R.2d 228 (7th Cir. 1963) (en banc), cert. denied 375 U.S. 929, 84 S.Ct. 330, 11 L.Ed.2d 262 (1963), rev'g 207 F.Supp. 771 (N.D.Ill.1962), aff'd on rehearing 209 F.Supp. 321 (N.D.Ill.1962); Philadelphia v. Westinghouse Electric Corp., 210 F.Supp. 483 (E.D.Pa.1962); Ford Motor Co. v. O. W. Burke Co., 59 Misc.2d 543, 299 N.Y.S.2d 946 (Sup.Ct.1969) (memorandum prepared by house counsel held entitled to same attorney-client privilege immunity as one prepared by outside counsel); Fischer v. Wolfinbarger, 45 F.R.D. 510 (D.Ky.1968) (attorney-corporate client privilege held not available against plaintiff-shareholder); Brereton, Pye & Withrow, "The Attorney-Corporate Client Privilege", 24 Record of N.Y.C.B.A. 230 (1969); Burnham, "The Attorney-Client Privilege in the Corporate Arena", 24 Bus.Law. 901 (1969); Maurer, "Privileged Communications and the Corporate Counsel", 28 Ala. Law. 352 (1967); Schaeffer, "The Attorney-Client Privilege in the Modern Business Corporation", 20 Bus.Law. 989 (1965); Haight, "Keeping the Privilege Inside the Corporation", 18 Bus.Law. 551 (1963); McLanahan, "Privileged Communications and Investigations by Federal Agencies", 18 Bus. Law. 683 (1963); Miller, "The Challenge to the Attorney-Client Privilege", 49 Va.L.Rev. 262 (1963); Maurer, "Privileged Communications and the Corporate Counsel", 16 Bus.Law. 959 (1961). But see Garner v. Wolfinbarger, 280 F.Supp. 1018 (N.D.Ala. 1968) (holding there was no attorney-client privilege between corporation's attorney and corporation when shareholders' action alleged directors have violated law); Pattie Lea, Inc. v. District Court, 161 Colo. 493, 423 P.2d 27 (1967) (semble, accountant-client privilege).

8.   Diplomat Electric, Inc. v. Westinghouse Electric Supply Co., 378 F.2d 377 (5th Cir. 1967) (imputations of lack of credit, insolvency, and financial difficulties); W. Prosser, Handbook of the Law of Torts 762 (3d ed. 1964).

9.   W. Prosser, Handbook of the Law of Torts § 122 (3d ed. 1964).

10.   United States v. Morton Salt Co., 338 U.S. 632, 652, 70 S.Ct. 357, 368, 94 L.Ed.2d 401, 416 (1950); Vassar College v. Loose-Wiles Biscuit Co., 197 F. 982 (W.D.Mo.1912). See also Jaggard v. R. H. Macy & Co., 176 Misc. 88, 26 N.Y.S.2d 829 (Sup.Ct. 1941), aff'd mem., 265 App.Div. 15, 37 N.Y.S.2d 570 (1st Dep't 1942) (denying corporation statutory right of privacy in favor of "any living person").

11.   N.Y.Const. art. X, § 4; 28 U.S.C.A. § 1654. But see McKinney's N.Y. CPLR, § 321(a) (requiring corporation or voluntary association to appear by attorney).

12.   United States v. 9.19 Acres of Land, 416 F.2d 1244 (6th Cir. 1969); Shapiro, Bernstein & Co. v. Continental Record Co., 386 F.2d 426 (2d Cir. 1967); Simbraw, Inc. v. United States, 367 F.2d 373 (3d Cir. 1966); Oliner v. Mid-Town Promoters, Inc., 2 N.Y.2d 63, 156 N.Y.S.2d 833, 138 N.E.2d 217 (1956); Nicholson Supply Co. v. First Fed. Savings & Loan Ass'n, 184 So.2d 438, 19 A.L.R.3d 1067 (Fla.Dist.Ct.App. 1966). See Ramada Inns, Inc. v. Lane & Bird Advertising, Inc., 102 Ariz. 127, 426 P.2d 395 (1967) (answer by president rather than licensed attorney held excusable neglect, not to prevent corporation from defending Arizona action on merits where president had relied on house counsel, admitted elsewhere, and Arizona courts had never specifically ruled against corporate appearance other than through licensed attorney); Dixon v. Reliable Loans, Inc., 112 Ga.App. 618, 145 S.E.2d 771 (1965) (corporation allowed to sue without licensed attorney); Prudential Ins. Co. of America v. Small Claims Court, 76 Cal.App.2d 379, 173 P.2d 38, 167 A.L.R. 820 (1946) (allowing small claims court appearance by corporation without licensed attorney). But see Remole Soil Service, Inc. v. Benson, 68 Ill.App.2d 234, 215 N.E.2d 678 (1966) (judgment for corporation in small claims court secured by non-attorney office manager set aside). See also Cotner, "May a Corporation Act as Its Own Attorney?", 16 Clev.-Mar.L.Rev. 173 (1967); Wexler, "The Right to Appear in Proper Person in the Federal Courts", 38 N.Y.U.L.Rev. 758 (1963); Annot., 19 A.L.R.3d 1073 (1968).

13.   E. g., Honolulu Lumber Co. v. American Factors, Ltd., 265 F.Supp. 578 (D.Hawaii 1966) (corporation held not person under *in forma pauperis* statute); State of Oregon v. Pacific Powder Co., 226 Or. 502, 360 P.2d 530, 83 A.L.R.2d 1111 (1961) (construing word "person" in involuntary manslaughter statute as not including corporation).

To treat the corporation as a person does not solve the problems of defining such personality from the point of view of domicile, residence, citizenship, nationality, etc. The question remains to what extent such characteristics of the individual members will be attributed to the corporation for various legal purposes, to assign it an appropriate place in our system of jurisprudence [14]—a process which involves the aggregate rather than the entity approach.

C. CORPORATION AS "DOMICILIARY"

CORPORATION AS "DOMICILIARY"

81. **The corporation, to the extent that domicile is a relevant concept, has its "legal" domicile in its jurisdiction of incorporation, but may also have a "commercial" domicile where it has its principal place of business. Such concepts have been used to uphold various taxes on, and regulation of, corporations by the jurisdictions of both domiciles. Modern cases tend to apply the "protection", "benefit" or "contact" theory in determining the validity of such taxes and regulation attacked for lack of due process or as an undue burden on interstate commerce. Multiple taxation and regulation often result.**

Domicile is an important concept with respect to natural persons, and once was more relevant to corporations than it is now.

The Restatement of Conflict of Laws originally provided that every person has at one time one and only one domicile,[1] and that a corporation is domiciled in the jursidiction where it was incorporated and cannot acquire a domicile outside that jursidiction.[2] A subsequent proposed official draft provides that a domicile, if and when attributed to a corporation, is in the jurisdiction of its incorporation, appending the comment that no useful purpose is served by attributing domicile to a corporation.[3]

The earlier cases on state taxation of personal property which had not acquired a permanent situs anywhere upheld such taxes by the jurisdiction of domicile of the corporation on the theory of *mobilia personam sequuntur*. The jurisdiction of incorporation was, of course, regarded as the "legal" domicile, but the jurisdiction where it had its principal place of business came to be regarded as the "commercial" domicile,[4] thus in effect avoiding the rule that a person could have only one domicile, and justifying multiple taxation—although the United States Supreme Court reserved decision on the latter point for some time.

The modern approach is reflected in two Supreme Court cases: State Tax Commission of Utah v. Aldrich,[5] and Braniff Airways, Inc. v. Nebraska State Board of Equalization and Assessment.[6] The Aldrich case

---

14. Rutledge, J., in United States v. Scophony Corp., 333 U.S. 795, 803, 68 S.Ct. 855, 859, 92 L.Ed. 1091, 1098 (1948): "The process of translating group or institutional relations in terms of individual ones, and so keeping them distinct from the nongroup relations of the people whose group rights are thus integrated, is perennial, not only because the law's norm is so much the individual man, but also because the continuing evolution of institutions more and more compels fitting them into individualistically conceived legal patterns."

1. Restatement of Conflict of Laws § 11 (1934).

2. Id. § 41. The comment stated that no unincorporated association of natural persons has a domicile. A. Farnsworth, The Residence and Domicil of Corporations (1939).

3. Restatement, Second, of Conflict of Laws § 11 (Proposed Official Draft, May 2, 1967).

4. The term "commercial domicile" is defined in the Uniform Division of Income for Tax Purposes Act § 1 as "the principal place from which the trade or business of the taxpayer is directed or managed."

5. 316 U.S. 174, 62 S.Ct. 1008, 86 L.Ed. 1358, 139 A. L.R. 1436 (1942) (7–2), citing Curry v. McCanless, 307 U.S. 357, 59 S.Ct. 900, 83 L.Ed. 1339, 123 A.L.R. 162 (1939) (4–1–4).

6. 347 U.S. 590, 74 S.Ct. 757, 98 L.Ed. 697 (1954) (5–1–1–1–1). Accord, Flying Tiger Line, Inc. v. Los Angeles County, 51 Cal.2d 314, 333 P.2d 323 (1958), cert. denied, 359 U.S. 1001, 79 S.Ct. 1140, 3 L.Ed.2d 1031 (1959). See Ott v. Mississippi Valley Barge Line Co., 336 U.S. 169, 69 S.Ct. 432, 93 L.Ed. 585

espoused as an additional standard of jurisdiction to tax the "protection" or "benefit" theory—if a jurisdiction confers some benefit or protection it enjoys a power to tax growing out of the same. In the Braniff Airways case, a jurisdiction which was neither the jurisdiction of incorporation nor the principal place of business was allowed to levy an apportioned *ad valorem* tax on flight equipment of an interstate air carrier. The basis of the holding was that the carrier's regular stops within the jurisdiction were enough "contact" to establish the jurisdiction's power to tax, and that interstate instrumentalities are not immune from paying a nondiscriminatory share of the local tax burden.

While it is sometimes possible to characterize a particular taxing scheme in more than one way, the general rules seem to be: (a) taxes on real property or on tangible personal property which has acquired a permanent situs may be levied by the jurisdiction of the situs and not by other jurisdictions; (b) taxes relating to other personal property, tangible or intangible, may be lev-

ied on the whole value thereof by the jurisdiction of incorporation and by the jurisdiction of the principal place of business and on an apportioned basis by any jurisdiction which confers "protection" or "benefit" thereon, or has "contact" therewith, in reasonable proportion to such protection, benefit, or contact without violating the due process or commerce clauses.

Multiple taxation often results. For example, ownership of shares may be taxed by the legal and commercial domiciles of the issuer and of the owner, and by the jurisdiction where the share certificate is physically located.[7]

Some states limit their taxing powers by their own constitutions.[8] Only about one-fourth of the states tax shares.[9]

The "protection", "benefit", or "contact" theories, used to sustain a state's power to tax, also supports other aspects of a state's legislative jurisdiction, such as a state's power to regulate corporations doing business within the state even though they may be incorporated in another jurisdiction.[10]

D. CORPORATION AS "RESIDENT"

CORPORATION AS "RESIDENT"— IN GENERAL

82. Corporate residence is relevant for various purposes. The problem of determining corporate residence or nonresidence is usually one of construing legislative intent.

Corporate residence is relevant for various purposes, including jurisdiction over the subject matter,[1] jurisdiction over the person,[2] venue,[3] forum non conveniens,[4] and statutes of limitations,[5] and in connection with other problems.[6]

(1949). Cf. Miller Bros. Co. v. Maryland, 347 U.S. 340, 74 S.Ct. 535, 98 L.Ed. 744 (1954), reh. denied 347 U.S. 964, 74 S.Ct. 708, 98 L.Ed. 1106 (1954) (tax held denial of due process for lack of minimum contact between state and corporation).

7. For a related problem with respect to escheat, see section 179 infra.

8. E. g., Del.Const. art. IX, § 6; N.Y.Const. art. XVI, § 3.

9. "Exemption of Shares of Stock", 19 Corp.J. 103 (1950).

10. See section 99 infra.

[§ 82]

1. See sections 83, 353 infra.

2. See sections 84, 97, 354 infra. Wilen Mfg. Co. v. Standard Products Co., 409 F.2d 56 (5th Cir. 1969) (construing term "nonresident" in Georgia long-arm statute reference to "any nonresident, or his executor or administrator" to include foreign corporation with principal place of business in jurisdiction of incorporation).

3. See sections 85, 355 infra.

4. See sections 86, 356 infra.

5. See sections 87, 357 infra.

6. E. g., reciprocal exemption of nonresident from motor vehicle registration. State v. Garford Truck-

Statutes rarely use the term "domicile",[7] but frequently use "residence"—an ambiguous term. "Residence" is often used in a sense equivalent to domicile; occasionally it means something more than domicile, e. g., a domicile at which a person actually dwells; or it may mean something else than domicile, e. g., a place of dwelling without the necessary intention of making a home there.[8] Residence also provides the basis for state citizenship.[9]

The problem of determining corporate residence or nonresidence is usually one of construing legislative intent. As a general rule, whether or not a corporation acquires residence for one purpose or another outside of its state of incorporation, it usually remains a resident of its state of incorporation, and the localization of its residence within the state may be determined by its articles of incorporation.[10] Similarly, the residence within the state of a foreign corporation may be determined by its application for a certificate of authority.[11]

CORPORATION AS "RESIDENT"—JURISDICTION OVER SUBJECT MATTER

83. **The corporation, for purpose of jurisdiction over the subject matter, may have its state of incorporation given recognition similar to that of the residence of natural persons.**

For purposes of one important aspect of federal court jurisdiction over the subject matter—diversity-of-citizenship—the *residence* of natural persons and *state or states of incorporation and principal place of business* of artificial persons are the tests of citizenship.[1]

Similar tests, although not phrased in terms of citizenship, may apply to some aspects of state court jurisdiction over the subject matter.[2]

CORPORATION AS "RESIDENT"—JURISDICTION OVER PERSON

84. **The corporation, for purposes of jurisdiction over the person, if domestic, is treated like the resident natural person. In personam jurisdiction over the foreign corporation involves various complications. Former requirements of joinder of, and personal service upon, all members of unincorporated enterprises, at least where liability was joint, have been somewhat relaxed by statute or judicial decision.**

Similar tests apply to jurisdiction over the person in the sense of amenability to process. In the case of the resident natural person or the domestic corporation, jurisdiction over the person thereof is usually obtained without much difficulty by compliance with the applicable service-of-process requirements.[1]

[§ 83]

ing, Inc., 4 N.J. 346, 72 A.2d 851, 16 A.L.R.2d 1407 (1950). Requirement that chattel mortgage be filed in county of mortgagor's residence. Matter of Norma Footwear Corp., 2 N.Y.2d 887, 161 N.Y.S.2d 143, 141 N.E.2d 628 (1957); nonresident motorist statute. McKinney's N.Y. Vehicle & Traffic Law, § 253; Sease v. Central Greyhound Lines, Inc., 306 N.Y. 284, 117 N.E.2d 899 (1954).

7. See section 81 supra. But see McKinney's N.Y. CPLR, § 302 ("non-domiciliaries").

8. Restatement, Second, of Conflict of Laws § 11, comment k (Proposed Official Draft, May 2, 1967). See A. Farnsworth, The Residence and Domicil of Corporations (1939).

9. U.S.Const. amend. XIV, § 1.

10. See section 129, n. 1 infra.

11. See section 136, n. 9 infra.

1. See section 88 infra.

2. E. g., McKinney's N.Y.Bus.Corp.Law, § 1314 (actions against foreign corporations by foreign corporations assimilated to those by nonresidents); Gibbs v. Young, 242 S.C. 217, 130 S.E.2d 484 (1963).

[§ 84]

1. Domestic business corporations are suable regardless of where the cause of action arose or whether the corporation is doing business in the state. Most jurisdictions require the appointment of a "resident agent" for service of process on the corporation, either in the articles of corporation or in a separate document. ABA–ALI Model Bus.Corp. Act § 11. A few require appointment of some state official, such as the secretary of state. West Virginia provides that that the state auditor shall be attorney in fact for every corporation to accept service of process without any appointment on the part of the corporation.

Acquiring in personam jurisdiction over the foreign corporation may involve various complications which will be discussed later.[2]

In personam jurisdiction over unincorporated enterprises once required, at least when liability was joint, joinder of, and personal service on, all members, which was often impossible. By statute or decision, these requirements have been somewhat relaxed.[3]

CORPORATION AS "RESIDENT"— VENUE

85. The corporation, for purposes of federal court venue, may be treated as a resident of the places where it is incorporated, qualified to do business, or doing business, subject to various special venue provisions; the unincorporated association is treated as a resident of the place where it has its principal place of business; in a class action, the residence of the class representatives might be controlling. The transfer-of-venue provision incorporates forum non conveniens principles. Venue objections can be waived by not being timely asserted or by the express designation of an agent for service of process in the jurisdiction. The corporation, for purposes of state court venue, may be treated as a resident of the place designated in its articles of incorporation or application for certificate of authority as the place of its principal place of business.

Venue requirements are frequently defined by statutes in terms of residence, with or without express reference to situations involving corporations.

Federal Court Venue

In the federal venue statute, the corporation, at least as a defendant, receives explicit treatment. The general requirements are that, except as otherwise provided by law: where jurisdiction is founded only on diversity, the proper district is where all plaintiffs or all defendants reside, or in which the claim arose; otherwise where all defendants reside, or in which the claim arose; followed

2. See section 97 infra.

3. See sections 18, 19, 28, 41, 49, 50, 58, 68 supra, section 369 infra.

by a provision that a corporation may *be sued* in any district where it is incorporated, or licensed to do business, or is doing business, and such district shall be regarded as the residence of such corporation for venue purposes.[1]

1. 28 U.S.C.A. § 1391; Farmers Elevated Mut. Ins. Co. v. Carl J. Austad & Sons, 343 F.2d 7 (8th Cir. 1965) (holding § 1391(c) satisfied if defendant corporation was doing business in district at time cause of action arose). The meaning of "doing business" for venue under § 1391(c) is uncertain: (a) The federal circuits are divided on whether the meaning of "doing business" is governed by state or federal law; the third, fifth, and seventh circuits are committed to a state test while the second and sixth circuits apply a federal test [see Note, 56 Colum.L.Rev. 394, 398 (1956)]; (b) The courts are in disagreement as to the quantitative meaning of "doing business". In Steiner v. Dauphin Corp., 208 F.Supp. 104 (E.D.Pa.1962), the courts held that the quantitative activity must meet the stricter state test of "doing business" for purposes of amenability to process notwithstanding that there were sufficient minimum contacts for federal constitutional purposes. In Remington Rand, Inc. v. Knapp-Monarch Co., 139 F.Supp. 613 (E.D.Pa.1956), the court equated the meaning of "doing business" in § 1391(c) to the standard of whether the corporation ought formally to have qualified and expressly to have appointed a resident agent. Accord, Farr's, Inc. v. National Shoes, Inc., 191 F.Supp. 803 (E.D. Pa.1960); Rensing v. Turner Aviation Corp., 166 F. Supp. 790 (N.D.Ill.1958); Bar's Leaks Western, Inc. v. Pollock, 148 F.Supp. 710 (N.D.Cal.1957). Other courts have equated "doing business" in § 1391(c) with the constitutional tests used in determining in personam jurisdiction [Champion Spark Plug Co. v. Karchmar, 180 F.Supp. 727 (S.D.N.Y.1960); Satterfield v. Lehigh Valley R. R., 128 F.Supp. 669 (S.D. N.Y.1955); H. Fins, Federal Jurisdiction and Procedure 82 (1960)]. See Annot., 2 A.L.R. Fed. 995 (1969) ("doing business" as of time of action or of accrual of claim).

Under § 1391(c), there is, besides the meaning of "doing business", a second unsettled question as to whether it applies to corporate plaintiffs as well as to corporate defendants. The trend is negative. Gould v. Brick, 358 F.2d 437 (5th Cir.1966); Robert E. Lee & Co. v. Veatch, 301 F.2d 434, 96 A.L.R.2d 619 (4th Cir. 1961), cert. denied 371 U.S. 813, 83 S.Ct. 23, 9 L.Ed.2d 55 (1962); United Artists Theatre Circuit, Inc. v. Nationwide Theatres Inv. Co., 269 F. Supp. 1020 (S.D.N.Y.1967). Comment, "The Corporate Plaintiff and Venue under Section 1391(c) of the Judicial Code", 28 U.Chi.L.Rev. 112 (1960); Note, 19 Okla.L.Rev. 197 (1966); Note, 76 Harv.L. Rev. 641 (1963); Note, 48 Va.L.Rev. 968 (1962). There are also particular venue provisions for several federal substantive law areas, many of which are based on a "doing business" variation: (a) Copyright infringement actions may be brought in any district in which the defendant is found [28 U. S.C.A. § 1400(a)]; (b) Patent infringement actions

By way of additional venue is the special provision on shareholder's derivative actions: [2]

"Any civil action by a stockholder on behalf of his corporation may be prosecuted in any judicial district where the corporation might have sued the same defendants."

Where the venue is laid pursuant to this section, and possibly otherwise, extraterritorial service of process on the corporation is authorized.[3]

The residence of an unincorporated association for purposes of venue is the district where it has its principal place of business.[4]

A class action against an unincorporated association could have the venue tested by the residence of the representative defendant or defendants.[5]

Improper venue once meant dismissal. Today by statute an action laying venue in the wrong district may, in the interest of justice, be transferred to any district where it could have been brought.[6] Another provision, combining venue and forum non conveniens, authorizes transfer of any civil action, for the convenience of parties and witnesses, in the interest of justice, to any other district where it might have been brought.[7]

Venue objections can be waived by not being timely asserted.[8]

An express designation of an agent in the state for service of process has been held to constitute a consent to be sued (and waiver of any venue objection) anywhere in the state [9]—a rule of more importance for the noncorporate than the corporate defendant

---

may be brought where the defendant resides or where the defendant has committed acts of infringement and has a regular and established place of business [28 U.S.C.A. § 1400(b)]; (c) Actions under the Federal Employers Liability Act may be brought in whatever district the defendant is doing business [45 U.S.C.A. § 56]; (d) The Jones Act permits actions in the district of defendant's residence or principal place of business [46 U.S.C.A. § 688; Pure Oil Co. v. Suarez, 384 U.S. 202, 86 S.Ct. 1394, 16 L.Ed.2d 474 (1966) (incorporating broadened concept of corporate residence in section 1391(c)); Note, 62 Mich.L.Rev. 817 (1964)]; (e) Actions under the Clayton Act may be brought against a corporation in any district in which it is transacting business [15 U.S.C.A. § 22; Comment, 1962 Wash.U.L.Q. 261]; (f) Actions to enforce any liability or duty under the Securities Exchange Act, 1934, may be brought in the district wherein any act or transaction constituting the violation occurred or in the district wherein the defendant is found or is an inhabitant or transacts business [15 U.S.C.A. § 78aa; Zorn v. Anderson, 263 F.Supp. 745 (S.D.N.Y.1966) (mailing of proxy held sufficient to sustain venue)]. For other examples of special venue requirements, see Note, 56 Colum.L.Rev. 394 (1956).

2. 28 U.S.C.A. § 1401. See Guth v. Groves, 44 F. Supp. 855 (S.D.N.Y.1942), aff'd per curiam 129 F.2d 325 (2d Cir.1942), cert. denied 318 U.S. 758, 63 S.Ct. 531, 87 L.Ed. 1131 (1943). As to whether such theoretical realignment for venue purposes affects diversity-of-citizenship jurisdiction, compare Dowd v. Front Range Mines, Inc., 242 F.Supp. 591 (D.Colo. 1965), with Schoen v. Mountain Producers Corp., 170 F.2d 707, 5 A.L.R.2d 1226 (3d Cir.1948), cert. denied 69 S.Ct. 746, 336 U.S. 937, 93 L.Ed. 1095 (1949).

3. 28 U.S.C.A. § 1695. See Note "Doing Business as a Test of Venue and Jurisdiction over Foreign Corporations in the Federal Courts", 56 Colum.L.Rev. 394 (1956).

4. Denver & Rio Grande Western R. R. v. Brotherhood of Railroad Trainmen, 387 U.S. 556, 87 S.Ct. 1746, 18 L.Ed.2d 954 (1967) (unincorporated labor

union assimilated to corporation); Sperry Products, Inc. v. Association of American Railroads, 132 F.2d 408, 145 A.L.R. 694, (2d Cir. 1942), cert. denied 319 U.S. 744, 63 S.Ct. 1031, 87 L.Ed. 1700 (1943) (nondiversity case). Concerning general partnerships, limited partnerships, and joint ventures, there is a split of authority. Joscar Co. v. Consolidated Sun Ray, Inc., 212 F.Supp. 634 (E.D.N.Y.1963); Goldberg v. Wharf Constructors, 209 F.Supp. 499 (N.D.Ala. 1962); Marshall v. Mole Constructors, 193 F.Supp. 617 (W.D.Pa. 1961). J. Moore's Judicial Code 193 (1949). See Williams, "Federal Court Venue: Residence of an Unincorporated Association", 33 Tenn. L.Rev. 507 (1966); Comment, 13 Okla.L.Rev. 206 (1960); Note, 8 Stan.L.Rev. 708 (1956).

5. Fed.R.Civ.P. 23, 23.2; Kaplan, "Suits Against Unincorporated Associations under the Federal Rules of Civil Procedure", 53 Mich.L.Rev. 945, 957–958 (1955).

6. 28 U.S.C.A. § 1406(a).

7. 28 U.S.C.A. § 1404(a); Norwood v. Kirkpatrick, 349 U.S. 29, 75 S.Ct. 544, 99 L.Ed. 789 (1955); Skilling v. Funk Aircraft Co., 173 F.Supp. 939 (W.D.Mo. 1959); Note, 54 Nw.U.L.Rev. 489 (1959). See section 86, nn. 3–8 infra.

8. Annot., 5 L.Ed.2d 1056 (1961).

9. Neirbo Co. v. Bethlehem Shipbuilding Corp., 308 U.S. 165, 60 S.Ct. 153, 84 L.Ed. 167 (1939) (6–3) (diversity case); Roger v. A. H. Bull & Co., 170 F.2d 664 (2d Cir.1948) (federal question); Comment, "The Aftermath of the Neirbo Case", 42 Ill.L.Rev. 780 (1948).

today. An implied designation however, is not a waiver of the federal venue privilege.[10]

State Court Venue

In contrast, state general venue statutes for transitory actions may be less explicit than the federal provisions, requiring that the action be tried in the county of the residence of the plaintiff or of the defendant.[11] The residence of a domestic corporation for venue purposes has been held to be the county designated as the location of its principal office in its articles of incorporation; of an authorized foreign corporation the county so designated in its application for certificate of authority.[12] By qualifying to do

business in another jurisdiction, it does not cease to be a resident of its state of incorporation; conversely, a foreign corporation qualifying to do local business, or doing local business, might continue to be deemed a nonresident for venue purposes.[13]

Venue for an unqualified corporation can be anywhere in the state.[14]

A partnership or individual proprietor, for venue purposes, is deemed a resident of any county where the business has its principal office or where the partner or individual proprietor suing or being sued actually resides.[15]

CORPORATION AS "RESIDENT"— FORUM NON CONVENIENS

86. The corporation, for purposes of the doctrine of forum non conveniens, might be able to assert, especially if it is a foreign corporation, that a trial elsewhere would better serve the convenience of the parties and witnesses and the interest of justice, or that the court should not interfere with the "internal affairs" of a foreign corporation.

Residence, or more accurately, nonresidence of the parties, is also a factor under the doctrine of forum non conveniens. Forum non conveniens is, in a sense, the judicial counterpart of statutory venue requirements. It involves the exercise by a court, which has jurisdiction over the subject matter and the person with proper venue, of discretion to refuse a case on the ground that another forum would be more convenient.[1]

10. Olberding v. Illinois Central Ry., 346 U.S. 338, 74 S.Ct. 83, 98 L.Ed. 39 (1953) (7–2). Contra, Knott Corp. v. Furman, 163 F.2d 199 (4th Cir.1947), cert. denied, 332 U.S. 809, 68 S.Ct. 111, 92 L.Ed. 387 (1947), reh. denied, 332 U.S. 826, 68 S.Ct. 164, 92 L.Ed. 401 (1947).

11. E. g., McKinney's N.Y. CPLR § 503(a).

12. McKinney's N.Y. CPLR § 503(c) (deeming domestic or authorized foreign corporation to be resident of county in which principal office is located); McKinney's N.Y.Bus.Corp.Law, § 102(a) (10) defining "office of a corporation" as that stated in articles of incorporation of domestic corporation or in application for authority of foreign corporation, regardless of where business activities are conducted); Wegorzewski v. Macrose Lumber & Trim Co., 28 A.D.2d 713, 280 N.Y.S.2d 994 (2d Dep't 1967) (domestic corporation); General Precision, Inc. v. Ametek, Inc., 24 A.D.2d 757, 263 N.Y.S.2d 470 (2d Dep't 1965) (foreign corporation); Dependable Ins. Co. v. Gibbs, 218 Ga. 305, 127 S.E.2d 454 (1962) (upholding statutory definition of corporate residence as county where insured property located or insured resident under state constitutional venue provision based on residence); Singuefield v. General Oglethorpe Hotel Co., 113 Ga.App. 326, 148 S.E.2d 92 (1966); Gutierrez v. Superior Court, 243 Cal.App.2d 710, 52 Cal.Rptr. 592 (1966); Note, "Corporation Residence for Purposes of Venue in Missouri", 29 Mo.L.Rev. 209 (1964); Note, "Constitutional Problem of Providing Venue Classification for Foreign Corporations in Texas", 18 Sw.L.J. 291 (1964). To discourage litigation or to try to have rural juries, corporations sometimes designate rural counties in remote areas as the location of their principal place of business. Where a corporation was required to state in its articles of incorporation not only its principal place of business but also the location at which its business was to be conducted, both were held to be its legal residence for purposes of venue. Yonkers Raceway, Inc. v. National Union Fire Ins. Co., 9 Misc.2d 412, 170 N.Y.S.2d 205 (Sup.Ct.1957), aff'd mem., 6 A.D.2d 846, 176 N.Y.S.2d 241 (2d Dep't

1958), aff'd mem., 6 N.Y.2d 756, 186 N.Y.S.2d 656, 159 N.E.2d 203 (1959) (parimutuel racing corporation).

13. Nash Kelvinator Sales Corp. v. Clark, 276 App. Div. 1056, 96 N.Y.S.2d 354 (4th Dep't 1950). But see McKinney's N.Y. CPLR § 503(c)—note 12 supra.

14. Semler v. Cook-Waite Lab., Inc., 203 Or. 139, 278 P.2d 150 (1954). See McKinney's N.Y. CPLR § 503(a) (if no party resides in state venue lies in any county designated by plaintiff).

15. E. g., McKinney's N.Y. CPLR § 503(c).

1. The doctrine properly assumes the existence of an alternative forum. Comment, "Requirement of a Second Forum for Application of Forum Non Con-

One aspect of the doctrine is the "internal affairs" rule, i. e., that a court should not interfere with the internal affairs of a foreign corporation.

Under the doctrine of forum non conveniens, regulation of the internal affairs of a foreign corporation, size of the plaintiffs' interest, and location of books, records, and witnesses, etc., have also been considered relevant. The ultimate judicial test, under federal law, is where the trial will best serve the convenience of the parties and the ends of justice.[2]

In 1948, a federal statute was passed, providing that:[3]

"For the convenience of parties and witnesses, in the interest of justice, a district court may transfer any civil action to any other district or division where it might have been brought."

The United States Supreme Court construed the statute as permitting transfer upon a lesser showing of inconvenience than would have resulted in a dismissal of the action (with attendant possibility of an expiring statute of limitations) under the strict doctrine of forum non conveniens.[4]

Questions have arisen as to whether a district court could transfer the action to a district in which the defendant would not be amenable to process or in which venue was lacking. Obviously, in all jurisdictions in which the venue requirements of section 1391(c) are satisfied as to a defendant corporation (e.g., district in which it is incorporated, licensed to do business, or doing business), it would also be subject to personal jurisdiction.

In Hoffman v. Blaski,[5] where venue and personal jurisdiction requirements were both satisfied in the district where the action had been brought and the defendants moved to transfer the action to a district where neither requirement would have been satisfied, the United States Supreme Court held, 6–3, that the phrase in section 1404(a), "where it might have been brought", refers to the time when the action was originally commenced, thereby apparently precluding transfer under section 1404(a) to a district where venue would have been improper and service of process unlikely.

In Goldlawr, Inc. v. Heinman,[6] the Supreme Court held, 7–2, that section 1406(a) authorized transfer of an action in which both venue and personal jurisdiction over the defendant were defective to a district where venue was proper and personal jurisdiction could be obtained. The same result has been reached under section 1404(a).[7]

In Van Dusen v. Barrack,[8] the Supreme Court held that the state law governing di-

veniens", 43 Minn.L.Rev. 1199 (1959); Note, "The Convenient Forum Abroad", 20 Stan.L.Rev. 57 (1967).

2. Koster v. Lumbermens Mutual Casualty Co., 330 U.S. 518, 67 S.Ct. 828, 91 L.Ed. 1067 (1947) (5–4); Gulf Oil Corp. v. Gilbert, 330 U.S. 501, 67 S.Ct. 839, 91 L.Ed. 1055 (1947) (5–4); Williams v. Green Bay & Western R. R., 326 U.S. 549, 66 S.Ct. 284, 90 L. Ed. 311 (1946); Rogers v. Guaranty Trust Co. of New York, 288 U.S. 123, 53 S.Ct. 295, 77 L.Ed. 652 (1933) (6–3). See Comment, "Development of the Doctrine of Forum Non Conveniens", 8 DePaul L. Rev. 350 (1959); Note "Forum Non Conveniens as a Substitute for the Internal Affairs Rule", 58 Colum.L.Rev. 234 (1958); Dainow, "The Inappropriate Forum", 29 Ill.L.Rev. 871 (1935).

3. 28 U.S.C.A. § 1404(a); Annot., 93 L.Ed. 1218 (1949); 99 L.Ed. 799 (1955); 11 L.Ed.2d 1222 (1964); 1 A.L.R. Fed. 15 (1969).

4. Norwood v. Kirkpatrick, 349 U.S. 29, 75 S.Ct. 544, 99 L.Ed. 789 (1955) (6–3). See section 85, n. 7 supra.

5. 363 U.S. 335, 80 S.Ct. 1084, 4 L.Ed.2d 1254 (1960); Comment, "Transfer in the Federal Court in the Absence of Personal Jurisdiction", 61 Colum.L.Rev. 902 (1961).

6. 369 U.S. 463, 82 S.Ct. 913, 8 L.Ed.2d 39 (1962). Ackert v. Bryan, 299 F.2d 65 (2d Cir.1962) (2–1), upheld the transfer of a private action for violation of a federal statute to a district in a circuit which had previously denied a private action (with concomitant extraterritorial service of process) for a similar claim.

7. United States v. Berkowitz, 328 F.2d 358 (3d Cir. 1964), cert. denied 379 U.S. 821, 85 S.Ct. 42, 13 L. Ed.2d 32 (1964).

8. 376 U.S. 612, 84 S.Ct. 805, 11 L.Ed.2d 945 (1964); Edwards, "The Erie Doctrine in Foreign Affairs

versity-of-citizenship cases transferred to a district in another state should be that which would have governed absent the transfer.

In the federal courts, the internal affairs rule of the forum is not necessarily binding, even in diversity-of-citizenship cases.[9]

In state courts, the doctrine also exists although its primary emphasis often has been on the "internal affairs" rule.[10]

The Delaware courts have been reluctant to apply forum non conveniens arguments to dismiss actions involving corporation law issues, thus fostering Delaware court decisional law and requiring representation by Delaware attorneys.[11]

Cases", 42 N.Y.U.L.Rev. 674 (1967); Comment, "Internal Affairs Rule in the Federal Courts—the Erie Problem", 115 U.Pa.L.Rev. 973 (1967); Note, "Erie, Forum Non Conveniens and Choice of Law in Diversity Cases", 53 Va.L.Rev. 380 (1967); Note, "Choice of Law After Transfer of Venue", 75 Yale L.J. 90 (1965). See also Comment, "Transfer of Quasi in Rem Actions under 28 U.S.C. § 1404(a): A Study in the Interpretation of 'Civil Action'", 31 U.Chi.L.Rev. 373 (1964).

9. Lapides v. Doner, 248 F.Supp. 883 (E.D.Mich.1965).

10. O'Brien v. Virginia-Carolina Chemical Corp., 44 N.J. 25, 206 A.2d 878 (1965), cert. denied 389 U.S. 825, 88 S.Ct. 65, 19 L.Ed.2d 80 (1967) (yielding to jurisdiction of incorporation on issue of redemption of preferred shares without payment of accrued dividends); Dudley v. Jack Waite Mining Co., 49 Wash.2d 867, 307 P.2d 281 (1957); Nothiger v. Carroon & Reynolds Corp., 293 N.Y. 682, 56 N.E.2d 296 (1944); Universal Adjustment Corp. v. Midland Bank, Ltd., 281 Mass. 303, 184 N.E. 152 (1933). Cf. Plum v. Tampax, Inc., 399 Pa. 553, 160 A.2d 549 (1960) (2–1); See Trautman, "Forum Non Conveniens in Washington: A Dead Issue?", 35 Wash.L. Rev. 88 (1960); Comment, 26 Fordham L.Rev. 534 (1957); cf. Royal China, Inc. v. Regal China Corp., 304 N.Y. 309, 107 N.E.2d 461 (1952). See Note, "Conflicts—Forum Non Conveniens in North Carolina", 45 N.C.L.Rev. 717 (1967); Note, "Jurisdiction of Actions Involving Internal Affairs of Foreign Corporations", 42 Iowa L.Rev. 90 (1956); Note, "The Development of the 'Internal Affairs Rule' and its Future Under Erie v. Tompkins", 46 Colum.L.Rev. 413 (1946); Note, "Interference with the Internal Affairs of a Foreign Corporation", 31 Mich.L.Rev. 682 (1933).

11. Parvin v. Kaufmann, 43 Del.Ch. 461, 236 A.2d 425 (Sup.Ct.1967); Kolber v. Holyoke Shares, Inc., —— Del.Ch. ——, 213 A.2d 444 (Sup.Ct.1965). But see General Foods Corp. v. Cryo-Maid, Inc., 41 Del. Ch. 474, 198 A.2d 681 (Sup.Ct.1964).

State law appears to be coalescing with federal law to the effect that a state will not exercise jurisdiction if it is a seriously inconvenient forum for the trial of the action provided that a more appropriate forum is available to the plaintiff.[12]

CORPORATION AS "RESIDENT"— STATUTES OF LIMITATIONS

87. **The corporation, for purposes of statutes of limitations, might be treated as a resident of its state of incorporation and possibly also where it is doing business or is otherwise amenable to process. Tolling of statutes of limitations might occur while the foreign corporation is absent from the jurisdiction, at least so long as it is not amenable to process there.**

Residence might also be a factor in applying the statute of limitations. Statutes of limitations generally, apart from the Erie-Tompkins rule, are procedural limitations on the remedy and governed by the law of the forum regardless of where the cause of action arose. Some statutes provide that foreign causes of action are barred if barred by the law of the place where the cause of action arose; other statutes provide that a cause of action against a nonresident is barred if barred by the law of the defendant's domicile or residence. If the latter type prescribes domicile or construes "residence" as domicile,[1] the law of the corporate defendant's state of incorporation would control.[2] If residence is the test, either the

12. Restatement, Second, of Conflict of Laws § 84 (Proposed Official Draft, May 2, 1967); Lonergan v. Crucible Steel Co. of America, 37 Ill.2d 599, 229 N.E.2d 536 (1967) (applying doctrine of forum non conveniens and refusing to apply internal affairs rule to postpone shareholders' meeting of foreign corporation with out-of-state principal place of business).

1. See section 81 supra.

2. Vandevoir v. Southeastern Greyhound Lines, 152 F.2d 150 (7th Cir.1945), cert. denied 327 U.S. 789, 66 S.Ct. 811, 90 L.Ed. 1016 (1946).

result could be the same or the corporation could be deemed to have a residence wherever it was doing business or otherwise amenable to process.[3]

The New York provision states that a foreign cause of action is controlled by the shorter of the statute of limitations of New York or of the jurisdiction where the cause of action arose, except that where such cause of action originally accrued in favor of a New York resident, it is governed by the New York statute.[4] For purposes of these provisions, a foreign corporation qualified to do business in New York was held not to be a New York resident.[5]

Somewhat similar problems arise in construing provisions tolling the statute of limitations while the defendant is absent from the jurisdiction.[6] As part of their tolling statutes, some jurisdictions expressly provide that there shall be no tolling while the designation of an agent for service of process remains in force, while a foreign corporation has someone in the state upon whom process may be served, or while jurisdiction over the person of the defendant can be obtained without personal service within the state.[7] By implication in other jurisdictions, the result is the same;[8] but the increased difficulty of serving an absconding or concealed corporate defendant, notwithstanding its amenability to process, might prevent the statute of limitations from tolling.[9]

E. CORPORATION AS "CITIZEN"

CORPORATION AS "CITIZEN"—FEDERAL DIVERSITY–OF–CITIZENSHIP JURISDICTION

88. The corporation for federal diversity-of-citizenship jurisdiction, is deemed a citizen of any state, including the territories, the District of Columbia, and Puerto Rico, by which it has been incorporated, and of the state, etc., where it has its principal place of business. The cases represent ingenious doctrinal development from Chief Justice Marshall's holding that a corporation was certainly not a citizen within the meaning of the diversity-of-citizenship clause. Unincorporated business enterprises are not deemed citizens for diversity purposes, but in class actions, the citizenship of the representatives of the class might alone be controlling.

Whether or not a corporation is a "citizen", and if so, the method of determining its citizenship, depends upon the problem involved. In the American constitutional sys-

3. Hartmann v. Time, Inc., 64 F.Supp. 671 (E.D.Pa. 1946).

4. McKinney's N.Y. CPLR, § 202; Fullmer v. Sloan's Sporting Goods Co., 277 F.Supp. 995 (S.D.N.Y.1967) (borrowing shorter period of limitations from foreign statute but refusing to toll it under foreign law where defendant was suable there under long-arm statute).

5. American Lumbermens Mutual Casualty Co. of Illinois v. Cochrane, 129 N.Y.S.2d 489 (Sup.Ct.1954), aff'd mem., 284 App.Div. 884, 134 N.Y.S.2d 473 (1st Dep't 1954), aff'd mem., 309 N.Y. 1017, 133 N.E.2d 461 (1956).

6. See Moss v. Standard Drug Co., 94 Ohio App. 269, 115 N.E.2d 48 (1952), aff'd 159 Ohio St. 464, 112 N. E.2d 542 (1953); Kenny v. Duro-Test Corp., 91 F. Supp. 633 (D.N.J.1950).

7. E. g., McKinney's N.Y. CPLR, § 207. Topp v. Casco Products Corp., 10 N.Y.2d 833, 221 N.Y.S.2d 725, 178 N.E.2d 428 (1961) (unqualified foreign corporation failing to designate process agent and neither doing business nor amenable to process held, 3–2, to lose benefit of tort statute of limitations).

8. Dedmon v. Falls Products Inc., 299 F.2d 173 (5th Cir.1962); Thompson v. Horvath, 10 Ohio St.2d 247, 227 N.E.2d 225 (1967); Norton v. Dartmouth Skis, Inc., 147 Colo. 436, 364 P.2d 866 (1961); Note, "Limitation of Action: Non-tolling Effect of 'Long Arm' Statute", 20 Okla.L.Rev. 211 (1967).

9. Coates Capitol Corp. v. Superior Court, 251 Cal. App.2d 125, 59 Cal.Rptr. 231 (1967).

tem, state citizenship is dependent upon residence.[1]

Under Article III of the United States Constitution, the federal judicial power extends to controversies between citizens of different states.[2]

Although early cases assumed that a corporation was a citizen of its state of incorpo-

1. U.S.Const. amend. XIV.

2. U.S.Const. art. III, § 2, cl. 1. Complete diversity between parties plaintiff and defendant has long been required. Strawbridge v. Curtiss, 7 U.S. (3 Cranch) 267, 2 L.Ed. 435 (1806). The federal judicial power also extends to cases arising under the laws of the United States. In Bank of the United States v. Deveaux, 9 U.S. (5 Cranch) 61, 3 L.Ed. 38 (1809), it was argued, without success, that the federal charter of the first bank (1791–1811) conferred federal jurisdiction and as such raised a federal question. In a case involving the second Bank of the United States (1816–1836), Osborn v. Bank of the United States, 22 U.S. (9 Wheat.) 738, 6 L.Ed. 204 (1824), Marshall, C. J., found that the second bank's charter had specifically authorized actions in the federal courts and that corporate capacity was an ingredient of the action and, being federal law, presented a federal question. Not until the Act of 1875 was federal question jurisdiction generally granted to the federal courts by statute. 28 U.S.C.A. § 1331. Following the Act of 1875, the "ingredient theory" gave federal corporations access to the federal courts. Union Pacific R.R. Removal Cases, 115 U.S. 1, 5 S.Ct. 1113, 29 L.Ed. 319 (1885). Cf. Gully v. First Nat'l Bank, 299 U.S. 109, 57 S.Ct. 96, 81 L.Ed. 70 (1936); The Fair v. Kohler Die & Specialty Co., 228 U.S. 22, 33 S.Ct. 410, 57 L.Ed. 16 (1913) (federal cause of action test); Mishkin, "The Federal 'Question' in the District Courts", 53 Colum.L.Rev. 157 (1953). In 1882, Congress provided that national banks were not subject to federal jurisdiction solely on the basis of federal incorporation. 28 U.S.C.A. § 1348. In 1915, Congress passed similar legislation concerning federally-incorporated railroads. 38 Stat. 804 (1915). In 1925, Congress provided that the federal courts have no jurisdiction in civil actions on the ground that the corporation is organized under federal law unless the United States is the owner of more than one-half of the corporation's capital stock. 28 U.S.C.A. § 1349. The federal judicial power similarly extends to controversies to which the United States shall be a party. Presumably in Bank of the United States v. Deveaux, the court, if the allegations had been accurate, could have found the United States, as a 20 percent shareholder, to have been a party to the controversy. The federal judicial power likewise extends to controversies between a state and citizens of another state but not vice versa. U.S.Const. art. III; amend. XI. An action by a citizen of one state against a corporation wholly-owned by another state was held barred as an action against a state. North Dakota v. Nat'l Milling & Cereal Co., 114 F.2d 777 (8th Cir.1940).

ration for such purposes, the issue was raised for the first time in Bank of the United States v. Deveaux.[3] Involved was the first Bank of the United States (1791–1811), incorporated by the federal government, located in Philadelphia, with 20 percent of its shares held by the federal government, and the rest held privately by residents of various states, including Georgia. The action was against Georgia residents for trespass in the federal circuit court of Georgia by "The President, Directors and Company of the Bank of the United States", alleging that they, the corporation, were citizens of Pennsylvania. The lower court (Johnson, J., of the United States Supreme Court, riding circuit, and Stephens, D. J.) held that a corporation was not a citizen and dismissed the action for lack of federal jurisdiction. On appeal, the United States Supreme Court (per Marshall, C. J.) unanimously held with the lower court that a corporation was certainly not a citizen within the meaning of the diversity-of-citizenship clause but concluded that the controversy was in fact between the Bank's shareholders, who allegedly were citizens of Pennsylvania, and the defendants, who allegedly were Georgia citizens, and hence, in substance there was a controversy between citizens of different states.

The allegations, not controverted, were that the Bank consisted of citizens of Pennsylvania; actually 20 percent of its shares were held by the Federal Government, some 60 percent by foreign investors, and the rest by residents of various states, including Georgia, the residence of the defendants.

In subsequent cases from 1809 to 1844 the courts looked behind the corporation to the citizenships of its members and dismissed cases for lack of complete diversity.[4] Later the Supreme Court avoided such results by

3. 2 Fed.Cas. 692, No. 916 (C.C.D.Ga.1808), rev'd 9 U. S. (5 Cranch) 61, 3 L.Ed. 38 (1809).

4. E.g., Commercial and R. R. Bank of Vicksburg v. Slocomb, 39 U.S. (14 Pet.) 60, 10 L.Ed. 354 (1840).

resorting to a fiction and holding that a corporation was "deemed" to be a citizen of its state of incorporation for diversity purposes,[5] or that there was a conclusive irrebuttable presumption that a corporation's shareholders were citizens of its state of incorporation.[6]

In Hawes v. Oakland,[7] the Supreme Court, concerned with the collusive possibilities of a shareholder, whose citizenship was diverse from that of the defendants, suing derivatively in behalf of a corporation which could not have sued directly in the federal court on the basis of diversity, ruled that the complaint had to allege that the action was not a collusive one to confer on a federal court jurisdiction over a case of which it could otherwise have no cognizance.

In Doctor v. Harrington,[8] New Jersey shareholders of a New York corporation brought a derivative action against New York alleged wrongdoers, on a state-law cause of action in behalf of the New York corporation, joining the New York corporation as nominal party defendant. The lower court dismissed for lack of diversity jurisdiction on the alternative grounds that the plaintiff shareholders were conclusively presumed to be of the same citizenship as their corporation (New York citizens vs. New York corporation and New York citizens), or that recognizing the plaintiffs as New Jersey citizens, the corporation must be realigned as plaintiff (New Jersey citizens and New York corporation vs. New York citizens), on either of which grounds there would be no diversity. The Supreme Court reversed, saying that the presumption was a

fiction for a special purpose to give the corporation status and not to take from a citizen a right given to him by the Constitution, and that realignment was improper because the corporation involved was under a control antagonistic to the plaintiffs.[9]

For purposes of *constitutional* construction, today, a corporation is deemed a citizen of its state of incorporation for diversity purposes.[10] By statute, a District of Columbia corporation is deemed a citizen of the District; [11] territorial corporations citizens of their respective territories (or state when the territory is admitted to the Union).[12] However, a state-owned corporation might be treated as the state rather than deemed a citizen thereof.[13]

In 1958, Congress provided that for diversity purposes, including removal, a corporation shall be deemed a citizen of *any* state including the territories, the District of Columbia, and Puerto Rico, by which it has been incorporated *and* of the state, etc.,

9. For the present realignment rule, see Smith v. Sperling, 354 U.S. 91, 77 S.Ct. 1112, 1 L.Ed.2d 1205, 68 A.L.R.2d 805 (1957), and Swanson v. Traer, 354 U.S. 114, 77 S.Ct. 1116, 1 L.Ed.2d 1221, 68 A.L.R.2d 820 (1957), discussed in section 353 infra.

10. See notes 5, 8 supra.

11. Food Machinery & Chemical Corp. v. Marquez, 139 F.Supp. 421 (D.N.M.1956); Patterson v. American Nat'l Red Cross, 101 F.Supp. 655 (S.D.Fla.1951). Since 1940 [28 U.S.C.A. § 1332(d)], the statute has included in diversity jurisdiction, controversies between citizens of different states, the territories, and the District of Columbia, over which Congress has additional powers. U.S.Const. art. IV, § 3, cl. 2, art. I, § 8, cl. 17. While these may not be "states" within the meaning of Article III [New Orleans v. Winter, 14 U.S. (1 Wheat.) 91, 4 L.Ed. 44 (1816); Hepburn v. Ellzey, 6 U.S. (2 Cranch) 445, 2 L.Ed. 332 (1805) (statutory construction)], the extension of federal jurisdiction over controversies between their citizens and citizens of the various states has been sustained by the Supreme Court by "conflicting minorities in combination". National Mut. Ins. Co. v. Tidewater Transfer Co., 337 U.S. 582, 69 S.Ct. 1173, 93 L.Ed. 1556 (1949) (5[3–2]–4).

12. 1 W. Fletcher, Private Corporations § 123 (1963 rev. vol.). With the admission of Alaska and Hawaii, this rule had current significance.

13. North Dakota v. Nat'l Milling & Cereal Co., 114 F.2d 777 (8th Cir. 1940).

5. Louisville, Cincinnati & Charleston R.R. v. Letson, 43 U.S. (2 How.) 497, 11 L.Ed. 353 (1844).

6. Marshall v. Baltimore & Ohio R.R., 57 U.S. (16 How.) 314, 329, 14 L.Ed. 953, 959 (1854). See McGovney, "A Supreme Court Fiction: Corporations in the Diverse Citizenship Jurisdiction of the Federal Courts", 56 Harv.L.Rev. 853, 1090, 1225 (1943).

7. 104 U.S. 450, 26 L.Ed. 827 (1882); see Fed.R.Civ. P. 23.1.

8. 196 U.S. 579, 25 S.Ct. 355, 49 L.Ed. 606 (1905).

where it has its principal place of business.[14]
The primary purpose of this and accompany-

ing amendments was to restrict the diversity
jurisdiction of the federal courts over controversies involving corporations.[15]

Since the 1958 amendments, the complaint
or any removal petition should allege the
"state" of incorporation and that the corporation's principal place of business is in that
"state" or in a "state" other than the
"state(s)" of the citizenship(s) of the opposing party or parties.[16]

Where a corporation was incorporated in
more than one state, the question arose as to
whether there was one or more corporations
and which state or states counted for purposes of diversity.[17] Where reincorporation

14. 28 U.S.C.A. §§ 1331, 1332, 1441; Eldridge v. Richfield, 247 F.Supp. 407 (S.D.Cal.1965), aff'd 364 F.2d
909 (9th Cir. 1966), cert. denied 385 U.S. 1020, 87 S.
Ct. 750, 17 L.Ed.2d 556 (1967) (upholding constitutionality of 1958 amendment); Moore & Weckstein,
"Corporations and Diversity of Citizenship Jurisdiction: A Supreme Court Fiction Revisited", 77
Harv.L.Rev. 1426 (1964); Scott, "Dual Citizenship
of Corporations, and Their Principal Place of Business", 23 Fed.B.J. 103 (1963); Phillips & Christen-
son, "Should Corporations Be Regarded as Citizens
Within the Diversity Jurisdiction Provisions?", 48
A.B.A.J. 435 (1962); Kessler, "Corporations and the
New Federal Diversity Statute: A Denial of Jus-
tice", 1960 Wash.U.L.Q. 239; Doub, "An Old Problem: The Federal Diversity Jurisdiction", 45 A.B.
A.J. 1273 (1959); Friedenthal, "New Limitations on
Federal Jurisdiction", 11 Stan.L.Rev. 213 (1959);
Cowen, "Federal Jurisdiction Amended", 44 Va.L.
Rev. 971 (1958); Massey, "New Limitations on Federal Jurisdiction—The 1958 Amendment to the Judicial Code", 11 U.Miami L.Rev. 63 (1958); Ticktin,
"'Principal Place of Business' of Corporation Under Diversity of Citizenship Jurisdiction Statute",
140 N.Y.L.J. No. 102, 4 (1958); Comment, "A Corporation's Principal Place of Business for Federal Diversity Jurisdiction", 38 N.Y.U.L.Rev. 148 (1963);
Notes, 44 Minn.L.Rev. 308 (1959); 72 Harv.L.Rev.
391 (1958). Some cases have held that a corporation's place of business is the state of its executive
offices and where its operations are directed and
not in the state where its principal operations are
conducted. Riley v. Gulf, Mobile & Ohio R.R., 173
F.Supp. 416 (S.D.Ill.1959); Scott Typewriter Co.
v. Underwood Corp., 170 F.Supp. 862 (S.D.N.Y.
1959). Place of principal operations was stressed in
Mattson v. Cuyuna Ore Co., 180 F.Supp. 743 (D.
Minn.1960); place of actual operating control in
Leve v. General Motors Corp., 246 F.Supp. 761 (S.
D.N.Y.1965). The principal tests are known as the
"nerve center" test and the "operational" test. See
also Chemical Transp. Corp. v. Metropolitan Pe-
troleum Corp., 246 F.Supp. 563 (S.D.N.Y.1964) (1958
amendment held inapplicable to alien corporation);
Eisenberg v. Commercial Union Assur. Co., 189
F.Supp. 500 (S.D.N.Y.1960) (holding alternatively
1958 inapplicable to alien corporation and princi-
pal place of business in world, not in United
States, controlling); but see ALI Study of the
Division of Jurisdiction between State and Federal
Courts 10 (1969) (proposal to add "or foreign state"
after "State"). See Pugh, "Federal Jurisdiction and
Practice", 36 N.Y.U.L.Rev. 142, 147 (1961); Note,
"The Corporate Place of Business: A Resolution
and Revision", 34 Geo.Wash.L.Rev. 780 (1966);
Note, "A Corporation's Principal Place of Business
for Federal Diversity Jurisdiction", 38 N.Y.U.L.Rev.
148 (1963). For an illuminating discussion of what
constitutes a corporation's "principal place of business" under the 1958 amendment and an appendix
of cases decided thereunder, see Kelly v. United
States Steel Corp., 284 F.2d 850, 855 (3d Cir. 1960).
See also Briggs v. American Flyers Airline Corp.,
262 F.Supp. 16 (N.D Okl.1966) (location of corpora-

tion's principal place of business held to be factual
question to be determined on case-by-case basis
through review of corporation's total activity).

15. H.R.Rep.No. 1706, 85th Cong., 2d Sess. (1958);
Jaconski v. McCloskey & Co., 167 F.Supp. 537 (E.D.
Pa.1958) (diversity held lacking in action by Pennsylvania citizen vs. Delaware corporation with principal place of business in Pennsylvania); Moesser
v. Crucible Steel Corp., 173 F.Supp. 953 (W.D.Pa.
1959); Harker v. Kapp, 172 F.Supp. 180 (N.D.Ill.
1959). The 1958 amendment also raised the jurisdictional amount to $10,000 from $3,000, and permitted the court to tax costs against the plaintiff
recovering less than $10,000, in cases covered by the
amendment. See Abernathy v. Consolidated Cab
Co., 169 F.Supp. 831 (D.Kan.1959); Lorraine Motors, Inc. v. Aetna Cas. & Surety Co., 166 F.Supp.
319 (E.D.N.Y.1958); Lomax v. Duchow, 163 F.Supp.
873 (D.Neb.1958). In the past 20 years, diversity
cases had more than tripled, with some two-thirds
of them involving corporate parties. Shareholder
derivative actions increasingly present federal questions; otherwise federal jurisdiction over them is
dependent upon diversity. Legislative proposals
have been made to make the corporation a citizen
of every state in which it does business, H.R.1987,
82d Cong., 1st Sess. (1951); to limit diversity jurisdiction to individual citizens, H.R. 2516, 85th Cong.,
1st Sess. (1957); to deem the corporation a citizen
of any state by which it has been incorporated and
of any state where it is qualified to do business,
H.R. 1834, 88th Cong., 2d Sess. (1963). Marden, "Re-
shaping Diversity Jurisdiction: A Plea for Study
by the Bar", 54 A.B.A.J. 453 (1968); Handy v. Uni-
royal Inc., 298 F.Supp. 301 (D.Del.1969).

16. Browne v. Hartford Fire Ins. Co., 168 F.Supp.
796 (N.D.Ill.1959); Roseberry v. Fredell, 174 F.
Supp. 937 (D.Ky.1959); Note, 13 Okla.L.Rev. 73
(1960). See Form 2, Federal Rules of Civil Procedure (as amended, effective July 1, 1966).

17. Note, "Federal Jurisdiction—Diversity of Citizenship—Effect of Multi-state Incorporation", 3 U.C.
L.A.L.Rev. 98 (1955); Annot., 27 A.L.R.2d 745

was not free and voluntary, it might have been ignored for purposes of diversity; otherwise among the possible alternatives were the state where the action was brought (if incorporated there),[18] the state alleged as the state of incorporation of the corporation in the complaint,[19] the state alleged as the state of first incorporation or final incorporation,[20] the state where the cause of action arose (if incorporated there),[21] or every state of incorporation.[22]　　The Supreme Court's per curiam affirmance of Jacobson v. New York, N. H. & H. R. R.,[23] although appearing to favor the rule that, in the case of multiple incorporation, in each state of incorporation the corporation must be regarded as solely incorporated therein, was in fact an affirmance of a denial of federal jurisdiction; such a rule, moreover, fails to solve

the problem when the forum is not one of the states of incorporation.

The easiest solution, treating the multi-state corporation(s) as having the citizenship of every state of incorporation (as well as of its principal place of business) and thereby limiting federal diversity jurisdiction, was apparently enacted by the 1958 amendment.[24]

Multiple incorporation, of course, must be distinguished from a corporation's dissolving in one state and incorporating in another. While such a corporation would have only one state of incorporation and would ordinarily be deemed a citizen thereof (and of its principal place of business) for diversity purposes, the new citizenship might be ignored as collusive. More important in the days of forum-shopping under Swift v. Tyson,[25] than since Erie R. R. v. Tompkins,[26] was incorporation for the purpose of achieving diversity for the advantage of a more favorable federal law. Such incorporation was found collusive in some earlier cases,[27] but was later upheld.[28]

(1953). See also Foley, "Incorporation, Multiple Incorporation and the Conflict of Laws", 42 Harv.L. Rev. 516 (1929); Note, "Multiple Incorporation as a Form of Railroad Organization", 46 Yale L.J. 1370 (1937).

18.　Seavey v. Boston & Maine R.R., 197 F.2d 485 (1st Cir. 1952). The "state of suit" rule was followed in the first, second, fourth, sixth, seventh, and eighth circuits, and rejected in the third circuit. Accord, Muller v. Dows, 94 U.S. 444, 24 L.Ed. 207 (1876).

19.　Gavin v. Hudson & M.R.R., 185 F.2d 104, 27 A.L. R.2d 739 (3d Cir. 1950) ("alleged state" rule), overruled in Di Frischia v. N. Y. Central R.R., 279 F.2d 141 (3d Cir. 1960).

20.　See Louisville, N. A. & C. Ry. v. Louisville Trust Co., 174 U.S. 552, 563, 19 S.Ct. 817, 821, 43 L.Ed. 1081, 1087 (1899); Memphis & Charleston R.R. v. Alabama, 107 U.S. 581, 2 S.Ct. 432, 27 L.Ed. 518 (1882) (corporation ceases to be corporation of first state when incorporated in second).

21.　Murphy v. Hudson & M. R. R., 45 F.Supp. 720 (E.D.N.Y.1942). See Patch v. Wabash R.R., 207 U. S. 277, 28 S.Ct. 80, 52 L.Ed. 204 (1907) (question left open).

22.　Waller v. N. Y. N. H. & H. R. R., 127 F.Supp. 863 (S.D.N.Y.1955), approved in Note, 3 U.C.L.A. L. Rev. 98, 101 (1955).

23.　347 U.S. 909, 74 S.Ct. 474, 98 L.Ed. 1067 (1954), citing with approval Patch v. Wabash R. R., supra note 21 (state where cause of action arose), Memphis & Charleston R. R. v. Alabama, supra note 20 (corporation ceases to be corporation of first state when incorporated in second), and Seavey v. Boston & Maine R. R., supra note 18 ("state-of-action" rule).

24.　J. Moore, Federal Practice ¶ 0.78[2] (2d ed. 1964); Weckstein, "Multi-State Corporations and Diversity of Citizenship: A Field Day for Fictions", 31 Tenn.L.Rev. 195 (1964); Hardymon, "Federal Jurisdiction—Diversity of Citizenship—Corporation's Principal Place of Business—Multiple Incorporation", 40 N.C.L.Rev. 122 (1961); Note, "Citizenship of Multi-State Corporations for Diversity Jurisdiction Purposes", 48 Iowa L.Rev. 410 (1963). Cf. Diesing v. Vaughn Wood Products, Inc., 175 F.Supp. 460 (W.D.Va.1959). The committee report is silent on the multi-state corporation problem. H.R.Rep. No.1706, 85th Cong., 2d Sess. (1958). See Fitzgerald v. Southern Ry., 176 F.Supp. 445, 446 (S.D.N.Y. 1959); Jaconski v. McCloskey & Co., 167 F.Supp. 537, 540 (E.D.Pa.1958) (dicta that 1958 amendment does not affect multiple incorporated corporations); Form 2, supra note 16.

25.　41 U.S. (16 Pet.) 1, 10 L.Ed. 865 (1842).

26.　304 U.S. 64, 58 S.Ct. 817, 82 L.Ed. 1188, 114 A.L. R. 1487 (1938).

27.　Miller & Lux, Inc. v. East Side Canal & Irrigation Co., 211 U.S. 293, 29 S.Ct. 111, 53 L.Ed. 189 (1908) (formation of subsidiary of diverse citizenship without dissolving parent which had already commenced similar action in state court).

28.　Black & White Taxicab & Transfer Co. v. Brown & Yellow Taxicab & Transfer Co., 276 U.S. 518, 48 S.Ct. 404, 72 L.Ed. 681, 57 A.L.R. 426 (1928) (6–3)

Multiple incorporation must also be distinguished from the relatively more common situation where a corporation incorporated in one state formally qualifies to do business in another or without qualification carries on such business. In such situation, the corporation is deemed to be a citizen only of its state of incorporation and principal place of business but otherwise not of the other state.[29] A federally-incorporated corporation has been held not to be deemed a citizen of the state where its business is carried on.[30] However, by statute, national banks for purposes of private actions are deemed citizens of the states where located.[31]

An alien nonresident foreign corporation having no assets in the United States has been held to have no standing to sue in the federal courts.[32]

The presumption of citizenship in the case of corporations has not been applied to unincorporated enterprises, even when enjoying various other corporate characteristics.[33]

In class actions,[34] however, only citizenship of the representatives might be relevant and they might be selected with an eye to achieving or avoiding diversity.[35]

CORPORATION AS "CITIZEN"—PRIVILEGES-AND-IMMUNITIES-OF-CITIZENS

89. The corporation, for purposes of privileges-and-immunities-of-citizens, is not a citizen. As a result, the states were allowed to exclude foreign corporations from doing local intrastate business or to impose constitutional

(plaintiff corporation dissolved in state of common citizenship and incorporated in state of diverse citizenship). See Bradbury v. Dennis, 310 F.2d 73 (10th Cir. 1962), cert. denied 372 U.S. 928, 83 S.Ct. 874, 9 L.Ed.2d 733 (1963) (insolvent resident corporation's assignment of claim against resident to nonresident sole shareholder held to establish diversity juridiction notwithstanding assignment might be attacked under state law).

29. Doten v. Halvy, 252 F.Supp. 830 (E.D.Tenn.1965); Nyberg v. Montgomery Ward & Co., 123 F.Supp. 599 (W.D.Mich.1954) (citizenship for purposes of diversity and of right of removal).

30. Bankers Trust Co. v. Texas & Pac. Ry., 241 U.S. 295, 36 S.Ct. 569, 60 L.Ed. 1010 (1916). But see Feuchtwanger Corp. v. Lake Hiawatha Federal Credit Union, 272 F.2d 453, 456 (3d Cir. 1959) (dictum that under 1958 amendment federally-incorporated corporation should be deemed citizen of state where it has its principal place of business).

31. 28 U.S.C.A. § 1348.

32. Kukatush Mining Corp. v. Securities and Exchange Commission, 309 F.2d 647, 114 U.S.App.D.C. 27 (1962).

33. United Steelworkers of America v. R. H. Bouligny, Inc., 382 U.S. 145, 86 S.Ct. 272, 15 L.Ed.2d 217 (1965) (unincorporated labor union). Compare Brocki v. American Express Co., 279 F.2d 785 (6th Cir. 1960), cert. denied 364 U.S. 871, 81 S.Ct. 113, 5 L.Ed.2d 92 (1960), with Mason v. American Express

Co., 334 F.2d 392 (2d Cir. 1964) (joint-stock company); Arbuthnot v. State Auto Ins. Ass'n, 264 F.2d 260 (10th Cir. 1959) (unincorporated interinsurance exchange); Great Southern Fireproof Hotel Co. v. Jones, 177 U.S. 449, 20 S.Ct. 690, 44 L.Ed. 842 (1900) (statutory partnership association), 193 U.S. 532, 24 S.Ct. 576, 48 L.Ed. 778 (1904); Ex parte Edelstein, 30 F.2d 636 (2d Cir. 1929), cert. denied 279 U.S. 851, 49 S.Ct. 347, 73 L.Ed. 994 (1929) (holding prior rule not changed by United Mine Workers of America v. Coronado Coal Co., 259 U.S. 344, 42 S.Ct. 570, 66 L. Ed. 975, 27 A.L.R. 762 (1922) (unincorporated labor union held suable in union name for action under federal law). Cf. Puerto Rico v. Russell & Co., 288 U.S. 476, 53 S.Ct. 447, 77 L.Ed. 903 (1933) (Puerto Rico sociedad en comandita); Note, "Federal Procedure—Diversity Jurisdiction Over a Louisiana Partnership", 27 La.L.Rev. 348 (1967); Swan v. First Church of Christ Scientist in Boston, 225 F.2d 745 (9th Cir. 1955); Comment, "Diversity Jurisdiction for Unincorporated Associations", 75 Yale L.J. 138 (1965); Comment, "Citizenship of Unincorporated Associations for Diversity Purposes", 50 Va.L.Rev. 1135 (1964). Under federal law, controversies involving unincorporated associations, such as labor unions, might be within the federal question jurisdiction of the federal courts. 29 U.S.C.A. § 185(b); Note, 37 N.C.L.Rev. 500 (1959). Such federal jurisdiction might not be exclusive. Note, 46 Va.L.Rev. 349 (1960). The American Law Institute has proposed that a "partnership or other unincorporated association capable of suing or being sued as an entity in the State in which an action is brought shall be deemed a citizen of the State or foreign state where it has its principal place of business." ALI Study of the Division of jurisdiction between State and Federal Courts 10 (1969); Symposium: "The American Law Institute's Proposals on the Division of Jurisdiction between State and Federal Courts", 17 S.C.L. Rev. 659 (1965); Comment, "Unincorporated Associations: Diversity Jurisdictions and the ALI Proposal", 1965 Duke L.J. 329.

34. Fed.R.Civ.P. 23.2.

35. Supreme Tribe of Ben-Hur v. Cauble, 255 U.S. 356, 41 S.Ct. 338, 65 L.Ed. 673 (1921); Kaplan, "Suits Against Unincorporated Associations under the Federal Rules of Civil Procedure", 53 Mich.L. Rev. 945, 958–961 (1955).

conditions on their admission. Modern emphasis is on the reasonable exercise of the state's police power over activities within the state, thus permitting reasonable regulation of unincorporated as well as incorporated forms of business enterprise, even those engaging in interstate and foreign commerce so long as there is no undue burden on such commerce.

The United States Constitution provides that "The Citizens of each State shall be entitled to all Privileges and Immunities of Citizens in the several States,"[1] thereby forbidding any state to discriminate against the citizens of other states in favor of its own. In Bank of Augusta v. Earle,[2] the Supreme Court held that a foreign corporation was not a citizen for such purposes and refused to look behind it to allow the foreign shareholders thereof to exercise in other states through the agency of the corporation such corporate privileges and immunities as the citizens thereof enjoyed.

In a second case, Paul v. Virginia,[3] the court reiterated that corporations were not citizens within the meaning of the privileges-and-immunities-of-citizens clause, despite the fact that they were deemed citizens under the diversity-of-citizenship clause. After emphasizing that the privileges and immunities secured to citizens of each state in the several states meant those common to the citizens of the latter states and not the special privileges enjoyed in the former, the court pointed out that a corporation was "the mere creation of local law" and could "have no legal existence beyond the limits of the sovereignty where created," and, as a foreign corporation, could, absent considerations of interstate commerce, be excluded entirely or admitted on such terms and conditions as each state may think proper to impose.

Subsequently, the court limited the discretion of the states in this regard, barring them not only from excluding foreign corporations engaged in interstate or foreign commerce but also from attaching unconstitutional conditions on the admission of foreign corporations.[4]

State control of foreign corporations later came to be approached as questions of reasonable exercise of the police power over activities within the state, regardless of whether such activities were by incorporated or unincorporated enterprises, rather than of application of the privileges-and-immunities clause,[5] and regardless of interstate or foreign commerce so long as such regulation did not constitute an undue burden on such commerce.[6]

Whether or not a corporation is a "citizen" for various purposes is a question which continues to arise.[7]

Modern corporate statutes provide that: (a) Corporations formed thereunder shall have power to conduct their business in any state, territory, district, or possession of the United States or in any foreign country;[8] and (b) Foreign corporations shall not do any business in the state without having procured a certificate of authority therefor.[9]

1. U.S.Const. art. IV, § 2.

2. 38 U.S. (13 Pet.) 519, 10 L.Ed. 274 (1839).

3. 75 U.S. (8 Wall.) 168, 19 L.Ed. 357 (1868). A second holding of the case was that insurance did not constitute interstate commerce—a holding since overruled in United States v. South-Eastern Underwriters Ass'n, 322 U.S. 533, 64 S.Ct. 1162, 88 L.Ed. 1440 (1944). But see McCarran-Ferguson Act, 15 U.S.C.A. §§ 1011 et seq.

4. See sections 96, 98, 100, 101 infra.

5. Hemphill v. Orloff, 277 U.S. 537, 48 S.Ct. 577, 72 L.Ed. 978 (1928); Campbell, "Jurisdiction over Non-resident Individuals and Foreign Corporations; The Privileges and Immunities Clause", 36 Tul.L. Rev. 663 (1962).

6. See sections 96–100 infra.

7. Pilgrim Real Estate, Inc. v. Superintendent of Police of Boston, 330 Mass. 250, 112 N.E.2d 796 (1953) (corporation held not "citizen" qualified to sue to enforce ordinance); Matter of Oneida County Forest Preserve Council v. Wehle, 309 N.Y. 152, 128 N.E.2d 282 (1955) (membership corporation held "citizen" for purposes of N.Y.Const. art. XIV, § 4). See B. Mukerjee, Indian Decisions on Corporate Citizenship (1961).

8. ABA–ALI Model Bus.Corp.Act § 4(j).

9. ABA–ALI Model Bus.Corp.Act § 99. See section 100 infra.

F. CORPORATION AS "NATIONAL"

CORPORATON AS "NATIONAL"

90. Nationality, an important concept for many purposes, is usually easily determined for natural persons. For corporations, two principal tests have been applied for determining foreignness or domesticness: (a) The aggregate test, looking to the nationality, domicile, or residence of the individuals controlling the corporation; and (b) The entity test, looking to the nation where it was incorporated, where its shareholders or board of directors meetings are held, or where it has its principal place of business.

The corporation, for purposes of trading with the enemy legislation, might have its nationality determined by those in control, thus looking behind the corporation and seizing the corporate assets of enemy-controlled corporations, or by its place of incorporation, thus looking only to the entity; shares held by enemy interests would be subject to seizure. During World War I, Great Britain followed the former aggregate approach; the United States the latter entity approach. During World War II, the United States adopted the former aggregate approach with some variations.

Nationality is an important concept for many purposes.

Although nationality of natural persons is usually easily determined, attributing nationality to corporations is more difficult.

Two principal tests have been applied for determining foreignness or domesticness: (a) The aggregate test, looking to the nationality, domicile, or residence of the individuals who control the corporation; and (b) The entity test, looking to the nation where it was incorporated, where its shareholders or board of directors meetings are held, or where it has its principal place of business.[1]

The nationality of a corporation has been relevant under the Trading with the Enemy Acts of the two World Wars. Where the statutory language is not explicit, statutory construction can involve choosing between entity and aggregate theories which can lead to different results.

In Daimler Co. v. Continental Tyre & Rubber Co. (Great Britain),[2] and English subsidiary of a German corporation was found to be German, by the "control test" (i. e., predominant character of its shareholders, directors, and managers), and hence enemy for purposes of the British World War I Act. The British World War II Act adopted the same "control test".

In contrast, the American Act of 1917 followed a different scheme based on the entity theory. With respect to the corporation's status and seizure of its property, its place of incorporation or of doing business, and not enemy ownership or control, was the test; each shareholder's enemy status was determined on its own merits with respect to the seizure of his shares.[3]

In 1941, the Act was amended to give the President flexible powers to vest in the Enemy Property Custodian "any property or interest of any foreign country or national thereof," but enabling nonenemies to reclaim property without enemy taint. The 1941 amendment was construed as calling for the piercing of the corporate veil to see if there is enemy control,[4] and to sever the nonenemy interests from enemy interests in the seized corporate assets of a foreign corporation found to be nonenemy.[5]

1. Vagts, "The Corporate Alien: Definitional Questions in Federal Restraint on Foreign Enterprise", 74 Harv.L.Rev. 1489 (1961); Comment, "The 'Nationality' of International Corporations under Civil Law and Treaty", 74 Harv.L.Rev. 1429 (1961).

2. [1916] 2 A.C. 307, citing Bank of the United States v. Deveaux, discussed in section 88 supra.

3. Behn, Meyer & Co. v. Miller, 266 U.S. 457, 45 S.Ct. 165, 69 L.Ed. 374 (1925).

4. Clark v. Uebersee Finanz-Korporation, A.G., 332 U.S. 480, 68 S.Ct. 174, 92 L.Ed. 88 (1947); Uebersee Finanz-Korporation, A.G. v. McGrath, 343 U.S. 205, 72 S.Ct. 618, 96 L.Ed. 888 (1952).

5. Kaufman v. Société Internationale, 343 U.S. 156, 72 S.Ct. 611, 96 L.Ed. 853 (1952). N. Lattin, The

G. CORPORATION AS "STATE"

GOVERNMENT–OWNED CORPORATIONS

91. Government-owned corporations pose the question of the extent to which governmental immunity from suit and taxation, or other governmental characteristics, will be afforded such corporations. The various court holdings cannot always be reconciled.

The earliest corporations were governments themselves, e.g., the Roman Republic, the English—later British—Crown, the Corporation of the City of London. English law saw the development of the great chartered overseas trading companies which enjoyed not only trading privileges but governmental powers in the colonies or "plantations", e.g., British East India Company, Virginia Company, Massachusetts Bay Company.

Government-owned corporations, at all levels of government, either wholly-owned by the government or "mixed" with governmental and private capital,[1] exercising so-called "governmental" or "proprietary" functions or both, have multiplied,[2] receiving impetus from World War I, the "Great Depression", World War II, and modern technology, e.g., the first and second Banks of the United States,[3] Panama Canal Company, Defense Supplies Corporation, Tennessee Valley Authority, Federal Deposit Insurance Corporation, Port of New York Authority,[4] St. Lawrence Seaway Development Corporation,[5] Communications Satellite Corporation.[6]

The advantages of the government-owned corporation are to employ usual business rather than governmental procedures in doing business, such as negotiating its purchases and resolving its funds, although the latter has been limited by the Government Corporation Control Act of 1945.[7]

Until 1945, most federal government corporations were formed under state law, usually Delaware, but since then there has been some trend in favor of federal incorporation. State government corporations, of course, are formed under state law.

Where the statute creating the government corporation is not explicit, problems arise as to when such a corporation should or should not enjoy various sovereign privileges. Sovereign immunity from suit has been denied such corporations on at least

---

Law of Corporations § 11 (1959); Fink, "That Pierced Veil—Friendly Stockholders and Enemy Corporations", 51 Mich.L.Rev. 651 (1953); Domke, "The Control of Corporations—Application of the Enemy Test in the United States of America", 3 Int'l & Comp.L.Q. 52–59 (1950).

[§ 91]

1. The Federal National Mortgage Association ("FNMA" or "Fannie Mae"), a "mixed" corporation which pays taxes, distributes dividends and has its shares publicly traded, in 1968 bought back its preferred shares held by the federal government and became entirely privately-owned. See Amdursky, "The New York Urban Development Corporation", 40 N.Y.St.B.J. 100 (1969).

2. U. S. General Accounting Office, Reference Manual of Government Corporations, S.Doc.No. 86, 75th Cong., 1st Sess. (1945, Supp. 1947); see Lillienthal & Marquis, "The Conduct of Business Enterprises by the Federal Government", 54 Harv.L.Rev. 545 (1941).

3. See section 88, n. 2 supra.

4. Edelstein, "The Authority Plan—Tool of Modern Government", 28 Cornell L.Q. 177 (1943).

5. 33 U.S.C.A. §§ 981–990.

6. Schwartz, "Governmentally Appointed Directors in a Private Corporation——The Communications Satellite Act of 1962", 79 Harv.L.Rev. 350 (1965); Shrader, "Communications Satellite Corporation: A New Experiment in Government and Business", 53 Ky.L.J. 732 (1965). Committee on Administrative Law, "Protection of the Public Interest in the Structure and Operations of the Communications Satellite Corporation", 18 Record of N.Y.C.B.A. 630 (1963).

7. 31 U.S.C.A. §§ 841–860 (listing some 40 wholly-owned government corporations). Before 1945, congressional control was very limited over such wholly-government-owned corporations as the Reconstruction Finance Corporation, Commodity Credit Corporation, Export-Import Bank, Federal Housing Authority, and the Tennessee Valley Authority. The 1945 Act required that all corporations "wholly owned" by the United States government submit annual "business-type" budgets, to form part of the President's executive budget and thus come under review of the Budget Bureau and examination of congressional appropriations committees.

four different grounds, two predicated on the aggregate theory and two on the entity theory: (a) the action is against the sovereign but the latter has waived its immunity by doing business in the business world in the corporate form; (b) not all shares are held by the sovereign; (c) the corporation as a separate entity does not enjoy the immunity of its sovereign shareholder; and (d) the corporation as agent of the sovereign does not enjoy the principal's immunity.[8]

A combination of the separate-entity theory and business-world theory usually provides the basis for denial of immunity. Some cases found waiver of immunity against contract but not tort claims. Sovereign immunity might be upheld where the corporation is found to be an agency of the state performing governmental, as distinguished from proprietary, functions.[9] The governmental-proprietary distinction, ancient in origin, is difficult to apply to the modern "welfare state".

The United Kingdom post office became a government corporation in 1968. Similar proposals have been made for the United States Post Office Department.[10]

Cities have been moving into a growing variety of businesses, often in direct competition with private enterprise.[11]

Immunity from taxation also is a problem, such immunity often being allowed.

Apart from the foregoing are other procedural problems, involving the government corporation, such as liability for court costs, amenability to supplementary proceedings, ability to plead the statute of limitations, etc., and problems in other areas as varied and manifold as the activities undertaken by such corporations.

The various court holdings can not always be reconciled.[12]

---

8. Jaffe, "Suits Against Governments and Officers: Sovereign Immunity", 77 Harv.L.Rev. 1 (1963); Comment, "Sovereign Immunity of States Engaged in Commercial Activities", 65 Colum.L.Rev. 1086 (1965); Comment, "Remedies Against the United States and Its Officials," 70 Harv.L.Rev. 827, 840–846 (1957). See Defense Supplies Corp. v. United States Lines Co., 148 F.2d 311 (2d Cir. 1945), cert. denied 326 U.S. 746, 66 S.Ct. 43, 90 L.Ed. 446 (1945) (action by one federal-government-owned corporation against another held an action by the United States against the United States not contemplated by statute).

9. See Easley v. New York State Thruway Authority, 1 N.Y.2d 374, 153 N.Y.S.2d 28, 135 N.E.2d 572 (1956) (upholding statute conferring upon court of claims jurisdiction over all claims against Authority under state constitution provision conferring on court jurisdiction over claims against state; dissenting opinion taking view that Authority was entity independent of state). But see B. W. King, Inc. v. Town of West New York, 49 N.J. 318, 230 A.2d 133 (1967).

10. Siegel, "The United States Post Office Incorporated: A Blueprint for Reform", 66 Mich.L.Rev. 615

(1968); Comment, "Project: Post Office", 41 S.Cal. L.Rev. 643 (1968).

11. Gordon, "Cities in Business", 158 Wall Street Journal, No. 52, 1 (Sept. 14, 1961).

12. Small Business Administration v. McClellan, 364 U.S. 446, 81 S.Ct. 191, 5 L.Ed.2d 200 (1960) (SBA held part of government entitled to priority of United States in bankruptcy proceeding); North Dakota v. Nat'l Milling & Cereal Co., 114 F.2d 777 (8th Cir. 1940) (holding state-created North Dakota Mill and Elevator Association under state statute not separate entity or agent but part of state itself and therefore immune from suit, even if liability arose out of commercial venture as distinguished from governmental function, by citizen of another state under U.S.Const., amend. XI, and not citizen of North Dakota); Note, 72 Dick.L.Rev. 296 (1968); Everett v. Riverside Hose Co. No. 4, 261 F.Supp. 463 (S.D.N.Y. 1966) (blackballing of negro for membership in corporate local volunteer fire department held to be state deprivation of civil rights); United States v. Anasae International Corp., 197 F.Supp. 926 (S.D.N.Y. 1961) (holding Commodity Credit Corporation, wholly-owned agency of United States, not indispensable party to Government's action to recover overpayments made by Corporation); Matter of New York Post Corp. v. Moses, 10 N.Y.2d 199, 219 N.Y.S.2d 7, 176 N.E.2d 709 (1961) (holding state-chartered Triborough Bridge and Tunnel Authority neither agent of New York City nor "public office" and its records not "public records" open to inspection by any member of public under McKinney's N.Y.Gen.Mun.Law, § 51); Osterman & Robinson, Comment, "Sovereignty of State Corporations", 42 Cornell L.Q. 540 (1957). See Abel, "The Public Corporation in the United States" in W. Friedmann, The Public Corporation 338–373 (1954). The term "public corporation" in this sense should not be confused with its broader meaning (see section 14 supra) or the English term "public company". See section 259 infra.

CHAPTER 4

SELECTION OF JURISDICTION OF INCORPORATION

FACTORS IN SELECTION

92. Selection of the jurisdiction of incorporation, if incorporation is found desirable, requires consideration of various factors which run the whole gamut of corporation law. Incorporation of a local business is usually best effected in the local jurisdiction. In the case of multi-state business, the impact not only of incorporation but also of qualification and other doing business requirements of the several jurisdictions involved must be compared. Separating the business into separate corporations in the same or different jurisdictions might offer advantages.

The problem of selecting the jurisdiction of incorporation for a proposed business corporation is discussed in this chapter. In Chapter 2, the corporation and other forms of business enterprise were compared. Both subjects in practice would have to be considered together since any comparison of the relative advantages and disadvantages of the various forms of business enterprise must take into account the applicable laws of the jurisdiction or jurisdictions involved in the comparison.

While competition among the states in attracting corporations and the most recent influence of the Model Business Corporation Act have tended to enhance uniformity among state corporation statutes,[1] many significant variations continue to exist.

Choice, of course, is not always possible. Many jurisdictions, for example, limit awards of contracts for public construction projects to domestic corporations, and sometimes only to them if they have their principal office and place of business in the state.

If a business enterprise is to be localized within a single jurisdiction, doing business and holding property only there (except possibly for doing exclusively interstate or foreign commerce business elsewhere), it should usually be incorporated, if incorporation is found desirable, in that jurisdiction. It might even split its business among two or more corporations to avoid the federal corporate surtax or accumulated earnings tax.[2] However, to incorporate elsewhere will subject it to the corporation laws, suability, regulation, and taxation not only of the state of incorporation, but also of the jurisdiction of its business activity as a "foreign corporation."[3]

1. See section 12 supra.

2. See section 76 supra and section 339 infra.

3. See sections 96–99 infra. The proposed North Carolina Business Corporation Act had special pro-

131

Where the business enterprise is doing, or is to do, business in more than one jurisdiction, the initial question also arises as to whether there should be one or more corporations. Perhaps a separate corporation in each jurisdiction might offer advantages.[4]

When a single corporation is to be formed to engage in multi-state activities, choice of

visions applicable to North Carolina businesses which incorporated elsewhere, but these were eliminated. Latty, "Pseudo-Foreign Corporations", 65 Yale L.J. 137 (1955). For a case imposing a higher duty on directors than that imposed by the law of the jurisdiction of incorporation, see Mansfield Hardwood Lumber Co. v. Johnson, 268 F.2d 317 (5th Cir. 1959), cert. denied 361 U.S. 885, 80 S.Ct. 156, 4 L.Ed.2d 120 (1959), reh. denied 361 U.S. 926, 80 S.Ct. 290, 4 L.Ed.2d 241 (1960). The New York Business Corporation Law subjects foreign corporations doing business in the state to various regulatory provisions (Article 13) but exempts them from some of those provisions if they are authorized to do business in the state and either have shares listed on a national securities exchange or have less than one-half of their business income allocable to the state for franchise tax purposes. McKinney's N.Y. Bus.Corp.Law, § 1320; see Note, 47 Cornell L.Q. 273 (1962).

4. See section 76 supra. In recent years, manufacturing affiliates have been formed in Puerto Rico under that commonwealth's "Operation Bootstrap". Puerto Rico residents pay no federal taxes, and various manufacturing enterprises are exempted from various local taxes for periods up to 10 years; low labor costs and the fact that Puerto Rico is part of the United States offer additional advantages. See O'Connor & Dobroski, "Tax Shelter in Puerto Rico Today: How to Select the Most Advantageous Form for Operating", 29 J.Taxation 248 (1968); Mihaly, "Recent Developments Affecting Taxation of Business Operations in Puerto Rico", 18 Stan.L.Rev. 823 (1966); "Puerto Rico Tax Haven?", 24 Corp.J. 223 (1965); Mihaly, "The Advantages of Doing Business in Puerto Rico", 16 Stan.L.Rev. 75 (1963); Friedman & Silbert, "The Inter-relationship of Puerto Rican and United States Income Tax", N.Y. U. 21st Inst. on Fed.Tax. 807 (1963); Francis, "Foreign Corporations Doing Business in the Commonwealth of Puerto Rico", 26 Rev.Jur.U.P.R. 347 (1957); Comment, "Tax Incentives in Puerto Rico", 48 Texas L.Rev. 198 (1969). The Bahamas, with their lack of income taxes and low inheritance taxes, have also attracted businesses, especially locally-incorporated overseas sales subsidiaries of distributor-holding companies. 1 P–H Corp. Rep. ¶ 25,146; Mason, "Bahamas Companies", 1961 J.Bus.L. 148; Hughes, "Tax Incentives of Manufacturing in the Caribbean: An Analysis of Four Jurisdictions", 21 J.Taxation 180 (1964). See also Beardwood, "Sophistication Comes to the Tax Havens", 79 Fortune, No. 2, 95 (Feb.1969); Norr, "Monaco: Biography of a Tax Haven", 19 Tax L.Rev. 469 (1964); Nolan & Blair, "Business in Monaco under the New Treaty with France", 19 Bus.Law. 661 (1964); Torem & Du-Vivier, "Corporation and Tax Laws of Monaco", 16

Bus.Law. 1053 (1961); Weissman, "Tax Advantages of the Netherlands Antilles for Motion Picture Companies", 32 S.Cal.L.Rev. 391 (1959); Marias, "Liechtenstein—A Corporate Home Away From Home", 12 Bus.Law. 405 (1957); Rudick, "Foreign Domiciles for Corporations—Advantages Offered by the Republic of Liberia", 12 Bus.Law. 257 (1957). For bibliography and references, see Elsman, "Helpful Publications for Lawyers with International Business Problems", 50 A.B.A.J. 857 (1964); J. Deniau, The Common Market (4th rev. ed. 1967); W. Feld, The European Common Market and the World (1967); W. Jackson, The Common Market (1967); W. Jensen, The Common Market (1967); P. Garland, A Businessman's Introduction to Brazilian Law and Practice (1966); P. Proehl, Foreign Enterprise in Nigeria, Laws and Policies (1965); S. Guevara, Business Organization in the Philippines (1965); A. Raedler, Corporate Taxation in the Common Market (1964–); V. Venturini, Company Law Reform in Malaysia (1964). See also M. Wasserman, The Common Market and American Business (1964); CCH Dominion Companies; W. Surrey & C. Shaw, A Lawyer's Guide to International Business Transactions (1963); A Lawyer's Guide to International Business (ABA 1963); E. Lovell, Managing Foreign Base Corporations (1963); C. Oberdorfer, Common Market Cartel Law (1963); R. Weigand, Doing Business in Japan (1963); A. Campbell & D. Thompson, Common Market Law—Texts and Commentaries (1962); A. Fatouros, Government Guarantees to Foreign Investors (1962); H. Landau, Doing Business Abroad (PLI 1962) (2 vols.); R. Martinez de Escobar Vargos, How to do Business in Mexico (1961); J. Allen, The European Common Market and the GATT (1960); E. Stein & T. Nicholson, American Enterprise in the European Common Market (1960) (2 vols.); H. Moreau et al., French Corporations (Sociétés Anonymes) (1956); Bruno, "Checklist for Formation of a Foreign Subsidiary", 24 Bus.Law. 493 (1969); Morris, "The New Regulations Governing Direct Foreign Investment—An Early Appraisal", 23 Bus.Law. 701 (1968); Hall & Mann, "United States Income Tax Problems in Doing Business Abroad", 3 Tex.Int'l L.F. 21 (1967); Steefel & von Falkenhausen, "The New German Stock Corporation Law", 52 Cornell L.Q. 518 (1967); Roberts & Goldberg, "The new income tax in Mexico: how it affects business operations there", 26 J.Taxation 164 (1967); Westberg, "The Joint Stock Company in Iran", 23 Bus.Law. 147 (1967); Kalish, "Tax Considerations in Organizing for Business Abroad", 44 Taxes 71 (1966); Poser, "Securities Regulation in Developing Countries: The Brazilian Experience", 52 Va.L.Rev. 1283 (1966); Steta, "Mexican Taxes on United States Corporations Doing Business in or With Mexico", 19 ABA Sect.Tax Bull. 50 (1966); Krause, "To Incorporate Abroad", 1965 U. Ill.L.F. 453; Symposium: "Organizing and Financing Businesses in Latin America", 21 Bus.Law. 5 (1965); Batiza, "Current Attitudes on Mexico's Treatment of the Foreign Enterprise", 17 Rutgers L.Rev. 365 (1963); Calhoun & Hoashi, "Japanese

jurisdiction of incorporation becomes important. Sound selection requires comparison of the features involved not only in incorporating in one jurisdiction or another but also in doing business (and often formally qualifying) in the jurisdiction or jurisdictions other than the jurisdiction of incorporation.[5]

Various factors might be relevant in the selection process.

Corporate statutes which are "enabling", "liberal", "permissive", and flexible, along with legislative, judicial and administrative attitudes sympathetic to business corporations—so-called "corporate climate", are the prime choice of corporate management and corporate counsel.[6]

Jurisdictions with well-developed bodies of corporate law are obviously preferable as jurisdictions of incorporation to those whose statutes and decisions offer less certainty and predictability.[7]

Tax System from the Standpoint of Foreign Business", 18 Bus.Law. 503 (1963); Christensen, "Japanese Equity Financing", 38 Wash.L.Rev. 105 (1963); Clubb & Vance, "Incentives to Private U. S. Investment Abroad Under the Foreign Assistance Program", 72 Yale L.J. 475 (1963); J. Gibson, South African Mercantile and Company Law (1963); Kust, "Treatment of Foreign Enterprise in India", 17 Rutgers L.Rev. 351 (1963); Laylin, "Legal Climate for Private Enterprise under the Alliance for Progress", 41 N.C.L.Rev. 364 (1963); Owens, "United States Income Tax Treaties: Their Role in Relieving Double Taxation", 17 Rutgers L.Rev. 428 (1963); "Selected Literature on European Common Market", 18 Record of N.Y.C.B.A. 308 (1963), 17 id. 263 (1962); Weiss, "Private Investment in French-Speaking Africa", 17 Rutgers L.Rev. 335 (1963); Angulo, "Comments on the Status of Foreign Business Corporation under the Commercial Codes of Argentina and Venezuela", 4 Inter-Am.L.Rev. 159 (1962); Bradshaw, "Selected Legal Aspects of Business in Japan", 14 Stan.L.Rev. 639 (1962); Brundo, "Practical Aspects of Incorporating and Doing Business Abroad", U.So.Cal.1962 Tax Inst. 345; Fagan & Calhoun, "Japanese Corporations", 17 Bus. Law. 346 (1962); Lang, "American Investment in Ireland and the European Common Market", 17 Record of N.Y.C.B.A. 557 (1962); Rice, "Foreign Companies in Great Britain", 1962 J.Bus.L. 155; McQuade, "The Development Corporation in Africa", 10 Am.J.Comp.L. 188 (1961); Pennington, "Company Law in Ghana", 105 Sol.J. 717, 735 (1961); Baker, "The Formation and Operation of a Venezuelan Corporation", 31 Tul.L.Rev. 261 (1957); Comment, "Regulation of American Business Interests in Peru—Basic Information for American Attorneys", 15 Catholic U.L.Rev. 93 (1966); Bibliography, "Selected English Language Materials on Doing Business in Latin America", 16 Record of N.Y.C.B.A. 286 (1961); Note, "Soviet Corporations", 5 Int'l & Comp.L.Q. 597 (1956).

5. E. g., the minimum organization taxes and initial filing fees for incorporating and minimum initial license, filing, and recording fees for qualifying as a foreign corporation in Delaware and New York are:

Incorporation: $ 35   (Delaware) $ 60   (New York)
Qualification: 120   (New York)   63   (Delaware)
    $155 $123

Thus the initial minimum cost of incorporation in New York and qualifying in Delaware is less than the initial cost of incorporating in Delaware and qualifying in New York. The recurrent New York franchise tax (7 percent) and Delaware income tax (5 percent on business carried on and property lo-

cated in Delaware) are the same for domestic and foreign corporations. The comparison between Nevada and California would be:
Incorporation: $ 39 (Nevada) $122 (California)
Qualification: 457 (California)   43 (Nevada)
    $496 $165
Statutory Costs of Domestic and Foreign Corporations in 50 States 7, 10, 31, 35 (United States Corporation Company 1968). See Restatement, Second, of Conflict of Laws ch. 13 (Business Corporations) (Proposed Official Draft, Pt. III, Apr. 22, 1969); Kaplan, "Foreign Corporations and Local Corporate Policy", 21 Vand.L.Rev. 433 (1968); Reese & Kaufman, "Law Governing Corporate Affairs: Choice of Law and the Impact of Full Faith and Credit", 58 Colum.L.Rev. 1118 (1958).

6. As distinguished from "regulatory" or "paternalistic" provisions which regulate business or "external affairs" or interfere with the "internal affairs" of a foreign corporation. See Henn, "The Philosophies of the New York Business Corporation Law of 1961", 11 Buffalo L.Rev. 439 (1962). The larger corporation's preference for Delaware has been described as follows:

"Its popularity results not only from its provisions but also from the state's sympathetic attitude toward business corporations. So long as that attitude continues, Delaware will probably remain the number one domicile for larger corporations. Other states, such as New Jersey, have in past years occupied that position only to see it lost when they failed to keep their laws up to date and their attitude toward business corporations sympathetic, and it is unfortunate that New York in the 1961–3 revisions of its corporation laws saw fit to adopt only a political compromise document, instead of correcting fully the policies and attitudes which for many years have encouraged larger than average businesses to incorporate elsewhere." G. Seward, Basic Corporate Practice 5–6 (ALI rev. 1966).

7. See section 93 infra.

For close corporations,[8] the statutes of Delaware, Florida, New York, and North Carolina are especially accommodating; for specialized types of corporations, (e.g., open-end investment companies or "mutual funds"), some jurisdictions may have special enabling legislation.

Counsel here can be aided substantially by retaining correspondent counsel in the other jurisdictions or requesting the assistance of one of the corporation service companies.

Relative advantages and disadvantages may change from time to time. One possibility might be to dissolve, liquidate, and reincorporate in another jurisdiction. A preferable alternative might be to form a new corporation in the other jurisdiction and then merge, tax-free, into it.[9]

Among the more relevant factors are:[10]

(1) Are there express provisions for preincorporation share subscriptions?

---

8. See section 259 infra.

9. In 1965, United States Steel Corporation, incorporated in New Jersey in 1901, created a wholly-owned Delaware subsidiary, merged tax-free into it, and had the subsidiary change its name to "United States Steel Corporation", thus becoming a Delaware corporation, and permitting exchange of 4–⅝% subordinated debentures for unredeemable 7% cumulative preferred shares on a 1–¾ to 1 basis. As a result the debenture interest deduction resulted in a tax saving of over $10,000,000. The common shares of the New Jersey corporation were exchanged for shares of the Delaware corporation on a 1 for 1 basis without the necessity of exchanging share certificates. As a result, New Jersey, the "mother of corporations" in the late 19th century, until succeeded by Delaware, enacted a very "permissive" statute in 1968. In 1969, Delaware made further revisions.

10. For Checklist—Selection of the Incorporating State, see 1 G. Hornstein, Corporation Law and Practice § 86 (1959); C. Rohrlich, Organizing Corporate and Other Business Enterprises 266–286 (4th ed. 1967); G. Seward, Basic Corporate Practice 39–42 (ALI rev. 1966); C. Israels, Corporate Practice 159–167 (PLI 2d ed. 1969); W. Beaman, Paying Taxes to Other States; State and Local Taxation of Non-Resident Businesses (1963); Willmarth, "Choice of Corporate Domicile", 49 Calif.L.Rev. 518 (1961) (comparison of California, Delaware, and Nevada); Garrett, "Where to Incorporate?", 37 Ill. B.J. 386 (1949).

---

(2) May a corporation be formed for perpetual or limited duration?

(3) How restrictive are the provisions concerning corporate names?

(4) Are there express provisions permitting use of a similar corporate name with the consent of the existing corporation? In the case of affiliated corporations? Otherwise?

(5) Is reservation of a corporate name possible? By express statutory provisions? By administrative courtesy?

(6) For what period may a corporate name be reserved?

(7) What renewals of reservation of corporate name are possible?

(8) Is a single incorporator permissible?

(9) Are there any requirements that the incorporator or incorporators subscribe for shares? What are the qualifications required of an incorporator or incorporators with respect to: Residence? Citizenship? Age? Otherwise?

(10) May a corporation serve as an incorporator?

(11) Are there express provisions for informal action by the incorporator(s)?

(12) For what purposes may a corporation be incorporated?

(13) Are broad purposes permissible?

(14) Must specified purposes be set forth in the articles of incorporation?

(15) Are there any constitutional or statutory restrictions on corporate ownership of real property? Agricultural land? Personal property? Shares in other corporations? Are there any constitutional or statutory debt limitations?

(16) Are there express provisions on the ultra vires doctrine?

(17) How broad are the statutory general corporate powers? Do they include power to make charitable contributions irrespective of corporate benefit? To carry out retirement, incentive and benefit plans for directors, officers, and employees? To be a partner? To adopt emergency by-laws? Must the statutory general corporate powers be set forth in the articles of incorporation?

(18) What are the fees for filing or recording the articles of incorporation?

(19) What are the organization taxes? Other initial taxes?

(20) Do such taxes discriminate against shares without par value?

(21) Are filings subject to close administrative scrutiny and conservatism, with resulting filing delays?

(22) Is there a state stamp tax on the issuance of securities?

(23) Are "blue sky" law requirements burdensome?

(24) What, if any, is the minimum authorized or paid-in capital requirement? Must evidence of compliance be filed? Who are liable, and to what extent, for noncompliance?

(25) What qualitative and quantitative consideration requirements apply to par value shares? To shares without par value? With respect to the valuation of property or services, does the "true value" or "good faith" rule apply? Do preincorporation services satisfy such consideration requirements?

(26) To what extent may a portion of the consideration received for shares be allocated to capital surplus? Within what period after the issuance of the shares may this be done?

(27) May partly-paid shares be issued? May certificates for partly-paid shares be issued?

(28) Are there express provisions for fractions of shares? Scrip?

(29) What provisions may be made with respect to: Dividend preferences? Liquidation preferences?

(30) When two or more classes of shares are authorized, must the provisions concerning them be stated or summarized on the share certificates?

(31) Are express provisions made for issuing preferred or other "special" classes of shares in series? What are the limitations on permissible variations between series of the same class?

(32) To what extent may preferred shares be made redeemable? To what extent may common shares be made redeemable?

(33) To what extent may shares be made convertible?

(34) What are the record date provisions? Are bearer shares permissible? What rights attach to them?

(35) What are the express statutory provisions for, and judicial and administrative attitudes toward, close corporations?

(36) To what extent may voting rights of shareholders be denied or limited? Absolutely? Contingently? May shares carry multiple votes? Fractional votes?

(37) What are the minimum quorum requirements for shareholder action?

(38) Are there express provisions permitting greater-than-normal requirements for: Shareholder quorum? Shareholder vote?

(39) Are there express provisions for holding shareholder meetings outside the state? On dates to be set by board of directors? What are the notice requirements?

(40) Are there express provisions for informal action by shareholders?

Unanimously? By required percentages?

(41) Is cumulative voting permissive or mandatory?

(42) What are the provisions for shareholder class voting for directors?

(43) Are there express provisions for shareholder voting agreements?

(44) Are there express provisions permitting shareholder control of directors?

(45) Are there express provisions for irrevocable proxies?

(46) Are there express provisions for voting trusts, permitting closed voting trusts and renewals?

(47) Are there express provisions for purchase and redemption by the corporation of its own shares, including use of stated capital if the purchase is made for specified purposes?

(48) Are there provisions concerning the validity and enforceability of agreements by the corporation to purchase its own shares?

(49) Is insolvency, in either the equity or the bankruptcy sense, a limitation on the redemption or purchase by the corporation of its own shares?

(50) Are there express provisions for rights and options to purchase shares, including the issuance of shares, and the share certificates therefor, even partly-paid, to directors, officers and employees? What are the judicial attitudes with respect thereto?

(51) Is shareholder approval required for the issuance of share options, either generally or to directors, officers and employees?

(52) Do preemptive rights exist or not exist absent provision in the articles of incorporation? Are they adequately defined? May they be denied, limit-

ed, amplified, or altered in the articles of incorporation?

(58) What is the minimum number of authorized directors?

(59) What are the qualifications required of directors with respect to: Residence? Citizenship? Shareholding? Age? Otherwise?

(60) May the board of directors be classified? Staggered?

(61) What are the minimum quorum requirements for board of directors action?

(62) Are there express provisions permitting greater-than-normal requirements for: Board of directors quorum? Board of directors vote?

(63) Are there express provisions for holding board of directors meetings outside the state?

(64) Are there express provisions for informal action by the board of directors? By means of conference telephone or some comparable communication technique:

(65) What are the provisions for removal of directors? For cause? Without cause?

(66) Are there express provisions for filling vacancies on the board of directors? By shareholder action? By board of directors action?

(67) Are there provisions for increasing the size of the board of directors? By shareholder action? By board of directors action?

(68) Are there provisions for filling newly-created directorships? By shareholder action? By board of directors action?

(69) Are there express provisions for executive committees of the board of directors? Other committees of the board of directors? Informal action by committees? What powers may be

exercised by committees? What is the minimum number of committee members?

(70) Are there express interested directors/officers provisions?

(71) What corporate officers are required?

(72) May the same person hold more than one office?

(73) What are the required qualifications of the various officers with respect to: Residence? Citizenship? Shareholding? Being a director? Age? Otherwise?

(74) Are there provisions for the election of officers by shareholders? For the removal of officers by shareholders?

(75) To what standards are directors and officers held accountable? Standard of care? Fiduciary standards? Statutory duties? What are the possible liabilities of directors? Officers?

(76) To what extent may directors immunize themselves from liability by filing their written dissents? By reliance on records?

(77) What are the express provisions for deadlock, arbitration, and dissolution, and the judicial attitudes concerning the same?

(78) Are cash and property dividends payable out of surplus? Capital surplus? Earned surplus? Net profits?

(79) Is insolvency, in either the equity or the bankruptcy sense, a limitation on cash or property dividends?

(80) Are unrealized appreciation and depreciation recognized in computing surplus? Capital surplus? Earned surplus?

(81) Are there express "wasting assets" corporation dividend provisions?

(82) Are there express provisions for share dividends? Share splits? Other share distributions?

(83) To what extent do statutory requirements of notice or disclosure to shareholders apply in the event of: Cash or property dividends or other distributions from sources other than earned surplus? Share distributions? Reduction of stated capital by cancellation of reacquired shares? Reduction of stated capital made by board of directors? Elimination of deficit in earned surplus account by application of capital surplus ("quasi-reorganization")? Conversion of shares? Who are liable for noncompliance? Corporation? Directors or officers for subjecting corporation to liability?

(84) What are the provisions for shareholder class voting for extraordinary corporate matters? May filings effecting extraordinary corporate matters have delayed effective dates?

(85) What shareholder approval is required for a sale, lease, exchange, or other disposition of corporate assets?

(86) What shareholder approval is required for a corporate mortgage or pledge?

(87) What shareholder approval is required for a corporate guaranty?

(88) Do the statutory provisions provide for expeditious amendment of the articles of incorporation? Including elimination of preemptive rights? Elimination of cumulative voting? Elimination of cumulative preferred dividend arrearages? Making nonredeemable shares redeemable? Are there provisions for "restated" articles of incorporation?

(89) What are the statutory provisions permitting merger or consolidation?

(90) Are there provisions for short-merger of a subsidiary into a parent corpora-

tion? Of a parent into a subsidiary corporation?

(91) What are the statutory provisions concerning nonjudicial dissolution?

(92) What are the statutory provisions concerning judicial dissolution?

(93) How extensive are the appraisal remedies afforded dissenting shareholders? To what extent are appraisal remedies exclusive?

(94) What are the express provisions relating to shareholder derivative actions?

(95) Are there express provisions for derivative actions by a director? By an officer? By a creditor? By others?

(96) Is there statutory differentiation between shareholder derivative actions and other actions brought by shareholders?

(97) What are the provisions for indemnification for litigation expenses of directors? Of officers? Of other corporate personnel? Are there provisions for insurance?

(98) Are the statutory indemnification provisions exclusive or not with respect to directors? Officers? Other corporate personnel?

(99) What books and records must be kept within the state?

(100) What are the requirements with respect to annual and other reports?

(101) What are the annual franchise tax rates?

(102) What are the state share transfer tax rates?

(103) Are nonresident security holders subject to local taxes? Personal property taxes? Inheritance taxes?

(104) Are there express provisions to accommodate small business investment companies?

(105) Are there express provisions to accommodate open-end investment companies ("mutual funds")?

(106) To what extent are foreign corporations doing business in the state subject to the corporate statute's regulatory provisions? Local "blue sky" laws? Local fees and taxes?

(107) To what extent has the corporate statute been construed by the courts? Are judicial and administrative attitudes sympathetic?

(108) Does the state have a statute or regulations similar to Subchapter S?

These factors run the whole gamut of corporation law.

ADVANTAGES AND DISADVANTAGES OF DELAWARE INCORPORATION

93. Delaware has been the most popular jurisdiction of incorporation for multi-state corporations. Its many advantages outweigh its few disadvantages for such corporations. While many other jurisdictions offer many similar advantages, no other jurisdictions are as fully accommodating to corporations, especially corporate management, as Delaware.

Delaware has been the mecca of numerous large American corporations since its general corporation law was first "modernized" in 1899.[1] For example, approximately one-third of the corporations listed on the New York Stock Exchange are incorporated in Delaware.[2]

1. See sections 1, 12 supra. When the federal government formed its corporations under state law, it usually did so in Delaware. Nevada has an advantageous corporation law for western multi-state businesses. The same phenomenon is found in other legal systems. In Europe, Liechtenstein, with its accommodating corporation code drafted by Swiss lawyers who ingeniously combined American and continental advantages (e. g., bearer shares), has humorously been said to have more corporate persons than natural persons. Luxembourg, Monaco, Liberia, Bahamas, and Isle of Jersey have had their attractions. See section 92, n. 4 supra.

2. E. g., Bethlehem Steel Corporation, Chrysler Corporation, Ford Motor Company, General Motors Corporation, J. C. Penney Company, Radio Corpora-

Drafted by corporation lawyers, with ample advice from Wall Street corporate lawyers and more recently the corporate laws committee of the American Bar Association, the Delaware corporation statute is designed to be attractive to corporations, corporate management, and their counsel. Those who favor the statute state that its construction by "a judiciary of corporate specialists" generally has been "sound and fair", resulting in a wealth of precedents, well-settled law with unique predictability, and a flexible and modern basis for corporate action.[3] Legislative changes, requiring a two-thirds vote of all members of each house of the General Assembly,[4] reflecting a sympathetic attitude toward corporate enterprise, are made upon the advice and with the cooperation of the Delaware Bar.

With the 1967 revision and the 1968 and 1969 amendments of the Delaware General Corporation Law, incorporation in Delaware has been made more advantageous to corporate management than ever before—"the very best which American corporation law can offer" !

Among the avowed advantages of the Delaware corporation are:[5]

(1) Perpetual or limited existence;

(2) Reservation of name (by administrative courtesy);[6]

(3) Broad purposes, permitting incorporation for any lawful business or purpose, without further specification; extensive powers, including broad charitable contribution provision; power to be partner; power to set up fringe benefits; partial elimination of ultra vires doctrine;

(4) Moderate filing fees and organization and annual taxes;[7]

(5) No state stamp tax on issues and transfers of securities;

tion of America, Southern Pacific Company, Standard Oil Company of California, Transamerica Corporation, Warner Bros. Pictures, Inc., not to mention E. I. du Pont de Nemours & Co. United States Steel Corporation moved to Delaware from New Jersey in 1965. See section 92, n. 9 supra.

3. For comparisons of New York Business Corporation Law, Delaware Corporation Law, and Model Business Corporation Law, prepared by Professor Ernest L. Folk III, see C. Israels, Corporate Practice 651–722 (PLI 2d ed. 1969). Many important areas were almost untouched by the statute, at least prior to 1967, and the Delaware case law, e. g., preemptive rights; indemnification of directors, officers, and other corporate personnel; interested director/officer transactions. Arsht & Stapleton, "Delaware's New General Corporation Law: Substantive Changes", 23 Bus.Law. 75 (1967). In two other important areas, the Delaware decisions have been confusing and replete with rehearings, modifications, reversals, and remands: (a) "Shareholder agreements": see, e. g., Abercrombie v. Davies, 36 Del.Ch. 371, 130 A.2d 338 (Sup.Ct.1937), rev'g 36 Del.Ch. 102, 125 A.2d 588, 35 Del.Ch. 599, 123 A.2d 893 (Ch.1956), on remand 36 Del.Ch. 445, 131 A.2d 822 (Ch.1957); Ringling Bros.-Barnum & Bailey Combined Shows, Inc. v. Ringling, 29 Del.Ch. 610, 53 A.2d 441 (Sup.Ct.1947), rev'g 29 Del.Ch. 318, 49 A.2d 603 (Ch.1946); (b) Share options: see, e. g., Beard v. Elster, 39 Del.Ch. 153, 160 A.2d 731 (Sup. Ct.1960), Gottlieb v. Heyden Chemical Corp., 32 Del.Ch. 231, 83 A.2d 595 (Ch.1951), rev'd 33 Del.Ch. 82, 90 A.2d 660 (Sup.Ct.1952), 33 Del.Ch. 177, 91 A. 2d 57 (Sup.Ct.1952), 34 Del.Ch. 84, 99 A.2d 507 (Ch. 1953); Kerbs v. California Eastern Airways, Inc., 32 Del.Ch. 219, 83 A.2d 473 (Ch. 1951), rev'd 33 Del.Ch. 69, 90 A.2d 652, 34 A.L.R.2d 839 (Sup.Ct. 1952), petition for reargument denied 33 Del.Ch. 174, 91 A.2d 62, 34 A.L.R.2d 850 (Sup.Ct.1952), 33 Del.Ch. 395, 94 A.2d 217 (Ch.1953).

4. Del.Const. art. IX, § 1.

5. E. Folk, The Red Book Digest of the New Delaware Corporation Law—1967, iv (Corporation Service Company, 45th ed. 1968); E. Folk, Amendments to the Delaware General Corporation Law (effective July 15, 1969) and Technical Amendments Act (effective January 2, 1968); Arsht & Stapleton, "Delaware General Corporation Law: 1969", 25 Bus. Law 287 (1969).

6. Reservation of name by statutory provision is, of course, preferable to reservation by administrative courtesy.

7. Only as late as January 1, 1958, did a Delaware income tax become effective. The rate is 5 percent of taxable income from business carried on and property located in Delaware. The law exempts corporations maintaining a statutory corporate office but not doing business in Delaware and those whose activities in Delaware are solely the maintenance and management of their intangible investments and collection and distribution of income from such investments or from tangible property physically located outside of Delaware. The law applies to foreign as well as domestic corporations.

(6) No "blue sky" law; [8]

(7) Provision for single incorporator; corporation eligible as incorporator, no residence or share-ownership requirement for incorporator(s);

(8) Very expeditious incorporation;

(9) Provision permitting single director; no residence or share-ownership requirement for directors;

(10) Provision enabling board of directors to adopt, amend, or repeal bylaws; to fill vacancies on board and newly-created directorships; provision authorizing emergency bylaws;

(11) No minimum capital requirement;

(12) Express provision for conferring voting rights and inspection rights on bondholders;

(13) Express provision for issuing preferred, special, or other class of shares in series, fractions of shares, scrip, convertible securities, and options;

(14) Elimination of preemptive rights unless otherwise provided in articles of incorporation;

(15) Express provision for executive committee and other committees of board of directors, with full power of board of directors; committee may consist of no more than one director;

(16) Express provision for holding shares and securities in other corporations;

(17) Issuance of shares (par value or no par value), for cash, property, or services (with director's valuation of consideration conclusive in absence of fraud, and with directors empowered to allocate consideration for no par shares between stated capital and surplus), with or without voting power and preferences, etc. Preferences,

etc., need not be printed on share certificates;

(18) Permissive cumulative voting;

(19) Express provision for purchase of corporation's own shares or redemption of its preferred shares, including use of capital for redeemable preferred shares;

(20) Interested director/officer provisions; approval by disinterested majority, even though less than quorum;

(21) Express provisions for holding directors' or shareholders' meetings outside state; power of board of directors to fix date of annual meeting, if any; express provisions for informal action by directors, committees, and shareholders (by required percentages of shareholders); provision for meetings by means of conference telephone;

(22) Limited liability of shareholders (although articles of incorporation may state extent to which private property of shareholders is subject to payment of corporate debts);

(23) "America's most advanced provision for indemnification" of directors, officers, and other corporate personnel; statutory provisions nonexclusive; even broader insurance powers;

(24) Restrictions on shareholder derivative actions;

(25) Simple annual reports which do not disclose corporation's financial affairs;

(26) Authorization of voting trusts;

(27) Provision permitting electronic record keeping; no requirement for keeping books and records (except copy of any voting trust agreement) within state;

(28) Expeditious amendment by majority vote of articles of incorporation (including recapitalization); provision

---

8. Until 1953, Delaware had an anti-fraud provision which was then dropped by the Delaware codifiers as superfluous.

for "restated" articles of incorporation; majority shareholder approval of sale of assets; mortgage without necessity of shareholder approval; broad merger and consolidation provisions, including short-form procedure for merger of subsidiary into parent *and vice versa*, dissolution; provision for delayed effective dates; limited dissenting shareholder appraisal rights;

(29) Liberal dividend rules, permitting payment out of surplus, or net profits for current or preceding fiscal year; express provision for share dividends; provision protecting directors who rely on records;

(30) No taxation upon shares held by non-residents and no inheritance tax upon nonresident holders; [9]

(31) Provisions allowing severe share transfer restrictions;

(32) Special subchapter dealing exclusively with close corporations.

Possible disadvantages in Delaware are relatively minor: its requirement of the appointment of a resident agent for service of process and maintenance of registered office; its liberal attachment of shares provisions [10] and the hesitancy of Delaware courts to apply the forum non conveniens doctrine,[11] thus promoting corporate litigation in the courts in Delaware. The Delaware Constitution limits consideration for shares to money paid, labor done, or personal property, or real estate or leases thereof actually acquired by the corporation.[12] Delaware has not included in its income tax pro-

visions similar to those of Subchapter S of the Internal Revenue Code. There is the possible disadvantage of distance between Delaware and the place or places of the corporation's principal business activities. Finally, many of the provisions of the 1967 revision and the 1968 and 1969 amendments remain to be court-tested and judicially construed.

While many other jurisdictions offer many similar advantages, no other jurisdictions are as fully accommodating to corporations as Delaware.

Why other jurisdictions maintain stricter standards for their domestic corporations, and allow foreign corporations to do business free from such standards is difficult to justify.

Nonmembers of the Delaware Bar should not presume to handle Delaware incorporation or other corporate problems without the assistance of Delaware correspondent counsel or one of the corporation service companies.

ADVANTAGES AND DISADVANTAGES OF NEW YORK INCORPORATION

94. New York has a modern Business Corporation Law, which became effective in 1963. It replaced a tier of complex and poorly-organized corporate statutes, known as the General Corporation Law and Stock Corporation Law. Several of its provisions also apply to foreign corporations doing business in New York and hence cannot be avoided by out-of-state incorporation, except to some extent if the foreign corporation is authorized to do business in New York and either has shares listed on a national securities exchange or has less than one-half of its total business income allocable to New York for franchise tax purposes. A very substantial body of decisional law exists for the guidance of corporate practitioners. In the New York Bar are the most sophisticated corporation lawyers, many of them retained by larger corporations but others aggressively representing dissident minority shareholders.

---

9. The Delaware constitution bars such tax. Del. Const. art. IX, § 6. Some jurisdictions do impose such a tax. Of these, a number of jurisdictions limit the tax to decedents who were residents of jurisdictions which do not come within the reciprocal exemption statute.

10. See sections 97, 176 infra.

11. See section 86, n. 11 supra.

12. Del.Const. art. IX, § 3.

New York, like Delaware, has a modern corporate statute, the Business Corporation Law, which became effective in 1963, after several years of intensive study.[1] It replaced a tier known as the General Corporation Law and Stock Corporation Law.[2]

Unlike the Delaware 1967 revision which retained the organization, sectioning and much of the language of the 1899 Delaware statute, the New York revision resulted in a well-organized statute employing the most modern formulations.

Several of the New York statute's provisions also apply to foreign corporations doing business in New York and hence cannot be avoided by out-of-state incorporation,[3] except to some extent if the foreign corporation is authorized to do business in New York and either has shares listed on a national securities exchange or has less than one-half of its total business income allocable to New York for franchise tax purposes.[4]

For the guidance of corporate practitioners, a very substantial body of decisional law

exists, including many divided Court of Appeals decisions with majority, sometimes concurring, and dissenting opinions analyzing corporation law principles to a degree not attained elsewhere.[5]

In the New York Bar are the most sophisticated corporation lawyers, many of them retained by larger corporations[6] but others aggressively representing dissident minority shareholders.[7]

Advantages of New York Incorporation

Among the possible advantages and disadvantages (depending on one's point of view) of New York incorporation are:[8]

(1) Express provision for preincorporation share subscriptions;[9]

(2) Corporation formable for perpetual or limited existence;[10]

---

1. The New York revision program, under the Joint Legislative Committee to Study Revision of Corporation Laws, began in 1957 and continued beyond the September 1, 1963 effective date of the new Business Corporation Law with some technical amendments thereof, and revisions concerning stock corporations other than business corporations and nonstock and not-for-profit corporations. As of 1969, it had cost more than $750,000. Beginning in 1964, Delaware appropriated $25,000 for review and study of its corporation law. Its revisions became effective July 3, 1967, with additional amendments effective January 2, 1968 and July 15, 1969. See Opinion of the Justices, —— Del.Ch. ——, 232 A.2d 103 (Sup.Ct. 1967).

2. See text accompanying section 14, nn. 22–24 supra.

3. See Henn, Appendix 4, Checklist 10, "Foreign Corporations", in 2 N.Y.Bus.Corp.Law 636–643 (McKinney 1963).

4. See 1 G. Hornstein, Corporation Law and Practice § 94 (Supp.1968); Henn, "The Philosophies of the New York Business Corporation Law of 1961", 11 Buffalo L.Rev. 439, 453–455 (1962); Lightstone, "Foreign Corporations in New York State", 18 N.Y. U.Intra.L.Rev. 257 (1967); Note, "Corporations: Domestic Regulation of Foreign Corporations: Concept of 'Domiciled Foreign Corporation': New York Business Corporation Law of 1961", 47 Cornell L.Q. 273 (1962).

5. See, e. g., Matter of Staklinski (Pyramid Electric Co.), 6 N.Y.2d 159, 188 N.Y.S.2d 541, 160 N.E.2d 78 (1959); Matter of Cohen v. Cocoline Products, Inc., 309 N.Y. 119, 127 N.E.2d 906 (1955); Rosenfeld v. Fairchild Engine & Airplane Corp., 309 N.Y. 168, 128 N.E.2d 291, 51 A.L.R.2d 860 (1955), reh. denied 309 N.Y. 807, 130 N.E.2d 610 (1955); Matter of Radom & Neidorff, Inc., 307 N.Y. 1, 119 N.E.2d 563 (1954); Auer v. Dressel, 306 N.Y. 427, 118 N.E. 2d 590, 48 A.L.R.2d 604 (1954); Gordon v. Elliman, 306 N.Y. 456, 119 N.E.2d 331 (1954); Schwarz v. General Aniline & Film Corp., 305 N.Y. 395, 113 N. E.2d 533 (1953); Long Park, Inc. v. Trenton-New Brunswick Theatres Co., 297 N.Y. 174, 77 N.E.2d 633 (1948) motion denied 298 N.Y. 856, 84 N.E.2d 324 (1949); Benintendi v. Kenton Hotel, Inc., 294 N.Y. 112, 60 N.E.2d 829, 159 A.L.R. 280 (1945); Clark v. Dodge, 269 N.Y. 410, 199 N.E. 641 (1936); McQuade v. Stoneham, 263 N.Y. 323, 189 N.E. 234 (1934), reargument denied 264 N.Y. 460, 191 N.E. 514 (1934); Berkey v. Third Avenue Ry., 244 N.Y. 84, 155 N.E. 58, 50 A.L.R. 599 (1926), reargument denied 244 N.Y. 602, 155 N.E. 914 (1927).

6. M. Mayer, The Lawyers (1967); E. Smigel, The Wall Street Lawyer: Professional Organization Man? (1964).

7. Klaw, "Abe Pomerantz Is Watching You", 74 Fortune, No. 2, 144 (Feb. 1968).

8. C. Israels, Corporate Practice 651–722 (PLI 2d ed. 1969) (New York-Delaware-Model Act comparison); Henn, Appendix 4, Checklist 1, "Advantages and Disadvantages of New York Incorporation", 2 N.Y. Bus.Corp.Law 586–591 (McKinney 1963).

9. McKinney's N.Y.Bus.Corp.Law, § 503.

10. McKinney's N.Y.Bus.Corp.Law, §§ 202(a) (1), 402(a) (9).

(3) Reservation of name (by express provision) (60 days—two renewals); [11]

(4) Broad permissible purposes; [12]

(5) No constitutional or statutory restrictions on corporate ownership of real property;

(6) Broad general powers, including powers to adopt emergency bylaws; to make charitable contributions irrespective of corporate benefit; to carry out retirement, incentive and benefit plans for directors, officers, and employees; and to be partner; statutory powers need not be set forth in articles of incorporation; [13]

(7) Moderate filing fee ($50); [14] moderate minimum organization tax ($10); [15]

(8) No state stamp tax on issue of securities;

(9) Limited security registration provisions (anti-fraud and broker-dealer-registration type of "blue sky" law); [16]

(10) Tax on transfer of securities in New York corporations owned by nonresidents and nonresident decedents, subject to reciprocal exemption; [17]

(11) Single incorporator permissible; no requirement that incorporator or incorporators subscribe to shares; [18]

(12) No qualifications for incorporator or incorporators (other than that incorporator be natural person of age of 21 years or over); [19]

(13) Express provision for informal action by incorporator(s); [20]

(14) Authorized board of directors of one director in one-shareholder corporation and of two directors in two-shareholder corporation permissible; [21]

(15) No residence, citizenship, shareholding requirements or other qualifications for director (other than that director be at least 21 years of age; [22]

(16) Express provision for classified board of directors; [23]

(17) Express provision for removal of directors, with or without cause; [24]

(18) Express provision for filling director vacancies; [25]

(19) Express provision for filling newly-created directorships; [26]

(20) Express provision for increasing size of board of directors by board of directors action; [27]

(21) No minimum authorized or paid-in capital requirement;

(22) Issuance of shares (par value shares or shares without par value) for money or other property, tangible or intangible, labor or services actually received by or performed for corporation or for its benefit or in its formation or reorganization (with valuation of consideration by board of directors conclusive in absence of fraud); [28]

11. McKinney's N.Y.Bus.Corp.Law, § 303.

12. McKinney's N.Y.Bus.Corp.Law, § 201.

13. McKinney's N.Y.Bus.Corp.Law, §§ 202(a), 402(b).

14. McKinney's N.Y.Exec.Law, § 96(9) (a).

15. McKinney's N.Y.Tax Law, § 180.

16. McKinney's N.Y.Gen.Bus.Law, §§ 352–359(h).

17. McKinney's N.Y.Tax Law, §§ 248, 248–p. See N.Y.Const. art. XVI, § 3 (securities within state not employed in carrying on any business therein deemed to be located at domicile of owner for purpose of taxation).

18. See McKinney's N.Y.Bus.Corp.Law, § 401.

19. See McKinney's N.Y.Bus.Corp.Law, § 401.

20. McKinney's N.Y.Bus.Corp.Law, § 404(b).

21. McKinney's N.Y.Bus.Corp.Law, § 702(a).

22. McKinney's N.Y.Bus.Corp.Law, § 701.

23. McKinney's N.Y.Bus.Corp.Law, §§ 617, 704.

24. McKinney's N.Y.Bus.Corp.Law, § 706.

25. McKinney's N.Y.Bus.Corp.Law, § 705.

26. McKinney's N.Y.Bus.Corp.Law, § 705.

27. McKinney's N.Y.Bus.Corp.Law, § 702(b).

28. McKinney's N.Y.Bus.Corp.Law, § 504(a).

(23) Board of directors empowered within 60 days, subject to specified limitations, to allocate consideration for shares without par value between stated capital and capital surplus; [29]

(24) Authorized shares with or without voting power, and wide variations of preferences, etc., permissible; [30]

(25) Preferences, etc., need not be stated on share certificates; [31]

(26) No constitutional or statutory debt limitations;

(27) Permissive cumulative voting; [32]

(28) Express provision for redeemable common shares (if corporation has outstanding class of common shares not subject to redemption); [33]

(29) Express provision for purchase and redemption by corporation of its own shares, including use of stated capital, absent insolvency, if purchase is made for specified purposes; [34]

(30) Express provision for issuing preferred shares in series (with only slight limitations on permissible variations between series of same class); [35]

(31) Express provision for rights and options to purchase shares, including issue of share certificates, even when partly-paid, to directors, officers and employees; [36]

(32) Express provision for fractions of shares and scrip; [37]

(33) Express provision for convertible shares and convertible bonds; [38]

(34) Express provision for conferring inspection and shareholder voting rights on bondholders; [39]

(35) Statutory formulation of preemptive rights; may be denied, limited, amplified or altered in articles of incorporation; [40]

(36) Express provision relating to earned surplus in case of merger, consolidation or combination; [41]

(37) Express provision for quasi-reorganization; [42]

(38) Cash and property dividends payable out of surplus; [43] recognition of unrealized appreciation and depreciation in computing capital surplus; [44] express "wasting assets" corporation exception; [45]

(39) Express provision for share distributions (without express reference to "share dividend" or "share split"); [46]

(40) Express provision for irrevocable proxies; [47]

(41) Express provision for voting trusts, permitting closed voting trusts and renewals; [48]

(42) Express provisions for holding shareholder and board of directors meetings outside New York; [49]

---

38. McKinney's N.Y.Bus.Corp.Law, § 519.

39. McKinney's N.Y.Bus.Corp.Law, § 518(c).

40. McKinney's N.Y.Bus.Corp.Law, § 622.

41. McKinney's N.Y.Bus.Corp.Law, § 517(a) (1) (B).

42. McKinney's N.Y.Bus.Corp.Law, § 517(a) (4).

43. McKinney's N.Y.Bus.Corp.Law, § 510.

44. See McKinney's N.Y.Bus.Corp.Law, § 102(a) (2), (6), (13).

45. McKinney's N.Y.Bus.Corp.Law, § 510(b).

46. McKinney's N.Y.Bus.Corp.Law, § 511.

47. McKinney's N.Y.Bus.Corp.Law, § 609.

48. McKinney's N.Y.Bus.Corp.Law, § 621.

49. McKinney's N.Y.Bus.Corp.Law, §§ 602, 710.

29. McKinney's N.Y.Bus.Corp.Law, § 506(b).

30. McKinney's N.Y.Bus.Corp.Law, § 501.

31. McKinney's N.Y.Bus.Corp.Law, § 508(b).

32. McKinney's N.Y.Bus.Corp.Law, § 618.

33. McKinney's N.Y.Bus.Corp.Law, § 512(c).

34. McKinney's N.Y.Bus.Corp.Law, § 513.

35. McKinney's N.Y.Bus.Corp.Law, § 502.

36. McKinney's N.Y.Bus.Corp.Law, § 505.

37. McKinney's N.Y.Bus.Corp.Law, § 509.

(43) Express provision for executive committee and other committees of board of directors; [50]

(44) Express interested directors provision; [51]

(45) Express provisions for close corporations; [52]

(46) Express provision for informal action by shareholders; [53]

(47) Express provision for shareholder voting agreements; [54]

(48) Express authorization for articles of incorporation provisions as to control of directors; [55]

(49) Express authorization for articles of incorporation provisions fixing greater-than-normal quorum and/or voting requirements for shareholder and/or board of directors action; [56]

(50) Express provision for dual office-holding; [57]

(51) No residence, citizenship, shareholding, directorship requirements or other qualifications for officers; [58]

(52) Express provision for election and removal of officers by shareholders; [59]

(53) Express provision for nonjudicial dissolution under articles of incorporation provision; [60]

(54) Liberal express provisions for deadlock and judicial dissolution; [61]

(55) Express restrictions on shareholder derivative actions to secure judgment in favor of corporation; [62]

(56) Express provision for director and officer derivative actions; [63]

(57) Indemnification of litigation expenses of corporate personnel other than directors and officers left to common law and contract; [64]

(58) Express liberal provisions for indemnification of litigation expenses of directors and officers; provision for insurance; [65]

(59) Expeditious amendment of articles of incorporation (including elimination of preemptive rights, of cumulative voting, of cumulative preferred dividend arrearages), sale of assets, mortgage, guaranty, merger or consolidation, including short-merger of subsidiary into parent, nonjudicial and judicial dissolution; [66]

(60) No requirement of shareholder approval for mortgage or pledge of, or security interest in corporate property; [67]

(61) Reformulated, detailed appraisal procedures; [68]

(62) No requirement for keeping books and records (except record of shareholders and voting trust records) within New York; [69]

(63) Express provisions for open-end investment companies ("mutual funds"); [70]

---

50. McKinney's N.Y.Bus.Corp.Law, § 712.

51. McKinney's N.Y.Bus.Corp.Law, § 713.

52. See section 259 infra.

53. McKinney's N.Y.Bus.Corp.Law, § 615.

54. McKinney's N.Y.Bus.Corp.Law, § 620(a).

55. McKinney's N.Y.Bus.Corp.Law, §§ 620, 701.

56. McKinney's N.Y.Bus.Corp.Law, §§ 616, 709.

57. McKinney's N.Y.Bus.Corp.Law, § 715(e).

58. See McKinney's N.Y.Bus.Corp.Law, § 715.

59. McKinney's N.Y.Bus.Corp.Law, §§ 715(b), 716(a).

60. McKinney's N.Y.Bus.Corp.Law, § 1002.

61. McKinney's N.Y.Bus.Corp.Law, §§ 1104, 1105, 1111.

62. McKinney's N.Y.Bus.Corp.Law, §§ 626, 627.

63. McKinney's N.Y.Bus.Corp.Law, § 720(b).

64. McKinney's N.Y.Bus.Corp.Law, § 721.

65. McKinney's N.Y.Bus.Corp.Law, §§ 722–726.

66. McKinney's N.Y.Bus.Corp.Law, §§ 801, 803, 804, 909, 911, 202(a) (7), 908, 901–907, arts. 10, 11.

67. McKinney's N.Y.Bus.Corp.Law, § 911.

68. McKinney's N.Y.Bus.Corp.Law, § 623.

69. McKinney's N.Y.Bus.Corp.Law, §§ 621, 624.

70. McKinney's N.Y.Bus.Corp.Law, §§ 302(b) (5), 512(b), (c).

(64) Express provisions for small business investment companies; [71]

(65) State income tax treatment parallel to Subchapter S election under Internal Revenue Code.

Disadvantages of New York Incorporation

(1) Provisions restricting use of corporate names (applicable also to foreign corporations); [72]

(2) No express general provision permitting use of similar name with consent of prior user, even in cases of affiliated corporations; [73]

(3) Relatively high organization tax rates which discriminate against shares without par value (license fee rates on foreign corporations somewhat parallel); [74]

(4) Substantial annual franchise tax (applicable also to foreign corporations); [75]

(5) State share transfer tax (applicable also to foreign corporations); [76]

(6) Disqualification of corporation as incorporator (obviated by use of "accommodation" or "dummy" incorporator(s)); [77]

(7) Requirement that purposes be set forth in articles of incorporation; [78]

(8) Close administrative scrutiny and conservatism, with resulting filing delays;

(9) Unlimited personal liability of 10 largest beneficial shareholders for wages (very broadly defined to include fringe benefits) of wage earners employed by corporation (applicable only to closely-held domestic corporations); [79]

(10) No provision for informal board of directors action; [80]

(11) Equity insolvency as limitation on cash, bond, or property dividends and distributions and on purchase by corporation of its own shares [81] (applicable only to domestic corporations and foreign corporations doing business in New York not exempted under § 1320); [82]

(12) Presumption of concurrence by director (applicable only to domestic corporations and foreign corporations doing business in New York not exempted under § 1320); [83]

(13) Notice and disclosure requirements (applicable only to domestic corporations and foreign corporations doing business in New York not exempted under § 1320); [84]

(14) Extensive appraisal remedies; [85]

71. McKinney's N.Y.Bus.Corp.Law, § 302(b) (4).

72. McKinney's N.Y.Bus.Corp.Law, §§ 301, 302.

73. Cf. McKinney's N.Y.Bus.Corp.Law, § 302(b).

74. The New York organization tax rates equate one no par value share with $100 par value of par value shares; 1/20 of 1 percent of the par value (or 5 cents per $100 par value) of authorized par value shares; 5 cents per authorized no par value share. McKinney's N.Y.Tax Law, §§ 180, 181. In contrast, the Delaware rates for authorized par value shares are 1 cent per $100 par value up to $2,000,000, 1/2 cent per $100 par value over $2,000,000 and up to $20,000,000, and 1/5 cent per $100 par value over $20,000,000; for authorized no par value shares, 1/2 cent per share up to 20,000 shares, 1/4 cent per share over 20,000 shares to 2,000,000 shares, and 1/5 cent per share over 2,000,000 shares. Del.Gen. Corp.Law § 391 (1967). Both New York and Delaware have a $10 minimum organization tax.

75. McKinney's N.Y.Tax Law, § 210.

76. McKinney's N.Y.Tax Law, § 270.

77. McKinney's N.Y.Bus.Corp.Law, § 401.

78. McKinney's N.Y.Bus.Corp.Law, § 402(a) (2); cf. § 1304(a) (3).

79. McKinney's N.Y.Bus.Corp.Law, § 630.

80. See McKinney's N.Y.Bus.Corp.Law, § 708.

81. See McKinney's N.Y.Bus.Corp.Law, §§ 102(a) (8), 510(a), 513, 719(a) (1), (2).

82. See McKinney's N.Y.Bus.Corp.Law, §§ 1317, 1320.

83. McKinney's N.Y.Bus.Corp.Law, §§ 719(b), 1317, 1320.

84. McKinney's N.Y.Bus.Corp.Law, §§ 510, 511(f), (g), 515(d), 516(c), 517(a) (4), 519(f), 520, 1318, 1320.

85. See McKinney's N.Y.Bus.Corp.Law, §§ 806(b) (6), 910, 1005(a) (3) (A), 623.

(15) Exclusivity of statutory provisions for indemnification of directors and officers (applicable only to domestic corporations and foreign corporations doing business in New York not exempted under § 1320) ; [86]

(16) New statute, with elaborately detailed provisions, not yet construed by courts.

ADVANTAGES AND DISADVANTAGES OF INCORPORATION IN JURISDICTIONS FOLLOWING MODEL BUSI- BUSINESS CORPORATION ACT

95. The Model Business Corporation Act was well drafted to balance the interests of the public, corporations, shareholders, and management. Its original thesis was not to sacrifice sound principles in order to attract incorporation thereunder. In more recent years, revisions have tended to be more "permissive" or management-oriented. While some uniformity has been achieved, the biennial revisions and alternative and optional provisions of the Model Act, as well as the modifications introduced by jurisdictions which have followed it, require caution in making generalizations as to the advantages and disadvantages of incorporation in such jurisdictions.

The Model Business Corporation Act was well drafted from the point of view of language, coordination, style, and arrangement, codifying current laws and practices found to be sound in principle.

The Model Act does not preserve local recording requirements, use of the corporate seal, residential and other qualifications for directors, holdings of meetings within the state, conditions that might result in a *de facto* corporation, and most of the *ultra vires* doctrine. Until 1969, it required minimum paid-in capital of at least $1,000 before commencing business, and at least three persons as directors. For extraordinary corporate matters, shareholders once enjoyed mandatory voting rights, under certain circumstances as a class. Various accounting terms are defined.

Dividends payable in cash or property are restricted to unreserved earned surplus, with some exceptions, with alternative nimble-dividend provision. All other distributions in cash or property are treated as distributions from capital surplus.

Flexibility is achieved by permitting various provisions for the regulation of the corporation's internal affairs either in the articles of incorporation or in the bylaws, providing for waiver of notices and informal shareholder and board of directors action.

All in all, the original thesis of the Model Act was to attempt to preserve in proper balance the interests of the public, corporations, shareholders, and management, and not to seek to attract local incorporation business.[1] It expressly provides that nothing therein should be construed as authorizing the state to regulate the organization or the internal affairs of foreign corporations —a provision which may encourage out-of-state incorporation. Some uniformity has been achieved by the Model Act.

However, the Model Act has been revised from time to time and came to include alternative provisions (e. g., preemptive rights, cumulative voting, nimble-dividend provision) and optional provisions (e. g., share rights and options, emergency bylaws, removal of directors, actions by directors without a meeting, provisions relating to actions by shareholders, amendment of articles of incorporation in reorganization proceedings, merger of subsidiary corporation).[2] Even apart from these, jurisdictions follow-

---

86. McKinney's N.Y.Bus.Corp.Law, §§ 721, 1319, 1320.

1. See Garrett, Preface to 1950 Revision, Model Business Corporation Act, Handbook A, Committee on Continuing Legal Education, American Law Institute iv–x. But see Harris, "The Model Business Corporation Act: Invitation to Irresponsibility?", 50 Nw.U.L.Rev. 1 (1955). See C. Israels, Corporate Practice 651–722 (PLI 2d ed. 1969) (New York-Delaware-Model Act comparison).

2. See biennial addenda of revisions, alternative provisions, and optional sections.

ing the Model Act have introduced various modifications. Hence the making of generalizations concerning the advantages and disadvantages of incorporation in Model Act jurisdictions requires caution.[3]

In recent years, the philosophies underlying the Model Act revisions have become increasingly "permissive" or management-oriented, as witness the collaboration of its current draftsmen with the Delaware revisers and the co-drafting of a joint provision for indemnification of, and liability insurance for, directors, officers, and other corporate personnel—"America's most advanced provision for indemnification of officers and directors"!

DOING BUSINESS AS FOREIGN CORPORATION—IN GENERAL

96. The consequences of doing business in jurisdictions other than the jurisdiction of incorporation must be considered in selecting the jurisdiction of incorporation. By doing such business, the foreign corporation becomes subject to local litigation, regulation, and taxation, including requirements of formal admission. Various sanctions are imposed for noncompliance with admission requirements.

The judicial jurisdiction and legislative jurisdiction of the states over corporations and other forms of business enterprise are tending to be governed by the same ultimate constitutional standard: whether the state's contacts with a person, thing, or occurrence are sufficient to make the state's action reasonable. If reasonable there is no denial of due process or undue burden on interstate commerce. Practical considerations determine the extent to which a state will actually exercise the jurisdiction which it constitutionally may. Tending to similar effect are tests of venue and forum non conveniens.

A corporation "doing business" (or "transacting business") in jurisdictions other than its jurisdiction of incorporation be-

comes, to a greater or less extent, subject to the laws of such jurisdictions.[1]

Hence, the consequences of doing business in jurisdictions other than the jurisdiction of incorporation are factors relevant in the selection of the jurisdiction of incorporation.

By doing business or even engaging in an isolated transaction in a jurisdiction or having some contact with such jurisdiction, a foreign corporation theoretically enjoys the benefit and protection of the laws of such jurisdiction, and thereby becomes reasonably subject to such laws. This is the constitutional basis for making such foreign corporations amenable to process in such jurisdiction at least with respect to a cause of action which arises in such jurisdiction out of such activity and, where there is sufficient local activity, with respect to any cause of action.[2] A similar theory justifies subjecting such foreign corporation to reasonable taxation and regulation by such jurisdiction.[3]

When a foreign corporation does business in another jurisdiction, it can be required by the latter, as a condition on its admission, to qualify formally to do such business. This is so even when the business done involves interstate or foreign commerce, so long as there is some element of intrastate commerce.[4] State qualification statutes constitutionally may not require qualification

[§ 96]

1. See section 81 supra and sections 97, 98, 99 infra. W. Beaman, Doing Business in Other States (United States Corporation Company 1963); What Constitutes Doing Business in States Foreign to the State of its Creation (Corporation Trust Company 1968); 21 Corp.J. 3 (1954); 16 Corp.J. 101 (1944); Annot., 59 A.L.R.2d 1131 (1958).

2. See section 97 infra.

3. See sections 98, 99 infra.

4. Eli Lilly & Co. v. Sav-On-Drugs, Inc., 366 U.S. 276, 81 S.Ct. 1316, 6 L.Ed.2d 288 (1961), reh. denied 366 U.S. 978, 81 S.Ct. 1913, 6 L.Ed.2d 1268 (1961); Union Brokerage Co. v. Jensen, 322 U.S. 202, 64 S. Ct. 967, 88 L.Ed. 1227, 152 A.L.R. 1072 (1944). But see International Textbook Co. v. Pigg, 217 U.S. 91, 30 S.Ct. 481, 54 L.Ed. 678 (1910); International Text Book Co. v. Tone, 220 N.Y. 313, 115 N.E. 914

[§ 95]

3. Model Business Corporation Act Annotated (1960, Supp. 1962, 1964, 1966) (3 vols.). See section 3, n. 6 supra.

when the business done is exclusively inter-state or foreign commerce.[5]

Such qualification requirements have been constitutionally upheld under the privileges-and-immunities-of-citizens clause (because a corporation is not a citizen for such purpose),[6] under the interstate commerce clause (where qualification is reasonable and not a discriminatory or undue burden on in-terstate commerce), and under the due proc-ess clause (as a reasonable exercise of state police power).[7] Admission and domestica-tion procedures are hereinafter treated.[8]

Modern-day jurisdiction, whether legislative[9] or judicial,[10] is tending to be governed by the same ultimate standard: whether a state's contacts with a person, thing, or occurrence are sufficient to make the state's action reasonable.[11] If reason-able, there is no *un*due process or *un*due bur-den on interstate commerce.

Of course, what is reasonable for one pur-pose may not be for another.[12] While de-grees of regulation and rates of taxation (with possibilities of apportionment) are in-finite, suability can only be denied, limited to causes of action related to the local activi-ty or contact, or not so limited. Further-more, standards of reasonableness change with the times.

Most significantly of all, the rules govern-ing jurisdiction are tending to be the same for individuals, partnerships, other unincor-porated associations, and corporations.[13]

The extent to which a state will exercise such jurisdiction, within constitutional limi-tations, depends on the interplay of a variety of nonlegal considerations. As a result, dif-ferent states react differently with respect to subjecting the foreign business enterprise to litigation (including method of service of process, venue privilege, and doctrine of fo-rum non conveniens—the tests for which are increasingly resembling the tests of jurisdiction[14]), income tax, privilege or franchise tax, sales and use taxes, gross re-ceipts taxes, personal property (tangible and intangible) taxes, unemployment insurance taxes, occupation taxes, special licenses, an-nual and other reports, qualification, etc.

DOING BUSINESS AS FOREIGN COR-PORATION—AMENABILITY TO PROCESS

97. The corporation which qualifies as a foreign corporation in another state becomes subject to the in personam judicial jurisdiction of such state, which must afford reasonable notice and opportunity to be heard.

(1917). Quaere, whether a state can require qualifi-cation of a foreign corporation which is to carry out a federal contract in a federal area. U.S.Const. art. I, § 8, cl. 17; 22 Corp.J. 43 (1957–58). See also Seaboard Air Lines R. R. v. Daniel, 333 U.S. 118, 68 S.Ct. 426, 92 L.Ed. 580 (1948).

5. But see Harlan, J., concurring in Eli Lilly & Co. v. Sav-On-Drugs, Inc., 366 U.S. 276, 284, n. 1, 81 S. Ct. 1316, 1321 n. 1, 6 L.Ed.2d 288, 295 n. 1 (1961).

6. See section 89 supra. See, e. g., ABA–ALI Model Bus.Corp. Act § 141 ("The provisions of this Act shall apply to commerce with foreign nations and among the several states only in so far as the same may be permitted under the provisions of the Con-stitution of the United States").

7. See sections 98, 100 infra.

8. See sections 100, 136, 137 infra.

9. See sections 98, 99 infra.

10. See section 97 infra.

11. Restatement, Second, of Conflict of Laws § 42(1) (Proposed Official Draft, May 2, 1967), §§ 43c, 43f (Tentative Draft No. 3, Apr. 19, 1956). But see Eli Lilly & Co. v. Sav-On-Drugs, 366 U.S. 276, 81 S.Ct. 1316, 6 L.Ed.2d 288 (1961), reh. denied 366 U.S. 978, 81 S.Ct. 1913, 6 L.Ed.2d 1268 (1961).

12. Comparable to the fact that under older tests, "doing business" did not mean the same thing for

suability, regulation, taxation, and qualification. "Three Kinds of Doing Business", 23 Corp.J. 163 (1961–62). See Douglas, Frankfurter, Whittaker & Stewart, JJ., dissenting in Eli Lilly & Co. v. Sav-On-Drugs, Inc., 366 U.S. 276, 288, 81 S.Ct. 1316, 1324, 6 L.Ed.2d 288, 297 (1961).

13. Restatement, Second, of Conflict of Laws § 40 (Proposed Official Draft, May 2, 1967).

14. See sections 85, 86 supra and sections 97, 98, 99 infra. See Leflar, Cleary, Cowen, Schlesinger & Ehrenzweig, Round Table: "Transient Jurisdiction —Remnant of Pennoyer v. Neff", 9 J.Pub.L. 281 et seq. (1960); "Symposium on Conflicts of Law in Oklahoma", 18 Okla.L.Rev. 379 (1965).

The corporation, even though it has not qualified in another state, by engaging in any activity therein which can be imputed to it, becomes subject to that state's in personam jurisdiction over any cause of action arising from such activity. In a foreign state, the corporation might also have to answer for activity outside that state, provided the contact with that state is sufficiently substantial to make such result reasonable. Reasonableness depends upon such considerations as the nature of the contact with the forum state, convenience of the forum to the parties, and benefit and protection conferred by the law of the forum on such a corporation. Reasonable notice and opportunity to be heard must be afforded. Under such circumstances, the exercise of judicial jurisdiction is consistent with due process and not an undue burden on interstate or foreign commerce, and therefore constitutional under the federal constitution.

A state need not exercise its judicial jurisdiction to the full extent permitted by the federal constitution. The extent of a state's exercise of judicial jurisdiction is dependent upon the scope thereof as determined by applicable state statutes and court decisions which do not exceed the foregoing constitutional limitations.

In all cases, process on the corporation must be served in the manner prescribed by applicable statute or court rule.

The corporation can also be subject to in rem or quasi-in-rem jurisdiction under state and federal law.

The nature of the corporation has also created theoretical difficulties in litigation involving foreign corporations.

That a corporation is entitled to the protection of the due process clauses of the Fifth and Fourteenth Amendments and of the equal-protection-of-the-laws clause of the Fourteenth Amendment of the United States Constitution has already been shown.[1] So also has the rule that a corporation, unlike an unincorporated association, is deemed a citizen for purposes of federal diversity-of-citizenship jurisdiction.[2] Some detailed discussion of the corporation for purposes of

jurisdiction over the subject matter, jurisdiction over the person, venue, forum non conveniens, statutes of limitations, etc., is found in the context of the treatment of the corporation as a resident.[3]

One of the most perplexing corporate litigation problems has been the extent of a state's judicial jurisdiction over foreign corporations.[4]

Judicial jurisdiction grew out of a state's de facto power over persons and things within its territory. Hence for natural persons, physical presence—whether permanent or transitory—became the key test of in personam jurisdiction; appearance or consent would also suffice.[5]

3. See sections 82–87 supra.

4. Elder, "Jurisdiction over a Foreign Corporation", 19 S.C.L.Rev. 806 (1968); "Jurisdiction over Foreign Corporations", 25 Corp.J. 291 (1968); Developments in the Law, "State-Court Jurisdiction", 73 Harv.L.Rev. 909, 919–935 (1960). For a case permitting departure from the traditional rule requiring service of process on a foreign corporation within the state, see Meyer v. Indian Hill Farm, Inc., 258 F.2d 287 (2d Cir.1958).

5. See National Equipment Rental, Ltd. v. Szukhent, 375 U.S. 311, 84 S.Ct. 411, 11 L.Ed.2d 354 (1964); "Designation of Agent by Contract", 24 Corp.J. 83 (1964). The presence of a res within a jurisdiction itself, of course, may provide a basis for in rem or quasi-in-rem jurisdiction, as distinguished from in personam jurisdiction. Attachment of shares in a domestic corporation might provide sufficient basis; the Delaware share attachment provisions are especially liberal in this respect. Del.Gen.Corp. Law § 325 (1967). See sections 176, 354 infra. Developments in the Law, "State-Court Jurisdiction", 73 Harv.L.Rev. 909, 948–966 (1960). The classic case on in personam jurisdiction is the pre-14th amendment decision, Pennoyer v. Neff, 95 U.S. 714, 735, 24 L.Ed. 565, 573 (1878), which significantly contained the following dictum: "Neither do we mean to assert that a State may not require a non-resident entering into a partnership or association within its limits, or making contracts enforceable there, to appoint an agent or representative in the State to receive service of process and notice in legal proceedings instituted with respect to such partnership, association, or contracts, or to designate a place where such service may be made and notice given, and provide, upon their failure to make such appointment or to designate such place, that service may be made upon a public officer designated for that purpose, or in some other prescribed way, and that judgments rendered upon such service may not be binding upon the non-residents both within and without the State."

1. See section 80 supra.

2. See section 88 supra.

Domestic corporations are suable regardless of where the cause of action arose or whether the corporation is transacting any business in the state.[6] Usually as part of the incorporation procedure, the corporation must designate an agent for the service of process.[7] The principal federal constitutional inhibition is the due process requirement, in the sense of reasonable notice and opportunity to be heard.[8]

In personam jurisdiction over *foreign* corporations involves far more complications.[9]

Constitutionally there must be not only reasonable notice and opportunity to be heard,[10] but also observance of the additional federal due process requirement that there be sufficient basis for the exercise of judicial jurisdiction by the state. Furthermore, prosecution of an action may not, under the interstate commerce clause of the federal constitution, constitute an undue burden on interstate or foreign commerce.[11]

In the absence of other traditional common law requisites of *in personam* jurisdiction—local incorporation, express consent, or general appearance—"presence" of the corporation within the state was prerequisite to *in personam* jurisdiction over it. In the early days, the theory that a foreign corporation had no existence outside of its state of incorporation was a complicating factor.[12]

Later, activity within the forum by corporate agents was imputed to the corporation and, if found quantitatively sufficient, was denominated "doing business" (or "transacting business")[13] and held to provide ade-

6. Developments in the Law, "State-Court Jurisdiction", 73 Harv.L.Rev. 909, 933–934 (1960).

7. E.g., McKinney's N.Y.Bus.Corp. Law, § 304 (statutory designation of secretary of state), id. § 305 (optional additional designation of registered agent). See section 129 infra. Note, 4 Brooklyn L.Rev. 197 (1934). But see Berkman v. Weckerling, 247 Minn. 277, 77 N.W.2d 291 (1956) (requiring plaintiff to notify corporation's nonresident sole shareholder if plaintiff knows of his interest and his address, besides serving secretary of state). Statutes or court rules also often authorize service on domestic corporations through designated corporate officers or other personnel. See Annot., 71 A.L.R.2d 178 (1960).

8. Restatement, Second, of Conflict of Laws §§ 24, 41 (Proposed Official Draft, May 2, 1967); Developments in the Law, "State-Court Jurisdiction", 73 Harv.L.Rev. 909, 987–991 (1960).

9. 18 W. Fletcher, Private Corporations §§ 8709–8794 (rev. 1955, Supp.1968); Developments in the Law, "State-Court Jurisdiction", 73 Harv.L.Rev. 909, 919–933, 934–935 (1960); Comment, "State Jurisdiction over Foreign Corporations", 11 Hast.L.J. 460 (1960).

10. Chassis-Trak, Inc. v. Federated Purchaser, Inc., 179 F.Supp. 780 (D.N.J.1960); Speir v. Robert C. Herd & Co., 189 F.Supp. 432 (D.Md.1960).

11. Boyd v. Warren Paint & Color Co., 254 Ala. 687, 49 So.2d 559 (1950) (unlicensed foreign corporation engaged in interstate commerce in state held ame-

nable to process); Schlesinger v. Italian Line, 303 N.Y. 994, 106 N.E.2d 69 (1952); Banque de France v. Supreme Court, 287 N.Y. 483, 41 N.E.2d 65 (1942), appeal dismissed and cert. denied 316 U.S. 646, 62 S.Ct. 1279, 86 L.Ed. 1730 (1942); Matter of Baltimore Mail Steamship Co. v. Fawcett, 269 N.Y. 379, 199 N.E. 628, 104 A.L.R. 1068 (1936) (undue burden usually found where foreign cause of action by nonresident original claimant against foreign common carrier corporation); Restatement, Second, of Conflict of Laws § 47, Comment h (Proposed Official Draft, May 2, 1967); Developments in the Law, "State-Court Jurisdiction", 73 Harv.L.Rev. 909, 983–987 (1960).

12. See section 89 supra.

13. Developments in the Law, "State-Court Jurisdiction", 73 Harv.L.Rev. 909, 932–933 (1960). Transient presence has traditionally been sufficient for in personam jurisdiction over individuals. Where the alleged local activity of a foreign corporation was carried on by a subsidiary or affiliated corporation, the courts might disregard the corporate entities ("alter ego"), or recognize the entities and find an agency (rather than independent contractor status), and thus find the foreign corporation to be doing business. Cannon Mfg. Co. v. Cudahy Packing Co., 267 U.S. 333, 45 S.Ct. 250, 69 L.Ed. 634 (1925); Public Adm'r of County of New York v. Royal Bank of Canada, 19 N.Y.2d 127, 278 N.Y.S.2d 378, 224 N.E.2d 877 (1967); Bolger v. Dial-A-Style Leasing Corp., 159 Colo. 44, 409 P.2d 517 (1966); Botwinick v. Credit Exchange, Inc., 419 Pa. 65, 213 A.2d 349 (1965); Taca International Airlines, S.A. v. Rolls-Royce of England, Ltd., 15 N.Y.2d 97, 256 N.Y.S.2d 129, 204 N.E.2d 329 (1965); Empire Steel Corp. v. Superior Court, 56 Cal.2d 823, 17 Cal.Rptr. 150, 366 P.2d 502 (1961); see Cardozo, "A New Footnote in Erie v. Tompkins: 'Cannon, Is Overruled'", 36 N.C.L.Rev. 181 (1958); Comment, "Jurisdiction over Parent Corporations", 51 Calif.L.Rev. 574 (1963); Note, "Foreign Parent Held Subject to State Jurisdiction where Subsidiary was Operating within Forum", 37 N.Y.U.L.Rev. 760 (1962); Note, 56 Mich. L.Rev. 812 (1958); "Parent and Subsidiary Corporations", 19 Corp.J. 263 (1951); Annot., 18 A.L.R.2d 187 (1951); Buechner v. Farbenfabriken Bayer Ak-

quate jurisdictional basis. "Doing business" was rationalized, for conformity to the older theories, as tantamount to "presence" or "implied consent"—additional fictions to becloud further the fictitious corporate entity.

"Doing business" cases became legion. Generally, "doing business", for purposes of judicial jurisdiction, meant the doing of a series of similar acts for the purpose of thereby realizing pecuniary profit, or otherwise accomplishing an object, or doing a single act for such purpose with the intention of thereby initiating a series of such acts.[14] The courts often confused "doing business" for one purpose with "doing business" for another.[15]

A few legislatures or legislative draftsmen attempted at least partial definition for one or more purposes.[16]

Where "doing business" was found, the foreign corporation was held to be amenable to process on causes of action related to such business and, if the doing of business was of sufficient quantum, possibly even causes of action unrelated to such business.[17]

In most of the states, the doing of business by an unqualified foreign corporation constitutes an *implied* designation of the secretary of state or some other official or board designated by the statute as the corporation's agent for service of process. In states which do not have such a provision,[18]

<hr/>

tiengesellschaft, 38 Del.Ch. 490, 154 A.2d 684 (Sup. Ct.1959). For discussion of disregard of separate corporate entities for purposes of liability, see sections 146–148 infra. Where foreign partnerships or other unincorporated associations are defendants, "doing business" is not required if proper service within the jurisdiction can be effected. See note 36 infra.

14. Restatement, Second, of Conflict of Laws § 47, Comment a (Proposed Official Draft, May 2, 1967). One traditional distinction was between "mere solicitation", which did not constitute doing business, and "solicitation plus" (see note 33 infra), which did. "Mere solicitation" involved local solicitation by salesmen of a foreign corporation of orders for goods to be shipped from out of the state, terms F.O.B. shipping point (with title passing out of the state upon shipment), such orders being accepted by the corporation out of the state. Such a practice kept local activity to a minimum and interstate commerce to a maximum.

15. See W. Beaman, Doing Business in Other States (United States Corporation Company 1963); What Constitutes Doing Business in States Foreign to the State of its Creation (Corporation Trust Company 1968); "'Doing Business' Confusion", 24 Corp.J. 363 (1966); Caplin, "Doing Business", 5 Prac.Law. 72 (Oct.1959). The least local activity is necessary to subject the foreign corporation to service of process (exposing the corporation to suit as a defendant); more local activity is required to subject it to local taxation; the most local activity is required to subject it to qualification (nonqualification when required often limiting the corporation from suing as a plaintiff). 2 G. Hornstein, Corporation Law and Practice § 581 (1959); Comment, "Doing Business: A Re-Examination", 12 W.Res.L. Rev. 89 (1960).

16. To avoid the constitutional problems of affirmative definitions of "doing business", the statutory formulations have usually been negative, stating what does not constitute "doing business". ABA–ALI Model Bus.Corp.Act § 99 (specification of activities which do not constitute transacting business for purposes of qualification and tax sections, but no specification of activities which may or may not subject foreign corporation to service of process). About one-half of the jurisdictions contain somewhat similar definitions. Cf. Pa.Bus.Corp.Law § 1011 (1966); Shoultz v. Revolvator Co., 186 F.Supp. 61 (E.D.Pa.1959) (repeal of § 1011 (c) construed as reverting to common-law definition of doing business for service of process purposes). The provision was reenacted in 1959. See also Adams v. Boyer Chemical Co., 188 F.Supp. 815 (W.D.Pa.1960); Ravner v. Blank, 189 F.Supp. 471 (E.D.Pa.1960).

17. Perkins v. Benguet Consolidated Mining Co., 342 U.S. 437, 72 S.Ct. 413, 96 L.Ed. 485 (1952), reh. denied 343 U.S. 917, 72 S.Ct. 645, 96 L.Ed. 1332 (1952) (holding that federal constitution neither prevented state from exercising jurisdiction over foreign cause of action nor required it to do so). Quaere, as to effect of state constitutional provisions making corporations suable in like cases as natural persons. See section 14 supra. Shoffner v. Glenshaw Glass Co., 173 F.Supp. 850 (W.D.Pa.1959) (jurisdiction denied over foreign cause of action); Tauza v. Susquehanna Coal Co., 220 N.Y. 259, 115 N.E. 915 (1917) (jurisdiction asserted over foreign corporation for foreign cause of action); Restatement, Second, of Conflict of Laws § 47 (Proposed Official Draft, May 2, 1967). See section 86 supra.

18. "Unlicensed Foreign Corporations—Service on State Officials", 22 Corp.J. 303 (1960). New York, Since 1963, has provided for such implied designation. McKinney's N.Y.Bus.Corp. Law, § 307. The Delaware Constitution provides that "No foreign corporation shall do any business in this State through or by branch offices, agents or representatives located in this State, without having an au-

the result is that, in most cases,[19] service ordinarily can only be effected in the state if a corporate officer, director, or managing agent can be found and served in the state.[20]

Even after a corporation ceases to do business, it remains theoretically subject to suit for any cause of action related to the business which it did,[21] but service of process might prove impossible where there is no agent in the state upon whom process might be served.

Of course, if the foreign corporation formally qualifies to do business in the state,[22] a frequent requirement of such qualification is that the corporation *expressly* designate the secretary of state or some other person

for service of process in any action or proceeding against the corporation.[23] Even after formal surrender of its authority to do business in the state, the corporation would remain suable on causes of action arising in the state prior to such withdrawal. The statutory provisions vary greatly in detail.[24]

With the decisional law so developing, state legislatures began by statute to subject nonresidents doing certain acts within the state to increasing amenability to process for causes of action arising out of such acts. Most of the statutes related to specific activities with substantial public interest; Maryland, however, went almost the whole way.[25] Some of the statutes expressly applied only to nonresident natural persons;[26] others specifically covered nonresident natural persons and foreign corporations;[27] still others were less explicit, applying to nonresidents and leaving to the courts the assimilation of foreign corporations to nonresidents for purpos-

thorized agent or agents in the State upon whom legal process may be served." Del.Const. art. IX, § 5.

19. New York, like many states, has additional statutes impliedly designating the secretary of state as agent as the result of prescribed conduct: McKinney's N.Y.Vehicle & Traffic Law, § 52 (nonresident motorist or motor vehicle owner); McKinney's N.Y.Gen.Bus.Law § 250 (nonresident aviator or aircraft owner); Peters v. Robin Airlines, 281 App. Div. 903, 120 N.Y.S.2d 1 (2d Dep't 1953) (construed as applicable only to accidents within the state); McKinney's N.Y.Gen.Bus.Law, § 352-b (nonresident securities dealers); or requiring express designation by certain persons; McKinney's N.Y.Real Prop. Law, § 442-g (nonresident real estate brokers or salesmen); McKinney's N.Y.Gen.Bus.Law, § 352-a (foreign corporations offering their securities for sale in state). See also McKinney's N.Y.Bank.Law, § 34; McKinney's N.Y.Gen.Ass'ns Law, § 19; McKinney's N.Y.Ins.Law § 59; McKinney's N.Y.Soc. Welfare Law § 482. A federal statute might require designation of a process agent: 49 U.S.C.A., § 321 (motor carriers); Esperti v. Cardinale Trucking Corp., 263 App.Div. 46, 31 N.Y.S.2d 253 (2d Dep't 1941); or otherwise make one amenable to suit: Warsaw Convention, Berner v. United Airlines, Inc., 2 Misc.2d 260, 149 N.Y.S.2d 335 (Sup.Ct.1956), aff'd 3 A.D.2d 9, 157 N.Y.S.2d 884 (1st Dep't 1956), aff'd 3 N.Y.2d 1003, 170 N.Y.S.2d 340, 147 N.E.2d 732 (1957).

20. E.g., former N.Y.Civ.Prac.Act § 229 (repealed, effective Sept. 1, 1963).

21. French v. Gibbs Corp., 189 F.2d 787 (2d Cir. 1951); Confidential, Inc. v. Superior Court, 157 Cal.App.2d 75, 320 P.2d 546 (1958); Eure v. Morgan, Jones & Co., 195 Va. 678, 79 S.E.2d 862 (1954). Restatement, Second, of Conflict of Laws § 48 (Proposed Official Draft, May 2, 1967).

22. See sections 98, 100, 136 infra.

23. E.g., McKinney's N.Y.Bus.Corp.Law, § 304 (statutory designation of secretary of state), id. § 305 (optional additional designation of registered agent). See section 136 infra.

24. ABA–ALI Model Bus.Corp. Act § 112; Snyder v. Eastern Auto Distributors, Inc., 357 F.2d 552 (4th Cir.1966), cert. denied 384 U.S. 987, 86 S.Ct. 1889, 16 L.Ed.2d 1004 (1966); Jay's Stores, Inc. v. Ann Lewis Shops, Inc., 15 N.Y.2d 141, 256 N.Y.S.2d 600, 204 N. E.2d 638 (1965); Munch v. United Air Lines, Inc., 184 F.2d 630 (7th Cir.1950); DeBoard v. B. Perini & Sons, 140 W.Va. 833, 87 S.E.2d 462 (1955); Foster v. Morrison, 226 S.C. 149, 84 S.E.2d 344 (1954); "Suits Against Withdrawn Companies", 20 Corp.J. 283 (1953–54). Cf. Robinson Brick & Tile Co. v. Copperstate Supply Co., 100 Ariz. 28, 410 P.2d 96 (1966) (delayed tax clearance held to preserve corporation's suability); Apache Tank Lines, Inc. v. Beall Pipe & Tank Corp., 19 Utah 2d 104, 426 P.2d 623 (1967) (revocation of certificate of authority for failure to file reports held to end suability in like manner as formal withdrawal).

25. Md.Gen.Corp. Law, § 88(b) (1951) (enacted 1937), infra note 36.

26. E.g., former N.Y.Civ.Prac.Act § 229 (enacted 1940) (nonresident natural person doing business in state).

27. E.g., Iowa R.Civ.P. 56(g) (first enacted 1851) (corporation, company, or individual having, for transaction of any business, office or agency in any county other than in which principal resides).

es thereof.[28]   Except for the relatively few statutes phrased in terms of "doing business",[29] such concept was ignored. Hence for the first time, nonresident natural persons and foreign corporations were treated alike for purposes of judicial jurisdiction.

In a series of United States Supreme Court cases, such extensions of jurisdiction were upheld as nonviolative of the federal constitutional due process and interstate commerce clauses.[30]

Statutory extensions received impetus from the Supreme Court's opinion in International Shoe Co. v. State of Washington.[31] The defendant was a Delaware corporation, with its principal place of business in Missouri, which did little in the state of Washington except maintain a dozen or so salesmen whose authority was limited to the solicitation of orders. The defendant corporation failed to contribute to the state unemployment compensation fund with respect to the salesmen's services within the state. Notice of assessment was personally served upon one of the defendant's salesmen within the state, and a copy thereof was sent via registered mail to the corporation's Missouri office.[32] The corporation made a special appearance to object to jurisdiction. The Washington administrative agencies and state courts ruled that the corporation should pay the unpaid contributions on the ground that the local activity was at least

within the "solicitation plus" rule.[33]   On appeal to the United States Supreme Court, the corporation assigned as error that the state statutes as applied infringed the due process and commerce clauses.

The Supreme Court, per Stone, C. J., first disposed of the commerce clause argument by citing the federal statute authorizing the states to collect unemployment compensation funds notwithstanding that the employer or employee be engaged in interstate commerce.

With respect to the due process argument, the Supreme Court expressly repudiated the "presence" and "implied consent" theories, stating that the due process clause:

"requires only that in order to subject a defendant to a judgment in personam, if he be not present within the territory of the forum, he have certain minimum contacts with it such that the maintenance of the suit does not offend 'traditional notions of fair play and substantial justice.'"

"Minimum contacts", reasonableness, and "estimate of the inconvenience" were, according to the opinion, the relevant considerations. Even single or occasional acts of a corporate agent in the state might provide a basis for jurisdiction; the test was not quantitative but qualitative.

The "benefit" theory[34] also was expressed:

"to the extent that a corporation exercises the privilege of conducting activities within a state, it enjoys the benefits and protection of the laws of that

28. E.g., McKinney's N.Y.Vehicle & Traffic Law § 253 (enacted 1928) (nonresident motorist or motor vehicle owner). See section 87 supra.

29. E.g., Vt.Stat.Ann. tit. 12, § 855 (1959). See note 37 infra.

30. Hess v. Pawloski, 274 U.S. 352, 47 S.Ct. 632, 71 L.Ed. 1091 (1927) (nonresident motorist statute); Henry L. Doherty & Co. v. Goodman, 294 U.S. 623, 55 S.Ct. 553, 79 L.Ed. 1097 (1935) (sustaining Iowa statute, supra note 27).

31. 326 U.S. 310, 66 S.Ct. 154, 90 L.Ed. 95, 161 A.L.R. 1057 (1945).

32. Such procedure for substitute service was upheld as consistent with due process in the sense of reasonable notice and opportunity to be heard.

33. In the words of Stone, C. J., the Supreme Court of Washington was "of opinion that there was sufficient additional activities shown to bring the case within the rule frequently stated, that solicitation within a state by the agents of a foreign corporation plus some additional activities there are sufficient to render the corporation amenable to suit brought in the courts of the state to enforce an obligation arising out of its activities there." [italics added]. See note 14 supra.

34. See section 81 supra.

state. The exercise of that privilege may give rise to obligations; and, so far as those obligations arise out of or are connected with the activities within the state, a procedure which requires the corporation to respond to a suit brought to enforce them can, in most instances, hardly be said to be undue."

Applying these reformulated criteria to the rather systematic and continuous activity carried on in behalf of the defendant corporation in the state of Washington, the Supreme Court concluded that both the maintenance of the action and the imposition of the tax liability were consistent with due process.

Black, J., dissented on the ground that the appeal should have been dismissed as "frivolous". He objected to the majority's criteria of "fair play", "justice", and "reasonableness", and saw:

> "no reason for reading the due process clause so as to restrict a State's power to tax and sue those whose activities affect persons and businesses within the State provided proper service can be had."

The holding in the International Shoe Co. case was reasonably consistent with the prevailing rules. The case's significance lies in the court's express repudiation of the "doing business" (and "presence" and "implied consent") concepts. Substituted was the "traditional notions of fair play and substantial justice" test: that the defendant have "certain minimum contacts" with the forum in order that the maintenance of the action does not offend such notions. Shorn of its natural law verbalization, the test has come to be known as the "minimum contact" test. To some extent, it is a manifestation of the "benefit" theory: when state law protects a person, in some activity, the person should suffer any reasonable burden along with the benefit and answer for the legal consequences of such activity in the courts of the state. Such a reasonable burden can be nei-

ther *un*due process nor an *un*due burden on interstate commerce.[35]

With this authoritative relaxation of the federal constitutional restrictions on state exercise of judicial jurisdiction, some states began to expand their exercise of such jurisdiction.

Maryland had anticipated the trend, by providing as early as 1937 that every foreign corporation was subject to suit in the state by a resident of the state on any cause of action arising out of a contract made within the state or liability incurred for acts done within the state, whether or not such foreign corporation was doing or had done business in the state.[36]

Vermont, in 1947, had passed a statute in effect equating the making of a contract with a resident of the state to be performed wholly or partly in the state or the commission of a tort against a resident of the state with doing business for purposes of causes of action arising therefrom.[37]

A few other states enacted somewhat similar statutes.[38] The Illinois statute,[39] in par-

35. For a similar holding subjecting a foreign partnership to jurisdiction on basis of fair play, see Lewis Mfg. Co. v. Superior Court in and for Los Angeles County, 140 Cal.App.2d 245, 295 P.2d 145 (1956).

36. Md.Ann.Code art. 23, § 92(d) (1957) (superseded by Md.Ann.Code art. 75, §§ 94–100 (1965)). See Pan-American Consulting Co. v. Corbu Industrial, S. A., 219 Md. 564, 150 A.2d 251 (1959) (unqualified foreign corporation held not suable on contract when last act necessary to make contract binding occurred without the state).

37. Vt.Stat.Ann. tit. 12, § 855 (1959); Notes, 18 U. Chi.L.Rev. 792 (1951); 16 U.Chi.L.Rev. 523 (1949); 23 St. John's L.Rev. 126 (1948).

38. E.g., Illinois, Minnesota, North Carolina, West Virginia. See Dahlberg Co. v. American Sound Products, Inc., 179 F.Supp. 928 (D.Minn.1959); Comment, "Problems Created by Statutory Definitions of the Scope of State Court Jurisdiction in Suits Against Foreign Corporations", 106 U.Pa.L. Rev. 1049 (1948); Note, "Recent Interpretations of 'Doing Business' Statutes", 44 Iowa L.Rev. 345 (1959).

39. Ill.Rev.Stat.1957, c. 110, § 17, sustained in Nelson v. Miller, 11 Ill.2d 378, 143 N.E.2d 673 (1957); National Gas Appliance Corp. v. A B Electrolux, 270

ticular, was singled out for considerable comment.[40]

With minor exceptions,[41] these statutes were upheld by state and lower federal courts.[42]

Meanwhile, the Supreme Court in three opinions in a single case, expressed approval, although four justices joined in a dissenting opinion which seemed to lapse into pre-International Shoe Co. emphasis on "presence".[43]

Not until late in 1957 in McGee v. International Life Insurance Co.,[44] was the dictum in the International Shoe Co. case applied by the Supreme Court to a far-reaching state statutory provision. In the McGee case, a California insured purchased, presumably through the mail, a life insurance policy from an Arizona corporation which maintained no office and had no agents in California. Thereafter, the defendant, International Life Insurance Company, a Texas corporation without office or agents in California, was by mail substituted as insurer. There was no evidence that the defendant had ever solicited or done any insurance business in California apart from this policy. Upon the death of the insured, his beneficiary sued the defendant in a California court, effecting service by registered mail on the defendant at its principal office in Texas, pursuant to the California unauthorized insurer statute.[45] The defendant did not appear in the California action, and default judgment was taken against it. The beneficiary then sought to enforce this judgment in Texas. The Texas court dismissed, primarily on the ground that the California statute was enacted after the issuance of the policy and could not be retroactively applied.

The Supreme Court unanimously reversed, holding (per Black, J.) that the "permissible scope of state jurisdiction over foreign corporations and other non-residents" was expanding, in part attributable to the fundamental transformation of the national economy over the years, and did not preclude California from exercising jurisdiction over the contract in litigation since the contract had a "substantial connection" with California. This connection was delineated: delivery of the contract there; mailing of premiums there, residence of insured in California

---

F.2d 472 (7th Cir.1959), cert. denied, 361 U.S. 959, 80 S.Ct. 584, 4 L.Ed.2d 542 (1960); Haas v. Fancher Furniture Co., 156 F.Supp. 564 (N.D.Ill.1957).

40. See Comment, "Section 17(1) (a) of the Illinois Civil Practice Act and the Limits of Due Process", 55 Nw.U.L.Rev. 238 (1960); Comment, "Jurisdiction Over Non-residents Under Section 17 of the Illinois Civil Practice Act", 53 Nw.U.L.Rev. 79 (1958); Note, 54 Mich.L.Rev. 1026 (1956).

41. See Hanson v. Denckla, infra note 47; Trippe Mfg. Co. v. Spencer Gifts, Inc., 270 F.2d 821 (7th Cir.1959); L. D. Reeder Contractors v. Higgins Indus., 265 F.2d 768 (9th Cir.1959); Mueller v. Steelcase, Inc., 172 F.Supp. 416 (D.Minn.1959); Grobark v. Addo Mach. Co., 16 Ill.2d 426, 158 N.E.2d 73 (1959); Erlanger Mills, Inc., v. Cohoes Fibre Mills, Inc., 239 F.2d 502 (4th Cir.1956) (sale of goods); Putnam v. Triangle Publications, Inc., 245 N.C. 432, 96 S.E.2d 445 (1957) (tortious conduct). But see Shepard v. Rheem Mfg. Co., 249 N.C. 454, 106 S.E.2d 704 (1959) (upholding application of statute). Sobeloff, "Jurisdiction of State Courts Over Non-Residents in Our Federal System", 43 Cornell L.Q. 196 (1957); Cardozo, "The Reach of the Legislature and the Grasp of Jurisdiction", 43 Cornell L.Q. 210 (1957).

42. Hutchinson v. Boyd & Sons Press Sales, Inc., 188 F.Supp. 876 (D.Minn.1960); Atkins v. Jones & Laughlin Steel Corp., 258 Minn. 571, 104 N.W.2d 888 (1960); Beck v. Spindler, 256 Minn. 543, 99 N.W. 2d 670 (1959); Compania de Astral, S.A. v. Boston Metals Co., 205 Md. 237, 107 A.2d 357, 108 A.2d 372 (dissenting opinion), 49 A.L.R.2d 646 (1954), cert. denied, 348 U.S. 943, 75 S.Ct. 365, 99 L.Ed. 738 (1955); Smyth v. Twin State Improvement Corp., 116 Vt. 569, 80 A.2d 664 (1951); Davis-Wood Lumber Co., Inc. v. Ladner, 210 Miss. 863, 50 So.2d 615 (1951); Johns v. Bay State Abrasive Products Co., 89 F. Supp. 654 (D.Md.1950). See Evans, "Expanding Jurisdiction Over Foreign Corporations", 37 Cornell L.Q. 458 (1952); Comment, 22 U.Chi.L.Rev. 674 (1955).

43. Travelers Health Ass'n v. Virginia, 339 U.S. 643, 70 S.Ct. 927, 94 L.Ed. 1154 (1950). (The dissenters contended that minimum contact required at least activity within the state by a corporate agent).

44. 355 U.S. 220, 78 S.Ct. 199, 2 L.Ed.2d 223 (1957) (8–0). There was no issue of lack of notice or opportunity to be heard.

45. West's Ann.Cal.Ins.Code §§ 1610–1620 (1955) (service also of two copies of process on California insurance commissioner).

when he died. To require that the action be brought elsewhere, said the court would have been inconvenient to California residents; to require the foreign corporation to defend in California was not so inconvenient or unreasonable as to amount to a denial of due process. Retroactive application of the statute was upheld as remedial.[46]

Subsequent to the McGee case, the Supreme Court impressed one limitation on its relaxation of constitutional requirements. In Hanson v. Denckla,[47] the Court held that it was essential that there be some act by which the foreign corporate defendant has *purposefully* availed itself "of the privilege of conducting activities within the forum State, thus invoking the benefits and protections of its laws". In that case, the local contacts resulted from a settlor's moving to Florida, having the defendant foreign corporation remit trust funds to her there, and her exercising powers of appointment under the trust agreement there.

Despite the authoritative relaxation of the constitutional limitations in the International Shoe Co. and McGee cases, many courts

continued to apply the old "doing business" test,[48] on the ground that such changes in the state law should be effected by legislation and not by judicial decision.[49]

As previously indicated, some state statutes had attempted to stretch judicial jurisdiction as fully as constitutional limitations permitted.[50]

Practically all of the states have enacted so-called "long-arm" or "single-act" statutes.[51] The language in which they are couched varies.[52] In each case, of course,

46. See Reese, "Judicial Jurisdiction over Non-Residents; The Impact of McGee v. International Life Insurance Company", 13 Record of N.Y.C.B.A. 139 (1958); Hoffman, "The Plastic Frontiers of State Judicial Power over Non-Residents: McGee v. International Life Insurance Company", 24 Brooklyn L.Rev. 291 (1958); Freeman, "McGee v. International Life Insurance Co. and the Amenability of Foreign Corporations to Suit", 13 Bus.Law. 515 (1958); Developments in the Law, "State-Court Jurisdiction", 73 Harv.L.Rev. 909, 919–933, 934–935 (1960). Lower court cases have gone even further. Schutt v. Commercial Travelers Mutual Accident Ass'n, 229 F.2d 158 (2d Cir.1956); Zacharakis v. Bunker Hill Mut. Ins. Co., 281 App.Div. 487, 120 N.Y.S.2d 418 (1st Dep't 1953) (McKinney's N.Y.Ins.Law, § 59–a); Pugh v. Oklahoma Farm Bureau Mutual Insurance Co., 159 F.Supp. 155 (E.D.La.1958) (Oklahoma insurance corporation held suable in Louisiana under nonresident motorist statute by Texas resident injured by Oklahoma insured in Louisiana highway accident on basis of sole contact of insurance coverage of risk at time of accident).

47. 357 U.S. 235, 78 S.Ct. 1228, 2 L.Ed.2d 1283 (1958) (5–4); Kurland, "The Supreme Court, the Due Process Clause and the In Personam Jurisdiction of State Courts: From Pennoyer to Denckla: A Review", 25 U.Chi.L.Rev. 569 (1958).

48. Bomze v. Nardis Sportswear, Inc., 165 F.2d 33 (2d Cir.1948). Compare WSAZ, Inc. v. Gearhart, 254 F.2d 242 (6th Cir.1958) (transmitting television program into state in fulfillment of contracts for advertising within state held to constitute doing business by television station in state for substituted service purposes), with McGriff v. Charles Antell, Inc., 123 Utah 166, 256 P.2d 703 (1953) (advertiser soliciting orders through local television station held not to be doing business within state).

49. Ames v. Senco Products, Inc., 1 A.D.2d 658, 146 N.Y.S.2d 298, (1st Dep't 1955), appeal granted 1 A.D.2d 774, 149 N.Y.S.2d 212 (1st Dep't 1956).

50. Comment, "Problems Created by Statutory Definitions of the Scope of State Court Jurisdiction in Suits Against Foreign Corporations", 106 U.Pa.L. Rev. 1049 (1958). Under the federal constitution, a state need not exercise the full scope of judicial jurisdiction permissible under the due process and commerce clauses; quaere, as to possible application of state constitutional provisions. See note 17 supra.

51. For list of statutes, see "Jurisdiction over Foreign Corporations", 25 Corp.J. 291 (1968). Johnson, "How Minimum Is 'Minimum Contact'? An Examinaton of 'Long Arm' Jurisdiction", 9 S. Tex.L.J. 184 (1967); Comment, "Long-Arm Jurisdiction Over Publishers: To Chill A Mocking Word", 67 Colum.L.Rev. 342 (1967); " 'Long-Arm' Statutes", 24 Corp.J. 291 (1966); Annot., 27 A.L.R.3d 397 (1969); 24 A.L.R.3d 532 (1969) (torts); 24 A.L.R.3d 551 (1969) (contracts); 20 A.L.R.3d 957, 1201 (1968).

52. Jacobsen, "Enlargement of Jurisdiction Over Unlicensed Foreign Corporations in Missouri—The 'Single-Act Statute' ", 31 U.Kan.City L.Rev. 292 (1967); Weissman, "The Georgia Long Arm Statute: A Significant Advance in the Concept of Personal Jurisdiction", 4 Ga.St.B.J. 13 (1967); Comment, "Interpretive Problems of Ohio's Long-Arm Statute", 19 Case W. Res.L.Rev. 347 (1968); Comment, "Personal Jurisdiction over Nonresidents— The Louisiana 'Long-Arm' Statute", 40 Tul.L.Rev. 366 (1966); Comment, "Expanded Basis of Jurisdiction—An Examination of Tennessee's New 'Long-Arm' Statute", 18 Vand.L.Rev. 1484 (1965); Comment, "South Dakota's Single Act Statute: In Per-

the exercise of *in personam* jurisdiction depends upon the sufficiency of contracts between the defendant and the forum state.[53]

As the result of studies begun in 1958, the Uniform Interstate and International Procedure Act[54] was approved by the National Conference of Commissioners on Uniform State Laws in 1962.

Section 1.03 of the Uniform Act [Personal Jurisdiction Based upon Conduct] reads:

"(a) A court may exercise personal jurisdiction over a person, who acts directly or by an agent, as to a [cause of action] [claim for relief] arising from the person's

(1) transacting any business in this state;

(2) contracting to supply services or things in this state;

(3) causing tortious injury by an act or omission in this state;

(4) causing tortious injury in this state by an act or omission outside this state if he regularly does or solicits business, or engages in any other persistent course of conduct, or derives substantial revenue from goods used or consumed or services rendered, in this state; [or]

(5) having an interest in, using, or possessing real property in this state[; or

(6) contracting to insure any person, property, or risk located within this state at the time of contracting].

(b) When jurisdiction over a person is based solely upon this Section, only a [cause of action] [claim for relief] arising from acts enumerated in this Section may be asserted against him."

The New York statute became effective in 1963 and was revised in 1966. As to a cause of action arising from any of the acts enumerated in the statute, it confers personal jurisdiction over any non-domiciliary, who in person or through an agent: (1) transacts any business within the state, or (2) commits a tortious act within the state (except defamation), or (3) commits a tortious act outside the state causing injury to a person or property within the state (except defamation) if he (i) regularly does or solicits business, or engages in any other persistent course of conduct, or derives substantial revenue from goods used or consumed or services rendered in the state, or (ii) expects or should reasonably expect the act to have consequences in the state and derives substantial revenue from interstate or international commerce; or (4) owns, uses or possesses any real property situated within the state.[55] Litigation concerning its application has flooded the courts.[56]

sonam Jurisdiction Over Foreign Corporations", 9 S.D.L.Rev. 188 (1964); Note, "Jurisdiction under New Ohio 'Long-Arm' Statute—Problems of Interpretation and Application", 35 U.Cin.L.Rev. 157 (1966); Note, "The Virginia 'Long Arm' Statute", 51 Va.L.Rev. 719 (1965).

53. Duple Motor Bodies, Ltd. v. Hollingsworth, 417 F.2d 231 (9th Cir. 1969); Gelfand v. Tanner Motor Tours, Ltd., 385 F.2d 116 (2d Cir.1967); Curtis Pub'g Co. v. Golino, 383 F.2d 586 (5th Cir.1967); Buckley v. New York Post Corp., 373 F.2d 175 (2d Cir.1967); New York Times Co. v. Connor, 365 F.2d 567 (5th Cir.1966); Elliott v. Edwards Engineering Corp., 364 F.2d 991 (10th Cir.1966); Buckley v. New York Times Co., 338 F.2d 470 (5th Cir.1964); Insull v. New York World-Telegram Corp., 273 F.2d 166 (7th Cir. 1959), cert. denied 362 U.S. 942, 80 S.Ct. 807, 4 L.Ed. 2d 770 (1960); Marshall Egg Transport v. Bender-Goodman Co., 275 Minn. 534, 148 N.W.2d 161 (1967); O'Brien v. Lanpar Co., 399 S.W.2d 340 (Tex.Sup.Ct. 1966); Pavalon v. Fishman, 30 Wis.2d 228, 140 N.W. 2d 263 (1966); Golden Gate Hop Ranch v. Velsicol Chemical Corp., 66 Wash.2d 469, 403 P.2d 351 (1965), cert. denied 382 U.S. 1025, 86 S.Ct. 644, 15 L.Ed.2d 539 (1966); Andersen v. National Presto Industries, Inc., 257 Iowa 911, 135 N.W.2d 639 (1965); Byham v. National Cibo House Corp., 265 N.C. 50, 143 S.E. 2d 225 (1965); Abney Mills, Inc. v. Tri-State Motor Co., 265 N.C. 61, 143 S.E.2d 235 (1965); Roy v. North American Newspaper Alliance, Inc., 106 N.H. 92, 205 A.2d 844 (1964); Nixon v. Cohn, 62 Wash.2d 987, 385 P.2d 305 (1963); Gray v. American Radiator & Standard Sanitary Corp., 22 Ill.2d 432, 176 N. E.2d 761 (1961).

54. 9B U.L.A. 307 (1966); approved 1962; adopted in Arkansas, Michigan, Nebraska, Oklahoma, and the Virgin Islands.

55. McKinney's N.Y. CPLR § 302.

56. Standard Wine & Liquor, Inc. v. Bombay Spirits Co., 20 N.Y.2d 13, 281 N.Y.S.2d 299, 228 N.E.2d 367 (1967); Platt Corp. v. Platt, 17 N.Y.2d 234, 270 N.

Whether or not a state's "long-arm" or "single-act" statute is substantive and therefore entirely prospective in application only to claims arising after its effective date,[57] or procedural and therefore applicable to actions commenced after its effective date on preexisting claims,[58] is a matter of construction.[59]

In federal diversity cases, the federal courts have tended to apply the rule of the state where they are sitting on the ground that Rule 4 of the Federal Rules of Civil Procedure [60] refers to the "manner" of service

to state law or that jurisdiction over the person is substantive.[61]

From the Supreme Court cases, it seems clear that any activity within a state which can be imputed to a foreign corporation can constitutionally subject the corporation to that state's in *personam* jurisdiction over any cause of action arising from such activity. This seems reasonable; if the act of someone within the state can be imputed to the corporation for purposes of the alleged liability, the lesser consequence of the corporation's being answerable in the local courts for trial of the issue of liability should follow; in short, burden and benefit under the law of the state should go together. The corporation might also have to answer for out-of-state activity which as a consequence wrongs someone within the jurisdiction, provided the local contact is sufficiently substantial to make such result reasonable. Here the "benefit" theory loses some of its support. As stated in the proposed revision of the Restatement of Conflict of Laws, judicial jurisdiction exists, assuming a state by statute or decisions exercises it, whenever the state's contacts with a person, thing, or occurrence are sufficient to

Y.S.2d 408, 217 N.E.2d 134 (1966) (tort "committed" by omission—failure of nonresident director to attend board of directors meetings in New York—held not within New York long-arm statutory reference to commission of "tortious act within the state"); Longines-Wittnauer Watch Co. v. Barnes & Reinecke, Inc., Feathers v. McLucas, Singer v. Walker, 15 N.Y.2d 443, 261 N.Y.S.2d 8, 209 N.E.2d 68 (1965); Bryant v. Finnish Nat'l Airline, 15 N.Y.2d 426, 260 N.Y.S.2d 625, 208 N.E.2d 439 (1965); Frummer v. Hilton Hotels International, Inc., 19 N.Y.2d 533, 281 N.Y.S.2d 41, 227 N.E.2d 851 (1967), cert. denied 389 U.S. 923, 88 S.Ct. 241, 19 L.Ed.2d 266 (1967); Katz & Son Billiard Products, Inc. v. G. Correale & Sons, 20 N.Y.2d 903, 285 N.Y.S.2d 871, 232 N.E.2d 864 (1967), aff'g 26 A.D.2d 52, 270 N.Y. S.2d 672 (1st Dep't 1966); Saratoga Harness Racing Ass'n v. Moss, 20 N.Y.2d 733, 283 N.Y.S.2d 55, 229 N.E.2d 620 (1967), aff'g 26 A.D.2d 486, 275 N.Y. S.2d 888 (3d Dep't 1967). Compare Liquid Carriers Corp. v. American Marine Corp., 375 F.2d 951 (2d Cir.1967), with McKee Electric Co. v. Rauland-Borg Corp., 20 N.Y.2d 377, 283 N.Y.S.2d 34, 229 N.E.2d 604 (1967) (negotiation of contract in state). See also Bard v. Steele, 28 A.D.2d 193, 283 N.Y.S.2d 930 (3d Dep't 1967) (listed New York telephone number for New York customers' use held sufficient); Homburger, "The Reach of New York's Long-Arm Statute: Today and Tomorrow", 15 Buffalo L.Rev. 61 (1965); Meisel, "Expanded Jurisdiction over Foreign Corporations—The Single Act Concept under CPLR Section 302", 36 N.Y.St.B.J. 424 (1964).

57. State ex rel. Clay Equipment Corp. v. Jensen, 363 S.W.2d 666 (Mo.1963); Krueger v. Rheem Mfg. Co., 260 Iowa 678, 149 N.W.2d 142 (1967).

58. Carvette v. Marion Power Shovel Co., 157 Conn. 92, 249 A.2d 58 (1968); Kilbreath v. Rudy, 16 Ohio St.2d 70, 242 N.E.2d 658 (1968); Simonson v. International Bank, 14 N.Y.2d 281, 251 N.Y.S.2d 433, 200 N.E.2d 427 (1964); Kilian v. Allegheny County Distributors, Inc., 409 Pa. 344, 185 A.2d 517 (1962).

59. Comment, "Retroactive Expansion of State Court Jurisdiction over Persons", 63 Colum.L.Rev. 1105 (1963); Annot., 19 A.L.R.3d 138 (1968).

60. Fed.R.Civ.P. 4(d) (3), 4(d) (7). See Comment, "Federal Jurisdiction over Foreign Corporations

and the *Erie* Doctrine", 64 Colum.L.Rev. 685 (1964); Comment, "Personal Jurisdiction over Foreign Corporations in Diversity Actions: A Tiltyard for the Knights of *Erie*", 31 U.Chi.L.Rev. 752 (1964); "Service of Process in Diversity Cases", 23 Corp.J. 63 (1961); Annot., 6 A.L.R.3d 1103 (1966). In 1963, Fed.R.Civ.P. 4 was expanded in three respects: (a) Permitting service beyond the state within 100 miles; (b) Incorporation by reference of state jurisdictional laws; and (c) Incorporation by reference of state quasi-in-rem jurisdiction. Vestal, "Expanding the Jurisdictional Reach of the Federal Courts: The 1963 Changes in Federal Rule 4", 38 N.Y.U.L. Rev. 1053 (1963); Comment, "Use of State Statutes by Federal District Courts in Extraterritorial Service of Process", 27 U.Chi.L.Rev. 751 (1960).

61. Arrowsmith v. United Press International, 320 F.2d 219, 6 A.L.R.3d 1072 (2d Cir.1963) (en banc), overruling Jaftex Corp. v. Randolph Mills, Inc., 282 F.2d 508 (2d Cir.1960); Walker v. General Features Corp., 319 F.2d 583 (10th Cir. 1963); Partin v. Michaels Art Bronze Co., 202 F.2d 541 (3d Cir.1953); Graham & Ross Mercantile Co. v. Sprout, Waldron & Co., 174 F.Supp. 551 (D.Mont.1959); Shoultz v. Revolvator Co., 186 F.Supp. 61 (E.D.Pa.1959).

make an action based thereon reasonable.[62] Reasonableness, in turn, depends upon such considerations as the nature of the contact, convenience of the forum to the parties,[63] and benefit conferred by local law. Finally, the same rules should apply to all parties— individuals, partnerships, other unincorporated associations, and corporations.[64]

In all cases, process on the corporation, of course, must be served in the manner prescribed by applicable statute or court rule.[65]

The corporation might also be subject to in rem or quasi-in-rem jurisdiction under state and federal law.[66]

62. Restatement, Second, of Conflict of Laws §§ 28–39, 42–52 (Proposed Official Draft, May 2, 1967).

63. Kilpatrick v. Texas & Pacific Ry., 166 F.2d 788 (2d Cir.1948), cert. denied 335 U.S. 814, 69 S.Ct. 32, 93 L.Ed.2d 369 (1948). See section 86 supra.

64. Restatement, Second, of Conflict of Laws §§ 24, 25, 27–40 (Proposed Official Draft, May 2, 1967). See note 17 supra. But see section 50, n. 7 supra.

65. E. g., Fed.R.Civ.P. 4; McKinney's N.Y. CPLR, §§ 311, 313; McKinney's N.Y.Bus.Corp.Law, §§ 304, 305, 307, 402(a) (8), 1304(a) (5), (6); McDonald v. Ames Supply Co., 22 N.Y.2d 111, 291 N.Y.S.2d 328, 238 N.E. 2d 726 (1968) (delivery of summons to proper person by another upon whom served held insufficient); Erdman v. Nat'l Indemnity Co., 180 Neb. 133, 141 N. W.2d 753 (1966); Miller v. Kiamesha-Concord, Inc., 420 Pa. 604, 218 A.2d 309 (1966); First Jackson Securities Corp. v. B. F. Goodrich Co., 253 Miss. 519, 176 So.2d 272 (1965); Richards v. Hamon, 54 Del. Ch. 323, 178 A.2d 140 (Sup.Ct.1962); Annot., 17 A. L.R.3d 625 (1968), 9 A.L.R.3d 738 (1966), 11 L.Ed.2d 1036 (1965). See Port Chester Electrical Co. v. Ronbed Corp., 28 A.D.2d 1008, 284 N.Y.S.2d 9 (2d Dep't 1967) (service of single summons upon officer of corporate defendant who was also individual defendant held effective service on both defendants). As to enforceability of default judgment against corporation failing to receive notice from person served, see Marquez v. Rapid Harvest Co., 99 Ariz. 363, 409 P.2d 285 (1965); Dunn v. Royal Brothers Co., 111 Ga.App. 322, 141 S.E.2d 546 (1965). See note 13 supra. The corporation should, of course, keep current its filings as to registered agent and address for forwarding of process served on secretary of state. See Meadis v. Atlantic Construction & Supply Co., 212 A.2d 613 (D.C.Ct.App.1965); Cascione v. Acme Equipment Corp., 23 A.D.2d 49, 258 N.Y.S.2d 234 (1st Dep't 1965).

66. See sections 176, 354 infra.

DOING BUSINESS AS FOREIGN COR-PORATION—REGULATION

98. **The domestic corporation is subject to the legislative jurisdiction of its state of incorporation, subject to some constitutional limitations.**

The foreign corporation can be excluded by a state from engaging in local intrastate business or admitted subject to constitutional conditions, including requirements of formal qualification. Even foreign corporations and other forms of business enterprise which cannot constitutionally be excluded or required to qualify can be subjected to reasonable regulation under the state police power, without violating due process of law or constituting an undue burden on interstate commerce. No state has exercised more than minor aspects of its constitutional power to regulate foreign corporations doing business in the state.

Theories of corporate personality have been complicating factors in defining the constitutional limitations on state regulation and taxation of foreign corporations.[1]

Since a corporation was regarded as a creation of law, and law was territorial, the corporation was first thought to have no existence outside of its jurisdiction of incorporation. Since it was not a citizen for purposes of the privileges-and-immunities-of-citizens clause of the federal constitution,[2] it could be excluded from other states or admitted

1. See G. Henderson, The Position of Foreign Corporations in American Constitutional Law (1918). Regulation and taxation of domestic corporations is not without constitutional limitations, especially the due process and equal protection of the laws clauses of the 14th amendment, which require that any exercise of the state police power be reasonable, and the provision against state impairment of the obligation of contracts. A practical limitation is that onerous regulation or taxation of domestic corporations will stimulate incorporation or reincorporation in other states. From the point of view of local presence, domicile, residence, consent, activity, consequences, contact, or things, legislative jurisdiction over domestic corporations is well based. Restatement, Second, of Conflict of Laws § 43f (Tentative Draft No. 3, Apr. 19, 1956). See Walker "Foreign Corporation Laws: The Loss of Reason", 47 N.C.L.Rev. 1 (1968); Walker, "Foreign Corporation Laws: Current Account", 47 N.C.L.Rev. 733 (1969).

2. See section 89 supra.

subject to conditions. However, it could not be excluded from engaging in interstate or foreign commerce,[3] and the conditions imposed on its admission to do intrastate business could not be unconstitutional conditions.[4] If it could not be excluded, it could not be required to qualify. This was the orthodox approach in defining the constitutional limitations on a state's legislative jurisdiction over foreign corporations (as distinguished from judicial jurisdiction previously discussed[5]). The result was that state statutes required formal qualification (with attendant regulation) by foreign corporations engaging in intrastate commerce ("doing business" for such purposes being quantitatively greater than "doing business" for purposes of amenability to process), but not by either foreign unincorporated business enterprises similarly engaged or foreign corporations engaging in interstate or foreign commerce.

The symmetry of these rules was first disturbed by states' extending their formal qualification requirements to unincorporated associations which resembled corporations, like the business trust and joint-stock company,[6] and the United States Supreme Court's approval thereof.[7]

Analogous Supreme Court cases placed even less reliance on whether or not the business enterprise was a citizen for purposes of the privileges-and-immunities-of-citizens clause. The view developed that even if persons constitutionally could not be excluded, they could be reasonably regulated. The test became whether or not the regulation was a reasonable exercise of the state police power.[8] As a result, nonresident individuals, partnerships, and other unincorporated associations were regulated and sometimes even required to secure licenses to do local business or to engage in certain local activities, or rarely to qualify.[9]

Meanwhile, engaging in interstate or foreign commerce ceased to immunize a foreign

---

3. Congress, of course, could consent to state jurisdiction over phases of interstate or foreign commerce or even preempt the same. In the case of foreign corporations engaging in interstate and intrastate commerce, a state could regulate the latter if it did not unduly burden the former. A foreign corporation, however, could not be excluded from performing federal governmental functions in a state. See Leslie Miller, Inc. v. Arkansas, 352 U.S. 187, 77 S.Ct. 257, 1 L.Ed.2d 231 (1956). These rules have remained fairly constant.

4. E. g., A state constitutionally could not, as a condition on admission, exact an advance agreement by the foreign corporation not to resort to the federal courts (Insurance Co. v. Morse, 87 U.S. (20 Wall.) 445, 22 L.Ed. 365 (1874)), nor revoke authority for resorting to the federal courts (Terral v. Burke Construction Co., 257 U.S. 529, 42 S.Ct. 188, 66 L. Ed. 352, 21 A.L.R. 186 (1922)). The theory was that corporations had a constitutional right to resort to the federal courts (cf. section 88 supra). However, compulsory local reincorporation was upheld even though this might preclude diversity-of-citizenship between the corporation and local residents (see section 88 supra, with respect to multiple incorporation) (Railway Express Agency, Inc. v. Virginia, 282 U.S. 440, 51 S.Ct. 201, 75 L.Ed. 450, 72 A.L.R. 102 (1931)). Nor could the conditions violate the corporation's rights to due process (unreasonable exercise of police power), or the equal protection of the laws (see section 80 supra), although the latter permitted reasonable classification of corporations into "domestic" and "foreign" and even retaliatory provisions against foreign corporations whose states of incorporation were not kindly disposed toward local corporations doing business there. Pembina Consol. Silver Mining & Milling Co. v. Pennsylvania, 125 U.S. 181, 8 S.Ct. 737, 31 L.Ed. 650 (1888); Annot., 91 A.L.R. 975 (1934). Finally, the conditions imposed could not constitute impairment of the obligation of contracts.

5. See section 97 supra.

Henn Corporations 2d Ed. HB—11

6. See Mich.Gen.Corp.Act § 21.98 (Supp.1968). Cf. more limited construction of New York foreign corporation statutes, discussed in section 59, nn. 3, 4 supra.

7. Hemphill v. Orloff, 277 U.S. 537, 48 S.Ct. 577, 72 L.Ed. 978 (1928) (sustaining application of Michigan statute, supra note 6). Even in Paul v. Virginia, 75 U.S. (8 Wall.) 168, 19 L.Ed. 357 (1868), the Supreme Court had stressed that the privileges-and-immunities-of-citizens clause secured only those privileges and immunities common to all citizens and not special privileges.

8. Henry L. Doherty & Co. v. Goodman, 294 U.S. 623, 55 S.Ct. 553, 79 L.Ed. 1097 (1935), discussed in section 97, n. 12 supra.

9. E. g., nonresident securities brokers and dealers; real estate brokers and dealers; insurers; N.H. Rev.Stat.Ann. c. 305–A (1965) (requiring qualification of foreign partnerships); Note, 52 Cornell L.Q. 157 (1966).

corporation from reasonable qualification requirements and regulation, even though such corporation constitutionally could not be excluded. Even as the concept of interstate commerce expanded (e. g., "stream of commerce" theory), reasonable exercise of the state police power over foreign corporations, which did not discriminate against such corporations engaged in interstate or foreign commerce, in the absence of congressional preemption of the field, was found to constitute no undue burden on interstate commerce.[10]

Constitutionally, for qualification requirements to apply, a very small degree of intrastate commerce will suffice, even though the mass of business being done is in interstate commerce. Only if the foreign corporation does *solely* interstate business, is it immune from admission requirements under the traditional rule.[11]

No state has exercised more than minor aspects of its constitutional power to regulate foreign corporations doing business in the state.

The United States Constitution prohibits a state from denying to any person (construed to include corporation) within its jurisdiction the equal protection of the laws.[12] State constitutions[13] and statutes[14] prohibit foreign corporations from transacting business within the state on more favorable conditions than are prescribed by law to similar domestic corporations. Yet the foreign corporation traditionally is either not subject to,[15] or is exempted from,[16] most of the regulatory features of the corporate statute applicable to domestic corporations.[17]

Occasionally, a court will refuse to follow the law of the state of incorporation when

---

10. Union Brokerage Co. v. Jensen, 322 U.S. 202, 64 S.Ct. 967, 88 L.Ed. 1227, 152 A.L.R. 1072 (1944) (7–2). The court ruled that the commerce clause "does not imply relief to those engaged in interstate or foreign commerce from the duty of paying an *appropriate share* for maintenance of the various state governments. Nor does it preclude a State from giving needful protection to its citizens in the course of their *contacts* with businesses conducted by outsiders when the legislation by which this is accomplished is general in its scope, is not aimed at interstate or foreign commerce, and involves merely burdens incident to effective administration." [italics added]. But see International Textbook Co. v. Pigg, 217 U.S. 91, 30 S.Ct. 481, 54 L.Ed. 678 (1910); International Text Book Co. v. Tone, 220 N.Y. 313, 115 N.E. 914 (1917).

11. Eli Lilly & Co. v. Sav-On-Drugs, Inc., 366 U.S. 276, 81 S.Ct. 1316, 6 L.Ed.2d 288 (1961), reh. denied 366 U.S. 978, 81 S.Ct. 1913, 6 L.Ed.2d 1268 (1961) (Harlan, J., concurring, indicated that there was no need to consider the traditional rule—restated as dictum by the majority—since the foreign corporation was found to have engaged in local business).

12. U.S.Const. amend. XIV, § 1. See section 13, n. 21 supra. See WHYY, Inc. v. Borough of Glassboro, 393 U.S. 117, 89 S.Ct. 286, 21 L.Ed.2d 242 (1968) (holding New Jersey statute denying tax exemption to foreign nonprofit corporations owning property in state on basis of foreign incorporation unconstitutional denial of equal protection of laws to persons within state).

13. E. g., Ariz.Const. art. XIV, § 5; Calif.Const. art. XII, § 15; Va.Const. art. XII, § 163; Ariz.Op. Att'y Gen. No. 65–9, May 7, 1965; Mich.Op.Atty Gen. No. 3652, Oct. 18, 1965.

14. E. g., ABA–ALI Model Bus.Corp.Act §§ 100, 141.

15. E. g., ABA–ALI Model Bus.Corp.Act § 99.

16. E. g., McKinney's N.Y.Bus.Corp.Law § 1320. See Restatement, Second, of Conflict of Laws ch. 12 (Agency and Partnerships), ch. 13 (Business Corporations) (Proposed Official Draft, Pt. III, Apr. 22, 1969); Kaplan, "Foreign Corporations and Local Corporate Policy", 21 Vand.L.Rev. 433 (1968).

17. E. g., ABA–ALI Model Bus.Corp.Act § 99 (nothing in act to be construed to authorize state "to regulate the organization or the internal affairs" of foreign corporation); Baraf, "The Foreign Corporation—A Problem in Choice-of-Law Doctrine", 33 Brooklyn L.Rev. 219 (1967); Kaplan, "Foreign Corporations and Local Corporate Policy", 21 Vand.L. Rev. 433 (1968); Latty, "Pseudo-Foreign Corporations", 65 Yale L.J. 137 (1955); Note, "Corporations —State Regulations of Foreign Corporations—Interstate v. Intrastate", 19 Ala.L.Rev. 193 (1966); Note, "The Entry and Regulation of Foreign Corporations under New Mexico Law and under the Model Business Corporation Act", 6 Natural Resources J. 617 (1966); Note, "Corporations: Domestic Regulation of Foreign Corporations: Concept of 'Domiciled Foreign Corporation': New York Business Corporation Law of 1961", 47 Cornell L.Q. 273 (1962); Note, "Pseudo Foreign Corporations and the Internal Affairs Rule", 1960 Duke L.J. 477. Hausman v. Buckley, 299 F.2d 696, 93 A.L.R.2d 1340 (2d Cir. 1962), cert. denied 369 U.S. 885, 82 S.Ct. 1157, 8 L.Ed.2d 286 (1962); Levine v. Milton, 42 Del.Ch. 597, 219 A.2d 145 (Ch. 1966) (holding law of jurisdiction of incorporation controlling, as substantive, on right of shareholder to maintain derivative action).

there is little contact between the corporation and such state, and the only contact is the "naked fact of incorporation." [18]

California in recent years has regulated foreign corporations with substantial California contacts under its "blue sky" laws. The California Corporation Commissioner, by denying securities permits, has enjoined Delaware corporations from eliminating cumulative voting for directors [19] and has asserted broad jurisdiction over changes in securities held by California residents.[20] A California court has intervened to wind up and dissolve a foreign corporation.[21]

DOING BUSINESS AS FOREIGN CORPORATION—TAXATION

99. The domestic corporation is subject to taxation by its state of incorporation.

The foreign corporation is subject to taxation by states where any of its activities enjoy benefit or protection or involve sufficient minimum contact, even though such activities involve interstate or foreign commerce, so long as the tax is commensurate with the corporation's activities in such states, subject to the limitations of the Federal Interstate Income Law of 1959.

A state's power to tax is, along with its police power, an aspect of its legislative jurisdiction. Here, too, corporate theories have loomed large.[1]

State jurisdiction to tax domestic corporations is subject to few constitutional limitations.[2]

The development of state jurisdiction to tax, from reliance on theories of situs of the property and corporate domicile to the formulation of the "doing business", "benefit" and "contact" theories, has already been traced.[3] The "traditional notions of fair play and substantial justice", "reasonableness", "minimum contact", and "benefit" tests promulgated in the International Shoe Co. case [4] were as applicable to the state's legislative jurisdiction to levy the unemployment tax there involved as to the state's judicial jurisdiction to sue to collect it.[5]

Requiring a foreign corporation engaged in interstate or foreign commerce in a state

---

18. Mansfield Hardwood Lumber Co. v. Johnson, 268 F.2d 317, 321 (5th Cir. 1959), cert. denied 361 U.S. 885, 80 S.Ct. 156, 4 L.Ed.2d 120 (1959), reh. denied 361 U.S. 926, 80 S.Ct. 290, 4 L.Ed.2d 241 (1960); Blazer v. Black, 196 F.2d 139 (10th Cir. 1952). A foreign corporation with substantial local contacts is sometimes called "pseudo-foreign corporation", "domiciled foreign corporation", "tramp corporation", "nominal foreign corporation".

19. People ex rel. Sobieski v. Western Air Lines, Inc., 258 Cal.App.2d 213, 66 Cal.Rptr. 316 (1968); Western Air Lines, Inc. v. Sobieski, 191 Cal.App.2d 399, 12 Cal.Rptr. 719 (1961). See Comment, "Jurisdiction of the California Corporations Commissioner over Delaware Short Form Mergers", 52 Calif.L. Rev. 1016 (1964).

20. See former California Securities Regulations § 367.1 (effective Nov. 11, 1959), repealed, effective Jan. 2, 1969.

21. In re Mercantile Guaranty Co., 238 Cal.App.2d 426, 48 Cal.Rptr. 589, 19 A.L.R.3d 1267 (1965).

1. The federal corporate income tax of 1909 was framed in terms of a franchise tax based on income and hence escaped the fate of the individual income tax which was declared unconstitutional because not apportioned among the states. The apportionment requirement for federal income tax was obviated by the 16th amendment, ratified in 1913.

2. E. g., Central R. R. v. Pennsylvania, 370 U.S. 607, 82 S.Ct. 1297, 8 L.Ed.2d 720 (1962), reh. denied 371 U.S. 856, 83 S.Ct. 15, 9 L.Ed.2d 93 (1962) (upholding power of state of incorporation to levy annual property tax on total value of most of corporation's freight cars absent proof that they had acquired tax situs elsewhere); Matson Navigation Co. v. State Board of Equalization, 297 U.S. 441, 56 S.Ct. 553, 80 L.Ed. 791 (1936), reh. denied 297 U.S. 728, 56 S.Ct. 666, 80 L.Ed. 1011 (1936) (allowing state of incorporation to tax entire corporate income). See Cheney v. Stephens, Inc., 231 Ark. 541, 330 S.W.2d 949 (1960) (income tax on out-of-state income of corporations with local income held unconstitutional in view of complete exemption from tax of corporations having only out-of-state income).

3. See section 81 supra. See also W. Beaman, Paying Taxes to Other States; State and Local Taxation of Non-Resident Businesses (1963); Roesken, "Doing Business in Other States: Taxation Problems", 23 Corp.J. 40 (1960).

4. See section 97 supra.

5. Annot., 161 A.L.R. 1068 (1946). "Convenience of forum" considerations obviously apply only to judicial jurisdiction. Conversely, situs, while relevant for taxation, is not for in personam jurisdiction, although it is for in rem and quasi-in-rem jurisdiction.

to pay an appropriate share of the state tax burden does not amount to an undue burden on interstate or foreign commerce.[6]

The Federal Interstate Income Act of 1959 granted immunity from state income tax to income derived within a state by any person (except a domestic corporation) from interstate commerce if the only business activities within such state by or in behalf of such person during the taxable year are either or both of the following:[7]

"(1) the solicitation of orders by such person, or his representative, in such State for sales of tangible personal property, which orders are sent outside the State for approval or rejection, and, if approved, are filled by shipment or delivery from a point outside the State; and

"(2) the solicitation of orders by such person, or his representative, in such State in the name of or for the benefit of a prospective customer of such person, if orders by such customer to such person to enable such customer to fill orders resulting from such solicitation are orders described in paragraph (1)."

Multiple state taxation remained a problem requiring further solution.[8] Possible relief has been urged in the form of interstate

6. General Motors Corp. v. Washington, 377 U.S. 436, 84 S.Ct. 1564, 12 L.Ed.2d 430 (1964), reh. denied 379 U.S. 875, 85 S.Ct. 14, 13 L.Ed.2d 79 (1964) (upholding privilege tax on foreign corporation measured by gross wholesale sales delivered in state); Northwestern States Portland Cement Co. v. Minnesota, Williams v. Stockham Valves & Fittings, Inc., 358 U.S. 450, 79 S.Ct. 357, 3 L.Ed.2d 421 (1959) (6–3) (upholding application of Minnesota and Georgia income taxes imposed upon income derived from exclusively interstate commerce "fairly apportioned to business activities within the taxing State"). Compare Scripto, Inc. v. Carson, 362 U.S. 207, 80 S.Ct. 619, 4 L.Ed.2d 660 (1960) (8–1) (upholding Florida use tax on sales by Georgia corporation to Florida residents), with National Bellas Hess, Inc. v. Illinois, 386 U.S. 753, 87 S.Ct. 1389, 18 L.Ed.2d 505 (1967) (foreign interstate catalog sellers held not required to collect and remit tax imposed on consumers who buy goods for use within state). Cf. Miller Bros. Co. v. Maryland, 347 U.S. 340, 74 S.Ct. 535, 98 L.Ed. 744 (1954), reh. denied 347 U.S. 964, 74 S.Ct. 708, 98 L.Ed. 1106 (1954). Compare Railway Express Agency, Inc. v. Virginia, 358 U.S. 434, 79 S.Ct. 411, 3 L.Ed. 2d 450 (1959) (7–2), with Railway Express Agency, Inc. v. Virginia, 347 U.S. 359, 74 S.Ct. 558, 98 L.Ed. 757 (1954) (5–4) and Spector Motor Service, Inc. v. O'Connor, 340 U.S. 602, 71 S.Ct. 508, 95 L.Ed. 573 (1951); Roadway Express, Inc. v. Division of Taxation, 50 N.J. 471, 236 A.2d 577 (1967). Failure by the foreign corporation to apportion its income might result in taxation on the whole amount. Monaghan v. Seismograph Service Co., 236 Miss. 278, 108 So.2d 721 (1959), appeal dismissed 361 U.S. 35, 80 S.Ct. 137, 4 L.Ed.2d 111 (1959). Contra, Seismograph Service Corp. v. Bureau of Internal Revenue, 61 N.M. 16, 293 P.2d 977 (1956). See also Flying Tiger Co. v. Los Angeles County, 51 Cal.2d 314, 333 P.2d 323 (1958), cert. denied 359 U.S. 1001, 79 S.Ct. 1140, 3 L.Ed.2d 1031 (1959); Braniff Airways, Inc. v. Nebraska State Board of Equalization and Assessment, 347 U.S. 590, 74 S.Ct. 757, 98 L.Ed. 697 (1954) (5–1–1–1–1) (upholding apportioned ad valorem tax on flight equipment of foreign interstate air carrier). Katz, "State Taxation of Interstate Income", 32 N.Y.St.B.Bull. 127 (1960); Kust, "State Taxation of Income from Interstate Commerce: New Dimensions of an Old Problem", 14 Sw.L.J. 1 (1960); Comment, 46 Va.L.Rev. 297 (1960); Note, 108 U.Pa.L.Rev. 1077 (1960); Cox, "The Impact of the Stockham Decision", 37 Taxes 299 (1959); Farrell, "State Taxation of Interstate Commerce", 31 N.Y.St.B.Bull. 316 (1959); Annot., 67 A.L.R.2d 1322 (1959). See also "A Symposium on State Taxation of Interstate Commerce", 46 Va.L.Rev. 1051 (1960).

7. 15 U.S.C.A. §§ 381–384; Comment, 44 Minn.L.Rev. 999 (1960); Notes, 35 N.Y.U.L.Rev. 572 (1960); 46 Va.L.Rev. 297 (1960); "Federal Interstate Income Law", 22 Corp.J. 283 (1960). The Act has been held constitutional in Smith, Kline & French Labs. v. Tax Comm'n, 241 Or. 50, 403 P.2d 375 (1965); International Shoe Co. v. Cocreham, 246 La. 244, 164 So.2d 314 (1964), cert. denied 379 U.S. 902, 85 S.Ct. 193, 13 L.Ed.2d 177 (1964); State ex rel. Ciba Pharmaceutical Prods., Inc. v. State Tax Comm'n, 382 S.W.2d 645 (Mo.1964).

8. Barrett, "State of the States in Taxing Multi-State Income", 48 A.B.A.J. 35 (1966); Dane, "A New Look at State Taxation of Income from Interstate Commerce", 52 A.B.A.J. 651 (1966); Del Duca & Wagner, "Uniformity or Preferential Immunity for Multi-State Firms—Tax Equity and Federal-State Relations", 70 Dick.L.Rev. 283 (1966); Barnes, "State Taxation of Interstate Commerce: Chaos and New Hope", 16 W.Res.L.Rev. 859 (1965); Barber, "State Taxation of Net Income Derived from Interstate Commerce", 48 A.B.A.J. 1133 (1962); Developments in the Law: "Federal Limitations on State Taxation of Interstate Business", 75 Harv.L.Rev. 953 (1962); Comment, "State Taxation of Multistate Businesses", 74 Yale L.J. 1259 (1965).

compacts,[9] uniform state legislation,[10] federal constitutional amendment, or centralized federal collection of state supplemental taxes.

A five-year study by Congress resulted in a report in 1965 [11] and proposed legislation.[12]

ADMISSION AS FOREIGN CORPORATION

100. The foreign corporation is generally required to qualify to do business within a jurisdiction. A foreign corporation usually may not do business which a domestic corporation is not permitted to do. Regulation of the organization and internal affairs of a foreign corporation is expressly negated by the typical corporate statute. Qualification involves various formalities and undeniably subjects the corporation to service of process and various regulatory and tax provisions applicable to foreign corporations.

A foreign corporation is generally required to qualify (or to secure authority or a certificate, permit, or license) to do any

9. "Multistate Tax Compact", 25 Corp.J. 125 (1967). Some two-fifths of the states have adhered to the Multistate Tax Compact: Alabama, Arkansas, Colorado, Florida, Hawaii, Idaho, Illinois, Kansas, Michigan, Missouri, Montana, Nebraska, Nevada, New Mexico, North Dakota, Oregon, Texas, Utah, Washington, Wyoming.

10. See Uniform Division of Income for Tax Purposes Act, 9A U.L.A. 153 (1965), approved in 1957; adopted in Alaska, Arkansas, California, Hawaii, Idaho, Kansas, New Mexico, North Dakota, Oregon, South Carolina, Utah. Keesling & Warren, "California's Uniform Division of Income for Tax Purposes Act", 15 U.C.L.A.L.Rev. 655 (1968); Note, "Uniform Division of Income for Tax Purposes Act", 8 B.C.Ind. & Com.L.Rev. 114 (1966). See "State Taxation of Interstate Business: An Evaluation of Developments During the Past Decade", 41 N.Y.St. B.J. 558, 662 (1969).

11. Report of the Special Subcommittee on State Taxation of Interstate Commerce of the Committee on the Judiciary, H.R.Rep.No.952, 89th Cong., 1st Sess., 1135–38 (1965); Taylor, "Willis Report on Interstate Taxation: New Laws to Make Sweeping Changes", 23 J.Taxation 374 (1965).

12. H.R. 11,798, 89th Cong., 1st Sess. (1965); H.R. 16,491, 89th Cong., 2d Sess. (1966); H.R. 2,158, 90th Cong., 2d Sess. (1968); H.R. 7906, 91st Cong., 1st Sess. (1969); "H.R. 11798—The Interstate Taxation Act", 24 Corp.J. 315 (1966); Note, 19 Vand.L. Rev. 523 (1966).

intrastate business within a jurisdiction, notwithstanding that it is also there doing interstate business as well.[1] In rare instances the foreign corporation might be required to reincorporate.[2]

Statutes often specify various activities which do not constitute transacting business for purposes of qualification requirements.[3]

1. Eli Lilly & Co. v. Sav-On-Drugs, Inc., 366 U.S. 276, 81 S.Ct. 1316, 6 L.Ed.2d 288 (1961), reh. denied 366 U.S. 978, 81 S.Ct. 1913, 6 L.Ed.2d 1268 (1961); Walker, "Foreign Corporation Laws: The Loss of Reason", 47 N.C.L.Rev. 1 (1968); Comment, "Corporate Registration: A Functional Analysis of 'Doing Business'", 71 Yale L.J. 575 (1962); Note, "State Regulation of Foreign Corporations: Qualification: Interstate v. Intrastate Business", 47 Cornell L.Q. 300 (1962).

2. See National Ass'n for Advancement of Colored People v. Alabama, 377 U.S. 288, 84 S.Ct. 1302, 12 L.Ed.2d 325 (1964) (Alabama qualification requirement to do business held inapplicable to foreign membership corporation formed by individuals exercising freedom to associate for collective advocacy of ideas); Anti-Defamation League of B'Nai B'rith v. American Italian Anti-Defamation League, Inc., 54 Misc.2d 830, 283 N.Y.S.2d 828 (Sup.Ct.1967) (nonprofit corporation held not required to qualify under Business Corporation Law); Note, "Qualification of Foreign Partnerships", 52 Cornell L.Q. 157 (1966). Federal corporations are not required to qualify, although the statutory definitions of "foreign corporation" might not be explicit. ABA–ALI Model Bus. Corp.Act § 2(b). See Home Owners' Loan Corp. v. Gordon, 36 Cal.App.2d 189, 97 P.2d 845 (1939). A few jurisdictions, e. g., Florida, Wisconsin, bar a foreign corporation from acquiring, holding, or disposing of property in the jurisdiction until it has qualified; Massachusetts requires a foreign corporation owning real property in the jurisdiction without a usual place of business there to qualify. 21 Corp.J. 183 (1956). Statutes in different jurisdictions variously refer to "admission" as "qualification", "authorization", "registration", "licensing", or "domestication" (Oklahoma, Tennessee), although "domestication" more strictly denotes a foreign corporation's becoming a domestic corporation (without surrendering its corporate charter) (Georgia, Mississippi, Nebraska)—see section 137 infra.

3. ABA–ALI Model Bus.Corp.Act § 99:

(a) Maintaining or defending any action or suit or any administrative or arbitration proceeding, or effecting the settlement thereof or the settlement of claims or disputes.

(b) Holding meetings of its directors or shareholders or carrying on other activities concerning its internal affairs.

(c) Maintaining bank accounts.

(d) Maintaining offices or agencies for the transfer, exchange and registration of its securities, or ap-

The typical corporate statute provides that (a) A foreign corporation is not entitled to qualify to transact in the state business which a domestic corporation is not permitted to transact; (b) A foreign corporation is not to be denied qualification because the laws of its jurisdiction of incorporation governing its organization and internal affairs differ from such statute; and (c) Nothing in such statute should be construed to authorize regulation of the organization or internal affairs of the foreign corporation.[4]

In doubtful situations, it is probably better to qualify, since the foreign corporation would in any event be amenable to local process, regulation, and taxation, although qualification prevents the corporation from taking the position that it is not doing business in the jurisdiction.[5] Failure to qualify when necessary might prevent the corpora-

tion from learning of actions against it and might subject it to various penalties.[6]

Qualification usually involves some filing of applications or certificates setting forth certain appropriate information (often with a copy of the articles of incorporation and any amendments thereto appended),[7] the payment of filing fees,[8] and the designation of a resident agent or the secretary of state, as the foreign corporation's agent for service of process. Qualification also means that the foreign corporation is undeniably subject to service of process and the various corporation law, regulatory, and tax provisions applicable to foreign corporations. Filings of reports are also required.[9]

About one-fifth of the states require the annual filing of a list of resident shareholders; a few states also require the inclusion of nonresident as well as resident shareholders.[10]

SANCTIONS FOR NONCOMPLIANCE WITH ADMISSION REQUIREMENTS

101. For failure to qualify as required, different jurisdictions impose various sanctions, the most significant penalties being to disable the unqualified foreign corporation from suing either generally or on contracts made within the jurisdiction. Other sanctions include fines against the corporation and corporate person-

pointing and maintaining trustees or depositaries with relation to its securities.

(e) Effecting sales through independent contractors.

(f) Soliciting or procuring orders, whether by mail or through employees or agents or otherwise, where such orders require acceptance without this State before becoming binding contracts.

(g) Creating evidences of debt, mortgages or liens on real or personal property.

(h) Securing or collecting debts or enforcing any rights in property securing the same.

(i) Transacting any business in interstate commerce.

(j) Conducting an isolated transaction completed within a period of 30 days and not in the course of a number of repeated transactions of like nature. New York lists only the first four. McKinney's N.Y.Bus.Corp.Law § 1301(b). See Ross Construction Co., Inc. v. U. M. & M. Credit Corp., 214 So.2d 822 (Miss.1968); "Qualification and the Sale of Securities", 25 Corp.J. 243 (1968); "Free Port Laws—Effect on Qualification Requirements", 24 Corp.J. 143 (1964); "Isolated Transactions", 23 id. 243 (1962); "Unusual Doing Business Activities", 23 id. 223 (1962); "'Doing Business' Definitions", 23 id. 183 (1962). The California attorney general has ruled that foreign baseball corporations entering California to play professional baseball games are transacting intrastate business and must qualify. Cal. Op.Att'y Gen. No. 64–178 (Jan. 20, 1964).

4. ABA–ALI Model Bus.Corp.Act § 99.

5. Farmingdale Steer-Inn, Inc. v. Steer Inn Realty Corp., 51 Misc.2d 986, 274 N.Y.S.2d 379 (Sup.Ct. 1966).

6. See section 101 infra.

7. The need to file copies of the articles of incorporation has been eliminated in a growing number of jurisdictions, which require instead a certificate from the jurisdiction of incorporation that the corporation is existing and in good standing. E. g., Cal.Gen.Corp.Law § 6403 (1947); McKinney's N.Y. Bus.Corp.Law, § 1304(b); Pa.Bus.Corp.Law § 1004 (1966).

8. 2 Model Business Corporation Act Annotated §§ 120–122 (1960).

9. E. g., ABA–ALI Model Bus.Corp.Act §§ 99–131. The Model Act expressly provides that nothing therein shall be construed to authorize the state to regulate the organization or the internal affairs of foreign corporations. Id. § 99.

10. "State 'Information' Reports", 23 Corp.J. 263 (1962).

nel involved; **personal liability of directors, officers, or agents involved; rendering contracts made within state "void"; disability to defend litigation or to plead statute of limitations; injunction; imposition of regulatory features; reciprocal penalties.**

Various sanctions are imposed for failure to qualify as required: [1]

(a) Fine or penalty on corporation; [2]

(b) Fine and/or imprisonment of corporate agents; [3]

(c) Fine and/or imprisonment of directors and/or officers; [4]

(d) Corporation's contracts made within state "void"; [5]

(e) Corporation's contracts made within state "unenforceable"; [6]

(f) Corporation's disability to sue or defend; [7]

(g) Corporation's disability to sue; [8]

(h) Denial of benefits to corporation of statute of limitations; [9]

(i) Directors/officers/agents personally liable on contracts made within state; [10]

(j) Injunctions against corporation; [11]

(k) Imposition of specified regulatory features; [12]

(l) Reciprocal penalties.[13]

1. For state-by-state tabulation, see 1 P-H Corp.Rep. ¶ 858. Kansas alone provides no express sanctions, but denies benefits of statute of limitations. Note, "Sanctions for Failure to Comply with Corporate Qualification Statutes: An Evaluation", 63 Colum. L.Rev. 117 (1963); Note, "The Legal Consequences of Failure to Comply with Domestication Statutes", 110 U.Pa.L.Rev. 241 (1961). Sometimes qualification is prerequisite to securing certain licenses. The foreign corporation might thus be denied access to the courts on failure to be licensed as well as to have qualified. "Access to Courts 'Doubly Barred' ", 24 Corp.J. 183 (1965).

2. E. g., ABA–ALI Model Bus.Corp.Act § 117 (amount equal to all fees and franchise taxes plus penalties); all jurisdictions except Arizona, Kansas, Maine, Massachusetts, and Virginia provide for fines or penalties against the corporation ranging up to $10,000 in Indiana and Ohio.

3. E. g., California, Maryland.

4. E. g., Maryland, Oklahoma.

5. E. g., Alabama (corporation expressly estopped from asserting such defense), Arizona, Arkansas, Michigan; quaere, Montana, Tennessee. Advance Industrial Security, Inc. v. William J. Burns I. D. Agency, 377 F.2d 236 (5th Cir. 1967) (Alabama law); Columbus Services, Inc. v. Preferred Building Maintenance, Inc., 270 F.Supp. 875 (W.D.Mich.1967) (Michigan law); Pacific Nat'l Bank v. Hernreich, 240 Ark. 114, 398 S.W.2d 221 (1966) (innocent purchaser held incapable of becoming holder in due course). See note 22 infra.

6. E. g., Idaho and Vermont provide that a prequalification contract made within the state may not be enforced; Massachusetts, New Jersey, and Pennsylvania prohibit the corporation from suing on a contract made within the state until it qualifies. Cf. note 8 infra.

7. E. g., Alabama, Hawaii, Idaho, Maryland, Nevada, Wisconsin. See "Right to Defend Suits", 23 Corp.J. 343 (1963), 23 Corp.J. 43 (1961). The disability under the Model Act is "in any court of this state", language which suggests that the disability does not extend to actions in the federal courts sitting in the state. See note 29 infra.

8. E. g., ABA–ALI Model Bus.Corp.Act § 117, Alaska, California, Illinois, New York, North Carolina, Ohio. See notes 14, 15 infra.

9. E. g., Hawaii (civil and criminal), Idaho, Kansas, Maryland, Nevada, and Wisconsin; Globig v. Greene & Gust Co., 193 F.Supp. 544 (E.D.Wis.1961) (forbidding plea of statute of limitations under disability to defend); Moss v. Standard Drug Co., 159 Ohio St. 464, 112 N.E.2d 542 (1953). Contra, Clawson v. Boston Acme Mines Development Co., 72 Utah 137, 269 P. 147, 59 A.L.R. 1318 (1928); see Annot., 59 A.L.R. 1336 (1929), 122 A.L.R. 1194 (1939).

10. E. g., Virginia (officers, directors, agents), Idaho (officers, agents, representatives), Massachusetts (officers, agents), Arkansas (officers, agents); Mountain Home Redi-Mix v. Conner Homes, Inc., 91 Idaho 612, 428 P.2d 744 (1967) (limiting liability to participants in negotiations); Texaco, Inc. v. Bosche, 242 Md. 334, 219 A.2d 80 (1966) (indicating Virginia statute, if compensatory to creditors and not penal, might be enforced by Maryland courts); Bachman v. Doerrie, 70 N.M. 277, 372 P.2d 951 (1962) (enforcing then Utah statute imposing personal liability on contract made by agent).

11. E. g., Indiana, New Hampshire, New York.

12. McKinney's N.Y.Bus.Corp.Law, §§ 1316(e), 1317(a) (1), 1318, 1319(a) (4), 1320, imposing liabilities on directors of foreign corporations for unlawful dividends and other distributions, corporate purchase of its shares and loans to directors, and liabilities on foreign corporation for failure to comply with specified notice and disclosure requirements. Only *qualified* foreign corporations are eligible for exemption from such provisions under section 1320.

13. E. g., New Jersey (prior to 1963); Eli Lilly & Co. v. Sav-On Drugs, Inc., 57 N.J.Super. 291, 154 A.2d

The most prevalent sanction is to bar the maintenance of any action, suit, or proceeding in any court of the state by a foreign corporation transacting business in the state without a certificate of authority or any successor or assignee.[14] Noncompliance usually does not impair the validity of any contract or act of such corporation or prevent it from defending litigation.[15]

Statutes which state that a corporation may not "maintain" an action "until" it shall have qualified are usually construed as permitting an unqualified corporation to "commence" suit so long as it thereafter qualifies.[16] Where the legislature barred

maintenance of the action but deleted from the bill the phrase "until such corporation shall have obtained a certificate of authority", qualification after the claim accrued was held to be too late.[17]

Instead of imposing a general disability to sue—which is applicable to tort as well as contract claims regardless of where the contract was made—some jurisdictions bar actions on contracts made in the jurisdiction prior to qualification.[18]

Of legislation affecting local contracts, most bar maintenance of any action before qualification and are construed to suspend enforcement, permitting enforcement after qualification (with possible penalties for tardy qualification in some cases).[19] A few statutes make the local contract unenforcea-

650 (1959) (application of more stringent Indiana rule barring corporation from suing on any claims), aff'd 31 N.J. 591, 158 A.2d 528 (1960), aff'd on other grounds 366 U.S. 276, 81 S.Ct. 1316, 6 L.Ed.2d 288 (1961), reh. denied 366 U.S. 978, 81 S.Ct. 1913, 6 L. Ed.2d 1268 (1961). Georgia, prior to 1969 also had a retaliatory provision. Textile Banking Co. v. Colonial Chemical Corp., 285 F.Supp. 824 (N.D.Ga. 1967); Duncan Cleaners, Inc. v. Shuman Co., 119 Ga.App. 128, 166 S.E.2d 387 (1969); Sherman Stubbs Realty & Ins., Inc. v. American Institute of Marketing, Inc., 117 Ga.App. 829, 162 S.E.2d 240 (1968) (all under former Georgia retaliatory provision); "Enforcement of Contracts: Retaliatory Provisions", 25 Corp.J. 339 (1968–69).

14. ABA–ALI Model Bus.Corp.Act § 117; McKinney's N.Y.Bus.Corp.Law § 1312; Comment, "Section 1312 of the Business Corporation Law: The Dilemma of Legislative History and Judicial Interpretation", 30 Fordham L.Rev. 331 (1961). When New York changed its statutory provision barring any action on a contract made by it in the state unless before the making it shall have qualified (former N.Y.Gen.Corp.Law, § 218) to a general disability to sue until qualified—McKinney's N.Y.Bus. Corp.Law, § 1312 (effective Sept. 1, 1963), the prior sanction was held to apply to causes of action accruing prior to September 1, 1963. Garden State Brickface & Stone Co. v. Oradell Construction Corp., 44 Misc.2d 22, 252 N.Y.S.2d 790 (App.T. 2d Dep't 1964); Tetreault v. State, 50 Misc.2d 170, 269 N.Y.S.2d 812 (Ct.Cl.1966). "Unlicensed Foreign Corporations: Maintenance of Suit by Assignees", 20 Corp.J. 43 (1951–52); Annot., 80 A.L.R.2d 465 (1961). An innocent purchaser of a negotiable instrument which is void cannot become a holder in due course. Pacific Nat'l Bank v. Hernreich, 240 Ark. 114, 398 S.W.2d 221 (1966).

15. ABA–ALI Model Bus.Corp.Act § 117. "Right to Defend Suits", 23 Corp.J. 343 (1963); "Unlicensed Foreign Corporations: Right to Defend Suits", 23 Corp.J. 43 (1961); see note 7 supra.

16. Inn Operations, Inc. v. River Hills Motor Inn Co., —— Iowa ——, 152 N.W.2d 808 (1967); Video

Engineering Co. v. Foto-Video Electronics, Inc., 207 Va. 1027, 154 S.E.2d 7 (1967); J. R. Watkins Co. v. Floyd, 119 So.2d 164 (La.Ct.App.1960); Annot., 6 A. L.R.3d 326 (1966).

17. Parker v. Lin-Co. Producing Co., 197 So.2d 228 (Miss.1967) (where prior law barred subsequent qualification).

18. E. g., New Jersey, Rhode Island, Vermont. "Unlicensed Foreign Corporations Contract Sanctions", 24 Corp.J. 243 (1965); "Statutory Restrictions on Enforcement of Contracts", 23 Corp.J. 323 (1963); "Unlicensed Foreign Corporations: Enforcement of Contracts", 23 Corp.J. 23 (1960). Such a formulation does not bar enforcement of contracts not made in the state. Brown Broadcast, Inc. v. Pepper Sound Studios, Inc., 242 Ark. 701, 416 S.W.2d 284 (1967); Kemp v. Darke County Farm Bureau Co-op. Ass'n, 115 Ohio App. 1, 184 N.E.2d 103 (1961). But see Allen Industries, Inc. v. Exquisite Form Brassiere, Inc., 31 Misc.2d 673, 221 N.Y.S.2d 619 (Sup.Ct.1961), aff'd 15 A.D.2d 760, 224 N.Y.S.2d 579 (1st Dep't 1962) (contractual provision stating that contract was deemed to have been made in Michigan held not to establish as matter of law that defense of nonqualification had been waived). Where the contract was unenforceable, the enforcement of a mechanic's lien has been held barred. Greene Plumbing & Heating Co. v. Morris, 144 Mont. 234, 395 P.2d 252 (1964); Berkshire Engineering Corp. v. Scott-Paine, 29 Misc.2d 1010, 217 N.Y.S.2d 919 (Columbia County Ct. 1961). Foreclosure of mortgage has also been barred. B. & P., Inc. v. Norment, 241 Ark. 1092, 411 S.W.2d 506 (1967).

19. New England Die Co. v. General Products Co., 92 R.I. 292, 168 A.2d 150 (1961); Day v. Stokes, 97 N. J.Eq. 378, 127 A. 331 (1925); Spokane Merchants' Ass'n v. Olmstead, 80 Idaho 166, 327 P.2d 385 (1958); Annot., 75 A.L.R. 446 (1931).

ble in the courts of the state even though the corporation later qualifies.[20] Statutory provisions often prohibit an assignee from enforcing the contract until the assignor corporation qualifies.[21]

Other problems of statutory construction arise from the particular statutory language employed: the meaning of "void" or "unenforceable";[22] the effect of the statute when the unqualified foreign corporation is sued on the contract so far as the plaintiff's enforcement or a counterclaim by the corporation is concerned;[23] the effect of the statute on contracts made within the state preparatory to doing business.[24] Actions on contracts arising from interstate transactions[25] or to assert federal rights[26] are allowed.

The corporation's disability to sue must be promptly asserted to avoid waiver of the defense.[27] Dismissal of a corporation's action for failure to qualify has been held to be not for want of jurisdiction but an adjudication on the merits and hence *res judicata*.[28]

The statute frequently affects the status of local contracts in the state or in the courts of the state. Whatever restrictions apply to the state courts' treatment of such contracts will be applied by federal courts

20. Calvert Iron Works, Inc. v. Algernon Blair, Inc., 284 Ala. 655, 227 So.2d 424 (1969); Wolf Creek v. Haas, 116 F.Supp. 37 (D.Mont.1953); Foreman & Clark Mfg. Co. v. Bartle, 125 Misc. 759, 211 N.Y.S. 602 (Sup.Ct.1925). Where the statute barred "any action", arbitration *proceedings* on contracts made within the state have been allowed. Tugee Laces, Inc. v. Mary Muffet, Inc., 273 App.Div. 756, 75 N.Y.S.2d 513 (1st Dep't 1947), aff'd mem., 297 N.Y. 914, 79 N.E.2d 744 (1948). Quasi-contractual liability might also be enforced by the corporation. Thurston v. Cedric Sanders Co., 80 S.D. 426, 125 N.W.2d 496 (1963); American Middle East Corp. v. Barouk, 13 A.D.2d 919, 215 N.Y.S.2d 843 (1st Dep't 1961). Evyan Perfumes, Inc. v. Hamilton, 20 Misc.2d 950, 195 N.Y.S.2d 869 (Sup.Ct.1959). So also might fair trade actions against nonsignatories. Max Factor & Co. v. Janel Sales Corp., 298 F.2d 511 (2d Cir. 1962); Gillette Co. v. Master, 408 Pa. 202, 182 A.2d 734 (1962).

21. E. g., Rhode Island, Vermont. Where the defense goes to enforceability and not validity, a holder in due course may sue on the contract. Allison Hill Trust Co. v. Sarandrea, 134 Misc. 566, 236 N. Y.S. 265 (Sup.Ct.1929), modified on other grounds, 236 App.Div. 189, 258 N.Y.S. 299 (3d Dep't 1932). See note 14 supra.

22. Compare Carolin Mfg. Corp. v. George S. May, Inc., 312 Mich. 487, 20 N.W.2d 283 (1945), with Douglass v. Standard Real Estate Loan Co., 189 Ala. 223, 66 So. 614 (1914).

23. Burley Newspapers, Inc. v. Mist Publishing Co., 90 Idaho 515, 414 P.2d 460 (1966); James Howden & Co. v. American Condenser & Engineering Corp., 194 App.Div. 164, 185 N.Y.S. 159 (1st Dep't 1920), aff'd mem., 231 N.Y. 627, 132 N.E. 915 (1921) (counterclaims by corporations allowed).

24. Worcester Felt Pad Corp. v. Tucson Airport Authority, 233 F.2d 44 (9th Cir. 1956) (construing Arizona statute as not voiding such contracts).

25. Textile Fabrics Corp. v. Roundtree, 39 Ill.2d 122, 233 N.E.2d 376 (1968); Shulton v. Consumer Value Stores, Inc., 352 Mass. 605, 227 N.E.2d 482 (1967); Vernon Co. v. Reed, 78 N.M. 554, 434 P.2d 376 (1967); Warner Electric Brake & Clutch Co. v. Bessemer Forging Co., 343 S.W.2d 471 (Tex.Civ.App. 1961); Pratt Laboratories v. Teague, 160 F.Supp. 176 (W.D.Ark.1958); Gilliland & Echols Farm Supply & Hatchery v. Credit Equipment Corp., 269 Ala. 190, 112 So.2d 331 (1959); Remington Arms Co. v. Lechmere Tire & Sales Co., 339 Mass. 131, 158 N.E.2d 134 (1959); East Coast Discount Corp. v. Reynolds, 7 Utah 2d 362, 325 P.2d 853 (1958); Superior Concrete Accessories v. Kemper, 365 Mo. 512, 284 S.W.2d 482 (1955).

26. Embassy Pictures Corp. v. Hudson, 226 F.Supp. 421 (D.Tenn.1964); Overstreet v. Frederick B. Cooper Co., 134 So.2d 225 (Fla.1961); William G. Roe & Co. v. State, 43 Misc.2d 417, 251 N.Y.S.2d 151 (Ct. Cl.1964). See also Matter of Leeds Homes, Inc. v. Nat'l Acceptance Co. of America, 322 F.2d 648 (6th Cir. 1964), cert. denied sub nom. Tate, Trustee v. Nat'l Acceptance Co. of America, 379 U.S. 836, 85 S.Ct. 71, 13 L.Ed.2d 43 (1964) (allowing in Chapter X proceeding corporation's claim on contract unenforceable under state law); Okin v. A. D. Gosman, Inc., 70 N.J.Super. 26, 174 A.2d 650 (1961) (permitting corporation's trustee-in-bankruptcy to enforce contract unenforceable under state law).

27. Elnat of California, Inc. v. Wilkinson Sword, Inc., 44 Cal.Rptr. 256 (Cal.Dist.Ct.App.1965); Outdoor Electric Advertising Co. v. Saurage, 207 La. 344, 21 So.2d 375 (1945). See Hulburt Oil & Grease Co. v. Hulburt Oil & Grease Co., 371 F.2d 251 (7th Cir. 1966) (allowing action by nonqualified foreign corporation doing business in jurisdiction against former agent, who, instead of qualifying corporation, formed competing domestic corporation with same name, which name barred foreign corporation's qualification), cert. denied 386 U.S. 1032, 87 S. Ct. 1482, 18 L.Ed.2d 594 (1967); Dari-Delite, Inc. v. Priest & Baker, Inc., 50 Misc.2d 654, 271 N.Y.S.2d 355 (Sup.Ct.1966) (burden on party challenging corporation's capacity).

28. J. R. Watkins Co. v. Kramer, 250 Iowa 947, 97 N.W.2d 303 (1959).

sitting in diversity jurisdiction in the state. In the leading case, Woods v. Interstate Realty Co.,[29] the United States Supreme Court held that a contract which by state statute was made "unenforceable" by the unqualified foreign corporation in any of the courts of the state was unenforceable in the federal court sitting in diversity cases in the state. The majority reiterated the rule that for purposes of diversity, the federal court is "in effect, only another court of the state" and concluded that such a state statute, by the "outcome" test, was substantive under the Erie-Tompkins dichotomy. A fortiori, the results are the same where the state statute makes the contract "void".[30]

When a qualified foreign corporation ceases to do business in the state, or is dissolved in its state of incorporation, it should formally withdraw by surrendering its certificate of authority.[31] Such surrender minimizes taxes and other requirements, often reduces its suability, and might restrict its ability to sue.[32]

29. 337 U.S. 535, 69 S.Ct. 1235, 93 L.Ed. 1524 (1949) (6–3).

Cf. Harms, Inc. v. Tops Music Enterprises, Inc., 160 F.Supp. 77 (S.D.Cal.1958) (unqualified foreign corporation held not barred from suing on federal question by California disability-to-sue statute).

30. See Advance Industrial Security, Inc. v. William J. Burns I. D. Agency, 377 F.2d 236 (5th Cir. 1967);

Hutterian Brethren v. Haas, 116 F.Supp. 37 (D. Mont.1953).

31. Some jurisdictions required the certificate of authority to be surrendered physically or accounted for. Georgia, Hawaii, Kansas, Pennsylvania, Utah, and West Virginia require publication of notice of withdrawal.

32. Robinson Brick & Tile Co. v. Copperstate Supply Co., 100 Ariz. 28, 410 P.2d 96 (1966) (holding certificate of authority to remain in full force until certificate of withdrawal issued); Note, 40 Cornell L. Q. 610 (1955); 22 Corp.J. 123 (1958). The Texas attorney general found no constitutional objection to a statute requiring applications for certificates of withdrawal to state that all known creditors or claimants have been provided for and that the applicant "is not involved in or threatened with litigation in any court in this State." Tex.Op.Att'y Gen.No. C–663, Apr. 26, 1966.

CHAPTER 5

PREINCORPORATION PROBLEMS

A. PROMOTERS

A. PROMOTERS

PROMOTERS—IN GENERAL

102. Promoters form and set in motion the corporation, frequently continuing in control. Promotion activities include discovery of the business opportunity, investigating its economic feasibility, and assembling the necessary resources, property and personnel. Promoters usually are treated as in a joint venture, and are in a fiduciary relationship among themselves. Especially troublesome are the problems of their own compensation and preincorporation agreements made with third persons in behalf of the then nonexistent corporation, including preincorporation share subscriptions.

A corporation does not spring into being spontaneously, but results from planning and preliminary arrangements by promoters, the creative force behind the corporate enterprise or the midwife of the business. The corporation is formed and set in motion by promoters, who frequently continue in control after the corporation achieves legal existence.[1]

1. C. Rohrlich, Organizing Corporate and Other Business Enterprises 53–72 (4th ed. 1967); 1 A. Dewing, The Financial Policy of Corporations 402–420 (5th ed. 1953); H. Guthmann & H. Dougall, Corporate Financial Policy 247–268 (4th ed. 1962); M. Ehrich, The Law of Promoters (1916); Ehrich & Bunzl "Promoters' Contracts", 38 Yale L.J. 1011 (1929). Promoters, of course, promote business enterprises other than corporations, but the promotion of corporations causes the most complex problems. The promoters themselves may serve as the incorporators, or use "dummy" or "accommodation" incorporators. See sections 131, 185 infra.

The term "promoter" has been described as a product of business, rather than of law.[2] In some respects it carries an unfavorable connotation in the public mind, a perhaps unwarranted stigmatization in view of the fact that a promoter usually serves a useful social purpose.

Promotional activities may be divided into three general steps:[3]

(a) Discovery;

(b) Investigation;

(c) Assembly.

Discovery consists of finding the business opportunity to be developed. Investigation entails an analysis of the proposed business to determine whether or not it is economically feasible. Finally, assembly encompasses the bringing together of the necessary personnel, property, and money to set the business in motion. It also includes the secondary details of setting up the corporation itself.

While reaching their objectives, promoters must protect the basic ideas involved and the means for implementing them. Promoters may require the services of professional experts such as lawyers, accountants, engineers, bankers, etc. Commitments must be made for financing the enterprise, employing the necessary experts, securing necessary options, patents, licenses, leases, other property, and contracts for services, and possibly engaging persons to serve as officers and employees of the corporation after its formation.

Since the corporation during the promotional stage is usually not in existence, binding contractual arrangements usually cannot be made without personally binding the promoters. For undertaking such risks and for the expenditure of his time, skill, and judgment, the promoter understandably expects to be compensated by the corporation after it has been launched. Compensation may be in the form of cash, shares, share options, and/or salaried position in the corporation. All of these usually involve problems of evaluating the services which the promoter has performed for the corporation or the property or options which the promoter has turned over to the corporation. In addition, any issue of shares or share options often encounters the statutory requirement that the only lawful consideration for shares is property, cash or services rendered to the corporation (i. e., after incorporation); advance commitments concerning corporate salaries might infringe on the managerial function of the board of directors. Permeating the entire situation is the problem of self-dealing.

Prior to incorporation, promoters usually occupy the status of joint venturers.[4] As such, there is a fiduciary relationship among them. Involved in the relationship is the fact that the ultimate goal is incorporation, which injects the corporation into the relationship as a complicating factor. A major aspect of the problem is defining the scope of the fiduciary duties owed by the promoters *inter se*,[5] to the corporation,[6] and to shareholders and creditors of the corporation.[7] A few statutes have attempted to deal with the problem.[8]

The legal approach to these various ramifications has never fully crystallized. Since the promoter was unknown to the common law, the courts have had to improvise. They borrowed heavily from agency, trusts,

2. Whaley Bridge Calico Printing Co. v. Green & Smith, 5 Q.B.D. 109, 111 (1879). For administrative definitions of the term "promoter", see S.E.C. Rule 405; Regulation A, Rules 251–263. The Ghana Companies Code, 1963, drafted by Professor L.C.B. Gower, defines a promoter as any person engaged or interested in the formation of a company, except a person acting in a professional capacity for persons engaged in procuring the formation of the company. Ghana Companies Code § 12.(1) (1963).

3. H. Guthmann & H. Dougall, Corporate Financial Policy 248 et seq. (4th ed. 1962).

4. See section 49 supra.

5. See section 103 infra.

6. See section 104 infra.

7. See section 105 infra.

8. See section 106 infra.

partnerships, and contracts, producing a body of decisions, occasionally implemented by statute or administrative regulation, not reducible to any legal common denominator.[9]

The dilemma affecting preincorporation agreements because of the then nonexistence of the corporation is resolved in various ways.[10] Preincorporation share subscriptions pose a subsidiary problem.[11]

Reference has already been made to certain matters of preincorporation planning in Chapters 2 and 3. Other matters of such planning in connection with incorporation, admission, and domestication procedures will be considered in Chapter 6 and in connection with the special problems of close corporations in Chapter 10.

B. DUTIES AND LIABILITIES OF PROMOTERS

PROMOTERS' DUTIES AND LIABILITIES INTER SE

103. During promotion, the promoters are in a fiduciary relationship to each other, as in a joint venture. After the corporation is formed, the joint venture relationship is usually terminated and replaced by corporate relationships.

Understanding the scope of the fiduciary duties of promoters requires analysis of when the fiduciary relationship begins and ends (including its replacement by the corporate relationships), to whom the fiduciary duties are owed before and after incorporation, and what consequences are thereby involved with respect to (a) the other promoters, (b) the corporation,[1] and (c) any other shareholders or creditors.[2]

While it may be difficult to determine when the promotion begins,[3] it is clear that once it begins, the promoters occupy a fiduciary relationship to each other. The rules which apply to the beginning and end of the

relationship, and the respective rights and duties, are those of the joint venture.[4]

After the corporation is formed, or when the promotional plan is completed, the joint venture relationship is usually terminated and replaced by corporate relationships.[5]

PROMOTERS' DUTIES AND LIABILITIES TO CORPORATION

104. Promoters owe fiduciary duties to the corporation, including duties of good faith, fair dealing, and full disclosure. To avoid secret profits, full disclosure must be made to an independent board of directors and to all persons interested in the corporation. Where there is full disclosure to all persons presently interested but other investors are contemplated as part of the promotional scheme, there is a split of authority, but the trend appears to allow recovery of the promoters' profits. The measure of recovery depends upon whether the property transferred to the corporation was acquired by the promoters during their fiduciary relationship to the corporation or prior thereto.

9. Bloche, "A Primer for Corporate Promoters", 9 Prac.Law. 13 (Jan. 1963); Isaacs, "The Promoter: A Legislative Problem", 38 Harv.L.Rev. 887 (1925).

10. See sections 108–114 infra. Agreements made in behalf of a corporation after its incorporation but before its compliance with the conditions precedent to doing business (see section 143 infra) present some of the problems of preincorporation agreements. Kenyon v. Holbrook Microfilming Service, Inc., 155 F.2d 913 (2d Cir. 1946).

11. See section 115 infra.

1. See section 104 infra.

2. See section 105 infra.

3. Shore Terrace Co-op., Inc. v. Roche, 25 A.D.2d 666, 268 N.Y.S.2d 278 (2d Dep't 1966). Compare Haskins v. Ryan, 71 N.J.Eq. 575, 64 A. 436 (1906), aff'd 75 N.J.Eq. 623, 73 A. 1118 (1909), with Brown v. Leach, 189 App.Div. 158, 178 N.Y.S. 319 (1st Dep't 1919), appeal dismissed 228 N.Y. 612, 127 N.E. 909 (1920).

4. See section 49 supra. Annot., 118 A.L.R. 640 (1939), 8 A.L.R.2d 722 (1949).

5. Compare Old Dominion Copper Mining & Smelting Co. v. Lewisohn, 210 U.S. 206, 28 S.Ct. 634, 52 L.Ed. 1025 (1908), with Old Dominion Copper Mining & Smelting Co. v. Bigelow, 203 Mass. 159, 89 N.E. 193 (1909), aff'd 225 U.S. 111, 32 S.Ct. 641, 56 L.Ed. 1009 (1912), both discussed in section 104 infra. See section 49, nn. 12, 13 supra.

Upon incorporation,[1] promoters owe fiduciary duties to the corporation. The gist of such duties are obligations of good faith and fair dealing. Among such duties is the duty of full disclosure to the corporation. For violation of such duties, such as the promoter's pocketing of secret profits, the corporation has a cause of action which it, someone standing in its stead, or a shareholder in a derivative action, may assert. Any wronged shareholder or creditor might also have personal remedies.[2]

Where the corporation is set up with an independent board of directors and there is full disclosure to such board, there obviously can be no wrong to the corporation by the promoters for nondisclosure.

Where, however, as is usually the situation, no independent board of directors is elected, full disclosure to *all* shareholders is required by the fiduciary concept. Subscription with knowledge or subsequent unanimous shareholder ratification with knowledge, absent fraud on creditors, is sufficient. Where disclosure is only to some of the shareholders (say, the controlling shareholders) and not to existing innocent shareholders or subscribers, the corporation has a cause of action for breach of the fiduciary duty.[3] On the other hand, if the promoters

or other holders of all of the contemplated shares take them with full knowledge, the corporation traditionally has no cause of action even if such shares are thereafter sold by such holders to the public without disclosure.[4]

A split of authority arises when there is full disclosure to all present shareholders and subscribers but additional shareholders are contemplated as part of the promotional scheme and are not informed.

Two cases involving the same promotion, one in the federal courts and the other in the Massachusetts courts, highlight the difference. The facts were as follows: Bigelow and Lewisohn, the two promoters organized a syndicate to acquire the shares of a Baltimore mining concern and some other mining property. In 1895, they formed the Old Dominion Copper Mining & Smelting Co. with 40 shares at $25 par value ($1,000), elected a dummy board of directors, increased the capitalization from $1,000 to $3,750,000 (150,000 shares) and sold the interests they had acquired (for which they had paid no more than $1,000,000, and which were worth at the time of transfer to the corporation be-

---

1. Topanga Corp. v. Gentile, 249 Cal.App.2d 681, 58 Cal.Rptr. 713 (1967); Adamson v. Lang, 236 Or. 511, 389 P.2d 39 (1964); Frick v. Howard, 23 Wis. 2d 86, 126 N.W.2d 619 (1964). Even prior to incorporation, a proposed corporation may be the beneficiary of a trust relationship. 1 Restatement, Second, Trusts § 112, comment e, § 116 (1959). Compare Old Dominion Copper Mining & Smelting Co. v. Bigelow, 203 Mass. 159, 89 N.E. 193 (1909), aff'd 225 U. S. 111, 32 S.Ct. 641, 56 L.Ed. 1009 (1912); Henderson v. Plymouth Oil Co., 16 Del.Ch. 347, 141 A. 197 (Sup.Ct.1928); Erlanger v. New Sombrero Phosphate Co., L.R. 3 App.Cas. 1218 (H.L.1878), with Mason v. Carrothers, 105 Me. 392, 74 A. 1030 (1909); Bigelow v. Old Dominion Copper Mining & Smelting Co., 74 N.J.Eq. 457, 71 A. 153 (1908); In re Oklahoma Texas Trust, 2 S.E.C. 764 (1937).

2. See section 105 infra.

3. Davis v. Las Ovas Co., 227 U.S. 80, 33 S.Ct. 197, 57 L.Ed. 426 (1913); Pipelife Corp. v. Bedford, 37 Del.Ch. 467, 145 A.2d 206 (Ch.1958), 38 Del.Ch. 276, 150 A.2d 319 (Ch.1959); cf. Gladstone v. Bennett, 38

Del.Ch. 391, 153 A.2d 577 (Sup.Ct.1959); Erlanger v. New Sombrero Phosphate Co., L.R. 3 App.Cas. 1218 (H.L.1878), aff'g L.R. 5 Ch.D. 73 (1872). See also Hughes v. Cadena De Cobre Min. Co., 13 Ariz. 52, 108 P. 231 (1910) (corporate cause of action allowed where single uninformed shareholder sold shares to corporation after transaction).

4. Fountainview Ass'n v. Bell, 203 So.2d 657 (Fla. Dist.Ct.App.1967), cert. discharged 214 So.2d 609 (Fla.1968); Piggly Wiggly Delaware, Inc. v. Bartlett, 97 N.J.Eq. 469, 129 A. 413 (1925); Hays v. The Georgian, Inc., 280 Mass. 10, 181 N.E. 765 (1932). Quaere, whether elements of usurpation of corporate opportunity might not be involved. Theoretically, the result would be the same even if such holders donate some of the shares back to the corporation for resale by the corporation of the shares as treasury shares. See Arn v. Dunnett, 93 F.2d 634 (10th Cir. 1938), cert. denied 304 U.S. 577, 58 S. Ct. 1046, 82 L.Ed. 1540 (1938); see also Bronson v. Bagdad Copper Corp., 38 Del.Ch. 340, 151 A.2d 677 (Sup.Ct.1959). Furthermore, the transferees of such shares would be bound by the assent of the original holders and would not be able to satisfy any "contemporaneous-share-ownership" requirement. See note 8 infra. Annot., 85 A.L.R. 1262 (1933). See also note 11 infra.

tween $1,000,000 and $2,000,000) to the corporation for 130,000 shares of the par value of $3,250,000. For the shares of the Baltimore mining concern, they received 100,000 shares, and for the other property 30,000 shares. Of the 130,000 shares, 80,000 shares were divided among the syndicate members; the remaining 50,000 shares went to Bigelow and Lewisohn alone. When the purchasers of the remaining 20,000 shares, who paid full par value ($500,000), learned of these transactions several years later, actions were begun by the corporation against Lewisohn in the federal court in New York and against Bigelow in the Massachusetts state court. In each case, the defendant demurred.

In the Massachusetts case against Bigelow, the demurrer was overruled.[5]

Thereafter, in the federal court case against the other principal promoter, Lewisohn, the demurrer was unanimously sustained by the United States Supreme Court.[6] Here the theory was, as expressed by Holmes, J., that any duty was to the corporation as it then existed and not as it was contemplated. Since there was full disclosure to all persons having a present interest in the corporation, there could be no wrong to the corporation. Even if there had been a technical wrong, it was condoned. If the later shareholders were defrauded, they could sue in their own behalf. The Supreme Court indicated that to charge one promoter for the alleged wrong to the corporation, in which $13/15$ of the shareholders participated, and allow a corporate recovery for benefit of any guilty and innocent alike, would be manifestly unjust.

Meanwhile, a $2,000,000 recovery was allowed by the lower Massachusetts court. On appeal, the Supreme Judicial Court of Mas-

sachusetts sustained the recovery, rejecting the approach of the United States Supreme Court.[7] The Massachusetts court's theory was that the promoter's duties to the corporation were coextensive with the promotional plan. Disclosure had to be to the corporation not only as it existed but as it was contemplated, and the entity could be looked behind to see if there had been such full disclosure. Disclosure to all of the existing shareholders, when originally-authorized shares were reserved as part of the promotional plan for additional shareholders to whom there was no disclosure, did not constitute full disclosure to the corporation. While this was a wrong to the corporation, as a practical matter there was no one to enforce it until innocent shareholders came in, when either the corporation (if freed from the control of the promoters) or shareholders in a derivative action might.[8] The Massachusetts court brushed aside the argument that requiring repayment by one promoter would benefit guilty ($13/15$) and innocent ($2/15$) alike, by pointing out that the promoter's real interest was $8/17$ or $4/17$, and that the presence of some wrongdoing shareholders does not prevent a corporate recovery.[9] Since there was found to be no fiduciary relationship when the promoters first acquired the property, the measure of damages was held to be the value of the shares, found to be par value, less the market value of the property at the time of transfer to the corporation, rather than the value of the shares less the cost of the property to the promoters.[10]

---

5. Old Dominion Copper Mining & Smelting Co. v. Bigelow, 188 Mass. 315, 74 N.E. 653 (1905).

6. Old Dominion Copper Mining & Smelting Co. v. Lewisohn, 210 U.S. 206, 28 S.Ct. 634, 52 L.Ed. 1025 (1908).

7. Old Dominion Copper Mining & Smelting Co. v. Bigelow, 203 Mass. 159, 89 N.E. 193 (1909), aff'd 225 U.S. 111, 32 S.Ct. 641, 56 L.Ed. 1009 (1912) (lack of denial of full faith and credit to federal court judgment).

8. See discussion of "contemporaneous-share-ownership" requirement in section 362 infra. Arn v. Operators Royalty & Producing Co., 13 F.Supp. 769 (N.D.Okl.1936), aff'd sub nom. Arn v. Dunnett, 93 F.2d 634 (10th Cir. 1938), cert. denied 304 U.S. 577, 58 S.Ct. 1046, 82 L.Ed. 1540 (1938).

9. See sections 363, 373 infra.

10. See Du Pont v. United Oil & Fuel Corp., 109 A. 136 (Del.Ch.1920) (measure of promoters' liability

Under either the Bigelow or the Lewisohn rules, where all of the originally intended shareholders have knowledge, the subsequent issue of shares to uninformed outsiders makes no difference. The corporation has no cause of action, as previously stated.[11]

In a subsequent United States Supreme Court case, McCandless v. Furlaud,[12] where mortgage bonds and notes, and shares without par value were taken by the promoters for overvalued property and then resold to the public, the promoters were sued not by the corporation but by a receiver. The Court of Appeals, relying on the Lewisohn case, held that the corporation, new shareholders, and receiver were bound by the corporate assent, and left open the question of action by a defrauded creditor. In the Supreme Court, four justices contended that the action was by the receiver in the right of the corporation and that, on the authority of the Lewisohn case, there was no corporate cause of action. For the majority, Cardozo, J., does not analyze the nature of the receiver's action,[13] but distinguishes the Lewisohn case on the grounds that there was in that case no evidence that the effect of the transaction was to make the corporation insolvent,[14] to work a fraud upon its creditors, to divert the assets to forbidden

uses, or to violate a statute.[15] Even unanimous shareholder assent, concluded the majority, was ineffective where creditors' rights or statutory policy was involved; furthermore, the amounts paid by the public to the promoters for the bonds and notes constituted a "trust fund" in the hands of the promoters.

A possibly sounder theory in support of a corporate recovery might have been to estop the promoters from denying the impression given to the public by the prospectus that the bonds and notes were being issued by the corporation and the proceeds thereof were going to the corporation to pay for property additions and development, whereas they were actually being resold by the promoters and the proceeds, to the extent of the promoters' profits, were not devoted to the corporation.[16]

The latter theory, of course, would be limited to cases where similar false impressions were given to the public. A recovery of the profits realized by the promoters on the resale of the bonds and notes and bonus shares —the latter on the theory that the transaction, being a unit, was infected with a common vice—was allowed. Reserved were questions of any rights of action of the corporation or of individual defrauded creditors, and the effect of the receiver's recovery in mitigation of damages in any other actions.

The Furlaud case qualified the authority of the Lewisohn case, if it did not, as contended by the minority in the Furlaud case, overrule it. In 1957, a federal court case followed the Bigelow case rather than the

held to be difference between value of property and market (not par) value of shares); Densmore Oil Co. v. Densmore, 64 Pa. 43 (1870); Note, 7 U.Chi.L. Rev. 534 (1940). As to the commencement of the fiduciary relationship with respect to the corporation, see section 103, n. 5 supra.

11. Jeffs v. Utah Power & Light Co., 136 Me. 454, 12 A.2d 592 (1940); Continental Securities Co. v. Belmont, 168 App.Div. 483, 154 N.Y.S. 54 (2d Dep't 1915), aff'd 222 N.Y. 673, 119 N.E. 1036 (1918); In re British Seamless Paperbox Co., L.R. 17 Ch.D. 467 (1881). See note 4 supra.

12. 296 U.S. 140, 56 S.Ct. 41, 80 L.Ed. 121 (1935).

13. The receiver was appointed in an action consolidating two actions: one by the mortgage trustee, and the other by a shareholder. The majority expressly refrained from discussing the corporation's right of action.

14. As a matter of fact, the lower court in the Furlaud case made no finding with respect to insolvency.

15. The statute implemented a Pennsylvania constitutional provision that bonds and shares may be issued by a corporation only for money, labor done, or property actually received, and that all fictitious increase of shares or indebtedness shall be void. See section 14, nn. 7, 8 supra, sections 167, 168, 171 infra. See Pipelife Corp. v. Bedford, 37 Del.Ch. 467, 145 A.2d 206 (Ch.1958), 38 Del.Ch. 276, 150 A.2d 319 (Ch.1959).

16. See Piggly Wiggly Delaware, Inc. v. Bartlett, 97 N.J.Eq. 469, 129 A. 413 (1925).

Lewisohn case, and the New York Court of Appeals cited the Lewisohn case but qualified the reference by rephrasing the rule of the Bigelow case without citing the latter.[17]

North Carolina expressly deals with promoters' secret profits in its corporation statute. Disclosure of such profits is also required by certain rules and regulations of the Securities and Exchange Commission under certain circumstances.[18]

PROMOTERS' DUTIES AND LIABILITIES TO SHAREHOLDERS AND CREDITORS

105. Promoters are liable, apart from any liability to the corporation, to any defrauded shareholders and creditors, who would recover either individually or in behalf of their class and not derivatively in behalf of the corporation.

Promoters presumably owe fiduciary duties not only to the corporation but also to the prospective investors thereof: the shareholders and possibly creditors. If the promoters serve as directors, officers, or in a control position, they might be subject to fiduciary duties in such capacity.

Apart from any corporate cause of action are the claims of innocent shareholders who have been defrauded by the promoters. Their remedies would be asserted in direct

actions by themselves rather than direct actions by the corporation or derivative actions by shareholders.[1]

Similarly, if creditors are defrauded, their remedies could be asserted in direct actions against the promoters. Fraud could result from positive misrepresentation or failure to disclose all the material facts when under a duty to disclose.[2]

STATUTORY DEVELOPMENTS CONCERNING PROMOTERS' DUTIES AND LIABILITIES

106. Statutes affecting promoters' duties and liabilities are relatively rare. Recognition of shares without par value minimizes to some extent the problem of evaluation of the property transferred to the corporation by the promoters. North Carolina, by statute, deals expressly with promoters' profits. The Federal Securities Act of 1933 and state "blue sky" statutes, along with administrative regulations thereunder, have some application.

An early statutory development which to some extent minimized the problem of evaluation of the property transferred to the corporation by the promoters for shares was the statutory recognition of shares without par value. Such shares may be issued only for money, labor done,[1] or property transfer-

17. San Juan Uranium Corp. v. Wolfe, 241 F.2d 121 (10th Cir. 1957) (2–1); Northridge Cooperative Section No. 1, Inc. v. 32nd Avenue Construction Corp., 2 N.Y.2d 514, 161 N.Y.S.2d 404, 141 N.E.2d 802 (1957); see also Bovay v. H. M. Byllesby & Co., 27 Del.Ch. 381, 38 A.2d 808, 174 A.L.R. 1201 (Sup.Ct. 1944). See generally McCrea, "Disclosure of Promoters' Secret Profits", 3 U.B.C.L.Rev. 183 (1968); McGowan, "Legal Control of Promoters' Profits", 25 Geo.L.J. 269 (1937); Brockelbank, "The Compensation of Promoters", 13 Ore.L.Rev. 195 (1934); Berle, "Compensation of Bankers and Promoters Through Stock Profits", 42 Harv.L.Rev. 748 (1929); Weston, "Promoters' Liability: Old Dominion v. Bigelow", 30 Harv.L.Rev. 39 (1916); Little, "Promoters' Frauds in the Organization of Corporations: The Old Dominion Copper Mining Cases", 5 Ill.L. Rev. 87 (1910); Gold, "The Liability of Promoters for Secret Profits in English Law", 5 U.Toronto L. J. 21 (1943).

18. See section 106 infra.

Henn Corporations 2d Ed. HB—12

[§ 105]
1. See Killeen v. Parent, 23 Wis.2d 244, 127 N.W.2d 34 (1964); Opdyke v. Kent Liquor Mart, Inc., 40 Del.Ch. 316, 181 A.2d 579 (Sup.Ct.1962); Arn v. Operators Royalty & Producing Co., 13 F.Supp. 769 (N.D.Okl.1936), aff'd sub nom. Arn v. Dunnett, 93 F.2d 634 (10th Cir. 1938), cert. denied 304 U.S. 577, 58 S.Ct. 1046, 82 L.Ed. 1540 (1938); Downey v. Byrd, 171 Ga. 532, 156 S.E. 259, 72 A.L.R. 345 (1930) (class action). Creditors' rights sometimes limit shareholders' rights of rescission for fraud. Obviously, a derivative action protects creditors better than individual shareholders' direct actions.

2. See McCandless v. Furlaud, 296 U.S. 140, 56 S.Ct. 41, 80 L.Ed. 121 (1935) (5–4), reh. denied 296 U.S. 664, 56 S.Ct. 304, 80 L.Ed. 473 (1936), discussed in section 104 supra; Frick v. Howard, 23 Wis.2d 86, 126 N.W.2d 619 (1964).

[§ 106]
1. See section 113 infra. Preincorporation services might be sufficient in a growing number of jurisdictions.

red to the corporation, but the quantity of such consideration for shares without par value is not usually subject to the minimum standards which generally exist for par value shares.[2] Even in the case of shares without par value, the property must be assigned a value for purposes of the books of account, and overvaluation should be avoided, and the promoter's interest should be adequately disclosed.[3]

Otherwise, statutes bearing upon "the chrysalis stage of corporate existence" are almost nonexistent.[4]

The 1955 revised North Carolina corporation statute deals expressly with promoters' profits. It combines principles of promoters' liability and those of share-watering liability,[5] by establishing a broad concept of "watered stock". When the recipient of shares gets more than that to which he is entitled in the light of his contribution to the corporation and his relationship to the venture and those in control, he may be required either to make an additional contribution or to surrender some of his shares.[6]

Securities legislation and administrative regulations by the states and federal government require full disclosure concerning promoters. Many state "blue sky" laws[7] and the Federal Securities Act of 1933[8] have such provisions applicable to the public offering of securities; some of the state statutes in addition impose "fair, equitable, and just" tests, or require that securities issued to promoters be placed in escrow. These provisions, along with tax provisions[9] and

(c) compensate the company for any loss suffered by it by reason of his failure so to do.

(3) A promoter who acquires any property or information in circumstances in which it was his duty as a fiduciary to acquire it on behalf of the company shall account to the company for such property and for any profit which he may have made from the use of such property or information.

(4) Any transaction between a promoter and the company may be rescinded by the company unless, after full disclosure of all material facts known to the promoter, the transaction shall have been entered into or ratified on behalf of the company,

(a) if all the company's directors are independent of the promoter, by the company's board of directors; or

(b) by all the members of the company; or

(c) by the company at a general meeting at which neither the promoter nor the holders of any shares in which he is beneficially interested shall have voted on the resolution to enter into or ratify that transaction.

(5) No period of limitation shall apply to any proceedings brought by a company to enforce any of its rights under this section; but in any such proceedings the Court may relieve a promoter in whole or in part and on such terms as it thinks fit from liability hereunder if in all the circumstances, including lapse of time, the Court thinks it equitable so to do."

---

2. See Piggly Wiggly Delaware, Inc. v. Bartlett, 97 N.J.Eq. 469, 129 A. 413 (1925).

3. See section 104, n. 10 supra, section 168 infra.

4. 1 G. Hornstein, Corporation Law and Practice § 93 (1959).

5. See section 171 infra.

6. N.C.Bus.Corp.Act § 55–53 (1957); Latty, "Some Miscellaneous Novelties in the New Corporation Statutes", 23 Law & Contemp.Prob. 363, 366–367 (1958). The North Carolina statute was drafted by law professors. The Ghana Companies Code, 1963, was drafted by Professor L. C. B. Gower. Section 12. (1) reads:

"12. (1) Any person who is or has been engaged or interested in the formation of a company shall be deemed to be a promoter of that company:

Provided that a person acting in a professional capacity for persons engaged in procuring the formation of the company shall not thereby be deemed to be a promoter.

(2) Until the formation of a company is complete and its working capital has been raised, the promoter shall,

(a) stand in a fiduciary relationship to the company;

(b) observe the utmost good faith towards the company in any transaction with it or on its behalf; and

7. See sections 305–307 infra. See Holmberg v. Marsden, 39 Cal.2d 592, 248 P.2d 417 (1952); Bernard v. Shure, 111 Cal.App.2d 920, 245 P.2d 370 (1952).

8. 15 U.S.C.A. § 77a et seq.; S.E.C. Form S–1, Item 11; Regulation A, Rules 251, 253; Form 1–A, Items 3, 9(d).

9. E. g., the long-term capital gain advantage to the promoter of postponing sale of his securities until after six months, and of deferred receipt of promotional expenses to spread the income.

other requirements,[10] tend to encourage the promotion of economically-sound enter- prises.[11]

C. PREINCORPORATION AGREEMENTS

KINDS OF PREINCORPORATION AGREEMENTS

107. Preincorporation agreements, in a broad sense, are of four kinds: (a) Agreements between promoters for the formation of a corporation; (b) Shareholder agreements; (c) Agreements of association; and (d) Agreements between promoters and third persons, including preincorporation share subscriptions. Only the fourth kind is discussed in this chapter, with the others reserved for subsequent treatment.

"Preincorporation agreement" is a broad term which encompasses at least four distinguishable kinds of agreements: [1]

(a) Agreements between promoters for the formation of the corporation;

(b) "Shareholder agreements";

(c) "Agreements of association"; and

(d) Agreements between promoters and third persons.

Agreements between promoters for the formation of the corporation do not always contemplate that the corporation will acquire rights or liabilities thereunder. When they do contemplate this, they resemble agreements between promoters and third persons [2] and will be so treated herein. Such preliminary agreements usually deal with where and how the corporation is to be formed, the respective contributions of each associate to the initial assets, the source of future funds if needed, the allocation of shares and other securities, and such intracorporate provisions as voting control, the names of the directors and officers, and their salaries, the taking over of the property assembled by the promoters for the business and adoption of outstanding preincorporation agreements with third persons, shareholder agreements, employment contracts, share transfer restrictions, etc. They may be only "binders" or complete agreements. [3]

"Shareholder agreements" are often executed by those interested in close corporations, may be made before (when the term "shareholder" would be technically a misnomer) or after incorporation, and may or may not involve the corporation as a party. [4] Sometimes provisions common to agreements between promoters for the formation of the corporation and those typically found in "shareholder agreements" are combined in a single instrument. While there is nothing wrong with this, it would appear preferable in most cases to separate the former, to the extent that they cease to be relevant after the corporation is launched, from the latter, which are relevant after incorporation.

"Agreement of association" (or "articles of agreement") is the term for a formal preliminary instrument required by statute in a

---

10. E. g., violation of S.E.C. Rule 10b–5, Stevens v. Vowell, 343 F.2d 374 (10th Cir. 1965) (agreement to form corporation held "security" under Federal Securities Exchange Act 1934); Frohling, "The Promoter and Rule 10b–5: Basis for Accountability", 48 Cornell L.Q. 274 (1963); Note, "Individual Recovery for Promoter's Fraud—Procedural Problems under S.E.C. Rule 10b–5", 51 Calif.L.Rev. 939 (1963). Recapture of short-swing insider profits realized within a six-month period by directors, officers, or more than 10 percent beneficial holders of corporations with registered equity securities, Securities Exchange Act, 1934, § 16(b), 15 U.S.C.A. § 78p(b), discussed in section 298 infra.

11. Bruenner & Gilley, "Promoters and Their Profits", 13 Bus.Law. 429 (1958).

1. See C. Rohrlich, Organizing Corporate and Other Business Enterprises §§ 302, 801–805 (4th ed. 1967).

2. Air Traffic & Service Corp. v. Fay, 196 F.2d 40 (D.C.Cir. 1952).

3. See sections 260, 284 infra. See 1 G. Hornstein, Corporation Law and Practice § 96 (1959) (Form— Agreement to Organize Corporation).

4. See sections 198, 213, 267, 275, 287 infra.

few jurisdictions as part of the incorporation procedure.[5]

When preincorporation agreements between promoters and third parties are made, there is no corporation in existence. Absent statute or provision in the articles of incorporation, the corporation is not automatically bound when it is incorporated. Apart from the legal theories is the practical concern over having the corporation come into being saddled with obligations. Obviously, such an approach affects both rights and liabilities not only of the corporation, but also of the promoters and third parties involved.

TYPES OF PREINCORPORATION AGREEMENTS BETWEEN PROMOTERS AND THIRD PERSONS

108. **Preincorporation agreements between promoters and third persons in behalf of proposed corporations are of five types: (a) Agreement constituting revocable "offer" to proposed corporation; (b) Contract constituting irrevocable "offer" to proposed corporation; (c) Contract initially binding promoter and continuing to bind him even if corporation is formed and becomes bound; (d) Contract binding promoter until corporation is formed and becomes bound; and (e) Preincorporation share subscription. Whether the agreement, other than a preincorporation share subscription, falls in the first, second, third, or fourth category depends upon the construction of the agreement as a whole, although the judicial tendency is to find a contract binding the promoter, at least initially. Many construction problems can be avoided by sound draftsmanship of the agreement.**

Preincorporation agreements—an "agreement" may or may not amount to a contract —between promoters and third persons in behalf of proposed corporations are of five types:[1]

(a) Agreement constituting revocable "offer" to proposed corporation, to result in contract if corporation is formed and accepts offer prior to its revocation;[2]

(b) Contract constituting irrevocable "offer" to proposed corporation, irrevocable for limited time, supported by promoter's promise to form corporation and use his best efforts to cause it to accept offer;[3]

(c) Contract initially binding promoter and, even though corporation is formed and becomes bound, continuing to bind promoter, either primarily or as surety for performance of corporation's obligations;[4]

(d) Contract binding promoter, but with understanding that his liability terminates if corporation is formed and becomes bound;[5] and

(e) Preincorporation share subscription.[6]

Problems of Construction

Whether the agreement, putting aside for separate discussion the preincorporation share subscription, falls in one category or another are matters of interpretation on the individual facts and of construction of the agreement as a whole. How the parties are designated in the agreement,[7] what the re-

---

(Centennial Edition 1967); Nicholson, "Contract and Non-Existent Companies", 7 Austl.Law. 3 (1967); Lücke, "Contracts Made by Promoters on behalf of Companies Yet to be Incorporated", 2 Adelaide L.Rev. 388 (1966); Kessler, "Promoters' Contracts: A Statutory Solution", 25 Rutgers L. Rev. 567 (1961); Ehrich & Bunzl, "Promoters' Contracts", 38 Yale L.J. 1011 (1929); Note, "Preincorporation Contracts", 5 Sydney L.Rev. 486 (1967); Note, "Preincorporation Agreements", 11 Sw.L.J. 509 (1957).

2. See section 109 infra.

3. See section 110 infra.

4. See section 111 infra.

5. See section 112 infra.

6. See section 115 infra.

7. Carle v. Corhan, 127 Va. 223, 103 S.E. 699 (1920); Weiss v. Baum, 218 App.Div. 83, 217 N.Y.S. 820 (2d

[§ 107]
5. See section 117 infra.

[§ 108]
1. 2 Restatement, Second, Agency § 327, comment b (1958); Getz, "Pre-incorporation Contracts: Some Proposals", U.B.C.L.Rev.-Les Cahiers de Droit 381

citals state, how the various undertakings are phrased and their timing,[8] and the form of the signatures,[9] are among the relevant factors in such construction. When the language is ambiguous, parol evidence is admissible to clarify it. Very often the courts hesitate to categorize the agreement, and instead decide the case on alternative constructions.[10] The courts tend, however, to find a contract binding the promoter.[11]

Drafting Technique

Many problems can be avoided if the instrument explicitly manifests the intention of the parties with respect to: whether one or more contracts or agreements and/or offers are involved; whether the promoter is to be initially bound; what are to be his rights and obligations; what are to be the rights and obligations of the contemplated corporation; what are to be the consequences if the contemplated corporation is not formed (either where a different corporation is formed or no corporation at all is formed); what are to be the consequences where the corporation as contemplated is formed and repudiates the agreement, does nothing with respect thereto, accepts benefits thereunder, or expressly ratifies or adopts the agreement; and what effect does such corporate action have on any initial liability of the promoter (novation or not). In

addition, the instrument should clearly set forth that the corporation is nonexistent,[12] and negative any unintended representations, warranties, and promises which might otherwise be implied with respect to the formation of the corporation.[13] Finally, any applicable statutory provisions [14] should be carefully considered in drafting the instrument.[15]

AGREEMENT BETWEEN PROMOTER AND THIRD PERSON CONSTITUTING REVOCABLE "OFFER" TO PROPOSED CORPORATION

109. An agreement between a promoter and a third person made in behalf of a proposed corporation and intended not to bind the promoter is not a contract but at most a "gentlemen's agreement" involving a revocable "offer" to be communicated to the proposed corporation after its formation. The promoter neither enjoys rights, nor suffers liabilities, absent misrepresentation or breach of warranty, under the agreement. If the "offer" is not revoked

Dep't 1926); Macy Corp. v. Ramey, 144 N.E.2d 698 (Ohio C.P.1957). But see Kelner v. Baxter, L.R. 2 C.P. 174 (1866); Abbott v. Hapgood, 150 Mass. 248, 22 N.E. 907 (1889).

8. O'Rorke v. Geary, 207 Pa. 240, 56 A. 541 (1903). See section 113 infra.

9. See note 7 supra.

10. O'Rorke v. Geary, 207 Pa. 240, 56 A. 541 (1903).

11. R. Stevens, Handbook on the Law of Private Corporations 210–213 (2d ed. 1949). The courts readily infer an intention of the third party and the promoter to contract with each other even though the language used in the agreement would, when used by an agent in behalf of an existing corporation, be sufficient to repel an inference of intention to bind the agent. See Note, "Preincorporation Agreements", 11 Sw.L.J. 509 (1957). See note 7 supra.

12. See Macy Corp. v. Ramey, 144 N.E.2d 698 (Ohio C.P.1957).

13. When a promoter agrees in behalf of the corporation, he might be liable to the third person on several theories other than as an intended party to the contract. If the promoter gives the third person the impression that he as agent is agreeing in behalf of an *existing* corporation, the promoter might be liable: (a) For breach of implied warranty of the existence of the principal; or (b) For breach of implied warranty of authority from the principal. If the promoter makes it clear that he is acting in behalf of a corporation *to be* formed, the otherwise implied warranties of the existence of the principal or of authority from the principal would be negatived. However, the promoter might be liable, if the corporation is not formed, for: (a) Misrepresentation that the corporation was being formed; (b) Breach of promise to form the corporation; or (c) Breach of warranty that the corporation would be formed. See Weiss v. Baum, 218 App.Div. 83, 217 N.Y.S. 820 (2d Dep't 1926). Whether the theory of liability is contract, warranty, or tort may affect the outcome, e. g., statute of limitations, measure of relief. On breach of contract to incorporate, see Kirschmann v. Lediard & Ree, 61 Barb. 573 (N.Y.1872) (damages); for limitations on equitable relief, see Brown v. Swarthout, 134 Mich. 585, 96 N.W. 951 (1903); Bunzl & Ehrich, "Promoters' Contracts", 38 Yale L.J. 1011 (1929).

14. See section 114 infra.

15. See R. Kessler, New York Close Corporations ch. 6 (1968).

and the corporation is formed and accepts it, a contract then arises between the corporation and the third person. In case of revocation of the offer or nonacceptance by the corporation, no contract ever arises. The courts tend to avoid this construction on the ground that the agreement contemplated legally-effective consequences.

When a promoter agrees with a third person in behalf of a proposed corporation without being personally bound, there is, of course, no contract. At most, such a "gentlemen's agreement" is a revocable offer when communicated to the contemplated corporation after its formation.[1] Regardless of what, if any, action the corporation takes with respect thereto, the promoter never enjoys the rights[2] nor suffers the liabilities[3] thereunder. If unrevoked by the other party in the interim, such offer may be accepted by the corporation. If the corporation is not formed,[4] or if formed, does not accept, no contract ever arises. Upon acceptance, express or implied, there is a contract between the corporation and such other party under which the corporation enjoys such rights and is subject to such liabilities as are provided therein.

Because such an agreement initially can have a nugatory effect, the courts avoid this construction on the ground that the promoter and third person intended immediate le-

gally-effective consequences. For this reason, only reasonably clear express or implied manifestations of intention that the promoter is not to be bound personally will be recognized by the courts.[5]

While the promoter never becomes a party to an agreement construed as of this type, he might become liable for misrepresentation or breach of warranty, depending on the reasonable impressions he has created in the mind of the third person.[6]

CONTRACT BETWEEN PROMOTER AND THIRD PERSON CONSTITUTING IRREVOCABLE "OFFER" TO PROPOSED CORPORATION

110. An agreement between a promoter and a third person made in behalf of a proposed corporation is a contract, constituting an irrevocable "offer" to the proposed corporation, irrevocable for a limited time, supported by the promoter's promise to form the corporation and to use his best efforts to cause it to accept the offer. The promoter is bound to perform such promise but not otherwise, absent misrepresentation or breach of warranty, under the contract. If the corporation accepts the "offer", a contract then arises between the corporation and the third person, but not otherwise.

When a promoter agrees with a third person in behalf of a proposed corporation, promising, expressly or impliedly, to form the corporation and to use his best efforts to cause it to accept the agreement, the promoter becomes personally bound to perform such promise, and there can be a contract, construed as an irrevocable "offer"[1] to the

[§ 109]

1. See R. A. C. Realty Co. v. W. O. U. F. Atlanta Realty Corp., 205 Ga. 154, 52 S.E.2d 617 (1949) (option for corporation to be formed adjudged revocable); Strause v. Richmond Woodworking Co., 109 Va. 724, 65 S.E. 659 (1909). An offer must be communicated to the offeree. 1 Restatement of Contracts § 23 (1932). Quaere, whether prior to incorporation there can be an "offer" to the corporation. For discussion of preincorporation share subscriptions treated as revocable offers, see section 115 infra.

2. Newborne v. Sensolid (Great Britain) Ld., L.R. [1954] 1 Q.B. 45.

3. Quaker Hill, Inc. v. Parr, 148 Colo. 45, 364 P.2d 1056 (1961).

4. Stewart Realty Co. v. Keller, 118 Ohio App. 49, 193 N.E.2d 179 (1962); Weiss v. Baum, 218 App. Div. 83, 217 N.Y.S. 820 (2d Dep't 1926).

5. See section 108, n. 11 supra.

6. See section 108, n. 13 supra.

[§ 110]

1. Technically, the third person's promises are construable as an agreement to communicate such "offer" to the contemplated corporation after its formation, and not to revoke it for a reasonable time. Quaere, whether an offer can exist until communicated to the offeree. See section 109, n. 1 supra. Cf. also McKinney's N.Y.Gen.Obl.Law § 5–1109. For discussion of preincorporate share subscription

proposed corporation, irrevocable for a limited time.

If the contemplated corporation is not formed, the promoter might be liable for breach of his promise to form it. If the corporation is formed but does not accept the "offer", the promoter might be subject to liability for failing to use his best efforts to cause the corporation to accept.

If the corporation is not formed, or if formed, does not accept, no contract between it and the third person ever arises.

Upon acceptance by the corporation, there is a contract between the corporation and the third person under which the corporation enjoys such rights and is subject to such liabilities as are provided therein.

While the promoter's liabilities as a party to an agreement construed as of this type are limited to his promises—to form the corporation and to use his best efforts to cause it to accept—he might also be liable for any misrepresentation or breach of warranty.[2]

CONTRACT BETWEEN PROMOTER AND THIRD PERSON BINDING PROMOTER EVEN IF CORPORATION BOUND

111. A contract between a promoter and a third person made in behalf of a proposed corporation and intended to bind the promoter is initially a contract between the promoter and the third person and remains so if the corporation is never formed or, if formed, does nothing with respect to the contract. If the corporation takes some action under the contract, the effect thereof on its, the promoter's, and the third person's rights and liabilities depends upon the legal theory applied. The possible theories, recognized in varying degrees in different jurisdictions, include: (a) Ratification; (b) Adoption; (c) Assignment; (d) Novation; (e) Implied continuing "offer" to corporation; (f) Third party beneficiary; (g) Beneficiary of trust; (h) Alter ego; (i) Quantum meruit;

(j) Estoppel; and (k) Statutory. Even apart from such theories, the promoter might be liable for misrepresentation, breach of warranty, or breach of promise to form the corporation.

When a promoter contracts with a third person in behalf of a proposed corporation, they, of course, are initially the parties to the contract,[1] and remain so if the contemplated corporation is never formed.

If the contemplated corporation is formed, various legal theories might come into play which affect the respective rights and liabilities of the corporation, the promoter, and the third person. To a considerable extent, these respective rights and liabilities are interdependent, and also are affected by actions which the corporation takes with respect to the contract. Obviously if the corporation does nothing with respect to the promoter's contract, the promoter's liabilities under the contract continue. If the corporation takes some action, the effect may be to vest rights in the corporation only, or to make the corporation liable as well. Even when the corporation becomes liable under most of the theories, it does not follow that the promoter's liabilities are released. Quite apart from the promoters' liabilities as parties to the main undertakings of the contract, they might be liable for misrepresentation, breach of warranty, or breach of promise to form the corporation.[2]

The respective rights and liabilities of the corporation, promoter, and third person vary under the several legal theories applicable to promoters' contracts made in behalf of a proposed corporation. These theories, which

with a double aspect treated as an irrevocable offer, see section 115 infra.

2. See section 108, n. 13 supra.

[§ 111]

1. O'Rorke v. Geary, 207 Pa. 240, 56 A. 541 (1903). Otherwise, there could be no contract. See Kelner v. Baxter, L.R. 2 C.P. 174 (1866). The courts also apply the agency rule that a person who purports to act as agent for a nonexistent principal is liable as principal. 2 Restatement, Second, Agency § 326 (1958).

2. See section 108, n. 13 supra. See Annot., 17 A.L. R. 452 (1922), 49 A.L.R. 673 (1927), 123 A.L.R. 726 (1939), 41 A.L.R.2d 477 (1955). For discussion of indemnification of corporate personnel, see sections 379, 380 infra.

are recognized in varying degrees in different jurisdictions, are:

(a) Ratification;

(b) Adoption;

(c) Assignment;

(d) Novation;

(e) Implied continuing "offer" to corporation;

(f) Third-party beneficiary;

(g) Beneficiary of trust;

(h) *Alter ego*;

(i) *Quantum meruit*;

(j) Estoppel;

(k) Statutory.

Ratification

The corporation is treated as having power to ratify the act of the promoter. The theoretical basis for this theory is the agency rule which allows a principal to ratify the unauthorized acts of one purporting to act as his agent. Such ratification, in agency law, relates back to the time the purported agent acted and is deemed equivalent to prior authority.[3] The difficulty of applying such a rule to the preincorporation agreement is that at the time of the making of the contract, there was no principal (i. e., the corporation) in existence. Despite such theoretical difficulty,[4] many courts continue to espouse the ratification theory. Ratification may be express or implied.[5] Its effect

is to make the corporation a party to the original contract as of the date of such contract (*nunc pro tunc*) for purposes of rights and liabilities.

In a very few jurisdictions, notably England [6] and Massachusetts,[7] the corporation may not become a party to the contract by ratification. Of course, the corporation could enter into a new contract with the third person, provided there was adequate new consideration. Or the promoter, third person, and corporation could make a novation substituting the corporation for the promoter as party to the contract. Otherwise under the ratification theory the contract remains one between the promoter and third person.[8]

---

3. 1 Restatement, Second, Agency § 82 (1958).

4. This theoretical difficulty is somewhat obviated where the corporation at the time of the making of the contract had a de facto existence (see section 140 infra). Since ratification amounts to a fiction, as does the corporate entity, the courts could theoretically indulge in the additional fiction that the corporation was in existence when the contract was made, or stated differently, that relation back is equivalent not only to prior authority but also to prior existence of the ratifier.

5. Express ratification could result from a resolution of the board of directors to such effect. Or the articles of incorporation possibly could provide for

ratification ipso facto upon incorporation. Implied ratification occurs when the corporation accepts the benefits of the promoter's contract with knowledge of the terms thereof. Chartrand v. Barney's Club, Inc., 380 F.2d 97 (9th Cir.1967); Graham v. First Nat'l Bank of Dickinson, 175 F.Supp. 81 (D.N.D. 1959); European Motors, Ltd. v. Oden, 75 Nev. 401, 344 P.2d 195 (1959); Benton-Bauxite Housing Co-op, Inc. v. Benton Plumbing, Inc., 228 Ark. 798, 310 S.W.2d 483 (1958). The benefit must be traced to the corporation. Glass v. Newport Clothing Co., 110 Vt. 368, 8 A.2d 651 (1939). The corporation must also know or be charged with knowledge of the terms of the contract. If the board of directors of the corporation is aware of the terms, as it would be where the terms were communicated to the board or where it was composed of promoters with such knowledge, the knowledge of the board of directors, absent a conflict of interest between them as promoters and as directors (C. & H. Contractors, Inc. v. McKee, 177 So.2d 851 (Fla.Dist.Ct.App. 1965); Clifton v. Tomb, 21 F.2d 893 (4th Cir.1927)), is deemed to be the knowledge of the corporation. Involved are problems of imputing knowledge to the corporation and of constructive knowledge. Where the arrangements of the promoters with third persons are divisible into two or more contracts, the corporation's acceptance of the benefits under one of such contracts might be regarded as an acceptance only of that contract and not of the related contracts. Weatherford, M. W. & Nw. Ry. v. Granger, 86 Tex. 350, 24 S.W. 795 (1894); Maryland Apartment House Co. v. Glenn, 108 Md. 377, 70 A. 216 (1908); Application of Jacoby, 33 N.Y.S.2d 621 (Sup.Ct.1942).

6. Kelner v. Baxter, L.R. 2 C.P. 174 (1866).

7. Abbott v. Hapgood, 150 Mass. 248, 22 N.E. 907 (1889).

8. See note 12 infra.

Adoption

Because of the relation-back connotation of "ratification", some courts, and most commentators, prefer the term "adoption".[9] Adoption, like ratification, may be express or implied.[10] The theory is that as part of the contract between the promoter and third person, there is an implied continuing "offer" to the corporation to adopt the contract after its incorporation. The effect of the adoption is to make the corporation a party to the contract as of the time of adoption.[11] Adoption alone does not end the liability of the promoter to the third-party.[12] However, if the promoter is found liable, he might seek indemnification from the corporation. Of course, under the adoption theory, absent adoption, the corporation would not become a party and the contract would remain one between the promoter and third person.[13]

In jurisdictions adhering to the English-Massachusetts rule, the same approach which precludes ratification bars adoption.[14]

Assignment

If the contract is assignable[15] and the promoter assigns it to the corporation after its formation, the corporation becomes the assignee of the promoter's rights under the original contract. If the corporation accepts delegation of the promoters' duties, it usually becomes liable under the contract.[16] In the latter case, the promoter usually remains liable,[17] but could seek indemnification from the corporation with respect to such liability.

Novation

When there is a novation, the corporation is substituted for the promoter as a party to the contract in all respects. In such a novation, the third person, promoter, and corporation would agree to such substitution. The consideration for the release of the promoter is the assumption of the promoter's duties by the corporation.[18] The novation may be express or, except possibly in jurisdictions like England and Massachusetts, implied.[19] Some courts tend to find an implied continuing offer to the corporation to such a novation.[20] In effect, the promoter-third person contract is treated as a "stop-gap" arrangement. Other courts, however, still favor the view that even after the corporation becomes bound, the double security of liability of promoter and corporation was intended.

9. McCrillis v. A & W Enterprises, Inc., 270 N.C. 637, 155 S.E.2d 281 (1967) (adoption of entire agreement, not only of parts formalized in resolutions, found). The difference may be more than semantic. For example, where the one-year statute of frauds is involved, a ratified (related-back) contract might be within the statute whereas an adopted contract (no relation-back) might not. McArthur v. Times Printing Co., 48 Minn. 319, 51 N.W. 216 (1892).

10. See note 5 supra. McEachin v. Kingman, 64 Ga. App. 104, 12 S.E.2d 212 (1940); Morgan v. Bon Bon Co., 222 N.Y. 22, 118 N.E. 205 (1917).

11. Speedway Realty Co. v. Grasshoff Realty Corp., 248 Ind. 6, 216 N.E.2d 845 (1966) (contract adopted by corporation held not enforceable by promoter); McArthur v. Times Printing Co., 48 Minn. 319, 51 N.W. 216 (1892); Wiley v. Borough of Towanda, 26 F. 594 (W.D.Pa.1886) (adoption held to bar action by promoter against third person).

12. Allen Steel Supply Co. v. Bradley, 89 Idaho 29, 402 P.2d 394 (1965), petition denied 89 Idaho 43, 403 P.2d 859 (1965); Akel v. Dooley, 185 So.2d 491 (Fla. Dist.Ct.App.1966); Stanley J. How & Associates v. Boss, 222 F.Supp. 936 (S.D.Iowa 1963); Van Duker v. Fritz, 222 Cal.App.2d 228, 35 Cal.Rptr. 55 (1963); Randolph Foods, Inc. v. McLaughlin, 253 Iowa 1258, 115 N.W.2d 868 (1962); O'Rorke v. Geary, 207 Pa. 240, 56 A. 541 (1903); Ennis Cotton-Oil Co. v. Burks, 39 S.W. 966 (Tex.Civ.App.1897).

13. Air Traffic & Service Corp. v. Fay, 196 F.2d 40 (D.C.Cir.1952).

14. See notes 6–7 supra.

15. See 1 Restatement of Contracts §§ 151 et seq (1932).

16. 1 Restatement of Contracts §§ 160, 164 (1932).

17. 1 Restatement of Contracts §§ 160, 165 (1932).

18. 2 Restatement of Contracts §§ 424 et seq. (1932).

19. See note 5 supra. There can be an implied "ratification" or adoption without an implied novation. See note 12 supra.

20. See section 112 infra.

Implied Continuing "Offer" to Corporation

Often referred to as a separate theory, the implied "offer" theory merely provides the theoretical basis for adoption and implied novation, previously discussed. Presumably, such "offer" becomes such when communicated to the corporation after it is formed.[21]

Third-Party Beneficiary

The corporation is regarded as the third-party beneficiary of the contract between the promoter and the third person. A third-party beneficiary need not be in existence at the time a contract is made for its benefit.[22] Absent rejection by the corporation of such rights, the corporation would enjoy them under the original contract; the corporation would not suffer any concomitant liability; the liability would remain in the promoters.

Beneficiary of Trust

The corporation is regarded as the beneficiary of a trust (assuming that the corporation has such capacity under applicable law), whose *res* is the contract and whose trustee is the promoter. A beneficiary of a trust need not be in existence at the time of the creation of the trust.[23] Absent rejection by the corporation of such benefits, the corporation would enjoy them under the original contract. When it accepts such benefits, the trust would presumably terminate and the corporation would become liable under the contract, with the promoter possibly discharged as trustee.[24]

Alter Ego

The promoters and the corporation are viewed as identical—the corporate entity being disregarded.[25]

Quantum Meruit

Where the corporation accepts benefits it might be liable, where for one reason or another it is not liable under the promoter's contract, for the reasonable value of such benefits (*quantum meruit*) on the theory of inferred-in-fact contract [26] or implied-in-law contract (quasi-contract).[27]

Estoppel

When the third-party suffers a loss in reliance upon the corporation's representation of fact, the corporation might be estopped from denying liability for such loss. Principles of estoppel might otherwise affect the promoters and/or third persons.[28]

Statutory

A few jurisdictions, by statute, have attempted to legislate on preincorporation agreements.[29]

CONTRACT BETWEEN PROMOTER AND THIRD PERSON BINDING PROMOTER UNTIL CORPORATION BOUND

112. A contract between a promoter and a third person made in behalf of a proposed corporation and intended to bind the promoter is initially a contract between the promoter and the third person. Only in case of a valid ex-

---

21. See section 109, n. 1 supra.

22. 1 Restatement of Contracts § 139 (1932). See Application of Jacoby, 33 N.Y.S.2d 621 (Sup.Ct. 1942).

23. 1 Restatement, Second, Trusts § 112, comment e (1959). See also 1 id. § 116.

24. See 2 Restatement, Second, Trusts § 334 (1959).

25. Home News, Inc. v. Goodman, 182 Md. 585, 35 A. 2d 442 (1945) (corporation and promoters bound). See sections 146–153 infra.

26. 1 Restatement of Contracts § 5 (1932).

27. Van Duker v. Fritz, 222 Cal.App.2d 228, 35 Cal. Rptr. 55 (1963); Restatement of Restitution §§ 1, 2 (1937).

28. See Patch v. Stahly, 135 F.2d 269 (7th Cir.1943), cert. denied 320 U.S. 750, 64 S.Ct. 54, 88 L.Ed. 446 (1943); McArthur v. Times Printing Co., 48 Minn. 319, 51 N.W. 216 (1892); Application of Jacoby, 33 N. Y.S.2d 621 (Sup.Ct.1942).

29. See section 114 infra.

press or implied novation after incorporation substituting the corporation for the promoter, with the corporation's assuming the promoter's rights and liabilities in consideration for the release of the promoter's liabilities under the contract does the promoter cease to be bound under the contract.

When a promoter contracts with a third person in behalf of a proposed corporation, the promoter and the third person are initially the parties to the contract.[1]

Absent a valid novation, the promoter and the third person continue as the parties. In case of a valid express or implied novation after incorporation[2] substituting the corporation for the promoter, the corporation takes the place of the promoter as party to the contract, and the promoter is divested of his rights and released of his liabilities.[3]

Otherwise, under the various theories previously discussed, except in the case of a valid assignment to the corporation after its formation, the promoter retains his rights under the contract. Where there is such an assignment, the corporation takes over the promoter's rights; if the corporation as assignee also assumes the liabilities, it becomes subject to such liabilities, but the promoter would nevertheless remain liable in the absence of a novation. The corporation, however, might agree to indemnify the promoter.

Of course, the promoter might also be liable for any misrepresentation or breach of warranty.[4]

[§ 112]

1. Annot., 41 A.L.R.2d 477 (1955); see section 111 supra.

2. 1 Restatement, Second, Agency § 104, comment c (1958).

3. Decker v. Juzwik, 255 Iowa 358, 121 N.W.2d 652 (1963); Frazier v. Ash, 234 F.2d 320 (5th Cir.1956); McEachin v. Kingman, 64 Ga.App. 104, 12 S.E.2d 212 (1940); Johnson & Carlson v. Montreuil's Estate, 291 Mich. 582, 289 N.W. 262 (1939) (based on Michigan statute discussed in section 114 infra); Ehrich & Bunzl, "Promoters' Contracts", 38 Yale L. J. 1011 (1929).

4. See section 108, n. 13 supra.

PREINCORPORATION SERVICES

113. At the time of any preincorporation services, the corporation is not in existence, and the only possible present contract is with the promoters. After incorporation, the corporation can, expressly or sometimes impliedly, assume responsibility for such services. Preincorporation services in most jurisdictions do not qualify as valid consideration for the issue of shares since the services were not rendered the corporation as required. Some statutes permit the corporation to pay or allow reasonable organizational expenses out of the consideration received by it for its shares without thereby rendering such shares not fully paid or assessable.

Where a person performs services in forming a corporation, whether such person be a promoter, attorney, other expert, or some other third person, he usually expects to be compensated for such services.

Since the corporation is not then in existence, the only possible present contract is with the promoters. Upon the formation of the corporation, the courts are, as has been discussed, reluctant to impose automatic liability on the corporation. In the absence of appropriate provision in statute or the articles of incorporation, the corporation's liability for preincorporation services usually depends upon the various theories previously discussed.[1]

Where the corporation *expressly* attempts to assume responsibility (e. g., *express* ratification, adoption, assumption of liabilities, novation, acceptance of continuing offer), the corporation would become liable, with possible release or indemnification of the promoter. *Implied* assumption of liability from acceptance of the benefits of preincorporation services, however, is usually not inferred because the corporation is not in a position to reject such benefits without in effect unincorporating itself.[2] However,

[§ 113]

1. See sections 109–112 supra.

2. See Bishop v. Parker, 103 Utah 145, 134 P.2d 180 (1943); Indianapolis Blue Print & Mfg. Co. v. Kennedy, 215 Ind. 409, 19 N.E.2d 554 (1939). Post-incor-

where the corporation has a choice and with the knowledge of the arrangements accepts post-incorporation services it may become liable for any related preincorporation services as well. Thus, for example, where an attorney performs preincorporation and post-incorporation services which are integrated to each other, the corporation's acceptance of the latter constitutes acceptance of the indivisible contract or offer covering both pre- and post-incorporation services.[3] Hence the corporation would be liable for the fees set forth in the contract or if no fee were prescribed for the reasonable value of the services (*quantum meruit*) on a theory of inferred-in-fact contract.[4]

Apart from the corporation's liability for preincorporation services, when its shares are to be issued to compensate for such services, there arises a second problem resulting from the frequent statutory requirement[5] that a corporation may issue its shares only for cash, property, or labor done or services rendered the corporation. In most jurisdictions, preincorporation services are not considered services rendered the corporation.[6]

A few jurisdictions by statute or decisional law permit shares to be issued for preincorporation services or other organizational expenses.[7]

In some jurisdictions, statutes permit the corporation to pay or allow reasonable organizational expenses out of the consideration received by it in payment of its shares without thereby rendering such shares not fully-paid or assessable.[8]

Even under the orthodox view, the issue of the shares might be construed as having been for property rather than for promotional services,[9] or the contract to issue shares construed to call for the issue after services had been rendered to the corporation after its formation.[10]

Besides the qualitative requirement applicable to consideration for shares, any quantitative requirements would require compliance.[11]

STATUTORY DEVELOPMENTS CONCERNING PREINCORPORATION AGREEMENTS BETWEEN PROMOTERS AND THIRD PERSONS

114. Only a few jurisdictions, notably Michigan and Kansas, have enacted legislation affecting preincorporation agreements between promoters, subscribers, and incorporators and

poration services follow closely preincorporation services. See section 117 infra. The promoters or their attorneys, directly or through "accommodation" or "dummy" personnel, are usually in control of the corporation during the initial stages of organization.

3. Ramsey v. Brooke County Building & Loan Ass'n, 102 W.Va. 119, 135 S.E. 249, 49 A.L.R. 668 (1926); Kridelbaugh v. Aldrehn Theatres Co., 195 Iowa 147, 191 N.W. 803 (1923). See Berk v. Twentynine Palms Ranchos, Inc., 201 Cal.App.2d 625, 20 Cal. Rptr. 144 (1962). Compare Ong Hing v. Arizona Harness Raceway, Inc., 10 Ariz.App. 380, 459 P.2d 107 (1969) (upholding summary judgment against attorney retained by promoters as general counsel for corporation to be formed, despite payment by corporation of reasonable fees for 20 months' postincorporation services for corporation).

4. Quasi-contractual recovery, however, would not be allowed. See section 111, nn. 26, 27 supra.

5. E. g., ABA–ALI Model Bus.Corp.Act § 18; Del. Gen.Corp.Law, § 152 (1967); Note, 55 Harv.L.Rev. 1365 (1942).

6. E. g., Triplex Shoe Co. v. Rice & Hutchins, Inc., 17 Del.Ch. 356, 152 A. 342, 72 A.L.R. 934 (Sup.Ct. 1930); Annot., 8 A.L.R.2d 722 (1949).

7. See McKinney's N.Y.Bus.Corp.Law, § 504 (services performed for corporation's benefit or in its formation); English Companies Act, 1948, 11 & 12 Geo. 6, c. 38, § 53(1) (b); Grafton v. Masteller, 232 F.2d 773 (3d Cir.1956), cert. denied 352 U.S. 832, 77 S.Ct. 47, 1 L.Ed.2d 52 (1956); Blish v. Thompson Automatic Arms Corp., 30 Del.Ch. 538, 64 A.2d 581 (Sup.Ct.1948); Shore v. Union Drug Co., 18 Del.Ch. 74, 156 A. 204 (Ch.1931), 159 A. 371 (Del.Ch.1932); United German Silver Co. v. Bronson, 92 Conn. 266, 102 A. 647 (1917); Fitzpatrick v. O'Neill, 43 Mont. 552, 118 P. 273 (1911).

8. E. g., ABA–ALI Model Bus.Corp.Act § 20; McKinney's N.Y.Bus.Corp.Law, § 507.

9. Nastasi v. Moore, 7 Misc.2d 226, 156 N.Y.S.2d 521 (Sup.Ct.1956).

10. Grafton v. Masteller, 232 F.2d 773 (3d Cir.1956), cert. denied 352 U.S. 832, 77 S.Ct. 47, 1 L.Ed.2d 52 (1956); Morgan v. Bon Bon Co., 222 N.Y. 22, 118 N.E. 205 (1917).

11. See sections 167, 168, 171 infra.

third persons, other than preincorporation share subscriptions.

A few jurisdictions have enacted legislation on the subject of preincorporation agreements.[1]

The Michigan statute [2] refers to "incorporators", whereas the Kansas statute [3] refers to promoters, subscribers, and incorporators.

PREINCORPORATION SHARE SUBSCRIPTIONS

115. Preincorporation share subscriptions, in the absence of statute, are usually revocable until accepted by the corporation after its formation. As to the revocability of a subscription with a double aspect, that is, where there is a contract among two or more subscribers with the mutual subscriptions providing consideration for each other, there is a split of authority. Common-law devices to prevent premature revocation or otherwise solve the problem include: (a) Irrevocable power of attorney by subscriber to promoter; (b) Designation of promoter as trustee for corporation; (c) Irrevocable option; (d) Third-party beneficiary contract; (e) Escrow deposit of subscription price; and (f) Underwriting agreements. Modern statutes tend to provide for preincorporation subscriptions, usually making them irrevocable for a stated period and/or providing for automatic acceptance upon incorporation, and sometimes requiring all subscriptions to be in writing and signed by the subscriber.

A preincorporation share subscription is an agreement by a person to take and pay for original, unissued shares of a corporation *to be formed*.[1]

Obviously, there is some practical advantage to a corporation to start out with sufficient capital or assurance of sufficient capital. Legally, some jurisdictions require that certain minimum capital be either subscribed or paid in as a condition precedent to doing business.[2] On the other hand, subscribers require some protection.

General Rules

A preincorporation share subscription in the articles of incorporation,[3] assuming that all the essential elements of an enforceable obligation, including price, are set forth,[4]

[§ 114]

1. See Kessler, "Promoter's Contracts: A Statutory Solution", 15 Rutgers L.Rev. 566 (1961). The Ghana Companies Code, 1963, provides for preincorporation contracts as follows:

"Any contract or other transaction purporting to be entered into by the company prior to its formation or by any person on behalf of the company prior to its formation may be ratified by the company after its formation and thereupon the company shall become bound by and entitled to the benefit thereof as if it had been in existence at the date of such contract or other transaction and had been a party thereto.

"Prior to ratification by the company the person or persons who purported to act in the name or on behalf of the company shall in the absence of express agreement to the contrary be personally bound by the contract or other transaction and entitled to the benefit thereof."

Ghana Companies Code § 13 (1963). For statutes affecting preincorporation share subscriptions, see section 115 infra.

2. Mich.Gen.Corp.Act § 21.8 (1948); Bil-Gel Co. v. Thoma, 345 Mich. 698, 77 N.W.2d 89 (1956) (corporation awarded specific performance on preincorporation agreement); Johnson & Carlson v. Montreuil's Estate, 291 Mich. 582, 289 N.W. 262 (1939); see Glover, "Preincorporation Contracts of Michigan Corporations", 16 U.Det.L.J. 113 (1953).

3. Kan.Gen.Corp.Code § 17–2807 (1949). See 54 Harv.L.Rev. 154 (1940).

[§ 115]

1. Only the problem arising from the nonexistence of the corporation will be discussed here. Preincorporation arrangements for debt financing often present the same problem. A subscriber is one who subscribes for shares in a corporation, whether before or after incorporation. ABA–ALI Model Bus. Corp.Act § 2(e). Other problems of the preincorporation share subscription and problems of the post-incorporation share subscription are reserved for later treatment. See section 169 infra. See Winton, "Private Corporate Stock Subscription Agreements", 33 So.Calif.L.Rev. 388, 390 (1960) (California law); Note, "Legal Effect of Preincorporation Subscription Agreements in California", 19 Hastings L.J. 1418 (1968).

2. E. g., ABA–ALI Model Bus.Corp.Act § 51 (minimum paid-in $1,000 capital requirement), eliminated by 1969 Model Act revision. See section 70, n. 1 supra, section 126 infra.

3. Modern statutes tend to drop the requirement that incorporators subscribe to shares. See section 131, n. 14 infra.

4. Where no price is set forth in the articles of incorporation, the par value or stated value, if any, might supply a guide. In the case of shares without par value without stated value, even this guide would be lacking. Where two or more classes of

probably is irrevocable and becomes binding upon incorporation.[5]

Otherwise, apart from statute, a preincorporation share subscription may be a simple one or one with a double aspect.

The simple preincorporation share subscription is at most an offer when communicated to the corporation and does not become a contract until accepted by the corporation. In the interim, like any other offer, it is revocable.[6]

The preincorporation share subscription with a double aspect is a binding contract among two or more subscribers, the subscription of one being the consideration to support the subscription of the other. Even such a preincorporation subscription, with a double aspect, it has been contended, is revocable by the subscriber prior to its acceptance by the corporation, despite the fact that such revocation without the consent of the other subscribers might constitute a breach of contract with the other subscribers.[7] Others have contended that such a preincorporation subscription is irrevocable.[8]

Common-Law Devices

Apart from statute, various devices might be used, alone or in combination, to try to keep the subscription in effect until the corporation can be formed and has an opportunity to accept.[9]

(a) "Irrevocable" power of attorney by the subscriber to the promoter to consummate the subscription after the corporation is formed. Such a power is irrevocable in most jurisdictions if "coupled with an interest".[10]

(b) Designation of the promoter as trustee for the corporation; a beneficiary of a trust need not be in existence when the trust is created.[11]

(c) "Irrevocable" option; if in the form of a contract among subscribers with an "offer" to the corporation, such subscription with a double aspect is revocable or irrevocable depending on the jurisdiction involved; an "offer" under seal or a written "irrevocable offer", per statute,[12] is conceptually troublesome until the offeree is incor-

shares are authorized, not only the number of shares but the class of shares for which the subscription is made should be specified.

5. Samia v. Central Oil Co., 339 Mass. 101, 158 N.E. 2d 469 (1959); Phoenix Warehousing Co. v. Badger, 67 N.Y. 294 (1876).

6. Collins v. Morgan Grain Co., 16 F.2d 253 (9th Cir. 1926) (revocable by withdrawal, death, or any other basis for revocation of an offer under contract law principles); Brown v. United Community Nat'l Bank, 282 F.Supp. 781 (D.D.C.1968); Schwenk, "Pre-Incorporation Subscriptions: The Offer Theory and—What Is an Offer?", 29 Va.L.Rev. 460 (1943); Morris, "Legal Effect of Pre-Incorporation Stock Subscriptions", 34 W.Va.L.Q. 219 (1928); Annot., 61 A.L.R. 1463 (1929), 71 A.L.R. 1345 (1931).

7. See Collins v. Morgan Grain Co., 16 F.2d 253 (9th Cir.1926); Eden v. Miller, 37 F.2d 8 (2d Cir.1930) (2–1); Lake Ontario, etc. Ry. v. Curtiss, 80 N.Y. 219 (1880). The subscriber has the power but not the right to revoke; the remedy of damages to the other subscribers is often unsatisfactory.

8. Minneapolis Threshing Mach. Co. v. Davis, 40 Minn. 110, 41 N.W. 1026 (1889); see Coleman Hotel Co. v. Crawford, 3 S.W.2d 1109, 61 A.L.R. 1459 (Tex.Com.App.1928). Generally, of course, subscribers can rescind their subscriptions for fraud, at least when creditors are not prejudiced. See sec-

tion 169 infra. The corporation as formed must be the one contemplated by the subscription. Dorris v. Sweeney, 60 N.Y. 467 (1875). Implicit is the condition that the corporation be a de jure corporation (see sections 139 et seq. infra). Tonge v. Item Pub. Co., 244 Pa. 417, 91 A. 229 (1914). See Frey, "Modern Developments in the Law of Pre-Incorporation Subscriptions", 79 U.Pa.L.Rev. 1005 (1931). See Welborne v. Preferred Risk Ins. Co., 232 Ark. 828, 340 S.W.2d 586 (1960) (subscriber denied specific performance of four-year old preincorporation share subscription where shares had greatly appreciated in value).

9. See Note, 34 W.Va.L.Q. 76 (1927). Preincorporation share subscriptions are usually formally accepted at the first meeting of the board of directors (see section 135 infra), which generally occurs promptly after incorporation, but they can be impliedly accepted.

10. Pole's Case, [1920] 2 Ch. 341, aff'g [1920] 1 Ch. 582; Electric Welding Co. v. Prince, 195 Mass. 242, 81 N.E. 306 (1907) (English company); Carmichael's Case, [1896] 2 Ch. 643.

11. Drake Hotel Co. v. Crane, 210 Mo.App. 452, 240 S.W. 859 (1922); Horseshoe Pier Amusement Co. v. Sibley, 157 Cal. 442, 108 P. 308 (1910).

12. E. g., McKinney's N.Y.Gen.Obl.Law § 5–1109.

porated and the "offer" communicated to it.

(d) Contract among the subscribers for the benefit of the proposed corporation; a third-party beneficiary of a contract need not be in existence when the contract is made. Since the development of the modern third-party beneficiary doctrine, this device appears to offer the most common-law protection to the corporation with respect to preincorporation share subscriptions.

(e) Escrow deposit of the subscription price pending the organization of the corporation; such actual deposit avoids some of the problems of executory preincorporation share subscriptions by executing them, so far as the subscriber is concerned, in escrow prior to incorporation.

(f) Underwriting agreements;[13] while a binding agreement between the underwriters and the corporation presents the usual difficulties prior to incorporation, the underwriters could enter into binding agreements with security dealers and investors whereby the latter would commit themselves to buy the shares, conditional upon the formation of the corporation and the issue of the shares.

Statutory Treatment

Many jurisdictions have enacted legislation relating to preincorporation share sub-

scriptions. Some require that all subscriptions be in writing and signed by the subscriber.[14] One approach is to make subscriptions irrevocable for a stated time in order to give the contemplated corporation an opportunity to accept;[15] another approach, sometimes combined with the former approach, is to provide for automatic acceptance upon incorporation of the contemplated corporation[16]—an approach which could lead to oversubscription or shareholders not desired by the corporation. Subscribers are protected against overreaching by recognition of their equitable defenses.

Relief might also be possible under federal securities legislation and state "blue sky" laws.[17]

---

13. See section 292 infra.

14. E. g., Arkansas, Idaho, Louisiana, New York, Oklahoma, North Carolina, Washington.

15. E. g., ABA–ALI Model Bus.Corp.Act § 16 (preincorporation subscription irrevocable for six months unless otherwise provided by terms of subscription agreement or unless all subscribers consent to revocation); Md.Gen.Corp.Law § 19 (1951) (three months); Wash.Bus.Corp.Act § 23A.08.140 (1967) (six months); Minn.Bus.Corp.Act § 301.17 (1961) (irrevocable for 60 days after issuance of certificate of incorporation or one year after first subscription if such certificate not issued during such period; void thereafter). The New York Business Corporation Law provides that preincorporation subscriptions shall be irrevocable for three months except with the consent of all other subscribers or the corporation. McKinney's N.Y.Bus.Corp.Law, § 503(a).

16. E. g., Ill.Bus.Corp.Act § 16 (1933); Pa.Bus.Corp. Law & 604 (1966). See Zemke, "Pre-Incorporation Subscription Contracts in Michigan", 34 U.Det.L.J. 662 (1957).

17. Securities Act § 17(a), 15 U.S.C.A. § 77q(a); Securities Exchange Act § 10(b), 15 U.S.C.A. § 78j(b).

CHAPTER 6

INCORPORATION, ADMISSION, AND DOMESTICATION

A. INTRODUCTION

A. INTRODUCTION

INCORPORATION, ADMISSION, AND DOMESTICATION—IN GENERAL

116. Incorporation procedures in the selected jurisdiction of incorporation, and qualification procedures in other jurisdictions where the corporation is to do business, should be followed only after full understanding of all relevant facts concerning the proposed enterprise and applicable corporation laws. Such procedures vary in different jurisdictions. Primarily involved is the drafting of articles of incorporation, bylaws, forms of share certificates, shareholder and other agreements in close corporations, and agenda or minutes for any required organization meetings.

After resolving the two concurrent inquiries of the most suitable form of business enterprise [1] and, assuming that incorporation is deemed best, the most advantageous jurisdiction in which to incorporate,[2] the next steps after the promotional stage [3] are to comply with the required incorporation procedures in the selected jurisdiction of incorporation and admission procedures in other jurisdictions where the corporation is to do business.[4]

Sound incorporation requires a thorough understanding and appreciation of many relevant facts concerning the proposed enterprise. Many of these facts should have already been considered in selecting the form of enterprise and jurisdiction of incorporation, in anticipation of the problems of complying with the incorporation and admission procedures.

1. See Chapter 2 supra.

2. See Chapter 4 supra.

3. See Chapter 5 supra.

4. See C. Rohrlich, Organizing Corporate and Other Business Enterprises 287–317 (4th ed. 1967); G. Seward, Basic Corporate Practice 25–55 (ALI rev. 1966); C. Israels, Corporate Practice 172–266 (PLI 2d ed. 1969); Jones, "Formation of Corporations", in Advising California Business Enterprises 341–402 (1958); Greene, "Formation of a New Hampshire Business Corporation", 6 N.H.B.J. 105 (1964); Trammell, "Organizing the Corporation with an Eye to the Tax Future", 17 Ark.L.Rev. 409 (1964); Bristow, "Organization of Corporations: Chapter 1.4", 15 S.C.L.Rev. 346 (1963): Richardson, "Formation of Corporations in Florida", 11 U.Fla.L.Rev. 395 (1958); "Incorporating a Business—A Short Course Given", 4 Bus.Law. 278 (May 1949); Stallwitz, "Organization of Private Corporations for Profit", 17 J.B.A.Kan. 11 (1948); Moses, "A Guide to the Formation of Corporations under the Business Corporation Act of Louisiana", 19 Tul.L.Rev. 566 (1945); Note, "Incorporation under the Civil Code of Montana, Chapter 42", 7 Mont.L.Rev. 49 (1946); Cookston, "Organizing a Corporation in Ohio", 26 Clev.B.A.J. 183 (1955); see also 1 G. Hornstein, Corporation Law and Practice § 50 (1959) (Checklist: How to Incorporate—Federal Tax Factors Only); McKee, "Income Tax Aspects of Organizing Corporations", in Advising California Business Enterprises 443–463 (1958). Compliance with federal and state securities legislation and securities exchange requirements might also be required. See sections 294–308 infra. Assistance of accountants is usually required, and possibly also tax counsel.

In general, counsel must know all the information relevant to drafting the articles of incorporation, bylaws, shareholder agreements, minutes of organization meetings, form(s) of share certificates, and any other papers relevant to the financing and management of the corporation. This might require some prodding of the client, who has probably not worked out in his own mind all the legally-significant details. Obviously, counsel should be thoroughly conversant with applicable corporation and other relevant laws.

The corporation service companies can provide substantial help for counsel. Among the organization services provided by the corporation service companies are assistance in selecting the jurisdiction of incorporation, clearance and possible reservation of corporate name, supplying forms and precedents, drafting articles of incorporation, filing and/or recording of articles and other papers, conduct of organization meetings, and preparation of bylaws.[5]

Informal conferences with state officials who handle incorporation might prove helpful in more unusual situations, although even this might be delegated to a corporation service company which obviously has long-established contacts with such officials.

In this chapter, the various steps in the incorporation procedures of American jurisdictions are first outlined in general terms.[6]

5. In addition, such companies also assist with respect to admission as a foreign corporation, statutory representation, amendment of articles of incorporation, dissolution, withdrawal, merger, consolidation, reorganization, reduction of capital, "blue-skying", as transfer agent, holding shareholders meetings. Some even furnish corporate outfits (minute book, seal, share ledger, and book of share certificates). The leading corporation service companies, sometimes called service companies, lawyer's service companies, incorporation companies, and corporation companies, are The C. T. Corporation System, The Prentice-Hall Corporation System, Inc., United States Corporation Company, Corporation Service Company.

6. See section 117 infra.

Thereafter, the general problems involved in drafting the articles of incorporation,[7] the bylaws,[8] and the form(s) of share certificates [9] are treated. Then, the organization meetings, their agenda and minutes, are discussed.[10] Finally, admission and domestication procedures are outlined.[11] Problems encountered in drafting preincorporation agreements between promoters and third persons [12] and preincorporation share subscriptions [13] have already been discussed. Drafting problems unique to the close corporation, including the drafting of close corporation provisions for the articles of incorporation and bylaws, shareholder and other agreements, and share certificate legends, are reserved for fuller treatment in the context of the discussion of the special problems of close corporations.[14]

STEPS IN INCORPORATION PROCEDURES

117. Incorporation procedures involve various steps in different jurisdictions. Some of such steps are regarded as mandatory; others as directory; some as conditions precedent to incorporation or to the doing of business; others as conditions subsequent. Corporate existence begins at different steps of the incorporation procedure in different jurisdictions depending upon applicable statutes and decisional law, most usually upon the filing of the articles of incorporation or upon the issue of a formal "certificate of incorporation".

Different American jurisdictions prescribe various steps as part of the incorporation procedure. A composite listing will be discussed in this section. No jurisdiction pre-

scribes all of these steps, and different jurisdictions prescribe varying combinations of some of the steps in different chronological order.[1]

(a) Selection and clearance of corporate name; [2] reservation or registration of

---

7. See sections 118–132 infra.

8. See section 133 infra.

9. See section 134 infra.

10. See section 135 infra.

11. See sections 136, 137 infra.

12. See sections 108–114 supra.

13. See section 115 supra.

14. See Chapter 10 infra.

1. See 1 I. Kantrowitz & S. Slutsky, White on New York Corporations ¶¶ 401.01–404.04 (13th ed. 1968); Henn, Appendix 4, Checklist 2, "Incorporation Procedure", 2 N.Y.Bus.Corp.Law 591–594 (McKinney 1963) (New York procedures).

2. ABA–ALI Model Bus.Corp.Act § 7 requires the corporate name to contain the word "corporation", "company", "incorporated", or "limited", or an abbreviation thereof; prohibits the use of any word or phrase indicating that the corporation is organized for any purpose other than its purposes as stated in its articles of incorporation; and provides that the name shall not be the same as, or deceptively similar to, the name of any domestic corporation or of any qualified foreign corporation, or to any reserved or registered name. Many jurisdictions do not recognize the word "company" or its abbreviation as a sufficient indication of corporateness. 1 I. Kantrowitz & S. Slutsky, White on New York Corporations ¶ 301.02 (13th ed. 1968); United Verde Copper Co. v. Hugo, 181 App.Div. 149, 168 N. Y.S. 80 (3d Dep't 1917). A few jurisdictions have special provisions concerning use of the word "company". For example, Maryland allows the corporate name to contain or end with the word "company" if such word is not preceded by the word "and" or any symbol therefor. In Colorado, initials included in corporate names must be separated by a full typewriter space or have a period after each one. Generally, the name is not expressly required to be in the English language, but some jurisdictions expressly require it to be in English letters or characters. In some jurisdictions, the name of a business corporation may not contain, except in specified instances or with specified approval, various proscribed words or phrases, e. g., "acceptance", "annuity", "assurance", "bank", "benefit", "board of trade", "bond", "casualty", "chamber of commerce", "court", "doctor", "endowment", "fidelity", "finance", "guaranty", "housing", "indemnity", "insurance", "investment" (except possibly by a "small business investment corporation" under the Federal Small Business Investment Act of 1958), "lawyer", "loan", "Mason", "mortgage", "savings", "state police", "state trooper", "surety", "title", "trust", "underwriter", "union", "labor", "trades council", "industrial organization"; see also McKinney's N.Y. Gen.Bus.Law § 138 ("army", "navy", "marine corps", "marines", "coast guard", "government", "post exchange", "P.X.", "G.I."), § 139 ("trust", "bank", "banking", "insurance", "assurance", "indemnity", "guarantee", "guaranty", "savings", "investment", "loan", "benefit"), § 135 (deceptive use of name of New York benevolent, humane, or charitable corporation); § 141 ("United Nations"); McKinney's N.Y. Educ.Law, § 224 ("university", "college", "school"), § 7209 ("engineers", "engineering"), § 7302 ("architects", "architecture"); N.Y.Op.Att'y Gen. 48 State

name, if possible, under statute or administrative practice, in jurisdiction or jurisdictions where enterprise is to be incorporated and business is to be

Dep't Rep. 151, July 15, 1933 ("surveyors"); 18 U.S. C.A. § 706 ("Red Cross"), § 709 ("national", "Federal", "United States", "reserve"); 36 U.S.C.A. § 27 ("Boy Scouts"), § 48 ("American Legion"), § 67–p ("Amvets"), § 117 ("Veterans of Foreign Wars"). Other names will not be allowed as a matter of public policy, if they suggest that the corporation is to be engaged in a business which it lawfully could not pursue, or is to be a form of public agency, or is to be affiliated with some organization with which there is in fact to be no affiliation. Some jurisdictions expressly permit use of similar corporate names with the consent of the existing corporation. E. g., Arizona, Massachusetts, Nevada, New Hampshire, Texas. Even in the absence of express statutory provision therefor, related corporations might be allowed to use somewhat similar names upon submission of a certified copy of a resolution of the board of directors of the existing corporation that the proposed name, in the opinion of the board, does not so nearly resemble the name of its corporation as to be calculated to deceive. For form of resolution, see N.Y. Rules of Corporations Bureau § 147.2 (1969). Since the purpose of the restriction is to prevent deception of the public, the secretary of state can reject the name notwithstanding the resolution. The availability of the proposed name should be checked in advance, usually with the secretary of state. The search is often made only of the corporation name records. See Barber Co. v. Department of State, 277 N.Y. 55, 12 N.E.2d 790 (1938); Steakley v. Braden, 322 S.W.2d 363 (Tex. Civ.App.1959) (likelihood of deception or unfair competition held immaterial). The secretary of state in some jurisdictions exercises judicial discretion in determining the availability of corporate names. Gross v. New York, —— A.D.2d ——, 306 N.Y.S.2d 28 (3d Dep't 1969) (holding state not liable to corporation for damages because of error of secretary of state in checking availability of corporate name, on ground secretary was performing discretionary act for which state could not be liable). Brooks Clothing v. Flynn, 232 App.Div. 346, 250 N.Y.S. 69 (3d Dep't 1931). Contra, Rixford v. Jordan, 214 Cal. 547, 6 P.2d 959 (1932). Some statutes expressly provide that their corporate name provisions do not derogate from the law of unfair competition. E. g., Idaho, Louisiana, Minnesota, Oklahoma, Pennsylvania, Washington. Some statutes expressly authorize injunctions against the use of corporate names despite their approval by the secretary of state. E. g., California, Massachusetts, Pennsylvania, Washington. Even in jurisdictions without such provisions, approval by the secretary of state is no defense to claims of unfair competition or trademark infringement. Sears, Roebuck & Co. v. Johnson, 219 F.2d 590 (3d Cir.1955); Great Atlantic & Pacific Tea Co. v. A. & P. Trucking Co., 29 N.J. 455, 149 A.2d 595 (1959); Dunkin' Donuts of American, Inc. v. Dunkin Donuts, Inc., 8 A.D.2d 228, 188 N.Y.S.2d 132 (3d Dep't 1959); Sullivan v. Ed Sullivan Radio & T. V., Inc., 1 A.D.2d 609, 152 N.Y.S.2d 227 (1st Dep't 1956). Care should be taken to avoid such violations of the rights of others in names by checking relevant telephone directories, trade directories, county clerk's files, and trademark records. Annot., 26 A.L.R.3d 994 (1969). To avoid invasion of right of privacy (e. g., McKinney's N.Y.Civ. Rights Law, §§ 50, 51 (prohibiting use of name of living person for purposes of trade without prior written consent), such written consent when necessary should be obtained. Gilson, "Tortious Incorporation: Trap for the Unwary", 24 Bus.Law. 237 (1968). Any necessary clearance should also be secured from any other governmental authorities which might have authority over the particular corporation. Corporate names may come under the scrutiny of the Federal Trade Commission, and, more recently of the Securities and Exchange Commission, especially of words like "nuclear", "missile", "space", "nucleonics", "electronics", in connection with the registration of securities. Where a registrant is substantially, but not principally, engaged in a line of activity indicated by its name, it may be sufficient to disclose this fact under the registrant's name on the cover of the prospectus. Leeway is allowed for established firms which over the years, have changed the character of their business. SEC Securities Act Release No. 5005 (Sept. 17, 1969) (guide relating to misleading character of certain registrants' names). If the corporation intends to do business in other jurisdictions, the name should also be cleared, and reserved or registered if possible, in such jurisdictions. Where the name is cleared only as "presently available", with no provision for reservation or registration, a name available at the time of inquiry might not be available when the articles of incorporation are offered for filing. Under such circumstances supplies bearing the name, such as signs, stationery, corporate seal, share ledger, share certificates, minute book(s), etc., should not be ordered (although they should probably be in the process of preliminary preparation) until the articles of incorporation have been filed. Within the permissible legal limitations, selection of the corporate name should be based on several practical considerations, which obviously vary in importance in different situations, such as the name's appropriateness to the corporate business, present and prospective, its impression on the public, its advertising potentialities, its availability and protectability as a trade name or trademark, or the desirability of featuring the name of some person who might later not be associated with the corporation. See United States Trademark Association: Trademark Selection: The Management Team Method (1960); Yarbrough, "Protection of Territorial Rights in Corporate Names and Trade Names", 19 Bus.Law. 925 (1964); Worthey, "Corporate Names: Their Selection and Use", 52 Trademark Rep. 91 (1962). Note, 56 Trademark Rep. 391 (1966). See also David B. Findlay, Inc. v. Findlay, 18 N.Y.2d 12, 271 N.Y.S.2d 652, 218 N.E.2d 531 (1966), cert. denied 385 U.S. 930, 87 S.Ct. 289, 17 L.Ed.2d 212 (1966). Some jurisdictions once required the corporation to display its name. See generally Comment, 44 Ky.L.J. 439 (1956). Use by

done;[3]

(b) Securing of subscriptions to shares;[4]

(c) Drafting and signing of preliminary articles of agreement;[5]

(d) First (or organization) meeting of subscribers (to adopt bylaws and to designate incorporators, directors, officers); preparation of record of meeting;[6]

(e) Subscription and/or payment of minimum capital; filing of affidavits in proof thereof;[7]

(f) Publication of notice of intention to incorporate; filing of proof of publication;[8]

(g) Application for approval of court or state official;[9]

(h) Drafting of articles of incorporation;[10]

(i) Filing of properly executed, acknowledged (or verified) and endorsed articles of incorporation (single, duplicate, or triplicate) in state and/or local office(s) (e. g., office of secretary of state and/or county, town, or court files where principal office is to be located, real property to be held, business to be carried on);[11]

Payment of filing fees and organization tax;[12]

Filing of any required additional papers (e. g., statement of paid-in capital, designation of agent for service of process, officers' oaths, antitrust affidavit);[13]

Issue of "certificate of incorporation";[14]

(j) Drafting of bylaws (if not done previously);[15]

(k) Post-filing publication of notice of incorporation; filing of affidavit of publication;[16]

(l) Securing necessary governmental authority (state and/or federal) to issue securities;[17]

---

corporations of fictitious names or trade names is regulated by statute in some jurisdictions. E. g., Colorado, Georgia, Indiana, Illinois, North Carolina, Pennsylvania, Virginia. Such assumed or fictitious name statutes often exempt from filing corporate names but not trade names used by corporations. Sparks v. Porter, 270 F.Supp. 953 (N.D.Fla.1967) (noncomplying corporation barred from defending or maintaining action); Admiral Corp. v. Trio Sales & Service, Inc., 138 Colo. 157, 330 P.2d 1106 (1958). But see Stanley v. State, 145 Tex.Crim. 32, 165 S. W.2d 456 (1942) (assumed name statute held inapplicable to corporations). See also Miami Credit Bureau, Inc. v. Credit Bureau, Inc., 276 F.2d 565 (5th Cir.1960). Oregon permits a corporation to register an assumed name whether or not it contains a corporate designation. Ore.Op.Att'y Gen. No. 5986, June 9, 1965. Rolston & Adler, "New Law of Corporate Trade Names", 2 Osgoode Hall L.Soc'y J. 191 (1961). In an era of conglomerates, even long-established corporate names are being changed to nondescriptive names.

3. ABA–ALI Model Bus.Corp.Act § 8 (reservation of corporate name for 120 days). The majority of states have such statutory provisions, with time periods ranging from 10 days to 12 months, with possible renewals. In several jurisdictions without such statutes, administrative officials as a matter of courtesy will reserve names under varying terms and conditions. Some jurisdictions by statute authorize "registration" of corporate names, effective until the end of the calendar year, with possible annual renewals. ABA–ALI Model Bus.Corp. Act §§ 9, 10. Where the name may not be reserved, "name-saver" corporations are sometimes formed for the purpose. McDermitt & Manetti, "Protection of Discontinued Company Names", 22 Bus.Law. 423 (1967).

4. See section 115 supra.

5. E. g., Maine. See section 107 supra.

6. E. g., Indiana, Maine, Massachusetts, New Hampshire.

7. See section 115 supra. For potential personal liability for noncompliance, see section 143 infra.

8. E. g., Georgia (until 1969).

9. E. g., Alabama, Georgia.

10. See sections 118–131 infra.

11. See section 132 infra.

12. See section 132 infra.

13. Affidavits or certificates of paid-in capital are required, e. g., in Indiana, Virginia, Washington. For potential personal liability for noncompliance, see section 143 infra.

14. E. g., ABA–ALI Model Bus.Corp.Act § 49.

15. See section 133 infra.

16. E. g., Arizona, Georgia, Mississippi.

17. See sections 295, 305–307 infra.

(m) Ordering of corporation outfit (i. e., corporate seal, share ledger, minute book, and form(s) of share certificate) [18] from law stationer;

(n) First (or organization) meeting of incorporators; [19]

(o) First (or organization) meeting of board of directors; [20]

(p) Payment of share subscriptions; [21]

(q) Issue of shares; payment of applicable issue taxes (affixation and cancellation of tax stamps) ; [22]

(r) Post-organization filings (e. g., lists of shareholders, directors, officers; statement of location of office; designation of agent; acceptance of state constitution) ; [23]

Share transfer tax certificate.[24]

Some of the foregoing steps are regarded as mandatory; others as directory. Some are regarded as conditions precedent either to incorporation or to the doing of business; others as conditions subsequent.[25]

De jure corporate existence begins at different stages of the incorporation procedure in particular jurisdictions depending upon the applicable statutes and decisional law. Some statutes expressly provide that corporate existence shall begin upon the filing of the articles of incorporation in the office of the secretary of state [26] or some other public office.[27] Other statutes provide that corporate existence begins upon the issue by the secretary of state or other public official of a formal "certificate of incorporation".[28] Still other statutes are less explicit.

B. ARTICLES (OR CERTIFICATE) OF INCORPORATION

DRAFTING ARTICLES (OR CERTIFICATE) OF INCORPORATION— IN GENERAL

118. The basic instrument which upon filing usually creates the corporation is called in most jurisdictions "articles of incorporation" or "certificate of incorporation". The contents thereof are prescribed in the general incorporation statutes. In many jurisdictions, official forms are also prescribed. In most jurisdictions, corporate existence begins with the filing, usually with the secretary of state, of the articles or certificate of incorporation. In some jurisdictions, duplicate articles of incorporation are filed, and corporate existence begins with the issue of a formal certificate appended thereto called a "certificate of incorporation". Various conditions precedent to doing business might also be imposed.

Most business corporations are organized today under general incorporation statutes.[1] The basic instrument is often called the "articles of incorporation" or "certificate of incorporation",[2] which is filed in a pre-

---

18. See note 2 supra, section 135 infra.

19. See section 135 infra.

20. See section 135 infra.

21. See section 169 infra.

22. See section 158 infra.

23. Miss.Bus.Corp.Act § 150 (1963) (applicable only to nonprofit and nonshare corporations).

24. E. g., McKinney's N.Y.Tax Law § 275-a.

25. See section 139 infra.

26. E. g., McKinney's N.Y.Bus.Corp.Law § 403.

27. E. g., Kansas, Tennessee.

28. ABA–ALI Model Bus.Corp.Act § 50.

1. See section 12 supra.

2. The Model Business Corporation Act (see § 2(c)) and most jurisdictions use the term "articles of incorporation"; Alabama, Connecticut, Delaware, Georgia (since 1969), New Jersey, New York, Tennessee, Wyoming, and Puerto Rico call the instrument "certificate of incorporation" (not to be confused with the formal "certificate of incorporation" issued in Model jurisdictions upon the filing of the articles of incorporation); Georgia until 1969 employed the term "charter"; Hawaii, Rhode Island, and Vermont, "articles of association"; Maine, "certificate of organization"; Massachusetts, "articles of organization"; New Hampshire, "articles of agreement"; West Virginia, "agreement of incorporation". For ease of reference herein, the term "articles of incorporation" will be used to refer to such instrument regardless of local nomenclature.

scribed public office, usually the office of the state secretary of state,[3] and possibly also in some local office. In several jurisdictions, "official" forms are prescribed.[4] Sample forms and precedents are supplied, usually without charge, by the corporation service companies.

Traditionally, three or more natural persons of the age of 21 years or more have been required to act as incorporators[5] for a business corporation, which may be formed for any lawful purpose or purposes with specified and possibly other exceptions.[6]

3. Alabama and Georgia require court orders for incorporation; Maine, and New Hampshire require approval of the state attorney general. See section 132 infra.

4. E. g., ABA–ALI Model Bus.Corp.Act § 135 (forms to be furnished by secretary of state upon request, but their use, unless otherwise specifically prescribed in the Act, not to be mandatory).

5. ABA–ALI Model Bus.Corp.Act § 47. The 1969 Model Act revision permitted one person or a domestic or foreign corporation to act as incorporator. The three-incorporator requirement had its counterpart in Roman law (see section 5 supra) but is on the wane. See section 131 infra.

6. ABA–ALI Model Bus.Corp.Act § 3 ("for any lawful purpose or purposes, except for the purpose of banking or insurance"). Prior to the 1969 revision the purpose or purposes had to be set forth more specifically. See section 121 infra.

7. ABA–ALI Model Bus.Corp.Act § 48. See Official Forms for use under the Model Business Corporation Act, Revised 1969, Form No. 11 (ALI 1970). R. Kessler, New York Close Corporations chs. 10–12, §§ 14.01, 14.02 (1968); K. Pantzer & R. Deer, The Drafting of Corporate Charters and Bylaws (ALI rev. 1968); G. Seward, Basic Corporate Practice 118–137 (ALI rev. 1966) (form for Delaware); C. Israels, Corporate Practice 496–523 (PLI 2d ed. 1969) (annotated form for New York); Henn, Appendix 4, Checklist 3, "Certificate of Incorporation", in 2 N.Y.Bus.Corp.Law 595–600 (McKinney 1963); 1 G. Hornstein, Corporation Law and Practice §§ 137, 138 (1959) (checklist and form for New York); Kessler, "Certificate of Incorporation for a New York Close Corporation: A Form", 33 Fordham L.Rev. 541 (1965), ". . . An Addendum", 35 id. 111 (1966); Greene, "Formation of a New Hampshire Business Corporation", 6 N.H.B.J. 105 (1964); Trammell, "Organizing the Corporation with an Eye to the Tax Future", 17 Ark.L.Rev. 409 (1964); Bristow, "Organization of Corporations: Chapter 1.4", 15 S.C.L. Rev. 346 (1963); Kessler, "A Close Corporation Checklist for Drafting the Certificate of Incorporation under the New York Business Corporation Law", 31 Fordham L.Rev. 323 (1962); Gordon, "Certificate of Incorporation under the New Stock

Typical requirements for articles of incorporation are found in the Model Business Corporation Act:[7]

Corporation Law", 35 Conn.B.J. 58 (1961); Sugarman, "Incorporation Techniques: Planning Today for Tax Advantages Tomorrow", 12 W.Res.L.Rev. 182 (1961); O'Neal, "Molding the Corporate Form to Particular Business Situations: Optional Charter Clauses", 10 Vand.L.Rev. 1 (1956); Slover, "Drafting Articles of Incorporation under the Texas Business Corporation Act", 8 Baylor L.Rev. 127 (1956). See N.Y. Rules of Corporations Bureau 5 et seq. 16 (1969). Some statutes expressly require that the articles of incorporation be in the English language [McKinney's N.Y.Bus.Corp. Law § 104(a)] and bear a prescribed title "Certificate of incorporation of .... [name of corporation] under **section 402 of the Business Corporation Law**, **id.** § 402(a). New York no longer requires endorsement by statute but does by administrative rule. See N.Y. Rules of Corporations Bureau § 150.1 (1969). Obviously the title and any endorsement should be identical and the inserted name should be identical with the name stated in the text of the articles. Wisconsin requires the name of the drafter to appear thereon. Wis.Bus.Corp.Law, § 59.513(3) (Supp.1968). For form books, see Prentice-Hall, Inc., Corporation Forms Guide; W. Fletcher, Fletcher's Corporate Forms Annotated (1957–   ); 1A & 1B S. Eager, Bender's Forms for the Consolidated Laws of New York: Business Corporation (1965); 7 & 8 M. Fogelman, West's McKinney's Forms: Business Corporation Law (1965). Because both co-authors have long been associated with the New York Department of State Division of Corporations, New York attorneys intending to deliver certificates or other instruments to the Department for filing should consult I. Kantrowitz & S. Slutsky, White on New York Corporations (13th ed. 1963–   ). See also Davis & Simon, "The New York Business Corporation Law and the Department of State", 36 St. John's L.Rev. 205 (1962). On choice between tax-free and taxable incorporation, see Int.Rev.Code of 1954, 26 U.S.C.A. § 351. Where property has appreciated, a taxable transfer might be advantageous, notwithstanding the capital gains tax on the transfer, since a new higher basis for depreciation is established for the corporation which can now deduct annual depreciation on such basis from income taxable at ordinary income rates. A taxable transfer can be achieved by not meeting the requirements of section 351 that "property" be transferred to a corporation "solely" in exchange for its "stock or securities" and the transferor(s) "control" [80 percent test] "immediately" after the exchange. B. Bittker & J. Eustice, Federal Income Taxation of Corporations and Shareholders ch. 3 (2d ed. 1966); Fisher, "The Conversion of Ordinary Income to Capital Gain by Intentionally Avoiding Section 351 of the Internal Revenue Code of 1954", 32 Mo.L.Rev. 421, 443 (1967); Weiss, "Problems in the Tax-Free Incorporation of a Business", 41 Ind.L.J. 666 (1966); Adelson, "Selected Problems under Section 351", 15 W.Res.L.Rev. 305 (1964); Note, "Section 351 Transfers to Controlled Corporations: The Forgotten Terms—'Securities'",

(a) The name of the corporation; [8]

(b) The period of duration, which may be perpetual; [9]

(c) The purpose or purposes for which the corporation is organized which may be stated to be, or to include, the transaction of any or all lawful business for which corporations may be incorporated under the Act; [10]

(d) The aggregate number of shares which the corporation shall have authority to issue; if such shares are to consist of one class only, the par value of each of such shares, or a statement that all of such shares are without par value; or, if such shares are to be divided into classes, the number of shares of each class, and a statement of the par value of the shares of each such class or that such shares are to be without par value; [11]

(e) If the shares are to be divided into classes, the designation of each class and a statement of the preferences, limitations and relative rights in respect of the shares of each class; [12]

(f) If the corporation is to issue the shares of any preferred or special class in series, then the designation of each series and a statement of the variations in the relative rights and preferences as between series in so far as the same are to be fixed in the articles of incorporation, and a statement of any authority to be vested in the board of directors to establish series and fix and determine the variations in the relative rights and preferences as between series; [13]

(g) A statement that the corporation will not commence business until consideration of the value of at least one thousand dollars has been received for the issuance of shares; [14]

(h) If any preemptive right is to be granted to shareholders, the provisions therefor; or, alternatively, any provision limiting or denying to shareholders the preemptive right to acquire additional or treasury shares of the corporation; [15]

(i) Any provision, not inconsistent with law, which the incorporators elect to set forth in the articles of incorporation for the regulation of the internal affairs of the corporation, including

114 U.Pa.L.Rev. 314 (1965). Organizational expenses (e. g., legal services incident to incorporation, such as drafting the articles of incorporation, bylaws, minutes of organization meetings, original share certificates; accounting services; incorporation fees) are a deferred expense, and may be amortized, for federal income tax purposes, ratably over a period of not less than 60 months, upon proper election. If such expenditures were amortized over five years, one-fifth would be deducted (credited) from the deferred expense (asset) account and debited (or charged) to the appropriate expense (liability) account. Int.Rev.Code of 1954, 26 U.S.C.A. § 248; Bay Sound Transportation v. United States, 20 Am.Fed.Tax R.2d 5418 (S.D.Tex.1967) (election held not timely). Absent election to so amortize, such expenditures are deductible as a loss upon dissolution. Carruthers, "How to Treat the Expenses of Organization, Reorganization and Liquidation", N.Y.U. 24th Inst. on Fed.Tax. 1055 (1966). For other than tax purposes, the corporation might amortize on a different basis. As to assumption of any predecessor's liabilities, see Diamond Fruit Growers, Inc. v. Goe Co., 242 Or. 397, 409 P.2d 909 (1966); Plaza Express Co. v. Middle States Motor Freight, Inc., 40 Ill.App.2d 117, 189 N.E.2d 382 (1963); Ryder Truck Rental, Inc. v. Ace Sales Co., 368 S.W.2d 869 (Tex.Civ.App.1963). Persons incorporating their business might continue to be personally liable to persons who reasonably believed that the business was being carried on as an individual proprietorship or partnership. American Smelting & Refining Co. v. Ridgeway, 412 S.W.2d 675 (Tex.Civ.App.1967); Central Islip Plumbing Supply, Inc. v. John Capparelli Plumbing Co., 151 N.Y.L.J. No. 84, 20 (Sup.Ct.1964).

8.   See section 119 infra.

9.   See section 120 infra.

10. See section 121 infra.

11. See section 123 infra.

12. See section 124 infra.

13. See section 125 infra.

14. Eliminated in 1969 Model Act revision. See section 126 infra.

15. See section 127 infra.

any provision restricting the transfer of shares and any provision which under the Act is required or permitted to be set forth in the bylaws; [16]

(j) The address of its initial registered office, and the name of its initial registered agent at such address; [17]

(k) The number of directors constituting the initial board of directors and the names and addresses of the persons who are to serve as directors until the first annual meeting of shareholders or until their successors be elected and qualify; [18]

(l) The name and address of each incorporator. [19]

It is not necessary to set forth in the articles of incorporation any of the corporate powers enumerated in the Model Act.[20]

Some jurisdictions require the articles of incorporation to be entitled and possibly endorsed or to contain the drafter's name as prescribed by statute.[21]

CORPORATE NAME

119. The articles of incorporation must set forth the name of the corporation. Subsequent display and other use of the name should be consistent with the name set forth in the articles.

All jurisdictions require the articles of incorporation to set forth the name of the corporation.[1] Requirements applicable to corporate names, and their clearance and possible advance reservation, or registration, have been previously discussed.[2] In setting forth the corporate name, it should be done precisely, with correct spelling, capitalization, punctuation, inclusion of the definite article, "The", if desired, use of abbreviations where desired (e. g., "Corp.", "Co.", "Ltd."), and use of the ampersand, "&", for "and" if desired. Obviously, the name as set forth in the articles of incorporation should conform to its use in any required title or endorsement of the articles.[3] Subsequent display and other use of the name should be consistent with the name set forth in the articles.

CORPORATE DURATION

120. Most jurisdictions require that the articles of incorporation set forth the duration of the corporation, at least when it is not to be perpetual. Some jurisdictions impose constitutional or statutory limitations on corporate duration, which should be observed in setting forth the duration in the articles of incorporation.

Most jurisdictions require either that the period of duration be stated in the articles of incorporation,[1] or that the duration be stated if it is not to be perpetual.[2] While most jurisdictions permit any desirable duration, a few still impose constitutional or statutory limitations.[3] Obviously, the duration as set forth in the articles of incorporation should be consistent with such limitations.[4]

16. See section 128 infra.

17. See section 129 infra.

18. See section 130 infra.

19. See section 131 infra.

20. ABA–ALI Model Bus.Corp.Act § 48. See section 121 infra.

21. See note 7 supra.

[§ 119]
1. E. g., ABA–ALI Model Bus.Corp.Act § 48(a); see also id. §§ 7, 8, 9, 10; Del.Gen.Corp.Law § 102(a) (1) (1967); McKinney's N.Y.Bus.Corp.Law § 402(a) (1).

2. See section 117, nn. 2, 3 supra.

3. See section 118, n. 7 supra.

[§ 120]
1. E. g., ABA–ALI Model Bus.Corp.Act § 48(b); see also id. § 4(a).

2. E. g., Del.Gen.Corp.Law § 102(b) (5) (1967); McKinney's N.Y.Bus.Corp.Law § 402(a) (9).

3. See section 14, n. 11, section 75, nn. 1, 3 supra.

4. For discussions of extension and revival of corporate existence, see sections 144, 344 infra; of dissolution, see sections 348, 381, 382 infra.

CORPORATE PURPOSES

121. **All jurisdictions require that the articles of incorporation set forth the corporate purposes, within constitutional and statutory limitations on permissible purposes. Most jurisdictions still require the statement to be reasonably definite. Ordinarily, undue specificity should be avoided in drafting the statement.**

All jurisdictions require the articles of incorporation to set forth the corporate purposes or objects, the two terms being synonymous.[1]

Wyoming until 1960 barred the formation of a corporation for more than a single purpose.[2] Oklahoma and Puerto Rico have constitutional limitations on incorporation for the purpose of dealing in real estate.[3]

Most jurisdictions permit incorporation of business corporations for "any lawful business" or "any lawful purpose or purposes", subject to various exceptions.[4] Some bar corporations from engaging in certain activities, such as practicing professions, in their corporation statutes, other statutes, or by case law.[5] Most exceptions are stated in terms of specific classes of corporations or corporations formable under other statutes or both, and often refer to banks and trust companies, loan companies, insurance companies, public utilities, and railroads.[6] Mon-

tana, until 1969, enumerated 32 specific purposes and provided that no corporation could be formed "for any other purpose than those mentioned".[7]

A growing number of modern statutes allow the articles of incorporation to set forth either specific purposes or a general statement that the corporation may pursue any and all lawful purposes under the statute.[8]

In other jurisdictions, the statement of purposes must be reasonably clear and definite; a mere paraphrase of the broad statutory language is usually not sufficient, although an omnibus-purpose clause following a more specific statement might be acceptable; however, its future construction would be conjectural. The usual practice is to define the principal business actually contemplated in the main purpose clause, and thereafter enumerate additional activities related and unrelated thereto, often without differentiation between purposes and powers.[9]

1. E. g., ABA–ALI Model Bus.Corp.Act § 48(c); see also id. § 3; Del.Gen.Corp.Law § 102(a) (3) (1967); McKinney's N.Y.Bus.Corp.Law § 402(a) (2).

2. Wyo.Const. art. X, § 6 (amendment effective Dec. 2, 1960).

3. Okl.Const. art. XXII, § 2; Puerto Rico Const. art. VI, § 14. See Le Force v. Bullard, 454 P.2d 297 (Okl.1969) (upholding power of farming corporations to own real estate outside limits of incorporated cities and towns).

4. E. g., ABA–ALI Model Bus.Corp.Act § 3; Comment, "Inclusion of Non-Licensable Business Activity Precludes Issuance of Corporate Charter", 12 U. Kan.L.Rev. 578 (1964).

5. See section 17, nn. 8, 9 supra.

6. E. g., ABA–ALI Model Bus.Corp.Act § 3. The New York formulation is very complicated:

"(a) A corporation may be formed under this chapter for any lawful business purpose or purposes except to do in this state any business for which forma-

tion is permitted under any other statute of this state unless such statute permits formation under this chapter. If, immediately prior to the effective date of this chapter, a statute of this state permitted the formation of a corporation under the stock corporation law for a purpose or purposes specified in such other statute, such statute shall be deemed and construed to permit formation of such corporation under this chapter, and any conditions, limitations or restrictions in such other statute upon the formation of such corporation under the stock corporation law shall apply to the formation thereof under this chapter.

. . .

"(c) In time of war or other national emergency, a corporation may do any lawful business in aid thereof, notwithstanding the purpose or purposes set forth in its certificate of incorporation, at the request or direction of any competent governmental authority." McKinney's N.Y.Bus.Corp.Law § 201.

7. Former Mont.Gen.Corp.Law § 15–104 (1947).

8. E. g., Delaware, Iowa, Maine, Nevada, Oregon, Pennsylvania, Wisconsin (all-purpose clauses); 1969 Model Act revision ("The purpose or purposes for which the corporation is organized which may be stated to be, or to include, the transaction of any or all lawful business for which corporations may be incorporated under this Act.").

9. Berkoff, "The Object Clause in Corporate Articles", 4 Wis.L.Rev. 424 (1928). See text accompanying note 12 infra.

The purpose clause or clauses should express the nature and scope of the business and risk as agreed upon among the shareholders. Therefore, the purpose clause or clauses should be so drafted as to be definite enough to curb excursions into unauthorized ventures and yet sufficiently general to permit reasonable operations and expansion without the necessity of future amendment of the articles of incorporation. Careful drafting of the purpose clause or clauses, using available forms and precedents as a checklist,[10] is highly desirable from several points of view.[11] In most situations, a relatively general statement of purposes to the extent permissible is preferable to specific enumeration.

The purpose clause might state that the purposes shall be construed as powers as well as purposes, and the matters expressed in any clause shall in nowise be limited by reference to or inference from the terms of any other, but shall be regarded as independent purposes and powers; and the enumeration of specific purposes and powers shall not be construed to limit or restrict in any manner the meaning of general terms of the general powers; nor shall the expression of one thing be deemed to exclude another not expressed, although it be of like nature.[12]

The extent to which the stated purposes will be carried out is within the discretion of the board of directors.[13]

CORPORATE POWERS

122. The articles of incorporation are usually not required to set forth corporate powers. Some modern statutes expressly provide that the articles need not or should not set forth the powers. However, a frequent practice is to include numerous power clauses, often commingling them with purpose clauses. Powers clauses should contain any desired lawful limitations on powers conferred by statute or implied apart from statute and any lawful provision for desired powers which exist only if provision is made for them in the articles.

In contrast to purpose clauses, which define the nature of the business, power clauses serve to empower the corporation to effectuate the purposes. Usually, there is no statutory requirement that the articles of incorporation set forth the corporation's powers.[1] Some modern statutes even expressly provide that the articles need not or should not set forth the corporate powers enumerated in the statute.[2] A frequent practice in jurisdictions where not prohibited, however, is to include numerous power clauses, often commingling them with purpose clauses.[3]

10. E. g., 1 M. Fogelman, West's McKinney's Forms: Business Corporation Law 106–190 (1965).

11. Not only are the purpose clauses supposed to protect shareholders, management, and the public by defining the line between intra vires and ultra vires corporate activity. See section 184 infra. The wording of purpose clauses might be decisive in determining whether one corporation may merge into another; whether a sale of corporate assets is within or without the regular course of business for purposes of shareholder consent requirements; whether certain property qualifies as consideration for issue of shares; whether certain property may be acquired by the corporation; whether the corporation is eligible for bankruptcy [11 U.S.C.A. § 22].

12. But see Cal.Gen.Corp.Law, § 301 (1947) (requiring statement in separate paragraph identifying specific business in which corporation is primarily to engage). The addition of the clause "and any and all other lawful business purposes" to a statement of specific purposes runs the risk of the application of

the maxim, Expressio unius est exclusio alterius, or being held improper as an all-purpose or omnibus clause in a jurisdiction which does not permit such clause.

13. Matter of Ideal Mutual Ins. Co., 18 Misc.2d 127, 190 N.Y.S.2d 887 (Sup.Ct.1959), aff'd 9 A.D.2d 60, 190 N.Y.S.2d 895 (1st Dep't 1959). For further discussion of purposes and objects, see section 181 infra.

1. 2 Model Business Corporation Act Annotated § 48 (1960).

2. ABA–ALI Model Bus.Corp.Act § 48; McKinney's N.Y.Bus.Corp.Law § 402(b).

3. The practice of inserting various power clauses arose to avoid the risk of strict construction of purpose and power clauses, somewhat as an historical vestige from the period when the ultra vires doctrine had more serious consequence, but probably more as a matter of professional practice and precedent. The practice tends to make the articles of incorporation a more reasonably self-contained

Frequently there are catch-all clauses empowering the corporation to have and to exercise all the powers presently or thereafter conferred by law upon corporations, to do any or all things to the same extent as natural persons might or could do,[4] and to enjoy all powers necessary and proper to effectuate the purposes of the corporation. To these power clauses are sometimes prefixed or added clauses that the power clauses should be construed both as purposes and as powers,[5] and that the enumeration of specific powers should not be held to limit or restrict in any manner the powers of the corporation.[6]

The extent to which power clauses should be included in the articles of incorporation is a much debated question and varies with the prospective needs of the business.

The law from which the powers derive may be statutory (with the more specific statute controlling in the event of inconsistency) or nonstatutory, the major difference being that it is more difficult to determine the validity and scope of powers without a statutory source. From the draftsman's viewpoint, the practical distinctions are that certain powers exist without apparent exception, others exist unless otherwise provided in the articles of incorporation, while still others do not exist in the absence of their mention in the articles of incorporation.

Modern statutes usually enumerate corporate powers, in a reasonably logical arrangement.[7] Older statutes often had scattered, poorly-drafted powers provisions.[8]

Apart from statute, implied power not inconsistent with statute or the "statutory norm" will be recognized to do all things reasonably necessary to enable the corporation to carry out its purposes and powers.[9] Besides such implied powers, which defy cataloguing,[10] are incidental powers or traditional corporate attributes:[11]

(a) To have existence independent of the death or withdrawal of members;

(b) To sue and be sued in the corporate name;

(c) To acquire, hold, and convey property for corporate purposes in the corporate name;

(d) To have a seal;

(e) To make bylaws—

all of which may be said to inhere in a corporation as a legal entity or in corporateness as such.

Statutory powers which are conferred without apparent exception, statutory powers which exist unless otherwise provided in the articles of incorporation, and implied or

---

document, and to provide assurances to title companies, loaning institutions, vendees, mortgagees, other creditors, and authorities and persons in any foreign jurisdiction where the corporation intends to do business.

4. Such clauses comprehend powers now or hereafter conferred upon corporations by law, statutory and nonstatutory; assimilate the artificial corporate person to a natural person; and spell out what is otherwise implied or set forth in statutes. The clauses are sometimes expressly qualified by the phrase "to the extent lawful".

5. To avoid the risk of a construction delimiting the powers by the purposes. See section 121, n. 12 supra.

6. To avoid the risk of the application of the maxim, Expressio unius est exclusio alterius, when any powers are spelled out in the articles of incorporation. But see Williams v. United Most Worshipful St. John's Grand Lodge, 140 So.2d 206 (La.Ct.App. 1962).

7. E. g., ABA–ALI Model Bus.Corp.Act § 4 (with only a few of the powers expressly limited to corporate purposes). New York has an even more comprehensive enumeration, but expressly limits them to corporate purposes. McKinney's N.Y.Bus. Corp.Law § 203.

8. E. g., N.Y.Const. art. X, § 4; McKinney's N.Y. Gen.Corp.Law, §§ 13, 14, 16, 17, 18, 34, 35 (no longer applicable to stock corporations); former McKinney's N.Y.Stock Corp.Law, §§ 14, 16, 18, 19, 20, 28, 29, 60, 69.

9. See Gause v. Commonwealth Trust Co., 196 N.Y. 134, 89 N.E. 476 (1909).

10. For an excellent summary, see R. Stevens, Handbook on the Law of Private Corporations §§ 48–61 (2d ed. 1949).

11. 6 W. Fletcher, Private Corporations § 2485 (rev. 1968).

incidental powers apart from statute clearly exist in the absence of any contrary provision in the articles of incorporation; statutory powers which exist only if mentioned in the articles of incorporation clearly do not exist unless so mentioned. The extent to which any of the several types of powers may be amplified, limited, or denied in the articles of incorporation may present unresolved problems of statutory construction. Certainly, they should not be amplified beyond the bounds prescribed by statute such as statutes which prohibit a corporation from possessing or exercising any powers unless given by law or necessary to the powers so given.[12] By construing the term "law" to include nonstatutory as well as statutory law and the word "necessary" in a broad sense, provisions in the articles of incorporation within such bounds should be upheld; in fact, it could be contended, by way of affirmative inference to be drawn from such a statute, that every corporation enjoys all powers given by law (except powers which exist only if mentioned in the articles of incorporation) or necessary to the powers so given in the absence of any lawful limitations in the articles of incorporation. "Limitations" in the articles of incorporation may be expressly permitted by statute so long as the corporation is not exempted from the performance of any obligation or duty imposed by law.[13] The matter, is obfuscated by the fact that a few of the statutory formulations of powers expressly provide that such formation shall not disturb any powers apart from statute, or that the powers so formulated shall exist in the absence of any contrary provision in the articles of incorporation, or both. So long as such problems remain unresolved, the cautious procedure might be to refrain from enumerating in the articles of incorporation, statutory powers which exist without apparent exception, statutory powers which exist unless otherwise provided in the articles of incorporation, and implied or incidental powers apart from statute, or, if enumeration appears desirable for practical considerations, to paraphrase closely the statutory language or to stay well within the permissible bounds of amplification or limitation, qualifying the same by resort to such phrases as "to the extent lawful", and adding suitable catchall and concluding clauses.[14]

For the corporation to enjoy powers which exist only if mentioned in the articles of incorporation, enumeration would be necessary. Here, too, enumeration should be within the bounds of statute and "statutory norms", and care should be taken that the enumeration is so drafted as not to exclude desired powers which would otherwise exist without mention.

In summary, then, the powers clauses in the articles of incorporation should, at least contain any desired denials or limitations on the powers conferred by statute or implied apart from statute and any provision for desired powers which exist only if provision is made for them in the articles, but in all such cases only to the extent lawful.

AUTHORIZED SHARES

123. All jurisdictions require that the articles of incorporation set forth the number of authorized shares, the number of shares in each class if shares are classified, and the par value of any par value shares, and if there are to be shares without par value a statement to such effect. Choice between par value shares

12. E. g., McKinney's N.Y.Gen.Corp.Law, § 13(1) (no longer applicable to stock corporations).

13. E. g., McKinney's N.Y.Gen.Corp.Law, § 13(2) (no longer applicable to stock corporations).

14. An additional complication may result from the fact that the various statutory sections sometimes provide that any corporation "shall have" certain powers; "may" do certain things; "has power" to do certain things. Even paraphrasing of statutory language might prove undesirable in the light of future statutory revision, although embarrassment could be minimized by an appropriate catchall clause. Enumeration might be construed as exhaustive, thereby negativing powers not mentioned —a construction which can possibly be avoided by appropriate clauses.

and shares without par value is usually based upon applicable requirements of consideration for their issue; rates of organization and capital, issue, and transfer taxes; and the desirability of allocating part of the consideration to capital surplus. Some jurisdictions require the articles of incorporation to include certain prescribed statements concerning stated capital.

The articles of incorporation in all jurisdictions are required to set forth the number of authorized shares, the number of shares in each class if shares are classified, and the par value of any par value shares, and if there are to be shares without par value a statement to such effect.[1]

Where there is only one class of shares, such shares, regardless of designation, are in effect "common shares". Such shares hold the voting rights, are entitled to such dividends as are distributed, and receive in the event of liquidation the net assets remaining after the payment of all creditor claims.

Par Value; Without Par Value (With or Without Stated Value)

Shares may be par value shares or shares without par value;[2] in some jurisdictions, shares without par value may have a stated value.[3] The choice is usually based on several factors, which in a given situation may or may not be significant: (a) the requirements of consideration for their issue; (b) the rates of organization and capital issue, and transfer taxes; and (c) the desirability of allocating part of the consideration to capital surplus.

Consideration Requirements

The requirements of consideration for the issue of shares are both qualitative and quantitative.

Qualitatively, the consideration requirement is usually the same for par value shares and shares without par value, viz., money, services, or property.[4]

Quantitatively, such consideration for par value shares usually may be no less than par value.[5]

For shares without par value, the consideration in many jurisdictions may be fixed from time to time by the board of directors unless the articles of incorporation reserve to the shareholders the right to fix the

---

1. ABA–ALI Model Bus.Corp.Act § 48(d); see also id. § 14. Usually, statutes prescribe no limitations on the amount of authorized shares, and the amount, of course, can be increased in the future, upon proper authorization, by the filing of an amendment of the articles of incorporation and payment of any capital taxes and filing fees. In most cases, the maximum amount covered by the minimum organization tax might well be initially authorized even though less than all of such shares are to be issued initially. Sufficient authorized and unissued shares should be reserved for the exercise of any subsisting conversion privileges or share options.

2. The par value multiplied by the number obviously should equal the amount. Besides having to be stated in the articles of incorporation, the par value is also often indicated as part of the designation of the shares, e. g., "$_____ Par Value Capital Shares", "Capital Shares—$_____ Par Value", "Capital Shares ($_____ Par Value)". Shares listed on the New York Stock Exchange, moreover are required to indicate the par value on the face of the share certificate. N.Y.S.E. Company Manual § A12. Shares without par value were first authorized in New York by statute in 1912. N.Y.Sess. Laws 1912, ch. 351. Nebraska and England do not permit shares without par value. Par value is a

value arbitrarily set—the statutes prescribe no limitations—and in a going concern is not necessarily synonymous with book value, market value, or the consideration received for the shares. The par value should be set sufficiently low in relation to its probable market value to be salable at a price which will satisfy the requirement that par value shares not be sold for less than par value and will create any desired capital surplus. The trend has been in favor of low par value shares because of tax considerations. The New York attorney general has ruled that par value can be fixed at one mill per share. 1959 N.Y.Op.Att'y Gen. 87. Nebraska requires that all shares in a corporation except preferred shares be of the same par value.

3. Stated value, unlike par value, is often not indicated on the share certificate. The setting of stated value is based on the same factors as the setting of par value, the only possible difference being different applicable tax rates. But see note 19 infra.

4. ABA–ALI Model Bus.Corp.Act § 18; see sections 167, 168 infra.

5. ABA–ALI Model Bus.Corp.Act § 17; see section 167 infra.

consideration.[6] Older statutes sometimes required that consideration be (a) prescribed
in the articles of incorporation, (b) equivalent to the fair market value, (c) fixed by
the board of directors pursuant to authority
conferred in the articles, or (d) approved by
a majority of the shareholders entitled to
vote thereon at a duly-called meeting.[7] In
the case of shares without par value which
have a stated value, such consideration also
should not be less than the stated value.[8]
Where a minimum capital provision is included in the articles of incorporation, either
as required or as permitted,[9] the capital represented by the shares originally issued
should satisfy such minimum capital
requirement.[10] All shares so issued are
deemed fully paid and nonassessable.[11]

*Organization and Capital, Issue, and Trans-
fer Tax Rates*

In some jurisdictions, there are organization taxes and capital taxes on *authorized*
shares, taxes on the *issue* of shares, and/or
taxes on the *transfer* of shares. Sometimes,
the rates of these taxes in effect discriminate against shares without par value by
equating each share without par value for
the purposes of such taxes to $100 of par
value.[12] In the case of organization and capital taxes, there is usually a minimum tax,
but when such minimum is exceeded, the authorization of par value shares might in-

volve a substantial tax saving over the authorization of shares without par value.[13]

Capital Surplus

The desirability of creating capital surplus
at the outset of corporate existence stems
principally from restrictions against impairment of stated capital by means of
dividends[14] or expenditure of the corporation's funds to purchase or redeem its own
shares.[15] In many such jurisdictions, capital
surplus, as distinguished from stated capital,
may be distributed as dividends or so expended. In such jurisdictions, the existence
of capital surplus gives the corporation a
flexibility it would not otherwise enjoy.
Capital surplus can be created at the outset
by issuing par value shares for more than
par value (allocating the par value to capital
and the excess or premium to capital surplus), and by allocating a part of the consideration received for shares without par value
to capital surplus, with the balance allocated
to stated capital.[16] Under the Model Business
Corporation Act, any portion (prior to 1957,
not more than 25 percent) of the consideration received for shares without par value
may be allocated to capital surplus, but no allocation to capital surplus may be made of
any portion of the consideration received for
shares without par value having a preference in the assets of the corporation in the
event of involuntary liquidation except the
amount, if any, of such consideration in excess of such preference.[17] In New York,
prior to 1963, the total consideration re-

6. E. g., ABA–ALI Model Bus.Corp.Act § 17; Mc-
Kinney's N.Y.Bus.Corp.Law, § 504(d). Several jurisdictions expressly authorize the incorporators to fix
the consideration for shares without par value up
to the time of incorporation. See section 168 infra.

7. See former McKinney's N.Y.Stock Corp.Law § 12.

8. See former McKinney's N.Y.Stock Corp.Law §
12(4) (A) (many pre-1963 New York corporations
still have no par value shares with stated value).

9. See section 126 infra.

10. See sections 126, 143 infra.

11. E. g., ABA–ALI Model Bus.Corp.Act § 18. See
section 171 infra.

12. See section 158 infra.

13. For example, under McKinney's N.Y.Tax Law, §
180, each share without par value is taxed as
equivalent to par value shares aggregating $100 par
value, at the rate of five cents, with a $10 mini-
mum tax. Such minimum tax would cover $20,000
par value of par value shares (e. g., 2,000 shares at
$10 par value each or 20,000,000 shares at one mill
par value each) or 200 shares without par value.

14. See sections 320–323 infra.

15. See section 336 infra.

16. E. g., Del.Gen.Corp.Law § 154 (1967).

17. ABA–ALI Model Bus.Corp.Act § 19.

ceived for shares without par value without stated value had to be allocated to capital,[18] but any consideration received for shares without par value with stated value in excess of such stated value could have been allocated to capital surplus (the stated value being allocated to stated capital).[19]

18. Former McKinney's N.Y.Stock Corp.Law §§ 12(4) (B), 13. The present New York Business Corporation Law follows the Model Act provision, supra note 17. McKinney's N.Y.Bus.Corp.Law § 506(b).

19. Former McKinney's N.Y.Stock Corp.Law, §§ 12(4) (A), 13. The present New York Business Corporation Law does not provide for shares without par value with stated value. Previously, New York, where shares without par value were being authorized, regardless of whether par value shares were also being authorized, had a somewhat unique provision requiring the articles of incorporation to include one of two statements *in haec verba*. See former McKinney's N.Y.Stock Corp.Law, §§ 5(3), 12(4) (A), (B):

A. "The capital of the corporation shall be at least equal to the sum of the aggregate par value of all issued shares having par value, plus . . . dollars (the blank space being filled in with some number representing one dollar or more) in respect to every issued share without par value, plus such amounts as, from time to time, may be transferred thereto.

B. "The capital of the corporation shall be at least equal to the sum of the aggregate par value of all issued shares having par value, plus the aggregate amount of consideration received by the corporation for the issuance of shares without par value, plus such amounts as, from time to time, may be transferred thereto."

Statement A was used for shares without par value which had a stated value; Statement B for shares without par value which did not have a stated value. The principal differences were that Statement A imposed an additional quantitative consideration requirement with respect to shares without par value, i. e., shares might not be issued for less than the stated value, and provided an additional means of creating capital surplus, i. e., shares might be issued for more than the stated value and the stated value allocated to stated capital and the excess or premium to capital surplus. In contracts, Statement B imposed no quantitative consideration requirement, and required that the total consideration received for shares without par value be allocated to capital. So far as par value shares and the transfer by the board of directors of additional amounts to stated capital were concerned, Statements A and B were identical.

Many articles of incorporation of New York corporations formed prior to 1963 retain Statement A or Statement B.

Required Statements Concerning Stated Capital

Some jurisdictions require the articles of incorporation to include minimum stated capital provisions.[20]

CLASSIFICATION OF SHARES

124. All jurisdictions require that the articles of incorporation, if the shares are to be divided into classes, set forth the designation of each class and a statement of the preferences, limitations, and relative rights in respect of the shares of each class. Preferences may exist with respect to dividends and/or net assets upon liquidation. Dividend preferences may be cumulative, cumulative-to-the-extent-earned, or noncumulative, and participating or nonparticipating. Liquidating preferences may or may not include any preferred dividend arrearages, and may be participating or nonparticipating. The articles of incorporation may usually deny or limit the voting rights, absolutely or conditionally, of some classes; provide for the redemption by the corporation of preferred shares; make shares convertible by the holder into other securities; contain protective or other provisions for preferred or other shares; and authorize the issue of share warrants. Apart from shares and other equity securities, debt securities, such as bonds, debentures, and notes, may be issued.

The articles of incorporation in all jurisdictions are required, if the shares are to be divided into classes, to set forth the designation of each class and a statement of the preferences, limitations, and relative rights in respect of the shares of each class.[1]

20. E. g., ABA–ALI Model Bus.Corp.Act, § 48(g) (eliminated in 1969 Model Act revision). See section 126 infra.

1. E. g., ABA–ALI Model Bus.Corp.Act, § 48(e); see also id. § 14; Del.Gen.Corp.Law, § 102(a) (4) (1967); McKinney's N.Y.Bus.Corp.Law, § 402(a) (5); Spoerri, "What Goes in the Stock Clauses?", 37 Ill.B.J. 422 (1949). Where shares with differing preferences, privileges or voting powers are desired, it is necessary to divide the shares into separately designated classes. Such classification cannot be legally accomplished by a bylaw provision. Gaskill v. Gladys Belle Oil Co., 16 Del.Ch. 289, 146 A. 337 (Ch.1929); Christal v. Petry, 275 App.Div. 550, 90 N.Y.S.2d 620 (1st Dep't 1949), aff'd 301 N.Y. 562, 93

Many jurisdictions also permit the articles of incorporation to authorize the issuance of preferred or special classes of shares in series.[2]

Designation

Shares may be designated in any manner which seems appropriate or descriptive, except that no shares which are entitled to a preference in the distribution of dividends or net assets should be designated as "common", and no shares without such a preference should be designated as "preferred".[3]

Normal Rights

Except as otherwise provided in the articles of incorporation, all shares enjoy equal rights. Chief among these are: (a) the right to participate ratably in earnings by way of dividends when, as and if declared by the board of directors, usually in the exercise of discretion,[4] out of legally available funds; [5] (b) the right to participate ratably in net assets (after satisfying liabilities to creditors) upon liquidation; [6] (c) the right to participate ratably (one vote per share) in control; [7] and (d) the preemptive rights to preserve ratably the foregoing rights.[8]

Dividend Preferences

For any class to enjoy a preference as to dividends, the articles of incorporation must so provide.[9] Such dividend preference may be expressed in terms of monetary amounts in any year in which legal funds are available. But courts will not construe a provision to deprive the board of directors of discretion in dividend declarations in the absence of a clear and express mandatory provision. See section 327 infra.

N.E.2d 450 (1950). Two or more classes with similar rights might be authorized where flexibility as to quantity of consideration and allocation of consideration between stated capital and capital surplus is desired or where directors are to be classified. For share certificate requirements where more than one class of shares is authorized, see section 134 infra.

2. See section 125 infra.

3. E. g., McKinney's N.Y.Bus.Corp.Law, § 501(b). Such designations as "Class A", "Class B", etc., differentiate the classes but are not otherwise descriptive. Shares which are entitled to preference in the distribution of dividends or net assets, or both, are frequently designated as "preferred" or "preference". Where two or more classes of preferred shares with different preferences are authorized, they are commonly differentiated by such titles as "first preferred", "second preferred", "prior preferred", etc., indicating relative priority. Other designations denoting one or more features of the shares are often employed, e. g., "cumulative preferred", "participating preferred", "——% preferred", "$—— preferred", "voting preference", "capital shares", "common shares ($—— par value)".

4. The board of directors may declare such dividends as seem appropriate in their business judgment, and the courts are loath to find an abuse of discretion. See section 327 infra. A few statutes have mandatory dividend provisions. In addition, discretion is limited when the articles of incorporation contain "mandatory" dividend provisions, as where shares expressly are to receive designated dividends

5. See section 320 infra. In New York, no limitation or definition of dividend rights shall be effective unless at the time one or more classes of outstanding shares, singly or in the aggregate, are entitled to unlimited dividend rights, and there may be no denial of dividend rights. McKinney's N.Y.Bus. Corp.Law, § 501(a). See also 35 N.C.Op.Att'y Gen. 21, Feb. 12, 1960. Absent a statutory requirement that all shares have liquidation rights, a second class of shares without any liquidation rights has been held valid. Halo Metal Products, Inc. v. Randall, 419 F.2d 1068 (7th Cir. 1969) (construing Illinois law which expressly requires that all shares have voting rights).

6. See sections 381, 382 infra. In New York, no limitation or definition of liquidation rights shall be effective unless at the time one or more classes of outstanding shares, singly or in the aggregate, are entitled to unlimited liquidation rights, and there may be no denial of liquidation rights. McKinney's N.Y.Bus.Corp.Law, § 501(a). See also 35 N.C.Op. Att'y Gen. 21, Feb. 12, 1960. Absent a statutory requirement that all shares have dividend rights, a second class of shares without any dividend rights has been held valid. Halo Metal Products, Inc. v. Randall, 419 F.2d 1068 (7th Cir. 1969) (construing Illinois law which expressly requires that all shares have voting rights).

7. See section 189 infra.

8. See sections 127, 172–175 infra.

9. Buxbaum, "Preferred Stock—Law and Draftsmanship", 42 Calif.L.Rev. 243, 243–257 (1954). See sections 324–326 infra. The articles of incorporation constitute the contract between the corporation and the shareholders, and their dividend rights must be determined by the language thereof. Gaskill v. Gladys Belle Oil Co., 16 Del.Ch. 289, 146 A. 337 (Ch. 1929); Roberts v. Roberts-Wicks Co., 184 N.Y. 257, 77 N.E. 13 (1906).

or percentage of par value,[10] and may be cumulative, cumulative-to-the-extent-earned, or noncumulative; beyond the dividend preference, such preferred shares may or may not participate in further dividends.

Cumulative; Cumulative-to-the-extent-earned; Noncumulative. The difference between a cumulative and noncumulative dividend preference is that, under the former, unpaid dividends for all prior fiscal periods accumulate and must be paid in full, along with the dividend for the current fiscal period, before any dividend may be distributed on shares having subordinate dividend rights. Under the latter, dividends unpaid in the past do not accumulate and need not be paid before a dividend distribution on other shares, so long as the dividend preference for the current fiscal period is satisfied. Noncumulative dividends not declared in any period lapse and are not thereafter payable.[11] A hybrid variety of dividend preference is the cumulative-to-the-extent-earned type, under which unpaid dividends accumulate during past fiscal periods only to the extent that there were then funds legally available to pay such dividends.[12] If any dividend preference is intended, the articles of incorporation should clearly indicate the type thereof.[13] While a cumulative dividend preference might enhance the marketability of the preferred shares, embarrassment can result eventually from any dividend arrearages, although such arrearages can often be eliminated by reclassification or similar procedures.[14]

Participating; Nonparticipating. Whether the dividend preference is cumulative, cumulative-to-the-extent-earned, or noncumulative, the preferred shares may or may not participate in further dividends with another class or classes of shares. Shares may participate in a variety of ways: equally or in a fixed ratio, immediately after the payment of preferred dividends or after the payment of a prescribed dividend upon another class or classes of shares, or only in the event of a specified contingency. Preferred shares with nonparticipating dividend rights receive no dividends beyond their dividend preference.[15] The articles of incorporation should provide whether the dividend preference is intended to be participating or nonparticipating, and if the former, should spell out the participation formula.[16]

In recent years, nonparticipating preferred shares convertible into common shares has tended to replace participating preferred shares.

Liquidation Preference

For any class of shares to enjoy a preference as to assets, the articles of incorporation must so provide.[17] Such liquidation

10. Preference of $——— or ———% of par value per annum, payable annually, semi-annually, or quarterly, or on designated dividend payment dates. A dividend preference can be most easily likened to a negative covenant: a promise not to pay dividends on any class of shares with a junior or no dividend preference until the preference is satisfied.

11. See section 325 infra.

12. Some articles of incorporation may be so construed; rare statutes so provide; New Jersey has applied the "dividend credit theory" to noncumulative preferred shares, treating a noncumulative preference as a cumulative-to-the-extent-earned preference. See section 325 infra.

13. "Cumulative" or "noncumulative" is usually sufficient. Silence leads to problems of construction. See section 325, n. 8 infra.

14. See section 325 infra.

15. See section 326 infra.

16. The question of participation in further dividends, where the articles of incorporation are silent on the matter, has not been fully resolved. The importance of having a specific provision in the articles of incorporation is, therefore, obvious. See Buxbaum, "Preferred Stock—Law and Draftsmanship", 42 Calif.L.Rev. 243, 245–247 (1954). If nonparticipation is intended, the articles of incorporation should provide for payment of the stated dividend preference "and no more". In addition, or alternatively, the articles of incorporation could provide for the payment of the dividend preference and then provide that after the payment thereof, all remaining dividends should be payable to and distributed ratably among the holders of record of the common shares.

17. Buxbaum, "Preferred Stock—Law and Draftsmanship", 42 Calif.L.Rev. 243, 257–262 (1954). See section 382 infra.

preference is usually expressed in terms of par value [18] or of monetary amount,[19] with or without provisions for unpaid dividend arrearages in the case of cumulative preferred shares; [20] sometimes such preference is greater in amount for voluntary than for involuntary dissolution.[21]

The articles of incorporation should also define what events give rise to the liquidation preference.[22] The provision might expressly negate any right to the liquidation preference in event of merger, consolidation, sale, lease or conveyance of assets—all of which in fact may involve complete or partial liquidation.

Beyond the liquidation preference, such preferred shares may or may not participate

further in the distribution of net assets. On the subject of participation, the articles of incorporation should be explicit,[23] indicating whether or not participation is intended and if so, to what extent.[24] Participation by classes of shares may be equal or in a stated ratio, may commence at once after the satisfaction of the liquidation preference or be limited to commence after designated payments to the shares of another class or classes, may be limited to a fixed amount, or may be created in any combination of the foregoing.

Voting Rights

So far as voting rights are concerned, every shareholder is entitled to one vote per share of record unless otherwise provided in the articles of incorporation.[25] The articles of incorporation may usually deny or limit the voting rights, absolutely or conditionally, of some classes.[26] Every corporation, howev-

---

18. E. g., "106% of the par value thereof", "full par value plus 6% thereof", etc.

19. E. g., "one hundred and six dollars ($106.00) per share."

20. See sections 325, 382 infra. A provision including unpaid dividend arrearages in the liquidation preference of cumulative preferred shares must be carefully drawn. See section 325, nn. 16, 17 infra. The term "dividend arrearage" or "accumulation" should be defined to include unpaid amounts regardless of whether the corporation shall have surplus available for dividends or whether there shall have been a declaration of dividends. Better still, to avoid the implication that "dividends" (even in arrears) are limited to legally available funds, a reference to the accumulation of unpaid or undeclared "dividends" might be avoided as follows: Upon dissolution, liquidation, or winding up, the holder of each share of cumulative preferred shares shall be entitled to an amount equal to the par value (or $——— per share) plus ——— percent (or $———) [annual dividend preference] per year for each year in which the share has been issued and outstanding, less the sum of any dividends paid thereon." See Shanik v. Empire Power Corp., 58 N.Y.S.2d 176 (Sup.Ct.1945), aff'd mem., 270 App.Div. 925, 62 N.Y.S.2d 760 (1st Dep't 1946), aff'd mem., 296 N.Y. 664, 69 N.E.2d 818 (1946). It is sounder to refer to the years of issue than to specify a date. See Blandin v. United North & South Development Co., 35 Del.Ch. 471, 121 A.2d 686 (Ch.1956), aff'd 36 Del.Ch. 538, 134 A.2d 706 (Sup.Ct.1957) (provision for payment of dividends on cumulative preferred shares to begin March 15, 1938 held not to require payment of dividends on some shares issued in 1945 for period prior to such issuance).

21. See section 382 infra.

22. Buxbaum, "Preferred Stock—Law and Draftsmanship", 42 Calif.L.Rev. 243, 260–261 (1954).

23. See section 382 infra. Silence, or ambiguous language, raises problems of construction. 2 I. Kantrowitz & S. Slutsky, White on New York Corporations ¶ 501.04[3] (13th ed. 1968).

24. The problem is one of construing the articles of incorporation. Where the articles of incorporation stated that the preferred shares should be "paid in full at par value before any amount shall be paid on account of the common shares", it was held there was no participation beyond the stated preference. Williams v. Renshaw, 220 App.Div. 39, 220 N.Y.S. 532 (3d Dep't 1927). If nonparticipation is intended, the articles of incorporation should provide for the payment of the liquidation preference "and no more" and that after the payment thereof, all of the remaining assets should be payable to and distributed ratably among the holders of record of the common shares. If participation is intended, the method of participation should be spelled out. Nonparticipation is usually desired.

25. E. g., ABA–ALI Model Bus.Corp.Act § 31; McKinney's N.Y.Bus.Corp.Law, § 612; see section 189 infra. Shareholders by agreement usually can bind themselves in advance to vote as shareholders on matters subject to shareholder action. See section 198 infra.

26. ABA–ALI Model Bus.Corp.Act § 31; McKinney's N.Y.Bus.Corp.Law, §§ 501, 613. In a few jurisdictions, constitutional or statutory provisions prohibit nonvoting shares. See section 189 infra. Under the Model Business Corporation Act, all shareholders are entitled to notice of extraordinary actions or transactions such as merger, consolidation, sale of assets not in the regular course of business, and

er, must have full voting rights.[27]

The articles of incorporation often are silent as to the voting rights of common shares (thereby granting unlimited voting rights) and provide that preferred shares either are nonvoting or have contingent voting rights.[28] Contingent voting rights typically arise upon the default of a specified number of dividend payments [29] and may follow any one of several patterns.[30] Provision for the return to normal voting after the curing of the default should be made in the articles of incorporation.[31]

Voting is straight unless otherwise provided by state constitution, statute, or the

articles of incorporation.[32] If class voting for directors or otherwise,[33] or cumulative voting for directors in jurisdictions where cumulative voting exists only where there is provision therefor in the articles of incorporation,[34] is desired, appropriate provision for either or both should be included in the articles of incorporation. Class voting is a means for assuring any desirable representation of the class on the board of directors; cumulative voting is a form or proportional representation to assure any desirable minority representation on the board.[35]

Preemptive Rights

To preserve the shareholder's proportionate dividend, liquidation, and voting rights, preemptive rights are usually recognized, but their existence and scope can be affected by provisions in the articles of incorporation.[36]

Redemption

A frequently-desired feature of preferred shares [37] is a redemption (or call) provision,

voluntary dissolution, often regardless of whether or not such shares are entitled to vote thereon by the articles; the vote required is of the shareholders entitled to vote thereon; for amendments of the articles of incorporation altering the rights, preferences, or relative status of shares of any class, the shares of that class are entitled to vote as a class regardless of the articles. ABA–ALI Model Bus. Corp.Act §§ 55, 67, 71, 77, 82. Under New York law, mandatory class voting rights exist in any class of shares with respect to certain amendments of the articles of incorporation.

27. In New York, no denial, limitation or definition of voting rights shall be effective unless at the time one or more classes of outstanding shares or bonds, singly or in the aggregate, are entitled to full voting rights. McKinney's N.Y.Bus.Corp.Law, § 501(a).

28. In order to be acceptable for listing on the New York Stock Exchange, common shares must be voting and preferred shares must have certain minimum (contingent) voting rights. N.Y.S.E. Company Manual § A15. See sections 189, 316 infra.

29. E. g., the right of preferred shareholders to elect one less than a majority of the board of directors upon default of six quarterly dividends, consecutive or nonconsecutive.

30. The preferred shareholders, upon happening of the contingency, may be empowered to elect a given number of directors, one less than a majority, an established proportion, or all of the directors. Buxbaum, "Preferred Stock—Law and Draftsmanship", 42 Calif.L.Rev. 243, 290–292 (1954).

31. The articles of incorporation should provide for the retention of voting control by the preferred shares until the dividend arrearages are paid in full. Such a provision will avoid constant shifts in voting rights. In any event, the articles of incorporation should be specific as to what event triggers the return to normal voting.

32. See section 189 infra.

33. See section 189 infra. Provision might be made in the articles of incorporation for each class of shares to elect a certain number of directors, or for a specified class to have several votes per share or fractional votes per share. Where there is doubt as to the validity of multiple or fractional votes, more or fewer shares for a proportionately smaller or greater consideration, respectively, can accomplish the same purpose, with appropriate adjustment in the other rights.

34. See section 189 infra.

35. The normal cumulative voting provision grants to each share as many votes as there are directors to be elected, the shareholder being permitted to distribute the votes in any way he sees fit. Where cumulative voting is authorized in jurisdictions with permissive, as distinguished from mandatory, provisions, any quorum provision must be contained in the articles of incorporation. McKinney's N.Y. Bus.Corp.Law, § 618. The tie-in between cumulative voting and class voting, classified board of directors, removal of directors, and decreasing the size of the board of directors should be considered.

36. See section 127 infra.

37. The preferential feature of shares is often necessary to attract capital investment at the outset of

empowering the corporation to acquire the shares from the holder. Absent a redemption provision in the articles of incorporation, the corporation would not have such power.

Redemption provisions may be mandatory[38] or optional[39] and may provide for partial as well as total redemption.[40]

The redemption price (including redemption premium) should be clearly defined in terms of par value or monetary amount;[41]

if the preferred shares are cumulative, and the redemption price is intended to include dividend arrearages, the drafting problem resembles that encountered in drafting the liquidation preference to include dividend arrearages.[42]

The redemption dates (if there is to be such limitation), the procedure for the giving of notice of redemption, any deposit arrangements, and the effect of redemption on any conversion privilege should also be set forth.[43]

Provision might also be made for a sinking fund for the redemption or repurchase of the preferred shares.[44]

Conversion

Preferred shares might be made more attractive to investors by a conversion privilege. Absent a conversion provision in the articles of incorporation, the shareholder would enjoy no such privilege. Such provision would provide that the shares be convertible at a designated ratio, at the option of the holder, into shares of another class, shares of any other series of the same class, or other securities. Thus, conversion may be "downstream" or "upstream", that is, to a junior or senior security.[45]

---

corporate existence. When the corporation settles down into a going concern and funds become more readily available, it is often desirable for the corporation to be able to remove some of the equities superior to the common shares or to refinance the preferred shares at a lower dividend rate. Usually, common shares may not have a redemption feature. American Hair & Felt Co. v. Starring, 21 Del.Ch. 431, 2 A.2d 249 (Sup.Ct.1937), aff'g 21 Del.Ch. 380, 191 A. 887 (Ch.1937). Contra, Lewis v. H. P. Hood & Sons, 331 Mass. 670, 121 N.E.2d 850, 48 A.L.R.2d 383 (1954). In New York, common shares may be redeemable so long as at their time of issuance and redemption the corporation has other common shares outstanding of a class not subject to redemption. McKinney's N.Y.Bus.Corp.Law, § 512(c). Redemption, however, should be distinguished from (a) an option on the part of the corporation to purchase its shares in the event of specified contingencies; (b) purchase by the corporation of its shares through negotiation; (c) elimination from authorized capital of reacquired ("treasury") shares; (d) restoration of reacquired shares to authorized but unissued status. Corporate action concerning reacquired shares may depend on provisions in the articles of incorporation. E. g., ABA–ALI Model Bus. Corp.Act § 61.

38. Mandatory redemption lacks flexibility and is seldom used except in connection with a sinking fund provision.

39. Redemption is usually in the discretion of the board of directors, and the articles of incorporation should so state. Shares simply denominated "redeemable" create problems of construction. See Fox v. Johnson & Wimsatt, Inc., 127 F.2d 729 (D.C. Cir. 1942) (Delaware corporation).

40. Where partial redemption is provided for, the articles of incorporation should prescribe that the shares chosen for redemption will be selected by lot, in sequence, or pro rata, to prevent discrimination among shareholders. See Buxbaum, "Preferred Stock—Law and Draftsmanship", 42 Calif.L.Rev. 243, 265–266 (1954). See sections 172, 173, 316 infra.

41. The redemption price might be, say, 105 percent for $100 par value shares or $105 for shares without par value, thus including in either case a $5 redemption premium. See Bowman v. Armour & Co., 17 Ill.2d 43, 160 N.E.2d 753 (1959). Redemption is

dependent upon the legal availability of funds for such purpose. As a general rule, in most jurisdictions, corporations may not redeem (or purchase) their own shares except out of surplus, except, subject to various safeguards, the redemption (or purchase) of redeemable preferred shares out of stated capital. See ABA–ALI Model Bus.Corp.Act §§ 5, 60; see section 336 infra.

42. Liebschutz v. Schaffer Stores, Inc., 279 App.Div. 96, 101, 108 N.Y.S.2d 476, 482 (3d Dep't (1951) (dictum). See note 20 supra.

43. Buxbaum, "Preferred Stock—Law and Draftsmanship", 42 Calif.L.Rev. 243, 275–276 (1954). Notice of redemption usually can be given by publication or mailing.

44. See Buxbaum, "Preferred Stock—Law and Draftsmanship", 42 Calif.L.Rev. 243, 268–275 (1954).

45. Common, as well as preferred, shares may have a convertible feature. In the vernacular, "downstream" is conversion to a junior security (e. g., preferred shares into common shares), while "upstream" is conversion to a senior security (e. g.,

Whenever shares convertible into a different series or class of shares are authorized, the corporation should reserve sufficient shares of the latter as authorized and unissued to satisfy any subsisting conversion privilege.[46]

Appropriate "anti-dilution" provisions should be included to safeguard the conversion privilege by readjusting the ratio whenever additional shares of the shares into which the convertible shares may be converted are issued at less than the conversion price, or the number of such shares is increased by a share dividend or share split-up, or the corporation is merged or consolidated, or the like.[47]

Any conversion provision should be coordinated with any redemption provision, since the redemption feature may be employed to cut off the conversion privilege which has become valuable.[48]

Other Shares Provisions

Various other protective provisions for the preferred and other shares might also be included in the articles of incorporation.[49]

Share Warrants

Besides classes of shares, the articles of incorporation might also authorize the issue of share warrants.[50]

Debt Securities

Apart from shares and other equity securities, debt securities (such as bonds, debentures, and notes) may be issued by the corporation. Such debt securities usually may be issued even in the absence of any provision in the articles of incorporation authorizing them.[51]

"Leverage". The possibilities of financing by debt as well as by shares should not be overlooked. When the corporation borrows funds from non-shareholders, "trading on equity" or "leverage" with its concomitant advantages and disadvantages, becomes possible.[52]

"Thin Incorporation". Even shareholders, especially of the close corporation, might be better off if they invest in both debt securities and shares. Their debt securities provide, to the extent thereof, the relative safety of creditor status;[53] their shares preserve their proportionate interest in the corporation with respect to control, earnings, and net assets. In addition, various tax advantages may result from investments in both debt securities and shares.[54] The ratio of debt shares, however, should be realistic. A disproportionate ratio (say, more than 3:1) might be found to be "too-thin incorporation" and lead to tax and other

common shares into preferred shares or preferred shares into debt security). Upstream share conversion provisions are often expressly prohibited by statute. E. g., McKinney's N.Y.Bus.Corp.Law, § 519(a).

46. Such a requirement must be considered when provision is made for the authorization of each class of security.

47. Buxbaum, "Preferred Stock—Law and Draftsmanship", 42 Calif.L.Rev. 243, 282–287 (1954); Irvine, "Some Comments Regarding 'Anti-Dilution' Provisions Applicable to Convertible Securities", 13 Bus.Law. 729 (1958). See section 158 infra.

48. Provision is sometimes made that the conversion privilege shall expire when the share is called for redemption. For provisions protecting against destruction of the conversion privilege, see Buxbaum "Preferred Stock—Law and Draftsmanship", 42 Calif.L.Rev. 243, 287–289 (1954).

49. E. g., provisions prohibiting the declaration of common share dividends unless certain ratios are maintained, giving to preferred shares veto powers over future issues of bonds or other debt securities or other preferred shares, limitations on indebtedness, etc. See 1 A. Dewing, The Financial Policy of Corporations 158–159 (5th ed. 1953).

50. E. g., McKinney's N.Y.Bus.Corp.Law, § 505.

51. E. g., ABA–ALI Model Bus.Corp.Act § 4(h). See section 156 infra and note 56 infra.

52. H. Guthmann & H. Dougall, Corporate Financial Policy 167–170 (4th ed. 1962). See section 165 infra.

53. Assuming absence of a basis for disregarding the corporate entity or equitable grounds of subordination of claim in bankruptcy (see sections 152, 164 infra). Of course, the creditor status of insiders is often expressly subordinated to the claims of outsider creditors.

54. See section 166 infra.

embarrassments.[55] So also would resort to hybrid securities combining various features of debt and shares.[56]

ISSUANCE OF CLASS IN SERIES

125. Most jurisdictions permit the articles of incorporation to authorize the issue of a class or classes in series, as provided therein or as fixed from time to time by the board of directors. Various limitations may limit the variations between series of the same class.

The articles of incorporation in most jurisdictions may authorize "series" or "blank" stock by providing that shares of a class or classes may be divided into and issued in series, as provided therein or as fixed from time to time by the board of directors.[1] Variations in the relative rights and preferences as between different series (i. e., rate of dividend, redemption, liquidation rights, sinking fund, conversion) may, subject to limitations in most of such jurisdictions,[2] be fixed in the articles of in-

corporation or by the board of directors when so authorized. In the latter case, the corporation files, usually in the office of the secretary of state, a statement of the relative rights and preferences of the series involved prior to the issue thereof.[3] Upon filing, such a statement becomes, in effect, part of the articles of incorporation.

MINIMUM PAID-IN CAPITAL

126. The articles of incorporation in some jurisdictions are required to state that the corporation will not commence business until a minimum capital, usually $1,000, has been paid in.

The articles of incorporation in some jurisdictions are required to state that the corporation will not commence business until consideration of the value of a specified minimum amount has been received for the issuance of shares.[1]

Even in jurisdictions which may not require such statement in the articles, minimum paid-in capital might be required before commencing business.

Most of the jurisdictions which require minimum paid-in capital specify $1,000;[2] a few set the minimum at $500;[3] Arkansas

---

55. See section 166 infra.

56. See sections 162–165 infra. In California, Delaware, Kansas, Louisiana, Maryland, Michigan, Minnesota, New York, Oklahoma, Pennsylvania, and Virginia, the articles of incorporation may attach voting rights to debt securities. New York authorizes the articles of incorporation to confer upon the holders of secured and unsecured bonds, debentures, and notes, issued or to be issued, rights to inspect the corporate books and records and to vote in the election of directors and on any other matters on which shareholders of the corporation may vote. McKinney's N.Y.Bus.Corp.Law, §§ 102(a) (1), 518(c).

[§ 125]

1. E. g., ABA–ALI Model Bus.Corp.Act § 48(f) (preferred or special class or classes); see id. § 15.

2. Wide variety is permitted in Arkansas, California, Delaware, Florida, Indiana, Kansas, Louisiana, and Puerto Rico. The Model Act requires that all shares of the same class be identical except for the following permissible variations between different series: rate of dividend, price and terms and conditions of redemption, amount payable in event of involuntary liquidation, amount payable in amount of voluntary liquidation, sinking fund provisions for redemption or purchase, and terms and conditions of any conversion privilege. The 1969 Model Act revision added voting rights to the permissible variations between different series. New York authorizes series of preferred, but not of special classes, "subject to the limitation that, if the stated dividends and amounts payable on liquidation are not

paid in full, the shares of all series of the same class shall share ratably in the payment of dividends including accumulations, if any, in accordance with the sums which would be payable on such shares if all dividends were declared and paid in full, and in any distribution of assets other than by way of dividends in accordance with the sums which would be payable on such distribution if all sums payable were discharged in full."

3. Except Florida, Ohio.

[§ 126]

1. E. g., ABA–ALI Model Bus.Corp.Act § 48(g); see also id. § 51. The 1969 Model Act revision dropped this requirement. Comment, "Statutory Minimum Capitalization Requirements", 5 Williamette L.J. 331 (1969).

2. Alabama, Alaska, Connecticut, Delaware, Hawaii, Illinois, Indiana, Kansas, Kentucky, Michigan, Minnesota, Mississippi, New Jersey, New Mexico, North Dakota, Oregon, South Carolina, South Dakota, Tennessee, Texas, Utah, Virginia, West Virginia, the District of Columbia, and Puerto Rico.

3. Florida, Georgia, Missouri, Ohio, Oklahoma, Vermont, Washington, and Wisconsin.

prescribes $300; [4] some statutes set no dollar amount but require that the amount stated in the articles of incorporation be paid in or subscribed before commencing business.[5]

Some older statutes required the filing of an affidavit or certificate evidencing compliance.[6]

For doing business without compliance with minimum capital requirements, the directors might be personally liable to the extent of the amount unpaid [7] or otherwise.[8] Similar liability might also be imposed on officers,[9] shareholders,[10] incorporators under certain circumstances,[11] or even others.[12]

Payment of the required minimum capital, of course, is no assurance against personal liability of the associates for launching an inadequately financed business.[13]

PREEMPTIVE RIGHTS

127. Most jurisdictions expressly permit the articles of incorporation to deny or limit preemptive rights. In several other jurisdictions, preemptive rights exist unless otherwise provided in the articles of incorporation. In other jurisdictions, preemptive rights exist only to the extent that provision is made for them in the articles of incorporation. As a general rule, preemptive rights might be avoided in corporations whose shares are to be widely held, especially those with complicated share structures, but secured in the case of close corporations.

The articles of incorporation in most jurisdictions are expressly authorized to deny or limit preemptive rights.[1] In several other jurisdictions, preemptive rights exist unless otherwise provided in the articles of incorporation.[2] In other jurisdictions, preemptive rights exist only to the extent that provision is made for them in the articles of incorporation.[3]

If preemptive rights, as they exist in a particular jurisdiction in the absence of provision concerning them in the articles of incorporation,[4] are not desired, appropriate provision should be included in the articles of incorporation, which may usually deny, create, limit, amplify, or otherwise define preemptive rights.[5] Where a corporation intends to issue more than one class of shares having different voting, dividend, and liquidation rights, the well-drafted articles of incorporation should anticipate any apportionment problems which might arise on the future issue of shares, share options, or securities convertible into shares. Any applicable statutory definitions [6] of preemptive rights might offer a convenient checklist to avoid possible pitfalls.

As a general rule, preemptive rights might well be avoided in the case of widely-held

[§ 126]

4. Ark.Bus.Corp.Act §§ 64–502, 64–504 (1966).

5. E. g., North Carolina.

6. 2 Model Business Corporation Act Annotated § 51, ¶ 2.02(3) (a) (1960, Supp.1966).

7. E. g., ABA–ALI Model Bus.Corp.Act § 43(e).

8. E. g., without limitation on liability, e. g., Indiana, Kentucky, Louisiana, Vermont.

9. E. g., Idaho, Indiana, Kansas, Minnesota, Washington.

10. E. g., Arkansas.

11. E. g., Hawaii, Ohio.

12. E. g., Georgia. See section 143 infra.

13. See sections 146–148 infra.

[§ 127]

1. ABA–ALI Model Bus.Corp.Act § 48(h); see also id. § 24; Alabama, Alaska, Arkansas, Colorado, Hawaii, Illinois, Kansas, Kentucky, Louisiana, Michigan, Minnesota, Missouri, Montana, Nebraska, North Carolina, North Dakota, Oregon, Texas, Virginia, West Virginia, Wisconsin, District of Columbia, and Puerto Rico.

2. ABA–ALI Model Bus.Corp.Act § 24—but see note 3 infra; Connecticut, Florida, Georgia, Idaho, Maine, Maryland, Nevada, New Jersey, New York, Ohio, Rhode Island, and Tennessee.

3. ABA–ALI Model Bus.Corp.Act § 24 (alternative provision); California, Delaware, Indiana, Massachusetts (in the articles or bylaws), Oklahoma, and Pennsylvania. The 1969 Model Act revision denies preemptive rights unless otherwise provided in the articles; the new alternative provision recognizes them unless denied or limited in the articles.

4. See sections 174, 175 infra.

5. E. g., S.C.Bus.Corp.Act § 12–16.21 (1964).

6. E. g., McKinney's N.Y.Bus.Corp.Law, § 622.

corporations, especially those with complicated share structures, but secured in the case of close corporations.

In connection with the financing of a corporation's operations outside the United States, because of the United States balance of payments of program, American corporations have been amending their articles of incorporation to waive preemptive rights, within prescribed limitations, to securities issued and sold in connection with the financing of such operations.

ADDITIONAL PROVISIONS

128. Most jurisdictions expressly permit the articles of incorporation to include provisions, not inconsistent with law, for the regulation of the internal affairs of the corporation. Some jurisdictions also provide that the articles of incorporation may include any provision required or permitted to be set forth in the bylaws. Many statutory substantive provisions are expressly subject to variation by provisions in the articles of incorporation or bylaws.

The articles of incorporation in most jurisdictions are expressly authorized to include provisions, not inconsistent with law, for the regulation of the internal affairs of the corporation.[1] Some jurisdictions also provide that the articles of incorporation may include any provision required or permitted to be set forth in the bylaws.[2]

Apart from such general provisions, many substantive sections of the corporation statutes make various provisions subject to variation in the articles of incorporation or bylaws.

In any given jurisdiction, the corporation statutes and possibly related statutes, court decisions, and rulings of the state attorney-general, determine the extent to which various additional provisions are permissible and desirable to effectuate a desired corporate structure.

Such additional provisions,[3] include provisions as to place of shareholder meetings,[4] place of board of directors meetings,[5] greater-than-normal quorum requirement for shareholder meetings,[6] greater-than-normal

---

1. E. g., ABA–ALI Model Bus.Corp.Act § 48(i). Rather typical is the Delaware provision: "Any provision for the management of the business and for the conduct of the affairs of the corporation, and any provisions creating, defining, limiting and regulating the powers of the corporation, the directors, and the stockholders, or any class of the stockholders . . .; if such provisions are not contrary to the laws of this State." Del.Gen. Corp.Law, § 102(b) (1) (1967). Compare Sterling v. Mayflower Hotel Corp., 33 Del.Ch. 293, 93 A.2d 107, 38 A.L.R.2d 425 (Sup.Ct.1952), with State ex rel. Cochran v. Penn-Beaver Oil Co., 34 Del. 81, 143 A. 257 (Ct. in Banc 1926). Any compromise or arrangement provision is required to follow the statutory language concerning such provision *in haec verba.* Del.Gen.Corp.Law, § 102(b) (2) (1967).

2. ABA–ALI Model Bus.Corp.Act § 48(i); Alaska, Colorado, Delaware, Maryland, New York, North Carolina, North Dakota, Ohio, Oregon, Texas, Wisconsin, and District of Columbia.

3. Additional provisions, to which the Model Business Corporation Act specifically refers, include those providing that the articles of incorporation may authorize indemnification of directors and officers (§ 4(o)); may permit the purchase by the corporation of its own shares to the extent of available unreserved and unrestricted capital surplus (§ 5); may reserve to shareholders the right to fix the consideration for shares without par value (§ 17); may contain provisions with respect to share rights and options (§ 18A); may fix the shareholder quorum at less than a majority (but not less than one-third), or require greater than majority shareholder vote or class vote (§ 30); may prescribe residence or other qualifications for directors (§ 33); may provide for two or three classes of directors where the board of directors has nine or more members (§ 35); may require greater than majority board of directors quorum and vote (§ 37); may provide for executive or other committees (§ 38); may provide otherwise with respect to action by directors without a meeting (§ 39A); may restrict the declaration and payment of dividends in cash, property, or its own shares (§ 40); may permit a "wasting assets" corporation to pay cash dividends out of its depletion reserve (§ 40(b)); may permit share dividends of a different class (§ 40(e)); may permit distributions out of capital surplus (§ 41(b)); may contain provisions restricting the transfer of shares and any provision which is required or permitted to be set forth in the bylaws (§ 48); may prohibit reissue of redeemed or purchased shares, thereby requiring cancellation (§ 61); may require greater vote or concurrence of shares or of any class or series thereof (§ 136). For comprehensive listing under New York law, see Henn, Appendix 4, Checklist 3, "Certificate of Incorporation", in 2 N.Y. Bus.Corp.Law 595–600 (McKinney 1963).

4. See section 191 infra.

5. See section 209 infra.

6. See sections 191, 266 infra.

vote requirement for shareholder action,[7] greater-than-normal quorum requirement for board of directors meetings,[8] greater-than-normal vote requirement for board of directors action,[9] executive and other committees,[10] transactions involving interested directors,[11] removal of directors without cause,[12] filling of director vacancies,[13] share transfer restrictions,[14] management compensation,[15] indemnification of directors, officers, and other corporate personnel for reasonable litigation expenses incurred by them as such in defending litigation,[16] and deadlock and dissolution.[17]

So far as the additional provisions which may be inserted in the articles of incorporation are concerned, some may be left to the bylaws, resolutions, or shareholders' agreements. Like the articles of incorporation, none of these may contravene the statutes or "statutory norms"; unlike the others, the articles of incorporation are subject to acceptance for filing by the secretary of state, upon filing become a matter of public record, and are subject to amendment only

7. See sections 191, 266 infra.

8. See sections 209, 274 infra.

9. See sections 209, 274 infra.

10. See section 212 infra.

11. See section 238 infra.

12. See sections 192, 205, 276 infra. Any removal provision, of course, should be correlated with any class voting, cumulative voting, classified or variable-size board of directors provisions. Absent provisions to the contrary, the majority of shareholders have inherent power to remove a director for cause despite a provision for cumulative voting. Campbell v. Lowe's Inc., 36 Del.Ch. 563, 134 A.2d 852 (Ch.1957).

13. See section 205 infra.

14. See sections 281–282 infra.

15. See sections 243–256 infra. Fixing compensation in the articles of incorporation reduces flexibility but obviates self-dealing by the board of directors in fixing their own compensation as directors or officers.

16. See sections 282–283 infra.

17. See sections 269, 277, 280 infra.

by the requisite shareholder vote and filing with the secretary of state. The bylaws are subject to no administrative scrutiny, and are usually more easily amendable by the board of directors or shareholders. A resolution can be changed by subsequent resolution; a shareholders' agreement by consent of the parties thereto. While the articles of incorporation, bylaws, and any resolutions must comply with the statutes or "statutory norms", in the event of any conflict among themselves, the articles of incorporation would prevail over the bylaws and any resolutions; the bylaws over any resolutions. Any shareholders' agreement would govern the voting by the parties thereto on the corporate matters covered by the agreement, but all within the framework of the articles of incorporation, bylaws, and any resolutions. A shareholders' agreement can be more personal in its references and application, and can deal with some matters more effectively than can the articles of incorporation, bylaws, or any resolution, but ordinarily binds only the parties thereto. These, along with such considerations as having the articles of incorporation and bylaws reasonably self-contained documents and following local practice, are among the more important factors which must be considered in determining whether a particular desirable provision which may be inserted in the articles of incorporation or elsewhere should be included in the articles of incorporation.[18]

REGISTERED OFFICE AND AGENT

129. All jurisdictions require the articles of incorporation to set forth the address of the registered office or place of business of the corporation. Several jurisdictions also require the designation of a registered agent for service of process upon the corporation, either in the articles or in a separate instrument.

The articles of incorporation in all jurisdictions are required to set forth the address

18. See O'Neal, "Molding the Corporate Form to Particular Business Situations: Optional Charter Clauses", 10 Vand.L.Rev. 1, 46–52 (1956).

of the registered office or place of business of the corporation.[1] Several jurisdictions also require the articles to designate a registered agent for service of process upon the corporation.[2]

[§ 129]

1. E. g., ABA–ALI Model Bus.Corp.Act § 48(j). As to constitutional requirements of maintenance of place of business and process agent in state, see Ariz. Const. art. XIV, § 8; Del.Const. art. IX, § 5; Ky. Const. § 194; S.C.Const. art. IX, § 4; Utah Const. art. XII, § 9. New York requires the articles of incorporation to state the city, incorporated village or town, and the county, within the state in which the office of the corporation is to be located. McKinney's N.Y.Bus.Corp.Law, §§ 402(a) (3), 102(a) (10), 104(b). Cf. Matter of Daughters of Bilitis of New York, Inc., 52 Misc.2d 1075, 277 N.Y.S.2d 709 (Sup.Ct.1966) (omission of county of New York City held fatally defective). The New York Legislative Manual lists all cities, towns, and villages in New York, as well as unincorporated communities with the names of the towns and counties in which they are located. The designated county can be important, so far as requirements for the perfecting of security interests are concerned. Uniform Commercial Code § 9–401(1) (d). See Matter of J. & J. Baking Co., 18 App.Div. 691, 236 N.Y.S.2d 17 (2d Dep't 1962). A corporation has been held to reside in the county designated in the articles of incorporation, notwithstanding that its principal place of business may be elsewhere or its office may have been physically moved. Matter of Norma Footwear Corp., 2 N.Y.2d 887, 161 N.Y.S.2d 143, 141 N.E.2d 628 (1957); In re Merrymeeting Products Corp., 139 F.Supp. 625 (D.Me.1956) (conditional sale filing). The county designation may also be determinative in matters of taxation, venue, and keeping of books. McKinney's N.Y.Bus.Corp.Law, § 624(a). Also in determining the county clerk to whom a copy of the articles of incorporation is transmitted by the secretary of state. When process forwarded by the secretary of state to the designated address is not received because of the fault of the corporation, especially when no meritorious defense is offered, default judgment against the corporation will not be vacated. Cascione v. Acme Equipment Corp., 23 A.D.2d 49, 258 N.Y.S.2d 234 (1st Dep't 1965). To list a post office box as registered office, or address for forwarding of process, is ill-advised.

2. E. g., ABA–ALI Model Bus.Corp.Act § 48(j). In some jurisdictions, the designation of the registered agent is by a separate instrument filed along with the articles of incorporation. New York requires designation in the articles of incorporation of the secretary of state as agent of the corporation for service of process. McKinney's N.Y.Bus.Corp.Law, § 402(a) (7). New York, in addition to such requirement, permits the articles of incorporation to designate also a resident agent. Id. § 402(a) (8). West Virginia requires no designation but provides for the implied appointment of the state auditor. Many jurisdictions provide for additional methods of serving the corporation. E. g., ABA–ALI Model

Some jurisdictions require the corporation to have and to maintain continuously in the state a registered office, which may but need not be the same as its place of business, and a registered agent whose business office is identical with such registered office.[3]

Provision is often made for changing the corporation's registered office or registered agent without the necessity of amending the articles of incorporation.[4]

INITIAL DIRECTORS

130. Many jurisdictions require the articles of incorporation to name the initial director or directors. Some jurisdictions require the articles to set forth the number of directors. In several jurisdictions, the articles of incorporation may prescribe qualifications for directors, or possibly dispense with certain requirements. Most jurisdictions allow classification of the directors, subject to some limitations.

The articles of incorporation in many jurisdictions are required to name the initial director or directors.[1] Tennessee provides that the incorporators are the first directors.[2]

Older statutes required the articles of incorporation to state the number of directors

Bus.Corp.Act § 13. See Meadis v. Atlantic Construction & Supply Co., 212 A.2d 613 (D.C.Ct.App. 1965) (default judgment against corporation failing to receive notice because of death of registered agent vacated).

3. E. g., ABA–ALI Model Bus.Corp.Act § 11.

4. E. g., ABA–ALI Model Bus.Corp.Act § 12. Several jurisdictions expressly require amendment of the articles of incorporation to change the registered office. E. g., Georgia, Ohio. Amendment is required in California only if the corporation moves to another county. New York permits, as alternative to amendment, "changes" in location of office, address to which secretary of state shall mail process against corporation served on him, and registered agent and address thereof, by board of directors action. McKinney's N.Y.Bus.Corp.Law, § 803(b).

[§ 130]
1. E. g., ABA–ALI Model Bus.Corp.Act § 48(k) (names and addresses of initial directors). Several jurisdictions, including Delaware and New York, have no such requirement.

2. Tenn.Gen.Corp.Law, § 48–8.03 (1969).

or that the number of directors shall be not less than a stated minimum, usually no less than three, or more than a stated maximum.[3]

The articles of incorporation or bylaws usually may state qualifications for directors,[4] occasionally, compliance with certain qualification requirements must be stated in the articles of incorporation.[5] Under older statutes, directors had to be shareholders unless otherwise provided;[6] today, directors need be shareholders only if so required.[7]

Older statutes imposed citizenship[8] and residence[9] requirements.

Most jurisdictions allow classification of the directors, subject to some limitations.[10]

If directors are designated by some other name (e. g., "trustees", "governors", "managers"), this possibly should be explained in the articles of incorporation.[11]

Frequently, the initial directors are "dummy" or "accommodation" personnel used to satisfy local qualifications and carry out the rituals required. Nevertheless, their actions or omissions are subject to the standards imposed on directors and the liabilities resulting therefrom.[12]

INCORPORATOR(S)

131. Most jurisdictions require the articles of incorporation to set forth the names and addresses of the incorporators. Traditionally, at least three adult natural persons are required as incorporators, but a growing number of jurisdictions permit one incorporator, or even a corporate incorporator. Some jurisdictions impose citizenship or residence requirements; a few still require that the incorporators subscribe to shares, sometimes in the articles of incorporation.

The articles of incorporation in all jurisdictions are required to be signed by the in-

3. E. g., former McKinney's N.Y.Stock Corp.Law, § 5(7) (leaving to bylaws determination of number within such limits). Delaware and some other jurisdictions leave the size of the board of directors entirely to the bylaws. Rockford Life Ins. Co. v. Production Press, Inc., 15 Ill.App.2d 50, 145 N.E.2d 276 (1957); Gow v. Consolidated Coppermines Corp., 19 Del.Ch. 172, 165 A. 136 (Ch.1933). The Model Act leaves the size of the board of directors, except for the initial board, to the bylaws. ABA–ALI Model Bus.Corp.Act § 34. A growing number of jurisdictions permit less than three directors in corporations with less than three shareholders, allowing two directors in a two-shareholder corporation and one director in a one-shareholder corporation. The 1969 Model Act revision and Delaware allow a board of directors to consist of one or more directors. See section 204 infra.

4. E. g., ABA–ALI Model Bus.Corp.Act § 33; McKinney's N.Y.Bus.Corp.Law, § 701.

5. E. g., former McKinney's N.Y.Stock Corp.Law, § 5(10) (statement that at least one of the persons named as a director is a citizen of the United States and a resident of New York state); see also McKinney's N.Y.Gen.Corp.Law, § 27 (all directors to be of full age). Such statements, no longer required by New York law, are found in articles of incorporation of New York corporations incorporated prior to 1963.

6. See section 204 infra.

7. E. g., ABA–ALI Model Bus.Corp.Act § 33 (directors need not be shareholders unless articles or bylaws so require). Most jurisdictions, including New York, adopt this approach.

8. Arkansas, Florida, and Nevada required, and New York until 1963 required, that at least one director be a United States citizen; Indiana required that a majority of the directors be United States citizens. Missouri required at least one director to be a bona fide citizen of the state.

9. South Dakota still does. Missouri (unless otherwise provided in the bylaws), New York, and Utah required at least one director to be a state resident. Vermont required at least two residents; Hawaii required no less than one-third of the directors to be residents. Several jurisdictions provide that directors need not be residents unless so required by the articles or bylaws. E. g., ABA–ALI Model Bus.Corp.Act § 33.

10. See sections 204, 205 infra. E. g., ABA–ALI Model Bus.Corp.Act § 35 (up to three classes, as equal in number as possible, where board consists of at least nine members). New York permits up to four classes, requiring at least three directors in each class. McKinney's N.Y.Bus.Corp.Law, § 704. Of course, the articles of incorporation can provide for the election of one or more classes of directors by one or more classes of shares.

11. See McKinney's N.Y.Bus.Corp.Law, § 102(a) (5).

12. Minton v. Cavaney, 56 Cal.2d 576, 15 Cal.Rptr. 641, 364 P.2d 473 (1961); Note, "Corporations: Liability of Accommodation Directors", 5 Santa Clara L.Rev. 202 (1965); Note, "Corporations: Use of Accommodation Incorporators, Directors, Officers: Potential Liability of Accommodation Personnel", 47 Cornell L.Q. 443 (1962).

corporator or incorporators.[1] In most jurisdictions, the articles must set forth the names and addresses of the incorporator or incorporators.[2]

Older statutes required three or more incorporators;[3] Mississippi requires only two incorporators.[4] A growing number of jurisdictions permit one incorporator.[5] Utah until 1962 required not less than five incorporators.[6]

Most jurisdictions require that incorporators be at least 21 years of age or of "full age".[7] Usually only "natural persons" are eligible;[8] a growing number of jurisdictions

permit a corporation to be an incorporator;[9] a natural person, corporation, or partnership.[10]

Older statutes imposed citizenship[11] or residence[12] requirements; or required that incorporators be subscribers to shares.[13] In several jurisdictions, the articles of incorporation must set forth the number of shares subscribed by each incorporator.[14]

1. E. g., ABA–ALI Model Bus.Corp.Act § 47.

2. E. g., ABA–ALI Model Bus.Corp.Act § 48(1) (name and address of each incorporator); Del.Gen. Corp.Law § 103(a) (1) (1967). New York no longer imposes such requirement, but pre-1963 articles of incorporation contain such provisions.

3. See 1 Model Business Corporation Act Annotated § 47 (1960, Supp.1966).

4. Miss.Bus.Corp.Act § 52 (1963).

5. E. g., ABA–ALI Model Bus.Corp.Act § 47. Delaware specifies "Any person, partnership, association or corporation, singly or jointly with others." Del. Gen.Corp.Law § 101(a) (1967). New York specifies one or more natural persons of the age of 21 years or over. McKinney's N.Y.Bus.Corp.Law, § 401. A single incorporator is permitted in a growing number of jurisdictions, e. g., Arizona, Arkansas, Connecticut, Delaware, Illinois, Iowa, Kentucky, Michigan, Minnesota, Missouri, Nebraska, New York, Oregon, Pennsylvania, Washington, Wisconsin, Wyoming. See Garrett, "Joe Doe Incorporates Himself", 19 Bus.Law. 535 (1964).

6. Former Utah Code Ann. § 16–2–3 (1953) (repealed, effective Jan. 1, 1962).

7. E. g., ABA–ALI Model Bus.Corp.Act § 47; former McKinney's N.Y.Gen.Corp.Law, § 7 ("of full age"). In New York, the articles, prior to 1963, had to state that all of the subscribers thereto were of full age. Former McKinney's N.Y.Stock Corp.Law, § 5(10). Such statement is no longer required by the New York law. Presumably under the "contract theory" (see section 78 supra), incorporators should be competent to contract. An age requirement excludes corporate incorporators even when the statute does not expressly require natural persons as incorporators. Kentucky permits persons 18 years old or older to serve as incorporators.

8. Ibid.

9. ABA–ALI Model Bus.Corp.Act § 47; Arizona, Delaware, Illinois, Iowa, Kentucky, Michigan, Pennsylvania, Washington.

10. Del.Gen.Corp.Law, § 101(a) (1967); Mich.Gen. Corp.Act § 21.2(c) (1948).

11. Idaho, and Washington require, and New York prior to 1963 required, that two-thirds of the incorporators be United States citizens; Ohio requires a majority to be United States citizens; Texas requires that two incorporators be Texas citizens. In New York, the articles once had to state that at least two-thirds of the subscribers thereto were United States citizens.

12. Mississippi requires two incorporators to be United States residents; South Dakota requires, and New York prior to 1963, required one to be a resident of the state; Vermont requires two to be state residents. In New York, the articles once had to state that at least one of the subscribers thereto was a New York resident.

13. E. g., Louisiana, Pennsylvania, Washington.

14. E. g., Kentucky, Louisiana, Pennsylvania, Washington, West Virginia. New York dropped such requirement in 1963. In jurisdictions with such requirement, every incorporator is a subscriber in two senses: to the articles of incorporation, and to shares. Where classes of shares are authorized, the articles should indicate to which class the share subscription applies. For minimum liability for share transfer tax and on the share subscription, "dummy" or "accommodation" incorporators should subscribe for only the minimum of one share each. The subscription in the articles (assuming price is stated or can be ascertained) is deemed accepted ipso facto upon the creation of the corporation. Phoenix Warehousing Co. v. Badger, 67 N.Y. 294 (1876). In contrast, other subscriptions may not become binding until accepted by act of the corporation. See section 115 supra. The subscriptions of the incorporators might have to be paid in before the incorporators become exempt from liabilities for debts incurred. The use of "dummy" or "accommodation" incorporators, despite the prevalent custom, usually has no legal sanction. The incorporators might be bound in their own right, rather than as agents for the promoters. See Note, "Corporations: Use of Accommodation Incorporators, Directors, Officers: Potential Liability of Accommodation Personnel", 47 Cornell L.Q. 443 (1962). See also sections 107–112 supra.

EXECUTION AND FILING

132. All jurisdictions require the incorporator or incorporators to sign the articles of incorporation. Acknowledgment or verification is usually required. Some jurisdictions require the filing of duplicate originals of the articles of incorporation. Local filings might also be required, as well as occasional other formalities. Upon the filing of the articles or possibly upon the issue of a "certificate of incorporation" corporate existence usually begins. Other requirements might be imposed, usually as conditions precedent to doing business rather than to incorporation.

The articles of incorporation in all jurisdictions must be signed by the incorporator or incorporators.[1] Some jurisdictions require verification;[2] others acknowledgment.[3]

In most jurisdictions only the original articles must be filed, usually with the secretary of state.[4] In some jurisdictions, duplicate originals of the articles must be delivered to the secretary of state, who, upon finding that they conform to law and that all fees and taxes have been paid, files one of the duplicate originals and issues a "certificate of incorporation" to which is affixed the other duplicate original.[5]

Some jurisdictions also require either prior[6] or subsequent[7] recording or filing in some county office or offices. In a few jurisdictions, the state official with whom the articles are filed is required to attend to the local recording or filing.[8]

1. E. g., ABA–ALI Model Bus.Corp.Act § 47. Personal signatures of the incorporators are usually required. New York requires that the name and address of each incorporator be stated beneath or opposite his signature. McKinney's N.Y.Bus.Corp. Law, § 402(a). If "dummy" or "accommodation" incorporators are employed, they must usually sign in their personal rather than their representative capacities. The signatures should conform in every particular to the names, if any, listed as incorporators in the articles (see section 131 supra).

2. 2 Model Business Corporation Act Annotated § 47 (1960, Supp.1966). Verification is no longer required by the Model Act; acknowledgment never was required.

3. E. g., McKinney's N.Y.Bus.Corp.Law, § 402(a). Absent provision for a composite instrument, all of the incorporators should sign the same articles, but there may be separate acknowledgments or verifications with different venues and notaries for the different incorporators. In New York, only one incorporator need acknowledge the articles of incorporation. N.Y.Bus.Corp.Law § 104(d). The names listed in the acknowledgments or verifications should conform in every particular to the signatures of the incorporators. Neither an incorporator nor any named initial director (see section 130 supra) should act in the capacity of notary in taking the acknowledgments or verifications. Erie R. R. Co. v. Board of R. R. Comm'rs, 105 App.Div. 273, 93 N.Y.S. 584 (3d Dep't 1905); 1934 N.Y.Op.Att'y Gen. 222. See also N.Y.Bus.Corp.Law § 104(d): "In lieu of being signed and verified or acknowledged, the certificate may be subscribed by such person and affirmed by him as true under the penalties of perjury."

4. E. g., Del.Gen.Corp.Law, §§ 101(a), 103(c) (1) (1967) (together with duplicate copy); McKinney's N.Y.Bus.Corp.Law, § 402(a). The secretary of state is the state officer in all jurisdictions except Alaska (commissioner of commerce), Arizona (corporation commission), District of Columbia (commissioner of the District of Columbia), Hawaii (state treasurer), Maryland (state tax commission), Massachusetts (secretary of the commonwealth), New Mexico (state corporation commission), Oregon (corporation commissioner), Pennsylvania (department of state), Virginia (state corporation commission). 1 P–H Corp.Rep., ¶ 9001–A. For ease of reference, the term "secretary of state" is used herein. New York imposes a $50 filing fee. McKinney's N.Y.Exec. Law, § 96(9) (b). Organization taxes are also required in several jurisdictions based upon authorized shares, but with a minimum tax. See section 158 infra. Payment of applicable filing fees and taxes is usually required before filing. In jurisdictions where a formal "certificate of incorporation" is not issued, local practice often is to order certified copies of the articles either by presenting copies for certification or ordering certified duplicated copies.

5. E. g., ABA–ALI Model Bus.Corp.Act §§ 49, 50, 120, 121. With respect to filings in the office of the secretary of state, the Model Act uniformly requires the delivery of duplicate originals, one to be filed and the other to be returned to the corporation or those acting in its behalf. For several purposes, duplicate "articles" of incorporation or otherwise are delivered one being filed and the other appended to a "certificate" of incorporation or otherwise and returned. See ABA–ALI Model Bus.Corp. Act § 49 (articles of incorporation); § 57 (articles of amendment); § 68 (articles of merger or consolidation); § 86 (articles of dissolution).

6. E. g., Louisiana.

7. E. g., Arkansas, California, Delaware, Illinois, Michigan, North Carolina, Washington, Wisconsin.

8. E. g., Minnesota, New York, Virginia. In New York, the secretary of state microfilms the original

Court orders,[9] approval of the state attorney general [10] is sometimes required. Publication is occasionally required.[11]

Upon the filing of the articles,[12] or possibly upon the issue of a "certificate of incorporation",[13] corporate existence usually begins. The "certificate of incorporation" or other specified evidence of incorporation might be conclusive [14] or presumptive [15] evidence of compliance with all conditions precedent to incorporation.

Some jurisdictions impose various conditions precedent to the doing of business.[16]

Where filing of the articles of incorporation is refused by the secretary of state or other official, mandamus or its modern equivalent is the usual remedy to test such refusal in the courts.[17]

There are often statutory provisions for the correction of articles of incorporation.[18]

The articles of incorporation are subject to amendment. Such amendments require shareholder consent (with possible appraisal right to dissenting shareholders), and involve filing fees and other expenses.[19]

articles of incorporation and retains the microfilm as the original in his files, forwarding the original as a "copy" to the appropriate county clerk for filing there. See McKinney's N.Y.Pub. Officers Law § 65–a; 1952 N.Y.Op.Att'y Gen. 170.

9. E. g., Alabama, Georgia.

10. E. g., Maine, New Hampshire (attorney general).

11. E. g., Arizona, Georgia, Minnesota, Texas. See Gay Harris & Son, Inc. v. E. H. Schlather & Sons, 423 S.W.2d 467 (Tex.Civ.App.1968) (liability unlimited for failure to publish required newspaper notice).

12. McKinney's N.Y.Bus.Corp.Law, § 403. Meanwhile, the bylaws (see section 133 infra) should be drafted. As soon as the articles of incorporation have been filed, but not before where it is impossible to reserve the corporate name (see section 117, n. 3 supra), the share certificate (see section 135 infra), corporate seal (see section 136 infra), minute book or books for shareholder, board of directors, and committee meetings, and share ledger should be ordered from the legal stationer. The next step is to draft advance minutes to serve as agenda for the organization meeting or meetings to be held after the filing of the articles of incorporation. See section 135 infra. Compliance should also be had in other jurisdictions where the corporation is to do business. See sections 136, 137 infra.

13. E. g., ABA–ALI Model Bus.Corp.Act § 50. Timing can be significant. Delaying incorporation until after a particular date might enable a corporation to postpone for up to a year the filing of reports and payment of taxes.

14. Ibid. (except as against direct state attack); see also ABA–ALI Model Bus.Corp.Act § 134; McKinney's N.Y.Bus.Corp.Law, § 403 (except against attorney general).

15. E. g., superseded McKinney's N.Y.Gen.Corp.Law, § 8(2).

16. E. g., minimum subscribed or paid-in capital and possibly filings of affidavits or certificate thereof. See section 126 supra. A few other jurisdictions require election of directors or officers and adoption of bylaws. See section 143 infra.

17. Some jurisdictions provide for appeal from the secretary of state. E. g., ABA–ALI Model Bus. Corp.Act § 133. The secretary of state is under a duty to reject articles which contain illegal or improper provisions. His acts in receiving and filing the articles are ministerial in nature, and may be reviewed by the courts. Va.Const. art. XIII, § 154; Association for the Preservation of Choice, Inc. v. Shapiro, 9 N.Y.2d 376, 214 N.Y.S.2d 388, 174 N.E.2d 487 (1961), reargument denied 11 N.Y.2d 662, 225 N. Y.S.2d 740, 180 N.E.2d 898 (1962). Gross v. New York, —— A.D.2d ——, 306 N.Y.S.2d 28 (3d Dep't 1969) (holding state not liable to corporation for damages because of error of secretary of state in checking availability of corporate name, on ground secretary was performing discretionary act for which state could not be liable). Cf. Dwight, "Objections to Judicial Approval of Charters of Non-Profit Corporations", 12 Bus.Law. 454 (1957); Comment, "Judicial Approval as Prerequisite to Incorporation of Non-Profit Organizations in New York and Pennsylvania", 55 Colum.L.Rev. 380 (1955). To be compared is possible judicial discretion in determining the availability of a corporate name. See section 117, n. 2 supra. See also ABA–ALI Model Bus.Corp.Act § 132. Quaere, as to constructive notice effect to third persons of filed articles of incorporation as public record. See R. Kessler, New York Close Corporations 329 (1968).

18. E. g., McKinney's N.Y.Bus.Corp.Law, § 105.

19. See section 345 infra.

C. DRAFTING BYLAWS

DRAFTING BYLAWS

133. Bylaws are usually not filed in any public office, as are the articles of incorporation, and hence avoid any administrative scrutiny. Bylaws must be consistent with the articles of incorporation, and applicable statutory and constitutional provisions. Statutes vary in different jurisdictions as to the required and permissible content of bylaws, and as to who has the power to adopt or amend them. In practice, bylaws range from the briefest statement of rules to comprehensive manuals. A provision which is invalid as a bylaw might be enforced as a contract among the shareholders who approved it.

Bylaws are the rules and regulations or private laws enacted by the corporation to regulate, govern, and control its own actions, affairs, and concerns, and its shareholders, directors, and officers.[1]

Unlike the articles of incorporation, bylaws are usually not filed in any public office, and hence avoid any administrative scrutiny. Bylaws, like the articles of incorporation, must be consistent with constitutional[2] and statutory provisions and "stat-

utory norms"[3] and, in addition, with any valid provisions in the articles of incorporation.[4]

While it is often said that every corporation as such has power to make bylaws, this

---

48 N.E. 1069 (1897); Note, 31 Notre Dame Law. 699 (1956).

1. 8 W. Fletcher, Private Corporations §§ 4166–4211 (perm. ed. rev. 1966); 1 G. Hornstein, Corporation Law and Practice § 267 (Checklist: Preparation of By-Laws), § 268 (Form) (1959). For draft of bylaws for Delaware, New York, and Model Act jurisdiction corporation, see G. Seward, Basic Corporate Practice 145–198 (ALI rev. 1966); for New York corporations, see C. Israels, Corporate Practice 524–563 (PLI 2d ed. 1969); R. Kessler, New York Close Corporations ch. 13 (1968); Henn, Appendix 4, Checklist 4, "By-Laws", 2 N.Y.Bus.Corp.Law 602–607 (McKinney 1963); for Model Business Corporation Act, see Official Forms for use under the Model Business Corporation Act, Revised 1969, Form Nos. 51, 52 (ALI 1970). For drafting suggestions, see K. Pantzer & R. Deer, The Drafting of Corporate Charters and Bylaws 73–89, 170–232 (ALI rev. 1968).

2. See section 116 supra. State ex rel. Syphers v. McCune, 143 W.Va. 315, 101 S.E.2d 834 (1958) (bylaw providing for election of directors on staggered basis and bylaw requiring proxyholder to be shareholder held repugnant to West Virginia constitution and statute requiring cumulative voting); Commonwealth ex rel. Laughlin v. Green, 351 Pa. 170, 40 A.2d 492 (1945). See generally People ex rel. McIlhany v. Chicago Live-Stock Exchange, 170 Ill. 556,

3. See section 116 supra. Mook v. Berger, 7 A.D.2d 726, 180 N.Y.S.2d 400 (1st Dep't 1958), aff'd mem., 6 N.Y.2d 833, 188 N.Y.S.2d 219, 159 N.E.2d 702 (1959) (bylaw of Connecticut corporation requiring approval of six of seven directors for board of directors action held invalid under Connecticut law); Automatic Steel Products, Inc. v. Johnston, 31 Del.Ch. 469, 64 A.2d 416, 6 A.L.R.2d 170 (Sup.Ct.1949) (bylaw providing for filling of newly-created directorships by remaining directors held invalid under Delaware statute granting shareholders such right); Kaplan v. Block, 183 Va. 327, 31 S.E.2d 893 (1944) (bylaw requiring shareholder approval for all board of directors action held invalid under Virginia law); Steigerwald v. A. M. Steigerwald Co., 9 Ill. App.2d 31, 132 N.E.2d 373 (1955) (bylaw authorizing president to appoint three reputable businessmen as members of executive committee held invalid under Illinois statute requiring appointment of directors to committee by board of directors); Matter of Crown Heights Hospital, Inc., 183 Misc. 563, 49 N.Y.S.2d 658 (Sup.Ct.1948) (bylaw prohibiting shareholder from voting for more than one director held invalid under New York statute providing for one vote per share unless otherwise provided in articles of incorporation). But cf. Blair v. Bishop's Restaurants, Inc., 202 Okl. 648, 217 P.2d 161 (1950) (upholding bylaw of close corporation authorizing secretary-treasurer to declare dividend without mention of Oklahoma statute vesting management in board of directors); Matter of Buckley (Rickerson), 183 Misc. 189, 50 N.Y.S.2d 54 (Sup.Ct.1944) (upholding bylaw adopted by less than all shareholders prohibiting board of directors from removing chairman of board or president despite statute providing for election and removal of officers by board of directors).

4. See section 116 supra. Christal v. Petry, 275 App.Div. 550, 90 N.Y.S.2d 620 (1st Dep't 1949), aff'd 301 N.Y. 562, 93 N.E.2d 450 (1950). But see Rockford Life Ins. Co. v. Production Press, Inc., 15 Ill. App.2d 50, 145 N.E.2d 276 (1957); Gow v. Consolidated Coppermines Corp., 19 Del.Ch. 172, 165 A. 136 (Ch.1933) (bylaws allowed to change number of directors fixed in articles of incorporation where statute authorized bylaws to fix number). Ohio provides a formal distinction between "regulations" adopted by shareholders and "bylaws" adopted by directors. The latter must be consistent with the regulations as well as the articles of incorporation. Ohio Gen.Corp.Law, § 1701.59 (1955).

is frequently confirmed by statute.[5]

Many jurisdictions provide that bylaws may contain any provision for the regulation and management of the affairs of the corporation not inconsistent with law or the articles of incorporation.[6] Some jurisdictions spell out by statute those matters which must or may be regulated by bylaws.[7]

Formulation of the initial bylaws is a power variously enjoyed in different jurisdictions by the incorporators,[8] the shareholders,[9] or the board of directors.[10] Power to adopt, amend, and repeal the bylaws is sometimes vested in the shareholders,[11] or

board of directors,[12] or left to treatment in the articles of incorporation or in the bylaws themselves.[13]

A growing number of jurisdictions empower the board of directors to adopt emergency bylaws, subject to repeal or change by shareholders, to be operative, notwithstanding contrary provisions elsewhere in the corporate statutes, or in the articles of incorporation or bylaws, during any emergency in the conduct of the business of the corporation resulting from an attack on the United States or any nuclear or atomic disaster.[14]

---

5. E. g., ABA–ALI Model Bus.Corp.Act § 4(1); Del. Gen.Corp.Law § 122(6) (1967); McKinney's N.Y. Bus.Corp.Law, § 202(a) (11). Quaere, as to whether bylaws are technically required. See Benintendi v. Kenton Hotel, Inc., 294 N.Y. 112, 120, 60 N.E.2d 829, 832, 159 A.L.R. 280, 284 (1945).

6. E. g., ABA–ALI Model Bus.Corp.Act §§ 25, 52 (at organization meeting of board of directors).

7. E. g., California, Hawaii, Indiana, Louisiana, Maine, Ohio, Vermont, West Virginia.

8. E. g., Delaware, Massachusetts, New Hampshire, New York, Rhode Island, Vermont. In New York, as a matter of practice, prior to 1963, the initial bylaws were adopted by the incorporators and confirmed by the board of directors at their respective organization meetings. See section 136 infra.

9. E. g., Alabama, Ohio (regulations), West Virginia; Illinois, Indiana, District of Columbia (if articles of incorporation so provide).

10. E. g., ABA–ALI Model Bus.Corp.Act § 25; Alaska, Indiana, Montana, North Carolina, South Dakota.

11. Shareholders are held to have inherent power to adopt and amend bylaws, Rogers v. Hill, 289 U.S. 582, 53 S.Ct. 731, 77 L.Ed. 1385, 88 A.L.R. 744 (1933) (bylaw provision for amendment by directors held not to prevent shareholder amendment); Auer v. Dressel, 306 N.Y. 427, 118 N.E.2d 590, 48 A.L.R.2d 604 (1954). Statutes provide for shareholder amendment in Connecticut, Delaware, Hawaii, Idaho, Kentucky, Louisiana, Maine, Maryland, Minnesota, Missouri, Nebraska, New Jersey, New York, Ohio (regulations), Oklahoma, Pennsylvania, Rhode Island, South Dakota, Texas, Vermont, Washington, West Virginia, and Wyoming. New York requires that certain provisions be authorized in the articles of incorporation or the specific provisions of a bylaw adopted by shareholders. McKinney's N.Y.Bus. Corp.Law, §§ 601(a), 704, 705(b), 706(a).

12. E. g., ABA–ALI Model Bus.Corp.Act § 25 (unless power reserved to shareholders in articles of incorporation); Kansas, Ohio (bylaws subject to regulations and articles of incorporation). Some statutes expressly limit, to some extent, amendment by the board of directors of bylaws affecting directors. E. g., Louisiana, Minnesota, Oklahoma. Even where the bylaws expressly authorize their amendment by the board of directors, such amendment power might not be construed as permitting the amendment of a bylaw limiting board action. Matter of Buckley (Rickerson), 183 Misc. 189, 50 N.Y.S.2d 54 (Sup.Ct.1944). New York, after providing that the initial bylaws shall be adopted by the incorporator or incorporators, provides that thereafter bylaws may be adopted, amended, or repealed by vote of the shareholders entitled to vote in the election of directors and by the board of directors under authority granted by the articles of incorporation or a bylaw adopted by the shareholders, expressly preserving the power of the shareholders to amend or repeal bylaws adopted by the board of directors. Otherwise, where the power is vested in the board of directors, shareholder amendment might be precluded. State ex rel. Daubenspeck v. Day, 189 Ind. 243, 123 N.E. 402 (1919). The better view, however, is to recognize the inherent power of shareholders to adopt, amend, and repeal bylaws.

13. E. g., Massachusetts, New Hampshire. Amendment may be by the shareholders or board of directors in California, Michigan, New York (see notes 11, 12 supra), North Carolina, Wisconsin. But see Model, Roland & Co. v. Industrial Acoustics Co., 16 N.Y.2d 703, 261 N.Y.S.2d 896, 209 N.E.2d 553 (1965) (holding ineffective bylaw requirement of two-thirds shareholder vote to amend bylaws because not in articles of incorporation); cf. Benintendi v. Kenton Hotel, Inc., 294 N.Y. 112, 60 N.E. 829, 159 A.L.R. 280 (1945) (upholding bylaw requirement of unanimous shareholder vote under prior law).

14. E. g., ABA–ALI Model Bus.Corp.Act § 25A. Similar provisions have been enacted in Arkansas, Colorado, Delaware, Illinois, Iowa, Missouri, New York, Ohio (emergency bylaws and code of regulations), Pennsylvania, South Carolina, South Dakota,

Bylaws range from the briefest statement of rules for the internal management of the corporation to what almost amounts to a manual (*vade mecum*) of such rules which includes a restatement of the applicable statutes and provisions in the articles of incorporation for the guidance of corporate personnel. A compromise approach is to include such statutes and other provisions in a memorandum or addendum to the bylaws proper.[15]

Some jurisdictions provide that any provision required or permitted to be set forth in the bylaws may instead be set forth in the articles of incorporation,[16] but in the absence of such a provision the bylaws should provide for: penalties for failure to pay installments or calls for subscriptions for shares;[17] place of holding meetings of shareholders and time of holding annual meeting of shareholders;[18] number of directors, except as to first board of directors;[19] division of directors into classes having different terms;[20] fixing of quorum of directors at a number greater

than a majority thereof, and requiring action of the board to be taken by vote of more than a majority of a quorum;[21] notice of directors' meetings;[22] and election or appointment of officers.[23]

Certain other provisions either may be prescribed in the bylaws or the articles of incorporation or may be omitted entirely: calling special meetings of shareholders in a manner other than as provided for by statute;[24] fixing record dates;[25] qualifications of directors;[26] and creation of an executive committee.[27]

The bylaws, as discussed, should be consistent with applicable statutes and provisions of the articles of incorporation. Certain practical considerations must also receive attention. In fixing the date of the annual meeting of shareholders, for example, the bylaws should refer to day of week of month (e. g., first Tuesday in May) rather than date of month (taking care to avoid holidays) to avoid complications of the latter's falling on weekends. The date should be set sufficiently later than the ending of the fiscal year to ensure the availability before or at the meeting of the financial data for such year. The fiscal year, in turn, should be its natural business year and not necessarily the calendar year.

A few cases have recognized that the bylaws constitute a contract among shareholders, which might not be amendable over objection of any shareholder.[28]

Virginia, Washington. New York provides that the state defense council may order the effectiveness, for a period of attack, of previously-adopted emergency bylaws. Such emergency bylaws may provide for board of directors quorum and vote, special elections of directors, filling director vacancies by the board of directors, and the interim management of the corporation's affairs. McKinney's N.Y.Bus. Corp.Law § 202(a) (11); McKinney's N.Y.Unconsol. Laws, tit. 26, art. 2; Gibson, "Corporate Management During Nuclear Attack", 17 Bus.Law. 249 (1962). See Continuity of Corporate Management in Event of Nuclear Attack (American Society of Corporate Secretaries, Inc. 1963).

15. See G. Seward, Basic Corporate Practice 51 (ALI rev. 1966). Such memorandum or addendum can easily reflect legislative changes or amendments of the articles of incorporation.

16. ABA–ALI Model Bus.Corp.Act § 48(i); Del.Gen. Corp.Law, § 102(b) (1) (1967); McKinney's N.Y.Bus. Corp.Law, § 402(b). In most corporation statutes there are scattered references as to various rules absent provision to different effects in the articles of incorporation or bylaws.

17. E. g., ABA–ALI Model Bus.Corp.Act § 16.

18. E. g., ABA–ALI Model Bus.Corp.Act § 26.

19. E. g., ABA–ALI Model Bus.Corp.Act § 34.

20. E. g., ABA–ALI Model Bus.Corp.Act § 35.

21. E. g., ABA–ALI Model Bus.Corp.Act § 37. See section 274 infra.

22. E. g., ABA–ALI Model Bus.Corp.Act § 39.

23. E. g., ABA–ALI Model Bus.Corp.Act § 44.

24. E. g., ABA–ALI Model Bus.Corp.Act § 26.

25. E. g., ABA–ALI Model Bus.Corp.Act § 28.

26. E. g., ABA–ALI Model Bus.Corp.Act § 33.

27. E. g., ABA–ALI Model Bus.Corp.Act § 38.

28. State of Washington v. Alaska Airlines, Inc., 68 Wash.2d 297, 413 P.2d 352 (1966); Bechtold v. Coleman Realty Co., 367 Pa. 208, 79 A.2d 661 (1951).

Bylaws can be adopted or amended impliedly as well as expressly, but the burden is on the party asserting such implied adoption or amendment.[29]

Occasionally, upon sufficient proof, a court will order reformation of the bylaws to reflect representations among the shareholders.[30]

Where two bylaws are inconsistent, the more specific should override the more general, and any later one should prevail over any earlier one.[31]

A provision which is invalid as a bylaw might be enforced as a contract among the shareholders who approved it.[32]

D. FORM(S) OF SHARE CERTIFICATES

FORM(S) OF SHARE CERTIFICATES

134. The share certificate is the instrument which evidences the shareholder's interest (or share or stock) in the corporation. Statutes usually require the issuance of share certificates, at least when shares have been fully paid for, and regulate their form and content. Securities exchange regulations prescribe standards for certificates for securities listed on the exchange. Appropriate legends on the share certificates might be necessary where there are greater-than-normal quorum or voting requirements for shareholder or board of directors action, share transfer restrictions, shareholder voting agreements, voting trusts, irrevocable proxies, partly-paid shares, articles of incorporation provisions for nonjudicial dissolution or as to control of directors, etc.

The share certificate, or stock certificate, is the instrument which evidences the shareholder's interest (or share or stock) in the corporation. Such interest, of course, may exist even though no share certificate is issued. The share certificate serves to identify the shareholder and to facilitate the transfer of his interest.

Statutes usually require the issue of share certificates,[1] and regulate their form and content.[2]

29. Compare Hinckley v. Swaner, 13 Utah 2d 93, 368 P.2d 709, 3 A.L.R.3d 620 (1962), with Olincy v. Merle Norman Cosmetics, Inc., 200 Cal.App.2d 260, 19 Cal.Rptr. 387 (1962) (no implied amendment for lack of notice); Magnus v. Magnus Organ Corp., 71 N.J.Super. 363, 177 A.2d 55 (1962); Pioneer Specialties, Inc. v. Nelson, 161 Tex. 244, 339 S.W.2d 199 (1960); Dixie Glass Co. v. Pollak, 341 S.W.2d 530, 91 A.L.R.2d 662 (Tex.Civ.App.1960), error ref. n.r.e. 162 Tex. 440, 347 S.W.2d 596 (1961); Bay City Lumber Co. v. Anderson, 8 Wash.2d 191, 111 P.2d 771 (1941); Taylor's Adm'r v. Taylor, 301 S.W.2d 579 (Ky.1957); In re Brandywine Fibre Products Co., 33 Del.Ch. 327, 92 A.2d 708 (Ch.1952); Elliott v. Lindquist, 356 Pa. 385, 52 A.2d 180 (1947); Belle Isle Corp. v. MacBean, 29 Del.Ch. 261, 49 A.2d 5 (Ch.1946), reargument denied 30 Del.Ch. 373, 61 A. 2d 699 (Ch.1948); In re Ivey & Ellington, Inc., 28 Del.Ch. 298, 42 A.2d 508 (Ch.1945); Comment, "Informal By-Law Amendment By Inconsistent Employment Contracts", 1961 Duke L.J. 619.

30. Katcher v. Ohsman, 26 N.J.Super. 28, 97 A.2d 180 (Ch.Div.1953).

31. New England Trust Co. v. Penobscot Chemical Fibre Co., 142 Me. 286, 50 A.2d 188 (1946).

32. Palmer v. Chamberlain, 191 F.2d 532, 27 A.L.R.2d 416 (5th Cir.1951), reh. denied 191 F.2d 859 (5th Cir.1951); First Nat'l Bank v. Shanks, 73 N.E.2d 93 (Ohio C.P.1945). Contra, Benintendi v. Kenton Hotel, Inc., 294 N.Y. 112, 60 N.E.2d 829, 159 A.L.R. 280 (1945) (4–3). See also Sensabaugh v. Polson Plywood Co., 135 Mont. 562, 342 P.2d 1064 (1959); Matter of American Fibre Chair Seat Corp., 241 App. Div. 532, 272 N.Y.S. 206 (2d Dep't 1934), aff'd 265 N.Y. 416, 193 N.E. 253 (1934), reargument denied 266 N.Y. 500, 195 N.E. 171 (1935); Note, "Enforcement of an Invalid By-Law as a Contract Among the Shareholders", 15 Wyo.L.J. 207 (1961).

1. E. g., ABA–ALI Model Bus.Corp.Act § 21; Cal. Gen.Corp.Law, § 2400 (1947); Del.Gen.Corp.Law, § 158 (1967); McKinney's N.Y.Bus.Corp.Law, § 508; Ohio Gen.Corp.Law, § 1701.24 (1955); Pa.Bus. Corp.Law, § 607 (1966). Quaere, whether all the falderol concerning share certificates, or even their continued use, is really necessary. The handling and transfer of share certificates by brokerage firms has become a Herculean problem. Smaller punch card share certificates, retaining engraved and other anticounterfeiting features, have been developed, to promote automatic processing. See Jolls, "Can We Do Without Stock Certificates? A Look at the Future", 23 Bus.Law. 909 (1968); Kendall, "The Certificateless Society: A Realistic Appraisal", 24 Bus.Law. 141 (1968).

2. See 11 W. Fletcher, Private Corporations § 5163 (1958 rev.). For form of share certificate for Delaware, New York, and Model Act jurisdiction corporations, see G. Seward, Basic Corporate Practice 199–201 (ALI rev. 1966); for New York, see C. Israels, Corporate Practice 275–279 (PLI 2d ed. 1969);

Regulations of the securities exchanges prescribe standards for certificates for securities listed thereon. Share certificates range from simple typewritten ones to engraved certificates, as required by the New York Stock Exchange to minimize the risk of counterfeiting and to facilitate clearance.

Since the usual share certificate is only approximately 8 by 12 inches in size, it can hardly state more than minimal matters without resorting to microscopic type. The importance of requiring comprehensive statements on the share certificate is counterbalanced by the fact that amendments to the articles of incorporation might render obsolete such statements on the share certificate.

Printed or engraved forms of share certificates may be obtained from or through legal stationers, corporation service companies, or banknote companies. Such certificates can be obtained in a bound book, containing numbered certificates and stubs, which for the small corporation can serve as the share ledger or record of shareholders. The stubs can state all relevant data and have affixed thereto any required original issue tax stamps.

Only the form and content of share certificates will be discussed in this section. Share transfer problems will be discussed later.[3]

Statutory Requirements

Most jurisdictions provide that shares of a corporation shall be represented by certificates signed[4] by two of several designated officers of the corporation, usually the president or a vice-president and the secretary or an assistant secretary of the corporation, and *may* be sealed with the seal of the corporation or a facsimile thereof.[5]

Certificates representing shares issued by a corporation which is authorized to issue shares of more than one class are often required to set forth upon the face or back of the certificate, or to state that the corporation will furnish to any shareholder upon request and without charge, a full [or summary] statement of the designations, preferences, limitations, and relative rights of the shares of each class authorized to be issued and, if the corporation is authorized to issue any preferred or special class in series, the variations in the relative rights and preferences between the shares of each such series so far as the same have been fixed and determined and the authority of the board of directors to fix and determine the relative rights and preferences of subsequent series.[6]

Furthermore, each share certificate usually is required to state upon its face:[7]

(a) That the corporation is organized under the laws of the state;

Henn, Appendix 4, Checklist 6, "Share Certificate", in 2 N.Y.Bus.Corp.Law 609–612 (McKinney 1963).

3. See section 177 infra.

4. Such signatures often may be facsimiles if the share certificate is countersigned by a transfer agent, or registered by a registrar, other than the corporation itself or an employee of the corporation. Such facsimiles suffice even though any officer involved has ceased to be such before such certificate is issued. E. g., ABA–ALI Model Bus. Corp.Act § 21. Facsimile signatures are not expressly authorized in Arizona. Of the jurisdictions which authorize facsimile signatures, no provision for former officers is made in Idaho, Minnesota, New Hamsphire, Vermont, and Washington.

5. E. g., ABA–ALI Model Bus.Corp.Act § 21. New York also permits the chairman or vice-chairman of the board. Affixation of the corporate seal is no longer mandatory in New York. McKinney's N.Y. Bus.Corp.Law, § 508.

6. E. g., ABA–ALI Model Bus.Corp.Act § 21. A growing number of jurisdictions dispense with the necessity of stating or summarizing the rights of the on-the-share certificate and permit the certificate to indicate where such a statement or summary can be had. New York no longer requires a full statement or summary. McKinney's N.Y.Bus.Corp. Law, § 508.

7. E. g., ABA–ALI Model Bus.Corp.Act § 21. New York follows the Model Act but does not require any statement concerning par value. Arizona has no statutory provision prescribing the content of share certificates, and in many other jurisdictions, such statutory provisions are fragmentary. Custom and possibly the bylaws often affect the content of share certificates, as do applicable securities exchange requirements.

(b) The name of the person to whom issued;

(c) The number and class of shares, and the designation of the series, if any, which such certificate represents;

(d) The par value of each share represented by such certificate, or a statement that the shares are without par value.

Some jurisdictions prohibit the *issue* of any share certificate for any share until such share is fully paid.[8]

Furthermore a share certificate should contain appropriate legends where greater-than-normal quorum and/or voting requirements for shareholder and/or director action apply,[9] or where the shares it represents are subject to transfer restrictions,[10] shareholder voting agreement,[11] voting trust,[12] or irrevocable proxy,[13] are not fully paid,[14] or are subject to articles of incorporation provisions for nonjudicial dissolution[15] or as to control of directors,[16] etc.

Modern share certificates often contain explanatory legends of abbreviations used to describe limitations on ownership or special types of ownership.[17]

New York Stock Exchange Listing Requirements

To safeguard against fraudulent duplication of publicly owned securities, the New York Stock Exchange has adopted minimum standards with respect to the form of listed securities.[18]

Share certificates for listed shares must be issued in 100-share and less-than-100-share denominations.[19]

The text of their face must indicate ownership, number of shares, whether shares are full-paid and nonassessable, class, and, when required by law, par value.

Where a company is authorized to issue more than one class or series of shares, the share certificates of each class or series must *either* (a) show the office or agency of the company from which shareholders may obtain a copy of the provisions of authorized

---

8. E. g., ABA–ALI Model Bus.Corp.Act § 21. Several jurisdictions, including California, Delaware, Indiana, Michigan, and Virginia, permit the issuance of certificates for partly-paid shares, with the amount paid or due shown thereon. New York bars the issuance of certificates for partly-paid shares, except in the case of employee share plans. McKinney's N.Y.Bus.Corp.Law, §§ 504(h), 505(e).

9. E. g., McKinney's N.Y.Bus.Corp.Law, §§ 616(c), 709(c).

10. E. g., Uniform Commercial Code § 8–204. An issuer's lien upon a security is valid against a purchaser only if the right of the issuer to such lien is noted conspicuously on the security. Id. § 8–103.

11. E. g., McKinney's N.Y.Bus.Corp.Law, § 620(a); Wohl v. Miller, 145 N.Y.S.2d 84 (Sup.Ct.1955), modified on other grounds, 5 A.D.2d 126, 169 N.Y.S.2d 233 (1st Dep't 1958), reargument denied 5 A.D. 2d 823, 170 N.Y.S.2d 991 (1st Dep't 1958). See also Trefethen v. Amazeen, 93 N.H. 110, 36 A.2d 266 (1944) (transferee of shares with notice of agreement held bound thereby). Cf. Nickolopoulos v. Sarantis, 102 N.J.Eq. 585, 141 A. 792 (1928) (shareholder agreement for voting contrary to articles of incorporation and bylaws held unlawful as secret agreement).

12. E. g., McKinney's N.Y.Bus.Corp.Law, § 621(a).

13. E. g., McKinney's N.Y.Bus.Corp.Law, § 609(h).

14. McKinney's N.Y.Bus.Corp.Law, § 505(e).

15. E. g., McKinney's N.Y.Bus.Corp.Law, § 1002(c).

16. E. g., McKinney's N.Y.Bus.Corp.Law, § 620(g). "Close corporations", designated as such in the articles of incorporation and otherwise subject to recent close corporation statutes—see section 359, n. 23 infra—must state such fact on the share certificate. The share certificates of Texas corporations should set forth at length or in summary any denial or limitation of preemptive rights. Tex.Bus. Corp.Act art. 2.22 (1955).

17. New York Clearing House Association, Uniform Procedures for Stockholder Descriptions and Addressing (1961), reprinted in B. Rogers, Forms of Registration for Corporate Stock (Chase Manhattan Bank, rev. ed. 1961). See sections 176, 177 infra.

18. N.Y.S.E. Company Manual § A12. Comparable requirements apply to listed securities other than shares.

19. In addition, provision may be made for issuance of certificates for more than 100 shares for the convenience of those having larger holdings. Brokers, however, need not accept such certificates in settlement of a contract made on the Exchange.

shares, or (b) contain a statement (verbatim or preferably a reasonable summarization) of the rights and preferences of all classes of authorized shares.[20]

All share certificates must be signed by a transfer agent and by a registrar.[21] Share certificates transferable in other cities as well as in New York City must name all such cities.

Share certificates must carry the prescribed form of assignment. Provision for a witness to the assignment is no longer required, and the Exchange recommends that there be no such provision.

The face of a listed security in definitive form [22] must be printed from at least two engraved steel plates: (a) a border and tint plate, and (b) a hand-engraved face plate containing the vignette and the descriptive portion of the security, printed in black. The printing of different classes and denominations of securities must be in distinctive colors, to make them readily distinguishable from each other.

The nature of these and other Exchange requirements with respect to the form of listed securities, the submission of models, proofs, and specimens, and the certifications and agreements required of the banknote company suggest the desirability of having listed securities prepared by banknote companies familiar with Exchange requirements and procedures.

E. ORGANIZATION MEETING(S)

ORGANIZATION MEETING(S)

135. **Organization meetings of the incorporators or the directors, or both, are usually held to get the corporation under way. At such meetings, usually bylaws are adopted, the corporate seal is approved, the forms of share certificates are approved, share subscriptions are accepted, preincorporation agreements are adopted, corporate officers are elected, a bank is selected as the depositary for the corporation's funds, and any required formal application for admission in other jurisdictions is authorized.**

In most jurisdictions, after the filing of the articles of incorporation, organization meeting or meetings are held to get the corporation under way. The usual practice is to draft advance minutes to serve as agenda for any meetings.[1]

Of the jurisdictions with express statutory requirements concerning organization meetings, most require only an organization meeting of the incorporators.[2] Some jurisdictions require only an organization meeting of the directors; [3] others impose vari-

20. For securities having a right of conversion not exercisable through the entire life of the security, the word "convertible" may not be used as part of the designation and an appropriate subheading is required.

21. For Exchange requirements with respect to transfer agents and registrars, see N.Y.S.E. Company Manual § A1.

22. Temporary use of temporary share certificates or overprinted (stamped) certificates, which comply with less-exacting requirements, is permitted by the Exchange; the title line of preferred share certificates and any showing of par value may be surface printed.

1. The minutes of each meeting should be signed by the secretary thereof or by those in attendance. See Matter of Teperman v. Atcos Baths, Inc., 6 Misc.2d 162, 163 N.Y.S.2d 221 (Sup.Ct.1957), aff'd 7 A.D.2d 854, 182 N.Y.S.2d 765 (2d Dep't 1959). For Delaware practice and forms of minutes for organization meetings of a Delaware corporation, see G. Seward, Basic Corporate Practice 53, 202–216 (ALI rev. 1966); for New York corporation, see 1 G. Hornstein, Corporation Law and Practice §§ 243–244, 251–252 (1959); Henn, Appendix 4, Checklist 5, "Organization Meeting(s)", in 2 N.Y.Bus.Corp.Law 607–608 (McKinney 1963).

2. E. g., Arkansas, Connecticut, Kansas, Maine, Massachusetts, Michigan, Nebraska, New Hampshire, New Jersey, New York, Oklahoma, Rhode Island, Vermont, West Virginia.

3. E. g., ABA–ALI Model Bus.Corp.Act § 52; Alabama, Colorado, Mississippi, New Mexico, North Carolina, North Dakota, Oregon, Pennsylvania, South Carolina, Texas, Virginia, District of Columbia.

ous requirements for organization meetings of subscribers, incorporators, shareholders, or directors.[4]

In jurisdictions without statutes on the subject, a common cautious practice is to hold post-incorporation organization meetings of both the incorporators and the directors.[5] The practice often resembles a ritual, with "dummies" or "accommodation" personnel, paper meetings, and, when required, token share subscriptions.

Any organization meetings should be held on proper call [6] and with proper notice,[7] and with due observance of applicable quorum and other requirements.

The procedures at the organization meetings are rather standardized and follow various patterns, depending on the extent to which "dummy" or "accommodation" incorporator(s) and/or dummy or accommoda-

tion directors are used. As a general rule, dummies should not be expected to assume responsibility for other than formal matters. The turnover by the dummies to the real parties in interest should be timed not only to leave the determination of substantial matters to the real parties in interest but also to comply with applicable quorum and other requirements.

The older practice was to use dummy incorporators and dummy initial directors.[8]

For the first meeting of the incorporators (assuming the presence of a quorum), the agenda is approximately as follows:

(a) Election of chairman and secretary of meeting;

(b) Filing of waiver(s) of notice of meeting;

(c) Presentation and filing in minute book of certificate of incorporation or certified copy of articles of incorporation and receipt for payment of filing fee and organization tax;

(d) Adoption of bylaws;

(e) Election of initial directors if not named in articles of incorporation; resignation of any accommodation or dummy initial directors and replacement, seriatim, where permissible by action of incorporator(s);

(f) Authorization to board of directors to issue shares;

(g) Presentation and filing of transfers of any subscriptions from accommodations or dummy incorporator(s) (with affixation and cancellation of any required share transfer tax stamps);

(h) Transaction of any other business where permissible by incorporator(s).

---

4. E. g., Delaware (incorporator(s) or director(s)); Illinois and Kentucky (shareholders and directors); Indiana (directors and possibly shareholders); Missouri (directors and shareholders); Wisconsin (directors and possibly subscribers).

5. Such was the New York practice until 1963. The New York Business Corporation Law requires only an organization meeting of the incorporator(s), for the purpose of adopting bylaws, electing directors, and the transaction of such other business as may come before the meeting; it permits incorporator(s) to act by written consent without a meeting. McKinney's N.Y.Bus.Corp.Law, § 404. To get the corporation more fully organized, the board of directors must, of course, meet, even though such initial meeting is not called an "organization meeting". An organization meeting of shareholders might sometimes be necessary to complete organization of the corporation.

6. By the majority of the directors for the board of directors meeting under the 1969 Model Act revision and in Illinois, Indiana, Kentucky, North Carolina, Pennsylvania, Wisconsin, District of Columbia; by a majority of the incorporators under ABA–ALI Model Bus.Corp.Act § 52 and in Alaska, Colorado, Illinois and Kentucky (for shareholders meeting), Indiana (for shareholders meeting when required), North Dakota, Oregon, Texas, Virginia, Wisconsin (for subscribers meeting when required); by any incorporator in New York.

7. One day's notice in Kentucky and Illinois (for board of directors meeting, three days' notice for shareholders meeting); reasonable notice in Virginia; three days' notice in several jurisdictions; five days' notice in New York. Notice usually must be "in writing". The usual practice is to waive notice.

8. When the initial directors were more frequently named in the articles of incorporation, under older statutes, dummy initial directors were more common. Today, the initial directors are often elected at the organization meeting of incorporators or shareholders to serve until the first annual shareholders meeting.

At the first meeting of the board of directors (assuming the presence of a quorum), the order of business is approximately the following:

(a) Election of chairman and secretary of meeting;

(b) Filing of waivers of notice of meeting;

(c) Resignation of any accommodation or dummy initial directors and replacement, seriatim, where permissible by action of board of directors;

(d) Approval of minutes of first meeting of incorporator(s);

(e) Approval, ratification and confirmation of all action taken at first meeting of incorporator(s);

(f) Approval of bylaws;

(g) Approval of corporate seal [9] (and affixation of seal to margin of minute book page);

(h) Approval of form(s) of share certificate, with appropriate legends;

(i) Adoption of resolution under Internal Revenue Code for "section 1244 stock";

(j) Acceptance of transfers of subscriptions from any accommodation or dummy incorporator(s);

(k) Acceptance of share subscriptions;

(l) Authorization of issue of shares; fixing of consideration; valuation of any property consideration; allocation, where permissible, of portion of consideration to capital surplus;

(m) Authorization for payment or reimbursement of incorporation expenses and legal fees;

(n) Adoption of any preincorporation agreements;

(o) Election of corporate officers per statute (e. g. president might have to be a director) and bylaws, bonding of officers, and fixing of compensation thereof;

(p) Adoption of any employment agreements; acceptance of transfers of property; making of leases;

(q) Bank resolution (form supplied by bank and appropriately modified); [10]

---

9. The power to adopt and use a corporate seal or common seal, is incidental to every corporation. Leggett v. New Jersey Mfg. & Banking Co., 1 N.J. Eq. 541 (1832). Modern statutes confirm this power. E. g., ABA–ALI Model Bus.Corp.Act § 4(c). Such provisions have been construed as permissive rather than mandatory. Collins v. Tracy Grill & Bar Corp., 144 Pa.Super. 440, 19 A.2d 617 (1941). The fact that an instrument bears a corporate seal might not make it a sealed instrument. Sigler v. Mt. Vernon Bottling Co., 158 F.Supp. 234 (D.Colo. 1958). The makeup of the corporate seal is generally not prescribed by statute, but usually consists of the corporate name, the words "Corporate Seal", and the date and jurisdiction of incorporation. See McKinney's N.Y.Gen.Constr.Law, §§ 43, 45 on the affixing of a corporate seal and the use of a private seal as the corporate seal. While a seal might not be directly required, the corporate seal might be required to be affixed to share certificates. A corporate acknowledgment might have to refer to either the corporate seal or the fact that the corporation has no corporate seal. McKinney's N.Y.Real Prop.Law, § 309. An informal opinion of the New York attorney general to the counsel to the County Clerk, New York, April 8, 1968, has ruled that New York law does not require that a corporate seal be of a particular form, shape, or substance and, so long as there is a proper form of corporate acknowledgment, an instrument bearing a free-hand drawing of the purported seal may be accepted for filing by a county clerk. The presence of a corporate seal on a written instrument purporting to be executed by authority of the corporation sometimes constitutes prima facie evidence that the instrument was so executed. McKinney's N.Y.Bus.Corp.

Law, § 107. Except as otherwise provided by law, the seal is without legal effect. McKinney's N.Y. Gen.Constr.Law, § 44–a.

10. The Comptroller of the Currency has ruled that national banks may accept corporate savings accounts. However, the Board of Governors of the Federal Reserve System had stated that its Regulation Q prohibits national banks from accepting other than time or demand deposits from corporations operated for a profit. See 1 G. Hornstein, Corporation Law and Practice § 254 (1959); Maley v. East Side Bank of Chicago, 361 F.2d 393 (7th Cir. 1966); Huber Glass Co. v. First Nat'l Bank of Kenosha, 29 Wis.2d 106, 138 N.W.2d 157 (1965); Weaver Construction Co. v. Farmers Nat'l Bank, 253 Iowa 1280, 115 N.W.2d 804 (1962); Berdane Furs, Inc. v. First

(r) Adoption of resolution under Internal Revenue Code for Subchapter S election;

(s) Authorization of filing of any required share transfer tax certificate;

(t) Authorization of application for admission or qualification of corporation as foreign corporation in any other jurisdiction(s) where corporation is to do business;

(u) Authorization of appointment of resident agent or agents;

(v) Authorization of designation of corporation's general counsel and accountant, and setting up of corporate records, including record of shareholders;

(w) Transaction of any business where permissible by action of board of directors.

Where dummy directors, as well as dummy incorporators, are used,[11] the resignations of the dummy directors and the election of their successors can take place either near the end of the first meeting of the incorporators or after the disposition of the formal matters at the first meeting of the board of directors.

In issuing the shares, applicable requirements of the Federal Securities Act, state "blue sky" laws, and securities exchange listing requirements, should be observed. Any required state share issue stamps should be affixed and cancelled. Obviously, shares should be issued only for proper consideration.

Appropriate action should also be taken to authorize application for admission of the corporation in other jurisdictions where business is planned, including the appointment of any required resident agents and the designation of any required registered officers.

Provision might also be made for the designation of the corporation's general counsel and accountant, and the setting up of the corporate records, including the share ledger or record of shareholders.

The corporation may elect to amortize its organizational expenditures over a five-year period for federal income tax purposes.[12]

The minute book should contain, usually in the front thereof, a certified copy of the articles of incorporation,[13] or the formal "certificate of incorporation" if one has been issued, and a copy of the bylaws certified by the secretary of the organization meeting or other meeting at which the bylaws were adopted.

Pennsylvania Banking & Trust Co., 190 Pa.Super. 639, 155 A.2d 465 (1959); Commercial Trading Co. v. Trade Bank & Trust Co., 286 App.Div. 722, 146 N.Y.S.2d 570 (1st Dep't 1955).

11. See note 8 supra.

12. Int.Rev.Code of 1954, 26 U.S.C.A. § 248.

13. Such a certified copy can be ordered from the office of the secretary of state at the time of the filing of the articles of incorporation.

F. ADMISSION AND DOMESTICATION PROCEDURES

ADMISSION PROCEDURES

136. Formal qualification of a corporation to transact business in a jurisdiction other than the jurisdiction of its incorporation usually involves the filing with the secretary of state and/or specified public officials of an application for a certificate of authority, with required supporting documentation. By formal qualification in a jurisdiction, the corporation becomes undeniably subject to service of process there and to the jurisdiction's laws and taxes applicable to foreign corporations. Additional filings are required in the event of various corporate changes. If the corporation ceases to transact business in the jurisdiction or is dissolved, it should formally withdraw and surrender its certificate of authority. Various grounds usually are specified for revocation of a foreign corporation's certificate of authority.

To transact business in a jurisdiction other than the jurisdiction of its incorporation, a corporation is, as previously discussed,[1] generally required to qualify in such other jurisdiction as a foreign corporation.

Generally, a foreign corporation is not entitled to qualify to transact in a jurisdiction any business which a domestic corporation would not be permitted to transact,[2] or any business not authorized in its articles of incorporation.[3] In some jurisdictions, foreign corporations are subject to certain disabilities with respect to real property or land.[4]

Admission (or qualification, authorization, licensing, securing a permit, registration, or domestication) of a foreign corporation usually involves the filing with the secretary of state and/or other specified public official [5] of a formal application for a certificate of authority.[6]

The contents of the application vary in different jurisdictions.[7] Often the application must state the corporate name,[8] juris-

---

1. See sections 98, 100 supra. Some statutes provide a nonexclusive listing of local activities that do not constitute transacting business for purpose of qualification requirements. E. g., ABA–ALI Model Bus. Corp.Act § 99; Alaska, Hawaii, Montana, North Dakota, Oregon. Similar listings are found in the Maryland, North Carolina, Texas, Utah, and Wisconsin statutes. Other jurisdictions with listings include California, Delaware, Kansas, New York, Ohio, Tennessee, Vermont, District of Columbia. Except to the extent that the matter is clarified by statute, the necessity of qualification depends on judicial holdings. See W. Beaman, Doing Business in Other States (United States Corporation Company 1963); What Constitutes Doing Business in States Foreign to the State of its Creation (Corporation Trust Company 1968).

2. E. g., ABA–ALI Model Bus.Corp.Act § 99.

3. See note 11 infra. See section 121 supra.

4. E. g., Georgia, Indiana.

5. E. g., ABA–ALI Model Bus.Corp.Act § 103. Local filings in the county where the corporation is to have its principal office or place of business within the jurisdiction are also sometimes required. E. g., Idaho, Indiana, Kansas, Nebraska, Nevada, West Virginia. Delaware and Minnesota require the state official to forward to the county officer copies of the filed documents. Corporation service companies, with offices in the jurisdictions involved, can be most helpful in assisting counsel in qualifying the corporation there.

6. E. g., ABA–ALI Model Bus.Corp.Act § 103 (requiring verified application to be made on forms prescribed and furnished by secretary of state and to be executed in duplicate by the corporation by designated corporate officers). Such officers should secure appropriate corporate authorization from the board of directors to make such application. A statement that such authorization has been obtained might have to appear in the application itself. E. g., Minnesota. Or a copy of the board of directors resolution authorizing such filing might have to accompany the application. E. g., Kansas, Louisiana. For New York authorization procedures, see Henn, Appendix 4, Checklist 11, "Qualification Procedure", in 2 N.Y.Bus.Corp.Law 644–645 (McKinney 1963); McKinney's N.Y.Exec.Law, § 96(9)(a) ($110 filing fee); McKinney's N.Y.Tax Law, § 181 (minimum $10 license fee).

7. E. g., ABA–ALI Model Bus.Corp.Act § 103.

8. The corporate name must comply with applicable requirements which are often the same as those applicable to domestic corporations. See section 117, n. 2 supra. Many jurisdictions require that the name contain a sufficient indication of corporateness, or require the corporation to agree to add to its name as used in the jurisdiction a word or abbreviation indicative of corporateness. Sufficient indication of corporateness is usually found in the

diction of incorporation, date of incorporation, duration of corporation, address of the principal office of the corporation in its jurisdiction of incorporation, address of registered office within the jurisdiction,[9] name of registered agent within the jurisdiction for service of process upon the corporation,[10]

various foreign corporate designations: English: "Ltd." (limited company, "Pty.Ltd." ("proprietary limited" for Australian and South African private company), "N.L." (no liability for Australian mining company); German: "A.G." (Aktiengesellschaft), "G.m.b.H." (Gesellschaft mit beshränkter Haftung); French: "S.A." (société anonyme), "S.A.R.L." (société á responsibilite limiteé); Spanish: "S.A." (sociedad anonomina), "S.R.L." (sociedad de responsabilidad limitada), "S.A.C.I." or "S.A.I.C." (sociedad de capital e industria); Italian: "S.p.A." (societa per azioni), "S.A.R.L." (societa a responsibilita limitada); Portuguese: "S.A." (sociedade anonima), "Ltda." (sociedade limitade por cotas); Japanese: "K.K." (Kabushiki-Kaisha), "Y.K." (Yugen-Kaisha); Dutch: "N.V." (naamloze vennootschap); Swedish: "A.B." (Aktiebolag); Afrikaans: "B.pk." (beperk), "Edms." (eiensdoms). Statutes often prohibit words or phrases implying that the corporation is organized for purposes other than those stated in its articles of incorporation; and prohibit names which are the same as or deceptively similar to the names of existing domestic corporations or qualified foreign corporations or to names duly reserved or registered in the jurisdiction. E. g., ABA–ALI Model Bus.Corp.Act §§ 101, 103(b). But see Blackstone, "Permitting Qualification of Corporations under Similar Names: A Change in the Model Business Corporation Act", 23 Bus.Law. 885 (1968). Appropriate endorsements might be required in connection with the use of certain names. Where a corporation expects to transact business in particular jurisdictions, advance reservation or registration of the name there, where possible, is desirable. In this respect, corporation service companies can be helpful. Statutes often contain provisions respecting changes of name of foreign corporations. E. g., ABA–ALI Model Bus.Corp.Act § 102.

9. E. g., ABA–ALI Model Bus.Corp.Act §§ 103(e), 106(a). Purely formal offices maintained by corporation service companies are often used to satisfy such requirements. For changing the registered office, see ABA–ALI Model Bus.Corp.Act § 107.

10. E. g., ABA–ALI Model Bus.Corp.Act §§ 103(e), 106(b). For changing the registered agent, see ABA–ALI Model Bus.Corp.Act § 107. A few jurisdictions do not require a resident agent, but provide for the appointment or require the designation of the secretary of state or some other official as agent for service of process against the corporation within the jurisdiction. E. g., Georgia, Massachusetts, New York, West Virginia. New York permits an optional designation of a registered agent in addition to the required designation of the secretary of state. McKinney's N.Y.Bus.Corp.Law, § 307.

purposes proposed to be pursued within the jurisdiction,[11] names and addresses of officers and directors, amount of authorized or issued shares or stated capital, and estimate of value of property and amount of first year's business within or without the jurisdiction.

Some jurisdictions require the application to be accompanied by other documentation, such as certified or authenticated copies of the articles of incorporation and all amendments thereof,[12] certificate from official of jurisdiction of incorporation that the corporation is an existing corporation there,[13] designation of agent for service of process,[14] copy of resolution of board of directors authorizing applications,[15] antitrust affidavit,[16] etc.

A few jurisdictions require publication of certain information concerning the application.[17]

If the application conforms to law, and all taxes and fees have been paid,[18] several ju-

11. E. g., ABA–ALI Model Bus.Corp.Act § 103(f). See notes 2–4 supra.

12. E. g., ABA–ALI Model Bus.Corp.Act § 104. Such requirements are no longer imposed in California, Nebraska, New Hampshire, New York; all but New Hampshire require instead a certificate by the proper public officer of the state of incorporation to the effect that the corporation is an existing corporation there. For requirements where articles of incorporation are subsequently amended, see ABA–ALI Model Bus.Corp.Act § 109.

13. E. g., California, Nebraska, New York.

14. E. g., Mississippi.

15. E. g., Kansas, Louisiana.

16. E. g., Texas.

17. E. g., Arizona, Pennsylvania.

18. See ABA–ALI Model Bus.Corp.Act §§ 120, 121, 124, 126. The initial fees and taxes for qualifying a foreign corporation vary in the different jurisdictions. New Jersey imposes a $125 filing fee and a recording fee depending on the length of the documentation ($10 and upwards, depending upon length). Until 1963, New Jersey exacted a reciprocally-higher filing fee from corporations from jurisdictions which imposed more than the then fee for the admission in New Jersey of foreign corporations.

risdictions provide for issuance of a receipt or formal certificate of authority.[19]

Upon the issuance of the receipt or certificate of authority where there is provision therefor and presumably upon the filing of the application in the absence of such provision, the corporation becomes authorized to transact business in the jurisdiction for the purposes set forth in the application.[20]

A qualified foreign corporation usually enjoys in the jurisdiction where qualified such powers as are permitted by the laws of the jurisdiction of its incorporation but no greater powers than domestic corporations formed for the business set forth in the application.[21]

By formally qualifying, the corporation undeniably becomes subject to service of process within the jurisdiction,[22] and presumably cannot deny that it is doing business and thereby has become subject to the applicable laws and taxes of the jurisdiction where qualified.[23] A few jurisdictions require the corporation to state expressly that it accepts their laws governing foreign corporations[24] or that it accepts their constitutions.[25]

The sanctions for transacting business in a jurisdiction without having secured the required certificate of authority have been previously discussed.[26]

Also specified in the various statutes dealing with the admission of foreign corporations are procedures to amend the certificate of authority,[27] to be followed in the event of a merger of such corporation,[28] or amendment of its articles of incorporation,[29] or other changes,[30] and for formal withdrawal of such corporation and surrender of the certificate of authority.[31]

Various grounds are usually also specified for revocation by the secretary of state or other designated public official of a foreign corporation's certificate of authority.[32]

---

19. E. g., ABA–ALI Model Bus.Corp.Act § 104. The Model Act, in keeping with its consistent pattern, requires duplicate originals of the application, one to be filed and the other to be affixed to a formal certificate of authority and returned to the corporation or its representatives.

20. E. g., ABA–ALI Model Bus.Corp.Act § 105. Delaying qualification until after a particular date might enable a corporation to postpone for up to a year the filing of certain reports and payment of certain taxes.

21. See ABA–ALI Model Bus.Corp.Act § 100. See section 122 supra. But see note 4 supra.

22. See section 97 supra.

23. Some statutes expressly provide that nothing therein should be construed to regulate the organization or the internal affairs of qualified foreign corporations. E. g., ABA–ALI Model Bus.Corp.Act § 99; Alaska, Colorado, Illinois, Iowa, Michigan, Missouri, North Dakota, Oklahoma, Oregon, Pennsylvania, Virginia, Wisconsin, District of Columbia. Cf. section 321 infra. See section 98 supra.

24. E. g., West Virginia.

25. E. g., Wyoming.

26. See section 101 supra.

27. E. g., ABA–ALI Model Bus.Corp.Act § 111.

28. E. g., ABA–ALI Model Bus.Corp.Act § 110.

29. E. g., ABA–ALI Model Bus.Corp.Act § 109.

30. E. g., ABA–ALI Model Bus.Corp.Act § 102 (change of name), § 107 (change of registered office or registered agent).

31. E. g., ABA–ALI Model Bus.Corp.Act §§ 112, 113. Usually required is the filing of a formal application for withdrawal, with provision for service of process upon the corporation by serving the secretary of state in any action, suit, or proceeding based upon any cause of action arising within the jurisdiction during the time the corporation was authorized to transact business there. Publication of notice of withdrawal might be required. E. g., Georgia, Hawaii, Kansas, Pennsylvania, West Virginia. Some jurisdictions require a copy of the resolution of the board of directors authorizing withdrawal. E. g., Georgia, Michigan, New Hampshire. Obviously, a corporation should formally withdraw whenever it ceases to do business in a jurisdiction or when it is dissolved. See section 348 infra.

32. E. g., ABA–ALI Model Bus.Corp.Act §§ 114, 115 (for failure to file annual reports or pay taxes when due; failure to maintain within the jurisdiction the required registered agent; failure to file statement of change of registered office or registered agent as required in the event of such change; failure to file amendments of articles of incorporation or articles of merger as required; or any material misrepresentation in any application, report, affidavit, or other document submitted by the corporation).

DOMESTICATION PROCEDURES

137. **A few jurisdictions require or permit "domestication" of foreign corporations to do business. Effects of "domestication" vary, from practically reincorporation as a domestic corporation to the usual consequences of admission.**

A few jurisdictions provide that a foreign corporation, in lieu of admission or qualification to do business in the state, or a qualified foreign corporation, may "domesticate".[1] Two other jurisdictions use the term "domestication" merely to denote admission or qualification.[2]

Domestication results in the corporation's being bound by the state's corporation statute with respect to its property and business operations within the state and possibly its becoming a domestic corporation or body corporate of such state.[3]

Some statutes provide that domesticated corporations shall no longer have that power of removing cases to the federal courts which inheres in foreign corporations.[4]

---

1. Georgia, Mississippi, Nebraska. See Note, "The Legal Consequences of Failure to Comply with Domestication Statutes", 110 U.Pa.L.Rev. 241 (1961).

2. Oklahoma, Tennessee. See Doten v. Halby, 252 F.Supp. 830 (E.D.Tenn.1965) (holding that domestication of Delaware corporation, with all rights and liabilities of Tennessee domestic corporation under Tennessee law, did not confer Tennessee citizenship on corporation for federal diversity-of-citizenship purposes).

3. See text accompanying section 88, nn. 17–24 supra.

4. See section 98, n. 4 supra.

CHAPTER 7

RECOGNITION OR DISREGARD OF CORPORATENESS

A. INTRODUCTION

A. INTRODUCTION

RECOGNITION OR DISREGARD OF CORPORATENESS— IN GENERAL

138. Recognition of corporateness for the purpose of one or more corporate attributes sometimes is afforded despite the corporation's having been defectively incorporated or is withheld despite technically correct incorporation. The two corollary sets of problems have received extensive judicial treatment with the former implemented in recent years by legislation.

Whether the focus be on the corporation as an artificial legal person or on the corporate personality of the natural legal persons who compose it,[1] the question occasionally arises as to whether corporateness, or the corporate entity or corporate personality, should be recognized or disregarded for the purpose of one or more corporate attributes.[2]

Such recognition sometimes is afforded despite the corporation's having been defectively incorporated or is withheld despite technically correct incorporation. These two corollary sets of problems have received extensive judicial treatment; the former has been implemented in recent years by legislation. The traditional rules relating to these problems will be summarized in this chapter: first, the problems of defective incorporation,[3] and then the problems of disregard of corporateness.[4]

2. See section 79 supra.

3. See sections 139–145 infra.

4. See sections 146–153 infra.

1. See section 78 supra.

B. DEFECTIVE INCORPORATION

CONDITIONS PRECEDENT TO INCORPORATION

139. Steps in incorporation procedures have been classified by the courts as (a) mandatory or directory; (b) conditions precedent to incorporation or conditions subsequent to incorporation; (c) conditions precedent to incorporation or conditions precedent to doing business, the latter often being also conditions subsequent to incorporation. When there is substantial compliance with all mandatory conditions precedent to incorporation, and its corporateness is generally immune from both direct and collateral attack on the basis of incorporation defects, a de jure corporation exists. In the absence of de jure incorporation consideration must be given to the de facto doctrine, "corporation by estoppel" principles, and certain statutory provisions, to determine whether or not, despite such defective incorporation, corporateness will be recognized, and if not, the consequences of such lack of recognition.

Corporateness, or the corporate entity or corporate personality, carries with it limited liability and the various other corporate attributes. Whenever there is a failure to comply with the statutory incorporation procedure in a given jurisdiction,[1] the question arises as to whether incorporation may be successfully attacked (a) *directly* in an action—e. g., *quo warranto* proceeding— brought by the state to prevent an illegal exercise of corporate powers, or (b) *directly* or *collaterally* by a party other than the state [2] or *collaterally* by the state.

Where there is substantial compliance with all steps necessary for incorporation, there is a so-called *de jure* corporation whose incorporation is generally insulated from both direct and collateral attack on the basis of incorporation defects.[3]

Since the various steps prescribed by incorporation statutes vary in importance in different jurisdictions, the fact that substantial compliance with a given statutory condition is lacking does not always deprive the corporation of its *de jure* character. In this regard the courts have devised the following distinctions:

(a) *Mandatory* vs. *Directory*: Failure to comply with a relatively inconsequential provision (i. e., directory) which results in no prejudice to public interests does not destroy the *de jure* character of a corporation. Whether a statutory incorporation provision is mandatory or directory depends upon construction of legislative intent.[4]

(b) *Condition precedent to incorporation* vs. *Condition subsequent to incorporation*: While failure to perform a condition subsequent to incorporation may result in revocation of its corporateness, a valid *de jure* corporation exists from the time that the mandatory conditions precedent to incorporation are met. The filing in a public office or public offices of the articles of incorporation, and concomitant payment of incorporation taxes and

---

1. See section 117 supra.

2. Such is the language frequently employed in discussions on the subject. The question might be better phrased in terms of vulnerability of incorporation to attack (a) directly by the state, or (b) otherwise. Direct attack by parties other than the state has been denied on principles akin to those applied to denial of collateral attack. Baum v. Baum Holding Co., 158 Neb. 197, 62 N.W.2d 864 (1954) (declaratory judgment action). See also Flash Cleaners, Inc. v. Columbia Appliance Corp., 156 Cal.App.2d 455, 319 P.2d 454 (1957); Wells v. Hiskett, 288 S. W.2d 257 (Tex.Civ.App.1956). An attacking party other than the state might be associates or outsiders. Dunham v. Natural Bridge Ranch Co., 115

Mont. 579, 147 P.2d 902 (1944); Temple Enterprises, Inc. v. Combs, 164 Or. 133, 100 P.2d 613, 128 A.L.R. 856 (1940). See Warren, "Collateral Attack on Incorporation", 20 Harv.L.Rev. 456 (1907); Annot., 55 A.L.R. 510 (1928).

3. But even a so-called de jure corporation might be subject to direct attack by the state (or others in a rare jurisdiction) (see note 10 infra) for noncompliance with a condition subsequent to incorporation.

4. R. Stevens, Handbook on the Law of Private Corporations § 22 (2d ed. 1949).

fees, are usually treated as conditions precedent to valid incorporation,[5] whereas compliance with a minimum paid-in capital requirement [6] or filing of certain reports or statements required by law [7] is sometimes regarded as a condition subsequent rather than a condition precedent.

(c) *Condition precedent to incorporation* vs. *Condition precedent to carrying on business*: The corporation assumes a *de jure* character once there is substantial compliance with all mandatory conditions precedent to corporateness—such as filing the articles of incorporation. This is true even though conditions classified as conditions precedent to carrying on business—such as election of directors,[8] or subscription and/or payment of

minimum capital [9]—are not met. Conditions precedent to doing business might also constitute conditions subsequent to incorporation.[10]

By the foregoing approach, a *de jure* corporation exists whenever there is substantial compliance with all mandatory conditions precedent to incorporation.[11] When such a finding cannot be made, consideration must be given to the *de facto* doctrine, "corporation by estoppel" principles, and certain statutory provisions, to determine whether or not, despite such defective incorporation, corporateness will be recognized, and if not, the consequences of such lack of recognition.

DE FACTO DOCTRINE

140. **Under the de facto doctrine, a corporation which is not de jure for failure to comply substantially with all mandatory conditions precedent to incorporation may nevertheless be recognized as a corporation for most purposes, except in a direct attack on its existence by the state. The traditional elements of the de facto doctrine are (a) existence of a statute under which the corporation might have been validly incorporated; (b) colorable attempt in good faith to comply with such statute; and (c) some user or exercise of corporate privileges. Where the required elements are found, the application of the doctrine also depends on the nature of the case and the fairness to the par-**

5. See section 132 supra. Pullum Window Corp. v. Feldstein, 357 Mich. 82, 97 N.W.2d 762 (1959); Matter of Planz, 282 App.Div. 552, 125 N.Y.S.2d 750 (3d Dep't 1953) (failure to file in office of secretary of state); Burks v. Cook, 225 Ark. 756, 284 S.W.2d 855 (1955); Doggrell v. Great Southern Box Co., 206 F. 2d 671 (6th Cir. 1953) (2–1), rev'd on other grounds on rehearing, 208 F.2d 310 (6th Cir. 1953) (2–1); Baker v. Bates-Street Shirt Co., 6 F.2d 854 (1st Cir. 1925) (failure to file in local office); Tisch Auto Supply Co. v. Nelson, 222 Mich. 196, 192 N.W. 600 (1923); Moe v. Harris, 142 Minn. 442, 172 N.W. 494 (1919); Annot., 22 A.L.R. 376 (1923), 37 A.L.R. 1319 (1925).

6. Matter of Hardin, —— Miss. ——, 218 So.2d 889 (1969) (corporation held de facto and not subject to collateral attack for noncompliance with minimum paid in capital requirement denominated as condition subsequent); Temple Enterprises, Inc. v. Combs, 164 Or. 133, 100 P.2d 613, 128 A.L.R. 856 (1940). See note 9 infra. But see Beck v. Stimmel, 39 Ohio App. 510, 177 N.E. 920 (1931).

7. Compare Werner v. Hearst, 177 N.Y. 63, 69 N.E. 221 (1903), with Connecticut Flour Corp. v. Kelly Bakery, Inc., 19 Conn.Supp. 211, 111 A.2d 20 (Super.Ct.1954). See also Hoss v. Purinton, 229 F.2d 104 (9th Cir. 1955), cert. denied 350 U.S. 997, 76 S. Ct. 548, 100 L.Ed. 861 (1956).

8. Cf. Dunham v. Natural Bridge Ranch Co., 115 Mont. 579, 147 P.2d 902 (1944); Kardo Co. v. Adams, 231 F. 950 (6th Cir. 1916). See Shaffer v. Buxbaum, 137 Mont. 397, 352 P.2d 83 (1960) (corporate entity held in abeyance while corporation had only two shareholders eligible to serve on required three-man board of directors).

9. See section 126 supra. Matter of Hardin, —— Miss. ——, 218 So.2d 889 (1969) (corporation held de facto and not subject to collateral attack for noncompliance with minimum paid in capital requirement denominated as condition subsequent); Temple Enterprises, Inc. v. Combs, 164 Or. 133, 100 P.2d 613, 128 A.L.R. 856 (1940). See note 6 supra.

10. Noncompliance with such conditions subsequent may usually be invoked by the state but not by others. Temple Enterprises, Inc. v. Combs, 164 Or. 133, 100 P.2d 613, 128 A.L.R. 856 (1940). But see Eastern Products Corp. v. Tennessee Coal, Iron & R. R., 151 Tenn. 239, 269 S.W. 4, 40 A.L.R. 1483 (1924) (holding corporation to be de jure but without capacity to do business, and such lack of capacity to be invocable by private party).

11. But such a de jure corporation might be subject to attack (see note 6 supra) for noncompliance with a condition subsequent to incorporation (including a condition precedent to doing business or a directory condition precedent to incorporation construed as a condition subsequent to incorporation).

ties under the circumstances. The de facto doctrine is also sometimes applied to corporations whose charters have expired or been terminated and then revived or reinstated with respect to activities during the interim period.

A corporation which fails to qualify as *de jure* may nonetheless assume a *de facto* corporate character under various circumstances.[1]

The significance of the *de facto* doctrine [2] —which is a product of judicial decision—is that it operates to prevent collateral attack upon corporateness even though substantial compliance with all mandatory conditions precedent to incorporation (necessary to create a *de jure* corporation) is lacking. The *de facto* doctrine may not be used to deny a direct attack by the state in the nature of a *quo warranto* proceeding.

The courts have been somewhat hesitant in resorting to the *de facto* doctrine, since it is used to bridge a legal gap where corporate privileges have been exercised by a corporation which has failed to comply with statutory incorporation requirements. Balanced against such unauthorized assumption of corporateness are interests of justice to the parties and of security in business dealings with "corporations". However, it has been recognized that the *de facto* doctrine serves certain public policy considerations: [3]

(a) The merits of the controversy seldom are affected by the corporate existence of a party to the action, where the *de facto* doctrine is applicable;

(b) If any rights and franchises have been usurped, they are rights and franchises of the state, and the state alone can object.

In any event, three traditional elements must exist before a *de facto* corporation may be recognized: [4]

(a) The existence of a statute under which the corporation might have been validly incorporated;

(b) Colorable attempt to comply with such statute; and

(c) Some user or exercise of corporate privileges.

In addition, some cases and commentators have added good faith of corporation or associates as a fourth element.[5] It is often omitted, however, because a colorable compliance with the incorporation statute usually encompasses a good faith attempt to incorporate.[6]

The third element—some user of corporate privileges—is rarely placed in issue, since the case would seldom arise absent this element. However, to meet this requirement more is demanded than a mere showing of corporate organization by the election of officers and the passage by directors of resolutions purely executory in nature.[7]

The first element—the existence of a law under which the corporation could be

---

1. R. Stevens, Handbook on the Law of Private Corporations §§ 26–27 (2d ed. 1949). Von Bodungen, "Defective Corporation in American and German Law", 15 Am.J.Comp.L. 313 (1967).

2. The de facto doctrine has been called an example of legal conceptualism at its worst. Frey, "Legal Analysis and the 'De Facto' Doctrine", 100 U.Pa.L. Rev. 1153, 1180 (1952). The de facto doctrine, as applied to defective incorporation, should not be confused with the principles of the same name sometimes applied to uphold the actions of irregular corporate directors or officers. See sections 206, 222 infra.

3. See Note, 53 Mich.L.Rev. 283, 284 (1954).

4. Pearson Drainage District v. Erhardt, 239 Mo. App. 845, 201 S.W.2d 484 (1947); R. Stevens, Handbook on the Law of Private Corporations § 27 (2d ed. 1949). Cf. Uniform Limited Partnership Act § 2(2): "A limited partnership is formed if there has been substantial compliance in good faith with the requirements [for forming a limited partnership]". See Giles v. Vette, 263 U.S. 553, 44 S.Ct. 157, 68 L. Ed. 441 (1924); Carpenter, "De Facto Corporations", 25 Harv.L.Rev. 623 (1912).

5. United Sewing Machine Distributors, Inc. v. Calhoun, 231 Miss. 390, 95 So.2d 453 (1957); H. Ballantine, Ballantine on Corporations § 24 (rev. ed. 1947); Frey, "Legal Analysis and the 'De Facto' Doctrine", 100 U.Pa.L.Rev. 1153, 1156 (1952).

6. Note, 53 Mich.L.Rev. 283, 284, n. 3 (1954).

7. Emery v. DePeyster, 77 App.Div. 65, 78 N.Y.S. 1056 (1st Dep't 1902).

formed has been most often before the courts where a statute under which a corporation was formed was later held to be unconstitutional. While the older cases were against applying the *de facto* doctrine in these cases, on the traditional ground that an unconstitutional statute is a nullity, there is a growing tendency to apply the *de facto* doctrine.[8]

While colorable compliance [9] is not easily defined, it usually is intended to mean an actual *bona fide* attempt to incorporate under the incorporation statute.

In a 1954 Nebraska case,[10] the corporate defendant was organized as a holding company in 1922, even though holding companies were not authorized by the legislature as a holding company until the time of the until 1941. The defendant continued to act litigation in 1954, at no time attempting to incorporate as a holding company under the 1941 statute. In a declaratory judgment action challenging the defendant's corporate existence, the court held that the defendant became a *de facto* corporation in 1941. Although a finding of "colorable compliance" was duly made, the court used the term to connote business activity rather than an actual attempt to incorporate under the 1941 statute. The suggestion has been advanced that this decision stands for a modification of the colorable compliance requirement in Nebraska, since apparently an attempt to in-

corporate prior to the statute authorizing incorporation is sufficient.[11]

In addition to the existence of the aforesaid three (or four) elements, the nature of the case itself (fairness to parties under circumstances) has some bearing as to whether the *de facto* doctrine will be applied in a given case, although some courts have emphasized the elements alone.

In contract cases, the doctrine is generally applied whenever the parties had prior dealings which were made on a corporate basis.[12] The same result has been reached where the parties had no prior dealings but each assumed a valid corporation. Such holdings effectuate the reasonable expectations of the parties.[13]

In tort cases, the doctrine has been more liberally employed where the corporation in question was the plaintiff,[14] and there is a growing tendency to afford the same treatment to the corporate defendant. On the other hand, when a criminal statute requiring strict construction is involved, the *de facto* doctrine is generally not applied.[15]

The courts have been liberal in their approach to cases involving a defectively-formed corporation in the chain of title, thus preserving the security of title demanded in real property transactions. As a general

---

8. Gwynne v. Board of Education, 259 N.Y. 191, 198, 181 N.E. 353, 356 (1932); Annot., 136 A.L.R. 187 (1942). See also Town of Maysville v. Magnolia Petroleum Co., 272 F.2d 806 (10th Cir. 1959) (holding there can be no de facto municipal corporation absent law authorizing de jure one).

9. The quantum of compliance is relevant as probably is the quality of good faith (see notes 5, 6 supra). Obviously, colorable compliance is short of substantial compliance which would result in a de jure corporation. Cf. Harrill v. Davis, 168 F. 187 (8th Cir. 1909) (articles of incorporation not filed; therefore no colorable compliance).

10. Baum v. Baum Holding Co., 158 Neb. 197, 62 N. W.2d 864 (1954).

11. Note, 53 Mich.L.Rev. 283 (1954). See Kiamesha Development Corp. v. Guild Properties, Inc., 4 N.Y. 2d 378, 388, 175 N.Y.S.2d 63, 70, 151 N.E.2d 214, 219 (1958): "Without any exercise of corporate functions, without any colorable attempt to comply with the statutes governing incorporation . . . ., without any certificate of incorporation having been even prepared or acknowledged, it cannot be said that Guild Properties, Inc. was a *de facto* corporation on that date."

12. See Beck v. Stimmel, 39 Ohio App. 510, 177 N.E. 920 (1931).

13. Tisch Auto Supply Co. v. Nelson, 222 Mich. 196, 192 N.W. 600 (1923). But see Harrill v. Davis, 168 F. 187 (8th Cir. 1909).

14. Evasion of liability by the wrongdoer is thus prevented. See Kardo Co. v. Adams, 231 F. 950 (6th Cir. 1916).

15. But see People v. Carter, 122 Mich. 668, 81 N.W. 924 (1900).

rule, collateral attack is denied in such cases whenever the three (or four) elements exist.[16]

On the other hand, there is some question as to the place of the *de facto* doctrine when a defectively-formed corporation attempts to exercise the power of eminent domain. Collateral attack is foreclosed under the majority rule, but the New York view is uncertain because of a case limiting the exercise of the power of eminent domain to a *de jure* corporation.[17]

While the cases sometimes tend to concentrate on the three (or four) elements and deemphasize the circumstances, the possible relevancy of the latter point up that a defective corporation treated as a corporation under the *de facto* doctrine for some purposes might not be for all purposes.[18] Hence to speak of such a corporation as a *"de facto corporation"* or a *"corporation in fact"*, as distinguishable from a *"de jure corporation"* or *"corporation in law"*, can lead to overgeneralization unless it is recognized that the *"de facto* corporation" or "corporation in fact" might have hybrid characteristics. In any event, the *de facto* doctrine represents some triumph of substance over form and, in a sense, some relaxation of the concession theory approach.

One of the more frequent causes of defective incorporation is failure to file the articles of incorporation as required in a public office or public offices.

Some cases hold that absent filing with the secretary of state, there has not been even colorable compliance and hence there can be no *de facto* corporateness.[19] Other cases excuse non-filing at least where there has been some drafting of the articles of incorporation.[20] In jurisdictions which have corporate existence begin on filing with the secretary of state, *de jure* corporateness usually then arises, and other required local filing requirements are usually construed as conditions subsequent to incorporation.[21]

A minority approach was represented by the Arkansas decisions. Under pre-1966 Arkansas law,[22] a corporation did not become a corporation *de jure* until the articles of incorporation were filed with the secretary of state and the county clerk of the county in which the corporation's principal office or place of business was located. Failure to file with the county clerk resulted in the corporation's being only a *de facto* corporation; the organizers or shareholders of a *de facto* corporation were personally liable as partners for the debts of the corporation.[23]

16. See Annot., 20 A.L.R.2d 1084 (1951).

17. New York Cable Co. v. Mayor, 104 N.Y. 1, 10 N. E. 332 (1887).

18. Some cases have recognized that a de facto corporation may be sued as such but may not sue. Rogers v. Toccoa Power Co., 161 Ga. 524, 131 S.E. 517, 44 A.L.R. 534 (1926); Note, "Defective Formation and Suits in Corporate Name," 84 U.Pa.L.Rev. 514 (1936). See cases cited in section 352, n. 1 infra. A subscriber to corporate shares can defend on the ground that incorporation was not de jure.

Tonge v. Item Pub. Co., 244 Pa. 417, 91 A. 229 (1914). But cf. Blumenthal v. Reiner, 247 F.2d 461 (4th Cir. 1957), cert. denied 355 U.S. 903, 78 S.Ct. 331, 2 L.Ed.2d 260 (1957) (buyer of shares denied damages for fraud where sellers had failed to form corporation properly since no loss to buyer was shown). See also Hoss v. Purinton, 229 F.2d 104 (9th Cir. 1955), cert. denied 350 U.S. 997, 76 S.Ct. 548, 100 L.Ed. 861 (1956) (allowing plaintiff to affirm and deny corporate existence with respect to same contract).

19. Harrill v. Davis, 168 F. 187 (8th Cir. 1909); Allen Steel Supply Co. v. Bradley, 89 Idaho 29, 402 P.2d 394 (1965), petition denied 89 Idaho 43, 403 P.2d 859 (1965); Annot., 22 A.L.R. 376 (1923), 37 A.L.R. 1319 (1925). See section 142 infra.

20. Kiamesha Development Corp. v. Guild Properties, Inc., 4 N.Y.2d 378, 175 N.Y.S.2d 63, 151 N.E.2d 214 (1958); Cottentin v. Meyer, 80 N.J.L. 52, 76 A. 351 (1910). See Vincent Drug Co. v. Utah State Tax Comm'n, 17 Utah 2d 202, 407 P.2d 683 (1965) (initial filing rejected for technical defect). See also Conway v. Samet, 59 Misc.2d 666, 300 N.Y.S.2d 243 (Sup.Ct.1969) (retaining and paying attorney to incorporate held insufficient; attorney's malpractice no defense).

21. Tarutis v. United States, 354 F.2d 546 (8th Cir. 1965); Jolley v. Idaho Securities, Inc., 90 Idaho 373, 414 P.2d 879 (1966).

22. The pre-1966 holdings are expressly overruled by Ark.Bus.Corp.Act § 64–117(B) (1966).

23. Gazette Publishing Co. v. Brady, 204 Ark. 396, 162 S.W.2d 494 (1942).

Where the articles of incorporation were not filed with the county clerk until the day of the trial, the court held that the corporation was a *de facto* corporation only and that the shareholders were individually liable as partners.[24]

A federal court held that the defendant, an incorporator and original shareholder residing in Tennessee, could be personally liable for the debts of the corporation under Arkansas law because of failure to file articles of incorporation with the county clerk even though the defendant had no knowledge of the corporation's noncompliance with the statute and was an inactive member of the corporation.[25]

The Tennessee Supreme Court refused to enforce the Arkansas law regarding the liability of shareholders in a *de facto* corporation. The court held that while Tennessee usually applies the law of the state in which the corporation is domiciled, here Arkansas law was repugnant to the public policy of Tennessee, where shareholders of a *de facto* corporation are not personally liable for the debts of the corporation, and that Arkansas law was "penal" in nature and therefore not entitled to full faith and credit.[26]

Thereafter, the federal court, on rehearing, reversed its prior holding on the ground that the Tennessee Supreme Court holding was controlling.[27]

The prevalent approach is followed in New York which requires filing of the articles of

incorporation and provides that corporate existence shall begin upon such filing. In a 1953 New York case,[28] the articles of incorporation were not filed until one month after they had been duly executed. During the interim an officer of the "corporation" executed a chattel mortgage, the validity of which was placed in issue by the litigation. The court held that there had been a valid mortgage, giving as alternative bases for its decision the *de facto* doctrine (there was a law under which there could be incorporation, as well as an attempt to incorporate, and an exercise of corporate powers) and ratification of a promoter's contract by the corporation's post-incorporation acceptance of benefits (use of property) with knowledge (the signer of the mortgage being also one of the incorporators).[29]

Somewhat analogous would be the failure to file with the secretary of state an approved amendment to the articles of incorporation. A New York decision in effect applied the *de facto* doctrine to such a case.[30] The shareholders unanimously approved a resolution calling for an amendment of the articles of incorporation to permit cumulative voting. The officers of the corporation, however, failed to file the amendment as directed, and the majority of the shareholders later objected when one of their number attempted to vote cumulatively. The shareholder who favored cumulative voting brought suit to enforce his vote, and the other shareholders based their defense on the requirement that a provision for cumulative voting must appear in the articles of incorporation or duly filed amendment thereof.[31] The court upheld the petitioner's right to vote cumulatively, on the ground that all the

24. Whitaker v. Mitchell Mfg. Co., 219 Ark. 779, 244 S.W.2d 965 (1952).

25. Doggrell v. Great Southern Box Co., 206 F.2d 671 (6th Cir. 1953).

26. Paper Products Co. v. Doggrell, 195 Tenn. 581, 261 S.W.2d 127, 42 A.L.R.2d 651 (1953), reh. denied 195 Tenn. 581, 261 S.W.2d 130 (1953). The Supreme Court of Arkansas in Burks v. Cook, 225 Ark. 756, 284 S.W.2d 855 (1955), again held that the organizers or shareholders of a de facto corporation were personally liable as partners but excepted those who withdrew from the corporation before the debt was incurred.

27. Doggrell v. Great Southern Box Co., 208 F.2d 310 (6th Cir. 1953).

28. Matter of Planz, 282 App.Div. 552, 125 N.Y.S.2d 750 (3d Dep't 1953).

29. See sections 111, 112 supra.

30. Matter of American Fibre Chair Seat Corp., 265 N.Y. 416, 193 N.E. 253 (1934).

31. Former McKinney's N.Y.Stock Corp.Law, § 49; see McKinney's N.Y.Bus.Corp.Law, § 618.

shareholders had agreed to the resolution, thus making their objection purely technical. In by-passing the statutory requirement, the court emphasized that the rights of third parties and interests of the state were not involved.

The *de facto* doctrine has been applied to mergers, consolidations, and dissolutions.[32]

The *de facto* doctrine also has been employed in situations where corporations have expired or been dissolved, especially when they have been subsequently revived or reinstated.[33]

It should be noted that the *de facto* doctrine may serve as a valuable shield to associates in a defective corporation who are sued in their individual capacities.[34] Cases of this nature arise most frequently when the corporation in question has become judgment-proof or is not subject to the court's jurisdiction.

Statutory provisions are being enacted increasingly to reduce the uncertainties in cases of defective incorporation.[35] The Model Business Corporation Act has been construed as having abolished the *de facto* doctrine.[36]

"CORPORATION BY ESTOPPEL"

141. Even when the de facto doctrine does not apply, collateral attack on corporateness might be barred on principles of estoppel, provided the necessary elements of holding out and reliance are present, to achieve a just result. In such cases, the term "corporation by estoppel", although somewhat misdescriptive, is sometimes employed. The Model Business Corporation Act has been construed as abolishing "corporation-by-estoppel" principles.

32. Provident Security Life Ins. Co. v. Gorsuch, 323 F.2d 839 (9th Cir. 1963), cert. denied 376 U.S. 950, 84 S.Ct. 966, 11 L.Ed.2d 970 (1964); Christensen v. Boss, 179 Neb. 429, 138 N.W.2d 716 (1965).

33. See section 144 infra.

34. See section 145 infra.

35. See section 142 infra.

36. Robertson v. Levy, 197 A.2d 443 (D.C.Ct.App. 1964).

"Corporation-by-estoppel" principles must be distinguished from the *de facto* doctrine, although, in a given case, one or both may be applied to achieve identical results.

Estoppel is an important consideration in cases involving defective incorporation, mainly because it supplements the *de facto* doctrine. Whenever there is no *de jure* corporation and defects are so serious as to preclude application of the *de facto* doctrine, collateral attack may nonetheless be barred provided elements of holding out and reliance are present.[1]

The term "corporation by estoppel" is itself misleading, since collateral attack may be denied even when there is no corporation at all, as well as where there is an irregular corporation which has not acquired corporate status generally. Third parties, associates, and the purported corporation itself are each subject to estoppel. One who has dealt with a "corporation" may be estopped from denying the latter's corporateness, or associates who held themselves out as a corporation may be estopped from claiming otherwise.[2]

Estoppel does not arise out of every case of holding out and reliance. In the final analysis, the circumstances and equities of a particular case control.

The Model Business Corporation Act has been construed as having abolished "corpo-

1. H. Ballantine, Ballantine on Corporations §§ 31, 32 (rev. ed. 1946); Comment, "Estoppel to Deny Corporate Existence", 31 Tenn.L.Rev. 336 (1964).

2. June v. Vibra Screw Feeders, Inc., 6 Mich.App. 484, 149 N.W.2d 480 (1967); Cranson v. International Business Mach. Corp., 234 Md. 477, 200 A.2d 33 (1964); Brandtjen & Kluge, Inc. v. Biggs, 205 Or. 473, 288 P.2d 1025 (1955); Kingsley v. English, 202 Minn. 258, 278 N.W. 154, 115 A.L.R. 654 (1938); Lowell-Woodward Hardware Co. v. Woods, 104 Kan. 729, 180 P. 734 (1919); Commercial Bank v. Pfeiffer, 108 N.Y. 242, 15 N.E. 311 (1888). Cf. Kidd v. Hilton of San Juan, Inc., 251 F.Supp. 465 (D.P.R. 1966); Frontier Refining Co. v. Kunkel's Inc., 407 P.2d 880 (Wyo.1965); Baker v. Bates-Street Shirt Co., 6 F.2d 854 (1st Cir. 1925). See Annot., 20 A.L.R.2d 1084 (1951). Compare partnership by estoppel, section 37 supra.

ration-by-estoppel" principles (as well as the *de facto* doctrine).[3]

CONSTITUTIONAL AND STATUTORY DEVELOPMENTS

142. **Constitutional and statutory provisions sometimes deal with one or more phases of defective incorporation: (a) by stating when corporate existence begins—thus classifying incorporation requirements as conditions precedent or conditions subsequent to incorporation; (b) by providing that the articles of incorporation, upon filing, or the formal "certificate of incorporation" when issued, constitutes conclusive evidence, presumptive or prima facie evidence, or evidence of incorporation, except possibly in certain direct proceedings by the state; (c) by eliminating dual filing, minimum stated capital, and other requirements; and (d) by defining the sanctions for noncompliance with various statutory requirements.**

Many jurisdictions have attempted by statute, and occasionally by constitutional provision, to deal with one or more phases of the problem of defective incorporation. Some statutes purport to codify the *de facto* doctrine so as to deny any collateral attack against corporateness whenever there has been a bona fide attempt to incorporate under an existing statute. Under rarer constitutional and statutory provisions, defective incorporation may not be raised as a defense. Under the several types of provisions, the state usually expressly preserves its own power to bring a direct action whenever corporate privileges are usurped.[1]

Several statutes provide that corporate existence begins upon the issuance of the "certificate of incorporation", and that such certificate is conclusive evidence that all conditions precedent to corporateness have been performed—except in so far as a direct action by the state is concerned.[2] Such statutes, at least in combination with statutes imposing personal liability on all persons assuming to act as a corporation without authority,[3] have been construed as abolishing both the *de facto* doctrine and corporation-by-estoppel principles.[4]

Statutes, by indicating when corporate existence begins, of course, tend to classify requirements as precedent or subsequent to incorporation. Besides the statutes providing that corporate existence begins upon the issue of a formal "certificate of incorporation" by the state, statutes variously provide that corporate existence begins upon the filing of the articles of incorporation with the secretary of state,[5] or with the court when such

[§ 141]
3. Robertson v. Levy, 197 A.2d 443 (D.C.Ct.App.1964).

[§ 142]
1. E. g., Arizona, Iowa, Kansas. See Ariz.Const. art. XIV, § 13 (prohibiting want of legal organization as defense); Del.Gen.Corp.Law, § 329 (1967) (prohibiting defective organization of corporation as defense). See also, e. g., Mont.Gen.Corp.Law, § 15–808 (1947) (due incorporation of any company, claiming in good faith to be corporation under law, and doing business as such, or its right to exercise corporate powers, shall not be inquired into collaterally in any private action to which such de facto corporation may be party, but such inquiry may be had at suit of state on information of attorney general), discussed in Dunham v. Natural Bridge Ranch Co., 115 Mont. 579, 147 P.2d 902 (1944). The

Montana statute also provides that one who assumes an obligation to an ostensible corporation, as such, cannot resist the obligation on the ground that there was in fact no such corporation until that fact has been adjudged in a direct proceeding for the purpose. Mont.Gen.Corp.Law, § 15–806 (1947). The new Montana Business Corporation Act, effective December 31, 1968, follows the Model Business Corporation Act.

2. ABA–ALI Model Bus.Corp.Act § 50; Arizona, Idaho, Indiana, Kentucky, Maryland, Minnesota, Mississippi, Montana, Nevada, Oklahoma, Rhode Island, South Carolina, South Dakota, Utah, Washington, West Virginia. Idaho and Kentucky require recording of such certificate before the transaction of any business. Some statutes make no express exception in favor of the state in a direct proceeding.

3. See note 13 infra.

4. Robertson v. Levy, 197 A.2d 443 (D.C.Ct.App.1964). Because a colorable and apparent compliance with the law is generally a requisite of "de facto" corporate existence, and because it is unlikely that any steps short of securing a certificate of incorporation would be held to constitute apparent compliance. See Comment, ABA–ALI Model Bus.Corp.Act § 50.

5. E. g., Hawaii, Maine, Massachusetts, New Jersey, New Mexico, New York, Ohio, Pennsylvania; see also Arkansas, California, Connecticut, Delaware, Missouri, Nebraska.

is the procedure,[6] or upon local filing in a few of the several jurisdictions requiring local filing.[7]

In some jurisdictions, the filing of the articles of incorporation amounts only to evidence or presumptive evidence of incorporation.[8]

Furthermore, modern corporate legislation has tended to minimize the area of defective incorporation by eliminating dual filing[9] or minimum stated capital[10] requirements, or by defining the sanctions for noncompliance with various statutory provisions.[11]

As a result, cases involving defective incorporation have been decreasing.[12]

In several jurisdictions, statutes expressly provide that persons assuming to act as a corporation without authority so to do shall be jointly and severally liable for all debts and liabilities incurred or arising as a result thereof.[13]

---

6. E. g., Alabama, Georgia.

7. E. g., Louisiana, Tennessee, Wisconsin.

8. *Evidence:* E. g., Delaware, Florida, Maryland, Missouri, Nebraska, New Jersey, New Mexico, Rhode Island, Utah, West Virginia, Wyoming. *Presumptive evidence* or *prima facie evidence:* E. g., Alabama, California, Connecticut, Idaho, Montana, Nevada, South Dakota. New York in 1963 changed the effect of filing from presumptive evidence to conclusive evidence.

9. See section 132 supra.

10. See section 126 supra.

11. See section 143 infra.

12. Frey, "Legal Analysis and the 'De Facto' Doctrine", 100 U.Pa.L.Rev. 1153, 1180, n. 96 (1952).

13. ABA–ALI Model Bus.Corp.Act § 139; Alaska, Colorado, Illinois, Montana, North Dakota, Oregon, Wyoming, District of Columbia. The Model Act comment reads: "The issuance of the certificate of incorporation, nothing more, nothing less, is the authority creating the existence of a corporation." The Model Act provisions have been construed as abolishing the de facto doctrine and corporation-by-estoppel principles. Robertson v. Levy, 197 A.2d 443 (D.C.Ct.App.1964). See also Frontier Refining Co. v. Kunkel's Inc., 407 P.2d 880 (Wyo.1965); Kinney v. Bank of Plymouth, 213 Iowa 267, 236 N.W. 31 (1931).

CONDITIONS PRECEDENT TO DOING BUSINESS

143. Several jurisdictions require that a corporation, before doing any business, have a minimum paid-in stated capital, or comply with various other requirements. Noncompliance subjects the designated corporate personnel to personal liability for corporate obligations either to the extent of the deficiency in the stated capital or without such limitation.

Statutes in several jurisdictions impose various requirements as conditions precedent to a corporation's doing any business.[1]

The most frequent provision prohibits a corporation from transacting any business or incurring any indebtedness, except such as shall be incidental to its organization or to obtaining subscriptions to or payment for its shares, until there has been paid in for the issuance of shares consideration of at least the value prescribed in the statute[2] or in the articles of incorporation.[3]

Other conditions precedent to doing business include local filings of the articles of incorporation,[4] filing of affidavits or certificates as to payment of required considera-

---

1. See Note, "Corporations—Conditions Precedent to Beginning Business—Personal Liability of Officers or Directors", 9 Kan.L.Rev. 446 (1961); Annot., 50 A.L.R. 1030 (1927).

2. E. g., ABA–ALI Model Bus.Corp.Act § 51 ($1,000), eliminated in 1969 Model Act revision; Illinois, Mississippi, North Dakota, Texas ($1,000); South Carolina ($1,000, $500 in cash); Vermont, Washington, Wyoming ($500); Arkansas ($300). Until 1967, Delaware had a $1,000 minimum paid-in capital requirement. New York, prior to 1963, permitted the articles of incorporation to set forth a minimum stated capital.

3. E. g., Indiana, Kansas, Kentucky, Louisiana, Tennessee ($1,000); Florida, Ohio, Oklahoma ($500 minimum); North Carolina (no minimum amount). The Oklahoma attorney general has ruled that insofar as consideration received for shares exceeds their par value, it must be allocated to paid-in surplus rather than to stated capital, and that therefore only the aggregate par value could be computed in determining compliance with the $500 minimum stated capital requirement. Okl.Op.Att'y Gen.No.63–125, Jan. 31, 1963.

4. E. g., Indiana, Kentucky, Louisiana.

tion for shares,[5] election of directors,[6] designation of registered office and agent,[7] etc.

Liable under the various statutory formulations are officers,[8] directors,[9] or other corporate personnel,[10] or at least those who participate,[11] assent,[12] or fail to dissent.[13]

5. E. g., Kansas, Oklahoma, Vermont.

6. E. g., Kentucky.

7. E. g., Arizona, Kentucky.

8. E. g., Kansas, Kentucky, Louisiana (prior to 1969), Vermont (president), Wisconsin. Temple Iron Works, Inc. v. Reburn Oil & Gas, Inc., 187 So.2d 160 (La.Ct.App.1966), writ refused 249 La. 472, 187 So.2d 446 (1966) (holding president of Louisiana corporation personally liable on corporate note for more than $9,000 where amount of capital stated in articles of incorporation had not been paid in).

9. E. g., ABA–ALI Model Bus.Corp.Act § 43(e); Alaska, Arkansas, Florida, Idaho, Kansas, Kentucky, Louisiana, North Carolina, Ohio, South Carolina, Texas. Sulphur Export Corp. v. Carribean Clipper Lines, Inc., 277 F.Supp. 632 (E.D.La.1968) (participating officers and nondissenting directors of Louisiana corporation held personally liable for more than $25,000 for corporation's failure to have $1,000 cash paid in as capital). Construction Engineering Co. v. Village Shopping Center, Inc., 168 So.2d 826 (La.Ct.App.1964), writ refused 247 La. 261, 170 So.2d 512 (1965) (holding promoters-shareholders-directors personally liable for $19,000 for failure to satisfy $1,000 minimum capital requirement even though they spent more than $1,000 for fees and lease for corporation); Tri-State Developers, Inc. v. Moore, 343 S.W.2d 812 (Ky.Ct.App.1961) (officer-director, who paid in $500, of $1,000 minimum stated capital required by Kentucky law, held personally liable for more than $10,000).

10. E. g., Ohio (incorporators), South Carolina (promoters, incorporators, shareholders, subscribers), Wisconsin (incorporators, subscribers for shares, shareholders). Fike v. Bauer, 90 Idaho 442, 412 P. 2d 819 (1966) (defendant who was not director, or officer held not liable).

11. E. g., Kansas, Kentucky, Louisiana (prior to 1969), Ohio, South Carolina.

12. E. g., ABA–ALI Model Bus.Corp.Act § 43(e); Alaska, Arkansas, North Carolina, Texas. See Blair v. Mueller, 299 F.2d 385 (10th Cir. 1962) (director of bankrupt Kansas corporation which had failed to file required treasurer's affidavit of paid-in capital held not personally liable for unsatisfied corporate indebtedness of $78,488 since he had become director after indebtedness had been incurred).

13. E. g., Idaho, Kansas, Kentucky, Louisiana (prior to 1969).

In some jurisdictions, such corporate personnel are subject to joint and several *unlimited* personal liability.[14]

Under other statutes, personal liability is limited to the unpaid part of the consideration prescribed in the statute or in the articles of incorporation.[15]

Such statutory liability usually will be enforced by the courts of another state by characterization of the statute as "remedial".[16]

Corporate transactions are usually not invalidated for commencing business before receipt of the minimum stated capital.[17]

EXPIRED/DISSOLVED/REVIVED/REINSTATED CORPORATION

144. Between expiration and revival of corporate existence de facto corporateness is usually recognized. If a charter is forfeited and later reinstated by the state, de facto corporateness during the interim is sometimes recognized.

Corporations of limited duration,[1] which are becoming increasingly rare, expire upon the termination of their period of duration unless previously extended or subsequently revived.[2]

14. E. g., Idaho, Kansas, Kentucky, Louisiana (prior to 1969), South Carolina.

15. E. g., ABA–ALI Model Bus.Corp.Act § 43(e); Alaska, Arkansas, Florida, North Carolina, Texas, Wisconsin.

16. In re Jensik's Estate, 34 Ill.App.2d 130, 180 N.E. 2d 740 (1963), cert. denied 372 U.S. 953, 83 S.Ct. 952, 9 L.Ed.2d 977 (1963) (Kansas statute held remedial and to survive defendant's death and to be enforceable in Illinois); Pullum Window Corp. v. Feldstein, 357 Mich. 82, 97 N.W.2d 762 (1959) (Indiana statute held remedial).

17. Ohio Gen.Corp.Law, § 1701.12 (1955); Allen v. Thompson, 248 Miss. 544, 158 So.2d 503 (1963) (grant of real property to Mississippi corporation before required $500 capital paid in upheld on ground corporation "was duly incorporated at least as a de facto corporation able to do business").

1. See section 120 supra.

2. See sections 345, 347 infra.

Statutes usually provide for effecting dissolution by corporate action without judicial proceedings, known as "nonjudicial dissolution", and for dissolution by judicial proceedings, known as "judicial dissolution".[3] Even absent statutory authorization, a court might dissolve a corporation for mismanagement [4] or even deadlock,[5] statutes often also provide for dissolution, or annulment or forfeiture of charter, in the event of various contingencies, such as failure to file required reports or to pay certain taxes.[6]

The *de facto* doctrine has been employed in cases involving corporations whose charters have expired.[7] If a charter expires and revival [8] is effected under a lawful provision authorizing the same, the corporation is usually deemed to have a *de facto* character in the interim between expiration and revival.[9]

A more difficult problem arises when the corporation continues its activity after the expiration of its charter without any attempt at revival. The courts have not been consistent in their treatment of such problems.[10]

3. See sections 348, 381 infra.

4. See section 375 infra.

5. See section 280 infra.

6. ABA–ALI Model Bus.Corp.Act §§ 87, 128.

7. Corporations having limited durations were common in the 19th century. Most modern corporations are formed with theoretically perpetual existence. See section 12, n. 13, section 75, n. 1, section 120 supra.

8. "Revival" occurs after expiration of the charter (or duration specified in the articles of incorporation or special act of the legislature creating the corporation), in contrast to "extension", which takes place before expiration. See section 347 infra.

9. See McKinney's N.Y.Gen.Corp.Law, § 49 (inapplicable to business corporations since 1963); Garzo v. Maid of the Mist Steamboat Co., 303 N.Y. 516, 104 N.E.2d 882 (1952); Elson v. Schmidt, 140 Neb. 646, 1 N.W.2d 314, 138 A.L.R. 641 (1941); Note, 19 St. John's L.Rev. 72 (1944); Annot., 13 A.L.R.2d 1220 (1950). But see Fla.Op.Att'y Gen.No.059–104 (June 4, 1959).

10. See Annot., 47 A.L.R. 1288 (1927), 97 A.L.R. 477 (1935); see also, e. g., Hall v. Kimsey, 48 Ga.App.

A similar problem occurs where the corporation has been dissolved or its charter forfeited by the state for failure to file required reports or pay required taxes, and is later reinstated. Some holdings recognize a *de facto* existence in the interim,[11] while others do not.[12] Absent any reinstatement, of course, corporateness is usually not recognized.[13]

A statute precluding collateral attack upon the existence of a defectively-organized

605, 173 S.E. 437 (1934); In re Solomon, 16 N.Y.S. 2d 472 (Sup.Ct.1939).

11. A. A. Sutain, Ltd. v. Montgomery Ward & Co., 22 A.D.2d 607, 257 N.Y.S.2d 724 (1st Dep't 1965), aff'd mem., 17 N.Y.2d 776, 270 N.Y.S.2d 626, 217 N. E.2d 674 (1966) (reinstated after dissolution by mistake); Industrial Coordinators, Inc. v. Artco, Inc., 366 Mich. 313, 115 N.W.2d 123 (1962); Spector v. Hart, 139 So.2d 923 (Fla.Dist.Ct.App.1962); Joseph A. Holpuch Co. v. United States, 58 F.Supp. 560 (Ct.Cl.1945); J. B. Wolfe, Inc. v. Salkind, 3 N.J. 312, 70 A.2d 72, 13 A.L.R.2d 1214 (1949); Note, 19 Md.L.Rev. 144 (1959). Reinstatement, of course, might expressly be nunc pro tunc or backdated. Colo.Op.Att'y Gen.No.60–3440 (Sept. 9, 1960). See Pacific Northwest Bell Tel. Co. v. Rivers, 88 Idaho 240, 398 P.2d 63 (1964) (temporary loss of charter held not to cost corporation its name).

12. New Hampshire Fire Ins. Co. v. Virgil & Frank's Locker Service, Inc., 302 F.2d 780 (8th Cir. 1962) (deed held void and not revived retroactively by reinstatement); City Nat'l Bank v. Jay Miles, Inc., 227 Cal.App.2d 837, 39 Cal.Rptr. 184 (1964); Moore v. Rommel, 223 Ark. 989, 350 S.W.2d 190 (1961); Dominion Oil Co. v. Lamb, 119 Colo. 62, 201 P.2d 372 (1948); see also Jorgensen v. Baker, 21 Ill.App. 2d 196, 157 N.E.2d 773 (1959); Poritzky v. Wachtel, 176 Misc. 633, 27 N.Y.S.2d 316 (Sup.Ct.1941). But see Gano v. Filter-Aid Co., 414 S.W.2d 480 (Tex. Civ.App.1967) (holding that corporate assets, on forfeiture of charter, vested proportionately in shareholders, and that reinstatement under subsequently enacted revival statute cannot constitutionally deprive nonconsenting shareholders of such rights).

13. Borbein, Young & Co. v. Cirese, 401 S.W.2d 940 (Mo.Ct.App.1966); Matter of Hare, 205 F.Supp. 881 (D.Md.1962) (partnership found for purposes of Federal Bankruptcy Act); R. V. McGinnis Theatres v. Video Independent Theatres, Inc., 386 F. 592 (10th Cir. 1967) (erroneous reinstatement under state law ignored); Comment, "Liability of Officers and Directors Who Continue the Business of a Corporation After Forfeiture of Its Charter", 1967 Wash. U.L.Q. 222. Cf. Vlasic Foods Co. v. Russek, 7 Mich.App. 359, 151 N.W.2d 872 (1967) (officers of corporation with *void* charter held not liable under statute rendering officers of *suspended* corporation personally liable for its debts contracted during period of delinquency).

corporation has been held limited to defects in incorporation and inapplicable to cases of forfeiture of the charter of a properly-organized corporation.[14]

CONSEQUENCES OF TOO DEFECTIVE INCORPORATION

145. When corporateness is successfully challenged because of defective incorporation, some cases have held that the enterprise was a partnership and the associates personally liable. Modern cases tend not to find a partnership. Alternative theories are breach of implied warranty of authority or joint venture, which limit personal liability to those who authorize, participate in, or ratify the acts upon which the asserted liability is predicated.

If a party is successful in collaterally attacking corporateness—because the "corporation" neither is *de jure* nor is protected against such attack by the *de facto* doctrine or corporation-by-estoppel principles—the consequences of such attack must be determined. The cases most often involve the problem of personal liability on the part of the associates in the too-defectively-incorporated enterprise.[1]

Under the old rule, all of the associates were held liable as partners, the theory being that the associated group was either a corporation or a partnership with its mutual agency.[2] This viewpoint failed to take into account the differentiation between active and inactive members of the group, as well as the objection that the shareholders did not intend to act as a partnership.

The more modern approach has been to examine each situation and thereby determine whether the too-defectively-incorporated enterprise should be treated as a partnership. Associates who assumed an inactive role and who believed that they were members of a valid corporation ought not to be held liable as partners.[3] Factors such as vesting authority in a "board of directors" and the absence of any holding out as partners (which might give rise to estoppel) assume importance under the modern view.

There are other theories upon which associates may be held liable by creditors.[4] For

14. Bland v. Knox Concrete Products, Inc., 207 Tenn. 206, 338 S.W.2d 605 (1960). But see Frederic G. Krapf & Son v. Gorson, —— Del.Ch. ——, 243 A.2d 713 (Sup.Ct.1968) (holding forfeiture of Delaware corporation's charter for inadvertent failure to pay franchise taxes not to render officer personally liable on contract he made in corporation's behalf after forfeiture of which he had no knowledge).

1. N. Lattin, The Law of Corporations 168 (1959); Dodd, "Partnership Liability of Stockholders in Defective Corporations", 40 Harv.L.Rev. 521 (1927); Magruder, "A Note on Partnership Liability of Stockholders in Defective Corporations", 40 Harv. L.Rev. 733 (1927); Carpenter, "Are the Members of a Defectively Organized Corporation Liable as Partners?", 8 Minn.L.Rev. 409 (1923); Lewinsohn, "Liability to Third Persons of Associates in Defectively Incorporated Associations", 13 Mich.L.Rev. 271 (1915); Baldwin, "Partnership Liability of Stockholders in De Facto Corporations", 8 Ill.L. Rev. 246 (1913); Burdick, "Are Defectively Incorporated Associations Partnerships?", 6 Colum.L.Rev. 1 (1906); Annot., 115 A.L.R. 658 (1938); Note, "Liability Under Defectively Organized Corporations", 26 Md.L.Rev. 354 (1966).

2. Gazette Publishing Co. v. Brady, 204 Ark. 396, 162 S.W.2d 494 (1942); Bonfils v. Hayes, 70 Colo. 336, 201 P. 677 (1921); Meyer v. Brunson, 104 S.C. 84, 88 S.E. 359 (1916); Smith v. Schoodoc Bond Packing Co., 109 Me. 555, 84 A. 268 (1912); Harrill v. Davis, 168 F. 187 (8th Cir. 1909). Noncompliance with the dual filing requirements of the Arkansas statute [Ark.Bus.Corp.Act §§ 64–102 to 64–104 (1957), repeal effective Jan. 1, 1966] had been construed as resulting in such liability, even when most other jurisdictions would apply the de facto doctrine. See, e. g., Burks v. Cook, 225 Ark. 756, 284 S.W.2d 855 (1955) (all associates, except those who withdrew prior to debt, held liable where articles of incorporation filed with secretary of state but not with county clerk); Whitaker v. Mitchell Mfg. Co., 219 Ark. 779, 244 S.W.2d 965 (1952). But cf. Paper Products Co. v. Doggrell, 195 Tenn. 581, 261 S.W.2d 127, 42 A.L.R.2d 651 (1953), reh. denied 195 Tenn. 581, 261 S.W.2d 130 (1953) (such liability in de facto corporation held penal in nature and not enforceable outside state); Doggrell v. Great Southern Box Co., 206 F.2d 671 (6th Cir. 1953) (2–1), rev'd on other grounds on rehearing, 208 F.2d 310 (6th Cir. 1953) (2–1) (ruling by Tennessee Supreme Court held controlling on federal court under Erie-Tompkins rule, and neither full faith and credit clause nor comity required Tennessee to enforce Arkansas penalties). See section 142, n. 11 supra. For other liabilities resulting from noncompliance with statutes, see sections 142, 143 supra.

3. Beck v. Stimmel, 39 Ohio App. 510, 177 N.E. 920 (1931); Baker v. Bates-Street Shirt Co., 6 F.2d 854 (1st Cir. 1925); Fay v. Noble, 61 Mass. (7 Cush.) 188 (1851).

4. R. Stevens, Handbook on the Law of Private Corporations §§ 31, 32 (2d ed. 1949).

instance, there is a possibility that an action may lie for breach of an implied warranty of authority brought against those who have acted on behalf of the supposed corporation. The same is true of an action based on a theory of joint venture against those who have acted or who have authorized or ratified such acts (there being no, or at most a, limited implied mutual agency in a joint venture).

In many jurisdictions, legislation has been enacted so that actions may be based upon statutory liability expressly imposed on certain persons acting for a too-defectively-incorporated enterprise,[5] or even for a *de jure* corporation which has failed to comply with prescribed conditions precedent to doing business.[6]

A very distinguished commentator, after analyzing more than 200 cases involving the question of the liability of associates in defectively-incorporated enterprises, has demonstrated that their holdings are irreconcilable.[7]

C. DISREGARD OF CORPORATENESS

"PIERCING THE CORPORATE VEIL"

146. Disregard of corporateness in various cases of technically-correct incorporation—often called "piercing the corporate veil"—is the converse of the recognition of corporateness in instances of defective incorporation. The general rule, subject to exceptions, is that corporateness, with attendant corporate attributes, will be recognized and not disregarded. Corporateness will not be recognized to produce unjust or undesirable consequences inconsistent with the purpose of the concept.

Incorporation for the purpose of achieving limited liability is recognized in most jurisdictions on the theory that limited liability is one of the principal objectives of incorporation. Limited liability is enjoyed even by a controlling shareholder where corporate formalities are observed, initial financing is reasonably adequate, the corporation is not formed to evade an existing obligation or a statute, or to cheat or to defraud.

Corporate property is usually regarded as belonging to the corporation and not to the shareholders, although exceptions are occasionally made when creditors or other shareholders are not prejudiced.

Under corporate contracts, ordinarily the corporation, and not the shareholders, enjoys the rights and suffers the liabilities. Guaranties present some unusual problems. When the corporate entity is recognized, a shareholder may become a creditor of the corporation, secured or unsecured, by loaning it money, performing services for it, transferring property to it, etc., subject to certain limitations. Directors and officers who cause their corporation to breach its contract with a third party are usually not liable for inducing breach of contract.

The converse of the recognition of corporateness in some instances of defective incorporation [1] is the disregard of corporateness in various cases of technically-correct incorporation. Such disregard, in terms of metaphor, is often called "piercing the corporate veil".[2]

---

5. See section 142, n. 13 supra; ABA–ALI Model Bus.Corp.Act § 139: "All persons who assume to act as a corporation without authority so to do shall be jointly and severally liable for all debts and liabilities incurred or arising as a result therefrom." See also former Iowa Gen.Corp.Law, § 491.-22 (1950, repealed 1959) (failure to comply substantially with incorporation requirements renders individual property of shareholders liable for corporate debts), discussed in Kenney v. Bank of Plymouth, 213 Iowa 267, 236 N.W. 31 (1931). See also Pullum Window Corp. v. Feldstein, 357 Mich. 82, 97 N.W.2d 762 (1959), discussed in section 142, n. 16 supra; Annot., 50 A.L.R. 1030 (1927).

6. See section 143 supra.

7. Frey, "Legal Analysis and the 'De Facto' Doctrine", 100 U.Pa.L.Rev. 1153, 1174 (1952).

1. See sections 139–145 supra.

2. The judicial opinions indulge in verbal characterizations, epithets, and metaphors: "mere adjunct", "agent", "alias", "alter ego", "alter", "idem", "arm", "blind", "branch", "buffer", "cloak", "coat", "corporate double", "cover", "creature", "curious remini-

Theories of corporate personality,[3] of course, are relevant [4] in determining when, in a particular case, one or more of the normal corporate attributes [5] will not be recognized. The entity theory—that the corporation is a separate entity, distinct from its shareholders—provides the traditional basis for the concept of limited liability, as well as the corporation's capacity to hold property, to contract not only with outsiders but also with its own shareholders, to sue and to be sued, and to enjoy continued existence notwithstanding changes in its membership.

General Rule; Exceptions

The rest of this chapter discusses the extent to which courts have gone in upholding corporateness and, conversely, in what situations they have seen fit to disregard corporateness or to "pierce the corporate veil".[6]

scence", "delusion", "department", "dry shell", "dummy", "fiction", "form", "formality", "fraud on the law", "instrumentality", "mouthpiece", "name", "nominal identity", "phrase", "puppet", "screen", "sham", "simulacrum", "snare", "stooge", "subterfuge", "tool". See E. Latty & G. Frampton, Basic Business Associations: Cases, Text and Problems 721 (1963). Various terms are often combined in artful phraseology. As Cardozo, J., wrote in Berkey v. Third Avenue Ry., 244 N.Y. 84, 94–95, 155 N. E. 58, 61, 50 A.L.R. 599, 604–605 (1926), reargument denied 244 N.Y. 602, 155 N.E. 914, 50 A.L.R. 610 (1927): "The whole problem of the relation between parent and subsidiary corporations is one that is still enveloped in the mists of metaphor. Metaphors in law are to be narrowly watched, for starting as devices to liberate thought, they end often by enslaving it. We say at times that the corporate entity will be ignored when the parent corporation operates a business through a subsidiary which is characterized as an 'alias' or a 'dummy'. All this is well enough if the picturesqueness of the epithets does not lead us to forget that the essential term to be defined is the act of operation. Dominion may be so complete, interference so obtrusive, that by the general rules of agency the parent will be a principal and the subsidiary an agent. Where control is less than this, we are remitted to the tests of honesty and justice. . . ." In In re Clark's Will, 204 Minn. 574, 578, 284 N.W. 876, 878 (1939), Stone, J., said: "Many cases present avowed disregard of corporate entity. . . . But they all came to just this—courts simply will not let interposition of corporate entity or action prevent a judgment otherwise required. Corporate presence and action no more than those of an individual will bar a remedy demanded by law in application to facts. Hence the process is not accurately termed one of disregarding corporate entity. It is rather and only a refusal to permit its presence and action to divert the judicial course of applying law to ascertained facts. The method neither pierces any veil nor goes behind any obstruction, save for its refusal to let one fact bar the judgment which the whole sum of facts requires. For such reasons, we feel that the method of decision known as 'piercing the corporate veil' or 'disregarding the corporate entity' unnecessarily complicates decision. It is dialectically ornate and correctly guides understanding, but over a circuitous and unrealistic trail. The objective is more easily attainable over the direct and unencumbered route followed herein."

3. After a thorough review of various theories of corporate personality, Bijur, J., in Farmers' Loan & Trust Co. v. Pierson, 130 Misc. 110, 119, 222 N.Y.S. 532, 543–544 (Sup.Ct.1927), concluded: "The concrete import of these views is that a corporation is more nearly a method than a thing, and that the law in dealing with a corporation has no need of defining it as a person or an entity, or even as an embodiment of functions, rights and duties, but may treat it as a name for a useful and usual collection of jural relations, each one of which

must in every instance be ascertained, analyzed and assigned to its appropriate place according to the circumstances of the particular case, having due regard to the purposes to be achieved. . . ." The United States Court of Appeals for the Fifth Circuit expressed the idea this way: "It is one thing to observe the corporate fiction as if the fiction were the truth—when the fiction is not abused. It is quite a different thing when the sole stockholder either ignores the corporation as a separate entity or uses the corporate fiction as an instrument of deceit. Here the corporation and the individual owner were two sides of a single false coin". Mayo v. Pioneer Bank & Trust Co., 270 F.2d 823, 830 (5th Cir. 1959), reh. denied, 274 F.2d 320 (5th Cir. 1960), cert. denied, 362 U.S. 962, 80 S.Ct. 878, 4 L.Ed.2d 877 (1960).

4. See section 78 supra.

5. See section 79 supra.

6. W. Hamilton, On the Composition of the Corporate Veil (1946); W. Anderson, Limitations of the Corporate Entity: A Treatise of the Law Relating to the Overriding of the Corporate Fiction (1931); I. Wormser, Disregard of the Corporate Fiction and Allied Corporation Problems (1927); Kaufer, "Pleading Facts Sufficient to Disregard the Corporate Entity", 40 L.A.B.Bull. 131 (1965); Samuels, "Lifting the Veil", 1964 J.Bus.L. 107; Hughes, "Piercing the Veil: A Clue to Legal Thought", 11 U.Kan.L.Rev. 527 (1963); Cohn & Simitris, " 'Lifting the Veil' in the Company Laws of the European Continent", 12 Int. & Comp.L.Q. 189 (1963); Berle, "The Theory of Enterprise Entity", 47 Colum.L.Rev. 342 (1947); Ke Chin Wang, "The Corporate Entity Concept (or Fiction Theory) and the Modern Business Organization", 28 Minn.L.Rev. 341 (1944); Horowitz, "Disregarding the Entity of Private Corporations", 14 Wash.L.Rev. 285 (1939); Latty, "The Corporate Entity as a Solvent of Legal Problems",

In cases involving government-owned corporations, the courts sometimes have treated the corporation as an entity apart from the government, and other times have disregarded the entity, in determining whether or not sovereign privileges should be afforded to the activity carried on by such corporation.[7]

Corporate privileges—such as limited liability—vanish whenever corporateness is disregarded. At the same time, however, the shareholder may directly benefit in certain cases if corporateness is disregarded.[8]

The general rule, subject to exceptions, is that corporateness—with attendant corporate attributes—will be recognized and will not be disregarded: [9]

"If any general rule can be laid down, in the present state of authority, it is that a corporation will be looked upon as a legal entity as a general rule, and until sufficient reason to the contrary appears; but, when the notion of legal entity is used to defeat public convenience, justify wrong, protect fraud, or defend crime, the law will regard the corporation as an association of persons. * * *"

This general rule, with its exceptions, has been applied as a form of judicial regulation of corporations, both large and small, notwithstanding their full compliance with statutory incorporation requirements. The test is simply whether or not recognition of corporateness would produce unjust or undesirable consequences inconsistent with the purpose of the concept.[10]

The concept will be sustained only so long as it is invoked and employed for legitimate purposes. Perversion of the concept to improper uses and dishonest ends (e. g., to perpetuate fraud, to evade the law, to escape obligations), on the other hand, will not be countenanced. In between are various situations where the courts might disregard corporateness to achieve a just result.[11]

While the same principles for disregarding corporateness apply whether the corporation has one shareholder or many shareholders,[12] the facts necessary for the application of such principles are most frequently encountered in cases of one-man, family, and other close corporations,[13] and subsidiary or other affiliated corporations.[14]

Liability Aspects

Apart from corporation law principles, a shareholder, whether a natural person or a corporation, may be liable on the ground that such shareholder's activity resulted in the liability. Such a result might follow where a contract is construed as having been made by or in behalf of such shareholder or where a tort is committed by such shareholder or by a servant, employee, or agent of such shareholder (*respondeat superior*). If a corporation conveys its assets to a shareholder in fraud of creditors, the assets may

---

34 Mich.L.Rev. 597 (1936). See also Schifferman, "The Alter Ego Doctrine in California", in Advising California Business Enterprises 785–807 (1958); Comment, "Alternative Methods Of Piercing The Corporate Veil In Contract And Tort Cases", 48 B.U.L.Rev. 123 (1968); Comment, "Piercing the Corporate Veil in Wyoming", 17 Wyo.L.J. 63 (1962); Comment, "Piercing the Corporate Veil", 78 L.Q.Rev. 472 (1962); Note, "Piercing the Corporate Veil under International Law", 16 Syracuse L.Rev. 779 (1965); Note, "Piercing the Corporate Veil in Illinois", 6 DePaul L.Rev. 244 (1957).

7. See section 91 supra.

8. Courts are reluctant to disregard corporateness for the benefit of shareholders. See section 149 infra.

9. Sanborn, J., in United States v. Milwaukee Refrigerator Transit Co., 142 F.2d 247, 255 (C.C.E.D. Wis.1905).

10. R. Stevens, Handbook on the Law of Private Corporations § 18 (2d ed. 1949). While generalizations are dangerous, it is probably fair to polarize the New York courts as recognizers of corporateness and the Texas courts as disregarders of corporateness.

11. Cataldo, "Limited Liability With One-Man Companies and Subsidiary Corporations", 18 Law & Contemp.Prob. 473, 480–482 (1953).

12. The general rule becomes less subject to exceptions as the number of shareholders increases.

13. See section 147 infra.

14. See section 148 infra.

be reached on principles of fraudulent conveyance.[15]

Incorporation for the purpose of avoiding unlimited liability is recognized in most jurisdictions, on the theory that limited liability is one of the principal objectives of incorporation.[16] While there are holdings to the contrary, suggesting that such incorporation is a fraud in law, such cases have usually involved inadequate initial financing or other factors.[17]

The prevailing rule is that where corporate formalities are substantially observed, initial financing reasonably adequate, and the corporation not formed to evade an existing obligation or a statute or to cheat or to defraud, even a controlling shareholder enjoys limited liability.[18]

Contract Liability

Initially, a contract might give rise to a construction problem as to the intended undertakings, persons to perform them, and liability for default.[19] By the general rule,

contractual obligations of a corporation subject it, but not its shareholders, to liability thereon. After all, a contractual obligee can select his obligor, and the law thus effectuates the reasonable expectation of the parties.[20]

However, where the corporation is launched with inadequate finances,[21] or

---

parole evidence rule might preclude going behind a written instrument. Wagner v. Manufacturers' Trust Co., 237 App.Div. 175, 261 N.Y.S. 136 (1st Dep't 1932), aff'd mem. 261 N.Y. 699, 185 N.E. 799 (1933). But see First Western Bank & Trust Co. v. Bookasta, 267 Cal.App.2d 910, 73 Cal.Rptr. 657 (1968).

20. Contractors Heating & Supply Co. v. Scherb, 163 Colo. 584, 432 P.2d 237 (1967) (absence of corporate formalities alone held no basis for imposing personal liability on president-shareholder of family corporation); Fisser v. International Bank, 282 F.2d 231 (2d Cir. 1960) (contracting corporation held not alter ego of defendant corporation); Bartle v. Home Owners Cooperative, Inc., 309 N.Y. 103, 127 N.E.2d 832 (1955) (6–1); Kingston Dry Dock Co. v. Lake Champlain Transp. Co., 31 F.2d 265 (2d Cir. 1929); New York Trust Co. v. Carpenter, 250 F. 668 (6th Cir. 1918). Compare Olympic Capital Corp. v. Newman, 276 F.Supp. 646 (C.D.Cal.1967) (holding "alter ego" doctrine limited to disregard corporate entity to reach individuals and not vice versa), with American Petroleum Exchange, Inc. v. Lord, 339 S. W.2d 213 (Tex.Civ.App.1966). Comment, "Disregarding the Corporate Entity: Contract Claims", 28 Ohio St.L.J. 441 (1967).

21. Francis O. Day Co. v. Shapiro, 105 U.S.App.D.C. 392, 267 F.2d 669, 673 (1959) ("An obvious inadequacy of capital, measured by the nature and magnitude of the corporate undertaking"); Riddle v. Leuschner, 51 Cal.2d 574, 335 P.2d 107 (1959); Holland v. Joy Candy Mfg. Co., 14 Ill.App.2d 531, 145 N.E.2d 101 (1957). But see Associates Development Corp. v. Air Control Products, Inc., 392 S.W.2d 542 (Tex.Civ.App.1965) (recovery against shareholder denied where seller dealt only with corporation and its capitalization was matter of public record). Financial inadequacy is measured by the nature and magnitude of the corporate undertaking or the reasonableness of the cushion for creditors at the time of the inception of the corporation. Inadequate financing appears to be stressed more in the subsidiary or other affiliated corporation cases than in the one-man family, or other close corporation cases. Note, "Inadequately Capitalized Subsidiaries", 19 U.Chi.L.Rev. 872, n. 1 (1952). For recent discussions of financial inadequacy, see Automotriz del Golfo de California, S. A. v. Resnick, 47 Cal.2d 792, 306 P.2d 1 (1957). Obviously, initially adequate finances can dwindle under the pressure of competition or bad times. Arnold v. Phillips, 117 F.2d 497 (5th Cir. 1941), cert. denied, 313 U.S. 583, 61 S.Ct. 1102, 85 L.Ed. 1539 (1941); Luckenbach S. S. Co. v. W. R. Grace & Co., 267 F. 676 (4th Cir. 1920), cert.

---

15. Zaist v. Olson, 154 Conn. 563, 227 A.2d 552 (1967); World Broadcasting System, Inc. v. Bass, 160 Tex. 261, 328 S.W.2d 863 (1959); Loughran v. Reynolds, 53 Cal.App.2d 250, 127 P.2d 586 (1942). See Note, 71 Harv.L.Rev. 1122, 1123–1124 (1958).

16. Ramey v. Koons, 230 F.2d 802 (5th Cir. 1956); Elenkrieg v. Siebrecht, 238 N.Y. 254, 144 N.E. 519, 34 A.L.R. 592 (1924); Buckner v. Dillard, 184 Okl. 586, 89 P.2d 326 (1939); Sayers v. Navillus Oil Co., 41 S.W.2d 506 (Tex.Civ.App.1931).

17. Dixie Coal Mining & Mfg. Co. v. Williams, 221 Ala. 331, 128 So. 799 (1930); Goldberg v. Engelberg, 34 Cal.App.2d 10, 92 P.2d 935 (1939). Inadequate initial financing is stressed in the California decisions.

18. Garrett & Garrett, "Choosing the Form of Business Enterprise", 1954 Ill.L.F. 359, 367. See also Dix, "Adequate Risk Capital: The Considerations for the Benefits of Separate Incorporation", 53 Nw.U.L.Rev. 478 (1958); Annot., 63 A.L.R.2d 1051 (1959). Adequate initial financing should not be confused with formal minimum paid-in capital requirements applicable in several jurisdictions. See sections 126, 143 supra. Cf. Beall v. Pacific Nat. Bank, 55 Wash.2d 210, 347 P.2d 550 (1959) (contract by 88 percent shareholder to sell corporate assets held invalid).

19. Klekamp v. Blaw-Knox Co., 179 F.Supp. 328 (S. D.Cal.1959); Weisser v. Mursam Shoe Corp., 127 F.2d 344 (2d Cir. 1942). The statute of frauds or

where its financial resources are drained off by the controlling shareholder or shareholders,[22] or where other of the factors previously mentioned are present, there is more justification for holding the latter liable. Of course, if a shareholder guarantees a corporate obligation, such shareholder would be secondarily liable thereon according to principles of contract law.[23]

Tort Liability

A victim of tort in the usual case can hardly be said to have selected his tort-feasor. Nevertheless, shareholders as such are, according to the general rule, not liable for corporate torts,[24] but they might be where formalities are not substantially observed, initial financing was not adequate, etc.[25]

Property Aspects

Under the general rule, the corporate property is treated as belonging to the corporation and not to the shareholders.[26] It, through its duly-constituted board of directors and officers, acquires, holds, and conveys its property. Corporate creditors may enforce their claims against corporate property; creditors of the shareholders enforce their claims against the individual property of the shareholders, including the shares owned by the latter in the corporation, but not against corporate property.[27] Corporate claims are asserted by the corporation or in

---

denied, 254 U.S. 644, 41 S.Ct. 14, 65 L.Ed. 454 (1920). See also Temple v. Bodega Bay Fisheries, Inc., 180 Cal.App.2d 279, 384, 4 Cal.Rptr. 300, 304 (1960) ("unencumbered capital reasonably adequate for the prospective liabilities").

22. E. g., by causing payment of unwarranted dividends, exacting unreasonable management charges, forcing corporation to do business with controlling shareholder at loss. See Note, 71 Harv.L.Rev. 1122, 1129 (1958).

23. See text accompanying section 150, nn. 26, 27 infra.

24. Zubik v. Zubik, 384 F.2d 267 (3d Cir. 1967), cert. denied 390 U.S. 988, 88 S.Ct. 1183, 19 L.Ed.2d 1291 (1968). See footnote 14, 384 F.2d at 273: Counsel have been unable to cite a case where the corporate entity was disregarded to make an individual liable for tort. Elenkrieg v. Siebrecht, 238 N.Y. 254, 144 N.E. 519, 34 A.L.R. 592 (1924); Berkey v. Third Avenue Ry., 244 N.Y. 84, 155 N.E. 58, 50 A.L.R. 599 (1926); Chesapeake Stone Co. v. Holbrook, 168 Ky. 128, 181 S.W. 953 (1916).

25. Sisco-Hamilton Co. v. Lennan, 240 F.2d 68 (7th Cir. 1957); Ross v. Pennsylvania R. R., 106 N.J.L. 536, 148 A. 741 (1930); Costan v. Manila Electric Co., 24 F.2d 383 (2d Cir. 1928); Walkovszky v. Carlton, 18 N.Y.2d 414, 276 N.Y.S.2d 585, 223 N.E.2d 6 (1966) (holding, 5 to 2, shareholder of 10 corporations, each owning two mortgaged cabs, valuable but judgment-proof medallions, and with required minimum $10,000 liability insurance per cab, allegedly operated as a single business with respect to financing, supplies, repairs, employees, garaging, not personally liable, absent allegation that he was conducting business in his individual capacity, on remand 29 A.D.2d 763, 287 N.Y.S.2d 546 (2d Dep't 1968) (4–1), aff'd mem. 23 N.Y.2d 714, 296 N.Y.S.2d 362, 244 N.E.2d 55 (1968) (upholding amended complaint against shareholder as sufficiently alleging

he and others were conducting business of taxicab fleet in their individual capacities as opposed to use of corporate form); Mangan v. Terminal Transp. System, 247 App.Div. 853, 286 N.Y.S.2d 666 (3d Dep't 1936), motion for leave to appeal denied, 272 N.Y. 676 (1936) (where four taxicab corporations were under common control with fifth corporation which serviced, inspected, repaired, and dispatched cabs and whose name appeared on all cabs, fifth corporation held liable for negligent operation of cab owned and operated by one of four other corporations). Turner v. Andrea Service Corp., 157 N.Y. L.J. No. 92, 17 (Sup.Ct.1967) (holding not liable principal shareholder and brother-sister taxicab corporations of corporation whose employee was negligent, even though he had personally guaranteed the corporations' debts and property of corporations but not his own were commingled, in the absence of personal negligence by him in management of business); Robinson v. Chase Maintenance Corp., 20 Misc.2d 90, 190 N.Y.S.2d 773 (Sup.Ct.1959) (complaint for injury from taxicab owned by two-cab corporation sustained against parent corporation which owned all shares of it and 50 other two-cab corporations but dismissed against individual sole shareholder of parent corporation); Mull v. Colt Co., 31 F.R.D. 154 (S.D.N.Y.1962) (allowing pedestrian injured by cab belonging to one of 100 two-cab multiple corporations to proceed against all corporations and their shareholders, based on allegations of inadequate capitalization and common centralized garaging, maintenance, and operations); Atkins, "The Impact of the Growth of Enterprise Liability on the Theory of Damages in Accident Cases", 20 La.L.Rev. 50 (1959); Comment, "Should Shareholders Be Personally Liable for the Torts of Their Corporations?", 76 Yale L.J. 1190 (1967); Note, "Piercing the Taxi Medallion", 19 N.Y.U.Intra.L.Rev. 1 (1963).

26. Parker v. Bethel Hotel Co., 96 Tenn. 252, 34 S.W. 209 (1896); Button v. Hoffman, 61 Wis. 20, 20 N.W. 667 (1884).

27. But see Shamrock Oil and Gas Co. v. Ethridge, 159 F.Supp. 693 (D.Colo.1958) (judgment against controlling shareholder enforced against corporate property).

its behalf (e. g., in a shareholder's *derivative* action) but not by the shareholder in a direct action.[28]

Where a fiduciary controls a corporation through shares in the trust estate, he might, in the interest of full disclosure, be required to account not only with respect to the shares but also for his administration of corporate affairs as a corporate director or officer.[29]

Contractual Aspects

An occasion for disregarding corporateness may arise when a shareholder attempts to contract for the corporation without first observing the necessary formalities (e. g., approval by the board of directors). Courts have sustained such contracts, holding that the corporation is the *"alter ego"* of the shareholder, or that a sole shareholder's authority is coextensive with that of the board of directors. In any event, any requirement that contracts must first be approved by the board of directors will not necessarily control.

Guaranty

Guaranties present some unusual problems, and inconsistent judicial holdings. The Supreme Court of California held that a guaranty to pay for the goods supplied an individual proprietorship ("Joe Goldberg, doing business under the name of 'Home Builders Supply Co.' ") covered goods supplied to the business after it became a one-man corporation,[30] while the Supreme Judicial Court of Massachusetts held that a guaranty given to a partnership for bills

contracted "at your house" did not survive the transition of the latter to a close corporation.[31]

Status of Shareholder as Creditor

Since the corporation, under the general rule, is a separate legal person from its shareholders, it may *bona fide* contract with them. The share contract itself is an obvious example. The shareholder may also become a creditor of his corporation, by loaning it money,[32] performing services for it,[33] transferring property to it,[34] etc.

Miscellaneous

The technical separateness of the corporation from its directors and officers is not recognized when they, acting properly in such capacity, cause the corporation to breach its contract with a third person. Accordingly, they are usually not liable to such third person for inducing breach of contract,[35] but they will be subjected to such liability when they cause the breach in their own rather than the corporation's interest.[36]

---

28. Wolf v. S. H. Wintman Co., 87 R.I. 156, 139 A.2d 84 (1958).

29. Matter of Hubbell, 302 N.Y. 246, 97 N.E.2d 888, 47 A.L.R.2d 176 (1951); Farmers' Loan & Trust Co. v. Pierson, 130 Misc. 110, 222 N.Y.S. 532 (Sup.Ct. 1927). See also In re Herrick's Estate, 161 N.Y.S. 2d 690 (Sur.Ct.1957). Cf. Matter of Greenberg, 208 Misc. 279, 143 N.Y.S.2d 226 (Sur.Ct.1955).

30. D. N. & E. Walter & Co. v. Zuckerman, 214 Cal. 418, 6 P.2d 251, 79 A.L.R. 329 (1931).

31. Jordan Marsh Co. v. Beals, 201 Mass. 163, 87 N. E. 471 (1909).

32. The corporation's giving of security for past loans may be suspect or constitute a preference. As to security for contemporaneous loan, see Annot., 31 A.L.R.2d 663 (1953). In an inadequate capitalization situation, such loans might be treated as capital contributions. See Arnold v. Phillips, 117 F.2d 497 (5th Cir. 1941), cert. denied 313 U.S. 583, 61 S.Ct. 1102, 85 L.Ed. 1539 (1941). The converse—loans by the corporation to shareholders—is sometimes barred by statute.

33. Such services, of course, should be *bona fide* and charged at their reasonable value. Accrued salary claims may be suspect. Pepper v. Litton, 308 U.S. 295, 60 S.Ct. 238, 84 L.Ed. 281 (1939). See section 152 infra.

34. Such transfers and valuations of the property should satisfy the test of an arm's-length bargain. Transfers or distributions of corporate property to shareholders are subject to various restrictions. See Chapter 12 infra.

35. See section 234, n. 28 infra.

36. Ehrlich v. Alper, 145 N.Y.S.2d 252 (Sup.Ct.1955), aff'd mem. 1 A.D.2d 875, 149 N.Y.S.2d 562 (1st Dep't 1956).

ONE–MAN, FAMILY, AND OTHER CLOSE CORPORATIONS

147. Corporateness of one-man, family, or other close corporations will be recognized, in the absence of illegitimate purpose, if (a) the business is conducted on a corporate and not on a personal basis, and (b) the enterprise was established on an adequate financial basis.

One-man, family, and other close corporations[1] have long been popular since they afford a means of combining limited liability with the degree of control found in an individual proprietorship or partnership. With the possibility of avoiding double federal income taxation under the Technical Amendments Act of 1958,[2] such corporations should prove even more popular. While there is considerable doubt as to whether the concept of corporateness was originally intended to embrace these enterprises, they have nevertheless received judicial sanction and approval.[3] At the same time, however,

a body of law has developed, governing the instances in which their corporateness may be disregarded.

A growing number of jurisdictions permit less than three incorporators.[4] Even the older requirements, however, do not pose a serious obstacle to the person interested in controlling a one-man corporation (or two persons with respect to a family or other close corporation) and thereby obtaining the benefits of limited liability, perpetual duration, possibly minimized taxes, possible avoidance of usury statutes, and other corporate attributes. A common practice is to employ "accommodation" or "dummy" incorporators, and then to obtain all outstanding subscriptions and/or shares (except possibly for qualifying shares).[5]

Once the one-man, family, or close corporation has been set in motion, various problems involving corporateness may arise, the basic question being whether for this or that purpose the enterprise will be treated as a corporation or as an individual proprietorship or partnership.

It is a well-settled rule that ownership of all or almost all the shares by one individual or a few individuals does not afford sufficient grounds for disregarding corporateness. However, the rule that corporateness will be sustained only so long as it is used for legitimate purposes has special signifi-

---

1. Latty, "A Conceptualistic Tangle and the One-or Two-Man Corporation", 34 N.C.L.Rev. 471 (1956); Cataldo, "Limited Liability With One-Man Companies and Subsidiary Corporations", 18 Law & Contemp.Prob. 473 (1953); Fuller, "The Incorporated Individual: A Study of the One-Man Company", 51 Harv.L.Rev. 1373 (1938); Comment, "Corporations: Preserving the Separate Entity of the Oklahoma Close Corporation", 21 Okla.L.Rev. 205 (1968); Note, "Theory of the Corporate Entity and the One-Man Corporation in Louisiana", 38 Tul.L.Rev. 738 (1964); Note, "One-Man Corporations—Scope and Limitations", 100 U.Pa.L.Rev. 853 (1952).

2. See section 76 supra and section 262 infra.

3. In the famous case of Salomon v. Salomon & Co., [1897] A.C. 22, Salomon in 1892 had incorporated his business, conveying its assets to the new company in return for one hundred £100 debentures (English floating-charge type) and 20,001 shares (the other six shares being allotted to his wife and five children to satisfy the then English law requirement of at least seven associates). When the company failed in 1893, the general creditors contended *arguendo* no entity, that such incorporation to escape personal liability was fraudulent, and, *arguendo* entity, that the company was an agent or trustee for Salomon. The House of Lords upheld the principal shareholder's right to become a secured corporate creditor and thereby not only escape personal liability to, but as such creditor acquire priority over, unsecured creditors. The fact that Salomon had incorporated for the purpose of achieving limited liability was deemed immaterial on the ground that it was a legitimate and permissible objective of incor-

poration. Accord, Robertson v. Roy L. Morgan Production Co., 411 F.2d 1041 (10th Cir. 1969).

4. See section 131 supra.

5. See sections 131, 135 supra. Older statutes required that each director own at least one share of stock; others imposed such a requirement unless the articles of incorporation or bylaws dispensed with it; still others permitted the corporation to impose such requirement. See section 130 supra. See Park Terrace, Inc. v. Phoenix Indem. Co., 243 N.C. 595, 91 S.E.2d 584 (1956) (sole shareholder held necessary party plaintiff in action by corporation), overruled by N.C.Bus.Corp.Act § 55–3.1 (1957). In England, the members of a public company become severally liable for company debts when the business is carried on with fewer than seven members; the members of a private company with less than two members.

cance when applied to the one-man, family, or other close corporation. Such an enterprise concentrates control and superior knowledge in the principal shareholder or shareholders and thereby lends itself to illegitimate use. Even absent illegitimate purposes, the courts have conditioned recognition of corporateness on compliance with two requirements: [6]

    (a) Business must be conducted on a corporate and not on a personal basis;

    (b) The enterprise must be established on an adequate financial basis.

Sound policy considerations support these requirements. The shareholder who refuses to draw a line between his individual and corporate affairs is in a poor position to ask that the court effect what he failed to do.[7] Moreover, there is an obvious reason for demanding an adequate financial structure as part of the price for the privilege of limited liability.

There is little or no problem in the case where a sole shareholder uses corporate property for private purposes, provided that the rights of creditors are not involved. Such transactions are usually upheld.[8] The same is not true, of course, if the corporation is insolvent. In such a case, moreover, the recipient of any corporate property may be compelled to return what he received on the ground that the payment constituted an unauthorized disposition of a corporate asset.[9] Some courts, however, have refused to apply this rule where the corporation was solvent when the third-party received the property.[10]

A perplexing problem arises whenever a sole shareholder attempts to dispose of corporate property in his will. There is authority for the proposition that such a bequest may be sustained, provided the corporation was simply used as a convenience in connection with the shareholder's financial operations.[11] On the other hand, if the corporation was expected to continue after the testator's death, the rights of existing and future creditors may be involved. Rather than impair corporate assets by complying with the testator's wishes, the corporate entity will be upheld. Of course, this result may not follow where there are no corporate creditors, or where there are corporate creditors but the corporation is nonetheless solvent.[12]

Where the plaintiff sold all the shares of a corporation to the defendants without disclosing that he owed the corporation a debt, the defendants were not allowed to set off against the claim for the purchase price for

6. Cataldo, "Limited Liability With One-Man Companies and Subsidiary Corporations", 18 Law & Contemp.Prob. 473, 482–483 (1953).

7. *Recognizing corporateness:* Zubik v. Zubik, 384 F.2d 267 (3d Cir. 1967), cert. denied 390 U.S. 988, 88 S.Ct. 1183, 19 L.Ed.2d 1291 (1968); Contractors Heating & Supply Co. v. Scherb, 163 Colo. 584, 432 P.2d 237 (1967); Associates Development Corp. v. Air Control Products, Inc., 392 S.W.2d 542 (Tex. Civ.App.1965); *Disregarding Corporateness:* Segan Construction Corp. v. Nor-West Builders, Inc., 274 F.Supp. 691 (D.Conn.1967); Schoenberg v. Romike Properties, 251 Cal.App.2d 154, 59 Cal.Rptr. 359 (1967); Platt v. Billingsley, 234 Cal.App.2d 577, 44 Cal.Rptr. 476 (1965).

8. Colorado Fed. S. & L. Ass'n v. Beery, 141 Colo. 45, 347 P.2d 146 (1959) (bank held not liable for issuing check on corporate account to president-general manager in his own name when he and his wife were sole shareholders); Zurlin v. Hotel Levitt, 5 A.D.2d 945, 172 N.Y.S.2d 427 (3d Dep't 1958), reargument and appeal denied 6 A.D.2d 734, 174 N.Y.S.2d 971 (3d Dep't 1958); State v. Stites, 5 Utah 2d 101, 297 P.2d 227 (1956) (officer-director-owner of all but four shares of corporation convicted of misapplying

corporate funds regardless of injury to creditors or other shareholders); Telis v. Telis, 132 N.J.Eq. 25, 26 A.2d 249 (1942) (wife held entitled to dower in husband's corporation's realty where corporate entity never really observed). But see Poillon v. Poillon, 90 App.Div. 71, 85 N.Y.S. 689 (1st Dep't 1904) (corporation used to avoid dower rights); Annot., 32 A.L.R.2d 705 (1953).

9. Garrow v. Fraser, 98 Wash. 88, 167 P. 75 (1917).

10. Sweet v. Lang, 14 F.2d 758 (D.Minn.1924).

11. Matter of Stukalo, 7 Misc.2d 1042, 166 N.Y.S.2d 478 (Sur.Ct.1957); Matter of Bush, 124 Misc. 674, 209 N.Y.S. 776 (Sur.Ct.1925).

12. Fuller, "The Incorporated Individual: A Study of the One-Man Company", 51 Harv.L.Rev. 1373, 1397–1401 (1938).

the shares the amount which the plaintiff owed the corporation, on the ground that the one-man corporation was a separate entity from its sole shareholder.[13]

SUBSIDIARY AND OTHER AFFILIATED CORPORATIONS

148. Separate corporateness of subsidiary and other affiliated corporations will be recognized, in the absence of illegitimate purposes, where (a) their respective business transactions, accounts, and records are not intermingled; (b) the formalities of separate corporate procedures for each corporation are observed; (c) each corporation is adequately financed as a separate unit in the light of its normal obligations foreseeable in a business of its size and character; and (d) the respective enterprises are held out to the public as separate enterprises. Where one corporation dominates another, the acts of the latter, on principles of agency law, might be attributed to the former.

While a corporation still in many jurisdictions may not be an incorporator, a dummy or dummies may serve in its stead.[1] Under modern law, a corporation may own shares issued by another corporation.[2]

Affiliated corporations may be parent-subsidiary or brother-sister corporations.

Generally-speaking, the principles governing one-man, family, and other close corporations[3] are applicable to subsidiary and other affiliated corporations.[4] Thus, the parent corporation and its subsidiary are treated as separate and distinct legal persons even though the parent owns all the shares in the subsidiary and the two enterprises have

identical directors and officers.[5] Such control, after all, is no more than a normal consequence of controlling share ownership.

In the case of subsidiary or other affiliated corporations, the separate corporate entities or personalities will be recognized, absent illegitimate purposes, unless:[6]

  (a) The business transactions, property, employees, bank and other accounts and records of the corporations are intermingled;

  (b) The formalities of separate corporate procedures for each corporation are not observed (where the directors and officers of each corporation are common, separate meetings and delineation of the respective capacities in which the common directors and officers are acting should be observed);

  (c) The corporation is inadequately financed as a separate unit from the point of view of meeting its normal obligations foreseeable in a business

---

Subsidiary", 39 Yale L.J. 193 (1929); Ballantine, "Separate Entity of Parent and Subsidiary Corporations", 14 Calif.L.Rev. 12 (1925); Note, "Liability of a Corporation for Acts of a Subsidiary or Affiliate", 71 Harv.L.Rev. 1122 (1958); Annot., 7 A.L. R.3d 1343 (1966).

5.   Brown v. Margrande Compania Naviera, 281 F. Supp. 1004 (E.D.Va.1968); Garrett v. Southern Ry., 173 F.Supp. 915 (E.D.Tenn.1959), aff'd 278 F.2d 424 (6th Cir. 1960), cert. denied 364 U.S. 833, 81 S.Ct. 49, 5 L.Ed.2d 59 (1960); Thompson v. Sinkler, 295 S.W. 2d 508 (Tex.Civ.App.1956).

6.   Cataldo, "Limited Liability With One-Man Companies and Subsidiary Corporations", 18 Law & Contemp.Prob. 473, 492–498 (1953). See Markow v. Alcock, 356 F.2d 194, 197–198 (5th Cir. 1966). *Recognizing separate corporate entities:* Blackwell Industrial Foundation, Inc. v. Texstar Corp., 387 F.2d 708 (10th Cir. 1968); My Bread Baking Co. v. Cumberland Farms, Inc., 353 Mass. 614, 233 N.E.2d 748 (1968); Bell Oil & Gas Co. v. Allied Chemical Corp., 431 S.W.2d 336 (Tex.1968); Washington & Old Dominion Users Ass'n v. Washington & Old Dominion R. R., 208 Va. 1, 155 S.E.2d 322 (1967). *Disregarding separate corporate entities:* Lopp v. Peerless Serum Co., 382 S.W.2d 620 (Mo.1964); Acton Plumbing & Heating Co. v. Jared Builders, 368 Mich. 626, 118 N.W.2d 956 (1962). Annot., 7 A.L.R.3d 1343 (1966). Whether or not the one corporation was organized by the other or taken over as a going concern is a factor sometimes mentioned, especially if the latter, to support recognition of corporateness.

---

13.   McLendon v. Galloway, 216 Ga. 261, 116 S.E.2d 208 (1960).

1.   See section 131 supra and sections 182, 183, 185 infra.

2.   See sections 182, 183 infra.

3.   See section 147 supra.

4.   E. Latty, Subsidiaries and Affiliated Corporations (1936); F. Powell, Parent and Subsidiary Corporations 103–111 (1931); Cataldo, "Limited Liability With One-Man Companies and Subsidiary Corporations", 18 Law & Contemp.Prob. 487 (1953); Douglas & Shanks, "Insulation From Liability through

of its size and character, because of either initial inadequate financing or having its earnings drained off so as to keep it in a condition of financial dependency;

(d) The respective enterprises are not held out to the public as separate enterprises; [7]

(e) The policies of the corporation are not directed to its own interests primarily but rather to those of the other corporation.

These conditions obviously parallel those previously discussed in connection with the one-man, family, or other close corporation. Where one corporation is under the domination of another, the separate corporate entities or personalities might be recognized, treating the latter as principal and the former as agent, thus making the acts of the latter in effect the acts of the former.[8]

---

7.   See Walsh v. Hotel Corp. of America, —— Del.Ch. ——, 231 A.2d 458 (Sup.Ct.1967). Compare Berkey v. Third Avenue Ry., 244 N.Y. 84, 155 N.E. 58, 50 A.L. R. 599 (1926), reargument denied 244 N.Y. 602, 155 N.E. 914 (1927), with Ross v. Pennsylvania R. R., 106 N.J.L. 536, 148 A. 741 (1930).

8.   Wyoming Construction Co. v. Western Casualty & Surety Co., 275 F.2d 97 (10th Cir. 1960), cert. denied 362 U.S. 976, 80 S.Ct. 1061, 4 L.Ed.2d 1011 (1960); Van Pelt v. Paull, 6 Mich.App. 618, 150 N.W.2d 185 (1967) (corporation which franchised dance schools held liable under bankrupt licensee's contract on ground corporation's retention of control over licensee made latter its agent); Majestic Factors Corp. v. Latino, 15 Misc.2d 329, 184 N.Y.S.2d 658 (Sup.Ct. 1959). The cases also speak in terms of "divisions" and "departments", suggesting disregard of the corporate entity or personality of the subsidiary. National Labor Relations Board v. Deena Artware, Inc., 359 U.S. 983, 80 S.Ct. 441, 3 L.Ed.2d 932 (1960). See Herman v. Mobile Homes Corp., 317 Mich. 233, 26 N.W.2d 757 (1947); The Willem Van Driel, Sr., 252 F. 35 (4th Cir. 1918). See also Miller v. Bethlehem Steel Corp., 189 F.Supp. 916 (S.D.W.Va.1960); Michaud v. P & M Mfg. Co., 103 N.H. 60, 164 A.2d 566 (1960). For converse holding that the unincorporated divisions of a single corporation are legally and factually capable of entering into a horizontal Sherman Act conspiracy with each other, see Hawaiian Oke & Liquors, Ltd. v. Joseph E. Seagram & Sons, 272 F.Supp. 915 (D.Hawaii 1967), rev'd 416 F.2d 71 (9th Cir. 1969). See also Cliff Food Stores, Inc. v. Kroger, Inc., 417 F.2d 203 (5th Cir. 1969).

Apart from liability, for purposes of service of process on a corporation itself not amenable to service within the jurisdiction, questions arise as to the sufficiency of serving an affiliated corporation amenable to service by disregarding the separate corporate entities or by recognizing them and treating the affiliated corporation as an agent of the defendant.[9]

DISREGARD OF CORPORATENESS FOR BENEFIT OF SHAREHOLDER

149.   **Although there are various exceptions to the general rule of recognizing corporateness when it is to the benefit of shareholders, corporateness is rarely disregarded for their benefit.**

A general rule may be observed that the persons who choose to become incorporated may not evade the consequences of corporateness when that would suit their convenience.[1]

Thus, it has been held that when one has been induced to incorporate in order to obtain a loan as to which a corporation is denied the defense of usury, he may not plead that defense on the contention that, in reality, the loan was made to him.[2]

Several affiliated clothing distributors drew down upon themselves a cease and desist order as a result of calling themselves "tailoring companies" and advertising "We Tailor Every Garment", and that all middlemen's profits were eliminated by selling from maker to wearer. They defended on the ground that the tailoring was done by a wholly-owned and controlled corporation. The court refused to disregard the separate corporateness to relieve the petitioners from

---

9.   See section 97, n. 13 supra and section 151, n. 2 infra.

1.   See Comment, "Corporations: Disregard of the Corporate Entity for the Benefit of Shareholders", 1963 Duke L.J. 722.

2.   See section 150 infra.

the consequences of their misleading advertising.[3]

Under rent control regulations which permit the owner or purchaser to take possession at the end of a lease if the purpose is to occupy the premises himself, a department store corporation bought a building for its own use, but took title in the name of a wholly-owned subsidiary organized for the purpose of acquiring the realty. The tenant in possession refused to leave, and the court held that the purchaser was not entitled to possession, since the corporation seeking possession was a different person from the corporation which held title to the property.[4]

A subsidiary of Schenley Distillers Corporation applied for a contract carrier permit, which was denied by the Interstate Commerce Commission. The Supreme Court of the United States held that the parent corporation, as owner of all the shares of the subsidiary, had no standing to bring an action to set aside the order and was not a person aggrieved by it.[5]

Under the same principle, the owner of a corporation may not as an individual bring an action to enforce a right which belongs to the corporation.[6] Nor will the sole shareholder be upheld in his assertion that his individual property, though used by the corporation and treated by him as corporate property, is corporate property so as to defeat the claims of his individual creditors.[7]

Where a parcel of land owned by a husband and wife was condemned by eminent domain, they claimed severance damages on the basis of an adjacent parcel owned by a corporation wholly-owned by the husband and his two sons. The court refused to disregard corporateness, holding that separate ownership precluded treating the two parcels together and finding a partial taking of the combined whole.[8]

In an unusual case, an individual borrowed $50,000 from a bank and directed the bank to credit this amount to a corporation of which he was the sole shareholder. With this credit, the corporation was able to secure a bond for the performance of its building contracts. This accomplished, the individual paid back the loan by a check drawn by him, as president of the corporation. The court held the individual and the corporation to be one and the same and that there was, therefore, no fraudulent conveyance by the corporation recoverable by its trustee-in-bankruptcy from the bank.[9]

Where a father was driving a car belonging to a corporation of which he was president, when his 15-year-old daughter, a passenger in the car, was hurt, and she sued the corporation, the car's owner, for her father's negligence, the corporation raised the defense that a minor daughter could not sue her father. The court upheld the corporate entity, refusing to dismiss both the daughter's action and the corporation's action over against the father.[10]

Where an automobile was totally wrecked in collision with a train, the court held that the husband of the driver could not recover damages for its replacement value and loss

3. Progress Tailoring Co. v. Federal Trade Commission, 153 F.2d 103 (7th Cir. 1946).

4. Goldberg v. Friedman, 186 Misc. 983, 61 N.Y.S.2d 222 (N.Y.C.Mun.Ct.1946), motion for leave to appeal denied 270 App.Div. 939, 62 N.Y.S.2d 751 (2d Dep't 1946).

5. Schenley Distillers Corp. v. United States, 326 U.S. 432, 66 S.Ct. 247, 90 L.Ed. 181 (1946).

6. W. E. Hedger Transp. Corp. v. Ira S. Bushey & Sons, 186 Misc. 758, 61 N.Y.S.2d 876 (Sup.Ct.1945), aff'd 270 App.Div. 912, 61 N.Y.S.2d 882 (2d Dep't 1946); Green v. Victor Talking Machine Co., 24 F.2d 378, 59 A.L.R. 1091 (2d Cir.1928), cert. denied 278 U.S. 602, 49 S.Ct. 9, 73 L.Ed. 530 (1928).

7. In re Sun Cab Co., 67 F.Supp. 137 (D.D.C.1946).

8. Jonas v. State, 19 Wis.2d 638, 121 N.W. 235, 95 A.L.R.2d 880 (1963). Accord, Sams v. Redevelopment Authority, 431 Pa. 240, 244 A.2d 779 (1968).

9. Mayo v. Pioneer Bank & Trust Co., 270 F.2d 823 (5th Cir.1959), reh. denied 274 F.2d 320 (5th Cir. 1960), cert. denied 362 U.S. 962, 80 S.Ct. 878, 4 L.Ed.2d 877 (1960).

10. Winnick v. Kupperman Const. Co., 29 A.D.2d 261, 287 N.Y.S.2d 329 (2d Dep't 1968).

of use where it was not owned by the husband but was owned in the name of a corporation of which the husband was president and sole shareholder.[11]

Recognition and disregard of corporateness in tax cases, in which the taxpayer may not gain the advantages but usually suffers the disadvantages of the form of business enterprise adopted, are reserved for later treatment.[12]

CONSTITUTIONAL, STATUTORY AND OTHER CONSTRUCTION ASPECTS

150. In the construction of constitutions, statutes, and other writings, recognition or disregard of the corporate entity is usually a question of determining intention. Generally, the corporate entity will be recognized, but it will not be permitted as a device to defeat public policy. As is to be expected, the holdings are not consistent.

Where constitutions, statutes, and other writings are involved, frequent questions arise as to whether recognition or disregard of corporateness is consistent with the underlying intention. Where the language is not clear, the problem is essentially one of construction.

Problems of constitutional construction have previously been treated.

For purposes of federal diversity-of-citizenship jurisdiction, Marshall, C. J., in Bank of the United States v. Deveaux,[1] disregarded the corporate entity and ruled that the citizenship of the shareholders was determinative. Later cases and statutes evolved the rule, recognizing the corporate entity, that a corporation is deemed a citizen of its "state" of incorporation and "state" of its principal place of business.[2]

Constitutional Construction

For purposes of the privileges-and-immunities-of-citizens clause of the Federal Constitution, the Supreme Court has consistently refused to disregard the corporate entity.[3]

Holdings that a corporation itself is a "person" for purposes of the due-process-of-law and equal-protection-of-the-laws clauses of the Federal Constitution have recognized the corporate entity in such cases.[4]

However, a sole shareholder may not avail himself of the privilege against self-incrimination of the Fifth Amendment, available to natural persons but not to corporations, in refusing to produce his corporation's books and records.[5]

Statutory Construction

Many cases can be explained on the elementary principle that, apart from any general theory about corporateness, if there is legislative intention to treat the owner as distinct from the corporation, or as the *alter ego* of the corporation, so as to accomplish the broad purposes of the legislation, that intention should be allowed to control.

As previously discussed, for purposes of defining nationality of a corporation under the British trading-with-the-enemy statute, the House of Lords, in Daimler Co. v. Continental Tyre & Rubber Co. (Great Britain),[6] disregarded the corporate entity and looked to the nationality of those in control of the corporation. On the other hand, the American trading-with-the-enemy act of 1917 was

---

11.   Riesberg v. Pittsburgh & Lake Erie R. R., 407 Pa. 434, 180 A.2d 575 (1962).

12.   See section 153 infra.

1.   9 U.S. (5 Cranch) 61, 3 L.Ed. 38 (1809), discussed in section 88 supra.

2.   Louisville, Cincinnati & Charleston R. R. v. Letson, 43 U.S. (2 How.) 497, 11 L.Ed. 353 (1844); Doc-

tor v. Harrington, 196 U.S. 579, 25 S.Ct. 355, 49 L. Ed. 606 (1905); 28 U.S.C.A. § 1332. See section 88 supra.

3.   See Bank of Augusta v. Earle, 38 U.S. (13 Pet.) 519, 10 L.Ed. 274 (1839); Paul v. Virginia, 75 U.S. (8 Wall.) 168, 19 L.Ed. 357 (1868). See section 89 supra.

4.   See section 80 supra.

5.   Wild v. Brewer, 329 F.2d 924 (9th Cir. 1964), cert. denied 379 U.S. 914, 85 S.Ct. 262, 13 L.Ed.2d 185 (1964); United States v. Guterma, 272 F.2d 344 (2d Cir. 1959).

6.   [1916] 2 A.C. 307, discussed in section 90 supra.

construed by the United States Supreme
Court as requiring an entity approach;[7] the
1941 amendment as requiring disregard of
the corporate entity in determining the
question of "enemy taint".[8]

Where a union and small corporation had
a bargaining agreement, and the small corporation merged into a larger corporation,
the latter was held bound by the agreement
to arbitrate with the union. Said the United
States Supreme Court:[9]

> "While the principles of law governing or-
> dinary contracts would not bind to a con-
> tract an unconsenting successor to a con-
> tracting party, a collective bargaining
> agreement is not an ordinary contract.
> * * * We do not hold that in every
> case in which the ownership or corporate
> structure of an enterprise is changed the
> duty to arbitrate survives. . . .
> [T]here may be cases in which the lack of
> any substantial continuity of identity in
> the business enterprise before and after a
> change would make a duty to arbitrate
> something imposed from without, not rea-

sonably to be found in the particular bargaining agreement and the acts of the parties involved".

Where an individual proprietor transferred his business to a corporation and he
and his wife owned 90 percent of the corporation, which built a new plant, and supervi-
sory personnel were brought over to the new
plant, and equipment of the old plant was
purchased by the new corporation and transferred to the new location, and the corporation continued in the same line of business,
the corporation was the alter ego of the individual proprietorship and was liable for
unfair labor practices based on dismissal of
employees of the individual proprietorship
because of union activity when business was
transferred to the new location.[10]

It has been held that when a family corporation discharges its union employees and its
shareholders replaced them and the union
picketed the plant, the corporate entity
would not be disregarded to permit a finding
that there was no employer-employee relationship; the corporation was still an employer and there was a labor dispute within
the state anti-injunction statute.[11]

The federal income tax laws permit the
corporation to deduct for reasonable salaries, and even fringe benefits, to employees
even though they are also shareholders.[12]

7. Behn, Meyer & Co. v. Miller, 266 U.S. 457, 45 S.Ct. 165, 69 L.Ed. 374 (1925), discussed in section 90 supra.

8. Clark v. Uebersee Finanz-Korporation, A.G., 332 U.S. 480, 68 S.Ct. 174, 92 L.Ed. 88 (1947); Uebersee Finanz-Korporation, A. G. v. McGrath, 343 U.S. 205, 72 S.Ct. 618, 96 L.Ed. 888 (1952), discussed in section 90 supra.

9. John Wiley & Sons v. Livingston, 376 U.S. 543, 550, 84 S.Ct. 909, 914–915, 11 L.Ed.2d 898, 904–905 (1964); Patrick, "Implications of the John Wiley Case for Business Transfers Collective Agreements, and Arbitration", 18 S.C.L.Rev. 413 (1966). See also National Labor Relations Board v. Royal Oak Tool & Machine Co., 320 F.2d 77 (6th Cir. 1963) (original corporation and spun-off corporation held single employee for bargaining purposes despite tax-free spin-off). A new corporation formed to avoid obligations under the National Labor Relations Board Act was held liable as agent for the old corporation. National Labor Relations Board v. Hopwood Retinning Co., 89 F.2d 97 (2d Cir. 1938). Compare National Labor Relations Board v. Tupelo Garment Co., 122 F.2d 603 (5th Cir. 1941); Berry v. Old South Engraving Co., 283 Mass. 441, 185 N.E. 601 (1933); Boro Park Sanitary Live Poultry Market, Inc. v. Heller, 280 N.Y. 481, 21 N.E.2d 687 (1939). See Fulner, "Assumption by a Purchasing, Merging, or Consolidating Corporation of Labor Contract Obligations of Its Predecessor", 17 N.Y.U.Intra.L.Rev. 228 (1962).

10. Reynolds Pallet & Box Co. v. National Labor Relations Bd., 324 F.2d 833 (6th Cir. 1963).

11. Boro Park Sanitary Live Poultry Market, Inc. v. Heller, 280 N.Y. 481, 21 N.E.2d 687 (1939).

12. See sections 76, 77 supra and section 153 infra. See Stark v. Flemming, 283 F.2d 410 (9th Cir. 1960) (where elderly widow formed corporation of her assets and was elected president and treasurer at $400 monthly salary, exact amount to earn maximum social security benefits, resigning without any successor as soon as qualified, corporate entity recognized and claim for social security benefits allowed, subject to review as to reasonableness of amount of salary); Brannon v. Ribicoff, 200 F. Supp. 697 (D.Mont.1961); Enke v. Ribicoff, 197 F. Supp. 319 (S.D.Fla.1961). See also Sabbagha v. Celebrezze, 345 F.2d 509 (4th Cir. 1965); Eastman v. Celebrezze, 240 F.Supp. 142 (N.D.Ohio 1965), rev'd and dismissed sub nom. Eastman v. Gardner, 373

In a prosecution under a World War II price control statute, the defendants, as individuals, had accepted "cash on the side", while their solely-owned corporation, the legal owner of the goods, accepted the ceiling price. The defense was that the price regulation had not been violated, since the corporate owner had received only the selling price, and the individuals, who had received the additional payment, could hardly sell what they did not own. A jury convicted the individuals, but not the corporation. The judgment was affirmed on appeal.[13]

In the antitrust and trade regulation area, the holdings have varied, depending on the statutory policies involved.[14]

While statutory obligations and prohibitions cannot be evaded, they can be avoided. An example of the former is Anderson v. Abbott,[15] where a holding company was formed to acquire double liability shares in banks. When the banks failed and the holding company was unable to satisfy the double liability assessed against it, the banking authorities proceeded against the shareholders of the holding company, most (but not all) of whom had received their "nonassessable" shares in the holding company in exchange for their double-liability bank shares. The United States Supreme Court, 5 to 4, disregarded the holding company and held that all of the shareholders of the holding company were subject to double liability.

Where a statute prohibited a life insurance company from engaging in the fire and casualty business in the state, it was held that a foreign life insurance company, licensed to do business in the state, could acquire a controlling interest in a foreign fire and casualty company, also licensed to do business in the state. It was reasoned that it should be assumed that the subsidiary would respect the mandate of the statute and would conduct the fire and casualty business as a separate business and not as agent for the parent.[16]

Under workmen's compensation statutes, wage earners are entitled to benefits notwithstanding that they are also shareholders of the corporation.[17]

F.2d 481 (6th Cir. 1967), cert. denied 389 U.S. 844, 88 S.Ct. 91, 19 L.Ed.2d 110 (1967).

13. United States v. Hare, 153 F.2d 816 (7th Cir. 1946), cert. denied 328 U.S. 836, 66 S.Ct. 982, 90 L. Ed. 1612 (1946). Copartners, enjoined from price-cutting, were found guilty of contempt when they formed a corporation which engaged in price-cutting. Mead Johnson & Co. v. Rosen, 16 A.D.2d 337, 228 N.Y.S.2d 204 (1st Dep't 1962).

14. Perma Life Mufflers, Inc. v. International Parts Corp., 376 F.2d 692 (7th Cir. 1967), cert. granted 389 U.S. 1034, 88 S.Ct. 770, 19 L.Ed.2d 821 (1968) (holding parent and subsidiaries, which carried on business as single business unit, could be guilty of conspiracy to violate antitrust laws); Reines Distributors, Inc. v. Admiral Corp., 257 F.Supp. 619 (S.D.N.Y.1965) (holding corporate subsidiary or unincorporated division is not "customer" or "purchaser" for Federal Robinson-Patman Act purposes); Joseph E. Seagram & Sons v. Hawaiian Oke & Liquors, Ltd., 416 F.2d 71 (9th Cir. 1969) (corporation's unincorporated divisions held immune for conspiracy charges); Willis & Pitofsky, "Antitrust Consequences of Using Corporate Subsidiaries", 43 N.Y. U.L.Rev. 20 (1968).

15. 321 U.S. 349, 64 S.Ct. 531, 88 L.Ed. 793 (1944), reh. denied 321 U.S. 804, 64 S.Ct. 845, 88 L.Ed. 1090 (1944). See Annot., 151 A.L.R. 1165 (1944).

16. Connecticut General Life Ins. Co. v. Superintendent of Insurance, 10 N.Y.S.2d 42, 217 N.Y.S.2d 39, 176 N.E.2d 63 (1961). For similar reasoning, see Berkey v. Third Avenue Ry., 244 N.Y. 84, 155 N.E. 58, 50 A.L.R. 599 (1926), reargument denied 244 N.Y. 602, 155 N.E. 914 (1927).

17. Marlin Electric Co. v. Industrial Comm'n, 33 Wis.2d 651, 148 N.W.2d 74 (1967); Henk v. Eastern Air Taxi, Inc., 91 N.J.Super. 317, 220 A.2d 200 (1966); Matter of Skouitchi v. Chic Cloak & Suit Co., 230 N.Y. 296, 130 N.E. 299, 15 A.L.R. 1285 (1921). Accord, Goldman v. Johanna Farms, Inc., 26 N.J.Super. 550, 98 A.2d 142 (1953) (holding that a corporate entity would not be disregarded because the petitioner for workman's compensation was a shareholder in a close corporation). But in Bendix v. Bendix Co., 217 Minn. 439, 14 N.W.2d 464 (1944), the court said that workmen's compensation statutes are intended to benefit, not executive officers, but employees, i. e., those who render services for wages. Conceding that it is difficult to formulate a rule for determining whether an officer is also an employee, it held that Bendix was not an employee because he was practically the sole shareholder, he devoted most of his time to sales and executive management, and he was in complete control and had no boss and no one with authority to discharge him. For a fuller discussion, see 1 A. Larson, Law of Workmen's Compensation §§ 54.00–54.23 (1960).

Where a claimant employed by a duly organized and existing corporation wanted to pierce the corporate veil and saddle responsibility for his claim on the shareholders and others associated with the corporate employer, the court held that the state industrial commission had no jurisdiction to disregard the legal existence of a corporation, and that the claimant could only do so in an appropriate court action.[18]

Comparable problems arise in the application of unemployment compensation statutes under which contributions are assessed against an employer to provide benefits for his employees if he employs a minimum number of employees, usually eight or more. In a case where the defendant split his business into four corporations controlled by him, the court held that the four corporations remained as one employing unit for the purpose of subjecting the corporations with less than eight employees to the statute but that the successor corporations were not entitled to the benefits of the favorable corporation rates of the predecessor business.[19]

On the other hand, where a partnership business was parcelled among three corporations under control of the same interest, the corporations were held to be distinct from the partnership so as to deny them the benefit of the statutory deduction in the rate of contribution which the partnership would have been entitled to based upon its past experience.[20]

18. Roberts' Fish Farm v. Spencer, 153 So.2d 718 (Fla.1963).

19. State v. Dallas Liquor Warehouse No. 4, 147 Tex. 495, 217 S.W.2d 654 (1949). See Shultz v. Mack Farland & Sons Roofing Co., 413 F.2d 1296 (5th Cir. 1969) (holding two corporations under common control as single enterprise subject to wage-hour coverage despite separateness in finance and operation).

20. El Queno Distributing Co. v. Christgau, 221 Minn. 197, 21 N.W.2d 601 (1946). Contra, James v. Consolidated Steel Corp., 195 S.W.2d 955 (Tex.Civ. App.1946) (holding that parent corporation was entitled to lower rate because its subsidiary had had three years' experience). Schell v. Unemployment Compensation Board of Review, 202

Avoidance of usury statutes by incorporation has almost been invited by the usury statutes of many American jurisdictions,[21] which specifically prohibit corporations from interposing the defense of usury. A leading case, Jenkins v. Moyse,[22] the owner of real estate was unable to get a mortgage loan at

Pa.Super. 77, 195 A.2d 189 (1963), held that the president and treasurer, each a one-third shareholder, laid off by their own corporation, were not entitled to collect unemployment compensation.

21. E. g., McKinney's N.Y.Gen.Obl.Law, § 5–421.

22. 254 N.Y. 319, 172 N.E. 521, 74 A.L.R. 205 (1930). Accord, Hoffman v. Lee Nashem Motors, Inc., 20 N.Y.2d 513, 285 N.Y.S.2d 68, 231 N.E.2d 765 (1967); Leader v. Dinkler Management Corp., 20 N.Y.2d 393, 283 N.Y.S.2d 281, 230 N.E.2d 120 (1967); Monmouth Capital Corp. v. Holmdel Village Shops, Inc., 92 N.J.Super. 480, 224 A.2d 35 (1966); Indian Lake Estates, Inc. v. Ten Individual Defendants, 121 U. S.App.D.C. 305, 350 F.2d 435 (1965), cert. denied 383 U.S. 947, 86 S.Ct. 1199, 16 L.Ed.2d 209 (1966) (District of Columbia statute prohibiting corporations from pleading usury held applicable to both domestic and qualified foreign corporations); Country Motors, Inc. v. Friendly Finance Corp., 13 Wis.2d 475, 109 N.W.2d 137 (1961), Holland v. Gross, 89 So.2d 255, 63 A.L.R.2d 920 (Fla.Sup.Ct.1956); Carozza v. Federal Finance & Credit Co., 149 Md. 223, 131 A. 332, 43 A.L.R. 1 (1925). But see 418 Trading Corp. v. Oconefsky, 14 N.Y.2d 676, 249 N.Y.S.2d 876, 198 N. E.2d 907 (1964) (where loan was device to extract usurious interest from individual borrowing for personal purposes); Gilbert v. Doris R. Corp., 111 So. 2d 682 (Fla.Dist.Ct.App.1959); Lesser v. Strubbe, 56 N.J.Super. 274, 152 A.2d 409 (1959); In re Greenberg, 21 N.J. 213, 121 A.2d 520 (1956); H. A. S. Loan Service, Inc. v. McColgan, 21 Cal.2d 518, 133 P.2d 391, 145 A.L.R. 349 (1943). If the corporate borrower may not plead usury as a defense, some courts have not allowed its individual accommodation endorser to make such a plea. Reynolds v. Service Loan & Finance Co., 116 Ga.App. 740, 158 S.E.2d 309 (1967); A. J. Armstrong Co. v. Janburt Embroidery Corp., 97 N.J.Super. 246, 234 A.2d 737 (1967); All Purpose Finance Corp. v. D'Andrea, 427 Pa. 341, 235 A.2d 808 (1967); Dahmes v. Industrial Credit Co., 261 Minn. 26, 110 N.W.2d 484 (1961); Pardee v. Fetter, 345 Mich. 548, 77 N.W.2d 124 (1956); Stewart v. Bramwell, 74 N.Y. 85 (1878). However, an individual comaker might be allowed to make such a plea even though the corporate comaker may not. Grove v. Chicago Title & Trust Co., 25 Ill.App.2d 402, 166 N.E.2d 630 (1960). Where the shareholder-guarantor owned only 25 percent of the shares, benefit to him from the guarantee was found too remote and his oral promise not enforced because of the statute of frauds. Acme Equipment Co. v. Allegheny Steel Corp., 207 Pa.Super. 436, 217 A.2d 791 (1966). See also Comment, "Incorporation to Avoid the Usury Laws", 68 Colum.L.Rev. 1390 (1968); Note, "Usury Laws and the Corporate Exception", 23 Md.L.Rev. 51 (1963).

the lawful six percent rate. He incorporated as "John F. Jenkins Company, Inc." transferring the real estate to it, and received a $27,000 loan for its six percent $45,000 second mortgage note. The court upheld the foreclosure, stating: "Here the corporate entity has been created because the statute permits a corporate entity to make a contract which would be illegal if made by an individual. The law has not been evaded but has been followed meticulously in order to accomplish a result which all parties desired and which the law does not forbid." [23]

State licensing and other statutes, especially when they employ the phrase "directly or indirectly", tend to be construed as covering activity in a personal or corporate capacity.[24]

Rent control statutes permitting owners to evict tenants to make the premises available for occupancy by such owners have been construed as requiring recognition of corporateness. Thus if a corporation owns the premises, it might be able to get possession for its own occupancy but not for occupancy by its shareholders or affiliated corporation.[25]

Where a shareholder agrees to answer for the debt of his corporation, the question arises whether or not such an agreement is subject to the statute of frauds provision requiring an agreement by one person to answer for the debt of *another* to be in writing. There is authority to support the rule that the corporate entity may be disregarded in such case.[26] By treating the shareholder and the corporation as one and the same, the promise is no longer a guaranty of another's obligation, and thus the statute of frauds does not apply. Contrariwise, some jurisdictions have held that ownership of all or substantially all of the shares by the promisor is not sufficient reason to pierce the corporate veil.[27]

---

23. To cope with the practices of lenders who required small home owners to incorporate so that higher rates of interest might be lawfully exacted on loans to such owners, the New York statute has undergone a series of amendments. In its present form, the statute permits a corporation whose principal asset is a one or two-family dwelling to raise the defense of usury on a loan secured by a mortgage on such dwelling, provided that within six months prior to the execution of the loan, the corporation was formed or a controlling interest was acquired therein. Statutory amendments expanding the corporate defense of usury have been applied retroactively. Yaffee v. International Co., 80 So.2d 910 (Fla.Sup.Ct.1955); Sohmer Factors Corp. v. 187–20 Tioga Drive Corp., 8 A.D.2d 847, 190 N.Y.S. 2d 555 (2d Dep't 1959), appeal denied 9 A.D.2d 629, 191 N.Y.S.2d 367 (2d Dep't 1959).

24. Beneficial Finance Co. v. Miskell, 424 S.W.2d 482 (Tex.Civ.App.1968) (upholding denial of loan license to subsidiary of foreign corporation which already held directly or through subsidiaries 60 licenses under statute prohibiting any person, directly or indirectly, or through subsidiaries or holding companies, to hold or have an interest in more than 60 licenses, the business thereof, or any interest in such license); E. J. Korvette, Inc. v. State Liquor Auth., 26 A.D.2d 439, 275 N.Y.S.2d 161 (1st Dep't 1966), aff'd 21 N.Y.2d 766, 288 N.Y.S.2d 239, 235 N.E.2d 223 (1968) (upholding denial of retail liquor license to minority shareholder of corporation whose subsidiary held license under statute barring licensee from being interested, directly or indirectly in any premises selling liquor, by share ownership, etc.); New Hampshire Wholesale Beverage Ass'n v. New Hampshire State Liquor Comm'n, 100 N.H. 5, 116 A.2d 885 (1955). Compare Nu-Brass Plumbing & Heating, Inc. v. Wiener, 29 A.D.2d 172, 286 N.Y. S.2d 922 (1st Dep't 1968) (denying collateral attack

on corporation engaging in plumbing trade on basis of share ownership of 51 percent of its shares by licensed plumber).

25. Hirsch v. Coleman, 190 Misc. 809, 78 N.Y.S.2d 685 (App.T. 1st Dep't 1948); Goldberg v. Friedman, 186 Misc. 983, 61 N.Y.S.2d 222 (N.Y.C.Mun.Ct.1946), motion for leave to appeal denied, 270 App.Div. 939, 62 N.Y.S.2d 751 (2d Dep't 1946); Tishman Realty & Constr. Co. v. Wolf, 185 Misc. 317, 57 N.Y.S.2d 73 (App.T. 1st Dep't 1945). See also Hotel Esplanade, Inc. v. Herman, 21 Misc.2d 1030, 197 N.Y.S.2d 579 (Sup.Ct.1960), appeal denied 24 Misc.2d 1086, 200 N. Y.S.2d 157 (Sup.Ct.1960).

26. Michael Distributing Co. v. Tobin, 225 Cal.App.2d 655, 37 Cal.Rptr. 518 (1964) (holding that oral promise by majority-shareholder-president of corporation for materials furnished to corporation was not subject to statute of frauds since his main purpose was to benefit himself). Donovan v. Purtell, 216 Ill. 629, 75 N.E. 334 (1905). See Annot., 35 A.L.R.2d 906 (1954).

27. Bulkley v. Shaw, 289 N.Y. 133, 44 N.E.2d 398 (1942). See also Acme Equipment Co. v. Alleghany Steel Corp., 207 Pa.Super. 436, 217 A.2d 791 (1966) (statute of frauds applied to promise by 25 percent shareholder to pay corporate obligation).

Under criminal statutes, the corporate entity is usually recognized,[28] but is occasionally disregarded.

Conspiracy cases, especially, have raised problems in both criminal and civil actions.[29]

The New York Civil Rights Law has been construed as not permitting incorporation of a recreation facilities corporation as a membership corporation to avoid anti-discrimination regulation while the same persons receive income as owners of the premises.[30]

On avoidance of dower rights, the corporate entity of the corporation holding the real property had sometimes been recognized to defeat such rights,[31] and occasionally disregarded to allow dower.[32] Under a statute abolishing dower and curtesy, and empowering the surviving spouse to elect an intestate share against a will which did not leave such spouse $2,500 absolutely plus an amount in trust for life at least equal to the intestate

share,[33] a bequest of $2,500 plus a one-third interest in the decedent's holdings in closely-held corporations was held, 5 to 2, to preclude election under the will.[34] The widow had argued that the trust was "illusory" since dividends could be withheld on the entrusted shares during her lifetime by those in control of the corporations.

Construction of Contracts, Wills, and Other Writings

Contracts, wills, and other writings pose similar problems of construction.[35]

LITIGATION ASPECTS

151. In litigation, the corporate entity is usually recognized but occasionally disregarded under certain circumstances for purposes of

---

28. People v. Schmidt, 147 Cal.App.2d 222, 305 P.2d 215 (1956) (sole shareholder held not able to escape criminal liability for taking corporate property by defense that corporation was his alter ego); People v. Dalsis, 5 A.D.2d 28, 168 N.Y.S.2d 549 (4th Dep't 1957) (corporate entity upheld to bar indictment of sole shareholder-president for larceny of automobiles entrusted to his corporation absent showing that he was personally involved in the taking); United States v. Kemmel, 160 F.Supp. 718 (M.D.Pa.1958) (held that corporation may be guilty of conspiring with its own officers, directors, and shareholders to commit criminal fraud. See also State v. Harris, 147 Conn. 589, 164 A.2d 399, 83 A.L.R.2d 783 (1960) (sole shareholder held guilty of embezzling from his corporation); Annot., 83 A.L.R.2d 791 (1962).

29. Pearson v. Youngstown Sheet & Tube Co., 332 F.2d 439 (7th Cir. 1964), cert. denied 379 U.S. 914, 85 S.Ct. 262, 13 L.Ed.2d 185 (1964) (holding corporation cannot be liable for conspiracy with one of its own employees since it as principal and employee as agent constitute only a single party); Cott Beverage Corp. v. Canada Dry Ginger Ale, Inc., 146 F.Supp. 300 (S.D.N.Y.1956), appeal dismissed 243 F.2d 795 (2d Cir. 1957) (held that corporation cannot conspire with its own officers and directors). See note 14 supra.

30. Matter of Castle Hill Beach Club, Inc. v. Arbury, 2 N.Y.2d 596, 162 N.Y.S.2d 1, 142 N.E.2d 186 (1957).

31. Poillon v. Poillon, 90 App.Div. 71, 85 N.Y.S. 689 (1st Dep't 1904); Annot., 32 A.L.R.2d 705 (1953).

32. Telis v. Telis, 132 N.J.Eq. 25, 26 A.2d 249 (1942).

33. McKinney's N.Y. EPTL, § 5–1.1. For the widow in question, the intestate share was one-third. Id. § 4–1.1.

34. Matter of Shupack, 1 N.Y.2d 482, 154 N.Y.S.2d 441, 136 N.E.2d 513 (1956).

35. Northern Propane Gas Co. v. Cole, 395 F.2d 1 (5th Cir. 1968) (provision in contract that corporation would not compete with buyer of business held not binding on corporation's president and sole shareholder who signed contract as president of corporation); Aetna Cas. & Sur. Co. v. Stover, 327 F.2d 288, 7 A.L.R.3d 655 (8th Cir. 1964) (insurance policy issued to William T. Stover with coverage excluding operation of watercraft "owned by" or "rented to" insured held to apply to boat owned by William T. Stover, Inc.); Savage v. Royal Properties, Inc., 4 Ariz.App. 116, 417 P.2d 925 (1966) (director's option to purchase corporate assets held not to survive sale of assets to wholly-owned subsidiary with his approval); Jolles v. Holiday Builders, Inc., 222 Ga. 358, 149 S.E.2d 814 (1966) (holding neither corporation nor president liable for specific performance to convey land owned by president under contract signed by president as agent of corporation); North Gate Corp. v. National Food Stores, Inc., 30 Wis.2d 317, 140 N.W.2d 744 (1966) (corporate lessor's covenant that "neither Lessor nor its heirs or legal representatives, or its beneficiaries, subsidiaries, successors or assigns, or any entity in which they or any of them have an interest" will lease to any other retail store within one mile of leased premises held not binding on one of six shareholders of close corporation which owned other real estate within one mile). Nash v. Gay Apparel Corp., 9 A.D.2d 345, 193 N.Y.S.2d 246 (1st Dep't 1959), aff'd per curiam 8 N.Y.2d 978, 204 N.Y.S.2d 545, 169 N.E.2d 126 (1960) (construing contract permitting inspection of corporation's books and records as including inspection of books and records of affiliated corporations).

service of process, "double" or other multiple derivative actions, setoffs, statutes of limitations, enforcing a judgment against the corporation against its dominant shareholders, res judicata, etc.

Under the general rule, of course, the corporation sues on its claims against others and is subject to suit by those having claims against it.[1]

Problems of recognizing or disregarding the corporate entities also occur in cases of service of process on one corporation for the alleged wrongdoing of an affiliated corporation,[2] and of derivative actions[3] or of so-called "double" derivative actions, i. e., derivative actions brought by a shareholder of one corporation in the right of an affiliated corporation.[4]

Generally-speaking, shareholder obligations may not be set off against corporate obligations, and *vice versa*.[5] The basis for this rule is simply that demands must be mutual and subsisting between the same parties. However, the rule is sometimes relaxed in cases involving one-man corporations for the express purpose of avoiding circuity of action.[6] Of course, setoff is not permitted when it would impair stated capital or prejudice the rights of corporate creditors.

Where statutes of limitations are involved, the traditional approach is that the commencement of an action against the wrong party does not toll the running of the statute against the proper defendant unless there

1. Erlich v. Glasner, 418 F.2d 226 (9th Cir. 1969) (plaintiff, who with wife owned all shares of corporation, held not entitled to sue for damages to corporation); London v. Bruskas, 64 N.M. 73, 324 P. 2d 424 (1958); Wolf v. S. H. Wintman Co., 87 R.I. 156, 139 A.2d 84 (1958); Miller & Lux, Inc. v. Nickel, 141 F.Supp. 41 (N.D.Cal.1956). But see Fontainebleau Hotel Corp. v. Crossman, 286 F.2d 926 (5th Cir. 1961), 323 F.2d 937 (5th Cir. 1963) (sole shareholder allowed to enforce lease and agreement executed in name of corporation); Park Terrace, Inc. v. Phoenix Indem. Co., 243 N.C. 595, 91 S.E.2d 584 (1956); Note, "Actions by a Sole Shareholder of a Corporation", 15 Clev.-Mar.L.Rev. 598 (1966). Nor can the sole shareholders ordinarily defend in their own names an action against the corporation. Malcolm v. Stondall Land & Inv. Co., 129 Mont. 142, 284 P.2d 258 (1955). See Inn Operations, Inc. v. River Hills Motor Inn Co., —— Iowa ——, 152 N.W.2d 808 (1967) (unqualified foreign parent corporation held disabled from suing despite fact that its wholly-owned subsidiaries were domestic corporations). Intervention of shareholders in corporate litigation is sometimes allowed. For treatment of corporate litigation (including derivative actions), see Chapter 14 infra.

2. Overmyer Warehouse Co. v. W. C. Caye & Co., 116 Ga.App. 128, 157 S.E.2d 68 (1967) (service on sole shareholder held not to constitute service on corporation); Taca International Airlines, S.A. v. Rolls-Royce of England, Ltd., 15 N.Y.2d 97, 256 N.Y.S.2d 129, 204 N.E.2d 329 (1965) (American subsidiary held "separately incorporated department or instrumentality" of British parent; service on former held to constitute service on latter); Botwinick v. Credit Exchange, Inc., 419 Pa. 65, 213 A.2d 349 (1965) (holding that New York parent was not served by process served on Pennsylvania subsidiary; common president, similar name and business activity, close business relationship, use of similar letterheads and business forms, and 100% share ownership were not sufficient to establish that subsidiary was mere alter ego of its parent, especially where corporations each maintained integrity of their separate corporate existence; nor was there showing that parent so dominated and controlled subsidiary as to render it mere instrumentality of itself). Delray Beach Aviation Corp. v. Mooney Aircraft, Inc.,

332 F.2d 135 (5th Cir. 1964), cert. denied 379 U.S. 915, 85 S.Ct. 262, 13 L.Ed.2d 185 (1964). Brunzell Const. Co. v. Harrah's Club, 225 Cal.App.2d 734, 37 Cal.Rptr. 659 (1964) (alter ego theory). See section 97 supra. See also State ex rel. Grinnel Co. v. MacPherson, 62 N.M. 308, 309 P.2d 981 (1957), cert. denied 355 U.S. 825, 78 S.Ct. 32, 2 L.Ed.2d 39 (1957) (upholding service on two unqualified foreign corporations by service on qualified foreign corporation where all three corporations had similar names, common boards of directors, and acted as one corporation).

3. Wright v. H. E. Clark Interests, Inc., Del.Ch. Ct.Civ.No.2075 (Mar. 17, 1966) (minority shareholder in derivative action allowed to examine related corporation's records).

4. Painter, "Double Derivative Suits and Other Remedies with Regard to Damaged Subsidiaries", 30 Ind.L.J. 143 (1961). See section 361 infra. See also Home Fire Ins. Co. v. Barber, 67 Neb. 644, 93 N.W. 1024 (1903) (corporation suing for equitable relief held barred by fact that its shareholders, who would be the real beneficiaries of any award, were without standing in equity).

5. McLendon v. Galloway, 216 Ga. 261, 116 S.E.2d 208 (1960).

6. State Trust & Savings Bank v. Hermosa Land and Cattle Co., 30 N.M. 566, 240 P. 469 (1925). See Pauley Petroleum, Inc. v. Continental Oil Co., 43 Del.Ch. 366, 231 A.2d 450 (Ch.1967) (refusing to enjoin Delaware parent corporation from maintaining actions in Mexico in name of Mexican subsidiary against plaintiffs suing it in Delaware action).

are grounds for disregarding the separateness of the parties.[7]

If the corporate plaintiff prevails, judgment is awarded in its favor, and any recovery goes into its treasury. Where the corporate defendant loses, the judgment is against it and its property is subject to attachment, levy, and execution.[8] However, where a principal shareholder strips the corporation of its assets immediately following an injury to the plaintiff, such shareholder may be held personally liable on the judgment against the corporation.[9]

The corporate entity has also been disregarded for purposes of *res judicata*. To prevent relitigation of issues already adjudicated, the practice has been to pierce the corporate veil and thereby establish privity between the corporation and its sole shareholder, with the result that the corporation may not relitigate an issue already litigated by the sole shareholder and *vice versa*.[10] This principle has been extended to a family corporation situation, with the court's holding that the litigation by all of the shareholders of the family corporation precluded litigation of the same issue by the corporation.[11]

BANKRUPTCY ASPECTS

152. Claims of shareholders as creditors of their corporations in receivership, bankruptcy, arrangement, and corporate reorganization proceedings may be allowed, subordinated to the claims of others, or disallowed, depending on their validity and fairness. Various other problems of recognition or disregard of corporate entities occur in bankruptcy administra-

7. B–W Acceptance Corp. v. Spencer, 268 N.C. 1, 149 S.E.2d 570 (1966) (holding action by subsidiary is not same as action by parent and counterclaim against subsidiary does not toll statute of limitations against parent, absent excessive domination by parent); Martz, Jr. v. Miller Bros. Co., 244 F. Supp. 246 (D.Del.1965) (action against Millers Brothers Co. two days before running of statute of limitations; substitution of proper defendant, Miller Brothers of Newark, refused); Stauffer v. Isaly Dairy Co., 4 Ohio App.2d 15, 211 N.E.2d 72 (1965) (permitting substitution of affiliated corporation where intermingling and estoppel); Food Fair Stores Corp. v. Vari, 55 Del. 280, 191 A.2d 257 (Sup.Ct.1963) (disallowing amendment of complaint against Food Fair Stores Corporation on claim against Food Fair Stores, New Castle, notwithstanding advice from Delaware secretary of state office that there was only one Delaware corporation with words "Food Fair" in its name when in fact there were nine such corporations—all subsidiaries of Food Fair Stores, Inc., a Pennsylvania corporation), —— Del. ——, 205 A.2d 529, 13 A.L.R.3d 844 (Sup.Ct.1964) (disallowing second action).

8. See William A. King, Inc. v. Ritchie Building Co., 20 Misc.2d 357, 191 N.Y.S.2d 42 (Sup.Ct.1959) (in action on contract against Ritchie Building Co., Inc., service of process and attachment against Ritchie Construction Co., Inc. vacated). Compare Shamrock Oil & Gas Co. v. Ethridge, 159 F.Supp. 693 (D.Colo. 1958) (judgment against dominant shareholder enforced against corporate property), with Campbell v. Birch, 53 Cal.App.2d 399, 128 P.2d 120 (1942) (judgment against sole shareholder refused against corporation); see also Thomas v. E. C. Mutter Const. Co., 405 Pa. 509, 178 A.2d 570 (1961) (president held not subject to body attachment to enforce judgment against corporation); Eaton Factors Co. v. Double Eagle Corp., 17 A.D.2d 135, 232 N.Y.S.2d 901 (1st Dep't 1962) (attachment warrant against property of three officer-shareholders of family corporation held not to prevent them from disposing of property of corporation).

9. Thoni Trucking Co. v. Foster, 243 F.2d 570 (6th Cir. 1957). Albre v. Sinclair Construction Co., 345 Mass. 712, 189 N.E.2d 563 (1963), upheld the appointment of receivers of the property of three cor-

porations, the assets and affairs of which allegedly had become entangled. The court held that such appointment was under the general equity powers of the court to appoint receivers of domestic corporations, and that the creditor of one of the corporations had standing to petition for appointment of receivers not only of his corporation but also of the other two corporations.

10. McNamara v. Powell, 256 App.Div. 554, 11 N.Y. S.2d 491 (4th Dep't 1939), reargument denied 257 App.Div. 913, 12 N.Y.S.2d 773 (4th Dep't 1939). Cf. Troy Lumber Corp. v. Hunt, 251 N.C. 624, 112 S.E.2d 132 (1960) (denial of recovery to chairman of the board-president-controlling shareholder, injured while driving corporation's automobile, in action against third person held not res judicata with respect to subsequent action by corporation against third person for damages to its automobile, since corporation had other shareholders). See Ely Valley Mines, Inc. v. Lee, 385 F.2d 188 (9th Cir. 1967) (corporations barred from relitigating action against their president); cf. Minton v. Cavaney, 56 Cal.2d 576, 15 Cal.Rptr. 641, 364 P.2d 473 (1961) (holding director could not be held personally liable on judgment against corporation for negligence without opportunity to relitigate issues of corporation's negligence and amount of damages where director was not party to action against corporation and did not control litigation).

11. Matter of Shea, Matter of Grainger, 309 N.Y. 605, 132 N.E.2d 864 (1956); Annot., 81 A.L.R.2d 1323 (1962).

tion, the primary concern being the equitable distribution of each corporation's assets among its respective claimants.

Since under the general rule there can be *bona fide* transactions between a corporation and its principal shareholder, including those which result in the shareholder's becoming a creditor of the corporation, the question often arises in receivership, bankruptcy, arrangement, or corporate reorganization proceedings, as to the treatment to be given to such claims when the corporation is insolvent.[1] The court, of course, should carefully scrutinize such a claim, since it must decide whether to allow or disallow it and, if allowed whether or not to subordinate it to one or more other classes of claims.

At one time the courts resolved the question by determining whether the corporate-debtor had been a "mere instrumentality" of the shareholder-claimant.

In the leading case of Taylor v. Standard Gas & Electric Co.,[2] known familiarly as the "Deep Rock" case because the subsidiary in reorganization was named Deep Rock Oil Corporation, the United States Supreme Court offered an additional new standard based upon "fairness" and the equities of the case. In that case, the parent corporation owned the common shares in the subsidiary, which had also issued preferred shares to the public. The parent filed a claim of sev-

eral million dollars as the open account balance due it on numerous intercorporate transactions. The Supreme Court allowed the parent corporation to participate in the reorganization plan of its subsidiary, but subordinated its creditor claims, to the subsidiary's preferred shareholders' interests. Such result was thought to be warranted under the "fairness" test since the subsidiary was found to have been launched originally by the parent with inadequate capital and thereafter to have been managed in the interests of the parent rather than of the subsidiary. Claims so subordinated are sometimes described as "deep-rocked".

A subsequent United States Supreme Court decision, Pepper v. Litton,[3] applied the "fairness" test in a straight bankruptcy proceeding involving a one-man corporation.

There apparently is no subordination of the shareholder's creditor claim under the "fairness" test unless the corporation's creditors or minority shareholders have been unjustly prejudiced.[4] It has been pointed out

3. 308 U.S. 295, 60 S.Ct. 238, 84 L.Ed. 281 (1939). Accord, Costello v. Fazio, 256 F.2d 903 (9th Cir. 1958); Comment, "Classification of Claims in Debtor Proceedings", 49 Yale L.J. 881 (1940).

4. Small v. Williams, 313 F.2d 39 (4th Cir. 1963) (upholding secured creditor claim of majority shareholder who took security contemporaneously with his advances of funds to corporation in good faith); In Spach v. Bryant, 309 F.2d 886, 889 (5th Cir. 1962), the two sole shareholders/officers each drew $50,000 salary from the corporation and immediately returned such amounts to the corporation. The subordination by the referee-in-bankruptcy of claims for such amounts was overruled by the trial judge. On appeal, the court of appeals held that there was no basis for subordination of the claims, saying:
"In circumstances where there are only two stockholders and two officers, it is obvious that salaries must be fixed by the persons receiving them. . . . The salaries paid were not unreasonable in view of the work and responsibility involved." But see Bankers Life & Casualty Co. v. Kirtley, 338 F.2d 1006 (8th Cir. 1964) (subordination of claims of dominating shareholders upheld). In state receivership proceedings, shareholders who have loaned money in good faith to their corporations are allowed to participate as creditors. But see Weyerhauser Co. v. Clark's Material Supply Co., 90 Idaho 455, 413 P.2d 180 (1966) (shareholder who mortgaged own property as security for loan

1. Bass v. Shutan, 259 F.2d 561 (9th Cir. 1958) (upholding corporate entity to give priority in corporation's bankruptcy to wage claims assigned to its sole shareholder).

2. 306 U.S. 307, 59 S.Ct. 543, 83 L.Ed. 669 (1939); Jennings, "Mr. Justice Douglas: His Influence on Corporate and Securities Regulation", 73 Yale L.J. 920 (1964). Stroia, "Deep Rock—A Post Mortem", 34 U.Det.L.J. 279 (1957); Sprecher, "The Conflict of Equities under the 'Deep Rock' Doctrine", 43 Colum.L.Rev. 336 (1943); Krotinger, "The 'Deep Rock' Doctrine: A Realistic Approach to Parent-Subsidiary Law", 42 Colum.L.Rev. 1124 (1942); Israels, "The Implications and Limitations of the 'Deep Rock' Doctrine", 42 Colum.L.Rev. 376 (1942); Note, "The Deep Rock Doctrine: Inexorable Command or Equitable Remedy", 47 Colum.L.Rev. 800 (1947).

that while the Deep Rock decision was intended to produce the most equitable result, the ultimate losers may be the shareholder's creditors, themselves equally innocent parties.[5] Such a result was reached in a case which applied the "fairness" test and thereby allowed pledgees of the subsidiary's shares to prevail over the unsecured creditors of the wrongdoing parent.[6]

Receivership, bankruptcy, arrangement, and corporate reorganization proceedings give rise to another class of problems which, to a limited extent, involve disregard of the corporate entity. Suppose the parent corporation, but not the subsidiary, becomes insolvent. While the latter's assets may be administered in the proceeding involving the parent, the rights of the subsidiary's creditors may not be impaired; a special fund for their benefit usually is established with any balance going to satisfy the parent's creditors.[7] If only the subsidiary is insol-

vent, the creditors of the subsidiary are not permitted to jeopardize the rights of the parent's creditors.[8]

A more difficult problem arises when both corporations become insolvent. Courts have arrived at various solutions, usually recognizing the separate corporate entities[9] but occasionally approving common pooling of the assets of both corporations, with all creditors sharing proportionately—a result which involves disregard of the corporate entities.[10]

A case has disregarded the separate entities of affiliated corporations in holding that a transfer by one corporation to a bank to pay an overdraft of its affiliated corporation did not constitute a voidable transfer.[11]

TAXATION ASPECTS

153. For federal income tax purposes, the corporate entity is usually recognized, although it will be disregarded when used as a tax-evasion device. Ordinarily, the taxpayer will not be permitted to disavow the corporate entity for his own benefit. Similar cases have arisen with respect to state and local taxation.

For purposes of the federal income tax the corporate entity is generally upheld but may be disregarded in unusual cases. Under the "business activity" test the determining factor is whether the corporation was formed —or functioned—for a proper business pur-

to corporation but used loan proceeds for himself causing corporation's insolvency denied creditor status); Erie Drug Co. Case, 416 Pa. 41, 204 A.2d 256 (1964); Entwistle v. Enjaco Corp., 97 R.I. 224, 197 A.2d 271 (1964); Obre v. Alban Tractor Co., 228 Md. 291, 179 A.2d 861 (1962).

5. R. Stevens & A. Larson, Cases and Materials on the Law of Corporations 57 (2d ed. 1955); Annot., 51 A.L.R.2d 989 (1957).

6. In re Commonwealth Light and Power Co., 141 F. 2d 734 (7th Cir. 1944).

7. Commerce Trust Co. v. Woodbury, 77 F.2d 478 (8th Cir. 1935), cert. denied 296 U.S. 614, 56 S.Ct. 134, 80 L.Ed. 435 (1935). In Matter of Gibraltor Amusements, Ltd., 291 F.2d 22 (2d Cir. 1961), cert. denied 368 U.S. 925, 82 S.Ct. 360, 7 L.Ed.2d 190 (1961), the question was whether a wholly-owned subsidiary of the alleged bankrupt corporation had standing as one of the three required petitioning creditors. Under ordinary principles of corporate law, the court held that disregard of the subsidiary's corporate identity was not warranted. Smith & Moore, Cir. JJ., literally construed the Bankruptcy Act definition of "creditor" as "anyone" who owns a provable claim, as including a wholly-owned subsidiary. Friendly, Cir. J., dissented, leaving open the question as to whether a wholly-owned subsidiary with independent creditors might be deemed separate from its parent in a case where, as a result of its own financial difficulties, the subsidiary was in effect acting for its creditors rather than for its shareholders.

8. Note, 46 Harv.L.Rev. 823 (1933); see Fox Jewelry Co. v. Lee, 264 F.2d 720 (5th Cir. 1959), cert. denied 361 U.S. 815, 80 S.Ct. 55, 4 L.Ed.2d 62 (1959).

9. Anaconda Bldg. Materials Co. v. Newland, 336 F.2d 625 (9th Cir. 1964).

10. Stone v. Eacho (In re Tip Top Tailors, Inc.), 127 F.2d 284 (4th Cir. 1942), reh. denied 128 F.2d 16 (4th Cir. 1942), cert. denied 317 U.S. 635, 63 S.Ct. 54, 87 L.Ed. 512 (1942). See Cataldo, "Limited Liability with One-Man Companies and Subsidiary Corporations", 18 Law & Contemp.Prob. 473, 500–503 (1953).

11. Mayo v. Pioneer Bank & Trust Co., 270 F.2d 823 (5th Cir. 1959), reh. denied 274 F.2d 320 (5th Cir. 1960), cert. denied 362 U.S. 962, 80 S.Ct. 878, 4 L. Ed.2d 877 (1960).

pose other than minimizing taxes.[1] In the last analysis this test turns upon *bona fides* and tax avoidance as well as business purpose.[2]

The "business activity" test controls even though in operation there is "substantial identity" between the corporation and its principal shareholders.

The decision of the United States Supreme Court in Higgins v. Smith [3] permitted the federal taxing authorities, under a statutory provision which was then silent on the point, to disregard the separate corporate entity of a one-man corporation for the purpose of denying to the shareholder the deduction of a loss arising from the sale by him to the corporation of securities (notwithstanding inconsistent treatment of capital gains).[4]

The decision established two bold generalizations: first, that the government may disregard sham corporations whenever that would best serve the purpose of a tax statute, and second, that a taxpayer who himself has chosen to do business as a corporation *must* accept any tax disadvantages of that

form and so will not be heard to deny the separate existence of the very corporation he himself has created.

As to the first generalization it is generally agreed that an exemption or qualification is to be recognized when the corporation is in fact carrying on a *bona fide* business, and is not merely a device created for the *ad hoc* purpose of avoiding a tax burden.[5]

As to the second generalization of Higgins v. Smith: the government has consistently argued since the Smith case that the corporate entity should never be disregarded at the request and for the benefit of the taxpayer, but the Supreme Court has not always stressed this ground.[6] However, cases in which the corporate entity is disregarded for the benefit of the taxpayer are not common, and usually involve some special circumstances or statutory policy. On the other hand, cases refusing to allow the owner to disavow the separate existence of his corporation are numerous.

A common example is the attempt by the owner or parent to deduct on his own return the losses of a wholly-owned or subsidiary corporation.[7]

1. Moline Properties, Inc. v. Comm'r, 319 U.S. 436, 63 S.Ct. 1132, 87 L.Ed. 1499 (1943); Nelson v. Comm'r, 281 F.2d 1 (5th Cir. 1960).

2. Balter, "Stockholder's Dealings with 'His' Closely Held Corporation", 46 Taxes 387 (1968); Chirelstein, "Learned Hand's Contribution to the Law of Tax Avoidance", 77 Yale L.J. 440, 442–452 (1968) (business purpose and corporate entity); Thrower, "Tax Risks in Dealings between Corporations and Their Officers or Stockholders", N.Y.U. 25th Inst. on Fed.Tax. 441 (1967); Eustice, "Tax Problems Arising from Transactions between Affiliated or Controlled Corporations", 23 Tax.L.Rev. 451 (1968), 16 Tul.Tax Inst. 57 (1966); Samuels, "Disregard of the Corporate Entity for the Taxpayer's Benefit: A Case Study", 5 Santa Clara L.Rev. 145 (1965); Watts, "Tax Problems of Regard for the Corporate Entity", N.Y.U. 20th Inst. on Fed.Tax 867 (1962); Tamaki, "Lifting the Corporate Veil in Canadian Income Tax Law", 8 McGill L.J. 159 (1962); Levitt, "Disregarding the Corporate Entity in Tax Cases", 22 Taxes 457 (1944); Cleary, "The Corporate Entity in Tax Cases", 1 Tax L.Rev. 3 (1945); Note, "Disregard of Corporate Entity in Federal Taxation— the Modern Approach", 30 Va.L.Rev. 398 (1944).

3. 308 U.S. 473, 60 S.Ct. 355, 84 L.Ed. 406 (1940).

4. Burnet v. Commonwealth Improvement Co., 287 U.S. 415, 53 S.Ct. 198, 77 L.Ed. 399 (1932) (recognizing gain).

5. Moline Properties, Inc. v. Comm'r, 319 U.S. 436, 63 S.Ct. 1132, 87 L.Ed. 1499 (1943); Standard Oil Co. v. United States, 63 F.Supp. 48 (N.D.Ohio 1945), rev'd sub nom. United States v. Standard Oil Co., 158 F.2d 126 (6th Cir. 1946), cert. denied 331 U.S. 836, 67 S.Ct. 1519, 91 L.Ed. 1849 (1947), reh. denied 332 U.S. 786, 68 S.Ct. 33, 92 L.Ed. 369 (1948). Compare Tomlinson v. Miles, 316 F.2d 710 (5th Cir. 1963), cert. denied 375 U.S. 828, 84 S.Ct. 71, 11 L. Ed.2d 60 (1963), reh. denied 375 U.S. 926, 84 S.Ct. 263, 11 L.Ed.2d 169 (1963) (holding corporation, formed to hold real property for use of shareholders and to facilitate local taxes and contemplated conveyances, subject to federal income taxes, despite trial court's finding of trust and agency), with Delaney v. Gardner, 204 F.2d 855 (1st Cir. 1953) (holding transfer of property to charitable corporation sham and including it as part of transferor's taxable estate).

6. Moline Properties, Inc. v. Comm'r, 319 U.S. 436, 63 S.Ct. 1132, 87 L.Ed. 1499 (1943).

7. Dodd v. Comm'r, 298 F.2d 570 (4th Cir. 1962); Raffold Process Corp. v. Comm'r, 153 F.2d 168 (1st Cir. 1946); Interstate Transit Lines v. Comm'r, 130 F.2d 136 (8th Cir. 1942), aff'd 319 U.S. 590, 63 S.Ct. 1279, 87 L.Ed. 1607 (1943), reh. denied 320 U.S. 809,

The Internal Revenue Code allows the Commissioner to allocate income and deductions among two or more enterprises controlled by the same interest when this is necessary to prevent evasion of taxes or clearly to reflect income.[8]

The principal statutory exceptions to the general principle of treating the corporation as wholly independent of its shareholders or affiliated corporations under the Internal Revenue Code have been listed as follows: [9]

  (a) Section 267, forbidding the deduction of certain losses, expenses, and interest incurred in transactions between a corporation and certain of its shareholders (see also sections 1235(d), 1237(a) (2) (A), 1239(a) (2));

  (b) Section 269, disallowing certain tax benefits if control of a corporation is acquired for the principal purpose of tax avoidance;

  (c) Section 401(a) (4), providing that a share bonus, pension, or profit-sharing plan will qualify for certain tax benefits only if it does not discriminate in favor of, *inter alia*, shareholders;

  (d) Section 531, imposing an additional tax on a corporation that is formed or availed of for the purpose of avoiding the income tax on shareholders by accumulating instead of distributing its earnings;

  (e) Section 541, imposing an additional tax on personal holding companies, which are defined in part by reference to the number of shareholders;

  (f) Section 382, limiting or disallowing the net operating loss carry over in cases where share ownership shifts in specified ways;

  (g) Section 341(c) (5) (A), which for certain purposes treats the corporation's assets as noncapital assets if they would have this character in the hands of a shareholder;

  (h) Sections 267(c) (1), 318(a) (2) (C), 544(a) (1), which for certain purposes treat shares owned by a corporation as though they were owned by the corporation's shareholders (and, under section 318(a) (3) (C), vice versa);

  (i) Section 1501, permitting an "affiliated" group of corporations to file a consolidated return.

Tax problems relating to disregard of the corporate entity have also arisen on the state and local levels, and have been accorded somewhat similar treatment.[10] This is especially true in the case of a person who seeks to deny corporate existence after choosing to do business as a corporation.[11]

---

64 S.Ct. 26, 88 L.Ed. 489 (1943); Menihan v. Comm'r, 79 F.2d 304 (2d Cir. 1935), cert. denied 296 U.S. 651, 56 S.Ct. 368, 80 L.Ed. 463 (1935).

8. Int.Rev.Code of 1954, 26 U.S.C.A. § 482; Pomeroy, "Allocation of Income, Deductions, Credits, and Allowances Among Related Taxpayers", 15 W.Res.L. Rev. 250 (1964).

9. B. Bittker & J. Eustice, Federal Income Taxation of Corporations and Shareholders 13–14 (2d ed. 1966).

10. Lewis Trucking Corp. v. Virginia, 207 Va. 23, 147 S.E.2d 747 (1966) (disregarding newly-formed Delaware corporation (as "*alter ego*, alias, stooge or dummy") to which interstate trucking operator in Virginia had transferred tractors to avoid higher Virginia license fees by paying lower Delaware fees under reciprocity agreement between two states); Orda v. State Tax Comm'n, 25 A.D.2d 332, 269 N.Y.S.2d 544 (3d Dep't 1966), aff'd 19 N.Y.2d 636, 278 N.Y.S.2d 611, 225 N.E.2d 205 (1967) (hotel owned by partnership and operated by corporation formed for purpose treated as capital asset of partnership subject to capital loss treatment).

11. See, e. g., Superior Coal Co. v. Dep't of Finance, 377 Ill. 282, 36 N.E.2d 354 (1951); Legion Clubhouse v. Madison, 248 Wis. 380, 21 N.W.2d 668 (1946).

CHAPTER 8

CORPORATE FINANCIAL STRUCTURE

A. INTRODUCTION

J. RECORD OWNERSHIP OF SECURITIES

A. INTRODUCTION

SOURCES OF CORPORATE FUNDS

154. **The finances necessary to launch and operate the corporation, at least initially, are obtained principally from investors who receive in return securities issued by the corporation evidencing the security holders' rights in or against the corporation. After the corporation is launched, corporate funds may be derived from various sources: reserves and retention of earnings, trade credits, short-term borrowing, accounts receivable financing, inventory financing, field warehousing, trust receipts financing, sales and leasebacks, leasing and installment purchasing, tax reserves, acquisition of tax-loss corporations, depreciation and depletion deductions, government sources. Less than one-fifth of corporate funds currently are derived from the issue of bonds, debentures, long-term notes, preferred shares, and common shares.**

The finances necessary to launch and operate the corporation are obtained principally, at least initially, from "investors" who receive in return "securities" issued by the corporation evidencing the security holders' rights in or against the corporation.[1]

The issue of securities is the usual initial method of raising corporate funds. After the corporation is launched, corporate funds might be derived from other sources. Of the latter, provision for depreciation and depletion and retention of earnings for working capital and business expansion are the most significant.[2] Other sources are trade credits (accounts payable), short-term borrowing, accounts receivable financing, inventory financing, field warehousing, trust receipts financing, sales and leasebacks, leasing and installment purchasing, acquisition of tax-loss corporations, government sources

64 Colum.L.Rev. 995 (1964); Dillenbeck, "The European Investment Bank", 17 Bus.Law. 568 (1962); Cole, Morley & Scott, "Corporate Financing in Great Britain", 12 Bus.Law. 321 (1957). For financing close corporations, see sections 261, 262 infra. See also P. Van Arsdell, Corporation Finance; Policy, Planning, Administration (1968).

2. Sometimes known as "ploughing-back" profits, i. e., earnings retained after dividend and tax payments. Tangible evidence of such reinvestment is sometimes given to shareholders in the form of share dividends or other share distributions. See section 329 infra. Internal funds of business corporations, including depreciation—liberalized under the Revenue Act of 1962—rose from $17,900,000,000 in 1950 to $58,700,000,000 in 1966. General Motors Corporation, from 1917 to 1962, retained 33 percent of its total earnings, distributing 67 percent to its shareholders; in 1962, almost $600,000,000 was retained, more than $800,000,000 being distributed. Sloane, "The Fabulous Growth Story", 69 Fortune, No. 2, 123, 125 (Feb.1964). Depreciation accounting is a method of allocating the cost of a capital asset over its useful life with the yearly amount allocated (depreciation) debited to depreciation expense and credited to allowance for depreciation (negative asset). As an expense it is deductible for federal income tax purposes and reduces net income and earned surplus, the funds usually legally available for dividends. See section 320 infra. The net effect is that the annual allowances for depreciation remain in the corporation.

1. See generally 2 A. Dewing, The Financial Policy of Corporations 1019–1061 (5th ed. 1953); H. Guthmann & H. Dougall, Corporate Financial Policy 224–268, 438–503 (4th ed. 1962); W. Husband & J. Dockeray, Modern Corporation Finance 313–336 (5th ed. 1962); Prentice-Hall Federal Aids to Financing; Business Financing 1–371 (American Bar Association 1963); J. Childs, Long-Term Financing (1961); McBrien, "Methods of Financing Corporate Business", in Advising California Business Enterprises 465 (1958); Conroy, Broach, Faherty, Sowle, Suss, Werner & Garrett, "Where to Look for Money", 9 Prac.Law. 15 (May 1963), 9 id. 65 (Oct.1963); Becker & Becker, "Financing a Business Enterprise", 112 J. Accountancy 42 (Dec.1961). See also C. Ashley & J. Smyth, Corporate Finance in Canada (1956); Blondeel, "A New Form of International Financing: Loans in European Units of Account",

(e. g., Federal Small Business Administration, local development corporations), etc.[3]

A survey for the 1946–53 period revealed that of $150 billion expended for capital expenditures by non-moneyed corporations, almost two-thirds came from internal corporate sources (retained earnings capitalized by the declaration of share dividends and reserves). Half of the remaining third came from current, usually bank, borrowing. Only slightly more than one-sixth was derived from the issue of investment securities, of which probably somewhat more than half of the issues were publicly offered and the other issues privately placed.[4] The approximate breakdown of investment securities was $18 billion (12 percent) in the form of debt securities (bonds, debentures, long-term notes) and $9 billion (6 percent) by way of shares (preferred shares and common shares).[5]

Since 1953, the pattern has fluctuated, with internal sources continuing to exceed external sources.[6]

TYPES OF SECURITIES

155. The term "securities" covers a wide variety of corporate paper issued to evidence the rights of holders in and against the corporation, ranging from the most senior type to the most junior type. Securities are not necessari-

---

3. Internal financing is also possible through sale of unneeded assets, redeployment of assets, reduction of working capital. See Williams, "Role of the Commercial Lease in Corporate Finance", 22 Bus. Law. 751 (1967); Kripke, Fairberg, Kemperich, Levinson & Whiteside, "Getting Down to Earth on Equipment Leasing Transactions", 12 Prac.Law. 9 (Jan.1966); Johnston, "Legal Aspects of Aircraft Finance", 29 J.Air L. & Com. 161 (1963); Lambert, "Survey of Domestic and International Aspects of Aircraft Equipment Financing", 18 Bus.Law. 627 (1963); Witherby, "Personal Property Lease Financing—The Lender's Point of View", 1963 Duke L.J. 98; Boothe, "The Practical Pros and Cons of Leasing", 1962 U.Ill.L.F. 1; Adkins & Bardos, "The Leasing Transaction", id. 16; Dean, "The Economics of Equipment Leasing", id. 33; Theiss, "Security Aspects of Equipment Leasing", id. 77; Wilkinson, "Borrower's Contracts as Long Term Loan Security", 17 Bus.Law. 1018 (1962); Comment, "Federal Income Tax Treatment of Equipment Lease-or-Purchase Agreements", 52 Va.L.Rev. 1336 (1966); Comment, "Taxation—Federal Income Taxation—The Three-Party Sale and Lease-Back", 61 Mich.L. Rev. 1140 (1963); Note, "Financing the Dealer's Inventory", 51 Ky.L.J. 142 (1962); Note, "Financing Inventory Through Field Warehousing", 69 Yale L. J. 663 (1960); In State of Florida v. Clay County Development Authority, 140 So.2d 576 (Fla.1962), an agreement by the County Development Authority to construct an industrial plant and then lease it to a private corporation, the cost of construction to be financed through the issue of revenue certificates payable solely from amounts to be paid by the corporation over the period of the lease was held to be invalid as a violation of Fla.Const. art. 9, § 10, which states that "the credit of the State should not be pledged or loaned to any individual, company, corporation or association. . . ."

4. Prior to 1929, more than 95 percent of corporate security issues were publicly offered. Since then, "direct or private placement" has become increasingly important in the financing of American business. In recent years, more than 40 percent of se-

curity issues have been privately placed with institutional investors, primarily insurance companies and, secondarily, pension funds. (Often there are legal restrictions as to the securities in which such investors may invest. See, e. g., Legal Investment Laws, CCH Blue Sky L.Rep.) The growth of private placement resulted from the poor public securities market during the great depression of the 1930's and received impetus from the Federal Securities Act of 1933, under which issues privately placed are exempt from the Act's registration and prospectus requirements with their attendant complexities, delays, and expenses. For a medium-size issue, the costs of public offering might be more than twice as large as those of private placement. See section 292, n. 10 infra.

5. A. Berle, The 20th Century Capitalist Revolution 37–39 (1954). Professor Berle asserts that "this is representative of the real pattern of the twentieth-century capitalism. The capital is there; and so is capitalism. The waning factor is the capitalist. . . . In his place stand the boards of directors of corporations, chiefly large ones, who retain profits and risk them in expansion of the business along lines indicated by the circumstances of their particular operation. Not the public opinion of the market place with all the economic world from which to choose, but the directoral opinion of corporate managers as to the line of greatest opportunity within their own concern, now chiefly determines the application of risk capital. Major corporations in most instances do not seek capital. They form it themselves." Id. at 39–40.

6. See Statistical Abstract of the United States 1969, 482 (U.S. Dep't of Commerce). In 1968, corporate funds of more than $113 billion were derived as follows:

Internal sources (undistributed profits, depreciation)	$64.1 billion
External sources (including $13 billion from bonds and $-.3 billion from shares)	$49.5 billion

ly secured in the legal sense. **The two main types of securities, each with many variants, are (a) debt securities, which create a debtor-creditor relationship between the corporation and the holder, and (b) equity securities, which create or contemplate the creation of a shareholder relationship. The selection of the capital structure, with various types of debt securities and equity securities, for any corporation depends upon numerous factors.**

The term "securities" covers a wide variety of corporate paper issued to evidence the rights of holders of such paper in and against the corporation,[1] ranging from the most senior type (first mortgage bonds) to the most junior (common shares). "Securities" are not necessarily secured in the legal sense.

Modern corporate statutes have become increasingly comprehensive in the treatment of the corporate financial structure.[2]

In addition to corporate statutes, the Uniform Commercial Code has substantial application to corporate securities.[3]

---

1. The term "securities" is often more broadly defined to include issues of noncorporate business enterprises and even nonbusiness issuers, whether evidenced by a written instrument or not. See, e. g., Federal Securities Act of 1933, § 2(1); 15 U.S.C.A. § 77b(1). See also L. Loss & E. Cowett, Blue Sky Law 349–352 (1958). Cf. Uniform Commercial Code § 1–201(37), defining "security interest" as "an interest in personal property or fixtures which secures payment or performance of an obligation. * * *" The certificate or other instrument evidencing the security holder's rights often has some of the qualities of negotiable paper (see section 177 infra). The holder's intentional destruction of a bond, even when thinking it worthless, might discharge the issuer's obligation. State Street Trust Co. v. Muskogee Electric Traction Co., 204 F.2d 920 (10th Cir.1953). Conversion of a share certificate has been held to constitute conversion of the shares represented thereby. Pierpont v. Hoyt, 260 N.Y. 26, 182 N.E. 235, 83 A.L.R. 1195 (1932). To qualify for listing on national securities exchanges, certificates evidencing debt securities or shares might have to conform to certain formal requirements. See N.Y.S.E. Company Manual § A12. Statutes frequently define the content or share certificates. See section 134 supra. See generally J. Boland, Federal Income Taxation of Securities (ALI 1965); C. Curtis, The Modern Prudent Investor —What the General Practitioner Should Know About Investments (ALI rev. 1961).

2. See Kummert, "Financial Provisions of the New Washington Business Corporation Act", 43 Wash.L. Rev. 337 (1967); deCapriles, "New York Business Corporation Law: Article 5—Corporate Finance", 11 Buffalo L.Rev. 461 (1962); deCapriles & McAniff, "Financial Provisions of the New (1961) New

York Business Corporation Law", 36 N.Y.U.L.Rev. 1239 (1961); Comment, 13 Syracuse L.Rev. 93 (1961).

3. U.L.A. (1969) (5 vols.); approved in 1951; revised in 1957, adopted in all states except Louisiana, and in District of Columbia, Virgin Islands. See Uniform Commercial Code § 8–102(1): "In this Article unless the context otherwise requires

(a) A 'security' is an instrument which

   (i) is issued in bearer or registered form; and

   (ii) is of a type commonly dealt in upon securities exchanges or markets or commonly recognized in any area in which it is issued or dealt in as a medium for investment; and

   (iii) is either one of a class or series or by its terms is divisible into a class or series of instruments; and

   (iv) evidences a share, participation or other interest in property or in an enterprise or evidences an obligation of the issuer."

Section 8–102 of the Code provides that a writing which is a security is governed by Article 8—Investment Securities and not by Article 3—Commercial Paper even though it also meets the requirements of Article 3. Article 8 is neither a corporate statute nor a "blue sky" law [see sections 305–307 infra], but more like a negotiable instruments law applicable to securities. Article 8 deals with bearer debt securities, formerly covered by the Uniform Negotiable Instruments Act, and with registered bonds, not previously covered by any uniform act. It also covers share certificates formerly provided for by the Uniform Stock Transfer Act, and additional types of investment paper not now covered by any uniform act. Comment, Uniform Commercial Code, § 8–101. Jolls, "Investment Securities", 23 Bus.Law. 849 (1968); Folk, "Article Eight: A Premise and Three Problems", 65 Mich.L.Rev. 1379 (1967); Folk, "Article Eight: Investment Securities", 44 N.C.L.Rev. 654 (1966); Wozencraft, "Investment Securities Under the Uniform Commercial Code—Guidelines for Business Lawyers", 44 Texas L.Rev. 669 (1966); Coogan, Kripke & Weiss, "The Outer Fringes of Article 9: Subordination Agreements, Security Interests in Money and Deposits, Negative Pledge Clauses, and Participation Agreements", 79 Harv.L.Rev. 229 (1965); Israels, "Investment Securities Problems—Article 8 of the UCC", 11 How.L.J. 120 (1965); Coogan, "Relationship of Article 9 of the Uniform Commercial Code to Pre-Code Chattel Security Law", 51 Va.L.Rev. 853 (1965); Lane, "Article 8—Investment Securities", 43 Neb.L.Rev. 792 (1964); Coogan, "A Suggested Analytical Approach to Article 9 of the Uniform Commercial Code", 63 Colum.L.Rev. 1 (1963); Coogan & Gordon, "The Effect of the Uniform Commercial Code upon Receivables Financing—Some Answers and Some Unresolved Problems", 76 Harv.L.Rev. 1529 (1963); Coogan, "Lazy Lawyer's Guide to Secured Transactions under the Code", 60 Mich.L.Rev. 685 (1962), 80 Banking L.J. 195 (1963); Gilmore,

The two main types of securities (each having many variants, some of which are "hybrids" [4]) are (a) debt securites, and (b) equity securities.

Debt securities create a debtor-creditor relationship between the corporation and holder, and as obligations owed by the corporation are part of its liabilities.

"The Purchase Money Priority", 76 Harv.L.Rev. 1333 (1963); Israels, "Investment Securities in New York: Statutory Text and Commercial Practice", 48 Cornell L.Q. 108 (1963); Sutkowski, "Inventory Financing Under the U.C.C., the Secured Creditor's Dream?", 68 Com.L.J. 95 (1963); Coogan, "How to Create Security Interests Under The Code—And Why", 48 Cornell L.Q. 131 (1962); Craig, "Accounts Receivable Financing: Transition From Variety To Uniform Commercial Code", 42 B.U.L.Rev. 187 (1962); Kripke & Felsenfeld, "Secured Transactions: A Practical Approach to Article 9 of The Uniform Commercial Code", 17 Rutgers L.Rev. 168 (1962); Guttman, "Article 8—Investment Securities", 17 Rutgers L.Rev. 136 (1962); Guttman, "Investment Securities Under the Uniform Commercial Code", 11 Buffalo L.Rev. 1 (1961); Comment, "Conflicting Perfected Security Interests in Proceeds Under Article 9 of the Uniform Commercial Code", 66 Mich.L.Rev. 517 (1968); Comment, "After-Acquired Property Security Interests in Bankruptcy: A Substitution of Collateral Defense of the U.C.C.", 77 Yale L.J. 139 (1967); Comment, "The Corporate Mortgage Under Article 9 of the Uniform Commercial Code and the New York Solution", 63 Mich.L. Rev. 1045 (1965); Comment, "The Status of an Investment Security Holder under Article 8", 33 Fordham L.Rev. 466 (1965); Comment, "Uniform Commercial Code Article 9 Filing Procedures for Railroad, Utility, and Other Corporate Debtors: Some Suggestions", 62 Mich.L.Rev. 865 (1964); Annot., 21 A.L.R.3d 268 (1968).

4. See sections 162–164 infra. See also Frank, Book Review, 42 Yale L.J. 989, 992 (1933): "[M]ore and more, the position of the bondholder and of the stockholder of large corporations are merging. It is true that the stockholder has no right to fixed income while the holder of an ordinary corporate bond seems to have a right to fixed income and to ultimate payment of a definite amount of principal. But the processes of reorganization can deprive the bondholder of those rights. If an ordinary corporate bond were realistically worded, it would perhaps advise the bondholder that the corporation was agreeing either (1) to pay him a stated sum of money with interest at stated periods, or (2) if the corporation finds itself financially embarrassed, then, at the option of those in control, to give him new securities which might take the form of non-voting stock in a new corporation. And in so far as a bondholder has an income bond the principal of which is payable at a long distant date, he is in substantially the same position as a non-voting stockholder."

Debt Securities

Corporations usually enjoy implied, if not express, powers to borrow funds for corporate purposes.[5] The articles of incorporation rarely expressly authorize issues of debt securities except in the most general terms.

Debt security holders, as creditors, obviously have a claim on corporate assets prior to shareholders.[6] Debt securities are frequently called "bonds",[7] whether the obligation is secured or not, although the term "bond" is also used to denote that the obligation is secured by a mortgage or lien on real or personal property or both.

The principal amount owed is the "principal"; the date when repayment of the principal is due is termed the "maturity date"; the periodic payments for the loan constitute "interest" (the rate of interest being often called the "coupon rate").

Debt securities may be issued for consideration equivalent to their principal amount, or for a greater consideration ("premium"), or for a lesser consideration ("discount").

In several jurisdictions, limitations may exist with respect to the consideration re-

5. E. g., ABA–ALI Model Bus.Corp.Act § 4(h). The New York Business Corporation Law is more comprehensive than most statutes in having a full section devoted to corporate bonds, debentures, and long-term notes. McKinney's N.Y.Bus.Corp.Law § 518. There are sometimes state constitutional or statutory limitations on corporate indebtedness. See, e. g., section 14, n. 8 supra.

6. For rights of debt security holders in bankruptcy of corporate reorganization, see sections 383–388 infra.

7. McKinney's N.Y.Bus.Corp.Law, § 102(a) (1) (defining "bonds" as including "secured and unsecured bonds, debentures and notes"). The term "bond" is sometimes defined as a formal promise (engraved or printed, signed, sealed) to pay a specific sum ("principal") at a fixed future time ("maturity date") and fixed interest ("coupon rate") periodically. Bonds are not always so formal; their maturities can be foreshortened by acceleration-in-event-of-default, redemption, or conversion features; the interest payments are not always fixed but may be dependent upon income. Some statutes expressly authorize facsimile signatures of corporate officers.

ceived by the corporation for debt securities.[8]

Some jurisdictions expressly authorize the articles of incorporation to confer voting rights on debt security holders.[9] A few jurisdictions permit other rights of shareholders to be conferred on debt security holders.[10]

Some debt securities are listed on one or more national securities exchanges, although such exchanges are frequently called "stock exchanges", but most are traded over-the-counter. Usually issued in denominations of $1,000 or multiples thereof, debt securities are quoted in terms of percentage of principal amount.

Debt securities are often issued under an indenture or agreement, to which the issuer and a trustee (usually a financial institution) are parties. The securities held by the security holders follow the form prescribed for them in the indenture. Such forms spell out the more important terms of the indenture, and usually in general language make reference to the indenture or agreement for any properties mortgaged or pledged, the na-

ture and extent of any security, the rights of the security holders and of the trustee and of the issuer in respect of any security, and the terms and conditions upon which the bonds are and are to be secured.[11] Modern indentures often confer voting rights on indenture security holders with respect to the indenture and the trustee's administration of the trust, but such voting rights should not be confused with rights to vote with respect to corporate affairs.[12] The trustee is supposed to safeguard the interests of the usually widely scattered security holders. With various exceptions, the issue of debt securities to the public may be subject to the Federal

8. E. g., Nebr.Const. art. XII, § 6; Tex.Const. XII, § 6 ("No corporation shall issue stock or bonds except for money paid, labor done or property actually received, and all fictitious increase of stock or indebtedness shall be void"); Lanpar Co. v. Stull, 405 S.W.2d 235 (Tex.Civ.App.1966); Langdeau v. Dick, 356 S.W.2d 945 (Tex.Civ.App.1962); McKinney's N.Y.Bus.Corp.Law, § 518 ("No corporation shall issue bonds except for money or other property, tangible or intangible, or labor or services actually received by or performed for the corporation or for its benefit or in its formation or reorganization, or a combination thereof"). For minority construction, see In re Mifflenburg Body Co., 127 F.2d 59 (3d Cir.1942) (upholding bonds issued to secure antecedent debt). See Harper, "Liability of Directors for Creating Excessive Indebtedness", 9 Cornell L.Q. 269 (1924).

9. E. g., California, Delaware, Kansas, Louisiana, Maryland, Michigan, Minnesota, New York, Oklahoma, Pennsylvania, Virginia. Absent statutory authority, such voting rights presumably will not be accorded creditors. Tracy, "The Problem of Granting Voting Rights to Bondholders", 2 U.Chi. L.Rev. 208 (1935).

10. Delaware, Kansas, Michigan, Pennsylvania ("any other rights" of shareholders); California, New York (inspection rights).

11. Such references have raised questions as to whether there is sufficient incorporation by reference. Garber, "Incorporation by Reference of 'No-Action' Clauses in Bonds", 8 Duke B.A.J. 93 (1940); Annot., 108 A.L.R. 88 (1937), 174 A.L.R. 435 (1948). When there is sufficient incorporation by reference and the indenture contains a "no-action" clause more or less vesting remedies under the securities and indentures exclusively in the trustee, and restricting individual actions by the security holders, the courts have construed such clause as only applicable to the enforcement of remedies against any property mortgaged or pledged as security. Perry v. Darlington Fire-Proofing Co., 76 Ohio App. 101, 63 N.E.2d 222 (1945). Of course, if the issue is unsecured, such a construction is not possible. In such a case, the no-action clause has been held to bar an action to recover principal or interest or both. Gordon v. Conlon Corp., 323 Ill.App. 380, 55 N.E.2d 821 (1944). Even when the issue was secured, a no-action clause has been similarly construed. Aladdin Hotel Co. v. Bloom, 200 F.2d 627 (8th Cir.1953). Or construed literally and held void for ousting courts of their jurisdiction. First Wis. Nat'l Bank v. Brynwood Land Co., 245 Wis. 610, 15 N.W.2d 840 (1944); see also Quirke v. St. Louis-San Francisco Ry., 277 F.2d 705 (8th Cir.1960), cert. denied 363 U.S. 845, 80 S.Ct. 1615, 4 L.Ed.2d 1728 (1960), reh. denied 364 U.S. 855, 81 S.Ct. 35, 5 L. Ed.2d 80 (1960). The no-action clause might be held inoperative where the indenture trustee has an adverse interest. See Rabinowitz v. Kaiser-Frazer Corp., 111 N.Y.S.2d 539 (Sup.Ct.1952). The Federal Trust Indenture Act of 1939 provides that every indenture, to be qualified for registration, shall provide that the right and remedy (except against property subject to the lien of the indenture) of the indenture security holder to principal and interest (with some exceptions) shall not be impaired or affected without the consent of such holder. 15 U.S.C.A. § 77 ppp(b).

12. See note 9 supra. See Rothschild v. Jefferson Hotel Co., 56 F.Supp. 315 (E.D.Mo.1944).

Trust Indenture Act of 1939,[13] which requires a qualified indenture and an eligible trustee.

A few states impose issue taxes on the issuance of certain debt securities.[14]

The transfer of debt securities is governed by the Uniform Commercial Code.[15]

South Carolina appears to impose transfer taxes on the transfer of debt securities.[16]

Unclaimed principal, interest, and redemption prices on debt securities are often subject to state abandoned property or escheat provisions.[17]

Equity Securities

Equity securities[18] generally create or contemplate the creation of a shareholder (or stockholder) relationship, with the shareholders being, in a broad sense, "insiders" who "own" the corporation (as compared to the holders of debt securities who are "outsiders" "owed" by the corporation).

The consideration received by the corporation for its shares, or at least a portion thereof, constitutes stated capital. Stated capital, plus any surplus or less any deficit, represents the equity of the shareholders in the corporation.

Authorization for the issue of shares is found in the articles of incorporation.

The shareholder has a proportionate interest in the corporation with respect to earnings, assets, and control, and often preemptive rights to preserve such proportionate interest. The financial and related aspects will be discussed in this chapter; the control and related aspects in Chapter 9.[19]

The corporation generally is under no obligation to return to the shareholder the amount of his investment, although under certain conditions it might redeem or negotiate the purchase of the shares. In other words, shares generally have no fixed maturity (except for dissolution and possibly for a rare mandatory redemption provision). Recoupment of the investment is usually dependent upon the shareholder's selling his shares to another person or upon liquidation of the corporation following its dissolution. In dissolution, shareholders are, of course, subordinate to creditors.

Any return to the shareholders by way of "dividends" is dependent upon the existence of legally available funds (usually net profits or surplus) and is usually within the discretion of the board of directors.

Shares may be issued for the required consideration or for a greater consideration ("premium"), in any of which cases the shares are usually full-paid and nonassessable. To the extent that shares are issued for inadequate consideration, they are said to be "bonus", "discount", or "watered" shares.[20]

Many issues of publicly-traded shares of larger corporations are listed on one or more national securities exchanges, where they are traded in round-lot (usually 100 shares) or odd-lot transactions. Shares are quoted in terms of dollars (and eighths thereof). Numerous other issues are traded over-the-counter, on a bid-and-asked quotation basis.

Selection of Capital Structure

The totality of the corporation's debt securities and equity securities is known as the corporate "capital structure".

---

13. 15 U.S.C.A. §§ 77aaa–77bbbb. See section 300 infra. For listed debt securities, the securities exchanges may impose various requirements concerning the indenture, trustee, and other matters. E. g., N.Y.S.E. Company Manual §§ A1–A6, A10, A12, A16.

14. E. g., Florida, South Carolina.

15. See note 3 supra and section 177 infra.

16. S.C. Code 1962, §§ 65–681, 65–682.

17. See section 179 infra.

18. "Equity securities" usually has a somewhat broader meaning than the term shares. Securities convertible into shares or options to acquire shares might also be included. See Federal Securities Exchange Act of 1934, § 3(a) (11), 15 U.S.C.A. § 78c(11).

19. See sections 180–230 infra.

20. See section 171 infra.

Every business corporation must, of course, issue some shares. Depending upon various factors, the issue of debt securities, as well as of shares, might prove advantageous. "Trading on the equity" or "leverage" magnifies profits (and losses);[21] "thin incorporation" offers some possible advantages.[22]

The choice between various types of debt securities and of equity securities depends upon numerous considerations, such as market conditions (the current temper of the investing public, inflationary or deflationary trends, encouragement or discouragement of risk capital by tax system), stability of corporate earnings (availability for fixed interest charges or preferred dividends), interest rate level, nature of corporate assets (suitability as security), and amount of funds required (attraction to investors with different objectives: growth, income, safety).[23]

From the viewpoint of investors, everything else being equal, bonds generally offer no growth possibilities, very steady income, and high safety; preferred shares have variable growth potential, reasonably steady income, and relatively good safety; common shares are best from the point of view of possible growth, variable in income, and least safe. Of course, the senior secured bonds of one corporation can experience a poorer safety record than the most junior class of shares of another corporation.

B. DEBT SECURITIES

CLASSIFICATION OF DEBT SECURITIES

156. Debt securities can be classified in various ways, depending upon the features emphasized, as (a) Maturity—long-term or funded, short-term or unfunded; (b) Purpose—purchase-money, construction, extension, improvement; funding, refunding; consolidated; adjustment; (c) Security of principal—mortgage; bridge, dock, divisional, terminal; collateral trust; equipment obligations; debentures; long-term loans; subordinated debentures and notes; assumed; guaranteed; receiver's certificates; (d) Income—fixed interest; income; participating; (e) Payees of principal and interest—registered; coupon; registered coupon; (f) Manner of payment of principal—gold, silver, legal tender; redeemable; convertible.

Debt securities, as mentioned, usually involve the corporation's obligation to pay principal when due (the maturity can be from 30 days or less to 100 years or more), and interest (usually at a fixed rate) while the obligation is outstanding.

Debt securities can be classified in various ways, depending upon the feature or features being emphasized. Often the designation or title of the security will reflect one or more such features.[1]

One generally-accepted classification system for corporate debt securities is as to (a)

21. See section 165 infra.

22. See section 166 infra.

23. See M. Zausner, Corporate Policy and the Investment Community (1968); C. Rohrlich, Organizing Corporate and Other Business Enterprises 373–457 (4th ed. 1967); Stock, "Use of Corporate Stock and Securities to Raise Capital", 16 Tul.Tax Inst. 292 (1966); Aarons, "Debt v. Equity: Special Hazards in Setting Up the Corporate Capital Structure", 23 J. Taxation 194 (1965); Donaldson, "New Framework for Corporate Debt Policy", 40 Harv.Bus.Rev. 117 (Mar.–Apr.1962); Weyher, "Capital Structure of New Corporations", N.Y.U. 16th Inst. on Fed. Tax. 277 (1958). The capital structure serves the triple function of allocating control, earnings, and ultimately assets. For public utilities, enterprises with stable, predictable earnings, the Securities and Exchange Commission follows, as a working policy, 60 percent debt, 10 percent preferred shares, and 30 percent common shares. See Cook & Cohn, "Capital Structures of Electric Utilities under the Public Utility Holding Company Act", 45 Va.L.Rev. 981 (1959). See also B. Bittker & J. Eustice, Federal Income Taxation of Corporations and Shareholders ch. 4 (2d ed. 1966).

1. E. g., "First and Consolidated Mortgage Bonds"; "General Refunding Mortgage Bonds, 4% Series J, due June 1, 1988"; "4½% Convertible Debentures, due 1992"; "Equipment Trust, Series VV". The correct designation or title is found in the instrument and any indenture.

maturity, (b) purpose, (c) security of principal, (d) income, (e) payees of principal and interest, and (f) manner of payment of principal.[2]

As to Maturity

While debt securities, in a broad sense, can, from the point of view of maturity, be "short-time" (say, one year or less), "short-term" (say, five or 10 years or less), or "long-term" (say, more than five or 10 years)—there is little general agreement as to the precise lines of demarcation—the term debt securities is often reserved for obligations of more that "short-time" duration, i. e., for "short-term" or "long-term" obligations. Short-term obligations are sometimes referred to as "unfunded debt"; long-term obligations are often called "funded debt".

As to Purpose

The purpose of the issue, while usually not a very significant feature, provides a classification basis.

Purchase-money securities are those issued in direct payment for property acquired by the corporation. Such securities are often secured by a lien on such property.

Construction securities are those issued to finance construction of the corporation's physical property in the sense that the proceeds realized from their issue are intended to be applied to pay for construction. *Extension* securities involve the application of their proceeds to pay for extensions to physical property. *Improvement* securities are issued to raise funds for the improvement of existing physical property. Obviously, these terms have overlapping meanings.

Funding securities involve the creation of a long-term obligation where none existed before. The proceeds are often used to retire short-term obligations. *Refunding* securities involve the issue of long-term obligations to provide funds to retire other long-term obli-

gations. Neither term has any reference to sinking fund or other reserves.

Consolidated securities constitute an issue sufficiently large to provide the funds to retire two or more outstanding issues of debt securities.

Adjustment securities are those issued, usually in reorganization, in substitution for outstanding securities. The "adjustments" might involve lower interest charges, extended maturity, and/or decreased principal.

As to Security of Principal

Debt securities are also classifiable according to the mortgage, pledge, or other security, if any, enjoyed by the holder in addition to the personal obligation of the issuer or principal obligor. The holder of an unsecured debt security ranks equally with other general creditors. Even the holder of a secured debt security is, after exhaustion of the security, a general creditor with respect to any unsatisfied balance.

Mortgage securities are secured by a mortgage or lien on the property of the issuer. First mortgage bonds are generally the senior issue, although not necessarily a first lien on all the property. There might, for example, be prior tax liens, purchase-money obligations, or prior liens on small segments of the property. Junior mortgage bonds are secured by a second or subsequent lien on the property. While the designations for such a junior issue vary, "General Mortgage Bonds" is frequently used.

Mortgage bonds are usually issued under a several-hundred page mortgage trust indenture (sometimes called a deed of trust or trust agreement) between the corporate issuer (mortgagor) and a trustee or trustees (mortgagee(s)). The trustee, usually a financial institution, represents the frequently numerous, scattered, and sometimes unknown mortgage bondholders. The indenture may be "closed-end" (limited as to amount of bonds to be issued thereunder) or

---

2. See generally G. Harold, Corporation Finance 49–64 (3d rev.ed. 1956).

"open-end" (without such limit). In the latter case, the indenture will usually provide for the authentication by the trustee of the initial issue or issues merely upon the request of the issuer and for the authentication of additional bonds of later series (e. g., "Series B", etc., usually under supplemental indentures) on the basis of property additions, retirement of prior liens, refunding of bonds outstanding under the indenture, or the deposit of cash equal to the principal amount of the bonds authenticated. Bonds of the various series are all equally and ratably secured (except as to any sinking fund established for any particular series) by the indenture.[3]

Bridge, Dock, Divisional, or *Terminal* securities are issued to finance such special purpose properties, and are usually secured by a lien thereon.

Collateral trust securities involve a pledge of personal property, usually securities of other issuers, especially subsidiaries, owned by the obligor.[4] Such financing has the possible advantages of being on the credit of the holding company, which might be better known than the subsidiary, of avoiding after-acquired property clauses, and of permitting the holding company to retain any control, at least prior to default, over the subsidiary. Use of such methods resulted in pyramiding of holding company systems,[5] a practice now restricted in interstate gas and electric business by the Federal Public Utility Holding Company Act of 1935.[6]

Equipment obligations involve the issue of various types of securities (mortgage bonds, collateral trust bonds, preferred shares, certificates of beneficial interest), secured by equipment. Such financing has been most used with respect to railroad rolling stock, although it has been tried in other situations, including recently with respect to the aircraft of airlines.[7]

Railroad rolling stock, with its standard guage and design, mobility, and its essentiality to railroad operations, has proven over the years to provide excellent security, despite the frequent financial vicissitudes of the railroads. Serial reduction of the debt in advance of depreciation of the property provides a comfortable cushion of security.

"Equipment trust" plans are of various types. The most prevalent—at one time some 97 percent in vogue—is a lease arrangement known as the "Philadelphia Plan". Under the "Philadelphia Plan", the equipment is purchased from the manufacturer by a trustee which provides, say, three-fourths of the purchase price (the balance being paid by the railroad). The trustee then leases the equipment to the railroad. The "rental" paid by the railroad to

3. Riemer, "After-Acquired Property Clause Revisited", 70 Com.L.J. 334 (1965); Tesdell, "'Assumption' and 'Subject to' Clauses with Reference to Mortgages", 20 Bus.Law. 447 (1965); Gordon, "Why Benedict v. Ratner?", 21 Wash. & Lee L.Rev. 70 (1964); Coogan & Bok, "The Impact of Article 9 of the Uniform Commercial Code on the Corporate Indenture", 69 Yale L.J. 203 (1959); Friedman, "The Bankruptcy Preference Challenge to After-Acquired Property Clauses under the Code", 108 U.Pa.L.Rev. 194 (1959); Arnold, "After-Acquired Property as Mortgage Security in Maryland", 19 Md.L.Rev. 294 (1959); Wilson, "The New Haven Clock Case—Another Look at Benedict v. Ratner," 13 Bus.Law. 633 (1958); Cohen & Gerber, "The After-Acquired Property Clause", 87 U.Pa.L.Rev. 635 (1939); Comment, "Corporate Mortgage Under Article 9 of the Uniform Commercial Code and the New York Solution", 63 Mich.L.Rev. 1045 (1965). For New York Stock Exchange requirements concerning indentures, see N.Y.S.E. Company Manual § A5. For a description of a corporate trust indenture, see R. Stevens & H. Henn, Statutes, Cases and Materials on the Law of Corporations and Other Business Enterprises 412–420 (1965). Shareholder approval of certain corporate mortgages is required in some jurisdictions. See section 342 infra.

4. See Powell v. Maryland Trust Co., 125 F.2d 260 (4th Cir.1942), cert. denied 316 U.S. 671, 62 S.Ct. 1046, 86 L.Ed. 1746 (1942), reh. denied 316 U.S. 711, 62 S.Ct. 1274, 86 L.Ed. 1777 (1942) (trustee awarded

cash and share dividends on pledged shares of mortgagor).

5. R. Stevens & A. Larson, Cases and Materials on the Law of Corporations 240–242 (2d ed. 1955).

6. 15 U.S.C.A. §§ 79–79z–6. See section 299 infra.

7. Adkins & Billyou, "Developments in Commercial Aircraft Equipment Financing", 13 Bus.Law. 199 (1958).

the trustee consists of "interest", amortization for serial retirement—say one-fifteenth at the end of the first and each successive year, such serial reduction being in advance of depreciation of the property—and the trustee's fees. For tax purposes, deduction by the lessor for depreciation and deduction by the lessee of the rental are important factors. The railroad has an option to acquire title in the equipment from the trustee at the end of the last year of the plan for a nominal sum (e. g., $1.00). The railroad covenants to keep the equipment repaired and insured, to replace when necessary, to affix to the equipment appropriate nameplates indicating that title thereto is in the trustee, and, in the event of default, to deliver the equipment to the custody of the trustee. Investors who participate under the plan are issued equipment trust certificates by the trustee. The certificate holders are entitled to receive from the trustee such funds as the latter receives for such purpose from the railroad. Except to treat the equipment as security for the certificate holders, and to carry out its fiduciary duties under the plan, the trustee is not otherwise personally bound. The railroad guarantees the payment of principal and interest to the holders, thus becoming personally bound to the certificate holders.[8]

Other arrangements have traditionally involved conditional sale ("New York Plan"), equipment mortgage, mortgage collateral, or preferred shares.

Debentures (a term derived from the Latin word *"debentur"*, meaning "are due") are generally unsecured obligations, involving only the personal obligation of the obligor, in the United States.[9]

Debentures are often issued under an indenture (sometimes called a trust agreement or deed of trust) between the issuer and a trustee. Debenture indentures, of course, have no granting clauses, since they do not involve any lien or mortgage. For the same reason, since there is no problem of equal and ratable security for a series of issues usually the indenture is "closed-end" and there is a separate indenture for each issue of debentures.[10]

To protect debenture holders who rank as general creditors, the debentures and/or indenture might limit borrowing,[11] impose a current liabilities-assets margin requirement, restrict dividend payments, limit share redemption or purchase, require the maintenance of certain reserves, or restrict additional issues of securities. Common protective provisions are so-called "negative pledge" and similar covenants.[12]

the obligor's property. The general lien, in the event of default, becomes specific. Debentures of this type account for Salomon's secured creditor status in the leading English case of Salomon v. Salomon & Co., [1897] A.C. 22, discussed in section 147 supra. See Coogan, "Operating under Article 9 of the Uniform Commercial Code without Help or Hindrance of the 'Floating Lien' ", 15 Bus.Law. 373 (1960); Adkins & Billyou, "A Proposed New Form of Security for the Senior Debt of Our Airlines and Railroads: Floating Charges", 12 Bus.Law. 378 (1957). For discussion of subordinated debentures, see text accompanying note 14 infra.

10. Such indentures, of course, are subject to the applicable requirements of the Federal Trust Indenture Act of 1939. See section 300 infra. For listing, stock exchange requirements should be observed. E. g., N.Y.S.E. Company Manual § A5. The American Bar Foundation drafted model nonnegotiated provisions for a debenture indenture, leaving the other provisions to be negotiated, decided, and drafted for each issue. American Bar Foundation Corporate Debt Financing Project—Sample Incorporating Indenture and Model Debenture Indenture Provisions—All Registered Issues (1967); id. [both registered and coupon forms] (1966); Garrett, "A Borrower's View of the Model Corporate Debenture Indenture Provisions", 21 Bus.Law. 675 (1966); Rodgers, "The Corporate Trust Indenture Project", 20 Bus.Law. 551 (1965).

11. See Kelly v. Central Hanover Bank & Trust Co., 11 F.Supp. 497 (S.D.N.Y.1935), rev'd 85 F.2d 61 (2d Cir.1936).

12. Pledge clauses are of various types. The affirmative pledge clause involves a covenant by the is-

8. For discussion of the "equitable equipment lease" variation, see Adkins & Billyou, "Current Developments in Railroad Equipment Financing", 12 Bus. Law. 207 (1957).

9. When debentures are subordinated to the claims of other classes of creditors, the term "Subordinated Debenture" is often employed. In England, debentures frequently constitute "floating charges" on

Long-term loans from commercial banks and insurance companies have become frequent in recent years, a departure from the long-standing tradition in favor of short-term commercial bank loans. Since the issue involves no public offering, Securities and Exchange Commission requirements, with attendant complexities and expense, can be avoided. The loan agreement, compared to an indenture, is a relatively short (say 30 or so pages) and simple instrument. Several commercial banks might form a group to make the loan.[13]

Subordinated debentures and notes are obligations (sometimes called "subordinated debt," "junior debt", or "inferior debt") upon which the right to receive payment is subordinated by a "subordination agreement" or "subordination clause" in an indenture or agreement to the prior payment of certain other indebtedness (sometimes called "senior debt", "superior debt", "prior debt", or "bank debt") of the same debtor. Subordination might be "inchoate" (not operative until a voluntary or involuntary distribution

of assets by the debtor to its creditors) or "complete" (payment of principal and interest on "subordinated debt" deferred until obligations on "senior debt" satisfied). Such arrangements developed in the late 1930's, with issues by sales finance and small loan companies, spreading to the oil and chemical industries and other industrial concerns, most recently to public utilities. Valid as between the parties, the status of subordinated debt in bankruptcy has not yet been fully resolved.[14]

Assumed obligations are obligations originally issued by corporations involved in corporate mergers or consolidations. In such situations, the corporation emerging from the amalgamation assumes the obligations of the constituent corporations whose corporate existences end.

Guaranteed obligations are those issued by one corporation (primary obligor) and guaranteed as to payment of principal and/or interest by another corporation (guarantor—secondary obligor). Technically, there are two securities, the underlying one issued by the principal obligor and the guaranty issued by the guarantor. The common example are

---

suer to afford ratable security to the debentures if any secured debt is incurred. A conditional negative pledge clause is to the effect that the issuer will not incur any secured debt unless the debentures are ratably secured. An absolute no pledge clause is a covenant by the issuer not to mortgage or pledge any of its assets. For a lower court holding which both narrowly construed a negative pledge clause and restricted the available legal and equitable remedies for the violation of such a clause, to the detriment of the debenture holders, see Kelly v. Central Hanover Bank & Trust Co., 11 F.Supp. 497 (S.D.N.Y.1935), rev'd 85 F.2d 61 (2d Cir.1936). Jacobs, "The Effect of Provision for Ratable Protection of Debenture Holders in Case of Subsequent Mortgage", 52 Harv.L.Rev. 77 (1938). Comment, "Protection for Debenture Holders", 46 Yale L.J. 97 (1936). Sass v. New York Towers, Ltd., 23 A.D.2d 105, 258 N.Y.S.2d 765 (1st Dep't 1965) (upholding no action clause barring enforcement of payment of principal or interest unless 85 percent of debenture holders joined in action). See Colonial Realty Corp. v. Curtis Pub. Co., CCH Fed.Sec.L.Rep. ¶ 92,105 (S.D.N.Y.1967) (debenture holder held to have no standing to enjoin contemplated issuance of later issue of debentures under S.E.C. Rule 10b–5).

13. Oddie, "Bank Financing of Business Enterprise", in Advising California Business Enterprises 39 (1958). For discussion of subordinated notes, see text accompanying note 14 infra.

14. See Austin v. Nat'l Discount Corp., 322 F.2d 928 (4th Cir.1963) (upholding subordination provision in bankruptcy proceeding); In re Nat'l Discount Corp., 212 F.Supp. 929 (W.D.S.C.1963), aff'd 322 F.2d 928 (4th Cir. 1963) (upholding subordination provisions in bankruptcy proceedings). But see In re Joe Newcomer Finance Co., 226 F.Supp. 387 (D.Colo. 1964); Matter of Itemlab, Inc., 197 F.Supp. 194 (E.D. N.Y.1961); Calligar, "Purposes and Uses of Subordination Agreements", 23 Bus.Law. 33 (1967); Everett, "Analysis of Particular Subordination Provisions", 23 Bus.Law. 41 (1967); Leiby, "Enforcement and the UCC", 23 Bus.Law. 57 (1967); Lascher, "Subordination Clauses in Court: Is California Unfair to Unfairness?", 1 U.San Fernando Valley L.Rev. 1 (1967); Everett, "Subordinated Debt—Nature and Enforcement", 20 Bus.Law. 953 (1965); Everett, "Subordinated Debt—Nature, Objectives and Enforcement", 44 B.U.L.Rev. 487 (1964); Eisenhardt, "Subordination of Purchase-Money Security", 52 Calif.L.Rev. 157 (1964); Calligar, "Subordination Agreements", 70 Yale L.J. 376 (1961); Johnson, "Subordinated Debentures: Debt that Serves as Equity", 10 J.Fin. 1 (1955).

securities issued by a subsidiary and guaranteed by its parent.[15]

Receiver's certificates are generally issued by a corporation in financial difficulties to raise necessary working capital, pursuant to an order of the court having jurisdiction over insolvency, receivership, bankruptcy arrangement, or reorganization proceedings involving the corporation. Such certificates are usually given a sufficiently high claim priority to assure their repayment out of the assets of the corporation.[16]

As to Income

According to their provisions for income ("interest"), debt securities may be classified. Taxwise, interest on debt securities, unlike dividends on shares, has the advantage of being deductible for federal and state income tax purposes. In unusual situations, debt securities might be made noninterest-bearing.

Traditionally, debt securities have involved a *fixed* interest charge. Such interest (or "coupon") rate usually ranges from 2½ to 6 or more percent *per annum,* payable semi-annually.[17] The interest rate is usually fixed in one-eighth units with resulting adjustment in the price of the security, either at a discount or at a premium. The obligation to pay definite interest continues regardless of the financial status of the corporation, with the result that such a fixed charge can be embarrassing in hard times. In the latter event, "trading on equity" or "leverage" has the effect of magnifying losses.

Income obligations condition the obligation to pay interest, in whole or part, on corporate earnings.[18] Sometimes the obligation is entirely dependent upon earnings. On the other hand, there might be a fixed obligation to pay a stated percentage of interest regardless of earnings, with the rest of the interest dependent upon earnings. The interest provision, to the extent of its income-dependent feature, might be cumulative or noncumulative.

To the extent that interest is dependent upon earnings, such feature somewhat resembles the dividend feature of shares. However, to the extent of earnings, there is a definite obligation to pay, in contrast to the usual discretionary power of the corporation to declare dividends even when legally available funds are available.

Income obligations are usually issued to minimize the corporation's fixed charges in bad times. Such interest provisions are a common feature of adjustment obligations or obligations, usually junior in nature, issued under corporate reorganization plans.

Obligations which call for interest payments in addition to the interest rate are known as *"participating"* obligations. Such a profit-sharing feature is rare but may be used to sweeten securities with otherwise low interest rates or interest-dependent-upon-income features.

---

15. Both securities, therefore, must be issued, and any indentures relating thereto must be qualified, under applicable requirements of state "blue sky" statutes, the Federal Securities Act of 1933, and the Federal Trust Indenture Act of 1939. See sections 295, 300 infra.

16. Pemberton Lumber & Mill-Work Industries, Inc. v. Wm. G. Ridgway Constr. Co., 38 N.J.Super. 383, 118 A.2d 873 (1955).

17. Corporations often are not subject to state usury statutes. See section 150 supra. Because of the uncertainty of the validity of interest-on-interest provisions under state law [cf. Newburger-Morris Co. v. Talcott, 219 N.Y. 505, 114 N.E. 846, 3 A.L.R. 287 (1916) (provision void)], and the equitable disallowance of even a valid (under state law) claim for interest-on-interest in a federal bankruptcy or reorganization proceeding [Vanston Bondholders Protective Committee v. Green, 329 U.S. 156, 67 S.Ct. 237, 91 L.Ed. 162 (1946)], such provisions are often qualified by a phrase like "(to the extent that payment of such interest is enforceable under applicable law)".

18. Comment, "Bonds—Income Bonds—Rights of Bondholders and Deductibility of Interest for Federal Income Tax Purposes", 56 Mich.L.Rev. 1334 (1958).

Miscellaneous

Various other interest provisions are occasionally found.[19]

As to Payees of Principal and Interest

Debt securities are classifiable as to the payees of principal and interest into two types: (a) registered, and (b) coupon.[20] Traditionally, the same issue has been available, at the choice of any holder, in either form, and either form has been exchangeable for the other at the request of the holder. When such exchange privilege exists, the security is sometimes called "interchangeable" or "exchangeable".

A *registered* security bears the name of the owner, who is also registered as the owner with his address on the registry books maintained by the registrar for the issue. The principal, upon maturity, and interest, on the interest dates, are paid to such registered owner. Such securities are usually in denominations of $1,000 or any multiple thereof. Ownership is transferred by a duly-executed assignment either on the security itself or by separate instrument.[21] Reg-

istered securities are "negotiable instruments" under the Uniform Commercial Code, which defines a "bona fide purchaser" as a purchaser for value in good faith and without notice of any adverse claim who takes delivery of a security in bearer form or of one in registered form issued to him or indorsed to him or in blank.[22]

A *coupon* security usually provides for the payment of principal to the bearer thereof, and for payment of an installment of interest to the bearer of the respective interest coupons upon presentation thereof upon their respective due dates. Coupon securities are usually in the denomination of $1,000. Ownership of the security and/or coupons is transferred by delivery thereof. Such a security is negotiable under the Uniform Commercial Code.[23]

Coupon securities often may be registered as to principal (sometimes called "*registered coupon*" form), in which case the principal is payable to the registered owner but the interest remains payable to the bearers of

---

19. The interest rate might be geared to the price index ("Stabilized Bonds"), or the issuer might undertake to pay some of the holder's income tax on such interest ("Tax-free Bonds"), which, of course, has a snowballing effect. "Tax-free Bonds" should not be confused with "Tax-exempt Bonds" (mainly municipal bonds).

20. Similar classifications sometimes list three categories: (a) "registered", (b) "coupon", (c) "registered coupon". The twofold categorization combines the last two. There is growing investor acceptance of registered bonds. More than half of the new bond issues are appearing only in registered form. Listed among the advantages of registered bonds are convenience, safety, better notice procedures, savings in manpower costs, storage costs and human effort, compared to the antiquated wasteful procedures involved in coupon bonds. Sebring, "Registered Bonds—A Brief Progress Report", 20 Bus.Law. 238 (1964); Waldbillig, "Coupon Bonds Have Advantages", 19 Bus.Law. 999 (1964); Sebring, " 'The Coupon Bond: A Costly Paradox'— A Postscript", 18 Bus.Law. 429 (1963); Sebring, "The Coupon Bond: A Costly Paradox", 17 Bus. Law. 844 (1962).

21. See Uniform Commercial Code § 8–102(1) (c), providing: "A security is in 'registered form' when it specifies a person entitled to the security or to the

rights it evidences and when its transfer may be registered upon books maintained for that purpose by or on behalf of an issuer or the security so states." This is comparable to the record ownership and transfer of shares. See sections 176, 177 infra.

22. Uniform Commercial Code §§ 8–105, 8–302. Under the former Uniform Negotiable Instruments Act, registered securities were not negotiable instruments because they were not negotiable in form. Landau v. Best, 41 Del.Ch. 1, 187 A.2d 75 (Sup.Ct.1962), appeal dismissed 375 U.S. 801, 84 S. Ct. 25, 11 L.Ed.2d 37 (1963). Compare Harr v. Market St. Title & Trust Co., 326 Pa. 410, 190 A. 903 (1957), with Reynolds v. Title Guarantee & Trust Co., 240 N.Y. 257, 148 N.E. 514 (1925). Steffen & Russell, "Registered Bonds and Negotiability", 47 Harv.L.Rev. 741 (1934); Steffen & Russell, "The Negotiability of Corporate Bonds", 40 Yale L.J. 261 (1930); Comment, "Negotiability of Corporate Bonds—Recent New York Legislation", 40 Yale L.J. 261 (1930).

23. Uniform Commercial Code §§ 8–105, 8–302. See id. § 8–102(1) (d), providing: "A security is in 'bearer form' when it runs to bearer according to its terms and not by reason of any indorsement." Under the former Uniform Negotiable Instruments Act, such securities, if in proper form, had been held negotiable. Enoch v. Brandon, 249 N.Y. 263, 164 N.E. 45 (1928). See note 22 supra.

the respective interest coupons. When a coupon security so registered is assigned in blank, it, of course, might be negotiable. If a coupon security so registered is made payable to bearer, principal would again become payable to the bearer of the security.

Obviously, the owners of bearer securities are often unknown to the issuer, any trustee, and the other security holders. This accounts for various provisions for publication of notices (e.g., redemption notice) and the difficulty of rounding up sufficient security holders to take effective action or to compel the trustee to act under certain circumstances.

As to Manner of Payment of Principal

A final way of classifying debt securities is by manner of payment of principal.

Debt securities in former years sometimes contained a "gold clause" ("*Gold* Bonds"), requiring payment of principal in "gold coin of the United States of the present standard of weight and fineness". The notorious *Gold Clause* cases in the United States Supreme Court [24] upheld the constitutionality of a joint congressional resolution (June 5, 1933) making such bonds dischargeable by payment of current legal tender United States money, and prohibiting such clauses in the future. *Silver* bonds, requiring payment of principal in silver or an amount of money measured thereby, have not been used in the United States. All debt securities in the United States, since the foregoing developments, have in effect been *legal tender* obligations.

One of the traditional features of debt securities is fixed maturity. The corporate issuer, like any other debtor, has no implied right of prepayment.[25]

A frequent provision, however, is a *redemption* provision permitting [26] the corporation to redeem or call the issue in whole or part [27] prior to maturity at the redemption price. The redemption price is often set forth as the face amount plus a redemption premium which is usually scaled from, say, five or so points above the face amount or public offering price on the first possible redemption date (often the first anniversary of the issue), down to zero on the maturity date, plus any accrued interest. The redemption procedure is prescribed and usually involves the giving of redemption notice by mail and/or publication,[28] and the deposit of the funds necessary for redemption no later than the redemption date. If there has been compliance with such procedure, the security holders on or after the redemption date lose all their rights except to receive the redemption price upon surrender of their securities. Sometimes the redemption feature is tied in with the operation of a sinking fund provision,[29] or a conversion feature.[30]

---

celeration-in-event-of-default provisions can operate to advance the maturity.

26. Redemption provisions are usually discretionary but can be mandatory. The option is usually in the issuer, but can be in the holder. For a case of abortive redemption of a convertible debenture, see Mueller v. Howard Aircraft Corp., 329 Ill.App. 570, 70 N.E.2d 203 (1946).

27. See Specht v. Eastwood-Nealley Corp., 25 N.J.Super. 69, 95 A.2d 485 (1953) (redemption of bonds held by majority shareholder who had agreed to sell them to plaintiff at substantial discount enjoined), aff'd 34 N.J.Super. 156, 111 A.2d 781 (1955). In case of partial redemption, the redemption might be proportionate or the securities to be redeemed can be selected by lot or some other fair manner.

28. Gampel v. Burlington Industries, Inc., 43 Misc.2d 846, 252 N.Y.S.2d 500 (Sup.Ct.1964) (upholding publication of notice of redemption of debentures in *The Wall Street Journal*).

29. Sinking funds are established to provide funds for the payment of principal not only by periodic partial redemption but also for the periodic retirement of serial bonds or for the payment of securities at maturity. Sinking funds are generally cre-

---

24. Norman v. Baltimore & Ohio R. R., United States v. Bankers Trust Co., 294 U.S. 240, 55 S.Ct. 407, 79 L.Ed. 885, 95 A.L.R. 1352 (1935). But see Bronson v. Rodes, 74 U.S. (7 Wall.) 229, 19 L.Ed. 141 (1868).

25. The corporation might, of course, purchase its securities by negotiating with holders thereof. Ac-

30. See note 30 on page 288.

Redemption before maturity might be desirable to the corporation to reduce fixed charges, improve credit standing, avoid high interest rates, free property from any mortgage or pledge, invest any sinking fund, refund or refinance at a lower interest rate, or forestall or promote exercise of any conversion privilege. The redemption premium is supposed to compensate the holder for delay in reinvesting his funds returned to him upon redemption and for any less advantageous market at such time.

A *convertible* debt security involves the privilege, usually at the option of the holder, of converting it into some other security. If the latter is a more senior debt security, the conversion is said to be "upstream"; if a junior debt security or shares, "downstream".

Debt securities convertible into shares have been frequently issued, because they combined safety (creditor status) with opportunity for possible speculative gain (increase in price of shares beyond conversion price), and result in retirement of debt, reduction of fixed charges, and substitution of equity interests.[31] Obviously, the corpora-

tion should have enough shares of authorized and unissued shares to take care of the exercise of any subsisting conversion privileges.

To prevent dilution of the conversion privilege during the conversion period, which may run from issue to maturity (subject to any prior redemption) or for a shorter period, so-called "anti-dilution" provisions [32] are included to make adjustments of the number of shares issuable upon exercise of the conversion privilege in certain instances, the most common being (a) issuance of shares for less than the conversion price, (b) issuance of rights to subscribe to or purchase shares or securities convertible into shares, (c) issuance of securities convertible into or exchangeable for shares, at a price less than the conversion price, (d) issuance of dividend of shares or securities convertible into shares, (e) share splits, (f) abnormally large

Kinney's N.Y.Bus.Corp.Law, § 519 (expressly authorizing bonds convertible into other bonds or shares of corporation, requiring that sufficient number of authorized but unissued shares be issued to satisfy any conversion privilege and that minimum consideration requirements applicable to shares be met). See generally C. Pilcher, Raising Capital with Convertible Securities (1955); Katzin, "Financial and Legal Problems in the Use of Convertible Securities", 24 Bus.Law. 359 (1969); Note, "Convertible Securities: Holder Who Fails to Convert Before Expiration of the Conversion Period", 54 Cornell L.Rev. 271 (1969). The Securities and Exchange Commission has not favored convertible securities. In the Matter of Public Service Co. of Indiana, Inc., 26 S.E.C. 338, 350–353 (1947). See Fleischer & Cary, "The Taxation of Convertible Bonds and Stock", 74 Harv.L.Rev. 473 (1961). The issue of securities convertible into shares sometimes is subject to preemptive rights. See sections 172–175 infra.

ated by contract which usually provide for the administration of the fund by a trustee, but in some instances, the corporation itself may retain control of the fund. The use of a sinking fund will increase the safety of an issue by reducing the amount of the bonds outstanding and by providing funds for their repayment. The amount of the periodic contribution to the fund will vary with the type of security and will usually be stipulated in the bond or trust indenture. The periodic contributions may be based on a percentage of annual earnings, the face value of the bonds divided by the duration of the bonds, or on an actuarial basis. Such amounts might be reduced by the earnings of the sinking funds.

Failure to meet the sinking fund requirements might constitute an event of default which would permit the trustee to accelerate the maturity of the principal.

30. Grace v. Sterling, Grace & Co., 30 A.D.2d 61, 289 N.Y.S.2d 632 (1st Dep't 1968) (subpledgee held liable for failure to convert debentures prior to redemption).

31. The New York Business Corporation Law devotes a section to convertible securities. Mc-

32. Absent provision to the contrary, a consolidation has been held to destroy a conversion privilege. Parkinson v. West End St. Ry., 173 Mass. 446, 53 N.E. 891 (1899). See C. Pilcher, Raising Capital with Convertible Securities (1955); Kaplan, "Some Further Comments on Anti-Dilution Clauses", 23 Bus.Law. 893 (1968); Ratner, "Dilution and Anti-Dilution: A Reply to Professor Kaplan", 33 U.Chi. L.Rev. 494 (1966); Kaplan, "Piercing the Corporate Boilerplate: Anti-Dilution Clauses in Convertible Securities", 33 U.Chi.L.Rev. 1 (1965); Irvine, "Some Comments Regarding 'Anti-Dilution' Provisions Applicable to Convertible Securities", 13 Bus.Law. 729 (1958); Hills, "Convertible Securities—Legal Aspects and Draftsmanship", 19 Calif.L.Rev. 1 (1930).

cash dividends, (g) distributions of assets, (h) subdivision or combination of shares or securities convertible into shares; and (i) reorganizations, reclassifications, mergers, or consolidations.[33]

A convertible security obviously has a triple aspect—involving three securities: itself,

the option, and the security into which it may be converted—which may be important for purposes of state "blue sky" statutes, Federal Securities Act of 1933, etc.

There are a few additional methods of classifying debt securities as to manner of payment of principal.[34]

C.　SHARES

SHARES—IN GENERAL

157.　Shares constitute a threefold interest in the corporation with respect to: (a) earnings, (b) net assets, and (c) control. The share certificate evidences such interests. Recognition of a shareholder's status often depends on record ownership. The shareholders' proportionate interests are protected, to some extent, by the fiduciary duties of corporate management and the doctrine of preemptive rights.

A shareholder owns shares[1] of stock in a corporation. Only in a loose sense does he own the corporation. Instead he has a three-fold proportionate interest in the corporation with respect to: (a) earnings, (b) net assets, and (c) control.[2] His interest,

assuming no complications from more than one class of issued shares, is in proportion to the number of shares he owns out of the total number of shares issued.

His share certificate evidences his share interest, although for most purposes, the corporation may rely on the record ownership disclosed by the record of shareholders which it maintains.[3]

To some extent, the shareholder's proportionate interest is protected by the fiduciary duties of corporate management, which apply to the issue of shares as well as to other corporate matters, and the doctrine of preemptive rights, which, when applicable, requires a pro rata offering of new shares to existing shareholders.[4]

The financial and related aspects of shares will be discussed in the rest of this chapter; the control and related aspects in Chapter 9.[5]

AUTHORIZED, ISSUED, OUTSTANDING SHARES

158.　Authorized shares are the shares of all classes which the corporation is authorized to issue in its articles of incorporation. Some taxes are based on authorized shares. Unless duly authorized, shares purportedly issued are void. Issued shares are such of the author-

---

33.　See B. S. F. Co. v. Philadelphia Nat'l Bank, 42 Del.Ch. 106, 204 A.2d 746 (Sup.Ct.1964).

34.　The amount of principal to be repaid might be geared to the price index ("Stabilized Bonds"). Comment, "The Probable Legal Consequences of Inserting Price-Index Clauses in Long-Term Corporate Obligations", 18 Hastings L.J. 959 (1967). Where the maturity date has been extended, the designation "Extended Bonds" might be used. If the security involves the operation of a sinking fund to provide funds for retirement, the phrase "Sinking Fund" might appear as part of the title of the issue, and provision might be made for different maturities. See Bankers Trust Co. v. Denver Tramway Co., 192 App.Div. 794, 183 N.Y.S. 326 (1st Dep't 1920), modified 233 N.Y. 604, 135 N.E. 936 (1922). For the different maturities, interest rate or price ("yield") might differ. "Perpetual Bonds" would describe debt securities, rare in practice, which have no maturity date.

1.　The term "Shares" has been defined to mean the units into which the proprietary interests in a corporation are divided. ABA–ALI Model Bus.Corp. Act § 2(d). See Ford, "Share Characteristics under the New Corporation Statutes", 23 Law & Contemp.Prob. 264 (1958).

2.　A financial editor has described the shareholder as having "three primary rights": (a) To throw out

management; (b) To sue management for misuse of power, gross mismanagement, fraud, or dishonesty; and (c) To sell his shares. J. Livingston, The American Stockholder 40–41 (1958).

3.　See sections 176–177 infra.

4.　See sections 172–175 infra.

5.　See sections 180–230 infra.

ized shares as have been issued to shareholders. Some taxes and the stated capital of a
corporation are generally computed on the
basis of issued shares. Outstanding shares are
such of the issued shares as are held by the
shareholders. Shares reacquired by the corporation are known as "treasury stock" or "treasury shares", and are deemed to be authorized
and issued but not outstanding. Reacquired
shares may and sometimes are required to be
restored to the status of unissued shares or
eliminated from authorized shares.

By definition a stock corporation is a corporation having shares of stock.[1]

Corporation statutes recognize the power
of the stock corporation to issue shares, but
usually require that the exercise of such
power be pursuant to proper authorization
in the articles of incorporation of the corporation involved.[2] The organization tax imposed by the jurisdiction of incorporation is
usually based on the authorized shares; so
also may be a capital tax, license fee on foreign corporations doing business in the
jurisdiction,[3] or franchise tax.[4] Unless the
shares purported to be issued are duly authorized, they are void.[5]

A few states[6] impose a tax on the issuance of shares.[7]

The capital of a corporation is generally
computed on the basis of the shares issued.[8]

Not all of the authorized shares, of course,
need be issued. Unissued shares might be
reserved for property additions, to secure
additional funds for share dividends, exercise of share options, or exercise of conversion privilege in securities convertible into
shares.

Shares which have been issued to the holders thereof are said to be outstanding.
When such shares are reacquired by the cor-

---

1. See, e.g., ABA–ALI Model Bus. Corp. Act §§ 2(d), 14. A business corporation is usually regarded as a type of stock corporation.

2. See, e.g., ABA–ALI Model Bus. Corp. Act §§ 2(g), 14, 48(d). See sections 123–125 supra.

3. See, e. g., ABA–ALI Model Bus. Corp. Act § 123; McKinney's N.Y. Tax Law, § 180 (organization tax); ABA–ALI Model Bus. Corp. Act § 124; McKinney's N.Y. Tax Law, § 181 (license fee on for-eign corporations).

4. See A. B. Frank Co. v. Latham, 145 Tex. 30, 193 S.W.2d 671 (1946); Jewel Tea Co. v. Rowe, 414 Ill. 495, 111 N.E.2d 568 (1953).

5. St. Thomas Jewelry, Inc. v. Comm'r of Finance, 255 F.Supp. 461 (D.V.I.1966); Triplex Shoe Co. v. Rice & Hutchins, Inc., 17 Del.Ch. 356, 152 A. 342, 72 A.L.R. 934 (Sup.Ct.1930); Mechanics' Bank v. New York & N. H. R. R., 13 N.Y. 599 (1856). One of the principal functions of the share registrar is to pre-vent the overissue of shares. Harris, "Is the Reg-istrar of Corporate Stock Necessary Today?", 47 Nw.U.L.Rev. 457 (1952). See Uniform Commercial Code § 8–104: (Effect of overissue; "overissue"), providing:

"(1) The provisions of this Article which validate a security or compel its issue or reissue do not apply

to the extent that validation, issue or reissue would result in overissue; but

(a) if an identical security which does not consti-tute an overissue is reasonably available for purchase, the person entitled to issue or vali-dation may compel the issuer to purchase and deliver such a security to him against surrender of the security, if any, which he holds; or

(b) if a security is not so available for purchase, the person entitled to issue or validation may recover from the issuer the price he or the last purchaser for value paid for it with in-terest from the date of his demand.

"(2) 'Overissue' means the issue of securities in ex-cess of the amount which the issuer has corporate power to issue."

See Note, "Original and Subsequent Purchases of 'Defective' Corporate Stock under the Uniform Commercial Code", 27 U.Pit.L.Rev. 857 (1966). The corporation may be liable in negligence for over-issue. New York & N. H. R. R. v. Schuyler, 34 N.Y. 30 (1865). See also Cal.Gen.Corp.Law, § 1307 (1947); McKinney's N.Y. Penal Law, § 190.35(2) (a) (misdemeanor for director or officer to participate in unauthorized issue).

6. *Florida: Par value:* 15 cents for each $100 or fraction thereof of actual value of share certifi-cate; *No par value:* 15 cents per $100 of actual value but not more than 15 cents per share. *South Carolina: Par value:* 10 cents on each $100 or fraction thereof of face value of certificate; *No par value:* Where actual value per share is $100–10 cents per share; Where actual value per share exceeds $100, 10 cents per $100 or fraction thereof; Where actual value per share is less than $100–1 cent per $10 or fraction thereof.

7. In small corporations, the stamps are usually af-fixed to the stubs in the share certificate book.

8. See, e. g., ABA–ALI Model Bus. Corp. Act § 19; McKinney's N.Y. Bus. Corp. Law, § 102(a) (12).

poration, by donation,[9] forfeiture,[10] purchase,[11] redemption,[12] conversion,[13] or otherwise, they are frequently called "treasury stock" or "treasury shares". The accounting treatment should be descriptively accurate from the point of view of the applicable corporation law.[14]

Legally, "treasury shares" are authorized and issued but not outstanding. However, the corporation may and, under certain circumstances, must restore the shares to unissued status or eliminate the shares from authorized shares by reducing the authorized capital.[15]

Treasury shares being somewhat in a state of limbo, have some unusual characteristics.[16] Even if otherwise voting, treasury shares may usually not be voted, since otherwise corporate management would be voting for themselves, or counted for purposes of determining a quorum or sufficient vote or consent of shareholders.[17] Nor do treasury shares participate in dividends or distributions of net assets upon dissolution, since such participation would result in circumgyration.[18] Nor is its reallotment usually subject to preemptive rights [19] or to consideration-for-shares requirements, at least where their original issue complied with such requirements.[20] For federal income tax purposes, with some exceptions, sales or purchases by a corporation of its own shares result in no taxable gain or deductible loss.[21]

PAR VALUE SHARES; SHARES WITHOUT PAR VALUE

159. Par value shares, without express limitations on assigned par value, and shares without par value are permitted in most jurisdictions. The principal differences between the different varieties are with respect to (a) rates of organization, capital, issue, transfer, and franchise taxes; (b) the desirability of allocating to capital surplus part of the consideration received for shares; and (c) the consideration requirements for the issue of shares. The

9. A surrender of shares to the issuing corporation by a shareholder (if not pro rata with holdings of other shareholders) can result in a fully deductible ordinary loss for such shareholder. Payne Housing Corp., P-H Tax Ct.Mem. ¶ 54,190.

10. See, e. g., ABA–ALI Model Bus. Corp. Act § 16. The Model Business Corporation Act does not permit the issue of partly-paid shares, but does expressly provide for fractions of shares. See section 161 infra.

11. A corporation may usually purchase its own shares out of surplus, and under certain circumstances and to a limited extent as allowed by statute out of capital. See section 336 infra.

12. If shares are redeemable, a corporation may redeem them out of surplus or, to the extent permitted by statute, out of capital. See sections 160, 336 infra.

13. See, e. g., ABA–ALI Model Bus. Corp. Act § 14 (conversion of preferred shares). See section 160 infra.

14. See Fultz v. Anzac Oil Corp., 240 F.2d 21 (5th Cir.1957); A. Shugerman, Accounting for Lawyers 470–472 (1952); Sprouse, "Accounting for Treasury Stock Transactions: Prevailing Practices and New Statutory Provisions", 59 Colum.L.Rev. 882 (1959); Randolph, "Accounting for Treasury Shares under the Model Business Corporation Act", 73 Harv.L. Rev. 323 (1959); Nemmers, "The Treasury Stock Sections of the Wisconsin Business Corporation Law", 1953 Wis.L.Rev. 480.

15. See, e. g., ABA–ALI Model Bus.Corp.Act § 2(h); see also ABA–ALI Model Bus.Corp.Act § 61 (cancellation of redeemable shares by redemption or purchase: restoration to unissued status or reduction of authorized shares), § 62 (cancellation of other reacquired shares), § 63 (reduction of stated capital). See Garrett, "Treasury Shares Under the Model Business Corporation Act", 15 Bus.Law. 916 (1960).

16. Ballantine, "The Curious Fiction of Treasury Shares", 34 Calif.L.Rev. 536 (1934); Glenn, "Treasury Stock", 15 Va.L.Rev. 625 (1929); Note, "The Legal Status of Treasury Shares", 85 U.Pa.L.Rev. 622 (1937). The consideration requirements applicable to the original issue of shares may not apply to the reallotment of treasury shares. See, e. g., ABA–ALI Model Bus.Corp.Act § 17. See sections 167–168 infra.

17. See, e. g., ABA–ALI Model Bus.Corp.Act § 31. See section 191 infra.

18. See Note, "The Legal Status of Treasury Shares", 85 U.Pa.L.Rev. 622 (1937).

19. Runswick v. Floor, 116 Utah 91, 208 P.2d 948 (1949); see also Sandler v. Schenley Industries, Inc., 32 Del.Ch. 46, 79 A.2d 606 (Ch.1951). See sections 174, 175 infra.

20. See sections 167, 168 infra.

21. Int.Rev.Code 1954, 26 U.S.C.A. § 1032; United States v. Anderson, Clayton & Co., 350 U.S. 55, 76 S.Ct. 25, 100 L.Ed. 43 (1955) (pre-1954 tax years).

trend has been in favor of shares of low par value.

Shares, as previously discussed,[1] may be par value shares or shares without par value. Shares without par value sometimes may have a stated value. Shares without par value with stated value resemble, in some respects, par value shares.[2] Shares without par value without stated value are sometimes called true no-par value shares.

Par value shares without express limitations on assigned par value and shares without par value are permitted in most jurisdictions.[3]

The principal differences between the varieties are with respect to (a) the rates of organization, capital, issue, transfer, and franchise taxes; (b) the desirability of allocating to capital surplus part of the consideration received for the shares; and (c) the consideration requirements for the issue of the shares.

Tax Rates

Many jurisdictions, as indicated, impose an *organization tax* based upon the authorized shares of a domestic corporation and payable at the time of the filing of the articles of incorporation.[4] With respect to foreign corporations doing business within the jurisdiction, a somewhat similar tax, sometimes called a *capital tax*, or license fee, based on authorized capital is imposed.[5] The rates of such taxes are sometimes fixed as so much per amount of par value for par value shares and so much per no-par value share—which discriminates against shares without par value; a minimum tax is usually prescribed.[6]

Two states—Florida and South Carolina—impose original *issue taxes*. In South Carolina, such tax is based on the par value of par value shares and on the actual value of shares without par value, thus to some extent discriminating against shares without par value.[7]

Two states—Florida and New York—impose *stock transfer taxes*. In Florida the transfer tax is a certain amount per $100 or fraction thereof of face value of the share certificate with respect to par value shares and so much per $100 of actual value of no-par value shares, thus to some extent dis-

---

1. See section 123 supra.

2. Except that the stated value might not appear on the share certificate as the par value usually would; and the statutes might not *expressly* prohibit the issue of stated value no par shares for less than the stated value. See section 168 infra. Israels, "Problems of Par and No-Par Shares: A Reappraisal", 47 Colum.L.Rev. 1279 (1947). The term "stated value" is also used in the sense of the amount of stated capital attributed to each share without par value.

3. See, e. g., ABA–ALI Model Bus.Corp.Act § 14; Del.Gen.Corp.Law, § 151 (1967); McKinney's N.Y. Bus.Corp.Law, § 501. The trend has been in favor of *low par value* shares because of tax savings, allocation of premium to capital surplus, attainment of wider distribution because low-priced, etc. G. Harold, Corporation Finance 35–36 (3d rev.ed.1956). Nebraska requires that all shares, except preferred shares, be of the same par value and prohibits shares without par value. England does not permit shares without par value. Quaere, as to the validity of no-par value shares in Oklahoma. Okla.Op. Att'y Gen. No. 69–102, Jan. 16, 1969 (ruling no-par value shares to be constitutional); Note, "Constitutionality of No-Par Stock in Oklahoma", 1 Okla.L. Rev. 76 (1948). See C. Wickersham, Stock Without Par Value (1927); Goodbar, "No-Par Stock—Its Nature and Use", 3 Miami L.Q. 1 (1948); Israels, "Problems of Par and No-Par Shares: A Reappraisal", 47 Colum.L.Rev. 1279 (1947); Berle, "Problems of No-Par Stock", 25 Colum.L.Rev. 43 (1925); Bonbright, "The Danger of Shares Without Par Value", 24 Colum.L.Rev. 449 (1924). Ghana requires that all new shares be of no par value and converts all previously issued shares into shares of no par value. Ghana Companies Code § 40 (1963).

4. See section 158, n. 3 supra.

5. See section 158, n. 3 supra.

6. For example, the New York organization tax is 5 cents per $100 par value for *par value shares*, and 5 cents per share *without par value*. Such discriminatory treatment of shares without par value becomes relevant, of course, only when shares are to be authorized in excess of those covered by the minimum fee, e. g., $10. The New Mexico attorney general has ruled that the New Mexico corporation commission may assign a value of $100 to each share without par value for the purpose of computing fees and taxes. N.M.Op.Att'y Gen. No. 63–65, June 12, 1963.

7. See section 158, n. 6 supra.

criminating against shares without par value.[8]

New York stock transfer tax[9] rates are the same per share regardless of whether the shares are par value or without par value.

Some *state franchise* taxes, on domestic corporations or foreign corporations doing business within the state, base their rates, sometimes as one of several alternative methods of computing such tax, on authorized or issued shares with or without par value.[10]

Capital Surplus

The desirability of creating capital surplus at the outset of corporate existence stems principally from restrictions which exist in many jurisdictions against using funds other than surplus for, or impairing stated capital, by means of dividends[11] or expenditure of the corporation's funds to purchase or redeem its own shares.[12] In many such jurisdictions, capital surplus, as distinguished from stated capital, may be distributed as dividends or so expended. In such jurisdictions, the existence of capital surplus gives the corporation a flexibility it would not otherwise enjoy.

Capital surplus can be created at the outset by issuing par value shares for more than par value (allocating the par value to capital and the excess or premium to capital surplus), and by allocating a part of the consideration received for shares without par value to capital surplus, with the balance allocated to stated capital.[13]

Under the Model Business Corporation Act,[14] any portion of the consideration received for shares without par value may be allocated to capital surplus, and no allocation to capital surplus may be made of any portion of the consideration received for shares without par value having a preference in the assets of the corporation in the event of involuntary liquidation except the amount, if any, of such consideration in excess of such preference.

Consideration Requirements

The consideration requirements for the issue of shares vary, depending on par value, lack of par value, stated value, minimum capital requirements, etc.[15]

At one time, the practice was to have $100 par value shares, and this practice has been somewhat retained for preferred shares. Shares without par value then became popular. The modern trend has been in favor of shares of low par value.[16]

CLASSIFICATION OF SHARES

160. **Shares of one or more classes may be authorized in the articles of incorporation. Where there is only one class, such shares are in effect common shares and hold the voting rights, are entitled proportionately to such dividends as are distributed, and receive proportionately in the event of liquidation the net assets remaining after the payment of all creditor claims. Where the articles of incorpora-**

---

8. *Florida: For par value shares*, 15 cents on each $100 of par or face value or fraction thereof; for *shares without par value*, 15 cents on each $100 of actual value or fraction thereof but not to exceed 15 cents per share.

9. McKinney's N.Y. Tax Law, § 270: For all shares, whether par value or without par value: 2½ cents per share if no sale involved; 1¼ cent per share sold for less than $5; 2½ cents per share sold for $5 or more and less than $10; 3¾ cents per share sold for $10 or more and less than $20; 5 cents per share sold for $20 or more. Special reduced rates (95% of regular rates) apply to transfers made in New York by nonresidents. There is also a maximum $2,500 tax on large block sales.

10. E. g., ABA–ALI Model Bus.Corp.Act §§ 125–128. See section 158 n. 4 supra.

11. See section 320 infra.

12. See section 336 infra.

13. See, e. g., Del.Gen.Corp.Law, § 154 (1967); McKinney's N.Y.Bus.Corp.Law, § 506(b).

14. ABA–ALI Model Bus.Corp.Act § 19 (such allocation to be made by the board of directors within 60 days after the issuance of the shares).

15. See sections 167, 168 infra.

16. See also section 123 supra.

tion authorize more than one class, the articles must set forth the designations, preferences, limitations, and relative rights of each class. Shares with a preference as to dividends or net assets or both are in effect preferred shares. Many jurisdictions permit the articles to authorize the issue of preferred or special classes of shares in series by board of directors action. All shares enjoy equal rights except as otherwise provided in the articles of incorporation. Dividend preferences may be cumulative, noncumulative, or cumulative-to-the-extent-earned; participating or nonparticipating. Liquidation preferences may be participating or nonparticipating, and may include cumulative preferred dividend arrearages. Voting rights, with some exceptions, may be limited or denied one or more classes provided they are enjoyed by another class or other classes. Preferred shares may usually be made redeemable. Shares may usually be made convertible, at least into a junior class or series of shares but usually not into debt or other senior securities. Other special protective provisions are also possible.

Shares of one or more classes may be authorized in the articles of incorporation.[1] Where there is only one class of shares, such shares, regardless of how the class is designated, are in effect "common shares".[2] Such shares hold the voting rights, are entitled proportionately to such dividends as are distributed, and receive proportionately in the event of liquidation the net assets remaining after the payment of all creditor claims.

Classes of Shares

Where more than one class is authorized the articles of incorporation must set forth the designations, preferences, limitations,

and relative rights of each class.[3] Shares of a class enjoying a preference with respect to earnings (dividends) or net assets (liquidation) or both are often called "preferred shares". Shares with either or both preferences should not be called "common shares" and, contrariwise, shares without either or both preferences should not be called "preferred shares".[4]

Series Shares

Many jurisdictions also permit the authorization of "blank" or "series" shares in the articles of incorporation. Shares of any preferred or special class may be divided into and issued in series. Variations in the relative rights and preferences as between different series (i.e., rate of dividend, redemption, liquidation rights, sinking fund, conversion) may, subject to limitations, be fixed in the articles of incorporation or by the board of directors when duly authorized. In the latter case, the corporation must file in the office of the secretary of state a statement of the relative rights and preferences of the series involved prior to the issue thereof.[5] Upon filing, such a statement becomes, in effect, part of the articles of incorporation.

3. See sections 123, 124 supra. For share certificate requirements in such a case, see section 134 supra. See generally Soldofsky, "Classified Common Stock", 23 Bus.Law. 899 (1968); Pickering, "Problems of the Preference Share", 26 Modern L.Rev. 499 (1963); Donaldson, "In Defense of Preferred Stock", 40 Harv.Bus.Rev. 123 (July-Aug.1962); Caplin, "Subchapter S and Its Effect on the Capitalization of Corporations", 13 Vand.L.Rev. 185 (1959); Buxbaum, "Preferred Stock—Law and Draftsmanship", 42 Calif.L.Rev. 243–309 (1954).

4. See, e. g., McKinney's N.Y.Bus.Corp.Law, § 501(b). See Ala.Const. art. 12, § 237: "No corporation shall issue preferred stock without the consent of the owners of two-thirds of the stock of said corporation."

5. See section 125 supra. Buxbaum, "Preferred Stock—Law and Draftsmanship", 42 Calif.L.Rev. 243, 247–249 (1954). See Ellerin v. Massachusetts Mutual Life Ins. Co., 167 F.Supp. 71 (S.D.N.Y.1959) ("class" as used in section 16(b) of Federal Securities Exchange Act held to mean class and not series), aff'd 270 F.2d 259 (2d Cir.1959).

1. See sections 123, 124 supra.

2. Except possibly in jurisdictions which permit a class of preferred shares to be issued in series and also permit the different series to have different preferences so that, say, one series may be preferred over another series as to dividends and the latter may be preferred over the former as to liquidation. Or in Delaware which does not limit series shares to class of preferred or special classes. See discussion of Series Shares infra.

Normal Rights

Except as otherwise provided in the articles of incorporation, all shares enjoy equal rights. Among these are the rights to participate ratably (a) in earnings by way of dividends when, as, and if declared by the board of directors, in the exercise of their discretion, out of legally available funds; (b) in net assets (after satisfying liabilities to creditors) upon liquidation; and (c) in control (voting rights).

Dividend Preferences

All classes of shares of a for-profit business corporation are theoretically entitled to dividends,[6] but one or more classes may be given a preference over another class or other classes of shares with respect to dividends. Full dividend rights must be given to one class or shared by two or more classes. Such dividend preference may be cumulative, noncumulative, or cumulative-to-the-extent earned. Beyond any dividend preference, such preferred shares may or may not participate in further dividends ("participating" or "nonparticipating").[7]

In recent years, new issues of preferred shares, except by utility corporations, have become relatively rare, because of the advantages of debt financing over financing by preferred shares.[8]

Dividends and other distributions are discussed more fully in Chapter 12.

Liquidation Preferences

All classes of shares are theoretically entitled to participate in net assets in the event of liquidation, but one or more classes of shares may be given a liquidation preference over another class or other classes of shares. Full liquidation rights must be given to one class or shared by two or more classes. Beyond any liquidation preference, such preferred shares may or may not participate further in net assets ("participating" or "nonparticipating").[9]

6. See, e. g., McKinney's N.Y.Gen.Corp.Law, § 3(5) (inapplicable to business corporations since 1963); Pierce v. Guaranty Laundry, 200 Okl. 395, 194 P.2d 875 (1948). See also McKinney's N.Y.Bus.Corp.Law, § 501(a): "The certificate of incorporation . . . may limit or otherwise define the dividend . . . rights of shares of any class, but . . . no such limitation or definition of dividend . . . rights shall be effective unless at the time one or more classes of outstanding shares, singly or in the aggregate, are entitled to unlimited dividend . . . rights". The New York language—compare voting provision quoted in note 12 infra—appears to preclude denial, as distinguished from limitation, of dividend rights to any class. Such denial may be possible under statutes which do not expressly or impliedly require that all shares have dividend rights. Halo Metal Products, Inc. v. Randall, 419 F.2d 1068 (7th Cir. 1969) (upholding second class of shares without any dividend rights under Illinois law which expressly requires that all shares have voting rights). All shares enjoy equal dividend rights unless otherwise provided, such provision, absent a statute to the contrary, being effective only if in the articles of incorporation. See Note, 15 Cornell L.Q. 284 (1930).

7. Buxbaum, "Preferred Stock—Law and Draftsmanship", 42 Calif.L.Rev. 243–257 (1954). Some states once fixed maximum dividend preferences.

8. 85 Forbes, No. 4, 24 (Feb. 15, 1960).

9. See A.B.A.-A.L.I. Model Bus.Corp.Act § 14(d), permitting the issue of shares of preferred or special classes having "preference in the assets of the corporation over any other class or classes of shares upon voluntary or involuntary liquidation of the corporation". See McKinney's N.Y.Bus.Corp. Law § 501(a): "The certificate of incorporation . . . may limit or otherwise define the . . . liquidation rights of any class, but . . . no such limitation or definition of . . . liquidation rights shall be effective unless at the same time one or more classes of outstanding shares, singly or in the aggregate, are entitled to unlimited . . . liquidation rights". The New York language—compare voting provision quoted in note 12 infra—appears to preclude denial, as distinguished from limitation, of liquidation rights to any class. Such denial may be possible under statutes which do not expressly or impliedly require that all shares have liquidation rights. Halo Metal Products, Inc. v. Randall, —— F.2d —— (7th Cir. 1969) (upholding second class of shares without any liquidation rights under Illinois law which expressly requires that all shares have voting rights). All shares enjoy equal liquidation rights unless otherwise validly provided. See Gaskill v. Gladys Belle Oil Co., 16 Del.Ch. 289, 146 A. 337 (Ch.1929) (denying validity of bylaw provision for liquidation preference); Note, 15 Cornell L.Q. 284 (1930). Buxbaum, "Preferred Stock—Law and Draftsmanship", 42 Calif.L. Rev. 243, 253–262 (1954). See note 6 supra.

Liquidation rights are discussed more fully in Chapter 15.[10] Whether or not preferred shares with a cumulative dividend preference with dividends in arrears are entitled to such arrearages in the event of liquidation depends upon the language defining the liquidation rights of such shares.[11]

Voting Rights

One or more classes of shares may hold the rights to vote at shareholder meetings or to give written consent to various corporate matters. While voting rights of a class may, with some exceptions, be limited or denied, full voting rights must exist in the corporation. Voting rights are discussed more fully in Chapter 9.[12]

Special Features

Apart from dividends, liquidation rights, and control, one or more classes of shares might be given special features.

Redemption. Absent appropriate provision in the articles of incorporation, a corporation may not redeem (or call) its shares. By such a provision, preferred shares may be made redeemable. Whether or not common shares may be made redeemable is still an open question in most jurisdictions. In the two reported American cases on the subject, Massachusetts permitted redeemable

common shares[13] and Delaware prohibited them.[14] The question in a particular jurisdiction is primarily one of statutory construction. In principle, no reason appears why common shares should not be redeemable so long as there remains some class of shares outstanding. Redemption provisions may be mandatory or optional, and may provide for partial as well as total redemption.[15]

As a general rule, in most jurisdictions, corporations may not redeem (or purchase) their own shares except out of surplus,[16] but modern statutes frequently permit, subject to various safeguards, the redemption (or purchase) of redeemable preferred shares out of stated capital.[17]

10. See especially sections 381, 382 infra.

11. See section 124 supra and sections 325, 381 infra.

12. See section 189 infra. See also McKinney's N.Y. Bus.Corp.Law, § 612(a) (one vote per share of record "unless otherwise provided in the certificate of incorporation"); see also id. § 501(a): "The certificate of incorporation may deny, limit or otherwise define the voting rights . . . of shares of any class, but no such denial, limitation or definition of voting rights shall be effective unless at the time one or more classes of outstanding shares or bonds, singly or in the aggregate, are entitled to full voting rights." "Deny" or "denied" are included for voting rights but not for dividend rights or liquidation rights. See notes 6, 8 supra.

13. Lewis v. H. P. Hood & Sons, 331 Mass. 670, 121 N.E.2d 850, 48 A.L.R.2d 383 (1954). See Comment, "Unqualified Redemption of Common Stock: A Question of Public Policy", 50 Nw.U.L.Rev. 558 (1955). New York provides that no redeemable common shares, other than shares of an investment company, shall be issued or redeemed unless the corporation, at the time, has outstanding a class of common shares not subject to redemption. McKinney's N.Y.Bus.Corp.Law, § 512(c). By drafting provisions for the corporation's reacquisition of shares in the form of share transfer restrictions with a corporate option to purchase or a buy-sell agreement—see sections 281, 282 infra—rather than a redemption provision, the desired result often can be achieved. In Matter of West Waterway Lumber Co., 59 Wash.2d 310, 367 P.2d 807 (1962).

14. American Hair & Felt Co. v. Starring, 21 Del.Ch. 431, 2 A.2d 249 (Sup.Ct.1937), aff'g 21 Del.Ch. 380, 191 A. 887 (Ch.1937).

15. See sections 172, 173 infra. The shareholder might have an option to "redeem" in an open-end investment company ("mutual fund"). See McKinney's N.Y.Bus.Corp.Law, § 512.

16. See section 336 infra. A mandatory redemption provision is usually construed to require redemption only when there are legally available funds for redemption and creditors would not be harmed; any other construction might render it invalid. Kraft v. Rochambeau Holding Co., 210 Md. 325, 123 A.2d 287 (1956); Mueller v. Kraeuter & Co., 131 N.J.Eq. 475, 25 A.2d 874 (1942).

17. See, e. g., ABA-ALI Model Bus.Corp.Act § 60; McKinney's N.Y.Bus.Corp.Law, § 513.

The redemption price,[18] dates,[19] notice requirements,[20] deposit arrangements,[21] effect of redemption on any conversion privilege,[22] and other aspects of the redemption procedure,[23] should be set forth in the articles of incorporation. Provision might also be made for a sinking fund for the redemption (or purchase) of the shares.

Conversion. A class of shares may be made more attractive by a conversion privilege. Absent a provision for such privilege in the articles of incorporation, of course, shares are not convertible. Such a privilege might enable the holder, at his option, to convert his shares at a designated ratio into shares of another class, shares of any other series of the same class, or rarely debt securities.[24] Conversion to a junior security is sometimes called "downstream"; to a senior security, "upstream".

Whenever shares are convertible into other shares, sufficient authorized (unissued or treasury) shares of the latter should be reserved for the exercise of such conversion privilege. The exercise of any conversion privilege should not impair or reduce stated capital. Appropriate "anti-dilution" provisions should be included to safeguard the conversion privilege by readjusting the ratio whenever the shares into which convertible shares may be converted is issued at less than the conversion price, or the number of the shares is increased by a share dividend

18. The redemption price might be, say, 105 percent for $100 par value shares or $105 for shares without par value, thus including in either case a $5 redemption premium. The redemption price ought to be drafted to allow for any dividend arrearages in the case of shares with cumulative dividend rights. Matter of Chandler & Co., 230 N.Y.S.2d 1012 (Sup. Ct.1962) (distinguishing between corporation functioning as going concern and corporation in dissolution); Leeds & Lippincott Co. v. Nevius, 51 N.J.Super. 343, 144 A.2d 4 (1958), modified, 30 N.J. 281, 153 A.2d 45 (1959); Liebschutz v. Schaffer Stores Co., 276 App.Div. 1, 93 N.Y.S.2d 125 (4th Dep't 1949) (3–2); see McKinney's N.Y.Bus.Corp.Law, § 513(d); "Upon a call for redemption, the amount payable by the corporation for shares having a cumulative preference on dividends may include the stated redemption price plus accrued dividends to the next dividend date following the date of redemption of such shares." See Buxbaum, "Preferred Stock—Law and Draftsmanship", 42 Calif.L.Rev. 243, 266–268 (1954). The redemption price should be in cash and not in other securities, e. g., debentures. Bowman v. Armour & Co., 17 Ill.2d 43, 160 N.E.2d 753 (1959).

19. E. g., on dividend payment dates.

20. E. g., by mailing and/or publication of redemption notice. Notice of redemption might mean the end of the rights and status of the shareholder as such. Statutes might deal with the redemption notice. See Cal.Gen.Corp.Law, §§ 1701–1702 (1947). Often the articles of incorporation provide for the notice, requiring in the case of convertible shares that attention be called to the conversion rights.

21. Deposit by the corporation of the redemption funds irrevocably with an agent "in trust" might end the shareholders' rights as such (except to receive the redemption price) even in advance of the redemption date. See Cal.Gen.Corp.Law, § 1703 (1947). The latter result is less likely when the corporation merely sets apart such funds. Even when the redemption notice is irrevocable [see Taylor v. Axton-Fisher Tobacco Co., 295 Ky. 226, 173 S.W.2d 377, 148 A.L.R. 834 (1943)], deposit, payment, and performance by the corporation of its other obligations with respect to redemption are prerequisite to termination of shareholder status. As a creditor, the former holder of redeemed shares might have a claim subordinate to the claims of other creditors.

22. Cf. Mueller v. Howard Aircraft Corp., 329 Ill. App. 570, 70 N.E.2d 203 (1946).

23. Buxbaum, "Preferred Stock—Law and Draftsmanship", 42 Calif.L.Rev. 243, 263–279 (1954). For securities exchange requirements applicable to redemption of listed shares, see N.Y.S.E. Company Manual § A10.

24. See A.B.A.–A.L.I. Model Bus.Corp.Act § 14(c), permitting the issue of shares of preferred or special classes "[c]onvertible into shares of any other class or into shares of any series of the same or any other class, except a class having prior or superior rights and preferences as to dividends or distribution of assets upon liquidation, but shares without par value shall not be converted into shares with par value unless that part of the stated capital of the corporation represented by such shares without par value is, at the time of conversion, at least equal to the aggregate par value of the shares into which the shares without par value are to be converted." Buxbaum, "Preferred Stock—Law and Draftsmanship", 42 Calif.L.Rev. 243, 279–290 (1954). Several statutes expressly provide for shares convertible into shares but not for shares convertible into debt securities. For express prohibition against conversion of shares into shares having superior preferences, see McKinney's N.Y.Bus.Corp. Law, § 519. See Fleischer & Cary, "The Taxation of Convertible Bonds and Stock", 74 Harv.L.Rev. 473 (1961). See also Soldofsky, "Convertible Preferred Stock: Renewed Life in an Old Form", 24 Bus.Law. 1385 (1969).

or share split-up, or the corporation is merged or consolidated, etc.[25]

When shares are convertible into debt securities, the shift from shareholder status to creditor status should not prejudice the rights of other creditors.[26]

Any conversion privilege should be coordinated with any redemption provision since the redemption feature may be employed to cut off the conversion privilege which has become valuable.[27]

Protective Provisions

Aside from possible sinking fund and other provisions mentioned above, various provisions might be included for the better protection of one or more classes of shares, e.g., prohibiting dividends on other classes of shares unless certain ratios are maintained, giving veto power over future issues of debt securities or shares except subordinate shares, limitations on indebtedness, etc.

FRACTIONS OF SHARES, SCRIP

161. A growing number of jurisdictions expressly authorize the issue of fractions of shares and scrip. Fractions of shares may create administrative and bookkeeping problems, and questions as to the rights of holders of fractions of shares where their rights are not clarified by statute. Scrip is a certificate exchangeable for a share when combined in whole units, or cash, usually before a specified date. A holder of scrip generally possesses none of the rights of shareholders.

A growing number of jurisdictions have statutory provisions expressly authorizing

the issuance of fractions of shares.[1] These statutes, while sanctioning fractions of shares, do not make their issuance mandatory. The issuance of fractions of shares may create administrative and bookkeeping problems for the issuing corporation. In connection with share dividends, odd share splits, reverse share splits, conversion, merger, consolidation, or corporate reorganizations, the issuance of fractions of shares might be desirable.[2] Where fractions of shares are issued, the rights of their holders with respect to dividends, net assets on liquidation, voting, preemptive rights, etc. having not always been adequately defined,[3] although modern statutes tend to clarify such rights.[4]

---

1. See, e. g., ABA–ALI Model Bus.Corp.Act § 22 (issuance of fractional shares or scrip); McKinney's N.Y.Bus.Corp.Law, § 509 (fractions of a share or scrip authorized "where necessary to effect share transfers, share distributions or reclassifications, mergers, consolidations or reorganizations, which shall entitle the holder, in proportion to his fractional holdings, to exercise voting rights, receive dividends and participate in liquidating distributions"); 19 W. Fletcher, Private Corporations § 9046 (perm.ed.rev.1959); 2 I. Kantrowitz & S. Slutsky, White on New York Corporations ¶ 504.01 (13th ed.1968). The 1969 Model Act revision amended the first sentence of section 22 to read as follows:

   "A corporation may (1) issue fractions of a share, (2) arrange for the disposition of fractional interests by those entitled thereto, (3) pay in cash the fair value of fractions of a share as of the time when those entitled to receive such fractions are determined, or (4) issue scrip in registered or bearer form which shall entitle the holder to receive a certificate for a full share upon the surrender of such scrip aggregating a full share."

2. For securities exchange requirements applicable to listed securities, see N.Y.S.E. Company Manual §§ A11, A14. See Sobieski, "Fractional Shares in Stock Dividends and Splits", 16 Bus.Law. 204 (1960).

3. Benson v. Eleven-Twenty St. Charles Co., 422 S. W.2d 297 (Mo.1967); Commonwealth ex rel. Cartwright v. Cartwright, 350 Pa. 638, 40 A.2d 30, 155 A.L.R. 1088 (1944) (fractional shares denied voting rights). Where the rights of fractions of shares are not defined, their issuance should be avoided.

4. See, e. g., McKinney's N.Y.Bus.Corp.Law, § 509(a) (holder entitled, in proportion to his fractional holdings, to exercise voting rights, receive dividends and participate in liquidating distributions); Roberts, "Fractional Corporate Shares", 47 Ky.L.J. 597 (1959).

---

25. For analogous provisions in debt securities convertible into shares, see section 156, n. 32 supra.

26. See, e. g., In re Phoenix Hotel Co. of Lexington, Ky., 83 F.2d 724 (6th Cir.1936), aff'g 13 F.Supp. 229 (D.Ky.1935) (preferred shares convertible into mortgage bonds denied secured creditor status and subordinated to general creditors in federal reorganization proceeding), cert. denied sub nom. Security Trust Co. v. Baker, 299 U.S. 568, 57 S.Ct. 31, 81 L. Ed. 418 (1936).

27. See note 22 supra.

Fractions of shares are probably sounder in concept than partly-paid shares.[5]

Where statutes are silent with respect to the issuance of fractions of shares, articles of incorporation, or amendment thereof, purporting to authorize the issuance of fractions of shares might not be accepted for filing by the secretary of state.[6]

Many statutes also authorize the issuance of scrip.[7]

Scrip is a certificate exchangeable for shares or cash, usually before a specified date. Issued for fractions of shares, sufficient scrip to represent a whole share may be combined and turned over to the corporation for a share. Scrip is usually transferable. A holder of scrip generally possesses none of the rights of shareholders.[8] Scrip is not traded on the New York Stock Exchange, which does specify minimum rights for scrip issued by listed companies.[9]

D. HYBRID SECURITIES

HYBRID SECURITIES—IN GENERAL

162. Hybrid securities, combining features of debt securities and of shares, often prove difficult to market and can lead to tax and other embarrassments. Resort to them is rarely justified since conventional securities are available in sufficient variety to reflect almost any desirable division of risk, income, and control.

Conventional types of securities are available in sufficient variety to reflect almost any desirable division or risk, income, and control.[1] Securities with hybrid features, combining features of debt securities and of shares might prove more difficult to market and might result in tax[2] and other embarrassments.[3]

5. See section 171, nn. 4–7 infra.

6. See, e. g., 1934 N.Y.Op.Att'y Gen. 237; 1946 N.Y. Op.Att'y Gen. 316. Since 1963, New York has expressly authorized certificates for fractions of shares as well as scrip.

7. See, e. g., ABA–ALI Model Bus.Corp.Act § 22.

8. See, e. g., McKinney's N.Y.Bus.Corp.Law, § 509(c), (d) (issuable in registered or bearer form, exchangeable as therein provided for full shares, not entitling holder to any rights of shareholder except as therein provided).

9. N.Y.S.E. Company Manual § A13. See S.E.C. Rule 152A.

[§ 162]
1. See sections 154–161 supra.
2. See section 163 infra.
3. See section 164 infra.

TAX ASPECTS OF HYBRID SECURITIES

163. Whether hybrid securities should be treated for tax purposes as debt securities, with the corporation allowed to deduct as interest periodic payments to the holders, or as shares, with such payments treated as dividends, has not received consistent judicial treatment. The principal tests are (a) fixed maturity in reasonable future time, (b) return fixed or dependent upon earnings, and (c) ranking with respect to general creditors. Where the maturity and return are both fixed, usually a debt obligation is found; absent both, usually shares; otherwise, the cases are in complete confusion.

Two leading United States Supreme Court cases, John Kelley Co. v. Comm'r and Talbot Mills v. Comm'r,[1] involved the deductibility as "interest", for purposes of federal income tax, of certain payments which the taxpayer corporations made to holders of certain securities. In both cases, the corporations had substantial investments of capital as shares (so that there was no question of too-thin-incorporation),[2] and the securities involved were issued as the result of recapitalizations.

In the John Kelley Co. case, "8% Noncumulative Income Debenture Bearer Bonds" were issued mainly to preferred shareholders

[§ 163]
1. 326 U.S. 521, 66 S.Ct. 299, 90 L.Ed. 278 (1946).
2. See section 166 infra.

in exchange for their preferred shares, with the balance being issued to common shareholders to the extent of their dividends. The "Bonds" provided for up to an eight percent annual return, depending on earnings; were in bearer form and transferable; had a 20-year maturity; were redeemable; were accelerable in event of default; had rights prior to the shares but were subordinate to the claims of all other creditors; and had no voting rights. The division of the Tax Court hearing the case, emphasizing the indicia of indebtedness,[3] ruled that the corporation properly deducted the annual amounts paid to holders of the "Bonds" as "interest". The Seventh Circuit, on appeal, reversed, holding that the payments constituted "dividends" and hence were not deductible.[4] The Supreme Court granted certiorari.[5]

In the Talbot Mills case, "10% Cumulative Income Registered Notes" were issued only to shareholders in exchange for $400,000 of the outstanding $500,000 shares. The "Notes" provided for a two percent fixed annual return and up to an additional eight percent annual return depending on earnings; were in registered form and assignable; had a 25-year maturity, had rights prior to the shares; had a provision whereby they could be subordinated to the claims of other creditors; and limited the corporation's right to mortgage its property. A different division of the Tax Court heard the case and ruled that the annual payments to the holders of the "Notes" constituted "dividends" and hence were not deductible.[6] This holding was affirmed on appeal by the First Circuit (2-1).[7] Certiorari was granted by the Supreme Court.[8]

In a single opinion, the Supreme Court upheld the Tax Court's findings of "interest" in the John Kelley Co. case (8-1) and of "dividends" in the Talbot Mills case (7-1) on the ground that the federal statutes, as then construed by the Supreme Court,[9] left to the final determination of the Tax Court all issues other than clear-cut questions of law, and that the Tax Court's determinations of the issues presented by the two cases were final, since there was some rational basis for such determinations and there was no clear-cut mistake of law. Rutledge, J., strongly dissented, urging that the Supreme Court should have resolved the inconsistency in the holdings of the two divisions of the Tax Court (characterizing them as "expert administrative fog") and contending, as did both Circuit Courts, that the payments in both cases should have been found to have been dividends. His position was that, despite some highly technical differences, the "Bonds" and "Notes" largely replaced preexisting shares and were held in the same proportion as such shares, and had substantially the same relative rights after the reclassification as the replaced shares had enjoyed before.

Similar issues have frequently been before the courts.[10] The principal tests most frequently applied have been: (a) fixed maturity in reasonable future time; (b) return fixed or dependent upon earnings, and (c) ranking with respect to general creditors. Where the hybrid security provides for fixed maturity and fixed return, it is usually

---

3. 1 T.C. 457 (1943).

4. 146 F.2d 466 (7th Cir.1944).

5. 325 U.S. 843, 65 S.Ct. 1084, 89 L.Ed. 1967 (1945).

6. 3 T.C. 95 (1944).

7. 146 F.2d 809 (1st Cir.1944).

8. 325 U.S. 844, 65 S.Ct. 1086, 89 L.Ed. 1968 (1945).

9. Dobson v. Comm'r, 320 U.S. 489, 64 S.Ct. 239, 88 L.Ed. 248 (1943), reh. denied 321 U.S. 231, 64 S.Ct. 495, 88 L.Ed. 691 (1944), abrogated a few years later by statute. See Int.Rev.Code 1954, 26 U.S.C.A. § 7482(a).

10. United States v. Snyder Brothers Co., 367 F.2d 980 (5th Cir.1966), cert. denied 386 U.S. 956, 87 S.Ct. 1021, 18 L.Ed.2d 104 (1967) (dividend); Utility Trailer Mfg. Co. v. United States, 212 F.Supp. 773 (S.D.Cal.1962) (interest); Security Finance & Loan Co. v. Koehler, 210 F.Supp. 603 (D.Kan.1962) (interest). See also Fellinger v. United States, 238 F. Supp. 67 (N.D. Ohio 1964), aff'd 363 F.2d 826 (6th Cir.1966) (repayment to holder held dividend).

found to be a debt obligation and the periodic payments to the holders are usually found to be interest. Where there is neither fixed maturity nor fixed return, the usual finding is that of equity security and dividend. Otherwise, the cases are in complete confusion.[11]

CREDITORS' RIGHTS WITH RESPECT TO HYBRID SECURITIES

164. Hybrid securities, even when not expressly subordinated to the claims of other creditors, are often treated as shares in relationship to creditors' claims.

The classification of securities as debt or shares is also important in the field of creditors' rights.[1]

Creditors' claims obviously come ahead of shareholder claims. Attempts to give preferred shares a lien on corporate property ahead of general creditors have generally not been upheld.[2]

Similarly rejected have been attempts to give preferred shareholders creditor status equivalent to the status of general creditors through redemption or conversion or otherwise.[3]

E. "TRADING ON EQUITY" AND "THIN INCORPORATION"

"TRADING ON EQUITY" (OR "LEVERAGE")

165. "Trading on equity" or "leverage" is the securing of funds ("trading") in return for debt securities (and possibly nonparticipating preferred shares), on the strength of the protective cushion of the common shares' "equity", at a rate of return lower than that expected to be yielded by the total investment in the business, thereby magnifying the rate of return, or, if earnings are poor, losses, on the common shares.

Financing by debt and shares, instead of by shares alone, offers possible advantages, which may differ, depending on whether the borrowing is from non-shareholders or from shareholders.[1]

Borrowing from "outsiders", on non-shareholders, permits "trading on equity" or "leverage".[2] So does issuing nonparticipating preferred shares to "outsiders".

---

11. R. Stevens & H. Henn, Statutes, Cases and Materials on the Law of Corporations and Other Business Enterprises 448–453 (1965). Compare Kraft Foods Co. v. Comm'r, 232 F.2d 118 (2d Cir.1956) (2–1), with Gooding Amusement Co. v. Comm'r, 236 F. 2d 159 (6th Cir.1956), cert. denied 352 U.S. 1031, 77 S.Ct. 595, 1 L.Ed.2d 599 (1957). Stone, "Debt-Equity Distinctions in the Tax Treatment of the Corporation and Its Shareholders", 42 Tul.L.Rev. 251 (1968); Note, "Two Courts Limit IRS Attack on Stockholder-Corporation Loans: Allow Interest Deductions", 27 J. Taxation 98 (1967); Comment, "Bonds-Income Bond-Rights of Bondholders and Deductibility of Interest for Federal Income Tax Purposes", 56 Mich.L.Rev. 1334, 1342–1352 (1958); Note, 3 Vill.L.Rev. 540 (1958). The Tax Reform Act of 1969 authorizes the Commissioner of Internal Revenue to issue regulations distinguishing debt from share interests in all situations arising under the tax law, with the following factors, inter alia, to be included in the new guidelines: (a) Whether there is a written unconditional promise to pay on demand or at a specified date a sum certain in money in return for adequate consideration, and to pay a fixed rate of interest; (b) Whether the alleged indebtedness is subordinated to or preferred over any other corporate indebtedness; (c) The ratio of debt to the corporation's equity; (d) Whether the alleged indebtedness is convertible into the issuing corporation's shares; (e) The relationship between alleged debt and actual share ownership in the issuing corporation.

[§ 164]

1. See Loiseaux, "Loans or Capital Contributions to the Close Corporation", 38 Ref.J. 4 (Jan.1964); Note, "Unorthodox Preferred Stock Provisions in Priority Litigation", 36 Mich.L.Rev. 96 (1937).

2. O'Neal v. Automobile Piston & Parts Co., 188 Ga. 380, 4 S.E.2d 40, 123 A.L.R. 850 (1939); Augusta Trust Co. v. Augusta, Hallowell & Gardiner R. R., 134 Me. 314, 187 A. 1 (1936).

3. Hurley v. Boston R. R. Holding Co., 315 Mass. 591, 54 N.E.2d 183 (1944); In re Fechheimer Fishel Co., 212 F. 357 (2d Cir. 1914), cert. denied 234 U.S. 760, 34 S.Ct. 777, 58 L.Ed. 1580 (1914).

[§ 165]

1. See section 166 infra.

2. Called "gearing" in England.

"Trading on equity" or "leverage" is the securing of funds ("trading") in return for debt securities (and possibly nonparticipating preferred shares) on the strength of the protective cushion of the common shares' "equity", at a rate of return lower than that expected to be yielded by the total investment in the business, thereby magnifying the rate of return on the common shares. Of course, if earnings are poor, losses are magnified.[3]

The following tabulation illustrates the advantages and disadvantages of such financing in good, average, poor, and very poor years:

A. Bonds   = $1,000,000
B. Shares   = 1,000,000
C. Total investment = $2,000,000

Leverage ratio = 2 [Total investment]: 1 [Shares]

	Very Poor Year	Poor Year	Average Year	Good Year
D. Earnings after taxes (before bond interest)	($10,000)	$50,000	$100,000	$200,000
E. Bond interest (5%)	50,000	50,000	50,000	50,000
F. Net earnings distributable to shareholders (D minus E)	(60,000)	0	50,000	150,000
G. Percentage earned on total investment (D divided by C)	(.5%)	2.5%	5%	10%
H. Percentage earned on shareholder investment (F divided by B)	(6%)	0	5%	15%

(———) = deficit

"THIN INCORPORATION"

166. "Thin incorporation" is the financing of a corporation by a thin, but not too-thin, ratio of shares compared to debt, primarily to enable the corporation to deduct the interest payments on the debt; to make the repayment of the investment taxfree; possibly to enable the shareholder to deduct any loss as a business bad debt, and to give creditor status to the holder of the debt. Today, Subchapter S election, by permitting avoidance of the corporate income tax, has reduced the incentive to maximize corporate deductions, and either the loss pass-through feature of Subchapter S or the tax treatment of losses on "section 1244 stock" makes financing solely or mainly by shares preferable to financing by debt and shares in ventures involving financial risk. When a corporation is too-thinly capitalized by shares, debts owing to shareholders are treated as con-

tributions to capital or shares. If a second class of shares is found, eligibility under Subchapter S ceases.

The financing of corporations by debt (where the debt is borrowed from nonshareholders) and shares, rather than shares alone, offering possibilities of "trading on equity" or "leverage", has been discussed.[1]

In the case of a *close* corporation, financing by debt and shares often offers advantages, especially tax advantages, over financing by shares alone.[2]

1. See section 165 supra.
2. See generally B. Bittker & J. Eustice, Federal Income Taxation of Corporations and Shareholders ch. 4 (2d ed. 1966); M. Lore, Thin Capitalization (1958); Horsley, "New Dimensions to the Thin Corporation", 9 Wm. & Mary L. Rev. 1066 (1968); Horsley, "When IRS Treats Debt as Equity Widespread Tax Problems Can Result", 29 J.Taxation 78 (1968); McLean, "Thin Incorporation—Advantages and Pitfalls", 14 Prac.Law. 81 (Nov.1968); Stone, "Debt-Equity Distinctions in the Tax Treat-

3. H. Guthmann & H. Dougall, Corporate Financial Policy 167–170 (4th ed. 1962); W. Husband & J. Dockeray, Modern Corporation Finance 216–220 (5th ed. 1962).

Prior to 1958, the tax situation was as follows. The corporation might deduct for interest paid or accrued on debt, but not for dividends on shares, thus partially minimizing the tax at the corporate level.[3] If the corporation were liquidated at a loss, a creditor, in a few situations, was allowed a greater deduction than a shareholder.[4] Furthermore, redemption of shares might have been taxable as ordinary income of the shareholder as a distribution essentially equivalent to a dividend,[5] whereas the repayment of a debt would not have been taxable on the ground that it was a return of capital to the creditor.

Also, the corporation can claim a stepped-up basis for assets received upon incorporating in exchange for certain short-term indebtedness, whereas if the corporation had issued only shares and securities, the transaction might be regarded as a tax-free exchange.[6]

After 1958, the tax situation was complicated by the Technical Amendments Act of

---

ment of the Corporation and its Shareholders", 42 Tul.L.Rev. 251 (1968); Garver, "Tax Factors Affecting Debt-Equity Financing for a New Small Corporation", 17 W.Res.L.Rev. 773 (1966); Hickman, "The Thin Corporation: Another Look at an Old Disease", 44 Taxes 883 (1966); Gerver, "De-emphasis of debt-equity test for thin corporations requires new defense tactics", 23 J. Taxation 28 (1965); Weissman, "Shareholder Advances: Debt or Equity", 7 Tax Coun.Q. 1 (1963); Weis, "The Labyrinth of the Thin Corporation", 40 Taxes 568 (1962); Webster, "Thin Corporations: The Ratio Test Is Not Enough", 35 L.A.B.Bull. 366 (1960); Wagman, "Protecting the Real Estate Corporation Against a Charge of Undue Thinness", 14 J.Taxation 186 (1961); Caplan, "The Caloric Count of a Thin Incorporation", 43 Marq.L.Rev. 31 (1959); Benjamin, "Thin Corporations—Whose 'Substance over Form'?", 34 Tul.L.Rev. 99 (1959); Comment, "Thin Incorporation: A Continuing Problem", 51 Marq.L.Rev. 158 (1967); Comment, "Taxation—Classification of Advances by Shareholders—Debt or Equity", 1964 Wis.L.Rev. 331; Comment, "Thin Capitalization and Tax Avoidance", 55 Colum.L. Rev. 1054 (1955); Note, 5 U.C.L.A.L.Rev. 275 (1958). See Dixon, "The Interest—Dividend Syndrome: What Are the Criteria Now?", N.Y.U. 24th Inst. on Fed.Tax. 1267 (1966).

3. Int.Rev.Code of 1954, 26 U.S.C.A. § 163(a). Of course, the individual receiving a dividend (but not interest) might be entitled to the $100-exclusion-from-gross-income. Int.Rev.Code of 1954, 26 U.S.C. A. § 116(a). Such saving to the individual shareholder is relatively minor when compared to the corporate tax-saving of 22 percent or 48 percent (depending on whether the corporation's net taxable income is more than $25,000). Int.Rev.Code of 1954, 26 U.S.C.A. § 11.

4. Where the creditor's loss involves no evidence of indebtedness and is classifiable as a business bad debt, it is deductible in full. Int.Rev.Code of 1954, 26 U.S.C.A. § 166(b). To qualify as business bad debt, the business of the corporation and that of the shareholder must be one and the same, or the shareholder must be principally engaged in the business of loaning money, or the shareholder must be engaged in organizing, promoting, and financing businesses on an extensive and continuous basis. Otherwise, it is nonbusiness bad debt and consequently limited as capital loss. Id. § 166(d). Shareholders tried to circumvent this rule through use of an outside-loan inside-guarantee, claiming their payments under the guarantee as a "transaction entered into for profit". Putnam v. Comm'r, 352 U.S.

82, 77 S.Ct. 175, 1 L.Ed.2d 144 (1956) plugged this loophole in ruling that "The loss sustained by the guarantor unable to recover from the debtor is by its very nature a loss from the worthlessness of a debt". See also Whipple v. Comm'r, 373 U.S. 193, 83 S.Ct. 1168, 10 L.Ed.2d 288 (1963), reh. denied 374 U.S. 858, 83 S.Ct. 1863, 10 L.Ed.2d 1082 (1963); Trent v. Comm'r, 291 F.2d 669 (2d Cir. 1961); Byerlite Corp. v. Williams, 286 F.2d 285 (6th Cir. 1960). Compare Murphy Logging Co. v. United States, 239 F.Supp. 794 (D.Or.1965), rev'd 378 F.2d 222 (9th Cir. 1967), with Fors Farms, Inc. v. United States, 17 Am. Fed.Tax.R.2d 222 (W.D.Wash.1965). H. Smith, Federal Tax Treatment of Bad Debts and Worthless Securities (1964); Comment, "Loss on Employee's Loan to Corporation Deductible as Business Bad Debt", 37 N.Y.U.L.Rev. 143 (1962); Note, "Guaranteed Shareholder Loans and Thin Capitalization", 70 W.Va.L. Rev. 52 (1967); Note, "Shareholder-Creditor Bad Debts under Section 166 of the Internal Revenue Code", 75 Harv.L.Rev. 589 (1962); Note, "Bad Debt Deduction Allowed for Shareholder's Loss on Advances to Wholly Owned Corporation Despite 18,-800:1 Debt—Equity Ratio", 61 Colum.L.Rev. 1164 (1961); Mays v. Comm'r, 272 F.2d 788 (6th Cir. 1959). Otherwise losses on shares, debt securities constituting capital assets, or nonbusiness bad debts are treated as capital losses, usually long-term in the case of shares or debt securities, short-term in the case of nonbusiness bad debts. Capital losses of individuals may be offset against capital gains and $1,000 of regular income, with indefinite carry over provision. See O'Neill v. Comm'r, 271 F.2d 44 (9th Cir. 1959). See also Worthy, "Stock Losses: Establishing Worthlessness", N.Y.U. 22d Inst. on Fed.Tax. 289 (1964).

5. See section 339 infra. Int.Rev.Code of 1954, 26 U.S.C.A. § 302; Fellinger v. United States, 363 F.2d 826 (6th Cir. 1966). Accumulating funds for repayment of debt can usually be justified as reasonable under the accumulated earnings tax.

6. Int.Rev.Code of 1954, 26 U.S.C.A. § 351. See section 118, n. 7 supra.

1958 and the Small Business Tax Revision Act of 1958.[7]

Under the Technical Amendments Act, a "small business corporation", as defined in Subchapter S,[8] may elect not to be taxed on its net income as a separate entity but to have its income, etc., passed through and taxed to its shareholders. Since such an election completely avoids the corporate income tax, the tax incentive of "thin incorporation" by maximizing corporate deductions is reduced to some extent and the loss pass-through feature provides more favorable treatment for losses.[9]

Under the Small Business Tax Revision Act, losses on "small business stock", as defined in section 1244 ("section 1244 stock"),[10] are treated more favorably than most losses on debts (assuming no Subchapter S election), since "section 1244 stock" losses are fully deductible as business losses up to $25,000 ($50,000 on a joint return) per year; as capital losses up to the extent of any excess.[11] For this reason, where the

venture involves financial risk, financing solely or mainly by shares would often be preferable to the older practice of financing by debt and shares.[12]

Apart from tax considerations, thin incorporation weakens the balance sheet and credit status, making it more difficult to obtain bona fide loans from outside creditors, at least without the insider debt being subordinated.[13]

Of course, the debt is subject to administrative and judicial scrutiny. If it has hybrid characteristics, it suffers the risk of being treated as shares.[14] Even if, on the basis of its characteristics, it is debt, it might nevertheless be regarded as shares if the ratio between debt and shares is such as to lead to the conclusion that the corporation is too-thinly capitalized by shares.[15]

---

7.   Int.Rev.Code of 1954, Subchapter S—Election of Certain Small Business Corporations as to Taxable Status, 26 U.S.C.A. §§ 1371–1377; id. § 1244.

8.   See section 16, n. 9 supra.

9.   The redemption of shares by an electing corporation is not expressly treated in Subchapter S but might have different tax consequences than would otherwise be the case. Frost, "New Election of Certain Corporations Not To Be Taxed As Such", 45 A.B.A.J. 81, 83 (1959). Quaere, whether the "too-thin incorporation" doctrine (infra note 15) will be applied to Subchapter S corporations for purposes of denying corporate "interest" deductions (with usually no adverse tax effect on recipient), taxing "debt retirement" as dividends (with adverse tax effect on recipient), and basis reduction when a loss has been incurred. Of course, if the debt is held to be in effect a second class of shares, the corporation would be ineligible for election under Subchapter S. See Henderson v. United States, 245 F.Supp. 782 (D.Ala.1965); Gamman v. Comm'r, 46 T.C. 1 (1966); Comment, "Application of the Thin Incorporation Doctrine to the Subchapter S One-Class-of-Stock Requirement", 1967 Duke L.J. 1202; Price, "The Small Business Tax Revision of 1958", 14 Bus.Law. 329, 343 (1959).

10.   See section 16, n. 11 supra.

11.   Int.Rev.Code of 1954, 26 U.S.C.A. § 1244(a), (b). Except for "section 1244 stock", treatment of losses

on shares and losses on debt has remained unchanged—usually as capital losses and subject to the limitations applicable to capital losses. See note 4 supra.

12.   Price, "The Small Business Tax Revision of 1958", 14 Bus.Law. 329, 351 (1959).

13.   See Obre v. Alban Tractor Co., 228 Md. 291, 179 A.2d 861 (1962) (upholding $35,548 creditor claim of one of two shareholders who contributed $65,548 in property for $10,000 par value of common shares, and $20,000 par value preferred shares, other shareholder having contributed $10,000 in property for $10,000 par value of common shares); Note, "Non-Tax Aspects of Thin Incorporation", 13 Vand.L.Rev. 751 (1960).

14.   See sections 162–164 supra.

15.   "Too-thin incorporation" has been the subject of numerous lower federal court cases. The debt-equity ratio is often mentioned as a criterion; also whether advances by shareholders-creditors are substantially proportionate to their shareholdings. Some commentators have suggested a 4:1 ratio as a rule of thumb. The equity element should be computed as including not only the shares accounts but also all surplus accounts; actual value rather than book value should be considered. All relevant factors are material in determining whether or not a bona fide debtor-creditor relationship exists. The United States Supreme Court has yet to be heard from on the subject, although its statement in John Kelley Co. v. Comm'r and Talbot Mills v. Comm'r, 326 U.S. 521, 526, 66 S.Ct. 299, 302, 90 L.Ed. 278, 281 (1946) discussed in section 163 supra, where the ratio approximated 4:1, that "As material amounts of capital were invested in stock, we need not consider the effect of extreme situations such as nomi-

There are various possible safeguards against too-thin incorporation: [16]

(a) Material amount of equity (at least sufficient to acquire the "core" assets);

(b) Realistic debt structure (payment of interest and repayment of principal, when due, should be feasible);

(c) Straightforward indebtedness (avoidance of hybrid securities);

(d) Collateral (to buttress idea of debt);

(e) Corporate formalities (to evidence intention to create debtor-creditor relationship);

(f) Identify consideration (respectively given for equity and debt);

(g) Avoid pro rata lending (loans should be disproportionate to shareholdings);

(h) Borrow in stages (to meet needs of business as they arise);

(i) Different types of indebtedness (to create more favorable climate for at least partial relief);

(j) Trust as lender (fiduciary relation buttresses *bona fides*);

(k) Guaranteed loans; [17]

(l) Business purpose (nontax reasons for issuing debt);

(m) Reasonable expectations of repayment (when loan is extended);

(n) Acting like a creditor (while loan is outstanding);

(o) Ratio (risks enlarged by debt:share ratios of 3:1 or more).

F. CONSIDERATION FOR SHARES

CONSIDERATION FOR PAR VALUE SHARES

167. The consideration requirements for the issue of shares are often both qualitative and quantitative. Qualitatively, the consideration for par value shares must be of the quality prescribed by applicable state constitutional provision and statute, usually limited to money, services rendered, and property received by the corporation. Quantitatively, the consideration of required quality may, with some exceptions, be no less than the par value. Applicable to the valuation of services and property are the so-called "True Value Rule" and "Good Faith Rule", with the latter often codified by statute.

The consideration requirements for the issue of shares are often both qualitative and quantitative. Such requirements must be considered not only when issuing shares, but when issuing securities convertible into shares or share options. While there is some variation among different jurisdictions, the same broad principles are generally recognized. The consideration requirements for par value shares differ from the consideration requirements for shares without par value.

General Rule

Qualitatively, the only lawful consideration for par value shares is not merely consideration in the contract law sense but only

nal stock investments and an obviously excessive debt structure", set the stage for what the lower federal courts have been doing. The concept of too-thin incorporation had already been before the Supreme Court in connection with the disallowance or subordination in bankruptcy or corporate reorganization of creditor claims of shareholders. See section 152 supra. In Gooding Amusement Co. v. Comm'r, 236 F.2d 159 (6th Cir. 1956), cert. denied 352 U.S. 1031, 77 S.Ct. 595, 1 L.Ed.2d 599 (1957), a 1:10 ratio was rejected. See Fin Hay Realty Co. v. United States, 261 F.Supp. 823 (D.N.J.1966) ($200,-000 debt: $20,000 shares rejected; reciting 16 indicia), aff'd 398 F.2d 694 (3d Cir. 1968) (1934 note, on which interest payments had been regularly paid, held in fact equity when issued because of high debt-equity ratio); Biritz Construction Co. v. Comm'r, 387 F.2d 451 (8th Cir. 1967) (upholding 2:1 ratio); Taft v. Comm'r, 314 F.2d 620 (9th Cir. 1963) ($107,000 debt: $1,410 shares upheld); Gilbert v. Comm'r, 248 F.2d 399 (2d Cir. 1957). For authorized regulations under the Tax Reform Act of 1969, see section 163, n. 11 supra.

16. Caplan, "The Caloric Count of a Thin Incorporation", 43 Marq.L.Rev. 31, 68–71 (1959).

17. But see Putnam v. Comm'r, supra note 4.

the consideration expressly permitted by the applicable state constitutional provision or corporation statute.

The constitutions which have such provisions and most statutes permit only money, services rendered, and property actually received for proper corporate purposes.[1]

Some statutes expressly exclude certain types of consideration,[2] or elaborate on permissible consideration.[3]

Services performed must be in the nature of services performed for the corporation;

hence neither future services[4] nor preincorporation services[5] would ordinarily suffice. Some jurisdictions permit the issue of shares for preincorporation services.[6] Property must be property in a rather strict sense in most jurisdictions, with the result that promissory notes,[7] forgiveness of debt owing

---

1. See, e. g., Ark.Const. art. XII, § 8; Del.Const. art. IX, § 3; Neb.Const. art. XII, § 6; ABA–ALI Model Bus.Corp.Act § 18; Del.Gen.Corp.Law, § 152 (1967). As Giffard, L. J., said in Drummond's Case, L.R. 4 Ch. 772, 779 (1869): "if a man contracts to take shares he must pay for them, to use a homely phrase, 'in meal or in malt;' he must either pay in money or in money's worth. If he pays in one or the other, that will be a satisfaction." For judicial constructions in favor of validity of consideration, see Highlights for Children, Inc. v. Crown, 43 Del. Ch. 323, 227 A.2d 118 (Ch.1967); Morgan v. Bon Bon Co., 222 N.Y. 22, 118 N.E. 205 (1917). But see United Steel Industries, Inc. v. Manhart, 405 S.W. 2d 231 (Tex.Civ.App.1966). Cash received by the corporation is, of course, debited to cash; the cost of the property is debited to the appropriate property account; and the cost of the services is debited to the appropriate salaries or wages expense account.

2. E. g., ABA–ALI Model Bus.Corp.Act § 18; Michigan, Montana, North Carolina, Ohio, Oklahoma, Tennessee (promissory notes, future services); Kentucky, Louisiana, Wisconsin (promissory notes); Maryland, Oregon, Virginia (future services); Kentucky, New York (obligations of subscriber and future services); Louisiana (uncertified check). Annot., 78 A.L.R.2d 834 (1961).

3. E. g., California, Hawaii, North Carolina, Oklahoma (cancellation of debts or securities); New Jersey, West Virginia (shares of another corporation); Massachusetts, New Hampshire (expenses); North Carolina (satisfaction of accrued dividends or dividend credits); New Hampshire, Vermont (franchises); New York (money or other property, tangible or intangible, or labor or services actually received by or performed for corporation or for its benefit or in its formation or reorganization, or combination thereof, but not obligations of subscriber for future payments or future services). A few statutes expressly deal with consideration requirements in connection with share dividends, share splits, exchanges, conversion, reclassification, consolidation. E. g., California, New York. See also ABA–ALI Model Bus.Corp.Act § 17. Cf. Young v. Bradford County Tel. Co., 341 Pa. 394, 19 A.2d 134 (1941).

4. See, e. g., ABA–ALI Model Bus.Corp.Act § 18 (holding shares may be issued for future services when all shareholders agree). Triplex Shoe Co. v. Rice & Hutchins, Inc., 17 Del.Ch. 356, 152 A. 342, 72 A.L.R. 934 (Sup.Ct.1930); cf. Petrishen v. Westmoreland Finance Corp., 394 Pa. 552, 147 A.2d 392 (1959); United Steel Industries, Inc. v. Manhart, 405 S.W.2d 231 (Tex.Civ.App.1966) (holding void entire issuance of shares for combined past and future services where corporation had made no allocation of shares between services rendered and future services). But see Don Johnston Drilling Co. v. Howard, 347 P.2d 640, 78 A.L.R.2d 824 (Okl.1959); Morgan v. Bon Bon Co., 222 N.Y. 22, 118 N.E. 205 (1917) (construed as not calling for issue of shares until after future services rendered); Ohio Gen.Corp.Law § 1701.18(C) (1955) (statute to similar effect). See Mertz, "Validity of a Contract to Issue Stock for Future Services", 2 Mont.L.Rev. 91 (1941).

5. See sections 113, 115 supra. Cf. Petrishen v. Westmoreland Finance Corp., 394 Pa. 552, 147 A.2d 392 (1959).

6. McKinney's N.Y.Bus.Corp.Law, § 504 (expressly permitting services actually performed for corporation's benefit or in its organization or reorganization); Blish v. Thompson Automatic Arms Corp., 30 Del.Ch. 538, 64 A.2d 581 (Sup.Ct.1948); Shore v. Union Drug Co., 18 Del.Ch. 74, 156 A. 204 (Ch. 1931); cf. Fitzpatrick v. O'Neill, 43 Mont. 552, 118 P. 273, Ann.Cas.1912C, 296 (1911); United German Silver Co. v. Bronson, 92 Conn. 266, 102 A. 647 (1917).

7. The cases are tending to uphold the validity of the notes, unless a statute dictates a contrary conclusion. See Haselbush v. Alsco of Colorado, Inc., 161 Colo. 138, 421 P.2d 113 (1967); Doyle v. Chladek, 240 Or. 598, 401 P.2d 18 (1965), modified reh. denied 240 Or. 598, 403 P.2d 381 (1965) (note held proper consideration but not to extinguish liability on share subscription); McCarty v. Langdeau, 337 S.W.2d 407 (Tex.Civ.App.1960); Thompson v. First State Bank of Amarillo, 109 Tex. 419, 211 S.W. 977 (1919). But see Roy v. Recker, 225 F.Supp. 743 (E.D.Ark.1963) (holding following Arkansas case law, that note ostensibly used to purchase shares was, like shares themselves under Arkansas Constitution, void, except in hands of holders in due course). General Beverages, Inc. v. Rogers, 216 F. 2d 413 (10th Cir. 1954) (note held unenforceable under applicable state law); State ex rel. Cullitan v. Stookey, 95 Ohio App. 97, 113 N.E.2d 254 (1953); Merchants Bank & Trust Co. v. Walker 192 Miss. 737, 6 So.2d 107 (1942); Cahall v. Lofland, 12 Del.Ch. 299, 114 A. 224 (Ch.1921); Sohland

by someone other than the corporation,[8] unpatented inventions, secret processes or formulas,[9] professional knowledge or goodwill (except goodwill of a profitable going concern),[10] etc., might not comply with the qualitative requirement.

Quantitatively, the consideration of required quality for par value shares may, with some exceptions, be no less than the par value.[11]

Money consideration, of course, involves no valuation problem, but consideration in the form of services or property often does. The stricter, minority rule, known as the *"True Value Rule"*, requires that the consideration at the time of the issue of the shares have a value no less than the par value.[12] The more liberal, majority rule, called the *"Good Faith Rule"*, requires only that such consideration be deemed by the board of directors in good faith to have a value no less than the par value.[13]

v. Baker, 15 Del.Ch. 431, 141 A. 277, 58 A.L.R. 693 (Sup.Ct.1927) (secured note with worthless security held insufficient). But see General Bonding & Cas. Ins. Co. v. Mosely, 110 Tex. 529, 222 S.W. 961 (1920) (secured note held sufficient). Paskus, " 'Illegal' Creation of Shares in Return for Notes", 39 Yale L.J. 706 (1930) ; Waterman, "Creation of Corporate Shares in Return for Promissory Notes", 7 Texas L.Rev. 215 (1929) ; Annot., 58 A.L.R. 708 (1929). See note 2 supra. Cf. McPhail v. L. S. Starrett Co., 157 F.Supp. 560 (D.Mass.1957), aff'd 257 F.2d 388 (1st Cir. 1958) ; Grafton v. Masteller, 232 F.2d 773 (3d Cir. 1956), cert. denied, 352 U.S. 832, 77 S. Ct. 47, 1 L.Ed.2d 52 (1956). Promised property, as distinguished from property received, does not suffice. United States Industries, Inc. v. Manhart, 405 S.W.2d 231 (Tex.Civ.App.1966).

8.   See Evans v. Ideal Brick & Brikcrete Mfg. Co., 287 P.2d 454 (Okl.1955) ; Whitwell v. Henry, 225 Ark. 987, 286 S.W.2d 852 (1956) ; Hodge v. Cuba Co., 142 N.J.Eq. 340, 60 A.2d 88 (1948) ; Brockett v. Winkle Terra Cotta Co., 81 F.2d 949 (8th Cir. 1936) ; cf. Graves, Inc. v. Comm'r, 202 F.2d 286 (5th Cir. 1953), cert. denied 346 U.S. 812, 74 S.Ct. 21, 98 L. Ed. 340 (1953). See note 3 supra.

9.   See Sterling Varnish Co. v. Sonom Co., 241 Miss. 810, 133 So.2d 624 (1961) (upholding assignment of contract for exclusive marketing rights of formula) ; Lichman v. Moore, 131 F.Supp. 434 (D.Mass. 1955) (upholding patent license even though terminable upon corporate insolvency) ; Trotta v. Metalmold Corp., 139 Conn. 668, 96 A.2d 798, 37 A.L.R.2d 906 (1953) (holding unpatented ideas not property) ; Scully v. Automobile Finance Co., 12 Del.Ch. 174, 109 A. 49 (Ch.1920) ; West v. Sirian Lamp Co., 28 Del.Ch. 398, 44 A.2d 658 (Ch.1945) (upholding patent rights as consideration) ; Annot., 37 A.L.R.2d 913 (1954). See note 3 supra. See Murray v. Murray Laboratories, 223 Ark. 907, 270 S.W.2d 927 (1954) (corporation which received unpatented formula for shares estopped from cancelling shares for lack of consideration).

10.   Linden Bros. v. Practical Electricity & Engineering Pub. Co., 309 Ill. 132, 140 N.E. 874 (1923) (holding goodwill of failing business insufficient) ; cf. Trotta v. Metalmold Corp., 139 Conn. 668, 96 A.2d 798, 37 A.L.R.2d 906 (1953) (upholding goodwill of going profitable concern as consideration) ; Brown v. Weeks, 195 Mich. 27, 161 N.W. 945 (1917) ; Washburn v. National Wall-Paper Co., 81 F. 17 (2d Cir. 1897). A lower court holding that knowledge and goodwill of employees of corporation rendering management consultant services constituted property "by modern usage" and hence was valid consideration for issued shares was rejected on appeal. Brown v. Watson, 124 N.Y.S.2d 504 (Sup.Ct.1953),

rev'd 285 App.Div. 587, 139 N.Y.S.2d 628 (1st Dep't 1955).

11.   See, e. g., ABA–ALI Model Bus.Corp.Act § 17 ; McKinney's N.Y.Bus.Corp.Law § 504(c) ; see Yasik v. Wachtel, 25 Del.Ch. 247, 17 A.2d 309 (Ch.1941). See also Joslin, "Stock Issue, The Above Par Problem", 12 J.Pub.L. 9 (1963).

12.   Van Cleve v. Berkey, 143 Mo. 109, 44 S.W. 743 (1898) ; Libby v. Tobey, 82 Me. 397, 19 A. 904 (1890) ; Adams, "Valuation of Property Paid for Stock: A Reappraisal", 3 Miami L.Q. 26 (1948) ; Note, "Valuation of Property or Services to a Corporation—the Ohio Treatment", 26 U.Cin.L.Rev. 611 (1957).

13.   Coit v. Gold Amalgamating Co., 119 U.S. 343, 7 S.Ct. 231, 30 L.Ed. 420 (1886) ; Johnson v. Louisville Trust Co., 293 F. 857, 36 A.L.R. 785 (6th Cir. 1923), cert. denied, 264 U.S. 585, 44 S.Ct. 334, 68 L. Ed. 862 (1923) ; Clinton Mining & Mineral Co. v. Jamison, 256 F. 577 (3d Cir. 1919) ; Henderson v. Plymouth Oil Co., 16 Del.Ch. 347, 141 A. 197 (Sup. Ct.1928). Several statutes appear to codify the good faith rule. E. g., ABA–ALI Model Bus.Corp. Act § 18. See Donald v. American Smelting & Refining Co., 62 N.J.Eq. 729, 48 A. 771 (1901) ; See v. Heppenheimer, 69 N.J.Eq. 36, 61 A. 843 (1905) (holding valuation by capitalizing future profits expected from property by price control of product through elimination of competition lacking good faith). But see Railway Review v. Groff Drill & Machine Tool Co., 84 N.J.Eq. 321, 91 A. 1021 (1914), aff'd mem. sub nom. Sloan, Rec'r v. Paul, 84 N.J. Eq. 508, 96 A. 1103 (1915) (upholding valuation based on capitalization of present earnings). Mass. Ann.Laws ch. 156, §§ 16, 36 (1959, Supp.1968) (inapplicable to most business corporations since 1965) ; former N.J.Gen.Corp.Law, § 14:8–16 (1937) ; Va. Stock Corp.Act § 13.1–16 (1957). For liabilities of officers and directors and other consequences of noncompliance, see Bay State York Co. v. Cobb, 346 Mass. 641, 195 N.E.2d 328 (1964) ; Sunrise Dairies v. Pierre's Steak House & Restaurant, Inc., 80 N.J.

If a minimum paid-in stated capital provision is applicable, the stated capital represented by the shares originally issued should satisfy such minimum stated capital requirement.[14]

Exceptions

The general quantitative requirement that par value shares be issued for no less than par value is subject, in some jurisdictions, to various exceptions.

Handley v. Stutz Doctrine. One exception was set forth by the United States Supreme Court in Handley v. Stutz.[15] The doctrine is stated in the syllabus:

"An active corporation, finding its original capital impaired by loss or misfortune, may, for the purpose of recuperating itself, and of producing new conditions for the successful prosecution of its business, issue new stock, and put it upon the market, and sell it for the best price that can be obtained: and in such case no such trust in favor of a creditor arises against the purchaser who, in good faith, buys for less than par."

It is doubtful if the Handley v. Stutz doctrine would have applied if a clear statute of the jurisdiction of incorporation had been found to apply. It has not been applied to newly-formed corporations.[16] Furthermore, since Erie R. R. v. Tompkins,[17] federal decisional law on the subject would appear to have little relevance.

Statutory Exceptions. A few jurisdictions have statutes more or less resembling the Handley v. Stutz doctrine which permit the issuance of par value shares for less than par value under prescribed circumstances.[18]

Some statutes expressly provide that the corporation may net less than the par value after deducting reasonable underwriting costs.[19]

State statutes sometimes exempt from the regular statutory consideration requirements shares which are issued under a reorganization plan confirmed by a federal reorganization court.[20]

Treasury Shares. With respect to the reallotment of treasury shares, the usual consideration requirements are ordinarily in-

16.   Harman v. Himes, 64 App.D.C. 252, 77 F.2d 375 (1935). See also Rickerson Roller-Mill Co. v. Farrell Foundry & Machine Co., 75 F. 554 (6th Cir. 1896); Utica Fire Alarm Tel. Co. v. Waggoner Watchman Clock Co., 166 Mich. 618, 132 N.W. 502 (1911).

17.   304 U.S. 64, 58 S.Ct. 817, 82 L.Ed. 1188, 114 A.L.R. 1487 (1938).

18.   E. g., California, Indiana, Kansas, Maryland, Rhode Island, West Virginia. Debt securities convertible into shares might be issued at a discount in most jurisdictions, but some jurisdictions prescribe limitations. See Ohio Gen.Corp.Law, §§ 1701.18(D), 1701.21 (1955); Cal.Gen.Corp.Law, § 1110(c) (1947).

19.   See e. g., ABA–ALI Model Bus.Corp.Act § 20. A growing number of statutes also permit deduction of organization expenses. See, e. g., Cal.Gen.Corp. Law, § 1900 (1947); McKinney's N.Y.Bus.Corp.Law, § 507.

20.   See, e. g., ABA–ALI Model Bus.Corp.Act § 59A; California, Delaware, Michigan, Ohio, Oklahoma, Virginia; id. § 26 (confirmed plan under Federal Bankruptcy Act § 26–a (under Federal Public Utility Holding Company Act of 1935). The New York provision refers to any court-confirmed corporate reorganization plan "under any applicable act of congress relating to reorganization of corporations". McKinney's N.Y.Bus.Corp.Law, § 808. See section 350 infra. For discussion of rule, absent statutory exception, see Brockett v. Winkle Terra Cotta Co., 81 F.2d 949 (8th Cir. 1936).

Super. 142, 193 A.2d 171 (1963); New Jersey Sign Erectors, Inc. v. Cocuzza, 72 N.J.Super. 269, 178 A. 2d 111 (1962); Hudson v. Clark, 200 Va. 325, 106 S. E.2d 133 (1958). Statutes sometimes require the filing of statements when shares are issued for property. Note, "Some Problems Raised by Issuing Stock for Overvalued Property and Services in Texas", 40 Texas L.Rev. 376 (1962).

14.   Cf. Livingston v. Adams, 226 Mo.App. 824, 43 S. W.2d 836 (1931). Israels, "Problems of Par and No-Par Shares: A Reappraisal", 47 Colum.L.Rev. 1279, 1285 (1947). See sections 126, 143 supra. Obviously, balance sheet inflation of the consideration received for shares should be avoided.

15.   139 U.S. 417, 11 S.Ct. 530, 35 L.Ed. 227 (1891). Clark v. Bever, 139 U.S. 96, 11 S.Ct. 468, 35 L.Ed. 88 (1891). Contra, Enright v. Heckscher, 240 F. 863 (2d Cir. 1917); New Haven Trust Co. v. Gaffney, 73 Conn. 480, 47 A. 760 (1901); Jackson v. Traer, 64 Iowa 469, 20 N.W. 764 (1884).

applicable, either by statute[21] or by court decision.[22]

Share Distributions. Consideration-for-shares requirements also apply to shares issued in the form of share distributions.[23]

Conversion. When shares are issued by exercise of conversion privileges, consideration-for-shares requirements apply.[24]

CONSIDERATION FOR SHARES WITHOUT PAR VALUE

168. Qualitatively, the consideration for shares without par value must conform to applicable state constitutional provisions and statutory requirements. Qualitatively, the consideration in many jurisdictions is required to be money, services rendered, or property. In different jurisdictions, the consideration for shares without par value is required to be determined in various manners, usually by the board of directors or shareholders, often depending upon provision therefor in the articles of incorporation. Quantitatively, such consideration should satisfy any applicable minimum paid-in stated capital requirement and be no less than any stated value assigned to the shares. Balance sheet inflation should be avoided. Contemporaneous issue of shares at different prices has been upheld under certain circumstances.

Constitutions, statutes, and cases, defining the consideration for shares without value are sometimes ambiguous.[1]

In most jurisdictions, the same qualitative requirement applicable to par value shares —usually money, services rendered, or property—applies to the issue of shares without par value.[2] Occasionally, it has been suggested without elaboration that any consideration prescribed in the articles of incorporation, or by the board of directors, or by shareholders, is sufficient.[3]

The consideration for shares without par value is determined in various manners in different jurisdictions, such as by the incorporators up to the time of incorporation,[4] by the board of directors unless the power is reserved to the shareholders in the articles of incorporation,[5] by the board unless otherwise provided in the articles,[6] by the shareholders unless the articles fix the consideration or authorize the board of directors to do so,[7] or by the shareholders or the board when so authorized by the shareholders absent contrary provision in the articles.[8]

Reappraisal", 47 Colum.L.Rev. 1279 (1947); Berle, "Problems of No-Par Stock", 25 Colum.L.Rev. 43 (1925); Bonbright, "The Dangers of Shares Without Par Value", 24 Colum.L.Rev. 449 (1924).

2. See section 167 supra. ABA–ALI Model Bus. Corp.Act § 18. See, e. g., Johnson v. Louisville Trust Co., 293 F. 857, 36 A.L.R. 785 (6th Cir. 1923), cert. denied 264 U.S. 585, 44 S.Ct. 334, 68 L.Ed. 862 (1923). Cf. Del.Gen.Corp.Law, §§ 152, 153 (1967). But see Speakman v. Bernstein, 59 F.2d 520 (5th Cir. 1932), cert. denied 287 U.S. 639, 53 S.Ct. 88, 77 L.Ed. 553 (1932) (gift of no par common shares of Delaware corporation upheld).

3. E. g., former McKinney's N.Y.Stock Corp.Law, §§ 12, 69. See also Norton v. Lamb, 144 Kan. 665, 62 P.2d 1311 (1936) (price per share fixed in articles of incorporation).

4. E. g., Idaho, Kentucky, New Hampshire, Pennsylvania.

5. E. g., ABA–ALI Model Bus.Corp.Act § 17. New York since 1963 has so provided. See note 9 infra.

6. E. g., California, Delaware, Kansas, Michigan, Missouri, Nevada, North Carolina. California expressly requires that the consideration be "reasonable". The duty of the board of directors has been held nondelegable to a non-director appraiser. Field v. Carlisle Corp., 31 Del.Ch. 227, 68 A.2d 817 (Ch.1949).

7. E. g., Indiana, Rhode Island, West Virginia.

8. E. g., Florida, Georgia, Hawaii, Maine.

21. E. g., ABA–ALI Model Bus.Corp.Act § 17; McKinney's N.Y.Bus.Corp.Law, § 504(e).

22. Highlights for Children, Inc. v. Crown, 43 Del. Ch. 323, 227 A.2d 118 (Ch.1967); Belle Isle Corp. v. MacBean, 30 Del.Ch. 373, 61 A. 699 (Ch.1948); Otter v. Brevoort Petroleum Co., 50 Barb. 247 (N.Y. Sup.Ct.1867).

23. E. g., ABA–ALI Model Bus.Corp.Act § 17. See sections 329, 330, 333 infra.

24. E. g., ABA–ALI Model Bus.Corp.Act § 17. See sections 156, 160 supra.

1. West v. Sirian Lamp Co., 28 Del.Ch. 90, 37 A.2d 835 (Ch.1944); Manne, "Accounting for Share Issues Under Modern Corporation Laws", 54 Nw.U.L. Rev. 285 (1959); Manne, "The American Law of No Par Value Shares", 1957 J.Bus.Law 431; Note, "No-Par Value Stock as a Measure of Shareholder Liability", 13 N.Y.U.Intra.L.Rev. 129 (1958); Israels, "Problems of Par and No-Par Shares: A

New York until 1963 provided that the consideration could be fixed in the articles of incorporation, the fair market value, that fixed by the board of directors pursuant to authority in the articles, or that fixed by the shareholders.[9]

Where a minimum paid-in stated capital requirement exists, the stated capital represented by the shares originally issued should satisfy such requirement.[10]

Where the shares without par value being issued have stated value, they should not be issued for less than such stated value.[11] To the extent that quantitative requirements are applicable, and there is a valuation problem with respect to the consideration received, the "True Value Rule" or "Good Faith Rule" might be applicable.[12] Balance sheet inflation should also be avoided.[13]

Some cases have upheld the contemporaneous issue of shares at different prices under certain circumstances.[14] A Minnesota statute prohibits the allotment of shares with or without par value for a cash consideration which is unfair to existing shareholders or for a consideration other than cash upon a valuation thereof which is unfair to such shareholders.[15]

G. SHARE SUBSCRIPTIONS AND OPTIONS

SHARE SUBSCRIPTIONS

169. Some statutes require that share subscriptions be in writing and signed by the subscriber. Statutory provisions for assessment and forfeiture in event of default also exist. Subscriptions may be rescinded for fraud. Share subscriptions are distinguishable from executory contracts for the purchase and sale of shares. The former results in immediate shareholder status while the latter postpones shareholder status until delivery of the share certificate and payment for the shares.

A person may become a shareholder in various ways, e. g., by (a) subscribing to shares in the articles of incorporation, (b) entering into a subscription for shares before or after incorporation,[1] or (c) taking shares by transfer from the holder thereof.[2]

9. Former McKinney's N.Y.Stock Corp.Law, § 12. New York now provides that shares without par value may be issued for such consideration as is fixed from time to time by the board of directors unless the articles of incorporation reserve to the shareholders the right to fix the consideration. McKinney's N.Y.Bus.Corp.Law, § 504(d).

10. Livingston v. Adams, 226 Mo.App. 824, 43 S.W.2d 836 (1931). See section 126 supra.

11. Some statutes expressly so provide. E. g., Kentucky, Maryland, Minnesota. See also Israels, "Problems of Par and No-Par Shares: A Reappraisal", 47 Colum.L.Rev. 1279, 1286-1287 (1947).

12. See section 167 supra.

13. For accounting purposes, value will have to be assigned to the consideration for all shares. See G. Loewus & Co. v. Highland Queen Packing Co., 125 N.J.Eq. 534, 6 A.2d 545 (1939); Brown-Wales Co. v. Barber, 88 N.H. 103, 184 A. 855 (1936); Crescent Mfg. Co. v. Hansen, 174 Wash. 193, 24 P.2d 604 (1933). Israels, "Problems of Par and No-Par Shares: A Reappraisal", 47 Colum.L.Rev. 1279, 1297-1300 (1947). An S.E.C. registration statement involving balance-sheet inflation might be "misleading" under the Federal Securities Act of 1933. In re Haddam Distillers Corp., 1 S.E.C. 37 (1934).

14. Bodell v. General Gas & Elec. Corp., 15 Del.Ch. 119, 132 A. 442 (Ch.1926), aff'd 15 Del.Ch. 420, 140 A. 264 (Sup.Ct.1927); Atlantic Refining Co. v. Hodgman, 13 F.2d 781 (3d Cir. 1926), cert. denied 273 U.S. 731, 47 S.Ct. 240, 71 L.Ed. 863 (1926); Milberg v. Baum, 25 N.Y.S.2d 451 (App.T. 1st Dep't 1941).

15. Minn.Bus.Corp.Act § 301.16 (1961).

1. ABA-ALI Model Bus.Corp.Act § 2(e). A corporation might issue unissued shares, or reallot treasury shares; or might issue shares upon the exercise of share options, or upon the exercise of a conversion privilege appertaining to securities convertible into shares or in the form of a share distribution. On share subscriptions, see generally Cataldo, "Conditions in Subscriptions for Shares", 43 Va.L. Rev. 353 (1957); Annot., 81 A.L.R. 198 (1932), 101 A.L.R. 231 (1936). For construction of share subscription, see Penn-Allen Broadcasting Co. v. Traylor, 389 Pa. 490, 133 A.2d 528 (1957). See also Winton, "Private Corporate Stock Subscription Agreements", 33 Calif.L.Rev. 388 (1960). Subscribers to shares whose subscriptions have been accepted sometimes exercise shareholder management functions where there are no shareholders of record. See McKinney's N.Y.Bus.Corp.Law, § 615(c).

2. See section 177 infra.

The special problems of preincorporation share subscriptions resulting from the fact that the corporation is not in existence at the time of such subscriptions have been discussed previously.[3]

Statutes tend to cover at least some aspects of the law of share subscriptions. Some of them require that subscriptions be in writing and signed by the subscriber.[4] Modern statutes are tending to be more comprehensive.[5]

Under the Model Business Corporation Act, share certificates representing partly paid shares may not be issued, but fractional shares may.[6]

If a share subscription is induced by fraud, the defrauded subscriber may rescind his subscription, subject to the rights of creditors and the other usual principles applicable to rescission.[7] Such rescission changes the defrauded subscriber's status from that of shareholder to creditor. In most jurisdictions, such rescission is permitted even after the insolvency of the corporation,[8] but a minority of jurisdictions preclude rescission after insolvency.[9]

Share subscriptions must be distinguished from executory contracts for the purchase and sale of shares.[10] Since both are contracts (assuming corporate acceptance of the share subscription),[11] the intention of the parties is controlling. In the case of a share subscription, the subscription might have to be in writing under the corporate statute [12] but usually is not subject to the statute of frauds provision requiring that a contract for the sale of goods be in writing; [13] the subscriber becomes a shareholder at the time of the making of the subscription; as a shareholder, the subscriber enjoys the rights and is subject to the liabilities of shareholders; [14] the delivery of the share

---

3. See section 115 supra.

4. See, e. g., Ky.Gen.Corp.Law, § 271.075 (1953) (preincorporation subscriptions); McKinney's N.Y. Bus.Corp.Law, § 503 and N.C.Bus.Corp.Act § 55–43 (1957) (pre- and post-incorporation subscriptions).

5. ABA–ALI Model Bus.Corp.Act § 16; McKinney's N.Y.Bus.Corp.Law, § 503. Upon forfeiture of a share subscription for default in payment, the shares subscribed for should be cancelled and restored to the status of authorized but unissued shares and all forfeited payments should be transferred to capital surplus ("Forfeiture surplus"). McKinney's N.Y.Bus.Corp.Law, § 503(d).

6. ABA–ALI Model Bus.Corp.Act §§ 21, 22. See section 161 supra.

7. Texas City Hotel Corp. v. Wilkenfeld, 410 S.W.2d 860 (Tex.Civ.App.1966); MacNamee v. Bankers' Union for Foreign Commerce & Finance, Inc., 25 F.2d 614 (2d Cir. 1928). R. Stevens, Handbook on the Law of Private Corporations § 90 (2d ed. 1949). Rogers v. Day, 230 Or. 564, 370 P.2d 624 (1962), motion denied 232 Or. 185, 375 P.2d 63 (1962) (minority shareholder allowed to recover consideration for his shares when majority "froze him out" by (a) not notifying him of meetings, (b) withholding dividends, (c) not informing him of corporate affairs, and (d) making him an officer but handing him a resignation form at the first meeting he attended).

8. Newton Nat'l Bank v. Newbegin, 74 F. 135 (8th Cir. 1896); Burningham v. Burke, 67 Utah 90, 245 P. 977, 46 A.L.R. 466 (1926); Gress v. Knight, 135 Ga. 60, 68 S.E. 834 (1910); Morrisey v. Williams, 74 W.Va. 636, 82 S.E. 509 (1914). Rescinding shareholders, while superior to non-rescinding shareholders, might have their claims deferred to the claims of other creditors. In re Morris Bros., 293 F. 294 (9th Cir. 1923).

9. Oakes v. Turquand, L.R. 2 H.L. 325 (1867); Annot., 41 A.L.R. 674 (1926), 46 A.L.R. 484 (1927).

10. See Minn.Bus.Corp.Act § 301.17(11) (1961): "Enforceable contracts to purchase shares from the corporation shall have the same status as accepted subscriptions."

11. Becker v. Tower Nat'l Life Inv. Co., 406 S.W.2d 553 (Mo.1966) (corporation held liable to subscriber on ground deposit of his payment in escrow account constituted acceptance of subscription by corporation).

12. See note 4 supra.

13. Rutenbeck v. Hohn, 143 Iowa 13, 121 N.W. 698 (1909); Mills v. Friedman, 111 Misc. 253, 181 N.Y.S. 285 (Sup.Ct.1920), aff'd 194 App.Div. 932, 184 N.Y.S. 613 (3d Dep't 1922), aff'd 233 N.Y. 517, 135 N.E. 899 (1922). If the subscription is not to be performed within a year, it might be required to be in writing. R. Stevens, Handbook on the Law of Private Corporations § 87 (2d ed. 1949).

14. Babbitt v. Pacco Investors Corp., 246 Or. 261, 425 P.2d 489 (1967) ($5,000 penalty against corporation and agent upheld for denial of inspection rights to share subscriber); Van Noy v. Gibbs, 7 Utah 2d 70, 318 P.2d 351 (1957); R. Stevens, Handbook on the Law of Private Corporations § 86 (2d ed. 1949). But see McKinney's N.Y.Bus.Corp.Law, § 504(i) ("When the consideration has been paid in full, the

certificate is not a concurrent condition; and the subscriber's duty to pay the subscription price survives the insolvency or bankruptcy of the corporation.[15] An executory contract for the purchase and sale of shares is usually subject to the statute of frauds;[16] the purchaser does not become a shareholder until the closing of the transaction;[17] The delivery of the share certificate is a concurrent condition; and not only is the purchaser's duty to pay cut off by the intervening insolvency or bankruptcy of the corporation, but the purchaser may

claim the refund of any payments he has made.[18]

Problems involved in the public offering of securities, the various types of underwriting agreements, and the application of federal securities legislation and state "blue sky" statutes are reserved for treatment in Chapter 11.[19]

SHARE OPTIONS

170. Share options usually may be issued by corporations, when supported by adequate consideration and consistent with preemptive rights. Share options usually are evidenced by share warrants. The option price should conform to applicable consideration requirements applicable to the optioned shares. Share options are currently most prevalent as forms of management and employee incentive compensation plans.

Corporations usually may issue share options.[1] Share options must be supported by consideration.[2] These are usually evidenced by certificates known as share warrants, and give their holders the right to buy a specified number of shares from the corporation[3] at a specified price[4] usually

subscriber shall be entitled to all the rights and privileges of a holder of such shares"). Berkowitz v. Linden Towers Cooperative No. 5, Inc., 35 Misc. 2d 219, 231 N.Y.S.2d 85 (Sup.Ct.1962) (holding that parties to a valid conditional subscription contract which required subscriptions for more than 90 percent of the dwelling units in a housing project before the share certificates would issue, were not shareholders when the subscriptions had not yet reached 90 percent); Cataldo, "Conditions in Subscriptions for Shares", 43 Va.L.Rev. 353 (1957); Ecorse Screw Mach. Prods. Co. v. Corp. & Sec. Comm'n, 1 Mich.App. 414, 136 N.W.2d 758 (1965), aff'd 378 Mich. 415, 145 N.W.2d 46 (1966) (unpaid share subscriptions held not "paid-up capital" or surplus subject to franchise fee).

15.   Allen v. Ryan, 219 App.Div. 634, 221 N.Y.S. 77 (4th Dep't 1927), aff'd mem., 246 N.Y. 609, 159 N.E. 671 (1927).

16.   Uniform Commercial Code § 8–319 (statute of frauds applicable to "contract for the sale of securities"). As a contract for the sale of goods of a certain value. Tisdale v. Harris, 20 Pick. (37 Mass.) 9 (1838). Older statutes of frauds required every contract for the sale of goods of a specified value or more to be in writing and signed by the party to be charged. Sales of shares were held covered by such statute. Samford v. Citizen's & Southern Nat'l Bank, 216 Ga. 215, 115 S.E.2d 517 (1960); Baron v. Schachter, 308 N.Y. 888, 126 N.E. 2d 565 (1955) (repurchase agreement); Agar v. Orda, 264 N.Y. 248, 190 N.E. 479, 99 A.L.R. 269 (1934); Rosenzweig v. Salkind, 5 A.D.2d 58, 169 N. Y.S.2d 213 (1st Dep't 1957). Contra, Porter v. Gibson, 25 Cal.2d 506, 154 P.2d 703 (1945); Duncuft v. Albrecht, 12 Sim. 189, 59 Eng.Rep. 1104 (V.C.1841). Some cases distinguished between a contract for the sale of shares to be issued and one for the sale of shares already issued.

17.   Graney v. United States, 258 F.Supp. 383 (S.D. W.Va.1966), aff'd 377 F.2d 992 (4th Cir. 1967), cert. denied 389 U.S. 1022, 88 S.Ct. 594, 19 L.Ed.2d 668 (1967) (holding period requirement for long-term capital gains treatment found not met); Bigelow v. Bicek, 298 Ill.App. 73, 18 N.E.2d 398 (1938).

18.   Stern v. Mayer, 166 Minn. 346, 207 N.W. 737, 46 A.L.R. 1167 (1926).

19.   See also Note, "Some Problems in Drafting and Enforcing Covenants in Stock Subscription Agreements for Subsequent Registration of the Stock", 13 N.Y.L.F. 368 (1967).

1.   See, e. g., ABA-ALI Model Bus.Corp.Act § 18A. The issuance of share options might be subject to preemptive rights. See sections 172–175 infra. The New York Business Corporation Law comprehensively deals with rights and options to purchase shares. McKinney's N.Y.Bus.Corp.Law, § 505. See Vernava, "Stock Options: Corporate, Regulatory and Related Tax Aspects", 30 U.Pitt.L.Rev. 197 (1968).

2.   See section 248 infra.

3.   Obviously, the corporation must be able to deliver the shares upon exercise of the option. For such purpose it may have sufficient shares reserved as authorized and unissued shares or as treasury shares, or acquire such shares from holders thereof, possibly on the open market. See Philipbar v. National Patent Development Corp., 157 N.Y.L.J. No. 78, 21 (Sup.Ct.1967) (holding that Delaware corporation's inability to reregister its shares for issuance upon exercise of warrants may have justified its refusal to honor warrants).

4.   The option price must conform to the consideration requirements applicable to the shares. See

within a specified time.[5] Two securities are involved: the option and the optioned shares.

Such "rights" [6] are often traded on securities exchanges or over-the-counter. They are frequently issued in rights offerings to shareholders who may let them expire, or sell them (assuming they are transferable as they usually are), or exercise them (possibly buying additional rights from other holders of rights and exercising the latter and former together).[7] Share options issued to corporate management and other personnel have become an increasingly popular form of management [8] and employee [9] incentive compensation. Securities convertible into shares, of course, involve share options.

H. SHAREHOLDERS' LIABILITIES ON "BONUS", "DISCOUNT", AND "WATERED" SHARES

SHAREHOLDERS' LIABILITIES ON "BONUS", "DISCOUNT", AND "WATERED" SHARES

171. Shares issued for full lawful consideration are usually fully-paid and nonassessable. Some statutes permit corporations to issue partly-paid shares, subject to calls or assessments until full lawful consideration has been paid. Shares issued as fully-paid and nonas-

sections 167, 168 supra. Elward v. Peabody Coal Corp., 9 Ill.App.2d 234, 132 N.E.2d 549 (1956). See also, G. Harold, Corporation Finance 108–112 (3d rev. ed. 1956). But see Gamble v. Penn Valley Crude Oil Corp., 34 Del.Ch. 359, 104 A.2d 257 (Ch. 1954) (perpetual option upheld, but question of denying specific performance on basis of unconscionableness left open). Bradford v. Crown-Bremson Industries, Inc., 255 F.Supp. 1009 (M.D.Tenn.1964) (holding that share warrant, which provided that upon its exercise and payment of price, corporation would issue and deliver share certificates, required corporation to issue and deliver shares only when warrant holder exercised option and paid option price and corporation, which was merely advised of warrant holder's desire to exercise warrants, did not breach contract by failing to register shares for issuance to warrant holder); Amdur v. Meyer, 15 A.D.2d 425, 224 N.Y.S.2d 440 (1st Dep't 1962), appeal dismissed 14 N.Y.2d 541, 248 N.Y.S.2d 639, 198 N.E.2d 30 (1964) (upholding board of directors reduction of employees' option price based on decrease in value of shares resulting from share dividends).

5. Philip v. Proydra, Inc., 28 A.D.2d 1100, 284 N.Y.S. 2d 309 (1st Dep't 1967). See Gamble v. Penn Valley Crude Oil Corp., 34 Del.Ch. 359, 104 A.2d 257 (Ch.1954); Kingston v. Home Life Ins. Co. of America, 11 Del.Ch. 258, 101 A. 898 (Ch.1917), aff'd per curiam 11 Del.Ch. 428, 104 A. 25 (Sup.Ct.1918).

6. A "New York right"—the term originated by the New York Stock Exchange—is the right enjoyed by one share; thus an option to acquire one share for each ten shares held would involve ten rights. The rarer term, "Philadelphia right", is the option to subscribe to one full share. Prior to the record date for determining the shareholders entitled to rights, the shares sell "rights-on" or "cum rights"; thereafter "ex-rights". H. Guthmann & H. Dougall,

Corporate Financial Policy 406–408 (4th ed. 1962). Rights have a market value whenever the subscription price is less than the market value of the shares. The warrant holder has several alternatives concerning his rights during the subscription period: (a) subscribe for the full amount of shares to which he is entitled, (b) subscribe for part of the shares and order the balance of his rights sold, (c) subscribe for more shares than he is entitled to, through the purchase of additional rights, (d) order all his rights sold, (e) transfer some or all of his rights to others, and (f) do nothing and let the rights expire.
Share rights issued by a corporation to its common shareholders to acquire additional shares are usually nontaxable. Int.Rev.Code of 1954, 26 U.S.C.A. § 304. The basis of the old shares is allocated among the old and new shares. Id. § 307. If the shareholder sells his rights, the holding period of the underlying shares may be tacked on in determining the holding period of the rights. Id. § 1223 (5). Antin, "Taxation of Stock Rights", 51 Calif. 146 (1963); Whiteside, "Income Tax Consequences of Distributions of Stock Rights to Shareholders", 66 Yale L.J. 1016 (1957). Distributions of share rights on preferred shareholders were made taxable in 1969.

7. The corporation in such a case might appoint and pay a broker, as agent of the rights holders, to handle orders of holders of fractional warrant or scrip to buy and sell, at nominal or no brokerage cost, to round out individual holdings into full shares. Such an arrangement is not a transaction involving an issuer (§ 4(1)) and is within the brokerage-transaction exemption (§ 4(2)) of the Federal Securities Act of 1933. 1 L. Loss, Securities Regulation 651–652 (2d ed. 1961). See N.Y.S.E. Company Manual §§ A7, A11; Note, "Stock Options under California Corporate Securities Law", 14 Hastings L.J. 162 (1962).

8. See section 248 infra.

9. See section 249 infra.

sessable for less than full lawful consideration are often called "bonus", "discount", or "watered" shares, and may be treated as void, voidable, assessable, or subject to creditor claims.

Liability on shares for which the full lawful consideration had not been received, depended, at common law, upon various theories: (a) Trust fund theory; (b) Holding out, Misrepresentation, or Fraud theory; (c) Implied promise theory; (d) Contract theory. Modern statutes variously codify to some extent one of the common-law theories or substitute statutory liability for any common-law theory, or add statutory liability to common-law liability.

Any liability on shares for which the full lawful consideration has not been paid inheres in the person to whom the shares are issued by the corporation. The liability of a transferee of such shares usually depends upon his belief that the shares were not fully-paid. Modern statutes often immunize from liability bona fide transferees, personal representatives, fiduciaries, pledgees, etc.

In General

Shares which are issued for full lawful consideration [1] are usually fully-paid and nonassessable. [2]

Shares which are issued for no consideration or for consideration which does not satisfy applicable qualitative and quantitative requirements are sometimes called "void" by state constitutional or statutory provisions. [3]

Some statutes permit corporations to issue shares as partly-paid, subject to calls or assessments thereon until the full lawful consideration has been paid. [4] If partly-paid

shares are duly authorized and issued, the holder is not liable to the corporation except for the unpaid consideration. [5]

The Model Business Corporation Act does not allow a share certificate to be issued for partly-paid shares. [6]

The issue of partly-paid shares when duly authorized (like an installment share subscription [7]) is to be distinguished from the issue of shares as fully-paid and nonassessable for less than the full lawful consideration. [8]

Shares which are issued as fully-paid and nonassessable for less than the full lawful consideration might be treated as void, voidable, assessable, or subject to creditor claims. In common parlance, such shares are said to be "bonus", "discount", or "watered" shares. [9]

---

§§ 504(h), 505(e), (f). See McPhail v. L. S. Starrett Co., 257 F.2d 388 (1st Cir. 1958).

5. Failure to pay installments when due can result in forfeiture of the shares and the previous payments. Forfeited shares might be reissued or reoffered for subscription. When certificates for shares for which the full consideration has not been paid may be issued, they are required to carry a legend indicating that fact.

6. ABA–ALI Model Bus.Corp.Act § 21. While the Model Act prohibits the issue of a share certificate for any share until such share is fully paid, installment subscriptions are expressly authorized. When shares are forfeited for nonpayment of any installment and sold by the corporation, the Model Act provides that the excess of proceeds realized over the amount due and unpaid on such shares shall be paid to the delinquent subscriber or to his legal representative. ABA–ALI Model Bus.Corp.Act § 16. See Annot., 83 A.L.R. 892 (1933).

7. See section 169 supra.

8. Liability under installment share subscriptions is contractual; liability for "bonus", "discount", or "watered" shares is usually of a tort nature. Comment, "Stockholders' Liability Upon Unpaid and Watered Stock Subscriptions", 24 Tenn.L.Rev. 584 (1956). See discussion in Spencer v. Anderson, 193 Cal. 1, 5, 222 P. 355, 356, 35 A.L.R. 822, 826 (1924).

9. The term "watered" shares is said to be derived from the practice of salting and then watering livestock before selling the livestock by weight. The term "watered" shares is often used as including "bonus" and "discount" shares. Occasionally, attempts are made to differentiate "bonus", "discount", and "watered" shares. Shares are called "bonus" shares when no lawful consideration is re-

---

1. See sections 167, 168 supra.

2. See, e. g., ABA–ALI Model Bus.Corp.Act § 18 ("fully-paid and nonassessable"); Del.Gen.Corp. Law, § 152 (1967) ("full paid stock and not liable to any further call"); McKinney's N.Y.Bus.Corp.Law, § 504(i) ("fully-paid and nonassessable").

3. See, e. g., Ark.Const. art. XII, § 8; Okl.Const. art. IX, § 39; Tex.Const. art. XII, § 6; Note, "'Watered Stock'—Shareholder's Liability to Creditors in Arizona", 8 Ariz.L.Rev. 327 (1967). See notes 10, 11 infra.

4. See, e. g., Del.Gen.Corp.Law, § 156 (1967). New York provides that certificates for shares may not be issued until the full amount of the consideration therefor has been paid, except in the case of employee option plans. McKinney's N.Y.Bus.Corp.Law,

If "bonus", "discount", or "watered" shares are void, in the strict sense, the holder thereof may enjoy no rights and be subject to no liabilities with respect thereto.[10] If voidable, such rights and liabilities might exist until his shareholder status is avoided by the corporation or others.[11]

Theories of Liability

With respect to liability on shares for which the full lawful consideration has not been received,[12] there are various theories which result in different conclusions in different cases. Four theories developed as a matter of decisional law: (a) Trust fund theory; (b) Holding out theory; (c) Implied promise theory; and (d) Contract theory. Many jurisdictions now have statutory provisions codifying to a greater or lesser extent one of the common-law theories,[13] or substituting statutory liability for any common-law theory,[14] or adding statutory liability to common-law liability.[15]

Trust Fund Theory

Under the Trust Fund Theory, first announced by a dictum of Story, J., while riding circuit in Maine in 1824,[16] the corporate assets, including unpaid consideration for shares, constitute a *res* or trust fund for the benefit of creditors. In such unpaid consideration, creditors have an equitable interest which they can pursue, in the event of corporate insolvency, against the subscriber. As an abstract proposition, the corporation should have the legal interest and recover on the same theory; if the corporation can recover, its trustee-in-bankruptcy or receiver, a shareholder in a derivative action, or a creditor by means of a creditor's bill, should be able also to recover in accordance with established procedures.[17]   The Trust Fund

ceived for them by the corporation; "discount" shares when the consideration received—usually money—is admittedly less than the full lawful consideration; and "watered" shares when the consideration received—usually property or services—purports to be but, usually because of overvaluation, is less than the full lawful consideration. Comment, "Discount, Bonus and Watered Stock in Colorado", 33 Rocky Mt.L.Rev. 197 (1961); Comment, "Shareholder Liability for Watered, Discount, or Bonus Stock Issued by a Kansas Corporation", 8 Kan.L. Rev. 644 (1960).

10.   Roy v. Recker, 225 F.Supp. 743 (E.D.Ark.1963) (holding following Arkansas case law, that note ostensibly used to purchase shares was, like shares themselves under Arkansas Constitution, void, except in hands of holder in due course). Stone v. Hudgens, 129 F.Supp. 273 (W.D.Okl.1955) (bankrupt corporation held not entitled to subscription price of shares issued without consideration in violation of Oklahoma constitution); Stone v. Young, 210 App.Div. 303, 206 N.Y.S. 95 (4th Dep't 1924) (unpaid installments on subscription for par value preferred shares at par value, with no par common shares included as bonus, held unenforceable by receiver of insolvent corporation because of illegality). See also General Beverages, Inc. v. Rogers, 216 F.2d 413 (10th Cir. 1954); Evans v. Ideal Brick & Brikcrete Mfg. Co., 287 P.2d 454 (Okl.1955). Cf. Oklahoma Gas & Electric Co. v. Hathaway, 192 Okl. 626, 138 P.2d 832 (1943) (issue of shares for less than par in violation of Oklahoma constitution held validated upon subsequent payment of balance). See also Crawford v. Erbsloh, 137 Misc. 790, 244 N.Y.S. 502 (Sup.Ct.1930).

11.   Murray v. Murray Laboratories, 223 Ark. 907, 270 S.W.2d 927 (1954); John W. Cooney Co. v. Arlington Hotel Co. (du Pont v. Ball), 11 Del.Ch. 430, 106 A. 39, 7 A.L.R. 955 (Sup.Ct.1918); Jeffery v. Selwyn, 220 N.Y. 77, 115 N.E. 275, 6 A.L.R. 1111 (1917); Bell v. Aubel, 151 Pa.Super. 569, 30 A.2d 617 (1943). Cf. Triplex Shoe Co. v. Rice & Hutchins, Inc., 17 Del.Ch. 356, 152 A. 342, 72 A.L.R. 934 (Sup.Ct.1930). In McCarty v. Langdeau, 337 S.W.2d 407 (Tex.Civ.App.1960), an installment note for shares, regardless of whether the shares were to be issued immediately or periodically as the note was paid, was held enforceable by the receiver of the corporation.

12.   See generally D. Dodd, Stock Watering (1930); Cataldo, "Limited Liability and Payment for Shares", 19 U.Pitt.L.Rev. 727 (1958).

13.   E. g., Cal.Gen.Corp.Law, § 1306 (1947), construed in Bing Crosby Minute Maid Corp. v. Eaton, 46 Cal.2d 484, 297 P.2d 5 (1956).

14.   See note 25 infra.

15.   John W. Cooney Co. v. Arlington Hotel Co. (du Pont v. Ball), 11 Del.Ch. 430, 106 A. 39, 7 A.L.R. 955 (Sup.Ct.1918).

16.   Wood v. Dummer, 30 F.Cas. 435, No. 17,944 (C.C. D.Me.1824); Scovill v. Thayer, 105 U.S. 143, 26 L. Ed. 968 (1882).

17.   Scovill v. Thayer, 105 U.S. 143, 26 L.Ed. 968 (1882); Livingston v. Adams, 226 Mo.App. 824, 43 S.W.2d 836 (1931); Williams v. Chamberlain, 123 Ky. 150, 94 S.W. 29 (1906). See Annot., 71 A.L.R. 103 (1931), 90 A.L.R. 1350 (1934). See note 21 infra.

Theory has been substantially repudiated,[18] but vestiges of it linger on. Some courts purport to apply it, but confuse it with the Holding Out Theory.

Holding Out Theory

Under the Holding Out Theory, sometimes called the Misrepresentation Theory or Fraud Theory, creditors who rely upon the representation of the amount of stated capital paid in or due and are deceived thereby to their detriment may sue the subscriber for the unpaid consideration.[19] Only subsequent creditors who became such without knowledge of the fact that the shares were not fully-paid for or who relied on the holding out may recover.[20] Neither the corporation, its receiver, shareholder in a derivative action, nor creditor asserting a corporate cause of action may succeed under this theory; *quaere*, whether the trustee-in-bankruptcy may.[21]

Implied Promise Theory

Under the Implied Promise Theory, the corporation's agreement to issue full paid and nonassessable shares for inadequate con-

sideration is *ultra vires*, and the acceptance of such shares by the subscriber raises an implied promise in equity to pay for them in full.[22] In the event of insolvency, if not otherwise, the corporation or those able to assert such a corporate claim may recover from the subscriber.[23]

Contract Theory

To be distinguished from the theories leading to liability is the Contract Theory, which recognizes the validity of the contract between the corporation and subscriber whereby the corporation agrees to issue the shares as fully-paid and nonassessable for inadequate consideration.[24] Absent supplementary statutory liability or liability for actual deception, the subscriber is not liable beyond the terms of the subscription contract. At common law, this theory prevailed in New York.[25]

Statutory Liability

Most jurisdictions today have statutes on the subject of liability on shares for which the full lawful consideration has not been paid.[26]

18. R. Stevens, Handbook on the Law of Private Corporations § 190 (2d ed. 1949); Johnson, "Is The Trust Fund Theory of Capital Stock Dead?", 34 Accounting Rev. 607 (1959); Hunt, "Trust Fund Theory, and Some Substitute for It", 12 Yale L.J. 63 (1902).

19. G. Loewus & Co. v. Highland Queen Packing Co., 125 N.J.Eq. 534, 6 A.2d 545 (1939); Rhode v. Dock-Hop Co., 184 Cal. 367, 194 P. 11, 12 A.L.R. 437 (1920); Courtney v. Georger, 228 F. 859 (2d Cir. 1915), cert. denied 241 U.S. 660, 36 S.Ct. 448, 60 L. Ed. 1226 (1916); Hospes v. Northwestern Mfg. & Car Co., 48 Minn. 174, 50 N.W. 1117 (1892). See Ballantine, "Stockholders' Liability in Minnesota", 7 Minn.L.Rev. 79 (1922); Note, " 'Watered Stock'— Shareholder's Liability to Creditors in Arizona", 8 Ariz.L.Rev. 327 (1967).

20. Bing Crosby Minute Maid Corp. v. Eaton, 46 Cal.2d 484, 297 P.2d 5 (1956); Annot., 7 A.L.R. 972 (1920), 69 A.L.R. 881 (1930).

21. Courtney v. Georger, 228 F. 859 (2d Cir. 1915), cert. denied 241 U.S. 660, 36 S.Ct. 448, 60 L.Ed. 1226 (1916) (denying recovery by trustee-in-bankruptcy). But see Federal Bankruptcy Act § 70(c), 11 U.S.C.A. § 110 ("strong-arm" provision), discussed in J. Moore, 4A Collier on Bankruptcy ¶ 70.29, n. 41 (14th ed. 1967).

22. John W. Cooney Co. v. Arlington Hotel Co. (du Pont v. Ball, 11 Del.Ch. 430, 106 A. 39, 7 A.L.R. 955 (Sup.Ct.1918). The defendants argued that the liabilities of the common shareholders to pay the debts of the corporation were not enforceable until the express subscriptions for the preferred shares had been collected, since such claims were legal assets of the corporation. The court rejected this contention, on the ground that there was a contractual relation in both cases, the promise being express in the case of the preferred share subscriptions and implied in the case of the common share subscriptions.

23. Ibid.

24. Southworth v. Morgan, 205 N.Y. 293, 98 N.E. 490 (1912); Christensen v. Eno, 106 N.Y. 97, 12 N.E. 648 (1887).

25. Jeffery v. Selwyn, 220 N.Y. 77, 115 N.E. 275, 6 A.L.R. 1111 (1917). For discussion of New York statutory provisions, see note 26 infra.

26. See, e. g., ABA–ALI Model Bus.Corp.Act § 23; Del.Gen.Corp.Law, § 162 (1967); McKinney's N.Y. Bus.Corp.Law, § 628. See, in addition, N.C.Bus. Corp.Act § 55–53(b) (1957), which provides: "Every original holder of watered shares ['watered shares'

Some of these statutory enactments more or less codify the above-described common-law theories. Whether or not statutory liability was intended to replace or merely to supplement the preexisting common-law theory might present problems of construction.[27]

Other problems of statutory construction might involve questions as to whether the subscribers' liability is joint or joint and

being very broadly defined in § 55–53(a)] shall be subject to:

"(1) Liability to the corporation for the excess of the par value of said shares over the price paid for their issuance or, as the case may be, for the amount of over-valuation of the consideration entered upon its books, unless the valuation so entered is conclusive under the provisions of G.S. 55–46(f), over and above the maximum valuation that could in good faith have been fixed therefor; but this liability exists

 "a. Only if there is reasonable ground to believe that creditors or shareholders may have relied on such excess or over-valuation and

 "b. Only to the extent necessary to pay the claims of such creditors or adjust the equities of such shareholders, or

"(2) Cancellation, in an action by the corporation, of such a number of shares as shall cure the dilution or breach of fiduciary duty which made the said shares watered shares; and if cancellation is impossible on the ground that such holder no longer retains the said number of shares, he shall be liable for such an amount in money as will fairly redress the injury to other shareholders occasioned by the said dilution or breach of fiduciary duty."

27. See notes 2, 3, 4 supra. See Minn.Bus.Corp.Act § 301.15(5) (1961) ("creditors shall not be presumed to have extended credit to the corporation relying upon the compliance by the corporation with the provisions of this section relating to allotment of shares and the consideration to be receiver therefor"); id. § 301.16 ("Directors or shareholders who, wilfully without reasonable investigation, either make an allotment of shares for a cash consideration which is unfair to the then shareholders or so over-value property or services received or to be received by the corporation as consideration for shares allotted, shall be jointly and severally liable to the corporation for the benefit of the then shareholders who did not assent to and are damaged by such action, to the extent of their damages . . ."). Colman & Finn, "Comparison of Business Corporation Law of Minnesota and Delaware", 22 Minn.L.Rev. 661, 667–668 (1938); Solether & Jennings, "The Minnesota Business Corporation Act", 12 Wis.L.Rev. 419, 445–446 (1937).

several;[28] whether the subscribers' liability is primary or secondary;[29] whether the corporation and those suing in its stead or creditors may enforce the statutory liability;[30] whether tort creditors as well as contract creditors may recover;[31] whether only subsequent creditors who became such without knowledge of the inadequacy of the consid-

28. See, e. g., Bottlers Seal Co. v. Rainey, 243 N.Y. 333, 153 N.E. 437 (1926) (liability held joint).

29. Return unsatisfied of execution of a judgment against the corporation is often expressly required as prerequisite to action against shareholders. See Del.Gen.Corp.Law, § 162 (1967). But see John W. Cooney Co. v. Arlington Hotel Co. (du Pont v. Ball), 11 Del.Ch. 430, 106 A. 39, 7 A.L.R. 955 (Sup.Ct.1918) (discussing two remedies: appointment of receiver under insolvency act (without necessity of prior judgment against corporation), and creditors' bill (requiring showing of inability to collect claim by legal process as evidenced by judgment and unsatisfied execution against corporation)). See also former McKinney's N.Y.Stock Corp.Law § 73. But see Bottlers Seal Co. v. Rainey, 243 N.Y. 333, 153 N.E. 437 (1926) (such requirement excused where corporation in bankruptcy and actions against bankrupt restrained by bankruptcy court).

30. See, e. g., ABA–ALI Model Bus.Corp.Act § 23 ("obligation to pay to the corporation the full consideration"); McKinney's N.Y.Bus.Corp.Law § 628(a), providing: "A holder of or subscriber for shares of a corporation shall be under no obligation to the corporation for payment for such shares other than the obligation to pay the unpaid portion of his subscription which in no event shall be less than the amount of the consideration for which such shares could be issued lawfully." Such liability can be enforced by the corporation, receiver, trustee-in-bankruptcy, or judgment creditor, for the benefit of shareholders as well as creditors. See Scully v. Automobile Finance Co., 12 Del.Ch. 174, 109 A. 49 (Ch.1920). Under former McKinney's N.Y.Stock Corp.Law, § 70: "Every holder of shares . . . not fully paid" was "personally liable to the creditors of the corporation, to an amount equal to the amount unpaid on the shares held by him for debts of the corporation contracted while such shares were held by him". See Brown v. Watson, 285 App.Div. 587, 139 N.Y.S.2d 628 (1st Dep't 1955) (trustee-in-bankruptcy held to have no cause of action against recipients of watered shares but to have cause of action against directors who authorized their issuance). But see note 21 supra.

31. Clinton Mining & Mineral Co. v. Beacom, 266 F. 621, 14 A.L.R. 263 (3d Cir. 1920), cert. denied 254 U.S. 637, 41 S.Ct. 9, 65 L.Ed. 450 (1920) ("debt" held not to include liability in tort even when reduced to judgment). Former McKinney's N.Y.Stock Corp. Law § 70 referred to the liability of a shareholder "for debts of the corporation *contracted* while such shares were held by him".

eration for the shares, or other creditors, may recover;[32] the procedural requirements for enforcing such liability.[33]

Persons Liable as Shareholders

Any liability on shares for which the full lawful consideration has not been paid inheres in the person to whom the shares are issued by the corporation.

The transferee of not fully paid shares who believed in good faith that the full consideration had been paid will not be liable for any unpaid balance.[34]

Some statutes expressly so provide.[35] Liability cannot be evaded by a transfer.[36]

Statutes also often provide that no executor, administrator, conservator, guardian, trustee, assignee for benefit of creditors, or receiver shall be personally liable, but that the estate or funds in his hands shall be, and that no pledgee or other holder of shares as collateral security shall be personally liable.[37]

I. PROTECTION OF SHAREHOLDERS' PROPORTIONATE INTERESTS

SHAREHOLDERS' PROPORTIONATE INTERESTS—IN GENERAL

172. Shareholders have threefold proportionate interests with respect to dividends, net assets, and control, which can be adversely affected by the non-proportionate issue of additional shares or by the non-proportionate reacquisition by the corporation of outstanding shares. With respect to the issue and reacquisition of shares, management is subject to fiduciary duties. Also protecting the shareholders' proportionate interests in the event of the issue of additional shares is the doctrine of preemptive rights.

As previously indicated, a shareholder has proportionate interests with respect to earnings, net assets, and control.[1] In most single class situations, such threefold interests will be proportionate to the shareholder's contribution, by way of cash, property, or services, to the corporation.[2]

Classification of shares into two or more classes, involving possible dividend or liquidation preferences or both and different vot-

32. See, e. g., John W. Cooney Co. v. Arlington Hotel Co. (du Pont v. Ball), 11 Del.Ch. 430, 106 A. 39, 7 A.L.R. 955 (Sup.Ct.1918) (creditors' knowledge held immaterial under Delaware statute); Bing Crosby Minute Maid Corp. v. Eaton, 46 Cal.2d 484, 297 P.2d 5 (1956) (California statute construed as codifying Holding Out Theory and requiring proof of reliance).

33. John W. Cooney Co. v. Arlington Hotel Co. (du Pont v. Ball), 11 Del.Ch. 430, 106 A. 39, 7 A.L.R. 955 (Sup.Ct.1918).

34. Under neither tort nor contract theories. Rhode v. Dock-Hop Co., 184 Cal. 367, 194 P. 11, 12 A.L.R. 437 (1920) (Holding Out Theory jurisdiction); Van Slochem v. Villard, 154 App.Div. 161, 163, 138 N.Y. S. 852, 853 (1st Dep't 1912), aff'd on other grounds 207 N.Y. 587, 101 N.E. 467 (1913). Gray Constr. Co. v. Fantle, 62 S.D. 345, 253 N.W. 464 (1934) (where shares acquired through corporation secretary were original issue and not transferred shares, as thought by purchasers, but were treated as latter by court). Transferees with notice are liable. Smith v. Donges, 73 F.2d 620 (3d Cir. 1934); Bonbright, "Shareholders' Defenses Against Liability to Creditors on Watered Stock", 25 Colum.L.Rev. 408, 418 (1925).

35. See, e. g., ABA–ALI Model Bus.Corp.Act § 23; Cal.Gen.Corp.Law, § 1303 (1947); Del.Gen.Corp. Law, § 162(c) (1967); McKinney's N.Y.Bus.Corp. Law, § 628. See also Diamond State Brewery, Inc. v. de la Rigaudiere, 25 Del.Ch. 257, 17 A.2d .313 (Ch.1941) (attempt by corporation to cancel shares issued for overvalued property and held by transferees alleging good faith purchase without notice;

burden of proof on such allegation held to be on transferees).

36. McKinney's N.Y.Bus.Corp.Law, § 628(b); id. § 629 (transfer of shares or subscription, if corporation's liabilities exceed its assets, made with intent to defraud creditors, not to relieve shareholder or subscriber of any liability).

37. E. g., ABA–ALI Model Bus.Corp.Act § 23.

1. See sections 157, 160 supra.

2. An agreement between subscribers whereby corporation issued 51 percent of its no par value shares to defendant for $500 and 49 percent to another subscriber for $1,700 was held not to be invalid so far as creditors were concerned. Milberg v. Baum, 25 N.Y.S.2d 451 (App.T. 1st Dep't 1941) (action by corporation's trustee-in-bankruptcy).

ing rights, obviously is a complicating factor.[3]

The shareholder's proportionate interests can be adversely affected by (a) the non-proportionate issue of additional shares, or (b) the non-proportionate reacquisition by the corporation of outstanding shares.

With respect to the issue and reacquisition of shares, management is subject to fiduciary duties.[4] Further possible protection of the shareholders' proportionate interests in the event of the issue of additional shares is provided by the doctrine of preemptive rights.[5]

FIDUCIARY DUTIES OF MANAGEMENT WITH RESPECT TO ISSUE AND RE-ACQUISITION OF SHARES

173. In issuing additional shares and in reacquiring outstanding shares, management is subject to fiduciary duties, whether or not preemptive rights exist. Use of corporate funds or credit to prevent a take over to reenforce management, or to buy out insurgents, in order to perpetuate management in control, can be wrongful unless justified by business judgment. Even if additional shares are offered to existing shareholders, the issue can be wrongful if new financing is unnecessary and the issue constitutes a fraudulent dilution of the shareholders' proportionate interests.

In issuing additional shares and in reacquiring outstanding shares, corporate management is, as in the case of any other corporate activity, under a fiduciary duty of taking corporate action according to the best interests of the corporation and not for personal advantage.[1] If the issuance[2] or

[§ 172]

3. See section 160 supra.

4. See section 173 infra.

5. See sections 174, 175 infra.

[§ 173]

1. See sections 236, 240 infra. For fraudulent dilution of a shareholder's proportionate interests, a derivative action might be the proper procedure, whereas an action for violation of a shareholder's preemptive rights might be brought by him on his share contract. See section 360 infra. See also Note, "Freezing Out Minority Shareholders", 74 Harv.L.Rev. 1630 (1961).

2. Condec Corp. v. Lunkenheimer Co., —— Del.Ch. ——, 230 A.2d 769 (Ch.1967); Wilson v. Jennings, 344

reacquisition[3] is otherwise, say, in favor of

Mass. 608, 184 N.E.2d 642 (1962); Gaines v. Long Mfg. Co., 234 N.C. 340, 67 S.E.2d 350, 38 A.L.R.2d 1359 (1951); Ross Transport, Inc. v. Crothers, 185 Md. 573, 45 A.2d 267 (1946); Schwab v. Schwab-Wilson Machine Corp., 13 Cal.App.2d 1, 55 P.2d 1268 (1936); Hammer v. Werner, 239 App.Div. 38, 265 N.Y.S. 172 (2d Dep't 1933) (breach of fiduciary duty found); Robinson v. Malheur Pub. Co., 272 F. Supp. 57 (D.Or.1967); Burnett v. Word, Inc., 412 S. W.2d 792 (Tex.Civ.App.1967) (upholding sale of treasury shares to trusted employee and his voting such shares in order to effect merger); Steven v. Hale-Haas Corp., 249 Wis. 205, 23 N.W.2d 620 (1946); Dunlay v. Avenue M Garage & Repair Co., 253 N.Y. 274, 170 N.E. 917 (1930); Standard International Corp. v. McDonald Printing Co., 159 N.E.2d 822 (Ohio C.P.1959); Berg v. United Board & Carton Corp., 106 N.Y.S.2d 658 (Sup.Ct.1951) (no breach of fiduciary duty found). For discussion of the nature of the duty of management with respect to the issue of shares subject to preemptive rights from the aspects of issuance price, notice to shareholders, exercise period, and disclosure of relevant facts, see Comment, "The Fiduciary Duty of Directors in the Issuance of Stock Subject to Preemptive Rights", 53 Mich.L.Rev. 595 (1955). For statutory prohibition on issue of shares for consideration unfair to existing shareholders, see Minn.Bus.Corp.Act § 301.-16 (1961). Absent fraud, bad faith, improper motive, or arbitrariness, shares may be issued at less than market value, when in the sound business judgment of the board of directors authorized to fix the consideration for shares. Bodell v. General Gas & Electric Corp., 15 Del.Ch. 420, 140 A. 264 (Sup. Ct.1927); Atlantic Refining Co. v. Hodgman, 13 F. 2d 781 (3d Cir. 1926), cert. denied 273 U.S. 731, 47 S.Ct. 240, 71 L.Ed. 863 (1926). See Note, "Judicial Control Over the Fairness of the Issue Price of New Stock", 71 Harv.L.Rev. 1133 (1958). Share dividends, even of shares of a class only to holders of shares of such class, and similarly share splits, can effect the shareholders' proportionate interests. A fortiori, shares dividends of shares of one class to holders of shares of a different class can. See Rowell, "Rights of Preferred Shareholders in Excess of Preference", 19 Minn.L.Rev. 406, 418 (1935). In Aiple v. Twin City Barge & Towing Co., 274 Minn. 38, 143 N.W.2d 374 (1966), a 30 percent shareholder financially interested in a competitor blocked an amendment of the articles of incorporation to increase the authorized shares to raise additional capital. The corporation transferred one of its divisions, some 11 percent of its assets, to a newly-formed subsidiary for the latter's shares which were then sold to raise the desired funds. Injunctive relief was granted, on the ground that the scheme, even if beneficial to the corporation, circumvented the statutory voting requirement and diluted the plaintiff's interest in the corporation. Warshaw v. Calhoun, 43 Del.Ch. 148, 221 A.2d 487 (Sup.Ct.1966), aff'g 42 Del.Ch. 437, 213 A.2d 539

3. See note 3 on page 320.

management, it is wrongful and can be enjoined, compensated in damages, or set aside, whether or not preemptive rights exist.

(Ch.1965), held that defendants, who were directors both of a personal holding company and its subsidiary insurance company, exercised reasonable business judgment in having the subsidiary issue new shares to obtain capital and to broaden public ownership and having the holding company sell its subscription rights to an underwriter rather than pass such rights on to its shareholders.

3. Redemption or other reacquisition can involve the total reacquisition of some class or series of shares or only a partial reacquisition of some class or series, and can unduly favor either the holders of the shares which are reacquired or the holders of the shares which remain outstanding. See Buss v. J. O. Martin Co., 241 Cal.App.2d 123, 50 Cal.Rptr. 206 (1966) (disallowing redemption to prevent involuntary dissolution); Vann v. Industrial Processes Co., 247 F.Supp. 14 (D.D.C.1965) (holding improper corporation's purchase of shares of brother of controlling shareholder absent showing of corporate purpose); Maggiore v. Bradford, 310 F.2d 519 (6th Cir. 1962), cert. denied 372 U.S. 934, 83 S.Ct. 881, 9 L. Ed.2d 766 (1963); Taylor v. Axton-Fisher Tobacco Co., 295 Ky. 226, 173 S.W.2d 377, 148 A.L.R. 834 (1943) (enjoining attempt by board of directors to rescind resolution redeeming Class A shares in action by Class B shareholders); Zahn v. Transamerica Corp., 162 F.2d 36, 172 A.L.R. 495 (3d Cir. 1947) (allowing holders of redeemed class of shares in direct action to recover from controlling shareholder whose class of shares remained outstanding and as result received large distribution of assets upon dissolution of corporation), 135 F.Supp. 176 (D.Del. 1955) (measure of damages), modified, 235 F.2d 369 (3d Cir. 1956); for 15-year history of litigation, see Comment, 54 Mich.L.Rev. 971 (1956); Allen v. Biltmore Tissue Corp., 2 N.Y.2d 534, 161 N.Y.S.2d 418, 141 N.E.2d 812, 61 A.L.R.2d 1309 (1957) (upholding corporation's option to reacquire shares at price originally paid to corporation for shares); Lewis v. H. P. Hood & Sons, 331 Mass. 670, 121 N.E.2d 850, 48 A.L.R.2d 383 (1954) (allowing redemption of common shares of former employee); Liebschutz v. Schaffer Stores Co., 276 App.Div. 1, 93 N.Y.S.2d 125 (4th Dep't 1949), reargument and appeal denied 276 App.Div. 944, 94 N.Y.S.2d 840 (4th Dep't 1950) (3-2) (upholding declaratory judgment action brought individually by minority shareholder whose preferred shares were called for redemption after he objected to proposed reorganization plan); Security Nat'l Bank v. Crystal Ice & Fuel Co., 145 Kan. 899, 67 P. 2d 527 (1937) (permitting corporate purchase of its own shares for retirement on non-pro rata basis). Contra, Currier v. Lebanon Slate Co., 56 N.H. 262 (1875). Redemption of shares to prevent inspection of the corporate books (see section 199 infra) has been held invalid. State ex rel. Waldman v. Miller-Wohl Co., 42 Del. 73, 28 A.2d 148 (Super.Ct. 1942); People ex rel. Colby v. Imbrie & Co., 126 Misc. 457, 214 N.Y.S. 53 (Sup.Ct.1926), aff'd on opinion below 216 App.Div. 713, 214 N.Y.S. 819 (1st Dep't 1926). Pro rata redemption or purchase, or

Use of corporate funds or credit to prevent the take over of a corporation by raiders, to reenforce management, or to buy out insurgents, in order to perpetuate management in control, is wrongful, unless under the business judgment rule, there are facts to justify such use of corporate funds.[4]

Even if additional shares are first offered to existing shareholders, those who are not estopped by acceptance might later claim that the new financing was unnecessary and a fraudulent dilution of their interest, especially where the price for the shares was inadequate.[5]

purchase in the open market, is more likely to be fair, and to avoid such abuses as entrenching management in control with corporate funds, bailing-out insiders from an unprofitable enterprise, or diluting the interest of remaining shareholders by payment of excessive prices for reacquired shares. New Jersey by statute had required that the purchase of shares for retirement be either on a pro rata basis or in the open market. Former N.J.Gen.Corp.Law, § 14:11–5 (1937). Delaware permits such purchases also "at private sale". Del.Gen.Corp.Law, § 244(a) (3) (1967), construed in Martin v. American Potash & Chemical Corp., 33 Del.Ch. 234, 92 A.2d 295, 35 A.L.R.2d 1140 (Sup.Ct.1952) (upholding private sale of block of shares, after merger plan collapsed, to eliminate managerial representatives of competitor and prevent dumping of shares on market); Dodd, "Purchase and Redemption By a Corporation of Its Own Shares", 89 U.Pa.L.Rev. 697 (1941). The New York Stock Exchange requires that partial redemption be pro rata or by lot. N.Y.S.E. Company Manual § A10.

4. Cheff v. Mathes, 41 Del.Ch. 494, 199 A.2d 548 (Sup.Ct.1964); SEC Securities Act Release No. 7434 (Oct. 1, 1964) (delisting of corporation's shares by New York Stock Exchange after three more years of losses); Kors v. Carey, 39 Del.Ch. 47, 158 A.2d 136 (Ch.1960). Cf. Bennett v. Propp, 41 Del.Ch. 14, 187 A.2d 405 (Sup.Ct.1962); Hendricks v. Mill Eng'r & Supply Co., 68 Wash.2d 490, 413 P.2d 811 (1966); Borden v. Guthrie, 23 A.D.2d 313, 260 N.Y.S.2d 769 (1st Dep't 1965), aff'd 17 N.Y.2d 571, 268 N.Y.S.2d 330, 215 N.E.2d 511 (1966); Brudney, "Fiduciary Ideology in Transactions Affecting Corporate Control", 65 Mich.L.Rev. 259, 263 (1966); Israels, "Corporate Purchase of Its Own Shares—Are There New Overtones?", 50 Cornell L.Q. 620 (1965); Israels, "Are Corporate Powers Still Held in Trust?", 64 Colum.L.Rev. 1446 (1964); Comment, "Buying Out Insurgent Shareholders with Corporate Funds", 70 Yale L.J. 308 (1960).

5. Relief was granted in Katzowitz v. Sidler, 24 N. Y.2d 512, 301 N.Y.S.2d 470, 249 N.E.2d 359 (1969) (6–1), rev'g 29 A.D.2d 955, 289 N.Y.S.2d 324 (2d Dep't 1968) (3-2); Browning v. C & C Plywood Corp., 248

Some preemptive rights statutes expressly preserve the fiduciary duties of management with respect to the issue of shares.[6]

PREEMPTIVE RIGHTS—JUDICIAL DEVELOPMENT

174. To protect the shareholder's proportionate interests in the event of the issue of additional shares, the doctrine of preemptive rights developed. The shareholder's preemptive right is his right to preempt or to purchase before others a new issue of shares in proportion to his present interests in the corporation. Usually not subject to preemptive rights are treasury shares, shares being issued for a non-cash consideration or in connection with a merger or consolidation, and shares originally authorized, at least when intended for present financing.

To protect the shareholder's proportionate interests in the event of the issue of additional shares, the doctrine of preemptive rights has developed in the United States.[1]

The development was initially by court decisions, as an application of the rule requiring corporate management to deal fairly with all the corporation's shareholders,[2] but statutory enactments on the subject have become increasingly frequent.[3]

The shareholder's preemptive right is his right to preempt (or to purchase before others) a new issue of shares in proportion to his present interests in the corporation. If the shares being issued are treasury shares,[4] or are being issued for a non-cash consideration,[5] or are being issued in connec-

---

Preemptive rights might be denied a shareholder with unclean hands. Heylandt Sales Co. v. Welding Gas Products Co., 180 Tenn. 437, 175 S.W.2d 557 (1943). Ex necessitu exceptions also exist. Todd v. Maryland Casualty Co., 155 F.2d 29 (7th Cir. 1946). See also Haakh, "Rights Offerings to Shareholders", 2 Prac.Law. 74 (Apr.1956). Even apart from preemptive rights, the board of directors of a corporation voluntarily could decide to offer new shares to its existing shareholders.

2. Gray v. Portland Bank, 3 Mass. 364 (1807); Eidman v. Bowman, 58 Ill. 444 (1871); Stokes v. Continental Trust Co., 186 N.Y. 285, 78 N.E. 1090 (1906); Miles v. Safe Deposit & Trust Co., 259 U.S. 247, 42 S.Ct. 483, 66 L.Ed. 923 (1922); Yoakam v. Providence Biltmore Hotel Co., 34 F.2d 533 (1st Cir. 1929); Fuller v. Krogh, 15 Wis.2d 412, 113 N.W.2d 25 (1962).

3. See section 175 infra.

4. See Fuller v. Krogh, 15 Wis.2d 412, 113 N.W.2d 25 (1962) (distinguishing treasury shares—authorized, issued, and not outstanding—from "canceled" shares—shares restored to unissued status); Runswick v. Floor, 116 Utah 91, 208 P.2d 948 (1949); Borg v. International Silver Co., 11 F.2d 147 (2d Cir. 1925). Gillette v. Noyes, 92 App.Div. 313, 86 N.Y.S. 1062 (1st Dep't 1904); Crosby v. Stratton, 17 Colo.App. 212, 68 P. 130 (1902). Cf. Hammer v. Werner, 239 App.Div. 38, 265 N.Y.S. 172 (2d Dep't 1933). See Note, "Shareholders' Rights of Preemption in Treasury Shares", 36 Yale L.J. 1181 (1927).

5. See Meredith v. New Jersey Zinc & Iron Co., 55 N.J.Eq. 211, 37 A. 539 (1897), aff'd 56 N.J.Eq. 454, 41 A. 1116 (1897) (property); cf. Wall v. Utah Copper Co., 70 N.J.Eq. 17, 62 A. 533 (1905). Issue of shares in payment of debt has been held not to be within the exception. Fuller v. Krogh, 15 Wis.2d 412, 113 N.W.2d 25 (1962); Hodge v. Cuba Co., 142 N.J.Eq. 340, 60 A.2d 88 (1948). When shares are to be optioned for services, and preemptive rights exist, the shares are usually excepted from such preemptive rights by appropriate amendment of the articles of incorporation. See note 18 infra. With respect to preemptive rights to shares issuable upon conversion, compare Wall v. Utah Copper Co., 70 N.J.Eq. 17, 62 A.

Or. 574, 434 P.2d 339 (1967); Bennett v. Breuil Petroleum Corp., 34 Del.Ch. 6, 99 A.2d 236 (Ch.1953); Gaines v. Long Mfg. Co., 234 N.C. 340, 67 S.E.2d 350, 38 A.L.R.2d 1359 (1951); Tashman v. Tashman, 13 Misc.2d 982, 174 N.Y.S.2d 482 (Sup.Ct.1958). Relief was refused in Greenbaum v. American Metal Climax, Inc., 27 A.D.2d 225, 278 N.Y.S.2d 123 (1st Dep't 1967); Maguire v. Osborne, 388 Pa. 121, 130 A.2d 157 (1957); Bellows v. Porter, 201 F.2d 429 (8th Cir. 1953); Hyman v. Velsicol Corp., 342 Ill. App. 489, 97 N.E.2d 122 (1951); Steven v. Hale-Haas Corp., 249 Wis. 205, 23 N.W.2d 620 (1946); Scheirich v. Otis-Hidden Co., 204 Ky. 289, 264 S.W. 755 (1924). See also Canada Southern Oils, Ltd. v. Manabi Exploration Co., 33 Del.Ch. 537, 96 A.2d 810 (Ch.1953) (waiver of preemptive rights by majority shareholder held not to permit sale of additional shares for primary purpose of depriving him of voting control); Gord v. Iowana Farms Milk Co., 245 Iowa 1, 60 N.W.2d 820 (1953) (waiver held ineffective).

6. E. g., N.C.Bus.Corp.Act § 55–56 (1957).

[§ 174]
1. 11 W. Fletcher, Private Corporations §§ 5135–5141 (perm. ed. rev. 1958); 2 G. Hornstein, Corporation Law and Practice §§ 623–626 (1959); R. Stevens, Handbook on the Law of Private Corporations § 111 (2d ed. 1949); H. Ballantine, Ballantine on Corporations § 209 (rev. ed. 1946); Drinker, "The Preemptive Right of Shareholders to Subscribe to New Shares", 43 Harv.L.Rev. 586 (1930); Frey, "Shareholders' Pre-emptive Rights", 38 Yale L.J. 563 (1929); Morawetz, "The Preemptive Right of Shareholders", 42 Harv.L.Rev. 186 (1928); Annot., 52 A.L.R. 220 (1928), 138 A.L.R. 526 (1942).

tion with a merger or consolidation,[6] the issue is not subject to preemptive rights. If the issue is of unissued shares originally authorized, preemptive rights in some jurisdictions do not attach, and in other jurisdictions attach or do not attach, depending upon whether such original authorization was for future or for present financing.[7]

The price offered to the shareholders should be fair,[8] and should be no less than any quantitative consideration requirements applicable to the shares involved.[9] A few early cases had required that the offer be at par value, even though the shares had a greater value.[10] Obviously, the price should be no more than any subsequent offer of the shares to others.

An equitable shareholder may be held entitled to preemptive rights.[11] However, a

holder of unexercised options to purchase shares has been denied the preemptive rights which would have attached to the optioned shares.[12]

Where there are two or more classes or series of shares outstanding with differing rights as to earnings, net assets, or voting, and additional shares of any of those classes or series or of a new class or series is being issued, a proportionate offering to existing shareholders presents substantial complications.[13] Apportionment of the new issue to preserve as nearly as possible the relative rights of the existing shareholders is the only alternative, absent advance anticipation of such problems when drafting or amending the articles of incorporation, but satisfactory apportionment is sometimes inherently impossible.[14]

If the corporation offers the new shares proportionately to existing shareholders, any shareholder who does not exercise such preemptive right, because financially unable to do so or otherwise, ordinarily cannot thereafter complain.[15] Otherwise, a minority shareholder unable or unwilling to sub-

---

533 (1905), with Todd v. Maryland Casualty Co., 155 F.2d 29 (7th Cir. 1946). See Hills, "Preemptive Rights as to Convertible Obligations", 19 Calif.L. Rev. 11 (1930); Berle, "Convertible Bonds and Stock Purchase Warrants," 36 Yale L.J. 649 (1927); Annot., 34 A.L.R.2d 852 (1954).

6. Thom v. Baltimore Trust Co., 158 Md. 352, 148 A. 234 (1930) (merger).

7. Dunlay v. Avenue M Garage & Repair Co., 253 N.Y. 274, 170 N.E. 917 (1930), restricting rule of Archer v. Hesse, 164 App.Div. 493, 150 N.Y.S. 296 (1st Dep't 1914); Yasik v. Wachtel, 25 Del.Ch. 247, 17 A.2d 309 (Ch.1941). Cf. Fuller v. Krogh, 15 Wis. 2d 412, 113 N.W.2d 25 (1962); Ross Transport, Inc. v. Crothers, 185 Md. 573, 45 A.2d 267 (1946).

8. See section 173, n. 5 supra.

9. See sections 167, 168 supra.

10. Hammond v. Edison Illuminating Co., 131 Mich. 79, 90 N.W. 1040 (1902); Cunningham's Appeal, 108 Pa. 546 (1885). Contra, McClanahan v. Heidelberg Brewing Co., 303 Ky. 739, 199 S.W.2d 127 (1947); Van Slyke v. Norris, 159 Minn. 63, 198 N.W. 409 (1924); Scheirich v. Otis-Hidden Co., 204 Ky. 289, 264 S.W. 755 (1924); Stokes v. Continental Trust Co., 186 N.Y. 285, 78 N.E. 1090 (1906). When new shares are issued for a fair price, the proportionate financial interests (earnings, net assets), but not voting rights, of existing shareholders, whether they subscribe pro rata or not, are theoretically preserved. See Note, "Judicial Control Over the Fairness of the Issue Price of New Stock", 71 Harv.L. Rev. 1133 (1958).

11. Samia v. Central Oil Co., 339 Mass. 101, 158 N. E.2d 469 (1959); cf. National Oil Co. v. Reeves, 228 Ark. 664, 310 S.W.2d 242 (1958).

12. Van Slyke v. Norris, 159 Minn. 63, 198 N.W. 409 (1924).

13. E. g., if there are two classes of shares outstanding—voting common and voting (nonparticipating) preferred—any additional issue of the voting common shares should be offered to both classes to preserve the proportionate voting rights, but only to the common shareholders to preserve their financial rights with respect to earnings and assets. Cf. Frey, "Shareholders' Pre-emptive Rights", 38 Yale L.J. 563, 564 (1929) (contending preemptive rights should be limited to voting shares). See Yoakam v. Providence Biltmore Hotel Co., 34 F.2d 533 (1st Cir. 1929); Riverside & Dan River Cotton Mills v. Thomas Branch & Co., 147 Va. 509, 137 S.E. 620, 52 A.L.R. 213 (1927); General Investment Co. v. Bethlehem Steel Corp., 88 N.J.Eq. 237, 102 A. 252 (1917); Hills, "Preemptive Right of Preferred Stockholders to Subscribe to New Stock", 5 N.Y.U.L.Q.Rev. 207 (1927); Note, "Preferred Stockholder's Right of Preemption", 26 Harv.L.Rev. 75 (1912).

14. Note, "Preemptive Rights: Importance of Drafting in Protecting Shareholders against Dilution of Interest and Compulsory Reinvestment", 40 Calif.L. Rev. 132 (1952).

15. Scheirich v. Otis-Hidden Co., 204 Ky. 289, 264 S. W. 755 (1924). But see section 173, n. 5 supra.

scribe could prevent the issue of additional shares. Such a holding has been justified on the ground that such holder can compensate for the decrease in his proportionate interest by selling his right to subscribe.[16] This justification gives more weight to the shareholder's proportionate financial than control interest, and ignores the problem of selling such right in a close corporation in which outsiders might not desire to become shareholders or might be prevented from becoming such by a share transfer restriction.[17]

When the corporation offers the new shares proportionately in accordance with preemptive rights, and some of the shareholders do not subscribe, the other shareholders have been held to enjoy no residual preemptive rights as to the unsubscribed shares.[18]

Where shares subject to preemptive rights are issued in violation of the preemptive rights of shareholders, it has been held that the corporation could not cancel the shares so issued, but that any complaining shareholders should have the right to purchase such of the shares as they would have been entitled to acquire under preemptive rights, and the corporation could recapture, upon adequate reimbursement, such shares from the persons not entitled to them who had purchased them only to the extent necessary to satisfy the preemptive rights of the original shareholders who wished to exercise such rights.[19]

When a corporation has securities listed on a securities exchange, the listing rules of the exchange sometimes impose various requirements.[20]

PREEMPTIVE RIGHTS—STATUTORY PROVISIONS

175. **Statutes on preemptive rights are of various patterns and comprehensiveness. Some provide that preemptive rights exist unless denied in the articles of incorporation; others that preemptive rights do not exist unless provided in the articles. Statutory definitions of preemptive rights exist in some jurisdictions, with some expressly applicable to the issue of securities convertible into shares or of rights to subscribe to shares as well as to the issue of shares themselves. Many jurisdictions provide for the sale of shares to employees free from otherwise applicable preemptive rights when approved by shareholder vote. Elimination of preemptive rights by amendment of the articles of incorporation is authorized in most jurisdictions. New York has the most comprehensive preemptive rights statutory formulation.**

Statutes on preemptive rights are of various patterns. Some provide that preemptive rights exist unless denied in the articles of incorporation;[1] others that preemptive

16. Quaere, if the rights are expressly nonassignable. Cf. Bennett v. Breuil Petroleum Corp., 34 Del.Ch. 6, 99 A.2d 236, 239 (Ch.1953).

17. See Steven v. Hale-Haas Corp., 249 Wis. 205, 226–228, 23 N.W.2d 620, 630–631 (1946); Comment, "Preemptive Rights in Close Corporations", 23 U. Chi.L.Rev. 697 (1956).

18. Dyer v. Securities and Exchange Commission, 290 F.2d 534 (8th Cir. 1961). Shareholders, of course, might be given the privilege of subscribing for additional shares which are not purchased by the shareholders to whom they were offered. This method might enable the corporation to sell the entire issue without resort to underwriters. An alternative arrangement for the corporation would be to enter into a stand-by agreement with underwriters who undertake to purchase whatever shares are not purchased by the shareholders to whom they were offered. See sections 292, 293 infra.

19. Barsan v. Pioneer Savings & Loan Co., 163 Ohio St. 424, 127 N.E.2d 614 (1955). Johnson v. Duensing, 351 S.W.2d 27 (Mo.1961) was a minority shareholder's derivative action to set aside the sale of treasury shares to a small group to give them control of the corporation at the price of the par value of the shares which was substantially less than market value. The court held that the sale by the directors constituted a breach of their fiduciary duties and upheld the rescission of the sale concluding that what should be done with the shares after their restoration to the corporation should be left to the sound discretion of the board of directors. See also Adams, "Remedy for Denial of the Stockholder's Preemptive Right", 6 N.Y.U.Intra.L. Rev. 126 (1951); Annot., 38 A.L.R.2d 1366 (1954).

20. N.Y.S.E. Company Manual § A11.

1. E. g., ABA–ALI Model Bus.Corp.Act §§ 24, 48(h); Florida, New York, North Carolina, Ohio. The 1969 Model Act revision provided that there shall be no preemptive rights "except to the extent, if

rights do not exist unless otherwise provided in the articles of incorporation; [2] still others attempt to codify more or less the judicially-developed doctrine of preemptive rights, in affirmative language [3] or by enumerating exceptions [4] or both, or make only passing reference to preemptive rights.[5] Massachusetts, prior to 1965, expressly provided only for preemptive rights in corporations other than business corporations, but now denies preemptive rights except to the extent provided in the articles of incorporation or in a bylaw adopted by and subject to amendment only by the shareholders.[6] Several jurisdictions have no statutory provisions relating to preemptive rights.[7] Some of the statutes

---

2. E. g., ABA–ALI Model Bus.Corp.Act § 24 (alternative provision), which under the 1969 Model Act revision, became *the* main section; California, Delaware, Indiana, Missouri, New Jersey, Oklahoma, Pennsylvania. The 1967 Delaware revision permits the articles of incorporation to contain "Such provisions as may be desired granting to the stockholders, or any class of them, the preemptive right to subscribe to any or all additional issues of stock of the corporation of any or all classes; otherwise, no stockholders shall have any preemptive right to subscribe to an additional issue of stock. This paragraph (3) shall not apply to any corporation whose certificate of incorporation, as in effect on the effective date of this Act, does not contain a provision limiting or denying to its stockholders the preemptive right to subscribe to any additional issues of its stock". Del.Gen.Corp.Law, § 102(b) (3) (1967). Previously, preemptive rights existed in Delaware corporations unless otherwise provided in the articles of incorporation. The Delaware cases defining preemptive rights leave much to be desired. Note, "Elimination of Preemptive Rights under Missouri's New Corporation Law", 34 U.Mo.Kan. City L.Rev. 382 (1966).

any, that such rights is provided in the articles of incorporation", and added as an alternative section:

"Except to the extent limited or denied by this section or by the articles of incorporation, shareholders shall have a preemptive right to acquire unissued or treasury shares or securities convertible into shares or carrying a right to subscribe to or acquire shares.

"Unless otherwise provided in the articles of incorporation,

"(a) No preemptive right shall exist

(1) to acquire any shares issued to directors, officers or employees pursuant to approval by the affirmative vote of the holders of a majority of the shares entitled to vote thereon or when authorized by and consistent with a plan theretofore approved by such a vote of shareholders; or (2) to acquire any shares sold other than for money.

"(b) Holders of shares of any class that is preferred or limited as to dividends or assets shall not be entitled to any preemptive right.

"(c) Holders of shares of common stock shall not be entitled to any preemptive right to shares of any class that is preferred or limited as to dividends or assets.

"(d) Holders of common stock without voting power shall have no preemptive right to shares of common stock with voting power.

"(e) The preemptive right shall be only an opportunity to acquire shares or other securities under such terms and conditions as the board of directors may fix for the purpose of providing a fair and reasonable opportunity for the exercise of such right."

3. E. g., Florida, North Carolina, Ohio. Typically, such statutes provide that unless otherwise provided in the articles of incorporation, every shareholder shall, upon the sale for cash of any new shares of the same class as that which he already holds, have the right to purchase his pro rata shares at the price at which it is offered to others, which price, in case of shares having par value, may be in excess of par value if the board of directors shall so determine. Note, "Shareholder Preemptive Rights in Florida", 13 U.Fla.L.Rev. 221 (1960); see also Minn.Bus.Corp.Act § 301.04(9) (1961).

4. E. g., Connecticut, North Carolina, Ohio. The common exceptions are (a) shares issued for consideration other than money, that is, for property or services; (b) treasury shares; (c) shares to be issued upon conversion; (d) shares to be issued upon exercise of options or warrants; (e) shares to be issued upon merger or consolidation; (f) shares released from preemptive rights by shareholder action; (g) shares offered to and not taken by shareholders; (h) shares originally authorized, shares issued within a specified time from incorporation, or shares needed to initiate the business; (i) shares issued as a share dividend; (j) shares to be issued to employees; (k) shares issued pursuant to federal reorganization plan. See Comment, "Corporation Law: Exceptions to Stockholder's Preemptive Right", 35 U.Colo.L.Rev. 482 (1963).

5. Del.Gen.Corp.Law, § 102(b)(3) (1967) (articles of incorporation to set forth such provisions as may be desired granting to shareholders, or any class of them, preemptive right to subscribe to any or all additional issues of shares of any or all classes; inapplicable to any corporation whose articles of incorporation, as in effect on July 3, 1967, does not contain provision limiting or denying to its shareholders preemptive right to subscribe to any additional issues of its shares).

6. Mass.Bus.Corp.Law, § 20 (1965); Mass.Gen.Corp. Law, ch. 155, § 20, ch. 156, § 41 (1932). See Samia v. Central Oil Co., 339 Mass. 101, 158 N.E.2d 469 (1959).

7. E. g., Arizona, New Hampshire, Vermont.

recognize preemptive right to securities convertible into shares or to rights to subscribe to shares.[8]

The majority of jurisdictions expressly authorize the articles of incorporation to deny or limit preemptive rights,[9] and the same result would presumably exist by implication in most other jurisdictions.[10]

Many jurisdictions provide for the sale of shares to employees free from otherwise applicable preemptive rights when approved by shareholder vote.[11]

A few statutes expressly provide that the offering price of par value shares pursuant to preemptive rights may be in excess of par value.[12]

Kansas accords special rights to shareholders if par value shares are issued at less than par value.[13] Minnesota prohibits the allotment of shares with or without par value for a cash consideration which is unfair to existing shareholders or for a consideration other than cash upon a valuation thereof which is unfair to such shareholders.[14]

If preemptive rights exist in a particular corporation, their elimination by amendment of the articles of incorporation is possible if such amendment is authorized by the laws of the jurisdiction of incorporation, no viola-tion of fiduciary duties is involved and the procedures required to effectuate such amendment are followed.[15] Dissenting shareholders might have a right of appraisal.[16]

The New York preemptive rights statute is the most comprehensive formulation.[17] It provides for preemptive rights except as otherwise provided in the articles, and comprehensively defines them, distinguishing between "equity shares" and "voting shares". "Equity shares" are defined as shares of any class, whether or not preferred as to dividends or assets, having "unlimited dividend rights", i. e., the right without limitation as to amount either to all or to a share of the balance of current or liquidating dividends after the payment of dividends on any shares entitled to preference. "Voting shares" are defined as any shares of any class having "voting rights" (but not including bonds on which voting rights are conferred), i.e., the noncontingent right to vote for election of one or more directors. Holders of "equity shares" have the right to purchase proportionately any issue of "equity shares", securities convertible into "equity shares", or options to acquire "equity shares" if such issue would adversely affect their "unlimited dividend rights". Holders of "voting shares" have the right to purchase proportionately any issue of "voting shares", securities convertible into "voting shares", or options to acquire "voting

---

8. E. g., McKinney's N.Y.Bus.Corp.Law § 622; N.C. Bus.Corp.Act § 55–56 (1957).

9. E. g., Illinois, North Carolina.

10. 1 G. Hornstein, Corporation Law and Practice § 128 (1959). Texas requires that any denial or limitation of preemptive rights to be effective must be set forth at length or in summary on each share certificate.

11. Some jurisdictions require a two-thirds vote. E. g., California, Illinois, Texas. Others, however, require only a majority shareholder vote. E. g., ABA–ALI Model Bus.Corp.Act § 24; Michigan, New York, Ohio, Pennsylvania. New York requires majority approval of those with preemptive rights to shares being issued or optioned to directors, officers, and employees.

12. E. g., Alabama, Florida, Illinois, Nevada, Tennessee.

13. Kan.Gen.Corp.Code § 17–3211 (1949).

14. Minn.Bus.Corp.Act § 301.16 (1961).

15. See, e. g., ABA–ALI Model Bus.Corp.Act §§ 53(p), 55(i); Cal.Gen.Corp.Law § 3601(f) (1947); Del.Gen. Corp.Law § 242 (1967), construed in Gottlieb v. Heyden Chemical Corp., 33 Del.Ch. 82, 90 A.2d 660 (Sup.Ct.1952), reargument denied in part, 33 Del.Ch. 177, 91 A.2d 57 (Sup.Ct.1952), adhered to 33 Del.Ch. 283, 92 A.2d 594 (Sup.Ct.1952); McKinney's N.Y. Bus.Corp.Law, § 801(b) (12); Mobile Press Register, Inc. v. McGowin, 271 Ala. 414, 124 So.2d 812 (1960); Milwaukee Sanitarium v. Lynch, 238 Wis. 628, 300 N.W. 760, 138 A.L.R. 521 (1941). See section 340 infra.

16. E. g., McKinney's N.Y.Bus.Corp.Law, § 806(b) (6) (C).

17. McKinney's N.Y.Bus.Corp.Law, § 622.

shares" if such issue would adversely affect their "voting rights."

Expressly not subject to preemptive rights are shares or other securities if they are: (a) issued or optioned to effect a merger or consolidation or for a non-cash consideration;[18] (b) issued or optioned to directors, officers, or employees;[19] (c) issued to satsify subsisting conversion or option rights;[20] (d) treasury shares;[21] (e) originally authorized in the articles of incorporation and issued, sold, or optioned within two years from the date of filing such articles;[22] or (f) issued or optioned pursuant to approved federal corporate reorganization plan.[23]

If each share entitled to preemptive rights does not have the same "voting rights" or the same "unlimited dividend rights", the new shares or other securities should be apportioned among the shareholders to preserve as far as practicable the relative "unlimited dividend rights" and "voting rights" of the respective holders. Any such apportionment by the board of directors, absent

fraud or bad faith, is binding on all shareholders.[24]

Notice is required to be mailed to each shareholder of record entitled to preemptive rights, making the offer and stating various information, at least 15 days prior to the expiration of the period during which the shareholder shall have the right to purchase.[25]

If the shareholder does not purchase the shares or securities offered to him, the corporation may sell them, during the succeeding one-year period, to anyone at a price (without deduction for such reasonable expenses of and compensation for underwriters or dealers as may lawfully be paid by the corporation) not less than that at which they were offered to shareholders. If such shares or securities be not sold or optioned during such one-year period, they thereafter again become subject to preemptive rights.[26]

Unless otherwise provided in the articles of incorporation, holders of bonds on which voting rights are conferred have no preemptive rights.[27]

J. RECORD OWNERSHIP OF SECURITIES

SIGNIFICANCE OF RECORD OWNERSHIP

176. The record ownership of securities is conclusive evidence of such ownership for many purposes.

As to ownership of debt and other securities in registered form, as well as shares, the Uniform Commercial Code permits the issuer (or any indenture trustee) to treat the registered owner as the person exclusively entitled to all the rights and powers of an owner.

have been subject to preemptive rights. See note 18 supra.

21. McKinney's N.Y.Bus.Corp.Law, § 622(e) (4).

22. McKinney's N.Y.Bus.Corp.Law, § 622(e) (5).

23. McKinney's N.Y.Bus.Corp.Law, § 622(e) (5) ("under a plan of reorganization approved in a proceeding under any applicable act of congress relating to reorganization of corporations"); see also id. § 808, discussed in section 350 infra.

24. McKinney's N.Y.Bus.Corp.Law, § 622(e).

25. McKinney's N.Y.Bus.Corp.Law, § 622(f), (g). The New York Stock Exchange normally requires a subscription period of at least 16 days. N.Y.S.E. Company Manual § A11.

26. McKinney's N.Y.Bus.Corp.Law, § 622(h).

27. McKinney's N.Y.Bus.Corp.Law, § 622(i).

18 McKinney's N.Y.Bus.Corp.Law, § 622(e) (1). The language would suggest that options issued for services or other non-cash consideration would be exempt from preemptive rights. See note 20 infra. But see Hyman v. Behar, 39 Misc.2d 617, 241 N.Y. S.2d 625 (Sup.Ct.1963) (holding that issuance of shares to employees or management upon basis of past services did not come within statutory exception applicable to shares issued or optioned for a non-cash consideration).

19. McKinney's N.Y.Bus.Corp.Law, § 622(e) (2); id. § 505(d).

20. McKinney's N.Y.Bus.Corp.Law, § 622(e) (3). The issue of such convertible securities or options might

Ownership of securities by minors has been simplified by the Uniform Gifts to Minors Act, permitting securities to be held by or in the registered name of a "custodian".

As to ownership of shares, statutes often require corporations to keep records of their shareholders, sometimes known also as the share book or share ledger. For various purposes, the corporation may rely on record ownership of shareholder status, fixing a reasonable record date or, under older statutes, closing the share transfer books temporarily for such determination. Statutory references to shareholders are not always clear as to whether they refer only to shareholders of record or also to the beneficial owners of shares. Substantial amounts of shares are held by brokers in their own names or in the names of their nominees (known as "street names") in behalf of their customers. Some statutes also require corporations to prepare voting lists based on record ownership before elections of directors. Because of the significance of record ownership, the recording of share transfers is an important function.

The record ownership of securities, both debt and other securities in registered form, as well as shares, is conclusive evidence of such ownership for many purposes.

The almost universally adopted Uniform Commercial Code [1] provides:

"Prior to due presentment for registration of transfer of a security in registered form the issuer or indenture trustee may treat the registered owner as the person exclusively entitled to vote, to receive notifications and otherwise to exercise all the rights and powers of an owner." [2]

Recent statutes have modernized the law respecting infant security holders. Because of the legal disability of a minor at common law, gifts of securities to minors involved

awkward complications,[3] which were best avoided by the troublesome alternatives of formal legal guardianship or trust. Recent gifts-to-minors legislation in a growing number of American jurisdictions [4] authorizes a

---

1. The Uniform Commercial Code has been adopted by all of the states except Louisiana and by the District of Columbia and the Virgin Islands. See section 155, n. 3 supra. See also C. Israels & E. Guttman, Modern Securities Transfers (1967).

2. Uniform Commercial Code § 8–207. For former Uniform Stock Transfer Act formulation, see note 9 infra.

3. Casey v. Kastel, 237 N.Y. 305, 142 N.E. 671, 31 A. L.R. 995 (1924) (corporation upheld where transfer completed in accordance with infant's directions). Cf. Hurley v. Southern California Edison Co., 183 F.2d 125 (9th Cir.1950) (forgery of infant's signature). Younger, "The Infant Stockholder in New York", 12 N.Y.U.Intra.L.Rev. 10 (1956); Annot., 3 A.L.R.2d 881 (1949). See also McKinney's N.Y.Bus. Corp.Law, § 625 (providing corporation may treat infant shareholder and bondholder as having capacity unless, in case of shares, corporate officer responsible for maintaining list of shareholders or transfer agent, or, in case of bonds, treasurer or paying officer or agent has received written notice that such holder is infant; infant shareholder or bondholder to have no right to disaffirm or avoid, as against corporation, specified acts on his part, unless prior thereto, written notice that such holder was infant was so received; foregoing provisions not to limit any other statute which authorizes any corporation to deal with infant or limits right of infant to disaffirm his acts).

4. The Uniform Gifts to Minors Act, 9B U.L.A. 231 (1966), approved in 1956, revised in 1965 and 1966, has been adopted in Alabama, Alaska, Arizona, Arkansas, California, Colorado, Connecticut, Delaware, Florida, Hawaii, Maine, Maryland, Massachusetts, Michigan, Minnesota, Mississippi, Missouri, Montana, Nebraska, Nevada, New Hampshire, New Jersey, New Mexico, New York, North Carolina, North Dakota, Ohio, Oklahoma, Oregon, Pennsylvania, Rhode Island, South Carolina, South Dakota, Tennessee, Texas, Utah, Vermont, Virginia, Washington (as amended), West Virginia, Wisconsin (as amended), Wyoming (as amended), District of Columbia, and the Virgin Islands. It replaced the narrower Model Gifts of Securities to Minors Act, sponsored by the New York Stock Exchange and the Association of Stock Exchange Firms, and adopted by about one-fourth of the states and the District of Columbia. When the gift is properly made, the donor may include it in his lifetime federal gift tax exemption and may exclude the first $3,000 ($6,000 for gift from both parents) given annually to each donee. Int.Rev.Code of 1954, 26 U. S.C.A. § 2503(c). The income (including interest, dividends, or any capital gain) from the securities, assuming it is not used to discharge a legal obligation to support the donee, is taxable to the minor, not to the donor or custodian. Income up to $1,000 a year (standard deduction of $300, personal exemption of $600 and $100 dividend exclusion) may be tax-free. The parent, no matter what his income, can take his $600 dependency exemption if the child is under 19 or in school. However, if the parent uses the income for the child's support, the income is taxable to the parent. Ordinarily, the securities would not be included in the donor's estate for estate tax purposes, unless the donor is a parent and dies before the child reaches 21. Shiney, "Gifts to

new method for making and administering such gifts by permitting the holding of the securities by a "custodian" and the registration of securities in the name of such "custodian".[5]

In the case of debt and other securities in registered form, as well as shares, any limitation on ownership or special type of ownership should be properly described not only in the corporate records but also on the face of the securities.

As to ownership of shares, statutes usually require corporations to keep records of their shareholders, sometimes known as share books or share ledgers (showing names and addresses, number and class of shares held).[6]

The record of shareholders is usually open to reasonable inspection by shareholders and possibly others.[7]

To protect the corporation in determining who its shareholders are, for various purposes, statutes permit the corporation to rely, to some extent, on the record ownership as shown in the record of shareholders (share ledger, share transfer book, or share certificate book). For all or specified purposes, record ownership is accepted as conclusive and binding on the courts.[8]

Statutes permit the corporation to rely on such record ownership in determining the shareholders entitled to be sent notices, to vote or otherwise participate in control, to receive dividends, etc.[9] For such purposes, a

Minors: Tax Considerations", 5 Washburn L.Rev. 218 (1966); Aland, "Tax and Substantive Aspects of Gifts to Minors", 18 Ala.L.Rev. 82 (1965); Rume, "Basis: A Prognosis of Potential Double Tax Liability Under the Model and Uniform Gift to Minors Acts", 17 N.Y.U.Intra.L.Rev. 279 (1962); Ehrlich, "Tax Aspects of Gifts to Minors", 46 Mass.L.Q. (Dec. 1961). The number of infant shareholders in the United States has been estimated to exceed 1,500,000.

5. Poland, "Gifts to Minors-Conservatorship-Trusteeship-Custodianship", 5 Washburn L.J. 29 (1965). Several jurisdictions, including New York, first adopted the Model Gifts of Securities to Minors Act. Former McKinney's N.Y.Pers.Prop.Law, §§ 265–270; Notes, 25 Fordham L.Rev. 390 (1956); 32 N.Y.U.L.Rev. 203 (1957). Effective July 1, 1959, these provisions were superseded by the Uniform Gifts to Minors Act. McKinney's N.Y. EPTL, §§ 7–4.1 to 7–4.9. The latter provides that it should apply to all gifts made under the prior statute "except so far as such substitution may impair constitutionally vested rights", McKinney's N.Y. EPTL, § 7–4.9. The Act is not limited to shares but also applies to gifts of other securities and money. See also Uniform Securities Ownership by Minors Act, 9A U.L.A. 85 (Supp.1967), approved in 1960, adopted in five jurisidictions, and withdrawn in 1967 because of similar provisions in the Uniform Commercial Code.

6. E. g., ABA–ALI Model Bus.Corp.Act § 46 (record of shareholders); Del.Gen.Corp.Law, § 219 (1967) (stock ledger); McKinney's N.Y.Bus.Corp.Law, §§ 624, 1315 (record of shareholders). In smaller corporations, the share certificate book, with its stubs, serves as a record of shareholders. Many statutes require share certificates to state on their face the name of the person to whom issued. See section 134 infra. See C. Israels & E. Guttman, Modern Securities Transfers (1967); F. Christy, The Transfer of Stock (4th ed.1967) (2 vols. looseleaf). Form-

er McKinney's N.Y.Pers.Prop.Law, §§ 186 to 186–c, replaced by McKinney's N.Y.U.C.C. §§ 8–101 et seq., on bearer shares, are expressly declaratory of existing law, and presumably apply to bearer shares issued by foreign corporations incorporated in jurisdictions whose laws authorize their issuance. For discussion of bearer shares of foreign corporations, see R. Schlesinger, Comparative Law: Cases-Text-Materials 425–443 (2d ed.1959); on limited recognition of bearer shares of American corporations, see Note, "Corporations: Bearer Shares in the United States: Civil Law Contrast: Connecticut and Montana Statutes Authorizing Issuance", 48 Cornell L. Q. 174 (1962). Montana has since repealed its provision.

7. See sections 199, 216 infra.

8. See Del.Gen.Corp.Law, § 219(c) (1967) (shareholder inspection right and right to vote conclusively determined by share ledger). But see Rosenfield v. Standard Electric Equipment Corp., 32 Del.Ch. 238, 83 A.2d 843 (Ch.1951). McKinney's N.Y.Bus.Corp. Law § 612(i) ("corporation shall be protected in treating the persons in whose names shares stand on the record of shareholders as the owners thereof for all purposes"). For New York cases under prior statute, see Matter of Doeskin Products, Inc., 7 A.D.2d 42, 180 N.Y.S.2d 760 (1st Dep't 1958) (3–2), citing Matter of William Faehndrich, Inc., 2 N.Y.2d 468, 161 N.Y.S.2d 99, 141 N.E.2d 597 (1957); Matter of A. Bruder & Son, Inc., 302 N.Y. 52, 96 N.E.2d 84 (1950) (share books held conclusive on validity of issuance of shares voted in summary proceeding under McKinney's N.Y.Gen.Corp.Law, § 25 (not applicable to business corporation since 1963) to review election). Cf. Matter of George Ringler & Co., 204 N.Y. 30, 97 N.E. 593 (1912) (share books held not conclusive on ownership of required qualifying shares by directors in summary proceeding to set aside their election).

9. See Uniform Commercial Code § 8–207, note 2 supra, replacing Uniform Stock Transfer Act § 3:

reasonable record date may be fixed or, under more old-fashioned statutes, the record of shareholders temporarily closed for transfers. The more modern statutory provisions are very comprehensive concerning the fixing of record dates and the time for determining shareholders if no record date is fixed.[10]

Implementing provisions are frequently found in bylaws,[11] and occasionally in articles of incorporation.

For voting purposes, statutes sometimes expressly permit administrators, executors, guardians, conservators, committees, and other fiduciaries, except trustees, and receivers when so authorized by court order, to vote shares held by them without their having become shareholders of record.[12]

The corporation statutes in their various substantive provisions sometimes refer to shareholders of record and/or beneficial owners of shares [13] but most frequently refer only to shareholders or members,[14] raising the question as to whether shareholders of record or beneficial owners or both are intended.[15]

Substantial amounts of shares are held by brokers in their own names or the names of their nominees ("street name") in behalf of their customers either on margin accounts or for the convenience of such customers.[16]

A growing number of jurisdictions require that corporations, besides maintaining records of their shareholders, prepare before every election of directors a voting list, containing the names and addresses of all shareholders of record.[17]

Because of the significance of record ownership, the recording of share transfers on the record of shareholders is an important function.[18]

The old rule that a holder's shares could be attached and levied upon by proceedings against the corporation, on the basis of its control of the record of shareholders, was

---

"Nothing in this act shall be construed as forbidding a corporation, (a) to recognize the exclusive right of a person registered on its books as the owner of shares to receive dividends, and to vote as such owner, or (b) to hold liable for calls and assessments a person registered on its books as the owner of shares". Read literally, this provision created no new rule, but preserved preexisting rules with respect to reliance on record ownership. See Lindner v. Utah Southern Oil Co., 3 Utah 2d 302, 283 P.2d 605 (1955); Bogardus v. Kentucky State Bank, 281 S.W.2d 904 (Ky.1955); Bay City Bank v. St. Louis Motor Sales Co., 255 Mich. 261, 238 N.W. 241 (1931). Provisions in articles of incorporation and bylaws may also affect permissible reliance on record ownership. Record ownership may affect escheat or attachment of shares. Note, "The Lost Shareholder", 62 Harv.L.Rev. 295 (1948). See sections 179, 354 infra.

10. E. g., ABA–ALI Model Bus.Corp.Act § 28; McKinney's N.Y.Bus.Corp.Law § 604 (record date not more than 50 days prior to any action; not less than 10 days before shareholder meeting); Maidman, "Voting Rights of After-Record-Date Shareholders: A Skeleton in a Wall Street Closet", 71 Yale L.J. 1205 (1962); Comment, "The After-Record-Date Stockholder Problem", 1 U. San Fernando Valley L.Rev. 183 (1968); Note, 45 Cornell L.Q. 111 (1959).

11. E. g., By-Laws, art. II, § 5, Official Forms for Use Under the Model Business Corporation Act, Form No. 47 (ALI rev. 1953).

12. McKinney's N.Y.Bus.Corp.Law, § 612(c), (d).

13. See, e. g., ABA–ALI Model Bus.Corp.Act § 27 (notice of shareholders' meetings to shareholders of record); § 46 (inspection rights of shareholders of record); § 23 (liability of subscribers and shareholders).

14. See, e. g., ABA–ALI Model Bus.Corp.Act § 2(f) ("unless context otherwise requires . . . 'Shareholder' means one who is a holder of record of shares in a corporation"); McKinney's N.Y.Gen. Corp.Law, § 3(15) (inapplicable to business corporations since 1963 or any other stock corporations since 1967) ("The term 'member of a corporation' as applied to a stock corporation includes a stockholder of record having the right to vote").

15. Attix, "Rights of Equitable Owners of Corporate Shares", 99 U.Pa.L.Rev. 999 (1951); Note, 45 Cornell L.Q. 111 (1959). See sections 199, 349, 361, 362 infra.

16. With respect to which the securities exchange might impose some rules. See, e. g., N.Y.S.E. Rules 870–875. See also American Hardware Corp. v. Savage Arms Corp., 37 Del. 59, 136 A.2d 690 (Sup. Ct.1957); In re Universal Pictures Co., 28 Del.Ch. 72, 37 A.2d 615 (Ch.1944).

17. E. g., ABA–ALI Model Bus.Corp.Act § 29; Del. Gen.Corp.Law § 219 (1967); McKinney's N.Y.Bus. Corp.Law, § 607.

18. See section 177 infra.

abolished in nearly all jurisdictions by the Uniform Stock Transfer Act, such abolition being continued by the Uniform Commercial Code.[19]

TRANSFER OF SECURITIES

177. A debt security in bearer form is transferred by delivery of the certificate to the transferee. A debt security in registered form or a share is transferred by delivery of the certificate duly assigned by the registered owner to the transferee or in blank.

The Uniform Commercial Code governs the transfer, negotiability, and registration of transfer of securities. The transferee of a security acquires the rights in the security which his transferor had or had actual authority to convey, and, if a "bona fide purchaser", free of any "adverse claim". In registering transfers, the corporation has been held responsible if the transfer was not authorized by the registered owner or if the transfer was negligently registered in breach of the interests of beneficial owners. The corporation's responsibilities in the latter respect have been relaxed by modern statutes, especially the Uniform Act for Simplification of Fiduciary Security Transfers and the Uniform Commercial Code. Depending upon the scope of the corporation's duty in recording transfers, various documentation might be required to evidence the propriety of proposed transfers. Wrongful refusal to record a transfer subjects the corporation to liability to the transferee. The corporation also has responsibilities under tax statutes, including the affixation and cancellation of any required transfer stamps.

The Uniform Commercial Code governs the transfer, negotiability, and registration of transfer of securities, including bonds, debentures, and other debt securities, and shares.[1]

The transferee of a security acquires the rights in the security which his transferor had or had actual authority to convey and, if a "bona fide purchaser",[2] also acquires the security free of any "adverse claim".[3]

Transfer of Bonds, Debentures, and Other Debt Securities

Bonds, debentures, and other debt securities, whether in bearer form or registered form, usually are freely transferable.[4] Provisions in the securities, or in applicable indentures or agreements under which they were issued, sometimes permit the formal exchange of a security issued in bearer form for one in registered form and vice versa.[5]

A bond, debenture, or other security in bearer form is transferred by delivery of the certificate representing the same. A debt security in registered form is transferred by

Transfer Act which had applied to the transfer of shares, and miscellaneous statutory provisions in different jurisdictions. F. Christy, The Transfer of Stock (4th ed. 1967) (2 vols. looseleaf) is the classic work in the field, now in a two-volume looseleaf fourth edition. Since its initial publication in 1929, it has become known as the "Bible of the Stock Transfer Agents". See also C. Israels & E. Guttman, Modern Securities Transfers (1967); J. Morley & J. Lynch, Handbook on Stock Transfers: An Outline of Basic Transfer Procedures and a Brief Summary of the Law Involved (Association of Stock Exchange Firms 1962); CCH Stock Transfer Guide; Prentice-Hall Stock Transfer Reports. See also Weiss, "Investment and Control Securities— Problems of Transfer Agents and Transfer Departments", 12 N.Y.L.F. 555 (1966).

2. "Bona fide purchaser" is defined as "a purchaser for value in good faith and without notice of any adverse claim who takes delivery of a security in bearer form or of one in registered form issued to him or endorsed to him in blank".

3. Uniform Commercial Code § 8–301. "Adverse claim" is defined to include a claim that a transfer was or would be wrongful or that a particular adverse person is the owner of or has an interest in the security. Ibid.

4. See Uniform Commercial Code § 8–105, making all securities governed by Article 8 thereof "negotiable instruments".

5. See Uniform Commercial Code § 8–310. Under the terms of their issuance, debt securities in bearer form can be registered as to principal but not as to interest. Debt securities in registered form, of course, can be assigned in blank.

19. Delaware adheres still to the older rule, rendering shareholders in Delaware corporations amenable to quasi-in-rem jurisdiction in Delaware. See section 354 infra.

1. Uniform Commercial Code, art. 8, §§ 8–101 to 8–406 ("Investment Securities"). See section 155, n. 3 supra. The Code replaced a large body of decisional law, the former Uniform Negotiable Instruments Act which had been held to apply to debt securities in negotiable form, the former Uniform Stock

the delivery of the certificate duly assigned by the registered owner to the transferee or in blank.[6]

Debt securities in registered form often contain on their backs a printed form of assignment. However, the assignment may be made in a separate instrument.[7]

Involved in the registration of transfers of securities of larger issues are persons, usually financial institutions, acting as authenticating trustees, transfer agents, registrars, etc.[8] In the case of issues listed on a securities exchange, the exchange often imposes various requirements.[9] In smaller corporations, transfers are often handled by the treasurer or secretary.

The issuer or any indenture trustee may treat the registered owner of a security in registered form as the person exclusively entitled to all the rights and powers of an owner.[10]

Transfer of Shares

Shares, absent valid provisions to the contrary, are freely transferable. However, share transfer restrictions can be imposed by intracorporate provisions, and frequently are in close corporations.[11] Where such a restriction is in a shareholders' agreement to which the corporation is not a party, the corporation has not been permitted to decline recordation of a transfer in violation of such restriction.[12] Shares are transferred by delivery of the certificate representing the same, accompanied by a form of assignment duly executed by or in behalf of the transferor in favor of the transferee or in blank.[13] Share certificates usually contain on their backs a printed form of assignment (with power of attorney running in favor of the transfer clerk).[14] However, a separate assignment (in substantially the same form and known as a "stock power" or "fly power") may be used.

The bylaws often contain provisions regulating the transfer of shares.[15]

The recording of transfers, cancellation of the surrendered certificates, and issuance of the new certificates in the name of the transferee are functions assigned to an agent (known as the "Transfer Agent"), or to a department of the corporation (known, e. g., as the "Stock Bureau"), or to an employee of the corporation (known as the "Transfer Clerk").[16] In a small corporation, the secretary frequently performs this function. If the shares are listed on a securities exchange, the rules of the exchange might impose requirements with respect to share transfer functions and those who perform them, and might require the appointment of a bank or trust company (other than the transfer agent) as "Stock Registrar" whose principal duty is to prevent overissue of the

6. Uniform Commercial Code § 8–302.

7. Uniform Commercial Code § 8–308.

8. Uniform Commercial Code §§ 8–208, 8–406.

9. E. g., N.Y.S.E. Company Manual § A5.

10. Uniform Commercial Code § 8–207. See section 176 supra.

11. See sections 281, 282 infra.

12. Matter of Argus Co., 138 N.Y. 557, 34 N.E. 388 (1893).

13. Uniform Commercial Code § 8–302. Cf. Greenspun v. Greenspun, 194 S.W.2d 134 (Tex.Civ.App. 1946), aff'd 145 Tex. 374, 198 S.W.2d 82 (1947). See Reynolds v. Reynolds, 54 Cal.2d 669, 7 Cal.Rptr. 737, 355 P.2d 481 (1960). See Matter of Szabo, 10 N.Y.2d 94, 217 N.Y.S.2d 593, 176 N.E.2d 395 (1961) (holding not valid inter vivos gift of joint ownership interest in shares for lack of recordation of transfer).

14. See section 134 supra.

15. E. g., McKinney's N.Y.Bus.Corp.Law, § 508(d) (stating shares transferable in manner provided by law and in bylaws); By-Laws, art. VI, §§ 1, 2, Official Forms for Use Under the Model Business Corporation Act, Form No. 47 (ALI rev. 1953). See Komar v. General Elec. Co., 17 Misc.2d 24, 183 N.Y. S.2d 762 (Sup.Ct.1959).

16. For an excellent discussion of the detailed procedures followed by a share transfer bureau with respect not only to share transfers but also to the mailing of notices, solicitation of proxies, processing of dividend checks, etc., see J. Foster & B. Rodey, Public Utility Accounting 635–650 (1951).

shares and to countersign the new share certificates.[17]

Usually before the corporation need recognize a transferee as a shareholder, the transfer must be recorded on the corporation's record of shareholders. As previously mentioned, statutes often give substantial weight to record ownership and permit the corporation to rely to a considerable extent on record ownership.[18]

Registration of Transfers of Securities

When securities were presented for registration of transfer, the issuer, in the absence of statutory provisions to the contrary, faced two different kinds of potential liability if it registered the transfer. First, if the person porporting to assign was not the owner or lacked authority to transfer the securities, the transfer was void and the issuer was liable in conversion to the legal owner of the securities, whether or not it exercised due care.[19] Second, if the transferor had authority, but the transfer was in breach of a fiduciary relationship, the issuer, in the absence of statutory provisions to the contrary, was liable to beneficial owners for participation in the breach of trust unless it exercised due care.[20]

The burden of inquiry on corporations and transfer agents transferring securities registered in the name of a fiduciary has been substantially reduced by modern statutes,[21] especially the Uniform Act for Simplification of Fiduciary Security Transfers and the Uniform Commercial Code.

Uniform Act for Simplification of Fiduciary Security Transfers

The Uniform Act for Simplification of Fiduciary Security Transfers,[22] adopted in

---

17. E. g., N.Y.S.E. Company Manual § A1.

18. See section 176 supra.

19. 1 F. Christy, The Transfer of Stock ch. XIX (4th ed. 1967); Frye v. Commonwealth Inv. Co., 107 Ga. 739, 131 S.E.2d 569 (1963), aff'd 219 Ga. 498, 134 S. E.2d 39 (1964) (forged power of attorney); Teiser, "The Transfer of Corporate Stock Under An Unauthorized Assignment", 2 Bus.Law. 18, 24 (Apr.1947); Note, "Apparent Authority of Agent To Transfer Stock Owned by Principal", 22 Md.L.Rev. 154 (1962).

20. 1 F. Christy, The Transfer of Stock ch. XXI (4th ed. 1967). The source of this rule is traceable to an unfortunate statement by Taney, C.J., while riding circuit in Maryland in 1848. Lowry v. Commercial & Farmers' Bank, 15 F.Cas. 1040, 1047, No. 8,581 (C.C.D.Md.1848). Klein v. Inman, 298 Ky. 122, 182 S.W.2d 34 (1944) (equities not evident from share certificate but corporation had knowledge). See also Christy, "Responsibilities in the Transfer of Stock", 53 Mich.L.Rev. 701 (1955); Annot., 56 A.L. R. 1199 (1928), 139 A.L.R. 273 (1942), 7 A.L.R.2d 1240 (1949), 75 A.L.R.2d 746 (1961). An indirect

meeting of the problem was the enactment of so-called "nominee" or "exoneration" statutes in most American jurisdictions. Such statutes authorize a fiduciary to cause shares or other securities held by such fiduciary to be registered or held in the name of a nominee without disclosure of the fiduciary relationship. See, e. g., McKinney's N.Y. EPTL, § 11–1.1(10); Comment, 56 Mich.L.Rev. 963 (1958). Since the trust does not appear on the corporation's records, the corporation is not bound to inquire into the terms of the trust even though it may know that the registered owner is in fact a nominee and that the securities are presumably held in a fiduciary capacity. See also Hartford Accident & Indemnity Co. v. Walston & Co., 21 N.Y.S.2d 219, 287 N.Y.S.2d 58, 234 N.E.2d 230 (1967), aff'd on rehearing 22 N.Y.2d 672, 291 N.Y.S.2d 366, 238 N.E.2d 754 (1968); Jolls, "Fictitious Registration of Stock Ownership—Hartford v. Walston Examined", 24 Bus.Law. 1085 (1969).

21. The Uniform Fiduciaries Act, 9B U.L.A. 24 (1966), approved in 1922, and adopted or followed in some 25 jurisdictions has in effect been replaced by the Uniform Act for Simplification of Fiduciary Security Transfers and the Uniform Commercial Code. It was designed to mitigate the corporate duty to beneficial interests and imposed liability only when the registration of the transfer was made with actual or constructive knowledge that the fiduciary was committing a breach of his trust. Transfer agents had not relied upon the Act to any great extent, especially where the transaction had multistate implications and involved the law of a jurisdiction which had not adopted the Act. See Israels, "Article 8—Investment Securities", 16 Law & Contemp.Prob. 249, 264 (1951).

22. 9C U.L.A. 88 (Supp.1967), approved in 1958; adopted in Alabama, Arizona, California, Colorado, Delaware, District of Columbia, Florida, Georgia, Hawaii, Idaho, Illinois, Indiana, Kansas, Louisiana, Maine, Maryland, Michigan, Minnesota, Mississippi, Missouri, Montana, Nebraska, Nevada, New Jersey, New York, North Carolina, North Dakota, Rhode Island, South Carolina, South Dakota, Tennessee, Texas, Utah, Virginia, Washington, West Virginia, Wisconsin, Wyoming. When adopting the Uniform Commercial Code, New York expressly retained the Uniform Act for Simplification of Fiduciary Security Transfers, providing that in the event of any in-

three-fourths of the states, provides that a corporation or transfer agent may register a security in the name of a fiduciary without inquiring into the existence or extent of the fiduciary relationship, and that they are not charged with notice of or bound to examine any court record or document relating to the fiduciary relationship or assignment, even though the record or document is in their possession.[23]

Under the Uniform Commercial Code,[24] where a security in registered form is presented to the issuer for registration of transfer, the issuer is under a duty to register the transfer if:

(a) the security is endorsed by the appropriate person or persons; [25]

consistency, the latter should control. McKinney's N.Y.U.C.C. §§ 10–104.

23. Transfers out of the name of a fiduciary thus can be accomplished in most cases upon presentation of an assignment by the fiduciary, with signature guarantee, and any necessary estate or inheritance tax waivers, and payment of any applicable state transfer taxes. Where the shares are in the name of a decedent, a certified copy or short-form certificate of letters testamentary or letters of administration should complete the documentation required. Jolls, "Simplified Securities Transfers", 104 Trusts & Estates 113 (1965); Hamburger, "New Departure in Fiduciary Security Transfers", 17 Bus.Law. 428 (1962); Partridge, "Help Wanted: Operation Simplification", 45 A.B.A.J. 476 (1959); Braucher, "Security Transfers by Fiduciaries", 43 Minn.L.Rev. 193 (1958); Conard, "A New Deal for Fiduciaries' Stock Transfers", 56 Mich.L.Rev. 843 (1958). There is also a Model Fiduciaries' Securities Transfer Act, sponsored by the American Bar Association and the Illinois Bar Association. See Christy, "The Model Fiduciaries' Securities Transfer Act", 29 N.Y.St.B.Bull. 434 (1957); Note, 35 N.D.L.Rev. 225 (1959).

24. Uniform Commercial Code § 8–401(1); Israels & Guttman, "The Transfer Agent and The Uniform Commercial Code", 83 Banking L.J. 941 (1966); Israels, "How to Handle Transfers of Stock, Bonds and Other Investment Securities", 19 Bus.Law. 90 (1963); Jolls, "Registration of Transfers of Securities under Article 8 of the Uniform Commercial Code", 50 Ill.B.J. 1014 (1962); Kelley, "New Rules for Security Transfers: Uniform Commercial Code Provisions Explained", 100 Trusts & Estates 400 (1961); Israels, "Investment Securities as Negotiable Paper—Article 8 of the Uniform Commercial Code", 13 Bus.Law. 676 (1958); Note, "Duties and Liabilities of the Stock Transfer Agent under the Uniform Commercial Code", 103 U.Pa.L.Rev. 209 (1954).

25. Uniform Commercial Code § 8–308.

(b) reasonable assurance is given that those indorsements are genuine and effective; [26]

(c) the issuer has no duty to inquire into adverse claims or has discharged any such duty; [27]

(d) any applicable law relating to the collection of taxes has been complied with; [28] and

(e) the transfer is in fact rightful or is to a bona fide purchaser.

Functions of Transfer Agent

The examination by the transfer agent is quite rigorous, extending to the validity of the surrendered certificate, the signature of the transferor on the assignment, the conformity of the latter to the name on the face of the certificate, the signature of the guarantor of the transferor's signature, the name and address of the transferee, the affixation and cancellation of any required transfer tax stamps, the date of transfer, etc. Where the assignment form is signed by an agent or one in some other representative capacity, appropriate evidence might be required to ascertain such person's authority and otherwise to support the propriety of the proposed transfer.

26. Uniform Commercial Code § 8–402.

27. Uniform Commercial Code § 8–403.

28. Where the transfer is out of the name of a decedent, the transfer agent must require the submission of any applicable state inheritance or estate tax waivers. The transfer agent is required by statute to police the affixation and cancellation of any applicable transfer stamps, which in appropriate denominations are purchasable at designated agencies. Transfer taxes are currently imposed on the transfer of shares by Florida (for par value shares: 15 cents per $100 par or face value or fraction thereof; for shares without par value; 15 cents on each $100 of actual value or fraction thereof but not to exceed 15 cents per share); State ex rel. Florida Light & Power Co. v. Green, 166 So.2d 146 (Fla.1964) and New York (2.5 cents per share if no sale involved; 1.25 cents per share sold for less than $5; 2.5 cents per share sold for $5 or more and less than $10; 3.75 cents per share sold for $10 or more and less than $20; 5 cents per share sold for $20 or more).

Typical of the documentation which, to a greater or less extent, might be required by the transfer agent, for various common situations, are: [29]

(a) Certificate properly assigned for transfer;

(b) Signature guarantee by a commercial bank or trust company having a local office or correspondent or a securities exchange firm on file with the transfer agent;

(c) Court certificate of recent date showing appointment of any representative seeking transfer (e. g., executor, administrator, trustee, guardian, conservator, committee);

(d) Certified copy of any relevant will;

(e) Affidavit as to legal residence;

(f) Affidavit that taxes and debts of estate have been paid or provided for;

(g) Certified copy of any relevant birth certificate;

(h) Certified copy of any relevant death certificate;

(i) Certified copy of any appropriate court order;

(j) Copy of any relevant power of attorney adequately certified to the effect that it is a true and complete copy of the original and is still in full force and effect and that the maker is still alive;

(k) Copy of any relevant trust instrument (with any amendments) adequately guaranteed to be a true and complete copy of the original and to be in full force and effect at the present time;

(l) Where the transferor is a corporation, certified copy of resolution of the board of directors of such corporation authorizing the transfer;

(m) Any applicable transfer stamps;

(n) Any applicable state inheritance or estate tax waivers; etc.

The required documentation has, as indicated, been substantially reduced by recent statutes.

In doubtful situations, the corporation may delay recording the transfer pending opinion of counsel.[30] However, if the proposed transferee has a right to have the transfer recorded, and the transfer agent unreasonably delays or refuses registration, its principal, the corporation, may be liable to such transferee for nonrecognition of his rights,[31] and the transfer agent may in turn be liable to the corporation.[32]

---

29. See Note, "Duties and Liabilities of the Stock Transfer Agent under the Uniform Commercial Code", 103 U.Pa.L.Rev. 209, 210 (1954); David, "The Decedent's Securities and Their Transfer", 1 Prac.Law. 50 (Apr.1955).

30. Travis Inv. Co. v. Harwyn Publishing Corp., 288 F.Supp. 519 (S.D.N.Y.1968) (holding that issuer on notice of potential Federal Securities Act violation by transfer of shares by persons in control relationship—see section 295, n. 19 infra—was justified in refusing transfer for reasonable period pending receipts of information requested by it on ownership and control); Spangenberg v. Nesbitt, 22 Cal.App. 274, 134 P. 343 (1913). See Kentucky Utilities Co. v. Skaggs, 293 Ky. 622, 169 S.W.2d 809 (1943) (upholding corporation's right to declaratory judgment concerning transfer). See Annot., 116 A.L.R. 571 (1938), 75 A.L.R.2d 746 (1961). Compare Claude Neon, Inc. v. Birrell, 177 F.Supp. 706 (S.D.N.Y. 1959), with Bartlett v. General Motors Corp., 36 Del.Ch. 131, 127 A.2d 470 (Ch.1956) (rights of judgment creditors to shares).

31. Uniform Commercial Code § 8–401(1); Jones v. Boyd Transfer & Storage Co., 323 F.2d 998 (8th Cir.1963); Security-First Nat'l Bank of Los Angeles v. Lutz, 297 F.2d 159 (9th Cir.1961) (corporations held liable for conversion); Prudential Petroleum Corp. v. Rauscher, Pierce & Co., 281 S.W.2d 457 (Tex.Civ.App.1955) (corporation held liable for conversion of shares for wrongful closing of share transfer books). See also Kanton v. United States Plastics, Inc., 248 F.Supp. 353 (D.N.J.1965) (granting mandatory injunction to compel corporation to register transfer of shares); Hertz v. Record Pub. Co., 219 F.2d 397 (3d Cir.1955), cert. denied 349 U.S. 912, 75 S.Ct. 601, 99 L.Ed. 1247 (1955) (mandatory injunction to corporation to record transfer granted). See Devine v. Rayette-Faberge, Inc., 285 F.Supp. 1006 (D.Minn.1968) (improper transfer by transfer agent held conversion when new share certificates issued and not later recordation of transfer on record of shareholders, for purposes of statute of limitations).

32. See Lenhart Altschuler Associates v. Benjamin, 28 Misc.2d 602, 215 N.Y.S.2d 541 (Sup.Ct.1961) (hold-

Not only should the name and address and description, if any, of the proposed transferee be correct, but in any situation where there might be problems of future transfer from such transferee such problems should be anticipated and avoided so far as possible.[33]

The New York Stock Exchange in 1966 introduced a "Central Certificate Service" (CCS), an automated program for the delivery of shares between clearing members by computerized bookkeeping entries rather than physical delivery of certificates by Stock Clearing Corporation, an Exchange subsidiary that recorded, confirmed and net-balanced the daily transactions between the Exchange's some 300 clearing firms.[34]

REPLACEMENT OF LOST, DESTROYED, AND STOLEN CERTIFICATES

178. Replacement of lost, destroyed, or stolen certificates representing securities subjects the corporation to possible liability if the original certificate later turns up in the hands of a bona fide purchaser. The Uniform Commercial Code governs replacement of certificates representing securities—debt and otherwise—in most jurisdictions. Occasional other statutes and bylaws apply to the replacement of certificates representing shares. Replacement is usually conditioned upon the posting of an adequate bond to indemnify the corporation.

If certificates are lost, destroyed, or stolen, their replacement by the corporation might subject it to liability if the original certificate later turns up in the hands of a *bona fide* purchaser.

The Uniform Commercial Code governs the replacement of lost, apparently destroyed, and wrongfully taken certificates representing securities—debt and otherwise—in most jurisdictions.[1]

Where a security has been lost, apparently destroyed, or wrongfully taken, and the owner has failed to notify the issuer within a reasonable time after he has notice, and the issuer registers a transfer of the security before receiving such notification, the owner is precluded from asserting against the issuer any claim for registering the transfer or any claim to a new security.[2]

Where the owner of a security claims that the security has been lost, destroyed, or wrongfully stolen, the issuer must replace the original security if the owner (a) so requests before the issuer has notice that the security has been acquired by a bona fide purchaser; (b) files with the issuer a sufficient indemnity bond;[3] and (c) satisfies any other reasonable requirements imposed by the issuer.[4]

If, after the issue of the new security, a bona fide purchaser of the original security

---

ing no action would be against transfer agent or officer for wrongful refusal to register transfer of shares); Mears v. Crocker First Nat'l Bank, 97 Cal.App.2d 482, 218 P.2d 91 (1950) (holding transfer agent's duty owing only to principal, the corporation, and not to shareholder for wrongful refusal to record transfer); Annot., 22 A.L.R.2d (1952).

33. See Ward v. Jersey Central Power & Light Co., 136 N.J.Eq. 181, 41 A.2d 22 (1945); Orgain, "Texas Joint Tenancy in Corporate Shares: Problems of the Stock Transfer Agent", 16 Baylor L.Rev. 99 (1964). Abbreviations are often used to denote the nature of the ownership. Uniform Procedures for Stockholder Descriptions and Addressing (The New York Clearing House Association 1961). See also section 176 supra.

34. Silberman, "New Bookkeeping Plan Reduces Brokers' Need to Remain in New York; Simple Entries Will Replace Physical Transfer of Stock Now Done by Messengers", 167 The Wall Street Journal, No. 107, 1 (June 2, 1966). See Uniform Commercial Code § 8–320.

1. See section 176, n. 1 supra. Louisiana has not adopted the Code, retaining, for shares, the Uniform Stock Transfer Act—see note 6 infra. A few other jurisdictions have retained some older statutory provisions—see note 10 infra. See C. Israels & E. Guttman, Modern Securities Transfers ch. 13 (1967); 1 F. Christy, The Transfer of Stock ch. 20 (4th ed. 1967).

2. Uniform Commercial Code § 8–405(1).

3. See Graham v. Commercial Credit Co., 41 Del.Ch. 580, 200 A.2d 828, 16 A.L.R.3d 1009 (Sup.Ct.1964) (holding share certificates resulting from 2 for 1 share split delivered by corporation to shareholder when received by latter's maid, and corporation not responsible for replacing certificates which thereafter disappeared). Many corporations, or their transfer agents, now carry group, or blanket, bonds covering lost securities, available at lower premium than individual indemnity bonds.

4. Uniform Commercial Code § 8–405(2).

presents it for registration of transfer, the issuer must register the transfer unless registration would result in overissue.[5] In addition to any rights on the indemnity bond, the issuer may recover the new security from the person to whom it was issued or any person taking under him except a bona fide purchaser.[6]

Before the adoption of the Uniform Commercial Code, the replacement of lost or destroyed certificates representing shares, but not other securities, was governed by the Uniform Stock Transfer Act,[7] once in force in all states but since replaced by the Code in all states, except Louisiana, and in the District of Columbia, and the Virgin Islands.

Corporate statutes are usually silent concerning the replacement of lost, destroyed, or stolen certificates.[8]

Bylaws often provide for replacement of certificates representing shares.[9]

Besides the Uniform Commercial Code, New York has two other statutory provisions applicable to the replacement of lost or destroyed certificates representing shares: (a) A provision that a court may order replacement of a lost or destroyed share certificate, requiring, as appears to the court, a bond sufficient to indemnify the corporation against any liability or expense which it may incur by reason of the original certificate's remaining outstanding, and limiting such liability of the corporation to the amount of the bond;[10] (b) A provision that the board of directors may require a bond sufficient to indemnify the corporation against any claim that may be made against it on account of the alleged loss or destruction or issuance of any new share certificate.[11]

Prior to due presentment for registration of transfer of a security in registered form, the issuer or any indenture trustee may treat the registered owner as the person exclusively entitled to exercise all the rights and powers of an owner.[12]

---

5. See Uniform Commercial Code § 8–104, discussed in section 158, n. 5 supra.

6. Uniform Commercal Code § 8–405(3).

7. 6 U.L.A. § 17 (1922) approved in 1909; Annot., 125 A.L.R. 997 (1940). Although New York had adopted the Uniform Stock Transfer Act, it had its own provision relating to lost or destroyed share certificates. Former McKinney's N.Y.Pers.Prop.Law, § 178; [1940] N.Y.L. Rev'n Comm'n Rep.1940 Legis. Doc.No. 65(B) 41–89. The New York procedure, being limited to corporations incorporated in New York or in states with consistent laws and limiting the corporation's liability to the amount of any posted bond, has been held inapplicable to a situation where the shares involved were issued by a corporation whose state of incorporation required an open-penalty bond and did not relieve the corporation from any liability. Matter of Hughes, 2 Misc.2d 122, 150 N.Y.S.2d 717 (Sup.Ct.1956). See also Davis v. Fraser, 307 N.Y. 433, 121 N.E.2d 406 (1954) (5–2) (refusal to order issuance of new land trust certificate ($1,280,000 value) to replace lost certificate and payment of declared dividends ($102,500), on ground claimant (successor to brokerage firm registered as owner 66 years before) failed to prove ownership). See also Mastellone v. Argo Oil Corp., 46 Del. 102, 82 A.2d 379 (Sup.Ct.1951) (three-year statute of limitations on claim of bona fide purchaser of old certificate held to run from time of issue of replacement certificate and not from time of demand for transfer).

8. E. g., ABA–ALI Model Bus.Corp.Act. But see McKinney's N.Y.Bus.Corp.Law, § 508(e)—see note 11 infra.

9. E. g., By-Laws, art. VI, § 1, Official Forms for Use Under the Model Business Corporation Act, Form No. 47 (ALI rev. 1953). See Komar v. General Elec. Co., 17 Misc.2d 24, 183 N.Y.S.2d 762 (Sup. Ct.1959) (bylaw requirement of bond as condition to issuance of replacement certificate held inapplicable where share certificate did not set forth such requirement and such requirement was adopted by executive committee of board of directors).

10. McKinney's N.Y.Gen.Bus.Law, § 394, following former McKinney's N.Y.Pers.Prop.Law, § 178, discussed in note 7 supra. Section 394 provides that in case of conflict between it and Uniform Commercial Code § 8–405, section 394 should control. Section 394 also provides that: "The issuance of a new certificate under an order of the court shall not relieve the corporation from liability in damages to a transferee of the original certificate in good faith and for value. The corporation shall not be liable to any such transferee in an amount in excess of the amount of the bond or the amount of the security required to be deposited."

11. McKinney's N.Y.Bus.Corp.Law, § 508(e).

12. Uniform Commercial Code § 8–207. The Uniform Stock Transfer Act § 3, had provided that nothing therein should "be construed as forbidding a corpo-

The replacement of lost, destroyed, or stolen share certificates is usually handled by the transfer agent, bureau, or clerk or, in the case of a small corporation, by the secretary.

MISSING SECURITY HOLDERS

179. Most states, under the common-law escheat doctrine, have sought to take over abandoned or unclaimed property, including shares, dividends, distributions, interest, principal, and properties due holders of securities.

After a series of vacillating rulings, the federal constitutional rule has emerged that in the case of a missing security holder, the state of the holder's last known address as shown by the issuer's records may escheat all securities and sums held for such holder—with supplementary rules. Under the Uniform Disposition of Unclaimed Property Act, the state of incorporation and of last known record address of the missing security holder may claim shares, dividends, other distributions, interest, principal or other sums due such security holder, with the latter state prevailing if the corporation is subject to such state's jurisdiction and such state has a reciprocal provision. The latest development is an interstate unclaimed property compact. Under some statutes, the state merely takes custody of the property until claimed by the rightful owner; under others, the state escheats or cuts off the claim of even the rightful owner who fails to claim the property during the prescribed period.

Corporations, as well as other business enterprises, often hold substantial properties belonging to persons whose present whereabouts are unknown. This is especially true of missing security holders to whom are entitled payments of principal, redemption proceeds, or interest on debt securities or dividends, other current and liquidating distributions, and redemption proceeds on shares.[1]

Increasingly, the states—as successors to the British Crown under the common-law doctrine of escheat—have tried to take over such property.[2] Unclaimed funds relating to corporate securities amount to untold hundreds of millions of dollars. For the states, escheat provides a source of ready and easily-collectible revenue.

Federal Constitutional Principles

Multiple claims by two or more states to escheat the same property resulted in increasing litigation within the original jurisdiction of the United States Supreme Court over controversies "between two or more States".[3]

After a series of strongly-pronounced but vacillating rulings,[4] the Supreme Court, in

1. Malabre, "Unclaimed Money; States Step Up Efforts To Grab Mounting Pile Of Abandoned Property; Banks, Firms and U.S. Hold $15 Billion in Tax Refunds, Dividends, Forgotten Items; Hunt for 2,000 Stockholders", 159 The Wall Street Journal, No. 15, 1, 18 (Jan. 22, 1962).

2. Note, "Origins and Development of Modern Escheat", 61 Colum.L.Rev. 1319 (1961). See Maryland Nat'l Bank v. Baltimore, No. A47433 (Cir.Ct. Baltimore City 1966) (city ordinance purporting to escheat unclaimed property held unconstitutional as usurpation of sovereign power belonging only to state).

3. U.S.Const. art. III, § 2, cl. 5.

4. Western Union Telegraph Co. v. Pennsylvania, 368 U.S. 71, 82 S.Ct. 199, 7 L.Ed.2d 139 (1961) (holding that corporation may resist escheat, on due process grounds, where there is risk of double recovery for lack of joinder of all interested states, and suggesting complete joinder by rival state claimants to achieve judgment binding on all by invoking Supreme Court's original jurisdiction); Standard Oil Co. v. New Jersey, 341 U.S. 428, 71 S.Ct. 822, 95 L. Ed. 1078 (1951) (upholding exercise of jurisdiction asserted over unclaimed intangible property by state of incorporation, and stating that corporation cannot be subjected to double recovery, since such multiple escheat would be barred by full faith and credit clause of the United States Constitution). Accord, Anderson Nat'l Bank v. Luckett, 321 U.S. 233, 64 S.Ct. 599, 88 L.Ed. 692, 151 A.L.R. 824 (1943); Security Savings Bank v. California, 263 U. S. 282, 44 S.Ct. 108, 68 L.Ed. 301, 31 A.L.R. 391 (1923). Presumably, a state where a foreign corporation has its principal place of business would also have had sufficient contact. See dissenting opinion

ration . . . To recognize the exclusive right of a person registered on its books as the owner of shares to receive dividends and to vote as such owner." See Lindner v. Utah Southern Oil Co., 3 Utah 2d 302, 283 P.2d 605 (1955) (3–2) (corporation held liable to bona fide purchaser of original certificate for having paid dividends in good faith to apparent transferee of replaced certificate from record owner). The Uniform Stock Transfer Act term "dividends" has been held not to include liquidating dividends. Cf. Bogardus v. Kentucky State Bank, 281 S.W.2d 904 (Ky.1955).

Texas v. New Jersey [5] in 1965, enunciated the rule that the right and power to escheat intangible property should be accorded to the state of the creditor's last known address as shown by the debtor's books and records. Where (a) there is no record of any address or (b) the state of last known address does not provide for escheat, the property is subject to escheat by the "State of corporate domicile", subject to the right of another state to recover the escheated property upon proof that the last-known address was within its borders.

Justifying the rule, Black, J., wrote: [6]

"Adoption of such a rule involves a factual issue simple and easy to resolve, and leaves no legal issue to be decided . . . [It] will tend to distribute escheats among the States in the proportion of the commercial activities of their residents. And by using a standard of last known address, rather than technical legal concepts of residence and domicile administration and application of escheat laws should be simplified."

of Douglas, J., Connecticut Mutual Life Ins. Co. v. Moore, 333 U.S. 541, 68 S.Ct. 682, 92 L.Ed. 863 (1948), reh. denied 334 U.S. 810, 68 S.Ct. 1014, 92 L. Ed. 1741 (1948) (held by foreign corporation of last known residence of missing owner).

5.   379 U.S. 674, 85 S.Ct. 626, 13 L.Ed.2d 596 (1965), 380 U.S. 518, 85 S.Ct. 1136, 14 L.Ed.2d 49 (1965) (final decree), motion denied 381 U.S. 931, 85 S.Ct. 1762, 14 L.Ed.2d 698 (1965), motion denied 381 U.S. 948, 85 S.Ct. 1795, 14 L.Ed.2d 723 (1965).

6.   379 U.S. 674, 681, 85 S.Ct. 626, 630, 13 L.Ed.2d 596, 601 (1965), 380 U.S. 518, 85 S.Ct. 1136, 14 L.Ed. 2d 49 (1965) (final decree), motion denied 381 U.S. 931, 85 S.Ct. 1762, 14 L.Ed.2d 698 (1965), motion denied 381 U.S. 948, 85 S.Ct. 1795, 14 L.Ed.2d 723 (1965). The Court considered and rejected the "most-significant-contacts" rule urged by Texas, the "domicile of the debtor" rule urged by New Jersey as the state of incorporation, and the "principal place of business" rule urged by Pennsylvania. Florida, possibly because it is a retirement haven, had suggested the "last-known-address-of-the-creditor-as-shown-by-the-debtor's-books-and-records" rule. Stewart, J., dissented in favor of the state of the debtor's incorporation, on the ground that "Adherence to settled precedent seems to me far better than giving the property to the State within which is located the one place where we know the creditor is not."

Extrapolating, to apply the rule to shares, the primary right to escheat is enjoyed by the state of the shareholder's address on the corporation's record of shareholders—presumably the last-known record address—but if such state has no escheat laws, then by the state of incorporation, subject to recovery from the latter state by the former state if and when its law made provision for escheat of such property.

State escheat statutes obviously must conform to such federal constitutional principles as well as to paramount law.[7]

State Escheat Statutes

Many states have enacted statutes authorizing the escheat of unclaimed or abandoned property, sometimes expressly enumerating shares, dividends, distributions, interest,

7.   Overton, "Constitutional Problems and Policy Decisions in Drafting an Escheat Statute for Tennessee", 34 Tenn.L.Rev. 173 (1967); Lynch, "Interstate Conflicts Over the Escheat of Intangibles", 40 L.A. B.Bull. 414 (1965); Sentell, "Escheat, Unclaimed Property and the Supreme Court", 17 W.Res.L.Rev. 50 (1965); Lake, "Escheat, Federalism and State Boundaries", 24 Ohio St.L.J. 322 (1963); Lane, "Western Union v. Pennsylvania or Whose Mink was Gored?", 18 Bus.Law. 311 (1962); Ely, "Escheats: Perils and Precautions," 15 Bus.Law. 791 (1960); McBride, "Unclaimed Dividends, Escheat Statutes and the Corporation Lawyer", 14 Bus.Law. 1062 (1959); "Escheat", 23 Corp.J. 203 (1962); Comment, "Escheat of Corporate Intangibles: Will the State of the Stockholder's Last Known Address Be Able to Enforce Its Rights?", 41 Notre Dame Law. 559 (1966); Comment, "Escheat—Abandoned Property—Full Faith and Credit As a Bar to Multiple Escheat of Intangibles", 59 Mich.L.Rev. 756 (1961); Note, "Personal Property: Oklahoma's New Unclaimed Property Law", 21 Okla.L.Rev. 96 (1968); Note, "Disposition of Unclaimed Dividends and Shares—Distributions from Interstate Business Associations", 17 Vand.L.Rev. 1354 (1964); Note, "Escheat of Corporate Dividends", 65 Harv.L.Rev. 1408 (1952); Note, "Escheat of Corporate Stocks and Dividends", 27 Ind.L.J. 113 (1951); Note, "Unclaimed Dividends and Shares of Stock", 46 Ill.L. Rev. 82 (1951); Note, "The Lost Shareholder", 62 Harv.L.Rev. 295 (1948); Annot., 7 L.Ed.2d 871 (1962). See in the Matter of Standard Gas & Electric Co., 301 F.Supp. 1382 (D.Del.1969) (upholding plan of liquidation for distribution of unclaimed shares to public utility company's remaining shareholders as "fair and equitable" and not barred by state escheat laws, over which federal law was paramount).

principal and other properties due holders of securities.[8]

Such statutes, called escheat laws, abandoned property laws, or unclaimed property laws, usually provide for (a) the escheat to the state of such property after having remained unclaimed for a specified time; (b) the filing of reports by the corporation with the state; (c) the state's giving notice of escheat to the corporation and publishing the names of holders of securities being escheated; (d) the release of the corporation from liability to the holders of securities escheated; (e) the right of the state to the escheat-

ed property, subject only to the real owner's interest.

Such statutes are of two types: (a) those under which the state merely takes custody of the property until claimed by the rightful owner,[9] and (b) those under which the state escheats or cuts off the claim of even the rightful owner who fails to claim the property during the prescribed period.[10]

Uniform Disposition of Unclaimed Property Act

Under the Uniform Disposition of Unclaimed Property Act, custodial in nature, adopted in a growing number of jurisdictions,[11] both the state of incorporation and shares, dividends, other distributions, interest, principal, and other sums due such security holder, with the latter state prevailing if the corporation is subject to such state's jurisdiction and such state has a reciprocal provision.[12] Such reciprocal provision was included to preclude the "race of diligence" possible under the earlier United States Supreme Court holdings.[13]

Interstate Unclaimed Property Compact

An unclaimed property compact has been drafted and recommended for enactment by the states by the Council of State

8. 2 CCH Corp. Law Guide ¶6630; 1 P-H Corp. Rep. ¶ 2179; Comment, "A Survey of State Abandoned or Unclaimed Property Statutes", 9 St. Louis L.Rev. 85 (1964). The Model Business Corporation Act, unlike most other corporate statutes, deals with missing shareholders but only with respect to their liquidation distributions. ABA–ALI Model Bus.Corp.Act § 97. State v. Amsted Industries, 48 N.J. 544, 226 A.2d 715 (1967) (holding state of incorporation had no power to escheat property of persons notwithstanding their last-known addresses were in states where corporation was not amenable to process, stating that state of last-known address with escheat statute could assert its claim against corporation in courts of state of incorporation). Accord, Central Light & Power Co. v. Texas, 410 S. W.2d 18 (Tex.Civ.App.1966), cert. denied 389 U.S. 933, 88 S.Ct. 297, 19 L.Ed.2d 286 (1967); Texas v. Texas Osage Royalty Pool, Inc., 394 S.W.2d 241 (Tex.Civ.App.1965) (holding state can escheat unclaimed shares even though shares which were to be issued in exchange for rights in prior trust had never been issued because owners never made such exchange); Occidental Life Ins. Co. v. Cranston, 237 Cal.App.2d 482, 47 Cal.Rptr. 37 (1965) (permitting corporation to recover unclaimed property erroneously deposited with state where statute of limitations had lapsed on effective date of state escheat statute); Tex.Op.Att'y Gen.No. C–475, July 30, 1965 (ruling property not subject to escheat by state because of federal law or expiration of states own statute of limitations nevertheless subject to state's reporting requirements); Ore.Op.Att'y Gen. No. 5982, June 3, 1965 (ruling that qualified foreign corporation did not have to turn over unclaimed property of persons whose last-known addresses were out of state, even though transactions were within state; that reports were required notwithstanding expiration of statute of limitations, and that turning over to state of its pro rata share of corporation's nationwide unclaimed property was not proper); Mo.Op.Att'y Gen.No. 203, Nov. 29, 1967 (holding assets of liquidated corporation belonging to shareholder missing for 25 years, whose last-known address was out of state, to escheat to state under common law).

9. E. g., Ky.Rev.Stat. §§ 393.010 et seq. (1962); McKinney's N.Y.Aband.Prop.Law, §§ 500 et seq.

10. E. g., Mass.Ann.Laws ch. 200A, § 5 (Supp.1968) (after 14 years).

11. 9A U.L.A. 412 (1965); approved 1954; revised 1966; adopted in Arizona, California, Florida, Idaho, Illinois, Indiana, Iowa, Maryland, Minnesota, Montana, New Mexico, Nebraska, Oklahoma, Oregon, Utah, Virginia, Washington, West Virginia. Annot., 98 A.L.R.2d 304 (1964).

12. Uniform Disposition of Unclaimed Property Act §§ 5, 10. Although a dual jurisdictional test is set up in section 5, the reciprocity clause of section 10 prevents multiple liability. See State of California v. State Tax Commission, 55 Wash.2d 155, 346 P.2d 1006 (1959) (6–3).

13. Quaere, as to whether the Uniform Disposition of Unclaimed Property Act, even as revised in 1966, is entirely consistent with the constitutional principles enunciated by the United States Supreme Court in Texas v. New Jersey, note 5 supra.

Governments.[14] It provides for the taking of unclaimed intangible personal property: (a) where the holder of such property is subject to the jurisdiction of only one state, by such state only; (b) otherwise, by the state of last known address of the person entitled to such property (presumptively as shown by the records of the holder); or (c) if the person entitled to such property is unknown, or has no last known address or the laws of the state of last known address do not subject such property to taking, by the state (or states equally in case of multiple incorporation) of incorporation of the corporate holder.

The interstate unclaimed property compact, of course, follows the constitutional principles promulgated by the United States Supreme Court. The compact also provided refinements in such principles, requires the signatory states to exchange information concerning escheatable property, and preserves the *status quo ante* Texas v. New Jersey with respect to property escheated or received before that decision.

---

14. To date the compact has been signed only by New Jersey, to become effective upon adherence by another state. 32 N.J.Stat.Ann. ch. 28 (Supp.1969). The Unclaimed Property Compact §§ 32:28–1 to 32:28–10 (Supp.1969).

CHAPTER 9

CORPORATE MANAGEMENT STRUCTURE

A. INTRODUCTION

A. INTRODUCTION

CORPORATE MANAGEMENT STRUCTURE—IN GENERAL

180. The scope of corporate powers and the consequences of acting beyond such powers ("ultra vires"); the distribution of management functions respecting such powers among various corporate organs and personnel—incorporators, shareholders, board of directors, and officers; the duties of corporate management; and management compensation are the subjects of this chapter.

A corporation must be organized and managed by natural persons. Their qualifications, functions, and procedures are often prescribed by a hierarchy of constitutions, statutes, and administrative rules and regulations,[1] and a substatutory, intracorporate hierarchy of provisions, in the form of articles of incorporation, bylaws, shareholder resolutions, and board of directors resolutions,[2] as well as "shareholder agreements",[3] voting trust agreements,[4] indentures and loan agreements,[5] proxies,[6] etc. This chain of powers and authority to the corporation and the distribution of functions under it among various corporate organs and personnel will be treated in this chapter.

The scope of corporate powers and the consequences of acting beyond such powers *("ultra vires")* will be first discussed.[7]

Various functions in the organization and management of corporations are performed by: (a) promoters, (b) incorporators, (c) subscribers, (d) shareholders, (e) directors, (f) officers, (g) other employees and agents, and occasionally (h) creditors. Often the same person will function in two or more such capacities. Directors and officers are collectively called "management".

The functions, rights, and liabilities of *promoters*, both before and after incorporation, have been discussed in Chapter 5. *Incorporators*, and subscribers who subscribe as incorporators, have been mentioned[8] but will receive further treatment.[9] *Subscribers* have already been discussed;[10] to the extent that subscribers are shareholders, their management functions are the same as shareholders and will be covered by the sections on *shareholders*.[11] Such management functions as creditors have on rare occasion will be mentioned during the discussion of shareholders. *Directors*[12] and *officers*[13] are then discussed seriatim. Concluding the survey of corporate management structure will be sections on the duties of management[14] and management compensation.[15]

8. See section 131 supra.

9. See section 185 infra.

10. See sections 115, 131, 169 supra.

11. See sections 186–202 infra.

12. See sections 203–218 infra.

13. See sections 219–230 infra.

14. See sections 231–242 infra.

15. See sections 243–256 infra. See generally H. Stieglitz & C. Wilkerson, Corporate Organization Structures (National Industrial Conference Board 1968).

1. See sections 13, 14 supra.

2. See section 15 supra.

3. See sections 198, 213, 267, 275, 287 infra.

4. See section 197 infra.

5. See section 156 supra.

6. See sections 196, 297 infra.

7. See sections 181–184 infra.

B. PURPOSES (OR OBJECTS) AND POWERS

PURPOSES (OR OBJECTS)

181. Business corporations usually may be formed for any lawful business purposes, with some exceptions, but are required to state their purposes in the articles of incorporation. Such purposes (or objects) clauses define the nature of the authorized business, for the protection of shareholders, management, and third parties. The stated purposes usually limit the corporate powers, which exist to effectuate such purposes.

Statutes usually permit incorporation for any lawful business purposes, with some exceptions,[1] but usually require that the articles of incorporation set forth the purposes (or objects) of the corporation involved.[2]

The purposes (or objects) clauses of the articles of incorporation define the authorized business, for the better protection of shareholders, management, and third parties. The stated purposes usually limit the powers, which are expressed in statute or the articles of incorporation or implied, and which exist to effectuate the purposes/objects.[3]

EXPRESS POWERS

182. Express corporate powers exist pursuant to statute or the articles of incorpora-

tion. Some statutes expressly provide that it is not necessary to set forth in the articles of incorporation the corporate powers enumerated in the statute. In practice, articles of incorporation often contain complicated powers clauses. Powers exist to effectuate corporate purposes and are usually limited by them.

Corporate powers, generally speaking, may be (a) statutory, (b) expressed in the articles of incorporation, or (c) implied.

Statutory Powers

Frequently, statutes grant expressly to corporations, as such, various powers.[1]

The Model Business Corporation Act provides that each corporation shall have power:

(a) To have perpetual succession by its corporate name unless a limited period of duration is stated in its articles of incorporation;[2]

(b) To sue and be sued, complain and defend, in its corporate name;[3]

(c) To have a corporate seal which may be altered at pleasure, and to use the same by causing it, or a facsimile thereof, to be impressed or affixed or in any other manner reproduced;[4]

(d) To purchase, take, receive, lease, or otherwise acquire, own, hold, improve, use and otherwise deal in and with,

[§ 181]

1. See section 121 supra.

2. See section 121 supra. A growing number of statutes no longer require the articles of incorporation to set forth the corporate purposes, in which case the corporation may pursue all purposes lawful for business corporations, but permit corporations with limited purposes to be formed by designating such purposes in the articles of incorporation. E. g., 1969 Model Act revision, Delaware, Iowa, Maine, Nevada, New Jersey, Oregon, Pennsylvania, Wisconsin.

3. Some statutory enumerations of powers are not so qualified. E. g., ABA–ALI Model Bus.Corp.Act § 4. Implied powers. by definition, must be in furtherance of the corporate purposes. Sometimes articles of incorporation clauses which are in the nature of powers clauses are expressly stated to be purposes clauses in order to avoid any limiting construction. See section 122 supra.

[§ 182]

1. See, e. g., ABA–ALI Model Bus.Corp.Act §§ 4(a)–(r), 4A, 5; Del.Gen.Corp.Law, §§ 121, 122(1)–(16) (1967); McKinney's N.Y.Bus.Corp.Law, § 202(a) (1)–(16); Blackwell, "General Provisions and Corporate Purposes and Powers", 15 S.C.L.Rev. 444 (1963).

2. As for corporate duration, see section 120 supra; as for corporate name, see section 117, n. 3 and section 119 supra.

3. As for capacity to sue and to be sued, see section 352 infra.

4. As for effect of corporate seal, see section 228 infra.

real or personal property, or any interest therein, wherever situated; [5]

(e) To sell, convey, mortgage, pledge, lease, exchange, transfer and otherwise dispose of all or any part of its property and assets; [6]

(f) To lend money to its employees other than its officers and directors, and otherwise assist its employees, officers and directors; [7]

(g) To purchase, take, receive, subscribe for, or otherwise acquire, own, hold, vote, use, employ, sell, mortgage, lend, pledge, or otherwise dispose of, and otherwise use and deal in and with, shares or other interests in, or obligations of, other domestic or foreign corporations,[8] associations, partnerships [9] or individuals, or direct or indirect obligations of the United States or of any other government, state, territory, governmental district or municipality or of any instrumentality thereof;

(h) To make contracts and guarantees [10] and incur liabilities, borrow money at such rates of interest as the corpora-

tion may determine, issue its notes, bonds, and other obligations, and secure any of its obligations by mortgage or pledge of all or any of its property, franchises and income; [11]

(i) To lend money for its corporate purposes, invest and reinvest its funds, and take and hold real and personal property as security for the payment of funds so loaned or invested;

(j) To conduct its business, carry on its operations, and have officers and exercise its granted powers in any state, territory, district, or possession of the United States, or in any foreign country; [12]

(k) To elect or appoint officers and agents of the corporation, and define their duties [13] and fix their compensation; [14]

(l) To make and alter bylaws, not inconsistent with its articles of incorporation or with the laws of the state, for the administration and regulation of the affairs of the corporation; [15]

(m) To make donations for the public welfare or for charitable, scientific or educational purposes; and in time of war to make donations in aid of war activities; [16]

(n) In time of war to transact any lawful business in aid of the United States in the prosecution of the war; [17]

---

5. As for corporate power to take and hold property, see section 183 infra; Comment, "Restrictions Upon Corporate Ownership of Real Property", 13 Mercer L.Rev. 410 (1962).

6. As for sale, lease, exchange, or other disposition of corporate assets, see section 341 infra.

7. Broadened by 1969 Model Act revision. As for corporate power to lend corporate funds, see section 183 infra.

8. As for corporate power to acquire and hold shares and other securities issued by other corporations, see section 183 infra. See also Jamieson v. Chicago Title & Trust Co., 33 Ill.App.2d 477, 179 N.E.2d 844 (1962), appeal dismissed, cert. denied 371 U.S. 232, 83 S.Ct. 325, 9 L.Ed.2d 494 (1963), reh. denied 372 U.S. 925, 83 S.Ct. 717, 9 L.Ed.2d 731 (1963) (holding 1933 Illinois statute empowering Illinois corporations to deal in shares of other domestic and foreign corporations applied to Illinois corporation incorporated prior to 1933).

9. As for corporate power to be a joint venturer or partner, see section 183 infra.

10. As for corporate power to guaranty, see sections 183, 343 infra.

11. As for corporate power to borrow money, issue obligations, and mortgage property, see sections 155–170 supra and sections 183, 342 infra.

12. See sections 96–101, 136–137 supra.

13. See sections 219–230 infra.

14. See sections 243–256 infra.

15. See section 133 supra.

16. As for corporate power to contribute to charity, see section 183 infra.

17. New York includes a similar provision in its purposes, rather than general powers, section. McKinney's N.Y.Bus.Corp.Law, § 201(b). The 1969 Model Act revision eliminates the reference to "war" and broadly authorizes "any corporate business which the board of directors shall find will be in aid of governmental authority." Thus, efforts

(o) To indemnify any director or officer or former director or officer of the corporation, or any person who may have served at its request as a director or officer of another corporation in which it owns shares of capital stock or of which it is a creditor, against expenses actually and reasonably incurred by him in connection with the defense of any action, suit or proceeding, civil or criminal, in which he is made a party by reason of being or having been such director or officer, except in relation to matters as to which he shall be adjudged in such action, suit or proceeding to be liable for negligence or misconduct in the performance of duty to the corporation; and to make any other indemnification that shall be authorized by the articles of incorporation or by any bylaw or resolution adopted by the shareholders after notice; [18]

(p) To pay pensions and establish pension plans, pension trusts, profit-sharing plans, stock bonus plans, stock option plans and other incentive plans for any or all of its directors, officers and employees; [19]

(q) To cease its corporate activities and surrender its corporate franchise; [20] and

(r) To have and exercise all powers necessary or convenient to effect any or all of the purposes for which the corporation is organized.[21]

The Model Business Corporation Act contains numerous other sections granting powers (although not always stated in terms of "power").[22]

The express statutory powers might or might not otherwise be implied as normal incidents of corporateness.[23] Some statutes also expressly provide that it is not necessary to set forth in the articles of incorporation the corporate powers enumerated in the statute.[24]

Articles of Incorporation Powers Clauses

In practice, powers are often confirmed, spelled out, limited, or enlarged in the articles of incorporation.[25] Of course, there are limitations on the permissible powers.[26]

---

dealing with the elimination of poverty, disease, and civil strife would be within the corporate powers.

18. Replaced by more comprehensive indemnification and insurance provision in 1969 Model Act revision. As for corporate indemnification of, or insurance for, litigation expenses of directors, officers, and other corporate personnel in corporate litigation (including derivative actions), see sections 379, 380 infra. The New York general powers provision reads: ". . . to indemnify corporate personnel." McKinney's N.Y.Bus.Corp.Law, § 202(a) (10). However, very detailed, exclusive provisions deal with indemnification of directors and officers, as distinguished from other corporate personnel. Id. §§ 721–726, 1319(a) (4), 1320.

19. See sections 243–256 infra.

20. Eliminated as superfluous by 1969 Model Act revision. See section 144 supra and sections 348, 381, 382 infra.

21. As for implied powers, see section 183 infra.

22. ABA–ALI Model Bus.Corp.Act § 4A (indemnification of officers, directors, employees and agents; insurance); § 5 (right of corporation to acquire and dispose of its own shares); § 14 (authorized shares ("power to create and issue")); [optional] § 18A (stock rights and options ("may create and issue")); § 22 (issuance of fractional shares or scrip ("may . . . issue")); § 25 (bylaws ("power")); [optional] § 25A (bylaws and other powers in emergency ("may adopt")); § 40 (dividends ("may declare and . . . pay dividends")); § 41 (distributions from capital surplus ("may . . . distribute")); § 53 (right to amend articles of incorporation); § 65 (procedure for merger ("may merge")); § 66 (procedure for consolidation ("may consolidate")); § 71 (sale of assets in regular course of business and mortgage or pledge of assets ("may be made")); § 72 (sale of assets other than in regular course of business ("may be made")); § 75 (voluntary dissolution by incorporators ("may be voluntarily dissolved")); § 76 (voluntary dissolution by consent of shareholders ("may be voluntarily dissolved")); § 77 (voluntary dissolution by act of corporation ("may be dissolved")).

23. See section 79 supra.

24. See, e. g., ABA–ALI Model Bus.Corp.Act § 48. See section 122 supra.

25. See section 122 supra.

26. See, e. g., ABA–ALI Model Bus.Corp.Act § 48(i); Del.Gen.Corp.Law, § 121(b) (1967); McKinney's N. Y.Bus.Corp.Law, § 202(a).

Powers, as previously mentioned, are usually limited by the corporate purposes, since they exist in theory to effectuate such purposes.[27]

Implied Powers

Besides express powers pursuant to statute or the articles of incorporation, corporations enjoy various implied powers.[28]

IMPLIED POWERS

183. Corporations generally have implied powers to do all things reasonably necessary to enable them to carry out their purposes, including implied powers (a) To take and hold property; (b) To borrow money, issue obligations, mortgage property, and make guaranties; (c) To loan corporate funds; (d) To acquire and hold shares and other securities or other corporations; (e) To reacquire its own shares; (f) To contribute to charity; (g) To be a joint venturer but not a partner. Such implied powers are often confirmed or elaborated by statute or the articles of incorporation.

To Take and Hold Property

Absent statutory limitations or provisions in the articles of incorporation to the contrary, corporations generally have implied powers to do all things reasonably necessary to enable them to carry out their purposes (or objects).[1]

A corporation's implied power to take and hold property, real and personal, legal or equitable, by grant, gift, purchase, devise, or bequest is generally recognized today.[2]

Statutes often confirm such power.[3]

Older statutes occasionally placed some limitations upon such power.[4] Obviously, a corporation may not take property beyond its capacity to do so.[5]

A corporation may, of course, sell, lease, or exchange its property in the regular course of business for cash or credit, but a sale, lease or exchange of all or substantially all of its property not in the regular course of business often requires shareholder

---

27. See section 181, n. 3 supra. Some statutes expressly limit the powers to furthering the corporate purposes; others do not. Still other statutes contain two listings of powers, one expressly limited to corporate purposes, and the other not so limited. McKinney's N.Y.Bus.Corp.Law, § 202 (General Powers), contains the following introductory paragraph: "(a) Each corporation, subject to any limitations provided in this chapter or any other statute of this state or its certificate of incorporation, shall have power in furtherance of its corporate purposes: . . ." See Ind.Gen.Corp.Act § 25–202 (1967) (General powers), which provides: "(a) Each corporation shall have the capacity to act possessed by natural persons, but shall have authority to perform only such acts as are necessary, convenient or expedient to accomplish the purposes for which it is formed and such as are not repugnant to law. . . ." The Ghana Companies Code confers on companies, "for the furtherance of its objects and of any business carried on by it and authorized in its Regulations, all the powers of a natural person of full capacity." Ghana Companies Code § 24 (1963).

28. See section 183 infra.

1. See Sutton's Hospital, 10 Coke 23a, 77 Eng.Rep. 960 (K.B. 1612); Jacksonville M. P. Ry. & Nav. Co. v. Hooper, 160 U.S. 514, 16 S.Ct. 379, 40 L.Ed. 515 (1896). For confirming statutory provisions, see ABA–ALI Model Bus.Corp.Act § 4(r); Del.Gen. Corp.Law § 121 (1967); McKinney's N.Y.Bus.Corp. Law, § 202(a) (16). See also John B. Waldbillig, Inc. v. Gottfried, 16 N.Y.2d 773, 262 N.Y.S.2d 498, 209 N.E.2d 818 (1965) (upholding practice of engineering by corporation with building, construction, and contracting powers).

2. R. Stevens, Handbook on the Law of Private Corporations § 49 (2d ed. 1949); Case v. Kelly, 133 U.S. 21, 10 S.Ct. 216, 33 L.Ed. 513 (1890) (corporation held unable to acquire real property not necessary to its business, even by donation, absent authorization in charter); Matter of DeForest, 147 Misc. 82, 263 N.Y.S. 135 (Sur.Ct.1933) (corporation held, absent express power, not eligible to be beneficiary of testamentary trust). But see Alcoma Corp. v. Ackerman, 26 Misc.2d 678, 207 N.Y.S.2d 137 (Sup.Ct. 1960).

3. See section 182, n. 5 supra.

4. E. g., former McKinney's N.Y.Deced.Est.Law, § 12 (prohibiting devise of real property to corporation unless expressly authorized to take by devise in articles of incorporation or statute). Cf. McKinney's N.Y. EPTL, § 3–1.3(a) (providing testamentary disposition of property may be made to any person having capacity to acquire and hold such property). Various state constitutional and federal and state statutory provisions sometimes limit corporations in holding property, especially rural real property. See section 14, n. 6 supra. See also 30 U.S.C.A. § 381; 48 U.S.C.A. §§ 302a, 1501.

5. See Matter of McGraw, 111 N.Y. 66, 19 N.E. 233 (1888), aff'd sub nom. Cornell University v. Fiske, 136 U.S. 152, 10 S.Ct. 775, 34 L.Ed. 427 (1889).

approval.[6] Transfers of corporate property to shareholders, directors, and officers, except for full cash consideration, when the corporation is in default on any obligation, or preferential transfers to creditors when the corporation is insolvent or its insolvency is imminent, are barred by some statutes.[7]

To Borrow Money, Issue Obligations, Mortgage Property, and Make Guaranties

The implied power to borrow money, issue obligations, and mortgage property is often confirmed and elaborated by statute,[8] which might require shareholder approval for the making of corporate mortgages [9] or guaranties.[10]

To Loan Corporate Funds

A corporation usually has implied power to loan idle funds with interest, or to loan funds or extend credit to customers or another corporation in which it owns shares or with which it has contractual relations, but no implied power to extend credit, make a loan, or pledge its assets as accommodation for others.[11]

Statutes often mention such power.[12]

6. See section 341 infra.

7. See, e. g., Uniform Fraudulent Conveyance Act. State debtor-creditor laws and federal bankruptcy provisions are also relevant.

8. See section 182, n. 11 supra.

9. See section 342 infra.

10. In New York, the general power to "give guarantees" is qualified by the limitation that such guarantees be in furtherance of the corporate purposes; guarantees not in furtherance of the corporate purposes and any mortgage, pledge, or creation of a security interest securing the same, require authorization by the vote of the holders of two-thirds of all outstanding shares entitled to vote thereon. McKinney's N.Y.Bus.Corp.Law, §§ 202(a) (7), 908. See section 343 infra.

11. R. Stevens, Handbook on the Law of Private Corporations § 55 (2d ed. 1949); Sun Oil Co. v. Redd Auto Sales, Inc., 339 Mass. 384, 159 N.E.2d 111 (1959); Wasserman v. National Gypsum Co., 335 Mass. 240, 139 N.E.2d 410 (1957); Ketcham v. Mississippi Outdoor Displays, Inc., 203 Miss. 52, 33 So.2d 300 (1948).

12. See section 182, n. 10 supra.

Statutes sometimes expressly prohibit a nonbanking corporation from exercising banking powers; [13] or prohibit corporations from making loans to directors or officers,[14]

13. See, e. g., former McKinney's N.Y.Bank.Law § 131 (prohibiting nonbanking corporations from engaging in banking business, including "making of discounts", and providing that any notes for the payment of money loaned or discounted contrary to such provisions shall be "void"); Meserole Securities Co. v. Cosman, 253 N.Y. 130, 170 N.E. 519 (1930). In Miller v. Discount Factors, Inc., 1 N.Y. 2d 275, 152 N.Y.S.2d 273, 135 N.E.2d 33, (1956) (5–2), the term "discount" was construed to include any charge for a loan deducted in advance, whether called interest, compensation, bonus, or premium, the 6% notes were found void, and the indorser released. The majority said that any other result would have been inconsistent with the usury statutes which limit banks of discount to six percent charges. See Kupfer, "The Impacts of Miller v. Discount Factors, Inc.", 12 Record of N.Y.C.B.A. 30 (Jan.1957); Kripke, "Illegal 'Discounts' by Non-Banking Corporations in New York", 56 Colum.L. Rev. 1183 (1956). Even if the notes be invalid, a mortgage securing them would not be thereby invalidated. Amherst Factors, Inc. v. Kochenburger, 4 N.Y.2d 203, 173 N.Y.S.2d 570, 149 N.E.2d 863 (1958); County Industrial Corp. v. Francia, 4 N.Y.2d 988, 177 N.Y.S.2d 507, 152 N.E.2d 530, (1958); New York Credit Men's Adjustment Bureau, Inc. v. Samuel Breiter & Co., 253 F.2d 675 (2d Cir.1958). In 1958, the New York statutory provisions were amended to exclude the provision that discounted notes were void and to include a provision that the purchase or other acquisition on original issue or subsequent transfer for less than the principal amount thereof or otherwise at a discount of any evidences of indebtedness or other obligations for the payment of money shall not by reason of such discount be or be deemed to be a violation of such sections. McKinney's N.Y.Bank.Law, § 131(1); Sigman v. Claar Bros., 291 F.2d 820 (2d Cir.1961); Bishop, "More on 'Discounts' under New York's Banking Law: Antiquarian Research Inspired by Contemporary Legislation", 68 Yale L.J. 269 (1958). See also First Thrift & Loan Ass'n v. State, 62 N.M. 61, 304 P.2d 582 (1956); Greenfield & Kelley, "New Kind of Banking: The Small Business Investment Company", 22 Shingle 159 (1959).

14. Cf. ABA–ALI Model Bus.Corp.Act §§ 4(f), 42. The 1969 Model Act revision removes the prohibition in both sections and adds a new definitional provision (§ 2(o)) to include officers as part of the definition of employees. New York prohibits loans to directors except with disinterested majority shareholder approval, stating that such prohibited loans are not for such reason void and unenforceable but constitute a violation of the duty to the corporation by the directors approving such loans. McKinney's N.Y.Bus.Corp.Law, §§ 714, 719(a) (4), 1317(a) (1), 1320. See also M. Feuer, Personal Liabilities of Corporate Officers and Directors ch. 15 (1961).

loans secured by its own shares,[15] or loans to shareholders.[16]

To Acquire and Hold Shares and Other Securities of Other Corporations

The general rule once was that a corporation could not purchase shares of another corporation.[17] If the purposes (or objects) of the two corporations were different, the corporation holding the shares became involved in a different business; if the purposes (or objects) were similar, the combination might tend toward monopoly. Various exceptions, however, developed.[18]

Modern corporation statutes recognize the power of a corporation, subject to limitations, to acquire and hold shares (and other securities) of other corporations and other business enterprises, at least where such acquisition is incidental to the corporation's business.[19]

This power to acquire shares in another corporation makes possible parent-subsidiary relationships[20] and holding companies[21] with their attendant problems. Share acquisitions or holdings might, of course, be unlawful under antitrust legislation[22] or the Federal Public Utility Holding Company Act of 1935.[23]

To Reacquire Its Own Shares

While at one time it was questionable whether or not a corporation had implied power to purchase or otherwise reacquire its own shares,[24] modern statutes expressly empower corporations to do so.[25]

Probably the power to do so exists today apart from statute and any provision in the articles of incorporation. The latter will often spell out such power. Generally, a corporation may not purchase (or redeem, if the shares are redeemable[26]) its shares except out of surplus. Statutes often express this limitation,[27] or limit purchases to earned surplus,[28] but provide for various exceptions. Purchases while the corporation is insolvent or purchases which would render

15. ABA–ALI Model Bus.Corp.Act § 42, eliminated in 1969 Model Act revision. Such prohibition appeared anomalous, since loans to shareholders unsecured by shares were not prohibited. See Annot., 80 A.L.R. 1338 (1932).

16. E. g., Mississippi, Missouri, Montana, New Hampshire.

17. Robotham v. Prudential Ins. Co., 64 N.J.Eq. 673, 53 A. 842 (1903).

18. R. Stevens, Handbook on the Law of Private Corporations § 59 (2d ed. 1949).

19. See Jamieson v. Chicago Title & Trust Co., 33 Ill. App.2d 477, 179 N.E.2d 844 (1962), appeal dismissed, cert. denied 371 U.S. 232, 83 S.Ct. 325, 9 L.Ed.2d 494 (1963), reh. denied 372 U.S. 925, 83 S.Ct. 717, 9 L. Ed.2d 731 (1963) (upholding application of broadened statutory power to preexisting corporations). See also section 182, n. 8 supra; Freedland, "History of Holding Company Legislation in New York State: Some Doubts as to the 'New Jersey First' Tradition", 24 Fordham L.Rev. 369 (1955). Articles of incorporation, in an era of conglomerates, are being amended to empower a corporation to acquire shares in another corporation irrespective of whether the powers or business of any such other corporation be in whole or in part similar or dissimilar to the powers or business of the corporation.

20. See section 148 supra. See also R. Stevens, Handbook on the Law of Private Corporations § 17 (2d ed. 1949).

21. H. Ballantine, Ballantine on Corporations § 182 (rev. ed. 1946).

22. See section 311 infra.

23. See section 299 infra.

24. R. Stevens, Handbook on the Law of Private Corporations § 60 (2d ed. 1949); Loomis, "Purchase by a Corporation of its Own Securities", 22 Record of N.Y.C.B.A. 275 (1967), Nemmers, "The Power of a Corporation to Purchase Its Own Stock", 1942 Wis.L.Rev. 161. See Bookman v. R. J. Reynolds Tobacco Co., 138 N.J.Eq. 312, 48 A.2d 646 (1946); Pace v. Pace Bros. Co., 91 Utah 132, 59 P.2d 1 (1936); Grasselli Chemical Co. v. Aetna Explosives Co., 258 F. 66 (S.D.N.Y.1918); Richards v. Wiener Co., 207 N.Y. 59, 100 N.E. 592 (1912).

25. ABA–ALI Model Bus.Corp.Act § 5; Del.Gen. Corp.Law, § 160 (1967); McKinney's N.Y.Bus.Corp. Law, §§ 202(a) (14), 513.

26. See sections 124, 160 supra.

27. See, e. g., Del.Gen.Corp.Law, § 160 (1967); McKinney's N.Y.Bus.Corp.Law, § 513.

28. See, e. g., ABA–ALI Model Bus.Corp.Act § 5.

the corporation insolvent usually are expressly prohibited.[29]

To Contribute to Charity

Since the primary purpose of a business corporation has traditionally been to make profits, the early cases held that a corporation had no implied power to contribute generally to charity.[30]

Under the common-law "corporate benefit" rule, the courts found implied power to contribute in cases where there was some resulting corporate benefit, e. g., employee benefits (notwithstanding incidental benefits to others), cultivating good will and promoting business, aid to education when there was some tie-in such as the educational institution's training students who might provide a pool of personnel for the corporation.[31]

Modern statutes have been enacted expressly empowering corporations to make donations for the public welfare or for charitable, scientific, or educational purposes.[32]

The leading case of A. P. Smith Mfg. Co. v. Barlow [33] involved a charitable gift by a New Jersey manufacturing corporation to Princeton University. The court held the gift to be *intra vires* despite lack of authorization in the articles of incorporation, on the alternative bases of (a) a "broad concept" of public policy,[34] thus going beyond the "corporate benefit" rule, (b) the "corporate benefit" rule, and (c) the New Jersey statute, enacted after the formation of the corporation, authorizing charitable contributions.[35]

Statutes often prohibit political contributions by corporations.[36]

---

29. See sections 335–337 infra.

30. R. Stevens, Handbook on the Law of Private Corporations § 52–54 (2d ed. 1949); Dodge v. Ford Motor Co., 204 Mich. 459, 170 N.W. 668, 3 A.L.R. 413 (1919); Annot., 3 A.L.R. 443 (1919).

31. See Note, 39 Cornell L.Q. 122 (1953). For a case, in a jurisdiction without a charitable contribution statute, upholding a corporation's implied power to contribute to a foundation it had set up for charitable purposes, see Union Pacific R. R. v. Trustees, Inc., 8 Utah 2d 101, 329 P.2d 398 (1958).

32. See, e. g., ABA–ALI Model Bus.Corp.Act § 4(m); McKinney's N.Y.Bus.Corp.Law, § 202(a) (12) ("To make donations, irrespective of corporate benefit, for the public welfare or for community fund, hospital, charitable, educational, scientific, civic or similar purposes, and in time of war or other national emergency in aid thereof);" 12 U.S.C.A. § 24 (national banks); J. Holder, Corporate Support Programs to Institutions of Higher Learning (1967); J. Watson, Company Contributions in Canada (1963); R. Eells, Corporation Giving in a Free Society (1956); F. Andrews, Corporate Giving (1952); Garrett, "Corporate Donations", 22 Bus. Law. 297 (1967); Kelso, "Corporate Benevolences or Welfare Distribution?", 15 Bus.Law. 259 (1960); Gibson, "Corporate Contributions to Charity and Enabling Legislation", 14 Bus.Law. 434 (1959); Garrett, "Corporate Contributions", 8 Bus.Law. 22 (Jan.1953); de Capriles & Garrett, "Legality of Corporate Support to Education: A Survey of Current

Developments", 38 A.B.A.J. 209 (1952); Bell, "Corporate Support for Education, The Legal Basis", 38 A.B.A.J. 119 (1952); Bleicken, "Corporate Contributions to Charities: The Modern Rule", 38 A.B.A.J. 999 (1952); Comment, "Corporate Conscience: Charitable Donations", 9 Ariz.L.Rev. 421 (1968); Annot., 39 A.L.R.2d 1192 (1955).

33. 13 N.J. 145, 98 A.2d 581, 39 A.L.R.2d 1179 (1953), appeal dismissed 346 U.S. 861, 74 S.Ct. 107, 98 L.Ed. 373 (1953). In 25 years, corporate giving has risen from $33,000,000 to $1,000,000,000 annually, which is still less than two percent of corporate income before taxes. For federal income tax purposes, corporate charitable contributions may be deducted up to five percent of taxable income with five-year carryover provision. Int.Rev.Code of 1954, 26 U.S.C.A. § 170(b) (2); The Citizens & Southern Nat'l Bank v. United States, 243 F.Supp. 900 (W.D.S.C.1965).

34. Under modern conditions, according to the court, individual citizens are no longer an adequate source of contributions, as a result of both the increasing concentration of wealth under corporate control and heavy taxes which prevent accumulation of individual fortunes; therefore, corporations, like individuals, are required to "acknowledge and discharge social as well as private responsibilities as members of the community within which they operate". 13 N.J. at 153, 98 A.2d at 586.

35. Holding retroactive application of statute to preexisting corporations constitutional. 13 N.J. at 160, 98 A.2d at 589. See section 340 infra.

36. Federal Corrupt Practices Act, 18 U.S.C.A. § 610; Federal Hatch Act, 18 U.S.C.A. § 608; Annot., 1 L. Ed.2d 1918 (1957); McKinney's N.Y. Election Law, § 460; Mo.Laws 1961, H.B. 119 (allowing corporations to campaign for or against changes in any law which would directly affect their businesses); United States v. Lewis Food Co., 366 F.2d 710 (9th Cir.1966) (corporation's payment for advertisements rating candidates held jury question under Federal Corrupt Practices Act); Lustwerk v. Lytron, Inc., 344 Mass. 647, 183 N.E.2d 871 (1962) (upholding power of corporation to expend corporate funds for advertising for the purpose of influencing voters to

For federal income tax purposes, corporate charitable contributions may be deducted up to five percent of taxable income (with five-year carryover provision).[37]

To Be a Partner or Joint Venturer

Corporations have been held to have no implied power to be general partners, on grounds that it was *ultra vires* their corporate powers and would divest their board of directors of the management of corporate affairs.[38]

Isolated cases have allowed a corporation to be a limited partner[39] or a member of a mining partnership.[40]

Corporations have been allowed to be parties to joint ventures, with the courts sometimes straining partnership principles to find a joint venture.[41]

vote against proposed graduated income tax amendment to state constitution and not to violate statutory prohibition on political contribution which expressly excepted election questions materially affecting any of the property, business, or assets of corporation); State ex rel. Corrigan v. Cleveland-Cliffs Iron Co., 169 Ohio St. 42, 157 N.E.2d 331 (1959) (holding corporation cannot make contributions to influence voters for or against issues presented at election); State v. Joe Must Go Club of Wisconsin, Inc., 270 Wis. 108, 70 N.W.2d 681 (1955) (criminal statute prohibiting corporations *doing business* in Wisconsin from contributing for political purposes held not applicable to corporation formed to effect recall of Senator McCarthy since corporation not doing business; conviction and $4,200 fine set aside). Or.Op. Att'y Gen.No. 5582, Feb. 7, 1963 (ruling corporation may expend funds in lobbying with respect to relevant legislation but not support of any political party). E. Epstein, Corporations, Contributions, and Political Campaigns: Federal Regulation in Perspective (1968); E. Epstein, The Corporation in American Politics (1969); A. Heidenheimer & F. Langdon, Business Associations and the Financing of Political Parties: A Comparative Study of the Evolutions of Practices in Germany, Norway and Japan (1968); Wood, "Corporations and Politics", 22 Bus.Law. 775 (1967); Smith, "Corporate Political Contributions: The Law and the Practice", 41 L.A.B.Bull. 547 (1966); Lambert, "Corporate Political Spending and Campaign Finance", 40 N.Y.U.L.Rev. 1033 (1965); Haley, "Limitations on Political Activities of Corporations", 9 Vill.L.Rev. 593 (1964); Cherington & Gillen, "The Company Representative in Washington", 39 Harv. Bus.Rev. 109 (May-June 1961); Farr, "Political Contributions by Corporations in Federal Elections", 19 Bus.Law. 789 (1964); Barton, "Corporations in Politics: How Far Can They Go Under the Law?", 50 A.B.A.J. 228 (1954); King, "Corporate Political Spending and the First Amendment", 23 U.Pitt.L.Rev. 847 (1962); Wood, "Corporate Political Activity", 15 Bus.Law. 112 (1959); Garrett, "Corporate Contributions for Political Purposes", 14 Bus.Law. 365 (1959); Comment, "Political Act: Its Application To Annexation, Third Party Attack, and Corporate Authority", 47 Marq.L.Rev. 71 (1963); Comment, "Corporate Political Affairs Program", 70 Yale L.J. 821 (1961); 24 Mo.L.Rev. 528 (1959); 31 Rocky Mt.L.Rev. 370 (1959); 27 Fordham L.Rev. 599 (1958–59).

37. Int.Rev.Code of 1954, 26 U.S.C.A. § 170(b) (2). See Theodora Holding Corp. v. Henderson, —— Del.

Ch. ——, 257 A.2d 398 (Ch.1969) (contribution of over $500,000 upheld as reasonable on ground, inter alia, within five percent limitation on deductibility).

38. Whittenton Mills v. Upton, 76 Mass. (10 Gray) 582 (1858); Cox v. Hickman, 8 H.L.Cas. 268, 11 Eng.Rep. 431 (1860); Marine Bank of Chicago v. Ogden, 29 Ill. 248 (1862); Burke v. Concord R. R., 61 N.H. 160 (1881); Mallory v. Hananer Oil Works, 86 Tenn. 598, 9 S.W. 396 (1888); People v. North River Sugar Refining Co., 121 N.Y. 582, 24 N.E. 834 (1890); Frieda Popkov Corp. v. Stack, 198 Misc. 826, 103 N.Y.S.2d 507 (Sup.Ct.1950); Mich.Op.Att'y Gen.No. 3652, Oct. 18, 1965; 111 Ala.Op.Att'y Gen. 17, Apr. 6, 1963; 1938 N.Y.Op.Att'y Gen. 340; 1935 N.Y.Op.Att'y Gen. 230. Contra, Kitchell Corp. v. Hermansen, 8 Ariz.App. 424, 446 P.2d 934 (1968) (upholding power of corporation to act as general partner in limited partnership); Memphis Natural Gas Co. v. Pope, 178 Tenn. 580, 161 S.W.2d 211 (1941), aff'd sub nom. Memphis Natural Gas Co. v. Beeler, 315 U.S. 649, 62 S.Ct. 857, 86 L.Ed. 1090 (1942); Ariz.Op.Att'y Gen. No. 66–9–L (R–43), Jan. 11, 1966 (if expressly authorized by articles of incorporation and if entire business is entrusted to it); Ohio Op.Att'y Gen. No. 1847, Sept. 15, 1952 (construction of Uniform Partnership Act); Philip Allen & Sons v. Woonsocket Co., 11 R.I. 288 (1876) (estoppel); Armstrong, "Can Corporations be Partners?", 20 Bus.Law. 899 (1965); Comment, "Corporations: Partnerships: The Corporate Partner", 17 Okla.L.Rev. 183 (1964); Comment, "May a Corporation Be a Partner?", 17 Bus.Law. 514 (1962); Rowley, "The Corporate Partner", 14 Minn.L.Rev. 769 (1930); Notes, 10 Okla.L.Rev. 207 (1957); 1955 Wash.U.L.Q. 76; 25 Tul.L.Rev. 272 (1951); Annot., 60 A.L.R.2d 917 (1958). See also Kelly v. Bell, —— Del.Ch. ——, 254 A.2d 62 (Ch.1969); "Corporate Partners", 26 Corp.J. 27 (1969).

39. Port Arthur Trust Co. v. Muldrow, 155 Tex. 612, 291 S.W.2d 312, 60 A.L.R.2d 913 (1956).

40. Sturm v. Ulrich, 10 F.2d 9 (8th Cir.1925).

41. American Pac. Dairy Prod. v. Siciliano, 235 F.2d 74 (9th Cir.1956); Excelsior Motor Mfg. & Supply Co. v. Sound Equipment, Inc., 73 F.2d 725 (7th Cir. 1934), cert. denied, 294 U.S. 706, 55 S.Ct. 352, 79 L. Ed. 1241 (1935); Milton Kaufman, Inc. v. Superior Court, 94 Cal.App.2d 8, 210 P.2d 88 (1949); Carmer v. J. Leo Johnson, Inc., 38 Del.Ch. 303, 150 A.2d 621 (Ch.1959), aff'd 38 Del.Ch. 579, 156 A.2d 499 (Sup. Ct.1959); Pan Am. Trade & Inv. Corp. v. Commercial Metals Co., 38 Del.Ch. 435, 154 A.2d 151 (Ch.

Provisions in articles of incorporation authorizing the corporation to be a partner have sometimes been upheld,[42] although such a partnership might divest the board of directors of management functions.[43]

Modern statutes tend expressly to empower corporations to be partners.[44]

ULTRA VIRES DOCTRINE

184. **The legal effect of ultra vires corporate acts has changed substantially in recent years, during which statutes circumscribing the defense of ultra vires have been enacted in most American jurisdictions.**

Apart from statute, fully-executed ultra vires contracts are usually not disturbed; entirely executory ultra vires contracts are usually subject to the defense of ultra vires; in the case of ultra vires contracts performed by one party, the other party is estopped in the majority of jurisdictions from asserting the defense of ultra vires, but a minority of jurisdictions hold such contracts void subject to possible quasi-

contractual recovery against the party benefited.

Corporations are usually responsible for torts, crimes, and contempt attributable to them, regardless of whether the tortious, criminal, or contemptuous activity was ultra vires.

For ultra vires activity, the state might enjoin such activity or dissolve the corporation; the corporation or some one in its behalf might recover damages against its responsible personnel; or a shareholder might enjoin such activity when threatened.

Statutory provisions on ultra vires vary considerably. The most typical statutes abolish the "doctrine of ultra vires", except for shareholder injunction proceedings against the corporation, actions by the corporation or those suing in its behalf against its personnel, or proceedings by the state to dissolve or to enjoin the corporation.

The approach to *ultra vires* acts [1] has undergone a drastic change over the years. As a result, the *Ultra Vires* Doctrine is no longer as important as it once was.[2]

Traditional Approach

In times past, corporations were formed with more limited purposes (or objects) and powers,[3] and these were more strictly con-

1959), remanded 39 Del.Ch. 234, 163 A.2d 264 (Sup. Ct.1960); Red Robin Stores, Inc. v. Rose, 274 App. Div. 462, 84 N.Y.S.2d 685 (1st Dep't 1948); Nolan v. J. & M. Doyle Co., 338 Pa. 398, 13 A.2d 59 (1940); Comment, "The Corporate Partner: An Exercise in Semantics", 35 N.Y.U.L.Rev. 548 (1960); Annot., 60 A.L.R.2d 917 (1958). Many corporations today engage in joint ventures. See section 49 supra.

42. Universal Pictures Corp. v. Roy Davidge Film Lab., Ltd., 7 Cal.App.2d 366, 45 P.2d 1028 (1935); Morgan v. Child, Cole & Co., 47 Utah 417, 155 P. 451 (1916); News Register Co. v. Rockingham Pub. Co., 118 Va. 140, 86 S.E. 874 (1915). The New York secretary of state, prior to 1963, would not accept articles of incorporation purporting expressly to empower a corporation to be a partner. 1935 N.Y. Op.Att'y Gen. 230; nor would Michigan admit a foreign corporation authorized to be a partner since a Michigan corporation could not be formed for such a purpose and a foreign corporation was subject to such limitation. Mich.Op.Att'y Gen. No. 3652, Oct. 18, 1965.

43. See Bates v. Coronado Beach Co., 109 Cal. 160, 41 P. 855 (1895) (upholding contract between corporation and individual to share profits and losses of business where entire management of business was entrusted to corporation itself); Ariz.Op.Att'y Gen. No. 66–9–L (R–43), Jan. 11, 1966.

44. See section 182, n. 9 supra. See McKinney's N. Y.Bus.Corp.Law, § 202(a) (15) ("To be a promoter, partner, member, associate or manager of other business enterprises or ventures, or to the extent permitted in any other jurisdiction to be an incorporator of other corporations of any type or kind").

1. Ultra vires acts are sometimes confused with illegal acts, or with acts within the power of the corporation but exercised either by the improper corporate organ or by the proper corporate organ without complying with required procedures. See Wiley & Foss, Inc. v. Saxony Theatres, Inc., 335 Mass. 257, 139 N.E.2d 400 (1957) (using "ultra vires" to characterize act within corporate powers but beyond actual authority of officer purporting to act in behalf of corporation). McDermott v. Bear Film Co., 219 Cal.App.2d 607, 610, 33 Cal.Rptr. 486, 489 (1963): ". . . In its true sense the phrase ultra vires describes action which is beyond the purpose or power of the corporation. . . . Some courts have inflated the phrase to characterize acts which are within corporate purpose or power but performed in an unauthorized manner or without authority."

2. See J. Street, The Doctrine of Ultra Vires (1930); S. Brice, Doctrine of Ultra Vires (3d ed. 1893).

3. See section 12 supra. However, the powers of crown corporations were coextensive with those of natural persons. Bonanza Creek Gold Mining Co. v. Rex, [1916] 1 A.C. 566; British So. Africa Co. v. DeBeers Consolidated Mines, Ltd., [1910] 1 Ch. 354. Corporations formed under parliamentary act were construed to have limited capacity. Ashbury Ry.

strued. By the traditional theories,[4] a corporation was deemed to be an artificial entity created by the state with limited capacity. Any corporate act beyond such capacity was deemed *ultra vires*, void, illegal, and a nullity.[5]

If the transaction was beyond the scope of the business as defined in the articles of incorporation, some cases have suggested that the other party was chargeable with knowledge of lack of corporate authority, since this appeared as a matter of public record (the filed articles of incorporation).[6]

Modern Approach

By the more modern approach, an *ultra vires* act if not a public wrong is not illegal. The question is not one of "capacity" but of powers. While the corporation may not exceed its powers, it can in fact do so and suffer the consequences.[7]

Ultra Vires Corporate Contracts

Contracts fully-executed on both sides, although *ultra vires*, form a firm foundation for rights acquired under them.[8] Under contracts entirely executory, *ultra vires* is a good defense by either party.[9] The controversial area is that of partially-executed contracts.[10]

The old-fashioned federal rule, followed by a minority of state courts, was that an *ultra vires* contract is void, and cannot be the foundation of any rights. Where the contract is wholly executory or fully executed, no action lies. Where there is performance by one party to the benefit of the other, the former might have a quasi-contractual remedy for the reasonable value of the benefits received by the other.[11]

The more modern majority rule is that an *ultra vires* contract not otherwise illegal is not void, but is enforceable under certain circumstances, viz., where one party has received benefits and is therefore estopped from setting up the defense of *ultra vires*.[12]

Of course, under either rule, an illegal contract, whether also *ultra vires* or not, would be void on the ground of illegality. *Ultra vires* character does not of itself make a contract illegal. The frequent occurrence of contracts both illegal and *ultra vires* has added to the confusion.[13]

Corporate Responsibility for Torts

The early thinking was that a corporation had no capacity to commit tort; therefore the tortious acts of its agents were *ultra vires*; therefore the corporation was not responsible.[14]

Carriage & Iron Co. v. Riche, L.R. 7 H.L. 653 (1875).

4. See section 78 supra.

5. R. Stevens, Handbook on the Law of Private Corporations §§ 62, 63 (2d ed. 1949).

6. Id. § 155.

7. Bissell v. Michigan Southern & Northern Indiana Railroad Companies, 22 N.Y. 258 (1860); R. Stevens, Handbook on the Law of Private Corporations § 73 (2d ed. 1949).

8. See N. Lattin, The Law of Corporations 198–200 (1949).

9. R. Stevens, Handbook on the Law of Private Corporations §§ 66, 67 (2d ed. 1949). But see Harris v. Independence Gas Co., 76 Kan. 750, 763, 92 P. 1123, 1127 (1907) (ultra vires held no defense on wholly executory contract).

10. R. Stevens, Handbook on the Law of Private Corporations §§ 66, 67 (2d ed. 1949).

11. Central Transportation Co. v. Pullman's Palace Car Co., 139 U.S. 24, 11 S.Ct. 478, 35 L.Ed. 55 (1891); Herbert v. Sullivan, 123 F.2d 477 (1st Cir. 1941) (2–1); R. Stevens, Handbook on the Law of Private Corporations § 70 (2d ed. 1949).

12. State Bank of Commerce of Brockport v. Stone, 261 N.Y. 175, 184 N.E. 750, 87 A.L.R. 1449 (1933); Whitney Arms Co. v. Barlow, 63 N.Y. 62 (1875); Zion's Sav. Bank & Trust Co. v. Tropic & East Fork Irr. Co., 102 Utah 101, 126 P.2d 1053 (1942). Where a national bank is involved, majority-rule jurisdictions apply the minority rule. Appleton v. Citizens' Cent. Nat'l Bank of New York, 190 N.Y. 417, 83 N.E. 470 (1908), aff'd 216 U.S. 196, 30 S.Ct. 364, 54 L.Ed. 443 (1910).

13. R. Stevens & A. Larson, Cases and Materials on the Law of Corporations 169 (2d ed. 1955). See also Lurie v. Arizona Fertilizer & Chemical Co., 101 Ariz. 482, 421 P.2d 330 (1966) (holding directors personally liable on ultra vires contract in violation of law).

14. R. Stevens, Handbook on the Law of Private Corporations § 64 (2d ed. 1949).

Today, it is well settled that a corporation is liable vicariously for the torts committed by its agents in the course of employment under the rule of *respondeat superior* whether the activity is *intra vires* or *ultra vires*.[15]

This is so even in jurisdictions which follow the minority rule applicable to *ultra vires* contracts.[16]

Such vicarious liability, of course, comprehends compensatory damages.[17]

Where the agent's act is willful, wanton, or malicious, there is a split of authority on corporate vicarious liability for punitive damages. Some jurisdictions hold the corporation liable for any punitive damages attributable to the agent.[18] Other jurisdic-

tions do not hold the corporation liable for such punitive damages unless the act of the agent was authorized or ratified by the corporation.[19]

Corporate Responsibility for Crime

The traditional early common-law view was that a corporation was incapable of the criminal intent required as an element of the then recognized crimes since it had no mind. Since it had no body, it could not be imprisoned. Therefore, a corporation could not be guilty of crime.[20]

The modern cases tend to make the corporation criminally responsible for criminal conduct of its agents attributable to it.

Some modern crimes, such as "public welfare" offenses, do not require criminal in-

---

15. Mrachek v. Sunshine Biscuit, Inc., 308 N.Y. 116, 123 N.E.2d 801 (1954) (corporation held liable for negligence of physician acting as agent in blood test required by corporation to determine whether plaintiff, prospective employee, was suffering from communicable disease); Hannon v. Siegel-Cooper Co., 167 N.Y. 244, 60 N.E. 597 (1901) (corporation engaging in ultra vires practice of dentistry held liable for malpractice of its apparent employee dentists). To allow the corporation to escape liability for its torts on the ground that the activity involved was ultra vires would exonerate it for a double wrong. See Symposium: "Corporation Tort Problems", 12 Clev.-Mar.L.Rev. 100 (1963).

16. National Bank v. Graham, 100 U.S. 699, 25 L.Ed. 750 (1879); Merchants' Bank v. State Bank, 77 U.S. (10 Wall.) 604, 645, 19 L.Ed. 1008, 1018 (1870).

17. R. Stevens, Handbook on the Law of Private Corporations § 64 (2d ed. 1949). The corporation is not responsible for the wrongful acts of its officers or agents not acting for the benefit of the corporation within the scope of their authority. Asphalt Industries, Inc. v. Comm'r, 384 F.2d 229 (3d Cir. 1967).

18. Equitable Life & Casualty Ins. Co. v. Lee, 310 F. 2d 262 (9th Cir.1962) (construing Oregon law and holding that corporation could be liable for punitive damages even though corporation did not knowingly authorize or ratify fraud so long as agents who committed fraud in soliciting orders for defendant's profit-sharing policies were acting within scope of their authority); Boise Dodge, Inc. v. Clark, 92 Idaho 902, 453 P.2d 551 (1969); Amos v. Prom, Inc., 115 F.Supp. 127 (N.D.Iowa 1953); Tietjens v. Gen. Motors Corp., 418 S.W.2d 75 (Mo.1967) (holding corporation liable for punitive damages resulting from its manager's false statements to prospective dealers of its products, even though no punitive damages assessed against manager); Peak v. W. T. Grant Co., 386 S.W.2d 685 (Mo.Ct.App.1964); Goddard v. Grand Trunk Ry. of Canada, 57 Me. 202 (1869). See Silliman, "Punitive Damages Against Corporation—

A Continuation", 18 Fed'n of Ins. Counsel Q. 10 (Fall 1967); Silliman, "Punitive Damages Related to Multiple Litigation Against a Corporation", 16 id. 91 (Spring 1966); Comment, "The Assessment of Punitive Damages against an Entrepreneur for the Malicious Torts of His Employees", 70 Yale L.J. 1296 (1961); Note, "Damages: Corporations: Corporate Liability for Exemplary Damages", 63 W. Va.L.Rev. 183 (1961).

19. Lake Shore & Michigan Southern Ry. v. Prentice, 147 U.S. 101, 13 S.Ct. 261, 37 L.Ed. 97 (1893); United States Steel Corp. v. Fuhrman, 407 F.2d 1143 (6th Cir.1969); Parris v. St. Johnsbury Trucking Co., 395 F.2d 543 (2d Cir.1968); Great Atlantic & Pacific Tea Co. v. Lethcoe, 279 F.2d 948 (4th Cir. 1960); Wooley v. Southwestern Portland Cement Co., 272 F.2d 906 (5th Cir.1959); General Motors Acceptance Corp. v. Froelich, 273 F.2d 92 (D.C.Cir. 1959); Petition of Den Norske Amerikalinje, 276 F.Supp. 163 (N.D.Ohio 1967); Smith v. Little, Brown & Co., 273 F.Supp. 870 (S.D.N.Y.1967); Kelleher v. Detroit Motors, 52 N.J.Super. 247, 145 A.2d 335 (1958); Corrigan v. Bobbs-Merrill Co., 228 N.Y. 58, 126 N.E. 260, 10 A.L.R. 662 (1920); Teofilo v. Mego Corp., 29 A.D.2d 693, 287 N.Y.S.2d 122 (2d Dep't 1968) (setting aside verdict against corporation for punitive damages for employee's assault); see 4 Restatement of Torts § 909 (1939) (imposing punitive damages on principal (a) where the principal has authorized the agent's acts, (b) where an unfit agent has been recklessly employed, (c) where a managerial employee has acted within the scope of his employment, or (d) where the principal has ratified the agent's acts); Fisher v. Carrousel Motor Hotel, Inc., 424 S.W.2d 627 (Tex.1967) (upholding punitive damage award against manager attempting to enforce management rule).

20. R. Stevens, Handbook on the Law of Private Corporations § 80 (2d ed. 1949).

tent. Even when intent is required, the intent of the corporation's agent might be imputed to the corporation.[21]

The New York Penal Law provides that a corporation is guilty of an offense when:[22]

"(a) The conduct constituting the offense consists of an omission to discharge a specific duty of affirmative performance imposed on corporations by law; or

"(b) The conduct constituting the offense is engaged in, authorized, solicited, requested, commanded, or recklessly tolerated by the board of directors or by a high managerial agent acting within the scope of his employment and in behalf of the corporation; or

"(c) The conduct constituting the offense is engaged in by an agent of the corporation while acting within the scope of his employment and in behalf of the corporation and (i) the offense is a misdemeanor or a violation, or (ii) the offense is one defined by a statute which clearly indicates a legislative intent to impose such criminal liability on a corporation."

Of course, whether or not the criminal statute was intended to apply to corporations sometimes presents a question of construction.[23]

Another factor of increasing importance is whether the agent stands high enough in the corporate hierarchy to justify the assumption that his acts are, without any special proof of authorization of the particular conduct, the acts of the corporation. This is known as the "Superior Agent" rule.[24]

Vicarious corporate criminal liability is tending to be governed by the same test applicable to vicarious corporate tort liability: whether the act was within the scope of the

---

21. United States v. Carter, 311 F.2d 934 (6th Cir. 1963), cert. denied sub nom. Felice v. United States, 373 U.S. 915, 83 S.Ct. 1301, 10 L.Ed.2d 415 (1963), reh. denied 373 U.S. 954, 83 S.Ct. 1677, 10 L.Ed.2d 708 (1963); United States v. American Stevedores, Inc., 310 F.2d 47 (1962), cert. denied 371 U.S. 969, 83 S.Ct. 552, 9 L.Ed.2d 539 (1963); Standard Oil Co. v. United States, 307 F.2d 120 (5th Cir. 1962); United States v. Chicago Express, Inc., 273 F.2d 751 (7th Cir.1960); Korholz v. United States, 269 F.2d 897 (10th Cir. 1959), cert. denied 361 U.S. 929, 80 S.Ct. 367, 4 L.Ed.2d 352 (1960); Rex v. I. C. R. Haulage, Ltd., [1944] 1 K.B. 551; Moore v. I. Bressler, Ltd., [1944] 2 All E.R. 515 (K.B.); Hamilton, "Corporate Criminal Liability in Texas", 47 Texas L.Rev. 60 (1968); Fisse, "Distinction between Primary and Vicarious Corporate Criminal Liability", 41 Austl.L.J. 203 (1967); Burns, "Test of Vicarious Criminal Liability", 1967 Crim.L.Rev. (Eng.) 702; Yarosky, "Criminal Liability of Corporations", 10 McGill L.J. 142 (1964); Campbell, "The Vicarious Liability of a Corporation for the Criminal Acts of Its Agents", 9 St. Louis B.J. 5 (June 1962); Mueller, "Mens Rea and the Corporation—A Study of the Model Penal Code Provision on Corporate Criminal Liability", 19 U.Pitt.L.Rev. 21 (1957); Winn, "The Criminal Responsibility of Corporations", 3 Camb. L.J. 398 (1929); Lee, "Corporate Criminal Responsibility", 28 Colum.L.Rev. 1, 181 (1928); Edgerton, "Corporate Criminal Responsibility", 36 Yale L.J. 827 (1927); Canfield, "Corporate Responsibility for Crime", 14 Colum.L.Rev. 469 (1914); Comment, "Corporate Criminal Liability for Acts in Violation of Company Policy", 50 Geo.L.J. 566 (1962); Comment, "Increasing Community Control Over Corporate Crime—A Problem in the Law of Sanctions", 71 Yale L.J. 280 (1961).

22. McKinney's N.Y. Penal Law § 20.20(2). "High managerial agent" is defined to mean "an officer of a corporation or any other agent in a position of comparable authority with respect to the formulation of corporate policy or the supervision in a managerial capacity of subordinate employees." "Agent" is defined to mean "any director, officer or employee of a corporation, or any other person who is authorized to act in behalf of the corporation." Id. § 20.20(1). The statute goes on to provide that "A person is criminally liable for conduct constituting an offense which he performs or causes to be performed in the name of or in behalf of a corporation to the same extent as if such conduct were performed in his own name or behalf." Id. § 20.25.

23. State of Oregon v. Pacific Powder Co., 226 Or. 502, 360 P.2d 530, 83 A.L.R.2d 1111 (1961); People v. Rochester Railway & Light Co., 195 N.Y. 102, 88 N.E. 22 (1909) (homicide statute, defining homicide as the killing of one human being by another, held inapplicable to corporation); Thompson v. Stauffer Chemical Co., 348 S.W.2d 274 (Tex.Civ.App.1961) (where code of criminal procedure provided no statutory procedure for prosecuting corporations).

24. See McKinney's N.Y.Penal Law, § 20.20, supra note 22; Continental Baking Co. v. United States, 281 F.2d 137 (6th Cir.1960); Holland Furnace Co. v. United States, 158 F.2d 2 (6th Cir.1946); C. I. T. Corp. v. United States, 150 F.2d 85 (9th Cir.1945); People v. Canadian Fur Trappers Corp., 248 N.Y. 159, 161 N.E. 455, 59 A.L.R. 372 (1928). But see United States v. George F. Fish, Inc., 154 F.2d 798 (2d Cir.1946), cert. denied 328 U.S. 869, 66 S.Ct. 1377, 90 L.Ed. 1639 (1946) ("public-necessity" exception).

agent's authority. Such common approach, of course, ignores the policy differences between criminal and tort responsibility: deterring and punishing offensive conduct in the former; compensating and distributing loss, in the latter.[25] This problem is to some extent highlighted in the aforementioned cases involving claims for punitive damages for torts committed by corporate agents.

Corporate Responsibility for Contempt

Although a corporation, of course, may not be imprisoned, it may be fined for civil or criminal contempt.[26]

Other Aspects of Ultra Vires Doctrine

Ultra vires questions are also relevant in other situations. Where a corporation is engaging in ultra vires activity, the state, by a quo warranto proceeding, might enjoin such activity or even compel corporate dissolution.[27]

If a corporation suffers damage from an ultra vires transaction, it, or someone in its behalf, such as a shareholder in a derivative action, might be allowed to recover against its agent responsible for the same, at least where the agent was negligent in failing to ascertain the limitations on corporate authority.[28]

A nonassenting shareholder, unless estopped or barred by laches, may, in a direct action, sue the corporation (and its management) to enjoin a threatened ultra vires transaction.[29] The reason why a direct ac-

tion is possible before, but not after, the consummation of an ultra vires transaction is that in the former case the shareholder is theoretically seeking to prevent the breach of the term of his membership contract defining the scope of corporate business, whereas in the latter case the claim is theoretically that of the corporation for loss resulting from breach of duty to it, and any recovery should go to the corporation for the better protection of its whole body of creditors and shareholders rather than to the complaining shareholder.[30]

The ultra vires acquisition of property by a corporation does not, in the absence of statutory policy to the contrary, enable anyone to attack the corporation's title to the property.[31]

Statutory Developments

Modern statutes deal with the ultra vires doctrine.[32]

The Model Business Corporation Act has abolished the ultra vires doctrine, except for shareholder injunction proceedings against

ment Co. v. Laurel Grove Memorial Park, Inc., 43 N.J.Super. 244, 128 A.2d 281 (1957) (holding third parties cannot enjoin corporation from exercising ultra vires powers).

30. R. Stevens, Handbook on the Law of Private Corporations 786, n. 7 (2d ed. 1949). See section 360 infra.

31. R. Stevens, Handbook on the Law of Private Corporations § 65 (2d ed. 1949).

32. Ham, "Ultra Vires Contracts under Modern Corporate Legislation", 46 Ky.L.J. 215 (1958); Barton & Ruwart, "Relaxed Approach to the Problem of Ultra Vires", 34 U.Det.L.J. 297 (1956); Stevens, "Ultra Vires Transactions under the New Ohio General Corporation Act", 4 U.Cin.L.Rev. 419 (1930); Comment, "Ultra Vires in Georgia", 16 Mercer L.Rev. 320 (1964); Comment, "Ultra Vires under the Texas Business Corporation Act", 40 Texas L.Rev. 677 (1962); Note, "Ultra Vires as a Defense in Ohio", 12 W.Res.L.Rev. 634 (1961). Quaere, as to effect of constitutional prohibitions against corporations engaging in businesses not expressly authorized by their articles of incorporation. E. g., Alabama, North Dakota, Pennsylvania, South Dakota, Utah. See also Baxt, "Doctrine of Ultra Vires and the Uniform Companies Act", 7 Austl.Law. 38 (Apr. 24, 1967); Thompson, "Ultra Vires Doctrine and the Jenkins Report", 1963 J.Bus.L. 143; Sangal, "Ultra Vires and Companies: The Indian Experience", 12 Int'l & Comp.L.Q. 967 (1963).

25. R. Stevens & A. Larson, Cases and Materials on the Law of Corporations 171–172 (2d ed. 1955).

26. United States v. Kormel, Inc., 230 F.Supp. 275 (D.Nev.1964) (corporation held guilty of criminal contempt); R. Stevens, Handbook on the Law of Private Corporations § 81 (2d ed. 1949).

27. R. Stevens, Handbook on the Law of Private Corporations § 69 (2d ed. 1949).

28. R. Stevens, Handbook on the Law of Private Corporations § 155 (2d ed. 1949). See section 234 infra.

29. R. Stevens, Handbook on the Law of Private Corporations § 68 (2d ed. 1949); Paterson Monu-

the corporation, actions by the corporation or those suing in its behalf against its officers or directors, or proceedings by the state to dissolve or to enjoin the corporation.[33]

C. INCORPORATOR(S)

INCORPORATOR(S)

185. **Incorporators formally incorporate the corporation, and in some jurisdictions are required to subscribe to shares, thereby becoming initial shareholders. Formal meetings of incorporations are sometimes required either before but more often after incorporation, possibly to adopt the initial bylaws, authorize the board of directors to issue shares, and elect directors. In some jurisdictions under certain circumstances, the incorporators may amend the articles of incorporation, dissolve the corporation, or manage the corporation prior to the election of directors.**

Incorporators are the persons who formally incorporate the corporation. Requirements as to the number and qualifications of incorporators have been previously discussed.[1]

"Dummy" or "accommodation" incorporators satisfying applicable qualification requirements are frequently used for convenience or where the real parties in interest are ineligible to serve as incorporators.

The articles of incorporation usually must set forth the names and addresses of the incorporators,[2] whose signatures must be affixed thereto. Statutes often require acknowledgment or verification.[3]

Older statutes required that the incorporators also subscribe in the articles of incorporation to at least one share;[4] such subscription usually becomes effective upon the filing of the articles of incorporation, unlike the usual subscription which requires post-incorporation acceptance by the corporation.[5]

In many jurisdictions, formal meetings of the incorporators are held. Sometimes these are required before incorporation; more frequently after incorporation. Sometimes, they are held as a matter of well-established practice despite the lack of any express statutory requirement. Any post-incorporation organization meeting of the incorporators is held, usually promptly after the filing of the articles of incorporation and before the first (or organization) meeting of the board of directors.[6] At the meeting of the incorporators, the bylaws are usually adopted,[7] the board of directors is authorized to issue shares, transfers of share subscriptions from any dummy incorporators are filed, and possibly any dummy directors

33. ABA–ALI Model Bus.Corp.Act § 6. Most American jurisdictions have statutes dealing with the "defense of ultra vires". Similar to the Model Act is McKinney's N.Y.Bus.Corp.Law, § 203, except for the insertion in the latter of an express exception of the defense of illegality, as distinguished from ultra vires. Such statutes largely codified preexisting case law, but changed case law by sustaining devises and bequests to corporations beyond their power to take and with respect to ultra vires contracts wholly executory on both sides by eliminating the defense of ultra vires to the parties. See 711 Kings Highway Corp. v. F. I. M.'s Marine Repair Service, Inc., 51 Misc.2d 373, 273 N.Y.S.2d 299 (Sup.Ct.1966) (holding New York statute captioned "Defense of ultra vires" not limited to raising ultra vires as defense). See also McKinney's N.Y.Bus. Corp.Law, § 109 (actions or special proceedings by attorney general). See Matter of B–F Building Corp. v. Coleman, 284 F.2d 679 (6th Cir.1960) (under Ohio ultra vires statute). Stevens, "Ultra Vires Transactions Under the New Ohio General Corporation Act", 4 U.Cin.L.Rev. 419 (1930); see also Stevens, "A Proposal as to the Codification and Restatement of the Ultra Vires Doctrine", 36 Yale L. J. 297 (1927).

1. See section 131 supra.

2. See section 131 supra.

3. See section 132 supra.

4. See section 131, nn. 13, 14 supra.

5. See section 115 supra.

6. See section 135 supra. Modern statutes expressly permit incorporators to act by written consent without a meeting.

7. See section 133, nn. 8–12 supra.

named in the articles of incorporation are replaced and initial directors are elected.[8] Under the Model Business Corporation Act, the incorporators do not meet, but call, by majority action, the first meeting of the board of directors.[9]

Incorporators with binding share subscriptions are shareholders. Otherwise, absent shareholders, they are the closest thing to shareholders. Under prescribed circumstances, such as if shares have not been issued or directors have not been elected, the incorporators are sometimes given certain powers by statute, such as acting to amend the articles of incorporation,[10] to dissolve the corporation,[11] or to take any action that shareholders are required or permitted to take by vote.[12] Incorporators sometimes are given the power to manage the corporation prior to the election of directors.[13]

D. SHAREHOLDER(S)

SHAREHOLDER(S)—IN GENERAL

186. **Management and related functions of shareholders are discussed in the next several sections. Financial and related aspects of shares have been previously discussed, including some topics relevant to both financial and management aspects. Any one with capacity to own property usually may own shares.**

The financial and related aspects of shares have been outlined in Chapter 8.[1] The next several sections will discuss the management functions of shareholders and related topics.[2] The extent to which shareholders are subject to fiduciary duties akin to those of directors and officers will be treated later.[3] Some topics which are relevant to shareholders in both financial and control aspects have been the subject of previous sections.[4]

Generally speaking, anyone with capacity to own property is capable of owning shares. One corporation usually may own shares in another corporation subject to some restrictions, or may purchase or acquire its own shares.[5] Treasury shares have been discussed previously.[6]

The estimated number of individuals owning shares in publicly-held corporations in the United States in 1970 was 26,500,000. An estimated 100,000,000 Americans were indirect owners whose savings were invested, in part, in savings banks, pension funds, insurance companies, and other financial institutions which, in turn, invest in shares.[7]

Recent years have witnessed a significant shift in the ownership of larger corporations from individuals to institutions, e. g., life in-

8. See section 205 infra.

9. See section 135 supra. Under the 1969 Model Act revision, the call is by the majority of the directors.

10. See, e. g., Del.Gen.Corp.Law, § 241 (1967).

11. See, e. g., ABA–ALI Model Bus.Corp.Act § 75.

12. See, e. g., McKinney's N.Y.Bus.Corp.Law, § 615(c): "When there are no shareholders of record, such action [which, under the statute, shareholders are required or permitted to take by vote] may be taken on the written consent signed by a majority in interest of the subscribers for shares whose subscriptions have been accepted or their successors in interest or, if no subscription has been accepted, on the written consent signed by the incorporator or a majority of the incorporators. When there are two or more incorporators, if any dies or is for any reason unable to act, the other or others may act. If there is no incorporator able to act, any person for whom an incorporator was acting as agent may act in his stead, or if such other person also dies or is for any reason unable to act, his legal representative may act."

13. See, e. g., Del.Gen.Corp.Law, § 107 (1967). See Tenn.Gen.Corp.Law, § 48–402 (1956) (incorporators constitute initial board of directors).

1. See sections 157–179 supra.

2. See sections 187–202 infra.

3. See sections 231, 232, 239–241, 340 infra.

4. See sections 158, 161, 169, 170, 172–179 supra.

5. See section 183 supra.

6. See section 158 supra.

7. Understanding the New York Stock Exchange 42–44 (New York Stock Exchange rev. ed. 1969).

surance companies,[8] banks, investment companies,[9] foundations, corporate and governmental pension funds, university and college endowment funds, and their potential control over corporate management. This development is no less significant than the decline of family ownership in favor of publicly-held corporations a half century ago.

The existence of large institutional investors is a relatively recent phenomenon. Their role in corporate management is only beginning to develop. Their influence is bound to be profound.[10]

CO-OWNERSHIP AND SPLIT OWNERSHIP OF SHARES

187. Shares, like other personal property, may be subject to co-ownership and split ownership. Types of co-ownership include tenancy in common, joint tenancy, tenancy in partnership, community property, and possibly tenancy by the entirety. Types of split ownership include trustee-beneficiary, committee or conservator—incompetent, executor or administrator —estate of deceased shareholder, guardian— ward, receiver—party in receivership, "custodian"—minor, pledgor—pledgee. Phases of such relationships involving shares are sometimes governed by corporation statutes.

Before taking up the management functions of shareholders, some of the problems of co-ownership and split ownership of shares will be surveyed.

8. M. Keller, The Life Insurance Enterprise, 1885–1910: A Study in the Limits of Corporate Power (1963).

9. Louis, "The Mutual Funds Have the Votes", 75 Fortune, No. 5, 150 (May 1967). See section 301 infra.

10. For a pioneer study in this area, see D. Baum & N. Stiles, The Silent Partners: Institutional Investors and Corporate Control (1965) (estimating that by 1970 institutional investors will hold one-third of all New York Stock Exchange listed securities). Congress has authorized an in-depth investigation of the impact of institutional investment on the operation of the nation's securities markets. S.J.Res. 160, 90th Cong., 2d Sess. (1968). See also E. Cox, Trends in the Distribution of Stock Ownership (1963); Enstam & Kamen, "Control and the Institutional Investor", 23 Bus.Law. 289 (1968).

Co-ownership

Shares, like other personal property, are subject to co-ownership; tenancy in common, joint tenancy,[1] tenancy in partnership, community property,[2] and tenancy by the entirety in jurisdictions which recognize the same in personal property, each with the respective normal incidents thereof.[3]

Split Ownership

The most obvious example of split ownership of shares would be a trust, with legal title in the trustee and the equitable interest in the beneficiary. Ordinarily, the trustee would be the record owner and receive dividends, be entitled to notices and to vote, receive any distributions of assets, etc.[4] Statutes often deal with shares held by a trustee, providing that a trustee may vote the shares only if the trustee is the record owner or sometimes without such qualification.[5]

In a voting trust, the voting trustees are the holders of record, and the beneficial

1. See Ark.Stat.Ann. §§ 50–110, 50–111 (Supp.1967); English v. United States, 270 F.2d 876 (7th Cir.1959) (jointly held shares held entirely includible in husband's estate for federal estate tax purposes).

2. See Messersmith v. Messersmith, 229 La. 495, 86 So.2d 169 (1956); Note, "Community Property Problems Relative to Stocks and Bonds", 33 Tul.L.Rev. 811 (1959).

3. See Frey v. Wubbena, 26 Ill.2d 62, 185 N.E.2d 850 (1962) (registration of shares on corporate books in appropriate language held to create joint tenancy); Townsend Corp. v. Davidson, 40 Del.Ch. 295, 181 A. 2d 219 (Ch.1962) (holding shares owned by husband and wife as joint tenants could be sequestered as separate property of one of them); Edwards & Woods, "Joint Ownership of Corporate Securities in North Carolina", 44 N.C.L.Rev. 290 (1966); Rogers, "Joint Ownership of Corporate Stock", 13 U.Pitt.L. Rev. 498 (1952); Annot., 134 A.L.R. 989 (1941).

4. See section 176 supra.

5. See, e. g., ABA–ALI Model Bus.Corp.Act § 31; McKinney's N.Y.Bus.Corp.Law, § 612(c) (only if record owner); Del.Gen.Corp.Law, § 217 (1967) (even if not record owner). Cleveland Trust Co. v. Eaton, 11 Ohio Misc. 151, 229 N.E.2d 850 (C.P.1967) (disallowing corporation from voting its own shares held by it as fiduciary); Note, "The Corporate Fiduciary's Power to Vote its Own Stock", 68 Colum. L.Rev. 116 (1968).

owners are issued voting trust certificates by the voting trustees.[6]

Other types of split ownership of shares involving fiduciary relationships generally have the same incidents where shares are involved as where other types of personal property are: Committee or Conservator—incompetent; Executor or Administrator—persons having an interest in the shares under the will or rules of intestate distribution; Guardian—ward; Receiver—party in receivership; "Custodian"—minor; Pledgor—pledgee.

Statutory provisions often provide that shares held by committees or conservators, executors, administrators, and guardians may be voted by them even when they are not the record owners, and that shares held by receivers may be voted by them, even when not the record owners, if so authorized by appropriate court order.[7]

In recent years, rather elaborate gifts-to-minors legislation has authorized the holding of shares for minors by informally-appointed "custodians".[8]

Statutes might also provide that shares held by two or more fiduciaries may be voted by a majority of them, in event of disagreement, or pursuant to appropriate court order, in the event of deadlock, absent relevant provisions in the instrument or order of appointment.[9] Statutes frequently also provide that fiduciaries who hold shares are not personally liable as shareholders, but that the funds in their hands are so liable.[10]

Where shares are pledged as collateral security, the pledgee gets possession of the shares. He thus has a possessory security interest, with the pledgor remaining the legal and beneficial owner. If the pledgee becomes the record owner, he would combine the legal title with his security interest. In either event, the pledgor would be the beneficial owner, absent foreclosure of the pledge in the event of default of the obligation secured.[11] Statutes often provide that the pledgor is entitled to vote the shares pledged, except where the pledgee or his nominee has become the record owner.[12]

---

6. See section 197 infra.

7. See e. g., ABA–ALI Model Bus.Corp.Act § 31; Del.Gen.Corp.Law, § 217 (1967); McKinney's N.Y. Bus.Corp.Law, § 612(c), (d); Matter of Pitman, 156 N.Y.L.J. No. 19, 8 (Sup.Ct.1966) (upholding executors' voting of shares in name of decedent notwithstanding disagreement with beneficial owners). See Annot., 114 A.L.R. 1057 (1938), 41 A.L.R.2d 1082 (1955), 7 A.L.R.3d 629 (1966). Rogers v. First Nat'l Bank of St. George, 410 F.2d 579 (4th Cir.1969) (allowing natural guardian to vote shares despite noncompliance with Uniform Gift to Minors Act).

8. See sections 176, 177 supra.

9. See, e. g., McKinney's N.Y.Bus.Corp.Law, § 612(h); Note, 21 Albany L.Rev. 156 (1957).

10. See, e. g., ABA–ALI Model Bus.Corp.Act § 23.

11. In a case involving default where pledged shares of small unknown corporations were sold at public auction under broad provisions authorizing public or private sale and waiving advertisement, etc., and the advertisement and auctioneer's catalog merely listed such shares and the pledgee bid in the shares, the sale was invalidated on the ground that the pledgee had not satisfied its equitable obligation of good faith which included, in the case of an auction sale, appropriate notice by advertisement. Matter of Kiamie, 309 N.Y. 325, 130 N.E.2d 745 (1955). Cf. Taylor v. Banks, 392 S.W.2d 856 (Tex.1965); Perkins v. Meyer, 302 N.Y. 139, 96 N.E.2d 744 (1951); General Phoenix Corp. v. Cabot, 300 N.Y. 87, 89 N.E.2d 238 (1949).

12. See, e. g., ABA–ALI Model Bus.Corp.Act § 31; McKinney's N.Y.Bus.Corp.Law, § 612(e). In Raible v. Puerto Rico Industrial Development Co., 392 F.2d 424 (1st Cir. 1968), the guarantor of a claim up to $42,000 pledged 60,000 $10 par value preference shares, which were virtually worthless, on the understanding that in the event of the pledgee's taking over such shares, they should be valued at par. The pledgee, with neither notice to nor knowledge of the pledgor, exercised rights of ownership in the shares by voting them in favor of a merger resulting in the exchange of each preference share for one one-cent par value common share. The court held that the pledgee was entitled to a $10 credit per preference share, which extinguished his obligation. In Beraksa v. Stardust Records, Inc., 215 Cal.App.2d 708, 30 Cal.Rptr. 504 (1963), substantially all of the shares of a corporation were pledged under an agreement whereby the pledgee could transfer the shares to his name in the event of default in payment of a note due him from the pledgor. After the pledgor defaulted in payment, the pledgee did not transfer the shares into his name but instead called a shareholders' meeting and voted the shares to elect a board of directors, which in turn appointed a new president, who then executed

Even where the pledgee has become the record owner, he or his proxy might be entitled to vote only if in the transfer on the books of the corporation the pledgor has expressly empowered the pledgee to vote.[13] Statutes might also provide that no pledgee shall be personally liable as a shareholder but the pledgor shall be deemed the shareholder and liable as such.[14]

The ordinary proxy involves simply an agency from the shareholder to the proxy holder to vote the shares. If the proxy is coupled with an interest in the shares, the proxy holder, to the extent of such interest, may be said to have some ownership along with the shareholder giving the proxy.[15]

Where shares are held in the name of a broker ("street name"), the broker is the holder of record. If this is done as a matter of convenience, the broker in effect holds the shares for the customer as undisclosed principal. An agency relationship, rather than split ownership, is thus involved, even though the customer is often said to be the beneficial owner. When the shares are held by a broker or his hypothecatee on a margin account, a pledgor-pledgee situation is involved. The Federal Securities Exchange Act of 1934, makes it unlawful for any member of a national securities exchange, or any broker or dealer transacting a business in securities through such member, to give a proxy, consent, or authorization in respect of any registered security carried for the account of a customer in contravention of S.

E. C. rules and regulations.[16] Securities exchanges sometimes also regulate their member brokers in this respect.[17]

SHAREHOLDERS' MANAGEMENT FUNCTIONS—IN GENERAL

188. Shareholder management functions usually take the form of voting at shareholder meetings or giving of written consents with respect to (a) election and removal of directors; (b) adoption, amendment, and repeal of by-laws; (c) shareholder resolutions, including ratification of board of directors action; and (d) extraordinary corporate matters. Traditionally, shareholders elect the board of directors, who manage the corporation by determining corporate policy and appointing officers to execute such policy. Separation of ownership (in the shareholders) and management (in the board of directors) is inherent in such approach, presenting different problems in the larger corporations, with occasional lip service to "shareholder democracy", and in the close corporation where identity of ownership and management is often desired as in the case of the individual proprietorship or partnership.

In a strict sense, management of a corporation is vested in its board of directors and shareholders have no functions of management as such. In the broader sense of participation in control, shareholders have various management functions.

Shareholder control generally takes the form of voting at shareholder meetings or giving of written consents[1] with respect to: (a) election, and possibly removal, of directors;[2] (b) adoption, amendment, and repeal of bylaws;[3] (c) shareholder resolutions, including ratification of action of board of directors;[4] and (d) extraordinary

---

an option agreement to sell the corporation's business to an optionee who entered into possession of the business. The pledgor's widow, as administratrix, elected a different board which appointed her as president. She demanded and repossessed the business from the optionee. The optionee was allowed to recover from the pledgee and his "president" the option price of $8,000, additional compensatory damages, $2,000 exemplary damages, and against such "president" $1,000 for breach of express warranty of authority.

13. See, e. g., Del.Gen.Corp.Law, § 217(a) (1967).

14. See, e. g., ABA–ALI Model Bus.Corp.Act § 23.

15. See section 196 infra.

16. Federal Securities Exchange Act of 1934, § 14(b), 15 U.S.C.A. § 77n(b). See section 297, nn. 29–30 infra.

17. See section 297, n. 31 supra.

1. See sections 189–191 infra.

2. See section 192 infra.

3. See section 193 infra.

4. See section 194 infra.

corporate matters.[5] In broad theoretical outline, shareholders elect the board of directors, who manage the corporation [6] by determining corporate policy and appointing officers to execute such policy; [7] can intrude on the managerial discretion of the board only to a limited extent; and control such extraordinary matters as are beyond the scope of ordinary management. In short, the shareholders' management functions are theoretically significant at both extremes of management, where such functions are sometimes shared with the board of directors, and the large middle ground of management is vested in the board of directors.[8]

Inherent, then, in the corporate setup is the idea that the shareholders "own" the corporation, but the board of directors manages it. In the large corporation, this sepa-ration of ownership and control has been the subject of considerable comment, especially in the 1930's.[9]

Professors Berle & Means, in their classic work, *The Modern Corporation and Private Property*, in 1933, discussing the large "quasi-public" corporations, emphasized the phenomenon of owners who do not manage, and managers without appreciable ownership, and this divorcement of control from ownership as "a characteristic product of the corporate system." [10]

The monographs published by the Temporary National Economic Committee ("T.N. E.C."), a special committee established by joint congressional resolution, echoed the same themes in the 1939–1941 period.[11]

Current best sellers re-echo identical themes.[12]

In effect, the commentators were pointing out that shareholders were not, in any effec-

---

5. See section 195 and Chapter 13 infra.

6. See sections 203–218 infra.

7. See sections 219–230 infra. See Meck, "Employment of Corporate Executives by Majority Stockholders", 47 Yale L.J. 1079 (1938).

8. See Chase, J., in Continental Securities Co. v. Belmont, 206 N.Y. 7, 16–17, 99 N.E. 138, 141 (1912): "As a general rule stockholders cannot act in relation to the ordinary business of a corporation. The body of stockholders have certain authority conferred by statute which must be exercised to enable the corporation to act in specific cases, but except for certain authority conferred by statute, which is mainly permissive or confirmatory, such as consenting to the mortgage, lease or sale of real property of the corporation, they have no express power given by statute. They are not by any statute in this state given general power of initiative in corporate affairs. Any action by them relating to the details of the corporate business is necessarily in the form of an assent, request or recommendation. Recommendations by a body of stockholders can only be enforced through the board of directors, and indirectly by the authority of the stockholders to change the personnel of the directors at a meeting for the election of directors." 1 G. Hornstein, Corporation Law and Practice § 185 (1959) (Checklist: Distribution of Power Between Directors and Shareholders); Jones, "Common Operating Aspects of California Corporations", in Advising California Business Enterprises 641–668 (1958); Berle, "Control in Corporate Law", 58 Colum.L.Rev. 1212 (1958); Hornstein, "The Future of Corporate Control", 63 Harv.L.Rev. 476 (1950); Hornstein, "Corporate Control and Private Property Rules", 92 U. Pa.L.Rev. 1 (1943). See also Eisenberg, "The Legal Roles of Shareholders and Management in Modern Corporate Decisionmaking", 57 Calif.L.Rev. 1 (1969).

9. A. Berle & G. Means, The Modern Corporation and Private Property (1933); T. Arnold, The Folklore of Capitalism (1937). See also J. Burnham, The Managerial Revolution (1941); J. Sears, The New Place of the Stockholder (1929); W. Ripley, Main Street and Wall Street (1927); Hetherington, "Fact and Legal Theory: Shareholders, Managers, and Corporate Responsibility", 21 Stan.L.Rev. 248 (1969). See also Eckert, "Shareholder and Management: A Comparative View on Some Corporate Problems in the United States and Germany", 46 Iowa L.Rev. 12 (1960).

10. A. Berle & G. Means, The Modern Corporation and Private Property 69–70 (1933); see A. Berle, Power Without Property: A New Development in American Political Economy (1959).

11. TNEC Monograph 11, Bureaucracy and Trusteeship in Large Corporations 19–21 (1940); TNEC Monograph 29, The Distribution of Ownership in the Two Hundred Largest Non-Financial Corporations (1940).

12. J. Galbraith, The New Industrial Society (1967). Professor Galbraith states that corporate decision-making power is in an autonomous "technostructure" (management, specialists, technicians) free from outside interference, whether from shareholders, financial institutions, government agencies, unions. The large corporations determine their products and prices and create the market's demand for such products. Emphasis is on growth rather than profits, with growth financed largely through retained earnings. Parallel to the industrial technostructure is the technostructure of government, with corresponding goals.

tive manner, exercising such control functions as they legally enjoyed. This should not becloud the fact that the corporation inherently involves a separation of ownership (in the shareholders) and management (in the board of directors).

Other commentators have been promoting "shareholder democracy"[13] and people's capitalism".[14] Resort to such terms has been subjected to deserving criticism.[15]

In the close corporation where the entrepreneur or associates want to carry on business as a "one-man corporation" or an "incorporated partnership", the inherent separation of ownership and management has presented frequent problems.[16]

SHAREHOLDERS' VOTING RIGHTS

189. Each share is usually entitled to one vote absent provision to the contrary. Voting rights, subject to jurisdictional and other variations, may be (a) straight, (b) cumulative, (c) class, (d) contingent, (e) disproportionate, (f) nonvoting.

In straight voting, each share carries one vote for each matter, including one vote for each director to be elected.

Cumulative voting, which is mandatory under some state constitutions or statutes and permissive in most other jurisdictions, gives each share as many votes as there are directors to be elected, the shareholder being permitted to distribute his votes among the candidates in any way he desires. Cumulative voting is a form of proportional representation to assure minority representation on the board of directors. Various devices exist to minimize the effect of cumulative voting.

Class (or series) voting involves the separate voting by classes (or series) of shares for separate classes of directors or in connection with other matters. Statutes often require class voting in connection with specified matters.

Contingent voting rights are dependent upon the happening of a stated contingency, often the default of specified dividends, with provision for return to original status when the contingency is over.

Disproportionate voting rights usually involve fractional or multiple votes per share of specified classes or series where permissible.

Nonvoting shares are permissible in most jurisdictions, provided voting rights reside in one or more other classes of shares or possibly debt securities. Even shares which are nominally nonvoting might have mandatory voting rights, often by class, with respect to certain matters adversely affecting such shares. Voting shares, under certain circumstances, might not vote. Securities exchanges might require minimum voting rights with respect to shares of companies having securities listed on such exchanges.

Shareholder rights with respect to control are traditionally asserted by voting at shareholder meetings, but under modern statutes may often be asserted, at least to some extent, by written consent without a meeting.[1]

With respect to voting rights as with other shareholder rights, the starting premise is that all shares are equal unless otherwise provided. Absent provisions to the contrary, each share of record is entitled to one

13. See, e. g., L. Gilbert, Dividends and Democracy (1956); Caplin, "Proxies, Annual Meetings and Corporate Democracy; The Lawyer's Role", 37 Va.L. Rev. 653 (1951).

14. Understanding the New York Stock Exchange 42–44 (New York Stock Exchange rev. ed. 1969). Some 26,500,000 persons were estimated in 1970 to own shares in publicly-held corporations. The most widely-held shares were American Telephone & Telegraph Co. (3,410,000 shareholders), General Motors Co. (1,391,000), Standard Oil of New Jersey (775,-000), General Electric Co. (535,000), Ford Motor Company (391,000). See J. Livingston, The American Stockholder 14–21 (1958). An estimated 100,-000,000 Americans, of course, have indirect ownership in shares owned by banks, insurance companies, investment companies, and pension funds.

15. J. Livingston, The American Stockholder 17–21, 68–80 (1958); Garrett, "Attitudes on Corporate Democracy: A Critical Analysis", 51 Nw.U.L.Rev. 310 (1956).

16. See Chapter 10 infra.

1. See section 190 infra. See generally Sneed, "The Stockholder May Vote as He Pleases: Theory and Fact", 22 U.Pitt.L.Rev. 23 (1960).

vote.[2] Thus shareholders for most purposes generally vote *pro rata* and not *per capita*.[3]

Provisions for different voting rights, subject to some limitations, may usually be included in the articles of incorporation, but, absent a statutory provision to such effect, ordinarily may not be validly effected in the bylaws or by shareholder resolution.[4] Even in the case of a proxy, a voting trust, or a shareholder agreement affecting voting, the voting rights exist according to the articles of incorporation but are exercised, respectively, by the holder of the proxy as voting agent for the shareholder,[5] by the voting trustees as shareholders of record pursuant to the voting trust agreement,[6] or by the shareholder pursuant to the shareholder agreement.[7]

Apart from such modern-day rarities as *per capita* and sliding-scale voting,[8] voting rights may, subject to jurisdictional or other variations, be (a) straight, (b) cumulative, (c) class, (d) contingent, (e) disproportionate, (f) nonvoting. In every stock corporation, voting rights must reside in one or more classes of shares, or possibly debt securities.[9]

2. See, e. g., ABA–ALI Model Bus.Corp.Act § 31; Del.Gen.Corp.Law § 212 (1967); McKinney's N.Y. Bus.Corp.Law, § 612. As to determination of shareholders of record, see section 176 supra.

3. General per capita voting provisions might be permissible in the articles of incorporation. 1910 N.Y. Op.Att'y Gen. 406. Otherwise, voice voting, unless challenged, would obviously be per capita. For older per capita practice, see E. Dodd, American Business Corporations Until 1860, 203, 231 (1954).

4. Matter of Schack (Crown Heights Hospital, Inc), 183 Misc. 563, 49 N.Y.S.2d 658 (Sup.Ct.1944).

5. See section 196 infra.

6. See section 197 infra.

7. See section 198 infra.

8. See, e. g., L. Gower, The Principles of Modern Company Law 325 (2d ed. 1957).

9. See Cal.Gen.Corp.Law, § 2216 (1947); Okl.Bus. Corp.Act § 68(b) (1961). New York provides that the articles of incorporation "may deny, limit or otherwise define the voting rights . . . of shares of any class, but no such denial, limitation or definition of voting rights shall be effective un-

Straight Voting

In straight voting, each share carries one vote for each matter, including one vote for each director to be elected.[10]

Thus in a corporation with a single class of shares, a plurality of the shares generally would elect all of the directors and the other shares would elect no director. If there are two or more classes of outstanding voting shares, each vote usually counts the same regardless of class. If the common shares are numerically greater than the preferred shares, the combined votes of the common shareholders will outvote the preferred shareholders. Straight voting is the normal method of shareholder voting for all corporate matters, except where cumulative voting is in effect with respect to the election of directors; in the latter case, straight voting would be the normal method except in the election of directors.

Cumulative Voting

In cumulative voting, which applies only to the election of directors, each share carries as many votes as there are vacancies to be filled, the shareholder being permitted to distribute the votes for all his shares among the candidates in any way he desires.[11]

less at the time one or more classes of outstanding shares or bonds, singly or in the aggregate, are entitled to full voting rights. . . ." McKinney's N.Y.Bus.Corp.Law, § 501.

10. N. Lattin, The Law of Corporations § 3 (1959). See State ex rel. Swanson v. Perham, 30 Wash.2d 368, 191 P.2d 689 (1948) (majority's right to straight voting held vested right under saving clause of 1933 legislation creating cumulative voting).

11. C. Williams, Cumulative Voting for Directors 6–7 (1951). Campbell, "The Origin and Growth of Cumulative Voting for Directors", 10 Bus.Law. 3 (Apr.1955). The formula for cumulating votes most effectively (assuming one vote per share) is:

$$X = \frac{Y \times N^1}{N+1} + 1$$

X = number of shares needed to elect a given number of directors

Y = total number of voting shares at meeting

N^1 = number of directors desired to elect

N = total number of directors to be elected

Cumulative voting is a form of proportional representation to assure any desirable minority representation on the board.[12]

Cumulative voting is required by state constitutions in some jurisdictions [13] and by statutes in some others,[14] and by federal statute for national banking corporations [15] (known as "mandatory cumulative voting").[16] Elsewhere, cumulative voting exists, in some jurisdictions, absent a provision to the contrary in the articles of incor-

poration or bylaws,[17] or does not exist, in other jurisdictions, unless there is a provision in the articles of incorporation or bylaws providing for cumulative voting (known as "permissive cumulative voting").[18]

Some statutes require that where cumulative voting is authorized, any shareholder intending to vote cumulatively must first announce such intention before doing so.[19] Until the results have been announced by the chairman, a shareholder may change his vote.[20]

The right to vote cumulatively can often be diluted by decreasing the number of vacancies to be filled, by reducing the size of the board of directors, or classifying the board and having a stagger system of election.[21]

See Mills, "Mathematics of Cumulative Voting", 1968 Duke L.J. 28; Cole, "Legal and Mathematical Aspects of Cumulative Voting", 2 S.C.L.Q. 225 (1950); Gerstenberg, "The Mathematics of Cumulative Voting", 9 J.Accountancy 177 (1910).

12. Cumulative voting for directors was introduced in Illinois in 1870; it is analogous to proportional representation in the political area. The inspiration came from John Stuart Mill's Essay on Representative Government published in 1861. Note, "Cumulative Voting, Classified Boards and Proportional Representation", 55 Mich.L.Rev. 997 (1957).

13. Ariz.Const. art. XIV, § 10; Idaho Const. art. XI, § 4; Ill.Const. art. XI, § 3; Ky.Const. art. 207; Miss.Const. art. 7, § 194; Mo.Const. art. XI, § 6; Mont.Const. art. XV, § 4; Neb.Const. art. XII, § 5; N.D.Const. art. VII, § 135; Pa.Const. art. XVI, § 4; S.C.Const. art. IX, § 11; S.D.Const. art. XVII, § 5; W.Va.Const. art. XI, § 4; Hanks v. Borelli, 2 Ariz. App. 589, 411 P.2d 27 (1966) (renewal of corporate charter held to constitute acceptance of constitutional mandatory cumulative voting provision adopted after its original incorporation). See Annot, 43 A.L.R.2d 1322 (1955).

14. E. g., ABA–ALI Model Bus.Corp.Act § 31; Alaska, Arkansas, California, Hawaii, Idaho, Illinois, Kansas, Michigan, Missouri, North Carolina, North Dakota, Ohio, Washington, West Virginia, Wyoming. See State ex rel. Starkey v. Alaska Airlines, Inc., 68 Wash.2d 318, 413 P.2d 352 (1966) (holding application of 1964 Alaska statute changing cumulative voting from mandatory to permissive to preexisting corporation impairment of contract in violation of United States Constitution, unless approved by minority shareholders holding sufficient votes to elect director by cumulative voting); People ex rel. Sobieski v. Western Air Lines, Inc., 258 Cal.App.2d 213, 66 Cal.Rptr. 316 (1968) (enjoining articles of incorporation amendment to eliminate cumulative voting permitted under law of jurisdiction of incorporation of foreign corporation whose principal place of business was in California and large proportion of shareholders lived there).

15. 12 U.S.C.A. § 61.

16. Campbell, "The Origin and Growth of Cumulative Voting for Directors", 10 Bus.Law. 3, 8–10 (Apr. 1955).

17. E. g., ABA–ALI Model Bus.Corp.Act § 31 (alternative provision); Minn.Bus.Corp.Act § 301.26 (1961). See Note, "Right of Cumulative Voting Provided for in By-Laws But Not in Charter", 48 Harv.L.Rev. 509 (1934).

18. E. g., ABA–ALI Model Bus.Corp.Act § 31 (alternative provision); Del.Gen.Corp.Law, § 214 (1967); N.J.Gen.Corp.Law 14:10–15 (1937); McKinney's N.Y.Bus.Corp.Law, § 618 (provision in articles of incorporation); cf. Matter of American Fibre Chair Seat Corp., 265 N.Y. 416, 193 N.E. 253 (1934) (failure to file duly-approved amendment of articles of incorporation to provide for cumulative voting held technical omission and cumulative voting permitted); cf. Matter of Schack (Crown Heights Hospital, Inc.), 183 Misc. 563, 49 N.Y.S.2d 658 (Sup.Ct. 1944) (bylaw provision for variation of cumulative voting held ineffective). See also N.C.Bus.Corp.Act §§ 55–67 (1957); State ex rel. Kearns v. Rindsfoos, 161 Ohio St. 60, 118 N.E.2d 138 (1954) (cumulative voting held not permissible in Ohio banking corporations because of failure of state's banking statute to authorize it expressly).

19. E. g., Minn.Bus.Corp.Act § 301.26 (1961); Ohio Gen.Corp.Law, § 1701.55 (1955). See Commonwealth ex rel. Laughlin v. Green, 351 Pa. 170, 40 A.2d 492 (1945).

20. Zachary v. Milin, 294 Mich. 622, 293 N.W. 770 (1940); State ex rel. David v. Dailey, 23 Wash.2d 25, 158 P.2d 330 (1945). See Grip v. Buffelen Woodworking Co., 73 Wash.2d 219, 437 P.2d 915 (1968) (holding person announced to have been elected ninth director of nine-man board was not elected where recount after adjournment showed that he had tied for ninth position; quaere as to power of board of directors to fill such vacancy).

21. C. Williams, Cumulative Voting for Directors 48–56 (1951). The Illinois and West Virginia con-

If directors are removable without cause by a simple majority vote of shareholders, a director elected by a minority of shareholders could be removed by the majority of shareholders.[22]

Where the right of cumulative voting exists pursuant to a provision in the articles of incorporation or bylaws, the right might be eliminated by proper amendment thereof, which might require no more than majority vote or a vote which the minority could not muster sufficient opposing votes to block.[23]

Arguments in favor of [24] and against [25] cumulative voting are raised periodically.

stitutional provisions requiring cumulative voting have been construed as requiring that all of the directors be elected annually, and prohibiting classification of directors by terms. Wolfson v. Avery, 6 Ill.2d 78, 126 N.E.2d 701 (1955) (6–1); State ex rel. Syphers v. McCune, 143 W.Va. 315, 101 S.E.2d 834 (1958). For contrary constructions of the Pennsylvania and Arizona constitutional provisions, see Stockholders Committee for Better Management of Erie Technological Products, Inc. v. Erie Technological Products, Inc., 248 F.Supp. 380 (W.D.Pa.1965) (upholding bylaw amendment classifying board into three classes, each of not less than two nor more than three directors); Janney v. Philadelphia Transportation Co., 387 Pa. 282, 128 A.2d 76 (1956); Bohannan v. Corporation Commission, 82 Ariz. 299, 313 P.2d 379 (1957). The Ohio Supreme Court construed statutes requiring cumulative voting and permitting classified board of directors as allowing a three-class classification of a three-man board of directors so that one director would be elected annually. Humphrys v. Winous Co., 165 Ohio St. 45, 133 N.E.2d 780 (1956) (4–2). Since then the Ohio statute has been amended to require that at least 3 directors be elected annually. Ohio Gen.Corp.Law, § 1701.57 (1955). See also McDonough v. Copeland Refrigerator Corp., 277 F.Supp. 6 (E.D.Mich.1967) (upholding bylaw amendment changing nine-director board elected annually to nine-director classified board with three directors elected each year). Reduction in the size of the board by appropriate amendment of the articles of incorporation or bylaws is often allowed, despite its adverse effect on cumulative voting. See Bond v. Atlantic Terra Cotta Co., 137 App.Div. 671, 122 N.Y.S. 425 (1st Dep't. 1910). Some statutes regulate such reductions. Cal.Gen.Corp.Law, § 3640 (1947); Note, "Classified Boards in Missouri", 32 Mo.L.Rev. 251 (1967). Other means of restricting cumulative voting are nonvoting shares, voting trusts, and voting agreements. Sensabaugh v. Polson Plywood Co., 135 Mont. 562, 342 P.2d 1064 (1959); E. K. Buck Retail Stores v. Harkert, 157 Neb. 867, 62 N.W.2d 288, 45 A.L.R.2d 774 (1954). The influence of minority directors can be minimized by informal director discussion, scheduling board meetings at times inconvenient for minority directors, or delegating functions to committees to which minority directors are not appointed. See Minn.Bus.Corp.Act § 301.28(4), (8) (1961).

22. Campbell v. Loew's, Inc., 36 Del.Ch. 563, 134 A.2d 852 (Ch.1957) (majority of shareholders held to have inherent power to remove director for cause despite articles of incorporation provision for cumulative voting). But cf. Matter of Rogers Imports, Inc., 202 Misc. 761, 116 N.Y.S.2d 106 (Sup.Ct.1952) (articles of incorporation amendment providing for cumulative voting held to invalidate preexisting bylaw provision for removal of directors without cause by majority of shareholders). Note, "Rela-

tionship between Cumulative Voting and Removal Provisions", 51 Mich.L.Rev. 744 (1953). A few jurisdictions by statute have attempted to remedy this loophole by providing that removal of a director, absent removal of the entire board, can be blocked by vote of the number of shares sufficient to elect such a director cumulatively. E. g., ABA–ALI Model Bus.Corp.Act § 36A (optional section); Cal.Gen.Corp.Law § 810 (1947); Mich.Gen.Corp.Act § 21.13 (1948); Minn.Bus.Corp.Act § 301.29 (1933); McKinney's N.Y.Bus.Corp.Law, § 706(c) (1); Ohio Gen.Corp.Law, § 1701.58 (1955); Pa.Bus.Corp.Law, § 405 (1966). See also Wilder v. Brace, 223 F.Supp. 703 (D.Me.1963) (upholding bylaw authorizing directors to fill vacancies on staggered board for full unexpired terms).

23. Maddock v. Vorclone Corp., 17 Del.Ch. 39, 147 A. 255 (Ch.1929) (amendment of articles of incorporation); Matter of New York Hanseatic Corp. (Kings Co. Lighting Co.), 200 Misc. 530, 103 N.Y.S.2d 698 (Sup.Ct.1951) (amendment of articles of incorporation; dissenters allowed appraisal remedy); Quilliam v. Hebbronville Utilities, Inc., 241 S.W.2d 225 (Tex.Civ.App.1951) (amendment of bylaw); Matter of Rogers Imports, Inc., 202 Misc. 761, 116 N.Y.S.2d 106 (Sup.Ct.1952); C. Williams, Cumulative Voting for Directors 57–59 (1951).

24. The Securities and Exchange Commission has favored cumulative voting whenever it could exert pressure, e. g., under the Federal Public Utility Holding Company Act of 1935, Chapter X of the Federal Bankruptcy Act, and Federal Investment Company Act of 1940. The California Commissioner of Corporations, under the California "blue sky" law, views with disfavor common shares issued by foreign corporations without cumulative voting (cumulative voting being mandatory for California corporations under statute). 15 Bus.Law. 70 (1959); see section 306 infra; Sobieski, "In Support of Cumulative Voting", 15 Bus.Law. 316 (1960); Steadman, "Should Cumulative Voting for Directors be Mandatory?—A Debate", 11 Bus.Law. 9 (Nov. 1955); Young, "The Case for Cumulative Voting", 1950 Wis.L.Rev. 49.

25. Sturdy, "Mandatory Cumulative Voting: An Anachronism", 16 Bus.Law. 550 (1961); Gibson, "Should Cumulative Voting for Directors be Mandatory?—A Debate", 11 Bus.Law. 22 (Nov.1955); Axley, "The Case against Cumulative Voting", 1950 Wis.L.Rev. 278.

Class (Series) Voting

In class (or series) voting, which obviously is possible only where two or more classes (series) of shares outstanding, each class (series) of shares votes as a separate unit for one or more purposes. The board of directors might be classified, with one class (series) of shares voting for its class of directors and another class (series) of shares separately voting for its class of directors.[26]

Either along with or apart from class (series) voting for directors, class voting for other matters might exist under statute or the articles of incorporation. Where such class voting exists, a sufficient vote of each class might be required,[27] or a sufficient vote generally plus a sufficient class vote of any class adversely affected by the matter being voted on.[28] Sometimes such a sufficient class vote might be required even though the shares are otherwise nonvoting.[29]

Contingent Voting

Contingent voting rights, which obviously exist only where two or more classes (or series) of shares are outstanding, are those which arise upon the happening of a stated contingency, such as the default of specified dividends. Once the contingency is over, such as the payment of dividend arrearages, a class (series) of shares with contingent voting rights usually reverts to its former voting status.[30] The requirement is occasionally found that preferred shares have at least minimum contingent or class voting rights.[31]

Disproportionate Voting

Disproportionate voting, which is possible only where two or more classes (or series) are outstanding, exists when one class (series) of shares is validly given greater or less votes per share than another class (series). An example would be where one class (series) has normal voting rights and the shares of another class (series) carry multiple or fractional votes.[32]

26. ABA–ALI Model Bus.Corp.Act § 136; e. g., Mc-Kinney's N.Y.Bus.Corp.Law, § 703(a); Standard Power & Light Corp. v. Investment Associates, 29 Del.Ch. 593, 51 A.2d 572 (Sup.Ct.1947). C. Williams, Cumulative Voting for Directors 18–19 (1951); class voting for a classified board of directors, under constitutions and statutes requiring cumulative voting, might not be valid since shareholders would not be able to vote for all directors to be elected and their voting power could be disproportionate to their number of votes. Mo.Op.Att'y Gen.No.238, Aug. 24, 1964. Provisions for removal of directors, where there is such class (series) voting for directors, should prescribe that directors may only be removed by the class (series) of shareholders which elected them. Statutes sometimes so provide. E. g., Cal.Gen.Corp.Law, § 810 (1947); Mich.Gen.Corp. Act § 21.13 (1948); McKinney's N.Y.Bus.Corp.Law, § 706(c) (2); Ohio Gen.Corp.Law, § 1701.58 (1955). See section 125 supra.

27. See, e. g., ABA–ALI Model Bus.Corp.Act § 55; Del.Gen.Corp.Law, § 242 (1967); McKinney's N.Y. Bus.Corp.Law, § 617.

28. See, e. g., McKinney's N.Y.Bus.Corp.Law, § 804(a) (overall majority and majority of class (or series) for certain amendments of articles of incorporation adversely affecting class); id. § 903(a) (2) (overall two-thirds vote and majority of class (or series) for certain mergers or consolidations); Hartford Accident & Indemnity Co. v. W. S. Dickey Clay Mfg. Co., 26 Del.Ch. 16, 21 A.2d 178 (Ch.1941), aff'd 26 Del.Ch. 411, 24 A.2d 315 (Sup.Ct.1942).

29. ABA–ALI Model Bus.Corp.Act § 55. See note 37 infra. Securities exchange listing requirements might prescribe minimal class voting rights for oth-

erwise nonvoting preferred shares. See note 38 infra. See Buxbaum, "Preferred Stock—Law and Draftsmanship", 42 Calif.L.Rev. 243, 294–295 (1954).

30. See Ellingwood v. Wolf's Head Oil Refining Co., 27 Del.Ch. 356, 38 A.2d 743, 154 A.L.R. 406 (Sup.Ct. 1944); State ex rel. Cullitan v. Campbell, 135 Ohio St. 238, 20 N.E.2d 366 (1939); Annot., 154 A.L.R. 418 (1945).

31. Federal Public Utility Holding Company Act of 1935, § 7(c), 15 U.S.C.A. § 79g(c); Public Utility Holding Company Act Release No. 13,106 (Feb. 16, 1956); Federal National Housing Act § 608, 12 U. S.C.A. § 1743; Sarner v. Mason, 130 F.Supp. 829 (D.N.J.1955), aff'd 228 F.2d 176 (3d Cir. 1955), cert. denied 351 U.S. 924, 76 S.Ct. 781, 100 L.Ed. 1454 (1956). Securities exchange listing requirements sometimes prescribe minimal contingent and class voting rights for otherwise nonvoting preferred shares. See note 50 infra. See Buxbaum, "Preferred Stock—Law and Draftsmanship", 42 Calif.L.Rev. 243, 290–293 (1954).

32. Garnier v. Garnier, 248 Cal.App.2d 255, 56 Cal. Rptr. 247 (1967) (holding fractional voting of shares not authorized by statute, articles of incorporation, or bylaws). Some statutes expressly permit multiple or fractional voting provisions. E. g., Va.Stock Corp.Act § 13.1–32 (1957). See 1969 Model Act revision. Presumably such provisions are permissible in most jurisdictions which provide for one vote per

Nonvoting Shares

Except for a few jurisdictions which require that all shares have voting rights,[33] nonvoting shares may usually be authorized and issued, so long as voting rights reside in one or more classes (or series) of outstanding shares or possibly debt securities.[34]

Statutes sometimes impose limitations on the issue of nonvoting shares.[35]

Even shares which are nominally nonvoting might have mandatory voting rights with respect to certain matters adversely affecting such shares or otherwise.[36]

Shares of a class otherwise entitled to voting rights, under certain circumstances, might not be voted or counted in determining the total number of outstanding shares.[37]

share except as otherwise provided in the articles of incorporation. 1910 N.Y.Op.Att'y Gen. 406. Illinois permits no variation from one vote per share. Ill.Bus.Corp.Act § 28 (1933). By issuing different classes of shares for different considerations, disproportionate voting on the basis of investment is still possible even within the one-vote per share limitation. For discussion of fractions of shares, see section 161 supra. See Seamans & Barger, "Multiple Votes Per Share", 16 Bus.Law. 400 (1961).

33. Constitutional and statutory provisions requiring cumulative voting have sometimes been construed as requiring that all shares be entitled to vote for directors. Ill.Const. art. XI, § 3; People ex rel. Watseka Telephone Co. v. Emmerson, 302 Ill. 300, 134 N.E. 707, 21 A.L.R. 636 (1922); W.Va.Const. art. XI, § 4; State ex rel. Dewey Portland Cement Co. v. O'Brien, 142 W.Va. 451, 96 S.E.2d 171 (1956) (4–1), since overruled by 1958 amendment of W.Va. Const. art. XI, § 4; Diamond v. Parkersburg-Aetna Corp., 146 W.Va. 543, 122 S.E.2d 436 (1961) (applying 1958 amendment to preexisting corporation). Contra, Mo.Const. art. XI, § 6; Shapiro v. Tropicana Lanes, 371 S.W.2d 237 (Mo.1963) (nonvoting common shares); State ex rel. Frank v. Swanger, 190 Mo. 561, 89 S.W. 872 (1905) (nonvoting preferred shares). See Comment, "Non-Voting Shares —The Code and the Constitution", 16 S.C.L.Rev. 657 (1964); Comment, "Corporations: Is Non-Voting Common Stock Legal in Missouri?", 27 U.Kan. City L.Rev. 234 (1959); Note, "Non-Voting Common Stock: State Constitutional Prohibitions" 7 Duke L.J. 105 (1958); Note, "Status of Non-Voting Stock in Nebraska", 33 Neb.L.Rev. 636 (1954); Note, "The Right of Non-Voting Common Stockholders to Vote for Directors or Managers in Missouri", 17 U.Kan. City L.Rev. 66 (1948). By statute, Illinois requires that all shares enjoy one vote for all matters requiring shareholder action. Ill.Bus.Corp.Act § 28 (1933). Ghana prohibits denial to a shareholder to vote but permits multiple votes to some extent. Ghana Companies Code §§ 31, 49, 50 (1963).

34. See, e. g., ABA–ALI Model Bus.Corp.Act § 31; Del.Gen.Corp.Law, § 151 (1967); New York apparently permits all shares to be nonvoting so long as outstanding debt securities enjoy full voting rights. See note 9 supra and note 36 infra. Ambiguous provisions in the articles of incorporation might require court construction. Gottschalk v. Avalon Realty Co., 249 Wis. 78, 23 N.W.2d 606 (1946); State ex rel. Cullitan v. Campbell, 135 Ohio St. 238, 20 N.E.2d 366 (1939). See Matter of North European Oil Corp., 36 Del.Ch. 290, 129 A.2d 259 (Ch.1957) (court approval of reorganization of solvent corporation unable to locate majority of its shareholders providing for missing shares to be nonvoting until

holders located, with corporation appointed trustee for missing shareholders with duty to try to locate them). In New York, prior to September 1, 1951, shareholders had the right, absent *specific* exclusion, to vote in connection with corporate mortgages, guarantees, sales of assets, establishing priorities or creating preferences, consolidation, voluntary dissolution, or change of name. Such language is often found in pre-1951 articles of incorporation. Since then a general denial of voting rights denies the right to vote for such matters. The 1951 amendment does not affect voting rights of shares issued or authorized before September 1, 1951.

35. See note 33 supra. Federal Public Utility Holding Company Act of 1935, § 7(c), 15 U.S.C.A. § 79g(c); Federal Bankruptcy Act § 216(12), 11 U.S. C.A. § 612(12); Investment Company Act of 1940, § 18, 15 U.S.C.A. § 80a–18; Dodd, "The Modern Corporation, Private Property and Recent Federal Legislation", 54 Harv.L.Rev. 917 (1941).

36. See, e. g., pre-1966 ABA–ALI Model Bus.Corp.Act § 55 (certain amendments of articles of incorporation), § 67 (certain mergers or consolidations); Del.Gen.Corp.Law, § 242 (1967); McKinney's N.Y. Bus.Corp.Law, § 804(a) (certain amendments of articles of incorporation adversely affecting class (or series)); id. § 903(a) (2) (certain mergers or consolidation adversely affecting class (or series)). See section 340 infra.

37. See, e. g., McKinney's N.Y.Bus.Corp.Law, § 612(b) (treasury shares; its shares held by any other corporation if majority of shares entitled to vote in election of directors of such other corporation is held by it); id. § 612(f) (shares called for redemption if redemption proceeds have been irrevocably deposited); ABA–ALI Model Bus.Corp.Act § 31. The former Delaware statutory provision that shares of a corporation's own capital shares belonging to it should not be voted "directly or indirectly" had been construed as precluding not only the corporation from voting treasury shares but also the corporation's subsidiary from voting shares it held in the corporation. Continental-Midwest Corp. v. Hotel Sherman, Inc., 13 Ill.App.2d 188, 141 N.E.2d 400 (1957); Italo Petroleum Corp. of America v. Producers Oil Corp. of America, 20 Del.Ch. 283, 174 A. 276 (Ch.1934); see also Atterbury v. Consolidated Coppermines Corp., 26 Del.Ch. 1, 20 A.2d 743 (Ch.1941). But cf. Dal-Tran Serv. Co. v. Fifth Ave. Coach Lines, Inc., 14 A.D.2d 349, 220 N.Y.S.2d 549

The New York Stock Exchange, since 1926, has barred the listing of nonvoting common shares, and, since 1940, has barred and prohibits a listed company from having nonvoting common shares outstanding in public hands,[38] the listing of nonvoting preferred shares which do not have the right, as a class, to elect at least two directors when six quarterly dividends, consecutive or nonconsecutive, are in default, or where a two-thirds class vote of such shares is not required for any change adversely affecting such shares.[39]

Voting Debt Securities

Some statutes, as previously mentioned, expressly permit voting rights to be con-

(1st Dep't 1961) (contrary result absent statute); Vanderlip v. Los Molinos Land Co., 56 Cal.App.2d 747, 133 P.2d 467 (1943). See also Leffert v. Jackman, 227 N.Y. 310, 125 N.E. 446 (1919); Comment, "The Voting of Stock Held in Cross Ownership", 76 Harv.L.Rev. 1642 (1963). Note, "Voting Rights in the Stock of a Parent Corporation Held by a Subsidiary", 28 U.Chi.L.Rev. 151 (1960). As for a corporation's voting its own shares held by it in a fiduciary capacity, see Del.Gen.Corp.Law, § 160 (1967); Cleveland Trust Co. v. Eaton, 11 Ohio Misc. 151, 229 N.E.2d 850 (C.P.1967); Graves v. Security Trust Co., 369 S.W.2d 114 (Ky.1963); 36 N.C.Op. Att'y Gen. 13, Sept. 27, 1960.

38. N.Y.S.E. Company Manual § A15. See United Funds, Inc. v. Carter Prods., Inc., No. 102A/450A4288 (Cir.Ct. Baltimore City 1963), 151 The Daily Record (Baltimore) 2 (Sept. 23, 1963) (enjoining issuance of new nonvoting common shares which would have resulted in delisting of present listed publicly-held common shares whose prospectus at time of their offering had represented that they would be listed, where no business justification for such issuance was shown). In 1925, Dodge Brothers, Inc. set up a capital structure of bonds, preferred shares, and two classes of common shares, under which the preferred shares and four-fifths of the common shares were nonvoting, with the result that an investment of less than $2,-250,000 controlled a $130,000,000 concern. This device was criticized in W. Ripley, Main Street and Wall Street 86–87 (1927). Cf. listing by the New York Stock Exchange of common shares of The Ford Motor Company in 1956, despite the fact that the Class B shares held by the Ford family were, by provisions for increasing such shares' voting rights per share, to retain 40 percent of the voting power with only 5.1 percent of the equity. For criticism of the latter device, see J. Livingston, The American Stockholder 166–177 (1958).

39. N.Y.S.E. Company Manual § A15.

Henn Corporations 2d Ed. HB—24

ferred on holders of bonds, debentures, and other debt securities.[40] To the extent such voting rights are conferred, shareholder control is, of course, diluted.

FORMALITIES OF SHAREHOLDER ACTION

190. **Shareholder voting rights are traditionally asserted at shareholder meetings, but modern statutes expressly permit shareholder action by a writing signed by all, or occasionally less than all, shareholders entitled to vote thereon in lieu of the required vote at a meeting.**

As previously indicated, shareholder rights with respect to control are traditionally asserted by voting at shareholder meetings.

Modern statutes now provide that written shareholder consent without a meeting, where unanimous or as otherwise prescribed, constitutes shareholder action in lieu of the required vote at a shareholder meeting.[1]

Sometimes, even in the absence of statute, shareholder informal action has been upheld by the courts where the rights of minority shareholders were not prejudiced.[2]

40. See section 154 supra. New York apparently permits all voting rights to be conferred on the holders of secured and unsecured bonds, debentures, and notes. McKinney's N.Y.Bus.Corp.Law, § 501(a). See note 9 supra.

1. E. g., ABA–ALI Model Bus.Corp.Act § 138 (any action required to be or which may be taken at a shareholder meeting may be taken without such meeting by unanimous written consent of all shareholders entitled to vote with respect to such matter); Alabama, Alaska, Arkansas, California, Colorado, Connecticut, Delaware, Hawaii, Idaho, Illinois, Iowa, Kansas, Kentucky, Louisiana, Maryland, Massachusetts, Minnesota, Mississippi, Montana, Nebraska, Nevada, New Jersey, New Mexico, New York, North Carolina, North Dakota, Ohio, Oklahoma, Oregon, Pennsylvania, South Carolina, South Dakota, Texas, Utah, Virginia, Washington, West Virginia, Wisconsin, Wyoming, District of Columbia. New Jersey permits shareholder action without a meeting by less than all of the shareholders if the articles of incorporation specifically so provide. Delaware permits the same even if the articles of incorporation do not so provide. Nevada permits such action by majority consent unless the action is such as would require a larger vote. See note 2 infra.

2. Philadelphia Life Ins. Co. v. Crosland-Cullen Co., 234 F.2d 780 (4th Cir. 1956). See Annot., 51 A.L.R.

SHAREHOLDERS' MEETINGS

191. Shareholder meetings are of two principal types: (a) annual and (b) special. Corporations are usually required to hold annual shareholder meetings, primarily for the election of directors. Some states still require shareholder meetings of domestic corporations to be held within the state, but modern statutes expressly permit such meetings to be held within or without the state. Advance written notice of the meeting, unless waived, is required to be given to shareholders. To transact business at a shareholder meeting, the required quorum must be present, and action, absent a greater requirement, is by majority vote. Shareholders for voting purposes are usually determined by the record of shareholders or voting list compiled therefrom. Inspectors of elections are sometimes appointed to supervise corporate elections. Court proceedings are usually available to compel or enjoin the holding of shareholder meetings, or to review corporate elections as provided by statute. Post-meeting reports, giving an account of the annual meeting, are sometimes mailed by corporations to their shareholders shortly after such meeting to promote better shareholder relations.

Shareholder meetings are of two principal types: (a) annual and (b) special. Where the incorporators-subscribers are shareholders, the organization meetings of incorporators can be considered as an additional type.[1]

Shareholders of record are entitled to receive notice of, and to be represented in person or by proxy at, such meetings. The corporation, usually through its secretary, should keep minutes of all meetings.[2] Such minutes are among the corporate records open to reasonable shareholder inspection.[3]

Shareholder meetings, like other meetings, should be conducted with due regard for parliamentary rules.[4]

Annual Meetings

Corporations are usually required to hold annual shareholder meetings.[5] The bylaws

---

941 (1927). But see Matter of Louisiana Investment & Loan Corp., 224 F.Supp. 274 (E.D.La.1963) (holding informal get-together of shareholders no meeting and no compliance with strictly-construed unanimous consent requirements of Louisiana statute); Note, "Corporations—Close Corporations—Strictness of Requirements at Meetings of Shareholders and Directors", 14 S.C.L.Q. 408 (1962).

[§ 191]

1. See section 135 supra. On shareholder meetings, see generally F. Shackleton, The Law and Practice of Meetings (5th ed. 1967); W. Craig, The Law and Procedure of Meetings in Canada (1966); L. Doris & E. Friedman, Encyclopedia of Corporate Meetings, Minutes and Resolutions (1958); Wetzel, "Conduct of a Stockholders' Meeting", 22 Bus.Law. 303 (1967); Kerr & Wolf, "Shareholder's Meetings Under The Texas Business Corporation Act", 43 Texas L.Rev. 713 (1965); Mahoney, "Will the Annual Meeting *Please* Come to Order!", 71 Fortune, No. 5, 140 (May 1965); Kelly, "Preparing for Shareholders Meetings", 52 Ill.B.J. 926 (1964); Monaghon, "Annual Stockholders' Meetings: Some

Legal and Practical Problems", 16 Baylor L.Rev. 129 (1964); Gilbert, "Annual Shareholders' Meeting and the Corporate Lawyer: Theory and Reality", 4 Corp.Prac.Comm. 56 (Feb. 1963); Caplin, "Proxies, Annual Meetings and Corporate Democracy: The Lawyer's Role", 37 Va.L.Rev. 653 (1951). See also L. Gilbert & J. Gilbert, First/Twenty-Ninth Annual Reports of Stockholder Activities at Corporation Meetings (1940/1968).

2. Statutes sometimes expressly require the keeping of corporate minutes. E. g., ABA-ALI Model Bus. Corp.Act § 46; Cal.Gen.Corp.Law § 3000 (1947); McKinney's N.Y.Bus.Corp.Law, § 624. Absent entry in the minute book of a shareholder resolution, oral evidence thereof is admissible. Handley v. Stutz, 139 U.S. 417, 11 S.Ct. 530, 35 L.Ed. 227 (1891). For case permitting corporate minutes to be signed nunc pro tunc, see Matter of Teperman v. Atcos Baths, Inc., 6 Misc.2d 162, 163 N.Y.S.2d 221 (Sup.Ct.1957), aff'd 7 A.D.2d 854, 182 N.Y.S.2d 765 (2d Dep't 1959); L. Doris & E. Friedman, Encyclopedia of Corporate Meetings, Minutes and Resolutions (1958); Annot., 66 A.L.R. 1328 (1938), 48 A.L.R.2d 1259 (1956).

3. Under common law principles or, where statutes give shareholders a statutory right to inspect the minutes, under such statutes. See section 199 infra.

4. 1 G. Hornstein, Corporation Law and Practice § 335 (1959). A standard manual on parliamentary rules should be used as a reference. E. g., A. Sturgis, Sturgis Standard Code of Parlimentary Procedure (2d ed. 1966); L. Cushing, Modern Rules of Order (1964 ed.); H. Robert, Robert's Rules of Order Revised (75th ed. 1951). See also Grady, "Role of the CPA at Stockholder Meetings", 101 J. Accountancy 31 (1956). For securities exchange rules applicable to shareholder meetings, see N.Y.S.E. Company Manual § A8.

5. See, e. g., ABA-ALI Model Bus.Corp.Act § 26; Del.Gen.Corp.Law, § 211 (1967); McKinney's N.Y. Bus.Corp.Law, § 602(b). But see Del.Gen.Corp.Law, § 228 (1967) (permitting any shareholder action without meeting by unanimous written consent or, if authorized by articles of incorporation, by written consent of holders of percentage of shares spec-

frequently fix the time for such meetings, usually in the spring.[6] At such meetings, the most important business is usually the election of all or some of the directors.[7]

The agenda may include reports of management, the amendment or repeal of by-laws, resolutions introduced in behalf of management or shareholders, extraordinary corporate matters, or other matters which may properly come before such meetings. The notice of the meeting will usually set forth the purposes thereof.[8] Statutes sometimes provide procedures for special meetings to elect directors when the required election has not been held.[9]

Special Meetings

Special shareholder meetings, between the annual meetings, may usually be called pur-

suant to applicable statutes,[10] the articles of incorporation, or more likely the bylaws,[11] for appropriate purposes.[12] The business transacted at a special meeting should be confined to the purposes set forth in the call.[13] There might even be special meetings of particular classes of shares if duly authorized and called for appropriate purposes.[14]

10. E. g., ABA–ALI Model Bus.Corp.Act § 26; McKinney's N.Y.Bus.Corp.Law, § 602(c) (callable by board of directors and by such person or persons as may be so authorized by articles of incorporation or bylaws).

11. See Cummings v. United Artists Theatre Circuit, Inc., 237 Md. 1, 204 A.2d 795 (1964) (5 to 2) (denying relief against consummation of transaction despite board of directors wrongful refusal to call special meeting on proper request of 25 percent of shareholders); Republic Corp. v. Carter, 15 N.Y.2d 661, 255 N.Y.S.2d 875, 204 N.E.2d 206 (1964) (call of meeting by president held not cancelable by board of directors or his successor after his proper removal from office by board of directors); Richman v. DeVal Aerodynamics, Inc., 40 Del.Ch. 389, 183 A.2d 569 (Ch.1962) (holding that "request" by majority of shareholders of record entitled to vote as of time of delivery of request to corporation could compel president to call special shareholder meeting); Smith v. Upshaw, 217 Ga. 703, 124 S.E.2d 751 (1962) (holding bylaw requirement that call of meeting be by 10 percent in number of shareholders not met by subsequent ratification by 10 percent of shareholders); Josephson v. Cosmocolor Corp., 31 Del.Ch. 46, 64 A.2d 35 (Ch.1949). Compare Moon v. Moon Motor Car Co., 17 Del.Ch. 176, 151 A. 298 (Ch.1930), with Permagon Press, Inc. v. Ross, — Misc.2d —, 306 N.Y.S.2d 103 (Sup.Ct.1969).

12. E. Aranow & H. Einhorn, Proxy Contests for Proxy Control 67 et seq. (2d ed. 1968). For discussion of propriety of purposes, see Campbell v. Loew's, Inc., 36 Del.Ch. 563, 134 A.2d 852 (Ch.1957); Auer v. Dressel, 306 N.Y. 427, 118 N.E.2d 590, 48 A.L.R.2d 604 (1954), infra note 14. Propriety of subject for action by shareholders is also relevant under the proposals-of-security-holders provisions of the S.E.C. Proxy Rules. See section 297 infra. On sufficiency of notice of special shareholder meeting which failed to specify that bylaw requiring two-thirds quorum was invalid and would be treated as such, see Matter of William Faehndrich, Inc., 2 N.Y.2d 468, 161 N.Y.S.2d 99, 141 N.E.2d 597 (1957).

13. E. g., McKinney's N.Y.Bus.Corp.Law, § 602(c) (only such business may be transacted which is related to purpose or purposes set forth in notice).

14. Auer v. Dressel, 306 N.Y. 427, 118 N.E.2d 590, 48 A.L.R.2d 604 (1954). Matter of R. Hoe & Co., Inc., a New York corporation had two classes of outstanding shares: Class A and Common. Its arti-

ified in articles of incorporation but not less than minimum percentage of total vote required by law for proposed corporate action; consents may be obtained by proxies—id. § 212; notice of action taken must be sent promptly to all shareholders—id. § 228); Matter of Mansdorf v. Unexcelled, Inc., 28 A.D.2d 44, 281 N.Y.S.2d 173 (1st Dep't 1967) (upholding power of board of directors to fix date of annual meeting only nine months after prior annual meeting); Wilder v. Brace, 223 F.Supp. 703 (D.Me.1963) (upholding bylaw of Maine corporation permitting board of directors fo fill vacancies on classified board for term extending beyond next annual shareholders meeting); Penn-Texas Corp. v. Niles-Bement-Pond Co., 34 N.J.Super. 373, 112 A.2d 302 (1955) (holding that attempt by directors to amend bylaws for later annual shareholder meeting (thus extending their term of office) violated New Jersey statute for annual election of directors and their holding office for one year).

6. The date of the annual meeting should be set so as to allow time for the preparation of the financial audit and annual report between the end of the fiscal year and such meeting. The most common months for shareholder meetings are April and May. See N. McLaren, Annual Reports to Stockholders (1947).

7. See, e. g., ABA–ALI Model Bus.Corp.Act § 26; Del.Gen.Corp.Law § 211(b) (1967); McKinney's N.Y.Bus.Corp.Law, § 602(b); Matter of Dollinger v. Dollinger Corp., 51 Misc.2d 802, 274 N.Y.S.2d 285 (Sup.Ct.1966) (upholding election of directors at shareholder meeting, duly called and concerned, with quorum present, after president unilaterally adjourned meeting and shareholders elected successor chairman).

8. E. g., ABA–ALI Model Bus.Corp.Act § 27.

9. E. g., McKinney's N.Y.Bus.Corp.Law, § 603.

cles of incorporation provided for an 11-man board of directors, nine of whom were to be elected by the Class A shareholders, and two of whom were to be elected by the Common shareholders; that the voting rights with respect to all matters, other than the election of directors, were to be in the holders of Class A shares; that the board of directors could remove directors for cause; and that vacancies in the board of directors occurring during the term should be filled by the majority vote of the remaining directors. The bylaws provided that they could be amended either by a majority of the board of directors or by the shareholders at a special meeting called for that purpose. A majority of the Class A shareholders requested the president to call a special meeting of the Class A shareholders, pursuant to a bylaw provision requiring the president to call a special meeting upon the request of shareholders owning a majority of the shares entitled to vote at such meeting, for the following purposes: (a) To vote on a resolution indorsing the administration of the former president and demanding his reinstatement; (b) To amend the articles of incorporation and bylaws to provide that vacancies on the board of directors arising from the removal of a director by the shareholders be filled only by shareholders of the class theretofore represented by the directors so removed; (c) To consider and vote on charges to remove four Class A directors for cause and to elect their successors; and (d) To amend the bylaws to reduce the quorum requirement for board of directors action. The president refused to call the meeting on the ground, among others, that the foregoing purposes were not proper subjects for a Class A shareholder meeting. The Court of Appeals split, 5 to 2, holding that the meeting should be called: Purpose (a)—Majority: Proper, since Class A shareholders could legally vote thereon, thus putting the directors, who were empowered to appoint and remove officers, on notice of the attitude of the shareholders; Minority: Improper, since any vote of Class A shareholders on officers would be an "idle gesture" and have no direct effect, inasmuch as appointment and removal of officers are board of directors functions; Purpose (b)—Majority: Proper, since Class A shareholders could vote effectively thereon; Minority: Improper, since dilution of power of Common directors to share in filling director vacancies constituted reclassification of voting rights adversely affecting Common shares and thereby afforded mandatory voting rights to the holders of such shares, thereby making Class A share vote alone ineffective; Purpose (c)—Majority: Proper, since shareholders who elect directors retain, under the circumstances involved, inherent power to remove directors for cause; Minority: Improper, since the articles of incorporation provisions granting removal power to directors precluded shareholders from exercising such power and contemplated procedure involved prejudging by proxy holders; Purpose (d) —Majority: not discussed; Minority: Improper, since implementing improper proposals. See also Liese v. Jupiter Corp., —— Del.Ch. ——, 241 A.2d 492 (Ch.1968); Starr v. Tomlinson, 7 Misc.2d 916, 166 N.Y.S.2d 629 (Sup.Ct.1957) (holding corporate owners should not be deprived of right to determine basic corporate policy).

Place of Shareholder Meetings

Some statutes still require that shareholder meetings be held in the state of incorporation, but modern statutes expressly permit such meetings to be held within or without the state.[15]

The articles of incorporation, or more likely the bylaws, might designate the place of meeting.[16]

Notice of Shareholder Meetings

Written notice of a shareholder meeting is usually required to be sent to shareholders sufficiently in advance of the meeting. There are usually statutory requirements, often implemented by bylaw provisions.[17]

Such notice, under the Model Business Corporation Act, for example, must state the place, day, and hour of the meeting and, in case of a special meeting, the purpose or purposes for which the meeting is called, and must be served on or mailed to each shareholder of record[18] entitled to vote at

15. E. g., ABA–ALI Model Bus.Corp.Act § 26; Cal. Gen.Corp.Law, § 2210 (1947); Del.Gen.Corp.Law, § 211 (1967) (as bylaws provide); Ill.Bus.Corp.Act § 26 (1933); Mich.Gen.Corp.Act § 21.38 (1948).

16. McKinney's N.Y.Bus.Corp.Law, § 602(a) (shareholder meetings to be held at such place, within or without state, as may be provided in bylaws, or as may be fixed, from time to time, by board of directors pursuant to authority conferred by bylaws; otherwise at office of corporation within state). Several corporations rotate the sites of their shareholder meetings and have regional meetings tied together by closed circuit television. The 1969 Model Act revision permits the bylaws to prescribe the manner of determining the time and place of meetings and the persons who may call them.

17. See, e. g., ABA–ALI Model Bus.Corp.Act § 27.

18. ABA–ALI Model Bus.Corp.Act § 27. See Merrion v. Scorup-Somerville Cattle Co., 134 F.2d 473 (10th Cir. 1943), cert. denied 319 U.S. 760, 63 S.Ct. 1317, 87 L.Ed. 1712 (1943). For fixing of record date or closing of share transfer books, see section 176 supra. See also Pacific Discount Co. v. Jackson, 37 N.J. 169, 179 A.2d 745 (1962) (certified mail held to satisfy registered mail requirement); Berger v. Amana Society, 253 Iowa 378, 111 N.W.2d 753 (1961) (statement of purposes held insufficient); Grant v. Hartman Ranch Co., 193 Cal.App.2d 497, 14 Cal. Rptr. 531 (1961) (setting aside action where notice omitted hour of meeting); Starrett Corp. v. Fifth Ave. & Twenty-Ninth St. Corp., 1 F.Supp. 868, 874–

such meeting not less than 10 nor more than 50 days before the date of meeting.[19]

Notice may be waived in writing before or after a meeting.[20]

If due notice is not given, the meeting, absent waiver or estoppel,[21] is a nullity.[22]

Quorum and Action at Shareholder Meetings

The quorum requirements for shareholder meetings are fixed, within statutory limitations,[23] by the articles of incorporation[24] or

---

875 (S.D.N.Y.1932) (holding telephone or other oral advice insufficient under statute requiring notice "in writing").

19. ABA–ALI Model Bus.Corp.Act § 27; cf. ABA–ALI Model Bus.Corp.Act § 67 (at least 20 days' notice for shareholder meeting called to act upon plan of merger or consolidation); McKinney's N.Y.Bus. Corp.Law, § 605 (requiring notice, when proposed action would afford appraisal remedy, to contain statement of purpose of meeting and to effect that proposed action, if taken, would entitle shareholders fulfilling statutory requirements to appraisal remedy. See American Hardware Corp. v. Savage Arms Corp., 37 Del. 59, 136 A.2d 690 (Sup.Ct.1957); Humphrys v. Winous Co., 165 Ohio St. 45, 133 N.E. 2d 780 (1956); Bryan v. Western Pacific R.R., 28 Del.Ch. 13, 35 A.2d 909 (Ch.1944); Robinson, "The Stockholder's Common Law Right to Notice of Business to be Transacted at Meetings", 5 Duke B. J. 1 (1955); Note, "Notice and Quorum Requirements of Shareholders Meetings", 24 U.Cin.L.Rev. 578 (1955). In MacCrone v. American Capital Corp., 51 F.Supp. 462 (D.Del.1943), the plaintiff argued that, although the minimum statutory notice had been given, the problem involved was of such complexity that the shareholders could not inform themselves of the issues within the 20-day minimum statutory notice period, and that, therefore, the vote should be set aside by the court in the exercise of its equitable powers. The court rejected the contention, pointing out that if judges were to substitute their judgment for that of the management on the length of notice, the directors would be in an intolerable position each time they were confronted with the decision of length of notice. Articles of incorporation or bylaw provisions requiring specified times for notices, if within the statutory time limits, are valid. Davison v. Parke, Austin & Lipscomb, Inc., 165 Misc. 32, 299 N.Y.S. 960 (Sup. Ct.1937), modified on other grounds 256 App.Div. 1071, 12 N.Y.S.2d 358 (1st Dep't 1939). Proper notice for a shareholder meeting has been held sufficient for an adjournment thereof. Matter of Bushwick & L. Ass'n, 189 Misc. 316, 70 N.Y.S.2d 478 (Sup.Ct.1947). Some statutes expressly deal with effectiveness of notice in cases of adjourned meetings. E. g., McKinney's N.Y.Bus.Corp.Law, § 605(b).

20. ABA–ALI Model Bus.Corp.Act § 137; Del.Gen. Corp.Law § 229 (1967); McKinney's N.Y.Bus.Corp. Law, § 606 (by waiver of notice, signed by any shareholder in person or by proxy, whether before or after meeting; attendance of any shareholder at meeting, in person or by proxy, without protesting prior to conclusion of meeting lack of notice of such meeting, to constitute waiver of notice by him).

21. Andrews v. Precision Apparatus, Inc., 217 F. Supp. 679, 685 (S.D.N.Y.1963); Kearneysville Creamery Co. v. American Creamery Co., 103 W.Va. 259, 137 S.E. 217, 51 A.L.R. 938 (1927), (estoppel by participation at meeting of all shareholders). Cf. Matter of 74 Tremont Ave. Corp., 10 Misc.2d 662, 173 N.Y.S.2d 154 (Sup.Ct.1958) (where factions in litigation, shareholders' actual knowledge of purpose of meeting held not to constitute waiver); "Sinnova" v. American Alcolac Corp., 8 Misc.2d 166, 171 N.Y.S.2d 149 (Sup.Ct.1957) (giving of general proxy held no waiver of notice of future meetings). See McKinney's N.Y.Bus.Corp.Law, § 606, discussed in note 20 supra. Camp v. Shannon, 162 Tex. 515, 348 S.W.2d 517 (1961) held that where all shareholders were present either in person or by proxy at a disputed shareholders' meeting called to order and presided over by the respondent, he could not complain because the meeting was not held on the date fixed by the bylaws or because notice of the meeting was inadequate. If notice is defective and not waived, an absent shareholder can invalidate the action taken at the meeting. Grant v. Hartman Ranch Co., 193 Cal.App.2d 497, 14 Cal.Rptr. 531 (1961).

22. 5 W. Fletcher, Private Corporations §§ 2006–2011 (rev. vol. 1967); E. Aranow & H. Einhorn, Proxy Contests for Corporate Control 62 (2d ed. 1968). Statutes may excuse lack of notice where delivery of the notice would be unlawful. Del.Gen.Corp.Law § 230 (1967); McKinney's N.Y.Bus.Corp.Law, § 108 (when notice or lapse of time unnecessary; notices dispensed with when delivery prohibited).

23. E. g., McKinney's N.Y.Bus.Corp.Law, § 608 (holders of majority of shares entitled to vote at meeting (or of class or series of shares when specified item of business is required to be voted on by class or series); lesser quorum not less than one-third of shares entitled to vote may be provided for in articles of incorporation or bylaws; greater quorum may be provided for in articles of incorporation; shareholders present may adjourn meeting despite absence of quorum). Quaere, whether at common law a quorum required no more than one or two shareholders. Morrill v. Little Falls Mfg. Co., 53 Minn. 371, 55 N.W. 547 (1893) (immaterial whether number only one or more than one); Sharp v. Dawes, 2 Q.B.D. 26 (1876); Montreal Trust Co. v. Oxford Pipe Line Co., 3 D.L.R. 619 (Ont.Ct.App. 1942), (at least two required for meeting). As to what shares may be counted toward required quorum, see Atterbury v. Consolidated Coppermines Corp., 26 Del.Ch. 1, 20 A.2d 743 (Ch.1941). The New York Stock Exchange requires a quorum of not less than a majority of all outstanding shares. N.Y.S.E. Company Manual § A15.

24. See, e. g., ABA–ALI Model Bus.Corp.Act § 30.

more usually by the bylaws.[25]

Once a quorum is present, it is questionable whether or not it can be broken by a walk out.[26] However, opposing shareholders by absenting themselves might prevent a quorum.[27]

If a quorum is present, the majority vote of the shares represented is usually sufficient to carry a matter unless a greater vote is required by statute[28] or a valid provision in the articles of incorporation or bylaws.[29]

In New York, the articles of incorporation may impose higher quorum or voting requirements for shareholder meetings.[30] Bylaw provisions purporting to impose such requirements are ineffective in New York.[31]

Record of Shareholders—Voting Lists

Statutes frequently require a corporation to keep at its principal office,[32] or at the office of its transfer agent or registrar,[33] a record of its shareholders, giving the names and addresses of all shareholders and the number and class (or series) of the shares held by each.[34] In addition, statutes sometimes require the preparation of a voting list before each shareholder meeting.[35]

Such record of shareholders and voting list are among the corporate records open to reasonable shareholder inspection.[36] Such record ownership is usually conclusively binding on the inspectors of election, and on the courts in certain kinds of court proceedings.

Inspectors (or Judges or Tellers) of Election

Inspectors (or judges or tellers) of election are, ideally, impartial supervisors of a corporate election. Usually the number is either one or three.[37]

Obviously, a small number facilitates decision; an odd number avoids a stalemate. In close corporations, especially, use of inspectors is a burdensome formality frequently disregarded in practice. Statutes do not make their use mandatory but require them

25. E. g., Note, "Notice and Quorum Requirements of Shareholders Meetings", 24 U.Cin.L.Rev. 578 (1955).

26. Textron, Inc. v. American Woolen Co., 122 F. Supp. 305 (D.Mass.1954); Duffy v. Loft, Inc., 17 Del.Ch. 140, 151 A. 223 (Ch.1930), aff'd 17 Del.Ch. 376, 152 A. 849 (Sup.Ct.1930); Hexter v. Columbia Baking Co., 16 Del.Ch. 263, 145 A. 115 (Ch.1929). New York expressly provides that when a quorum is once present to organize a meeting, it is not broken by the subsequent withdrawal of any shareholders, and that the shareholders present may adjourn the meeting despite the absence of a quorum. McKinney's N.Y.Bus.Corp.Law, § 608(c), (d).

27. Matter of Pioneer Drilling Co., 36 Del.Ch. 386, 130 A.2d 559 (Ch.1957). The corporation's 1,000 outstanding shares were held by B (500), T (300), and Mrs. T (200). The annual shareholder meeting followed T's death but before letters testamentary were issued Mrs. T as T's executrix. She requested adjournment for a month without success. Mrs. T absented herself from the meeting, preventing a quorum (majority: 501 shares), thereby avoiding being outvoted by B (500–200). Mrs. T, after qualifying as executrix, was held to have the right to insist that the annual meeting be held.

28. E. g., ABA–ALI Model Bus.Corp.Act § 30.

29. See, e. g., ABA–ALI Model Bus.Corp.Act § 136 (articles of incorporation); Del.Gen.Corp.Law, § 216 (1967) (articles of incorporation or bylaws); McKinney's N.Y.Bus.Corp.Law, § 616 (articles of incorporation). See section 266 infra.

30. McKinney's N.Y.Bus.Corp.Law, § 616.

31. Model, Roland & Co. v. Industrial Acoustics Co., 16 N.Y.2d 703, 261 N.Y.S.2d 896, 209 N.E.2d 553 (1965); Matter of William Faehndrich, Inc., 2 N.Y. 2d 468, 161 N.Y.S.2d 99, 141 N.E.2d 597 (1957); Benintendi v. Kenton Hotel, Inc., 294 N.Y. 112, 60 N.E. 2d 829, 159 A.L.R. 280 (1945). But see Pawley v.

Ostrowsky, 155 N.Y.L.J. No. 113, 17 (Sup.Ct.1966) (confirming arbitrator's award directing amendment of articles of incorporation to include greater-than-normal voting requirements).

32. E. g., ABA–ALI Model Bus.Corp.Act § 46; McKinney's N.Y.Bus.Corp.Law, § 624.

33. Ibid.

34. For determination of shareholders entitled to vote, and fixing of record date or closing of share transfer books, see section 176 supra.

35. E. g., ABA–ALI Model Bus.Corp.Act § 29; Del. Gen.Corp.Law § 219 (1967); McKinney's N.Y.Bus. Corp.Law, § 607. See E. Aranow & H. Einhorn, Proxy Contests for Corporate Control 40 et seq. (2d ed. 1968).

36. See section 199 infra.

37. Cal.Gen.Corp.Law, § 2232 (1947); Pa.Bus.Corp. Law, § 512 (1966); Missouri requires not less than two. Mo.Gen. & Bus.Corp.Law, § 351.235 (1963).

pursuant to shareholder request [38] or bylaw requirement.[39]

Shareholders traditionally have the right to appoint the inspectors, but statutes or by-laws might provide for appointment by directors or the presiding officer of the meeting.[40] An inspector need not be a shareholder. Some statutes forbid the appointment of candidates, directors or officers.[41] Despite lack of express statutory prohibition, an impartial inspector is preferable. A few statutes require the inspectors to be sworn; [42] even when not required, oaths are frequently used in practice.

Inspectors determine the number of shares outstanding and the voting power of each, the shares represented at the meeting, the existence of a quorum, the validity and effect of proxies, shall receive votes, ballots or consents, hear and determine all challenges and questions arising in connection with the right to vote, count and tabulate all votes, ballots or consents, determine the result, and do such acts as are proper to conduct the election or vote with fairness to all shareholders. They become important functionaries in cases of proxy contests.[43] The

presiding officer of the meeting must accept the inspectors' certification.[44]

Inspectors' duties are mainly ministerial, but in practice they make quasi-judicial decisions.[45] Their rulings are subject to court review.[46]

Court Proceedings

To compel or enjoin the holding of a shareholder meeting, various judicial remedies are available.[47] Mandamus (or its statutory counterpart) [48] or injunction [49] are the traditional remedies. In several jurisdictions, special court proceedings are authorized.[50] Exhaustion of remedies within the corporation, such as demand and refusal, has sometimes been required as a prerequisite to judicial relief.[51]

Statutes also authorize summary judicial proceedings to review corporate elections upon the petition of any aggrieved shareholder.[52] Depending upon the statuto-

ery Ward Proxy Contest", 11 Bus.Law. 98 (Nov. 1955).

44. State v. Hohmann, 248 S.W.2d 49 (Mo.1952). See also McKinney's N.Y.Bus.Corp.Law, § 611 (any report or certificate of inspectors to be prima facie evidence of facts stated and of vote as certified by them).

45. 5 W. Fletcher, Private Corporations § 2018 (rev. vol. 1967); E. Aranow & H. Einhorn, Proxy Contests for Corporate Control 407 et seq. (2d ed. 1968); Comment, "Judicial Actions of Inspectors of Election", 48 Mich.L.Rev. 483 (1950).

46. McGoldrick v. Rotwein, 127 N.Y.L.J. No. 26, 508 (Sup.Ct.1952).

47. Annot., 48 A.L.R.2d 615 (1956).

48. People ex rel. Miller v. Cummings, 72 N.Y. 433 (1878); Auer v. Dressel, 306 N.Y. 427, 118 N.E.2d 590, 48 A.L.R.2d 604 (1954).

49. Penn-Texas Corp. v. Niles-Bement-Pond Co., 34 N.J.Super. 373, 112 A.2d 302 (1955).

50. E. g., McKinney's N.Y.Bus.Corp.Law, § 619; Aranow & Einhorn, "State Court Review of Corporate Elections", 56 Colum.L.Rev. 155 (1956).

51. Annot., 48 A.L.R.2d 615, 630–632 (1956).

52. E. g., Del.Gen.Corp.Law, § 225 (1967); McKinney's N.Y.Bus.Corp.Law, § 619; Aranow & Einhorn, "State Court Review of Corporate Elections", 56 Colum.L.Rev. 155 (1956).

38. Cal.Gen.Corp.Law, § 2232 (1947); Mich.Gen.Corp. Act § 21.41 (1948); McKinney's N.Y.Bus.Corp.Law, § 610 (only if required by bylaws); Ohio Gen.Corp. Law, § 1701.50 (1955); Pa.Bus.Corp.Law, § 512 (1966). See [1953] N.Y.L.Rev'n Comm'n Rep. 1953 Legis.Doc.No. 65 (J) 437–462.

39. Mo.Gen. & Bus.Corp.Law, § 351.235 (1963).

40. Cal.Gen.Corp.Law, § 2232 (1947); Mo.Gen. & Bus.Corp.Law, § 351.235 (1963); Ohio Gen.Corp. Law, § 1701.50 (1955); Pa.Bus.Corp.Law, § 512 (1966).

41. Mo.Gen. & Bus.Corp.Law, § 351.235 (1963); N.J. Bus.Corp.Law § 14A:5–25 (1969); Pa.Bus.Corp.Law, § 512 (1966).

42. Mo.Gen. & Bus.Corp.Law, § 351.240 (1963); McKinney's N.Y.Bus.Corp.Law, § 610.

43. E. g., McKinney's N.Y.Bus.Corp.Law, § 610; E. Aranow & H. Einhorn, Proxy Contests for Corporate Control 436–441 (2d ed. 1968). See Cal.Gen. Corp.Law, § 2233 (1947); Ohio Gen.Corp.Law, § 1701.50 (1955); Pa.Bus.Corp.Law, § 512 (1966); Doty, "Tabulating Proxies at Meetings of Stockholders", 24 Bus.Law. 887 (1969); Sprowl, "The Work of the Inspectors of Election in the Montgom-

ry language, the court's power in such proceedings might be limited to confirming the election, ordering a new election, or granting a temporary stay,[53] and might not extend to the determination of various issues [54] or permit the court to go beyond the record ownership.[55]

Post-Meeting Reports

In recent years, some of the larger corporations have prepared and mailed to their shareholders post-meeting reports to promote better shareholder relations. Prepared shortly after the annual shareholder meeting, such a report gives an account thereof.[56]

SHAREHOLDER ELECTION AND RE-MOVAL OF DIRECTORS AND OFFICERS

192. **Initial directors are usually named in the articles of incorporation or elected by the incorporators at their organization meeting. At the annual shareholder meeting, directors are elected. Vacancies on the board of directors and newly-created directorates are filled by shareholders or otherwise as provided by statute. Shareholders have inherent power to remove directors for cause, subject to possible court review, but may remove directors without cause only if such power was reserved at the time of the election of such directors. Shareholder agreements to elect certain persons as directors are usually enforceable so long as the directors are on good behavior, thereby precluding their removal without cause but not their removal for cause. Some modern statutes permit shareholder election and removal of officers.**

Initial Directors

The initial directors to serve until the first annual meeting, or until successors are elected, are sometimes required to be named in the articles of incorporation,[1] or are elected by the incorporators at their organization meeting.[2] Tennessee provides that the incorporators are the initial directors.[3]

Election of Directors

At the annual shareholder meeting, all or some of the directors are elected by the shareholders. Directors usually hold over

53. Aranow & Einhorn, "State Court Review of Corporate Elections", 56 Colum.L.Rev. 155, 165–171 (1956) (under McKinney's N.Y.Gen.Corp.Law § 25) (inapplicable to business corporations since 1963), court had power only to confirm election or to order new election, setting date of election, fixing record date, and imposing notice requirements in latter case. Cf. Del.Gen.Corp.Law, § 225 (1967) (". . . make such order or decree in any such case as may be just and proper"); Empire Southern Gas Co. v. Gray, 29 Del.Ch. 95, 46 A.2d 741 (Ch.1946). N.C.Bus.Corp.Act § 55.71 (1957). The language of the present New York Business Corporation Law is broader than the predecessor statute which gave the reviewing court only two alternatives: (a) to confirm the election, or (b) to order a new election. See Unbekant v. Bohl Tours Travel Agency, Inc., 21 A.D.2d 317, 250 N.Y.S.2d 397 (3d Dep't 1964) ("Under section 619 the Supreme Court is not limited to confirmation or the ordering of a new election but may also 'take such other action as justice may require.' We construe this language to have broadened the authority of the Supreme Court in a proceeding of this nature to allow it to decide or make arrangement for the decision of all necessary issues, including the question of stock ownership. (See comment following section 619 in McKinney's.)"), appeal dismissed, 14 N.Y.2d 959, 253 N.Y.S.2d 996, 202 N.E.2d 377 (1964). See also Matter of Elias v. Artistic Paper Box Co., 29 A.D.2d 118, 286 N.Y.S.2d 371 (2d Dep't 1967) (ordering consolidation of special proceeding to review election and derivative action).

54. Cf. Matter of William Faehndrich, Inc., 2 N.Y.2d 468, 161 N.Y.S.2d 99, 141 N.E.2d 597 (1957); Rosenfield v. Standard Electric Equipment Corp., 32 Del. Ch. 238, 83 A.2d 843 (Ch.1951) (issue of true ownership of shares); Matter of A. Bruder & Son, Inc., 302 N.Y. 52, 96 N.E.2d 84 (1950); Matter of Doeskin Products, Inc., 7 A.D.2d 42, 180 N.Y.S.2d 760 (1st Dep't 1958) (3–2) (issue of validity of issuance of shares); Matter of George Ringler & Co., 204 N.Y. 30, 97 N.E. 593 (1912) (issue of ownership by directors of required qualifying shares).

55. Aranow & Einhorn, "State Court Review of Corporate Elections", 56 Colum.L.Rev. 155, 161–163, 176–178 (1956). See Matter of Doeskin Products, Inc., 7 A.D.2d 42, 180 N.Y.S.2d 760 (1st Dep't 1958) (3–2); Rosenfield v. Standard Electric Equipment Corp., 32 Del.Ch. 238, 83 A.2d 843 (Ch.1951).

56. L. Gilbert & J. Gilbert, First/Twenty-Ninth Annual Reports of Stockholder Activities at Corporation Meetings (1940/1968).

1. E. g., ABA–ALI Model Bus.Corp.Act § 48(k). See section 130 supra.

2. E. g., Del.Gen.Corp.Law, § 107 (1967); McKinney's N.Y.Bus.Corp.Law, § 404.

3. Tenn.Gen.Corp.Law, § 48–803 (1969).

until their successors are elected.[4] However, if the required election is not held, a special meeting might be called.[5]

Vacancies on the board of directors are filled in accordance with statute or the bylaws.[6] Absent any controlling provision, vacancies are filled by the shareholders.[7]

Newly-created directorates are filled by shareholders in the absence of statute[8] or under some statutes which so provide.[9] A growing number of statutes authorize the board of directors to fill newly-created directorates.[10]

Removal of Directors

Shareholders have inherent power to remove a director for cause.[11] Such removal for cause is subject to court review.[12]

However, shareholders may not remove a director without cause unless power to remove without cause was reserved at the time of the election of the director.[13] Any

4. E. g., ABA–ALI Model Bus.Corp.Act § 34.

5. E. g., McKinney's N.Y.Bus.Corp.Law, § 603. See Reedy v. Alderman, 242 S.C. 552, 131 S.E.2d 689 (1963) (refusing to order overdue election of directors where bylaws failed to specify number of directors, size had varied over years, and shareholders could not agree on number).

6. E. g., ABA–ALI Model Bus.Corp.Act § 36; McKinney's N.Y.Bus.Corp.Law § 705(b), (vacancies occurring by reason of removal of directors without cause to be filled only by vote of shareholders, unless articles of incorporation or specific provision of bylaw adopted by shareholders provide that such vacancies shall be filled by board of directors). The Illinois Constitution mandatory cumulative voting provision has been construed as requiring that vacancies can be filled only by shareholders. People ex rel. Weber v. Cohn, 339 Ill. 121, 171 N.E. 159 (1930) (6–1) (statute providing for filling of vacancies by board of directors held unconstitutional).

7. 2 W. Fletcher, Private Corporations § 286 (perm. ed. rev. 1954). See section 205 infra.

8. 2 W. Fletcher, Private Corporations § 286 (perm. ed. rev. 1954); Note, "Applications to Newly Created Directorships of Statutory Provisions for Filling Vacancies", 47 Mich.L.Rev. 378 (1949).

9. E. g., ABA–ALI Model Bus.Corp.Act § 36; Ill. Bus.Corp.Act § 36 (1933); Ind.Gen.Corp.Act § 25–208 (1967).

10. E. g., Cal.Gen.Corp.Law, §§ 806, 808 (1947); Del. Gen.Corp.Law, § 223 (1967); McKinney's N.Y.Bus. Corp.Law § 705 (unless articles of incorporation or bylaws provide for shareholder vote); Ohio Gen. Corp.Law, § 1701.58 (1955). Cf. Automatic Steel Products, Inc. v. Johnston, 31 Del.Ch. 469, 64 A.2d 416, 6 A.L.R.2d 170 (Sup.Ct.1949) (bylaw providing for filling of newly-created directorship by remaining directors held invalid as repugnant to then Delaware statute granting shareholders such right).

11. Matter of Koch, 257 N.Y. 318, 178 N.E. 545 (1931); Fox v. Cody, 141 Misc. 552, 252 N.Y.S. 395 (Sup.Ct.1930). To remove a director for cause, there must be service of specific charges, adequate notice, and full opportunity to meet the accusations. Auer v. Dressel, 306 N.Y. 427, 118 N.E.2d 590, 593, 48 A.L.R.2d 604, 612 (1954); Matter of Norman v. Roosevelt Democratic Club, 17 Misc.2d 219, 184 N. Y.S.2d 980 (Sup.Ct.1959); Matter of Pegg v. United Mutual Life Ins. Co., 6 Misc.2d 600, 167 N.Y.S.2d 486 (Sup.Ct.1957). The inherent power of the majority of shareholders to remove a director for cause has been recognized despite cumulative voting. Campbell v. Loew's, Inc., 36 Del.Ch. 563, 134 A.2d 852 (Ch.1957). The court in the Campbell case also held that any proxy solicitation for shareholder votes to remove a director for cause must, either before or contemporaneously therewith, give such director the opportunity to present his defense to shareholders at the expense of the corporation. Wrongfully resisting removal might subject the director to liability to the corporation for its expenses. Mook v. Merdinger, 14 Misc.2d 639, 179 N. Y.S.2d 554 (Sup.Ct.1958). See Note, "Removal of Directors for Cause", 27 U.Cinc.L.Rev. 92 (1958).

12. See section 205 infra.

13. Travers, "Removal of the Corporate Director During His Term of Office", 53 Iowa L.Rev. 389 (1967). Statutes sometimes provide for removal with or without cause. See, e. g., ABA–ALI Model Bus.Corp.Act § 36A (optional section); Frank v. Anthony, 107 So.2d 136 (Fla.Dist.Ct.App.1958). New York permits the articles of incorporation or bylaws to provide that, subject to safeguards in the case of cumulative or class voting situations, any or all of the directors may be removed without cause by the shareholders, and also permits the articles of incorporation or the specific provisions of a bylaw adopted by shareholders, subject to the same safeguards, to provide for removal of directors for cause upon action by the board of directors. McKinney's N.Y.Bus.Corp.Law, § 706. Power to remove directors without cause can be conferred in the articles of incorporation or bylaws. See Essential Enterprises Corp. v. Automatic Steel Products, Inc., 39 Del.Ch. 93, 159 A.2d 288 (Ch.1960) (holding bylaw permitting removal of director with or without cause by majority vote of shareholders void for inconsistency with articles of incorporation provision for staggered three-year terms for directors); Matter of Rogers Imports, Inc., 202 Misc. 761, 116 N.Y.S.2d 106 (Sup.Ct.1952) (articles of incorporation amendment providing for cumulative voting held to

removal power may be exercised notwithstanding the existence of class or cumulative voting, subject to safeguards in statutes, articles of incorporation, or bylaws,[14] but would require a majority vote or any greater vote required by a valid provision in the articles of incorporation or bylaws.[15]

A shareholder agreement might require the parties to vote for certain directors. Such a provision is usually enforceable so long as the directors involved are on good behavior, and would preclude removal without cause but not removal for cause.[16]

Some modern statutes permit the articles of incorporation to provide that all or specified officers be elected by shareholders instead of by the board of directors.[17] Such statutes often add that any officer so elected may be removed, with or without cause, only by the shareholders, but his authority to act as an officer may be suspended by the board of directors for cause.[18]

SHAREHOLDER ADOPTION, AMENDMENT AND REPEAL OF BYLAWS

193. Initial bylaws are adopted in different jurisdictions by the incorporators, shareholders, or board of directors. Notwithstanding any power in the board of directors to amend

invalidate preexisting bylaw provision for removal of directors without cause by majority of shareholders). Absent such statute, such power in the articles of incorporation or bylaws should be given only prospective effect. See Matter of Singer, 189 Misc. 150, 70 N.Y.S.2d 550 (Sup.Ct.1947), aff'd 273 App.Div. 755, 75 N.Y.S.2d 514 (1st Dep't 1947); Abberger v. Kulp, 156 Misc. 210, 281 N.Y.S. 373 (Sup. Ct.1935). See Jacobson v. Backman, 16 Utah 2d 356, 401 P.2d 181 (1965) (holding directors could not be removed by less than two-thirds shareholder vote required by articles of incorporation since statutory provision requiring only majority vote could not constitutionally apply to preexisting corporation).

14. See section 205 infra.

15. See Matter of Burkin (Katz), 1 N.Y.2d 570, 572, 154 N.Y.S.2d 898, 900, 136 N.E.2d 862, 864 (1956).

16. See section 205 infra.

17. E. g., McKinney's N.Y.Bus.Corp.Law, § 715.

18. E. g., McKinney's N.Y.Bus.Corp.Law, § 716.

or repeal the bylaws, shareholders usually retain inherent power to do so. Statutes sometimes require shareholder approval for certain bylaws.

The bylaws, as discussed, may contain provisions, not inconsistent with law or the articles of incorporation, for the management and regulation of the corporations.[1]

The bylaws are initially adopted, in different jurisdictions, by the incorporators, shareholders, or board of directors.[2]

Notwithstanding any power in the board of directors to amend or repeal the bylaws,[3] the shareholders usually retain inherent power to do so.[4]

Statutes sometimes make a distinction between bylaws adopted by the shareholders and bylaws.[5]

Whether bylaws may be amended or repealed by the holders of the majority of outstanding shares or by a greater proportion depends upon the applicable statutes and judicial attitudes.[6]

Even bylaws unanimously adopted by shareholders may not provide for the man-

1. See section 133 supra.

2. See section 133 supra.

3. See section 214, n. 2 infra.

4. Rogers v. Hill, 289 U.S. 582, 53 S.Ct. 731, 77 L.Ed. 1385, 88 A.L.R. 744 (1933). Cf. Auer v. Dressel, 306 N.Y. 427, 118 N.E.2d 590, 48 A.L.R.2d 604 (1954). Bylaws might be impliedly amended, at least when shareholder action inconsistent with a bylaw is authorized by procedures consistent with those required to amend the bylaws. See section 132 supra.

5. McKinney's N.Y.Bus.Corp.Law, § 601. Bylaws adopted by the board of directors may be amended or repealed by the shareholders entitled to vote thereon.

6. See section 266 infra. But see Keating v. K–C–K Corp., 383 S.W.2d 69 (Tex.Civ.App.1964) (requiring three-fourths shareholder vote required by bylaws to amend bylaws). See also Model, Roland & Co. Industrial Acoustics Co., 16 N.Y.2d 703, 261 N.Y.S. 2d 896, 209 N.E.2d 553 (1965) (holding two-thirds shareholder vote requirement in bylaws to amend bylaws invalid since not in articles of incorporation as required by McKinney's N.Y.Bus.Corp.Law §§ 601, 614(b), 616(a) (2), 702(b)).

agement and regulation of the corporation in a manner inconsistent with law.[7]

SHAREHOLDER RESOLUTIONS

194. Shareholder resolutions can relate to a wide variety of matters, so long as they are proper subjects for action at shareholder meetings. For various extraordinary matters, shareholder approval is often required. Shareholders occasionally act as a substitute corporate organ for the board of directors. Where shareholders purport to ratify some matter, various questions arise, such as fullness of disclosure, ratifiability of matter, effect of ratification, burden of proof, counting of interested shareholders. Shareholder ratification may estop ratifying shareholders from thereafter complaining, assuming full disclosure. The S. E.C. Proxy Rules and securities exchange listing requirements sometimes also apply.

Shareholder resolutions can deal with a great variety of matters, so long as they are proper subjects for action at shareholder meetings.[1]

In the case of extraordinary corporate matters requiring shareholder approval, statutes often expressly require sufficient vote at a shareholders' meeting or possibly written shareholder consent without a meeting approving such matters.[2] Occasional statutory references to shareholder resolutions may be found.[3]

[§ 193]

7. Benintendi v. Kenton Hotel, Inc., 294 N.Y. 112, 60 N.E.2d 829, 159 A.L.R. 280 (1945). Cf. Matter of Buckley (Rickerson), 183 Misc. 189, 50 N.Y.S.2d 54 (Sup.Ct.1944) (bylaw upheld notwithstanding slight impingement on statutory norms and adoption by less than all shareholders).

[§ 194]

1. See section 191 supra. See generally I. Drummond, Corporate Resolutions ch. 1 (rev. ed. 1948); L. Doris & E. Friedman, Encyclopedia of Corporate Meetings, Minutes and Resolutions (1958). See also Frankel v. Donovan, 35 Del.Ch. 433, 120 A.2d 311 (Ch.1956) (charter clause that any contract, transaction or act of the corporation which shall be ratified by a majority of the shareholders shall be as valid and as binding as though ratified by every shareholder held not to cover gift of corporate assets by granting share options without consideration).

2. See Chapter 13 infra.

3. See, e. g., Model Bus.Corp.Act § 4(o) (resolution adopted by shareholders after notice authorizing indemnification of director or officer).

Shareholders occasionally act as a substitute corporate organ for the board of directors, such as where the board is incapable of effective action[4] or in close corporations where the shareholders want to exercise management functions as fully as possible.[5]

When shareholders purport to ratify the acts of the directors or officers, or other corporate transactions, various questions arise.

A favorable shareholder vote obviously can have no meaning in the absence of full disclosure to the shareholders.[6]

As to what matters may be ratified by shareholders, the votes required for ratification, and the effect of ratification, there are conflicting views.[7]

Matters which could have been authorized by shareholders may usually be ratified by a similar shareholder vote.[8]

4. Point Trap Co. v. Manchester, 98 R.I. 49, 199 A.2d 592 (1964) (requiring shareholder approval of all contracts and other transactions, even though "fair" to corporation, under interested directors and officers statute). See sections 209, 238, 366 infra.

5. See, e. g., McKinney's N.Y.Bus.Corp.Law, § 620(b) (provision in articles of incorporation as to control of directors). See sections 198, 213, 267, 275 infra.

6. Hudson v. American Founders Life Ins. Co. of Denver, 151 Colo. 54, 377 P.2d 391 (1963); Bowker v. Nashua Textile Co., 103 N.H. 242, 169 A.2d 630 (1961). Approval and ratification by the shareholders present in person or by proxy at the annual meeting of all of the acts of the directors and officers during the past year is an outmoded ritual. Colorado Management Corp. v. American Founders Life Ins. Co. of Denver, Colorado, 145 Colo. 413, 359 P.2d 665 (1961) ("ratification can never exist unless it is clearly shown that the party charged with ratification has full knowledge of all material facts, and thereafter knowingly accepts and approves").

7. Leavell, "Shareholders as Judges of Alleged Wrongdoers by Directors", 35 Tul.L.Rev. 331 (1961); Sneed, "The Factors Affecting the Validity of Stockholder Votes in Adverse Interest", 13 Okla.L. Rev. 373 (1960); Comment, "Shareholder Validation of Directors' Frauds: The Non-Ratification Rule v. The Business Judgment Rule", 58 Nw.U.L.Rev. 807 (1964).

8. Triplett v. Grundy Electric Cooperative, Inc., 389 S.W.2d 401 (Mo.Ct.App.1965) (holding unanimous vote not required for shareholders to ratify voidable action which they could have authorized by lesser vote).

Usually not subject to shareholder ratification are illegal acts,[9] ultra vires acts,[10] or fraudulent acts such as breaches of the fiduciary duties of management.[11]

Some courts permit breaches of the duties of due care of management to be ratified by less than all of the shareholders,[12] although the sounder view is not to allow such exoneration for negligence.[13]

Shareholder ratification sometimes neutralizes adverse inferences which might otherwise arise from transactions involving the fiduciary duties of management,[14] or relaxes the burden of proof imposed on the defendants,[15] or even shifts the burden on the defendants to prove fairness to a burden on the plaintiffs to show unfairness.[16]

The extent to which interested shareholders should be counted in cases of alleged shareholder ratification is ignored in some opinions.[17] Other cases, taking the view that shares are private property which may be voted in the shareholder's self-interest, do not require disinterested shareholder ratification.[18] Still other cases require that ratification be by independent shareholders.[19]

---

9. Rogers v. American Can Co., 305 F.2d 297 (3d Cir. 1962).

10. In the sense of being beyond the purposes (or objects) and powers of the corporation. See section 184 supra.

11. Braunstein v. Devine, 337 Mass. 408, 149 N.E.2d 628 (1958); Gottlieb v. Heyden Chemical Corp., 33 Del.Ch. 82, 90 A.2d 660 (Sup.Ct.1952) reargument denied in part 33 Del.Ch. 177, 91 A.2d 57 (Sup.Ct.1952), adhered to 33 Del.Ch. 283, 92 A.2d 594 (Sup.Ct.1952); Keenan v. Eshleman, 23 Del.Ch. 234, 2 A.2d 904, 120 A.L.R. 227 (Sup.Ct.1938) (fraudulent misapplication of corporate funds held not subject to shareholder ratification); Continental Securities Co. v. Belmont, 206 N.Y. 7, 18, 99 N.E. 138, 142 (1912) ("authority in stockholders to ratify and conform the acts of boards of directors is confined to acts voidable by reason of irregularities in the make up of the board or otherwise or by reason of the directors or some of them being personally interested in the subject-matter of the contract or act, or for some other similar reason which makes the action of the directors voidable. No such authority exists in case of an act of the board of directors which is prohibited by law or which is against public policy. . . . In any case where action is taken by stockholders confirming and ratifying a fraud and misapplication of the funds of the corporation by the directors or others the action is binding only by way of estoppel upon such stockholders as vote in favor of such approval"). Contra, Claman v. Robertson, 164 Ohio St. 61, 128 N.E.2d 429 (1955) ("a disinterested majority of the shareholders of a corporation have the power to ratify directors' frauds provided there is no actual fraud in either inducing or effecting such ratification").

12. Smith v. Brown-Borhek Co., 414 Pa. 325, 200 A.2d 398 (1964) (holding breaches by directors and officers of their duties of due care ratified, upon full disclosure, by majority of shareholders, including votes cast by directors and officers voting their own shares and shares for which they held proxies, even after shareholder derivative action had been commenced).

13. See Alcott v. Hyman, 42 Del.Ch. 233, 208 A.2d 501 (Sup.Ct.1965); Continental Securities Co. v. Belmont, 206 N.Y. 7, 99 N.E. 138 (1912).

14. Gottlieb v. Heyden Chemical Corp., 33 Del.Ch. 82, 90 A.2d 660 (Sup.Ct.1952), reargument denied in part 33 Del.Ch. 177, 91 A.2d 57 (Sup.Ct.1952), adhered to 33 Del.Ch. 283, 92 A.2d 594 (Sup.Ct.1952).

15. Alcott v. Hyman, 42 Del.Ch. 233, 208 A.2d 501 (Sup.Ct.1965).

16. Olson Bros. v. Englehart, 42 Del.Ch. 348, 211 A.2d 610 (Ch.1965) (shareholder ratification held to shift burden to objecting party—here the corporation itself—that business judgment was not exercised); Saxe v. Brady, 40 Del.Ch. 474, 184 A.2d 602 (Ch.1962) (upholding independent shareholder ratification, of interested directors transaction, on findings that had proven full disclosure, that such ratification relieved defendants from proving *fairness* of transaction, and that plaintiffs had failed to sustain burden of establishing *unfairness* of transaction).

17. See Alcott v. Hyman, 42 Del.Ch. 233, 208 A.2d 501 (Sup.Ct.1965) (discussing effect of shareholder ratification on burden of proof on defendants, and expressing no views on possible disqualification of interested controlling shareholder, since greater burden discharged).

18. Smith v. Brown-Borhek Co., 414 Pa. 325, 200 A.2d 398 (1964); Wiberg v. Gulf Coast Land & Development Co., 360 S.W.2d 563 (Tex.Civ.App.1962) (upholding ratification, after full disclosure, by holders of 80 percent of shares, majority of which were owned by directors, of contract approved by three-man board of directors, two of whom were other parties to contract, where contract was fair to corporation); Bjorngaard v. Goodhue County Bank, 49 Minn. 483, 52 N.W. 48 (1892) (upholding ratification of controlling interested shareholders of corporation's purchase of their real property authorized by them as majority directors, absent showing that minority was defrauded).

19. Pappas v. Moss, 393 F.2d 865 (3d Cir. 1968) (interested majority shareholder ratification held ineffective to shift defendants' burden of showing fairness of contract under New Jersey corporation's articles of incorporation interested-directors provision); Brundage v. New Jersey Zinc Co., 48 N.J.

Corporate reimbursement of successful insurgents of their proxy contest expenses has been upheld on the basis of shareholder approval of such reimbursement.[20] In any event, shareholders who, with knowledge, join in ratifying a transaction might be estopped from thereafter complaining about such transaction.[21]

When ratification is solicited from holders of shares listed on a securities exchange or registered under the Federal Securities Exchange Act of 1934, the S.E.C. Proxy Rules are applicable.[22]

Securities exchanges, in their listing requirements, sometimes encourage or require shareholder approval for various corporate matters.[23]

SHAREHOLDER APPROVAL OF EXTRAORDINARY CORPORATE MATTERS

195. Shareholder approval is required for various extraordinary corporate matters, such as amendments of the articles of incorporation, sale or lease of assets not in the regular course of business, merger, consolidation, dissolution, etc. These are more fully treated in Chapter 13.

450, 226 A.2d 585 (1967); Bowker v. Nashua Textile Co., 103 N.H. 242, 169 A.2d 630 (1961). See Abelow v. Symonds, 40 Del.Ch. 36, 173 A.2d 167 (Ch.1961) (questioning 97 percent shareholder ratification of sale of assets by subsidiary corporation to parent corporation, where 96 percent of votes were cast by parent corporation, and some one percent (302 shares) by disinterested shareholders); S. Solomont & Sons Trust, Inc. v. New England Theatres Operating Corp., 326 Mass. 99, 93 N.E.2d 241 (1950) (disinterested shareholder vote). See also Rogers v. American Can Co., 305 F.2d 297 (3d Cir. 1962); Bastian v. Bourns, Inc., — Del.Ch. —, 256 A.2d 680 (Ch.1969) (approval by two-thirds of disinterested shareholders regarded as less significant because of relatively small number of disinterested voters).

20. See section 196 infra.

21. See section 363 infra. But see Gottlieb v. McKee, 34 Del.Ch. 537, 107 A.2d 240 (Ch.1954). See also Lowman v. Harvey R. Pierce Co., 276 Pa. 382, 120 A. 404 (1923).

22. See section 297 infra.

23. N.Y.S.E. Company Manual § A15.

Shareholders invest in the corporate enterprise as defined in the articles of incorporation with the expectation that the board of directors will manage the enterprise so far as its ordinary business is concerned.

Amendments of the articles of incorporation involve, to a greater or less extent, organic changes in the corporation; extraordinary transactions are beyond the ordinary business whose management is delegated to the board of directors.

At common law, such extraordinary matters required unanimous shareholder approval. Statutes today permit such matters when approved by a prescribed vote or consent of shareholders (such vote or consent requirements possibly varying for different matters), with or without concurrent board of directors action; dissenting shareholders under such circumstances often enjoy the right to have their shares appraised and purchased by the corporation.

Typically, such extraordinary matters include amendments of the articles of incorporation (including reclassification), sale or lease of assets outside of the corporation's regular course of business, merger, consolidation, and dissolution, etc.

Such extraordinary matters will be fully explored in Chapter 13.

PROXIES

196. Many statutes provide that shareholders entitled to vote at a shareholder meeting have the right to be present and to vote in person or by proxy. The proxy holder is the shareholder's agent for voting purposes. Many statutes require that proxies be in writing and signed by the shareholder. In larger corporations, management's control of the proxy machinery tends to perpetuate management in office.

Different durations are fixed for proxies in different jurisdictions, 11 months being the most typical.

Proxies are revocable like other agencies unless "coupled with an interest" or "given as se-

curity" or as provided by irrevocable proxy statutory provisions.

A general proxy authorizes the proxy holder to vote on all matters properly coming before the shareholder meeting.

The proxy holder is under a duty to exercise it as contemplated by the agency.

Corporate funds may be used by management to inform shareholders of corporate matters, to give notice of shareholder meetings, to obtain a quorum, and to solicit proxies so long as policy (rather than personnel) issues are involved and the expenses are reasonable, whether management is successful or unsuccessful. Successful insurgents have been allowed reimbursement of their reasonable expenses by the corporation where policy issues were involved and there was a corporate benefit or reimbursement was approved by shareholders.

In General

The term "proxy" sometimes causes initial confusion because of its various meanings: (a) the *authority* given by the shareholder to his agent; (b) the *instrument* evidencing such authority; (c) the *agent* (called the proxy holder); and (d) the *exercise* of authority by the agent ("voting, etc., by proxy"). In the following discussion, the meaning of the term will vary in different contexts.

Many statutes provide that shareholders entitled to vote at a shareholders meeting have the right to be present and to vote at such meeting in person or by proxy.[1] The proxy holder usually need not be a shareholder, but must have the legal capacity to be an agent.[2]

1. E. g., ABA–ALI Model Bus.Corp.Act § 31; Del. Gen.Corp.Law, § 212 (1967); McKinney's N.Y.Bus. Corp.Law, § 609; 12 U.S.C.A. § 61 (national banks). See generally Oulahan, "Some Practical Problems Involved in Proxy Solicitation and Counting under Virginia Law", 8 Wm. & Mary L.Rev. 185 (1967); Garrett, "Proxies and Reorganizations", 16 Baylor L.Rev. 211 (1964); Goodsill, "Corporation Law— Proxy Solicitation", 1 Hawaii B.J. 1 (Feb.1963); Axe, "Corporate Proxies", 41 Mich.L.Rev. 38, 225 (1942); Note, "Voting By Proxy", 46 Iowa L.Rev. 136 (1961). See also Oleck, "Proxy Voting in Non-Profit Organizations", 14 Clev.-Mar.L.Rev. 273 (1965). See generally B. Rogers, Proxy Guide for Meetings of Stockholders (1969).

2. Axe, "Corporate Proxies", 41 Mich.L.Rev. 38, 50– 51 (1942). A bylaw requirement that only a share-

Under certain circumstances, courts might compel a shareholder of record to deliver a proxy to the real or beneficial owner.[3]

Securities exchanges may have rules regulating the giving of proxies by their members who hold shares in the "street name".[4]

Of course, when shares are sold "ex-voting rights" the seller retains the voting rights for the forthcoming election.[5]

Statutes also provide that every proxy must be in writing and signed by the shareholder or his duly authorized attorney-in-fact.[6]

To sell a vote or proxy might be unlawful.[7] Until 1967, New York had pro-

holder may be a proxy holder has been held invalid. State ex rel. Syphers v. McCune, 143 W.Va. 315, 101 S.E.2d 834 (1958). For detailed statutory treatment of proxies, see Minn.Bus.Corp.Act § 301.26 (1961); McKinney's N.Y.Bus.Corp.Law, § 609.

3. In re Giant Portland Cement Co., 26 Del.Ch. 32, 21 A.2d 697 (Ch.1941). See also McKinney's N.Y. Bus.Corp.Law, § 609(d) (obligation to deliver proxy to pledgor or owner, upon demand and payment of necessary expenses, where record holder holds shares as pledgee or otherwise as security or which belong to another, except when other provision shall have been made by written agreement between parties).

4. E. g., N.Y.S.E. Rules 870–875. See Schott v. Climax Molybdenum Co., 38 Del.Ch. 450, 154 A.2d 221 (Ch.1959).

5. Bunker v. Gruntal, 129 N.Y.L.J., No. 66, 1137 (Sup.Ct.1953).

6. E. g., ABA–ALI Model Bus.Corp.Act § 31; Robbins v. Beatty, 246 Iowa 80, 67 N.W.2d 12 (1954); McLain v. Lanova Corp., 28 Del.Ch. 176, 39 A.2d 209 (Ch.1944). Where shares are registered in an individual name, the proxy should be signed exactly in such name; where registered jointly, all registered holders must sign; where registered in the names of one or more trustees, executors, administrators, or other fiduciaries, at least a majority should sign under their proper and full title; where registered in a corporate name, the duly authorized officer or officers of such corporation should sign; if registered in a partnership name, the duly authorized partner or partners must sign. See "Presumptions for Determining the Validity of Proxies", 11 Bus.Law. 127 (Nov.1955).

7. E. g., McKinney's N.Y.Bus.Corp.Law, § 609(e) (except as authorized in §§ 609 and 620). See also Pa. Bus.Corp.Law, § 504 (1966). Lurie v. Kaplan, 31 A. D.2d 93, 295 N.Y.S.2d 493 (1st Dep't 1968), held, 4 to 1, that an agreement to sell shares of a Pennsylvania corporation at a premium, with payment and

vided that the sale of a vote or a proxy was a misdemeanor.[8]

Duration

In larger corporations, management by its control of the proxy machinery is able to keep itself in power and gain shareholder ratification of its actions. Any fraud or illegality in procuring proxies, of course, is subject to appropriate relief.

Statutes in different jurisdictions fix different periods of duration for proxies.[9] In most jurisdictions, such period is applicable only where no time is fixed in the proxy;[10] in some jurisdictions, a maximum allowable period is fixed by statute.[11]

Typical of the former would be a statutory provision that no proxy shall be valid after 11 months from the date of its execution unless its duration is specified in the proxy.[12]

Revocation

A proxy is revocable like any other agency—at the will or upon the loss of capacity or death of the shareholder (principal)—unless it is "coupled with an interest" or "given as security".[13]

delivery deferred, and the immediate delivery of an irrevocable proxy to vote the shares, did not constitute a sale of votes in violation of the Pennsylvania statute.

8. Former McKinney's N.Y.Penal Law, Appendix § 668(1).

9. Usually 11 months. See e. g., ABA–ALI Model Bus.Corp.Act § 31; McKinney's N.Y.Bus.Corp.Law, § 609(b). Delaware fixes three years. Del.Gen. Corp.Law, § 212 (1967).

10. E. g., ABA–ALI Model Bus.Corp.Act § 31; Del. Gen.Corp.Law, § 212 (1967); McKinney's N.Y.Bus. Corp.Law § 609(b); Stein v. Capital Outdoor Advertising, Inc., 273 N.C. 77, 159 S.E.2d 351 (1968) (proxy specifying neither time of its expiration nor limitation to particular meeting held to expire automatically 11 months after date of execution).

11. E. g., Cal.Gen.Corp.Law, § 2226 (1947) (seven years); N.C.Bus.Corp.Act § 55–68 (1957) (10 years); Okl.Bus.Corp.Act § 60 (1961) (seven years).

12. E. g., McKinney's N.Y.Bus.Corp.Law, § 609(b).

13. Axe, "Corporate Proxies", 41 Mich.L.Rev. 225, 256–260 (1942); Comment, "Voting Trusts and Irrevocable Proxies", 41 Temp.L.Q. 480 (1968); Com-

Thus, notifying the corporation of revocation or the giving of a second proxy revokes the earlier one;[14] when the shareholder attends and participates at the meeting in person, his proxy is revoked.[15] Revocation is effective, unless "coupled with an interest" or "given as security" or irrevocable under statutes, even if the proxy is expressly "irrevocable" and the revocation is in breach of contract.[16]

ment, "Irrevocable Proxies", 43 Texas L.Rev. 733 (1965); Abercrombie v. Davies, 35 Del.Ch. 599, 123 A.2d 893, 906–907 (Ch.1956) (holding proxies given as part of binding shareholder pooling agreement, supported by legal consideration, to implement arbitration provision of agreement, especially where strong element of reliance, to involve more than principal-agent relationship and to be irrevocable), rev'd on other grounds, 36 Del. 371, 130 A.2d 338 (Sup.Ct.1957); Deibler v. Charles H. Elliot Co., 368 Pa. 267, 81 A.2d 557 (1951) (corporate office and interest as pledgee of shares to secure performance of contract to employ proxy holder for life as president held sufficient interest); Ecclestone v. Indiatlantic, Inc., 319 Mich. 248, 29 N.W.2d 679 (1947) (corporate office held sufficient interest); State ex rel. Everett Trust & Savings Bank v. Pacific Waxed Paper Co., 22 Wash.2d 844, 157 P.2d 707, 159 A.L.R. 297 (1945) (interest in control and right of first refusal found sufficient interest). See also State ex rel. Breger v. Rusche, 219 Ind. 559, 39 N.E.2d 433 (1942). Older cases required that the "interest" of the proxy holder be in the shares themselves. In re Public Industrial Corp. (Chilson), 19 Del.Ch. 398, 168 A. 82 (Ch.1933). The concept of agency "coupled with an interest" as irrevocable stems primarily from Marshall, C. J., in Hunt v. Rousmanier's Adm'rs, 21 U.S. (8 Wheat.) 174, 5 L.Ed. 589 (1823). For definition of a power "given as security," see 1 Restatement, Second, Agency § 138 (1958); W. Seavey, Studies in Agency 109 (1949); Note, "The Irrevocable Proxy and Voting Control of Small Corporations", 98 U.Pa.L.Rev. 401 (1950); Note, "Voting Trusts and Irrevocable Proxies", 36 Calif.L.Rev. 281 (1948); Annot., 159 A.L.R. 307 (1945).

14. Schott v. Climax Molybdenum Co., 38 Del.Ch. 450, 154 A.2d 221 (Ch.1959); Axe, "Corporate Proxies", 41 Mich.L.Rev. 225, 259 (1942). In the New York Central Railroad proxy contest, some proxies were found to have been revoked as many as 11 times. 50 Fortune, No. 2, 87 (Aug.1954).

15. State ex rel. Breger v. Rusche, 219 Ind. 559, 39 N.E.2d 433 (1942); Axe, "Corporate Proxies", 41 Mich.L.Rev. 225, 259 (1942). But not where shareholder giving proxy is physically present at meeting for purpose, among others, of confirming rather than of revoking proxy. Matter of Manacher v. Central Coal Co., 205 Misc. 513, 133 N.Y.S.2d 265 (Sup.Ct.1954), aff'd mem., 283 App.Div. 1048, 131 N.Y.S.2d 914 (1st Dep't 1954).

16. Distinction is made between the power of the agent, which the principal can revoke, and the con-

Statutes sometimes provide that a proxy is not revoked by the incompetence or death of the shareholder executing the same unless before its exercise the corporation or a designated officer received written notice thereof.[17]

In New York, every proxy is revocable at the pleasure of the person executing it, except as otherwise provided.[18] The ambiguous terminology "coupled with an interest" or "given as security" has been avoided by the New York statute,[19] which limits irrevocable proxies to five types of proxy holders: (a) a pledgee; (b) one who has purchased or agreed to purchase the shares; (c) a creditor who extends or continues credit to the corporation[20] in consideration of the proxy if the proxy (i) so states, (ii) gives the amount thereof, and (iii) names the creditor; (d) one who has contracted to perform services as an officer of the corporation,[21] if the employment contract provides for the proxy and the proxy (i) so states, (ii) names the employee, and (iii) states the period of employment; and (e) one designated by or under a signed written

shareholder voting agreement.[22] In each case, the proxy must be entitled "Irrevocable Proxy" and state that it is irrevocable; the irrevocability is not enforceable against the purchaser of the shares without knowledge unless the existence of the proxy and its irrevocability is noted conspicuously on the face or back of the share certificate. Irrevocability ends in the case of the pledgee when the pledge is redeemed (thus ending the pledgor-pledgee relationship); in the case of the executory sale contract, upon performance (the proxy holder thus becoming the shareholder); in the case of the creditor, when the debt of the corporation is paid; in the case of the officer, upon the termination of the stated period of employment; and in the case of shareholder voting agreement, upon the termination of such agreement. In the case of the creditor or officer, irrevocability cannot extend beyond three years after the date the proxy was given unless the period of irrevocability is renewed by the execution of a new irrevocable proxy.[23]

Scope of Proxy

A general proxy authorizes the proxy holder to vote on all matters properly coming before the meeting, even though the matter is not enumerated in the notice of the meeting. While such a vote may be counted (at least on a matter not introduced by management), a Delaware court has held that such vote does not estop the shareholder giving the proxy from later bringing a derivative action to challenge the action of the

---

tract with the agent, which the principal may not revoke. M. Ferson, Principles of Agency § 190 (1954); Brady v. Mexican Gulf Sulphur Co., 32 Del.Ch. 372, 88 A.2d 300 (Ch.1952).

17. E. g., Minnesota, New York, North Carolina, Ohio, Oklahoma, Pennsylvania. [1957] N.Y.L.Rev'n Comm'n Rep.1957 Legis.Doc.No.65(I) 283–313.

18. McKinney's N.Y.Bus.Corp.Law, § 609(b).

19. [1953] N.Y.L.Rev'n Comm'n Rep. 1953 Legis.Doc. No. 65(G) 233–262. Since 1967 Delaware has provided that a proxy may be irrevocable if it states that it is irrevocable and if, and only as long as, it is coupled with an interest sufficient in law to support an irrevocable power; and that a proxy may be made irrevocable regardless of whether the interest with which it is coupled is an interest in the shares themselves or an interest in the corporation generally. Del.Gen.Corp.Law § 212(c) (1967). Presumably such an interest would support an irrevocable proxy held by a pledgee, one who has purchased or agreed to purchase shares, a creditor, an officer, or a shareholder under a voting agreement.

20. Added by N.Y.Laws 1953, ch. 863.

21. Ibid.

22. Added by McKinney's N.Y.Bus.Corp.Law, § 609(f) (4).

23. McKinney's N.Y.Bus.Corp.Law, § 609(f), (g), (h); De Masi v. Demasi Schematics, Inc., 146 N.Y.L.J. No. 37, 6 (Sup.Ct.1961) (upholding power of pledgee of majority of shares with irrevocable proxy to remove pledgor and his brother as directors under bylaw authorizing removal of directors without cause by shareholders). A shareholder agreement requiring inactive shareholders to give irrevocable proxies to active shareholder has been ruled to create a second class of shares disqualifying Subchapter S election. Rev.Rul. 63–226, 1963–2 Cum.Bull. 341.

directors which the vote was cast to ratify.[24] The case involved management's mailing to shareholders before the meeting of a proxy statement which, in accord with the Securities and Exchange Commission Proxy Rules,[25] stated that management knew of no matters which would come before the meeting other than those stated in the notice of the meeting, but that if any other matter properly came before the meeting, the proxy would be exercised in accordance with the best judgment of the proxy holder.

An earlier Delaware case had permitted management to whom a general proxy had been given to make a substitution in the slate of directors in the absence of fraud or misrepresentation in solicitation.[26]

Exercise of Proxy

Where the proxy is held by two or more persons, they function by majority vote.[27] They are usually given express power of substitution.

While it has been said that a proxy holder, like any other agent, can always abandon his agency at the risk of incurring whatever liability might ensue,[28] the better view would seem to be that the proxy holder is under a duty to exercise the proxy.[29] Otherwise, the shareholder giving the proxy is disenfranchised. In any event, the presence at the meeting of the proxy holder as such constitutes the presence of the shares represented by the proxy for purposes of quorum.[30]

Where management solicits proxies in its favor and receives an adverse proxy, it should return the proxy promptly to the shareholder to avoid any duty of exercising it.[31]

Where the proxy solicitation is subject to the S.E.C. Proxy Rules,[32] a ballot-type form of proxy is required for all matters intended to be acted upon, other than elections to office. The Rules prescribe that the form of proxy shall state that the shares represented by the proxy will be voted and that, if the shareholder marks the ballot, they will be voted in accordance therewith;[33] and prohibit false and misleading statements in connection with any solicitation subject to such Rules.[34]

Some statutes require filing of proxies; in England, they must be lodged before the meeting.[35]

24. Gottlieb v. McKee, 34 Del.Ch. 537, 107 A.2d 240 (Ch.1954). See also State ex rel. Pertuit v. Pioneer Petroleum Corp., 193 So.2d 286 (La.Ct.App.1967), writ refused 250 La. 271, 195 So.2d 148 (1967) (holding proxy holder's authority limited to voting shares and not to extend to defending action involving ownership of shares); Jaquith & Co. v. Island Creek Coal Co., 47 N.J. 111, 219 A.2d 514 (1966) (proxy vote against merger held sufficient written notice of dissent for purposes of appraisal remedy).

25. See section 297 infra

26. Hauth v. Giant Portland Cement Co., 33 Del.Ch. 496, 96 A.2d 233 (Ch.1953). See also McKee v. Home Savings & Trust Co., 122 Iowa 731, 98 N.W. 609 (1904) (general proxy held not to extend to extraordinary corporate matters).

27. Callister v. Graham-Paige Corp., 146 F.Supp. 399 (D.Del.1956).

28. Duffy v. Loft, Inc., 17 Del.Ch. 140, 147, 151 A. 223, 227 (Ch.1930), aff'd 17 Del.Ch. 376, 152 A. 849 (Sup.Ct.1930).

29. Second Consolidated Trust, Ltd. v. Ceylon Amalgamated Tea and Rubber Estates, Ltd., [1943] 2 All (letters) E.R. 567 (Ch.). Cf. In re Giant Portland Cement Co., 26 Del.Ch. 32, 21 A.2d 697 (Ch.1941). The proxy holder, as an agent, has been held subject to fiduciary duties. Blair v. F. H. Smith Co., 18 Del.Ch. 150, 156 A. 207 (Ch.1931); see also Matter of Ideal Mutual Ins. Co., 18 Misc.2d 127, 190 N.Y.S.2d 887 (Sup.Ct.1959), aff'd 9 A.D.2d 60, 190 N.Y. S.2d 895 (1st Dept's 1959).

30. Duffy v. Loft, Inc., 17 Del.Ch. 140, 151 A. 223 (Ch.1930), aff'd 17 Del.Ch. 376, 152 A. 849 (Sup.Ct. 1930); Textron, Inc. v. American Woolen Co., 122 F.Supp. 305 (D.Mass.1954).

31. Dean, "Noncompliance with Proxy Regulations", 24 Cornell L.Q. 483, 493 (1939); see Comment, "Regulation of Proxy Solicitation by the S.E.C.", 33 Ill.L.Rev. 914, 928–929 (1939).

32. See section 297 infra.

33. S.E.C. Rule 14A–4(e).

34. S.E.C. Rule 14A–9.

35. N.J.Stat.Ann. § 17:9A–90 (1963) (banks); Barclay v. First Nat'l Bank of Highstown, 81 N.J.Super. 472, 196 A.2d 13 (1963); L. Gower, The Principles of Modern Company Law 442–443 (2d ed. 1957)

Incidence of Proxy Contest Expenses

Proxy contests occasionally occur and usually involve widespread publicity.[36] The expenses of management and insurgent groups in waging proxy fights have been very substantial.[37] To what extent corporate funds may be expended to pay or reimburse such expenses is a not yet settled question.

Management may clearly use corporate funds to inform shareholders of corporate matters, to give notice of the shareholders' meeting, and to obtain a quorum,[38] since management is under a duty to perform such functions. Some cases permit further use of corporate funds by management, even for proxy solicitation, so long as a policy (rather than personnel) issue is involved and the expenses are reasonable, whether

management wins [39] or loses.[40] The policy vs. personnel distinction has been criticized.[41]

Where *insurgents* are *successful*, one case allowed them to recover reasonable expenditures in a proxy contest involving policy on the ground that they had conferred a benefit on the corporation—change of management —and, by analogy to a successful shareholder's derivative action, should be allowed to recover the expenses incurred in creating that benefit.[42] In a more recent case, by a sharply-divided court, successful insurgents were allowed to recover their expenses on the basis of shareholder approval of such reimbursement.[43] Neither the benefit theory nor the shareholder approval approach (shareholder approval being so easily obtainable by means of proxies) provides a very satisfactory criterion.[44]

Reimbursement to *unsuccessful insurgents* has not been allowed in any reported case, largely because successful management has never reimbursed them.[45] Under the shareholder approval approach, such approval

(called "battle of circulars" in England); Skora v. Great Sweet Grass Oils Ltd., 30 Misc.2d 572, 205 N.Y.S.2d 98 (Sup.Ct.1960), appeal dismissed 12 A.D. 2d 596, 214 N.Y.S.2d 713 (1st Dep't 1960) (Ontario corporation).

36. E. g., American Woolen Co.; Decca Records, Inc.; Fairbanks, Morse & Co.; Penn-Texas Corp.; Loew's, Inc.; Libby, McNeil & Libby Co.; Montgomery Ward & Co.; New York Central R. R.; New York, New Haven & Hartford R. R.; Thermoid Co.; Boston & Maine R. R. See E. Aranow & H. Einhorn, Proxy Contests for Corporate Control (2d ed. 1968); Barnhill, "The Corporate Raider: Contesting Proxy Solicitations and Take Over Offers", 20 Bus.Law. 763 (1965); Stephan, "Highlights of the Montgomery Ward Proxy Contest from a Lawyer's Viewpoint", 11 Bus.Law. 86 (Nov.1955). See generally Emerson & Latcham, "Proxy Contests: A Study in Shareholder Sovereignty", 41 Calif.L.Rev. 393 (1953); Comment, "Buying Out Insurgent Shareholders with Corporate Funds", 70 Yale L.J. 308 (1960).

37. E. g., allegedly some $550,000 by management and $1,300,000 by insurgents in New York Central R. R. proxy fight; some $700,000 by management and $500,000 by insurgents in Montgomery Ward & Co. proxy fight. There are even large professional proxy-solicitation firms. Where a corporate shareholder helped to finance a proxy fight in another corporation, the directors of the corporate shareholder were surcharged for misuse of corporate funds. Kaufman v. Wolfson, 153 F.Supp. 253 (S.D. N.Y.1957).

38. Lawyers' Advertising Co. v. Consolidated Ry. Lighting and Refrigerating Co., 187 N.Y. 395, 80 N. E. 199 (1907); see Rascovor v. American Linseed Co., 135 F. 341 (2d Cir.1905).

39. Levin v. Metro-Goldwyn-Mayer, Inc., 264 F.Supp. 797 (S.D.N.Y.1967); Hall v. Trans-Lux Daylight Picture Screen Corp., 20 Del.Ch. 78, 171 A. 226 (Ch. 1934); Pell v. London and North Western Ry., [1907] 1 Ch.Div. 5.

40. Steinberg v. Adams, 90 F.Supp. 604 (S.D.N.Y. 1950).

41. See Note, 41 Cornell L.Q. 714, 715, n. 8 (1956).

42. Steinberg v. Adams, 90 F.Supp. 604 (S.D.N.Y. 1950). Shareholder ratification was found incapable of curing any defects of improper reimbursement except possibly to estop shareholders who had voted for ratification. See section 377 infra.

43. Rosenfeld v. Fairchild Engine & Airplane Corp., 309 N.Y. 168, 128 N.E.2d 291, 51 A.L.R.2d 860 (1955), reh. denied, 309 N.Y. 807, 130 N.E.2d 610 (1955). See Machtinger, "Proxy Fight Expenditures of Insurgent Shareholders", 19 Case W.Res.L.Rev. 212 (1968); Comment, "Proxy Contests: Corporate Reimbursement of Insurgents' Expenses", 23 U.Chi.L. Rev. 682 (1956).

44. Note, 41 Cornell L.Q. 714, 717–718 (1956).

45. Cf. Phillips v. United Corp., Civ.No. 40–497 (S.D. N.Y.1948) (claim by unsuccessful insurgent), appeal dismissed, 171 F.2d 180 (2d Cir. 1948); Grodetsky v. McCrory Corp., 49 Misc.2d 322, 267 N.Y.S.2d 356 (Sup.Ct.1966), aff'd mem., 27 A.D.2d 646, 276 N.Y.S. 2d 841 (1st Dep't 1966).

would be most unlikely; under the benefit theory, the benefit of change in management could not be shown. Occasional commentators have advocated some reimbursement of unsuccessful insurgents.[46]

Probably the leading case on the subject of proxy contest expenses is Rosenfeld v. Fairchild Engine & Airplane Corp.,[47] decided by the New York Court of Appeals in 1955. There the contest revolved around an employment contract which the incumbent board of directors had awarded to an officer-director. In the resulting proxy contest, both management and insurgent factions employed legal counsel, public relations experts, and proxy solicitors. Management, while still in office, charged most of its expenses to the corporation. The successful insurgents, on taking office, had the corporation pay the balance of the management expenses and, after getting overwhelming shareholder approval, had the corporation reimburse their own proxy contest expenses.

A minority shareholder[48] brought a derivative action against the former and present directors to recover the corporate funds so expended. The complaint was dismissed on the merits after trial; the Appellate Division unanimously affirmed.[49] On appeal, the Court of Appeals split 3–1–3, affirming the judgment, leaving the New York law in considerable confusion.[50]

Three judges sustained the expenditure of corporate funds by management on the ground that the proxy contest involved a policy issue and the expenses were reasonable; and the reimbursement of the successful insurgents on the basis of shareholder approval.[51] Desmond, J., concurred in the result on the ground that the plaintiff had failed to sustain his burden of proof.[52] The three dissenting judges rejected the policy-issue criterion as meaningless, and instead suggested that the corporation be responsi-

---

46. See, e. g., Comment, 23 U.Chi.L.Rev. 682, 690, 692 (1956); Emerson & Latcham, "Proxy Contests: A Study in Shareholder Sovereignty", 41 Calif.L.Rev. 393, 496 (1953). The formula suggested is:

$$\frac{X \text{ (allowable insurgent expenses)}}{\text{Votes secured by insurgents}} = \frac{\text{Management expenses allowed}}{\text{Votes secured by management}}$$

47. 309 N.Y. 168, 128 N.E.2d 291, 51 A.L.R.2d 860 (1955), reh. denied 309 N.Y. 807, 130 N.E.2d 610 (1955).

48. Plaintiff, an attorney who with his attorney in the case had collected in many actions of such character, owned 25 of the 2,308,817 shares of the corporation. Of the 10,245 shareholders, 750 had joined the plaintiff in the action. 284 App.Div. 201, 202–203, 132 N.Y.S.2d 273, 275 (2d Dep't 1954).

49. 284 App.Div. 201, 132 N.Y.S.2d 273 (2d Dep't 1954).

50. After the Appellate Division holding in favor of reimbursement of both management and insurgents (the latter on the basis of shareholder ratification), 284 App.Div. 201, 132 N.Y.S.2d 273 (2d Dep't 1954), the successful insurgents in the New York Central R. R. proxy contest secured shareholder ratification in favor of their reimbursement by the corporation, presumably on the basis of such holding. The affirmance of such holding by the Court of Appeals, 3–1–3, with Desmond, J., concurring on the ground that the plaintiff had failed to sustain his burden of proof, cast obvious doubts on the validity of the New York Central R. R. reimbursement. Eventually, claims against the defeated New York Central management, which spent some $550,000 of corporate funds in waging the proxy fight, were settled for $125,000; claims against the successful insurgents for more than $1,300,000 were settled for $300,000. See generally M. Feuer, Personal Liabilities of Corporate Officers and Directors ch. 13 (1961); E. Aranow & H. Einhorn, Proxy Contests for Corporate Control ch. 20 (2d ed. 1968); Machtinger, "Proxy Fight Expenditures of Insurgent Shareholders", 19 Case W.Res.L.Rev. 212 (1968); Stifel, "Shareholder Proxy Fight Expenses", 8 Clev.-Mar.L.Rev. 339 (1959); Aranow & Einhorn, "Corporate Proxy Contests: Expenses of Management and Insurgents", 42 Cornell L.Q. 4 (1956); Friedman, "Expenses of Corporate Proxy Contests", 51 Colum.L.Rev. 951 (1951); Note, "Use of Corporate Funds to Thwart the Control Ambitions of the Corporate Raider—Time for a Reappraisal?", 35 U.Mo.Kan.City L.Rev. 335 (1967); Annot., 51 A.L. R.2d 873 (1957).

51. The three judges, Froessel, J., joined by Conway, Ch. J. & Burke, J., neither cited Steinberg v. Adams, supra note 42, nor accepted the benefit theory of that case.

52. 309 N.Y. at 174, 128 N.E.2d at 293 (1955).

ble only for management expenses in informing shareholders, giving notice of the shareholder meeting, and obtaining a quorum, but not for their campaign expenses (which served no corporate purpose and were *ultra vires*); and rejected the benefit theory as speculative, and contended that the corporation should never pay any of the expenses of insurgents (at least in the absence of unanimous shareholder ratification of such *ultra vires* act).[53]

In cases involving the use of corporate funds for various proxy contest expenses, involving as they do nice questions of policy vs. personnel, corporate purpose, corporate benefit, and reasonableness, the placing of the burden of proof might be determinative. If the corporation has expended its funds, the burden of proof would be on the plaintiff seeking to restore such funds to the corporation; if the corporation has not paid the expenses and is sued by a plaintiff seeking payment or reimbursement, the burden of proof would be on such plaintiff. Ordinarily what the corporation does or does not do is protected by the "business judgment" rule.[54] However, where the management engages in self-dealing or has a conflicting interest, an adverse inference arises which shifts the burden of going forward with the evidence to the defenders of the management action, unless either such action is ratified by shareholders or an appropriate provision authorizing corporate transactions in which the directors have a personal interest is contained in the articles of incorporation.[55]

Deductibility of proxy contest expenses for federal income tax purposes has recently been recognized.[56] The prior government po-

sition had been severely criticized.[57]

Regulation of Proxies

Proxies can become involved in court proceedings and, to the extent that the Securities and Exchange Commission has jurisdiction, subject to the S.E.C. Proxy Rules.

A wide variety of controversies concerning proxies can become involved in court proceedings.[58] Where the solicitation of proxies was misleading because of nondisclosure or misstatement, appropriate legal or equitable relief, either before or after the election, might be sought in the courts.[59]

---

ordinary and necessary nonbusiness expenses under Int.Rev.Code of 1954, 26 U.S.C.A. § 212; Surasky v. United States, 325 F.2d 191 (5th Cir. 1963) (expenses of unsuccessful insurgent held deductible as ordinary and necessary nonbusiness expenses under Int. Rev.Code of 1954, 26 U.S.C.A. § 212); Locke Mfg. Cos. v. United States, 237 F.Supp. 80 (D.Conn.1964) (successful corporation's expenses held deductible as ordinary and necessary business expenses under Int.Rev.Code of 1954, 26 U.S.C.A. § 162); Central Foundry Co. v. Comm'r, 49 T.C. No. 25 (1967) (holding corporate payment of expenses both of successful insurgents and of ousted management deductible as ordinary and necessary business expenses under Int.Rev.Code, 26 U.S.C.A. § 162). But cf. Dyer v. Comm'r, 352 F.2d 948 (8th Cir. 1965) (expenditures incurred by lawyer-minor shareholder engaging in unrealistic legal struggle over corporate control and continuous proxy crusade held not deductible business or nonbusiness expenses). See Rev.Rul. 67–1, Int.Rev.Bull. No. 1 at 5. Rev.Rul. 64–236, 1964–2 Cum.Bull. 64 (upholding deduction under Int.Rev. Code of 1954, 26 U.S.C.A. §§ 162, 212 where expenses were incurred primarily over corporate policy and not to benefit personal interests). See also Note, "Internal Revenue—Corporate Deductions— Insurgent Proxy Expenditures", 20 Case W.Res.L. Rev. 270 (1968).

57. Webster, "Proxy Fight Expenses: Problems of Tax Deduction", 43 Va.L.Rev. 891 (1957).

58. See generally E. Aranow & H. Einhorn, Proxy Contests for Corporate Control ch. 19 (2d ed. 1968).

59. Willoughby v. Port, 277 F.2d 149 (2d Cir. 1960); Lonergan v. Crucible Steel Co. of America, 37 Ill.2d 599, 229 N.E.2d 536 (1967); Berendt v. Bethlehem Steel Corp., 108 N.J.Eq. 148, 154 A. 321 (1931) (proxies allowed to be voted but announcement of results enjoined); Empire Southern Gas Co. v. Gray, 29 Del.Ch. 95, 46 A.2d 741 (Ch.1946) (solicitation of proxies enjoined); Skora v. Great Sweet Grass Oils Ltd., 30 Misc.2d 572, 205 N.Y.S.2d 98 (Sup.Ct.1960), appeal dismissed, 12 A.D.2d 596, 214 N.Y.S.2d 713 (1st Dep't 1960) (holding that where committee of shareholders solicited proxies but failed to inform shareholders of activities of committee creator, who

---

53. 309 N.Y. at 176, 128 N.E.2d at 295 (1955) (Van Voorhis, Dye & Fuld, JJ.). See Kent v. Quicksilver Mining Co., 78 N.Y. 159 (1879); Continental Securities Co. v. Belmont, 206 N.Y. 7, 99 N.E. 138 (1912).

54. See section 242 infra.

55. See section 238 infra.

56. Graham v. Comm'r, 326 F.2d 878 (4th Cir. 1964) (expenses of successful insurgent held deductible as

Where the proxy solicitation is not subject to the S.E.C. Proxy Rules, the party aggrieved is limited to remedies under state law which are often less than adequate.[60]

Where the solicitation is subject to the S. E.C. Proxy Rules, additional remedies are available. The Securities and Exchange Commission, when its informal attempts to secure compliance with its rules fail, may resort to court action for injunction,[61] mandamus,[62] or criminal penalties.[63] Furthermore, despite the silence of the congressional legislation on the subject, private persons have been held entitled to seek court

was under indictment by federal grand jury for fraudulent sale of securities, committee had breached its duty to inform other shareholders and failure in that duty could not be relieved by information sent to shareholders from management or other sources; enjoining voting of such proxies obtained by reason of fraudulent representations or fraudulent omissions of material facts; and holding that where fraudulently obtained proxies have already been voted for some matter, the carrying out of the matter can be enjoined); Wyatt v. Armstrong, 186 Misc.2d 216, 59 N.Y.S.2d 502 (Sup.Ct. 1945) (election set aside); Matter of Scheuer, 59 N.Y. S.2d 500 (Sup.Ct.1942) (new election ordered). Because of exclusive federal court jurisdiction over S. E. C. Proxy Rules enforcement, state courts refuse to consider their application. Gordon Holdings, Ltd. v. Mohawk Business Machines Corp., 13 Misc.2d 1024, 179 N.Y.S.2d 33 (Sup.Ct.1958) (temporary stay of meeting denied), 13 Misc.2d 1044, 179 N.Y.S.2d 33 (Sup.Ct.1958) (setting aside of proxies denied). See also Matter of R. Hoe & Co., 137 N.Y.S.2d 142 (Sup.Ct.1954) (allowing a "certain amount of innuendo, misstatement, exaggeration and puffing . . . as a natural by-product of a bitter campaign"), aff'd mem., 285 App.Div. 927, 139 N.Y.S.2d 883 (1st Dep't 1955), aff'd mem., 309 N.Y. 719, 128 N.E.2d 420 (1955) (aftermath of Auer v. Dressel, 306 N.Y. 427, 118 N.E.2d 590, 48 A.L.R. 2d 604 (1954)). See also Levin v. Metro-Goldwyn-Mayer, Inc., 43 Del.Ch. 168, 221 A.2d 499 (Ch.1966); Comment, "Standards of Disclosure in Proxy Solicitation of Unlisted Securities", 1960 Duke L.J. 623.

60. E. Aranow & H. Einhorn, Proxy Contests for Corporate Control 529 et seq. (2d ed. 1968).

61. Id. at 455 et seq. For discussion of SEC enforcement of its proxy rules generally, see id. at 450–462; Aranow & Einhorn "Corporate Proxy Contests: Enforcement of SEC Proxy Rules by the Commission and Private Parties", 31 N.Y.U.L.Rev. 875 (1956).

62. E. Aranow & H. Einhorn, Proxy Contests for Corporate Control 455 et seq. (2d ed. 1968).

63. Id. at 460–462.

enforcement of the S.E.C. Proxy Rules.[64] A number of cases have held that a state court is without jurisdiction to consider violations of the S.E.C. Proxy Rules, on the ground that the federal legislation gives the federal courts exclusive jurisdiction on violations of the Securities and Exchange Act of 1934.[65]

The Securities and Exchange Commission has power to regulate proxies and proxy solicitations under three federal acts: Securities Exchange Act of 1934, Public Utility Holding Company Act of 1935, and Investment Company Act of 1940.[66]

Securities exchanges sometimes require proxy solicitation in the case of listed securities, thus bringing into play the S.E.C. Proxy Rules.[67]

VOTING TRUSTS

197. Voting trusts are trusts created by the transfer of voting shares by shareholders to voting trustees to hold such shares of record and to vote them during the duration of the voting trust pursuant to the voting trust agreement. Voting trusts are valid in most jurisdictions, many of which have enacted voting trust statutes. Voting trusts inconsistent with such statutes are usually void. In exchange for the entrusted shares, the voting trustees issue voting trust certificates to the transferor-shareholders. Statutes often limit the duration of

64. J. I. Case Co. v. Borak, 377 U.S. 426, 84 S.Ct. 1555, 12 L.Ed.2d 423 (1964); Aranow & Einhorn, "Corporate Proxy Contests: Enforcement of SEC Proxy Rules by the Commission and Private Parties", 31 N.Y.U.L.Rev. 875, 883–893 (1956).

65. Eliasberg v. Standard Oil Co., 23 N.J.Super. 431, 92 A.2d 862 (1952), aff'd mem., 12 N.J. 467, 97 A.2d 437 (1953); Standard Power & Light Corp. v. Investment Associates, 29 Del.Ch. 593, 51 A.2d 572 (Sup.Ct.1947), aff'g 29 Del.Ch. 225, 48 A.2d 501 (Ch. 1946). See E. Aranow & H. Einhorn, Proxy Contests for Corporate Control 480–495, 529–532 (2d ed. 1968).

66. See sections 297, 299, 301, especially section 297 infra.

67. N.Y.S.E. Company Manual § A8. See also Procedure for Soliciting Proxies from Shareholders with Stock in Brokers' Names (Joint Report of American Society of Corporate Secretaries, Inc., Association of Stock Exchange Firms, New York Stock Exchange, 1961).

voting trusts, usually to 10 years, sometimes providing for permissible extensions. Voting trusts are usually irrevocable except by the mutual consent of all parties. Voting trustees are subject to the usual fiduciary duties of trustees. Voting trustees may vote for the election of directors, otherwise exercise the ordinary voting rights of the entrusted shares, and even vote with respect to extraordinary corporate matters when so authorized by the voting trust agreement. Some statutes require that all voting trusts be open to accession by all shareholders, but other statutes permit closed voting trusts. The shareholder status of voting trust certificate holders for various purposes depends upon applicable statutes and court construction.

In General

The voting trust is a trust created by the transfer of voting shares by shareholders to a voting trustee or voting trustees, to hold and vote them, until the purpose is fulfilled or for a specified period, usually pursuant to a voting trust agreement.[1] It is a device to concentrate shareholder control in one or a few persons who, primarily through the election of directors, can control corporate affairs.[2] Numerically, corporate reorgani-

zation is the most important occasion for the use of a voting trust, where it may be used to give control to creditors.[3] It might also be used by incorporators to retain control, or in the close corporation to distribute voting power disproportionately to share ownership.[4]

Validity

The older cases found voting trusts to be illegal irrespective of purpose on the ground that the separation of voting power from beneficial interest was repugnant to the concept of corporation law.[5] Absent an illegal object, such as monopoly, many modern courts would probably uphold a voting trust even in the absence of statute.[6] Many jurisdictions authorize voting trusts by statutes.[7]

---

1. J. Leavitt, The Voting Trust (1941); H. Cushing, Voting Trusts (2d ed. 1927); Gose, "Legal Characteristics and Consequences of Voting Trusts", 20 Wash.L.Rev. 129 (1945); Ballantine, "Voting Trusts —Their Abuses and Regulation", 21 Texas L.Rev. 139 (1942); Comment, "Voting Trusts and Irrevocable Proxies", 41 Temp.L.Q. 480 (1968); Note, "The Voting Trust", 34 N.Y.U.L.Rev. 290 (1959); Note, "Voting Trust: Drafting Suggestions", 42 N.Y.U.L. Rev. 349 (1967); Note, "The Voting Trust: California Erects a Barrier to a Rational Law of Corporate Control", 18 Stan.L.Rev. 1210 (1966); Note, "Corporate Purchase of Voting Trust Certificates", 24 U.Pitt.L.Rev. 587 (1963); Annot., 98 A.L.R.2d 376 (1964). On occasion, voting trustees have held the shares of more than one corporation for monopolistic purposes, e. g., Standard Oil Trust. As a result, antimonopoly legislation is usually referred to as antitrust laws. See sections 309–315 infra. Quaere, as to merger of legal and equitable interests. See Grogan v. Grogan, 159 Tex. 392, 322 S. W.2d 514 (1959).

2. J. Leavitt, The Voting Trust 3 (1941) As a control device, the voting trust is becoming less popular (although sanctioned by an increasing number of statutes—see note 7 infra), since other less cumbersome and more effective methods of control are available.

3. J. Leavitt, The Voting Trust 5, 78–85 (1941). See 11 U.S.C.A. §§ 616(11), 621(5); In re Lower Broadway Properties, 58 F.Supp. 615 (S.D.N.Y.1945); Rittenberg v. Murnighan, 381 Ill. 267, 44 N.E.2d 913 (1942) (voting trust of shares issued to voting trustees in exchange for bonds under federal reorganization plan held not to violate Illinois constitutional requirement that all shares have right to vote cumulatively).

4. J. Leavitt, The Voting Trust 6 (1941); Note, "The Voting Trust", 34 N.Y.U.L.Rev. 290, 299–301 (1959). See sections 270, 288 infra.

5. Shepaug Voting Trust Cases (Bostwick v. Chapman), 60 Conn. 553, 24 A. 32 (1890); Harvey v. Linville Improvement Co., 118 N.C. 693, 24 S.E. 489 (1896); Warren v. Pim, 66 N.J.Eq. 353, 59 A. 773 (1904); Luthy v. Ream, 270 Ill. 170, 110 N.E. 373 (1915) (voting trust held to violate Illinois constitutional requirement that all shares have right to vote cumulatively); Burke, "Voting Trusts Currently Observed", 24 Minn.L.Rev. 347 (1940). Voting trusts are not favored by the Interstate Commerce Commission and the Securities and Exchange Commission.

6. Brightman v. Bates, 175 Mass. 105, 55 N.E. 809 (1900). See Grogan v. Grogan, 159 Tex. 392, 322 S. W.2d 514 (1959); State ex rel. Johnson v. Keystone Life Ins. Co., 93 So.2d 565 (La.App.1957) (trust to perpetuate person as officer held improper); Annot., 105 A.L.R. 123 (1936).

7. See, e. g., ABA–ALI Model Bus.Corp.Act § 32; Del.Gen.Corp.Law, § 218 (1967); McKinney's N.Y. Bus.Corp.Law § 621. See Adams v. Clearance Corp., 35 Del.Ch. 459, 121 A.2d 302 (Sup.Ct.1956) (upholding under Delaware statute 10-year voting trust of subsidiary's shares (principal asset of parent corporation) set up by parent corporation's directors with themselves as voting trustees). See Watkins, "The Development of Voting Trust Legis-

Voting trusts inconsistent with such statutes are generally void.[8]

Procedure for Setting Up Voting Trusts

To set up a voting trust, a voting trust agreement is usually executed among the voting trustees, such shareholders as desire to become parties, and possibly the corporation whose shares are involved. The shareholders than transfer their shares to the voting trustees;[9] the transfers are recorded, with notation of the voting trust, on the corporation's record of shareholders, making the voting trustees the record holders; new share certificates usually bearing an appropriate legend (to preclude the shares being acquired by *bona fide* purchasers free of the voting trust) are issued by the corporation to the voting trustees; and voting trust certificates are issued by the voting trustees to the shareholders in exchange for their shares.

Voting Trust Certificates

The voting trust certificates represent equitable interests in the shares transferred and any shares subsequently allotted as share dividends, and entitle the certificate holders to a ratable distribution of any cash or property dividends paid by the corporation to the voting trustees, and to receive share certificates evidencing the shares, plus any share distribution thereon, in exchange for the voting trust certificates upon the termination of the voting trust.

Voting trust certificates, like share certificates, are usually registered in the names of

lation", 35 U.Det.L.J. 595 (1958); Horne, "Voting Trust Agreements in Indiana", 19 Ind.L.J. 225 (1944); Comment, "Voting Trusts in Texas", 12 Sw.L.J. 85 (1958); Note, "Voting Trusts in Iowa", 11 Drake L.Rev. 140 (1962); Notes, 17 U.Chi.L.Rev. 103 (1949); 42 Ill.L.Rev. 401 (1947); Holmes v. Sharretts, 228 Md. 358, 180 A.2d 302, 98 A.L.R.2d 363 (1962) was an action for the cancellation of a Maryland voting trust agreement, the stated termination of which was five years, after the happening of an uncertain and contingent event. The petition claimed that the voting trust was invalid because (a) it could extend beyond the 10-year statutory limit; (b) it failed to state any proper business purpose; and (c) it failed to the extent a voting trustee owned shares because of the merger of legal and equitable title thereto. The court stated that such an agreement, because it incorporated the applicable statute both as a matter of law and because it was so stated in the agreement, had a 10-year limitation; that the statute did not require a voting trust to state a proper business purpose; and that the statute impliedly permits a voting trustee to be a shareholder.

8. Abercrombie v. Davies, 36 Del.Ch. 371, 130 A.2d 338 (Sup.Ct.1957), 36 Del.Ch. 445, 131 A.2d 822 (Ch. 1957) (on remand). The shareholder pooling arrangement involved (a) the divorce of the voting rights of the pooled shares from the beneficial ownership retained by the shareholders; (b) the transfer of the voting rights of fiduciaries (called "agents"); (c) the giving of "irrevocable proxies" for 10 years; and (d) the pooling of all voting rights in the "agents" with the shareholders retaining no voting rights; for (e) the principal object of controlling the corporation. The arrangement also provided for its possible future formal transformation into a voting trust by the following: "agents" to become "voting trustees"; shares with "irrevocable proxies" held by agents to be transferred of record to agents as voting trustees; and voting trust certificates to be issued in substitution for receipts held by shareholders. The defendants contended that there was no intent to set up a present voting trust (the future formal transformation not having occurred); that the agents were not voting trustees; and that the agents had not been vested with legal title to the shares. The Supreme Court of Delaware, reversing the Chancellor, ruled that the arrangement involved all of the elements of a voting trust; and was void for noncompliance with the Delaware voting trust statute as a

secret voting trust inasmuch as the shares were not transferred on the corporate stock books to the voting trustees and the voting trust agreement was not on file at the office of the corporation. See Lehrman v. Cohen, 43 Del.Ch. 222, 222 A.2d 800 (Sup.Ct. 1966) (issue of one share of class to two-family corporation's counsel to elect fifth director to vote in case of tie held not to constitute voting trust, since no separation of voting rights from other attributes of share ownership). See also Matter of Morse, 247 N.Y. 290, 160 N.E. 374 (1928); DeMarco v. Paramount Ice Corp., 102 N.Y.S.2d 692 (Sup.Ct.1950); Hirschwald v. Erlebacher, Inc., 27 Del.Ch. 43, 29 A. 2d 798 (Ch.1943); Perry v. Missouri-Kansas Pipe Line Co., 22 Del.Ch. 33, 19 A. 823 (Ch.1937).

9. See 1 G. Hornstein, Corporation Law and Practice § 221 (1959) (form of voting trust agreement). Compare Abercrombie v. Davies, 36 Del.Ch. 371, 130 A. 2d 338 (Sup.Ct.1957); Smith v. Biggs Boiler Works Co., 33 Del.Ch. 183, 91 A.2d 193, 34 A.L.R.2d 1125 (Ch.1952) (requiring recorded transfer), with Boericke v. Weise, 68 Cal.App.2d 407, 156 P.2d 781 (1945) (not requiring recorded transfer). See State ex rel. Johnson v. Keystone Life Ins. Co., 93 So.2d 565 (La.App.1957). See also Gamson v. Robinson, 284 App.Div. 945, 135 N.Y.S.2d 505 (1st Dep't 1954) (transfer to voting trustees held not barred by share transfer restriction).

the holders thereof. Such certificates, absent a valid transfer restriction, are transferable.[10]

The voting trustees usually maintain voting trust certificate books, which are generally open to inspection by voting trust certificate holders and possibly other shareholders.[11]

Duration

Statutes frequently specify the maximum duration of voting trusts, usually to 10 years. Depending on the statutory language, an attempt to set up a voting trust for an excessive period might be completely void[12] or only invalid as to the excess.[13] Statute sometimes also provide for permissible extensions.[14]

Until its purposes have been achieved or achievement becomes impossible, the voting trust is usually irrevocable except by the mutual consent of all parties.[15]

Powers and Duties of Voting Trustees

As in the case of more conventional trusts, the voting trustees, absent a provision to the contrary, usually act by majority vote.[16] In the event of deadlock, resort to the courts for appropriate relief is possible.[17] Voting trustees may be removed for cause by appropriate court proceedings.[18] In functioning as voting trustees, they are subject to the

---

10. See Lawson v. Household Finance Corp., 17 Del. Ch. 343, 152 A. 723 (Sup.Ct.1930) (upholding reasonable restriction on transfer of voting trust certificates). See Orpheum Building Co. v. Anglion, 127 F.2d 478 (9th Cir. 1942) (transfer of voting trust certificates held subject to share transfer tax as shares in "association").

11. See, e. g., ABA–ALI Model Bus.Corp.Act § 32; Del.Gen.Corp.Law, § 218 (1967); McKinney's N.Y. Bus.Corp.Law, §§ 621, 1316. See section 199 infra.

12. Perry v. Missouri-Kansas Pipe Line Co., 22 Del. Ch. 33, 19 A. 823 (Ch.1937) (under statute providing that voting trust not exceeding X years is valid). A fortiori, a statute providing that no voting trust for more than X years shall be valid is logically construable as invalidating in toto any voting trust of excessive duration.

13. A statute providing that a voting trust not exceeding X years is valid (see note 12 supra) might be construed as invalidating only the excess duration, depending on whether the statute was intended to limit or expand the situation at common law. See Christopher v. Richardson, 394 Pa. 425, 147 A. 2d 375 (1959) (voting trust with possible duration in excess of period held void); Kittinger v. Churchill Evangelistic Ass'n, 151 Misc. 350, 271 N.Y.S. 510 (Sup.Ct.1934), aff'd 244 App.Div. 876, 281 N.Y.S. 680 (4th Dep't 1935). A statute providing that no voting trust shall be valid for more than X years is construable as sustaining for the permissible period the voting trust of excessive duration. See Note, "Corporations—Validity of Voting Trust Where Created for Longer Than Statutory Period", 38 Colum.L.Rev. 508 (1938).

14. See, e. g., Del.Gen.Corp.Law, § 218 (1967). New York provides that at any time within six months before the expiration of such voting trust agreement as originally fixed or as extended, one or

more holders of voting trust certificates may, by agreement in writing, extend the duration of such voting trust agreement, nominating the same or substitute trustee or trustees, for an additional period not exceeding 10 years, but that such extension agreement shall not affect the rights or obligations of persons not parties thereto and shall in every respect comply with and be subject to all the statutory provisions applicable to the original voting trust agreement. McKinney's N.Y.Bus.Corp.Law, § 621; Belle Isle Corp. v. Corcoran, 29 Del.Ch. 554, 49 A.2d 1 (Sup.Ct.1946); Oppenheimer v. Cassidy, 345 Ill. App. 212, 102 N.E.2d 678 (1951).

15. Thomas v. Kliesen, 166 Kan. 337, 201 P.2d 663 (1949); Herman v. Dereszewski, 312 Mich. 244, 20 N.W.2d 176 (1945); Alderman v. Alderman, 178 S.C. 9, 181 S.E. 897 (1935). Cf. Selig v. Wexler, — Mass. —, 247 N.E.2d 567 (1969) (voting trust held terminated by frustration of purposes because of lack of independence of two "impartial" trustees); H. M. Bylesby & Co. v. Doriot, 25 Del.Ch. 46, 12 A. 2d 603 (Ch.1940) (sole beneficiary of voting trust allowed to revoke after failure of purpose of trust). For attempts by voting trustees to extend their powers beyond period of trust, see Brown v. McLanahan, 148 F.2d 703, 159 A.L.R. 1058 (4th Cir. 1945); Friedberg v. Schultz, 312 Ill.App. 171, 38 N.E.2d 182 (1941). Cf. Matter of Atlantic City Ambassador Hotel Corp., 62 N.Y.S.2d 62 (Sup.Ct. 1946). In contrast, most proxies are revocable. In California, a proxy is limited to only seven years, a voting trust to 21 years. Cal.Gen.Corp.Law, §§ 2226, 2231 (1947).

16. R. Stevens, Handbook on the Law of Private Corporations § 121, n. 79 (2d ed. 1949). Del.Gen. Corp.Law, § 218 (1967); McKinney's N.Y.Bus.Corp. Law, § 612(h). See Hirschwald v. Erlebacher, Inc., 27 Del.Ch. 180, 33 A.2d 148 (Ch.1943), aff'd per curiam sub nom. Erlebacher v. Hirschwald, 27 Del. Ch. 343, 36 A.2d 167 (Sup.Ct.1944).

17. See McKinney's N.Y.Bus.Corp.Law, § 612(h).

18. Moore v. Bowers, 8 Cal.2d 162, 64 P.2d 423 (1937); Lippard v. Parish, 22 Del.Ch. 25, 191 A. 829 (Ch.1937); Annot., 33 A.L.R.2d 1136 (1954).

usual fiduciary duties of trustees.[19] For breach of trust, any aggrieved voting trust certificate holder may sue directly since the duty breached was to him and not to the corporation.[20]

Voting trustees may usually vote in the election of directors and otherwise exercise the ordinary voting rights enjoyed by the entrusted shares. Whether they may vote the shares for extraordinary matters depends upon any applicable statutes and the construction of the voting trust agreement. Voting trustees cannot vote in derogation of the trust.[21] Accordingly, absent a rather clear showing of authority, they cannot vote to affect adversely the voting rights of the entrusted shares [22] or for the sale of corporate assets or the dissolution of the corporation.[23]

Even when the voting trustees have the power to vote for some matter, it is questionable whether they can delegate their discretion by giving proxies to others, at least where any statute or the voting trust agreement does not expressly provide for proxy voting by them.[24] Even where a statute or voting trust agreement permits voting trustees to vote by proxy, an irrevocable proxy, absent a provision authorizing such a proxy in the statute or the voting trust agreement, would probably not be recognized as irrevocable.[25]

Other Statutory Requirements

Older statutes sometimes required that every voting trust be open to accession by all shareholders.[26] Modern statutes permit a

---

19. Stone v. Massa, 351 Mass. 264, 218 N.E.2d 583 (1966); Brown v. McLanahan, 148 F.2d 703, 159 A. L.R. 1058 (4th Cir. 1945); 5 W. Fletcher, Private Corporations § 2091.1 (rev. vol. 1967).

20. Greater Iowa Corp. v. McLendon, 378 F.2d 783 (8th Cir. 1967); Eisner v. Davis, 109 N.Y.S.2d 504 (Sup.Ct.1951), aff'd mem., 279 App.Div. 1003, 112 N. Y.S.2d 672 (1st Dep't 1952). Cf. Gottschlak v. Avalon Realty Co., 249 Wis. 78, 23 N.W.2d 606 (1946) (voting trust held designed to protect preferred shareholders and bondholders who dominated trust and not common shareholders who had no substantial equity); Koplar v. Rosset, 355 Mo. 496, 196 S. W.2d 800 (1946).

21. Brown v. McLanahan, 148 F.2d 703, 159 A.L.R. 1058 (4th Cir. 1945). But express delegation of voting power with respect to extraordinary corporate matters has been upheld. Tompers v. Bank of America, 217 App.Div. 691, 217 N.Y.S. 67 (1st Dep't 1926); Annot., 159 A.L.R. 1067 (1945).

22. Brown v. McLanahan, 148 F.2d 703, 159 A.L.R. 1058 (4th Cir. 1945).

23. Clarke Memorial College v. Monaghan Land Co., —— Del.Ch. ——, 257 A.2d 234 (Ch.1969) (holding that voting trustees could vote in favor of sale of substantially all of real estate corporation's assets, since such sale would not in effect destroy entrusted shares or voting trust, or compel dissolution of corporation, in view of broad language concerning voting power of trustees in voting trust agreement); Stone v. Massa, 351 Mass. 264, 218 N.E. 2d 583 (1966) (finding breach of duties by voting trustees in selling corporate assets); Gould v. District Nat'l Securities Corp., 278 F.2d 34 (D.C.Cir. 1960) (laches); Jesser v. Mayfair Hotel, Inc., 316 S.W.2d 465 (Mo.1958) (sale of assets); Matter of Bacon (Susquehanna Silk Mills), 287 N.Y. 1, 38

N.E.2d 105 (1941) (dissolution). But cf. Taft Realty Corp. v. Yorkhaven Enterprises, Inc., 146 Conn. 338, 150 A.2d 597 (1959) (upholding long-term lease of corporate property approved by directors who as voting trustees had elected themselves to board of directors).

24. Chandler v. Bellanca Aircraft Corp., 19 Del.Ch. 57, 162 A. 63 (Ch.1932) (where voting trust agreement expressly permitted voting trustees to vote by proxy at shareholder meetings). See also Del.Gen. Corp.Law, § 218 (1967) (expressly permitting voting trustees to vote shares by proxy).

25. Brady v. Mexican Gulf Sulphur Co., 32 Del.Ch. 372, 88 A.2d 300 (Ch.1952).

26. See, e. g., Connecticut, Maryland, New York (prior to 1963). See Matter of Morse, 247 N.Y. 290, 160 N.E. 374 (1928). Open voting trusts may constitute a continuing offer of voting trust certificates under the Federal Securities Act of 1933. See also Greater Iowa Corp. v. McLendon, 378 F.2d 783 (8th Cir. 1967) (holding corporation and shareholders cannot under antifraud provisions of Federal Securities Act, sue other shareholders soliciting membership in voting trust, purpose of which was to gain control of corporation, since complainants were neither "purchasers" nor "sellers"; nor could they challenge legality of voting trust agreement under Federal Securities Exchange Act or Federal Investment Company Act, since they were not parties to agreement; but they could sue to enforce compliance with S.E.C. Proxy Rules, if court found that invitation to membership in voting trust, with its accompanying literature, constituted proxy solicitation); Dunning v. Rafton, CCH 1964-1966 Fed.Sec. L.Rep. ¶91,660 (N.D.Cal.1965) (letters to holders of voting trust certificates urging actions on termination held subject to S.E.C. Proxy Rules); Boericke v. Weise, 68 Cal.App.2d 407, 156 P.2d 781 (1945) (necessity of approval of voting trust by California Corporation Commissioner).

closed voting trust.[27] Statutes often require that copies of any voting trust agreement be on file at the principal office of the corporation or with the voting trustees, and be open to reasonable inspection by voting trust certificate holders and other shareholders.[28]

The existence of a voting trust can have some serious tax consequences.[29]

Status of Voting Trust Certificate Holders as Shareholders

Voting trust certificate holders are the beneficial owners, but not the record owners, of the shares. The corporation may usually rely on the record ownership, and treat the voting trustees as shareholders for most purposes. Whether the voting trust certificate holders are shareholders for the purpose of appraisal rights,[30] shareholder inspection rights,[31] and other shareholder rights,[32] depends upon applicable statutory language and judicial holdings.

"SHAREHOLDER AGREEMENTS"

198. **Shareholders usually may agree in advance to exercise their voting rights in certain ways, absent oppression of minority shareholders or some other illegal object. The most important function of shareholders is to elect directors. Since corporate management is vested in the board of directors, any shareholder wishing to exercise influence at the board of directors level must have sufficient representation on the board or control over the directors, the latter being usually accomplished to some extent by "director agreements". Shareholder agreements requiring the parties to vote for certain directors are usually enforceable so long as the directors involved are on good behavior, and would ordinarily preclude removal without cause but not removal for cause. Shareholder agreements binding the parties to vote or consent under certain circumstances for specified extraordinary corporate matters requiring shareholder approval should also be upheld when consistent with the fiduciary duties of controlling shareholders to minority shareholders. Shareholder agreements often contain arbitration clauses, or are subject to the remedies of declaratory judgment, damages, injunction, and specific performance.**

In most jurisdictions,[1] shareholders may agree in advance to exercise their voting rights [2] in certain ways. The basis for such holdings is that shareholders are generally under no fiduciary duties, and may do collectively what they may do individually, assuming lack of fraud by controlling shareholders against minority shareholders or some other illegal object. By such a shareholder agreement, the shareholders usually agree either to cast their votes in a certain way for various matters or to pool their votes and cast

27. See, e. g., ABA–ALI Model Bus.Corp.Act § 32; Del.Gen.Corp.Law, § 218 (1967); McKinney's N.Y. Bus.Corp.Law, § 621.

28. ABA–ALI Model Bus.Corp.Act § 32. Noncompliance with such filing requirement might invalidate the voting trust. Abercrombie v. Davies, 36 Del. 371, 130 A.2d 338 (Sup.Ct.1957), 36 Del.Ch. 445, 131 A.2d 822 (Ch.1957) (on remand). See also McKinney's N.Y.Bus.Corp.Law, § 621; DeMarco v. Paramount Ice Corp., 102 N.Y.S.2d 692 (Sup.Ct. 1950).

29. A. & N. Furniture & Appliance Co. v. United States, 271 F.Supp. 40 (S.D.Ohio 1967) (holding invalid U. S. Treas. Reg. § 1.1371–1(e) (1960), treating voting trust of all shares as second class and voting trust as disqualifying shareholder thus barring Subchapter S election). Voting trusts can have other tax consequences depending upon requirements of "voting stock" or "control". See Maxwell Hardware Co. v. Comm'r, 343 F.2d 713 (9th Cir. 1965).

30. Matter of Bacon (Susquehanna Silk Mills), 287 N.Y. 1, 38 N.E.2d 105 (1941) (appraisal allowed petitioning voting trust certificate holders where voting trustees had voted in favor of sale of corporate assets but at prior meeting of certificate holders petitioners had voted against proposal). But see Scott v. Arden Farms Co., 26 Del.Ch. 283, 28 A.2d 81 (Ch. 1942) (appraisal denied voting trust certificate holder whose shares had been voted in favor of merger).

31. See section 199 infra.

32. E. g., petitioning for review of corporate election. Chandler v. Bellanca Aircraft Corp., 19 Del.Ch. 57, 162 A. 63 (Ch.1932) (compliance with voting trust);

Smith v. Biggs Boiler Works Co., 33 Del.Ch. 183, 91 A.2d 193, 34 A.L.R.2d 1125 (Ch.1952) (validity of voting trust). See also sections 361, 362 infra.

1. See section 267 infra.

2. See section 189 supra. Any arbitrator should be given express irrevocable proxies to vote the parties' shares when they fail to agree. See section 196 supra.

them jointly as they agree or as an arbitrator determines.[3]

The most important traditional function of shareholders is to elect the directors.[4] Shareholders also have inherent power to remove directors for cause, and, when such power is conferred upon them, have power to remove, even without cause, directors thereafter taking office.[5]

Since management of a corporation is vested in its board of directors, any shareholder who wishes to exercise influence at the board of directors level must either have sufficient representation on the board or have sufficient control over the directors. The former can be accomplished by "shareholder agreements" predetermining the personnel of the board; the latter, to some extent, by "director agreements".[6] Broad shareholder removal-without-cause power is often desirable as an adjunct to such agreements with respect to any non-shareholder directors.

A shareholder agreement requiring the parties to vote for certain directors is usually enforceable so long as the directors involved are on good behavior, and would ordinarily preclude removal without cause but not removal for cause.[7]

While any shareholder action in connection with the election or removal of directors, absent a greater-than-normal quorum/voting requirement for shareholder action, would require only a majority vote of shareholders, where such a requirement is in force, effective shareholder action is possible only by compliance therewith.[8]

Shareholder approval is also usually required for extraordinary corporate matters.[9] While controlling shareholders are, with respect to such matters, under some fiduciary duties,[10] they probably can agree to exercise their voting rights with respect to such matters in a predetermined manner, absent breach of such fiduciary duties. Hence, a shareholder agreement to vote for or consent to dissolution of the corporation in the event of deadlock or other stated contingencies should be enforced by the courts.[11]

Shareholder agreements often contain arbitration clauses, which would subject arbitrable controversies among the parties to arbitration.[12]

Shareholder agreements, unlike irrevocable proxies[13] and voting trusts,[14] are not self-executing. Absent required arbitration, a declaratory judgment might lie; for breach of a shareholder agreement, the other party or parties to the agreement could seek damages, injunction, or specific performance.[15]

Where a *bona fide* purchaser takes shares subject to a shareholder agreement without notice thereof, he usually would not be bound by such agreement.[16] Accordingly sound practice requires that the share certificates involved bear an appropriate legend referring to the shareholder agreement.

SHAREHOLDER INSPECTION RIGHTS

199. **Shareholders apart from statute have qualified rights to inspect the corporate books and records for proper purposes enforceable by the discretionary remedy of mandamus.**

3. Such shareholder voting agreements are expressly authorized in a growing number of statutes. See section 259 infra.

4. See section 188 supra.

5. See section 192 supra.

6. See sections 213, 267, 275 infra.

7. Fells v. Katz, 256 N.Y. 67, 175 N.E. 516 (1931).

8. Matter of Burkin (Katz), 1 N.Y.2d 570, 154 N.Y.S. 2d 898, 136 N.E.2d 862 (1956).

9. See Chapter 13 infra.

10. See section 240 infra.

11. See sections 269, 277 infra.

12. Ibid.

13. See section 196 supra and sections 270, 288 infra.

14. See section 197 supra and sections 270, 288 infra.

15. See section 267, n. 42 infra.

16. See section 267, n. 44 infra.

Most jurisdictions have enacted statutes defining shareholder inspection rights with respect to specified books and records, leaving common-law inspection rights unaffected with respect to other books and records and possibly even the books and records specified in the statute. Under statutes, shareholder inspection rights are absolute or qualified, and are often limited to shareholders of record who hold more than a stated percentage of outstanding shares or who have been shareholders for a minimum period or both. Some jurisdictions have statutes defining the inspection rights of voting trust certificate holders and possibly also of creditors. The usual remedies to compel inspection are mandamus or injunction; various penalties exist for the denial of statutory inspection rights. Several jurisdictions also provide for inspection of voting lists and possibly of certain corporate reports.

Under the Federal Securities Exchange Act, a corporation having securities registered thereunder might be required to furnish a list of security holders to a security holder desiring to communicate with other security holders. The existence of such federal remedy should not affect shareholder inspection rights under state law.

Common-Law Inspection Rights

Shareholders enjoyed at common law qualified rights to inspect the corporate books and records, such as the record of shareholders, books of account, bylaws, minutes of board of directors, executive committee, and shareholder meetings, other records, including contracts, correspondence, and tax returns, and even the physical plant.[1]

The qualification was that shareholder inspection be at proper times and places and for proper purposes. The burden of proof in the earlier cases was on the shareholder to establish the propriety of his purpose,[2] possibly aided in the later cases by a presumption of propriety,[3] but in some more recent cases has been shifted to the corporation to show improper purpose.[4]

Purposes proper with respect to a particular book or record might be improper with respect to a different one. Examples of proper purposes (so far as inspection of books of account is concerned) might be to ascertain the financial condition of the corporation, the propriety of dividends, the value of the shares, the existence of mismanagement,[5] or information in aid of legitimate litigation; or (with respect to examination of the record of shareholders) to ascertain the names and addresses of other

1. 2 G. Hornstein, Corporation Law and Practice § 612 (1959); Freed, "Providing by Statute for Inspection of Corporate Computer and Other Records not Legible Visually—A Case Study on Legislating for Computer Technology", 23 Bus.Law. 457 (1968); Blades, "Inspecting Corporate Books and Records: The Stockholder's Uncertain Right", 35 J.B.A.Kan. 293 (1965); Bartels & Flanagan, "Inspection of Corporate Books and Records in New York by Stockholders and Directors", 38 Cornell L.Q. 289 (1953); Comment, "Right of Stockholder to Inspect the Corporate Books", 18 La.L. Rev. 337 (1958); Comment, "Shareholder Inspection Rights", 12 Sw.L.J. 61 (1958); Comment, "Inspection of Corporate Books and Records in Delaware", 41 Va.L.Rev. 237 (1955); Annot., 22 A.L.R. 24

(1923), 43 A.L.R. 783 (1926), 59 A.L.R. 1373 (1929), 80 A.L.R. 1502 (1932), 174 A.L.R. 262 (1948), 15 A.L. R.2d 11 (1951), 19 A.L.R.3d 869 (1968). See Ochs v. Washington Heights Fed. S. & L. Ass'n, 17 N.Y.2d 82, 268 N.Y.S.2d 294, 215 N.E.2d 485 (1966) (recognizing common-law rights to inspect membership lists of federal savings and loan associations); Durnin v. Allentown Fed. S. & L. Ass'n, 218 F. Supp. 716 (E.D.Pa.1963).

2. Breswick & Co. v. Greater N. Y. Industries, Inc., 308 N.Y. 1041, 127 N.E.2d 871 (1955), rev'g 285 App. Div. 804, 137 N.Y.S.2d 616 (1st Dep't 1955); Albee v. Lamson & Hubbard Corp., 320 Mass. 421, 69 N.E. 2d 811 (1946); State ex rel. Miller v. Loft, Inc., 34 Del. 538, 156 A. 170 (Super.Ct.1931).

3. Klein v. Scranton Life Ins. Co., 139 Pa.Super. 369, 11 A.2d 770 (1940).

4. See 5 W. Fletcher, Private Corporations §§ 2213, 2219, 2253.1 (rev. vol. 1967); Hagy v. Premier Mfg. Corp., 404 Pa. 330, 172 A.2d 283 (1961); Matter of Hausner v. Hopewell Products, Inc., 10 A.D.2d 876, 201 N.Y.S.2d 252 (2d Dep't 1960).

5. 5 W. Fletcher, Private Corporations §§ 2222–2224 (rev. vol. 1967). The right to inspect to discover possible mismanagement is not dependent upon a showing of mismanagement in most American jurisdictions. Matter of Durr v. Paragon Trading Corp., 270 N.Y. 464, 1 N.E.2d 967 (1936); cf. Matter of Martin v. Columbia Pictures Corp., 307 N.Y. 922, 123 N.E.2d 572 (1954) (4–3) (necessity of showing reasonable grounds for suspecting mismanagement).

shareholders in order to communicate with them concerning corporate affairs.[6]

Typical of improper purposes, with respect to one record or another, would be to learn business secrets to aid a competitor of the corporation, to secure prospects for personal business or "sucker lists", or to find technical defects in corporate transactions in order to bring "strike suits" for purposes of blackmail and extortion.[7]

Obviously, the line between proper and improper purposes is not always clear, with the result that the placing of the burden of proof and possible recognition of presumptions with respect to propriety of purpose are sometimes determinative. The common-law remedy to enforce shareholder inspection rights was mandamus, the granting of which was subject to the discretion of the courts.[8]

In making inspections, the shareholders usually may have the assistance of their attorneys, accountants, etc.,[9] and may make reasonable extracts.[10]

Common-law shareholder inspection rights are not necessarily abrogated by statutes creating statutory shareholder inspection rights, especially with respect to subjects of examination not covered by the statute, and possibly also, depending on the statutory language, with respect even to subjects of examination covered by the statute, on the theory that the statute was intended to enlarge and not to restrict common-law rights.[11]

6. 5 W. Fletcher, Private Corporations § 2225 (rev. vol. 1967). A shareholder might want to try to persuade sufficient other shareholders to join him in a derivative action to avoid having to post security for expenses. See Baker v. Macfadden Publications, Inc., 300 N.Y. 325, 90 N.E.2d 876 (1950); Sivin v. Schwartz, 22 A.D.2d 822, 254 N.Y.S.2d 914 (2d Dep't 1964); Weitzen v. Friedman, 157 N.Y.L.J. No. 6, 17 (Sup.Ct.1967) (staying posting of security for expenses pending inspection). But see Greenstein v. Paul, 157 N.Y.L.J. No. 58, 16 (Sup.Ct.1967) (ordering posting of security for expenses and denying inspection because less than two percent of shares worth less than $50,000 were owned by persons other than defendant). Federal courts in the past had denied inspection on grounds of lack of power. Neuwirth v. Merin, 267 F.Supp. 333 (S.D.N.Y.1967). But see note 8 infra. See section 372 infra.

7. 5 W. Fletcher, Private Corporations §§ 2226–2226.4 (rev. vol. 1967). See State ex rel. Thiele v. Cities Service Co., 31 Del.Ch. 514, 115 A. 773, 22 A.L.R. 8 (Sup.Ct.1922); Slay v. Polonia Pub. Co., 249 Mich. 609, 229 N.W. 434 (1930).

8. Or under equivalent statutory procedures. E. g., McKinney's N.Y. CPLR §§ 7801 et seq.; Matter of Martin v. Columbia Pictures Corp., 307 N.Y. 922, 132 N.E.2d 572 (1954); Matter of Durr v. Paragon Trading Corp., 270 N.Y. 464, 1 N.E.2d 967 (1936); Wallace v. Miller Art Co., 12 Misc.2d 793, 173 N.Y. S.2d 364 (Sup.Ct.1958). The fact that the shareholder already has available the information he is seeking might be ground for denying inspection for lack of good faith. See People ex rel. Giles v. Klauder-Weldon Dyeing Mach. Co., 180 App.Div. 149, 167 N.Y.S. 429 (3d Dep't 1917). Prior to 1968, federal courts refused to order inspection on the

grounds that they lacked original jurisdiction to issue writs of mandamus, but sometimes afforded relief by injunctions. These holdings were overruled by Stern v. South Chester Tube Co., 389 U.S. 911, 88 S.Ct. 242, 19 L.Ed.2d 259 (1968) (holding federal courts may compel inspection, in cases within their jurisdiction—quaere as to ascertainment of any jurisdictional amount requirement—under traditional equity power, regardless of whether state law characterizes such relief "mandamus" or mandatory injunction, at least where state law recognizes inspection rights and remedies).

9. 5 W. Fletcher, Private Corporations § 2233 (rev. vol. 1967).

10. 5 W. Fletcher, Private Corporations § 2241 (rev. vol. 1967).

11. ABA–ALI Model Bus.Corp.Act § 46 ("Nothing herein contained shall impair the power of any court of competent jurisdiction, upon proof by a shareholder of proper purpose, irrespective of the period of time during which such shareholder shall have been a shareholder of record, and irrespective of the number of shares held by him, to compel the production for examination by such shareholder of the books and records of account, minutes, and record of shareholders of a corporation."); 2 G. Hornstein, Corporation Law and Practice § 611 (1959); Texas Infra-Red Radiant Co. v. Erwin, 397 S.W.2d 491 (Tex.Civ.App.1965) (recognizing common-law inspection rights of beneficiary of trust); Sivin v. Schwartz, 22 A.D.2d 822, 254 N.Y.S.2d 914 (2d Dep't 1964) (recognizing common-law inspection rights of shareholder not of record); Black v. Thermasol, Ltd., 21 A.D.2d 645, 249 N.Y.S.2d 389 (1st Dep't 1964); Bishop's Estate of Antilles Enterprises, Inc., 252 F.2d 498 (3d Cir. 1958) (Virgin Islands statutory right held not to have restricted common-law right); Matter of Baczkowska v. 2166 Operating Corp., 304 N.Y. 811, 109 N.E.2d 470 (1952) (voting trust certificate holder allowed inspection of corporation's books of account); Sanders v. Neely, 197 Miss. 66, 19 So.2d 424 (1944); Matter of Schnepf, 84 N.Y.S.2d 416 (Sup.Ct.1948); People ex rel. Ven-

Shareholder inspection rights should not be confused with director's inspection rights which in some jurisdictions are stated to be absolute.[12]

Statutory Inspection Rights

Most jurisdictions have enacted statutes affecting, in some or more respects, the shareholder's inspection rights.

Statutes usually do not deal with all the corporate books and records,[13] thus preserv-

ing the shareholder's common-law rights of inspection with respect to those books and records not covered by the statute.[14] Thus, in such jurisdictions, the record of shareholders may be subject to the statutory inspection right, while the books of account, minutes of board of directors or shareholder meetings, bylaws, or other records, may remain subject to the common-law inspection right.

The shareholder's statutory rights of inspection might be absolute;[15] absolute, so far as penalties are concerned, but qualified as to the availability of any mandamus remedy;[16] or qualified (codification of common-law right),[17] perhaps with the corpora-

ner v. N. Y. Life Ins. Co., 111 App.Div. 183, 97 N. Y.S. 465 (1st Dep't 1906); State ex rel. Armour & Co. v. Gulf Sulphur Corp., —— Del.Ch. ——, 233 A.2d 457 (Super.Ct.1967), aff'd —— Del.Ch. ——, 231 A.2d 470 (Sup.Ct.1967) (denying inspection of confidential merger information supplied by other corporation which was potential competitor of shareholder); Matter of Steinberg, 157 N.Y.L.J. No. 29, 15 (Sup.Ct.1967) (refusing to require corporation to organize its records for shareholder inspection); Tucson Gas & Electric Co. v. Schantz, 5 Ariz.App. 511, 428 P.2d 686 (1967) (granting inspection of proxies and ballots on ground statute was only partially declaratory of common law); Weck v. District Court, 158 Colo. 521, 408 P.2d 987 (1965) (denying inspection of confidential worksheets of accountant under accountant-client privilege); State ex rel. Jones v. Ralston Purina Co., 358 S.W.2d 772 (Mo.1962) (denying inspection of internal memoranda and worksheets). McKinney's N.Y.Bus.Corp.Law, § 624(f) (expressly provide that nothing therein shall impair power of courts to compel production for examination of corporate books and records).

12. See section 216 infra.

13. ABA–ALI Model Bus.Corp.Act § 46 (books and records of account, minutes, and record of shareholders; quaere as to bylaws, etc.; "relevant" inserted by 1969 Model Act revision); Cal.Gen.Corp. Law, §§ 3003, 3005 (1947) (share or duplicate share register, books of account, minutes of shareholder, board of directors, and executive committee meetings, property and funds of corporation); Del.Gen. Corp.Law, §§ 218, 219, 220 (1967) (voting trust agreement, voting list, stock ledger, list of shareholders, and other books and records); McKinney's N.Y.Bus.Corp.Law, § 624 (record of shareholders and minutes of proceedings of shareholders); Ohio Gen.Corp.Law, § 1701.37(C) (1955) (articles of incorporation, regulations, bylaws, books and records of account, minutes and record of shareholders, voting trust certificates on file); Holdsworth v. Goodall-Sanford, Inc., 143 Me. 56, 55 A.2d 130, 174 A.L.R. 257 (1947) (statutory right of inspection held limited to share book and records of meetings); Matter of Steinway, 159 N.Y. 250, 53 N.E. 1103 (1899). New York requires every domestic corporation to keep correct and complete books and records of account, minutes of proceedings of its shareholders, board of directors and executive committee, if any, and to

keep at the office of the corporation in New York or at the office of its transfer agent or registrar in New York the prescribed record of shareholders—in written form or capable of being converted into written form within a reasonable time. McKinney's N.Y.Bus.Corp.Law, § 624(a). The 1969 Model Act revision provides that any books, records and minutes may be in written form or in any other form capable of being converted into written form within a reasonable time. See Freed, "Providing by Statute for Inspection of Corporate Computer and Other Records Not Legible Visually—A Case Study on Legislating for Computer Technology", 23 Bus.Law. 457 (1968).

14. See note 11 supra.

15. Jurisdictions which once granted such absolute rights have tended to qualify them in recent years. See, e. g., Mich.Gen.Corp.Act § 21.45 (1948); Wis. Bus.Corp.Law, § 180.43(2) (1951). Cf. Slay v. Polonia Pub. Co., 249 Mich. 609, 229 N.W. 434 (1930) (prior Michigan statute). When the right is made absolute by statute, there might be some question of the statute's effect on the court's traditional discretion in granting mandamus or equivalent remedy. See note 16 infra.

16. Guthrie v. Harkness, 199 U.S. 148, 26 S.Ct. 4, 50 L.Ed. 130 (1905); Morris v. United Piece Dye Works, 137 N.J.L. 262, 59 A.2d 660 (1948); Slay v. Polonia Pub. Co., 249 Mich. 609, 229 N.W. 434 (1930); State ex rel. Thiele v. Cities Service Co., 31 Del. 514, 115 A. 773, 22 A.L.R. 8 (Sup.Ct.1922). See State ex rel. Dempsey v. Werra Aluminum Foundry Co., 173 Wis. 651, 182 N.W. 354, 22 A.L.R. 1 (1921) (intimation under absolute right statute that court might prevent shareholder from improperly using information).

17. E. g., California, Idaho, Louisiana, Michigan, New Hampshire, Ohio, Pennsylvania, Texas, Utah, Virginia, Washington. See 5 W. Fletcher, Private Corporations §§ 2247, 2253 (rev. vol. 1967). Nationwide Corp. v. Northwestern Nat'l Life Ins. Co., 251

tion subject to the burden of showing improper purpose.[18]

Minn. 255, 87 N.W.2d 671, 73 A.L.R.2d 884 (1958); Bundy v. Robbins & Myers, Inc., 38 Ohio Op. 77, 75 N.E.2d 717 (Ct.App.1947), reh. denied 76 N.E.2d 312 (Ct.App.1947).

See also State ex rel. Wolfner v. Fairfax Shipside Storage, Inc., 93 So.2d 336 (La.App.1957) (allowing inspection to shareholder without right to vote in corporate affairs); Willard v. Harrworth Corp., 258 Del.Ch. 914, 258 A.2d 914 (Ch.1969) (holding dissolution of corporation, notwithstanding three-year winding up period, precluded proper purpose for shareholder inspection). Shareholder inspection of the record of shareholders by a shareholder planning either to make a tender offer to other shareholders for their shares or to resist a take over by others has been held to be a proper purpose. NVF Co. v. Sharon Steel Corp., 294 F.Supp. 1091 (W.D.Pa.1969); Mite Corp. v. Heli-Coil Corp., —— Del.Ch. ——, 256 A.2d 855 (Ch.1969).

18. Northwest Industries, Inc. v. B. F. Goodrich Co., —— Del.Ch. ——, 260 A.2d 428 (Sup.Ct.1969) (denying inspection on grounds of lack of "proper purpose" where actual purpose was to block impending take over and maintain incumbent management); General Time Corp. v. Talley Industries, Inc., 43 Del.Ch. 531, 240 A.2d 755 (Sup.Ct.1968) (holding burden of proof to show improper purpose was on corporation, and if primary purpose was proper, any secondary purpose was immaterial): Matter of Waldman v. Eldorado Towers, Ltd., 25 A.D.2d 836, 270 N.Y.S. 2d 216 (1st Dep't 1966), aff'd mem., 19 N.Y.2d 843, 280 N.Y.S.2d 407, 227 N.E.2d 320 (1967) (holding shareholder entitled to inspection absent showing of bad faith); Lake v. Buckeye Steel Castings Co., 2 Ohio 2d 101, 206 N.E.2d 566 (1965) (holding corporation had not satisfied burden of proof to show improper purpose, and holding statement of purpose to communicate with other shareholders "regarding the affairs of the corporation" to be sufficient); Matter of Mook v. American Fabrics Co., 24 A.D.2d 971, 265 N.Y.S.2d 589 (1st Dep't 1965), aff'd mem., 17 N.Y.2d 756, 270 N.Y.S.2d 215, 217 N.E.2d 39 (1966) (holding that holders of 49.78 percent of shares should be granted inspection "unless very cogent reasons are presented for denying such relief"); Smith v. Flynn, 275 Ala. 392, 155 So.2d 497 (1963) (burden of proof on officers refusing inspection); Goldman v. Trans-United Industries, Inc., 404 Pa. 288, 171 A.2d 788 (1961) (permitting corporation to have opportunity to prove general assertions of improper purpose). Compare Morris v. Broadview, Inc., 385 Ill. 228, 52 N.E.2d 769 (1944) (holding statutory inspection dependent upon allegation and proof of proper purpose), with Dines v. Harris, 88 Colo. 22, 291 P. 1024 (1930) (burden of proof to show improper purpose on corporation). See 5 W. Fletcher, Private Corporations § 2253.1 (rev. vol. 1967). Compare Murchison v. Alleghany Corp., 27 Misc.2d 290, 210 N.Y.S.2d 153 (Sup.Ct. 1960), aff'd 12 A.D.2d 753, 210 N.Y.S.2d 975 (1st Dep't 1960), appeal denied 12 A.D.2d 903, 212 N.Y. S.2d 997 (1st Dep't 1961) and Matter of Houston Oil Field Material Co., 157 N.Y.L.J. No. 49, 17 (Sup.Ct.

Qualifying the statutory inspection right in some jurisdictions are various specified defenses, such as improper use of a list of shareholders or information secured in a prior inspection of any corporation by the shareholder during a previous specified period, lack of good faith, or improper purpose.[19]

Some statutes, to safeguard the corporation, impose various conditions, such as that the shareholder own at least a minimum amount of shares,[20] or that he have been a

1967) (ordering inspection by shareholder making takeover offer where management communicated with shareholders urging rejection of offer), with Matter of Laidlaw & Co. v. Pacific Ins. Co., 52 Misc. 2d 122, 275 N.Y.S.2d 125 (Sup.Ct.1966) (denying inspection to shareholders seeking to acquire additional shares). Compare Donaldson v. Boston Herald-Traveler Corp., 347 Mass. 274, 197 N.E.2d 671 (1964) (no constitutional right to jury trial), with Uvalde Rock Asphalt Co. v. Loughridge, 423 S.W.2d 602 (Tex.Civ.App.1968) (improper denial of jury trial).

19. ABA-ALI Model Bus.Corp.Act § 46; McKinney's N.Y.Bus.Corp.Law, § 624(c) (refusal to furnish affidavit that inspection is not desired for purpose which is in interest of business or object other than business of corporation and that person seeking inspection has not within five years sold or offered for sale any list of shareholders of any corporation of any type or kind, whether or not formed under laws of New York, or aided or abetted any person in procuring any such record of shareholders for any such purpose).

20. ABA-ALI Model Bus.Corp.Act § 46 (holder of record of at least five percent of all outstanding shares), Alaska, Colorado, Florida, Idaho, New York (any person holding at least five percent of any class of outstanding shares), North Carolina, North Dakota, Oregon, Texas, Virginia, Wisconsin. New York, North Carolina, and West Virginia expressly permit shareholders to aggregate their shares to meet the percentage requirement. Under the former New York statute, it was held that an owner of at least five percent of all the outstanding shares did not have to be a holder of record. See Monitor Co. v. Confianza Furniture & Appliance Corp., 142 N.Y.S.2d 140 (Sup.Ct.1955) (judgment creditor succeeding to rights of pledgee, who was record owner, held entitled to inspection). See also Babbitt v. Pacco Investors Corp., 246 Or. 261, 425 P.2d 489 (1967) (subscriber for unpaid shares without certificate held to be shareholder of record entitled to inspection where minutes showed his participation at shareholder meetings and his election as director); Barnett v. Barnett Enterprises, Inc., 182 So.2d 728 (La.Ct.App.1966) (denying inspection to shareholder who had sought appraisal remedy on ground demand for appraisal ended shareholder status); George v. International Breweries, Inc., 1 Mich.App. 129, 134 N.W.2d 381 (1965) (construing shareholder who now owned required percentage but had owned

shareholder for a minimum period,[21] or both,[22] possibly adding a proviso that a court might order an inspection even when such conditions are not satisfied.[23]

Statutes often limit the statutory shareholder inspection rights to shareholders of record,[24] but might have separate provisions for inspection by voting trust certificate

holders,[25] or even judgment creditors, creditors, or holders of debt securities.[26]

Some statutes require a written demand by the shareholder seeking inspection, stating the purposes of the inspection.[27]

Statutes sometimes also expressly provided that the inspection may be by the shareholder or by his agent or attorney.[28]

of record smaller percentage for three months as meeting statutory requirements); DeRosa v. Terry Steam Turbine Co., 26 Conn.Supp. 131, 214 A.2d 684 (1965) (upholding inspection rights of employees who held single shares as nominees of union desiring to communicate with shareholders).

21. ABA–ALI Model Bus.Corp.Act § 46 (shareholder of record for at least six months); Alaska, Arkansas, Colorado, Florida, Illinois, New York, North Carolina, North Dakota, Oregon, Texas, Virginia, Wisconsin. Hence under the former New York statute, a petitioner owning less than five percent who had pledged his shares to a pledgee who became the record owner was held not entitled to inspection under the statute. Neisloss v. Alleghany Corp., 141 N.Y.S.2d 732 (Sup.Ct.1955) (notwithstanding repayment of loan). See Joannou v. Joannou Cycle Co., 6 A.D.2d 592, 180 N.Y.S.2d 141 (1st Dep't 1958).

22. E. g., Louisiana, Maryland, Michigan. Louisiana expressly permits shareholders to aggregate their shares to meet the statutory requirements.

23. E. g., ABA–ALI Model Bus.Corp.Act § 46.

24. E. g., ABA–ALI Model Bus.Corp.Act § 46; Del. Gen.Corp.Law, § 220 (1967); State ex rel. Rogers v. Sherman Oil Corp., 31 Del. 570, 117 A. 122 (Sup.Ct. 1922) (shareholder allowed examination of his corporation, but not of almost wholly-owned subsidiary); cf. Donna v. Abbotts Dairies, Inc., 399 Pa. 497, 161 A.2d 13 (1960) (compelling inspection only of records covered by statute); Brecker v. Nielsen, 21 Conn.Supp. 33, 143 A.2d 463 (1958) (inspection denied beneficiary of trust holding shares in corporation); State ex rel. Crowder v. Sperry Corp., 41 Del. 84, 15 A.2d 661 (Super.Ct.1940) (mandamus denied voting trust certificate holder but possibility of equitable relief suggested). Compare Matter of Baczkowska v. 2166 Operating Corp., 304 N.Y. 811, 109 N.E.2d 470 (1952), with Brentmore Estates, Inc. v. Hotel Barbizon, Inc., 263 App.Div. 389, 33 N.Y.S. 2d 331 (1st Dep't 1942). See McKinney's N.Y.Bus. Corp.Law, § 624 (entitling to statutory inspection rights (a) Any person who shall have been shareholder of record of corporation for at least six months immediately preceding his demand, or (b) Any person holding, or thereunto authorized in writing by holders of, at least five percent of any class of corporation's outstanding shares, and (c) Providing that holders of voting trust certificates representing shares of corporation to be regarded as shareholders for such purposes).

25. E. g., 1969 Model Act revision; Cal.Gen.Corp. Law, § 3003 (1947); Md.Gen.Corp.Law, § 51(c) (1951); Wis.Bus.Corp.Law, § 180.43(3) (1951) (granting broad inspection rights to voting trust certificate holders). Cf. ABA–ALI Model Bus.Corp.Act § 32 (deposited voting trust agreement counterpart open to inspection by voting trust certificate holders and shareholders); Del.Gen.Corp.Law, § 218 (1967) (voting trust agreement open to inspection by voting trust certificate holders and shareholders); McKinney's N.Y.Bus.Corp.Law, § 621(c) (voting trust agreement and record of voting trust certificate holders open to inspection by shareholders of record and holders of voting trust certificates). Voting trust certificate holders had previously been denied the right to inspect the names and addresses of voting trust certificate holders on the grounds that the statutory right to inspect the share list had been granted only to shareholders of record and that certain proceeding could only be brought against corporations and their officers to enforce a clear legal right and not against voting trustees to enforce mere contract rights. Brentmore Estates, Inc., v. Hotel Barbizon, Inc., 263 App.Div. 389, 33 N.Y.S.2d 331 (1st Dep't 1942). But see Matter of Baczkowska v. 2166 Operating Corp., 304 N.Y. 811, 109 N.E.2d 470 (1952) (voting trust certificate holder allowed inspection of corporation's book of accounts).

26. E. g., Arkansas, Florida, Hawaii, Nevada, New Hampshire, New York (judgment creditors); Louisiana, Oklahoma (creditors per bylaws); Delaware (holders of debt securities per articles of incorporation); Maine ("all persons interested"). See La. Const. art. XIII, § 4 (inspection by shareholders, officers, and public). New York permits the articles of incorporation to confer inspection rights upon bondholders and also authorizes inspection of the record of shareholders by wage earners with claims against shareholders. McKinney's N.Y.Bus.Corp. Law, §§ 548(c), 624(b), 630(b).

27. E. g., ABA–ALI Model Bus.Corp.Act § 46; McKinney's N.Y.Bus.Corp.Law, § 624(b) (at least five days' written demand); Hanrahan v. Puget Sound Power & Light Co., 332 Mass. 586, 126 N.E.2d 499 (1955).

28. E. g., ABA–ALI Model Bus.Corp.Act § 46; McKinney's N.Y.Bus.Corp.Law, § 624(b) (in person or by agent or attorney).

Some statutes expressly provide that extracts may be made in connection with any inspection.[29]

Shareholder statutory inspection rights may not be limited by provisions in the articles of incorporation or bylaws.[30] Reasonable restrictions therein concerning the time, place, and conditions of inspection and provisions enlarging shareholders' inspection rights are probably valid.[31]

To compel inspection, the usual remedies are mandamus or its modern statutory equivalent,[32] or mandatory injunction.[33]

Penalties for wrongful refusal of inspection vary in the different jurisdictions. The most common is to make the corporation or any officer or agent denying inspection liable to the shareholder for a penalty equal to 10 percent of the value of the shareholder's shares in addition to any other damages or remedies available.[34] Some jurisdictions impose a fine payable to the state,[35] or impose a penalty payable to the shareholder.[36] In a few jurisdictions, willful denial of inspection right constitutes a misdemeanor.[37]

Statutes might also provide for inspection of voting lists in connection with shareholder meetings [38] and various reports and information.[39]

29. E. g., ABA–ALI Model Bus.Corp.Act § 46; McKinney's N.Y.Bus.Corp.Law, § 624(b); Matter of Baker, 158 N.Y.L.J. No. 21, 12 (Sup.Ct.1967) (allowing shareholder to make copies on Xerox machine at corporation's principal office); Brandt Glass Co. v. New Orleans Housing Mart, 193 So.2d 321 (La. Ct.App.1966) (allowing shareholder to remove designated corporate records of domestic corporation to his attorney's office for copying since latter's copying device was better than corporation's); Matter of Mencher v. Seminole Oil & Gas Corp., 20 Misc.2d 56, 194 N.Y.S.2d 162 (Sup.Ct.1959) (transfer agent equipped to make desired extracts at shareholder's expense ordered to do so).

30. State ex rel. Cochran v. Penn-Beaver Oil Co., 34 Del. 81, 143 A. 257 (Ct. in Banc 1926) (articles of incorporation); Loew's Theatres, Inc. v. Commercial Credit Co., — Del.Ch. —, 243 A.2d 78 (Ch.1968); Donaldson v. Boston Herald-Traveler Corp., 347 Mass. 274, 197 N.E.2d 671 (1964) (bylaw requiring board of directors approval of inspection held invalid); State ex rel. Miller v. Loft, Inc., 34 Del. 538, 156 A. 170 (Super.Ct.1931) (bylaws). The articles of incorporation, or possibly the bylaws, might contain provisions limiting the shareholder's common-law inspection rights (books of account, bylaws, minutes, etc.). Limitations of statutory rights are probably not acceptable either in the articles of incorporation or in the bylaws. See Cal.Gen.Corp. Law § 3003 (1947) (right of shareholders to inspect corporate records not to be limited in articles of incorporation or bylaws).

31. See Koenigsberg, "Provisions in Charters and By-Laws Governing Inspection of Books by Stockholders", 30 Geo.L.J. 227 (1942).

32. See note 8 supra. E. g., McKinney's N.Y. CPLR § 217 (requiring proceeding to be brought within four months of refusal); Matter of Cravatts v. Klozo Fastener Corp., 205 Misc. 781, 133 N.Y.S.2d 235 (Sup.Ct.1954) (absent express refusal, refusal deemed to occur upon expiration of time fixed by shareholder; otherwise within reasonable time after demand).

33. See Bergman v. Orkin Exterminating Co., 213 Ga. 561, 100 S.E.2d 267 (1957); Gavin v. Purdy, 335 Mass. 236, 139 N.E.2d 397 (1957).

34. E. g., ABA–ALI Model Bus.Corp.Act § 46; Alabama, Colorado, Illinois, North Carolina, North Dakota, Oregon, Wisconsin. See Sterling v. City Nat'l Bank & Trust Co., 17 Ill.App.2d 340, 149 N.E.2d 789 (1959) (transfer agent held to have only custody of record of shareholders, subject to control of corporation, and hence not liable for such penalty).

35. E. g., Nevada, New Mexico.

36. Smith v. Flynn, 275 Ala. 392, 155 So.2d 497 (1963) (upholding penalty against president of $23,740, under statute providing for penalty of 10 percent of value of shares owned by shareholder, even though such penalty clearly exceeded shareholder's actual damage); Babbitt v. Pacco Investors Corp., 246 Or. 261, 425 P.2d 489 (1967) (upholding $5,000 penalty against corporation and its registered agent for wrongfully refusing inspection). Compare McCormick v. Statler Hotels Delaware Corp., 30 Ill.2d 86, 195 N.E.2d 172 (1963) (upholding $2,000 penalty under Illinois law against Delaware corporation qualified to do business in Illinois), with Schaeffer v. H. B. Green Transp. Line, 232 F.2d 415 (7th Cir. 1956) (Illinois penalty provision held penal, rather than remedial, and not applicable in case of Iowa corporation doing business in Illinois).

37. E. g., Arizona.

38. E. g., ABA–ALI Model Bus.Corp.Act § 29; Alabama, Colorado, Connecticut, Delaware, Illinois, Indiana, Iowa, Kansas, Louisiana, Michigan, Missouri, Nebraska, New Jersey, New York, North Carolina, North Dakota, Ohio, Oklahoma, Oregon, Pennsylvania, Texas, Virginia, Wisconsin. See also Magill v. North American Refractories Co., 36 Del. 185, 128 A.2d 233 (Sup.Ct.1956) (voting list required to contain shareholders' addresses and number of shares held), 36 Del. 305, 129 A.2d 411 (Sup.Ct.1957) (penalty of disqualification for office held inapplicable to directors refusing inspection of voting list since refusal was not willful, but in good faith and upon advice of counsel); Womsley, "Shareholder

39. See Note 59 on page 402.

Inspection of foreign corporation has been allowed under statutes which expressly so provide [40] or are construed to apply to foreign corporations doing business within the jurisdiction,[41] or on general principles.[42]

Federal Securities Exchange Act of 1934 and Securities Exchange Requirements

Under the S.E.C. Proxy Rules, a security holder of a corporation whose management makes a solication with respect to a registered security, who desires to communicate with other security holders, might demand a list of security holders from the corporation. The corporation may elect not to disclose the list but to handle the mailing for him.[43]

The existence of such federal remedy has been held not to affect the shareholders' inspection rights under state law.[44]

Other provisions of the 1934 Act require the filing with the Securities and Exchange Commission and national securities exchanges of various reports.[45]

Securities exchanges sometimes require corporations having listed securities to file and send to shareholders annual reports and to publish interim statements of earnings.[46]

Voting List Statutes—Are They Effective?", 26 U. Cin.L.Rev. 288 (1957).

39. E. g., ABA–ALI Model Bus.Corp.Act § 46 (requirement that corporation mail to any shareholder, upon written request, its most recent financial statements); McKinney's N.Y.Bus.Corp.Law, § 624(e) (upon written request of any person who shall have been shareholder of record for at least six months immediately preceding his request, or any person holding, or thereunto authorized in writing by holders of, at least five percent of any class of corporation's outstanding shares, corporation shall give or mail to such shareholder annual balance sheet and profit and loss statement for preceding fiscal year, and, if any interim balance sheet or profit and loss statement has been distributed to its shareholders or otherwise made available to public, most recent such interim balance sheet or profit and loss statement; corporation to be allowed reasonable time to prepare such annual balance sheet and profit and loss statement); Okl.Const. art. 9, § 43 (list of shareholders, officers, and directors); McKinney's N.Y.Bus.Corp.Law, § 718 (availability for inspection of current list of names and addresses of corporation's directors and officers by shareholder or creditor of corporation or state official. See E. Floyd, Preparing the Annual Report (1960); N. McLaren, Annual Reports to Stockholders (1947); Bryant, "How's the Annual Report Coming?", 69 Fortune, No. 1, 104 (Jan. 1964); Girdler, "18,000,000 Books Nobody Reads", 46 Saturday Review, No. 15, 71 (Apr. 13, 1963).

40. McKinney's N.Y.Bus.Corp.Law, § 1315 (subjecting record of shareholders of foreign corporation doing business in New York to inspection by any New York resident who shall have been shareholder of record for at least six months immediately preceding his demand, or by any New York resident holding, or thereunto authorized in writing by holders of, at least five percent of any class of corporation's outstanding shares, with resident holders of voting trust certificates representing shares of foreign corporation to be regarded as shareholders for such purpose, at office of foreign corporation in New York or at office of its transfer agent or registrar in New York or at such other place in county in New York in which foreign corporation is doing business as may be designated by foreign corporation. See also id. § 1316 (voting trust records). Matter of Crane Co. v. Westinghouse Air Brake Co., 56 Misc.2d 538, 288 N.Y.S.2d 984 (Sup.Ct.1968) (scope of res judicata).

41. Toklan Royalty Corp. v. Tiffany, 193 Okl. 120, 141 P.2d 571 (1943).

42. See Donna v. Abbotts Dairies, Inc., 399 Pa. 497, 161 A.2d 13 (1960); Sanders v. Pacific Gamble Robinson Co., 250 Minn. 265, 84 N.W.2d 919 (1957);

Kahn v. American Cone & Pretzel Co., 365 Pa. 161, 74 A.2d 160 (1950); Matter of Beryl v. United States Smelting Refining & Min. Co., 34 Misc.2d 382, 228 N.Y.S.2d 394 (Sup.Ct.1962); Wyman v. Sombrerete Min. Co., 32 Misc.2d 276, 222 N.Y.S.2d 996 (Sup.Ct.1959); Matter of Mencher v. Seminole Oil & Gas Corp., 20 Misc.2d 56, 194 N.Y.S.2d 162 (Sup.Ct.1959); Comment, "Shareholder's Right to Inspect Books of Foreign Corporations", 39 Calif.L. Rev. 133 (1951); Note, "Right of Stockholders in a Foreign Corporation to Inspect Books", 31 Ill.L. Rev. 677 (1937); Annot., 19 A.L.R.3d 869 (1968).

43. See section 297 infra. For state court cases suggesting a similar approach, see Crouse v. Rogers Park Apts., Inc., 343 Ill.App. 319, 99 N.E.2d 404 (1951); Javits v. Investors League, Inc., 92 N.Y.S. 2d 267 (Sup.Ct.1949).

44. Wood, Walker & Co. v. Evans, 300 F.Supp. 171 (D.Colo.1969); Alabama Gas Corp. v. Morrow, 265 Ala. 604, 93 So.2d 515 (1957); Matter of Ditisheim, 96 N.Y.S.2d 622 (Sup.Ct.1950).

45. See section 296 infra. Reports are also required under other federal statutes, e. g., Public Utility Holding Company Act of 1935 (see section 299 infra); Trust Indenture Act of 1939 (see section 300 infra); Investment Company Act of 1940 (see section 301 infra); Int.Rev.Code of 1954, 26 U.S.C.A. § 6103(c) (all bona fide shareholders of record owning one percent or more of outstanding shares of any corporation to be allowed to examine annual income returns of such corporation and of its subsidiaries).

46. E. g., N.Y.S.E. Company Manual § A4.

SHAREHOLDER RIGHTS OF ACTION

200. Shareholder rights of action can be (a) direct, as when the shareholder is suing the corporation to enforce his shareholder contract, or (b) derivative, as when the shareholder is suing in behalf of the corporation against persons allegedly wronging it. Derivative and other actions are discussed in Chapter 14.

To enforce his shareholder contract, the shareholder may sue in a direct individual action; to enforce a corporate right, he may under prescribed conditions, commence a derivative action in behalf of the corporation against persons, within or without the corporation, who allegedly are wronging it or have wronged it. The subject will be more fully explored in Chapter 14.

MISCELLANEOUS SHAREHOLDER RIGHTS

201. Other rights of shareholders include the rights to have their shares recorded on the corporation's record of shareholders, to transfer their shares, and to have their shares appraised when they dissent from certain extraordinary corporate matters.

To complete the catalog of shareholder rights, cross-reference should be made to the rights of shareholders to have their shares recorded on the corporation's record of shareholders and, subject to applicable reasonable restrictions, to transfer their shares,[1] and to the appraisal remedy when they dissent from certain extraordinary corporate matters.[2]

SHAREHOLDER LIABILITIES

202. Statutes often provide that a shareholder is under no obligation to the corporation or its creditors with respect to his shares other than the obligation to pay to the corporation the full lawful consideration for such shares.

Nevertheless, the holders of "fully paid and nonassessable" shares are not entirely immune

[§ 201]

1. See sections 176, 177 supra, and sections 281, 282 infra.

2. See section 349 infra.

from corporate obligations, such as in cases of too-defective incorporation, disregard of corporateness, noncompliance with conditions precedent to doing business, receiving unlawful dividends or other distributions, relieving the board of directors of their corporate management functions.

Two states—New York and Wisconsin—impose personal liability on shareholders for wages due to corporate employees, even though the shares are "fully paid and nonassessable."

The limited liability of shareholders is probably the most significant attribute of the modern corporation.[=]

Statutes often provide that a shareholder is under no obligation to the corporation or its creditors with respect to his shares other than the obligation to pay to the corporation the full lawful consideration for such shares.[2]

If the full lawful consideration has been received by the corporation, the shares are said to be "fully paid and nonassessable."[3] Nevertheless, the holders of "fully paid and nonassessable" shares are not entirely immune from personal liability for corporate obligations.[4]

[§ 202]

1. See sections 73, 79 supra.

2. E. g., ABA–ALI Model Bus.Corp.Act § 23. This section also provides that a bona fide transferee of shares or of subscriptions for shares, without knowledge that full consideration therefor has not been paid, shall not be personally liable for the amount unpaid; that an executor, administrator, conservator, guardian, trustee, etc., shall not be personally liable as a shareholder but that the estate and funds in his hands shall be so liable; and that no pledgee or other holder of shares as collateral security shall be personally liable as a shareholder. Similar is McKinney's N.Y.Bus.Corp.Law, § 628. See also Or.Const. art. XI, § 3. See section 171 supra.

3. E. g., ABA–ALI Model Business Corporation Act § 18.

4. If a shareholder becomes a party to a corporate contract, by signing individually as a principal party or as surety or guarantor, his liability thereon would result from such personal obligation. Brown v. Goldsmith, 39 Okl. 198, 437 P.2d 247 (1968) (holding one 50 percent and two 25 percent shareholders, who jointly and severally guaranteed $20,971 corporate debts, liable in proportion to their respective share ownership). For his own torts, too, he would be personally liable, even though the corporation

If the corporation is too-defectively incorporated, the shareholders, or at least those who authorized, participated in, or ratified the acts upon which liability is predicated, may be subject to personal liability.[5]

Even in the case of technically-correct incorporation, shareholders can be personally liable where there are grounds for "piercing the corporate veil" or disregarding corporateness.[6]

Under statutes in a few jurisdictions, for commencing business without complying with conditions precedent to doing business, such as payment of minimum stated capital, shareholders are personally liable for corporate obligations either to the extent of the deficiency in the stated capital or without such limitation.[7]

Shareholders who knowingly receive unlawful dividends or other distributions can be required to return them to the corporation; knowledge would be irrelevant if the corporation were insolvent.[8]

To the extent that shareholders relieve the board of directors of their discretion and powers in their management of corporate affairs, such shareholders, under some statutes, become subject to the liability for managerial acts and omissions which is imposed on directors.[9]

might be liable respondeat superior. Comment, "Should Shareholders Be Personally Liable for the Torts of Their Corporations?", 76 Yale L.J. 1190 (1967). See also Felsen v. Sol Mfg. Corp., 24 N.Y.2d 682, 301 N.Y.S.2d 610, 249 N.E.2d 459 (1969) (shareholder held privileged to induce corporation to breach employment contract between it and employee, absent malice or use of illegal means).

5. See section 145 supra.

6. See sections 146, 147, 148 supra.

7. See section 143, n. 10 supra.

8. E. g., ABA–ALI Model Bus.Corp.Act § 43; Drew v. United States, 177 Ct.Cl. 458, 367 F.2d 828 (1966) (holding shareholders, who received liquidation distributions without adequate provision for liabilities, personally liable for unpaid taxes). See sections 323, 381 infra.

9. E. g., McKinney's N.Y.Bus.Corp.Law, § 620(f).

Shareholder Liabilities to Wage Earners

Two states—New York[10] and Wisconsin[11]—have statutory provisions subjecting shareholders to personal liability for wages due corporate employees, even though the shares are "fully paid and nonassessable."[12] Several jurisdictions have repealed similar provisions.[13]

The New York statutory provision[14] is the most far-reaching of the few remaining statutes. It imposes unlimited joint and several personal liability on the 10 largest beneficial shareholders[15] of business corporations, no shares of which are publicly traded,[16] for debts, wages, and salaries due

10. McKinney's N.Y.Bus.Corp.Law, § 630—discussed in text accompanying notes 15–25 infra.

11. Wis.Bus.Corp.Law, § 180.40(6) (1951) (liability limited to par value or issue price of no-par shares, for not exceeding six months' service); In re Supreme Tool & Mfg. Co., 3 Wis.2d 554, 89 N.W.2d 292 (1958).

12. Annot., 104 A.L.R. 765 (1936).

13. Michigan in 1964 repealed a similar constitutional provision and Tennessee in 1969, Massachusetts in 1965, and Pennsylvania in 1966 repealed similar statutory provisions. See Stull v. Bellefonte Stone Prods. Corp., 205 Pa.Super. 40, 205 A.2d 677 (1964) (holding president entitled to recovery of his unpaid salaries under statutory language "salaries and wages due and owing to its laborers and employees").

14. McKinney's N.Y.Bus.Corp.Law, § 630; derived from N.Y.Laws 1848, ch. 40, § 18, derived in turn from N.Y.Laws 1811, Sess. 34, ch. 67, § 7. Liability for "fringe benefits" was added in 1952. N.Y.Laws ch. 794. Comment, "Shareholder Liability for Wages: Section 630 of the New York Business Corporation Law", 30 Fordham L.Rev. 471 (1962).

15. The 10 largest shareholders are determined by the fair value of their beneficial interest as of the beginning of the period during which the unpaid services were performed. See McKinney's N.Y.Bus. Corp.Law, § 624 (allowing any person to whom shareholder may be liable for unpaid wages right to examine in person or by agent record of shareholders and to make extracts therefrom). Quaere, as to how the record of shareholders will necessarily reveal the 10 largest shareholders as determined by the fair value of their beneficial interest?

16. The statutory provision applies to every domestic business corporation (other than an investment company registered under the Federal Investment Company Act of 1940) no shares of which are listed on a national securities exchange or regularly quoted in an over-the-counter market by one or more

laborers, servants and employees, other than contractors, of such corporations, including such "fringe benefits" as overtime, vacation, holiday and severance pay, insurance and welfare benefits, and payments due pension and annuity funds.[17] There are procedural limitations and contribution provisions: (a) The employee must give to the shareholder written notice, within 90 days [18] after the termination of his services, that he intends to hold the shareholder liable; (b) An action against the shareholder must be commenced within 90 days after the return of an execution unsatisfied against the corporation upon a judgment recovered against it for such services; (c) A shareholder who has paid more than his pro rata share [19] is entitled to contribution with respect to the excess from the other shareholders liable under the statute, and may seek recovery

against them in a separate action; (d) Such shareholder must, unless the other shareholders have been given notice by the employee, give them written notice, within 20 days after the notice was given to him by the employee. The New York statute has been held not to apply to a foreign corporation even though it is doing business in New York, the employee's services were rendered in New York, and the contract of employment was made in New York.[20] The repeal of the New York provision has been urged on the grounds that it is obsolete and contrary to the basic corporate concept of limited liability, that under it shares of a closely-held New York business corporation are never fully paid and nonassessable,[21] that it constitutes a "bobby trap" for shareholders,[22] that it fosters discrimination against New York as a jurisdiction of incorporation,[23] and that employees are adequately protected by other provisions.[24]

members of a national or an affiliated securities association.

17. Including but not limited to salaries, overtime, vacation, holiday and severance pay; employer contributions to or payments of insurance or welfare benefits; employer contributions to pension or annuity funds; any other moneys properly due or payable for service rendered by such employee. Lindsey v. Winkler, 52 Misc.2d 1037, 277 N.Y.S.2d 768 (Nassau County Dist.Ct.1967) (dismissing action against one of 10 largest shareholders where plaintiff failed to allege nonpayment to her by corporation of unpaid wages but relied on prior judgment against corporation for wrongful dismissal under employment contract); Tessler v. Suskind, 42 Misc. 2d 27, 274 N.Y.S.2d 537 (Nassau Co.Dist.Ct.1964) (sustaining action by union against shareholder for sums owing by corporation under union contract requiring welfare, pension, and sick leave funds); Greenberg v. Corwin, 31 Misc.2d 736, 222 N.Y.S.2d 80 (Sup.Ct.1961) (holding shareholder personally liable under predecessor statute to union, which was bargaining agent for employees of corporation, for amounts due from corporation to union's health and welfare fund and retirement benefits fund, but refraining from deciding union's capacity to sue for amounts due as basic wages to several named employees); Corenti v. Kulik, 36 Misc.2d 996, 234 N. Y.S.2d 28 (Sup.Ct.1962); Harris v. Lederfine, 196 Misc. 410, 92 N.Y.S.2d 645 (Sup.Ct.1949) (holding director-officer not to be "laborer, servant, or employee" within meaning of predecessor statute).

18. Or 60 days after employee's examination of record of shareholders. See note 16 supra.

19. "Pro rata" is defined to mean in proportion to beneficial share interest. See note 16 supra.

20. Armstrong v. Dyer, 268 N.Y. 671, 198 N.E. 551 (1935). See McKinney's N.Y.Bus.Corp.Law, § 102(a) (4) (defining "corporation" as domestic business corporation).

21. Prior to 1963, all shareholders of all New York business corporations were jointly and severally liable for all moneys due employees for their services, without provision for contribution from other shareholders. Such potential liability raised questions as to whether shares of New York business corporations could be legally purchased by trustees, insurance companies, pension funds, and similar investors, or whether counsel in an offering of shares subject to the Federal Securities Act of 1933 could give an unqualified opinion of counsel that the shares when sold will be fully paid and nonassessable. See S.E.C. Form S–9, Instructions as to Exhibits 6.

22. Rogers & McManus, "Stockholders' Booby-Trap: Partnership Liabilities of Stockholders under Section 71, New York Stock Corporation Law," 28 N. Y.U.L.Rev. 1149 (1953) ($130,000 claims for severance pay filed against 20 of over 2,300 shareholders, including some who had contributed to corporation without realizing they were becoming shareholders, settled for some $70,000).

23. Brownell, "The Not-So-Limited Liability of Stockholders of New York Corporations", 27 N.Y. St.B.Bull. 58, 60 (1955). See note 21 supra.

24. See, e. g., McKinney's N.Y. Debt. & Cred.Law, § 22 (claims for wages and "fringe benefits" due employee of assignor for benefit of creditors up to $1000 earned within three months prior to assign-

E. DIRECTOR(S)

DIRECTOR(S)—IN GENERAL

203. Shareholders traditionally elect from their ranks directors who, as a board, direct or manage the corporation, through officers. The balance of this chapter will discuss the management functions of directors and officers, the duties of management, and management compensation.

Traditionally, the shareholders elect from their ranks directors (sometimes called trustees, managers, or governors) [1] who, as a

board, direct or manage the corporation, through the officers. The balance of this chapter will discuss the management functions of directors,[2] the management functions of officers,[3] the duties of management,[4] and management compensation,[5] respectively. Before taking up the management functions of directors, the number and qualifications,[6] and election, tenure, and removal of directors [7] will first be considered.

DIRECTOR(S)—NUMBER AND QUALIFICATIONS

204. Until recently, nearly all statutes required that there be at least three directors; many such statutes now permit one or two

ment given top priority); McKinney's N.Y.Bus. Corp.Law, § 1210 (wage claims given top priority in receivership of New York corporation doing business in New York); McKinney's N.Y.Labor Law, § 191 (frequency of wage payments); McKinney's N.Y.Labor Law, § 198(1–a) (employee prevailing upon wage claim entitled to reasonable attorney's fees and, upon finding that failure was willful, additional 25 percent of wages due as liquidated damages); McKinney's N.Y.Labor Law, § 198–a (officers knowingly permitting corporation to fail to pay employee wages guilty of misdemeanor—$100–$10,000 fine and/or up to one-year imprisonment); People v. D. H. Ahrend Co., 308 N.Y. 112, 123 N.E.2d 799 (1954); People v. Vetri, 206 Misc. 640, 133 N.Y.S.2d 431 (Ct.Spec.Sess.1954), aff'd mem., 285 App.Div. 1089, 141 N.Y.S.2d 505 (2d Dep't 1955), rev'd 309 N.Y. 401, 131 N.E.2d 568 (1955) ("wages" held to include vacation pay); Federal Bankruptcy Act § 17, 11 U.S.C.A. § 35 (wages earned within three months of date of bankruptcy not dischargeable); Federal Bankruptcy Act § 64–a, 11 U.S.C.A. § 104–a (wage claims up to $600 per claimant earned within three months before bankruptcy given second priority). Straus-Duparquet, Inc. v. Local Union No. 3, I. B. of E. W., 386 F.2d 649 (7th Cir. 1967) (holding severance pay, and vacation pay, to extent of latter's accrual from date of bankruptcy to termination of employment, entitled to first priority as expense of administration in bankruptcy); Arabian v. Coleman, 338 F.2d 41 (6th Cir. 1964) (holding vacation pay entitled to second bankruptcy priority only for portion accruing during three months prior to date of bankruptcy and severance pay entitled to no priority since it did not constitute "earned" wages on day of termination or within three months prior thereto); Riemer, "Treatment of Vacation Pay and Severance Pay in Bankruptcy", 70 Com.L.J. 228 (1965).

1. See generally Poor's Register of Corporations, Directors and Executives (1970); S. Vance, The Corporate Director—A Critical Evaluation (1968); W. McDougall & G. Fogelberg, Corporate Boards in Canada: How Sixty-Four Boards Operate (1968); H. Koontz, The Board of Directors and Effective Management (1967); H. Friedman, Corporate Management Guide; Rights, Duties, and Liabilities of Managers, Officers, and Directors (1967); J. Juran & J. Louden, The Corporate Director (American

Management Association 1966); M. Feuer, Handbook for Corporate Directors (1965); The Corporate Director and The Investing Public (New York Stock Exchange 1965); Corporate Directorship Practices (National Industrial Conference Board, Inc. and American Society of Corporate Secretaries, Inc. 1962); P. Jackson, Corporate Management (The Directors and Executives) (1955); J. Baker, Directors and Their Functions (1945); W. Grange & T. Woodbury, Corporation Law: Operating Procedures for Officers and Directors (2d ed. 1964); H. Spellman, Corporate Directors (1931); see also Directorate Analysis in the Corporation (American Institute of Management 1959); Symposium: "Company Directors", 5 Melbourne U.L.Rev. 395 (1967); Israels, "A New Look at Corporate Directorship", 24 Bus.Law. 727 (1969); Loomis, "A Squeeze on the Directors", 79 Fortune, No. 6, 146 (May 15, 1969); McSweeney, "The Director's Dilemma", 51 Saturday Review, No. 23, 72 (June 8, 1968); Chamberlain, "Why It's Harder and Harder to Get a Good Board", 66 Fortune, No. 5, 108 (Nov.1962).

See also C. Datta, Company Directors (1967). Some states do not require a board of directors, especially in close corporations. Kessler, "The Statutory Requirement of a Board of Directors: A Corporate Anachronism", 27 U.Chi.L.Rev. 696, 712, n. 76 (1960). See also 1 Restatement, Second, Agency, § 14C (1958) (neither board of directors nor individual director of business is, as such, agent of corporation or of its members).

2. See sections 207–218 infra.

3. See sections 219–230 infra.

4. See sections 231–242 infra.

5. See sections 243–256 infra.

6. See section 204 infra.

7. See sections 205, 206 infra.

directors in corporations with one or two shareholders; only a few prescribe a maximum number. The number of directors is usually stated in the articles of incorporation or bylaws. Some statutes permit a variable number.

Some statutes require that directors be of "full age". Older statutes imposed residence, citizenship, or shareholding requirements, although such requirements have been eliminated in the more modern statutes. Other qualifications for directors may be prescribed in the articles of incorporation or bylaws.

Number

Until recently, nearly all statutes required that there be at least three directors, but many of such statutes now permit one or two directors in corporations with one or two shareholders.[1] The number is usually stated in the articles of incorporation[2] or bylaws,[3] either at a fixed number or at not less than a certain minimum (within statutory limitation) and not more than a certain maximum.[4] Where an indefinite number or no number is stated in the articles of incorporation, the number is fixed in the bylaws.[5]

The number can be changed, within any controlling limitations, by amendment of the articles of incorporation or bylaws.[6]

To lessen the chance of deadlock, authorization of an odd number of directors is the more common practice except where an even split is desired.[7]

Qualifications

Some statutes expressly require that directors be at least 21 years of age or of

1. See, e. g., ABA–ALI Model Bus.Corp.Act § 34 ("not less than three"; the 1969 Model Act revision allows a board of directors to consist of one or more directors). So does Delaware. Jurisdictions which provide that where all the shares are owned beneficially and of record by less than three shareholders, the number of directors may be less than three, but not less than the number of shareholders, include Arkansas, Connecticut, Illinois (of record), Minnesota, Nebraska (of record), Nevada, New York, North Carolina, North Dakota, Oregon, South Carolina, Virginia, West Virginia, and Wyoming. Iowa, Kentucky, and Missouri authorize one or more directors without reference to the number of shareholders. Rudolph, "Further Thoughts on the One and Two Director Statutes", 20 Bus.Law. 781 (1965). In the case of a classified board of directors with staggered terms, statutes often require at least three directors in each class, thus requiring six, nine, or 12 directors where there are two, three or four classes. In England, no more than two directors are required in a public company; no more than one director in a private company. L. Gower, The Principles of Modern Company Law 240 (2d ed. 1957). Only North Dakota prescribes a maximum number of directors (15). Sizes of boards of directors of larger corporations vary, up to approximately 30 in a few corporations, 12 being the current average.

2. E. g., ABA–ALI Model Bus.Corp.Act §§ 34, 48(k) (number of initial board of directors; "or in the manner" provided in the articles of incorporation or bylaws—1969 Model Act revision). See note 5 infra.

3. E. g., ABA–ALI Model Bus.Corp.Act § 34 (except that number of initial board of directors shall be fixed in articles of incorporation); Del.Gen.Corp. Law, § 141(b) (1967); McKinney's N.Y.Bus.Corp.

Law, § 702(a); Rockford Life Ins. Co. v. Production Press, Inc., 15 Ill.App.2d 50, 145 N.E.2d 276 (1957); Gow v. Consolidated Coppermines Corp., 19 Del.Ch. 172, 165 A. 136 (Ch.1933).

4. E. g., California.

5. E. g., McKinney's N.Y.Bus.Corp.Law, § 702(a) (fixed by bylaws, or by action of board of directors or shareholders under specific provisions of bylaw adopted by shareholders; if not so fixed, number to be three).

6. E. g., ABA–ALI Model Bus.Corp.Act § 34; Del. Gen.Corp.Law, § 141(b) (1967); McKinney's N.Y. Bus.Corp.Law, § 702(b); Model, Roland & Co. v. Industrial Acoustics Co., 16 N.Y.2d 703, 261 N.Y.S.2d 896, 209 N.E.2d 553 (1965) (5–2) (holding that number of directors could not be increased by shareholder resolution under statute which authorized increase or decrease by amendment of bylaws or by action of board of directors or shareholders under specific provisions of bylaw adopted by shareholders, where there was no such bylaw, and that bylaw requiring two-thirds vote was invalid). In Hinckley v. Swaner, 13 Utah 2d 93, 368 P.2d 709, 3 A.L.R.3d 620 (1962), an action for a declaratory judgment on the question of the validity of the addition of a fifth director to the board of directors, the court held that when the bylaws permitted from four to six directors, with the number to be four unless otherwise determined by the shareholders, the addition of the fifth was valid by majority shareholder vote even though bylaw amendment required a two-thirds vote.

7. Even when an odd number is authorized, a vacancy results in an even number which might deadlock. Greater-than-majority quorum or voting requirements enhance the probability of deadlock. See section 277 infra.

"full age".[8] Statutes do not prescribe a maximum age.[9]

Statutory residence [10] or citizenship requirements,[11] once common, are becoming rarer.[12]

Similarly, statutory requirements that directors be shareholders, prevalent in the past,[13] are tending to disappear.[14]

Other qualifications for directors may be prescribed in the articles of incorporation or bylaws.[15]

Some boards of directors are composed entirely or largely of "insiders", i. e., directors who are also officers of the corporation or of other corporations affiliated with it; [16]

---

8. E. g., Florida, Georgia, Nevada, New York, Tennessee. Oklahoma requires that directors be legally competent to enter into contracts. Myott v. Greer, 204 Mass. 389, 90 N.E. 895 (1910) (holding that absent age requirement, directors may be minors). In England, unlike the United States, another company may be a director. L. Gower, The Principles of Modern Company Law 120 (2d ed. 1957). Ineligible directors acting as such in a de jure position can be treated as de facto directors. See section 206 infra.

9. But see L. Gower, The Principles of Modern Company Law 120 (2d ed. 1957). Many corporations have introduced a retirement age for directors, usually from 65 to 72. Some corporations have established the post of "director emeritus" or "honorary director" who may attend meetings, participate in discussion, and enjoy all of the rights and privileges of a director except that he may not vote. Retiring directors might also be retained as consultants for life. See Osborne v. Locke Steel Chain Co., 153 Conn. 527, 218 A.2d 526 (1966). According to a recent survey of larger corporations, some 70 percent were over 50 about one percent over 80, less than one-half percent 30 or younger. Some corporations have mandatory retirement ages, usually in the lower 70's. In college background, the Ivy League colleges had the most listed management personnel; approximately one-third never attended any college. Less than two percent were women.

10. E. g., South Dakota (at least one director required to be resident of state); Vermont (at least two directors required to be residents of state); Hawaii (no less than one-third of directors required to be residents of state). See 12 U.S.C.A. § 72 (at least three-fourths of directors of national bank required to be residents of state or of area within 50 miles of bank).

11. E. g., Florida, Nevada. New York dropped its requirements in 1963.

12. E. g., ABA–ALI Model Bus.Corp.Act § 33 (directors need not be residents of jurisdiction unless so required by articles of incorporation or bylaws).

13. E. g., Vermont (directors except during initial period required to be shareholders). New York completely eliminated such requirements in 1963. See Kaye v. Kentucky Public Elevator Co., 295 Ky. 661, 175 S.W.2d 142 (1943); Lippman v. Kehoe Stenograph Co., 11 Del.Ch. 412, 102 A. 988 (Sup.Ct.1918); Matter of George Ringler & Co., 204 N.Y. 30, 97 N.

E. 593 (1912) (holding directors to whom shares had been transferred of record and retransferred to transferors without recording such retransfers not to be shareholders; record ownership not to be conclusive on court in proceeding to review corporate election, and elections by directors as well as by shareholders to be reviewable by court in such proceeding. Even the older New York statute was construed as not requiring that the directors named in the articles of incorporation be shareholders. Davidson v. Westchester Gas-Light Co., 99 N.Y. 558, 2 N.E. 892 (1885).

14. E. g., ABA–ALI Model Bus.Corp.Act § 33 (directors need not be shareholders unless so required by articles of incorporation or bylaws). See Maidman v. Drescher, 158 N.Y.L.J. No. 16, 9 (Sup.Ct.1967) (construing bylaw requirement that directors be shareholders as requiring share ownership before assuming duties, not before election). A few large corporations, e. g., E. I. du Pont de Nemours, have "proprietary" boards made up mainly by family members and large shareholders. Less than five percent of directors own no shares in the corporation; some 10 percent own less than 100 shares; a majority own more than 1,000 shares; in some corporations, the directors in the aggregate own less than one percent of the shares. In close corporations, the president or controlling shareholders tend to dominate the board.

15. ABA–ALI Model Bus.Corp.Act § 33; McKinney's N.Y.Bus.Corp.Law, § 701. Typical are requirements that a prescribed number of majority of directors be residents of the jurisdiction of incorporation. Rubin v. Chicago South Shore & South Bend R. R., 217 F.2d 177 (7th Cir.1954), cert. denied 348 U.S. 972, 75 S.Ct. 534, 99 L.Ed. 757 (1955); McKee & Co. v. First Nat'l Bank, 265 F.Supp. 1 (S.D.Cal.1967) (upholding bylaws requiring that directors be residents of county for at least one year prior to election, that no director be attorney for or connected with any other banking institution, and that certain information concerning nominees be furnished). See also McKinney's N.Y.Ins.Law, § 48(8) (c); 15 U. S.C.A. § 80a–9.

16. E. g., Anderson, Clayton & Co., Bethlehem Steel Corp, International Shoe Co., Standard Oil Co. of New Jersey ("Esso"). See 70 Time, No. 10, 66 (Sept. 2, 1957) (noting shift from inside to outside directors). In 1966, Frederick R. Kappel, Chairman of the board of American Telephone and Telegraph Company, and Julius A. Stratton, retiring president of Massachusetts Institute of Technology and chairman of the board of the Ford Foundation, became

some other boards consist mainly of "outsiders", i. e., non-officers; however, most boards are mixed. Periodically, the advantages and disadvantages of "insider" or "full-time" directors, and "outsider" or "part-time" directors, are reviewed.[17]

In any event, the chairman of the board, who might be an important executive officer, obviously must be a director, and in many jurisdictions so must the president.[18]

Interlocking directorships on the boards of directors of competing corporations is prohibited by the Federal Clayton Act.[19] More extensive statutory prohibition of management interlocks has been urged.[20] Only since 1963 have federal judges been prohibited from serving as directors of business corporations.[21] A similar prohibition was

imposed on New York State judges in 1964.[22] Quaere, also as to the customs of attorneys,[23] accountants, brokers,[24] academic administrators,[25] and others with possible conflicts of interests, serving on boards of directors.

DIRECTOR(S)—ELECTION, TENURE, AND REMOVAL

205. Initial directors are usually named in the articles of incorporation or elected by the incorporators, and serve until the first annual shareholder meeting or their successors are elected and qualified. Absent a classified board of directors, directors serve for one year. Most statutes permit a classified board, often imposing conditions as to minimum size of board, minimum number of directors to be elected annually, maximum number of classes, or maximum term; most prevalent are nine-men boards equally divided into three classes.

the first directors of Standard Oil Company (New Jersey) who were not employees of the corporation or its affiliates.

17. Towl, "Outside Directors Under Attack", 43 Harv.Bus.Rev. 135 (Sept.–Oct.1965). In larger corporations, on the average, some 40 percent of directors are "insiders", 60 percent "outsiders". "One of the functions of a good board is to act as a microcosm of business, enabling a company to get a quick reading on the stage of business in general." Chamberlain, "Why It's Harder and Harder to Get a Good Board", 66 Fortune, No. 5, 109 (Nov.1962); "Management: Inside the Board Room", 83 Time, No. 9, 96 (Feb. 28, 1964). Honoraria for "outsider" directors range from $10 to $1,250 for each board meeting attended and from $10 to $1,000 for each committee meeting attended, with or without annual retainers ranging from $400 to $12,500, with payment sometimes deferred for tax reasons. "Public directors" to protect the interests of customers, employees, and the public generally, have also been urged. See N.Y.S.E. Company Manual § B1. Occasional statutes empower corporations to provide for employee representation on the board of directors. E. g., Mass.Bus.Corp.Law, § 49 (1965).

18. See section 220 infra.

19. See section 312 infra.

20. See Interlocks in Corporate Management, A Staff Report to the Antitrust Committee (Subcommittee No. 5) of the Committee on the Judiciary, H.R. 89th Cong., 1st Sess. (Mar. 12, 1965).

21. Some federal judges had received higher income from their directorships than their judicial salaries. Landauer, "Judges in Business: Ethics Debate Stirred by Federal Jurists Who Sit on Company Boards; Directors of Illinois Banks, Equitable Life

Say They Avoided Interest Conflicts; But Bar Associations Frown", 161 The Wall Street Journal, No. 86, 1 (May 2, 1963).

22. By direction of the New York State Judicial Council, applicable to judges or justices of the Court of Appeals, Appellate Division, Supreme Court, Court of Claims, County Courts and Civil and Criminal Courts of New York City.

23. Many reputable law firms and accounting firms have policies against their members and associates serving on boards of directors of corporations, even, or perhaps especially, when the corporations are their clients. See Aine v. Power, 146 N.Y.L.J., No. 115, 13 (Sup.Ct.1961) (*"This court is aware of the practice of corporate attorneys serving as officers and directors of their clients. The desirability of this practice and the extent to which it prevails, are matters which require reexamination by bench and bar, as well as by the community generally"*— emphasis in original).

24. See Kohlmeier, "Stiff Restrictions on Brokers Doubling As Corporate Directors Studied by SEC", 161 The Wall Street Journal, No. 112, 1 (June 10, 1963); Cony, "Brokers Under Fire; Some Stir Criticism By Sitting on Boards of Traded Companies; Exchange Warns of Possible Conflicts of Interest; Some Houses Defend Practice", 160 The Wall Street Journal, No. 56, 1 (Sept. 19, 1962).

25. The presence on the governing bodies of universities and colleges of directors and officers of business corporations and on the boards of directors of business corporations of academic administrators raises various unresolved problems, such as the propriety of corporate contributions to such educational institutions and the use of inside information in academic endowment investments.

Vacancies on the board and newly-created directorships are usually filled by shareholders except as otherwise provided by statutes.

Directors hold office for the terms for which they were elected or until successors are elected and have qualified. Directors elected to fill vacancies serve for the unexpired terms.

Directors are removable for cause by shareholders, even if such power is also validly conferred on the board of directors. Before being removed for cause, the director is entitled to notice of the charges against him and reasonable opportunity to be heard. Shareholder agreements to keep named persons as directors do not preclude removal for cause by the required shareholder vote. Directors usually may not be removed without cause, unless advance power to do so was reserved at the time the director commenced his term. Statutes, the articles of incorporation, or bylaws may confer such power on shareholders. Modern statutes often deal with removal of directors for cause or without cause, frequently with provisions to protect any applicable cumulative voting rights or class voting rights.

Election

The initial directors are usually named in the articles of incorporation or elected at the organization meeting of incorporators.[1] Directors named in the articles of incorporation sometimes are accommodation or dummy directors and are replaced by the real initial directors at one of the organization meetings.[2] The initial directors serve until the first annual meeting of shareholders, or until their successors are elected and qualified.[3]

At the first annual meeting of shareholders, and at each annual meeting thereafter, the shareholders elect directors to serve until the next succeeding annual meeting,[4] except where directors are divided into classes with one class elected each year as permitted by law.[5]

Most statutes expressly permit such classification,[6] often imposing conditions that there be at least a certain number of

ensuing year", in accordance with bylaws, where most other annual meetings had been held in February and March), with Silverman v. Gilbert, 185 So.2d 373 (La.Ct.App.1966), writ refused 249 La. 384, 186 So.2d 630 (1966) (holding board of directors, empowered by articles of incorporation to fix date of annual meeting, could not perpetuate themselves in office by postponing annual meeting without consent of shareholders). In some jurisdictions, the articles of incorporation might authorize election of directors by bondholders. E. g., California, Connecticut, Delaware, Kansas, Louisiana, Maryland, Michigan, Minnesota, Nebraska, New Jersey, New York, Oklahoma, Pennsylvania, Virginia, and Puerto Rico. A few jurisdictions authorize election of directors by employees. E. g., Massachusetts. Provisional directors might be judicially appointed to break a deadlock. E. g., California, Delaware, Missouri. See also Poirier v. Welch, 233 F.Supp. 436 (D.D.C.1964) (denying preliminary injunction to enjoin shareholders meeting because board of directors of Communications Satellite Corporation were seeking proxies for reelection of six incumbents).

5. Adkins, "Corporate Democracy and Classified Directors", 11 Bus.Law. 31 (Nov.1955). The stagger system is barred by statutes requiring annual elections of all directors in some states [Cal.Gen.Corp. Law, § 805 (1947)], and by constitutional provisions requiring cumulative voting in some others [Ill. Const. art. XI, § 3; Wolfson v. Avery, 6 Ill.2d 78, 126 N.E.2d 701 (1955) (6–1); W.Va.Const. art. XI, § 4; State ex rel. Syphers v. McCune, 143 W.Va. 315, 101 S.E.2d 834 (1958). Cf. Janney v. Philadelphia Transportation Co., 387 Pa. 282, 128 A.2d 76 (1956); Bohannan v. Corporation Commission, 82 Ariz. 299, 313 P.2d 379 (1957) (stagger system held not to violate constitutional cumulative voting requirement)]. Comment, "Classified Boards in Missouri", 32 Mo.L.Rev. 251 (1967). For discussion of class voting for directors, see section 189, n. 26 supra.

6. E. g., ABA–ALI Model Bus.Corp.Act § 35; Alabama, Colorado, Delaware, Florida, Georgia, Indiana, Iowa, Kentucky, Louisiana, Maine, Maryland, Massachusetts, Michigan, Missouri, Montana, Nebraska, New Jersey, New Mexico, New York, North Carolina, North Dakota, Ohio, Pennsylvania, Tennessee, Texas, Utah, Virginia, Wisconsin, District of Columbia. Hawaii, Idaho, Minnesota, New Hampshire, Oklahoma, Vermont, Washington (by implication from provision authorizing articles of incorporation or bylaws to fix terms of directors). Some jurisdictions also expressly provide that classes or series of shares or bonds may be authorized to elect their own classes of directors. E. g., Louisiana, Massachusetts, New Jersey, New York, Virginia.

---

1. See sections 130, 135 supra.

2. See section 135 supra.

3. E. g., ABA–ALI Model Bus.Corp.Act § 34.

4. Compare Matter of Mansdorf v. Unexcelled, Inc., 28 A.D.2d 44, 281 N.Y.S.2d 173 (1st Dep't 1967) (allowing board of directors to fix date of annual meeting less than nine months after previous annual meetings, when directors were elected "for the

directors on the board [7] or a certain minimum number elected annually,[8] or fixing maximum number of classes [9] or maximum terms.[10] Most prevalent in corporations where the stagger system is in effect are three classes, which means that one-third are elected annually to serve three-year terms (except at the start when the three classes are elected to serve one-year, two-year, and three-year terms, respectively).[11] Annual election of less than one-fifth of the board is rare.[12]

Any vacancy occurring in the board of directors, absent provision to the contrary, is filled by the shareholders.[13] Statutes often provide that such vacancies, except possibly vacancies resulting from removal without cause, shall be filled as prescribed in the articles of incorporation or the bylaws, or by the remaining directors.[14]

Where the number of directors is increased by appropriate amendment of the articles of incorporation or bylaws, any newly-created directorship, absent provision to the contrary, is filled by the shareholders.[15] Statutes sometimes codify this rule with or without variations.[16] A growing number of

---

7. E. g., ABA–ALI Model Bus.Corp.Act § 35 (two or three classes, each class to be as nearly equal in number as possible); Alabama, North Carolina, North Dakota, Texas (at least nine-man board of directors). New York permits two, three, or four classes, all in as nearly equal number as possible and no class to include less than three directors.

8. E. g., Florida, Nevada, New York (at least three).

9. E. g., Alabama, Colorado, Delaware, Iowa, North Carolina, North Dakota, Oregon, Texas, Virginia, Wisconsin, District of Columbia (maximum of three classes); New York (maximum of four classes).

10. E. g., Indiana, Ohio, Tennessee (three years); Pennsylvania (four years); Maryland, Massachusetts, New Jersey (five years).

11. E. g., ABA–ALI Model Bus.Corp.Act § 35 (permitting two or three classes where board consists of nine or more members). For effect of stagger system on cumulative voting, see section 189 supra. Cf. Humphrys v. Winous Co., 165 Ohio St. 45, 133 N.E.2d 780 (1956) (4–2) (construing former Ohio statute as permitting classification of three-man board so that only one director would be elected annually, despite statutory requirement of cumulative voting).

12. Adkins, "Corporate Democracy and Classified Directors", 11 Bus.Law. 31 (Nov.1955).

13. See section 192, n. 7 supra.

14. E. g., ABA–ALI Model Bus.Corp.Act § 36 (by remaining directors through less than a quorum); Del.Gen.Corp.Law, § 223 (1967) (by remaining directors then in office) (prior to 1967, by remaining directors unless otherwise provided in articles of in-

corporation or bylaws); McKinney's N.Y.Bus.Corp. Law, § 705 (vacancies occurring for any reason except removal without cause may be filled by majority of directors then in office, though less than quorum exists, unless articles of incorporation or bylaws provide that such vacancies be filled by shareholders; unless articles of incorporation or specific provisions of bylaw adopted by shareholders provide that board may fill vacancies by reason of removal without cause, such vacancies may be filled only by shareholders); Matter of Caplan v. Lionel Corp., 20 A.D.2d 301, 246 N.Y.S.2d 913 (1st Dep't 1964), aff'd mem., 14 N.Y.2d 679, 249 N.Y.S.2d 877, 198 N.E.2d 908 (1964) (holding remaining directors, even though less than usual quorum for board of directors action, may fill vacancies, absent provision in articles of incorporation or bylaws that shareholders should fill such vacancies); Avien, Inc. v. Weiss, 50 Misc.2d 127, 269 N.Y.S.2d 836 (Sup.Ct.1966) (upholding action by three directors of five-man board, where one of three had been elected by two of three remaining directors, in unanimously removing other remaining director from his position as president of corporation); Ivancevic v. Milton, 153 N.Y.L.J. No. 112, 16 (Sup.Ct.1965) (holding that where there are two vacancies on seven-man board of directors, four of five remaining directors may fill them, even though bylaws set quorum of five, especially when fifth director deliberately absents himself). Any statute or bylaw providing for the filling of vacancies by the board of directors should specify that this can be effected by a majority of "the remaining directors" or of "the directors then in office" "though less than a quorum". Compare Cirrincione v. Polizzi, 14 A.D.2d 281, 220 N.Y. S.2d 741 (4th Dep't 1961), with Continental Television Corp. v. Caster, 42 Ill.App.2d 122, 191 N.E.2d 607 (1963). The Illinois Constitution has been construed as requiring that vacancies can be filled only by shareholders. People ex rel. Weber v. Cohn, 339 Ill. 121, 171 N.E. 159 (1930) (6–1) (statute providing for filling of vacancies by board of directors held unconstitutional); Hacket v. Diversified Chemicals, Inc., 180 So.2d 831 (La.Ct.App.1965) (holding power of directors to fill vacancies did not encompass power to fill directorship newly-created by board of directors under its power to determine number of directors); Automatic Steel Products, Inc. v. Johnston, 31 Del.Ch. 469, 64 A.2d 416, 6 A.L. R.2d 170 (Sup.Ct.1949) (then Delaware statute authorizing directors to fill vacancies construed as inapplicable to newly-created directorships).

15. See section 192, n. 8 supra.

16. See section 192, n. 10 supra.

statutes authorize the board of directors to fill newly-created directorships.[17]

Tenure

As indicated, the initial directors usually serve until replaced at one of the organization meetings or at the first annual meeting of shareholders. The term of office of directors elected at any annual or special meeting of shareholders usually runs until the next annual meeting, unless the board of directors is classified, in which case the directors' terms, on a staggered basis, except for the first class during the first year, run for more than one year.[18]

Each director holds office for the term for which he is elected, and until his successor shall have been elected and qualified (such director holding over beyond his term being sometimes called a "holdover director").[19]

Any director elected to fill a vacancy is elected for the unexpired term of his predecessor in office.[20]

Until 1945 in England, life directors were permitted.[21]

Removal

Removal of a director during his term of office was known at common law as "amotion."

Directors may be removed *for cause* by shareholders, but not by the board of directors absent a provision in the articles of incorporation or bylaws conferring such power.[22] Even when such power is conferred on the board of directors, the shareholders retain inherent power to remove directors for cause.[23]

Any shareholder agreement to elect and keep certain persons as directors is subject to the condition of good behavior on the part of such persons and therefore would not preclude removal for cause by the shareholders who are parties to such agreement.[24]

17. ABA–ALI Model Bus.Corp.Act § 36 (for term of office continuing only until next election of directors by shareholders); Del.Gen.Corp.Law, § 223 (1967); McKinney's N.Y.Bus.Corp.Law, § 705 (newly-created directorships resulting from increase in number of directors may be filled by majority of directors then in office, although less than quorum exists, unless articles of incorporation or bylaws provide that such newly-created directorships shall be filled by shareholders).

18. See notes 6–12 supra.

19. E. g., ABA–ALI Model Bus.Corp.Act § 34; Del. Gen.Corp.Law, § 141(b) (1967). Compare Du Bois v. Century Cement Products Co., 119 N.J.Eq. 472, 183 A. 188 (1936) (director's unqualified resignation, absent provision to contrary, effective without acceptance), with Lippman v. Kehoe Stenograph Co., 11 Del.Ch. 190, 98 A. 943 (Ch.1916), aff'd 11 Del.Ch. 412, 102 A. 988 (Sup.Ct.1918); Young v. Janas, 34 Del.Ch. 287, 103 A.2d 299 (Ch.1954) (director's resignation not effective until accepted). Some statutes provide that if a director resigns, the resignation to take effect at a later date, the board or the shareholders may elect a successor to take office when the resignation becomes effective. E. g., Cal.Gen.Corp.Law, § 809 (1947); Del.Gen.Corp.Law, § 223 (1967); N.C. Bus.Corp.Act § 55-27 (1957); S.C.Bus.Corp.Act § 12–18.6(c) (1964). See Crespinel v. Color Corp. of America, 160 Cal.App.2d 386, 325 P.2d 565 (1958); Note, "Resignation by Directors and Officers of Private Corporations", 83 U.Pa.L.Rev. 1006 (1935). In resigning, directors are subject to certain duties. See section 242 infra. See Ming v. Simpkins, 59 Misc.2d 853, 300 N.Y.S.2d 805 (Sup.Ct.1968).

20. E. g., ABA–ALI Model Bus.Corp.Act § 36. Wilder v. Brace, 223 F.Supp. 703 (D.Me.1963) (upholding bylaw providing for board of directors to fill vacancies on classified board with staggered terms for full unexpired term of vacancies where statute generally requires annual election of directors but permits classified board of directors with longer terms and authorizes board to fill vacancies).

21. Life directors of private companies holding office on July 18, 1945 are excepted from the prohibition. L. Gower, The Principles of Modern Company Law 120 (2d ed. 1957).

22. See section 192, n. 11 supra.

23. Matter of Grace v. Grace Institute, 19 N.Y.2d 307, 279 N.Y.S.2d 721, 226 N.E.2d 531 (1967) (4–3) (upholding removal of life member and trustee of charitable corporation for cause under inherent power, after hearing, upon basis of evidence); Auer v. Dressel, 306 N.Y. 427, 118 N.E.2d 590, 48 A.L.R.2d 604 (1954). See Frank v. Anthony, 107 So.2d 136 (Fla.Dist.Ct.App.1958) (absent charter or bylaw authority, president-sole shareholder held not able to remove directors without cause or notice before regular shareholders' meeting).

24. Matter of Burkin (Katz), 1 N.Y.2d 570, 154 N.Y. S.2d 898, 136 N.E.2d 862 (1956); Fells v. Katz, 256 N.Y. 67, 175 N.E. 516 (1931); Matter of Katz (Fulton-Washington Corp.), 2 Misc.2d 325, 143 N.Y.S.2d 282 (Sup.Ct.1955), aff'd mem., 1 A.D.2d 657, 147 N. Y.S.2d 10 (1st Dep't 1955).

However, a statute or valid provision in the articles of incorporation or bylaws requiring a certain vote for any shareholder action would preclude removal for cause by less than such required vote of shareholders.[25] In Matter of Burkin (Katz),[26] even when the minority shareholder voting against removal was the director whose removal for cause was at issue, the New York Court of Appeals so held, and also found that, since the required shareholder vote had not effected removal, there was no arbitrable controversy under the arbitration clause in the agreement among the shareholders.

Directors may not be removed *without cause* unless the power to do so was reserved at the time the director commenced his term.[27]

Power to remove a director without cause operates only prospectively with respect to directors thereafter taking office.[28] Such power may be conferred by the articles of incorporation or bylaws on shareholders,[29] but not on the board of directors.[30]

A shareholder agreement to elect and keep certain persons as directors would preclude their removal without cause by the shareholders who are parties to such agreement.[31]

Removal of directors for cause is subject to court review.[32]

Absent provision to the contrary, any removal by shareholders is by majority vote, even when the director in question was elected by cumulative voting.[33]

A growing number of jurisdictions have enacted statutes with respect to the removal of directors for cause and without cause.[34]

25. Idaho requires a two-thirds shareholder vote for removal of directors. See also Matter of Burkin (Katz), 1 N.Y.2d 570, 154 N.Y.S.2d 898, 136 N.E.2d 862 (1956) (unanimous shareholder action required by articles of incorporation provision under former New York statute). Cf. Matter of Stylemaster Department Store, Inc., 7 Misc.2d 207, 154 N.Y.S.2d 58 (Sup.Ct.1956) (bylaw removal provision requiring 70 percent shareholder vote held valid except as to supra-majority requirement).

26. 1 N.Y.2d 570, 154 N.Y.S.2d 898, 136 N.E.2d 862 (1956). In New York the question of whether or not a controversy is arbitrable no longer depends upon the justiciable character of the controversy. McKinney's N.Y.CPLR, § 7501. Furthermore, justiciability has been introduced by the statutory provision for judicial removal in an action brought by the holders of 10 percent of the outstanding shares. See note 38 infra.

27. Travers, "Removal of the Corporate Director During His Term of Office", 53 Iowa L.Rev. 389 (1967). See section 192, n. 13 supra.

28. See Abberger v. Kulp, 156 Misc. 210, 281 N.Y.S. 373 (Sup.Ct.1935). Cf. Matter of Schwartz, 119 Misc. 387, 196 N.Y.S. 679 (Sup.Ct.1922) (bylaw provision for removal of directors without cause adopted after director's election held enforceable against director who as director and shareholder had voted for such provision). See also Pilat v. Broach Systems, Inc., 108 N.J.Super. 88, 260 A.2d 13 (1969).

29. Cuppy v. Stollwerck Bros., 216 N.Y. 591, 111 N.E. 249 (1916) (articles of incorporation); Matter of Singer, 189 Misc. 150, 70 N.Y.S.2d 550 (Sup.Ct.1947), aff'd 273 App.Div. 755, 75 N.Y.S.2d 514 (1st Dep't 1947) (bylaws). Cf. Essential Enterprises Corp. v. Automatic Steel Products, Inc., 39 Del.Ch. 93, 159 A.2d 288 (Ch.1960).

30. 3 I. Kantrowitz & S. Slutsky, White on New York Corporations ¶ 706.03 (13th ed. 1968) (refusal of New York secretary of state to accept articles of incorporation provision for removal of directors without cause by board of directors).

31. Matter of Burkin (Katz), 1 N.Y.2d 570, 154 N.Y.S.2d 898, 136 N.E.2d 862 (1956); Matter of Katz (Fulton-Washington Corp.), 2 Misc.2d 325, 143 N.Y.S.2d 282 (Sup.Ct.1955), aff'd mem., 1 A.D.2d 657, 147 N.Y.S.2d 10 (1st Dep't 1955). Such agreement, however, would not preclude non-reelection for cause or removal for cause.

32. E. g., Matter of Grace v. Grace Institute, 19 N.Y.2d 307, 279 N.Y.S.2d 721, 226 N.E.2d 531 (1967); Matter of Koch, 257 N.Y. 318, 178 N.E. 545 (1931); Matter of Teperman v. Atcos Baths, Inc., 4 Misc.2d 738, 158 N.Y.S.2d 391 (Sup.Ct.1956).

33. Campbell v. Loew's, Inc., 36 Del.Ch. 563, 134 A.2d 852 (Ch.1957). Cf. Matter of Rogers Imports, Inc., 202 Misc. 761, 116 N.Y.S.2d 106 (Sup.Ct.1952) (holding that articles of incorporation amendment providing for cumulative voting invalidated preexisting bylaw provision for removal of directors without cause by majority of shareholders). Statutes sometimes deal with removal to implement cumulative voting provisions. See notes 34, 35 infra. Of course, a greater quorum or vote might be required and thus preclude majority removal. A shareholder agreement might bind the parties to keep named persons as directors.

34. E. g., ABA-ALI Model Bus.Corp.Act § 36A (optional section). McKinney's N.Y.Bus.Corp.Law, § 706 (any or all directors removable for cause by

Such statutes often protect cumulative voting rights [35] and class voting rights.[36]

Some statutes authorize the board of directors to remove a director by declaring his office vacant on designated grounds.[37]

Statutes sometimes empower the state, by appropriate court proceedings, to suspend or remove directors for cause.[38]

shareholders; articles of incorporation or specific provisions of bylaw adopted by shareholders may provide for such removal by action of board of directors, except in case of any director elected by cumulative voting, or by holders of shares of any class or series, or holders of bonds, voting as a class, when so entitled by articles of incorporation; if articles of incorporation or bylaws so provide, any or all of directors may be removed without cause by shareholders. See Jacobson v. Backman, 16 Utah 2d 356, 401 P.2d 181 (1965) (removal of directors held governed by "repealed" corporate statute in effect at time of articles of incorporation since such articles constituted contract between corporation and its shareholders not alterable under state's reserved power).

35. E. g., ABA–ALI Model Bus.Corp.Act § 36A, Colorado, Minnesota, New York, North Carolina, North Dakota, Ohio, Oklahoma, Pennsylvania, Virginia, Washington (unless entire board of directors is removed, any director elected by cumulative voting may not be removed if vote cast against his removal would have been sufficient to elect him by cumulative voting); Michigan, Nevada and New York provide protection even when entire board is removed.

36. E. g., ABA–ALI Model Bus.Corp.Act § 36A, California, New York, North Carolina, North Dakota, Ohio, Virginia (class or series vote required to remove director elected by class or series). New York also includes bonds voting as a class. See Essential Enterprises Corp. v. Automatic Steel Products, Inc., 39 Del.Ch. 93, 159 A.2d 288 (Ch.1960) (holding that bylaw providing for removal, either with or without cause, of director by majority of shareholders was inconsistent with provision of articles of incorporation calling for staggered three-year terms for directors, and removal of three of six directors at one time before expiration of their terms was invalid and their successors were not validly elected and were not directors).

37. E. g., California, North Carolina, Ohio, Oklahoma, Pennsylvania.

38. E. g., California, New York, North Carolina, Pennsylvania. New York provides that an action to procure a judgment removing a director for cause may be brought by the attorney general or by the holders of 10 percent of the outstanding shares, whether or not entitled to vote, and that the court may bar from reelection any director so removed for a period fixed by the court. McKinney's N.Y. Bus.Corp.Law, § 706(d). See Brown v. North Ven-

Removal provisions in well-drafted articles of incorporation and bylaws are correlated with any class voting, cumulative voting, and classified or variable size board of directors provisions.

If the director removed is the chairman of the board,[39] or president in jurisdictions which require that the president be a director,[40] such person would cease to be eligible to continue to serve as such officer.[41]

If under an arrangement with a person acquiring registered securities by a tender offer subject to the Federal Securities Exchange Act, a majority of the directors are to be designated otherwise than at a meeting of security holders, the corporation is required to file with the Securities and Exchange Commission and send to all holders of record of its securities information substantially equivalent to that contained in a proxy statement under the S.E.C. Proxy Rules.[42]

DE FACTO DIRECTORS

206. **Persons (a) exercising the functions of directors (b) under some color of office, despite their lack of de jure status, are de facto directors who may bind the corporation and whose status usually is subject to direct attack but not to collateral attack.**

tura Road Development Co., 216 Cal.App.2d 227, 30 Cal.Rptr. 568 (1963) (holding that, since directors occupied position of trust, judicial power to remove them for cause existed apart from statute).

39. Cf. Matter of Buckley (Rickerson), 183 Misc. 189, 50 N.Y.S.2d 54 (Sup.Ct.1944).

40. See section 220 infra.

41. Cf. Young v. Janas, 34 Del.Ch. 287, 103 A.2d 299 (Ch.1954); Miller v. Vanderlip, 285 N.Y. 116, 33 N. E.2d 51 (1941). But see Realty Acceptance Corp. v. Montgomery, 51 F.2d 636 (3d Cir. 1930) (removal of complainant as director thereby disqualifying him as president held breach of implied condition not to do anything to prevent performance). Presumably, the status of the complainant as president, on such removal as director, would have changed from de jure to de facto. See section 222 infra.

42. Federal Securities Exchange Act § 14(f), 15 U.S. C.A. § 78n(f). See section 297 infra.

Persons (a) exercising the functions of directors (b) under some color of office, despite their lack of proper qualifications, election, or other requirements necessary to constitute them *de jure* directors, or despite even their removal, may nevertheless bind the corporation under the so-called *de facto* doctrine.[1] This doctrine should not be confused with the doctrine of the same name applicable to cases of defective incorporation.[2] The doctrine is not limited to cases of estoppel.

The *de facto* doctrine does not preclude direct attack,[3] and does not under all circumstances preclude collateral attack[4] on the validity of the acts of the *de facto* directors. Since the *de facto* doctrine is to protect innocent persons, it may not be invoked by a person who has wrongfully assumed to act as director.[5]

Anyone assuming to act as director is subject to the duties of a director.[6]

DIRECTORS' MANAGEMENT FUNCTIONS—IN GENERAL

207. **Directors are not agents of the shareholders who elect them, but are sui generis. As persons in control of the property of others, directors are fiduciaries, with their duties running primarily to the corporation. Under the concession theory, directors' powers are derived from the state, not delegated by the shareholders. Most statutes vest in the board of directors the management of the corporation.**

In the exercise of their management functions, the directors, usually as a board, are required to use their best judgment and independent discretion, and are responsible for the determination and execution of corporate policy, usually including (a) policy decisions with respect to products, services, prices, wages, labor relations; (b) selection, supervision, and removal of officers and possibly other executive personnel; (c) fixing of executive compensation, pension, retirement, etc. plans; (d) determination of dividends, financing, and capital changes; (e) delegation of authority for administrative and possibly other action; (f) possible adoption, amendment, and repeal of bylaws; (g) possible participation, along with shareholders, in approving various extraordinary corporate matters; and (h) supervision and vigilance for the welfare of the whole enterprise.

Although elected by the shareholders[1] and removable by them for cause and possibly without cause, the directors are not the agents of the shareholders. Nor are directors, in the strict sense, trustees. Their position is *sui generis*.[2] They are fiduciaries,

[§ 206]

1. Morse v. Fall River Line Pier, Inc., 345 Mass. 681, 189 N.E.2d 512 (1963) (holding that directors elected by directors, instead of by members as required, were de facto directors whose action could bind corporation on contract with pier manager, a key employee, who did not know of such defect); Prickett v. American Steel & Pump Corp., —— Del.Ch. ——, 253 A.2d 86 (Ch.1969) (directors elected under invalid bylaw held to be de facto directors replaceable at valid election). See 2 W. Fletcher, Private Corporations §§ 372–390 (perm. ed. 1968).

2. See section 140 supra.

3. Young v. Janas, 34 Del.Ch. 287, 103 A.2d 299 (Ch. 1954); Matter of Salnor Realty Corp., 141 N.Y.L.J. No. 29, 12 (Sup.Ct.1959) (directors elected pursuant to invalid bylaw purporting to increase size of board of directors beyond that authorized in articles of incorporation held not de jure directors and removable by de jure directors); R. Stevens, Handbook on the Law of Private Corporations § 160 (2d ed. 1949).

4. Matter of George Ringler & Co., 204 N.Y. 30, 97 N.E. 593 (1912) (holding directors appointed by de facto directors are also de facto (not de jure) and hence are subject to direct attack—in effect collateral attack on appointing de facto directors).

5. R. Stevens, Handbook on the Law of Private Corporations 744 (2d ed. 1949).

6. Ibid. See sections 231–242 infra.

[§ 207]

1. See section 192 supra.

2. Continental Securities Co. v. Belmont, 206 N.Y. 7, 99 N.E. 138 (1912); New York Dock Co. v. McCollum, 173 Misc. 106, 16 N.Y.S.2d 844 (Sup.Ct. 1939); R. Stevens, Handbook on the Law of Private Corporations § 143 (2d ed. 1949); Note, "Position of Corporate Directors as Sui Generis", 35 Minn.L.Rev. 564 (1951). In the early English joint-stock companies, property was actually transferred to the directors as trustees by deeds of settlement. L. Gower, The Principles of Modern Company Law 471 (2d ed. 1957). As persons in control of corporate affairs and hence of property belonging to others, directors are, broadly speaking, "trustees" and occasionally are so designated.

their duties primarily running to the corporation.[3]

The powers of the directors, under the concession theory,[4] are deemed to be derived from the state,[5] not delegated by shareholders.[6]

In most jurisdictions, management is vested in the board of directors by statute.[7]

While statutes often expressly permit the articles of incorporation or bylaws to contain provisions limiting the powers of the directors, or otherwise for the regulation and management of the corporation, such permission is usually qualified by the limitation that such provisions be not inconsistent with law.[8]

In the exercise of their duty of management, the directors, usually as a board,[9] are required to use their best judgment and independent discretion,[10] and are responsible for the determination and execution of corporate policy. Their management functions usually include: (a) policy decisions with respect to products, services, prices, wages, labor relations, (b) selection, supervision, and removal of officers and possibly other executive personnel,[11] (c) fixing of executive compensation, pension, retirement, etc., plans,[12] (d) determination of dividends, financing, and capital changes,[13] (e) delegation of authority for administrative and possibly other action,[14] (f) possible adoption,

3. See sections 231–242 infra.

4. See section 78 supra.

5. Comstock, J., in Hoyt v. Thompson's Executor, 19 N.Y. 207, 216 (1859); Manson v. Curtis, 223 N.Y. 313, 322, 119 N.E. 559, 562 (1918); Continental Securities Co. v. Belmont, 206 N.Y. 7, 99 N.E. 138 (1912). For criticism of this approach, see R. Stevens, Handbook on the Law of Private Corporations § 143 (2d ed. 1949).

6. Ibid. Cf. Automatic Self-Cleansing Filter Syndicate Co. v. Cuninghame, [1906] 2 Ch. 34; Brownell v. Schering Corp., 120 F.Supp. 879 (D.N.J.1955) (absent creditors' intervening rights, otherwise valid director action cannot be rescinded because taken under compulsion of sole shareholder).

7. E. g., ABA–ALI Model Bus.Corp.Act § 33. Cf. 1969 Model Act revision (except as may be otherwise provided in articles of incorporation); Del. Gen.Corp.Law, § 141(a) (1967) (except as in statute of articles of incorporation otherwise provided). The older Iowa statute has no such provision and apparently does not require that there be a board of directors. But see McKinney's N.Y.Bus.Corp. Law, § 701 (business of corporation to be managed by its board of directors, subject to valid provision in articles of incorporation as to control of directors or for election of officers by shareholders); N.C.Bus.Corp.Act § 55–24a (1957) ("Subject to the provisions of the charter, the bylaws or agreements between the shareholders otherwise lawful, the business and affairs of a corporation shall be managed by a board of directors").

The board of directors is so much an organ of the corporation that directors can authorize the corporation to breach its contracts without personal liability for inducing breach of contract if in pursuit of corporate (not personal) interests. Avins, "Liability for Inducing a Corporation to Breach Its Contract", 43 Cornell L.Q. 55 (1957). Provision in a corporation's contract for arbitration by its board of directors has been held invalid. Matter of Cross & Brown Co. (Nelson), 4 A.D.2d 501, 167 N.Y.S.2d 573 (1st Dep't 1957). See generally H. Koontz, The Board of Directors and Effective Management (1967); Corporate Directorship Practices (National Industrial Conference Board, Inc. and American Society of Corporate Secretaries, Inc. 1962); Directorate Analysis in the Corporation (American Institute of Management 1959); P. Jackson, Corporate Management (The Directors and Executives) (1955); A. Towl & M. Copeland, Board of Directors and Business Management (1947); J. Baker, Directors

and Their Functions (1945); R. Gordon, Business Leadership in the Large Corporation (1961); H. Spellman, Corporate Directors (1931); Freeman, "Directors and Officers", 15 S.C.L.Rev. 396 (1963); Gilmore & Brandenburg, "Anatomy of Corporate Planning", 40 Harv.Bus.Rev. 61 (Nov.-Dec. 1962); Hoffman, "The Status of Shareholders and Directors Under New York's Business Corporation Law: A Comparative View", 11 Buffalo L.Rev. 496 (1962); Kessler, "The Statutory Requirement of a Board of Directors: A Corporate Anachronism", 27 U.Chi. L.Rev. 696 (1960); Weinberg, "A Corporate Director Looks at His Job", 27 Harv.Bus.Rev. 586 (Sept. 1949); Comment, "The Board of Directors Under the Utah Business Corporation Act", 7 Utah L.Rev. 503 (1961).

8. E. g., ABA–ALI Model Bus.Corp.Act § 48(i). Del. Gen.Corp.Law § 102(b) (1) (1967); McKinney's N.Y. Bus.Corp.Law, § 402(b); N.C.Bus.Corp.Act § 55–7(g) (1957).

9. See sections 208, 209 infra.

10. See section 213 infra.

11. See section 210 infra.

12. See sections 211, 243–256 infra.

13. See section 211 and Chapter 12 infra.

14. See section 212 infra.

amendment, and repeal of bylaws,[15] (g) participation, along with shareholders, in effecting various extraordinary corporate matters,[16] and (h) supervision and vigilance for the welfare of the whole enterprise.[17]

In many larger corporations, in practice, the officers in effect manage corporate affairs, and the board of directors may be reduced to a body which does little more than ratify, or "rubber-stamp", executive decisions.[18]

FORMALITIES OF BOARD OF DIRECTORS ACTION

208. **Traditionally, directors can exercise their management functions only when duly convened as a board. Directors vote per capita and, except under a rare statute, may not vote by proxy. The vesting of management in the board, rather than in the directors individually, is usually justified on grounds of the value of consultation, deliberation, and collective judgment. Even absent statutory exceptions, courts have sometimes upheld informal director action, especially in close corporations. A growing number of statutes provide that directors may act without a meeting by unanimous written consent. Such statutes vary widely in language and have been strictly construed.**

Traditionally, the directors could exercise their management functions only when duly convened as a board, and several statutes still so provide.[1]

15. See section 214 infra.

16. See section 215 and Chapter 13 infra.

17. See sections 216, 217, 218, 235 infra

18. TNEC Monograph 11, Bureaucracy and Trusteeship in Large Corporations 23–37 (1940); TNEC Monograph 29, The Distribution of Ownership in the 200 Largest Nonfinancial Corporations 22 et seq. (1940). Executive and finance committees often exercise considerable control, especially between the periodic (say annually, quarterly, or monthly) board of directors meetings.

1. E. g., ABA–ALI Model Bus.Corp.Act §§ 33, 37, 39. But see note 6 infra. Alabama, Alaska, Arizona, Arkansas, California, Georgia, Hawaii, Kansas, Louisiana, Maine, New Hampshire, New Jersey, New York, North Dakota, Tennessee, Utah, Vermont. See Gumpert v. Bon Ami Co., 251 F.2d 735

Unlike shareholders, directors always vote *per capita,* and except for a rare statute to the contrary,[2] may not vote by proxy.[3]

The vesting of management in the board, rather than in the directors individually, is usually justified on the grounds of the value of consultation, deliberation, and collective judgment. Even in jurisdictions where the statutes make no apparent exceptions to the meeting requirement, some exceptions have been recognized by the courts, especially in close corporations.[4]

A growing number of statutes expressly provide that directors may act without a meeting if they unanimously consent in writing.[5] The Model Business Corporation Act now has an optional section, introduced in 1966, which provides that:[6] "Unless other-

(2d Cir.1958) (individual director and member of executive committee held to have no authority to hire officers, such authority resting in board or committee as a body); Audenreid v. East Coast Milling Co., 68 N.J.Eq. 450, 59 A. 577 (1904) (holding invalid articles of incorporation provision for informal board of directors action).

2. See, e. g., La.Bus.Corp.Law, § 12:81 (1969) (represented by other director or shareholder if articles of incorporation so provide). Arkansas had a similar provision but since 1966 has expressly prohibited directors from voting by proxy.

3. Greenberg v. Harrison, 143 Conn. 519, 124 A.2d 216 (1956); Lippman v. Kehoe Stenograph Co., 11 Del.Ch. 80, 95 A. 895 (Ch.1915).

4. Philadelphia Life Ins. Co. v. Crosland-Cullen Co., 234 F.2d 780 (4th Cir.1956); Linwood State Bank v. Lientz, 413 S.W.2d 248 (Mo.1967); Columbia Stamping & Mfg. Co. v. Reich, 28 Wis.2d 297, 137 N.W.2d 45 (1965) (upholding agreement, not formally approved at board of directors meeting, when made at meeting at which all directors and shareholders were present and none objected to informality); Matter of Stylemaster Department Store, Inc., 7 Misc.2d 207, 154 N.Y.S.2d 58 (Sup.Ct.1956); Matter of Kartub, 7 Misc.2d 72, 152 N.Y.S.2d 34 (Sup.Ct. 1956), aff'd mem., 3 A.D.2d 896, 163 N.Y.S.2d 938 (1st Dep't 1957); Simonson v. Helburn, 198 Misc. 430, 97 N.Y.S.2d 406 (Sup.Ct.1950). But cf. Brent v. Advance Scale Mfg. Co., 66 Ohio L.Abs. 262, 116 N.E.2d 761 (Ct.App.1952); Hurley v. Ornsteen, 311 Mass. 477, 42 N.E.2d 273 (1942) (no acquiescence by third director).

5. See note 1 supra; Kessler, "The Statutory Requirement of a Board of Directors: A Corporate Anachronism", 27 U.Chi.L.Rev. 696 (1960).

6. ABA–ALI Model Bus.Corp.Act § 39A. Of the jurisdictions which permit shareholder action by writ-

wise provided by the articles of incorporation or by-laws, any action required by this Act to be taken at a meeting of the directors of a corporation, or any action which may be taken at a meeting of the directors or of a committee, may be taken without a meeting if a consent in writing, setting forth the action so to be taken, shall be signed before such action by all of the directors, or all of the members of the committee, as the case may be. Such consent shall have the same effect as a unanimous vote."

Such statutes are subject to strict construction, and informal board of directors action which might have been sustained under preexisting case law [7] runs the risk of being held ineffective because of noncompliance with the statutory provisions.[8]

---

ten consent in lieu of a meeting—see section 190, n. 1 supra—only Alabama, Alaska, Arkansas, California, Hawaii, Kansas, New York, North Dakota, and Utah do not allow board of directors action by written consent without a meeting.

7. See note 4 supra.

8. Considerable variation is found in the language of such statutes. Such informal action is variously allowed if the articles of incorporation or bylaws so provide, if the articles so provide, or if the bylaws so provide, or if not prohibited or by the articles or bylaws, or by the articles, by the bylaws. Most statutes require prior written consent; a few permit the written consent to be before or after the action. Requirements as to filing of the written consent with the corporation also vary. Village of Brown Deer v. City of Milwaukee, 16 Wis.2d 206, 114 N.W.2d 493 (1962), cert. denied 371 U.S. 902, 83 S.Ct. 205, 9 L.Ed.2d 164 (1962), held that the corporation's president, who was also its majority shareholder and one of its 11 directors and had been accustomed to resolving corporate problems himself with only infrequent board of directors meetings, had no authority to sign an annexation petition in its behalf, where he had failed to obtain the written consent of all of the directors required by the Wisconsin statute permitting board of directors action without a meeting. The court construed the statute as preempting the field and prohibiting corporations from acting informally without complying with the statute. Cf. Acampora v. Birkland, 220 F.Supp. 527 (D.Colo.1963), where a director was absent from the board meeting but later sent in a letter in which he attempted to ratify and cast his vote in favor of the proceedings of the meeting. The court held that while the procedure was not identically the same as that authorized by the Maryland statute the purported ratification was not invalid under Maryland law. A few statutes express-

---

MEETINGS OF BOARD OF DIRECTORS

209. Boards of directors may meet at regular or special meetings, which are often regulated by bylaw provisions.

Board of directors meetings usually may be held within or without the jurisdiction of incorporation unless otherwise provided in the articles of incorporation or bylaws.

Notice requirements for regular and special meetings often differ, depending on statutes, bylaws, and usages within the corporation. The presence and participation of directors at a meeting might constitute a waiver of notice. Statutes sometimes provide for written waiver of notice before or after meetings.

A quorum for board of directors meetings, absent provision to the contrary, is usually a majority of the whole number of directors. Statutes sometimes permit the fixing of a lesser quorum, possibly with a one-third minimum, or greater quorum. Board of directors action usually requires a majority vote of directors present at a meeting at which a quorum is present, but statutes sometimes permit the fixing of a greater vote requirement. As to the counting for quorum or voting purposes of directors personally interested in the corporate matter involved, in the absence of a controlling statute, there are conflicting basic views, variously affected by such factors as an interested-directors provision in the articles of incorporation or possibly in the bylaws, or shareholder ratification.

The board of directors may meet in regular or special meetings.[1] The bylaws often

---

ly combine the Model Act features of unanimous written consent of directors with the informalities usually permitted by decisional law, such as where all shareholders knew and acquiesced, or where informal action is customary and such custom is generally known to shareholders and all of the directors knew of the action in question and did not make prompt objection thereto. N.C.Bus.Corp.Act § 55–29 (1957). See also S.C.Bus.Corp.Act § 12–18.12 (1964).

1. ABA–ALI Model Bus.Corp.Act § 39. Minutes are sometimes required by statute. E. g., ABA–ALI Model Bus.Corp.Act § 46. Sanctions for noncompliance are not prescribed. Minutes of the meetings are not always required. National Labor Relations Board v. Crosby Chemicals, Inc., 274 F.2d 72 (5th Cir.1960). However, some official record of proceedings has evidentiary value. Eremic v. East Pittsburgh Airport, Inc., 429 Pa. 328, 240 A.2d 522 (1968); Whitley v. Pacific Industries, Inc., 28 A.D.2d

set the times for regular meetings and the procedures for calling special meetings.[2] An organization meeting of the board of directors is also common practice.[3]

Place of Board Meetings

Statutes generally do not require that meetings of the board of directors be held within the state, unless the articles of incorporation or bylaws provide otherwise.[4]

Notice of Board Meetings

For *regular* meetings of the board of directors, the time is often fixed in the bylaws, or a standing resolution, or by usage. Accordingly, absent provision to the contrary, no notice of such meetings usually need be given to directors. For special meetings, absent provision to the contrary, reasonable advance notice is usually required. For ordinary business matters, any required notice may be general, but any extraordinary matters should be enumerated in the notice.[5]

Any required notice is probably waived where all of the directors are present and participate.[6] Statutes often so provide[7] or provide that the attendance of any director waives his lack of notice except where he attends for the express purpose of objecting to the lack of notice.[8] Some statutes also generally provide that written waiver of notice by any director entitled to notice, whether before or after the event, is equivalent to the giving of notice.[9]

147, 283 N.Y.S.2d 525 (1st Dep't 1967) (upholding minutes despite subsequent approval thereof); Koepplin v. Pfister, 179 Neb. 423, 138 N.W.2d 637 (1965); Levine v. Randolph Corp., 150 Conn. 232, 188 A.2d 59, 98 A.L.R.2d 349 (1963); Santa Fe Hills Golf & Country Club v. Safehi Realty Co., 349 S.W.2d 27 (Mo.1961); Matter of Teperman v. Atcos Baths, Inc., 6 Misc.2d 162, 163 N.Y.S.2d 221 (Sup.Ct.1957), aff'd 7 A.D.2d 854, 182 N.Y.S.2d 765 (2d Dep't 1959); Annot., 66 A.L.R. 1328 (1938), 48 A.L.R.2d 1259 (1956). The minutes usually record actions proposed and taken, but not the discussion except possibly in brief outline. See Field v. Oberwortmann, 16 Ill. App.2d 376, 148 N.E.2d 600 (1958), cert. denied 358 U.S. 833, 79 S.Ct. 55, 3 L.Ed.2d 71 (1958); Brewer & Solberg, "Corporate Minutes: What Should They Include?", 20 Bus.Law. 745 (1965); Annot., 64 A.L. R. 712 (1929).

2. See, e. g., By-Laws, art. III, §§ 3, 4, Official Forms for Use Under the Model Business Corporation Act, Form No. 47 (ALI rev. 1953).

3. See section 135 supra.

4. E. g., ABA–ALI Model Bus.Corp.Act § 39; Del. Gen.Corp.Law, § 141(g) (1967); McKinney's N.Y. Bus.Corp.Law, § 710.

5. See Matter of William Faehndrich, Inc., 2 N.Y.2d 468, 161 N.Y.S.2d 99, 141 N.E.2d 597 (1957) (holding that if the purpose of the meeting be clearly stated, there generally is no duty to specify the course of conduct contemplated by the directors after their election, no requirement to explain consequences thereof, and no necessity of indicating that bylaw provisions with respect to two-thirds quorum requirement would be treated as invalid); Fay v. Charles Michel & Sons, 147 N.Y.L.J. No. 38, 15 (Sup.Ct.1962) (notice of special board meeting stating purpose "to consider adjustment of the salary of the Secretary . . . and such other matters as relate thereto" held insufficient to support doubling of salaries of other officers); see McKinney's N.Y.Bus.Corp.Law, § 712(b) (notice need not specify purpose of any regular or special meeting unless required by bylaws). Action taken at a meeting for which notice was neither given nor waived is void. Kendall v. Henry Mountain Mines, Inc., 78 Nev. 408, 374 P.2d 889 (1962); Cirrincione v. Polizzi, 14 A.D.2d 281, 220 N.Y.S.2d 741 (4th Dep't 1961).

6. Columbia Stamping & Mfg. Co. v. Reich, 28 Wis. 2d 297, 137 N.W.2d 45 (1965); Zachary v. Milin, 294 Mich. 622, 293 N.W. 770 (1940) (holding presence involves physical presence and assent to holding of meeting). Notice might be excused where the director is too distant to attend, in cases of emergency, or where notice is prohibited by law. Paducah & Illinois Ferry Co. v. Robinson, 161 Ky. 485, 171 S. W. 171 (1914). Or where directors customarily met without notice without objection by any shareholder or director. Scott v. Cord, 75 Nev. 179, 336 P.2d 773 (1959).

7. E. g., McKinney's N.Y.Bus.Corp.Law, § 711(c).

8. E. g., ABA–ALI Model Bus.Corp.Act § 39; McKinney's N.Y.Bus.Corp.Law, § 711(c) (by attendance of any director at meeting without protesting, prior thereto or at its commencement, lack of notice to him).

9. E. g., ABA–ALI Model Bus.Corp.Act § 137; Del. Gen.Corp.Law, § 229 (1967); McKinney's N.Y.Bus. Corp.Law, § 711(b), (c); as for adjournments see id. § 711(d). Matter of Seminole Oil & Gas Corp., 38 Del.Ch. 549, 155 A.2d 887 (Ch.1959). Absent statute, *subsequent* waiver of notice might be ineffective. Hill Dredging Corp. v. Risley, 18 N.J.Super. 501, 114 A.2d 697 (1955); United States v. Interstate R. R., 14 F.2d 328 (W.D.Va.1926); Holcombe v. Trenton White City Co., 80 N.J.Eq. 122, 82 A. 618 (1912), aff'd mem., 82 N.J.Eq. 364, 91 A. 1069 (1913). Notices may be dispensed with when delivery is prohibited. McKinney's N.Y.Bus.Corp.Law, § 108.

Quorum and Action at Board Meetings

A majority of the whole number of directors, absent any contrary provision, usually constitutes a quorum at a board of directors meeting.[10] Statutes sometimes permit the fixing, say in the bylaws, of a quorum of less than a majority but not less than a prescribed minimum, say one-third of the number.[11] Statutes often also permit a quorum of more than a majority to be required by the articles of incorporation or bylaws.[12] In New York, provisions requiring greater-than-majority quorum are valid if in the articles of incorporation[13] but not if in the bylaws.[14]

A few jurisdictions permit directors to participate in meetings by means of conference telephone or some comparable communication technique.[14a]

Unless directors may act by proxy, the director must be present in person. In Louisiana, which alone permits directors to act by proxy providing that the proxy holder is a shareholder or another director and the articles of incorporation so provide, presence by proxy would be sufficient.

A California case has held that a director could not bring his own attorney to a board meeting over the objection of the board.[15]

Where directors absent themselves from a meeting to prevent a quorum, they may or may not be estopped from questioning the validity of the action taken at the meeting.[16]

The act of the majority of the directors present at a meeting at which a quorum is present usually constitutes the act of the board. Statutes might permit the articles of incorporation or bylaws to require more than a majority vote.[17] New York permits a greater-than-majority vote requirement in the articles of incorporation, but does not permit such requirement to be imposed by the bylaws.[18]

Whether or not directors who are personally interested in a transaction with their

10. E. g., ABA–ALI Model Bus.Corp.Act § 37; Del. Gen.Corp.Law, § 141(b) (1967); McKinney's N.Y. Bus.Corp.Law, § 702(a) (majority of "entire board" —defined as total number of directors which corporation would have if there were no vacancies); Belle Isle Corp. v. MacBean, 29 Del.Ch. 261, 49 A.2d 5 (Ch.1946), reargument denied 30 Del.Ch. 373, 61 A.2d 699 (Ch.1948); Despatch Line of Packets v. Bellamy Man. Co., 12 N.H. 205 (1841). Cf. Twisp Mining & Smelting Co. v. Chelan Mining Co., 16 Wash.2d 264, 133 P.2d 300 (1943), cert. denied and appeal dismissed 320 U.S. 705, 64 S.Ct. 58, 88 L.Ed. 413 (1943), cert. denied 320 U.S. 716, 64 S.Ct. 258, 88 L.Ed. 420 (1943), cert. denied and appeal dismissed 325 U.S. 837, 65 S.Ct. 1401, 89 L.Ed. 1964 (1945). Action purported to be taken without a quorum is void. Olincy v. Merle Norman Cosmetics, Inc., 200 Cal.App.2d 260, 19 Cal.Rptr. 387 (1962); Lyons, "The Validity or Invalidity of Corporate Directors' Action and the Quorum Requirement", 15 Kan.L. Rev. 366 (1967); Blewer, "Quorum and Voting Requirements", 6 Prac.Law 79 (Dec.1960).

11. E. g., Del.Gen.Corp.Law, § 141(b) (1967) (not less than one-third); McKinney's N.Y.Bus.Corp.Law § 707 (not less than one-third).

12. E. g., ABA–ALI Model Bus.Corp.Act § 37 (articles of incorporation or bylaws). See section 274 infra.

13. McKinney's N.Y.Bus.Corp.Law, § 709(a) (1) (articles of incorporation).

14. See section 274 infra.

14a. E. g., Delaware, New Jersey.

15. Burt v. Irvine Co., 224 Cal.App.2d 50, 36 Cal. Rptr. 270 (1964).

16. In Matter of Gearing v. Kelly, 11 N.Y.2d 201, 227 N.Y.S.2d 897, 182 N.E.2d 391 (1962), a New York close corporation had a four-director board, a majority being required for a quorum. After one of the directors resigned, one of the directors, who with her mother owned 50 percent of the shares, absented herself from a board meeting to prevent a quorum to fill the vacancy. The court, 5 to 2, held that where a director intentionally and deliberately refused to attend a meeting for the purpose of preventing a quorum from assembling, neither such director nor an associated shareholder could then seek to set aside the election of a director on the ground that a quorum was not present. Accord, Avien, Inc. v. Weiss, 50 Misc.2d 127, 269 N.Y.S.2d 836 (Sup.Ct.1966); Ivancevic v. Milton, 153 N.Y.L.J. No. 112, 16 (Sup.Ct.1965). Cf. Tomlinson v. Loew's, Inc., 36 Del.Ch. 516, 134 A.2d 518 (Ch.1957), reargument denied 37 Del.Ch. 8, 135 A.2d 136 (Ch.1957) (holding minority directors had right to absent themselves to prevent quorum for election of directors to fill vacancies because they felt that shareholders should fill such vacancies).

17. E. g., ABA–ALI Model Bus.Corp.Act § 37 (articles of incorporation or bylaws). See section 274 infra.

18. See section 274 infra.

corporation may count for quorum or voting purposes, in the absence of a statute permitting such practice, presents questions not yet fully resolved.[19] Modern statutes permit such practice but provide safeguards to try to assure that the transaction is "fair" to the corporation.[20] In the absence of such statutes, interested directors may be counted in some jurisdictions[21] but not in others.[22] Even in the latter jurisdictions, they usually may be counted if there are valid provisions to such effect in the articles of incorporation or possibly in the bylaws.[23]

Shareholder ratification has different effects in different jurisdictions depending upon the presence of the previously mentioned factors and the differing judicial attitudes toward the same. Thus, shareholder ratification can replace action by a board of directors which cannot muster a disinterested quorum.[24] It might at least estop any shareholders who voted for such ratification from complaining,[25] or shift the burden of proof or the burden of going forward with the evidence,[26] or even validate an otherwise voidable transaction.[27]

BOARD OF DIRECTORS SELECTION, SUPERVISION, AND REMOVAL OF OFFICERS

210. The board of directors selects the officers in most jurisdictions, although a growing number of statutes permit election of all or specified officers by shareholders.

Piccard v. Sperry Corp., 48 F.Supp. 465 (S.D.N.Y. 1943), aff'd per curiam 152 F.2d 462 (2d Cir.1946), cert. denied 328 U.S. 845, 66 S.Ct. 1024, 90 L.Ed. 1619 (1946). In New York and other jurisdictions where the courts allowed interested directors to be counted even in the absence of statute—see note 21 supra—interested-director provisions in articles of incorporation were given the effect of neutralizing any adverse inferences which might be drawn because of such conflict of interests. Everett v. Phillips, 288 N.Y. 227, 43 N.E.2d 18 (1942), reargument denied 289 N.Y. 625, 43 N.E.2d 841 (1942), reargument denied 289 N.Y. 675, 45 N.E.2d 176 (1942). Accord, Spiegel v. Beacon Participations, Inc., 297 Mass. 398, 8 N.E.2d 895 (1937). Contra, Abeles v. Adams Engineering Co., 35 N.J. 411, 173 A.2d 246 (1961). Note, "Effect of a Provision in Articles of Incorporation Permitting the Counting of Interested Directors for Quorum Purposes", 52 Mich.L. Rev. 295 (1953).

19. Fountain v. Oreck's, Inc., 245 Minn. 202, 71 N. W.2d 646 (1955); Munson v. Syracuse, Geneva & Corning R. R., 103 N.Y. 58, 8 N.E. 355 (1886). Contra, Gallaher v. Texagon Mills, Inc., 267 F.Supp. 845 (S.D.N.Y.1946) ("Under the [pre-1969] law of New Jersey, the director of a corporation whose interest in a matter disqualifies him from voting upon a resolution concerning the same, cannot be counted for the purpose of ascertaining whether a quorum is present when the vote is taken. A director so disqualified by personal interest losses, pro hac vice, his character as a director and so cannot be counted"); Blish v. Thompson Automatic Arms Corp., 30 Del.Ch. 538, 64 A.2d 581 (Sup.Ct. 1948). Cf. Martin Foundation, Inc. v. North American Rayon Corp., 31 Del.Ch. 195, 68 A.2d 313, (Ch. 1949) (disqualifying director from counting toward quorum under express articles of incorporation provision to such effect); Salton v. Seaporcel Metals, Inc., 27 Misc.2d 301, 208 N.Y.S.2d 60 (Sup.Ct. 1960). Whether or not any interested director may count toward a quorum or vote is the procedural question treated at this point. Assuming that the contract or transaction has been approved by the board of directors, there remains the substantive question as to whether or not the corporation may avoid the contract or transaction. See section 238 infra. See also Goldman, "Self-Dealing by Directors under Illinois Law: Transactions between Corporations Having Common Directors", 53 Ill.B.J. 1068 (1965); Note, "Dealings Between Directors and Their Corporations—A Discussion of the 'Disinterested Quorums' Rule under Present Statutory Limitations in Michigan", 34 U.Det.L.J. 43 (1956).

20. E. g., Cal.Gen.Corp.Law, § 820 (1947); Del.Gen. Corp.Law, § 144 (1967); McKinney's N.Y.Bus.Corp. Law, § 713. Such statutes deal with both the procedural and substantive problem distinguished in note 19 supra. The Model Business Corporation Act contained no such provision prior to the 1969 revision.

21. Fountain v. Oreck's, Inc.; Munson v. Syracuse, Geneva & Corning R. R., supra note 19.

22. Gallaher v. Texagon Mills, Inc.; Blish v. Thompson Automatic Arms Corp., supra note 19.

23. Sterling v. Mayflower Hotel Corp., 33 Del.Ch. 293, 93 A.2d 107, 38 A.L.R.2d 425 (Sup.Ct.1952);

24. Wiberg v. Gulf Coast Land & Development Co., 360 S.W.2d 563 (Tex.Civ.App.1962); Crass v. Budd, 157 N.Y.L.J. No. 47, 16 (Sup.Ct.1967). See section 366 infra.

25. Cf. Gottlieb v. McKee, 34 Del.Ch. 537, 107 A.2d 240 (Ch.1954).

26. Alcott v. Hyman, 42 Del.Ch. 233, 208 A.2d 501 (Sup.Ct.1965); Gottlieb v. Heyden Chemical Corp., 33 Del.Ch. 177, 91 A.2d 57 (Sup.Ct.1952). See section 194 supra. Where fiduciaries are charged with having violated their fiduciary duties, the burden of proving fairness should be on those who would sustain the transaction. Shlensky v. South Parkway Bldg. Corp., 19 Ill.2d 268, 166 N.E.2d 793 (1960).

27. See section 238 infra.

Officers have such authority as inheres in their offices and as is delegated to them by the bylaws or by the board of directors. Directors are under a duty of due care in supervising officers.

Removal of officers is usually at the pleasure of the board of directors, subject to some restrictions when officers are elected by shareholders, even though removal is in breach of any valid employment contract between the officer and the corporation and might subject the corporation to liability for wrongful removal.

As indicated, the traditional theory was that the board of directors determined the policies of the corporation, and delegated to officers appointed by and answerable to it the execution and administration of such policies.

Selection of Officers

Most statutes provide for election of the corporate officers—at least the president, vice-presidents, secretary, and treasurer—by the board of directors, sometimes providing that other officers and assistant officers, agents, and employees may be elected or appointed by the board or chosen as prescribed in the bylaws.[1]

Some statutes require that the president be elected from among the directors; others

provide.[2] That any two offices may be held by the same person with stated exceptions.[3]

A growing number of statutes permit the officers to be elected by shareholders.[4]

Supervision of Officers

Corporate officers have such authority and duties in the management of the corporation as inhere in their offices and as may be provided in the bylaws or as determined by resolution of the board of directors not inconsistent with the bylaws.[5]

Directors are under a duty of due care in supervising the officers.[6]

Removal of Officers

Removal of officers is usually at the pleasure of the board of directors.[7]

2. See section 220 infra.

3. See section 219, nn. 6–8 infra.

4. E. g., Delaware, Nebraska, New Jersey, New Mexico (by directors or shareholders as bylaws direct); New York (by directors unless otherwise provided in articles of incorporation); Connecticut, Maryland, Pennsylvania (by directors unless otherwise provided in bylaws); Georgia, Hawaii, Indiana (as provided in bylaws); Oklahoma (as provided in bylaws or determined by board of directors); Maine (president by board of directors; other officers per bylaws); Massachusetts (president by directors; treasurer and clerk by shareholders); New Hampshire (initial clerk by incorporators, thereafter by shareholders or per articles of incorporation or bylaws); Vermont (president and treasurer by directors; clerk by shareholders).

5. E. g., ABA–ALI Model Bus.Corp.Act § 44; McKinney's N.Y.Bus.Corp.Law, § 715(g). See sections 224–228 infra.

6. Ordinarily, directors are personally liable for the wrong of an officer only where they participated in the wrong, failed to exercise due care in the selection of the officers, or failed to exercise due care in the supervision of the officer. Graham v. Allis-Chalmers Mfg. Co., 41 Del.Ch. 78, 188 A.2d 125 (Sup.Ct.1963); Foster v. Bowen, 311 Mass. 359, 41 N.E.2d 181 (1942); Lowell Hoit & Co. v. Detig, 320 Ill.App. 179, 50 N.E.2d 602 (1943). See section 235 infra.

7. E. g., ABA–ALI, Model Bus.Corp.Act § 45; McKinney's N.Y.Bus.Corp.Law, § 716(a). Such power is sometimes expressly restricted with respect to officers elected by shareholders. McKinney's N.Y. Bus.Corp.Law, § 716(a) (removable, with or without cause, only by vote of shareholders (but his authority to act as officer may be suspended by board of directors for cause)).

1. E. g., ABA–ALI Model Bus.Corp.Act § 44; Del. Gen.Corp.Law, § 142 (1967); McKinney's N.Y.Bus. Corp.Law, § 715(a). Jennings v. Ruidoso Racing Ass'n, 79 N.M. 144, 441 P.2d 42 (1968) (upholding board of directors' authority to employ "comptroller" for period longer than next annual meeting despite bylaw requirement of annual election of "treasurer", because of different functions of two officers); Streett v. Laclede-Christy Co., 409 S.W.2d 691 (Mo.1966) (upholding five-year contract for employment of president as "general manager and chief operating officer", with respect to general managership); DeAngeles v. Roos Bros., 244 Cal. App.2d 434, 52 Cal.Rptr. 783 (1966) (subjecting corporation to damages where executive vice-president was discharged for taking business trip in violation of instructions of chairman of board that such trip was ill-advised because of ill-health of such officer). Osborne v. Locke Steel Chain Co., 153 Conn. 527, 218 A.2d 526 (1966) (upholding agreement, made one year before retirement, to pay former chairman of board $15,000 per year for rest of his life, on basis of consideration not to compete and to be available for consultation). See section 219 infra.

Even when an officer has a valid employment contract[8] with the corporation, he cause.[9] Any such removal is without prejumay usually be removed with or without dice, however, to his right to recover damages for any wrongful removal in breach of such contract.[10]

MANAGEMENT COMPENSATION; DECLARATION OF DIVIDENDS

211. **Executive compensation is usually fixed by the board of directors. Some statutes empower the board of directors to fix their own compensation except as otherwise provided in the articles of incorporation. Management compensation will be treated later in this chapter.**

The declaration of dividends is usually within the discretion of the board of directors. Dividends will be discussed in Chapter 12.

Management Compensation

Executive compensation, absent provision to the contrary, is usually fixed by the board of directors.[1]

Some statutes expressly empower the board also to fix the compensation of directors unless otherwise provided in the articles of incorporation.[2]

The various problems of management compensation are reserved for later treatment.[3]

Declaration of Dividends

Absent relatively rare mandatory provisions, and subject to any preferences and other restrictions, the declaration of divi-

dends (limited, of course, to funds legally available for dividends) is within the discretion of the board of directors. The whole subject of dividends will be explored in Chapter 12.

DELEGATION OF AUTHORITY BY BOARD OF DIRECTORS

212. **The board of directors, to some extent, may delegate management authority, the most common instances being to officers and to executive and other committees of the board. Delegation of authority to officers is generally recognized by statute. Many statutes expressly authorize, subject to prescribed limitations, delegation of authority to executive and other committees. Unduly broad delegation is treated as an unlawful abdication by the board of its management functions. Delegation of authority to outsiders, such as management companies or arbitrators in the event of director deadlock, has been difficult to sustain. Delegation of authority does not relieve the directors of their legal responsibilities, unless otherwise provided by statute.**

To some extent, at least, the board of directors may delegate management authority. Delegation of authority to officers and other agents and employees is common.[1]

---

8. See section 221, n. 9 infra.

9. See section 221, n. 8 infra. See also Stevenot v. Norberg, 210 F.2d 615 (9th Cir.1954) (where bylaw requiring shareholder approval of discharge of shareholder-employee repealed and shareholder discharged, bylaw amendment held valid and, in any event, specific performance denied).

10. See section 221, n. 9 infra.

[§ 211]

1. E. g., ABA–ALI Model Bus.Corp.Act § 4(k).

2. E. g., ABA–ALI Model Bus.Corp.Act § 33.

3. See sections 243–256 infra.

[§ 212]

1. E. g., ABA–ALI Model Bus.Corp.Act § 44. See generally Comment, "Delegating the Managerial Functions of Corporate Directors", 5 S.Tex.L.J. 293 (1960); Note, "Delegation of Duties by Corporate Directors", 47 Va.L.Rev. 278 (1961). But see Clarke Memorial College v. Monaghan Land Co., —— Del.Ch. ——, 257 A.2d 234 (Ch.1969) (delegation to officers by board of directors of power to fix terms and conditions for sale of corporate assets when such power given to board of directors by shareholders held improper); Brown v. Grayson Enterprises, Inc., 401 S.W.2d 653 (Tex.Civ.App.1966) (board of directors power to employ employees for life held nondelegable to officers or agents); Long Park, Inc. v. Trenton-New Brunswick Theatres Co., 297 N.Y. 174, 77 N.E.2d 633 (1948), motion denied 298 N.Y. 856, 84 N.E.2d 324 (1949); Marvin v. Solventol Chemical Products, Inc., 298 Mich. 296, 298 N.W. 782 (1941). Employment contracts for periods extending beyond the terms of the board of directors authorizing the contracts are subject to statutes and cases permitting removal of the officer or employee with or without cause at any time by the board of directors, without prejudice to his contract rights, if any. See Phoenix Sav. & Loan, Inc. v. Aetna Cas. & Sur. Co., 302 F.Supp. 832 (D.Md.1969).

The exercise by the officers, etc., of the authority delegated to them is subject to the supervision of the board of directors.

Modern statutes also expressly permit delegation by the board of directors of at least some of its more discretionary authority to committees composed of directors with power to act at least during the intervals between meetings of the whole board of directors.[2]

The Model Business Corporation Act, for example, authorizes an executive committee and one or more other committees composed of two or more directors to exercise all of the authority of the board of directors in the management of the corporation, subject to stated limitations.[3]

2. Most of the statutes require that members of executive and other committees of the board of directors, as distinguished from administrative committees, be directors. Under such statutes, nondirectors may not be appointed. Steigerwald v. A. M. Steigerwald Co., 9 Ill.App.2d 31, 132 N.E.2d 373 (1955); Mylander, "Management by Executive Committee", 33 Harv.Bus.Rev. 51 (May-June 1955). The chairman of the executive committee might be an important officer of the corporation, besides presiding over executive committee sessions. Broad use of board of directors committees might limit the effectiveness of minority directors elected under cumulative voting. Committees are governed by the rules applicable to the board of directors. Peurifoy v. Loyal, 154 S.C. 267, 151 S.E. 579 (1930).

See Halliday, "Corporation Executive Committees", 16 Clev.-Mar.L.Rev. 167 (1967); Aurell, "The Corporate Executive Committee: A Dilemma for the Nonmember Director", 17 U.Fla.L.Rev. 525 (1965); TNEC Monograph 11, Bureaucracy and Trusteeship in Large Corporations 23–37 (1940); Note, "Executive Committees—Creation, Procedures, and Authority", 1967 Wash.U.L.Q. 42.

3. ABA–ALI Model Bus.Corp.Act § 38. The executive or other committees must be authorized in the articles of incorporation or bylaws and by a resolution of a majority of the full board of directors, which must define the authority delegated. No committee may exercise the authority of the board with respect to amendments of the articles of incorporation, mergers, consolidations, sales, etc., of all or substantially all corporate assets other than in the regular course of business, voluntary dissolutions or revocation thereof, and bylaw amendments. The Model Act does not expressly require the keeping of minutes by such committees, and permits a committee as well as the board of directors to act by prior written consent without a meeting. ABA–ALI Model Bus.Corp.Act § 39A. See section 208 supra. See also Doyle v. Chladek, 240 Or. 598, 401 P.

Older corporate statutes made no or only oblique references to committees of the board.[4]

Absent statutory authorization, delegation of authority to committees is usually strictly construed,[5] and any broad delegation runs the risk of being treated as an unlawful abdication by the board of its management functions.[6]

2d 18 (1965), modified, reh. denied 240 Or. 598, 403 P.2d 381 (1965) (setting aside purported rescission of share subscription by executive committee on which bylaws conferred "administrative and ministerial authority in the management of the corporation").

4. McKinney's N.Y.Gen.Corp.Law, § 31 (inapplicable since 1963 to business corporations) (reference in waiver of notice provision to "board of directors or any committee thereof"). Despite the lack of statute, executive committees of New York corporations had been upheld by the courts. Sheridan Elec. Light Co. v. Chatham Nat'l Bank, 127 N.Y. 517, 28 N.E. 467 (1891). Hoyt v. Thompson's Executor, 19 N.Y. 207, 216 (1859). The New York Business Corporation Law provides rather full treatment of executive and other committees. New York permits executive and other committees, each consisting of three or more directors, if the articles of incorporation or bylaws so provide, when authorized by a majority of the entire board of directors, and specifically prohibits the delegation to committees of certain powers: (a) To submit to shareholders any action requiring shareholder approval; (b) To fill vacancies among directors or in any committee of directors; (c) To fix compensation of the directors for serving on the board or on any committee; (d) To adopt, amend, or repeal bylaws; (e) To amend, or repeal any resolution of the board which by its terms shall not be so amendable or repealable; New York also provides for alternative members. McKinney's N.Y.Bus.Corp.Law, § 712; Comment, "Corporate Management by an Executive Committee: Proposed New York Business Corporation Act", 25 Albany L.Rev. 93 (1961).

5. 2 W. Fletcher, Private Corporations § 550 (perm. ed. rev. 1954).

6. Under the early rule, "ministerial" but not "discretionary" functions could be delegated. Fensterer v. Pressure Lighting Co., 85 Misc. 621, 149 N.Y.S. 49 (N.Y.C.City Ct.1914). For statement in support of broader delegation, see Manson v. Curtis, 223 N.Y. 313, 322, 119 N.E. 559, 562 (1918). The modern rule seems to allow delegation of "discretionary" as well as "ministerial" functions, but not "extraordinary" powers (e. g., initiation of extraordinary corporate matters (see Chapter 13 infra)). See Hayes v. Canada, Atlantic & Plant S. S. Co., 181 F. 289 (1st Cir. 1910) (broad delegation construed limited to ordinary business transactions). Cf. Kennerson v. Burbank Amusement Co., 120 Cal.App.2d 157, 260 P.2d 823 (1953) (holding delegation of exclusive manage-

Delegation of authority to outsiders, such as management companies [7] or even arbitrators in the event of deadlock of the board,[8] unless minor in scope, is even more difficult to sustain.[9]

Delegation of authority to committees or others does not relieve the directors of their responsibilities imposed by law,[10] unless otherwise provided by statute.[11]

"DIRECTOR AGREEMENTS"

213. Agreements unduly depriving directors of their discretion in managing the corporation according to its best interests are invalid.

As previously mentioned,[1] shareholders, even though they are also directors, and possibly other persons interested in a corpora-

tion can, to some extent, agree to cooperate with respect to various matters. When they bind themselves in their capacity as shareholders, the agreement, absent fraud on the minority or illegal purposes, etc., is valid in most jurisdictions.

However, even when purporting to agree as shareholders, if they bind themselves in their capacity as directors to the extent of *unduly* depriving themselves of their discretion in managing the corporation according to its best interests, such purported commitments are invalid.[2]

Modern statutes [3] are tending to permit provisions otherwise prohibited by law as improperly restricting the board of directors in the management of the corporate business if properly included in the articles of incorporation [4] or an agreement to which all shareholders have assented.[5] Such provisions usually are permissible only in closely-held or close corporations.[6]

BOARD OF DIRECTORS ADOPTION, AMENDMENT, AND REPEAL OF BYLAWS

214. The board of directors in some jurisdictions adopts the initial bylaws, and in most jurisdictions may amend or repeal bylaws, except possibly bylaws limiting the powers of the board of directors or bylaws specifically requiring shareholder approval.

In some jurisdictions, the board of directors adopts the initial bylaws.[1]

ment to one director illegal). But cf. Union Pacific Ry. v. Chicago, R. I. & P. Ry., 163 U.S. 564, 595–598, 16 S.Ct. 1173, 1185–1186, 41 L.Ed. 265, 276–277 (1895) (upholding broad delegation to executive committee where federal charter did not commit exclusive control in board but preserved common-law management functions of shareholders); Blair v. Bishop's Restaurants, Inc., 202 Okl. 648, 217 P.2d 161 (1950) (upholding bylaw delegation to secretary-treasurer of close corporation of power to declare dividends). Comment, 42 Mich.L.Rev. 133 (1943); Note, 35 Ky.L.J. 156 (1947); Note, 6 Ark.L. Rev. 486 (1952).

7. Sherman & Ellis, Inc. v. Indiana Mut. Casualty Co., 41 F.2d 588 (7th Cir. 1930), cert. denied 282 U.S. 893, 51 S.Ct. 107, 75 L.Ed. 787 (1930); Long Park, Inc. v. Trenton-New Brunswick Theatres Co., 297 N.Y. 174, 77 N.E.2d 633 (1948); State ex rel. National Mut. Ins. Co. v. Conn, 115 Ohio St. 607, 155 N.E. 138, 50 A.L.R. 473 (1927).

8. O'Neal, "Resolving Disputes in Closely Held Corporations: Intra-Institutional Arbitration", 67 Harv.L.Rev. 786, 797–803 (1954). See section 277 infra.

9. See R. Stevens, Handbook on the Law of Private Corporations § 144 (2d ed. 1949).

10. E. g., ABA–ALI Model Bus.Corp.Act § 38; McKinney's N.Y.Bus.Corp.Law, § 712(c) (designation of any executive or other committee and delegation thereto of authority not alone to relieve any director of his duty to corporation).

11. E. g., McKinney's N.Y.Bus.Corp.Law, § 620(f) (relieving directors and imposing on shareholders liability for managerial acts and omissions under articles of incorporation provision as to control of directors).

[§ 213]
1. See section 198 supra.

2. See sections 267, 275 infra.

3. See section 259 infra.

4. McKinney's N.Y.Bus.Corp.Law, §§ 701, 620(b)–(g).

5. N.C.Bus.Corp.Act §§ 55–24, 55–73 (1957).

6. See Chapter 10 infra.

[§ 214]
1. E. g., ABA–ALI Model Bus.Corp.Act § 52. See section 133 supra. In some jurisdictions, the practice (sometimes not formalized by statute) is shortly after incorporation to have the incorporators at their organization meeting adopt the initial bylaws, and the board of directors at its organization meeting also approve and adopt such bylaws. See section 135 supra.

In such cases, or even when the initial by-laws are adopted by incorporators or shareholders and a statute, the articles of incorporation, or bylaws so provide the board may amend or repeal the bylaws.[2] Notwithstanding any such power in the board, the shareholders retain inherent power to amend or repeal the bylaws.[3]

Furthermore, bylaws limiting the power of the board of directors,[4] or bylaws specifically requiring shareholder approval might be capable of adoption, amendment, or repeal only by shareholders.[5] Bylaws limiting the power of directors or otherwise affecting corporate management in a manner inconsistent with law, even when unanimously adopted by shareholders, are void.[6]

BOARD OF DIRECTORS INITIATION OF EXTRAORDINARY COR-PORATE MATTERS

215. Board of directors action, as well as shareholder action, is in some jurisdictions required for extraordinary matters, such as amendments of the articles of incorporation, sale or lease of all or substantially all corporate assets not in the regular course of business, merger, consolidation, dissolution. Even in jurisdictions without such requirements, the

[§ 215]

2. E. g., ABA–ALI Model Bus.Corp.Act § 25 (unless such power is reserved to shareholders by articles of incorporation); Del.Gen.Corp.Law, § 109 (1967) (if power conferred on board of directors in articles of incorporation); McKinney's N.Y.Bus.Corp.Law, § 601 (when so provided in articles of incorporation or bylaw adopted by shareholders). Compare Matter of Mansdorf v. Unexcelled, Inc., 28 A.D.2d 44, 281 N.Y.S.2d 173 (1st Dep't 1967) (upholding power of board of directors to fix date of annual meeting only nine months after prior annual meeting), with Penn-Texas Corp. v. Niles-Bement-Pond Co., 34 N.J. Super. 373, 112 A.2d 302 (1955) (holding that attempt by directors to amend bylaws for later annual shareholder meeting (thus extending their term of office) violated New Jersey statute for annual election of directors and their holding office for one year).

3. See section 193 supra.

4. See section 193, n. 5 supra.

5. Ibid.

6. See section 193, n. 7 supra.

board of directors usually initiates such extraordinary matters, which are discussed in Chapter 13.

Extraordinary corporate matters, such as amendments of the articles of incorporation or transactions beyond the ordinary business, such as sale or lease of all or substantially all corporate assets not in the regular course of business, merger, consolidation, dissolution, are beyond the scope of management delegated to the board of directors.

Shareholder approval is generally required for such extraordinary matters.[1] Some statutes expressly require board of directors approval as well.[2] Even in the jurisdictions which do not require board of directors action, the board of directors as a practical matter usually initiates such extraordinary matters.

Extraordinary corporate matters will be discussed in Chapter 13.

DIRECTOR'S INSPECTION RIGHTS

216. Directors as individuals enjoy, on common-law principles, a right, termed "absolute" in some and "qualified" in other jurisdictions, to inspect the corporate books and records, as corollary to their duties to keep informed on corporate matters. Such rights are rarely affected by statutes. Removal of the director ends his director status, and with it any unqualified inspection rights. After removal, the director has been held to enjoy a qualified right to inspect records covering the period of his incumbency to protect his "personal responsibility interest".

To subserve the supervision and vigilance functions of the board of directors in managing the corporation, even directors, as indi-

[§ 216]

1. See section 195 supra.

2. E. g., ABA–ALI Model Bus.Corp.Act §§ 54, 65, 66, 72, 77; Del.Gen.Corp.Law, §§ 242, 251, 271, 275 (1967); McKinney's N.Y.Bus.Corp.Law, § 902 (adoption of plan of merger or consolidation by board of directors); id. § 909 (authorization of proposed sale, lease, exchange, or other disposition of assets, requiring shareholder approval, by board of directors).

viduals, are afforded certain powers, such as their rights to inspect corporate books and records, to bring a derivative action in behalf of the corporation, etc.

Because of the duties imposed on directors, including the duty of keeping informed on corporate matters,[1] directors enjoy, on common-law principles, a right, termed "absolute"[2] in some and "qualified"[3] in other jurisdictions, to inspect corporate books and records, to make reasonable extracts,[4] and to have any necessary assistance of attorneys, accountants, or others.[5]

Such inspection rights of directors have only rarely been affected by statutes.[6]

While the remedy to compel inspection is theoretically discretionary with the court, such remedy is usually granted upon a showing that the petitioner is a director, made a demand for inspection, and was refused, and that, where there the right is qualified, no basis for disqualification exists.[7]

Improper purpose, ulterior motive, etc., may or may not provide a defense even when the right is termed "absolute".[8]

1. See section 235 infra. See Lariscy v. Hill, 117 Ga.App. 152, 159 S.E.2d 443 (1968) (director's inspection rights held available to protect director buying shares from insiders).

2. State ex rel. Watkins v. Cassell, 294 S.W.2d 647 (Mo.Ct.App.1956); Matter of Cohen v. Cocoline Products, Inc., 309 N.Y. 119, 127 N.E.2d 906 (1955); McLaughlin, "The Director's Right to Inspect the Corporate Books and Records—Absolute or Otherwise", 22 Bus.Law. 413 (1967); Bartels & Flanagan, "Inspection of Corporate Books and Records in New York by Stockholders and Directors", 38 Cornell L.Q. 282, 312–319 (1953); Note, "Right of Directors to Inspect Corporate Books and Records", 11 Vill.L.Rev. 578 (1966).

3. Henshaw v. American Cement Corp., —— Del.Ch. ——, 252 A.2d 125 (Ch.1969); State ex rel. Farber v. Seiberling Rubber Co., 53 Del. (3 Storey) 295, 168 A.2d 310 (Super.Ct.1961); State ex rel. Paschall v. Scott, 41 Wash.2d 71, 247 P.2d 543 (1952); Strassburger v. Philadelphia Record Co., 335 Pa. 485, 6 A.2d 922 (1939); Note, "Inspection of Corporate Books and Records in Delaware", 41 Va.L.Rev. 237, 242 (1955).

4. Maidman v. Central Foundry Co., 27 A.D.2d 923, 279 N.Y.S.2d 365 (1st Dep't 1967) (corporation ordered to supply available daily information on share transfers to director who has already received list of shareholders); Kunin v. Forman Realty Corp., 21 Ill.App.2d 221, 157 N.E.2d 785 (1959), appeal dismissed 17 Ill.2d 543, 162 N.E.2d 401 (1959) (holding director entitled to receive copy of report where corporation had multiple copies available); Matter of Pacent v. Fourth Fed. Sav. & Loan Ass'n, 9 Misc.2d 37, 167 N.Y.S.2d 550 (Sup.Ct. 1957).

5. State ex rel. Dixon v. Missouri-Kansas Pipe Line Co., 42 Del. (3 Terry) 423, 36 A.2d 29 (Super.Ct. 1944). But see Matter of Wachman v. Artistic Leather Goods Mfg. Co., 22 A.D.2d 900, 255 N.Y.S.2d 396 (2d Dep't 1964) (requiring director to be present with his attorney or accountant for at least one hour of each day during inspection); Bero v. Bero Const. Corp., 36 Misc.2d 453, 233 N.Y.S.2d 150 (1962) (requiring director to be present with his attorney-

auditor for at least one-half hour each day during inspection); Matter of Grossman v. Central Coal Co., 11 Misc.2d 834, 173 N.Y.S.2d 423 (Sup.Ct.1958) (allowing director-attorney assistance of accountant but not of attorney); Matter of Pacent v. Fourth Fed. Sav. & Loan Ass'n, 9 Misc.2d 37, 167 N.Y.S.2d 550 (Sup.Ct.1957) (director denied assistance of his personal outside attorney and accountant absent showing of corporate mismanagement); Dandini v. Superior Court, 38 Cal.App.2d 32, 100 P.2d 535 (1940).

6. Cal.Gen.Corp.Law, § 3001 (1947) (books of account); Fla.Gen.Corp.Law, § 608.39 (1953) (stock ledger); W.Va.Gen.Corp.Law, § 3086 (1943) (books and records of corporation at all times subject to examination by any director).

7. Davis v. Keilsohn Offset Co., 273 App.Div. 695, 79 N.Y.S.2d 540 (1st Dep't 1948) (3–2); People ex rel. Leach v. Central Fish Co., 117 App.Div. 77, 101 N. Y.S.2d 1108 (1st Dep't 1907); Matter of Smith v. Republic Pictures Corp., 144 N.Y.S.2d 142 (Sup.Ct. 1955), aff'd mem., 286 App.Div. 1000, 145 N.Y.S.2d 311 (1st Dep't 1955), appeal denied 286 App.Div. 1089, 147 N.Y.S.2d 674 (1st Dep't 1955). See People ex rel. Bartels v. Borgstede, 169 App.Div. 421, 155 N. Y.S. 322 (2d Dep't 1915) (dummy director); Hartman v. Hollingsworth, 255 Cal.App.2d 579, 63 Cal.Rptr. 563 (1967) (holding director's status and inspection right ended with filing of winding-up certificate of dissolved corporation); Matter of Bellman, People ex rel. v. Standard Match Co., 208 App.Div. 4, 202 N. Y.S. 840 (2d Dep't 1924) (holding director's right not absolute after dissolution of corporation). See also Edelman v. Goodman, 47 Misc.2d 8, 261 N.Y.S.2d 618 (Sup.Ct.1965) (director successful in proceeding to compel inspection held not entitled to reimbursement for reasonable attorneys' fees by corporation).

8. Matter of Dewar v. Cigarette Service, Inc., 5 A. D.2d 764, 170 N.Y.S.2d 89 (1st Dep't 1958); Matter of Grossman v. Central Coal Co., Inc., 11 Misc.2d 834, 173 N.Y.S.2d 423 (Sup.Ct.1958). But see Matter of Liberman, 146 N.Y.L.J. No. 84, 13 (Sup.Ct.1961) (inspection denied inactive director who was suing corporation for unfair competition and who had not interested himself in corporation); State ex rel. Paschall v. Scott, 41 Wash.2d 71, 247 P.2d 543 (1952) (inspection denied hostile director by analogy

Removal of the director ends his status as a director, and with it his "absolute" inspection right. Even if the removal occurs after the director has commenced a proceeding to compel inspection, his "absolute" right ends.[9] Furthermore, the inspection proceeding might even be stayed pending the removal of the director;[10] the issue of the validity of any removal is not triable in the inspection proceeding.[11]

A former director has been held to have a qualified right to inspect records covering the period of his incumbency to protect his "personal responsibility interest . . . the protection of which could very well inure to the benefit of the stockholders by a disclosure to them of any derelictions by other directors or officers", as is likely where a director of long service "unexpectedly fails of re-election just at a time when he was about to undertake an investigation in his capacity as director".[12]

Absent some showing that he has been charged or may reasonably be charged with some act or failure to act during his incumbency for which he may be held personally responsible, inspection has been denied a former director.[13]

A former director who is also a shareholder would, of course, enjoy such shareholder inspection rights as exist.[14]

Where a Delaware corporation maintained its principal business office in New York where many of its books and records were located and its directors met, an order compelling inspection both of the books and records physically located within New York and of those kept in an office outside the state was affirmed by the New York Court of Appeals over the objection that such inspection would interfere with the internal affairs of a foreign corporation.[15]

DIRECTOR'S DERIVATIVE ACTIONS

217. Directors as individuals may in a few jurisdictions bring certain derivative actions in behalf of their corporations. Such derivative actions are not subject to the various restrictions imposed on derivative actions by shareholders. Once such an action has been commenced by a director, his subsequent failure of reelection or removal has been held not to abate the action.

to shareholder inspection right); Matter of Posen v. United Aircraft Products Co., 201 Misc. 260, 111 N.Y.S.2d 261 (Sup.Ct.1952) (inspection by director of corporation engaged in national defense work held subject to his federal security clearance); Melup v. Rubber Corp., 181 Misc. 826, 828, 43 N.Y.S.2d 444, 447 (Sup.Ct.1943); Hemingway v. Hemingway, 58 Conn. 443, 19 A. 766 (1890). Cf. Javits v. Investors League, Inc., 92 N.Y.S.2d 267 (Sup.Ct.1949) (distinguishing between books and records and membership list, and holding director of membership corporation has no absolute right to inspect and copy latter, since corporation can mail to the members any communication submitted by director).

9. Matter of Cohen v. Cocoline Products, Inc., 309 N.Y. 119, 127 N.E.2d 906 (1955). Cf. Matter of Hyman, 155 N.Y.L.J. No. 107, 18 (Sup.Ct.1966) (director's inspection right held to survive non-reelection after court order for inspection delayed by corporation's dilatory tactics).

10. Overland v. Le Roy Foods, Inc., 304 N.Y. 573, 107 N.E.2d 74 (1952).

11. Matter of Cohen v. C-C Clubs, Inc., 10 Misc.2d 57, 171 N.Y.S.2d 873 (Sup.Ct.1958).

12. Matter of Cohen v. Cocoline Products, Inc., 309 N.Y. 119, 127 N.E.2d 906 (1955) (4–3) (remanding case to trial court to determine in its discretion whether inspection is necessary to protect former directors' personal responsibility interest as well as interest of shareholders). See note 13 infra.

13. Matter of Cohen v. C-C Clubs, Inc., 10 Misc.2d 57, 171 N.Y.S.2d 873 (Sup.Ct.1958); Matter of Cohen v. Cocoline Products, Inc., 14 Misc.2d 720, 179 N.Y.S.2d 262 (Sup.Ct.1958) (on remittitur from Court of Appeals, supra note 12) (finding additional basis for denial of qualified right on ground of bad faith).

14. See section 199 supra.

15. Matter of Newmark v. C & C Super Corp., 3 N. Y.2d 790, 164 N.Y.S.2d 42, 143 N.E.2d 796 (1957); Matter of Morris, 151 N.Y.L.J. No. 63, 14 (Sup.Ct. 1964) (ordering inspection of qualified foreign's books and records in state and those of wholly-owned subsidiary where businesses commingled); Gresov v. Shattuck Denn Mining Corp., 29 Misc.2d 324, 215 N.Y.S.2d 98 (Sup.Ct.1961) (holding director of qualified Delaware corporation to have absolute, unqualified inspection right, and motive to oust management not act of bad faith detrimental to corporate interests).

Where the corporation has been wronged, it, of course, has a cause of action against the wrongdoer. If a wrong against the corporation is threatened, it may seek an injunction.

Actions by and in the name of the corporation usually are commenced and maintained as authorized by the board of directors in the exercise of their business judgment. Sometimes, the bylaws or a resolution of the board of directors might confer such power on an officer.[1]

If the board of directors negligently[2] or in violation of their fiduciary duties[3] fail to assert a corporate cause of action or claim, to the damage of the corporation, they would be liable for breach of their duties to the corporation.

A few jurisdictions by statute authorize director derivative actions.[4]

The New York provisions, for example, authorize a director, among others, to bring an action against one or more of the directors or officers of the corporation to compel them to account and pay over to the corporation for breach of their duties to the corporation, or to set aside or enjoin an unlawful transfer of corporate property, or to bring an action against directors who vote for or concur in any declaration of any unlawful dividends or other distributions, any unlawful purchase of shares of the corporation, any unlawful liquidation distributions, or any unlawful loans to directors.[5] Such a derivative action by an individual director is not subject to the various restrictions imposed on derivative actions by shareholders.[6]

Once such an action is commenced by a director, his subsequent failure of reelection as director (or by analogy, removal) has been held not to abate the action or affect his standing to sue.[7]

Where majority shareholders and directors voted against the corporation's interposing a defense in an action against it by a third person, a dissenting director has not been allowed to interpose a defense in behalf of the corporation.[8]

DIRECTOR'S LIABILITIES

218. Directors can be liable for their individual as well as their collective actions. A director who personally participates in a tort is personally liable to the victim, even though the corporation might be vicariously liable. Directors who guaranty corporate obligations are subject to the liability of guarantors. Statutes often provide for personal liability for assuming to act as a corporation without authority. Personal liability is also a possible consequence of too-defective incorporation. Directors (and officers) are subject to three-fold duties under decisional law, often complemented by statute. State corporate statutes increasingly deal with directors' liabilities, imposing personal liability for noncompliance with various requirements. Criminal penalties are also imposed. Additional liabilities exist

1. See section 225 infra.

2. See section 234 infra.

3. See sections 235, 242 infra.

4. See also Mich.Gen.Corp.Act § 21.47 (1948) (actions against agents as well as against directors or officers); McKinney's N.Y.Bus.Corp.Law, § 720(b); Okl.Bus.Corp.Act § 28(b) (1961) (actions against shareholders as well as against directors or officers).

5. McKinney's N.Y.Bus.Corp.Law, §§ 719(a), 720. Note, "Director's Statutory Action in New York", 36 N.Y.U.L.Rev. 99 (1961).

6. See Chapter 14 infra. On the other hand, director derivative actions are more limited as to the corporate causes of action they can assert. Williams v. Robinson, 9 Misc.2d 774, 169 N.Y.S.2d 811 (Sup.Ct. 1957) (holding directors who ratified or acquiesced in wrong to corporation by defendant directors not estopped from maintaining action); Katz v. Braz, 188 Misc. 581, 66 N.Y.S.2d 722 (Sup.Ct.1946), aff'd mem. 271 App.Div. 970, 69 N.Y.S.2d 324 (1st Dep't 1947) (holding prior demand on board of directors not required); Green v. Compton, 41 Misc. 21, 83 N.Y.S. 588 (Sup.Ct.1903) (corporation held not indispensable party).

7. Tenney v. Rosenthal, 6 N.Y.2d 204, 189 N.Y.S.2d 158, 160 N.E.2d 463 (1959) (non-abatement because of "stewardship obligation" of director), aff'g 6 A. D.2d 510, 179 N.Y.S.2d 728 (1st Dep't 1958), rev'g 13 Misc.2d 393, 176 N.Y.S.2d 1009 (Sup.Ct.1958). Cf. Kehaya v. Axton, 32 F.Supp. 266 (S.D.N.Y.1940); Singer v. State Laundry, Inc., 188 Misc. 583, 68 N. Y.S.2d 808 (Sup.Ct.1947).

8. Hertz v. Quinn & Kerns, Inc., 21 Misc.2d 227, 195 N.Y.S.2d 907 (Sup.Ct.1959).

under federal tax, antitrust and trade regulation, and securities legislation. Indemnification by the corporation of the director is often available.

Directors, qua directors, do not act for the corporation individually, but collectively as the board of directors.[1]

Liability of directors, however, can result from their individual as well as their collective actions.

For any tort committed by a director against his corporation,[2] his fellow directors or officers,[3] shareholders,[4] creditors,[5] or others,[6] he can be personally liable, whether he was acting in behalf of the corporation or on his own, under traditional tort law principles,[7] buttressed by trust law fiduciary principles.[8]

For breach of corporate contracts, a director is not usually personally liable, under traditional contract law principles, unless he has personally bound himself thereunder as party, surety, or guarantor, assuming compliance with any applicable statute of frauds.[9]

Statutes often provide that all persons (whether purporting to act as directors or otherwise) who assume to act as a corporation without authority to do so shall be jointly and severally liable for all debts and liabilities incurred or arising as a result thereof.[10]

As a consequence of too-defective incorporation, those who purport to act in behalf of the business, whether as directors or otherwise, can be personally liable for the obligations of the business.[11]

Apart from, although increasingly complemented by, statutes,[12] directors (and officers) are subject to duties (a) to act intra vires and within their respective authority,[13] (b) to exercise due care,[14] and (c) to observe applicable fiduciary duties.[15] Most of these duties are owed to the corporation, but

1. See sections 208, 209 supra. See Symposium: "Duties and Liabilities of Corporate Directors", 22 Bus.Law. 29 (1966); Conway, "Directors' Duties in N.Y. under the Corporation Law", 159 N.Y.L.J. No. 13, 1, No. 14, 1, No. 15, 1 (1968); Mayer, "Civil and Criminal Liability of Directors of California Banks and Savings and Loan Associations", 41 Calif.St.B.J. 881 (1966); Adkins & Janis, "Some Observations on Liabilities of Corporate Directors", 20 Bus.Law. 817 (1965); Davies, "Personal Liability of 'Directors' of Non-Existent Companies", 6 U.West.Austl.L.Rev. 400 (1964); Note, "Corporate Director Liability—The Utah Law in Theory and Practice", 1966 Utah L. Rev. 660.

2. See sections 235–241 infra. For wrongs against the corporation, it may sue directly or the claims may be asserted derivatively in its behalf. Compare Underwood v. Stafford, 270 N.C. 700, 155 S.E. 2d 211 (1967), with Sutton v. Reagan & Gee, 405 S. W.2d 828 (Tex.Civ.App.1966). See section 360 infra.

3. See Avins, "Liability for Inducing a Corporation to Breach Its Contract", 43 Cornell L.Q. 55 (1957).

4. See sections 239–241 infra.

5. Acroglide Corp. v. Zeh, 301 F.2d 420 (2d Cir.1962) (holding personally liable for conversion directors who voted for chattel mortgage on property owned by plaintiff, even though they were unaware of plaintiff's title under unfiled conditional sale contract).

6. Allied Bldg. Credits, Inc. v. Damicus, 167 Neb. 390, 93 N.W.2d 210 (1958); Kathleen Foley, Inc. v. Gulf Oil Corp., 12 A.D.2d 644, 208 N.Y.S.2d 781 (2d Dep't 1960), aff'd mem. 10 N.Y.2d 859, 222 N.Y.S.2d 691, 178 N.E.2d 913 (1961).

7. See M. Feuer, Personal Liabilities of Corporate Officers and Directors ch. 20 (1961). See section 235 infra.

8. See sections 236–241 infra. See also Gould v. Jacobs, 44 Misc.2d 990, 256 N.Y.S.2d 20 (Sup.Ct.1965),

aff'd per curiam 24 A.D.2d 934, 263 N.Y.S.2d 1004 (1st Dep't 1965) (including in money judgment against director recital to provide basis for contempt proceedings on grounds of willful dereliction of duty while acting in fiduciary relationship under McKinney's N.Y. CPLR, § 5105.

9. First Nat'l Bank of Hopkins v. Int'l Machs. Corp., 279 Minn. 188, 156 N.W.2d 86 (1968); Alberts v. Schneiderman, 182 So.2d 50 (Fla.Dist.Ct.App.1966), aff'd per curiam 186 So.2d 784 (Fla.1966); Nation Wide, Inc. v. Scullin, 256 F.Supp. 929 (D.N.J.1966), aff'd per curiam 377 F.2d 554 (3d Cir.1967).

10. E. g., ABA–ALI Model Bus.Corp.Act § 139. See section 142 supra.

11. See section 145 supra.

12. See section 232 infra.

13. See section 234 infra.

14. See section 235 infra. Being an accommodation or dummy director is no defense. See Note, "Corporations: Use of Accommodations Incorporators, Directors, Officers: Potential Liability of Accommodation Personnel", 47 Cornell L.Q. 443 (1962).

15. See sections 236–241 infra.

some are owed to shareholders [16] and possibly creditors.[17]

State corporate statutes increasingly deal with directors' liabilities,[18] especially with respect to improper dividends or distributions,[19] improper purchase by corporation of its own shares,[20] improper loans to directors, officers, or shareholders,[21] preferential transfers,[22] commencing business without compliance with conditions precedent to doing business,[23] failure to comply with consideration requirements for shares,[24] failure to file accurate required reports or pay required fees,[25] continuing to carry on business after expiration of corporate existence,[26] forfeiture of charter,[27] or dissolution.[28]

Directors can also be liable under other state statutes, such as criminal codes or penal laws [29] or "blue sky" laws.[30]

Directors' liabilities, in addition, are imposed by several federal statutes, such as the Internal Revenue Code,[31] antitrust and trade regulation statutes,[32] and federal securities legislation.[33]

Indemnification by the corporation of directors' litigation expenses, including payment of liabilities, judgments, settlement

16.   See sections 239–241 infra.

17.   E. g., Henry F. Michell Co. v. Fitzgerald, 353 Mass. 318, 231 N.E.2d 373 (1967).

18.   See section 232 infra.

19.   See sections 323, 381 infra.

20.   Burton Mill & Cabinet Works, Inc. v. Truemper, 422 S.W.2d 825 (Tex.Civ.App.1967). See section 336 infra.

21.   See section 183 supra.

22.   E. g., Alberts v. Schneiderman, 182 So.2d 50 (Fla.Dist.Ct.App.1966), aff'd per curiam 186 So.2d 784 (Fla.1966).

23.   E. g., Ky.Gen.Corp.Law, § 271.095 (1953) (several liability of officers and nondissenting directors for debts of corporation transacting business before filing of articles of incorporation with clerk of county court, receipt of specified amount of capital, election of first board of directors by shareholders, and designation by corporation of registered office and process agent). See section 143 supra.

24.   E. g., Mass.Ann.Laws ch. 156, §§ 16, 36 (1959, Supp.1968) (inapplicable to business corporations since 1965); Henry F. Michell Co. v. Fitzgerald, 353 Mass. 318, 231 N.E.2d 373 (1967); Bay State York Co. v. Cobb, 346 Mass. 641, 195 N.E.2d 328 (1964); Brown v. Watson, 285 App.Div. 587, 139 N.Y.S.2d 628 (1st Dep't 1955). See sections 167, 168 supra.

25.   E. g., ABA–ALI Model Bus.Corp.Act § 129; Mountain States Supply, Inc. v. Mountain States Feed & Livestock Co., 149 Mont. 198, 425 P.2d 75 (1967). But see Arcouet v. Papp, 21 Misc.2d 294, 190 N.Y.S.2d 549 (Sup.Ct.1959) (refusing to enforce Colorado statutory penalty for failure to file annual reports).

26.   See section 144 supra.

27.   Borbein Young & Co. v. Cirese, 401 S.W.2d 940 (Mo.Ct.App.1966); Sheffield v. Nobles, 378 S.W.2d 391 (Tex.Civ.App.1964). Compare Vlasic Foods Co. v. Russek, 7 Mich.App. 359, 151 N.W.2d 872 (1967), with People v. Parker, 30 Ill.2d 486, 197 N.E.2d 30 (1964). See section 144 supra.

28.   See section 144 supra and sections 348, 381 infra.

29.   E. g., McKinney's N.Y.Penal Law, § 190.35 (misconduct by corporate official). See People v. Knapp, 206 N.Y. 373, 99 N.E. 841 (1912) (upholding indictment of directors on ground that when corporation itself is forbidden to do an act, prohibition extends to board of directors and to each director, separately and individually).

30.   See sections 305–308 infra.

31.   Int.Rev.Code of 1954, 26 U.S.C.A. §§ 6671(b), 6672 (making liable for tax any person who willfully fails to collect or pay over tax); United States v. Graham, 309 F.2d 210 (9th Cir.1962) (holding director might be personally liable for nonpayment of corporate taxes).

32.   E. g., Federal Sherman Antitrust Act § 1, 15 U.S.C.A. § 1 ($50,000 fine or up to one-year imprisonment or both). See section 310 supra. Federal Clayton Act § 14, 15 U.S.C.A. § 24 ($5,000 fine or one-year imprisonment). See section 312 supra. United States v. Wise, 370 U.S. 405, 82 S.Ct. 1354, 8 L.Ed.2d 590 (1962); Rooks, "Personal Liabilities of Officers and Directors for Antitrust Violations and Securities Transactions", 51 Ill.B.J. 626 (1963); Kramer, "Liability of Corporate Officers and Directors under the Antitrust Laws", 17 Bus.Law. 897 (1962).

33.   E. g., Federal Securities Act §§ 5, 11, 17 U.S.C.A. §§ 77f, 77k, 77q; Escott v. BarChris Construction Corp., 283 F.Supp. 643, 2 A.L.R.Fed. 86 (S.D.N.Y. 1968) (new outside director held liable for misstatements in prospectus). See M. Feuer, Personal Liabilities of Corporate Officers and Directors chs. 16–18 (1961). See section 295 supra. Federal Securities Exchange Act §§ 10(b), 16(b), 15 U.S.C.A. §§ 78j, 78p. See section 298 infra.

sums, fines, as well as attorneys' fees, and insurance covering the same, exist, subject to limitations, on common-law principles, under articles of incorporation or bylaw provisions, pursuant to board of directors resolutions, and under modern corporate statutes.[34]

F. OFFICERS

OFFICERS—IN GENERAL

219. Officers traditionally are selected and removed by the board of directors, which delegates to them authority to execute and administer the policies determined by the board of directors. Some statutes provide for the selection of all or some officers by shareholders. Officers are agents of the corporation, and as such are governed by the principles of agency law. As agents and as delegatees of the board of directors, officers are fiduciaries of the corporation. Statutes often prescribe that a corporation must or may have specified officers. The bylaws often enumerate the officers, typically president, one or more vice-presidents, treasurer, and secretary, and define their authority. The chief executive officer is usually the president but occasionally the chairman of the board of directors. Many corporations have a general manager, either so designated or under the title of some other office, most frequently president.

Traditionally, officers[1] are selected, and are removable, by the board of directors, which delegates to them authority to execute and administer the policies determined by the board of directors. Some statutes provide for selection of officers by shareholders.[2]

Unlike directors, who, as has been seen, are *sui generis*, officers are agents of the corporation, and, as such, subject to the usual principles of agency law, including the fiduciary duties of agents.[3]

Also as delegatees of the board of directors, officers are fiduciaries of the corporation subject to the same fiduciary duties as are directors within the scope of their delegated management functions.[4]

Statutes often prescribe that a corporation must or may have certain officers.[5]

34. See sections 379, 380 infra.

1. See generally Poor's Register of Corporations, Directors and Executives (1968); H. Friedman, Corporate Management Guide; Rights, Duties, and Liabilities of Managers, Officers, and Directors (1967); W. Grange, Manual for Corporation Officers (1967); W. Grange & T. Woodbury, Corporation Law: Operating Procedures for Officers and Directors (2d ed. 1964); R. Manley & S. Manley, The Age of the Manager (1963); L. Appley, The Management Evolution (1963); P. Jackson, Corporate Management (The Directors and Executives) (1955); see also O. Elliott, Men at the Top (1960); A. Harrington, Life in the Crystal Palace (1959); The World of The Wall Street Journal 75–116 (C. Preston, ed. 1959); W. Whyte, The Organization Man (1957); W. Warner & J. Abegglen, Big Business Leaders in America (1956); M. Newcomer, The Big Business Executive, The Factors That Made Him, 1900–1950 (1956); The Executive Life (1956); R. Gordon, Business Leadership in the Large Corporation (1961); Freeman, "Directors and Officers", 15 S.C.L.Rev. 396 (1963); Miles, "The Management Politician", 39 Harv.Bus.Rev. 99 (Jan.-Feb. 1961); Woodman, "What the Executive Expects of the Corporate Law Department", 13 Bus.Law. 461 (1958).

2. See section 210, n. 4 supra.

3. Kempin, "The Corporate Officer and the Law of Agency", 44 Va.L.Rev. 1273 (1958) (distinguishing the "executive officer" (officer with purely internal powers) and the "officer of the business" (agent-officer with some external duties and therefore subject to agency rules)). The 1969 Model Act revision in its definition of "employee" includes officers.

4. See sections 231–242 infra.

5. *Mandatory* provisions: E. g., ABA–ALI Model Bus.Corp.Act § 44; Alaska, California, Colorado, Illinois, Iowa, New Mexico, North Carolina, North Dakota, South Dakota, Texas, Virginia, Wisconsin, District of Columbia (president, one or more vice-presidents, secretary, treasurer); Delaware, Florida, Georgia, Idaho, Indiana, Kansas, Louisiana, Maine, Maryland, Massachusetts, Michigan, Minnesota, Nebraska, Nevada, New Jersey, Ohio, Oklahoma, Pennsylvania, Tennessee, Washington, West Virginia (president, secretary (or clerk), treasurer); Missouri (president, secretary); New Hampshire (clerk, treasurer).

Permissive provisions: E. g., New York (president, one or more vice-presidents, secretary, treasurer). Various statutes expressly authorize vice-presidents, secretaries, treasurers, assistant secretaries, assistant treasurers, chairmen of the board of directors.

In any event, the bylaws often enumerate the officers and make some references to their respective authority.[6]

The usual officers are president, one or more vice-presidents, treasurer, secretary, and, in the case of a banking corporation, cashier, and in the case of some New England corporations, clerk. Numerous other varieties of officers exist: chairman of the board, vice-chairman of the board, chairman of the executive committee, executive vice-presidents, senior vice-presidents, administrative vice-presidents, division vice-presidents,[7] comptroller (or controller), assistant presidents, assistant vice-presidents, assistant treasurers, assistant secretaries, assistants to the president, general counsel, general solicitor, etc. Many corporations have a general manager, either so designated or under the title of some other office. In a strict sense, only the more important of such executive personnel are "officers";[8] the inferior grades of executive personnel are not.

Problems involved in the compensation of officers will be discussed along with those of compensation to directors.[9]

OFFICERS—QUALIFICATIONS

220. **Statutes sometimes require that the president be a director, and impose various qualifications for other designated officers. An officer, like any other agent, should have the legal capacity required of agents. Dual office-holding is usually permitted, subject to some limitations, at common law or under statutes.**

Older statutes require that the president be chosen from among the directors.[1]

Some statutes impose various qualifications for designated officers.[2]

Obviously, where there is a chairman of the board, he should be a director.[3]

Presumably if a general counsel is appointed, he should be a duly qualified attorney at law.

Obviously, any officer, like any other agent, should have the legal capacity required of agents under the principles of agency.

---

6. See, e. g., By-Laws, art. IV, §§ 1, 5–9, Official Forms for Use Under the Model Business Corporation Act, Form No. 47 (ALI rev. 1953).

7. Some corporations have a hierarchy of more than 100 vice-presidents, classified into executive vice-presidents, senior vice-presidents, administrative vice-presidents, vice-presidents, division vice-presidents, etc. The Executive Life 149–162 (1956).

8. Evans v. General Ins. Co., 390 S.W.2d 818 (Tex. Civ.App.1965) (president held not "employee" under insurance policy exclusion); Gruber Personnel Services, Inc. v. Indemnity Ins. Co., 212 Pa.Super. 120, 239 A.2d 880 (1968) (employee with title "vice-president" found to be officer for purposes of insurance policy exclusion); Alldritt v. Kansas Centennial Global Exposition, Inc., 189 Kan. 649, 371 P.2d 181 (1962) (holding general manager to be "officer" and therefore barred from wage preference upon corporation's insolvency); cf. County Nat'l Bank v. U. S. Fidelity & Guaranty Co., 41 F.R.D. 293 (S.D. N.Y.1966) (honorary chairman of board of directors held not subject to pretrial examination as officer or managing agent, even though he had been president, absent showing of his involvement in corporation's day-to-day affairs). See note 3 supra.

9. See sections 243–256 infra.

Henn Corporations 2d Ed. HB—28

1. E. g., Florida, Idaho, Indiana, Kansas, Maine, Massachusetts, Michigan, Minnesota, Oklahoma, Vermont, Virginia, West Virginia. See Young v. Janas, 34 Del.Ch. 287, 103 A.2d 299 (Ch.1954); Miller v. Vanderlip, 285 N.Y. 116, 33 N.E.2d 51 (1941). Minnesota and Oklahoma provide that a president retains his office until a successor has been selected and has qualified even though he ceases to be a director. Shareholder removal of a president might be effectuated by removing him as a director. But see Realty Acceptance Corp. v. Montgomery, 51 F. 2d 636 (3d Cir.1930) (removal of plaintiff as director thereby disqualifying him as president held breach of implied condition of employment contract not to do anything to prevent performance—quaere as to de facto doctrine—see section 222 infra).

2. E. g., Idaho, Michigan (express provisions that vice-president may not succeed to office of president unless a director); Oklahoma (expressly requiring officers to be legally competent to contract); Massachusetts, New Hampshire, Vermont (requiring clerk to be state resident). Oklahoma and Pennsylvania expressly permit a corporation to be a treasurer.

3. Sometimes the chairman of the board, instead of the president, is the chief executive officer.
   Removal as a director by shareholders thus would disqualify the chairman of the board from serving in such office. This approach was not considered in Matter of Buckley (Rickerson), 183 Misc. 189, 50 N.Y.S.2d 54 (Sup.Ct.1944).

Some statutes expressly provide for oaths to be taken by officers,[4] or for their being bonded.[5]

Dual office-holding, absent provision to the contrary, is usually permissible if the offices are not incompatible;[6] this subject is sometimes treated in statutes[7] or bylaw provisions.[8]

[§ 220]

4. E. g., Kansas, New Hampshire.

5. E. g., Delaware, Kansas, Maine, Massachusetts, New Jersey, New York, Oklahoma, Pennsylvania, South Carolina, West Virginia.

6. See 2 W. Fletcher, Private Corporations § 310 (perm. ed. rev. 1954).

7. Most jurisdictions expressly permit dual office-holding, with some limitations, the most typical being against the same person holding the offices of president and secretary. E. g., ABA–ALI Model Bus.Corp.Act § 44. Hawaii deleted its provision permitting two or more offices to be held by the same person. Some jurisdictions permit dual office-holding only if the bylaws so provide. E. g., Illinois, Indiana, Maryland, Missouri, Pennsylvania, West Virginia, District of Columbia. Michigan allows dual office-holding unless the bylaws otherwise provide. Idaho, Kansas, and Kentucky permit combinations of the offices of vice-president, secretary, and treasurer. Washington permits two of the offices of vice-president, secretary, and treasurer to be combined in one person, thus precluding the president from also serving as treasurer. Wash.Op.Att'y Gen. 61–62, No. 179, Nov. 27, 1962. There would seem little purpose in having the same person serve as president and vice-president. Such combination is expressly prohibited in some jurisdictions. E. g., Maryland, Michigan, Minnesota, Nebraska, Oklahoma, West Virginia, Wisconsin. Under statutes contemplating the execution of certain documents by the president and the secretary, having different persons in the two offices would appear desirable. Some statutes limit a dual office-holder to a single capacity in connection with the execution, acknowledgment, and verification of corporate instruments. E. g., Florida, Maryland, Michigan, North Carolina, Ohio, Oklahoma, West Virginia. Law firms sometimes place their passed-over or about to be passed-over associates, and more rarely their partners, with client corporations to serve as officers, often as an assistant secretary, as secretary, or as members of the legal department. Sometimes the corporation's counsel or accountant, or both, might serve as officers of the corporation. Many reputable law firms and accounting firms have policies against their members and associates serving as officers of corporations, even, or perhaps especially, when such corporations are their clients. See Aine v. Power, 140 N.Y.L.J., No. 115, 13 (Sup. Ct.1961). See section 204, nn. 20–25 supra.

8. See, e. g., By-Laws, art. IV, § 1, Official Forms for Use Under the Model Business Corporation Act, Form No. 47 (ALI rev. 1953).

OFFICERS—APPOINTMENT OR ELECTION, TENURE, AND REMOVAL

221. Officers are usually appointed by the board of directors. Statutes often require board of directors appointment of at least the more important officers. A growing number of statutes provide for shareholder election of officers.

Tenure of officers is usually at the pleasure of the board of directors. A few statutes limit the terms of officers, usually to one year.

Officers are usually removable, with or without cause, by the board of directors, even where there is a valid employment contract between the officer and the corporation. Removal without cause in breach of such contract usually subjects the corporation to liability for damages. A valid shareholder or director agreement binding directors to keep certain persons in office usually precludes such parties from voting for removal of such officers without cause. Some statutes empower the state or shareholders to remove officers for cause.

Appointment

The officers are usually appointed by the board of directors. Statutes often require the selection of the more important officers, e. g., president, vice-president(s), treasurer, and secretary, by the board.[1]

Under statutes in a growing number of jurisdictions, officers may be elected by shareholders.[2]

Inferior officers, assistant officers, and other agents and employees, pursuant to statute or bylaws, are usually appointed by the more senior officers.[3]

Tenure

Officers, and other corporate agents and employees, usually serve at the pleasure of the board of directors.[4] This is usually so

[§ 221]

1. E. g., ABA–ALI Model Bus.Corp.Act § 44.

2. See section 210, n. 4 supra.

3. E. g., ABA–ALI Model Bus.Corp.Act § 44 (elected or appointed by board of directors or chosen in such manner as may be prescribed by the bylaws).

4. E. g., ABA–ALI Model Bus.Corp.Act § 45 (election or appointment of officer or agent not of itself to

even when there is a valid employment contract between them and the corporation.

A few statutes expressly limit the terms of officers.[5]

Removal

Officers, and other corporate agents and employees, in most jurisdictions, are usually removable, with or without cause, by the board of directors.[6]

In such jurisdictions, when there is a valid employment contract between them and the corporation,[7] the board may be said usually

create contract rights). See Atwood v. Curtiss Candy Co., 22 Ill.App.2d 369, 161 N.E.2d 355 (1959) (annual salary for president held not to create annual employment); Winslow v. Roberts Numbering Machine Co., 17 Misc.2d 18, 183 N.Y.S.2d 817 (Sup.Ct. 1959).

5. E. g., Ohio (all officers limited to one-year terms unless otherwise provided in articles of incorporation or bylaws); Maryland (all officers limited to one-year terms unless otherwise provided in bylaws); New Hampshire, Vermont (clerk to hold office for one-year); Tennessee (all officers limited to two-year terms). New York fixes the term until the meeting of the board of directors following the next annual meeting of the shareholders or, in the case of officers elected by shareholders, until the next annual meeting of shareholders, unless otherwise provided in the articles of incorporation or bylaws, and provides that each officer shall hold office for the term for which he was elected or appointed, and until his successor has been elected or appointed and qualified.

6. E. g., ABA–ALI Model Bus.Corp.Act § 45; McKinney's N.Y.Bus.Corp.Law, § 716(a) (any officer elected or appointed by board of directors removable by board with or without cause; officer elected by shareholders removable, with or without cause, only by vote of shareholders, but his authority to act as officer suspendible by board of directors for cause). See note 13 infra.

7. A long-term contract might require board of directors or shareholder ratification. See Miller v. Vanderlip, 285 N.Y. 116, 33 N.E.2d 51 (1941); Grossman v. Redi-Food Co., 142 N.Y.S.2d 724 (App.T. 1st Dep't 1955), rev'd, 2 A.D.2d 670, 152 N.Y.S.2d 624 (1st Dep't 1956) (so long as employee or wife held shares in corporation); Horan v. John F. Trommer, Inc., 129 N.Y.S.2d 539 (Sup.Ct.1954), aff'd mem., 283 App.Div. 774, 128 N.Y.S.2d 595 (1st Dep't 1954); Pullman Co. v. Ray, 201 Md. 268, 94 A.2d 266 (1953) (for life of employee). See also Streett v. Laclede-Christy Co., 409 S.W.2d 691 (Mo.1966) (upholding five-year contract, authorized by board of directors, to employ plaintiff as "general manager and chief operating officer", severing such provision from another provision for him to be president for five

to have the power, but not the right, to remove an officer without cause.[8] Any such

years); Magnus v. Magnus Organ Corp., 71 N.J.Super. 363, 177 A.2d 55 (1962) (finding implied bylaw amendment by shareholder ratification of five-year contract of employment of president); Dixie Glass Co. v. Pollak, 341 S.W.2d 530, 91 A.L.R.2d 662 (Tex.Civ.App.1960), error ref. n. r. e. 162 Tex. 440, 347 S.W.2d 596 (1961) (implied amendment of bylaw for one-year term found where board of directors and shareholders unanimously approved five-year contract of employment of comptroller). An oral contract of employment for life has been construed as for an indefinite period and therefore terminable at will by either party. Marin v. Jacuzzi, 224 Cal. App.2d 549, 36 Cal.Rptr. 880 (1964). An employment contract delegating substantially all management functions to the employee has been held void. Kennerson v. Burbank Amusement Co., 120 Cal. App.2d 157, 260 P.2d 823 (1953). See Good v. Modern Globe, Inc., 346 Mich. 602, 78 N.W.2d 199 (1956) (upholding five-year consulting contract with officer-director, who was retiring from active management and agreed to refrain from working for any competitor, as within power of board, not violative of fiduciary duties of directors in dealing with fellow director, and not unlawful restraint of employment). But see Revlon, Inc. v. Kurtzman, 157 N.Y. L.J. No. 79, 17 (Sup.Ct.1967) (refusing to enforce covenant not to compete for six months after termination of employment by merchandising director absent showing of trade secrets or that employee was unique and extraordinary). See Matter of Cross & Brown Co. (Nelson), 4 A.D.2d 501, 167 N.Y.S.2d 573 (1st Dep't 1957) (provision in employment contract for arbitration by corporate employer's board of directors held invalid). See Stevenot v. Norberg, 210 F.2d 615 (9th Cir.1954) (where bylaw requiring shareholder approval of discharge of shareholder-employee repealed and shareholder discharged, held: bylaw amendment valid; in any event, no specific performance). An employment agreement might be invalid for lack of authority of officer or other person negotiating it. Gumpert v. Bon Ami Co., 251 F.2d 735 (2d Cir.1958) (2–1); Annot., 28 A.L.R.2d 929 (1953). Or for noncompliance with the statute of frauds requiring agreements not to be performed within one year to be in writing. McLaughlin v. Ford Motor Co., 269 F.2d 120 (6th Cir.1959). But see White Lighting Co. v. Wolfson, 68 Cal.2d 347, 66 Cal.Rptr. 697, 438 P.2d 345 (1968) (enforcing oral employment for unspecified term for base salary plus percentage of annual profits as agreement terminable at will and therefore performable within one year). See also Heyler, "Corporate Employment Contracts", in Advising California Business Enterprises 669–685 (1958); Meck, "Employment of Corporate Executives by Majority Stockholders", 47 Yale L.J. 1079 (1938).

8. See note 7 supra. However, if the officer is an agent coupled with an interest, his agency might be irrevocable. See Lane Mortgage Co. v. Crenshaw, 93 Cal.App. 411, 269 P. 672 (1928); Hunt v. Rousmanier's Adm'rs, 21 U.S. (8 Wheat.) 174, 5 L.Ed. 589 (1823). Specific performance of a contract of employment is usually denied for lack of mutuality

removal in breach of contract usually subjects the corporation to damages.[9]

The directors, however, are not liable for inducing breach of the corporation's contract if they exercise such removal power according to their business judgment.[10]

Where there is a valid provision in a shareholder or director agreement to keep certain persons as officers, the directors who are parties to such agreement are usually bound to such commitment so long as such officers are faithful, efficient, and competent in the performance of their duties.[11]

Statutes might also empower the state to suspend or remove a corporate officer for cause,[12] or enable the shareholders to remove officers.[13]

In most jurisdictions, shareholders have no power to remove officers,[14] except indi-

of remedy. If the officer's employment contract has an arbitration clause per the American Arbitration Association form (whose rules let arbitrator "grant any remedy or relief . . . including . . . specific performance of a contract"), the arbitrator may compel reinstatement in office. Matter of Staklinski (Pyramid Electric Co.), 6 N.Y. 2d 159, 188 N.Y.S.2d 541, 160 N.E.2d 78 (1959) (3–1–3) (11-year employment contract); Chayes, "Madame Wagner and the Close Corporation", 73 Harv. L.Rev. 1532 (1960). Union protection or labor legislation might also protect the employee-officer.

9. E. g., ABA–ALI Model Bus.Corp.Act § 45 (removal to be without prejudice to contract rights, if any, of person so removed; election or appointment not of itself to create contract rights); United Producers & Consumers Co-op v. Held, 225 F.2d 615 (9th Cir.1955); In re Paramount Publix Corp., 90 F.2d 441, 111 A.L.R. 889 (2d Cir.1937); Dennis v. Thermoid Co., 128 N.J.L. 303, 25 A.2d 886 (1942); Hansen v. Columbia Breweries, Inc., 12 Wash.2d 554, 122 P.2d 489 (1942). See also Nelson v. Pioneer Specialties, Inc., 325 S.W.2d 924 (Tex.Civ.App.1959) (action on former president's two-year employment contract, to extent of damages for period between removal and end of first year, sustained despite by-law limitation of officers' terms to one year). Whitley v. Pacific Industries, Inc., 28 A.D.2d 147, 283 N.Y.S.2d 525 (1st Dep't 1967) (holding minutes, not formally approved until after discharge, supported removal of president with or without cause); Goldberg v. Valve Corp. of America, 89 Ill.App.2d 383, 233 N.E.2d 85 (1967) (question of wrongfulness of removal held properly triable in action for damages for breach of contract not in declaratory judgment action); DeAngeles v. Roos Bros., 244 Cal.App.2d 434, 52 Cal.Rptr. 783 (1966) (removal for cause held not justified); Freeman v. King Pontiac Co., 236 S.C. 335, 114 S.E.2d 478 (1960) (upholding removal for cause). See also Cox v. Berry, 19 Utah 2d 352, 431 P.2d 575 (1967) (sustaining directors' agreement, made to induce his resignation, to indemnify president against liability on his personal note for property later turned over by him to corporation). See Note, "Removal Without Cause of Corporate Executives Under Agreement", 109 U.Pa.L.Rev. 224 (1960).

10. Wrigley v. Nottingham, 111 Ga.App. 404, 141 S. E.2d 859 (1965) (holding dominant shareholder-president-director liable for persuading board of directors to discharge officer, but refusing to hold director liable in absence of malice), rev'd sub nom. Nottingham v. Wrigley, 221 Ga. 386, 144 S.E.2d 749 (1965), conformed to 112 Ga.App. 622, 145 S.E.2d 829 (1966) (finding that director acted with malice); Terry v. Zachary, 272 S.W.2d 157 (Tex.Civ.App. 1954); Lager v. Su Su Fashions, Inc., 10 A.D.2d

832, 199 N.Y.S.2d 169 (1st Dep't 1960); Ehrlich v. Alper, 145 N.Y.S.2d 252 (Sup.Ct.1955), aff'd mem., 1 A.D.2d 875, 149 N.Y.S.2d 562 (1st Dep't 1956). However, the officer is personally liable to the third person when he induces the corporation to breach its contract to benefit himself or to the detriment of the corporation. Rendich v. Preferred Mutual Fire Ins. Co., 274 App.Div. 800, 79 N.Y.S.2d 501 (2d Dep't 1948), appeal and reargument denied 274 App.Div. 892, 83 N.Y.S.2d 234 (2d Dep't 1948). Cf. Burr v. American Nat'l Theatre & Academy, 103 N.Y.S.2d 589 (Sup.Ct.1951), aff'd mem., 278 App.Div. 908, 105 N.Y.S.2d 901 (1st Dep't 1951) (officer acting for own personal interest held not liable because not adverse to interests of corporation). The officer might also be liable for inducing breach of contract to the third person when accompanied by an independent tort. Carpenter v. Williams, 41 Ga.App. 685, 154 S.E. 298 (1930); see also Dickerson v. Dickerson, 197 La. 907, 2 So.2d 643 (1941); Avins, "Liability for Inducing a Corporation to Breach Its Contract", 43 Cornell L.Q. 55 (1957).

11. See sections 198, 213 supra. Matter of Burkin (Katz), 1 N.Y.2d 570, 154 N.Y.S.2d 898, 136 N.E.2d 862, 64 A.L.R.2d 638 (1956); Fells v. Katz, 256 N.Y. 67, 175 N.E. 516 (1931); Matter of Katz (Fulton-Washington Corp.), 2 Misc.2d 325, 143 N.Y.S.2d 282 (Sup.Ct.1955), aff'd mem., 1 A.D.2d 657, 147 N.Y.S.2d 10 (1st Dep't 1955). Quaere, as to whether an agreement to keep a person in office will be specifically enforced. Chayes, "Madame Wagner and the Close Corporation", 73 Harv.L.Rev. 1532 (1960). See note 8, supra. See note 8 supra.

12. E. g., Michigan, Minnesota, New York, Tennessee, Wisconsin.

13. See McKinney's N.Y.Bus.Corp.Law, § 716 (removal by shareholders of officers elected by them; action to remove officer for cause may be brought by attorney general or by holders of 10 percent of outstanding shares, whether or not entitled to vote; court may bar from reelection or reappointment any officer so removed for period fixed by court).

14. McKinney's N.Y.Bus.Corp.Law, § 716(a) (officers elected by shareholders removable, with or without cause, only by vote of shareholders).

rectly where the officer in question must be a director and is removed as a director by the shareholders.[15]

In rare instances, courts have in effect removed corporate officers by enjoining them from continuing as officers [16] or ordering those with power to remove such officers to exercise such power.[17]

DE FACTO OFFICERS

222. A person, although not a de jure officer, who (a) exercises some corporate office (b) under some color of title is often treated as a de facto officer, thus giving legal effect to such person's official acts and precluding collateral, but not direct, attack on his officer status.

A person, although not a *de jure* officer, who (a) exercises some corporate office (b) under some color of title is often treated as a *de facto* officer,[1] thus giving legal effect to such person's official acts and precluding collateral attack on his officer status. Direct attack by *quo warranto* or possibly injunction usually is countenanced.[2]

This *de facto* doctrine also applies to directors,[3] but is to be distinguished from the doctrine of the same name applicable in some cases of defective incorporation.[4]

15. See section 220, nn. 6–8 supra.

16. See United States v. Grinnell Corp., 384 U.S. 563, 579, 86 S.Ct. 1698, 1708, 16 L.Ed.2d 778, 791 (1966).

17. Jacksonville Terminal Co. v. Florida East Coast Ry., 363 F.2d 216 (5th Cir. 1966), cert. denied 385 U.S. 950, 87 S.Ct. 321, 17 L.Ed.2d 227 (1966).

[§ 222]

1. Georgia Casualty & Surety Co. v. Seaboard Surety Co., 210 F.Supp. 644 (N.D.Ga.1962), aff'd per curiam 327 F.2d 666 (5th Cir.1964) (director usurping power of officer held not de facto officer and not within insurance policy covering loss through fraudulent act of "employee"). See also Permagon Press, Inc. v. Ross, —— Misc.2d ——, 306 N.Y.S.2d 103 (Sup.Ct.1969).

2. See Schepp v. Evansville Television, Inc., 236 Ind. 472, 141 N.E.2d 437 (1957).

3. See section 206 supra.

4. See section 140 supra.

OFFICERS' MANAGEMENT FUNCTIONS —IN GENERAL

223. Officers have such management functions as are delegated to them by the board of directors, pursuant to statute, the articles of incorporation, bylaws, and resolutions of the board. Apart from such express delegation, officers have implied authority arising out of their office.

Officers have such management functions as are delegated to them by the board of directors pursuant to statute, the articles of incorporation, the bylaws, and resolutions of the board. Usually, the bylaws and board resolutions are the most relevant in this respect. Apart from such express delegation, officers have implied authority arising out of their office. To support broad delegation of authority of officers, or when some conflicting interest of directors-officers is involved, shareholder ratification is important.[1]

Mention has already been made of the fact that in many larger corporations, the board does little more than ratify, or "rubber-stamp", the actions and even policy decisions of the officers.[2]

OFFICERS' ACTUAL AUTHORITY— EXPRESS

224. The authority of corporate officers may be (a) actual (express or implied), (b) apparent, or (c) derived from ratification of an act beyond the officer's power. Express authority stems from statute, the articles of incorporation, or, as is more usually the case, the bylaws or resolutions of the board of directors.

The authority of corporate officers,[1] like that of agents generally, may be (a) actual

[§ 223]

1. See section 194 supra and section 238 infra.

2. See section 207, n. 18 supra.

[§ 224]

1. The authority of corporate officers is discussed in this and the next succeeding sections on the assumption that such authority is within the purposes (or objects) and powers of the corporation, that is, intra vires and not ultra vires. See section 184 supra.

(express or implied[2]), or (b) apparent,[3] or (c) derived from ratification of an act beyond the officer's power.[4]

Actual authority may be express or implied. Where there is actual authority, holding out by the corporation or reasonableness of reliance by a third party is immaterial. The emphasis is on the relationship between the corporation and its officer. —the manifestation of consent by the corporation to the officer that he should act on its behalf and subject to its control.

Express authority stems from statute,[5] the articles of incorporation,[6] or, as is more usually the case, the bylaws,[7] or resolutions of the board of directors.[8]

For example, the bylaws might enumerate the various officers and define their respective authority. In this connection, the president is usually named as the chief executive officer, but sometimes the chairman of the board is.

2. See section 225 infra.

3. See section 226 infra.

4. See section 227 infra.

5. Statutory provisions are rare. See, e. g., Del. Gen.Corp.Law, § 142(a) (1967) (secretary to record all proceedings of meetings of shareholders and directors in book to be kept for that purpose, and perform such other duties as shall be assigned to him). Most statutes merely provide that the officers shall have such authority as may be provided in the bylaws or as may be determined by resolution of the board of directors not inconsistent with the bylaws. E. g., ABA–ALI Model Bus.Corp.Act § 44.

6. Provisions in the articles of incorporation are rare. See W. Grange & T. Woodbury, Corporation Law: Operating Procedures for Officers and Directors 315 (2d ed. 1964).

7. E. g., ABA–ALI Model Bus.Corp.Act § 44. See, e. g., By-Laws, art. IV, §§ 5–9, Official Forms for Use Under the Model Business Corporation Act, Form No. 47 (ALI rev. 1953). See DePova v. Camden Forge Co., 254 F.2d 248 (3d Cir. 1958), cert. denied 358 U.S. 816, 79 S.Ct. 26, 3 L.Ed.2d 59 (1958).

8. E. g., ABA–ALI Model Bus.Corp.Act § 44 (as may be determined by resolution of the board of directors not inconsistent with the bylaws).

OFFICERS' ACTUAL AUTHORITY— IMPLIED

225. Actual authority other than express authority is called "implied", "presumptive", or "inherent" authority, or authority "by virtue of office".

The president traditionally presides at board of directors and shareholder meetings. The older cases tended to find that he had no implied authority by virtue of his office to bind the corporation. The more modern cases tend to recognize the authority of the president by virtue of his office to act for the corporation, at least with respect to its ordinary business transactions. Where the president is in fact general manager, he has the implied authority inhering in the general manager.

Vice-presidents have no authority by virtue of their office to bind the corporation, but act in the place of the president in case of the latter's absence, disability, resignation, or death.

The treasurer in most jurisdictions has no authority by virtue of his office to bind the corporation. As the corporation's fiscal officer in charge of its treasury, he receives and keeps the corporate moneys and disburses corporate funds as authorized.

The secretary is without authority by virtue of his office to bind the corporation. The secretary usually attends and keeps the minutes of corporate meetings, gives notices, certifies corporate records, and keeps and attests the corporate seal.

The general manager has implied authority to do any act in behalf of the corporation, at least with respect to its ordinary business transactions. No formal appointment is required; any person allowed by the corporation to act as general manager, whether the president or some other officer or not, has such authority.

The cashier, as general agent of a banking corporation, has rather broad implied powers in dealing with customers with respect to ordinary banking business.

So far as instituting corporate litigation or arbitration in the corporate name is concerned, the president or any other officer or person acting as general manager usually has implied authority to do so, but such implied authority, like other implied authority, can be negatived by provisions in the articles of incorporation or bylaws or by resolution of the board of directors.

Implied authority, as the term will be used in this discussion, means actual authority other than express authority. Implied authority may be said to be "presumptive", "inherent", or exist "by virtue of office",[1] or it might result from general custom or the practice of the particular corporation (with the acquiescence of directors or shareholders).

By virtue of office, some officers enjoy some implied authority.[2]

President

Traditionally, the president was one of several directors, whose principal function was to preside at board of directors and shareholder meetings, and who had no authority by virtue of his office to bind the corporation.[3]

The growing tendency of the modern cases is to recognize the authority of the president to act by virtue of his office for the corporation, at least in connection with its ordinary business transactions.[4]

1. See, e. g., Bankers' Trust Co. v. International Ry., 207 App.Div. 579, 587, 202 N.Y.S. 561, 568 (1st Dep't 1924) ("implied"), aff'd mem., 239 N.Y. 619, 147 N.E. 220 (1924); Comment, "Inherent Power as a Basis of a Corporate Officer's Authority to Contract", 57 Colum.L.Rev. 868 (1957); Comment, "Inherent Powers of Corporate Officers: Need for a Statutory Definition", 61 Harv.L.Rev. 867 (1948); Martin v. Webb, 110 U.S. 7, 14, 3 S.Ct. 428, 532, 28 L.Ed. 49, 52 (1884) ("by virtue of office").

2. Annot., 161 A.L.R. 1443 (1946), 28 A.L.R.2d 929 (1953), 34 A.L.R.2d 290 (1954), 50 A.L.R.2d 447 (1956), 62 A.L.R.2d 712 (1958).

3. Pattelena v. Segel, 346 Mass. 726, 195 N.E.2d 900 (1964); Hale-Georgia Minerals Corp. v. Hale, 83 Ga.App. 561, 63 S.W.2d 920 (1951); Black v. Harrison Home Co., 155 Ala. 121, 99 P. 494 (1909); Myers, "The Inherent Powers of Corporation Presidents", 23 Wash.U.L.Q. 117 (1937); Note, "Authority of a Corporation President to Bind the Corporation by Virtue of His Office", 50 Yale L.J. 348 (1940).

4. Parks v. Midland Ford Tractor Co., 416 S.W.2d 22 (Mo.App.1967); Meyer v. Glenmoor Homes, Inc., 246 Cal.App.2d 242, 54 Cal.Rptr. 786 (1966), reh. denied 246 Cal.App.2d 273, 55 Cal.Rptr. 502 (1967); Kolodney v. Kolodney Bros., 21 Conn.Supp. 308, 154 A.2d

In effect, when the president acts as general manager, he enjoys the implied authori-

531 (1959); Lee v. Jenkins Bros., 156 F.Supp. 858 (D.Conn.1957); Jaffe v. Chicago Warehouse Lumber Co., 4 Ill.App.2d 514, 124 N.E.2d 618 (1954); Jeppi v. Brockman Holding Co., 191 P.2d 534 (Cal.Dist.Ct. 1948), rev'd 34 Cal.2d 11, 206 P.2d 847, 9 A.L.R.2d 1297 (1949) (4–3); Johnson v. Sengstacke, 334 Ill. App. 620, 79 N.E.2d 761 (1948); Beck v. Edwards & Lewis, 141 N.J.Eq. 326, 57 A.2d 459 (1948); Mosell Realty Corp. v. Schofield, 183 Va. 782, 33 S.E.2d 775, 159 A.L.R. 786 (1945); Joseph Greenspan's Sons Iron & Steel Co. v. Pecos Valley Gas Co., 34 Del. 567, 156 A. 350 (Super.Ct.1931); George E. Lloyd & Co. v. Matthews, 223 Ill. 477, 79 N.E. 172 (1906); R. Stevens, Handbook on the Law of Private Corporations 768–769 (2d ed. 1949). The cases on implied authority "fall generally into three groups: (a) those stating the president has no more power by virtue of his office than any other director; (b) those expressing the view that a corporation president has, by virtue of his office, the power to make any contract for the corporation, so long as it concerns that corporation's ordinary or everyday course of business; and (c) those holding that a president has the power to make any contract for the corporation which the board of directors could authorize or ratify" [English rule—see Royal British Bank v. Turquand, 5 El. & Bl. 248, 119 Eng.Rep. 474 (Q.B. 1855)]. Comment, "Inherent Power as a Basis of a Corporate Officer's Authority to Contract", 57 Colum.L.Rev. 868, 869 (1957). Earlier New York cases stated that the president has prima facie authority to make any contract which the board of directors could have authorized or ratified, especially where the president was also acting as general manager. Twyeffort v. Unexcelled Mfg. Co., 263 N.Y. 6, 188 N.E. 138 (1933); Patterson v. Robinson, 116 N.Y. 193, 22 N.E. 372 (1889); cf. Hastings v. Brooklyn Life Ins. Co., 138 N.Y. 473, 34 N.E. 289 (1893) (secretary acting as general agent). Accord, Sun Printing & Publishing Ass'n v. Moore, 183 U.S. 642, 22 S.Ct. 240, 46 L.Ed. 366 (1902). Subsequent New York cases have tended to follow the "ordinary course of business" rule. Liebermann v. Princeway Realty Corp., 13 N.Y.2d 999, 245 N.Y.S.2d 390, 195 N.E.2d 57 (1963); Pettit v. Doeskin Products, Inc., 270 F.2d 95 (2d Cir. 1959), reh. denied 270 F.2d 699 (2d Cir. 1959), cert. denied 362 U.S. 910, 80 S.Ct. 660, 4 L.Ed.2d 618 (1960); Schwartz v. United Merchant & Manufacturers, Inc., 72 F.2d 256 (2d Cir. 1934); O'Connor v. Bankers Trust Co., 159 Misc. 920, 946, 289 N.Y.S. 252, 283 (Sup.Ct.1936), aff'd mem., 253 App.Div. 714, 1 N.Y.S.2d 641 (1st Dep't 1937), aff'd mem., 278 N.Y. 649, 16 N.E.2d 302 (1938). But see Best-Site Associates v. Ventrice, 245 App.Div. 758, 280 N.Y.S. 583 (2d Dep't 1935) (citing Hastings v. Brooklyn Life Ins. Co., supra); cf. Ralph Klonick Corp. v. Berkshire Life Ins. Co., 277 App.Div. 1158, 101 N.Y.S.2d 633 (4th Dep't 1950). See Annot., 53 A.L.R.2d 1421 (1957). Implied authority can be inferred from express authority. Aimonetto v. Rapid Gas, Inc., 80 S.D. 453, 126 N.W.2d 116 (1964) (authority to draw checks to pay for pipe inferred from express authority to purchase pipe). As to authority and power of president to execute commercial pa-

ty traditionally inhering in the general manager.[5]

Vice-President

There is often more than one vice-president. Some corporations have over a hundred, classified into executive vice-presidents, senior vice-presidents, administrative vice-presidents, vice-presidents, division vice-presidents, and the like.[6]

Vice-presidents have no authority by virtue of their office.[7]

The vice-president acts *vice* (in the place of) the president. In the event of the absence, disability, resignation, or death of the president, the appropriate vice-president might exercise whatever authority the president enjoyed.[8]

Succession to the presidency usually depends upon the bylaws or resolution of the board of directors,[9] and the vice-president's eligibility for the office of president.[10]

---

per, see Annot., 96 A.L.R.2d 549 (1964). Wishnow v. Kingsway Estates, Inc., 26 A.D.2d 61, 270 N.Y.S.2d 834 (1st Dep't 1966) (holding that president's alleged lack of authority to sell realty did not bar finding that president had authority to hire brokers to find purchaser). In Yucca Mining & Petrol. Co. v. Howard C. Phillips Oil Co., 69 N.M. 281, 365 P.2d 925 (1961), rescission of a contract was not granted to a corporation which claimed, inter alia, that its president, a member of the board of directors, did not have the authority to modify an oil well drilling contract not in the usual course of business. The court stated that ordinarily only the board of directors can authorize acts out of the usual course of business, but that under the circumstances, where the disputed modified contract was made for the benefit of the corporation, it could not claim lack of authority when it turned out that no oil was struck and there was no benefit. The court stated that "with the swift pace of modern business life, it is impossible to expect action by the directors in every transaction, even though it may be termed 'unusual' ", without determining under which of the various agency theories of "apparent authority," "implied authority," "waiver," or "estoppel," or ratification or acquiescence, the result was reached. See also Doody v. John Sexton & Co., 411 F.2d 1119 (1st Cir. 1969). Bentall v. Koening Brothers, Inc., 140 Mont. 339, 372 P.2d 91 (1962), held that the president of a corporation and manager of its business, where the corporation was in immediate need of money to cover current operating expenses, had implied authority to execute a corporate note. In close corporations, implied authority is often found in officers in sufficiently controlling positions to create the necessary authority. Mutual Life Ins. Co. of New York v. Mooreman, 366 F.2d 686 (9th Cir. 1966), cert. denied 386 U.S. 959, 87 S.Ct. 1030, 18 L.Ed.2d 109 (1967); Air Technical Development Co. v. Arizona Bank, 101 Ariz. 70, 416 P.2d 183 (1966). See also Rednor & Kline, Inc. v. Department of Highways, 43 Pa. 119, 196 A.2d 355 (1964) (authority of president of close corporation to sign corporation's formal demand for damages in condemnation proceedings). As to president's power to confess judgment, compare Craven v. Gazza, 36 Misc.2d 493, 232 N.Y.S.2d 896 (Sup.Ct.1962), modified 19 A.D.2d 646, 241 N.Y.S.2d 897 (2d Dep't 1963), motion granted 14 N.Y.2d 542, 248 N.Y.S.2d 640, 198 N.E.2d 31 (1964), with Prestressed Structures, Inc. v. Bargain City, U.S.A., Inc., 413 Pa. 262, 196 A.2d 338 (1964); Annot., 92 A.L.R.2d 952 (1963). Principles of promissory estoppel might also be applied. Hessler, Inc. v. Farrell, —— Del.Ch. ——, 226 A.2d 708 (Sup.Ct.1967). Whatever authority the president had ends upon the appointment of a receiver for the corporation. Malone v. Voges Mfg. Co., 271 F.2d 230 (2d Cir. 1959). See also National Surety Corp. v. Inland Properties, Inc., 416 F.2d 457 (8th Cir. 1969).

5. Arkansas Valley Feed Mills, Inc. v. Fox De Luxe Foods, Inc., 171 F.Supp. 145 (W.D.Ark.1959); Fletcher Oil Co. v. Bay City, 346 Mich. 411, 78 N.

W.2d 205 (1956); Petition of Mulco Products, Inc., 50 Del. 28, 123 A.2d 95 (Super.Ct.1956); Memorial Hospital Ass'n v. Pacific Grape Products Co., 277 P.2d 878 (Cal.App.1954), aff'd 45 Cal.2d 634, 290 P. 2d 481, 50 A.L.R.2d 634 (1955): Hobbs v. Homes, Inc., 246 Iowa 1195, 71 N.W.2d 592 (1955); Rothberg v. Manhattan Coil Co., 84 Ga.App. 528, 66 S.E. 2d 390 (1951); Lewin v. Proehl, 211 Minn. 256, 300 N.W. 814 (1941). See discussion of General Manager, infra.

6. The Executive Life 149–162 (1956).

7. Nelson v. Central Metropolitan Bank, 185 Minn. 449, 241 N.W. 585 (1932). But see Milwaukee Trust Co. v. Van Valkenburgh, 132 Wis. 638, 112 N.W. 1083 (1907). Chesapeake & Potomac Telephone Co. of Baltimore City v. Murray, 198 Md. 526, 84 A.2d 870 (1951) (holding vice-president had no implied authority to bind corporation by contract for lifetime employment to assistant fired after 25 years of service).

8. Smith v. Smith, 62 Ill. 493 (1872); Aaronson v. David Meyer Brewing Co., 26 Misc. 655, 56 N.Y.S. 387 (N.Y.C.City Ct.1899), rev'd 29 Misc. 289, 60 N.Y. S. 523 (App.T.1899). See also Stammelman v. Interstate Co., 111 N.J.L. 122, 166 A. 724 (1933), rev'd 112 N.J.L. 342, 170 A. 595 (1934).

9. In recent years, corporations, aware of the danger of nuclear warfare, have been adopting bylaws that surviving directors may succeed to the presidency in order of seniority and surviving directors, with less than a quorum, may fill vacancies on the board.

10. See section 220 supra.

A vice-president who acts as general manager or manager of the business, or some phase thereof, might have the implied authority of a general manager or manager.[11]

Treasurer

In most jurisdictions, the treasurer [12] has no authority by virtue of his office to bind the corporation.[13]

As the fiscal officer of the corporation, however, he is in charge of the corporate treasury, receiving and keeping the moneys of the corporation and disbursing corporate funds as authorized.[14]

In Massachusetts, the treasurer of a manufacturing or trading corporation is clothed by virtue of his office with authority to accept, endorse, issue, and negotiate notes and bills of exchange in behalf of the corporation.[15]

Secretary

The secretary [16] is without authority by virtue of his office to bind the corporation.[17]

The secretary is a ministerial officer, who usually attends meetings of shareholders, the board of directors, and any committees thereof, and keeps the minutes of such meetings, gives notices, prepares any necessary certified copies of corporate records, and keeps and attests the corporate seal.[18]

General Manager

The general manager has implied authority to make any contract or to do any other act appropriate in the ordinary business of the corporation.[19]

11. Gillian v. Consolidated Foods Corp., 424 Pa. 407, 227 A.2d 858 (1967). See discussion of General Manager, infra.

12. Fidelity Bankers Trust Co. v. Chapman Drug Co., 366 S.W.2d 528 (Tenn.Ct.App.1963); Boston & Maine R. R. v. Howard Hardware Co., 123 Vt. 203, 186 A.2d 184 (1962); L. Doris, Corporate Treasurer's and Controller's Handbook (1956). The treasurer's role has increased immeasurably in prestige during recent years, sometimes being ranked as financial vice-presidents just below the president in authority. Financial men head many large corporations. 81 Time, No. 10, 85 (Mar. 8, 1963). For allocation of responsibilities between treasurer and comptroller, see P–H Corp. Forms ¶ 39, 112(e).

13. Slavin v. Passaic Nat'l Bank & Trust Co., 114 N. J.L. 341, 176 A. 339 (1935); Hoberg v. Sofranscy, 248 N.Y. 141, 161 N.E. 449 (1928); Millward-Cliff Cracker Co.'s Estate, 161 Pa. 157, 28 A. 1072 (1894); Matter of Spinner v. Graulich, Inc., 159 N.Y.L.J. No. 54, 17 (Sup.Ct.1968); American Can Co. v. Penn-Kraut, Inc., 158 N.Y.S.2d 236 (Sup.Ct.1956). Cf. Boston & Maine R. R. v. Howard Hardware Co., 123 Vt. 203, 186 A.2d 184 (1962) (treasurer's authority to execute lease confirmed and ratified).

14. H. Ballantine, Ballantine on Corporations § 55 (rev. ed. 1946).

15. Merchants' Nat'l Bank v. Citizens' Gas Light Co., 159 Mass. 505, 34 N.E. 1083 (1893); Jewett v. West Somerville Co-operative Bank, 173 Mass. 54, 52 N.E. 1085 (1899); New Hampshire Nat'l Bank v. Garage & Factory Equipment Co., 267 Mass. 483, 166 N.E. 840 (1929). But cf. Kagan v. Levenson, 334 Mass. 100, 134 N.E.2d 415 (1956) (no implied authority to execute chattel mortgage).

16. B. Miller, Manual and Guide for the Corporate Secretary (1969) (3 vols.); The Corporate Secretary's Handbook (Prentice-Hall, Inc. 1964); L. Doris & E. Friedman, Corporate Secretary's Encyclopedia (1958); L. Doris, E. Friedman & H. Spellman, Corporate Secretary's Manual and Guide (rev. ed. 1949); T. Bolton, Duties of a Company Secretary (3d ed. 1967) (English).

17. H. Ballantine, Ballantine on Corporations § 54 (rev. ed. 1946).

18. Del.Gen.Corp.Law, § 142(a) (1967) (secretary to record all proceedings of meetings of shareholders and directors in book to be kept for that purpose); Matter of Drive-In Development Corp., 371 F.2d 215 (7th Cir. 1966) (corporation held bound by secretary's certified resolution falsely supporting vice-president's authority). For discussion of secretary's duties in keeping minutes, see Field v. Oberwortmann, 16 Ill.App.2d 376, 148 N.E.2d 600 (1958), cert. denied 358 U.S. 833, 79 S.Ct. 55, 3 L.Ed.2d 71 (1958); Choka, "Six Check Lists for the Corporate Secretary", 5 Prac.Law. 85 (Jan.1959).

19. 1 Restatement, Second, Agency § 73 (1958); Gillian v. Consolidated Foods Corp., 424 Pa. 407, 227 A. 2d 858 (1967) (vice-president-general manager); Binkowski v. Tech Plaza, Inc., 369 Mich. 333, 119 N.W. 2d 589 (1963); R. H. Kyle Furniture Co. v. Russell Dry Goods Co., 340 S.W.2d 220, 85 A.L.R.2d 428 (Ky. Ct.App.1960) (general manager of store); Local Joint Executive Board v. Nationwide, 229 F.Supp. 413 (D.Mo.1964) (holding that general manager with authority to hire employees could bind corporation to union contract). Extraordinary matters, such as lifetime contracts, are usually beyond the implied authority of the general manager. Porshin v. Snider, 349 Mass. 653, 212 N.E.2d 216 (1965); Mannion v. Campbell Soup Co., 243 Cal.App.2d 317, 52 Cal. Rptr. 246 (1966) (personal manager); Freeman v. River Farms Co., 5 Cal.2d 431, 55 P.2d 199 (1936); Matson v. Alley, 141 Ill. 284, 31 N.E. 419 (1892); Rathbun v. Snow, 123 N.Y. 343, 25 N.E. 379 (1890). Some cases suggest that the general manager can

No formal appointment is necessary; the fact that a person is permitted to act as general manager is sufficient to clothe him with such authority. Such person may hold a different office—usually but not necessarily president—but such formal designation does not limit his authority as general manager.[20]

These rules account, at least to some extent, for the more modern cases broadening the implied authority of presidents who act as chief executive officers [21] and the occasional case recognizing unusual implied authority in other officers.[22]

Cashier

The cashier, as a general agent of a banking corporation, has rather broad implied powers in dealing with customers with respect to ordinary banking business.[23]

Implied Authority of Corporate Officers to Institute Litigation or Arbitration in Name of Corporation

The implied authority of corporate officers to institute litigation or arbitration in the name of the corporation has been the subject of four noteworthy opinions of the New York Court of Appeals, more signifi-

cant for their reasoning than for their actual rather limited holdings.

The first of the Court of Appeals cases was Sterling Industries, Inc. v. Ball Bearing Pen Corp.[24] Sterling Industries, Inc. was formed by Ball Bearing Pen Corp. and a group of individuals. The articles of incorporation contained an interested-director provision to the effect that no corporate contract or other transaction should be invalidated because any director was personally interested therein or was a director or officer of any other corporation having any interest therein. The bylaws contained no reference to any authority on the part of the president or any other officer to institute litigation.[25] The Class A shares were issued to the group of individuals, who elected two directors; the Class B shares to two representatives of the pen company who were elected the other two directors. One of the Class A directors was elected president. The corporation and the pen company then made an oral contract which the pen company failed to perform. At a special meeting of the board of directors called to consider an action by the corporation against the pen company for breach of the contract, the Class A directors voted in favor of the action; the Class B directors (the pen company representatives) opposed it. The president, a Class A director, stated that in view of the 2–2 tie vote, the motion authorizing the action had failed to be carried. Without further board action, the president caused an action to be brought by the corporation against the pen company for breach of contract.[26] The complaint contained no allega-

---

do anything which the board of directors can authorize or ratify, but this is subject to qualifications. R. Stevens, Handbook on the Law of Private Corporations 769 (2d ed. 1949). See note 4 supra.

20. Lydia E. Pinkham Medicine Co. v. Gove, 298 Mass. 53, 9 N.E.2d 573 (1937); Ceeder v. H. M. Loud & Sons Lumber Co., 86 Mich. 541, 49 N.W. 575 (1891); Annot., 5 A.L.R. 1488 (1920).

21. R. Stevens, Handbook on the Law of Private Corporations 769 (2d ed. 1949). See note 4 supra.

22. See Gillian v. Consolidated Foods Corp., 424 Pa. 407, 227 A.2d 858 (1967) (vice-president); Rothman & Schneider, Inc. v. Beckerman, 2 N.Y.2d 493, 161 N.Y.S.2d 118, 141 N.E.2d 610 (1957) (secretary-treasurer); Wallach v. Hadley Co., 339 Mass. 699, 122 N.E.2d 355 (1955) (treasurer); Hastings v. Brooklyn Life Ins. Co., 138 N.Y. 473, 34 N.E. 289 (1893) (secretary); cf. Jersey Carpenters, Inc. v. Schmittmeyer, 6 A.D.2d 700, 174 N.Y.S.2d 97 (2d Dep't 1958); Grossman v. Redi-Food Co., 2 A.D.2d 670, 152 N.Y.S.2d 624 (1st Dep't 1956) (vice-president).

23. R. Stevens, Handbook on the Law of Private Corporations 770 (2d ed. 1949); H. Ballantine, Ballantine on Corporations 146 (rev. ed. 1946).

24. 298 N.Y. 483, 84 N.E.2d 790, 10 A.L.R.2d 694 (1949).

25. The bylaws also required a majority note of the entire board for any board of directors action. Cf. Benintendi v. Kenton Hotel, Inc., 294 N.Y. 112, 60 N.E.2d 829, 159 A.L.R. 280 (1945).

26. 75 N.Y.S.2d 475 (Sup.Ct.1947), aff'd 273 App.Div. 460, 77 N.Y.S.2d 691 (1st Dep't 1948), appeal granted, 273 App.Div. 1007, 79 N.Y.S.2d 880 (1st Dep't 1948). But see Conlee Construction Co. v. Cay Construction Co., 221 So.2d 792 (Fla.Dist.Ct.App.1969)

tion that the corporation's existence was threatened or that its business could not continue normally.

The Court of Appeals unanimously held [27] that a president of a corporation may not institute a corporate action under the alleged circumstances after he has sought permission from the board of directors and has been refused.[28] The court stated that the president had no express authority to commence corporate litigation; that the two representatives of the pen company on the board were allowed to vote and their votes were presumptively proper in view of the interested-director provision of the articles of incorporation; [29] that the submission and failure of the motion at the special board meeting was a negation of any implied authority to sue; [30] that, therefore, the president had no actual authority to sue; that the question of apparent authority to sue was irrelevant since there was no reliance by third persons; that there was no corporate emergency threatening immediate injury to the corporation; and that the proper remedy was a shareholder derivative action which would not saddle the corporation with the expense of probably unsuccessful litigation.[31]

The second Court of Appeals case was Rothman & Schneider, Inc. v. Beckerman.[32]

Rothman and Schneider organized the plaintiff corporation. Each, with his respective wife, owned 50 percent of the corporate shares, and all four were directors. Rothman was president; Schneider was secretary-treasurer. In the practical operations of the corporation, no board of directors meetings were held and either one, as president or as secretary, signed corporate papers indiscriminately, verifying complaints or answers in litigation without any question ever having been raised. The corporation employed Beckerman, the son-in-law of Rothman, as a salesman. Thereafter, Rothman and Schneider agreed to dissolve the corporation, with Schneider in charge of the liquidation.[33] Rothman, as a practical matter, retired from the business. Thereupon, Schneider hired an attorney to defend two actions against the corporation. The corporation was not formally dissolved. At the instance of Schneider, the corporation sued Beckerman for conversion of corporate assets. Asserting that the institution of a corporate action required the consent of the majority of the board and that the Rothmans opposed the action, the defendants moved to dismiss.

On appeal, the Court of Appeals held that, under the circumstances of the case, the secretary-treasurer had authority to institute the action.[34] The Sterling Industries, Inc.

(holding invalid bylaw which prevented institution of action by president when directors were deadlocked).

27. Rev'g 273 App.Div. 460, 77 N.Y.S.2d 691 (1st Dep't 1948) (3–2).

28. 298 N.Y. 483, 84 N.E.2d 790, 10 A.L.R.2d 694 (1949).

29. See section 238 infra.

30. Quaere, if there were implied authority, how a tie vote could constitute a negation thereof.

31. A derivative action by the president-director qua director or qua officer would not lie in New York since the New York statutory provisions concerning such actions are limited to certain corporate claims against the corporation's own officers or directors. See section 217 supra and section 229 infra.

32. 2 N.Y.2d 493, 161 N.Y.S.2d 118, 141 N.E.2d 610 (1957). See Annot., 64 A.L.R.2d 900 (1959).

33. The parties agreed that Schneider could announce Rothman's retirement and that Schneider would operate the business formerly conducted by the corporation and receive and handle all corporate correspondence. Neither party, however, was to "settle or compromise any claim or controversy in favor of or against the corporation" unless by their mutual consent. See Image and Sound Service Corp. v. Altec Service Corp., 148 F.Supp. 237 (D.Mass.1956) (upholding corporate action instituted by director-treasurer-general managing agent on basis of general manager capacity).

34. Aff'g 1 A.D.2d 154, 148 N.Y.S.2d 396 (1st Dep't 1956), aff'g 142 N.Y.S.2d 668 (Sup.Ct.1955). See Jersey Carpenters, Inc. v. Schmittmeyer, 6 A.D.2d 700, 174 N.Y.S.2d 97 (2d Dep't 1958) (upholding vice-president's authority to cause corporation to sue on notes).

case was distinguished as involving an action against "insiders" and an actual refusal by the board of directors, when requested to act, to authorize the president to institute the action; and was characterized as not meaning that a corporation may not sue without formal authorization by the board. Cases holding that the president, absent direct prohibition by the board, has presumptive authority, in the discharge of his duties, to defend and prosecute suits in the corporate name, were cited with approval. Recognizing that in the normal course the implied authority vested in an actively functioning president would not devolve upon a secretary or treasurer, the court concluded that such officer would have such implied authority when he was the one actually managing the corporate business.

In the third case, Matter of Paloma Frocks, Inc. (Shamokin Sportswear Corp.),[35] the Court of Appeals was presented with the question: When a contract between two corporations includes a general arbitration clause, may the president of one corporation without specific authorization from his directors commence an arbitration of an alleged dispute, when half of the directors of his corporation represent the other contracting party on his corporation's board and presumably would not vote in favor of bringing the dispute before arbitrators?

The Court of Appeals refused to stay the arbitration,[36] distinguishing the Sterling Industries, Inc. case on the basis that in that case the directors had refused the president's requested permission to bring the action, and that in the instant case the president was carrying out arbitration pursuant to an arbitration clause in a contract entered into by the president in behalf of the corporation and authorized by the board of directors: [37]

"We do not suggest that the board of directors could not forbid a particular arbitration but there was no prohibition here. Even as to lawsuits, 'Where there has been no direct prohibition by the board . . . the president has presumptive authority, in the discharge of his duties, to defend and prosecute suits in the name of the corporation.' "

In the fourth case, West View Hills, Inc. v. Lizau Realty Corp.,[38] the president, director, and one-third shareholder brought an action in the name of the corporation against the two other directors and two-thirds shareholders (the majority of the board of directors) for alleged breach of fiduciary duty in improperly paying out corporate funds. The defendant directors took no official board action to deny such authority of the president plaintiff, but moved to dismiss the complaint on the ground that he had no standing to sue.

---

35. 3 N.Y.2d 572, 170 N.Y.S.2d 509, 147 N.E.2d 779 (1958). See Annot., 65 A.L.R.2d 1321 (1959).

36. Rev'g 1 A.D.2d 640, 152 N.Y.S.2d 652 (1st Dep't 1956).

37. 3 N.Y.2d at 575, 170 N.Y.S.2d at 509, 147 N.E.2d at 779 (1958). See also John W. Daniel & Co. v. Janaf, Inc., 169 F.Supp. 219 (E.D.Va.1958), aff'd per curiam 262 F.2d 958 (4th Cir. 1959).

38. 6 N.Y.2d 344, 189 N.Y.S.2d 863, 160 N.E.2d 622 (1959) (5–2). Accord, Durfee & Canning, Inc. v. Canning, 78 R.I. 385, 82 A.2d 615 (1951); Berma Management Corp. v. 140 W. 42nd Realty, Inc., 21 Misc.2d 571, 197 N.Y.S.2d 18 (Sup.Ct.1960). Compare Gottlieb v. Gross, 159 N.Y.L.J. No. 88, 17 (Sup. Ct.1968) and Celia Realty Corp. v. Tenenbaum, 158 N.Y.L.J. No. 37, 12 (Sup.Ct.1967), with Schillinger & Albert, Inc. v. Myral Hats, Inc., 55 Misc.2d 178, 284 N.Y.S.2d 780 (N.Y.C.Civ.Ct.1967). See also Glenmark, Inc. v. Carity, 38 Misc.2d 980, 239 N.Y.S.2d 440 (Sup.Ct.1963) (denying motion to substitute attorneys, in action brought by corporation by its president for breach of contract, by corporation controlled by defendants who had meanwhile acquired a majority of shares of plaintiff corporation); Goebel, "The Authority of the President over Corporate Litigation: A Study in Inherent Agency", 37 St. John's L.Rev. 29 (1962); Note, "Presidential Power to Institute Corporate Litigation", 50 Ky.L.J. 93 (1961); Comment, "Corporations: President's Power to Sue: New York View on Failure to Observe Formal Requirements of Corporate Laws: Derivative Suits", 6 N.Y.L.F. 212 (1960). See N.C. Bus.Corp.Act § 55–34(c) (1957).

Affirming a denial of the motion to dismiss, the Court of Appeals stated that the lower courts had: [39]

" . . . correctly stated the accepted principle that when there has been no direct prohibition ' . . . the president has presumptive authority in the discharge of his duties to defend and prosecute suits in the name of the corporation' [citing Rothman & Schneider, Inc. v. Beckerman and Matter of Paloma Frocks, Inc.]."

The court recognized that there was no danger of deadlock as in the two prior cases cited, but held that the same principle controlled "for it is the corporation whose interests are affected, and it was for the purpose of protecting and preserving the corporate interest that prompted the president to institute this suit." [40]

The two dissenting judges would have limited the Rothman & Schneider, Inc. v. Beckerman and Matter of Paloma Frocks, Inc. cases to deadlock situations, contending that finding implied authority in a president to bring an action in the corporate name where a majority of the board of directors "unquestionably oppose such action" divests the board of directors of the management vested in it by statute.[41]

OFFICERS' APPARENT AUTHORITY/ESTOPPEL

226. Apparent authority, sometimes called ostensible authority, exists when a corporation manifests to a third person that an "officer" or "agent" may act in its behalf, and such third person in good faith believes that such "authority" exists. In such a case, lack of actual authority, express or implied, is no defense. In certain cases, the corporation may be estopped

from denying the "authority" of the "officer" or "agent".

Apparent authority, sometimes called ostensible authority, exists when a corporation manifests to a third person (rather than to the agent in the case of actual authority) that an "officer" or "agent" may act in its behalf, and such third person in good faith believes that such "authority" exists.[1]

Apparent authority may or may not involve principles of estoppel.[2]

Where a corporation clothes an officer or agent with apparent authority, which is reasonably relied upon a good faith by a third person, the corporation and possibly such third person are estopped from denying such authority.[3]

1. 1 Restatement, Second, Agency § 8 (1958); Minnesota Amusement Co. v. Larkin, 299 F.2d 142 (8th Cir. 1962); Walker v. Pacific Mobile Homes, Inc., 68 Wash.2d 347, 413 P.2d 3 (1966); Hessler, Inc. v. Farrell, — Del.Ch. —, 226 A.2d 708 (Sup. Ct.1967); Geyer v. Walling Co., 175 Neb. 456, 122 N.W.2d 230 (1963). Cf. Mannion v. Campbell Soup Co., 243 Cal.App.2d 317, 52 Cal.Rptr. 246 (1966). For authority of managing directors under British law, see Rice, "Ostensible Authority of Company Directors", 1965 J.Bus.L. 317; Frenkel, "Ostensible Authority of Managing Directors", 5 Austl.L.Rev. 134 (1964).

2. M. Ferson, Principles of Agency §§ 141, 143–145 (1954); Cook, "Agency by Estoppel", 5 Colum.L. Rev. 35, 38 (1905).

3. Matter of Drive-In Development Corp., 371 F.2d 215 (7th Cir. 1966); Doric Co. v. Leo Jay Rosen Associates, 303 F.2d 817 (5th Cir. 1962); Georgia Broilers, Inc. v. Western Reserve Foods, Inc., 154 F.Supp. 211 (N.D.Ohio 1957); Kimball v. Kimball Bros., 143 Ohio St. 500, 56 N.E.2d 60 (1944); Winslow v. Roberts Numbering Machine Co., 17 Misc.2d 18, 183 N.Y.S.2d 817 (Sup.Ct.1959); Petition of Mulco Products, Inc., 50 Del. 28, 123 A.2d 95 (Super.Ct. 1956). Cf. Hermusic, Ltd. v. Reverse Producers Corp., 254 F.Supp. 502 (S.D.N.Y.1965); Clubb Testing Service v. Singletary, 395 S.W.2d 956 (Tex.Civ. App.1965); Colish v. Brandywine Raceway Ass'n, 49 Del. 493, 119 A.2d 887 (Super.Ct.1955). The elements necessary for estoppel are "(a) act or negligence of the principal creating an appearance of authority in the principal; (b) actual reliance by a third party upon the appearance so created; (c) reasonableness of this reliance; (d) consequent detriment to the third party". Note, 55 Mich.L.Rev. 447, 448 (1957). But cf. 1 Restatement, Second, Agency § 8 (1958) (change of position in reliance by third person element of estoppel but not of apparent authority; estoppel estops principal but not third person from denying authority). See also Naz

39. 6 N.Y.2d at 346, 189 N.Y.S.2d at 864, 160 N.E.2d at 623 (1959).

40. 6 N.Y.2d at 347, 189 N.Y.S.2d at 865, 160 N.E.2d at 624 (1959).

41. 6 N.Y.2d at 352, 189 N.Y.S.2d at 869, 160 N.E.2d at 627 (1959).

Where there is apparent authority, the absence of actual authority, express or implied, is immaterial.[4]

The relationship stressed is that between the corporation and the person transacting business with its purported agent.

RATIFICATION OF ACT BEYOND OFFICER'S POWER

227. Acts of officers beyond their powers may be ratified by the board of directors. Ratification relates back and is equivalent to a prior authority, subject to possible intervening rights of third persons. Ratification may be express, such as by resolution of the board of directors or implied, such as by acceptance of benefits of the unauthorized act with knowledge of the facts.

Acts of officers beyond their powers, which could have been previously authorized by the board of directors, may be thereafter ratified by the board of directors.[1]

Ratification relates back and is equivalent to a prior authority, subject to possible intervening rights of third persons.

Ratification may be express (e. g., resolution of board of directors) or implied. An implied ratification usually results from acceptance of benefits with knowledge of the facts.[2] When knowledge of a director or officer should be imputed to the corporation sometimes presents a nice abstract problem.[3]

Agency, Inc. v. United States Fidelity & Guaranty Co., 277 F.2d 640 (6th Cir. 1960).

4. Newton v. Johnston Organ & Piano Mfg. Co., 180 Cal. 185, 180 P. 7 (1919).

[§ 227]

1. 1 Restatement, Second, Agency §§ 84–104 (1958); H. Ballantine, Ballantine on Corporations § 60 (rev. ed. 1946).

2. See Tee Mining Corp. v. Nat'l Sales, Inc., 76 N.M. 677, 417 P.2d 810 (1966); Collins v. Collins Fruit Co., 189 So.2d 262 (Fla.Dist.Ct.App.1966); Boston & Maine R. R. v. Howard Hardware Co., 123 Vt. 203, 186 A.2d 184 (1962); McCook Livestock Exchange Co. v. State Dep't of Roads, 173 Neb. 766, 115 N.W.2d 147 (1962); Rachelle Enterprises, Inc. v. United States, 169 F.Supp. 266 (Ct.Cl.1959); Roth v. Embotelladora Nacional, Inc., 2 N.Y.2d 864, 161 N.Y.S.2d 128, 141 N.E.2d 617 (1957); Farmers &

EFFECT OF CORPORATE SEAL

228. The presence of a corporate seal on an instrument purporting to be executed by authority of the corporation, in some jurisdictions, constitutes prima facie evidence that the instrument was so executed. Occasional statutes recognize the binding effect of written corporate instruments executed by designated officers notwithstanding actual limitations on authority.

The presence of a corporate seal[1] on a written instrument purporting to be executed by authority of the corporation, in some jurisdictions, constitutes prima facie evidence that the instrument was so executed.[2] This may be so even in jurisdictions which have otherwise provided that the presence or absence of a seal is without legal effect.[3]

A few statutes go even further and provide that, notwithstanding bylaw provisions to the contrary, any corporate writing signed by two officers shall be held to have been properly executed for and in behalf of the corporation, unless the other persons had actual knowledge of such bylaws.[4]

Merchants Bank of St. Clair v. Burns & Hood Motor Co., 295 S.W.2d 199 (Mo.1956); Annot., 7 A.L.R. 1446 (1920). Cf. Julien J. Studley, Inc. v. Gulf Oil Corp., 282 F.Supp. 748 (S.D.N.Y.1968). See also E. Edelmann & Co. v. Amos, 277 F.Supp. 105 (N.D.Ga. 1967) aff'd per curiam Transonic Corp. v. E. Edelmann & Co., 386 F.2d 996 (5th Cir. 1967) (finding ratification by shareholder resolution approving all acts of officers for previous year on theory knowledge was imputed to corporation).

3. H. Ballantine, Ballantine on Corporations § 61 (rev. ed. 1946).

[§ 228]

1. See section 135, n. 9 supra.

2. E. g., New York, Oklahoma (by statute); Munroe v. Harriman, 85 F.2d 493 (2d Cir. 1936); Bryant v. Lakeside Galleries, Inc., 402 Ill. 466, 84 N.E.2d 412 (1949); Robertson v. Burstein, 105 N.J.L. 375, 146 A. 355, 65 A.L.R. 324 (1929). Cf. Corvino v. 910 South Boston Realty Co., 332 P.2d 15 (Okl.1958). See 1968 N.Y.Op.Att'y Gen. 67.

3. E. g., McKinney's N.Y.Gen.Constr.Law, § 44–a; McKinney's N.Y.Bus.Corp.Law, § 107.

4. Pa.Bus.Corp.Law, § 305 (1966); N.C.Bus.Corp.Act § 55–36 (1957); Prestressed Structures, Inc. v. Bargain City, U. S. A., Inc., 413 Pa. 262, 196 A.2d 338 (1964) (upholding $397,425 judgment on cognovit note executed in behalf of corporation by president,

OFFICER'S DERIVATIVE ACTIONS

229. Officers may in a few jurisdictions bring certain derivative actions in behalf of their corporations. Such derivative actions are not subject to the various restrictions imposed on derivative actions by shareholders.

A few jurisdictions expressly authorize derivative actions in behalf of a corporation by its officers,[1] at least against one or more of the directors or officers of the corporation.[2]

Such a derivative action by an officer may not be subject to the various restrictions imposed on derivative actions by shareholders.[3] Presumably, once such an action is commenced by an officer, his subsequent removal from office would not abate the action.[4]

OFFICER'S LIABILITIES

230. Officers purporting to contract in behalf of a corporation without authority might be personally liable to the third person on the contract on the theory that one who purports to contract in behalf of a principal is liable if the principal is not, or for breach of implied warranty of authority. Even authorized officers might be liable on contracts if they do not indicate that they are contracting only as agents for the corporation. Officers who personally guaranty their corporation's obligations are subject to the liability of guarantors. An officer who personally participates in a tort is personally liable to the victim, even though the corporation might also be liable under respondeat superior. Various statutes, at the federal and state levels, make corporate officers liable for corporate debts, taxes, crimes, etc., under

certain circumstances. Indemnification by the corporation of the officer is often available.

Officers who without authority purport to contract in behalf of a corporation might be personally liable to the other contracting party on the theory that one who purports to contract as agent for a principal is bound by the contract if the principal is not, or for breach of implied warranty of authority.[1]

Officers even when authorized to contract in behalf of the corporation might be personally liable on contracts if they do not indicate that they are contracting as agents for their undisclosed or even disclosed corporate principal.[2] In the case of a written contract which on its face appears to bind the officer personally, either alone or along with the corporation, parol evidence is usually inadmissible to relieve the officer from personal liability.[3]

---

on ground that statute, while importing validity to any instrument executed by two officers as prescribed therein, did not preclude corporations from following other forms of execution).

[§ 229]

1. E. g., Michigan, New York, Oklahoma.

2. McKinney's N.Y.Bus.Corp.Law, §§ 719(a), 720.

3. See Chapter 14 infra. On the other hand, officer's derivative actions are more limited as to the corporate causes of action they can assert. See note 2 supra. See section 217 supra.

4. Peets v. Manhasset Civil Engineers, Inc., 4 Misc. 2d 683, 68 N.Y.S.2d 338 (Sup.Ct.1946). Cf. Tenney

v. Rosenthal, 6 N.Y.2d 204, 189 N.Y.S.2d 158, 160 N. E.2d 463 (1959) (director's derivative action).

[§ 230]

1. Walton v. Hudson, 82 Ohio App. 330, 79 N.E.2d 921 (1947); Moore v. Maddock, 251 N.Y. 420, 167 N. E. 572, 64 A.L.R. 1189 (1929) (holding that corporate officer who purported to contract in name of corporation without authority was liable for breach of implied warranty of authority to plaintiff as other contracting party, that such was a continuing one, and that cause of action arose when defendant wrote terminating plaintiff's services). M. Ferson, Principles of Agency §§ 289–291 (1954).

2. Carranza v. Noroian, 240 Cal.App.2d 481, 49 Cal. Rptr. 629 (1966); Betz v. Bank of Miami Beach, 95 So.2d 891 (Fla.1957); Chesebro, Robbins & Graham, Inc. v. Leadbetter, 19 Conn.Supp. 422, 110 A.2d 578 (1955); Jahncke Service v. Heaslip, 76 So.2d 463 (La.Ct.App.1954). Compare Meyer v. Redmond, 205 N.Y. 478, 98 N.E. 906 (1912), with Air Waves, Inc. v. Link, 89 So.2d 422 (La.Ct.App.1956). See also Crawford Door Sales Co. v. Kowalik, 4 Ill.App.2d 32, 123 N.E.2d 111 (1954); Riemer, "Personal Liability of Corporate Officer for Purchases Made Without Disclosure of His Representative Capacity", 72 Com.L.J. 5 (1967).

3. Ricker v. B–W Acceptance Corp., 349 F.2d 892 (10th Cir. 1965) (holding president who signed as "president" personally liable on corporation's guaranty when guaranty clearly indicated he was to be bound personally); Harris v. Milam, 389 P.2d 638

An officer who personally guarantees his corporation's obligations, is, of course, personally liable on the guarantee, assuming compliance with any applicable statute of frauds.[4]

If an officer commits or participates in the commission of a tort he, of course, is personally liable to the victim for any resulting damage. When the tort is committed during the officer's scope of employment, the corporation would also be liable under the doctrine of *respondeat superior*.[5]

(Okl.1964) (parol evidence allowed to show note signed "W. T. Milam

> Braniff Eng'r Corp.,
> President
> C. J. Crim
> Braniff Engineering Corp.,
> Sec'y-Treasurer"

was sole obligation of corporation); Bell v. Dornan, 203 Pa.Super. 562, 201 A.2d 324 (1964) (officer held liable on corporate contract signed

> "Chet D. Earle, Inc.
> James G. Dornan [corporate seal]").

Compare Warren-Connolly Co. v. Saphin, 283 App.Div. 391, 128 N.Y.S.2d 272 (1st Dep't 1954), with Mencher v. Weiss, 306 N.Y. 1, 114 N.E.2d 177 (1953) (5–2). See also Norman v. Beling, 58 N.J.Super. 575, 157 A.2d 17 (1959), rev'd 33 N.J. 237, 163 A.2d 129 (1960).

4. Linwood State Bank v. Lientz, 413 S.W.2d 248 (Mo.1967); Presley v. American Guarantee & Liability Ins. Co., 237 Miss. 807, 116 So.2d 410 (1959); Ware v. Rankin, 97 Ga.App. 837, 104 S.E.2d 555 (1958); Womack v. Ballard Sales Co., 411 S.W.2d 956 (Tex.Civ.App.1967) (holding president liable on oral promise to pay corporate debt for merchandise furnished on his credit); Salzman Sign Co. v. Beck, 10 N.Y.2d 63, 217 N.Y.S.2d 55, 176 N.E.2d 74 (1961) (holding that officer, by his single signature:

> "Leslie 575 Corp. L.S.
> Irving Beck, pres L.S."

had not signed as guarantor, as required by statute of frauds, but only as president in behalf of corporation, despite statement in contract purporting to bind signing officer individually); London Leasing Corp. v. Interfina, Inc., 157 N.Y.L.J. No. 74, 21 (Sup.Ct.1967) (president, who had both signed corporate note as president and personally endorsed it, held to have consented to extension as endorsed where he signed extension as president); cf. Cohn v. Lionel Corp., 21 N.Y.2d 559, 289 N.Y.S.2d 404, 236 N.E.2d 634 (1968) (officer held entitled to indemnification from corporation for liability on personal guaranty that certain shares exchanged by corporation would continue to be worth at least a specified amount).

5. Where a tort is committed by a corporate officer, the officer, as a tortfeasor, is individually liable to the injured person whether or not the officer was

Various statutes, at the federal and state levels, make corporate officers liable for corporate debts,[6] taxes,[7] crimes,[8] etc., under certain circumstances.

acting within the scope of his employment. Alabama Music Co. v. Nelson, 282 Ala. 517, 213 So.2d 250 (1968); Herring v. Mathis Certified Dairy, 118 Ga.App. 132, 162 S.E.2d 863 (1968), modified sub nom. Bourn v. Herring, 225 Ga. 67, 166 S.E.2d 89 (1969). If the tort is committed by the officer within the scope of his employment, the corporation is also liable—vicariously or secondarily under the doctrine of respondeat superior; the officer, of course, remains primarily liable, and might enjoy a right to indemnification. If the tort is committed by the officer outside the scope of his employment, the corporation, of course, is not liable; only the officer is liable. See Solo Cup Co. v. Paper Machinery Corp., 240 F.Supp. 126 (E.D.Wis.1965) (trade secrets), aff'd on this ground, 359 F.2d 754 (7th Cir. 1966); Wampler v. Palmerton, 250 Or. 65, 439 P.2d 601 (1968) (president held not liable for inducing corporation to breach contract); Nottingham v. Wrigley, 221 Ga. 386, 141 S.E.2d 859 (1965) (maliciously inducing breach of contract); Weather-Tite Co. v. Lepper, 25 Wis.2d 70, 130 N.W.2d 198 (1964) (conversion); Borochoff v. Russell, 108 Ga.App. 266, 132 S.E.2d 861 (1963) (negligence); Hirsch v. Phily, 4 N.J. 408, 73 A.2d 173 (1950) (conversion); Burke v. Musarra, 46 Misc.2d 933, 261 N.Y.S.2d 314 (Sup. Ct.1965) (false imprisonment and malicious prosecution); M. Feuer, Personal Liabilities of Corporate Officers and Directors ch. 20 (1961); Avins, "Liability for Inducing a Corporation to Breach Its Contract", 43 Cornell L.Q. 55 (1957). Absent personal participation, an officer is usually not liable for the torts of other corporate personnel. Martin v. Wood, 400 F.2d 310 (3d Cir. 1968); Lemmons v. Zurich Ins. Co., 403 F.2d 512 (5th Cir. 1968). See discussion of Corporate Responsibility for Torts in section 184 supra.

6. E. g., ABA–ALI Model Bus.Corp.Act § 139 (all persons assuming to act as corporation without authority so to do jointly and severally liable for all debts and liabilities incurred or arising as result thereof) —see sections 142, 145 supra. For personal liabilities of officers of corporations whose charters have expired or been forfeited, and possible application of the de facto doctrine to interim period in cases where revival is effected or forfeiture rescinded, see section 144 supra. Ky.Gen.Corp.Law, § 271.095 (1953) (providing for several liability of officers and nondissenting directors for debts of corporation transacting business before filing of articles of incorporation with clerk of county court, receipt of specified amount of capital, election of first board of directors by shareholders, and designation by corporation of registered office and process agent) —see section 143 supra; Ala.Bus.Corp.Act § 10.05.-

---

7. See note 7 on Page 449.

8. See note 8 on Page 449.

Officers also risk potential civil and criminal liability under federal antitrust and

trade regulation laws [9] and under federal securities laws.[10]

243 (1959) (officer wrongfully denying shareholder inspection rights subject to penalty of 10 percent of value of shares owned by shareholder). In Smith v. Flynn, 275 Ala. 392, 155 So.2d 497 (1963), the president refused to let a shareholder examine the books and records. The court ruled that the burden of proof was on the officer to show that the shareholder's demand was improper or that he had reasonable cause for refusal to allow the inspection, and upheld a penalty claim of the shareholder for $23,740, under the statute providing for a penalty of 10 percent of the value of the shares owned by the shareholder, even though such penalty clearly exceeded the shareholder's actual damage. Enforcement of the penalty would not, the court stated, be an unconstitutional taking of property without due process of law. McCormick v. Statler Hotels Delaware Corp., 30 Ill.2d 86, 195 N.E.2d 172 (1963), involved the application to a Delaware corporation which had qualified to do business in Illinois of the provision of the Illinois Business Corporation Act under which a $2,000 penalty had been imposed against the corporation and its secretary for wrongfully refusing shareholder inspection of the shareholders' lists. The court, finding that there was no debatable constitutional issue, refused to entertain a direct appeal. No denial of due process of law or failure to give full faith and credit to the Delaware inspection statute was found. See section 199 supra. McKinney's N.Y.Bus.Corp.Law § 720 (actions against directors and officers)—see section 232 infra; Mich.Gen.Corp.Act § 21.87 (1948) (officers of corporation in default more than 10 days in filing reports and paying fees liable for all corporate debts contracted during such period of suspension of corporate powers). Radio Electronics Supply Co. v. Smith, 372 Mich. 393, 126 N.W.2d 729 (1964) (holding president personally liable on corporate note made during period when annual report not filed; defective report failing to list names of directors and give change of address of corporation was not accepted for filing by state whose request for correction was not heeded by president); Ebert's Cadillac Co. v. Miller, 372 Mich. 172, 125 N.W.2d 306 (1963) (holding vice-president and secretary personally liable on $9,800 corporate debts contracted during period when annual report not filed; two-year statute of limitations held not to run until after 10-day grace period). But cf. Vlasic Foods Co. v. Russek, 7 Mich.App. 359, 151 N.W.2d 872 (1967) (section 21.87 held not to apply corporation whose charter had become void for failure to file reports and pay fees for two consecutive years); Arcouet v. Papp, 21 Misc.2d 294, 190 N.Y.S.2d 549 (Sup.Ct.1959) (refusing to enforce penalty under Colorado statute for failure to file annual reports). Tex.Tax.Gen.Ann. art. 12.14 (1960) (partnership-type liability for debts, including franchise taxes and penalties, imposed on approving directors and officers of corporation whose right to do business has been forfeited); First Nat'l Bank of Boston v. Silberstein, 398 S.W.2d 914 (Tex.1966); Sheffield v. Nobles, 378 S.W.2d 391 (Tex.Civ.App.1964).

7. Int.Rev.Code of 1954, 26 U.S.C.A. §§ 6671–6674 (officers, etc., responsible for withholding and paying

over federal income and social security taxes liable for failure); Spivak v. United States, 370 F.2d 612 (2d Cir. 1967), cert. denied 387 U.S. 908, 87 S.Ct. 1690, 18 L.Ed.2d 625 (1967); United States v. Leuschner, 336 F.2d 246 (9th Cir. 1964); Seaton v. United States, 254 F.Supp. 161 (D.Mo.1966) (officer's resignation two weeks before deadline for turning over federal income withholding and social security taxes held no defense); Yudkin, "Corporate Officers in Increasing Numbers Face Penalties for Defaults on Withholding Tax", 18 J.Taxation 248 (1963); Scholder, "Personal Liability of Corporate Officers for Taxes Withheld or Collected by the Corporation", 46 A.B.A.J. 1355 (1960); Schwartz, "Personal Liability of Corporate Officers for Unpaid, Withheld or Collected Taxes", 12 Tax L.Rev. 343 (1957).

8. United States v. Andreadis, 366 F.2d 423 (2d Cir. 1966), cert. denied 385 U.S. 1001, 87 S.Ct. 703, 17 L.Ed.2d 541 (1967) (upholding conviction of corporate president for 46 counts of mail and wire fraud, conspiracy, and misbranding); ABA–ALI Model Bus. Corp.Act § 129 (misdemeanor for officer or director to fail to answer truthfully and fully interrogatories propounded by secretary of state or knowingly to file false document, subject to $500 fine); McKinney's N.Y.Labor Law, § 198(a) (providing fines of up to $10,000 and jail sentences of up to one year for officers who knowingly permit corporation to fail to pay wages); People v. D. H. Ahrend Co., 308 N.Y. 112, 123 N.E.2d 799 (1954); McKinney's N.Y.Labor Law, § 198(c) (making designated corporate officers guilty of misdemeanor for not paying fringe benefits due under collective bargaining agreements); People v. Trapp, 20 N.Y.2d 613, 286 N.Y.S.2d 11, 233 N.E.2d 110 (1967) (upholding statute as limited to officers standing in such relation to corporation that he presumptively knew or should have known of and taken steps to prevent nonpayment of benefits); Annot., 68 A.L.R.2d 1269 (1959).

9. United States v. Wise, 370 U.S. 405, 82 S.Ct. 1354, 8 L.Ed.2d 590 (1962) (corporate officer, acting solely for corporation, held criminally liable for $50,000 fine under Sherman Act); Forte, "Liabilities of Corporate Officers for Violations of Fiduciary Duties Concerning the Antitrust Laws", 40 Ind.L.J. 313 (1965); Rooks, "Personal Liabilities of Officers and Directors for Antitrust Violations and Securities Transactions", 18 Bus.Law. 579 (1963), 51 Ill.B.J. 626 (1963); Whiting, "Criminal Antitrust Liability of Corporation Representatives", 51 Ky.L.J. 434 (1963); Whiting, "Antitrust and the Corporate Executive", 47 Va.L.Rev. 929 (1961), 48 Va.L.Rev. 1 (1962); Kramer, "Liability of Corporate Officers and Directors under the Antitrust Laws", 17 Bus. Law. 897 (1962); Comment, "The Antitrust Laws and the Corporate Executive's Civil Damage Liability", 18 Vand.L.Rev. 1938 (1965). See sections 309–314 infra.

10. See sections 295–298 infra.

Other liabilities of corporate officers are treated in connection with duties of management in succeeding sections.[11]

Indemnification by the corporation of officers' litigation expenses, including payment of liabilities, judgments, settlement sums, fines, as well as attorneys' fees, and insurance covering the same, exist, subject to limitations, on common-law principles, under articles of incorporation or bylaw provisions, pursuant to board of directors resolutions, and under modern corporate statutes.[12]

G. DUTIES OF MANAGEMENT

DUTIES OF MANAGEMENT— IN GENERAL

231. Management, meaning directors, officers, and sometimes controlling shareholders, owe various duties to their corporation and sometimes to the community of corporate interests: the shareholders and, possibly at least when the corporation is insolvent, the creditors. Broadly speaking, the duties of management are (a) to act intra vires and within their respective authority, (b) to exercise due care, and (c) to observe applicable fiduciary duties.

Management is the collective term used to refer to directors and officers and possibly other policy-makers—the "technostructure" of the modern corporation. In the broad sense of the term, controlling shareholders might also be covered by such reference. In any event, controlling shareholders are subject to duties akin to the duties imposed on directors and officers.[1]

Since directors occupy a *sui generis* position,[2] are expected as directors to devote only part of their time to the affairs of the corporation, often without compensation, and, as a board, are usually vested with the management of the corporation, and since officers are agents of the corporation, usual-ly full-time and for compensation, with such management functions as are delegated to them, there are, as one would expect, some differences between the duties of directors[3] and the duties of officers.[4]

However, directors, with their powers and responsibilities for managing the property of another, i. e., the corporation and officers, as agents for a principal, i. e., the corporation, are in a fiduciary relationship with the corporation.

The various duties of directors, officers, and controlling shareholders are owed clearly to the corporation as an entity and sometimes to the community of corporate interests: the shareholders and, possibly at least

---

11. See sections 231–242 infra.

12. See sections 379, 380 infra.

1. Comments, "Fiduciary Duties of Majority or Controlling Shareholders", 44 Iowa L.Rev. 734 (1959); "Fiduciary Duty of Controlling Shareholders", 7 W.Res.L.Rev. 467 (1956).

2. See section 207, n. 2 supra. Analogies are frequently drawn to agents, mandatories, trustees, managing partners, but can be misleading. The duties of directors are the same, whether the directors are called directors, trustees, managers, or governors in the particular business corporation.

3. M. Feuer, Personal Liabilities of Corporate Officers and Directors (1961); H. Spellman, Corporate Directors chs. X, XI (1931); P. Jackson, Corporate Management (The Directors and Executives) ch. XV (1955); Bishop, "Sitting Ducks and Decoy Ducks: New Trends in the Indemnification of Corporate Directors and Officers", 77 Yale L.J. 1078 (1968); Wallace, "Liabilities of Directors and Officers: Facts and Fallacies", 158 N.Y.L.J. No. 49, 1, No. 50, 1, No. 51, 1 (Sept. 11, 12, 13, 1967); Neilsen, "Directors' Duties Under Anglo-American Law", 43 U. Det.L.J. 605 (1966); Pasley, "Non-Profit Corporations—Accountability of Directors and Officers", 21 Bus.Law. 621 (1966); Cary, "Corporate Standards and Legal Rules", 50 Calif.L.Rev. 408 (1962); Cary, "The Case for Higher Corporate Standards", 40 Harv.Bus.Rev. 53 (Sept.-Oct.1962); Feuer, "Liabilities of Directors and Officers", 5 N.Y.L.F. 127, 235 (1959). See, e. g., Wilson, "Responsibilities of a Bank Director", 10 Bus.Law. 45 (Apr.1955); Duties and Liabilities of Directors of National Banks (Treasury Dept. Form 1417) (rev. 1956). See also Comment, "Duty of Corporate Officers and Directors in Louisiana", 29 La.L.Rev. 691 (1969).

4. See Bates v. Dresser, 251 U.S. 524, 40 S.Ct. 247, 64 L.Ed. 388 (1920) (holding president-director but not other directors liable for misconduct of employee).

when the corporation is insolvent, the creditors.[5]

Broadly speaking, the duties of management are threefold in nature: (a) obedience, (b) diligence, and (c) loyalty. When management fulfills such duties, by acting *intra vires* and within their respective authority,[6] by exercising due care,[7] and by observing applicable fiduciary duties,[8] the transaction is usually immune from attack, and management is usually immune from liability under the so-called "business judgment" rule.[9]

In most jurisdictions, these rules have been primarily developed by court decision, with or without significant statutory implementation.[10]

DUTIES OF MANAGEMENT—STATUTORY PROVISIONS

232. Statutory provisions deal with some aspects of management duties. Broadly-worded statutes leave ample room for desirable judicial flexibility. Some statutes impose liabilities for improper dividends or distributions, payment for corporation's own shares out of improper funds, unlawful loans to directors, officers, or shareholders, commencing business without required minimum paid-in stated capital, false financial statements. Some federal statutes also deal with liability of corporate officers and directors. Decisional law, however, remains the more significant in defining management duties. Statutes sometimes impose criminal penalties with respect to various corporate matters.

The duties of corporate management have been defined mainly by decisional law, especially by courts of equity which developed and have been expanding the fiduciary concept in corporate relations. Statutes deal with some aspects, but decisional law remains the most significant.

A growing number of jurisdictions have attempted general formulation, in a broadly-worded statute, which still leaves ample room for desirable judicial flexibility:[1]

> "Officers and directors shall be deemed to stand in a fiduciary relationship to the corporation, and shall discharge the duties of their respective positions in good faith and with that diligence, care and skill which ordinarily prudent men would exercise under similar circumstances in their personal business affairs."

North Carolina provides that the duties run in favor not only of the corporation but also of shareholders.[2]

Sometimes the statute is noncommittal as to whom the directors, and officers' duties are owed.[3]

5. Pepper v. Litton, 308 U.S. 295, 306–307, 60 S.Ct. 238, 245, 84 L.Ed. 281, 289–290 (1939) ("standard of fiduciary obligation is designed for the production of the entire community of interests in the corporation—creditors as well as stockholders"); McCandless v. Furlaud, 296 U.S. 140, 56 S.Ct. 41, 80 L.Ed. 121 (1935); New York Credit Men's Adjustment Bureau, Inc. v. Weiss, 305 N.Y. 1, 110 N.E.2d 397 (1953). But see Sutton v. Reagan & Gee, 405 S.W.2d 828 (Tex.Civ.App.1966). The duties (the relations between corporation and shareholder, corporate officer or director and shareholder, and between shareholders inter sese) are defined by the law of the jurisdiction of incorporation; the quantum of breach of duty by the law of the place of the alleged wrong. Zahn v. Transamerica Corp., 162 F.2d 36, 172 A.L.R. 495 (3d Cir.1947); Otis & Co. v. Pennsylvania R. R., 61 F.Supp. 905 (E.D.Pa.1945), aff'd mem., 155 F.2d 522 (3d Cir.1946). But see Mansfield Hardwood Lumber Co. v. Johnson, 268 F.2d 317 (5th Cir.1959) (holding law of forum, where corporation had all contacts except formal incorporation, to define duties of management absent express provisions in corporate charter or statutes of jurisdiction of incorporation), cert. denied 361 U.S. 885, 80 S.Ct. 156, 4 L.Ed.2d 120 (1959), reh. denied 361 U.S. 926, 80 S.Ct. 290, 4 L.Ed.2d 241 (1960).

6. See section 233 infra.

7. See section 234 infra.

8. See sections 235–241 infra.

9. See section 242 infra.

10. See section 232 infra.

1. E. g., Pa.Bus.Corp.Law, § 408 (1966); Idaho, Kentucky, Louisiana, Minnesota, Washington. See Lutherland, Inc. v. Dahlen, 357 Pa. 143, 53 A.2d 143 (1947); Bailey v. Jacobs, 325 Pa. 187, 189 A. 320 (1937); Weiss, "Standard of Diligence of Corporate Directors in Pennsylvania", 10 U.Pitt.L.Rev. 370 (1949). For an unusually comprehensive formulation of the duties of directors, see Ghana Companies Code § 203 (1963).

2. N.C.Bus.Corp.Act § 55–35 (1957).

3. Cal.Gen.Corp.Law, § 820 (1947) ("Directors and officers shall exercise their powers in good faith, and

Some statutes state the standard of care in terms of that of the ordinary director ("in like position"),[4] or of the ordinary man ("in own affairs")[5] while others are even more vague.[6]

In this connection, the Model Business Corporation Act[7] provides that, in addition to any other liabilities imposed by law upon directors of a corporation, they shall be jointly and severally liable to the corporation[8] for (a) improper dividends or other distribution of corporate assets;[9] (b) purchase of shares of the corporation out of improper funds;[10] (c) distribution of assets to shareholders in the event of liquidation without providing for all known debts, obli-

gations, and liabilities of the corporation;[11] (d) loans to any officer or director or any loan secured by shares of the corporation;[12] and (e) commencing business without $1,000 minimum paid-in stated capital.[13] Exonerated from liability are directors who file their written dissent,[14] or who, with respect to dividends, purchase of shares, or liquidation distributions, rely in good faith upon financial statements represented to be correct by the officer in charge of the books of account or properly certified by an independent public accountant, or who, with respect to dividends or distributions, consider assets at book value.[15] Any director found liable is entitled to contribution from his fellow directors and, in the case of dividends or distributions, proportionately from the shareholders who received the same with knowledge of their impropriety.[16]

with a view to the interests of the corporation."); McKinney's N.Y.Bus.Corp.Law, § 717 ("Directors and officers shall discharge the duties of their respective positions in good faith and with that degree of diligence, care and skill which ordinarily prudent men would exercise under similar circumstances in like positions.").

4. E. g., McKinney's N.Y.Bus.Corp.Law, § 717 (see 1960 version of comment: "In the case of the ordinary business corporation, this [ordinary man] standard may be too severe."); N.C.Bus.Corp.Act § 55–35 (1957) ("with that diligence and care which ordinarily prudent men would exercise under like circumstances in like positions.").

5. Pa.Bus.Law, § 408 (1966) ("with that diligence, care and skill which ordinarily prudent men would exercise under similar circumstances in their personal business affairs")—supra note 1; Selheimer v. Manganese Corp. of America, 423 Pa. 563, 224 A. 2d 634 (1966).

6. Cal.Gen.Corp.Law, § 820 (1947)—supra note 3. See also McKinney's N.Y.Bus.Corp.Law, § 723 (providing corporation may indemnify "if such director or officer acted, in good faith, for a purpose which he reasonably believed to be in the best interests of the corporation".).

7. ABA–ALI Model Bus.Corp.Act § 43; see also McKinney's N.Y.Bus.Corp.Law, § 719; id. § 720 (actions against directors and officers for misconduct; section not to affect any liability otherwise imposed by law upon any director or officer).

8. In New York, the joint and several liability of the directors is "to the corporation for the benefit of its creditors or shareholders, to the extent of any injury suffered by such persons, respectively, as a result of such action." McKinney's N.Y.Bus.Corp. Law, § 719(a).

9. See sections 319, 323 infra.

10. See section 336 infra.

11. See section 381 infra.

12. See ABA–ALI Model Bus.Corp.Act § 42, deleted to conform with other amendments in 1969 Model Act revision. See section 183, nn. 14, 15 supra.

13. See section 143 supra. Deleted to conform with elimination of minimum paid-in stated capital requirement in 1969 Model Act revision.

14. ABA–ALI Model Bus.Corp.Act § 43 (providing that director present at meeting of board of directors at which action on any corporate matter is taken shall be presumed to have assented to action taken unless his dissent shall be entered in minutes of meeting or unless he shall file his written dissent to such action with person acting as secretary of meeting before adjournment thereof or shall forward such dissent by registered mail to secretary of corporation immediately after adjournment of meeting, but that such right to dissent shall not apply to director who voted in favor of such action). The New York provision also applies to committees of the board of directors and to absent directors. McKinney's N.Y.Bus.Corp.Law, § 719(b).

15. ABA–ALI Model Bus.Corp.Act § 43. Cf. McKinney's N.Y.Bus.Corp.Law, § 717 (general provision that in discharging their duties, directors and officers, when acting in good faith, may rely upon financial statements of corporation represented to them to be correct by president or officer of corporation having charge of its books of accounts, or stated in written report by independent public or certified public accountant or firm of such accountants fairly to reflect financial condition of such corporation). See sections 319, 323 infra.

16. ABA–ALI Model Bus.Corp.Act § 43. The New York provisions are more sophisticated providing

Statutes permitting shareholder provisions interfering with the discretion of the board of directors usually impose the statutory liabilities of directors on the consenting shareholders,[17] sometimes expressly relieving the directors of such liabilities.[18]

Some federal statutes also deal with the liability of corporate directors and officers.[19]

In addition, various acts of directors and officers might be criminal offenses.[20]

DUTIES TO ACT INTRA VIRES AND WITHIN AUTHORITY

233. **Directors and officers are under duties to act intra vires and within their respective authority. For any loss to the corporation resulting from their engaging the corporation in ultra vires activity, they are, in some jurisdictions, absolutely liable, and in other jurisdictions, liable only if they were negligent as to the scope of the corporate powers.**

Directors and officers should not presume to act as such in behalf of their corporation in *ultra vires* transactions,[1] or beyond the

powers or authority of their respective positions.[2]

For any loss to the corporation resulting from their engaging the corporation in an *ultra vires* transaction, they are, by one view, liable absolutely,[3] and by another view, liable only where they have been negligent as to the scope of the corporate powers.[4]

In a broad sense, when directors or officers act in violation of statute, they are acting *ultra vires*.[5]

Negligence precludes application of the "business judgment" rule.[6]

DUTIES OF DUE CARE

234. **Directors and officers owe duties of due care to their corporation. A growing number of statutes in general terms define such duties of due care. When the required duty of due care has not been observed, management is liable to the corporation only for such corporate damage as was caused by such negligence. Liability of the directors for negligence includes negligence in selecting and supervising officers. For actionable negligence, the tortfeasors are jointly and severally liable.**

Directors and officers are liable to the corporation for negligence to it in the performance of their corporate duties. They can be negligent in acting or in failing to

---

for contribution among directors, subrogation to rights of corporation, or rescission of purchase of shares.

17. N.C.Bus.Corp.Act § 55–73 (1957).

18. McKinney's N.Y.Bus.Corp.Law, § 620(f).

19. E. g., Federal Securities Act of 1933, § 11, 15 U. S.C.A. § 77k; Int.Rev.Code of 1954, 26 U.S.C.A. §§ 6671–6674 (officers, etc., liable for failure to withhold or pay over tax). See sections 218, 230 supra.

20. E. g., McKinney's N.Y.Penal Law, §§ 170.00–170.-15 (Falsifying business records); id. § 190.35 (Directors: Unlawful declaration of dividends; Unauthorized reduction of capital; Prohibited loans to shareholders; Purchase of shares except out of legally available funds. Officers and directors: Issue of shares in excess of shares authorized; Sale of shares by nonowner); McKinney's N.Y.Election Law, § 460 (Making political contributions from corporation funds); McKinney's N.Y.Labor Law, § 198–a (Officers knowingly permitting corporation to fail to pay wages); McKinney's N.Y.Gen.Bus.Law, § 352 (Fraudulent practices with respect to securities).

1. See sections 181–184 supra.

2. See for directors, sections 207–215 supra, and for officers, sections 223–227 supra.

3. 2 Restatement, Second, Agency § 383, Comment b (1958); W. Fletcher, Private Corporations §§ 1021–1028 (rev. vol. 1965).

4. Leppaluoto v. Eggleston, 57 Wash.2d 393, 357 P.2d 725 (1960); Litwin (Rosemarin) v. Allen, 25 N.Y.S. 2d 667 (Sup.Ct.1940).

5. Gilbert v. Burnside, 197 N.Y.S.2d 623 (Sup.Ct. 1959), rev'd on other grounds 13 A.D.2d 982, 216 N.Y.S.2d 430 (2d Dep't 1961), aff'd mem. 11 N.Y.2d 960, 229 N.Y.S.2d 10, 183 N.E.2d 325 (1962); Cowin v. Jonas, 43 N.Y.S.2d 468 (Sup.Ct.1943), aff'd mem. 267 App.Div. 947, 48 N.Y.S.2d 460 (1st Dep't 1944), aff'd mem. 293 N.Y. 838, 59 N.E.2d 436 (1944) (holding good faith no defense); 3 W. Fletcher, Private Corporations § 1046 (rev. vol. 1965).

6. See section 242 infra.

act.[1] However, they are not insurers and are not liable for errors of judgment or mistakes while acting with reasonable skill and prudence.

Persons who accept directorships as "accommodation" or "dummy" directors,[2] or as sinecures for lending their prestige to boards of directors,[3] are liable for any corporate losses resulting from their passive, as well as active, negligence.[4]

Directors should attend meetings of the board of directors, have their dissents entered on the minutes of the meetings, keep well-informed on corporate matters, familiarize themselves with the financial statements prepared by the corporation's accountants and the legal advice rendered by corporate counsel, and resign when they are unable to carry out their responsibilities.

Directors can be held liable when the corporation suffers a loss as a result of the directors' failure to assert a corporate claim.[5]

The standard of care has been variously described as that of a "reasonably prudent man",[6] or of an ordinarily prudent director

---

1. Charitable Corp. v. Sutton, 2 Atkyns 400, 26 Eng. Rep. 642 (Ch.1742) ("acts of commission or omission, of malfeasance or nonfeasance"); Barnes v. Andrews, 298 F. 614 (S.D.N.Y.1924); Dyson, "Director's Liabilities for Negligence", 40 Ind.L.J. 341 (1965); Comment, "Factors That Limit the Negligence Liability of a Corporate Executive or Director", 1967 U.Ill.L.F. 341; Note, 71 Dick.L.Rev. 668 (1967). See Sutton v. Reagan & Gee, 405 S.W.2d 828 (Tex.Civ.App.1966) (holding directors did not owe duty of due care to creditors of corporation, but only to corporation). See also Trebilcock, "The Liability of Company Directors for Negligence", 32 Modern L.Rev. 499 (1969).

2. See Minton v. Cavaney, 56 Cal.2d 576, 15 Cal.Rptr. 641, 643, 364 P.2d 473, 475 (1961): "It is immaterial whether or not he accepted the office of director as an 'accommodation' with the understanding that he would not exercise any of the duties of a director. A person may not in this manner divorce the responsibilities of a director from the statutory duties and powers of that office." See Note, "Corporations: Use of Accommodation Incorporators, Directors, Officers: Potential Liability of Accommodation Personnel", 47 Cornell L.Q. 443 (1962).

3. See 80 Time, No. 14, 96 (Oct. 5, 1962): "In Britain, where a company's list of directors often reads like a tear sheet from Burke's Peerage, many a titled tycoon sits on more boards than he can count. Lord Boothby, 62, a longtime Tory backbencher who is one of this happy breed himself (he has 'eight or nine' directorships), explained last week just what directors do in return for adding prestige to corporate letterheads. 'No effort of any kind is called for,' he told an audience of Yorkshire clubwomen. 'You go to a meeting once a month in a car supplied by the company. You look both grave and sage, and on two occasions say "I agree," say "I don't think so" once, and if all goes well, you get $1,440 a year. If you have five of them, it is total heaven, like having a permanent hot bath.' "

4. Neese v. Brown, 218 Tenn. 686, 405 S.W.2d 577 (1964) (upholding negligence action by corporation's trustee-in-bankruptcy against inattentive director; "directors must be something more than figureheads"). See also Lariscy v. Hill, 117 Ga.App. 152, 159 S.E.2d 443 (1968) (denying relief to inactive director who alleged other directors misrepresented corporate data when selling him their shares);

Burt v. Irvine Co., 237 Cal.App.2d 828, 47 Cal.Rptr. 392 (1965) (dismissing action against passive directors who acquiesced in sale of corporate assets for inadequate price on ground claim was based on negligence, not fraud, and therefore subject to two-year statute of limitations for negligence).

5. Walker v. Man, 142 Misc. 277, 253 N.Y.S. 458 (Sup.Ct.1931). Cf. Trunede v. Universal Pictures Co., 76 F.Supp. 465 (S.D.N.Y.1948). See Simon, "Must We Sue?", 17 Bus.Law. 888 (1962), which reviews the question as to when corporate management should sue to recover treble damages for antitrust violations especially when the government has already been successful in a parallel action, and suggests four factors to be considered;

(a) The likelihood of success in the proposed litigation;

(b) The direct and indirect costs of such litigation, measured against the probable recovery;

(c) The possible non-monetary gains, such as an injunction to enjoin a competitively unlawful practice; and the value to the corporation in possibly settling the law in an unclear area; and

(d) The likelihood of commercial disadvantages to the corporation arising from the impairment of friendly commercial relations with the defendants, or the industry of which the defendants are members.

6. Anderson v. Akers, 7 F.Supp. 924 (W.D.Ky.1934), modified sub nom. Atherton v. Anderson, 86 F.2d 518 (6th Cir.1936), modified sub nom. Anderson v. Atherton, 302 U.S. 643, 58 S.Ct. 53, 82 L.Ed. 500 (1937); Cf. Medford Trust Co. v. McKnight, 292 Mass. 1, 197 N.E. 649 (1935) (gross negligence standard, at least where directors serve without compensation); Spiegel v. Beacon Participations, Inc., 297 Mass. 398, 8 N.E.2d 895 (1937); Murphy v. Hanlon, 322 Mass. 683, 79 N.E.2d 292 (1948); Swentzel v. Penn Bank, 147 Pa. 140, 23 A. 405 (1892) ("only liable for fraud, or such gross negligence as amounts to fraud").

in similar business,[7] or "the same degree of fidelity and care as an ordinarily prudent man would exercise in the management of his own affairs of like magnitude and importance".[8]

The Pennsylvania statutory formulation defines the standard of care as "that diligence, care and skill which ordinarily prudent men would exercise under similar circumstances in their personal business affairs";[9] the North Carolina statute as "that diligence and care which ordinarily prudent men would exercise under similar circumstances in like positions".[10]

In applying the standard of due care, the courts have indulged in subjective as well as objective considerations. Whether the director is part-time or full-time,[11] whether or not he is being compensated,[12] whether distant residence causes his absence,[13]

whether or not he has special background,[14] his health and state of mind,[15] have been recognized by the courts in determining his negligence. The standard also varies depending upon the nature of the business.[16]

Directors and officers are required to act carefully in the light of their actual knowledge and such knowledge as they should have gained by reasonable care and skill.[17] Reasonable reliance on others is consistent with such requirement.[18]

---

7. Atherton v. Anderson, 99 F.2d 883 (6th Cir.1938); Anderson v. Bundy, 161 Va. 1, 171 S.E. 501 (1933). See note 10 infra.

8. Simon v. Socony-Vacuum Oil Co., 179 Misc. 202, 38 N.Y.S.2d 270 (Sup.Ct.1942), aff'd mem., 267 App. Div. 890, 47 N.Y.S.2d 589 (1st Dep't 1944). Litwin (Rosemarin) v. Allen, 25 N.Y.S.2d 667, 677–678 (Sup.Ct.1940); Straus v. United States Fidelity & Guaranty Co., 63 F.2d 174 (4th Cir.1933); Burkhart v. Smith, 161 Md. 398, 157 A. 299 (1931); Martin v. Hardy, 251 Mich. 413, 232 N.W. 197 (1930); Kavanaugh v. Commonwealth Trust Co., 223 N.Y. 103, 119 N.E. 237 (1918). See note 9 infra.

9. Pa.Bus.Corp.Law, § 408 (1966); Selheimer v. Manganese Corp. of America, 423 Pa. 563, 224 A.2d 634 (1966); Idaho, Kentucky, Louisiana, Minnesota, Washington. See note 4 supra.

10. N.C.Bus.Corp.Act §§ 55–35 (1957); McKinney's N.Y.Bus.Corp.Law, § 717. See note 3 supra.

11. Anderson v. Akers, 7 F.Supp. 924 (W.D.Ky.1934), modified sub nom. Atherton v. Anderson, 86 F.2d 518 (6th Cir.1936), modified sub nom. Anderson v. Atherton, 302 U.S. 643, 58 S.Ct. 53, 82 L.Ed. 500 (1937).

12. Anderson v. Akers, 7 F.Supp. 924 (W.D.Ky.1934), modified sub nom. Atherton v. Anderson, 86 F.2d 518 (6th Cir.1936), modified sub nom. Anderson v. Atherton, 302 U.S. 643, 58 S.Ct. 53, 82 L.Ed. 500 (1937); Medford Trust Co. v. McKnight, 292 Mass. 1, 197 N.E. 649 (1935).

13. Compare Bowerman v. Hammer, 250 U.S. 504, 39 S.Ct. 549, 63 L.Ed. 1113 (1919) (absent nonresident banker of standing held liable to receiver for bank's

excessive loans), Dinsmore v. Jacobson, 242 Mich. 192, 218 N.W. 700 (1928) (jury charge that jury consider distance between main office of corporation and address of director held error), and Kavanaugh v. Commonwealth Trust Co., 223 N.Y. 103, 119 N.E. 237 (1918), with Wallach v. Billings, 277 Ill. 218, 115 N.E. 382 (1917), cert. denied 244 U.S. 659, 37 S. Ct. 745, 61 L.Ed. 1376 (1917) (absent nonresident directors elected and reelected by shareholders held to lesser degree of care than resident directors in derivative action by shareholders). See Note, 5 U. Chi.L.Rev. 668 (1938).

14. Barnes v. Andrews, 298 F. 614 (S.D.N.Y.1924).

15. Anderson v. Akers, 7 F.Supp. 924 (W.D.Ky.1934), modified sub nom. Atherton v. Anderson, 86 F.2d 518 (6th Cir.1936) (directors of unsound mind exonerated), modified sub nom. Anderson v. Atherton, 302 U.S. 643, 58 S.Ct. 53, 82 L.Ed. 500 (1937); Gamble v. Brown, 29 F.2d 366 (4th Cir.1929), cert. denied 279 U.S. 839, 49 S.Ct. 253, 73 L.Ed. 986 (1928) (age and infirmity of director held no excuse).

16. 3 W. Fletcher, Private Corporations § 1035 (rev. vol. 1965).

17. Barnes v. Andrews, 298 F. 614 (S.D.N.Y.1924); Commercial Bank of Menominee v. Weidman, 301 Mich. 405, 3 N.W.2d 323 (1942).

18. Pool v. Pool, 22 So.2d 131 (La.Ct.App.1945) (directors who relied on certified public accountant and attorney held not liable for federal surtax imposed on corporation for improper accumulation of earnings); Winkelman v. General Motors Corp., 39 F. Supp. 826 (S.D.N.Y.1940), 44 F.Supp. 960, 48 F.Supp. 485, 48 F.Supp. 500, 48 F.Supp. 504 (S.D.N.Y.1942), aff'd per curiam sub nom. Singer v. General Motors Corp., 136 F.2d 905 (2d Cir.1943); Epstein v. Schenck, 35 N.Y.S.2d 969 (Sup.Ct.1939) (permitting directors to rely on independent accountants or auditors). Cf. Gallin v. National City Bank, 155 Misc. 880, 281 N.Y.S. 795 (Sup.Ct.1935) (directors held liable for excess payments under profit bonus plan in relying on false figures prepared by personnel under supervision of officers receiving bonuses). Compare People v. Marcus, 261 N.Y. 268, 185 N.E. 97 (1933) (director's reliance on advice of counsel held no defense), with Spirt v. Bechtel, 232 F.2d 241 (2d Cir. 1956) (director's reliance on advice of counsel held good defense).

Even when the required duty of care has not been exercised, the directors, officers, or controlling shareholders are only liable, under the causation rules of negligence law, for such loss to the corporation as was caused by their negligence.[19]

If officers, agents, or employees violate their duties to the corporation, they are, of course, liable to it. In such a case, the directors or officers might also be liable to the corporation for the misconduct of the officer, agent, or employee if they were negligent in selecting[20] or supervising him.[21]

In a leading Delaware case,[22] shareholders brought a derivative action for damages against the directors and major officers of a Delaware corporation for breach of their fiduciary duty by failing to prevent minor corporate officials from price-fixing in violation of the federal antitrust laws. The corporation had been convicted and paid a fine and allegedly was subject to treble damage actions and suffered irreparable damage to its business reputation and good will. The court held that in absence of proof that the officers and directors knew or had reason to know of the violations or were negligent in their selection and supervision of the wrongdoing subordinate officials, the officers and directors of such a large, complex corporation could not be held liable.[23]

Negligence on the part of corporate personnel toward a third person might be attributed to the corporation and preclude a corporate claim against the third person.[24]

Obviously, if directors or officers (or other corporate agents or employees) act negligently to persons other than the corporation and cause or threaten damage to such persons or commit other torts against such

---

19. Barnes v. Andrews, 298 F. 614 (S.D.N.Y.1924); Allied Freightways v. Cholfin, 325 Mass. 630, 91 N. E.2d 765 (1950).

20. 3 W. Fletcher, Private Corporations §§ 1065, 1079 (rev. vol. 1965).

21. See Olin Mathieson Chemical Corp. v. Planters Corp., 236 S.C. 318, 328, 114 S.E.2d 321, 326 (1960): "An officer . . . of a corporation cannot be held responsible for losses resulting from the wrongful acts or omissions of other officers . . . unless the loss is a consequence of his own neglect of duty in failing to supervise the business with the degree of care which ordinarily prudent and diligent men would exercise under similar circumstances. What may be negligence in one case may not be want of ordinary care in another, and the question of negligence is, therefore, ultimately a question of fact. An officer of a corporation will not be shielded from liability because of a want of knowledge of wrongdoing of another officer if that ignorance is the result of such officer's negligence and inattention to the business." See also 3 W. Fletcher, Private Corporations §§ 1070–1071 (rev. vol. 1965). See Bates v. Dresser, 251 U.S. 524, 40 S.Ct. 247, 64 L.Ed. 388 (1920) (president-director, not other directors, held liable); Groel v. United Electric Co. of New Jersey, 70 N.J.Eq. 616, 61 A. 1061 (1905). Cf. Foster v. Bowen, 311 Mass. 359, 41 N.E.2d 181 (1942) (directors held not liable in minority shareholder's action for wrongs of officer); Lowell Hoit & Co. v. Detig, 320 Ill.App. 179, 50 N.E.2d 602 (1943); Cohen v. Maus, 297 Pa. 454, 147 A. 103 (1929) (directors held not liable to third person for officer's torts). See Annot., 2 A.L.R. 867 (1919).

22. Graham v. Allis-Chalmers Mfg. Co., 41 Del.Ch. 78, 188 A.2d 125 (Sup.Ct.1963).

23. Compare Smiles v. Elfred, 149 N.Y.L.J. No. 35, 14 (Sup.Ct.1963) (dismissing complaint for failure to allege net loss); Borden v. Cohen, 231 N.Y.S.2d 902 (Sup.Ct.1962) (dismissing complaint alleging $50,000 fine on plea of nolo contendere and threat of treble damage actions); Knopfler v. Bohen, 15 A.D.2d 922, 225 N.Y.S.2d 609 (2d Dep't 1962) (upholding complaint in shareholder derivative action against directors and two other corporations for damages for fines and subjection to treble damage actions for antitrust violations); Premselaar v. Chenery, Civ.No. 6151 (N.Y.Sup.Ct.1963) ($60,000 fine, costs of litigation, potential treble damage liability, loss of good will, and loss of time of corporate employees, held sufficient allegations of damages). See Turner, "Some Comments with Respect to the Rule of Outside Counsel in a Corporate Antitrust Compliance Program", 19 Record of N.Y.C.B. A. 143 (1964); Withrow, "Antitrust Compliance Programs", 19 id. 151; Rooks, "Personal Liabilities of Officers and Directors for Antitrust Violations and Securities Transactions", 18 Bus.Law. 579 (1963), 51 Ill.B.J. 626 (1963); Anderson, "Effective Antitrust Compliance Programs and Procedures (An Outline)", 18 Bus.Law. 739 (1963); Whiting, "Criminal Antitrust Liability of Corporation Representatives", 51 Ky.L.J. 434 (1963); Kramer, "Liability of Corporate Officers and Directors under the Antitrust Laws," 17 Bus.Law. 897 (1962); Withrow, "Making Compliance Programs Work", 17 Bus.Law. 877 (1962); Whiting, "Antitrust and Corporate Executive", 47 Va.L.Rev. 929 (1961), 48 id. 1 (1962).

24. Manheim Dairy Co. v. Little Falls Nat'l Bank, 54 N.Y.S.2d 345 (Sup.Ct.1945).

persons,[25] such corporate personnel would be responsible to such third persons according to the ordinary principles of tort law, and if such acts were committed during the scope of corporate activity, the corporation would be vicariously responsible to such third persons under the doctrine of *respondeat superior*.[26] Such torts might or might not involve breach of duty to the corporation. Depending on the circumstances, the corporation might implead any corporate personnel who has subjected it to such liability, seek indemnification from such wrongdoer, or be required or permitted to indemnify such corporate personnel.[27]

Directors and officers are usually not liable to any third person for inducing the corporation, in the exercise of their business judgment to breach its contract with such third person.[28]

Negligence to the corporation precludes application of the "business judgment" rule.[29]

The burden of proof, of course, is on the plaintiff to establish negligence, causation, and damage.[30] In a law action such issues would usually be decided by a jury.[31] Even in an equity action, such as a derivative action or where equitable relief is sought, the issue of negligence might be referred to a jury.[32]

For actionable negligence, the tortfeasors responsible are jointly and severally liable.[33]

FIDUCIARY DUTIES—IN GENERAL

235. **Directors, officers, and possibly controlling shareholders, owe fiduciary duties to their corporation and possibly to other shareholders. A growing number of statutes provide in general terms that directors and officers are in a fiduciary relationship to their corporation and possibly to shareholders. Fiduciary duties require good faith and fair dealing. Cases involving fiduciary duties can be**

---

25. New England Box Co. v. Gilbert, 100 N.H. 257, 123 A.2d 833 (1956). See Bystrom v. Villard, 175 App.Div. 433, 162 N.Y.S. 100 (1st Dep't 1916), appeal dismissed 220 N.Y. 765, 116 N.E. 1038 (1917) (directors held liable to purchaser for misrepresentations inducing purchase of shares; Von Au v. Magenheimer, 126 App.Div. 257, 110 N.Y.S. 629 (2d Dep't 1908), aff'd mem., 196 N.Y. 510, 89 N.E. 1114 (1909) (directors held liable to shareholder for misrepresentation inducing sale of shares and for manipulating and depressing value of shares). See also Evans v. Rohrbach, 35 N.J.Super. 260, 113 A.2d 838 (1955) (directors and officers held not liable for accident to corporate employee injured performing hazardous act for corporation).

26. Douglas, "Vicarious Liability and Administration of Risk", 38 Yale L.J. 584, 720 (1929); Laski, "The Basis of Vicarious Liability", 26 Yale L.J. 105 (1916).

27. See sections 379, 380 infra.

28. Marin v. Jacuzzi, 224 Cal.App.2d 549, 36 Cal. Rptr. 880 (1964); Wampler v. Palmerton, 250 Or. 65, 439 P.2d 601 (1968); A. S. Rampell, Inc. v. Hyster Co., 3 N.Y.2d 369, 165 N.Y.S.2d 475, 144 N.E. 2d 371 (1957); Potter v. Minskoff, 2 A.D.2d 513, 156 N.Y.S.2d 872 (4th Dep't 1956), aff'd mem., 4 N.Y.2d 695, 171 N.Y.S.2d 88, 148 N.E.2d 303 (1958); Horan v. John F. Trommer, Inc., 124 N.Y.S.2d 217 (Sup. Ct.1953), 129 N.Y.S.2d 539 (Sup.Ct.1954), aff'd mem., 283 App.Div. 774, 128 N.Y.S.2d 595 (1st Dep't 1954). However, directors and officers are liable for inducing breach of contract when they do so for personal gain. Ehrlich v. Alper, 145 N.Y.S.2d 252 (Sup.Ct. 1955), aff'd mem., 1 A.D.2d 875, 149 N.Y.S.2d 562 (1st Dep't 1956); Buckley v. 112 Central Park South, Inc., 285 App.Div. 331, 136 N.Y.S.2d 233 (1st

Dep't 1954). See Avins, "Liability for Inducing a Corporation to Breach Its Contract", 43 Cornell L. Q. 55 (1957). Cf. Emmert v. Drake, 224 F.2d 299 (5th Cir.1955) (directors held personally liable for corporation's not paying notes with first proceeds from sale of shares as provided in notes).

29. See section 242 infra.

30. Anderson v. Akers, 7 F.Supp. 924 (W.D.Ky.1934), modified sub nom. Atherton v. Anderson, 86 F.2d 518 (6th Cir.1936), modified sub nom. Anderson v. Atherton, 302 U.S. 643, 58 S.Ct. 53, 82 L.Ed. 500 (1937); Barnes v. Andrews, 298 F. 614 (S.D.N.Y. 1924).

31. See Regional Land Corp. v. McLaughlin, 334 Mass. 276, 135 N.E.2d 24 (1956).

32. E. g., McKinney's N.Y.Gen.Corp.Law, § 61 (inapplicable since 1963 to business corporations). See also Ross v. Bernhard, —— U.S. ——, 90 S.Ct. 733, —— L.Ed.2d —— (1970) (holding shareholders in federal court derivative action are guaranteed jury trial on issues triable by jury if corporation were suing directly); DePinto v. Provident Security Life Ins. Co., 323 F.2d 826 (9th Cir.1963), cert. denied 376 U.S. 950, 84 S.Ct. 965, 11 L.Ed.2d 969 (1964); Richland v. Crandall, 259 F.Supp. 274 (S.D.N.Y.1966); Comment, "The Right to a Jury Trial in a Stockholder's Derivative Action", 74 Yale L.J. 725 (1965).

33. Absent a joint judgment, there might be no right of contribution.

traditionally classified into those involving **(a) competing with the corporation, (b) usurping corporate opportunity, (c) having some interest which conflicts with the interest of the corporation, (d) insider trading, (e) oppression of minority shareholders, and (f) sale of control,** but such situations do not exhaust the possible corporate applications of fiduciary concepts.

Corporate managerial powers, being powers in trust, must be exercised honestly and in good faith. The director or officer

"owes loyalty and allegiance to the corporation—a loyalty that is undivided and an allegiance that is influenced in action by no consideration other than the welfare of the corporation. Any adverse interest of a director will be subjected to a scrutiny rigid and uncompromising. He may not profit at the expense of his corporation and in conflict with its rights; he may not for personal gain divert unto himself the opportunities which in equity and fairness belong to his corporation. He is required to use his independent judgment. In the discharge of his duties a director must, of course, act honestly and in good faith . . . ." [1]

In the words of a leading case, which actually involved a joint venture rather than a corporation, but which is frequently cited in cases involving alleged breaches of fiduciary duties by corporate directors, officers, or controlling shareholders: [2]

"Joint adventurers, like copartners, owe to one another, while the enterprise continues, the duty of the finest loyalty. Many forms of conduct permissible in a workaday world for those acting at arm's length, are forbidden to those bound by fiduciary ties. A trustee is held to something stricter than the morals of the market place. Not honesty alone, but the punctilio of an honor the most sensitive, is

then the standard of behavior. As to this there has developed a tradition that is unbending and inveterate. Uncompromising rigidity has been the attitude of courts of equity when petitioned to undermine the rule of undivided loyalty by the 'disintegrating erosion' of particular exceptions . . . Only thus has the level of conduct for fiduciaries been kept at a level higher than that trodden by the crowd. It will not consciously be lowered by any judgment of this court."

While analogies to fiduciary principles applied to trustees, partners, joint venturers, agents, and others in fiduciary positions may be helpful, such principles are not always strictly applicable to the director, officer, and controlling shareholder. Of course, the officers are agents of the corporation, subject to all of the fiduciary rules of agency, but both the directors, being usually part-time with other business interests and often serving gratuitously, and the controlling shareholders, whose shares are traditionally their own private property to enjoy as they will, are not always subjected to the strictest rules applicable to fiduciaries like trustees.

To say that directors, officers, and controlling shareholders are fiduciaries is then, only the first step in any analysis. As stated by Frankfurter, J.: [3]

---

1. Litwin (Rosemarin) v. Allen, 25 N.Y.S.2d 667, 677–678 (Sup.Ct.1940).

2. Cardozo, J., in Meinhard v. Salmon, 249 N.Y. 458, 463–464, 164 N.E. 545, 546, 62 A.L.R. 1, 4–5 (1928).

3. Securities and Exchange Commission v. Chenery Corp., 318 U.S. 80, 85–86, 63 S.Ct. 454, 458, 87 L.Ed. 626, 631–632 (1943). Tarver, "Arrogance of Corporate Power: A Study of the Evolution of the Fiduciary Duty Owed by Management to the Corporation or Its Shareholders", 42 Tulane L.Rev. 155 (1967); Sealy, "The Director as Trustee", 1967 Camb.L.J. 83; Brudney, "Fiduciary Ideology in Transactions Affecting Corporate Control", 65 Mich.L.Rev. 259 (1966); Israels, "Are Corporate Powers Still Held in Trust?", 64 Colum.L.Rev. 1446 (1964). See Bayne, "The Fiduciary Duty of Management: The Concept in the Courts", 35 U. Det.L.J. 561 (1958); Tilden, "The Fiduciary Duty of Corporation Directors in Massachusetts", 28 B.U.L. Rev. 265 (1948); Dodd, "For Whom Are Corporate Managers Trustees?", 45 Harv.L.Rev. 1145 (1932); Berle, "Corporate Powers as Powers in Trust", 44 Harv.L.Rev. 1049 (1931); Comment, "Fiduciary Duties of Directors and Officers of Private Corpora-

". . . But to say that a man is a fiduciary only begins analysis; it gives direction to further inquiry. To whom is he a fiduciary? What obligations does he owe as a fiduciary? In what respects has he failed to discharge these obligations? And what are the consequences of his deviation from duty?"

A growing number of statutes restate in general terms the rule that directors and officers are in a fiduciary relationship to their corporation,[4] and perhaps to shareholders as well.[5]

Breach of a fiduciary duty precludes application of the "business judgment" rule.[6]

Fiduciary duties and their correlative rights are an abstraction unless defined in terms of their persons of inherence and of incidence, their subject matter, and the acts or forbearances they require.

To the extent that fiduciary duties are applicable to any situation, they generally require good faith and fair dealing. Cases involving the fiduciary duties of directors, officers, and controlling shareholders can be traditionally classified into those involving (a) competing with the corporation,[7] (b) usurping a corporate opportunity,[8] (c) having some interest which conflicts with the interest of the corporation,[9] (d) insider

trading,[10] (e) authorizing some corporate transaction which oppresses minority shareholders,[11] and (f) sale of control.[12] These situations, of course, do not exhaust the possible corporate applications of fiduciary concepts.

FIDUCIARY DUTIES—COMPETING WITH CORPORATION

236. **Directors and officers, as fiduciaries of their corporation, are subject to the rule of undivided loyalty which, inter alia, restricts their competing with their corporation. Directors and officers are not necessarily precluded from engaging in other businesses, but may not use their corporate positions to prevent the corporation from competing with them, use corporate personnel, facilities, or funds for their other businesses, disclose corporate trade secrets to others, lure away corporate business or personnel, receive secret commissions on corporate transactions, improperly profit by acquiring claims against their corporation, or breach reasonable covenants not to compete. Many cases of fiduciaries' competing with their corporations can be subclassified into situations involving what is known as "usurpation of corporate opportunity" or "conflicting interest", although the various situations often tend to merge.**

Directors and officers, because of their fiduciary relationship with their corporation, are subject to the rule of undivided loyalty. This rule, *inter alia* restricts the fiduciary from competing with his corporation.[1]

However, a director or officer, besides his corporate activities, has personal interests to advance. Hence, too strict an application of the rule of undivided loyalty would tend to restrict freedom of enterprise and to dis-

tions", 27 Tenn.L.Rev. 284 (1960). See also United States v. Liner, 300 F.Supp. 996 (D.Mass.1969) (holding that former director/officer was under no fiduciary duty to corporation).

4. See section 232 supra. Some statutes are noncommittal as to whom the fiduciary duties are owed.

5. See section 232 supra, and sections 298, 301 infra; Greene, "Fiduciary Standards of Conduct under the Investment Company Act of 1940", 28 Geo.Wash.L. Rev. 266 (1959).

6. Steinberg v. Altschuler, 158 N.Y.S.2d 411 (Sup.Ct. 1956); Bayer v. Beran, 49 N.Y.S.2d 2 (Sup.Ct.1944). See section 242 infra.

7. See section 236 infra.

8. See section 237 infra.

9. See section 238 infra.

10. See sections 239, 298 infra.

11. See section 240 infra.

12. See section 241 infra.

1. Newman, "Formation of Competing Enterprise by Corporate Fiduciary", 3 Houston L.Rev. 221 (1965); Ramsey, "Director's Power to Compete with his Corporation", 18 Ind.L.J. 293 (1943); Note, 50 Mich.L.Rev. 471 (1952); Note, 26 St.John's L.Rev. 116 (1951).

courage competent men from serving in corporate directorships or offices, especially the former, which are generally part-time and often involve no or only nominal compensation.

The general rule is that directors and officers, especially directors, may engage in independent business, but if such business competes with the business of the corporation, equitable limitations apply.[2]

The fiduciary may not, for example, use his corporate position to prevent the corporation from competing with himself;[3] use corporate personnel, facilities, or funds for his own business;[4] disclose trade secrets of his corporation to others;[5] lure away corporate business[6] or personnel;[7] or receive, unknown to his corporation, a commission on a corporate transaction.[8]

Where a fiduciary competes with his corporation in breach of his fiduciary duties, the corporation is entitled to damages to itself or profits realized by the fiduciary and may be able to attach a constructive trust to any property acquired by the fiduciary.[9]

Plans; Secretary Spies on Employees of Electronics Company: How to Guard Toy Designs; Barrage of Suits and Denials", 160 The Wall Street Journal, No. 68, 1 (Oct. 5, 1962).

2.   Guth v. Loft, Inc., 23 Del.Ch. 255, 280, 5 A.2d 503, 514 (Sup.Ct.1939); Red Top Cab Co. v. Hanchett, 48 F.2d 236 (N.D.Cal.1931); Fuller, "Restrictions Imposed by the Directorship Status on the Personal Business Activities of Directors", 26 Wash.U.L.Q. 189 (1940). Of course, by agreement, the corporation could restrict outside competitive activities on the part of corporate personnel. Corporations often impose reasonable restrictions on competitive activities after a person leaves the corporation. See notes 10–16 infra.

3.   Singer v. Carlisle, 26 N.Y.S.2d 172 (Sup.Ct.1940), aff'd mem., 261 App.Div. 897, 26 N.Y.S.2d 320 (1st Dep't 1941), motion for leave to appeal denied 261 App.Div. 956, 27 N.Y.S.2d 190 (1st Dep't 1941).

4.   Guth v. Loft, Inc., 23 Del.Ch. 255, 5 A.2d 503 (Sup.Ct.1939).

5.   Components For Research, Inc. v. Isolation Products, Inc., 241 Cal.App.2d 726, 50 Cal.Rptr. 829 (1966); Schulenburg v. Signatrol, 33 Ill.2d 379, 212 N.E.2d 865 (1965), cert. denied 383 U.S. 959, 86 S.Ct. 1225, 16 L.Ed.2d 302 (1966) (injunction restraining use of trade secrets limited to period which would have been required for lawful duplication of product); Beaudette v. Graham, 267 Mass. 7, 165 N.E. 671 (1929). Cf. Hudson Valley Propane Corp. v. Byrne, 24 A.D.2d 908, 264 N.Y.S.2d 416 (3d Dep't 1965) (where employee previously knew some customers); R. Ellis, Trade Secrets (1953); Harding, "Trade Secrets and the Mobile Employee", 22 Bus. Law. 395 (1967); Leydig, "Protecting Trade Secrets When Employees Move", 21 Bus.Law. 325 (1966); Drummond, "Trade Secrets and Agreements Not to Compete: A Bibliography", 6 Corp.Prac.Comm. 92 (May 1964); Comment, "The Obligation of a High-Level Employee to His Former Employer: The *Standard Brands* Case", 29 U.Chi.L.Rev. 339 (1962). See also Carley, "The Secret Stealers; Firms Seek to Curb Job Hoppers Who Take Their Confidential

6.   Hoggan & Hall & Higgins, Inc. v. Hall, 18 Utah 2d 3, 414 P.2d 89 (1966); Hayes v. Schweikarts Upholstering Co., 402 S.W.2d 472 (Tenn.Ct.App.1966); Raines v. Toney, 228 Ark. 1170, 313 S.W.2d 802 (1958); Duane Jones Co. v. Burke, 306 N.Y. 172, 117 N.E.2d 237 (1954); Battle Creek Food Co. v. Kirkland, 298 Mich. 515, 299 N.W. 167 (1941); Coleman v. Hanger, 210 Ky. 309, 275 S.W. 784 (1924).

7.   Bancroft-Whitney Co. v. Glen, 64 Cal.2d 327, 49 Cal.Rptr. 825, 411 P.2d 921 (1966); Hoggan & Hall & Higgins, Inc. v. Hall, 18 Utah 2d 3, 414 P.2d 89 (1966); Duane Jones Co. v. Burke, 306 N.Y. 172, 117 N.E.2d 237 (1954).

8.   Wilshire Oil Co. v. Riffe, 381 F.2d 646 (10th Cir.1967), cert. denied 389 U.S. 822, 88 S.Ct. 50, 19 L.Ed.2d 75 (1968) (holding transfer of shares of competing concern to children of executive vice-president of corporation was breach both of latter's fiduciary duties to corporation and of his contract providing that he would not invest in competing concern, etc.); Flynn v. Zimmerman, 231 Ill.App.2d 467, 163 N.E.2d 568 (1960); Knox Glass Bottle Co. v. Underwood, 228 Miss. 699, 89 So.2d 799 (1956), cert. denied, 353 U.S. 977, 77 S.Ct. 1060, 1 L.Ed.2d 1137 (1957).

9.   Bancroft-Whitney Co. v. Glen, 64 Cal.2d 327, 49 Cal.Rptr. 825, 411 P.2d 921 (1966) (damages against disloyal former president and competitor and its president who induced breach of president's fiduciary duties); Sequoia Vacuum Systems v. Stransky, 229 Cal.App.2d 281, 40 Cal.Rptr. 203 (1964) (recovery of $1,600 in lost profits and $5,000 punitive damages against double-dealing corporate officer); Hussong Dyeing Mach. Co. v. Morris, 89 A. 249 (N. J.Ch.1913). But see Lincoln Stores, Inc. v. Grant, 309 Mass. 417, 34 N.E.2d 704 (1941); cf. Durfee v. Durfee & Canning Inc., 323 Mass. 187, 80 N.E.2d 522 (1948); Eccles v. Sylvester, 131 Colo. 296, 281 P.2d 1006 (1955) (failure of case for lack of proof of damage to corporation). See also Maclary v. Pleasant Hills, Inc., 35 Del.Ch. 39, 109 A.2d 830 (Ch. 1954).

Covenants not to compete [10] will be enforced when reasonable as to time [11] and area.[12] Such covenants, because they limit competition and a person's ability to pursue his livelihood, are usually strictly construed.[13] Where covenants are too restrictive, some courts "blue pencil" the restrictions by narrowing them to reasonable scope,[14] while other courts treat them as entirely invalid.[15]

For breach of valid covenants not to compete, a panoply of remedies is available to the employer.[16]

Many cases of fiduciaries' competing with their corporations can be subclassified into situations involving what is known as "usurpation of corporate opportunity" [17] or "conflicting interest",[18] although the various situations often tend to merge.[19]

10. Blake, "Employee Agreements Not to Compete", 73 Harv.L.Rev. 625 (1960); Note, "Antitrust Significance of Covenants Not to Compete", 64 Mich.L.Rev. 503 (1966). See also Redmond, "Corporate Recruiting—Unfair Competition Considerations", 24 Bus. Law. 459 (1969).

11. Brenner v. Barco Chemicals Division, Inc., 209 So.2d 277 (Fla.Dist.Ct.App.1968).

12. Taylor Freezer Sales Corp. v. Sweden Freezer E. Corp., 224 Ga. 160, 160 S.E.2d 356 (1968).

13. Purchasing Associates v. Weitz, 13 N.Y.2d 267, 246 N.Y.S.2d 600, 196 N.E.2d 245 (1963) (refusing to enforce employee's covenant not to compete because his services were not unique and there was no sale of business—no assets, only know-how, transferred). Compare Engineering Associates v. Pankow, 268 N. C. 137, 150 S.E.2d 56 (1966) (holding covenant not to compete made after start of employment would have required additional consideration), with Beneficial Finance Co. of Lebanon v. Becker, 422 Pa. 531, 222 A.2d 873 (1966) (upholding covenant not to compete signed by employee two days after employment started and accepted by employer's parent foreign corporation nine days later, even though employment contract terminable by either party on five days' notice).

14. Credit Bureau Mgmt. Co. v. Hine, 254 F.Supp. 547 (E.D.Ark.1966) (reforming unreasonable five-year term to two years where out-of-state covenant had specific clause that if its restrictions should be found legally enforceable they could be reduced to enforceable limits).

15. House of Vision, Inc. v. Hiyane, 37 Ill.2d 32, 225 N.E.2d 21 (1967) (reversing trial court's modification of covenant not to compete within 30-mile radius without time limitation to 20-mile radius with five-year limitation, and directing dismissal of complaint); Baker v. Starkey, 259 Iowa 480, 144 N.W. 2d 889 (1966) (refusing to narrow too-broad restrictions on ground too-restrictive covenants often are observed by former employees, and to allow employers to use broad language and then to enforce such covenants to extent reasonable would give employers unconscionable advantage over employees).

16. Capelonto v. Orkin Exterminating Co., 183 So.2d 532 (Fla.1966), appeal dismissed 385 U.S. 11, 87 S.

Ct. 78, 17 L.Ed.2d 10 (1966), reh. denied 385 U.S. 964, 87 S.Ct. 390, 17 L.Ed.2d 310 (1966) (upholding injunction against competing former employee for two years from decree where covenant not to compete was for two years following termination of employment); U-Haul Co. of North Carolina v. Jones, 269 N.C. 284, 152 S.E.2d 65 (1967) (holding provision for liquidated damages not to preclude injunctive relief); Mansfield v. B & W Gas, Inc., 222 Ga. 259, 149 S.E.2d 482 (1966) (enforcing covenant not to compete, found reasonable as to time and area, against employee even if he were wrongfully discharged, where covenant read "regardless of who was at fault"); S. Tepfer & Sons v. Zscheler, 25 A. D.2d 786, 269 N.Y.S.2d 552 (2d Dep't 1966) (requiring former employees to turn back salaries paid for time they spent in planning to set up competing business); Haggerty v. Burkey Mills, Inc., 211 F. Supp. 835 (E.D.N.Y.1962) (holding back commissions of disloyal employee). But see Advance Industrial Security, Inc. v. William J. Burns I. D. Agency, 377 F.2d 236 (5th Cir.1967) (holding unenforceable covenant not to compete made in state by foreign corporation prior to qualification in Alabama).

17. See section 237 infra.

18. See section 238 infra.

19. Ramsey, "Director's Power to Compete with his Corporation", 18 Ind.L.J. 293, 304 (1943). Cases involving the acquisition by a corporate fiduciary of claims against his corporation, in a sense, may involve competing with the corporation and usurping a corporate opportunity. Weissman v. A. Weissman, Inc., 374 Pa. 470, 97 A.2d 870 (1953) (president-director held to hold corporate mortgage he purchased on corporate property as constructive trustee for corporation), 382 Pa. 189, 114 A.2d 797 (1955) (president-director allowed to foreclose mortgage on corporate property to extent of his personal advances to former mortgagees); Mothershead v. Douglas, 215 Ark. 519, 221 S.W.2d 424 (1949). Cf. Manufacturers Trust Co. v. Becker, 338 U.S. 304, 70 S.Ct. 127, 94 L.Ed. 107 (1949) (claims of directors who acquired bankrupt corporation's debentures at discount allowed). See also Matter of People (Bond & Mtge. Guar. Co.), 303 N.Y. 423, 103 N.E.2d 721 (1952) (liquidation trustee's attorney who acquired claims against corporation required to surrender them and to account for any profit realized); Securities and Exchange Commission v. Chenery Corp., 332 U.S. 194, 67 S.Ct. 1575, 67 S.Ct. 1760, 91 L.Ed. 1995 (1947) (management not allowed to benefit from shares traded during reorganization under Federal Public Utility Holding Company Act of 1935); Securities and Exchange Commission v. Dumaine, 218 F.2d 308 (1st Cir.1954) (compensation denied reorganization committee member because wife traded in securities of corporation), cert. denied sub

FIDUCIARY DUTIES—USURPATION OF CORPORATE OPPORTUNITY

237. The "corporate opportunity" doctrine, an aspect of the undivided loyalty rule, precludes corporate personnel from diverting unto themselves opportunities in which the corporation has a right, property interest, or expectancy, or which in justice should belong to the corporation. If the corporation rejects the opportunity, at least by a disinterested vote of the board of directors after full disclosure, it usually ceases to be a corporate opportunity, although some cases apply the undivided loyalty rule strictly. For usurpation of a corporate opportunity, the corporation can recover any damages to it or profits realized by the fiduciary or attach a constructive trust for its benefit on any traceable subject matter of the opportunity.

Another of the several aspects of the rule of undivided loyalty, imposed on fiduciaries, is the so-called doctrine of "corporate opportunity".[1] Corporate personnel may not for personal gain divert unto themselves the opportunities which in equity and fairness belong to their corporation.[2]

The critical question is whether the opportunity is a corporate one or one within the legitimate scope of the individual interests of the director or officer. The answer is dependent upon the facts and circumstances of the specific situation.[3]

The opportunity is a corporate opportunity if the corporation has a right, property interest, or expectancy in the opportunity,[4]

nom. Dumaine v. Securities and Exchange Commission, 349 U.S. 929, 75 S.Ct. 771, 99 L.Ed. 1259 (1955); 11 U.S.C.A. § 649 (barring compensation or reimbursement to Chapter X reorganization committee member or attorney acquiring claims or shares in debtor corporation). See Comment, "Purchases of Corporate Indebtedness by a Fiduciary", 1960 Duke L.J. 613.

1. See generally M. Feuer, Handbook for Corporate Directors ch. 9 (1965); Slaughter, "Corporate Opportunity Doctrine", 18 Sw.L.J. 96 (1964); Wadmond, "Seizure of Corporate Opportunity", 17 Bus. Law. 63 (1961); Walker, "Legal Handles Used to Open or Close the Corporate Opportunity Door", 56 Nw.U.L.Rev. 608 (1961); Carrington & McElroy, "The Doctrine of Corporate Opportunity as Applied to Officers, Directors and Stockholders of Corporations", 14 Bus.Law. 957 (1959); Comment, "The Doctrine of Corporate Opportunity: Has It Meaning in Arizona?", 9 Ariz.L.Rev. 59 (1967); Comment, "Liability of Directors and Other Officers for Usurpation of Corporate Opportunities", 26 Fordham L.Rev. 528 (1957); Comment, "The Doctrine of Corporate Opportunity", 26 U.Cin.L.Rev. 104 (1957); Comment, "A Survey of Corporate Opportunity", 45 Geo.L.J. 99 (1956); Comment, "The Doctrine of Corporate Opportunities", 31 Calif.L.Rev. 188 (1943); Note, "Corporate Opportunity in the Close Corporation—A Different Result?", 56 Geo. L.J. 381 (1967); Notes, 10 Wyo.L.J. 143 (1956); 74 Harv.L.Rev. 765 (1961).

2. Knutsen v. Frushour, 92 Idaho 37, 436 P.2d 521 (1968) (real property); Schildberg Rock Products

Co. v. Brooks, 258 Iowa 759, 140 N.W.2d 132 (1966) (lease); Hubbard v. Pape, 2 Ohio App.2d 326, 203 N.E.2d 365 (1964) (competing business); General Automotive Mfg. Co. v. Singer, 19 Wis.2d 528, 120 N.W.2d 659 (1963) (holding former general manager of corporation liable for secret profits realized from orders which he diverted to corporation's competitors); Zampetti v. Cavanaugh, 406 Pa. 259, 176 A. 2d 906 (1962) (shareholder action by one-third shareholder in corporation, holding two directors who diverted corporate opportunity to their new corporation, to account to first corporation as constructive trustees regarding new corporation's earnings and ordering each of them to turn over one-sixth of their shares in new corporation to plaintiff); Ragnar Benson, Inc. v. Kassab, 325 F.2d 591 (3d Cir. 1963) (holding director of corporation liable for diversion to himself of corporate opportunity with respect to construction contract, but exonerating other party to contract because corporation by its silence had mislead such party into believing that it had consented to director's making such contract); American Investment Co. of Ill. v. Lichtenstein, 134 F.Supp. 857 (E.D.Mo.1955); Durfee v. Durfee & Canning, Inc., 323 Mass. 187, 199, 204, 80 N.E.2d 522, 529, 531–532 (1948); Turner v. American Metal Co., 36 N.Y.S.2d 356 (Sup.Ct.1942), modified on other grounds 268 App.Div. 239, 50 N.Y.S.2d 800 (1st Dep't 1944), appeal dismissed 295 N.Y. 822, 66 N.E. 2d 591 (1946); Litwin (Rosemarin) v. Allen, 25 N. Y.S.2d 667, 677–678 (Sup.Ct.1940).

3. Burg v. Horn, 380 F.2d 897 (2d Cir. 1967); Irving Trust Co. v. Deutsch, 73 F.2d 121 (2d Cir. 1934), cert. denied 294 U.S. 708, 55 S.Ct. 405, 79 L.Ed. 1243 (1935), petition for reh. denied 294 U.S. 733, 55 S.Ct. 514, 79 L.Ed. 1242 (1935).

4. Burg v. Horn, 380 F.2d 897 (2d Cir. 1967) (2–1) (holding that since defendant corporate directors of corporation operating low rent housing buildings spent most of their time in unrelated enterprises and already owned other corporations holding similar properties when corporation in which plaintiff was shareholder was formed—facts well known to plaintiff—no duty to offer corporation all such low rent buildings coming to their attention could be implied absent further evidence of agreement to such effect); Liddell v. Smith, 65 Ill.App.2d 352, 213 N.E.2d 604 (1965) (upholding receivership where controlling shareholder advanced personal funds for development and took title in own name of realty which corporation could have bought); Higgins v. Shenango Pottery Co., 256 F.2d 504 (3d Cir. 1958); Fayes, Inc. v. Kline, 136 F.Supp. 871 (S.D.N.Y.

or the opportunity is one which in justice should belong to the corporation.[5]

Obviously, if the corporation has been seeking such an opportunity,[6] or the opportunity has been offered to it,[7] or its funds have been involved in financing the opportunity [8] or its facilities or personnel have been used in developing the opportunity,[9] the opportunity in justice should belong to the corporation.

However, when the opportunity unexpectedly appears,[10] is offered personally to a person who happens to be a director or officer,[11] and corporate funds are not involved,[12] it need not be regarded as a corporate opportunity.

The opportunity might involve multiple aspects, only part of which might be construed as involving a corporate opportunity.[13]

1955); Guth v. Loft, Inc., 23 Del.Ch. 255, 5 A.2d 503 (Sup.Ct.1939); Singer v. Carlisle, 26 N.Y.S.2d 172 (Sup.Ct.1940), aff'd mem., 261 App.Div. 897, 26 N.Y. S.2d 320 (1st Dep't 1941), motion for leave to appeal denied 261 App.Div. 956, 27 N.Y.S.2d 190 (1st Dep't 1941); Weissman v. A. Weissman, Inc., 374 Pa. 470, 97 A.2d 870 (1953). See also Meinhard v. Salmon, 249 N.Y. 458, 164 N.E. 545, 62 A.L.R. 1 (1928). Cf. Blaustein v. Pan American Petroleum & Transport Co., 293 N.Y. 281, 56 N.E.2d 705 (1944). Opportunities to speculate in commodities have been held not to constitute corporate opportunities where the corporation was not engaged in such activities. Lancaster Loose Leaf Tobacco Co. v. Robinson, 199 Ky. 313, 250 S.W. 997 (1923) (tobacco); Broderick v. Blanton, 59 N.Y.S.2d 136 (Sup.Ct.1945) (whiskey). Compare Irving Trust Co. v. Deutsch, 73 F.2d 121 (2d Cir. 1934), cert. denied 294 U.S. 708, 55 S.Ct. 405, 79 L.Ed. 1243 (1935), petition for reh. denied, 294 U.S. 733, 55 S.Ct. 514, 79 L.Ed. 1242 (1935), with Litwin (Rosemarin) v. Allen, 25 N.Y.S. 2d 667 (Sup.Ct.1940) (share speculation). Compare Howell v. McCloskey, 375 Pa. 100, 99 A.2d 610 (1953) (no corporate interest in own shares with balance of power), with Brown v. Dolese Bros. Co., 38 Del.Ch. 471, 154 A.2d 233 (Ch.1959), aff'd, 39 Del.Ch. 1, 157 A.2d 784 (Sup.Ct.1960) (corporate option to reacquire shares). See also Vulcanized Rubber & Plastics Co. v. Scheckter, 400 Pa. 405, 162 A. 2d 400 (1960) (secret purchase of controlling shares held no usurpation of corporate opportunity). Compare Faraclas v. City Vending Co., 232 Md. 457, 194 A.2d 298 (1963). See also Brophy v. Cities Service Co., 31 Del.Ch. 241, 70 A.2d 5 (Ch.1949). But see Northern Trust Co. v. Essaness Theatres Corp., 348 Ill.App. 134, 108 N.E.2d 493 (1952).

5. Comment, "Liability of Directors and Other Officers for Usurpation of Corporate Opportunities", 26 Fordham L.Rev. 528, 529 (1957).

6. Irving Trust Co. v. Deutsch, 73 F.2d 121 (2d Cir. 1934), cert. denied 294 U.S. 708, 55 S.Ct. 405, 79 L. Ed. 1243 (1935), petition for reh. denied, 294 U. S. 733, 55 S.Ct. 514, 79 L.Ed. 1242 (1935); Guth v. Loft, Inc., 23 Del.Ch. 255, 5 A.2d 503 (Sup.Ct.1939). Cf. Johnston v. Greene, 35 Del.Ch. 479, 121 A.2d 919 (Sup.Ct.1956), rev'g Greene v. Allen, 35 Del.Ch. 242, 114 A.2d 916 (Ch.1955).

7. Irving Trust Co. v. Deutsch, 73 F.2d 121 (2d Cir. 1934), cert. denied, 294 U.S. 708, 55 S.Ct. 405, 79 L. Ed. 1243 (1935), petition for reh. denied, 294 U.S. 733, 55 S.Ct. 514, 79 L.Ed. 1242 (1935); McClure v. Law, 161 N.Y. 78, 55 N.E. 388 (1899).

8. Paulman v. Kritzer, 74 Ill.App.2d 284, 219 N.E.2d 541 (1966), aff'd 38 Ill.2d 101, 230 N.E.2d 262 (1967);

Brown v. Dolese Bros. Co., 38 Del.Ch. 471, 154 A.2d 233 (Ch.1959), aff'd 39 Del. 1, 157 A.2d 784 (Sup.Ct. 1960); Samia v. Central Oil Co., 339 Mass. 101, 158 N.E.2d 469 (1959); Broadway Federal S. & L. Ass'n v. Howard, 133 Cal.App.2d 382, 285 P.2d 61 (1955); Guth v. Loft, Inc., 23 Del.Ch. 255, 5 A.2d 503 (Sup. Ct.1939).

9. Ibid.

10. Johnston v. Greene, 35 Del.Ch. 479, 121 A.2d 919 (Sup.Ct.1956).

11. Equity Corp. v. Milton, 42 Del.Ch. 425, 221 A.2d 494 (Sup.Ct.1966) (upholding reacquisition by officer-director of 1,800,000 shares of investment company, where (a) opportunity came to him personally, and (b) corporation had no policy to acquire its own shares); Johnston v. Greene, 35 Del.Ch. 479, 121 A.2d 919 (Sup.Ct.1956); cf. Litwin (Rosemarin) v. Allen, 25 N.Y.S.2d 667 (Sup.Ct.1940). Of course, a fiduciary who takes an opportunity and resells it to the corporation and realizes a secret profit could be compelled to account. New York Trust Co. v. American Realty Co., 244 N.Y. 209, 155 N.E. 102 (1926); cf. Tower Recreation, Inc. v. Beard, —— Ind.App. ——, 231 N.E.2d 154 (1967) (holding that director who innocently acquired property could resell it to corporation for profit); Dravosburg Land Co. v. Scott, 340 Pa. 280, 16 A.2d 415 (1940). If the fiduciary has been authorized to negotiate in behalf of the corporation he usually cannot regard the opportunity as a personal one. 1 F. Mechem, Agency § 1224 (2d ed. 1914); Irving Trust Co. v. Deutsch, 73 F.2d 121 (2d Cir. 1934), cert. denied 294 U.S. 708, 55 S.Ct. 405, 79 L.Ed. 1243 (1935), petition for reh. denied, 294 U.S. 733, 55 S.Ct. 514, 79 L.Ed. 1242 (1935); Procario v. 74 & 76 West Tremont Ave. Corp., 3 N.Y.2d 973, 169 N.Y.S.2d 39, 146 N.E. 2d 795 (1957).

12. Johnston v. Greene, 35 Del.Ch. 479, 121 A.2d 919 (Sup.Ct.1956); Litwin (Rosemarin) v. Allen, 25 N. Y.S.2d 667 (Sup.Ct.1940). Cf. Irving Trust Co. v. Deutsch, 73 F.2d 121 (2d Cir. 1934), cert. denied 294 U.S. 708, 55 S.Ct. 405, 79 L.Ed. 1243 (1935), petition for reh. denied 294 U.S. 733, 55 S.Ct. 514, 79 L.Ed. 1242 (1935).

13. Litwin (Rosemarin) v. Allen, 25 N.Y.S.2d 667 (Sup.Ct.1940) (underwriting and post-underwriting

If the corporation is unable to accept the opportunity, such as, for example, because its exploitation of the opportunity would be *ultra vires,* it might be found not to constitute a corporate opportunity.[14] Even under such circumstances, however, at least one case has held that the opportunity was a corporate opportunity which management could not accept personally but should be shared by the shareholders proportionately.[15]

If the opportunity is rejected by the corporation, at least by a disinterested vote of the board of directors after full disclosure, the opportunity usually ceases to be a corporate opportunity.[16]

If the corporation is unable to finance the opportunity, the directors and officers are, of course, not required to advance their personal funds to enable the corporation to finance it.[17] However, the directors and officers should use their best efforts to secure the necessary financing. If they fail to do their best and personally take the opportunity, they cannot defend on the ground that the opportunity ceased to be a corporate opportunity because the corporation could not finance it.[18] Even if the directors and officers use their best efforts to raise the necessary funds for the corporation and are unable to do so, and they thereafter personally take the opportunity, or even such portion thereof as the corporation is unable to finance, some cases, applying the strict rule of undivided loyalty, have found that they have usurped a corporate opportunity.[19]

Shareholder ratification might estop shareholders who, after full disclosure, joined in the ratification,[20] but in most juris-

opportunities). Compare Johnston v. Greene, 35 Del.Ch. 479, 121 A.2d 919 (Sup.Ct.1956) (shares-patents), with Irving Trust Co. v. Deutsch, 73 F.2d 121 (2d Cir. 1934), cert. denied 294 U.S. 708, 55 S.Ct. 405, 79 L.Ed. 1243 (1935), petition for reh.denied 294 U.S. 733, 55 S.Ct. 514, 79 L.Ed. 1242 (1935) (patents-shares).

14. Black v. Parker Mfg. Co., 329 Mass. 105, 106 N. E.2d 544 (1952); Urban J. Alexander Co. v. Trinkle, 311 Ky. 635, 224 S.W.2d 923 (1949); Alger v. Brighter Days Mining Corp., 63 Ariz. 135, 160 P.2d 346 (1945). Cf. Irving Trust Co. v. Deutsch, 73 F.2d 121 (2d Cir. 1934), cert. denied 294 U.S. 708, 55 S.Ct. 405, 79 L.Ed. 1243 (1935), petition for reh. denied 294 U.S. 733, 55 S.Ct. 514, 79 L.Ed. 1242 (1935) (share speculation); Annot., 153 A.L.R. 663 (1944). But see Faraclas v. City Vending Co., 232 Md. 457, 194 A.2d 298 (1963).

15. Young v. Columbia Oil Co. of West Virginia, 110 W.Va. 364, 58 S.E. 678 (1931); see also Dravosburg Land Co. v. Scott, 340 Pa. 280, 16 A.2d 415 (1940).

16. Northwestern Terra Cotta Corp. v. Wilson, 74 Ill.App.2d 38, 219 N.E.2d 860 (1966); Gaynor v. Buckley, 203 F.Supp. 620 (D.Or.1962), aff'd on other grounds 318 F.2d 432 (9th Cir. 1963) (holding that officer had not diverted corporate opportunity where he had urged corporation to accept opportunity, had fully disclosed his interest, and independent board of directors had rejected opportunity); Franco v. J. D. Streett & Co., 360 S.W.2d 597 (1962) (holding directors not liable for profits made from another corporation they acquired which transported their corporation's goods since opportunity was offered to and rejected by their corporation, acquisition was approved by all shareholders, and rates were fair). Robinson v. Brier, 412 Pa. 255, 194 A. 2d 204 (1963), held that a director of a corporation had not usurped a corporate opportunity by permitting a corporation in which he had an interest to sell goods to the former instead of having the former make such goods itself where it was unable to make such goods and therefore unable to avail itself of such opportunity. Cowell v. McMillin, 177

F. 25 (9th Cir. 1910); American Investment Co. of Ill. v. Lichtenstein, 134 F.Supp. 857 (E.D.Mo.1955); cf. Johnston v. Greene, 35 Del.Ch. 479, 121 A.2d 919 (Sup.Ct.1956) (where dominant director was at board meeting but refrained from voting). But see Wilshire Oil Co. v. Riffe, 381 F.2d 646 (10th Cir. 1967), cert. denied 389 U.S. 822, 88 S.Ct. 50, 19 L. Ed.2d 75 (1968) (holding director-officer liable where he received secret profits from those who took over deal on grounds he had breached his fiduciary duties and violated provision in employment contract barring him from investing in shares of competing corporation); Procario v. 74 & 76 West Tremont Ave. Corp., 3 N.Y.2d 973, 169 N.Y.S.2d 39, 146 N.E.2d 795 (1957).

17. Santarelli v. Katz, 270 F.2d 762 (7th Cir. 1959); Urban J. Alexander Co. v. Trinkle, 311 Ky. 635, 224 S.W.2d 923 (1949); Alger v. Brighter Days Mining Corp., 63 Ariz. 135, 160 P.2d 346 (1945).

18. Irving Trust Co. v. Deutsch, 73 F.2d 121 (2d Cir. 1934), cert. denied 294 U.S. 708, 55 S.Ct. 405, 79 L. Ed. 1243 (1935), petition for reh. denied 294 U.S. 733, 55 S.Ct. 514, 79 L.Ed. 1242 (1935); News-Journal Corp. v. Gore, 147 Fla. 217, 2 So.2d 741 (1941).

19. Regal (Hastings), Ltd. v. Gulliver, [1942] 1 All E.R. 378 (H.L.).

20. Cf. Gottlieb v. McKee, 34 Del.Ch. 537, 107 A.2d 240 (Ch.1954).

dictions would not condone the usurpation of the corporate opportunity.[21]

For usurpation of a corporate opportunity, the corporation can recover any damages to it [22] or profits realized by the fiduciary [23] or attach a constructive trust for its benefit on the subject matter of the opportunity.[24]

FIDUCIARY DUTIES—CONFLICTING INTEREST

238. **When a corporate fiduciary has in a corporate transaction an interest which conflicts with that of his corporation—another aspect of the undivided loyalty rule—the transaction might be voidable by or in behalf of the corporation on the basis, in different jurisdictions, of the conflicting interest alone or plus the additional element of fraud or bad faith or unfairness to the corporation, possibly with the burden of proof on the proponents of the transaction or with the transaction subject to an adverse inference. The more modern cases tend to apply the "fairness" test: Would an independent corporate fiduciary in an arm's length bargain bind his corporation to such a transac-**

tion? **Whether interested directors may count toward a quorum or vote depends upon applicable common-law rules, statutes, or articles of incorporation provisions. Shareholder ratification of the transaction, especially if by disinterested shareholders after full disclosure, usually, if unanimous, bars avoidance, or, if not unanimous, estops ratifying shareholders from complaining or neutralizes any adverse inference.**

Another situation involving the application of the rule of undivided loyalty is when the corporate fiduciary has in a corporate transaction an interest which conflicts with that of his corporation. This conflicting interest might be personal, as in the case of a transaction between his corporation and himself personally, or might involve a fiduciary relationship with another, as in the case of a transaction between his corporation and another corporation of which he is an officer, director, or controlling shareholder, with the rules possibly being stricter for the transaction between a corporation and one of its directors than for the transaction between two corporations having common directors.[1]

---

21. Remillard Brick Co. v. Remillard-Dandini Co., 109 Cal.App.2d 405, 241 P.2d 66 (1952). Cf. Rosenblum v. Judson Engineering Corp., 99 N.H. 267, 109 A.2d 558 (1954).

22. International Bankers Life Ins. Co. v. Holloway, 368 S.W.2d 567 (Tex.1963) (upholding award of punitive damages against directors whose sale of their shares were found to have usurped corporate opportunity to sell its shares); Raines v. Toney, 228 Ark. 1170, 313 S.W.2d 802 (1958); Dunlop's Sons, Inc. v. Spurr, 285 N.Y. 333, 34 N.E.2d 344 (1941).

23. Higgins v. Shenango Pottery Co., 256 F.2d 504 (3d Cir. 1958); Irving Trust Co. v. Deutsch, 73 F.2d 121 (2d Cir. 1934), cert. denied 294 U.S. 708, 55 S.Ct. 405, 79 L.Ed. 1243 (1935), petition for reh. denied 294 U.S. 733, 55 S.Ct. 514, 79 L.Ed. 1242 (1935); Regal (Hastings), Ltd. v. Gulliver, [1942] 1 All E.R. 378 (H.L.); Sialkot Importing Corp. v. Berlin, 295 N.Y. 482, 68 N.E.2d 501 (1946). Cf. Mason v. Richardson, 289 N.Y. 541, 43 N.E.2d 526 (1942).

24. Guth v. Loft, Inc., 23 Del.Ch. 255, 5 A.2d 503 (Sup.Ct.1939); Weissman v. A. Weissman, Inc., 374 Pa. 470, 97 A.2d 870 (1953); Equity Corp. v. Groves, 294 N.Y. 8, 60 N.E.2d 19 (1945); Beatty v. Guggenheim Exploration Co., 225 N.Y. 380, 122 N.E. 378 (1919); Bosworth v. Allen, 168 N.Y. 157, 61 N.E. 163 (1901). Compare Winger v. Chicago City Bank & Trust Co., 394 Ill. 94, 67 N.E.2d 265 (1946), with Equity Corp. v. Groves, 294 N.Y. 8, 60 N.E.2d 19 (1945) (4–2) (tracing problems). See also Potter v. Walker, 276 N.Y. 15, 11 N.E.2d 335 (1937).

1. Compare Munson v. Syracuse, Geneva & Corning R.R., 103 N.Y. 58, 8 N.E. 355 (1886) (holding contract between corporation and dominant one of its 10 directors voidable by corporation regardless of its fairness), with Everett v. Phillips, 288 N.Y. 227, 43 N.E.2d 18 (1942), reargument denied 289 N.Y. 625, 43 N.E.2d 841 (1942), reargument denied 289 N.Y. 675, 45 N.E.2d 176 (1942) (holding contract between two corporations with common directors not voidable on that ground alone). M. Feuer, Personal Liabilities of Corporate Officers and Directors chs. 6, 10 (1961); Barrow, "Dealings of Directors and Officers With Their Corporation and Its Shareholders", in Advising California Business Enterprises 809 (1958); Prochnow, "Conflict of Interest and the Corporate Trustee", 22 Bus.Law. 929 (1967); Goldman, "Self-Dealing by Directors under Illinois Law: Transactions between Corporations Having Common Directors", 53 Ill.B.J. 1068 (1965); Davis, "Conflicts of Interest between Corporations and Their Directors, Officers, Employees and Agents", 8 Rocky Mt. M.L.Inst. 191 (1963); Wadmond, "Conflict of Interest", 21 N.Y. County Law. Ass'n B.Bull. 120 (1963); Kaplan, "Conflict of Interests: Corporate Directors", 50 Ill.B.J. 1072 (1962); Krashowiecki, "Existing Rules of Trust Administration: A Stranglehold on the Trustee-Controlled Business Enterprise", 110 U. Pa.L.Rev. 506, 816 (1962); Watt, "Conflicts of Interest: Formalizing the Corporate Policy and Minimiz-

If the interested fiduciary makes full disclosure to the board of directors, and the transaction is authorized by the board, on the basis of required quorum and vote, the transaction usually would be properly autho-

ing Exposure to Conflicts of Interest", 17 Bus.Law. 42 (1961); Wadmond, "Conflicts of Business Interests", 17 Bus.Law. 48 (1961); Ward, "Some Notes on Transactions Involving Interested and Interlocking Directors in Pennsylvania", 23 Temp.L.Q. 107 (1949); Comment, "Dealings Between Directors and Their Corporations in Argentine and American Law", 5 Am.J.Comp.L. 497 (1956). See also Ripley v. International Railways of Central America, 8 N. Y.2d 430, 209 N.Y.S.2d 289, 171 N.E.2d 443 (1960) (upholding recovery, in derivative action by minority shareholders of railroad, of difference between inadequate freight rates charged fruit company, which controlled railroad, and fair and reasonable value of transportation services rendered fruit company by railroad).

The conflict of interest of a director may arise not only out of his personal business interests or his directorship in another corporation; it may also stem from a desire to favor friends, relatives, or business associates. In Johnson v. Radio Station WOW, Inc., 144 Neb. 406, 13 N.W.2d 556 (1944), the president leased the radio station to a close personal friend at an average annual rental of $74,000, although the station's average net income for seven years had been $194,000. The court, 4 to 3, struck down the contract on the ground that the unfairness of its terms added to the evidence that the president was zealously trying to secure the future welfare of his friend (who had contributed much to the success of the station) amounted to constructive fraud. But in Bayer v. Beran, 49 N.Y.S.2d 2 (Sup. Ct.1944), the court was not impressed by an argument that the president of Celanese Corporation had expended large sums on the "Celanese Hour", a radio program, in order to provide a vehicle for the talents of his wife, Miss Jean Tennyson, one of the singers on the program. The complainants also evidently put forward the argument that it was a betrayal of trust to choose a program of classical music as an advertising medium rather than a variety program.

As for conflicting duties of persons who serve both as directors and as trustees holding shares of a corporation, compare Matter of McLaughlin, 164 Misc. 539, 299 N.Y.S. 559 (Sur.Ct.1937) and Matter of Adler, 164 Misc. 544, 299 N.Y.S. 542 (Sur.Ct.1937), with Matter of Doelger, 254 App.Div. 178, 4 N.Y.S.2d 334 (1st Dep't 1938), rev'g 164 Misc. 590, 290 N.Y.S. 565 (Sur.Ct.1936). See also Cashman v. Petrie, 14 N.Y. 2d 426, 252 N.Y.S.2d 447, 201 N.E.2d 24 (1964). For discussion of provision against interlocking directorates in Federal Clayton Antitrust Act, see section 312 infra. Prohibitions on corporate loans to directors and officers [see section 183 supra], and problems of directors fixing their own compensation as directors or officers [see sections 243–245 infra] or indemnifying themselves for litigation expenses [see sections 379, 380 infra] are common situations involving conflicting interests.

rized, but with the burden of sustaining the transaction possibly on its proponents.[2]

In the event of such a conflicting interest, the transaction is not void but at most voidable by or in behalf of the corporation.[3]

There is a three-way split of authority as to whether such a transaction is voidable on the basis of the conflicting interest alone,[4] on the basis of the conflicting interest plus the additional element of fraud or bad faith,[5] or on the basis of the conflicting interest plus the additional factor of unfairness to

2.   Colorado Management Corp. v. American Founders Life Ins. Co. of Denver, Colorado, 145 Colo. 413, 359 P.2d 665 (1961); Twin-Lick Oil Co. v. Marbury, 91 U.S. 587, 23 L.Ed. 328 (1876); Johnston v. Greene, 35 Del. 479, 121 A.2d 919 (Sup.Ct.1956); 3 W. Fletcher, Private Corporations §§ 931, 932 (rev. vol. 1965). Cf. Globe Woolen Co. v. Utica Gas & Electric Co., 224 N.Y. 483, 121 N.E. 378 (1918) (refusal to vote by fiduciary with conflicting interest held to give to transaction form and presumption of propriety, but transaction held unfair and voidable by corporation). But see United States Rolling Stock Co. v. Atlantic & G. W. R.R., 34 Ohio St. 450 (1878) (transaction held not voidable); Cuthberg v. McNeill, 103 N.J.Eq. 199, 142 A. 819 (1928) (transaction held voidable by corporation regardless of fairness). As for required quorum and vote, see notes 9, 10 infra.

3.   Annot., 33 A.L.R.2d 1060, 1064–1065 (1954). For different use of term "void", see note 18 infra.

4.   Cathedral Estates, Inc. v. Taft Realty Corp., 228 F.2d 85 (2d Cir. 1955) (Connecticut law); Landstreet v. Meyer, 201 Miss. 826, 29 So.2d 653 (1947); Johnson v. Duensing, 351 S.W.2d 27 (Mo.1961); Hotaling v. Hotaling, 193 Cal. 368, 224 P. 455, 56 A.L. R. 734 (1924); Alabama Fidelity Mortgage & Bond Co. v. Dubberly, 198 Ala. 545, 73 So. 911 (1917); Munson v. Syracuse, Geneva & Corning R.R., 103 N.Y. 58, 8 N.E. 355 (1886); Pearson v. Concord R. R. Corp., 62 N.H. 537 (1883); Stewart v. Lehigh Valley R.R., 38 N.J.L. 505 (1875); Aberdeen Ry. v. Blaikie Bros., 1 Macq. 461 (H.L.1854); cf. Everett v. Phillips, 288 N.Y. 227, 43 N.E.2d 18 (1942), reargument denied 289 N.Y. 625, 43 N.E.2d 841 (1942), reargument denied 289 N.Y. 675, 45 N.E.2d 176 (1942); Globe Woolen Co. v. Utica Gas & Electric Co., 224 N. Y. 483, 121 N.E. 378 (1918); Annot., 114 A.L.R. 306 (1938). For different use of term "voidable", see note 18 infra.

5.   Sanders v. E–Z Park, Inc., 57 Wash.2d 474, 358 P.2d 138 (1960); Skelly v. Dockweiler, 75 F.Supp. 11 (S.D.Calif.1947); Briggs v. Scripps, 13 Cal.App. 2d 43, 56 P.2d 277 (1936); G O S Cattle Co. v. Bragaw's Heirs, 38 N.M. 105, 28 P.2d 529 (1933); Boston Acme Mines Development Co. v. Clawson, 66 Utah 103, 240 P. 165 (1925).

the corporation.[6] The more modern cases tend to apply the "fairness" test: Would an independent corporate ficuciary in an arm's length bargain bind his corporation to such a transaction? [7]

Where some additional element or factor, besides the conflicting interest itself, is prerequisite to the avoidance of the transaction, many courts have recognized presumptions that the transaction is fraudulent or unfair thereby placing the burden of sustaining the transaction on those who would sustain it.[8]

At common law there was a split of authority as to whether directors with conflicting interests could count toward a quorum and vote.[9]

Some jurisdictions, by statute, expressly authorize interested directors to count toward quorum and to vote.[10]

6. Piccard v. Sperry Corp., 48 F.Supp. 465 (S.D.N.Y. 1943), aff'd per curiam, 152 F.2d 462 (2d Cir. 1946), cert. denied, 328 U.S. 845, 66 S.Ct. 1024, 90 L.Ed. 1619 (1946); Crawford v. Mexican Petroleum Co., 130 F.2d 359 (2d Cir. 1942); Ransome Concrete Machinery Co. v. Moody, 282 F. 29 (2d Cir. 1922); Wyman v. Bowman, 127 F. 857 (8th Cir. 1904); Hill v. Erwin Mills, Inc., 239 N.C. 437, 80 S.E.2d 358 (1954); Sterling v. Mayflower Hotel Corp., 33 Del. Ch. 293, 93 A.2d 107, 38 A.L.R.2d 425 (Sup.Ct.1952); Everett v. Phillips, 288 N.Y. 227, 43 N.E.2d 18 (1942), reargument denied 289 N.Y. 625, 43 N.E.2d 841 (1942), reargument denied 289 N.Y. 675, 45 N.E.2d 176 (1942); Nicholson v. Kingery, 37 Wyo. 299, 261 P. 122 (1927); Globe Woolen Co. v. Utica Gas & Electric Co., 224 N.Y. 483, 121 N.E. 378 (1918); Evansville Public Hall Co. v. Bank of Commerce, 144 Ind. 34, 10 N.E. 1097 (1896); cf. Munson v. Syracuse, Geneva & Corning R.R., 103 N.Y. 58, 8 N.E. 355 (1886). See note 7 infra.

7. Murphy v. Washington American League Base Ball Club, Inc., 324 F.2d 394 (D.C.Cir. 1963); Holloway v. Int'l Bankers Life Ins. Co., 354 S.W.2d 198 (Tex.Civ.App.1962), rev'd on other grounds 368 S.W. 2d 567 (Tex.1963); Wiberg v. Gulf Coast Land & Development Co., 360 S.W.2d 563 (Tex.Civ.App.1962); Colorado Management Corp. v. American Founders Life Ins. Co. of Denver, Colorado, 145 Colo. 413, 359 P.2d 665 (1961); Johnston v. Greene, 35 Del. 479, 121 A.2d 919 (Sup.Ct.1956); Note, "The Fairness Test of Corporate Contracts with Interested Directors", 61 Harv.L.Rev. 335 (1948); Annot., 33 A.L.R.2d 1060 (1954); State ex rel. Hayes Oyster Co. v. Keypoint Oyster Co., 64 Wash.2d 388, 391 P.2d 979 (1964), reiterated the court's abolition of the mechanical rule whereby any transaction between a corporation and an interested director was voidable at the option of the corporation, and stated that such a transaction cannot be avoided if the director can show that the transaction was fair to the corporation but that nondisclosure of his interest by the director is, in itself, unfair. Voss Oil Co. v. Voss, 367 P.2d 977, 979 (Wyo.1962) ("One of the tests of 'fairness' in transactions of this kind is whether there has been a full disclosure").

8. Taussig v. Wellington Fund, Inc., 313 F.2d 472 (3d Cir. 1963), cert. denied 374 U.S. 806, 83 S.Ct. 1693, 1695, 10 L.Ed.2d 1031 (1963); Elie v. Pullias, 407 F.2d

615 (6th Cir. 1969); Alcott v. Hyman, 42 Del.Ch. 233, 208 A.2d 501 (Sup.Ct.1965) (absent disinterested director approval, burden on directors to show utmost good faith and scrupulous fairness; suggestion that shareholder ratification would have reduced burden to showing of exercise of business judgment); Mardel Securities, Inc. v. Alexandria Gazette Corp., 183 F.Supp. 7 (E.D.Va.1960), aff'd 320 F.2d 890 (4th Cir. 1963); Shlensky v. South Parkway Bldg. Corp., 19 Ill.2d 268, 166 N.E.2d 793 (1960); Geominerals Corp. v. Grace, 232 Ark. 524, 338 S.W.2d 935 (1960). Cf. Case v. New York Cent. R.R., 15 N.Y.2d 150, 256 N.Y.S.2d 607, 204 N.E.2d 643 (1965) (showing of faithlessness of subsidiary's directors to its corporate interests held not demonstrated to warrant judicial interference with challenged corporate decision). Annot., 33 A.L.R.2d 1060, 1072–1075 (1954).

9. See section 209 supra. The question discussed in this section is, assuming that the transaction has been authorized by the corporation, whether by the board of directors, with or without disinterested quorum or vote, or by the majority of shareholders, whether or not disinterested, the voidability of the transaction and the incidence of the burden of proof with respect thereto. In particular jurisdictions, the rules with respect to voidability and burden of proof vary, depending upon the starting point of the rule applicable with respect to corporate authorization of the transaction.

10. See section 209 supra. Such statutes typically provide that:

"No contract or other transaction between a corporation and one or more of its directors, or between a corporation and any corporation, firm, or association in which one or more of its directors are directors or are financially interested, is either void or voidable because such director or directors are present at the meeting of the board of directors or a committee thereof which authorizes or approves the contract or transaction, or because his or their votes are counted for such purpose, if the circumstances specified in any of the following subdivisions exist:

"(a) The fact of the common directorship or financial interest is disclosed or known to the board of directors or committee and noted in the minutes, and the board or committee authorizes, approves, or ratifies the contract or transaction in good faith by a vote sufficient for the purpose without counting the vote or votes of such director or directors.

"(b) The fact of the common directorship or financial interest is disclosed or known to the shareholders, and they approve or ratify the contract or

Even in jurisdictions which might adhere to the stricter rule, and, *a fortiori,* in other jurisdictions, provisions in articles of incorporation authorizing interested directors to count toward a quorum and to vote have been upheld.[11]

transaction in good faith by a majority vote or written consent of shareholders entitled to vote.

"(c) The contract or transaction is just and reasonable as to the corporation at the time it is authorized or approved.

"Common or interested directors may be counted in determining the presence of a quorum at a meeting of the board of directors or a committee thereof which authorizes, approves, or ratifies a contract or transaction."

Cal.Gen.Corp.Law, § 820 (1947). Similar are 1969 Model Act revision, Conn.Stock Corp.Act § 42 (1961); McKinney's N.Y.Bus.Corp.Law, § 713; Comment, "The 'Unfair' Interested Directors' Contract under the New York Business Corporation Law", 16 Buffalo L.Rev. 840 (1967). In the case of shareholder approval, shares of the interested director or directors are apparently shares entitled to vote for such purpose. Despite full disclosure and either disinterested board of directors or shareholder approval, the contract or other transaction presumably should be just and reasonable to the corporation at the time of such approval. See Remillard Brick Co. v. Remillard-Dandini Co., 109 Cal.App.2d 405, 241 P.2d 66 (1952) (holding that despite disclosure of common directorships to shareholders and ratification by majority shareholders who had issued proxy and contracted to sell shares to common directors in technical compliance with § 820, transactions which are unfair and unreasonable to corporation may be avoided). See also Mich.Gen.Corp. Act § 21.13(5) (1948), providing:

" . . . 5. No contract of any corporation made with any director of such corporation or with a partnership or other group or association of which any such director shall be a member or with any other corporation of which such a director may be a member or director and no contract between corporations having common directors shall be invalid because of such respective facts alone. When the validity of any such contract is questioned, the burden of proving the fairness to the contracting parties of any such contract shall be upon such director, partnership, other group or association or corporation who shall be asserting the validity of such contract."

Note, "Dealings Between Directors and Their Corporations—A Discussion of the 'Disinterested Quorum' Rule under Present Statutory Limitations in Michigan", 34 U.Det.L.J. 43 (1956). See also N.C. Bus.Corp.Act § 55–30(b) (1) (1957) (no corporate transaction in which director has adverse interest to be either void or voidable, if knowledge on part of other directors of such adverse interest, transaction is approved in good faith by majority, not less than two, of disinterested directors present even though less than quorum, irrespective of participation of adversely interested director in approval). Smith v. Robinson, 343 F.2d 793 (4th Cir. 1965) (construing "corporate transaction" to apply to situation where corporate director is dealing directly with corporation). See also R.I.Gen.Corp.Law, § 7–4–7 (1956), providing:

"Any corporation may contract for any lawful purpose with one or more of its directors or with any corporation having with it a common director or directors, if the contract is entered into in good faith, if it is approved or ratified by vote of the holders of a majority in interest of its stock or by a majority vote at any meeting of its board of directors excluding any vote by the contracting or common director or directors and if the contracting or common director or directors shall not be necessary for a quorum at the meeting for this purpose. A contract made in compliance with the foregoing provisions shall be voidable by the corporation complying with the said provisions only in case it would be voidable if made with a stranger. A contract not otherwise void or voidable shall not be rendered void or voidable merely because not approved or ratified in accordance with the foregoing provisions."

See Point Trap Co. v. Manchester, 98 R.I. 49, 199 A. 2d 592 (1964) (refusing to enforce director's contract for purchase of surplus property from corporation for fair price because of lack of shareholder approval). See also W.Va.Gen.Corp.Law, § 308 (1943). In Duncan Shaw Corp. v. Standard Machinery Co., 196 F.2d 147 (1st Cir. 1952), the court had before it a contract between corporations having common directors which had not been approved by a disinterested board of the defendant Rhode Island corporation. The court said it was in doubt whether under Rhode Island decisions such a contract was void or only voidable, but held that the provision was for the protection of shareholders and that the shareholders, having accepted the benefits of the contract, the defense was waived and the defendant liable for a breach of the contract. See also Ghana Companies Code § 207 (1963).

11. Piccard v. Sperry Corp., 48 F.Supp. 465 (S.D.N.Y.1943), aff'd per curiam, 152 F.2d 462 (2d Cir. 1946), cert. denied 328 U.S. 845, 66 S.Ct. 1024, 90 L. Ed. 1619 (1946) (Delaware law); Sterling v. Mayflower Hotel Corp., 33 Del.Ch. 293, 93 A.2d 107, 38 A.L.R.2d 425 (Sup.Ct.1952); Kaufman v. Shoenberg, 33 Del.Ch. 211, 91 A.2d 786 (Ch.1952); Spiegel v. Beacon Participations, Inc., 297 Mass. 398, 8 N. E.2d 895 (1937); Sterling Industries, Inc. v. Ball Bearing Pen Corp., 298 N.Y. 483, 84 N.E.2d 790, 10 A.L.R.2d 694 (1949); Everett v. Phillips, 288 N.Y. 227, 43 N.E.2d 18 (1942), reargument denied 289 N.Y. 625, 43 N.E.2d 841 (1942), reargument denied 289 N.Y. 675, 45 N.E.2d 176 (1942) (4–3). See Matter of Burkin (Katz), 1 N.Y.2d 570, 154 N.Y.S.2d 898, 136 N. E.2d 862 (1956); Martin Foundation v. North American Rayon Corp., 31 Del.Ch. 195, 68 A.2d 313 (Ch. 1949).

The effect of such provisions varies depending on whether they are in derogation of the common-law rule existing in some jurisdictions that interested directors may not count toward a quorum or vote or supplement the common-law rule existing in oth-

Such provisions, whether in the statute or articles of incorporation, enable the directors to act, but do not preclude setting aside the transaction for fraud or unfairness [12] or subjecting the fiduciary to liability for breach of his fiduciary duty to his corporation.[13] Some cases have held that such provisions neutralize the adverse inferences which would otherwise arise,[14] thus subjecting those seeking to set aside the transaction or to surcharge the fiduciaries to the burden of showing any required fraud or unfairness.[15]

At least one case has recognized a double standard, permitting the transaction to be avoided but exonerating the interested fiduciaries from personal liability.[16]

Unanimous shareholder ratification of the transaction generally precludes avoidance of the transaction by the corporation, at least where creditors are not prejudiced. Even in the case of less-than-unanimous shareholder ratification, a few cases have barred avoidance of the transaction by the corporation or minority shareholders.[17] Most of the cases, however, take the position that less-than-unanimous shareholder ratification does not bar avoidance,[18] but has the effect possibly of providing any necessary corporate authorization for the transaction, estopping those shareholders who voted for the ratification [19] or of neutralizing the adverse inference which would otherwise arise.[20] Obviously, shareholder ratification, to have

---

er jurisdictions that interested directors may count toward a quorum and vote. The problem of interested directors counting toward a quorum and voting is obviously more acute in the case of transactions between corporations with common directors than in the case of transactions between a director personally and the corporation of which he is a director.

12. Remillard Brick Co. v. Remillard-Dandini Co., 109 Cal.App.2d 405, 241 P.2d 66 (1952) (under California statute supra note 10); Chelrob, Inc. v. Barrett, 293 N.Y. 442, 57 N.E.2d 825 (1944) (articles of incorporation provision).

13. See Everett v. Phillips, 288 N.Y. 227, 43 N.E.2d 18 (1942), reargument denied 289 N.Y. 625, 43 N.E.2d 841 (1942), reargument denied 289 N.Y. 675, 45 N.E. 2d 176 (1942); see also Carp, "Effect of Directors' Adverse Interest or Conflicting Duties to Invalidate Contracts: California Civil Code Section 311", 29 Calif.L.Rev. 480, 482–483 (1941). But see Breswick & Co. v. Harrison-Rye Realty Corp., 2 A.D.2d 769, 154 N.Y.S.2d 625 (2d Dep't 1956), aff'd mem., 4 N.Y. 2d 685, 171 N.Y.S.2d 81, 148 N.E.2d 299 (1958).

14. Spiegel v. Beacon Participations, Inc., 297 Mass. 398, 8 N.E.2d 895 (1937); Everett v. Phillips, 288 N.Y. 227, 43 N.E.2d 18 (1942), reargument denied 289 N.Y. 625, 43 N.E.2d 841 (1942), reargument denied 289 N.Y. 675, 45 N.E.2d 176 (1942). But see Abeles v. Adams Engineering Co., 35 N.J. 411, 173 A.2d 246 (1961) (holding that, notwithstanding express sanction in the corporation's charter authorizing contracts between two corporations having common directors or officers, even assuming the validity of such a provision, the burden of proof remained on the interested director to demonstrate the fairness of the agreement); Sterling v. Mayflower Hotel Corp., 33 Del.Ch. 293, 93 A.2d 107, 38 A.L.R.2d 425 (Sup.Ct. 1952) (burden on those who would sustain transaction). See Note, "Effect of a Provision in Articles of Incorporation Permitting the Counting of Interested Directors for Quorum Purposes", 52 Mich.L. Rev. 295 (1953).

15. La Vin v. La Vin, 283 App.Div. 809, 128 N.Y.S.2d 518 (2d Dep't 1954), aff'd mem., 307 N.Y. 790, 119 N.Y.S.2d 573, 121 N.E.2d 620 (1954).

16. Chelrob, Inc. v. Barrett, 293 N.Y. 442, 57 N.E.2d 825 (1944).

17. See Rosenfeld v. Fairchild Engine & Airplane Corp., 309 N.Y. 168, 128 N.E.2d 291, 51 A.L.R.2d 860 (1955), reh. denied 309 N.Y. 807, 130 N.E.2d 610 (1955); Claman v. Robertson, 164 Ohio St. 61, 128 N.E.2d 429 (1955); United States Steel Corp. v. Hodge, 64 N.J.Eq. 807, 54 A. 1 (1903); North-West Transp. Co. v. Beatty, 12 App.Cas. 589 (P.C.1887) (ratification by interested shareholder). See section 194 supra.

18. Seagrave Corp. v. Mount, 212 F.2d 389 (6th Cir. 1954). See Continental Securities Co. v. Belmont, 206 N.Y. 7, 99 N.E. 138 (1912). See section 194 supra. The terms "voidable" or "void" are sometimes used to distinguish between transactions which can be validated by less than all the shareholders and transactions which cannot. Piccard v. Sperry Corp., 48 F.Supp. 465 (S.D.N.Y.1943), aff'd per curiam, 152 F.2d 462 (2d Cir. 1946), cert. denied, 328 U.S. 845, 66 S.Ct. 1024, 90 L.Ed. 1619 (1946). Cf. other usages of terms "voidable" and "void" (see notes 3, 4 supra).

19. Sarner v. Fox Hill, Inc., 151 Conn. 437, 199 A.2d 6 (1964) (lack of authorization). Cf. Gottlieb v. McKee, 34 Del.Ch. 537, 107 A.2d 240 (Ch.1954) (estoppel).

20. Alcott v. Hyman, 42 Del.Ch. 233, 208 A.2d 501 (Sup.Ct.1965) (shareholder ratification said to reduce burden to that of showing exercise of business judgment); Gottlieb v. Heyden Chemical Corp., 33 Del.Ch. 177, 91 A.2d 57 (Sup.Ct.1952); cf. Sterling v. Mayflower Hotel Corp., 33 Del.Ch. 293, 93 A.2d 107, 38 A.L.R.2d 425 (Sup.Ct.1952) (burden on proponents of transaction); Eliasberg v. Standard Oil Co., 23 N.J.Super. 431, 92 A.2d 862 (1952), aff'd mem., 12 N.J. 467, 97 A.2d 437 (1953).

any effect, presupposes full disclosure to the shareholders in soliciting their votes or proxies.[21]

Transactions between affiliated corporations with common directors inherently involve conflicting interests.

Under the Internal Revenue Code of 1954,[22] each affiliated corporation retains any tax-saving resulting from the filing of a consolidated return. A New York case [23] is one of the few reported cases involving elections to file consolidated federal income tax returns challenged because most of the resulting tax savings to the subsidiary were, by agreement approved by common directors of the parent and subsidiary, paid over to the parent. The court appeared to assume that interested directors could count toward a quorum and vote. Under the agreement, the subsidiary in effect saved $268,725 in taxes and the parent received $3,556,992. The trial court had found the contract fair but a majority of the intermediate appellate court, 3 to 2, had found the contract unfair to the subsidiary.[24] On appeal, the court of appeals held that no such faithlessness of the majority of the subsidiary's directors had been demonstrated as to warrant judicial interference with the challenged corporate decision.

Corporations increasingly impose rules to prevent conflicts of interests on the part of their personnel.

FIDUCIARY DUTIES—INSIDER TRADING

239. Insider trading traditionally involved no fiduciary duties since the directors', officers', and controlling shareholders' fiduciary duties are owed to the corporation, not to individual shareholders, with respect to corporate transactions, not with respect to personal dealings in shares. For fraud or misrepresentation, defrauded persons enjoy the usual remedies therefor.

Under the "majority rule", insider trading is not subject to fiduciary duties to shareholders of disclosure of any inside information to the selling shareholder.

Under the "special facts rule", insider trading is subject to fiduciary duties to shareholders of disclosure when special facts or circumstances justify exception to the "majority rule".

Under the "minority rule", insider trading is subject to fiduciary duties to shareholders of disclosure regardless of special facts or circumstances.

Insider trading is regulated to some extent by federal statutes, primarily the Securities Exchange Act of 1934.

The treatment of fiduciary duties so far has dealt primarily with the fiduciary duties which directors and officers owe to the corporation with respect to corporate affairs. Discussion of insider trading requires analysis of the fiduciary duties which directors

21. See Heilbrunn v. Sun Chemical Corp., 37 Del.Ch. 552, 146 A.2d 757 (Ch.1958), aff'd 38 Del.Ch. 321, 150 A.2d 755 (Sup.Ct.1959); Eliasberg v. Standard Oil Co., 23 N.J.Super. 431, 92 A.2d 862 (1952), aff'd mem., 12 N.J. 467, 97 A.2d 437 (1953) (alleged failure of full disclosure in proxy solicitation); Berendt v. Bethlehem Steel Corp., 108 N.J.Eq. 148, 154 A. 321 (1931).

22. Int.Rev.Code of 1954, 26 U.S.C.A. §§ 1501–1505, 1561–1563.

23. Case v. New York Cent. R. R., 15 N.Y.2d 150, 256 N.Y.S.2d 607, 204 N.E.2d 643 (1965), rev'g 19 A. D.2d 383, 243 N.Y.S.2d 620 (1st Dep't 1963).

24. See Alliegro v. Pan American Bank, 136 So.2d 656 (Fla.Dist.Ct.App.1962), cert. denied 149 So. 2d 45 (Fla.1963). A parent and subsidiary filed and used consolidated federal income tax returns and agreed that the resulting tax savings to either should be paid to the other. Such payment by the subsidiary to the parent was held to violate the rights of the minority shareholders of the subsidiary who had not approved such a procedure and to constitute an improper "dividend" recoverable against the parent in a shareholder derivative action. See Comment, "Corporate Fiduciary Doctrine in the Context of Parent-Subsidiary Relations", 74 Yale L.J. 338 (1964). Until 1968 the few reported cases involved a loss-parent and a profitable subsidiary. But see Meyerson v. El Paso Natural Gas Co., —— Del.Ch. ——, 246 A.2d 789 (Ch.1968) (minority shareholders of loss-subsidiary corporation acquired by parent corporation for tax advantages denied right to compel profitable parent corporation to share resulting tax savings with such subsidiary corporation).

and officers owe to individual shareholders with respect to their shares.

Traditionally, trading in shares as such involved no fiduciary duties, even when one of the parties to the purchase or sale was a director, officer, or controlling shareholder. Of course, up to the time of any purchase by a corporate insider, the seller was a shareholder. However, in the case of a sale by an insider, the purchaser had not become a shareholder until after the negotiations had been completed.[1]

Corporate theory has shaped the judicial approach to such problems. The orthodox view was that a director or officer occupied a fiduciary relationship to the corporation and its shareholders as a body with respect to corporate business and property. Since shares were private property and a director or officer as such had no control over them, dealings in shares were not corporate transactions and directors and officers owed shareholders no fiduciary duties with respect thereto. Even if a director or officer violated his duty to the corporation by dealing in its shares, the claim would belong to the corporation, not to the individual shareholder; any recovery would go to the corporation, to the indirect benefit of all its present shareholders, including the directors or officers who wrongfully purchased shares if they had not ceased to be shareholders, but would not benefit former shareholders, who had sold their shares.[2]

Where a director or officer purchases shares from a shareholder, and commits fraud or utters half truths or makes other misrepresentations in connection therewith, such director or officer is, of course, responsible to such shareholder for fraud and misrepresentation and subject to the usual remedies for such wrongdoing.[3]

However, where a director or officer avoids fraud or misrepresentation but merely fails to disclose to the shareholder facts which he has as the result of his position in the corporation, the director or officer is responsible for such nondisclosure only if he is under a duty to the shareholder to disclose.

"Majority Rule"

At common law, the "majority rule" was that a director or officer owed no fiduciary

1. See Joseph v. Farnsworth Radio & Television Corp., 99 F.Supp. 701 (S.D.N.Y.1951); Birnbaum v. Newport Steel Corp., 98 F.Supp. 506 (S.D.N.Y.1951), aff'd 193 F.2d 461 (2d Cir. 1952), cert. denied 343 U.S. 956, 72 S.Ct. 1051, 96 L.Ed. 1356 (1952). H. Manne, Insider Trading and the Stock Market (1966); Schotland, "Unsafe at Any Price: A Reply to Manne, 'Insider Trading and the Stock Exchange' ", 53 Va.L.Rev. 1425 (1967); Hetherington, "Insider Trading and the Logic of the Law", 1967 Wis.L.Rev. 720; Brudney, "Fiduciary Ideology in Transactions Affecting Corporate Control", 65 Mich.L.Rev. 259 (1966); Johnston & Coles, "Wall Street Trading Firms as Securities 'Insiders' ", 12 Clev.-Mar.L.Rev. 369 (1963); Miller, "Purchase of Outstanding Stock by Insiders", 12 Neb.St.B.J. 87 (July 1963); Brudney, "Insider Securities Dealings During Corporate Crises", 61 Mich.L.Rev. 1 (1962); Conant "Duties of Disclosure of Corporate Insiders Who Purchase Shares", 46 Cornell L.Q. 53 (1960); Weisbrod, "Trading in Business Ownership", 1954 Ill.L.F. 465; Berle, "Publicity of Accounts and Directors' Purchasers of Stock", 25 Mich.L.Rev. 827 (1927); Walker, "The Duty of Disclosure by a Director Purchasing Stock from His Stockholders", 32 Yale L.J. 637 (1923); Smith, "Purchase of Shares of a Corporation by a Director from a Shareholder", 19 Mich.L.Rev. 698 (1921); Laylin "The Duty of a Director Purchasing Shares of Stock", 27 Yale L.J. 731 (1918); Wilgus, "Purchase of Shares of a Corporation by a Director from a Shareholder", 8 Mich.L.Rev. 267 (1910); Note, "Insider Trading without Disclosure—Theory of Liability", 28 Ohio St.L.J. 472 (1967); Note, "Insider Liabilities Examined", 18 Syracuse L.Rev. 803 (1967).

2. R. Stevens, Handbook on the Law of Private Corporations § 150 (2d ed. 1949); Barrow, "Dealings of Directors and Officers with Their Corporation and Its Shareholders", in Advising California Business Enterprises 809–831 (1958).

3. Amen v. Black, 234 F.2d 12 (10th Cir. 1956), cert. denied 352 U.S. 888, 77 S.Ct. 127, 1 L.Ed.2d 84 (1956); Speed v. Transamerica Corp., 99 F.Supp. 808, 828 (D.Del.1951) (sustaining common-law count for fraud and deceit on basis of misrepresentations); Quinn v. Forsyth, 116 Ga.App. 611, 158 S.E. 2d 686 (1967); Judson v. Peoples Bank & Trust Co., 25 N.J. 17, 134 A.2d 761 (1957); Llewellyn v. Queen City Dairy, Inc., 187 Md. 49, 48 A.2d 322 (1946); Hobart v. Hobart Estate Co., 26 Cal.2d 412, 159 P. 2d 958 (1945); Von Au v. Magenheimer, 126 App. Div. 257, 110 N.Y.S. 629 (2d Dep't 1908), aff'd mem., 196 N.Y. 510, 89 N.E. 1114 (1909); Note, "Majority Shareholders' Fraud in the Purchase of Stock", 50 Mich.L.Rev. 743 (1952).

duty to a shareholder with respect to transactions in the shares of the corporation. Hence, a director or officer with inside information could engage with impunity in such transactions without disclosing such information so long as he avoided fraud or misrepresentation.[4]

"Special Facts Rule"

Later the "special facts rule" or "special circumstances rule" developed, which subjected a director or officer engaging in share transactions to a fiduciary duty to disclose any inside information to the selling shareholder when special facts or circumstances justified exception to the "majority rule".[5]

4. Cundick v. Broadbent, 383 F.2d 157 (10th Cir. 1967), cert. denied 390 U.S. 948, 88 S.Ct. 1037, 19 L. Ed.2d 1139 (1968) (Wyoming "majority rule"); Geller v. Transamerica Corp., 53 F.Supp. 625 (D. Del.1943), aff'd per curiam 151 F.2d 534 (3d Cir. 1945) (concluding Kentucky follows "majority rule"); Speed v. Transamerica Corp., 71 F.Supp. 457 (D.Del.1947) (summary judgment granted defendant on common-law count for fraud and deceit on authority of Geller case), ruling reconsidered, 99 F.Supp. 808, 828 (D.Del.1951) (sustaining common-law count for fraud and deceit on basis of misrepresentations); Gladstone v. Murray Co., 314 Mass. 584, 50 N.E.2d 958 (1943) (stating and appearing to accept premises of "majority rule", but also negativing the existence of special facts and circumstances; inferring that their existence might have changed result; stating that shareholder had not relied on defendant; and questioning value of shares found by master); Hauben v. Morris, 255 App.Div. 35, 5 N.Y.S.2d 721 (1st Dep't 1938), aff'd mem., 281 N.Y. 652, 20 N.E.2d 1016 (1939); Board of Commissioners of Tippicanoe County v. Reynolds, 44 Ind. 509 (1873); Carpenter v. Danforth, 52 Barb. 581 (N.Y.Sup.Ct.1868). See Hyland v. Auspitzer, 5 N.Y. 2d 743, 177 N.Y.S.2d 720, 152 N.E.2d 674 (1958) (4-3). Cf. Fischer v. Guaranty Trust Co., 259 App.Div. 176, 18 N.Y.S.2d 328 (2d Dep't 1940), aff'd mem., 285 N.Y. 679, 34 N.E.2d 379 (1941). Although it has become habitual to speak of the harsh rule denying the existence of any duty on the part of the director or officer toward the shareholder as the "majority rule", it is probably time to abandon this terminology in favor of a more realistic appraisal of the current state of the law. In the last 50 years, although the strict rule has been announced as a starting point in many cases, it has actually been applied in pure form in very few. In all others, the court has either gone on to accept the "special facts" exception (see note 5 infra) or has reached a result identical to that which would have been reached under the "special facts" exception or the "minority rule" (see note 7 infra).

5. Strong v. Repide, 213 U.S. 419, 29 S.Ct. 521, 53 L. Ed. 853 (1909) introduced the "special facts rule" on

Among the special facts or circumstances which the courts came to recognize were: that the shares were closely-held with no

the ground that the case involved more than "the bare relationship between director and shareholder". The special facts and circumstances justifying exception to the "majority rule" were detailed in the opinion. Oddly, the case arose in a civil law jurisdiction, the Philippine Islands. Since Erie R. R. v. Tompkins, 304 U.S. 64, 58 S.Ct. 817, 82 L.Ed. 1188, 114 A.L.R. 1487 (1938), a federal rule would have no application in a diversity-of-citizenship case. However, it would be relevant in federal-question cases such as those defining "fraud or deceit" under S.E.C. Rule 10b–5; Taylor v. Wright, 69 Cal.App.2d 371, 159 P.2d 980 (1945) (allowing exemplary damages); Agatucci v. Corradi, 327 Ill. App. 153, 63 N.E.2d 630 (1945); Nicol v. Sensenbrenner, 220 Wis. 165, 263 N.W. 650 (1935); Saville v. Sweet, 234 App.Div. 236, 254 N.Y.S. 768 (1st Dep't 1932), aff'd mem., 262 N.Y. 567, 188 N.E. 67 (1933) (close corporation); Cochran v. Channing Corp., 211 F.Supp. 239 (S.D.N.Y.1962) was a federal diversity-of-citizenship case purporting to apply New York law where the defendants, a controlling corporate shareholder and three of its directors who were also directors of the controlled New York corporation, allegedly reduced the latter's dividends in order to depress the market price of the latter's shares to permit the controlling corporate shareholder to acquire more of such shares at depressed prices. The plaintiff sold some 500 such shares at the resulting depressed prices, not to the defendants but to others, suffering $8,000 damages. The court concluded that New York adhered to the "special facts rule", which under the complaint stated a cause of action for "active concealment" in favor of the plaintiff who was among the class of persons expected to rely on the dividend reduction as evidence of decreased valuation of his shares. The case is noteworthy because one of the defendants was a controlling shareholder and the sale of shares was not to the defendants. In Low v. Wheeler, 207 Cal.App.2d 477, 24 Cal.Rptr. 538 (1962), dividends were withheld and the plaintiff minority shareholders lost their representative on the board of directors. A third party desired to buy the assets of the corporation, which was not disclosed to the plaintiffs, but the defendant majority shareholders-directors desired to sell their shares. The plaintiffs sold their 250 shares to the third party for $1,250 per share; the defendants sold their 750 shares for $1,700 per share. The jury awarded the plaintiff the difference between $1,250 and $1,587.-50, namely, $337.50 per share, a total of $28,012.50. On appeal, the judgment was affirmed, the appellate court concluding that the "special facts rule", was as applicable to such a sale of shares by directors as it would be if the directors had purchased the plaintiffs' shares without full disclosure. Berger v. Fogarty, 51 Misc.2d 628, 273 N.Y.S.2d 620 (Sup.Ct.1965) (granting defendants' motion for summary judgment in shareholder derivative action against Texas Gulf Sulphur Co. insiders and their "tipees" for profits made by buying and selling shares on open market on ground "major sharehold-

readily ascertainable market value, that the director or officer had inside access to information, that the shareholder lacked business experience or acumen, that the director or officer instigated the transaction, that the director or officer used an intermediary who did not disclose his principal, that the shareholder raised questions concerning the value of the shares.[6]

"Minority Rule"

Eventually, as fiduciary concepts and business ethics became more refined, the "minority rule" was recognized by the courts. Under it, directors and officers are subjected to a fiduciary duty to shareholders with respect to insider trading. Nondisclosure of inside information, regardless of "special facts", constitutes a breach of such fiduciary duty to the shareholder.[7]

The "special facts rule" by its expanding recognition of types of special facts, has tended to merge into the "minority rule", relegating the "majority rule" to decreasing application.

Even under the "special facts rule" or "minority rule", the nondisclosure must be of fact, as distinguished from opinion,[8] and there must be reliance thereon by the plaintiffs.[9] Such reliance is lacking where the transaction occurs on a securities exchange,[10] or where the shareholder makes an independent investigation and relies thereon.[11]

A few cases have held that the use of inside information by a corporate insider in selling or buying shares breached such insider's fiduciary duty to the corporation ena-

---

ers" are not fiduciaries and scienter not sufficiently alleged).

6. R. Stevens & A. Larson, Cases and Materials on the Law of Corporations 356 (2d ed. 1955).

7. Mansfield Hardwood Lumber Co. v. Johnson, 268 F.2d 317 (5th Cir. 1959) (applying Louisiana law rather than law of jurisdiction of incorporation), cert. denied, 361 U.S. 885, 80 S.Ct. 156, 4 L.Ed.2d 120 (1959), reh. denied 361 U.S. 926, 80 S.Ct. 290, 4 L.Ed.2d 241 (1960); Blazer v. Black, 196 F.2d 139 (10th Cir. 1952) (applying Kansas law rather than law of jurisdiction of incorporation of dissolved corporation); Jacobson v. Yaschik, 249 S.C. 577, 155 S.E.2d 601 (1967) (holding majority shareholder had duty to disclose special facts known to him, which enhanced shares' value, to minority shareholder who neither knew such facts nor could have ascertained them by inspection of corporation's books and records); Hotchkiss v. Fischer, 136 Kan. 530, 16 P.2d 531 (1932) (involving less than candid representations and some special facts and circumstances, where appellate court assimilated director-president to trustee and stated "minority rule"); Sautter v. Fulmer, 258 N.Y. 107, 179 N.E. 310 (1932) (close corporation), motion for reargument denied 259 N.Y. 508, 182 N.E. 157 (1932); Stewart v. Harris, 69 Kan. 498, 77 P. 277 (1904) (actually involving half-truth response); Oliver v. Oliver, 118 Ga. 262, 45 S.E. 232 (1903) (actually involving fraudulent financial report and officer's serving as shareholder's agent in connection with shares). Many cases characterized as involving the "minority rule" actually involved active fraud, or a fiduciary duty arising from some other source. For the "minority rule" in its pure form, see Jacquith v. Mason, 99 Neb. 509, 156 N.W. 1041 (1916); Dawson v. National Life Ins. Co., 176 Iowa 362, 157 N.W. 929 (1916). In

close corporations, especially, fiduciary relationships are sometimes extended by analogy to partnership law. As to duties of closely-held corporation, its directors, officers, and majority shareholders in acquiring shares of minority shareholders, see Annot., 7 A.L.R.3d 500 (1966). See also Lank v. Steiner, 43 Del.Ch. 262, 224 A.2d 242 (Sup.Ct.1966) (director of close corporation held not required to remind selling shareholder of facts known to latter).

8. Little v. Haas, 68 F.Supp. 545 (N.D.Ga.1946); Fox v. Cosgriff, 66 Idaho 371, 159 P.2d 224 (1945); Fox v. Heatherton, 281 App.Div. 748, 118 N.Y.S.2d 156 (2d Dep't 1953).

9. Such requirements are akin to the requisites of fraud or deceit. See Collings v. Bush Manufacturing Co., 256 F.2d 573 (2d Cir. 1958). See note 11 infra.

10. Goodwin v. Agassiz, 283 Mass. 358, 186 N.E. 659 (1933). See also Joseph v. Farnsworth Radio & Television Corp., 99 F.Supp. 701 (S.D.N.Y.1951).

11. Fischer v. Guaranty Trust Co., 259 App.Div. 176, 18 N.Y.S.2d 328 (2d Dep't 1940), aff'd mem., 285 N.Y. 679, 34 N.E.2d 379 (1941). See Lariscy v. Hill, 117 Ga.App. 152, 159 S.E.2d 443 (1968) (finding no breach of duty of disclosure by active directors who sold shares to inactive director who could have ascertained facts by inspection of corporate books and records); Jacobson v. Yaschik, 249 S.C. 577, 155 S.E.2d 601 (1967) (suggestion that duty of disclosure owed by majority shareholder to minority shareholder did not extend to facts ascertainable by inspection of corporate books and records). See also Schine v. Schine, 250 F.Supp. 822 (S.D.N.Y. 1966) (general release, containing clause covering claims for fraud, held not, as matter of law, to bar action for nondisclosure).

bling the corporation to recover against such insider.[12]

Where insiders acquire shares on the basis of inside information, some argument might be made that they are profiting by the use of something belonging to the corporation and thereby usurping a corporate opportunity.[13] However, a corporation which purchases its own shares without full disclosure to its selling shareholders would presumably be liable therefor or the sale would be subject to rescission.[14]

12. Diamond v. Oreamuno, 24 N.Y.2d 494, 301 N.Y.S. 2d 78, 248 N.E.2d 910 (1969), aff'g 29 A.D.2d 285, 287 N.Y.S.2d 300 (1st Dep't 1968) (insiders held accountable on agency law principles to corporation in shareholder derivative action for difference between selling price and eventual declined market value where they sold shares on over-the-counter market on basis of inside information concerning prospective loss in corporation's earnings); Brophy v. Cities Service Co., 31 Del.Ch. 241, 70 A.2d 5 (Ch. 1949) (secretary to president held accountable to corporation on profits where he bought shares on basis of inside information that corporation would soon seek to reacquire substantial number of shares on market). See also Black v. Shearson, Hammill Co., —— Cal.App.2d ——, 72 Cal.Rptr. 157 (1968) (director of corporation who as broker-dealer advised customers to buy its shares when he knew business was very poor and shares of little value held liable for punitive, as well as compensatory, damages to customer, despite defense that disclosure of corporate information would have violated his duties to corporation).

13. du Pont v. du Pont, 242 F. 98 (D.Del.1917), aff'd 256 F. 129 (3d Cir. 1919), cert. denied 250 U.S. 642, 39 S.Ct. 492, 63 L.Ed. 1185 (1919). But see Steven v. Hale-Haas Corp., 249 Wis. 205, 23 N.W.2d 620 (1946) (upholding purchase by officer as involving no corporate opportunity since corporation's purchase without full disclosure would have been actionable). See section 237 supra. In Beggy v. Deike, 413 Pa. 74, 196 A.2d 179 (1963), the corporation had the right-of-first refusal with respect to an officer's shares. When he offered his shares to the corporation, the two principal officers (who were also the majority shareholders) purchased the shares for themselves and their families without disclosure that they, and not the corporation, were the purchasers. Confidential government contracts involving the corporation were then being negotiated. Rescission was ordered on the ground that the defendants had, without disclosure to and consent of the plaintiff, availed themselves of a contractual option not granted to them.

14. Northern Trust Co. v. Essaness Theatres Corp., 348 Ill.App. 134, 108 N.E.2d 493 (1952); Wood v. MacLean Drug Co., 266 Ill.App. 5 (1932); MacGill v. MacGill, 135 Md. 384, 109 A. 72 (1919). Cf. Kors

Statutory Insider Trading Provisions and Securities Exchange Requirements

Statutes exert increasing influence in this area. The Uniform Securities Act makes unlawful "fraud" or "deceit" (defined as being "not limited to common-law deceit") in connection with the offer, sale, or purchase of any security.[15]

Several federal statutes deal with insider trading, the most significant being the Federal Securities Exchange Act of 1934, which will be discussed in Chapter 11.[16]

With respect to shares listed on a securities exchange, exchange policies might require timely disclosure of favorable and unfavorable developments, such as acquisitions, mergers, share splits, changes in dividend rates or earnings, new contracts, products, or discoveries, etc.[17]

v. Carey, 39 Del.Ch. 47, 158 A.2d 136 (Ch.1960) (directors authorizing corporate purchase held to have no special knowledge of future appreciation of shares); Gladstone v. Murray Co., 314 Mass. 584, 50 N.E.2d 958 (1943) (duty of directors or officers buying shares for corporation held to extend only to corporation and not to sellers of shares).

15. See section 307 infra.

16. S.E.C. Rule 10b–5 is an administrative rule having overwhelming impact. Although it was promulgated under Section 10b of the Federal Securities Exchange Act of 1934, its application is not limited to the purchase or sale of registered securities. It applies whenever interstate commerce (broadly defined), the mails, or a national securities exchange facility is used. Section 16b of the Act requires certain disclosure of insider trading in equity securities of registered issuers, and provides that any profits realized by an officer or director of a registered issuer or more than 10 percent beneficial owner of any equity security, in connection with a purchase or sale, or sale and purchase within six months, of any equity security of such issuer, regardless of the use of insider information, may be recovered by such issuer or any of its security-holders suing in its behalf—known as "recapture" of "short-swing profits"—in the federal courts. See section 298 infra. The Federal Bankruptcy Act § 249, 11 U.S.C.A. § 649, denies to a "fiduciary" or "representative" any compensation or reimbursement if at any time during the corporate reorganization proceeding he trades in the claims against, or shares of, the debtor. See Wolf v. Weinstein, 372 U.S. 633, 83 S.Ct. 969, 10 L.Ed.2d 33 (1963). See also Rubin & Feldman, "Statutory Inhibitions Upon Unfair Use of Corporate Inside Information", 95 U.Pa.L.Rev. 468 (1947).

17. E. g., N.Y.S.E. Company Manual § A2.

FIDUCIARY DUTIES—OPPRESSION OF MINORITY SHAREHOLDERS

240. **Since directors, with respect to their exercise of their management functions, owe fiduciary duties to the corporation to exercise unbiased judgment in the best interests of the corporation as a whole, any attempt by directors to favor one intracorporate group to the detriment of another breaches such duties to the corporation and, in a sense, violates the implied term in the share contract between the corporation and any oppressed shareholder to the effect that corporate affairs will be managed in the best interests of the corporation.**

Controlling shareholders, especially when approving extraordinary corporate matters requiring shareholder approval, are usually subjected to fiduciary duties. Such fiduciary duties preclude "fraud on the minority" or "oppression of the minority", or fraudulent, bad faith, or unfair results. In close corporations, some fiduciary duties among the shareholders, possibly analogous to those among partners, have been recognized.

In the preceding discussion of fiduciary duties, the emphasis has been on the fiduciary duties of directors and officers, rather than of controlling shareholders.

In discussing fiduciary duties applicable to the authorization of corporate transactions detrimental to some shareholders, it should be recalled that various corporate transactions may be authorized by the board of directors or shareholders or both. This obviously requires further definition of the respective fiduciary duties which directors and controlling shareholders owe to minority shareholders.[1]

Directors

Since directors, with respect to their exercise of their management functions,[2] owe fiduciary duties to the corporation to exercise unbiased judgment in the best interests of the corporation as a whole, any attempt by directors to favor one intracorporate group to the detriment of another breaches such duties to the corporation and, in a sense, violates the implied term in the share contract between the corporation and any oppressed shareholder to the effect that corporate affairs will be managed in the best interests of the corporation.

If directors offer additional shares to freeze out the minority, regardless of the application and even technical observance of preemptive rights, the directors have breached their fiduciary duties.[3] Contrariwise, any redemption or other reacquisition by the corporation of some of its outstanding shares which unduly favors one group of shareholders over another constitutes a breach of the directors' fiduciary duties.[4]

Stated more generally, any actions by the directors with respect to corporate affairs, whether solely within the management function of directors or involving coaction by shareholders, such as possibly in the case of merger or consolidation,[5] sale or lease of

Minn.L.Rev. 537 (1961); Comment, "Oppression as a Statutory Ground for Corporate Dissolution", 1965 Duke L.J. 128; Note, "Remedies for Oppression in Close Corporations in Indiana", 41 Ind.L.J. 256 (1966). See also Afterman, "Statutory Protection for Oppressed Minority Shareholders: A Model for Reform", 55 Va.L.Rev. 1043 (1969).

2. See section 207 supra.

3. See section 173 supra.

4. Ibid.

5. Hottenstein (Moore) v. York Ice Machinery Corp., 136 F.2d 944 (3d Cir. 1943), petition for leave to file bill of review denied 146 F.2d 835 (3d Cir. 1944), cert. denied 325 U.S. 886, 65 S.Ct. 1573, 89 L.Ed. 2000 (1945); Sterling v. Mayflower Hotel Corp., 33 Del.Ch. 293, 93 A.2d 107, 38 A.L.R.2d 425 (Sup.Ct. 1952); Porges v. Vadsco Sales Corp., 27 Del.Ch. 127, 32 A.2d 148 (Ch.1943); Cole v. Nat'l Cash Credit Ass'n, 18 Del.Ch. 47, 156 A. 183 (Ch.1931); Juvi-

1. See generally F. O'Neal & J. Derwin, Expulsion or Oppression of Business Associates: "Squeeze-Outs" in Small Enterprises § 5.15 (1961); Fales, "Judicial Attitudes Towards the Rights of Minority Stockholders", 22 Bus.Law. 459 (1967); Shandling, "Corporate Freezeouts and the Protection of Minority Shareholders in Alberta Companies", 4 Alberta L.Rev. 395 (1966); Boyle, "Minority Shareholder in the Nineteenth Century: A Study in Anglo-American Legal History", 28 Modern L.Rev. 317 (1965); McPherson, "Oppression of Minority Shareholders", 36 Austl.L.J. 404 (1963); Harey, "Shareholder's Petition in Cases of Oppression", 36 Austl.L.J. 187 (1962); O'Neal, "Arrangements Which Protect Minority Shareholder Against 'Squeeze-Outs'", 45

major corporate assets,[6] mortgaging of corporate property,[7] dissolution,[8] or amendment of the articles of incorporation,[9] are subject to fiduciary duties.[10]

ler v. Unitronics Corp., 8 Misc.2d 1033, 166 N.Y.S.2d 770 (Sup.Ct.1957). See discussion of consolidations and mergers in section 346 infra.

6. Eisenberg v. Central Zone Property Corp., 306 N. Y. 58, 115 N.E.2d 652 (1953); Ribakove v. Rich, 13 Misc.2d 98, 173 N.Y.S.2d 306 (Sup.Ct.1958). Cf. Gomberg v. Midvale Co., 157 F.Supp. 132 (E.D.Pa. 1955); Scott v. Stanton Heights Corp., 388 P. 628, 131 A.2d 113 (1957); Cottrell v. Pawcatuck Co., 36 Del. 169, 128 A.2d 225 (Sup.Ct.1956), 36 Del. 296, 129 A.2d 263 (Sup.Ct.1957), cert. denied 355 U.S. 12, 78 S.Ct. 54, 2 L.Ed.2d 20 (1957); Baron v. Pressed Metals of America, Inc., 35 Del.Ch. 325, 117 A.2d 357 (Ch.1955), aff'd 35 Del.Ch. 581, 123 A.2d 848 (Sup.Ct.1956); Schiff v. RKO Pictures Corp., 34 Del.Ch. 329, 104 A.2d 267 (Ch.1954); Klopot v. Northrup, 131 Conn. 14, 37 A.2d 700 (1944); Kirwan v. Parkway Distillery, Inc., 285 Ky. 605, 148 S.W. 2d 720 (1941). See discussion of sales and leases of corporate assets in section 341 infra.

7. Farmers Co-operative Ass'n v. Kotz, 222 Minn. 153, 23 N.W.2d 576 (1946). See discussion of mortgaging of corporate property in section 342 infra.

8. Lebold v. Inland Steel Co., 125 F.2d 369 (7th Cir. 1941), cert. denied 316 U.S. 675, 62 S.Ct. 1045, 86 L. Ed. 1749 (1942); Eisenberg v. Central Zone Property Corp., 306 N.Y. 58, 115 N.E.2d 652 (1953); Shrage v. Bridgeport Oil Co., 31 Del.Ch. 305, 71 A. 2d 882 (Ch.1950); Weisbecker v. Hosiery Patents, Inc., 356 Pa. 244, 51 A.2d 811 (1947); Kavanaugh v. Kavanaugh Knitting Co., 226 N.Y. 185, 123 N.E. 148 (1919); Ribakove v. Rich, 13 Misc.2d 98, 173 N.Y.S. 2d 306 (Sup.Ct.1958). Cf. Kirwan v. Parkway Distillery, Inc., 285 Ky. 605, 148 S.W.2d 720 (1941). See Sprecher, "The Right of Minority Stockholders to Prevent the Dissolution of a Profitable Enterprise", 33 Ky.L.J. 150 (1945). For discussion of the converse situation, see Hornstein, "A Remedy for Corporate Abuse—Judicial Power to Wind Up a Corporation at the Suit of a Minority Shareholder", 40 Colum.L.Rev. 220 (1940). See Note, "Freezing Out Minority Stockholders", 41 Va.L.Rev. 77 (1955). See discussion of dissolution in section 348 infra.

9. Barrett v. Denver Tramway Corp., 53 F.Supp. 198 (D.Del.1944), aff'd 146 F.2d 701 (3d Cir. 1944); McNulty v. W. & J. Sloane, 184 Misc. 835, 54 N.Y. S.2d 253 (Sup.Ct.1945); Lehrman v. Godchaux Sugars, Inc., 207 Misc. 314, 138 N.Y.S.2d 163 (Sup.Ct. 1955); Becht, "Changes in the Interests of Classes of Stockholders by Corporate Charter Amendments Reducing Capital, and Altering Redemption, Liquidation and Sinking Fund Provisions", 36 Cornell L. Q. 1 (1950); Latty, "Fairness—The Focal Point in Preferred Stock Arrearage Elimination", 29 Va.L. Rev. 1 (1942); Dodd, "Fair and Equitable Recapitalizations", 55 Harv.L.Rev. 780 (1942); Curran, "Minority Shareholders and the Amendment of Corporate Charters", 32 Mich.L.Rev. 743 (1934); Lat-

Shareholders

The extent to which shareholders, in exercising their management functions,[11] are subject to fiduciary duties, presents a more difficult question.

Shares, after all, are the private property of the shareholders who traditionally are allowed to vote the shares as they desire. This has essentially remained the rule with respect to the election of directors—as indicated by the upholding in most jurisdictions of shareholder agreements binding the par-

tin, "Equitable Limitations on Statutory or Charter Powers Given to Majority Stockholders", 30 Mich. L.Rev. 645 (1932); Note, "Limitations on Alteration of Shareholders' Rights by Charter Amendment", 69 Harv.L.Rev. 538 (1956). See discussion of amendments of articles of incorporation in section 345 infra.

10. Whether such fiduciary duties are to the corporation and/or to the minority shareholders has not received much attention by the courts. But see Lebold v. Inland Steel Co., 125 F.2d 369 (7th Cir. 1941), cert. denied 316 U.S. 675, 62 S.Ct. 1045, 86 L. Ed. 1749 (1942) (dissolution—duty to minority shareholders); Lehrman v. Godchaux Sugars, Inc., 207 Misc. 314, 138 N.Y.S.2d 163 (Sup.Ct.1955) (action by minority shareholder to enjoin unfair capitalization held to be direct and not derivative); see discussion of distinction between derivative and individual shareholder actions in section 360 infra. The Pennsylvania statute [Pa.Bus.Corp.Law § 408 (1966)] refers to officers and directors standing in a fiduciary relationship to the corporation, but the North Carolina statute [N.C.Bus.Corp.Act § 55–35 (1957)] refers to their fiduciary relation to the corporation *and to its shareholders.* Most of the cases have involved attempts by minority shareholders suing in a direct class action in behalf of themselves and all other shareholders similarly situated to enjoin the proposed transaction. E. g., Eisenberg v. Central Zone Property Corp., 306 N.Y. 58, 115 N. E.2d 652 (1953) (direct class action). Dissenting shareholders enjoy some protection under the appraisal remedy when applicable (see section 349 infra).

11. See section 188 supra. See Sneed, "Stockholder Votes Motivated by Adverse Interest: The Attack and the Defense", 58 Mich.L.Rev. 961 (1960); Comment, "Rights of Minority Shareholders in Tennessee", 27 Tenn.L.Rev. 261 (1960); Torem & Focsaneanu, "Minority Stockholders' Rights under French Law", 15 Bus.Law. 331 (1960); Note, "Fiduciary Duties of Majority or Controlling Stockholders", 44 Iowa L.Rev. 734 (1959); Note, "Fiduciary Duty of Controlling Shareholders", 7 W.Res.L.Rev. 467 (1956); Note, 14 U.Chi.L.Rev. 92 (1946).

ties in advance to vote for certain persons as directors.[12]

However, when shareholders vote for or consent to extraordinary corporate matters, which require shareholder approval,[13] they are subject to fiduciary duties.[14]

The fiduciary duties imposed on controlling shareholders with respect to corporate affairs have been predicated on two bases: (a) a *direct* approach, based on equitable principles that one who holds a position of superiority and influence over the interests of others is a fiduciary, concluding that the relationship of controlling shareholders to minority shareholders is a fiduciary relationship, or (b) an *indirect* approach to the effect that if the officers and directors owe fiduciary duties, the controlling shareholders who dominate the corporation through their

influence over the directors and officers are subject to identical duties.[15]

While such fiduciary duties of controlling shareholders do not disqualify them from exercising their voting rights with respect to various matters, the result may not amount to "fraud on the minority" or "oppression of the minority"[16] or be "unfair".[17] Some courts seem to emphasize "fraud" without further explanation,[18] or talk in terms of "good faith" or "bad faith";[19] most apply the test of "fairness",[20] sometimes equating

12. See section 198 supra.

13. See Chapter 13 infra.

14. Kavanaugh v. Kavanaugh Knitting Co., 226 N.Y. 185, 123 N.E. 148 (1919); Farmers' Loan & Trust Co. v. New York and Northern Ry., 150 N.Y. 410, 44 N.E. 1043 (1896). The courts have not yet fully resolved the question of whether such fiduciary duties of controlling shareholders are to the corporation and/or to the minority shareholders. Some cases have held or suggested that the duties are to the minority shareholders. Southern Pacific Co. v. Bogert, 250 U.S. 483, 39 S.Ct. 533, 63 L.Ed. 1099 (1919) (controlling shareholders held answerable to minority shareholders in direct action by latter in behalf of themselves and other minority shareholders without necessity of joinder of corporation as a party); Zahn v. Transamerica Corp., 162 F.2d 36, 172 A.L.R. 495 (3d Cir. 1947) (action against controlling shareholder held to be direct and not derivative); Lebold v. Inland Steel Co., 125 F.2d 369 (7th Cir. 1941), cert. denied 316 U.S. 675, 62 S.Ct. 1045, 86 L.Ed. 1749 (1942). But see Perlman v. Feldmann, 219 F.2d 173, 50 A.L.R.2d 1134 (2d Cir. 1955), cert. denied 349 U.S. 952, 75 S.Ct. 880, 99 L.Ed. 1277 (1955) (action against controlling shareholder held to be derivative but individual recovery allowed); Greenfield v. Denner, 6 N.Y.2d 867, 188 N.Y.S.2d 986, 160 N.E.2d 118 (1959) (4–3) (finding only derivative corporate cause of action for improper dissolution), rev'g mem., 6 A.D.2d 263, 175 N.Y.S.2d 918 (1st Dep't 1958). See Sneed, "The Stockholder May Vote as He Pleases: Theory and Fact", 22 U.Pitt.L.Rev. 23 (1960). Dissenting shareholders enjoy some protection under any applicable appraisal remedy. See section 349 infra.

15. Finch & Long, "The Fiduciary Relation of the Dominant Shareholder to the Minority Shareholders", 9 Hastings L.J. 306, 307 (1958). In Pepper v. Litton, 308 U.S. 295, 306, 60 S.Ct. 238, 245, 84 L.Ed. 281, 289 (1939), the Court referred to corporate powers as "powers in trust"; in Zahn v. Transamerica Corp., 162 F.2d 36, 46, 172 A.L.R. 495, 508 (3d Cir. 1947), the court referred to the "puppet-puppeteer relationship" between the corporate directors and the dominant controlling shareholder.

16. Baron v. Pressed Metals of America, Inc., 35 Del.Ch. 325, 117 A.2d 357 (Ch.1955), aff'd 35 Del.Ch. 581, 123 A.2d 848 (Sup.Ct.1956).

17. See note 21 infra.

18. Hottenstein (Moore) v. York Ice Machinery Corp., 136 F.2d 944 (3d Cir. 1943), petition for leave to file bill of review denied 146 F.2d 835 (3d Cir. 1944), cert. denied 325 U.S. 886, 65 S.Ct. 1573, 89 L.Ed. 2000 (1945); Krantman v. Liberty Loan Corp., 152 F.Supp. 705 (N.D.Ill.1956), aff'd 246 F.2d 581 (7th Cir. 1957); Barrett v. Denver Tramway Corp., 53 F.Supp. 198 (D.Del.1944), aff'd 146 F.2d 701 (3d Cir. 1944); Cole v. Nat'l Cash Credit Ass'n, 18 Del. Ch. 47, 156 A. 183 (Ch.1931); Kirwan v. Parkway Distillery, Inc., 285 Ky. 605, 148 S.W.2d 720 (1941); Kavanaugh v. Kavanaugh Knitting Co., 226 N.Y. 185, 123 N.E. 148 (1919); Ribakove v. Rich, 13 Misc.2d 98, 173 N.Y.S.2d 306 (Sup.Ct.1958).

19. Lebold v. Inland Steel Co., 125 F.2d 369 (7th Cir. 1941), cert. denied 316 U.S. 675, 62 S.Ct. 1045, 86 L.Ed. 1749 (1942); Cole v. Nat'l Cash Credit Ass'n, 18 Del.Ch. 47, 156 A. 183 (Ch.1931) (conscious abuse of discretion); Kavanaugh v. Kavanaugh Knitting Co., 226 N.Y. 185, 123 N.E. 148 (1919); Gamble v. Queens County Water Co., 123 N.Y. 91, 25 N.E. 201 (1890); Ribakove v. Rich, 13 Misc.2d 98, 173 N.Y.S. 2d 306 (Sup.Ct.1958); Juviler v. Unitronics Corp., 8 Misc.2d 1033, 166 N.Y.S.2d 770 (Sup.Ct.1957).

20. Hottenstein (Moore) v. York Ice Machinery Corp., 136 F.2d 944 (3d Cir. 1943), petition for leave to file bill of review denied 146 F.2d 835 (3d Cir. 1944), cert. denied 325 U.S. 886, 65 S.Ct. 1573, 89 L.Ed. 2000 (1945); Lebold v. Inland Steel Co., 125 F.2d 369 (7th Cir. 1941), cert. denied 316 U.S. 675, 62 S.Ct. 1045, 86 L.Ed. 1749 (1942); Cathedral Estates, Inc. v. Taft Realty Corp., 157 F.Supp. 895 (D.Conn.

the term "fraud" (in the sense of constructive fraud) with unfairness.[21]

In close corporations, some fiduciary duties among the shareholders, possibly analogous to those among partners, have been recognized.[22]

When management functions are transferred to one or more shareholders or others, under articles of incorporation provi-

sions authorized by shareholders, as permitted by some modern statutes, the usual responsibilities of directors are imposed upon the shareholders authorizing the same so long as the discretion or powers of the board of directors in its management of corporate affairs is controlled by any such provision.[23]

FIDUCIARY DUTIES—PURCHASE OR SALE OF CONTROL

241. In selling control, controlling shareholders owe to the corporation duties of due care and fiduciary duties, being liable for any resulting damage to the corporation and any profits realized by them for control in connection with the sale of their controlling shares, on the theory that those in control hold control as fiduciaries for the corporation and all of the shareholders and may not treat it as their own personal property to dispose of as they wish. Where the sale of control involves a breach of duty to the minority shareholders, they can recover their proportionate interest in any profits.

Sale of control, while it can involve the turning over of directorships and offices by the directors and officers alone,[1] usually involves the sale of control, along with a controlling block of shares,[2] by a shareholder or

---

1954), aff'd 228 F.2d 85 (2d Cir. 1955); Gomberg v. Midvale Co., 157 F.Supp. 132 (E.D.Pa.1955); Barrett v. Denver Tramway Corp., 53 F.Supp. 198 (D. Del.1944), aff'd 146 F.2d 701 (3d Cir. 1944); Porges v. Vadsco Sales Corp., 27 Del.Ch. 127, 32 A.2d 148 (Ch.1943); McNulty v. W. & J. Sloane, 184 Misc. 835, 54 N.Y.S.2d 253 (Sup.Ct.1945).

21. Pepper v. Litton, 308 U.S. 295, 60 S.Ct. 238, 84 L.Ed. 281 (1939); Hottenstein (Moore) v. York Ice Machinery Corp., 136 F.2d 944 (3d Cir. 1943), petition for leave to file bill of review denied 146 F.2d 835 (3d Cir. 1944), cert. denied 325 U.S. 886, 65 S.Ct. 1573, 89 L.Ed. 2000 (1945); Lebold v. Inland Steel Co., 125 F.2d 369 (7th Cir. 1941), cert. denied 316 U.S. 675, 62 S.Ct. 1045, 86 L.Ed. 1749 (1942); Barrett v. Denver Tramway Corp., 53 F.Supp. 198 (D. Del.1944) ("gross unfairness"), aff'd 146 F.2d 701 (3d Cir. 1944); Krantman v. Liberty Loan Corp., 152 F.Supp. 705 (N.D.Ill.1956), aff'd 246 F.2d 581 (7th Cir. 1957); Cole v. Nat'l Cash Credit Ass'n, 18 Del.Ch. 47, 156 A. 183 (Ch.1931) (conscious abuse of discretion); Kaye v. Kentucky Public Elevator Co., 295 Ky. 661, 175 S.W.2d 142 (1943); Kavanaugh v. Kavanaugh Knitting Co., 226 N.Y. 185, 123 N.E. 148 (1919); Walter, "Fairness in State Court Recapitalization Plans—A Disappearing Doctrine", 29 B.U.L. Rev. 173 (1948). In Note, "Limitations on Alteration of Shareholders' Rights by Charter Amendment", 69 Harv.L.Rev. 538, 545–551 (1956), "fairness" is considered in the context of specific charter amendments (recognizing that the cumulative effect of all proposed changes is relevant): amendments to eliminate accrued dividends and the right to future accruals; amendments to authorize an issue of prior preferred; amendments to reduce capital; amendment of provisions for redemption and sinking funds; amendments of liquidation preferences; amendments of voting and preemptive rights; and merger and consolidation as a means of avoiding limitations on charter amendments.

22. Helms v. Duckworth, 249 F.2d 482 (D.C.Cir. 1957) (shareholder agreement); Efron v. Kalmanovitz, 226 Cal.App.2d 546, 38 Cal.Rptr. 148 (1964) (sale of assets); Sautter v. Fulmer, 258 N.Y. 107, 179 N.E. 310 (1932), motion for reargument denied 259 N.Y. 508, 182 N.E. 157 (1932) (insider share trading); Kavanaugh v. Kavanaugh Knitting Co., 226 N.Y. 185, 123 N.E. 148 (1919) (dissolution); Ribakove v. Rich, 13 Misc.2d 98, 173 N.Y.S.2d 306 (Sup.Ct.1958) (dissolution and sale); Gottfried v. Gottfried, 197 Misc. 562, 73 N.Y.S.2d 692 (Sup.Ct.1950) (action to compel declaration of dividends).

23. See section 259, n. 7 infra.

1. Mitchell v. Dilbeck, 10 Cal.2d 341, 74 P.2d 233 (1937). Generally, it is illegal to sell corporate office or management control by itself, that is, accompanied by no transfer of shares or insufficient shares to carry voting control. See Greene, "Directors' Surrender of Office for Pecuniary Consideration", 28 U.Cin.L.Rev. 380 (1959).

2. Such a controlling block of shares could, of course, involve a majority of the voting shares. Gerdes v. Reynolds, 28 N.Y.S.2d 622 (Sup.Ct.1941); Ballantine v. Ferretti, 28 N.Y.S.2d 668 (Sup.Ct. 1941). However, a smaller block might carry de facto control. Perlman v. Feldmann, 219 F.2d 173, 50 A.L.R.2d 1134 (2d Cir. 1955) (2–1), cert. denied 349 U.S. 952, 75 S.Ct. 880, 99 L.Ed. 1277 (1955) (37 percent); Insuranshares Corporation of Delaware V. Northern Fiscal Corp., 35 F.Supp. 22 (E.D.Pa. 1940) (27 percent). Cf. Essex Universal Corp. v. Yates, 305 F.2d 572, 13 A.L.R.3d 346 (2d Cir. 1962) (questioning 28 percent as carrying de facto control); Matter of Caplan v. Lionel Corp., 14 N.Y.2d

group of shareholders.[3]

Thus, the question usually raised is the scope of the duties which controlling shareholders owe with respect to corporate control. Shareholders generally, except when they are subject to valid share transfer restrictions,[4] may sell their shares for whatever price they can get, and a controlling block of shares as a practical matter usually can be sold at a higher price per share than other shares. The dilemma, arising from the rules that duties attach to the sale of

control—on the theory that those in control hold control as fiduciaries for the corporation and all of the shareholders and may not treat directorships and offices as their own personal property to dispose of as they wish —but not to the sale of the shares, is that a controlling block of shares cannot be severed from its appurtenant control and the price realized from the sale of such block cannot readily be allocated between the payment for such shares *per se* and any premium for appurtenant control.[5]

679, 249 N.Y.S.2d 877, 198 N.E.2d 908 (1964), aff'g 20 A.D.2d 301, 246 N.Y.S.2d 913 (1st Dep't 1964) (vacating election of seven substituted directors pursuant to sale of three percent of outstanding shares, since sale involved less than majority of shares or even such percentage as gave working control, and holding their vacancies were to be filled by majority of three directors remaining in office in accordance with their judgment and duties to shareholders and corporation); Annot., 13 A.L. R.3d 361 (1967).

3. Essex Universal Corp. v. Yates, 305 F.2d 572, 13 A.L.R.3d 346 (2d Cir. 1962) (three concurring opinions showing inability of federal court to determine how New York law would decide question whether contract for sale of 28 percent of shares of New York corporation (for $8 per share when market price approximated $6 per share) is invalid as against public policy solely because it included clause giving purchaser option to require majority of existing directors to replace themselves, by process of seriatim resignation, with majority designated by purchaser); where directorships and offices are relinquished as part of a deal involving the sale by the incumbents of their shares for a bonus for such positions, the corporation may recover such bonus. Moulton v. Field, 179 F. 673 (7th Cir. 1910); Heineman v. Marshall, 117 Mo.App. 546, 92 S.W. 1131 (1905); McClure v. Law, 161 N.Y. 78, 55 N.E. 388 (1899); Gerdes v. Reynolds, 28 N.Y.S.2d 622 (Sup.1941); Ballantine v. Ferretti, 28 N.Y.S.2d 668 (Sup.Ct.1941). Cf. Benson v. Braun, 141 N.Y.S.2d 286 (Sup.Ct.1955), aff'd mem., 286 App.Div. 1098, 145 N.Y.S.2d 711 (1st Dep't 1955) (upholding complaint), 8 Misc.2d 67, 155 N.Y.S.2d 824 (Sup.Ct. 1956) (dismissal after trial); Seagrave Corp. v. Mount, 212 F.2d 389 (6th Cir. 1954) (voiding agreement to acquire controlling shares at premium and to retain minority directors in office). See also Crespinel v. Color Corp. of America, 160 Cal.App.2d 386, 325 P.2d 565 (1958) (upholding director's agreement with corporation to resign upon request of board of directors); Barnes v. Brown, 80 N.Y. 527 (1880) (upholding agreement between buyers and sellers of controlling shares for resignation of sellers as directors upon sale). See also Matter of Carter, 21 A.D.2d 543, 251 N.Y.S.2d 378 (1st Dep't 1964).

4. See sections 281, 282 infra.

5. See Bayne, "The Sale-of-Control Premium: The Disposition", 57 Calif.L.Rev. 615 (1969); Bayne, "The Sale-of-Control Premium: The Intrinsic Illegitimacy", 47 Texas L. Rev. 215 (1969); Bayne, "The Sale-Of-Control Premium: The Definition", 53 Minn.L.Rev. 485 (1969); Brudney, "Fiduciary Ideology in Transactions Affecting Corporate Control", 65 Mich.L.Rev. 259 (1966); Bayne, "Sale-of-Control Quandry", 51 Cornell L.Q. 49 (1965); Berle, "The Price of Power: Sale of Corporate Control", 50 Cornell L.Q. 628 (1965); Bayne, "Sale of Corporate Control", 33 Fordham L.Rev. 583 (1965); Bayne, "Corporate Control as a Strict Trustee", 53 Geo.L.J. 543 (1965); Bayne, "Definition of Corporate Control", 9 St. Louis U.L.J. 445 (1965); Newman & Pickering, "Premium for Control", 28 Tex.B.J. 735 (1965); Boyle, "Sale of Controlling Shares: American Law and the Jenkins Committee", 13 Int. & Comp.L.Q. 185 (1964); Bayne, "A Philosophy of Corporate Control", 112 U.Pa.L.Rev. 22 (1963); Hill, "The Sale of Controlling Shares", 70 Harv.L.Rev. 986 (1957); Katz, "The Sale of Corporate Control", 38 Chi.B.Rec. 376 (1957); Leech, "Transactions in Corporate Control", 104 U.Pa.L. Rev. 725 (1956); Jennings, "Trading in Corporate Control", 44 Calif.L.Rev. 1 (1956); Weisbrod, "Trading in Business Ownership", 1954 Ill.L.F. 465, 477–479; Comment, "Corporate Control and the Corporate Asset Theory", 27 Mont.L.Rev. 153 (1966); Comment, "Sales of Corporate Control and the Theory of Overkill", 31 U.Chi.L.Rev. 725 (1964); Note, "The Sale of Corporate Control: The Berle Theory and the Law", 25 U.Pitt.L.Rev. 59 (1963); Annot., 13 A.L.R.3d 361 (1967); Fenestra, Inc. v. Gulf American Land Corp., 377 Mich. 565, 141 N. W.2d 36 (1966) (upholding delivery of control to majority shareholder where no breach of duty by such shareholder or damage to corporation); Goode v. Powers, 97 Ariz. 75, 397 P.2d 56 (1964) (upholding agreement for sale of 25 percent of shares and for turning over proxies from other shareholders, even though price was generous, absent showing that there was premium for delivery of control). Absent negligence or breach of fiduciary duty, the sale of shares at a price reflecting the control factor has been upheld. Stanton v. Schenck, 140 Misc. 621, 251 N.Y.S. 221 (Sup.Ct.1931); Keely v. Black, 91 N. J.Eq. 520, 111 A. 22 (1920) (sale to competitor). Sale of control has been upheld where there was no secrecy concerning terms or discrimination against

In selling control, controlling shareholders owe to the corporation [6] duties of due care [7] and fiduciary duties.[8] For negligence, the controlling shareholders are liable to the

the minority shareholders. Mayflower Hotel Stockholders Protective Committee v. Mayflower Hotel Corp., 193 F.2d 666 (D.C.Cir. 1951). Purchase of controlling shares at more than twice the price paid to minority shareholders was upheld in Tryon v. Smith, 191 Or. 172, 229 P.2d 251 (1951). Some commentators have suggested that a sale of controlling shares should be accompanied by a general offer for all shares at the same price. Andrews, "The Stockholder's Right to Equal Opportunity in the Sale of Shares", 78 Harv.L.Rev. 505 (1965); Javaras, "Equal Opportunity in the Sale of Controlling Shares: A Reply to Professor Andrews", 32 U. Chi.L.Rev. 420 (1965). The Interstate Commerce Commission has taken such approach. Buffalo, R. & P. Ry. Co. Control, 158 I.C.C. 656, 664 (1930). See Federal Securities Exchange Act § 14(d), 15 U.S.C.A. § 78n(d) (requiring filing with SEC of information concerning tender offers for any equity security registered under Act or any equity security issued by registered investment company, where offeror would, after consummation, become beneficial owner of more than 10 percent of such class of equity security; requiring pro rata acceptance in case of response greater than tender offer. See also Federal Securities Exchange Act § 14(f), 15 U.S.C.A. § 78n(f) (requiring filing with SEC and transmission to holders of securities entitled to vote for directors of information substantially equivalent to that required by S.E.C. Proxy Rules, where under arrangement with persons acquiring securities under section 14(d), etc., any persons are to be elected or designated as directors constituting majority of directors, otherwise than at meeting of security holders).

6. Essex Universal Corp. v. Yates, 305 F.2d 572, 13 A.L.R.3d 346 (2d Cir. 1962); Perlman v. Feldmann, 219 F.2d 173, 50 A.L.R.2d 1134 (2d Cir. 1955), cert. denied 349 U.S. 952, 75 S.Ct. 880, 99 L.Ed. 1277 (1955) (shareholder derivative action); Insuranshares Corporation of Delaware v. Northern Fiscal Corp., 35 F.Supp. 22 (E.D.Pa.1940) (action by corporation).

7. Oil Shares, Inc. v. Kahn, 94 F.2d 751 (3d Cir. 1938), rev'd on other grounds per curiam sub nom. Oil Shares, Inc. v. Commercial Trust Co., 304 U.S. 551, 58 S.Ct. 1059, 82 L.Ed. 1522 (1938); Field v. Western Life Indemnity Co., 166 F. 607 (N.D.Ill. 1908), aff'd 179 F. 673 (7th Cir. 1910), cert. denied 219 U.S. 586, 31 S.Ct. 470, 55 L.Ed. 347 (1911); Insuranshares Corporation of Delaware v. Northern Fiscal Corp., 35 F.Supp. 22 (E.D.Pa.1940) (where without any investigation, controlling shareholders sold their shares to others, turning over the directorships and offices to them, despite fact that corporation—an investment company with a portfolio of readily-marketable securities—had previously been looted by insiders, that price paid was substantially higher than the value of shares, that the purchasers (without apparent financial resources) were known to be planning to convert many of the corporation's securities into cash on the closing date, and that counsel had warned the controlling

shareholders, the court held that "the owners of control are under a duty not to transfer it to outsiders if the circumstances surrounding the proposed transfer are such as to awaken suspicion and put a prudent man on his guard—unless a reasonably adequate investigation discloses such facts as would convince a reasonable person that no fraud is intended or likely to result"); Bosworth v. Allen, 168 N.Y. 157, 61 N.E. 163 (1901); McClure v. Law, 161 N.Y. 78, 55 N.E. 388 (1899); Keystone Guard v. Beaman, 264 Pa. 397, 107 A. 835 (1919). The rationale is that directors and officers cannot abandon their positions and responsibilities to irresponsible persons or profit from the sale of their positions. Cf. Ryder v. Bamberger, 172 Cal. 791, 158 P. 753 (1916); Smith v. Gray, 50 Nev. 56, 250 P. 369 (1926); Barnes v. Brown, 80 N.Y. 527 (1880); Levy v. Feinberg, 29 N.Y.S.2d 550 (Sup.Ct.1941), rev'd sub nom. Levy v. American Beverage Corp., 265 App. Div. 208, 38 N.Y.S.2d 517 (1st Dep't 1942); Stanton v. Schenck, 140 Misc. 621, 251 N.Y.S. 221 (Sup.Ct. 1931) (where, absent conspiracy, old directors and officers retained their positions until replaced at next annual shareholder meeting when new controlling shareholders elected new directors who in turn appointed new officers).

8. Perlman v. Feldmann, 219 F.2d 173, 50 A.L.R.2d 1134 (2d Cir. 1955), cert. denied 349 U.S. 952, 75 S.Ct. 880, 99 L.Ed. 1277 (1955), rev'g 129 F.Supp. 162 (D. Conn.1952). The case involved a sale for a price ($20) substantially in excess of the over-the-counter market price ($12) and book value of the shares ($17) of a controlling block of shares (37 percent) by the dominant shareholder—president—chairman of the board—director, who expressly agreed to deliver the resignations of all the directors, to a group of end-users of steel who thereafter bought the entire steel output of the corporation (at prevailing prices), thereby frustrating two corporate possibilities during the steel shortage resulting from the Korean crisis—interest-free loans from customers for plant modernization and development of good will among local customers. The district court had ruled that the plaintiffs had failed to satisfy their burden of proving that the sales price was not a fair price for the shares per se. The court of appeals ruled that the burden of proof was always on the fiduciaries to establish the fairness of their dealings with trust property, and remanded the case to determine the value of the defendants' shares "without the appurtenant control" over the corporation's steel output. Swan, J. vigorously dissented. On remand, the district court computed the "enterprise value" at $14.67 per share and the premium for control at $5.33 per share. Perlman v. Feldmann, 154 F.Supp. 436 (D.Conn. 1957). The total recovery on such basis would have been $2,126,280, reduced to a pro rata individual recovery for innocent shareholders (53 percent) of $1,339,770. The case was eventually settled for $1,150,000, and plaintiffs' counsel fees of $450,000 and $38,000 disbursements awarded from such sum. Perlman v. Feldmann, 160 F.Supp. 310 (D.Conn. 1958).

corporation for any resulting damage.[9] For breach of fiduciary duties, they might be liable to the corporation for any resulting damages [10] or, as is more frequently the case, for any profits realized by them,[11] usually the premium for control.[12]

Since the looting cases have often involved investment companies,[13] the Federal Investment Company Act of 1940 contains provisions requiring honest and unbiased management of investment companies subject to the Act.[14]

A corporate officer and director has been allowed to *acquire* control through the purchase of most of the few remaining shares held by outsiders, on the ground that he owed no fiduciary duty as a shareholder and was not bound by the agreement among the other insider shareholders to try to acquire the shares held by outsiders and either to divide such shares among the parties to the agreement or to have them cancelled by the corporation.[15]

Where two directors and officers acquired sufficient shares to *prevent* a prospective purchaser from acquiring control, the shareholders who thereby lost the opportunity to sell their shares to such prospective purchaser were held to have no cause of action against such directors and officers on the ground that the mere ownership of shares involves no fiduciary relationship among shareholders.[16]

Where the sale of control involves a breach of duty to the minority shareholders, they can recover their proportionate interest in any profits.[17]

9. Insuranshares Corporation of Delaware v. Northern Fiscal Corp., 42 F.Supp. 126 (E.D.Pa.1941) (fixing amount of damages); Gerdes v. Reynolds, 28 N.Y.S.2d 622 (Sup.Ct.1941); Ballantine v. Ferretti, 28 N.Y.S.2d 668 (Sup.Ct.1941); see also Gerdes v. Reynolds, 30 N.Y.S.2d 755 (Sup.Ct.1941) (confirming referee's report). Cf. Levy v. Feinberg, 29 N.Y.S.2d 550 (Sup.Ct.1941), rev'd sub nom. Levy v. American Beverage Co., 265 App.Div. 208, 38 N.Y.S.2d 517 (1st Dep't 1942) (looting by purchasers not reasonably foreseeable by sellers).

10. Dale v. Thomas H. Temple Co., 186 Tenn. 69, 208 S.W.2d 344 (1948) (holding liable both sellers and purchasers of controlling shares at premium where both knew purchase would be financed in part out of corporate assets). Cf. Algonac Marine Hardware Co. v. Cline, 10 Mich.App. 158, 159 N.W.2d 150 (1968).

11. Gabriel Industries, Inc. v. Defiance Industries, Inc., 22 N.Y.2d 405, 293 N.Y.S.2d 65, 239 N.E.2d 706 (1968) ($283,712 recovery of profits for illegal sale of control of board of directors); Annot., 50 A.L.R. 2d 1146–1156 (1956).

12. See note 8 supra.

13. Insuranshares Corporation of Delaware v. Northern Fiscal Corp., 35 F.Supp. 22 (E.D.Pa.1940); Gerdes v. Reynolds, 28 N.Y.S.2d 622 (Sup.Ct.1941); Ballantine v. Ferretti, 28 N.Y.S.2d 668 (Sup.Ct. 1941).

14. § 16(a), 15 U.S.C.A. § 80a–16(a); Securities and Exchange Commission v. Insurance Securities, Inc., 254 F.2d 642 (9th Cir. 1958), cert. denied 358 U.S. 823, 79 S.Ct. 38, 3 L.Ed.2d 64 (1958); Jaretski, "The Investment Company Act of 1940", 26 Wash.U.L.Q. 303, 323–324 (1941); Comment, "Protecting the Interests of Mutual-Fund Investors in Sales of Management-Corporation Control (or Policing the Traffic in Other People's Money)", 68 Yale L.J. 113 (1958).

15. Howell v. McCloskey, 375 Pa. 100, 99 A.2d 610 (1953). Quaere, as to the defendant's using as his agent to acquire the remaining shares one of the other insiders who was a party to the agreement, the terms of which were known to the defendant. See also King Mfg. Co. v. Clay, 216 Ga. 581, 118 S. E.2d 581 (1961) (holding corporation had no cause of action for purchase of control by certain directors); Vulcanized Rubber & Plastics Co. v. Scheckter, 400 Pa. 405, 162 A.2d 400 (1960). For cases sanctioning use of corporate funds to keep management in control by the corporation's buying-out the insurgents' shares, see Cheff v. Mathes, 41 Del.Ch. 494, 199 A. 2d 548 (Sup.Ct.1964); Bennett v. Propp, 41 Del.Ch. 14, 187 A.2d 405 (Sup.Ct.1962); Kors v. Carey, 39 Del.Ch. 47, 158 A.2d 136 (Ch.1960); Hendricks v. Mill Eng'r & Supply Co., 68 Wash.2d 490, 413 P.2d 811 (1966) (4–3) (upholding board of directors redemption of voting preferred shares to avoid shift of control to minority common shareholders who had acquired sufficient preferred shares to muster majority vote). Cf. Kullgren v. Navy Gas & Supply Co., 110 Colo. 454, 135 P.2d 1007 (1943) (sale of treasury shares to directors to perpetuate themselves in control held wrongful despite broad authorization to them to sell such shares in their discretion). See section 242, n. 4 infra.

16. Mairs v. Madden, 307 Mass. 378, 30 N.E.2d 242, 132 A.L.R. 256 (1940). The persons who had sold their shares to the two directors and officers were not complaining. Quaere, as to the fiduciary duties of directors and officers with respect to the use of inside information.

17. Dunnett v. Arn, 71 F.2d 912 (10th Cir. 1934) (where offer was for all of the outstanding shares and, unknown to rest of shareholders, president and secretary, who owned majority of shares, sold their shares for higher price per share than rest of

If, in connection with any transfer of more than 10 percent of the outstanding shares of a corporation subject to the Federal Securities Exchange Act, there is any arrangement or understanding by which a majority of the directors are to be changed without a vote of shareholders, the corporation must file with the Securities and Exchange Commission and send to its shareholders, before any of the new directors are installed, information substantially equivalent to that which would have to be filed and sent if those persons were nominees for election as directors at a shareholder meeting.[18]

"BUSINESS JUDGMENT" RULE

242. The "business judgment" rule sustains corporate transactions and immunizes management from liability where the transaction is within the powers of the corporation (intra vires) and the authority of management, and involves the exercise of due care and compliance with applicable fiduciary duties.

Corporate management is vested in the board of directors. If in the course of management, directors arrive at a decision, within the corporation's powers (*intra vires*) and their authority,[1] for which there is a reasonable basis,[2] and they act in good faith, as the result of their independent discretion and judgment, and uninfluenced by any consideration other than what they honestly believe to be the best interests of the corporation,[3] a court will not interfere with internal management and substitute its judgment for that of the directors to enjoin or set aside the transaction or to surcharge the directors for any resulting loss.[4]

3. See sections 232, 235–241 supra.

4. Shlensky v. Wrigley, 95 Ill.App.2d 173, 237 N.E.2d 776 (1968) (declining to interfere with business judgment of board of directors of Chicago Cubs, a Delaware corporation, against night home games); Olson Bros. v. Englehart, 42 Del.Ch. 348, 211 A.2d 610 (Ch.1965) (holding shareholder ratification shifted to objecting party burden of proof as to exercise of sound business judgment); Otis & Co. v. Pennsylvania R. R., 61 F.Supp. 905 (E.D.Pa.1945), aff'd mem., 155 F.2d 522 (3d Cir. 1946) (allegations of unfavorable underwriting); Casey v. Woodruff, 49 N.Y.S.2d 625 (Sup.Ct.1944) (similar facts); Rous v. Carlisle, 261 App.Div. 432, 26 N.Y.S.2d 197 (1st Dep't 1941), aff'd mem., 290 N.Y. 869, 50 N.E.2d 250 (1943) (allegations of excessive underwriting fees and prices for power plants); New York Credit Men's Adjustment Bureau, Inc. v. Weiss, 305 N.Y. 1, 110 N.E.2d 397 (1953) (directors held liable to creditors for failure to get full value for assets of insolvent corporation at public auction rather than resorting to permissive methods of dissolution under court supervision); Glassberg v. Boyd, 35 Del. Ch. 293, 116 A.2d 711 (Ch.1955) (directors held not liable for good faith payment of out-of-state taxes subsequently invalidated as unconstitutional); Conviser v. Simpson, 122 F.Supp. 205 (D.Md.1954) (directors of investment company whose retention of realized capital gain, rather than distributing it to shareholders along with investment income, resulted in $3,500,000 federal capital gains tax on corporation held not liable under "business judgment" rule); Foster v. Bowen, 311 Mass. 359, 41 N.E.2d 181 (1942); Pollitz v. Wabash R. R., 207 N.Y. 113, 124, 100 N.E. 721, 723 (1912); November v. National Exhibition Co., 10 Misc.2d 537, 173 N.Y.S.2d 490 (Sup.Ct.1958); Diston v. Loucks, 62 N.Y.S.2d 138 (Sup.Ct.1941) (allegations of inadequate sales price for shares in subsidiary). See also Hornstein v. Paramount Pictures, Inc., 292 N.Y. 468, 55 N.E.2d 740 (1944) (4–3) (upholding "business judgment" of directors in paying racketeers in violation of labor-relations statute); Abrams v. Allen, 297 N.Y. 52, 74 N.E.2d 305 (1947) (allegations of relocation of plants to punish employees) (complaint held to state cause of action), 113 N.Y.S.2d 181 (Sup.Ct.1952) (complaint dismissed after trial); Garwin v. Anderson, 334 Mich. 287, 54 N.W.2d 667 (1952) (settlement of controversy); Western Pac. R. R. v. Western Pac. Ry., 197 F.2d 994 (9th Cir. 1951) (consolidated tax returns), rev'd on other grounds, 345 U.S. 247, 73 S. Ct. 656, 97 L.Ed. 986 (1953), 205 F.2d 374 (9th Cir. 1953), 206 F.2d 495 (9th Cir. 1953), cert. denied 346

shareholders). Sautter v. Fulmer, 258 N.Y. 107, 179 N.E. 310 (1932), motion for reargument denied 259 N.Y. 508, 182 N.E. 157 (1932); McMynn v. Peterson (Richardson-Phenix Co.), 186 Wis. 442, 201 N.W. 272 (1924). Cf. McCord v. Martin, 47 Cal.App. 717, 191 P. 89 (1920) (no deception of minority shareholders); R. Stevens, Handbook on the Law of Private Corporations 793 (2d ed. 1949). Compare McDaniel v. Painter, 418 F.2d 545 (10th Cir. 1969) (majority held entitled to premium for control), with Jones v. H. F. Ahmanson & Co., 1 Cal.3d 93, 81 Cal.Rptr. 592, 460 P.2d 464 (1969) (majority shareholders' exchange of control block of corporation's unmarketable shares for holding company shares, excluding minority from ownership of marketable holding company shares, held breach of fiduciary responsibility to minority).

18. Federal Securities Exchange Act of 1934, § 14(f), 15 U.S.C.A. § 78n(f). See section 297 infra.

1. See section 233 supra.

2. See sections 232, 234 supra.

Business judgment thus, by definition, presupposes an honest, unbiased judgment

U.S. 910, 74 S.Ct. 241, 98 L.Ed. 407 (1953), 216 F.2d 513 (9th Cir. 1954) (appeal dismissed). Comment, "Reliance on Advice of Counsel", 70 Yale L.J. 978 (1961); Note, "Continuing Viability of the Business Judgment Rule as a Guide for Judicial Restraint", 35 Geo.Wash.L.Rev. 562 (1967); Note, "The Business Judgment Rule: A Guide to Corporate Directors' Liability", 7 St.Louis U.L.J. 151 (1962). As to the use of corporate funds by incumbent management to buy out insurgents, thus perpetuating present management, see Cheff v. Mathes, 41 Del. Ch. 494, 199 A.2d 548 (Sup.Ct.1964) (upholding directors' use of borrowed corporate funds for corporation to purchase at excessive prices its shares held by outsider seeking control, on ground directors had satisfied burden of showing reasonable grounds to believe danger to corporate policy and effectiveness existed by presence of such share ownership); Bennett v. Propp, 41 Del.Ch. 14, 187 A.2d 405 (Sup.Ct. 1962) (holding chairman of board and president liable for damages resulting from corporation's purchase with borrowed funds of its shares to retain control, threatened by letter indicating interest in acquiring corporation, where they failed to prove substantial threat to control and probability of injury to corporation if control were lost, but exonerating directors who in emergency ratified fait accompli); Kors v. Carey, 39 Del.Ch. 47, 158 A.2d 136 (Ch.1960) (upholding corporation's purchase of its shares to retain control where it was being actively sought by another concern whose business policies, arguably, were in violation of Robinson-Patman Act). Cheff v. Mathes has been criticized as the "third of the unholy trio" of Delaware cases: "It would be ostrich-like to deny that Delaware is responsible for the public's image of the moral chaos in the public-issue corporation. The standards (i. e., absence of standards) to which Delaware complaisantly and complacently accedes and then foists upon the rest of the country have generated an understandable distrust of the corporate system and unfair condemnation of it as simply legalized wrongdoing. This year has confirmed the now too-familiar theme—complete judicial abdication of authority to curtail abuse of management (directorial) power. For the third time in five years, the factual setup posed the same issue, and the results command respect only for their consistency". Hornstein, "Corporations", in 1964 Annual Survey of American Law 462 (1965). "Business judgment" is also the test in cases alleging that failure timely to assert a corporate claim resulted in a corporate loss. Walker v. Man, 142 Misc. 277, 253 N.Y.S. 458 (Sup.Ct.1931) (complaint based on directors' refusal to sue held to state claim against them); Epstein v. Schenck, 35 N.Y.S.2d 969 (Sup.Ct.1939) (upholding directors' refusal to sue); Druckerman v. Harbord, 31 N.Y.S.2d 867, 871 (Sup.Ct.1940) (rejecting contention that directors' refusal to sue was new cause of action which prevented statute of limitations from barring action); Truncale v. Universal Pictures

(compliance with fiduciary duty) reasonably exercised (due care), and compliance with other applicable requirements.[5]

Although the "business judgment" rule is usually stated in terms of director functions, it is no less applicable to officers in the exercise of their authority and may be applicable to controlling shareholders when they exercise their more extraordinary management functions.[6]

Co., 76 F.Supp. 465 (S.D.N.Y.1948) (refusing to surcharge directors for inaction in allowing statute of limitations to run on corporation's claim). See Groel v. United Electric Co. of New Jersey, 70 N.J. Eq. 616, 61 A. 1061 (1905). See section 234 supra. See also Heimann v. American Express Co., 53 Misc.2d 749, 279 N.Y.S.2d 867 (Sup.Ct.1967) (upholding settlement for some $60,000,000 of $130,000,000 claims arising out of field warehousing business conducted by two wholly-owned subsidiaries); Issner v. Aldrich, 254 F.Supp. 696 (D.Del.1966) (holding that exercise of business judgment by board of directors refusing to sue barred shareholder derivative action)—see section 365 infra. See also Kelly v. Bell, —— Del.Ch. ——, 254 A.2d 62 (Ch.1969) (upholding payment of tax without any statutory basis in return for favorable legislation).

5. Gilbert v. Burnside, 13 A.D.2d 982, 216 N.Y.S.2d 430 (2d Dep't 1961), aff'd mem., 11 N.Y.2d 960, 229 N.Y.S.2d 10, 183 N.E.2d 325 (1962) (refusing to surcharge directors for corporate losses resulting from invalidated merger where directors had in good faith relied on advice of counsel); Foster v. Arata, 74 Nev. 143, 325 P.2d 759 (1958). Modern corporate statutes providing for reimbursement of corporate personnel for litigation expenses and intracorporate provisions attempting to stay within the statutory prohibitions on reimbursement in cases where such personnel were "adjudged liable for negligence or misconduct in the performance of their duties", often provide that a conviction or judgment shall not be deemed an adjudication of liability for negligence or misconduct in the performance of one's duties if one were acting in good faith in what one considered to be the best interests of the corporation—in effect a paraphrase of the "business judgment" rule. See Simon v. Socony-Vacuum Oil Co., 179 Misc. 202, 38 N.Y.S.2d 270 (Sup.Ct.1942), aff'd mem., 267 App.Div. 890, 47 N.Y.S.2d 589 (1st Dep't 1944) (upholding directors' exercise of business judgment despite antitrust conviction and use of corporate funds to pay counsel fees and fines of convicted corporate personnel).

6. 3 W. Fletcher, Private Corporations § 1039 (rev. vol. 1965) (directors and officers); Cole v. Nat'l Cash Credit Ass'n, 18 Del.Ch. 47, 156 A. 183 (Ch. 1931) (controlling shareholders' approval of merger).

H. MANAGEMENT COMPENSATION

MANAGEMENT COMPENSATION— IN GENERAL

243. **Management compensation involves various practical factors, especially the fair allocation of corporate earnings among labor, management, the various taxing levels of government, and shareholders. Tax factors have become increasingly relevant. Hence, management compensation is predicated upon two sets of legal considerations: (a) those of corporation law, and (b) those of taxation, especially federal income taxation. With respect to corporation law aspects, the rules applicable to directors present some features not applicable to officers.**

Compensating those who manage the corporation involves various practical factors, especially the fair allocation of corporate earnings among labor, management, the government (federal, state, and local), and shareholders.[1]

As taxation increases, tax factors become increasingly relevant,[2] resulting in forms of compensation, often somewhat complicated, to minimize taxes, at both corporate and recipient levels. Taxation of the corporation is minimized by deducting its payments as legitimate business expense and, where plans are funded, avoiding income to itself. The recipient of the compensation usually wants (a) to avoid a tax on illusory benefit, (b) to spread his compensation over a period to obtain continued income and to avoid higher

---

1. See generally G. Washington, V. Rothschild, T. Ness & R. Sobernheim, Compensating the Corporate Executive (3d ed. 1962) (2 vols.); B. Bryson & T. Lefevre, Tax Aspects of Executives' Compensation (PLI 1955); Small, "Compensating Corporate Executives", in Advising California Business Enterprises 717–783 (1958); Bibliography: "Selected Materials on the Legal Aspects of Executive Compensation", 21 Record of N.Y.C.B.A. 328 (1966); Klaus, "A Corporate Quandry: Search for an Adequate Method of Executive Compensation", 4 Tulsa L.Rev. 197 (1967); J. Lasser, Tax Protected Compensation for the Executive (1965); Steadman, "Capital Gains as Applied to Executive Compensation", 16 Bus.Law. 643 (1961); Trimble, "Executive Compensation: Corporate Transactions", 6 Prac.Law. 45 (Dec.1960); Murphy, "Introduction to Management Compensation", 1958 U.Ill.L.F. 1; Comment, "The Tax Bargain in Executive Compensation", 47 Texas L.Rev. 405 (1969). See also Sager & Weinberg, "State Taxation of Employee Retirement and Death Benefits", 31 Fordham L.Rev. 413 (1963); Kramer, "Employee Benefits and Federal Estate and Gift Taxes", 1959 Duke L.J. 341. For application of federal securities legislation to management compensation, see 2 G. Washington, V. Rothschild, T. Ness & R. Sobernheim, op. cit. supra, ch. 17. Salaries and other compensation for directors and officers of corporations abroad are rarely disclosed and are modest by American standards. "Management: Who Gets What", 86 Time, No. 7, 68 (Aug. 13, 1965).

2. Indicative of tax impact is the fact that the president of E. I. du Pont de Nemours and Co. in 1923 received a salary of $78,570 ($60,843 net after taxes), and in 1947 received a salary of $175,000 ($48,251 net after taxes)—thus after 25 years the holder of the office was netting $12,500 less (in dollars of decreased purchasing power). 1 G. Washington, V. Rothschild, T. Ness & R. Sobernheim, op. cit. supra note 1, at 9–10. In 1959, the chief executive officer of General Motors Corporation received $670,350 in compensation, in the form of $201,350 in salaries and fees, $351,750 in bonuses, and $117,250 in contingent credits (on share options); his estimated income after taxes was $111,782. The 1967 compensation of the chief executive officer of General Motors Corporation (salary, bonus, "contingent credit", share options, pension plan, life insurance) approximated $950,000 before taxes. Main, "An Expanding Executive Pay Package", 77 Fortune, No. 7, 166, 167 (June 15, 1968). Since World War II, while salaries and wage payments have almost tripled, fringe benefits have sextupled, exceeding $20,000,000,000 annually, compared to $22,800,000,000 annual dividends. If the trend continues the basic salaries and wages may become the fringe area. 161 The Wall Street Journal, No. 94, 1 (May 14, 1963). See Frommer, "Compensation and Its Fringes", N.Y.U. 21st Inst. on Fed.Tax. 375 (1963); Shelmerdine, "Executive Fringe Benefits", N.Y.U. 20th Inst. on Fed.Tax. 371 (1962); Foegen, "Product Mix for Fringe Benefits", 39 Harv.Bus.Rev. 64 (July-Aug.1961); Weisbard, "Executives Compensation Package Can Have Many Benefits, Save Him Much Money", 10 J.Taxation 54 (1959). Corporations with welfare or retirement plans covering at least 26 participants, including former employees drawing benefits, are subject to the Federal Welfare and Pension Plans Disclosure Act, adopted in 1958 and substantially revised in 1962. 29 U.S.C.A. §§ 301–309; Comment, "The Welfare and Pension Plans Disclosure Act: Its History, Operation and Amendment", 30 Geo.Wash.L.Rev. 682 (1962); "How To Operate under the *New* Disclosure Law" (Prentice-Hall, Inc. 1962).

tax brackets, and (c) to reduce his estate tax.[3]

Today, management compensation must be determined not only on the basis of various practical factors, largely economic, but on two sets of legal considerations: first, those of corporation law, and second, those of taxation, especially federal income taxation because of its high rates.[4]

With respect to corporation law aspects, the rules applicable to directors [5] present some features not applicable to officers.[6]

COMPENSATION OF DIRECTORS

244. Directors, in theory, as representative shareholders with a substantial financial stake in the corporation, traditionally are supposed to attend to corporate affairs without compensation absent a valid prearrangement with the corporation. Directors lack inherent authority to fix their own compensation. Even when such authority is expressly conferred on the board of directors, the exercise of such authority inevitably involves self-dealing with the usual legal consequences. Increasingly, provision for director compensation is being made in statutes, articles of incorporation, bylaws adopted by shareholders, and resolutions of shareholders.

The traditional view was that the director was, in theory, a representative shareholder whose share holdings and dividends therefrom justified his special attention to corpo-

rate affairs without further reward.[1] Then, too, directors were without inherent authority to fix their own compensation, and even when authority to do so was expressly conferred on the board of directors, the exercise of such authority inevitably involved self-dealing by fiduciaries with the usual legal consequences.[2] Many cases reiterate the presumption that directors perform their duties without compensation unless they have a valid prearrangement with the corporation.[3] The reward of the director *qua* director, however, was essentially social and business prestige and, until his fiduciary duties were tightened, occasional inside opportunities for financial again.[4]

With the increasing prevalence of directors with little or no share ownership, attitudes in favor of compensating directors developed. Increasingly, provision for such compensation was made in articles of incorporation, bylaws adopted by shareholders, and resolutions of shareholders.[5]

These either fixed the compensation, set forth a formula for fixing it, or authorized the board to fix it. Shareholder participation in such process helped to minimize the problems of authority and self-dealing; an interested director provision in the articles of incorporation might tend to supply the necessary authority and to neutralize an otherwise adverse inference. Some modern

---

[§ 243]

3. 1 G. Washington, V. Rothschild, T. Ness & R. Sobernheim, op. cit. supra note 1, at 31–34; Kramer, "Employee Benefits and Federal Estate and Gift Taxes", 1959 Duke L.J. 341.

4. Rudick "Compensation of Executives under the 1954 Code", 33 Taxes 7 (1955). Prior to the income tax (or franchise tax based on income), whether corporate funds were used in the form of salaries, interest, dividends (from income or otherwise), redemption payments, etc., was, of course, governed by principles of corporation law alone.

5. See section 244 infra.

6. See section 245 infra.

[§ 244]

1. 1 G. Washington, V. Rothschild, T. Ness & R. Sobernheim, Compensating the Corporate Executive 257–261 (3d ed. 1962).

2. See section 238 supra.

3. 1 G. Washington, V. Rothschild, T. Ness & R. Sobernheim, op. cit. supra note 1, at 203; Lofland v. Cahall, 13 Del.Ch. 384, 118 A. 1 (Sup.Ct.1922). The presumption would be inapplicable to a director who performed extraordinary or special services, which he would be doing in some capacity other than as director. Rocky Mountain Powder Co. v. Hamlin, 73 Nev. 87, 310 P.2d 404 (1957).

4. See sections 237, 239 supra.

5. 1 G. Washington, V. Rothschild, T. Ness & R. Sobernheim, op. cit. supra note 1, at 255–261.

statutes expressly provide that the board of directors shall have authority to fix the compensation of directors unless otherwise provided in the articles of incorporation or possibly the bylaws.[6]

Many corporations still do not compensate their directors as such. Most others provide a nominal honorarium, say $50 or $100, per meeting, the modern counterpart of the traditional $20 gold piece. A growing number of larger American corporations provide for rather substantial compensation to directors, a practice prevalent in English companies.[7]

Since directors are subject to very substantial duties,[8] reasonable compensation to them, especially when they are neither substantial shareholders with a financial stake in the enterprise nor officers receiving compensation in such capacity, certainly can be justified.

COMPENSATION OF OFFICERS

245. Officers who are also directors are traditionally presumed to serve gratuitously, at least with respect to "usual" matters, absent a valid salary prearrangement with the corporation; non-director officers, even in the absence of such prearrangement, are entitled to reasonable compensation on principles of implied contract or quantum meruit. Forms of executive compensation to supplement fixed salaries include (a) profit-sharing plans, (b) share bonuses, (c) share options, (d) share purchase plans, (e) deferred compensation plans, (f) pension plans, (g) annuity plans, (h) tax reimbursement plans, and (i) other fringe benefits.

Executive compensation must be reasonable in amount and based on services performed for the corporation, and should usually be determined before the services are rendered, with a minimum of self-dealing on the part of those involved and, when appropriate, ratified by shareholders.

The traditional view was that officers who were also directors were presumed to have served gratuitously, absent a valid prearrangement with the corporation.[1] The non-director officer, absent such prearrangement, was usually not bothered by such presumption, and was awarded reasonable compensation under the principles of implied contract or quantum meruit. Even in the case of the director-officer, the presumption was not controlling where the officer was found to have performed more than the "ordinary" or "usual" duties of his office— which was not infrequent when express authority was not spelled out and implied authority was narrowly construed.[2]

6. E. g., ABA–ALI Model Bus.Corp.Act § 33; Alabama, Alaska, Colorado, Indiana, Illinois, Iowa, New York, North Carolina, North Dakota, Ohio, Oregon, Virginia, Wisconsin. See Note, "Problems in Fixing or Increasing Compensation of Directors", 38 Calif.L.Rev. 906 (1950).

7. In the United States, at least in larger corporations, directors' fees range from $10 to $1,250 per board meeting and $10 to $1,000 per committee meeting, sometimes along with annual retainers from $400 to $12,500. See also 1 G. Washington, V. Rothschild, T. Ness & R. Sobernheim, op. cit. supra note 1, at 256–258. See Bank of New Smyrna v. United States, 4 AFTR2d 5183 (S.D.Fla.1959) ($5,000 compensation paid to each of five bank directors in 1953 upheld as reasonable in light of their services in 1953 and prior years). Fees paid to directors are not subject to withholding or the payment of social security or unemployment taxes. See Blanton v. Comm'r, 379 F.2d 558 (5th Cir. 1967) (disallowing deduction to director for paying back to corporation director's fees determined to be excessive by Internal Revenue Service under voluntary agreement with corporation to do so). The English system has its share of critics. It has tended to produce some directors, often indigent peers, whose function seemed to be merely to add an appearance of respectability to the board of directors by lending it their names or titles and who are called, from the old practice of paying them in guineas and providing lunch, "guinea pig" directors. L. Gower, The Principles of Modern Company Law 129 (2d ed. 1957).

8. See sections 231–242 supra. Some cases have suggested higher duties for directors paid for devoting their whole time to the corporate business than for part-time directors serving gratuitously ("gratuitous mandatories"). R. Stevens, Handbook on the Law of Private Corporations § 151 (2d ed. 1949).

1. Alexander v. Lindsay, 152 So.2d 261 (La.Ct.App. 1963), writ refused 244 La. 897, 154 So.2d 767 (1963); Savage v. Lorraine Corp., 217 F.2d 378 (9th Cir.1954).

2. Security-First Nat'l Bank of Los Angeles v. Lutz, 322 F.2d 348 (9th Cir. 1963). See sections 224, 225 supra.

Not until the 20th century did a professional executive class begin to emerge and to receive substantial compensation. The entrepreneurs of the late 19th century looked for their rewards toward profits from expansion and promotion and not from salaries. In the period from World War I to the Great Depression (1914–1929), executive compensation took the form of fixed salary, with or without expense accounts and profit-sharing bonus, often in very substantial amounts, and usually without much disclosure. As an aftermath of the depression, much publicity was given to high corporate executive compensation (occasionally over $1,000,000 a year), as the result of shareholder derivative actions, receivership, bankruptcy, government investigation, tax returns, and Securities and Exchange Commission full disclosure requirements.[3]

New forms of executive compensation to supplement fixed salaries, along with more liberal expense accounts,[4] developed: (a)

profit-sharing plans,[5] (b) share bonuses,[6] (c) share options,[7] (d) share purchase plans,[8] (e) deferred compensation plans,[9] (f) pension plans,[10] (g) annuity plans,[11] (h) tax reimbursement plans,[12] and (i) other fringe benefits.[13]

Modern statutes often expressly empower the corporation to fix the compensation of officers,[14] and to establish and carry out pension, profit-sharing, share bonus, share purchase, share option, savings, thrift, and other retirement, incentive, and benefit plans for any or all of its directors, officers, and employees.[15]

General Principles

Regardless of the form of executive compensation, it should be reasonable in

3. 1 G. Washington, V. Rothschild, T. Ness & R. Sobernheim, Compensating the Corporate Executive 5–11 (3d ed. 1962); Klaus, "Corporate Quandary: Search for an Adequate Method of Executive Compensation", 4 Tulsa L.J. 197 (1967); Business Week, No. 1812, 81 (May 23, 1964) (listing compensation of the executives of 122 corporations); Patton, "Executive Compensation Here and Abroad", 40 Harv. Bus.Rev. 144 (Sept.-Oct. 1962); Patton, "What is an Executive Worth?", 39 Harv.Bus.Rev. 65 (Mar.-Apr. 1961). The 45-year bonus program of incentive compensation of General Motors Corp. has been called absolutely indispensable to the corporation's historic success. A. Sloan, My Years with General Motors (1963).

4. Main, "An Expanding Executive Pay Package", 77 Fortune, No. 7, 166 (June 15, 1968); Palestin, "Travel and Entertainment Expenses Under the 1962 Revenue Act", 20 N.Y. County Law. Ass'n B. Bull. 203 (1963); Farrell, "New Drive on Expense Accounts", 32 N.Y.St.B.Bull. 123 (1960); Cantrall, "Expense Accounts in 1960", 6 Prac.Law. 61 (Apr. 1960); Rothschild & Sobernheim, "Expense Accounts for Executives", 67 Yale L.J. 1363 (1958). The corporation may deduct reasonable amounts which it provides for ordinary and necessary expenses; the employee realizes no income if the expenses were incurred for the convenience of the employer.

5. See section 246 infra.

6. See section 247 infra.

7. See section 248 infra.

8. See section 249 infra.

9. See section 250 infra.

10. See section 251 infra.

11. See section 252 infra.

12. See section 253 infra.

13. See section 254 infra.

14. E. g., ABA–ALI Model Bus.Corp.Act § 4(k).

15. E. g., ABA–ALI Model Bus.Corp.Act § 4(p); Alaska, Colorado, Illinois, Iowa, New York, North Carolina, North Dakota, Virginia; Oregon, Texas (for officers and employees); Georgia, Hawaii, Maryland, Michigan, Minnesota, Mississippi, New Jersey, Ohio, Oklahoma, Pennsylvania, Washington (employee welfare plans); Pennsylvania (plans for dependents of directors, officers, employees); Hawaii (plans for dependents of employees). See Mehler, "The Colorado Corporation Act of 1959: Some Aspects of Private Industrial Incentive Plans", 32 Rocky Mt.L.Rev. 164 (1960).

amount [16] and based on services performed for the corporation.[17] Furthermore, it should be determined before the services are rendered, with a minimum of self-dealing on the part of those involved and, when appropriate, ratified by shareholders.

Prearrangement

To avoid any presumption of gratuitous services and perhaps limited recovery on implied contract or *quantum meruit* principles, an advance arrangement fixing the compensation is desirable. If any such arrangement proves unsatisfactory, it can be modified for the future by mutual consent of the parties.

Retroactive compensation for past services is usually regarded as without consideration and a gift of corporate assets.[18] However,

---

16. The reasonableness of compensation is relevant for two purposes: (a) To negative waste or gift of corporate assets; and (b) To justify the corporation's deduction thereof for federal income tax purposes as a business expense.

As to the first, the whole package of compensation, current and deferred, must be assayed in the light of probable benefits to the corporation. Where compensation is excessive, the directors authorizing the same may be liable if they do not stay within the "business judgment" rule. So also would the recipients of such compensation. Heller v. Boylan, 29 N.Y.S.2d 653 (Sup.Ct.1941), aff'd mem., 263 App. Div. 815, 32 N.Y.S.2d 131 (1st Dep't 1941), motion for leave to appeal or reargument denied 263 App. Div. 852, 32 N.Y.S.2d 1011 (1st Dep't 1942); M. Feuer, Personal Liabilities of Corporate Officers and Directors Ch. 7 (1961). See section 242 supra. Corporate personnel who breach their duties to the corporation may be denied compensation or be required to disgorge it to the corporation. Teren v. Howard, 322 F.2d 949 (9th Cir. 1963) (allowing recovery of profits from exercise of share options instead of difference between cost of options and then market value of shares). Cf. Security-First Nat'l Bank of Los Angeles v. Lutz, 322 F.2d 348 (9th Cir. 1963) (holding officer entitled to salary since his breaches were not of duties owed corporation). Payments of salaries to executives and employees while in military service, provided they intend to return, raise some problems in this area, as do payments to widows of executives and employees. See note 22 infra. As to the corporation's federal income tax deduction, Int.Rev.Code of 1954, 26 U.S.C.A. § 162(a) (1), permits the deduction of "a reasonable allowance for salaries or other compensation for personal services actually rendered". C. Halsey & M. Peloubet, Federal Taxation and Unreasonable Compensation (1964); Meyer, "Reasonableness of Compensation—A Tabular Review", N.Y.U. 26th Inst. on Fed.Tax. 1121 (1968); Swift, "Reasonable Compensation: A Question of Fact", 52 A.B.A.J. 384 (1966); Brodsky, "What Is Reasonable Compensation?", 14 Tul.Tax Inst. 389 (1965); Dixon, "Planning Reasonable Compensation", N.Y.U. 19th Inst. on Fed.Tax. 181 (1961); Wolder, "How the Tax Court Treats Reasonable Compensation", 39 Taxes 473 (1961); Brodsky, "What Constitutes Reasonable Compensation: Contingent Compensation Plans: Factors in Proving Reasonableness of Compensation", N.Y.U. 19th Inst. on Fed.Tax. 169 (1961); Graichen, "Reasonable Compensation", N.Y.U. 17th Inst. on Fed.Tax. 117 (1959); Annot., 10 A.L.R.3d 125 (1966). Attempts to maximize salary payments and minimize dividends for tax advantages are most common in close corporations.

17. See Comm'r v. Duberstein, Stanton v. United States, 363 U.S. 278, 80 S.Ct. 1190, 4 L.Ed.2d 1218 (1960). Compensation in proportion to the share-

holdings of the recipients usually cannot, on corporation law principles, be regarded as payment for services (nor as a dividend if not distributed proportionately to all shareholders of the same class or series). Scott v. P. Lorillard Co., 108 N.J.Eq. 153, 154 A. 515 (1931), aff'd per curiam, 109 N.J.Eq. 417, 157 A. 388 (1931); Godley v. Crandall & Godley Co., 212 N.Y. 121, 105 N.E. 818 (1914). But cf. Bookman v. R. J. Reynolds Tobacco Co., 138 N.J.Eq. 312, 48 A.2d 646 (1946) (upholding bonus based on shares held by employees under former N.J.Gen. Corp.Law 14:9–1 (1937)). When excessive compensation corresponds to shareholdings, and is found to be a distribution of earnings or profits, the excessive payments will be treated as a dividend. R. J. Reynolds Tobacco Co. v. United States, 138 Ct.Cl. 1, 149 F.Supp. 889 (1957), cert. denied 355 U.S. 893, 78 S.Ct. 266, 2 L.Ed.2d 191 (1957).

18. Glenmore Distilleries Co. v. Seideman, 267 F. Supp. 915 (E.D.N.Y.1967); Hurt v. Cotton States Fertilizer Co., 159 F.2d 52 (5th Cir. 1947), cert. denied 331 U.S. 828, 67 S.Ct. 1351, 91 L.Ed. 1843 (1947); Spaeth v. Journal Printing Co., 16 Alaska 149, 139 F.Supp. 188 (1956); Heise v. Earnshaw Publications, Inc., 130 F.Supp. 38 (D.Mass.1955); Beacon Wool Corp. v. Johnson, 331 Mass. 274, 119 N.E. 195 (1954); Godley v. Crandall & Godley Co., 212 N.Y. 121, 105 N.E. 818 (1914); Note, 64 Dick.L.Rev. 65 (1959). Cf. Tennessee Products & Chemical Corp. v. United States, 199 F.Supp. 885 (M.D.Tenn.1961) (recognizing corporate liability for salary cut of former officer on condition that it should be repaid from return of property); DaPrato v. DaPrato, 346 Mass. 763, 190 N.E.2d 869 (1963) (refusing to enjoin distribution, pursuant to shareholders' vote in 1958, of 188 shares, notes, and cash in satisfaction of "open account" credits purporting to represent "officers' salaries" unpaid for period 1924–1937).

some exceptions have been recognized, such as when the compensation is stated in terms of a fixed amount plus such additional amounts as may be determined by the board,[19] when the additional compensation added to the original compensation is still within the limits of reasonableness,[20] or when pension plans operate retroactively.[21]

Payments to the estate or survivors of a deceased executive usually will be upheld if made under a statute or preexisting legal duty;[22] otherwise, they might be held to constitute a waste of corporate assets.[23]

Self-Dealing

Especially acute in the case of board of directors composed of insiders but present whenever an officer is a member of the board is the problem of self-dealing, i. e., voting as director for one's own compensation as officer. Such officer-director's membership on, or even presence at, the board meeting is of little concern unless such officer-director's presence is necessary for a quorum or his vote is required for board action.[24] "Cross-voting" is equivalent to self-dealing.[25] The usual consequences of

---

19. Holmes v. Republic Steel Corp., 84 Ohio App. 442, 84 N.E.2d 508 (1948), modifying 69 N.E.2d 396 (Ohio C.P.1946).

20. Hurt v. Cotton States Fertilizer Co., 159 F.2d 52 (5th Cir.1947, cert. denied 331 U.S. 828, 67 S.Ct. 1351, 91 L.Ed. 1843 (1947); Blish v. Thompson Automatic Arms Corp., 30 Del.Ch. 538, 64 A.2d 581 (Sup.Ct. 1948). See also Lucas v. Ox Fibre Brush Co., 281 U.S. 115, 50 S.Ct. 273, 74 L.Ed. 733 (1930).

21. 1 G. Washington, V. Rothschild, T. Ness & R. Sobernheim, op. cit. supra note 3, at 245. But see Fogelson v. American Woolen Co., 170 F.2d 660 (2d Cir. 1948).

22. In re Wood's Estate, 299 Mich. 635, 1 N.W.2d 19 (1941). Statutes sometimes expressly authorize corporate payments to estates, families, dependents, or beneficiaries of deceased directors, officers, and employees on account of prior services rendered to the corporation by such decedents. Wis.Bus.Corp.Law § 180.31 (1951); Annot., 29 A.L.R.2d 1262 (1953).

The Internal Revenue Code of 1954 permits the widow to deduct $5,000 as a death benefit, Int.Rev.Code of 1954, 26 U.S.C.A. § 101(b), and limits deductions for any business "gift" under Int.Rev.Code of 1954, 26 U.S.C.A. § 102, to $25.

See Comm'r v. Duberstein, Stanton v. United States, 363 U.S. 278, 80 S.Ct. 1190, 4 L.Ed.2d 1218 (1960) (holding that whether "dominant reason" for payment was compensation or kindness and sympathy is for trier of facts). If the payment to the widow is, by agreement or otherwise, additional compensation for past services, it is deductible by the corporation as a business expense, and taxable to the widow, at ordinary income tax rates. Cronheim v. Comm'r, 327 F.2d 706 (8th Cir. 1963). If the payment is held to be dividend, it is taxable to the widow as ordinary income but not deductible by the corporation. If the payment is held to be a gift it is neither taxable to the widow nor deductible by the corporation.

See Simmons, "Voluntary Death Payments Face Taxability", 48 A.B.A.J. 678 (1962); Polisek, "Voluntary Payment to Widows of Corporate Officers and Employees: A Second Look", 45 Marq.L.Rev. 366 (1961–62); Crown, "Payments to Corporate Executives' Widows", N.Y.U. 19th Inst. on Fed.Tax. 815 (1961); Comment, "Voluntary Payments to Widows of Corporate Executives: Gifts or Income", 62 Mich.L.Rev. 1216 (1964); Comment, "Payments to Widows of Corporate Executives and Employees—Gifts or Income?", 49 Va.L.Rev. 74 (1963); Comment, "Payments to Widows of Deceased Executives: Gift or Income?", 4 B.C.Ind. & Com.L.Rev. 145 (1962); Comment, "Gifts v. Compensation: Still an Enigma", 29 U.Cin.L.Rev. 483 (1960); Annot., 95 A.L.R.2d 520 (1964).

23. Adams v. Smith, 275 Ala. 142, 153 So.2d 221 (1963); Moore v. Keystone Macaroni Mfg. Co., 370 Pa. 172, 87 A.2d 295, 29 A.L.R.2d 1256 (1952) (payments enjoined); Dwyer v. Tracey, 118 F.Supp. 289 (N.D.Ill.1954) (director-general manager surcharged for payments). See Salesky v. Hat Corp. of America, 20 A.D.2d 114, 244 N.Y.S.2d 965 (1st Dep't 1963) (president's widow held to have no vested rights as third-party donee beneficiary in agreement between him and corporation, ratified by shareholders, to pay her $10,000 per year for life, and subsequently amended by him and corporation, without shareholder ratification, to substitute his sister for widow).

24. Kerbs v. California Eastern Airways, Inc., 33 Del.Ch. 69, 90 A.2d 652, 34 A.L.R.2d 839 (Sup.Ct. 1952), petition for reargument denied 33 Del.Ch. 174, 91 A.2d 62, 34 A.L.R.2d 850 (Sup.Ct.1952). Bins v. St. Louis Hide & Tallow Co., 378 S.W.2d 228 (Mo.Ct.App.1964).

25. Stoiber v. Miller Brewing Co., 257 Wis. 13, 42 N. W.2d 144 (1950); Indurated Concrete Corp. v. Abbott, 195 Md. 496, 74 A.2d 17 (1950); Sagalyn v. Meekins, Packard & Wheat Inc., 290 Mass. 434, 195 N.E. 769 (1935); Baker v. Cohn, 42 N.Y.S.2d 159

self-dealing by directors—viz., that the transaction is "void" or "voidable"—can be relieved to some extent by statute, "interested-director" provisions in the articles of incorporation, or shareholder ratification.[26]

Shareholder Ratification

Shareholder ratification of executive compensation can serve three purposes: (a) It can confirm action by the board of directors when the board acted on the borderline of its authority; (b) It, substituting for the board of directors, can provide the necessary corporate authorization; and (c) It can ratify the voidable action of the board, such as where self-dealing is involved.[27]

PROFIT–SHARING PLANS

246. Profit-sharing plans are a form of incentive compensation, providing for cash bonus, share bonus, or some other reward, depending upon improvement in corporate profits, dividends, sales, or other factor, and can be on an individual or group basis. For federal income tax purposes, profit-sharing retirement plans may be "qualified" or "nonqualified".

Profit-sharing plans are a form of incentive compensation, providing for cash bonus, share bonus, or some other reward, depending upon improvement in corporate profits, dividends, sales, or some other factor. Profit-sharing plans can be either on an individual or on a group basis.

Profit-sharing plans can add to current compensation, or serve as a retirement plan, as an alternative to a pension plan.

(Sup.Ct.1942), modified 266 App.Div. 715, 40 N.Y.S. 2d 623 (1st Dep't 1943), aff'd mem., 292 N.Y. 570, 54 N.E.2d 689 (1944). See Annot., 175 A.L.R. 577 (1948).

26. See section 238 supra.

27. 1 G. Washington, V. Rothschild, T. Ness & R. Sobernheim, op. cit. supra note 3, at 225–232; Kerbs v. California Eastern Airways, Inc., 33 Del.Ch. 395, 94 A.2d 217 (Ch.1953). See sections 194, 238 supra.

Assuming that the plan is properly authorized,[1] a problem which occasionally occurs is the propriety of the computation of the base figures upon which the bonus is based. While the directors have broad discretion with respect to fixing executive compensation, they are accountable for miscomputation where they have been negligent in relying upon computations prepared by others, especially if such persons are not disinterested.[2]

Whether an employee enjoys a contractual right to a bonus depends upon express contract or inferred-in-fact contract based upon statements to the employee and corporate practices.[3]

1. Chambers v. Beaver-Advance Corp., 392 Pa. 481, 140 A.2d 808 (1958); Bruton, "Profit-Sharing Plan", 5 S.C.L.Q. 201 (1952); Note, "Corporate and Officer Authority in Granting Pensions and Bonuses", 17 Brooklyn L.Rev. 310 (1950); Annot., 40 A.L.R. 1423 (1926), 88 A.L.R. 751 (1934), 164 A.L.R. 1125 (1946).

2. Heller v. Boylan, 29 N.Y.S.2d 653 (Sup.Ct.1941), aff'd mem., 263 App.Div. 815, 32 N.Y.S.2d 131 (1st Dep't 1941), motion for leave to appeal or reargument denied 263 App.Div. 852, 32 N.Y.S.2d 1011 (1st Dep't 1942); Gallin v. National City Bank, 152 Misc. 679, 273 N.Y.S. 87 (Sup.Ct.1934). Good faith reliance on the computation of a reputable disinterested firm has been held sufficient. Winkelman v. General Motors Corp., 39 F.Supp. 826, 833 (S.D.N.Y.1940); Epstein v. Schenck, 35 N.Y.S.2d 969 (Sup.Ct.1939). See L. Rice, Basic Pension and Profit-Sharing Plans (ALI rev. 1961); Annot., 49 A.L.R.2d 1129 (1956). See also Fry v. National Rejectors, Inc., 306 S.W.2d 465 (Mo.1957); Maguire v. Osborne, 384 Pa. 430, 121 A.2d 147 (1956) (construing "net profits" in bonus plan as profits before income and profits taxes); Beacon Wool Corp. v. Johnson, 331 Mass. 274, 119 N.E.2d 195 (1954) (directors surcharged for bonuses continued after death of corporation's key man despite rapidly deteriorating condition of business).

3. In Re Alloy Mfg. Co. Employees Trust, 411 Pa. 492, 192 A.2d 394 (1963), the corporation's profit-sharing plan provided that the employee's interest in the plan would vest after he had contributed to the plan for six years or earlier if he terminated his employment because of "physical or mental disability". Reading the entire instrument, the court construed the latter phrase to mean total and permanent disability and not to encompass partial disability as well. Compare Marvin Turner Engineers v. Allen, 326 S.W.2d 200 (Tex.Civ.App.1959) (employee discharged shortly before distribution of

Bonuses, along with other compensation, must be reasonable in amount in the light of the services rendered to the corporation.[4]

For federal income tax purposes, profit-sharing retirement plans may be "qualified" or "nonqualified".

In the case of "qualified" plans (which require broad coverage and limited benefits to qualify, with approval of the Internal Reve-

nue Service not required but usually sought), the corporation may deduct any amounts it sets aside for employees out of profits, the employee pays no tax until he receives payment, any employee who receives his entire bonus within a single year because of separation from service is entitled to treat such bonus as a capital gain, and any earnings of the fund are tax-free.[5]

The "nonqualified" funded plan does not allow a corporate deduction if the employee's interests are forfeitable, results in immediate tax on the employee whose interests are nonforfeitable, and provides no tax exemption for the earnings of the fund.[6]

The "unfunded" plan postpones the corporation's deductions until payments are

year-end bonus awarded 11/12 of bonus which he would have received at end of year, where bonus was incentive measure explained to employee when hired, bonuses were regularly paid, other employees received bonuses without working to end of year, and employee's name was on bonus list), with Borden v. Skinner Chuck Co., 21 Conn.Supp. 184, 150 A.2d 607 (1958) (employee held to enjoy no contractual right to year-end bonus on basis of statement in company booklet and references on pay slips to company's contributions, where booklet referred to board of directors discretion concerning bonuses, past bonus practices were not consistent, and there was no showing that any representations concerning bonuses induced employee to remain in company's employ). See also Porter v. Pepsi-Cola Bottling Co., 247 S.C. 370, 147 S.E.2d 620 (1966), cert. denied 385 U.S. 827, 87 S.Ct. 61, 17 L.Ed.2d 63 (1966) (employee held to forfeit profit-sharing benefits for conduct prejudicial to employer); First Nat'l Bank of Birmingham v. Adams, 281 Ala. 404, 203 So.2d 124 (1967) (merger held not to constitute "dissolution" resulting in termination of profit-sharing trust with immediate distribution of vested funds to employees); Rankin v. Kellam, 388 S.W.2d 306 (Tex. Civ.App.1965) (corporation's relocation of plant, resulting in many employees refusing to move, held not to terminate profit-sharing plan). In Fernekes v. CMP Industries, Inc., 13 N.Y.2d 217, 246 N.Y.S.2d 201, 195 N.E.2d 884 (1963). CMP Industries, Inc. operated two divisions and had a noncontributory retirement and profit-sharing plan, which provided for the distribution of the assets of the plan in the event of discontinuance of the plan. After one division was sold to Midland-Ross Corporation, two former employees of such division, who became employees of Midland-Ross Corporation, sought an adjudication of their rights under the plans. The court held, 4 to 3, that since CMP Industries, Inc., as an entity, and the plan, continued in existence, plaintiffs were not entitled to any distribution and enjoyed no other rights under the plan. The dissent argued that each division should have been regarded as a separate corporation for the purposes of administering the plan. Annot., 81 A.L.R.2d 1066 (1962).

4. Rogers v. Hill, 289 U.S. 582, 53 S.Ct. 731, 77 L.Ed. 1385, 88 A.L.R. 744 (1933); Smith v. Dunlap, 269 Ala. 97, 111 So.2d 1 (1959).

5. Int.Rev.Code of 1954, 26 U.S.C.A. §§ 401 et seq.; D. Rothman, Understanding Pension and Profit-Sharing Plans (ALI 1967); R. Holzman, Guide to Pension and Profit Sharing Plans (3d ed. 1969); L. Rice, Basic Pension and Profit-Sharing Plans (ALI rev. 1961); Brooks, "The Attorney's Role in Pension and Profit-Sharing Plans: The Challenge to Learn, Innovate and Advise", 22 Sw.L.J. 417 (1968); Knisel & Brott, "Profit Sharing for the Medium-Sized Corporation", 38 N.Y.St.B.J. 339 (1966); Taylor, "Principal Advantages and Features of Profit Sharing Retirement Plans", 21 U.Pitt.L.Rev. 493 (1960); Goldstein, "Pension and Profit-Sharing Plans: Fallacies and Facts", 38 Taxes 71 (1960); Lurie, "Plastic Contributions for Pensions and Profit-Sharing", 67 Yale L.J. 1003 (1958); Comment, "Profit-Sharing Method of Providing for Employee Retirement Income", 41 Iowa L.Rev. 277 (1956). See also Mundheim & Henderson, "Applicability of the Federal Securities Laws to Pension and Profit-Sharing Plans", 29 Law & Contemp.Prob. 795 (1964); Craig, "Securities Aspects of Pension, Profit-Sharing, and Stock Bonus Plans", 17 Sw.L.J. 444 (1963). See section 251 infra.

6. Int.Rev.Code of 1954, 26 U.S.C.A. §§ 404(a) (5), 402(b). In the case of a funded arrangement with forfeitable rights, the Internal Revenue Service takes the position that the corporate deduction is permanently lost since section 404(a) (5) allows a deduction only "in the taxable year when paid". Treas.Reg. § 1.404(a)–12 (1960). The court of claims has rejected this interpretation and allowed the deduction when paid to the employee. Mississippi River Fuel Corp. v. United States, 161 Ct.Cl. 237, 314 F.2d 953 (1963); Russell Mfg. Co. v. United States, 146 Ct.Cl. 833, 175 F.Supp. 159 (1959).

made, when they constitute income to the employee.[7]

SHARE BONUSES

247. **Share bonuses are a form of profit-sharing arrangement. Share bonuses do not reduce the corporation's cash but dilute the shareholders' interests. Applicable consideration requirements for the issue of shares and preemptive rights must be observed. Many modern statutes expressly authorize the issue of shares to corporate employees, sometimes requiring shareholder approval.**

Share bonuses are awarded as additional incentive compensation on the basis of improvement of the corporation according to some predesignated index. One advantage of a share bonus is that the corporation's cash is usually not reduced; a concomitant disadvantage is the dilution of the shareholders' interests. The awarding of share bonuses must, of course, follow the formula of the plan[1] and must comply with applicable consideration requirements for the issue of shares[2] and may not violate any preemptive rights.[3] Many modern statutes expressly authorize the issue of shares to corporate employees, sometimes requiring shareholder approval.[4]

With respect to listed shares, securities exchanges sometimes require shareholder approval of share bonus plans not applicable to all employees.[5]

SHARE OPTIONS

248. **Share options are a form of incentive compensation based on the idea that good management results in higher share prices which render the share option valuable. They usually result in the corporation's gaining additional funds, if the options are exercised, and in no corporate expenditure of funds, unless the corporation has to purchase shares to cover the exercise of the options. Share options must be authorized by law, and be supported by adequate consideration. The option price must conform to the consideration requirements applicable to the issue of shares. Observance of applicable preemptive rights is also required. For federal income tax purposes, share options are "qualified" or "nonqualified", with favorable tax treatment afforded to "qualified" share options.**

Share option plans have become increasingly prevalent, at least until 1964, when their federal income tax advantages were de-

7. B. Bryson & T. Lefevre, Tax Aspects of Executives' Compensation 35–36 (PLI 1955).

1. Frey v. Geuder, Paeschke & Frey Co., 4 Wis.2d 257, 90 N.W.2d 765 (1958).

2. See sections 167, 168 supra.

3. See sections 172–175 supra.

4. See, e. g., ABA–ALI Model Bus.Corp.Act § 24; Wells v. J. C. Penney Co., 250 F.2d 221 (9th Cir. 1957) (sustaining plan for issue of shares to retiring employees over objection that it involved illegal wager, lottery, or tontine). Cochran, "A Do-It-Yourself Kit for Drafting a Stock-Bonus Trust", 45 Calif.L.Rev. 607 (1957). For discussion of "shareless" share bonus plans, see section 250 infra. Compensation in the form of shares protects the cash position of the corporation and permits a business expense deduction for the full fair market val-

ue of the shares. Even if the corporation's basis for treasury shares is lower, it would pay no tax on the gain. The employees pay tax, at the ordinary rates, on the fair market value of the shares received, but on subsequent sale for an appreciated price would enjoy capital gains treatment. The corporation could even include sufficient additional shares roughly equivalent to the federal income taxes on key employees' salaries, deducting the full fair market value, and in effect providing "tax-free" salaries. See Comm'r v. Fender Sales, Inc., 338 F.2d 924 (9th Cir.1964), cert. denied 382 U.S. 813, 86 S.Ct. 29, 15 L.Ed.2d 61 (1965) (holding that shares received in lieu of salary by shareholders-employees, without change in proportionate interests, constituted taxable income). Share bonus plans may or may not be "qualified" for federal income tax purposes. Int.Rev.Code of 1954, 26 U.S. C.A. § 401 (qualified pension, profit-sharing, and share bonus plans). See section 246 supra and section 251 infra. For possible requirements under the Federal Securities Act of 1933, see SEC Securities Act Release No. 4844 (Aug. 5, 1966); S.E.C. Form S–8.

5. E. g., N.Y.S.E. Company Manual § B1.

creased. They usually result in the corporation's gaining additional funds, if the options are exercised, and in no corporate expenditure of funds, unless the corporation has to purchase shares to cover the exercise of the options.[1] In theory, they are a form of incentive compensation based on the idea that good management results in higher share prices which render the share option valuable. The principal advantage to the executive is the favorable tax treatment afforded to share options of the "qualified" type.[2]

A share option, to be valid, must be permissible under applicable law [3] and support-

ed by adequate consideration.[4] Binding the optionee by an employment contract will suffice,[5] but is not required if there is other consideration, such as the exercise of the option being dependent upon continued employment.[6] The issue of the share upon

1. Compare Truncale v. Universal Pictures Co., 76 F.Supp. 465 (S.D.N.Y.1948), with Eliasberg v. Standard Oil Co., 23 N.J.Super. 431, 92 A.2d 862 (1952), aff'd mem., 12 N.J. 467, 97 A.2d 437 (1953).

2. See generally 2 G. Washington, V. Rothschild, T. Ness & R. Sobernheim, Compensating the Corporate Executive ch. 11 (3d ed. 1962); B. Bryson & T. Lefevre, Tax Aspects of Executives' Compensation 56–65 (PLI 1955); Silbert & Rosenberg, "Non-Statutory Stock Options and Restricted Stock The New Proposed Regulations", N.Y.U. 27th Inst. on Fed. Tax. 51 (1969); Hancock, "The Non-Qualified Stock Option Plan and the Shadow Stock Plan", 24 Bus. Law. 1245 (1969); Vernava, "Stock Options: Corporate, Regulatory and Related Tax Aspects", 30 U. Pitt.L.Rev. 197 (1968); Baker, "Employee Stock Option Plans Under the Revenue Act of 1964", 20 Tax L.Rev. 77 (1964); Baker, "Stock Options at the Crossroads", 41 Harv.Bus.Rev. 22, 164 (Jan.-Feb. 1963); Scull, "Deferred Compensation and Stock Options", 41 Taxes 20 (1963); Griswold, "The Mysterious Stock Option", 51 Ky.L.J. 246 (1962); Hacker, "Choosing between Stock Options and Outright Sales", 15 W.Res.L.Rev. 325 (1964); Moore, "Stock Options for Directors in Small Corporations", 11 Clev.-Mar.L.Rev. 396 (1962); Ford, "Stock Options are in the Public Interest", 39 Harv.Bus.Rev. 45 (July-Aug. 1961); Ware, "Stock Options", 41 Barron's, No. 25, 5 (June 19, 1961); Steadman, "Increasing Management's Real Income Through Deferral and Stock Options", 15 Bus.Law. 764 (1960); Grossman & Herzel, "Employee Stock Options", 1958 U.Ill.L.F. 45; Dean, "Employee Stock Options", 66 Harv.L.Rev. 1403 (1953); Garfinkle, "Stock Option Plans for Executives", 41 Calif.L. Rev. 535 (1953); Note, "Shareholder Attack Against Stock Options for Corporate Executives", 62 Yale L.J. 84 (1952). See section 170 supra and note 15 infra.

3. ABA–ALI Model Bus.Corp.Act § 18A (requiring majority shareholder approval for issuance of share

options to directors, officers, and employees). Under Oklahoma law, options to purchase shares are valid only in limited situations, e. g., share subscriptions, share dividends. Okl.Bus.Corp.Act §§ 2(12), 29, 46 (1961); Emerson v. Labor Investment Corp., 284 F.2d 946 (10th Cir.1960). In Gaynor v. Buckley, 318 F.2d 432 (9th Cir.1963), the corporation entered into a share option agreement with one of its officers which was ratified by the board of directors and approved by shareholders at the annual meeting. Two conditions limiting the option were not disclosed to the shareholders. Thereafter, the board of directors waived the conditions. The court held that since the conditions were never ratified, the board of directors could waive them without consulting the shareholders. The rules of the New York Stock Exchange, on which the shares were listed, requiring, with some exceptions, shareholder approval of share options, were held not to limit the power of the board of directors to authorize the options under the law of the state of incorporation. Brooklyn Union Gas Co. v. Public Service Commission, 8 A.D.2d 210, 187 N.Y.S.2d 207 (3d Dep't 1959) aff'd mem., 8 N.Y.2d 815, 202 N.Y.S.2d 322, 168 N.E.2d 390 (1960) (holding public utility corporation without power to adopt share option plan for certain officers and key personnel). Cf. McKinney's N.Y.Bus.Corp.Law §§ 202(a) (13), 505.

4. ABA–ALI Model Bus.Corp.Act § 18A; Saigh v. Busch, 403 S.W.2d 559 (Mo.1966); Olson Bros. v. Englehart, 42 Del.Ch. 348, 211 A.2d 610 (Ch.1965) (where shareholder ratification held to shift burden to objecting party to show lack of business judgment); Stemerman v. Ackerman, 40 Del.Ch. 431, 184 A.2d 28 (Ch.1962); Amdur v. Meyer, 15 A.D.2d 425, 224 N.Y.S.2d 440 (1st Dep't 1962) appeal dismissed 14 N.Y.2d 541, 248 N.Y.S.2d 639, 198 N.E.2d 30 (1964); Kerbs v. California Eastern Airways, Inc., 33 Del.Ch. 69, 90 A.2d 652, 34 A.L.R.2d 839 (Sup.Ct.1952), petition for reargument denied 33 Del.Ch. 174, 91 A.2d 62, 34 A.L.R.2d 850 (Sup.Ct. 1952), 33 Del.Ch. 395, 94 A.2d 217 (Ch.1953); Frankel v. Donovan, 35 Del.Ch. 433, 120 A.2d 311 (Ch. 1956). See generally Ward, "Two-Contract Analysis May Imperil Stock Option Plans", 52 Mich.L.Rev. 849 (1954); Annot., 34 A.L.R.2d 852 (1954).

5. Kaufman v. Shoenberg, 33 Del.Ch. 211, 91 A.2d 786 (Ch.1952).

6. Gruber v. Chesapeake & Ohio Ry., 158 F.Supp. 593 (N.D.Ohio 1957); Holthusen v. Edward G. Budd Mfg. Co., 52 F.Supp. 125 (E.D.Pa.1943), 53 F.Supp. 488 (E.D.Pa.1944); Beard v. Elster, 39 Del.Ch. 153, 160 A.2d 731 (Sup.Ct.1960); Eliasberg v. Standard

the exercise of the option must comply with any consideration requirements applicable to the issue of shares.[7] Observance of preemptive rights might also be required.[8]

Discharge of the optionee, especially for cause, might terminate his right to exercise the option.[9]

In addition to the requirements of state corporate statutes applicable to the issuance of share options to corporate personnel, other requirements of federal laws, such as the Federal Securities Act of 1933,[10] Federal Securities Exchange Act of 1934,[11] and Federal Investment Company Act of 1940,[12] and of

---

Oil Co., 23 N.J.Super. 431, 92 A.2d 862 (1952), aff'd mem., 12 N.J. 467, 97 A.2d 437 (1953); Gottlieb v. Heyden Chemical Corp., 32 Del.Ch. 231, 83 A.2d 595 (Ch.1951), rev'd 33 Del.Ch. 82, 90 A.2d 660 (Sup.Ct. 1952), 33 Del. 177, 91 A.2d 57 (Sup.Ct.1952), 34 Del. Ch. 84, 99 A.2d 507 (Ch.1953), on motion for counsel fees, 34 Del.Ch. 436, 105 A.2d 461 (Sup.Ct.1954); Sandler v. Schenley Industries, Inc., 32 Del.Ch. 46, 79 A.2d 606 (Ch.1951). The value of the consideration must be commensurate with the value of the option. Clamitz v. Thatcher Mfg. Co., 158 F.2d 687 (2d Cir. 1947), cert. denied 331 U.S. 825, 67 S.Ct. 1316, 91 L.Ed. 1841 (1947); Wyles v. Campbell, 77 F.Supp. 343 (D.Del.1948); Rosenthal v. Burry Biscuit Corp., 30 Del.Ch. 299, 60 A.2d 106 (Ch.1948). A typical statute is ABA–ALI Model Bus.Corp.Act § 18A, providing that in the absence of fraud, the judgment of the board of directors shall be conclusive as to the adequacy of consideration for share options. See Note, "Stock Option Plans and the Business Judgment Rule in Delaware", 53 Colum.L. Rev. 283 (1953). Cf. McPhail v. L. S. Starrett Co., 157 F.Supp. 560 (D.Mass.1957), aff'd 257 F.2d 388 (1st Cir. 1958) (upholding issue of short-term options at their market without consideration to nearly all employees). See Wharton v. Fidelity-Baltimore Nat'l Bank, 222 Md. 177, 158 A.2d 887 (1960) (director held not employee for required purposes of share option plan).

7. ABA–ALI Model Bus.Corp.Act § 18A. See sections 167, 168 supra. Edward v. Peabody Coal Co., 9 Ill.App.2d 234, 132 N.E.2d 549 (1956) (holding option invalid on ground $3 option price was less than $5 par value). See McPhail v. L. S. Starrett Co., 157 F.Supp. 560 (D.Mass.1957), aff'd, 257 F.2d 388 (1st Cir. 1958) (upholding plan whereby up to half of price of nonpar value shares could be made by crediting of dividends paid on shares purchased).

8. See sections 174, 175 supra. See McKinney's N. Y.Bus.Corp.Law, § 505(d) (provision for release of any preemptive rights, if there are such under articles of incorporation, as to shares being optioned to directors, officers, or other employees, by vote or written consent of holders of majority of shares entitled to exercise such preemptive rights); id. § 622(e) (1) (excepting from preemptive rights, unless otherwise provided in articles of incorporation, shares or options issued for non-cash consideration); id. § 622(e) (2) (exception of share options under § 505(d)); cf. ABA–ALI Model Bus.Corp.Act § 24; Ohio Gen.Corp.Law, §§ 1701.24, 1701.40(C) (1955). See also Gottlieb v. Heyden Chemical Corp., 33 Del.Ch. 82, 90 A.2d 660 (Sup.Ct.1952).

9. In Ellis v. Emhart Mfg. Co., 150 Conn. 501, 191 A.2d 546 (1963), a share option plan provided that

the board of directors' interpretation of the terms and provisions thereof should be final, binding and conclusive. The court held that any attempt by the board of directors to interpret the plan so as to alter or impair the rights already acquired under the contract would not be binding on the plaintiff.

Maytag Co. v. Alward, 253 Iowa 455, 112 N.W.2d 654 (1962), held that where an employee voluntarily left employment within the period for which he had promised to stay in consideration of the employer's offering share options was a repudiation and breach of contract entitling the employer to rescind and recover the shares already sold to the employee upon the exercise of the option. The agreement expressly provided that in the event of such a violation, any options held by the employee, to the extent not theretofore exercised, should forthwith terminate. The court construed this provision to apply only to unexercised options since an option which has been exercised is no longer an option, leaving the usual remedies for breach of contract to apply to exercised options. See also Freeman v. Copper Range Co., 248 F.2d 20 (7th Cir.1957) (employee discharged prior to time during which option could be exercised held to have no right to buy shares since right had not accrued at time of discharge); Shipman v. General Transistor Corp., 22 Misc.2d 632, 198 N.Y.S.2d 852 (Sup.Ct.1960), aff'd 12 A.D.2d 529, 207 N.Y.S.2d 734 (2d Dep't 1960) (share option agreement held subject to implied covenant of good faith and fair dealing barring exercise of option by employee discharged for cause); Annot., 96 A.L.R.2d 176 (1964).

10. Wheat, "Securities Regulation Aspects of Employee Stock Options under the 1964 Revenue Act", U.So.Cal.1965 Tax Inst. 151. "Investment letters" to the effect that the shares purchased under the option are for purposes of investment and not for resale and share certificate legends that the shares had not been registered under the Federal Securities Act of 1933 and might not be transferred except in compliance with such act are often required. See Altman v. American Foods, Inc., 262 N.C. 671, 138 S.E.2d 526 (1964); Int.Rev.Serv. Ruling (67–102). See also SEC Securities Act Release No. 4844 (Aug. 5, 1966). See section 295 infra.

11. Kelly & Green, "Application of Section (16)b of the Securities and Exchange Act of 1934 to Insiders' Transactions under Employee Stock Option Plans", 17 Bus.Law. 402 (1962). See sections 296–298 infra.

12. State Bond & Mortgage Co., Variable Annuity Life Ins. Co. of America ("Valic"), Inv.Co.Act Re-

other state statutes, such as state "blue sky" laws,[13] should be observed, as should any applicable securities exchange requirements.[14]

For federal income tax purposes, distinction must be made between "qualified" share options (including share options under employee share option plans and pre-1964 "restricted" share options) and "unqualified" share options.

"Qualified" Share Options

A "qualified" share option is an option granted to an employee by his employer corporation or its parent or subsidiary corporation to purchase shares of any of such corporations, but only if (a) the option is granted pursuant to a prescribed plan approved by the shareholders of the granting corporation within 12 months before or after the date such plan is adopted; (b) the option is granted within 10 years from the date of adoption or approval, whichever is earlier; (c) the option by its terms is not exercisable after five years after the grant of the option; (d) the option price, with some exceptions, is not less than the fair market value of the shares at the time the option is granted; (e) the option by its terms is not exercisable while specified older options held by the grantee are outstanding; (f) the option by its terms is not transferable by the grantee otherwise than by will or the laws of descent and distribution, and is exercisable, during his lifetime, only by him; and (g) the grantee, immediately after the

grant of the option, does not own more than five percent (or 10 percent in certain small businesses) of the total combined voting power or value of all classes of shares of the employer corporation or its parent or subsidiary corporation.[15]

As a general rule, an employee does not realize taxable income upon the exercise of a "qualified" share option, the corporation enjoys no deduction, and no amount other than the price paid under the option is considered to have been received by the corporation for the shares.[16]

The Revenue Act of 1964 all but eliminated the future use of "restricted" share options [17] and substituted "qualified" share options and options issued under employee share purchase plans. As to "qualified" share options, bargain purchase tax advantages were practically eliminated. However, in the case of employee share purchase plans, the old law relating to "restricted" share options was continued with some modification. To qualify for treatment under the employee share purchase plans, various conditions were imposed to require that

lease No. 4685, 4686 (Aug. 25, 1966) (barring share option plans for registered investment companies). See section 301 infra.

13. Haddad v. Electronic Production & Development, Inc., 219 Cal.App.2d 137, 33 Cal.Rptr. 89 (1963) (declaring invalid share option agreement for failure to obtain required permit under "blue sky" law). See sections 305–307 infra.

14. These sometimes require shareholder approval for share option plans not open to all employees. N.Y.S.E. Company Manual § B1.

15. Int.Rev.Code of 1954, 26 U.S.C.A. § 422(b) (1)–(7). McKinney's N.Y. Tax Law, § 358–c. B. Bryson & T. Lefevre, Tax Aspects of Executives' Compensation 56–58 (PLI 1955); Prentice-Hall 1968 Federal Tax Course ¶1327; Rubenfeld, "Qualified Stock Options: Some Developing Problems Under the 1964 Revenue Act", 21 J. Taxation 140 (1964); Rothschild, "The New Stock Option: Problems of the Smaller Company", 33 Fordham L.Rev. 393 (1965); Note, "Stock Options—Validity and Federal Tax Requirements", 44 N.C.L.Rev. 1111 (1966). Share option plans have been criticized as (a) requiring large borrowings by an executive without accumulated wealth, (b) necessitating large liquidation of any option exercised to take care of such borrowing, (c) subjecting the executive to risks during the six-months' period—the long-term capital gain period and insider-trading period, and (d) putting the executive in the speculative market. The Executive Life 129 (1956).

16. Int.Rev.Code of 1954, 26 U.S.C.A. § 421.

17. Int.Rev.Code of 1954, 26 U.S.C.A. § 424.

plans, with specified exceptions, be open to all employees.[18]

The corporation may not take a deduction on account of either granting the option or its exercise by the employee.[19]

To provide relief in the event of a serious decline in the value of the shares, modifications, extensions, and renewals of "qualified" share options are to some extent possible, in effect being treated as the granting of a new option.[20]

Problems concerning share options arise in cases of corporate take-overs, mergers, consolidations, reorganizations, etc.[21]

"Nonqualified" Share Options

In the case of the "nonqualified" share option, any bargain-purchase element has been held to be compensation taxable as ordinary income.[22] Such an option does not enjoy the

same income deferral, capital gains, and holding period treatment as the "qualified" share option.

SHARE PURCHASE PLANS

249. **Share purchase plans involve the offer of shares in the corporation to its employees, usually at a favored price payable in installments, giving them a stake in the corporation. Applicable consideration requirements for the issue of shares and preemptive rights must be observed. Modern statutes often provide for employee share purchase plans, sometimes requiring shareholder approval thereof. Employee share purchase plans sometimes require or permit the corporation to repurchase the shares upon the employee's cessation of employment by the corporation. For federal income tax purposes, profit-sharing plans may be "qualified" or "nonqualified".**

Under such plans, employees are offered shares in the corporation, usually at a favored price, giving them a stake in the corporation. Acceptance by the employee binds him to pay for the shares, usually in installments. Relatively common before 1929, such plans proved unpopular after the stock market crash, which meant that employees were continuing to pay for shares at a price far in excess of the then market price.[1] In more recent years, such plans have been revived with substantial escape clauses for the employees.[2]

18. Int.Rev.Code of 1954, 26 U.S.C.A. § 423. See also Tax Reform Act of 1969. See section 249 infra.

19. See notes 2, 15 supra.

20. Sheehan, "The Stir over Stock Options", 66 Fortune, No. 4, 131 (Oct.1962); Klinck, "Hedging the Restricted Stock Option", 14 J.Am.Soc'y C.L.U. 457 (1960); Webster, "Restricted Stock Options in a Declining Market", 44 A.B.A.J. 68 (1958). One way of hedging against market declines between the exercise of the option and the disposition of the shares would be, contemporaneously with the exercise of the option, to purchase a "put" (right to sell the shares at a specified price within a specified period) to sell the shares at the option price after the expiration of the period during which disposition would not be consistent with "qualified" share option requirements.

21. Musto, "What To Do About Stock Options of a Merging Corporation", 24 J. Taxation 246 (1966).

22. Treas.Reg. § 1.421–6 (1966). Comm'r v. Lo Bue, 351 U.S. 243, 76 S.Ct. 800, 100 L.Ed. 1142 (1956), petition for reh. denied 352 U.S. 859, 77 S.Ct. 21, 1 L. Ed.2d 69 (1956) (5–2–2), on remand 28 T.C. 1317 (1957), aff'd 256 F.2d 735 (3d Cir. 1958); Horwich, "A Tale of Two Dicta: The Non-Restricted Stock Option", 18 U.Miami L.Rev. 596 (1964); Willis, "Non-Restricted Stock Options", 101 Trusts & Estates 1146 (1962). Lefevre, "Nonrestricted Stock Options", N.Y.U. 20th Inst. on Fed.Tax. 353 (1962);

Chapman & De Kosmian, "Federal Income Tax Consequences of Non-Restricted Stock Options", 8 Bus.Law, 321 (1961). Kempler, "Non-Restricted Stock Option Plans", 16 Tax L.Rev. 339 (1961).

1. 2 G. Washington, V. Rothschild, T. Ness & R. Sobernheim, Compensating the Corporate Executive 613–614 (3d ed. 1962).

2. See 66 Time, No. 16, 102 (Oct. 17, 1955); Baker, "Purchases by a Corporation of Its Own Shares for Employee Benefit Plans", 22 Bus.Law. 439 (1967); Cohen, "Stock Purchase Plans and Stock Bonus Plans", N.Y.U. 21st Inst. on Fed.Tax. 545 (1963); Sobernheim & Brown, "Collective Bargaining on Stock Purchase Plans: What Price Employee Stock Ownership?", 55 Colum.L.Rev. 1000 (1955); Parker, "Stock Purchase Plans for the Rank and File Employee", 27 St. John's L.Rev. 234 (1953).

Here again applicable consideration requirements for the issue of shares[3] and preemptive rights must be observed.[4]

Modern statutes often contain provision for employee share purchase plans, sometimes requiring shareholder approval thereof.[5]

An employee share purchase plan has been upheld whereby selected employees were allowed to buy a limited number of shares upon a small down payment and a pledge of the shares to the corporation as security for the unpaid balance, with the employee's obligation to be met out of payroll deductions, dividends on the shares, and cash payments according to a specified schedule.[6]

Employee share purchase plans sometimes require or permit the corporation to repurchase the shares upon the employee's cessation of employment by the corporation.[7]

Eventual employee control of even large corporations is possible under such plans.[8]

Employee share purchase plans may be "qualified" or "nonqualified" under the Internal Revenue Code.[9] The "qualified" employee share purchase plan, introduced in 1964, represents an admixture of "qualified" share options and "qualified" pension, profit-sharing, and share bonus plans.[10]

Employee share purchase plans are subject to the Federal Securities Act of 1933[11] and other governmental regulations.[12]

DEFERRED COMPENSATION PLANS

250. **Deferred compensation plans include pension plans and annuity plans, as well as deferred compensation contracts, providing that payment of some of the executive's compensation for current services be deferred and paid later as either a retirement or other future allowance to the executive, when presumably his income would be lower, or death benefit to his survivors.**

In a broad sense, such plans include pension plans[1] and annuity plans,[2] as well as deferred compensation contracts. The deferred compensation plan provides that the payment of some of the executive's compensation for current services be deferred, to be paid later as either a retirement or other future allowance to the executive, when presumably his income would be lower, or death benefit to his survivors.[3] At the time of

[§ 249]

3. See sections 167, 168 supra.

4. See sections 174, 175 supra.

5. E. g., ABA–ALI Model Bus.Corp.Act § 24. See Krantman v. Liberty Loan Corp., 152 F.Supp. 705 (N.D.Ill.1956), aff'd 246 F.2d 581 (7th Cir. 1957).

6. McPhail v. L. S. Starrett Co., 157 F.Supp. 560 (D. Mass.1957), aff'd 257 F.2d 388 (1st Cir. 1958).

7. See Evans Production Corp. v. Shaw, 276 F.2d 313 (5th Cir. 1960), reh. denied 277 F.2d 927 (5th Cir. 1960), cert. denied 364 U.S. 819, 81 S.Ct. 54, 5 L.Ed. 2d 50 (1960); A. Guild, D. Davis & D. Hoxie, Stock-Purchase Agreements & the Close Corporation (1960). See sections 281, 282 infra.

8. As a result of the Sears, Roebuck and Co. employee share purchase plan, almost 100,000 employees now own some 23 percent of the corporation's outstanding shares—some 36,000,000 shares having a market value of over $2,600,000,000.

9. Int.Rev.Code of 1954, 26 U.S.C.A. § 423; Truitt, "The Employee Stock Purchase Plan", 52 A.B.A.J. 879 (1966).

10. See sections 246, 247 supra and section 251 infra.

11. See SEC Securities Act Release No. 4,790 (July 13, 1965) (employee share purchase plans).

12. See Friedman, "Financing of Employee Stock Purchase Plans under New Regulation G", 23 Bus. Law. 947 (1968).

[§ 250]

1. See section 251 infra.

2. See section 252 infra.

3. E. Wood, Tax Aspects of Deferred Compensation (2d ed. 1969); C. Habighurst, Deferred Compensation for Key Employees: A Planning Guide for Small Businessmen and Lawyers (1964); Rustigan, "A Deferred Income Plan for the Corporate Executive", 54 A.B.A.J. 506 (1968); Hancock, "Planning and Drafting Nonqualified Deferred Compensation Arrangements", 19 Case W.Res.L.Rev. 921 (1968); Nolan, "Deferred Compensation Planning: Special

payment, the corporation should be entitled to a deduction and the recipient would realize income, presumably spread over a series of lower tax brackets.[4]

"Shareless" share bonus plans, under which employees receive the financial (but not voting) benefits of share ownership without owning any shares, have been introduced in recent years. Under such plans, the employee is assigned "units", each unit being valued at the then market price of a share of the corporation. When the employee retires, he receives any increase in the market value of the shares. The corporation adds to the employee's account increments per unit equivalent to the dividends per share, which the employee can take currently or accumulate until he retires.[5]

PENSION PLANS

251. Pension plans are a form of old-age security to encourage a life-time career with the corporation. They may be unfunded or funded. If funded, whether "trusteed" in the form of a pension trust or "insured" by an annuity, pension plans may be "qualified" or "nonqualified" for federal income tax purposes. Pension plans, including money-purchase plans, and profit-sharing retirement plans are the two types of retirement plans eligible for qualification.

Pension plans are a form of old-age security to encourage a life-time career with the corporation. High taxes and expenses for the rising executive often preclude his accumulating any substantial capital. Pension plans, if properly set up, can result in several tax advantages.[1]

Situations for Individuals in Large and Small Corporations", N.Y.U. 23d Inst. on Fed.Tax. 217 (1965); Steadman, "Increasing Management's Real Income Through Deferral and Stock Options", 15 Bus.Law. 764 (1960); Neal, "Deferred Compensation Plans: Qualifying for Non-Qualified Treatment", 13 Vand. L.Rev. 461 (1960); Durkin, "Non-Qualified Deferred Compensation Plans", 29 U.Cin.L.Rev. 68 (1960); Nims, "Deferred Compensation Agreements", 45 A. B.A.J. 1204 (1959); Bergen, "Deferred Compensation", N.Y.U. 17th Inst. on Fed.Tax. 879 (1959); Hamblen, "Précis of Deferred Compensation Arrangements", 4 Prac.Law. 58 (Nov. 1958); Farwell, "Deferred Compensation", 1958 U.Ill.L.F. 25; Johnson, "Work Now and Be Paid Later", N.Y.U. 16th Inst. on Fed.Tax. 15 (1958); Long, "Deferred Compensation for Executives", 24 Tenn.L.Rev. 285 (1956); Comment, "The Taxation of Qualified Annuity Plans and Deferred Compensation Agreements to the Employee and His Beneficiary", 34 St. John's L.Rev. 249 (1960).

4. Drysdale v. Comm'r, 277 F.2d 413 (6th Cir. 1960); Rev.Rul. 60–31, 1960–1 Cum.Bull. 174; B. Bryson & T. Lefevre, Tax Aspects of Executives' Compensation 39–43 (PLI 1955); Rice, "The New Tax Policy on Deferred Compensation", 59 Mich.L.Rev. 381 (1961).

5. Lieberman v. Becker, 38 Del.Ch. 540, 155 A.2d 596 Sup.Ct.1959) (upholding plan attacked on ground retirement benefits bore no relation to value of employee's services). Contra, Berkwitz v. Humphrey, 163 F.Supp. 78 (N.D.Ohio 1958) (plan held invalid on ground retirement payments did not bear any relation to value of employee's services); Shelmerdine, "Shadow Stock Deferred Compensation Arrangements", N.Y.U. 17th Inst. on Fed.Tax. 933

(1959); Comment, "Phantom Stock Plans", 76 Harv.L.Rev. 619 (1963); Comment, "Deferred Compensation: The Phantom Stock Plan Materializes", 12 W.Res.L.Rev. 63 (1960); Note, "Phantom Stock Plans: An Increasingly Popular Form of Executive Compensation", 22 J. Taxation 342 (1965).

1. See generally CCH Pension Plan Guide (2 vols.); P–H Pension and Profit Sharing; P–H Profit Sharing & Pension Forms; D. Rothman, Establishing Pension & Profit Sharing Plans & Trust Funds (ALI 1967); W. Kolodrubetz, Private Pension Plan Benefits (1966); E. Hicks, Accounting for the Cost of Pension Plans (1965); R. Holzman, Guide to Pension and Profit Sharing Plans (3d ed. 1969); M. Bernstein, Future of Private Pensions (1964); H. Biegel, Pensions and Profit Sharing (1964); D. McGill, Fundamentals of Private Pensions (1964); 2 G. Washington, V. Rothschild, T. Ness & R. Sobernheim, Compensating the Corporate Executive 634–706 (3d ed. 1962); L. Rice, Basic Pension and Profit-Sharing Plans (ALI rev. 1961); Taft, "Tax Effect of Corporate Reorganizations on Pension Plans", 41 Notre Dame Law. 471 (1966); Young, "Miscellaneous Problems Involving Suspension and Termination of Pension Plans", 15 W.Res.L.Rev. 667 (1964); Bernstein, "Employee Pension Rights When Plants Shut Down: Problems and Some Proposals", 76 Harv.L.Rev. 952 (1963); Rothschild, "Problems of Employer Cost and Coverage: Trusteed Plans", N.Y.U. 21st Inst. on Fed.Tax. 589 (1963); Peril, "The Uses of Pension and Profit-Sharing Plans for Small or Medium-Sized Businesses", 66 Dick.L.Rev. 143 (1962); Spector, "Pension and Profit Sharing Plans: Coverage and Operation for Closely-Held Corporations and Professional Associations", 7 Vill.L.Rev. 335 (1962). See Croom, "Retirement Plan Check List", 24 Bus.Law 1325 (1969).

Corporations have implied power to establish pension plans;[2] modern statutes often expressly confirm such power.[3] Within the corporation, pensions must be authorized by the proper corporate body, usually the board of directors.[4]

Pension plans must be reasonable,[5] and are enforceable by the employee in cases of express contract[6] or inferred-in-fact

2. Heinz v. Nat'l Bank of Commerce, 237 F. 942 (8th Cir.1916); People ex rel. Metropolitan Life Ins. Co. v. Hotchkiss, 136 App.Div. 150, 120 N.Y.S. 649 (3d Dep't 1909).

3. E. g., ABA–ALI Model Bus.Corp.Act § 4(p). See section 245 supra.

4. See, e. g., Teich v. Nat'l Castings Co., 201 F.Supp. 451 (N.D.Ohio 1962) (permitting shareholder-approved pension plan to be amended by board of directors alone when shareholders had delegated their power in this respect to board and such delegation had been confirmed by statute); Kolodney v. Kolodney Bros., 21 Conn.Supp. 308, 154 A.2d 531 (1959) (president held to have no implied authority to bind corporation by contract to pay pension for life).

5. Good v. Modern Globe, Inc., 346 Mich. 602, 78 N. W.2d 199 (1956); Osborne v. United Gas & Improvement Co., 354 Pa. 57, 46 A.2d 208, 164 A.L.R. 1119 (1946); cf. Fogelson v. American Woolen Co., 170 F.2d 660 (2d Cir.1948) (pension plan established during president's final year providing an annual $54,-220 pension to him for life held subject to court's scrutiny; case settled for pension not to exceed $27,000 per year). See section 245 supra.

6. Murphy v. R. J. Reynolds Tobacco Co., 260 Iowa 422, 148 N.W.2d 400 (1967) (holding retirement board not indispensable party in action by employee against employer for disability benefits under retirement plan); National Outdoor Advertising Co. v. Kalkhurst, 418 P.2d 661 (Okl.1966) (letter advising employee of his retirement at $200 per month nor corporate resolution authorizing such payments held not to create binding pension agreement); Teren v. First Nat'l Bank of Chicago, 243 Or. 251, 412 P.2d 794 (1966) (upholding discretionary determination by pension committee denying early retirement benefits to discharged president); Lano v. Rochester Germicide Co., 261 Minn. 556, 113 N.W.2d 460 (1962); Gediman v. Anheuser Busch, Inc., 299 F.2d 537 (2d Cir.1962), held that the failure of the corporate employer's pension consultants, in advising an employee that election to take cash distribution at a later date would reduce enormously the death benefit in the event of employee's death prior to such date, provided no basis for recovery from the employer on the theory of negligent communica-

contract[7] or on principles of promissory estoppel.[8]

tion; Loengard v. Metal & Thermit Corp., 204 F. Supp. 74 (S.D.N.Y.1962), held that the good faith participation of a shareholder in a proxy contest could not be deemed detrimental to the corporation's interests and constitute ground for terminating retirement benefits under an agreement authorizing termination for conduct detrimental to the corporation's interest. See Specht v. Eastwood-Nealley Corp., 34 N.J.Super. 156, 111 A.2d 781 (1955) (pension granted former general manager on express condition that he would not willfully interfere with or prejudice corporation held revocable as result of his suing corporation without probable cause). See Annot., 76 A.L.R.2d 568 (1961), 18 A.L. R.3d 1248 (1968). Cantor v. Berkshire Life Ins. Co., 171 Ohio St. 405, 171 N.E.2d 518 (1960), held that where an employee had complied with all the conditions of his employment contract relating to retirement benefits under a noncontributory retirement plan and had reached the retirement age specified in the contract, his retirement rights became vested, and the employer could not, in the absence of one of the specified causes set forth in the contract for the divestiture of retirement benefits, divest him of such rights by the exercise of a provision in the contract allowing termination thereof without cause. Compare Muggill v. Reuben H. Donnelley Corp., 62 Cal.2d 239, 42 Cal.Rptr. 107, 398 P.2d 147, 18 A.L.R.3d 1241 (1965), with Kristt v. Whelan, 5 N.Y.2d 807, 181 N.Y.S.2d 205, 155 N.E.2d 116 (1958) (validity of provision for forfeiture of pension rights by retired employees working for competitor). Austin v. House of Vision, Inc., 385 F.2d 171 (7th Cir.1967) (holding that clause for forfeiture of pension rights for accepting position with competitor might provide employee with claim under Federal Sherman Antitrust Act).

7. Sparta v. Lawrence Warehouse Co., 368 F.2d 227 (3d Cir.1966) (holding that former employee whose employment ended before revision of pension plan which reduced period of employment prerequisite to pension eligibility so that he would have been covered if employed and which set date before his employment ended as effective date of amended scheme had no right to benefits in view of plan provisions that interest of participating employee ceased if employment were terminated before completion of specified period of service and that, in effect, interest should be used to increase interests of remaining employees); Hablas v. Armour & Co., 270 F.2d 71 (8th Cir.1959) (35-year employee discharged without cause one year before reaching retirement age held not entitled to pension under contributory plan which provided for return of employees' contributions in case of voluntary resignation or dismissal and preserved corporation's right to discharge employees, where references to advantages of pension plan made no promise of continued employment).

8. Feinberg v. Pfeiffer Co., 322 S.W.2d 163 (Mo.App. 1959).

Pension plans discriminating against union members have been held to constitute unfair labor practices in violation of the Federal National Labor Relations Act.[9]

Various federal and state statutes provide for disclosure and supervision of employee pension and welfare plans.[10]

Pension plans and profit-sharing retirement plans are the two types of retirement plans eligible for qualification for federal income tax purposes. In the former, except for money-purchase plans, the benefits are fixed (ascertainable in the case of money-purchase plans) based upon contributions of up to 10 percent of salaries; in the latter, the contributions are fixed at a certain percentage of profits.

Pension plans may be unfunded or funded. If unfunded, corporate deductions are postponed until payments are made, when they constitute income to the recipient.

If funded, whether "trusteed" in the form of a pension trust or "insured" by an annuity, the pension plan may be "qualified" or "nonqualified" for federal income tax purposes.

"Qualified" Pension Plans

Qualification requires broad coverage and limited benefits, which render them less satisfactory, despite their tax advantages, than unfunded plans for application to top executives. Approval of the Internal Revenue Service, while not prerequisite to qualification, is often sought.[11]

In the case of a "qualified" pension plan, which must be funded, no tax is imposed on the employee, even if his interests are nonforfeitable, until benefits are received, when presumably his income is less and he is in a lower tax bracket; part of such receipts might enjoy capital gain treatment; the corporation may deduct its contributions to the fund; and the earnings of the fund are exempt from income tax.

"Nonqualified" Pension Plans

In the case of a funded "nonqualified" pension plan, the corporation may take a deduction only if the interests of the employees are nonforfeitable; payments to the fund, if the employees' interests are nonforfeitable, are immediately taxable to the employees, and the earnings of the fund are not tax exempt.[12]

---

9. Jim O'Donnell, Inc., 123 N.L.R.B. No. 201 (1959).

10. Mundheim & Henderson, "Applicability of the Federal Securities Laws to Pension and Profit-Sharing Plans", 29 Law & Contemp.Prob. 795 (1964); Craig, "Securities Aspects of Pension, Profit-Sharing, and Stock Bonus Plans", 17 Sw.L.J. 444 (1963); Isaacson, "Employee Welfare and Pension Plans: Regulation and Protection of Employee Rights", 59 Colum.L.Rev. 96 (1959); Scaife, "Problems of Compliance with the Welfare and Pension Plans Disclosure Act", 14 Bus.Law. 762 (1959); Scaife, "The Welfare and Pension Plans Disclosure Act", 14 Bus.Law. 162 (1958). See Cox v. Superior Court, 52 Cal.2d 855, 346 P.2d 15 (1959) (federal jurisdiction over administration of employee trust funds held not exclusive).

11. Int.Rev.Code of 1954, 26 U.S.C.A. §§ 401–407. "Qualified" pension plans may provide for payments of sickness, accident, hospitalization and medical expenses of retired employees and their families. Crafts, "Qualified Retirement Plans", in Advising California Business Enterprises 618–715 (1958); Frei & Archer, "Taxation and Regulation of Pension Plans under the Internal Revenue Code", 1967 U.Ill.L.F. 691; Surrey, "Government Thinking on Pension Plan Reform Revealed", 27 J. Taxation 48 (1967); Lurie, et al., "Case Study of the Planning and Execution of a Qualified Employees' Retirement Plan", N.Y.U. 21st Inst. on Fed.Tax. 625 (1963); McCarthy, "Problems of Employer Cost and Coverage: Insured Plans", id., 603; Alexander, "Rules Governing Qualification of Pension and Profit-Sharing Plans", id., 661; Childs, "Tax Problems Regarding Retirement of Corporate Executives", 41 Taxes 753 (1963); Levy, "Taxation of Distributions from Qualified Pension or Profit-Sharing Plans", 39 Taxes 819 (1961); Kearns, "Protecting Qualified Plans with Mutual Funds", 37 Taxes 1023 (1959).

12. B. Bryson & T. Lefevre, Tax Aspects of Executives' Compensation 24–31 (PLI 1955).

ANNUITY PLANS

252. Annuity plans are a form of funded pension plan which may "qualify" or not with differing federal income tax consequences.

Annuity plans, as a form of funded pension plan, may "qualify" or not with differing federal income tax consequences.[1]

TAX REIMBURSEMENT PLANS

253. Tax reimbursement plans, whereby the corporation undertakes to pay or reimburse the employee for the taxes on his salary, are in disfavor since such payments have been held to be additional taxable income to the employee and some states have enacted statutory prohibitions against such plans.

Such plans called for the corporation either to pay the tax in the first instance or to reimburse the employee for the taxes on his salary. A United States Supreme Court holding that any allowance for the tax was also taxable as income to the employee,[1] with snowballing effect, and state statutes barring such plans,[2] obviously discouraged the use of such plans.

OTHER FRINGE BENEFITS

254. Other fringe benefits often include life insurance, annuities, accident and health insurance, meals, lodging, etc.

Other common fringe benefits include life insurance, annuities, accident and health insurance, meals, lodging, etc.[1]

[§ 252]

1. B. Bryson & T. Lefevre, Tax Aspects of Executives' Compensation 37–39 (PLI 1955). See Detroit Greyhound Employees Federal Credit Union v. Aetna Life Ins. Co., 7 Mich.App. 430, 151 N.W.2d 852 (1967) (holding invalid attempted assignment to creditor by employee of his rights under group annuity contracting containing nonassignment clause); Bresnick v. Home Title Guaranty Co., 175 F.Supp. 723 (S.D.N.Y.1959). See also section 251 supra.

[§ 253]

1. Old Colony Trust Co. v. Comm'r, 279 U.S. 716, 49 S.Ct. 499, 73 L.Ed. 918 (1929).

If the corporation pays the premiums on life insurance on the life of its employee, and

2. See, e. g., McKinney's N.Y. Tax Law, § 385.

[§ 254]

1. B. Bryson & T. Lefevre, Tax Aspects of Executives' Compensation 22–23 (PLI 1955). See Int. Rev.Code of 1954, 26 U.S.C.A. § 101(b) (employee's death benefits not exceeding $5,000 excludable from gross income). See also id. § 104 (compensation for injuries or sickness); § 105 (amounts received under accident and health plans); § 106 (contributions by employer to accident and health plans). Other miscellaneous fringe benefits include country club memberships [one corporation has its own 700-acre employee country club with four golf courses, 18 tennis courts, and staff of more than 100], executive dining rooms or free meals [Int.Rev.Code of 1954, 26 U.S.C.A. § 119—one corporation has been serving almost 20,000 free lunches daily at an annual cost of $7,500,000], substantial discounts on corporation's products, home financing programs, moving expenses, medical checkups, medical reimbursement plans [see Larkin v. Comm'r, 394 F.2d 494 (1st Cir.1968)], educational opportunities, recreational facilities, guest houses, conventions, health resorts, fishing and hunting lodges, summer camps, overseas inspection trips, savings plans, limousines and chauffeurs, yachts and crews. Wolf, "Fringe Benefits: The Use of Corporation Facilities (Nonfinancial) by Officers and Stockholders", N.Y.U. 26th Inst. on Fed.Tax. 1159 (1968); Walker, "Employee Meals, Lodging and Moving Expenses", N.Y.U. 25th Inst. on Fed.Tax. 529 (1967); Taynor, "Nonmonetary Fringe Benefits for Corporate Executives", 38 Taxes 711 (1960). Int.Rev.Code of 1954, 26 U.S.C.A. § 274 disallows deductions for entertainment, amusement, and recreation expenses in the absence of their close relationship to the active conduct of the taxpayer's trade or business, for any business "gift" in excess of $25 per donee, and for traveling not allocable to such trade or business, and requires substantiation for any allowable deductions. 1 G. Washington, V. Rothschild, T. Ness & R. Sobernheim, Compensating the Corporate Executive ch. 7 (3d ed. 1962); Palestin, "Travel and Entertainment Expenses Under the 1962 Revenue Act", 20 N.Y. County Law. Ass'n B.Bull. 203 (1963); Lipoff, "Entertainment of Related Expenses Under Legislature Attack", 17 Texas L.Rev. 183 (1962); Wakely, "Some New Thoughts on Travel and Entertainment Expenses", N.Y.U. 20th Inst. on Fed.Tax. 505 (1962); Comment, "IRS, Expense Accounts and the Cohan Rule: An Exercise in Loophole-Closing", 42 Neb.L.Rev. 644 (1963). See Mississippi River Fuel Corp. v. Koehler, 266 F.2d 190 (8th Cir. 1959) cert. denied 352 U.S. 916, 77 S.Ct. 213, 1 L.Ed.2d 122 (1956) (employer's contributions to savings plan held not deductible for federal income tax purposes); see also medical benefits, such as hospital care under basic Medicare and doctors' bills under supplementary Medicare, should be excluded from plans with respect to employees eligible for such Medicare benefits. Plans providing medical, surgical, or hospital care of benefits, or benefits on sickness, accident, disability, death, or unemployment are sub-

is not the beneficiary, such premiums are deductible by the corporation and constitute income to the employee.[2] Premiums for group life insurance policies, if forfeitable except for possible conversion power, are, subject to limitations, deductible by the corporation and do not constitute income to the employees.[3]

[§ 254]

ject to the Federal Welfare and Pension Plans Disclosure Act, 29 U.S.C.A. §§ 301–309. Note, "Federal Income Taxation—Tax-Free Health Benefits—Application of Health Plans to Stockholder-Employees", 16 Kan.L.Rev. 254 (1968). Note, "Taxation—Payment of Health Insurance Proceeds as a Pension for Disability Retirement", 4 Vill.L.Rev. 567 (1959).

2. Corporations often insure the lives of key personnel—some $40,000,000,000 being in force at present—with the proceeds payable to the corporation on death to cushion the loss of the executive or to retire his shares, or on his retirement to finance his pension, or to his family. 2 G. Washington, V. Rothschild, T. Ness & R. Sobernheim, Compensating the Corporate Executive chs. 13, 15 (3d ed. 1962); Goldstein, "Tax Aspects of Corporate Business Use of Life Insurance", 18 Tax L.Rev. 133 (1963); Sneed, "A Defense of the Tax Court's Result in Prunier and Casale", 43 Cornell L.Q. 339 (1958); Comment, "Corporation's Insuring Employees' Lives", 17 Vand.L.Rev. 1264 (1964); Comment, "Taxation—Insurance Premiums Paid by Corporation, as Taxable Income to the Insured", 33 N.Y.U. L.Rev. 89 (1958). See Prudential Ins. Co. of America v. Gray Mfg. Co., 328 F.2d 438 (2d Cir.1964) (wife, beneficiary of $100,000 under policy until January 1, 1963, held entitled to proceeds when executive committed suicide on December 31, 1962). See section 282 infra. See Morgan v. E. J. Evans Co., 266 F.2d 423, 72 A.L.R.2d 1306 (5th Cir.1959) (corporation held not entitled to cash surrender value of endowment life insurance contract for director secured by corporation upon director's severing connection with corporation and refusing to consent to surrender).

3. Int.Rev.Code of 1954, 26 U.S.C.A. § 79 (premium for amount in excess of $50,000 of insurance included in gross income of employee); First Nat'l Bank of Birmingham v. United States, 358 F.2d 625 (5th Cir.1966); McAleer v. McNally Pittsburg Mfg. Co., 329 F.2d 273 (3d Cir.1964) (holding, under Pennsylvania law, value of group life insurance coverage not element of damages for breach of employment agreement, since employee survived term of employment); Elfstrom v. New York Life Ins. Co., 67 Cal.2d 503, 63 Cal.Rptr. 35, 432 P.2d 731 (1967); Walker v. Occidental Life Ins. Co., 67 Cal.2d 518, 63 Cal.Rptr. 45, 432 P.2d 741 (1967); Humphrey v. Equitable Life Assurance Society, 67 Cal.2d 527, 63 Cal.Rptr. 50, 432 P.2d 746 (1967). For termination of coverage under group policy with regard to termination of employment, see Annot., 68 A.L.R.2d 8 (1959).

For fringe benefits due from the corporation, shareholders are sometimes personally liable to corporate employees classifiable as wage earners.[4]

LIABILITY OF DIRECTORS AND OFFICERS

255. Directors or officers who improperly expend corporate funds as management compensation are liable to the corporation when they are recipients of such funds and sometimes even when they are not recipients. The recipients themselves might be required to refund such compensation as is found to be improper or, in cases of serious misconduct, the entire sums received.

Where directors or officers improperly expend corporate funds as management compensation, they are liable to the corporation, directly or derivatively, for waste of corporate assets, where they are recipients of such funds [1] and sometimes even when they are not recipients.[2] The recipients them-

4. See McKinney's N.Y.Bus.Corp.Law, § 630(b) (liability of shareholders for wages due to laborers, servants or employees), defining "wages or salaries" to mean "all compensation and benefits payable by an employer to or for the account of the employee for personal services rendered by such employee. These shall specifically include but not be limited to salaries, overtime, vacation, holiday and severance pay; employer contributions to or payments of insurance or welfare benefits; employer contributions to pension or annuity funds; and any other moneys properly due or payable for services rendered by such employee." See section 202 supra.

[§ 255]

1. Smith v. Dunlap, 269 Ala. 97, 111 So.2d 1 (1959); Hackley v. Oltz, 105 So.2d 20 (Fla.Dist.Ct.App. 1958); Godley v. Crandall & Godley Co., 212 N.Y. 121, 105 N.E. 818 (1914); Heller v. Boylan, 29 N.Y. S.2d 653 (Sup.Ct.1941), aff'd mem., 263 App.Div. 815, 32 N.Y.S.2d 131 (1st Dep't 1941), motion for leave to appeal or reargument denied 263 App.Div. 852, 32 N.Y.S.2d 1011 (1st Dep't 1942).

2. Dwyer v. Tracey, 118 F.Supp. 289 (N.D.Ill.1954); Beacon Wool Corp. v. Johnson, 331 Mass. 274, 119 N.E.2d 195 (1954); Haberman v. New York Ambassador, Inc., 272 App.Div. 375, 71 N.Y.S.2d 196 (1st Dep't 1947); cf. Matter of Horowitz, 272 App.Div. 942, 72 N.Y.S.2d 67 (2d Dep't 1947) (directors voting excessive salaries to others but not selves held not liable); Heller v. Boylan, 29 N.Y.S.2d 653 (Sup.Ct. 1941), aff'd mem., 263 App.Div. 815, 32 N.Y.S.2d 131 (1st Dep't 1941), motion for leave to appeal or rear-

selves, whether they were involved in authorizing the expenditure[3] or not,[4] might be liable to refund either such compensation as is found to be improper[5] or, in cases of serious misconduct, the entire sums they have received.[6]

MISCELLANEOUS REQUIREMENTS

256. Miscellaneous requirements applicable to management compensation include various requirements under the Federal Securities Act of 1933 and Federal Securities Exchange Act of 1934. In the close corporation, with its merger of the roles of shareholders, directors, and officers, management compensation often involves problems unique to such an enterprise.

Apart from regular corporation law principles and tax considerations, management compensation is subject to various miscellaneous requirements, including full disclosure whenever securities of the corporation are subject to the registration (and prospectus) requirements of the Federal Securities Act of 1933,[1] a proxy statement of the corporation is required by the Federal Securities Exchange Act of 1934,[2] such securities are registered under such Act,[3] or reports of securities trading by insiders are required.[4]

If any compensation plan involves the nonexempt (e. g., public) *offering*[5] of a nonexempt *security* (e. g., shares of a business corporation under share option, share purchase, pension, or profit-sharing plans), the shares, options, of plan itself might require registration under the Securities Act.[6] If shares subject to the registration requirements of the Securities Exchange Act are involved (e. g., share bonus, share option, or share purchase plan), registration of the shares thereunder is, of course, required.[7] If shares or other equity securities of a corporation having equity securities registered under such act are involved in any compensation plan, the trading of such shares or

[§ 255]

gument denied 263 App.Div. 852, 32 N.Y.S.2d 1011 (1st Dep't 1942) (holding only recipient directors-officers liable for miscomputation of corporate treasurer); Carr v. Kimball, 153 App.Div. 825, 139 N. Y.S. 253 (1st Dep't 1913), aff'd mem., 215 N.Y. 634, 109 N.E. 1068 (1915) (directors held liable for voting excessive salaries to selves but not to others).

3. Glenmore Distilleries Co. v. Seideman, 267 F.Supp. 915 (E.D.N.Y.1967); Godley v. Crandall & Godley Co., 212 N.Y. 121, 105 N.E. 818 (1914).

4. Flight Equipment & Engineering Corp. v. Shelton, 103 So.2d 615 (Fla.1958). See 5 W. Fletcher, Private Corporations §§ 2170–2185 (rev. vol. 1967); Annot., 16 A.L.R.2d 467 (1951), 88 A.L.R.2d 1437 (1963).

5. Teren v. Howard, 322 F.2d 949 (9th Cir.1963) (requiring return of salary to extent excessive, cancellation of deferred compensation plans if unreasonable, and return in full of, profits from share options if unreasonable); Glenmore Distilleries Co. v. Seideman, 267 F.Supp. 915 (E.D.N.Y.1967) (directors-officers of insolvent corporation held personally liable for excessive salaries, they paid themselves); Spaeth v. Journal Printing Co., 139 F. Supp. 188 (D. Alaska 1956); Bachelder v. Brentwood Lanes, Inc., 369 Mich. 155, 119 N.W.2d 630 (1963) (requiring repayment to corporation of excessive portion of salary); Godley v. Crandall & Godley Co., 212 N.Y. 121, 105 N.E. 818 (1914).

6. Richardson v. Blue Grass Mining Co., 29 F.Supp. 658 (E.D.Ky.1939), aff'd mem. 127 F.2d 291 (6th Cir.1942), cert. denied 317 U.S. 639, 63 S.Ct. 30, 87 L.Ed. 515 (1942); Production Mach. Co. v. Howe, 327 Mass. 372, 99 N.E.2d 32 (1951); Backus v. Finkelstein, 23 F.2d 531 (D.Minn.1924) (forfeiture of entire salaries for breach of fiduciary duties). Cf. Special Term holding in Godley v. Crandall & Godley Co., rev'd, 153 App.Div. 697, 139 N.Y.S. 236 (1st Dep't 1912), modified on other grounds 212 N.Y. 121, 105 N.E. 818 (1914).

[§ 256]

1. See generally 2 G. Washington, V. Rothschild, T. Ness & R. Sobernheim, Compensating the Corporate Executive ch. 17 (3d ed. 1962); Feldman & Rothschild, "Executive, Compensation and Federal Securities Legislation", 55 Mich.L.Rev. 1115, 1143–1144 (1957). See section 295 infra.

2. Feldman & Rothschild, "Executive Compensation and Federal Securities Legislation", 55 Mich.L.Rev. 1115, 1144–1145 (1957). See section 297 infra.

3. Feldman & Rothschild, "Executive Compensation and Federal Securities Legislation", 55 Mich.L.Rev. 1115, 1145–1146 (1957). See section 296 infra.

4. Feldman & Rothschild, "Executive Compensation and Federal Securities Legislation", 55 Mich.L.Rev. 1115, 1147–1148 (1957). See section 298 infra.

5. See section 295 infra.

6. Feldman & Rothschild, "Executive Compensation and Federal Securities Legislation", 55 Mich.L.Rev. 1115, 1116–1140 (1957).

7. Id. at 1140–1143.

other equity securities by any insider (director, officer, or more than 10 percent beneficial owner) during any six months might run afoul of such act.[8]

In the close corporation, with its merger of the roles of shareholders, directors, and officers, management compensation often involves problems unique to such an enterprise.[9] To minimize double taxation, maximum salary deductions are desirable but this can encounter tax embarrassment or complaints from any shareholders who are not receiving such management compensation.

Statutes to protect the wage claims of employees are usually not construed to extend to the compensation claims of executives.[10]

---

8. See section 298, n. 40 infra.

9. 2 G. Washington, V. Rothschild, T. Ness & R. Sobernheim, Compensating the Corporate Executive ch. 18 (3d ed. 1962). See sections 261, 262 infra.

10. Compare Stull v. Bellefonte Stone Prods. Corp., 205 Pa.Super. 40, 205 A.2d 677 (1964) (holding president entitled to recovery of his unpaid salary under statutory language "salaries and wages due and owing to its laborers and employees"), with Lindsey v. Winkler, 52 Misc.2d 1037, 277 N.Y.S.2d 768 (Nassau County Dist.Ct.1967) (dismissing action against one of 10 largest shareholders where plaintiff failed to allege nonpayment to her by corporation of unpaid wages but relied on prior judgment against corporation for wrongful dismissal under employment contract). See section 202 supra.

CHAPTER 10

SPECIAL PROBLEMS OF CLOSE CORPORATIONS

A. INTRODUCTION

B. INCORPORATION

C. FINANCIAL STRUCTURE

D. MANAGEMENT STRUCTURE

E. SHARE TRANSFER RESTRICTIONS

F. DRAFTING TECHNIQUES

A. INTRODUCTION

"CLOSE CORPORATION"

257. The "close corporation" is a corporation whose shares, or at least voting shares, are held by a single shareholder or closely-knit group of shareholders. Most but not all close corporations are relatively small business enterprises. In the close corporation, usually there are no public investors; its shareholders are active in the conduct and management of the business, and favor the principle of delectus personae with respect to additional associates; and the emphasis is on simplified and informal procedures with all participating, with attendant possible risk of deadlock. The close corporation is formed to achieve certain corporate advantages, usually limited liability and corporate tax advantages, at the same time preserving many of the internal attributes of an individual proprietorship or a partnership.

Small businesses in the United States employ some 30,000,000 persons and account for some 40 percent of the total American business activity. Of some 3,512,000 reporting units for social security purposes, some 1,885,000 employed from one to three employees, some 685,000 employed four to seven employees, some 550,000 employed eight to 19 employees, some 320,000 employed 20 to 99 employees, and some 72,000 employed 100 or more employees. Of some 1,490,000 corporations filing federal income tax returns, some 507,000 reported no net income, most of them probably as the result of maximizing deductions, especially for salaries. Nearly 175,000 "small business corporations" elected under Subchapter S. More than two-fifths of the 1,424,000 active corporations reported assets of less than $50,000; approximately three-fifths reported assets of less than $100,000.[1] Some 9,087,000 individ-

ual proprietorships and 923,000 partnerships, many of them potential close corporations, make up most of the balance of small businesses.[2]

The "close corporation", "closed corporation" or "closely-held corporation"—or "one-man corporation", "family corporation", "incorporated partnership", or "chartered partnership", as it is variously called[3] —is, as its name implies, a corporation whose shares are held by a single sharehold-

1. Statistical Abstract of the United States 1969, 475–478 (U.S. Dep't. of Commerce); Int.Rev.Serv., Report, Statistics of Income—1965–1966, Corporation Income Tax Returns 2, 4, 33 (1968). In England there are some 553,237 private companies compared with some 16,583 public companies. Whitaker's Almanack 1219 (101st ed. 1969).

2. See sections 18–36 supra.

3. A subsidiary corporation generally is a close corporation, although rarely referred to by such term. See section 148 supra. See generally R. Kessler, New York Close Corporations (1968); F. O'Neal, Close Corporations: Law and Practice (1958) (2 vols.); Symposium: "Close Corporations", 1969 U. Ill.L.F. 1; Tenney, "The Potential of the Closed Corporation: An Analysis of its Economic Future", 14 How.L.J. 241 (1968); Hodge & Smith, "The Close Corporation and the Colorado Lawyer", 39 U.Colo. L.Rev. 299 (1967); Seward, "Special Problems of Closely Held Corporations", 12 Prac.Law. 57 (Nov. 1966); Foley, "Small Business—Can It Adjust to the 1970's? The 1990's?", 18 U.Fla.L.Rev. 191 (1965); Olson, "Guidelines for Advising a Small Close Corporation in North Dakota", 42 N.D.L.Rev. 7 (1965); O'Neal, "Developments in the Regulation of the Close Corporation", 50 Cornell L.Q. 641 (1965); Symposium: "A Symposium for the General Practitioner Advising Small Business Concerns", 18 Bus.Law. 99 (1962); Ham, "The Close Corporation Under Kentucky Law", 50 Ky.L.J. 125 (1961–1962); Symposium on the Legal Problems of the Small Business, 8 Kan.L.Rev. 519 (1960); Small Business: A Symposium, 24 Law & Contemp.Prob. 1 et seq. (1959); Scott, "Close Corporation in Contemporary Business", 13 Bus.Law. 741 (1958); Steiner, "Closely Held Corporation", 22 Albany L.Rev. 102 (1958); Close Corporation: A Symposium, 52 Nw.U.L.Rev. 345 et seq. (1957); Panel Discussion: Problems of Closely Held Corporations, 10 Bus.Law. 9 et seq. (Nov. 1954); Hornstein, "Judicial Tolerance of the Incorporated Partnership", 18 Law & Contemp.Prob. 435 (1953); Note, "Corporation—Definition of the Close Corporation", 16 Vand.L. Rev. 1267 (1963). One commentator has suggested the terms "endocratic corporation" (large, publicly-held corporation, whose shares are scattered in small fractions among thousands of shareholders) and "exocratic corporation" (any other corporation, large or small, which is controlled by ownership of substantial blocks of voting shares by a small number of shareholders). Rostow, "To Whom and for What Ends is Corporate Management Responsible?", in E. Mason, The Corporation in Modern Society 303 (1960).

er or by a closely-knit group of shareholders. It differs from the public-issue corporation in that there is no public issue or trading of its voting shares.

Although the corporation is generally thought of as a small business enterprise, no distinction between the close corporation and the public-issue corporation along such lines can be drawn in all cases. Not all large business corporations have publicly-held voting shares outstanding.[4] Most close corporations, however, are relatively small business enterprises. Numerically, the vast majority of business corporations are closely-held.[5]

The close corporation desires to function and does function very differently from the larger corporations with public shareholders. In the close corporation, there are usually no public investors;[6] its shareholders are active in the conduct and management of the business (with resulting coincidence of control and management); the insiders want to keep out outsiders (*delectus personae*); and the emphasis is on simplified and informal procedures with all participating, with attendant possible risk of deadlock. In short, its member or members desire to gain certain corporate advantages, such as limited liability[7] and certain corporate tax consequences (with minimization of double taxation),[8] at the same time preserving many of the internal attributes of an individual proprietorship[9] or partnership.[10]

In contrast with the close corporation, larger corporations with public shareholders and other investors necessarily involve substantial separation of ownership and control, have a form of representative government-by-the-majority, with management delegated to a board of directors, following rather formal procedures, and operate in a relatively institutionalized and depersonalized manner, which is not susceptible to deadlock. The transfer of its shares is usually not only free from transfer restrictions but is facilitated by securities exchange listing or an active over-the-counter market.

Despite the basic differences between the close corporation and the larger corporation with public shareholders, all are organized under and governed in the various American jurisdictions by the same corporation statutes,[11] which only in recent years have shown concern for the basic interests of the close corporation.[12]

---

4. The Ford Motor Company, for example, was closely-held until January, 1956 when The Ford Foundation made a public offering of some of its shares, which was nonvoting in its hands but acquired voting rights upon sale. Practically overnight, 10,-200,000 shares of common shares were sold to the public (known as "going public"), with the result that the Ford family shareholders of Class B shares were joined by more than 250,000 other shareholders of common shares. In 1959, some 4,000,000 additional shares were sold to the public by the Foundation, which retained some 32,000,000 shares of what in its hands remained nonvoting Class A shares. Again in 1961, 1962, 1963, and 1965, some 15,000,000 additional shares were sold to the public by the Foundation, reducing its holdings from some 88 percent to some 25 percent and diversifying its investments. The Ford family held some 6,500,000 shares of Class B shares, with 40 percent of the total voting power. In April, 1959, The Great Atlantic & Pacific Tea Co. (A. & P.), which previously had listed on the American Stock Exchange nonvoting preferred and common shares which were then split and reclassified into voting shares, became publicly-held when the A. & P. heirs (Hartfords) sold an aggregate of 1,800,000 of their voting shares to the public, continuing to hold substantial shares. In these two situations, secondary distributions by existing shareholders rather than primary distributions by the issuers resulted in the shares ceasing to be closely-held. See Owen, "Should a Small Business Go Public?", 6 Law Notes 4 (Oct. 1969).

5. In England, which formally distinguishes between public and private companies, private companies are 33 times more numerous than public companies. See note 1 supra.

6. Or at least no voting shares in the hands of the public. Public holdings of debt securities, nonvoting preferred shares, or even nonvoting common shares, would not keep a corporation from being a close corporation.

7. See sections 73, 146–148 supra.

8. See section 76 supra.

9. See section 18 supra.

10. See sections 19–26 supra.

11. See sections 3, 14 supra.

12. See section 259 infra.

This chapter will concentrate on the peculiar problems of close corporations, first exploring the practical distinctions between the "one-man corporation" and the "incorporated partnership";[13] then enumerating the growing number of provisions in modern American corporate statutes to accommodate them to the special needs of close corporations, with some comparison of the express differentiation between close and other corporations in foreign legal systems;[14] then highlighting the problems of incorporating the close corporation[15] and the typical deviations of close corporations from the statutory norms with respect to financial structure,[16] management structure,[17] and transferability of shares;[18] and concluding with a summary of the drafting problems involved in obtaining the desired individual proprietorship or partnership attributes within the permissible theoretical and practical limitations of the corporate mold.[19]

The unique problems of larger corporations, resulting from the superimposition on the state corporate statutes of substantial regulation, governmental (at federal and state levels) and nongovernmental, are reserved for treatment in Chapter 11.

"ONE–MAN CORPORATION"; "INCORPORATED PARTNERSHIP"

258. A "one-man corporation" is a corporation with a single shareholder, except for possible nominal shareholdings in others when necessary to qualify them to serve as directors. Where the sole shareholder is itself a corporation, a parent-subsidiary relationship arises. Two or more subsidiaries of a common parent corporation are sometimes called "brother-sis-

13. See section 258 infra.
14. See section 259 infra.
15. See section 260 infra.
16. See sections 261, 262 infra.
17. See sections 263–280 infra.
18. See sections 281, 282 infra.
19. See sections 283–290 infra.

ter corporations." When two more persons are involved, the resulting close corporation is sometimes called an "incorporated partnership" or "chartered partnership", or when family members are involved, a "family corporation", or when corporations or corporations and individuals combine for some enterprise, a "joint venture corporation".

One, two, or more individuals might desire to form a business corporation.

Where one person is involved, except for possible nominal shareholdings in others when necessary to qualify them to serve as directors, incorporation results in a "one-man corporation".[1]

If the sole shareholder is itself a corporation, a parent-subsidiary relationship arises. Two or more subsidiaries of a common parent corporation—siblings—are sometimes called "brother-sister corporations."

Where two or more persons are involved, the resulting close corporation is sometimes loosely called an "incorporated partnership" or "chartered partnership". The associates might all be members of the same family, giving rise to the term "family corporation"; or members of two or more families; individuals who are completely unrelated; or even a combination of corporations or of corporations and individuals (including so-called "joint venture" corporations).[2]

1. Note, "One Man Corporations—Scope and Limitations", 100 U.Pa.L.Rev. 853 (1952); see section 147 supra. The English House of Lords case of Salomon v. Salomon & Co., [1897] A.C. 22, discussed in section 147, n. 3 supra, dramatized the potentialities of the one-man corporation as a device to give its shareholder status as a creditor (there secured) of the corporation and immunity against personal liability for corporate obligations. The "one-man corporation" should not be confused with the "corporation sole". See section 6 supra.

2. Scott, "The Close Corporation in Contemporary Business", 13 Bus.Law. 741 (1958). Examples of large well-known corporations owned by two or more other corporations are Arabian-American Oil Co., Bahrein Petroleum Co., Chemstrand Corporation, Ethyl Corporation, Pan American Grace Airways, Standard Vacuum Oil Corporation. See Adkins, Gilpatric & Abraham, "Corporate Joint Ventures in Operation", 14 Bus.Law. 285 (1959).

The close corporation might involve the incorporation either of a new business or of a preexisting business enterprise, usually an individual proprietorship or partnership.[3]

The associate or associates of a close corporation often desire to carry on the business with the external attributes of the corporate form (primarily limited liability), certain tax consequences (minimizing double taxation), and the internal attributes of the individual proprietorship or partnership, i. e., informality of organization and operation, flexibility of financing and distribution of profits, active participation in management, *delectus personae,* and easy dissolution, termination, and liquidation of the business.[4]

STATUTORY DIFFERENTIATION

259. In all American jurisdictions, close and other corporations are organized and operate under corporate statutes equally applicable to all corporations. The older statutes were drafted with no particular concern for the special problems of close corporations. Some modern statutes have a separate subchapter or group of sections applicable to such eligible close corporations as elect to become subject thereto. Several modern statutory provisions, while theoretically available to all corporations, are invocable as a practical matter only by close corporations, such as provisions permitting the fixing of greater-than-normal quorum or voting requirements for shareholders or directors, or permitting informal action by shareholders or directors. Rare statutes permit shareholders to divest the board of directors of its traditional management functions or to provide for shareholder dissolution at will or upon the occurrence of a specified event. Court decisions occasionally afford some tolerance to close corporations. Ingenuity in drafting arrangements for the close corporation has

3. See discussion on incorporating a partnership in 2 J. Barrett & E. Seago, Partners and Partnerships: Law and Taxation 417–442 (1956).

4. See Weisman v. Awnair Corp. of America, 3 N.Y. 2d 444, 165 N.Y.S.2d 745, 144 N.E.2d 415 (1957); Funk v. Spalding, 74 Ariz. 219, 246 P.2d 184 (1952); Seitz v. Michel, 148 Minn. 80, 181 N.W. 102, 12 A.L. R. 1060 (1921); Jackson v. Hooper, 76 N.J.Eq. 599, 75 A. 568 (1910); Smith v. San Francisco & N. P. Ry., 115 Cal. 584, 47 P. 582 (1897).

enabled close corporations to achieve most of their legitimate objects within present statutory frameworks. Federal statutes occasionally differentiate close corporations from larger corporations. Foreign legal systems often afford separate statutory treatment to close corporations, known as "private companies" or "limited responsibility companies". Periodically, separate statutory treatment of the close corporation in the United States is urged, but the problem of satisfactorily distinguishing the close corporation from other corporations in the drafting of such statutes presents difficulties.

In every American jurisdiction, close and other corporations are organized and operate under the corporate statutes which are equally applicable to all corporations. The older statutes were not drafted with particular concern for the special problems of close corporations.[1]

1. For a historical statement concerning the early New York general incorporation statute, see Spencer, Ch.J., in Slee v. Bloom, 19 Johns. *456, *473 (N.Y.1822): "The object and intention of the legislature in authorizing the association of individuals for manufacturing purposes, was, in effect, to facilitate the formation of partnerships, without the risks ordinarily attending them, and to encourage internal manufactures." The Model Business Corporation Act was drawn to be equally applicable to the needs of both large and small incorporated business enterprises. Campbell, "The Model Business Corporation Act", 11 Bus.Law. 98, 104–106 (July 1956). The Model Business Corporation Act presently has seven provisions helpful to close corporations: Section 47, permitting one or more incorporators; Section 138, permitting shareholder action by prior unanimous written consent without a meeting; Section 30, permitting the articles of incorporation to require greater-than-normal quorum for shareholder meetings and permitting the articles of incorporation or bylaws to require greater-than-normal vote for shareholder action; Section 136, recognizing the effectiveness of provisions in the articles of incorporation requiring greater-than-normal vote for shareholder action; Optional Section 39A, permitting board of directors action by prior unanimous written consent without a meeting (1964 addendum); Section 37, permitting the articles of incorporation or bylaws to require greater-than-normal quorum for board of directors meetings and greater-than-normal vote for board of directors action; and Section 90, authorizing judicial dissolution in event of deadlock. The 1969 Model Act revision expressly recognizes (a) shareholder voting agreements, free from voting trust provisions, (b) articles of incorporation provisions for management of the business and affairs of corporations by a person or persons other than the board of directors,

Typically, American corporation statutes have prescribed at least three directors, formal meetings of incorporators, directors, and shareholders, management (including election and removal of officers) vested in the board of directors (who derive their authority from the state, who vote per capita, and whose primary duties are to the corporation), majority quorum and vote (except for extraordinary corporate matters), and free transferability of shares, and have only sparingly authorized judicial dissolution.

Some modern statutes have a separate subchapter or group of sections applicable to such eligible close corporations as elect to become subject thereto.[2]

Several modern statutory provisions, while theoretically available to all corporations, are as a practical matter invocable only by close corporations.

Statutory provisions enacted primarily for close corporations include those permitting the fixing of greater-than-normal quorum and voting requirements for shareholder action [3] or board of directors action,[4] permitting greater informality on the part of shareholders [5] and directors,[6] and, in fewer jurisdictions, permitting rather substantial impingement by shareholders of close corporations on the management functions traditionally vested in the board of directors,[7]

and (c) a board of directors of a single director. The New York Business Corporation Law has more than 20 provisions helpful to close corporations. Henn, Appendix 4, Checklist 9, "Close Corporations", in 2 N.Y.Bus.Corp.Law 626–635 (McKinney 1963); Hetherington, "Trends in Legislation for Close Corporations: A Comparison of the Wisconsin Business Corporation Law of 1951 and the New York Business Corporation Law of 1961", 1963 Wis.L. Rev. 92; Stevens, "Close Corporations and the New York Business Corporation Law", 11 Buffalo L.Rev. 481 (1962); Kessler, "A Close Corporation Checklist for Drafting the Certificate of Incorporation Under the New York Business Corporation Law", 31 Fordham L.Rev. 323 (1962); Hoffman, "New Horizons for the Close Corporation in New York under Its New Business Corporation Law", 28 Brooklyn L. Rev. 1 (1961); Kessler, "The New York Business Corporation Law", 36 St. John's L.Rev. 1, 42–67 (1961). See also O'Neal, "Developments in the Regulation of the Close Corporation", 50 Cornell L.Q. 641 (1965); Myers, "The Close Corporation Under the New South Carolina Corporation Law", 16 S.C. L.Rev. 577 (1965); Ham, "Suggestions for Modernizing the Kentucky General Corporation Law to Meet the Needs of Close Corporations", 52 Ky.L.J. 527 (1964); O'Neal, "The Small Corporation and the Proposed Arkansas Corporation Code", 17 Ark. L.Rev. 356 (1964); Latty, "The Close Corporation and the North Carolina Business Corporation Act", 34 N.C.L.Rev. 432 (1956). Reasonable share transfer restrictions were recognized by the former Uniform Stock Transfer Act in 1922, 6 U.L.A. § 15 (1922), and currently by the Uniform Commercial Code § 8–204. See sections 281, 282 infra.

2. Florida, in 1963, enacted a Close Corporations Act, Fla.Laws, 1963, ch. 63–379, §§ 1–6 (providing that close corporation could elect to bring itself within provisions by written consent of owners of majority of voting shares; for articles of incorporation provision as to control of directors; for informal shareholder and board of directors action; for shareholder agreements, whether in articles of

incorporation, bylaws, or side agreement, "relating to any phase of the affairs of the corporation"; and for judicial dissolution in cases of deadlock. Dickson, "The Florida Close Corporation Act: An Experiment That Failed", 21 U.Miami L.Rev. 842 (1967); Comment, "Statutory Recognition of the Close Corporation in Florida", 16 U.Fla.L.Rev. 569 (1964); Legis., 77 Harv.L.Rev. 1551 (1964). In 1967, Maryland passed a somewhat similar statute, Md. Gen.Corp.Law, §§ 100–111 (1967), permitting a close corporation so to designate itself in its articles of incorporation (and share certificates), and thereby be able to include provisions in its articles of incorporation for management by shareholders without having a board of directors, to have shareholder agreements similar to those permitted under the Florida statute, to dispense with annual shareholder meetings, and to provide for dissolution or continuance of business in case of shareholder or director deadlock. Hall, "The New Maryland Close Corporation Law", 27 Md.L.Rev. 341 (1967). In 1967, Delaware enacted similar provisions. Del.Gen. Corp.Law §§ 341–356 (1967); Bradley, "A Comparative Evaluation of the Delaware and Maryland Close Corporation Statutes", 1968 Duke L.J. 525; Comment, "Delaware's Close-Corporation Statute", 63 Nw.U.L.Rev. 230 (1968). Pennsylvania, in 1968, followed. Comment, "The Close Corporation Comes of Age in Pennsylvania: Article III, Chapter B of the Business Corporation Law", 73 Dick.L.Rev. 272 (1969). See also Hughes, "Close Corporations", 36 Tenn.L.Rev. 352 (1969); Bowman, "An Introduction to the New Georgia Corporation Law", 4 Ga.St.B.J. 419 (1968); Comment, "A Comparison of the Close Corporation Statutes of Delaware, Florida and New York", 23 U.Miami L.Rev. 515 (1969); See note 21 infra.

3. See section 266 infra.

4. See section 274 infra.

5. See section 190 supra and section 265 infra.

6. See section 208 supra and section 273 infra.

7. The prime early departure from the more traditional approach was the 1955 revision of the North

permitting provision for shareholder dissolution at will or upon the occurrence of a spec-

ified event.[8]

Most court decisions have required close corporations to adhere to the statutory norm,[9] but occasionally greater judicial tol-

Carolina corporation statute. See O'Neal, "Recent Legislation Affecting Close Corporations", 23 Law & Contemp.Prob. 341 (1958); Latty, "The Close Corporation and the North Carolina Business Corporation Act", 34 N.C.L.Rev. 432 (1956); Latty, Powers & Breckenridge, "The Proposed North Carolina Business Corporation Act", 33 N.C.L.Rev. 26 (1954). See especially N.C.Bus.Corp.Act § 55–73 (1957), providing that (a) an otherwise valid contract between two or more shareholders that the shares held by them shall be voted as a unit for the election of directors shall, if in writing and signed by the parties, be valid and enforceable as between the parties, but not for longer than 10 years from the date of its execution; (b) where shares of the corporation are not publicly-traded, no written agreement to which all of the shareholders have actually assented, whether embodied in the charter or bylaws or in any side agreement in writing and signed by all the parties thereto, and which relates to any phase of the affairs of the corporation, whether to the management of its business or division of its profits or otherwise, shall be invalid as between the parties thereto, on the ground that it is an attempt by the parties thereto to treat the corporation as if it were a partnership or to arrange their relationships in a manner that would be appropriate only between partners, and that a transferee of shares covered by such agreement who acquires them with knowledge thereof is bound by its provisions; and (c) an agreement between all or less than all of the shareholders, whether solely between themselves or between one or more of them and a party who is not a shareholder, is not invalid, as between the parties thereto, on the ground that it so relates to the conduct of the affairs of the corporation as to interfere with the discretion of the board of directors, but the making of such an agreement shall impose upon the shareholders who are parties thereto the liability for managerial acts that is imposed by the statute upon directors; § 55–24(a), providing that "Subject to the provisions of the charter, the bylaws or agreements between the shareholders otherwise lawful, the business and affairs of a corporation shall be managed by a board of directors". See also McKinney's N.Y.Bus.Corp. Law § 620(b) (articles of incorporation provision otherwise prohibited by law because it improperly restricts board of directors in its management of business of corporation, or improperly transfers to one or more shareholders or to one or more persons or corporations to be selected by him or them, all or any part of such management otherwise within authority of board of directors under statute shall nevertheless be valid: (a) if all incorporators or holders of record of all outstanding shares, whether or not having voting power, have authorized such provision in articles of incorporation or amendment thereof; and (b) if, subsequent to adoption of such provision, shares are transferred or issued only to persons who had knowledge or notice thereof or consented in writing to such provision); id. § 620(c) (such provision to be valid only so long as no shares of corporation are listed on national securities exchange or regularly quoted in over-the-coun-

ter market by one or more members of national or affiliated securities association); id. §§ 620(d), (e) (striking out provision authorized by § 620(b) to be authorized at meeting of shareholders by vote of holders of two-thirds of all outstanding shares entitled to vote thereon or by holders of such greater proportion of shares as may be required by **articles** of incorporation for that purpose); id. § 620(f) (effect of such provision to relieve directors from and impose upon shareholders authorizing same or consenting thereto liability for managerial acts or omission that is imposed on directors by statute to extent that and so long as discretion or powers of board of directors in its management of corporate affairs is controlled by any such provision); id. § 620(g) (existence of such provision to be noted conspicuously on face or back of every share certificate issued by corporation). See also id. § 715(b) (articles of incorporation may provide that all or specified officers shall be elected by shareholders instead of by board of directors); id. § 716 (any officer elected by shareholders removable, with or without cause, only by vote of shareholders, but his authority to act as officer suspendible by board of directors for cause). The 1969 Model Act revision allows an articles of incorporation provision to vest the management of the business and affairs of a corporation in a person or persons other than the board of directors.

8. In 1947, California, to meet situations of dissension and deadlock, enacted provisions for the judicial appointment of a provisional director and for buying out a shareholder seeking judicial dissolution. Cal. Gen.Corp.Law, § 819 (1947). See sections 269, 277, 280 infra. See N.C.Bus.Corp.Act § 55–125(a) (3) (1957), providing for judicial dissolution in an action by a shareholder upon a showing that all of the present shareholders are parties to, or are transferees or subscribers of shares with actual notice of a written agreement, whether embodied in the charter or separate therefrom, entitling the complaining shareholder to liquidation or dissolution of the corporation at will or upon the occurrence of some event which has subsequently occurred. See also McKinney's N.Y.Bus.Corp.Law, § 1002 (providing that articles of incorporation may contain provision that any shareholder, or holders of any specified number or proportion of all or any class or series of shares may require dissolution of corporation at will or upon occurrence of specified event).

9. E. g., Mook v. Berger, 7 A.D.2d 726, 180 N.Y.S.2d 400 (1st Dep't 1958), aff'd mem., 6 N.Y.2d 833, 188 N.Y.S.2d 219, 159 N.E.2d 702 (1959) (Connecticut law); Matter of William Faehndrich, Inc., 2 N.Y.2d 468, 161 N.Y.S.2d 99, 141 N.E.2d 597 (1957); Benintendi v. Kenton Hotel, Inc., 294 N.Y. 112, 60 N.E.2d 829, 159 A.L.R. 280 (1945) (invalidating greater-than-normal quorum/voting requirements) (see sections 266, 274 infra); Hurley v. Ornsteen, 311

erance of the close corporation has been afforded.[10]

Ingeniousness on the part of counsel in drafting arrangements for the formation and operation of close corporations has, notwithstanding lack of statutory and judicial differentiation, enabled close corporations to achieve most of their legitimate objects thereby rendering the present situation tolerable to numerous small business corporations.[11] An extensive body of literature on the subject is available to assist the practitioner.[12]

At the federal regulatory level, the statutes have been drafted for primary application to larger corporations issuing their securities to the public[13] or engaging in activities with substantial impact on the economy.[14]

Also at the federal level, tax relief has been provided to certain small business corporations.[15]

The Federal Small Business Investment Act of 1958 was enacted to promote small business enterprises.[16]

Outside of the United States, separate statutory treatment is afforded the close corporation.

Since 1908, England has distinguished between the "private company" and the "public company",[17] defining the "private company" as a company which has not more than 50 members (exclusive of employees and ex-employees), has made no public offering of its securities, and has share transfer restrictions. The private company, which is much more prevalent than the public company[18] and has largely replaced the lim-

Mass. 477, 42 N.E.2d 273 (1942) (requiring formal board of directors action) (see section 208 supra and section 273 infra); Abercrombie v. Davies, 36 Del. 371, 130 A.2d 338 (Sup.Ct.1957), rev'g on other grounds, 35 Del.Ch. 599, 123 A.2d 893 (Ch.1956); Long Park, Inc. v. Trenton-New Brunswick Theatres Co., 297 N.Y. 174, 77 N.E.2d 633 (1948); McQuade v. Stoneham, 263 N.Y. 323, 189 N.E. 234 (1934) (7–2); Manson v. Curtis, 223 N.Y. 313, 119 N.E. 559 (1918) (invalidating shareholder agreements impinging on management functions of board of directors) (see sections 198, 213 supra and sections 267, 275, 287 infra).

10.   E. g., Hornstein, "Judicial Tolerance of the Incorporated Partnership", 18 Law & Contemp.Prob. 435 (1953); Ripin v. United States Woven Label Co., 205 N.Y. 442, 98 N.E. 855 (1912) (upholding articles of incorporation provision requiring unanimous shareholder vote to change number of directors); Matter of Stylemaster Department Store, Inc., 7 Misc.2d 207, 154 N.Y.S.2d 58 (Sup.Ct.1956) (upholding informal director action); Galler v. Galler, 32 Ill.2d 16, 203 N.E.2d 577 (1964), 95 Ill.App.2d 340, 238 N.E.2d 274 (1968) (upholding unanimous shareholder agreement); Clark v. Dodge, 269 N.Y. 410, 199 N.E. 641 (1936) (upholding unanimous "shareholder" agreement); Matter of Buckley (Rickerson), 183 Misc. 189, 50 N.Y.S.2d 54 (Sup.Ct.1944) (upholding less than unanimous "shareholder" agreement); Sautter v. Fulmer, 258 N.Y. 107, 179 N.E. 310 (1932), motion for reargument denied 259 N.Y. 508, 182 N.E. 157 (1932); Kavanaugh v. Kavanaugh Knitting Co., 226 N.Y. 185, 123 N.E. 148 (1919); Helms v. Duckworth, 249 F.2d 482 (D.C.Cir. 1957) (recognizing fiduciary relationship between shareholders of close corporation); see also Wabash Ry. v. American Refrigerator Transit Co., 7 F.2d 335 (8th Cir. 1925), cert. denied 270 U.S. 643, 46 S.Ct. 208, 70 L.Ed. 776 (1926) (upholding agreement giving corporation partnership attributes).

11.   See sections 283–290 infra.

12.   See especially F. O'Neal, Close Corporations: Law and Practice (1958) (2 vols.); C. Rohrlich, Organizing Corporate and Other Business Enterprises 123–176 (4th ed. 1967); Oppenheim & Zatz, "Closer Look at the Close Corporation", 46 Chi.B.Rec. 249

(1965); Ham, "Close Corporation Under Kentucky Law", 50 Ky.L.J. 125 (1961–62); Cross, "Close Corporation in Connecticut", 35 Conn.B.J. 432 (1961); Neef & Sullivan, "Close Corporation in Michigan", 39 Mich.St.B.J. 8 (1960); Powers, "Cross Fire on the Close Corporation: Norms Versus Needs", 11 U.Fla.L.Rev. 433 (1958); Symposium: "The Close Corporation", 52 Nw.U.L.Rev. 345 (1957); Panel Discussion: "Problems of Closely Held Corporations", 10 Bus.Law. 9 (Nov.1954); Symposium: "The Close Corporation", 18 Law & Contemp.Prob. 433 (1953); Note, "Montana's Close Corporations—Victims of a Statutory Strangle Hold?", 25 Mont. L.Rev. 213 (1964). See note 1 supra.

13.   See sections 292–308, and especially section 261, n. 4 infra.

14.   See sections 309–315 infra.

15.   See section 76 supra and section 262 infra.

16.   15 U.S.C.A. § 631 et seq. See section 261 infra.

17.   The English term "public company" should not be confused with American references to "public corporation". See sections 14, 91 supra.

18.   As of Dec. 31, 1956, there were 11,107 public companies and 290,889 private companies. The aggregate paid-up capital of the public companies was £4,421,000,000; of the private companies £2,541,000,-

ited partnership in England, need not have more than two incorporators and one director, as compared with the requirement that a public company must have at least seven incorporators or members and two directors. The shortcoming of the English Companies Act is that it does not specify which of its provisions do or do not apply to the private company.[19]

The British Commonwealth nations have similar systems.[20]

In continental Europe and under other foreign legal systems, there is more complete separate statutory treatment of the close corporation, which is there known as the limited responsibility company.[21]

The new Israeli companies law was drafted primarily with the close corporation in mind.[22]

Periodically, greater separate statutory treatment of the close corporation in the United States is urged.[23]

One problem of statutory differentiation is the statutory definitions to be given the two types of corporations.[24]

000. L. Gower, The Principles of Modern Company Law 13, n. 49 (2d ed. 1957). See Note, "Conversion of Private Companies into Public Companies", 103 Sol.J. 192 (1959). By 1966, there were 16,500 public companies and 540,000 private companies.

19. S. Borrie, Private Companies: Their Management and Statutory Obligations (7th ed. 1954); A. Balcombe, Law and Practice Relating to Exempt Private Companies (1953); McFadyean, "The American Close Corporation and Its British Equivalent", 14 Bus.Law. 215 (1958); Gower, "The English Private Company", 18 Law & Contemp.Prob. 535 (1953).

20. II Rev.Stat. of Canada, c. 53, § 3(j); Campbell, "The Future of Limited Liability Companies and Their Administration", 41 Austl.L.J. 348 (1967); New Brunswick Rev.Stat. c. 33, § 77 (1952); Macindoe, "Proprietary Companies", 31 L.Inst.J. 260 (1957–58). In Australia, the private or "proprietary company" must include as part of its name the word "Proprietary" or abbreviation "Pty." immediately before the word "Limited" or abbreviation "Ltd.".

21. E. g., "société à responsabilité limitée" ("SARL") in France or Switzerland; "Gesellschaft mit beschrankter Haftung" ("G.mitb.H" or "GmbH") in Germany or Switzerland; "sociedad de responsabilidad limitada" ("SRL" or "SdeRL") in Spanish Latin America; "sociedade limitada por cotas" ("Ltda") in Brazil; "société de personnes à responsabilité limitée" ("SPRL") in Belgium; "societa a responsibilita limitada" ("SARL") in Italy; "Yugen-Kaisha" ("YK") in Japan; "proprietary limited" ("Pty.Ltd.") or "eiensdoms" ("Edms.") in Republic of South Africa. See E. Church, Business Associations under French Law (1960); De Bries & Juenger, "Limited Liability Contract: The GmbH", 64 Colum.L.Rev. 866 (1964); Becker, "The Société Anonyme and the Société À Responsibilité Limitée in France", 38 N.Y.U.L.Rev. 835 (1963); Haskell, "The American Close Corporation and Its West German Counterpart: A Comparative Study", 21 Ala.

L.Rev. 287 (1969); Schneider, "The American Close Corporation and Its German Equivalent"; Houwink, "The American Close Corporation and Its Dutch Equivalent"; Reverdin & Homburger, "The American Close Corporation and Its Swiss Equivalent"; 14 Bus.Law. 228 (1958); Treillard, "The Close Corporation in French and Continental Law", 18 Law & Contemp.Prob. 546 (1953).

22. Yadin, "Proposed New Israeli Companies Law", 13 Bus.Law. 277 (1958).

23. Wolen, "A Round Peg—A Square Hole: The Close Corporation and the Law", 22 Sw.L.J. 811 (1968); Bradley, "Toward a More Perfect Close Corporation—The Need for More and Improved Legislation", 54 Geo.L.J. 1145 (1966); Adickes, "A 'Closed Corporation Law' for California", 54 Calif. L.Rev. 1990 (1966); Oppenheim, "The Close Corporation in California—Necessity of Separate Treatment", 12 Hastings L.J. 227 (1961); Winer, "Proposing a New York 'Close Corporation Law'", 28 Cornell L.Q. 313 (1943) (with draft of Close Corporation Law as appendix); Weiner, "Legislative Recognition of the Close Corporation", 27 Mich.L. Rev. 273 (1929); Comment, "The Failure of the Ohio General Corporation Law to Adequately Provide for Close Corporations—Proposals for Change", 37 U.Cin.L.Rev. 620 (1968); Comment, "A Plea for Separate Statutory Treatment of the Close Corporation", 33 N.Y.U.L.Rev. 700 (1958); Note, "Statutory Assistance for Closely Held Corporations", 71 Harv.L.Rev. 1498 (1958); Note, "Desirability of a 'Close Corporation Act'", 52 Nw.U.L.Rev. 297 (1957). See note 2 supra.

24. 1 F. O'Neal, Close Corporations: Law and Practice § 1.02 (1958). See Winer, "Proposing a New York 'Close Corporation Law'", 28 Cornell L.Q. 313, 314 (1943), defining "close corporation" in the appended draft of close corporation law as "any stock corporation in which the stock is owned by not more than five persons who elect to incorporate under this law . . ." Id. at 335–336. "Small business corporation" is defined differently for purposes of Subchapter S election and for purposes of favorable tax treatment of "section 1244 stock" losses under the Internal Revenue Code. See section 16, especially nn. 8 and 10, and sections 17, 76, 166 supra and section 262 infra. See N.C.Bus. Corp.Act § 55.73(b) (1957) (whether shares of corporation are "generally traded in the markets maintained by securities dealers or brokers"); McKinney's N.Y.Bus.Corp.Law, §§ 620(c), 630(a) (wheth-

B. INCORPORATION

INCORPORATION OF CLOSE CORPORATION

260. The close corporation must comply with the same incorporation formalities as are required of corporations generally, but the drafting problems in organizing a close corporation are substantially greater than those involved in other incorporations. Prior to incorporating the close corporation, complete agreement should be reached on all matters, and all the necessary implementing documentation drafted and executed.

Requirements as to number and qualifications of incorporators can be observed, when desirable, by the use of "dummy" or "accommodation" incorporators to be replaced after incorporation by the real party or parties in interest.

Shares should be authorized and issued to reflect the desired interests with respect to earnings, net assets, and control, and the shareholders should bind themselves by an appropriate shareholders agreement. Appropriate provision should be made to exclude others from becoming shareholders.

At the board of directors level, provision should be made, so far as permissible, for the control of the board, by the real party or parties in interest.

Officers should be selected, employed, authorized, and compensated to carry out the wishes of the real party or parties in interest.

The close corporation must comply with the same incorporation formalities as are required of corporations generally.[1]

Frequently, the drafting problems entailed in setting up a close corporation are substantially greater than those involved in other incorporations. Molding the corporate form to meet the needs of the situation, within the permissible limitations of corporation law, involves the drafting of the usual articles of incorporation [2] and bylaws (but with various special provisions relevant to close corporations),[3] share certificate forms,[4] and minutes of organization meetings of incorporators and board of directors,[5] and often, in addition, preincorporation agreements,[6] "shareholder agreements" [7] and appropriate legends for the share certificates.[8] Prior to incorporation,[9] complete agreement should be reached on all matters, and all the necessary implementing documentation drafted and executed.

A business corporation may involve either a new business or the incorporation of an

2. O'Neal, "Molding the Corporate Form to Particular Business Situations: Optional Charter Clauses", 10 Vand.L.Rev. 1 (1956). See section 285 infra.

3. See section 286 infra.

4. See section 290 infra.

5. See generally section 135 supra.

6. See section 284 infra.

7. See sections 198, 213 supra and sections 267, 275, 287 infra.

8. See section 290 infra.

9. See, e. g., R. Kessler, New York Close Corporations (1968); J. Abbott, Organizing Small Michigan Business Enterprises (Institute of Continuing Legal Education 1962); L. Sarner & G. Shinehouse, Organizational Problems of Small Businesses (ALI rev. 1961); Schwarzer, "Practical Problems of Organizing Closely Held Corporations", in Advising California Business Enterprises 403–441 (1958); Kessler, "Setting Up a Close Corporation in New York", 17 Buffalo L.Rev. 237 (1968); Borini, "Problems Upon Incorporation of the Family Business", N.Y.U. 25th Inst. on Fed.Tax. 229 (1967); Robinson, "'Tax Free' and Taxable Incorporations", 18 U.Fla. L.Rev. 207 (1965); Hare, "Consideration in Incorporating Farm Businesses", 18 U.Fla.L.Rev. 221 (1965); Cary, "How Illinois Corporations May Enjoy Partnership Advantages: Planning for the Closely Held Firm", 48 Nw.U.L.Rev. 427 (1953).

er shares of corporation are "listed on a national securities exchange or regularly quoted in an over-the-counter market by one or more members of a national or affiliated securities association"); Fla. Laws 1963, ch. 63–379, § 1(2) (whose shares are generally not traded in markets maintained by securities dealers or brokers); Del.Gen.Corp.Law, § 342(a) (1)–(3) (1967) (if articles of incorporation recite that (a) it is close corporation; (b) maximum number of shareholders must be stated, not to exceed 30 (actually 60); (c) all shares must be subject to some transfer restriction; and (d) no shares may be subject to public offering within meaning of Federal Securities Act of 1933). See also Md.Gen.Corp.Law, § 100 (1967).

1. See Chapter 6 supra. See generally R. Kessler, New York Close Corporations ch. 5 (1968).

existing business previously conducted as an individual proprietorship or partnership, etc.[10]

Incorporator(s)

One, two, or more individuals, or one or more corporations, desiring to form a close corporation, must comply with the applicable requirements as to number and qualifications of incorporators, under older statutes at least three natural persons.[11]

In jurisdictions where each incorporator must subscribe for shares,[12] there obviously must be at least as many incipient shareholders as any required minimum number of incorporators.

These older requirements are easily observed by the extra-legal use of "dummy" or "accommodation" incorporators-subscribers who promptly after incorporation transfer any of their subscriptions to the real party or parties in interest.[13]

Shareholder(s)

Obviously, shares should be authorized and issued so as to create the desired share interests with respect to earnings, net assets, and control (with due attention to tax considerations); shareholder functions and procedures should be formally established (e. g., control over directors by broad removal provisions, quorum or voting requirements) to approximate as closely as legally permissible

what the parties desire; shareholders should bind themselves, by an agreement *inter sese*, so far as lawfully possible, to exercise their respective functions to carry out their intentions (e. g., voting for directors and other matters);[14] and an appropriate provision should be made to exclude others from becoming shareholders and for cases of deadlock at the shareholder level.

Board of Director(s)

A board of directors of at least three individual directors must be authorized under older corporate statutes, relieved by some modern corporate statutes permitting one-director or two-director boards, at least in one-shareholder or two-shareholder corporations.[15]

In a close corporation composed of two equal interests held by two individuals, families, or groups, an even-numbered board is often established to reflect the 50–50 share ownership. Where at least a three-man board of directors must be authorized, as under older statutes, and directors are required to be shareholders (an even less prevalent modern requirement), the qualification of at least three directors is dependent upon there being no less than three shareholders, with at least nominal interest. Although the initial directors named in the articles of incorporation who attend to the initial formal arrangements at the outset, can be "accommodation" or "dummy" directors,[16] the duties imposed on management[17] militate against the use of "accommodation" or "dummy" directors in a going concern.[18] In the case of

10. 2 J. Barrett & E. Seago, Partners and Partnerships: Law and Taxation 417–442 (1956).

11. See sections 131, 185 supra.

12. Ibid.

13. Cf. Park Terrace, Inc. v. Phoenix Indemnity Co., 243 N.C. 595, 91 S.E.2d 584 (1956) (holding that corporation under statute was association of three or more persons and lesser number would not suffice), overruled by N.C.Bus.Corp.Act § 55-3.1 (1957); Lester Bros. v. Pope Realty & Ins. Co., 250 N.C. 565, 109 S.E.2d 263 (1959) (refusing to apply later statute retroactively). Articles of incorporation with a provision requiring incorporators to assign their subscription upon incorporation, however, were denied filing by the New York Secretary of State. 7 I. Kantrowitz & S. Slutsky, White on New York Corporations ¶5.11 (12th ed. 1953).

14. Hornstein, "Stockholders' Agreements in the Closely Held Corporation", 59 Yale L.J. 1040 (1950).

15. See sections 130, 204 supra. The 1969 Model Act revision and Delaware permit a single director.

16. See sections 130, 135 supra.

17. See sections 231–242 supra.

18. Cf. N.C.Bus.Corp.Act § 55-73(c) (1957) providing that the making of a shareholder agreement divesting the board of directors of management functions shall impose upon the shareholders who are parties to such agreement the liability for managerial acts

two equal shareholders, one practical solution under older statutes might be to authorize a three-man board but after the initial formalities are completed have the board carry on with each of the two shareholders as a director and with one vacancy.[19]

Another device, where permissible, would be to have an executive committee composed of the real parties in interest with as much authority delegated to it as applicable law permits.[20]

Obviously, in a parent-subsidiary situation, the parent corporation cannot itself be on the board and perforce must be represented, if at all, by its designee or designees, usually chosen from among its own officers or directors.[21]

So far as the board of directors is concerned, desired representation on it of the shareholders (by themselves or their designees) should be assured; its functions and procedures formally circumscribed so far as lawful, and the individual directors subjected to maximum shareholder control by, for example, appropriate removal provisions in the

articles of incorporation or bylaws, and in "shareholder agreements" binding the parties, as directors, so far as legally possible, to exercise their director functions (e. g., voting for officers and other matters) to effectuate the legitimate interests of the parties; and appropriate provision made for deadlock at the board of directors level.

Officers ·

At the time of incorporation, some thought must also be given to the corporate officers, who in most jurisdictions are appointed and serve at the pleasure of the board of directors.[22]

The bylaws should provide for the desired offices, delimit the authority of the respective officers[23] to the extent desired, and make appropriate provision for their compensation.[24]

Here, the parties' intentions can be implemented by provisions in "shareholder agreements", employment contracts between each officer and the corporation, and the actual appointment of the officers by the directors promptly after incorporation.

In short, practically all of the problems involved not only in formal incorporation but also in the operation and dissolution of the corporation should be considered at the time of incorporation. While such problems might later be resolved it is usually far more practical to anticipate and resolve them in advance, before difficulties and dissension arise. More detailed treatment of these problems, along functional lines, is found in the succeeding sections of this chapter.

that is imposed by the statute upon directors. Such a provision might better have provided that, to the extent that directors are "dummified" by valid shareholder agreements, the shareholders who are parties to such agreements should be liable and the directors should be relieved from liability pro tanto. See McKinney's N.Y.Bus.Corp.Law, § 620(f) (articles of incorporation provision as to control of directors effective to relieve directors and impose upon shareholders authorizing same or consenting thereto liability for managerial acts or omissions that is imposed on directors by statute to extent that and so long as discretion or powers of board of directors in its management of corporate affairs is controlled by any such provisions).

19. But see Dunham v. Natural Bridge Ranch Co., 115 Mont. 579, 147 P.2d 902 (1944).

20. See section 212 supra.

21. See section 147 supra. England permits a corporation to serve as a director. L. Gower, The Principles of Modern Company Law 120 (2d ed. 1957).

22. See section 221 supra.

23. See sections 224–226 supra.

24. See sections 243–256 supra.

C. FINANCIAL STRUCTURE

FINANCIAL STRUCTURE OF CLOSE CORPORATION—NONTAX ASPECTS

261. The financial structure of the close corporation can follow a wide variety of patterns, the basic feature being that its voting shares are closely held and not in the hands of the public. The goal is to minimize risk and maximize profits. Financing by debt as well as by shares alone might be desirable from the point of view of "leverage" or "trading on equity" or "thin incorporation". More than a single class of shares might be desirable, subject to limitations where Subchapter S election is desirable for various reasons. The initial financial structure should be protected against future changes which would disturb the initial scheme, which often is based on various provisions at the shareholder level binding the shareholders and through them the directors and officers. Grounds for disregarding corporateness or regarding the corporation as an instrumentality of the shareholders, thereby subjecting the shareholders to personal liability, arise more frequently in close corporations than in other corporations.

The financial structure of the close corporation can follow a wide variety of patterns, the basic difference between such financial structure and those of other corporations is that the voting shares of the close corporation are closely held and not in the hands of the public. Of course, certain considerations are more relevant to the close corporation than to other corporations, and will be stressed in this section and the next section. Otherwise, the general discussion of corporate financial structure in Chapter 8 is equally applicable to the close corporation.

In setting up the financial structure, the goal obviously is to minimize risk and maximize profits.[1]

The close corporation may be financed by borrowing (and possibly issuing debt securities to evidence such obligations) or the issuance of equity securities. To the extent that it borrows from non-shareholders,[2] the

1. R. Kessler, New York Close Corporations ch. 5 (1968); "Venture Capital Financing for Small Business—A Symposium", 24 Bus.Law. 935 (1969); Mayer & Goldstein, "Small Business Growth and Survival During the First Two Years", 18 Vand.L.Rev. 1749 (1965); Howell, "Financing—A Major Problem of Small Businesses", 18 Vand.L.Rev. 1683 (1965);

Symposium: "Small Business Financing", 20 Bus. Law. 185 (1964); Barker, "Financing Small Businesses", 18 Bus.Law. 113 (1962); Herwitz, "Allocation of Stock Between Services and Capital in the Organization of a Close Corporation", 75 Harv.L.Rev. 1098 (1962); Hea, "Capitalization of the Close Corporation", 34 Notre Dame Law. 335 (1959); Seminar: "What the General Practitioner Should Know about Sources and Methods of Financing Small Business", 13 Bus.Law. 296 (1958); Riely & Talbert, "Financing the Small Business", 13 Bus.Law. 768 (1958); Herold, "Financing Closely Held Corporations", 47 Ill.B.J. 288 (1958); Abrahams, "Advising the Small Business to Expand", 4 Prac.Law. 59 (Oct.1958); Funk, "Secured Borrowing by Small Business", 13 Bus.Law. 335 (1958); Symposium: "The Close Corporation", 52 Nw.U.L.Rev. 345, 365–375 ("Capitalization") (1957); Garrett & Garrett, "Financing a Small Business", 2 Prac.Law. 23 (Feb.1956).

2. The lender, of course, might insist that the principal shareholder or shareholders personally guarantee the corporate obligation. Commercial Credit Corp. v. Sorgel, 274 F.2d 449 (5th Cir. 1960). See section 147 supra. Financial aid from the federal government might be possible. The Small Business Investment Act of 1958 [15 U.S.C.A. §§ 631 et seq.] fosters the incorporation of small business investment companies, primarily under state laws, or by the Federal Small Business Administration upon a determination that such companies cannot be formed under state law and operate in accordance with the purposes of the Act. Through the Act, Congress has facilitated access of small business concerns to equity capital and long-term loans, and has supplemented other federal loan programs in aid of small business. With the approval of the Small Business Administration, small business investment companies become vehicles for the making of loans directly to small business concerns or for the purchasing of debentures of such firms. In its first 15 years, the Small Business Administration made more than 85,000 loans for $3,800,000,000, more than 1,800 local development company loans for $375,000,000, and some 75,000 loans for some $650,000,000; distributed more than 41,000,000 management publications, sponsored more than 11,000 conferences and workshops, and offered advice to some 565,000 small businessmen. See Small Business Investment Companies, Law-Regulations-Explanation (New Financing for Small Business) (Commerce Clearing House, Inc. 1959); Noone, "The 1968 Model SBIC", 23 Bus.Law. 1214 (1968); Zeidman, "The Small Business Investment Company—A Tool for Economic Self-Help", 21 Bus.Law. 947 (1966); Conwill, "Protection or Oppression? The Investment Company Impact on the Publicly

advantages and concomitant disadvantages of "leverage" or "trading on equity" exist.[3]

Debt securities, nonvoting preferred shares, and even nonvoting classes of common shares might even be issued to the public, and traded actively on the over-the-counter market and possibly on a national securities exchange.[4] Public financing, however,

is the exception rather than the general practice in the case of close corporations.[5]

Where the financing comes from persons who are shareholders, such financing may be by shares alone or by a combination of debt and shares—"thin incorporation". The possible advantages of "thin incorporation", taxwise [6] and from the point of view of creditor status,[7] have been previously discussed.

Held SBIC", 19 Bus.Law. 345 (1964); Powers, "Small Business Investment Companies—A Place in Our Economy?", 17 J.Am.Soc'y C.L.U. 166 (1963); Parris, "Small Business Investment Company Program", 42 Mich.St.B.J. 45 (1963); Sullivan, "Newly Formed 'Equity' Banks: Financing 'via' an SBIC", 35 Wis.B.Bull. 47 (1962); Suss, "SBA Small Business Financing Programs: A Joint Undertaking by Government and Private Institutions", 18 Bus.Law. 120 (1962); Bowman, "Small Business Investment Companies", 17 Bus.Law. 1005 (1962); Stewart, "Small Investment Companies: An Introduction", 32 N.Y.St.B.Bull. 391 (1961); Gilbertson, "Small Business Financing Under the Small Business Act and the Small Business Investment Act of 1958", 8 Kan.L.Rev. 538 (1960); Murphy & Netter, "Small Business Investment Act of 1958", 19 Fed.B.J. 162 (1959); McCallum, "The Small Business Investment Act of 1958—Its First Year of Operation", 45 Va.L. Rev. 1039 (1959); Evans, "A Review of Small Business Financing", 14 Bus.Law. 568 (1959); McCallum, "Loans by the Small Business Administration", 13 Bus.Law. 349 (1958); Osterman, "How the United States Department of Commerce Helps Small Business", 63 Com.L.J. 199 (1958); Sturdy, "Federal Aids to Small Business", 11 Bus.Law. 39 (Apr.1956). Comment, "Showdown at Equity Gap: A Decade of the Small Business Investment Act", 54 Va.L.Rev. 772 (1968); Comment, "The Small Business Investment Company: An Attempt to Fill the Equity Gap", 9 Vill.L.Rev. 109 (1963). See Small Business Administration v. McClellan, 364 U.S. 446, 81 S.Ct. 191, 5 L.Ed.2d 200 (1960) (holding Small Business Administration is not separate legal entity from United States, but is integral part of governmental mechanism created to accomplish what Congress deemed to be of national importance, and where Administration joined private bank in loan, and borrower became bankrupt, Administration was entitled to priority of United States in bankruptcy proceeding, even though it agreed to share any money collected with bank).

3. Garver, "Tax Factors Affecting Debt-Equity Financing for a New Small Corporation", 17 W.Res. L.Rev. 773 (1966); Loiseaux, "Loans or Capital Contribution to the Close Corporation", 38 Ref.J. 4 (1964); Comment, "Taxation—Classification of Advances to Close Corporations by Shareholders—Debt or Equity", 1964 Wis.L.Rev. 331; Comment, "Financing of Small Corporations: Debt or Equity?", 42 Marq.L.Rev. 387 (1959). See section 165 supra.

4. E. g., American Stock Exchange listing of nonvoting preferred and common shares of The Great At-

lantic & Pacific Tea Co. prior to 1959. The New York Stock Exchange does not currently list nonvoting shares. Where securities are publicly issued or traded, they and their issuers become subject to extensive federal and state regulation (see sections 292–308 infra). Relevant to close corporations are the "private offering" and "intrastate" exemptions from the registration (and prospectus) requirements and Regulation A under the Federal Securities Act of 1933 (see section 295 infra), and § 10(b) and S.E. C. Rule 10b–5 under the Federal Securities Exchange Act of 1934 (see section 298 infra). R. Kessler, New York Close Corporations ch. 18 (1968); Owen, "The Private Offering and Intrastate Exemptions Under the Securities Act of 1933", Law Notes: Corporate (July 1967), in H. Wander & W. Grienenberger, Selected Articles on Federal Securities Law 165 (ABA 1968); Duff, "First Public Financing of a Closely-Held Corporation: Securities Act of 1933 Aspects", 34 U.Mo.Kan.City L.Rev. 242 (1966). Orrick, "Non-Public Offerings of Corporate Securities—Limitations on the Exemptions under the Federal Securities Act", 21 U.Pitt.L.Rev. 1 (1959); Lane, "Securities Exemptions for Small Corporations", 8 Clev.-Mar.L.Rev. 152 (1959); Gadsby, "The Securities and Exchange Commission and the Financing of Small Business", 14 Bus.Law. 144 (1958); Latty, "The Aggrieved Buyer or Seller or Holder of Shares in a Close Corporation Under the S.E.C. Statutes", 18 Law & Contemp.Prob. 505 (1953); Note, "Federal Control Over Small Issues of Securities", 70 Harv.L.Rev. 1438 (1957).

5. Most close corporations, being small, do not require outside investment. Outside investors, furthermore, hesitate to invest in close corporations because of the risk involved, and lack of a ready market for the sale of such securites. Lack of a ready market makes valuation of the shares of close corporations difficult for estate and gift tax purposes. See Kascle, "Valuation of Closely Held Corporations", 43 Taxes 454 (1965); Panel Discussion: "Problems in Valuing Stock of a Close Corporation", N.Y.U. 23d Inst. on Fed.Tax. 1261 (1965); Kragen, "Some Thoughts on the Valuations of Closely Held Business Interests", 43 Calif.L.Rev. 781 (1955).

6. See M. Lore, Thin Capitalization (1958); Comment, "Financing of Small Corporations: Debt or Equity?", 42 Marq.L.Rev. 387 (1959). See section 165 supra. Hybrid securities might be treated as shares for tax purposes (see section 163 supra).

7. Creditor status of a shareholder might be denied and his loans treated as capital contributions (i. e.,

To the extent of financing by shares, the possible advantages of classification into two or more classes (or series) should be considered. As a general rule, of course, where shares are to be issued proportionately to the consideration and received by the corporation therefor and to the desired shareholder participation in control, dividends, and net assets, authorization and issue of a single class will ordinarily suffice. Otherwise, or even under such circumstances when class voting might be desirable in connection with the election of classes of directors (thus assuring representation of each class of shares on the board of directors) or shareholder voting for other purposes (thus assuring each class of shares a veto), or for tax advantages (e. g., preferred shares "bailout"), two or more classes (or series) of shares might better be authorized and issued.[8]

In setting up the initial financial structure, it not only should meet the needs of the situation, but in addition should be protected by safeguards to assure against future changes adversely affecting the minority, such as increases of the authorized shares, issue of originally authorized but unissued, shares, reacquisition or redemption of shares, reissue of such shares, and recapitalizations, which would disturb the initial scheme, which often is based on various provisions at the shareholder level binding the shareholders and through them the directors and officers. The usual rules to protect the shareholder's proportionate interest—fiduciary duties of management and doctrine of preemptive right—might afford some but less than adequate protection to the minority.[9]

Limited liability is as much an attribute of the close corporation as of other corporations. However, grounds for disregarding corporateness or regarding the corporation as an instrumentality of the shareholders, thereby subjecting the shareholders to personal liability, arise far more frequently in the case of close corporations than in other corporations.[10]

FINANCIAL STRUCTURE OF CLOSE CORPORATION—TAX ASPECTS

262. Taxwise, the close corporation offers greater flexibility and pitfalls, and greater possibility of tax avoidance and evasion, than other corporations. As a result, financial transactions of close corporations (with their frequent shareholder-director-officer merger) are subject to the close scrutiny of taxing authorities.

Taxwise, there are more potential flexibility and pitfalls in the close corporation than in other corporations, and greater possibility of tax avoidance and evasion.[1] As a result,

---

shares) in cases of inadequate capitalization (i. e., too-thin financing by shares) (see section 146 supra). In receivership, bankruptcy, and corporate reorganization proceedings, courts might disallow creditor claims of shareholders or disallow them to one or more other classes of claims (see section 152 supra). See section 165 supra. Hybrid securities might be held to be shares rather than debt securities (see section 164 supra). The lender, of course, might insist that corporate obligations to inside creditors be expressly subordinated to his loan. Inadequate financing might result in disregard of corporateness (see section 146 supra).

8. For purposes of eligibility for Subchapter S election, a small business corporation may not have more than one class of shares, but only issued and outstanding shares are counted. The issued shares must be identical as to rights, interest, and preferences, but different groups of shares can qualify as one class if they are identical except for the right of each group to elect a proportionate number of directors. Treas.Reg. § 1.1371–1(g) (1959). See also section 270 infra (voting trust and irrevocable proxy). See also Reed, "Advantages of a Preferred Stock Recapitalization in Closely Held Corporation Situations", 45 Taxes 596 (1967); Henderson, "The Use of Different Classes of Stock in Maintaining Control in the Close Corporation", N.Y.U. 24th Inst. on Fed.Tax. 531 (1966); Herwitz, "Allocation of Stock Between Services and Capital in the Organization of a Close Corporation", 75 Harv.L.Rev. 1098 (1962).

9. Honikman v. Ruedd, Inc., 363 F.2d 839 (5th Cir. 1966) (permitting holders of majority of outstanding shares to approve amendment of articles of incorporation for issuance of additional shares). See sections 172–175 supra.

10. See sections 146–148 supra.

1. R. Kessler, New York Close Corporations ch. 17 (1968); T. Ness & E. Vogel, Taxation of the Closely-Held Corporation (1967); Tax Guide For Small Business (Int.Rev.Serv.1959); Tillinghast, "Prob-

financial transactions of close corporations (with their frequent shareholder-director-officer merger) are subject to the close scrutiny of taxing authorities.

The current federal income tax is only 22 percent at the corporate level on the first $25,000 of taxable corporate income (normal tax), becoming 48 percent (22 percent normal tax and 26 percent surtax on such income in excess of $25,000. The corporation, taxwise, offers possible advantages through capital gains treatment and employee fringe benefits.[2]

A small business corporation might come under statutory taxing provisions not applicable to other corporations: (a) Subchapter S election not to be taxed at the corporate level (thus avoiding double taxation and achieving a tax status somewhat resembling that of a partnership), if the corporation has a single class of shares, is closely-held, and otherwise meets the qualifications of Subchapter S and makes the necessary

lems of the Small or Closely Held Corporation Under the Revenue Act of 1962", N.Y.U. 22d Inst. on Fed.Tax. 697 (1964); Kess, "Tax Planning for the Closely Held Business", 40 Taxes 590 (1962); McDowell, "Gift Tax Problems in Organization and Reorganization of Family Corporations", N.Y.U. 20th Inst. on Fed. Tax. 213 (1962); Andrews, Friedland & Shapiro, "Working-Capital Financing of Small Business", 24 Law & Contemp.Prob. 68 (1959).

2. See Murdock, "Primer for Compensating Executives in Closely-Held Corporations", 50 Chi.B.Rev. 146 (Dec.1968); Davidson, "Tax Considerations in the Close Corporation" 3 U.B.C.L.Rev. 143 (Dec. 1968); Sweeney, "Deferred Compensation Plans for the Close Corporation and Subchapter S Corporation", N.Y.U. 26th Inst. on Fed.Tax. 1103 (1968); Ridley, "Employee Benefit Plans for the Close Corporation", 1967 Ins.L.J. 273; Byron, "Profit-Sharing Plans for the Closely Held Corporation", 40 Taxes 47 (1962); Moore, "Stock Options for Directors in Small Corporations", 11 Catholic U.L.Rev. 396 (1962); Peril, "The Uses of Pension and Profit-Sharing Plans for Small or Medium-Sized Businesses", 66 Dick.L.Rev. 143 (1962); Specter, "Pension and Profit Sharing Plans; Coverage and Operation for Closely Held Corporations and Professional Associations", 7 Vill.L.Rev. 335 (1962); Vesely, "Compensation Arrangements in Smaller Corporations—Compensation Through the Use of Corporate Stock", 29 U.Cin.L.Rev. 52 (1960); Note, "Stock Options for Directors in Small Corporations", 11 Clev.-Mar.L.Rev. 396 (1962). See section 76 supra.

unanimous shareholder election;[3] and (b) "Section 1244 stock" provisions liberalizing

3. Int.Rev.Code of 1954, 26 U.S.C.A. §§ 1371–1378. A Subchapter S or tax-option corporation is not subject to the corporate income tax, the accumulated earnings tax, or the personal holding company tax. The corporate income, whether distributed or not, is taxed to the shareholders—as ordinary income except for excess of long-term capital gain over short-term capital loss. Any corporate net operating loss is passed through to the shareholders to the extent of their respective aggregate investment in the corporation in shares or indebtedness, with carry back and carry forward provisions. Byrne v. Comm'r, 361 F.2d 939 (7th Cir. 1966) (shareholder held not entitled to any deduction for net operating losses of tax-option corporation since basis of his shares had been reduced to zero and, for such purpose, retained earnings and profits accumulated were not contributions by taxpayer to corporation's capital and did not serve to increase such basis); Perry v. Comm'r, 392 F.2d 458 (8th Cir. 1968) (holding shareholder's personal guaranties of corporate indebtedness, prior to their performance, did not increase maximum amount of corporate losses deductible by him); Roob v. Comm'r, 50 T.C. No. 90 (1968) (salary of executive of Subchapter S corporation who with wife and eight children each owned one-tenth of shares held too low, and dividends reallocated in order to reflect his services). Eligibility requirements must be maintained to avoid termination of tax-option status. Crumbley, "Avoid Unintentional Disqualifications of Subchapter S Corporations", 44 Taxes 374 (1966). Reasonable share transfer restrictions should be imposed to prevent the number of shareholders from exceeding 10, and to prevent ineligible shareholders, such as nonresident aliens or trusts, from becoming shareholders. See sections 281, 282 infra. See Old Virginia Brick Co. v. Comm'r, 367 F.2d 276 (4th Cir. 1966) (executors of estate kept open for 18 years held in effect testamentary trustees and ineligible shareholder). No more than one class of shares (except for classes with proportionate rights to elect classes of directors) should be outstanding. Pollack v. Comm'r, 392 F.2d 409 (5th Cir. 1968). The mere issuance of share options, warrants, or convertible debentures does not affect eligibility. Rev.Rul. 67–269, 1967 Int.Rev.Bull.No. 34, at 20. Even where only one class of shares is authorized in the articles of incorporation, more than one class of shares, for purposes of Subchapter S eligibility, can result from shareholder voting agreements. Comment, "Shareholder Agreements and Subchapter S Corporations", 19 Tax L.Rev. 391 (1964). Or from some shares being subject to irrevocable proxies. Rev.Rul. 63–226, 1963–2 Cum.Bull. 341. Or possibly from some shares being subject to voting trusts. But see A. & N. Furniture & Appliance Co. v. United States, 271 F.Supp. 40 (S.D.Ohio 1967). Or from loans by shareholders to their corporation which, if hybrids, might be treated as a second class of shares—see sections 162–164 supra —or which, in the case of too-thin incorporation— see section 166 supra—might be treated as a second class of shares or, when owned substantially in the same proportion as shares, as contributions to capital rather than a second class of shares. Treas.

deductions for losses on such shares, if the corporation financially is within prescribed

limitations and otherwise meets the tests and has the requisite "plan" under Section 1244.[4] These provisions have been previously discussed.[5]

Payments by a close corporation to its shareholder-"officers" of large "salaries"[6]

Reg. § 1.1371-1 (1966); Portage Plastics, Inc. v. United States, — F.Supp. — (W.D.Wis.1969); Brock, "The Dangers of Stockholder Loans to Subchapter S Corporations", 53 A.B.A.J. 670 (1967); Comment, "Shareholder Lending and Tax Avoidance in the Subchapter S Corporation", 67 Colum. L.Rev. 495 (1967). Formation of a subsidiary resulting in membership in an affiliated group, terminates Subchapter S ineligibility. Coca-Cola Bottling Co. v. United States, — F.Supp. — (D.N. M.1969). See generally Silverman, "Continued Problems May Lie Ahead in Subchapter S Second Class of Stock Area", 45 Taxes 639 (1967); McGaffey, "Requirement That a Subchapter S Corporation May Have Only One Class of Stock", 50 Marq. L.Rev. 365 (1966); Note, "Application of the Thin Incorporation Doctrine to the Subchapter One-Class-of-Stock Requirement", 1967 Duke L.J. 1202. See Hall v. Secretary of Health, Education & Welfare, CCH Corp. L. Guide ¶11,861 (D.Okl.1965) (holding earnings of tax-option corporation allocated but not actually distributed to retired shareholder did not impair his right to collect social security benefits); Wilhelm v. United States, 257 F.Supp. 16 (D.Wyo. 1966) (holding that employee-shareholders, like other employees, may exclude from their taxable income food and lodging furnished for convenience of their tax-option corporation). See generally I. Schreiber, Subchapter S; Planning and Operations (1967); B. Bittker & J. Eustice, Federal Income Taxation of Corporations and Shareholders §§ 14.-01-14.10 (2d ed. 1966); I. Schreiber, Subchapter S; Its Opportunities and Pitfalls (1965); Braverman, "Special Subchapter S Situations—Regulations Run Rampant", 114 U.Pa.L.Rev. 680 (1966); Gadon, "Subchapter S—After Election Then What?", 38 Temp.L.Rev. 392 (1965); Hrusoff, "Election, Operation and Termination of a Subchapter S Corporation", 11 Vill.L.Rev. 1 (1965); Levi, "The Subchapter S Election: Friend or Foe?", 32 Mo.L.Rev. 185 (1965); Ward & Bradford, "Section 1244 and Subchapter S—Two Allies of the Close Corporation", 18 U.Fla.L.Rev. 270 (1965); Calkins, "How to Use Subchapter S and Section 1244 Without Running Into Trouble", 15 W.Res.L.Rev. 349 (1964); Note, "Tax Planning With Subchapter S in 1967: Problems and Prospects", 53 Va.L.Rev. 1161 (1967); Note, " 'Locked-in Earnings'—How Serious a Problem Under Subchapter S?", 49 Va.L.Rev. 1516 (1963); Plowden-Wardlaw, "Subchapter S and Partnerships as Vehicles Governing Family Business", N.Y.U. 21st Inst. on Fed.Tax. 981 (1963); Peden, "Problems Resulting from the Death of the Principal Partner or Principal Shareholder of Subchapter S Corporation", id., 1051; Caplin, "Subchapter S—Election of Small Business Corporations", 51 Ky.L.J. 308 (1962); Lourie, "Subchapter S After Three Years of Operation", 18 Tax L.Rev. 99 (1962); Bersch, "A Roadmap of Subchapter S", 3 Wm. & Mary L.Rev. 99 (1961); Swietlik, "Subchapter S: What Is It and How Does It Work", 44 Marq. L.Rev. 470 (1961); Willis, "Subchapter S: A Lure to Incorporate Proprietorships and Partnerships", 6 U.C.L.A.L.Rev. 505 (1959), 11 J.Taxation 66 (1959); Comment, "Stockholder Agreements and

Subchapter S Corporations", 19 Tax L.Rev. 391 (1964); Comment, "Subchapter S: A New Concept in the Tax Status of Business Associations", 44 Cornell L.Q. 560 (1959). In considering Subchapter S election, the effect of state taxation of the income of the corporation and of the shareholders should be considered. Relevant are such questions as (a) state-tax law provision for similar election; (b) the deductibility by the corporation for federal income taxes in computing its state income tax when the corporation avoids federal taxes under Subchapter S, and (c) the deductibility by the shareholders for federal income taxes they paid on the corporation's undistributed income. Matter of Garlin v. Murphy, 51 Misc.2d 477, 273 N.Y.S.2d 374 (Sup.Ct.1966); Note, "Double State Tax on Subchapter S Corporation", 27 J.Taxation 254 (1967). Some 12 percent of active American corporations, 173,000 out of 1,424,000, are currently electing Subchapter S taxation. See also D. Kahn, Basic Corporate Taxation 284 et seq. (ICLE 1970).

4. Int.Rev.Code of 1954, 26 U.S.C.A. § 1244; B. Bittker & J. Eustice, Federal Income Taxation of Corporations and Shareholders § 4.09 (2d ed. 1966); Johnston, "Small Business Stock", 54 A.B.A.J. 922 (1968); Ward & Bradford, "Section 1244 and Subchapter S—Two Allies of the Close Corporation", 18 U.Fla.L.Rev. 270 (1965); Calkins, "How to Use Subchapter S and Section 1244 Without Running Into Trouble", 15 W.Res.L.Rev. 349 (1964); Farrell, "Losses on Small Business Stock", 31 N.Y.St.B.Bull. 98 (1959); Moore & Sorlien, "Adventures in Subchapter S and Section 1244", 14 Tax L.Rev. 453 (1959); Price, "The Small Business Tax Revision of 1958", 14 Bus.Law. 329 (1959); Wright & Libin, "Impact of Recent Tax Stimulants on Modest Enterprises: A 'New Look' for Messrs. Small and Smaller Business", 57 Mich.L.Rev. 1131 (1959). See also D. Kahn, Basic Corporate Taxation 267 et seq. (ICLE 1970); White, "Recurring and New Problems Under Subchapter S", N.Y.U. 27th Inst. on Fed.Tax 755 (1969); Rosenkranz, "Subchapter S: The Presidential Proposals", 55 A.B.A.J. 1181 (1969).

5. See section 76 supra.

6. See Int.Rev.Code of 1954, 26 U.S.C.A. § 162 (allowing as deduction reasonable allowance for salaries or other compensation for personal services actually rendered). "The basic factors bearing on reasonableness of compensation in such cases are generally said to be: the executive's qualifications; the nature and scope of his work; the size and complexities of the business; comparison of the compensation paid with gross income, with net income, with dividends paid, with prevailing rates of compensation in comparable corporations, with

or to its shareholder-"creditors" of "interest" on debt or hybrid securities [7] might not be allowed as a corporate tax deduction, or such payments, as well as payments for certain redemptions of corporate shares,[8] might be treated as dividends for tax purposes.[9]

amounts paid by the same corporation in previous years, and with the prior earning capacity of the executive; and general economic conditions", 2 G. Washington, V. Rothschild, T. Ness & R. Sobernheim, Compensating the Corporate Executive 863 (3d ed. 1962); C. Halsey & M. Peloubet, Federal Taxation and Unreasonable Compensation (1964); Fullmer, "Compensation for Employee-Shareholders of Closely Held Corporations", 17 W. Res.L.Rev. 807 (1966); Hawkins, "Tax Factors in Balancing the Interests of Investor-Shareholders and Officer-Shareholders", 12 W.Res.L.Rev. 215 (1961); Boehm, "Compensation Arrangements in Smaller Countries: Ordinary Compensation Arrangements for the Closely Held Corporation", 29 U.Cin.L.Rev. 157 (1960); Note, "Excessive Salaries in a Closely Held Corporation", 18 Clev.-Mar.L.Rev. 188 (1969); Note, "Worth of a Man: A Study of Reasonable Compensation in Close Corporations", 38 Calif.L.Rev. 269 (1965). The maxim to be followed is: Maximum amount payable at the minimum tax cost to the parties. Excessive salaries can disqualify shareholder-employees from social security retirement benefits. Johnson v. Celebrezze, Civ.No. 1–65–16 (D.Idaho 1965). Or result in an operating loss in excess of the owner's basis for his shares and corporate indebtedness to such owner. **Byrne v. Comm'r**, 361 F.2d 939 (7th Cir.1966). More than 35 percent of American corporations, 509,000 out of 1,424,000 report no taxable income, many as the result of deductions for salaries. One approach to setting reasonable compensation is to estimate reasonable dividends and allow the balance for salaries. See sections 243–256 supra.

7. Int.Rev.Code of 1954, 26 U.S.C.A. § 163 (allowing as deduction all interest paid within taxable year on indebtedness).

8. Cavitch, "Costly Traps in Corporate Stock Purchases from Shareholders", 15 W.Res.L.Rev. 338 (1964); Note, "Stock Redemptions in Close Corporations: A Plan for Taxation", 67 Yale L.J. 112 (1957). See section 339 infra.

9. Gurtman v. United States, 353 F.2d 212 (3d Cir. 1965); Zipp v. Comm'r, 259 F.2d 119 (6th Cir. 1958), cert. denied 359 U.S. 934, 79 S.Ct. 649, 3 L.Ed.2d 636 (1959); Cohen, "Taxation in Stockholders' Forgiveness of Accrued Salaries", 9 Clev.-Mar.L.Rev. 362 (1960); Brafford, "The Constructive Receipt of Dividends by Stockholders of a Closely Held Corporation", 46 Ky.L.J. 515 (1958), 47 Ky.L.J. 17 (1958), 47 Ky.L.J. 378 (1959); Note, "Stock Redemptions in Close Corporations: A Plan for Taxation", 67 Yale L.J. 112 (1957). See section 339 infra.

Obviously, the application of the federal personal holding company tax should be avoided.[10]

In most close corporation situations, the federal penalty tax on improper accumulation of earnings poses no serious problem because of its $100,000 lump-sum credit.[11]

Life insurance plans to fund agreements for disposition of a deceased shareholder's interest,[12] gifts to closely-held corporations,[13] and the valuation of inactively-traded shares in closely-held corporations for estate, inheritance, and gift tax purposes, pose several problems.[14]

10. See section 76, n. 22 supra. Closely-held non-investment corporations (at least 50 percent of whose shares are owned by not more than five persons) with some income from investments, personal service contracts, etc., can become subject to the tax if other operations result in a loss or insufficient income. See section 339 infra.

11. Int.Rev.Code of 1954, 26 U.S.C.A. §§ 531–537. See section 76 supra and section 339 infra.

12. See section 282, n. 30 infra.

13. See Note, "Taxation of Gifts to Closely Held Corporations", 57 Colum.L.Rev. 240 (1957).

14. C. Bosland, Estate Tax Valuation in the Sale or Merger of Small Firms (1963); Norris, "Valuation of Stock of Closely Held Corporations for Estate Tax Purposes", 46 Taxes 183 (1968); Drymalski, "Valuation of Stock of a Subchapter S Corporation", 56 Ill. B.J. 672 (1968); Griffith, "The Use of Subchapter S in the Sale of a Corporate Business", 53 A.B.A.J. 87 (1967); Sneed & Will, "Family Corporation Uses in Estate Planning", 20 Okla.L.Rev. 243 (1967); Kascle, "Valuation of Closely Held Corporations", 43 Taxes 454 (1965); Panel Discussion: "Problems in Valuing Stock of a Close Corporation", N.Y.U. 23d Inst. on Fed.Tax. 1261 (1965); Butala, "Valuation of Securities of Closely-Held Corporations", 14 W. Res.L.Rev. 193 (1963); Crowe, "Retention or Disposal of a Close Corporation Interest at Death", 17 J.Am.Soc'y C.L.U. 355 (1962); Weed, "Technique in Valuation of Close Corporations", N.Y.U. 20th Inst. on Fed.Tax. 597 (1962); Kragen, "Some Thoughts on the Valuation of Closely-Held Business Interests", 43 Calif.L.Rev. 781 (1955); Comment, "The Estate and Gift Tax Valuation of Closely-Held Holding Company Stock", 50 Va.L.Rev. 337 (1964); Note, "The Estate and Gift Tax Valuation of Closely Held Holding Company Stock", 50 Va.L.Rev. 337 (1964); Note, "Taxation-Valuation of Securities in a Close Corporation for Federal Estate Tax Purposes", 8 Vill.L.Rev. 92 (1962). See Int.Rev.Code of 1954, 26 U.S.C.A. § 303 (Distribution in redemption of stock to pay death taxes); id., § 6166 (Extension of time for payment of estate tax where estate consists largely of interest in closely held business).

D.   MANAGEMENT STRUCTURE

MANAGEMENT STRUCTURE OF CLOSE CORPORATION—IN GENERAL

263. The management structure of the close corporation can follow a variety of patterns, depending on the extent to which the person or persons concerned desire to function in ways different from the normal corporate pattern. In setting up the management structure, the respective traditional managerial functions of shareholders, directors, and officers must be considered. In many close corporation situations, centralizing managerial functions as fully as possible in shareholders (as such, as directors, and as officers) may be desirable, despite the traditional separation of ownership (in shareholders) and management (in board of directors and officers) in the corporation.

The management structure of the close corporation can follow a variety of patterns, depending on whether the close corporation is to be a "one-man corporation", subsidiary, affiliated corporation, "family corporation", etc., and the extent to which those concerned desire to function in ways different from the normal corporate pattern. The considerations especially applicable to the close corporation will be stressed in this section and succeeding sections, in contrast to the more traditional corporate management structure outlined in Chapter 9.

In setting up the management structure, the respective traditional managerial functions of shareholders, directors, and officers must be considered.[1] Under the "concession theory", corporations are created by the state and must conform to the "statutory norms", which may or may not have built-in flexible provisions. At the opposite extreme is the idea, often expressed but too infrequently applied, that shareholders may agree among themselves to do what they want so long as there is no damage to creditors or others.[2]

In many close corporation situations, centralizing managerial functions as fully as permissible in shareholders (as such, as directors, and as officers) may be desirable, despite the traditional separation of ownership (in shareholders) and management (in board of directors and officers) in the corporation.

SHAREHOLDERS—INITIAL AND SUBSEQUENT

264. The initial shareholders, and their respective interests, are fixed at the time of incorporation. Subsequent changes can be controlled by appropriate share transfer restrictions and limitations on the authorization and issue of additional shares. To the extent that any close corporation managerial setup is based on arrangements among shareholders in one capacity or another, changes in the identity and proportionate holdings of shareholders might dislocate such managerial setup.

At the time of incorporation, the initial shareholder group, and their respective share interests, are fixed. Subsequent changes can be controlled by appropriate share transfer restrictions (along with options) relating to issued shares[1] and by appropriate limitations on the authorization and issue of additional shares.

Obviously, to the extent that any close corporation managerial setup is based on arrangements among shareholders in one capacity or another, changes in the identity of

---

[§ 263]

1. See, e. g., Basil, "Managerial Problems of the Enterprise", 18 Vand.L.Rev. 1733 (1965); Logan, "Methods to Control the Closely Held Kansas Corporation", 7 Kan.L.Rev. 405 (1959); Ballard, "Arrangements for Participation in Corporate Management Under the Pennsylvania Business Corporation Law", 25 Temp.L.Q. 131 (1951). See also Lipman, "Anticipating Disagreement in a Close Corporation", 41 N.Y.St.B.J. 497 (1969).

2. For a trenchant criticism of the "concession theory", see R. Stevens, Handbook on the Law of Private Corporations § 146 (2d ed. 1949).

[§ 264]

1. See sections 281, 282 infra.

shareholders or in their proportionate interests might dislocate such managerial setup.[2]

SHAREHOLDERS' VOTING RIGHTS

265. Shares, absent provision to the contrary, carry one vote each. Shareholders, under modern statutes, can act by a unanimous writing in lieu of a meeting. While cumulative voting is a means of assuring minority shareholder representation on the board of directors, there are often more satisfactory alternative methods of achieving such result in the close corporation. There are often also more satisfactory alternatives in the close corporation to class voting, contingent voting rights, disproportionate voting rights, and nonvoting shares.

Where shares are to be issued in proportion to consideration received and to the desired respective interests of the shareholders, a single class of shares would ordinarily be authorized. Such shares would carry one vote per share for each matter, unless cumulative voting were in effect with respect to elections of directors.

Formalities of Shareholder Action

A growing number of modern statutes permit shareholder action to be taken by unanimous written consent in lieu of the otherwise required shareholder vote at a duly-convened shareholder meeting.[1]

Cumulative Voting

Cumulative voting is mandatory in some jurisdictions, permissive in others.[2] In the latter jurisdictions, a provision authorizing cumulative voting can be inserted in the articles of incorporation.[3]

Cumulative voting is a form of proportional representation to assure any desirable minority representation on the board. In the usual close corporation situation, where the board of directors is of small size, holders of small minority interests would not be assured of any representation on the board by cumulative voting.[4]

More satisfactory methods of assuring representation on the board by minority shareholders in close corporations than cumulative voting are shareholder agreements requiring the parties to vote for certain persons as directors[5] or sufficiently high greater-than-normal quorum/voting requirements for shareholder election of directors to render ineffective any such election without the concurrence of minority shareholders.[6]

Class Voting

Another means of assuring representation on the board of directors of different shareholders is to authorize classes of shares and a classified board of directors, so that each class of shares elects its class of directors.[7] In all other respects, the rights of the holders of the different classes can be identical. Or class voting requirements can in effect

[§ 264]

2. McKeon v. Santa Claus of California, Inc., 230 Cal.App.2d 359, 41 Cal.Rptr. 43 (1964) (defendant, who owned one-half of majority interest and required some additional shares from a minority shareholder, ordered to offer one-half of such additional shares to plaintiff, who owned other half of majority interest, where plaintiff and defendant had agreed to preserve status quo); O'Neal, "Arrangements Which Protect Minority Shareholders Against 'Squeeze-Outs'", 45 Minn.L.Rev. 537 (1961).

[§ 265]

1. Comment, "Corporations: Close Corporations: Strictness of Requirements at Meetings of Shareholders and Directors", 14 S.C.L.Q. 408 (1962). See section 190 supra. Delaware permits shareholders action by less-than-unanimous written consent without a meeting unless prohibited by the articles of incorporation.

2. See section 189 supra.

3. E. g., McKinney's N.Y.Bus.Corp.Law, § 618.

4. C. Williams, Cumulative Voting for Directors ch. VIII (1951).

5. See section 267 infra. Even where cumulative voting is in effect, shareholders can nevertheless agree among themselves to vote in a certain way for directors. Sensabaugh v. Polson Plywood Co., 135 Mont. 562, 342 P.2d 1064 (1959); E. K. Buck Retail Stores v. Harkert, 157 Neb. 867, 62 N.W.2d 288, 45 A.L.R.2d 774 (1954).

6. See section 266 infra.

7. See section 189 supra.

give a veto power to a class, which might consist of only a single shareholder.[8] As indicated in connection with cumulative voting, there are often satisfactory alternative methods of achieving the same results.

Miscellaneous

Where shares are classified because of financial considerations,[9] there is normally no need in the close corporation for authorizing shares with contingent voting rights, shares with disproportionate voting rights, or non-voting shares.[10]

SHAREHOLDER QUORUM/VOTING REQUIREMENTS

266. Greater-than-normal shareholder quorum/voting requirements in effect enable minority shareholders to veto action at the shareholder level. Such requirements, like direct shareholder veto provisions, are inconsistent with majority rule and, if broad in application, might be invalid except as sanctioned by statute. Modern statutes tend to permit such requirements when imposed by the articles of incorporation or possibly the bylaws. Such requirements often enhance the probability of deadlock and other paralysis at the shareholder level.

There are two ways of giving a minority shareholder protection against his fellow shareholders' doing something objectionable to such shareholder: (a) shareholder veto provisions, and (b) greater-than-normal quorum/voting requirements for shareholder action. Both devices, unlike "shareholder agreements" which are often positive in terms, are negative.

Shareholder veto provisions are inconsistent with the idea of corporate-government-by-the-majority and, unless of rather limited scope, run the risk of invalidity.[1]

8. See Aldridge v. Franco Wyoming Oil Co., 24 Del. Ch. 349, 14 A.2d 380 (Sup.Ct.1940).

9. See section 261 supra.

10. See section 189 supra.

1. See Matter of William Faehndrich, Inc., 2 N.Y.2d 468, 161 N.Y.S.2d 99, 141 N.E.2d 597 (1957); Benin-

Greater-than-normal quorum/voting requirements for shareholder action are also

tendi v. Kenton Hotel, Inc., 294 N.Y 112, 60 N.E.2d 829, 159 A.L.R. 280 (1945). Cf. Roland Park Shopping Center, Inc. v. Hendler, 206 Md. 10, 109 A.2d 753 (1954); Katcher v. Ohsman, 26 N.J.Super. 28, 97 A.2d 180 (Ch.Div.1953); Ripin v. United States Woven Label Co., 205 N.Y. 442, 98 N.E. 855 (1912).

In the Benintendi case, the plaintiff held one-third of the shares; the defendant two-thirds. They unanimously adopted four bylaws requiring:

Bylaw # 1. Unanimous vote of all shareholders for shareholder action (or unanimous vote of shareholders present in person or by proxy if 30 days' notice of the meeting were given);

Bylaw # 2. Unanimous vote of all shareholders to elect the three-man board of directors;

Bylaw # 3. Unanimous vote of all directors for board of directors action;

Bylaw # 4. Unanimous vote of all shareholders to amend the bylaws.

The New York Court of Appeals held, 4–3 (with the majority adhering to the "concession theory"), that bylaw # 1 violated the statutory scheme of corporate government with various powers of decision lodged in the majority or prescribed fractions of shareholders; that bylaw # 2 violated the statutory policy in favor of election of directors by a plurality of shareholder votes; that bylaw # 3 flouted the statutory purpose of vesting management in the board acting by majority vote, subject to a majority (one-third) quorum requirement; and that bylaw # 4 was not violative of statutory or public policy; and indicated that even if such provisions had been in the articles of incorporation the result would have been the same. The invalid bylaw provisions were held unenforceable as a unanimous shareholder agreement. The three dissenting judges, contending that holders of all the shares of a corporation "may do with it as they will, even to giving it away, provided the rights of creditors are not involved and the public policy of the State is not offended", agreed that bylaws # 1 and # 2 were invalid as bylaws (but could be enforced as a shareholder agreement), contended that bylaw # 3 came within express statutory exceptions and should have been upheld, and agreed that bylaw # 4 was valid.

In Model, Roland & Co. v. Industrial Acoustics Co., 16 N.Y.2d 703, 261 N.Y.S.2d 896, 209 N.E.2d 553 (1965) (holding that *bylaw* requiring two-thirds shareholder vote to amend certain bylaws, including one fixing number of directors, was ineffective under McKinney's N.Y.Bus.Corp.Law, §§ 601(a), 614(b), 616(a)(2) providing for adoption, amendment, or repeal of bylaws by majority shareholder vote unless greater vote is required by *articles of incorporation*).

In Roland Park Shopping Center, Inc. v. Hendler, supra, a charter requirement of unanimous vote for shareholder action was held valid.

The New Jersey court in Katcher v. Ohsman, supra, held that a bylaw of a New York corporation requiring 90 percent shareholder approval for all shareholder and board of directors action was valid

inconsistent with majority rule, but are being sanctioned by statutes in a growing number of American jurisdictions.[2]

Prior to the adoption of the New York statute, a greater-than-normal quorum/voting requirement of sufficiently limited application for specified shareholder action, especially when in the articles of incorporation, might have been upheld,[3] but any such requirement of broad application, whether in the articles of incorporation [4] or bylaws,[5] was invalid.

> on common-law principles (the New York law not having been put in evidence). While the corporation had no such bylaw, the other shareholders had represented to the plaintiff when he bought one-third of the shares that there was such a bylaw, and the court ordered the bylaws reformed to include such a provision. For refusal of court to order reformation of articles of incorporation to include unanimous quorum/voting requirement for shareholder and board of directors action, see Green v. Karlson Associates, 159 N.Y.S.2d 245 (Sup. Ct.1957). But see Pawley v. Ostrowsky, 155 N.Y.L. J. No. 113, 17 (Sup.Ct.1966) (confirming arbitrator's award ordering amendment of articles of incorporation to include provision requiring unanimous shareholder and board of directors vote, where shareholders had agreed for such requirement in bylaws where it would have been ineffective).

In the Ripin case, supra, the New York Court of Appeals unanimously upheld an articles of incorporation provision of limited scope—requiring unanimous shareholder consent to amend the articles of incorporation to change the size of the four-man board of directors.

See also O'Neal, "Giving Shareholders Power to Veto Corporate Decisions: Use of Special Charter and By-Law Provisions", 18 Law & Contemp.Prob. 451 (1953).

2. See, e. g., ABA–ALI Model Bus.Corp.Act § 30 (per articles of incorporation or bylaws); Del.Gen.Corp. Law, § 216 (1967) (per articles of incorporation or bylaws); McKinney's N.Y.Bus.Corp.Law, § 616 (per articles of incorporation).

3. Ripin v. United States Woven Label Co., discussed supra note 1.

4. Matter of Boulevard Theatre & Realty Co., 195 App.Div. 518, 186 N.Y.S. 430 (1st Dep't 1921), aff'd mem., 231 N.Y. 615, 132 N.E. 910 (1921); see also Benintendi v. Kenton Hotel, Inc., discussed supra note 1.

5. Benintendi v. Kenton Hotel, Inc., discussed supra note 1.

In 1948, New York adopted section 9 of the former Stock Corporation Law [6] expressly authorizing provisions in the articles of incorporation specifying:[7] (a) that the number of shares necessary to constitute a quorum for the transaction of any business or of any specified item of business at a shareholder meeting shall be a number greater than the majority or plurality prescribed by law in the absence of such provision; and (b) that the number of shareholder votes or consents necessary for the transaction of any business or of any specified item of business at a shareholder meeting, including amendments of the articles of incorporation, or the giving of any consent, shall be a number greater than the proportion prescribed by law in the absence of such provision.

Section 9 was subsequently amended in 1949 and 1951, and replaced by the Business Corporation Law in 1963.[8]

Under present New York law, such a provision can be included in the original articles of incorporation or can be inserted by amending the articles of incorporation by appropriate shareholder action [9] and filing in the office of the secretary of state.

6. [1948] N.Y.L.Rev'n Comm'n Rep. 1948 Legis.Doc. No. 65(K) 381–427; Israels, "The Close Corporation and the Law", 33 Cornell L.Q. 488 (1948).

7. Former McKinney's N.Y.Stock Corp.Law, § 9(1) (c), (d).

8. McKinney's N.Y.Bus.Corp.Law, § 616; see also id. § 709 (greater-than-normal board of directors quorum/voting requirements), discussed infra section 274. [1951] N.Y.L.Rev'n Comm'n Rep. 1951 Legis.Doc.No. 65(H) 251–318; Israels, "The Commission and the Corporation Laws", 40 Cornell L.Q. 686, 692–693 (1955).

9. Amendments of the articles of incorporation adding, changing, or striking out such provision, must be authorized at a meeting of shareholders by vote of the holders of two-thirds of all outstanding shares entitled to vote thereon, or of such greater proportion of shares or class or series of shares as may be provided *specifically* in the articles of incorporation for adding, changing or striking out such provision. McKinney's N.Y.Bus.Corp.Law, § 616(b).

Where there is a greater-than-normal quorum/voting requirement, New York law requires that notice of the existence of such provision be noted conspicuously on the face or back of each share certificate issued by the corporation.[10]

Under present New York law, greater-than-normal quorum/voting requirements for shareholder action are valid only if they are in the articles of incorporation. Where they appear only in the bylaws, they are invalid.[11]

Obviously, greater-than-normal quorum/voting requirements preclude any shareholder action without the required quorum or vote, which means that any shareholder whose holdings are sufficiently large can in effect veto such action by absenting himself from any shareholder meeting or by not voting in favor of or by voting against such action. Where 100 percent quorum or vote is required for shareholder action, each holder of voting shares enjoys in effect such a veto at the shareholder level.

Greater-than-normal quorum/voting requirements, of course, often enhance the probability of deadlock and other paralysis at the shareholder level, such as might result from the incapacity of a shareholder. The latter possibility suggests coupling a moderate quorum requirement with a high or even unanimous voting requirement based on those present or represented at the meeting.

10. McKinney's N.Y.Bus.Corp.Law, § 616(c).

11. Globe Slicing Machine Co. v. Hasner, 223 F.S. 589 (S.D.N.Y.1963), aff'd on other grounds 333 F.2d 413 (2d Cir. 1964), cert. denied 379 U.S. 969, 85 S.Ct. 666, 13 L.Ed.2d 562 (1965); Model, Roland & Co. v. Industrial Acoustics Co., 16 N.Y.2d 703, 261 N.Y.S. 2d 896, 209 N.E.2d 553 (1965); Matter of William Faehndrich, Inc., 2 N.Y.2d 468, 161 N.Y.S.2d 99, 141 N.E.2d 597 (1957). Cf. Roland Park Shopping Center, Inc. v. Hendler, 206 Md. 10, 109 A.2d 753 (1954); Matter of American Fibre Chair Seat Corp., 265 N.Y. 416, 193 N.E. 253 (1934).

"SHAREHOLDER AGREEMENTS" GOVERNING SHAREHOLDER FUNCTIONS

267. Shareholder agreements purporting to bind the parties, as shareholders, to vote as therein provided are, absent fraud on the minority or other illegal object, valid in nearly all jurisdictions. When such agreements purport to bind the parties, as directors, in exercising their discretion in the management of the corporation, such agreements have been upheld by some courts if they do not unduly impinge on such discretion or injure creditors, at least when all shareholders are parties to such agreements. Even unanimous agreements which substantially impinge on the directors' discretion or other "statutory norms" are invalid, in the absence of express statutory recognition of such agreements. For breach of valid provisions, specific performance is the most adequate remedy. A transferee of any shares without notice of such agreement would take the shares free from the obligations of such agreement.

Because of the traditional separation of ownership and control in the corporation, shareholders of close corporations often agree among themselves to vote collectively in certain matters.

An agreement among shareholders to combine in the exercise of their shareholder functions is valid in the majority of jurisdictions, on the ground that shareholders are generally under no fiduciary duties, and what they may do individually they may do collectively,[1] assuming lack of fraud by con-

1. Ringling Bros.-Barnum & Bailey Combined Shows, Inc. v. Ringling, 29 Del.Ch. 610, 53 A.2d 441 (Sup. Ct.1947); McQuade v. Stoneham, 263 N.Y. 323, 189 N.E. 234 (1934); Annot., 45 A.L.R.2d 799 (1956). In Sensabaugh v. Polson Plywood Co., 135 Mont. 562, 342 P.2d 1064 (1959), a bylaw requiring straight voting was held to violate the Montana constitution requiring cumulative voting. Two of the five judges indicated that a contract among the shareholders to such effect would be valid but that the bylaw could not be enforced as such a contract. One judge concurred in the result only. The fourth judge held that the bylaw should be enforced as a contract among the shareholders who approved the bylaw but not as against dissenters. The fifth judge held that such a contract violated public policy.

See Trefethen v. Amazeen, 93 N.H. 110, 36 A.2d 266 (1944) (shareholders' agreement not to vote upheld);

trolling shareholders against minority shareholders[2] or some other illegal object. By such a shareholder agreement, the shareholders usually agree either to cast their votes in a certain way for various matters[3]

or to pool their votes and cast them jointly as they agree or an arbitrator determines.[4]

Such agreements usually do not run afoul of prohibitions on shareholders' selling their votes or proxies.[5]

Under a few older cases in some jurisdictions, such an agreement, especially when all shareholders were not parties, was unlawful since it limited in advance the shareholders in voting their shares in the best interests of the corporation and separated voting power from ownership.[6]

Nickolopoulos v. Sarantis, 102 N.J.Eq. 585, 141 A. 792 (1928) (shareholders agreement to vote disproportionately to voting rights invalid as secret agreement). See R. Kessler, New York Close Corporations ch. 8 (1968); 1 G. Hornstein, Corporation Law and Practice §§ 157–165 (1959); 1 F. O'Neal, Close Corporations: Law and Practice §§ 5.01–5.30 (1958); Morganstern, "Agreements for Small Corporation Control", 17 Clev.-Mar.L.Rev. 324 (1968); Elson, "Shareholder Agreements: A Shield for Minority Shareholders of Close Corporations", 22 Bus.Law. 449 (1967); Logan, "Methods to Control the Closely Held Kansas Corporation", 7 Kan.L.Rev. 405 (1959); O'Neal, "Protecting Shareholders' Control Agreements Against Attack", 14 Bus.Law. 184 (1958); Sturdy, "Significance of 'Form' and 'Purpose' in Determining the Effectiveness of Agreements Among Stockholders to Control Corporate Management", 13 Bus.Law. 283 (1958); Johnston, "Shareholders Agreements in Closely Held Corporations", 47 Ill.B.J. 330 (1958); Cary, "How Illinois Corporations May Enjoy Partnership Advantages: Planning for the Closely Held Firm", 48 Nw.U.L.Rev. 427 (1953); Ballard, "Arrangements for Participation in Corporate Management Under the Pennsylvania Business Corporation Law", 25 Temp.L.Q. 131 (1951); Hornstein, "Stockholders' Agreements in the Closely Held Corporation", 59 Yale L.J. 1040 (1950); Comment, "Corporations—Shareholders' Voting Agreements—Drafting Precautions", 46 Mich.L.Rev. 70 (1947); Comment, "'Shareholders' Agreements' and the Statutory Norm", 43 Cornell L.Q. 68 (1957). For court holdings that a fiduciary relationship exists between shareholders who are parties to such agreements, see Helms v. Duckworth, 101 U.S.App.D.C. 390, 249 F.2d 482 (1957); Williams v. Fitting, 157 N.Y.L.J. No. 12, 18 (Sup. Ct.1967). See notes 6, 27 infra. For statutory formulations on "shareholder agreements", see Del. Gen.Corp.Law, § 218 (1967); Fla.Gen.Corp.Law, Part II, Close Corporations § 608.0105 (1963); Md. Gen.Corp.Law, § 45 (1951); McKinney's N.Y.Bus. Corp.Law, § 620; N.C.Bus.Corp.Act § 55–73 (1957) (10 year limitation). See notes 28, 31, 41–42 infra. The 1969 Model Act revision provides that agreements among shareholders regarding the voting of their shares shall be valid and enforceable in accordance with their terms and shall not be subject to the provisions regarding voting trusts.

2. See section 240 supra.

3. See, e. g., Clark v. Dodge, 269 N.Y. 410, 199 N.E. 641 (1936). In agreeing to vote for named persons as directors, they are bound to do so only so long as such directors act faithfully and competently. Fells v. Katz, 256 N.Y. 67, 175 N.E. 516 (1931); Brightman v. Bates, 175 Mass. 105, 55 N.E. 809 (1900).

4. See, e. g., Stein v. Capital Outdoor Advertising, Inc., 273 N.C. 77, 159 S.E.2d 351 (1968) (holding that proxy, without specified duration, expired after 11 months); Ringling Bros.-Barnum & Bailey Combined Shows, Inc. v. Ringling, 29 Del.Ch. 610, 53 A. 2d 441 (Sup.Ct.1947) (finding no implied irrevocable proxy from recalcitrant shareholder in favor of other shareholder); Smith v. San Francisco & N. P. Ry., 115 Cal. 584, 47 P. 582 (1897) (finding implied irrevocable proxy). See McKinney's N.Y.Bus.Corp. Law, § 609(f) (5) (authorizing irrevocable proxy to person designated by or under written shareholder voting agreement under § 620(a) or his nominee).

5. But cf. Morgenstern v. Cohon, 2 N.Y.2d 302, 160 N.Y.S.2d 633, 141 N.E.2d 314 (1957) (sustaining defense of illegality under former McKinney's N.Y. Stock Corp.Law, § 47 of agreement to indemnify person for loss on resale of shares purchased by person to vote for reelection of directors); Reilly v. Korholz, 137 Colo. 20, 320 P.2d 756 (1958) (New York law). But see McKinney's N.Y.Bus.Corp.Law, § 609(e) (prohibiting shareholder from selling his vote or issuing proxy to vote to any person for any sum of money or anything of value, except as authorized in § 609 (proxies) and § 620 (shareholder voting agreements; articles of incorporation provisions as to control of directors)).

6. Thomas v. Sanborn, 172 So.2d 841 (Fla.Dist.Ct. App.1965) (holding shareholder voting pool within voting pool to violate Florida public policy because it denied to member of first pool excluded from second pool free exercise of judgment by his fellow voting pool members). Compare Burnett v. Word, Inc., 412 S.W.2d 792 (Tex.Civ.App.1967) (upholding agreement provisions binding parties in exercise of their shareholder functions but not with respect to functions as directors). Roberts v. Whitson, 188 S. W.2d 875 (Tex.Civ.App.1945) (agreement also held revocable). See also Stott v. Stott, 258 Mich. 547, 242 N.W. 747 (1932); Creed v. Copps, 103 Vt. 164, 152 A. 369 (1930); Palmbaum v. Magulsky, 217 Mass. 306, 104 N.E. 746 (1914); Gage v. Fisher, 5 N.D. 297, 65 N.W. 809 (1895). Quaere, as to validity of agreement among controlling but not all shareholders to vote with respect to extraordinary corporate matters under circumstances when controlling shareholders might be subject to fidu-

"Shareholder agreements" often have provisions dealing with matters other than the exercise of shareholder voting rights, such as matters within the proper purview of the management functions of the board of directors or share transfer restrictions, deadlock, and arbitration provisions, etc.

If an agreement among shareholders binds them with respect not only to their shareholder functions but also to any director functions they might have, the agreement can be said to be one among directors as well as among shareholders. If such a "shareholder agreement" (it being to such an extent a "director agreement") contains provisions limiting the discretion of the board of directors in managing the corporation in the best interests of the corporation, such provisions might be invalid.[7] Such

"shareholder agreements" have been before the New York courts more often than before the courts of any other jurisdiction. Four opinions of the New York Court of Appeals are leading cases on the subject.

The first case, Manson v. Curtis,[8] involved an agreement entered into by the holders of a majority, but not all, of the shares. The parties provided that each was to name three directors; one of the parties, the plaintiff, was to be continued in his present position of general manager for a year and, as such, was to manage the business of the corporation and shape its policy; the president was to be only the nominal head. The court said that, standing alone, the provision concerning the election of directors was innocent and legal, but went on to find the agreement invalid on the ground that its fundamental and dominant intent and pur-

ciary duties. Leventhal v. Atlantic Finance Corp., 316 Mass. 194, 55 N.E.2d 20, 154 A.L.R. 260 (1945) (shareholder agreement between two sole shareholders for dissolution in event of stated contingencies and prohibiting parties from otherwise causing dissolution held to waive statutory right to file petition for dissolution); Apfelbaum v. American Binder Co., 10 Misc.2d 899, 173 N.Y.S.2d 753 (Sup.Ct. 1958); Matter of Hega Knitting Mills, Inc., 124 N.Y.S.2d 115 (Sup.Ct.1953) (but requiring all shareholders to be parties to such agreement); cf. Flanagan v. Flanagan, 273 App.Div. 918, 77 N.Y.S.2d 682 (2d Dep't 1948), aff'd mem., 298 N.Y. 787, 83 N.E.2d 473 (1948). Hornstein, "Judicial Tolerance of the 'Incorporated Partnership'", 18 Law & Contemp. Prob. 433, 448 (1953). See section 240 supra and section 340 infra.

7. For liberal statutory treatment of such agreements, see N.C.Bus.Corp.Act § 55–73 (1957); McKinney's N.Y.Bus.Corp.Law, § 620 (shareholder agreements; provision in articles of incorporation as to control of directors); 1969 Model Act revision (business and affairs of corporation to be managed by board of directors except as may be otherwise provided in articles of incorporation). Florida, Maryland, and Delaware have close corporation statutes permitting sterilization or even abolition of the board of directors. See section 259, n. 2 supra. Compare Manson v. Curtis, 223 N.Y. 313, 323, 119 N.E. 559, 562 (1918) ("Clearly the law does not permit the stockholders to create a sterilized board of directors"); Anderson & Lesher, "The New Business Corporation Law", 33 N.Y.St.B.J. 308, 428 (1961). Analogous are situations where the directors transfer their corporation's shares in a subsidiary to themselves (and others) as voting trustees. Adams v. Clearance Corp., 35 Del.Ch. 459, 121 A.2d 302 (Sup.Ct.1956) (voting trust upheld). Or where shareholders attempt to control corporate policy by

will. D'Arcangelo v. D'Arcangelo, 137 N.J.Eq. 63, 43 A.2d 169 (1945) (provisions held void). Or where testator sets up voting trust or testamentary trust of shares. Matter of Burns, 40 Misc.2d 377, 243 N.Y.S.2d 96 (Sur.Ct.1963), aff'd 22 A.D.2d 912, 255 N.Y.S.2d 655 (2d Dep't 1964), aff'd mem., 15 N.Y.2d 1008, 260 N.Y.S.2d 20, 207 N.E.2d 614 (1965) (holding that will which directed executrix to incorporate testator's business, leaving particulars of incorporation to her, and directed issue of 25 percent of corporation's shares to herself and 75 percent to two employees, did not empower her to include in articles of incorporation permissive provisions requiring unanimity for shareholder and board of directors action). In Matter of Hirshon, 13 N.Y.2d 787, 242 N.Y.S.2d 218, 192 N.E.2d 174 (1963), the majority shareholder of a corporation by will transferred his shares to trustees, providing that they should be elected directors of the corporation, that two of them should be elected president and secretary, that his wife or daughter was to serve as chairman of the board and receive a certain salary, and that certain business policies should be followed. The court, 5 to 2, upheld the trust except for the provisions requiring the trustees to elect and compensate the wife or daughter as chairman of the board. The two dissenting judges contended that the entire trust was invalid. Compare Billings v. Marshall Furnace Co., 210 Mich. 1, 177 N.W. 222, 9 A.L.R. 1239 (1920) (trust held invalid), with In re Pittock's Will, 102 Or. 159, 199 P. 633, 17 A.L.R. 218 (1921) (trust upheld, but testator's directions to trustee construed as precatory). Or management contracts. Kennerson v. Burbank Amusement Co., 120 Cal.App.2d 157, 260 P.2d 823 (1953); Marvin v. Solventol Chemical Products, Inc., 298 Mich. 296, 298 N.W. 782 (1941).

8. 223 N.Y. 313, 119 N.E. 559 (1918).

pose was to vest management solely and exclusively in the plaintiff.[9] So construed, the latter provisions were found to deprive the directors of their statutory duty to manage the corporation.[10]

Manson v. Curtis was significant not only for its holding, but also for its dictum on the permissible purview of "shareholders' agreements": [11]

"An ordinary agreement, among a minority in number, but a majority in shares, for the purpose of obtaining control of the corporation by the election of particular persons as directors is not illegal. Shareholders have the right to combine their interests and voting powers to secure such control of the corporation and the adoption of and adhesion by it to a specific policy and course of business. Agreements upon a sufficient consideration between them, of such intendment and effect, are valid and binding, if they do not contravene any express charter or statutory provision or contemplate any fraud, oppression or wrong against other stockholders or other illegal object."

The Manson case also contained dictum which was to become more important in later years: [12]

"The rule that all stockholders by their universal consent may do as they choose with the corporate concerns and assets, provided the interests of creditors are not affected, because they are the complete owners of the corporation, cannot be invoked here."

In the second case, McQuade v. Stoneham,[13] the court was again presented with an agreement made, not between all shareholders, but between the holder of the majority of the shares and two other shareholders. The agreement stated that the parties were to use their best efforts to keep one another in office as directors and officers, and that salaries, amount of capital, number of shares, bylaws or policy were not to be changed except by unanimous consent of the parties to the agreement.[14] The court held the agreement invalid, the majority [15] stating: [16]

"The power to unite is . . . limited to the election of directors and is not extended to contracts whereby limitations are placed on the power of the directors to manage the business of the corporation by the selection of agents at defined salaries."

In the third case, Clark v. Dodge,[17] the parties to the agreement, rather than representing less than all the shares, held *all* of the shares in the corporation. The agreement provided that Dodge was to vote in his capacity as shareholder for Clark as director, and to vote in his capacity as director for Clark as general manager, so long as Clark proved faithful, efficient, and

---

9. The agreement was found to be non-severable, and invalid in toto.

10. 223 N.Y. at 323, 119 N.E. at 562 (1918). Even this aspect of the agreement would have been valid if the agreement had specified or the court had inferred the qualification "subject to the discretion of the board of directors." See Lorillard v. Clyde, 86 N.Y. 384 (1881).

11. 223 N.Y. at 319–320, 119 N.E. at 561 (1918).

12. 223 N.Y. at 325, 119 N.E. at 562 (1918), cited with approval in Clark v. Dodge, 269 N.Y. 410, 415, 199 N.E. 641, 643 (1936).

13. 263 N.Y. 323, 189 N.E. 234 (1934).

14. Selection of officers, fixing officers' salaries, and determining corporate policies are obviously board of directors, not shareholder, functions. Even they might have been upheld if the agreement had specified or the court had inferred the qualification "subject to the discretion of the board of directors" (and "so long as they remained faithful, efficient, and competent" with respect to the officers' tenure).

15. The agreement was held illegal on the additional ground that the plaintiff, as a city magistrate, was prohibited from engaging in business. Lehman & Crouch, JJ., concurred solely on such additional ground, pointing out that a combination of the majority shareholders, except for an illegal object, was not against public policy.

16. 263 N.Y. 323, 329, 189 N.E. 234, 236 (1934).

17. 269 N.Y. 410, 199 N.E. 641 (1936).

competent.[18] It was further agreed that Clark was to receive one-fourth of the profits, and this right was strengthened by a provision that no unreasonable salaries which would tend to decrease profits were to be paid. The court [19] held that the complaint for specific enforcement of the agreement stated a cause of action; the court avoided the broad language of the McQuade case by saying that if there was any invasion of the statutory powers of directors, such impingement was slight. In giving validity to the instrument, the court in a unanimous opinion discounted the restrictions on the discretion of directors: [20]

> "There was no attempt to sterilize the board of directors, as in the Manson and McQuade cases. The only restrictions on Dodge were (a) that as a stockholder he should vote for Clark as a director—a perfectly legal contract; (b) that as director he should continue Clark as general manager, so long as he proved faithful, efficient and competent—an agreement which could harm nobody; (c) that Clark should always receive as salary or dividends one-fourth of the 'net income'. For the purpose of this motion, it is only just to construe that phrase as meaning whatever was left for distribution after the direc-

tors had in good faith set aside whatever they deemed wise; (d) that no salaries to other officers should be paid, unreasonable in amount or incommensurate with services rendered—a beneficial and not a harmful agreement.

> "If there was any invasion of the powers of the directorate under that agreement, it is so slight as to be negligible; and certainly there is no damage suffered by or threatened to anybody."

The test of validity was described as follows: [21]

> "If the enforcement of a particular contract damages nobody—not even, in any perceptible degree, the public—one sees no reason for holding it illegal, even though it impinges slightly upon the broad provision of section 27 [which vested management in the board of directors]. Damage suffered or threatened is a logical and practical test, and has come to be the one generally adopted by the courts. . . . Where the directors are the sole stockholders, there seems to be no objection to enforcing an agreement among them to vote for certain people as officers."

This case has been characterized as standing for the proposition that: [22]

> " . . . an agreement which damages no one is valid and enforceable. There was no damage to the public, for the court found that the impingement on the statutory norm was, at the most, slight. There apparently was no damage to the creditors of the corporation, for no creditor was found to be involved. There was no damage to shareholders for all of them were parties to the agreement. Presumably this 'no damage' test would not be satisfied if there were more than a slight impingement on the statutory norm, if creditors were aggrieved, or if there were

---

18. Such a qualification, even if not expressed in the agreement, might have been inferred by the court. Fells v. Katz, 256 N.Y. 67, 175 N.E. 516 (1931).

19. The unanimous opinion was written by Crouch, J., who had concurred with Lehman, J., in McQuade v. Stoneham, supra note 15. Clark v. Dodge actually involved two New Jersey corporations, but the court considered the agreement from the point of view of the New York statutory norms. See also Gramatan Clothes, Inc. v. Rose, 159 N.Y.L.J. No. 16, 16 (Sup.Ct.1968) (enforcing as valid under law of forum agreement involving foreign corporation despite possible violation of law of state of incorporation). It has been indicated that at common law, management rests with the shareholders. Union Pacific Ry. v. Chicago, R. I. & P. Ry., 163 U.S. 564, 595–598, 16 S.Ct. 1173, 1185–1186, 41 L.Ed. 265, 276–277 (1895). Cf. Katcher v. Ohsman, 26 N.J.Super. 28, 97 A.2d 180 (Ch.Div.1953) (common law applied by New Jersey court to situation involving New York corporation where New York law was not introduced in evidence).

20. 269 N.Y. at 417, 199 N.E. at 643 (1936).

21. 269 N.Y. at 415, 199 N.E. at 642 (1936).

22. Comment, " 'Shareholders' Agreements' and the Statutory Norm", 43 Cornell L.Q. 68, 72–73 (1957).

shareholders who were not parties to the agreement."

In the fourth case, Long Park, Inc. v. Trenton-New Brunswick Theatres Co.,[23] the court was faced with an agreement involving *all* shareholders, as in Clark v. Dodge, with provisions to the effect that one of the corporate parties was to be termed "manager" and was to be given "full authority and power to supervise and direct the operation and management" of the principal business of the corporation.[24] The court found that such a vesting of management operated to sterilize the board of directors.[25] The agreement was held invalid as being a clear violation of the statute placing the duty of management in the hands of the directors. It was felt that the agreement went far beyond the provisions in Clark v. Dodge.

From these four cases and a host of lower court cases, the following general conclusions may be drawn: [26]

Agreements by shareholders *qua* shareholders (absent fraud on the minority or other illegal object) involve no impingement on the "statutory norms" and are valid. Agreements which go beyond this and only slightly impinge on the "statutory norms" are, under the "no damage" test of Clark v. Dodge, valid if they do not injure creditors, the public, or the shareholders; the public is not damaged by slight impingements on the "statutory norms"; shareholders clearly are not damaged if they *all* are parties to the agreement, and possibly are not damaged even when less than all of the shareholders are parties.[27] Agreements which involve

23. 297 N.Y. 174, 77 N.E.2d 633 (1948). See also Kennerson v. Burbank Amusement Co., 120 Cal. App.2d 157, 260 P.2d 823 (1953).

24. 297 N.Y. at 177, 77 N.E.2d at 634 (1948).

25. Such construction would have been avoided by the court's inferring the qualification "subject to the discretion of the board of directors".

26. Comment, " 'Shareholders' Agreements' and the Statutory Norm", 43 Cornell L.Q. 68, 74–76 (1957). Careful amendment of the articles of incorporation and bylaws, along with a "shareholder agreement", might validly effectuate the wishes of those involved in the corporation. Simonson v. Helburn, 198 Misc. 430, 97 N.Y.S.2d 406 (Sup.Ct.1950). In Miller v. Vanderlip, 285 N.Y. 116, 33 N.E.2d 51 (1941), some unnamed shareholders of a Michigan corporation in financial difficulties approached the plaintiff who in turn approached the defendants. The complaint did not allege that the plaintiff and defendants were then shareholders or directors of the corporation. Plaintiff and defendants set up a plan to rehabilitate the corporation, to try to increase the size of the board of directors, and to urge the plan on the board insofar as within their power lay. The plan called for the election of the plaintiff as president and general manager for $9,000 annual salary and share options. The defendants cooperated only to the extent of increasing the size of the board of directors. The Court of Appeals, 4–3, upheld the cause of action for breach of contract. The majority stated that, there being no allegation that the parties were directors, there was no attempt to influence the discretion of the direc-

tors; agreeing to urge the plan was not illegal; even if the parties were shareholders, they may agree to combine their votes; and that even if the Michigan statute were the same as the then New York statute requiring the president to be a director and barring a three-year engagement as president, the plaintiff could still be the general manager. The dissenting opinion by Lehman, C. J. (compare his concurring opinion in McQuade v. Stoneham, supra note 15) contended that it was against public policy to permit one seeking the presidency of a corporation to obtain from others (directors, officers, etc.), who can influence the board of directors, a binding promise to advocate his employment at a previously agreed upon compensation. In accord with Clark v. Dodge, supra note 17, are Cohen v. Wacht, 124 N.Y.S.2d 207 (Sup.Ct.1953), aff'd mem., 282 App.Div. 1054, 126 N.Y.S.2d 910 (2d Dep't 1953), appeal denied, 283 App. Div. 660, 127 N.Y.S.2d 820 (2d Dep't 1954); Martocci v. Martocci, 2 Misc.2d 330, 42 N.Y.S.2d 222 (Sup. Ct.1943), aff'd mem., 266 App.Div. 840, 43 N.Y.S.2d 516 (1st Dep't 1943); Simonson v. Helburn, supra. Cf. Matter of Hega Knitting Mills, Inc., 124 N.Y.S. 2d 115 (Sup.Ct.1953) (requiring all shareholders to be parties to agreement binding shareholders qua shareholders). In accord with Long Park, Inc. v. Trenton-New Brunswick Theatres Co., supra note 23, is Abbey v. Meyerson, 274 App.Div. 389, 83 N.Y. S.2d 503 (1st Dep't 1948), aff'd mem., 299 N.Y. 557, 85 N.E.2d 789 (1949).

27. Matter of Buckley (Rickerson), 183 Misc. 189, 50 N.Y.S.2d 54 (Sup.Ct.1944); Johnston, J., dissenting in Flanagan v. Flanagan, 273 App.Div. 918, 77 N.Y. S.2d 682 (2d Dep't 1948), aff'd mem., 298 N.Y. 787, 83 N.E.2d 473 (1948); Lehman & Crouch, JJ., concurring in McQuade v. Stoneham, 263 N.Y. 323, 333, 189 N.E. 234, 238 (1934). Contra, Rochester v. Bergen, 265 App.Div. 547, 39 N.Y.S.2d 840 (2d Dep't 1943), aff'd mem., 291 N.Y. 656, 51 N.E.2d 933 (1943). See also, Matter of Lockley v. Robie, 301 N.Y. 371, 93 N.E.2d 895 (1950), reargument denied 301 N.Y. 731, 95 N.E.2d 409 (1951) (where parties to agreement when made did not own but later acquired all outstanding shares); Matter of Hega

substantial impingements on the "statutory norms", even when all shareholders are parties thereto as in Long Park, Inc. v. Trenton-New Brunswick Theatres Co., thereby precluding damage to them, are invalid because of damage to the public.

The New York Business Corporation Law, effective in 1963, expressly provides that an agreement between two or more shareholders, if in writing and signed by the parties thereto, may provide that in exercising any voting rights, the shares held by them shall be voted as therein provided, or as they may agree, or as determined in accordance with a procedure agreed upon by them.[28]

The statute also validates a provision in the articles of incorporation, when authorized by all shareholders,

> "otherwise prohibited by law because it improperly restricts the board in its management of the business of the corporation, or improperly transfers to one or more shareholders or to one or more persons or corporations to be selected by him or them, all or any part of such management otherwise within the authority of the board." [29]

The New York Business Corporation Law also expressly permits the articles of incorporation to provide for shareholder election of all or specified officers,[30] in which case such officers would be removable, with or without cause, only by shareholder vote.[31]

In a leading Delaware case, Abercrombie v. Davies,[32] a rather elaborate "shareholder agreement" was at issue. In 1947, a Delaware corporation was formed, to exploit an Arabian oil and gas concession. It had 10 shareholders, eight of whom were corporations and two of whom were individuals. Under an organization agreement, each shareholder was allowed to name one director for each 5,000 shares held. The articles of incorporation provided for cumulative voting. The number of directors was 15, elected proportionately.

In 1954, five of the corporate shareholders and one individual shareholder, who was also the president and a director of the

Knitting Mills, Inc., 124 N.Y.S.2d 115 (Sup.Ct.1953) (holding, if agreement is among all of the holders of the outstanding shares, the fact that the corporation has additional authorized and unissued shares is immaterial). Quaere, whether all shareholders need be parties where shareholder voting governed by agreement is subject to fiduciary duties. See section 240 supra and section 340 infra.

28. McKinney's N.Y.Bus.Corp.Law, § 620(a); Kessler, "Drafting a Shareholders' Agreement for a New York Close Corporation", 35 Fordham L.Rev. 625 (1967). Presumably, oral shareholder voting agreements, if valid under preexisting case law, would be valid under the statute. Quaere, as to irrevocable proxies implementing an oral shareholder voting agreement. See McKinney's N.Y.Bus.Corp.Law, § 609(f) (5).

29. McKinney's N.Y.Bus.Corp.Law, § 620(b). Such provision, because of the limitations that it must have unanimous consent of all shareholders, whether or not entitled to vote, and that the shares of the corporation must not be publicly listed or quoted either at the time of the agreement or thereafter, can be practically used only in close corporations.

The statute expands the ruling in Clark v. Dodge, 269 N.Y. 410, 199 N.E. 641 (1936), and, to the extent therein provided, overrules Long Park, Inc. v. Trenton-New Brunswick Theatres Co., 297 N.Y. 174, 77 N.E.2d 633 (1948). Manson v. Curtis, 223 N.Y. 313, 119 N.E. 559 (1918), and McQuade v. Stoneham, 263 N.Y. 323, 189 N.E. 234 (1934). Notice of the existence of such articles of incorporation provision must be stated on the share certificates. Agreements not "otherwise prohibited by law" under preexisting case ought to be valid under the statute even if not contained in the articles of incorporation. Compare Gramatan Clothes, Inc. v. Rose, 159 N.Y.L.J. No. 16, 16 (Sup.Ct.1968) (upholding agreement between majority shareholder and minority shareholder for their retention as directors and officers, concluding that such agreement did not bar removal for cause but that cause for removal had not been shown), with Solon v. Held, 152 N.Y.L.J. No. 121, 11 (Sup.Ct.1964) (nullifying oral agreement binding directors to retain one of parties as president at specified salary, on ground such agreement was "improperly restrictive" of board of directors discretion and therefore was invalid since not included in articles of incorporation with consent of all shareholders).

30. McKinney's N.Y.Bus.Corp.Law, § 715(b).

31. McKinney's N.Y.Bus.Corp.Law, § 716(a).

32. 36 Del. 371, 130 A.2d 338 (Sup.Ct.1957), rev'g 36 Del.Ch. 102, 125 A.2d 588, 35 Del.Ch. 599, 123 A.2d 893 (Ch.1956), 36 Del.Ch. 445, 131 A.2d 822 (Ch 1957) (on remand); see also 35 Del.Ch. 354, 118 A.2d 358 (Ch.1955).

corporation, holding together a majority of the shares, executed a so-called "Agents' Agreement" among themselves and seven others. This Agreement designated the individual shareholder and the seven others, who were the designee directors of the five corporate shareholders—in other words, eight of the 15 directors—as "agents". The Agreement provided that the shareholder parties should deposit their share certificates, accompanied by appropriate endorsement or share powers, with the agents, who would deposit them with a bank in escrow; that the shareholder parties would give their "irrevocable" proxies to the agents; that the agents should vote such proxies and should vote as directors as any seven of the eight determined or, in the event of no such determination, as directed by a disinterested arbitrator. Each corporate shareholder party reserved the right to remove its agents without cause and designate successors; the individual shareholder party's successor as agent was to be selected by a majority of the remaining agents (the agents at all times to be the same persons as the directors). The Agreement was stated to be irrevocable for 10 years unless either seven agents voted to terminate it or less than 50 percent of the outstanding shares of the corporation remained subject to the Agreement. There was also a provision whereby the Agreement could be transformed, upon the request of seven agents, into a formal voting trust.

Subsequently, at a meeting of the board of directors, a resolution amending the bylaws to authorize the board to remove any officer without cause received the affirmative votes of nine directors, but two of them voted in violation of the Agreement. In an action in California, the two agents, and their principal who had violated the Agreement were enjoined from doing so. Meanwhile, the plaintiffs, who were the other individual shareholder and two of the other corporate shareholders who were not parties to the Agreement, brought an *in rem* action

against the corporation and the parties to the Agreement to have the Agreement declared invalid under Delaware law, and for ancillary injunctive relief,[33] on the ground that it deprived the board of directors of their management function by placing control in a minority of the board or an arbitrator, or because the meetings of the board became a mere sham.

The Chancellor, citing Manson v. Curtis, Clark v. Dodge, Long Park, Inc. v. Trenton-New Brunswick Theatres Co., and other cases, first ruled that the Agreement was invalid as an unlawful attempt by certain shareholders to encroach upon the statutory power and duties imposed on directors by the Delaware corporation law.[34]

On reargument, the Chancellor found that the shareholder provisions of the Agreement were severable from such of the director provisions as were invalid, and sustained the validity of the shareholder provisions.[35]

In a supplemental opinion, the Chancellor held that the Agreement was not a voting trust (and hence invalid for noncompliance with the Delaware voting trust statutory provision), since legal title to the shares had not passed to the agents; that the Agreement was a valid pooling agreement not rendered illegal because the voting was done by agents, or by their seven-eighths vote, or by an arbitrator; and that the proxies were irrevocable since there was the requisite legal consideration and reliance.[36] In a subsequent fourth opinion, the Chancellor modified his supplemental opinion in minor respects.[37]

33. 35 Del.Ch. 354, 118 A.2d 358 (Ch.1955) (holding that appearance by nonresident defendants, not served personally would not subject them to personal liability, even if complaint be thereafter amended).

34. 35 Del.Ch. 599, 123 A.2d 893 (Ch.1956).

35. 35 Del.Ch. 599, 123 A.2d 893, 900 (Ch.1956).

36. 35 Del.Ch. 599, 123 A.2d 893 (Ch.1956).

37. 36 Del.Ch. 102, 125 A.2d 588 (Ch.1956).

On appeal, the Supreme Court of Delaware found that the Agreement was in substance a voting trust, that it did not comply with Delaware voting trust statutory requirements that the shares be transferred on the record of shareholders and that a copy of it be filed in the corporation's principal office in Delaware, and that for such non-compliance it was void as an illegal voting trust.[38]

A few corporate statutes include a special subchapter or set of sections to which eligible close corporations may elect to be subject.[39] Such close corporations remain subject to the other provisions of the corporate statute to the extent that they are not inconsistent with the close corporation sections. Expressly permitted in close corporations are written shareholder agreements, whether embodied in the articles of incorporation, bylaws, or side agreement: [40]

"relating to any phase of the affairs of the corporation, including, but not limited to, the following:

(a) Management of the business of the corporation.

(b) Declaration and payment of dividends or division of profits.

(c) Who shall be officers or directors, or both, of the corporation.

(d) Restrictions on transfer of stock.

(e) Voting requirements, including the requirements of unanimous voting of stockholders or directors.

(f) Employment of stockholders by the corporation.

(g) Arbitration of issues as to which the stockholders are deadlocked in voting power or as to which the directors are deadlocked and the stockholders are unable to break the deadlock."

Reflecting the slight development of the law concerning the special problems of close corporations in many American jurisdictions is Galler v. Galler,[41] an Illinois case, which is especially significant because the Illinois Business Corporation Act was the basis for the Model Business Corporation Act. The agreement was held valid in all respects, including the provisions for the election of certain persons to specified offices for a period

---

38. 36 Del. 371, 130 A.2d 338 (Sup.Ct.1957), 36 Del. Ch. 445, 131 A.2d 822 (Ch.1957) (on remand).

39. Pa.Bus.Corp.Law, §§ 371–386 (1968); Del.Gen. Corp.Law, §§ 341–355 (1967); Fla.Gen.Corp.Law, Part II, Close Corporations §§ 608.0100–608.0107 (1963); Md.Gen.Corp.Law, §§ 100–111 (1951).

40. Fla.Gen.Corp.Law, Part II, Close Corporations § 608.0105 (1963). North Carolina (1957) was the forerunner of such statutes. See N.C.Bus.Corp.Act § 55–73 (1957) (Shareholders' agreements) which provides: "(a) An otherwise valid contract between two or more shareholders that the shares held by them shall be voted as a unit for the election of directors shall, if in writing and signed by the parties thereto, be valid and enforcible as between the parties thereto, but for not longer than ten years from the date of its execution. . . .

"(b) Except in cases where the shares of the corporation are at the time or subsequently become generally traded in the markets maintained by securities dealers or brokers, no written agreement to which all of the shareholders have actually assented, whether embodied in the charter or bylaws or in any side agreement in writing and signed by all the parties thereto, and which relates to any phase of the affairs of the corporation, whether to the management of its business or division of its profits or

otherwise, shall be invalid as between the parties thereto, on the ground that it is an attempt by the parties thereto to treat the corporation as if it were a partnership or to arrange their relationships in a manner that would be appropriate only between partners. . . . A transferee of shares covered by such agreement who acquires them with knowledge thereof is bound by its provisions.

"(c) An agreement between all or less than all of the shareholders, whether solely between themselves or between one or more of them and a party who is not a shareholder, is not invalid, as between the parties thereto, on the ground that it so relates to the conduct of the affairs of the corporation as to interfere with the discretion of the board of directors, but the making of such an agreement shall impose upon the shareholders who are parties thereto the liability for managerial acts that is imposed by this chapter upon directors."

41. 32 Ill.2d 16, 203 N.E.2d 577 (1964), 95 Ill.App.2d 340, 238 N.E.2d 274 (1968); Oppenheim & Katz, "A Closer Look at the Close Corporation—The Supreme Court Takes a Realistic View of Shareholder-Director Agreements", 46 Chi.B.Rec. 249 (1965). See also Klausman v. Rosenberg, 221 Ga. 59, 143 S. E.2d 164 (1965).

of years, for the mandatory declaration of at least $50,000 dividends annually so long as $500,000 earned surplus was maintained, and for salary continuation of two years' salary of a deceased executive to his widow over a five-year period contingent upon such payments being income-tax-deductible by the corporation. The court construed that the agreement was to continue as long as one of the parties was living. Specific performance of the agreement was decreed.

Shareholder agreements, unlike irrevocable proxies and voting trusts, are not self-executing. For breach of valid provisions, the most adequate remedy is usually specific performance.[42] Damages are usually inadequate. Special statutory proceedings are generally not available to enforce such an agreement.[43]

If the shares are transferable, as they would be absent a valid share transfer restriction, a transferee without notice would take them free from the obligations of any shareholder agreement.[44] Accordingly,

sound practice requires that the share certificates involved bear an appropriate legend referring to the shareholder agreement.

The agreement should have an ascertainable duration to avoid its being construed as terminable at will,[45] and should be sufficiently definite to prevent its invalidity for vagueness.[46]

Other aspects of "shareholder agreements" in the close corporation, such as share transfer restrictions, deadlock and ar-

42. Chayes, "Madame Wagner and the Close Corporation", 73 Harv.L.Rev. 1532 (1960); Note, "Corporations—Specific Enforcement of Shareholder Agreements", 45 N.C.L.Rev. 228 (1966); Note, "Specific Enforcement of Shareholder Voting Agreements", 15 U.Chi.L.Rev. 738 (1948). Such a relief was granted in Galler v. Galler, 32 Ill.2d 16, 203 N.E.2d 895 (1950), reargument denied 301 N.Y. 731, 95 N.E.2d 409 (1951) (holding that derivative claim to (1968); Matter of Lockley v. Robie, 301 N.Y. 371, 93 N.E.2d 895 (1950), reargument denied 301 N.Y. 731, 95 N.E.2d 409 (1951) (4–3); Clark v. Dodge, 269 N.Y. 410, 199 N.E. 641 (1936); Clark v. Dodge, 28 N.Y.S.2d 442 (Sup.Ct.1939), aff'd mem., 261 App.Div. 1086, 28 N.Y.S.2d 464 (2d Dep't 1941) aff'd mem., 287 N.Y. 833, 41 N.E.2d 102 (1942) (except decree for reinstatement as director and officer). In Ringling Bros.-Barnum & Bailey Combined Shows, Inc. v. Ringling, 29 Del.Ch. 610, 53 A.2d 441 (Sup.Ct.1947), specific performance was not sought.

43. Matter of Lockley v. Robie, 301 N.Y. 371, 93 N.E.2d 895 (1950), reargument denied 301 N.Y. 731, 95 N.E.2d 409 (1951) (holding that derivative claim to surcharge officer could not be asserted in individual action for specific performance of shareholder agreement). See section 360 infra. Matter of Heller v. Clark Merchandisers, Inc., 9 Misc.2d 106, 154 N.Y.S.2d 150 (Sup.Ct.1955).

44. Wohl v. Miller, 145 N.Y.S.2d 84 (Sup.Ct.1955) (construing former McKinney's N.Y.Pers.Prop.Law, § 176), modified on other grounds, 5 A.D.2d 126, 169

N.Y.S.2d 233 (1st Dep't 1958), reargument denied 5 A.D.2d 823, 170 N.Y.S.2d 991 (1st Dep't 1958). See also Trefethen v. Amazeen, 93 N.H. 110, 36 A.2d 266 (1944) (transferee of shares with notice of agreement held bound thereby). Cf. Nickolopoulos v. Sarantis, 102 N.J.Eq. 585, 141 A. 792 (1928) (shareholder agreement for voting contrary to articles of incorporation and bylaws held unlawful as secret agreement). The New York statute does not expressly require notice of a shareholder voting agreement to be on the certificates reporting shares subject to such agreement.

45. See Weil v. Beresth, 154 Conn. 12, 220 A.2d 456 (1966) (upholding voting agreement under which each of four shareholders agreed to vote his shares to elect themselves as directors, etc., for so-long-as-he-is-shareholder); Galler v. Galler, 32 Ill.2d 16, 203 N.E.2d 577 (1964), 95 Ill.App.2d 340, 238 N.E.2d 274 (1968); Tschirgi v. Merchants Nat'l Bank, 253 Iowa 682, 113 N.W.2d 226 (1962) (enforcing shareholder agreement to elect directors against representative of one of shareholders); Roberts v. Whitson, 188 S.W.2d 875 (Tex.Civ.App.1945); 721 Corp. v. Morgan Guaranty Trust Co., 40 Misc.2d 395, 243 N.Y.S.2d 198 (Sup.Ct.1963), involved the sale of the majority of the shares of Tiffany and Company, a very well-known jewelry concern upon the condition that the buyers would use their best efforts to have two nominees of the seller, which operated the adjacent Bonwit Teller department store, elected to the board of directors, without any time limitation. Two years later, the buyers gave notice that they would refuse to comply with such provision. The court held the voting agreement enforceable.

46. Glazer v. Glazer, 374 F.2d 390 (5th Cir. 1967), cert. denied 389 U.S. 831, 88 S.Ct. 100, 19 L.Ed.2d 90 (1967), on remand 278 F.Supp. 476 (E.D.La.1968) (upholding jury finding in favor of plaintiff's rights to continued compensation as directors and officers of corporation under agreement that they would continue their present relationship, to carry on their various business enterprises successfully, and that they would refrain from unnecessarily interfering with welfare or duties of each other, and that they would make every effort to create good, healthy, and harmonious relationship); Most Worshipful Prince Hall Grand Lodge of Free and Accepted Masons v. Hiram Grand Lodge Masonic Temple, Inc., 32 Del.Ch. 85, 80 A.2d 294 (Ch.1951).

bitration provisions, etc., will be explored more fully later.[47]

FIDUCIARY RELATIONSHIP AMONG SHAREHOLDERS OF CLOSE CORPORATION

268. Relationships among shareholders of close corporations have been held to a higher fiduciary standard than is recognized in other corporations.

In the close corporation, not only do the normal fiduciary duties of controlling shareholders apply,[1] but in addition the courts are prone to require a higher standard of fiduciary responsibility.[2]

PROVISION AGAINST SHAREHOLDER DEADLOCK

269. Shareholder deadlock can be dealt with by three alternative methods: (a) buy-out arrangements, (b) arbitration, and (c) dissolution.

Deadlock buy-out arrangements provide for one faction to be bought out, thus preserving the corporation as a going concern and assur-

ing a fair price to those whose interests are bought out.

Provision for arbitration of future controversies among shareholders is more or less possible in several jurisdictions. Arbitration clauses, when desirable, are probably best inserted in shareholder and other agreements.

Dissolution in the event of shareholder deadlock might possibly be effected either with or without judicial proceedings. Dissolution without judicial proceedings in case of deadlock might be achieved pursuant to an advance agreement among the necessary shareholders to vote for or consent to such dissolution. Dissolution with judicial proceedings in case of deadlock, even when expressly authorized by statute, is subject to various restrictions.

Wherever shareholders are equally divided, enjoy a veto, or are subject to greater-than-normal quorum/voting requirements, the likelihood of deadlock at the shareholder level is increased.[1]

Generally, there are three alternative methods of dealing with deadlock: (a) buy-out arrangements, (b) arbitration, and (c) dissolution.

Buy-Out Arrangements

Apart from buy-out arrangements in connection with share transfer restrictions, which will be discussed later,[2] are provisions, usually in shareholder agreements, whereby in the case of deadlock (as well as other contingencies), one faction can be bought out, thus preserving the corporation as a going concern and assuring a fair price to those whose interests are bought out.[3]

---

47. See sections 269, 277, 280, 281, 282 infra.

[§ 268]
1. See sections 240, 241 supra.

2. Helms v. Duckworth, 101 U.S.App.D.C. 390, 249 F.2d 482 (1957); Manis v. Miller, 19 N.Y.S.2d 875, 280 N.Y.S.2d 675, 227 N.E.2d 596 (1967); Mendelson v. Blatz Brewing Co., 9 Wis.2d 487, 101 N.W.2d 805 (1960) (general manager held to have cause of action for squeeze-out by majority of shareholders to give job to inexperienced son of one of majority shareholders and to pressure him to sell his shares at unfair price); O'Neal & Moeling, "Problems of Minority Shareholders in Michigan Close Corporations", 14 Wayne L.Rev. 723 (1968); Hancock, "Minority Interests in Small Business Entities", 17 Clev.-Mar.L.Rev. 130 (1968); Susman, "Use of Rule 10b–5 as a Remedy for Minority Shareholders of Close Corporations", 22 Bus.Law. 1193 (1967); O'Neal, "Arrangements Which Protect Minority Shareholders Against 'Squeeze-Outs'", 45 Minn.L. Rev. 537 (1961); Conway, "The New York Fiduciary Concept in Incorporated Partnerships and Joint Ventures", 30 Fordham L.Rev. 297 (1961). See section 240, n. 22 supra. But see Bridge v. Newridge Chemical Co., 88 Ill.App.2d 337, 232 N.E.2d 551 (1967); Illinois Rockford Corp. v. Kulp, 88 Ill. App.2d 458, 232 N.E.2d 190 (1967); Boss v. Boss, 98 R.I. 146, 200 A.2d 231 (1964).

[§ 269]
1. Lehrman v. Cohen, 43 Del.Ch. 222, 222 A.2d 800 (Sup.Ct.1966) (upholding third class of one share without dividend or liquidation rights, to elect fifth director, with each of two other classes electing two directors each); R. Kessler, New York Close Corporations chs. 15, 16 (1968); Huberman, "Methods of Resolving Intra-Corporate Disputes", 3 U.B. C.L.Rev. 1 (Dec.1968); Note, "Close Corporations: Voting Trust Legislation and Resolution of Deadlocks", 67 Colum.L.Rev. 590 (1967).

2. See sections 281, 282 infra.

3. See Matter of Astey, 19 Misc.2d 1059, 189 N.Y.S.2d 2 (Sup.Ct.1959); 2 F. O'Neal, Close Corporations: Law and Practice § 9.05 (1958). In West Virginia,

Arbitration

Provision for arbitration of future controversies among shareholders is more or less possible in several jurisdictions. In some states, the enforcement of agreements to arbitrate future disputes is precluded by common-law rules or by limited statutory arbitration provisions.[4] Under the rather liberal New York arbitration statute, controversies to be arbitrable, since 1963, need no longer be capable of being the subject of an action (i. e., justiciable).[5]

Arbitration clauses, when desirable, are probably best inserted in shareholder and other agreements. Problems of drafting such clauses can be formidable.[6]

the holders of at least one-fifth of the outstanding shares may petition for judicial dissolution, in which event the holders of the majority of the outstanding shares enjoy the option of avoiding dissolution by purchasing the petitioners' shares at their face value. W.Va.Gen.Corp.Law § 3093 (1943). California permits the holders of 50 percent or more of the outstanding shares to avoid judicial dissolution by purchasing the petitioners' shares. Cal.Gen. Corp.Law § 4658 (1947); Brodsky v. Seaboard Realty Co., 206 Cal.App.2d 504, 24 Cal.Rptr. 61 (1962) (holding that deadlock buy-out provision of California statute applied even when no shares had been issued and were outstanding and that shareholder who had elected to purchase under statute could be relieved of his election within discretion of trial court); Comment, "Unusual Statutory Remedies for the Deadlocked Corporation in California: Voluntary Dissolution and the Provisional Director", 48 Calif.L.Rev. 272 (1960). See also England v. Christensen, 243 Cal.App.2d 413, 52 Cal.Rptr. 402 (1966) (construing California statute permitting purchase of its shares out of stated capital as applicable to controversy between corporation and shareholder and not among shareholders themselves).

4. Uniform Arbitration Act, 9 U.L.A. 76 (1957); approved in 1955; adopted in Arizona, Illinois, Maine, Maryland, Massachusetts, Michigan, Minnesota, Texas, Wyoming. Pirsig, "Arbitrability under the Uniform Act", 19 Bus.Law. 763 (1964); Carb, "The Need for Uniform Laws of Arbitration", 15 Bus. Law. 37 (1959). See American Arbitration Association Commercial Arbitration Rules § 42, providing: "The Arbitrator may grant any remedy or relief which he deems just and equitable and within the scope of the agreement of the parties, including, but not limited to, specific performance of a contract." See also Annot., "Power of Arbitrators to Award Injunction or Specific Performance", 70 A. L.R.2d 1055 (1960).

5. McKinney's N.Y.CPLR, § 7501 (effect of arbitration agreement): "A written agreement to submit any controversy thereafter arising or any existing controversy to arbitration is enforceable without regard to the justiciable character of the controversy and confers jurisdiction on the courts of the state

to enforce it and to enter judgment on an award." See also McKinney's N.Y.CPLR, §§ 3031–3037 (simplified procedure for court determination of disputes); Legis., 75 Harv.L.Rev. 1666 (1962). Matter of Vogel v. Lewis, 25 A.D.2d 212, 268 N.Y.S.2d 237 (1st Dep't 1966), aff'd 19 N.Y.2d 589, 278 N.Y.S.2d 236, 224 N.E.2d 738 (1967) (requiring arbitration); R. Kessler, New York Close Corporations ch. 16 (1968); Kessler, "Arbitration of Intra-Corporate Disputes under New York Laws", 19 Arb.J. 1, 85 (1964); Falls, "Arbitration Under the Civil Practice Law and Rules in New York", 9 N.Y.L.F. 335 (1963); Comment, "Arbitration as a Means of Settling Disputes Within Close Corporations", 63 Colum.L.Rev. 267 (1963); Note, "Arbitration in Close Corporations in New York", 18 N.Y.U.Intra.L.Rev. 157 (1963). Compare former N.Y.Civ.Prac.Act § 1448. Quaere, if the controversy could have been the subject of a declaratory judgment action. See Matter of Burkin (Katz), 1 N.Y.2d 570, 154 N.Y.S.2d 898, 136 N.E.2d 862, 64 A.L.R.2d 638 (1956). See section 267 supra.

6. Moskowitz v. Surrey Sleep Products, Inc., 30 A.D. 2d 820, 292 N.Y.S.2d 748 (2d Dep't 1968) (arbitration of deadlocked issue under arbitration clause in shareholder agreement enforced and dissolution denied); Matter of Herrman, 155 N.Y.L.J.No.10, 14 (Sup.Ct.1966) (provision for arbitration of all controversies "in connection with or arising out of" shareholder agreement construed not to cover dispute arising out of articles of incorporation). See 2 F. O'Neal, Close Corporations: Law and Practice §§ 9.08–9.25 (1958); Hornstein, "Controversies Under Stockholders' Agreements", 5 Arb.J. (n.s.) 62 (1950); Hornstein, "Arbitration Provisions in Stockholders' Agreements", 10 Arb.J. (n.s.) 67 (1956); Hornstein, "Arbitration in the 'Incorporated Partnership'", 12 Arb.J. (n.s.) 28 (1957); Note, "Arbitration and Unanimity Agreements in the Close Corporation", 30 St.John's L.Rev. 262 (1956); Annot., 64 A.L.R.2d 643 (1959). Cf. Matter of Burkin (Katz), 1 N.Y.2d 570, 154 N.Y.S.2d 898, 136 N.E.2d 862, 64 A.L.R.2d 638 (1956) (holding that where articles of incorporation required unanimous shareholder action, removal of director for cause required unanimous shareholder vote, absent which no litigable (and therefore arbitrable) controversy concerning same could be arbitrated under arbitration clause in shareholder agreement). See G. Seward, Basic Corporate Practice 82 (ALI 1966): "The criticism of arbitration is that it is a rough and ready remedy which often results not in a careful determination of rights but rather in a compromise". An alternative in New York is the simplified procedure possible under N.Y. CPLR, §§ 3031–3037, which may be incorporated by reference in an agreement as the means for settling disputes thereunder.

Dissolution

Dissolution in the event of shareholder deadlock might possibly be effected either with or without judicial proceedings.[7]

Dissolution without judicial proceedings in case of deadlock might be achieved pursuant to an advance agreement among the necessary shareholders to vote for or consent to such dissolution.[8]

New York has a statutory provision that the articles of incorporation may provide that any shareholder, or the holders of any specified number or proportion of shares, or of any class or series of shares, may require the dissolution of the corporation at will or upon the occurrence of a specified event.[9]

Dissolution with judicial proceedings is rarely ordered by a court in the absence of enabling legislation. Even where there is such legislation, as under the Model Business Corporation Act,[10] dissolution in the event of deadlock will be ordered only if the court is satisfied "that irreparable injury to the corporation is being suffered or is threatened by reason" of such deadlock. This subject will be explored more fully later.[11]

VOTING TRUST AND IRREVOCABLE PROXY IN CLOSE CORPORATION

270. Voting trusts, while self-executing, suffer from several disadvantages which, coupled with the fact that desired control of close corporations can be achieved in less cumbersome and more effective ways, have relegated voting trusts to relatively minor roles in close corporations.

7. See section 348 infra.

8. R. Stevens & H. Henn, Statutes, Cases and Materials on the Law of Corporations and Other Business Enterprises 881 (1965) (shareholder agreement provision implemented by irrevocable proxy). See section 267 supra and section 280 infra.

9. McKinney's N.Y.Bus.Corp.Law, § 1002. See note 3 supra.

10. ABA–ALI Model Bus.Corp.Act § 90.

11. See section 280 infra.

Irrevocable proxies, available only in limited situations, sometimes may be useful in close corporations as a means of insuring performance of voting obligations of shareholders under shareholder agreements, since irrevocable proxies, unlike shareholder agreements, are self-executing.

Voting Trusts

The voting trust is a device for concentrating shareholder voting rights, at least for the permissible duration of voting trusts, in the hands of one or more persons—the voting trustees.[1]

The principal disadvantages of the voting trust are the expenses of setting it up and exchanging the shares for voting trust certificates, the necessity of strict compliance with technical statutory requirements, the problems of selecting the voting trustees, and its limited maximum duration—10 years. Despite the fact that the voting is self-executing, these disadvantages, coupled with the fact that desired control can be achieved in less cumbersome and more effective ways, have relegated the voting trust to a relatively minor role in close corporations.[2]

Where shares are held in a voting trust, the share certificates should refer to such fact.[3]

Irrevocable Proxies

Irrevocable proxies also provide a means, sometimes for a shorter period than that allowed for a voting trust, of enabling one or more persons—the proxyholders, as agents of the shareholders giving the proxies—to exercise the voting rights belonging to such shareholders. To be irrevocable, a proxy must either be "coupled with an interest" or

1. See section 197 supra.

2. See 1 F. O'Neal, Close Corporations: Law and Practice §§ 5.31–5.35 (1958); Comment, "Voting Trusts and Irrevocable Proxies", 41 Temp.L.Rev. 480 (1968); Note, "The Voting Trust", 34 N.Y.U.L. Rev. 290, 299–301 (1959); Note, "Close Corporations: Voting Trust Legislation and Resolution of Deadlocks", 67 Colum.L.Rev. 590 (1967).

3. E. g., Del.Gen.Corp.Law, § 218 (1967); McKinney's N.Y.Bus.Corp.Law, § 621.

"given as security" in jurisdictions which adhere to such concept or comply with statutory requisites in jurisdictions with statutes governing irrevocable proxies.[4]

Available only in limited situations, irrevocable proxies sometimes may be useful in a close corporation as a means of insuring performance of voting obligations of shareholders under a shareholders' agreement, since irrevocable proxies, unlike shareholders' agreements, are self-executing.[5]

If the share certificate on its face refers to the proxy and its irrevocability, the irrevocable proxy should be effective against any purchaser of the shares.[6]

DIRECTORS—IN GENERAL

271. Corporate management being vested in the board of directors, the associates in a close corporation in order to exercise the desired control must assure themselves of such control at the board of directors level as well as at the shareholder level. Shareholder control over board of directors action can be achieved by (a) giving minority shareholders a veto over board of directors action; (b) giving directors who represent minority shareholders a veto over board of directors action; and (c) binding directors in advance to act in prescribed ways.

Since corporate management is vested in the board of directors, the associates in a close corporation, in order to exercise the control they desire, must assure themselves of such control at the board of directors level as well as at the shareholder level.

Shareholder control over board of directors action can be achieved in several ways: (a) giving minority shareholders a veto over board of directors action; (b) giving directors who represent minority shareholders a veto over board of directors action; and (c) binding the directors in advance to act in prescribed ways.

While giving a minority shareholder a veto over board of directors action would appear to be the most simple and direct approach, any such veto provision sufficiently broad in scope to accomplish the purpose might well be held invalid as unduly impinging on the statutory norm vesting management in the board of directors.[1]

Giving a minority director a veto over board of directors action might run counter to a statutory policy that board of directors action should be by a majority of directors present (assuming a quorum).[2]

A possible variation is to have classified directors, with each class of directors elected by a different class of shares, and to require approval of each class of directors for any board of directors action. The validity of

---

4. See section 196 supra.

5. E. g., McKinney's N.Y.Bus.Corp.Law, § 609(f) (5). See generally 1 F. O'Neal, Close Corporations: Law and Practice §§ 5.36–5.37 (1958); Comment, "Voting Trusts and Irrevocable Proxies", 41 Temp.L.Rev. 480 (1968); Note, "The Irrevocable Proxy and Voting Control of Small Business Corporations", 98 U. Pa.L.Rev. 401 (1950). Compare Ringling Bros.-Barnum & Bailey Combined Shows, Inc. v. Ringling, 29 Del.Ch. 610, 53 A.2d 441 (Sup.Ct.1947), with Smith v. San Francisco & N. P. Ry., 115 Cal. 584, 47 P. 582 (1897).

6. E. g., McKinney's N.Y.Bus.Corp.Law, § 609(h).

1. Kaplan v. Block, 183 Va. 327, 31 S.E.2d 893 (1944) (invalidating requirement of unanimous *shareholder* approval for all shareholder *and board of directors* action because (a) departure from statutory norm, (b) private business corporation without a board of directors is "an impossible concept", and (c) promotive of deadlock); see also Long Park, Inc. v. Trenton-New Brunswick Theatres Co., 297 N.Y. 174, 77 N.E.2d 633 (1948). But see Ripley v. Storer, 1 Misc.2d 281, 139 N.Y.S.2d 786 (Sup.Ct.1955) (sustaining validity of proposed bylaws, to be adopted by majority of shareholders, providing (a) that no contract for more than a year should be valid unless approved by a majority of the shareholders; (b) that no director shall be eligible to vote on the ratification of a contract from which he derives a financial benefit; and (c) that no resolution which provides for the payment of a bonus to any officer in excess of five percent of the corporation's net income shall be valid unless approved by a majority of the shareholders), aff'd 286 App.Div. 844, 142 N. Y.S.2d 269 (1st Dep't 1955), modified on other grounds 309 N.Y. 506, 132 N.E.2d 87 (1956). See section 275, n. 1 infra.

2. Benintendi v. Kenton Hotel, Inc., 294 N.Y. 112, 60 N.E.2d 829, 159 A.L.R.2d 280 (1945).

such provisions, when broad in scope, is questionable in many jurisdictions.

A sounder approach, in jurisdictions which permit, is to impose sufficiently greater-than-normal quorum/voting requirements for board of directors action, thereby giving a director who absents himself from a board meeting, or who does not vote in favor of any board of directors action, an effective veto.[3]

Any such director veto approach, of course, protects a minority shareholder only if he or his obedient representative is a director. Methods of assuring shareholder representation on the board have been previously discussed.[4]

Attempts to bind the directors to act in advance in prescribed ways encounter two major difficulties. The first is the legal barrier against unduly fettering (or "sterilizing") the board of directors; the second difficulty is the practical one of anticipating in advance matters which will require board of directors action in the future.[5]

DIRECTORS—NUMBER, ELECTION, AND REMOVAL

272. **A statutory minimum of three directors once had to be authorized, but modern statutes permit two directors in a two-shareholder corporation and one director in a one-shareholder corporation. The size of the board in the close corporation possibly ought to be fixed to give each shareholder a representative on the board, or otherwise to reflect proportionate share interests. In the case of two-man or one-man corporations, or in a parent-subsidiary situation, there are various ways of controlling non-shareholder directors. Where a managerial setup is predicated upon an assumption of a certain size board, safeguards should be imposed to assure against changes in the size of the board. In assuring shareholder representation on the board, the corollary prob-**

lem of removing recalcitrant directors, especially those without a financial interest in the corporation, should not be overlooked.

The number of directors is usually fixed in the articles of incorporation or bylaws.[1] In American jurisdictions, a statutory minimum of three directors generally once had to be authorized, but modern statutes increasingly permit two directors in a two-shareholder corporation and one director in a one-shareholder corporation.[2]

Where a managerial setup is predicated upon an assumption of a certain size board of directors, safeguards should be imposed to assure against changes in the size of the board.[3] Provision in articles of incorpora-

[§ 272]

1. See sections 130, 204 supra.

2. E. g., ABA–ALI Model Bus.Corp.Act § 34. The 1969 Model Act revision allows a board of directors to consist of one or more directors. Del.Gen.Corp. Law, § 141(b) (1967, Supp.1969) (board of directors to consist of one or more directors); McKinney's N.Y.Bus.Corp.Law, § 702 (permitting one or two directors in one- or two-shareholder corporation); Rudolph, "Further Thoughts on the One and Two Director Statutes", 20 Bus.Law. 781 (1965). In jurisdictions still requiring an authorized board of at least three directors, possible approaches in a two-shareholder corporation are to authorize four directors, with each shareholder electing two, either as the result of cumulative or class voting or mutual necessity where the shares are held on a 50-50 basis; or to authorize a three-man board and either remove the third initial director or have him resign without bothering to fill the vacancy, or, where permissible, establish a two-man executive committee composed of the two shareholders with the broadest possible delegated authority. See section 212 supra. In a "one-man corporation", a similar approach might succeed with respect to the second and third directors, especially in jurisdictions which, while requiring that a three-man board be authorized, permit a provision fixing a board of directors quorum at one-third. See Ray v. Homewood Hospital, 223 Minn. 440, 27 N.W.2d 409 (1947) (contract between incorporators and two outsiders for latter to serve on board of directors but take no active part in corporate affairs held void as against public policy). See Shaffer v. Buxbaum, 137 Mont. 397, 352 P.2d 83 (1960) (entity held to be in abeyance when less than three directors). England permits a single director in a private company. I. Gower, The Principles of Modern Company Law 118 (2d ed. 1957).

3. Ripley v. Storer, 1 Misc.2d 281, 139 N.Y.S.2d 786 (Sup.Ct.1955), aff'd 286 App.Div. 844, 142 N.Y.S.2d 269 (1st Dep't 1955) (4–1), modified on other

[§ 271]

3. See section 274 infra.

4. See section 267 supra.

5. See section 275 infra.

tion requiring unanimous shareholder consent to any change in the size of the board of directors should be upheld.[4]

Election and removal of directors have previously been discussed.[5]

In assuring shareholder representation on the board, the corollary problem of removing any director who is not carrying out the wishes of the shareholder or shareholders who elected him should not be overlooked. Classified directors, with any class of shareholders empowered to remove, with or without cause, any director elected by such class, is one possible solution. Advance power to remove directors without cause is probably most important where any director has no financial interest in the corporation, such as in the case of directors serving as representatives of a parent corporation on the board of its subsidiary,[6] of the required two additional directors in a "one-man corporation", or of the required third director in a two-shareholder corporation.[7]

FORMALITIES OF DIRECTOR ACTION

273. Under a growing number of statutes, unanimous written director consent without a meeting is effective in lieu of a board meeting. Even in jurisdictions without any statutory exception to the board meeting requirement, informal action by directors of close corporations without a meeting has been upheld by the courts.

Under a growing number of statutes, unanimous written director consent without

a meeting is effective in lieu of a board meeting.[1]

Even in jurisdictions without any statutory exception to the board meeting requirement,[2] informal action by directors of close corporations without a meeting has been upheld by the courts in some cases.[3]

DIRECTOR QUORUM/VOTING REQUIREMENTS

274. Greater-than-normal board of directors quorum/voting requirements in effect enable minority directors to veto action at the board of directors level. Such requirements, if broad in application, might be invalid except as sanctioned by statute. Modern statutes tend to permit such requirements when imposed by the articles of incorporation or possibly the by-laws. Such requirements often enhance the probability of deadlock at the board of directors level.

Greater-than-normal quorum/voting requirements for board of directors action can give a minority director an effective veto. Absent express statutory authorization for such requirements, their validity depends on judicial attitudes toward statutory norms.[1] Apart from statute, such requirements, at least when of broad scope, have been held

[§ 273]

1. See section 208 supra. Such statutes often provide that the articles of incorporation or bylaws can preclude board of directors action without a meeting. Such statutes are construable as preempting the field and prohibiting corporations from acting informally without complying with the statute. Village of Brown Deer v. City of Milwaukee, 16 Wis.2d 206, 114 N.W.2d 493 (1962), cert. denied 371 U.S. 902, 83 S.Ct. 205, 9 L.Ed.2d 164 (1962).

2. E. g., McKinney's N.Y.Bus.Corp.Law, § 708 ("at a meeting of the board").

3. Comment, "Corporations: Close Corporations: Strictness of Requirements at Meetings of Shareholders and Directors", 14 S.C.L.Q. 408 (1962). See section 208 supra.

[§ 274]

1. Many statutes in general terms expressly authorize provisions in articles of incorporation or bylaws not inconsistent with law. See section 128 supra. See O'Neal, "Giving Shareholders Power to Veto Corporate Decisions: Use of Special Charter and By-Law Provisions", 18 Law & Contemp.Prob. 451 (1953).

grounds 309 N.Y. 506, 132 N.E.2d 87 (1956), motion denied 309 N.Y. 976, 132 N.E.2d 335 (1956).

4. E. g., Ripin v. United States Woven Label Co., 205 N.Y. 442, 98 N.E. 855 (1912). See section 266 supra.

5. See section 192 supra.

6. England realistically permits a corporation to serve as a director. L. Gower, The Principles of Modern Company Law 120 (2d ed. 1957).

7. See note 2 supra. See Note, "Removal of Directors in Closely Held Corporations", 12 U.Fla.L.Rev. 332 (1959). One frequent device is to have directors without a financial interest in the corporation sign undated resignations effective upon acceptance.

invalid.[2] New York, in 1948[3] enacted a statute subsequently revised in 1949, 1951, and 1963, as part of the Business Corporation Law,[4] expressly authorizing provisions in the articles of incorporation specifying any or all of the following:[5] (a) that the number of directors necessary to constitute a quorum for the transaction of any business or of any specified item of business at a board of directors meeting shall be such number greater than a majority as may be specified; and (b) that the number of directors' votes necessary for the transaction of any business or of any specified item of business at any board of directors meeting shall be such number greater than a majority as may be specified. Similar provisions in the bylaws alone are presumably invalid.[6]

If the articles of incorporation contain any such provision, notice thereof is required to be noted conspicuously on the face or back of every share certificate issued by the corporation.[7]

A high director quorum requirement might preclude board of directors action during the absence or incapacity of a di-

rector. Furthermore, greater-than-normal quorum/voting requirements for board of directors action obviously enhance the probability of deadlock at the board of directors level.

"DIRECTOR AGREEMENTS"

275. Any agreement to bind directors in advance to vote in a certain way is in effect a "director agreement" although the parties might have entered into the agreement nominally as shareholders. The validity of such agreements depends upon applicable statutes and judicial attitudes toward "statutory norms". Such agreements completely fettering the discretion of the directors so as to result in a "sterilized" board ordinarily are found invalid. Agreements to keep named persons as named officers so long as faithful, efficient, and competent, to pay them reasonable salaries, to pay reasonable dividends, etc., especially when all shareholders are parties to the agreement, have been upheld.

Any agreement to bind directors in advance to vote in a certain way is, as previously discussed, in effect a "director agreement" although the parties might have entered into the agreement nominally as shareholders ("shareholder agreement"); the validity of "director agreements" depends on applicable statutes and judicial attitudes toward "statutory norms".[1]

2. Mook v. Berger, 7 A.D.2d 726, 180 N.Y.S.2d 400 (1st Dep't 1958), aff'd mem., 6 N.Y.2d 833, 188 N.Y.S.2d 219, 159 N.E.2d 702 (1959) (Connecticut law); Benintendi v. Kenton Hotel, Inc., 294 N.Y. 112, 60 N.E.2d 829, 159 A.L.R. 280 (1945).

3. [1948] N.Y.L.Rev'n Comm'n Rep.1948 Legis.Doc. No.65(K) 381–427; Israels, "The Close Corporation and the Law", 33 Cornell L.Q. 488 (1948).

4. McKinney's N.Y.Bus.Corp.Law, § 709; see id. § 616 (greater-than-normal shareholder quorum/voting requirements, discussed in section 266 supra); [1951] N.Y.L.Rev'n Comm'n Rep.1951 Legis.Doc.No. 65(H) 251–318.

5. Former McKinney's N.Y.Stock Corp.Law, § 9(1) (a), (b).

6. See Matter of William Faehndrich, Inc., 2 N.Y.2d 468, 161 N.Y.S.2d 99, 141 N.E.2d 597 (1957). Quaere, whether the formal amendment of the articles of incorporation should be required in all situations. Matter of American Fibre Chair Seat Corp., 265 N.Y. 416, 193 N.E. 253 (1934). Or whether reformation of the articles of incorporation will be ordered. Compare Pawley v. Ostrowsky, 155 N.Y.L.J. No. 113, 17 (Sup.Ct.1966), with Green v. Karlson Associates, 159 N.Y.S.2d 245 (Sup.Ct.1957).

7. McKinney's N.Y.Bus.Corp.Law, § 709(c).

1. See sections 198, 213, 267 supra. Burnstein, "Restrictions on Directors in Close Corporations", 126 N.Y.L.J. 768 (Oct. 8, 1951), id. at 786 (Oct. 9, 1951), id. at 802 (Oct. 10, 1951); Delaney, "The Corporate Director: Can His Hands Be Tied in Advance", 50 Colum.L.Rev. 52 (1950); Hornstein, "Stockholders' Agreements in the Close Corporation", 59 Yale L.J. 1040 (1950); Comment, " 'Shareholders' Agreements' and the Statutory Norm", 43 Cornell L.Q. 68 (1957). Most statutes vest management in the board of directors and make no exceptions for close corporations. The first notable exception was the North Carolina Business Corporation Act (enacted in 1955, effective in 1957): "Subject to the provisions of the charter, the business and affairs of a corporation shall be managed by a board of directors". N.C. Bus.Corp.Act § 55–24(a) (1957). The Act also deals specifically with "shareholders' agreements" in close corporations. N.C.Bus.Corp.Act § 55–73(b) (1957). The Florida, Maryland, and Delaware close corporation statutes also expressly permit "shareholder agreements", whether in the articles of incorporation, bylaws, or a side agreement, restricting

Although it has been said that the directors derive their authority from the shareholders,[2] statutes impose conditions as to the manner in which that authority may be exercised.

One of these conditions is that the directors generally may not bargain away the discretion vested in them. An agreement which purports to bind a director to vote in a certain manner so as to result in a "sterilized" board of directors ordinarily will be held invalid. On the other hand, all agreements affecting the power of directors do not result in "sterilization".[3]

In the leading case of Clark v. Dodge,[4] the New York Court of Appeals was faced with an agreement between all of the shareholders in which the defendant promised to vote as director, and to influence the other directors he controlled, to elect the plaintiff as an officer of the corporation, so long as he should "remain faithful, efficient and competent", and further promised to cause one-fourth of the net profits to be distributed to him. As his defense to an action for specific performance, the defendant claimed that the agreement resulted in sterilization of the

board of directors and was therefore void. The court rejected the argument and held that where the enforcement of an agreement would damage no one—not even the public—the impingement on the statutory norm was so slight that no public policy would be frustrated by upholding the contract.

Unfortunately, the "no damage" test is not easy of application. The validity of the agreement would seem to depend upon the number and the importance of the functions taken from the board.[5] Thus, if the agreement in effect gives broad management powers to specified shareholders it will constitute a substantial impingement upon the "statutory norms" and will therefore be void.[6]

But Clark v. Dodge illustrates that agreements to elect named persons as officers, so long as they are faithful, efficient, and competent,[7] and to fix dividends, subject to

the discretion or powers of the directors of electing close corporations. See also 1969 Model Act revision ("except as may be otherwise provided in the articles of incorporation"); McKinney's N.Y.Bus. Corp.Law, § 701 (subject to any provision in articles of incorporation authorized by § 620(b) as to control of directors or by § 715 for election of officers by shareholders, business of corporation shall be managed by its board of directors); id. § 620(b) (articles of incorporation provision as to control of directors); id. § 715(b) (articles of incorporation provision for shareholder election of officers); id. § 716 (shareholder removal of officers elected by shareholders). See section 259, note 7 supra.

2. R. Stevens, Handbook on the Law of Private Corporations § 143 (2d ed. 1949).

3. See sections 198, 213, 267 supra.

4. 269 N.Y. 410, 199 N.E. 641 (1936). Such holding, and the validity of similar agreements should not be affected by McKinney's N.Y.Bus.Corp.Law, § 620(b)–(g), supra note 1, since such agreements do not "improperly" restrict the board of directors in its management functions or "improperly" transfer all or any part of such management.

5. See Abercrombie v. Davies, 35 Del.Ch. 599, 608, 123 A.2d 893, 898 (Ch.1956), modified 36 Del.Ch. 102, 125 A.2d 588 (Ch.1956), rev'd on other grounds 36 Del.Ch. 371, 130 A.2d 338 (Sup.Ct.1957): "This means that our corporation law does not permit actions or agreements by shareholders which would take all power from the board to handle matters of substantial management policy . . . Even unanimous stockholder action in this field has limitations."

6. Long Park, Inc. v. Trenton-New Brunswick Theatres Co., 297 N.Y. 174, 77 N.E.2d 633 (1948), motion denied 298 N.Y. 856, 84 N.E.2d 324 (1949), overruled by McKinney's N.Y.Bus.Corp.Law, § 620(b)–(g) if provision is in articles of incorporation in compliance with such statutory requirements.

7. Such qualification, even if not expressed in the agreement, might be implied by the court to sustain the agreement. Fells v. Katz, 256 N.Y. 67, 175 N.E. 516 (1931); Matter of Katz (Fulton-Washington Corp.), 2 Misc.2d 325, 143 N.Y.S.2d 282 (Sup.Ct. 1955), aff'd mem., 1 A.D.2d 657, 147 N.Y.S.2d 10 (1st Dep't 1955). See also Slonim v. Brodie, 109 N.Y.S. 2d 440 (Sup.Ct.1951), aff'd mem., 281 App.Div. 861, 119 N.Y.S.2d 916 (1st Dep't 1953); Eisenberg v. Rodless Decorations, Inc., 106 N.Y.S.2d 822 (Sup.Ct. 1951) (agreements affecting payment of salaries). See Klausman v. Rosenberg, 221 Ga. 59, 143 S.E.2d 164 (1965) (upholding preincorporation agreement that neither of two 50 percent shareholders would employ any person objectionable to other); Galler v. Galler, 32 Ill.2d 16, 203 N.E.2d 577 (1964), 95 Ill. App.2d 340, 238 N.E.2d 274 (1968) (upholding provisions for election of certain persons to specified officers for period of years, and for salary continua-

the discretion of the board of directors,[8] might be upheld, as well as agreements relating to other corporate matters,[9] at least where unanimously adopted by the shareholders. Some cases have upheld such agreements even though all of the shareholders were not parties to the agreement.[10]

Because of the risk of invalidity of provisions binding directors in the exercise of their discretion, such provisions must be carefully drafted in the light of applicable statutes and case law. To prevent the whole agreement from being invalidated because one or more of its provisions are found invalid,[11] any such agreement should clearly indicate, if such is the parties' intention, that its various provisions are severable.

tion of two-years salary of deceased executive to his widow over five-year period contingent upon such payments being income-tax-deductible by corporation).

8. Such qualification was not expressed in the agreement involved in Clark v. Dodge but was implied by the court. See also M. Groh's Sons v. Groh, 80 App.Div. 85, 80 N.Y.S. 438 (1st Dep't 1903), rev'd on other grounds 177 N.Y. 8, 68 N.E. 992 (1903), reargument denied 177 N.Y. 554, 69 N.E. 1127 (1904); Harris v. 42 E. 73rd St., Inc., 145 N.Y.S. 2d 361 (Sup.Ct.1955) (agreements affecting distribution of profits). Galler v. Galler, 32 Ill.2d 16, 203 N.E.2d 577 (1964), 95 Ill.App.2d 340, 238 N. E.2d 274 (1968) (upholding provision for mandatory declaration of at least $50,000 dividends annually so long as $500,000 earned surplus maintained). Contractual limitations on dividends in indentures and loan agreements are usually upheld without any serious question. See section 322 infra.

9. E. g., Cohen v. Wacht, 124 N.Y.S.2d 207 (Sup.Ct. 1953), aff'd mem., 282 App.Div. 1054, 126 N.Y.S.2d 910 (2d Dep't 1953), appeal denied 283 App.Div. 660, 127 N.Y.S.2d 820 (2d Dep't 1954); Martocci v. Martocci, 2 Misc.2d 330, 42 N.Y.S.2d 222 (Sup.Ct.1943), aff'd mem., 266 App.Div. 840, 43 N.Y.S.2d 516 (1st Dep't 1943), appeal denied 266 App.Div. 917, 42 N. Y.S.2d 517 (1st Dep't 1943); Simonson v. Helburn, 198 Misc. 430, 97 N.Y.S.2d 406 (Sup.Ct.1950).

10. See section 267, n. 27 supra.

11. Compare Manson v. Curtis, 223 N.Y. 313, 119 N. E. 559 (1918) (provisions found inseverable), and McQuade v. Stoneham, 263 N.Y. 323, 189 N.E. 234 (1934), reargument denied 264 N.Y. 460, 191 N.E. 514 (1934) (provisions found inseverable), with Abercrombie v. Davies, 35 Del.Ch. 599, 123 A.2d 893 (Ch. 1956) (provisions found severable), rev'd on other grounds, 36 Del.Ch. 371, 130 A.2d 338 (Sup.Ct.1957)

FIDUCIARY DUTIES OF DIRECTORS

276. Directors of close corporations might be held to higher fiduciary duties than those applicable to directors of other corporations.

Directors of a close corporation are, of course, subject to the usual fiduciary duties,[1] and might even be held to a higher fidiciary standard.[2]

PROVISION AGAINST DIRECTOR DEADLOCK

277. Board of directors deadlock can be dealt with by three alternative methods: (a) arbitration, (b) appointment of provisional director, and (c) dissolution.

Arbitration of director deadlock involves, besides the usual problems of arbitration, the problem of delegating managerial discretion to the arbitrator.

A few statutes authorize court appointment, under prescribed circumstances, of a disinterested provisional director when the corporation is deadlocked by an equally-divided even-numbered board.

Judicial dissolution in case of deadlock, even when expressly authorized by statute, is subject to various restrictions.

Where there is an even-numbered board of directors, a veto provision, or a greater-than-normal quorum/voting requirement for

(whole arrangement invalidated as illegal voting trust).

1. See sections 231–242 supra.

2. E. g., Matter of Gearing v. Kelly, 11 N.Y.2d 201, 227 N.Y.S.2d 897, 182 N.E.2d 391 (1962) (holding that where director of close corporation absented herself from board of directors meeting to prevent quorum to fill vacancy, neither such director nor her associate shareholder could then seek to set aside election of director on ground quorum was not present); Sautter v. Fulmer, 258 N.Y. 107, 179 N.E. 310 (1932), motion for reargument denied 259 N.Y. 508, 182 N.E. 157 (1932) (subjecting director of close corporation who engaged in insider trading to fiduciary duty in jurisdiction then purporting to follow "majority rule", discussed in section 239 supra); Elder, "Statutory Remedies of Minority Shareholders in Close Corporations", 2 U.B.C.L.Rev. 440 (1966); Grissom & King, "Liabilities of Directors of Closely-Held Corporations", 36 U.Colo.L.Rev. 95 (1963); Note, "Corporate Opportunity in the Close Corporation—A Different Result?", 56 Geo. L.J. 381 (1967).

board of directors action, the probability of deadlock at the director level is increased.[1]

Three methods of resolving such deadlock are (a) arbitration, (b) appointment of provisional director, and (c) dissolution.[2]

Arbitration

Besides the usual problems of arbitration, previously discussed in connection with the arbitration of shareholder deadlock,[3] arbitration of deadlock at the director level presents the additional problem of delegating managerial discretion—a responsibility vested by statute in the board of directors—to someone else—the arbitrator.[4] For example, articles of incorporation containing a provision that in the event of deadlock among the directors their differences will be arbitrated might not be accepted for filing by the secretary of state.[5] The problem is

analogous to binding in advance the directors' discretion.[6]

Appointment of Provisional Director

A few jurisdictions by statute provide for the court appointment, under prescribed circumstances, of a disinterested "provisional director" when the corporation has an even number of directors who are equally divided and cannot agree as to management of its affairs.[7] Quite apart from some disfavor against a court-appointee's running a business corporation—with its overtones of political patronage, even though his decisions require the concurrence of half of the directors, such statutes suffer from the shortcoming of being limited to director deadlock situations caused by an equally-divided even-numbered board.

Dissolution

Where the board of directors is deadlocked, courts hesitate to order such a drastic remedy as dissolution absent statutory authorization to do so.[8] Even when there is a statute, the courts might tend to construe it strictly. The Model Business Corporation Act authorizes judicial dissolution in the

1.   Callahan, "Corporations: The Incorporated Partnership and the Problem of the Deadlocked Board", 3 Vill.L.Rev. 196 (1958).

2.   In some situations, an issue upon which the board of directors is deadlocked might be resolved by shareholders. See Boss v. Boss, 98 R.I. 146, 200 A. 2d 231 (1964); Kentucky Package Store, Inc. v. Checani, 331 Mass. 125, 117 N.E.2d 139 (1954).

3.   See section 269 supra.

4.   O'Neal, "Resolving Disputes in Closely-Held Corporations: Intra-Institutional Arbitration", 67 Harv.L.Rev. 786 (1954); O'Neal, "Arbitration in Closely-Held Corporations", 9 Arb.J. (n. s.) 31 (1954); Note, "Arbitration and Unanimity Agreements in the Close Corporation", 30 St. John's L. Rev. 262 (1956); Annot., 64 A.L.R.2d 643 (1959). Cf. note 8 infra.

5.   E. g., 7 S. Slutsky, White on New York Corporations ¶ 8.18 (12th ed. 1953, Supp.1960). But see McKinney's N.Y.Bus.Corp.Law, § 620(b) (permitting articles of incorporation provision transferring to one or more persons to be selected by shareholders all or any part of management otherwise within authority of board of directors); Lehrman v. Cohen, 43 Del.Ch. 222, 222 A.2d 800 (Sup.Ct.1966) (upholding third class of one share without dividend or liquidation rights but with right to elect fifth director where two other classes of shares, with dividend and liquidation rights, each had right to elect two directors. See also Matter of Uddo, 21 A.D.2d 402, 250 N.Y.S.2d 645 (1st Dep't 1964) (construing provision for arbitration where board of directors was unable to take effective action as not making arbitrable question whether board of directors had voted effectively).

6.   See sections 212, 275 supra. A few modern statutes permit broad delegation of the management functions of the directors, at least in close corporations, by provisions in the articles of incorporations (New York), or in the articles of incorporation, by-laws or a side agreement (North Carolina, Florida, Maryland, Delaware). See section 259 supra.

7.   Cal.Gen.Corp.Law, § 4655 (1947); Del.Gen.Corp. Law, § 353 (1967) (electing close corporation); Ga. Bus.Corp.Code § 22–608 (1963); Mo.Gen. and Bus. Corp.Law, § 351.323 (1963). See Matter of Jamison Steel Corp., 158 Cal.App.2d 27, 322 P.2d 246 (1958); Comment, "Unusual Statutory Remedies for the Deadlocked Corporation in California: Voluntary Dissolution and the Provisional Director", 48 Calif. L.Rev. 272 (1960). Note, "Provisional Director Statute", 31 Mo.L.Rev. 536 (1966). Even in the absence of a provisional director statute, one court experimented with the appointment of a "special fiscal agent". Roach v. Margulies, 42 N.J.Super. 243, 126 A.2d 45 (1956).

8.   A possible interim remedy would be receivership. See Farrar v. Pesterfield, 216 Ga. 311, 116 S.E.2d 229 (1960) (receiver appointed to manage corporation until deadlock broken). Cf. note 4 supra.

event of director deadlock which cannot be resolved by the shareholders if "irreparable injury to the corporation is being suffered or is threatened by reason thereof".[9]

Since the same dissolution statutes usually deal with director and shareholder deadlock, they will be treated together in a more comprehensive manner in a later section.[10]

OFFICERS

278. Statutes increasingly permit shareholders to elect officers, a practice better suited to close corporations than to other corporations. More frequently, officers are appointed and are removable by the board of directors. Director agreements for the appointment of named persons as named officers and fixing their compensation, especially when all shareholders are parties to such agreements, have been upheld by the courts. Employment contracts between the corporation and various officers are also possible, but usually do not preclude removal of the officers with or without cause, although in the latter case the corporation would usually be liable to the officer for damages for breach of contract. Salaries to officers of close corporations are subject to close scrutiny by taxing authorities. Inequities as between salary and dividend policies arise most frequently in close corporations.

A growing number of statutes permit officers to be elected by shareholders,[1] a practice better suited to close corporations than to other corporations. However, in most jurisdictions, officers are appointed and are removable by the board of directors. Yet, in the close corporation, shareholders often want to designate the officers and even fix their salaries.

Preincorporation agreements or "shareholder agreements" binding the parties as directors to keep in office a particular person so long as he is faithful, efficient, and competent, have been upheld, at least where all the future or present shareholders were parties to such agreement.[2] Whether such an agreement is specifically enforceable is not altogether clear.[3]

The corporation, of course, can enter into an employment contract with various officers. Such a contract would not preclude the directors from removing the officer for cause and ordinarily would not preclude their removing him without cause. In the latter case, the officer would have a cause of action for breach of contract and could recover damages from the corporation but ordinarily would not be awarded specific performance.[4]

Of course, once a person is installed in office, his removal is usually possible only by board of directors action which might be subject to a veto provision or a greater-than-normal quorum/voting requirement for board of directors action in lieu of the normal majority rule.

Salaries and other compensation of officers are subject to the usual rules relating to executive compensation.[5] Such compensa-

---

9. ABA–ALI Model Bus.Corp.Act § 90. See section 269, n. 3 supra.

10. See section 280 infra.

1. See section 221 supra.

2. See sections 198, 213, 267, 275 supra. See Montgomery Pipe & Tube Co. v. Mann, 205 So.2d 660 (Fla.Dist.Ct.App.1968) (action by removed president seeking reinstatement and restoration of salary benefits); Gramatan Clothes, Inc. v. Rose, 159 N.Y.L.J. No. 16, 16 (Sup.Ct.1968) (issues of whether shareholder agreement to retain defendant as officer was valid under law of Massachusetts, state of incorporation, and whether there was cause for removal); Klausman v. Rosenberg, 221 Ga. 59, 143 S.E.2d 164 (1965) (breach of preincorporation agreement that person hired must be acceptable to plaintiff); Wilson v. McClenny, 262 N.C. 121, 136 S.E.2d 569 (1964), appeal after remand 269 N.C. 399, 152 S.E.2d 529 (1967) (breach of preincorporation agreement to keep plaintiff as president for five years); Meck, "Employment of Corporate Executives by Majority Stockholders", 47 Yale L.J. 1079, 1097 (1938).

3. See section 267, n. 42 supra.

4. See section 221, nn. 7, 8, 9 supra.

5. Havighurst, "The Continuing Utility of Employee Stock Options in Closely Held Businesses", 18 U.Fla L.Rev. 251 (1965); Vesely, "Compensation Arrangements in Smaller Corporations—Compensation Through the Use of Corporate Stock", 29 U.Cin.L. Rev. 52 (1960); Goodwin, "Hiring an Executive—A Case Study of the Incentives a Smaller Corporation

tion is usually determined by the board of directors in its discretion. However, it could be fixed in the articles of incorporation or bylaws, or even in a "shareholder agreement", at least where all the shareholders are parties to such agreement. To be deductible by the corporation as an operating expense for federal income tax purposes, compensation must be reasonable in amount.[6] In close corporations, especially, salaries to shareholder-officers are subject to close scrutiny by taxing authorities. Inequities might also develop where some shareholders are active in the business, receiving salaries, and others are not, having dividends as their only source of income from the business.[7]

MAINTENANCE OF MANAGEMENT STRUCTURE

279. To maintain the desired management structure against dislocation by changes in shareholdings, composition of the board of directors, or officers, and by amendments of the articles of incorporation or bylaws, etc., various devices are available which tend to preserve the status quo absent unanimous agreement by those involved in favor of any proposed change.

Once the desired management structure is set up, it might be subject to serious dislocation by changes in shareholdings, composition of board of directors, or officers, amendments of the articles of incorporation or bylaws, or merger, consolidation, dissolution, etc.[1]

Share transfer restrictions, provisions in any agreements binding personal representatives, heirs, and assigns, appropriate share certificate legends, sufficiently greater-than-normal quorum/voting requirements for shareholder and director actions, including amendments of the articles of incorporation and bylaws, and extraordinary corporate matters, should tend to preserve the *status quo* absent unanimous agreement by those involved in favor of any proposed change.

DISSOLUTION OF DEADLOCKED CORPORATION

280. Dissolution of a deadlocked corporation is possible without judicial proceedings if sufficient shareholders consent thereto. Otherwise, dissolution only by judicial proceedings may be possible. Absent an applicable statute, courts are reluctant to compel dissolution. Deadlock statutes often limit judicial dissolution to specified deadlock situations where there exists or is threatened irreparable injury or where dissolution would be beneficial to shareholders. Where such limitations on judicial dissolution exist, a shareholder agreement, especially among all shareholders, binding the parties to consent to non-judicial dissolution in event of deadlock is a possible means of avoiding such limitations.

In the event of deadlock, one drastic remedy is dissolution.

Where all or a sufficient number of shareholders, otherwise deadlocked, vote for or consent to dissolution, voluntary dissolution without judicial proceedings can easily be effectuated.[1]

Can Offer", 12 Bus.Law. 126 (Jan. 1957); Lubick, "Designing a Deferred Compensation Profit Sharing Plan for a Small Company", 3 Buffalo L.Rev. 222 (1954). See sections 243–256 supra.

6. See sections 243–245 supra.

7. See Notes, 14 N.Y.U.Intra.L.Rev. 140 (Jan.1959); 10 Rutgers L.Rev. 723 (1956).

[§ 279]
1. F. O'Neal & J. Derwin, Expulsion or Oppression of Business Associates: "Squeeze-Outs" in Small Enterprises (1961); Steadman, "Maintaining Control of Close Corporations", 14 Bus.Law. 1077 (1959).

[§ 280]
1. E. g., ABA–ALI Model Bus.Corp.Act §§ 75–86; Del.Gen.Corp.Law, § 275 et seq. (1967); McKinney's N.Y.Bus.Corp.Law, § 1002 (permitting articles of incorporation provision for shareholder dissolution at will or upon occurrence of specified event). See F. O'Neal & J. Derwin, Expulsion or Oppression of Business Associates; Squeeze-Outs in Small Enterprises (1961); McKinney's N.Y.Bus.Corp.Law, art. 10; J. Tingle, The Stockholder's Remedy of Corporate Dissolution (1959); Hornstein, "Voluntary Dissolution—A New Development in Intra-Corporate Abuse", 51 Yale L.J. 64 (1941); Note, "Minority

However, where the required shareholder vote or consent for such dissolution cannot be mustered, the only alternative method of achieving possible dissolution is by court proceedings. Absent an applicable statute, courts are reluctant to compel dissolution.[2]

Statutory provisions for judicial dissolution might or might not meet the needs of deadlock situations, depending upon the statutory formulation and the court's construction thereof.

The Model Business Corporation Act, for example, empowers a court to liquidate the assets and business of a corporation, *inter alia*, in an action by a shareholder when it is established: [3]

"That the directors are deadlocked in the management of the corporate affairs and the shareholders are unable to break the deadlock, and that irreparable injury to the corporation is being suffered or is threatened by reason thereof; or

"That the acts of the directors or those in control of the corporation are illegal, oppressive or fraudulent; [4] or

"That the shareholders are deadlocked in voting power, and have failed, for a period which includes at least two consecutive annual meeting dates, to elect successors to directors whose terms have expired or would have expired upon the election of their successor; or

"That the corporate assets are being misapplied or wasted."

Under a statutory judicial dissolution provision requiring that dissolution be "beneficial to the stockholders . . . and not injurious to the public",[5] deadlock alone has been held insufficient.[6]

Dissolution of the Close Corporation", 35 Geo. Wash.L.Rev. 1068 (1967); Note, "Dissolution and Minority Shareholder Protection in the Close Corporation", 1966 Wis.L.Rev. 1232; Note, "Dissolution of the Close Corporation", 41 St. John's L.Rev. 239 (1966); Note, "Deadlock and Dissolution in Close Corporations", 45 Iowa L.Rev. 767 (1960). See section 348 infra.

2. Hall v. John S. Isaacs & Sons Farm, Inc., 39 Del. Ch. 244, 253, 163 A.2d 288, 293 (Sup.Ct.1960) ("Mere dissension among corporate stockholders seldom, if ever, justifies the appointment of a receiver for a solvent corporation. The minority's remedy is withdrawal from the corporate enterprise by the sale of its stock"); Hepner v. Miller, 130 Colo. 243, 274 P.2d 818 (1954); 2 F. O'Neal, Close Corporations: Law and Practice § 9.27 (1958); Israels, "The Sacred Cow of Corporate Existence: Problems of Deadlock and Dissolution", 19 U.Chi.L.Rev. 778 (1952); Hornstein, "A Remedy for Corporate Abuse—Judicial Power to Wind Up a Corporation at the Suit of a Minority Shareholder", 40 Colum. L.Rev. 220 (1940). But see Levant v. Kowal, 350 Mich. 232, 86 N.W.2d 336 (1957); Annot., 13 A.L.R. 2d 1260 (1950), 47 A.L.R.2d 365 (1956).

3. ABA-ALI Model Bus.Corp.Act § 90(a) (1), (3). The New York Business Corporation Law authorizes petition for judicial deadlock on any one of three broad grounds, and also authorizes the articles of incorporation to provide that any shareholder or holders of any percentage of shares may enforce dissolution at will or upon the occurrence of any specified event. McKinney's N.Y.Bus.Corp.Law, §§ 1104, 1002. See Howe, "Corporate Divorce: Deadlocks in the Close Corporation", 22 Bus.Law. 469 (1967); Note, "Corporations—Election Deadlock as Ground for Dissolution in the Close Corporation", 35 Temp.L.Q. 338 (1962); Note, "Deadlock and Dissolution: Problems in the Closely Held Corporation in Illinois", 56 Nw.U.L.Rev. 525 (1961). See also section 269, n. 3 supra.

4. Gidwitz v. Lanzit Corrugated Box Co., 20 Ill.2d 208, 170 N.E.2d 131 (1960), construing the Illinois statutory judicial dissolution provision which was the basis for the Model Business Corporation Act § 90, held, where equal shareholders had been deadlocked for 10 years, that it was not necessary to show fraud, illegality, or loss to prove "oppression" and decreed dissolution where the president and his family had operated the corporation to the exclusion of the holders of the other half of the shares; Comment, "Oppression as a Statutory Ground for Corporate Dissolution", 1965 Duke L.J. 128.

5. McKinney's N.Y.Gen.Corp.Law, § 117 (inapplicable to business corporations since 1963). If the parties want a dissolution proceeding discontinued, the court must dismiss such proceeding. Matter of Fine Sound, Inc., 5 A.D.2d 973, 172 N.Y.S.2d 200 (1st Dep't 1958), amended in other respect 6 A.D.2d 777, 175 N.Y.S.2d 15 (1st Dep't 1958).

6. Matter of Radom & Neidorff, Inc., 307 N.Y. 1, 119 N.E.2d 563 (1954). In re Collins-Doan Co., 3 N.J. 382, 70 A.2d 159, 13 A.L.R.2d 1250 (1949), the New Jersey Supreme Court, interpreting a statutory provision similar to the New York provision, found that for several years there had been a deadlock in the board of four directors, that the two factions of shareholders had been unable to elect directors with the consequence that business had been conducted by a manager without board supervision, and that the primary cause of the stalemate was the failure to pay dividends although the profits had been sufficient for such payment. Affirming an order of

In Matter of Radom & Neidorff, Inc.,[7] two brothers-in-law had been in business together for 30 years, each owning 80 of the 160 shares of their corporation. In 1950, one died, with the result that his widow (the survivor's sister) acquired his 80 shares. The widow and her brother—the president of the corporation—were at odds: she brought a derivative action against him, refused to sign his salary checks ($25,000 per year), and refused to sell him her shares. A third director could not be elected, although the widow offered to submit to arbitration the election of the third director; no dividends were declared. The corporation, however, was solvent and its operations successful. The brother, as the holder of one-half the shares, petitioned for judicial dissolution on the ground of deadlock. The New York Court of Appeals, 4–3, held that

under the circumstances dissolution would not be "beneficial to the stockholders". The dissenting judges contended that neither insolvency nor actual irreparable injury was required by the statute.

Regardless of the inherent power of courts of equity to dissolve corporations, the statutory provision might be held to be exclusive.[8]

On the other hand, one case ordered judicial dissolution of a prosperous deadlocked corporation on the ground that the two associates had so slightly observed corporate formalities that they should be treated as a partnership.[9]

dissolution, the court said that there was want of that community of interest essential to corporate operation, that dissolution would serve the interests of the shareholders as well as public policy, and, if dissolution were not granted, there would be no alternative corrective remedy.

7. 307 N.Y. 1, 119 N.E.2d 563 (1954); accord, Jackson v. Nicolai-Neppach Co., 219 Or. 560, 348 P.2d 9 (1959). See also Paulman v. Kritzer Radiant Coils, Inc., 37 Del.Ch. 348, 143 A.2d 272 (Ch.1958); Comment, "Rights of the Minority Shareholders to Dissolve the Closely Held Corporation", 43 Calif.L.Rev. 514 (1955). The New York Business Corporation Law now provides that in a special proceeding brought by directors or shareholders, the benefit to the shareholders of a dissolution is of paramount importance, and that in a special proceeding brought by shareholder petition in case of deadlock among directors or shareholders, "dissolution is not to be denied merely because it is found that the corporate business has been or could be conducted at a profit." McKinney's N.Y.Bus.Corp. Law § 1111(b). See Matter of Nelkin, 25 N.Y.2d 543, —— N.Y.S.2d ——, —— N.E.2d —— (1969). Matter of Sheridan Construction Corp., 22 A.D.2d 390, 256 N.Y.S.2d 210 (4th Dep't 1965), aff'd per curiam 16 N.Y.2d 680, 261 N.Y.S.2d 300, 209 N.E.2d 290 (1965) (ordering dissolution where brothers developed such intense discord that efficient management had become impossible); Matter of Steig, 155 N.Y.L.J. No. 95, 16 (Sup. Ct.1966) (deadlock and feud held insufficient basis for dissolution which would have benefited petitioner who had set up competing business). The New York Supreme Court motion and trial term decisions on dissolution for deadlock form no discernible pattern. See 28–—— Clark's Digest-Annotator 350.1104 (1964– ——). See also Matter of Gordon & Weiss, Inc., 32 A.D.2d 279, 301 N.Y.S.2d 839 (1st Dep't 1969).

8. Compare Kruger v. Gerth, 16 N.Y.2d 802, 263 N.Y. S.2d 1, 210 N.E.2d 355 (1965), with Leibert v. Clapp, 13 N.Y.2d 313, 247 N.Y.S.2d 102, 196 N.E.2d 540 (1963); Cachules v. Finkelstein, 279 App.Div. 173, 109 N.Y.S.2d 272 (1st Dep't 1951), reargument and appeal denied 279 App.Div. 778, 109 N.Y.S.2d 360 (1st Dep't 1952) (denying an action for dissolution under general equity powers of court). The court quoted Hitch v. Hawley, 132 N.Y. 212, 217, 30 N.E. 401, 403 (1892); "Whether courts of equity have inherent power to dissolve corporations . . . is unnecessary for us to consider, as the method of effecting corporate dissolution, when prescribed by statute, as in this state, is exclusive and must be substantially followed."

9. In Matter of Pivot Punch & Die Corp., 15 Misc.2d 713, 182 N.Y.S.2d 459 (Sup.Ct.1959), the petitioner and the respondent each owned one-half of the shares. For three years there had been dissension and an inability to elect directors. The respondent, as manager, had been controlling corporate policy and had been receiving a substantial return for his services and upon his investment and the petitioner had been receiving nothing. The court pointed out that under partnership law, when loyalty and confidence between partners cease, the true partnership ceases, and, by analogy, when those characteristics no longer exist between the shareholders of a close corporation, the corporation ceases to be beneficial to the deadlocked shareholders. It distinguished the Radom case on the ground that here the corporation was weak and declining and held that dissolution was needed for the good of the shareholders and of the public. Accordingly, it ordered the appointment of a referee to determine the facts. In 9 A.D.2d 861, 193 N.Y.S.2d 34 (4th Dep't 1959), the order was modified by directing that the hearing be before the court and not a referee. Flemming v. Heffner & Fleming, 263 Mich. 561, 248 N.W. 900 (1933) likened a close corporation to a partnership and held that in such case a court had inherent power to appoint a receiver for the liquidation of the corporation. See also Stark v. Reingold, 18 N.

In jurisdictions where judicial dissolution in the event of deadlock is not readily available, alternative provisions for dealing with deadlock—buy-out arrangements to eliminate a shareholder faction, arbitration, shareholder agreement to vote for or consent to non-judicial dissolution—should be seriously considered.[10]

Provisions in articles of incorporations for dissolution in the event of deadlock have been held invalid as contrary to law.[11]

Although not free from doubt, provisions in shareholder agreements, at least when all shareholders are parties thereto, binding the parties to vote for dissolution in the event of deadlock, should be sustained.[12]

Some jurisdictions are becoming increasingly liberal in ordering judicial dissolution of the deadlocked corporation.[13]

Modern statutes tend to deal more realistically with judicial dissolution of deadlocked corporations.[14]

J. 251, 113 A.2d 679 (1955); Casey v. Harrington, 136 N.Y.L.J. No. 101, 13 (Sup.Ct.1956).

10. See Barkin, "Deadlock and Dissolution in Florida Closed Corporations: Litigating and Planning", 13 U.Miami L.Rev. 395 (1959); Comment, "Unusual Statutory Remedies for the Deadlocked Corporation: Voluntary Dissolution and the Provisional Director", 48 Calif.L.Rev. 272 (1960); Note, "Some Experimental Parallels to the Deadlocked Close Corporation", 13 U.Fla.L.Rev. 232 (1960). See sections 269, 277 supra.

11. A few modern statutes expressly permit articles of incorporation provisions for nonjudicial dissolution by any or some shareholders at will or upon the occurrence of a specified event. E. g., McKinney's N.Y.Bus.Corp.Law, § 1002; S.C. Bus.Corp. Act § 12.14 (1964) (dissolution pursuant to provision in articles of incorporation; provision valid only so long as shares of corporation not traded on any national securities exchange or regularly traded in any over-the-counter market maintained by one or more brokers or dealers in securities). 2 F. O'Neal, Close Corporations: Law and Practice § 9.06 (1958); Comment, 43 Calif.L.Rev. 514, 519–522 (1955).

12. Fish v. Nebraska City Barb-Wire Fence Co., 25 F. 795 (C.C.D.Neb.1885); Matter of Hega Knitting Mills, Inc., 124 N.Y.S.2d 115 (Sup.Ct.1953) (requiring unanimous shareholder agreement); Matter of Block, 186 Misc. 945, 60 N.Y.S.2d 639 (Sup.Ct.1946). But see Flanagan v. Flanagan, 273 App.Div. 918, 77 N.Y.S.2d 682 (2d Dep't 1948), aff'd mem., 298 N.Y. 787, 83 N.E.2d 473 (1948). Some jurisdictions require not only shareholder action but also board of directors action to effectuate non-judicial dissolution (see section 348 infra), in which case any such agreement would constitute a "director agreement" as well as a "shareholder agreement". For statuto-

ry provisions expressly authorizing shareholder voting agreements, see section 267, nn. 28, 42 supra.

13. Reynolds v. Special Projects, Inc., 260 Cal.App.2d 518, 67 Cal.Rptr. 374 (1968) (dissolution ordered on basis of shareholder dissension and lack of business reason for continuation of business after expiration of license); Laskey v. L. & L. Manchester Drive-In, Inc., — Me. —, 216 A.2d 310 (1966) (judicial dissolution ordered under statute permitting same "if equity so requires"); Gidwitz v. Lanzit Corrugated Box Co., 20 Ill.2d 208, 170 N.E.2d 131 (1960); In re Security Finance Co., 49 Cal.2d 370, 317 P.2d 1 (1957); Strong v. Fromm Laboratories, 273 Wis. 159, 77 N.W.2d 389 (1956); Krall v. Krall, 141 Conn. 325, 106 A.2d 165 (1954); In re Collins-Doan Co., 3 N.J. 382, 70 A.2d 159, 13 A.L.R.2d 1250 (1949). But see Johnston v. Livingston Nursing Home, Inc., 282 Ala. 309, 211 So.2d 151 (1968) (dissolution denied, despite shareholder deadlock, where business could be managed by two of three directors); In re Lakeland Development Corp., 277 Minn. 432, 152 N.W.2d 758 (1967) (deadlock, unless permanently irreconcilable, held insufficient ground for dissolution). For tax consequences of dissolution under deadlock statute, see Dear Publication & Radio, Inc. v. Comm'r, 274 F.2d 656 (3d Cir. 1960). As for use of corporate name after dissolution, see Warren v. Summit, 151 N.Y.L.J. No. 41, 19 (Sup.Ct.1964).

14. One of the two principal statutory approaches is to provide for judicial dissolution in the event of specified deadlocks. Del.Gen.Corp.Law § 229 (1967) (with authorization of appointment of "custodian"); Fla.Gen.Corp.Law, Part II, Close Corporations § 608.0107 (1963); McKinney's N.Y.Bus.Corp.Law, §§ 1101–1117; N.C.Bus.Corp.Act § 55–125(a) (1), (2) (1957). A few of such statutes include provisions whereby the shares of any shareholder opposing dissolution can purchase the shares of any shareholder seeking dissolution. E.g., Cal.Gen.Corp.Law, §§ 4651, 4658 (1947); W.Va.Gen.Corp.Law, § 3093 (1943). The second principal statutory approach is to provide for dissolution by one or more shareholders at will or upon the occurrence of a specified event. E. g., Del.Gen.Corp.Law, § 355 (1967) (nonjudicial dissolution under such provision in articles of incorporation); id. § 352 (appointment of "custodian" for "close corporation"); McKinney's N.Y.Bus.Corp.Law, § 1002 (nonjudicial dissolution under such provision in articles of incorporation); N.C. Bus.Corp.Act § 55–125(a) (3) (1957) (judicial dissolution under such provision in written agreement whether embodied in articles of incorporation or separate therefrom). Judicial dissolution might be made conditional on one side's buying the other's shares. Compare Matter of Astey, 19 Misc.2d 1059, 189 N.Y.S.2d 2 (Sup.Ct.1959), with Matter of Ulrich (Schulman), 145 N.Y.L.J. No. 11, 12 (Sup.Ct.1961).

E. SHARE TRANSFER RESTRICTIONS

SHARE TRANSFER RESTRICTIONS— RULES AS TO VALIDITY

281. Share transfer restrictions serve two primary functions in the close corporation: (a) securing of delectus personae; and (b) preservation of management structure.

Share transfer restrictions to be valid must be adopted for a lawful purpose, such as preventing outsiders from becoming shareholders and maintaining the proportionate interests of shareholders. Share transfer restrictions cannot be an unreasonable restraint on alienation. Most common are provisions that a shareholder must offer his shares to the corporation and/or proportionately to other shareholders before transferring the shares to an outsider, or for an absolute option in, or a binding buy-sell agreement with, the corporation and/or other shareholders exercisable upon a specified event.

The Uniform Commercial Code provides that unless noted conspicuously on the security a restriction on transfer imposed by the issuer even though otherwise lawful is ineffective except against a person with actual knowledge of it.

In General

Shares in a close corporation, at least shares with voting rights, are by definition closely-held. Mutual agreement, usually is the means of selecting the original shareholders and their respective interests.

Since shares in a close corporation are rarely traded, much less listed on a securities exchange, their value is usually difficult to determine, and there is, as a practical matter, very little market for such shares. Besides the practical difficulties, the shares in most close corporations are usually subjected to the legal limitations of share transfer restrictions.[1]

The prime function of share transfer restrictions is to keep the corporation close, and to achieve in the corporate form of business the partnership principle of *delectus personae*. Apart from such transfer restrictions, corporate shares are usually freely alienable; in fact, ready transferability of interest is one of the traditional attributes of a corporation. Corporate statutes generally provide that shares are transferable in the manner provided by law and in the bylaws.

Share transfer restrictions also help to preserve the management structure of a close corporation which is often predicated on the assumption that certain persons will be holders of certain share interests and should control the business as shareholders, directors, and officers. Shifts in shareholding, by changing the respective proportionate interests or introducing outsiders, can seriously dislocate the initial desires of the associates.

Share transfer restrictions also tend to maintain relative secrecy in corporate affairs, since the requirements of corporation law do not require substantial public disclo-

1. R. Kessler, New York Close Corporations ch. 9 (1968); A. Guild, D. Davis & D. Hoxie, Stock-Purchase Agreements & the Close Corporation (1960); 2 F. O'Neal, Close Corporations: Law and Practice ch. VII (1958); Coates, "Share Transfer and Transmission Restrictions in the Close Corporation", 3 U.B.C.L.Rev. 96 (Dec. 1968); Barron, "Arrangements: Validity and Enforcement of Restrictions on Share Transfer and Buy-out Various Types of Restrictions in Ohio", 31 U.Cin.L.Rev. 266 (1962); Childs, "Control of Transfer of Business Interests", 1958 U.Ill.L.F. 79; O'Neal, "Restrictions on Transfers of Stock in Closely-Held Corporations: Planning and Drafting", 65 Harv.L.Rev. 773 (1952); Cataldo, "Stock Transfer Restrictions and the Closed Corporation", 37 Va.L.Rev. 229 (1951); Hornstein, "Stockholders' Agreements in the Closely Held Corporation", 59 Yale L.J. 1040, 1047–1051 (1950); Comment, "Close Corporation Stock Purchase Agreements", 11 W.Res.L.Rev. 278 (1960); Note, "Corporations: Restriction on Transfer of Shares", 48 Mass.L.Q. 86 (1963); Note, 44 Cornell L.Q. 133 (1958). To achieve a similar result in a two-man corporation, most of the shares can be issued equally to the two associates with a few shares representing the balance of control held by an escrow agent or trustee subject to the agreement affecting the transfer of the shares, or held by them as joint tenants with right of survivorship subject to the express provision that both joint tenants must join in any transfer.

sure of information in most close corporation situations.

Of course, share transfer restrictions are not limited to close corporations. Such restrictions are occasionally adopted by public-issue corporations to serve somewhat different purposes. For example, they may be used to restrict the ownership of one class of shares to a given group, such as employees. These shares may be used as an incentive for increased production if they participate only in the higher earnings of the corporation. Such shares may remain freely transferable among members of the restricted class.[2] Or restrictions might be adopted to prevent the corporation from becoming subject to securities regulation or to prevent share ownership from passing to persons which might destroy Subchapter S election or to aliens or other groups as business needs may dictate.

Validity of Restrictions

The question of the validity of share transfer restrictions is sometimes confused by the fact that shares have both contractual and property aspects.[3] The freedom to restrain the alienation of shares thus can vary, depending on whether the contract or property rule be applied.[4] However, shares should be regarded as *sui generis* and neither rule should control.[5] Thus, the validity of share transfer restrictions turns upon corporation law rules developed by the courts with or without the aid of statute.

Generally, restrictions to be valid must be adopted for a lawful purpose.[6]

The purposes of preventing outsiders from obtaining ownership in the corporation and of maintaining the proportionate interests of shareholders are ordinarily recognized as proper.[7]

The nature of the business being conducted may have some bearing upon the validity of a restriction.[8] This is particularly true where special statutes control the business being conducted, as in the case of banking corporations. The special statutory rules are likely to differ from the general principles determining the validity of restrictions.[9]

The type of restraint employed is the most important factor in determining the validity of a transfer restriction. It is now generally accepted that a share transfer restriction will be upheld if it does not constitute an unreasonable restraint on alienation.[10] An absolute restraint on alienation would be unreasonable *per se* and therefore void.[11] On the other hand, absolute restraints have been upheld where they are to last only for a limited period.[12] However, restrictions

---

2. See, e. g., Lawson v. Household Finance Corp., 17 Del.Ch. 343, 152 A. 723 (Sup.Ct.1930).

3. See Painter, "Stock Transfer Restrictions: Continuing Uncertainties and a Legislative Proposal", 6 Vill.L.Rev. 48 (1960); Gower, "Some Contrasts Between British and American Corporation Law", 69 Harv.L.Rev. 1369, 1376–1377 (1956). O'Neal, "Restrictions on Transfer of Stock in Closely Held Corporations: Planning and Drafting", 65 Harv.L.Rev. 773, 789 (1952); Annot., 65 A.L.R. 1159 (1930), 138 A.L.R. 647 (1942), 61 A.L.R.2d 1318 (1958).

4. For a discussion of the result under the property rule, see Sparks, "Future Interests", in 1957 Survey of New York Law, 32 N.Y.U.L.Rev. 1434, 1441 (1957), and in 1958 Survey of American Law, 33 N.Y.U.L.Rev. 398 (1958).

5. See Note, 44 Cornell L.Q. 133, 134–135 (1958).

6. Greene v. E. H. Rollins & Sons, 22 Del.Ch. 394, 2 A.2d 249 (Ch.1938); Royal China, Inc. v. Regal China Corp., 279 App.Div. 515, 110 N.Y.S.2d 718 (1st Dep't 1952), rev'd on other grounds 304 N.Y. 309, 107 N.E.2d 461 (1952) (dictum).

7. See, e. g., Longyear v. Hardman, 219 Mass. 405, 106 N.E. 1012 (1914).

8. See Lawson v. Household Finance Corp., 17 Del. Ch. 343, 152 A. 723 (Sup.Ct.1930), where the court was impressed with the fact that the maintenance of a closely-knit group of shareholders was essential to the type of business being conducted.

9. See, e. g., Wentworth v. Russell State Bank, 167 Kan. 246, 205 P.2d 972 (1949); Quinn v. Ellenson, 236 Wis. 627, 296 N.W. 82 (1941).

10. 2 I. Kantrowitz & S. Slutsky, White on New York Corporations ¶ 508.03 (13th ed. 1968); Annot., 61 A.L.R.2d 1318 (1958).

11. Greene v. E. H. Rollins & Sons, 22 Del.Ch. 394, 2 A.2d 249 (Ch. 1938).

12. E. g., W. O. Barnes Co. v. Folsinski, 337 Mich. 370, 60 N.W.2d 302 (1953); Williams v. Montgomery, 148 N.Y. 519, 43 N.E. 57 (1896).

having a limited duration are not usually desirable and the draftsmen will rarely employ them.

By far the most common restriction is that making use of an option provision. Typically, they provide that a shareholder must offer his shares to the corporation and/or proportionately to the other shareholders before transferring the shares to an outsider. They might also provide for an absolute option in, or a binding buy-sell agreement with, the corporation and/or other shareholders exercisable upon a specified event. Such provisions are generally held to be reasonable and therefore valid.[13]

A less common restraint is the "consent" restriction, which requires the consent of the board of directors or of the remaining shareholders as a prerequisite to the transfer of the shares. While these restrictions are valid in some states,[14] they operate virtually to bar the alienation of the shares and are more likely to be considered unreasonable.[15] Consent restrictions when adopted by corporations running cooperative apartment houses have been upheld on the ground that the restriction is similar to a provision in a lease against assignment.[16]

However, other uses of consent restrictions will at least invite litigation, with no assurances that the restriction will be upheld.

Despite the hostility of some courts to consent restrictions, other restraints of a more severe type have been upheld.[17]

In the absence of special factors demanding a different type of restriction, the wisest course would seem to be to adopt restrictions of the option type, buy-sell type, or of another type whose validity is beyond question in the jurisdiction involved.

Uniform Commercial Code

In addition to the common-law rules affecting the validity—or enforceability—of a restraint, there is also one widely adopted statute[18]—section 8–204 of the Uniform Commercial Code.[19]

Section 8–204 provides that unless noted conspicuously on the security a restriction on transfer imposed by the issuer even though otherwise lawful is ineffective except against a person with actual knowledge of it.

The predecessor statute, section 15 of the Uniform Stock Transfer Act, provided that there should be no restriction upon the transfer of shares by virtue of any bylaws or otherwise unless the restriction was stated upon the share certificate.

Section 8–204 of the Uniform Commercial Code is generally in accord with section 15 of the Uniform Stock Transfer Act but extends to debt securities as well as shares, is limited to restrictions imposed by the issuer, adds an exception for persons with actual knowledge and requires that the restriction be "noted conspicuously" rather than "stated" upon the share certificate.

13.   See, e. g., Allen v. Biltmore Tissue Corp., 2 N.Y. 2d 534, 161 N.Y.S.2d 418, 141 N.E.2d 812, 61 A.L.R. 2d 1309 (1957); Hassel v. Pohle, 214 App.Div. 654, 212 N.Y.S. 561 (2d Dep't 1925). Contra, Victor G. Bloede Co. v. Bloede, 84 Md. 129, 34 A. 1127 (1896).

14.   See, e. g., Del.Gen.Corp.Law, § 202(a) (3) (1967) (permitting restriction which requires corporation or holders of any class of securities to consent to any proposed transfer); Colbert v. Hennessey, 351 Mass. 131, 217 N.E.2d 914 (1966) (upholding shareholder agreement not to transfer shares without consent of other shareholders); Longyear v. Hardman, 219 Mass. 405, 106 N.E. 1012 (1914).

15.   See, e. g., Rafe v. Hindin, 29 A.D.2d 481, 288 N.Y.S.2d 662 (2d Dep't 1968) (share transfer restriction barring transfer unless with consent of other shareholder held unreasonable; evidence of oral agreement that consent would not be withheld unreasonably barred by parole evidence rule); Tracey v. Franklin, 31 Del.Ch. 477, 67 A.2d 56, 11 A.L.R.2d 990 (Sup.Ct.1949); People ex rel. Malcolm v. Lake Sand Corp., 251 Ill.App. 499 (1929).

16.   Weisner v. 791 Park Avenue Corp., 6 N.Y.2d 426, 190 N.Y.S.2d 70, 160 N.E.2d 720 (1959) (6–1); Pent-

house Properties, Inc. v. 1158 Fifth Ave., Inc., 256 App.Div. 685, 11 N.Y.S.2d 417 (1st Dep't 1939).

17.   2 F. O'Neal, Close Corporations: Law and Practice § 7.05 (1958).

18.   All American states, excepting Louisiana, have adopted the Uniform Commercial Code.

19.   Uniform Commercial Code § 8–204 (1962).

The restriction must be "noted" but need not be set forth in full on the share certificate; incorporation by adequate reference is sufficient.[20]

The Uniform Commercial Code, by excepting the ineffectiveness of a share transfer restriction not noted conspicuously on the security as against a person with actual knowledge of it, avoided the question under the Uniform Stock Transfer Act of whether section 15 went to the validity or merely to the enforceability of a restriction as against persons who were not parties to the original restriction. The majority view was that unless the restriction was stated on the share certificate it was invalid, even though the transferees had actual notice of such restriction.[21] The minority view was that a failure to state such restriction affected only its enforceability against *bona fide* purchasers of the shares.[22] Even in the same juris-diction, the holdings were not always consistent.[23]

Even under the majority view, however, a restriction may have had some binding effect despite the absence of any reference to it on the share certificate. Thus, it has been held that a restriction by way of an option provision may be considered as a continuing offer to the optionee which may be accepted until its withdrawal by the shareholder.[24]

Since the Uniform Commercial Code provision is limited to transfer restrictions imposed by the issuer, such as in the articles of incorporation, the bylaws, or an agreement to which the corporation is a party, and the Uniform Stock Transfer Act has been repealed by the Code, the lack of reference on the share certificate should now affect the enforceability of the transfer restriction only against bona fide purchasers without knowledge or notice.

However, share transfer restrictions imposed prior to the repeal of the Uniform Stock Transfer Act by the Code, and not

20. Allen v. Biltmore Tissue Corp., 2 N.Y.2d 534, 161 N.Y.S.2d 418, 141 N.E.2d 812, 61 A.L.R.2d 1309 (1957) (upholding legend "Issued subject to restrictions in sections 28, 29, and 30 of the By-laws" as sufficient statement). A restriction is sufficiently "stated" by a legend noting that the shares are "issued subject to restriction" and specifying where its full text may be found.

21. Strait's Transit, Inc. v. Union Terminal Piers, 370 Mich. 274, 121 N.W.2d 679 (1963); Security Life & Acc. Ins. Co. v. Carlovitz, 251 Ala. 508, 38 So.2d 274 (1949); Sorrick v. Consolidated Tel. Co. of Springport, 340 Mich. 463, 65 N.W.2d 713 (1954); Age Publishing Co. v. Becker, 110 Colo. 319, 134 P.2d 205 (1943); Costello v. Farrell, 234 Minn. 453, 48 N.W.2d 557, 29 A.L.R.2d 890 (1951); Hopwood v. Topsham Tel. Co., 120 Vt. 97, 132 A.2d 170 (1957); Magnetic Mfg. Co. v. Manegold, 201 Wis. 154, 229 N.W. 544 (1930). Cf. Hoosier Chemical Works, Inc. v. Brown, 200 Ind. 535, 165 N.E. 323 (1929), where under the facts the transferee must have had knowledge of the restriction but the issue was not discussed by the court. Uniform Commercial Code § 8–204 first adopted the majority view as to the knowledge of the transferee. However, the 1957 Official Text rejected this position in its version of the Code by adding to § 8–204 the express provision that a restriction not noted upon the share certificate is ineffective "except against a person with actual knowledge of it." See Note, "Uniform Stock Transfer Act: Effect of Notice on Restriction on Transfer", 8 Vand.L.Rev. 640 (1955); Annot., 29 A.L.R.2d 901 (1953).

22. State v. Clarks Hill Telephone Co., 218 N.E.2d 154 (Ind.App.1966); Baumohl v. Goldstein, 95 N.J.

Eq. 597, 124 A. 118 (1924); Doss v. Yingling, 95 Ind.App. 494, 172 N.E. 801 (1930).

23. Compare Allen v. Biltmore Tissue Corp., 2 N.Y.2d 534, 161 N.Y.S.2d 418, 141 N.E.2d 812, 61 A.L.R.2d 1309 (1957) (sufficiency of share certificate legend considered in enforcing restriction against executor of deceased shareholder), with Tomoser v. Kamphausen, 307 N.Y. 797, 121 N.E.2d 622 (1954) (transferee with actual knowledge of restriction held bound thereby). For lower court holdings applying majority view, see H. M. R. Enterprises, Inc. v. National Offset, Inc., 12 Misc.2d 997, 177 N.Y.S.2d 797 (Sup.Ct.1958); Peets v. Manhasset Civil Engineers, Inc., 4 Misc.2d 683, 68 N.Y.S.2d 338 (Sup.Ct.1946). See also General Development Corp. v. Catlin, 139 So.2d 901 (Fla.Dist.Ct.App.1962) (upholding corporation's implied right where shares were issued "for investment and not with a view to distribution", to affix to share certificates legend reading "These shares have been issued on the condition that they will be held for investment purposes only and not for distribution"); cf. Altman v. American Foods, Inc., 262 N.C. 671, 138 S.E.2d 526 (1964).

24. Larson v. Superior Auto Parts, Inc., 207 Wis. 613, 72 N.W.2d 316 (1955). Cf. Costello v. Farrell, 234 Minn. 453, 48 N.W.2d 557, 29 A.L.R.2d 890 (1951), in which it was stated in a dictum that the Uniform Stock Transfer Act could not be used by the transferee to avoid a contractual obligation.

stated upon the certificate, can be invalid under the majority construction of that Act, even though attempted enforcement of the restriction occurs after such repeal.[25]

The Delaware corporate statute, since 1967, has contained a comprehensive provision on restrictions on transfer of securities.[26] Restrictions may be imposed by the articles of incorporation, the bylaws, or an agreement among security holders or between them and the corporation. Permissible transfer restrictions include rights of first refusal, options, buy-sell agreements, consent requirements, "not manifestly unreasonable" prohibitions on transfers to designated persons or classes, restrictions to maintain Subchapter S eligibility, and any other lawful restriction. No restrictions are effective against previously issued securities without their holders' consent.[27]

25.　Goodar Inv. Co. v. Detroit Bank & Trust Co., 4 Mich.App. 218, 144 N.W.2d 649 (1966) (holding invalid share transfer restriction not stated on share certificate under Uniform Stock Transfer Act, since replaced by Uniform Commercial Code).

26.　Del.Gen.Corp.Law, § 202 (1967); Note, "Section 202 of the Delaware Corporations Law—Per Se Rules for Stock Transfer Restrictions", 9 B.C.Ind. & Com.L.Rev. 405 (1968). See also Painter, "Stock Transfer Restrictions: Continuing Uncertainties and a Legislative Proposal", 6 Vill.L.Rev. 48 (1960); Note, "Stock Transfer Restrictions and the Close Corporation—A Statutory Proposal", 17 Hastings L.J. 583 (1966). See also Md. Gen.Corp.Law § 101 (1967); Pa.Bus.Corp.Law §§ 372, 613.1 (1968).

27.　Tu-Vu Drive-In Corp. v. Ashkins, 61 Cal.2d 283, 38 Cal.Rptr. 348, 391 P.2d 828 (1964), held that a bylaw amendment restricting share transfers was valid as applied to a shareholder who neither knew of nor consented to such amendment. Cf. Bechtold v. Coleman Realty Co., 367 Pa. 208, 79 A.2d 661 (1951), which held that a shareholder had a "vested right" in a bylaw restricting share transfers until an offer to sell, at book value, had been made to the corporation or to other shareholders proportionately. See Mueller v. Merz, 23 Wis.2d 588, 127 N. W.2d 774 (1964) (allowing purchaser of shares to rescind sale where notice of special meeting of shareholders to repeal bylaw share transfer restriction failed to state purpose of meeting as required). Tobin v. Cody, 343 Mass. 716, 180 N.E.2d 652, 65 A.L. R.2d 502 (1962), held that when two shareholders who together owned 50 percent of the shares and were actively engaged in a Massachusetts close corporation sold all of their shares to the two other shareholders, all of their interest, including good

SHARE TRANSFER RESTRICTIONS— DRAFTING PROBLEMS

282.　Drafting share transfer restrictions involves such factors as (a) scope of restriction, (b) optionees and parties, (c) price, (d) location of restriction, and (e) enforcement of restriction.

The restriction should be sufficiently comprehensive to proscribe the various types of transfers, inter vivos, testamentary, and by operation of law, intended to be restricted.

The optionees in most cases, to achieve maximum flexibility, should be the corporation and, if the option is not exercised by the corporation, the other shareholders proportionately or otherwise as such other shareholders desirous of acquiring more shares may agree.

The price in an option-type restriction or buy-sell agreement must be definite or capable of ascertainment. Price can be based on book value, capitalization of earnings, fixed price (with or without provision for its periodic redetermination), appraisal, arbitration. "right-of-first refusal" option, etc.

Share transfer restrictions can be set forth in the articles of incorporation, bylaws, or shareholders' agreement.

Share transfer restrictions should be sufficiently definite and fair as to assure their enforcement in equity by injunction or specific performance.

In drafting the restriction, various factors must be considered: (a) scope of restriction, (b) optionees and parties, (c) price, (d) location of restriction, and (e) enforcement of restriction.[1]

---

will, was transferred, and along with good will were implied covenants against competition. Levin, "Implied Covenants Against Competition Created by Transactions in Corporate Stock: Some Thoughts on Tobin v. Cody", 43 B.U.L.Rev. 20 (1963).

1.　See A. Guild, D. Davis & D. Hoxie, Stock-Purchase Agreements & the Close Corporation (1960); 1 G. Hornstein, Corporation Law and Practice §§ 201–203 (1959); Cavitch, "Costly Traps in Corporate Stock Purchases from Shareholders", 15 W. Res.L.Rev. 338 (1964); Stoeber, "Stock Redemption v. Cross-Purchase Agreements in Closely-Held Corporations", 17 J.Am.Soc'y C.L.U. 212 (1963); Weyher & Noall, "Providing for Succession Through Buy-Sell Agreements and Recapitalization", N.Y.U. 21st Inst. on Fed.Tax. 445 (1963); Huberman, "Buy and Sell Agreements for Canadian Close Corporations", 41 Can.B.Rev. 538 (1963); Polasky, "Plan-

Scope of Restriction

The restriction should be sufficiently comprehensive to proscribe the various types of transfers which it is intended to restrict. In this respect the draftsman is faced with the basic proposition that restraints on alienation will be strictly construed and not extended beyond their express provisions. Thus, for example, if the restriction is silent as to the following transfers, the restriction might not be construed to apply to them: (a) transfers by will;[2] (b) transfers by

intestacy;[3] (c) transfers by operation of law;[4] (d) transfers for security purposes;[5] (e) transfers to voting trustees;[6] (f) transfers between shareholders;[7] (g) transfers

ning for the Disposition of a Substantial Interest in a Closely Held Business—The Corporation: Stock-Purchase Agreements and Redemption of Shares", 46 Iowa L.Rev. 516 (1961); Jones, "Stockholders' Buy-Sell Agreements: Six Guideposts for Proper Planning", 33 N.Y.St.B.J. 38 (1961); Note, "Closer Look at Disability 'Buy-outs' for the Close Corporation", 52 Minn.L.Rev. 483 (1967); Note, "Buy and Sell Agreements and the Widow's Rights", 114 U.Pa.L.Rev. 1006 (1966). See Murphy v. Royal American Industries, Inc., 188 So.2d 884 (Fla.Dist.Ct.App.1966), cert. denied 389 U.S. 953, 88 S.Ct. 336, 19 L.Ed.2d 362 (1967) (holding "investment letters" did not modify corporation's obligation to buy back shares if they were not listed on securities exchange within specified time); Dickson v. Hausman, 68 Wash.2d 368, 413 P.2d 378 (1966) (construing "retirement" in buy-sell agreement to mean leaving active work after substantial number of years); McLeod v. Keith, 69 Wash.2d 201, 417 P.2d 861 (1966) (specific performance of buy-sell agreement); Meyer v. Confab Corp., 239 Ark. 524, 393 S.W.2d 253 (1965) (enforcing buy-sell agreement, applicable upon termination of employment "for any reason", against corporation, where employment ended prematurely by mutual consent).

2. Vogel v. Melish, 46 Ill.App. 465, 196 N.E.2d 402 (1964), aff'd 31 Ill.2d 620, 203 N.E.2d 411 (1965) (holding that agreement was silent with respect to shares in event of death of either party and that it had terminated on death of first party to die, despite general language purporting to bind parties' administrators, executors, heirs, and personal representatives); Globe Slicing Machine Co. v. Hasner, 333 F.2d 413 (2d Cir. 1964), cert. denied 379 U.S. 969, 85 S.Ct. 666, 13 L.Ed.2d 562 (1965) (holding bylaw prohibiting "sale or disposition" of shares without first giving corporation or other shareholders opportunity to purchase inapplicable to transfer consequent upon death of shareholder). See Ward v. City Drug Co., 235 Ark. 767, 362 S.W.2d 27 (1963) (holding agreement among all shareholders that they should be bound by bylaw which permitted corporation to acquire at book value shares pledged and not redeemed prior to maturity of debt, to be binding on shareholder's trustee-in-bankruptcy). Card v. Stirnweis, 232 Or. 123, 374 P.2d 472 (1962) (involving agreement between two shareholders giving survivor option to acquire deceased

shareholder's shares; one of parties sold his shares to other; upon death of latter, former shareholder sought to exercise option; held that option was subject to implied condition that optionee be shareholder at time of its exercise); Stern v. Stern, 79 U.S.App.D.C. 340, 146 F.2d 870 (1945); Taylor's Adm'r v. Taylor, 301 S.W.2d 579 (Ky.1957).

3. Lane v. Albertson, 78 App.Div. 607, 79 N.Y.S. 947 (2d Dep't 1903).

4. See, e. g., Brigham v. M & J Corp., 352 Mass. 674, 227 N.E.2d 915 (1967) (holding deceased shareholder's administrator bound by buy-sell agreement); Matter of Trilling and Montague, 140 F.Supp. 260 (E.D.Pa.1956); McDonald v. Farley & Loetscher Mfg. Co., 226 Iowa 53, 283 Wis. 261 (1939) (not binding on trustee-in-bankruptcy); Messersmith v. Messersmith, 229 La. 495, 86 So.2d 169 (1956) (not applicable to transfers as community property); cf. Magnetic Mfg. Co. v. Manegold, 201 Wis. 154, 229 N.W. 544 (1930) (not applicable to transfer by shareholder to his undisclosed principal). See also Fanchon & Marco, Inc. v. Paramount Pictures, Inc., 133 F.Supp. 839 (S.D.N.Y.1955).

5. Compare Taylor v. Banks, 392 S.W.2d 856 (Tex. 1965), with Westbury Electronic Corp. v. Anglo-American Totalisator Co., 52 Misc.2d 1060, 277 N.Y.S.2d 553 (Sup.Ct.1967), rev'd 28 A.D.2d 683, 280 N.Y.S.2d 762 (2d Dep't 1967) (duty of corporation—pledgee of shares subject to transfer restrictions—to invite bids from outsiders on foreclosure of pledge with disclosure of such provisions); Monotype Composition Co. v. Kiernan, 319 Mass. 456, 66 N.E.2d 565 (1946); Good Fellows Associates, Inc. v. Silverman, 283 Mass. 173, 186 N.E. 48 (1933); Crescent City Seltzer & Mineral Water Mfg. Co. v. Deblieux, 40 La.Ann. 155, 3 So. 726 (1888).

6. Colbert v. Hennessey, 351 Mass. 131, 217 N.E.2d 914 (1966) (bylaw transfer restriction held applicable to shares and voting trust certificates representing shares); Gamson v. Robinson, 284 App.Div. 945, 135 N.Y.S.2d 505 (1st Dep't 1954).

7. Campbell v. Campbell, 198 Kan. 181, 422 P.2d 932 (1967) (restriction on transfers to outsiders held not to prevent transfer to one shareholder without offering shares to all other shareholders); Birmingham Artificial Limb Co. v. Allen, 280 Ala. 445, 194 So.2d 848 (1967) (share transfer restriction held inapplicable to transfers between shareholders); Lank v. Steiner, 43 Del.Ch. 262, 224 A.2d 242 (Sup.Ct.1966) (share transfer restriction applicable only to transfers to others than existing shareholders); Casteel v. Gunning, 402 S.W.2d 529 (Tex. Civ.App.1966) (bylaw share transfer restriction held inapplicable to transfers between shareholders); Gibbon v. 3920 Lake Shore Drive Building Corp., 310 Ill.App. 385, 34 N.E.2d 109 (1941); Serota v. Serota, 168 Misc. 27, 5 N.Y.S.2d 68 (Sup.Ct.1938). See also E. I. Du Pont de Nemours & Co. v. Pathe

without consideration.[8]

Optionees and Parties

In the case of an option restriction, the option usually runs in favor of the corporation, the other shareholders proportionately or otherwise as such other shareholders desirous of acquiring more shares may agree, or both in whatever order is specified, although other variations are possible.[9]

Making the corporation the sole optionee is generally undesirable. In the first place, the corporation may not have funds legally available to purchase the shares at the time the option is to be exercised.[10] Secondly, if

the corporation assumes the absolute duty to buy on a named event, the restriction might be void for want of mutuality since the promise of the corporation is illusory in that there is no assurance that it will have the funds legally available to make the purchase.[11] Even if the corporation takes out insurance on the lives of its shareholders (which would provide funds to acquire shares only of a deceased shareholder),[12]

Film Corp., 25 F.Supp. 850 (S.D.N.Y.1938) (restriction held inapplicable to distribution of shares by corporate shareholder).

8. Magnetic Mfg. Co. v. Manegold, 201 Wis. 154, 229 N.W. 544 (1930).

9. See, e. g., Palmer v. Chamberlain, 191 F.2d 532, 27 A.L.R.2d 416 (5th Cir. 1951) (2–1) (option in favor of directors), reh. denied, 191 F.2d 859 (5th Cir. 1951). Where option referred to the "ten shares assigned to me", and the assignee had received 30 more shares as share dividends on the 10 shares, the option was construed to cover only the first 10 shares. Smith v. Stowell, 256 Iowa 165, 125 N.W.2d 795 (1964). Redemption provisions, optional or mandatory, dependent on a contingency or otherwise, might also be possible. Analogous to options in favor of the corporation are shares redeemable by the corporation, whether optional or mandatory, or dependent on some contingency or otherwise. See Lewis v. H. P. Hood & Sons, 331 Mass. 670, 121 N.E.2d 850, 48 A.L.R.2d 383 (1954) (permitting redeemable common shares). Contra, American Hair & Felt Co. v. Starring, 21 Del.Ch. 431, 2 A.2d 249 (Sup.Ct.1937), aff'g 21 Del.Ch. 380, 191 A. 887 (Ch.1937); Annot., 43 A.L.R.2d 392 (1956). See also McKinney's N.Y.Bus.Corp.Law, § 512(a), (c) (authorizing corporation to provide in its articles of incorporation for one or more classes or series of shares to be redeemable, in whole or in part, at option of corporation at such price or prices and under such conditions as are stated in articles of incorporation, except that no redeemable common shares shall be issued or redeemed unless corporation at time has outstanding class of common shares not subject to redemption).

10. Sanchez v. Centro Mexicano of Sacramento, 1 Cal.App.3d 756, 81 Cal.Rptr. 875 (1969) (failure to offer shares to corporation without necessary surplus excused). Assuming that a corporation has power to acquire its own shares, it may usually do so only out of surplus, but there are some exceptions. Lewis v. Powell, 203 So.2d 504 (Fla.Dist.Ct. App.1967) (enforcing buy-sell agreement, even though

statute prohibits corporate purchase except out of surplus, lacking evidence that creditors or other shareholders would be defrauded). See section 336 infra.

11. But see McKinney's N.Y.Bus.Corp.Law, § 514 (agreement for purchase by corporation of its own shares enforceable by shareholder and corporation to extent such purchase is permitted at time of purchase by id. § 513; possibility that corporation may not be able to purchase its shares under § 513 not to be ground for denying to either party specific performance of agreement for purchase by corporation of its own shares, if at time for performance corporation can purchase all or part of such shares under § 513), overruling Topken, Loring & Schwartz, Inc. v. Schwartz, 249 N.Y. 206, 163 N.E. 735, 66 A.L.R. 1179 (1928) (holding, where only consideration for shareholder's promise to sell shares to corporation was corporation's promise to buy them, that corporation's promise was illusory in that there was no assurance that it would have funds legally available to make purchase, and that therefore there was no mutuality of consideration or remedy). But see Matter of Farah, 13 N.Y.2d 909, 243 N.Y.S.2d 858, 193 N.E.2d 641 (1963) (holding corporation's agreement to buy deceased shareholder's shares, by applying proceeds of life insurance policies corporation carried on his life and by paying balance out of other funds, valid irrespective of existence of funds legally available for corporation's purchase of its own shares at time of purchase); Cross v. Beguelin, 252 N.Y. 262, 169 N.E. 378 (1929) (holding corporate buy-sell agreement to be valid when made, since funds legally available for purchase then existed, but rendered unenforceable against corporation because of current lack of such funds). Buy-sell agreements, of course, involve a commitment on the part of both buyer and seller, in contrast to options, which bind only the offeror of the shares. See Tiedje v. Aluminum Taper Milling Co., 46 Cal.2d 450, 296 P.2d 554 (1956); Cunningham, "Stock 'Buy-Out' Plans: Selection and Drafting", 18 Md.L.Rev. 277 (1958). See also Zimmerman, "Buy-Sell Agreements in Close Corporations—A Summary for the New York Lawyer", 10 Buffalo L.Rev. 1 (1960).

12. Marion v. Orson's Camera Centers, Inc., 29 Wis. 2d 339, 138 N.W.2d 733 (1966) (corporation held to have option, not duty, to purchase shares of deceased employee, even though it had procured life insurance on employee for approximate value of shares). The insured in life insurance to fund

such funds still might not be legally available for use by the corporation to acquire its own shares. Thirdly, corporate exercise of its option might be prevented by the holder of the shares involved or his representatives at meetings of the board of directors or shareholders, unless provision is made in advance to exclude them from voting thereon.[13]

In lieu of an option in favor of the corporation, the option might run in favor of the other shareholders proportionately, possibly with a provision to the effect that if any of the other shareholders do not exercise their option, the rest may acquire the balance of the shares involved proportionately, etc.

The plan which probably offers the most flexibility is to have the option run to the corporation and, if not exercised by the corporation, to the other shareholders proportionately or otherwise as such other share-

holders desirous of acquiring more shares may agree.[14] Obviously, it is probably better to have the optionees as parties to any such arrangement, such as when such arrangement takes the form of a shareholder agreement, rather than to rely on their being able to assert their option rights as third party beneficiaries of any such contract. Even if the corporation is not an optionee, it should be a party to the restriction in order that it can be enforced against it.[15]

Price

In the case of an option-type restriction or buy-sell agreement, the price must be definite or capable of ascertainment; otherwise an essential term of the option or agreement would be lacking and the restriction would be too indefinite to be enforceable.[16]

Selection of the price or price-fixing technique is a challenging problem to the drafts-

buy-sell agreements should retain no incidents of ownership, lest the proceeds be included in his gross estate for estate tax purposes. First Nat'l Bank of Birmingham v. United States, 358 F.2d 625 (5th Cir. 1966) (finding life insurance proceeds were earmarked for purchase of shares and hence were not part of estate of deceased shareholder); Estate of Fuchs, 47 T.C. 199 (1966); Sarner, "Uses of Life Insurance in Buy-Sell Agreements: Stockholder-Corporation Obligations in Buy-Sell Agreements", N.Y.U. 24th Inst. on Fed.Tax. 591 (1966); Jones, "How Insurance Is Used by Closely Held Corporations", 32 N.Y.St.B.Bull. 13 (1960).

13. Boss v. Boss, 98 R.I. 146, 200 A.2d 231 (1964), illustrates the problem which exists when the corporation is the sole offeree. An offer of six shares (representing the future balance of power) to the corporation, as required by the articles of incorporation, was rejected by the shareholders (64 votes to 3 votes) and board of directors (1 to 1, the principal defendant abstaining). The principal defendant thereupon purchased the six shares. The court held that the complaint stated no cause of action, since the corporation had validly rejected the offer of the shares, which thereupon were freed from the share transfer restriction.

Where directors secretly bought shares for themselves from a shareholder who offered them to the corporation under its first refusal option, the shareholder was allowed to rescind the sale because of the directors' breach of their fiduciary duties. Beggy v. Deike, 413 Pa. 74, 196 A.2d 179 (1963). Irwin v. Prestressed Structures, Inc., 420 S.W.2d 491 (Tex.Civ.App.1967) (shareholders allowed to vote against corporation's exercise of option to purchase shares). Kentucky Package Store, Inc. v. Checani, 331 Mass. 125, 117 N.E.2d 139 (1954).

14. Helmly v. Schultz, 219 Ga. 201, 131 S.E.2d 924 (1963), held that a proportionate offer of shares by a retiring shareholder to other shareholders, as required by the bylaws, was not accepted by one of six other shareholders agreeing to take his proportion plus such shares as the other shareholders failed to take. In effect, according to the opinion, unless every shareholder agreed to buy his proportion of the offered shares, there could be no acceptance, and the offered shares could be transferred without restriction. See also Phillips v. Newland, 166 So.2d 357 (La.App.1964), cert. denied 246 La. 872, 167 So.2d 679 (1964) (remaining shareholders' option to purchase proportionately shares of holder desiring to sell all his shares held not accepted by one of remaining shareholders agreeing to buy his proportionate amount).

15. Compare Black & White Cabs of St. Louis, Inc. v. Smith, 370 S.W.2d 669 (Mo.Ct.App.1963) (holding nonparty corporation third party beneficiary of share transfer agreement), with Smith v. Doctors' Service Bureau, Inc., 49 Ill.App.2d 243, 199 N.E.2d 831 (1964); Matter of Argus Co., 138 N.Y. 557, 34 N.E. 388 (1893).

16. Forde v. Vernbro Corp., 218 Cal.App.2d 405, 32 Cal.Rptr. 577 (1963) ("fair valuation as agreed by the attorneys" held sufficiently definite to be enforceable); Hardin v. Rosenthal, 213 Ga. 319, 98 S. E.2d 901 (1957) ("market value or true value"). But see Bendalin v. Delgado, 406 S.W.2d 897 (Tex. 1966) (inferring reasonable price and reasonable time in oral agreement which specified neither); Bailey v. Smith, 268 Ala. 456, 107 So.2d 868 (1959) (sufficient shares to give survivor voting control at twice its book value).

man of such an arrangement,[17] which must be presently framed for application at some future time when circumstances may be substantially different. Closely-held shares rarely have an ascertainable market value.

Basing the price on "book value" is deceptively simple, and can lend itself to subtle manipulation by the board of directors.[18] Although frequently used, "book value" is more of an historical cost than current value concept, and often involves questions as to the conclusiveness of the corporation's books of account and financial reports.[19] An ex-

ample of such a case is Aron v. Gillman,[20] where the price was prescribed as the "book value . . . as determined by the most recent audit", and such audit, as of July 31, included an "estimated" ($12,000) inventory (in contrast to $51,000 actual value) and expressly noted that it was subject to federal and state income taxes and year-end adjustments. The New York Court of Appeals held, 5 to 2, that the value of the inventory should have been based on a physical count rather than on the estimated basis actually used in such audit and that income taxes should be allocated for the January 1–July 31 period ($53,000).[21]

Other price-fixing techniques are capitalization of earnings, fixed price (with or without provision for its periodic redetermination), appraisal, arbitration, "right-of-first-refusal" option, etc.

Capitalization of earnings involves multiplying the average annual net earnings of the close corporation by some figure designated as the rate of capitalization. The arithmetic is simple once the base figure and multiplier are determined, but the latter is most difficult.

A fixed price has the advantage of certainty but can lead to inequities with changes in the fortunes of the business. Provision for periodic redetermination of the price by the parties can be used to minimize unfairness.[22]

---

17. C. Rohrlich, Organizing Corporate and Other Business Enterprises § 4.23 (4th ed. 1967); Page, "Setting the Price in a Close Corporation Buy-Sell Agreement", 57 Mich.L.Rev. 655 (1959); Stern, "Determination of Price in Close Corporation Stock Purchase Arrangements", 13 Rutgers L.Rev. 293 (1958).

18. Corbett v. McClintock-Marshall Corp., 17 Del.Ch. 165, 151 A. 218 (Ch.1930); Druchlieb v. Harris, 209 N.Y. 211, 102 N.E. 599 (1913).

19. See Home Development of St. Petersburg v. Bursani, 178 So.2d 113 (Fla.1965) (book value or market value whichever be higher); Jones v. Harris, 63 Wash.2d 559, 388 P.2d 539 (1964) (enforcing "book value" plus 20 percent of depreciation as price set forth in buy-sell agreement); Chadwick v. Cross, Abbott Co., 124 Vt. 325, 205 A.2d 416 (1964) ("book value based on sound and accepted accounting principles" held not limited to specific method used by corporation in computing taxes and bonuses); Natelson v. Sharp, 152 N.Y.L.J. No. 119, 14 (Sup.Ct. 1964) (requiring surviving shareholder to purchase shares at book value or in no case for less than life insurance proceeds—such proceeds being payable to corporation—notwithstanding insolvency of corporation); Covey v. Covey's Little America, Inc., 378 P. 2d 506 (Wyo.1963) (upholding determination of "book value" in accordance with sound accounting practices by accountants which made no adjustment for market value under agreement providing that accountants' determination of book value was to be binding on all parties); S. C. Pohlman Co. v. Easterling, 211 Cal.App.2d 466, 27 Cal.Rptr. 450 (1962) (upholding determination of "book value" by accountants which excluded unrealized profits on outstanding contracts and excess of market value over book value of securities owned by corporation where agreement provided that accountants' determination was to be conclusive); Piedmont Publishing Co. v. Rogers, 193 Cal.App.2d 171, 14 Cal.Rptr. 133 (1961) ("total book value" held to include fair market value of good will not recorded in corporation's books of account); Schaffer v. Below, 174 F. Supp. 505 (D.V.I.1959), aff'd 278 F.2d 619 (3d Cir. 1960); Block, "Book Value Pitfalls in Buy-Sell Agreements", 95 Trust & Estates 408 (1956); Staus

& Goldert, "What Is Book Value?", 99 J. Accountancy 38 (1955); Annot., 51 A.L.R.2d 606 (1957).

20. 309 N.Y. 157, 128 N.E.2d 284, 51 A.L.R.2d 598 (1955).

21. Desmond & Fuld, JJ., dissented in part, agreeing that the "book value . . . as determined by the most recent audit" necessarily involved a deduction for the estimated amount of taxes to become due on business already done, but contending that the audit estimate of the inventory should be controlling.

22. See Ginsberg v. Coating Products, Inc., 152 Conn. 592, 210 A.2d 667 (1965) (holding refusal of younger shareholders to redetermine value of share to be arbitrable controversy). Where the shareholders fixed the option price for the corporation's acquisition of

Appraisal and arbitration are other means for fixing a fair price. Each delegates the fixing of the price to a third party—initially in the case of appraisal,[23] or after the parties have been unable to agree in the case of arbitration. Such valuation problems may be arbitrable under arbitration statutes even though the controversy is nonjusticiable in nature.[24]

Another possible method, limited to sale situations, is a "right-of-first-refusal" option, under which the shares may not be sold to another without giving the optionee the right to acquire the shares at the proposed price. Obviously, this method is feasible only for situations where an offer for the shares has been made by or is being made to a third person.[25]

Various combinations of price-fixing methods are possible, either by limiting one method by another or by having different methods apply to different situations.

Leaving the price to mutual agreement in the future, without more, would involve only an agreement to agree and not give rise to a valid contract.[26]

One case has held that where the agreement between two sole shareholders, one 33 years older than the other, fixed a price, subject to its being redetermined annually by written mutual consent, and one shareholder died eight years later with no redetermination having been made or requested, the value of the shares having increased eight-fold in the interim, the shareholders were in a fiduciary relationship to each other and the failure of the surviving shareholder to disclose his intention never to consent to any redetermination would constitute a breach of his fiduciary duty and would, standing alone, warrant cancellation of the agreement upon the request of the administratrix of the deceased shareholder.[27]

While discrepancy between the price and value of the shares will ordinarily not invalidate the arrangement, a wide discrepancy might cause a court to refuse to enforce such arrangement as unconscionable.[28]

Recent cases tend both to sustain the restraint as reasonable and to enforce buy-sell agreements and options despite substantial disparity between the price and the value of the shares.[29]

---

the shares of one of them for the first year and provided for annual mutual redetermination and, if they failed to agree, by an arbitrator, and then did nothing for several years, the executor of such shareholder was held entitled to arbitration on the ground that his death did not terminate the right to arbitration. Kolmer-Marcus, Inc. v. Winer, 32 A.D.2d 763, 300 N.Y.S.2d 952 (1st Dep't 1969). See also note 27 infra.

23. E. g., Ginsberg v. Coating Products, Inc., 152 Conn. 592, 210 A.2d 667 (1965) (ordering arbitration of controversy over annual revaluation); Matter of Colletti, 23 A.D.2d 245, 260 N.Y.S.2d 130 (1st Dep't 1965) (holding arbitrators could fix different valuations for shares of different shareholders where agreement required valuations "fair and equitable to all"); Shumaker v. Utex Exploration Co., 157 F. Supp. 68 (D.Utah 1957); see Warren v. Baltimore Transit Co., 220 Md. 478, 154 A.2d 796 (1959).

24. E. g., former N.Y.Civ.Prac.Act § 1448. But see McKinney's N.Y. CPLR, §§ 7501 et seq.

25. Huber v. Mullan, 350 F.2d 872 (4th Cir. 1965) ("right-of-first-refusal" option limited to outside offer "for cash only" held inapplicable to outside offer for cash and installment notes); Sankin v. 5410 Connecticut Ave. Corp., 281 F.Supp. 524 (D.D.C. 1968) (fraudulent outside offer); Addiego v. Hill, 238 Cal.App.2d 842, 48 Cal.Rptr. 240 (1965) ("right-of-first-refusal" option "on the same terms" construed to permit other shareholders to purchase shares for cash equivalent to unique property being offered by outsider).

26. See note 16 supra.

27. Helms v. Duckworth, 101 U.S.App.D.C. 390, 249 F.2d 482 (1957). See note 22 supra.

28. E. g., Greene v. E. H. Rollins & Sons, 22 Del.Ch. 394, 2 A.2d 249 (Ch.1938); cf. McIntyre v. States Marine Corp., 283 App.Div. 651, 127 N.Y.S.2d 2 (1st Dep't 1954), appeal denied 283 App.Div. 783, 129 N.Y.S.2d 226 (1st Dep't 1954) (upholding corporation's option to reacquire shares at par value ($100,000) from employee on termination of employment for any cause, despite shares having present value of $2,000,000, without prejudice to former employee-shareholder's seeking appropriate equitable relief).

29. Mather Estate, 410 Pa. 361, 189 A.2d 586 (1963), upheld and specifically enforced a buy-sell agreement in a Pennsylvania close corporation for the purchase by the surviving shareholder of a deceased shareholder's shares at $1 per share, in the face of the contention that the agreement was an

To provide funds to enable the optionee to exercise the option, at least in survivorship situations, life insurance is frequently taken out by the corporation or shareholders on the latters' lives.[30] Tax consequences of such arrangements should be anticipated.[31]

Option-type restrictions and buy-sell agreements involve various significant tax aspects which are beyond the scope of this discussion.[32]

Location of Restriction

The location of the restriction is also of some importance to the draftsman. The restriction might be set forth in the articles of incorporation, the bylaws, and/or a shareholders' agreement.[33]

invalid restraint on alienation because the price of $1 was grossly unfair for shares then worth $1,060 per share. Cutter Laboratories, Inc. v. Twining, 221 Cal.App.2d 302, 34 Cal.Rptr. 317 (1963), upheld the corporation's buy-sell agreement with respect to 1,800 shares at $20 per share, the fair value at the time the agreement was made, despite the fact that in the intervening 20 years the value of the 1,800 shares had increased from $36,000 to $800,000. In Allen v. Biltmore Tissue Corp., 2 N.Y.2d 534, 161 N.Y.S.2d 418, 141 N.E.2d 812, 61 A.L.R.2d 1309 (1957), the court held specifically enforceable as no unreasonable restraint the corporation's option to reacquire the shares on death from the shareholder's personal representative for the same price which the corporation had received originally for the shares, five of which were issued for $5 per share, five issued as a share dividend, and 10 issued at $10 per share (the corporation was offering $20 per share), and also upheld a share certificate legend reading "Issued subject to restrictions in sections 28, 29, and 30 of the By-laws" as sufficient compliance with Uniform Stock Transfer Act § 15.

30. A. Guild, D. Davis & D. Hoxie, Stock-Purchase Agreements & the Close Corporation (1960); E. White, Business Insurance: Insured Business Continuation Plans for Proprietorships, Partnerships, and Close Corporations (2d ed. 1956). See Land & Simmons Co. v. Arconti, 223 Md. 204, 162 A.2d 478, 163 A.2d 455 (1960) (3–2) (life insurance policy proceeds held includable in assets of corporation in computing "book value" of shares).

31. Ducros v. Comm'r, 272 F.2d 49 (6th Cir. 1959) (insurance proceeds on policy bought by corporation held not taxable to surviving shareholder named as beneficiary of policy; quaere, as to taxability of premiums paid by corporation or cash surrender value). See Prunier v. Comm'r, 248 F.2d 818 (1st Cir. 1957); Casale v. Comm'r, 247 F.2d 440 (2d Cir. 1957) (holding that where corporation owned life insurance policies, premiums it paid did not constitute income to shareholders); Doran v. Comm'r, 246 F.2d 934 (9th Cir. 1957) (holding that where shareholders owned policies, their receipt of proceeds (used to purchase shares of deceased shareholder) were exempt from taxation as life insurance proceeds). To minimize federal income taxes where the corporation pays the premiums, its ownership of the policy should be made clear, and when it uses the proceeds to acquire the shares of the deceased shareholder, it should cancel them; Sneed, "A Defense of the Tax Court's Result in Prunier and Casale", 43 Cornell L.Q. 339 (1958). Goldstein, "Tax Aspects of Corporate Business Use of Life Insurance", 18 Tax Law Rev. 133 (1963); Zox, "Stock Redemption Funded by Life Insurance", 23 Ohio St.L.J. 532 (1962); Comment, "Taxability of Life

Insurance Proceeds Paid to Stockholders of Closely-Held Corporation", 37 Ind.L.J. 246 (1962); Comment, "The Use of Group Insurance to Fund a Buy-Sell Agreement", 8 U.C.L.A.L.Rev. 428 (1961). See also Sarner, "Uses of Life Insurance in Buy-Sell Agreements: Stockholder-Corporation Obligations in Buy-Sell Agreements", N.Y.U. 24th Inst. on Fed. Tax. 591 (1966).

32. Sneed, "Stockholders' Restrictive Agreements and Their Tax Consequences", 38 Okla.B.A.J. 1111 (1967); Weinstock, "Stock Purchase Agreements", 40 Taxes 561 (1962); Crawford, "Redemptions: Buy-Sell Agreements; Long-Term Payouts; Realignment of Family Interests; Other New Developments", N.Y.U. 19th Inst. on Fed.Tax. 567 (1961); Note, "Stock Redemptions from Close Corporations under Section 302", 47 Minn.L.Rev. 853 (1963). The price fixed in the option or agreement may be relevant but not controlling for federal estate tax and state inheritance tax purposes. Mathers v. United States, 226 F.Supp. 1003 (E.D.N.Y. 1964); In re Estate of Kennedy, 173 Ohio St. 379, 182 N.E.2d 624 (1962); Butala, "Valuation of Securities in Closely-Held Corporations", 14 W.Res.L. Rev. 193 (1963); Comment, "Drafting an Effective Buy-Sell Agreement with Emphasis on Estate Tax Valuation of Close Corporate Stock", 53 Ky.L.J. 373 (1965); Comment, "Taxation: Valuation of Securities in a Close Corporation for Federal Tax Purposes", 8 Vill.L.Rev. 92 (1962). Strecher, "Corporate Buy-Sell Agreements: Tax Problems in Drafting", 15 Wash. & Lee L.Rev. 18 (1958); Page, "Setting the Price in a Close Corporation Buy-Sell Agreement", 57 Mich.L.Rev. 655, 679–684 (1959); Tauber, "Tax Aspects of Corporate Buy and Sell Agreements", 57 Wash. & Lee L.Rev. 578 (1959); Buschmann & Carr, "The Corporate Buy-and-Sell Agreement", 45 A.B.A.J. 292 (1959); Note, "Stock Redemption Agreements and the Accumulated Earnings Tax", 44 Marq.L.Rev. 96 (1960). D. Kahn, Basic Corporate Taxation 179 et seq. (ICLE 1970); Abrams, "Tax Planning for Agreements Disposing of a Shareholder's Closely Held Stock at Death", 57 Geo.L.J. 1211 (1969); Cannon, "Buy-Sell Agreements: Form of Purchase Price Received by Seller", N.Y.U. 24th Inst. on Fed.Tax. 607 (1966); Corneel, "Valuation Techniques in Buy-Sell Agreements: Effect on Gift and Estate Taxes", N.Y.U. 24th Inst. on Fed.Tax. 631 (1966).

33. Some authorities suggest that setting forth the share transfer restriction in all possible places is

The articles of incorporation and bylaw provision will insure the binding effect of the restriction on future shareholders, regardless of how they obtain their shares.[34] While the articles of incorporation and bylaws normally might be amended by less than a unanimous vote, absent greater-than-normal quorum-vote requirements, the shareholders agreement cannot be. Any provision in the articles of incorporation, and possibly in the bylaws, usually ought to be impersonal in language. The fact that the restriction is set forth in full on the share certificate alone is usually not sufficient,[35] although in all cases it should be "noted conspicuously" on the share certificate.[36]

Enforcement of Restriction

Share transfer restrictions are generally not self-executing, apart from the corporations withholding transfer of record ownership, and therefore an action for injunction or specific performance may be necessary if a shareholder balks at living up to the share transfer provisions. Since an action at law is manifestly inadequate, care must be taken to avoid the adoption of a restriction which is too indefinite or will operate so harshly as to cause equitable relief to be denied. For example, in the case of an option restriction, if the option price is so low as to work a forfeiture, the court may leave the corporation and its shareholders to the remedy at law.[37] However, the mere fact that the option price is below the fair value of the shares will not alone cause a court of equity to deny relief.[38]

---

the sounder approach. 2 F. O'Neal, Close Corporations: Law and Practice § 7.14 (1958). Obviously, all such insertions should be consistent with each other. Although the Uniform Stock Transfer Act referred to share transfer restrictions in the bylaws "or otherwise", the Uniform Commercial Code refers to securities transfer restrictions imposed by the corporation. See text accompanying section 281, nn. 18–25 supra. Statute of frauds requirements should be satisfied. Previti v. Rubenstein, 156 N.Y.L.J. No. 81, 18 (Sup.Ct.1966) (shares of close corporation subject to transfer restrictions held "security" under Uniform Commercial Code § 8–102); Konsuvo v. Netzke, 91 N.J.Super. 353, 220 A.2d 424 (1966); Smith v. Doctors' Service Bureau, Inc., 49 Ill.App.2d 243, 199 N.E.2d 831 (1964); Hunt v. Doliner, 26 A.D.2d 41, 270 N.Y.S.2d 937 (1st Dep't 1966) (oral conditions allowed as "consistent additional items" under Uniform Commercial Code § 2–202 to modify written option); Hunt Foods & Industries v. Doliner, 26 A.D.2d 41, 270 N.Y.S.2d 937 (1st Dep't 1966) (allowing evidence of "consistent" oral conditions on written option agreement). Oral evidence to explain a written option or other agreement might be inadmissible under the parol evidence rule).

34. The amendment of share transfer restrictions in the articles of incorporation has been upheld. Silva v. Coastal Plywood & Timber Co., 124 Cal.App.2d 276, 268 P.2d 510 (1954) (Nevada corporation). Amendment or imposition of such restrictions in bylaws by less than unanimous shareholder approval has been held ineffective. Bechtold v. Coleman Realty Co., 367 Pa. 208, 79 A.2d 661 (1951); Cowles v. Cowles Realty Co., 201 App.Div. 460, 194 N.Y.S. 546 (1st Dep't 1922); see also Sandor Petroleum Corp. v. Williams, 321 S.W.2d 614 (Tex.Civ.App. 1959) (first option bylaw restriction adopted after initial issue of shares held inapplicable to outstanding shares).

35. Union Bank of Brooklyn v. United States Exchange Bank, 143 App.Div. 128, 127 N.Y.S. 661 (2d Dep't 1911).

36. See section 281, nn. 18–25 supra.

37. Palmer v. Chamberlin, 191 F.2d 532, 27 A.L.R.2d 416 (5th Cir. 1951) (2–1), reh. denied 191 F.2d 859 (5th Cir. 1951) (dictum). Cf. Penthouse Properties, Inc. v. 1158 Fifth Ave., Inc., 256 App.Div. 685, 11 N.Y.S.2d 417 (1st Dep't 1939) (dictum that consent restriction will not be enforced if consent withheld unreasonably). As to defense of lack of mutuality of remedy, compare Murphy v. George Murphy, Inc., 7 Misc.2d 647, 166 N.Y.S.2d 290 (Sup.Ct.1957), with Topken, Loring & Schwartz, Inc. v. Schwartz, 249 N.Y. 206, 163 N.E. 735, 66 A.L.R. 1179 (1928). See McKinney's N.Y.Bus.Corp.Law, § 514(b) (specific performance not deniable merely because corporation's promise might become unenforceable by reason of insolvency or lack of surplus).

38. See e. g., Taylor's Adm'r v. Taylor, 301 S.W.2d 579 (Ky.1957) (book value less 10 percent). See notes 28, 29 supra.

F. DRAFTING

DRAFTING TECHNIQUES— IN GENERAL

283. The sound formation of close corporations essentially involves challenging problems of draftsmanship—to attain in the corporate form so far as legally permissible the desired attributes of the individual proprietorship or partnership. Prior to incorporation, agreement on all matters should be reached and implemented as fully as possible by appropriate documentation in various instruments: (a) preincorporation agreements; (b) articles of incorporation; (c) bylaws; (d) "shareholder agreements"; (e) voting trusts; (f) irrevocable proxies; (g) employment contracts; and (h) share certificate legends.

As previously mentioned, the sound formation of a close corporation essentially involves problems of draftsmanship—to attain in the corporate form so far as legally permissible the desired attributes of the individual proprietorship or partnership. In this respect, the formation of a close corporation on a sound basis is usually far more challenging to the draftsman than the incorporation of other corporations despite the fact that the latter might have substantially greater financial interests.

Prior to incorporation of the close corporation, when relations are generally harmonious, it is generally desirable to reach agreement on all matters and to implement such agreement as fully as possible by appropriate documentation.

Some provisions may be effective if included in any one of various instruments; others are effective only if included in a particular instrument; still others are unacceptable in certain instruments; finally, some provisions which are effective only if included in a particular instrument may be repeated elsewhere. Where the same provision appears in more than one place, each should be consistent with the other. In addition, the overall draftsmanship should be on a consistent basis.

The drafting problems [1] involve or may involve the following: (a) preincorporation agreements; [2] (b) articles of incorporation (with various special provisions relevant to close corporations); [3] (c) bylaws (with appropriate special provisions); [4] (d) "shareholder agreements"; [5] (e) voting trusts; [6] (f) irrevocable proxies; [7] (g) employment contracts; [8] and (h) share certificate legends.[9]

So far as the location of various provisions is concerned, the draftsman sometimes has a choice. No such provisions may, of course, contravene applicable statutes or "statutory norms". Articles of incorporation are subject to administrative scrutiny, usually by the secretary of state, who might take a strict view of provisions which may be included therein, and upon filing become matters of public record; other instruments usually are not subject to administrative scrutiny and do not become matters of public record.

Articles of incorporation are subject to amendment by the requisite shareholder and/or board of directors action and filing with the secretary of state; bylaws are amendable by directors or shareholders as provided by statute or therein, although there may be some limitations on the power of the directors to amend the bylaws and the shareholders might retain inherent power to

1. For specimen provisions, see R. Kessler, New York Close Corporations (1968); 2 F. O'Neal, Close Corporations: Law and Practice ch. X (1958).
2. See section 284 infra.
3. See section 285 infra.
4. See section 286 infra.
5. See section 287 infra.
6. See section 288 infra.
7. See section 288 infra.
8. See section 289 infra.
9. See section 290 infra.

amend the bylaws; "shareholder agreements", voting trusts, irrevocable proxies, and employment contracts usually can be changed only with the unanimous consent of the parties thereto.

While all instruments must be reasonably consistent with applicable statutes or "statutory norms", in the event of any conflict among themselves, the articles of incorporation would ordinarily prevail over the bylaws (and any director or shareholder resolutions); the bylaws over any resolutions. Any "shareholders' agreement" would govern the exercise of voting rights by the parties thereto with respect to the corporate matters covered thereby, but all within the framework of the articles of incorporation, bylaws, and any resolutions. A "shareholder agreement" can be more personal in its references and application, and can deal with some matters more effectively than other instruments, but binds only the parties thereto (and possibly their representatives and assigns and any third party beneficiaries). These, along with such considerations as having the articles of incorporation and bylaws, especially the latter, reasonably self-contained documents and following local practice, are among the more important factors which must be considered in determining the location or locations of various desirable provisions.

DRAFTING TECHNIQUES—PREINCORPORATION AGREEMENT

284. The preincorporation agreement among the associates is an agreement among them for the formation of the corporation, which sometimes takes the form of a simple binder but preferably formulates the entire financial and management structure of the contemplated close corporation by its own provisions and provisions of various documents appended thereto.

The preincorporation agreement among the associates is an agreement among them for the formation of the corporation[1] and is to be distinguished from agreements between promoters and third persons, which have been previously discussed.[2]

Sometimes the preincorporation agreement among the associates includes provisions typically found in "shareholder agreements". It would appear preferable in most cases to separate the latter, which are relevant after incorporation, from the former, to the extent that its provisions cease to be relevant after the corporation is launched.

The preincorporation agreement among the associates can take the form of a simple binder, but the more careful practice is to draft a relatively elaborate and detailed agreement,[3] in which the persons interested in the enterprise agree (a) on the persons who are to serve as incorporators and as initial directors; (b) to execute and acknowledge and cause to be filed the articles of incorporation in the form attached; (c) to subscribe to shares and/or debt securities for prescribed consideration; (d) at the organization meetings of the incorporators and of the board of directors (i) to vote to adopt the bylaws in the form attached, (ii) to authorize the acceptance of any subscriptions and the issue of any debt securities and of shares, (iii) to approve the form(s) of the share certificates with legends in the forms attached, (iv) to appoint certain persons to certain offices at certain salaries, (v) to approve the execution by the corporation of any desired employment contracts with certain persons in the forms attached, and (vi) to authorize the payment by the corporation of a certain fee to the attorney for his fees and disbursements in connection with the or-

1. See section 107 supra. For form of agreement to organize corporation, see 1 G. Hornstein, Corporation Law and Practice § 96 (1959). See also Moss v. Waytz, 4 Ill.App.2d 296, 124 N.E.2d 91 (1955); Mansfield v. Lang, 293 Mass. 386, 200 N.E. 110 (1936).

2. See sections 108–112 supra.

3. See generally 1 F. O'Neal, Close Corporations: Law and Practice § 2.23 (1958).

ganization of the corporation. If there are any accommodation or dummy subscribers, they can agree to transfer any of their subscriptions as the real parties in interest desire. Those with a continuing interest in the enterprise can also agree to enter into a "shareholder agreement" in the form attached, either among themselves or among themselves and the corporation.

Since the above method contemplates attaching copies of the various documents as appendices to the preincorporation agreement, the entire financial and management structures would be formulated in advance on an integrated basis.

DRAFTING TECHNIQUES—ARTICLES OF INCORPORATION

285. **The articles of incorporation, besides stating the various matters required by statute for all corporations, should usually include additional provisions specifically or generally authorized by statute. Generally authorized by statute may be provisions regulating the business of the corporation, the conduct of its affairs, its rights or powers, or the rights or powers of its shareholders or directors, not inconsistent with law, including possibly any provision required or permitted to be set forth in the bylaws. Such general authorization is often narrowly construed by the courts and administrative officials, such as the secretary of state, in reviewing articles of incorporation for filing. Some special close corporation provisions which may not be inserted in the articles might validly be included in other documents. Statutes which give greater recognition to the special problems of the close corporation afford more flexibility.**

The articles of incorporation must state the various matters required by statute,[1] and may include other provisions not inconsistent with law.[2]

1. See sections 118–127, 129–131 supra.

2. R. Kessler, New York Close Corporations chs. 10–12, §§ 14.01, 14.02 (1968); Kessler, "Certificate of Incorporation for a New York Close Corporation: A Form", 33 Fordham L.Rev. 541 (1965). See section 128 supra.

Such additional provisions may be specifically or generally authorized by statute.[3]

Among the provisions which in some jurisdictions may be specifically authorized by statute are those (a) authorizing cumulative or class voting; [4] (b) providing that directors need not be shareholders; [5] (c) requiring that meetings of the board of directors be held only within the state; [6] (d) requiring that shareholder meetings be held only within the state; [7] (e) imposing greater-than-normal quorum/voting requirements for shareholder [8] and/or board of directors action; [9] (f) permitting action by unanimous written consent in lieu of a meeting by shareholders; [10] (g) permitting action by unanimous written consent in lieu of a meeting by directors; [11] providing for shareholder election of officers; [12] (h) imposing control over directors; [13] (i) requiring shareholder approval for corporate mortgages; [14] (j) requiring indemnification of directors, officers, and employees by the corporation for reasonable litigation expenses incurred by them as such in defending litigation; [15] (k) providing

3. E. g., ABA–ALI Model Bus.Corp.Act §§ 17 (second paragraph), 24 (second paragraph), 25 (second sentence), 30 (second sentence), 31 (first paragraph), 33 (second sentence), 33 (last sentence), 34 (second sentence), 37 (first sentence), 37 (second sentence), 38 (first sentence), 40 (first sentence), 40(b), 40(e), 43(a), 61 (second sentence), 136 (specific references), 48(i) (general provision).

4. See sections 124, 189 supra.

5. See sections 130, 204 supra.

6. See section 209 supra.

7. See section 191 supra.

8. See section 266 supra.

9. See section 274 supra.

10. See section 190 supra.

11. See section 208 supra.

12. See section 192 supra.

13. E. g., McKinneys N.Y.Bus.Corp.Law, § 620(b)-(g). See sections 198, 213, 267, 275 supra.

14. See section 342 infra.

15. See sections 379, 380 infra. As alternatives to insertion in the articles of incorporation, such provisions may take the form of a shareholder bylaws

for nonjudicial dissolution by a shareholder or the holders of a specified number of proportion of shares at will or upon the occurrence of a specified event;[16] and (1) restricting the power of shareholders to petition for judicial dissolution in the event of deadlock.[17]

Generally authorized by statute may be provisions regulating the business of the corporation, the conduct of its affairs, its rights or powers, or the rights or powers of its shareholders or directors, not inconsistent with law, including possibly any provision required or permitted to be set forth in the bylaws. The initial language of such authorization is very broad, but the "not inconsistent with law" concluding clause is often construed by the courts as restrictive, permitting no more than possibly slight impingement on the "statutory norms".[18]

Among provisions which may be included in the articles of incorporation are: those to the effect that any transaction between the corporation and another shall not be affected because one or more of its directors has a personal interest in the transaction or is connected with such other person;[19] provisions authorizing shareholder removal of directors without cause;[20] provisions rea-

sonably restricting the transfer of shares;[21] provisions fixing the compensation for directors or officers or authorizing the board of directors to fix their own compensation.[22]

Examples of special provisions which might not be allowed in articles of incorporation by the secretary of state are: provisions that the incorporators shall assign their subscriptions immediately after incorporation; provisions delegating management of the business to an individual or another corporation; provisions purporting to authorize the sale of corporate assets or other extraordinary matters beyond the statutes governing such matters; absolute prohibitions on share transfers, or provisions making transfer contingent upon the consent of directors or shareholders, or provisions barring employees from transferring their shares and requiring them to sell their shares to the corporation upon termination of their employment; provisions that preferred shares shall be redeemed out of surplus at a stated time, but if surplus is insufficient, steps shall be taken to reduce stated capital in order to create surplus for such purpose; provisions giving shareholders an all-inclusive power to veto board of directors action;[23] provisions requiring greater-than-normal quorum/vote for shareholder action in terms of number of shares rather than percentage; provisions authorizing various matters upon less-than-normal vote or con-

---

or shareholder resolution, thereby possibly achieving broader indemnification than is possible under the standards applied by the secretary of state in accepting for filing articles of incorporation containing such provisions.

16. See section 280 supra and section 348 infra.

17. See section 280 supra.

18. See generally O'Neal, "Molding the Corporate Form to Particular Business Situations: Optional Charter Clauses", 10 Vand.L.Rev. 1, 10–13 (1956). See section 128 supra.

19. Everett v. Phillips, 288 N.Y. 227, 43 N.E.2d 18 (1942), reargument denied 289 N.Y. 625, 43 N.E.2d 841 (1942), reargument denied 289 N.Y. 675, 45 N.E. 2d 176 (1942). Such an interested director provision may be important in a close corporation where a director's approval might be required for matters personally affecting him, such as appointment to office, salary, loans by him to the corporation, etc. Quaere, whether such a provision, if inserted only in the bylaws, would be valid. See section 238 supra.

20. Such a removal provision might validly be included in the bylaws, even without a parallel provision in the articles of incorporation.

21. Instead of being inserted in the articles of incorporation, or paralleling insertion therein, such restriction might be included in the bylaws and/or shareholders' agreement. In the event of multiple insertion, consistency should be maintained. Because the articles of incorporation and bylaws are impersonal in nature, any share transfer restriction or options of a more personal type should be effected by a shareholders' agreement. See sections 281, 282 supra.

22. In lieu of insertion in the articles of incorporation, such provisions can be included in the bylaws or a shareholder resolution or, except for possible self-dealing complications, board of directors resolution.

23. However, a type of veto which empowers shareholders or a class of shareholders to overrule board action in *particular* matters may be acceptable.

sent of shareholders; provisions authorizing removal of directors without cause by the board of directors; provisions authorizing directors to act otherwise than collectively as a board or giving certain directors more than one vote; provisions that if the directors disagree or are evenly divided, their differences should be arbitrated; provisions for the unqualified delegation of powers of the board of directors to an executive committee; provisions that the right of the directors to manage the business shall be subject to the bylaws, provisions limiting the powers of directors to appoint or remove officers and authorizing the shareholders to fix the compensation of officers; provisions conferring on the board excessively broad powers to amend the bylaws; provisions for reimbursement of litigation expenses incurred by corporate personnel where the litigation is settled without court approval, or except where such person is adjudged "guilty of wilful malfeasance or misfeasance in the performance of his duties".

Thus, in jurisdictions with less modern statutes or where administrative officials adhere strictly to traditional notions, there are many restrictions on the special close corporation provisions which may be inserted in the articles of incorporation. Some such provisions which may not be inserted in the articles of incorporation might validly be included in other documents. Statutes which give greater recognition to the special problems of the close corporation [24] afford more flexibility.

DRAFTING TECHNIQUES—BYLAWS

286. The bylaws may contain any provisions for the regulation and management of corporate affairs not inconsistent with law or the articles of incorporation. Bylaw provisions escape the administrative scrutiny of the secretary of state. Bylaws often might contain provisions parallel to those in the articles in order that the bylaws will be a reasonably self-con-

tained manual for the guidance of corporate personnel. As a matter of practice, the bylaws deal with many aspects of the administration and regulation of corporate affairs not covered by the articles, such as provisions relating to corporate affairs, share certificates (with possible reference to appropriate legends), share transfer matters (including restrictions), amendment of the bylaws, etc.

The bylaws may contain any provisions for the regulation and management of corporate affairs not inconsistent with law or the articles of incorporation.[1]

As a general proposition, the limitations applicable to provisions in the articles of incorporation also apply to bylaw provisions, although the latter escape the administrative scrutiny of the secretary of state who might apply more exacting standards than some court when a bylaw provision might become the subject of litigation.

Even when a particular optional provision must be in the articles of incorporation to be effective, a parallel provision can also be inserted in the bylaws—not to add to the legal effectiveness of such provision but to make the bylaws a reasonably self-contained manual (or *vade mecum*) for the guidance of corporate personnel.

Some provisions, of course, are effective if in the bylaws alone, at least when adopted by shareholders.

An occasional provision is required to be in the bylaws.

As a matter of practice, the bylaws deal with many aspects of the administrative and regulation of corporate affairs which are not covered by the articles of incorporation, such as provisions relating to the corporate officers, share certificates (with possible reference to appropriate legends), share transfer matters (including restrictions), amendment of the bylaws, etc.

---

24. See sections 259 and 275, n. 1 supra.

1. E. g., ABA–ALI Model Bus.Corp.Act § 25. See section 133 supra. See R. Kessler, New York Close Corporations ch. 13, § 14.03 (1968).

DRAFTING TECHNIQUES—"SHAREHOLDER AGREEMENTS"

287. In "shareholder agreements" in close corporations, the parties can in most jurisdictions, subject to some limitations, bind themselves to do or to refrain from doing certain things, e. g., at the shareholder level: reasonably restricting the transfer of shares, combining to elect directors, voting concerning specified extraordinary corporate matters, such as nonjudicial dissolution, arbitrating their differences; at the board of directors level: having certain persons as officers, paying certain salaries, declaring certain dividends, and following other specified corporate policies, so long as the board of directors is not "sterilized". The sounder practice is to have all shareholders and the corporation as parties, and to make the agreement expressly binding on the shareholders' heirs, representatives, and assigns. The agreement should be definite as to its terms and duration, usually with an express severability provision. Reference to such agreements should be made on all certificates representing shares covered thereby.

"Shareholder agreements" are executed by those interested in close corporations, may be made before (when the term "shareholder" would be technically a misnomer) or after incorporation, and may or may not, but usually should, involve the corporation as a party.[1]

In "shareholder agreements", the parties can, in most jurisdictions, subject to some limitations, bind themselves as shareholders or as directors or as both to do or to refrain from doing certain things.[2]

Shareholders can by agreement reasonably restrict the transfer of their shares, thus achieving *delectus personae*. The most common methods are to give the corporation or the other shareholders or both an option to buy such shares, or to make such purchase mandatory by "buy-sell agreements".[3]

Shareholders, in voting for directors, are usually subject to no fiduciary duties, and hence some or all may agree in advance to vote for certain persons as directors or to pool their votes for directors and cast them jointly as they agree or an arbitrator determines. Such agreements ordinarily do not run afoul of prohibitions on shareholders' selling their votes or proxies, but might if consideration other than mutual promises, such as payment of money, is involved.[4] In a minority of jurisdictions, such an agreement is unlawful since it limits in advance the shareholders in voting their shares in the best interests of the corporation and separates voting power from ownership.[5]

Shareholders, in voting for extraordinary corporate matters, are subject to fiduciary duties. While less than all might validly agree in advance to vote in certain ways with respect to such matters, the more cautious practice is to have all shareholders as parties to such agreements.[6]

Provisions binding shareholders to vote for dissolution in the event of deadlock, if carried out by the parties or enforced by the courts, are a practical means of achieving dissolution of a deadlocked corporation with-

1. The corporation would not be bound by the agreement unless a party. Matter of Argus Co., 138 N.Y. 557, 34 N.E. 388 (1893). Even if the corporation is not a party, it might be able to enforce the agreement on third-party beneficiary principles, or it might be bound on the basis of adoption. Weber v. Sidney, 19 A.D.2d 494, 244 N.Y.S.2d 228 (1st Dep't 1963), aff'd mem., 14 N.Y.2d 929, 252 N.Y.S.2d 327, 200 N.E.2d 867 (1964); Moss v. Waytz, 4 Ill.App.2d 296, 124 N.E.2d 91 (1955). The agreement should be in writing, not only for purposes of any applicable statute of frauds requirements, but also for evidentiary purposes, certainty, and psychological effect. See Weber v. Sidney, supra; Williams v. Fitting, 157 N.Y.L.J. No. 12, 18 (Sup.Ct.1967). Specific performance of a written agreement might be granted more readily than of an oral agreement; Aldridge v. Franco Wyoming Oil Co., 24 Del.Ch. 126, 141, 7 A.2d 753, 761 (Ch.1939), aff'd 24 Del.Ch. 349, 14 A. 2d 380 (Sup.Ct.1940).

2. See sections 198, 213, 267, 275 supra.

3. See sections 281, 282 supra.

4. See sections 198, 267 supra.

5. See sections 198, 267 supra.

6. E. g., Matter of Hega Knitting Mills, Inc., 124 N. Y.S.2d 115 (Sup.Ct.1953). See sections 198, 240, 267 supra.

out encountering the difficulties of judicial dissolution of solvent corporations.[7]

Provisions binding the parties to arbitrate their future differences as shareholders might also be included, making sure, of course, to avoid any inconsistency between arbitration and dissolution provisions, and to comply with applicable local restrictions on arbitration.[8]

To the extent that extraordinary matters in some jurisdictions require concurrent board of directors.[11]
ble to "director agreements" also apply.

Provisions binding directors with respect to their management functions can also be included where they do not unduly infringe on the discretion of directors, especially where all shareholders are parties to such "director agreements".[10] Such provisions might bind directors to appoint and keep in office certain persons so long as they are faithful, efficient, and competent, to pay certain salaries to officers, to declare certain dividends, and to follow other corporate policies, but such commitments should be properly qualified to allow some continued exercise of director discretion with respect to such policies, thus avoiding a "sterilized" board of directors.[11]

The drafting of provisions for arbitration of director deadlocks finds fewer guideposts in the decided cases.[12]

Since the "shareholder agreement", when properly drafted, can effectuate the intentions of the associates in a close corporation, its preparation should be carefully consid-ered in the light of current developments, including any applicable statutes.[13]

Although it can be argued that an invalid provision in the articles of incorporation or bylaws should be construed as an agreement among the shareholders who approved the same, drafting such provisions in the form of a "shareholder agreement" is much more likely to assure court enforcement.[14]

The sounder practice is to have all of the shareholders, even preferred shareholders, as parties to "shareholder agreements" and often also the corporation itself. The agreement should be made expressly binding on the parties' heirs, executors, administrators, representatives, successors, and assigns.[15]

The provisions of agreement should be sufficiently definite for purposes not only of validity but also of specific performance by a court of equity.[16]

Sometimes a partial self-executing feature can be built into a shareholder agreement by appropriate provisions for irrevocable proxies.[17]

13. R. Kessler, New York Close Corporations ch. 8 (1968); 1 F. O'Neal, Close Corporations: Law and Practice §§ 5.01–5.30 (1958); Kessler, "Drafting a Shareholder's Agreement for a New York Close Corporation", 35 Fordham L.Rev. 625 (1967); O'Neal, "Protecting Shareholders' Control Agreements against Attack", 14 Bus.Law. 184 (1958); Hornstein, "Stockholders' Agreements in the Closely Held Corporation", 59 Yale L.J. 1040 (1950); Redfern, "Shareholders' Voting Agreements—Drafting Precautions", 46 Mich.L.Rev. 70 (1947); Strecher, "Corporate Buy-Sell Agreements: Tax Problems in Drafting", 15 Wash. & Lee L.Rev. 18 (1958); Winton, "Tax Traps in Stockholders' Agreements", 2 Prac.Law. 78 (Mar.1956); Comment, "'Shareholder Agreements' and the Statutory Norm", 43 Cornell L.Q. 68 (1957). For form of shareholders' agreement, see C. Israels, Corporate Practice 472–488 (PLI 2d ed. 1969).

14. See section 267 supra.

15. Storer v. Ripley, 12 Misc.2d 669, 178 N.Y.S.2d 7 (Sup.Ct.1958). Also, in community property states, the shareholders' spouses should be parties.

16. Most Worshipful Prince Hall Grand Lodge of Free & Accepted Masons v. Hiram Grand Lodge Masonic Temple, Inc., 32 Del.Ch. 85, 80 A.2d 294 (Ch.1951).

17. McKinney's N.Y.Bus.Corp.Law, § 609(f) (5). Compare Ringling Bros.-Barnum & Bailey Combined Shows, Inc. v. Ringling, 29 Del.Ch. 610, 53 A.

7. See section 280 supra.

8. Matter of Herrman, 155 N.Y.L.J. No. 10, 14 (Sup. Ct.1966) (agreement providing for arbitration of all controversies "arising out of agreement" held not to cover controversies arising out of violation of articles of incorporation). See section 269 supra.

9. See section 215 supra and Chapter 13 infra.

10. See sections 267, 275 supra.

11. See sections 267, 275 supra.

12. See section 277 supra.

The duration of the agreement should also be specified, such as so long as any of the individual parties are shareholders of the corporation or are alive.[18]

Because of judicial attitudes toward such agreements and the risk that the invalidation of part of the agreement will void the rest,[19] there might well be an express provision that in the event any part of the agreement is held invalid, such invalid part shall be deemed severable from the balance of the agreement, and such balance shall be deemed to constitute the agreement of the parties.

Appropriate reference to any shareholder agreement should be made on all certificates representing shares covered thereby.[20]

DRAFTING TECHNIQUES—VOTING TRUST AND IRREVOCABLE PROXY

288. Drafting voting trusts and irrevocable proxies for close corporations presents no problems different from those in corporations generally. Possible complications of federal securities legislation are not present in close corporation as they are in public-issue corporations.

Voting Trusts

Voting trusts in the close corporation are subject to the same requirements which are applicable to voting trusts generally. These requirements have been previously discussed.[1]

Voting trusts in the close corporation, of course, would not be subject to the registra-

tion (and prospectus) requirements of the Federal Securities Act of 1933, as voting trusts in public-issue corporations might.[2]

Irrevocable Proxies

Irrevocable proxies in the close corporation pose no special problems, and are governed by the same rules previously mentioned in the general discussion thereof.[3] The question is whether the desired proxy can be made irrevocable in the particular jurisdiction. Proxies in close corporations, of course, are not subject to the S.E.C. Proxy Rules.[4]

DRAFTING TECHNIQUES—EMPLOYMENT CONTRACTS

289. Employment contracts can be entered into by the close corporation with its officers and other employees promptly after incorporation. Once a person is in office his removal can be forestalled by greater-than-normal quorum/voting requirements, in effect requiring his consent to his removal. An officer removed in breach of a valid employment contract usually may not have specific performance by a court decree but might be reinstated by an arbitrator's award where appropriate provision is made for arbitration.

Employment contracts can be entered into by the corporation promptly after its formation with the persons who are intended to occupy the various positions. Such a contract can specify the intended salary of the officer and, if authorized by appropriate corporate action, can provide that such employment is to continue so long as the employee remains a shareholder of the corporation or for some other specified period.[1]

Once a person is in office, it might be difficult for others to replace him, especially if a greater-than-normal quorum/vote require-

2d 441 (Sup.Ct.1947), with Smith v. San Francisco & N. P. Ry., 115 Cal. 584, 47 P. 582 (1897). See section 196 supra.

18. Weil v. Beresth, 154 Conn. 12, 220 A.2d 456 (1966); Galler v. Galler, 32 Ill.2d 16, 203 N.E.2d 577 (1964), 95 Ill.App.2d 340, 238 N.E.2d 274 (1968); Boatright v. Steinite Radio Corp., 46 F.2d 385 (10th Cir. 1931); Ohlstein v. Hillcrest Paper Co., 22 Misc.2d 405, 199 N.Y.S.2d 88 (Sup.Ct.1960).

19. See sections 198, 213, 267, 275 supra.

20. See section 290 infra.

[§ 288]
1. See sections 197, 270 supra. See also Comment, "The Voting Trust: Drafting Suggestions", 42 N.Y. U.L.Rev. 349 (1967).

2. See section 295 infra.

3. See sections 196, 270 supra.

4. See section 297 infra.

[§ 289]
1. See section 221 supra. See also Harl, "Selected Aspects of Employee Status in Small Corporations", 13 Kan.L.Rev. 23 (1964). For form of employment

ment for board of directors action (possibly along with an interested director provision [2]) gives him the power as director to veto his removal as an officer with or without cause and a greater-than-normal quorum/vote requirement for shareholder action enables him as shareholder to veto his removal as a director with or without cause.[3]

If an officer has been removed in breach of a valid employment contract, such contract is usually not specifically enforced by the courts but might be reinstated by an arbitrator's award where appropriate provision is made for arbitration.[4]

DRAFTING TECHNIQUES—SHARE CERTIFICATE LEGENDS

290. Share certificates representing shares subject to such close corporation provisions as greater-than-normal quorum/voting requirements for shareholder or board of directors action, share transfer restrictions, "shareholder agreements", voting trusts, irrevocable proxies, provisions as to control of directors, or for nonjudicial dissolution at will or upon the occurrence of any specified event, etc., should contain appropriate legends referring thereto to avoid the risk of such provisions being held void or unenforceable against transferees of the share certificates. "Close corporations", designated as such in their articles of incorporation and otherwise subject to recent close corporation statutes must state such fact on their share certificates.

In the close corporation, where the shares are subject to various provisions, the share certificates representing such shares should contain appropriate legends referring to such provisions, to avoid the risk of such provisions being held void or unenforceable against transferees of the share certificates.

The share certificate, for example, should contain appropriate legends where greater-than-normal quorum/voting requirements for board of directors or shareholder action apply,[1] or the shares it represents are subject to transfer restrictions [2] or a lien of the corporation, "shareholder agreements",[3] voting trusts,[4] or irrevocable proxies,[5] or are not fully paid,[6] or where the articles of incorporation contain a provision as to control of directors,[7] or for dissolution at will or upon the occurrence of any specified event,[8] etc.

Such legends should at least indicate that there are such provisions and specify where their full text may be found.[9]

"Close corporations", designated as such in their articles of incorporation and otherwise subject to recent close corporation statutes [10] must state such fact on their share certificates.

[§ 290]

1. E. g., McKinney's N.Y.Bus.Corp.Law, §§ 616(c), 709(c) (to be noted conspicuously on face or back of every share certificate issued by corporation).

2. Uniform Commercial Code § 8–204 (to be noted conspicuously on security). Certificates representing shares subject to any agreement for their repurchase by the corporation ought to refer to such agreement. See McKinney's N.Y.Bus.Corp.Law, § 514.

3. See section 267, n. 44 supra. See McKinney's N.Y.Bus.Corp.Law, § 620(a) (shareholder voting agreement).

4. E. g., McKinney's N.Y.Bus.Corp.Law, § 621(a) (share certificates issued to voting trustee(s) to state that they are issued under voting trust agreement).

5. E. g., McKinney's N.Y.Bus.Corp.Law, § 609(h) (to be noted conspicuously on face or back of certificate representing shares subject to irrevocable proxy).

6. E. g., McKinney's N.Y.Bus.Corp.Law, § 505(e) (to be noted conspicuously on face or back of certificate representing partly-paid shares).

7. E. g., McKinney's N.Y.Bus.Corp.Law, § 620(g) (to be noted conspicuously on face or back of every share certificate issued by corporation).

8. E. g., McKinney's N.Y.Bus.Corp.Law, § 1002(c) (to be noted conspicuously on face or back of every share certificate issued by corporation).

9. See section 281, nn. 18–25 supra. See Allen v. Biltmore Tissue Corp., 2 N.Y.2d 534, 161 N.Y.S.2d 418, 141 N.E.2d 812, 61 A.L.R.2d 1309 (1957).

10. See section 259, n. 23 supra.

[§ 289]

agreement, see C. Israels, Corporate Practice 489–495 (PLI 2d ed. 1969).

2. See section 238 supra.

3. Matter of Burkin (Katz), 1 N.Y.2d 570, 154 N.Y.2d 898, 136 N.E.2d 862, 64 A.L.R.2d 638 (1956).

4. See sections 221, 278 supra.

CHAPTER 11

SPECIAL PROBLEMS OF LARGER
CORPORATIONS

A. INTRODUCTION

A. INTRODUCTION

SPECIAL PROBLEMS OF LARGER CORPORATIONS—IN GENERAL

291. Larger corporations issuing their securities to the public and engaging in activities seriously affecting the economy are subject to substantial governmental regulation, not under state corporate statutes as such, but under separate regulatory legislation at the federal level, largely based on federal power over interstate and foreign commerce and the mails, and at the state level, based on state police power. Extragovernmental regulation is also significant.

As previously indicated, business corporations in the United States are generally incorporated under state corporate statutes

573

which have been drafted, with minor exceptions, primarily for larger corporations, many of which, by today's standards, are medium-size corporations.

The problems of organizing and operating close corporations under such statutes have already been discussed.[1]

Larger corporations issuing their securities to the public[2] or engaging in activities which have or can have significant effects on the economy[3] have become subject to substantial governmental regulation, not under the state corporate statutes as such, but under separate regulatory legislation at federal and state levels.[4]

The exercise of federal regulation is based largely on federal power over interstate and foreign commerce[5] and the mails.[6]

State regulation is based on state police power.

To the extent that corporations are subject to rules and regulations of securities exchanges or other nongovernmental associations, such extragovernmental or self-regulation also must be taken into account.[7]

In this chapter, the regulation, at federal and state levels, of securities will be treated first,[8] followed by a brief discussion of antitrust and trade regulation aspects.[9] Rules and regulations of securities exchanges and other nongovernmental associations will then be briefly outlined.[10]

B. SECURITIES REGULATION

PUBLIC ISSUE OF SECURITIES

292. For the public issue of securities, especially larger issues, investment bankers or underwriters are usually involved. They usually combine to form a purchase or underwriting group to share the underwriting risk and to effect successful public distribution of the issue, and also form a more widespread "selling group" to join in the distribution. The underwriters are usually selected as the result of private negotiation with the issuer, but some administrative agencies require competitive bidding. Basically, there are three types of underwriting: (a) "Stand-by" underwriting; (b) "Firm commitment" underwriting; and (c) "Best efforts" underwriting. Most frequently, there are three agreements involving the underwriters: (a) "Agreement among" underwriters; (b) Underwriting agreement (or purchase contract); and (c) Selected dealers agreement (or selling agreement).

Securities regulation developed first at the state level, starting about 50 years ago, and

1. See Chapter 10 supra.

2. See sections 292–308 infra.

3. See sections 309–315 infra.

4. In continental Europe, such regulation has been integrated into the corporation provisions of the commercial codes. In countries without a federal system, of course, distribution-of-powers problems do not exist as they do in the United States. Even in other countries with a federal system (e. g., Brazil, Canada, Mexico, West Germany), the federal government enjoys substantially broader powers over incorporation itself than does the federal government in the United States. See sections 8, 12–14 supra.

5. U.S.Const. art. I, § 8, cl. 3. Obviously, as the federal power over commerce has been enlarged by United States Supreme Court cases expanding the concept of interstate and foreign commerce, intrastate commerce, traditionally subject to state regulation, has been reduced in scope. See E. Corwin, The Commerce Power Versus States Rights (1936). Of course, the states may regulate aspects of interstate or foreign commerce within their respective borders (or by interstate compact) to the extent that Congress has not exercised its powers with respect to such aspects and provided such state regulation does not constitute an undue burden on interstate or foreign commerce.

6. U.S.Const. art. I, § 8, cl. 7. Over the years, the federal government has exercised some degree of control through the postal laws and regulations, especially the mail fraud statutes.

7. See sections 316, 317 infra.

8. See sections 292–308 infra.

9. See sections 309–315 infra.

10. See sections 316, 317 infra.

then, when state regulation proved less than fully effective, at the federal level.[1]

In order to understand securities regulation, knowledge of the practical operations involved in the public issue and trading of securities is prerequisite.[2]

When a corporation in bygone days desired to issue its securities to the public, it traditionally bore the risk alone and distributed its securities by agents selling on a commission basis. Since then, beginning after the Civil War but accelerating after World War I in the United States, the investment banking industry evolved.

The investment banker came to perform a series of interrelated services, including the formulation of the plan and method to be pursued in raising the money, the undertaking of the risk, and the distribution of the security issue as a whole. As issues grew in size, underwriters combined in connection with a larger issue and formed a purchase or underwriting group (pool or syndicate) to share the underwriting risk and to effect successful public distribution of the issue and formed a larger, more widespread "selling group" (or syndicate) to join in the distribution, with the underwriting group serving as wholesalers and the selling group as retailers.[3]

The Banking Act of 1933 (Glass-Steagall Act)[4] required divorcement of investment banking functions, on the one hand, from commercial and deposit banking, on the other.[5]

Corporations interested in raising funds, of course, do not always use the services of an investment banker. Typical of such transactions are:[6]

    (a) A direct public offering by the issuer without an investment banker;

    (b) A direct offering to existing security holders without an investment banker;

    (c) A direct private placement without an investment banker;

---

1. See generally L. Loss, Securities Regulation (2d ed. 1961) (3 vols.) (1969 Supp., 3 vols.); E. McCormick, Understanding the Securities Act and the S.E.C. (1948); A. Choka, An Introduction to Securities Regulation (1958); Symposium: "Securities Regulation", 16 W.Res.L.Rev. 9 (1964).

2. For discussion of public trading of securities, see section 293 infra. See also Adkins, "Practice of Corporate Financial Law", 4 Stud.Law. 6 (Apr.1959).

3. For an excellent history of investment banking, see opinion of Medina, Cir. J., in United States v. Morgan, 118 F.Supp. 621, 635–655 (S.D.N.Y.1953). See H. Guthmann & H. Dougall, Corporate Financial Policy ch. 18 (4th ed. 1962); Stuebner, "The Role of the Investment Banker in Arranging Private Financing", 16 Bus.Law. 377 (1961). See 1 L. Loss, Securities Regulation 159 et seq. (2d ed. 1961); C. Israels & G. Duff, When Corporations Go Public (PLI 1962); G. Robinson, Going Public: Successful Securities Underwriting (1961); E. Winter, A Complete Guide to Making a Public Stock

Offering (1962); H. Guthmann & H. Dougall, Corporate Financial Policy ch. 18 (4th ed. 1962); "Going Public: A Panel Discussion of Certain Factual Situations", N.Y.U. 21st Inst. on Fed.Tax. 1497 (1963); Symposium: "Current Problems of Securities Underwriters and Dealers", 18 Bus.Law. 27 (1962); Sterling, "Legal Audit Upon Going Public: Non-Securities Law Aspects", 22 Bus.Law. 765 (1967); Spencer & Sullivan, "An Introduction to 'Going Public'", 42 Mich.S.B.J. 11 (Feb.1963); Burns, Parker & Peder, "How to Evaluate the Complex Tax Problems and Opportunities in 'Going Public'", 18 J.Taxation 66 (1963); Rotberg, "The 'Hot Issue'", 17 Bus.Law. 360 (1962); Kahn, Harris, West & Forer, "Going Public as a Means of Expansion", N.Y.U. 19th Inst. on Fed.Tax. 453 (1961); Backus, "Timetable for Public Financing", 7 Prac.Law. 13 (Oct.1961); Fleischer & Meyer, "What Treatment for Non-Employee Stock Options? Underwriters Position Difficult", 14 J.Taxation 274 (1961). See Wing, "Guidelines for Underwriter Activity", 25 Bus.Law. 397 (1970).

4. 48 Stat. 162 (1933), 12 U.S.C.A. § 227.

5. Institutions engaged in both investment banking and commercial and deposit banking had to elect prior to June 16, 1934 which of the two functions they would pursue to the exclusion of the other. J. P. Morgan & Co., then a partnership, elected to cease investment banking, eventually incorporating as J. P. Morgan & Co. Incorporated, merged in 1959 into Guaranty Trust Co. of New York with name changed to Morgan Guaranty Trust Co. of New York. Some of the partners of J. P. Morgan & Co. later resigned and organized Morgan Stanley & Co. to engage in investment banking. Investment bankers are not "bankers" in the usual sense. See I. Friend, et al., Investment Banking and the New Issues Market (1967); J. Hazard & M. Christie, The Investment Business: A Condensation of the SEC Report (1964).

6. Medina, Cir. J., in United States v. Morgan, 118 F.Supp. 621, 651 (S.D.N.Y.1953).

(d) A public sealed bidding transaction without the assistance of an investment banker; and

(e) Term bank loans, commercial mortgage loans, leasebacks and equipment loans by commercial banks, life insurance companies, and other institutions.

Typical of the transactions involving the services of an investment banker are: [7]

(a) A negotiated underwritten public offering;

(b) An underwritten public offering awarded on the basis of publicly invited sealed bids, an investment banker having been retained on a fee basis to shape up the issue;

(c) A negotiated underwritten offering to existing security holders. Here the investment banker enters into a commitment to "stand by" until the subscription or exchange period has expired, at which time the investment banker must take up the securities not subscribed or exchanged;

(d) An underwritten offering to existing security holders awarded on the basis of publicly invited sealed bids, an investment banker having been retained on a fee basis to render the necessary assistance;

(e) A non-underwritten offering to existing security holders, with an investment banker acting as agent of the seller on a negotiated basis; and

(f) A private placement with an investment banker acting as agent of the seller on a negotiated basis.

Some of the foregoing transactions, with or without an investment banker, involve a public offering and others do not. Every case of competitive bidding [8] necessarily in-

volves a public offering by the issuer, and, if the successful bidder or bidders purchase and reoffer the securities to the public, a public offering by them. Transactions by an issuer not involving any public offering are exempt from the registration (and prospectus) requirements of the Federal Securities Act of 1933,[9] with their attendant complexities, delays, and expenses. For a medium-size issue, the costs of public offering might be more than twice as large as those of private placement.[10]

Basically, there are, in a broad sense,[11] three types of underwriting: [12]

as the Interstate Commerce Commission, Federal Power Commission, Securities and Exchange Commission in connection with the issue of securities of registered companies under the Public Utility Holding Company Act of 1935, and New York Public Service Commission. 1 L. Loss, Securities Regulation 388–396 (2d ed. 1961). In cases of competitive bidding, the "bidding papers" usually consist of a public invitation for bids for the purchase of the securities, a statement of terms and conditions relating to bids, a form of bid, and a purchase contract (for execution by the issuer and the successful bidder or bidders). Independent counsel to represent the interests of the successful bidders are selected by the issuer. Such counsel, inter alia, prepare the "Blue Sky Survey" and, when relevant, "Legal Investments Survey".

9. See section 295 infra.

10. One estimate of an issuer's expenses—private placement vs. public offering—for an $8,000,000 bond issue is as follows:

	Private Placement	Public Offering
Underwriting (or Agency) Fee	$40,000	$ 90,000
S.E.C. Registration Fee	–	1,616
Trustee Fees	–	7,500
Counsel Fees	12,000	20,000
Auditing Fees	–	10,000
Printing indentures, etc.	1,500	
Printing registration statement and prospectus	–	25,000
Printing securities	500	2,000
Blue Sky & Legality Fees	–	8,000
Miscellaneous	1,000	5,884
Totals	$55,000	$170,000

11. A. Choka, An Introduction to Securities Regulation 8–10 (1958).

12. The term "underwriting", in a strict insurance sense, means underwriting or assuming a risk. The term "underwriter" is broadly defined in the Federal Securities Act of 1933 to include a person who engages in underwriting of any of the three types.

7. Ibid.

8. Competitive bidding has been favored, and often required by such regulatory administrative agencies

(a) *"Stand-by" Underwriting* (or strict, "old-fashioned", traditional, English underwriting):[13] The issuer, either directly or through an "issuing house", makes a public offering of the securities (often to existing shareholders, whether pursuant to preemptive rights or otherwise) and the underwriter makes a firm commitment (subject to "market out" clause) to take up the unsubscribed portion of the issue. The underwriter usually gets a "stand-by" fee and additional sums based on the amount of the securities taken up, subject to limitations. "Stand-by" underwriting is rarely used in the United States except in connection with rights offerings.

(b) *"Firm Commitment" Underwriting:*[14] The issuer sells the entire issue to the underwriter who then resells the securities. Technically, this is not underwriting in the insurance sense, but a purchase-and-sale arrangement; it is the most prevalent type of underwriting in the United States. The underwriting fee is usually the difference between what the underwriter pays the issuer for the securities and what the underwriter realizes from the resale of the securities (known as the "underwriting spread").

(c) *"Best Efforts" Underwriting:*[15] The underwriter is bound only to use his best efforts to sell the securities as agent for the issuer, receiving a commission for such services. Strictly speaking, this is not always underwriting but sometimes is more of an agency relationship.[16] It is used for smaller or less established corporations or more speculative issues when no underwriter is willing to assume the risk with respect to the issue.

Sometimes "firm commitments" and "best efforts" underwritings are used in combined form.

In the case of "firm commitment" or "stand-by" underwriting, the underwriters usually enter into three agreements:[17]

(a) *Agreement Among Underwriters* (known as the "agreement among"):[18] The underwriters agree among themselves on their proportionate several (not joint) participation, designate one or more representatives (or managers) from their number, authorize the latter to execute and perform the Underwriting Agreement in behalf of all of them, and agree to compensate (in proportion to their several participation) the representatives for serving as such. The "agreement among" contains numerous ancillary provisions. In practice, the representatives usually bring together the participating underwriters to form the underwriting group. These underwriters who sign the "agreement among" and through the execution of the underwriting agreement come in privity with the issuer

13. For form of "stand-by" underwriting agreement, see Modern Legal Forms § 2992 (rev. ed. 1966).

14. For form of "firm commitment" underwriting agreement, see C. Israels & G. Duff, When Corporations Go Public 372 (PLI 1962); G. Robinson, Going Public: Successful Securities Underwriting 63 (1961); 7 J. Rabkin & M. Johnson, Current Legal Forms With Tax Analysis, Form 18.44 (1968); Modern Legal Forms § 2994 (rev. ed. 1966).

15. For form of "best efforts" underwriting agreement, see C. Israels & G. Duff, When Corporations Go Public 293 (PLI 1962).

16. See Demarco v. Edens, 390 F.2d 836 (2d Cir. 1968) (holding "best efforts" underwriter not to be under issuer's control by agency for purposes of § 12 of Securities Act, where underwriting agreement provided that fee was "discount" rather than "commission" suggesting purchase and resale, that issuer would deliver shares for account of underwriter, and that underwriter was not under control of issuer).

17. 1 L. Loss, Securities Regulation 159–178 (2d ed. 1961).

18. For form of agreement among underwriters, see 2 Lassers, Fletcher Corporation Forms Annotated § 1560 (3d rev. ed. 1958); Modern Legal Forms § 2999 (rev. ed. 1966).

are sometimes called the "principal underwriters" to distinguish them from dealers who participate in the distribution and hence are underwriters but are not in privity with the issuer.

(b) *Underwriting Agreement (or Purchase Contract):* [19] This is an agreement between the issuer of the securities and the underwriters (executed by their representatives) for the sale by the issuer and the purchase by the underwriters severally (and not jointly) at a prescribed price of a stated percentage of the entire issue (in the case of "firm commitment" underwriting) or of the securities unsubscribed by the public (in the case of "stand-by" underwriting). Numerous additional provisions deal with many matters. In preliminary negotiations, tentative agreement on all details except price is usually achieved. No firm commitment is usually made until a day or two before the effective date of the registration statement. The so-called "market out" clause—usually broader than a *force majeure* or "act of God" clause—often permits termination of the agreement "by the Representative at any time prior to the expiration of 24 hours after the Registration Statement shall become effective (but not after the commencement of the public offering of the Securities by the Underwriter), if the market for securities in general or the market for the Securities or political, financial and economic conditions shall have so materially and adversely changed after the date of this agreement and within the time set forth above as, in the judgment of the Representative, would render it

inadvisable to make a public offering of the Securities".[20]

(c) *Selected Dealers Agreement (or Selling Agreement):* [21] These agreements between selected dealers and the underwriters (by their representatives) invite orders from such dealers for the securities (subject to the confirmation of the representatives). The dealers pay the public offering price less a so-called "dealer's concession" and a small discount (if a National Association of Securities Dealers member or foreign dealer agreeing to conform to the N.A.S.D. Rules of Fair Practice).[22]

20. Another widely-used "termination-of-agreement" provision reads:

"This agreement may be terminated by the Representative with the consent of the Underwriters (including the Representative) who have agreed to purchase in the aggregate 50 percent or more of the aggregate principal amount of the Securities agreed to be purchased hereunder, at any time prior to the time of Purchase, if the Company shall have sustained a substantial loss by fire, flood, accident, or other calamity which, in the judgment or discretion of the Representative, shall render it impracticable to resell the Securities agreed to be purchased hereunder, whether or not such loss shall have been insured. If the Underwriters shall have advised the Company that they propose to make a public offering of the Securities purchased hereunder, this agreement may be terminated at any time prior to the expiration of 24 hours after the Post-Effective Amendment shall become effective (but not after the public offering of the Securities) by the Representative with like consent, if trading in securities on the New York Stock Exchange shall have been suspended or limited, or minimum prices shall have been established on such Exchange, or a banking moratorium shall have been declared by either Federal or State authorities." See Richard Bruce & Co. v. J. Simpson & Co., 40 Misc.2d 501, 243 N.Y.S. 2d 503 (Sup.Ct.1963) (holding that "market out" provision of underwriting agreement stating that underwriter could terminate agreement if, in its "absolute discretion", it determined that market conditions or prospects of public offering were such as to make it inadvisable, granted underwriter only discretion based on fair dealing and good faith, reasonable discretion, to be understood in light of nature of risks with respect to compensation on "all-or-none" basis for its services, and such "market out" clause did not render agreement illusory).

21. For form of selected dealers agreement, see Modern Legal Forms § 2998 (rev. ed. 1966).

19. For forms of underwriting agreements, see notes 13, 14, 15 supra.

22. See section 317 infra.

PUBLIC TRADING OF SECURITIES

293. **Public trading in securities involves the transfer or secondary distribution from one holder to another of outstanding securities, as distinguished from the primary distribution of new issues of securities by the issuer directly or indirectly through an underwriter. Securities are traded either on a securities exchange, as listed or admitted to unlisted trading, or off a securities exchange ("over-the-counter"). Securities exchanges, their members, listed and other large publicly-held companies, and over-the-counter brokers and dealers are subject to substantial governmental and nongovernmental regulation.**

Trading in securities involves the transfer or secondary distribution (from one holder to another) of outstanding securities as distinguished from the primary distribution of new issues of securities by the issuer directly or indirectly through an underwriter. Securities are publicly traded in the United States either on or off a securities exchange (often called "stock exchange", although other securities, such as bonds, debentures, and warrants, are also traded thereon).[1]

If traded on a securities exchange,[2] the securities may either be listed or admitted to unlisted trading.[3]

The exchanges themselves, their members, and the companies whose securities are traded thereon, are subject to substantial governmental regulation[4] and their own internal regulation.[5]

If traded off a securities exchange, the securities are said to be traded "over-the-counter" or "off board". Involved is personal selling and the use of the mails, telephone, telegraph, and teletype; the marketing of new securities by underwriters as well as trading in existing securities. Most bonds (United States government and corporate), almost all state and municipal bonds, real estate issues, and securities of "open-end" investment companies ("mutual funds") and of smaller corporations are traded over-the-counter.[6]

Brokers and dealers on the over-the-counter market and large publicly-held companies are subject to governmental[7] and nongovernmental regulation.[8]

4. See sections 296–298 infra.

5. See section 316 infra.

6. L. Loll & J. Buckley, The Over-the-Counter Securities Markets: A Review Guide (2d ed. 1967); Over the Counter Markets Study (Booz, Allen & Hamilton, Inc. 1966); H. Guthmann & H. Dougall, Corporate Financial Policy 381 (4th ed. 1962); I. Friend, G. Hoffman & W. Winn, The Over-the-Counter Securities Market (1958); Over the Counter Securities Markets—An Active Partner in Corporate Progress (N.A.S.D.); Understanding the Over-the-Counter Securities Market (1966); Burns, "Over-the-Counter Market Quotations: Pink, Yellow, Green and White Sheets—A Gray Area in the Law of Evidence", 52 Cornell L.Q. 262 (1967); Polakoff & Sametz, "Third Market—The Nature of Competition in the Market for Listed Securities Traded Off-Board", 11 Antitrust Bull. 191 (1966); Loomis & Rotberg, "Over-the-Counter Market Quotations", 62 Mich.L.Rev. 589 (1964); Frey, "Federal Regulation of the Over-the-Counter Securities Market", 106 U.Pa.L.Rev. 1 (1957).

7. E. Weiss, Registration and Regulation of Brokers and Dealers (1965); Sowards & Mofsky, "Securities Industry: Regulatory Control over Entry", 8 Corp. Prac.Comm. 99 (Aug.1966); Levin & Evan, "Professionalism and the Stockbroker", 21 Bus.Law. 337 (1966); Comment, "Churning by Securities Dealers", 80 Harv.L.Rev. 869 (1967). See sections 296, 305–308 infra.

8. Cary, "Self-Regulation in the Securities Industry", 49 A.B.A.J. 244 (1963). See sections 316, 317 infra.

1. E. Willett, Fundamentals of Securities Markets (1968); S. Robbins, The Securities Markets: Operations and Issues (1966); G. Leffler & L. Farwell, The Stock Market (3d ed. 1963); B. Shultz, The Securities Market—And How It Works (rev. ed. 1963); Woodside, "Resumé of the Special Study of Securities Markets and the Commission's Legislative Proposals", 19 Bus.Law. 463 (1964); Stigler, "Public Regulation of the Securities Markets", 19 Bus.Law. 721 (1964); Hodes, "Some Pros and Cons of Listing on a Securities Exchange", 10 Prac.Law. 41 (Apr.1964). See also Execution of Odd-Lot Orders on the New York Stock Exchange (Carlisle & Jacquelin 1966).

2. For a readable summary of the operations of a national securities exchange, see Understanding the New York Stock Exchange (New York Stock Exchange rev. ed. 1969); see also The Language of Investing: A Glossary (New York Stock Exchange rev. ed. (1969).

3. In 1910, the New York Stock Exchange abolished unlisted trading. Since 1936, unlisted trading on exchanges has been subject to rigorous SEC regulation. 15 U.S.C.A. § 78l(f); 2 L. Loss, Securities Regulation 1132–1149 (2d ed. 1961).

FEDERAL SECURITIES LEGISLATION— IN GENERAL

294. Federal securities legislation consists of seven statutes, enacted between 1933 and 1940, following the great depression. Six of these statutes, all based on federal power over interstate and foreign commerce and the mails, are administered by the Securities and Exchange Commission: (a) Securities Act, 1933; (b) Securities Exchange Act, 1934; (c) Public Utility Holding Company Act, 1935; (d) Trust Indenture Act, 1939; (e) Investment Company Act, 1940; and (f) Investment Advisers Act, 1940. Under Chapter X of the Bankruptcy Act, 1938, the S.E.C. has certain advisory functions.

At the federal level, seven securities regulation statutes were enacted during the seven-year period, 1933–1940, following the great depression. Six of these statutes, all based on federal power over interstate and foreign commerce and the mails, are administered by the Securities and Exchange Commission (S.E.C.), established in 1934.[1]

1. Prior to the establishment of the Securities and Exchange Commission by the Securities Exchange Act of 1934, the Securities Act of 1933 was administered by the Federal Trade Commission (F.T.C.). The S.E.C. is an independent, bipartisan, quasi-judicial agency of the federal government, composed of five commissioners, appointed by the President with the advice and consent of the Senate, for rotating five-year terms. Not more than three commissioners may be members of the same political party. One of the commissioners is designated by the President as the chairman. The S.E.C. has a staff of some 1,400 employees divided into several "offices" and three "divisions": Corporation Finance, Trading and Markets, and Corporate Regulation. The principal offices of the S.E.C. are in Washington, D.C. There are nine regional offices, the largest being in New York City, and several branch offices. In 1934, shares listed on the New York Stock Exchange had a value of $34 billion; twenty-five years later, the value had risen to $350 billion, subsequently to more than $500 billion; new corporate issues had risen from $400 million to $10 billion annually, subsequently to some $20 billion; the number of shareholders had risen to some 20,000,000. See generally R. DeBedts, The New Deal's SEC: The Formative Years (1964); H. Black, Watchdogs of Wall Street (1962); Cary, "Administrative Agencies and the Securities and Exchange Commission", 29 Law & Contemp.Prob. 653 (1964); Hopper, "The Securities and Exchange Commission as It Affects the General Practitioner", 36 U.Colo.L.Rev. 36 (1963); North & Focht, "What You Should Know About the Securities and Exchange Commission", 6 Stud.Law. 7 (June, 1967); Dean, "Twenty-Five Years of Federal Securities Regulation by the Secu-

The six statutes are the Securities Act, rities and Exchange Commission", 59 Colum.L.Rev. 697 (1959); Gadsby, "Historical Development of the S.E.C.—The Government View", 28 Geo.Wash.L. Rev. 6 (1959); Freeman, "A Private Practioner's View of the Development of the Securities and Exchange Commission", 28 Geo.Wash.L.Rev. 18 (1959); Wheat, "Federal Regulation of Corporate Securities", in Advising California Business Enterprises 581–637 (1958); Dunton, "Selected Bibliography, Including Legislative History of the Securities and Exchange Commission and the Statutes It Administers", 28 Geo.Wash.L.Rev. I (1959). In July 1, 1966–June 30, 1967, new registered securities issues totaled $34,218,000,000; 1, 649 registration statements were filed, 440 or 24 percent by companies which had not previously filed registration statements; 363 indentures qualified; volume of trading on securities exchanges was approximately $150,-000,000,000, involving close to 4,000,000,000 shares; there were 4,175 registered brokers and dealers, 216 registered public utility holding companies and subsidiaries, 775 registered investment companies, and 1,732 registered investment advisers; 90,525 customer's men, or registered representatives were registered with the National Association of Securities Dealers, Inc. See generally L. Loss, Securities Regulation (2d ed. 1961) (3 vols.) (1969 Supp., 3 vols.); L. Rappaport, SEC Accounting Practice and Procedure (2d ed. 1963); H. Wander & W. Grienenberger, Selected Articles on Federal Securities Law (ABA 1968); R. Jennings & H. Marsh, Securities Regulation: Cases and Materials (2d ed. 1968); H. Sowards, The Federal Securities Act (1968); H. Bloomenthal, Cases and Materials on Securities Law (1966); R. Knauss, Securities Regulation Sourcebook (1965-) (looseleaf); P. Tyler, Securities, Exchanges and the SEC (1965); H. Guthermann & H. Dougall, Corporate Financial Policy (4th ed. 1962); C. Israels & G. Duff, When Corporations Go Public (PLI 1962); G. Robinson, Going Public: Successful Securities Underwriting (1961); A. Choka, An Introduction to Securities Regulation (1958); CCH Federal Securities Law Reports (4 vols.); P–H Securities Regulation (2 vols.); M. Feuer, Personal Liabilities of Corporate Officers and Directors chs. 16–18 (1961); J. Williamson, Securities Regulation in Canada (1960); "Conference on Codification of the Federal Securities Laws", 22 Bus.Law. 793 (1967); Symposium: "Securities Regulation", 20 Sw. L.J. 431 (1966); Symposium: "Federal and State Regulation of Securities", 34 U.Mo.Kan.City L.Rev. 172 (1966); Symposium: "Securities Acts Amendments of 1964", 20 Bus.Law. 265 (1965); Crossland & Sehr, "The Gods of the Market Place: An Examination of the Regulation of the Securities Business", 48 B.U.L.Rev. 515 (1968); Haack, "Corporate Responsibility to the Investing Public", 23 Record of N.Y.C.B.A. 336 (1968); Knauss, "Disclosure Requirements—Changing Concepts of Liability", 24 Bus. Law. 43 (1968); Schneider, "An Administrative Program for Reforming the Federal Securities Laws", 23 Bus.Law. 737 (1968); Morton & Booker, "The Paradoxical Nature of Federal Securities Regulations", 44 Denver L.J. 479 (1967); Schneider, "Reform of the Federal Securities Laws", 115 U.Pa.L. Rev. 1023 (1967); Shipley, "The SEC's Amicus Cur-

1933;[2] Securities Exchange Act, 1934;[3] Public Utility Holding Company Act, 1935;[4] Trust Indenture (Barkley) Act, 1939;[5] Investment Company Act, 1940;[6] and Investment Advisers Act, 1940.[7]

Specific federal securities legislation has largely replaced the application of the federal mail-fraud statutes to securities transactions.

In addition, the Securities and Exchange Commission has certain advisory functions

under Chapter X of the Federal Bankruptcy (Chandler) Act, 1938.[8]

FEDERAL SECURITIES LEGISLATION— SECURITIES ACT, 1933

295. **The Securities Act, 1933, deals mainly with the initial (or primary) distribution of securities by the issuer, imposing (a) registration (and prospectus) requirements, and (b) anti-fraud provisions.**

Under the registration (and prospectus) requirements, no security may be offered or sold through the mails or interstate or foreign commerce without compliance with such requirements unless either the security is exempt or the transaction is exempt. Under the "small-issues" exemption, a simplified procedure for issues not exceeding $300,000, involving the filing of a notification and possibly use of an offering circular, is provided by Regulation A and related regulations. Otherwise, the requirements involve the advance filing of a registration statement with the Securities and Exchange Commission, where it becomes a matter of public record, and the furnishing of a prospectus to each purchaser of the securities. Different activities are permissible during the pre-filing period, the waiting period, and the post-effective period.

Even though a security or transaction is exempt from registration, the civil and criminal liabilities for misrepresentation and anti-fraud provisions of the Act apply if interstate or foreign commerce or the mails are involved in the offer or sale of securities.

The Securities Act, 1933,[1] or "Truth-in-securities" act, deals mainly with the initial

iae Aid to Plaintiffs in Mutual Fund Litigation", 52 A.B.A.J. 337 (1966); Loomis & Eisenberg, "The SEC as *Amicus Curiae* in Shareholder Litigation—A Reply", 52 A.B.A.J. 749 (1966); Poser, "Securities Regulation in Developing Countries: The Brazilian Experience", 52 Va.L.Rev. 1283 (1966); Fleischer, "'Federal Corporation Law': An Assessment", 78 Harv.L.Rev. 1146 (1965); Cary, "A Review of the Work of the Securities and Exchange Commission— 1961–4", 19 Record of N.Y.C.B.A. 458 (1964); Jennings, "Mr. Justice Douglas: His Influence on Corporate and Securities Regulation", 73 Yale L.J. 920, 934 (1964); Knauss, "A Reappraisal of the Role of Disclosure", 62 Mich.L.Rev. 607 (1964); Stigler, "Public Regulation of the Securities Markets", 19 Bus.Law. 721 (1964); Woodside, "Resumé of the Report of the Special Study of Securities Markets and the Commission's Legislative Proposals", 19 Bus. Law. 463 (1964); Jackson, "Public Offerings: A Comparative Study of Disclosure in Western Europe and the United States", 16 W.Res.L.Rev. 44 (1964); Kaplan, "Corporation Law and Securities Regulation", 18 Bus.Law. 867 (1963); Killbride, "The British Heritage of Securities Legislation in the United States", 17 Sw.L.J. 258 (1963); North, "Implied Liability Cases Under the Federal Securities Laws", 4 Corp.Prac.Comm. 1 (May, 1962); Simpson, "Investors' Civil Remedies under the Federal Securities Laws", 12 DePaul L.Rev. 71 (1962); Windels, "Our Securities Markets—Some S.E.C. Problems and Techniques", 8 N.Y.L.F. 169 (1962); Note, "Regulation of Nonissuer Transactions under Federal and State Securities Registration Laws", 78 Harv.L.Rev. 1635 (1965); Loss, "The American Law Institute's Federal Securities Code Project", 25 Bus. Law. 27 (1969).

2. 15 U.S.C.A. §§ 77a–77aa. See section 295 infra.

3. 15 U.S.C.A. §§ 78a–78jj. See sections 296–298 infra.

4. 15 U.S.C.A. §§ 79–79z–6. See section 299 infra.

5. 15 U.S.C.A. §§ 77aaa–77bbbb. See section 300 infra.

6. 15 U.S.C.A. §§ 80a–1–80a–52. See section 301 infra.

7. 15 U.S.C.A. §§ 80b–1–80b–21. See section 302 infra.

8. 11 U.S.C.A. §§ 501–676. See sections 386–389 infra. The S.E.C. also has some duties with respect to the Bretton Woods Agreement Act and under Int.Rev.Code of 1954, 26 U.S.C.A. § 851.

1. 15 U.S.C.A. §§ 77a–77aa; M. Parrino, Truth in Securities: An Introductory Guide to the Securities Act of 1933 (1968); H. Sowards, The Federal Securities Act (1968); J. Flom, B. Garfinkle & J. Freund, Disclosure Requirements of Public Corporations & Insiders (1967); 1 L. Loss, Securities Regulation ch. 3 (2d ed. 1961); E. Thomas, Federal Securities Act Handbook (ALI rev. 1969); A. Choka, An Introduction to Securities Regulation 8–32 (1958); 1 CCH Fed.Sec.L.Rep. ¶¶ 1 et seq.; Wheat, "'Truth in Securities' Three Decades Later", 13 How.L.J. 100 (1967); Cohen, "'Truth in Se-

(or primary) distribution of securities by the issuer rather than with subsequent trading in such securities by the owners thereof.[2]

curities' Revisited", 79 Harv.L.Rev. 1340 (1966); Pasmas, "Securities Issuance and Regulation: Securities Law", 38 Ind.L.J. 38 (1962); Landis, "The Legislative History of the Securities Act of 1933", 28 Geo.Wash.L.Rev. 29 (1959); Stevenson, "Legal Aspects of the Public Offering of Foreign Securities in the United States", 28 Geo.Wash.L.Rev. 194 (1959); Chilgren, "The Federal Securities Act," 40 Chi.B.Record 103 (Dec.1958).

2. Secondary distributions of securities by persons in a control relationship with the issuer of the securities where such distribution involves an underwriter are, with some exceptions, subject to the registration requirements of the 1933 Act. This consequence follows from the provision in the statutory definition of "underwriter" to the effect that persons in a control relationship with an issuer should be regarded as issuers for the purposes of such definition (see note 19 infra). See Brooks, "A Reporter at Large: This Way to Sign Up for Ford, Boys!", 31 New Yorker, No. 52, 39 (Feb. 11, 1956). See also Securities and Exchange Commission v. Guild Films Co., 279 F.2d 485 (2d Cir. 1960), cert. denied, 364 U.S. 819, 81 S.Ct. 52, 5 L.Ed.2d 49 (1960) (foreclosure pledgee selling pledged shares to public held "underwriter"); Haynes, "Guild Films: A Solution under the Intrastate Exemption", 24 Wash. & Lee L.Rev. 49 (1967); C. Israels, et al., S.E.C. Problems of Controlling Stockholders and in Underwritings (PLI 1962); Newlin, "Control Stock: Disposition without Registration under the Securities Act of 1933", 24 Bus.Law. 773 (1969); Rice, "The Effects of Registration Requirements on the Disposition of Pledged Securities", 21 Stan.L.Rev. 1607 (1969); Frank, "Sale of Securities by 'Controlling Persons' under the Federal Securities Act", 14 Hastings L.J. 137 (1962); Israels, Throop & Kennedy, "Offerings of Outstanding Securities", 18 Bus.Law. 59 (1962); Bromberg, "Corporate Liquidation and Securities Law: Problem in the Distribution of Portfolio Securities", 3 B.C.Ind. & Com.L.Rev. 1 (1961); Pierce, "Securities and Exchange Commission v. Guild Films Co., Inc.", 16 Bus.Law. 603 (1961); Sargent, "The Guild Films Case: The Effect of 'Good Faith' in Foreclosure Sales of Unregistered Securities Pledged as Collateral", 46 Va.L.Rev. 1573 (1960); Sargent, "Pledges and Foreclosure Rights Under the Securities Act of 1933", 45 Va.L.Rev. 885 (1959); Comment, "Pledge of Unregistered Securities in Bona Fide Loan Transactions: The Guild Films Legacy", 47 B.U.L.Rev. 85 (1967); Comment, "Banks and the Securities Act of 1933", 52 Va.L.Rev. 117 (1966). See Travis Investment Co. v. Harwyn Publishing Corp., 288 F.Supp. 519 (S.D.N.Y.1968) (S.E.C. notification to issuer that shares might be presented for transfer by persons in control relationship with issuer held to justify issuer's refusal to authorize transfer to pledgee of shares attempting to foreclose upon default); Flanagin, "Federal Securities Act and the Locked-in Stockholder", 63 Mich.L.Rev. 1139 (1965); Note, "The Investment-Intent Dilemma in Secondary Transactions", 39 N.Y.U.L.Rev. 1043 (1964).

The 1933 Act imposes (a) registration requirements (involving (i) registration statement and (ii) prospectus) and (b) anti-fraud provisions.

Registration (and Prospectus) Requirements

No "security" may be "offered" or "sold" through the mails or instrumentalities of interstate or foreign commerce [3] without compliance with the registration (and prospectus) requirements unless either the security is exempt or the transaction is exempt.

The term "security" is very comprehensively defined for purposes of the 1933 Act as embracing every conceivable type of interest or instrument with investment characteristics.[4]

3. I. e., the constitutional bases for the exercise of such federal power. See United States v. Re, 336 F.2d 306 (2d Cir. 1964), cert. denied 379 U.S. 904, 85 S.Ct. 188, 13 L.Ed.2d 177 (1964) (holding floor of securities exchange instrumentality of interstate commerce); McCauley, "Intrastate Securities Transactions under the Federal Securities Act", 107 U.Pa. L.Rev. 937 (1959). As to whether or not telephone is instrumentality of interstate commerce when used for intrastate call, compare Pawgan v. Silverstein, 265 F.Supp. 898 (S.D.N.Y.1967) and Nemitz v. Cunny, 221 F.Supp. 571 (N.D.Ill.1963), with Rosen v. Albern Color Research, Inc., 218 F.Supp. 473 (E.D. Pa.1963).

4. § 2(1), 15 U.S.C.A. § 77b(1). In the case of preorganization certificate or subscription, the issuers would be the promoters, but the issuer of the shares pursuant thereto would be the corporation. The term "investment contract" is somewhat of a catch-all, embracing any contract, transaction, or scheme whereby a person invests his money in a common enterprise and is led to expect profits solely from the efforts of the promoter or a third person. Securities and Exchange Commission v. W. J. Howey Co., 328 U.S. 293, 66 S.Ct. 1100, 90 L.Ed. 1244 (1946); Securities and Exchange Commission v. Joiner Leasing Corp., 320 U.S. 344, 64 S.Ct. 120, 88 L.Ed. 88 (1943); Los Angeles Trust Deed & Mortgage Exchange v. Securities and Exchange Commission, 285 F.2d 162 (9th Cir. 1960), cert. denied 366 U.S. 919, 81 S.Ct. 1095, 6 L.Ed.2d 241 (1961); Continental Marketing Corp. v. Securities and Exchange Commission, 387 F.2d 466 (10th Cir. 1967) (contracts for "sale, care, management, replacement or resale of live beaver for breeding purposes" held investment contract); Roe v. United States, 287 F.2d 435 (5th Cir. 1961) (oil leases); Blackwell v. Bentsen, 203 F.2d 690 (5th Cir. 1953), cert. granted 346 U.S. 908, 74 S.Ct. 240, 98 L.Ed. 406 (1953), cert. dismissed 347 U.S. 925, 74 S.Ct. 528, 98 L.Ed. 1078 (1954); Securities and Exchange Commission v. Latta, 250 F.Supp. 170 (N.D.Calif.1965),

"Sale" and "offer" were defined identically until 1954, when separate definitions of each term were inserted in the Act.[5]

aff'd per curiam 356 F.2d 103 (9th Cir. 1966), cert. denied 384 U.S. 940, 86 S.Ct. 1459, 16 L.Ed.2d 539 (1966) (undivided distributive shares in claims to estate of decedent administered in 1883); Securities and Exchange Commission v. Orange Grove Tracts, 210 F.Supp. 81 (D.Mass.1962) (efforts of third person). In the case of a voting trust required by state law to be open to all shareholders, a continuous offer of voting trust certificates to shareholders who have not transferred their shares to the voting trustee(s) is involved; the issuers of the voting trust certificates would be the voting trustee(s). In the case of a convertible security three securities may be involved; the convertible security, the option, and the security into which it may be converted; in the case of a guaranty or warrant, two securities may be involved: the security guaranteed and the guaranty; the warrant and the security for which it may be exercised. See generally H. Filer, Put and Call Options (1959). Although insurance policies and annuity contracts are not expressly included within the definition of "security", they are expressly exempted from the registration requirements (see note 13 infra). Variable annuities have been held to be securities under the Act. Securities and Exchange Commission v. Variable Annuity Life Ins. Co., 359 U.S. 65, 79 S.Ct. 618, 3 L.Ed.2d 640 (1959); In re Prudential Ins. Co. of America, Inc., SEC Investment Company Act Release No. 3620 (Jan. 22, 1963) aff'd 326 F.2d 383 (2d Cir. 1964), cert. denied 377 U.S. 953, 84 S.Ct. 1629, 12 L.Ed. 497 (1964); Kern, "Variable Annuities", 54 A.B.A.J. 144 (1968); Shipley, "SEC's Expanding Definition of a Security", 37 N.Y.St.B.J. 521 (1965); Securities and Exchange Commission v. United Benefit Life Ins. Co., 387 U.S. 202, 87 S.Ct. 1557, 18 L.Ed.2d 673 (1967) (holding flexible fund annuity contract to be investment contract); Johnson, "The Variable Annuity: Insurance, Investment, or Both?", 48 Geo. L.J. 641 (1960); Jones, "A Discussion and Analysis of the Valic Decision", 5 Vill.L.Rev. 407 (1960); Shea, "Implementation of the Valic Decision", 5 Vill.L.Rev. 426 (1960); Dorsey, "The Place of 'Variable Annuities' in Law and Economics", 34 Notre Dame Law. 489 (1959); Mearns, "The Commission, the Variable Annuity and the Inconsiderate Sovereign", 45 Va.L.Rev. 831 (1959); Comment, "The Flexible Fund Annuity: VALIC Revisited", 115 U.Pa.L.Rev. 600 (1967); Comment, "The Expanding Jurisdiction of the Securities and Exchange Commission: Variable Annuities and Bank Collective Investment Funds", 62 Mich.L.Rev. 1398 (1964); Note, "Regulation of Variable Annuity Sales: The Aftermath of SEC v. VALIC", 1959 Wash.U.L.Q. 206; Annot., 18 L.Ed.2d 1557 (1968). See also Tcherepnin v. Knight, 389 U.S. 332, 88 S. Ct. 548, 19 L.Ed.2d 564 (1967) (withdrawable capital share in savings and loan association held security).

5.   § 2(3), 15 U.S.C.A. §§ 77b(3); Demmler & Armstrong, "The Federal Securities Law: The Scope and Effect of the New Amendments", 41 A.B.A.J. 133 (1955); Forer, "A Comment on the Amendments

Securities exempted from the registration requirements of the Act are: (a) Securities offered to the public within 60 days after the enactment of the Act;[6] (b) Securities of domestic governments and banks;[7] (c) Commercial paper (financing for current transaction, not more than nine months maturity, similarly-limited renewal);[8] (d) Securities of charitable organizations;[9] (e) Securities of building and loan associations or farmers' cooperative associations;[10] (f) Securities of carriers where the issuance is subject to Interstate Commerce Commission;[11] (g) Certificates issued by receiver or trustee-in-bankruptcy with court ap-

to the Federal Securities Acts", 103 U.Pa.L.Rev. 1020 (1955). Excluded from such definitions are preliminary negotiations or agreements between an issuer and any underwriter or among underwriters who are or are to be in privity of contract with an issuer. By the "no sale" theory of Rule 133, securities issued in connection with certain mergers, consolidations, reclassifications, and transfers of assets, pursuant to required shareholder approval, were exempt from the registration requirements but the rule has since been tightened by SEC Securities Act Release No. 4892 (Jan. 9, 1968) and SEC Securities Act Release No. 4115 (July 16, 1959). The S.E. C. has proposed that Rule 133 be revised to provide that the submission to shareholders of a proposal for certain mergers, consolidations, reclassifications of securities or transfers of assets be deemed to involve an offering of securities to the security holders of the corporation being merged or consolidated or whose securities are being reclassified or assets transferred to another person on the theory that when such matters are submitted to the vote of shareholders, each such shareholder is being asked to determine whether or not he wishes to surrender the security he then holds for a new security or, in effect, is being offered the new security. SEC Securities Act Release No. 5012 (Oct. 9, 1969).

6.   § 3(a) (1), 15 U.S.C.A. § 77c(a) (1).

7.   § 3(a) (2), 15 U.S.C.A. § 77c(a) (2).

8.   § 3(a) (3), 15 U.S.C.A. § 77c(a) (3); SEC Securities Act Release No. 4412 (Sept. 21, 1961).

9.   § 3(a) (4), 15 U.S.C.A. § 77c(a) (4). See Securities and Exchange Commission v. Children's Hospital, 214 F.Supp. 883 (D.Ariz.1963) (holding bonds issued by hospital should have been registered where promoters became salaried directors and officers and were to keep 10 percent of proceeds from sale and also profit from construction of hospital facilities).

10.   § 3(a) (5), 15 U.S.C.A. § 77c(a) (5).

11.   § 3(a) (6), 15 U.S.C.A. § 77c(a) (6).

proval; [12] and (h) Insurance policies and annuity contracts issued by a corporation subject to the supervision of a state insurance commissioner, etc.[13] Also exempted from the registration requirements are the following "securities" (although more like transaction exemptions): (i) "Any security exchanged by the issuer with its existing security holders exclusively where no commission or other remuneration is paid or given directly or indirectly for soliciting such exchange"; [14] (j) Reorganization securities issued and exchanged with court or other governmental approval; [15] and (k) "Any security which is part of an issue offered and sold only to persons resident within a single State or Territory, where the issuer of such security is a person resident and doing business within, or, if a corporation, incorporated by and doing business within such State or Territory".[16]

12. § 3(a) (7), 15 U.S.C.A. § 77c(a) (7).

13. § 3(a) (8), 15 U.S.C.A. § 77c(a) (8). Insurance policies and annuity contracts are not expressly included within the definition of "security" (see note 4 supra). Variable annuities, developed in recent years, have been held subject to the registration requirements of the Act. Securities and Exchange Commission v. Variable Annuity Life Ins. Co., 359 U.S. 65, 79 S.Ct. 618, 3 L.Ed.2d 640 (1959) (5–4), rev'g 257 F.2d 201 (D.C.Cir.1958), 155 F.Supp. 521 (D.D.C. 1957) (holding that variable annuities were not subject to the 1933 Act and their issuers were not subject to the Investment Company Act of 1940, relying on the McCarran-Ferguson Act of 1945, 15 U.S.C.A. §§ 1011–1015 (1964), leaving the regulation of insurance to the states). See note 4 supra.

14. § 3(a) (9), 15 U.S.C.A. § 77c(a) (9); SEC Securities Act Release No. 1495 (July 1, 1937); SEC Securities Act Release No. 627 (Class C) (Mar. 15, 1956); Sargent, "Questionable Uses of the 'Exchange' to Securities Registration: A Caveat", 44 Va.L.Rev. 703 (1958).

15. § 3(a) (10), 15 U.S.C.A. § 77c(a) (10).

16. § 3(a) (11), 15 U.S.C.A. § 77c(a) (11). This exemption, known as the "intrastate exemption" applies when interstate or foreign commerce or the mails are involved; if neither is involved, the 1933 Act does not apply at all. If a single offeree or purchaser, whether direct or indirect, as of the time of ultimate distribution, does not reside within such state or territory, the exemption is lost. SEC Securities Act Release No. 4434 (Dec. 6, 1961); Owen, "The Private Offering and Intrastate Exemptions Under the Securities Act of 1933", in H.

Under section 3(b),[17] the so-called "small-issues" exemption, the S.E.C. is empowered to exempt securities issues provided the aggregate amount at which such issue is offered to the public does not exceed $300,000. Pursuant to section 3(b), the S.E.C. has promulgated several regulations, the most important of which is Regulation A.[18]

Wander & W. Grienenberger, Selected Articles on Federal Securities Law 165 (ABA 1968); Sosin, "The Intrastate Exemption: Public Offerings and the Issue Concept", 16 W.Res.L.Rev. 110 (1964); Bloomenthal, "The Federal Securities Act Intra-State Exemption: Fact or Fiction?", 15 Wyo.L.J. 121 (1961); McCauley, "Intrastate Securities Transactions under the Federal Securities Act", 107 U. Pa.L.Rev. 937 (1959); Hertz, "Federal Securities Act of 1933—The Intrastate Exemption of Section 3(a) (11)—Fact or Fiction?", 34 Dicta 289 (1957); Note, 31 Rocky Mt.L.Rev. 186 (1959). For sample investment letter, see G. Robinson, Going Public: Successful Securities Underwriting 114 (1961); Delaney, "The Whys and Wherefores of Investment Letters", 30 Fordham L.Rev. 267 (1961). See Chapman v. Dunn, 414 F.2d 153 (6th Cir. 1969) (2–1) (holding that sales of securities by Michigan resident to other Michigan resident are not exempt when all income-producing property to which securities applied was located outside of Michigan).

17. § 3(b), 15 U.S.C.A. § 77c(b).

18. S.E.C. Rules 251–262; 17 C.F.R. §§ 230.251–230.-263 (1968); 1 CCH Fed.Sec.L.Rep. ¶¶ 4251–4262, 7325–7332. Regulation A applies to almost all Canadian and domestic issuers, individuals or associations. The maximum amount that may be offered in any one year by the issuer and all of its "affiliates" (certain persons in a control relationship with the issuer) may not exceed $300,000 in the case of a primary offering (by an issuer) or $100,000 in the case of a secondary offering (by an affiliate) ($300,000 total maximum by all concerned). No exemption is available for the securities of any issuer if such issuer, any of its predecessors, or any affiliated issuer has been subjected to any one of a number of specified judicial or administrative proceedings involving the issue of securities within a limited period of time. Aside from total exclusion from the exemption there are special rules which apply to offerings by issuers organized in the last year which have not had a net income from operations, or issuers which have not had a net income from operations of the character in which the issuer intends to engage for at least one of the last two fiscal years. Such offerings may be made only for the account of the issuer and an offering circular (see infra) must be used even if the amount of the offering is less than $50,000. Securities may not be offered under Regulation A until 10 days after the filing of a notification on Form 1-A [see P–H Sec. Reg. ¶ 4101], at the regional office of the S.E.C., unless the S.E.C., in its discretion, agrees to an acceleration. Where the offering is made on behalf

Four transactions exempted from the registration requirements of the Act are: (a) "Transactions by any person other than an issuer, underwriter, or dealer"—the so-called "nonprofessional" exemption; [19] (b) "trans-

actions by an issuer not involving any public offering"—the so-called "private offering" exemption; [20] (c) the so-called "dealer"

of an affiliate, both the issuer and the affiliate must sign the notification. Aside from the notification, no written offer or sale of securities shall be made unless: (1) an offering circular (updated every nine months, or in the case of employee purchase plans, every 12 months) containing the information specified in Schedule I of Form 1–A is concurrently or previously given or previously sent to the offeree; (2) where the transaction is on an exchange, copies are left with the exchange; or (3) the aggregate offering is under $50,000 and the specified conditions (see supra) are complied with. The S.E.C. also requires the filing of additional selling material prior to the use thereof and certain reports. See generally 1 CCH Fed.Sec.L.Rep. ¶¶ 4,251–4,262, 7,325–7,332; 1 P–H Sec.Reg. ¶¶ 2031 et seq., 1 L. Loss, Securities Regulation 605 (2d ed. 1961); C. Israels & G. Duff, When Corporations Go Public 23 (PLI 1962); G. Robinson, Going Public: Successful Securities Underwriting 149 (1961); A. Choka, An Introduction to Securities Regulation 29 (1958); Parrino, "Acquiring Equity Capital for Small Businesses Pursuant to a 'Regulation A' Filing", 39 N.Y.St.B.J. 517 (1967); Weiss, "Regulation A Under the Securities Act of 1933—Highways and Byways", 8 N.Y.L.F. 3 (1962); Frank, "Processing of Small Issues of Securities Under Regulation A", 1962 Duke L.J. 507; Erickson, "The Federal Securities Act of 1933: Some Recurring Problems Found in Regulation A", 36 Dicta 402 (1959); Glavin & Purcell, "Securities Offerings and Regulation A— Requirements and Risks", 13 Bus.Law. 303 (1958); Bennett, "Financing Speculative Corporations under Regulation 'A' of the Federal Securities Act of 1933", 5 Utah L.Rev. 44 (1956). The potential liabilities under Regulation A are not as broad as those in the case of full-dress registration.

In the year ending June 30, 1968, 515 notifications were filed under Regulation A, covering proposed offerings of $112,318,744. Approximately 60 percent were for offerings between $200,000 and $300,000; some 20 percent were for offerings of $100,000 or less. Underwriters were used in 144 of the offerings. The offerors were the issuers in 486 of the offerings, shareholders ("affiliates") in 22 offerings, and issuers and shareholders jointly in 7 offerings. 34 SEC Ann.Rep. 32 (1969).

19. § 4(1), 15 U.S.C.A. § 77d(1). This exemption brings into play the statutory definitions of "issuer", "underwriter", and "dealer". "Underwriter" is defined to include, with some exceptions, any participant in the distribution of a security *by an issuer* [encompassing "firm commitments" (purchase and resale), "stand-by", and "best efforts" underwriting, discussed in section 292 supra]. § 2(11). The last sentence of the definition of "underwriter" broadens the definition of "issuer" for the purpose of defining the term "underwriter", and is the basis for the application of the registration requirements

of the Act to secondary distributions of securities by persons in a control relationship with the issuer of the securities where such distribution involves an underwriter (see note 2 supra). United States v. Wolfson, 282 F.Supp. 772 (S.D.N.Y.1967), aff'd 405 F.2d 779 (2d Cir. 1968), cert. denied 394 U.S. 946, 89 S.Ct. 1275, 22 L.Ed.2d 479 (1969); Gilchrist & Hanna, "Secondary Distribution of Corporate Securities", 13 Sw.L.J. 1 (1959). The last sentence, however, does not carry over into the definition of "issuer" in § 2(4). The term "dealer" is defined to include (besides a dealer in the usual sense) "broker" (§ 2(12)), whereas at common law and in the Securities Exchange Act of 1934, "dealer" denotes one who trades as principal for his own account; "broker", one who trades as agent for another. Securities Exchange Act, 1934, § 3(a) (4), (5), 15 U.S.C.A. § 77c(a) (4), (5). See generally Williams, "Exempted Transactions under Section 4(1)", 15 Bus.Law. 138 (1959); Note, "Distribution of Exempt Securities Under Section 4(1) of the Securities Act of 1933", 16 U.Miami L.Rev. 319 (1961). Prior to the 1964 amendments, the exemptions now found in section 4(1), (2), and (3), were in three clauses of section 4(1).

20. § 4(2), 15 U.S.C.A. § 77d(2) (formerly § 4(1) (second clause)). Factors to be considered in determining the availability of this exemption are the number of offerees and their relationship to each other and to the issuer, the number of units offered, the size of the offering, and the manner of offering. Opinion of General Counsel, SEC Securities Act Release No. 285 (Jan. 24, 1935), 1 CCH Fed.Sec.L.Rep. ¶ 2740. A rule-of-thumb developed for administrative convenience is that an offer to no more than 25 persons is not public. In the case of a private offering, there is no distribution and therefore no underwriter. To be public, an offering need not be open to the entire world; offerings to employees or shareholders may be public. The only United States Supreme Court case construing this exemption is Securities and Exchange Commission v. Ralston Purina Co., 346 U.S. 119, 73 S.Ct. 981, 97 L.Ed. 1494 (1953) (6–2). There, shares were offered to a large number of employees of the issuer. The Court stated that the number of employees was not determinative, and applied the so-called "needs test"—whether or not the offerees have such knowledge as not to need the protection of full disclosure under the registration (and prospectus) requirements of the Act:

". . . The design of the statute is to protect investors by promoting full disclosure of information thought necessary to informed investment decisions. The natural way to interpret the private offering exemption is in light of the statutory purpose. Since exempt transactions are those as to which 'there is no practical need for . . . application', the applicability of § 4(1) should turn on whether the particular class of persons affected needs the protection of the Act. An offering to those who are shown to be able to fend for them-

exemption; [21] and (d) the so-called "bro- kers' transactions" exemption.[22]

selves is a transaction 'not involving any public offering'. . . .

". . . Indeed nothing prevents the commission, in enforcing the statute, from using some kind of numerical test in deciding when to investigate particular exemption claims. But there is no warrant for superimposing a quantity limit on private offerings as a matter of statutory interpretation.

"The exemption, as we construe it, does not deprive corporate employees, as a class, of the safeguards of the Act. We agree that some employee offerings may come within § 4(1), e. g., one made to executive personnel who because of their position have access to the same kind of information that the act would make available in the form of a registration statement. Absent such a showing of special circumstances, employees are just as much members of the investing 'public' as any of their neighbors in the community. . . . "

See United States v. Custer Channel Wing Corp., 376 F.2d 675 (4th Cir. 1967), cert. denied 389 U.S. 850, 88 S.Ct. 38, 19 L.Ed.2d 119 (1967), reh. denied 389 U.S. 998, 88 S.Ct. 458, 19 L.Ed.2d 503 (1967) (sale of shares with share transfer restrictive legend to three "associates" as conduits for 136 individuals and 19 other individuals, all of whom signed investment letters, held public offering); Gilligan, Will & Co. v. Securities and Exchange Commission, 267 F. 2d 461 (2d Cir. 1959), cert. denied 361 U.S. 896, 80 S.Ct. 200, 4 L.Ed.2d 152 (1959); SEC Securities Act Release No. 4552 (Nov. 6, 1962). See Commission's footnote 2: Reference is made to the so-called "investment clubs" which have been organized under claim of an exemption from the registration provisions of the Securities Act of 1933 as well as the Investment Company Act of 1940. It should not be assumed that so long as the investment club, which is an investment company within the meaning of the latter Act, does not *obtain* more than 100 members, a public offering of its securities, namely the memberships, will not be involved. An investment company may be exempt from the provisions of the Investment Company Act if its securities are owned by not more than 100 persons *and* it is not making and does not presently propose to make a public offering of its securities. (Section 3(c) (1)). Both elements must be considered in determining whether the exemption is available. In re Crowell-Collier Pub. Co., SEC Securities Act Release No. 3825 (Aug. 12, 1957); S. E.C. Rule 155, SEC Securities Act Release No. 4450 (Feb. 7, 1962); Owen, "The Private Offering and Intrastate Exemptions under the Securities Act of 1933", in H. Wander & W. Grienenberger, Selected Articles on Federal Securities Law 165 (ABA 1968); Kennedy, "The Case of the Scarlet Letter or The Easy Way Out on Private Offerings", 23 Bus.Law. 23 (1967); Cohan, "Should Direct Placements Be Registered?", 43 N.C.L.Rev. 298 (1965); Steffen, "Private Placements Should be Registered", 43 N.C. L.Rev. 548 (1965); Richardson, "Private Placement Method of Financing", 45 Chi.B.Rec. 328 (1964); Steffen, "The Private Placement Exemption: What to Do About a Fortuitous Combination in Restraint of Trade", 30 U.Chi.L.Rev. 211 (1963); Fooshee &

McCabe, "Questions as to SEC's Legislative Authority to Adopt Rule 155, and of Its Constitutionality", 15 Bus.Law. 508 (1960); Lund, "Private Placements and Proposed Rule 155: General Comments", 15 Bus.Law. 516 (1960); Gadsby, "Private Placement of Convertible Securities", 15 Bus.Law. 470 (1960); Fooshee & McCabe, "Private Placements—Resale of Securities: The Crowell-Collier Case", 15 Bus.Law. 72 (1959); Sterling, "Possible Solutions to Problems in the Private Placement of Convertible Securities and Warrants under the Federal Securities Act", 15 Bus.Law. 145 (1959); Israels, "Some Commercial Overtones of Private Placement", 45 Va.L.Rev. 851 (1959); Victor & Bedrick, "Private Offering: Hazards for the Unwary", 45 Va.L.Rev. 869 (1959); Orrick, "Non-Public Offerings of Corporate Securities —Limitations on the Exemption under the Federal Securities Act", 21 U.Pitt.L.Rev. 1 (1959). As to use of investment letters and restrictive share transfer legends on share certificates to avoid public distribution, see Murphy v. Royal American Industries, Inc., 188 So.2d 884 (Fla.Dist.Ct.App.1966), cert. denied, 389 U.S. 953, 88 S.Ct. 336, 19 L.Ed.2d 362 (1967); Altman v. American Foods, Inc., 262 N. C. 671, 138 S.E.2d 526 (1964); General Development Corp. v. Catlin, 139 So.2d 901 (Fla.Dist.Ct.App.1962).

21. § 4(3), 15 U.S.C.A. § 77d(1) (formerly § 4(1) (third clause)).

22. § 4(4), 15 U.S.C.A. § 77d(2) (1964) (formerly § 4 (2)); "brokers' transactions executed upon customers' orders on any exchange or in the open or counter market, but not the solicitation of such orders". See S.E.C. Rule 154, 1 CCH Fed.Sec.L.Rep. ¶¶ 2272, 4154, SEC Securities Act Release No. 4814 (Jan. 21, 1966). See also Matter of Ira Haupt & Co., 23 S.E.C. 589 (1956) (broker *distributing* securities for person in control relationship with issuer ruled underwriter). Where an issuer appoints (and even pays) a broker to handle orders of holders of fractional warrants or scrip, at nominal or no brokerage cost to them, to round out individual holdings into full shares, and the arrangements make such broker the agent of such holders and not of the issuer, the transaction should both fall within the brokerage-transaction exemption and not involve an issuer within the meaning of the nonprofessional exemption (see note 19 supra). 1 L. Loss, Securities Regulation 697–707 (2d ed. 1961). Rifkind, "Securities Problems of the 'Locked-in' Estate", 25 Bus.Law. 169 (1969); Flanagin, "The Federal Securities Act and the Locked-In Stockholder", 63 Mich.L.Rev. 1139 (1965); Hill, "Rule 154 Under the Securities Act of 1933 and Related Problems— A Proposed Solution", 20 Bus.Law. 335 (1965); Sowards, "Sales of Shares by Controlling Persons and Rule 154", 18 U.Miami L.Rev. 88 (1963); Comment, "The Ramifications of SEC Rule 154", 23 U. Miami L.Rev. 768 (1969); Comment, "Broker's Exemption under Rule 154: Ira Haupt Plus Two Decades", 14 How.L.J. 395 (1969); Comment, "Secondary Distributions and the Brokers' Exemption", 36 U.Colo.L.Rev. 404 (1964). For listed securities, the New York Stock Exchange requires the issuer to maintain in Manhattan an office or agency where

Section 5 is the heart of the Act so far as the registration (and prospectus) requirements are concerned.[23]

Under section 5, different activities are permissible during the period prior to the filing of the registration statement, the waiting period, and the post-effective period.[24]

During the pre-filing period, the issuer may make preliminary negotiations with an underwriter or among underwriters who are to be in privity of contract with the issuer (thus, the underwriting group but not the selling group may be formed); investors' indications of interest may be solicited; and in connection with a rights offering, shareholders may be notified of the issuer's intention along prescribed lines.[25]

During the waiting period (from filing to effective date of the registration statement), *oral* offers (and acceptances but not written confirmations of sales) may be made, copies of preliminary or "red-herring" prospectuses (so-called because of their red-ink caption)[26] may be distributed; "tombstone

ads" may be used;[27] and a summary-type prospectus may be used.[28]

After the effective date of the registration statement, a full-fledged selling effort may be made. A final prospectus, unless previously supplied, must accompany the delivery of securities or confirmation of the sale, whichever occurs first. Supplemental selling literature may be used under prescribed conditions during the post-effective period.[29]

The S.E.C. does not approve the securities; it attempts to assure full and complete disclosure of information concerning the issuer, underwriters, and securities.[30]

A registration statement[31] is filed with the S.E.C. where it becomes a matter of pub-

---

scrip for such securities will, during the period provided for consolidation thereof, be accepted for such purpose. N.Y.S.E. Company Manual § A1.

23. The real effect of § 5 (assuming no exemption) has been summarized as follows:
"Unless a Registration Statement is filed, securities may not be sold to the public by the issuing corporation, by underwriters for the issuing corporation, or by persons in control of the issuing corporation. No dealer in securities may sell them for 40 days after they are issued, or, if the dealer is part of the underwriting group, he may not sell them at all, unless a Registration Statement is in effect."

A. Choka, An Introduction to Securities Regulation 27 (1958). See also, Shade, "Compliance with the Registration Provisions of the Securities Act of 1933—An Outline", 25 Bus.Law. 437 (1970).

24. SEC Securities Act Release No. 4697 (May 28, 1964).

25. S.E.C. Rule 134(d); S.E.C. Rule 135. See Securities and Exchange Commission v. Arvida Corp., 169 F.Supp. 211 (S.D.N.Y.1958); In re Carl M. Loeb, CCH Fed.Sec.L.Rep. ¶ 76,635 (pre-filing press releases and press conferences); Demmler, "Problems Inherent in Pre-Filing Publicity", 15 Bus.Law. 132. (1959). See also Chris-Craft Industries, Inc. v. Bangor Punta Corp., — F.2d — (2d Cir. 1969).

26. See S.E.C. Rule 433.

27. § 2(10) (b), 15 U.S.C.A. § 77b(10) (b); S.E.C. Rule 134.

28. § 2(10) (a), 15 U.S.C.A. § 77b(10) (a); S.E.C. Rule 434A.

29. For an amusing account of a rights offering and underwriting of General Motors Corporation shares, see Brooks, "A Reporter at Large: The Adventure", 30 New Yorker, No. 10, 84 (Apr. 23, 1955).

30. Every prospectus on the outside front cover page must state, in boldface capital letters: "THESE SECURITIES HAVE NOT BEEN APPROVED OR DISAPPROVED BY THE SECURITIES AND EXCHANGE COMMISSION NOR HAS THE COMMISSION PASSED UPON THE ACCURACY OR ADEQUACY OF THIS PROSPECTUS. ANY REPRESENTATION TO THE CONTRARY IS A CRIMINAL OFFENSE." S.E.C. Rule 425. The function of the S.E.C. with respect to new issues of corporate securities registered for sale is to assure compliance by the issuing corporation, the underwriters and others concerned with the offering with the full disclosure and anti-fraud provisions of the 1933 Act. See Heller, "Disclosure Requirements under Federal Securities Regulation", 16 Bus.Law. 300 (1961).

31. In general, Schedule A of the Act specifies the information and documents to be contained in the registration statement of a corporation or other private issuer. Required are such matters as the names of persons who participate in the direction, management, or control of the issuer's business; their security holdings and remuneration and the options or bonus and profit-sharing privileges allotted to them; the character and size of the business enterprise, its capital structure, past history and earnings, and its financial statements, certified by independent accountants; underwriters' commissions; payments to promoters made within two years or intended to be made; the interest of directors, officers and principal stockholders in material transactions; pending or threatened legal proceed-

lic record, subject to a 20-day waiting period before it becomes effective; [32] a prospectus (containing much of the information in the registration statement) [33] must be furnished each purchaser of the securities. For engaging in transactions in unregistered securities which should have been registered and for false statements or material omissions in

ings; and the purpose to which the proceeds of the offering are to be applied. Flexibility is provided by power in the S.E.C. to prescribe registration statements varying in their disclosure requirements so as to provide maximum disclosure of the essential facts pertinent in a given type of case while at the same time minimizing the burden and expense of compliance with the Act. For most issues, the registration form is Form S–1. It consists mainly of two parts: Part I (prospectus), containing the information, in textual form and tabular form when prescribed, required by 21 items, and Part II (information not required in prospectus) containing answers under items 22–31 and captions; followed by an undertaking to file reports, signatures of the registrant, its principal executive, accounting, and financial officers, and a majority of its board of directors, consents of experts, opinion and consent of independent public accountants, financial schedules, and exhibits. Guides for Preparation and Filing of Registration Statements, SEC Securities Act Release No. 4936 (Dec. 9, 1968); 1 CCH Fed.Sec.L. Rep. ¶¶ 7121–7129. For issues of nonconvertible, fixed-interest debt securities, meeting prescribed requirements, Form S–9 may be used. It is much shorter than Form S–1, and consists mainly of two parts: Part I (prospectus), answering only five items, and Part II (information not required in prospectus), containing answers under items 6–9 and captions, etc. 1 CCH Fed.Sec.L.Rep. ¶¶ 7198–1— 7198–9. For equity or debt securities offered for cash by listed companies and other domestic issuers which have complied with certain provisions of the Securities Exchange Act and meet certain earnings and management standards, a simplified Form S–7 was prescribed in 1968. 1 CCH Fed.Sec.L.Rep. ¶ 7190. Other forms are also prescribed. See also L. Rappaport, SEC Accounting Practice and Procedure (2d ed. 1963). In the year ending June 30, 1968, 2,417 registration statements for securities aggregating $54,100,000,000 became effective. Of these 69 percent were for the account of issuers for cash sale; 25 percent were for the account of issuers other than for cash sale; and 6 percent ($3,137,000,000) were for the account of others. Of cash sales for the account of issuers, some 42 percent were for bonds, debentures, and notes; 4 percent for preferred shares; and 66 percent for common shares. 34 SEC Ann.Rep. 27, 177 (1969).

32. A registration statement becomes effective on the twentieth day after its filing. During such period, the S.E.C. sends to the registrant a memorandum (or letter) of comment (popularly called a "deficiency letter"), enumerating suggestions for changing the registration statement. See In re Doman Helicopters, Inc., SEC Securities Act Release No. 4594 (Mar. 27, 1963) (stop order issued despite S.E. C. failure to issue letter of comment). The registrant will then file a delaying amendment to start anew a 20-day waiting period and prevent the registration statement from becoming effective in a defective state. A subsequent amendment curing

any defects is then filed by the registrant with request for acceleration of the effective date. As a matter of discretion the S.E.C. may grant such acceleration. For S.E.C. acceleration policy, see S.E. C. Rule 460; Mulford, " 'Acceleration' under the Securities Act of 1933—A Postscript", 22 Bus.Law. 1087 (1967); Garrett & Gadsby, " 'Acceleration' under the Securities Act of 1933—A Comment on the A.B.A.'s Legislative Proposal", 13 Bus.Law. 718 (1958). See also Woodside, "Development of S.E.C. Practices in Processing Registration Statements and Proxy Statements", 24 Bus.Law. 375 (1969); Hodes, "Shelf Registration: The Dilemma of the Securities and Exchange Commission", 49 Va.L.Rev. 1106 (1963); Rappaport, "S.E.C. Procedures and Problems in Going Public", N.Y.U. 21st Inst. on Fed.Tax. 1341 (1963); Israels, Throop, Cohen, Loomis & Blackstone, Panel Discussion: "Offering of New Securities", 18 Bus.Law. 37 (1962); Wheat & Blackstone, "Guideposts for a First Public Offering", 15 Bus. Law. 539 (1960). As to withdrawal by registrant of registration statement prior to effective date, see Columbia General Investment Corp. v. Securities and Exchange Commission, 265 F.2d 559 (5th Cir. 1959). See also S.E.C. Rules 473, 478 (optional procedure to avoid filing successive delaying amendments). To reduce its backlog of registrations, the S.E.C. in 1968 adopted three procedures: (a) Refusal to review seriously defective ones; (b) Cursory review; and (c) "Regular review". See Maloney, "Avoiding Delays in Processing Registration Statements under the Securities Act of 1933", 24 Bus. Law. 1143 (1969).

33. For discussion of drafting a prospectus, see C. Israels & G. Duff, When Corporations Go Public 177 (PLI 1962). The prospectus is Part I of the registration statement. Whereas the registration statement is on file with the S.E.C. and is a matter of public record, a final prospectus is required to be made available to every purchaser of the securities no later than either the written confirmation of the sale or the delivery of the security. To cover transactions in the securities on a national securities exchange, copies of the prospectus are furnished such exchange. S.E.C. Rule 153. A listed company might be required to send copies of any prospectus to the national securities exchange. See N.Y.S.E. Company Manual § A6. A so-called "tombstone ad" is a notice, circular, advertisement, letter or communication which states from whom a written prospectus meeting the requirements of section 10 may be obtained and, in addition, does no more than identify the security, state the price thereof, state by whom orders will be executed, and contain such other information as the Commission by rules or regulations may permit. § 2(10); S.E.C. Rule 134.

a registration statement or prospectus, various sanctions are imposed.[34]

34. Liability extends to every director of the issuer at the time of registration, every person who signed the registration statement, every expert as to the part he "expertized", every underwriter, every person named as about to become a director, and the issuer. Section 12(1) imposes absolute liability for relief in the form of rescission or damages in favor of innocent purchasers; section 12(2) affords the defense of due care to the seller. See Escott v. Barchris Construction Corp., 283 F.Supp. 643 (S.D. N.Y.1968) (holding "due diligence" defenses not available to underwriters and their counsel, "outside" directors, and accountants who relied on general information and assurances of officers without verifying data); also Securities and Exchange Commission v. Frank, 388 F.2d 486 (2d Cir. 1968) (liability of attorney who prepared offering circular or prospectus); United States v. Benjamin, 328 F.2d 854 (2d Cir. 1964), cert. denied, 377 U.S. 953, 84 S.Ct. 1631, 12 L.Ed.2d 497 (1964) (holding accountant liable for false information in "pro forma" balance sheet); Globus v. Law Research Service, Inc., 418 F.2d 1276 (2d Cir. 1969) (reversing allowance of punitive damages under 1933 Act § 17(a) and holding void as against public policy agreement by issuer to indemnify underwriter); Beale, "Punitive Damages Under Section 17(a) of the Securities Act: A Myopic View of Congressional Intent", 15 Wayne L.Rev. 792 (1969); Derdiarian v. Futterman Corp., 223 F.Supp. 265 (S.D.N.Y.1963), settlement approved 38 F.R.D. 178 (S.D.N.Y.1965) (liabilities held not to abate on officer-director's death). Liability is only in favor of purchasers of the shares covered by the registration statement. Barnes v. Osofsky, 373 F.2d 269 (2d Cir. 1967); Colonial Realty Corp. v. Brunswick Corp., 257 F.Supp. 875 (S.D.N.Y.1966). See Institute: "The Barchris Case: Prospectus Liability", 24 Bus.Law. 523 (1969); Panel Discussion: "Barchris: A Dialogue on a Bad Case Making Hard Law", 57 Geo.L.J. 221 (1968); Folk, "Civil Liabilities under the Federal Securities Acts: The *Barchris* Case—Part I—Section 11 of the Securities Act of 1933", 55 Va.L.Rev. 1 (1969); Folk, "Civil Liabilities under the Federal Securities Acts: The *Barchris* Case—Part II—The Broader Implications", 55 Va.L.Rev. 199 (1969); "Barchris and Related Cases—A Lawyer's View and Overview", 41 N.Y.St.B.J. 189 (1969); Kurland, "Accountant's Legal Liability—Ultramares to Barchris", 25 Bus. Law. 155 (1969); Jordan, "Barchris and the Registration Process", 22 Sw.L.J. 790 (1968); Solomon, "Pro Forma Statements, Projections and the S.E.C.", 24 Bus.Law. 389 (1969); Hayes, "Tort Liability for Misstatements or Omissions in Sales of Securities", 12 Clev.-Mar.L.Rev. 100 (1963); Simpson, "Investors Civil Remedies under the Federal Securities Laws", 12 DePaul L.Rev. 71 (1962); Comment, " 'Due Diligence' and the Expert in Corporate Securities Registration", 42 S.Cal.L.Rev. 293 (1969); Note, "New and Comprehensive Duties of Securities Sellers to Investigate, Disclose, and Have an 'Adequate Basis' for Representations", 62 Mich. L.Rev. 880 (1964); Note, "Civil Remedies Available to Buyers and Sellers under the 1933 Federal Se-

Anti-Fraud Provisions

Even though the security or transaction is exempt from registration, the civil and criminal liability for misrepresentation[35] and anti-fraud provisions[36] of the 1933 Act apply if interstate or foreign commerce or the mails are involved in the offer or sale of securities.[37]

Expressly preserved in the 1933 Act was state jurisdiction over securities.[38]

Under the 1933 Act, the S.E.C. has promulgated various rules and regulations.[39]

curities Laws", 38 Wash.L.Rev. 627 (1963). For indemnification, see C. Israels & G. Duff, When Corporations Go Public (PLI 1962); Note, "Indemnification of Underwriters and Section 11 of the Securities Act of 1933", 72 Yale L.J. 406 (1962). As to statute of limitations applicable to interveners, see Escott v. Barchris Construction Corp., 340 F.2d 731 (2d Cir. 1965).

35. §§ 11, 12, 16, 15 U.S.C.A. §§ 77k, 77l, 77p. Compare United States v. Dardi, 330 F.2d 316 (2d Cir. 1964), cert. denied 379 U.S. 845, 85 S.Ct. 50, 13 L.Ed.2d 50 (1964), with United States v. Crosby, 294 F.2d 928 (2d Cir. 1961), cert. denied sub nom. Mittleman v. United States, 368 U.S. 984, 82 S.Ct. 599, 7 L.Ed.2d 523 (1962) (criminal liability of broker-dealer for willfully selling large block of unregistered securities for controlling person). See Stim, "Criminal Liability Provisions of the Securities Act of 1933", 6 Crim.L.Rev. (Man.) 31 (1959); Shulman, "Civil Liability and the Securities Act", 43 Yale L.J. 227 (1933). Legal expenses incurred in an unsuccessful defense of a business-related criminal prosecution for violation of the Securities Act has been held deductible as an ordinary and necessary and business expense under Int.Rev.Code of 1954, 26 U.S. C.A. § 162(a). Comm'r v. Tellier, 383 U.S. 687, 86 S.Ct. 1118, 16 L.Ed.2d 185 (1966).

36. § 17, 15 U.S.C.A. § 77q.

37. Blackwell v. Bentsen, 203 F.2d 690 (5th Cir. 1953), cert. granted, 346 U.S. 908, 74 S.Ct. 240, 98 L.Ed. 406 (1953), cert. dismissed, 347 U.S. 925, 74 S.Ct. 528, 98 L.Ed. 1078 (1954).

38. § 18, 15 U.S.C.A. § 77r. See Millonzi, "Concurrent Regulation of Interstate Securities Issues: The Need for Congressional Reappraisal", 49 Va.L. Rev. 1483 (1963); Cowett, "Federal-State Relationships in Securities Regulation", 28 Geo.Wash.L.Rev. 287 (1959); Hayes, "State 'Blue Sky' and Federal Securities Laws", 11 Vand.L.Rev. 659 (1958). See sections 305–307 infra.

39. § 19, 15 U.S.C.A. § 77s. Rules under the 1933 Act are designated by Arabic numerals. E. g., Rule 151 (excluding certain offerings of shares of small business investment companies from definition of "public offering"), also designated "230." followed by the rule number to conform to 17 C.F.R. § 230.—,

FEDERAL SECURITIES LEGISLATION— SECURITIES EXCHANGE ACT, 1934—IN GENERAL

296. The Securities Exchange Act, 1934, deals mainly with the secondary distribution of securities. The Act provides for registration with the Securities and Exchange Commission of securities exchanges; Commission supervision over their rules and practices; the filing of various reports by issuers of registered securities with the Commission and any exchange where listed; Commission regulation of proxy solicitation with respect to registered securities; limitations on insider-trading of registered equity securities; registration of over-the-counter brokers and dealers; registration of national securities associations; prohibition of fraud and manipulation in connection with the sale or purchase of securities; enforcement of the margin rules set by the Board of Governors of the Federal Reserve System.

The Securities Exchange Act, 1934,[1] deals mainly with the secondary distribution of securities. Besides establishing the S.E.C.,[2] the main purposes of the Act were to afford some disclosure to buyers and sellers of securities, to regulate the securities markets (both exchanges and "over-the-counter"), and to control the credit in such markets. The provisions of the Act relate to registration with the S.E.C. of securities exchanges;[3] S.E.C. supervision over their rules and practices;[4] the filing by listed is-

suers of listing applications, the registration by listed and certain other issuers of their listed securities and certain other equity securities, and the filing by such issuers of annual and periodic reports with the S.E.C. and any exchange where listed;[5] S.E.C. regulation of proxy solicitation with respect to registered securities;[6] limitations on insider-trading of registered equity securities;[7] registration of over-the-counter brokers and dealers;[8] registration of national securities associations;[9] prohibition of fraud and manipulation in connection with sale or purchase of securities;[10] enforcement of the

e. g., 230.151 or simply Rule 151. All S.E.C. rules are officially reported in 17 C.F.R. ch. II, §§ 200 et seq. (1969) and in the daily issues of the Federal Register.

1. 15 U.S.C.A. §§ 78a–78jj; 2 L. Loss, Securities Regulation 784 et seq. (2d ed. 1961); E. Gadsby, Federal Securities Exchange Act of 1934 (1964); A. Choka, An Introduction to Securities Regulation chs. 6–8 (1958); 2 CCH Fed.Sec.L.Rep. ¶¶ 12, 101 et seq.; Loomis, "The Securities Exchange Act of 1934 and the Investment Advisers Act of 1940", 28 Geo. Wash.L.Rev. 214 (1959).

2. See section 294, n. 1 supra.

3. § 6, 15 U.S.C.A. § 78f (as "national securities exchanges"). See section 316 infra.

4. § 19, 15 U.S.C.A. § 78s; Comment, "Stock Exchange Regulation of Non-member Brokers", 71 Yale L.J. 748 (1962).

5. §§ 12, 13, 15 U.S.C.A. §§ 78*l*, 78m. E. g., Form 10, Form 10–K. Some 2,500 issuers having approximately 4,000 issues, of which some 70 percent were shares and some 30 percent bonds, listed and registered on national securities exchanges. Under § 12(g) (effective July 1, 1964), up to 3,000 additional issuers (including some 600 banks), which had not listed their securities had to register certain classes of their equity securities. See note 14 infra. Registration brings into play the periodic reporting requirements of § 13, proxy rules under § 14, and insider trading provisions of § 16. See United States v. Simon, —— F.2d —— (2d Cir.1969) (upholding conviction of independent auditors under 1934 Act for not reporting uncollectibility of substantial receivable).

6. § 14, 15 U.S.C.A. § 78n. See section 297 infra.

7. § 16, 15 U.S.C.A. § 79p. See section 298 infra.

8. § 15, 15 U.S.C.A. § 78o. See Greene, "Regulation of Entry into the Securities Business", 20 Bus.Law. 307 (1965); Fishman, "Stockbrokers and the Public Investor: Civil Remedies", 53 Ill.B.J. 992 (1965); Bloomenthal, "The Case of the Subtle Motive and the Delicate Art: Control and Domination in Over-the-Counter Securities-Markets", 1960 Duke L.J. 196; Comment, "A Symptomatic Approach to Securities Fraud: The SEC's Proposed Rule 15C2–6 and Boiler Room", 72 Yale L.J. 1411 (1963); Note, 62 Mich.L.Rev. 880 (1964); Note, 8 Utah L.Rev. 382 (1963). Denial, suspension, and revocation of broker/dealer registration's are powerful enforcement weapons of the S.E.C. As of June 30, 1968, 4,397 broker-dealers and 2,007 investment advisers were registered. 34 SEC Ann.Rep. 79 (1969).

9. § 15A, 15 U.S.C.A. § 78o–3. Only one such association has registered, the National Association of Securities Dealers, Inc. ("N.A.S.D."). See Section 317 infra.

10. §§ 9, 10, 15 U.S.C.A. §§ 78i, 77j. See Foshay, "Market Activities of Participants in Securities Distributions", 45 Va.L.Rev. 907 (1959). See section 298 infra.

margin rules set by the Board of Governors of the Federal Reserve System.[11]

Under the 1934 Act, the S.E.C. has promulgated various rules and regulations.[12]

In 1964, long-standing proposals to regulate companies in addition to companies whose shares were traded on a national securities exchange under the Act [13] were enacted. The legislation brought under the 1934 Act companies engaged in interstate or foreign commerce, or whose securities are traded by use of the mails or interstate or foreign commerce, with assets in excess of $1,000,000, and with a class of equity security held of record by at least 500 persons, subject to specified exemptions,[14] and result-

ed in some 3,000 large unlisted companies having to file registration statements, annual and other periodic reports, having to comply with the S.E.C. Proxy Rules, and becoming subject to the insider-trading provisions of the 1934 Act.

Jurisdiction of violations of the 1934 Act is exclusively in the federal courts,[15] with broad venue and provisions for extraterritorial service of process.[16]

FEDERAL SECURITIES LEGISLATION— SECURITIES EXCHANGE ACT, 1934— PROXY REGULATION

297. Proxy regulation under the Securities Exchange Act, 1934, is limited to proxies, consents, and authorizations with respect to securities registered under the Act. The S.E.C.

amended, every unlisted company, subject to specified exemptions, which is engaged in interstate commerce, or whose securities are traded by use of the mails or interstate commerce, must file a registration statement—if it has (a) total assets exceeding $1 million, and (b) a class of "equity security" held by 500 or more shareholders of record. Under § 12(i), every national and state-chartered bank which (a) has its deposits insured by the Federal Deposit Insurance Corporation, and (b) meets the statutory tests as to assets and number of shareholders must comply with the registration and disclosure provisions of the 1934 Act. However, administration and enforcement of such provisions is vested in the appropriate federal banking agency and not in the S.E.C. Gray & Rosen, "Section 12(g) and Blue Sky Laws", 20 Bus.Law. 1075 (1965); Meeker, "Extending Disclosure to Nonlisted Companies", 20 Bus.Law. 265 (1965); Sowards, "The Securities Acts Amendments of 1964: New Registration and Reporting Requirements", 19 U.Miami L.Rev. 33 (1964); Phillips & Shipman, "An Analysis of the Securities Acts Amendments of 1964", 1964 Duke L.J. 706; Comment, "The Securities Acts Amendments of 1964: Effect on the Over-the-Counter Market", 39 St.John's L.Rev. 111 (1964).

11. §§ 7, 8, 15 U.S.C.A. §§ 78g, 78h; see Regulation T (credit by brokers, dealers, and members of national securities exchanges), 12 C.F.R. §§ 220.1 et seq. (1969); Regulation U (loans by banks for purpose of purchasing or carrying registered shares), 12 C.F.R. §§ 221.1 et seq. (1969); Regulation G (credit by others); 12 C.F.R. §§ 207.1 et seq. (1969); Kelly & Webb, "Credit and Securities: The Margin Requirements", 24 Bus.Law. 1153 (1969).

Margin requirements since 1934 have varied from 40 to 100 percent. New York Stock Exchange 1968 Fact Book 35 (1968). In addition to federal regulation of credit, securities exchanges also may impose certain credit requirements. Comment, "Application of Margin Requirements to the Case Tender Offer", 116 U.Pa.L.Rev. 103 (1967); Comment, "Credit Regulation in the Securities Market: An Analysis of Regulation T", 62 Nw.U.L.Rev. 587 (1967); Comment, "Securities Exchange Act of 1934 —Civil Remedies Based Upon Illegal Extension of Credit in Violation of Regulation T", 61 Mich.L. Rev. 940 (1963); Note, "Federal Margin Requirements as a Basis for Civil Liability", 66 Colum.L. Rev. 1463 (1966).

12. Rules under the 1934 Act were designated "X" followed by the number of the section of the Act and the chronological number of the rule thereunder, e. g., Rule X–14A–11; the letter prefix has been dropped and they are now designated "240." followed by numbers to conform to 17 C.F.R. § 240.—, e. g., 240.14a–11, or simply Rule 14a–11. A. Choka, An Introduction to Securities Regulation ch. 8 (1958).

13. Special Study of the Securities Markets (SEC 1963); Frey, "Federal Regulation of the Over-the-Counter Securities Market", 106 U.Pa.L.Rev. 1 (1957); Comment, "The Fulbright Bill: Extension of Investor Protection to Unlisted Securities", 71 Harv.L.Rev. 1337 (1958).

14. Securities Acts Amendments of 1964, Pub.L. 88–467, 78 Stat. 565. Under § 12(g) of the 1934 Act as

15. § 27, 15 U.S.C.A. § 78aa. But see Colonial Realty Corp. v. Bache & Co., 358 F.2d 178 (2d Cir. 1966), cert. denied, 385 U.S. 817, 87 S.Ct. 40, 17 L. Ed.2d 56 (1966) (holding violation of margin rules of securities exchange does not necessarily create federal civil liability); Goodbody & Co. v. Penjaska, 8 Mich.App. 64, 153 N.W.2d 655 (1967), appeal dismissed, cert. denied 393 U.S. 16, 89 S.Ct. 47, 21 L. Ed.2d 15 (1968), reh. denied 393 U.S. 971, 89 S.Ct. 390, 21 L.Ed.2d 386 (1968) (allowing state court action for breach of margin contract notwithstanding violation of margin rules of securities exchange and of 1934 Act).

16. Ibid.

Proxy Rules prescribe requirements for the proxy statement and form of proxy, require various filings, facilitate communication among security holders, and provide for security holder proposals. Solicitation in proxy contests involving the election or removal of directors is subject to special provisions. In the absence of any management proxy solicitation, information substantially equivalent to the information required in connection with such solicitation must be filed with the S.E.C. and sent to security holders before any meeting thereof. Disclosure is also required in connection with any attempt to acquire a substantial block of equity securities by a cash tender offer or through open market or privately negotiated purchases, and with any corporation's repurchase of its own equity securities. The S. E.C. Proxy Rules also apply with respect to securities of registered public utility holding companies and their subsidiaries under the Public Utility Holding Company Act, 1935, and, along with some additional rules, to securities of registered investment companies under the Investment Company Act, 1940.

Proxy regulation under the Securities Exchange Act, 1934, is authorized by section 14 thereof,[1] which is limited to proxies, consents, and authorizations in respect of securities (other than exempted securities) registered under the Act. Section 14 contains six subsections.

Subsection (a) prohibits any person from soliciting or permitting the use of his name in soliciting any such proxy or consent or authorization in contravention of any S.E.C. rules and regulations prescribed thereunder.[2] Under this subsection, the S.E.C. has promulgated Regulations 14A, 14B, 14C, and 14D (known as the "S.E.C. Proxy Rules").[3]

The S.E.C. Proxy Rules are composed of 23 rules (Rules 14a–1 to 14a–12, 14c–1 to 14c–7, and 14d–1 to 14f–1) and four schedules (Schedules 14A, 14B, 14C, and 14D). They apply, with some exceptions, to every solicitation of a proxy with respect to securities registered under the Act.[4]

1. 15 U.S.C.A. § 78n; Giroir, "Proxy and Inside-Trading Regulation: Federal-State Cooperation in the Protection of Investors", 19 Ark.L.Rev. 308 (1966); Sowards & Mofsky, "Federal Proxy Regulation: Recent Extension of Controls", 41 St. John's L.Rev. 165 (1966); Kennedy, "Proxy Regulation", 20 Bus.Law. 273 (1965); Green, "Soliciting Proxies Under the SEC's Rules", 11 Prac.Law. 29 (Dec. 1965); Aranow & Einhorn, "Proxy Regulation: Suggested Improvements", 28 Geo.Wash.L.Rev. 306 (1959); Brey, "A Synopsis of the Proxy Rules of the Securities & Exchange Commission", 26 U.Cin.L.Rev. 58 (1957); Aranow & Einhorn, "Corporate Proxy Contests: Enforcement of SEC Proxy Rules by the Commission and Private Parties", 31 N.Y.U.L.Rev. 875 (1956). See Sawyer v. Pioneer Mill Co., 190 F. Supp. 21 (D.Hawaii 1960) (shares listed but not registered on S.E.C.-exempted Honolulu Stock Exchange and traded, though unlisted, on San Francisco Division of Pacific Coast Stock Exchange held not subject to S.E.C. Proxy Rules). Compare Brown v. Chicago, Rock Island & Pacific R. R., 328 F.2d 122 (7th Cir. 1964) (newspaper advertisement stating advantages of advertising railroad's merger offer to Rock Island & Pacific R. R. and disadvantages of other railroad's offer, published before calling of shareholders' meeting, held not to be proxy solicitation), with Union Pacific R. R. v. Chicago and North Western Ry., 226 F.Supp. 400 (N.D. Ill.1964) (brokerage-firm's research report on offer asking for proxies against merger, sent to shareholders of Rock Island & Pacific R. R. after calling of shareholders' meeting, held proxy solicitation).

2. 15 U.S.C.A. § 78n(a). Prior to 1964, section 14 applied only to securities listed on a national securities exchange. See Comment, "Standards of Disclosure in Proxy Solicitation of Unlisted Securities", 1960 Duke L.J. 623.

3. 2 CCH Fed.Sec.L.Rep. ¶¶ 24,001 et seq.; upheld in Securities and Exchange Commission v. May, 229 F.2d 123, 55 A.L.R.2d 1123 (2d Cir. 1956). During the year ending June 30, 1968, 5,244 proxy statements in definitive form were filed, all but 20 by management, with respect to the following types of matters: election of directors, 4,473; mergers, consolidations, acquisitions of businesses, purchases and sales of property, and dissolutions, 634; authorizations of new or additional securities, modifications of existing securities, recapitalization plans (other than mergers, consolidations, etc.), 1,420; employee pension and retirement plans (including amendments to existing plans, 75; bonus, profit-sharing plans and deferred compensation arrangements (including amendments to existing plans and arrangements), 87; share option plans (including amendments to existing plans), 687; shareholder approval of selection by management of independent auditors, 1,666; miscellaneous amendments to articles of incorporation and bylaws, and miscellaneous other matters (excluding above), 1,790. In addition, 110 information statements were filed. 34 SEC Ann.Rep. 41–42 (1969).

4. Rule 14a–2. The S.E.C. Proxy Rules do not require proxy solicitation; since 1964, absent solicitation the information required in the proxy statement must be given to security holders. In 1959, the New York Stock Exchange instituted a program calling for mandatory solicitation by all actively

A written *proxy statement,* containing the information specified in Schedule 14A, but not in the item and sub-item form thereof, is required to precede or accompany any solicitation.[5] When any solicitation is on behalf of management for the annual meeting, an annual report must usually precede or accompany the solicitation.[6]

The *form of proxy* must indicate in boldface type whether or not the proxy is solicited on behalf of management, must provide a specifically designated blank space for dating the proxy, and must identify clearly and impartially each matter to be acted upon, whether proposed by management or by security holders.[7] With respect to each such matter, other than elections to office, the form of proxy shall provide the security holder an opportunity to specify by ballot approval or disapproval. If no choice is specified, the proxy may be voted for or against any such matter if the form of proxy so states in boldface type.[8] The proxy may confer discretionary authority with respect to other matters which may come before the meeting and of which the persons soliciting the proxy are unaware provided a specific statement to that effect is made in the proxy statement or form of proxy.[9] No proxy shall confer authority to vote for the election of any person to any office for which a bona fide nominee is not named in the proxy statement, or to vote at any annual meeting other than the next annual meeting (or any adjournment thereof) following the proxy statement and form of proxy.[10] The proxy statement or form of proxy must provide that the shares represented thereby will be voted and, if any ballot choice is made by the security holder, will be voted in accordance with such choice.[11]

Various *filings* are required. Five preliminary copies of the proxy statement, form of proxy, and any other soliciting material must be filed in advance with the S.E.C. (at least 10 days for original material; at least two days for subsequent material). The printing of definitive copies for distribution to security holders should be deferred until the comments of the S.E.C. staff have been received and considered. Informal methods, especially by "letters of comment", have been the best deterrent to violation of the S.E.C. Proxy Rules. Eight definitive copies must also be filed with the S.E.C. and three copies with any national securities exchanges on which the security is listed. In the case of any personal solicitation, copies of any written instructions or other material furnished the solicitors must be filed in advance with the S.E.C. While copies of soliciting material in the form of speeches, press releases, and radio or television scripts need not be filed in advance, definitive copies thereof must be when used.[12]

Where management makes or intends to make any solicitation, any security holder entitled to vote is given the opportunity *to communicate with other security holders.* Upon written request, the corporation must either handle the mailing of such communication, including any proxy statement and proxy, furnished by such security holder, or furnish such security holder with a reasonably current list of the names and addresses of security holders of record, etc. The corporation is entitled to be defrayed its rea-

---

operating companies with securities listed on the Exchange.

5.   Rules 14a–3, 14a–5.

6.   Rule 14a–3(b).

7.   Rule 14a–4(a).

8.   Rule 14a–4(b).

9.   Rule 14a–4(c).

10.   Rule 14a–4(d).

11.   Rule 14a–4(e).

12.   Rule 14a–6. See Millimet v. George F. Fuller Co., 2 CCH Fed.Sec.L.Rep. ¶¶ 22,781 et seq. (D.C. N.Y.1965) (S.E.C. clearance of proxy statement held no defense to shareholder derivative action claiming false and misleading proxy statement).

sonable expenses, and is not responsible for such communication.[13]

Proposals of security holders (except with respect to elections to office or counter proposal to management proposals) may be submitted by any security holder entitled to vote a prescribed time before the solicitation is made, accompanied by notice of his intention to present the proposal for action at the meeting. Except under specified circumstances, management must set forth the proposal in its proxy statement and identify it and provide a ballot with respect to it in its form of proxy.[14] If management opposes the proposal, it must, on request of the proponent, include in its proxy statement his statement of not more than 100 words in support of the proposal.[15] Management may omit the proposal and supporting statement if (a) under the laws of the corporation's domicile, it is not a proper subject for action by security holders;[16] (b) it appears clearly to have been submitted primarily to enforce a personal claim or redress a personal grievance or for the purpose of promoting general economic, political, racial, religious, social,

or similar causes;[17] (c) the proposal had been included in the management proxy statement and form of proxy at the request of the security holder for either of the last two annual meetings, or any special meeting during such period, and such security holder has failed without good cause to present the proposal at the meeting; (d) substantially the same proposal had been included in the management proxy statement and form of proxy relating to any meeting during the past five years (provided the last meeting of submission was within three years) and received less than various stated percentages (three, six, ten percent) of votes cast at such meeting or meetings;[18] or (e) the proposal relates to the conduct of the ordinary business operations of the corporation.[19] Where management asserts that a proposal and supporting statement may properly be omitted from its proxy statement and form of proxy, it must submit the matter in advance to the S.E.C. and notify the proponent of its intention to omit the proposal and a statement of its reasons.[20] Contrary to expectations, the security holder proposal rule has resulted in neither a field day for crackpots nor a millenium in shareholder democracy.[21]

---

13. Rule 14a–7; Rosen v. Alleghany Corp., 133 F. Supp. 858 (S.D.N.Y.1955). The rule has been held not to constitute federal preemption, precluding shareholder inspection under state law. Wood, Walker & Co. v. Evans, 300 F.Supp. 171 (D.Colo. 1969). See section 199 supra.

14. Rule 14a–8(a); Chilgren, "A Plea for Relief from Proxy Rule 14a–8", 19 Bus.Law. 303 (1963).

15. Rule 14a–8(b).

16. Rule 14a–8(c) (1). See Dyer v. Securities and Exchange Commission, 289 F.2d 242 (8th Cir. 1961) (proposal to censure and declare ineligible for reelection directors who were candidates for reelection at forthcoming meeting); Securities and Exchange Commission v. Transamerica Corp., 163 F.2d 511 (3d Cir. 1947), cert. denied 332 U.S. 847, 68 S.Ct. 351, 92 L.Ed. 418 (1948) (holding security holder's proposals for employment of independent auditors, for elimination of certain notice requirements tending to block shareholder amendment of bylaws, and sending post-meeting reports to all shareholders, to be proper subjects for action by shareholders within S.E.C. rule). Cf. Auer v. Dressel, 306 N.Y. 427, 118 N.E.2d 590, 48 A.L.R.2d 604 (1954) See "Proper Subject: A Symposium", 34 U.Det.L.J. 520 (1957); Comment, "Proper Subject Revisited", 9 St. Louis U.L.J. 530 (1965).

17. Rule 14a–8(c) (2). See Peck v. Greyhound Corp., 97 F.Supp. 679 (S.D.N.Y.1951) (proposal for abolition of segregated seating system in corporation's buses in the South). Brooks v. Standard Oil Co., —— F.Supp. —— (S.D.N.Y.1969) (resolution that corporation encourage undersea exploration and promote international organization to control operations held inappropriate for shareholder action and inclusion in proxy statement).

18. Rule 14a–8(c) (4).

19. Rule 14a–8(c) (5). See Curtin v. American Telephone and Telegraph Co., 124 F.Supp. 197 (S.D.N.Y. 1954) (proposal by shareholder union for increased employee pension benefits).

20. Rule 14a–8(d).

21. Security holder proposals appear in approximately three percent of proxy statements filed with the S.E.C., some three-fourths of the proposals coming from the same three or four sources. Such proposals, despite their frequent merit, are almost always defeated overwhelmingly by the management proxy machinery. Clusserath, "The Amended Stockholder Proposal Rule: A Decade Later", 40 Notre Dame

False and misleading statements in connection with any solicitation are prohibited,[22] as is the solicitation of undated or postdated proxies, etc.[23]

Solicitations in proxy contests involving the election or removal of directors have been subject to special provisions since 1956.[24] Information required by Schedule 14B must be filed with the S.E.C. and any national securities exchanges on which the security is listed in behalf of each "participant" in such solicitation.[25] The term "participant" is broadly defined.[26] The information required by Schedule 14B of each participant is very extensive.[27] The use of reprints or reproductions of any previously published material is subject to detailed regulation.[28]

Subsection (b) prohibits registered brokers, dealers, etc., in contravention of any S.E.C. rules and regulations prescribed thereunder to give or refrain from giving a proxy, consent, or authorization in respect of any security registered under the Act and carried for the account of a customer (i. e., in "street name").[29] Although the S.E.C. has proposed rules under subsection (b),[30] none has yet been promulgated. The securities exchanges, however, have rules on the subject governing their own members with respect to both listed and unlisted securities.[31]

Subsection (c) requires issuers of securities registered under the Act, where there is no proxy solicitation by or in behalf of management in accordance with the S.E.C. Proxy Rules, before any meeting of the holders of such securities, to file with the S. E.C. and transmit to all holders of record of such securities, in accordance with the S.E. C. rules and regulations prescribed thereunder, information substantially equivalent to the information which would be required to be transmitted if a solicitation were made.[32]

In 1968, the so-called "Takeover Bid Law" was enacted to put cash tender offers and other block acquisitions to the same disclosure footing as proxy contests for control.

Law. 13 (1964). In the year ending June 30, 1968, 254 proposals were submitted. The 162 included proposals involved 115 corporations by 34 proponents. Some 92 proposals were omitted for the following reasons: (a) 18 proposals were withdrawn by proponents; (b) 10 proposals related to the ordinary conduct of the corporation's business; (c) 11 proposals were not a proper subject matter under state law; (d) 11 proposals were not timely submitted; (e) 33 proposals concerned a personal grievance against the corporation; (f) six proposals were outside the scope of the rules; and (g) three proposals were the converse of management proposals. 34 SEC Ann.Rep. 42 (1969).

22. Rule 14a–9. See Swanson v. American Consumer Industries, Inc., 415 F.2d 1326 (7th Cir. 1969) (nondisclosure of material facts in proxy statement concerning merger held actionable by minority shareholders despite fact that dominating shareholders of corporation had more than enough votes to approve merger).

23. Rule 14a–10.

24. Rule 14a–11; Note, "Securities and Exchange Commission Regulation of Proxy Contests", 69 Harv.L.Rev. 1462 (1956); Bayne & Emerson, "The Virginia-Carolina Chemical Corporation Proxy Contest: A Case-Study of the SEC's New Rule 240.-14a–11 and Schedule 14B", 57 Colum.L.Rev. 801 (1957). For the pre-1956 situation, see Armstrong, "The Role of the Securities and Exchange Commission in Proxy Contests of Listed Companies", 11 Bus.Law. 110 (Nov.1955). In 1967–68 there were 27 proxy contests: 21 for control of the board of directors; 6 for representation on the board, with indifferent results for the insurgents. Some 536 persons filed statements as participants.

25. Rule 14a–11(c).

26. Rule 14a–11(b).

27. See Schedule 14B.

28. Rule 14a–11(h).

29. 15 U.S.C.A. § 78n(b).

30. 2 CCH Fed.Sec.L.Rep. ¶ 24,181.

31. E. g., N.Y.S.E. Rules 450–460. See Procedure for Soliciting Proxies from Shareholders with Stock in Brokers' Names (Joint Report of American Society of Corporate Secretaries, Inc., Association of Stock Exchange Firms, New York Stock Exchange 1961); E. Aranow & H. Einhorn, Proxy Contests for Corporate Control 240 et seq. (2d ed. 1968); Aranow & Einhorn, "Corporate Proxy Contests: Solicitation and Validity of Brokers' Proxies", 23 U.Chi.L.Rev. 640 (1956).

32. § 14c, 15 U.S.C.A. § 78n(c); Regulation 14C, 2 CCH Fed.Sec.L.Rep. ¶¶ 24,201 et seq. Some 110 information statements were filed in 1968.

Involved were amendments to sections 13 and 14 of the Act.

Subsection (d) requires the filing of a statement by any person who makes a tender offer for any class of securities registered under the Act if, after consummation of the offer, he would be the beneficial owner of more than 10 percent of the class. Such statement must be filed with the S.E.C., and a copy sent to the issuer at the time that the tender offer is first made public.[33] The S.E.C. is authorized to adopt rules and regulations with respect to solicitations or recommendations to accept or reject tender offers or requests or invitations for tenders.[34]

Subsection (e) prohibits any misstatement or omission of a material fact, or any fraudulent or manipulative acts or practices, in connection with any tender offer, whether for cash, securities, or other consideration, or in connection with any solicitation of security holders in opposition to or in favor of any tender offer.[35]

Subsection (f) provides that if any persons are to be elected directors of the issuer without a shareholder vote, pursuant to any arrangement with persons acquiring securities in a transaction subject to subsection (d) or section 13(d), and the persons so designated would constitute a majority of the board of directors, the issuer must file with the S.E.C. and transmit to all shareholders information substantially equivalent to the information which would be required by subsection (a) or subsection (c), if such persons were to be elected directors at a shareholder meeting.[36]

The S.E.C. Proxy Rules also apply to proxies, etc., with respect to securities of registered public utility holding companies and their subsidiaries under the Federal Public Utility Holding Company Act of 1935 [37] and securities of registered investment companies under the Federal Investment Company Act of 1940.[38]

For violations of the 1934 Act and the rules and regulations thereunder, the federal courts have exclusive jurisdiction; there are liberal venue provisions; and provisions for extraterritorial service of process.[39]

---

33. § 14(d), 15 U.S.C.A.; Electronic Specialty Co. v. International Controls Corp., 409 F.2d 937 (2d Cir. 1969) (permitting "target" corporation of cash tender offer to challenge tender offer under S.E.C. tender offer rules); B. F. Goodrich Co. v. Northwest Industries, Inc., 406 F.2d 755 (2d Cir. 1969); Armour & Co. v. General Host Corp., 296 F.Supp. 470 (S.D.N.Y.1969); E. Aranow & H. Einhorn, Proxy Contests for Corporate Control ch. 23 (2d ed. 1968); Schneider, "Acquisitions under the Federal Securities Acts—A Program for Reform", 116 U.Pa.L.Rev. 1323 (1968); Schmults & Kelly, "Disclosure in Connection with Cash Take-Over Bids: The New Regulations", 24 Bus.Law. 19 (1968); Lockwood, "Corporate Acquisitions and Actions Under Section 10(b) and 14 of the Securities Exchange Act of 1934", 23 Bus.Law. 365 (1968); Sowards & Mofsky, "Corporate Take-Over Bids: Gap in Federal Securities Regulation", 41 St. John's L.Rev. 499 (1967), 9 Corp.Prac.Comm. 207 (1967); Fleischer & Mundheim, "Corporate Acquisition by Tender Offer", 115 U.Pa.L.Rev. 317 (1967); Stephan, "Acquisition Trouble Spots", 21 Bus.Law. 401 (1966). Subsection (d) is composed of eight detailed paragraphs. Implementing subsection (d) is section 13(d), which requires the filing of a statement by any person who acquires the beneficial ownership of any equity security registered under the Act if after such acquisition he beneficially owns more than 10 percent of the securities of that class. Such statement must be sent to the issuer and to each securities exchange where the security is traded and filed with the S.E.C.

34. See 17 C.F.R. §§ 240.14d–1 to 240.14d–4 (1969); Schedule 13D; Schedule 14D; SEC Securities Exchange Act Release No. 8510 (Jan. 31, 1969).

35. § 14(e), 15 U.S.C.A. § 78n(e). Section 13(e) authorizes the S.E.C. to adopt regulations requiring appropriate disclosures when corporations repurchase their own shares.

36. § 14(f), 15 U.S.C.A. § 78n(f); 17 C.F.R. § 240.14f–1 (1969), 2 CCH Fed.Sec.L.Rep. ¶ 24,302; Ratner, "Section 14(f): A New Approach to Transfers of Corporate Control", 54 Cornell L.Rev. 65 (1968).

37. § 12(e); 15 U.S.C.A. § 79(e); 17 C.F.R. §§ 250.60–250.65 (1969).

38. § 20(a); 15 U.S.C.A. § 80a–20(a); 17 C.F.R. §§ 270.20a–1 to 270.20a–3 (1969). For additional investment company proxy rules, see SEC Investment Company Act Release No. 2978 (Feb. 26, 1960).

39. § 27, 15 U.S.C.A. § 78aa; Webster v. Steinberg, 84 Nev. 426, 442 P.2d 894 (1968) (refusing to enjoin shareholder meeting on allegation of false and misleading proxy statements, because of exclusive jurisdiction of federal courts to enforce S.E.C. Proxy Rules); Loss, "The SEC Proxy Rules in the Courts", 73 Harv.L.Rev. 1041 (1960); Loss, "The

The United States Supreme Court has held that private parties enjoy an implied right of action, directly and derivatively, for violation of the S.E.C. Proxy Rules, in soliciting proxies for a merger under state law which was later consummated, and that all necessary remedial relief was within the power of the federal courts.[40] This decision represents a further advance in the growing area of federal corporation law, presaging relief in the federal courts with respect to matters traditionally governed by state law, when there has been a violation of the S.E.C. Proxy Rules, without the possible restric-

SEC Proxy Rules and State Law", 73 Harv.L.Rev. 1249 (1960).

40. J. I. Case Co. v. Borak, 377 U.S. 426, 84 S.Ct. 1555, 12 L.Ed.2d 423 (1964); cf. Securities and Exchange Commission v. Nat'l Securities, Inc., 393 U. S. 453, 89 S.Ct. 564, 21 L.Ed.2d 668 (1969) (McCarran-Ferguson Act, which generally exempts insurance companies from federal regulation, held not to prevent S.E.C. from challenging merger of two insurance companies for deficient proxy materials used by one constituent company, on ground federal policy of full disclosure to protect shareholders and Arizona policy to protect policyholders not incompatible); Mills v. Electric Autolite Co., 403 F.2d 429 (7th Cir. 1968) (finding issue of fact as to causal relationship between proxy statement deficiency and challenged merger), rev'd —— U.S. ——, 90 S.Ct. 616, —— L.Ed.2d —— (1970) (holding such issue irrelevant); General Time Corp. v. Talley Industries, Inc., 403 F.2d 159 (2d Cir. 1968) (standard of materiality); Studebaker Corp. v. Gittlin, 360 F.2d 692 (2d Cir. 1966) (upholding standing of corporation to assert in federal court claim for injunctive relief against use of authorizations received from 42 other shareholders solicited allegedly in violation of S.E.C. Proxy Rules to support exercise of statutory shareholder inspection rights available to any person holding, or authorized in writing by holders of, at least five percent of any class of outstanding shares); Barnett v. Anaconda Co., 238 F.Supp. 766 (S.D.N.Y.1965) (denying relief under S.E.C. Proxy Rules, where defendant held sufficient shares to authorize dissolution, for lack causal connection between alleged violation of Rules and minority shareholders' alleged damage); Demmler, "Private Suits Based on Violation of the Proxy Rules", 20 U.Pitt.L.Rev. 587 (1959); Comment, "Private Actions and the Proxy Rules: The Basis and the Breadth of the Federal Remedy", 31 U.Chi.L.Rev. 328 (1964); Note, "Violation of S.E.C. Proxy Rules—Federal Jurisdiction to Invalidate Corporate Merger," 39 Wash. & Lee L.Rev. 297 (1964).

tions imposed by state law on such litigation.[41]

FEDERAL SECURITIES LEGISLATION— SECURITIES EXCHANGE ACT, 1934— INSIDER TRADING

298. The Securities Exchange Act, 1934, has two insider trading provisions, buttressing to the extent applicable, the court-developed "majority rule", "special facts rule", and "minority rule."

Section 10(b), implemented by S.E.C. Rule 10b–5, makes unlawful any manipulative or deceptive device or contrivance, including frauds or deceits, in connection with the purchase or sale of any security, whether listed or not on an exchange, in interstate commerce, through the mails, or by any national securities exchange facility. Violations have been construed as resulting in civil liability, enforceable by any aggrieved person in the federal courts.

Section 16 requires certain disclosure of insider trading in equity securities of issuers of any equity security registered under the Act, and provides that any profits realized by an officer or director of such issuer or more than 10 percent beneficial owner of a registered equity security, in connection with a purchase or sale, or sale and purchase, within six months, of any equity security of such issuer, regardless of the use of inside information, may be recovered by such issuer or any of its security holders suing in its behalf—known as "recapture" of "short-swing profits"—in the federal courts.

Other federal insider trading statutory provisions are found in the Public Utility Holding Company Act, 1935, and Investment Company Act, 1940.

Three federal statutes deal with insider trading of securities, the most significant being the Securities Exchange Act, 1934, which has two applicable provisions, thus

41. Kaplan, "Shareholder Attacks on Mergers and Acquisitions Under Federal Securities Laws", 50 Chi.B.Rec. 441 (1969); Elson, "The Meaning of J. I. Case Co. v. Borak—Remedies Available for Violations of Proxy Rules Under the Federal Securities Act", 23 Sw.L.J. 609 (1969); Fleischer, " 'Federal Corporation Law': An Assessment", 78 Harv.L.Rev. 1146 (1965).

buttressing, to the extent applicable, the court-developed "majority rule", "special facts rule", and "minority rule" previously discussed.[1]

One of the provisions, section 10b, implemented by S.E.C. Rule 10b–5, not only buttresses and expands the common-law rules against insider share trading but also applies to situations in addition to insider share trading.

Section 10(b) of Securities Exchange Act, 1934; S.E.C. Rule 10b–5

Section 10(b) of the 1934 Act makes it unlawful for any person, directly or indirectly, by the use of interstate commerce or the mails or any facility of any national securities exchange to use or employ, in connection with the purchase or sale of any security, whether listed or not on an exchange, any manipulative or deceptive device or contrivance in contravention of S.E.C. rules and regulations.[2]

In 1942, the Securities and Exchange Commission promulgated under section 10(b) Rule X–10B–5, later designated Rule 10b–5, and known as the "anti-fraud rule", which provides: [3]

"It shall be unlawful for any person, directly or indirectly, by the use of any means or instrumentality of interstate commerce, or of the mails, or of any facility of any national securities exchange,

"(1) to employ any device, scheme, or artifice to defraud,

"(2) to make any untrue statement of a material fact or to omit to state a material fact necessary in order to make the statements made, in the light of the cir-

---

1. See section 239 supra. See also W. Painter, Federal Regulation of Insider Trading (1969); Symposium: "Insider Trading in Stocks", 21 Bus.Law. 1009 (1966); Conant, "Duties of Disclosure of Corporate Insiders Who Purchase Shares", 46 Cornell L.Q. 53 (1960); Rubin & Feldman, "Statutory Inhibitions upon Unfair Use of Corporate Inside Information", 95 U.Pa.L.Rev. 468 (1947).

2. 15 U.S.C.A. § 78j(b). A somewhat similar provision in the Federal Securities Act of 1933 deals with fraud and misrepresentation in the interstate sale of securities. § 17, 15 U.S.C.A. § 77q. "The language of Rule 10b–5 is broader in several respects than that of section 17(a) of the Securities Act. Thus, while section 17(a) prohibits fraudulent or deceptive practices 'in the offer or sale' of any security, section 17(a) makes it unlawful 'to obtain money or property by means of' false or misleading statements, while Rule 10b–5 provides, that it is unlawful 'to make any such statements.' Rule 10b–5 specifically refers to the use 'of any facility of any national securities exchange,' language not contained in section 17(a). A national securities exchange, however, is one of the facilities of interstate commerce." Matter of Cady, Roberts & Co., 40 S.E.C. 907, n. 11 (1961). Punitive damages apparently are not recoverable under Rule 10b–5. Green v. Wolf Corp., 406 F.2d 291 (2d Cir. 1968), cert. denied 395 U.S. 977, 89 S.Ct. 2131, 23 L.Ed.2d 766 (1969). But see de Haas v. Empire Petroleum Co., 302 F.Supp. 647 (D.Colo.1969) (allowing punitive damages for tort of fraud under Rule 10b–5. See Myzel v. Fields, 386 F.2d 718 (8th Cir. 1967),

cert. denied 390 U.S. 951, 88 S.Ct. 1043, 19 L.Ed.2d 1143 (1968) (use of telephone even though only for intrastate calls in purchase of shares of close corporation held to involve instrumentality of interstate commerce). Accord, Nemitz v. Cunny, 221 F.Supp. 571 (N.D.Ill.1963). Contra, Rosen v. Albern Color Research, Inc., 218 F.Supp. 473 (E.D.Pa.1963). See also Derdiarian v. Futterman Corp., 223 F.Supp. 265 (S.D.N.Y.1963), settlement approved 38 F.R.D. 178 (S.D.N.Y.1965) (cause of action under anti-fraud provisions of 1933 and 1934 Acts held to survive death of officer-director). See also Lowenfels, "Rule 10b–13, Rule 10b–7, and Purchase of Target Company Securities During an Exchange Offer", 69 Colum.L.Rev. 1392 (1969); Krasik, "Tender Offers: The Target Company's Duty of Disclosure", 25 Bus. Law. 455 (1970).

3. SEC Securities Exchange Act Release No. 3230 (May 21, 1942); A. Bromberg, Securities Law Fraud: SEC Rule 10b–5 (1967); Jacobs, "Trading and Disclosure Under Rule 10b–5", 1 P–H Corp.Rep. ¶ 26,005 (1969); Cohen, "The Development of Rule 10b–5", 23 Bus.Law. 593 (1968); Lowenfels, "The Demise of the Birnbaum Doctrine: A New Era for Rule 10b–5", 54 Va.L.Rev. 268 (1968); Marsh, "What Lies Ahead under Rule 10b–5?", 24 Bus. Law. 69 (1968); Painter, "Insider Information Growing Pains for the Development of Federal Corporation Law Under Rule 10b–5", 65 Colum.L.Rev. 1361 (1965); Comment, "Negligent Misrepresentations Under Rule 10b–5", 32 U.Chi.L.Rev. 824 (1965); Ruder, "Pitfalls in the Development of a Federal Law of Corporations by Implications through Rule 10b–5", 59 Nw.U.L.Rev. 185 (1964); Whitney, "Rule 10b–6: The Special Study's Rediscovered Rule", 62 Mich.L.Rev. 567 (1964); Lohf, "Corporation Law of the Securities Acts: Federal Rights of Corporations", 36 U.Colo.L.Rev. 76 (1963); Frohling, "The Promoter and Rule 10b–5: Basis for Accountability", 48 Cornell L.Q. 274 (1963); Annot., 22 A.L.R.2d 793 (1968).

cumstances under which they were made, not misleading, or

"(3) to engage in any act, practice, or course of business which operates or would operate as a fraud or deceit upon any person,

"in connection with the purchase or sale of any security."

Rule 10b–5 has been construed as creating implied civil liability,[4] enforceable only in the federal courts,[5] and can afford relief in situations where none would be available on applicable common-law principles.[6]

---

4. Kardon v. Nat'l Gypsum Co., 73 F.Supp. 798 (E.D. Pa.1947), supplemented 83 F.Supp. 613 (E.D.Pa.1947) (involving close corporation with only four shareholders; holding burden of proving profits, unlike burden of proving damages for common-law deceit, not on plaintiffs; extraterritorial service of process upheld); Dystra, "Civil Liability Under Rule 10b–5", 1967 Utah L.Rev. 207; Susman, "Use of Rule 10b–5 As a Remedy for Minority Shareholders of Close Corporations", 22 Bus.Law. 193 (1967); Klein, "Extension of a Private Remedy to Defrauded Securities Investors Under SEC Rule 10B–5", 20 U.Miami L.Rev. 81 (1965); Lowenfels, "Rule 10b–5 and the Stockholder's Derivative Action", 18 Vand.L.Rev. 893 (1965); Ruder, "Civil Liability Under Rule 10b–5: Judicial Revision of Legislative Intent?", 57 Nw.U.L.Rev. 627 (1963); Comment, "Measurement of Damages in Private Actions under Rule 10b–5", 1968 Wash.U.L.Q. 165; Comment, "Rule 10b–5: Elements of a Private Right of Action", 43 N.Y.U.L.Rev. 541 (1968); Comment, "Fiduciary Suits Under Rule 10b–5", 1968 Duke L.J. 791; Comment, "Ancillary Relief in SEC Injunction Suits for Violation of Rule 10b–5", 79 Harv.L.Rev. 656 (1966); Comment, "Shareholders' Derivative Suit to Enforce a Corporate Right of Action Against Directors Under SEC Rule 10b–5", 114 U. Pa.L.Rev. 578 (1966); Comment, "Individual Recovery for Promoter's Fraud—Procedural Problems Under S.E.C. Rule 10b–5", 51 Calif.L.Rev. 939 (1963). See notes 15–17 infra.

5. 15 U.S.C.A. § 78aa.

6. Presumably, the duty to disclose under Rule 10b–5 is never less than that required by the federal "special facts rule". Reed v. Riddle Airlines, 266 F.2d 314 (5th Cir. 1959); Speed v. Transamerica Corp., 99 F.Supp. 808 (D.Del.1951); Matter of Ward La-France Truck Corp., 13 S.E.C. 373 (1943). See also Speed v. Transamerica Corp., 135 F.Supp. 176 (D. Del.1955) (measure of damages), modified 235 F.2d 369 (3d Cir. 1956); Note, 54 Mich.L.Rev. 971 (1956). Compare Geller v. Transamerica Corp., 53 F.Supp. 625 (D.Del.1943), aff'd per curiam 151 F.2d 534 (3d Cir. 1945) (judgment for defendant under Kentucky common-law "majority rule"), with Speed v. Transamerica Corp., 71 F.Supp. 457 (D.Del.1947) (uphold-

---

Assuming use of any means or instrumentality of interstate commerce or the mails, or any facility of any national securities exchange, almost any kind of "fraud"[7] would seem to suffice so long as it was "in connection with the purchase or sale of any security".[8] Scienter,[9] deception,[10] reliance,[11]

---

ing claims for violation of Rule 10b–5). See also Connelly v. Balkwill, 174 F.Supp. 49 (N.D.Ohio 1959), aff'd on opinion below, 279 F.2d 685 (6th Cir. 1960) (holding that state court action in Ohio, whose law was construed as imposing same broad and exacting duty of disclosure as existed under Rule 10b–5, was res judicata in later federal court action between same parties on same transaction).

7. Securities and Exchange Commission v. Electrogen Industries, Inc., CCH Fed.Sec.L.Rep. ¶ 92,156 (E.D.N.Y.1968) (enjoining continued use of allegedly false statements concerning products after corporation commenced public offering of shares); Entel v. Allen, 270 F.Supp. 60 (S.D.N.Y.1967) (upholding claim that controlling shareholder caused sale of corporation's shares at insufficient price to second corporation dominated by such controlling shareholder); O'Neill v. Maytag, 339 F.2d 764 (2d Cir. 1964) (construing "fraud" under Rule 10b–5 as having to involve deception relating to purchase or sale of security, and not including constructive fraud in sense of breach of general duties of management in exchanging shares at unfavorable ratio to retain control).

8. Purchase and sale are not limited to their meanings in the commercial law of sales. Securities and Exchange Commission v. Nat'l Securities, Inc., 393 U.S. 453, 89 S.Ct. 564, 21 L.Ed.2d 668 (1969) (misleading proxy statement in merger of two insurance companies held to involve purchase of securities under Rule 10b–5 even though violation of S.E.C. Proxy Rules also involved); Mader v. Armel, 402 F. 2d 158 (6th Cir. 1968), cert. denied 394 U.S. 930, 89 S.Ct. 1188, 22 L.Ed.2d 459 (1969) (exchange of shares in merger, effected through allegedly misleading proxy statements, held to constitute sale under Rule 10b–5); Dasho v. Susquehanna Corp., 380 F.2d 262 (7th Cir. 1967), cert. denied 389 U.S. 977, 88 S.Ct. 480, 19 L.Ed.2d 470 (1967) (statutory merger held to involve purchase or sale of securities under Rule 10b–5); Vine v. Beneficial Finance Co., 374 F.2d 627 (2d Cir. 1967), cert. denied 389 U. S. 970, 88 S.Ct. 463, 19 L.Ed.2d 460 (1968) (dissenting shareholder, with only choice between cash offered and appraisal, in merger corporation in short form merger, alleged effected by fraud, held seller); Ruckle v. Roto American Corp., 339 F.2d 24 (2d Cir. 1964) (held, in shareholder derivative action, that issuance by corporation of its own shares constituted "sale" under Rule 10b–5, and that nondisclosure of relevant information by defendants, who were principal officers and constituted majority of board of directors, to remaining directors, constituted "fraud" upon corporation under Rule 10b–5); Hoop-

---

9, 10, 11. See notes 9, 10, 11 on page 600.

and privity,[12] apparently are no longer required. The term "insider", a judicial gloss

er v. Mountain States Securities Corp., 282 F.2d 195 (5th Cir. 1960), cert. denied 365 U.S. 814, 81 S.Ct. 695, 5 L.Ed.2d 693 (1961) (upholding action by corporation's trustee-in-bankruptcy under Rule 10b–5 on theory that corporation issuing shares for spurious assets was "seller" thereunder even though it was not investor since 1934 Act authorized rules "in the public interest or for the protection of investors"); Iroquois Industries, Inc. v. Syracuse China Corp., 417 F.2d 963 (2d Cir. 1969) (tender offeror held not defrauded purchaser or purchaser who relied on alleged fraudulent statements issued by defendant target corporation to its shareholders, under Rule 10b–5).

9. Heit v. Weitzen, 402 F.2d 909 (2d Cir. 1968), cert. denied 395 U.S. 903, 89 S.Ct. 1740, 23 L.Ed.2d 217 (1969) (allegedly inflated earnings statements, in reliance on which plaintiffs bought shares and convertible debentures, held, 2 to 1, actionable, despite lack of any intent to deceive and of any trading by corporation or its insiders); Meisenholder, "Scienter and Reliance as Elements in Buyer's Suit Against Seller Under Rule 10b–5", 4 Corp.Prac. Comm. 27 (Feb. 1963); Note, "Proof of Scienter Necessary in a Private Suit Under SEC Anti-Fraud Rule 10b–5", 63 Mich.L.Rev. 1070 (1965).

10. Note, "Securities—Rule 10b–5—Purchaser-Seller and Deception Elements Held Not Strict Prerequisites to Liability in Civil Action under SEC Rule 10b–5", 42 N.Y.U.L.Rev. 978 (1967).

11. List v. Fashion Park, Inc., 340 F.2d 457 (2d Cir. 1965), cert. denied 382 U.S. 811, 86 S.Ct. 23, 15 L. Ed.2d 60 (1965), reh. denied 382 U.S. 933, 86 S.Ct. 305, 15 L.Ed.2d 344 (1965) (defining test of "materiality" as whether reasonable man would have been influenced to act differently if insider had disclosed to him undisclosed fact, and test of "reliance" as whether minority shareholder would have been influenced to act differently than he did if insider had disclosed to him undisclosed fact); Britt v. Cyril Bath Co., 290 F.Supp. 934 (N.D.Ohio 1968) (nondisclosure of fraudulent diversion of profits found to lack causal connection with plaintiff's purchase or sale of shares; no federal jurisdiction over claim for mismanagement). See also Crane Co. v. Westinghouse Air Brake Co., 419 F.2d 787 (2d Cir. 1969) (corporate shareholder which cooperated with target corporation's management to defeat competitor's tender offer, through undisclosed market manipulations that drove price of target corporation's shares high enough to discourage tenders, is liable to unsuccessful tender offeror under Rule 10b–5, even though defeated offeror did not rely upon manipulator's nondisclosure).

12. Cochran v. Channing Corp., 211 F.Supp. 239 (S. D.N.Y.1962) (reduction of dividends to deflate price of corporation's shares to depress price to enable corporation to repurchase shares at depressed value held actionable under Rule 10b–5 by shareholders who sold shares, without proving privity of contract with corporation or directors); Comment, "The Purchaser-Seller Rule: An Archaic Tool for

on the statute to find fiduciary duties where they would not otherwise exist, has come to include any person with material information not disclosed to the public.[13]

The scope of Rule 10b–5 has not yet been fully defined, but its growing implications are outstanding.[14]

The Securities and Exchange Commission itself has been the initiator in three landmark cases under Rule 10b–5.

In the first,[15] the corporation's board of directors decided to reduce its quarterly div-

Determining Standing Under Rule 10b–5", 56 Geo. L.J. 1177 (1968); Comment, "Civil Liability Under Section 10B and Rule 10B–5: A Suggestion for Replacing the Doctrine of Privity", 74 Yale L.J. 658 (1965); Note, "The Purchaser-Seller Limitation to SEC Rule 10b–5", 53 Cornell L.Rev. 684 (1968).

13. Securities and Exchange Commission v. Texas Gulf Sulphur Co., 401 F.2d 833 (2d Cir. 1968) (en banc), cert. denied 394 U.S. 976, 89 S.Ct. 1454, 22 L.Ed.2d 756 (1969), infra note 16; Ross v. Licht, 263 F.Supp. 395 (S.D.N.Y.1967) (employee-shareholders and persons closely tied by blood or association with management held insiders and liable as "tip-

14. Schoenbaum v. Firstbrook, 405 F.2d 200 (2d Cir. 1968) (2–1), modified 405 F.2d 215 (2d Cir. 1968) (en banc) (7–3); Securities and Exchange Commission v. Great American Industries, Inc., 407 F.2d 453 (2d Cir. 1968) cert. denied 295 U.S. 920, 89 S.Ct. 1770, 23 L.Ed.2d 237 (1969) (sale of land to corporation for shares, where five-sixths thereof were to go to finder without disclosure to corporation, enjoined, 7 to 1, under Rule 10b–5). Symposium: "Rule 10b–5: Developments in the Law", 63 Nw.U.L.Rev. 452 (1968); Ruder, " 'Challenging Corporate Action under Rule 10b–5' ", 25 Bus.Law. 75 (1969); Patrick, "Rule 10b–5, Equitable Fraud and Schoenbaum v. Firstbrook: Another Step in the Continuing Developing of Federal Corporation Law", 21 Ala.L.Rev. 457 (1969); Hamilton, "Some Reflections on Cash Tender Offer Legislation", 15 N.Y.L.F. 269 (1969); Loomis, "Purchases by a Corporation of Its Own Securities", 22 Record of N.Y.C.B.A. 275 (1967); Comment, "Rule 10b–5 and Purchase by a Corporation of Its Own Shares", 61 Nw.U.L.Rev. 307 (1966); Comment, "The Regulation of Corporate Tender Offers Under Federal Securities Law: A New Challenge for Rule 10b–5", 33 U.Chi.L.Rev. 359 (1966); Note, "Corporate Stock Repurchases Under the Federal Securities Laws", 66 Colum.L.Rev. 1292 (1966); Latty, "The Aggrieved Buyer or Seller or Holder of Shares in a Close Corporation under the S.E.C. Statutes", 18 Law & Contemp.Prob. 505 (1953); Comment, "The Prospects for Rule X–10B– 5: An Emerging Remedy for Defrauded Investors", 59 Yale L.J. 1120, 1143 (1950).

15. Matter of Cady, Roberts & Co., 40 S.E.C. 907 (1961); Daum & Phillips, "The Implications of Cady, Roberts", 17 Bus.Law. 939 (1962); Comment,

idend, but notice of such action to the New York Stock Exchange and Dow Jones News Ticker Service was inadvertently delayed. One director, who was a member of a brokerage firm, thinking the information had been released, during a subsequent recess in the board meeting, informed one of his partners who in behalf of the firm's customers actively traded in the shares of the corporation. Realizing that the release of the information had been delayed, the second broker sold 7,000 shares "short" (at approximately 40) on the exchange, such shares being in the firm's discretionary accounts and in his wife's account. The shares closed at 34⅞. In S.E.C. suspension proceedings against the broker who sold the shares, the S.E.C. ruled that he was under a duty (even to nonshareholders) to disclose such information before effecting a sale on a national securities exchange, and his nondisclosure amounted to a fraud or deceit upon the purchasers. Any fiduciary duties to his clients could not excuse use of inside information at the expense of the public. The broker was suspended for 20 days by the S.E.C. (having already been fined $3,000 by the New York Stock Exchange) for willful violation of section 10(b) and Rule 10b–5 under the Securities Exchange Act and of section 17(a) of the Securities Act. No sanctions were imposed against the registrant brokerage firm.

In the second,[16] the S.E.C. sued Texas Gulf Sulphur Co., and several of its directors, officers, and employees, charging, under Rule 10b–5, that they had purchased large

"Insider Liability under Securities Exchange Act Rule 10b–5: The Cady, Roberts Doctrine", 30 U. Chi.L.Rev. 121 (1962); Comment, "Broker Silence and Rule 10b–5: Expanding the Duty to Disclose", 71 Yale L.J. 736 (1962).

16.   Securities and Exchange Commission v. Texas Gulf Sulphur Co., 401 F.2d 833 (2d Cir. 1968) (en banc), cert. denied 394 U.S. 976, 89 S.Ct. 1454, 22 L.Ed.2d 756 (1969). More than 100 former shareholders also sued the corporation for their losses in selling their shares prematurely and for punitive damages. Prior to public disclosure, the corporation acquired lands adjacent to the test bores. Several of the sellers of such lands also asserted claims against the corporation. Welles, "SEC vs. Texas Gulf raises sticky questions . . . Bonanza Trouble", 59 Life, No. 6, 29 (Aug. 6, 1965).

See Sunray DX Oil Co. v. Helmerich & Payne, Inc., 398 F.2d 447 (10th Cir. 1968) (exclusion from proxy statement in connection with proposed merger of exploratory information of uncertain nature upheld on ground it would have greatly enlarged statement and would not have helped average investor); Kuehnert v. Texstar Corp., 286 F.Supp. 340 (S.D. Tex.1968), aff'd 412 F.2d 700 (5th Cir. 1969) (2–1) (Rule 10b–5 construed as intended to protect ordinary persons buying and selling securities based upon information generally available to investing public and not "tippee" who used material inside information to his detriment); Bromberg, "Corporate Information: Texas Gulf Sulphur and Its Implications", 22 Sw.L.J. 731 (1968); Jennings, "Insider Trading in Corporate Securities: A Survey of Hazards and Disclosure Obligations Under Rule 10b–5", 62 Nw.U.L.Rev. 809 (1968); Ruder, "Texas Gulf Sulphur—The Second Round: Privity and State of Mind in Rule 10b–5 Purchase and Sale Cases", 63 Nw.U.L.Rev. 423 (1968); Wiesen, "Disclosure of Insider Information—Materiality and *Texas Gulf Sulphur*", 28 Md.L.Rev. 189 (1968); Liles, "How and When Does Corporate Insider Information Become 'Public'?, A Consideration of the Views of the District Court in the Texas Gulf Sulphur Case", 28 Ala.Law. 111 (1967); Ruder, "Corporate Disclosures Required by the Federal Securities Laws: the Codification Implications of Texas Gulf Sulphur", 61 Nw.U.L.Rev. 872 (1967); Mundheim, "Texas Gulf Sulphur Complaint: A Major Step in Restricting Insider Trading in Corporate Securities", 1966 J.Bus.L. 284; Fleischer, "Securities Trading and Corporate Information Practices: The Implications of the Texas Gulf Sulphur Proceedings", 51 Va.L.Rev. 1271 (1965); Kennedy & Wander, "Texas Gulf Sulphur, a Most Unusual Case", 20 Bus.Law. 1057 (1965); Comment, "Texas Gulf Sulphur: Expanding Concepts of Corporate Disclosure under SEC Rule 10b–5", 43 St. John's L. Rev. 425 (1968), 43 id. 655 (1969); Note, "SEC Enforcement of the Rule 10b–5 Duty to Disclose Material Information—Remedies and the Texas Gulf Sulphur Case", 65 Mich.L.Rev. 944 (1967); Note, "The Downstairs Insider: The Specialist and Rule 10b–5", 42 N.Y.U.L.Rev. 695 (1967). See also Reynolds v. Texas Gulf Sulphur Co., —— F.Supp. —— (D.Utah 1969) (corporation held liable for deceptive news release to former shareholders who sold their shares as result); Astor v. Texas Gulf Sulphur Co., 306 F.Supp. 1333 (S.D.N.Y.1969) (withholding by corporation of information upheld on ground disclosure would have interfered with acquisition of lands adjoined to drill sites). Securities and Exchange Commission v. Texas Gulf Sulphur Co., —— F.Supp. —— (S.D.N.Y.1970) (on remand) (holding that corporation's April 12, 1964 press release was made without due diligence and was misleading, and requiring insiders to give up to corporation their and their tipee's estimated profits— but not the estimated profits of a tippee of a tippee —to be held in escrow for three or more years subject to disposition by court order upon application by the SEC or other interested person, with any undisposed money then to go to the corporation).

amounts of the corporation's shares or calls thereon, had accepted share options without disclosure to the board of directors, and passed out "tips" before announcing the corporation's rich ore discovery in November, 1963, in Timmins, Ontario, to the public on April 16, 1964, and that the corporation prior to such date had issued "materially false and misleading" information discounting the richness of the strike, and demanding rescission in favor of the sellers of the shares to the defendants and the "tippees". Judgment was granted to the effect that the information was material and the transactions of all of the insiders who knew of it had violated Rule 10b–5, even though the transactions were on a national securities exchange; that the conduct of the "tippees", who were not parties, was equally reprehensible; that the options should be rescinded; and that the issues of the deceptiveness of the press release and the remedies should be decided on remand.

In the third,[17] where one of the nation's most prominent broker-dealers and its employees in connection with a prospective un-derwriting, which it was to manage, received material information concerning a substantial decline in earnings of the prospective issuer, and disclosed such information to some of its favored institutional and other large customers who effected sales and short sales of the securities of the issuer, disciplinary sanctions were imposed upon the broker-dealer and its employees for violation of Rule 10b–5. Meanwhile, other customers of the broker-dealer, without disclosure to them, were retaining or purchasing such securities.

In actions under the 1934 Act, the venue requirements are liberal and nationwide service of process is authorized.[18] The most relevant statute of limitations of the forum controls,[19] with its commencing to run being subject to the federal discovery-of-the-fraud rule.[20] Class actions are possible;[21] limitations on derivative actions in the forum, such as security-for-expenses statutes, are inapplicable.[22] Under the doctrine of pendent jurisdiction, state law claims can be adjudicated by the federal courts.[23]

---

17. Matter of Merrill Lynch, Pierce, Fenner & Smith, Inc., SEC Securities Exchange Act Release No. 8459 (Nov. 25, 1968) (public censure, temporary closing of certain offices, suspension without pay of certain officers and employees). Quaere, as to liability of "tippees" who made sales or short sales without disclosure to purchasers, on theory that "tippees" are in same position, with same duties, as "tippors". See Financial Industrial Fund, Inc. v. Merrill Lynch, Pierce, Fenner & Smith, Inc., —— F. Supp. —— (D.Colo.1969) (action to recover losses alleged to approximate $2,000,000 plus interest). Quaere, as to the firm's conflicting interests as underwriter, broker, dealer, mutual fund. See Matter of Van Alstyne, Noel & Co., SEC Securities Exchange Act Release No. 8511 (Feb. 3, 1969). See also "Expanded Policy on Timely Disclosure" (New York Stock Exchange 1969); Leavell, "Investment Advice and the Fraud Rules", 65 Mich.L.Rev. 1569 (1967); Manne, "Insider Trading and the Stock Market", 42 N.Y.U.L.Rev. 212 (1967); Schotland, "Unsafe At Any Price: A Reply to Manne, 'Insider Trading and the Stock Market'", 53 Va.L.Rev. 1425 (1967); Comment, "An Investment Company's Duty to Its Customers Versus Its Duty to the Public Under Rule 10b–5: A Conflict of Interest?", 1969 Utah L.Rev. 212; Note, "A Suggested Locus of Recovery in National Exchange Violations of Rule 10b–5", 54 Cornell L.Rev. 306 (1969).

18. 15 U.S.C.A. § 78aa.

19. Charney v. Thomas, 372 F.2d 97 (6th Cir. 1967) (action under Rule 10b–5 held not subject to local "blue sky" law statute of limitations); Schulman, "Statutes of Limitation in 10b–5 Actions: Complication Added to Confusion", 13 Wayne L.Rev. 635 (1967).

20. Janigan v. Taylor, 344 F.2d 781 (1st Cir. 1965), cert. denied 382 U.S. 879, 86 S.Ct. 163, 15 L.Ed.2d 120 (1965) (applying federal concept that claim for fraud does not arise until discovery, thereby tolling state statute of limitations, in action under Rule 10b–5).

21. Green v. Wolf Corp., 406 F.2d 291 (2d Cir. 1968), cert. denied 395 U.S. 977, 89 S.Ct. 2131, 23 L.Ed.2d 766 (1969) (one of 2,300 similarly situated shareholders held to have standing to bring class action to enforce Rule 10b–5 under Fed.R.Civ.P. 23); Esplin v. Hirschi, 402 F.2d 94 (10th Cir.1968), cert. denied 394 U.S. 928, 89 S.Ct. 1194, 22 L.Ed.2d 459 (1969).

22. McClure v. Borne Chemical Co., 292 F.2d 824 (3d Cir. 1961), cert. denied 368 U.S. 939, 82 S.Ct. 382, 7 L.Ed.2d 339 (1961) (holding that state security-for-expenses statute does not apply to claim arising under federal law).

23. Ellis v. Carter, 291 F.2d 270 (9th Cir. 1961) (upholding federal pendent jurisdiction over nonfederal

Section 16 of Securities Exchange Act, 1934

The second relevant provision of the 1934 Act, section 16,[24] dealing with insider trading, is composed of five subsections, and is subject to various exemptions.[25]

Subsection (a) requires that each officer and director of an issuer with equity securities registered under the Act, and each beneficial owner of more than 10 percent of any class of registered equity security, file with the exchange and the S.E.C. an initial report showing his holdings in such issuer's equity securities [26] and an additional report for

each month thereafter in which changes occur in his holdings.

Subsection (b) provides that any profits realized by such an officer,[27] director,[28] or more than 10 percent beneficial owner,[29] in

---

claims); Trussell v. United Underwriters, Ltd., 228 F.Supp. 757 (D.Colo.1964) (denying extraterritorial service for pendent state claims).

24. 15 U.S.C.A. § 78p.

25. Lowenfels, "Section 16(b): A New Trend in Regulating Insider Trading", 54 Cornell L.Rev. 45 (1968); Wu, "Economist Looks at Section 16 of the Securities Exchange Act of 1934", 68 Colum.L.Rev. 260 (1968); Manne, "Insider Trading and the Administrative Process", 35 Geo.Wash.L.Rev. 473 (1967); Munter, "Section 16(b) of the Securities Exchange Act of 1934: An Alternative to 'Burning Down the Barn in Order to Kill the Rats' ", 52 Cornell L.Q. 69 (1966); Kramer, "An Examination of Section 16(b)", 21 Bus.Law. 183 (1965); Michaely & Lee, "Put and Call Options: Criteria for Applicability of Section 16(b) of the Securities Exchange Act of 1934", 40 Notre Dame Law. 239 (1965); Painter, "The Evolving Role of Section 16(b)", 62 Mich.L. Rev. 649 (1964); Meeker & Cooney, "The Problem of Definition in Determining Insider Liabilities Under Section 16(B)", 45 Va.L.Rev. 949 (1959); Cole, "Insiders' Liabilities under the Securities Exchange Act of 1934", 12 Sw.L.J. 147 (1958); Cook & Feldman, "Insider Trading Under the Securities Exchange Act", 66 Harv.L.Rev. 385, 612 (1953); Comment, "Securities Regulation: Insider Status in Legal Fiction and Financial Fact—A Proposed Revision to Section 16(b)", 50 Calif.L.Rev. 500 (1962); Note, "The Role of the Securities and Exchange Commission under Section 16(b)", 52 Va.L.Rev. 668 (1966); Note, "Short-Swing 'Purchase and Sales' Under the Securities Exchange Act", 61 Nw.U.L. Rev. 448 (1966); Note, "Securities Regulation—Short Swing Profits—Pragmatic Approach to Section 16(b)", 41 Tul.L.Rev. 194 (1966).

26. The term "equity security" is defined by the 1934 Act as "any stock or similar security; or any security convertible, with or without consideration, into such a security, or carrying any warrant or right to subscribe to or purchase such a security; or any such warrant or right; or any other security which the Commission shall deem to be of similar nature . . ." § 3(a) (11), 15 U.S.C.A. § 78c(a) (11). For definition of "officer", see 17 C.F. R. § 240.3b–2 (1969). See United States v. Guterma,

272 F.2d 344 (2d Cir. 1959) (criminal conviction for failure to file insider reports). Ownership reports are available for public inspection at the Washington, D. C. office of the S.E.C. and also at any exchange where filed. Monthly, the S.E.C. publishes its "Official Summary of Security Transactions and Holdings" which has more than 24,000 subscribers. Some 93,823 ownership reports were filed during the year ending June 31, 1968, of which 14,893 were initial statements of ownership, and 78,930 were statements of changes in ownership. 34 SEC Ann. Rep. 43 (1969).

27. See Lee Nat'l Corp. v. Segur, 281 F.Supp. 851 (E.D.Pa.1968) (officer of wholly-owned subsidiary held not officer of parent issuer where he performed no functions for latter and no fraud or subterfuge was involved); Colby v. Klune, 178 F.2d 872 (2d Cir. 1949); Lockheed Aircraft Corp. v. Campbell, 110 F.Supp. 282 (S.D.Calif.1953); Lockheed Aircraft Corp. v. Rathman, 106 F.Supp. 810 (S.D.Calif.1952).

28. See Feder v. Martin Marietta Corp., 406 F.2d 260 (2d Cir. 1969), cert. denied —— U.S. ——, —— S.Ct. ——, —— L.Ed.2d —— (1970) (imposing liability on person who was director at time of purchase but not at time of sale); Adler v. Klawans, 267 F.2d 840 (2d Cir. 1959) (imposing liability on person who was director at time of sale but not at time of purchase). A broker who serves as a corporate director is subject to potential conflicts of interests: his duties to the corporation not to divulge corporate information vs. his duties to his clients to disclose. The matter is of serious concern to the S.E.C., the national securities exchanges, and the National Association of Securities Dealers, Inc., 161 The Wall Street Journal, No. 112, 4 (June 10, 1963); Blau v. Lehman, 368 U.S. 403, 82 S.Ct. 451, 7 L.Ed.2d 403 (1962) (limiting recovery to partner-director's proportionate share of his brokerage partnership's profits, on ground partner was not sitting as director to represent his partnership and profits were realized by partnership without any advice or information from such director); Feder v. Martin Marietta Corp., supra (applying "deputization theory" to sustain recovery of short-swing profits from corporation whose officer sat as its alter ego on board of directors of issuer); Wagner, "Deputization under Section 16(b): The Implications of Feder v. Martin Marietta Corporation", 78 Yale L.J. 1151 (1969); Johnston & Coles, "Wall Street Trading Firms as Securities 'Insiders' ", 12 Clev.-Mar.L.Rev. 369 (1963).

29. Chemical Fund, Inc. v. Xerox Corp., 377 F.2d 107 (2d Cir. 1967) (holding that investment company holding more than 10 percent of corporation's convertible debentures which if converted would have resulted in ownership of 2.72 percent of corporation's common shares was not beneficial owner of more than 10 percent of any class of any equity se-

connection with a purchase and sale, or sale and purchase,[30] within six months [31] in equi-

ty securities of such issuer may be recovered by such issuer—known as "recapture" of "short-swing profits". Use of inside information is immaterial; [32] transactions on an exchange are covered; and the profit goes to such issuer,[33] not the person to whom the insider sold or from whom the insider purchased.[34]

If the issuer fails to sue the insider within 60 days after requested to do so,[35] or fails to prosecute diligently, any security holder of the issuer may sue in behalf of the issuer.[36]

curity); SEC Securities Exchange Act Release No. 8325 (June 9, 1968); SEC Securities Exchange Act Release No. 7793 (Jan. 19, 1966) (person generally is to be regarded as beneficial owner of securities held in name of his or her spouse and their minor children); SEC Securities Exchange Act Release No. 7824 (Feb. 14, 1966); S.E.C. Rule 16a–2 (class deemed to consist of all outstanding securities of class exclusive of securities held by or for account of issuer or any subsidiary in computing more than 10 percent beneficial ownership). Compare Stella v. Graham-Paige Motors Corp., 132 F.Supp. 100 (S.D. N.Y.1955), modified on other grounds 232 F.2d 299 (2d Cir. 1956) (2–1), cert. denied 352 U.S. 831, 77 S.Ct. 46, 1 L.Ed.2d 52 (1956), with Arkansas Louisiana Gas Co. v. W. R. Stephens Inv. Co., 141 F. Supp. 841 (W.D.Ark.1956). See also Ellerin v. Massachusetts Mutual Life Ins. Co., 270 F.2d 259 (2d Cir. 1959) (distinguishing series from class of securities); Shreve, "Beneficial Ownership of Securities Held by Family Members", 22 Bus.Law. 431 (1967); Feldman & Teberg, "Beneficial Ownership Under Section 16 of the Securities Exchange Act", 17 W.Res.L.Rev. 1054 (1966).

30. Compare Ferraiolo v. Newman, 259 F.2d 342 (6th Cir. 1958), cert. denied 359 U.S. 927, 79 S.Ct. 606, 3 L.Ed.2d 629 (1959) (holding conversion of preferred shares called for redemption into common shares of equivalent value, sold within six months after conversion, not purchase), with Park & Tilford v. Schulte, 160 F.2d 984 (2d Cir. 1947), cert. denied 332 U.S. 761, 68 S.Ct. 64, 92 L.Ed. 347 (1947) (conversion held purchase where redemption was authorized by defendants who controlled corporation). See note 24 infra. Shaw v. Dreyfus, 172 F.2d 140 (2d Cir. 1949), cert. denied 337 U.S. 907, 69 S.Ct. 1048, 93 L. Ed. 1719 (1949); Truncale v. Blumberg, 80 F.Supp. 387 (S.D.N.Y.1948); Comment, " 'Purchase' and 'Sale' under Section 16(B) of the Securities Exchange Act", 10 Syracuse L.Rev. 296 (1959). See also Roberts v. Eaton, 212 F.2d 82 (2d Cir. 1954), cert. denied 348 U.S. 827, 75 S.Ct. 44, 99 L.Ed. 652 (1954) (reclassification of shares held not to constitute "purchase" by shareholders of reclassified shares); Silverman v. Landa, 306 F.2d 422 (2d Cir. 1962) (simultaneous issue of matched puts and calls by director held not sale and purchase where calls never exercised and puts not exercised until after six months); Miller v. General Outdoor Advertising Co., 223 F.Supp. 790 (S.D.N.Y.1963) (extension of call on shares held not purchase), rev'd 337 F.2d 944 (2d Cir. 1964). See also Newmark v. RKO General, Inc., 294 F.Supp. 358 (S.D.N.Y.1968) (exchange of surviving corporation's shares for merging corporation's shares and debentures that had been purchased, to facilitate merger, by majority shareholder of other merging corporation held "sale", making majority shareholder liable to surviving corporation for insider's profits); Lang & Katz, "Liability for 'Short Swing' Trading in Corporate Reorganization", 20 Sw.L.J. 472 (1966).

31. Booth v. Varian Associates, 334 F.2d 1 (1st Cir. 1964) cert. denied 379 U.S. 961, 85 S.Ct. 651, 13 L.

Ed.2d 556 (1965) (holding date of closing in June, 1959, when shares were actually transferred, to be date of purchase rather than January, 1954, date of execution of agreement which deferred fixing of price and number of shares to day before closing date); Stella v. Graham-Paige Motors Corp., 132 F. Supp. 100 (S.D.N.Y.1955), modified on other grounds, 232 F.2d 299 (2d Cir. 1956), cert. denied, 352 U.S. 831, 77 S.Ct. 46, 1 L.Ed.2d 52 (1956); Perfect Photo, Inc. v. Grabb, 205 F.Supp. 569 (E.D.Pa. 1962) (offerer-director held liable for short-swing profits from sale of shares which had been listed between their purchase and sale).

32. Magida v. Continental Can Co., 231 F.2d 843 (2d Cir. 1956), cert. denied 351 U.S. 972, 76 S.Ct. 1037, 100 L.Ed. 1490 (1956).

33. Ibid.

34. Double liability under common law (see section 239 supra) or Rule 10b–5 and under § 16(b) would probably be avoided by reducing the profit realized for the purpose of recovery in one action by the amount of any profit recovered in the other action, more likely if the prior recovery were in the common-law or Rule 10b–5 action.

35. The 60-day period is for the benefit of the issuer. Grossman v. Young, 72 F.Supp. 375 (S.D.N.Y.1947). See Note, "Insider Trading: The Issuer's Disposition of an Alleged 16(b) Violation", 1968 Duke L.J. 94.

36. Blair v. Lamb, 314 F.2d 618 (2d Cir. 1963) (holding person who bought shares on margin account held in "street name" was "owner" with standing to bring action for recovery of short-swing profits); Molybdenum Corp. of America v. International Mining Corp., 32 F.R.D. 415 (S.D.N.Y.1963) (allowing minority shareholder to intervene in action by corporation to recover short-swing profits where shareholders contended corporation might be dominated by defendants); Silverman v. Re, 194 F.Supp. 540 (S.D.N.Y.1961) (motion by corporation in whose behalf shareholder action to recover short-swing profits was brought to be realigned as plaintiff rather than nominal defendant, to insure vigorous prosecution, granted, despite fact that new action by corporation would have been barred by two-year statute of limitations).

A two-year federal statute of limitations applies.[37] Jurisdiction is exclusively in the federal courts.[38]

Determining the profit realized by matching the lowest-priced purchases against the highest-priced sales within the preceding or following six months has been upheld.[39]

Options, warrants, and convertible securities have presented troublesome questions as to characterization and as to time and price of purchase and sale.[40]

The courts have been very generous in awarding counsel fees to security holders who have assisted in achieving recoveries of short-swing profits.[41]

Unlike minority shareholders suing derivatively who are subject to "contemporaneous-share-ownership" requirements in many jurisdictions or under Fed.R. Civ.P. 23.1, formerly 23(b), the security holder suing under § 16(b) probably need not have been one at the time the cause of action arose. Dottenheim v. Murchison, 227 F.2d 737 (5th Cir. 1955), cert. denied 351 U.S. 919, 76 S.Ct. 712, 100 L.Ed. 1451 (1956); Blau v. Mission Corp., 212 F.2d 77 (2d Cir. 1954), cert. denied 347 U.S. 1016, 74 S.Ct. 872, 98 L.Ed. 1138 (1954); Pellegrino v. Nesbit, 203 F.2d 463, 37 A.L.R.2d 1296 (9th Cir. 1953); Blau v. Oppenheim, 250 F.Supp. 881 (S.D.N.Y.1966); Benisch v. Cameron, 81 F.Supp. 882 (S.D.N.Y.1948). Nor do security-for-expenses statutes, applicable to derivative actions, apply. Blau v. Albert, 157 F.Supp. 816 (S.D. N.Y.1957). See sections 362, 372 infra. See also Epstein v. Shindler, 26 F.R.D. 176 (S.D.N.Y.1960) (barring counterclaim against corporation for past services in action by shareholder to recover short-swing profits). See also Western Auto Supply Co. v. Gamble-Skogmo, Inc., 348 F.2d 736 (8th Cir. 1965), cert. denied 382 U.S. 987, 86 S.Ct. 556, 15 L. Ed.2d 475 (1966) (non-abatement because action non-penal and remedial); Epstein v. Shindler, 200 F. Supp. 836 (S.D.N.Y.1961) (shareholder action to recover short-swing profits, since section 16(b) more remedial than penal, held not to abate on death of defendant insider).

37. Delay in filing the reports required by § 16(a) might delay the running of the two-year period of limitations. See Blau v. Albert, 157 F.Supp. 816 (S.D.N.Y.1957); Carr-Consolidated Biscuit Co. v. Moore, 125 F.Supp. 423 (M.D.Pa.1954); Fistel v. Beaver Trust Co., 94 F.Supp. 974 (S.D.N.Y.1950); Grossman v. Young, 72 F.Supp. 375 (S.D.N.Y.1947).

38. § 27, 15 U.S.C.A. § 78aa; American Distilling Co. v. Brown, 295 N.Y. 36, 64 N.E.2d 347, 165 A.L.R. 1228 (1945).

39. Gratz v. Claughton, 187 F.2d 46 (2d Cir. 1951), cert. denied 341 U.S. 920, 71 S.Ct. 741, 95 L.Ed. 1353 (1951) (judgment against defendant for $300,000 profits on basis of such method of computation, despite $300,000 actual loss). As to problem of partnership realization of profits from trading in securities of corporation in which a partner was an insider, see note 28 supra; Rattner v. Lehman, 98 F. Supp. 1009 (S.D.N.Y.1951), aff'd 193 F.2d 564 (2d Cir.1952). Profits have been held recoverable even though the sale agreement granted the purchaser an option to rescind the sale within a two-year period. Lewis v. Mason, CCH Fed.Sec.L.Rep. ¶ 90,915 (S.D.N.Y.1959). See also Volk v. Zlotoff, 285 F.Supp. 650 (S.D.N.Y.1968) (mutual rescission of purchase held not to avoid liability for short-swing

profits); Newmark v. RKO General, Inc., 305 F. Supp. 310, (S.D.N.Y. 1969) (premium for control included in computing profits).

40. Cook & Feldman, "Insider Trading under the Securities Exchange Act", 66 Harv.L.Rev. 612 (1953); Comment, "Put and Call Options under Section 16 of the Securities Exchange Act", 69 Yale L.J. 868 (1960). Former Rule X–16B–3 exempted *acquisitions* of certain securities under bonus, profit-sharing, retirement, share option, thrift, savings, or similar plans, but not the *sale* of such securities, from section 16. Greene v. Dietz, 247 F.2d 689 (2d Cir. 1957) (2–1) (expressing doubt on validity of rule but exonerating insider who had relied on it); Van Aalten v. Hurley, 176 F.Supp. 851 (S.D.N.Y.1959); Perlman v. Timberlake, 172 F.Supp. 246 (S.D.N.Y. 1959) (holding Rule X–16B–3 invalid). But see Continental Oil Co. v. Perlitz, 176 F.Supp. 219 (S.D. Tex.1959); Gruber v. Chesapeake & Ohio Ry., 158 F.Supp. 593 (N.D.Ohio 1957). Rule X–16B–3 was amended on May 26, 1960 to limit the exemption. Halleran, "The Impact of Section 16(b) of the Securities Exchange Act of 1934 on Restricted Stock Options", 15 Bus.Law. 158 (1959); Comment, "Background and Impact of the Proposed Amendment to Rule X–16B–3 of the Securities and Exchange Commission", 7 U.C.L.A.L.Rev. 495 (1960). By S.E.C. Rule 16b–9, effective February 17, 1966, ordinary conversion transactions were exempted from section 16(b). The trend of court decisions has been against finding that conversion was a "sale" of the convertible security and a "purchase" of the security into which converted. Petteys v. Northwest Airlines, Inc., 367 F.2d 528 (8th Cir. 1966), cert. denied 385 U.S. 1006, 87 S.Ct. 712, 17 L.Ed.2d 545 (1967); Blau v. Lamb, 363 F.2d 507 (2d Cir. 1966), cert. denied 385 U.S. 1002, 87 S.Ct. 707, 17 L.Ed.2d 542 (1967). But see Heli-Coil Corp. v. Webster, 352 F. 2d 156 (3d Cir. 1965); Parke & Tilford, Inc. v. Schulte, 160 F.2d 984 (2d Cir. 1947), cert. denied 332 U.S. 761, 68 S.Ct. 64, 92 L.Ed. 347 (1947). See Lynam v. Livingston, 276 F.Supp. 104 (D.Del.1967); Davis, "Conversions as Purchases and Sales Under Section 16(b) of the Securities and Exchange Act of 1934"; 24 Bus.Law 1109 (1969); Hamilton, "Convertible Securities and Section 16(b): The End of an Era", 44 Texas L.Rev. 1447 (1966). See also Hemmer, "Insider Liability for Short-Swing Profits pursuant to Mergers and Related Transactions", 22 Vand.L.Rev. 1101 (1969); Annot., 1 A.L.R.Fed. 719 (1969).

41. Blau v. Rayette-Faberge, Inc., 389 F.2d 469 (2d Cir. 1968) (holding that where statute of limitations had run on first series of officer-director's insider

Many challenging tax questions are also involved.[42]

Subsection (c) of section 16 prohibits insiders from selling any equity security of the issuer, if the person selling the security or his principal (a) does not own the security sold, or (b) if owning the security, fails, without excuse, to deliver it against such sale within 20 days thereafter, or does not within five days after such sale deposit it in the mails or other usual channels of transportation.[43]

Subsection (d) of section 16 provides that subsection (b) shall not apply to any purchase and sale, or sale and purchase, and subsection (c) shall not apply to any sale, of an equity security not then or theretofore held by him in an investment account, by a dealer in the ordinary course of his business and incident to the establishment or maintenance by him of a primary or secondary market (otherwise than on a national securi-

ties exchange or an exempted exchange for such security).[44]

Subsection (e) provides that section 16 shall not apply to foreign or domestic arbitrage transactions unless made in contravention of any S.E.C. rules and regulations.[45]

Other Federal Insider Trading Statutory Provisions

Besides the Securities Exchange Act of 1934, two other federal statutes, the Public Utility Holding Company Act of 1935[46] and the Investment Company Act of 1940,[47] regulate insider trading in the case of securities of registered public utility companies and subsidiaries and of registered investment companies, respectively.

FEDERAL SECURITIES LEGISLATION— PUBLIC UTILITY HOLDING COMPANY ACT, 1935

299. The Public Utility Holding Company Act, 1935, regulates holding companies and their subsidiaries engaged in the interstate electric utility business or in the interstate retail distribution of gas. Under the Act, the regulatory powers of the Securities and Exchange Commission are very comprehensive.

The Public Utility Holding Company Act, 1935,[1] regulates holding companies and their

---

profits transactions and 18 months of two-year limitation period had run on second series at time shareholder's attorney informed corporation by letter of transactions and demanded that corporation bring action within 60 days or attorney would file action and corporation settled case with officer-director without filing action, shareholder's attorney was entitled to attorney's fee even though he did not bring action on behalf of corporation); Gilson v. Chock Full O'Nuts Corp., 331 F.2d 107 (2d Cir. 1964) (shareholder whose investigation by attorney resulted in corporation's successful action to recover short-swing profits allowed reasonable attorney's fees); Blau v. Brown and Western Nuclear, Inc., CCH Fed.Sec.L.Rep. ¶ 92,263 (S.D.N.Y.1968) (awarding $7,500, or 20 percent of short-swing profits recovered for corporation to attorney who did no more than file routine complaint).

42. The insider whose profits are recaptured has been denied either a business expense or a loss deduction for federal income tax purposes. However, a business deduction was allowed an insider who disgorged his profits voluntarily. Marks v. Comm'r, 27 T.C. 464 (1956); Int.Rev.Bull. 1966–23; Rev.Rul. 61–115; Darrell, "The Tax Treatment of Payments under Section 16(b) of the Securities Exchange Act of 1934", 64 Harv.L.Rev. 80 (1950). Insider profits recovered by the issuer are taxable as gross income of the issuer. General American Investors Co. v. Comm'r, 348 U.S. 434, 75 S.Ct. 478, 99 L.Ed. 504 (1955). See Treas.Reg. § 1.1341–1 (1964).

43. See Silverman v. Landa, 306 F.2d 422 (2d Cir. 1962).

44. See Painter, "Section 16(d) of the Securities Exchange Act: Legislative Compromise or Loophole", 113 U.Pa.L.Rev. 358 (1965); Note, "§ 16(d) Market-Making Exemption", 18 Stan.L.Rev. 1418 (1966).

45. Falco v. Donner Foundation, Inc., 208 F.2d 600, 40 A.L.R.2d 1340 (2d Cir. 1953).

46. § 17, 15 U.S.C.A. § 79q. See section 299 infra.

47. § 30(f), 15 U.S.C.A. § 80a–29. See section 301 infra.

1. 15 U.S.C.A. §§ 79–79z–6; 1 L. Loss, Securities Regulation 131 (2d ed. 1961); A. Choka, An Introduction to Securities Regulation 2, 120–121 (1958); 3 CCH Fed.Sec.L.Rep. ¶¶ 25,101 et seq. Rules under this Act were designated "U" followed by the consecutive number of the rule. E. g., Rule U–50; the letter prefix has been dropped and they are now designated "250." Followed by numbers to conform to 17 C.F.R. 250.—, e. g., 250.46, or simply Rule 46. In 1968, there were 25 registered holding

subsidiaries engaged in the interstate electric utility business or in the interstate retail distribution of manufactured or natural gas. Under the Act, the regulatory powers of the Securities and Exchange Commission are very comprehensive. Besides its requirements relating to geographical integration and corporate simplification, the Act regulates such companies in the issuance of their securities (competitive bidding rule), filing of reports, solicitation of proxies, trading by corporate insiders, accounting practices, acquisition of securities and assets, dividend payments, and services performed for subsidiaries.[2]

FEDERAL SECURITIES LEGISLATION— TRUST INDENTURE ACT, 1939

300. The Trust Indenture Act, 1939, requires that bonds or other debt securities offered to the public by the mails or interstate commerce, unless exempt, be secured by an indenture qualified under the Act.

The Trust Indenture Act, 1939,[1] requires that bonds, debentures, notes, and other debt securities, other than exempted securities, offered to the public by the mails or interstate commerce be secured by an indenture qualified under the Act. Among the exemptions are issues of not more than $250,000 within a period of 12 consecutive months otherwise than under an indenture, and issues of not more than $1,000,000 within a period of 36 consecutive months under an indenture.

To be qualified the indenture must contain provisions for an independent institutional trustee which is subject to affirmative duties and other provisions to protect the indenture security holders. Outlawed are exculpatory provisions formerly used to limit the liability of the trustee. Imposed on the trustee, after default, is the duty to use the same degree of care and skill "in the exercise of the rights and powers invested in it by the indenture" as a prudent man would use in

[§ 300]

companies; in the 17 active systems were 89 electric and/or gas utility subsidiaries, 47 nonutility subsidiaries, and 15 inactive companies, or a total of 172 system companies, with aggregate assets approximating $16,785,000,000. 34 SEC Ann.Rep. 131–132 (1969).

2. See Securities and Exchange Commission v. New England Electric System, 384 U.S. 176, 86 S.Ct. 1397, 16 L.Ed.2d 452 (1966), on remand, 376 F.2d 107 (1st Cir. 1967), rev'd 390 U.S. 207, 88 S.Ct. 916, 19 L.Ed.2d 1042 (1968); United Gas Corp. v. Pennzoil Co., 248 F.Supp. 449 (S.D.N.Y.1965), aff'd 354 F.2d 1002 (2d Cir. 1965) (denying injunction against corporations acquiring 10 percent or more of common shares of plaintiff gas utility which would have required both plaintiff and defendant to register under 1935 Act); R. Ritchie, Integration of Public Utility Holding Companies (1954); Brudney, "The Investment-Value Doctrine and Corporate Adjustments", 72 Harv.L.Rev. 645 (1959); Cook & Cohen, "Capital Structures of Electric Utilities under the Public Utility Holding Company Act", 45 Va.L.Rev. 981 (1959); Ferber, Blasberg & Katz, "Conflicts of Interest in Reorganization Proceedings under the Public Utility Holding Company Act of 1935 and Chapter X of the Bankruptcy Act", 28 Geo.Wash.L. Rev. 319 (1959); Annot., 16 L.Ed.2d 1218 (1966). See section 350 infra.

1. Sometimes called the "Barkley Act". 15 U.S.C.A. §§ 77aaa to 77bbbb; C. Israels & G. Duff, When Corporations Go Public 60 (PLI 1962); G. Robinson, Going Public: Successful Securities Underwriting 112 (1961); 1 L. Loss, Securities Regulation 719–753 (2d ed. 1961); A. Choka, An Introduction to Securities Regulation ch. 5 (1958); 1 CCH Fed. Sec.L.Rep. ¶¶ 7,001 et seq.; 1 P-H Sec.Reg. ¶¶ 9125 et seq.; R. Stevens, Handbook on the Law of Private Corporations 196 (2d ed. 1949); McKeehan, "Duties of the Trustee of a Mortgage Given to Secure Bondholders", 49 Dick.L.Rev. 1 (1944); Comment, "The Trust Indenture Act of 1939", 25 Cornell L.Q. 105 (1939). Rules under the Act were designated "T" followed by the number of the section of the Act and the consecutive number of the rule under such section, e. g., Rule T–10B–1; the letter prefix has been dropped and they are now designated "260." followed by numbers to conform to 17 C. F.R. 260.—, e. g., 260.10b–1, or simply Rule 10b–1. When a pre-1939 indenture is amended, in connection with the issue of a new series of securities thereunder, to qualify under this Act, it is said to be "Barkleyized". Cf. Katz, "The Protection of Minority Bondholders in Foreclosures and Receiverships", 3 U.Chi.L.Rev. 517 (1936); Payne, "Exculpatory Clauses in Corporate Mortgages and Other Instruments", 19 Cornell L.Q. 171 (1934); Posner, "Liability of the Trustee Under the Corporate Indenture", 42 Harv.L.Rev. 198 (1928). During the year ending June 30, 1968, 564 indentures, filed with the S.E.C., were awaiting disposal. 34 SEC Ann.Rep. 61 (1969).

the conduct of his own affairs. The required "boiler-plate" provisions add substantially to the length and expense of indentures.[2] These include indenture provisions concerning the persons eligible for appointment as trustee, disqualification of trustee, preferential collection of claims against obligor, indenture security holders lists, reports by indenture trustee, reports by obligor, evidence of compliance with indenture provisions, duties and responsibilities of trustee, prohibition of impairment of indenture security holder's right to payment, special powers of trustee, duties of paying agents, and effect of prescribed indenture provisions.

FEDERAL SECURITIES LEGISLATION— INVESTMENT COMPANY ACT, 1940

301. **The Investment Company Act, 1940, regulates investment companies, that is, companies which invest, reinvest, hold, and trade in the securities of other companies. Investment companies, under the Act, are classified as face-amount certificate companies, unit investment trusts, or management companies. Management companies may be "closed-end" or "open-end" ("mutual funds"); "diversified" or "nondiversified".**

The Investment Company Act, 1940,[1] regulates so-called investment companies or investment trusts, i. e., companies primarily engaged in the business of investing, reinvesting, holding, and trading in the securities of other issuers.[2] The Act classifies them as follows:

(a) Face-amount certificate companies;

(b) Unit investment trusts, including small business investment companies;

(c) Management companies (whose certificates or shares are equity securities representing a fluctuating interest in a fund):

(i) "Closed-end" or "Open-end" ("Mutual funds");[3]

An Introduction to Securities Regulation ch. 10 (1958); 3 CCH Fed.Sec.L.Rep. ¶¶ 35,001 et seq. In 1968, there were some 862 investment companies registered under the Act, including 53 small business investment companies, with an estimated aggregate market value of assets approximating $69,-732,000,000. The total assets of mutual funds have been estimated to approximate $53,480,000,000. 34 SEC Ann.Rep. 113 (1969). Sheedy, "A Tangled Web? Some Peripheral Problems Under the Investment Company Act", 17 W.Res.L.Rev. 1011 (1966); Garrett, "When Is an Investment Company?", 37 U.Det.L.J. 355 (1959); Kerr, "The Inadvertent Investment Company: Section 3(a) (3) of the Investment Company Act", 12 Stan.L.Rev. 29 (1959); Choka, "An Introduction to Investment Companies", 3 Prac.Law. 48 (Feb. 1957); Jaretzki, "The Investment Company Act of 1940", 26 Wash. U.L.Q. 303 (1941). Variable annuity companies, small business investment companies, real estate investment trusts, and bank-operated collective investment funds are subject to the Act. See also SEC Investment Company Act Release No. 4538 (Mar. 9, 1966); Comment, "Regulation of Bank-Operated Collective Investment Funds—Judicial or Legislative Resolution of, an Administrative Controversy?", 73 Yale L.J. 1249 (1964); Comment, "The Expanding Jurisdiction of the Securities and Exchange Commission: Variable Annuities and Bank Collective Investment Funds", 62 Mich.L.Rev. 1398 (1964); Comment, "The Regulation by the Investment Company Act of 1940 of Small Business Investment Companies Established Under the Small Business Investment Act", 46 Minn.L.Rev. 143 (1961). Rules under the Act were designated "N" followed by the number of the section of the Act and the consecutive number of the rule under such section, e. g., Rule N–SB–1: the letter prefix has been dropped and they are now designated "270.", followed by numbers to conform to 17 C.F.R. 270.—, e. g., 270.8b–1.

2. See H. Bullock, The Story of Investment Companies (1959). See also A. Wiesenberger, Investment Companies (1969 ed.).

3. "Open-end" investment companies, or "mutual funds", are called "open-end" because they do not

---

[§ 301]

2. Such "boiler-plate" provisions might just as well have been made terms of every indenture subject to the Act without the necessity of their being physically incorporated in the indenture. See Sample Incorporating Indenture (Demonstrating a Method of Incorporating by Reference Model Debenture Indenture Provisions—All Registered Issues—1967) and Model Debenture Indenture Provisions—All Registered Issues—1967 (American Bar Foundation 1967); Sample Incorporating Indenture (Demonstrating a Method of Incorporating by Reference Model Debenture Indenture Provisions) and Model Debenture Indenture Provisions—1965 (American Bar Foundation 1965); Rodgers, "The Corporate Trust Indenture Project", 20 Bus.Law. 551 (1965). See also Pohl, "Cautions in Drafting and Administering Corporate Trust Indentures", 36 Trust Bull. 19 (Apr.1957), 96 Trusts & Estate 247 (1957).

[§ 301]

1. 15 U.S.C.A. §§ 80a–1—80a–52; 1 L. Loss, Securities Regulation 144–153 (2d ed. 1961); A. Choka,

(ii) "Diversified" or "Nondiversified" (depending on degree of diversification of portfolio).

The Act, besides requiring registration of nonexempt "investment companies", prohibits such companies from changing the nature of their business or their investment policies without the approval of their shareholders, requires disclosure of their finances and investment policies, regulates the means of custody of the companies' assets, requires management contracts to be submitted to security holders for their approval, prohibits underwriters, investment bankers, and brokers from constituting more than a minority

of the directors of such companies, and prohibits transactions between such companies and their officers, directors, and affiliates except with the approval of the S.E.C.[4] The act also regulates the issuance of senior securities and requires face-amount certificate companies to maintain reserves adequate to meet maturity payments upon their certificates.

The securities of investment companies which are offered to the public are also required to be registered under the Securities Act, 1933, and the companies must file periodic reports. Such companies are also subject to the S.E.C. Proxy Rules to "insider" trading rules.

The Act has been held to have created a private federal remedy for violation thereof.[5]

Legislation has been proposed for stricter regulation of mutual funds, viz., imposition of a ceiling on sales charges, elimination of "front-end load" on contractual plans, fixing of standard of "reasonableness" for management fees, banning of mutual fund holding companies, etc.[6]

---

have a fixed capitalization; they sell their own new shares to investors, stand ready to buy back or "redeem" their old shares, and are not listed on securities exchanges. Such shares are "redeemable" at the option of the holder and out of the stated capital represented by such shares and surplus. "Closed-end" investment companies have fixed capitalization; their shares are sometimes listed on securities exchanges, and are traded like shares of other corporations. Wise, "The Double Play in Closed-End Funds", 66 Fortune, No. 4, 107 (Oct. 1962). See Prudential Ins. Co. of America v. Securities and Exchange Commissions, 326 F.2d 383 (2d Cir. 1964), cert. denied 377 U.S. 953, 84 S.Ct. 1629, 12 L.Ed.2d 497 (1964) (holding insurance company-sponsored variable annuity contracts subject to Investment Company Act, notwithstanding exemptions of insurance company as such); Securities and Exchange Commission v. Variable Annuity Life Ins. Co., 359 U.S. 65, 79 S.Ct. 618, 3 L.Ed.2d 640 (1959); J. Straley, What About Mutual Funds? (3d rev. ed. 1967); Bibliography: "Selected Materials on Mutual Funds", 22 Record of N.Y.C.B.A. 646 (1967); "The Mutual Fund Industry: A Legal Survey", 44 Notre Dame Law. 732 (1969); Anderson, "Rights and Obligations in the Mutual Funds: A Source of Law", 20 Vand.L.Rev. 1120 (1967); Modesitt, "Mutual Fund—A Corporate Anomaly", 14 U.C.L.A.L. Rev. 1252 (1967); Mundheim, "Some Thoughts on the Duties and Responsibilities of Unaffiliated Directors of Mutual Funds", 115 U.Pa.L.Rev. 1058 (1967); Sullivan, "Some Common Problems of Mutual Fund Shareholders", 13 Prac.Law. 23 (May, 1967); Jaretzki, "Duties and Responsibilities of Directors of Mutual Funds", 29 Law & Contemp. Prob. 777 (1964); Conwill, "The Minority Menace to Mutual Fund Selling", 18 Bus.Law. 1055 (1963); Salamy, "Federal Income Tax Aspects of Mutual Funds", 9 Prac.Law. 33 (Mar.1963); Lobell, "Rights and Responsibilities in the Mutual Fund", 70 Yale L.J. 1258 (1961); Lobell, "The Mutual Fund: A Structural Analysis", 47 Va.L.Rev. 181 (1961). For an amusing account of an investment-management firm specializing in mutual funds, see Brooks, "Profiles—The Happy Venture", 34 New Yorker, No. 3, 47 et seq. (Mar. 8, 1958).

4. Green, "Fiduciary Standards of Conduct under the Investment Company Act of 1940", 28 Geo.Wash.L. Rev. 266 (1959). See section 241 supra.

5. Esplin v. Hirschi, 402 F.2d 94 (10th Cir. 1968) cert. denied 394 U.S. 928, 89 S.Ct. 1194, 22 L.Ed.2d 459 (1969); Brown v. Bullock, 294 F.2d 415 (2d Cir. 1961) (holding that Investment Company Act creates implied private federal remedy for violation thereof); Brouk v. Managed Funds, Inc., 286 F.2d 901 (8th Cir. 1961), cert. granted 366 U.S. 958, 81 S.Ct. 1921, 6 L.Ed.2d 1252 (1961) (holding that failure of directors of investment company to discharge their duties in compliance with Investment Company Act did not give rise to private remedy for resulting damages to investment company), judgment vacated and case remanded with directions to dismiss, 369 U.S. 424, 82 S.Ct. 878, 8 L.Ed.2d 6 (1962); Eisenberg & Lehr, "An Aspect of the Emerging 'Federal Corporation Law': Directorial Responsibility under the Investment Company Act of 1940", 20 Rutgers L.Rev. 181 (1966); Eisenberg & Phillips, "Mutual Fund Litigation—New Frontiers for the Investment Company Act", 62 Colum.L.Rev. 73 (1962); Comment, "The Investment Company Act in the State Courts", 1962 Duke L.J. 423; Comment, "Private Rights of Action Under the Investment Company Act", 10 Clev.-Mar.L.Rev. 421 (1961).

6. Conference on Mutual Funds, 115 U.Pa.L.Rev. 659 (1967); Gopman, "Current Problems in the Regula-

FEDERAL SECURITIES LEGISLATION— INVESTMENT ADVISERS ACT, 1940

302. The Investment Advisers Act, 1940, regulates persons engaged for compensation in the business of rendering advice or issuing analyses or reports concerning securities.

The Investment Advisers Act, 1940,[1] regulates persons engaged for compensation in the business of rendering advice or issuing analyses or reports concerning securities, requiring their registration unless exempted

tion of Mutual Fund Selling Practices", 24 Bus.Law. 409 (1969); Werner "Protecting the Mutual Fund Investor: The SEC Reports on the SEC", 68 Colum.L.Rev. 1 (1968); Wymeersch, "Some Aspects of Management Fees of Mutual Funds", 17 Buffalo L. Rev. 747 (1968); Conwill, "Blight or Blessing? The Wharton School Study of Mutual Funds", 18 Bus.Law. 663 (1963); Lobell, "A Critique of the Wharton School Report on Mutual Funds", 49 Va. L.Rev. 1 (1963); Herman, "Lobell on the Wharton School Study of Mutual Funds: A Rebuttal", 49 Va.L.Rev. 938 (1963); Jaretzki, "The Investment Company Act: Problems Relating to Investment Advisory Contracts", 45 Va.L.Rev. 1023 (1959); Comment, "The Use of Brokerage Commissions to Promote Mutual Fund Sales: Time to Give Up the 'Give Up'", 68 Colum.L.Rev. 334 (1968); Comment, "Mutual Funds and the Investment Advisory Contract", 50 Va.L.Rev. 141 (1964); Comment, "Termination of Management Contracts under the Investment Company Act of 1940", 63 Colum.L.Rev. 733 (1963); Comment, "The Mutual Fund and Its Management Company: An Analysis of Business Incest", 71 Yale L.J. 137 (1961).

[§ 302]

1. 15 U.S.C.A. §§ 80b–1 to 80b–21. See Securities and Exchange Commission v. Capital Gains Research Bureau, Inc., 375 U.S. 180, 84 S.Ct. 275, 11 L.Ed.2d 257 (1963) (holding that "scalping" violates antifraud provisions of Investment Advisers Act, investment advisor being under affirmative duty to disclose his financial interest and intent to trade in security he recommends to his clients); 1 L. Loss, Securities Regulation 1392 et seq. (2d ed. 1961); A. Choka, An Introduction to Securities Regulation ch. 9 (1958); 3 CCH Fed.Sec.L.Rep. ¶¶ 44,001 et seq.; 2 P-H Sec.Reg. ¶¶ 25,251 et seq.; Comment, "The Regulation of Investment Advice: Subscription Advisers and Fiduciary Duties", 63 Mich.L.Rev. 1220 (1965); Leavell, "Investment Advice and the Fraud Rules", 65 Mich.L.Rev. 1569 (1967); Comment, "The Regulation of Investment Advisers", 14 Stan.L.Rev. 827 (1962). Rules under the Act were designated "R" followed by the number of the section of the Act and the consecutive number of the rule under such section, e. g., Rule R–203–1; the letter prefix has been dropped and they are now designated "275.", followed by such numbers to conform to 17 C.F.R. 275.—, e. g., 275.203–1. See Annot., 11 L.Ed. 2d 1017 (1965).

therefrom, e. g., where investment advice is given only to persons resident in the state in which adviser maintains his principal place of business so long as his advice does not concern securities listed on a national securities exchange or admitted to unlisted trading privileges thereon. It outlaws fraudulent, deceptive, or manipulative acts or practices on the part of registered advisers, giving the S.E.C. authority, by rules and regulations, to define and to prescribe means reasonably designed to prevent such acts and practices, prohibits profit-sharing arrangements, prevents assignment of an advisory contract without the client's consent, etc. Approximately 2,000 investment advisors are currently registered.

FEDERAL BANKRUPTCY ACT, 1938— CHAPTER X

303. Under Chapter X of the Federal Bankruptcy Act, which is administered by the federal courts, the functions of the Securities and Exchange Commission are advisory.

Under Chapter X (corporate reorganization) of the Federal Bankruptcy (Chandler) Act, which is administered by the federal courts, the S.E.C. has certain advisory functions.

The S.E.C. participates as a party to these proceedings, either at the request or with the approval of the courts. It renders independent, expert advice and assistance to the courts, which do not maintain their own staffs of expert consultants. In cases in which the scheduled liabilities of the debtor exceed $3,000,000, the plan of reorganization must be, and in other cases may be, referred by the court to the S.E.C. for preparation of an advisory report upon the fairness and feasibility of the plan.

Corporate reorganization is reserved for later treatment.[1]

[§ 303]

1. See sections 387–389 infra. During 1967–68, the S.E.C. was a party in 109 Chapter X reorganization proceedings, of which 22 were new proceedings and

MISCELLANEOUS FEDERAL SECURITIES LEGISLATION

304. **Under various statutes, federal administrative agencies other than the Securities and Exchange Commission regulate securities of issuers under their jurisdiction, in which event such securities are usually exempt from Securities and Exchange Commission regulation.**

Apart from the S.E.C., other federal administrative agencies regulate securities of issuers under their jurisdiction. In such situations, the securities and their issuers are usually exempt from most S.E.C. regulations.[1] Thus, for example, the issuance of securities by national banks and federal savings and loan associations is subject to the Comptroller of the Currency and Federal Home Loan Bank Board, respectively, etc.;[2] of interstate rail and motor carriers to the Interstate Commerce Commission;[3] and of electric utility companies engaged in interstate commerce to the Federal Power Commission.[4]

National and state-chartered banks whose deposits are insured by the Federal Deposit Insurance Corporation and which meet the assets and number of shareholders tests must comply with the registration and disclosure provisions of the Securities Exchange Act. Administration and enforcement are vested not in the Securities and Exchange Commission but in the case of National and District of Columbia banks, in the Comptroller of the Currency, in the case of state banks which are members of the Federal Reserve System, in the Federal Reserve Board, and in the case of other state banks, in the Federal Deposit Insurance Corporation.

Specific federal securities legislation has largely replaced the application of the federal mail-fraud statutes to securities transactions.

STATE "BLUE SKY" LAWS— IN GENERAL

305. **Nearly all states, under their police power, have enacted statutes, known as "blue sky" laws, regulating the issuance of securities. State jurisdiction over securities has been expressly preserved by the Federal Securities Act, 1933.**

State regulation of securities antedates federal regulation by many years. As early as 1852, Massachusetts began to regulate the issuance of securities by common carriers. In the early 20th century, the various states increasingly regulated the issuance of securities by public utilities. Beginning in 1910, the states began regulating the issuance of securities generally, under statutes which came to be known as "blue sky" laws.[1]

All of the states, except Delaware,[2] now have "blue sky" laws of one type or

17 were closed. 34 SEC Ann.Rep. 144 (1969). See Securities and Exchange Commission v. Templar, 405 F.2d 126 (10th Cir. 1969).

[§ 304]

1. See A. Choka, An Introduction to Securities Regulation ch. 13 (1958).

2. 12 U.S.C.A. §§ 51 et seq., 1464 et seq. See section 295, nn. 7, 10 supra.

3. 49 U.S.C.A. §§ 20a, 314; Alleghany Corp. v. Breswick & Co., 353 U.S. 151, 77 S.Ct. 763, 1 L.Ed.2d 726 (1957); United States v. New York, New Haven & Hartford R. R., 276 F.2d 525 (2d Cir. 1959), cert. denied sub nom. Tri-Continental Financial Corp. v. U. S., 362 U.S. 961, 80 S.Ct. 877, 4 L.Ed.2d 876 (1960); Adkins, "The New Haven Preferred Stock Cases: A Study in Judicial Legislation", 15 Bus.Law. 847 (1960). See section 295, n. 11 supra. Interstate motor carriers and freight forwarders are subject to the regulation of the Interstate Commerce Commission, but not so far as their issuance of securities is concerned. See Mechem, "Regulation of Motor Carrier Securities", 11 Vand.L.Rev. 1095 (1958).

4. 16 U.S.C.A. § 824c, but such regulation does not extend to a public utility organized and operating in a state under the laws of which its security issues are regulated by a state commission.

[§ 305]

1. The term "blue sky" laws is derived from the purpose of such enactments of preventing "speculative schemes which have no more basis than so many feet of 'blue sky'." Hall v. Geiger-Jones Co., 242 U.S. 539, 550, 37 S.Ct. 217, 220–221, 61 L.Ed. 480, 489 (1917).

2. Delaware had a simple anti-fraud provision until 1953 when it was dropped by the Delaware codifiers as superfluous.

another.[3] Such legislation has been enacted pursuant to the state's police powers.[4]

State jurisdiction over securities has been expressly preserved by the Federal Securities Act, 1933.[5]

STATE "BLUE SKY" LAWS—TYPES OF "BLUE SKY" LAWS

306. State "blue sky" laws differ widely. Conflicting philosophies of state regulation have resulted in three basic approaches which are sometimes found individually but more frequently exist in combination: (a) Fraud-type provisions; (b) Broker-dealer-registration provisions; and (c) Registration-of-securities provisions.

State securities regulation suffered from several shortcomings. Various attempts at greater uniformity have been tried, the most recent being the new Uniform Securities Act.

Provisions of state "blue sky" laws differ widely among different states. Conflicting philosophies of state regulation have resulted in three basic approaches which sometimes are found individually but more frequently exist in combination.[1]

3. See generally G. Calvert, A Primer on State Securities Regulation (Investment Bankers Association of America, rev. 1965); L. Loss & E. Cowett, Blue Sky Law (1958); 1 L. Loss, Securities Regulation 23 et seq. (2d ed. 1961); A Choka, An Introduction to Securities Regulation ch. 12 (1958); 1 CCH Blue Sky L.Rep. ¶¶ 501–518. The CCH Blue Sky Law Reports (2 vols.) also includes the legal investment laws. For sample of "Blue Sky memo", see C. Israels & G. Duff, When Corporations Go Public 317 (PLI 1962). See Symposium: "Blue Sky Laws", 17 W.Res.L.Rev. 1098 (1966); Hayes, "State Regulation of Securities Issues", 17 Drake L.Rev. 170 (1968); Manne & Mofsky, "What Price Blue-Sky? State Securities Laws Work Against Private and Public Interest Alike", 48 Barron's, No. 2, 5 (Aug. 5, 1968); Hoffman, "Blue Skying an Issue", 13 How.L.J. 108 (1967); Wolens, " 'Hidden Gold' in the Blue Sky Laws", 20 Sw.L.J. 578 (1966); Calvin, "A History of State Securities Regulation of Options and Warrants to Underwriters", 17 Bus.Law. 610 (1962); Sobieski, "State Securities Regulation of Real Estate Investment Trusts: The Midwest Position", 48 Va.L.Rev. 1069 (1962); Weinstein, "Problems in the Field of State Securities Regulation", 3 B.C.Ind. & Com.L.Rev. 381 (1962); Loss, "Developments in Blue Sky Laws", 15 Bus.Law. 1021 (1960), 14 Bus.Law. 1161 (1959); Brainin & Davis, "State Regulation of the Sale of Securities: Some Comments", 14 Bus.Law. 456 (1959); Jennings, "The Role of the States in Corporate Regulation and Investor Protection", 23 Law & Contemp.Prob. 193 (1958); Cowett, "Reorganizations, Consolidations, Mergers and Related Corporate Events under the Blue-Sky Laws", 13 Bus.Law. 418 (1958); Annot., 87 A.L.R. 42 (1933).

4. Hall v. Geiger-Jones Co., 242 U.S. 539, 37 S.Ct. 217, 61 L.Ed. 480 (1917); Caldwell v. Sioux Falls Stock Yards Co., 242 U.S. 559, 37 S.Ct. 224, 61 L.Ed. 493 (1917); Merrick v. N. W. Halsey & Co., 242 U.S. 568, 37 S.Ct. 227, 61 L.Ed. 498 (1917).

5. Securities Act, 1933, § 18, 15 U.S.C.A. § 77r; Allen, "Dissemination of Information under State Blue Sky Laws—A Shotgun Wedding", 18 Bus.Law. 763 (1963); Millonzi, "Concurrent Regulation of Interstate Securities Issues: The Need for Congressional Reappraisal", 49 Va.L.Rev. 1483 (1963); Cowett, "Problem in Jurisdiction of State Securities Laws", 1961 U.Ill.L.F. 300; Cowett, "Federal-State Relationships in Securities Regulation", 28 Geo.Wash.L.Rev. 287 (1959); Hayes, "State 'Blue Sky' and Federal Securities Laws", 11 Vand.L.Rev. 659 (1958); Armstrong, "The Blue Sky Laws", 44 Va.L.Rev. 713 (1958).

1. See Harum, "Needed Reform in Security Dealer Legislation", 12 U.Miami L.Rev. 75 (1957); Symposium: "The Operation and Effectiveness of Blue Sky Legislation", 15 Wayne L.Rev. 1401 (1969); Symposium: "Blue Sky Laws", 17 W.Res.L.Rev. 1098 (1966); Symposium: "Securities Regulation in Illinois", 1961 U.Ill.L.F. 205; Mofsky, "Blue Sky Restrictions on New Business Promotions", 1969 Duke L.J. 273; Basye, "A Glimpse of Oregon's Blue Sky Legislation: The Revision of 1967", 47 Ore. L.Rev. 403 (1968); Gray & Rosen, "Section 12(g) and Blue Sky Laws", 20 Bus.Law. 1075 (1965); Meer, "New Look at the Texas Securities Act", 43 Texas L.Rev. 680 (1965); Stevens, "Regulatory Aspects of the Illinois Securities Law; How the Illinois Securities Act of 1953 Differs from the Federal Securities Act of 1933", 54 Ill.B.J. 240 (1965); Bromberg, "Texas Exemptions for Small Offerings of Corporate Securities", 18 Sw.L.J. 537 (1964); Allen, "Dissemination of Information under the Securities Act of 1933 and under State Blue Sky Laws—A Shotgun Wedding", 18 Bus.Law. 763 (1963); Weinstein, "Problems in the Field of State Securities Regulation", 10 Catholic U.L.Rev. 1 (1961), 3 B.C.Ind. & Com.L.Rev. 381 (1962); Meer, "The Texas Securities Act: 1957 Mode: Facelift or Forward Look?", 36 Texas L.Rev. 429 (1958); Parthemos, "The New Georgia Securities Act", 9 Mercer L.Rev. 332 (1958); Robinton & Sowards, "Florida's Blue Sky Law: The Lawyer's Approach", 6 Miami L.Q. 525 (1952); Comment, "Dark Clouds in a Blue Sky: An Analysis of the Limited Offering Exemption", 23 U.Miami L.Rev. 568 (1969); Comment, "Take-over Bids in Virginia", 26 Wash. & Lee L.Rev. 323 (1969); Comment, "The South Dakota Blue Sky Law and the Need for a Private Offering Exemption", 12 S.D.L.Rev. 341 (1967); Comment, "Civil Remedies Available to Buyers Under the

Fraud-Type Provisions

Fraud-type provisions are the most simple. They prohibit fraud in the sale of securities, sometimes define "fraud" as not limited to common-law "deceit", and often provide for stronger sanctions than existed at common law,[2] such as more adequate remedies to defrauded persons, injunction proceedings by the state attorney general, criminal penalties. Some older statutes had only anti-fraud provisions.[3] Today, all statutes

Iowa Securities Law", 14 Drake L.Rev. 131 (1965); Legis., "Securities Legislation in Oklahoma", 21 Okla.L.Rev. 469 (1968). Virginia in 1968 enacted "take-over-bid" disclosure provisions similar to those inserted in the Federal Securities Exchange Act in 1968.

2. See Reno v. Bull, 226 N.Y. 546, 124 N.E. 144 (1919) (distinguishing fraud—representation, falsity, scienter, deception, injury—and negligence; measure of damages: difference between what plaintiff paid for shares and what shares were worth, not what value would have been if representation had been true). See Shulman, "Civil Liberty and the Securities Act", 43 Yale L.J. 227 (1933).

3. Delaware had only an anti-fraud provision until even it was eliminated in 1953.

New York had only anti-fraud provisions—so called "Martin Act"—until 1932 when broker-dealer registration provisions were added; in 1959, salesmen registration and in 1960 investment advisers provisions were added. McKinney's N.Y.Gen.Bus.Law, art. 23A, §§ 352–359–h. New York prescribes several filings: (a) "State Notice"; (b) "Further State Notice"; (c) "Dealer's Statement"; (d) "Supplemental Dealer's Statement"; (e) "Salesman's Statement"; (f) "Supplemental Salesman's Statement"; (g) "Investment Advisor's Statement", and (h) "Supplemental Investment Advisor's Statement".

No "dealer" or broker may offer for sale any security until a "state notice" is filed with the New York Department of State ($20 fee). Such notice contains the name and address of the dealer or broker, its state of incorporation, if a corporation, and the names of the partners, if a partnership. The "further state notice", filed in the New York Department of State ($20 fee), required unless the security is exempt, identifies each security offered by the "dealer" and gives the name, address, and state of incorporation of the issuer. The manager of an underwriting or selling syndicate with a New York office may file such notice in behalf of the entire syndicate. Every "dealer" must file a verified "dealer's statement" with the New York State Department of Law ($40 fee, $2 for each partner, officer, etc.), setting forth prescribed information. Where the dealer is a partnership or corporation, the same information must be given for all partners, officers, directors, and branch managers.

have such provisions along with more extensive regulatory provisions.

Broker-Dealer-Registration Provisions

Broker-dealer-registration provisions regulate securities by regulating the persons engaged in the securities business: brokers, dealers, salesmen, agents, etc. Only one state, for most securities, limits its regulation to such measures, implemented by anti-fraud provisions.[4]

The other states with "blue sky" laws go further, and have, besides broker-dealer-registration provisions, provisions for the registration of the securities.

Registration-of-Securities Provisions

Registration-of-securities provisions are combined with anti-fraud provisions and broker-dealer-registration provisions. Some of the registration-of-securities provisions require some or full disclosure,[5] somewhat along the lines of the Federal Securities Act of 1933, but with power in the state official to deny registration on specified grounds; many others, in theory if not in practice, in

Levy, "Securities Regulation in New York", 35 N. Y.St.B.J. 256 (1963). A verified "supplemental dealer's statement" must be filed with the New York State Department of Law ($5 fee), if any change occurs in the particulars given in the "dealer's statement". The fee for each "salesman's statement" is $10 and "supplemental salesman's statement" is $5. The fee for an "investment advisor's statement" is $100, with a $25 fee for each "supplemental investment advisor's statement".

In 1968, New York provided for the registration of intrastate offerings, i. e., securities other than those registered under the Federal Securities Act of 1933 and securities exempt from such registration under some provision other than § 3(a) (11) thereof (the so-called "intrastate exemption"). McKinney's N.Y. Gen.Bus.Law, § 359ff.1. Hochman, "Intra-State Financing Act of 1968 and Other New York Blue Sky Laws", 161 N.Y.L.J. No. 13, 1 (Jan 20, 1969), id. No. 14, 1 (Jan. 21, 1969).

Otherwise, New York, except for the registration of real estate and theatrical ventures, requires informational filings, supra, instead of registration of securities.

4. Connecticut (except for registration of mining and oil securities).

5. E. g., Massachusetts.

addition impose substantive criteria, often quite strict, for the securities [6]—tantamount

to approval of the securities—somewhat like the Federal Public Utility Holding Company Act of 1935 and Investment Company Act of 1940. Several states have two registration procedures: [7] (a) a relatively simple streamlined method for seasoned securities, known as registration "by notification" or "by description", resembling the registration under Regulation A of small-issues pursuant to Section 3(b) of the Federal Securities Act of 1933; and (b) full-dress registration, known as registration "by qualification" or "by application", analogous to full registration (except for possible additional substantive criteria) under the Federal Securities Act of 1933. Some jurisdictions have a special procedure for securities registered under the Federal Securities Act of 1933. [8]

Shortcomings of State Securities Regulation

State securities regulation suffered from several shortcomings.

In the first place, state regulation was often inadequate. As indicated, Delaware has no "blue sky" law; others with legislation impose less than sufficient regulation. Where the transactions involved more than one state, complicated conflict-of-laws prob-

---

6. E. g., California (fair, just, and equitable standard with burden on commissioner of showing that offering is unfair, unjust, and inequitable). Western Air Lines, Inc. v. Sobieski, 191 Cal.App.2d 399, 12 Cal.Rptr. 719 (1961), the corporation was a Delaware corporation with its principal place of business in California, and was successor to a California corporation. It proposed to amend its articles of incorporation to abolish cumulative voting. The court upheld, over objection of undue interference with the internal affairs of a foreign corporation, the refusal of the California commissioner of corporations to grant a permit to solicit proxies or hold a meeting for that purpose under provisions of the California corporation code that a corporation may not sell any security without a permit from the commissioner, "sell" being defined to include "any change in the rights, preferences, privileges or restrictions on outstanding securities". See also People ex rel. Sobieski v. Western Air Lines, Inc., 258 Cal.App.2d 213, 66 Cal.Rptr. 316 (1968) (holding that pseudo-foreign corporation would not be permitted to circumvent California public policy concerning cumulative voting for domestic and pseudo-foreign corporations by amending its articles of incorporation under laws of jurisdiction of incorporation so as to eliminate cumulative voting); Western Air Lines, Inc. v. Schutzbank, 258 Cal.App.2d 218, 66 Cal.Rptr. 293 (1968) (upholding fairness of administrative proceeding). The new California securities statute exempts from registration recapitalizations, mergers, consolidations, and sales of corporate assets unless 25 percent of the outstanding shares of any class involved are held by persons who have California addresses on the record of shareholders. H. Marsh & R. Volk, Practice under the California Corporate Securities Law of 1968 (1969); N. Schlei, State Regulation of Corporate Financial Practices: The California Experience (1962); Wheat, "Issuance of Securities Under the California Corporate Securities Law", in Advising California Business Enterprises 497–562 (1958); Rosenfeld, "Tax Aspects of Securing Permits and Issuing Stock in California", in Advising California Business Enterprises 563–580 (1958); Volk, "The California Corporate Securities Law of 1968—A Significant Change from Prior Law", 24 Bus.Law. 77 (1968); Sterling, "California Corporate Securities Law of 1968: Underwritings and Corporate Reorganizations", 23 Bus.Law. 645 (1968); Olson, "The California Corporate Securities Law of 1968", 9 Santa Clara Law. 75 (1968); Volk, "Fifty Years of Securities Regulation in California", 42 L.A.B.Bull. 569 (1967); Heath, "Administration of the California Corporate Securities Law", 13 U.C.L.A.L.Rev. 513 (1966); Sobieski, "Securities Regulation in California: Recent Developments", 11 U.C.L.A.L.Rev. 1 (1963); Small, "Changes in Rights, Preferences, Privileges and Restrictions on Outstanding Securities under the California Corporate Securities Law", 14 Hastings L.J. 94 (1962); Weinstein, "Problems in the Field of State Securities Regulation", 10 Catholic U.L.Rev. 1 (1961); Ellis & McCloskey, "The Future of Corporate Securities Regu-

lation in California—Effect of Proposed Uniform Act", 12 Hastings L.J. 256 (1961); Fields & Maron, "Escrow of Corporate Securities in California: Guideposts and Pitfalls", 34 L.A.B.Bull. 195 (1959); Pearce, "California Corporate Securities Law vs. Proposed Uniform Securities Law", 9 Hastings L.J. 1 (1957); Comment, "Noncomplying Securities in California: Judicial Protection of Interests Under Corporations Code, Sec. 26100", 18 Stan.L.Rev. 1184 (1966); Comment, "Jurisdiction of the California Corporations Commissioner Over Delaware Short Form Mergers", 52 Calif.L.Rev. 1016 (1964); Comment, "Alteration of Rights in California Public Securities", 53 Calif.L.Rev. 1081 (1965); Note, "Franchise Regulation under the California Corporate Securities Law", 5 San Diego L.Rev. 140 (1968); Note, "The Availability to the Syndicator of the Private Offering Exemption to the California Corporate Securities Law", 17 Hastings L.J. 792 (1966).

7. E. g., Ohio. Registration of securities "by notification" sometimes closely resemble registration of securities by "notice of intention" in some states tying in registration of securities with broker-dealer-registration. E. g., Massachusetts.

8. E. g., Tennessee.

lems arose, and enforcement against persons outside the jurisdiction was difficult. Where interstate or foreign commerce or the mails were involved, the Federal Securities Act of 1933 resulted in substantial federal regulation, in addition to such state regulation as existed.

In the second place, the problems of qualifying an issue for simultaneous sale in various states with different regulatory philosophies, statutory provisions, exemptions, and administrative procedures and forms were very complex.[9] In the interests of greater uniformity in such matters, various approaches were attempted. A Uniform Sale of Securities Act was approved in 1930 by the National Conference of Commissioners on Uniform State Laws, but was adopted in only a few states,[10] rendered obsolete by the Federal Securities Act of 1933, and withdrawn in 1943. Since the federal act, simultaneous compliance with its requirements and those of the applicable state "blue sky" laws has been necessary. The National Association of Securities Administrators, enlarged to include Canadian administrative officials and accordingly renamed the North American Securities Administrators ("N.A. S.A.") has tried to achieve some uniformity.[11]

9. Where the issuer is issuing securities subject to preemptive rights, the rights offering has to be made in whatever jurisdictions its shareholders reside, and the issue has to be "blue-skyed" (the securities qualified) for such jurisdictions. See Jacobson, "Exemptions in Securities Act Registration", 33 Fla.B.J. 69 (Feb.1959).

10. 9 U.L.A. 625 (1942); approved 1930; adopted in Hawaii and Louisiana, and with modifications in Alabama, Florida, Michigan, Oregon, and South Carolina; withdrawn 1943.

11. By drafting in 1941 a uniform application form designed for most corporate issues to be registered under the Federal Securities Act of 1933, and in 1942, in cooperation with the S.E.C., the several securities exchanges, and N.A.S.D., a rule and form for the filing of annual financial reports. Calvin, "New Uniform Blue Sky Forms", 19 Bus.Law. 538 (1964); Calvin, "Report on the Uniform Application to Register Securities", 18 Bus.Law. 297 (1962).

The most recent attempt at uniformity is the new Uniform Securities Act.[12]

STATE "BLUE SKY" LAWS—UNIFORM SECURITIES ACT

307. The Uniform Securities Act, adopted in a growing number of states, was drafted in such a way as to be acceptable, in part at least, to states with varying regulatory philosophies.

The new Uniform Securities Act[1] was approved by the National Conference of Com-

12. See section 307 infra.

1. 9C U.L.A. 86 (1957); approved 1956; adopted in Hawaii, Kansas; amended 1958; adopted (with some local variations in Alabama, Alaska, Arkansas, Colorado, Hawaii, Indiana, Kansas, Kentucky, Maryland, Michigan, Missouri, Montana, Nevada, New Jersey, Oklahoma, South Carolina, Utah, Virginia, Washington, Wyoming, and Puerto Rico). L. Loss & E. Cowett, Blue Sky Law 245–420 (1958) (with official comments and draftsmen's commentary); 1 CCH Blue Sky L.Rep. ¶¶ 4901–4953; Loss, "The Uniform Securities Act and the Bar", 13 Bus.Law 609 (1958); Sobieski, "The Uniform Securities Act", 12 Stan.L.Rev. 103 (1959); Bolliger, "The New Wisconsin Uniform Securities Law", 25 Bus.Law. 223 (1969); Logan, "Missouri's New Uniform Securities Act and Securities Regulations", 37 U.Mo.Kan.City L.Rev. 1 (1969); Newton, "Look at the Montana Securities Act and Its Relation to the Federal Securities Act", 26 Mont.L.Rev. 31 (1964); Bennett, "Securities Regulation in Utah: A Recap of History and the New Uniform Act", 8 Utah L.Rev. 216 (1963); Miller, "A Prospectus on the Maryland Securities Act", 23 Md.L.Rev. 289 (1963); Pasmas, "Securities Issuance and Regulation: The New Indiana Securities Law", 38 Ind.L.J. 38 (1962); Reckson, "Comparisons of the Florida and Uniform Securities Act", 16 U.Miami L.Rev. 351 (1962); Hill, "Some Comments on the Uniform Securities Act", 55 Nw.U.L.Rev. 661 (1961); Ellis & McCloskey, "The Future of Corporate Securities Regulation in California—Effect of Proposed Uniform Act", 12 Hastings L.J. 256 (1961); Edwards, "California Measures the Uniform Securities Act Against Its Corporate Securities Law", 15 Bus.Law. 814 (1960); Mulford, "The Proposed New Jersey Blue Sky Law", 15 Bus.Law. 810 (1960); Stewart, "Securities Act of 1959", 13 Ark.L.Rev. 323 (1959); Riely, "Virginia Securities Act: A Blue Sky Primer", 45 Va.L.Rev. 303 (1959); Lohf, "The Colorado Securities Law", 35 Dicta 271 (1958); Bennett, "Should Utah Adopt the New Uniform Securities Act?", 5 Utah L.Rev. 471 (1957); Comment, "Selling the Blue Sky Law in Mississippi—A Comparison of Mississippi Securities Act with the Uniform Securities Act", 35 Miss.L.Rev. 421 (1964); Note, "Securities Regulation in New Jersey", 17 Rutgers L.Rev. 602 (1963); Legis., "Montana Securities Law —Its Rules and Regulations", 25 Mont.L.Rev. 205

missioners on Uniform State Laws, endorsed by the American Bar Association, and approved qualifiedly by the National Association of Securities Administrators (N.A.S.A.) in 1956, and amended in 1958.[2]

Not intended for adoption as a whole by every state, it was drafted in such a way as to be acceptable, in part at least, to states with varying regulatory philosophies.

The New Uniform Securities Act is composed of four parts: Part I consists of *antifraud provisions*, prohibiting fraudulent practices in sales or purchases of securities or investment advisory services;[3] Part II

contains *broker-dealer registration provisions*; Part III provides for the *registration of securities*: "by notification"; "by qualification"; and "by coordination" (for use when the securities involved are being registered under the Federal Securities Act of 1933); Part IV deals with definitions, exemptions, procedures, and conflict-of-laws matters, accompanied by notations as to which portions of Part IV should be enacted along with the enactment of Parts I, II, and/or III, respectively.

STATE LAWS—MISCELLANEOUS SECURITIES REGULATION

308. **Various state statutes subject the securities of issuers regulated by various state administrative agencies to the regulation of such agencies. Such state regulation sometimes exempts the securities from federal or other forms of state regulation.**

The states also regulate the securities of intrastate carriers and public utilities,[1] insurance companies,[2] state banks,[3] etc., through regulatory commissions, superintendents or commissioners of insurance, superintendents or commissioners of banks, etc. Such state regulation sometimes exempts the securities from federal or other forms of state regulation.

[§ 307]
(1964); Legis., "Blue Sky Laws: Uniform Securities Act", 3 B.C.Ind. & Com.L.Rev. 218 (1962). The Uniform Securities Act should not be confused with the old Uniform Sale of Securities Act (1930) (withdrawn 1943)—see text accompanying section 306, n. 10 supra.

2. Subsequently, however, the N.A.S.A. qualified its resolution with respect to the Act. N.A.S.A. has since changed its name to North American Securities Administrators, Inc.

3. Uniform Securities Act § 101, copied from S.E.C. Rule 10b–5 without federal constitutional limitations, provides:

"It is unlawful for any person, in connection with the offer, sale, or purchase of any security, directly or indirectly.

(1) to employ any device, scheme, or artifice to defraud,

(2) to make any untrue statement of a material fact or to omit to state a material fact necessary in order to make the statements made, in the light of the circumstances under which they are made, not misleading, or

(3) to engage in any act, practice, or course of business which operates or would operate as a fraud or deceit upon any person".

Section 401 provides that " 'fraud,' 'deceit,' and 'defraud' are not limited to common-law deceit."

[§ 308]
1. See, e. g., McKinney's N.Y.Pub.Serv.Law, §§ 55, 62, 69, 82, 89–f.

2. See, e. g., McKinney's N.Y.Ins.Law, §§ 48(7), 51, 53.

3. See, e. g., McKinney's N.Y.Bank.Law, §§ 14, 96.

C. ANTITRUST AND TRADE REGULATION

FEDERAL ANTITRUST AND TRADE REGULATION—IN GENERAL

309. Federal antitrust and trade regulation legislation has been enacted to assure a competitive economy and fair conduct and fair practices on the part of business enterprises. The most significant federal antitrust and trade regulation statutes are the (a) Sherman Antitrust Act of 1890, (b) Federal Trade Commission Act of 1914, (c) Clayton Act of 1914, and (d) Robinson-Patman Act of 1935.

At both federal and state levels, various statutes have been enacted to assure a competitive economy and fair conduct and practices on the part of business enterprises.[1]

The most significant federal antitrust and trade regulation statutes are the Sherman Antitrust Act of 1890,[2] Federal Trade Commission Act of 1914,[3] Clayton Act of 1914,[4] and Robinson-Patman Act of 1935.[5]

Special exemptions are provided by miscellaneous legislation.[6] The same action or proceeding often involves allegations or counts of violation of two or more antitrust or trade regulation statutes.

Corporations, as the dominating business enterprises, and their directors, officers, and other personnel,[7] run the gamut of the antitrust and trade regulation statutes. To minimize risks of violation, many corporations have instituted compliance programs.[8] Even

---

1. See generally CCH Trade Regulation Reports (5 vols.); J. Van Cise, Understanding the Antitrust Laws (PLI rev. 1966); E. Kintner, An Antitrust Primer: A Guide to Antitrust and Trade Regulation Laws for Businessmen (1964); M. Hoffman, Antitrust Law and Techniques (1963) (3 vols.); G. Stocking, Workable Competition and Antitrust Policy (1961); A. Neale, The Antitrust Laws of the United States of America (1960); W. Fugate, Foreign Commerce and the Antitrust Laws (1958); H. Kronstein & J. Miller, Modern American Antitrust Law (1958); K. Brewster, Antitrust and American Business Abroad (1958); Sproul, "United States Antitrust Laws and Foreign Joint Ventures", 54 A.B.A.J. 889 (1968); Handler, "The Polarities of Antitrust", 60 Nw.U.L.Rev. 751 (1966); Bloom, "A Guide to Antitrust", 20 Bus.Law. 61 (1964); Friedmann, "Antitrust in Economically Underdeveloped Countries", 60Col trust Law and Joint International Business Ventures in Economically Underdeveloped Countries", 60 Colum.L.Rev. 780 (1960). See also Handler, "Antitrust: 1969", 24 Record of N.Y.C.B.A. 556 (1969); Handler, "Through The Antitrust Looking Glass", 23 Record of N.Y.C.B.A. 601 (1968); Handler, "The Twentieth Annual Antitrust Review—1967", 53 Va. L.Rev. 1667 (1967); Handler, "Some Misadventures in Antitrust Policymaking—Nineteenth Annual Review", 76 Yale L.J. 92 (1966); Handler, "Recent Antitrust Developments—1965", 40 N.Y.U.L.Rev. 823 (1965); Handler, "Recent Antitrust Developments—1964", 63 Mich.L.Rev. 59 (1964); Handler, "Recent Antitrust Developments", 112 U.Pa.L.Rev. 159 (1963); Handler, "Recent Antitrust Developments", 71 Yale L.J. 75 (1961). Shareholders might sue to enjoin antitrust violations, to recover for their corporation treble damages resulting from antitrust violations against their corporation by third parties, or to recover for the corporation from its management any loss suffered by the corporation because of its antitrust violations. See Graham v. Allis-Chalmers Mfg. Co., 41 Del.Ch. 78, 188 A.2d 125 (Sup.Ct.1963); Blake, "The Shareholders' Role in Antitrust Enforcement", 110 U.Pa.L.Rev. 143 (1961); Comment, 59 Mich.L.

Rev. 904 (1961). "The word 'trust' strictly used refers to a business form under which specified property is controlled by trustees in the interests of cestuis or beneficiaries. This form was frequently used in the United States in the late 19th century in order to avoid existing restrictions on intercorporate holdings, the corpus or property consisting of shares of the various corporations to be operated under unified management. Over time, the word came to have a wider connotation, being used to describe any large business combination, regardless of form." W. Baldwin, Antitrust and the Changing Corporation 4, n. 4 (1961). See also J. von Kalinowski, Antitrust Laws and Trade Regulation (1969) (2 vols.).

2. 15 U.S.C.A. §§ 1–7. See section 310 infra.

3. 15 U.S.C.A. §§ 41–58. See section 311 infra.

4. 15 U.S.C.A. §§ 12–27. See section 312 infra.

5. 15 U.S.C.A. §§ 15–21a. See section 313 infra.

6. Symposium: "Exemptions from Federal Antitrust Laws", 20 Fed.B.J. 3 (1960). See section 314 infra.

7. United States v. Wise, 370 U.S. 405, 82 S.Ct. 1354, 8 L.Ed.2d 590 (1962); Rooks, "Personal Liabilities of Officers and Directors for Antitrust Violations and Securities Transactions", 18 Bus.Law. 579 (1963); Kramer, "Liability of Corporate Officers and Directors under the Antitrust Laws", 17 Bus. Law. 892 (1962); Whiting, "Antitrust and the Corporate Executive", 47 Va.L.Rev. 929 (1961), 48 Va. L.Rev. 1 (1962). For discussion of criminal liabilities of corporations and their managements, see Watkins, "Electrical Equipment Antitrust Cases— Their Implications for Government and for Business", 29 U.Chi.L.Rev. 97 (1961).

8. Galgay, "Corporate Plans and Policies for Voluntary Antitrust Compliance", 19 Bus.Law. 637 (1964);

shareholders sometimes have a role in antitrust and trade regulation enforcement.[9]

Antitrust and trade regulation litigation and proceedings can be extremely time-consuming, distracting, and expensive for corporations and their directors, officers, and other personnel.[10] As a result, claims and cases, sometimes regardless of the merits, are often compromised or settled, in the case of criminal proceedings, by nolo contendere pleas.[11]

For antitrust violations, as distinguished from trade regulation violations,[12] actions by private persons for treble damages lie.[13] For antitrust or trade regulation violations, injunctive relief [14] may be available.[15]

FEDERAL ANTITRUST AND TRADE REGULATION—SHERMAN ANTITRUST ACT, 1890

310. The Sherman Antitrust Act, 1890, in broad language, prohibits unreasonable restraints upon and monopolization of trade in interstate or foreign commerce. It is enforced by the courts in actions brought by the Justice Department or by private persons. Some re-

Withrow, "Antitrust Compliance Programs", 19 Record of N.Y.C.B.A. 151 (1964); Anderson, "Effective Antitrust Compliance Programs and Procedures (An Outline)", 18 Bus.Law. 739 (1963); Withrow, "Making Compliance Programs Work", 17 Bus.Law. 877 (1962).

9. See note 1 supra.

10. Symposium: "The Trial of an Antitrust Action", 18 ABA Antitrust Section 13 (1961). See Comment, "The Antitrust Expediting Act—A Critical Reappraisal", 63 Mich.L.Rev. 1240 (1965).

11. Note, "Nolo Pleas in Antitrust Cases", 79 Harv. L.Rev. 1475 (1966).

12. Country Maid, Inc. v. Haseotes, 299 F.Supp. 633 (E.D.Pa.1968).

13. See section 312, n. 7 infra. See also Lasky, "Overview and Overkill: Private Enforcement of Antitrust Laws", 24 Bus.Law. 1221 (1969).

14. MacIntyre, "Injunctive Relief—A Private Antitrust Remedy Available to the Small Firm", 21 Bus.Law. 267 (1965).

15. Comment, "Consent Decrees and the Private Action: An Antitrust Dilemma", 53 Calif.L.Rev. 627 (1965).

straints, like price-fixing, are illegal per se, but the legality of others depends on the "rule of reason".

The Sherman Antitrust Act, 1890,[1] in broad language prohibits unreasonable restraints upon and monopolization of trade in interstate or foreign commerce. It is enforced by the courts in actions brought by the Department of Justice (Antitrust Division) or by private persons.[2]

The Sherman Act's most important provisions are found in sections 1 and 2.

Section 1 of the Sherman Act declares illegal "Every contract, combination in the form of trust or otherwise, or conspiracy, in restraint of trade or commerce among the several states, or with foreign nations". Although "contract", "combination", or "conspiracy" requires at least two persons acting

1. 15 U.S.C.A. §§ 1–7; J. Van Cise, Understanding the Antitrust Laws 19–30 (PLI rev. 1966); 1 CCH Trade Reg.Rep. ¶¶ 620–705; Keck, "The Schwinn Case", 23 Bus.Law. 669 (1968); Coons, "Non-Commercial Purpose as a Sherman Act Defense", 56 Nw.U.L.Rev. 705 (1962); Krause, "The Multi-Corporate International Business Under Section 1 of the Sherman Act—Intra-Enterprise Conspiracy Revisited", 17 Bus.Law. 912 (1962); Turner, "The Definition of Agreement under the Sherman Act: Conscious Parallelism and Refusals to Deal", 75 Harv. L.Rev. 655 (1962).

2. Violations may be the subject of criminal or civil action by the federal government. Injunctive relief may extend to divestiture of shares, or of divisions of an integrated corporation, or to dissolution. United States v. Paramount Pictures, Inc., 334 U.S. 131, 68 S.Ct. 915, 92 L.Ed. 1260 (1948); Northern Securities Co. v. United States, 193 U.S. 197, 24 S. Ct. 436, 48 L.Ed. 679 (1904); United States v. Pullman Co., 50 F.Supp. 123 (E.D.Pa.1943), 53 F.Supp. 908 (E.D.Pa.1944), 64 F.Supp. 108 (E.D.Pa.1946), aff'd per curiam 330 U.S. 806, 67 S.Ct. 1078, 91 L. Ed. 1263 (1947) (4–4). Private persons may sue for treble damages, petition for injunctive relief, and defend contract and patent and copyright infringement actions on the ground of antitrust violation. In such private actions, injured persons need not show independent injury to the public. Klor's, Inc. v. Broadway-Hale Stores, Inc., 359 U.S. 207, 79 S. Ct. 705, 3 L.Ed.2d 741 (1959). Incipient Sherman Act violations may be the subject of Federal Trade Commission proceedings. Criminal violations can entail imprisonment and fines for corporate officials as well as fines levied against the corporation. E. g., General Electric case. See Kennedy, "This Case Is a Reflection on All of Us", 50 Life, No. 8, 30 (Feb. 24, 1961).

in concert, corporations and their officials have been found to violate the Act because of concert of action between two or more officials [3] or affiliated corporations.[4]

Some restraints, like price fixing, are illegal *per se*; the legality of others depends on the "rule of reason".[5]

Section 2 of the Sherman Act declares that:

"Every person who shall monopolize, or attempt to monopolize, or combine or conspire with any other person or persons, to monopolize any part of the trade or commerce among the several states, or with foreign nations, shall be deemed guilty of a misdemeanor."

FEDERAL ANTITRUST AND TRADE REGULATION—FEDERAL TRADE COMMISSION ACT, 1914

311. The Federal Trade Commission Act, 1914, substantially amended in 1938, declares

unlawful **"unfair methods of competition in commerce and unfair or deceptive acts or practices in commerce"**, empowering the Federal Trade Commission to initiate proceedings, make findings of fact, decide questions of law, and issue orders to cease and desist.

The Federal Trade Commission Act, 1914,[1] substantially amended in 1938, declares unlawful "Unfair methods of competition in commerce, and, since the Wheeler-Lea Act of 1938, unfair or deceptive acts or practices in commerce," [2] empowering the Federal Trade Commission (F.T.C.) to initiate proceedings, make findings of fact, decide questions of law and issue orders to cease and desist. The Act also grants the Federal Trade Commission investigatory powers and authority to proceed against false advertising.[3]

[§ 311]

1. 15 U.S.C.A. §§ 41–58; J. Van Cise, Understanding the Antitrust Laws 30–35 (PLI rev. 1966); 1 CCH Trade Reg.Rep. ¶¶ 800–835. "Fifty Years of the Federal Trade Commission and Clayton Acts", 24 A.B.A.Antitrust Sect. 14 (1964); Symposium: "The Fiftieth Anniversary of the Federal Trade Commission", 64 Colum.L.Rev. 385 (1964); Dixon, "Practice and Procedure Before the Federal Trade Commission", 9 N.Y.L.F. 31 (1963); Baker & Boum, "Section 5 of the Federal Trade Commission Act: A Continuing Process of Redefinition", 7 Vill. L.Rev. 517 (1962); Dixon, "The Federal Trade Commission: Its Fact-Finding Responsibilities and Powers", 46 Marq.L.Rev. 17 (1962); Harkrader, "Fictitious Pricing and the FTC: A New Look at an Old Dodge", 37 St.Johns L.Rev. 1 (1962); Mueller, "Access to Corporate Papers Under the FTC Act", 11 Kan.L.Rev. 77 (1962); Rockefeller & Wald, "Antitrust Enforcement by the Federal Trade Commission and the Department of Justice: A Primer for Small Business", 66 Dick.L.Rev. 251 (1962); Oppenheim, "Guides to Harmonizing Section 5 of the Federal Trade Commission Act with the Sherman and Clayton Acts", 59 Mich.L.Rev. 821 (1961); Comment, "Per Se Rules and Section 5 of the Federal Trade Commission Act", 54 Calif.L.Rev. 2049 (1966); Note, "Small Business Before the Federal Trade Commission", 75 Yale L.J. 487 (1966); Note, "The Federal Trade Commission and Reform of the Administrative Process", 62 Colum.L.Rev. 671 (1962).

2. Federal Trade Commission Act § 5, 15 U.S.C.A. § 45. The power of the Federal Trade Commission to proceed against incipient Sherman Act violations as "unfair" has been upheld. Federal Trade Commission v. Motion Picture Adv. Service Co., 344 U.S. 392, 73 S.Ct. 361, 97 L.Ed. 426 (1953).

3. Prior to the Wheeler-Lea Act of 1938, 15 U.S.C.A. §§ 41–58, Federal Trade Commission control over advertising was limited to the food, drug, and cosmetic fields. Compare similar control in Secretary

3. Patterson v. United States, 222 F. 599 (6th Cir. 1915), cert. denied 238 U.S. 635, 35 S.Ct. 939, 59 L. Ed. 1499 (1915).

4. Joseph E. Seagram & Sons v. Hawaiian Oke & Liquors, Ltd., 416 F.2d 71 (9th Cir.1969), rev'g 272 F.Supp. 915 (D.Hawaii 1967). Kiefer-Stewart Co. v. Joseph E. Seagram & Sons, 340 U.S. 211, 71 S.Ct. 259, 95 L.Ed. 219 (1951), reh. denied 340 U.S. 939, 71 S.Ct. 487, 95 L.Ed. 678 (1951); Schine Chain Theatres, Inc. v. United States, 334 U.S. 110, 68 S.Ct. 947, 92 L.Ed. 1245 (1948).

5. Standard Oil Co. of New Jersey v. United States, 221 U.S. 1, 31 S.Ct. 502, 55 L.Ed. 619 (1911). See United States v. General Motors, 384 U.S. 127, 86 S.Ct. 1321, 16 L.Ed.2d 415 (1966); Bork, "The Rule of Reason and the Per Se Concept: Price Fixing and Market Division", 74 Yale L.J. 775 (1965), 75 id. 377 (1966); Loevinger, "The Rule of Reason in Antitrust Law", 50 Va.L.Rev. 23 (1964); Van Cise, "The Future of Per Se in Antitrust Law", 50 Va.L. Rev. 1165 (1964); Von Kalinowski, "The Per Se Doctrine—An Emerging Philosophy of Antitrust Law," 11 U.C.L.A.L.Rev. 569 (1964); Loevinger, "Rule of Reason in Antitrust Law", 7 Prac.Law. 17 (Nov. 1961); Comment, "Is Per Se the Rule for Boycotts?", 35 U.Colo.L.Rev. 577 (1963); Note, "Restricted Channels of Distribution under the Sherman Act", 75 Harv.L.Rev. 795 (1962); Rahl, "Per Se Rules and Boycotts under the Sherman Act: Some Reflections on the Klor's Case", 45 Va. L.Rev. 1165 (1959). See also United States v. Citizen Publishing Co., 394 U.S. 131, 89 S.Ct. 927, 22 L.Ed.2d 148 (1969).

FEDERAL ANTITRUST AND TRADE REGULATION—CLAYTON ACT, 1914

312. The Clayton Act, 1914, prohibits certain kinds of price and other discrimination; tying, exclusive dealing, and total requirements agreements; acquisitions by a corporation of the shares or assets of another corporation tending substantially to lessen competition in any line of commerce; and interlocking directorates. Various provisions are enforceable by the Justice Department, the Federal Trade Commission, and private parties.

The Clayton Act, 1914,[1] prohibits certain kinds of price and other discrimination (now covered by the Robinson-Patman Act), certain tying, exclusive dealing, and total requirements agreements involving commodities,[2] and, as amended by the Anti-Merger Act of 1950,[3] the acquisition by a corporation, in interstate or foreign commerce, of:

"the whole or any part of the stock or . . . assets of another corporation engaged also in commerce, where in any line

of commerce in any section of the country, the effect of such acquisition may be substantially to lessen competition, or to tend to create a monopoly." [4]

of Health, Education, and Welfare under federal food, drug, and cosmetic statutes. 21 U.S.C. §§ 301–392; CCH Food, Drug, and Cosmetic Law Report; "Developments in the Law: Deceptive Advertising", 80 Harv.L.Rev. 1005 (1967).

1. 15 U.S.C.A. §§ 12–27; J. Van Cise, Understanding the Antitrust Laws 35–43 (PLI rev. 1966); 1 CCH Trade Reg.Rep. ¶¶ 725–770; B. Bock, Mergers and Markets: A Guide to Economic Analysis of Case Law (3d ed. 1964); D. Martin, Mergers and the Clayton Act (1959); Buxbaum, "Boycotts and Restrictive Marketing Arrangements", 64 Mich.L.Rev. 671 (1966); Hausman, "Reciprocal Dealing and the Antitrust Laws", 77 Harv.L.Rev. 873 (1964); Stewart, "Antitrust Considerations Involved in Product Distribution", 19 Bus.Law. 967 (1964); Jordan, "Exclusive and Restricted Sales Areas Under the Antitrust Laws", 9 U.C.L.A.L.Rev. 111 (1962); Kramer, "How to Comply with the Clayton Act: The Problems of Small Business", 1959 Antitrust L.Sym. 125; Comment, "Tying Arrangements under the Antitrust Laws: The 'Integrity of the Product' Defense", 62 Mich.L.Rev. 1413 (1964).

2. Clayton Act §§ 2, 3, 15 U.S.C.A. §§ 13, 13a. Compare Standard Oil Co. (Calif.) v. United States, 337 U.S. 293, 69 S.Ct. 1051, 93 L.Ed. 1371 (1949), with Federal Trade Commission v. Motion Picture Adv. Service Co., 344 U.S. 392, 73 S.Ct. 361, 97 L.Ed. 426 (1953).

3. 15 U.S.C.A. § 18.

4. United States v. Von's Grocery Co., 384 U.S. 270, 86 S.Ct. 1478, 16 L.Ed.2d 555 (1966); Brown Shoe Co. v. United States, 370 U.S. 294, 82 S.Ct. 1502, 8 L.Ed.2d 510 (1962); B. Fox & E. Fox, Corporate Acquisitions and Mergers (1968); Symposium on Section 7 of the Clayton Act, 40 N.Y.U.L.Rev. 613 (1965); Davidow, "Conglomerate Concentration and Section Seven: The Limitations of the Anti-Merger Act", 68 Colum.L.Rev. 1231 (1968); Finkelstein & Friedberg, "The Application of an Entropy Theory of Concentration to the Clayton Act", 76 Yale L.J. 677 (1967); Reilly, "Conglomerate Mergers—An Argument for Action", 61 Nw.U.L.Rev. 522 (1966); Blackford, "Vertical Acquisition and Section 7 of the Clayton Act", 17 W.Res.L.Rev. 102 (1965); Turner, "Conglomerate Mergers and Section 7 of the Clayton Act", 73 Harv.L.Rev. 1313 (1965); Hrusoff, "Conglomerate Mergers, Joint Ventures, Market Extensions and Section 7 of the Clayton Act", 69 Dick.L.Rev. 113 (1965); Berghoff, "Analyzing a Proposed Acquisition under the Antitrust Laws", 19 Bus.Law. 373 (1964); Duke, "Scope of Relief under Section 7 of the Clayton Act", 63 Colum.L.Rev. 1192 (1963); von Kalinowski, "Section 7 and Competitive Effects", 48 Va.L.Rev. 827 (1962); Lewyn & Mann, "Ten Years Under the New Section 7 of the Clayton Act: A Lawyer's Practical Approach to the Case Law", 36 N.Y.U.L.Rev. 1067 (1961); Rowe, "Mergers and the Law: New Directions for the Sixties", 47 A.B.A.J. 1074 (1961); Steele, "Decade of the Celler-Kefauver Anti-Merger Act", 14 Vand. L.Rev. 1049 (1961); Mann & Lewyn, "The Relevant Market under Section 7 of the Clayton Act: Two New Cases—Two Different Views", 47 Va.L. Rev. 1014 (1961); Comment, "Section 5(b) of the Clayton Act: The Tolling Effect of Government Antitrust Actions on Unnamed Parties", 34 U.Chi. L.Rev. 906 (1967); Comment, "Divestiture of Illegally Held Assets: Observations on its Scope, Objective, and Limitations", 64 Mich.L.Rev. 1574 (1966); Comment, "Conglomerate Mergers under Section 7 of the Clayton Act", 72 Yale L.J. 1265 (1963); Comment, "Corporate Joint Ventures and Section 7 of the Clayton Act", 9 Vill.L.Rev. 94 (1963); Comment, "Federal Antitrust Law—Mergers—An Updating of the 'Failing Company' Doctrine in the Amended Section 7 Setting", 61 Mich.L. Rev. 566 (1963); Note, "Antitrust-Post-Acquisition Evidence and Conglomerate Mergers", 46 N.C.L.Rev. 366 (1968); Note, "Prosecutions for Attempts to Monopolize: The Relevance of the Relevant Market", 42 N.Y.U.L.Rev. 110 (1967); Note, "Section 5 of the Clayton Act and the Nolo Contendere Plea", 75 Yale L.J. 845 (1966); Note, "Preliminary Injunctions and the Enforcement of Section 7 of the Clayton Act", 40 N.Y.U.L.Rev. 771 (1965). The Department of Justice has announced guidelines for enforcing the Clayton Act's antimerger provisions with respect to horizontal, vertical, and conglomerate mergers. For 13-year litigation resulting in rulings that du Pont's acquisition of 63,000,000 shares

Additional provisions of the Clayton Act condemn interlocking directorates,[5] and grant certain exemptions from the antitrust laws to labor, agricultural, and horticultural organizations.

The various provisions of the Clayton Act are enforced by the Department of Justice, the Federal Trade Commission,[6] or private parties. The Act authorizes actions by private parties injured by antitrust violations for treble damages.[7]

—about 23 percent and worth some $3 billion—of General Motors common shares in 1917–1919 violated the then section 7 of the Clayton Act and requiring total divestment of such interest within 10 years, see United States v. E. I. du Pont de Nemours & Co., 126 F.Supp. 235 (N.D.Ill.1954), rev'd 353 U.S. 586, 77 S.Ct. 872, 1 L.Ed.2d 1057 (1957) (4–3), 177 F.Supp. 1 (N.D.Ill.1959) (on remand), rev'd, 366 U.S. 316, 81 S.Ct. 1243, 6 L.Ed.2d 318 (1961) (4–3). On remand, divestment within three years by du Pont, Christiana Securities Co.—du Pont family-controlled holding company with 29 percent interest in du Pont—and du Pont family members was ordered—in case of du Pont by distribution to its common shareholders. See Symposium: "The Du-Pont-General Motors Decision: The Merger Problem in a New Perspective", 46 Geo.L.J. 561 (1958); Pub.Law 87–403, 76 Stat. 4 (1962), Int.Rev.Code of 1954, 26 U.S.C.A. § 1111 (tax-relief for recipient shareholders). See also Proceedings, ABA National Institute, "Conglomerates and Other Modern Merger Movements", 25 Bus.Law. 555 (1970).

5. Clayton Act § 8, 15 U.S.C.A. § 19; United States v. W. T. Grant Co., 345 U.S. 629, 73 S.Ct. 894, 97 L.Ed. 1303 (1953); United States v. Sears, Roebuck & Co., 111 F.Supp. 614 (S.D.N.Y.1953). See Travers, "Interlocks in Corporate Management and the Antitrust Laws", 46 Texas L.Rev. 819 (1968); Lombard, "The Corporate Management Interlocks Bill", 21 Bus.Law. 879 (1966).

6. Federal Trade Commission v. Dean Foods Co., 384 U.S. 597, 86 S.Ct. 1738, 16 L.Ed.2d 802 (1966) (recognizing power of Federal Trade Commission to issue preliminary injunction pending completion of administrative proceedings); Kauper, "Cease and Desist: The History, Effect, and Scope of Clayton Act Orders of the Federal Trade Commission", 66 Mich.L.Rev. 1095 (1968); Symposium: "The Fiftieth Anniversary of the Federal Trade Commission", 64 Colum.L.Rev. 385 (1964); Rockefeller & Wald, "Antitrust Enforcement by the Federal Trade Commission and the Department of Justice: A Primer for Small Business", 66 Dick.L.Rev. 251 (1962); Oppenheim, "Guides to Harmonizing Section 5 of the Federal Trade Commission Act with the Sherman and Clayton Acts", 59 Mich.L.Rev. 821 (1961); Comment, "The FTC's Power to Seek Preliminary Injunctions in Anti-Merger Cases", 66 Mich.L.Rev. 142 (1967).

7. Clayton Act § 4, 15 U.S.C.A. § 15, authorizes any person injured by reason of the violation of any antitrust law to recover threefold the damages sustained and the cost of the action, including a reasonable attorney's fees. Hanover Shoe, Inc. v. United Shoe Machinery Corp., 392 U.S. 481, 88 S.Ct. 2224, 20 L.Ed.2d 1231 (1968) (holding competitor which passed on to customers increases in prices resulting from overcharges nevertheless could recover treble damages measured by such overcharges); Dailey v. Quality School Plan, Inc., 380 F.2d 484 (5th Cir. 1967) (upholding private antitrust action by adversely affected employees); Perryton Wholesale, Inc. v. Pioneer Distributing Co. of Kansas, Inc., 353 F.2d 618 (10th Cir. 1965), cert. denied 383 U.S. 945, 86 S.Ct. 1202, 16 L.Ed.2d 208 (1966) (ruling that treble damage action lies for inducing plaintiff's employees who had no term employment, to leave employment and for breach covenant not to compete); E. Timberlake, Federal Treble Damage Antitrust Actions (1965). As for federal income tax consequences, see Tax Reform Act of 1969, § 902(a), amending Int.Rev.Code of 1954, 26 U.S.C.A. § 162 (limiting deduction of treble damage awards or settlements paid to private persons in civil antitrust actions on account of criminal violations to compensatory amount, e. g., one-third of treble damages); Wright, "A Tax Formula to Restore the Historical Effects of the Antitrust Treble Damage Provisions", 65 Mich.L.Rev. 245 (1966); Note, "Payments of Treble Damages in Private Antitrust Suits Ruled Deductible as 'Ordinary and Necessary' Business Expenses", 113 U.Pa.L.Rev. 954 (1965). Legislation (S. 2479, 89th Cong., 1st Sess. (1965)) was subsequently introduced, but not passed, to treat such damage awards as nondeductible penalties. After 29 of the largest electrical manufacturers were convicted in 1961 on criminal antitrust charges, 1,912 civil actions were filed in 35 federal courts by public and private utilities and cooperatives, representing more than 25,000 treble damage claims for losses on "fixed" sales of some 20 different kinds of equipment. These cases quadrupled the normal antitrust litigation in the United States; the total claims exceeded $1,000,000,000. General Electric Co. has paid out or set aside some $250,000,000, Westinghouse Electric Corp. some $110,000,000, and Allis-Chalmers some $45,000,000. Neal & Goldberg, "The Electrical Equipment Antitrust Cases: Novel Judicial Administration", 50 A.B.A.J. 623 (1964); Wiprud, "Antitrust Treble Damage Suits Against Electrical Manufacturers: The Statute of Limitations and Other Hurdles", 57 Nw.U.L.Rev. 29 (1962); Pollock, "The 'Injury' and 'Causation' Elements of a Treble-Damage Antitrust Action", 57 Nw.U.L.Rev. 691 (1963); Comment, "Private Treble Damage Antitrust Suits: Measure of Damages for Destruction of All or Part of a Business", 80 Harv.L.Rev. 1566 (1967); Note, "Release of One Joint Tortfeasor in Private Antitrust Suit Held To Be Release of All", 41 N.Y.U.L.Rev. 627 (1966); Note, "Standing To Sue for Treble Damages Under Section 4 of the Clayton Act", 64

FEDERAL ANTITRUST AND TRADE REGULATION—ROBINSON–PATMAN ACT, 1935

313. The Robinson-Patman Act, 1935, prohibits certain discrimination in prices and practices in connection with the sale in interstate or foreign commerce of commodities, and provides for enforcement proceedings in the courts and before the Federal Trade Commission.

The Robinson-Patman Act, 1935,[1] enacted as an amendment to the Clayton Act, prohibits certain discrimination in prices and practices in connection with the sale in interstate or foreign commerce of commodities,[2] and provides for enforcement proceedings in the courts and before the Federal Trade Commission.

MISCELLANEOUS FEDERAL ANTITRUST AND TRADE REGULATION

314. Limited exemptions from the antitrust laws exist for industries supervised by various federal or state administrative agencies, for labor organizations, and for "fair-trade" agreements.

Limited exemptions from the antitrust laws exist for industries supervised by various federal or state administrative agencies,[1]

Colum.L.Rev. 570 (1964). Quaere, whether the defendant in a treble-damage action may refuse to deal with the plaintiff. Compare Bergen Drug Co. v. Parke, Davis & Co., 307 F.2d 725 (3d Cir. 1962), with House of Materials, Inc. v. Simplicity Pattern Co., 298 F.2d 867 (2d Cir. 1962).

In a treble-damage action, a final judgment in a criminal action, except a "consent judgment", constitutes prima facie evidence of the violation. Compare Commonwealth Edison Co. v. Allis-Chalmers Mfg. Co., 211 F.2d 712 (7th Cir. 1963) (judgment based on guilty plea held not "consent judgment"), with Gottesman v. General Motors Corp., 221 F. Supp. 488 (S.D.N.Y.1963), cert. denied 379 U.S. 882, 85 S.Ct. 144, 13 L.Ed.2d 88 (1964), reh. denied 379 U. S. 940, 85 S.Ct. 321, 13 L.Ed.2d 351 (1965), reh. denied 382 U.S. 875, 86 S.Ct. 17, 15 L.Ed.2d 118 (1965) (judgment based on nolo contendere plea held "consent judgment"). See Note, "Clayton Act—Admissibility of Criminal Conviction Entered on a Plea of Guilty as Prima Facie Evidence in Civil Suit for Treble Damages", 62 Mich.L.Rev. 326 (1963). For discussion of the "asphalt clause"—a clause in a civil antitrust case consent decree that the decree shall have a specified prima facie effect in favor of plaintiffs in certain subsequent private treble damage actions for the same violation, see Kaplan, "The Asphalt Clause—A New Weapon in Antitrust Enforcement", 3 B.C.Ind. & Com.L.Rev. 355 (1962); McHenry, "The Asphalt Clause—A Trap for the Unwary", 36 N.Y.U.L.Rev. 1114 (1961).

[§ 313]

1. 15 U.S.C.A. §§ 15–21a; J. Van Cise, Understanding the Antitrust Laws 43–52 (PLI rev. 1966); D. Baum, The Robinson-Patman Act: Summary and Comment (1964); W. Patman, Complete Guide to the Robinson-Patman Act (1963); A. Sawyer, Business Aspects of Pricing Under the Robinson-Patman Act (1963); F. Rowe, Price Discrimination Under the Robinson-Patman Act (1962); C. Edwards, The Price Discrimination Law: A Review of Experience (1959); 1 CCH Trade Reg.Rep. ¶¶ 180–190; C. Austin, Price Discrimination and Related Problems under the Robinson-Patman Act (ALI rev. 1959); W. Patman, The Robinson-Patman Act (1938); Millstein, "The Status of 'Availability' under Section 2(a) of the Robinson-Patman Act", 42 N.Y.U.L.Rev. 416 (1967); Symposium: "The Robinson-Patman Act", 41 Notre Dame Law. 285 (1966); Dilks, "A

Stepchild Gains Small Favor: The FTC and the Meeting Competition Defense under the Robinson-Patman Act", 21 Bus.Law. 481 (1966); Mezines, "Brokerage—When Is It Permitted Under the Robinson-Patman Act?", 7 B.C.Ind. & Com.L.Rev. 821 (1966); Tomlin, "Private Recovery under the Robinson-Patman Act—An Analysis and a Suggestion", 43 Texas L.Rev. 168 (1964); Barton, "Competitive Injury under the Robinson-Patman Act", 19 Bus. Law. 649 (1964); Kintner, "Robinson-Patman Act Dangers in Distribution and Pricing", 19 Bus.Law. 481 (1964); Suss, "Meeting Competition with Price Discrimination—A Legal Principle in Search of Maturity", 18 Bus.Law. 1017 (1963); Miller, "Sections 2(d) and 2(e) of the Robinson-Patman Act: Seller in a Quandary", 45 Marq.L.Rev. 511 (1962); Murray & Fixler, "Area Price Discrimination: A Workable Concept of Injury to Competition", 23 U.Pitt.L.Rev. 893 (1962); Rahl, "Price Competition and the Price Fixing Rule—Preface and Perspective", 57 Nw.U.L. Rev. 137 (1962); Barber, Private Enforcement of the Antitrust Laws: The Robinson-Patman Experience", 30 Geo.Wash.L.Rev. 181 (1961); Brooks, "Injury to Competition under the Robinson-Patman Act", 109 U.Pa.L.Rev. 777 (1961); Note, "Pricing Systems and the Meeting Competition Defense", 49 Va.L.Rev. 1325 (1963); Note, "Discouragement of Private Treble Damage Suits Through a Simple Refusal to Deal", 71 Yale L.J. 1565 (1962); Note, "Competitive Injury under the Robinson-Patman Act", 74 Harv.L.Rev. 1597 (1961).

2. See Reines Distributors, Inc. v. Admiral Corp., 257 F.Supp. 619 (S.D.N.Y.1965) (holding that alleged preferences to division, later wholly-owned subsidiary, not prohibited by Robinson-Patman Act).

[§ 314]

1. E. g., McCarran-Ferguson Act, 15 U.S.C.A. §§ 1011–1012 (insurance business declared subject to state regulation, provided that after June 30, 1958,

for labor organizations,[2] etc., and for "fair-trade" agreements.[3]

Sherman Act, Clayton Act, and Federal Trade Commission Act were to be applicable to insurance business to extent such business not regulated by state law), overruling United States v. South-Eastern Underwriters Ass'n, 322 U.S. 533, 64 S.Ct. 1162, 88 L. Ed. 1440 (1944). Industries regulated by the federal or state governments are often subject to special legislative and administrative provisions parelleling many of the antitrust prohibitions. J. Van Cise, Understanding the Antitrust Laws 52–56 (PLI rev. 1966); Symposium: "Exemptions from Federal Antitrust Laws", 20 Fed.B.J. 3 (1960); Hale & Hale, "Competition or Control VI: Application of Antitrust Laws to Regulated Industries", 111 U.Pa. L.Rev. 46 (1962); Hale & Hale, "Mergers in Regulated Industries", 59 Nw.U.L.Rev. 49 (1964); Note, "Antitrust and Regulated Industries: The *Panagra* Decision and Its Ramifications", 38 N.Y.U.L.Rev. 593 (1963); Note, "Administrative Law—Clayton Act—Mergers—Regulatory Agencies Cannot Grant Immunity from Antitrust Prosecutions by Approving Mergers", 24 U.Pitt.L.Rev. 168 (1962). As for railroads, airlines, and other carriers, see Foley & Fordham, "Mergers in Domestic Aviation: The Role of Competition", 5 B.C.Ind. & Com.L.Rev. 279 (1964); Fulda, "Antitrust Aspects of Recent Transportation Mergers", 48 Minn.L.Rev. 723 (1964); Morton, "Carrier Consolidation", 30 ICC Prac.J. 425 (1963); Adkins, "Roadblocks to Railroad Mergers", 17 Bus.Law. 519 (1962); Tucker & O'Brien, "The Public Interest in Railroad Mergers", 42 Boston U. L.Rev. 160 (1962); Phillips, "Railroad Mergers: Competition, Monopoly and Antitrust", 19 Wash. & Lee L.Rev. 1 (1962); Barber, "Airline Mergers, Monopoly, and the CAB", 28 J.Air.L. & Com. 189 (1961–62); Comment, The Role of Antitrust Law in Railroad Mergers—A Case Study: The Great Northern and Northern Pacific Merger", 41 N.D.L. Rev. 40 (1964); Comment, "Merger and Monopoly in Domestic Aviation", 62 Colum.L.Rev. 851 (1962); Note, "The American-Eastern Application: Crucial Test of CAB Merger Policy", 111 U.Pa.L.Rev. 195 (1962); Note, "Merger in the Domestic Air Transport Industry", 48 Va.L.Rev. 1428 (1962). As for banks, see United States v. Third Nat'l Bank, 390 U.S. 171, 88 S.Ct. 882, 19 L.Ed.2d 1015 (1968); United States v. First City Nat'l Bank, United States v. Provident Nat'l Bank, 386 U.S. 361, 87 S.Ct. 1088, 18 L.Ed.2d 151 (1967); United States v. First Nat'l Bank & Trust Co. of Lexington, 376 U.S. 665, 84 S. Ct. 1033, 12 L.Ed.2d 1 (1964) (holding elimination of competition between two merging banks violated Sherman Act § 1); United States v. Philadelphia Nat'l Bank, 374 U.S. 321, 83 S.Ct. 1715, 10 L.Ed.2d 915 (1963) (holding that merger of two banks, approved by Comptroller of the Currency, violated Clayton Act § 7); Via, "Antitrust and the Amended Bank Merger and Holding Company Acts: The Search for Standards", 53 Va.L.Rev. 1115 (1967); Seeley, "Banks and Antitrust", 21 Bus.Law. 917 (1966); Via, "The Administration of the Bank Merger and Holding Company Acts: Confusion Compounded", 51 Va.L.Rev. 1517 (1965); Dorset, "Bank Mergers and Holding Companies and the

STATE ANTITRUST AND TRADE REGULATION

315. State antitrust and trade regulation legislation typically proscribes monopolies and restraints of trade, and sanctions "fair trade" contracts. Antitrust and trade regulation proceedings at the state level have been relatively rare.

Enactment of state antitrust and trade regulation legislation was stimulated by the United States Supreme Court holding in 1894 in United States v. E. C. Knight Co.,[1]

Public Interest", 18 Bus.Law. 703 (1963); Fiechter, "Another Year of American Antitrust Law Regarding Bank Mergers", 17 Bus.Law. 906 (1962); Klebaner, "Federal Control of Commerical Bank Mergers", 37 Ind.L.J. 287 (1962); Wemple & Cutler, "Federal Bank Merger Law and Antitrust Laws", 79 Banking L.J. 461 (1962); Comment, "The 1966 Amendment to the Bank Merger Act", 20 Vand.L. Rev. 200 (1966); Comment, "Bank Mergers and the Six-Headed Monster", 15 Catholic U.L.Rev. 69 (1966); Comment, "The 1966 Amendment to the Bank Merger Act", 66 Colum.L.Rev. 764 (1966); Comment, "Government Regulation of Bank Mergers: The Revolving Door of Philadelphia Bank", 62 Mich.L.Rev. 990 (1964); Comment, "The Applicability of the Antitrust Laws to Combinations Approved Under the Bank Merger Act, Federal Power Act and Natural Gas Act", 37 N.Y.U.L.Rev. 735 (1962); Annot., 83 A.L.R.2d 374 (1962). Securities exchanges, despite the fact that they are already subject to substantial governmental regulation, are not exempt from the antitrust laws. Silver v. New York Stock Exchange, 373 U.S. 341, 83 S.Ct. 1246, 10 L.Ed.2d 389 (1963), reh. denied 375 U.S. 870, 84 S.Ct. 26, 11 L.Ed.2d 99 (1963).

2. Clayton Act § 6, 15 U.S.C.A. § 17; Norris-LaGuardia Anti-Injunction Act, 29 U.S.C.A. § 101; 1 CCH Trade Reg.Rep. ¶¶ 980–995; P. Boarman, Union Monopolies and Antitrust Restraints (1963); Comment, "Labor's Antitrust Exemption", 55 Calif. L.Rev. 254 (1967); Comment, "The Antitrust Laws and Labor", 30 Fordham L.Rev. 759 (1962).

3. Miller-Tydings Act, 1937, 15 U.S.C.A. § 1 (amendment to Sherman Act); McGuire Fair Trade Act, 1952, 15 U.S.C.A. § 45 (amendment to Federal Trade Commission Act). See section 315, n. 6 infra.

1. 156 U.S. 1, 15 S.Ct. 249, 39 L.Ed. 325 (1894). J. Flynn, Federalism and State Antitrust Regulation (1964); Arnold & Ford, "Uniform State Antitrust Act: Toward Creation of a National Antitrust Policy", 15 W.Res.L.Rev. 102 (1963); Mosk, "State Antitrust Enforcement and Coordination with Federal Enforcement", 51 Ky.L.J. 256 (1963); Note, "The Commerce Clause and State Antitrust Regulation", 61 Colum.L.Rev. 1469 (1961). See State v. Southeast Texas Chapter of Nat'l Elec. Contractor's Ass'n, 358 S.W.2d 711 (Tex.Civ.App.1962), cert. denied 372 U.S. 965, 83 S.Ct. 1089, 10 L.Ed.

that manufacture was not commerce, in effect returning antitrust and trade regulation to the various states. While many states have antitrust and trade regulation statutes,[2] proceedings under them have been relatively rare,[3] perhaps because of the expanding broad sweep of federal authority under the commerce clause to regulate monopoly and trade practices.

Some state constitutions have provisions prohibiting monopolies, trusts, and combinations in restraint of trade.[4]

State statutes typically declare illegal and void every contract, agreement, arrangement, or combination (with prescribed exceptions) for monopoly or in restraint of any business, trade, or commerce or in the furnishing of any service in the state. Remedies are damages, fines and/or imprisonment, and actions by the attorney general to restrain and prevent.[5] In addition many states have fair trade laws.[6]

D. "SELF–REGULATION" BY SECURITIES INDUSTRY

NATIONAL SECURITIES EXCHANGES

316. When securities are listed on a securities exchange, the issuer becomes subject both to such provisions of the Securities Exchange Act, 1934, as apply to listed securities and their issuer, and to the rules and regulations of such securities exchange. The latter, at least in the case of the New York Stock Exchange, are very comprehensive.

Besides being subject to federal and state regulation not applicable to smaller business enterprises, larger corporations often become subject to nongovernmental regulation.

When securities are listed on a securities exchange, the issuer becomes subject both to such provisions of the Securities Exchange Act as apply to listed securities and their issuers [1] and to the rules and regulations of such securities exchange. If securities are traded over-the-counter, the rules and regu-

---

2d 128 (1963) (holding federal antitrust laws had not preempted field and upholding state's action for civil remedies and forfeiture of charter for antitrust violations under state statute despite pending federal criminal antitrust action arising out of same facts).

2. See generally CCH Trade Regulation Reports (5 vols.); Symposium: "Trade Regulation", 15 W.Res. L.Rev. 9 (1963); Wilson, "The State Antitrust Laws", 47 A.B.A.J. 160 (1961); Note, "The Present Revival and Future Course of State Antitrust Enforcement", 36 N.Y.U.L.Rev. 575 (1963).

3. Report of the Special Committee to Study the New York Antitrust Laws of the New York State Bar Ass'n 89a–116a (1957).

4. E. g., Ala.Const. art. IV, § 103; S.D.Const. art. 7, § 20; Tex.Const. art. 1, § 26; Va.Const. art. 12, § 165. Some jurisdictions require corporations to file antitrust affidavits.

5. E. g., McKinney's N.Y.Gen.Bus.Law §§ 340–347, 350, 351; The Law of Competition in Illinois (Chicago Bar Ass'n Committee on Antitrust Law 1963); Mantzoros, "State Antitrust Statutes—Rules of Construction and Enforcement", 24 Record of N.Y. C.B.A. 425 (1969); Survey, "Trade Regulation in Ohio", 15 W.Res.L.Rev. 122 (1963); Barron, "California Antitrust—Legislative Schizophrenia", 35 S.Cal.L.Rev. 393 (1962); French, "The Minnesota Antitrust Law", 50 Minn.L.Rev. 59 (1965); Wilson,

"The State Antitrust Laws", 47 A.B.A.J. 160 (1961); Lefkowitz, "New York State Antitrust Activity— Another Year of Progress", 31 N.Y.St.B.Bull. 110 (1959); Kalinowski & Hanson, "The California Antitrust Laws: A Comparison with the Federal Antitrust Laws", 6 U.C.L.A.L.Rev. 533 (1959).

6. E. g., McKinney's N.Y.Gen.Bus.Law §§ 369–a to 369–e. See 2 CCH Trade Reg.Rep. ¶¶ 6000–6855; Conant, "Resale Price Maintenance: Constitutionality of Nonsigner Clauses", 109 U.Pa.L.Rev. 539 (1961); Herman, "Fair Trade: Origins, Purposes, and Competitive Effects", 27 Geo.Wash.L.Rev. 621 (1959); Comment, "Resale Price Maintenance: The Nature and Validity of Fair-Trade Laws", 1967 U.Ill.L.F. 307; Comment, "The Enforcement of Resale Price Maintenance", 69 Yale L.J. 168 (1959); Note, "The Constitutionality of the Virginia Fair-Trade Act", 47 Va.L.Rev. 626 (1961); Annot., 12 L. Ed.2d 1207 (1965). See section 314, n. 3 supra.

1. See section 296 supra. Some 125 unlisted corporations of the some 3,000 corporations brought under the Securities Exchange Act in 1934 are eligible for listing on the New York Stock Exchange; almost 700 more of them are eligible for listing on the American Stock Exchange.

lations of the National Association of Security Dealers, Inc. often apply.[2]

In the United States, there are 16 national securities exchanges,[3] each with its own rules

and regulations governing its members [4] and securities traded thereon.

The New York Stock Exchange, known as the "Big Board", is by far the most important exchange,[5] with the strictest rules. Its organization [6] and operation [7] are beyond the scope of this discussion, which will highlight the regulation by the exchange of its listed

2. See section 317 infra.

3. Of the 16 national securities exchanges in the United States, 13 are S.E.C.-registered exchanges: American Stock Exchange ("Amex") (formerly New York Curb Exchange), Boston Stock Exchange, Chicago Board of Trade, Cincinnati Stock Exchange, Detroit Stock Exchange, Midwest Stock Exchange, National Stock Exchange (formerly New York Mercantile Exchange), New York Stock Exchange, Pacific Coast Stock Exchange, Philadelphia-Baltimore-Washington Stock Exchange, Pittsburgh Stock Exchange, Salt Lake Exchange, and Spokane Stock Exchange; and those are exempt from S.E.C. registration: Colorado Springs Stock Exchange, Honolulu Stock Exchange, and Richmond Stock Exchange. See CCH New York Stock Exchange Guide (3 vols.); CCH American Stock Exchange Guide; G. Leffler & L. Farwell, The Stock Market (3d ed. 1963); D. Spray, The Principal Stock Exchanges of the World (1964); J. Walter, The Role of Regional Security Exchanges (1957); Halsted, "Rules and Regulations of the Midwest Stock Exchange", 1961 U. Ill.L.F. 257. See "Stock Markets: Those Other Exchanges", 86 Time, No. 10, 78 (Sept. 3, 1965); Note, "Securities Marketing and Stock Exchanges in Black Africa", 67 Colum.L.Rev. 892 (1967). See also Hodes, "Some Pros and Cons of Listing on a Securities Exchange", 10 Prac.Law. 41 (April 1964); Jennings, "Self-Regulation in the Securities Industry: The Role of the Securities and Exchange Commission", 29 Law & Contemp. Prob. 663 (1964); Cary, "Self-Regulation in the Securities Industry", 49 A.B.A.J. 244 (1963). See Report of the Special Study of Securities Markets (1963). See also Pettit v. American Stock Exchange, 217 F.Supp. 21 (S.D. N.Y.1963) (exchange held liable for not preventing members' fraud). Exempted from various regulatory provisions of the New York Business Corporation Law are qualified foreign corporations doing business in New York, their directors, officers, and shareholders, if when any such provision would otherwise apply, the "shares of such corporation were listed on a national securities exchange". McKinney's N.Y.Bus.Corp.Law § 1320. Listing might also provide exemption under state "blue sky" laws. See section 306 supra. Antitrust laws apply to national securities exchanges only to a limited extent because of their self-regulatory rôles under federal securities legislation. Silver v. New York Stock Exchange, 373 U.S. 341, 83 S.Ct. 1246, 10 L.Ed. 2d 389 (1963), reh. denied 375 U.S. 870, 84 S.Ct. 26, 11 L.Ed.2d 99 (1933); Thill Securities Corp. v. New York Stock Exchange, 283 F.Supp. 239 (E.D. Wis.1969); Kaplan v. Lehman Bros., 250 F.Supp. 562 (N.D.Ill.1966); Comment, "Antitrust and the Stock Exchange: Minimum Commission or Free Competition?", 18 Stan.L.Rev. 213 (1965). Sterling, "Stockbrokers Going Public: Antitrust Aspects of Exchange Rules", 13 U.C.L.A.L.Rev. 563 (1966);

Bicks, "Antitrust and the New York Stock Exchange", 21 Bus.Law. 129 (1965).

4. For a discussion of requirements of membership in the New York Stock Exchange, see A. Choka, An Introduction to Securities Regulation 98–101 (1958); see Constitution of the New York Stock Exchange; Rules of the Board of Governors of the New York Stock Exchange. See Lowenfels, "Implied Liabilities Based upon Stock Exchange Rules", 66 Colum. L.Rev. 12 (1966); Note, "Stock Exchange Regulation of Nonmember Brokers", 71 Yale L.J. 748 (1962).

5. F. Eames, The New York Stock Exchange (1968); R. Sobel, The Big Board: A History of the New York Stock Market (1965). Of the dollar volume of share-trading on the various exchanges, 80 percent occurs on the New York Stock Exchange, 12 percent on the American Stock Exchange, and the remaining eight percent on all of the other exchanges combined.

6. A voluntary association, it has an elected 33-man board of governors, salaried president, department of member firms, personnel department, floor department, real estate department, department of stock list, electronic systems center, research services, quotation services, and clearing house (through its subsidiary, Stock Clearing Corporation), a new facility of which is the Central Certificate Service with its electronic bookkeeping entries to transfer securities from one brokerage house to another without the physical delivery of certificates. It provides trading facilities for its members and allied members (brokers and dealers); it has 1366 "seats"; since May, 1953, corporations have been eligible for membership; seats can be bought only when available ranging, since 1929, from $17,000 to $515,000; the initiation fee is $7,500 and dues $1,500 annually. The members engage in various activities: as commission brokers, specialists, odd-lot dealers (to handle odd-lot transactions since only round-lot transactions (usually 100 shares) are carried out on the exchange), floor brokers, and the "bond crowd". A. Choka, An Introduction to Securities Regulation ch. 11 (1958); Understanding the New York Stock Exchange 10–17 (New York Stock Exchange rev. ed. (1969); Odd-Lot Manual (Carlisle & Jacquelin 1969); Jennings, "The New York Stock Exchange and the Commission Rate Struggle", 21 Bus.Law. 159 (1965), 53 Calif.L.Rev. 1119 (1965).

7. See Understanding the New York Stock Exchange (New York Stock Exchange rev. ed. (1969).

securities [8] and companies.[9]

Eligible companies might list some or all of their securities: Debt securities or equity securities of various classes or series. To be eligible, a company must meet the following minimum numerical standards: [10]

Number of shareholders:

Total 2,000
Holders of 100 shares or more.1,800

Number of shares:

Total outstanding 1,000,000
Publicly-held 800,000

Market value of publicly-held
    shares: $14,000,000
    (or $14,000,000 minimum
    net tangible assets)

Demonstrated earning power before federal income taxes
and under competitive
conditions:

Latest fiscal year ....$ 2,500,000
Each of preceding two
    years ....$ 2,000,000

Even if the company is otherwise eligible its securities might not be listed if the issuer has outstanding in public hands nonvoting shares, however designated, which by their terms are in effect common shares,[11] or has

fixed a quorum for its shareholder meetings at less than a majority of all outstanding shares.[12] Common shares without voting rights will not be listed; [13] nor will preferred shares without at least minimum voting rights; [14] Nor will voting trust certificates (except when the voting trust is established pursuant to a court-directed reorganization) or voting shares subject to a voting trust or irrevocable proxy.[15]

For a security to be listed, the issuer must file a "listing application" with the exchange.[16]

---

8. For a concise summary of the advantages of listing, see Advantages of Listing (American Stock Exchange 1967). Unlisted trading is not permitted by the New York Stock Exchange, but is permitted by the other exchanges, where it is subject to a rigorous S.E.C. regulation. 15 U.S.C.A. § 78*l*(f); 2 L. Loss, Securities Regulation 1132–1149 (2d ed. 1961).

9. See N.Y.S.E. Company Manual (containing general rules and regulations, practices, and procedures relating to listed companies and listed securities, and general listing procedure and directions for preparation of listing applications).

10. N.Y.S.E. Company Manual § B1. Other factors besides the numerical standards are taken into consideration. The company must be a going concern or the successor to a going concern. While the amount of assets and earnings and the aggregate market value are considerations, greater emphasis is placed on such questions as the degree of national interest in the company, the character of the market for its products, its relative stability and position in its industry, and whether or not it is engaged in an expanding industry with prospects for maintaining its position.

11. N.Y.S.E. Company Manual §§ A15, B1.

12. Id. at § A15.

13. Id. at §§ A15, B1. Such requirements were adopted in 1926. See section 189, n. 38 supra. See United Funds, Inc. v. Carter Prods., Inc., No. 102A/450A4288 (Cir.Ct. Baltimore City 1963), 151 The Daily Record (Baltimore) 2 (Sept. 23, 1963) (enjoining issuance of new nonvoting common shares which would result in delisting of present shares).

14. Nonvoting preferred shares will not be listed if such shares do not have the right, as a class, to elect at least two directors when six quarterly dividends are in default, or if a two-thirds class vote of such shares is not required for any change adversely affecting such shares. Such requirements were adopted in 1940.

15. Nor shares with or subject to unusual voting provisions.

16. N.Y.S.E. Company Manual §§ A2, B1–B3, reprinted in Listing Procedure (N.Y.S.E.). The objectives of the listing agreement are:

    (1) Timely disclosure, to the public and to the Exchange which may affect security values or influence investment decisions, and in which shareholders, the public, and the Exchange have a warrantable interest;

    (2) Frequent, regular, and timely publication of financial reports prepared in accordance with accepted accounting practice, and in adequate (but not burdensome) detail;

    (3) Providing the Exchange with timely information to enable it to perform, efficiently and expeditiously, its function of maintaining an orderly market for the company's securities and to enable it to maintain its necessary records;

    (4) Preclusion of certain practices not generally considered sound; and

    (5) Allowing the Exchange opportunity to make representations as to certain matters before they become accomplished facts.

N.Y.S.E. Company Manual § A2.

In preparing the listing application Exchange assistance is available. Concurrently with listing on the Exchange, the securities must be registered with

Listing is subject to the condition that the issuer enter into a "listing agreement" [17] with the exchange covering the listed securities and any additional securities of the same class. The listing agreement requires that listed companies do not issue share options to key employees and that they refrain from certain other matters except after approval by shareholders,[18] that they distribute annual consolidated balance sheets and income and surplus statements to shareholders and release quarterly earnings statements,[19] that they solicit proxies for every shareholder meeting,[20] that they handle any redemption of the securities in a prescribed way,[21] that they secure shareholder approval of certain matters,[22] that they follow certain practices with respect to dividends and interest,[23] share dividends,[24] share split-ups,[25] and share warrants,[26] record dates and closing of transfer books,[27] and indentures, trustees, and depositaries for listed bonds and other listed debt securities,[28] that they issue prompt publicity releases on various matters,[29] and that they make prescribed filings with the exchange.[30]

The form and workmanship of certificates representing listed securities, whether debt securities or shares, are subject to stringent rules to minimize the risk of counterfeiting and to facilitate the clearing of transactions in such certificates.[31]

Listed companies are also required to maintain qualified fiscal agents (transfer agent, registrar, paying agent) in the Manhattan financial district, but they may also have qualified fiscal agents elsewhere.[32]

Securities may be delisted by the issuer, with the approval of the Securities and Exchange Commission, the New York Stock Exchange, and the holders of the securities;[33] or for cause, by appropriate exchange action.[34]

In 1969, a computerized system for making large securities transactions, bypassing both brokers and securities exchanges, was offered to institutional investors, who own some 25 percent of the dollar value of shares listed on the New York Stock Exchange.

---

the S.E.C. under the Federal Securities Exchange Act, 1934. After listing has been authorized, 650 printed copies of the listing application are required by the Exchange for distribution to all member firms, and to others, including the general public, who may request a copy. See C. Israels & G. Duff, When Corporations Go Public 91 (PLI 1962); Rosenberry, "Listing and Delisting Securities on the New York Stock Exchange", 45 Va.L.Rev. 897 (1959).

17. N.Y.S.E. Company Manual §§ A2, B5.

18. Id. at §§ A7, B5.

19. Id. at. § A4.

20. Id. at § A8.

21. Id. at § A10.

22. Id. at § B1.

23. Id. at § A3.

24. Id. at § A13.

25. Id. at § A14.

26. Id. at § A11.

27. Id. at § A9.

28. Id. at § A5.

29. Id. at §§ A3 (dividends), A4 (financial statements), A10 (redemption), A11 (rights to subscribe), A13 (share dividends), A14 (share split-ups).

30. Id. at §§ A4, A6.

31. Id. at § A12. See section 134 supra.

32. Id. at § A1.

33. Id. at § B1.

34. Id. at § A16; Atlas Tack Corp. v. New York Stock Exchange, 246 F.2d 311, 66 A.L.R.2d 664 (1st Cir. 1957); Exchange Buffet Corp. v. New York Stock Exchange, 244 F.2d 507 (2d Cir. 1957); Rosenberry, "Listing and Delisting Securities on the New York Stock Exchange", 45 Va.L.Rev. 897 (1959); Annot., 66 A.L.R.2d 676 (1959). Companies may now be delisted if they fail to have (a) at least 400,000 publicly-held common shares; (b) average net earnings of at least $600,000 for the past three years; (c) at least $7,000,000 market value of outstanding shares or net tangible assets; (d) at least 900 round-lot holders; and (e) at least $4,000,000 market value of publicly-held shares. Id. § A16.

NATIONAL ASSOCIATION OF SECURITIES DEALERS, INC.

317. The National Association of Securities Dealers, Inc. (N.A.S.D.) is a nonprofit association of securities brokers and dealers. It has promulgated Rules of Fair Practice and a Uniform Practice Code for the over-the-counter market. It is the only such association registered with the Securities and Exchange Commission under the Securities Exchange Act, 1934.

The National Association of Securities Dealers, Inc. (N.A.S.D.) is the only association of securities dealers registered with the Securities and Exchange Commission under the Securities Exchange Act of 1934; a majority of securities brokers and dealers belong to the National Association of Securities Dealers, Inc.

The National Association of Securities Dealers, Inc. organized in 1939, is a nonprofit association of brokers and dealers engaged in the investment banking and securities business in the United States.[1]

It has promulgated Rules of Fair Practice, designed to promote and enforce just and equitable principles of trade in the securities business, and a Uniform Practice Code, designed to make uniform the rules developed by brokers and dealers to cover trading practice and the settlement of contracts in the over-the-counter market. It covers such technical matters as trading terms, deliveries, payments, dividends, rights, interest reclamations, when issued and when distributed trading, etc.[2]

A broker-dealer firm registered with the Securities and Exchange Commission, which is not a N.A.S.D. member, is known as a "SECO".

"The National Association of Securities Dealers: Continuing Government-Industry Cooperative Regulation in the Over-the-Counter Securities Industry", 7 Vill.L.Rev. 611 (1962); White, "National Association of Securities Dealers, Inc.", 28 Geo.Wash.L. Rev. 250 (1959); Note, "The NASD—An Unique Experiment in Cooperative Regulation", 46 Va.L.Rev. 1586 (1960). See also CCH NASD Manual.

2. A. Choka, An Introduction to Securities Regulation 66–70 (1958); The NASD and the Registered Representative (N.A.S.D.1964); Lowenfels, "Private Enforcement in the Over-the-Counter Securities Markets: Implied Liabilities Based on NASD Rules", 51 Cornell L.Q. 633 (1966).

1. Sterling, "National Association of Securities Dealers and the Securities Acts Amendments of 1964", 20 Bus.Law. 313 (1965); Report of the Special Study of Securities Markets ch. VII (1963); Rutter,

CHAPTER 12

DIVIDENDS AND OTHER DISTRIBUTIONS

A. INTRODUCTION

A. INTRODUCTION

DIVIDENDS—IN GENERAL

318. **Dividends distributable among its shareholders is a characteristic feature of the profit, stock, or business corporation. Most shareholders, especially in larger corporations, are more interested in the financial than the control aspects of their shares, desiring a periodic return on their investment in the form of dividends or capital gains or both. While stock corporations, including business corporations, usually are authorized by law to distribute dividends, they can only do so out of legally available funds, and then only in accordance with applicable dividend preferences and other rights. In most cases, the question of the extent to which the corporation should distribute or retain its profits is within the discretion of the board of directors.**

The term "dividend" includes distribution to shareholders of corporate earnings and profits, and is sometimes used to include distributions in partial liquidations or distributions from capital surplus, as well as distributions of earnings and profits. The principal kinds of dividends are (a) cash dividends; (b) property dividends; and (c) share dividends (to be distinguished from share splits). Analogous to dividends are redemption and purchase by the corporation of its own shares, to which rules similar to the rules applicable to dividends sometimes apply.

Dividends on listed shares are subject to securities exchange requirements.

The distinctive feature of profit or stock corporations, including business corporations, is that they have shares of stock and are usually expressly authorized by law to distribute dividends to the holders thereof.[1]

Generally speaking, stock or business corporations are corporations for profits,[2] as distinguished from "nonprofit" or "not-for-profit" corporations, in the sense of corporations no part of the income or profit of which is distributable to its members, directors, or officers.[3]

Most shareholders, especially in the larger corporations, are more interested in the financial than in the control aspects of their shares. This is so in the case of nonvoting preferred shares, but applies also to most of those who invest (or speculate) in common shares of larger corporations. Financially, shareholders desire a periodic return on their investment in the form of dividends or capital gains on their investment or both.

While stock or business corporations usually are authorized by law to distribute dividends, they can only do so out of legally available funds,[4] and then only in accordance with applicable dividend preferences and other rights.[5] In most cases, the question of the extent to which the corporation should distribute or retain its profits is within the discretion of the board of directors, whose management functions include the determination of financial policy.[6] In the small business corporation, retained earnings may be the only source of additional funds. Even in large corporations, the largest portion of funds expended for capital expenditures have been coming from internal corpo-

1. See generally D. Kehl, Corporate Dividends; Legal and Accounting Problems Pertaining to Corporate Distributions (1941). In New York, no limitation or definition of dividend rights is effective unless at the time one or more classes of outstanding shares, singly or in the aggregate, are entitled to unlimited dividend rights. Dividend rights apparently may not be denied any class. McKinney's N. Y.Bus.Corp.Law, § 501(a). Some two-thirds of the states require corporations to file annual reports of dividend payments made to shareholders to facilitate collection of state income and intangible property taxes.

2. See, e. g., ABA–ALI Model Bus.Corp.Act § 2(a).

3. See, e. g., ABA–ALI Model Non-Profit Corp.Act § 2(a), (c).

4. See sections 320–323 infra.

5. See sections 324–326 infra.

6. See sections 327, 328 infra. In 1968, corporate profits before taxes approximated $92,300,000,000; after taxes $51,000,000,000. Cash dividends totaled $24,600,000,000, leaving $26,300,000,000 undistributed profits. Statistical Abstract of the United States 1969, 483 (U.S. Dep't of Commerce). See also Loomis, "A Case for Dropping Dividends", 77 Fortune, No. 7, 181 (June 15, 1968).

rate sources (retained earnings capitalized by the declaration of share dividends and reserves)—some 10 times more than has been realized by the issue of additional shares.[7]

Before discussing the various legal problems relevant to dividends, the different kinds of dividends and distributions will be described, and the applicable accounting principles briefly outlined.[8]

Kinds of Dividends and Distributions

Corporate earnings and profits not retained in the business, when distributed among shareholders, are known as "dividends". In some jurisdictions, the term "dividends" is used to include distributions in partial liquidation or distributions from capital surplus, as well as distributions of earnings and profits. Special rules applicable to the distribution of capital surplus might not apply to a dividend, in its more restricted sense. In a growing number of jurisdictions, as under the Model Business Corporation Act, distinction is made between the two types of distribution and the term "dividend" is limited to the former.[9]

The principal kinds of dividends are (a) cash dividends, (b) property dividends, and (c) share dividends.

"Cash Dividend". A "cash dividend" — the most common—is distributed in cash, from legally available funds.

"Property Dividend". A "property dividend" is a distribution which does not consist of cash or shares in the same corporation. Examples include shares in a subsidi-

ary or other corporation, other securities, or other property. It is, in effect, a dividend-in-kind, usually subject to the same rules as are cash dividends. Both "scrip" and "bond" dividends are more or less special types of property dividends, although they are usually accorded separate treatment. Scrip is essentially a short-term promissory note which in effect divides profits but enables the corporation to postpone actual distribution of cash.[10] A bond dividend is extremely rare, perhaps because there is an obvious objection to distributing bonds among shareholders, where only the holders of certain classes of shares are the recipients.

"Share Dividend".[11] A "share dividend", or "stock dividend", entitles the shareholder to additional shares—usually a fraction thereof—for each share which he owns. The distribution is usually expressed as a ratio. Thus, a 10 percent distribution means that the shareholder receives one additional share for each 10 shares already held by him; if he owns only one share, it is possible that he might receive a share certificate evidencing ownership of one-tenth of one share in jurisdictions recognizing fractions of shares.[12] However, the usual practice is to award scrip (which can be combined with other scrip for a share) or even cash rather than fractions of shares. Such scrip is to be distinguished from the "scrip dividend" discussed above in connection with "property dividends". The dividend itself must consist of shares in the declaring corporation, usually but not necessarily of the same class or series. For example, when permissible, a holder of common shares might receive a dividend in the form of preferred shares, or *vice versa*. The share divi-

---

7. See section 154 supra. See generally H. Guthmann & H. Dougall, Corporate Financial Policy 527–550 (4th ed. 1962).

8. See section 319 infra.

9. ABA–ALI Model Bus.Corp.Act §§ 40, 41; see 2 G. Hornstein, Corporation Law and Practice § 937 (1959). Eastman Kodak Co., since 1912, has paid to employees a "wage dividend", based on cash dividends declared on the common shares, in recognition of employees' contributions to the corporation's success. Annual "wage dividends" have approximated $35 per $1,000 of wages during the preceding five years.

10. See Billingham v. E. P. Gleason Mfg. Co., 101 App.Div. 476, 91 N.Y.S. 1046 (1st Dep't 1905), aff'd mem., 185 N.Y. 571, 78 N.E. 1099 (1906), motion to amend remittitur denied, 185 N.Y. 598, 78 N.E. 1099 (1906) (scrip payable at corporation's "pleasure" held payable within reasonable time).

11. See section 329 infra.

12. See section 161 supra.

dend is not a true dividend, and may be subject to different rules from those applying to cash and property dividends. Since it increases stated capital, it cannot prejudice creditors. A "share split" resembles a share dividend but must be distinguished from it for various purposes.[13]

Miscellaneous. An "extra dividend" does not constitute a special kind of dividend in the strict sense of the word. It is simply a distribution in one form or another which is given in addition to the regular or usual dividend the corporation has been paying. A closely related distribution which occurs in rare instances is the "composite dividend." This is a combination of cash and shares, cash and property, shares and property, etc. Equally rare is the "optional dividend" which gives the shareholder a choice between two specified types of distributions.

Redemption and Purchase by Corporation of Own Shares. Analogous to dividends and distributions are redemption and purchase by the corporation of its own shares, to which such exchanges rules similar to the rules applicable to dividends sometimes apply.[14]

Securities Exchange Requirements

With respect to dividends on listed shares, securities exchange requirements are applicable. Such requirements relate to (a) some supervision of key accounts, (b) publicity and notice, (c) record and payment dates, etc., (d) "ex-dividend" dealings, and (e) share dividends. The New York Stock Exchange requirements are rather exacting.

Revaluation of Assets; Restatement of Stated Capital; Charges Against Capital Surplus. Where a corporation with listed securities revaluates its assets or restates its stated capital, certain notices to the exchange are required.[15]

Under the current form of listing agreement, no substantial charges against capital surplus may be made by a corporation or a subsidiary without notifying the exchange, which can require the corporation to submit such charges to the shareholders for approval or ratification.[16]

Publicity and Notice. The New York Stock Exchange requires that any action (or omission of action) in respect of dividends be given prompt publicity, and that the exchange be given prompt notice thereof, at least 10 days before the record date.[17]

Record and Payment Dates, etc. As indicated, the exchange requires at least 10 days' advance notice of the record date. Saturdays, Sundays, and holidays should be avoided as record dates. A short interval between record and payment dates is desirable. An office or agency in Manhattan must be maintained for payment of dividends.[18]

"Ex-Dividend" Dealings. Under the exchange rules, listed shares on which a dividend has been declared are usually dealt in on an "ex-dividend" basis on and after the fourth business day prior to the record date. "Ex-dividend" ("ex-d") means that the seller retains the right to receive and keep the dividend and the amount of the dividend is not included in the purchase price (with consequent adjustment in the quoted market price). The reason for such rule is that non-"cash" contracts for purchase and sale are usually settled by delivery of the share certificates on the fifth business day after the contract is made, making change in record ownership impossible prior to the record date.[19]

Share Dividends and Splits. The New York Stock Exchange imposes additional requirements with respect to share dividends

---

13.   See section 330 infra.

14.   See sections 335–338 infra.

15.   N.Y.S.E. Company Manual § A6.

16.   N.Y.S.E. Company Manual § B5, II, 5.

17.   N.Y.S.E. Company Manual § A3.

18.   Ibid.

19.   Ibid.

and split-ups. These will be outlined in the discussion of share dividends and splits.[20]

ACCOUNTING PRINCIPLES

319. **Accounting principles are relevant to the discussion of some of the legal rules governing dividends and other distributions. Some modern corporate statutes define the accounting terms used in their provisions.**

The double entry system of recording financial transactions requires, singly or in combination, for every debit or charge (left-side entry) a contra credit (right-side entry).

The basic accounting equation is: Assets = Liabilities + Shareholders' Equity (or Proprietorship or Net Worth) (stated capital plus surplus, earned and unearned), with expenses decreasing and income increasing net worth. "Working capital" is the excess of current assets over current liabilities. "Insolvency" has two meanings: (a) inability of the corporation to meet its debts as they mature— so-called "equity sense"—in short, insufficient working capital, and (b) excess of liabilities over assets—so-called "bankruptcy sense"—in short, when stated capital is more than fully impaired.

The two principal books of account are (a) the journal (book of original entry), and (b) the ledger (book of final entry, "posted" from the journal).

The two principal financial statements are (a) the balance sheet (Assets = Liabilities + Shareholders' Equity (or Proprietorship or Net Worth) at a particular time, usually at the end of an accounting period), and (b) the income statement, or profit and loss statement (Income minus Expenses during accounting period), with or without integrated or separate surplus statements.

The independent auditors' reports, based on their audits, may (a) be unqualified, (b) be qualified, (c) be adverse, or (d) involve a disclaimer of opinion.

To some extent, directors and officers may rely in good faith upon the corporation's financial records, with respect to various corporate matters, including dividends and other distributions.

Some knowledge of basic accounting principles is necessary in order to understand some of the legal rules governing dividends and other distributions.

Of the two most usual methods of accounting—(a) cash method, and (b) accrual method—the latter is employed by most commercial and industrial businesses.

For more adequate coverage of the applicable accounting principles, reference should be made to the excellent texts and other writings on legal accounting.[1]

20. See sections 329, 330 supra.

1. H. Bierman & A. Drebin, Financial Accounting, An Introduction (1968); B. Ferst & S. Ferst, Basic Accounting for Lawyers (ALI 2d ed. 1965); J. Dohr, G. Thompson, E. Phillips & W. Warren, Accounting and the Law: Cases and Materials (3d ed. 1964); H. Finney & H. Miller, Principles of Accounting—Introductory (6th ed. 1963); H. Finney & H. Miller, Principles of Accounting—Advanced (5th ed. 1960); R. Amory & C. Hardee, Materials on Accounting—An Introduction to the Problems and Practice of Financial Accounting for Students of Law (3d ed. by D. Herwitz & D. Trautman 1959); H. Finney & H. Miller, Principles of Accounting—Intermediate (5th ed. 1958); Symposium: "Uniformity in Financial Accounting", 30 Law & Contemp.Prob. 621 (1965); Lerner & Solomon, "Accounting and the Law Intertwined: A Case Study of the Need for Uniform Accounting Principles", 56 Geo. L.J. 670 (1968); Tucker, "The Lawyer's Role in Corporate Accounting Problems", 21 Bus.Law. 415 (1966); Hackney, "Accounting Principles in Corporation Law", 30 Law & Contemp.Prob. 791 (1965); de-Capriles, "Modern Financial Accounting", 37 N. Y.U.L.Rev. 1001 (1962), 38 N.Y.U.L.Rev. 1 (1963); Goldberg, "Accounting in a Nutshell: A Guide for Lawyers", 39 A.B.A.J. 467 (1953). See especially American Institute of Certified Public Accountants, APB Accounting Principles (CCH 1968) (2 vols.) Accounting Research and Terminology Bulletins, New York: American Institute of Certified Public Accountants (final ed. 1961). For current developments, see Bulletins of Committee on Accounting Procedure and of Committee on Auditing of American Institute of Certified Public Accountants. Different accounting procedures often exist for purposes of corporate records and reports to shareholders, income tax returns, and reports to regulatory agencies, which sometimes prescribe uniform systems of accounts. See S.E.C.Reg. S–X (form and content of financial statements), 3 CCH Fed.Sec.L.Rep. ¶¶ 61,-101 et seq.; 1 P–H Sec.Reg. ¶ 8,611; L. Rappaport, SEC Accounting Practice and Procedure (2d ed. 1963); L. Day, Tax Accounting Methods and Periods (PLI 1963); T. Keller, Accounting for Corporate Income Taxes (1961); Dixon, "Accounting Periods and Methods", N.Y.U. 21st Inst. on Fed.Tax. 1199 (1963); Hahn, "Methods of Accounting: Their Role in the Federal Income Tax Law", 1960 Wash. U.L. Q. 1; Barr & Koch, "Accounting and the S.E.C.",

Some of the more modern corporation statutes contain definitions of the accounting terms used in their provisions.[2]

Accounting is the art of recording, classifying, and summarizing in a significant manner and in terms of money, transactions and events which are, in part at least, of a financial character, and in interpreting the results thereof. Its function is to measure the resources held by the enterprise and to reflect the claims against and the interests in the enterprise; to measure the changes in such resources, claims, and interests; and to assign such changes to specifiable periods of time.

The accounting period is usually one year and, in any event, not more than one year. It may be the calendar year (January 1–December 31) or some other fiscal year ending on the last day of a specified month. Interim statements may be issued for lesser periods, such as one month, three months, six months, or nine months.

The postulate of accounting is that the business enterprise is a going concern. (In liquidation, assets frequently shrink in value, while liabilities remain relatively constant). Income and expenses are matched for the

accounting period to compute the profits or losses for such period.

The goal of accounting is to present the financial data to provide the basis for an informed judgment as to the financial position and results of operations of the business enterprise.

Accounting does not measure values, but allocates revenues and costs among accounting periods. It does not describe such valuable aspects as competent personnel, favorable sources of supply, and strong competitive position.

Double Entry System

Under the double entry system of recording transactions, each account has two sides. Changes that reflect an increase are recorded on one side and decreases on the other side, thus keeping the books in perpetual balance. The left side of an account is called "debit" (or "charge"); the right side is called "credit". For every debit there is an equivalent (or contra) credit (singly or in combination). Whether the debit or credit reflects an increase or decrease depends on the account. For example, a debit to an asset account represents an increase in assets, while a debit to a liability account represents a decrease in liabilities. (What is a liability to the debtor—a credit—is obviously an asset of the creditor—a debit or charge).

Thus, if a cash dividend (say, $100) were paid out of surplus, the net effect would be to credit cash (an asset account) and to debit (or charge) surplus (a shareholders' equity, proprietorship, or net worth account) (assuming simultaneous declaration and payment):

28 Geo.Wash.L.Rev. 176 (1959); Note, "Problems Arising From Changes in Tax-Accounting Methods", 73 Harv.L.Rev. 1564 (1960). See Watson v. Watson Seed Farms, Inc., 253 N.C. 238, 116 S.E.2d 716 (1960) (upholding corporation's accounting methods); CCH Accountancy Law Reports; Louis, "The Accountants Are Changing the Rules", 77 Fortune, No. 7, 177 (June 15, 1968) (description of 19-member AICPA Accounting Principles Board reviewing "generally accepted accounting principles"). See also Davidson, "Accounting and Financial Reporting in The Seventies", 128 J. Accountancy 29 (Dec. 1969).

2. ABA–ALI Model Bus. Corp. Act § 2(i), (j), (k), (l), (m), (n); McKinney's N.Y.Bus.Corp.Law § 102(a) (2), (6), (8), (9), (12), (13).

Assets	Liabilities, Stated Capital, and Surplus
Cash	Surplus
$500 $100 *	$100 * $200
$400	$100

(thus reducing the total assets
by $100 and the total liabilities,
stated capital, and surplus by $100).

———————

If a share dividend were distributed, again there would be a debit (or charge) of the appropriate amount (say $100) to surplus, but the credit would be to stated capital (another proprietorship or net worth account):

Assets	Liabilities, Stated Capital, and Surplus
	Stated Capital
	$400 100 *
	$500
	Surplus
	$100 * $200
	$100

(thus not changing the total assets
or total liabilities, stated
capital, and surplus).

———————

In short, what the corporation receives is debited (charged); what it pays out is credited.

Basic Accounting Equation

The basic accounting equation is:

Assets   = Liabilities   + Stated Capital and
                          Surplus [3]

(what corpo- = (what corpo- + (equity of sharehold-
ration owns)   ration owes   ers; "book value" of
             to creditors   shares)

Stated Capital and Surplus (sometimes called "shareholders' equity", "proprietor-

ship", "net worth") is made up of stated capital (sometimes called "capital", "capital stock", "capital shares", "legal capital") and surplus.

Stated capital has been defined as the sum of (a) the par value of all shares with par value that have been issued, (b) the amount of the consideration received for all shares without par value that have been issued, except such part of the consideration therefor as may have been allocated to surplus in a manner permitted by law, and (c) such other amounts as have been transferred to stated capital, whether upon the distribution of shares or otherwise, minus all reductions

---

3. Sometimes referred to as "Shareholders' Equity", "Proprietorship", or "Net Worth"; sometimes the term "liabilities" is used loosely to designate both liabilities (in the sense of amounts owed others) and stated capital. See, e. g., former McKinney's N.Y. Stock Corp.Law, § 58; cf. McKinney's N.Y. Bus.Corp.Law, § 102(a) (9) ("Stated capital and surplus are not liabilities").

from such sums as have been effected in a manner permitted by law [4] and surplus. Surplus,[5] in turn, may be either earned surplus (net accumulation of profits) or unearned surplus (capital surplus, paid-in surplus, etc.).[6] "Net assets" is a term used to mean assets minus liabilities.[7]

4. See, e. g., ABA–ALI Model Bus.Corp.Act §§ 2(j) ("stated capital"), 17, 19; Del.Gen.Corp.Law, §§ 154, 152–153 (1967); McKinney's N.Y.Bus.Corp.Law, §§ 102(a) (12), 504, 506, 517.

5. Surplus is the excess of net assets over stated capital. If the surplus balance is negative (i. e., its debits exceed its credits), there is said to be a deficit (indicated by a minus sign, or by red, or by parentheses).

6. Earned surplus is that portion of surplus that represents the net earnings, gains or profits, after deduction of all losses, that have not been distributed to the shareholders as dividends, or transferred to stated capital or capital surplus, or applied to other purposes permitted by law.

Earned surplus is computed from the date of incorporation, from the latest quasi-reorganization, from the time when earned surplus is first segregated from surplus, or from the time of any merger, consolidation, or combination of two or more corporations by purchase or otherwise. Earned surplus may be unrestricted or "restricted". A corporation may "restrict" earned surplus or capital surplus by creating "reserves" from its earned surplus or capital surplus for proper purposes, and may increase, decrease, or abolish any such reserve.

To the earned surplus account should be credited: (a) all profits realized in the ordinary course of business, whether recurring or nonrecurring; (b) all profits realized from extraordinary transactions not involving shares (even though such profits might be "capital gains" for federal income tax purposes); and (c) any "adjustments" to correct past understatements. Normally to be debited (charged) would be: (a) all losses suffered, whether ordinary or extraordinary; (b) any "adjustments" to correct past overstatements; (c) all reductions resulting from extraordinary transactions not involving shares; (d) all cash or property dividends representing distributions of earned surplus to shareholders; (e) all transfers of earned surplus to stated capital or capital surplus, whether by way of share distributions or resolution of the board of directors; and (f) all expenses of the corporation's reacquiring its own shares not properly attributable to reductions in stated capital or capital surplus.

All or part of the earned surplus may be transferred by the board of directors at any time to capital surplus or to stated capital.

Unearned surplus means the surplus other than earned surplus, and includes the following:

(a) Paid-in surplus—amounts contributed for or assigned to shares in excess of the stated capital

Thus, from the basic accounting equation:

Assets = Liabilities + Stated Capital and Surplus

the following equations can be derived:

Assets − Liabilities = Stated Capital and Surplus

Assets − Liabilities = Net Assets

Net Assets = Stated Capital and Surplus

Stated Capital and Surplus (or Net Assets) − Stated Capital = Surplus

Assets − Liabilities − Stated Capital = Surplus

Surplus = Earned Surplus + Unearned Surplus (or Capital Surplus)

Unearned Surplus (or Capital Surplus) = Surplus − Earned Surplus

Besides assets, liabilities, and stated capital and surplus (in one of which every account is reflected), two other concepts are relevant: income and expense. Income is the gain of the corporation from its operations, and is a positive surplus account (credit); the expenses are the costs of the corporation in connection therewith, and are a negative surplus account (debit). If assets are thought of as "unrecovered costs", the

applicable thereto, whether upon original issue of shares, lawful reduction of stated capital (sometimes called "reduction surplus"), or transactions by the corporation in its own shares;

(b) Revaluation surplus—surplus arising from a revaluation of assets above cost, usually in connection with a recapitalization (sometimes called "recapitalization surplus") or quasi-reorganization (sometimes called "reorganization surplus");

(c) Donated surplus—contributions other than for shares, whether from shareholders or others.

The terms "surplus", "capital surplus", "earned surplus", etc., in accounting procedures, are tending to be replaced by designations which emphasize the distinction between (a) legal capital, (b) capital in excess of legal capital, and (c) undivided profits. "Earned surplus", for example, is being replaced by such terms as "retained income", "retained earnings", "accumulated earnings", "earnings retained for use in the business", "accumulated capital", "undivided profits", etc.

7. ABA–ALI Model Bus.Corp.Act § 2(i).

reason for recording both assets and expenses as debits is clear. In terms of the five concepts, the basic accounting condition can be graphically displayed as: [8]

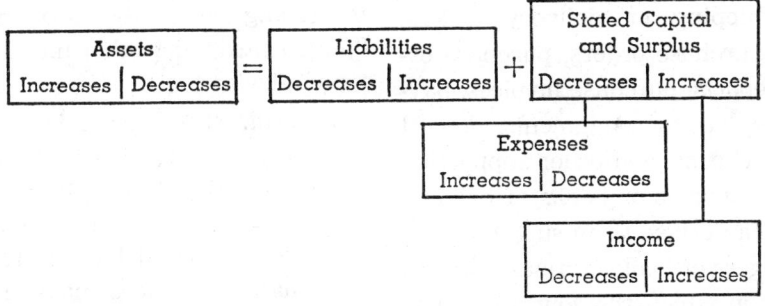

and summarized in terms of debits and credits as follows: [9]

DEBIT		CREDIT
Increase	Asset	Decrease
Decrease	Liability	Increase
Decrease	Stated Capital and Surplus	Increase
Decrease	Income	Increase
Increase	Expense	Decrease

Thus, assets and expenses are debits, and equal liabilities, income and stated capital and surplus, which are credits.

The income and expense accounts are temporary accounts in the ledger and provide data for the income statement. At the end of the accounting period, they are closed, and the net amount is transferred, by way of a profit and loss summary account, to earned surplus.

The term "working capital" has nothing to do with "capital" (or "stated capital"). "Working capital" is the excess of current assets over current liabilities, and is sometimes called "net current assets". "Quick assets" are cash and net receivables. The so-called "current position" or "current ratio" is the quotient resulting from dividing current assets by current liabilities. "Net quick assets" is the remainder resulting from subtracting inventories and current liabilities from current assets. Where there is no working capital, and current liabilities exceed current assets, the corporation would be unable to meet its debts as they mature and would be "insolvent" in the equity sense.

The term "insolvency" has two meanings: (a) inability of the corporation to pay its debts as they become due in the usual course of business—so-called "equity sense", and (b) excess of liabilities over assets—so-called "bankruptcy sense".[10] Thus, a corporation, loosely speaking, can be said to be "insolvent" in the equity sense when it is without working capital; "insolvent" in the bankruptcy sense when its stated capital is more than fully impaired.

As indicated, modern corporation statutes define the more important accounting terms used therein.[11]

8. B. Ferst & S. Ferst, Basic Accounting for Lawyers 16 (ALI 2d ed. 1965).

9. Ibid.

10. See Federal Bankruptcy Act § 1(19), 11 U.S.C.A. § 1(19).

11. ABA–ALI Model Bus.Corp.Act § 2; Kreidmann, "Dividends—Changing Patterns", 57 Colum.L.Rev. 372, 384–385 (1957). See also Garrett, "Capital and Surplus Under the New Corporation Statutes", 23 Law & Contemp.Prob. 239 (1958); Ballantine & Hills, "Corporate Capital and Restrictions Upon Dividends Under Modern Corporation Laws," 23 Calif.L.Rev. 229 (1935); Weiner, "Theory of Anglo-American Dividend Law: American Statutes and Cases", 29 Colum.L.Rev. 461 (1929). See also Basye, "Recent Amendments to Certain Financial

Financial Records

Financial records and books of account include (a) business papers, such as customers' orders, shipping or delivery orders, sales invoices, purchase orders, purchase orders received reports, purchase invoices, payrolls, cash receipt acknowledgments, deposit slips, vouchers, checks, and other supporting evidences; (b) journals or books of original entry of the data derived from such business papers; (c) ledgers or books of final entry, to the "accounts" in which the journal entries are "posted" (*i.e.*, transferred and classified); and (d) financial statements, reports, and analyses—the basic goal of accounting—based on the data in the general ledger derived through "worksheets" (or working papers) and "trial balances" which are abstracts of the general ledger.[12]

Books of Account

The two principal books of account are (a) the journal, and (b) the ledger. To an increasing extent, they are being replaced by "punch card" and other mechanical and electronic devices.

Journal. The journal is the book of original entry in which is chronologically recorded (*jour* = day) an analysis of a transaction in terms of increases and decreases of individual accounts, by "debits" and "credits" as the case may be. There may be a single journal, but where the volume of transactions is large, a general journal and specialized journals (e. g., cash receipts, cash disbursements, sales, purchases, voucher register, etc.) are common.

The journal entry for the $100 cash dividend (assuming simultaneous declaration and payment) would be as follows:

	Debit	Credit
[Date] Surplus, Dr. Cash, Cr. (Declaration and payment of dividend)	$ 100	$ 100

◆

Ledger. The ledger is the book containing the individual accounts on a classified basis where all changes therein are recorded, by "posting" from the journal. There may be only a general ledger, but a general (controlling) ledger and one or more subsidiary ledgers for such accounts as trade receivables, inventories, machinery and equipment, accounts payable, capital stock (sometimes called the "stock ledger" or "record of shareholders"), etc., are frequently used.

Provision of the Oregon Business Corporation Act", 47 Ore.L.Rev. 320 (1968); Hauptman, "Corporate Dividend Accounting under the New York Business Corporation Law", 34 Brooklyn L.Rev. 34 (1967); Kummert, "Financial Provisions of the New Washington Business Corporation Act", 43 Wash.L.Rev. 337 (1967); Hackney, "The Financial Provisions of the Model Business Corporation Act", 70 Harv.L. Rev. 1357 (1957); Mulford, "Corporate Distributions to Shareholders and Other Amendments to the Pennsylvania Corporation Law", 106 U.Pa.L.Rev. 536 (1958). See note 6 supra.

12. Statutes often require corporations to keep correct books of account. E. g., ABA–ALI Model Bus.

Corp.Act § 46. Modern statutes expressly permit corporate books and records to be kept in written form or in any other form capable of being converted into written form within a reasonable time.

Transport Indemnity Co. v. Seib, 178 Neb. 253, 132 N. W.2d 871, 11 A.L.R.3d 1368 (1965) (electronic computer tape business records); Annot., 11 A.L.R.3d 1377 (1967); Symposium: "Legal and Evidentiary Problems Arising Out of the Use of Computers and Electronic Data Processing Equipment", 17 Bus. Law. 94 (1961). Shareholders and possibly others enjoy common-law and statutory inspection rights. See section 199 supra.

The accounts in the ledger are used to prepare the financial statements.

The ledger accounts would reflect the $100 cash dividend as follows:

Cash

[Date]

	Debit	Credit	Balance
	$ 500	$	$ 500
		100	400

Surplus

[Date]

	Debit	Credit	Balance
	100		100
	$	$ 200	$ 200

———◆———

Financial Statements

The two principal financial statements are (a) the balance sheet, and (b) the income statement, with the latter often containing a surplus statement ("income and surplus statement"), or being supplemented by separate (c) "surplus statement", and (d) cash flow statement.[13]

13. See Accounting Research and Terminology Bulletins 15 (A.I.C.P.A. final ed. 1961); I. Kellogg, How to Use Financial Statements: A Handbook for Lawyers (1969); Arthur Andersen and Company, Auditors' Reports (2d ed. 1969); How To Read a Financial Report (Merrill Lynch, Pierce, Fenner & Smith, Inc. rev. 1968); L. Foster, Understanding Financial Statements and Corporate Annual Reports (rev. ed. 1968); R. Kennedy, Financial Statements: Form, Analysis, and Interpretation (4th ed. 1962); Scott Paper Company 1961 Annual Report (stud. ed. 1962); C. Stabler, How to Read the Financial News (9th ed. 1959); Wise, "How to Read a Balance Sheet", 18 J. Am. Soc'y C.L.U. 77 (1964). Affiliated corporations often prepare consolidated financial statements, eliminating intercompany items, to show the overall picture; they do not necessarily reflect the finances or dividend-paying ability of any of the affiliated corporations. Gormley, "The Pooling of Interests Principle of Accounting —A Lawyer's View", 23 Bus.Law. 407 (1968); Halvorson, "Accounting Aspects of Conglomerate Reporting", 23 Bus.Law. 549 (1968); Sommer, "Conglomerate Financial Reporting", 23 Bus.Law. 521 (1968); Sommer, "Conglomerate Disclosure: Friend or Foe?", 22 Bus.Law. 317 (1967); Hackney, "Financial Accounting for Parents and Subsidiaries, A New Approach to Consolidated Statements", 25 U. Pitt.L.Rev. 8 (1963). See also R. Mautz, Financial

Balance Sheet. The balance sheet (sometimes called statement of financial condition, statement of assets and liabilities, statement of worth, statement of financial position, etc.) is a statement of the position of the business in terms of the formula: Assets = Liabilities + Stated Capital and Surplus, as of a particular time, usually the end of an accounting period. As such, it is a look between successive income statements. It is a statement of facts largely historical in character and based on cost. Traditionally in the United States,[14] the assets are listed on the left (debit) side; the liabilities are listed on the right (credit) side, followed by the stated capital + earned surplus (or deficit) + any unearned surplus.

Reporting by Diversified Companies (1968). Corporate statutes sometimes entitle qualified shareholders, upon written request, to an annual balance sheet and profit and loss statement for the preceding fiscal year, and, if any interim balance sheet or profit and loss statement has been distributed to shareholders or otherwise made available to the public, the most recent such interim balance sheet or profit and loss statement. Federal statutes and securities exchange rules also require disclosure of financial data.

14. In England, assets are listed on the right (credit) side; liabilities and proprietorship (share capital) on the left (debit) side. L. Gower, The Principles of Modern Company Law 420 (2d ed. 1957).

The interrelationship of the financial statements—to one another and to the ac- counting period—has been shown graphical- ly as follows: [15]

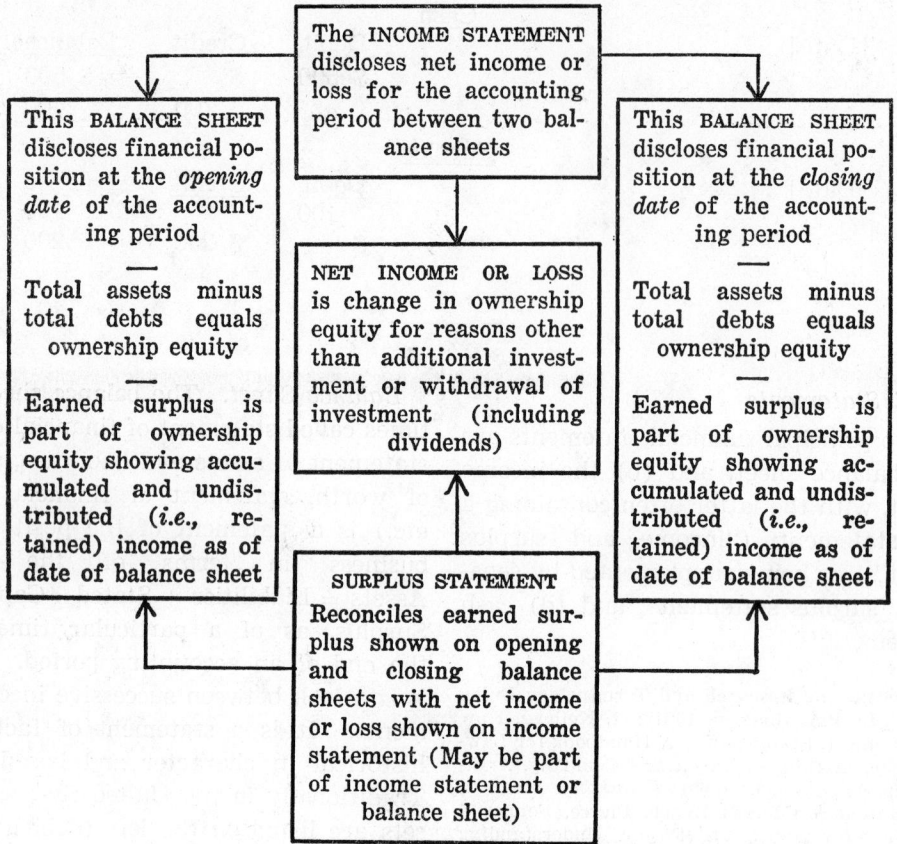

15. deCapriles, "Modern Financial Accounting", 38 N.Y.U.L.Rev. 1, 49 (1963).

The following is a simple, conventional form of balance sheet, dated as of the end of the accounting period:

[Corporate Name]

Balance Sheet—[Date]

Assets

Current Assets $

     Cash

     U.S. Bonds

     Marketable Securities
         (at cost)

     Accounts Receivable
         (less estimated losses in collection)

     Inventories (at lower of cost or market)

Fixed Assets

     Land

     Buildings (less accumulated
         depreciation)

     Equipment (less accumulated
         depreciation)

Prepaid Expenses and Deferred Charges

Good Will

            Total Assets $_____

Liabilities and Stated Capital and Surplus

Current Liabilities $

     Accounts Payable

     Notes Payable

     Accrued Taxes

Fixed Liabilities

     Mortgage Bonds

     Debentures

Stated Capital and Surplus

     Stated Capital

         5% Cumulative Preferred
            Shares ($100 par value)

         Common Shares ($10 par value)

     Unearned Surplus

     Earned Surplus

       Total Liabilities and $_____
          Stated Capital and
          Surplus

———◆———

The balance sheet lists assets and liabilities in decreasing order of liquidity. An asset represents an expenditure for an asset whose useful life is greater than one year or the accounting period, which expenditure is therefore said to be a "capital outlay" and to be "capitalized".

Current assets include cash, bank deposits, temporary investments, amounts due from trade creditors and others, inventories of merchandise or raw materials, goods in process of manufacture and finished goods, and current prepayments.

Fixed assets include land and land improvements, buildings and other structures, machinery and equipment, and good will.

Current liabilities include amounts owing for purchases of merchandise or raw materials, services, wages, interest, and taxes.

Fixed liabilities include bonds, debentures, and other long-term financial obligations whose maturities vary over periods in excess of one year.

Stated Capital and Surplus, as previously mentioned, include stated capital, capital (or unearned) surplus, and earned surplus.

Inventories are carried under one of several methods, e.g., First-in, first-out (FIFO), Last-in, first-out (LIFO), Simple average, Weighted average. Such entries can be at Market or at Cost or at Lower of Cost or Market ("cost or market, whichever is lower"), the last being the more conservative and widely prevalent.[16] The other asset

figures usually represent cost to the present owner, with deductions for estimated bad debts and depreciation,[17] and also repre-

"LIFO Cost or Market—Sound Accounting Principle or Tax Device?", 12 Nat'l Tax J. 367 (1959).

17. Land, generally, is not depreciable, but buildings and equipment are. "Depreciation" is the cost of the utilization of the service capacity of a fixed asset. It is a method for allocating cost and not for measuring decline in value.

There are several methods of depreciation accounting:

(a) Straight-line method (involving equal depreciation charges over the life of the asset);

(b) Accelerating (or declining-rate) methods:
    (a) Declining-balance method;
    (b) Sum-of-the-years-digits method;

(c) Usage methods:
    (1) Unit-of-production method;
    (2) Operating-day method;
    (3) Observed-usage method.

Under the straight-line method, the estimated net retirement loss (original cost to present owner less estimated scrap or salvage value) is spread by equal periodic debits (charges) to operating expenses over the estimated service life.

The accelerating methods recognize that depreciation is only one of the periodic expenses of using an asset, and assume that smaller depreciation charges in later years are balanced by greater maintenance expenses.

The declining-balance method assumes that an asset depreciates by a fixed percentage of the previous year's undepreciated balance. The charges become progressively smaller, leaving a small amount eventually to be written off arbitrarily. The so-called double declining balance (DDB) fixes such percentage at double the straight-line method rate.

Under the sum-of-the-years-digits method, the original cost of the asset is multiplied by a fraction whose numerator is the years of remaining life and whose denominator is the sum of the numbers representing the years of life of the property. If an asset has a five-year life, the first year's charge would be $5/15$, 5 being the number of remaining years, and 15 being the sum of 1/2/3/4/5. For the second year the charge would be $4/15$, etc.

The unit-of-production method provides equal depreciation per unit of work done by the machine, irrespective of time. For the operating-day method, days of operation are substituted for production units. The observed-usage method bases depreciation on observation.

A variation of straight-line depreciation is the sinking-fund reserve method, under which equal charges are made to operating expenses each accounting period in such amount that their accumulation at a specified rate of compound interest will equal the estimated net retirement loss.

Depreciation entries are debited (charged) as an expense and credited to the asset account of the property involved, usually a negative asset account called "accrued depreciation", which represents the

16. Inventory includes finished goods, work in progress, raw materials and supplies. Underlying FIFO is the assumption that the earliest goods acquired or produced are the first to be sold. Under the converse assumption of LIFO, the most recently incurred inventory costs are properly chargeable against revenues of the accounting period. For an excellent graphic description, see deCapriles, "Modern Financial Accounting", 37 N.Y.U.L.Rev. 1001, 1065 (1962). Obviously, the inventory accounting method employed can substantially affect tax liability and net income for the accounting period cleared at the end of such period to earned surplus. See R. Hoffman, Inventories: A Guide to Their Control, Costing, and Effect Upon Income and Taxes (1962); Accounting Research and Terminology Bulletins 27 (A.I.C.P.A. final ed. 1961); Hoffman, "Inventories", 48 Marq.L.Rev. 191 (1964); Summa, "Inventory Valuation Problems, Including Consideration of Related Tax and Accounting Treatment", N.Y.U. 21st Inst. on Fed.Tax. 1183 (1963); Barron,

sent good will (if more than nominal). Good will may involve substantial values (e. g., well-known trademarks or names), but is difficult to measure, and accounting practices vary. Some corporations list it at a nominal figure (say, $1) or not at all.

The term "reserve" has several meanings in accounting:

(a) The negative side of an asset account, such as "Reserve for Depreciation" and "Reserve for Bad Debts", preferably called, respectively, "Allowance for Depreciation" or "Less Accrued Depreciation" and "Allowance for Bad Debts" or "Less Estimated Losses in Collection";

(b) A liability account where the amount is estimated, such as "Reserve for Federal Income Taxes", preferably called "Estimated Federal Income Taxes";

portion of original cost charged to the revenues of past accounting periods. Obviously, the depreciation accounting method employed, especially if accelerated, can substantially affect tax liability and net income for the accounting period cleared at the end of such period to earned surplus.

Differences between the initial cost and higher replacement cost present problems not solved by any of the foregoing depreciation methods.

"Depletion" refers to the allocation of cost of "wasting assets" such as oil wells, mines, etc. "Amortization" measures the cost for the accounting period of such items as patents, copyrights, and improvements to leased property or the decline in value resulting solely from time rather than from wear and tear, and is applicable to prepaid expenses and deferred charges.

See W. Hogan, Depreciation Policies and Resultant Problems (1967).

(c) A surplus account, representing a portion usually of Earned Surplus, transferred to the reserve account, "reserved" or "restricted" for some purpose, usually to make such "reserved" or "restricted" earned surplus unavailable for dividends.

While the balance sheet shows the book surplus (or deficit), there is no necessary correlation between the balance sheet figures, which are based on costs and estimates, and current value, either on a going concern or liquidation basis. For the same reason, the "book value" of shares rarely reflects the value of shares.

Balance sheets often include comparative data as of the end of prior accounting periods.

Affiliated corporations often prepare consolidated financial statements, eliminating intercorporate items, to show the overall financial position and income of the group as an economic unit. Although consolidated statements do not necessarily reflect the finances or dividend-paying ability of any of the affiliated corporations, they do disclose in the parent corporation's financial statements the subsidiaries' assets, liabilities, and stated capital and surplus (instead of the amounts which the parent invested in the subsidiaries) and net income of the subsidiaries (instead of the portion thereof received by the parent in the form of dividends).

Very modern balance sheets sometimes look as follows:

[Corporate Name]

Consolidated Balance Sheet—[Date]

	[End of Accounting Period]	[End of Prior Accounting Period]
Current Assets:		
Cash	$	$
U. S. Bonds		
Marketable Securities at Cost (lower than market)		
Accounts Receivable (less estimated losses in collection)		
Inventories (at lower of cost or market)		
Total Current Assets	$	$
Current Liabilities:		
Accounts Payable	$	$
Notes Payable		
Taxes Payable		
Total Current Liabilities	$	$
Working Capital	$	$
Prepaid Expenses and Deferred Charges ..		
Land, Buildings, and Equipment (less Accrued Depreciation of $)........		
Goodwill		
	$	$
Mortgage Bonds	$	$
Debentures	$	$
Shareowners' Investment:		
5% Cumulative Preferred hSares ($100 par value)	$	$
Common Shares ($10 par value)		
Paid-in Capital in Excess of Par Value		
Accumulated Retained Earnings		
Total Shareowners' Equity	$	$

———◆———

Income Statement. The income statement (sometimes called profit and loss statement, income account, statement of operations, earnings statement, statement of income and expenses, etc.) shows the principal elements in the derivation of income or loss for the accounting period, rather than as of the date of the end of the accounting period like the balance sheet. In brief, it shows the income less the expenses, in effect, the net income or loss from the business operations during such period, per the books of account, often integrated with or supplemented by a surplus statement. As a measure of performance it is more important than the balance sheet.

The following is a simple, conventional form of income and earned surplus statement:

[Corporate Name]

Income Statement [Dates of Beginning and End of Accounting Period]

NET SALES		$
Cost of Sales and Other Operating Expenses		
Cost of Goods Sold	$	
Selling, Administrative and General Expenses		
Depreciation		
Maintenance and Repairs		
Taxes (Other Than Federal Income Taxes)	———	———
PROFIT FROM OPERATIONS		$
Other Income:		
Interest from U. S. Bonds	$	
Other Interest	———	
TOTAL INCOME		$
Less: Interest Charges:		
Interest on Mortgage Bonds	$	
Interest on Debentures		
Interest on Notes	———	———
Income Before Provision for Federal Income Taxes		$
Provision for Federal Income Taxes		———
NET INCOME FOR YEAR		$
Less: Dividends Paid		
On Preferred Shares ($ per share)	$	
On Common Shares ($ per share)		
Provision for Contingencies	———	———
Balance Carried to Earned Surplus		$
Earned Surplus—[Date of Beginning of Accounting Period]		———
EARNED SURPLUS—[Date of End of Accounting Period]		$———

———◆———

As of the end of the accounting period, the net income or loss is closed out and cleared to the earned surplus (or deficit) account of the balance sheet as of such date.

The income statement, like the balance sheet, often gives comparative data for prior accounting periods, and, in the case of affiliated corporations, may be on a consolidated basis.

Very modern income statements sometimes look as follows:

[Name of Corporation] and Consolidated Subsidiaries
Income Statement [Accounting Period]

	[Accounting Period]	[Prior Accounting Period]
Net Sales	$	$
Cost of Goods Sold		
Depreciation and Maintenance		
Selling and Administrative Expenses ..		
Taxes (Other than Federal Income Taxes)		
Operating Income	$	$
Non-operating Income		
Total Income	$	$
Interest		
Provision for Federal Income Taxes ...		
Net Income	$	$
Earned per Common Share	$	$
Dividends on 5% Cumulative Preferred Shares—$5 per Share	$	$
Dividends on Common Shares—$——— per Share	$	$
Balance Carried to Earned Surplus	$	$
Earned Surplus at Beginning of Period		
Earned Surplus at End of Period	$	$

Surplus Statement. The surplus statement reconciles the earned surplus shown in the balance sheets for the current and preceding accounting periods with the net income or loss for the accounting period as shown in the income statement. It (a) shows the earned surplus at the beginning of the accounting period; (b) adds the net income or loss for the period; (c) subtracts any dividends paid during the period, and (d) states the earned surplus at the end of the period.

Supplementary Information. Financial statements are sometimes accompanied by supplementary information showing the effects of changes in the value of the dollar due to inflation or deflation.

Independent Auditor's Report

The independent auditor's report,[18] by a certified public accountant or public ac-

18. Goldberg, "A Guide for Lawyers: How To Read CPA's Certificate and Report", 43 A.B.A.J. 227, 230 (1957). See also Ready, "The Auditor's Protection Against Liability Based on Client's Fraud", 16 Bus. Law. 1039 (1961); Wise, "The Auditors Have Arrived", 62 Fortune, No. 6, 144 (Dec.1960); Annot., 76 A.L.R.2d 1322 (1961). The New York Stock Exchange requires listed companies to notify it of any change of auditors. N.Y.S.E. Company Manual § A6. Accountants are potentially liable not only to their clients but also to others who may foreseeably rely on their reports. Escott v. BarChris Construction Corp., 283 F.Supp. 643, 2 A.L.R.Fed. 86 (S.D.N.Y. 1968); Rusch Factors, Inc. v. Levin, 284 F.Supp. 85 (D.R.I. 1968). But cf. Ultramares v. Touche & Co., 255 N.Y. 170, 174 N.E. 441, 74 A.L.R. 1139 (1931); Soloman, "Ultramares Revisited: A Modern Study of Accountants' Liability to the Public", 18 DePaul L.Rev. 56 (1968); Trueblood, "An Accountant Considers His Profession", 23 Bus.Law. 621 (1968);

countant or an accounting firm, states (a) the *scope* of the audit—whether the examination of the financial records, etc., has been made in accordance with generally accepted auditing standards; (b) the *conformity* of the financial statements—whether, in his or their opinion, the financial statements are presented in conformity with generally accepted principles of accounting; (c) the *consistency* of the financial statements—whether, in his or their opinion, such principles have been consistently applied in the preparation of the financial statements of the current accounting period in relation to those of the preceding period; and (d) his or their opinion on the fairness with which the financial statements present the financial position and results of operations.

Such opinion may be (a) Unqualified, with or without explanation; (b) Qualified, with or without explanation; or (c) Adverse (to the effect that the financial statements "do not" present fairly the financial position and results of operations); or may involve a (d) Disclaimer of opinion (to the effect that there was not available sufficient evidential matter upon which to base an opinion).

The most reliable is the unqualified report, certificate, or opinion, which reads substantially as follows:

We have examined the consolidated balance sheet of [Name of Corporation], as

of [Date of End of Current Accounting Period] and the related statement of consolidated income and earned surplus for the year then ended. Our examination was made in accordance with generally accepted auditing standards, and accordingly included such tests of the accounting records and such other auditing procedures as we considered necessary in the circumstances.

In our opinion, the accompanying consolidated balance sheet and statement of consolidated income and earned surplus present fairly the financial position of [Name of Corporation], at [Date of End of Current Accounting Period] and the results of its operations for the year then ended, in conformity with generally accepted accounting principles applied on a basis consistent with that of the preceding year.

[Date of Report]

> [Name of Certified Public Accountant, Public Accountant, or Firm]

Reliance by Directors and Officers on Financial Records

Modern statutes often permit directors and officers to rely in good faith upon financial records of the corporation, providing that under such circumstances the director shall not be liable for voting for or assenting to various corporate matters, including dividends.[19]

Katsoris, "Accountants' Third Party Liability—How Far Do We Go?", 36 Fordham L.Rev. 191 (1967); Hanson, "Responsibilities of Independent Public Accountants", 22 Bus.Law. 975 (1967); Comment, "Accountants' Liabilities to Third Parties Under Common Law and Federal Securities Law", 9 B.C.Ind. & Com. L.Rev. 137 (1967); Note, "Accountants' Liabilities for False and Misleading Financial Statements", 67 Colum.L.Rev. 1437 (1967). Some jurisdictions recognize an accountant-client privilege. Weck v. District Court, 158 Colo. 521, 408 P.2d 987 (1965); cf. Pattie Lea, Inc. v. District Court, 161 Colo. 493, 423 P.2d 27 (1967) (refusing to apply privilege in shareholder derivative action); Legis., 66 Mich.L.Rev. 1264 (1968). See Louis, "The Accountants Are Changing the Rules", 77 Fortune, No. 7, 177 (June 15, 1968).

19. ABA–ALI Model Bus.Corp.Act § 43 (expressly protecting director who in good faith in connection with dividends and other distributions considered assets to be of book value); Del.Gen.Corp. Law, §§ 172, 141(e) (1967) (expressly protecting director who in good faith relied on records and statements as to value and amount of assets, liabilities and/or net profits, etc., as to dividends, redemptions, and purchases); McKinney's N.Y.Bus.Corp.Law, § 717 (directors and officers, when acting in good faith, may rely upon financial statements, as "correct" or fairly reflecting "financial condition" of corporation). Gallagher v. New York Dock Co., 93 N.Y.L.J. No. 137, 3045 (Sup.Ct.1935).

B. FUNDS LEGALLY AVAILABLE FOR DIVIDENDS

STATUTORY LIMITATIONS ON SOURCES OF DIVIDENDS

320. Dividends are payable only from funds legally available for such purposes under the law of the jurisdiction of incorporation, subject to possible additional limitations. Distribution of dividends which would render the corporation insolvent is probably wrongful in most jurisdictions even apart from statutes expressing such limitation, on principles of the law of creditors' rights. Statutes sometimes differentiate between (a) "dividends" and (b) "distributions from capital surplus", or between (a) cash and property dividends, and (b) share dividends. Various different statutory formulations define the funds legally available for dividends, or at least for cash or property dividends, in terms of (a) Earned surplus, (b) Net profits or net earnings, (c) Surplus, (d) Nonimpairment of capital, or (e) Insolvency, or some combination thereof. Treatment of unrealized appreciation and depreciation, goodwill, so-called "wasting assets" corporations, and affiliated corporations varies in different jurisdictions.

Dividends are payable only from funds which are legally available for such purpose.[1] Most jurisdictions, influenced by the principle that the rights of creditors and shareholders alike must be protected, have limited the source of dividends to prescribed funds.

In all cases, of course, the limitations imposed by the law of the jurisdiction of incorporation cannot be exceeded. However, there might be additional limitations, imposed possibly by the laws of another jurisdiction in which the corporation is doing business, applicable federal law, administrative regulations,[2] the articles of incorporation, securities exchange rules, indentures, loan agreements, etc.[3]

Distribution of dividends which would render the corporation insolvent is probably wrongful in most jurisdictions, even apart from statutes expressing such limitation [4] on principles of the law of creditors' rights.[5] Even where statutes prescribe such limitation, additional statutory limitations usually exist.[6] As a practical matter, for cash dividends the corporation needs sufficient cash

---

1. Analogous limitations define the funds legally available to a corporation for the purchase or redemption of its own shares. See section 336 infra. The funds legally available for share dividends will be discussed more fully later. See section 329 infra.

2. See section 321 infra.

3. See section 322 infra.

4. E. g., ABA–ALI Model Bus.Corp.Act § 40. Such statutes do not always define the type of insolvency which they contemplate. See section 319, n. 10 supra. However, the Model Business Corporation Act defines "insolvent" as the "inability of a corporation to pay its debts as they become due in the usual course of its business". §§ 2(n), 40, 41. The New York statute uses better grammar in defining "insolvent" as "being unable to pay debts as they become due in the usual course of the debtor's business."

McKinney's N.Y.Bus.Corp.Law, § 102(a) (8). The California statute is also explicit, providing that a stock corporation shall not declare dividends payable in cash or property when there is reasonable ground for believing that thereupon the corporation's debts and liabilities would exceed its assets, or that it would be unable to meet its debts and liabilities as they mature. Cal.Gen.Corp.Law, § 1501 (1947). The North Carolina statute prohibits payment of a cash or property dividend if (a) there is reasonable ground for believing that the corporation would be unable to meet its obligations as they become due in the ordinary course of business, or (b) the liabilities of the corporation would exceed the fair present value of its assets, or (c) the highest aggregate liquidation preferences of shares entitled to such preference over the shares receiving the dividend would exceed the corporation's net assets. N.C.Bus.Corp.Act § 55–50(c) (1957).

5. E. g., Uniform Fraudulent Conveyance Act, 9B U. L.A. 70 (1966) (approved in 1918, adopted in Arizona, California, Delaware, Maryland, Massachusetts, Michigan, Minnesota, Montana, Nevada, New Hampshire, New Jersey, New Mexico, New York, North Dakota, Ohio, Oklahoma, Pennsylvania, South Dakota, Tennessee, Utah, Washington, Wisconsin, Wyoming, and the Virgin Islands). See also Federal Bankruptcy Act §§ 60, 67, 70, 11 U.S.C.A. §§ 96, 107, 110.

6. E. g., ABA–ALI Model Bus.Corp.Act § 40. The "insolvency" limitation is primarily to protect creditors; the other limitations to protect shareholders.

to pay them, so that its working capital is a relevant factor.[7]

Some more modern statutes expressly differentiate between "dividends" and "distributions from capital surplus" or "distributions in partial liquidation".[8] Some statutes differentiate between (a) cash and property dividends, and (b) share dividends,[9] but other statutes do not.[10] Various different statutory formulations define the funds legally available for dividends, or at least for cash and property dividends, in terms of: (a) Earned surplus; (b) Net profits or net earnings; (c) Surplus; (d) Nonimpairment of capital; or (e) Insolvency; or some combination thereof.[11]

Earned Surplus

Earned surplus, at least if unreserved and unrestricted, is available for dividends in all American jurisdictions, either by statute or decisional law. Earned surplus, in effect, consists of the undistributed net profits earned by the corporation since its formation or quasi-reorganization. Some statutes permit dividends only out of earned surplus;[12] but most statutes are less restrictive.

Net Profits or Net Earnings

Some statutes permit dividends out of "profits", "net profits", or "net earnings" without further definition.[13] Some cases equate such terms to "earned surplus";[14] other cases construe the terms literally and uphold dividends out of profits for the current year notwithstanding a previous deficit or capital impairment.[15]

---

7. The corporation might borrow cash to make lawful dividends, being careful to avoid insolvency in either bankruptcy or equity senses. Cf. West v. Hotel Pennsylvania, 148 Pa.Super. 373, 25 A.2d 593 (1942).

8. E. g., ABA–ALI Model Bus.Corp.Act § 40; Cal. Gen.Corp.Law, §§ 1500–1507 (1947); N.C.Bus.Corp. Act §§ 55–50, 55–51 (1957).

9. ABA–ALI Model Bus.Corp.Act §§ 40, 41; McKinney's N.Y.Bus.Corp.Law, §§ 510, 511; N.C.Bus. Corp.Act § 55–50 (1957).

10. E. g., Del.Gen.Corp.Law, § 173 (1967).

11. See generally D. Kehl, Corporate Dividends; Legal and Accounting Problems Pertaining to Corporate Distributions (1941); G. Hills, The Law of Accounting and Financial Statements 136–165 (1957); Hauptman, "Corporate Dividend Accounting Under the New York Business Corporation Law", 34 Brooklyn L.Rev. 34 (1967); Kummert, "The Financial Provisions of the New Washington Business Corporation Act: Part III", 43 Wash.L.Rev. 337 (1967); Williams, "Sources of Corporate Distributions", 17 Ark.L.Rev. 373 (1964); Hackney, "Financial Accounting for Parents and Subsidiaries—A New Approach to Consolidated Statements", 25 U. Pitt.L.Rev. 9 (1963); Knowlton, "Corporate Finance: Chapter 1.5, Part II: Dividends, Distributions and Corporate Accounting", 15 S.C.L.Rev. 370 (1963); Theobald, "The Distribution of Income in an Automated World", 40 U.Det.L.J. 473 (1963); Weisskopf, "Reform of Company Law and the Ethics of Distribution", id. at 490; Zeff, "Legal Dividend Sources—A National Survey and Critique", 31 N.Y.Cert.Pub.Acc't 741, 802 (1961); Buttiner, "Dividends and the Law", 34 Accounting Rev. 438 (1961); Kreidmann, "Dividends—Changing Patterns", 57 Colum.L.Rev. 372 (1957); Hackney, "The Financial Provisions of the Model Business Corporation Act", 70 Harv.L.Rev. 1357 (1957); Harris, "The Model Business Corporation Act: Invitation to Irresponsibility?", 50 Nw.U.L.Rev. 1 (1955); Seward, "Sources

of Distributions to Stockholders", 5 Baylor L. Rev. 242 (1953); Comment, "Corporate Distributions and the South Dakota Business Corporations Act", 12 S.D.L.Rev. 12 (1967); Comment, "Corporate Dividends in New Mexico", 5 Nat'l Res.J. 149 (1965); Note, "Common Stock Dividends in Iowa", 46 Iowa L.Rev. 582 (1961). See section 329 infra.

12. E. g., ABA–ALI Model Bus.Corp.Act § 40(a) (cash or property "dividends" out of unreserved and unrestricted earned surplus); § 41 ("distributions from capital surplus" or "distributions in partial liquidation"). After a quasi-reorganization by charging any deficit off to capital surplus, subsequent earnings become earned surplus available for dividends. See ABA–ALI Model Bus.Corp.Act §§ 2(1), 64; McKinney's N.Y.Bus.Corp.Law, § 517.

13. E. g., former N.J.Gen.Corp.Law, § 14:8–19 (1937) (surplus or net profits).

14. E. g., Lich v. United States Rubber Co., 39 F. Supp. 675 (D.N.J.1941), aff'd per curiam 123 F.2d 145 (3d Cir. 1941); Dohme v. Pacific Coast Co., 5 N.J.Super. 477, 68 A.2d 490 (1949) (both under former New Jersey statute). See Hamilton Mfg. Co. v. United States, 214 F.2d 644 (7th Cir. 1954) (construing "net profits" under Wisconsin statute, for purposes of federal accumulated earnings surtax, as earned surplus).

15. Goodnow v. American Writing Paper Co., 73 N. J.Eq. 692, 69 A. 1014 (1908) (holding that, while two funds existed for payment of dividends, "net profits" could be either annual profits, that is, gross earnings less operating expenses of the current year, or net profits upon whole of corporation's business from its organization, that is, excess of

Other statutes using "profits" or "net profits" terminology are more explicit. For example, the California statute permits cash or property dividends only out of (a) earned surplus, or (b) net profits earned during the preceding six-month-one year accounting period despite the fact that the net assets are less than the stated capital, providing that if the value of the net assets amounts to less than the stated capital attributed to shares having liquidation preferences no dividends shall be declared out of net profits *except upon such shares* until the stated capital ceases to be impaired.[16]

Delaware allows a corporation to declare and pay dividends (a) out of surplus, or (b) in case there shall be no such surplus, out of its net profits for the current or preceding fiscal year, but not if the stated capital represented by *any shares* having a liquidation preference is or would become impaired.[17]

North Carolina permits cash or property dividends out of (a) earned surplus, or (b) net profits earned during the current or preceding accounting period, regardless of any impairment of stated capital, etc.[18]

A provision allowing dividends out of net profits when stated capital is impaired is known as the "nimble dividend" rule.[19]

In "net profits" jurisdictions without the "nimble dividend" rule, the cautious practice where there is a deficit is to effect a reduction of stated capital by the required formal procedure,[20] and apply the resulting capital reduction surplus to eliminate the deficit.[21]

Surplus

Some jurisdictions permit dividends out of any kind of surplus, earned or unearned, without further limitation.[22] Even New York, in effect, did prior to 1963 while its principal statutory dividend provision read primarily in terms of nonimpairment of stated capital.[23] Several other jurisdictions ex-

fiscal year in Delaware; current or preceding accounting period in North Carolina; current fiscal year and next preceding fiscal year taken as a single period under the Model Business Corporation Act—without any reference to whether or not such declaration occurs "before such net profits are closed to the surplus account, i. e., charged against the accumulated deficit", as contended in Kreidmann, "Dividends—Changing Patterns", 57 Colum.L.Rev. 372, 374 (1957); Note, "Corporations: Consideration of 'Nimble Dividend' Statutes in Drafting Preferred Share Contracts", 44 Calif.L.Rev. 584 (1956); McCormick, "Nimble Dividends: Some States Do Permit Dividends Despite Deficits in Accumulated Earnings", 88 J.Accountancy 196 (1949); Note, 62 Harv. L.Rev. 130 (1948). Many jurisdictions use language construable as permitting dividends from lifetime or current net earnings despite impairment of stated capital. See note 12 supra. Current net earnings are a permitted source of dividends despite capital impairment in a growing number of jurisdictions. Introduced into the Model Business Corporation Act is alternative section 40(a): "Dividends may be declared and paid in cash or property only out of the unreserved and unrestricted earned surplus of the corporation, or out of the unreserved and unrestricted net earnings of the current year and the next preceding fiscal year taken as a single period."

20. See section 344 infra.

21. Kreidmann, "Dividends—Changing Patterns", 57 Colum.L.Rev. 372, 374 (1957). See ABA–ALI Model Bus.Corp.Act §§ 2(1), 64. See also Cal.Gen.Corp. Law, § 1500(c) (1947). See note 12 supra.

22. E. g., McKinney's N.Y.Bus.Corp.Law, § 510(b); Gibson, "Surplus, So What? The Model Act Modernized", 17 Bus.Law. 476 (1962).

23. Former McKinney's N.Y.Stock Corp.Law § 58. But cf. former McKinney's N.Y.Penal Law, Appendix § 664(1) ("except from surplus"). New York now defines "Capital surplus", "Earned surplus", "Insolvent", "Net assets", "Stated capital", "Surplus", see McKinney's N.Y.Bus.Corp.Law, § 2(a) (2), (6), (8), (9), (12), (13). Its financial provisions are very com-

value of present assets over value of actual assets with which corporation began business). See United States v. Riely, 169 F.2d 542 (4th Cir. 1948), cert. denied 335 U.S. 908, 69 S.Ct. 411, 93 L.Ed. 441 (1949) (construing "out of net earnings, or out of its net assets in excess of its capital", under former Virginia statute, for purposes of federal accumulated earnings surtax, as allowing two separate sources of dividends, permitting dividends out of net earnings for year, despite impairment in stated capital as result of deficits in prior years). See McDowell, "The Theory of Capital in Virginia: An Historical Comma and a Disjunctive Conjunction", 6 Wash. & Lee L.Rev. 35 (1949).

16. Cal.Gen.Corp.Law, § 1500(a), (b) (1947).

17. Del.Gen.Corp.Law, § 170 (1967).

18. N.C.Bus.Corp.Act § 55–50 (1957).

19. The word "nimble" has probably been adopted since directors must be "nimble" to declare dividends out of net profits for the permissible accounting period—preceding six-month to one-year accounting period in California; current or preceding

pressly permit dividends out of surplus arising from reduction of stated capital (when duly formalized),[24] or out of paid-in surplus,[25] or other variations of capital or unearned surplus,[26] but sometimes only under certain circumstances.[27]

The Model Business Corporation Act generally limits cash and property dividends to

prehensive. See also id. § 506 (Determination of stated capital); id. § 510 (Dividends or other distributions in cash or property); id. § 516 (Reduction of stated capital in certain cases); id. § 517 (Special provisions relative to surplus and reserves); id. § 802 (Reduction of stated capital by amendment); id. § 520 (Liability for failure to disclose required information), providing: "Failure of the corporation to comply in good faith with the notice or disclosure provisions of paragraph (c) of section 510 (Dividends or other distributions in cash or property), or paragraphs (f) and (g) of section 511 (Share distributions and changes), or paragraph (d) of section 515 (Reacquired shares), or paragraph (c) of section 516 (Reduction of stated capital in certain cases), or subparagraph (a) (4) of section 517 (Special provisions relative to surplus and reserves), or paragraph (f) of section 519 (Convertible shares and bonds), shall make the corporation liable for any damage sustained by any shareholder in consequence thereof." See deCapriles, "Article 5—Corporate Finance", 11 Buffalo L.Rev. 461, 467 (1962); Henn, "The Philosophies of the New York Business Corporation Law of 1961", 11 Buffalo L.Rev. 439, 453 (1962); deCapriles & McAniff, "The Financial Provisions of the New (1961) New York Business Corporation Law", 36 N.Y.U.L.Rev. 1239, 1253 (1961); Note, "Article V of the New York Business Corporation Law: Corporate Finance", 13 Syracuse L.Rev. 93, 97 (1961).

24.   E. g., Cal.Gen.Corp.Law, § 1500(c) (1947). Comment, "The Current Law Regarding Reduction of Capital: Its Methodology, Purposes and Dangers", 110 U.Pa.L.Rev. 723 (1962). Reduction of capital often requires shareholder consent. See notes 20, 21 supra.

25.   E. g., Cal.Gen.Corp.Law, § 1500(c) (1947).

26.   E. g., revaluation surplus, donated surplus, reorganization surplus.

27.   E. g., Cal.Gen.Corp.Law, § 1500(c) (1947) (limited to shares with dividend preference if any outstanding; requirement that shareholders receive notice of source of dividend); McKinney's N.Y.Bus.Corp. Law, § 510(c) (notice to shareholders required where any part of cash or property dividend is from sources other than earned surplus); id. § 520 (liability of corporation for nondisclosure; id. § 1318 (disclosure required of nonexempt foreign corporations doing business in New York); N.C.Bus.Corp. Act § 55–50(a) (3) (1957) (limited to shares with dividend preference, and then only if no earned surplus or net profits are available, provided source of dividend is disclosed to shareholders, § 55–50(g)).

"unreserved and unrestricted earned surplus",[28] but authorizes "distributions from capital surplus" or "distributions in partial liquidation" [29] to shareholders out of capital surplus [30] of a portion of the corporate assets, in cash or property, subject to several provisions.[31] Also authorized are distributions to holders of shares with a cumulative dividend preference of dividends payable in cash out of capital surplus, if at the time the corporation has no earned surplus and is not insolvent and would not thereby be rendered insolvent, and if such distribution, when made, is identified as a payment of cumulative dividends out of capital surplus.[32]

Nonimpairment of Capital

Nonimpairment of capital in some jurisdictions is the express limitation, either alone or along with insolvency.[33] Jurisdictions which authorized dividends only from surplus by implication prohibit the impairment of stated capital. Under such statutes, for example, dividends are payable if before and after such payment the net assets are not less than the stated capital; [34] in short, surplus of any kind is available for

28.   ABA–ALI Model Bus.Corp.Act § 40(a); see also § 2(1).

29.   Until the 1959 revision, distributions—until then designated "distributions in partial liquidation"— were redesignated as "distributions from capital surplus". See ABA–ALI Model Bus.Corp.Act § 2(j).

30.   See ABA–ALI Model Bus.Corp.Act § 2(m) (entire surplus other than earned surplus).

31.   ABA–ALI Model Bus.Corp.Act § 41. See Hackney, "The Financial Provisions of the Model Business Corporation Act", 70 Harv.L.Rev. 1357 (1957).

32.   Ibid.

33.   E. g., former McKinney's N.Y.Stock Corp. Law, § 58 (1951) (capital impairment sole limitation). Capital impairment is coupled with insolvency or with other tests in a few jurisdictions. Kreidmann, "Dividends—Changing Patterns", 57 Colum.L.Rev. 372, 375 (1957).

34.   E. g., McKinney's former N.Y.Stock Corp.Law, § 58 (1951). Quaere, as to whether time of declaration and/or time of payment controlled. Gallagher v. New York Dock Co., 93 N.Y.L.J. No. 137, 3045 (Sup.Ct.1935).

dividends [35]—earned surplus as well as the various types of unearned surplus: (a) paid-in surplus (from issue of shares for more than par value or stated value or resale of treasury shares for more than the stated capital represented thereby); [36] (b) capital reduction surplus; [37] (c) revaluation surplus; [38] (d) donated surplus; (e) reorganization surplus; etc.—any value remaining after deducting from assets both liabilities and stated capital.[39]

Old statutes forbade impairment of stated capital in addition to other limitations,[40] or restricted impairment beyond a prescribed limitation.[41]

Insolvency

As previously mentioned, several statutes expressly prohibit dividends where the corporation is or might thereby become "insolvent" (with or without further definition thereof), imposing such limitation in addition to other restrictions prescribed by the statute.[42] Even absent such statutes, insolvency would probably constitute a limitation in addition to any limitation mentioned in the statute. Massachusetts until 1965 was somewhat unique in that the only limitation

prescribed by its then statute was a provision making the directors liable, to the extent of such dividend for the debts of the corporation for declaring or assenting to a dividend if the corporation was or thereby was rendered bankrupt or insolvent.[43]

Miscellaneous Problems

Treatment of unrealized appreciation, depreciation, goodwill, so-called "wasting assets" or "consuming assets", corporations, and affiliated corporations sometimes presents problems under the various statutory formulations.

Unrealized Appreciation and Depreciation. Sometimes, statutes expressly bar the recognition of unrealized appreciation,[44] or require the recognition of depreciation in computing funds available for dividends.[45] Otherwise, the courts must resolve the problems of unrealized appreciation [46] and de-

---

35. Former McKinney's N.Y.Penal Law, Appendix § 664.

36. See McKinney's N.Y.Bus.Corp.Law, § 506; Equitable Life Assurance Society v. Union Pacific R. R., 212 N.Y. 360, 106 N.E. 92 (1914).

37. McKinney's N.Y.Bus.Corp.Act § 516. Cf. terms "reduction of capital" and "impairment of capital." Cf. Roberts v. Roberts-Wicks Co., 184 N.Y. 257, 77 N.E. 13 (1906) (former statute). See also Jay Ronald Co. v. Marshall Mortgage Corp., 291 N.Y. 227, 52 N. E.2d 108 (1943). See Comment, "Corporations: Distributing Reduction Surplus Under the California Corporations Code—The Secretary of State Adds His Own Requirement", 56 Calif.L.Rev. 215 (1968).

38. Randall v. Bailey, 23 N.Y.S.2d 173 (Sup.Ct.1940), aff'd mem., 262 App.Div. 844, 29 N.Y.S.2d 512 (1st Dep't 1941), aff'd 288 N.Y. 280, 43 N.E.2d 43 (1942).

39. For definition of stated capital, see notes 4, 6 supra.

40. See note 33 supra.

41. See notes 15, 16 supra.

42. See notes 4–6 supra.

43. Mass.Ann.Laws ch. 156, § 37 (1959).

44. E. g., Cal.Gen.Corp.Law, §§ 1502, 1505 (1947); Ind.Gen.Corp.Act § 25–211(a) (1967) (prohibiting cash or property dividends out of surplus due to or arising from unrealized appreciation in value or from revaluation of assets); N.C.Bus.Corp.Act § 55–49(d) (1957) (for purposes of earned surplus); but cf. § 55–49(e) (recognizing capital surplus arising from revaluation of assets when made in good faith upon demonstrably adequate bases of revaluation). Some other jurisdictions distinguish among various types of assets as to which unrealized appreciation might be recognized, usually current but not fixed assets. Michigan permits the recognition of unrealized appreciation only to the extent that it results from readjustments of previous reductions of value to correctly reflect the accounts of the corporation.

45. E. g., Idaho Bus.Corp.Act § 30–130 (1929); Minn. Bus.Corp.Act § 301.22 (1961); Wash.Bus.Corp.Act § 23.01.250 (1967); see also Cal.Gen.Corp.Law, § 1500(b) (1947); Del.Gen.Corp.Law, § 170 (1967); Vogtman v. Merchants Mortgage and Credit Co., 20 Del.Ch. 364, 178 A. 99 (Ch.1935).

46. See Randall v. Bailey, 23 N.Y.S.2d 173 (Sup.Ct. 1940), aff'd mem., 262 App.Div. 844, 29 N.Y.S.2d 512 (1st Dep't 1941), aff'd 288 N.Y. 280, 43 N.E.2d 43 (1942) (permitting recognition of unrealized appreciation in fixed assets). See McKinney's N.Y.Bus. Corp.Law, § 102(a) (6) ("Unrealized appreciation of assets is not included in earned surplus"; it would be capital surplus still available in New York for dividends if required disclosure made to recipient shareholders). Contra, Kingston v. Home Life Ins. Co. of America, 11 Del.Ch. 258, 101 A. 898 (Ch.

preciation [47] in the light of the applicable statutory language. A few statutes comprehensively deal with surplus, net profits, and the valuation of assets, applying "generally accepted principles of sound accounting practice." [48] Reliance in good faith by the directors on the corporation's books of account and financial statements, however, often protects them from liability. [49]

Goodwill. Goodwill, when found to have adequate basis, has been recognized in computing funds legally available for dividends. [50]

"Wasting Assets" Corporation. So-called "wasting assets" or "consuming assets" corporations [51] are sometimes expressly authorized by statute to distribute dividends without allowance for depletion [52] under certain circumstances. [53] Even absent such a

---

1917), aff'd per curiam 11 Del.Ch. 428, 104 A. 25 (Sup.Ct.1918) (holding unrealized appreciation of corporation's office building cannot be included in computing surplus available for dividends); Vogtman v. Merchants Mortgage and Credit Co., 20 Del. Ch. 364, 178 A. 99 (Ch.1935) (dictum). But see Morris v. Standard Gas & Electric Co., 31 Del.Ch. 20, 63 A.2d 577 (Ch.1949) (upholding board of directors' recognition of unrealized appreciation of shares held in other issuers, in concluding there was no diminution of stated capital represented by shares having liquidation preference for purposes of nimble dividend provision). See also Matter of Marx v. Bragalini, 6 N.Y.2d 322, 189 N.Y.S.2d 846, 160 N.E. 2d 611 (1959), rev'g 6 A.D.2d 393, 178 N.Y.S.2d 524 (3d Dep't 1958); Bugge, "Unrealized Appreciation as a Source of Shareholder Distributions under the Wisconsin Business Corporation Law", 1964 Wis.L. Rev. 292; Brightwell, "Depreciation Policy and Its Effect in Determining Earnings Available for Dividends", 36 U.Colo.L.Rev. 143 (1963); Gibson, "Surplus, So What? The Model Act Modernized", 17 Bus.Law. 476 (1962); Hackney, "The Financial Provisions of the Model Business Corporation Act", 70 Harv.L.Rev. 1357, 1380 (1959); Garrett, "Capital and Surplus Under the New Corporation Statutes", 23 Law & Contemp.Prob. 239, 259 (1958) (contending that under ABA–ALI Model Bus.Corp.Act § 2(i) (*l*), (m), criterion is "book value", with result that, absent write-up on books, neither "dividends" (per § 40) nor "distributions from capital surplus" (per § 41) lawfully may be paid out of unrealized appreciation); Carrington, "Experience in Texas with the Model Business Corporation Act", 5 Utah L. Rev. 292, 296–297 (1957); Seward, "Earned Surplus —Its Meaning and Use in the Model Business Corporation Act", 38 Va.L.Rev. 435, 440–443 (1952) (contending that criterion is "current value" and that unrealized appreciation, presumably whether or not recorded on books, increases "net assets" and constitutes "gains" within definition of "earned surplus" with result that "dividends" (per § 40—"only out of the unreserved and unrestricted earned surplus") lawfully may be paid out of unrealized appreciation); Note, "Cash Dividends Payable from Unrealized Appreciation of Fixed Assets—A Reconsideration of Randall v. Bailey," 20 U.Pitt.L.Rev. 632 (1959); Note, "Statutes, Case Law, and Generally Accepted Principles on the Write-Up of Physical Assets", 28 U.Cin.L.Rev. 79 (1959); Note, "May Nebraska Corporations Pay a Dividend from Surplus Including Unrealized Appreciation from Revaluation of Fixed Assets", 34 Neb.L.Rev. 531 (1955).

47. Randall v. Bailey supra note 46 (requiring recognition of depreciation); Vogtman v. Merchants Mortgage and Credit Co., 20 Del.Ch. 364, 178 A. 99 (Ch.1935) (holding that certain assets carried at cost were carried at too high amounts and there-

fore dividends on preferred shares were not out of surplus and preferred shareholders' contingent voting rights were exercisable); Gallagher v. New York Dock Co., 93 N.Y.L.J. No. 137, 3045 (Sup.Ct. 1935).

48. N.C.Bus.Corp.Act §§ 55–2(5), 55–49 (1957).

49. Randall v. Bailey supra note 46; Gallagher v. New York Dock Co. supra note 47; cf. Cowin v. Jonas, 43 N.Y.S.2d 468 (Sup.Ct.1943), aff'd mem., 267 App.Div. 947, 48 N.Y.S.2d 460 (1st Dep't 1944), aff'd mem., 293 N.Y. 838, 59 N.E.2d 436 (1944). The New York statute seems to afford less protection in relying on the records and statements for actual value than does the Model Business Corporation Act and the Delaware statute. See section 319, n. 19 supra.

50. Randall v. Bailey supra note 46.

51. Often defined to include corporations engaged in the business of exploiting natural resources. E. g., ABA–ALI Model Bus.Corp.Act § 40(b). The California statute refers to corporations formed to exploit mines, oil wells, gas wells, patents, and other wasting assets, or to liquidate specific assets. Cal.Gen. Corp.Law, § 1503 (1947).

52. "Depletion" represents an allowance for the assets extracted or consumed, is analogous to depreciation, and ordinarily would constitute a charge against earnings and a credit to depletion (an asset deduction).

53. ABA–ALI Model Bus.Corp.Act § 40(b) (if articles of incorporation so provide and there is disclosure to recipient shareholders); Cal.Gen.Corp.Law, § 1503 (1947) (if adequate provision is made for meeting debts and liabilities and any liquidation preferences of outstanding shares and shareholders are given notice that no allowance has been made for depletion); Del.Gen.Corp.Law § 170 (1967); Mc-Kinney's N.Y.Bus.Corp.Law, § 510(b) (if net assets remaining after dividend are sufficient to cover liquidation preferences of shares having such preferences in involuntary liquidation); N.C.Bus.Corp.Act § 55–50(d) (1957) (with required disclosure to shareholders). Most of the states have "wasting assets" dividend provisions of various types.

statute, such distributions have been upheld by court decision.[54]

APPLICABLE STATUTORY LIMITATIONS OTHER THAN OF JURISDICTION OF INCORPORATION

321. In addition to limitations on the funds legally available for dividends under the laws of the jurisdiction of incorporation, additional statutory or administrative limitations might be imposed (a) by other jurisdictions in which the corporation is doing business and (b) by applicable federal law, such as the Public Utility Holding Company Act of 1935 and the Investment Company Act of 1940.

As a general proposition, the law of the jurisdiction of incorporation determines the funds legally available for dividends. Two exceptions are (a) possible limitations in the law of another jurisdiction in which the corporation is doing business when such limitations are applicable to foreign corporations doing business within such jurisdiction, and (b) applicable federal law.

The Model Business Corporation Act dividend provisions apply to a "corporation",[1] but the Model Act defines "corporation", unless the context otherwise requires, as a domestic corporation.[2] Although the Model Act expressly states that nothing therein should be construed to authorized the state to regulate the organization or the "internal affairs" of a foreign corporation,[3] it also limits the powers of foreign corporations to those enjoyed by domestic corporations and,

except as otherwise provided, subjects foreign corporations "to the same duties, restrictions, penalties [4] and liabilities . . . imposed upon a domestic corporation of like character."

State dividend statutes applicable to foreign corporations doing business within the state are rare.

The present New York statute dividend provisions are made applicable to foreign corporations doing business in the state,[5] unless exempted.[6]

Prior to 1963, New York had a statutory provision expressly to the effect that the directors of a foreign stock corporation transacting business in the state were liable to the same extent as directors of a domestic corporation for the making of "Unauthorized dividends".[7]

A director of a New Jersey corporation authorized to do business in New York, having its principal business office in New

54. Mellon v. Mississippi Wire Glass Co., 77 N.J.Eq. 498, 78 A. 710 (1910); Excelsior Water & Mining Co. v. Pierce, 90 Cal. 131, 27 P. 44 (1891); Lee v. Neuchatel Asphalte Co., 41 Ch.Div. 1 (C.A.1889); see also People ex rel. United Verde Copper Co. v. Roberts, 156 N.Y. 585, 51 N.E. 293 (1898) (tax case). But see Wittenberg v. Federal Mining & Smelting Co., 15 Del.Ch. 147, 133 A. 48 (Ch.1926), aff'd 15 Del.Ch. 409, 138 A. 347 (Sup.Ct.1927) (requiring depletion deduction), 15 Del.Ch. 351, 138 A. 352 (Ch. 1927) (after enactment of Delaware statute).

1. ABA–ALI Model Bus.Corp.Act § 40.

2. Id. § 2(a).

3. Id. § 99.

4. Id. § 100.

5. McKinney's N.Y.Bus.Corp.Law, §§ 1317, 1318.

6. McKinney's N.Y.Bus.Corp.Law, § 1320 (exempted is any qualified foreign corporation if either (a) its shares are listed on national securities exchange or (b) less than one-half of its total business income for preceding three fiscal years, or such portion thereof as corporation was in existence, was allocable to New York for franchise tax purposes under New York Tax Law).

7. Former McKinney's N.Y.Stock Corp.Law, § 114(1) (except foreign moneyed or railroad corporation); see also former McKinney's N.Y.Penal Law, Appendix §§ 664(1), 667. See Stevens, "New York Business Corporation Law of 1961", 47 Cornell L.Q. 141, 172 (1962); Henn, "The Philosophies of the New York Business Corporation Law of 1961", 11 Buffalo L.Rev. 439, 453 (1962); Kessler, "The New York Business Corporation Law", 36 St.John's L.Rev. 1, 107 (1961). The original 1961 bill applied the same dividend standards to foreign corporations doing business in the state as were applicable to domestic corporations. As passed, this bill was amended so that such standards did not apply to foreign corporations other than a "domiciled foreign corporation", a concept abandoned before the law's effective date in favor of the exemption provisions of § 1320. See Note, "Domestic Regulation of Foreign Corporations: Concept of 'Domiciled Foreign Corporation': New York Business Corporation Law of 1961", 47 Cornell L.Q. 273 (1962). The New York Penal Law provisions were revised in 1967.

York, and holding most of its directors' meetings in New York, had been held liable by the New York Court of Appeals [8] under the former New York statute in a case where the dividends were "unauthorized" under both New York and New Jersey law.[9]

Cardozo, J., for a unanimous court, stated that the principal issue was one of statutory construction, and concluded that the dividend restrictions applicable to domestic corporations applied to foreign corporations doing business in the state. No constitutional impediment was found to such construction since foreign corporations coming into, and transacting business in, the state yield obedience to the laws of the state.[10]

Subsequently, a Delaware corporation authorized to do business in New York and having its principal office in New York, was held not liable under the federal accumulated earnings tax [11] for not distributing dividends which would have been lawful under the Delaware "nimble dividend" rule but which would have impaired capital in violation of the then New York non-impairment-of-capital rule.[12]

Two federal statutes which impose limitations on the source of dividends payable by corporations subject to such statutes are the Public Utility Holding Company Act of 1935 [13] and the Investment Company Act of 1940.[14]

In general, the former and the rules of the Securities and Exchange Commission promulgated thereunder prohibit dividends by registered public utility holding companies and some of their subsidiaries out of stated capital or unearned surplus, except with the approval of the Commission.[15] Registered investment companies may only distribute dividends from accumulated undistributed net income or net income for the current or preceding fiscal year unless accompanied by disclosure of source.[16]

NONSTATUTORY LIMITATIONS

322. In addition to statutory limitations on the funds legally available for dividends, additional limitations might be imposed by applicable securities exchange requirements, the articles of incorporation, indentures, loan agreements, resolutions, bylaws, or even "shareholder agreements".

Nonstatutory limitations on the source of dividends must also be considered.

Any applicable securities exchange rules must be considered with respect to listed shares. In general, these rules presently regulate several phases of dividends, but not their source, except possibly for share dividends.[1] The New York Stock Exchange

8. German-American Coffee Co. v. Diehl, 216 N.Y. 57, 109 N.E. 875 (1915).

9. The then New Jersey statutory remedy was in favor of shareholders and of the corporation only where the corporation was insolvent; the New York statute gave the remedy to the corporation, regardless of insolvency, or its creditors; there was no claim that the German-American Coffee Co. was insolvent.

10. See Reese & Kaufman, "Law Governing Corporate Affairs: Choice of Law and the Impact of Full Faith and Credit", 58 Colum.L.Rev. 1118, 1128 (1958); Latty, "Pseudo-Foreign Corporations", 65 Yale L.J. 137, 156 (1955); Coleman, "Corporate Dividends and the Conflict of Laws", 63 Harv.L.Rev. 433 (1950). See note 1 supra.

11. See discussion of Federal Accumulated Earnings Tax in section 339 infra.

12. International Ticket Scale Corp. v. United States, 165 F.2d 358 (2d Cir. 1948). Cf. Borg v. International Silver Co., 11 F.2d 147, 151 (2d Cir. 1925) (dictum).

13. § 12(c), 15 U.S.C.A. § 79l(c). See section 299 supra.

14. § 19, 15 U.S.C.A. § 80a–19. See section 301 supra.

15. 17 C.F.R. § 250.46 (1969), 3 CCH Fed.Sec.L.Rep. ¶ 36,573, 2 P–H Sec.Reg. ¶ 16,235. See Matter of Columbia Gas & Electric Corp., 3 S.E.C. 313 (1938), 4 S.E.C. 400 (1939).

16. 17 C.F.R. § 270.19–1 (1969), 3 CCH Fed.Sec.L.Rep. ¶ 48,077, 2 P–H Sec.Reg. ¶ 26,254. See also L. Rappaport, SEC Accounting Practice and Procedure 310 (2d ed. 1963); N.Y.S.E.Company Manual §§ A1, A4, A6.

1. N.Y.S.E. Company Manual § A13. But some key account changes are regulated. See discussion of Securities Exchange Requirements in section 318 supra.

requirement that the company maintain an office in Manhattan for the payment of dividends [2] might help to subject the corporation to the New York dividend statute.[3]

Restrictions contained in the articles of incorporation may also be imposed. Some statutes expressly so provide.[4] Even in the absence of such a statute, some such restrictions will usually be upheld.[5] However, the North Carolina statute provides that any future provision in any charter, or bylaws or resolutions or agreement of the shareholders purporting to make unavailable the sources mentioned in the North Carolina statute for the payment of dividends to shares with a dividend preference shall be null and void, but excepts any agreement between a corporation and its creditors restricting the payment of dividends.[6]

In drafting dividend provisions in the articles of incorporation, unless additional restrictions are desired, it is sound draftsmanship to provide that they shall be payable "out of funds legally available therefor".[7] Paraphrasing the current statute might prove embarrassing if the statute is amended.[8]

Indentures, loan agreements, etc., sometimes contain additional restrictions for the protection of creditors. Resolutions or even bylaws [9] possibly also do, for the protection not only of creditors but also of certain classes of shareholders.

"Shareholder agreements" arranging the distribution of earnings in a fixed manner have been upheld.[10]

LIABILITY FOR UNLAWFUL DIVIDENDS

323. For dividends out of funds not legally available under applicable statutes, directors are often made liable by statute to the corporation, or to its creditors or shareholders, and possibly also subjected to criminal penalties. Shareholders receiving such unlawful dividends with knowledge of such illegality, under statutes, or even apart from statute at least when insolvency is present or imminent, are often similarly liable or liable by way of contribution to directors found liable for such dividends. Statutes sometimes also impose liability on the corporation.

Various sanctions are imposed by statute for the declaration and payment of dividends out of funds not legally available under applicable statutes. The most common is to impose civil or criminal liability on the directors involved, subject to some exceptions; some statutes also deal with the shareholders who receive such dividends; or the corporation is sometimes liable for failing to give a required notice to the extent of any damage sustained by any shareholder in consequence thereof.

2. N.Y.S.E. Company Manual A–53.

3. See section 321, nn. 1–6 supra.

4. E. g., ABA–ALI Model Bus.Corp.Act § 40. North Carolina prohibits preferred dividend restrictions in the articles of incorporation. See note 6 infra.

5. Loftus v. Mason, 240 F.2d 428 (4th Cir. 1957), cert. denied 353 U.S. 949, 77 S.Ct. 860, 1 L.Ed.2d 858 (1957); Lich v. United States Rubber Co., 39 F. Supp. 675 (D.N.J.1941), aff'd per curiam 123 F.2d 145 (3d Cir. 1941).

6. N.C.Bus.Corp.Act § 55–50(b) (1957).

7. Buxbaum, "Preferred Stock—Law and Draftsmanship", 42 Calif.L.Rev. 243, 249 (1954). Such language might also relieve a debt obligation where the dividend is declared without a proper fund for payment.

8. See Weinberg v. Baltimore Brick Co., 34 Del.Ch. 586, 108 A.2d 81 (Ch.1954), aff'd 35 Del.Ch. 225, 114 A. 2d 812 (Sup.Ct.1955) (charter limitation to "net earnings" when statute read "surplus or net profits" construed as not restricted to earned surplus but including current earnings per later Delaware "nimble dividend" statute).

9. Quaere, as to validity of bylaw restrictions where the statute expressly recognizes the effectiveness of restrictions in the articles of incorporation.

10. Wabash Ry. v. American Refrigerator Transit Co., 7 F.2d 335 (8th Cir. 1925), cert. denied 270 U.S. 643, 46 S.Ct. 208, 70 L.Ed. 776 (1926); Galler v. Galler, 32 Ill.2d 16, 203 N.E.2d 577 (1964), 95 Ill. App.2d 340, 238 N.E.2d 274 (1968) (upholding provision for mandatory declaration of at least $50,000 dividends annually so long as $500,000 earned surplus maintained); Clark v. Dodge, 269 N.Y. 410, 199 N.E. 641 (1936).

Directors

For unlawful dividends, the directors are often made civilly or criminally liable by statute.[1]

For example, the Model Business Corporation Act makes directors who vote for or assent to unlawful dividends (or other distributions of assets) jointly and severally liable to the corporation for the amount thereof, unless they in good faith rely upon certain financial statements or in determining the amount available for such dividend (or distribution) considered the assets to be of their book value; any directors held liable are entitled to contribution against other directors who voted for or assented to the dividend (or distribution) and proportionately against shareholders who received the same with knowledge of its unlawfulness.[2]

The Model Act also provides that a director shall not be liable if he relied and acted in good faith upon financial statements of the corporation represented to him to be correct by the president or the officer of such corporation having charge of its books of account, or stated in a written report by an independent public or certified public accountant or firm of such accountants fairly to reflect the financial condition of such corporation, nor shall he be so liable if in good faith in determining the amount available

for any such dividend or distribution he considered the assets to be of their book value.[3]

The Delaware statute provides for joint and several liability of directors to the corporation and its creditors in case of willful or negligent payment of unlawful dividends.[4] However, the director is fully protected in relying in good faith on the corporation's books of account and financial statements as to value and the amount of the assets, liabilities and/or net profits or any other facts pertinent to the existence and amount of surplus or other funds from which dividends might properly be declared and paid or with which the corporation's shares might properly be purchased or redeemed.[5]

In New York, the civil liability provision excepts from liability directors who have had their dissents recorded or who under the circumstances discharged their duties to the corporation within the business judgment rule.[6] Any directors held to be liable are entitled to contribution from other directors who voted for or concurred in the unlawful

---

1. E. g., Cal.Gen.Corp.Law, § 1510 (1947). Some statutes give the remedy to creditors; others to the corporation; still others to the creditors and to the corporation or shareholders. Under some statutes, the remedy is limited to then-existing creditors. Some statutes limit recovery to the amount of actual loss to creditors or shareholders. See M. Feuer, Personal Liabilities of Corporate Officers and Directors ch. 14 (1961); Note, "The Statutory Responsibility of Directors for Payment of Dividends Out of Capital", 35 Yale L.J. 870 (1926).

2. ABA–ALI Model Bus.Corp.Act § 43; McKinney's N.Y.Bus.Corp.Law, § 719(a) (joint and several liability to corporation for benefit of its creditors or shareholders to extent of any injury suffered by them). See Aiken v. Peabody, 168 F.2d 615 (7th Cir. 1947) (liability for illegal dividend held to be statutory rather than sounding in tort and therefore not to abate upon death of director).

3. ABA–ALI Model Bus.Corp.Act § 43. Opinion of counsel might also be had. For example, in the case of a New York-centered corporation incorporated in Delaware and subject also to the New York dividend provisions, general counsel in New York might provide their opinion as to the propriety of the dividend under New York law and correspondent Delaware counsel might provide their opinion as to the propriety of the dividend under Delaware law. See Comment, "Reliance on Advice of Counsel", 70 Yale L.J. 978 (1961).

4. Del.Gen.Corp.Law, § 174 (1967).

5. Del.Gen.Corp.Law, §§ 172, 141(e) (1967).

6. McKinney's N.Y.Bus.Corp.Law, § 719(a), (b), (c); id. § 717 (in discharging their duties, directors and officers, when acting in good faith, may rely upon financial statements of corporation represented to them to be correct by president or officer of corporation having charge of its books of accounts, or stated in written report by independent public or certified public accountant or firm of such accountants fairly to reflect financial condition of such corporation). Absent from the New York statute is the Model Business Corporation Act language immunizing a director from liability "if in good faith in determining the amount available for any such dividend or distribution he considered the assets to be of their book value."

dividend and to be subrogated to the rights of the corporation against shareholders who received such dividend with knowledge of the facts.[7] As previously discussed, the directors of a foreign business corporation transacting business in New York, unless exempt, are liable to the same extent as directors of a domestic corporation for unlawful dividends.[8] In New York, a director of a stock corporation is guilty of misconduct for knowingly concurring in any vote or act by which it is intended to make a dividend except in the manner provided by law.[9] Deleted from the New York Penal Law in 1967 was the provision that the fact that the corporation was a foreign corporation, if it carried on business or kept an office therefor in the state, was no defense.[10]

Recipient Shareholders

Some statutes expressly provide that shareholders receiving dividends out of funds not legally available under applicable statutes with knowledge of facts indicating such illegality are liable to the corporation for the amount so received.[11] Others make recipient shareholders, who accept a dividend known to be unlawful, proportionately liable by way of contribution to directors

found liable for such dividend.[12] Even in jurisdictions without such statutory provisions, shareholders who accept unlawful dividends with knowledge thereof may be liable for such dividend,[13] at least where insolvency was present or imminent,[14] but innocent recipients need not return the dividend, unless the corporation is insolvent, in which case there would be a fraudulent conveyance to the shareholders, who, not having given value, would not be bona fide purchaser.[15]

Corporation

Statutes sometimes also provide that the corporation shall be liable for failing to give any required notice in connection with dividends to the extent of any damage sustained by any shareholder in consequence thereof.[16]

---

7. McKinney's N.Y.Bus.Corp.Law, § 719(c), (d).

8. See section 321 supra.

9. McKinney's N.Y.Penal Law, § 190.35(1).

10. Former McKinney's N.Y.Penal Law, Appendix § 667.

11. E. g., Cal.Gen.Corp.Law, § 1510 (1947).

12. E. g., ABA–ALI Model Bus.Corp.Act § 43; McKinney's N.Y.Bus.Corp.Law, § 1719(d) (1).

13. Cottrell v. Albany Card and Paper Mfg. Co., 142 App.Div. 148, 126 N.Y.S. 1070 (3d Dep't 1911); cf. Hannigan v. Italo Petroleum Corp., 45 Del. 593, 77 A.2d 209 (Sup.Ct.1949). See Uniform Fraudulent Conveyance Act.

14. United States v. Seyler, 142 F.Supp. 408 (W.D. Pa.1956); Quintal v. Adler, 146 Misc. 300, 262 N.Y. S. 126 (Sup.Ct.1933), aff'd mem., 239 App.Div. 775, 263 N.Y.S. 943 (1st Dep't 1933), aff'd mem., 264 N.Y. 452, 191 N.E. 509 (1934).

15. McDonald v. Williams, 174 U.S. 397, 19 S.Ct. 743, 43 L.Ed. 1022 (1899); Gallagher v. New York Dock Co., 93 N.Y.L.J. No. 137, 3045 (Sup.Ct.1935). See Fuld, "Recovery of Illegal and Partial Liquidating Dividends from Stockholders", 28 Va.L.Rev. 50 (1941); Note, "Actions Against Stockholders to Recover Illegal Dividends", 33 Colum.L.Rev. 481(1933); Note, "Shareholders' Responsibility For Improper Dividends", 81 U.Pa.L.Rev. 314 (1933). See also Fried v. Cano, 167 F.Supp. 625 (S.D.N.Y.1958) (recovery by trustee-in-bankruptcy of dividends paid to shareholder who had not paid for shares.

16. McKinney's N.Y.Bus.Corp.Law, §§ 520, 1318.

C. DIVIDEND PREFERENCES AND OTHER RIGHTS

BASIC DIVIDEND RULE

324. The basic dividend rule is that all shareholders participate ratably in dividends when, as, and if declared by the board of directors, in the exercise of their discretion, out of legally available funds, except as otherwise provided in the articles of incorporation. Dividend preferences may be expressed in terms of monetary amounts or percentage of par value. and may be cumulative, noncumulative, cumulative-to-the-extent-earned, etc., and participating or nonparticipating. Absent provision to the contrary, a dividend preference is capable of satisfaction only by cash. Dividend preferences are subject to change by amendment of the articles of incorporation, merger, etc.

The basic dividend rule is that all shareholders participate ratably in dividends when, as, and if declared by the board of directors, in the exercise of their discretion, out of legally available funds,[1] except as otherwise provided in the articles of incorporation.

Many variations may be provided in the articles of incorporation, but the usual practice, where dividends are not to be shared ratably, is to give to one or more classes of shares a dividend preference over another class or other classes.[2] Any class with such

a preference may and often is designated "preferred shares".[3]

For any class of shares to enjoy a preference as to dividends, the articles of incorporation must so provide.[4] Such dividend preference may be expressed in terms of monetary amounts or percentage of par value,[5] and may be cumulative, noncumulative, cumulative-to-the-extent-earned, etc.[6] Beyond the dividend preference, such preferred shares may or may not participate in further dividends.[7]

---

1. See Scott v. P. Lorillard Co., 108 N.J.Eq. 153, 154 A. 515 (1931), aff'd per curiam, 109 N.J.Eq. 417, 157 A. 388 (1931); Godley v. Crandall & Godley Co., 212 N.Y. 121, 105 N.E. 818 (1914). But cf. Wabash Ry. v. American Refrigerator Transit Co., 7 F.2d 335 (8th Cir. 1925), cert. denied, 270 U.S. 643, 46 S.Ct. 208, 70 L.Ed. 776 (1926) (sharing of profits dependent upon amount of business of subsidiary over three parents' lines, rather than share ownership, upheld). Accord, Seaboard Air Line R. R. v. Atlantic Coast Line R. R., 240 N.C. 495, 82 S.E.2d 771 (1954); Klein v. Greenstein, 24 N.J.Super. 348, 94 A.2d 497 (1953) (rebates to customer shareholders in proportion to purchases held not dividends); Bookman v. R. J. Reynolds Tobacco Co., 138 N.J.Eq. 312, 48 A.2d 646 (1946) (upholding bonus based on shares held by employees under then New Jersey statute).

2. Classes of shares, especially if they are preferred or special, may be subdivided into series, but each series of the same class is often required to have the same preference although they might differ as to rate of dividend. See ABA–ALI Model Bus. Corp.Act § 15. See section 125 supra.

3. Usually, "preferred shares" also enjoy a liquidation preference (see section 382 infra), but the term is properly applied to shares with either as well as both dividend preference and liquidation preference. Shares with any such preference should not be designated "common shares". See e. g., McKinney's N.Y.Bus.Corp.Law, § 501(b).

4. Gaskill v. Gladys Belle Oil Co., 16 Del.Ch. 289, 146 A. 337 (Ch.1929) (bylaw fixing preferences broader than those in articles of incorporation held invalid). The articles of incorporation constitute the contract between the corporation and the shareholders, and their dividend rights must be determined by the language thereof. Roberts v. Roberts-Wicks Co., 184 N.Y. 257, 77 N.E. 13 (1906). But see Gordon v. Elliman, 306 N.Y. 456, 119 N.E.2d 331 (1954) (4–3).

5. Preference of $———, or ———% of par value per annum, payable annually, semi-annually, or quarterly, or on designated dividend payment dates. Is the preference for the year ("per annum") or for any quarterly or other designated payment dates? Quaere, as to what the draftsmen intended. Dividend preferences were once limited by statute (analogous to usury laws) in some jurisdictions. E. g., New Jersey (8 percent), New Mexico (10 percent), Wyoming (7 percent). If the par value is changed by reclassification, a dividend preference stated in terms of percentage of par value is correspondingly changed. Cf. Sterling v. 16 Park Avenue, Inc., 132 N.Y.S.2d 921 (Sup.Ct.1954), modified 284 App.Div. 1033, 136 N.Y.S.2d 363 (1st Dep't 1954). Quaere, if the dividend preference is stated in terms of so much per year, despite provision for quarterly payment, whether dividends on subordinate shares must be deferred until the annual preference is fully satisfied. See generally Annot., 6 A.L.R. 802 (1920), 67 A.L.R. 765 (1930), 98 A.L.R. 1526 (1935), 133 A.L.R. 653 (1941).

6. See section 325 infra.

7. See section 326 infra.

Satisfaction of Dividend Preferences

A dividend preference, absent provision to the contrary, is usually capable of satisfaction only by cash, unless the recipient shareholders accept some other distribution in satisfaction.[8]

Changes in Dividend Preferences

In most jurisdictions, dividend preferences can be changed, with prospective effect, as to priority, rate of dividend, cumulative feature, participating feature, etc., either directly or indirectly by creation of prior preferred shares, merger, etc. Such changes are most commonly effected by amendment of the articles of incorporation.[9]

CUMULATIVE; NONCUMULATIVE; CUMULATIVE-TO-THE-EXTENT-EARNED

325. A cumulative dividend preference entitles the preferred shareholder to unpaid dividends for all prior and current fiscal periods before any dividend may be distributed on shares having subordinate dividend rights.

A noncumulative dividend preference entitles the preferred shareholder in most jurisdictions only to the dividend preference for the current fiscal period before any dividend may be distributed on shares having subordinate dividend rights.

A cumulative-to-the-extent-earned dividend preference entitles the preferred shareholder to unpaid dividends for the current fiscal period and all prior fiscal periods in which there were funds legally available to pay such dividends before any dividend may be distributed on shares having subordinate dividend rights.

Problems of construction arise unless dividend preferences are clearly defined. Where a dividend preference is not expressed as cumulative or noncumulative, some cases suggest a presumption in favor of a cumulative dividend preference.

Under the so-called "dividend credit theory", developed primarily in New Jersey, noncumulative preferred shares are treated as having a cumulative-to-the-extent-earned dividend preference. Even common shares have been held entitled under such theory to credits for funds legally available in prior fiscal periods for dividends thereon.

Cumulative dividend arrearages on liquidation depend upon the language defining the liquidation rights of the preferred shares and judicial attitudes concerning such arrearages.

Cumulative dividend arrearages in many jurisdictions, depending upon the jurisdictions reserved power and applicable statutes and absence of fraud, unfairness, or bad faith, can be eliminated directly or indirectly by amendment of the articles of incorporation or other procedures, such as merger or consolidation. Such procedures require shareholder approval and sometimes afford an appraisal remedy to dissenting shareholders.

Cumulative Dividend Preference

In the case of a cumulative dividend preference, unpaid dividends for all prior and the current fiscal periods accumulate and must be paid in full before any dividend may be distributed on shares having subordinate dividend rights.[1]

Of course, even cumulative preferred dividends, like any other dividends, are payable only out of legally available funds,[2] and

---

8. Strout v. Cross, Austin & Ireland Lumber Co., 283 N.Y. 406, 28 N.E.2d 890 (1940). Contingent voting rights often arise on nonpayment of dividend preferences. See section 189 supra. See Vogtman v. Merchants Mortgage and Credit Co., 20 Del.Ch. 364, 178 A. 99 (Ch.1935) (contingent voting rights held to arise when preferred dividends were paid out of improper funds).

9. See section 325, nn. 21–25 infra.

1. "The fundamental characteristic of cumulative dividends is that if the preferred dividend is not paid in full in any year, whether or not earned, the deficiency must be made up before any dividend may be paid on any common or other subordinate class of shares". 2 I. Kantrowitz & S. Slutsky, White on New York Corporations ¶ 501.04, n. 46 (13th ed. 1968); 11 W. Fletcher, Private Corporations § 5318 (perm. ed. rev. 1958). See Blandin v. United North & South Development Co., 35 Del.Ch. 471, 121 A.2d 686 (Ch.1956), aff'd 36 Del.Ch. 538, 134 A.2d 706 (Sup.Ct.1956) (provision for payment of dividends on cumulative preferred shares to begin March 15, 1938 held not to require payment of dividends on some shares issued in 1945 for period prior to such issuance); Roberts v. Roberts-Wicks Co., 184 N.Y. 257, 77 N.E. 13 (1906) (holding under prior law cumulative dividend preference did not extend to reduction surplus).

2. See sections 320–322 supra.

usually only in the discretion of the board of directors,[3] but the cumulative dividend preference must be fully satisfied before any dividends on subordinate shares.[4] While a cumulative dividend preference might enhance the marketability of preferred shares, embarrassment can result eventually from any dividend arrearages, although such arrearages can be eliminated by reclassification or other procedures.[5]

Noncumulative Dividend Preference

In the case of noncumulative dividend preferences, dividends unpaid in the past, even to the extent earned in most jurisdictions, do not accumulate and need not be paid before a dividend distribution on other shares, so long as the dividend preference for the current fiscal period is satisfied.[6]

Cumulative-to-the-Extent-Earned Dividend Preference

A hybrid variety or dividend preference is the cumulative-to-the-extent-earned type, under which unpaid dividends accumulate during fiscal periods only to the extent that

there were then funds legally available to pay such dividends.[7]

Problems of Construction

Dividend preferences, when intended, should be clearly defined in the articles of incorporation. Use of the terms "cumulative" or "noncumulative" is sufficient to indicate the meaning in such respect; sometimes these terms are also included as part of the designation of the class of shares. Ambiguous provisions may require court construction. Where a dividend preference is expressed without indicating whether it is intended to be cumulative or not, the cases tend to hold such a preference to be cumulative by indulging in a slight presumption that cumulative preferences were intended, but authority is sparse and unsatisfactory.[8]

"Dividend Credit Theory"

In most jurisdictions where a dividend preference is found to be noncumulative, the preference is applied only to the current fiscal period.[9]

However, New Jersey has applied the so-called "dividend credit theory" to noncumulative preferred shares, treating noncumulative preference as a cumulative-to-the-ex-

---

3. See sections 327, 328 infra. Contingent voting rights are often made to vest in preferred shareholders upon prescribed failures to pay dividends. See section 189 supra.

4. See section 324 supra.

5. See discussion of Elimination of Cumulative Dividend Arrearages, infra.

6. Wabash Ry. v. Barclay, 280 U.S. 197, 50 S.Ct. 106, 74 L.Ed. 368, 67 A.L.R. 762 (1930). Although in the Wabash Ry. case, the profits were "justifiably applied by the directors to capital improvements", a later attempt to limit it to situations where funds otherwise available for dividends were properly expended for additions and betterments, was rejected. Guttmann v. Illinois Central R. R., 189 F.2d 927, 27 A.L.R.2d 1066 (2d Cir. 1951), cert. denied 342 U. S. 867, 72 S.Ct. 107, 96 L.Ed. 652 (1951). See Hicks, "Rights of Non-Cumulative Preferred Stock—A Doubtful Decision by the United States Supreme Court", 5 Temp.L.Q. 538 (1931); Lattin, "Is Non-Cumulative Preferred Stock in Fact Preferred?", 25 Ill.L.Rev. 148 (1930); Annot., 27 A.L.R.2d 1073 (1953). In the case of the non-declaration of noncumulative preferred dividends, a court is more likely to award equitable relief. See section 328 infra.

7. 2 I. Kantrowitz & S. Slutsky, White on New York Corporations ¶ 501.04 (13th ed. 1968). See note 10 infra.

8. Hazel Atlas Glass Corp. v. Van Dyk & Reeves, Inc., 8 F.2d 716 (2d Cir. 1925), cert. denied, 269 U.S. 570, 46 S.Ct. 26, 70 L.Ed. 417 (1925). See Henry v. Great Northern Ry., 1 De G. & J. 606, 44 Eng.Rep. 858 (Ch.1857); Boardman v. Lake Shore & Michigan Southern Ry., 84 N.Y. 157 (1881); Lockhart v. Van Alstyne, 31 Mich. 76 (1875); Hazeltine v. Belfast & Moosehead Lake R. R., 79 Me. 411, 10 A. 328 (1887). Most of these cases involved "guaranteed" dividends. In the case of common shares, the presumption seems to be that the dividend is not cumulative. Lockwood v. General Abrasive Co., 210 App.Div. 141, 205 N.Y.S. 511 (4th Dep't 1924), aff'd mem., 240 N.Y. 592, 148 N.E. 719 (1925). See Ghana Companies Code § 51(2) (1963) (canon of construction that unless contrary intention appears, fixed preferential dividend payable on any class of shares is cumulative).

9. See note 6 supra.

-tent-earned preference.[10] The New Jersey cases also suggested that the "dividend credit theory" also applies to common shares.[11]

Under the North Carolina statute,[12] non-cumulative preferred shares are entitled to a

dividend credit,[13] and until such dividend credit is fully discharged, dividends may not be paid to junior shares.

Cumulative Dividend Arrearages on Liquidation

Whether or not preferred shares with a cumulative dividend preference with dividends in arrears are entitled to such arrearages in the event of liquidation depends upon the language defining the liquidation rights of such shares and the judicial attitudes concerning such arrearages.[14]

Except where the language suggests a contrary construction, most courts probably tend to construe the liquidation preference of cumulative preferred shares as including arrearages despite lack of funds legally available for current dividends, since dividends accrue on regular cumulative shares even if not earned.[15]

In New York, there are two troublesome cases. In the older case, the articles of incorporation provided that the holders of preferred shares should be entitled to receive, when and as declared, from the surplus of the corporation an eight percent annual cu-

10. According to the Comment to N.J.Bus.Corp.Act § 14A:7–1 (1969), the absence of specific definition of the rights of holders of noncumulative preferred shares should not preclude the application of equitable principles such as the dividend credit theory. Bassett v. U. S. Cast Iron Pipe & Foundry Co., 75 N.J.Eq. 539, 73 A. 514 (1909); Moran v. U. S. Cast Iron Pipe & Foundry Co., 95 N.J.Eq. 389, 123 A. 546 (1924), aff'd, 96 N.J.Eq. 698, 126 A. 329 (1924); Day v. U. S. Cast Iron Pipe & Foundry Co., 95 N.J.Eq. 389, 123 A. 546 (1924), aff'd 96 N.J.Eq. 736, 126 A. 302 (1924); National Newark and Essex Banking Co. v. Durant Motor Co., 124 N.J.Eq. 213, 1 A.2d 316 (1938), aff'd 125 N.J.Eq. 435, 5 A.2d 767 (1939); Lich v. United States Rubber Co., 39 F.Supp. 675 (D.N.J.1941), aff'd per curiam 123 F.2d 145 (3d Cir. 1941); Cintas v. American Car & Foundry Co., 131 N.J.Eq. 419, 25 A.2d 418 (1942), aff'd 132 N.J.Eq. 460, 28 A.2d 531 (1942); Agnew v. American Ice Co., 2 N.J. 291, 66 A.2d 330 (1949) (all involving shares issued prior to 1926 statutory amendment); Dohme v. Pacific Coast Co., 5 N.J.Super. 477, 68 A. 2d 490 (1949) (post-1926 shares); Sanders v. Cuba R. R., 21 N.J. 78, 120 A.2d 849 (1956). Leeds & Lippincott Co. v. Nevius, 30 N.J. 281, 153 A.2d 45 (1959), modifying 51 N.J.Super. 343, 144 A.2d 4 (1958). See Ashley, "The Future of the Law of Non-Cumulative Preferred Stock in New Jersey: A Raid on the Inarticulate", 5 Rutgers L.Rev. 358 (1951); Note, "Non-Cumulative Preferred Stock Dividends—The Persistence of the New Jersey Rule", 11 U.Pitt.L.Rev. 301 (1950). One commentator suggested that the New Jersey rule depended upon the language of the pre-1926 New Jersey statute. Allcorn, "Corporations", 5 Rutgers L.Rev. 190, 192–194 (1950). Another pointed out that the New Jersey cases narrowly construing the funds available for dividend credits and the Wabash Ry. case, on its facts (see note 6 supra), achieved the same result. Note, "Dividend Credits for Non-Cumulative Preferred Stock", 17 U.Chi.L.Rev. 740 (1950); Note, "Judicial Elaboration of the Dividend Credit Theory in New Jersey", 24 Temp.L.Q. 69 (1950).

11. Bassett v. U. S. Cast Iron Pipe & Foundry Co., 75 N.J.Eq. 539, 73 A. 514 (1909); Day v. U. S. Cast Iron Pipe & Foundry Co., 95 N.J.Eq. 389, 123 A. 546 (1924), aff'd 96 N.J.Eq. 736, 126 A. 302 (1924).

12. N.C.Bus.Corp.Act § 55–40(c), (d) (2) (1957). See comment: "Without some such provisions, non-cumulative preferred shares under one line of American authority enjoy little in the way of 'rights' because the directors, by not declaring dividends year after year despite earnings, can in a later year confer a huge 'windfall dividend' on the common, in a sense out of the pockets of the preferred shareholders. Non-cumulative preferred shares' basic legitimate function is to avoid piling up of 'arrearages'

in periods of no earnings; this function is preserved."

13. N.C.Bus.Corp.Act § 55–2(5) (1957).

14. Buxbaum, "Preferred Stock—Law and Draftsmanship", 42 Calif.L.Rev. 243, 258 (1954). Such arrearages on redemption pose a similar problem. See Liebschutz v. Schaffer Stores Co., 276 App.Div. 1, 93 N.Y.S.2d 125 (4th Dep't 1949) (3–2); Franzen v. Fred Rueping Leather Co., 255 Wis. 265, 38 N. W.2d 517 (1949), reh. denied 255 Wis. 265, 39 N.W. 2d 161 (1949). See Ghana Companies Code § 51(3) (1963) (canon of construction that unless contrary intention appears, in winding up arrears of any cumulative preferential dividend whether earned or declared or not are payable up to date to actual payment in winding up).

15. See, e. g., Hay v. Hay, 38 Wash.2d 513, 230 P.2d 791, 25 A.L.R. 776 (1951) (5–4); Fawkes v. Farm Lands Invest. Co., 112 Cal.App. 374, 297 P. 47 (1931); Penington v. Commonwealth Hotel Construction Corp., 17 Del.Ch. 394, 155 A. 514, 75 A.L. R. 1136 (Sup.Ct.1931); Willson v. Laconia Car Co., 275 Mass. 435, 176 N.E. 182 (1931); Johnson v. Johnson, 138 Va. 487, 122 S.E. 100 (1924); Annot., 25 A.L.R.2d 788 (1952).

mulative dividend, and that in case of liquidation or dissolution of the corporation, the surplus assets and funds of the corporation should be applied, first, to the payment in full par value of the preferred shares, and all accrued and unpaid dividends thereon, and no more. The corporation had no surplus for the six years preceding its dissolution, and no dividends were declared during such period. The court held that the preferred shareholders were entitled to receive only the par value of their shares.[16]

In the more recent case, the articles of incorporation provided that the holders of preferred shares should be entitled to cumulative dividends as and when declared, and that, upon dissolution, after payment of debts, the assets and funds of the corporation were first to be applied to payment of the par value of the preferred shares with any arrearage of dividends to which the holders of preferred shares may be entitled. Upon dissolution of the corporation, the court held that the holders of the preferred shares were entitled to receive only the par value of their shares, without any additional amount equal to the dividends which were not declared and paid on their shares.[17]

To avoid such results, the term "dividend arrearage" or "accumulation" is often defined to include unpaid amounts regardless of whether the corporation shall have funds available for dividends or whether there shall have been a declaration of dividends.[18]

The North Carolina statute [19] expressly provides that absent provision to the contrary, cumulative preferred shares are entitled to receive as part of any liquidation preference the amount of any "accrued dividends".[20]

Elimination of Cumulative Dividend Arrearages

In most jurisdictions, depending upon the jurisdiction's reserved power and statutory authorization and following prescribed procedures, which may require approval of the holders of any class of shares adversely affected thereby, cumulative dividend arrearages might be eliminated directly by amendment of the articles of incorporation (reclassification),[21] or indirectly by such

16. Michael v. Cayey-Caguas Tobacco Co., 190 App. Div. 618, 180 N.Y.S. 532 (1st Dep't 1920). But see Matter of Chandler & Co., 230 N.Y.S.2d 1012 (Sup. Ct. 1962) (construing term "accrued dividends" in liquidation preference, by holding that while right to payment of dividends in going concern accrues only after they are declared out of surplus, right to payment of dividends in corporation in liquidation can accrue by mere lapse of time out of corporate assets when articles of incorporation so provide).

17. Wouk v. Merin, 283 App.Div. 522, 128 N.Y.S.2d 727 (1st Dep't 1954) (3–2) (alternative holding).

18. See section 124, n. 20 supra.

19. N.C.Bus.Corp.Act § 55–40(b) (1) (1957). See also Cal.Gen.Corp.Law, § 114 (1947).

20. N.C.Bus.Corp.Act § 55–2(1) (1957) (defining "accrued dividend" to mean the amount by which aggregate cumulative dividend preferences pertaining to share for entire period during which share was outstanding and cumulative, exceeds all dividends actually paid thereon).

21. ABA–ALI Model Bus.Corp.Act § 53(k); O'Brien v. Socony Mobil Oil Co., 207 Va. 707, 152 S.E.2d 278 (1967), cert. denied 389 U.S. 825, 88 S.Ct. 65, 19 L. Ed.2d 80 (1967); Sherman v. Pepin Pickling Co., 230 Minn. 87, 41 N.W.2d 571 (1950); Western Foundry Co. v. Wicker, 403 Ill. 260, 85 N.E.2d 722, 8 A.L.R.2d 878 (1949); Franzblau v. Capital Securities Co., 2 N.J.Super. 517, 64 A.2d 644 (1949); Arstein v. Robert Reis & Co., 77 N.Y.S.2d 303 (Sup.Ct. 1946), aff'd mem., 273 App.Div. 963, 79 N.Y.S.2d 314 (1st Dep't 1948), leave to appeal denied, 298 N.Y. 931, 81 N.E.2d 335 (1948), cert. denied 335 U.S. 860, 69 S.Ct. 135, 93 L.Ed. 407 (1948); McNulty v. W. & J. Sloane, 184 Misc. 835, 54 N.Y.S.2d 253 (Sup.Ct. 1945). Contra, Schaad v. Hotel Easton Co., 369 Pa. 486, 87 A.2d 227 (1952); Schaffner v. Standard Boiler & Plate Iron Co., 150 Ohio St. 454, 83 N.E.2d 192 (1948); Wheatley v. A. I. Root Co., 147 Ohio St. 127, 69 N.E.2d 187 (1946); Wessel v. Guantanamo Sugar Co., 134 N.J.Eq. 271, 35 A.2d 235 (1944), aff'd sub nom. Murphy v. Guantanamo Sugar Co., 135 N.J.Eq. 506, 39 A.2d 431 (1944); Davison v. Parke, Austin & Lipscomb, Inc., 285 N.Y. 500, 35 N. E.2d 618 (1941) (under former statute); Keller v. Wilson & Co., 21 Del.Ch. 391, 190 A. 115 (Sup.Ct. 1936) (under former statute); Consolidated Film Industries, Inc. v. Johnson, 22 Del.Ch. 407, 197 A. 489 (Sup.Ct.1937) (under former statute); but see Harr v. Pioneer Mechanical Corp., 65 F.2d 332 (2d Cir. 1933), cert. denied 290 U.S. 673, 54 S.Ct. 92, 78 L. Ed. 581 (1933) (Delaware corporation). Since 1967, Delaware has expressly authorized the cancellation

amendment [22] or other procedures, such as merger or consolidation.[23]

Absent fraud, unfairness, or bad faith, the courts hesitate to enjoin or set aside such reclassifications, etc., when effected pursuant to statute.[24]

Shareholders objecting to such reclassification, etc., sometimes are afforded an appraisal remedy by statute.[25]

PARTICIPATING; NONPARTICIPATING

326. Beyond their dividend preference, preferred shares may or may not participate in further dividends with another class or classes of shares. Absent explicit provisions in the articles of incorporation, such as reference to the dividend preference, "and no more", quaere whether preferred shares are "participating" or "nonparticipating".

Whether the dividend preference is cumulative, cumulative-to-the-extent-earned, or noncumulative, the preferred shares may or may not participate in further dividends with another class or classes of shares. If such shares participate, they are said to be "participating"; otherwise, "nonparticipating".[1]

Shares may participate in a variety of ways: equally or in a fixed ratio, immediately after the payment of preferred dividends or after the payment of a prescribed dividend upon another class or classes of shares, or only in the event of a specified contingency. Preferred shares with nonparticipating dividend rights receive no dividends beyond their dividend preference.[2]

In recent years, nonparticipating preferred shares convertible into common shares have tended to replace participating preferred shares.

of "dividends which have accrued but have not been declared" by amendment of the articles of incorporation. Del.Gen.Corp.Law § 242(a) (4) (1967). See also Becht, "Alterations of Accrued Dividends", 45 Mich.L.Rev. 363, 565 (1951); Becht, "Changes in the Interests of Classes of Stockholders by Corporate Charter Amendments", 36 Cornell L.Q. 1 (1950); Campanella & Nakrin, "New York's Changing Concept of Vested Rights in Regard to Shareholders", 24 St. John's L.Rev. 90 (1949); "Rights in Unpaid Accrued Dividends", 20 Corp.J. 183 (1953); Annot., 8 A.L.R.2d 878 (1950).

22. Shanik v. White Sewing Mach. Corp., 25 Del.Ch. 371, 19 A.2d 831 (Sup.Ct.1941); Barrett v. Denver Tramway Corp., 53 F.Supp. 198 (D.Del.1944), aff'd, 146 F.2d 701 (3d Cir. 1944) (Delaware corporation) (creation of prior preferred shares).

23. See also Bove v. Community Hotel Corp., — R. I. —, 249 A.2d 89 (1969); Langfelder v. Universal Laboratories, Inc., 163 F.2d 804 (3d Cir. 1947) (Delaware corporation); Federal United Corp. v. Havender, 24 Del.Ch. 318, 11 A.2d 331 (Sup.Ct.1940); Porges v. Vadsco Sales Corp., 27 Del.Ch. 127, 32 A. 2d 148 (Ch.1943); Hottenstein (Moore) v. York Ice Machinery Corp., 136 F.2d 944 (3d Cir. 1943), petition for leave to file bill of review denied, 146 F.2d 835 (3d Cir. 1944), cert. denied 325 U.S. 886, 65 S.Ct. 1573, 89 L.Ed. 2000 (1945) (Delaware corporation); Anderson v. International Minerals & Chemical Corp., 295 N.Y. 343, 67 N.E.2d 573 (1946) (merger or consolidation). But see Allstate Ins. Co. v. Oxford Finance Companies, 275 F.Supp. 54 (D.Md.1967) (cumulative dividend arrearages held to survive merger where merger agreement did not deal with them). See generally Conard, "Manipulation of Share Priorities—The Record of 79 Listed Securities", 8 Vand.L.Rev. 55 (1954); Dodd, "Accrued Dividends in Delaware—From Vested Rights to Mirage", 57 Harv.L.Rev. 894 (1944).

24. Barrett v. Denver Tramway Corp., 53 F.Supp. 198 (D.Del.1944), aff'd 146 F.2d 701 (3d Cir. 1944) (Delaware law). But cf. Franzblau v. Capital Securities Co., 2 N.J.Super. 517, 64 A.2d 644 (1949); Kamena v. Janssen Dairy Corp., 133 N.J.Eq. 214, 31 A.2d 200 (1943), aff'd per curiam, 134 N.J.Eq. 359, 35 A.2d 894 (1944). See Note, "Limitations on Alteration of Shareholders' Rights by Charter Amendment", 69 Harv.L.Rev. 538 (1956); Becht, "Changes in Interests of Classes of Stockholders by Corporate Charter Amendments", 36 Cornell L.Q. 1 (1950); Walter, "Fairness—A Disappearing Doctrine", 29 B.U.L.Rev. 453 (1949); Latty, "Fairness—The Focal Point in Preferred Stock Arrearage Elimination", 29 Va.L.Rev. 1 (1942); Dodd, "Fair and Equitable Recapitalizations", 55 Harv.L.Rev. 780 (1942). See section 240 supra. The ultimate has perhaps been

reached in an action by a common shareholder to enjoin the corporation's issuing long-term notes to satisfy preferred dividend arrearages on the ground that such arrearages are not a vested right belonging to the preferred shareholders. Sinson v. Bowser, Inc., Civ.No. 59–C–1429 (N.D.Ill.1960).

25. See section 349 infra.

1. Liquidation preferences may also be "participating" or "nonparticipating". Just as preferred shares may have a preference with respect to dividends or liquidation or both, they may be "participating" or "nonparticipating" in either or both respects.

2. Equitable Life Assurance Society v. Union Pacific R. R., 212 N.Y. 360, 106 N.E. 92 (1914); 12 W. Fletcher, Private Corporations 266 (perm. ed. rev. 1957).

Ambiguous provisions may require court construction.[3] The question of participation in further dividends, where the articles of incorporation are silent on the matter, has not been resolved. One view is that a preference takes the place of the normal rule of equality and therefore impliedly precludes participation;[4] the contrary view is that a preference is in addition to such normal equality and does not preclude further participation.[5] The question does not seem to have been settled in many jurisdictions.[6]

The North Carolina statute expressly provides that, absent provision to the contrary preferred shares are nonparticipating.[7]

Problems of construction can be avoided by specific provision in the articles of incorporation.[8]

D. SHAREHOLDERS' "RIGHTS" TO DIVIDENDS

DISCRETION OF BOARD OF DIRECTORS

327. The distribution of dividends, even on shares with a dividend preference, is usually discretionary, within the business judgment of the board of directors. Only when such discretion is abused will courts order a distribution of dividends.

Where discretion is limited by a "mandatory" dividend provision, such provision will be enforced according to its terms whenever legal funds are available. Courts are reluctant to construe a dividend provision as mandatory. "Guaranteed" dividends are often construed as mandatory. A few statutes have or have had mandatory dividend requirements.

The normal rule in most jurisdictions is that shareholders receive dividends, in accordance with applicable dividend preferences and other rights,[1] out of legally available funds,[2] when, as, and if declared by the board of directors in the exercise of their discretion. This rule applies even when dividends are not mentioned in the articles of incorporation, as is usually the case when only a single class of shares is authorized.

"Discretionary Dividends"

In short, the distribution of dividends, even on shares with a dividend preference, is usually discretionary, within the business judgment of the board of directors.[3]

Only when abuse of discretion is shown will courts substitute their own judgment and order a distribution of dividends.[4]

3. See St. Louis Southwestern Ry. v. Meyer, 364 Mo. 1057, 272 S.W.2d 249, 46 A.L.R.2d 964 (1954), appeal dismissed 349 U.S. 942, 75 S.Ct. 871, 91 L. Ed. 1269 (1955), reh. denied 350 U.S. 856, 76 S.Ct. 38, 100 L.Ed. 761 (1955); Rowell, "Rights of Preferred Shareholders in Excess of Preference", 19 Minn.L. Rev. 406 (1935).

4. James F. Powers Foundry Co. v. Miller, 166 Md. 590, 171 A. 842 (1934); Tennant v. Epstein, 356 Ill. 26, 189 N.E. 864 (1934); Stone v. United States Envelope Co., 119 Me. 394, 111 A. 536 (1920).

5. St. Louis Southwestern Ry. v. Loeb, 318 S.W.2d 246 (Mo.1958); Englander v. Osborne, 261 Pa. 366, 104 A. 614, 6 A.L.R. 800 (1918); Sternbergh v. Brock, 225 Pa. 279, 74 A. 166 (1908).

6. E. g., 2 I. Kantrowitz & S. Slutsky, White on New York Corporations ¶ 501.04 (13th ed. 1968).

7. N.C.Bus.Corp.Act § 55–40(b)(2) (1957). See Ghana Companies Code § 51(4) (1963) (canon of construction that unless contrary intention appears, any class of shares with right to preferential dividend to have no further right to participate in dividends).

8. See section 124, n. 16 supra.

[§ 327]

1. See sections 324–326 supra.

2. See sections 320–323 supra.

3. Matter of Carlisle, 53 Misc.2d 546, 278 N.Y.S.2d 1011 (Sur.Ct.1967); Lippman v. New York Water Service Corp., 25 Misc.2d 267, 205 N.Y.S.2d 541 (Sup.Ct.1960), appeal dismissed 12 A.D.2d 611, 214 N.Y.S.2d 715 (1st Dep't 1960); 11 W. Fletcher, Private Corporations § 5325 (perm. ed. rev. 1958); R. Stevens, Handbook on the Law of Private Corporations § 99 (2d ed. 1949); H. Ballantine, Ballantine on Corporations § 231 (rev. ed. 1946). See Ghana Companies Code § 51(1) (1963) (canon of construction that unless contrary intention appears, no dividend is payable absent declaration).

4. Cashman v. Petrie, 14 N.Y.2d 426, 252 N.Y.S.2d 447, 201 N.E.2d 24 (1964) (trustee of majority share interest, who was also director of corporation, held to be under no fiduciary duty to distribute dividends to income beneficiaries of another trust hold-

Abuse of discretion is found only if there is evidence of fraud or bad faith or a clear case of unreasonableness.[5]

ing remaining shares); Farmers Warehouse of Pelham, Inc. v. Collins, 220 Ga. 141, 137 S.E.2d 619 (1964) (shareholder who had agreed to pay for his shares with dividends and services held entitled only to such dividends as were declared); Moskowitz v. Bantrell, 41 Del.Ch. 177, 190 A.2d 749 (Sup.Ct.1964) (upholding board of directors discretion in setting aside income of wasting-asset corporation for future development rather than in distributing such income as dividends); Leibert v. Grinnel Corp., 41 Del.Ch. 340, 194 A.2d 846 (Ch. 1963) (refusing to compel holding corporation, whose charter purpose was to hold securities of other corporations, to receive dividends and interest therefrom, and to distribute dividends, despite $3,500,000 accumulation, where no accumulated earnings surtax had been claimed by government and accumulation approximated amount needed to buy another corporation under long-standing negotiations); Berwald v. Mission Development Co., 40 Del.Ch. 509, 185 A.2d 480 (Sup.Ct.1962) (denying dissolution of holding company whose principal subsidiary in 1954 stopped paying cash dividends and in 1960 ceased distributing five percent share dividends, while holding company continued to purchase more shares of subsidiary, subsidiary being found to have embarked on expensive modernization program); Doherty v. Mutual Warehouse Co., 255 F.2d 489 (5th Cir. 1958) (affirming lower court's finding of no abuse of discretion in board of directors' adding earnings to surplus and not declaring a dividend); but cf. Dodge v. Ford Motor Co., 204 Mich. 459, 170 N.W. 668, 3 A.L.R. 413 (1919) ($19,275,386 dividend ordered); Patton v. Nicholas, 154 Tex. 385, 279 S.W.2d 848 (1955), 302 S.W.2d 441 (Tex.Civ. App.1957); see Wormser, "May the Courts Compel the Declaration of a Corporate Dividend", 3 So.L.Q. 281 (1918); Note, 64 Har.L.Rev. 299 (1950).

5. Whittemore v. Continental Mills, 98 F.Supp. 387 (D.Me.1951) (personal income tax status of dominant shareholder and director); Keough v. St. Paul Milk Co., 205 Minn. 96, 285 N.W. 809 (1939) (conversion of corporate property; fraudulent expense accounts). Indicative of abuse of discretion might be relatively high compensation compared to dividends, intense hostility, freeze-out or other oppression of the minority, danger of federal undistributed profits surtax (70 percent rule-of-thumb). See Schmitt v. Eagle Roller Mill Co., 199 Minn. 382, 272 N.W. 277 (1937); Jones v. Motor Sales Co., 322 Pa. 492, 185 A. 809 (1936); City Bank Farmers' Trust Co. v. Hewitt Realty Co., 257 N.Y. 62, 177 N.E. 309, 76 A. L.R. 881 (1931). Abuse of discretion will probably be found more readily where the complainants are preferred shareholders, especially those with noncumulative dividend preferences. See Guttmann v. Illinois Central R. R., 189 F.2d 927, 27 A.L.R.2d 1066 (2d Cir. 1951), cert. denied 342 U.S. 867, 72 S.Ct. 107, 96 L.Ed. 652 (1951) (where court assumed arguendo that standard of discretion in weighing propriety of non-declaration of noncumulative preferred shares was far stricter than that applicable to common

"Mandatory Dividends"

However, discretion is limited when the articles of incorporation contain a "mandatory" dividend provision, as where shares expressly are to receive designated dividends in any year in which legal funds are available.[6]

Absent a clear and express mandatory provision, the courts will not construe a provision to deprive the board of directors of its discretion in dividend declarations.[7]

shares, and Frank, Cir. J., stated: "But the preferred stockholders are not—like sailors or idiots or infants—wards of the judiciary"). Most of the successful cases to compel dividends have involved close corporations. See F. O'Neal & J. Derwin, Expulsion or Oppression of Business Associates: "Squeeze-Outs" in Small Enterprises §§ 3.03, 3.04 (1961); Comment, "Proposals to Help the Minority Shareholder Receive Fairer Dividend Treatment From the Closely Held Corporation", 56 Nw.U.L. Rev. 503 (1961); Note "Forcing Dividends from the Closely Held Corporation", 37 U.Det.L.J. 246 (1959); Note, "Minority Shareholder's Power to Compel Declaration of Dividends in Close Corporations", 10 Rutgers L.Rev. 723 (1956).

6. Arizona Western Insurance Co. v. L. L. Constantin & Co., 247 F.2d 388 (3d Cir. 1957), cert. denied 355 U.S. 905, 78 S.Ct. 332, 2 L.Ed.2d 260 (1957) (New Jersey corporation); but see L. L. Constantin & Co. v. R. P. Holding Corp., 56 N.J.Super. 411, 153 A.2d 378 (Ch.1959) (contrary holding involving same corporation based on bylaw not discussed in 1957 case); New England Trust Co. v. Penobscot Chemical Fibre Co., 142 Me. 286, 50 A.2d 188 (1946); Crocker v. Waltham Watch Co., 315 Mass. 397, 53 N.E.2d 230 (1944); Warburton v. John Wanamaker Philadelphia, 329 Pa. 5, 196 A. 506 (1938); Wood v. Lary, 47 Hun 550 (1st Dep't 1888), aff'd, 124 N.Y. 83, 26 N.E. 338 (1891); cf. Hassett v. S. F. Iszard Co., 61 N.Y.S.2d 451 (Sup.Ct.1945) (argument based on prospectus unsuccessful); Note, "Mandatory Dividend Provisions in Shareholders' Contracts", 9 Syracuse L.Rev. 239 (1958).

7. 11 W. Fletcher, Private Corporations § 5325 (perm. ed. rev. 1958). A "shareholder agreement" arranging the distribution of earnings in a fixed manner has been upheld. Wabash Ry. v. American Refrigerator Transit Co., 7 F.2d 335 (8th Cir. 1925), cert. denied 270 U.S. 643, 46 S.Ct. 208, 70 L.Ed. 776 (1926); see also Galler v. Galler, 32 Ill.2d 16, 203 N.E.2d 577 (1964), 95 Ill.App.2d 340, 238 N.E.2d 274 (1968); Clark v. Dodge, 269 N.Y. 410, 199 N.E. 641 (1936). Such "shareholder agreements" run the risk of being held invalid as undue interference with the discretion of the board of directors—a risk to which a "mandatory" dividend provision in the articles of incorporation does not seem to be subject. See also Blair v. Bishop's Restaurants, Inc., 202 Okl. 648, 217 P.2d 161 (1950) (upholding bylaw of

"Guaranteed" dividends are often construed as mandatory dividends.[8]

A few statutes require or have required the distribution of legally available funds as dividends, after allowance for working capital.[9]

ACTIONS TO COMPEL DISTRIBUTION OF DIVIDENDS

328. An action to compel the distribution of a "mandatory" dividend is by the shareholder, in behalf of himself and others similarly situated, against the corporation on the basis of his share contract.

An action to compel the distribution of a "discretionary" dividend has been held by most courts to be an action by the shareholder based on his share contract, but a closely-divided New York decision has held such an action to be a shareholder derivative action at least for certain statutory purposes, a result since overruled by statute.

In an action to compel the distribution of a "discretionary" dividend, directors are usually not indispensable parties but at most conditionally necessary parties.

The burden of proof is on the complaining shareholder to show abuse of discretion—an onerous burden.

Remedies are mandatory injunction, decree of specific performance, or declaratory judgment, possibly with the court retaining jurisdiction to prevent recurrence of the abuse of discretion.

There is little authority concerning the incidence of litigation expenses of actions to compel dividend distributions.

"Mandatory Dividends"

Enforcement of the relatively rare mandatory dividend provision should be had in a direct action by the shareholder, in behalf of himself and others similarly situated, against the corporation on the basis of his share contract.[1]

"Discretionary Dividends"

Where dividends are discretionary, as most are, and there are funds legally available for dividends which the board of directors refrains from distributing as dividends to shareholders, the primary resort of the shareholders is to sue to compel a dividend distribution. Wrongful withholding of proper dividends is the converse of distribution of improper dividends—both involve abuse of the discretion over dividends entrusted to directors, except that statutory regulation is largely directed only toward the latter.[2]

---

close corporation providing that "whenever the surplus profits of the company amount to one percent, or more, of the capital stock, the secretary-treasurer may declare a dividend on the shares", without mention of the Oklahoma statute vesting management in the board of directors). While bond indentures, loan agreements, etc., might limit the discretion of the board of directors with respect to dividends, such limitations are almost invariably negative rather than positive, thereby not arousing contentions that they unduly interfere with the discretion of the board of directors.

8. Burk v. Ottawa Gas & Electric Co., 87 Kan. 6, 123 P. 857 (1912); Belfast & Moosehead Lake R. R. v. Belfast, 77 Me. 445, 1 A. 362 (1885); Lockhart v. Van Alstyne, 31 Mich. 76 (1875); Boardman v. Lake Shore & Michigan Southern Ry., 84 N.Y. 157 (1881). Cf. Jones Valley Finance Co. v. Tennille, 40 Ala. App. 284, 115 So.2d 495 (1959), cert. denied 270 Ala. 738, 115 So.2d 504 (1959). "Guaranteed" dividends on shares cannot be guaranteed by the issuing corporation except conditionally upon the existence of funds legally available for dividends.

9. See N.C.Bus.Corp. Act § 55-50(i)-(k) (Supp.1969) (making compulsory dividend provision inapplicable to any corporation having assets of $1,000,000 or more or whose shareholders number 750 or more); New Jersey and New Mexico have repealed their mandatory dividend provisions. Nebel v. Nebel, 241 N.C. 491, 85 S.E.2d 876 (1955); Steele v. Locke Cotton Mills Co., 231 N.C. 636, 58 S.E.2d 620 (1950); cf. Gaines v. Long Mfg. Co., 234 N.C. 331, 67 S.E.2d 355, 38 A.L.R.2d 1359 (1951).

1. Boardman v. Lake Shore & Michigan Southern Ry., 84 N.Y. 157 (1881) (corporation only defendant); Koppel v. Middle States Petroleum Corp., 272 App.Div. 790, 69 N.Y.S.2d 784 (1st Dep't 1947). Cf. Rubens v. Marion-Washington Realty Corp., 116 Ind.App. 55, 59 N.E.2d 907 (1945) (holding that, where mandatory dividends were subject to certain conditions, shareholder's remedy was only in equity until dividend was actually declared); Malone v. Armor Insulating Co., 191 Ga. 146, 12 S.E.2d 299 (1940); Cannon v. Wiscasset Mills Co., 195 N.C. 119, 141 S.E. 344 (1928) (mandamus).

2. H. Ballantine, Ballantine on Corporations § 231 (rev. ed. 1946).

Direct or Derivative Action

An action to compel the distribution of discretionary dividends has been held by most courts to be a direct action by the shareholder, based on his share contract.[3] However, the New York Court of Appeals held, in a 4–3 decision, that such an action was derivative.[4] The majority reasoned that the action brought into question the duty of policy, and that the object of the action was to cause the court to perform a corporate function which the directors would have done except for their bad faith. Two dissenting judges contended that the right of a shareholder to receive dividends was part of his share contract, that this was a corporate obligation not a corporate right, that any recovery would be from and not to the corporation, that the majority in effect had the corporation suing itself, and that the majority's error would have been more manifest if the action had been to compel the declaration of a dividend on one of two or more classes of shares rather than on the only class of shares. A third judge dissented on the ground that the security-for-expenses provision was intended to be limited to actions against directors for money damages for wrongs done by them to their corporation.[5]

Of course, once a cash dividend is declared, it usually creates a debtor-creditor relationship between the corporation and the shareholders giving rise to a direct action on the debt.[6]

Joinder of Defendants

In an action to compel the distribution of a discretionary dividend, the corporation should, of course, be joined as defendant on the theory either that the share contract allegedly breached is between it and the shareholder or that a corporation is an indispensable party to a derivative action.[7] Since the court, if it grants relief, is in effect substituting its discretion for that of the directors, and can order the corporation, over which it has jurisdiction, to distribute the dividend, no logical reason appears why the directors need be joined in the action, except to compel them to engage in the empty ritual of formally declaring the dividend which the court orders. In other words, the action is to compel the corporation to distribute rather than to compel the directors to vote for the declaration. Several cases have held that the directors, in such an action, are not indispensable parties but are at most conditionally necessary parties.[8]

---

3. Knapp v. Bankers Securities Corp., 230 F.2d 717 (3d Cir. 1956) (for purposes of Pennsylvania security-for-expenses statute); Doherty v. Mutual Warehouse Co., 245 F.2d 609 (5th Cir. 1957) (for purposes of contemporaneous-share-ownership requirement of Fed.R.Civ.P. 23.1).

4. Gordon v. Elliman, 306 N.Y. 456, 119 N.E.2d 331 (1954) (for purposes of New York security-for-expenses statute) (overruled in effect by McKinney's N.Y.Bus.Corp.Law, § 627 (limiting application of security-for-expenses statute to shareholder derivative action brought in right of corporation to procure judgment *in its favor*)).

5. See section 360 infra.

6. See section 331 infra.

7. See section 369 infra.

8. Doherty v. Mutual Warehouse Co., 245 F.2d 609 (5th Cir. 1957); Kroese v. General Steel Castings Corp., 179 F.2d 760, 15 A.L.R.2d 1117 (3d Cir. 1950), cert. denied 339 U.S. 983, 70 S.Ct. 1026, 94 L.Ed. 1386 (1950) (Pennsylvania law); Whittemore v. Continental Mills, 98 F.Supp. 387 (D.Me.1951) (Maine law); Swinton v. W. J. Bush & Co., 199 Misc. 321, 102 N.Y.S.2d 944 (Sup.Ct.1951), aff'd mem., 278 App.Div. 754, 103 N.Y.S.2d 1019 (1st Dept. 1951); W. Q. O'Neall Co. v. O'Neall, 108 Ind. App. 116, 25 N.E.2d 656 (1940); see also Gordon v. Elliman, 306 N.Y. 456, 464, 119 N.E.2d 331, 337 (1954). Contra, Schuckman v. Rubenstein, 164 F.2d 952 (6th Cir. 1947), cert. denied 333 U.S. 875, 68 S.Ct. 905, 92 L.Ed. 1151 (1948) (Ohio law); Tower Hill Connellsville Coke Co. v. Piedmont Coal Co., 33 F.2d 703 (4th Cir. 1929), cert. denied, 280 U.S. 607, 50 S.Ct. 157, 74 L.Ed. 650 (1929). See N.C.Bus.Corp. Act § 55–50(k) (1957) (directors not necessary parties). Forum non conveniens might provide a useful defense if the action is against a foreign corporation. Compare Altman v. Central of Georgia Ry., 363 F.2d 284 (D.C.Cir.1966), cert. denied 385 U. S. 920, 87 S.Ct. 231, 17 L.Ed.2d 144 (1966), rev'g 254 F.Supp. 167 (D.D.C.1965), with Shulof v. Rockefeller, 326 F.2d 86 (2d Cir. 1963); Cohn v. Mishkoff-Costlow Co., 256 N.Y. 102, 175 N.E. 529 (1931); Frank v. Getty, 29 Misc.2d 115, 216 N.Y.S.2d 15 (Sup.Ct.1961).

Burden on Complaining Shareholder

As previously mentioned courts hesitate to substitute their judgment for the business judgment of the board of directors, to whom has been delegated dividend policy determination, and to order a dividend distribution; courts, however, will intervene upon a showing that the directors have acted in bad faith or are acting clearly unreasonably.[9] This places a heavy burden of proof on the complaining shareholder.[10] Of the many cases brought, relief has been granted in relatively few instances.[11]

9. See section 327 supra. See 1 G. Hornstein, Corporation Law and Practice § 479 (1959) (checklist for complaint or petition in action to compel declaration of dividends).

10. New York no longer imposes its onerous security-for-expenses requirement on smaller (but not other) shareholders bringing such an action. See note 4 supra and section 372 infra.

11. The classic case was the $19,275,386 dividend ordered in Dodge v. Ford Motor Co., 204 Mich. 459, 170 N.W. 668, 3 A.L.R. 413 (1919). The Ford Motor Co. was a close corporation controlled by Henry Ford I, who wanted to use profits to expand business to increase employment and to sell cars to the public at a reduced price of $360 per car (from $440, at which price the corporation could not meet the demand). The corporation had $132,000,000 assets, some $18,000,000 liabilities, $1,800,000 stated capital (mainly as the result of share dividends), $112,000,000 surplus, $60,000,000 annual net income, and some $54,000,000 in cash and municipal bonds. While $1,200,000 annual dividends were being paid, and $41,000,000 extra dividends were paid in 1911–1915, no extra dividend had been paid since October, 1915. The two Dodge brothers, who held one-tenth of the shares (on a $15,000 investment) sued to compel an extra dividend of at least three-fourths of the cash balance. In ordering a dividend of $19,275,386, the court stated: "We have no doubt that certain sentiments, philanthropic and altruistic, creditable to Mr. Ford, had large influence in determining the policy to be pursued by the Ford Motor Company . . . There should be no confusion (of which there is evidence) of the duties which Mr. Ford conceives that he and the stockholders owe to the general public and the duties which in law he and his codirectors owe to protesting, minority stockholders. A business corporation is organized and carried on primarily for the profit of the stockholders. The powers of the directors are to be employed for that end. The discretion of directors is to be exercised in the choice of means

Remedies

The traditional remedies, where abuse of discretion has been found, are mandatory injunction ordering a dividend, decree for specific performance, or declaratory judgment. Such relief does not prevent repetition of the same wrong in the future. Liquidation is a drastic remedy, productive of economic loss in the case of a solvent corporation. A more adequate remedy is for the court to order annual dividends consistent with sound business practice to retain jurisdiction for the next several years, thus assuring a reasonable dividend policy under threat of contempt or liquidation.[12]

Expenses of Action

If the shareholder is successful in suing to compel the declaration of a dividend, there is little authority concerning his right to recover his reasonable expenses incurred in the litigation. A possible solution is to pay him out of the dividend fund before distributing the balance proportionately among shareholders.[13]

to attain that end and does not extend to a change in the end itself, to the reduction of profits or to the nondistribution of profits among stockholders in order to devote them to other purposes." 204 Mich. at 505–507, 170 N.W. at 683–684, 3 A.L.R. at 440–441. The court-compelled distribution obviously left ample funds for expansion of the business. Ford later bought out the Dodge brothers, who then formed the Dodge Motor Co. See section 327, nn. 4, 5 supra.

12. Patton v. Nicholas, 154 Tex. 385, 279 S.W.2d 848 (1955), 302 S.W.2d 441 (Tex.Civ.App.1957) (ordering prompt reasonable dividend based on accumulated surpluses, and reasonable future dividends, and retaining jurisdiction to punish for contempt and to appoint liquidating receiver).

13. See Starring v. Kemp, 167 Va. 429, 188 S.E. 174 (1936), reh. denied 167 Va. 438, 190 S.E. 163 (1937) (allowing as counsel fees, in successful action to compel distribution of dividends on prior preference shares, award of two percent of $380,604, amount ordered to be distributed, or $7,612, to be deducted by corporation when the dividends were paid). See section 377 infra.

E. SHARE DISTRIBUTIONS

SHARE DIVIDENDS

329. Share dividends, or stock dividends, are distributions to shareholders of additional shares of stock of the corporation making the distribution. The dividend shares usually are of the same but sometimes may be of a different class (or series) from the shares upon which the dividend is declared. A share dividend results in a greater number of shares representing the same total equity, which means that each share's equity is diluted pro tanto. To the extent that surplus is capitalized, the stated capital is increased and the surplus correspondingly decreased, thus changing the nature of the equity. Statutes differ widely in their treatment of share dividends.

As to the funds legally available for share dividends, there must be, as a minimum, sufficient surplus, earned or unearned, to cover a sufficient transfer to stated capital to represent the new issued shares resulting from the share dividend.

The usual accounting treatment for a share dividend is to credit stated capital and debit surplus for the appropriate amount to represent the dividend shares issued—usually no less than the par value of any par value shares or the minimum allowed for shares without par value.

In the case of listed shares, securities exchange requirements, such as transferring from earned surplus to stated capital and capital surplus an amount equal to the fair value of such shares and sending a prescribed notice to shareholders, might also apply.

A share dividend, with some exceptions, is not taxable but requires adjustment in the holder's basis with respect to both his former shares and dividend shares.

Share dividends (or stock dividends, as they are often called) and share splits [1] are similar to each other in several respects, each being a type of share distribution, but nevertheless differ in certain respects. Hybrid share distributions have presented various problems.

Share dividends are distributions to shareholders of additional shares of stock of the corporation making the distribution. The dividend shares are usually of the same but may be of a different class (or series) from the shares upon which the dividend is declared, subject to any applicable limitations.

A share dividend, in effect, is not a real dividend, since it results in a greater number of shares representing the same total equity (or net worth or proprietorship), which means that each share's equity is diluted *pro tanto*. However, since some surplus is capitalized (except when treasury shares are distributed), the stated capital is increased and the surplus correspondingly decreased, thus changing the nature of the equity.[2]

Share dividends are second only to cash dividends in frequency and amount. Their principal purpose is to retain profits in the business and to give the shareholders some tangible evidence of such fact. Usually a share dividend is small, say, one to 10 percent. A five percent share dividend would give the holder one additional share for each 20 shares held; for holdings of less than 20 shares, fractions of shares, where lawful, or scrip might be issued or adjustments made in cash.[3]

---

2. M. Sussman, The Stock Dividend (1962). One share of Eastman Kodak Co. purchased in 1884 would, as the result of splits, share dividends, and other distributions, have grown by 1968 to 24,536.84 shares, and, if all warrants and rights had been exercised, to 37,113.96 shares. See Powell v. Maryland Trust Co., 125 F.2d 260 (4th Cir. 1942), cert. denied 316 U.S. 671, 62 S.Ct. 1046, 86 L.Ed. 1746 (1942), reh. denied 316 U.S. 711, 62 S.Ct. 1274, 86 L.Ed. 1777 (1942). Similar to a share dividend is a transfer from surplus to stated capital without the distribution of shares. While a share dividend, prior to the 1966 repeal of the tax, was subject to the federal issue tax, a capitalization of surplus alone was not. F. & M. Schaefer Brewing Co. v. United States, 256 F.2d 696 (2d Cir. 1958).

3. Sobieski, "Fractional Shares in Stock Dividends and Splits", 16 Bus.Law. 204 (1960); Waring, "Fractional Shares Under Stock Dividend Declarations", 44 Harv.L.Rev. 404 (1931). See section 161 supra.

1. See section 330 infra.

Share dividends, especially if large (so-called "melons"), reduce the market price per share (possibly bringing the shares into a more popular trading price range), and somewhat camouflage earnings per share— although a share split-up is a more common device to achieve such results. A share dividend may offer possible tax advantages to the recipient.[4]

Statutes differ widely in their treatment of share dividends. Some make no or only a passing reference to them.[5]

Even the Delaware corporation law continues to treat them in very general terms.[6]

Funds Legally Available for Share Dividends

The treatment of share dividends in the Model Business Corporation Act is rather substantial.[7] It prohibits share dividends (as well as cash or property dividends) when contrary to the articles of incorporation. In addition, the Model Act has provisions relating only to share dividends.[8]

Extensive treatment of share dividends is found in other modern corporation statutes, which sometimes expressly distinguish between share dividends, distributions of treasury shares, and share split-ups, and often allow share dividends out of types of un- earned surplus not available for cash or property dividends.[9]

When statutes are silent on the point, the question might arise as to whether share dividends may be distributed only when there are, by the general prevailing standard, funds legally available for dividends [10] which can be capitalized to the extent required. Presumably, as a minimum, there must be sufficient surplus, earned or unearned, to cover a sufficient transfer to stated capital to represent the new issued shares resulting from the share dividend. No share dividend itself can affect a corporation's insolvency in either equity or bankruptcy senses.

In the case of listed shares, securities exchange requirements might also apply.[11]

Accounting Treatment of Share Dividends

The more traditional accounting treatment for a share dividend was to credit the stated capital account and debit the surplus account for the appropriate amount to represent the dividend shares issued—usually no less than the par value of any par value shares or the minimum allowed for shares without par value.[12]

4. See H. Guthmann & H. Dougall, Corporate Financial Policy 543–546 (4th ed. 1962).

5. Comprehensive treatment is found in ABA–ALI Model Bus.Corp.Act § 40(c)–(e); McKinney's N.Y. Bus.Corp.Law, § 511 (notice requirement). Share dividends have been upheld even in the absence of statutory provision for them. Williams v. Western Union Tel. Co., 93 N.Y. 162 (1883). Except when additional shares for a share dividend need be authorized (see section 345 infra), no shareholder approval is necessary in most jurisdictions.

6. Del.Gen.Corp.Law, § 173 (1967). New York had no provision prior to 1963 when its very comprehensive provision became effective.

7. ABA–ALI Model Bus.Corp.Act § 40.

8. ABA–ALI Model Bus. Corp.Act, § 40(c), (d), (e). Increase in stated capital is the express test to distinguish a share dividend from a split-up under the Model Act.

9. E. g., Cal.Gen.Corp.Law, §§ 1504–1506 (1947); McKinney's N.Y.Bus.Corp.Law, § 511; N.C.Bus. Corp.Act § 55–51 (1957) (distinguishing distributions of treasury shares and share split-ups from share dividends). See deCapriles, "Article 5—Corporate Finance", 11 Buffalo L.Rev. 461, 476 (1962); deCapriles & McAniff, "The Financial Provisions of the New (1961) New York Business Corporation Law", 36 N.Y.U.L.Rev. 1239, 1266 (1961). The 1960 study bill contained the following provision which was soon deleted: "the term 'stock dividend' or 'share dividend', if used in such notice, shall be expressly stated to be applicable only to the number of distributed shares as to which a transfer has been made from earned surplus in an amount equal to their aggregate fair value as determined by the directors." (§ 5.12(a) (5)).

10. See sections 320–322 supra. Creditors can hardly be injured by the capitalization of surplus.

11. See discussion of Securities Exchange Requirements Applicable to Share Dividends, infra.

12. See Cal.Gen.Corp.Law, § 1506 (1947). Once capitalized, the former surplus is not available for dividends. Lich v. United States Rubber Co., 39 F. Supp. 675 (D.N.J.1941), aff'd per curiam 123 F.2d

More recently, accountants have suggested that, in the case of share distributions which are so small that they will not have any apparent effect upon the share market price, a publicly-held corporation should in the public interest account for the transaction by transferring from earned surplus to the category of permanent capitalization (represented by the stated capital and capital surplus accounts) an amount equal to the fair value of the shares issued.[13]

Securities Exchange Requirements Applicable to Share Dividends

Securities exchanges on which the shares participating in the share dividend is listed might impose certain requirements. For example, the New York Stock Exchange, to guard against possible misconception by the shareholders of the effect of share dividends on their equity and of their relation to current earnings, imposes for share dividends (and share split-ups in such range as well) involving less than 25 percent of the number of shares outstanding prior to such distribution the following requirements: [14]

(a) In respect of each such share so distributed, a transfer from *earned* surplus to the permanent capitalization (stated capital and capital surplus accounts) an amount equal to the fair value of such shares (with "fair value" approximating the current share market price adjusted to reflect issuance of the additional shares);

(b) Accompanying notice to shareholders advising them of the amount capitalized per share, the aggregate amount thereof, the relation of such aggregate amount to current undistributed earnings, the account or accounts to which such aggregate has been charged and credited, the reason for paying the share dividend, and that sale of the dividend shares would reduce their proportionate equity;

(c) Advance listing of any such shares distributed if of a listed class or series; and

(d) Equitable methods of settlement of fractional-share interests.

Other dividend rules of the exchange applicable to dividends in general also apply to share dividends.[15] In addition, share split-ups are subject to further securities exchange requirements.[16]

Tax Aspects of Share Dividends

Generally speaking, a share dividend, with some exceptions, is not taxable under the federal income tax laws, but requires adjustment in the holder's basis with respect to both his former shares and his dividend shares. Taxable share dividends since 1969 include share dividends on preferred shares

---

145 (3d Cir. 1941); Keough v. St. Paul Milk Co., 205 Minn. 96, 285 N.W. 809 (1939). However, a share dividend can be set aside when made fraudulently or unreasonably to forestall cash dividends. See Keough v. St. Paul Milk Co., supra.

13. See Accounting Research Bulletin No. 43, reprinted in Accounting Research and Terminology Bulletins 47 (A.I.C.P.A. final ed. 1961). See G. Hills, The Law of Accounting and Financial Statements 149–153 (1957). The Securities and Exchange Commission agrees with the share dividend accounting pronouncements of the American Institute of Certified Public Accountants that the issuer should charge its earned surplus account with the fair value of the shares issued as a share dividend. Proposed SEC Rule 10b–12, SEC Securities Exchange Act Release No. 8268 (Mar. 7, 1968). L. Rappaport, SEC Accounting Practice and Procedure 16.32 (2d ed. 1963).

14. N.Y.S.E. Company Manual § A13. This exchange policy might be applied to 25 or more but less than 100 percent distributions, but is not applicable to 100 percent or more distributions. The S.E.C. would subject to such requirements any issuer which publicly offers any class of shares or has outstanding any class of shares traded by use of the mails or interstate commerce or of any facility of any national securities exchange. See note 13

supra. In 1967, there were 234 distributions on shares listed on the New York Stock Exchange. Of these, 142 were less than 25 percent, 24 were 25 up to 100 percent, 62 were 2-for-1 to 2½-for-1, and 6 were 3-for-1 to 3½-for-1. New York Stock Exchange 1968 Fact Book 29 (1968).

15. See section 318 supra.

16. See section 330 infra.

and disproportionate distributions, including distributions of common shares to some shareholders and of preferred shares to other shareholders and distributions of convertible preferred shares to common shareholders.[17]

SHARE SPLITS

330. Share splits, or stock splits, may be (a) split-ups, where one share is split into a larger number of shares, or (b) reverse splits, or split-downs, where a number of shares are combined to form a smaller number of shares.

Share splits involve no transfer from surplus to stated capital or any changes except adjustments in par value or stated value per share, when applicable, so that the same stated capital which represented the issued shares before the split properly represents the changed number of shares after the split. A split-up requires not only board of directors action, but often requires advance shareholder approval as well when the articles of incorporation must be amended to change the par value or stated value of shares and also, when necessary, to authorize additional shares.

The usual accounting treatment for a share split is to do nothing except to reflect the different number of issued shares and any changes in par or stated value.

For split-ups of listed shares, applicable securities exchange requirements must be observed, including transfers to stated capital and capital surplus from earned surplus of the fair value of the new shares for certain distributions and avoidance of the word "dividend" in any reference to a share distribution not being covered by such a transfer.

Ordinarily for trust and estate purposes, shares resulting from share split-ups are part of the corpus.

There are no tax consequences to share splits except to divide (in the case of a split-up) or multiply (in the case of a reverse split) the base for each share.

Share splits, or stock splits, are of two types: (a) the usual share split-up, where one share is split into a larger number of shares; and (b) the so-called reverse split, or split-down, where a number of shares are combined to form one share (*quaere*, as to any resulting fractions of shares).

Statutes sometimes expressly provide that a split-up or division of the shares of any class into a greater number of shares of the same class without increasing the stated capital of the corporation shall not be construed to be a share dividend within the meaning of the statutory provision dealing with share dividends.[1]

A corporation by splitting-up its shares splits the price per share downward, thus possibly securing a more marketable price range, say $20 to $40 range, which is likely to increase the number of its shareholders and potential customers for its goods or services and for future issues of its securities. Split-ups also tend to disguise earnings per share, and increase brokerage commissions and taxes based on number of shares.[2]

---

17. See discussion of Share Dividends in section 339 infra. General Bancshares Corp. v. Comm'r, 326 F. 2d 712 (8th Cir. 1964), cert. denied 379 U.S. 832, 85 S.Ct. 62, 13 L.Ed.2d 40 (1964), held that expenses incurred by a corporation in issuing nontaxable share dividends were essentially capital expenditures and not deductible as ordinary and necessary business expenses. McKinney's N.Y.Tax Law, § 180, imposes a tax on changes of authorized shares. In 18 East 48th Street Corp. v. New York, 19 A.D.2d 940, 244 N.Y.S.2d 446 (3d Dep't 1963), the board of directors resolved to split the 200 originally authorized shares into 31,567 shares. The articles of amendment of articles of incorporation indicating an increase in the number of shares—not a share split—were filed with the secretary of state and a tax of $1,568.35 (five cents times 31,367 new shares) paid. If the articles of amendment had reflected a share split, only a $10 tax would have been due. Correction of the articles of amendment nunc pro tunc and a $1,558.35 tax refund were denied. See also Southern Spring Bed Co. v. State Corporation Commission, 205 Va. 272, 136 S.E.2d 900 (1964) (entrance fees on foreign corporation). Issue taxes may apply to share dividends but not share splits. See former 26 U.S.C.A. § 4303; Fla.Op.Att'y Gen. No. 63–7 (Jan. 23, 1963).

1. E. g., ABA–ALI Model Bus.Corp.Act § 40; N.C. Bus.Corp.Law, § 55–51(d), (e) (1957); see also Cal. Gen.Corp.Law, § 1507 (1947).

2. Barker, "A Clearer Picture of Effective Stock Splits", 34 Harv.Bus.Rev. 101 (Jan.-Feb. 1956); Note, "Manipulation of Voting Control—The Stock Split", 4 Stan.L.Rev. 575 (1952). See Smith v. Hoyle, —— Pa. ——, —— A.2d —— (——) (enforcing long-term contract to sell shares, requiring twice number of shares specified in contract on basis of

Split-ups also have a tendency to encourage speculation.

Legal Limitations

Share splits, in the legal sense, involve no transfers from surplus to stated capital or any changes except adjustments in par value or stated value per share, when applicable, so that the same stated capital which represented the issued shares before the split property represents the changed number of shares after the split.

A split-up requires not only board of directors action, but often requires advance shareholder approval as well when the articles of incorporation must be amended to change the par value of par value shares or any stated value of shares without par value and also, when necessary, to authorize additional shares.[3]

Accounting Treatment of Share Splits

The usual accounting treatment for a share split is to do nothing except to reflect

intervening two-for-one share split); cf. Merchants-Citizens Nat'l Bank & Trust Co. v. Mauser, 297 Pa. 399, 147 A. 90 (1929); Matter of American Chicle Co. v. State Tax Commission, 5 A.D.2d 318, 172 N.Y.S.2d 389 (3d Dep't 1958) (requiring additional tax on authorized capital when number of shares without par value increased); Rosenthal & Rosenthal, Inc. v. Wolfe, 54 Misc.2d 716, 283 N.Y.S.2d 315 (N.Y.C.Civ.Ct.1967) (allowing pledgee of 46 shares to sue his pledgor for conversion for latter's failure to turn over additional 46 shares resulting from share split); Ohio Op.Att'y Gen. 1367, May 19, 1960. Where a shareholder sold shares after a split, he was held liable for failure to deliver the new shares to his broker, even though no due bill for the new shares was requested at the time of sale, to the extent of the broker's expenses in making delivery. Smith v. Hilliard, 408 S.W.2d 440 (Ky.1966). See also Sobieski, "Fractional Shares in Stocks Dividends and Splits", 16 Bus.Law. 204 (1960); see also section 161 supra. If a person had invested $1,600 to buy 100 shares of Winn-Dixie Stores, Inc. in 1940, the number of his shares, as the result of four share splits would have increased, by 1965, to 5,400 shares, with a market value approximating $200,000. Meanwhile, almost $50,000 in cash dividends would have been received.

3.   See section 345 infra.

the different number of issued shares, indicating any change in par, and possibly stated, value.[4]

Securities Exchange Requirements Applicable to Share Split-Ups

The New York Stock Exchange requirements applicable to share dividends[5] apply also to share split-ups. However, the exchange discourages split-ups in a ratio of less than two shares for one, and split-ups when earnings of a corporation are unstable or the shares have not maintained a consistently high dollar-market-price. The small split-up is regarded by the exchange as in the nature of a share dividend and therefore is governed by its share dividend rules, applicable to up to 25 percent distributions and possibly applicable to 25–100 percent distributions, regardless of whether effected through the technique of a share dividend or that of a split-up and regardless of whether it is represented as a share dividend or as a split-up. The exchange also requires all possible avoidance of the word "dividend" in any reference to a share distribution not being "capitalized" at its fair value out of *earned* surplus.[6]

Allocation in Case of Share Split-Ups

Since split-ups, in a legal sense, do not change the shareholders' interests in any way except to give them additional shares which along with the previous shares represent the identical equity both in total and in proportion between stated capital and surplus, shares so distributed belong to corpus. However, a testator or settlor may provide

4.   See discussion of Securities Exchange Requirements Applicable to Share Split-Ups, infra.

5.   See discussion of Securities Exchange Requirements Applicable to Share Dividends in section 329 supra.

6.   N.Y.S.E. Company Manual § A14.

otherwise and his directions will be followed.[7]

Sometimes transactions denominated as a share dividend are to some extent a share split, or *vice versa,* requiring separation of the transaction into its share split and share dividend aspects.[8]

Tax Aspects of Share Splits

There are no federal income tax consequences to the share split except to divide (in the case of the split-up) or to multiply (in the case of the reverse split) the basis for each share.[9]

F. MISCELLANEOUS DIVIDEND AND RELATED PROBLEMS

DECLARATION OF DIVIDENDS

331. Before declaring a dividend, the board of directors must consider (a) the availability of legal funds for the dividends, (b) any applicable dividend preferences and other rights, (c) the corporation's working capital and cash position—all essentially legal considerations, and (d) various policy factors.

The usual practice, especially of larger corporations, is to declare a dividend payable to shareholders of record as of some future record date on a payment date subsequent to such record date.

The declaration of a cash or property dividend ordinarily creates a debtor-creditor relationship between the corporation and shareholder with respect to the dividend, and may not be revoked without shareholder consent. A share dividend ordinarily may be rescinded at any time before the actual issuance of the shares.

Before declaring a dividend, the board of directors must consider various factors, non-legal as well as legal.

Initially, the board of directors must consider (a) the availability of legal funds for the dividend, (b) any applicable dividend preferences and other rights, (c) the corporation's working capital and cash position—all essentially legal considerations, and (d) various policy factors, to some extent non-legal in nature.

Legally Available Funds

In all cases, directors must consider the availability of legal funds for the dividend, whether cash or property or shares, at the times of declaration and payment. The legal requirements in this respect for cash and property dividends sometimes differ from those for share dividends.

Dividend restrictions not only under the law of the jurisdiction of incorporation [1] but also under any other applicable laws, administrative regulations,[2] the articles of incorporation, securities exchange rules, indentures, loan agreements, etc., must be considered.[3] For distribution of dividends in excess of funds legally available under applicable statutes, the liabilities of the directors can be substantial.[4] Hence they should best rely on financial reports duly certified by qualified accountants and opinions of counsel admit-

7. Matter of Pearson, 13 Misc.2d 257, 176 N.Y.S.2d 891 (Sur.Ct.1958). Cf. Matter of Fosdick, 4 N.Y.2d 646, 176 N.Y.S.2d 966, 152 N.E.2d 228 (1958) (6–1); Matter of Hormann, Matter of Guggenheimer, 3 A. D.2d 5, 157 N.Y.S.2d 704 (1st Dep't 1956) (4–1).

8. Matter of Tealdi, 16 Misc.2d 685, 182 N.Y.S.2d 68 (Sup.Ct.1958). See section 333 infra.

9. Share splits can be subject to capital taxes when shares without par value are split if such tax is computed on the basis of a certain amount per share without par value, equating each such share to $100 of par value or $100 of actual value absent proof to the contrary. McKinney's N.Y.Tax Law, § 180; N.M.Op.Att'y Gen. No. 66–75, June 15, 1966. See Utah Op.Att'y Gen. No. 66–109, Nov. 14, 1966.

1. See section 320 supra.

2. See section 321 supra.

3. See section 322 supra.

4. See section 323 supra.

ted to practice in the jurisdiction or jurisdictions whose dividend laws might be applicable.

Applicable Dividend Preferences and Other Rights

Where more than a single class (or series) of shares is outstanding, applicable dividend preferences and other rights should be observed.[5]

Working Capital and Cash

The distribution of the dividend, even apart from statutory insolvency provisions, should not so deplete the working capital as to render the corporation unable to meet its obligations as they mature or cause other possible financial embarrassment. Where a cash dividend is contemplated, sufficient cash must of course, be available on the payment date.[6]

Policy Factors

Where dividends are discretionary, the directors should exercise sound business judgment. Various policy factors, nonlegal as well as legal in nature, must be considered.

For cash dividends, various factors are relevant.[7] In general, dividends except out of earned surplus, even when lawful, are best avoided, to preserve the integrity of the original investment; when derived from any source other than earned surplus, candor (if not applicable requirements as well) suggests disclosure of such fact to the recipient shareholders. Maintaining an adequate cash and working capital position is as important a practical as legal consideration; earnings

retention[8] is especially important if reducing debt, retiring senior shares, or expanding the business is contemplated, or where the earnings are cyclical or unstable. The dividend program should maximize the standing of the shares and credit of the corporation, which are usually enhanced by the regularity of dividends.[9] Finally, the effect of taxation, not only on the corporation but also on the shareholders of varying tax positions, as well as potential problems of allocation of dividends and share distributions, should be anticipated.[10]

Record and Payment Dates

Except in small corporations when declaration and payment of dividends are often simultaneous, the usual practice is for the board of directors to declare a dividend on a certain date payable to shareholders of record as of some date, say, 10 days in the future, with the payment date to follow the record date by, say, 30 days. In fact, securities exchanges require such a practice with respect to dividends on listed shares.[11]

Effect of Declaration

Upon declaration of a cash or property dividend, assuming it is lawful and proper, a debtor-creditor relationship usually arises between the corporation and the shareholder with respect to the dividend.[12] If the corpo-

---

5.   See section 325 supra.

6.   See New England Trust Co. v. Penobscot Chemical Fibre Co., 142 Me. 286, 50 A.2d 188 (1946).

7.   H. Guthmann & H. Dougall, Corporate Financial Policy 527–543 (4th ed. 1962). For policy factors applicable to share, property, and other types of dividends and distributions, see id. at 543–550.

8.   Declaration of a share dividend might, under such circumstances, be desirable. See Loomis, "A Case for Dropping Dividends", 77 Fortune, No. 7, 181 (June 15, 1968); Mendelson, "Payout Policy and Resource Allocation", 116 U.Pa.L.Rev. 377 (1968); Donaldson, "Financial Goals: Management vs. Stockholders", 41 Harv.Bus.Rev. 116 (May-June 1963); Spear, "Dividend Policies Under Changing Price Levels", 27 Harv.Bus.Rev. 612 (1949).

9.   Additional dividends are often labeled "extra" dividends.

10.   See sections 333, 339 infra.

11.   See discussion of Securities Exchange Requirements in section 318 supra. See G. Seward, Basic Corporate Practice 94 (ALI rev. 1966) (form of minutes).

12.   Godley v. Crandall & Godley Co., 212 N.Y. 121, 105 N.E. 818 (1914); Lowne v. American Fire Ins.

ration actually segregates the dividend fund, the latter becomes a trust fund for the shareholders.[13]

Once legally declared, a cash dividend may not be revoked without shareholder consent.[14] If declared out of funds not legally available for dividends, the declaration should be revocable.[15] Where the declaration was not disclosed to shareholders, a Massachusetts case has allowed revocation.[16]

A share dividend may be rescinded at any time before the actual issuance of the shares.[17]

If the declaration of a dividend is qualified or conditional, the debtor-creditor relationship does not thereby arise, and the declaration is revocable.[18]

PERSONS ENTITLED TO DIVIDENDS

332. Shareholders of record on the record date ordinarily are entitled to receive dividends, and the corporation ordinarily is protected in relying on record ownership at least where it is without notice of other interests in the shares. In some jurisdictions, dividends might be paid on partly-paid shares or fractions of shares. Apart from the question as to whom the corporation should pay the dividend, there may be two or more persons with interests in the shares, requiring the recipient to pay over the dividend to such other person or persons.

So far as the corporation is concerned, statutes often expressly allow it to fix a record date, or under older provisions, to close the transfer books, for the purpose of determining shareholders entitled to receive payment of any dividend.[1] The Uniform

Co., 6 Paige (N.Y.) 482 (1837); cf. Hunt v. O'Shea, 69 N.H. 600, 45 A. 480 (1899); Note, "Dividends—When They Become Finally Declared", 23 Minn.L. Rev. 831 (1939); Note, "Declaration of Dividends—Stockholders as Creditors", 28 Mich.L.Rev. 914 (1930). See Klein v. Compania Azucarera Vertientes-Camaguey de Cuba, 28 A.D.2d 142, 283 N.Y.S.2d 478 (1st Dep't 1967) (interest on declared dividend denied nonresident shareholder of Cuban corporation since dividend fund frozen in interim). Quaere, where the record date is in the future. Compare Ford v. Snook, 205 App.Div. 194, 199 N.Y.S. 630 (4th Dep't 1923), aff'd mem., 240 N.Y. 624, 148 N.E. 732 (1925) (date of declaration), with Richter & Co. v. Light, 97 Conn. 364, 116 A. 600 (1922) (record date). Ownership of the shares, even of record, may change between the date of declaration and the record date. Courts construing liquidation preferences for cumulative preferred shares as not encompassing arrearages for dividends undeclared in the past ignore the rule that a shareholder entitled to a *declared* cash dividend is a creditor with a claim superior in liquidation to any liquidation preference.

13. 11 W. Fletcher, Private Corporations § 5322 (perm. ed. rev. 1958); Searles v. Gebbie, 115 App. Div. 778, 101 N.Y.S. 199 (4th Dep't 1906), aff'd mem., 190 N.Y. 533, 83 N.E. 1131 (1907).

14. 11 W. Fletcher, Private Corporations § 5323 (perm. ed. rev. 1958); Note, "Declaration and Rescission of Cash and Stock Dividends", 16 Colum.L. Rev. 599 (1916). See Strout v. Cross, Austin & Ireland Lumber Co., 175 Misc. 826, 25 N.Y.S.2d 377 (Sup.Ct.1941), aff'd mem., 263 App.Div. 801, 32 N.Y.S.2d 127 (1st Dep't 1941) (resolution for dividend in amount of $22.75 per share, followed by resolution that payment should be $2.75 cash and remainder in property, construed to give shareholder no claim for $20 in cash).

15. Benas v. Title Guaranty Trust Co., 216 Mo.App. 53, 267 S.W. 28 (1924) (property dividend). Especially if the articles of incorporation limit dividends to legally available funds, although the law would seem to be as much a part of the share contract as the articles of incorporation. Quaere, if some adverse financial change between declaration and payment dates renders payment unlawful.

16. Ford v. Easthampton Rubber Thread Co., 158 Mass. 84, 32 N.E. 1036 (1893); cf. Brown v. Luce

Mfg. Co., 231 Mo.App. 259, 96 S.W.2d 1098 (1936); McLaren v. Crescent Planing Mill Co., 117 Mo. App. 40, 93 S.W. 819 (1906).

17. Malone v. Armor Insulating Co., 191 Ga. 146, 12 S.E.2d 299 (1940); Terry v. Eagle Lock Co., 47 Conn. 141 (1879); see also Staats v. Biograph Co., 236 F. 454 (2d Cir. 1916); 11 W. Fletcher, Private Corporations § 5323.1 (perm. ed. rev. 1958); Note, "Declaration and Rescission of Cash and Stock Dividends", 16 Colum.L.Rev. 599 (1916). A share dividend really involves no change until surplus is capitalized.

18. Dock v. Schlichter Jute Cordage Co., 167 Pa. 370, 31 A. 656 (1895); cf. United States v. Baldy, 108 F. 2d 591 (9th Cir. 1939) (conditional declaration); Taylor v. Axton-Fisher Tobacco Co., 295 Ky. 226, 173 S.W.2d 377, 148 A.L.R. 834 (1943) (redemption held irrevocable).

1. E. g., ABA–ALI Model Bus.Corp.Act § 28 (absent the closing of transfer books or fixing of record date, the date of declaration is deemed the record date). See Munro v. Mullen, 100 N.H. 128, 121 A.2d 312 (1956) (holding shareholder of record on record date, and not owner of shares at time preferred dividend, arrearages accrued, entitled to such arrearages).

Commercial Code expressly provides that prior to due presentment for registration of transfer of a security in registered form the issuer may treat the registered owner as the person exclusively entitled to exercise all the rights and powers of an owner.[2]

Where statutes allow the issue of partly-paid shares, dividends may be declared and paid thereon on the basis of the consideration paid for such shares.[3]

Apart from the question as to whom the corporation should pay the dividend, there may be two or more persons who between themselves have interests in the shares. For example, in the case of transfers of shares, absent provision to the contrary, dividends declared before the transfer belong to the transferor; those declared after the transfer being to the transferee.[4] Ordinarily, the pledgee, during the pledge of shares, is entitled to receive the dividends, to be applied on the debt or held subject to the pledge.[5] A specific legatee of shares is entitled to dividends declared after the testator's death.[6] A trustee receiving dividends may

have a problem of allocating them as between life tenants and remaindermen. This allocation problem is discussed in the next section.[7]

Dividends on shares declared after sequestration belong to the owner, even though the court order gives the sequestrator all the right, title, and interest in the shares.[8]

ALLOCATION OF DIVIDENDS AND SHARE DISTRIBUTIONS

333. As to the allocation of dividends between those entitled to income (life tenant) and corpus (remainderman) of a trust of shares, when the intention of the testator or settlor cannot be determined, there are three common-law rules. Share splits, absent a contrary intention, belong to the remainderman.

Under the "Massachusetts Rule" or "Majority Rule", codified in the Uniform Principal and Income Act and Restatement of Trusts, the test is the kind of the dividend, with all cash and property dividends out of profits going to the life tenant and all share dividends, regardless of source, belonging to the remainderman.

Under the "Pennsylvania Rule" or "American Rule", formerly codified in the Restatement of Trusts, the test is the source of the dividend, with any dividend—cash, property, or shares—out of profits subsequent to the establishment of the trust going to the life tenant and any distribution out of prior profits or not out of profits belonging to the remainderman.

Under the "Kentucky Rule", the test is the time of the declaration of the dividend, with any dividend—cash, property, or shares—out of profits declared during the life estate belonging to the life tenant; otherwise to the remainderman.

Statutes sometimes codify one rule or another, with or without variation, and with or without retroactive as well as prospective effect. The Uniform Principal and Income Act, approved in 1931 and revised in 1962, has been adopted in more than half the states.

A wide variety of rules have arisen as to the distribution or allocation of dividends

---

2. Uniform Commercial Code § 8–207. This provision does more than state affirmatively what the Uniform Stock Transfer Act § 3, 6 U.L.A. 9 (1922), stated negatively. The latter provided that nothing in the Uniform Stock Transfer Act should be construed to prevent a corporation from recognizing the exclusive rights of the record owner of shares to receive dividends. For cases thereunder, see Baar v. Fidelity & Columbia Trust Co., 302 Ky. 91, 193 S.W.2d 1011 (1946); Turnbull v. Longacre Bank, 249 N.Y. 159, 163 N.E. 135 (1928); Matter of Alling, 186 Misc. 192, 63 N.Y.S.2d 427 (Sur.Ct.1945) (corporation protected by record ownership only if without notice); Lindner v. Utah Southern Oil Co., 3 Utah 2d 302, 283 P.2d 605 (1955).

3. Cal.Gen.Corp.Law, § 1508 (1947); Del.Gen.Corp. Law, § 156 (1967); cf. McKinney's N.Y.Bus.Corp. Law, § 505(e). See also McPhail v. L. S. Starrett Co., 157 F.Supp. 560 (D.Mass.1957), aff'd 257 F.2d 388 (1st Cir. 1958). As to dividends on fractions of shares, see section 161 supra.

4. 11 W. Fletcher, Private Corporations §§ 5377–5381 (perm. ed. rev. 1958); Annot., 60 A.L.R. 703 (1929).

5. 11 W. Fletcher, Private Corporations § 5382 (perm. ed. rev. 1958).

6. 11 W. Fletcher, Private Corporations § 5383 (perm. ed. rev. 1958).

7. See section 333 infra.

8. Trans World Airlines, Inc. v. Hughes, 41 Del.Ch. 11, 187 A.2d 350 (Ch.1962).

between those entitled to the income (life tenant) and corpus (remainderman) of a trust of the shares, when the intention of the testator or settlor cannot be determined.

Apart from statute, these rules were known as the "Massachusetts Rule," "Pennsylvania Rule" (or "American Rule"), and "Kentucky Rule".[1]

There is often disagreement even as to statement of the respective rules. While these rules apply to all dividends, most of the cases have arisen with respect to share dividends.

These rules, it should be emphasized, are only rules of construction, or of presumed intention, applicable only when the intention of the testator or settlor cannot be determined. If the intention can be ascertained, it controls the distribution.[2]

1. 1 G. Hornstein, Corporation Law and Practice § 473 (1959); 12 W. Fletcher, Private Corporations §§ 5389–5418 (perm. ed. rev. 1957). On possible effect of statutes against accumulations, see 12 id. § 5392. Somewhat analogous problems are presented by share distributions in cases of share purchase agreements. Keller Industries, Inc. v. Fineberg, 203 So.2d 644 (Fla.Dist.Ct.App.1967); W. O. Barnes Co. v. Folsinksi, 337 Mich. 370, 60 N.W.2d 302 (1953). Or pledges of specified number of shares. Rosenthal & Rosenthal, Inc. v. Wolfe, 54 Misc.2d 716, 283 N.Y.S.2d 315 (N.Y.C.Civ.Ct.1967). Or bequests of shares stated in terms of a specified number of shares. Harlan National Bank v. Brown, 317 S.W. 2d 903 (Ky.1958); cf. Allen v. Nat'l Bank of Austin, 19 Ill.App.2d 149, 153 N.E.2d 260 (1958) (share split-up); Matter of Fitch, 281 App.Div. 65, 118 N. Y.S.2d 234 (3d Dep't 1952) (probable-intention-of-testator test). Some cases hold that a general legatee of shares takes neither share dividends nor share splits; a specific legatee of shares takes share splits but not share dividends. Greathead Estate, 428 Pa. 553, 236 A.2d 224 (1967) (legacy of 200 shares by testatrix who then held many more shares, most of them resulting from prior share splits, and who made 14 other bequests—all 15 bequests equally total number of shares she then held —held not to include additional shares resulting from share split between her execution of her will and her death); Matter of Howe, 15 A.D.2d 396, 224 N.Y.S.2d 992 (4th Dep't 1962), aff'd mem., 12 N. Y.2d 870, 237 N.Y.S.2d 343, 187 N.E.2d 794 (1962) (construing bequest of 500 shares—representing only small amount of testator's holdings in New Jersey corporation—as specific, and to include additional shares resulting from share split but not share dividends (by capitalization-of-earned-surplus-test)—distributed between testator's execution of his will and his death); Igoe v. Darby, 343 Mass. 145, 177 N.E.2d 676 (1961) (construing bequests of all of testatrix's shares as specific, rather than general, legacies, and to include additional shares resulting from three-for-one share split between her execution of will and her death); Matter of Helfman v. Lar Rieu, 193 Cal.App.2d 652, 14 Cal.Rptr. 482 (1961) (construing bequests of specified numbers of shares to include shares resulting from split between time will was executed and death of testatrix). Quaere, as to doctrine of ademption where property, as in case of share splits, loses its original identity. See Warren v. Shoemaker, 4 Ohio Misc. 15, 207 N.E.2d 419 (P.Ct.1965) (holding bequest of all of testator's shares in corporation to be specific but not to adeem, under "substantial identity doctrine", upon exchange of such shares for shares

of surviving corporation in merger). See also In re Schlosser's Estate, 277 F.2d 268 (3d Cir. 1960), cert. denied 364 U.S. 819, 81 S.Ct. 53, 5 L.Ed.2d 49 (1960) (share dividend distributed between date of death and alternative valuation date one year later held includable in gross estate for federal estate purposes where alternative valuation date elected by executor). Comment, "The Creation of General and Specific Bequests of Securities and the Rules for the Distribution of Accessions to Securities", 52 Marq.L.Rev. 271 (1968); Note, "Decedents' Estates: Increase Resulting from Stock Splits Prior to Testator's Death", 43 Marq.L.Rev. 115 (1959); Annot., 15 A.L.R.3d 1038 (1967); 7 A.L.R.2d 276 (1949). Where securities are convertible into shares, "anti-dilution" provisions should provide for adjustment in cases of share dividends, share splits, etc.

2. See, e. g., Matter of Hormann, Matter of Guggenheimer, 3 A.D.2d 5, 157 N.Y.S.2d 704 (1st Dep't 1956) (4-1); Matter of Grace, 51 Misc.2d 531, 273 N.Y.S.2d 514 (Sur.Ct.1966); Matter of Muller, 5 Misc.2d 83, 158 N.Y.S.2d 417 (Sur.Ct.1956); Matter of Appleby, 15 Misc.2d 200, 175 N.Y.S.2d 176 (Sur. Ct.1958). In Kirby v. Kirby, 68 S.D. 612, 5 N.W.2d 405 (1942), the testator left his estate, including 442 shares of a corporation, to a trustee to pay the balance of rents, dividends, and profits, after the payment of expenses, to his widow for life. The will provided that upon the death of the widow, the trustee should deliver to his son, the remainderman, "442 shares". While the widow was living, a share dividend of 294 shares (2-for-3) was declared on the 442 shares from earnings accrued after the death of the testator. The court held that the share dividend was part of the corpus to be added to the 442 shares and ultimately transferred to the remainderman. See generally Aronstein, "Common Stocks in Trust", 113 U.Pa.L.Rev. 228 (1964); Cohen, "Accounting Considerations of Apportionment by Trustees of Receipts from Stock", 36 Temple L.Q. 121 (1963); Flickinger, "A Trustee's Nightmare: Allocation of Stock Dividends Between Income and Principal", 43 B.U.L.Rev. 199 (1963); Grossman, "Mechanics of Apportionment of Receipts from Shares of Stock", 65 Dick.L.Rev. 179 (1961); Browning, "Problems of Fiduciary Accounting", 36 N.Y.U.L.Rev. 931, 936 (1961); Comment, "Effectuating the Settlor's Intent: A Formula for Providing More Income for the Life Beneficiary", 33 U.Chi.L. Rev. 783 (1966); Comment, "Allocation of Stock

"Massachusetts Rule" or "Majority Rule"

The "Massachusetts Rule" (or "Majority Rule") holds that all cash or property dividends out of profits go to the life tenant, and all share dividends, regardless of source, belong to the remainderman. The test is the *kind* of the dividend. This has been the Restatement of Trusts rule since 1947, has been codified in the Uniform Principal and Income Act, and was the statutory rule in New York from 1926 to 1965.[3]

"Pennsylvania Rule" or "American Rule"

Under the "Pennsylvania Rule" (or so-called "American Rule", because it was the majority rule before the Massachusetts Rule), or "intact value principle", any ordinary dividend declared during the life estate out of profits and any extraordinary dividend—cash, property, or shares—declared during such period out of profits subsequent to the establishment of the trust or the acquisition of the shares by the trustee go to the life tenant; any other distribution out of prior profits or not out of profits belongs to the remainderman. The test is the *source* of the dividend; it requires apportionment to preserve the value of the corpus as of the time the trust was established. This apportionment rule was the rule of the Restatement of Trusts prior to 1947.[4] Pennsylvania, by

statute, in 1945 adhered to the Massachusetts Rule, and in 1963 adopted the six percent rule.[5]

Dividends Between the Life Beneficiary and Remainderman", 1966 Wash.U.L.Q. 216; Comment, "Trustee's Dilemma in the Distribution of Dividends", 7 S.Tex.L.J. 294 (1965); Comment, "Trust Allocation of Dividends in Securities of Non-Declaring Corporations", 43 B.U.L.Rev. 303 (1963); Note, "Mutual Funds—Trusts and Trustees—Capital Gains Distributions From Mutual Funds: Income or Principal?", 65 Mich.L.Rev. 761 (1967). See revised Uniform Principal and Income Act § 2, 9B U.L.A. 573 (1966); McKinney's N.Y. EPTL, § 11–2.1(a) (1) (in accordance with terms of trust instrument, notwithstanding any contrary provisions in section).

3. Former McKinney's N.Y.Pers.Prop.Law, § 17–a, infra note 7.

4. 1 Restatement of Trusts § 236 (1935); Cohan & Dean, "Legal, Tax and Accounting Aspects of Fidu-

ciary Apportionment of Stock Proceeds: The Non-Statutory Pennsylvania Rules", 106 U.Pa.L.Rev. 157 (1957); Note, "Trusts—Apportionment of Stock Distributions under the Pennsylvania Rule", 63 Dick. L.Rev. 376 (1959). In preserving values, dollars are the measure, and the purchasing power of the dollar at the respective periods of time involved is not considered. Mercantile Safe-Deposit & Trust Co. v. Apponyi, 220 Md. 275, 152 A.2d 184 (1959).

5. Pa.Stat.Ann. Tit. 20, § 3470.5 (Purdon 1964) (corporate distributions to trustee in shares of distributing corporation, however described or designated by latter, to be deemed principal, but if number of shares of any class distributed to shareholders of such class is six percent or less of number of shares of that class outstanding on record date for such distribution, shares so distributed shall be deemed income. New York has a similar six percent rule; New Jersey a four percent rule. N.J. Rev.Stat. § 3A:14A–4 (Supp.1968). Pre-1945 trusts in Pennsylvania until 1961 were governed by the Pennsylvania Rule. Pennsylvania adopted the Uniform Principal and Income Act with an express retroactive provision. The Pennsylvania Supreme Court had held in 1949 (overruled in 1961) that such provision was unconstitutional since a life tenant had a vested interest in accumulated applicable earnings even though he was not entitled to them until they were distributed upon the happening of the apportionable event under the Pennsylvania Rule. But see In re Catherwood Trust, 405 Pa. 61, 173 A.2d 86 (1961) (holding under Pennsylvania Rule: "If a total stock distribution for the current year is payable at the rate of 6% or less of the corporation's outstanding shares before such distributions were made such distribution in stock of the distributing corporation should be treated as income"); Pew Trust, 398 Pa. 523, 158 A.2d 552 (1960) (1-for-4 share distribution, called by corporation 5-for-4 "split-up", without any transfer from earned surplus to stated capital, held hybrid transaction which had never been accorded recognition as an apportionable event and therefore was not apportionable). See also Brock Estate, 420 Pa. 454, 218 A.2d 281 (1966) (ruling that distribution by mutual fund or regulated investment company source of which was "realized capital gains", was allocable to principal, rather than to income, under Pennsylvania Principal and Income Act of 1947); Anthony Estate, 423 Pa. 401, 223 A.2d 857 (1966) (allocating to principal General Motors Corporation common shares distributed by E. I. du Pont de Nemours and Company to its shareholders under antitrust divestitive decree); Cunningham Estate, 395 Pa. 1, 149 A.2d 72 (1959) (4–2) (share distribution only partially capitalized out of earnings held not apportionable because of practicalities of situation, historical judicial restriction of rule to specified situations, and legislative enunciation of public policy contrary to rule).

"Kentucky Rule"

The "Kentucky Rule", no longer followed even there,[6] made the *time* of declaration of the dividend the test: any dividends, regardless of type, based on earnings or earned surplus declared during the life estate belonged to the life tenant; otherwise to the remainderman.

Statutory Enactments

Statutory enactments have been passed in many states in attempting to clarify the situation.[7]

Where such statutes do not operate retroactively, because of either concern for constitutional limitations or construction of legislative intention, preexisting trusts are governed by the prior rule or rules.[8] In New York, for example, the cases were very confusing prior to 1913[9] when the New York Court of Appeals adopted the Pennsylvania Rule.[10] In 1926, the New York Legislature substituted the Massachusetts Rule by statute, but only prospectively. Hence, trusts arising prior to 1926 continued to be governed by the Pennsylvania Rule; subsequent trusts by the statute.[11]

In 1965, a new statute, expressly retroactive to preexisting trusts, became effective in New York. Under it, subject to any clearly ascertainable intention of the testator or settlor to the contrary, any share distribution of six percent or less—regardless of how many per year is income, and the *entire* amount of any share distribution in excess of six percent is principal.[12]

---

6. See Farmers Bank & Capital Trust Co. v. Hulette, 293 S.W.2d 458 (Ky.1956). See Notes, 39 Mich.L.Rev. 338, 339 (1955); 6 Vand.L.Rev. 416, 418 (1953).

7. E. g., McKinney's N.Y. EPTL, § 11–2.1, former McKinney's N.Y.Pers.Prop.Law, §§ 17–a, 17–e.

8. In adopting the Uniform Principal and Income Act, Connecticut omitted the provision that the act "shall apply to all estates of tenants or remaindermen which become legally effective after that date"; New Mexico provided that the act should apply as well to preexisting estates (but not to receipts and expenses received or paid prior to its effective date); Virginia provided that the act should apply as well to preexisting estates (but not to affect or change any transactions which had previously taken place). Retroactive application, when provided by the statute, has been upheld in the more recent cases. In re Arens, 41 N.J. 364, 197 A. 2d 1 (1964); Will of Allis, 6 Wis.2d 1, 94 N.W.2d 226, 69 A.L.R.2d 1128 (1959); Matter of West, 289 N.Y. 423, 46 N.E.2d 501 (1943), aff'd sub nom. Demorest v. City Bank Farmers' Trust Co., 321 U.S. 36, 64 S.Ct. 384, 88 L.Ed. 526 (1944). Contra, Crawford's Estate, 362 Pa. 458, 67 A.2d 124 (1949), overruled by In Re Catherwood Trust, 405 Pa. 61, 173 A.2d 86 (1961) (retroactive applicability of statute to all audits then pending and henceforth). See King, "Uniform Principal and Income Act: § 5: Constitutionality of Its Retroactive Application", 1960 Wash.U.L.Q. 339; Annot., 69 A.L.R.2d 1137 (1960). Compare McKinney's N.Y. EPTL, § 11–2.1 (applicable to any distribution after effective date by any trust or decedent's estate, whether established before, on, or after effective date, and whether asset involved was acquired by trustee before, on, or after effective date), with predecessor McKinney's N.Y.Pers. Prop.Law, § 17–a (effective May 17, 1926) ("Unless otherwise provided in a will, deed or other instrument, which shall hereafter be executed and shall create or declare a trust . . ."), note 12 infra.

9. See Matter of Kernochan, 104 N.Y. 618, 11 N.E. 149 (1887).

10. Matter of Osborne, 209 N.Y. 450, 477, 103 N.E. 723, 731 (1913): "(1) Ordinary dividends, regardless of the time when the surplus out of which they are payable was accumulated, should be paid to the life beneficiary of the trust. (2) Extraordinary dividends, payable from the accumulated earnings of the company, whether payable in cash or stock, belong to the life beneficiary, unless they entrench in whole or in part upon the capital of the trust fund as received from the testator or maker of the trust or invested in the stock, in which case such extraordinary dividends should be returned to the trust fund or apportioned between the trust fund and the life beneficiary in such a way as to preserve the integrity of the trust fund." Such judicial change of rule obviously applied retroactively to preexisting trusts and wills.

11. Matter of Payne (Bingham), 7 N.Y.2d 1, 194 N.Y.S. 2d 465, 163 N.E.2d 301 (1959) (5–2) (under 1915 trust containing shares on which were made share distributions capitalized out of capital surplus (which could not be identified as arising from earnings) thereby exhausting capital surplus, and the balance out of earned surplus; allocation of such distributions to income and principal based on respective percentages capitalized out of earned surplus and out of capital surplus, on theory latter did not represent distribution of corporate earnings and was therefore not subject to apportionment under Osborne Rule, upheld; whether or not too much had been allocated to income not at issue since respondents, representing principal, had not appealed).

12. McKinney's N.Y. EPTL, §§ 11–2.1 et seq. Protection against claims of loss by an income benefi-

Uniform Principal and Income Act

The Uniform Principal and Income Act, approved in 1931 and revised in 1961, has been adopted, sometimes with variations, in several jurisdictions.[13] It follows the Massachusetts Rule distinction based on the form of the dividend, declaring, unless the trust otherwise provides, a share dividend to belong to corpus; other dividends to be treated as income.[14]

Restatement of Trusts (Second)

The present Restatement of Trusts (Second) rule [15] provides, with considerable elaboration, that, except as otherwise provided by the terms of the trust, cash and property dividends are income, and share dividends are principal.

Sometimes, transactions denominated as a share dividend are, to some extent a share split, or vice versa, in which cases, the transaction must be separated into its share

dividend and split aspects,[16] since the provision in the trust instrument or will or apportionment rule applicable to a share dividend might differ from that applicable to a share split-up, which ordinarily would be part of the corpus.[17]

UNCLAIMED DIVIDENDS

334. Unclaimed dividends and other distributions are subject to escheat, primarily by the state of the shareholder's address on the corpo-

---

ciary is given to a trustee who temporarily allocates a share distribution to principal pending an accounting because he is not certain whether it belongs in income or not, and subsequently receives a determination that it is income; income beneficiaries will not be able to claim a loss if such shares have been sold and thereafter increase in value, or have been held and decrease in value. The trustee looks to the terms of the instrument, then to the statute, and finally to considerations of what is reasonable and equitable. See Comment, "Principal and Income Allocation of Stock Distributions—The Six Per Cent Rule", 64 Mich.L.Rev. 856 (1966).

13. Uniform Principal and Income Act (1931), 9B U. L.A. 588 (1966) (adopted in Alabama, Arizona, Colorado, Connecticut, Florida, Illinois, Kansas, Kentucky, Louisiana, Montana, New Mexico, North Carolina, Oklahoma, Oregon, Pennsylvania, Tennessee, Texas, Utah, Vermont, Virginia, West Virginia, Wisconsin). Revised (1962), 9B U.L.A. 572 (1966) (adopted in Idaho, Kansas, Maryland, Michigan, Mississippi, South Carolina, Wyoming). New York has followed several provisions, but with variations.

14. E. Gamble, The Revised Uniform Principal and Income Act (1966); Barclay, "The Principal and Income Act", 33 Brooklyn L.Rev. 489 (1967); Bogert, "The Revised Uniform Principal and Income Act", 38 Notre Dame Law. 50 (1962); Comment, "The Revised Uniform Principal and Income Act—Progress But Not Perfection", 1963 Ill.L.F. 473.

15. 1 Restatement, Second, Trusts § 236 (1959).

16. The New York courts apply the "transfer of earned surplus" test. Matter of Fosdick, 4 N.Y.2d 646, 176 N.Y.S.2d 966, 152 N.E.2d 228 (1958) (6–1) (where 1918 deed of trust directed transfer of all share dividends to settlor or his residuary estate, exchange of three new shares of $5 par value for one old share without par value of $6.25 stated value, with transfer of $8.75 per three new shares from earned surplus to stated capital to cover increase over old stated value ($6.75) of new par value for shares issued (3 x $5 = $15), held to be $7/12$ ($8.75 ÷ $15) share dividend and $5/12$ ($6.25 ÷ $15) share split-up); Matter of Carlson, 16 A.D.2d 28, 224 N.Y.S.2d 985 (4th Dep't 1962), aff'd mem., 12 N. Y.2d 1047, 239 N.Y.S.2d 879, 190 N.E.2d 239 (1962) (holding that 1959 share distribution by New Jersey corporation of one additional $10 par value common share for each outstanding $10 par value common share, supported by transfer of $10 per new share from capital surplus to stated capital, did not constitute "share dividends" to be treated as income under express provision of will of decedent who died in 1956, since distribution was not supported by transfer from *earned* surplus to stated capital). Pew Trust, 398 Pa. 523, 158 A.2d 552 (1960); Matter of Parsley, 21 Misc.2d 461, 190 N.Y.S.2d 761 (Sup.Ct.1959). Matter of Payne (Bingham), supra note 11, did not involve the distinction between share dividends and share splits. Cf. New York Stock Exchange percentage distinction (see discussion of Securities Exchange Requirements Applicable to Share Dividends in section 329 supra). See Machen, "The Apportionment of Stock Distribution in Trust Accounting Practice", 20 Md.L.Rev. 89 (1960); Note, "New Light on Equitable Apportionment of Extraordinary Stock Distributions in New York and Elsewhere", 35 N.Y.U.L.Rev. 810 (1960); Dunham, "A Trustee's Dilemma as to Principal and Income", 26 U.Chi.L.Rev. 405 (1959); Niles, "Fosdick, Cunningham and Chaos: Ways Out of Apportionment Dilemma", 98 Trusts & Estates 924 (1959); Cohan, "Solving Apportionment Questions: New Approach Based on Recent Decisions", 98 Trusts & Estates 899 (1959); Cohan, "Pandora's Box Revisited: Recent Decisions on Stock Apportionment Call for New Formula", 98 Trusts & Estates 655 (1959). See also Comment, "Trust Apportionment of Stock Distributions: Stock Dividend v. Stock Split", 25 Albany L.Rev. 130 (1961).

17. Pew Trust, 398 Pa. 523, 158 A.2d 552 (1960); Pentland v. Pentland, 113 So.2d 872 (Fla.1959).

ration's record of shareholders—presumably the last known record address—but if such state has no escheat laws, then by the jurisdiction of incorporation, subject to recovery from the latter by the former if and when its laws should make provision for the escheat of such property. Most states now have escheat or abandoned or unclaimed property statutes of general application, either custodial in nature, such as the Uniform Disposition of Unclaimed Property Act, or applying strict escheat or forfeiture.

Unclaimed dividends or other distributions, that is, dividends or other distributions which are due missing shareholders whose present addresses are unknown, are subject to escheat by the state of the shareholder's last known address as shown by the record of shareholders.[1] Where there is no record of any address or the state of last known address does not provide for escheat, the property is subject to escheat by the jurisdiction of incorporation, subject to the right of another jurisdiction to recover the escheated property upon proof that the last known address was within its borders.[2]

Under the Uniform Disposition of Unclaimed Property Act, a "custodial escheat" statute, the state of incorporation and of last known record address of the missing shareholder may claim dividends and other distributions, with the latter state prevailing if the corporation is subject to such state's jurisdiction and such state has a reciprocal provision.[3]

Under some escheat or abandoned or unclaimed property statutes, the state merely takes custody of the property until claimed by the rightful owner;[4] under other statutes, the state "escheats" or cuts off the claim of even the rightful owner who fails timely to claim the property.[5]

G. REDEMPTION OR PURCHASE BY CORPORATION OF OWN SHARES

REDEMPTION OR PURCHASE— IN GENERAL

335. Redemption or purchase by a corporation of its own shares sometimes has an effect similar to a dividend, and is subject to analogous legal limitations and tax consequences. A corporation ordinarily has power to purchase or otherwise acquire its own shares or to issue redeemable preferred, and possibly common, shares. Redemption is usually at the option of the corporation and within the discretion of the board of directors but may be mandatory.

1. For more comprehensive discussion of missing security holders ,see section 179 supra.

2. Texas v. New Jersey, 379 U.S. 674, 85 S.Ct. 626, 13 L.Ed.2d 596 (1965), 380 U.S. 518, 85 S.Ct. 1136, 14 L.Ed.2d 49 (1965) (final decree), motion denied 381 U.S. 931, 85 S.Ct. 1762, 14 L.Ed.2d 698 (1965), motion denied 381 U.S. 948, 85 S.Ct. 1795, 14 L.Ed.2d 723 (1965).

3. See text accompanying section 179, nn. 11–13 supra.

4. See section 179, n. 9 supra.

5. See section 179, n. 10 supra.

Partial redemption may be authorized. Redemption might become irrevocable upon the board of directors resolution, the giving of the redemption notice, or the deposit of redemption funds. When effective, the status of the holder of redeemed shares shifts from that of shareholder to creditor.

A redemption or purchase by a corporation of its own shares sometimes has an effect similar to a dividend, in the sense that each involves the distribution of cash or other property by the corporation to its shareholders. In the case of a dividend, only a distribution is involved, whereas a redemption or purchase involves an exchange, the surrender by the shareholder to the corporation of some or all of his shares. A redemption or purchase is subject to legal limitations and tax consequences analogous to those applicable to dividends.

Statutes often expressly empower a corporation to purchase or otherwise to acquire its own shares.[1] So also do articles of incorporation. Even absent any such provision, a corporation might be held to have implied power to purchase or otherwise acquire its own shares.[2]

Statutes usually expressly[3] or otherwise impliedly[4] authorize a corporation to issue redeemable preferred shares.[5] However, absent a redemption provision in the articles of incorporation, a corporation does not have power to redeem any of its shares.[6] Redemption is usually at the option of the corporation within the discretion of the board of directors.[7]

Where partial redemption is provided for, the articles of incorporation should prescribe that the shares chosen for redemption should be selected by lot, in sequence, or pro rata, to prevent discrimination among shareholders.[8] In redeeming shares, the directors are subject to fiduciary duties.[9]

1. E. g., ABA–ALI Model Bus.Corp.Act § 5; Del. Gen.Corp.Law, § 160 (1967); McKinney's N.Y.Bus. Corp.Law, § 513; McKinney's N.Y.Penal Law, § 190.35(5). See generally Millikan, "Corporate Purchase of Own Shares", in Advising California Business Enterprises 881–908 (1958); Israels, "Limitations on the Corporate Purchase of Its Own Shares", 22 Sw.L.J. 755 (1968); Loomis, "Purchases by a Corporation of Its Own Securities", 22 Record of N.Y.C.B.A. 275 (1967); Ruder, "Dangers in a Corporation's Purchase of Its Own Shares", 13 Prac.Law. 75 (May 1967); Israels, "Corporate Purchase of Its Own Shares—Are There New Overtones?", 50 Cornell L.Q. 620 (1965); Zilber, "Corporate Tender Offers for Their Own Stock: Some Legal and Financial Considerations", 33 U.Cin.L. Rev. 315 (1964); Love, "Redemption of Stock by Corporation", 37 Mich.St.B.J. 41 (1958); Dodd, "Purchase and Redemption By a Corporation of Its Own Shares: The Substantive Law", 89 U.Pa.L. Rev. 697 (1941); Comment, "Buying Out Insurgent Shareholders with Corporate Funds", 70 Yale L.J. 308 (1960); [1947] N.Y.L.Rev'n Comm'n Rep.1947 Legis.Doc.No. 65(I) 167–223.

2. Grasselli Chemical Co. v. Aetna Explosives Co., 258 F. 66 (S.D.N.Y.1918); Richards v. Wiener Co., 207 N.Y. 59, 100 N.E. 592 (1912) (under prior New York law).

3. E. g., ABA–ALI Model Bus.Corp.Act §§ 14, 15; Del.Gen.Corp.Law, § 243 (1967); McKinney's N.Y. Bus.Corp.Law, § 512.

4. Former McKinney's N.Y.Stock Corp.Law, §§ 11, 28, 29.

5. As to whether or not common shares may be made redeemable, case authority is sparse. Compare Lewis v. H. P. Hood & Sons, 331 Mass. 670, 121 N.E.2d 850, 48 A.L.R.2d 383 (1954) (upholding redemption—essentially buy-sell arrangement—of common shares held by former employee), with American Hair & Felt Co. v. Starring, 21 Del.Ch. 431, 2 A.2d 249 (Sup.Ct.1937) (holding that common shares may not be redeemable). The distinction between redeemable common shares and common shares subject to reacquisition at the option of the corporation upon some contingency or otherwise, which is usually enforceable, raises a serious question as to traditional notions of the unredeemability of common shares. See Allen v. Biltmore Tissue Corp., 2 N.Y.2d 534, 161 N.Y.S.2d 418, 141 N.E.2d 812, 61 A.L.R.2d 1309 (1957). Some statutes expressly authorize open-end investment companies subject to the Investment Company Act of 1940 (see section 301 supra) to issue preferred, special, or common shares redeemable at the option of the holder at a price substantially equal to the share's proportionate interest in the net assets of the corporation. E. g., Maryland, New York. See McKinney's N.Y.Bus.Corp.Law, § 512 (no redeemable common share, other than shares of investment company, to be issued or redeemed unless corporation at time has outstanding class of common shares not subject to redemption).

6. 2 I. Kantrowitz & S. Slutsky, White on New York Corporations ¶ 512.02 (13th ed. 1968). A redemption provision can be inserted, changed, or deleted by amendment of the articles of incorporation if authorized by statute. See section 345 infra. See Bowman v. Armour & Co., 17 Ill.2d 43, 160 N.E.2d 753 (1959) (holding that where preferred shares were redeemable for cash, amendment of articles of incorporation to provide for redemption by issuance of 30-year subordinated cumulative income debentures was not authorized by statute). See also Annot., 70 A.L.R.2d 843 (1959).

7. Mandatory redemption lacks flexibility and is seldom used except in connection with a sinking fund provision. See Mueller v. Kraeuter & Co., 131 N.J. Eq. 475, 25 A.2d 874 (1942) (mandatory redemption provision held subject to implied condition not to injure creditors, even though sufficient surplus available). Sometimes "redemption" is at the option of the respective shareholders. See Fox v. Johnson & Wimsatt, Inc., 127 F.2d 729 (D.C.Cir. 1942). See note 5 supra.

8. See Buxbaum, "Preferred Stock—Law and Draftsmanship", 42 Calif.L.Rev. 243, 265–266 (1954). Snyder v. Memco Engineering & Mfg. Co., 23 A.D.2d 671, 257 N.Y.S.2d 213 (2d Dep't 1965) (4–1) (construing articles of incorporation against redemption of less than all outstanding preferred shares as permitting separate purchases of 852 of 1,000 outstanding shares at discount of less than one percent below redemption price).

9. Hendricks v. Mill Eng'r & Supply Co., 68 Wash.2d 490, 413 P.2d 811 (1966) (redemption to forestall threat of change in management held within business judgment rule). See section 173 supra.

Sometimes, partial redemption is authorized to be made only on the designated dividend dates.[10]

Whether or not cumulative preferred dividend arrearages are included in the redemption price—usually stated as a dollar amount or percentage of par value plus redemption premium with or without reference to dividend arrearages—depends upon the wording of the articles of incorporation and judicial attitudes toward cumulative preferred dividend arrearages.[11]

Redemption might become irrevocable upon the making of an unqualified redemption resolution by the board of directors,[12]

10. Hendricks v. Mill Eng'r & Supply Co., 68 Wash. 2d 490, 413 P.2d 811 (1966) (construing articles of incorporation provision for redemption "on any preferred stock dividend paying date, in such amounts and in such manner as may be determined by the board of trustees" as permitting redemption at any time so long as accumulated dividends to next paying date were included in redemption price).

11. See Franzen v. Fred Rueping Leather Co., 255 Wis. 265, 38 N.W.2d 517 (1949), reh. denied 255 Wis. 265, 39 N.W.2d 161 (1949) (where 6% cumulative preferred shares, on which dividends were payable on basis of previous fiscal year ending October 31, were redeemable on any dividend date (1st of January, April, July, and October) at $105 per share together with accrued earned dividends due thereon, redemption price for redemption on April 1, 1948 held to be $106.50 per share, and not $106.50 plus $3 for $1.50 quarterly dividends which would have been due on July 1, and October 1, 1948 and $2.50 for five-month period from November 1, 1947 to April 1, 1948); Matter of Chandler & Co., 230 N.Y. S.2d 1012 (Sup.Ct.1962) (dictum that "accrued dividends" in redemption provision "meant those which had been, or were required to be, declared"); Liebschutz v. Schaffer Stores Co., 276 App.Div. 1, 93 N.Y.S.2d 125 (4th Dep't 1949) (3–2), reargument and appeal denied 276 App.Div. 944, 94 N.Y.S.2d 840 (4th Dep't 1950) (where stated redemption price of cumulative preferred shares was $110, shareholder held not entitled to more than $110, despite $77 arrearages per share). See McKinney's N.Y.Bus.Corp. Law, § 513 (upon a call for redemption, amount payable by corporation for shares having cumulative preference on dividends may include stated redemption price plus accrued dividends to next dividend date following date of redemption). See also Allstate Ins. Co. v. Oxford Finance Companies, 275 F.Supp. 54 (D.Md.1967) (dividend arrearages held to accumulate after redemption of shares in merger not altering shareholder's rights).

12. Taylor v. Axton-Fisher Tobacco Co., 295 Ky. 226, 173 S.W.2d 377, 148 A.L.R. 834 (1943).

giving of the redemption notice,[13] or deposit of redemption funds,[14] possibly depending upon the language of the redemption provision in the articles of incorporation. When effective, assuming compliance with applicable requirements, the status of the holders of the redeemed shares shifts from that of shareholders to creditors.[15] This is partially analogous to the effect of declaration of a cash dividend.

FUNDS LEGALLY AVAILABLE FOR REDEMPTION OR PURCHASE

336. **The only funds legally available for redemption or purchase by a corporation of its own shares are surplus, earned surplus, or unreserved and unrestricted earned surplus and, if permitted by the articles of incorporation or approved by shareholders, unreserved and unrestricted capital surplus, excepting: (a) redeemable shares, (b) shares of dissenting shareholder pursuing their appraisal remedy, (c) reacquisitions collecting or compromising indebtedness to the corporation, (d) elimination of fractions of shares, (e) exercise by the corporation of an option or obligation to repurchase shares from an employee, such exceptions being subject to various limitations. Insolvency is often an additional general limitation.**

Generally speaking, the only funds legally available for redemption or purchase by a corporation of its own shares are surplus, earned surplus or unreserved and unrestricted earned surplus and, if permitted by the articles of incorporation or if approved by shareholders, unreserved and unrestricted capital surplus, with insolvency as an addi-

13. Borst v. East Coast Shipyards, Inc., 105 N.Y.S.2d 228 (Sup.Ct.1951) (New Jersey corporation).

14. E. g., McKinney's N.Y.Bus.Corp.Law, § 612(f); Mueller v. Howard Aircraft Corp., 329 Ill.App. 570, 70 N.E.2d 203 (1946).

15. E. g., ABA–ALI Model Bus.Corp.Act § 31 (ninth paragraph) (voting rights). In the case of redemption of convertible securities, the redemption notice should state the effect of redemption on the conversion privilege. See Note, "Convertible Securities: Holder Who Fails to Convert Before Expiration of the Conversion Period", 54 Cornell L.Rev. 271 (1969).

tional general limitation.[1] This is somewhat

analogous to the limitations on the funds legally available for dividends.[2] In the case of purchase, the price might not be allowed to exceed any redemption price.

Statutes, however, often set forth certain exceptions permitting redemption or purchase out of stated capital: (a) redeemable shares,[3] (b) shares of dissenting shareholders exercising their appraisal remedy,[4] (c) reacquisitions collecting or compromising indebtedness to the corporation,[5] (d) elimination of fractions of shares,[6] and (e) exercise by the corporation of an option or obligation to repurchase shares from an employee.[7] These exceptions, permitting redemption or purchase out of stated capital, do not apply when currently the corporation is insolvent or would thereby be made insolvent,[8] or when the redemption or purchase would prejudice prior or equal involuntary liquidation rights.[9]

In several jurisdictions, statutes expressly recognize the rights of shareholders in

1. E. g., ABA–ALI Model Bus.Corp.Act § 5 (unreserved and unrestricted earned surplus and possibly capital surplus); McKinney's N.Y.Bus.Corp.Law, § 513 (surplus). "Insolvency" is often defined by the corporate statutes, in the equity sense, to mean inability to pay debts as they become due. ABA–ALI Model Bus.Corp.Act § 2(n); McKinney's N.Y.Bus. Corp.Law, § 102(a) (8). See Herwitz, "Installment Repurchase of Stock: Surplus Limitations", 79 Harv.L.Rev. 303 (1965); deCapriles, "Article 5— Corporate Finance", 11 Buffalo L.Rev. 461, 473 (1962); deCapriles & McAniff, "The Financial Provisions of the New (1961) New York Business Corporation Law", 36 N.Y.U.L.Rev. 1239, 1244 (1961); Kessler, "Share Repurchasers Under Modern Corporation Laws", 28 Fordham L.Rev. 637 (1959–60). The redemption price is stated in terms of par value or monetary amount and usually includes a premium; in the case of cumulative preferred shares, provision might also be made for any arrearages. See note 2 infra. Even a mandatory redemption provision is subject to the implied condition that redemption does not render the corporation insolvent. Kraft v. Rochambeau Holding Co., 210 Md. 325, 123 A.2d 287 (1956). In the case of a corporation's agreement to repurchase its shares, the older cases required legally available funds both at the time the agreement was made and at the time of performance. The modern trend is to uphold such agreements as valid, regardless of the situation at the time of the making of the agreement, and to enforce them, even by specific performance, to the extent that the corporation has legally available funds at the time of repurchase. E. g., McKinney's N.Y.Bus.Corp.Law, § 514; McConnell v. Butler, 402 F.2d 362 (9th Cir. 1968); Brockington v. Scott, 381 F.2d 792 (4th Cir. 1967); Matter of Trimble Co., 339 F.2d 838 (3d Cir. 1964); Baxter v. Lancer Industries, Inc., 213 F.Supp. 92 (E.D.N.Y.1963), appeal dismissed 324 F.2d 286 (2d Cir. 1963) (also holding that existence of surplus was to be determined not solely by book values but by actual values conservatively applied); Tracy v. Perkins—Tracy Printing Co., 278 Minn. 159, 153 N.W.2d 241 (1967). See also Maley v. Carroll, 381 F.2d 147 (5th Cir. 1967) (upholding upward revaluation of assets to create surplus); In re Belmetals Mfg. Co., 299 F.Supp. 1290 (N.D.Cal.1969) (rejecting upward revaluation based on alleged over-depreciation in past); Cate v. Pagel-Clikeman Co., 87 Ill.App.2d 65, 230 N.E.2d 387 (1967) (rejecting downward revaluation of surplus to avoid agreement); La Voy Supply Co. v. Young, 84 Idaho 120, 369 P.2d 45 (1962). Shareholders who bought shares subject to repurchase agreements with corporation and received payment for shares when the corporation was insolvent have been required to repay the amounts received to the corporation's trustee-in-bankruptcy. Jackson v. Colagrossi, 50 Wash. 2d 572, 313 P.2d 697 (1957). See also Tiedje v. Aluminum Taper Milling Co., 291 P.2d 521 (Cal.App. 1955), rev'd, 46 Cal.2d 450, 296 P.2d 554 (1956). See Annot., 47 A.L.R.2d 758 (1956). The statutory restrictions on funds legally available for a corporation's redemption or purchase of its own shares sometimes apply to foreign corporations. McKin-

ney's N.Y.Bus.Corp.Law, §§ 1317(a) (1), 1318, 1319, 1320; but cf. ABA–ALI Model Bus.Corp.Act § 100.

2. See Huron Milling Co. v. Hedges, 257 F.2d 258 (2d Cir. 1958). Inclusion of cumulative preferred dividend arrearages as part of the redemption price poses problems analogous to the problem of including such arrearages as part of the liquidation preference. See section 235, n. 11 supra.

3. E. g., McKinney's N.Y.Bus.Corp.Law, § 513(c) (subject to any restrictions in articles of incorporation, absent insolvency or reduction of net assets below stated capital remaining after giving effect to cancellation of such redeemable shares).

4. E. g. McKinney's N.Y.Bus.Corp.Law, § 513(b) (3).

5. E. g., McKinney's N.Y.Bus.Corp.Law, § 513(b) (2); England v. Christensen, 243 Cal.App.2d 413, 52 Cal. Rptr. 402 (1966) (limiting provision to controversies between corporation and shareholders, not among shareholders).

6. E. g., ABA–ALI Model Bus.Corp.Act § 5; McKinney's N.Y.Bus.Corp.Law, § 513(b) (1). See section 161 supra.

7. E. g., Cal.Gen.Corp.Law, § 1706 (1947).

8. E. g., McKinney's N.Y.Bus.Corp.Law, § 513(b).

9. ABA–ALI Model Bus.Corp.Act § 5 (if articles of incorporation so permit or with affirmative vote of holders of at least two-thirds (majority under 1969 revision) of all shares entitled to vote thereon), § 60.

open-end investment companies,[10] within prescribed limitations, to withdraw their pro rata share of net assets.[11]

When shares are reacquired out of surplus, cash will be credited for the amount of the purchase price, and a negative earned surplus account, "Restricted Earned Surplus", often debited (or charged). The stated capital account, at the same time, can be debited (or charged), and a subsidiary stated capital account, "Treasury Shares", credited, or, in the alternative, the breakdown between treasury shares and outstanding shares can be disclosed.[12]

For unlawful redemptions or purchases, the directors assenting to the same,[13] and possibly the shareholders receiving the same, with knowledge or notice, are usually liable.[14]

STATUS OF REACQUIRED SHARES

337. Reacquired shares may be held as treasury shares or may, and sometimes must, be either restored to unissued status or eliminated from authorized shares.

Reacquired shares may be held as treasury shares [1] or may, and sometimes must, be either restored to unissued status or eliminated from authorized shares.[2] Restoration to unissued status or elimination from authorized shares may be effected by filings with the secretary of state of prescribed certificates, which might not require shareholder approval.[3] Elimination from authorized shares can, in the alternative, be effected by reducing stated capital [4] or amending the articles of incorporation, which requires shareholder approval.[5]

---

10. See section 301 supra.

11. E. g., Md.Gen.Corp.Law, § 32(b) (2) (1951); Minn.Bus.Corp.Act § 301.39(1) (1961); McKinney's N.Y.Bus.Corp.Law, § 512(b). The "redeemable shares" exception, if sufficiently broad, might achieve the same result where shares of open-end investment companies might be "redeemable" at the option of the holders. See note 3 supra.

12. See R. Amory & C. Hardee, Materials on Accounting—An Introduction to the Problems and Practice of Financial Accounting for Students of Law 324–331 (3d ed. by D. Herwitz & D. Trautman 1959) (par value method; cost method); G. Hills, The Law of Accounting and Financial Statements 141–143 (1957); Stanger, "Comparative Accounting Treatment Mandated by the Model Business Corporation Act and the New York Business Corporation Law Regarding Share Reacquisitions and the Related Effect on Surplus", 24 Bus.Law. 115 (1968). See ABA–ALI Model Bus.Corp.Act § 5 ("To the extent that earned surplus or capital surplus is used as the measure of the corporation's right to purchase its own shares, such surplus shall be restricted so long as such shares are held as treasury shares, and upon the disposition or cancellation of any such shares the restriction shall be removed pro tanto").

13. E. g., ABA–ALI Model Bus.Corp.Act § 43(b) (jointly and severally liable to corporation); McKinney's N.Y.Bus.Corp.Law § 719(a) (2); id. § 1318 (application to foreign corporations doing business in New York not exempted therefrom by id. § 1320). Liability also exists for failure to disclose information. Id. §§ 515(d), 516(c), 1318(c). Besides civil liabilities, statutes sometimes provide criminal penalties. McKinney's N.Y.Penal Law, § 190.35(5) (when purchase not "in the manner provided by law").

14. McKinney's N.Y.Bus.Corp.Law, § 719(d) (2); see also Uniform Fraudulent Conveyance Act; Reilly v. Segert, 31 Ill.2d 293, 201 N.E.2d 444 (1964) (statutory remedy against directors held not to preclude common-law liability of shareholders for selling their shares to corporation with knowledge of its insolvency).

1. See section 158 supra.

2. E. g., ABA–ALI Model Bus.Corp.Act § 61 (unless articles of incorporation prohibit reissue of cancelled redeemable shares, in which case authorized capital is reduced), § 62 (unless authorized shares are reduced by amendment of the articles of incorporation). See McKinney's N.Y.Bus.Corp.Law, § 515, to effect that shares that have been issued and have been purchased, redeemed, or otherwise reacquired by a corporation shall be cancelled if they are reacquired out of stated capital, or if they are converted shares, or if the articles of incorporation require that such shares be cancelled upon reacquisition. Where stated capital is reduced as the result of the cancellation of reacquired shares or otherwise, disclosure to shareholders is sometimes required. McKinney's N.Y.Bus.Corp.Law, §§ 515(d), 516(c), 1318(a); see also id. §§ 520, 1318 (liability of corporation for failure to disclose required information).

3. E. g., ABA–ALI Model Bus.Corp.Act §§ 61, 62.

4. See section 344 infra.

5. E. g., ABA–ALI Model Bus.Corp.Act § 63. See section 345 infra.

On the disposition or cancellation of treasury shares, any restriction imposed on the surplus account when the shares were reacquired removed "pro tanto".

MISCELLANEOUS REDEMPTION AND PURCHASE PROBLEMS

338. When listed shares are redeemed, applicable securities exchange requirements must be observed. In most cases, redemption and sale are treated alike for federal income tax purposes—as a sale of the shares by the shareholder to the corporation, subject to capital gains tax, except where redemption is a disguised dividend, in which case it is treated for tax purpose as a dividend (with adjustment of the basis of the remaining shares).

Securities Exchange Requirements Applicable to Redemption or Purchase

When listed shares are redeemed, applicable securities exchange requirements must be observed.

For example, the New York Stock Exchange requires prompt publicity of any redemption action and notice to the exchange thereof and of the record date. An agency in Manhattan must be maintained where the shares called for redemption may be presented for payment. The redemption procedure is regulated. In cases of partial redemption, the redeemed shares may not be selected otherwise than pro rata or by lot. Tender offers by the corporation for the purchase of its shares are required to be made to all shareholders to participate on equal terms.[1]

Tax Aspects of Redemption or Purchase

In most cases, redemption and purchase are treated alike for federal income tax purposes—as a sale of the shares by the shareholder to the corporation, subject to a capital gains tax.

However, to prevent the use of redemptions to disguise distributions of earnings (which in the form of a dividend would usually be taxable to the shareholder as ordinary income), redemption is treated as a dividend (with adjustment of the basis of the remaining shares) unless the redemption (a) is not essentially equivalent to a dividend, or (b) is substantially disproportionate and the shareholder owns less than 50 percent of the total voting power after redemption, or (c) is of all of the shareholder's shares in the corporation.[2]

H. DIVIDEND AND REDEMPTION TAX ASPECTS

DIVIDEND AND REDEMPTION TAX ASPECTS

339. The most significant taxes applicable to dividends are the federal income tax, the federal accumulated earnings tax, and the federal personal holding company tax.

The federal income tax statutes distinguish between (a) cash and property dividends, (b) liquidating dividends, and (c) share dividends. Cash or property dividends out of earnings and profits may not be deducted by the corporation and constitute ordinary income to recipient shareholders, subject ordinarily to $100 exclusion. Liquidation dividends are treated as a sale of shares, to which the capital gains rules apply. Redemption of shares is similarly treated if the redemption is not a disguised dividend, in which case it is treated as a dividend, with adjustment of the basis of remaining shares. Share dividends on common shares are not taxable unless the shareholder is given an election to take cash or other property in lieu of the dividend shares or the distribution is disproportionate.

To discourage the nonpayment of dividends to avoid income tax at the shareholder level, the federal accumulated earnings tax imposes, at the corporate level, a heavy surtax on unreasonable accumulations in excess of the "reasonable needs of the business", for which a $100,000 credit is allowed.

1. N.Y.S.E. Company Manual § A10. See also Federal Securities Exchange Act §§ 13(d), (f), 14(d), (e), 15 U.S.C.A. §§ 78m(d), (e), 78n(d), (e).

2. See section 339 infra.

Similarly, the federal personal holding company tax imposes, at the corporate level, a virtually confiscatory tax on undistributed "personal holding company income".

Also applicable to dividends are federal estate and gift taxes, and state income, inheritance, estate, and other taxes. Share dividends or splits are subject to state organization, capital, and franchise taxes, and any state issue taxes.

Directors who negligently or in breach of other duty subject the corporation to avoidable tax assessment might be personally liable to the corporation for the loss.

Of all the taxes applicable to dividends, the most significant are those imposed under federal law, especially the federal income tax, federal accumulated earnings tax, and federal personal holding company tax.

Federal Income Tax

The federal income tax statutes distinguish between (a) cash and property dividends, (b) liquidating dividends, and (c) share dividends.

Cash or Property Dividends. A "dividend" for federal income tax purposes is any distribution by a corporation to its shareholders, whether in cash or property, out of (a) earnings and profits accumulated after February 28, 1913,[1] or (b) earnings and profits for the taxable year. That portion of a cash or property distribution which is not a dividend usually is applied against and reduces the adjusted basis of the shares, and any excess is treated as gain from the sale or exchange of property.[2]

For the distribution of a dividend, neither gain nor loss is usually recognized, the corporation's earnings and profits are generally reduced, and most corporations are allowed no deduction;[3] and the shareholder receiving the dividend is subject to the tax thereon as ordinary income.[4] Property dividends

dating Distributions in Cash, Property, Stock, and Obligations", 5 How.L.J. 46 (1959); Andrews, "'Out of Its Earnings and Profits': Some Reflections on the Taxation of Dividends", 69 Harv.L.Rev. 1403 (1956); Wren, "The Income Taxation of Corporate Distributions Under the Internal Revenue Code of 1954", 43 Calif.L.Rev. 268 (1955), 44 Calif.L.Rev. 105 (1956) (Addendum); Cohen, Silverman, Surrey, Tarleau & Warren, "The Internal Revenue Code of 1954: Corporate Distributions, Organizations, and Reorganizations", 68 Harv.L.Rev. 393 (1955); Dean & Headly, "New Corporate Concepts Under the 1954 Revenue Code", 103 U.Pa.L.Rev. 491, 493–504 (1955). For state law analogy, see Matter of Marx v. Bragalini, 6 N.Y.2d 322, 189 N.Y.S.2d 846, 160 N.E.2d 611 (1959). See also D. Kahn, Basic Corporate Taxation 1 et seq. (ICLE 1970).

3. Int.Rev.Code of 1954, 26 U.S.C.A. §§ 311, 312. To try to achieve a deduction, corporate distributions sometimes assume the form of a "bargain purchase", rental and royalty arrangements, interest, compensation, life insurance, loan of credit to corporation, rebates, etc. Hash v. Comm'r, 273 F.2d 248 (4th Cir. 1959); Appleman v. United States, 176 F.Supp. 706 (S.D.N.Y.1959). See 2 G. Hornstein, Corporation Law and Practice § 934 (1959); Comment, "Disguised Dividends: A Comprehensive Survey", 3 U.C.L.A.L.Rev. 207 (1956). Subchapter S elections, limited to "small business corporations", might avoid the tax at the corporate level. See sections 76, 262 supra. For discussion of "thin incorporation", see section 166 supra.

4. However, the individual shareholder enjoys an exclusion of the first $100 in dividends of certain domestic corporations from gross income. Int.Rev. Code of 1954, 26 U.S.C.A. § 116; U.S.Treas.Reg. § 1.116 (1956). There might also be an additional credit for dividends under the retirement income credit. A corporation is taxable only on 15 percent of the dividends it receives from most domestic corporations. Int.Rev.Code of 1954, 26 U.S.C.A. §§ 243 et seq.; U.S.Treas.Reg. §§ 1.243 et seq. (1956). For attempts to achieve capital gain treatment or avoidance of tax at shareholder level by means of "bargain sale", rental and royalty arrangements, loans, gifts, payments to shareholder's family, life insurance, etc., and the possibility of constructive dividends, see Sullivan v. United States, 363 F.2d 724 (8th Cir. 1966), cert. denied 387 U.S. 905, 87 S.Ct. 1683, 18 L.Ed.2d 622 (1967), reh. denied 388 U.S. 924, 87 S.Ct. 2104, 18 L.Ed.2d 1378 (1967); Noble v. Comm'r, 368 F.2d 439, (9th Cir. 1966); Baum, "Effects of Stockholder Use of Corporate Property, Including Stockholder Borrowings Deemed Dividends in Relation to Section 1341", N.Y.U. 25th Inst. on

1. March 1, 1913 being the effective date of the Revenue Act of 1913, subsequent to the ratification of U.S.Const. Amend. 16. Prior to the amendment, the constitutionality of franchise taxes on corporations based on their income had been upheld. Flint v. Stone Tracy Co., 220 U.S. 107, 31 S.Ct. 342, 55 L.Ed. 389 (1911).

2. Int.Rev.Code of 1954, 26 U.S.C.A. §§ 316, 317, 301; B. Bittker & J. Eustice, Federal Income Taxation of Corporations and Shareholders §§ 5.01–5.24 (2d ed. 1966); D. Holland, Dividends Under the Income Tax (1962); Ball, "Tax Considerations of Corporate Distributions", 17 Ark.L.Rev. 434 (1964); Bittker, "Corporate Dividends and Other Non-Liqui-

are so taxed on the basis of their fair market value.[5]

Distributions in Partial Liquidation. Distributions in partial liquidation, sometimes loosely called "liquidating dividends", are distributions in cash or property which are treated as sales of shares, to which the capital gains rules usually apply.[6]

Redemption of Shares. Redemption of shares is treated as a sale of shares, subject to the capital gains rules, if the redemption (a) is "not essentially equivalent to a dividend", or (b) is "substantially disproportionate" and the shareholder owns less than 50 percent of the total voting power after redemption", or (c) is of all of the shareholder's shares in the corporation. Otherwise, redemption is treated as a dividend, with adjustment of the basis of remaining shares.[7]

Fed.Tax. 509 (1967); Nims, "Minimizing Constructive Dividend Exposure", 16 Tul.Tax Inst. 259 (1966); Hines, "Constructive Dividends—Ever-Present Threat", 50 A.B.A.J. 685 (1964); Cohen, "Loan or Dividend: A Common Tax Hazard for Controlling Shareholders", 36 Conn.B.J. 599 (1962); Comment, "Disguised Dividends: A Comprehensive Survey", 3 U.C.L.A.L.Rev. 207 (1956). See also Sneed, "A Defense of the Tax Courts Result in Prunier and Casale", 43 Cornell L.Q. 339 (1958); Note, 6 U.C.L.A.L.Rev. 107 (1959). Bills have been introduced in Congress to require corporations to withhold a 20 percent tax on cash dividends. In England, dividends are excluded from individual income tax, but not surtax; Canada allows a 20 percent dividend tax credit. Chommie, "Surtax Avoidance and Extra Taxation of Corporate Earnings in the United States, United Kingdom, and Canada", 12 Tax L.Rev. 279 (1957).

5. Int.Rev.Code of 1954, 26 U.S.C.A. § 301; Scott, "Taxation of Corporate Distributions in Kind", 12 Stan.L.Rev. 529 (1960). For tax relief afforded shareholders of E. I. du Pont de Nemours & Company upon distribution to them of shares of General Motors Corporation under an antitrust divestiture decree, see 26 U.S.C.A. §§ 301(f), 1111.

6. B. Bittker & J. Eustice, Federal Income Taxation of Corporations and Shareholders, §§ 7.60–7.63 (2d ed. 1966).

7. Int. Rev. Code of 1954, 26 U.S.C.A. § 302. Redemption is defined as an acquisition by a corporation of its shares from a shareholder in exchange for property (including cash), whether or not the shares so acquired are cancelled, retired, or held as treasury shares. Id. § 317(b). Thus "redemption", for tax purposes, includes purchases of shares, and resembles a "dividend" in the sense that each in-

There are special rules, applicable to redemptions to pay death taxes,[8] through use

volves a distribution of cash or property by a corporation to a shareholder, but differs from a "dividend" in the sense that the latter does not involve an exchange, i.e., the surrender of some or all of the shareholder's shares, as does a "redemption". There are complicated provisions on constructive ownership of shares, attributing shares owned by one person to another. See id. § 318. See generally D. Kahn, Basic Corporate Taxation 11 et seq. (ICLE 1970); B. Bittker & J. Eustice, Federal Income Taxation of Corporations and Shareholders §§ 7.20–7.25 (2 ed. 1966); J. Reeves, Tax Aspects of Corporate Mergers, Exchanges, Redemptions, Liquidations, and Reorganizations (1967); P. Seghers, et al., Essentially Equivalent to a Dividend (1960); 2 G. Hornstein, Corporation Law and Practice § 938 (1959); Goldstein, "Stock Redemptions and the Attribution Rules", N.Y.U. 27th Inst. on Fed. Tax. 793 (1969); Eisenberg, "Corporate Reorganization Problems With Redemption and Preferred Stock", 25 J. Taxation 278 (1966); Pomeroy, "Effect of Stock Redemptions Upon Tax Avoidance and the Reasonable Needs of the Business", 17 W.Res.L.Rev. 754 (1966); Robbins, "Cutting Down or Buying Out Stockholders in Close or Family Corporations: Disproportionate Redemptions and Complete Terminations", N.Y.U. 23d Inst. on Fed.Tax. 663 (1965); Cavitch, "Costly Traps in Corporate Stock Purchases from Shareholders", 15 W.Res.L.Rev. 338 (1964); Moore, "Dividend Equivalency—Taxation of Distributions in Redemption of Stock, 19 Tax L. Rev. 249 (1964); Greene, "Planning for Corporate Stock Redemptions Faces Many Potential Hazards", 19 J. Taxation 2 (1963); Odell, "Purchase by Redemption—A Proposed Solution for the Taxation of the Remaining Shareholder", 18 U.Miami L.Rev. 129 (1963); Clark, "Dangers Involved in Stock Redemptions", 11 Tul.Tax Inst. 123 (1962); Dean, "Redemptions: Liquidating and Non-liquidating; Kinds of Distributions", N.Y.U. 20th Inst. on Fed.Tax. 895 (1962); Bittker, "The Taxation of Stock Redemptions and Partial Liquidations", 44 Cornell L.Q. 299 (1959); Singer, "Tax Consequences of Stock Redemptions for Shareholders Whose Stock Is Not Redeemed", 38 Ore.L.Rev. 1 (1958). Cohen, "Redemptions of Stock Under the Internal Revenue Code of 1954", 103 U.Pa.L.Rev. 739 (1955); Comment, "Taxation—Constructive Ownership Rules Automatically Applied to Section 302(b) (1) Dividend Equivalency Test", 21 Vand.L.Rev. 399 (1968); Comment, "Redemptions and Partial Liquidations under the 1954 Internal Revenue Code: The Dividend Equivalence Test", 103 U.Pa.L.Rev. 936 (1955). "Accrued dividends" included in the redemption price have been held not to constitute dividends. Estate of Mathis v. Comm'r, 47 T.C. 248 (1966); 1967 Int. Rev. Bull. No. 23, at 6 (acquiescence). See Davis v. United States, 408 F.2d 1139 (6th Cir. 1969), cert. granted 396 U.S. 815, 90 S.Ct. 88, 24 L.Ed.2d 66 (1969).

8. Int. Rev. Code of 1954, 26 U.S.C.A. § 303; B. Bittker & J. Eustice, Federal Income Taxation of Corporations and Shareholders § 7.40 (2d ed. 1966); Massey, "Section 303 Stock Repurchase vs. Accumu-

of related corporations (including so-called "brother-sister corporations"),[9] "preferred shares bail-outs",[10] etc.

Quaere, as to the tax consequences in the case of Subchapter S election, since Sub-

chapter S does not expressly deal with redemption of shares by an electing corporation.[11]

Share Dividends. Share dividends may or may not be taxable.

Under the 1954 Code, until 1969, share dividends were not taxable, unless (a) paid to satisfy a dividend preference, or (b) the shareholder was given an election to take cash or other property in lieu of the dividend shares. If non-taxable, upon subsequent sale of the old or new shares, allocation of the basis of the old and new shares in proportion to the fair market values at the time of distribution is required; the holding period of the new shares includes the period for which the shareholder held the old shares. Taxable share dividends since 1969 include share dividends on preferred shares and disproportionate distributions, including distributions of common shares to some shareholders and of preferred shares to other shareholders and distributions of convertible preferred shares to common shareholders.[12]

---

lated Earnings Tax", 17 Clev.-Mar. L.Rev. 175 (1968); Stoeber, "Planning Section 303 Redemptions", 21 C.U.L.J. 65 (Jan. 1967); Horwich, "Stock Redemptions Under Section 303 and the Accumulated Earnings Tax", 10 Tax Coun.Q. 117 (1966). The Tax Reform Act of 1969 redefined "reasonable needs of the business" to include amounts necessary for section 303 redemptions to pay death taxes.

9. Int. Rev. Code of 1954, 26 U.S.C.A. § 304; Wiseman v. United States, 371 F.2d 816 (1st Cir. 1967); B. Bittker & J. Eustice, Federal Income Taxation of Corporations and Shareholders §§ 7.30, 7.31 (2d ed. 1966); Marans, "Section 304: The Shadowy World of Redemptions Through Related Corporations", 22 Tax L.Rev. 161 (1967); Kempf, "Section 304 of the Internal Revenue Code: Unmasking Disguised Dividends in Related Corporation Transactions", 33 U.Chi.L.Rev. 60 (1965); Lefevre, "Purchases of Stock by Related Corporations— Acquisitions or Redemptions?", 14 Tul. Tax Inst. 441 (1965); Baum, "Reshuffling of Stock Interests of Closely Held Brother-Sister Corporations", N.Y. U. 22d Inst. on Fed.Tax. 677 (1964). See also Comm'r v. Stickney, 399 F.2d 828 (6th Cir. 1968).

10. Int. Rev. Code of 1954, 26 U.S.C.A. § 306. If "section 306 stock" is sold or otherwise disposed of, the amount realized is ordinary income to the extent of the share's ratable share of earnings and profits at the time of distribution; the balance, if any, is applicable against the allocated basis of the shares, and any excess is treated as gain from the sale of the shares. If "section 306 stock" is redeemed, the amount received by the shareholder is to be treated as a § 301 distribution, *i. e.,* taxable as a dividend to the extent of the corporation's earnings and profits at the time of redemption; the balance, if any, as a return of capital under § 301(c) (2) and (3). See B. Bittker & J. Eustice, Federal Income Taxation of Corporations and Shareholders ch. 8 (2d ed. 1966); Metzer, "The Impact of Section 306, Stock upon Convertible Preferred Stock Issued in a Corporate Reorganization", 116 U. Pa. L.Rev. 755 (1968); Rosenberg, "Advantages of Using Convertible Preferred in Acquisitions: How to Avoid the 306 Problem", 26 J. Taxation 7 (1967); Kendal, "section 306 Stock: How to Remove the 'Taint' and Use it Effectively in Tax Planning", 24 J. Taxation 322 (1966); Trimble, "The Treatment of Preferred Stock Distributions in Reorganizations Under Section 306 of the Internal Revenue Code of 1954", 19 Tax L.Rev. 345 (1964); Diamond, "A View of Section 306 Or 'Taint' Necessarily So", 17 Bus. Law. 256 (1962); Alexander & Landis, "Bail-Outs and the Internal Revenue Code of 1954", 65 Yale L.J. 909 (1956). See Chamberlin v. Comm'r, 207 F.2d 462 (6th Cir. 1953), cert. denied 347 U.S. 918, 74 S.Ct. 516, 98 L.Ed. 1073 (1954) (pre-1954 Code).

11. See Frost, "New Election of Certain Corporations Not To Be Taxed As Such", 45 A.B.A.J. 81, 83 (1959).

12. Int. Rev. Code of 1954, 26 U.S.C.A. §§ 305, 306, 1223(5); B. Bittker & J. Eustice, Federal Income Taxation of Corporations and Shareholders §§ 5.60– 5.62 (2d ed. 1966); Lee, "Stock Dividends", 37 Taxes 959 (1959); Kumler, "Corporate Distributions of Stock: A Bird's Eye View of the New Code Provisions", 41 A.B.A.J. 29 (1955); see also Whiteside, "Tax Consequences of Distributions of Stock Rights to Shareholders", 66 Yale L.J. 1016 (1957). For pre-1954 Code rules, see Helvering v. Griffiths, 318 U.S. 371, 63 S.Ct. 636, 87 L.Ed. 843 (1943) (common share dividend on common shares held not taxable); Koshland v. Helvering, 298 U.S. 441, 56 S.Ct. 767, 80 L.Ed. 1268, 105 A.L.R. 756 (1936) (common share dividend on preferred shares changing shareholders' proportionate interests in net corporate assets held taxable); Eisner v. Macomber, 252 U.S. 189, 40 S. Ct. 189, 64 L.Ed. 521, 9 A.L.R. 1570 (1920) (common share dividend on common shares held not taxable); Strassburger v. Comm'r, 318 U.S. 604, 63 S.Ct. 791, 87 L.Ed.2d 1029, 144 A.L.R. 1335 (1943) (preferred share dividend declared by corporation having only common shares outstanding and received by person having all common shares held not taxable because distribution brought about no change whatsoever in shareholder's interest in corporation); Sprouse v. Comm'r, 122 F.2d 973, 143 A.L.R. 226 (9th Cir. 1941), aff'd sub nom. Helvering v. Sprouse, 318

Except in cases of redemptions through use of related corporations, "preferred share bail-outs", etc.,[13] the subsequent sale of the shares is subject to tax at the capital gains rates.

In the case of taxable share dividends, the old shares retain their original basis, and the new shares constitute income at their fair market value, which becomes their basis.

Federal Accumulated Earnings Tax

To discourage the nonpayment of dividends to avoid the income tax at the shareholder level on the receipt of dividends, the federal accumulated earnings tax was imposed in 1936. In addition to other corporate taxes, it is imposed on a corporation's "accumulated taxable income" at the rates of 27½ percent on the first $100,000 of such income and 38½ percent of such income in excess of $100,000. Included in the accumulated earnings credit are amounts "retained for the reasonable needs of the business". A minimum credit of $100,000 is allowed.[14]

U.S. 604, 63 S.Ct. 791, 87 L.Ed. 1029, 144 A.L.R. 1335 (1943) (share dividend of nonvoting common shares on voting common shares; taxability held dependent on whether shareholders' proportionate interests changed). As was stated in the landmark case of Eisner v. Macomber, supra, 252 U. S. at 202–203, 40 S.Ct. at 191, 64 L.Ed. at 527: A share dividend really takes nothing from "the property of the corporation and adds nothing in the interests of the shareholders. Its property is not diminished, and their interests are not increased . . . the proportional interest of each shareholder remains the same. The only change is in the evidence which represents that interest, the new shares and the original shares together representing the same proportional interests that the original shares represented before the issue of the new ones."

13. See notes, 9, 10 supra.

14. Int. Rev. Code of 1954, 26 U.S.C.A. §§ 531–537; The Tax on Accumulated Earnings (CCH 1968); S. Weithorn & R. Noall, The Accumulated Earnings Tax (PLI 1968); B. Bittker & J. Eustice, Federal Income Taxation of Corporations and Shareholders §§ 6.01–6.09 (2d ed. 1966); S. Weithorn & R. Noall, Penalty Taxes on Accumulated Earnings and Personal Holding Companies (1963); R. Holzman, The Tax on Accumulated Earnings (1956); R. Kilcullen, Taxing the Improper Accumulation of Corporate

Federal Personal Holding Company Tax

The federal personal holding company tax,[15] in addition to other corporate taxes, is

Surplus (PLI rev. 1956); Symposium: "The New Emphasis on Section 531: A Survey of the Penalty on Undisturbed Earnings", 17 W.Res.L.Rev. 704 (1966); Symposium: "531 Penalty Tax on Accumulated Earnings: How to Avoid It", 30 J. Taxation 130 (1964); Canty, "Accumulated Earnings Tax 1954 Reforms: An Appraisal", 2 U. San Francisco L. Rev. 242 (1968); Culverhouse & Anderson, "Recent Developments in the Accumulated Earnings Tax", 54 A.B.A.J. 612 (1968); Levitan, "Accumulated Earnings Tax—Defensive Planning", 2 Gonz.L.Rev. 19 (1967); Luria, "The Accumulated Earnings Tax", 76 Yale L.J. 793 (1967); Crampton, "Improper Accumulation of Surplus: Procedures for Handling the Case: Advance Planning; Audit; Litigation", N.Y.U. 24th Inst. on Fed.Tax. 843 (1966); Kushinsky, "Recent 531 Cases Show Sharper IRS Attack, But Also Refine Defenses to Penalty Tax", 26 J. Taxation 328 (1967); Whitmore, "Accumulated Earnings Tax: Where We Are—Major Developments 1965–1966", 16 Tul. Tax Inst. 230 (1966); Maxfield, "Recent Cases Forecast More Liberal Trend in Allowing Accumulations to Redeem Stock", 25 J. Taxation 43 (1966); Washington, "Can Earnings Still Be Accumulated to Finance Section 303 Redemptions?", 44 Taxes 43 (1966); Horvitz, " 'Operating Cycle' Test Provides Needed Guidelines for Measuring 531 Accumulations", 24 J. Taxation 326 (1966); Altman, "Improper Accumulation of Earned Surplus: Circumstances Which Invoke the Section 531 Penalty Tax: Business Needs; Purpose to Avoid Surtax; Multiple Corporations and Section 531", N.Y.U. 24th Inst. on Fed.Tax. 805 (1966); Latham, "Practical Aspects of Accumulated Earnings Tax", 15 W.Res.L.Rev. 363 (1964); Delaney, "What is 'Accumulation Beyond Reasonable Needs' of the Business", 39 Taxes 402 (1961); Herwitz, "Stock Redemptions and the Accumulated Earnings Tax", 74 Harv.L.Rev. 866 (1961); Boughner, "Careful Planning Prevents Serious Accumulated Earnings Problems", 15 J. Taxation 74 (1961); Holzman, "Why Taxmen Are Sore at '534' ", 39 Taxes 777 (1961); Weithorn, "What Constitutes a 'Reasonable' Corporate Accumulation?", N.Y.U. 17th Inst. on Fed.Tax. 299 (1959); Wallick, "§ 531 Penalty Tax: What Is an Unreasonable Accumulation?", 4 Prac.Law. 31 (Nov. 1958); Comment, "Accumulated Earnings Tax: Burdens of Proof of Reasonableness and Purpose", 54 Calif.L. Rev. 1050 (1966); Comment, "The Accumulated Earnings Tax and the Problems of Diversification", 64 Mich.L.Rev. 1135 (1966). See United States v. Donruss Co., 393 U.S. 297, 89 S.Ct. 501, 21 L.Ed.2d 495 (1969) (subjecting to tax corporation which accumulated earnings beyond reasonable needs of business where one, though not dominant, purpose of accumulation was tax avoidance). Prior to 1958, the lump-sum credit was $60,000. The lump-sum

15. See note 15 on page 693.

imposed on the "undistributed personal holding company income" of every "personal holding company" at the rate of 70 percent of such income. Two requirements must co-exist in order for a corporation to be a "personal holding company": (a) Adjusted ordinary gross income requirement (at least 60 percent of the corporation's adjusted ordinary gross income must be "personal holding company income", i. e., passive income, such as rents, royalties, interest, dividends, etc.), and (b) Share ownership requirement (at any time during last half of taxable year more than 50 percent in value of the corporation's outstanding shares is owned, directly or indirectly, by or for not more than five individuals). One of the purposes of the tax is to force distribution of accumulated investment income by such corporations, known as "incorporated pocketbooks".[16]

Miscellaneous Taxes

Besides the federal income tax, accumulated earnings tax, and personal holding company tax, the federal estate and gift taxes might also be applicable to dividends. So also state income, inheritance, estate, and other taxes.

Where share dividends (or splits) are involved, state organization or capital taxes on authorized capital and franchise taxes on outstanding shares,[17] and any state issue taxes [18] apply.

Directors' Tax Responsibilities

Directors in determining dividend policy should consider the tax aspects involved, in the interests of soundness, good shareholder relations, and their own potential personal liability for negligence or breach of fiduciary duty.

Where the corporation incurs avoidable tax assessments as the result of negligence or other breach of duty on the part of its directors, the directors may be held personally liable to the corporation for the loss, in an action by or in behalf of the corporation.[19]

credit in effect exempts very small corporations. Most of the cases, however, have involved close corporations. For the outstanding case involving a public-issue corporation, see Trico Products Corp. v. Comm'r, 46 B.T.A. 346 (1942), aff'd 137 F.2d 424 (2d Cir. 1943), cert. denied, 320 U.S. 799, 64 S.Ct. 369, 99 L.Ed. 482 (1943).

15. Int. Rev. Code of 1954, 26 U.S.C.A. §§ 541–547.

16. B. Bittker & J. Eustice, Federal Income Taxation of Corporations and Shareholders §§ 6.20–6.26 (2d ed. 1966); S. Weithorn & R. Noall, Penalty Taxes on Accumulated Earnings and Personal Holding Companies (1963); L. Hochberg, The Foreign Investors Tax Act: Its Impact on Personal Holding Companies (1967); Liles, "A New Look at Personal Holding Company Problems: The New Rules of the 1964 Act", N.Y.U. 24th Inst. on Fed.Tax. 863 (1966); Gannet, "Personal Holding Companies: The Special Relief Provisions of the 1964 Act", id. 889; Kockritz, "How to Minimize the Personal Holding Company Tax under the New Rules", 22 J. Taxation 2 (1965); Libin, "Personal Holding Companies and the Revenue Act of 1964", 63 Mich.L.Rev. 421 (1965); Lipoff, "Personal Holding Companies: A Waking Tiger", 18 U.Fla.L.Rev. 304 (1965); Vesely, "Adjusted Personal Holding Company Income Concepts Under the Revenue Act of 1964", 16 W.Res.L.Rev. 306 (1965); Fisher & Kohl, "1964 Act: Personal Holding Company Rules Tightened; More Corporations Vulnerable", 20 J. Taxation 258 (1964); Schmitt, "Personal Holding Companies", 13 Tul. Tax Inst. 264 (1964); Cuddihy, "Accumulated Earnings and Personal Holding Company Taxes", N.Y.U. 21st Inst. on Fed.Tax. 401 (1963). Every close corporation is a potential personal holding company. The effect of the tax can be minimized by the so-called "deficiency dividend" procedure.

17. See Matter of P. J. Garvey Carting & Storage, Inc. v. State Tax Commission, 27 A.D.2d 237, 279 N.Y.S.2d 508 (3d Dep't 1967); Matter of American Chicle Co. v. State Tax Commission, 5 A.D.2d 318, 172 N.Y.S.2d 389 (3d Dep't 1958), appeal denied 6 A.D.2d 948, 176 N.Y.S.2d 251 (3d Dep't 1958).

18. Cf. F. & M. Schaefer Brewing Co. v. United States, 256 F.2d 696 (2d Cir. 1958) (holding capitalization of surplus without distribution of shares is not subject to former federal share issue tax).

19. After Trico Products Corp. was subjected to a $7,300,000 federal accumulated earnings tax, a claim against directors for the loss was settled for $2,390,000. Mahler v. Trico Products Corp., No. A79948 (Sup.Ct. Erie County, N.Y.). Cf. Pool v. Pool, 22 So.2d 131 (La.Ct.App.1945) (directors who relied on certified public accountant and attorney held not liable for federal accumulated earnings tax imposed on corporation); Conviser v. Simpson, 122 F.Supp. 205 (D.Md.1954) (directors of investment company whose retention of realized capital gain, rather than distributing it to shareholders along with investment income, resulted in $3,500,000 federal capital gain tax on corporation held not liable under business judgment rule).

CHAPTER 13

EXTRAORDINARY CORPORATE MATTERS

EXTRAORDINARY CORPORATE MATTERS—IN GENERAL

340. **Shareholders invest in the corporate enterprise as defined in the articles of incorporation with the expectation that the board of directors will manage the enterprise so far as its ordinary business is concerned. Amendments of the articles of incorporation involve, to some extent, organic changes; extraordinary transactions transcend ordinary business matters delegated to the board of directors.**

Modern statutes authorize various extraordinary matters when approved by a prescribed vote or consent of shareholders. Typically, such extraordinary matters are sales, etc., of all or substantially all of the corporate assets other than in the regular course of business, amendments of the articles of incorporation, mergers and consolidations, nonjudicial dissolution, etc., with possible provision for voting even by shareholders not otherwise entitled to vote or for class voting.

Under the "contract theory", a corporate charter constitutes contracts between the corporation and the state, among the members, and between the members and the corporation —the obligation of contracts being protected against state impairment by the United States Constitution. Rights which could not be changed became known as "vested rights". By advance reservation of the power to change corporate statutes and charters, such reservation itself became a term of the contract between the corporation and the state, and, in most jurisdictions, of the contracts among the shareholders and between the shareholders and the corporation.

Extraordinary matters must (a) be authorized by law, (b) comply with required procedures, and (c) not exceed equitable limitations thereon. Dissenting shareholders sometimes enjoy an appraisal remedy.

Shareholders invest in the corporate enterprise as defined in the articles of incorporation with the expectation that the board of directors will manage the enterprise so far as its ordinary business is concerned. Amendments of the articles of incorporation involve, to a greater or lesser extent, organic changes in the corporation; extraordinary transactions are beyond the ordinary business whose management is delegated to the board of directors. At common law, such extraordinary matters required unanimous shareholder approval.[1]

1. Voeller v. Neilston Warehouse Co., 311 U.S. 531, 535, 61 S.Ct. 376, 377–378, 85 L.Ed. 322, 326, n. 6 (1941). N. Lattin, The Law of Corporations ch. 11 (1959); Lynch, "The Majority's Power to Effect Fundamental Changes in Shareholder Rights", 2 Corp.Prac.Comm. 1 (Feb. 1961); Freas, "Fundamental Corporate Changes: Merger, Consolidation, Sale of Assets, and Dissolution", 28 Tenn.L.Rev. 529 (1961). Lattin, "A Primer on Fundamental Corporate Changes", 1 W.Res.L.Rev. 3 (1949). See Carter v. Spencer, 4 Utah 2d 1, 286 P.2d 245 (1955).

"Vested Rights" Doctrine

Despite the "concession theory",[2] even the sovereign creator of the corporation has been held subject to constitutional restraints in the United States. The leading case is Trustees of Dartmouth College v. Woodward,[3] decided by the United States Supreme Court in 1819, which gave rise to the "contract theory". There, where the state by legislation attempted to amend the Dartmouth College crown charter, the Court held that a corporate charter was a contract between the state and the corporation which is protected by the United States Constitution against state impairment of the obligation of contracts.[4] Story, J., concurring, suggested a solution:

"Unless a power be reserved for this purpose, the crown cannot, in virtue of its prerogative, without the consent of the corporation, alter or amend the charter, . . .[5]

. . . If the legislature mean to claim such an authority, it must be reserved in the grant. The charter of Dartmouth College contains no such reservation; . . ."[6]

Subsequently, clauses reserving the power to alter, amend or repeal were inserted in charters issued by state legislatures in cases of special incorporation,[7] and as general incorporation statutes came into vogue, reserved power provisions were enacted into state constitutions[8] or such statutes[9] or both.[10] The reserved power itself thus became a term of the contract.[11]

2. See section 78 supra.

3. 17 U.S. (4 Wheat.) 518, 4 L.Ed. 629 (1819). See Marks, "The Dartmouth College Case", 14 N.Y.U.L. Center Bull. No. 2 and 3, 24 (Winter-Spring 1966), 15 id. No. 1, 13 (Fall 1966), 15 id. No. 2, 14 (Spring 1967), 15 id. No. 4, 13 (Summer 1967).

4. U.S.Const. art. I, § 10, cl. 1

5. 17 U.S. (4 Wheat.) at 675, 4 L.Ed. at 668 (1819).

6. 17 U.S. (4 Wheat.) at 712, 4 L.Ed. at 677 (1819).

7. Some earlier charters had contained reserved power clauses. Dodd, "Dissenting Stockholders and Amendments to Corporate Charters", 75 U.Pa.L. Rev. 588, 592 (1927).

8. E. g., Alabama, Arizona, Arkansas, Idaho, Kansas, Kentucky, Michigan, Mississippi, Ohio, Utah, Washington, Wisconsin. See also note 10 infra. The constitutional provision sometimes contains a proviso that no injustice be done to incorporators, corporators, or shareholders. E. g., Alabama, Arkansas, Colorado, Idaho, Mississippi, Oklahoma, Pennsylvania, South Dakota. Several constitutions provide that any domestic corporation by amending or renewing its articles of incorporation accepts the constitution and laws of the state.

9. E. g., ABA–ALI Model Bus.Corp.Act § 142; Alaska, Connecticut, Illinois, Louisiana, Minnesota, Missouri, New Hampshire, Oregon, Rhode Island, West Virginia, District of Columbia. See also note 10 infra.

10. E. g., N.Y.Const. art. X, § 1; McKinney's N.Y. Bus.Corp.Law, § 110; all jurisdictions except those named in notes 8 and 9 supra and Florida and Hawaii, which apparently have neither constitutional nor statutory reservation of power provisions. In State ex rel. Holekamp v. Holekamp Lumber Co., 340 S.W.2d 678 (Mo.1960), appeal dismissed 366 U.S. 715, 81 S.Ct. 1660, 6 L.Ed.2d 846 (1961), petition for reh. denied 368 U.S. 820, 82 S.Ct. 26, 7 L.Ed.2d 71 (1961), a Missouri corporation was incorporated in 1908 for 50 years, the then maximum duration. At that time, a three-fourths vote of shareholders was required to extend corporate existence. In 1943, the extension statute was amended to permit extension by majority shareholder vote, such amendment being expressly applicable to preexisting corporations. Extension of the corporation's existence by majority vote under the 1943 amendment was upheld on the ground that the Missouri Constitution of 1875, in effect in 1908, contained sufficient reserved power to permit the application of the 1943 amendment to the 1908 corporation. The Constitution of 1875 read: "No corporation, after the adoption of this Constitution, shall be created by special laws; nor shall any existing charter be extended, changed or amended by special laws, except those for charitable, penal or reformatory purposes, which are under the patronage and control of the State."
The Constitution of 1865 had previously read: "Corporations may be formed under general laws; . . . all general laws and special acts . . . may be altered, amended, and repealed . . . .." See Hanks v. Borelli, 2 Ariz.App. 589, 411 P.2d 27 (1966) (renewal of corporate existence construed as renegotiation of new contract, subject to laws then in effect). Midland Truck Lines, Inc. v. Atwood, 362 Mo. 397, 241 S.W.2d 903 (1951) (holding new statutory provision applicable to preexisting corporation which by statute in force at time of incorporation elected to be governed by new statute).

11. Mobile Press Register, Inc. v. McGowin, 271 Ala. 414, 124 So.2d 812 (1960) (upholding amendment of articles of incorporation eliminating preemptive

Not only was a corporate charter a contract between the corporation and the state; it also came to be recognized as a contract among the members and between the members and the corporation.[12] This three-contract analysis affected not only charter amendments, but sales of all or substantially all corporate assets, mergers, consolidations, dissolutions, etc. Under traditional contract law theory, changes in the contract required consent of all of the parties. The so-called "vested rights" doctrine developed,[13] which raised questions as to deprivation by the state, through the purported exercise of its police power,[14] of property without due process of law.[15]

Some authorities construed statutory reserved power provisions as applicable only to the contract between the corporation and the state, and not to the contract among the members and the contracts between the members and the corporations.[16] Under this strict approach, legislation specifically authorizing various fundamental changes could constitutionally operate only prospectively to corporations thereafter formed and not retroactively to corporations already in existence.[17] Apart from any constitutional question, the authorization might be construed as intended by the legislature to apply only prospectively.[18]

Courts also tended to construe legislation strictly, holding, for example, that power "to classify or reclassify" or to change "preferences . . . or other special rights" of

rights since term of articles was constitutional reserved power); Hudson-Harlem Valley Title & Mortgage Co. v. White, 251 App.Div. 1, 296 N.Y.S. 424 (3d Dep't 1937). The state may, under the reserved power, enact or amend statutes which in turn have the effect of amending or repealing corporate charters in either of two ways: (a) by changing the law under which the corporation was incorporated; (b) by enacting a law which allows a corporation to make changes, such as amending its articles of incorporation. Lord v. Equitable Life Assurance Society, 194 N.Y. 212, 87 N.E. 443 (1909). See Note, "Limitations on the Amending Power in the Corporate Contract", 18 U.Chi.L.Rev. 139 (1950).

12. Western Foundry Co. v. Wicker, 403 Ill. 260, 85 N.E.2d 722, 8 A.L.R.2d 878 (1949); Fuld, J., dissenting in Gordon v. Elliman, 306 N.Y. 456, 469, 471, 119 N.E.2d 331, 340, 341 (1954).

13. McNulty, "Corporations and the Intertemporal Conflict of Laws", 55 Calif.L.Rev. 12, 27 (1967); Gibson, "How Fixed Are Class Shareholder Rights?", 23 Law & Contemp.Prob. 283 (1959); Note, "Stockholder and Vested Rights in Virginia", 42 Va.L.Rev. 107 (1956); Note, "New York's Changing Concept of Vested Rights in Regard to Shareholders", 24 St. John's L.Rev. 90 (1949). See discussion of Decline of "Vested Rights" Doctrine in section 345 infra. For "vested rights" approach to by-law amendments, see Bechtold v. Coleman Realty Co., 367 Pa. 208, 79 A.2d 661 (1951). In most jurisdictions today, the question is not one of "vested rights" but whether the matter is one authorized by statute. Silva v. Coastal Plywood & Timber Co., 124 Cal.App.2d 276, 268 P.2d 510 (1954); Davison v. Parke, Austin & Lipscomb, Inc., 285 N.Y. 500, 509, 35 N.E.2d 618, 622 (1941).

14. U.S.Const. amend. X.

15. U.S.Const. amend. XIV, § 1.

16. Jacobson v. Backman, 16 Utah 2d 356, 401 P.2d 181 (1965) (reserved power held to permit alteration of contract between state and corporation and its shareholders but not contract between corporation and its shareholders); Wheatley v. A. I. Root Co., 147 Ohio St. 127, 69 N.E.2d 187 (1946); cf. Ohio State Life Ins. Co. v. Clark, 274 F.2d 771 (6th Cir. 1960), cert. denied 363 U.S. 828, 80 S.Ct. 1599, 4 L. Ed.2d 1523 (1960); Opdyke v. Security Savings & Loan Ass'n, 157 Ohio St. 121, 105 N.E.2d 9 (1952); see Zabriskie v. Hackensack & N. Y. R. R., 18 N.J. Eq. 178 (1867); Faunce v. Boost Co., 15 N.J.Super. 534, 83 A.2d 649 (1951). But see Boege v. American Sumatra Tobacco Corp., (1960) 192 F.Supp. 689, 692 (D.Del.1961) ("The [reserved] power applies to statutes dealing with the corporation vis-a-vis its stockholders and vis-a-vis the state."); Brundage v. New Jersey Zinc Co., 48 N.J. 450, 469, 226 A.2d 585, 595 (1967); Tu-Vu Drive-In Corp. v. Ashkins, 61 Cal.2d 283, 38 Cal.Rptr. 348, 391 P.2d 828 (1964); A. P. Smith Mfg. Co. v. Barlow, 13 N.J. 145, 98 A.2d 581, 39 A.L.R.2d 1179 (1953), appeal dismissed 346 U.S. 861, 74 S.Ct. 107, 98 L.Ed. 373 (1953); State ex rel. Swanson v. Perham, 30 Wash.2d 368, 191 P.2d 689 (1948). But see Detroit & Canada Tunnel Corp. v. Martin, 353 Mich. 219, 91 N.W.2d 525 (1958); Fenton v. Perry Land & Livestock Co., 3 Utah 2d 156, 280 P.2d 452 (1955); Hayes, "Extent of the Legislature's Reserve Power to Change Common Law Attributes of Corporations", 13 Vand.L.Rev. 261 (1959); Note, "Alteration of Shareholders' Rights: Scope of the Reserved Power", 3 Okla.L.Rev. 222 (1950).

17. See Metzger v. George Washington Memorial Park, 380 Pa. 350, 110 A.2d 425 (1955).

18. Janes v. Washburn Co., 326 Mass. 356, 94 N.E.2d 479 (1940). Sometimes, of course, the statute is expressly only prospective in affecting existing rights. Sutton v. Globe Knitting Works, 276 Mich. 200, 267 N.W. 815, 105 A.L.R. 1447 (1936); Schaad v. Hotel Easton Co., 369 Pa. 486, 87 A.2d 227 (1952).

shares did not permit making issued non-redeemable shares redeemable,[19] or the elimination of accrued but undeclared dividend arrearages.[20] Such holdings were sometimes cured by direct amendment of the articles of incorporation under a later statute authorizing such amendment,[21] or by the ingenuity of counsel in taking advantage of other statutory provisions as were already in effect.[22] Other courts, however, gave broad effect to generally worded legislation.[23]

Statutory Authorizations for Extraordinary Matters

Even when a particular extraordinary matter is authorized by statute, the required procedures as to board of directors and shareholder approval must be followed. The statute might also afford an appraisal remedy to dissenting shareholders.[24] Notwithstanding compliance with the statutory procedures, courts have also imposed equitable limitations on oppression of minority shareholders by controlling shareholders.[25]

Modern statutes authorize various extraordinary matters when approved by a prescribed vote or consent of shareholders, such vote or consent requirements in a particular jurisdiction sometimes varying for different matters.[26] Several jurisdictions require concurrent board of directors action.[27] In jurisdictions not requiring concurrent board of directors action,[28] extraordinary matters as a practical matter are usually initiated by the directors.

Typically, the extraordinary matters requiring shareholder approval include sale, lease, or exchange of all or substantially all the corporate assets outside of the corporation's regular course of business,[29] amend-

---

19. Breslav v. New York & Queens Electric Light & Power Co., 249 App.Div. 181, 291 N.Y.S. 932 (2d Dep't 1936), aff'd mem., 273 N.Y. 593, 7 N.E.2d 708 (1937).

20. Davison v. Parke, Austin & Lipscomb, Inc., 285 N.Y. 500, 35 N.E.2d 618 (1941); Consolidated Film Industries, Inc. v. Johnson, 22 Del.Ch. 407, 197 A. 489 (Sup.Ct.1937), aff'g 22 Del.Ch. 262, 194 A. 844 (Ch.1937). Compare Keller v. Wilson & Co., 21 Del. Ch. 391, 190 A. 115 (Sup.Ct.1936), rev'g 21 Del.Ch. 13, 180 A. 584 (Ch.1934), with Harr v. Pioneer Mechanical Corp., 65 F.2d 332 (2d Cir. 1933), cert. denied 290 U.S. 673, 54 S.Ct. 92, 78 L.Ed. 581 (1933) (Delaware corporation).

21. O'Brien v. Socony Mobil Oil Co., 207 Va. 707, 152 S.E.2d 278 (1967), cert. denied 389 U.S. 825, 88 S.Ct. 65, 19 L.Ed.2d 80 (1967) (upholding amendment of articles of incorporation which eliminated cumulative preferred share dividend arrearages under statute expressly authorizing such amendment enacted after issuance of such preferred shares, as not unconstitutionally depriving holders of such preferred shares of any vested property right); McNulty v. W. & J. Sloane, 184 Misc. 835, 54 N.Y.S.2d 253 (Sup.Ct.1945).

22. Barrett v. Denver Tramway Corp., 53 F.Supp. 198 (D.Del.1944), aff'd 146 F.2d 701 (3d Cir. 1944); Hottenstein (Moore) v. York Ice Machinery Corp., 136 F.2d 944 (3d Cir. 1943), petition for leave to file bill of review denied 146 F.2d 835 (3d Cir. 1944), cert. denied 325 U.S. 886, 65 S.Ct. 1573, 89 L.Ed. 2000 (1945).

23. McQuillen v. National Cash Register Co., 27 F. Supp. 639 (D.Md.1939), aff'd 112 F.2d 877 (4th Cir. 1940), cert. denied 311 U.S. 695, 61 S.Ct. 140, 85 L. Ed. 450 (1940), petition for reh. denied 311 U.S. 729, 61 S.Ct. 316, 85 L.Ed. 474 (1940); Sherman v. Pepin Pickling Co., 230 Minn. 87, 41 N.W.2d 571 (1950); Johnson v. Bradley Knitting Co., 228 Wis. 566, 280 N.W. 688 (1938).

24. See section 349 infra.

25. Sneed, "The Shareholder May Vote as He Pleases: Theory and Fact", 22 U.Pitt.L.Rev. 23 (1960); Sneed, "Stockholder Votes Motivated by Adverse Interest: The Attack and the Defense", 58 Mich.L. Rev. 961 (1960); Lattin, "Minority and Dissenting Shareholders' Rights in Fundamental Changes", 23 Law & Contemp.Prob. 307 (1958). See section 240 supra.

26. The necessary votes are usually rounded up in larger corporations by the corporate proxy machinery. Professional proxy solicitors might be retained. See section 196 supra. The disclosure requirements of the S.E.C. Proxy Rules might be applicable. See section 297 supra.

27. E. g., ABA–ALI Model Bus.Corp.Act §§ 54, 63, 67, 73, 77. McKinney's N.Y.Bus.Corp.Law, §§ 903 (merger or consolidation), 909 (sale, etc. of all or substantially all corporate assets not in regular course of business). See note 28 infra. Where both board of directors and shareholders action are required, the shareholders may either approve or disapprove but may not revise board of directors action.

28. E. g., McKinney's N.Y.Bus.Corp.Law, §§ 803 (amendment of articles of incorporation), 908 (guarantee), 1001 (nonjudicial dissolution). See note 27 supra.

29. See section 341 infra.

ments of the articles of incorporation and related matters,[30] merger or consolidation,[31] and nonjudicial or voluntary dissolution.[32]

In some jurisdictions, matters requiring shareholder approval also include expressly certain mortgages of corporate property,[33] some guarantees,[34] and certain other matters.[35]

In addition, extension or revival of corporate existence usually requires shareholder approval.[36]

When shareholder approval is required for any matter, the usual requirement is approval of only those shareholders entitled to vote on such a matter,[37] although broader approval is sometimes required by statute.

The Model Business Corporation Act required (besides board of directors action) for merger or consolidation,[38] sale, mortgage, or other disposition of substantially all corporate assets other than in the regular course of business,[39] nonjudicial or voluntary dissolution,[40] or revocation of such dissolution proceedings,[41] the unanimous written consent or a two-thirds vote (changed to majority vote by the 1969 revision) of the holders of all the outstanding shares entitled to vote thereon, and for various specified types of amendment of the articles of incorporation at least a two-thirds vote (also changed to majority vote by the 1969 revision) of any class of shares, as a class, even though such

shares are not otherwise entitled to vote thereon.[42] The various requirements of shareholder vote at a meeting under the Model Act may, under a general provision, be satisfied without a shareholder meeting by unanimous written consent of shareholders entitled to vote with respect to such matter.[43] The articles of incorporation may, with respect to any shareholder action, require the vote or concurrence of holders of a greater proportion of the shares, or any class or series, than is otherwise required by the Act.[44]

By way of summary, then, with respect to specific extraordinary matters, attention must be given to (a) the extent to which the matter is authorized by law; (b) the required procedures; (c) and the equitable limitations thereon. In short, the validity of any extraordinary corporate matter depends upon its being legal, regular, and equitable.

Finally, when shareholder approval is required, shareholders (usually limited to those entitled to vote on the matter) who do not assent and follow the prescribed procedure are, with respect to specified matters, given a right to dissent, i. e., the right to have their shares appraised and purchased, usually by the corporation.[45] When an appraisal remedy exists, the courts appear re-

30. See section 345 infra.

31. See section 346 infra.

32. See section 348 infra.

33. See section 342 infra.

34. See section 343 infra.

35. See section 344 infra.

36. See section 347 infra.

37. See section 189 supra.

38. ABA–ALI Model Bus.Corp.Act § 67.

39. ABA–ALI Model Bus.Corp.Act § 72.

40. ABA–ALI Model Bus.Corp.Act § 77.

41. ABA–ALI Model Bus.Corp.Act § 82.

42. ABA–ALI Model Bus.Corp.Act § 55. In some jurisdictions, the approval of the required vote of shareholders, whether or not otherwise entitled to vote on the matter, is required. In New York, prior to September 1, 1951, shareholders had the right, absent *specific* denial in the articles of incorporation, to vote in connection with corporate mortgages, guarantees, sales of assets, establishing priorities or creating preferences, consolidation, voluntary dissolution, or change of name. Since then a general denial of voting rights denies the right to vote for such matters. The 1951 amendment does not affect voting rights of shares issued or authorized before September 1, 1951. N.Y.Laws 1951, ch. 170, § 2.

43. ABA–ALI Model Bus.Corp.Act § 138. See section 190 supra.

44. ABA–ALI Model Bus.Corp.Act § 136. See sections 191, 266 supra.

45. See section 349 infra.

luctant to intervene on the basis of equitable considerations.

Different rules apply in cases of federal corporation reorganization.[46]

Different extraordinary corporate matters often can lead to the same or similar result with differing legal consequences.[47]

SALE, LEASE, EXCHANGE, OR OTHER DISPOSITION OF CORPORATE ASSETS

341. **Sales, leases, exchanges, or other dispositions of all or substantially all the assets of a corporation, other than in the regular course of business, usually require approval by the shareholders of such corporation. A majority of statutes afford an appraisal remedy to dissenting shareholders of such corporation.**

Sometimes, similar practical results to such a sale, lease, exchange, or disposition can be achieved by such alternatives as dissolution, merger, or consolidation, which may involve different legal procedures and impact of appraisal remedy or liquidation preferences and other rights.

A sale, lease, exchange or other disposition, even when duly authorized by shareholder approval, requires fairness and good faith.

Sales under plans of complete liquidation often can avoid gain or loss at the corporate level for federal income tax purposes.

Sales of corporate assets are to some extent regulated by antitrust laws.

Instead of sale and purchase of assets, all or controlling shares are purchased to take over the business. Often involved are take-over bids.

At common law, sales, leases, exchanges, or other dispositions by a solvent corporation of all or substantially all of its assets generally required unanimous shareholder approval.[1] Most states, by statute, have re-

duced the required percentage of shareholders who must approve such transactions, and either expressly provide or have been construed to mean that shareholder consent is not required of such a transaction when it is in the regular course of business of the corporation.[2] A majority of the statutes afford dissenting shareholders an appraisal remedy.[3]

---

46. See sections 350, 389 infra.

47. See section 341, n. 16 infra.

1. Geddes v. Anaconda Copper Mining Co., 254 U.S. 590, 41 S.Ct. 209, 65 L.Ed. 425 (1921); Carpenters Local Union v. Texas State Federation of Labor Bldg. Ass'n, 288 S.W.2d 874 (Tex.Civ.App.1956).

2. Delaware authorizes the sale, lease or exchange of all corporate assets, without distinction as to whether the disposition is within or without the regular course of business by board of directors action when authorized by the holders of a majority of the outstanding voting shares. Del.Gen.Corp. Law, § 271 (1967). See Van Buren v. Highway Ranch, Inc., 46 Wash.2d 582, 283 P.2d 132 (1955); Swift v. Southeastern Greyhound Lines, 294 Ky. 49, 171 S.W.2d 49 (1943). The common law recognized the "failing corporation exception". *Quaere*, whether the statutes will be construed as incorporating such exception. Compare Matter of MacDonald, 205 App.Div. 579, 199 N.Y.S. 873 (2d Dep't 1923) (dictum that sale by insolvent corporation requires compliance with statutory procedure), with Matter of Avard (Oneita Knitting Mills), 5 Misc.2d 817, 144 N.Y.S.2d 204 (Sup.Ct.1955), appeal dismissed 2 A.D. 2d 647, 156 N.Y.S.2d 970 (4th Dep't 1956) (sale by insolvent corporation held outside statute). See also Michigan Wolverine Student Co-Operative, Inc. v. Wm. Goodyear & Co., 314 Mich. 590, 22 N.W.2d 884 (1946) (dictum refusing to read "failing corporation exception" into Michigan statute). See generally D. Linowes, Managing Growth Through Acquisition (1968); A. Choka, Buying, Selling, and Merging Businesses (ALI rev. 1969); C. Scharf, Techniques for Buying, Selling, and Merging Businesses (1964); G. McCarthy, Acquisitions and Mergers (1963); Mulliner, "Purchase and Sale of a Business", in Advising California Business Enterprises 953–1024 (1958), 5 Prac.Law. 13 (Mar. 1959), 5 id. 37 (Apr.1959); Note, "Stockholder Consent to Sales of Integral Corporate Assets: Balancing Dissenter and Purchaser Interests", 67 Yale L.J. 1288 (1958); Note, "Necessity of Stockholders' Approval of Sale of Corporate Assets", 9 Syracuse L.Rev. 269 (1958); Note, "Necessity of Stockholder Consent to Sale of Corporate Assets", 28 N.Y.U.L.Rev. 1014 (1953); Annot., 79 A.L.R. 624 (1932). Applicable bulk sales requirements should also be observed. Annot., 16 A.L.R.2d 1315 (1951).

3. Delaware affords no appraisal remedy in such a case. Del.Gen.Corp.Law, § 271 (1967). McKinney's N.Y.Bus.Corp.Law, § 910(a) (1) (B) excepts from the appraisal remedy a "transaction wholly for cash where the shareholders' authorization thereof is conditioned upon the dissolution of the corporation and the distribution of substantially all of its net assets to the shareholders in accordance with their respective interests within one year after the date of such transaction." To the same effect is ABA– ALI Model Bus.Corp.Act § 73(b). For rights of dis-

Statutory Formulations

Statutes often provide that a corporation shall have power to sell, convey, lease, exchange, transfer and otherwise dispose of all or any part of its property and assets.[4] A sale, lease, exchange, or other disposition in the corporation's usual and regular course of business, even when of all or substantially all the corporate property and assets, usually requires only board of directors approval,[5] but sometimes needs shareholder approval as well.[6] For a sale, lease, exchange, or other disposition of all or substantially all the corporate property and assets other than in the usual and regular course of business, common requisites are a board of directors resolution and the prescribed approval of shareholders entitled to vote thereon [7] and in some jurisdictions whether or not entitled to vote thereon by the articles of incorporation.[8]

Whether or not a sale, lease, exchange, or other disposition is in the regular course of business should be tested by the purpose clauses of the articles of incorporation or by the business in which the corporation is actually engaged is an unresolved question in most jurisdictions.[9]

Some cases have held that a sale of assets by a corporation relocating its business does not require shareholder approval, and therefore affords no appraisal remedy.[10]

---

senting shareholders, see section 349 infra. Most states recognize the appraisal remedy for most mergers. In states which allow appraisal for merger but not for sale, the latter might be treated as a de facto merger giving rise to appraisal, etc. Compare Farris v. Glen Alden Corp., 393 Pa. 427, 143 A.2d 25 (1958), with Hariton v. Arco Electronics, Inc., 41 Del.Ch. 74, 188 A.2d 123 (Sup.Ct.1963) and Heilbrunn v. Sun Chemical Corp., 38 Del.Ch. 321, 150 A.2d 755 (Sup.Ct.1959), discussed in notes 22–24 infra. See also Troupiansky v. Henry Disston & Sons, 151 F.Supp. 609 (E.D.Pa.1957) (appraisal remedy in absence of appraisal statute).

4. E. g., ABA–ALI Model Bus.Corp.Act § 4(e).

5. E. g., ABA–ALI Model Bus.Corp.Act § 71; Santa Fe Hills Golf & Country Club v. Safehi Realty Co., 349 S.W.2d 27 (Mo.1961).

6. Del.Gen.Corp.Law, § 271 (1967) (any sale, lease, or exchange of all corporate property or assets). See Smith v. Good Music Station, Inc., 36 Del.Ch. 262, 129 A.2d 242 (Ch.1957).

7. The voting requirements range from majority (e. g., California, Delaware, Florida, Michigan, New Jersey (for post-1968 corporations), Pennsylvania, 1969 Model Act revision), to 60 percent (e. g., West Virginia), to two-thirds (e. g., ABA–ALI Model Bus. Corp.Act § 72, Alabama, Illinois, Massachusetts, New Jersey (for pre-1969 corporations), New York, Ohio, South Dakota, Texas, Washington), to three-fourths (e. g., Hawaii, Missouri).

8. E. g., ABA–ALI Model Bus.Corp.Act § 72 (prior to 1962). Class voting requirements (ibid) and greater voting requirements (id. § 136) of the articles of in-

corporation must be observed. Unanimous written consent will suffice in lieu of a vote at a meeting. Id. § 138.

9. Eisen v. Post, 3 N.Y.2d 518, 169 N.Y.S.2d 15, 146 N.E.2d 779 (1957) (5–2) (holding that actual business not authorized by articles of incorporation could not be deemed regular course of business within meaning of then statute requiring shareholder approval of sale of substantially all corporate assets outside regular course of business). See also Matter of Roehner v. Gracie Manor, Inc., 6 N.Y.2d 280, 189 N.Y.S.2d 644, 160 N.E.2d 519 (1959). See also then McKinney's N.Y.Gen.Corp.Law, § 3(17) defining "business of a corporation" as meaning "the operations for the conduct of which it is incorporated". But see McKinney's N.Y.Bus.Corp.Law, § 909(a) (test of "business actually conducted by such corporation"); Matter of McKay v. Teleprompter Corp., 19 A.D.2d 815, 243 N.Y.S.2d 591 (1st Dep't 1963), appeal dismissed 13 N.Y.2d 1058, 246 N.Y.S.2d 34, 195 N.E.2d 762 (1963); Boyer v. Legal Estates, Inc., 44 Misc.2d 1067, 255 N.Y.S.2d 955 (Sup.Ct.1964). See also McKinney's N.Y.Bus.Corp.Law, § 909(b) (recital to effect that property described in instrument does not constitute all or substantially all assets of corporation, or that disposition was made in usual or regular course of business of corporation, or that shareholders have duly authorized such disposition, to be presumptive evidence of facts so recited); id. § 909(c) (action to set aside instrument not to be maintained unless commenced and notice of pendency filed within one year after recordation of such instrument).

10. Murphy v. Washington American League Base Ball Club, Inc., 293 F.2d 552 (D.C.Cir. 1961); November v. National Exhibition Co., 10 Misc.2d 537, 173 N.Y.S.2d 490 (Sup.Ct.1958); Matter of Avard (Oneita Knitting Mills), 5 Misc.2d 817, 144 N.Y.S.2d 204 (Sup.Ct.1955), appeal dismissed 2 A.D.2d 647, 156 N.Y.S.2d 970 (4th Dep't 1956); Matter of Rudel (Eberhard Faber Pencil Co.), 2 Misc.2d 957, 146 N. Y.S.2d 498 (Sup.Ct.1955). See also Maffia v. American Woolen Co., 125 F.Supp. 465 (S.D.N.Y.1954) (holding sale with view to relocation not dissolution entitling preferred shareholders to liquidation preference); Treves v. Menzies, 37 Del.Ch. 330, 142 A. 2d 520 (Ch.1958), aff'd sub nom. Treves v. Servel, Inc., 38 Del.Ch. 483, 154 A.2d 188 (Sup.Ct.1959). As to employees' rights in event of relocation, see Od-

Shareholder approval can be in general terms, leaving the details to the board of directors.[11]

Notwithstanding shareholder authorization, the board of directors may abandon the sale, lease, exchange or other disposition of assets, subject to the rights of third parties under any contracts relating thereto.[12]

Where shareholder approval is required, dissenting shareholders enjoy an appraisal remedy in the majority of jurisdictions.[13] If the sale is not consummated but corporate action with respect thereto has not been re-scinded, the appraisal proceeding may continue.[14]

Where formal shareholder approval is required but not had, informal shareholder acquiescence or laches might prevent the raising of such defect.[15]

Camouflaged Sales

For various reasons, corporations sometimes try to camouflage a sale as something else or to camouflage something else as a sale. For example, dissolution followed by liquidation can have the same practical effect as a sale; a sale in exchange for shares of a purchasing corporation to be distributed among the shareholders of the selling corporation can be, for practical purposes, similar to a merger or consolidation. Yet in these and other situations, the required legal procedures and availability of the dissenting shareholders' appraisal remedy or liquidation preferences or other rights sometimes involve substantial differences.[16]

---

die v. Ross Gear & Tool Co., 305 F.2d 143 (6th Cir. 1962), cert. denied 371 U.S. 941, 83 S.Ct. 318, 9 L. Ed.2d 275 (1962); Zdanok v. Glidden Co., 288 F.2d 99 (2d Cir. 1961); Maddux, "Labor Law Implications in the Sale, Transfer or Discontinuance of All or Part of a Business Operation", 18 Bus.Law. 819 (1963).

11. Matter of Hake (Hake Mfg. Co.), 285 App.Div. 316, 136 N.Y.S.2d 817 (4th Dep't 1955), appeal dismissed 308 N.Y. 940, 127 N.E.2d 90 (1955); Mattiello v. Flagg-Utica Corp., 14 Misc.2d 597, 178 N.Y.S.2d 179 (Sup.Ct.1958). See Ward, "Legal Effect of Merger and Asset Sale Agreements Before Shareholder Approval", 18 W.Res.L.Rev. 780 (1967). But general shareholder authorization to sell "the group of lots" is inadequate. Downing Development Corp. v. Brazelton, 253 Md. 390, 252 A.2d 849 (1969). Nor can the board of directors delegate to corporate officers authority given to board by shareholders to sell all corporate assets "upon such terms and conditions as directors deem for best interest of corporation". Clarke Memorial College v. Monaghan Land Co., 147 Del.Ch. ——, 257 A.2d 234 (Ch.1969).

12. ABA–ALI Model Bus.Corp.Act § 72(d). See also Kirwan v. Parkway Distillery, Inc., 285 Ky. 605, 148 S.W.2d 720 (1941) (substitution of dissolution (and sale) for sale to avoid appraisal remedy (market value, but not less than book value) upheld); Matter of Hake (Hake Mfg. Co.), 285 App.Div. 316, 136 N.Y.S.2d 817 (4th Dep't 1955), appeal dismissed 308 N.Y. 940, 127 N.E.2d 90 (1955); Note, "Withdrawal of Fundamental Corporate Changes Before a Vote, an Unrecognized Complement to Abandonment—A Proposed Change in Ohio's Abandonment Statute", 32 U.Cin.L.Rev. 380 (1963).

13. E. g., ABA–ALI Model Bus.Corp.Act § 73(b). See note 3 supra. See also Matter of Bacon (Susquehanna Silk Mills), 287 N.Y. 1, 38 N.E.2d 105 (1941); Matter of Hurd, 5 Misc.2d 443, 159 N.Y.S.2d 895 (Sup.Ct.1957) (appraisal rights of voting trust certificate holders); Note, "Interplay of Rights of Stockholders Dissenting from Sale of Corporate Assets", 58 Colum.L.Rev. 251 (1958); Annot., 58 A.L. R.2d 784 (1958).

14. Matter of Hake (Hake Mfg. Co.), 285 App.Div. 316, 136 N.Y.S.2d 817 (4th Dep't 1955), appeal dismissed 308 N.Y. 940, 127 N.E.2d 90 (1955).

15. Kazlowski v. Seville Syndicate, Inc., 155 N.Y.L.J. No. 20, 16 (Sup.Ct.1966); Alhambra-Shumway Mines v. Alhambra Gold Mine Corp., 200 Cal.App.2d 322, 19 Cal.Rptr. 208 (1962). Long Construction Co. v. Empire Drive-In Theatres, Inc., 208 Cal.App.2d 726, 25 Cal.Rptr. 509 (1962), held that a corporate creditor could not attack a transfer of substantially all of the corporate assets made without required shareholder approval since such transfer was voidable and not void, could be validated by subsequent shareholder approval alone, and would require a rescission to set it aside. See Annot., "Who May Assert Invalidity of Sale, Mortgage, or Other Disposition of Corporate Property Without Approval of Stockholders", 58 A.L.R.2d 784 (1958).

16. Sales of assets often, in practical effect, resemble mergers, consolidations, and dissolutions. In the merger, the surviving corporation acquires the assets of the merged corporation; in the consolidation, the consolidated corporation acquires the assets of the constituent corporations; dissenting shareholders of the merged or constituent corporations, in most jurisdictions, enjoy an appraisal remedy. In the case of sale, the dissenting shareholders of the purchasing corporation enjoy no appraisal remedy; even the dissenting shareholders of the selling corporation, in most jurisdictions, enjoy no appraisal remedy. Sales of assets which very closely resemble mergers have been held to be de facto mergers subject to the merger statute and affording

In Eisenberg v. Central Zone Property Corp.,[17] those in control formulated a complicated reorganization plan for a New York corporation involving a sale of its sole asset to a Delaware corporation of identical capital structure, all of whose shares were to be issued to the New York corporation for such asset and deposited with voting trustees with broad powers to sell the entrusted shares, with a view to the "dissolution" of the New York corporation and the distribution to its shareholders of the voting trust certificates. Underlying the plan was the desire of those in control to gain certain tax advantages by selling all of the shares in the New York corporation as a unit, to which some minority shareholders objected. A minority shareholder sued to enjoin the plan, and the defendants answered that appraisal was the exclusive remedy. The New York Court of Appeals held that the injunction should have been granted, since the transaction was not authorized by the sale [18] or dissolution [19] provisions of the New York statute.

Where one corporation sells all of its assets to another corporation, which assumes the liabilities of the former, in exchange for shares of the latter to be distributed among shareholders of the former, the practical result is the same as if the former had merged into the latter. Statutes sometimes provide for an appraisal remedy in the case of a merger but not in the case of a sale,[20] or in the case of a merger afford an appraisal remedy to dissenting shareholders of both corporations but in the case of a sale afford such remedy only to dissenting shareholders of the selling corporation and not to shareholders of the purchasing corporation.[21] Some courts have held that such a sale is a de facto merger and can be set aside for noncompliance with the merger statute.[22] Subsequently, in one case, the directors were held not liable for the corporation's expenses in setting up and defending the transaction.[23] Contrariwise, the Delaware courts case have upheld such a transaction as a sale to which the merger statute had no application.[24]

Equitable Limitations

A sale, lease, exchange, or other disposition of corporate assets, even when authorized by appropriate shareholder approval, requires fairness and good faith on the part of controlling shareholders.[25]

---

appraisal remedies. See section 346 infra. Often sales of assets are followed by dissolution; dissolutions result in liquidation of assets and distribution either in kind or in the cash proceeds of the sale of assets. See section 348 infra. If a sale is to be followed by dissolution, shareholder might well be sought for both at the same time, especially if larger shareholder approval is needed for dissolution than for sale. Compare Del.Gen.Corp.Law, § 271 (1967) (majority approval for sale), with id. § 275 (two-thirds approval for dissolution). In the case of liquidation or dissolution, liquidation preferences and other rights apply. See section 382 infra. For discussion of federal tax consequences of various extraordinary corporate matters, see section 351 infra.

17. Eisenberg v. Central Zone Property Corp., 306 N.Y. 58, 115 N.E.2d 652 (1953).

18. Former McKinney's N.Y.Stock Corp.Law, § 20.

19. Former McKinney's N.Y.Stock Corp.Law, §§ 105–106. See section 348 infra.

20. Del.Gen.Corp.Law, § 262 (1967). See section 346 infra.

21. Pa.Bus.Corp.Law, § 908(A) (1933). In 1959, the Pennsylvania statute was amended expressly to afford an appraisal remedy to shareholders in a corporation which purchases the assets of another if the other corporation gets more than a majority of the voting shares in the purchasing corporation. Id. § 311(F). See section 346 infra.

22. Farris v. Glen Alden Corp., 393 Pa. 427, 143 A.2d 25 (1958). Accord, Applestein v. United Board & Carton Corp., 60 N.J.Super. 333, 159 A.2d 146 (1960), aff'd per curiam 33 N.J. 72, 161 A.2d 474 (1960). See also Rath v. Rath Packing Co., 257 Iowa 1277, 136 N.W.2d 410 (1965).

23. Gilbert v. Burnside, 13 A.D.2d 982, 216 N.Y.S.2d 430 (2d Dep't 1961), rev'g 197 N.Y.S.2d 623 (Sup.Ct. 1959) ($118,000 award), aff'd mem., 11 N.Y.2d 960, 229 N.Y.S.2d 10, 183 N.E.2d 325 (1962).

24. Hariton v. Arco Electronics, Inc., 41 Del.Ch. 74, 188 A.2d 123 (Sup.Ct.1963); Heilbrunn v. Sun Chemical Corp., 38 Del.Ch. 321, 150 A.2d 755 (Sup. Ct.1959). See Hills, "Consolidation of Corporations by Sale of Assets and Distribution of Stock", 19 Calif.L.Rev. 349 (1931).

25. Abelow v. Midstates Oil Corp., 41 Del.Ch. 145, 189 A.2d 675 (Sup.Ct.1963) (upholding sale price for

Tax Considerations

The risk that both a corporation and its shareholders would be subject to federal tax on gains attributable to sales of assets in connection with the liquidation of the corporation, has been largely alleviated under the 1954 Code.

In summary, section 337 of the 1954 Code [26] provides generally that no gain or loss shall be recognized to a corporation from the sale or exchange of property within a 12-month period beginning on the date the corporation adopts a plan of complete liquidation if, within that period, all of the assets of the corporation except assets retained to meet claims are distributed in complete liquidation.[27]

Section 334(b) [28] concerns the related problem of the purchaser's basis for assets where most of the shares of a corporation are acquired, and the latter is promptly liquidated. It provides that when all the conditions are met, the basis for the assets acquired is the purchase price of the shares rather than a carry over basis from the liquidated corporation.

Antitrust Aspects

The principal federal antitrust provision applicable to a corporation's sale of assets is the so-called Anti-Merger Act of 1950, an amendment to the Clayton Act. Its prohibitions extend to the acquisition by a corporation of the shares or assets of another corporation.[29]

Purchase of Assets or Shares

An alternative to the sale and purchase of assets is the sale and purchase of shares.[30] Often involved are take-over bids.[31]

---

assets, of subsidiary sold to parent corporation where price established by independent appraisals; for lack of disinterested shareholder approval, plaintiff minority shareholder of subsidiary not required to prove unfairness; defendants' burden to prove fairness held satisfied). Ribakove v. Rich, 13 Misc.2d 98, 173 N.Y.S.2d 306 (Sup.Ct.1958); cf. Marks v. Wolfson, 41 Del.Ch. 115, 188 A.2d 680 (Ch.1963) (holding that even where corporate action was allegedly taken to benefit majority shareholders, burden of proving bad faith rested on plaintiff, notwithstanding fiduciary duty owed minority by the majority, and concluding that plaintiff shareholders had not rebutted presumption in favor of proper directorial action); Baron v. Pressed Metals of America, Inc., 35 Del.Ch. 325, 117 A.2d 357 (Ch. 1955), aff'd 35 Del.Ch. 581, 123 A.2d 848 (Sup.Ct. 1956) (fact that some of directors and substantial shareholders were to be employed by purchaser held not to rebut presumption of good faith). See also Cottrell v. Pawcatuck Co., 35 Del.Ch. 309, 116 A.2d 787 (Ch.1955), aff'd 36 Del.Ch. 169, 128 A.2d 225 (Sup.Ct.1956), cert. denied 355 U.S. 12, 78 S.Ct. 54, 2 L.Ed.2d 20 (1957); Lebold v. Inland Steel Corp., 125 F.2d 369 (7th Cir. 1941), cert. denied 316 U.S. 675, 62 S.Ct. 1045, 86 L.Ed. 1749 (1942) (dissolution of subsidiary and sale of assets to parent); Kirwan v. Parkway Distillery, Inc., 285 Ky. 605, 148 S.W.2d 720 (1941) (no fraud alleged).

26. Int.Rev.Code of 1954, 26 U.S.C.A. § 337.

27. MacLean, "Taxation of Sales of Corporate Assets in the Course of Liquidation", 56 Colum.L.Rev. 641 (1956). See also Lanning, "Tax Erosion and the 'Bootstrap Sale' of a Business", 108 U.Pa.L.Rev. 623, 943 (1960); Valentine, "Some Unexpected Tax Results Where a Business is Acquired by Purchase of Stock", 15 Bus.Law. 732 (1960); Seplow, "Acquisition of Assets of a Subsidiary: Liquidation or Reorganization", 73 Harv.L.Rev. 484 (1960); Note, "Income Tax Consequences of Sales of Assets between Related Corporations", 60 Colum.L.Rev. 178

(1960); Bittker, "The Corporation and the Federal Income Tax: Transfers to a Controlled Corporation", 1959 Wash.U.L.Q. 1; Silverstein, "Section 337 and Liquidation of the Multi-Corporate Enterprise", N.Y.U. 16th Inst. on Fed.Tax. 429 (1958); Cohen, Gelberg, Surrey, Tarleau & Warren, "Corporate Liquidations under the Internal Revenue Code of 1954" 55 Colum.L.Rev. 37 (1955); Comment, "Watch Your Step on the Way Out: Tax Savings on Sale of Corporate Assets Under Section 337, 1954 I.R.C.", 24 Mo.L.Rev. 342 (1959); Note, "Twelve-Month Corporate Liquidations: Section 337 of the Internal Revenue Code", 10 Syracuse L.Rev. 103 (1958); "Corporate Liquidations Under the 1954 Internal Revenue Code", 41 A.B.A.J. 1158 (1955). See also Sealy, "Acquisitions and Mergers", 16 Bus.Law. 209 (1960).

28. Int.Rev.Code of 1954, 26 U.S.C.A. § 334(b) (2).

29. 15 U.S.C.A. § 18; Berghoff, "Analyzing a Proposed Acquisition Under the Antitrust Laws", 19 Bus.Law. 373 (1964). See section 312 supra.

30. The purchase of assets without assumption of liabilities is the cleanest from the purchaser's viewpoint. See Lamb v. Leroy Corp., —— Nev. ——, 454 P.2d 24 (1969) (holding corporation purchasing assets of another corporation not liable for liabilities of latter absent assumption, merger, mere change of name for business, or fraud). Compliance with bulk sales statutes will be necessary. The pur-

31. See note 31 on page 704.

MORTGAGING OF CORPORATE PROPERTY

342. Mortgaging or pledging of corporate property does not require shareholder approval in most jurisdictions. Some of the others limit their shareholder approval requirement to mortgages or pledges of all or substantially all

chaser will want the maximum part of the total purchase to be allocated to depreciable or amortizable assets, covenants not to compete, and inventory; the seller will want maximum allocation to capital assets. The purchaser achieves a stepped-up basis for depreciable items and inventory, any available investment credit, and initial 20 percent depreciation allowance. The corporation, under the 1962 recapture-of-depreciation rules [Int.Rev.Code of 1954, 26 U.S.C.A. § 1245] might have to take into income and pay tax on depreciable property to the extent that it covers depreciation after 1961, and might have to restore some of the investment credit claimed on retained assets. The sale of shares is the cleanest from the seller's viewpoint. His gain is usually capital gain. In purchasing shares, the purchaser indirectly assumes the corporation's liabilities and will seek protection by way of audit, representations, warranties, indemnity, or possibly escrow deposit of part of the purchase price. The purchaser would have to liquidate the corporation to achieve a stepped-up basis; meanwhile, the corporation would be subject to the recapture-of-depreciation and recapture-of-credit rules and any investment credit and initial 20 percent depreciation allowance might not apply. I. Schreiber, How to Buy and Sell a Business Taxwisely (1968); S. Hagendorf, Tax Guide for Buying and Selling a Business (1967); A. Choka, Buying, Selling, and Merging Businesses (ALI rev. 1965); R. Graichen, Buying, Selling and Merging (1965); C. Scharf, Techniques for Buying, Selling, and Merging Businesses (1964); C. Bosland, Estate Tax Valuation in the Sale or Merger of Small Firms (1963); G. McCarthy, Acquisitions and Mergers (1963); Mulliner, "Purchase and Sale of a Business", in Advising California Business Enterprises 593–1024 (1958); Lefevre, "Tax Check List for Acquisitions and Mergers", 25 Bus.Law. 355 (1969); Weiner, et al., "Tax and Other Considerations in the Sale of a Business: A Panel Discussion", N.Y.U. 27th Inst. on Fed.Tax. 471 (1969); Lefevre, et al., "Problems in Acquiring a Business: A Panel Discussion", N.Y.U. 26th Inst. on Fed.Tax. 815 (1968); Houston, "How Warranties Can Be Used to Control Tax Consequences in Corporate Acquisitions", 28 J.Taxation 22 (1968); Kripke, "Accounting for Corporation Acquisitions and the Treatment of Goodwill: An Alert Signal to All Business Lawyers", 24 Bus. Law. 89 (1968); Rockwell, "How To Acquire a Company", 46 Harv.Bus.Rev. 121 (Sept.-Oct. 1968); Willard, "Labor Law Aspects of Corporate Acquisitions", 36 U.Mo.Kan.City L.Rev. 241 (1968); Cavitch, Zolman & Hoehnen, "Buying or Selling a Corporate Business: Stock or Assets", 28 Ohio St.L.J. 614 (1967); Monyek & Kessler, "Tax Considerations in Buying and Selling a Corporate Business", 16 DePaul L.Rev. 28 (1966); Patrick, "Implications of the John Wiley Case for Business Transfers, Collective Agreements, and Arbitration", 18 S.C.L.

Rev. 413 (1966); Sebring, "Statutory Mergers and Asset Acquisitions", 21 Bus.Law. 799 (1966); Sogg, "Problem Areas in Buying and Selling a Corporate Business", 17 W.Res.L.Rev. 784 (1966); Stoloff, "Corporate Combinations: Mergers, Consolidations, Asset and Stock Purchases", 45 Ore.L.Rev. 161 (1966); Bryan, "Taxable Transfers of Corporate Businesses", 43 Taxes 880 (1965); Maddux, "Labor Law Problems Arising From Changes in Business Operations—A Re-Evaluation", 20 Bus.Law. 573 (1965); Sommer, "Mergers, Consolidations, Sales of Assets—Rule 133", 16 W.Res.L.Rev. 11 (1964); Holmes, "Buyer's Counsel Looks at Acquisitions", 18 Bus.Law. 755 (1963); Maddux, "Labor Law Implications in the Sale, Transfer or Discontinuance of All or Part of a Business Operation", 18 Bus. Law. 819 (1963); Anthoine, Elder, Weithorn, Englert, Beck & Freling, "Sale of a Corporate Business: A Panel Discussion of the Issues, Including Valuation and Assets vs. Stock Techniques", N.Y.U. 21st Inst. on Fed.Tax. 1143 (1963); Weithorn & Elder, "Buyer's and Seller's Points to Sale of Corporate Business: An Outline—Checklist", N.Y.U. 21st Inst. on Fed.Tax. 1065 (1963); Holmes, "Buyer's Counsel Looks at Acquisition", 18 Bus.Law. 755 (1963); Freling, "Tax Consequences of Nontax Motivated Aspects and Factors in the Sale of a Corporate Business", N.Y.U. 21st Inst. on Fed.Tax. 1107 (1963); Tufts, "Transfer of a Corporate Business to Another Corporation: Taxable Sale and Purchase of Stock or Assets", 3 Santa Clara Law. 43 (1962); Bierman, et al., "How to Buy and Sell a Business", N.Y.U. 17th Inst. on Fed.Tax. 717 (1959). The New York Stock Exchange requires listed companies to notify it of their acquisition or disposition of substantial assets otherwise than in the regular course of business. N.Y.S.E. Company Manuel § A6. For form of agreement to purchase assets, see G. Seward, Basic Corporate Practice 274 (ALI rev. 1966); for form of agreement to purchase all outstanding shares, see id. 259. Borden, "Drafting a Purchase Agreement for the Acquisition of a Closely Held Business", 12 Prac.Law. 9 (Feb. 1966).

31. Cohen, "Tender Offers and Takeover Bids", 23 Bus.Law. 611 (1968); Kennedy, "Tender Moment", 23 Bus.Law. 1091 (1968); Brudney, "A Note on Chilling Tender Solicitations", 21 Rutgers L.Rev. 609 (1967); Fleischer & Mundheim, "Corporate Acquisition by Tender Offer", 115 U.Pa.L.Rev. 317 (1967); Schmults & Kelly, "Cash Take-Over Bids—Defense Tactics", 23 Bus.Law. 115 (1967); Cohen, "Note on Takeover Bids and Corporate Purchases of Stock", 22 Bus.Law. 149 (1966); Manne, "Cash Tender Offers for Shares—A Reply to Chairman Cohen", 22 Bus.Law. 149 (1966); Penrose, "Some Aspects of the Development, Criticism and Control of the Take-Over Bid, Since 1945", 1964 Jurid.Rev. 128; Comment, "Regulation of Contested Cash Tender Offers", 46 Texas L.Rev. 915 (1968). See section 297, nn. 33, 34 supra. The Tax Reform Act of 1969 limits the amount of interest deductible on "corporation acquisition indebtedness" to acquire shares or two-thirds of all the operating assets (excluding cash) of another corporation.

the corporate property not in the regular course of business. Shareholders dissenting to a mortgage or pledge usually enjoy no appraisal remedy. Corporate mortgages subject to the Federal Trust Indenture Act of 1939 must observe its requirements.

Most jurisdictions expressly permit corporations to mortgage their property without requiring shareholder approval.[1] A decreasing number require shareholder approval.[2] Such requirements obviously are relevant when the corporation issues debt securities secured by a mortgage or pledge of its property.

Most of the statutes which require shareholder approval for a mortgage or pledge do not require such approval if the mortgage or pledge is not of all or substantially all the corporate property or is in the regular course of business.[3] Until 1963, New York required shareholder approval for any mortgage, except a purchase money mortgage, whether or not of all property and whether or not in the regular course of business.[4] Some states

require shareholder approval to increase the "bonded indebtedness".[5]

Absent express statutory provision governing shareholder approval for a mortgage or pledge, especially one of all or substantially all the corporate assets not in the regular course of business, a mortgage might be assimilated, at least in a title-theory jurisdiction as distinguished from a lien-theory jurisdiction, to a sale, and the statutory requirements applicable to a sale, lease, exchange, or other disposition of corporate assets applied.

Several statutes therefore expressly provide that no shareholder approval is required for the transfer of corporate assets by mortgage or pledge to secure indebtedness unless otherwise provided in the articles of incorporation.[6] Some statutes expressly

---

1. ABA-ALI Model Bus.Corp.Act § 71 (mortgage or pledge of any or all assets of corporation whether or not in usual or regular course of business). See Spoerri, "Statutory Requirements for Authorization of Corporate Mortgage", 18 Bus.Law. 731 (1963).

2. The Model Business Corporation Act, until 1962, adopted in several jurisdictions, expressly required shareholder approval for a mortgage or pledge of all or substantially all the corporate assets not in the regular course of business. Where shareholder approval is required, mortgagees should be sure that there has been compliance with such requirements.

3. E. g., Alabama, Alaska, Colorado, Illinois, North Dakota, Oregon, Wisconsin, District of Columbia.

4. Former McKinney's N.Y. Stock Corp.Law, § 16 (approval by holders of two-thirds of shares entitled to vote thereon given either in writing or at a shareholders' meeting). In re Cinemart International Corp., 117 F.Supp. 357 (S.D.N.Y.1953) (chattel mortgage to discharge mechanic's lien held not equivalent to purchase money mortgage); Reconstruction Finance Corp. v. Eastern Terra Cotta Realty Corp., 266 App.Div. 148, 41 N.Y.S.2d 569 (2d Dep't 1943) (New York statute held inapplicable to foreign corporation and to pledge since statute referred only to mortgage and was in derogation of common law). See also former McKinney's N.Y. Stock Corp. Law, § 51. Under it, a certificate evidencing such consent was required to be filed with the mortgage or, if none of the mortgaged property

was within the state, with the clerk of the county where the office of the corporation was located. Ibid. Rochester Savings Bank v. Averell, 96 N.Y. 467 (1884). See also McKinney's N.Y. Lien Law, § 190; Matter of Norma Footwear Corp., 2 N.Y.2d 887, 161 N.Y.S.2d 143, 141 N.E.2d 628 (1957). Until 1963, New York provided that if the mortgage affected property within the state, was authorized by the board of directors, recited that it had been authorized by shareholders, and had been duly recorded within the state, such recital was presumptive evidence of shareholder approval; after such mortgage had been recorded for more than one year, if it had been issued for consideration and the interest thereon had been paid, such recital was conclusive evidence of shareholder approval, unless attacked within one year of recordation, in which case such recital was presumptive evidence of shareholder approval; if the required consent was filed, it was conclusive evidence of shareholder approval in favor of *bona fide* purchasers of any obligations secured by such mortgage. Former McKinney's N.Y.Stock Corp.Law, § 17. Mortgages often include after-acquired property. MacDonnell v. Buffalo Loan, Trust & Safe Deposit Co., 193 N.Y. 92, 85 N.E. 801 (1908).

5. E. g., Arizona, Arkansas.

6. E. g., California, Florida, Georgia, Hawaii, Nevada, New York, North Carolina, Tennessee, Texas. Under such statutes, mortgagees or pledgees should be sure that shareholder approval for a mortgage or pledge is not required by the articles of incorporation. New York in 1963 eliminated its two-thirds shareholder approval requirement for all corporate mortgages—only purchase money mortgages were previously excepted. McKinney's N.Y.Bus.Corp. Law, § 911 (mortgage or pledge of, or creation of security interest in, all or any part of corporate property, or any interest therein, wherever situated,

provide that shareholder approval is not required for a mortgage or pledge,[7] or mortgage.[8]

The holdings are not consistent as to the necessity of strict compliance with the statutory requirements and who may challenge the mortgage for noncompliance.[9]

Where a broker procures a mortgage loan commitment, he has been held entitled to his commission notwithstanding that shareholders had not previously authorized the mortgage as then required.[10]

Notwithstanding shareholder approval, the board of directors need not go through with the mortgage.

Shareholders dissenting to the mortgage usually enjoy no appraisal remedy.

States sometimes have statutory provisions relating to trust indentures and interests therein.[11]

States also sometimes tax mortgages on real property situated therein.[12]

Federal Trust Indenture Act, 1939

In drafting corporate mortgages subject to the Federal Trust Indenture Act of 1939, its requirements must be observed.[13]

MAKING OF GUARANTY

343. Making of guarantees is expressly authorized by most statutes, few of which require shareholder approval of the guarantee. Shareholders entitled to vote on guarantees who object thereto usually enjoy no appraisal remedy.

Most statutes and sometimes articles of incorporation empower corporations to make guarantees.[1] Absent any such provision, the existence of such power to effectuate the corporation's stated purposes might be implied.[2] Power to make guarantees is often expressly limited by the corporation's stated purposes.[3] A few statutes require

---

may be authorized by board of directors without vote or consent of shareholders unless articles of incorporation provide otherwise). See also id. §§ 102(a) (5), (6), (14), 908.

7. E. g., Missouri, Virginia.

8. E. g., Kentucky, Maine, New Hampshire.

9. See Annot., 58 A.L.R.2d 784, 800–804 (1958) (majority view appearing to be that such requirements are for protection of shareholders and only they may complain in event of noncompliance). See United States v. Jones, 229 F.2d 84, 58 A.L.R.2d 778 (10th Cir. 1956), cert. denied 351 U.S. 939, 76 S.Ct. 835, 100 L.Ed. 1466 (1956); Leffert v. Jackman, 227 N.Y. 310, 125 N.E. 446 (1919); Black v. Ellis, 129 App.Div. 140, 113 N.Y.S. 558 (1st Dep't 1908), aff'd mem., 197 N.Y. 402, 90 N.E. 958 (1910).

10. Smith Bros. Plumbing Co. v. Engine Air Service, Inc., 307 N.Y. 903, 123 N.E.2d 254 (1954).

11. E. g., McKinney's N.Y.Real Prop.Law, §§ 124–130–k.

12. E. g., McKinney's N.Y.Tax Law, §§ 250 et seq.

13. See section 300 supra.

1. ABA-ALI Model Bus.Corp.Act § 4(h). The statutes vary widely as to what may be guaranteed, whose obligations or securities may be guaranteed, and under what conditions. See Bryant Realty Corp. v. Lorberbaum, 221 Ga.App. 820, 147 S.E.2d 420 (1966) (construing statute which provided that corporation may not make accommodation indorsements unless such power was contained in charter as permitting corporation which amended its articles of incorporation to provide therefor); Puerto Rico Industrial Development Co. v. J. H. Miller Mfg. Corp., 173 F.Supp. 596 (S.D.Ill.1959); Bayou Drilling Co. v. Baillio, 312 S.W.2d 705 (Tex.Civ. App.1958); Kriedmann, "The Corporate Guaranty", 13 Vand.L.Rev. 229 (1959); Report, "Guaranties Issued by Corporations", 11 Bus.Law. 67 (July 1956); Slover, "Enforceability of Guaranties Made by Texas Corporations", 10 Sw. L.J. 134 (1956); Warshaw, "Power of a Corporation to Act as Surety or Guarantor", 6 John Marshall L.J. 80 (1949); Comment, "Power of Corporations to Guarantee an Obligation to Pay Money", 13 Fordham L.Rev. 233 (1944); Annot., 11 A.L.R. 554 (1921).

2. See section 183 supra.

3. The New York statute generally empowers a corporation, in furtherance of its purposes, to give guarantees, and allows a guarantee although not in furtherance of the corporate purposes, when authorized by holders of two-thirds of the outstanding shares. McKinney's N.Y.Bus.Corp.Law, §§ 202(a) (7), 908. Compare H. S. Crocker Co. v. Lock-Lined, Inc., 155 N.Y.L.J. No. 122, 12 (Sup.Ct.1966) (upholding guarantee of customer's obligation made without shareholder approval), with 120 Jane Corp. v. Commercial Trading Co., 156 N.Y.L.J. No. 2, 10 (Sup.Ct.1966) (refusing to enforce guarantee of obligation of another corporation owned by relatives made without formal shareholder approval), rev'd 27 A.D.2d 533, 275 N.Y.S.2d 621 (1st Dep't 1966) (upholding guarantee on basis of informal shareholder approval). But see ABA-ALI Model Bus. Corp.Act § 4(h). See also E. Edelmann & Co. v. Amos, 277 F.Supp. 105 (N.D.Ga.1967), aff'd per curiam Transonic Corp. v. E. Edelmann & Co., 386 F.2d 996 (5th Cir. 1967) (upholding guaranty of subsidiary's debt made by vice president of parent corporation

shareholder approval, at least for certain guarantees.[4] Absent required shareholder approval, or estoppel, the corporation has been held not liable on its guarantee.[5]

Shareholders entitled to vote on guarantees who object thereto usually enjoy no appraisal remedy.

MISCELLANEOUS EXTRAORDINARY MATTERS

344. Miscellaneous extraordinary matters requiring shareholder approval in different jurisdictions include bylaws or resolutions for the indemnification of litigation expenses of corporate personnel, fixing the consideration for shares without par value, issuance of share rights and options to corporate personnel, reduction of stated capital, share dividends in shares of different class, purchase of the corporation's own shares out of capital surplus, distributions from capital surplus or in partial liquidation, provision for the conversion of debt securities or shares into shares, etc. Shareholders who dissent from such matters usually enjoy no appraisal remedy.

Besides the matters previously discussed and those reserved for treatment in the fol-

lowing sections, statutes might require shareholder approval for some other matters of a more or less extraordinary nature.

Under statutes in different jurisdictions, approval of the holders of at least a majority of the shares entitled to vote thereon may be required for a bylaw or resolution to indemnify corporate personnel for litigation expense,[1] to fix the consideration for shares without par value, depending upon the provision therefor in the articles of incorporation,[2] for the issuance of share rights and options to directors, officers, or employees,[3] or for certain cases of reduction of stated capital.[4]

[§ 344]

1. E. g., ABA-ALI Model Bus.Corp.Act § 4(o).

2. E. g., ABA-ALI Model Bus.Corp.Act § 17; McKinney's N.Y.Bus.Corp.Law, § 504(d).

3. E. g., ABA-ALI Model Bus.Corp.Act § 18A (optional section) (plus board of directors action); id. § 24 (preemptive rights); cf. alternative provision; but see 1969 Model Act revision; McKinney's N.Y.Bus. Corp.Law, § 505(d).

4. E. g., ABA-ALI Model Bus.Corp.Act, § 63 (plus board of directors resolution); McKinney's N.Y.Bus. Corp.Law, § 802.

A corporation may reduce its stated capital by amendment of its articles of incorporation by (a) reducing the par value of its issued shares; (b) changing the number of issued shares; or (c) eliminating treasury shares from authorized shares.

The board of directors may at any time reduce the stated capital by eliminating from stated capital amounts previously transferred by the board of directors from surplus to stated capital and not allocated to any designated class or series of shares, or by eliminating any amount of stated capital represented by issued shares having a par value which exceeds the aggregate par value of such shares, or by reducing the amount of stated capital represented by issued shares without par value. Id. § 516(a).

When any such reduction has been effected by the board of directors, the amount of such reduction shall be disclosed in the next financial statement covering the period in which such reduction is made that is furnished by the corporation to all its shareholders or, if practicable, in the first notice of dividend or share distribution that is furnished to the holders of each class or series of its shares between the date of such reduction and the next such financial statement, and in any event to all its shareholders within six months of the date of such reduction. Id. § 516(c).

No reduction of stated capital may be made unless thereafter the stated capital exceeds the aggregate preferential amounts payable upon involuntary liq-

[§ 343]

for latter where he was authorized to make ordinary contracts and shareholder resolution ratified all acts of its officers for year). Ultra vires guarantees, like other ultra vires acts which are not illegal, are ratifiable by all shareholders. Goodman v. Ladd Estate Co., 246 Or. 621, 427 P.2d 102 (1967); Empire Steel Corp. of Texas v. Omni Steel Corp., 378 S.W.2d 905 (Tex.Civ.App.1964) (enforcing ultra vires guarantee).

4. E. g., California, New York. See McKinney's N. Y.Bus.Corp.Law, § 908 (authorizing guarantee by corporation, although not in furtherance of its corporate purposes, when authorized at meeting of shareholders by vote of holders of two-thirds of all outstanding shares entitled to vote thereon. If authorized by like vote, such guarantee may be secured by mortgage or pledge of, or creation of security interest in, all or any part of corporate property, or any interest therein, wherever situated) § 615(c) (where there are no shareholders of record, by subscribers to shares whose subscriptions have been accepted or, if none, by incorporator(s)). See Commercial Trading Co. v. 120 Jane Corp., 27 A.D. 2d 533, 275 N.Y.S.2d 621 (1st Dep't 1966) (upholding guarantee not in furtherance of corporate purposes on basis of informal shareholder approval).

5. Rusch & Co. v. Syndicate First Corp., 7 Misc.2d 198, 155 N.Y.S.2d 369 (Sup.Ct.1956).

For a share dividend of shares of one class to shareholders of a different class, unless provided in the articles of incorporation, approval of the holders of a majority of the outstanding shares of the class in which the payment is made may be required.[5]

Purchase by the corporation of its own shares out of capital surplus, absent such provision in the articles of incorporation,[6] and restatement of the articles of incorporation may require, besides board of directors resolution, a vote of the holders of at least the required percentage of the outstanding shares entitled to vote thereon.[7]

Distributions from capital surplus or in partial liquidation, absent provision for them in the articles of incorporation, may require approval of the holders of a majority of the outstanding shares of each class whether or not entitled to vote thereon by the articles of incorporation.[8]

Shareholder approval might also be desirable for any provision for the conversion of debt securities or shares into shares, to facilitate the increase of authorized shares necessary to satisfy the conversion privileges.[9]

In connection with such matters, no appraisal remedy is usually provided dissenting shareholders.

AMENDMENT OF ARTICLES (OR CERTIFICATE) OF INCORPORATION

345. Amendments of articles (or certificate) of incorporation are authorized by statutes, either in general terms or by itemization

uidation upon all issued shares having preferential rights in the assets plus the par value of all other issued shares with par value. Id. §§ 516(b), 806(b).

5. E. g., ABA-ALI Model Bus.Corp.Act § 40(e) (plus board of directors declaration); McKinney's N.Y. Bus.Corp.Law, § 511(a) (3).

6. E. g., ABA-ALI Model Bus.Corp.Act § 5.

7. E. g., ABA-ALI Model Bus.Corp.Act § 59; McKinney's N.Y.Bus.Corp.Law, § 807.

8. E. g., ABA-ALI Model Bus.Corp.Act § 41.

9. E. g., McKinney's N.Y.Bus.Corp.Law, § 519(c).

of specific permissible changes. Amendments usually cannot transcend contemporary limitations on provisions in original articles of incorporation. The validity of amendments depends on the scope of the authorizing statute (from the point of view of both the changes it permits and its application to preexisting corporations), the judicial construction of the state's reserved power to authorize changes in the contracts between the shareholders and the corporation and among the shareholders, and judicial attitudes with respect to the fiduciary duties of controlling shareholders toward minority shareholders.

Amendments usually require shareholder action, often by class voting of any class adversely affected, and possibly also board of directors action. Dissenting shareholders enjoy an appraisal remedy in relatively few jurisdictions.

Most modern cases seem to find no constitutional objection to any amendment covered by the statute, although a few cases still follow the "vested rights" doctrine. Shareholder approval requirements, and the appraisal remedy where recognized, are thought to protect minority shareholders. The equitable limitations of the "good faith", "constructive fraud", or "unfairness" tests afford a modicum of protection against oppression of minority shareholders.

Under regulatory statutes, and to some extent under "blue sky" laws, administrative supervision might be exercised over corporate recapitalizations or reclassifications. Reclassifications, along with other corporate reorganizations, might be tax-free under the federal income tax laws.

Corporation statutes authorize, either in general terms or by itemization of specific changes, amendments of articles of incorporation. Such amendments usually cannot introduce provisions which would not be permissible in original articles of incorporation at the time of the amendments.[1] Such

1. For examples of amendments not allowed because they could not lawfully be contained in original articles of incorporation, see State v. Jefferson Lake Sulphur Co., 36 N.J. 577, 178 A.2d 329 (1962) (escheat provision inconsistent with escheat statute); Bowman v. Armour & Co., 17 Ill.2d 43, 160 N.E.2d 753, 70 A.L.R.2d 843 (1959) (redemption through issue of 30-year subordinated income debentures). As to provisions which might be lawfully contained in original articles of incorporation, see sections 118–131 supra.

amendments, however, can, and frequently do substantially limit or alter shareholders' rights.

The validity of amendments depends upon the scope of the authorizing statute (from the point of view of both the specific changes it permits and its application to preexisting corporations), the judicial construction of the state's reserved power to authorize changes in the contracts between the shareholders and the corporation and among the shareholders, and judicial attitudes with respect to the judiciary duties of controlling shareholders toward minority shareholders.[2]

As previously discussed, most states have reserved power provisions in their constitutions or corporate statutes or both [3]—a typical feature of state constitutions and corporate statutes since the Dartmouth College case.[4]

Statutory Authorization for Amendments

The Model Business Corporation Act provision authorizing amendment of the articles of incorporation is very comprehensive.[5]

Amendments of the articles of incorporation under the Model Act require board of directors resolution and shareholder approval. All amendments require at least either the affirmative vote at a meeting of the holders of at least two-thirds (majority under the 1969 revision) of the shares entitled to vote thereon, unless any class of shares is entitled to vote thereon as a class, in which event, the vote must be of at least two-thirds (majority under the 1969 revision) of the shares of each such class and of the total shares entitled to vote thereon,[6] or the

---

2. See sections 340, 240 supra. For an excellent discussion of the subject of this section, see Note, "Limitations on Alteration of Shareholders' Rights by Charter Amendment". 69 Harv.L.Rev. 538 (1956).

3. See section 340 supra.

4. 17 U.S. (4 Wheat.) 518, 4 L.Ed. 629 (1819), discussed in section 340 supra. See section 14 supra.

5. ABA-ALI Model Bus.Corp.Act § 53. Under the Model Act, reduction of capital is governed by separate provisions. Reduction of stated capital may be effected in certain cases by board of directors action without amendment of the articles of incorporation. See ABA-ALI Model Bus.Corp.Act § 63; Comment, "The Current Law Regarding Reduction of Capital: Its Methodology, Purposes and Dangers", 110 U.Pa. L.Rev. 723 (1962). Annot., 44 A.L.R. 11 (1926), 35 A. L.R.2d 1149 (1954). See section 344 supra. Older statutory authorizations to change the preferences, limitations, and relative rights had been construed, especially by the Delaware courts, as not authorizing amendments directly cancelling cumulative preferred share dividend arrearages. Keller v. Wilson & Co., 21 Del.Ch. 391, 190 A. 115 (Sup.Ct.1936); Consolidated Film Industries, Inc. v. Johnson, 22 Del.Ch. 407, 197 A. 489 (Sup.Ct.1937). Contra, Harr v. Pioneer Mechanical Corp., 65 F.2d 332 (2d Cir. 1933), cert. denied 290 U.S. 673, 54 S.Ct. 92, 78 L. Ed. 581 (1933) (Delaware corporation) (under pre-1967 Delaware statute). See also Davison v. Parke,

Austin & Lipscomb, Inc., 285 N.Y. 500, 35 N.E.2d 618 (1941) motion denied 286 N.Y. 673, 36 N.E.2d 910 (1941) (under pre-1943 New York statute). Such holdings did not preclude changing a dividend provision from cumulative to noncumulative for the future. Permitted under such authorization have been amendments to eliminate voting rights [Morris v. American Public Utilities Co., 14 Del.Ch. 136, 122 A. 696 (Ch.1923)], amendments to eliminate cumulative voting [Maddock v. Vorclone Corp., 17 Del.Ch. 39, 147 A. 255 (Ch.1929)], amendments to change dividend preferences [Morris v. American Public Utilities Co., supra], amendments to change liquidation preferences [Goldman v. Postal Telegraph, Inc., 52 F.Supp. 763 (D.Del.1943)], amendments to reduce the redemption price [Morris v. American Public Utilities Co., supra], amendments to abrogate preemptive rights [Gottlieb v. Heyden Chemical Corp., 33 Del.Ch. 82, 90 A.2d 660 (Sup.Ct.1952)]. Creation of prior preferred shares has been upheld, even where its effect was to cancel cumulative preferred share dividend arrearages. Shanik v. White Sewing Mach. Corp., 25 Del.Ch. 371, 19 A.2d 831 (Sup.Ct.1941); Barrett v. Denver Tramway Corp., 53 F.Supp. 198 (D.Del.1944), aff'd 146 F.2d 701 (3d Cir.1944); Becht, "Corporate Charter Amendments: Issues of Prior Stock and the Alterations of Dividend Rates", 50 Colum.L.Rev. 900 (1950); Schaaf, "Amendment of Articles to Eliminate Dividends Accrued on Cumulative Preferred Shares", 32 Cornell L.Q. 586 (1947); Dodd, "Accrued Dividends in Delaware Corporations—From Vested Rights to Mirage", 57 Harv.L.Rev. 894 (1944); Henley, "Amendment of Articles to Eliminate Dividends Accrued on Cumulative Preferred Shares", 25 Cornell L.Q. 431 (1940); Comment, "Elimination of Accrued Dividends—Comparison of New York and Delaware Law", 2 Buffalo L.Rev. 310 (1952).

6. ABA-ALI Model Bus.Corp.Act § 54 (shareholders must either adopt or reject an amendment submitted by the board of directors; they cannot revise it). Cf. 1969 Model Act revision; Del.Gen.Corp.Law § 242(1) (1967); McKinney's N.Y.Bus.Corp.Law, § 803 (majority of shareholders entitled to vote thereon). New York permits certain minor "changes", alternatively, by board of directors action alone. Id. § 805A. See also ABA-ALI Model Bus.Corp.Act § 12 (change of registered office or registered agent

unanimous written consent of the holders of all such shares without a meeting.[7] The holders of the outstanding shares of a class are entitled to vote as a class upon a proposed amendment, whether or not entitled to vote thereon by the articles of incorporation, if the amendment would make specified changes.[8]

Some statutes have specific provisions protecting greater-than-normal quorum or voting requirements by applying such requirements for voting on amendments thereof.[9] Otherwise, compliance with the

voting requirements for amendment might be deemed sufficient.[10]

Shareholders objecting to amendment of the articles of incorporation are afforded no appraisal remedy by the Model Act.[11]

In keeping with the Model Act filing procedures and nomenclature, duplicate originals of the "articles of amendment"[12] are delivered to the secretary of state who, if they conform to law (assuming all taxes and fees have been paid), files one in his office and appends the other to a "certificate of amendment" which is returned to the corporation or its representative.[13] Any amendment becomes effective upon the issuance of the "certificate of amendment" by the secretary of state.[14]

Articles of incorporation as theretofore amended may be restated at any time by appropriate board of directors and shareholder action and often by board of directors action alone, unless involving some amendment or change other than a change permitted by board of directors action alone.[15]

by board of directors action alone). See Aiple v. Twin City Barge & Towing Co., 274 Minn. 38, 143 N.W.2d 374 (1966); John P. King Mfg. Co. v. Clay, 218 Ga. 382, 128 S.E.2d 68 (1962); Berger v. Amana Society, 253 Iowa 378, 111 N.W.2d 753 (1962). Under pre-1963 New York law, different types of amendments required (a) majority vote of outstanding shares entitled to vote; (b) two-thirds vote of outstanding shares entitled to vote; and/or (c) two-thirds of outstanding shares of *each class* entitled to vote which would be *adversely affected* by certain amendments. Former McKinney's N.Y. Stock Corp.Law, § 37. See note 8 infra. Any proxy solicitation should provide full disclosure to shareholders and should comply with applicable S. E.C.Proxy Rules. See sections 196, 297 supra

7. See sections 190, 191, 266 supra.

8. ABA-ALI Model Bus.Corp.Act, § 55; Del.Gen. Corp.Law, § 242(1) (1967). Under McKinney's N.Y. Bus.Corp.Law, § 804, holders of shares of any class or series whose voting rights would be excluded or limited or who would be adversely affected by any specified classification or reclassification are entitled to vote regardless of any provision to the contrary in the articles of incorporation. Some statutes provide for amendment of the articles of incorporation before the receipt of payment for shares by the incorporators or directors. E. g., Del.Gen. Corp.Law, § 241 (1967). Shareholder approval of an amendment contingent upon further discretionary action of the board of directors has been upheld. Matter of McKinney (Bush Term. Bldgs. Co.), 306 N.Y. 207, 117 N.E.2d 256 (1954) (4–3); [1949] N.Y.L. Rev'n Comm'n Rep., 1949 Legis.Doc.No.65(F) 415– 608; [1950] N.Y.L.Rev'n Comm'n Rep.1950 Legis. Doc.No.65(N) 389–401.

9. In Ohio, when the articles of incorporation require a specified vote for some corporate action, any amendment thereof must be approved by such vote. Ohio Gen.Corp.Law, § 1701.71 (1955). In New York, adding, changing, or striking out a provision of the articles of incorporation for greater-than-normal quorum/voting requirements for board of directors or shareholder action authorized by Mc-Kinney's N.Y.Bus.Corp.Law, §§ 616, 709 is governed by those sections.

10. Warren v. 536 Broad St. Corp., 6 N.J.Super. 170, 70 A.2d 782 (1950). Cf. Sellers v. Joseph Bancroft & Sons Co., 23 Del.Ch.13, 2 A.2d 108 (Ch.1938).

11. New York is almost unique in affording appraisal remedies to shareholders who object to certain amendments of the articles of incorporation. Appraisal is authorized if the amendment would adversely affect a class of shares in a prescribed way. McKinney's N.Y.Bus.Corp.Law, § 806(b) (6).

12. ABA-ALI Model Bus.Corp.Act § 56. See section 117 supra.

13. ABA-ALI Model Bus.Corp.Act § 57. Some jurisdictions call the filed amendment a "certificate of amendment." E. g., McKinney's N.Y.Bus.Corp.Law, § 805.

14. ABA-ALI Model Bus.Corp.Act § 58. In some jurisdictions, amendments become effective upon the filing by the secretary of state of the "certificate of amendment" (see note 13 supra). E. g., McKinney's N.Y.Bus.Corp.Law, § 104(f).

15. ABA-ALI Model Bus.Corp.Act § 59; McKinney's N.Y.Bus.Corp.Law, § 807; [1948] N.Y.L.Rev'n Comm'n Rep., 1948 Legis.Doc.No.65(L) 429–519; [1949] N.Y.L.Rev'n Comm'n Rep.1949 Legis.Doc.No. 65(P) 857–884; [1951] N.Y.L.Rev'n Comm'n Rep.1951 Legis.Doc.No.65(I) 319–324. See 2 CCH Corp.L. Guide ¶ 9763.

Decline of "Vested Rights" Doctrine

Only in a minority of jurisdictions does the "vested rights" language of the earlier cases still persist.[16] Based on a strict construction of reserved power provisions in state constitutions or corporate statutes, a few jurisdictions refuse to apply to preexisting corporations statutory provisions authorizing the elimination of cumulative preferred share dividend arrearages.[17]

Most modern courts seem to find no constitutional objection to any amendment covered by the statute.[18]

Earlier cases narrowly construing less comprehensive earlier statutes sometimes engaged in the "vested rights" language fashionable at the time,[19] but such language

now appears to be passé in most jurisdictions.

As stated by Shientag, J., in McNulty v. W. & J. Sloane:[20]

"Decisions in other States and scholarly law review articles pointed out that the term 'vested right' in connection with the problem we are considering was, to use the language of Mr. Justice Cardozo, a 'deceptive label.' To characterize dividends, accumulating through lapse of time, but never declared, as a 'vested' interest is but to argue from a conclusion.

• • •

" 'Vested right' was indeed a term susceptible of many shades of meaning, a term which had not been clearly defined in the cases. Whenever the court was of the opinion that certain rights of stockholders could not be interfered with, they characterized those rights as 'vested.' The doctrine of vested rights was found to be inadequate as a general test."

Previously, Desmond, J., in the New York Court of Appeals had stated:[21]

"So it seems that only confusion results from saying that 'vested rights' are not within the contemplation of the statute. All preferential rights of stockholders are in a sense vested. They are all property rights founded upon contract. . . . The judicial problem is not whether a particular preferential right is vested or not,

---

16. See section 340 supra; Dodd, "Accrued Dividends in Delaware—From Vested Right to Mirage", 57 Harv.L.Rev. 894 (1944).

17. Schaad v. Hotel Easton Co., 369 Pa. 486, 87 A.2d 227 (1952); Schaffner v. Standard Boiler & Plate Iron Co., 150 Ohio St. 454, 83 N.E.2d 192 (1948); Wheatley v. A. I. Root Co., 147 Ohio St. 127, 69 N. E.2d 187 (1946); Wessel v. Guantanamo Sugar Co., 134 N.J.Eq. 271, 35 A.2d 235 (1944), aff'd sub nom. Murphy v. Guantanamo Sugar Co., 135 N.J.Eq. 506, 39 A.2d 431 (1944). But see Brundage v. New Jersey Zinc Co., 48 N.J. 450, 226 A.2d 585 (1967) (merger case).

18. O'Brien v. Socony Mobil Oil Co., 207 Va. 707, 152 S.E.2d 278 (1967), cert. denied 389 U.S. 825, 88 S.Ct. 65, 19 L.Ed.2d 80 (1967); Sherman v. Pepin Pickling Co., 230 Minn. 87, 41 N.W.2d 571 (1950); Western Foundry Co. v. Wicker, 403 Ill. 260, 85 N. E.2d 722, 8 A.L.R.2d 878 (1949) (elimination of cumulative preferred share dividend arrearages by amendment of articles of incorporation); Anderson v. International Minerals & Chemical Corp., 295 N. Y. 343, 67 N.E.2d 573 (1946) (upholding consolidation eliminating cumulative preferred share dividend arrearages); Arstein v. Robert Reis & Co., 77 N.Y.S.2d 303 (Sup.Ct.1948), aff'd mem., 273 App.Div. 963, 79 N.Y.S.2d 314 (1st Dep't 1948), leave to appeal denied 298 N.Y. 931, 81 N.E.2d 335 (1948), cert. denied 335 U.S. 860, 69 S.Ct. 135, 93 L.Ed. 407 (1948) (upholding amendment of articles of incorporation to eliminate cumulative preferred share dividend arrearages); McNulty v. W. & J. Sloane, 184 Misc. 835, 54 N.Y.S.2d 253 (Sup.Ct.1945) (upholding amendment of articles of incorporation to eliminate cumulative preferred share dividend arrearages).

19. Kent v. Quicksilver Mining Co., 78 N.Y. 159 (1879); Roberts v. Roberts-Wicks Co., 184 N.Y. 257, 77 N.E. 13 (1906); Breslav v. New York & Queens Electric Light & Power Co., 249 App.Div. 181, 291 N.Y.S. 932 (2d Dep't 1936), aff'd mem., 273 N.Y. 593,

7 N.E.2d 708 (1937) (holding then term "reclassify" too general to permit construction authorizing amendment making non-redeemable preferred shares redeemable at option of corporation). Cf. Davison v. Parke, Austin & Lipscomb, Inc., 285 N.Y. 500, 35 N.E.2d 618 (1941) (holding then statute did not authorize elimination of cumulative preferred share dividend arrearages or sinking fund rights by amendment of articles of incorporation). See Annot., 70 A.L.R.2d 843 (1960).

20. 184 Misc. 835, 841, 54 N.Y.S.2d 253, 259–260 (Sup.Ct.1945). Accord, O'Brien v. Socony Mobil Oil Co., 207 Va. 707, 152 S.E.2d 278 (1967), cert. denied 389 U.S. 825, 88 S.Ct. 65, 19 L.Ed.2d 80 (1967).

21. Davison v. Parke, Austin & Lipscomb, Inc., 285 N.Y. 500, 509, 35 N.E. 618, 622 (1941), motion denied 286 N.Y. 673, 36 N.E.2d 910 (1941).

but rather what was the legislative intent as to it."

In short, most courts now appear to sustain comprehensive legislative authorization for amending the articles of incorporation, recognizing that the legislature sought to protect minority shareholder interests by requiring sufficient vote and the approval of the holders of sufficient outstanding shares of each class of shares adversely affected thereby, and possibly by affording to objecting shareholders an appraisal remedy. The equitable limitation of the "good faith", "constructive fraud", or "unfairness" tests also confers some judicial protection against oppression of minority shareholders by controlling shareholders: [22]

> "There also exists the inherent power of a court of equity, a power limited generally to the test of good faith rather than a test objective in character, a power the exercise of which may be circumscribed, because too often what is an accomplished fact is presented to the court; but it is a significant, restraining influence nevertheless."

Even with the application of the "good faith", or "constructive fraud" or "unfairness", tests, only a few amendments have not been upheld by the courts.[23]

Miscellaneous

Amendments of the articles of incorporation are, of course, governed by the law of the jurisdiction of incorporation.[24]

Besides legislative and judicial requirements, California is unique in exercising general administrative supervision over corporate recapitalizations.[25] Its regulatory provisions, part of its "blue sky" laws, are unlike federal laws, which either concern only closely regulated industries [26] or are mere disclosure acts (which, however, might apply to securities issued in reclassifications).[27]

An attempt by the California Commissioner of Corporations to restrict articles of incorporation amendment by a foreign corporation qualified to do business in California has been upheld by the courts as involving a sale of securities and not "fair, just and equitable".[28] The California Commis-

---

22. McNulty v. W. & J. Sloane, 184 Misc. 835, 844–845, 54 N.Y.S.2d 253, 262 (Sup.Ct.1945). See also Becht, "Changes in the Interests of Classes of Stockholders by Corporate Charter Amendments". 36 Cornell L.Q. 1 (1950); Campanella & Nakrin, "New York's Changing Concept of Vested Rights in Regard to Shareholders", 24 St.John's L.Rev. 90 (1949); Comment, "A Standard of Fairness for Compensating Preferred Shareholders in Corporate Recapitalizations" 33 U.Chi.L.Rev. 97 (1965).

23. Faunce v. Boost Co., 15 N.J.Super. 534, 83 A.2d 649 (1951); Kamena v. Janssen Dairy Corp., 133 N.J.Eq. 214, 31 A.2d 200 (1943), aff'd per curiam 134 N.J.Eq. 359, 35 A.2d 894 (1944). But see Honigman v. Green Giant Co., 309 F.2d 667 (8th Cir. 1962), cert. denied 372 U.S. 941, 83 S.Ct. 934, 9 L.Ed.2d 967 (1963); Barrett v. Denver Tramway Corp., 53 F. Supp. 198 (D.Del.1944), aff'd 146 F.2d 701 (3d Cir. 1944); Franzblau v. Capital Securities Co., 2 N.J. Super. 517, 64 A.2d 644 (1949); Walter, "Fairness— A Disappearing Doctrine", 29 B.U.L.Rev. 453 (1949); Latty, "Fairness—The Focal Point in Preferred Stock Arrearage Elimination", 29 Va.L.Rev. 1 (1942);

Dodd, "Fair and Equitable Recapitalizations", 55 Harv.L.Rev. 780 (1942).

24. Foreign corporations may be required to comply with requirements of jurisdictions where they are authorized to transact business with respect to change of name, change of registered office or registered agent, or amendment of articles of incorporation, by means of amendment of their certificate of authority or otherwise. ABA-ALI Model Bus. Corp.Act §§ 102, 107, 109, 111.

25. Note, "Protection for Shareholder Interests in Recapitalization of Publicly Held Corporations", 58 Colum.L.Rev. 1031, 1048–1055 (1958). See generally Cowett, "Reorganizations, Consolidations, Mergers and Related Corporate Events under the Blue Sky Laws", 12 Bus.Law. 418, 760 (1958).

26. E. g., Interstate Commerce Act, 49 U.S.C.A. §§ 1 et seq.; United States v. New York, New Haven & Hartford R. R., 276 F.2d 525 (2d Cir. 1959), cert. denied sub nom. Tri-Continental Financial Corp. v. U. S., 362 U.S. 961, 80 S.Ct. 877, 4 L.Ed.2d 876 (1960); Public Utility Holding Company Act of 1935, 15 U.S.C.A. §§ 79–79z; Investment Company Act of 1940, 15 U.S.C.A. §§ 80a–1 to 80a–52; Federal Power Act § 204, 16 U.S.C.A. § 824c; Civil Aeronautics Act of 1938, § 408, 49 U.S.C.A. § 488.

27. Securities Act, 1933, 15 U.S.C.A. §§ 77a–77aa (see section 295 supra); See also Securities Exchange Act, 1934, 15 U.S.C.A. §§ 78a–78jj.

28. People ex rel. Sobieski v. Western Air Lines, Inc., 258 Cal.App.2d 213, 66 Cal.Rptr. 316 (1968); Western Air Lines, Inc. v. Sobieski, 191 Cal.App.2d 399, 12 Cal.Rptr. 719 (1961), rev'g Western Air

sioner of Corporations has also ruled that nonvoting or limited voting features of common shares, or absence of cumulative voting, would be unfavorable factors in the determination of the eligibility of the issuer for a permit covering the shares.[29] Reclassifications, as "Type E reorganizations", are often tax-free under the federal income tax laws.[30]

MERGER AND CONSOLIDATION

346. The traditional distinction between a merger and consolidation is that in the case of a merger one or more constituent corporations merge into another constituent corporation and cease to exist but such other corporation continues as the surviving corporation, whereas in the case of a consolidation two or more constituent corporations consolidate to form a new consolidated corporation and cease to exist.

All current statutes authorize mergers and consolidations approved by the required vote or consent of shareholders and possibly also by the board of directors.

Under so-called "short merger" statutes, substantially wholly-owned subsidiaries may be merged into their parent corporation, and sometimes vice versa, by action of the board of directors of the parent corporation alone, without shareholder approval.

Most statutes afford an appraisal remedy to dissenting shareholders, at least those of any nonsurviving corporation.

To protect minority shareholders against oppressive mergers or consolidations, courts apply equitable limitations, known as the "unfairness" or "good faith" tests.

Where foreign corporations are involved in a merger or consolidation, such corporations must comply also with the law of their jurisdiction of incorporation. Compliance with applicable federal securities laws and state "blue sky" laws is also required. Antitrust laws, both federal and state, are especially relevant

to such combinations as mergers and consolidations.

Distinction between Merger and Consolidation

The traditional distinction between a merger and consolidation is that in the case of a merger one or more constituent corporations merge into another constituent corporation, known as the surviving corporation, with the result that the former cease to exist and the latter's corporate existence continues, viz.:

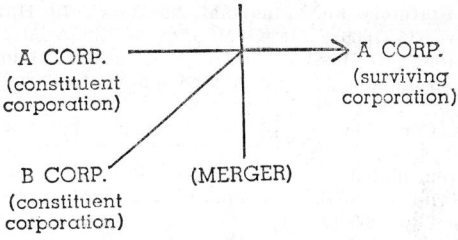

Whereas in the case of a consolidation the two or more constituent corporations cease to exist and a new consolidated corporation emerges, viz.:

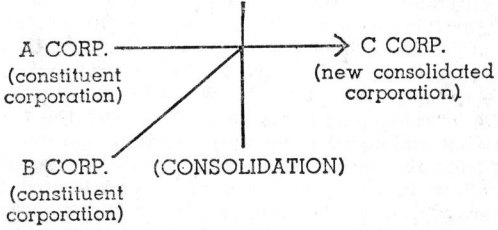

In either case, the surviving or consolidated corporation, as of the time of merger or consolidation, takes over the assets of the former constituent corporations and assumes their liabilities, and issues its shares, or pays consideration, on some fair basis, in exchange for the shares of the former constituent corporations.[1]

Lines, Inc. v. Stephenson, 2 CCH Blue Sky L.Rep. ¶ 70,396 (Cal.Super.Ct.1958).

29. "New California Rule Re Cumulative Voting in Foreign Corporations", 15 Bus.Law. 70 (1959).

30. See section 351 infra.

1. See generally B. Fox & E. Fox, Corporate Acquisitions and Mergers (1968); D. Linowes, Managing Growth Through Acquisition (1968); R. Short, Business Mergers, How and When to Transact Them (1967); A. Choka, Buying, Selling, and Merging Businesses (ALI revd. 1969); C. Scharf, Techniques for Buying, Selling, and Merging Busi-

Statutes Authorizing Mergers and Consolidations

All current statutes authorize mergers and consolidations without the necessity of unanimous approval of the shareholders involved; the statutes usually apply to preexisting corporations under the state's reserved power;[2] most statutes afford an appraisal remedy to dissenting shareholders, at least those of any nonsurviving corporation. Judicial requirements of "fairness" have also been imposed by the courts. Mergers or consolidations of domestic corporations under the Model Business Corporation Act require board of directors resolution and the approval at a meeting by the holders of at least two-thirds (majority under the 1969 revision) of the outstanding shares of each corporation entitled to vote thereon. If any class of such shares is entitled to vote as a class on such merger or consolidation the vote of at least two-thirds (majority under the 1969 revision) of the shares of such class is also required.[3]

nesses (1964); A. Little, Mergers and Acquisitions (1963); G. McCarthy, Acquisitions and Mergers (1963); M. Weinberg, Take-Overs and Amalgamations (1963); M. Mace, Management Problems of Corporate Acquisitions (1962); 15 W. Fletcher, Private Corporations §§ 7048–7074 (perm.ed.rev.1961); Clark, "Merger and Consolidation under California Law", in Advising California Business Enterprises 1027–1107 (1958); Kitching, "Why Do Mergers Miscarry?", 45 Harv.Bus.Rev. 84 (Nov.-Dec.1967); Braxton, "Mergers and Miscarriages", 13 Prac.Law. 55 (Oct.1967); Siegel, "When Corporations Divide: A Statutory and Financial Analysis", 79 Harv.L. Rev. 534 (1966); Hale, "Mergers of Financial Institutions", 21 Bus.Law. 211 (1965); Sealy, "Ohio Acquisition and Merger Amendments", 5 Corp.Prac. Comm. 366 (1964); Johnstone & Galloway, "Mergers, Consolidations and Asset Sales: Chapters 1.10 and 1.11", 15 S.C.L.Rev. 415 (1963); McCarthy, "Premediated Merger", 39 Harv.Bus.Rev. 74 (Jan.-Feb.1961); Sealy, "Acquisitions and Mergers", 16 Bus.Law. 209 (1960); Freedland, "Merger and Consolidation of New York Business Corporations: History of Enabling Legislation, 1776–1956", 25 Fordham L.Rev. 672 (1957). Since 1963, New York has defined "Merger" as a procedure whereby two or more corporations "Merge into a single corporation which shall be one of the constituent corporations"; "Constituent corporation" as "an existing corporation that is participating in the merger or consolidation with one or more other corporations"; "Surviving corporation" as "the constituent corporation into which one or more other constituent corporations are merged". McKinney's N.Y.Bus. Corp.Law, § 901. Prior to 1963, New York used the term "consolidation" to include not only the traditional consolidation but also the traditional merger except the merger of a 95–100 percent-owned subsidiary into a parent corporation and limited the term "merger" to such parent-subsidiary merger. Mergers and other acquisitions may be desirable to diversify—into new products, new lines of business, new geographic markets—especially by defense industries, or to acquire skilled management, working capital, or tax attributes. 163 The Wall Street Journal, No. 24, 1 (Feb. 4, 1964). Mergers and consolidations raise a host of problems. See John Wiley & Sons v. Livingston, 376 U.S. 543, 84 S.Ct. 909, 11 L.Ed.2d 898 (1964) (holding that corporate employer was required to arbitrate with union under collective bargaining agreement between union and another corporation which had merged into corporate employer where business entity had remained the same, there was wholesale transfer of merged employer's employees to corporate employer's plant and union had made its position known well before merger and never had departed from it); Note, "Assumption by a Purchasing, Merging or Consolidating Corporation of Labor Contract Obligations of Its Predecessor", 17 N.Y.U.Intra.L.Rev. 228 (1962); First Nat'l Bank of Birmingham v. Adams,

281 Ala. 404, 203 So.2d 124 (1967) (effect of merger on profit-sharing plan); Harrison, "Acquisitions and Qualified Pension Plans: Studies on Corporate Take-Overs", 15 J.Taxation 36 (1961); Rank v. United States, 345 F.2d 337 (5th Cir.1965) (effect of merger on share options); Musto, "What To Do About Stock Options of a Merging Corporation", 24 J.Taxation 246 (1966). See also Symposium: "Trademark Problems in Acquisitions and Mergers", 57 Trademark Rep. 743 (1967); Brufsky, "Trademarks: A Primer for the Merger-Minded", 3 Mergers & Acquisitions 18 (Aug.1968). For merger proceedings, see C. Israel, Corporate Practice 598–647 (PLI 2d ed. 1969).

2. Brundage v. New Jersey Zinc Co., 48 N.J. 450, 226 A.2d 585 (1967), involved the merger of a New Jersey corporation which was incorporated before the state's first merger statutes permitting merger with two-thirds shareholder approval. At the time of incorporation, both the state constitution and corporate statute expressly reserved the power to amend corporate charters. The court held that such reserved power was constitutionally adequate to sustain the application to preexisting corporations of the later statutes authorizing mergers with less than unanimous shareholder approval. See section 340 supra.

3. ABA-ALI Model Bus.Corp.Act §§ 65, 66; see also id. § 70 (merger or consolidation of domestic and foreign corporations). The 1969 Model Act revision requires the affirmative vote of the holders of a majority of the shares entitled to vote thereon, subject to any class voting requirements. Until 1962, authorization by the holders of two-thirds of all outstanding shares, whether or not otherwise entitled to vote, was required by the Model Act. Delaware and Pennsylvania permit a merger without approval of shareholders of the surviving corpora-

Any class of shares is entitled to vote as a class if the plan of merger or consolidation contains any provision which, if contained in a proposed amendment to the articles of incorporation,[4] would entitle such class of shares to vote as a class.

After such shareholder approval, at any time prior to the filing of the articles of merger or consolidation, the merger or consolidation may be abandoned pursuant to any provisions therefor set forth in the plan of merger or consolidation.[5]

The articles of incorporation may require greater shareholder approval.[6] Unanimous written shareholder consent without a meeting will suffice in lieu of the required vote at a meeting.[7]

"Short Merger" Statutes

Under the Model Act, a corporation owning at least 95 percent of the outstanding

shares of each class of another corporation may merge such other corporation into itself without the approval of the shareholders of either corporation—known as a "short merger".[8]

Miscellaneous

Dissenting shareholders are entitled under the Model Act to an appraisal remedy enforceable against the surviving or consolidated corporation, except shareholders of the surviving corporation in a merger where such corporation owns all the outstanding

---

tion if no more than a 15 percent share increase would be involved. Dell & Hackney, "A New Pennsylvania Statute: Tax-Free Reorganization by Merger Without Shareholder Vote", 30 U.Pitt.L.Rev. 309 (1968). "Short mergers" also dispense with shareholder approval requirements. See note 8 infra. Under a former merger statute which authorized the merger of corporations in the same or similar business a merger between a razor blade corporation and a pen and pencil corporation was enjoined. Imperial Trust Co. v. Magazine Repeating Razor Co., 138 N.J.Eq. 20, 46 A.2d 449 (1946).

4. New York requires, in addition to a two-thirds vote of all outstanding shares entitled to vote thereon, only a majority vote of the class or series entitled to vote as such. McKinney's N.Y.Bus. Corp.Law, § 903(a) (2). See also Moss Estate, Inc. v. Metal & Thermit Corp., 73 N.J.Super. 56, 179 A. 2d 54 (1962) (upholding merger increasing authorized shares under merger statute requiring two-thirds vote of all outstanding shares notwithstanding articles of incorporation requirement of two-thirds vote of each class to increase number of authorized shares). See section 345 supra.

5. ABA-ALI Model Bus.Corp.Act § 67. See also Note, "Withdrawal of Fundamental Corporate Changes Before a Vote, an Unrecognized Complement to Abandonment—A Proposed Change in Ohio's Abandonment Statute", 32 U.Cin.L.Rev. 380 (1963).

6. ABA-ALI Model Bus.Corp.Act § 136. See sections 191, 266 supra.

7. ABA-ALI Model Bus.Corp.Act § 138. See sections 190, 266 supra.

8. ABA-ALI Model Bus.Corp.Act § 68A (optional section); McKinney's N.Y.Bus.Corp.Law, § 905; see note 1 supra. The constitutionality of the New York "short merger" statute has been upheld. Beloff v. Consolidated Edison Co. of New York, 300 N.Y. 11, 87 N.E.2d 561 (1949). The Delaware "short merger" statute authorizes such merger not only of a 90 percent-owned subsidiary into a parent but vice versa, requiring in the case of a short merger of a parent into its subsidiary approval by the holders of a majority of the shares of the parent. Any dissenting shareholder of a subsidiary Delaware corporation party to a short merger is afforded an appraisal remedy against the surviving corporation. Where a subsidiary is "short merged" into its parent, the interest of minority shareholders can be terminated by the payment of cash, etc., instead of shares of the surviving corporation. Del.Gen. Corp.Law § 253 (1967); Coyne v. Park & Tilford Distillers Corp., 38 Del.Ch. 514, 154 A.2d 893 (Sup. Ct.1959) (involving 96 percent owned subsidiary formed when short merger statute required 100 percent ownership, statutory decrease of ownership requirement to 90 percent in 1957 being upheld under reserved power). In practice, probably the only alternative for objecting minority shareholders is the appraisal remedy which assures them a fair price, since the purpose of the short merger statute is to enable the parent to eliminate minority shareholders of its subsidiary leaving them with only a monetary claim. Stauffer v. Standard Brands, Inc., 41 Del.Ch. 7, 187 A.2d 78 (Sup.Ct.1962). Even before express statutory authorization, "down-stream" mergers had been upheld in Delaware, even when effected to eliminate cumulative preferred share dividend arrearages of the merged corporation. Federal United Corp. v. Havender, 24 Del.Ch. 318, 11 A.2d 331 (Sup.Ct.1940); Hottenstein (Moore) v. York Ice Machinery Co., 136 F.2d 944 (3d Cir.1943), petition for leave to file bill of review denied 146 F.2d 835 (3d Cir.1944), cert. denied 325 U.S. 886, 65 S.Ct. 1573, 89 L.Ed. 2000 (1945). Cf. Allstate Ins. Co. v. Oxford Finance Companies, 275 F.Supp. 54 (D.Md.1967). See also Joseph v. Wallace-Murray Corp., 354 Mass. 477, 238 N.E.2d 360 (1968); Comment, "The Short Merger Statute", 32 U.Chi.L.Rev. 596 (1965).

shares of the other corporations which are parties to the merger.[9]

In keeping with Model Act practice, duplicate originals of articles of merger or consolidation are filed. Upon the issuance to the surviving or consolidated corporation by the secretary of state of a certificate of merger or a certificate of consolidation (with the other duplicate original attached thereto), the merger or consolidation is effective.[10] In the case of a merger, the articles of incorporation of the surviving corporation might or might not be amended by the merger plan; in the case of a consolidation, the articles of consolidation constitute the articles of incorporation of the consolidated corporation.

In the case of de facto mergers or consolidations, without compliance with applicable statutory procedures and recognition of appraisal remedies, judicial relief is available;

furthermore, the directors who fail to exercise sound business judgment can be surcharged for the expenses involved [11] and the corporation can be dissolved by the state.[12]

To protect minority shareholders against oppressive mergers and consolidations, the courts apply equitable limitations, known as the "unfairness" test [13] and/or the "good faith" test.[14]

In cases of merger or consolidation of domestic and foreign corporations, there must be compliance not only with local law but also with the law of the jurisdiction of incorporation of the foreign corporation.[15]

9. ABA-ALI Model Bus.Corp.Act §§ 73, 74. The 1969 Model Act revision limited the availability of the appraisal remedy in mergers and consolidations. See section 349, n. 6 infra. Delaware affords dissenting shareholders of some corporations an appraisal remedy against the resulting or surviving corporation, limiting such remedy in the case of merger of parent and subsidiary to dissenting minority shareholders of any domestic subsidiary. Del.Gen. Corp.Law, § 262 (1967). Shareholders who are not entitled to vote—see note 3 supra—would enjoy no right to dissent. New York affords an appraisal remedy to dissenting shareholders of each corporation, except those of any surviving corporation unless the articles of consolidation effects one or more of the changes specified in McKinney's N.Y. Bus.Corp.Law, § 806(b) (6) in the rights of the shares held by such shareholder and except shareholders of the parent in a merger of a 95–100 percent owned subsidiary into such parent. McKinney's N.Y.Bus.Corp.Law, § 910. See Applestein v. United Board & Carton Corp., 60 N.J.Super. 333, 159 A.2d 146 (1960), aff'd per curiam 33 N.J. 72, 161 A.2d 474 (1960).

10. ABA-ALI Model Bus.Corp.Act §§ 68, 69. Del. Gen.Corp.Law, § 251 (1967) (filings in the office of the secretary of state and recording in the office of the recorder of deeds of the appropriate county, with the merger of consolidation becoming effective upon the former event); id. § 103. Where a Delaware corporation whose shares had been attached was merged into a New Jersey corporation, quasi-in-rem jurisdiction was held to have been lost. Union Chemical & Materials Corp. v. Cannon, 38 Del. Ch. 203, 148 A.2d 348 (Sup.Ct.1959).

11. See Blackwell Industrial Foundation, Inc. v. Texstar Corp., 387 F.2d 708 (10th Cir.1968); Spartans Industries, Inc. v. John Pilling Shoe Co., 263 F.Supp. 191 (D.Mass.1967), rev'd 385 F.2d 495 (1st Cir. 1967); Hoche Productions, S.A. v. Jayark Films Corp., 256 F.Supp. 291 (S.D.N.Y.1966); Jac See Packing Co. v. C. & F. Packing House Market, Inc., —— Miss. ——, 215 So.2d 704 (1968); Rath v. Rath Packing Co., 257 Iowa 1277, 136 N.W.2d 410 (1965). For possible recognition of appraisal remedy in case of de facto mergers or consolidations, see section 349 infra. For possible liability of management, see Gilbert v. Burnside, 197 N.Y.S.2d 623 (Sup.Ct.1959) ($118,000 damage award), rev'd on other grounds 13 A.D.2d 982, 216 N.Y.S.2d 430 (2d Dep't 1961) (on ground that directors had followed advice of eminent counsel), aff'd mem., 11 N.Y.2d 960, 183 N.E.2d 325, 229 N.Y.S.2d 10 (1962).

12. People v. North River Sugar Refining Co., 121 N.Y. 582, 24 N.E. 834 (1890).

13. Knauff v. Utah Construction & Mining Co., 408 F.2d 958 (10th Cir.1969), cert. denied —— U.S. ——, 90 S.Ct. 83, 24 L.Ed.2d 81 (1969); Levin v. Great Western Sugar Co., 406 F.2d 1112 (3d Cir.1969); David J. Greene & Co. v. Dunhill International Inc., —— Del.Ch. ——, 249 A.2d 427 (Ch.1968); Bruce v. E. L. Bruce Co., 40 Del.Ch. 80, 174 A.2d 29 (Ch.1961); Sterling v. Mayflower Hotel Corp., 33 Del.Ch. 293, 93 A.2d 107, 38 A.L.R.2d 425 (Sup.Ct.1952); Donohue v. Heuser, 239 S.W.2d 238 (Ky.1951); Cole v. Nat'l Cash Credit Ass'n, 18 Del.Ch. 47, 156 A. 183 (Ch.1931).

14. See Gilbert v. Burnside, 197 N.Y.S.2d 623 (Sup. Ct.1959), rev'd on other grounds, 13 A.D.2d 982, 216 N.Y.S.2d 430 (2d Dep't 1961), aff'd mem., 11 N.Y.2d 960, 229 N.Y.S.2d 10, 183 N.E.2d 325 (1962); Juviler v. Unitronics Corp., 8 Misc.2d 1033, 166 N.Y. S.2d 770 (Sup.Ct.1957).

15. See, e. g., ABA-ALI Model Bus.Corp.Act § 70; Del.Gen.Corp.Law, §§ 252, 253 (1967); McKinney's N.Y.Bus.Corp.Law, § 907. See Levin v. Mississippi River Fuel Corp., 386 U.S. 162, 87 S.Ct. 927, 17 L. Ed.2d 834 (1967). If the surviving corporation or

Compliance should be made with any applicable federal securities laws [16] and state "blue sky" laws,[17] as well as other regulatory measures.

Mergers and consolidations can be attacked in the federal courts for violation of the S.E.C. Proxy Rules [18] and of S.E.C. Rule 10b–5.[19]

Antitrust laws, both federal and state, are especially relevant to such combinations as mergers and consolidations.[20]

The tax aspects of mergers and consolidations, which can come within the 1954 Code definition of "reorganization", are especially complex, with such concepts as "boot", but statutory mergers or consolidations, as "Type A reorganizations", can be tax-free.[21]

EXTENSION AND REVIVAL OF CORPORATE EXISTENCE

347. Extension or revival of corporate existence is governed by specific statutory provisions in some jurisdictions, usually with no provision for appraisal remedy, whereas others often permit extension or revival by amendment of the articles of incorporation. Appraisal remedies are sometimes afforded dissenting shareholders. The basic difference between "extension" and "revival" (or "revivor" or "renewal") is that the former is effectuated prior to termination of corporate existence and the latter after such termination, but the term "ex-

consolidated corporation is a foreign corporation, it should comply with applicable qualification and filing requirements, and any nonsurviving constituent foreign corporations authorized to transact business should formally withdraw. See ABA-ALI Model Bus.Corp.Act §§ 110–113. Although the Delaware merger provisions do not apply to alien corporations, a Netherlands corporation which owned more than 90 percent of the shares of a Delaware subsidiary was allowed to form a subsidiary Delaware holding company, transfer all such shares to the latter, and then merge the former into the latter. Braasch v. Goldschmidt, 41 Del.Ch. 519, 199 A.2d 760 (Ch.1964). Under Florida law authorizing the merger of domestic corporations with corporations organized under the laws of "any other state or of the United States", the Florida attorney general has ruled Puerto Rican corporations were not covered. Fla.Op.Att'y Gen. No. 062–85 (June 18, 1962).

16. See sections 295, 297, 298 supra.

17. Cowett, "Reorganizations, Consolidations, Mergers and Related Corporate Events under the Blue Sky Laws", 13 Bus.Law. 418, 760 (1958). See sections 305–308 supra.

18. Securities and Exchange Commission v. Nat'l Securities, Inc., 393 U.S. 453, 89 S.Ct. 564, 21 L.Ed.2d 668 (1969) (S.E.C.Proxy Rules held applicable to insurance company merger); J. I. Case Co. v. Borak, 377 U.S. 426, 84 S.Ct. 1555, 12 L.Ed.2d 423 (1964) (upholding power of federal court to award damages and to invalidate merger allegedly approved because of misleading proxy statement in violation of S.E.C.Proxy Rules); Lockwood, "Corporate Acquisitions and Actions under Sections 10(b) and 14 of the Securities Exchange Act of 1934", 23 Bus.Law. 365 (1968); Birkholz, "Violations of S.E.C.Proxy Rules—Federal Jurisdiction to Invalidate Corporate Mergers", 39 Wash.L.Rev. 297 (1964). See section 297 supra.

19. Securities and Exchange Commission v. Nat'l Securities, Inc., 393 U.S. 453, 89 S.Ct. 564, 21 L.Ed.2d 668 (1969) (statutory merger of insurance company held to involve purchase of securities under S.E.C. Rule 10b–5); Dasho v. Susquehanna Corp., 380 F.2d 262 (7th Cir.1967), cert. denied 389 U.S. 977, 88 S.Ct. 480, 19 L.Ed.2d 470 (1967); Lockwood, "Corporate Acquisitions and Actions under Sections 10(b) and 14 of the Securities Exchange Act of 1934", 23 Bus.Law. 365 (1968); Comment, "The Effect of the Anti-Fraud Provisions of the Securities and Exchange Act upon the Corporate Merger", 13 N.Y.L.F. 349 (1967). See section 298 supra.

20. Burck, "The Merger Movement Rides High", 79 Fortune, No. 2, 79 (Feb.1969); Chaffetz, "What's Left of Mergers", 23 Bus.Law. 599 (1968). See sections 309–315 supra.

21. Int.Rev.Code of 1954, 26 U.S.C.A. §§ 361, 368(a) (1) (A); see also § 354; Libson Shops, Inc. v. Koehler, 353 U.S. 382, 77 S.Ct. 990, 1 L.Ed.2d 924 (1957), reh. denied 354 U.S. 943, 77 S.Ct. 1390, 1 L.Ed.2d 1542 (1957) ("continuity of business enterprise" theory applied to limit survival of net operating loss carryovers after statutory merger); B. Bittker & J. Eustice, Federal Income Taxation of Corporations and Shareholders §§ 12.12, 13.25 (2d ed. 1966); Cohen, "Conglomerate Mergers and Taxation", 55 A.B.A.J. 40 (1969); Fillman, "Cash and Property as Consideration in a Merger or Consolidation", 62 Nw.U.L.Rev. 837 (1968); Spillers & Shors, "The Role of the Statutory Merger in Corporate Acquisitions: A Legal and Financial Inquiry", 53 Iowa L. Rev. 121 (1967); Hellerstein, "Mergers, Taxes, and Realism", 71 Harv.L.Rev. 254 (1957); Darrell, "The Use of Reorganization Techniques in Corporate Acquisitions", 70 Harv.L.Rev. 1183 (1957); Manning, " 'In Pursuance of the Plan of Reorganization': The Scope of the Reorganization Provisions of the Internal Revenue Code", 72 Harv.L.Rev. 881 (1959); Lefevre, "Tax Check List for Acquisitions and Mergers", 25 Bus.Law. 355 (1969). See section 351 infra. The Tax Reform Act of 1969 limits the amount of interest deductible on "corporation acquisition indebtedness" to acquire shares or two-thirds of all the operating assets (excluding cash) of another corporation.

tension" is sometimes used to encompass both. In the case of revival, the corporation might have a de facto existence in the interim between termination and revival. Absent statutory provision for revival, reincorporation might afford the only means for carrying on the business.

Most modern corporations are formed for theoretically perpetual existence. In times past, corporations were often limited in their duration,[1] and even today some states limit corporate duration,[2] and in most of the states which permit perpetual existence, corporations of limited duration can be formed.[3]

When a corporation's existence is of limited duration, statutes often provide for extending or reviving its corporate existence. The basic distinction between "extension" and "revival" (or "revivor" or "renewal") is that "extension" is effectuated prior to termination of corporate existence, whereas "revival" occurs after such termination. Sometimes, the term "extension" is used to include both extension and revival. In the case of revival, the corporation might be said to have a *"de facto"* existence in the interim period between termination and revival.[4]

Older statutes have special extension or revival provisions;[5] others permit extension

or revival by amendment of the articles of incorporation;[6] a few jurisdictions afford appraisal remedies to dissenters.[7]

The Delaware statute contains rather elaborate provisions enabling corporations which have a limited duration, or whose articles of incorporation have become inoperative by law for nonpayment of taxes, or which have renewed their articles of incorporation in a defective manner, to procure extension, restoration, renewal or revival of their corporate existence. Shareholder approval, however, is not required.[8]

In the absence of a revival statute, a corporation whose duration has expired or whose existence has otherwise ended might have to be reincorporated in order that the business can be carried on.[9]

---

1. N. Lattin, The Law of Corporations 154 (1959).

2. See section 120 supra.

3. E. g., ABA-ALI Model Bus.Corp.Act §§ 4(a), 48(b); Del.Gen.Corp.Law, §§ 122(1), 102(b) (5) (1967); McKinney's N.Y.Bus.Corp.Law, § 402(a) (9).

4. Garzo v. Maid of the Mist Steamboat Co., 303 N. Y. 516, 104 N.E.2d 882 (1952). See discussion of de facto doctrine in section 140 supra and of expired, dissolved, and revived corporation in section 144 supra.

5. E. g., Arizona, California, Delaware, Georgia, Hawaii, Idaho, Iowa, Kansas, Maryland, Michigan, Minnesota, Montana, Nebraska, Nevada, North Carolina, Oklahoma, South Dakota. See also District of Columbia, Florida, Massachusetts, Washington (reinstatement or restoration provisions). To be distinguished from revival are provisions for revocation of voluntary dissolution proceedings. E. g., ABA-ALI Model Bus.Corp.Act §§ 81–84. See also [1943] N.Y.L.Rev'n Comm'n Rep.1943 Legis.Doc.No.

65(I) 349–408; [1944] N.Y.L.Rev'n Comm'n Rep. 1944 Legis.Doc. No. 65(A) 19–32; [1945] N.Y.L.Rev'n Comm'n Rep.1945 Legis.Doc. No. 65(D) 115–129. See Garzo v. Maid of the Mist Steamboat Co., 303 N.Y. 516, 104 N.E.2d 882 (1952) (holding then applicable McKinney's N.Y.Gen.Corp.Law, § 49 retroactive to corporations whose charters had expired prior to its enactment, and recognizing de facto corporation in interim); Kelley v. American Sugar Refining Co., 58 F.Supp. 242 (D.N.J.1944), aff'd per curiam 152 F.2d 280 (3d Cir.1945); cf. Lester Bros. v. Pope Realty & Ins. Co., 250 N.C. 565, 109 S.E.2d 263 (1959); Merges v. Altenbrand, 45 Mont. 355, 123 P. 21 (1912); Home Bldg. Ass'n v. Bruner, 134 Ky. 361, 120 S.W. 306 (1909). See also McKinney's N.Y. Tax Law, § 203–a(7) (annulment of dissolution for nonpayment of taxes); Annot., 108 A.L.R. 59 (1937).

6. E. g., ABA-ALI Model Bus.Corp.Act § 53(b); McKinney's N.Y.Bus.Corp.Law, § 801(b) (6). Delaware merely authorizes amendment of the articles of incorporation to "change the period of . . . duration" of a corporation. Del.Gen.Corp.Law § 242(a) (6) (1967). Pontiac Improvement Co. v. Leisy, 144 Neb. 705, 14 N.W.2d 384 (1944). See section 345 supra.

7. E. g., Idaho, Minnesota, Washington. See Note, "Dissenters' Rights and Corporate Survival: A Reexamination of Some Redemption Statutes", 62 Yale L.J. 497 (1953).

8. Del.Gen.Corp.Law, § 312 (1967).

9. Cf. Ark.Op.Att'y Gen., Sept. 24, 1958, Dec. 5, 1958. See also State ex rel. Holekamp v. Holekamp Lumber Co., 331 S.W.2d 171 (St. Louis Ct.App.1960), rev'd 340 S.W.2d 678 (Mo.1960), appeal dismissed 366 U.S. 715, 81 S.Ct. 1660, 6 L.Ed.2d 846 (1961), petition for reh. denied 368 U.S. 820, 82 S.Ct. 26, 7 L. Ed.2d 71 (1961) (extension).

DISSOLUTION

348. Dissolution by corporate action without judicial proceedings is usually provided by statutes, which also often provide for judicial dissolution. Even absent statutory authorization, courts sometimes can dissolve a corporation for mismanagement or even deadlock. Statutes often also provide for dissolution or annulment or forfeiture of charter in the event of various contingencies. Typically, for nonjudicial dissolution, shareholder approval is required, and no appraisal remedy is ordinarily provided. The shareholders, subject to any applicable liquidation preferences and other rights, share proportionately in the net assets remaining after the satisfaction of creditors. Courts will prevent dissolutions which are unduly oppressive of minority shareholders, especially where dissolution is effected to "squeeze out" or "freeze out" the minority. Statutes continue corporate existence after dissolution for various purposes, including suing and being sued. Corporate liquidations can avoid federal income tax consequences at the corporate level and sometimes be tax-free.

Corporate existence usually begins with the filing of articles of incorporation or issuance of a formal "certificate of incorporation" and, absent a provision for some duration other than perpetual, continues until dissolution or annulment of charter.

As stated by Cardozo, Ch. J.: [1]

"Neither bankruptcy . . . nor cessation of business . . . nor dispersion of stockholders, nor the absence of directors . . . nor all combined, will avail without more to stifle the breath of juristic personality. The corporation abides as an ideal creation, impervious to the shocks of these temporal viscissitudes. Not even the sequestration of the assets at the hands of a receiver will terminate its being."

Except in jurisdictions where dissolution is difficult, which difficulty sometimes encourages the formation of corporations of limited duration, or foreshortening duration by amendment of articles of incorporation, and except in jurisdictions which limit duration,[2] most corporations are formed for theoretically perpetual duration.

In the event of dissolution, in jurisdictions with a calendar taxable year, completion of dissolution prior to January 1st often involves substantial tax savings.[3]

A corporation formally qualified to do business in another jurisdiction, upon dissolution, should withdraw or surrender its certificate of authority, although it would thereafter, to some extent, remain amenable to process in such other jurisdiction.[4]

Statutes usually provide for effecting dissolution by corporate action without judicial proceedings, known as "nonjudicial dissolution", and for dissolution by judicial proceedings, known as "judicial dissolution".[5]

1. Petrogradsky Mejdunarodny Kommerchesky Bank v. Nat'l City Bank, 253 N.Y. 23, 31–32, 170 N.E. 479, 482 (1930), reargument denied 254 N.Y. 563, 173 N. E. 867 (1931), cert. denied 282 U.S. 878, 51 S.Ct. 82, 75 L.Ed. 775 (1931). At common law, upon dissolution, the corporation's real property reverted to the original grantor or his heirs; the personal property escheated to the state; all debts to and from the corporation were extinguished; and the corporation could neither sue nor be sued. 1 Blackstone, Commentaries *484.

2. See Tognizzini v. Jordan, 165 Cal. 19, 130 P. 879 (1913). See section 120 supra.

3. See Walker Center Corp. v. State Tax Commission, 20 Utah 2d 346, 437 P.2d 888 (1968).

4. ABA–ALI Model Bus.Corp.Act §§ 112, 113. See Dr. Hess & Clark, Inc. v. Metalsalts Corp., 119 F. Supp. 427 (D.N.J.1954). See section 97 supra.

5. H. Rumpf, Corporate Liquidations—For the Lawyer and Accountant (2d ed. 1965); J. Tingle, The Stockholder's Remedy of Corporate Dissolution (1959); Barker, "The Dissolution of Corporations Under California Law", in Advising California Business Enterprises 1109–1160 (1958). New York has separate articles for nonjudicial dissolution [McKinney's N.Y.Bus.Corp.Law, art. 10, §§ 1001–1010], and for judicial dissolution [id. art. 11, §§ 1107–1117], and also authorizes the articles of incorporation to provide that any shareholder or holders of any percentage of shares may enforce dissolution at will or upon the occurrence of any specified event [id. § 1002]. For discussion of nonjudicial dissolution under provision in articles of incorporation, and agreements among shareholders as to exercise of their voting rights to dissolve, see sections 269, 277, 280 supra. In re Mercantile Guaranty Co., 238 Cal.App.2d 426, 48 Cal.Rptr. 589, 19 A.L.R.3d 1267 (1965), held that the California

Even absent statutory authorization, courts sometimes can dissolve a corporation for mismanagement [6] or even deadlock.[7] Statutes often also provide for dissolution, or annulment or forfeiture of charter in the event of various contingencies.[8]

Typically, in cases of statutes providing for dissolution without judicial proceedings, shareholder approval is required, and no appraisal remedy is ordinarily provided. The shareholders, subject to any applicable liquidation preferences and other rights,[9] share proportionately in the net assets remaining after the satisfaction of corporate creditors.[10]

Courts will prevent dissolutions which are unduly oppressive of minority shareholders, especially where dissolution is effected to "squeeze out" or "freeze out" the minority.[11]

The statutes continue corporate existence after dissolution for various purposes, including suing and being sued; such statutory formulations exist in many variations.[12]

The Model Business Corporation Act has a separate section providing for voluntary dissolution of a corporation by its incorporators at any time within two years after the issuance of its "certificate of incorporation" if it has not commenced business and has not issued any shares.[13]

Otherwise under the Model Act, voluntary dissolution requires either unanimous written consent of all shareholders of the corporation,[14] or board of directors resolution and the affirmative vote at a shareholder meeting of the holders of at least two-thirds (majority under 1969 revision) of the outstanding shares of the corporation entitled to vote thereon. If class voting is prescribed in the articles, the vote must be

---

courts had jurisdiction to wind up the affairs of a Delaware corporation where all of its assets, books, and records were in California and all of its business had been conducted in California; to appoint a trustee to represent the defunct corporate shareholder; and to vote for dissolution. Sometimes corporations cease doing business and wind up and liquidate without the formality of dissolution.

6. Hornstein, "Voluntary Dissolution—A New Development in Intra-Corporate Abuse", 51 Yale L.J. 64 (1941). See section 375 infra.

7. See section 280 supra.

8. E. g., ABA–ALI Model Bus.Corp.Act §§ 87 et seq.; Cavanaugh, "'Automatic' Forfeiture of Corporate Charters", 16 Bus.Law. 676 (1961). See also Sheard, "Forfeiture of Non-Profit Corporation Charters", 14 Clev.-Mar.L.Rev. 253 (1965). See section 144 supra.

9. See section 382 infra.

10. See section 381 infra. In Kellogg v. Georgia-Pacific Paper Corp., 227 F.Supp. 719 (W.D.Ark.1964), a minority shareholder of The Crossett Company complained against a plan of liquidation and distribution whereby Georgia-Pacific Paper Corp., which had acquired 99.6 percent of the shares of The Crossett Company, took over practically all the latter's assets and business as its distributive share in liquidation, and the minority shareholders would receive their distributive share in cash at $54.85 per share, fixed by Georgia-Pacific Paper Corp. on basis of the book value of the shares. The court held that, under Arkansas law, Georgia-Pacific Paper Corp., in liquidating The Crossett Company, "had a right to distribute the assets in kind or to put them on the block for sale and divide the proceeds, in either case treating all stockholders alike. It had no right to take over The Crossett Company as a going business and eliminate plaintiffs' interests in that company by cash payments." See Commonwealth v. Passell, 422 Pa. 473, 223 A.2d 24 (1966) (holding that real property of corporation upon its dissolution passed by operation of law to its shareholders as tenants in common and subsequent deed was merely confirmatory); Hampton v. Hampton Beach

Improvement Co., 107 N.H. 89, 218 A.2d 442 (1966) (holding that lease made by corporation prior to revocation of its charter survived dissolution and, since assignable, passed to corporation's shareholders); Blanchard v. Commonwealth Oil Co., 116 So. 2d 663 (Fla.Dist.Ct.App.1959) (holding that demand of minority shareholders of dissolved corporation for distribution in kind rather than sale of assets and distribution of cash should have been honored absent showing of need for latter method). See McKinney's N.Y.Bus.Corp.Law, § 1005(a) (3) (A) (permitting corporation, with majority shareholder approval, to sell its remaining assets for shares, bonds, and other securities, or partly therefor and partly for cash, to be distributed among its shareholders, affording appraisal remedy to nonassenting shareholders).

11. See note 28 infra.

12. See Note, 40 Cornell L.Q. 610 (1955).

13. ABA–ALI Model Bus.Corp.Act § 75 (two-year limitation repealed in 1969 Model Act revision); Del. Gen.Corp.Law, § 274 (1967); McKinney's N.Y.Bus. Corp.Law, § 615(c) (by subscribers to shares whose subscriptions have been accepted or, if none, by incorporator(s), where there are no shareholders of record).

14. ABA–ALI Model Bus.Corp.Act § 76.

of two-thirds (majority under 1969 revision) of any such class as well as of the total outstanding voting shares.[15]

The articles of incorporation can require a greater vote for dissolution.[16] No appraisal remedy is provided dissenting shareholders.[17]

In keeping with the usual duplicate filing requirements of the Model Act, the procedure involves the delivery to the secretary of state of duplicate originals of a "statement of intent to dissolve", one of which is filed and the other returned to the corporation or its representative.[18] Thereupon, the corporation should wind up its business[19] and comply with the required procedures.[20]

The Model Act allows revocation of voluntary dissolution proceedings; such revocation requires appropriate shareholder approval.[21]

"certificate of dissolution" is filed, which should not be confused with the formal "certificate of dissolution" issued under the Model Act—see note 23 infra.

19. ABA–ALI Model Bus.Corp.Act § 79; Del.Gen. Corp.Law, §§ 278, 282 (1967) (continuation of corporation after dissolution for three years for purposes of suing and being sued and winding up affairs); McKinney's N.Y.Bus.Corp.Law, § 1006; United States v. Brakes, Inc., 157 F.Supp. 916 (S.D.N.Y. 1958) (criminal proceeding); Milton L. Ehrlich, Inc. v. Unit Frame & Floor Corp., 5 N.Y.2d 275, 184 N.Y.S. 2d 334, 157 N.E.2d 495, 71 A.L.R.2d 1115 (1959) (arbitration, prior to express statutory provision therefor). See Borbein, Young & Co. v. Cirese, 401 S.W. 2d 940 (Mo.Ct.App.1966) (directors and officers of dissolved corporation held personally liable on debt contracted by corporation during winding up period in violation of their duties as trustees to liquidate corporation). See Schoone, "Shareholder Liability upon Voluntary Dissolution of Corporation", 44 Marq.L.Rev. 415 (1961).

20. ABA–ALI Model Bus.Corp.Act § 80. In New York, the corporation, at any time after dissolution, may give notice requiring all creditors and claimants to present their claims at a specified place and by a specified day, which shall not be less than six months after the first publication of such notice; such notice to be published at least once a week for two successive weeks; on or before the date of first publication of the notice, the corporation shall mail a copy thereof to each person believed to be a creditor or claimant against the corporation whose name and address are known to or can with due diligence be ascertained by the corporation; claims, except tax claims and other claims of New York State and the United States, are required to be filed; claims not timely filed as provided in the notice, except claims in litigation on the date of first publication of the notice, and claims filed but disallowed by the court, are forever barred as against the corporation, its assets, directors, officers, and shareholders, except to the extent, if any, as the court may allow them against any remaining assets of the corporation. McKinney's N.Y.Bus. Corp.Law, § 1007.

21. ABA–ALI Model Bus.Corp.Act §§ 81, 82, 83, 84. Until 1962, revocation required the affirmative vote of the holders of at least two-thirds of the outstanding shares. See also ABA–ALI Model Bus. Corp.Act § 81 (Revocation of voluntary dissolution proceedings by consent of shareholders). Duplicate originals are delivered to the secretary of state for filing. ABA–ALI Model Bus.Corp.Act § 83. Revocation is effective upon such filing, "and the corporation may again carry on its business". ABA–ALI

15. ABA–ALI Model Bus.Corp.Act § 77. The 1969 Model Act revision requires only the affirmative vote of the holders of a majority of the shares entitled to vote thereon, subject to any class voting requirements. Until 1962, authorization by the holders of two-thirds of all outstanding shares, whether or not otherwise entitled to vote, was required. See also Del.Gen.Corp.Law, § 275 (1967); McKinney's N.Y.Bus.Corp.Law, § 1001 (two-thirds of outstanding shares entitled to vote thereon).

16. ABA–ALI Model Bus.Corp.Act § 136. See sections 191, 266 supra.

17. But see ABA–ALI Model Bus.Corp.Act § 73 (sale of assets in contemplation of merger subject to appraisal remedy); Flarsheim v. Twenty Five Thirty Two Broadway Corp., 432 S.W.2d 245 (Mo.1968) (sale of all assets in preparation for dissolution held subject to appraisal remedy applicable to sale of assets). In New York, no appraisal remedy is afforded dissenting shareholders, except that where its remaining assets are sold to another corporation for shares, bonds, or other securities of the latter, or partly therefor and partly for cash, to be distributed proportionately among shareholders of the dissolved corporation (when authorized by the holders of a majority of the outstanding shares of such corporation entitled to vote thereon), the dissenting shareholders of such corporation are entitled to appraisal. McKinney's N.Y.Bus.Corp.Law § 1005(a) (3) (A). See also Fla.Gen.Corp.Law, § 608.30(3) (b) (1953); N.C.Bus.Corp.Act § 55–119(b) (1957).

18. ABA–ALI Model Bus.Corp.Act § 78. Under the Model Act, the three stages are: (a) Statement of intent to dissolve, (b) Winding up or liquidation, and (c) "Dissolution". In some other jurisdictions, "dissolution" is the first stage, not the final stage: (a) "Dissolution", (b) Winding up or liquidation, and (c) "Termination"—the latter terminology being analogous to that of partnership law. See Uniform Partnership Act § 30; Del.Gen.Corp.Law, §§ 275, 278 (1967); former McKinney's N.Y.Stock Corp. Law, § 107. The Texas attorney general has ruled that the secretary of state need not accept a statement of intent to dissolve from a corporation which lists less than three directors. Tex.Op.Att'y Gen. No. C–773, Oct. 6, 1966. In some jurisdictions, a

Absent revocation, after payment or provision for all corporate debts, liabilities, and obligations, and distribution of the net assets to shareholders, duplicate originals of "articles of dissolution" are delivered to the secretary of state under the Model Act.[22]

Upon the issuance of a "certificate of dissolution", the existence of the corporation ceases, except for the purpose of actions, other proceedings, etc.[23]

Court supervision of liquidation in connection with nonjudicial dissolution is often provided.[24]

Other provisions in the Model Act deal with involuntary dissolution,[25] and judicial liquidation (in actions by a shareholder under limited circumstances, a creditor, or the attorney general, or upon application of a corporation which has filed a statement of intent to dissolve).[26]

Model Bus.Corp.Act § 84. In jurisdictions without such revocation provisions, to resume business a new corporation usually must be formed since the corporate extension and revival provisions usually do not apply to such a situation. In Delaware, voluntary dissolution may be revoked during the three-year winding up period with shareholder approval. Del.Gen.Corp.Law, § 311 (1967). In New York, once the articles of dissolution are filed, the corporation is dissolved and such dissolution cannot be revoked. See section 347 supra.

22. ABA–ALI Model Bus.Corp.Act §§ 85, 86. New York, prior to 1963, required the filing and publication of a "certificate of termination" to terminate corporate existence, except for pending actions.

23. ABA–ALI Model Bus.Corp.Act § 86; see also id. § 79. Melrose Distillers, Inc. v. United States, 359 U.S. 271, 79 S.Ct. 763, 3 L.Ed.2d 800 (1959); United States v. P. F. Collier & Son Corp., 208 F.2d 936, 40 A.L.R.2d 1389 (7th Cir. 1953); Marcus, "Liability of Dissolved Corporations—A Study in Interstate and Federal-State Relationships", 58 Harv.L.Rev. 675 (1945); Note, "Federal Criminal Actions Against Dissolved Corporations", 1959 Duke L.J. 292. However, the corporation cannot, by dissolution, avoid liability on long-term employment contracts [Martin v. Star Publishing Co., 48 Del. 106, 126 A.2d 238 (Sup.Ct.1956)], share options [Gamble v. Penn Valley Crude Oil Corp., 34 Del.Ch. 359, 104 A.2d 257 (Ch.1954)], or other contracts [In re Mosquito Hawks, Inc., 109 So.2d 815 (La.Ct.App.1959)]. Shareholders might be liable for dissolving the corporation and thus preventing it from performing its contracts. W. P. Iverson & Co. v. Dunham Mfg. Cir. 1963], remanded sub nom. Textile Workers Union of America v. Darlington Mfg. Co., 380 U.S. 263, 85 S.Ct. 994, 13 L.Ed.2d 827 (1965) (upholding right of corporation to close entire, but not part of, business to avoid dealing with union). As to dissolved corporation's rights and liabilities under various circumstances, see Hall v. Pilgrim Plywood Corp., 126 Vt. 224, 227 A.2d 285 (1967); Ainsley Realty Co. v. Kramer, 189 So.2d 609 (Fla.1966); Security Nat'l Bank v. Plymouth Cheese Co., 3 Wis.2d 4, 87 N.W.2d 780 (1958); Means v. Norwood, 319 S.W.2d 817 (Tex.Civ.App.1958); Addy v. Short, 47 Del. 157, 89 A.2d 136 (Sup.Ct.1952); K. & J. Markets, Inc. v. Martin Packing Corp., 18 N.J.Super. 124, 86 A.2d 715 (1952); Nardis Sportswear v. Simmons, 147 Tex. 608, 218 S.W.2d 451 (1949); Kay Furniture Co. v. Rovin, 312 Mich. 290, 20 N.W.2d

194 (1945). See also Annot., 75 A.L.R.2d 1399 (1961). See Christensen v. Boss, 179 Neb. 429, 138 N.W.2d 716 (1965) (holding dissolution not subject to collateral attack in action brought after five-year survival period after issuance of certificate of incorporation). The formal "certificate of dissolution" under the Model Act should not be confused with the instrument of the same name in other jurisdictions which is equivalent to the Model Act "statement of intent to dissolve"—see note 15 supra.

24. E. g., ABA–ALI Model Bus.Corp.Act §§ 90–98; Del.Gen.Corp.Law, § 279 (1967); McKinney's N.Y. Bus.Corp.Law, § 1008.

25. See ABA–ALI Model Bus.Corp.Act § 87 (Listing as grounds for action by attorney general for involuntary dissolution: (a) failure to file annual report or pay franchise tax; (b) procurement of articles of incorporation through fraud; (c) exceeding or abusing authority; (d) failure to appoint and maintain registered agent in state, or (e) failure to file statement of change of registered office or registered agent), § 88 (Notification by secretary of state to attorney general), § 89 (Venue and process). Such statutory enumeration of grounds for dissolution might be expressly stated as not excluding actions or special proceedings by the attorney general or other state officials for the annulment or dissolution of a corporation for other causes as provided in the corporate or other statutes. E. g., McKinney's N.Y.Bus.Corp.Law, § 1101(c).

26. See ABA–ALI Model Bus.Corp.Act § 90 (Jurisdiction of court to liquidate assets and business of corporation), § 91 (Procedure in liquidation of corporation by court), § 92 (Qualifications of receivers), § 93 (Filing of claims in liquidation proceedings), § 94 (Discontinuance of liquidation proceedings when established that cause for liquidation no longer exists), § 95 (Decree of involuntary dissolution), § 96 (Duty of court clerk to cause certified copy of dissolution decree to be filed with secretary of state), § 97 (Deposit with state treasurer of assets distributable to creditor or shareholder who is unknown, cannot be found or is under legal disability), § 98 (Survival of remedy after dissolution). New York, besides authorizing the attorney general to bring an action for judicial dissolution, authorizes the majority of the board of directors or a majority of the shareholders to petition for judicial dissolution where the corporation's assets are not sufficient to discharge its liabilities or where dissolution will be

Statutes often provide for dissolution of corporations for failure to file required reports or to pay certain taxes.[27]

The power of the controlling shareholders to dissolve is subject to equitable limitations.[28]

beneficial to the shareholders. McKinney's N.Y. Bus.Corp.Law, §§ 1101–1103. Petition by holders of one-half (or one-third when articles of incorporation provide for greater-than-normal board of directors or shareholder vote) of the shares entitled to vote at an election of directors is also allowed in specified cases of deadlock. Id. § 1104. The procedures involved and limitations on such judicial dissolution have been previously discussed (see section 280 supra). McKinney's N.Y.Bus.Corp.Law, § 1111(b) sets forth the following criteria for the court to consider in exercising its discretion to dissolve a corporation: "(1) In an action brought by the attorney-general, the interest of the public is of paramount importance. (2) In a special proceeding brought by directors or shareholders, the benefit to the shareholders of a dissolution is of paramount importance. (3) In a special proceeding brought under section 1104 (Petition in case of deadlock among directors or shareholders) dissolution is not to be denied merely because it is found that the corporate business has been or could be conducted at a profit." In contrast to nonjudicial dissolution, a judicial dissolution proceeding may be discontinued with the consent of all the interested parties. Matter of Fine Sound, Inc., 5 A.D.2d 973, 172 N.Y.S.2d 200 (1st Dep't 1958) amended in other respect 6 A.D. 2d 777, 175 N.Y.S.2d 15 (1st Dep't 1958). The New York statute also contains detailed receivership provisions. McKinney's N.Y.Bus.Corp.Law art. 12, §§ 1201–1218. Statutes usually authorize proceedings for forfeiture or annulment of corporate charters. Del.Gen.Corp.Law, §§ 283–284 (1967); 4 I. Kantrowitz & S. Slutsky, White on New York Corporations ¶ 1161.01 (13th ed. 1968).

27. E. g., McKinney's N.Y.Tax Law, § 203–a (failure to file tax reports or to pay taxes assessed for period of any three years). For reinstatement provision, see McKinney's N.Y.Tax Law, § 203–a(7) (nunc pro tunc upon payment of tax arrears and penalties). For nonpayment of taxes, some 5,000 corporations in New York (over 250,000 during the 10 depression years) and 3,000 corporations in Delaware are dissolved annually. Some corporations going out of business seem to prefer this method of "informal dissolution". A corporation between such dissolution and reinstatement might have a de facto existence but runs the risk of being treated as a partnership. Jones v. Young, 115 W.Va. 225, 174 S.E. 885 (1934). See Note, "Dissolution and Suspension as Remedies for Corporate Franchise Tax Delinquency: A Comparative Analysis", 41 N.Y.U.L. Rev. 602 (1966).

28. Lebold v. Inland Steel Co., 125 F.2d 369 (7th Cir. 1941), cert. denied 316 U.S. 675, 62 S.Ct. 1045, 86 L. Ed. 1749 (1942); Eisenberg v. Central Zone Property Corp., 306 N.Y. 58, 115 N.E.2d 652 (1953);

Miscellaneous

Corporate liquidations can avoid federal income tax consequences at the corporate level and sometimes be tax-free.[29]

DISSENTING SHAREHOLDER'S APPRAISAL REMEDY

349. The dissenting shareholder's appraisal remedy is essentially a statutory creation to enable shareholders who object to certain extraordinary matters to dissent and to require the corporation to buy their shares at the value immediately prior to the approval of such matter and thus to withdraw from the corporation. In different jurisdictions, the appraisal remedy often applies to sales of substantially all corporate assets other than in the regular course of business, mergers, and consolidations, more rarely to certain amendments of the articles of incorporation or miscellaneous matters, but usually not to dissolution. The appraisal remedy is often limited to shareholders of record entitled to vote on the matter. Where the matter is authorized by statute, the required intracorporate procedures are followed, and no fraud or inequity is involved, the appraisal remedy is often exclusive. To secure appraisal, the dissenting shareholder must timely file objection and demand for payment, submit his share certificates for appropriate notation, and, if no agreement can be reached as to the fair price of the shares, commence court appraisal proceedings. Shareholder status of the dissenting shareholders ends in different jurisdictions at different stages of the appraisal proceedings. Provisions differ as to assessment of the costs and expenses of the appraisal proceeding. Often there is no restriction on the funds available to the corporation to pur-

Shrage v. Bridgeport Oil Co., 31 Del.Ch. 305, 71 A. 2d 882 (Ch.1950), modifying 31 Del.Ch. 203, 68 A.2d 317 (Ch.1949). Kavanaugh v. Kavanaugh Knitting Co., 226 N.Y. 185, 123 N.E. 148 (1919); Ribakove v. Rich, 13 Misc.2d 98, 173 N.Y.S.2d 306 (Sup.Ct.1958). Cf. Kirwan v. Parkway Distillery, Inc., 285 Ky. 605, 148 S.W.2d 720 (1941). See F. O'Neal & J. Derwin, Expulsion or Oppression of Business Associates: "Squeeze-Outs" in Small Enterprises §§ 4.09 et seq. (1961); Sprecher, "The Right of Minority Stockholders to Prevent the Dissolution of a Profitable Enterprise", 33 Ky.L.J. 150 (1945). Cf. Matter of Roehner v. Gracie Manor, Inc., 6 N.Y.2d 280, 189 N.Y.S.2d 644, 160 N.E.2d 519 (1959).

29. See section 381 infra.

chase the shares of dissenting shareholders, short of insolvency.

The appraisal remedy is essentially a statutory creation[1] to enable shareholders who object to certain extraordinary corporate matters to dissent and to require the corporation to buy their shares at the value immediately prior to the approval of the matter and thus to withdraw from the corporation. Usually, no appraisal remedy is afforded shareholders in the event of dissolution.[2]

Some jurisdictions provide an appraisal remedy to dissenting shareholders in several situations. Most jurisdictions provide for an appraisal remedy at least in the event of the sale of substantially all the corporate assets other than in the regular course of business, merger, or consolidation.[3]

At the opposite extreme, at least one jurisdiction provides no statutory appraisal remedy for any extraordinary corporate matter.[4]

New York allows appraisal to dissenting shareholders in the event of any sale, lease, exchange or other disposition of all or substantially all the assets of a corporation which requires shareholder approval under the statute other than a transaction wholly for cash where shareholders' approval thereof is conditioned upon the dissolution of the corporation and distribution of substantially all of its net assets to shareholders in accordance with their respective interests within one year after the date of such transaction; any merger or consolidation to which a corporation is a party except for any shareholder of a surviving corporation in a short merger or any other merger unless such other merger has certain adverse effects on the shares held by such shareholder; any amendment of articles of incorporation adversely affecting specified rights of shares; any sale by a dissolved corporation of its remaining assets, or any part thereof, for shares, bonds or other securities or partly for cash and partly for shares, bonds or other securities, to be distributed among its shareholders according to their respective rights.[5]

---

1. Sometimes called the "right to dissent" or "right to receive payment for shares"—appraisal being the remedy only when the corporation and dissenting shareholders cannot agree on the fair price of the shares. Dissenting shareholders receiving cash for their shares may be subject to federal income tax; as to other shareholders, the reorganization would usually be tax-free. Shareholder given this information might be less likely to dissent. Manning, "The Shareholder's Appraisal Remedy: An Essay for Frank Coker", 72 Yale L.J. 223 (1962); Kaplan, "Problems in the Acquisition of Shares of Dissenting Minorities", 34 B.U.L.Rev. 291 (1954); Lattin, "A Reappraisal of Appraisal Statutes", 38 Mich.L. Rev. 1165 (1940); Comment, "Dissenting Minority Stockholder's Right of Appraisal", 4 B.C.Ind. & Com.L.Rev. 85 (1962); Comment, "The Right of Shareholders Dissenting From Corporate Combinations To Demand Cash Payment for Their Shares", 72 Harv.L.Rev. 1132 (1959); Comment, "Interplay of Rights of Stockholders Dissenting from Sale of Corporate Assets", 58 Colum.L.Rev. 251 (1958); see Troupiansky v. Henry Disston & Sons, 151 F.Supp. 609 (E.D.Pa.1957) (appraisal rights of shareholders objecting to sale of assets in absence of appraisal statute). Cf. Garzo v. Maid of the Mist Steamboat Co., 303 N.Y. 516, 104 N.E.2d 882 (1952).

2. But see section 348, n. 17 supra.

3. Most jurisdictions grant appraisal to dissenters from mergers (at least to shareholders of nonsurviving corporations) or consolidations; about half to dissenters from asset sales; a smaller number to dissenters from at least certain amendments of the articles of incorporation; a few to dissenters from extension or revival and miscellaneous other matters. Skoler, "Some Observations on the Scope of Appraisal Statutes", 13 Bus.Law. 240 (1958); Comment, "The Dissenting Shareholder: Appraisal and Other Rights Under the Texas Business Corporation Act", 17 Sw.L.J. 279 (1963); Comment, "The

Right of Shareholders Dissenting From Corporate Combinations To Demand Cash Payment for Their Shares", 72 Harv.L.Rev. 1132 (1959); Note, 67 Yale L.J. 1288, 1289, n. 6 (1958); Annot., 87 A.L.R. 597 (1933), 162 A.L.R. 1237 (1946), 174 A.L.R. 960 (1948). See notes 9, 10 infra.

4. West Virginia. See also Schwabacher v. United States, 334 U.S. 182, 68 S.Ct. 958, 92 L.Ed.2d 1305 (1948) (merger of interstate railroad corporations formed under state laws held subject to federal law, and rights granted to dissenting shareholders held not to survive merger approved by Interstate Commerce Commission as just and reasonable).

5. McKinney's N.Y.Bus.Corp.Law, §§ 910(a), 806(b) (6), 1005(a) (3) (A); Matter of McKay v. Teleprompter Corp., 19 A.D.2d 815, 243 N.Y.S.2d 591 (1st Dep't 1963), appeal dismissed 13 N.Y.2d 1058, 246 N.Y.S.2d 34, 195 N.E.2d 762 (1963) (where notice to shareholders stated that dissenting shareholders would enjoy appraisal remedy, corporation held estopped from denying appraisal on ground statute did not afford it to sale in question); Matter of Rosenshein,

The Model Business Corporation Act provides for appraisal in certain cases of merger or consolidation, or sale or exchange of all or substantially all the corporate assets other than in the regular course of business.[6]

Delaware limits appraisal to certain kinds of consolidation or merger.[7]

16 A.D.2d 537, 229 N.Y.S.2d 14 (1st Dep't 1962) (appraisal remedy held inapplicable where shareholder consent required for sale of corporate property by shareholder agreement). Amendments of articles of incorporation with the specified adverse effect are those altering or abolishing any preferential right of any outstanding shares having preferences, creating, altering or abolishing any provision or right in respect of the redemption of any outstanding shares, altering or abolishing any preemptive right of such holder to acquire shares or other securities, or excluding or limiting the right of such holder to vote on any matter, except as such right may be limited by voting rights given to new shares then being authorized of any existing or new class. The required adverse effect has been found in cases of reduction of stated capital but not the creation of prior preferred shares [Matter of Kinney, 279 N.Y. 423, 18 N.E.2d 645 (1939); Matter of Dresser, 247 N.Y. 553, 161 N.E. 179 (1928)], and reduction of par value resulting in decrease of liquidation preference geared to par value [Sterling v. 16 Park Avenue, Inc., 132 N.Y.S.2d 921 (Sup.Ct.1954), modified 284 App.Div. 1033, 136 N.Y.S.2d 363 (1st Dep't 1954)]. Enlarging voting rights of existing preferred shares or the abolition of cumulative voting has been held to involve the abolition of a voting right. Matter of Marcus (R. H. Macy & Co.), 297 N.Y. 38, 74 N.E.2d 228 (1947); Matter of New York Hanseatic Corp. (Kings Co. Lighting Co.), 200 Misc. 530, 103 N.Y.S.2d 698 (Sup.Ct.1951). But see McKinney's N.Y.Bus. Corp.Law, § 808. See section 350 infra.

6. ABA–ALI Model Bus.Corp.Act §§ 73, 74; see also § 68A (optional short merger provision). The 1969 Model Act revision provides that its appraisal section "shall not apply to the shareholders of the surviving corporation in a merger if such corporation is on the date of the filing of the articles of merger the owner of all outstanding shares of the other corporations, domestic or foreign, which are parties to the merger or if a vote of the shareholders of such corporation is not necessary to authorize such merger. Nor shall it apply to the holders of shares of any class or series if the shares of such class or series were registered on a national securities exchange on the date fixed to determine the shareholders entitled to receive notice of and to vote at the meeting of shareholders at which a plan of merger or consolidation or a proposed sale or exchange of property and assets is to be acted upon unless the articles of incorporation of the corporation shall otherwise provide." See Squires, "Dissenting Shareholder's Appraisal Remedy Under the Illinois Business Corporation Act", 53 Ill.B.J. 482 (1965).

7. Del.Gen.Corp.Law, § 262 (1967) (except, unless otherwise provided in articles of incorporation, share-

Different extraordinary corporate matters, as previously mentioned,[8] can have the same practical effect. In a few jurisdictions, purchases of substantially all assets, under complicated plans (a) where the effect was the same as that of a merger, have been held to be "de facto mergers" subject to the appraisal remedy applicable to mergers,[9] or

holders of surviving corporation in merger involving no more than 15 percent increase of corporation's outstanding shares, holders of shares listed on any national securities exchange, and holders of shares of any class held of record by not less than 2,000 shareholders, whether or not listed on any exchange—if shareholders under plan are to receive solely shares of surviving or consolidated corporations); id. § 253 (except shareholders of parent corporation when a 90-100 percent owned subsidiary merges into it or vice versa); Kerr & Letts, "Appraisal Procedures for Dissenting Delaware Stockholders", 20 Bus.Law. 1083 (1965). See also Pa.Bus. Corp.Law, § 908 (Supp.1969).

8. See section 340 supra.

9. Farris v. Glen Alden Corp., 393 Pa. 427, 143 A.2d 25 (1958) (enjoining "reorganization agreement" on ground that it was more than a simple purchase of assets, for which Pennsylvania law afforded no appraisal remedy to dissenting shareholder of *purchasing* corporation, but was (a) "de facto merger" for which Pennsylvania law afforded appraisal remedy to dissenting shareholders of corporations involved, and (b) "upside-down sale" in which selling corporation was in effect acquiring purchasing corporation's assets, for which Pennsylvania law afforded appraisal remedy to dissenting shareholders of *selling* corporation. See also Butze v. T. J. W. Corp., 29 F.R.D. 474 (M.D.Pa.1962); Troupiansky v. Henry Disston & Sons, 151 F.Supp. 609 (E. D.Pa.1957). Pa.Bus.Corp.Law, § 908(c) (Supp.1969), as amended in 1958 (effective Nov. 10, 1959), reads "Where a corporation acquires assets by purchase, lease or exchange, by the issuance of shares, evidences of indebtedness or otherwise, with or without assuming liabilities other than by the procedure for merger or consolidation prescribed in this Article IX, the rights, if any, of dissenting shareholders shall be governed by section 311 (Voluntary transfer of corporate assets) and not by this section 908." Applestein v. United Board & Carton Corp., 60 N.J.Super. 333, 159 A.2d 146 (1960), aff'd per curiam 33 N.J. 72, 161 A.2d 474 (1960) (exchange of all shares in corporation by sole shareholder for 40 percent of shares and control of board of directors of second corporation and complete absorption by second corporation of first corporation's business). But see Good v. Lackawanna Leather Co., 96 N.J.2d 439, 233 A.2d 201 (1967); Hariton v. Arco Electronics, Inc., 41 Del.Ch. 74, 188 A.2d 123 (Sup.Ct.1963), aff'g 40 Del.Ch. 326, 182 A.2d 22 (Ch.1962) (upholding sale as authorized by sale-of-assets statute, found to be independent of, and of equal dignity with, merger statute, and denying injunction sought

(b) where the effect was that of a sale of substantially all assets, held to be "upside-down sales" subject to the appraisal remedy applicable to sales of substantially all assets not in the regular course of business.[10]

In many cases, the appraisal remedy is limited to shareholders of record entitled to vote on the matter, but there are exceptions.[11]

The value which the dissenting shareholder is entitled to receive is variously defined

---

by dissenting shareholder of *selling* corporation who contended transaction constituted de facto merger entitling dissenting shareholders to appraisal remedy under Delaware law); Orzeck v. Englehart, 41 Del.Ch. 361, 195 A.2d 375 (Sup.Ct.1963) (holding purchase by inactive Delaware corporation of all shares of seven active California corporations, former becoming holding company, no de facto merger entitling minority shareholder of former to appraisal remedy); Alcott v. Hyman, 40 Del.Ch. 449, 184 A.2d 90 (Ch.1962), aff'd 42 Del.Ch. 233, 208 A.2d 501 (Sup.Ct.1965) (holding that sale by corporation of substantially all of its assets to corporation which had acquired most of its shares, for such shares and cash sufficient to redeem debt of selling corporation and pay $11.19 for shares which remained outstanding, where complaining minority shareholders continued to hold their shares in selling corporation, which was not to be dissolved for five years, did not constitute de facto merger entitling them to appraisal); Heilbrunn v. Sun Chemical Corp., 38 Del.Ch. 321, 150 A.2d 755 (Sup.Ct. 1959), aff'g 37 Del.Ch. 522, 146 A.2d 757 (Ch.1958) (holding that there was no de facto merger entitling dissenting shareholders of *purchasing* corporation to appraisal remedy); Folk, "De Facto Mergers in Delaware: Hariton v. Arco Electronics, Inc.", 49 Va.L.Rev. 1261 (1963). See also State of Washington ex rel. Carriger v. Campbell Food Markets, Inc., 60 Wash.2d 478, 374 P.2d 435 (1962) (holding that when control of corporation was purchased by another corporation and former retained its assets and continued its corporate business, there was no corporate merger or consolidation entitling objecting minority shareholder to appraisal remedy). Appraisal statutes might better emphasize the substantive effect a corporate act has on a shareholder instead of conditioning appraisal on form (i. e., merger, irregular sale of substantially all assets, etc.).

10. See Farris v. Glen Alden Corp., note 9 supra; Comment, "Corporations—Stockholders' Appraisal Rights—Dissenting Stockholders of Purchasing Corporation Protected by Ohio Statute", 35 U.Cin.L. Rev. 704 (1966).

11. See ABA-ALI Model Bus.Corp.Act §§ 67, 72; cf. § 55 (allowing holders of shares of class to vote as class on such matters regardless of voting rights conferred by articles of incorporation); Del.Gen. Corp.Law, § 262 (1967) (appraisal remedy to any shareholder who objected to merger or consolidation in writing and whose shares were not voted in favor thereof); cf. id. §§ 251(f), 262(k) (no shareholder

vote—and therefore no appraisal—required from shareholders of surviving corporation in merger which does increase corporation's outstanding shares by more than 15 percent); McKinney's N.Y. Bus.Corp.Law, §§ 806(b) (6), 910, 1005(a) (3) (A); see also § 613 (limitation on voting rights), § 804 (mandatory class voting on amendment of articles of incorporation), § 806(b) (6) (appraisal remedy of holder of any adversely affected shares), and § 909(a) (2) (notice to shareholders entitled to vote *or* to appraisal); Matter of Harwitz (Republic Pictures Corp.), 192 Misc. 91, 80 N.Y.S.2d 570 (Sup.Ct.1948). See also Matter of Bacon (Susquehanna Silk Mills), 287 N.Y. 1, 38 N.E.2d 105 (1941) (appraisal allowed voting trust certificate holders whose shares were not voted for sale); cf. Matter of Flagg-Utica Corp. v. Baselice, 14 Misc.2d 476, 178 N.Y.S.2d 860 (Sup. Ct.1958). See e. g., Ohio Gen.Corp.Law, §§ 1701.-76(C), 1701.81(B); cf. § 1701.74 (1955) ("whether or not entitled to vote"). See Pittman, "Corporations —Are Nonvoting Shares Entitled to Appraisal Rights?", 28 Mo.L.Rev. 246 (1963). Record ownership has been required as the basis for appraisal under several statutes. Lesch v. Chicago & Eastern Ill. R.R., 226 F.2d 687 (7th Cir. 1955) (construing Indiana statute); Abraham & Co. v. Olivetti Underwood Corp., 42 Del.Ch. 95, 204 A.2d 740 (Ch.1964) (upholding objection by shareholders of record without proof of their authority to act for beneficial owners); Carl M. Loeb, Rhoades & Co. v. Hilton Hotels Corp., 43 Del.Ch. 206, 222 A.2d 789 (Sup.Ct. 1966) (objection by beneficial owners of shares held in "street name" held insufficient, absent showing that they were acting as agents for shareholder of record; corporation held not estopped by treasurer's assurances); Coyne v. Schenley Industries, Inc., 38 Del.Ch. 535, 155 A.2d 238 (Sup.Ct.1959); In re Kreher, 379 Pa. 313, 108 A.2d 708 (1954); Era Co. v. Pittsburgh Consol. Coal Co., 355 Pa. 219, 49 A.2d 342 (1946); Salt Dome Oil Corp. v. Schenck, 28 Del.Ch. 433, 41 A.2d 583 (Sup.Ct.1945). See Nickles v. United Nuclear Corp., 41 Del.Ch. 234, 192 A. 2d 628 (Ch.1963), held that the Delaware statute did not require a dissenting shareholder to be a shareholder of record when he filed his written objection to a merger, it being sufficient that he be a shareholder of record before the taking of the vote (although after the record date). See also Bache & Co. v. General Instrument Corp., 42 N.J. 44, 198 A. 2d 759 (1964) (upholding objection by brokerage firm holding shares in "street name"); Bohrer v. United States Lines Co., 92 N.J.Super. 592, 224 A.2d 348 (1966) (upholding objection by beneficial owners of shares held in "street name"). New York cases, construing the New York statutory provisions, have allowed appraisal to shareholders not of record. Matter of Bacon (Susquehanna Silk Mills), 287 N.Y. 1, 38 N.E.2d 105 (1941); Matter of Deutschmann, 281 App.Div. 14, 116 N.Y.S.2d 578 (1st Dep't 1952); Matter of Friedman, 184 Misc. 639, 54 N.Y.S.2d 45 (Sup.Ct.1945), modified on other grounds 269 App. Div. 834, 56 N.Y.S.2d 516 (1st Dep't 1945); Matter of Bazar, 183 Misc. 736, 50 N.Y.S.2d 521 (Sup.Ct. 1944), aff'd mem., 271 App.Div. 1007, 69 N.Y.S.2d 910 (1st Dep't 1947). See Comment, "Corporations—

as "market value", "fair value", "value", or "fair cash value". In situations where there is a reliable market value, such value is, in some jurisdictions, presumptively controlling; [12] in other jurisdictions, market value is only one factor to be considered along with others, such as net asset value, dividends, earning prospects, the nature of the enterprise, etc. [13] Of course, even in the former jurisdictions, when there is no readily-ascertainable market value, various alternative indicia of value must be considered and weighted to determine what price would be fixed by the imaginary willing buyer and willing seller. [14]

Where the matter is authorized by statute, etc., and the required formal shareholder vote or consent secured, absent fraud or inequity, [15] the appraisal remedy is often exclusive, either expressly by statute [16] or by

Consolidation and Merger—Rights of Beneficial Owner Under the Appraisal Statutes", 49 Iowa L. Rev. 1309 (1963); Annot., 158 A.L.R. 983 (1945).

12. Warren v. Baltimore Transit Co., 220 Md. 478, 154 A.2d 796 (1959); Matter of Marcus (R. H. Macy & Co.), 191 Misc. 808, 77 N.Y.S.2d 529 (Sup.Ct.1948), modified 273 App.Div. 725, 79 N.Y.S.2d 76 (1st Dep't 1950), aff'd mem., 302 N.Y. 881, 100 N.E.2d 55 (1951), 303 N.Y. 711, 103 N.E.2d 338 (1951); Matter of Fulton, 257 N.Y. 487, 178 N.E. 766, 79 A.L.R. 608 (1931). If appraisal is aimed at market value, it is a meaningless remedy in corporations whose shares have an active market, since the dissatisfied shareholder can realize such value merely by selling his shares on such market. Recognizing this, the Delaware statute affords no appraisal remedy where shares are listed on a national securities exchange or where a class of shares, whether or not listed on an exchange, is held of record by not less than 2,000 shareholders. Del.Gen.Corp.Law, § 262(k) (1967). The appraised value should take into account the value of any corporate causes of action against management. Netter v. Ashland Paper Mills, Inc., 19 F.R.D. (S.D.N.Y.1957); Matter of Tabulating Card Co. v. Leidesdorf, 17 Misc.2d 573, 188 N.Y.S.2d 23 (Sup.Ct.1959); cf. Beloff v. Consolidated Edison Co. of New York, 300 N.Y. 11, 87 N.E. 2d 561 (1949). See Notes, 23 St.John's L.Rev. 325 (1949); 16 Brooklyn L.Rev. 86 (1949); 17 Fordham L.Rev. 259 (1948).

13. In re Olivetti Underwood Corp., —— Del.Ch. ——, 246 A.2d 800 (Ch.1968), held that, in valuing shares of a dissenting shareholder in a "short-form" merger, the elements considered should be weighted: (a) 25 percent for earnings and dividends for the past five years; (b) 25 percent for the value of the assets; and (c) 50 percent for the market value of the shares. See also Application of Delaware Racing Ass'n, 42 Del.Ch. 406, 213 A.2d 203 (Sup.Ct.1965) (going concern rather than liquidation value, book value, earnings, price to earnings, ratio, future prospects); Swanton v. State Guaranty Corp., 42 Del.Ch. 477, 215 A.2d 242 (Ch.1965) (asset value, earnings value, investment policy); Lucas v. Pembroke Water Co., 205 Va. 84, 135 S.E.2d 147 (1964); Matter of West Waterway Lumber Co., 59 Wash.2d 310, 367 P.2d 807 (1962); Tri-Continental Corp. v. Battye, 31 Del.Ch. 523, 74 A.2d 71 (Sup.Ct.1950); Felder v. Anderson, Clayton & Co., 39 Del.Ch. 76, 159 A.2d 278 (Ch.1960); Adams v. R. C. Williams & Co., 39 Del.Ch. 61, 158 A.2d 797 (Ch.1960); Sporborg v. City Specialty Stores, Inc., 35 Del.Ch. 560, 123 A.2d 121 (Ch.1956); Heller v. Munsingwear, 33

Del.Ch. 593, 98 A.2d 774 (Ch.1953); Jacques Coe & Co. v. Minneapolis-Moline Co., 31 Del.Ch. 368, 75 A. 2d 244 (Ch.1950) (weighting of market value, asset value, investment value); Lowry v. General Waterworks Corp., 26 D. & C.2d 154 (C.P.1962); cf. Matter of Kaufmann, Alsberg & Co. v. H. L. Green Co., 15 A.D.2d 468, 222 N.Y.S.2d 305 (1st Dep't 1961) (market price of actively traded listed shares held material and potent, but not controlling factor in determining value of shares). But see Poole v. N. V. Deli Maatschappij, 43 Del.Ch. 283, 224 A.2d 260 (Sup.Ct.1966), appeal after remand —— Del.Ch. ——, 243 A.2d 67 (Sup.Ct.1968). Cf. Phelps v. Watson-Stillman Co., 365 Mo. 1124, 293 S.W.2d 429 (1956). See Comment, "Valuation of Dissenters' Stock Under Appraisal Statutes", 79 Harv.L.Rev. 1453 (1966); Comment, 55 Mich.L.Rev. 689 (1957); Note, "Valuation of Dissenting Stockholders' Shares under an Appraisal Statute", 23 Mo.L.Rev. 223 (1958). See also Duddy v. Conshohocken Printing Co., 171 Pa. Super. 140, 90 A.2d 394 (1952).

14. Matter of Silverman, 282 App.Div. 252, 122 N.Y. S.2d 312 (1st Dep't 1953); Sporborg v. City Specialty Stores, Inc., 35 Del.Ch. 560, 123 A.2d 121 (Ch. 1956). See Annot., 38 A.L.R.2d 442 (1954).

15. See section 240 supra.

16. E. g., California (merger and consolidation), Connecticut, Michigan, Pennsylvania, Virginia, Washington, Wisconsin. Cf. Weckler v. Valley City Mill Co., 93 F.Supp. 444 (W.D.Mich.1950), aff'd 188 F.2d 367 (6th Cir. 1951) (construing Michigan statute). The New York and North Carolina statutes expressly preserve equitable remedies. E. g., McKinney's N.Y.Bus.Corp.Law, § 623(k) (enforcement of appraisal remedy not to exclude right of shareholder to bring or maintain appropriate action to obtain relief on ground corporate action would be or is unlawful or fraudulent as to him); Yoss v. Sacks, 26 A.D.2d 671, 272 N.Y.S.2d 387 (2d Dep't 1966) (holding that dissenting shareholder, who had initiated appraisal proceedings, was not thereby barred from suing for derivative and individual recovery for alleged wrongful and fraudulent acts of individual defendants upon proper showing that corporate action was fraudulent or unlawful as to him). Kentucky and Maine expressly provide that the appraisal remedy is nonexclusive. Ohio expressly provides for the stay of an appraisal proceeding during an injunction action, thus saving the

court decision,[17] but usually is not under other circumstances.

The procedures involved in asserting the appraisal remedy, of course, differ from jurisdiction to jurisdiction.[18] Required are

minority shareholder from the delicate choice between appraisal and injunction. See Matteson v. Ziebarth, 40 Wash.2d 286, 242 P.2d 1025 (1952) (then appraisal statute held exclusive remedy since it bound dissenting shareholders "with like force and effect" as though he had voted for merger, meaning that vote was binding unless secured by actual fraud). A few cases have allowed a shareholder to seek appraisal and injunction in the alternative. Victor Broadcasting Co. v. Mahurin, 236 Ark. 196, 365 S.W.2d 265 (1963); Robb v. Eastgate Hotel, Inc., 347 Ill.App. 261, 106 N.E.2d 848 (1952); Opelka v. Quincy Memorial Bridge Co., 335 Ill.App. 402, 82 N.E.2d 184 (1948). Compare Miller v. Steinbach, 268 F.Supp. 255 (S.D.N.Y.1967) (shareholder derivative action under federal law held not precluded by Pennsylvania appraisal statute); Voege v. American Sumatra Tobacco Corp., 241 F.Supp. 369 (D.Del.1965) (holding that shareholder's demand for appraisal made in ignorance of frauds resulting in merger was not election of remedies which barred action by such shareholder for relief under Federal Securities Exchange Act), with Vine v. Beneficial Finance Co., 252 F.Supp. 212 (S.D.N.Y.1966) (saving clause in New York statute held to preclude application of S.E.C. Rule 10b–5 applicable to purchase or sale of any security), rev'd 374 F.2d 627 (2d Cir. 1967), cert. denied 389 U.S. 970, 88 S.Ct. 463, 19 L.Ed.2d 460 (1968). See also Petry v. Harwood Elec. Co., 280 Pa. 142, 124 A. 302, 33 A.L.R. 1249 (1924); Lazenby v. International Cotton Mills Corp., 174 App.Div. 906, 160 N.Y.S. 1 (1st Dep't 1916). But see Johnson v. Baldwin, 221 S.C. 141, 69 S.E. 585 (1952) (pending derivative action held to abate when shareholder elected appraisal remedy); Pikor v. Cinerama Productions Corp., 25 F.R.D. 92 (S.D.N.Y. 1960); Blumner v. Federated Department Stores, Inc., 99 N.Y.S.2d 691 (Sup.Ct.1950) (where dissenting shareholder sought appraisal for 380 of his 381 shares, his derivative action was held to abate since appraisal remedy under then statute was exclusive remedy of shareholder under circumstances). See Vorenberg, "Exclusiveness of the Dissenting Stockholder's Appraisal Right", 77 Harv.L.Rev. 1189 (1964); Wolf, "Dissenting Shareholders: Is the Statutory Appraisal Remedy Exclusive?", 42 Texas L.Rev. 58 (1963). The exclusivity of the appraisal remedy is a question which should not be confused with the question of whether a dissenting shareholder seeking appraisal, where such remedy is not exclusive, may also maintain an action for relief against the extraordinary corporate matter involved. Compare Opelka v. Quincy Memorial Bridge Co., 335 Ill.App. 402, 82 N.E.2d 184 (1948) (action held maintainable), with Johnson v. Baldwin, 221 S.C. 141, 69 S.E.2d 585 (1952) (dissenting shareholder held to have made election at time of demand for payment). Shareholder status is lost at varying stages of the appraisal proceeding in different jurisdictions. See notes 24, 25 infra.

17. Stauffer v. Standard Brands, Inc., 41 Del.Ch. 7, 187 A.2d 78 (Sup.Ct.1962); Gordon v. Public Service Corp., 101 N.H. 372, 143 A.2d 428 (1958); Beloff v. Consolidated Edison Co. of New York, 300 N.Y. 11,

87 N.E.2d 561 (1949); Anderson v. International Mineral & Chemical Corp., 295 N.Y. 343, 67 N.E.2d 573 (1946); Liebschutz v. Schaffer Stores Co., 274 App.Div. 847, 80 N.Y.S.2d 771 (4th Dep't 1948). However, lacking statutory authorization [Eisenberg v. Central Zone Property Corp., 306 N.Y. 58, 115 N.E.2d 652 (1953)], or required shareholder approval [Matter of MacDonald, 205 App.Div. 579, 199 N.Y.S. 873 (2d Dep't 1923)], or fairness, the objecting shareholder is not limited to the appraisal remedy but may instead pursue other remedies such as injunction or action for damages. Starrett Corp. v. Fifth Ave. & Twenty-Ninth St. Corp., 1 F.Supp. 868 (S.D.N.Y.1932); Bown v. Ramsdell, 227 App.Div. 224, 237 N.Y.S. 573 (4th Dep't 1929). The availability of the appraisal remedy might be regarded as an adequate legal remedy precluding equitable relief. Katz v. R. Hoe & Co., 99 N.Y.S.2d 899 (Sup.Ct.1950), modified 277 App.Div. 966, 99 N.Y.S.2d 853 (1st Dep't 1950); Newman v. Arabol Mfg. Co., 41 Misc.2d 184, 245 N.Y.S.2d 442 (Sup.Ct.1963) (nonvoting shares).

18. ABA–ALI Model Bus.Corp.Act § 74; Del.Gen. Corp.Law, § 262 (1967); McKinney's N.Y.Bus.Corp. Law, § 623; Letts, "Appraisal Procedures for Dissenting Delaware Stockholders", 20 Bus.Law. 1083 (1965). Time schedules in enforcing the appraisal remedy can be critical. The time schedule under McKinney's N.Y.Bus.Corp.Law, § 623 is as follows:

Written objection by shareholder to proposed corporate action to be filed with corporation before meeting of shareholders at which action is submitted to vote or at such meeting but before vote (§ 623(a));

Written notice by corporation to be sent by registered mail to each objecting shareholder and each shareholder from whom written objection is not required, of shareholders' authorization of or consent to proposed corporate action within 10 days after such authorization or consent (§ 623(b));

Written notice of election to dissent by objecting shareholder to be filed with corporation within 20 days after giving of notice to him (§ 623(c));

Share certificates to be submitted by dissenting shareholder to corporation, or to its transfer agent, for notation at time of filing of notice of election to dissent or within one month thereafter (§ 623(f));

Written offer by corporation to be sent by registered mail to all dissenting shareholders to pay for shares at specified price, within seven days after expiration of period within which shareholders may file their notices of election to dissent, or within seven days after proposed corporate action is consummated, whichever is later (§ 623(g));

Payment for shares to be made within 60 days after making of such offer upon surrender of certificates representing such shares, if corporation and shareholder agree upon price within 30 days

timely objection and demand for payment,[19] submission of share certificates for appropri-

ate notation,[20] and commencement of appraisal proceeding in court.[21] Provisions

after making of written offer by corporation (§ 623(g));

    Institution of special proceeding in supreme court to determine rights of dissenting shareholders and to fix fair value of their shares (§ 623(h)).

H. Henn, Appendix 4, Checklist 8, "Appraisal Remedy", in 2 N.Y.Bus.Corp.Law 623, 624–625 (McKinney 1963). Quaere, as to standing of dissenting shareholders who had accepted corporation's offer to claim additional amounts based on any higher price determined in appraisal proceedings.

19. See Carl M. Loeb, Rhoades & Co. v. Hilton Hotels Corp., 43 Del.Ch. 206, 222 A.2d 789 (Sup.Ct. 1966) (holding that written objection filed with corporation prior to shareholder vote was not satisfied by written objection of beneficial shareholders absent showing that they were acting as agents for shareholder of record, by written objection of shareholder of record mailed two days before vote absent proof of actual delivery to corporation before vote, or by telephone conversation between employee of shareholder of record and corporation's secretary); Carl Marks & Co. v. Universal City Studios, Inc., 43 Del.Ch. 391, 233 A.2d 63 (Sup.Ct. 1967); Walsh v. Wollaston Golf Club, 353 Mass. 247, 230 N.E.2d 909 (1967) (appraisal demand held premature); Zeeb v. Atlas Powder Co., 32 Del.Ch. 486, 87 A.2d 123 (Sup.Ct.1952) (upholding objection signed by shareholder's alleged agent absent failure to show agency when questioned). See Schenley Industries, Inc. v. Curtis, 38 Del. 370, 152 A.2d 300 (Sup.Ct.1959); Spear v. Respro, 85 R.I. 272, 129 A. 2d 785 (1957); Duddy v. Conshohocken Printing Co., 163 Pa.Super. 150, 60 A.2d 394 (1948); Matter of O'Brien (American Locomotive Co.), 182 Misc. 577, 45 N.Y.S.2d 208 (Sup.Ct.1943).

The appraisal remedy is lost if the demand for payment is not timely made, even though the written objection was filed as required. Abraham & Co. v. Olivetti Underwood Corp., 42 Del.Ch. 95, 204 A.2d 740 (Ch.1964) ("statutory ceremony of objection and demand" ruled "mandatory"). Rank Organization, Ltd. v. Pathe Laboratories, Inc., 33 Misc.2d 748, 227 N.Y.S.2d 562 (Sup.Ct.1962), held that the parent corporation in a short merger was estopped to deny the sole minority shareholder, an English corporation which had an American representative known to the parent corporation, the right to statutory appraisal after the expiration of the statutory time for the filing of notice of dissent where the English corporation's only notice had been surface mailed and did not state the date of filing of the certificate of ownership.

Compare Jaquith & Co. v. Island Creek Coal Co., 47 N.J. 111, 219 A.2d 514 (1966) (holding that shareholders who had, prior to shareholder meeting, returned to management proxy marked "Against" proposed merger had sufficiently given written notice of dissent as required by appraisal statute), with F. S. Moseley & Co. v. Midland-Ross Corp., 40 Del.Ch. 245, 179 A.2d 295 (Sup.Ct.1965) ("no" proxy and accompanying letter of explanation held **insufficient**

demand). See also Apartment Properties, Inc. v. Luley, —— Ind.App. ——, 239 N.E.2d 403 (1968), aff'd —— Ind. ——, 247 N.E.2d 71 (1969); Shaffer v. General Grain, Inc., 133 Ind.App. 598, 182 N.E.2d 461 (1962).

20. Hamberg v. Pittsburgh Western Land Corp., 41 D. & C.2d 591 (C.P.1966). Compare Matter of Sasseen v. Danco Industries, Inc., 20 A.D.2d 657, 246 N.Y.S.2d 440 (2d Dep't 1964) (excusing less-than-two-months-tardy submission of share certificates); Matter of Wiedersum v. Transvision Electronics, Inc., 41 Misc.2d 936, 246 N.Y.S.2d 638 (Sup.Ct.1964) (denying relief where share certificates were submitted more than six months after statutory submission date).

Surrender of shares and acceptance of the award while appeal was pending on the ground that the award was less than the proper value has been held not to constitue waiver of right to appeal. Matter of Silverman (Hoe & Co.), 305 N.Y. 13, 110 N.E.2d 402 (1953) (5–2). See Booma v. Bigelow-Sanford Carpet Co., 330 Mass. 79, 111 N.E.2d 742 (1953). Appraisal might be denied if the shares were acquired after the proposed matter had been publicized. Matter of Leventall, 241 App.Div. 277, 271 N.Y.S. 493 (1st Dep't 1934); Matter of Dynamics Corp. v. Abraham & Co., 4 Misc.2d 50, 152 N.Y.S.2d 807 (Sup.Ct.1956), modified 1 A.D.2d 1005, 153 N.Y. S.2d 533 (1st Dep't 1956), appeal denied 2 A.D.2d 673, 153 N.Y.S.2d 554 (1st Dept. 1956).

21. Compare Matter of McKay v. Teleprompter Corp., 19 A.D.2d 815, 243 N.Y.S.2d 591 (1st Dep't 1963), appeal dismissed 13 N.Y.2d 1058, 246 N.Y.S.2d 34, 195 N.E.2d 762 (1963) (holding that corporation was estopped from denying appraisal on ground that sale was not extraordinary sale requiring shareholder approval), with Matter of McKinney (Bush Term.Bldgs.Co.), 306 N.Y. 207, 117 N.E.2d 256 (1954) (4–3) (appraisal proceedings started more than 50 days after demand held too late, even though recapitalization plan left to discretion of board of directors and board had not declared plan effective; Dissent: such delegation to directors was improper; in any event required action not complete until directors had acted); Matter of Stockwell, 210 App.Div. 753, 206 N.Y.S. 834 (2d Dep't 1924). Cf. Matter of Hake (Hake Mfg. Co.), 285 App.Div. 316, 136 N.Y.S.2d 817 (4th Dep't 1955), appeal dismissed 308 N.Y. 940, 127 N.E.2d 90 (1955) (appraisal allowed where shareholders approved sale, lease, or mortgage in directors' discretion but directors had not yet acted, unless shareholders promptly rescinded their approval). See Matter of Gordon, 160 N.Y.L.J. No. 50, 18 (Sup.Ct.1968) (stay of appraisal proceeding denied, even though corporation failed to file amendment of articles of incorporation). Compare R.I.Gen.Corp.Law, § 7–5–14 (1956) (expressly permitting any dissenting shareholder to withdraw his dissent and give his assent at any time prior to filing of appraiser's report).

differ as to the allowance of interest [22] and costs and expenses.[23]

Shareholder status of dissenting shareholders ends in some jurisdictions as of the time of the shareholder dissent, demand, or petition, sometimes subject to reinstatement,[24] and in others not until the conclusion of the appraisal.[25]

22. Interest in different jurisdictions runs from different times. Swanton v. State Guaranty Corp., 42 Del.Ch. 477, 215 A.2d 242 (Ch.1965) (from date of exception to appraiser's report); Meade v. Pacific Gamble Robinson Co., 30 Del.Ch. 509, 58 A.2d 415 (Sup.Ct.1948) (from date judgment entered); Martignette v. Sagamore Mfg. Co., 340 Mass. 136, 163 N.E.2d 9 (1959) (from 30 days after appraiser's finding); McKinney's N.Y.Bus.Corp.Law, § 623(h) (6) (from shareholders authorization date); Va.Stock Corp.Act § 13.1–75 (1957) (from day before vote). See Lowry v. General Waterworks Corp., 406 Pa. 152, 177 A.2d 82 (1962), where the appellate court held that the lower court had not exceeded its powers in not granting dissenting shareholders interest on their shares; Clarke v. Rockwood & Co., 18 Ohio Op.2d 414, 181 N.E.2d 59 (Ct.App.1960) (holding trial court had abused its discretion in awarding dissenting shareholder interest at six percent per annum on $1.44 per share where for three prior years dividends had been but five cents per share). McKinney's N.Y.Bus.Corp.Law, § 623(h) (6), provides: ". . . If the court finds that the refusal of any shareholder to accept the corporate offer of payment for his shares was arbitrary, vexatious or otherwise not in good faith, no interest shall be allowed to him." In re Janssen Dairy Corp., 2 N.J. Super. 580, 64 A.2d 652 (1949) (allowing no interest on award until expiration of statutory period within which corporation had to pay). Absent express statutory provision for interest, the latter rule would presumably apply. See General Grain, Inc. v. Goodrich, 140 Ind.App. 100, 221 N.E.2d 696 (1966).

23. In Delaware, the costs and expenses of any appraisal are taxed upon the parties thereto as appears equitable. Del.Gen.Corp.Law, § 262(h) (1967). Levin v. Midland-Ross Corp., 41 Del.Ch. 352, 194 A. 2d 853 (Ch.1963), held that dissenting shareholders in an appraisal proceeding who took no active part therein could not be required to contribute proportionately to the defraying of counsel and expert witness fees incurred by the other dissenting shareholders who participated actively in the proceeding, since the proceeding was not a class action and there was no fund in court. In re Janssen Dairy Corp., 2 N.J.Super. 580, 64 A.2d 652 (1949) (assessing appraisers' fees equally against corporation and petitioners, with assessment against petitioners being according to size of their respective share holdings). The New York statute provides that the costs and expenses of such proceeding shall be determined by the court and shall be assessed against the corporation, except that all or any part of such costs and expenses may be apportioned and assessed, as the court may determine, against any or all of the dissenting shareholders who are parties to the proceeding if the court finds that their refusal to accept the corporate offer was arbitrary, vexatious or otherwise not in good faith. Such expenses shall include reasonable compensation for and the reasonable expenses of the appraiser, but shall exclude the fees and expenses of counsel for and experts employed by any party unless the court, in its discretion, awards such fees and ex-

penses. In exercising such discretion, the court shall consider any of the following: (a) that the fair value of the shares as determined materially exceeds the amount which the corporation offered to pay; (b) that no offer was made by the corporation; and (c) that the corporation failed to institute the special proceeding within the period specified therefor. McKinney's N.Y.Bus.Corp.Law, § 623(h) (7); Matter of Dynamics Corp. v. Abraham & Co., 5 Misc.2d 652, 166 N.Y.S.2d 128 (Sup.Ct.1956), modified on other grounds, 6 A.D.2d 683, 174 N.Y. S.2d 952 (1st Dep't 1958) (costs and expenses of appraisal assessed against corporation where corporation offered $15 per share, shareholder demanded $32, and appraiser found $19); Note, "Appraisal of Corporate Dissenters' Shares: Apportioning the Proceedings' Financial Burdens", 60 Yale L.J. 337 (1951). The corporation's appraisal expenses may be deductible for federal income tax purposes. Hilton Hotels v. United States, 410 F.2d 194 (7th Cir. 1969); Smith Hotel Enterprises, Inc. v. Nelson, 236 F.Supp. 303 (E.D.Wis.1964). But see Woodward v. Comm'r, 410 F.2d 313 (8th Cir.1969), cert. granted, — U.S. —, 90 S.Ct. 153, 24 L.Ed.2d 133 (1969); Boulder Bldg. Corp. v. United States, 125 F.Supp. 512 (W.D.Okl.1954) (expenses held to be essentially share acquisition costs subject to capitalization but not current deduction). The conflicting decisions are being reviewed by the United States Supreme Court.

24. See, e. g., McKinney's N.Y.Bus.Corp.Law, § 623(e), reading ". . . Upon filing a notice of election to dissent, the shareholder shall cease to have any of the rights of a shareholder except the right to be paid the fair value of his shares and any other rights under this section. A notice of election may be withdrawn by the shareholder at any time before an offer is made by the corporation, as provided in paragraph (g), to pay for his shares. After such offer, withdrawal of a notice shall require the written consent of the corporation. If a notice of election is withdrawn, or the proposed corporate action is abandoned or rescinded, or a court shall determine that the shareholder is not entitled to receive payment for his shares, or the shareholder shall otherwise lose his dissenter's rights, he shall not have the right to receive payment for his shares and he shall be reinstated to all his rights as a shareholder as of the filing of his notice of election, including any intervening preemptive rights and the right to payment of any intervening dividend or other distribution or, if any such rights have expired or any such dividend or distribution other than in cash has been completed, in lieu

25. See note 25 on page 731.

There is in the Model Act no restriction on the funds available to the corporation to purchase the shares of dissenting shareholders, short of equity insolvency.[26]

thereof, at the election of the corporation, the fair value thereof in cash as determined by the board as of the time of such expiration or completion, but without prejudice otherwise to any corporate proceedings that may have been taken in the interim." See also Tex.Bus.Corp.Act § 5.13 (Supp.1968); Barnett v. Barnett Enterprises, Inc., 182 So.2d 728 (La. Ct.App.1966); Braasch v. Goldschmidt, 41 Del.Ch. 519, 199 A.2d 760 (Ch.1964) (holding that shareholders who sought appraisal of their shares had ceased to be shareholders capable of maintaining representative action complaining of merger); Gallois v. Stauffer Chemical Co., 221 Cal.App.2d 328, 34 Cal. Rptr. 411 (1963) (holding that dissenting shareholder of merged corporation was not entitled to cash and share dividends declared by surviving corporation during appraisal proceedings). Cf. Ohio Gen. Corp.Law, § 1701.85(E) (1955). Loss of shareholder status would preclude commencing or maintaining an equity action to enjoin the extraordinary corporate matter involved. A fairer solution would be to allow the dissenting shareholder to seek an injunction, with his appraisal proceedings stayed during the pendency of the injunction proceeding. See McKinney's N.Y.Bus.Corp.Law, § 623(k) (appraisal remedy not to exclude right of dissenting shareholder to bring or maintain appropriate action to obtain relief on ground that such corporate action will be or is unlawful or fraudulent as to him). Some statutes expressly do not require the shareholder to dissent and seek appraisal as to all his shares. E. g., ABA–ALI Model Bus.Corp.Act § 73. Cf. McKinney's N.Y.Bus.Corp.Law, § 623(d) (providing that shareholder may not dissent as to less than all of shares, held by him of record, that he owns beneficially, and that nominee or fiduciary may not dissent on behalf of any beneficial owner as to less than all of shares of such owner held of record by such nominee or fiduciary). See Olivetti Underwood Corp. v. Jacques Coe & Co., 42 Del.Ch. 588, 217 A.2d 683 (Sup.Ct.1966) (allowing broker holding shares in "street name" to assent as to some shares owned by some beneficial shareholders and to dissent as to others, indicating holding was limited to "short merger" but not to "street name" shareholders); Colonial Realty Corp. v. Reynolds Metals Co., 40 Del.Ch. 515, 185 A.2d 754 (Ch.1962) (holding that broker holding blocks of shares in "street name" for various beneficial owners, notwithstanding that it had voted some of shares for proposed merger, could seek appraisal as to other shares voted against merger, stating that practical consideration suggested desirability of permitting shareholder to split his shares in merger proceedings, aff'd sub nom. Reynolds Metals Co. v. Colonial Realty Corp., 41 Del.Ch. 183, 190 A.2d 752 (Sup.Ct.1963) (expressly confining decision to facts of case, i. e., case of beneficial owner and nominee); Bache & Co. v. General Instrument Corp., 42 N.J. 44, 198 A.2d 759 (1964) (where plaintiff, brokerage firm, held certain shares in "street name" for certain customer; under instructions from customer, it voted these shares against proposed merger, at same time voting other shares in its name in favor of merger; held: plaintiff was not precluded from demanding

FEDERAL CORPORATE REORGANIZATIONS

350. **Federal corporate reorganizations, under the Bankruptcy Act, and possibly under the Public Utility Holding Company Act of 1935 or under any other federal law, are expressly exempted by some state corporate statutes from the usual requirements of shareholder and board of directors action and possibly other requirements where the reorganization is confirmed by a court of competent jurisdiction.**

Where a corporation undergoes reorganization under the Federal Bankruptcy Act [1] or possibly under other federal laws,[2] some state corporation statutes expressly provide

appraisal of shares it voted against proposed merger, court finding it immaterial that plaintiff was not beneficial owner of shares and that plaintiff had voted other shares in favor of proposed merger; court treated shares held in "street name" as involving special situation). See also Sonnenschein v. Evans, 21 N.Y.2d 563, 289 N.Y.S.2d 609, 236 N.E. 2d 846 (1968) (upholding dissenting shareholder's right to settle for higher price per share than that paid consenting shareholders).

25. See, e. g., Cal.Gen.Corp.Law, § 4315 (1947); Del. Gen.Corp.Law, § 262 (1967) (shareholder voting and dividend rights suspended during appraisal); Ind. Gen.Corp.Act § 25–236 (1967); see also Fein v. Lanston Monotype Machine Co., 196 Va. 753, 85 S.E.2d 353 (1955). Quaere, as to unilateral dismissal of appraisal proceeding by dissenting shareholder in the event shares should appreciate during pendency of appraisal proceeding. See Bauman v. Advance Aluminum Castings Corp., 27 Ill.App.2d 178, 169 N. E.2d 382 (1960) (holding that dissenting shareholder pursuing appraisal remedy may not, even though judgment has not been entered, resume status as shareholder). See also Matter of Gordon, 160 N.Y. L.J. No. 50, 18 (Sup.Ct.1968) (denying stay of appraisal proceeding on motion of dissenting shareholder where corporation failed to file amendment of articles of incorporation).

26. ABA–ALI Model Bus.Corp.Act § 5. New York prohibits payment when the corporation is or would be rendered insolvent, in which event, the dissenting shareholder may, at his option, withdraw his notice of election, or retain his status as a claimant until payment lawfully can be made or until liquidation when his claim would be subordinated to the rights of creditors but superior to the rights of nondissenting shareholders. McKinney's N.Y.Bus.Corp.Law, § 623(j).

1. See sections 386–389 infra.

2. E. g., Public Utility Holding Company Act of 1935. See section 299 supra.

that the usual board of directors or shareholder action requirements, etc., do not apply.[3]

Some statutes specifically authorize amendments of the articles of incorporation, pursuant to a plan of reorganization confirmed by the court under federal law, so long as such amendments introduce provisions which might lawfully be then contained in the articles of incorporation, without any action thereon by the directors or shareholders of the corporation and with the same effect as if the amendments had been adopted by unanimous action of the directors and shareholders of the corporation.[4]

Some of the statutes apply to reorganization under any federal law;[5] a few statutes apply to reorganizations under the Federal Bankruptcy Act and reorganizations under the Federal Public Utility Holding Company

Act of 1935;[6] a few only to reorganizations under the Federal Bankruptcy Act.[7] The Maryland statute expressly applies to any reorganization.[8] In all cases, the necessity of court confirmation would tend to operate as an alternative protective safeguard in place of the normal safeguards of shareholder approval, etc.

FEDERAL TAX "REORGANIZATIONS"

351. **Federal tax "reorganizations", which may be tax-free under the Internal Revenue Code of 1954, include, besides mergers and consolidations, recapitalizations, and mere changes in identity, form, or place of organization, "Type B reorganization"—shares-for-shares swap, "Type C reorganization"—shares-for-assets, and "Type D reorganization"—to combine two or more affiliated corporations or to effect corporate separations by the three kinds of divisive reorganization commonly known as (a) "split-up", (b) "spin-off", and (c) "split-off".**

The term "reorganization", in tax parlance, has a different definition from its corporate law meaning, embracing a wide variety of overlapping corporate readjustments, only some of which have corporate law analogues.

Federal tax reorganizations, which may be tax-free under the Internal Revenue Code of 1954,[1] include, besides statutory mergers and

---

3. E. G., ABA–ALI Model Bus.Corp.Act § 59A (optional section); Arkansas, California, Colorado, Delaware, Iowa, Maine, Maryland, Michigan, Mississippi, Nebraska, New Jersey, New York, North Dakota, Ohio, Oklahoma, Oregon, Pennsylvania, Texas, Utah, Virginia, Washington.

4. E. g., ABA–ALI Model Bus.Corp.Act § 59A (optional section). Among the permissible amendments are to:

(a) Change the corporate name, period of duration or corporate purposes;

(b) Repeal, alter or amend the bylaws;

(c) Change the aggregate number of shares, or shares of any class, which the corporation has authority to issue;

(d) Change the preferences, limitations and relative rights in respect of all or any part of the shares, and classify, reclassify or cancel all or any part thereof, whether issued or unissued;

(e) Authorize the issuance of bonds, debentures or other obligations, whether or not convertible into shares of any class or bearing warrants or other evidences of optional rights to purchase or subscribe for shares of any class, and fix the terms and conditions thereof; and

(f) Constitute or reconstitute and classify or reclassify the board of directors, and appoint directors and officers in place of or in addition to all or any of the directors or officers then in office.

5. E. g., ABA–ALI Model Bus.Corp.Act § 59A (optional section); California, Colorado, Delaware, Iowa, Michigan, New York, North Dakota, Ohio, Oklahoma, Texas, Virginia.

6. E. g., New Jersey until 1969; New York until 1963. McKinney's N.Y.Bus.Corp.Law, § 808 authorizes the carrying out of a plan of reorganization, when confirmed by the court, in proceedings under any applicable act of Congress relating to reorganization of corporations, without action of the corporation's shareholders or board of directors, for which provision is made in any statute governing the corporation or is or might be lawfully made in the articles of incorporation or bylaws. Appraisal rights or payments to shareholders in connection therewith are expressly denied except as provided in such plan. The consideration requirements for the issue of shares, bonds, and other securities do not apply. Neither do preemptive rights. Id. § 622(e) (6).

7. E. g., Nebraska, Pennsylvania.

8. Md.Gen.Corp.Law, § 75 (1951).

1. Int.Rev.Code of 1954, 26 U.S.C.A. §§ 354–368; R. Holzman, Tax-Free Reorganizations (1967); J. Reeves, Tax Aspects of Corporate Mergers, Exchanges, Redemptions, Liquidations, and Reorganizations (1967); B. Bittker & J. Eustice, Federal Income Taxation of Corporations and Shareholders

consolidations,[2] recapitalizations,[3] and mere changes in identity, form, or place of organi-

zation, however effected,[4] three principal types of reorganization, known as "Type B reorganizations", "Type C reorganizations", and "Type D reorganizations".

"Type D reorganizations" are methods of combining two or more affiliated corporations or effecting a corporate separation by the so-called divisive reorganizations: (a) "Split-up"; (b) "Spin-off"; and (c) "Split-off".

"Type B reorganizations" involve the acquisition by one corporation, in exchange *solely* for all or a part of its voting shares, of shares of another corporation if, immediately after the acquisition, the acquiring corporation has "control" of such other corporation (whether or not such acquiring corporation had "control" immediately before the acquisition).[5]

chs. 11, 12 (2d ed. 1966); 2 G. Hornstein, Corporation Law and Practice § 972 (1959); Symposium: "Tax-Free Corporate Reorganizations Introduction", 19 Case W.Res.L.Rev. 974 (1968); Stark, "Non-Income Tax Aspects of Corporate Reorganizations: A Check List of the Issues and Problems Involved", N.Y.U. 24th Inst. on Fed. Tax. 1085 (1966); Saplenza, "Tax Considerations in Corporate Reorganizations and Mergers", 60 Nw.U.L.Rev. 765 (1966); Arnold, "Tax Considerations of Fundamental Corporate Changes", 17 Ark.L.Rev. 444 (1964); Cavitch, "Reorganization Techniques in Corporate Planning", 19 Bus.Law. 429 (1964); Kaufman & Loeb, "Corporate Reorganizations—Selected Securities, Corporate and Tax Law Considerations in Choice of Form", 16 So.Calif.Tax Inst. 199 (1964); Dauber, "Use of Reorganization Techniques to Avoid Collapsible Treatment", 49 A. B.A.J. 1214 (1963); Stutsman, "Status of Minority Stockholders in Corporate Acquisitions and Reorganization", 15 So.Calif.Tax Inst. 293 (1963); Note, "Exclusion from Section 306 Treatment in Unifying Reorganization", 76 Harv.L.Rev. 1627 (1963); Seplow, "Acquisition of Assets of a Subsidiary: Liquidation or Reorganization", 73 Harv.L.Rev. 484 (1960). Nonrecognition of taxpayers' gains from corporate reorganizations, even if sound for horizontal and vertical mergers, is questionable for conglomerate mergers in which the taxpayer's investment is changed both in form and in substance. Cohen, "Conglomerate Mergers and Taxation", 55 A.B.A.J. 40 (1969); Lipkind, "Gallagher Revisited: The Functionally Unrelated Corporate Reorganization", 13 Vill.L.Rev. 487 (1968). D. Kahn, Basic Corporate Taxation 115 et seq. (ICLE 1970).

2. Int.Rev.Code of 1954, 26 U.S.C.A. § 368(a) (1) (A) (sometimes called "Type A reorganizations"). Convertible preferred shares, voting or nonvoting, qualify as shares under § 368(a) (1) (A), and, if voting qualify as voting shares under § 368(a) (1) (B) or (c), whereas convertible debentures would not. See B. Bittker & J. Eustice, Federal Income Taxation of Corporations and Shareholders § 12.12 (2d ed. 1966); Lowenstein, "New Form of 'A' Reorganization Solves Many Corporate Acquisition Problems", 30 J.Taxation 168 (1969); Vesely, "'A' Reorganizations—Statutory Mergers and Consolidations", 19 Case W.Res.L.Rev. 975 (1968); Spillers & Shors, "Role of the Statutory Merger in Corporate Acquisitions: A Legal and Financial Inquiry", 53 Iowa L.Rev. 1 (1967). See section 346 supra.

3. Int.Rev.Code of 1954, 26 U.S.C.A. § 368(a) (1) (E) (sometimes called "Type E reorganizations"). See

also id. §§ 302, 354; B. Bittker & J. Eustice, Federal Income Taxation of Corporations and Shareholders § 12.16 (2d ed. 1966); Pugh, "The F Reorganization: Reveille for a Sleeping Giant?", 24 Tax L.Rev. 437 (1969). See section 345 supra.

4. Int.Rev.Code of 1954, 26 U.S.C.A. § 368(a) (1) (F) (sometimes called "Type F reorganizations"). See Davant v. Comm'r, 366 F.2d 874 (5th Cir. 1966), cert. denied 386 U.S. 1022, 87 S.Ct. 1370, 18 L.Ed.2d 460 (1967), reh. denied 389 U.S. 893, 88 S.Ct. 14, 19 L.Ed.2d 203 (1967); Reef Corp. v. Comm'r, 368 F.2d 125 (5th Cir. 1966), cert. denied 386 U.S. 1018, 87 S. Ct. 1371, 18 L.Ed.2d 454 (1967); B. Bittker & J. Eustice, Federal Income Taxation of Corporations and Shareholders § 12.17 (2d ed. 1966); Kasner, "F-Reorganization Enigma: What is a 'Mere' Change in Form or Place?", 29 J.Taxation 210 (1968); Grossberg, "Type F Reorganizations in the Fifth Circuit: The Mouse That Roared", 5 Houston L.Rev. 926 (1968); Nicholson, "Recent Developments in the Reincorporation Area", 19 Tax L.Rev. 123 (1964); Mayer, "Ramifications of the Treasury's Liquidation—Reincorporation Doctrine", 25 U.Pitt.L.Rev. 637 (1964); Comment, "(F) Reorganizations and Proposed Alternate Routes for Post-Reorganization Net Operating Loss Carrybacks", 66 Mich.L.Rev. 498 (1968).

5. Int.Rev.Code of 1954, 26 U.S.C.A. § 368(a) (1) (B); see also id. § 354. The "Type B reorganization" is a method of acquiring a subsidiary.

Type B Reorganization (shares-for-shares swap):

Compare Turnbow v. Comm'r, 368 U.S. 337, 82 S.Ct. 353, 7 L.Ed.2d 326 (1961), with Howard v. Comm'r, 238 F.2d 943 (7th Cir. 1956) (effect of "solely for voting stock" requirement on taxability of gain);

"Type C reorganizations" involve the acquisition by one corporation, in exchange solely for all or a part of its voting shares (or in exchange solely for all or a part of the voting shares of a corporation which is in control of the acquiring corporation), of substantially all of the properties of another corporation, but in determining whether the exchange is solely for shares the assumption by the acquiring corporation of a liability of the other, or the fact that property acquired is subject to a liability, shall be disregarded.[6]

"Type D reorganizations" involve a transfer by a corporation of all or a part of its assets to another corporation if immediately after the transfer the transferor, or one or more of its shareholders (including persons who were shareholders immediately before the transfer), or any combination thereof, is in "control" of the corporation to which the assets are transferred; but only if, in pursuance of the plan, shares or securities of the corporation to which the assets are transferred are distributed in a transaction which qualifies under section 354, 355, or 356 of the Code.[7]

"Type D reorganizations" of the divisive reorganization type, are known as (a) "split-ups", (b) "spin-offs", and (c) "split-offs".[8]

In a "split-up", the original corporation is split-up into two or more separate corporations, by distributing to its shareholders

---

Note 5.—Continued from page 733.

Mills v. Comm'r, 331 F.2d 321 (5th Cir. 1964) (holding cash payments in lieu of fractional shares did not disqualify transaction as "Type B reorganization"); Architectural Building Products, Inc. v. Cripples Products Corp., 221 F.Supp. 154 (E.D.Wis. 1963) (agreement to indemnify for any loss resulting from breach of warranties in contract for sale of shares, purportedly under § 368(a) (1) (B), held not to constitute assumption of liabilities); Mer-

ritt, " 'B' Reorganizations and the 'Solely' for Voting Stock Problem", 19 Case W.Res.L.Rev. 990 (1968); Toll, "Transfer of Boot in Stock-for-Stock Acquisitions", 15 U.C.A.L.Rev. 1347 (1968); Vernava, "Howard and Turnbow Cases and the 'Solely' Requirement of B Reorganizations", 20 Tax L.Rev. 387 (1965); Kanter, "Cash in a 'B' Reorganization: Effect of Cash Purchases on 'Creeping' Reorganization", 19 Tax L.Rev. 441 (1964).

---

6.   Int.Rev.Code of 1954, 26 U.S.C.A. § 368(a) (1) (C); see also id. §§ 35, 361. The "Type C reorganization" is a method of combining the assets of two or more corporations.

Type C Reorganization (shares-for-assets):

voting shares
$\longrightarrow$

Acquiring corporation   Controlled corporation

$\longleftarrow$

substantially all assets

See B. Bittker & J. Eustice, Federal Income Taxation of Corporations and Shareholders § 12.14 (2d ed. 1966); Leake, "Coping with the Problems Presented in a Stock-plus-Boot C Reorganization", 29 J.Taxation 354 (1968); Hertzog, "The Reincorporation Problem in Subchapter C. A Question of Seman-

tics?", 9 Wm. & Mary L.Rev. 928 (1968); Goldman, "C Reorganizations", 19 Tax L.Rev. 31 (1963); Comment, "Transferee Liability and the C Reorganization", 40 U.Colo.L.Rev. 380 (1968). See also Cohn v. Lionel Corp., 21 N.Y.2d 559, 289 N.Y.S.2d 404, 236 N.E.2d 634 (1968).

---

7.   Int.Rev.Code of 1954, 26 U.S.C.A. § 368(a) (1) (D); see id. §§ 355, 361. The "Type D reorganization" involves methods of combining two or more affiliated corporations or effecting corporate separations. See B. Bittker & J. Eustice, Federal Income Taxation of Corporations and Shareholders ch. 11, § 12.15 (2d ed. 1966); Morris, "Combining Divisive and Amalgamating Reorganizations—Section 355 Fails Again", 46 Texas L.Rev. 315 (1968).

8.   Whitman, "Draining the Serbonian Bog: A New Approach to Corporate Separations Under the 1954

Code", 81 Harv.L.Rev. 1194 (1968); Siegel, "When Corporations Divide: A Statutory and Financial Analysis", 79 Harv.L.Rev. 534 (1966); Lipnick, "Nontaxable Corporate Separations", 2 Houston L. Rev. 344 (1965); Simon, "Tax-Free Corporate Divisions: They Are Still a Danger Area After Ten Years", 23 J.Taxation 22 (1965); Comment, "Splitting the Small Corporation by Divisive Reorganization: Internal Revenue Code, Sections 355 and 368 (a) (1) (D)", 18 U.Fla.L.Rev. 330 (1965); Comment, "Divisive Reorganizations Under the Internal Revenue Code of 1954", 67 Yale L.J. 38 (1957).

shares in two or more existing or newly-created subsidiaries in its complete liquidation.[9]

In a "spin-off", the original corporation transfers part of its assets to a new corporation in exchange for the latter's shares and then immediately distributes such shares to the original corporation's shareholders, without the surrender by them of any of their shares in the original corporation. A "spin-off" might also occur through a distribution by a parent of an existing controlled subsidiary's shares.[10]

---

9. **"Split-up"** (complete liquidation of parent corporation):

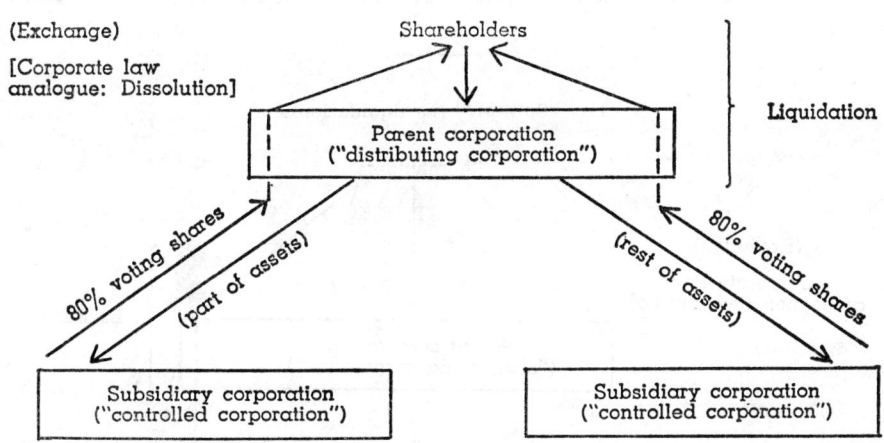

The parent corporation transfers all of its assets to at least two other corporations which have issued or then issue at least 80 percent of their voting shares to it and exchanges such shares for all of its outstanding shares in complete liquidation.

---

10. **"Spin-off"** (no liquidation):

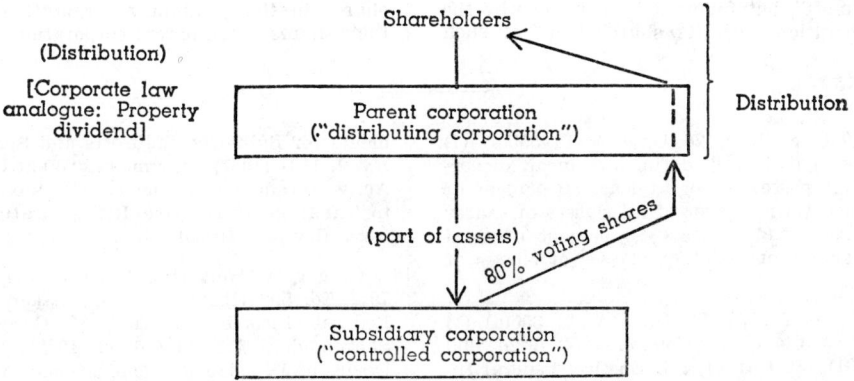

The parent corporation transfers part of its assets to an existing or newly-created subsidiary, and then distributes its shares in such subsidiary to its shareholders. See Comm'r v. Gordon, 391 U.S. 83, 88 S.Ct. 1517, 20 L.Ed.2d 448 (1968); Jacobs, "Anatomy of a Spin-Off", 1967 Duke L.J. 1; Sealy, "The Functions of Spin-Offs and Partial Liquidations", N.Y.U. 20th Inst. on Fed.Tax. 799 (1962); Comment, "Suggested Treatment of Spin-Off Reorganizations", 53 Cornell L.Rev. 700 (1968); Comment, "Spin-Off Spins in Two Directions", 43 Notre Dame Law. 389 (1968); Comment, "Variations on the Spin-Off as Non-Taxable Distributions", 67 Colum.L.Rev. 1544 (1967); Comment, "Income Tax—Reorganization—Spin-Offs—Spin-Off Pursuant to Plan of Merger Exempt Under Section 355 When Complete Transaction Has Business Purpose Other Than Tax Avoidance", 55 Geo.L.J. 948 (1967).

In a "split-off", the transaction is the same as in a "spin-off" except that the original corporation's shareholders surrender a portion of their shares in the original corporation.[11]

Divisive reorganizations must also meet the specified dual-control tests [12] and the so-called "actual business" requirement.[13]

Judicial restrictions on otherwise tax-free reorganizations include the "business pur-

pose", "continuity of interest",[14] and "step transaction" [15] doctrines.

In the case of a reorganization, generally, subject to the inevitable refinements, the corporation recognizes neither gain nor loss on the transfer of its property for shares or securities in another corporation which is a party to the reorganization; shareholders and creditors may exchange their shares and securities for new securities without recogni-

---

11. "Split-off" (no liquidation):

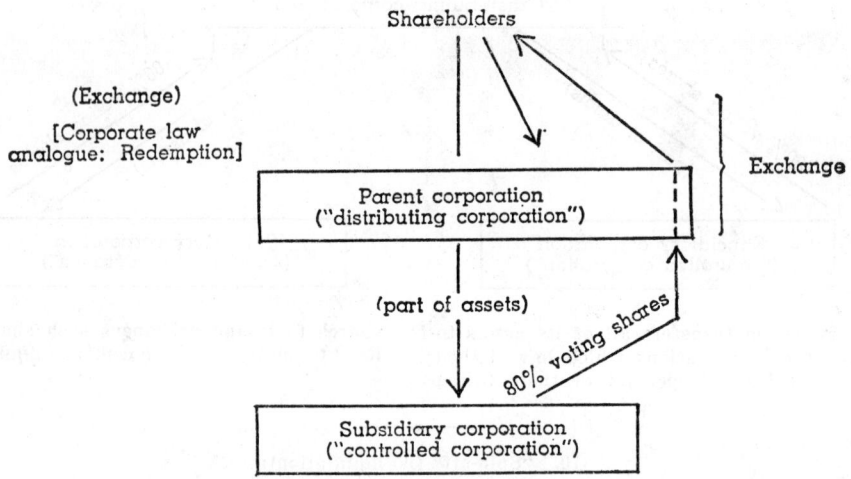

(Exchange)

[Corporate law analogue: Redemption]

Shareholders

Parent corporation ("distributing corporation")

Exchange

(part of assets)

80% voting shares

Subsidiary corporation ("controlled corporation")

Same as "spin-off", but followed by exchange by the parent corporation with its shareholders of such shares in the subsidiary corporation for some of their shares in the parent corporation.

---

12. Int.Rev.Code of 1954, 26 U.S.C.A. §§ 355(a) (1) (A), (D), 368(c) ("control" defined to mean ownership of shares possessing of at least 80 percent of total combined voting power of all classes of shares entitled to vote and at least 80 percent of total number of shares of all other classes of shares of corporation).

13. Int.Rev.Code of 1954, 26 U.S.C.A. §§ 355(a) (1) (C), (b). See Coady v. Comm'r, 289 F.2d 490 (6th Cir. 1961); B. Bittker & J. Eustice, Federal Income Taxation of Corporations and Shareholders § 11.04 (2d ed. 1966); Jacobs, "IRS Now Concedes That a Single Business May Be Divided Under Section 355", 21 J.Taxation 22 (1964); Jacobs, "Spin-Offs: The Pre-Distribution Two Business Rule— Edmund P. Coady and Beyond", 19 Tax L.Rev. 155 (1964); Simmons, "Corporate Separations and the Definition of Trade or Business'", 46 A.B.A.J. 667 (1960); "Section 355: Active Business Require-

ments for Spin-offs, Split-offs and Split-ups", 43 A.B.A.J. 1131 (1957); Comment, "What Constitutes an Active Trade or Business? A Flexible Approach to Taxation of Divisive Reorganizations", 16 Mercer L.Rev. 414 (1965).

14. Gregory v. Helvering, 293 U.S. 465, 55 S.Ct. 266, 79 L.Ed. 596 (1935). See B. Bittker & J. Eustice, Federal Income Taxation of Corporations and Shareholders § 12.19 (2d ed. 1966); Corder, "The Device of Divisive Reorganizations: An Analysis of Section 355(a) (1) (B) and Its Relation to Section 368(a) (1) (D) and the Doctrines of 'Continuity of interest' and 'Business Purpose'", 10 U.Kan.L.Rev. 21 (1961); Tarleau, "'Continuity of the Business Enterprise' in Corporate Reorganizations and Other Corporate Readjustments", 60 Colum.L.Rev. 792 (1960).

15. See id. § 12.20.

tion of gain or loss; the tax attributes (loss carry overs, earnings and profits, accounting methods, etc.) of a corporation whose assets are acquired by another corporation in the reorganization are usually inherited by the acquiring corporation; the receipt of "boot" [16] may result in recognition of some or all gain; and there is a carry over of basis.[17]

16. See id. § 11.10. "Boot" includes anything received other than "stock or securities" of a controlled corporation. "Boot" can disqualify a "Type C reorganization". See note 5 supra. In the case of a § 355 exchange (split-offs, split-ups), the tax results of the receipt of "boot" are governed by § 356(a)—gain is recognized but not in excess of the "boot"; in the case of a § 355 distribution (spin-off), § 356(b) treats the "boot" as an ordinary distribution subject to § 301. See Rosenzweig, "The 'Boot' Peril: What is 'Solely' Under Section 368 (a)?", 24 N.Y.U. 24th Inst. on Fed.Tax. 995 (1966); Comment, "Unexpected Disqualification of Reorganizations Under the Internal Revenue Code by the Inadvertent Transfer of Boot", 18 Vand.L.Rev. 1534 (1965).

17. See B. Bittker & J. Eustice, Federal Income Taxation of Corporations and Shareholders 499 (2d ed. 1966).

Henn Corporations 2d Ed. HB—47

The liquidation of a corporation followed by a transfer of some or all of its assets to a newly-organized corporation owned by the same shareholders—in effect, reincorporation—can be a tax-avoidance device.[18]

18. Surkin, "The Reincorporation Quandary Under Sections 368(a) (1) (d) and 354(b) (1): Comments on Moffatt v. Commissioner", 53 Cornell L.Rev. 575 (1968); Hjorth, "Liquidations and Reincorporations —Before and After Davant (Davant v. Comm'r, 366 F.2d 874)", 42 Wash.L.Rev. 737 (1967); Freling, " 'Boot-Strap' Purchase; Sections 302, 304 and 337; Reorganizations and Reincorporations", N.Y.U. 24th Inst. on Fed.Tax. 1229 (1966); Whitaker, "Liquidation and Reincorporation", U.So.Cal.1966 Tax Inst. 191; Hewitt, "Liquidations v. Reincorporations and Reorganizations: The Current Battle", 15 Tul.Tax Inst. 187 (1965); Harnack, "Liquidation—Reincorporation: It is Still Possible to Achieve an Earnings Bailout", 21 J.Taxation 84 (1964); Mayer, "Ramifications of the Treasury's Liquidation-Reincorporation Doctrine", 25 U.Pitt.L.Rev. 637 (1964); Comment, "Income Tax—Reincorporation and Liquidation", 69 W.Va.L.Rev. 206 (1967); Comment, "When Liquidations Become Reorganizations: The Elements of 'Control' ", 1965 Duke L.J. 764.

CHAPTER 14

CORPORATE LITIGATION
(INCLUDING DERIVATIVE ACTIONS)

A. GENERAL PROCEDURAL PROBLEMS

CAPACITY TO SUE AND TO BE SUED

352. The corporation can sue and be sued in the corporate name, one of the traditional attributes of the corporation. Upon dissolution, the corporation's capacity to sue or to be sued depends upon the law of the forum and of the jurisdiction of incorporation.

Corporate litigation can involve claims by or against the corporation. Corporate claims can be asserted by it or anyone standing in its stead, such as a trustee-in-bankruptcy; if not asserted by the corporation directly, such claim might be asserted by a shareholder, and possibly others, in a derivative action in behalf of the corporation. Claims against the corporation would include claims against it by a shareholder for breach of his membership contract, brought in his own right individually for himself and possibly for others similarly situated as well in a representative or class action.

One of the traditional attributes of a corporation, under the entity theory, is that it can sue and be sued in the corporate name.[1]

The capacity of a dissolved corporation in such respect depends upon the statutes and decisional law of the forum and of the jurisdiction of incorporation.[2]

In contrast, the unincorporated association, as such, in some jurisdictions has, and in others does not have, capacity to sue and to be sued.[3]

1. See section 79, n. 1 supra. More than one-fifth of the states constitutionally provide that corporations, sometimes broadly defining the term to include unincorporated associations with corporate characteristics, may sue and be sued in like cases as natural persons. E. g. Cal.Const. art. XII, § 4, N.Y.Const. art. X, § 4. The requirement of McKinney's N.Y. CPLR, § 321 that a corporation must appear only by a duly-licensed New York attorney at law has been held not to violate the New York constitutional provision. Oliner v. Mid-Town Promoters, Inc., 2 N.Y.2d 63, 156 N.Y.S.2d 833, 138 N.E. 2d 217 (1956). Under the same statute, a minority shareholder was allowed to sue derivatively pro se. Brooks v. Saxony Tobacco & Sales Corp., 20 Misc.2d 401, 188 N.Y.S.2d 384 (Sup.Ct.1959). Results are similar in the federal courts under 28 U. S.C.A. § 1654. Willheim v. Murchison, 206 F.Supp. 733 (S.D.N.Y.1962), appeal dismissed 312 F.2d 399 (2d Cir. 1963). Statutes almost universally authorize corporations to sue and to be sued. E. g., ABA–ALI Model Bus.Corp.Act § 4(b). Generally, corporations can only appear through duly-licensed attorneys. Simbraw, Inc. v. United States, 367 F.2d 373 (3d Cir. 1966); Flora Construction Co. v. Fireman's Fund Ins. Co., 307 F.2d 413 (10th Cir. 1962), cert. denied 373 U.S. 919, 83 S.Ct. 1296, 10 L.Ed.2d 419 (1963); Ashley-Cooper Sales Services, Inc. v. Brentwood Mfg. Co., 168 F.Supp. 742 (D.Md.1958); United States v. Crosby, 24 F.R.D. 15 (S.D.N.Y.1959) (court appointment of attorney to represent corporation which had defaulted in appearance). The rule is sometimes relaxed in courts not of record or

under limited statutory exceptions. Burgess v. Federated Credit Service, Inc., 148 Colo. 8, 365 P.2d 264 (1961); Prudential Ins. Co. of America v. Small Claims Court, 76 Cal.App.2d 379, 173 P.2d 38, 167 A.L.R. 820 (1946). But see Remole Soil Service, Inc. v. Benson, 68 Ill.App.2d 234, 215 N.E.2d 678 (1966). A nonparty officer has been allowed to serve the summons in an action brought by his corporation. Majal Corp. v. Ancora Productions, Inc., 154 N.Y.L.J. No. 40, 9 (Sup.Ct.1965). The Oregon attorney general has ruled that the statutory prohibition against a party serving his own process did not apply to the employee of a plaintiff corporation. Or.Op.Att'y Gen. No. 5942, Mar. 19, 1965. Even a de facto corporation can be sued and usually can sue (see section 140, n. 18 supra). Ross P. Beckstrom Co. v. Armstrong Paint & Varnish Works, 220 Ill.App. 598 (1921); First Baptist Church v. Branham, 90 Cal. 22, 27 P. 60 (1891). Corporate capacity to sue or to defend might be suspended for failure to file reports or pay franchise taxes. Compare Black River Associates, Inc. v. Koehler, 126 Vt. 394, 233 A.2d 175 (1967), with Erb v. Flower, 248 Cal.App.2d 499, 56 Cal.Rptr. 612 (1967). Cf. Traub Co. v. Coffee Break Service, Inc., 66 Cal.2d 368, 57 Cal.Rptr. 846, 425 P.2d 790 (1967). See section 144 supra. Or for failure of a foreign corporation to qualify in certain jurisdictions where required. See section 101 supra. In the federal courts, the capacity of a corporation to sue and to be sued is determined by the law of its jurisdiction of incorporation. Fed.R.Civ.P. 17(b). On pleading and raising issues as to such capacity, see Fed.R. Civ.P. 9(a); McKinney's N.Y. CPLR, Rule 3015(b).

2. Melrose Distillers, Inc. v. United States, 359 U.S 271, 79 S.Ct. 763, 3 L.Ed.2d 800 (1959); Marcus, "Suability of Dissolved Corporations—A Study in Interstate and Federal-State Relationships", 58 Harv.L.Rev. 675 (1945); Note, 40 Cornell L.Q. 610 (1955); Annot., 40 A.L.R.2d 1396 (1955). With respect to actions by a foreign corporation which has qualified and formally withdrawn or allowed its certificate of authority to be revoked, see Apache Tank Lines, Inc. v. Beall Pipe & Tank Corp., 19 Utah 2d 104, 426 P.2d 623 (1967); 22 Corp.J. 123 (1958).

3. In federal court cases, the capacity of a partnership or other unincorporated association to sue and be sued is determined by the law of the jurisdiction in which the district court is held, except that a

Corporate litigation can involve **(a)** claims by the corporation, and **(b)** claims against the corporation.

Claims by the corporation may be against its subscribers, shareholders, directors, officers, agents, or employees, or against outsiders. They may be asserted by the corporation itself (by authority of the board of directors or other proper authorization),[4] or anyone standing in its stead, such as an assignee, trustee-in-bankruptcy, or the like.

If not asserted by the corporation itself, any such claim of the corporation may, if certain conditions are met, be asserted by a shareholder, and possibly others, in a derivative action. While the corporation is joined as an indispensable party defendant in a derivative action, its claim is in effect being asserted derivatively and hence it is the real party plaintiff.

Claims against the corporation may be asserted by its subscribers, shareholders, other insiders or outsiders. Claims against the corporation by a shareholder as such are based on his membership contract with the corporation[5] and are asserted in a shareholder's direct individual action, as distinguished from a shareholder's derivative action.[6] Such direct action might be a representative or class action in the sense that it is also in behalf of other shareholders similarly situated.

JURISDICTION OVER SUBJECT MATTER

353. State court jurisdiction over the subject matter is very broad, but is subject to some limitations, especially in cases of actions by or against foreign corporations. Even within the scope of such jurisdiction, further limitations on its exercise result from lack of jurisdiction over the parties, improper venue, the doctrine of forum non conveniens (or "internal affairs rule"), and statutes of limitations or laches.

Although in some areas of federal law, state courts have concurrent jurisdiction with federal courts, other federal statutes provide that the federal courts' jurisdiction shall be exclusive.

Federal court jurisdiction is over two principal kinds of cases and controversies: (a) cases "arising under" federal law, including pendent jurisdiction over state law claims, and (b) controversies between citizens of different states.

For purposes of federal diversity-of-citizenship jurisdiction, the corporation is treated as a party defendant, whose citizenship (jurisdiction of incorporation and principal place of business) and that of the real defendants must be completely diverse from that of the plaintiff-shareholders, and there is no realignment of the corporation as a party whenever those in control of the corporation refuse to take action to undo the business transaction involved or so approve it that a demand would be futile.

State court jurisdiction over the subject matter, even in state courts of general jurisdiction, is subject to some limitations.[1] Within the scope of such jurisdiction, of course, limitations on its exercise can result from lack of jurisdiction over the parties,[2]

---

partnership or other unincorporated association without such capacity under such law may sue or be sued in its common name where a federal substantive right is involved. Fed.R.Civ.P. 17(b) (see sections 19, 41, 50, 58 supra). The federal substantive right exception codifies the court-developed rule in United Mine Workers of America v. Coronado Coal Co., 259 U.S. 344, 42 S.Ct. 570, 66 L.Ed. 975, 27 A.L.R. 762 (1922); Sturgis, "Unincorporated Associations as Parties to Actions", 33 Yale L.J. 383 (1924). See 29 U.S.C.A. § 185 (labor organization may sue and be sued as an entity; any judgment for money enforceable only against the organization and its assets). See also Marshall v. International Longshoremen's & Warehousemen's Union, 57 Cal.2d 781, 22 Cal.Rptr. 211, 371 P.2d 987 (1962).

4. See section 225 supra. Under certain circumstances, shareholders may intervene in corporate litigation to help protect the interests of the corporation. Note, 63 Harv.L.Rev. 1426 (1950).

5. See section 78 supra, for discussion of "contract" theory.

6. See section 360 infra.

1. E. g., McKinney's N.Y.Bus.Corp.Law, § 1313 (actions or special proceedings by foreign corporations); id. § 1314 (actions or special proceedings against foreign corporations); S.C.Code § 10–214 (1962) (foreign corporations as defendants); Gibbs v. Young, 242 S.C. 217, 130 S.E.2d 484 (1963). See section 83 supra.

2. See sections 84 and 97 supra and section 354 infra.

improper venue,[3] the doctrine of forum non conveniens (or "internal affairs rule"),[4] and statutes of limitations or laches.[5]

In several important areas of federal law, state courts have no jurisdiction over the subject matter because federal statutes provide that the federal courts' jurisdiction shall be exclusive.[6]

Federal court jurisdiction over the subject matter is over two principal kinds of cases and controversies: (a) cases "arising under" federal law, including pendent jurisdiction over state law claims, and (b) controversies between citizens of different states.

The growing body of federal corporation law is tending to become stricter as state law standards become more permissive.[7] In federal court litigation, whether jurisdiction be based on federal question or diversity of citizenship, the Federal Judicial Code [8] and Federal Rules of Civil Procedure apply in place of state procedural rules,[9] thus excluding some state law limitations restricting shareholder derivative actions.[10]

In many instances where shares or other securities are offered, sold, purchased, or exchanged, including issuance of securities, mergers and consolidations, involving the mails, interstate commerce, or the facility of a national securities exchange,[11] or shareholder approval is sought through proxy solicitation subject to the S.E.C. Proxy Rules,[12] claims under federal law exist even though there has been compliance with applicable state law or, even where state law violations coexist, federal remedies are more easily available. Federal law often imposes stricter standards for directors, officers, and other corporate personnel,[13] authorizes extraterritorial service of process,[14] and more liberal venue,[15] imposes federal contemporaneous-share-ownership requirements,[16] federal demand on board of directors and, when necessary, on shareholders,[17] federal settlement provisions,[18] avoids any state security-for-expenses requirement as to any claim under federal law,[19] and applies federal burden of proof [20] and statute of limitations concepts.[21]

Cases "arising under" Federal Law

Of the numerous federal laws under which corporation law "cases and controversies" are "arising", the more significant statutes are those regulating securities, especially the

---

3. See section 85 supra and section 355 infra.

4. See section 86 supra and section 356 infra.

5. See section 87 supra and section 357 infra.

6. E. g., Federal Securities Exchange Act § 27, 15 U.S.C.A. § 78aa. Cf. Federal Securities Act § 22, 15 U.S.C.A. § 77v (concurrent federal court and state court jurisdiction).

7. See section 12 supra. See also Fleischer, " 'Federal Corporation Law': An Assessment", 78 Harv.L. Rev. 1146 (1965); Friendly, "In Praise of Erie—and of the New Federal Common Law", 19 Record of N.Y.C.B.A. 64 (1964); Sullivan, "Federal Courts as an Effective Forum in Shareholders' Derivative Actions", 22 La.L.Rev. 580 (1962).

8. 28 U.S.C.A. §§ 1 et seq.

9. Hanna v. Plumer, 380 U.S. 460, 85 S.Ct. 1136, 14 L.Ed.2d 8 (1965).

10. See sections 361–367, 372 infra.

11. See section 298 supra.

12. See section 297 supra. See also Mills v. Electric Auto-Lite Co., —— U.S. ——, 90 S.Ct. 616, 24 L.Ed.2d 593 (1970); J. I. Case Co. v. Borak, 377 U.S. 426, 84 S.Ct. 1555, 12 L.Ed.2d 423 (1964).

13. See sections 297, 298 supra.

14. E. g., 28 U.S.C.A. § 1695; 15 U.S.C.A. § 78aa; Fed.R.Civ.P. 4; Puma v. Marriott, 294 F.Supp. 1116 (D.Del.1969). See sections 84, 97 supra.

15. E. g., 28 U.S.C.A. §§ 1391, 1392, 1401, 1404, 1406; 15 U.S.C.A. § 78aa. See section 85 supra and section 355 infra.

16. Fed.R.Civ.P. 23.1. See section 362 infra.

17. Fed.R.Civ.P. 23.1. See sections 364–367 infra.

18. Fed.R.Civ.P. 23.1. See section 374 infra.

19. See section 372 infra.

20. See, e. g., Kardon v. Nat'l Gypsum Co., 73 F. Supp. 798, 801–802 (E.D.Pa.1947), supplemented 83 F.Supp. 613 (E.D.Pa.1947).

21. See section 87 supra and section 357 infra.

Federal Securities Exchange Act of 1934 [22] and more particularly section 10b, and S.E. C. Rule 10b–5 thereunder,[23] and section 14, and the S.E.C. Proxy Rules thereunder.[24]

Pendent Jurisdiction

Where a federal court has jurisdiction over a claim arising under federal law, it also may determine closely related claims arising under state law.[25]

Federal Diversity-of-Citizenship Jurisdiction

In a shareholder derivative action, the claim asserted belongs to the corporation as does any eventual recovery. Only because the corporation itself has not brought the action [26] may the shareholder sue in its behalf. The corporation is an indispensable party,[27] in effect the real party plaintiff, but served and joined, as nominal party defendant, with the real defendant or defendants who have allegedly wronged it.

For purposes of federal diversity-of-citizenship jurisdiction, a corporation is deemed a citizen of its jurisdiction of incorporation and of its principal place of business.[28] Complete diversity between the plaintiffs and defendants is required for there to be a controversy between citizens of different states.

The problem of realignment of the corporation in federal diversity-of-citizenship cases is one example of the difficulties which arise because of the corporation's dual position in the litigation.

Suppose a New York resident who is a shareholder of a Pennsylvania corporation with principal place of business in Pennsylvania sues derivatively in a federal district court an alleged wrongdoer who is a citizen of Pennsylvania. If the corporation in this case is realigned as the real party plaintiff, there will be no diversity of citizenship, since a corporation is deemed to be a citizen of its jurisdiction of incorporation and principal place of business.[29]

For many years the federal courts held that the corporation must be realigned as a party plaintiff unless it was antagonistic to the plaintiff-shareholder in the sense that it was under the domination of the real defendant. The practice was to look behind the pleadings and thereby realign litigants in accordance with their real interests. This in

---

22. See sections 296–298 supra. See also Loomis & Eisenberg, "SEC as *Amicus Curiae* in Shareholder Litigation—A Reply", 52 A.B.A.J. 749 (1966); Shipley, "The SEC's *Amicus Curiae* Aid to Plaintiffs in Mutual Fund Litigation", 52 A.B.A.J. 337 (1966).

23. See section 298 supra. See also Securities and Exchange Commission v. Nat'l Securities, Inc., 393 U.S. 453, 89 S.Ct. 564, 21 L.Ed.2d 668 (1969).

24. See section 297 supra. See also Securities and Exchange Commission v. Nat'l Securities, Inc., 393 U.S. 453, 89 S.Ct. 564, 21 L.Ed.2d 668 (1969).

25. United Mine Workers of America v. Gibbs, 383 U.S. 715, 86 S.Ct. 1130, 16 L.Ed.2d 218 (1966); Hurn v. Oursler, 289 U.S. 238, 53 S.Ct. 586, 77 L.Ed. 1148 (1933); Osborn v. Bank of United States, 22 U.S. (9 Wheat.) 738, 6 L.Ed. 204 (1824); ALI Study of the Division of Jurisdiction between State and Federal Courts § 1313 (Tentative Draft No. 5, May 2, 1967). Compare Ellis v. Carter, 291 F.2d 270 (9th Cir. 1961) (upholding federal pendent jurisdiction over nonfederal claims), with Carliner v. Fair Lanes, Inc., 244 F.Supp. 25 (D.Md. 1965). As to extraterritorial service of process in connection with nonfederal claim, compare Puma v. Marriott, 294 F.Supp. 1116 (D.Del.1969), with Trussell v. United Underwriters, Ltd., 236 F.Supp. 801 (D.Colo.1964). See also Shakman, "The New Pendent Jurisdiction of the Federal Courts", 20 Stan. L.Rev. 262 (1968); Lowenfels, "Pendent Jurisdiction and the Federal Securities Acts", 67 Colum.L.Rev. 474 (1967); Ferguson, "Pendent Personal Jurisdiction in the Federal Court", 11 Vill.L.Rev. 56 (1965); Comment, "The Expanding Scope of Federal Pendent Jurisdiction", 34 Tenn.L.Rev. 413 (1966); Annot., 5 A.L.R.2d 1040 (1966).

26. See sections 364–367 infra.

27. See section 369 infra.

28. See section 88 supra.

29. The contention that the corporation is the real plaintiff and that therefore only diversity-of-citizenship between the corporation and the real defendants is required for federal diversity-of-citizenship (the minority shareholder plaintiff being analogized to a stakeholder-impleader) was rejected in J. R. A. Corp. v. Boylan, 30 F.Supp. 393 (S.D.N.Y.1939), aff'd per curiam, 109 F.2d 1018 (2d Cir. 1940); Annot., 18 A.L.R.2d 1022 (1951).

effect often meant a preliminary determination on the merits to resolve the jurisdictional issue.[30]

In 1957, the United States Supreme Court's decision in Smith v. Sperling,[31] a 5–4 holding, effected a substantial change in this approach. A new test was provided whereby the issue of antagonism was to be determined "on the face of the pleadings and by the nature of the controversy". Under this test there is no realignment whenever those in control of the corporation refuse to take action to undo the business transaction involved or so approve it that a demand to rescind is futile. However, collusion to satisfy jurisdictional requirements may still be shown to defeat diversity jurisdiction.[32]

The more-than-$10,000 jurisdictional amount requirement in a diversity-of-citizenship case is obviously satisfied if the plaintiff-shareholders' interest in the corporate claim meets that test. In a class action, it is not settled whether the claims of the class should be aggregated.[33] Perhaps the value of the shares owned by the plaintiff-shareholders should control.[34]

JURISDICTION OVER PARTIES

354. Over the corporation, in personam jurisdiction must be obtained, since neither quasi-in-rem nor in rem jurisdiction is sufficent to provide a basis for res judicata. Over the alleged wrongdoers, quasi-in-rem or in rem jurisdiction over the defendants' property, including shares owned by them, might be sufficient to satisfy a judgment for a sum of money. Some statutes provide for the implied appointment of the secretary of state as agent for service of process against directors of domestic corporations in any action relating to corporate affairs while they were directors. Under some federal statutes and in certain derivative actions in the federal courts, extraterritorial or nationwide service of process on the corporation is authorized. The Federal Rules of Civil Procedure facilitate service of process in the federal courts not only by their own liberal provisions but also by incorporating the local state procedures.

Since the corporation is an indispensable party and the alleged wrongdoers must be joined to secure an effectual judgment against them, jurisdictional requirements are extremely important.[1] In personam jurisdiction must be obtained over the corporation, and neither quasi-in-rem nor in rem jurisdiction is sufficient, since the resulting determination should be res judicata.[2] For recovery against alleged wrongdoers, in personam jurisdiction provides the most solid

30. Doctor v. Harrington, 196 U.S. 579, 25 S.Ct. 355, 49 L.Ed. 606 (1905); Carr v. Beverly Hills Corp., 237 F.2d 323 (9th Cir. 1956), rev'd per curiam, 354 U.S. 917, 77 S.Ct. 1375, 1 L.Ed.2d 433 (1957) (5–4). The jurisdictional issue was determined by federal law; the merits, since the Erie case, by applicable state law. Annot., 132 A.L.R. 193 (1941).

31. 354 U.S. 91, 77 S.Ct. 1112, 1 L.Ed.2d 1205, 68 A.L.R.2d 805 (1957) (5–4); Swanson v. Traer, 354 U.S. 114, 77 S.Ct. 1116, 1 L.Ed.2d 1221, 68 A.L.R.2d 820 (1957). Frankfurter, J., dissenting, contended that the majority flouted precedent, expanded federal diversity jurisdiction, and achieved an unconstitutional result. See Reed v. Robilio, 376 F.2d 392 (6th Cir. 1967); Note, "Diversity Requirements in Multi-Party Litigation", 58 Colum.L.Rev. 548 (1958); Annot., 68 A.L.R.2d 824 (1959). But cf. Levitan v. Stout, 97 F.Supp. 105 (W.D.Ky.1951) (corporate defendant realigned as plaintiff per Ky.Gen. Corp.Law § 271.605 (1953) (providing that corporation by shareholder or shareholders to be plaintiff, e. g., X Corporation by John Doe, Shareholder)).

32. See Fed.R.Civ.P. 23.1; Annot., 75 A.L.R.2d 717 (1961).

33. Compare Gas Service Co. v. Coburn, 389 F.2d 831 (10th Cir. 1968), with Alvarez v. Pan American Life Ins. Co., 375 F.2d 992 (5th Cir. 1967), cert. denied 389 U.S. 827, 88 S.Ct. 74, 19 L.Ed.2d 82 (1967). See Snyder v. Epstein, 290 F.Supp. 652 (E.D.Wis.1968); Twardzik v. Sepauley, 286 F.Supp. 346 (E.D.Pa.

1968). But see Vine v. Beneficial Finance Co., 252 F.Supp. 212 (S.D.N.Y.1966), modified 374 F.2d 627 (2d Cir. 1967), cert. denied 389 U.S. 970, 88 S.Ct. 463, 19 L.Ed.2d 460 (1968) (holding that $10,000 federal jurisdictional amount requirement was not satisfied in "spurious" class action, where alleged damage to class was $1,700,000, of which plaintiff's proportionate amount was only $273).

34. Twardzik v. Sepauley, 286 F.Supp. 346 (E.D.Pa. 1968). See Stern v. South Chester Tube Co., 390 U.S. 606, 88 S.Ct. 1332, 20 L.Ed.2d 177 (1968).

1. For discussion of judicial jurisdiction over corporations, see section 97 supra.

2. See Dean v. Kellogg, 294 Mich. 200, 292 N.W. 704 (1940).

basis, especially when implemented by any available provisional remedy of attaching property to satisfy any resulting judgment. Long-arm statutes promote service of process, not only on the indispensable corporate party, but also on the defendants who have allegedly wronged it,[3] they usually are subject to quasi-in-rem and in rem jurisdiction resulting from an attachment of any property they may have in the jurisdiction.[4] However, in many cases adequate property might not be available or an attachment might not be allowed. In some jurisdictions, for instance, an attachment is limited to an action for a money recovery, thereby excluding some forms of equitable relief.[5]

South Carolina was the first jurisdiction to provide an unusual solution to the problem where the alleged wrongdoers are nonresident directors of a domestic corporation. Under the South Carolina statute, a person who accepts election or appointment as a director of a domestic corporation is deemed to have appointed the Secretary of State of South Carolina as his agent for service of process in any action relating to corporate affairs arising while he was director.[6]

In some cases it may be possible to attach the shares registered in the name of the alleged wrongdoer and thereby obtain quasi-in-rem jurisdiction. However, the Uniform Commercial Code[7] prohibits an attachment or levy upon a security or any share or other interest evidenced thereby, which is outstanding, unless the security is actually seized by the officer making the attachment or levy, or the security has been surrendered to the issuer, under court order or otherwise.

Delaware, which has adopted the Uniform Commercial Code, has retained some older provisions, permits attachment of shares on the corporation's record of shareholders, and has extended this concept to reach the nonresident wrongdoer who is the equitable owner of shares in the jurisdiction.[8] This includes the case where the shares are registered on the corporate books in the "street name" of another person, usually the wrongdoer's broker. Seizure of equitable share interests is allowed only whenever the shares can be actually seized and identified so that the attachment can be noted in the corporation's record of shareholders.[9] However, Delaware has limited this procedure to an action for a sum of money only, and has refused to allow it where an injunction is sought.[10] As a result of such attachment

3. See section 97 supra. Platt Corp. v. Platt, 17 N. Y.2d 234, 270 N.Y.S.2d 408, 217 N.E.2d 134 (1966) (nonfeasance of absentee nonresident director held not to constitute tortious act within state under long-arm statute). But see Lawson v. Baltimore Paint & Chemical Corp., 298 F.Supp. 373 (D.Md. 1969) (directors held subject to service of process under long-arm statute for tortious act to corporation, even though they resided and held all of their meetings out of state, since their decisions were given effect by actions of officers and employees within state where principal office and plant were located).

4. Pomeroy v. Simon, 17 N.J. 59, 110 A.2d 19 (1954); Carrington, "The Modern Utility of Quasi in Rem Jurisdiction", 76 Harv.L.Rev. 303 (1962).

5. E. g., McKinney's N.Y. CPLR § 6201.

6. S.C.Bus.Corp.Act § 12–13.7 (1964); Wagenberg v. Charleston Wood Products, Inc., 122 F.Supp. 745 (E.D.S.C.1954) (upholding constitutionality of statute). Indiana, Michigan, and North Carolina have similar statutes.

7. Uniform Commercial Code § 8–317; see also McKinney's N.Y. CPLR, §§ 5201, 6202 (attachment). See Austin & Nelson, "Attaching and Levying on Corporate Shares", 16 Bus.Law. 336 (1961). See section 176 supra.

8. Del. Uniform Commercial Code § 8–317(1) (1967); Del.Gen.Corp.Law, § 324 (1967); Del.Code tit. 10, § 366 (1953); Hodson v. Hodson Corp., 32 Del.Ch. 76, 80 A.2d 180 (Ch.1951); see also First Western Financial Corp. v. Neumeyer, — Del.Ch. —, 240 A.2d 579 (Super.Ct.1968); Krizanek v. Smith, 32 Del.Ch. 513, 87 A.2d 871 (Sup.Ct.1952); Comment, "Attachment of Corporate Stock: The Conflicting Approaches of Delaware and the Uniform Stock Transfer Act", 73 Harv.L.Rev. 1579 (1960). Compare Tryon v. Silverstein, 10 Ariz.App. 25, 455 P.2d 474 (1969) (older garnishment statute held impliedly repealed by Uniform Stock Transfer Act).

9. Greene v. Johnston, 34 Del.Ch. 115, 99 A.2d 627, 42 A.L.R.2d 906 (Sup.Ct.1953).

10. Sands v. Lefcourt Realty Corp., 35 Del.Ch. 340, 117 A.2d 365 (Sup.Ct.1955). Cf. Lutz v. Boas, 38 Del.Ch. 563, 156 A.2d 96 (Ch.1959), aff'd sub nom.

provisions, directors and officers of Delaware corporations, who own shares therein, as well as other shareholders, are especially susceptible to the quasi-in-rem jurisdiction of the Delaware courts.

Whenever property, whether shares or otherwise, has been attached, the alleged wrongdoer may appear specially to raise jurisdictional objections, or he may make a general appearance which is a submission to the court's jurisdiction. But he cannot seek leave to appear for the purpose of contesting the claim, and then contend that his liability, if any, is limited to the value of the property seized.[11]

A more recent attachment technique would be available against directors and officers, if insurance had been secured to cover their litigation expenses, by attaching the policy if the insurer is amenable to process within the jurisdiction.[12]

Since jurisdictional problems in derivative actions arise whenever the corporation and the alleged wrongdoers are not amenable to process in the same state, it has been suggested that in any case where the corporation cannot be served, the derivative action should be allowed, with the judgment binding even the corporation.[13] Another partial solution to the problem, possible in the federal courts, is to permit nationwide service. When venue is laid pursuant to 28 U.S.C.A. § 1401, extraterritorial service upon the corporation is clearly possible.[14]

Service of process is facilitated in the federal courts by the Federal Rules of Civil Procedure, which not only have their own liberal provisions but also incorporate by

Rebstock v. Lutz, 39 Del.Ch. 25, 158 A.2d 487 (Sup. Ct.1960); Steinberg v. Shields, 38 Del.Ch. 423, 153 A.2d 599 (Ch.1959). Quasi-in-rem jurisdiction over the shares of nonresident directors of a Delaware corporation has been held lost when the Delaware corporation merged into a foreign corporation. Union Chemical & Materials Corp. v. Cannon, 38 Del. Ch. 203, 148 A.2d 348 (Sup.Ct.1959). Seizure of shares in a Delaware corporation held by a wholly-owned subsidiary of a parent German corporation has been vacated in an action against the parent corporation. Buechner v. Farbenfabriken Bayer Aktiengesellschaft, 38 Del.Ch. 329, 151 A.2d 125 (Ch.1959), aff'd 38 Del.Ch. 490, 154 A.2d 684 (Sup. Ct.1959).

11. McKinney's N.Y. CPLR, Rule 320(c); Lefcourt v. Sea Crest Hotel & Motor Inn, Inc., 54 Misc.2d 376, 282 N.Y.S.2d 896 (Sup.Ct.1967); Leftcourt Realty Corp. v. Sands, 35 Del.Ch. 164, 113 A.2d 428 (Ch.1955), aff'd 35 Del.Ch. 340, 117 A.2d 365 (Sup. Ct.1955).

12. Simpson v. Loehmann, 21 N.Y.2d 305, 287 N.Y.S. 2d 633, 234 N.E.2d 669 (1967); Seider v. Roth, 17 N. Y.2d 111, 269 N.Y.S.2d 99, 216 N.E.2d 312 (1966); Lefcourt v. Sea Crest Hotel & Motor Inn, Inc., 54 Misc.2d 376, 282 N.Y.S.2d 896 (Sup.Ct.1967). See section 380, n. 52 infra. See also Minichiello v. Rosenberg, 410 F.2d 106 (2d Cir. 1969) (en banc) (5–1–3), cert. denied 396 U.S. 844, 90 S.Ct. 69, 24 L. Ed.2d 94 (1969), reh. denied 396 U.S. 949, 90 S.Ct. 370, 24 L.Ed.2d 254 (1969) (upholding constitutionality of such omniforum rule); Stein, "Jurisdiction by Attachment of Liability Insurance", 43 N.Y. U.L.Rev. 1075 (1968).

13. A proposed bill in New York would have enabled a derivative action to proceed without joinder of the corporation. [1941] N.Y.L.Rev'n Comm'n Rep. 1941 Legis.Doc. No. 65(I) 209–236; Note, 50 Yale L. J. 1261 (1941). In Matter of Burge (Oceanic Trading Co.), 288 App.Div. 219, 122 N.Y.S.2d 232 (1st Dep't 1953), aff'd mem., 306 N.Y. 811, 118 N.E.2d 822 (1954), rev'g 203 Misc. 677, 118 N.Y.S.2d 23 (Sup.Ct. 1952), the appellate courts reversed the appointment, upon application of a minority shareholder, of a New York receiver of a Panamanian corporation to take over a corporate "asset" in New York —a cause of action against New York wrongdoing insiders—and to sue thereon. See Note, 44 Yale L. J. 1091 (1935) (suggesting receivership with receivers to sue wrongdoers where suable or mandatory injunction against corporation to sue). See Cohen v. Dana, 83 N.Y.S.2d 414 (Sup.Ct.1948), aff'd mem., 275 App.Div. 723, 87 N.Y.S.2d 614 (2d Dep't 1949), aff'd per curiam, 300 N.Y. 608, 90 N.E.2d 65 (1949); Levin v. Fisk Rubber Co., 30 Del.Ch. 31, 52 A.2d 741 (Ch. 1947); Cohen v. Dana, 287 N.Y. 405, 40 N.E.2d 227 (1942); Turner v. United Mineral Lands Corp., 308 Mass. 531, 33 N.E.2d 282 (1941); Dean v. Kellogg, 294 Mich. 200, 292 N.W. 704 (1940); Freeman v. Bean, 243 App.Div. 503, 276 N.Y.S. 310 (1st Dep't 1934), aff'd mem., 266 N.Y. 657, 195 N.E. 368 (1935). The problem is to some extent obviated by the increasing amenability to process of foreign corporations (see section 97 supra). See Keeffe, Levy & Donovan, "Lee Defeats Ben Hur", 33 Cornell L.Q. 327 (1948); Winer, "Jurisdiction over the Beneficiary Corporation in Stockholder's Suits", 22 Va. L.Rev. 153 (1935).

14. 28 U.S.C.A. § 1695; Lavin v. Lavin, 182 F.2d 870, 18 A.L.R.2d 1017 (2d Cir. 1950). Quaere, if venue is laid otherwise. Norte & Co. v. Huffines, 222 F.Supp. 90 (S.D.N.Y.1962), appeal dismissed 319 F.2d 336 (2d Cir. 1963). See also Comment, "Use of State Statutes by Federal District Courts in Extraterritorial Service of Process", 27 U.Chi.L.Rev. 751 (1960).

reference the local state procedures for achieving in personam and quasi-in-rem jurisdiction.[15]

VENUE

355. **State venue requirements often are tested by the plaintiff-shareholder's residence rather than by the corporation's residence. Venue in federal court cases is in the district where all the defendants reside or in which the claim arose or, if jurisdiction is based solely on diversity, also in the district where all the plaintiffs reside. A corporation may be sued in any district where it is incorporated, authorized to do business, or doing business, and such district is the residence of the corporation for venue purposes. A shareholder derivative action may be brought in any district where the corporation might have sued the same defendants. If the derivative action is brought in the federal district where the alleged wrongdoer resides, extraterritorial or nationwide service of process is authorized.**

In states where the required venue is the county of residence of plaintiff or defendant, the fact that the corporation is the real party plaintiff may not be enough to warrant a change of venue to the county of the corporation's principal business office, if the venue is originally laid in the county where the plaintiff-shareholder resides.[1]

A federal court action, where jurisdiction is founded only on diversity of citizenship, generally may be brought in the district where all plaintiffs or all defendants reside or in which the claim arose;[2] where, jurisdiction is not founded solely on diversity of citizenship, in the district where all defendants reside or in which the claim arose.[3] A corporation may be sued in any district in which it is incorporated or licensed to do

business or is doing business, and such district is to be regarded as the residence of such corporation for venue purposes.[4] Any shareholder derivative action may be brought in any district where the corporation might have sued the same defendants.[5]

As indicated, if the derivative action is brought in the federal district where the real party defendant resides, process may then be served upon the corporation in any district where it resides or may be found. This benefit of extraterritorial service of process is extremely important, and appears to have been intended, at least originally, to apply only when venue is laid in the district where the wrongdoer resides.[6]

FORUM NON CONVENIENS
356. **Forum non conveniens justifies the non-exercise of jurisdiction by a court in a forum which is seriously inconvenient for the trial of the action provided that a more appropriate forum is available. Analogous is the rule that a court should not interfere with the "internal affairs" of a foreign corporation. The effect is to relegate some corporate litigation to the courts of the jurisdiction of incorporation.**

Forum non conveniens is a doctrine which permits a court with jurisdiction over the subject matter and of the parties, with proper venue, in its discretion, to refuse to exercise its jurisdiction, if it is a seriously inconvenient forum for the trial of the action provided that a more appropriate forum is available.[1]

Since one important factor is that a court should not interfere with the "internal af-

15. Fed.R.Civ.P. 4. See section 176 supra.

[§ 355]
1. Feldmeier v. Webster, 208 Misc. 996, 145 N.Y.S.2d 365 (Sup.Ct.1955), aff'd mem., 1 A.D.2d 938, 150 N.Y.S.2d 581 (4th Dep't 1956). See section 85 supra.

2. 28 U.S.C.A. § 1391(a).

3. 28 U.S.C.A. § 1391(b).

4. 28 U.S.C.A. § 1391(c).

5. 28 U.S.C.A. § 1401. On the effect of such theoretical realignment of parties on diversity-of-citizenship jurisdiction, compare Schoen v. Mountain Producers Corp., 170 F.2d 707, 5 A.L.R.2d 1226 (3d Cir. 1948), cert. denied, 69 S.Ct. 746, 336 U.S. 937, 93 L.Ed. 1095 (1949), with Dowd v. Front Range Mines, Inc., 242 F.Supp. 591 (D.Colo.1965).

6. 28 U.S.C.A. § 1391. See section 354, n. 14 supra. See also section 85 supra.

[§ 356]
1. See section 86 supra.

fairs" of a foreign corporation, the doctrine is more frequently applied in corporate litigation when a foreign corporation is a real or nominal party defendant and there are issues of law of the jurisdiction of incorporation.[2]

The effect is to relegate some corporate litigation to the courts of the jurisdiction of incorporation, e.g., Delaware.

STATUTES OF LIMITATIONS; LACHES

357. **Statutes of limitations ordinarily bar derivative actions on corporate claims which if asserted by the corporation would have been barred. A few jurisdictions have special statutes of limitations applicable to at least certain kinds of derivative actions. In the absence of an applicable federal statute of limitations, the federal courts apply the most nearly applicable period of limitations of the forum. However, in cases of actual fraud, or even constructive fraud, the federal courts, at least in cases arising under federal law, will compute the period of limitations from the time of the discovery of the wrong rather than of the time of wrong. Even if commenced within the period of the applicable statute of limitations, an equitable action, such as an action for an injunction or a derivative action, can be barred by laches.**

Though a derivative action is in equity, the general tendency is to consider whether the corporate cause of action would have been barred by a statute of limitations had the action been brought by the corporation itself. Thus, if the corporation were seeking relief by way of rescission or an accounting, for example, the equitable period of limitations would be applicable. On the other hand, if the corporation were suing for negligence of the directors or waste, the applicable legal period of limitations would be applicable.

A cause of action for an accounting to recover not only losses resulting from alleged wrongful acts of directors but also to recover profits alleged to have been received by them has been held to be covered by the equitable period of limitations. A second cause of action stated in the same complaint based upon alleged negligence of directors and to recover for injury to the property of the corporation was held to be governed by a shorter period of limitations.[1]

State practice statutes usually have a series of periods of limitations applicable to different kinds of actions, thus requiring classification of the action to determine the applicable period.

Some jurisdictions have specific statutes of limitations applicable to at least certain kinds of derivative actions. The Michigan statute for example, provides in substance that a director shall not be held liable for any delinquency thereunder after six years from the date of such delinquency, or after two years from the time when such delinquency was discovered by one complaining thereof, whichever shall sooner occur.[2] New York in 1963 replaced a complex of provisions distinguishing between three-year, six-year, and 10-year derivative actions, with a uniform six-year period of limitations for an action by or on behalf of a corporation against a present or former director, officer, or shareholder for an accounting, or to procure a judgment on the ground of fraud, or to enforce a liability, penalty, or forfeiture, or to recover damages for waste or for an injury to property or for an accounting in conjunction therewith.[3]

[§ 356]

2. Compare Parvin v. Kaufmann, 43 Del.Ch. 461, 236 A.2d 425 (Sup.Ct.1967), with Lonergan v. Crucible Steel Co. of America, 37 Ill.2d 599, 229 N.E.2d 536 (1967).

[§ 357]

1. Potter v. Walker, 276 N.Y. 15, 11 N.E.2d 335 (1937). See also Burt v. Irvine Co., 237 Cal.App.2d 828, 47 Cal.Rptr. 392 (1965) (nonfeasance held negligence, not fraud, and therefore governed by two-year statute of limitations applicable to negligence actions). See section 87 supra.

2. Mich.Gen.Corp.Act § 21.47 (1948).

3. McKinney's N.Y. CPLR, § 213(8).

There are no general federal statutes of limitations, and most federal enactments do not contain their own statutes of limitations. The result is that the federal courts, in a case arising under a federal law without its own statute of limitations or in a diversity case,[4] must look to the most nearly applicable period of limitations of the forum to determine the period of limitations.[5]

The traditional theory is that statutes of limitations applicable to "actions at law" run from the time of wrong and that laches applicable to "suits in equity" run from the discovery of the wrong.

The period of limitations usually begins to run when the wrongs are committed, although in some cases it begins to run upon the "discovery" of the "fraud"—raising questions as to what wrongs constitute "fraud" and knowledge by whom constitutes "discovery".[6]

When there is actual fraud the statute of limitations does not begin to run until the facts are discovered. Here the knowledge of innocent directors or knowledge of shareholders as a class is determinative, rather than that of the plaintiff-shareholder.[7]

The federal courts, at least in federal question cases, and some state courts apply the same rule for actual fraud to cases involving constructive fraud.[8] A minority of jurisdictions refuse to equate concealment of the facts of the transaction with actual fraud. Hence, unless actual misrepresentation can be shown, the statute begins to run at the time the wrong is committed.[9]

It is arguable that their actual concealment of the wrong or their failure to have their corporation sue, or, as directors or officers, to sue the wrongdoers in timely actions, might itself constitute a new, separate wrong—"secondary fraud" or "secondary wrong"—subject to its own statute of limitations.[10]

Tolling of the statute of limitations is another problem which may arise in a derivative action. If the plaintiff-shareholder was under a disability at the time the corporate cause of action arose, for example, may he claim the benefit of tolling, even though the normal period of limitations on the corporate cause of action expired during his disability? This question arose in a federal diversity case which was decided under New York law. The plaintiff was the sole shareholder and this fact apparently prompted the court to answer the question in the affirmative.[11] Whether or not this same re-

---

4. See Guaranty Trust Co. of New York v. York, 326 U.S. 99, 65 S.Ct. 1464, 89 L.Ed. 2079, 160 A.L.R. 1231 (1945), reh. denied 326 U.S. 806, 66 S.Ct. 7, 90 L.Ed. 491 (1945) (state statute of limitations, whether characterized as "substantive" or "procedural" under state law, held under "outcome test" of Erie R. R. v. Tompkins to be "substantive" and to bar recovery in diversity case).

5. E. g., Janigan v. Taylor, 344 F.2d 781 (1st Cir. 1965), cert. denied 382 U.S. 879, 86 S.Ct. 163, 15 L. Ed.2d 120 (1965); Connelly v. Balkwill, 174 F.Supp. 49 (N.D.Ohio 1959), aff'd on opinion below 279 F.2d 685 (6th Cir. 1960). See generally Saylor v. Lindsley, 302 F.Supp. 1174 (S.D.N.Y.1969).

6. 2 G. Hornstein, Corporation Law and Practice § 718 (1959); N. Lattin, The Law of Corporations 388–393 (1959); Note, "Statute of Limitations and Shareholders' Derivative Actions", 56 Colum.L.Rev. 106 (1956); Hoffheimer, "Stockholders' Suits and the Statute of Limitations in Ohio", 18 U.Cin.L. Rev. 467 (1949); Annot., 123 A.L.R. 346 (1939).

7. See Lever v. Guaranty Trust Co., 289 N.Y. 615, 43 N.E.2d 837 (1942).

8. Janigan v. Taylor, 344 F.2d 781 (1st Cir. 1965), cert. denied 382 U.S. 879, 86 S.Ct. 163, 15 L.Ed.2d 120 (1965); Tobacco & Allied Stocks, Inc. v. Transamerica Corp., 143 F.Supp. 323 (D.Del.1956), aff'd 244 F.2d 902 (3d Cir. 1957). Quaere, as to the rule in a diversity case. See note 4 supra. See generally Saylor v. Lindsley, 302 F.Supp. 1174 (S.D.N.Y. 1969).

9. See Ebbert v. Plymouth Oil Co., 338 Pa. 272, 13 A.2d 42 (1942).

10. See Golding v. Golding, 4 A.D.2d 65, 163 N.Y.S.2d 118 (1st Dep't 1957); Forbes v. Finkelstein, 7 Misc. 2d 450, 164 N.Y.S.2d 742 (Sup.Ct.1957), aff'd per curiam 5 A.D.2d 825, 171 N.Y.S.2d 793 (1st Dep't 1958); Walker v. Man, 142 Misc. 277, 253 N.Y.S. 458 (Sup. Ct.1931).

11. Drews v. Eastern Sausage & Provision Co., 125 F.Supp. 289 (S.D.N.Y.1954); International Rys. of Central America v. United Fruit Co., 373 F.2d 408 (2d Cir. 1967), cert. denied 387 U.S. 921, 87 S.Ct. 2031, 2035, 18 L.Ed.2d 975 (1967), reh. denied, 389 U.S. 1059, 88 S.Ct. 757, 19 L.Ed.2d 861 (1968), held that the statute of limitations on a corpora-

sult would be reached where there were several shareholders seems somewhat doubtful.

Even if commenced within the period of the applicable statute of limitations, an equitable action, such as an action for an injunction or other equitable relief or a derivative action, can be barred by the equitable doctrine of laches.[12] While mere passage of time usually is not enough to constitute laches, inaction by the plaintiff-shareholder after acquiring knowledge of the wrong and the vesting of rights can be fatal.

B. INTRODUCTION TO DERIVATIVE ACTIONS

ORIGIN AND DEVELOPMENT OF DERIVATIVE ACTIONS

358. Equity developed the derivative action so that the shareholder "derivatively" or "secondarily" could enforce a corporate right against insiders or outsiders, where those in control of the corporation refused to have the corporation sue directly, and thereby protect the whole community of corporate interests— creditors and shareholders, including his own investment in the corporation. The plaintiff-shareholder in effect sues as guardian ad litem for the corporation, which although the real party plaintiff, is brought into the litigation as a nominal party defendant. The derivative action, because of its procedural development, is equitable in nature and besides often involves equitable issues of breach of fiduciary duty but can involve law issues of due care. While the derivative action serves a useful purpose, it is susceptible to abuse by "strike suits" when brought by small shareholders and their attorneys to gain private settlement and self-enrichment. Misuses of the derivative remedy led to various restrictions being placed upon it by statutes, rules of practice, and increased judicial recognition of the plaintiff-shareholder as guardian ad litem or fiduciary for the corporation.

Equity developed the derivative action so that the shareholder could enforce a corporate right or claim (that is, one derived from the corporation) and thereby indirectly protect his interest in the corporation.[1]

There is no need for such an equitable remedy except when those in control of the

derivative actions, such law has been held substantive and controlling, thus precluding any shareholder derivative action in behalf of such corporation. Hausman v. Buckley, 299 F.2d 696, 93 A.L.R. 2d 1340 (2d Cir. 1962), cert. denied 369 U.S. 885, 82 S. Ct. 1157, 8 L.Ed.2d 286 (1962); Levine v. Milton, 219 Del.Ch. 145, 219 A.2d 145 (Ch. 1966).

See Block, "Current Critical Points in Stockholder Litigation", 62 Nw.U.L.Rev. 181 (1967); Dykstra, "The Revival of the Derivative Suit", 116 U.Pa.L. Rev. 74 (1967); Hornstein, "Shareholder's Derivative Suit in the United States", 1967 J.Bus.L. 282; Prunty, "The Shareholder's Derivative Suit: Notes on Its Derivation", 32 N.Y.U.L.Rev. 980 (1957). See sections 361–363 infra. See Atwell v. Bide-A-Wee Home Ass'n, 59 Misc.2d 321, 299 N.Y.S.2d 40 (Sup. Ct.1969) (derivative action by member in right of membership corporation). Derivative actions are usually brought by minority shareholders since majority shareholders can usually prevail upon the corporation to sue in its own name. The existence of the possible resort to a derivative action can serve as a deterrent to such abuse of power. The current amount of such litigation for alleged breach of management duties and other wrongs is very extensive. As substitutes for derivative actions, some commentators have suggested administrative control. Hornstein, "A New Forum for Stockholders", 45 Colum.L.Rev. 35 (1945); Lasswell, "A Non-Bureaucratic Alternative to Minority Stockholders' Suits, A Proposal", 43 Colum.L.Rev. 1036 (1943); Dean, "A Reply", 43 Colum.L.Rev. 1040 (1943); Podell, "A Third Viewpoint", 43 Colum.L.Rev. 1045 (1943); Hornstein, "Legal Controls for Intracorporate Abuse—Present and Future", 41 Colum.L.Rev. 405 (1941). In 1965, the S.E.C. sued Texas Gulf Sulphur Co. and several of its officers, directors and employees, for alleged violations of S.E.C. Rule 10b–5 to recover profits in behalf of former shareholders who had sold their shares on the ground that information concerning the corporation's rich ore discovery in Canada had been withheld, etc. Securities and Exchange Commission v. Texas Gulf Sulphur Co., 401 F.2d 833 (2d Cir. 1968) (en banc), cert. denied 394 U.S. 976, 89 S.Ct. 1454, 22 L.Ed.2d 756 (1969). Other commentators have suggested increased attorney general action. Berlack, "Stockholders' Suits, A Possible Substitute", 35 Mich.L. Rev. 597 (1937); Pound, "Visitorial Jurisdiction Over Corporations in Equity", 49 Harv.L.Rev. 369

tion's claim against its controlling shareholder was not tolled on the basis of the latter's domination of the plaintiff since there was less than full, complete, and exclusive control.

12. Tobacco & Allied Stocks, Inc. v. Transamerica Corp., 143 F.Supp. 323 (D.Del.1956), aff'd 244 F.2d 902 (3d Cir. 1957).

1. If the law of the jurisdiction of incorporation of the corporation does not recognize shareholder

corporation refuse to sue in the corporate name. Hence a showing of the inadequacy of legal remedy by showing an unsuccessful demand that the corporation take steps to enjoin or redress the wrong is usually required before a shareholder may sue derivatively.[2]

' A wrong to the corporation is the basis for the action and any recovery usually goes into the corporate treasury for the protection of the whole community of corporate interests—creditors and shareholders.[3] In this sense, the derivative action is unique,

for the plaintiff-shareholder does not sue for his own direct benefit or in his own direct right but rather as a guardian ad litem for the corporation.[4]

The corporation, moreover, occupies a dual position in the litigation. Refusing to sue in its own name as party plaintiff, it is brought into the action as a nominal party defendant, but at the same time is the real party plaintiff. This gives rise to many procedural complications, since the ordinary procedural rules have not been framed with such a situation in mind, involving such matters as the shareholders standing to sue,[5] the necessity of exhausting intracorporate remedies before seeking judicial relief,[6] joinder of claims and counterclaims,[7] joinder of parties,[8] representation by counsel of the several parties,[9] permissible defenses by the various defendants,[10] nature of relief,[11] problems of settlement,[12] res judicata effect,[13] and incidence of litigation expenses.[14]

Since the corporation's cause of action is being asserted and any favorable judgment thereon will usually be in favor of the corporation,[15] the corporation is usually an indispensable party to the action.[16] Problems of serving it and the alleged wrongdoing defendants often occur.[17]

(1936). For statutory provisions for interrogatories by secretary of state, see ABA–ALI Model Bus. Corp.Act §§ 130, 131. See Tipon, "Shareholders' Derivative Suits in the Philippines: An Appraisal in the Light of Comparative Law and Practice", 43 Philippine L.J. 486 (1968); Cazorla, "Derivative Actions Under Spanish Corporation Law", 4 Tex.Int'l L.F. 359 (1968); Falkenhausen & Steefel, "Shareholders' Rights in German Corporations (AG and GMBH)", 10 Am.J.Comp.L. 407 (1961); Starr, "Protection of Stockholders' Rights in the French Societe Anonyme", 40 Tul.L.Rev. 57 (1965); Koessler, "Stockholder's Suit: A Comparative View", 46 Colum.L.Rev. 238 (1946). Analogous to derivative actions is the problem of shareholder intervention in litigation brought directly by or against the corporation. Pellegrino v. Nesbit, 203 F.2d 463, 37 A.L.R.2d 1296 (9th Cir. 1953); Rugee v. Hadley Products, Inc., 73 Ariz. 362, 241 P.2d 798, 33 A.L.R.2d 468 (1952); Thorman v. Dome Producing & Developing Co., 50 Cal.App.2d 201, 122 P.2d 927 (1942); Note, "Shareholder Intervention in Corporate Litigation", 63 Harv.L.Rev. 1426 (1950).

See Gower, "Some Contrasts Between British and American Corporation Law", 69 Harv.L.Rev. 1369, 1387–1389 (1956), discussing the power of the British Board of Trade to appoint an inspector to investigate the affairs of a company where, e. g., there are circumstances suggesting oppression of minorities, or fraud or misconduct by the directors, or failure to give the shareholders information which they might reasonably expect. The inspector (generally an independent barrister, solicitor, or accountant) reports to the Board. Normally, the report is published. As a result, the wrong may be remedied. In any event, the facts will have been discovered. The Board may institute civil or criminal proceedings, or petition for winding up or for the alternative remedy under section 210 of the Companies Act. Inspectors have been appointed in about 10 percent of the cases in which complaints have been made to the Board. In many other cases, preliminary discussions have brought about settlements agreeable to the complainants.

2. See sections 364–367 infra.

3. See section 373 infra.

4. See section 374 infra.

5. See sections 361–363 infra.

6. See sections 364–367 infra.

7. See section 368 infra.

8. See section 369 infra.

9. See section 370 infra.

10. See section 371 infra.

11. See sections 373, 375 infra.

12. See section 374 infra.

13. See section 376 infra.

14. See sections 377–380 infra.

15. See section 373 infra.

16. See section 369 infra.

17. See section 354 supra.

The wrong to the corporation may be perpetrated by either outsiders or insiders. The need for the derivative remedy is best illustrated when those in control of the corporation are the alleged wrongdoers, for they can compound their wrong by preventing an action by the corporation against themselves. Redress in the form of a separate action by each individual shareholder whenever the value of his shares is impaired by a wrong to the corporation would result in unnecessary multiplicity of actions and could prejudice creditors. Hence, the value of the derivative remedy is that it allows a single action brought by a shareholder for complete relief to the corporation as a whole, thus protecting both creditors and shareholders according to their respective interests.

If two or more derivative actions are commenced by different shareholders asserting the same corporate claims against a person or persons who have allegedly wronged the corporation, the later actions can be stayed pending the outcome of the earlier actions or the actions can be consolidated or the later actions dismissed by court order, in order to prevent undue harassment from multiplicity of actions.[18]

Derivative actions are sometimes referred to as actions "in the right of a corporation", "secondary actions by shareholders", or "actions to enforce a secondary right on the part of shareholders." There is even a further breakdown: "shareholders' derivative action brought in the right of the corporation to procure a judgment in its favor".

In a derivative action, the plaintiff-shareholder represents not only the corporation in behalf of whom and on whose claim he is suing but also the other shareholders similarly situated. In this sense, a derivative action is both a representative action and a class action.[19]

The derivative action, because of its procedural development, is equitable in nature [20] and besides often involves equitable issues of breach of fiduciary duty—traditionally tried without a jury—but can involve issues of due care and other issues traditionally triable by jury.[21]

18. Dresdner v. Goldman Sachs Trading Corp., 240 App.Div. 242, 269 N.Y.S. 360 (2d Dep't 1934). See Hamburg v. Dillon, Read & Co., 146 N.Y.L.J. No. 102, 13 (Sup.Ct.1961) (staying fifth shareholder derivative action after four prior actions on same corporate claims had been consolidated); Witmondt v. Shima, 151 N.Y.L.J. No. 90, 14 (Sup.Ct.1964) (ordering consolidation of three shareholder derivative actions and selecting plaintiff-shareholder's attorneys in first action as general counsel on grounds that first action was instituted more than month before other two, that some eight times more shares were represented in first action than in second action, and that attorney in third action favored such selection). See also section 370, n. 4 infra.

19. Snyder v. Harris, 394 U.S. 332, 89 S.Ct. 1053, 22 L.Ed.2d 319 (1969); Green v. Wolf Corp., 406 F.2d 291 (2d Cir. 1968), cert. denied, 395 U.S. 977, 89 S.Ct. 2131, 23 L.Ed.2d 766 (1969); Hohmann v. Packard Inst. Co., 399 F.2d 711 (7th Cir. 1968); Eisen v. Carlisle & Jacquelin, 391 F.2d 555 (2d Cir. 1968); Gas Service Co. v. Coburn, 389 F.2d 831 (10th Cir. 1968); Dolgow v. Anderson, 45 F.R.D. 470 (E.D.N.Y.1968); "The Class Action—A Symposium", 10 B. & C.Ind. & Com.L.Rev. 497 (1969); Bernfeld, "Class Actions and Federal Securities Laws", 55 Cornell L.Rev. 78 (1969); Simeone, "Procedural Problems of Class Suits", 60 Mich.L.Rev. 90 (1962); Comment, "The Jurisdiction and Venue of Federal Courts in Class Actions", 7 Washburn L.J. 347 (1968); Note, "Class Action Treatment of Securities Fraud Suits Under the Revised Rule 23", 36 Geo. Wash.L.Rev. 1150 (1968); Comment, "Spurious Class Actions Based Upon Securities Frauds Under the Revised Federal Rules of Civil Procedure", 35 Fordham L.Rev. 295 (1966); Note, "Proposed Rule 23: Class Actions Reclassified", 51 Va.L.Rev. 629 (1965).

20. United Copper Securities Co. v. Amalgamated Copper Co., 244 U.S. 261, 37 S.Ct. 509, 61 L.Ed. 1119 (1917) (holding that derivative action was equitable and therefore could not be maintained at law for damages for violation of Sherman Antitrust Act).

21. In Fanchon & Marco, Inc. v. Paramount Pictures, Inc., 202 F.2d 731, 36 A.L.R.2d 1336 (2d Cir. 1953), the court (2-1) allowed a shareholder to sue an alleged violator of the antitrust laws in a derivative action and thereby enforce the corporation's statutory cause of action; the court indicated that provision could be made under the merged procedure of the federal rules for reference to a jury, unless waived, of the issue of the violation of the antitrust laws causing damage to the corporation. The dissent contended that a shareholder derivative action could not be maintained in equity for treble damages under the antitrust laws. Prior to 1963, New York had a statutory provision for jury trial or any issue of negligence in derivative actions in behalf of business corporations. Superseded McKinney's N.Y.Gen.Corp. Law § 61. Until the

While the derivative action serves a useful purpose, it is susceptible to abuse by "strike-suits" or "blackmail by litigation" when brought by small shareholders and their attorneys primarily to enrich themselves. Derivative actions, whether legitimate or not, are often protracted, time-consuming for corporate management, and very expensive. Nuisance actions, private settlements with the corporation buying off the complainant,[22] and other misuses of the de-

rivative remedy led to various restrictions being placed upon it.[23] These restrictions, unique to the derivative action, require differentiation between derivative actions and nonderivative actions, giving rise to various problems of characterization.[24]

Early restrictions on derivative actions developed in the federal courts, which had the additional problem of collusive diversity-of-citizenship jurisdiction.[25] The rules set forth in Hawes v. Oakland [26] became Federal Equity Rule 94, Federal Equity Rule 27,[27] and later Federal Rule of Civil Procedure 23(b), and still later Federal Rule of Civil Procedure 23.1.[28]

1960's, it was usually assumed that there was no constitutional right to a jury trial in a shareholder derivative action under U.S.Const. Amend. VII, which preserves right to jury trial "in suits at common law", since a derivative action is a suit in equity. The United States Supreme Court has held that shareholders in federal court derivative actions are guaranteed trial by jury on issues on which the corporation, if it had sued directly, would have had a right to jury trial. Ross v. Bernhard, —— U.S. ——, 90 S.Ct. 733, —— L.Ed.2d —— (1970), rev'g 403 F.2d 909 (2d Cir. 1968); DePinto v. Provident Security Life Ins. Co., 323 F.2d 826 (9th Cir. 1963), cert. denied 376 U.S. 950, 84 S.Ct. 965, 11 L.Ed.2d 969 (1964) reh. denied 383 U.S. 973, 86 S.Ct. 1269, 16 L.Ed.2d 313 (1966) (holding that whether or not there was right to jury trial in shareholder derivative action depended upon whether any of claims asserted on behalf of corporation were of kind which, if asserted directly by corporation, would be cognizable in action at common law, such as claims for damages for negligence, as distinguished from claims for breach of fiduciary duties or for equitable relief). See also Richland v. Crandall, 259 F.Supp. 274 (S.D.N.Y.1966); Suesholtz v. Baruch-Foster Corp., 158 N.Y.L.J. No. 96, 22 (Sup. Ct.1967); Notes, 74 Yale L.J. 725 (1965); 49 Cornell L.Q. 664 (1964).

22. See section 374 infra. "Strike suit" has been defined as "an action brought in whole or in part for its nuisance value and whose primary motivation is not the welfare of the stockholders. Originally, its principal purpose was usually to obtain a settlement for the sole benefit of the complaining stockholder—the amount of the proposed settlement being far greater than any possible injury suffered by the complainant, whose equity in the corporation was typically (as the courts rarely failed to point out) minuscule. Today, with general acceptance of the principle that any recovery, including the proceeds of any settlement, must go to the corporation, the motivation of a strike suit is more likely to be the hope and expectation of the plaintiff's lawyer —often the actual instigator of the suit—that the court will allow him a generous fee out of any fund brought into court or out of the corporation's assets if the benefit resulting to the corporation from his efforts takes some form other than a cash recovery." G. Washington & J. Bishop, Indemnifying the Corporate Executive; Business, Legal, and Tax Aspects of Reimbursement for Personal Liabil-

ity (1963). "Strike litigation" is probably a better term. The whole purpose is to avoid an action. They are more like "strike campaigns".

23. Compare F. Wood, Survey and Report Regarding Stockholders' Derivative Suits (Chamber of Commerce of the State of New York 1944), with Hornstein, "The Death Knell of Stockholder's Derivative Suits in New York", 32 Calif.L.Rev. 123 (1944). See also Hornstein, "New Aspects of Stockholder's Derivative Suits", 47 Colum.L.Rev. 1 (1947); Note, Extortionate Corporate Litigation: The Strike Suit", 34 Colum.L.Rev. 1308 (1934). For an amusing account of Clarence H. Venner, a pioneer "strike-suitor" whose name is immortalized in some leading cases, see J. Livingston, The American Stockholder 50 et seq. (1958). "Venner was called a nuisance, but he was also a legal Robin Hood, a protector of the ignorant. By constantly challenging the proposals of companies, by demanding to have stock 'appraised out'—as the expression is—in mergers, by examining every legal loophole, he kept corporation officials and lawyers alert to their obligations to security owners. They had to observe the letter as well as the spirit of their charters and bylaws, or face Venner. He was like an auditing system in business, or a policeman on a beat—a restraint, on people who might be tempted. True, he would sell his nightstick—at a price. But the mere fact that he wore a coat of mail, often called black, produced higher corporate morality. He raised the level of the corporate conscience. He made such a nuisance of himself that the phrase 'strike suit' is associated with his name. And laws to protect corporations from strike suits have crystallized."

24. See section 360 infra.

25. Hawes v. Oakland, 104 U.S. 450, 452–453, 26 L. Ed. 827, 829 (1882). See section 359 infra.

26. 104 U.S. 450, 26 L.Ed. 827 (1882). See sections 362, 364–367 infra.

27. Fed.Eq.R. 27, 226 U.S. 656 (1912).

28. Fed.R.Civ.P. 23.1. See sections 362, 364–367 infra.

Beginning with New York in 1944, several states enacted statutes or promulgated rules of procedure, the latter usually patterned on the Federal Rules of Civil Procedure, regulating various phases of derivative actions.[29]

The interplay of local statutory provisions and the Federal Rules of Civil Procedure in derivative actions in the federal courts have created many problems.[30]

Judicial amelioration of derivative action abuses has also occurred, as witness the court holdings to the effect that the shareholder-plaintiff is a guardian ad litem or fiduciary and holds any recovery by settlement or otherwise as constructive trustee for the corporation.[31]

STATUTES AND RULES CONCERNING DERIVATIVE ACTIONS

359. **Early restrictions on shareholder derivative actions developed in the federal courts, primarily in Hawes v. Oakland, are now part of the Federal Rules of Civil Procedure. Rule 23.1, formerly 23(b), states the "contemporaneous-share-ownership" requirement, bars collusive actions, and requires prior exhaustion of intracorporate remedies. Rule 23.1, formerly 23(c), prohibits the dismissal or compromise of such actions without court approval. Some state statutes have imposed the "contemporaneous-share-ownership" requirement; required the small plaintiff-shareholder to post security for the corporation's litigation expenses, including attorneys' fees; provided for indemnifying corporate personnel for their litigation expenses; imposed a special statute of limitations for certain actions against directors or officers for mismanagement; or provided for reimbursement of the defendants' expenses by the plaintiffs even when security therefor has not previously been given. Several states which have patterned their rules of procedure on the Federal Rules of Civil Procedure have promulgated most of Rule 23.1.**

Early restrictions on derivative actions, as previously mentioned, developed in the federal courts, their principal source being the rules set forth in Hawes v. Oakland and carried into Federal Equity Rule 94, Federal Equity Rule 27, and later Federal Rule of Civil Procedure 23(b), presently 23.1.[1]

Under Federal Rule of Civil Procedure 23.1, formerly 23(b), the plaintiff must allege, in a verified complaint, that he was a shareholder at the time of the transaction of which he complains or that his share thereafter devolved on him by operation of law;[2] that the action is not a collusive one to confer jurisdiction on the federal court;[3] and, with particularity, the efforts of the plaintiff, if any, made to obtain the action he desires from the directors and, if necessary, from the shareholders, and the reasons for his failure to obtain the action or for not making the effort.[4] Rule 23.1, formerly 23(c), also prohibits dismissal or compromise without court approval, with such notice to other shareholders as the court may direct.[5] Under Rule 23.1 the derivative action may not be maintained if it appears that the plaintiff does not fairly and adequately represent the interests of the shareholders similarly situated in enforcing the right of the corporation.

---

29. See section 359 infra.

30. Erie R. R. v. Tompkins, 304 U.S. 64, 58 S.Ct. 817, 82 L.Ed. 1188, 114 A.L.R. 1487 (1938). See sections 361, 362, 365, 366, 372 infra.

31. See section 374 infra.

1. See section 358 nn. 25–28 supra.

2. See section 362 infra. Surowitz v. Hilton Hotels Corp., 383 U.S. 363, 86 S.Ct. 845, 15 L.Ed.2d 807 (1966), reh. denied 384 U.S. 915, 86 S.Ct. 1333, 16 L. E.2d 367 (1966), upheld a complaint in a derivative action brought by a small shareholder whose verification stated that some of the allegations were true and that "on information and belief" she thought the others were true, despite the fact that she did not understand the complaint, where the record showed that she, to protect her investment, acted in good faith on the basis of advice by her counsel and financial advisor son-in-law, and that there were grave fraud charges based on reasonable beliefs growing out of careful investigation. The case was subsequently settled for $825,000, paid by 13 directors to the corporation. 116 New York Times, No. 39,744 at 69, col. 6 (Nov. 17, 1966).

3. See section 353 supra.

4. See sections 364–367 infra.

5. See section 374 infra.

New York in its series of legislative enactments beginning in 1941, regulated various phases of derivative actions in a four-fold approach: (a) contemporaneous-share-ownership requirement; [6] (b) provision requiring the small plaintiff-shareholder to post security for expenses, including attorneys' fees, of the corporation upon application by the corporation; [7] (c) provisions for indemnifying corporate personnel for their litigation expenses; [8] and (d) a special six-year statute of limitations for certain actions brought by or in behalf of a corporation against its directors, officers, or shareholders.[9]

Prior to 1941, New York already had enacted its provision [10] authorizing actions for specified misconduct against a corporation by its officers or directors to be brought by the corporation, or a receiver or trustee-in-bankruptcy thereof,[11] or by an officer [12] or director [13] thereof, creditor thereof,[14] or, in a shareholder derivative action brought in the right of the corporation to procure a judgment in its favor,[15] by a shareholder, voting trust certificate holder, or the owner of a beneficial interest in shares thereof. Derivative actions by directors and officers are not subject to many of the various restrictions imposed on derivative actions by shareholders.[16]

6. See section 362 infra.

7. See section 372 infra.

8. See section 380 infra.

9. See section 357 supra.

10. McKinney's N.Y.Bus.Corp.Law § 720(a); id. § 1318 (applicable to directors and officers of domestic corporations and to directors and officers of foreign corporations doing business in New York not exempted therefrom by § 1320). On the earlier New York legislation, see generally Hornstein, "Rights of Stockholders in the New York Courts", 56 Yale L.J. 942 (1947); House, "Stockholders' Suits and the Coudert-Mitchell Laws", 20 N.Y.U.L.Q.Rev. 377 (1945); Hornstein, "The Death Knell of Stockholders' Derivative Suits in New York", 32 Calif.L.Rev. 123 (1944); Carson, "Further Phases of Derivative Actions against Directors", 29 Cornell L.Q. 431 (1944); Note, 30 Va.L.Rev. 656 (1944).

11. A receiver or trustee-in-bankruptcy would take over most corporate assets, including most corporate rights of action. See McKinney's N.Y.Bus. Corp.Law § 1206. Federal Bankruptcy Act § 70a(5), (6), 11 U.S.C.A. § 110a(5), (6); McKinney's N.Y.Pers.Prop.Law § 41; Annot., 66 A.L.R.2d 1217 (1959).

12. See section 229 supra.

13. See section 217 supra.

14. See McKinney's N.Y.Bus.Corp.Law, § 1201 (action by judgment creditor for sequestration). A creditor may pursue other procedures to reach corporate causes of action. See, e. g., McKinney's N.Y. CPLR, § 5201 (debt or property subject to enforcement; proper garnishee); § 5202 (judgment creditor's rights in personal property); § 5232 (levy upon personal property); § 6202 (debt or property subject to attachment; proper garnishee).

A judgment creditor's action, akin to the old creditor's bill, might enable the creditor to reach, under the general equity powers of the court, a cause of action not arising out of contract. Other statutes might give creditors standing to sue officers or directors, etc. Before a creditor may sue, judgment must be obtained and execution returned unsatisfied against the corporation. Buttles v. Smith, 281 N.Y. 226, 22 N.E.2d 350 (1939); Hyde v. Everett Van Kleeck & Co., 17 Misc.2d 375, 190 N.Y.S.2d 914 (Sup.Ct.1959); see also Goodwin v. Whitener, 262 N.C. 582, 138 S.E.2d 232 (1964) (requiring prior demand on corporation or its receiver and joinder of corporation); Capitol Wine & Spirit Corp. v. Pokrass, 277 App.Div. 184, 98 N.Y.S.2d 291 (1st Dep't 1950), aff'd on other grounds 302 N.Y. 734, 98 N.E. 2d 704 (1951), reargument denied 302 N.Y. 840, 100 N.E.2d 37 (1951); H. Ballantine, Ballantine on Corporations § 351 (rev. ed. 1946); Annot., 50 A.L.R. 462 (1927). Apart from statute, and the traditional creditors' bill, creditors may not sue directors or officers for breach of their duty to the corporation. Allen v. Cochran, 160 La. 425, 107 So. 292, 50 A.L. R. 459 (1926).

15. For restrictions of such a shareholder derivative action, see sections 361, 362, 365, 372–374 infra.

16. Where the director or officer who commences a derivative action ceases to remain such, the action does not abate, as would be the case when a shareholder bringing a shareholder derivative action ceases to remain a shareholder. Tenney v. Rosenthal, 6 N.Y.2d 204, 189 N.Y.S.2d 158, 160 N.E.2d 463 (1959) (director derivative action); Peets v. Manhasset Civil Engineers, Inc., 4 Misc.2d 683, 68 N.Y. S.2d 338 (Sup.Ct.1946) (officer derivative action). Contra, Kehaya v. Axton, 32 F.Supp. 266 (S.D.N.Y. 1940); Singer v. State Laundry, Inc., 188 Misc. 583, 68 N.Y.S.2d 808 (Sup.Ct.1947); Williams v. Robinson, 9 Misc.2d 774, 169 N.Y.S.2d 811 (Sup.Ct.1957) (holding directors who ratified or acquiesced in wrong to corporation by defendant directors not estopped from maintaining action); Katz v. Braz, 188 Misc. 581, 66 N.Y.S.2d 722 (Sup.Ct.1946), aff'd mem., 271 App.Div. 970, 69 N.Y.S.2d 324 (1st Dep't 1947) (holding prior demand on board of directors not required); Green v. Compton, 41 Misc. 21, 83 N.Y.S. 588 (Sup.Ct.1903) (corporation held not indispensa-

The Model Business Corporation Act, in an optional section,[17] sets forth a contemporaneous-share-ownership requirement; [18] a provision whereby the court in a shareholder derivative action found to have been brought without reasonable cause may require the plaintiff to pay the defendants the reasonable expenses, including attorneys' fees, incurred in the defense of the action; [19] and a security for expenses provision.[20] The provision for reimbursement of the defendants' expenses by the plaintiffs, even when security therefor has not previously been given, is the unique contribution of the Model Act.

Many jurisdictions adopted one or more of the foregoing provisions as part of their corporate statutes or rules of procedure.[21] Several jurisdictions which patterned their rules of procedure on the Federal Rules of Civil Procedure have promulgated most of Rule 23.1, formerly Rule 23(b) and (c),[22] which,

of course, apply in the federal courts, including the courts of the District of Columbia.

The Model Business Corporation Act also empowers a corporation to indemnify directors, officers, and other corporate personnel against litigation expenses.[23] This provision has undergone several revisions, each in favor of greater indemnification. The 1967 revision, worked out with the Delaware corporate law revisers, is overly permissive in authorizing indemnification, and extends itself even further in authorizing insurance.[24]

In 1968, New York enacted legislation relating to derivative actions by limited partners.[25]

DERIVATIVE ACTIONS DISTINGUISHED FROM OTHER ACTIONS

360. The shareholder derivative action involves the assertion by a shareholder of a corporate cause of action against persons, either within or without the corporation, who have allegedly wronged it, where the corporation has failed to enforce such claim directly. Such action is brought in the right of the corporation by the shareholder in behalf of himself and all other shareholders similarly situated. In contrast, the direct or individual shareholder action involves the enforcement by a shareholder of a cause of action belonging to such shareholder on the basis of his membership contract, against the corporation and possibly others, being brought by the shareholder either individually or in behalf of himself and all other shareholders similarly situated. The distinction between derivative and nonderivative actions is important because of various requirements which are applicable only to derivative actions. Classification is sometimes difficult because of the lack of precise definition of the person or persons in whose favor various intracorporate duties run and the inherent dilemma that one aspect of management's duty to the corporation is to carry out the corporation-

---

ble party in director's action). McKinney's N.Y. Bus.Corp.Law §§ 626, 627 apply only to shareholders' derivative actions brought in the right of the corporation to procure a judgment in its favor. The indemnification provisions (id. §§ 721–726) distinguish actions by or in the right of the corporation to procure a judgment in its favor, apparently assimilating for indemnification purposes such derivative actions by directors and officers to such derivative actions by shareholders, from other actions. Derivative actions by directors or officers are, of course, limited to actions for certain relief against directors and officers for specified misconduct. Note, "Director's Statutory Action in New York", 36 N.Y.U.L.Rev. 199 (1961). Michigan also authorizes derivative actions by directors or officers. Mich.Gen.Corp.Act § 21.47 (1948).

17. ABA–ALI Model Bus.Corp.Act § 43A (optional section). This provision was introduced in the 1957 revision. The original version of the Model Act contained no section on the subject of actions by shareholders.

18. See section 362 infra.

19. See sections 378, 380 infra.

20. See section 372 infra.

21. See Fleischmann, "Shareholders' Actions Against Corporations", in Advising California Business Enterprises 833–879 (1958).

22. E. g., Arizona, Colorado, Delaware, Minnesota, Nevada, New Jersey, New Mexico, North Dakota, Texas, Wyoming, and Puerto Rico.

23. ABA–ALI Model Bus.Corp.Act § 4(o).

24. ABA–ALI Model Bus.Corp.Act § 4A. See section 380 infra.

25. McKinney's N.Y.Part.Law §§ 91, 115, 115–a to 115–c; [1967] N.Y.L. Rev'n Comm'n Rep. 1967 Legis. Doc.No. 65(B) 101–148.

shareholder membership contract and converse-ly observation of management duties to the corporation is an implied term of the share-holder's membership contract. Shareholder ac-tions to enjoin threatened corporate wrongs are often allowed as direct actions, even though subsequent redress would have been available only in a derivative action. New York distinguishes between shareholder deriva-tive actions brought in the right of the corpo-ration to procure a judgment in its favor and other actions and proceedings.

The corporation may sue directly in its own name on a cause of action which ac-crues in its favor. This is what may be termed a direct action by the corporation. It may be maintained by the corporation or anyone standing in its stead, such as an as-signee, trustee-in-bankruptcy, or the like.

When the corporate cause of action is for some reason not asserted by the corporation itself, if certain conditions are met, the shareholder may resort to a derivative ac-tion and sue for the enforcement of the cor-porate claim.[1]

Contrasted with the corporate cause of ac-tion, which is the basis for both a direct ac-tion by the corporation and a derivative ac-tion by a shareholder, is a cause of action which accrues to the shareholder against the corporation and possibly others on the basis of his membership contract. This latter type of claim is enforced in a direct or indi-vidual action brought by the shareholder.

Derivative actions and shareholder's direct actions are often called "representative" or "class" actions: (a) the derivative action on the theory that it is brought by the share-holder as a representative of the corporation and all other shareholders similarly situated; [2] (b) the shareholder's direct ac-tion when brought by the shareholder for himself and as a representative for all other shareholders similarly situated.[3] Even when a choice is available to the shareholder to frame the complaint as a class action or not, suing in behalf of a class might give rise to a more favorable impression, would invite other shareholders of the class to intervene in the action to share expenses and to par-ticipate otherwise in the litigation, and could result in a larger judgment and resulting greater counsel fees for the plaintiff-share-holder's attorneys.

For purposes of jurisdictional amount in a shareholder derivative action in the federal courts, the damage asserted to have been sustained by the corporation and not the plaintiff's own financial stake is the test.[4] Under Federal Rule of Civil Procedure 23, in a "spurious" as distinguished from a "true" class action, only the claims of the actual plaintiffs, and not those of the rest of the class, were counted in computing the juris-dictional amount. Under revised Rule 23, which replaced the "true", "hybrid", and "spurious" class actions with a functional approach, the older court-developed stand-ards for determining when claims are joint and common, and therefore aggregable, and when they are separate and distinct, and therefore not aggregable, will probably be retained.[5]

---

1. The complaint in the shareholder derivative ac-tion should state (a) the corporation's claim as the corporation would have had to in a direct action by it on such claim, and (b) the facts entitling the shareholder-plaintiff to maintain the action in the right of the corporation. Continental Securities Co. v. Belmont, 206 N.Y. 7, 99 N.E. 138 (1912). In a sense, the shareholder derivative action involves a double wrong to the corporation: (a) the basic wrong to it, and (b) its not redressing such wrong directly. The derivative nature of the action is in-dicated not only by the statement of claim in the complaint but also by its caption and prayer for re-lief.

2. See Taormina v. Taormina Corp., 32 Del.Ch. 18, 78 A.2d 473 (Ch.1951) (sustaining derivative action in behalf of close corporation where all sharehold-ers other than the plaintiff participated in the wrong and holding that action did not thereby cease to be derivative). See also Fed.R.Civ.P. 23.1 (deriv-ative actions by shareholders).

3. See Witherbee v. Bowles, 201 N.Y. 427, 95 N.E. 27 (1911). See also Fed.R.Civ.P. 23 (class actions). See section 358, n. 19 supra.

4. Koster v. Lumbermens Mutual Casualty Co., 330 U.S. 518, 67 S.Ct. 828, 91 L.Ed. 1067 (1947).

5. Snyder v. Harris, 394 U.S. 332, 89 S.Ct. 1053, 22 L.Ed.2d 319 (1969); Ames v. Mengel Co., 190 F.2d

The use of the term "representative" to refer both to derivative actions and to shareholder's direct actions in behalf of a class, and of the term "individual actions" to refer to shareholder's direct actions whether in behalf of a class or not, sometimes causes confusion.[6]

The outcome of a given case may depend upon whether a derivative or an individual cause of action is being asserted by the shareholder. This is because of the strict requirements and limitations, discussed in subsequent sections, which have been placed upon the use of the derivative remedy, but which do not apply to the shareholder's direct or individual action. There are other practical reasons for distinguishing between derivative and direct or individual actions. For instance, since a derivative action is exclusively an equitable form of relief while a direct or individual action may be at law, the availability of a jury trial may to some extent depend upon the ultimate determination.[7]

No simple and foolproof method exists whereby a derivative action may be distinguished from a shareholder's direct or individual action.[8] But generally speaking, the breach of the shareholder's membership contract gives rise to a direct or individual action while a wrong to the incorporated group as a whole (i.e., breach of some duty to the corporation) is the basis for a derivative action. Problems of defining intracorporate duties, especially the person or persons in whose favor various duties run, are often very complex.[9]

The following have been held to be direct actions by the shareholder:

(a) to compel payment of lawfully declared dividends [10] or of mandatory dividends; [11]

(b) to enforce the right to inspect corporate books and records; [12]

9. See sections 231–242 supra. A director's misconduct may be a wrong to a shareholder as well as to the corporation, as where the plaintiff had pledged his shares with the defendants, who were directors, and they conspired to reduce the value of the shares, caused plaintiff to default, and bought the shares themselves. Ritchie v. McMullen, 79 F. 522 (6th Cir. 1897) cert. denied 168 U.S. 710, 18 S.Ct. 945, 42 L.Ed. 1212 (1897). In Matter of Auditore, 249 N.Y. 335, 164 N.E. 242, 62 A.L.R. 551 (1928), a fiduciary was held liable to the beneficiary for despoiling a corporation in which the fiduciary held shares, the fact that the beneficiary would also be liable to the corporation being held not to prevent recovery by the beneficiary for the loss in value of the shares. See also Matter of Shehan, 285 App. Div. 785, 141 N.Y.S.2d 439 (4th Dep't 1955) (trustee ordered to account to beneficiary for his acts as director and officer of corporation shares of which were held by him as trustee). By way of further complication, sole shareholders have sometimes been allowed to sue directly on claims belonging to their corporations, by disregarding corporateness. Compare Anderson v. King, 370 S.W.2d 775, 777 (Tex.Civ. App.1963) (not "preferable practice"), with Dale v. City Plumbing & Heating Supply Co., 112 Ga.App. 723, 146 S.E.2d 349 (1965). See sections 146–151 supra.

344 (2d Cir.1951); Giesecke v. Denver Tramway Corp., 81 F.Supp. 957 (D.Del.1949).

6. Kalven & Rosenfeld, "The Function of the Class Suit", 8 U.Chi.L.Rev. 684, 715–717 (1941); Note, "Shareholder Derivative Suits: Are They Class Actions?" 42 Iowa L.Rev. 568 (1957).

7. See section 358, n. 21 supra.

8. 2 G. Hornstein, Corporation Law and Practice § 601 (1959); Comment, "Distinguishing Between Direct and Derivative Suits", 110 U.Pa.L.Rev. 1147 (1962), 7 Corp.Prac.Comm. 176 (Aug.1965); Note, "Protection of Shareholders' Rights: Derivative v. Representative Suits", 46 Ill.L.Rev. 937 (1952); Note, "Derivative Actions: Policy Considerations Leading to Choice of Derivative Form", 40 Calif.L. Rev. 127 (1952). See McKinney's N.Y.Bus.Corp.Law §§ 626, 627, 722 et seq. (test for certain purposes: whether shareholder derivative action is brought in right of corporation to procure judgment in its favor). In Borak v. J. I. Case Co., 377 U.S. 426, 84 S.Ct. 1555, 12 L.Ed.2d 423 (1964), the United States Supreme Court recognized that the same allegations of fact in a complaint were capable of supporting either a derivative action or an individual cause of action by a minority shareholder.

10. Godley v. Crandall & Godley Co., 212 N.Y. 121, 105 N.E. 818 (1914); Matter of Booth, 139 Misc. 253, 248 N.Y.S. 264 (Sup.Ct.1931). In most cases, of course, the declaration of a cash dividend creates a debtor-creditor relationship between the corporation and the shareholders.

11. Boardman v. Lake Shore & Michigan Southern Ry., 84 N.Y. 157 (1881); Koppel v. Middle States Petroleum Corp., 272 App.Div. 790, 69 N.Y.S.2d 784 (1st Dep't 1947). Mandatory dividend provisions are relatively rare (see section 327 supra).

12. See section 199 supra.

(c) to protect preemptive rights [13] and possibly otherwise prevent fraudulent dilution of his proportionate interests; [14]

(d) to enforce the right to vote; [15]

(e) to proceed against voting trustees; [16]

(f) to enjoin an ultra vires act or other threatened wrong before its consummation; [17]

(g) to recover from insider who purchased shareholders' shares without proper disclosure; [18]

(h) to recover from controlling shareholder for wrongful redemption; [19]

(i) to sue for breach of a preincorporation agreement; [20]

(j) to sue for breach of a shareholder agreement; [21]

(k) to compel corporate dissolution.[22]

On the other hand, the following have been held to be wrongs to the corporation which give rise to derivative actions:

(a) to recover damages resulting from a consummated ultra vires act; [23]

(b) to enjoin directors, officers, and controlling shareholders from breaching their fiduciary duty to the corporation,[24] or to recover damages,

---

13. Borak v. J. I. Case Co., 317 F.2d 838 (7th Cir. 1963), aff'd 377 U.S. 426, 84 S.Ct. 1555, 12 L.Ed.2d 423 (1964); Ames v. Mengel Co., 190 F.2d 344 (2d Cir. 1951); Horwitz v. Balaban, 112 F.Supp. 99 (S. D.N.Y.1949); Saigh v. Busch, 403 S.W.2d 559 (Mo. 1966); Witherbee v. Bowles, 201 N.Y. 427, 95 N.E. 27 (1911). But see Andersen v. Albert & J. M. Anderson Mfg. Co., 325 Mass. 343, 90 N.E.2d 541 (1950); Hammer v. Werner, 239 App.Div. 38, 265 N.Y.S. 172 (2d Dep't 1933). See sections 172–175 supra.

14. Sheppard v. Wilcox, 210 Cal.App.2d 53, 26 Cal. Rptr. 412 (1963); Bennett v. Breuil Petroleum Corp., 34 Del.Ch. 6, 99 A.2d 236 (Ch.1953); Schwab v. Schwab-Wilson Machine Corp., 13 Cal.App.2d 1, 55 P.2d 1268 (1936); Adams, "Remedy for Denial of the Stockholder's Preemptive Right", 6 N.Y.U.Intra.L.Rev. 126 (1951). Cf. Shaw v. Empire Sav. & Loan Ass'n, 186 Cal.App.2d 401, 9 Cal.Rptr. 204 (1960) (action for fraudulent dilution of shareholder's proportionate interests in corporation held to be derivative action). But see Jones v. H. F. Ahmanson, 1 Cal.3d 93, 460 P.2d 464 (1969) (holding shareholder could maintain individual breach of fiduciary duty action even though injury to him might affect substantial number of shareholders).

15. Reifsnyder v. Pittsburgh Outdoor Advertising Co., 405 Pa. 142, 173 A.2d 319 (1961) (minority shareholder action to determine majority shareholder's right to vote on resolution authorizing purchase of latter's shares at allegedly excessive price held to be for protection of minority shareholders' voting rights and nonderivative); Horwitz v. Balaban, 112 F.Supp. 99 (S.D.N.Y.1949); Lazar v. Knolls Cooperative Section No. 2, Inc., 205 Misc. 748, 130 N.Y.S.2d 407 (Sup.Ct.1954). See section 189 supra.

16. Eisner v. Davis, 109 N.Y.S.2d 504 (Sup.Ct.1951), aff'd mem., 279 App.Div. 1003, 112 N.Y.S.2d 672 (1st Dep't 1952). Of course, voting trust certificate holders, as beneficial owners of shares, may bring shareholder derivative actions in many jurisdictions against persons who have wronged the corporation. See section 197 supra.

17. H. Ballantine, Ballantine on Corporations § 144 (rev. ed. 1946) (on theory that such wrongs may be treated as breach of contract or breach of trust, and that shareholders are ultimate beneficiaries for whom business is being conducted by their representatives). See section 184 supra. See also notes 23, 24 infra.

18. See section 239 supra. See Watson v. Button, 235 F.2d 235 (9th Cir. 1956) (allowing direct action by former 50 percent shareholder against other former 50 percent shareholder for misappropriation by latter of corporate assets prior to sale by them of all shares to third person who released all corporate claims against such wrongdoing shareholder, since creditors were not prejudiced and no other shareholders were involved).

19. Zahn v. Transamerica Corp., 162 F.2d 36, 172 A. L.R. 495 (3d Cir. 1947).

20. Dreben v. Belloise, 275 App.Div. 755, 87 N.Y.S.2d 572 (1st Dep't 1949).

21. Timely Drive-In Cleaning Corp. v. Jacobs, 21 Misc.2d 1052, 190 N.Y.S.2d 194 (Sup.Ct.1959).

22. Leibert v. Clapp, 13 N.Y.2d 313, 247 N.Y.S.2d 102, 196 N.E.2d 540 (1963); Fontheim v. Walker, 141 N. Y.S.2d 62 (Sup.Ct.1955); Lennan v. Blakely, 80 N. Y.S.2d 288 (Sup.Ct.1948).

23. Starbird v. Lane, 203 Cal.App.2d 247, 21 Cal. Rptr. 280 (1962); Morris v. Elyton Land Co., 125 Ala. 263, 28 So. 513 (1899). See note 184 supra.

24. Kavanaugh v. Kavanaugh Knitting Co., 226 N.Y. 185, 123 N.E. 148 (1919) (enjoining individual defendants as directors and controlling shareholders from dissolving corporation). However, actions to enjoin corporate transactions have frequently been allowed as direct actions, possibly influenced by the fact that they usually involved neither financial recovery to anyone nor financial motivation on the part of the shareholder plaintiff (compare note 17 supra). Southern Pacific Co. v. Bogert, 250 U.S. 483, 39 S.Ct. 533, 63 L.Ed. 1099 (1919); Eisenberg v.

or profits for breach of duty to the corporation, e. g., mismanagement of the business by directors or officers,[25] or misappropriation of corporate assets,[26] or opportunities,[27] or sale of control; [28]

(c) to enjoin issue of share options for inadequate consideration; [29]

(d) to recover improper dividends; [30]

(e) to enjoin outsiders from wronging the corporation or to recover for such wrong.[31]

Central Zone Property Corp., 306 N.Y. 58, 115 N.E. 2d 652 (1953). But see Bassett v. Battle, 253 App. Div. 893, 1 N.Y.S.2d 869 (2d Dep't 1938); November v. National Exhibition Co., 10 Misc.2d 537, 173 N.Y. S.2d 490 (Sup.Ct.1958); Selman v. Allen, 121 N.Y.S. 2d 142 (Sup.Ct.1953); Elster v. American Airlines, Inc., 34 Del.Ch. 94, 100 A.2d 219 (Ch.1953), 34 Del. Ch. 500, 106 A.2d 202 (Ch.1954) (holding share optionees indispensable parties). See sections 231–242 supra. Weinberg v. Baltimore Brick Co., 34 Del.Ch. 586, 108 A.2d 81 (Ch.1954), aff'd 35 Del.Ch. 225, 114 A.2d 812 (Sup.Ct.1955); Otis & Co. v. Pennsylvania R. R., 61 F.Supp. 905 (E.D.Pa.1945), aff'd mem., 155 F.2d 522 (3d Cir. 1946); Foster v. Bowen, 311 Mass. 359, 41 N.E.2d 181 (1942).

25. Litwin (Rosemarin) v. Allen, 25 N.Y.S.2d 667 (Sup.Ct.1940).

26. Heller v. Boylan, 29 N.Y.S.2d 653 (Sup.Ct.1941), aff'd mem., 263 App.Div. 815, 32 N.Y.S.2d 131 (1st Dep't 1941), motion for leave to appeal or reargument denied 263 App.Div. 852, 32 N.Y.S.2d 1011 (1st Dep't 1942). But see note 18 supra.

27. Greene v. Allen, 35 Del.Ch. 242, 114 A.2d 916 (Ch.1955), rev'd on other grounds sub nom. Johnston v. Greene, 35 Del.Ch. 479, 121 A.2d 919 (Sup.Ct. 1956); Singer v. Carlisle, 26 N.Y.S.2d 172 (Sup.Ct. 1940), aff'd mem., 261 App.Div. 897, 26 N.Y.S.2d 320 (1st Dep't 1941), motion for leave to appeal denied 261 App.Div. 956, 27 N.Y.S.2d 190 (1st Dep't 1941). See section 237 supra.

28. Perlman v. Feldmann, 219 F.2d 173, 50 A.L.R.2d 1134 (2d Cir. 1955), cert. denied 349 U.S. 952, 75 S. Ct. 880, 99 L.Ed. 1277 (1955) (derivative action with individual recovery to minority shareholders). See section 241 supra.

29. Selman v. Allen, 121 N.Y.S.2d 142 (Sup.Ct.1953).

30. Campbell v. Clark, 159 Cal.App.2d 432, 324 P.2d 51 (1958).

31. Fanchon & Marco, Inc. v. Paramount Pictures, Inc., 202 F.2d 731, 36 A.L.R.2d 1336 (2d Cir. 1953). See Sterling Industries, Inc. v. Ball Bearing Pen Corp., 298 N.Y. 483, 84 N.E.2d 790, 10 A.L.R.2d 694 (1949).

In the case of wrongs by outsiders, such wrongs can hardly be said to involve a breach of the shareholder's membership contract (apart from the possibility of maliciously inducing breach by the corporation of such contract), and are either wrongs to the corporation or individual wrongs to others who happen to be shareholders.

In categorizing actions as direct or derivative, theoretical difficulty is encountered, in greater or less degree, because inhering in the shareholder's membership contract is the provision that management will observe its duties to the corporation, or stated conversely, one aspect of management's duty to the corporation is to carry out the corporation-shareholder membership contract.

For instance, there is still a theoretical split of authority as to whether an action brought by a shareholder to compel the declaration of a discretionary dividend constitutes a derivative action.

In Gordon v. Elliman,[32] the effect of which has been overruled by statute, the New York Court of Appeals, in a 4–3 decision, held that such an action was derivative in nature so far as the New York security-for-expenses statute was concerned. The majority reasoned that the action brought into question the duty of good faith that the directors owed the corporation in maintaining a sound financial policy, and that the object of the action was to cause the court to perform a corporate function which the directors would have done except for their bad faith. Two dissenting judges contended that the right of a shareholder to receive dividends was part of his membership contract, that this was a corporate obligation not a corporate right, that any recovery would be from and not to the corporation, that the majority in effect had the corporation suing itself, and that the majority's error would have been more manifest if the action had been to compel the declaration of a dividend on one of two or

32. 306 N.Y. 456, 119 N.E.2d 331 (1954).

more classes of shares rather than on the only class of shares. A third judge dissented on the ground that the security-for-expenses provision was intended to be limited to actions against directors for money damages for wrongs done by them to their corporation.[33]

Contrary to Gordon v. Elliman is a better-reasoned federal case,[34] which held that an action to compel the declaration of discretionary dividends gives rise to a direct action by the shareholder, requiring no posting of security under the Pennsylvania statute. In arriving at this decision the federal court of appeals emphasized that the shareholders were the injured parties and they, and not the corporation, would benefit by any recovery.

Since 1963, New York has distinguished between shareholder derivative actions brought in the right of the corporation to procure a judgment in its favor and other actions and proceedings, thus in effect overruling the result, if not the theory, in Gordon v. Elliman.[35]

Another difficult question arises when a shareholder seeks to enjoin a proposed recapitalization because it is unfavorable to

one class of shares. In a lower court case,[36] the plaintiff alleged that a plan of recapitalization made substantial changes in the respective rights of the Class A and Class B shares, and that these changes were unfair to the Class A shareholders. The court held that the action constituted a direct action because it was simply a contest between two classes of shareholders. According to the court, the corporation's only interest in the matter was that the recapitalization be properly carried out.[37]

An action to compel the calling of a meeting for the election of directors to replace those named in the articles of incorporation has been held to be a direct action.[38]

Actions to enjoin a proposed merger or consolidation,[39] sale of corporate assets [40] or dissolution [41] have been permitted as deriva-

---

33. Textual support was found in superseded McKinney's N.Y.Gen.Corp.Law, § 60 for the proposition that an action to compel the declaration of a discretionary dividend was not an action in the right of the corporation within the meaning of the security-for-expenses statute. Superseded McKinney's N.Y.Gen.Corp.Law, § 61–b. See McKinney's N.Y. Bus.Corp.Law, § 627 (security-for-expenses requirement applicable in shareholders' derivative action brought in right of corporation to procure judgment in its favor).

34. Knapp v. Bankers Securities Corp., 230 F.2d 717 (3d Cir. 1956). To similar effect is Doherty v. Mutual Warehouse Co., 245 F.2d 609 (5th Cir. 1957) (holding such action to be direct rather than derivative and therefore not subject to contemporaneous-share-ownership requirement of then Fed.R.Civ.P. 23(b) (1), now 23.1) (see section 362 infra).

35. McKinney's N.Y.Bus.Corp.Law, § 627 (security for expenses required only in shareholder derivative action brought in right of corporation to procure judgment in its favor).

36. Lehrman v. Godchaux Sugars, Inc., 207 Misc. 314, 138 N.Y.S.2d 163 (Sup.Ct.1955).

37. See notes 17, 24 supra.

38. Lazar v. Knolls Cooperative Section No. 2, Inc., 205 Misc. 748, 130 N.Y.S.2d 407 (Sup.Ct.1954).

39. General Inv. Co. v. Lake Shore & M. S. Ry., 250 F. 160 (6th Cir. 1918), modified 260 U.S. 261, 43 S. Ct. 106, 67 L.Ed. 244 (1922); Goldberg v. Whittier Corp., 111 F.Supp. 382 (E.D.Mich.1953). The cases, to some extent, appear to turn on whether the proposal would injure the corporation as a whole or benefit one intracorporate group to the detriment of another or whether it is alleged to be unauthorized by or not to comply with applicable statutes or is alleged to be an inequitable exercise of statutory power. See notes 17, 24 supra.

40. Eisenberg v. Central Zone Property Corp., 306 N.Y. 58, 115 N.E.2d 652 (1953). Cf. Bassett v. Battle, 253 App.Div. 893, 1 N.Y.S.2d 869 (2d Dep't 1938) (rescission); November v. National Exhibition Co., 10 Misc.2d 537, 173 N.Y.S.2d 490 (Sup.Ct.1958). Abelow v. Symonds, 38 Del.Ch. 572, 156 A.2d 416 (Ch.1959), began as a shareholder action to enjoin a proposed sale of corporate assets for an allegedly inadequate price, but the action became moot when the corporation was liquidated and the plaintiffs tendered their shares for the preferred liquidation payments. The amended complaint sought damages and accounting for the plaintiff's alleged personal losses. The court upheld the amended complaint as stating a nonderivative class action. See note 39 supra.

41. Eisenberg v. Central Zone Property Corp., 306 N.Y. 58, 115 N.E.2d 652 (1953). Cf. Kavanaugh v. Kavanaugh Knitting Co., 226 N.Y. 185, 123 N.E. 148 (1919). See note 39 supra.

tive or direct actions. **They are hardly actions to procure a judgment in favor of the corporation.** Actions to compel dissolution have been termed direct actions.[42]

When a shareholder seeks only to appoint a receiver for the corporation during liquidation, there is authority for the finding that the action is direct.[43] However, when further relief is sought, the conclusion should depend on the nature of the remedies sought.

A shareholder has been allowed to sue an alleged violator of the antitrust laws in a derivative action and thereby enforce the corporation's statutory cause of action.[44] An individual shareholder's action has been denied as a general rule, since the wrong is to the corporation, rather than to shareholders as such. Jury reference on the issues of right to treble damages in the equitable derivative action was found to obviate the procedural difficulties.[45]

C. QUALIFICATIONS OF SHAREHOLDERS TO COMMENCE AND MAINTAIN DERIVATIVE ACTION

SHARE OWNERSHIP AT COMMENCEMENT AND DURING MAINTENANCE OF ACTION

361. The plaintiff in a derivative action ordinarily must be a shareholder in order to commence and to maintain such action. If he ceases to be a shareholder while the action is pending, the action will ordinarily be held to abate. Equitable ownership at the time of the action is usually sufficient. The owner of shares in a parent corporation may sue in behalf of a subsidiary in a so-called "double derivative action". Where there is a chain of proprietary interests, "triple" or other "multiple" derivative actions have been allowed. Some cases infer that the multiple derivative action is limited to situations where all the corporations involved are dominated by the alleged wrongdoers, but the modern trend seemingly favors a broader approach. Multiple derivative actions multiply the already complicated rules applicable to the ordinary derivative action. The effect of merger or consolidation on standing to sue poses several still unresolved problems. Shareholder intervention in derivative, as well as other, actions, also presents many problems, some of them still not settled.

Before he may sue derivatively, the shareholder must meet certain qualifications relating to his proprietary interest in the corporation whose cause of action he seeks to assert.

The plaintiff-shareholder's standing to sue depends upon his indirect interest in the outcome of the litigation. This is the reason for the rule that he must be a shareholder at the commencement and during the maintenance of the action.[1] The size of his holding

---

42. Leibert v. Clapp, 13 N.Y.2d 313, 247 N.Y.S.2d 102, 196 N.E.2d 540 (1963); Fontheim v. Walker, 141 N. Y.S.2d 62 (Sup.Ct.1955); Davidson v. Rabinowitz, 140 N.Y.S.2d 875 (Sup.Ct.1951). Cf. note 41 supra.

43. Davidson v. Bankers Bond & Mortgage Guaranty Co. of America, 38 F.Supp. 825 (E.D.Pa.1941).

44. Fanchon & Marco, Inc., v. Paramount Pictures, Inc., 202 F.2d 731, 36 A.L.R.2d 1336 (2d Cir. 1953); cf. Fleitman v. Welsbach Street Lighting Co., 240 U.S. 27, 36 S.Ct. 233, 60 L.Ed. 505 (1916); United Copper Securities Co. v. Amalgamated Copper Co., 244 U.S. 261, 37 S.Ct. 509, 61 L.Ed. 1119 (1917). See also Schechtman v. Wolfson, 141 F.Supp. 453 (S.D. N.Y.1956), aff'd, 244 F.2d 537 (2d Cir. 1957) (derivative action to enjoin interlocking directorate); Comment, "Stockholders' Suits and the Sherman Act", 5 Stan.L.Rev. 480 (1953).

45. Cf. note 7 supra.

1. See McKinney's N.Y.Bus.Corp.Law, § 626(a) (action may be brought in right of domestic or foreign corporation to procure judgment in its favor by holder of shares or of voting trust certificates or of beneficial interest in such shares or certificates). Most corporate statutes are less explicit. See Mayflower Hotel Stockholders Protective Committee v. Mayflower Hotel Corp., 73 F.Supp. 721 (D.D.C.1947), rev'd on other grounds 173 F.2d 416 (D.C.Cir. 1949); Everett v. Phillips, 288 N.Y. 227, 43 N.E.2d 18 (1942), reargument denied, 289 N.Y. 625, 43 N.E.2d 841 (1942), reargument denied 289 N.Y. 675, 45 N.E. 2d 176 (1942). To obviate such rule, courts occasionally allow a former shareholder to bring a nonderivative action even when the cause of action appears in theory to be derivative. Watson v. Button,

is immaterial in this regard, although it may be critical in determining whether or not security for expenses is required.[2]

Where the plaintiff-shareholder has ceased to be a shareholder after the commencement of the derivative action, the action has been held to abate.[3]

235 F.2d 235 (9th Cir. 1956); Morrison v. St. Anthony Hotel, 295 S.W.2d 246 (Tex.Civ.App.1956); Annot., 168 A.L.R. 906 (1947). For breach of the shareholder's agreement with the corporation, the shareholder might be allowed to sue even after he ceases to be a shareholder where he has retained the cause of action for such wrong. Morrison v. St. Anthony Hotel, supra; Hammer v. Werner, 239 App.Div. 38, 265 N.Y.S. 172 (2d Dep't 1933).

2. See section 372 infra.

3. Standing to sue must exist not only when the action is commenced but during its entire maintenance through entry of the final judgment. See Levy, J., in Sorin v. Shahmoon Industries, Inc., 30 Misc.2d 429, 432, 220 N.Y.S.2d 760, 783, 784 (Sup. Ct.1961):

"I have heretofore had occasion to point out that, under the established law on the subject—whether the matter be examined from the standpoint of the plaintiff's 'incapacity to sue' or of his 'having a cause of action'—'it is necessary [in an action such as this] for the plaintiff to show, in order that she may recover, that she was a "stockholder at the time of the transaction of which [s]he complains" . . . and that she was a stockholder as well at the time of the commencement of the action . . .' . . . I add here that it is equally well established that the plaintiff must also be a stockholder at the time of the trial. . . . "

"And I now add further—and I hold—that the plaintiff must also be a stockholder up to and including the time of the entry of the final judgment in the action."

As stated by Fuld, J., in Tenney v. Rosenthal, 6 N.Y. 2d 204, 211, 189 N.Y.S.2d 158, 163, 160 N.E.2d 463, 466–467 (1959):

"In a very real sense, in modern theory, the standing of the shareholder is based on the fact that, when he sues derivatively, he is defending his own interests as well as those of the corporation. If he disposes of his shares after initiating the derivative action, he destroys the technical foundation of his right to continue to prosecute the suit."

See Johnson v. Baldwin, 221 S.C. 141, 69 S.E.2d 585 (1952); Gleicher v. Times-Columbia Distributors, Inc., 283 App.Div. 709, 128 N.Y.S.2d 55 (1st Dep't 1954). For the rule that a director's derivative action does not abate upon the plaintiff-director's ceasing to be a director, see section 217 supra. Cf. Rademacher v. Russ, 131 F.Supp. 50 (D.Minn.1955) (where shareholder sued on two counts: (a) derivative, and (b) nonderivative for rescission of his shares purchase, derivative action stayed pending decision on rescission question); Helfand v. Gam-

Sufficiency of Equitable Share Ownership

Capacity to sue derivatively should depend upon the law of the forum and applicable real-parties-in-interest rules. Equitable ownership ordinarily should be recognized in an equity action such as a derivative action, in the absence of a contrary statute.[4]

Shares purchased on margin and held continuously by brokers usually constitute the purchaser a shareholder for purposes of a derivative action.[5]

bee, 37 Del.Ch. 51, 136 A.2d 558 (Ch.1957) (shareholder of old corporation reorganized under antitrust decree held not to have lost right to sue in behalf of it for wrong done to it). Some attorneys representing shareholders in derivative actions require the deposit of the shareholders' shares certificates with them while the action is pending to forestall their clients' ceasing to remain shareholders. Intervention by other shareholders also might prevent abatement by the initial shareholder's ceasing to remain a shareholder.

4. Unless otherwise mandated by statute or court rule referring to shareholder of record or defining "shareholder" as holder of record, beneficial or equitable owners of shares should have sufficient standing in equity to bring a derivative action. See Arfsten v. Higby, 150 Colo. 254, 372 P.2d 166 (1962) (holding that non-record minority shareholders with equitable title to 7-5/12 of 46 outstanding shares of corporation had standing to sue majority shareholders, corporation, and others, for alleged breaches of fiduciary duties owing to minority shareholders in administration of corporate affairs). Meltzer v. Wattles, 19 A.D.2d 871, 244 N.Y.S.2d 100 (1st Dep't 1963) (holding that custodian of shares under Uniform Gifts to Minors Act had standing to maintain shareholder derivative action). Even if the shareholder-plaintiff surmounts this requirement, he must qualify under any applicable "contemporaneous-share-ownership" requirement [see section 362 infra] which might require contemporaneous-share-ownership of record. See Matthies v. Seymour Mfg. Co., 270 F.2d 365 (2d Cir. 1959), cert. denied 361 U.S. 962, 80 S.Ct. 591, 4 L.Ed.2d 544 (1960) (holding one of several beneficiaries of active trust which held shares in corporation was not "shareholder" under Fed.R.Civ.P. 23.1, and could not bring action in behalf of such corporation. Cf. Sheppard v. Wilcox, 210 Cal.App.2d 53, 26 Cal.Rptr. 412 (1963) (holding that action could be maintained by plaintiffs, who were not record holders, but were beneficial owners, of their shares at time of alleged wrongs, for breach by directors of their fiduciary duties in issuing shares to their group to give them control of corporation).

5. Saks v. Gamble, 35 Del.Ch. 378, 118 A.2d 793 (Ch. 1955), aff'd sub nom. Gamble-Skogmo, Inc. v. Saks, 35 Del.Ch. 503, 122 A.2d 120 (Sup.Ct.1956).

However, the fact that a widow files an election and consents to receive certain shares as part of her statutory distributive share does not make her a legal or equitable owner of the shares prior to the actual distribution.[6] Moreover, a person who holds an interest in an estate as a statutory distributee has no right to maintain a derivative action based upon shares held by the administrator.[7]

"Multiple Derivative Actions"

The owner of shares in a parent corporation may sue on behalf of a subsidiary, giving rise to what has been termed a "double derivative action."[8] This type of derivative action has been allowed against any wrongdoer whom the subsidiary could sue, and to enforce any claim of the subsidiary.

Theoretically, this so-called "multiple derivative action" may involve unlimited multiples so long as there is a chain of proprietary interests. Thus, there may be a "triple derivative action" where three corporations are involved. This occurs when a shareholder in one corporation, which owns shares in a second corporation, which in turn owns shares in a third corporation, sues derivatively to enforce a cause of action belonging to the third corporation.[9]

Apparently, a multiple derivative action may lie even when the plaintiff-shareholder's corporation does not own a controlling interest in the corporation whose cause of action is the basis for the action.[10] While some cases have inferred that a multiple derivative action is limited to a situation where all the corporations involved are dominated by the alleged wrongdoer,[11] the modern trend seemingly favors a broader approach.

Multiple derivative actions multiply the already complicated rules applicable to the ordinary derivative action.[12]

Effect of Merger or Consolidation on Standing to Sue

Where a corporation has a claim against someone and then is merged or consolidated into another corporation, the surviving or consolidated corporation acquires such claim

---

6. Steuer v. Hector's Tavern, Inc., 1 Misc.2d 614, 148 N.Y.S.2d 402 (Sup.Ct.1955), rev'd on other grounds, 1 A.D.2d 1003, 151 N.Y.S.2d 830 (1st Dep't 1956).

7. Parrish v. Brantley, 256 N.C. 541, 124 S.E.2d 533 (1962), held that plaintiffs had no standing in a derivative action brought against the officers of the corporation for mismanagement, where the plaintiffs were next-of-kin of the deceased shareholder and alleged that the estate was insolvent and the corporation bankrupt, since the next-of-kin after death, and shareholders after dissolution of a corporation, share only after debts are paid. See also Faiello v. Li Castri, 2 A.D.2d 749, 153 N.Y.S.2d 247 (2d Dep't 1956).

8. See, e. g., Otis & Co. v. Pennsylvania R.R., 61 F. Supp. 905 (E.D.Pa.1945), aff'd mem., 155 F.2d 522 (3d Cir. 1946); Craftsman Finance & Mortgage Co. v. Brown, 64 F.Supp. 168 (S.D.N.Y.1945); Singer v. Allied Factors, Inc., 216 Minn. 443, 13 N.W.2d 378 (1944); Kaufman v. Wolfson, 1 A.D.2d 555, 151 N. Y.S.2d 530 (1st Dep't 1956); Note, "Minority Stockholders of a Subsidiary Corporation: How May They Redress Wrongs Perpetrated on Behalf of the Parent?", 13 U.Pitt.L.Rev. 358 (1952); Annot., 154 A.L.R. 1295 (1945).

9. Marcus v. Otis, 168 F.2d 649 (2d Cir. 1948); Kaufman v. Wolfson, 132 F.Supp. 733 (S.D.N.Y.1955) (where all corporations under control of alleged wrongdoers).

10. Birch v. McColgan, 39 F.Supp. 358 (S.D.Cal.1941).

11. Goldstein v. Groesbeck, 142 F.2d 422, 154 A.L.R. 1285 (2d Cir. 1944), cert. denied 323 U.S. 737, 65 S. Ct. 36, 89 L.Ed. 590 (1944); United States Lines, Inc. v. United States Lines Co., 96 F.2d 148 (2d Cir. 1938). See also Breswick & Co. v. Harrison-Rye Realty Corp., 280 App.Div. 820, 114 N.Y.S.2d 25 (2d Dep't 1952) (indicating that double derivative action could only be maintained in holding company-operating company or parent-subsidiary relationship).

12. E. g., share ownership at commencement and during maintenance of action, "contemporaneous-share-ownership" requirements [see section 362 infra], demands on board of directors and shareholders [see sections 364–367 infra], indispensability of corporations as parties [see section 369 infra], application of security-for-expenses statutes [see section 372 infra]. Painter, "Double Derivative Suits and Other Remedies With Regard to Damaged Subsidiaries", 36 Ind.L.J. 143 (1961); Note, "Examination of the Multiple Derivative Suit and Some Problems Involved Therein in Light of the Theory of the Single Derivative Suit", 31 N.Y.U.L.Rev. 932 (1956); Note, "Suits by a Shareholder of a Parent Corporation to Redress Injuries to the Subsidiary", 64 Harv.L.Rev. 1313 (1951).

by operation of law.[13] The effect of such merger or consolidation on the standing to assert derivatively such claim by a shareholder of any constituent corporation which ceases to exist upon merger or consolidation poses some still unresolved problems.[14]

Shareholder Intervention in Derivative and Other Actions

Intervention is the subject of statute and court rules.[15]

Shareholders sometimes seek to intervene in direct actions by or against their corporations, in order to help press its claims or defend the action.[16]

Shareholder intervention in shareholder derivative actions is also sought. If granted, the original plaintiff-shareholder usually retains control of the action.[17]

Authorities are in conflict as to whether intervening shareholders in a derivative action must be contemporaneous share owners, the trend apparently being that they should be.[18]

Intervention is often desirable to avoid the necessity of posting security for expenses applicable only when the plaintiff-shareholder(s) own less than a stated amount or percentage of shares.[19]

Intervention does not destroy federal diversity-of-citizenship jurisdiction.[20]

SHARE OWNERSHIP AT TIME OF ALLEGED WRONG ("CONTEMPORANEOUS – SHARE – OWNERSHIP" REQUIREMENT)

362. Shareholding at the time of the alleged wrong is required of a shareholder bringing a derivative action—the so-called "contemporaneous-share-ownership" requirement—by stat-

13. See section 346 supra.

14. Braasch v. Goldschmidt, 41 Del.Ch. 519, 199 A.2d 760 (Ch.1964) (holding shareholders of merged corporation could not sue derivatively in behalf of merged corporation, since asserted derivative rights had passed to surviving corporation); Niesz v. Gorsuch, 295 F.2d 909 (9th Cir. 1961) (holding that neither merged corporation nor one of its shareholders could maintain action after merger; remanded to provide opportunity for intervention by surviving corporation or, if it refused, by one of its shareholders including plaintiff if he was owner of shares in it, and joinder of it, an indispensable party, as nominal defendant). But see Nationwide Ins. Co. v. New York, Chicago & St. Louis R. Co., 4 Ohio App.2d 167, 211 N.E.2d 872 (Ct.App.1965) (under statutory provision that any claim existing against any of constituent corporations may be prosecuted as if merger or consolidation had not taken place); Platt Corp. v. Platt, 21 A.D.2d 116, 249 N.Y.S.2d 75 (1st Dep't 1964), aff'd per curiam 15 N.Y.2d 705, 256 N.Y.S.2d 335, 204 N.E.2d 495 (1965) (rejecting argument that merged corporation lost standing to maintain action against former president for dereliction because it no longer had any contemporaneous shareholders where merger agreement expressly provided that proceeds from such litigation should be distributed among merged corporation's Class A common shareholders); Miller v. Steinbach, 268 F.Supp. 255 (S.D.N.Y.1967) (upholding action by shareholder of merged corporation under federal securities laws, despite law of its jurisdiction of incorporation that merged corporation had lost any legal identity, and permitting action to proceed without joinder or corporation since any recovery could go directly to its shareholders).

15. See Fed.R.Civ.P. 24; McKinney's N.Y. CPLR, § 1012 (intervention as of right), § 1013 (intervention by permission); Annot., 84 A.L.R.2d 1412 (1962).

16. See Stadin v. Union Electric Co., 309 F.2d 912 (8th Cir. 1962), cert. denied 373 U.S. 915, 83 S.Ct. 1298, 10 L.Ed.2d 415 (1963) (denying minority shareholder intervention in treble-damage antitrust action brought by corporation); Molybdenum Corp. of America v. International Mining Corp., 32 F.R.D. 415 (S.D.N.Y.1963) (intervention by minority shareholder allowed in action by corporation against defendants with interlocking directors); Rugee v. Hadley Products, Inc., 73 Ariz. 362, 241 P.2d 798, 33 A.L.R.2d 468 (1952) (denying intervention by minority shareholder in action against corporation in order to present additional defenses).

17. See Duncan v. National Tea Co., 14 Ill.App.2d 280, 144 N.E.2d 771, 69 A.L.R.2d 546 (1957) (allowing intervention where original plaintiff-shareholder was of advanced age, and had, in interim between hearings on intervention, sold all her shares in corporation). As to selection of counsel, see section 370 infra.

18. Kaufman v. Wolfson, 136 F.Supp. 939 (S.D.N.Y. 1955); Richman v. Felmus, 8 A.D.2d 985, 190 N.Y. S.2d 920 (2d Dep't 1959). A proposed provision for the New York Business Corporation Law expressly allowing the intervention of noncontemporaneous owners was not enacted.

19. See section 372 infra.

20. See generally Hornstein, "Problems of Procedure in Stockholder's Derivative Suits", 42 Colum.L.Rev. 574 (1942); Note, "Shareholder Intervention in Corporate Litigation", 63 Harv.L.Rev. 1426 (1950).

ute, court rule, or case law in the majority of jurisdictions and the federal courts. To satisfy such requirement, the plaintiff must have been a shareholder at the time of the alleged wrong or the shares must have later devolved upon him by operation of law. Unless the contemporaneous-share-ownership provision by its terms requires contemporaneous ownership of record, contemporaneous equitable ownership usually has been held sufficient. The contemporaneous-share-ownership rule is probably procedural rather than substantive.

In a minority of jurisdictions, a noncontemporaneous shareholder, absent special circumstances, may sue derivatively on the premise that any corporate rights of action are part of the indivisible interest in the corporation represented by the share certificates and therefore transferable along with the share certificates.

In the case of "continuing wrongs", persons acquiring their shares during such wrongs might be regarded as contemporaneous owners.

The contemporary-share-ownership requirement of Federal Rule of Civil Procedure 23.1 has been held inapplicable to secondary actions to recover insider profits under federal securities legislation, especially the Federal Securities Exchange Act of 1934.

Where all shareholders are barred by the contemporaneous-share-ownership rule from suing derivatively, the corporation itself has been held barred from suing the wrongdoers directly. Recovery in a derivative action ordinarily is not reduced in proportion to the holdings of the noncontemporaneous shareholders, on the ground that even a diminished recovery to the corporation would inure proportionately to the benefit of subsequent shareholders and thereby reduce the share of the contemporaneous shareholders.

Majority Rule

Perhaps the most important qualification placed upon a plaintiff-shareholder is a derivative action [1] is that of "contemporaneous-share-ownership". It applies by stat-

ute,[2] court rule,[3] or case law [4] in the majority of jurisdictions, and the federal courts.[5]

To satisfy this requirement the plaintiff must have been a shareholder [6] at the time of the act of which he complains, or the shares must have later devolved upon him by operation of law.[7]

2. E. g., ABA–ALI Model Bus.Corp.Act § 43A (optional section); California, Delaware, Georgia, Illinois, Kentucky, New Jersey, New Mexico, New York, Ohio, Oklahoma, Pennsylvania, Wisconsin. New York applies its contemporaneous-share-ownership requirement to shareholders' derivative actions brought in the right of the corporation to procure a judgment in its favor. McKinney's N.Y.Bus.Corp. Law, § 626(b). See also McKinney's N.Y.Part.Law § 115–a(2).

3. E. g., Fed.R.Civ.P. 23.1 (formerly 23(b)); Arizona, Colorado, Delaware, Nevada, New Jersey, Pennsylvania, Washington. Federal Rule 23.1 applies in the District of Columbia.

4. E. g., Hawes v. Oakland, 104 U.S. 450, 26 L.Ed. 827 (1882); News-Journal Corp. v. Gore, 147 Fla. 217, 2 So.2d 741 (1941); Tevis v. Hammersmith, 31 Ind.App. 281, 66 N.E. 79 (1903); Mitchell v. Beachy, 110 Kan. 60, 202 P. 628 (1921); Von Schlemmer v. Keystone Life Ins. Co., 121 La. 987, 46 So. 991 (1903); Matthews v. Headley Chocolate Co., 130 Md. 523, 100 A. 645 (1917); Wagner Electric Corp. v. Hydraulic Brake Co., 269 Mich. 560, 257 N.W. 884 (1934); McKee v. Hogan, 145 Miss. 760, 110 So. 775 (1927); Reils v. Nicholas, 137 Neb. 19, 287 N.W. 853 (1939); Moore v. Silver Valley Min. Co., 104 N. C. 534, 10 S.E. 679 (1890); Jepson v. Peterson, 69 S.D. 388, 10 N.W.2d 749 (1943); Sanders v. Bank of Mecklenburg, 113 Va. 661, 75 S.E. 96 (1912).

5. See notes 8–10 infra.

6. Some of the provisions expressly refer to holders of voting trust certificates as well as to holders of shares. E. g., ABA–ALI Model Bus.Corp.Act § 43A (optional section); Colorado, Illinois, Iowa, New Jersey, North Dakota; the Ohio provision expressly includes an equitable owner. The California and Wisconsin provisions refer to "registered shareholder" or voting trust certificate holder. For definition of shareholder as "holder of record", see ABA–ALI Model Bus.Corp.Act, § 2(f). See McKinney's N.Y.Bus.Corp.Law, § 626(b) (holder of shares or of voting trust certificates or of beneficial interest in such shares or certificates).

7. Some provisions expressly require that in the case of devolution by operation of law, it be from a contemporaneous holder. E. g., ABA–ALI Model Bus. Corp.Act, § 43A (optional section); California, Colorado, Illinois, Iowa, North Dakota, Wisconsin. In California, Ohio, and Wisconsin, derivative actions are expressly allowed if the ownership was contemporaneous with the transaction complained of or "any part thereof". It would seem that the fact

1. Even a shareholder suing his corporation nonderivatively for breach of his membership contract would have to have been a shareholder at the time of the alleged wrong, or an assignee of the cause of action. But see Zahn v. Transamerica Corp., 162 F.2d 36, 172 A.L.R. 105 (3d Cir. 1947).

The rule originated in the federal courts as a means of preventing transfer of shares to a nonresident for the purpose of acquiring diversity jurisdiction.[8] However, it later took on a nonjurisdictional aspect and now applies even in nondiversity cases, formerly as a rule of equity [9] and now as a rule of procedure.[10]

that shares were acquired by devolution negative a motive, possibly inferable from a purchase of shares, namely, that the shares were acquired for the purpose of bringing the action. See Helfand v. Gambee, 37 Del.Ch. 51, 136 A.2d 558 (Ch.1957).

8. Hawes v. Oakland, 104 U.S. 450, 26 L.Ed. 827 (1882).

9. Fed.Eq.R. 27, 226 U.S. 656 (1912). See Venner v. Great Northern Ry., 209 U.S. 24, 34, 28 S.Ct. 328, 330, 52 L.Ed. 666, 670 (1908) ("principle of equity").

10. Fed.R.Civ.P. 23.1. The Rules Advisory Committee indicated in 1946 that whether predecessor Rule 23(b) (1) was a matter of substantive right or of procedure [an important question since Erie R.R. v. Tompkins, 304 U.S. 64, 58 S.Ct. 817, 82 L.Ed. 1188, 114 A.L.R. 1487 (1938), conformed to 98 F.2d 49 (2d Cir. 1938)] was a debatable question. See Comment, "Developments in the Law: Multiparty Litigation in the Federal Courts", 71 Harv.L.Rev. 874, 964 (1958). The more recent view tends to regard such rules as procedural and binding on the federal court regardless of the state rule. Hanna v. Plumer, 380 U.S. 460, 85 S.Ct. 1136, 14 L.Ed.2d 8 (1965); H. F. G. Co. v. Pioneer Pub. Co., 162 F.2d 536 (7th Cir. 1947); Piccard v. Sperry Corp., 36 F. Supp. 1006 (S.D.N.Y.1941), aff'd on opinion below, 120 F.2d 328 (2d Cir.1941); Elkins v. Bricker, 147 F.Supp. 609 (S.D.N.Y.1956); Kaufman v. Wolfson, 136 F.Supp. 939 (S.D.N.Y.1955); Perrott v. United States Banking Corp., 53 F.Supp. 953 (D.Del.1944); Winkelman v. General Motors Corp., 44 F.Supp. 960 (S.D.N.Y.1942). Contra, Gallup v. Caldwell, 120 F. 2d 90 (3d Cir. 1941); Fuller v. American Machine & Foundry Co., 95 F.Supp. 764 (S.D.N.Y.1951). Quaere, as to whether the rule should be similarly construed for purposes of the initial plaintiff shareholder, shareholders seeking intervention, and in cases of removal from a state court. In Cohen v. Beneficial Industrial Loan Corp., 337 U.S. 541, 69 S.Ct. 1221, 93 L.Ed. 1528 (1949), in which the United States Supreme Court (6-3) found the New Jersey security-for-expenses statute to be substantive [see section 372 infra], even the majority opinion recognized that then Federal Rule 23(b) and (c) [now 23.1] neither created nor exempted from liabilities, did not conflict with the New Jersey security-for-expenses statute, and might be observed by a federal court even if a similar rule were not applicable in the local state courts. See Siegel, "The Federal Rules in Diversity Cases: Erie Implemented, Not Retarded", 54 A.B.A.J. 172 (1968); Zabin, "The Federal Rules in Diversity Cases: Erie in Retreat", 53 A.B.A.J. 266 (1967); McCoid, "Hanna v. Plumer: The Erie Doctrine Changes Shape", 51 Va.L.Rev. 884 (1965).

The state courts and legislatures adopted the contemporaneous-share-ownership requirement to prevent a subsequent purchaser of shares from "speculating in litigation" or "litigating purchased grievances".

The constitutionality of contemporaneous-share-ownership statutes has been upheld.[11] In a case where the statute was not expressly retroactive, the requirement was held not applicable to shareholder derivative actions already pending at the time of the enactment of the statute.[12]

Unless the contemporaneous-share-ownership provision by its terms requires contemporaneous-share-ownership of record,[13] contemporaneous equitable ownership has usually been held sufficient.[14]

Minority Rule

The minority rule permits a shareholder, absent special circumstances,[15] to sue in behalf of the corporation because of a transaction consummated before he acquired his shares on the premise that any corporate rights of action are part of the indivisible interest in the corporation represented by the share certificates and therefore transferable by the transfer of such certificates.[16]

11. Myer v. Myer, 296 N.Y. 979, 73 N.E.2d 562 (1947).

12. Coane v. American Distilling Co., 298 N.Y. 197, 81 N.E.2d 87 (1948).

13. See note 6 supra.

14. Murdock v. Follansbee Steel Corp., 213 F.2d 570 (3d Cir. 1954); Craftsman Finance & Mortgage Co. v. Brown, 64 F.Supp. 168 (S.D.N.Y.1945); Brown v. Dolese Bros. Co., 38 Del.Ch. 471, 154 A.2d 233 (Ch. 1959), aff'd 39 Del.Ch. 1, 157 A.2d 784 (Sup.Ct.1960); Kimball v. Bangs, 321 Mich. 394, 32 N.W.2d 831 (1948); Law v. Alexander Smith & Sons Carpet Co., 271 App.Div. 705, 68 N.Y.S.2d 143 (1st Dep't 1947). Contra, Bookman v. R. J. Reynolds Tobacco Co., 133 N.J.Eq. 116, 30 A.2d 823 (1943), 138 N.J.Eq. 312, 48 A.2d 646 (1946).

15. For limitations imposed on such actions by the "dirty stock" or "tainted shares" rule, see section 363, n. 6 infra. Cf. Kenrich Corp. v. Miller, 377 F. 2d 312 (3d Cir. 1967) (assignment of claim against directors to former shareholder held champertous).

16. Pollitz v. Gould, 202 N.Y. 11, 94 N.E. 1088 (1911) [overruled by then applicable McKinney's N.Y.Gen. Corp.Law, § 61 in 1944; now in McKinney's N.Y.

"Continuing Wrong Theory"

In an effort to escape the effect of the contemporaneous-share-ownership rule, subsequent shareholders have at times advanced the theory of a "continuing wrong". A few statutes even expressly require contemporaneous-share-ownership only at the time of the wrong or "any part thereof".[17]

Where the plaintiff-shareholder acquired his shares after the initial allegedly wrongful transaction under which payments were continuing to be made by the corporation, the contemporaneous-share-ownership rule has been held satisfied.[18]

On the other hand, there may be times when the "transaction complained of" is not fully consummated when the subsequent shareholder acquires his interest. For example, the plaintiff may become a shareholder after the formulation of an alleged illegal plan but before the shareholders vote at a general meeting, their approval being necessary to give the plan legal effect.[19]

Unlike the federal courts, Delaware has adopted a liberal approach in applying the "continuing wrong" theory. It has permitted a derivative action where the shareholder became such after the alleged illegal authorization of shares but before its actual issuance, even though issuance of the shares is usually deemed a mere ministerial act.[20]

Secondary Actions under Federal Securities Legislation

The federal courts have not always reached similar results in applying the contemporaneous-share-ownership requirement in actions brought by shareholders under federal securities legislation, especially section 16(b) of the Securities Exchange Act to recover a corporate insider's "short-swing" trading profits.[21]

Actions to recover such profits may be brought by the issuer or, if the issuer fails to do so, by the owner of any security of the issuer in the name and in behalf of the is-

Bus.Corp.Law § 626(b)]. Accord, Craftsman Finance & Mortgage Co. v. Brown, 64 F.Supp. 168 (S. D.N.Y.1945) (shares registered in broker's name); Parson v. Joseph, 92 Ala. 403, 8 So. 788 (1891); Fortner v. Cornell, 66 Idaho 512, 163 P.2d 299 (1945); Peterson v. Hopson, 306 Mass. 597, 29 N.E. 2d 140, 132 A.L.R. 1 (1940); Forrester v. Boston & M. Consol. Copper & Silver Min. Co., 21 Mont. 544, 55 P. 229 (1898); Winsor v. Bailey, 55 N.H. 218 (1875); North v. Union Savings & Loan Ass'n, 59 Or. 488, 117 P. 824 (1911); Roberson v. Donnelly, 53 Utah 263, 178 P. 35 (1919); Bank of Mill Creek v. Elk Horn Coal Corp., 133 W.Va. 639, 57 S.E.2d 736 (1950); Bloxam v. Metropolitan Ry., 3 Ch.App. 337 (1868).

17. See note 7 supra.

18. Palmer v. Morris, 316 F.2d 649 (5th Cir. 1963). Compare Weinhaus v. Gale, 237 F.2d 197 (7th Cir. 1956), where a subsidiary corporation transferred a number of its preferred shares to the parent which sold them within a year at a considerable profit. The plaintiff acquired her interest in the subsidiary after the original transfer of the shares but before the later disposition of the shares by the parent corporation. She alleged that the shares were underpriced and that the parent made an unconscionable profit that rightfully belonged to the subsidiary. The court, however, rejected her attempt to circumvent the contemporaneous-share-ownership requirement by holding that any wrong occurred when the shares were first transferred to the parent, and that the later sale neither added to nor subtracted from the original act. See also Blau v. Brown and Western Nuclear, Inc., CCH Fed.Sec.L.Rep. ¶92,263 (S.D.N.Y.1968) (allowing $3,800 fee to attorney whose shareholder-plaintiff bought some shares after transaction in order to bring action under § 16(b), where recovery one month after commencement of action was $37,796); Henis v. Campania Agricola de Guatemala, 116 F.Supp. 223, 228–230 (D.Del.1953), aff'd 210 F.2d 950 (3d Cir. 1954); Bauer v. Servel, Inc., 168 F.Supp. 478 (S.D.N.Y. 1958). See also Bateson v. Magna Oil Corp., 414 F.2d 128 (5th Cir. 1969) (allowing action by long-time shareholder planning to sue who inadvertently sold his shares but purchased other shares before

suing, on ground wrong was continuing one and he was not estopped by knowledge of alleged wrong when he purchased latter shares).

19. Lavine v. Gulf Coast Leaseholds, Inc., 35 Del.Ch. 539, 122 A.2d 50 (Ch.1956). For unsuccessful attempts by the defendants to defeat shareholder derivative actions on the ground that the wrongs began before the shareholders acquired their shares, see Goldie v. Yaker, 78 N.M. 485, 432 P.2d 841 (1967); Wool v. Solar Aircraft Co., 47 Ill.App.2d 84, 197 N.E.2d 477 (1964); Gittleman v. Doyle, 21 Misc.2d 834, 194 N.Y.S.2d 401 (Sup.Ct.1959). The failure of the director to act on the old wrong might itself be actionable. See Gluck v. Unger, 25 Misc.2d 554, 557, 202 N.Y.S.2d 832, 834 (Sup.Ct.1960), appeal denied 10 A.D.2d 911, 203 N.Y.S.2d 1005 (1st Dep't 1960).

20. Maclary v. Pleasant Hills, Inc., 35 Del.Ch. 39, 109 A.2d 830 (Ch.1954).

21. See section 298 supra.

suer. After some differences of opinion by the federal courts on the question, with some courts holding that the statutory intent was that any shareholder could sue, and that this right should not be hobbled by a procedural rule,[22] and another, subsequently reversed, applying the contemporaneous-share-ownership rule on the ground that it would be inequitable to allow a subsequent purchaser who had no interest at the time of the transaction, to sue,[23] the definite trend is now against applying Rule 23.1 to such secondary actions.[24] As a matter of construction, it could be contended that section 16(b) of the Securities Exchange Act permits secondary actions thereunder by the owner of any security, that Rule 23.1 applies only to secondary actions by shareholders, and that therefore Rule 23.1 was not intended to apply to secondary actions by holders of securities under section 16(b).

The contemporaneous-share-ownership rule has been held inapplicable to actions under other federal securities legislation.[25]

Other "Contemporaneous-Share-Ownership" Requirement Problems

If all the shareholders are barred from suing derivatively because of the contemporaneous-share-ownership rule, may the corporation then bring a direct action to recover on the claim that could not be enforced derivatively?

In Capitol Wine & Spirit Corp. v. Pokrass,[26] the New York Court of Appeals unanimously affirmed a split decision of the appellate division [27] upon the ground that the contemporaneous-share-ownership rule barred the maintenance of a direct action by the corporation where its sole shareholder could not sue derivatively under the rule. Apparently the New York courts would apply a similar rule where there were several shareholders, all of whom were precluded from bringing a derivative action, some under the contemporaneous-share-ownership requirement and others on different grounds.[28]

Whether or not the federal courts would similarly apply Rule 23.1 remains to be decided.[29]

22. Benisch v. Cameron, 81 F.Supp. 882 (S.D.N.Y. 1948).

23. Dottenheim v. Murchison, 127 F.Supp. 790 (N.D. Tex.1956), rev'd 227 F.2d 737 (5th Cir. 1955), cert. denied 351 U.S. 919, 76 S.Ct. 712, 100 L.Ed. 1451 (1956).

24. Dottenheim v. Murchison, 227 F.2d 737 (5th Cir. 1955), cert. denied 351 U.S. 919, 76 S.Ct. 712, 100 L. Ed. 1451 (1956); Blau v. Mission Corp., 212 F.2d 77 (2d Cir. 1954), cert. denied 347 U.S. 1016, 74 S.Ct. 872, 98 L.Ed. 1138 (1954); Pellegrino v. Nesbit, 203 F.2d 463, 37 A.L.R.2d 1296 (9th Cir. 1953).

25. See also Entel v. Guilden, 223 F.Supp. 129 (S.D. N.Y.1963) (holding that "in view of the strongly expressed intent of the [Federal] Investment Company Act [of 1940] to benefit 'investors' and 'all classes of security holders' [see section 301 supra] the balance of economic policy" lay with permitting claim asserted by warrant holders in behalf of a registered investment company to be heard, and holding that § 17(e) of the Act created "a private right of action for the benefit of an investment company which may be exercised secondarily by plaintiffs as the holders of the warrants in question", notwithstanding then Fed.R.Civ.P. 23(b)).

26. 302 N.Y. 734, 98 N.E.2d 704 (1951), reargument denied 302 N.Y. 840, 100 N.E. 37 (1951); Ford Tank Maintenance Co. v. Ford, 24 Misc.2d 261, 203 N.Y. S.2d 542 (Sup.Ct.1960); cf. Platt Corp. v. Platt, 21 A.D.2d 116, 249 N.Y.S.2d 75 (1st Dep't 1964), aff'd per curiam 15 N.Y.2d 705, 256 N.Y.S.2d 335, 204 N.E.2d 495 (1965). See also Park Terrace, Inc. v. Burge, 249 N.C. 308, 106 S.E.2d 478 (1959).

27. 277 App.Div. 184, 98 N.Y.S.2d 291 (1st Dep't 1950) (2-1-2).

28. Ripley v. Colwell, 206 Misc. 46, 129 N.Y.S.2d 578 (Sup.Ct.1954). But see Comment, "Demise of the Doctrine of *Capital Wine and Spirit v. Pokrass*," 18 Buffalo L.Rev. 184 (1969).

29. Cf. Central Railway Signal Co. v. Longden, 194 F.2d 310 (7th Cir. 1952), indicating that the federal contemporaneous-share-ownership rule did not apply to an action by the corporation against a former officer for usurpation of corporate opportunity, against the contention that the recovery should not have been in favor of the corporation—more than 99 percent of whose shares were said to be held by a noncontemporaneous owner—but should have been for the benefit of only contemporaneous share owners.

If some of the shareholders are barred from suing derivatively because they cannot meet the contemporaneous-share-ownership requirement, should the damages recovered in a derivative action brought by those entitled to sue be reduced in proportion to the holdings of noncontemporaneous shareholders? Courts have usually rejected such efforts to reduce the recovery going to the corporate treasury, the reason being that even a diminished recovery to the corporation inures proportionately to the benefit of subsequent shareholders, and thereby reduces the share of the contemporaneous shareholders.[30]

OTHER DISQUALIFICATIONS TO COMMENCE AND MAINTAIN ACTION

363. The personal motives of a shareholder in bringing a derivative action are usually immaterial, at least where he is not acting to serve an adverse interest. Laches might bar the shareholder from suing derivatively. There is a split of authority as to whether the shareholder's participation in, ratification of, or acquiescence in the allegedly wrongful transaction will bar his derivative action where the corporation itself would not have been barred from suing the alleged wrongdoers directly. Some cases have applied the so-called "dirty stock" or "tainted shares" rule to bar a derivative action by a shareholder, except possibly a bona fide purchaser, who has acquired his shares from a party to the allegedly wrongful transaction.

Motives of Shareholder

In examining the qualifications of the plaintiff-shareholder, a further question arises. May the wrongful motive of the plaintiff-shareholder be employed as a defense to a derivative action? This question assumes importance when a minority shareholder brings a "strike suit", hoping to exploit its nuisance value and thereby force payment of a sum disproportionate to the value of his interest as a price for his discontinuance of the action. The general rule is that the plaintiff-shareholder is not disqualified from suing derivatively because of his motive to gain a settlement from the defendants or other personal motives.[1] But if it can be shown that he is acting to serve the interest of a rival concern which is not a shareholder, the action will be dismissed.[2]

Other Disqualifications

A defense that limits the right to recovery in a derivative action is laches on the part of the plaintiff-shareholder.[3]

There is a split of authority as to whether the plaintiff-shareholder's participation in the wrongful transaction, his ratification

---

30. E. g., Norte & Co. v. Huffins, 416 F.2d 1189 (2d Cir. 1969); Overfield v. Pennroad Corp., 48 F.Supp. 1008, 1018 (E.D.Pa.1943), rev'd on other grounds 146 F.2d 889 (3d Cir. 1944); Platt Corp. v. Platt, 21 A. D.2d 116, 249 N.Y.S.2d 75 (1st Dep't 1964), aff'd per curiam 15 N.Y.2d 705, 256 N.Y.S.2d 335, 204 N.E.2d 495 (1965) (rejecting argument that merged corporation lost standing to maintain action against former president for dereliction because it no longer had any contemporaneous shareholders where merger agreement expressly provided that proceeds from such litigation should be distributed among merged corporation's Class A Common shareholders); Keenan v. Eshleman, 23 Del.Ch. 234, 2 A.2d 904, 120 A.L.R. 227 (Sup.Ct.1938). But see section 373 infra.

1. R. Stevens, Handbook on the Law of Private Corporations § 172 (2d ed. 1949). See section 374 infra. See also Bowker v. Nashua Textile Co., 103 N.H. 242, 169 A.2d 630 (1961), dismissing action by shareholder who was suing as a "matter of principle", claiming damages for innocent shareholders but expressly waiving them for himself.

2. Quirke v. St. Louis-San Francisco Ry., 277 F.2d 705 (8th Cir. 1960) cert. denied 363 U.S. 845, 80 S. Ct. 1615, 4 L.Ed.2d 1728 (1960), reh. denied 364 U.S. 855, 81 S.Ct. 35, 5 L.Ed.2d 80 (1960); Forrest v. Manchester, Sheffield and Lincolnshire Ry., 4 De Gex, F. & J. 126, 45 Eng.Rep. 1131 (Ch.1861). See Globus, Inc. v. Jaroff, 271 F.Supp. 378 (S.D.N.Y. 1967). In Donavan v. Shaheen, 34 Misc.2d 525, 232 N.Y.S.2d 67 (Sup.Ct.1962), the court refused to dismiss a shareholder derivative action on the ground that the action was allegedly instigated by, and was under the control of and financed by, outside parties who were allegedly seeking to further ulterior motives and to seize control of the corporation.

3. Federal Home Loan Bank Board v. Elliott, 386 F. 2d 42, 54 (9th Cir. 1968) (finding three required elements of laches: (a) full knowledge of facts, (b) unreasonable delay in assertion of available remedy, and (c) intervening prejudice to another); Johnson v. King-Richardson Co., 36 F.2d 675, 67 A.L.R. 1465 (1st Cir. 1930); Saigh v. Busch, 403 S.W.2d 559 (Mo.1966); Annot., 10 A.L.R. 370 (1921).

thereof, or his acquiescence thereto, will estop him from maintaining a derivative action. Some cases conclude that such a shareholder is without standing in equity,[4] while others hold that the individual disqualification of the shareholder does not bar recovery for the corporation, where the corporation itself would not have been barred

from suing directly, since the shareholder is suing only in a representative capacity.[5]

Some cases have applied the so-called "dirty stock" or "tainted shares" rule to bar a derivative action by one who had acquired his shares, other than as a bona fide purchaser, from a party to the allegedly wrongful transaction.[6]

D. CONDITIONS PRECEDENT TO DERIVATIVE ACTION

EXHAUSTION OF INTRACORPORATE REMEDIES

364. The requirement of the exhaustion of intracorporate remedies—by prior demand on the board of directors and/or shareholders—as prerequisite to a shareholder derivative action originated in the courts of equity, and usually

applies even in the absence of express provision to such effect. Several jurisdictions by statute or court rule expressly require prior demand on the board of directors and, if necessary, on the shareholders, or sufficient reason for not making such demand.

In order to have standing to sue derivatively, the plaintiff-shareholder is generally required to seek relief initially through the corporate organization, or, in other words, to exhaust his intracorporate remedies before suing in equity. This affords the corporation an opportunity to conduct its own litigation, since it is the principal party in interest. Also, in certain cases shareholders may "ratify" the alleged wrong when given the opportunity to do so and thus rectify it or render it non-wrongful or exercise business judgment in behalf of the corporation that the litigation should not continue.

The requirement of the exhaustion of intracorporate remedies as prerequisite to a shareholder derivative action originated in the courts of equity,[1] and usually applies even in the absence of express provision to such effect.[2]

4. Hawkins v. Mall, Inc., 444 S.W.2d 369 (Mo. 1969) ; Swafford v. Berry, 152 Colo. 493, 382 P.2d 999 (1963) ; Chalverus v. Wilson Mfg. Co., 212 Ga. 612, 94 S.E.2d 736 (1956) ; Gottfried v. Gottfried, 112 N. Y.S.2d 431 (Sup.Ct.1952) ; Ohio Farmers' Co-operative Milk Ass'n v. Clover Meadow Creamery Co., 50 Ohio App. 261, 198 N.E. 53 (1934). In Diamond v. Diamond, 307 N.Y. 263, 120 N.E.2d 819 (1954), reargument denied 307 N.Y. 804, 121 N.E.2d 626 (1954), the court held that one of two sole shareholders who participated equally in and profited from a wrongful diversion of corporate funds was barred from suing the other in a derivative action under the rule that when shareholders are individually estopped from questioning wrongs done their corporation, they cannot redress such wrongs through an action brought directly by the corporation or derivatively by themselves for the corporation.

5. Liken v. Shaffer, 64 F.Supp. 432 (N.D.Iowa 1946) ; Kullgren v. Navy Gas & Supply Co., 112 Colo. 331, 149 P.2d 653 (1944) ; Atkinson v. McCabe Hanger Mfg. Co., 55 N.Y.S.2d 274 (Sup.Ct.1945). Alhambra-Shumway Mines v. Alhambra Gold Mine Corp., 200 Cal.App.2d 322, 19 Cal.Rptr. 208 (1962), held that the lease of a corporation's gold mine constituting substantially all of the corporate assets required shareholder approval, but that the corporation and a shareholder suing to cancel the lease four years after it was made and after the lessee had struck gold and had expended substantial sums in developing the mine, were barred by laches from contending that the lease was invalid for want of shareholder approval.

6. Erickson v. Hellekson-Vye Co. v. A. Wells Co., 217 Minn. 361, 15 N.W.2d 162 (1944) ; Parson v. Joseph, 92 Ala. 403, 8 So. 788 (1891) ; see also Russell v. Louis Melind Co., 331 Ill.App. 182, 72 N.E.2d 869 (1947) (barring even innocent transferee of "tainted shares" from bringing derivative action). See also Pollitz v. Gould, 202 N.Y. 11, 94 N.E. 1088 (1911).

1. Foss v. Harbottle, 2 Hare 461, 67 Eng.Rep. 189 (V.Ch.1843) ; Hawes v. Oakland, 104 U.S. 450, 26 L. Ed. 827 (1882) ; Wedderburn, "Shareholders' Rights and the Rule in Foss v. Harbottle", 1957 Camb.L.J. 194, 1958 Camb.L.J. 93.

2. E. g., Kowalski v. Nebraska-Iowa Packing Co., 160 Neb. 609, 71 N.W.2d 147 (1955). Where the corporation is in receivership, demand on the receiver is usually required. Lucking v. Delano, 117 F.2d 159 (6th Cir. 1941) ; Waller v. Waller, 187 Md. 185, 49 A.2d 449 (1946).

The required attempt at relief within the corporation usually must take the form of a demand on the board of directors[3] and/or shareholders.[4]

Several jurisdictions by statute[5] or court rule[6] expressly require prior exhaustion of intracorporate remedies, most frequently by requiring that the plaintiff in a shareholder derivative action must aver: (a) that he attempted to obtain redress from the board of directors and, if necessary, from the shareholders, and why such redress was not obtained, or (b) the reasons for not making such effort.[7]

[§ 364]

3. See section 365 infra.

4. See section 366 infra.

5. E. g., California, Georgia, Kentucky, New York, Oklahoma, Wisconsin.

6. E. g., Fed.R.Civ.P. 23.1; Arizona, Colorado, Delaware, Iowa, Minnesota, Nevada, New Jersey, North Dakota, Utah, Wyoming. The Federal Rules apply in the District of Columbia. Such requirements of Federal Rule 23.1 are presumably procedural. Hanna v. Plumer, 380 U.S. 460, 85 S.Ct. 1136, 14 L.Ed. 2d 8 (1965). But see Newman v. Baldwin, 13 Misc. 2d 897, 179 N.Y.S.2d 19 (Sup.Ct.1958).

7. California and Wisconsin do not expressly require an attempt to seek relief from the other shareholders. However, California and Wisconsin specify that the plaintiff must allege that he has either informed the corporation or the board of directors, in writing, of the ultimate facts of each cause of action against each defendant director or delivered to the corporation or board of directors a true copy of the complaint which he proposes to file. Pennsylvania requires an allegation of the efforts made to secure enforcement by the corporation or the reason for not making any such efforts. New York expressly requires the complaint, in a shareholder's derivative action brought in the right of the corporation to procure a judgment in its favor, to set forth with particularity the efforts of the plaintiff to secure the initiation of the action by the board of directors or the reasons for not making such effort. Apart from statute, New York had required demands on the board of directors and also on the shareholders in certain cases (see section 366, n. 2 infra). Quaere, as to the effect upon the demand-on-shareholders requirement of a statutory provision codifying only the demand-on-directors requirement, but omitting any demand-on-shareholders requirement. See also McKinney's N.Y.Part.Law § 115–a(3).

DEMAND ON BOARD OF DIRECTORS

365. Prerequisite to a shareholder derivative action is a demand by the shareholder on the board of directors for redress of the alleged wrong against the corporation, except when such a demand would be futile. If proper demand is made and refused, the shareholder may nevertheless be barred from suing derivatively if such refusal was made by the directors in the exercise of their sound business judgment.

As a general rule, the plaintiff must first make a demand on the board of directors that the corporation take the steps necessary to enforce its cause of action.[1]

However, where hostility on the part of the directors makes such a demand futile, it is excused.[2] The latter situation arises most often where the directors are the alleged wrongdoers,[3] or are under the control of the alleged wrongdoer,[4] or deny the occurrence

1. Hawes v. Oakland, 104 U.S. 450, 26 L.Ed. 827 (1882); Continental Securities Co. v. Belmont, 206 N.Y. 7, 99 N.E. 138 (1912); R. Stevens, Handbook on the Law of Private Corporations § 169 (2d ed. 1949). Such a demand on the board of directors is expressly required by statute or court rule in Arizona, California, Colorado, Delaware, Minnesota, Nevada, New Jersey, New Mexico, New York, North Dakota, Ohio, Oklahoma, Utah, Wisconsin, and Wyoming, and in the federal courts under Fed.R.Civ.P. 23.1 (formerly 23(b)). See Note, "Demand on Directors and Shareholders as a Prerequisite to a Derivative Suit", 73 Harv.L.Rev. 746 (1960).

2. E. g., Smith v. Sperling, 354 U.S. 91, 77 S.Ct. 1112, 1 L.Ed.2d 1205, 68 A.L.R.2d 805 (1957); Campbell v. Loew's, Inc., 36 Del.Ch. 563, 134 A.2d 852 (Ch.1957); cf. Balling v. Casabianca, 285 App.Div. 20, 135 N.Y. S.2d 211 (1st Dep't 1954).

3. Reed v. Norman, 48 Cal.2d 338, 309 P.2d 809 (1957); Eston v. Argus, Inc., 328 Mich. 554, 44 N. W.2d 154 (1950).

4. See Meltzer v. Atlantic Research Corp., 330 F.2d 946 (4th Cir. 1964), cert. denied sub nom. Scurlock v. Meltzer, 379 U.S. 841, 85 S.Ct. 78, 13 L.Ed.2d 47 (1964) (excusing demand on directors because they were dominated by alleged wrongdoers and demand on shareholders because defendants owned 40 percent of shares and remaining 60 percent was widely distributed and convening of sufficient number thereof for discussion and vote would not be feasible); Akin v. Mackie, 310 S.W.2d 164 (Tenn.1958).

of the alleged transaction,[5] or had approved it.[6]

If the directors comply with the plaintiff-shareholder's demand, there is no need for a derivative action. If the directors refuse to enforce the corporate right, the plaintiff-shareholder may nevertheless be barred from suing derivatively if such refusal was made by the directors in the exercise of their sound business judgment.[7] This, of course, assumes that the directors are fair-minded and have no personal interests in the matter, and exercise due diligence.[8]

DEMAND ON SHAREHOLDERS

366. Prerequisite to a shareholder derivative action is a demand, when necessary, by the plaintiff-shareholder on the other shareholders except when such a demand would be futile. Such demand is necessary when the other shareholders could effectively "ratify" the alleged wrong. There are three different views on the necessity of such a demand where the alleged wrong is not capable of ratification except by unanimous shareholder action: (a) Traditional or English view; (b) American

rule; and (c) Case-by-case approach. Effective shareholder ratification of the wrong eliminates the corporate claim. Even absent effective shareholder ratification, disapproval of the assertion of the claim by or in behalf of the corporation by disinterested shareholders in the exercise of their sound business judgment might bar the shareholder from suing derivatively.

The requirement of a demand on shareholders as a condition precedent to a derivative action is somewhat dependent on the substantive law regarding shareholder ratification of challenged acts.[1] Certain acts may be ratified by a mere majority of shareholders, while others such as waste of corporate assets or director's fraud usually require

---

5. Screven Oil Mill v. Hudmon, 214 Ga. 414, 105 S. E.2d 328 (1958).

6. Maas v. Tyler, 316 S.W.2d 211 (Ky.Ct.App.1958); American Life Ins. Co. v. Powell, 262 Ala. 560, 80 So.2d 487 (1954).

7. Ash v. International Business Machines, Inc., 353 F.2d 491 (3d Cir. 1965), cert. denied 384 U.S. 927, 86 S.Ct. 1446, 16 L.Ed.2d 531 (1966); Swanson v. Traer, 249 F.2d 854 (7th Cir. 1957); Issner v. Aldrich, 254 F.Supp. 696 (D.Del.1966); Brooks v. Brooks Pontiac, Inc., 143 Mont. 256, 389 P.2d 185 (1964); Rice v. Wheeling Dollar Savings & Trust Co., 130 N.E.2d 442 (Ohio C.P.1954); Findley v. Garrett, 109 Cal.App.2d 166, 240 P.2d 421 (1952). See Margolis v. Zale Corp., 159 N.Y.L.J.No. 60, 17 (Sup.Ct.1968) (allowing corporation with new disinterested board of directors, upon advice of independent counsel, to take over and discontinue shareholder derivative action).

8. Groel v. United Electric Co. of New Jersey, 70 N. J.Eq. 616, 61 A. 1061 (1905) (with "grave doubt" whether nominal corporate defendant, in whose behalf action was brought, should be permitted to raise issue of right of minority shareholder to sue in behalf of corporation by plea or answer denying such right instead of by petition). See section 242 supra.

1. Whether demand on shareholders is substantive or procedural is not clear. Even the express requirement of such demand is limited by the condition "if necessary". See Newman v. Baldwin, 13 Misc.2d 897, 179 N.Y.S.2d 19 (Sup.Ct.1958) (demand on shareholders held governed by law of jurisdiction of incorporation). Cf. Hanna v. Plumer, 380 U.S. 460, 85 S.Ct. 1136, 14 L.Ed.2d 8 (1965) (construing Federal Rules of Civil Procedure as procedural); Levitt v. Johnson, 334 F.2d 815 (1st Cir. 1964), cert. denied 379 U.S. 961, 85 S.Ct. 649, 13 L.Ed.2d 556 (1965) (state law held inapplicable to action under Federal Investment Company Act). Demand on shareholders, if necessary, or explanation for not making such demand, is expressly required by statute or court rule in Arizona, Colorado, Minnesota, Nevada, New Jersey, New Mexico, North Dakota, Oklahoma, Utah, and Wyoming, and in the federal courts under Federal Rule of Civil Procedure 23.1, formerly 23(b). See Leavell, "Shareholders as Judges of Alleged Wrongs by Directors", 35 Tul.L.Rev. 331 (1961); Stickells, "Derivative Suits—The Requirement of Demand Upon the Stockholders", 33 B.U.L.Rev. 435 (1953); Waterbury, "Shareholder's Derivative Suits —When Demand on Shareholders is a Prerequisite to Maintenance of Suit", 48 Mich.L.Rev. 87 (1949); Comment, "Shareholder Validation of Directors' Frauds: The Non-Ratification Rule v. The Business Judgment Rule", 58 Nw.U.L.Rev. 807 (1964); Comment, "Shareholder Demand as a Condition Precedent to Derivative Suit: A Proposed Compromise", 39 U.Cin.L.Rev. 196 (1961); Note, "The Nonratification Rule and the Demand Requirement: The Case for Limited Judicial Review", 63 Colum.L.Rev. 1086 (1963); Note, "Demand on Directors and Shareholders as a Prerequisite to a Derivative Suit", 73 Harv.L.Rev. 746 (1960); Note, "Derivate Suits—Requirement of Demand on Shareholders Where Unanimity is Necessary for Ratification", 33 N.Y.U.L. Rev. 71 (1958); Note, "Corporations—Stockholder's Suit—Necessity of Demand on Other Stockholders in Derivative Action", 55 Mich.L.Rev. 450 (1957); Annot., 72 A.L.R. 628 (1931).

unanimous shareholder action for ratification or condonation of the wrong.[2]

All courts apparently require the plaintiff-shareholder to make a demand or give sufficient excuse for not making a demand where a mere majority of the shareholders may ratify the alleged wrong, since such ratification would rectify the wrong.[3]

There are three different views on the necessity of a demand on shareholders where

the alleged wrong is not capable of ratification except by unanimous shareholder action: (a) Traditional or English view; (b) American rule; and (c) Case-by-case approach.[4]

Traditional or English View

The traditional or English view is that a demand is usually unnecessary when ratification would be effective only if unanimous, since presumably the complaining shareholder would not join in such ratification.[5] Under this traditional view, however, a demand may be required if the majority of the shareholders could effectively vote to bar the action, even though they could not ratify.[6]

2. Mayer v. Adams, 37 Del.Ch. 298, 141 A.2d 458 (Sup.Ct.1958) (holding that demand on shareholders is not necessary where ground of shareholder derivative action is alleged wrong of directors beyond ratification by majority of shareholders, and stating one instance of necessary demand is case involving only irregularity or lack of authority in directorate action), rev'g 37 Del.Ch. 1, 135 A.2d 119 (Ch.1957); Continental Securities Co. v. Belmont, 206 N.Y. 7, 99 N.E. 138 (1912) (holding that majority of shareholders, even if disinterested, may not ratify fraud of directors in misappropriating corporate shares and property, and therefore demand on shareholders was not condition precedent to shareholder derivative action based on such fraud). Delaware in 1962 deleted from its chancery court rule the phrase "and, if necessary, from the shareholders". New York, when it adopted McKinney's N.Y. Bus.Corp.Law, § 626(c) based on Fed.R.Civ.P. 23.1 (then 23(b)) omitted the similar phrase. See Syracuse Television, Inc. v. Channel 9, Syracuse, Inc., 51 Misc.2d 188, 273 N.Y.S.2d 16 (Sup.Ct.1966). But see Claman v. Robertson, 164 Ohio St. 61, 128 N.E. 2d 429 (1955) (holding derivative action, where disinterested majority of shareholders had ratified, not maintainable absent demand on shareholders, since disinterested majority of shareholders, with full disclosure (a) could ratify transaction—modifying lower court holding that unanimity of shareholders was required to ratify—which therefore required negation, or (b) could also decide, as matter of business judgment, to sue or not to sue) ["overruled" in 1956 by Ohio Rev.Code § 2307.311 (Supp. 1959), dispensing with express requirement of demand on shareholders]. See Smith v. Brown-Borhek Co., 414 Pa. 325, 200 A.2d 398 (1964) (holding that negligent failure of directors to exercise their duties, as distinguished from affirmative negligence or intentional wrongdoing, could be ratified by disinterested majority of shareholders). Even unanimous shareholder ratification of a transaction, if obtained without full disclosure, does not bar a shareholder derivative action attacking the transaction. Brown v. Dolese Bros. Co., 38 Del.Ch. 471, 154 A.2d 233 (Ch.1959), aff'd 39 Del.Ch. 1, 157 A.2d 784 (Sup.Ct.1960). Note, "Majority Stockholders Ratification of Directors' Frauds", 25 U.Cin.L.Rev. 354 (1956); Note, "Stockholder's Derivative Suit— Ratification of Fraud", 32 N.D.L.Rev. 125 (1956). See section 194 supra.

3. E. g., Pollitz v. Wabash R. R., 207 N.Y. 113, 100 N.E. 721 (1912).

4. Statutes and court rules on the subject do not resolve the problem since they expressly require such demand only "if necessary". See note 1 supra.

5. Foss v. Harbottle, 2 Hare 461, 67 Eng.Rep. 189 (V. Ch.1843); Hyams v. Calumet & Hecla Mining Co., 221 F. 529, 537 (6th Cir. 1915); Steinberg v. Adams, 90 F.Supp. 604, 609 (S.D.N.Y.1950); Saigh v. Busch, 396 S.W.2d 9 (Mo.Ct.App.1965), aff'd on other grounds 403 S.W.2d 559 (Mo.1966); Mayer v. Adams, 37 Del.Ch.298, 141 A.2d 458 (Sup.Ct.1958); Continental Securities Co. v. Belmont, 206 N.Y. 7, 99 N.E. 138 (1912). See note 2 supra.

6. American Life Ins. Co. v. Powell, 262 Ala. 560, 80 So.2d 487 (1954). The theory behind such a requirement is that disinterested shareholders, even though less than all might not ratify the wrong, might bar the corporation's claim from being asserted derivatively when they, as a substitute organ for interested directors, exercise their sound business judgment against the claim's being asserted by or in behalf of the corporation. See section 365, nn. 7, 8 supra. See also S. Solomont & Sons Trust, Inc. v. New England Theatres Operating Corp., 326 Mass. 99, 93 N.E.2d 241 (1950) (holding derivative action barred by disinterested majority shareholder vote in exercise of business judgment against maintenance of action); Cf. Braunstein v. Devine, 337 Mass. 408, 149 N.E.2d 628 (1958), where the plaintiff did not make a demand upon either the directors or the shareholders because a majority of the shareholders had ratified the acts of the directors. In reversing an order dismissing the bill, it was said that the majority shareholders cannot condone and ratify the fraud and breach of trust of the officers so far as their conduct disregards the right of the shareholders. See also Levitt v. Johnson, 334 F.2d 815 (1st Cir. 1964), rev'g 222 F.Supp. 805 (D.Mass.1963), cert. denied 379 U.S.961, 85 S.Ct. 649, 13 L.Ed.2d 556 (1965) (suggesting that Massachusetts law does not require demand on shareholders in every case where there is disinterested majority of shareholders). But see Rogers v. American Can Co., 305 F.2d

American Rule

Under the second view, which has been termed the "American rule", a demand is required in every case where a majority of shareholders are not wrongdoers.[7] However, this requirement may be dispensed with when the time does not permit, when it cannot be done, or when it is not reasonable to require it.[8]

Case-by-Case Approach

The third view assumes a middle position by employing a case-by-case method which balances such factors as size of the corporation, the motive of the plaintiff, the number of shareholders joining in the action, and the

imminence of the next shareholders' meeting.[9]

Effect of Shareholder Action After Demand

The courts seem undecided as to the effect to be given shareholder action after a demand is made. A vote by a disinterested majority of the shareholders against bringing an action may or may not amount to effective ratification of the wrong, thereby eliminating the corporate claim.[10] In any event, a ratification of the wrong, or a decision not to sue the wrongdoers, made by a majority of impartial shareholders may be binding on the minority.[11]

If there is no ratification but rather an accession to the demand to sue, the plaintiff-shareholder may proceed with the derivative action, except where the vote of the shareholders constitutes a binding demand on the directors to bring the action.[12]

PLEADING–OF–DEMAND REQUIREMENTS

367. The plaintiff-shareholder in his complaint must sufficiently allege the fact that a demand was made on the directors or the reasons why such demand would have been futile. Where a demand on shareholders is required, similar pleading rules apply.

In his complaint the plaintiff-shareholder must allege either the fact that a demand was made upon the directors or the reasons why such a demand would have been futile.

297 (3d Cir. 1962) (allowing shareholder derivative action under federal antitrust laws, despite disinterested majority shareholder vote against action, on ground such vote could not ratify violation of antitrust laws and could not bar action). Reasons suggested for requiring a demand on shareholders, even though their disinterested adverse vote would not be held to ratify the wrong or bar the action, were to encourage a satisfactory intracorporate settlement, to persuade the directors to have the corporation bring the action, or to have the shareholders take over the action themselves. Allowing a majority of the shareholders to bar the action but not to ratify appears to be a questionable distinction.

7. Carroll v. New York, N. H. & H. R. R., 141 F.Supp. 456 (D.Mass.1956); Pomerantz v. Clark, 101 F.Supp. 341 (D.Mass.1951); S. Solomont & Sons Trust, Inc. v. New England Theatres Operating Corp., 326 Mass. 99, 93 N.E. 241 (1950). Cf. Braunstein v. Devine, 337 Mass. 408, 149 N.E.2d 628 (1958); Rogers v. American Can Co., 187 F.Supp. 532 (D.N.J.1960), aff'd 305 F.2d 297 (3d Cir. 1962).

8. Hawes v. Oakland, 104 U.S. 450, 26 L.Ed. 827 (1882); Brewer v. Boston Theatre, 104 Mass. 378 (1870). But see Haffer v. Voit, 219 F.2d 704 (6th Cir. 1955); Pomerantz v. Clark, 101 F.Supp. 341 (D.Mass.1951). Halprin v. Babbitt, 303 F.2d 138 (1st Cir. 1962), was a shareholder derivative action in behalf of a Massachusetts corporation which alleged that the majority shareholder had refused to bring the action. Dismissal of the action on the ground that this was an insufficient allegation of demand on shareholders was reversed. The court indicated that the purposes of requiring a demand on the majority of the shareholders were twofold: (a) to permit the majority to take affirmative action itself; (b) to permit the majority to decide that no action be taken by anybody. If the majority does neither, the court stated, the minority is not powerless to proceed because of its failure to obtain "express authorization from the majority".

9. Compare Berg v. Cincinnati, N. & C. Ry., 56 F. Supp. 842 (E.D.Ky.1944), with Bruce & Co. v. Bothwell, 8 F.R.D. 45 (S.D.N.Y.1948), 9 F.R.D. 183 (S.D. N.Y.1947). See also Gottesman v. General Motors Corp., 268 F.2d 194 (2d Cir. 1959); Stone v. Holly Hill Fruit Products, Inc., 56 F.2d 553 (5th Cir. 1932); Dannmeyer v. Coleman, 11 F. 97 (C.C.D.Calif.1882); Stokes v. Knickerbocker Inv. Co., 70 N.J. Eq. 518, 61 A. 736 (1905).

10. See notes 2, 6 supra.

11. See note 6 supra.

12. But see Orlando Orangegroves v. Hale, 107 Fla. 403, 144 So. 674 (1932). See "Developments in the Law: Multiparty Litigation in the Federal Courts", 71 Harv.L.Rev. 874, 953–954 (1958).

Where a demand on shareholders is required, similar pleading rules apply. Rule 23.1, formerly 23(b), of the Federal Rules of Civil Procedure has been copied into the statutes or court rules of several states.[1]

Where the complaint charges fraudulent waste or corporate assets by the directors or fraud, conspiracy, or criminal conduct on the part of the directors, an allegation that demand on the directors would have been futile might constitute a sufficient particularization of "the reasons for not making such effort".[2]

An allegation that a demand upon the corporation would be futile because the individual defendant was the sole person in control has been held insufficient.[3] In such a case the plaintiff must show the makeup of the board of directors, or their implication in the matter, or that they would not comply with a demand.

E. PROCEDURAL PROBLEMS IN DERIVATIVE ACTION

CLAIMS, JOINDER, AND COUNTERCLAIMS

368. **A shareholder cannot join an individual or direct action with a derivative action by the traditional view. The modern cases tend to be more liberal. Some states, by statute, permit rather free joinder of causes of action.**

Counterclaims against the plaintiff-shareholder as an individual by the real defendants, by the traditional view, cannot be asserted in a derivative action, even when based on the same transaction which gave rise to the derivative action, since he is not suing in his own right.

This and the next succeeding sections discuss some of the procedural problems arising from derivative actions, viz., joinder of claims, counterclaims, joinder of parties[1]—jurisdiction over the person,[2] venue,[3] forum non conveniens,[4] and statutes of limitations

and laches[5] having already been discussed. Other considerations equally adjective in nature are treated in other sections. For example, the question of alignment of the corporation in a federal diversity-of-citizenship case was included in the discussion of jurisdiction over the subject matter,[6] while certain pleading requirements have been discussed in conjunction with conditions precedent to the derivative action.[7]

A shareholder cannot join an individual or direct action with a derivative action by the traditional view.[8]

The modern cases tend to be more liberal.[9] Some states, by statute, permit rather free joinder of causes of action.[10]

5. See section 357 supra.

6. See section 353 supra.

7. See sections 364–367 supra.

8. Schaffer v. Universal Rundle Corp., 397 F.2d 893 (5th Cir. 1968) (even where plaintiff-shareholder in derivative action was sole shareholder of corporation); Goodliffe v. Colonial Corp., 107 Utah 488, 155 P.2d 177 (1945). See also Shenberg v. De Garmo, 61 Cal.App.2d 326, 143 P.2d 74 (1943).

9. Bennett v. Breuil Petroleum Corp., 34 Del.Ch. 6, 99 A.2d 236 (Ch.1953). See also Conviser v. Simpson, 122 F.Supp. 205 (D.Md.1954).

10. E. g., McKinney's N.Y. CPLR, § 601 (plaintiff in complaint may join as many claims as he may have against adverse party; there may be like joinder of claims when there are multiple parties). Matter of Elias v. Artistic Paper Box Co., 29 A.D.2d 118, 286 N.Y.S.2d 371 (2d Dep't 1967) (upholding consolida-

[§ 367]
1. See section 364, nn. 5, 6, 7 supra.

2. Smith v. Sperling, 354 U.S. 91, 77 S.Ct. 1112, 1 L. Ed.2d 1205, 68 A.L.R.2d 805 (1957); Mayer v. Adams, 37 Del.Ch. 298, 306, 141 A.2d 458, 463 (Sup.Ct. 1958); Reed v. Norman, 48 Cal.2d 338, 309 P.2d 809 (1957).

3. Balling v. Casabianca, 285 App.Div. 20, 135 N.Y. S.2d 211 (1st Dep't 1954).

[§ 368]
1. See section 369 infra.

2. See section 354 supra.

3. See section 355 supra.

4. See section 356 supra.

The plaintiff-shareholder who sues derivatively is not subject to counterclaims against him as an individual by the alleged wrongdoers since he is not suing in his own right.[11]

This traditional view was premised on the rule that a counterclaim had to be on a claim against the plaintiff in the capacity in which he was suing. This is so even where the proposed counterclaim is based upon the same transaction which gave rise to the derivative action and alleges that the plaintiff-shareholder as a director wrongfully participated in the transaction.[12]

A lower court case presented a novel variation on this problem. The corporation sued a director for misconduct in office and the latter attempted to counterclaim against the corporation and certain other directors who allegedly had damaged the corporation by misconduct related to the transaction on which the original complaint was based. The counterclaim was dismissed on the ground it asserted a corporate right rather than a right of the defendant.[13]

JOINDER OF PARTIES

369. The corporation is ordinarily an indispensable party to a derivative action, since its claim is being litigated, and in order that the judgment may be res judicata and may be entered in favor of the corporation. Sufficient alleged wrongdoers should be joined as defendants to satisfy any resulting judgment against them or to enforce any equitable decree. In an action to compel the distribution of a dividend in nearly all jurisdictions, the directors are at most conditionally necessary parties. Intervention as plaintiffs by other qualified shareholders is permitted under various circumstances.

Pre-trial examination, ordinarily limited to examination of an opposing party, is complicated by the corporation's unique position as nominal party defendant and real party plaintiff. Whether the corporation may be examined by the plaintiff-shareholder and vice versa may depend upon the defenses interposed by the corporation. Examination of the corporation by the real party defendant might be justified, regardless of corporate defenses, on the ground

tion of shareholder special proceeding to review election of directors and shareholder derivative action); Young v. Taber, 284 App.Div. 829, 132 N.Y. S.2d 431 (4th Dep't 1954), aff'd mem., 308 N.Y. 687, 124 N.E.2d 322 (1954); De Baryshe v. Kidwell, 282 App.Div. 1104, 126 N.Y.S.2d 678 (3d Dep't 1953). Where there is doubt whether a cause of action is an individual or corporate one, the complaint may allege both and let the court treat one as surplusage. Where derivative and non-derivative claims are joined, the restrictions on derivative actions apply to the derivative claims.

11. Compare Berger v. Reynolds Metals Co., 39 F.R. D. 313 (E.D.Pa.1966), and Burg v. Horn, 37 F.R.D. 562 (E.D.N.Y.1965) (allowing individual counterclaims against plaintiff-shareholder in derivative action brought in behalf of close corporation), with Higgins v. Shenango Pottery Co., 99 F.Supp. 522 (W.D.Pa.1951) (barring individual counterclaims against plaintiff-shareholders in derivative action), and Epstein v. Shindler, 26 F.R.D. 176 (S.D.N.Y.1960) (barring counterclaim against corporation for past salary in action by shareholder to recover insider's "short-swing profits" under section 16(b) of Federal Securities Exchange Act). Fed.R.Civ.P. 13 permits counterclaims against an "opposing party". See also Valmart Food Buying Service, Inc. v. Sterngass, 30 A.D.2d 551, 290 N.Y.S.2d 671 (2d Dep't 1968) (dismissing derivative counterclaims in action based on noncorporate claim). See Annot., 1 A.L.R. Fed. 815, 818 (1969).

12. Shane v. Ohlstein, 24 A.D.2d 742, 263 N.Y.S. 2d 532 (1st Dep't 1965); Binon v. Boel, 271 App. Div. 505, 66 N.Y.S.2d 425 (1st Dep't 1946), aff'd mem., 297 N.Y. 528, 74 N.E.2d 466 (1947). Cf. Purdy v. Purdy, 146 N.Y.L.J. No. 68, 14 (Sup.Ct.1961) (shareholder derivative action in which complaint also stated cause of action for dissolution of corporation; defendant interposed counterclaim for prima facie tort against plaintiff-shareholder personally; interposition of counterclaim was upheld on theory that plaintiff-shareholder had combined in his complaint with derivative claims also claim for dissolution which was non-derivative). See also McKinney's N.Y. CPLR, § 601 (defendant in answer setting forth counterclaim or cross-claim may join as many claims as he may have against ad-

verse party; there may be like joinder of claims when there are multiple parties); McKinney's N.Y. CPLR, § 3019 (counterclaim may be any cause of action in favor of one or more defendants or person whom defendant represents against one or more plaintiffs, person whom plaintiff represents or plaintiff and other persons alleged to be liable; in action brought by trustee or in name of plaintiff who has no actual interest in contract upon which it is founded, claim against plaintiff shall not be allowed as counterclaim, but claim existing against person beneficially interested shall be allowed as counterclaim to extent of plaintiff's claim, if it might have been so allowed in action brought by person beneficially interested).

13. Orto Theatres Corp. v. Newins, 207 Misc. 414, 138 N.Y.S.2d 550 (Sup.Ct.1955).

that the claim involved does not thereby cease to be a corporate claim.

Since the derivative action asserts a corporate cause of action, the corporation is in reality the real party plaintiff. It enters the litigation as a nominal party defendant because of its failure to enforce the claim in its own right.[1]

In any event, the corporation is an indispensable party and without its presence the derivative action usually cannot proceed.[2] This requirement protects the alleged wrongdoers by making any determination of the controversy res judicata and permits judgment in favor of the corporation.

The same requirement applies upon dissolution of the corporation if the dissolved corporation is deemed to continue to exist under applicable law for such purposes. The corporation is not an indispensable party when its existence has completely terminated prior to commencement of the action.[3]

If a receiver has already been appointed, he must be joined.[4] If the state law prohibits the receiver from participating in the action, the action must fail for want of an indispensable party.

The alleged wrongdoers are generally tortfeasors and as such, apart from special statute, jointly and severally liable. One, some, or all may be joined as parties defendant, but enough should be joined to satisfy any resulting judgment against them.

Where an injunction is sought, it obviously is binding only on those personally served or having notice thereof. Where an injunction directed against the corporation would be effective, the directors might be at most conditionally necessary parties, where the court is substituting its discretion for theirs, as in an action brought to compel the distribution of a discretionary dividend.[5] The logical conclusion is that the absence of all the directors from the jurisdiction will not

---

1. See sections 364–367 supra. Cf. Ky.Gen.Corp.Law, § 271.605 (1953) (corporation by shareholder or shareholders to be plaintiff, e. g., X Corporation by John Doe, Shareholder).

2. Geer v. Mathieson Alkali Works, 190 U.S. 428, 23 S.Ct. 807, 47 L.Ed. 1122 (1903); Jordan v. Hartness, 230 N.C. 718, 55 S.E.2d 484 (1949); Dean v. Kellogg, 294 Mich. 200, 292 N.W. 704 (1940). See also Glover v. Diggs, 368 Mich. 430, 118 N.W.2d 278 (1963) (mutual insurance company held indispensable party to derivative action by policyholder); Carruthers v. Jack Waite Mining Co., 306 N.Y. 136, 116 N.E.2d 286 (1953) (holding complaint not dismissable under former N.Y.Civ.Prac.Act §§ 192–193 until opportunity had been provided to bring in indispensable party, even when such party was foreign corporation and any attempt to serve it would be futile). Cf. Green v. Compton, 41 Misc. 21, 83 N.Y.S.2d 588 (Sup.Ct.1903) (corporation held not indispensable party in director's action).

3. Weinert v. Kinkel, 296 N.Y. 151, 71 N.E.2d 445, 172 A.L.R. 688 (1947). Reed v. Norman, 48 Cal.2d 338, 309 P.2d 809 (1957), allowed a shareholder to maintain a derivative action against a corporation and its directors for alleged misconduct even though the corporation itself had had its franchises suspended for nonpayment of franchise tax and therefore itself could not engage in litigation. See also Castner v. First National Bank of Anchorage, 278 F.2d 376 (9th Cir. 1960).

4. Coyle v. Skirvin, 124 F.2d 934 (10th Cir. 1942), cert. denied 316 U.S. 673, 62 S.Ct. 1044, 86 L.Ed. 1748 (1942). Meyer v. Fleming, 327 U.S. 161, 66 S.Ct. 382, 90 L.Ed. 595 (1946), held that a shareholder derivative action was not abated where the corporation was adjudged bankrupt or when a receiver was appointed, but that the trustee or receiver might let the action continue under the shareholder's auspices, intervene in it, start a new action, settle the claim, reserve the claim for the reorganized corporation, or abate the action.

5. Doherty v. Mutual Warehouse Co., 245 F.2d 609 (5th Cir. 1957); Kroese v. General Steel Castings Corp., 179 F.2d 760, 15 A.L.R.2d 1117, (3d Cir. 1950), cert. denied, 339 U.S. 983, 70 S.Ct. 1026, 94 L.Ed. 1386 (1950); Whittemore v. Continental Mills, 98 F.Supp. 387 (D.Me.1951); Swinton v. W. J. Bush & Co., 199 Misc. 321, 102 N.Y.S.2d 994 (Sup.Ct.1951), aff'd mem., 278 App.Div. 754, 103 N.Y.S.2d 1019 (1st Dep't 1951); W. Q. O'Neall Co. v. O'Neall, 108 Ind. App. 116, 25 N.E.2d 656 (1940); see also Gordon v. Elliman, 306 N.Y. 456, 119 N.E.2d 331 (1954). Contra, Schuckman v. Rubenstein, 164 F.2d 952 (6th Cir. 1947), cert. denied, 333 U.S. 875, 68 S.Ct. 905, 92 L.Ed. 1151 (1948); Uccello v. Gold'n Foods, Inc., 325 Mass. 319, 90 N.E.2d 530, 16 A.L.R.2d 459 (1950). The correctness of the majority view appears more obvious if the action is thought of as one to compel the distribution of a dividend by the corporation rather than to compel the declaration of a dividend by the board of directors.

cause the discontinuance of an action to compel the distribution of a dividend.

On the plaintiff-shareholder side of the action, intervention by other shareholders, who are qualified under any applicable "contemporaneous-share-ownership" and other requirements,[6] is permitted under various circumstances.[7]

Pre-trial examination is another problem arising from the corporation's unique position as a nominal party defendant and real party plaintiff.

The corporation has been denied the right to examine the plaintiff-shareholder before trial, because it would allow the corporation to take a position antagonistic to the claim asserted in its behalf.[8] However, the plaintiff-shareholder was allowed to examine the corporation before trial where the latter became an active rather than a nominal party

by interposing an answer which placed in issue certain allegations of the complaint.[9]

Ordinarily, one defendant may not examine a co-defendant before trial unless the former seeks affirmative relief from the latter. However, where the corporation as nominal party defendant filed an answer which denied the essential allegations of the complaint, the alleged wrongdoers were allowed to examine the corporation, by its president, before trial with respect to affirmative defenses, on the ground that the essential character of the corporate cause of action remained the same, because any recovery would run in the corporation's favor.[10]

COUNSEL

370. **Common counsel may not properly represent both the corporation, whose claim is being asserted, and the alleged wrongdoers, in view of the conflicting and inconsistent interests involved. Where two or more shareholder derivative actions are consolidated, the court usually designates the counsel for one of the plaintiff-shareholders as general counsel for the plaintiffs.**

A nice question is whether in a derivative action brought against directors, officers, or shareholders, the corporation's attorney may properly represent both the alleged wrongdoers and the corporation. The courts in the past, usually failing to recognize the potential conflict of interests, have sometimes permitted common counsel.[1] Barring com-

---

6. See sections 361, 362 supra.

7. Duncan v. National Tea Co., 14 Ill.App.2d 280, 144 N.E.2d 771, 69 A.L.R.2d 546 (1957). Such intervention might forestall the imposition of a requirement that security for expenses be posted. See section 372 infra. It might also nullify personal defenses existing only against the original plaintiff. See section 363 supra. See Annot., 69 A.L.R.2d 562 (1960). Analogous is the consolidation of two or more pending shareholder derivative actions based on the same alleged wrong. Analogous to derivative actions is the problem of shareholder intervention in litigation brought directly by or against the corporation. Shlensky v. South Parkway Bldg. Corp., 44 Ill.App.2d 135, 194 N.E.2d 35 (1963) (allowing majority shareholder to intervene in derivative action even after entry of judgment upon showing subsequent proceedings threatened his interests and would deprive corporation of its recovery); System Meat Co. v. Stewart, 175 Neb. 387, 122 N.W.2d 1 (1963) (allowing intervention by shareholders in action by corporation and providing them with opportunity to be heard concerning proposed settlement); Note, "Shareholder Intervention in Corporate Litigation", 63 Harv.L.Rev. 1426 (1950). See also Lazar v. Merchants' Nat'l Properties, Inc., 22 A.D.2d 253, 254 N.Y.S.2d 712 (1st Dep't 1964) (corporation substituted for minority shareholder as plaintiff). But see Palmer v. Morris, 341 F.2d 577 (5th Cir. 1965) (elimination of original plaintiff-shareholder held not justified).

8. Carthage Paper Makers, Inc. v. Mutual Box Board Co., 159 N.Y.S.2d 659 (Sup.Ct.1956), aff'd mem., 3 A.D.2d 640, 158 N.Y.S.2d 790 (4th Dep't 1956).

9. Yaeger v. Moncrieff, 5 Misc.2d 970, 161 N.Y.S.2d 723 (Sup.Ct.1956), aff'd mem., 3 A.D.2d 650, 158 N.Y.S.2d 757 (1st Dep't 1956). For discussion of defenses interposable by corporation, see section 371 infra.

10. Chaplin v. Selznick, 186 Misc. 66, 58 N.Y.S.2d 453 (Sup.Ct.1945).

1. See Selama-Dindings Plantations, Ltd. v. Durham, 216 F.Supp. 104 (E.D.Pa.1963) (upholding joint representation absent express showing of conflict of interest or breach of trust); Otis & Co. v. Pennsylvania R. R., 57 F.Supp. 680 (E.D.Pa.1944). Occasionally, the issue has been raised in connection with the allowance of counsel fees. Compare Heller v. Boylan, 29 N.Y.S.2d 653 (Sup.Ct.1941), aff'd mem., 263 App.Div. 815, 32 N.Y.S.2d 131 (1st

mon counsel in such cases is the more cautious and usually sounder view.[2]   The problem is complicated by the complexity of what defenses are interposable by the corporation and by the real parties defendant.[3]

Where two or more shareholder derivative actions are consolidated, the court usually designates the counsel for one of the plaintiff-shareholders as general counsel for the plaintiffs.[4]   Because of his preeminent rôle, the general counsel, if successful, usually receives liberal allowances as attorney's fees.[5]

Dep't 1941), motion for leave to appeal or reargument denied 263 App.Div. 852, 32 N.Y.S.2d 1011 (1st Dep't 1942), with Kelley v. 74 & 76 West Tremont Ave. Corp., 24 Misc.2d 370, 198 N.Y.S.2d 721 (Sup. Ct.1960).   See sections 379, 380 infra.   See Tockman, "The Position of Corporate Counsel in Derivative Actions", 51 Ill.B.J. 654 (1963); Note, "Independent Representation for Corporate Defendants in Derivative Suits", 74 Yale L.J. 524 (1964).

2.   Marco v. Dulles, 169 F.Supp. 622 (S.D.N.Y.1959), appeal dismissed 268 F.2d 192 (2d Cir. 1959); Lewis v. Shaffer Stores Co., 218 F.Supp. 238 (S.D.N.Y. 1963) (holding corporation's counsel may not also represent alleged wrongdoing directors, officers, and controlling shareholders, no "insuperable difficulty" was found in fact that independent counsel would be selected by and accountable to corporation which was under the control of the alleged wrongdoing defendants); Langer v. Garay, 30 A.D.2d 942, 293 N. Y.S.2d 783 (1st Dep't 1968); Garlen v. Green Mansions, Inc., 9 A.D.2d 760, 193 N.Y.S.2d 116 (1st Dep't 1959), reargument denied, 10 A.D.2d 557, 196 N.Y.S. 2d 593 (1st Dep't 1959).   Committee on Professional Ethics of the Association of the Bar of the City of New York, Opinion No. 842, 15 Record of N.Y.C.B. A. 80 (1960).   In Kaplan v. Okun, 15 A.D.2d 848, 224 N.Y.S.2d 542 (3d Dep't 1962), minority shareholders sued to enjoin salary payments to corporation president and for other relief.   Counsel for the corporation was retained by consent of three of the four officers and directors.   The plaintiff and his brother held 30 percent of the shares and the brother was one of the four directors.   The articles of incorporation required an 85 percent vote for shareholder action and unanimous vote for board of directors action.   The court refused to strike out the appearance of counsel in view of the peculiar situation involved, pointing out that the retaining officers, as well as the retained attorneys, remained bound to serve only the best interests of the corporation.   Korman v. Matthias, 32 Ill.App.2d 341, 177 N.E.2d 720 (1961), upheld the appointment by the alleged wrongdoing directors of an attorney to represent the corporation in a shareholder derivative action against them, absent allegations that the attorney had been involved in the alleged transaction or had represented the individual directors and officers of the corporation.   Glenmark, Inc. v. Carity, 38 Misc.2d 980, 239 N.Y.S.2d 440 (Sup.Ct.1963), involved a corporate action, instituted by the president of the corporation, against the other two directors for alleged wrongs to the corporation.   The motion by the two defendant directors to substitute counsel selected by them for counsel selected by the president to represent the corporation in the action was denied.   See also Sorin v. Shahmoon Industries, Inc., 20 Misc.2d 149, 191 N.Y.S.2d 14 (Sup.Ct. 1959) (corporation held entitled to recover corporate papers delivered by defendant president-director to his attorney from such attorney who was asserting attorney's retaining lien); Willheim v. Murchison, 206 F.Supp. 733 (S.D.N.Y.1962), appeal dismissed, 312 F.2d 399 (2d Cir. 1963) (holding that under Federal Judicial Code, 28 U.S.C.A. § 1654, providing

that parties may plead and conduct "their own cases" in federal courts, shareholder, not lawyer, may bring derivative action and act pro se in proceedings on ground that derivative action is action of shareholder even though brought for benefit of corporation).   Accord, Brooks v. Saxony Tobacco & Sales Corp., 20 Misc.2d 401, 188 N.Y.S.2d 384 (Sup. Ct.1959) (derivative action commenced by non-attorney shareholder-plaintiff allowed, notwithstanding McKinney's N.Y. CPLR, § 321(a) requirement that corporation must appear by duly-licensed attorney at law).   See also Seifert v. Dumatic Industries, Inc., 413 Pa. 395, 197 A.2d 454 (1964) (former counsel for corporation allowed to represent plaintiff-shareholder in derivative action).

Jacuzzi v. Jacuzzi Bros., Inc., 218 Cal.App.2d 24, 32 Cal.Rptr. 188 (1963), held that it was not unethical for the former attorney of a California corporation to represent minority shareholders in a shareholder derivative action where there was no showing that the attorney would be called upon to breach a professional confidence previously entrusted to him by his former client, since the attorney here was acting for the benefit of the corporation he previously represented and therefore was not representing an adverse interest.   A former director was also allowed to represent the minority shareholders as counsel in their derivative action.

As to eligibility of corporate counsel, called as a witness, to continue to represent the corporation, see Phillips v. Liberty Mutual Ins. Co., 43 Del.Ch. 388, 232 A.2d 101 (Sup.Ct.1967).

3.   See section 371 supra.   See also Bank v. Masmo, Inc., 157 N.Y.L.J. No. 18, 22 (Sup.Ct.1967) (allowing the corporation's counsel to demand posting of security for expenses).

4.   Rich v. Reisini, 25 A.D.2d 32, 266 N.Y.S.2d 492 (1st Dep't 1966), involved four consolidated shareholder derivative actions.   On the "delicate question" of the designation of the general counsel to conduct the litigation in behalf of all the shareholders, the court stated that counsel for the shareholder who brought the first derivative action should be entitled to no special consideration, and that the guiding principle was to find among those eligible the one who would best serve the interests of the plaintiffs.   See also Witmondt v. Shima, 151 N.Y.L. J. No. 90, 14 (Sup.Ct.1964).

5.   See section 377 infra.

DEFENSES

371. The extent to which the corporation may interpose an answer to the plaintiff-shareholder's action asserting a corporate claim should depend upon the nature of the particular defense and the party whom such defense is designed to protect. Defenses have been classified into three types: (a) Conventional defenses to defeat the corporate claim on the merits—ordinarily not available to the corporation; to defeat a remedy against the corporation, e. g., receivership—available to the corporation; (b) Conventional defenses against the plaintiff-shareholder alleging his disqualification—presumably not available to the corporation; and (c) Defenses unique to derivative actions—ordinarily available to the corporation.

Another problem arising from the corporation's dual position is the right of the corporation to interpose an answer to the plaintiff-shareholder's assertion of a corporate claim.

Many courts fail to draw any distinction as to which party defendant may properly raise a given defense. The suggestion has been made that the proper party to invoke a particular defense should be the party whom the defense is designed to protect, and that a threefold classification of defenses aids such analysis.[1]

The first type of defense, a conventional defense which would defeat the corporate right of recovery, should be asserted only by the wrongdoers. The courts have generally followed this principle by precluding the corporation from defending on the merits where the issue was whether or not a wrong had been committed against it.[2] But they have allowed the corporation to defend where it was a real defendant as to some issue in the case, such as the appointment of a

receiver.[3] However, the corporation's use of conventional defenses is limited to those aspects of the case in which it is a real defendant.

A second category of defenses is the conventional defense against the plaintiff-shareholder such as laches, ratification, or similar conduct.[4] It can be argued that such defenses have no place in a three-party proceeding wherein the plaintiff-shareholder sues in the right of the corporation, but several court holdings permit the alleged wrongdoers to raise the plaintiff-shareholder's disability as a bar to the action.[5] While there does not appear to be any direct authority on the point, the probable rule is that the corporation is precluded from relying on such defenses against the plaintiff-shareholder.

A third class of defenses are those which are sui generis to derivative actions. Some of these have arisen from efforts to protect the interest of the corporation, such as the requirement that a demand be made on the board of directors.[6] Others such as the necessity for contemporaneous-share-ownership,[7] were created to curtail "strike suits" and to prevent collusive diversity jurisdiction. The corporation can raise such defenses as a general rule. Where the alleged wrongdoers are outsiders, there is a strong argument that they should not be permitted to rely upon a defense of this na-

3.   Godley v. Crandall & Godley Co., 181 App.Div. 75, 168 N.Y.S. 251 (1st Dep't 1917), aff'd mem., 227 N.Y. 656, 126 N.E. 908 (1920). But see Providential Investment Corp. v. Dibrell, 320 S.W.2d 415 (Tex.Civ. App.1959) (holding corporation could not post bond to set aside appointment of receiver pendente lite for it). See also Otis & Co. v. Pennsylvania R. R., 57 F.Supp. 680 (E.D.Pa.1944); Brown v. De Young, 167 Ill. 549, 47 N.E. 863 (1897).

4.   See section 363 supra.

5.   E. g., Johnson v. King-Richardson Co., 36 F.2d 675, 67 A.L.R. 1465 (1st Cir. 1930). Contra, Atkinson v. McCabe Hanger Mfg. Co., 55 N.Y.S.2d 274 (Sup.Ct.1945).

6.   See section 365 supra.

7.   See section 362 supra.

1.   Note, "Defenses in Shareholders' Derivative Suits —Who May Raise Them", 66 Harv.L.Rev. 342 (1952).

2.   E. g., Kartub v. Optical Fashions, Inc., 158 F. Supp. 757 (S.D.N.Y.1958); Slutsker v. Rieber, 132 N.J.Eq. 412, 28 A.2d 528 (1942).

ture unless it was designed to afford them certain protection. Unfortunately, there is no clear-cut answer on this point.[8]

The general rule differentiates between the interests of the corporation and the individual interests of the alleged wrongdoers, and allows the corporation to answer only when its own interests are affected by the suit. This rule is applied when a long standing financial policy of the corporation is put in issue, or where the plaintiff-shareholder seeks to have the corporation placed in the hands of a receiver. However, in such a case the corporation's answer is limited to those allegations involving its own interests.[9]

F. SECURITY FOR EXPENSES IN DERIVATIVE ACTION

SECURITY FOR EXPENSES IN DERIVATIVE ACTION

372. Statutory provisions permitting corporations in derivative actions to secure from the plaintiff-shareholders security for the corporate expenses in such litigation have been enacted in some jurisdictions. The typical security-for-expenses statute provides that in a shareholder action in the right of a corporation, the court might require the plaintiff shareholder or shareholders with less than prescribed holdings, upon application by the corporation, to give security for the corporation's litigation expenses, including attorneys' fees, not only the corporation's own expenses but also those indemnifiable by it. Such statutes, which both require the posting of a bond and create a new liability, despite their application only to small shareholders, have been upheld as constitutional. Intervention by sufficient other shareholders usually can avoid such security-for-expenses requirement, but such interveners can be limited to contemporaneous share owners where a contemporaneous-share-ownership requirement prevails. In the federal courts, any security-for-expenses statute of the state of the forum applies since such statutes have been held to be substantive.

Statutory provisions permitting corporations in derivative actions to secure from small plaintiff-shareholders security for the corporate expenses in such litigation have been adopted in several jurisdictions, beginning with New York in 1944,[1] as a device for eliminating some of the abuses of derivative actions. A comparatively recent development in the law, this statutory bond-posting requirement *and creation of new liability* have given rise to numerous problems.

8. See Note, "Defenses in Shareholders' Derivative Suits—Who May Raise Them", 66 Harv.L.Rev. 342, 346–347 (1952).

9. Otis & Co. v. Pennsylvania R. R., 57 F.Supp. 680 (E.D.Pa.1944); Brown v. De Young, 167 Ill. 549, 47 N.E. 863 (1897). See Rugee v. Hadley Products, Inc., 73 Ariz. 362, 241 P.2d 798, 33 A.L.R.2d 468 (1952) (denying intervention by minority shareholder in action against his corporation to interpose defense in behalf of corporation).

1. McKinney's N.Y.Bus.Corp.Law, § 627; ABA-ALI Model Bus.Corp.Act § 43A (optional section); California, Colorado, Florida, Maryland, New Jersey, New York, North Dakota, Pennsylvania, Wisconsin. All of the provisions include reasonable attorneys' fees within such expenses except Colorado and Maryland which expressly exclude attorneys' fees. Bowes, "Should New York's 'Security for Expenses' Act Be Amended?", 2 Syracuse L.Rev. 37 (1950); Milano, "Security for Expenses in Shareholders' Derivative Suits—Suggested Amendment to New York General Corporation Law", 5 N.Y.U.Intra.L. Rev. 196 (1950); Bolen, "Section 61–B of the General Corporation Law of New York: Its Constitutionality and Applicability in the Federal Courts", 23 St.John's L.Rev. 296 (1949); Ballantine, "Abuses of Shareholders' Derivative Suits: How Far is California's New 'Security for Expenses' Act Sound Regulation?", 37 Calif.L.Rev. 399 (1949); Zlinoff, "The American Investor and the Constitutionality of Section 61–B of the New York General Corporation Law", 54 Yale L.J. 352 (1945); Hornstein, "The Death Knell of Stockholders' Derivative Suits in New York", 32 Calif.L.Rev. 123 (1944); Note, "Security for Expenses in Shareholders' Derivative Suits: 23 Years Experience", 4 Colum.L.J. & Soc. Prob. 50 (Mar.1968); Note, "Security for Expenses Legislation—Summary, Analysis, and Critique", 52 Colum.L.Rev. 267 (1952); Note, "New York General Corporation Law Requiring Security for Expenses in Shareholders' Derivative Suits—Suggested Repeal of Section 61b", 24 N.Y.U.L.Q.Rev. 395 (1949); Note, " 'Security for Expenses' Requirement in Stockholders' Derivative Actions", 42 Ill.L.Rev. 667 (1947). See also McKinney's N.Y.Part.Law § 115–b.

The typical security-for-expenses statute provides that in a shareholder action in the right of a corporation [2] the court can require the plaintiff-shareholder or shareholders with less than certain prescribed holdings,[3]

2. Such statutes expressly apply to actions brought in the right of domestic or foreign corporations, except the Maryland statute which refers to an action in the right of "any corporation". Hence, they are inapplicable in nonderivative actions. New York limits its security-for-expenses provision to shareholders' derivative actions brought in the right of the corporation to procure a judgment in its favor. McKinney's N.Y.Bus.Corp.Law, § 627. See section 360 supra. Levine v. Bradlee, 378 F.2d 620 (3d Cir. 1967), held, 2 to 1, that the Pennsylvania security-for-expenses statute did not apply to a shareholder's claim for attorneys fees against the corporation arising from a derivative action, since such claim was a direct and separate action against the corporation based on quantum meruit. In Reifsnyder v. Pittsburgh Outdoor Advertising Co., 405 Pa. 142, 173 A.2d 319 (1961), the minority shareholder in a prior unsuccessful action had been required to give security for expenses on the theory that such action was derivative. The corporation was awarded some $70,000 for its expenses. On appeal, the Pennsylvania Supreme Court held that the prior action was nonderivative and hence not subject to the security-for-expenses statute, and therefore the corporation was not entitled to reimbursement of its expenses. In Gilbert v. Case, 3 A.D.2d 930, 163 N. Y.S.2d 179 (2d Dep't 1957), reargument and leave to appeal denied 4 A.D.2d 688, 164 N.Y.S.2d 995 (2d Dep't 1957), stay dismissed 3 N.Y.2d 876, 166 N.Y.S. 2d 498, 145 N.E.2d 176 (1957), a foreign corporation, named as defendant, entered a special appearance to attack the jurisdiction of the court over it on the ground that it was not doing business in the state, and moved for an order requiring the plaintiff to give security in the amount of $25,000 and for a stay until the security was given. It was held that since the corporation had not subjected itself to the jurisdiction of the court and was contending that no action was pending, it was not entitled to demand security under the New York statute.

3. E. g., where plaintiffs own less than five percent of outstanding shares or voting trust certificates unless the shares or voting trust certificates so held have a market value in excess of $25,000—ABA–ALI Model Bus.Corp.Act § 43A (optional section), Colorado, Maryland, New Jersey, North Dakota; less than five percent of any class of outstanding shares or voting trust certificates or beneficial interest in shares representing less than five percent of any class of such shares, unless market value of shares, voting trust certificates and beneficial interest is in excess of $50,000—New York; less than five percent of outstanding shares of any class or of voting trust certificates unless market value is in excess of $50,000—Pennsylvania; less than three percent of outstanding shares of any class, with no alternative dollar amount exception—Wisconsin. See Murdock v. Follansbee Steel Corp., 213

upon application by the corporation,[4] to give security for the corporation's litigation ex-

F.2d 570 (3d Cir. 1954) (holding that a beneficial owner of more than five percent of the corporation's shares registered for convenience in his broker's name was a "holder" of such shares within the meaning of the Pennsylvania security-for-expenses statute). Only the Model Act and the Colorado and North Dakota provisions provide that market value shall be determined as of the date that the plaintiff institutes the action or, in the case of an intervener, as of the date that he becomes a party to the action. The same rule should apply absent such provision. In Sorin v. Shahmoon Industries, Inc., 30 Misc.2d 429, 220 N.Y.S.2d 760, 783 (Sup.Ct.1961), the court construed the New York security-for-expenses statute as requiring that the unit market value of the share ownership of the plaintiff be ascertained as of the time of the institution of the action, that the unit market value of the share ownership of any intervener be ascertained as of the time of his application to intervene, and that the number of shares owned by the plaintiffs—whether original suitor or intervener—be counted as of the time of application for security. The quantum requirements are the same regardless of the number of derivative causes of action joined in the complaint. Perry v. Shahmoon Industries, Inc., 11 Misc.2d 137, 172 N.Y.S.2d 245 (Sup.Ct.1958), aff'd mem., 6 A.D.2d 1010, 178 N.Y.S. 2d 612 (1st Dep't 1958), appeal denied 7 A.D.2d 634, 179 N.Y.S.2d 846 (1st Dep't 1958). In determining whether or not the plaintiff-shareholder owns five percent of the outstanding shares, the shares held by the alleged wrongdoing defendant are to be included as outstanding shares. Trooper v. Bysshe, 4 N.Y.2d 397, 175 N.Y.S.2d 811, 151 N.E.2d 610 (1958) (where alleged wrongdoing corporate defendant owned 98 percent of outstanding shares and remaining shares had a value well below $50,000. See also Amdur v. Meyer, 22 A.D.2d 655, 253 N.Y.S.2d 65 (1st Dep't 1964) (ordering hearing to determine whether plaintiffs' share holdings in defendant corporation were disposed of to point where their value fell below $50,000 and, if so, how and when). Marks v. Seedman, —— F.Supp. —— (S.D.N.Y.1969) (redemption of plaintiff-shareholder's preferred shares, reducing his holdings below five percent, held to end security-free status, where complaint sought to compel redemption of such preferred shares), with Roach v. Franchises International, Inc., 32 A.D.2d 247, 300 N.Y.S.2d 630 (2d Dep't 1969) (holding that shareholders who had more than five percent of corporate shares prior to issuance of new shares for which they did not exercise their option to purchase and who brought action attacking purpose of issuance of new shares were not required to post security).

4. And not by others. Adler v. Adler, 138 N.Y.L.J. No. 85, 6 (Sup.Ct.1957). Application may be made at any time before final judgment except in California. See note 6 infra. All of the statutes expressly empower the court in its discretion to increase or decrease the amount of security required. Amdur v. Meyer, 36 Misc.2d 433, 233 N.Y.S.2d 15 (Sup.Ct.1962), aff'd 17 A.D.2d 571, 237 N.Y.S.2d 352

penses, not only its own but also those indemnifiable by it.[5]

California had adopted a different approach by permitting application for security not only by the corporation but also by a defendant director or officer and gives the

court power to set the amount of security required for expenses upon a showing by the defendants that (a) there is no reasonable possibility that the action will benefit the corporation or its security holders or (b) the defendants did not participate in any capacity in the transaction complained of. Such security for expenses can be sought regardless of the size of the plaintiff's holding of shares or voting trust certificates.[6]

The purpose behind security-for-expenses statutes is to curtail "strike suits" and thereby protect the corporation. Because of the quantum requirements, such statutes affect only the small plaintiff-shareholder, who may have to post security for all the expenses of the corporation, including amounts which the corporation might be required to pay to other defendants in reimbursement of their expenses in defending the action.[7]

While the small shareholder is not prevented from bringing a derivative action, the practical effect of such statutes is to bar him unless he posts the required bond which saddles him with the expenses of both sides of the litigation unless he is successful—an awesome and rather unique situation. On the other hand, there is no such restriction on the large shareholder who can meet the quantum requirements.[8] The theory behind

---

(1st Dep't 1963), aff'd per curiam 13 N.Y.2d 1089, 246 N.Y.S.2d 408, 196 N.E.2d 63 (1963), was a shareholder derivative action where security for expenses was fixed at $35,000, but later vacated when intervention by other plaintiffs resulted in combined shareholdings having a market value in excess of $50,000. After final judgment had been entered in favor of the defendants, the plaintiffs appealed to the court of appeals and the defendant corporation sought security for the expenses of such appeal. Meanwhile, the plaintiffs had disposed of some of their shares with the result that their holdings at the time of appeal had a market value well below $50,000. At no time had the plaintiffs' shares equated five percent of the total outstanding common shares of the defendant corporation. The court agreed that the right to security should not depend upon the vagaries of market value but that here the reduction in market value resulted from the plaintiffs' disposition of some of their shares. The right and power of the court to review the amount of security at any stage before final judgment was upheld.

5. Expenses expressly include attorneys' fees except in Colorado and Maryland, which exclude them. All of the statutes provide that security shall comprehend expenses of other defendants for which the corporation may become liable. See sections 379, 380 infra. In Auerbach v. Shafstor, Inc., 34 Misc. 2d 658, 229 N.Y.S.2d 927 (Sup.Ct.1962), aff'd 19 A. D.2d 531, 240 N.Y.S.2d 146 (2d Dep't 1963), appeal dismissed 13 N.Y.2d 891, 243 N.Y.S.2d 673, 193 N.E. 2d 501 (1963), where security-for-expenses in the amount of $75,000 was sought, the plaintiff resisted on the ground that the corporation was only a nominal party defendant and that its officers and directors, being also officers and directors of the alleged wrongdoing corporation, along with their attorneys, would incur expenses not in behalf of the corporation as a nominal party defendant but in an effort to absolve themselves as the real defendants from liability. The corporation claimed that proper, adequate participation in the case would involve the expenditure of funds for accounting services and doing a very substantial amount of accounting work. The court allowed security for expenses in the amount of $35,000. Sorin v. Shahmoon Industries, Inc., 34 Misc.2d 1008, 231 N.Y.S.2d 6 (Sup.Ct.1962), held that where the actual defendants would probably prevail as to some matters and lose as to some others, the corporation's security for expenses should cover expenses and attorney's fees of the actual defendants as to the former, since the corporation would probably be liable for them, and that security for expenses should cover not only future expenses but all expenses incurred in defense of the action prior to the application for posting of security.

6. Cal.Gen.Corp.Law, § 834(b) (1947). Ballantine, "Abuses of Shareholders' Derivative Suits: How Far is California's New 'Security for Expenses' Act Sound Regulation?", 37 Calif.L.Rev. 399 (1949). California requires application within 30 days after the commencement of the action with possible extension up to 60 days for good cause shown. See Oser v. Wilcox, 338 F.2d 886 (9th Cir. 1964); Koster v. Warren, 297 F.2d 418 (9th Cir. 1961); Suburban Water Systems v. Superior Court, 264 Cal.App. 2d 1094, 71 Cal.Rptr. 45 (1968); Woodman v. Ackerman, 249 Cal.App.2d 644, 57 Cal.Rptr. 687 (1967); Marble v. Latchford Glass Co., 205 Cal.App.2d 171, 22 Cal.Rptr. 789 (1962); Bailey v. Fosca Oil Co., 180 Cal.App.2d 289, 4 Cal.Rptr. 474 (1960); Olson v. Basin Oil Co., 136 Cal.App.2d 543, 288 P.2d 952 (1955); Wood v. Gordon, 112 Cal.App.2d 374, 246 P. 2d 84 (1952).

7. See sections 379, 380 infra.

8. See Isensee v. Long Island Motion Picture Co., 184 Misc. 625, 54 N.Y.S.2d 556 (Sup.Ct.1945) (holder of more than five percent of outstanding shares

this seemingly arbitrary classification is that a large shareholder is less inclined to make use of the derivative remedy for personal gain.

The constitutionality of this approach has been upheld by the United States Supreme Court, 6–3, as being within the reserved police powers of the states, even when construed to apply to future expenses in pending actions,[9] involving no impairment of obligation of contract, and not violating due process of law or the equal protection of the laws because of its singular treatment of small shareholders.[10]

who did not and could not be required to post security for expenses under New York statute held not liable for such expenses to successful corporation). See also Tyler v. Gas Consumers Ass'n, 35 Misc.2d 801, 231 N.Y.S.2d 15 (Sup.Ct.1962). A few statutes provide that a court, after final judgment in a shareholder derivative action and a finding that the action was brought without reasonable cause, may require the plaintiff or plaintiffs to pay to the defendants the reasonable expenses, including attorneys' fees, incurred by them in the defense of such action. ABA–ALI Model Bus.Corp.Act § 43A (optional section); North Dakota; Colorado (not including attorneys' fees).

9. Under New Jersey security-for-expenses statute which was expressly made applicable to all pending actions in which no final judgment had been rendered as well as to all future actions. N.J.Bus. Corp.Act § 14A:3–6 (1969). In Shielcrawt v. Moffett, 184 Misc. 1074, 56 N.Y.S.2d 134 (Sup.Ct.1945), the court rejected the argument that the expressly-retroactive New Jersey statute was substantive and therefore could be invoked by a defendant New Jersey corporation sued in the New York courts. Accord, Berkwitz v. Humphrey, 130 F.Supp. 142 (N.D. Ohio 1955) (refusing to apply in Ohio security-for-expenses statute of Pennsylvania, jurisdiction of incorporation of corporation). Shielcrawt v. Moffett, 294 N.Y. 180, 61 N.E.2d 435 (1945), the New York security-for-expenses statute was construed as not merely affecting the form of remedy but as interfering with antecedent rights of small shareholders and creating a new remedy and as not intended by the legislature to apply to actions pending when the statute went into effect.

10. Cohen v. Beneficial Industrial Loan Corp., 337 U.S. 541, 69 S.Ct. 1221, 93 L.Ed. 1528 (1949). Accord, Gaudiosi v. Mellon, 269 F.2d 873 (10th Cir. 1959), cert. denied 361 U.S. 902, 80 S.Ct. 211, 4 L. Ed.2d 157 (1959) (Pennsylvania statute); Beyerbach v. Juno Oil Co., 42 Cal.2d 11, 265 P.2d 1 (1954); Hogan v. Ingold, 38 Cal.2d 802, 243 P.2d 1, 32 A.L. R.2d 834 (1952) (California statute); Lapchak v. Baker, 298 N.Y. 89, 80 N.E.2d 751 (1948).

It should be emphasized that the security-for-expenses statute creates a liability. When a bond is posted and the derivative action is unsuccessful for any reason, including a failure on technical grounds that does not go to the merits, the corporation has recourse to the security for indemnification of its own litigation expenses and those expenses for which it might be ordered to reimburse its directors, officers, and employees by a court.[11] Contrariwise, there is no such right to indemnification from the plaintiff-shareholder in most jurisdictions when a bond is not required or posted.[12]

In most jurisdictions, the amount of the undertaking is fixed by the court, and may be increased or decreased from time to time upon a showing that it has or may become inadequate or excessive.[13] Security for expenses might well be hundreds of times greater than security for the customary court costs, e. g., $150,000[14] vs. $250.[15]

Some cases have ameliorated the harsh operation of the security-for-expenses requirement by the device of a conditional order permitting the plaintiff-shareholder to have other shareholders join him in the action and thereby bring in the necessary shares required to avoid the necessity for giving security.[16] In this regard the plain-

11. See sections 379, 380 infra.

12. See note 8 supra. See also Tyler v. Gas Consumers Ass'n, 35 Misc.2d 801, 231 N.Y.S.2d 15 (Sup. Ct.1962).

13. See note 4 supra.

14. See, e. g., Truncale v. Universal Pictures Co., 76 F.Supp. 465 (S.D.N.Y.1948) ($150,000); Cohen v. Beneficial Industrial Loan Corp., 337 U.S. 541, 69 S.Ct. 1221, 93 L.Ed. 1528 (1949) ($125,000); Koster v. Warren, 176 F.Supp. 459 (N.D.Calif.1959) ($100,- 000) (of course, the amounts would be substantially lower in jurisdictions [see note 1 supra] which do not include attorneys' fees).

15. See, e. g., Craftsman Finance & Mortgage Co. v. Brown, 64 F.Supp. 168 (S.D.N.Y.1945).

16. E. g., Baker v. Macfadden Publications, Inc., 300 N.Y. 325, 90 N.E.2d 876 (1950). Quaere, whether the plaintiff-shareholder can avoid posting security for expenses by acquiring additional shares. Compare Weinstein v. Behn, 68 N.Y.S.2d 199 (Sup.Ct.

tiff-shareholder may obtain a stay of the action and thereafter inspect the corporation's record of shareholders so that he may invite other shareholders to join as plaintiffs.[17] The shares owned by all the plaintiff-shareholders determine whether or not security is required. If an order for security was originally granted, it may be vacated when the additional shareholders join in the action.[18]

There is conflicting authority as to whether those shareholders who desire to intervene as plaintiffs in order to avoid a security-for-expenses requirement need to qualify under any prevailing contemporaneous-share-ownership requirement [19] so long as the original plaintiff is a contemporaneous-share-owner. The better view would seem to be that if the original plaintiff must be a contemporaneous-share-owner in order to bring a derivative action, persons desiring to intervene as plaintiffs should be subject to the same contemporaneous-share-ownership requirement.[20] However, a few cases have

not applied the contemporaneous-share-ownership requirement to interveners, on the ground that there is a substantial distinction between the contemporaneous-share-ownership and security-for-expenses requirements.[21] The problem is further complicated in the federal courts by Erie R. R. v. Tompkins.[22]

Under security-for-expenses statutes, the plaintiff-shareholder may avoid posting security only when he and his co-plaintiffs own the required amount of shares in the corporation whose cause of action is being asserted. Thus, when a derivative action involves two corporations and the plaintiff-shareholder meets the quantum requirements for but one, he is not absolved from posting security in respect to the other.[23] If a shareholder joins in a single action direct and derivative claims,[24] he may be required to post security only for the latter.[25]

There is no general provision requiring security for expenses in the federal courts when jurisdiction is based upon a federal

---

1947), aff'd mem., 272 App.Div. 1045, 75 N.Y.S.2d 284 (1st Dep't 1947), with Richman v. Felmus, 8 A.D.2d 985, 190 N.Y.S.2d 920 (2d Dep't 1959) and Purdy v. Humphrey, 187 Misc. 40, 60 N.Y.S.2d 535 (Sup.Ct.1946). In Tyler v. Gas Consumers Ass'n, 34 Misc.2d 947, 229 N.Y.S.2d 169 (Sup.Ct.1962), a shareholder derivative action, the plaintiff-shareholder was ordered either to post $40,000 security for expenses or to bring in additional shareholders in order to meet the five percent or more-than-$50,000 criteria of the statute. The plaintiff thereupon purchased additional shares to bring his holdings to more than five percent. The corporate defendant's motion to dismiss the complaint was granted on the ground that the shareholder had failed to fulfill the terms of the order for security.

17. Baker v. Macfadden Publications, Inc., 300 N.Y. 325, 90 N.E.2d 876 (1950). However, the statutory right to inspect the record of shareholders is sometimes afforded only to shareholders of record for at least the preceding six months or holders of at least five percent of all of the outstanding shares. See section 199 supra.

18. Neuwirth v. Wyman, 119 N.Y.S.2d 266 (Sup.Ct. 1953), aff'd 282 App.Div. 1044, 126 N.Y.S.2d 895 (1st Dep't 1953), reargument and appeal denied 283 App.Div. 708, 128 N.Y.S.2d 544 (1st Dep't 1954).

19. See section 362 supra.

20. Richman v. Felmus, 8 A.D.2d 985, 190 N.Y.S.2d 920 (2d Dep't 1959); Breswick & Co. v. Harrison Rye Realty Corp., 280 App.Div. 820, 114 N.Y.S.2d 25

(2d Dep't 1952). In Sorin v. Shahmoon Industries, Inc., 30 Misc.2d 429, 220 N.Y.S.2d 760, 783 (Sup. Ct.1961), the court ruled that, under the New York contemporaneous-share-ownership statute, one suing in a derivative action was required to be a contemporaneous owner, but that, under the New York security-for-expenses statute, it was not necessary for him—alone or in association with others—to have owned the required shares in number or value to avoid posting security for expenses at the time of the alleged wrongs. A provision in the proposed New York Business Corporation Law expressly allowing the intervention of noncontemporaneous owners was eliminated.

21. Perry v. Shahmoon Industries, Inc., 11 Misc.2d 137, 172 N.Y.S.2d 245 (Sup.Ct.1958), aff'd mem. 6 A.D.2d 1010, 178 N.Y.S.2d 612 (1st Dep't 1958), appeal denied 7 A.D.2d 634, 179 N.Y.S.2d 846 (1st Dep't 1958); Noel Associates, Inc. v. Merrill, 184 Misc. 646, 53 N.Y.S.2d 143 (Sup.Ct.1944).

22. 304 U.S. 64, 58 S.Ct. 817, 82 L.Ed. 1188, 114 A.L. R. 1487 (1938). See notes 28, 32–34 infra.

23. Altman v. Autocar Co., 133 N.Y.S.2d 535 (Sup.Ct. 1954).

24. See section 368 supra.

25. Davidson v. Rabinowitz, 140 N.Y.S.2d 875 (Sup. Ct.1951). See also Drews v. Eastern Sausage & Provision Co., 125 F.Supp. 289 (S.D.N.Y.1954).

question.[26] In a diversity case the federal courts must apply the state security-for-expenses statute on the ground that such statute under Erie R. R. v. Tompkins [27] created a new liability and so conditioned the shareholder's action as to be substantive rather than procedural,[28] but this rule applies only when the state of the forum has such a statute. The statute of a jurisdiction which is not the jurisdiction of the forum is not applied, since the liability it creates is not an essential ingredient of the cause of action.[29]

Where a complaint joins a claim under state law with a claim for violation of a federal statute, the state security-for-expenses requirement has been held applicable only to the nonfederal claim, whether based on pendent jurisdiction or diversity-of-citizenship jurisdiction.[30]

In a diversity case, jurisdiction is not defeated by the fact that intervening shareholders have the same citizenship as the defendant.[31]

On the question of whether interveners in shareholder derivative actions in the federal courts based on diversity of citizenship have to be contemporaneous-share-owners, most federal courts have held the federal contemporaneous-share-ownership rule to be procedural [32] and to require interveners to be contemporaneous-share-owners, thus barring intervention by noncontemporaneous-share-owners to avoid state security-for-expenses statutes, even though the state law [33] might permit the intervention of noncontemporaneous-share-owners for such purpose.[34]

26. Occasional federal legislation provides for posting of bond for costs, including attorneys' fees, and for assessment whether or not such bond has been required. E. g., Federal Securities Act of 1933, § 11(e), 15 U.S.C.A. § 77k(e); Federal Securities Exchange Act of 1934, § 9(e), 15 U.S.C.A. § 78i(e).

27. 304 U.S. 64, 58 S.Ct. 817, 82 L.Ed. 1188, 114 A.L.R. 1487 (1938).

28. Cohen v. Beneficial Industrial Loan Corp., 337 U.S. 541, 69 S.Ct. 1221, 93 L.Ed. 1528 (1949) (6–3: the dissent regarding the matter as procedural and hence governed only by the Federal Rules of Civil Procedure, which define the procedure for federal courts). See Hanna v. Plumer, 380 U.S. 460, 85 S. Ct. 1136, 14 L.Ed.2d 8 (1965).

29. Berkwitz v. Humphrey, 130 F.Supp. 142 (N.D. Ohio 1955).

30. Epstein v. Solitron Devices, Inc., 388 F.2d 310 (2d Cir. 1968); Phelps v. Burnham, 327 F.2d 812 (2d Cir. 1964); Fielding v. Allen, 181 F.2d 163 (2d Cir. 1950), cert. denied 340 U.S. 817, 71 S.Ct. 46, 95 L. Ed. 600 (1950); Mintz v. Allen, 254 F.Supp. 1012 (S.D.N.Y.1966). Levine v. Bradlee, 248 F.Supp. 395 (E.D.Pa.1965), a shareholder derivative action join-

ing a federal cause of action and a state-law claim based on diversity-of-citizenship, required security for costs, under the local court rule, with respect to the former and security for expenses, under the Pennsylvania statute with respect to the latter. See J. I. Case v. Borak, 377 U.S. 426, 84 S.Ct. 1555, 12 L.Ed.2d 423 (1964).

31. Weinstock v. Kallet, 11 F.R.D. 270 (S.D.N.Y. 1951).

32. See section 362, n. 10 supra.

33. See notes 20, 21 supra.

34. Piccard v. Sperry Corp., 36 F.Supp. 1006 (S.D.N.Y.1941), aff'd on opinion below, 120 F.2d 328 (2d Cir. 1941); Elkins v. Bricker, 147 F.Supp. 609 (S. D.N.Y.1956); Kaufman v. Wolfson, 136 F.Supp. 939 (S.D.N.Y.1955); Winkelman v. General Motors Corp., 44 F.Supp. 960 (S.D.N.Y.1942). Contra, Fuller v. American Machine & Foundry Co., 95 F.Supp. 764 (S.D.N.Y.1951) (holding that where local law permitted intervention of noncontemporaneous-share-owners for purpose of avoiding security for expenses under state statute, federal court should also since such statute was substantive); Note, "Stockholders' Derivative Actions: State Security-for-Expenses Statutes: Application of Federal Rules of Civil Procedure Rule 23(b) to Intervening Stockholders", 45 Calif.L.Rev. 80 (1957).

G. RECOVERY, SETTLEMENT, AND OTHER RELIEF IN DERIVATIVE ACTION

RECOVERY IN DERIVATIVE ACTION

373. Any recovery usually is of the full corporate loss and in favor of the corporation, thus adhering to the theory of derivative actions and protecting the interests of both creditors and shareholders in the unimpaired financial condition of the corporation. Pro rata recovery by minority shareholders might be allowed (a) to prevent the funds from reverting to the control of insider wrongdoers; (b) to prevent an indirect benefit to "guilty" shareholders or a windfall to purchasers from the wrongdoers; or (c) to facilitate the distribution of funds where the corporation is no longer a going concern. Pro rata recovery by some minority shareholders should not bar a later similar claim by other minority shareholders. Where a common fund is created for minority shareholders, reimbursement of the plaintiff-shareholder's litigation expenses can be awarded out of such fund.

Since a derivative action asserts a corporate rather than an individual right, the vast majority of cases hold that any recovery should be of the full corporate loss and inure to the corporation. This protects the interests of both shareholders and creditors in the unimpaired financial condition of the corporation.[1]

However, in limited instances courts have allowed individual shareholders to recover in derivative actions. It should be emphasized that this type of recovery is entirely different from that awarded in an individual or direct action brought by a shareholder.[2]

When there is an individual recovery by a shareholder in a derivative action, he receives a pro rata share of what the corporation normally would have received. Thus, a shareholder who owned 10 percent of the outstanding shares would be awarded 10 percent of what would have gone to the corporate treasury, had an individual recovery not been allowed.[3]

A pro rata recovery by shareholders has been permitted in three situations:[4]

(a) Where the derivative action is against insiders who have misappropriated

---

1. Liken v. Shaffer, 64 F.Supp. 432, 441 (N.D.Iowa 1946) (for protection of creditors and avoidance of tax problems, including changes in tax reports previously made, additional tax liability and payment of unpaid tax claims); Keenan v. Eshleman, 23 Del.Ch. 234, 2 A.2d 904, 120 A.L.R. 227 (Sup.Ct. 1938); see also Old Dominion Copper Mining and Smelting Co. v. Bigelow, 203 Mass. 159, 89 N.E. 193 (1909), aff'd 225 U.S. 111, 32 S.Ct. 641, 56 L.Ed. 1009 (1912). Notwithstanding the equitable nature of shareholder derivative actions, some courts have awarded exemplary or punitive damages. Globus v. Law Research Service, Inc., 287 F.Supp. 188 (S.D.N.Y.1968); Hedworth v. Chapman, 135 Ind.App. 129, 192 N.E.2d 649 (1963). Such damages, when supported by the evidence, should be awarded against the persons who have wronged the corporation, regardless of whether the action is by a shareholder in the right of the corporation or by the corporation. See Holloway v. Int'l Bankers Life Ins. Co., 354 S.W.2d 198 (Tex.Civ.App.1962), rev'd on other grounds 368 S.W.2d (Tex.1963); Annot., 20 A.L.R.3d 666 (1968).

2. See section 360 supra; see note 7 infra.

3. Perlman v. Feldmann, 219 F.2d 173, 50 A.L.R.2d 1134 (2d Cir.1955), cert. denied 349 U.S. 952, 75 S.Ct. 880, 99 L.Ed. 1277 (1955); Id., 154 F.Supp. 436 (D.Conn.1957) (63 percent of premium for control wrongfully sold by controlling minority shareholder); Di Tomasso v. Loverro, 250 App.Div. 206, 293 N.Y.S. 912 (2d Dep't 1937), aff'd mem., 276 N.Y. 551, 12 N.E.2d 570 (1937), motion for reargument or to amend remittitur denied 276 N.Y. 610, 12 N.E.2d 601 (1937); Id., 276 N.Y. 681, 13 N.E.2d 59 (1938). See McKinney's N.Y.Bus.Corp.Law, § 626(e) (provision that if any shareholder derivative action is successful, in whole or in part, or if anything is received by plaintiff or claimant as result of judgment, compromise or settlement of action or claim, court may award plaintiff or claimant reasonable expenses, including reasonable attorney's fees, and direct him to account to corporation for remainder of proceeds so received by him inapplicable to any judgment rendered for benefit of injured shareholders only and limited to recovery of loss or damage sustained by them).

4. See Grenier, "Prorata Recovery by Shareholders on Corporate Causes of Action as a Means of Achieving Corporate Justice", 19 Wash. & Lee L. Rev. 165 (1962); Note, "Corporations—Entity Theory—Derivative Actions—Pro Rata Individual Recovery", 5 B.C.Ind. & Com.L.Rev. 773 (1964); Note, "Shareholders' Right to Direct Recovery in Derivative Suits", 17 Wyo.L.J. 208 (1963); Note, "Individual Pro Rata Recovery in Stockholders' Derivative Suits", 69 Harv.L.Rev. 1314 (1956).

corporate assets; here an individual pro rata recovery prevents the funds from reverting to the control of the wrongdoers; [5]

(b) Where there are both "innocent" and "guilty" shareholders; hence a pro rata recovery may be limited to the "innocent" ones; [6]

(c) Where the corporation is no longer a going concern; here individual awards facilitate distribution of funds.[7]

As a general rule, a pro rata recovery by shareholders is not allowed when the rights of creditors are involved. In addition, some courts have refused to allow a pro rata recovery on the ground it does violence to the nature of the derivative remedy, while others have restricted its use because it "forces a dividend", and thereby operates against the business judgment of those in control of the corporation.

Where a pro rata recovery by the plaintiff-shareholder is allowed, the probable rule is that other shareholders who later sue for a similar award of their proportionate share of the damages are not barred by the plaintiff-shareholder's recovery.[8] This same principle applies where there is a court-approved settlement in the nature of a pro rata recovery.

At the same time, the general rule is that a pro rata recovery by the plaintiff-shareholder, absent substantial benefit to the corporation, precludes reimbursement for his expenses, unless he has created or protected a common fund for himself and other innocent shareholders.[9]

Other problems may arise in connection with the principle of individual shareholder pro rata recovery: (a) Precaution must be taken to insure that such recovery will not prejudice creditors; (b) There may be shareholders other than the plaintiff who may be entitled to pro rata recovery, a problem which can be ameliorated by making the action a class action or by intervention; (c) Could the existence of precedents for individual pro rata recovery be used to justify a private settlement between the individual defendant and the plaintiff even though the action was brought in the right of the corporation and on behalf of all other shareholders similarly situated?[10] Should not a judgment for pro rata recovery or court approval of the settlement be insisted upon?[11]

Analogous to the problem of individual shareholder pro rata recovery in a deriva-

5. Eaton v. Robinson, 19 R.I. 146, 32 A. 339 (1895); see also Backus v. Finkelstein, 23 F.2d 531 (D. Minn.1924); Dill v. Johnston, 72 Okl. 149, 179 P. 608 (1919).

6. Di Tomasso v. Loverro, 250 App.Div. 206, 293 N. Y.S. 912 (2d Dep't 1937), aff'd mem., 276 N.Y. 551, 12 N.E.2d 570 (1937), motion for reargument or to amend remittitur denied 276 N.Y. 610, 12 N.E.2d 601 (1937); Id., 276 N.Y. 681, 13 N.E.2d 59 (1938); Brown v. De Young, 167 Ill. 549, 47 N.E. 863 (1897). Pro rata recovery might also be allowed to prevent a windfall to purchasers from the wrongdoers. Perlman v. Feldmann, 219 F.2d 173, 50 A.L.R.2d 1134 (2d Cir.1955), cert. denied 349 U.S. 952, 75 S.Ct. 880, 99 L.Ed. 1277 (1955); Id., 154 F.Supp. 436 (D. Conn.1957); Joyce v. Congdon, 114 Wash. 239, 195 P. 29 (1921); Matthews v. Headley Chocolate Co., 130 Md. 523, 100 A. 645 (1917). See also Geltman v. Levy, 11 A.D.2d 411, 207 N.Y.S.2d 366 (1st Dep't 1960), reargument and appeal denied 12 A.D.2d 740, 211 N.Y.S.2d 695 (1st Dep't 1961).

7. Bailey v. Jacobs, 325 Pa. 187, 189 A. 320 (1937). For direct relief to minority shareholders other than pro rata recovery, see Samia v. Central Oil Co., 339 Mass. 101, 158 N.E.2d 469 (1959); Weinert v. Kinkel, 296 N.Y. 151, 71 N.E.2d 445, 172 A.L.R. 688 (1947) (corporation not necessary party). Watson v. Button, 235 F.2d 235 (9th Cir.1956), allowed a former owner of one-half of the shares to sue the former general manager and owner of the remaining shares in his own name for misappropriation of corporate funds where rights of creditors and other shareholders were not affected, since a former shareholder cannot bring a derivative action and since the value of his prior shareholdings had been reduced by the misappropriation.

8. See section 376 infra.

9. Perlman v. Feldmann, 160 F.Supp. 310 (D.Conn. 1958) (award of $450,000 attorneys' fees and $38,000 disbursements for $1,150,000 settlement). See section 377 infra.

10. See Hornstein, "Problems of Procedure in Stockholder's Derivative Suits", 42 Colum.L.Rev. 574, 583 (1942).

11. See section 374 infra.

tive action are questions as to (a) whether in such an action any corporate recovery should be reduced to the extent of the interests of shareholders involved in the wrongdoing or disqualified from suing, and (b) whether the action should not be treated as an individual rather than a derivative action.[12]

SETTLEMENT OF DERIVATIVE ACTION

374. Settlement of shareholder derivative actions can serve a useful social purpose in foreshortening litigation which can often be very protracted and expensive. However, the use of corporate funds to settle corporate claims against persons who have allegedly wronged the corporation and to enrich the complaining shareholder and his attorney compounds the initial wrong. Some jurisdictions do not require court approval of settlements, while others, like Federal Rule of Civil Procedure 23.1, formerly 23(c), do. Court approval of settlements requires consideration of various factors, primarily the amount of the proposed settlement in relation to the amount which the corporation would probably ultimately realize from the action. Courts are tending to regard the plaintiff-shareholder as a guardian ad litem in the litigation and to require him as a fiduciary of the corporation to turn over to the corporation any proceeds of the litigation, whether by private settlement as well as by court-approved settlement or judgment. Some statutes so provide or indirectly encourage court approval of settlements when not directly required.

Very often a derivative action is terminated by a settlement [1] or a dismissal. Reasonable settlements serve a useful social purpose in foreshortening litigation which can

often be very protracted and expensive. The expenses of the settlement should be paid by the alleged wrongdoers and not by the corporation, although the latter practice has not been uncommon, sometimes with the settlement taking the form of a purchase at a substantial premium of the shares of the plaintiff-shareholder, thus ending his standing to complain further. Along with such settlement, the parties usually enter into a stipulation of discontinuance; the action may or may not be dismissed as a matter of record. Obviously, the use of corporate funds to settle corporate claims against persons who have allegedly wronged the corporation and to enrich the complaining shareholder and his attorney compounds the initial wrong and in effect amounts to "double looting".

Jurisdictions differ as to what rôle the courts should play in the settlement and dismissal of derivative actions.

In some jurisdictions, the plaintiff-shareholder has full control of the action, and may compromise or discontinue it whenever he wishes without court approval.[2] If he chooses to compromise the action, he is per-

---

12. See Watson v. Button, 235 F.2d 235 (9th Cir. 1956), note 7 supra.

1. Haudek, "The Settlement and Dismissal of Stockholders' Actions", 22 Sw.L.J. 767 (1968), 23 Sw.L.J. 765 (1969). Where a corporation settles a shareholder derivative action, it may deduct the expenses of itself and those of others which it has reimbursed. B. T. Harris Corp., 30 T.C. 365 (1958). Directors and officers may also deduct their settlement expenses as necessary and ordinary expenses for production or collection of income. Int.Rev. Code of 1954, 26 U.S.C.A. § 212; Guttmann v. United States, 181 F.Supp. 290 (W.D.Pa.1960).

2. Manufacturers Mut. Fire Ins. Co. of Rhode Island v. Hopson, 176 Misc. 220, 25 N.Y.S.2d 502 (Sup.Ct.1940), aff'd mem., 262 App.Div. 731, 29 N.Y. S.2d 139 (1st Dep't 1941), aff'd mem., 288 N.Y. 668, 43 N.E.2d 71 (1942), involved a settlement, with neither court nor shareholder approval, of a shareholder derivative action for mismanagement and waste of corporate funds, with the moneys paid in settlement coming from the corporation or its subsidiaries. Several years later when other minority shareholders and the corporation's trustee-in-bankruptcy attempted to vacate the stipulation of discontinuance, the court denied their motion without prejudice to the institution of a plenary action for such relief, on the ground that the original action had been terminated although the corporate cause of action still survived which other shareholders could have prosecuted at any time thereafter until barred by the statute of limitations. But see Whitten v. Dabney, 171 Cal. 621, 154 P. 312 (1915) (holding that a derivative action could only be settled with court approval since the shareholder in bringing the action was in the position of a fiduciary to the corporation). Court approval of settlements might be prerequisite to corporate indemnification of defense expenses of corporate personnel. See sections 379–380 infra. Quaere, as to settlement of threatened actions.

sonally bound by the settlement agreement. The operation of the settlement as res judicata is discussed later.[3]

In contrast is Rule 23.1, formerly 23(c), of the Federal Rules of Civil Procedure, which has been copied by statutes or rules of procedure in many states,[4] and which requires court approval for the dismissal or compromise of a derivative action, and notice to other shareholders in such a manner as the court directs. This requirement is designed to discourage "strike suits" and prevent collusive settlements of actions instituted in good faith. In exercising its discretion, the court considers: [5]

(a) the size of the possible recovery by the corporation in relation to the amount of the proposed settlement;

(b) the probability of an ultimate victory; and

(c) the solvency of the defendants.

When a proposed settlement is brought before the court any shareholder may appear and voice his objection.[6] Similarly, if the settlement is approved, any shareholder may prosecute an appeal. But where the trial court exercised adequate supervision over the terms of a settlement, its findings bind the appellate court unless there is reversible error.

Rule 23.1, formerly 23(c), has been limited in its application to settlements before entry of final judgment. However, a settlement executed after final judgment may be collaterally attacked in a second derivative action on the ground of unfairness, if the alleged wrongdoers are those in control of the corporation.

Under the rule prescribed by the United States Supreme Court in Young v. Higbee,[7]

---

3. See section 376 infra.

4. Arizona, Colorado, Delaware, Iowa, Minnesota, Missouri, Nevada, New Jersey, New Mexico, New York, North Dakota, Texas, Utah, Washington, Wisconsin, Wyoming, District of Columbia. See [1942] N.Y.L.Rev'n Comm'n Rep.1942 Legis.Doc. No. 65(J) 471–563; [1945] N.Y.L.Rev'n Comm'n Rep.1945 Legis.Doc. No. 65(c) 75–114. See also Wolf v. Barkes, 348 F.2d 994 (2d Cir.1965), cert. denied 382 U.S. 941, 86 S.Ct. 395, 15 L.Ed.2d 351 (1965) (holding that rule does not preclude out-of-court settlement by corporation of claims which are subject of shareholder derivative action. Quaere, as to settlement of threatened actions. See also Fed.R.Civ.P. 23.1. See also McKinney's N.Y. Part. Law § 115–a(4).

5. Masterson v. Pergament, 203 F.2d 315 (6th Cir. 1953), cert. denied 346 U.S. 832, 74 S.Ct. 33, 98 L. Ed. 355 (1954); Ladd v. Brickley, 158 F.2d 212 (1st Cir.1946), cert. denied 330 U.S. 819, 67 S.Ct. 675, 91 L.Ed. 1271 (1947), reh. denied 330 U.S. 855, 67 S.Ct. 964, 91 L.Ed. 1297 (1947); Fox v. Glickman Corp., 253 F.Supp. 1005 (S.D.N.Y.1966) (approving settlement of derivative actions for $1,825,000, which was about 36 percent of potential maximum recovery, and allowed shareholders' attorneys fees totaling $285,000 or 16 percent of settlement figure); Heddendorf v. Goldfine, 167 F.Supp. 915 (D.Mass. 1958); Berger v. Dyson, 111 F.Supp. 533 (D.R.I. 1953); Goodman v. Futrovsky, 42 Del.Ch. 468, 213 A.2d 899 (Sup.Ct.1965), cert. denied 383 U.S. 946, 86 S.Ct. 1197, 16 L.Ed.2d 209 (1966), reh. denied 384 U.S. 934, 86 S.Ct. 1443, 16 L.Ed.2d 535 (1966); Hoffman v. Dann, 42 Del.Ch. 123, 205 A.2d 343 (Sup.Ct. 1964), cert. denied 380 U.S. 973, 85 S.Ct. 1332, 14 L. Ed.2d 269 (1965); Rome v. Archer, 41 Del.Ch. 404, 197 A.2d 49 (Sup.Ct.1964); Shlensky v. South Parkway Bldg. Corp., 44 Ill.App.2d 135, 194 N.E.2d 35 (1963); Karasik v. Pacific Eastern Corp., 21 Del. Ch. 81, 180 A. 604 (Ch. 1935).

6. Or even to participate actively in the negotiation of the settlement. See Breswick & Co. v. Briggs, 135 F.Supp. 397 (S.D.N.Y.1955); Note, "Corporations—Stockholders—Intervention in Settlement", 49 Iowa L.Rev. 581 (1964).

7. 324 U.S. 204, 65 S.Ct. 594, 89 L.Ed. 890 (1945). See also Whitten v. Dabney, 171 Cal. 621, 154 P. 312 (1915) (settlement and dismissal of shareholder derivative action held to require court approval since plaintiff-shareholder was suing in behalf of corporation as its fiduciary). In Dabney v. Levy, 191 F. 2d 201 (2d Cir. 1951), cert. denied 342 U.S. 887, 72 S. Ct. 177, 96 L.Ed. 665 (1951), reh. denied 342 U.S. 911, 72 S.Ct. 301, 96 L.Ed. 682 (1952), the individual defendants in a minority shareholders' action paid the plaintiff's attorney, out of the funds of a subsidiary of defendant corporation, $21,000 by way of a private settlement without judicial approval. The attorney paid plaintiffs $200 of this and paid his associate, an accountant, $6,000. Ten years later, the trustee-in-bankruptcy of the defendant corporation sued and recovered the $6,000 from the associate. It was held that the statute of limitations did not begin to run until the trustee could and did discover the misappropriation of corporate funds. See also Miller v. Steinbach, 268 F.Supp. 255, 281 (S.D.N.Y.1967) ("self-assumed obligator of corporate champion cannot be shed at will"—allowing attack on court-approved settlement, without notice to other shareholders of action attacking merger, seeking $25,000,000 compensatory damages and $25,000,000 punitive damages, where plaintiff-shareholder sold his 89,000 shares to surviving cor-

and the New York Court of Appeals in Clarke v. Greenberg,[8] another shareholder may bring a new derivative action against the original plaintiff-shareholder to recover the amount of the settlement he received.

New York and Wisconsin have codified this salutary rule by statute, which provides that if anything is recovered or obtained as the result of the action or claim, whether by compromise, settlement, or judgment, the court may, out of the proceeds, award the plaintiff-shareholder the reasonable expenses, including reasonable attorneys' fees, and may direct the plaintiff-shareholder to account to the corporation for the remainder of such proceeds.[9]

Where the plaintiff-shareholder may be compelled to pay into the corporation the amount he received as a settlement, there remains little opportunity to derive personal gain from a derivative action, thus seriously curbing "strike-suits", although such rules may encourage pre-litigation chicanery.

Even where court approval of settlements is not required, there may be indirect pressures upon the real party defendants to seek court approval of the settlement. For instance, reimbursement by the corporation of the litigation expenses of corporate personnel may not be allowed unless the settlement is court-approved;[10] the plaintiff-shareholder might also be denied allowance of his expenses unless he has benefited the corporation or created a common fund.[11] Perhaps more important is the fact that wrongdoers who wish the benefit of the settlement as res judicata must obtain court approval.[12]

OTHER RELIEF IN DERIVATIVE ACTION

375. Receivership during a shareholder derivative action is usually within the court's discretion. Courts are often reluctant to order a receivership of a solvent going concern for fear of harming the corporation's credit and good will. Statutes often deal with receivership.

Dissolution for mismanagement is sparingly afforded in shareholder derivative actions by

---

10. See section 380 infra.

11. Young v. Potts, 161 F.2d 597 (6th Cir.1947); Perrine v. Pennroad Corp., 29 Del.Ch. 423, 51 A.2d 327 (Ch. 1947), aff'd 30 Del.Ch. 517, 64 A.2d 412 (Sup. Ct.1948). See section 377 infra.

12. Just as a judgment in a derivative action normally bars a subsequent action in the corporate right, so a settlement with court approval embodied in the court order is res judicata. However, a private settlement without court participation ordinarily would leave open the possibility of derivative actions by other shareholders on the same corporate cause of action. The principal practical exception is the not uncommon case in which the private settlement in fact destroys all possibility of recovery in the corporate right because of the running of the statute of limitations against all other possible plaintiffs. Although a court-approved settlement constitutes res judicata, it would not bar a corporate claim against its directors for legal fees incurred by the corporation in connection with the settled litigation. Essential Enterprises Corp. v. Dorsey Corp., 40 Del.Ch. 343, 182 A.2d 647 (Ch. 1962). Setting aside of a court-approved settlement requires sufficient evidence of fraud. Alleghany Corp. v. Kirby, 218 F.Supp. 164 (S.D.N.Y.1963), aff'd 333 F.2d 327 (2d Cir. 1964) (2–1), aff'd on rehearing en banc 340 F.2d 311 (2d Cir. 1965) (4–4), cert. granted sub nom. Holt v. Alleghany Corp., 381 U.S. 933, 85 S.Ct. 1772, 14 L.Ed.2d 698 (1965), cert. dismissed 384 U.S. 28, 86 S.Ct. 1250, 16 L.Ed.2d 335 (1966), reh. denied 384 U.S. 967, 86 S.Ct. 1583, 16 L.Ed.2d 680 (1966). The sounder procedure is to have the settlement vacated by the court which approved it. See Sonnenschein v. Evans, 21 N.Y.2d 563, 289 N.Y.S.2d 609, 236 N.E.2d 846 (1968); Note, "Collateral Attack of Judicially-Approved Settlements of Shareholder's Derivative Suits", 74 Yale L.J. 1140 (1965). See section 376 infra.

---

poration for price allegedly in excess of their value).

8. 296 N.Y. 146, 71 N.E.2d 443, 169 A.L.R. 944 (1947) reargument denied 296 N.Y. 993, 73 N.E.2d 569, 169 A.L.R. 944 (1947), where the court said that the very nature of the derivative action by a plaintiff-shareholder suing in the corporation's behalf suggests the application of the fiduciary principle to the proceeds realized from such litigation whether received by way of judgment, by settlement with approval of the court, which presupposes shareholders' approval, or by private settlement and discontinuance of the action at any stage of the proceeding. Quaere, as to settlement of threatened actions.

9. McKinney's N.Y.Bus.Corp.Law, § 626(e) (excepting any judgment rendered for the benefit of injured shareholders only and limited to a recovery of the damage sustained by them). Wis.Bus.Corp.Law, § 180.405(3) (1951). See also McKinney's N.Y.Part. Law § 115-a(5).

courts of equity in the absence of statute. A receiver might be appointed with a proviso for dissolution in the event the situation does not improve. Some statutes expressly provide for judicial dissolution in a shareholder's action where management is acting illegally, oppressively, or fraudulently.

Shareholders in derivative actions sometimes seek the appointment of a receiver of the corporation pendente lite where the corporate management is breaching its duties to the corporation, or a permanent receiver to attend to the dissolution and liquidation of the corporation.[1] Not only does a receiver protect the corporation's assets and business; his appointment discourages dilatory tactics by the defendant. The appointment of receivers is usually within the court's discretion.[2]

Courts are often reluctant to order a receivership of a solvent going concern for fear of harming the corporation's credit and good will. One recent compromise—avoiding the stigma of receivership—was the court appointment of a "special fiscal agent" to overlook management and report any derelictions.[3] A more far-reaching remedy might be for the court to appoint a receiver under a proviso for dissolution if the situation did not improve.[4]

Statutes often deal with various phases of corporate receiverships.[5]

The more drastic remedy of dissolution for mismanagement, waste of corporate assets, etc., has been sparingly afforded by courts of equity in the absence of statute,[6] but some trend in favor of such relief has been observed.[7]

---

1. See notes 6–9 infra.

2. In Tate v. Philadelphia Transportation Co., 410 Pa. 490, 190 A.2d 316 (1963), the court refused to appoint a temporary receiver on the ground that the proper basis for the receivership of a solvent corporation had not been made out for lack of showing that the right to receivership was clear, irreparable damage was probable, the receivership would not substantially prejudice the rights of creditors and shareholders, greater damage would not result if a receiver were not appointed than would if one were, and the receivership would be in aid of some recognized presently existing right, or a showing that there had been such gross mismanagement or fraud or similar circumstances that a receivership was clearly required. Macon Lumber Co. v. Bishop & Collins, 229 F.2d 305 (6th Cir. 1956); Texarkana College Bowl, Inc. v. Phillips, 408 S.W.2d 537 (Tex. Civ.App.1966); Conlee Construction Co. v. Krause, 192 So.2d 330 (Fla.Dist.Ct.App.1966); Sandfield v. Goldstein, 29 A.D.2d 999, 289 N.Y.S.2d 733 (3d Dep't 1968); Weber v. Sutorius Bread Co., 185 Kan. 171, 341 P.2d 959 (1959); Hall v. John S. Isaacs & Sons Farms, Inc., 37 Del.Ch. 530, 146 A.2d 602 (Ch.1958), modified 39 Del.Ch. 244, 163 A.2d 288 (Sup.Ct. 1960); Sabella v. Sheepshead Bay U–Drives, Inc., 10 Misc.2d 312, 167 N.Y.S.2d 538 (Sup.Ct.1957); Nadrich v. Nagelberg, 8 Misc.2d 339, 165 N.Y.S.2d 166 (Sup.Ct.1957). Appointment of a receiver should be requested in the prayer for relief in the complaint. Pioche Mines Consol., Inc. v. Dolman, 333 F.2d 257 (9th Cir. 1964), cert. denied 380 U.S. 956, 85 S.Ct. 1081, 13 L.Ed.2d 972 (1965). For resort to receivership in attempt to have receiver assert corporate cause of action, see section 354, n. 13 supra. See Magnusson v. American Allied Ins. Co., 282 Minn. 287, 164 N.W.2d 867 (1969) (attorney who unsuccessfully opposed receivership of insolvent corporation denied preference for fee over general creditors).

3. Roach v. Margulies, 42 N.J.Super. 243, 126 A.2d 45 (1956).

4. Cf. Patton v. Nicholas, 154 Tex. 385, 279 S.W.2d 848 (1955), 302 S.W.2d 441 (Tex.Civ.App.1957).

5. E. g., McKinney's N.Y.Bus.Corp.Law, §§ 1201–1218.

6. Leibert v. Clapp, 13 N.Y.2d 313, 247 N.Y.S.2d 102, 196 N.E.2d 540 (1963) (unanimous decision as to inherent power of equity to dissolve corporation but divided 4 to 3 in favor of its exercise under facts). Cf. Kruger v. Gerth, 16 N.Y.2d 802, 263 N.Y.S.2d 1, 210 N.E.2d 355 (1965) (4–3 holding against exercise), aff'g 22 A.D.2d 916, 917, 255 N.Y.S.2d 498, 500 (2d Dep't 1964) (3–2) ("More is required to sustain an action to compel the dissolution of a corporation than to sustain a derivative stockholder's action for waste"). See also Matter of Nelkin, —— N.Y.2d ——, —— N.Y.S.2d ——, —— N.E.2d —— (1969); Rizzuto v. Onset Cafe, Inc., 330 Mass. 595, 116 N.E.2d 249 (1953); Fontheim v. Walker, 282 App.Div. 373, 122 N.Y.S.2d 642 (1st Dep't 1953), aff'd mem., 306 N.Y. 926, 119 N.E.2d 605 (1954); Lennan v. Blakely, 273 App.Div. 767, 75 N.Y.S.2d 331 (1st Dep't 1947); Miner v. Belle Isle Ice Co., 93 Mich. 97, 53 N.W. 218 (1892). See also Bellevue Gardens, Inc. v. Hill, 111 U.S.App.D.C. 343, 297 F.2d 185 (1961) (dissolution of foreign corporation under inherent power of equity court). An action by a shareholder for dissolution, as other than an action brought in the right of the corporation to procure a judgment in its favor, would not be subject to the several limitations on shareholder derivative actions. See section 360 supra.

7. N. Lattin, The Law of Corporations § 4 (1959); J. Tingle, The Stockholder's Remedy of Corporate Dissolution (1959); R. Stevens, Handbook on the Law of Private Corporations § 199 (2d ed. 1949); Comment, "Corporate Dissolution for Illegal, Oppres-

Some statutes expressly provide for judicial dissolution in a shareholder's action where management is acting illegally, oppressively, or fraudulently.[8]

RES JUDICATA EFFECT OF DERIVATIVE ACTION

376. A final judgment on the merits or a court-approved settlement of a shareholder derivative action, when due notice thereof has been given to all shareholders, ordinarily is res judicata. A settlement without court approval is at most binding only upon the immediate parties.

Subject to such limitations as contemporaneous-share-ownership,[1] exhaustion of intracorporate remedies,[2] and the need for se-

curity for expenses in certain cases,[3] a shareholder may initiate a derivative action. Other shareholders may subsequently intervene,[4] or bring other derivative actions based on the same facts.[5] However, a final judgment on the merits in one shareholder derivative action operates as res judicata for later shareholder derivative actions or a later action by the corporation based on the same claim, and bars any further litigation.[6] It has been pointed out that this affords the defendants the opportunity to litigate the basic issues in the action that appears most favorable to them, simply by employing dilatory tactics in the other actions.[7]

---

sive or Fraudulent Acts: the Maryland Solution", 28 Md.L.Rev. 360 (1968); Hornstein, "A Remedy for Intra-Corporate Abuse—Judicial Power to Wind up a Corporation at the Suit of a Minority Shareholder", 40 Colum.L.Rev. 220 (1940); Note, "Oppression as a Statutory Ground for Corporate Dissolution", 1965 Duke L.J. 128; Note, "Oppression as a Basis for Dissolving a Solvent Corporation", 30 U.Cin.L. Rev. 478 (1961); Note, "Rights of the Minority Shareholders to Dissolve the Closely Held Corporation", 43 Cal.L.Rev. 514 (1955).

8. E. g., ABA–ALI Model Bus.Corp.Act § 90; McKinney's N.Y.Bus.Corp.Law, § 1102 (directors' petition for judicial dissolution where assets of corporations are not sufficient to discharge its liabilities or that dissolution will be beneficial to shareholders); id. § 1103 (shareholders' petition for judicial dissolution where assets not sufficient to discharge its liabilities or shareholders deem dissolution to be beneficial to them); id. § 1111(b) (2) (criterion: benefit to shareholders of dissolution of paramount importance). See Gidwitz v. Lanzit Corrugated Box Co., 20 Ill.2d 208, 170 N.E.2d 131 (1960) (dissolution ordered on basis of oppressive conduct); Central Standard Life Ins. Co. v. Davis, 10 Ill.2d 566, 141 N.E.2d 45 (1957) (failure to pay dividends held not oppressive conduct). Polikoff v. Dole & Clark Bldg. Corp., 37 Ill.App.2d 29, 184 N.E.2d 792 (1962), held that equity has no jurisdiction to order liquidation of a corporation independent of any statutory authorization and strictly construed the Illinois statutory provision, stating that the remedy of liquidation was so drastic that it must be invoked with extreme caution lest one evil—oppression of the minority by the majority—would be merely eliminated by substituting a greater one—oppression of the majority by the minority. See sections 280, 348 supra.

1. See section 362 supra.

2. See sections 364–367 supra.

3. See section 372 supra.

4. Duncan v. National Tea Co., 14 Ill.App.2d 280, 144 N.E.2d 771, 69 A.L.R.2d 546 (1957).

5. Auerbach v. Cities Service Co., 37 Del.Ch. 381, 143 A.2d 904, 70 A.L.R.2d 1298 (Sup.Ct.1958); Dresdner v. Goldman Sachs Trading Corp., 240 App.Div. 242, 269 N.Y.S. 360 (2d Dep't 1934).

6. Saylor v. Lindsley, 391 F.2d 965 (2d Cir. 1968) (judgment dismissing complaint for failure to post security for expenses held not res judicata since not on merits); International Rys. of Central America v. United Fruit Co., 373 F.2d 408 (2d Cir. 1967), cert. denied 387 U.S. 921, 87 S.Ct. 2031, 18 L. Ed.2d 975 (1967), reh. denied 389 U.S. 1059, 88 S.Ct. 757, 19 L.Ed.2d 861 (1968) (federal court action by corporation under federal statute allowed on ground judgment in prior shareholder derivative action in state court not res judicata); Liken v. Shaffer, 64 F.Supp. 432 (N.D.Iowa 1946); McMenomy v. Ryden, 276 Minn. 55, 148 N.W.2d 804 (1967) (S.E.C. injunction action under Federal Investment Company Act held not res judicata in later shareholder derivative action seeking relief under act on ground parties and relief different); Bowker v. Nashua Textile Co., 103 N.H. 242, 169 A.2d 630 (1961) (dismissal of shareholder derivative action held bar to subsequent action by another shareholder); Gagnon Co. v. Nevada Desert Inn, 45 Cal.2d 448, 289 P.2d 466 (1955). Res judicata applies only if the judgment was "in bar" and not "in abatement". The rationale is that a judgment in a class action bars the class and that the corporate claim has been fully litigated. See Gottesman v. General Motors Corp., 222 F.Supp. 342 (S.D.N.Y.1963), cert. denied 379 U.S. 882, 85 S.Ct. 321, 13 L.Ed.2d 351 (1964) (comparing doctrine of preclusion against inconsistent positions with res judicata and collateral estoppel).

7. Note, " 'Enjoining' Res Judicata: The Federal-State Relationship and Conclusiveness of Settlements in Stockholders' Derivative Suits", 65 Yale L.J. 543 (1956).

A court-approved settlement ordinarily has the same effect as a final judgment.[8] But where there is no court approval, the settlement is, at most, binding only upon the immediate parties.[9] In applying for court approval, the plaintiff-shareholder may submit the settlement agreement without securing the consent of other shareholders who are suing separately on the same cause of action. Objecting shareholders, however, may intervene in the hearing and contest the propriety of the proposed settlement. In the federal courts and in states with similar rules, notice of the proposed settlement and the time of the hearing must be given to all shareholders as the court directs.[10] Where such practice is followed, whether or not mandatory, the settlement is ordinarily res judicata.[11]

A federal case has added one further condition necessary to give conclusive effect to a settlement decree by holding that all actively litigating shareholders must participate in negotiation of the settlement before a defendant could claim the benefit of the decree in a federal court.[12] To what degree "participation" is necessary remains an open question.

H. INCIDENCE OF EXPENSES OF CORPORATE LITIGATION

LITIGATION EXPENSES OF PLAINTIFF–SHAREHOLDER

377. The plaintiff-shareholder is entitled to be reimbursed by the corporation for his reasonable expenses, including attorneys' fees, where he has been successful in his derivative assertion of the corporation's claim with subsequent benefit—monetary or otherwise—to the corporation. Quaere, whether a shareholder should be allowed compensation as an attorney pro se in a derivative action. In the case of pro rata recovery, reimbursement should be awarded if a fund has been created for a class or if the corporation has been sufficiently benefited.

As discussed, a plaintiff-shareholder may in certain instances be required by statute to post security for the litigation expenses of the corporation.[1] Potential liability of the plaintiff-shareholder for the litigation expenses incurred by any defendant arises only because of the security, except in a few jurisdictions,[2] and may be enforced only when the plaintiff-shareholder is unsuccessful in pursuing his derivative remedy.

There are times, however, when the corporation may be compelled either to bear the initial burden for expenses incurred by other parties to the derivative action or to reimburse such parties for expenses they originally paid. The ultimate liability for such expenses resulting from the litigation to the plaintiff-shareholder is examined in this section; the incidence of the defendant corporation's own expenses are discussed in the

8. Stella v. Kaiser, 218 F.2d 64 (2d Cir. 1954), cert. denied 350 U.S. 835, 76 S.Ct. 71, 100 L.Ed. 745 (1955); Dana v. Morgan, 232 F. 85 (2d Cir. 1916); Boothe v. Baker Industries, Inc., 262 F.Supp. 168 (D.Del.1967) (settlement of prior shareholder derivative action held res judicata in later class action alleging derivative and nonderivative claims); Milvy v. Sperry Corp., 36 N.Y.S.2d 881 (Sup.Ct.1939); Comment, "Corporations: Settlement of Stockholders' Derivative Actions: Res Judicata", 38 N.C.L. Rev. 391 (1960).

9. Manufacturers Mut. Fire Ins. Co. of Rhode Island v. Hopson, 176 Misc. 220, 25 N.Y.S.2d 502 (Sup.Ct. 1940), aff'd mem., 262 App.Div. 731, 29 N.Y.S.2d 139 (1st Dep't 1941), aff'd mem., 288 N.Y. 668, 43 N.E.2d 71 (1942).

10. Fed.R.Civ.P. 23.1 (formerly 23(c)).

11. Nesbitt v. Hagan, 265 Ala. 213, 90 So.2d 217 (1956); Gerith Realty Co. v. Normandie National Securities Corp., 154 Misc. 615, 276 N.Y.S. 655 (Sup.Ct.1933), aff'd mem., 241 App.Div. 717, 269 N.Y.S. 1007 (1st Dep't 1934), aff'd mem., 266 N.Y. 525, 195 N.E. 183 (1934).

12. Breswick & Co. v. Briggs, 135 F.Supp. 397 (S.D. N.Y.1955).

1. See section 372 supra.

2. See section 372, n. 8 supra.

next section,[3] followed by a discussion of the incidence of the expenses of defendant corporate personnel at common law [4] and under statutes.[5]

As a general rule, the plaintiff-shareholder is entitled to be reimbursed by the corporation for his reasonable expenses where he has been successful in his derivative action, with consequent benefit to the corporation.[6]

"Reasonable expenses" usually include very liberal allowances for attorney's fees.[7]

Where the corporation receives the direct financial benefit resulting from the action, the reasoning behind such reimbursement is apparent. A monetary fund accruing to the corporation is sufficient to meet this requirement. However, courts have disagreed as to whether a non-fund benefit suffices. While some cases stand for the proposition that only a pecuniary benefit entitles the plaintiff-shareholder to reimbursement,[8] many jurisdictions go further and permit the plaintiff-shareholder to recover for his reasonable expenses in certain cases even where

---

3. See section 378 infra.

4. See section 379 infra.

5. See section 380 infra.

6. F. MacKinnon, Contingent Fees for Legal Services: A Study of Professional Economics and Responsibilities (1964); 2 G. Hornstein, Corporation Law and Practice § 732 (1959); Smith, "Recovery of Plaintiff's Attorney's Fees in Corporate Litigation", 40 L.A.B.Bull. 15 (1964); Hornstein, "Legal Therapeutics: The 'Salvage' Factor in Counsel Fee Awards", 69 Harv.L.Rev. 658 (1956); Hornstein, "The Counsel Fee in Stockholder's Derivative Suits", 39 Colum.L.Rev. 784 (1939); Note, 55 Mich. L.Rev. 595 (1957). New York and Wisconsin have statutory provisions, although oblique ones, on the subject. They provide that if anything is recovered or obtained as the result of a shareholder derivative action whether by means of a compromise and settlement or by a judgment, the court may, out of the proceeds, award the plaintiff the reasonable expenses of maintaining the action, including reasonable attorneys' fees, and may direct the plaintiff to account to the corporation for the remainder of such proceeds. McKinney's N.Y.Bus. Corp.Law, § 626(e); Wis.Bus.Corp.Law § 180.405(3) (1951); McKinney's N.Y.Part. Law § 115–a(5). See also McKinney's N.Y. CPLR, § 8303 (providing for allowance in addition to taxable disbursements in discretion of court to any party to difficult or extraordinary case, where defense has been interposed, sum not exceeding five percent of sum recovered or claimed, or of value of subject matter involved, and not exceeding $3,000); Annot., 8 L.Ed.2d 894 (1963).

7. E. g., Ripley v. International Railways of Central America, 16 A.D.2d 260, 227 N.Y.S.2d 64 (1st Dep't 1962), aff'd mem., 12 N.Y.2d 814, 236 N.Y.S.2d 64, 187 N.E.2d 131 (1962) (award of $1,500,000 fee plus $92,000 disbursements to general counsel for plaintiff-shareholder in shareholder derivative action resulting in actual recovery of $8,000,000 and other substantial benefits to corporation, $240,000 fee and disbursements to other counsel for plaintiffs, and $272,900 fees to various experts). The minority shareholder's attorneys sought a total of $8,500,000 legal fees and disbursements for their more-than-10-years work on a contingency basis; the general counsel sought $5,175,000. 110 N.Y. Times, No. 37,-751, 24 (June 3, 1961). Zenn v. Anzalone, 46 Misc.

2d 378, 259 N.Y.S.2d 747 (Sup.Ct.1965) ($1,876,000 plus disbursements allowed for counsel and consultants' fees for 10-year shareholder derivative litigation in federal and state courts, resulting in $3,-300,000 corporate recovery—"it is not necessary to fix any exact value to the speculative future benefits resulting from a stockholders' action, and it is sufficient to recognize the existence of some probable future benefit as an additional factor in the assessment of claimants' compensation"). Perlman v. Feldmann, 160 F.Supp. 310 (D.Conn.1958) (award to plaintiffs of $450,000 counsel fees (14,000 hours at $32 per hour) and $38,000 disbursements for achieving a $1,150,000 settlement in derivative action against former principal officer, director and controlling shareholder for fraudulent sale of control, where pro rata recovery payable to minority shareholders had been decreed in prior appeal); Waterman Corp. v. Johnston, 204 Misc. 587, 122 N.Y.S.2d 695 (Sup.Ct.1953) (award of $226,000 counsel fees), modified 283 App.Div. 768, 128 N.Y.S.2d 573 (1st Dep't 1954) (award reduced to $143,900 counsel fees because substantial part of services of several of the counsel was duplicative, unnecessary and productive of no ultimate benefit to corporation). National Bankers Life Ins. Co. v. Rosson, 400 S.W.2d 366 (Tex.Civ.App.1966), upheld a jury award of $200,000 to attorneys for minority shareholders in a derivative action found to have aided the corporation in the recovery of $1,025,000 from its former officer, as based upon evidence of the work and skill of the attorneys, the nature and character of the litigation, the time involved, and other factors. See Angoff v. Goldfine, 270 F.2d 185 (1st Cir. 1959); Aaron v. Parsons, 37 Del.Ch. 407, 144 A.2d 155 (Sup.Ct.1958); Braun v. Fleming-Hall Tobacco Co., 33 Del.Ch. 354, 93 A.2d 495 (Sup.Ct.1952); Annot., 56 A.L.R.2d 13, 176 (1957). See also Mardel Securities, Inc. v. Alexandria Gazette Corp. 278 F.Supp. 1010 (E.D.Va.1967) (awarding to successful plaintiff-shareholder's attorney $25,000 fee from corporation, despite original $7,500 retainer by shareholder, and requiring return to shareholder of amount of retainer paid to attorney); Klaw, "Abe Pomerantz Is Watching You", 77 Fortune, No. 2, 144 (Feb. 1968).

8. See, e. g., Shaw v. Harding, 306 Mass. 441, 28 N. E.2d 469 (1940).

the corporation receives no specific fund as the result of the litigation.[9] For example, reimbursement has been allowed where the action resulted in the avoidance of some threatened or illegal act.[10]

The same rules apply even though the derivative action is not pursued to final judgment, so long as the purpose of the action is accomplished. Thus, a settlement which results in a benefit to the corporation is sufficient for purposes of reimbursement.[11]

Also, merely bringing an action and obtaining a temporary injunction may produce the desired benefit.[12]

Where a shareholder or his attorney, by investigation, determined that a valid claim existed in favor of the corporation, and forthwith made a demand upon the board of directors which thereupon caused the corporation to bring a direct action and thereby enforced the corporate right, courts have awarded the shareholder and his attorney reasonable investigation expenses, on the ground that the demand produced a benefit to the corporation. Attorney's fees were included as a part of the reasonable investigation expenses.[13]

9. Fletcher v. A. J. Industries, Inc., 266 Cal.App.2d 329, 72 Cal.Rptr. 146 (1968); Bosch v. Meeker Cooperative Light & Power Ass'n, 257 Minn. 362, 101 N. W.2d 423 (1960); Bysheim v. Miranda, 45 N.Y.S.2d 473 (Sup.Ct.1943). Denney v. Phillips & Buttorff Corp., 331 F.2d 249 (6th Cir. 1964), upheld an award of $235,000 attorneys' fees and $6,225 disbursements, despite fact that judgment was for only $40,000 where there was additional benefit of some $2,700,000 to corporation from cancellation of purchase before court had opportunity to pass on case. See notes 10–13 infra.

10. Berger v. Amana Society, 257 Iowa 956, 135 N. W.2d 618 (1965) (award of $125,000 and disbursements for setting aside amendment of articles of incorporation authorizing additional shares); Bosch v. Meeker Cooperative Light & Power Ass'n, 257 Minn. 362, 101 N.W.2d 423 (1960); Yap v. Wah Yen Ki Tuck Tsen Nin Hue, 43 Hawaii 37 (1958); Abrams v. Textile Realty Corp., 97 N.Y.S.2d 492 (Sup.Ct.1949). See also Mills v. Electric Auto-Lite Co., — U.S. —, 90 S.Ct. 616, 24 L.Ed.2d 593 (1970) (shareholder who had established violation of federal securities law—illegal proxy statements promoting merger—held entitled to reimbursement from corporation).

11. In Maggiore v. Bradford, 310 F.2d 519 (6th Cir. 1962), cert. denied 372 U.S. 934, 83 S.Ct. 881, 9 L. Ed.2d 766 (1963), a minority shareholder brought a derivative action against majority shareholders and others to rescind a transaction whereby the latter financed the purchase of their shares with $2,700,000 corporate funds. While the action was pending, the majority shareholders themselves rescinded the transaction. The court held that this fact did not defeat the minority shareholder's right to compensation, stating that the rescission, without the necessity of a trial, would be taken into account in fixing the fees along with other relevant factors. See Dann v. Chrysler Corp., 42 Del.Ch. 508, 215 A.2d 709 (Ch.1965), aff'd 43 Del.Ch. 252, 223 A.2d 384 (Sup.Ct.1966) (where resulting change in corporation's incentive plan enabled it to attract higher quality personnel but at greater expense to corporation); Aaron v. Parsons, 37 Del.Ch. 407, 144 A.2d 155 (Sup.Ct.1958); Waterman Corp. v. Johnston, 204 Misc. 587, 122 N.Y.S.2d 695 (Sup.Ct.1953), modified 283 App.Div. 768, 128 N.Y.S.2d 573 (1st Dep't 1954); Perrine v. Pennroad Corp., 29 Del.Ch. 423,

51 A.2d 327 (Ch.1947), aff'd 30 Del.Ch. 517, 64 A.2d 412 (Sup.Ct.1948).

12. Martin Foundation, Inc. v. Phillips-Jones Corp., 204 Misc. 120, 123 N.Y.S.2d 222 (Sup.Ct.1953), modified 283 App.Div. 729, 127 N.Y.S.2d 649 (2d Dep't (1954), aff'd mem., 306 N.Y. 972, 120 N.E.2d 230 (1954).

13. Blau v. Rayette-Faberge, Inc., 389 F.2d 469 (2d Cir. 1968) (attorney who demanded that corporation recapture "short-swing" profits under Federal Securities Exchange Act, which it did without any further need for services of attorney, who in meantime had drafted complaint, held entitled to fee from corporation whose claims were being barred by statute of limitations); Gilson v. Chock Full O'Nuts Corp., 331 F.2d 107 (2d Cir. 1964) (attorney held entitled to fee for discovering claim for insider "short-swing" profits, demanding that corporation sue, and drafting complaint where corporation thereafter sued insiders); Blau v. Brown and Western Nuclear Inc., CCH Fed.Sec.L.Rep. ¶ 92,263 (S. D.N.Y.1968) ($7,500 fee awarded for filing routine complaint against insider for recapture of "short-swing" profits under Federal Securities Exchange Act—some 30 hours of work—where corporation recovered $37,795 profits). Shareholder litigation to recapture "short-swing" profits under the Federal Securities Exchange Act is often brought by Isadore Blau, represented by Morris J. Levy, Esq. Quaere, why should not anyone not only a security holder—who need not be a contemporaneous-shareowner—be able to recapture such profits if the corporation fails to do so.

In Blau v. Lehman, 368 U.S. 403, 82 S.Ct. 451, 7 L.Ed. 2d 403 (1962), a shareholder, in behalf of the corporation, sued to recover "short-swing profits" under the Federal Securities Exchange Act, 1934, seeking almost $100,000 from a brokerage firm one of whose partners was a director of the corporation. Recovery was allowed only against the director-broker in the amount of approximately $4,000. Subsequently, the court allowed the shareholder's

Where a plaintiff-shareholder acts as his own attorney in a derivative action, and the action results in a benefit to the corporation, may he recover the reasonable value of his professional services? This question has not been fully answered, but in at least one case recovery has been denied where the plaintiff-shareholder-attorney's interest in the corporation amounted to less than 1/40th of one percent of the outstanding shares.[14] An intermediate appellate court, whose decision was affirmed without opinion on appeal, held that the extremely limited interest of the shareholder cast considerable doubt upon his good faith in pursuing the derivative remedy, and by dictum expressed serious doubt as to whether a shareholder should be allowed compensation as attorney pro se in his own derivative action.[15] This dictum has added additional discouragement to derivative actions brought by a shareholder-attorney for the purpose of personal gain.

Where a shareholder-plaintiff proceeded by a derivative action rather than by an available and far less costly administrative remedy, his failure to invoke the administrative remedy before resorting to a derivative action was held not necessarily to prevent reimbursement.[16]

Where a shareholder had unsuccessfully attacked a share option plan and thereafter sought to recover reasonable expenses, the court rejected the plaintiff-shareholder's contention that the corporation had received the benefit of having its share option plan court-tested.[17]

In the case of a successful action to compel the distribution of a dividend for a class of shares, the reasonable expenses incurred by the plaintiff-shareholder ought to be payable out of the dividend fund before the balance is distributed proportionately among shareholders.[18]

If the corporation reimburses the plaintiff-shareholder who successfully made use

---

attorney one-third of the amount actually recovered, stating that neither the amount of his work nor his out-of-pocket expenses should be the measure of the fee since they related only partly to the amount recovered inasmuch as they related also to the unsuccessful effort to recover approximately $100,000 from the firm. Kaufman v. Shoenberg, 33 Del.Ch. 282, 92 A.2d 295 (Ch.1952). See also Matter of Pomerantz, 186 F.Supp. 412 (D.Mass. 1959).

14. Eisenberg v. Central Zone Property Corp., 1 A. D.2d 353, 149 N.Y.S.2d 840 (1st Dep't 1956), aff'd mem., 3 N.Y.2d 729, 163 N.Y.S.2d 968, 143 N.E.2d 516 (1957), cert. denied 355 U.S. 884, 78 S.Ct. 151, 2 L.Ed.2d 113 (1957) (but allowing award to non-shareholder attorney handling appeal).

15. See Giesecke v. Pittsburgh Hotels, Inc., 82 F. Supp. 64 (W.D.Pa.1949), aff'd 180 F.2d 65 (3d Cir. 1950). Contra, Ontjes v. MacNider, 234 Iowa 208, 12 N.W.2d 284 (1943) (upholding allowance of attorney's fees to plaintiff-shareholder-attorney). Dann v. Chrysler Corp., 42 Del.Ch. 508, 215 A.2d 709 (Ch. 1965), aff'd 43 Del.Ch. 252, 223 A.2d 384 (Sup.Ct. 1966), awarded $450,000 as fees for the plaintiff-shareholders' attorneys services for the benefit conferred on the corporation by change in a compensation plan as the result of a derivative action. The chancellor stated that the fact that one or more plaintiffs also acted as attorneys, in and of itself, was not an ethical block to recovery, but denied participation in the award by the principal plaintiff-shareholder because of his conduct during the litigation.

16. Schechtman v. Wolfson, 244 F.2d 537 (2d Cir. 1957) (but denying reimbursement because of lack of benefit to the corporation). The lower court, 141 F.Supp. 453 (S.D.N.Y.1956), had denied recovery for failure initially to invoke the administrative remedy.

17. Gottlieb v. Heyden Chemical Corp., 34 Del.Ch. 436, 105 A.2d 461 (Sup.Ct.1954). See also Grodetsky v. McCrory Corp., 49 Misc.2d 322, 267 N.Y.S.2d 356 (Sup.Ct.1966), aff'd mem., 27 A.D.2d 646, 276 N.Y.S. 2d 841 (1st Dep't 1966) (shareholder's attorney who conducted shareholder's proxy contest held not entitled to reimbursement by corporation, even though his efforts defeated corporation's proposed sale of certain assets and allegedly saved corporation millions of dollars, since (a) he was full-time salaried employee of shareholder, and (b) contest was conducted for shareholder's own purpose and not over matters of policy—see section 196 supra). Absent benefit to the corporation, the litigating plaintiff-shareholder must bear his own litigation expenses. Aiple v. Twin City Barge & Towing Co., 274 Minn. 38, 143 N.W.2d 374 (1967); Garfield v. Equitable Life Assurance Soc'y, 24 A.D.2d 74, 263 N.Y.S.2d 922 (1st Dep't 1965), aff'd 17 N.Y.2d 841, 271 N.Y.S.2d 281, 218 N.E.2d 322 (1966); Leppaluoto v. Eggleston, 57 Wash.2d 393, 357 P.2d 725 (1960).

18. See Harris v. Chicago Great Western Ry., 197 F.2d 829 (7th Cir. 1952); Starring v. Kemp, 167 Va. 429, 188 S.E. 174 (1936), reh. denied 167 Va. 438, 190 S.E. 163 (1937). See section 328 supra. See note 24 infra.

of the derivative remedy, the legal fees so paid may be deducted by the corporation as a business expense for tax purposes.[19] If the plaintiff-shareholder paid the attorney's fees and then attempted to deduct them, he might lose on the ground that the fees were a corporate expense, or that they were really capital contributions increasing the cost of his shares.

Where the plaintiff-shareholder brings a derivative action and is awarded a pro rata recovery in behalf of a class,[20] reimbursement of his reasonable expenses out of the recovery should be allowed.[21] Presumably if he recovers only his own proportionate damages, he should not be reimbursed [22] unless the action resulted in sufficient benefit to the corporation, in which event reimbursement by the corporation should be allowed.[23]

Where the shareholder brings a direct or individual action and recovers a fund in behalf of a class, he should be reimbursed from such fund.[24] Absent a class fund, presumably the normal rule that a litigant pays his own litigation expense should apply.[25]

LITIGATION EXPENSES OF DEFENDANT CORPORATION

378. The corporation must bear its own litigation expenses, and possibly those of defendant corporate personnel, in a derivative action, apart from statute. A few statutes permit the court to assess the plaintiff-shareholder for such expenses where the derivative action was brought without reasonable cause. Under security-for-expenses statutes, where security has been posted, the corporation may have recourse thereto in such amount as the court may determine upon the termination of the derivative action. Improper expenditure of corporate funds in defense of litigation give rise to a corporate cause of action which might be asserted against those responsible therefor either by or in behalf of the corporation.

---

19. Shoe Corp. of America v. Comm'r, 29 T.C. 297 (1957); Estate of Steckel v. Comm'r, 26 T.C. 600 (1956).

20. See section 373 supra.

21. Perlman v. Feldmann, 160 F.Supp. 310 (D.Conn. 1958).

22. Di Tomasso v. Loverro, 250 App.Div. 206, 293 N. Y.S. 912 (2d Dep't 1937), aff'd mem., 276 N.Y. 551, 12 N.E.2d 570 (1937), motion for reargument or to amend remittitur denied 276 N.Y. 610, 12 N.E.2d 601 (1937); Id., 276 N.Y. 681, 13 N.E.2d 59 (1938). But see May v. Midwest Refining Co., 121 F.2d 431 (1st Cir. 1941), cert. denied 314 U.S. 668, 62 S.Ct. 129, 86 L.Ed. 534 (1941).

23. Slayton v. Missouri Pacific R. R., 279 F.Supp. 525 (E.D.Mo.1968) (award against corporation of $548,161 fees and $41,926 disbursements to attorneys representing shareholders in class action challenging consolidation plan); Matter of Caplan v. Lionel Corp., 23 A.D.2d 655, 257 N.Y.S.2d 644 (1st Dep't 1965), aff'd mem., 18 N.Y.2d 945, 277 N.Y.S.2d 144, 223 N.E.2d 568 (1966) (award of $30,000 counsel fees from corporation for successful proceeding to set aside election of directors in sale of control situation). In Richman v. DeVal Aerodynamics, Inc., 40 Del.Ch. 548, 185 A.2d 884 (Ch.1962), a plaintiff-shareholder, in behalf of a group of shareholders, enjoined certain contemplated board of directors action and sought counsel fees from the corporation. The court stated that it was settled Delaware law that the characterization of an action as derivative or representative was immaterial for such purpose, the question being whether such benefits had been conferred either on the corporation or on the shareholders as would permit recovery of expenses from the corporation. A "substantial" benefit to the class of which plaintiff was a mem-

ber was found, requiring, in equity, payment by the class as a whole. Accordingly, plaintiff's counsel was awarded a fee of $5,000 plus disbursements from the corporation. See also Mencher v. Sachs, 39 Del.Ch. 366, 164 A.2d 320 (Sup.Ct.1960) (upholding allowance of $10,000 for compelling corporate election and of $30,000 for action to cancel shares where both proceedings were consolidated). In Sarner v. Sarner, 38 N.J. 463, 185 A.2d 851 (1962), two minority shareholders, each holding 10 percent of the shares, sued the other shareholder, owner of 80 percent of the shares, joining corporate claims and personal claims in the same action. After a substantial judgment was awarded in favor of the corporation and against the individual defendant, the plaintiff sought counsel fees. Under the New Jersey statutory provision that no fees for legal services should be allowed except "out of a fund in court", the court held that such a fund existed and justified an allowance of $25,000. The case was remanded for further proof as to the value of the services in connection with the derivative claim and those in connection with the non-derivative claim on the theory that no counsel fees should be allowed with respect to the enforcement of the litigants' personal rights.

24. Cherner v. Transitron Electronic Corp., 221 F. Supp. 55 (D.Mass.1963). See note 18 supra.

25. See Riddell v. Cascade Paper Co., 56 Wash.2d 663, 355 P.2d 3 (1960); Edelman v. Goodman, 47 Misc.2d 8, 261 N.Y.S.2d 618 (Sup.Ct.1965).

Attorneys' fees and other expenses of parties in litigation are, apart from statute, ordinarily borne by the respective parties themselves. General statutory provisions for assessment of costs by the winning party against the losing party usually include certain court costs and specified disbursements but not attorneys' fees.[1]

In a few jurisdictions, statutes provide that in a shareholder derivative action the court having jurisdiction, upon final judgment and a finding that the action was brought without reasonable cause, may require the plaintiff or plaintiffs to pay to the parties named as defendant the reasonable expenses, including attorneys' fees, incurred by them in the defense of such action.[2]

As previously discussed,[3] several jurisdictions have security-for-expenses statutes which enable the corporation in a shareholder derivative action to require small shareholder-plaintiffs[4] to post security for expenses. Where such security is posted, the corporation may have recourse thereto in such amount as the court may determine upon the termination of the action.

In jurisdictions without such statutes and in jurisdictions with security-for-expenses statutes where security has not been posted, because the plaintiff-shareholder either failed to do so on demand[5] or met the quantum requirement[6] or the corporation failed to make application for such security, the corporation must, regardless of the outcome of the litigation and whether it was brought with or without reasonable cause, bear its own expenses[7] and possibly the expenses of defendant directors, officers, and employees.[8]

Ordinarily in a derivative action the corporation should have counsel independent from the attorneys representing defendant directors, officers, and employees.[9] Otherwise, apart from problems of conflicting interests, the propriety of the payment of corporate funds to common counsel can lead to embarrassment.[10]

Where corporate management improperly expends corporate funds in defense or settlement of litigation, such mismanagement gives rise to a corporate cause of action which can be asserted against those responsible therefor either by or in behalf of the corporation.[11]

more than five percent of outstanding shares who did not and could not be required to post security for expenses under New York statute held not liable for such expenses to successful corporation).

7. See section 372, n. 8 supra. See also Byram Concretanks, Inc. v. Warren Concrete Products Co., 374 F.2d 649 (3d Cir. 1967).

8. See sections 379, 380 infra. As to deductibility by corporation of litigation expenses for federal income tax purposes, see Comm'r v. Tellier, 383 U.S. 687, 86 S.Ct. 1118, 16 L.Ed.2d 185 (1966); Iowa Southern Utilities Co. v. Comm'r, 333 F.2d 382 (8th Cir. 1964); Comm'r v. Longhorn Portland Cement Co., 148 F.2d 276 (5th Cir. 1945).

9. See section 370 supra.

10. Heller v. Boylan, 29 N.Y.S.2d 653 (Sup.Ct.1941), aff'd mem., 263 App.Div. 815, 32 N.Y.S.2d 131 (1st Dep't 1941), motion for leave to appeal or reargument denied 263 App.Div. 852, 32 N.Y.S.2d 1011 (1st Dep't 1942); cf. Otis & Co. v. Pennsylvania R. R., 57 F.Supp. 680 (E.D.Pa.1944); Esposito v. Riverside Sand & Gravel Co., 287 Mass. 185, 191 N.E. 363 (1934); Simon v. Socony-Vacuum Oil Co., 179 Misc. 202, 38 N.Y.S.2d 270 (Sup.Ct.1942), aff'd mem., 267 App.Div. 890, 47 N.Y.S.2d 589 (1st Dep't 1944); Kelley v. 74 & 76 West Tremont Ave. Corp., 24 Misc.2d 370, 198 N.Y.S.2d 721 (Sup.Ct.1960).

11. Wilson v. Jennings, 344 Mass. 608, 184 N.E.2d 642 (1962), held that two defendant shareholders-directors-officers sued by other shareholders in two actions—one derivative and the other in their own behalf—were properly ordered to reimburse the corporation for its counsel fees, costs and expenses in each case. See sections 231–236, 238 supra. See also Wilshire Oil Co. v. Riffe, 409 F.2d 1277 (10th

1. E. g., J. Weinstein, H. Korn & A. Miller, Weinstein-Korn-Miller Manual—CPLR ch. 33 (1967).

2. ABA–ALI Model Bus.Corp.Act § 43A (optional section); North Dakota, Rhode Island; a similar provision was deleted from the proposed New York Business Corporation Law. The Colorado provision expressly excludes attorneys' fees.

3. See section 372 supra.

4. See section 372, n. 3 supra. California does not limit its security-for-expenses provision to small shareholders.

5. Tyler v. Gas Consumers Ass'n, 35 Misc.2d 801, 231 N.Y.S.2d 15 (Sup.Ct.1962). See section 372 supra.

6. Isensee v. Long Island Motion Picture Co., 184 Misc. 625, 54 N.Y.S.2d 556 (Sup.Ct.1945) (holder of

LITIGATION EXPENSES OF DIRECTORS, OFFICERS, AND OTHER CORPORATE PERSONNEL—AT COMMON LAW

379. Directors, officers, and other corporate personnel are not entitled to indemnification by their corporation of their litigation expenses where their defense has been unsuccessful except possibly where such defense has benefited the corporation. Where their defense is successful, a few cases have recognized a common-law right of indemnification, while occasional other cases have held to the contrary at least where such defense has not benefited the corporation. With respect to a corporation's power to indemnify, apart from statute, the result depends on judicial attitudes toward indemnification, whether the expenses were incurred in a derivative or nonderivative action, the existence of an intracorporate provision authorizing indemnification, and the procedures followed in connection therewith. Where there is power to indemnify, the corporation can presumably agree, even in advance, to indemnify, thus in effect creating a duty to indemnify. The same principles should apply to corporate advances for litigation expenses, subject to recoupment if the indemnified defendants have been found to have wronged the corporation, as apply to reimbursement, and to the corporation's purchasing insurance covering the litigation expenses of itself and its personnel. Judicial hostility toward indemnification, and lack of any judicial authority in most jurisdictions, have resulted in increasing intracorporate provision for indemnification and statutory enactments. Even in jurisdictions with such statutes, the prior law remains relevant as to the construction of the statute and the validity of indemnification arrangements not affected by the statute.

In performing their functions, corporate directors, officers, and employees assume a certain financial risk, attributable not only to the existence of the derivative remedy but also to other potential litigation—criminal and nonderivative civil actions. When successful in a civil action asserting a corporate claim against them, they in effect defeat such corporate claim; when unsuccessful they have been found to have wronged the corporation.

Unlike the right to reimbursement possessed by the successful plaintiff-shareholder, the right of directors, officers, and employees to recover litigation expenses may often result from an indemnification statute or a right by way of articles of incorporation, bylaws, resolution, or agreement.

Under the common-law rule there is no right of indemnification accruing to a director, officer, or employee who is unsuccessful in his defense of an action. A possible exception to this rule exists where his defense, even though unsuccessful, substantially benefited the corporation.[1]

However, where the defense proves successful, there is a split of authority as to whether a common-law right of indemnification arises.[2] New Jersey[3] and Minnesota[4]

Cir. 1969); Esposito v. Riverside Sand & Gravel Co., 287 Mass. 185, 191 N.E. 363 (1934); Albrecht, Maguire & Co. v. General Plastics, Inc., 256 App.Div. 134, 9 N.Y.S.2d 415 (4th Dep't 1939), aff'd mem., 280 N.Y. 840, 21 N.E.2d 887 (1939).

1. Hornstein, "The Counsel Fee in Stockholders' Derivative Suits", 39 Colum.L.Rev. 784, 816 (1939); Comment, "Indemnification of Litigation Expenses", 52 Mich.L.Rev. 1023, 1025–26 (1954). See Godley v. Crandall & Godley Co., 153 App.Div. 697, 139 N.Y.S. 236 (1st Dep't 1912), modified 212 N.Y. 121, 105 N.E. 818 (1914), 181 App.Div. 75, 168 N.Y.S. 251 (1st Dep't 1917), aff'd mem., 227 N.Y. 656, 126 N.E. 908 (1920); Warnecke v. Forty Wall Street Bldg., Inc., 16 Misc.2d 467, 183 N.Y.S.2d 925 (Sup.Ct.1959), aff'd sub nom. Marine Midland Trust Co. of New York v. Forty Wall Street Corp., 13 A.D.2d 630, 215 N.Y.S. 2d 720 (1st Dep't 1961), reargument denied, 13 A.D. 2d 760, 216 N.Y.S.2d 674 (1st Dep't 1961), aff'd mem., 11 N.Y.2d 679, 225 N.Y.S.2d 755, 180 N.E.2d 909 (1962).

2. Indemnification of directors is, apart from statute, different from indemnification of officers and employees who, as agents of the corporation, might enjoy protection under principles of agency law. 2 Restatement, Second, Agency §§ 439 et seq. (1958); Cohn v. Lionel Corp., 21 N.Y.2d 559, 289 N.Y.S.2d 404, 236 N.E.2d 634 (1968) (upholding implied promise of indemnity by corporation to agent for damages resulting from good faith execution of agency). So far as directors are concerned, analogizing them to trustees who are entitled to equitable indemnification under principles of trust law would support a finding of a corporate duty to indemnify them, whereas treating directors as sui generis might not. See generally G. Washington & J. Bishop, Indemnifying the Corporate Executive; Business, Legal,

3, 4. See notes 3, 4 on page 801.

have recognized that such a common-law right exists, while New York [5] and England [6] have reached the opposite conclusion.

Illustrative of the conflicting views are the New York case of New York Dock Co. v. McCollum [7] and the New Jersey case of Solimine v. Hollander.[8]

and Tax Aspects of Reimbursement for Personal Liability (1963); Cheek, "Control of Corporate Indemnification: A Proposed Statute", 22 Vand.L. Rev. 255 (1969); Rogers, "Indemnification of Savings Association Officers and Directors," 32 Legal Bull. 135 (1966); Bishop, "Indemnification of Corporate Directors, Officers and Employees", 20 Bus. Law. 833 (1965); Frampton, "Indemnification of Insiders' Litigation Expenses", 23 Law & Contemp. Prob. 325 (1958); Hornstein, "Directors' Expenses in Stockholders' Suits", 43 Colum.L.Rev. 301 (1943); Bates & Zuckert, "Directors' Indemnity: Corporate Policy or Public Policy", 20 Harv.Bus.Rev. 244 (1942); Washington, "Litigation Expenses of Corporate Directors in Stockholders' Suits", 40 Colum.L. Rev. 431 (1940); Comment, "Indemnifying the Corporate Directors for Litigation Expenses", 28 U. Pitt.L.Rev. 114 (1966); Comment, "The Corporate Agent and His Right to Compel Reimbursement for Expenses Incurred in Defense of the Entity", 10 St.Louis U.L.J. 10 (1965); Note, "Right in Wisconsin of Directors, Officers and Employees to Indemnification by Their Corporation", 46 Marq.L.Rev. 94 (1962). As to indemnification of union officials, see Comment, "Counsel Fees for Union Officers under the Fiduciary Provision of Landrum-Griffin", 73 Yale L.J. 443 (1964); Annot., 152 A.L.R. 909 (1944), 39 A.L.R.2d 580 (1955). The New York statute limits its statutory indemnification provisions to directors and officers, expressly providing that nothing in the statute shall affect any rights to indemnification to which corporate personnel other than directors and officers may be entitled by contract or otherwise under law. See note 13 infra.

3. Solimine v. Hollander, 129 N.J.Eq. 264, 19 A.2d 344 (1941).

4. In re E. C. Warner Co., 232 Minn. 207, 45 N.W.2d 388 (1950). But cf. Tomash v. Midwest Technical Development Corp., 281 Minn. 21, 160 N.W.2d 273 (1968) (corporation held not required to indemnify former directors not entirely vindicated of misconduct in direct action brought against them by S.E. C.).

5. New York Dock Co. v. McCollum, 173 Misc. 106, 16 N.Y.S.2d 844 (Sup.Ct.1939); Bailey v. Bush Terminal Co., 46 N.Y.S.2d 877 (Sup.Ct.1943), aff'd mem., 267 App.Div. 899, 48 N.Y.S.2d 324 (1st Dep't 1944), aff'd mem., 293 N.Y. 735, 56 N.E.2d 739 (1944).

6. Tomlinson v. Liquidators of Scottish Amalgamated Silks, Ltd., 1935 Sess.Cas. 1 (H.L.).

7. 173 Misc. 106, 16 N.Y.S.2d 844 (Sup.Ct.1939) Crouch, Official Referee, who decided the case, was a retired New York Court of Appeals judge, which added to the significance of the holding.

8. 129 N.J.Eq. 264, 19 A.2d 344 (1941).

The New York case was an action for declaratory judgment, brought by the corporation against certain of its directors, alleging that a shareholder had previously brought a derivative action against the directors charging misconduct, and asking for the appointment of a receiver; that the action had been defeated; that the directors had demanded payment of their expenses by the corporation; and that the corporation sought a declaratory judgment that it was not legally obligated to pay or reimburse such expenses and could not properly do so. The court held that the directors were not entitled to reimbursement since (a) they derived their authority from the state, not from the corporation or its shareholders, and were not in the position of agents entitled to recovery for necessary expenses but were sui generis, and therefore the corporation was not "legally obligated" to reimburse them; (b) there were no equitable considerations, such as conserving some substantial corporate interest or bringing some definite benefit to the corporation, justifying reimbursement or payment; (c) no benefit to the corporation from the directors' defense had been shown, as the dismissal of the petition for a receivership was due to the efforts of the corporation's own counsel; (d) an argument for indemnity based upon public policy had to be rejected in view of the settled state of the law; and (e) if the directors had been entitled to reimbursement they should have applied to the judge who tried the shareholder's action.

In the New Jersey case, the directors had successfully defended a derivative action which alleged negligence, mismanagement, diversion of assets, fraud, and usurpation of corporate opportunities, and asked for an accounting. The court held that the directors, who were essentially trustees, should be entitled to expenses where their defense is sustained and it is adjudged that they have committed no breach of trust or duty. In so holding, the court added (a) that the directors and officers not only had a right but also were under a duty to stand their ground against all unjust attack and to resist the attempt to wrest the corporate trust estate from those hands to which the shareholders had previously committed it; (b) that their defense demonstrated to the investing public the honesty of the corporate management, thus not alone serving their own interests but also performing a duty owed to the beneficiaries of the trust—the shareholders; (c) that benefit to the corporation is not a necessary element of the directors' right to reimbursement or indemnification under such circumstances; and (d) that the same principle applies to the corporation's paying such expenses directly without putting the directors to the necessity of paying in the first instance.

It should be emphasized that the common-law approach has been more concerned with the right of corporate personnel to indemnification (or stated conversely, the duty of the corporation to indemnify), than the power of the corporation to indemnify the director, officer, or employee when it determines to do so.

With respect to the corporation's power to indemnify corporate personnel for litigation expenses, apart from statute, the result depends on judicial attitudes toward indemnification, whether the expenses were incurred in a derivative or nonderivative action, the existence of an intracorporate provision authorizing indemnification, and the procedures followed in connection therewith.

Courts obviously can recognize a power to indemnify, consistent with public policy, more extensive than the duty to indemnify.[9]

Expenses in actions by the corporation or in derivative actions are incurred by the director, etc., to defeat a corporate claim against him [10] whereas third party actions or criminal proceedings against the director, etc., as such do not involve such a factor.[11]

Whether or not the expenses were incurred by the director, etc., as such might also be an issue.[12]

9. Compare Bailey v. Bush Terminal Co., 46 N.Y.S.2d 877 (Sup.Ct.1943), aff'd mem., 267 App.Div. 899, 48 N.Y.S.2d 324 (1st Dep't 1944), aff'd mem., 293 N.Y. 735, 56 N.E.2d 739 (1944) (no duty to reimburse directors absent contract or statute), with New York Dock Co. v. McCollum, 173 Misc. 106, 16 N.Y. S.2d 844 (Sup.Ct.1939) (corporation not "legally obligated" to reimburse in action seeking declaratory judgment that it was not legally obligated and could not properly reimburse).

10. Figge v. Bergenthal, 130 Wis. 594, 109 N.W. 581 (1906) (upholding corporate power to indemnify directors and officers where defense successful, partly on statute of limitations, and indemnification voted by themselves as shareholders); Griesse v. Lang, 37 Ohio 553, 175 N.E. 222 (1931) (no power to indemnify successful directors absent shareholder authorization or benefit to corporation); New York Dock Co. v. McCollum, 173 Misc. 106, 16 N.Y.S.2d 844 (Sup.Ct.1939) (no power to indemnify successful directors absent benefit to corporation); cf. Bailey v. Bush Terminal Co., 46 N.Y.S.2d 877 (Sup.Ct.1943), aff'd mem., 267 App.Div. 899, 48 N.Y.S.2d 324 (1st Dep't 1944), aff'd mem., 293 N.Y. 735, 56 N.E.2d 739 (1944) (power to indemnify successful directors by contract).

11. Simon v. Socony-Vacuum Oil Co., 179 Misc. 202, 38 N.Y.S.2d 270 (Sup.Ct.1942), aff'd mem., 267 App. Div. 890, 47 N.Y.S.2d 589 (1st Dep't 1944), was decided after the adoption of the original New York indemnification statutes passed in 1941 but apparently concerned payments prior to their effective date, and does not refer to the McCollum or Bailey cases or the statutes. The Simon case was a derivative action against the directors of Socony-Vacuum Oil Company seeking to hold the directors liable (a) for damages suffered by the corporation as a result of its participation in a buying program which had been held to be in violation of the antitrust laws, (b) for expenses incurred in defending unsuccessfully the criminal proceedings against the corporation and the directors under the antitrust laws, and (c) for amounts paid by the corporation for the fines of two of the directors who pleaded nolo contendere. The court held for the defendant directors, saying, as to the expenses of the defense, that they had acted in good faith and with reasonable care and that the interests of the corporation were sufficiently threatened to warrant the payment of defense counsel, and, as to the fines paid for the directors who had pleaded nolo contendere, that the corporation benefited by such plea. The case epitomizes the "business judgment" rule. Its language has been carried over into modern statutes. See McKinney's N.Y.Bus.Corp.Law § 723. Also into intracorporate provisions. See Koster v. Warren, 297 F.2d 418 (9th Cir. 1961).

12. Jesse v. Four-Wheel Drive Auto Co., 177 Wis. 627, 189 N.W. 276 (1922). See Essential Enterprises Corp. v. Automatic Steel Products, Inc., 39 Del.Ch. 371, 164 A.2d 437, 82 A.L.R.2d 957 (Ch.1960) (litigation expenses in successfully contesting validity of removal as directors held incurred by reason of

The existence of an intracorporate provision authorizing indemnification might supply the power, especially if in the original articles of incorporation or in an amendment thereof, bylaws, resolution, or agreement approved by disinterested shareholders.[13]

If there is a power to indemnify, either on common-law principles prevailing in the jurisdiction or pursuant to an intracorporate provision therefor in the particular corporation, and such power is exercised to indemnify corporate personnel, questions can arise as to whether such exercise was proper. Involved can be problems of the self-interest of the directors, shareholder ratification, burden of proof, etc.[14]

Where there is power to indemnify, the corporation can presumably agree, even in advance, to pay the expenses, in articles of incorporation, bylaws, resolutions or agreements, thus in effect creating a corporate duty to indemnify.[15]

The same rules should apply to the corporation's advancing the expenses in the first instance, subject to the corporation's recouping such advances if the defendants are found to have wronged the corporation, as apply to corporate reimbursement after the director has paid them, since both are aspects of indemnification.[16] Similar rules should apply to the corporation's purchasing insurance covering the litigation expenses of itself and its personnel.

The cases are sometimes complicated by the difficulty of segregating the expenses of the director's defense from those of the corporation's defense, especially when there is common counsel.[17]

The reluctance of the courts to afford more adequate protection to corporate insiders, not to mention the complete lack of judicial authority on the subject in most jurisdictions, has brought about both intracorporate and statutory changes.

An increasingly large number of corporations have amended their articles of incorporation, passed bylaws, entered into agreements providing for indemnity, or purchased insurance, sometimes exceeding the bounds of propriety.[18]

During the past 20 years, the vast majority of jurisdictions have passed indemnification statutes designed to protect such parties by extending indemnification to expenses incurred in the not unsuccessful defense of actions involving them by reason of their corporate positions. Most of the statutes are drafted in terms of corporate power to in-

being director); Sorensen v. Overland Corp., 242 F. 2d 70 (3d Cir. 1957), aff'g 142 F.Supp. 354 (D.Del. 1956) (litigation expenses held not reimbursable since incurred by president-director in actions against him in individual capacity for conduct prior to his becoming director or officer); Mooney v. Willys-Overland Motors, Inc., 204 F.2d 888, 39 A.L. R.2d 566 (3d Cir. 1953), aff'g 106 F.Supp. 253 (D. Del.1952) (holding expenses incurred as director and officer).

13. Figge v. Bergenthal, 130 Wis. 594, 109 N.W. 581 (1906) (power recognized where approval was by interested shareholders); Griesse v. Lang, 37 Ohio 553, 175 N.E. 222 (1931) (power denied with court pointing out that payment had not been authorized by shareholders); Tomlinson v. Liquidators of Scottish Amalgamated Silks, Ltd., 1935 Sess.Cas. 1 (H. L.) (criminal litigation expenses held not covered by indemnity clause of articles of association). The agent indemnification rules apply only "unless otherwise agreed". 2 Restatement, Second, Agency §§ 439, 440 (1958). See note 2 supra.

14. See section 238 supra. A possible solution of the interested-directors problem is to appoint independent counsel to determine whether or not indemnification is warranted.

15. See Essential Enterprises Corp. v. Dorsey Corp., 40 Del.Ch. 343, 182 A.2d 647 (Ch.1962) (statutory scope of indemnification held restricted by bylaw with respect to partial liability and compromise); Mooney v. Willys-Overland Motors, Inc., 204 F.2d 888, 39 A.L.R.2d 566 (3d Cir. 1953), aff'g 106 F.Supp. 253 (D.Del.1952).

16. See Solimine v. Hollander, 129 N.J.Eq. 264, 19 A. 2d 344 (1941); New York Dock Co. v. McCollum, 173 Misc. 106, 16 N.Y.S.2d 844 (Sup.Ct.1939).

17. Esposito v. Riverside Sand & Gravel Co., 287 Mass. 185, 191 N.E. 363 (1934); Albrecht, Maguire & Co. v. General Plastics, Inc., 256 App.Div. 134, 9 N.Y.S.2d 415 (4th Dep't 1939), aff'd mem., 280 N.Y. 840, 21 N.E.2d 887 (1939). See section 370 supra.

18. Jervis, "Corporate Agreements to Pay Directors' Expenses in Stockholders' Suits", 40 Colum.L.Rev. 1192 (1940). See note 15 supra and note 20 infra.

demnify; several in terms of statutory right of indemnification; some both.[19]

The law in a jurisdiction prior to the statute remains relevant in construing the statute as being declaratory or in derogation of the common law and in determining the validity of indemnification arrangements expressly preserved by the statute or neither covered nor excluded by the statute.[20]

In principle, indemnification of corporate personnel appears sustainable where there has been no breach of duty to the corporation but not otherwise.

LITIGATION EXPENSES OF DIRECTORS, OFFICERS, AND OTHER CORPORATE PERSONNEL—UNDER STATUTES

380. Almost all jurisdictions have enacted statutes for the indemnification by the corporation of the litigation expenses incurred by directors, officers, and possibly other corporate personnel, in the defense of litigation brought against them as such. Most of the statutes are drafted in terms of corporate power to indemnify; several in terms of a statutory right of indemnification; some with both features. Most of the statutes are not limited to derivative actions, and expressly or impliedly permit broader indemnification than that provided by the statute, sometimes expressly requiring shareholder approval therefor. Usually indemnification is precluded only where the director, officer, etc., has been adjudged liable for negligence or misconduct in the performance of his duty, or of his duty to the corporation, or, by the most permissive formulation to date, where he had not acted in good faith and in a manner he reasonably believed to be in or not opposed to the best interests of the corporation. Several statutes expressly refer to settlements, some of them requiring court, disinterested board of directors, or shareholder approval. Recent highly permissive statutes empower corporations to purchase and maintain insurance for

their directors, officers, or other personnel, against any liability relating to their corporate positions, whether or not the corporation would have the power to indemnify such person against such liability.

Almost all American jurisdictions, beginning with New York in 1941,[1] have enacted statutes for the indemnification by corporation of the litigation expenses incurred by directors, officers, and possibly other corporate personnel, in the defense of litigation brought against them as such.[2]

1. Formerly McKinney's N.Y.Gen.Corp.Law §§ 27–a and 61–a, amended and consolidated in 1945 as McKinney's N.Y.Gen.Corp.Law, art. 6A; [1945] N.Y.L. Rev'n Comm'n Rep.1945 Legis.Doc.No.65(E) 131–175; [1957] N.Y.L.Rev'n Comm'n Rep.1957 Legis.Doc.No. 65(J) 315–345. In Hayman v. Morris, 37 N.Y.S.2d 884 (Sup.Ct.1942), when reimbursement was sought against a Virginia corporation under the original New York court-award-of-expenses statute, the statute was held to be constitutional on the grounds, among others, that attorney's fees could be assimilated to and awarded as costs, that such remedial legislation can operate retroactively to pending actions, and that the legislature can impose assessment upon foreign corporation as a condition on which the right to do business within the state depends. The present New York Business Corporation Law expressly authorizes advances by the corporation or court award of expenses pendente lite, subject to recoupment by the corporation where they exceed the amount to which the director or officer is ultimately entitled to indemnification; Professional Ins. Co. v. Barry, 60 Misc.2d 424, 303 N.Y.S. 2d 556 (Sup.Ct.1969). New York's indemnification provisions apply to domestic corporations and nonexempt foreign corporations. The 1967 Model Act revision also permits a corporation to advance expenses upon the recipient's undertaking to repay such amount unless it shall ultimately be determined that he was entitled to indemnification. ABA–ALI Model Bus.Corp.Act § 4A; Delaware, Georgia, Iowa, Kansas, Louisiana, Nevada, New Jersey, Pennsylvania, Tennessee (advances by corporation and court award of expenses pendente lite), Virginia.

2. E. g., ABA–ALI Model Bus.Corp.Act § 4(o), supplanted by § 4A, renumbered § 5. Six jurisdictions still lack statutes: Alabama, Idaho, Illinois, New Hampshire, Oklahoma, Vermont. See generally G. Washington & J. Bishop, Indemnifying the Corporate Executive; Business, Legal, and Tax Aspects of Reimbursement for Personal Liability (1963); Cheek, "Control of Corporate Indemnification: A Proposed Statute", 22 Vand.L.Rev. 255 (1969); Bishop, "Sitting Ducks and Decoy Ducks: New Trends in the Indemnification of Corporate Directors and Officers", 77 Yale L.J. 1078 (1968); Sebring, "Recent Legislative Changes in the Law of Indemnification of Directors, Officers and Others", 23 Bus.Law. (1967); Frampton, "Indemnification of In-

19. See section 380 infra.

20. E. g., ABA–ALI Model Bus.Corp.Act §§ 4(o), 4A; Connecticut, Maine, Missouri, New Jersey, New York, Rhode Island, Wisconsin. But see California. Mooney v. Willys-Overland Motors, Inc., 204 F.2d 888, 39 A.L.R.2d 566 (3d Cir. 1953), aff'g 106 F.Supp. 253 (D.Del.1952). See section 380, n. 7 infra.

Most of the statutes are drafted in terms of corporate power to indemnify;[3] several in terms of a statutory right of indemnification;[4] some with both features.[5]

Most indemnification statutes are not expressly limited to derivative actions; they often have different provisions applicable to actions by or in the right of the corporation (to procure a judgment in its favor) and to other actions and proceedings.[6]

Most of the statutes expressly[7] or impliedly permit broader indemnification than that

---

siders' Litigation Expenses", 23 Law & Contemp. Prob. 325 (1958); Bishop, "Current Status of Corporate Directors' Right to Indemnification", 69 Harv.L.Rev. 1057 (1956); Abrons, "Indemnification of Corporate Officers and Directors for Expenses Incurred in Litigation", 130 N.Y.L.J. No. 92, 1046 (Nov. 19, 1953); Hornstein, "Directors' Expenses in Stockholders' Suits", 43 Colum.L.Rev. 301 (1943); Ballantine, "California's 1943 Statute as to Directors' Litigation Expenses: An Exclusive Remedy for Indemnification of Directors, Officers, and Employees", 31 Calif.L.Rev. 515 (1943); Comment, "Statutory Reimbursement of Litigation Expenses of Director-Defendants in New York", 35 N.Y.U.L. Rev. 827 (1960); Comment, "Indemnification of Litigation Expenses", 52 Mich.L.Rev. 1023 (1954); Note, "Corporate Responsibility for Litigation Expenses of Management", 40 Calif.L.Rev. 104 (1952); Note, "Directors' Reimbursement for Litigation Expenses", 1950 Wis.L.Rev. 157; Annot., 39 A.L.R.2d 580 (1955). Of a different nature are a few statutes authorizing the court in a derivative action upon final judgment and a finding that the action was brought without reasonable cause, to require the plaintiff or plaintiffs to pay to the parties named as defendant the reasonable expenses, including attorney's fees, incurred by them in the defense of such action. ABA–ALI Model Bus.Corp.Act § 43A (optional section); North Dakota, Colorado (expressly excluding attorneys' fees). The California security-for-expenses statute permits not only the corporation but also defendant directors and officers to apply for security from the plaintiff. See section 372 supra. Absent express statutory authority, even successful directors and officers cannot recover their litigation expenses from the plaintiff. Shapiro v. Magaziner, 418 Pa. 278, 210 A.2d 890 (1965); De Mendez v. Davis, 153 N.Y.L.J. No. 107, 18 (Sup.Ct.1965).

3.   E. g., ABA–ALI Model Bus.Corp.Act § 4(o); Alaska, Arizona, California (limited to actions by third parties), Colorado, Connecticut (if authorized by bylaws or resolution adopted by shareholders), Delaware, Florida, Georgia, Hawaii, Indiana, Iowa, Kansas, Louisiana, Maine (if authorized in articles of incorporation or, when approved by shareholders, bylaws or resolution in specific case), Maryland, Michigan, Minnesota, Nebraska, Nevada, New Jersey, New Mexico, North Carolina (limited to nonderivative actions by third parties and criminal proceedings), North Dakota, Ohio, Oregon, Pennsylvania, Rhode Island (if authorized by bylaws), South Carolina, South Dakota, Texas, Utah, Virginia, Washington, West Virginia, Wisconsin, Wyoming, District of Columbia, Puerto Rico. Where there is power to indemnify, the corporation usually can agree in advance to do so (by articles of incorporation, bylaws, resolutions, agreements), thus in effect creating a duty to indemnify.

4.   E. g., Arkansas, California, Kentucky, Maryland, Missouri, Montana, New York, North Carolina, Tennessee.

5.   E. g., California (only with respect to actions by third parties), New York, North Carolina (only with respect to nonderivative actions by third parties and criminal proceedings). Corporate personnel successful on the merits or otherwise enjoy a right to indemnification under the latest Model Act revision and in Delaware, Georgia, Iowa, Kansas, Louisiana, Nevada, New Jersey, Pennsylvania, and Virginia. See notes 33, 34 infra. New York equates power and duty, by limiting court awards of indemnification (except for the general statutory limitations) only to prohibitions or limitations in preexisting intracorporate provisions in effect at the time of the accrual of the alleged cause of action asserted in the action in which the expenses were incurred. A few of the statutes expressly apply to nonexempt foreign as well as domestic corporations. E. g., California, New York, North Carolina. New York limits its indemnification provisions to domestic corporations and nonexempt foreign corporations.

6.   E. g., ABA–ALI Model Bus.Corp.Act §§ 4(o), 4A. Express references to criminal proceedings indicate that the statute is intended to apply to nonderivative actions as well as to actions by or in behalf of the corporation. In a nonderivative action corporate personnel might be held liable to the third party or subject to criminal penalties without having been guilty of negligence or misconduct in the performance of duty, at least to the corporation, and should under such a statute, when consistent with public policy, be indemnified by the corporation for such liability or penalties, as well as for his defense expenses. But see note 21 infra; cf. section 379, n. 11 supra for a case upholding indemnification on common-law principles. If the matter appears doubtful in a particular jurisdiction, it should be covered by appropriate provision in the articles of incorporation, bylaws, or resolutions, preferably with the approval of disinterested shareholders.

7.   E. g., ABA–ALI Model Bus.Corp.Act §§ 4(o), 4A; Alaska, Arizona, Colorado, Delaware, Georgia, Hawaii, Indiana, Iowa, Kansas, Louisiana, Maine, Maryland, Massachusetts, Minnesota, Mississippi, Missouri, Nebraska, Nevada, New Jersey, New Mexico, North Dakota, Ohio, Oregon, Pennsylvania, Rhode Island, South Dakota, Texas, Utah, Virginia,

provided by the statute,[8] sometimes expressly requiring shareholder approval therefor.[9] Such broader indemnification presumably is subject to public policy limitations,[10] and may be subject to the common-law indemnification rules prevailing in the particular jurisdiction.[11]

A typical example of a power-to-indemnify statute is found in the 1959 revision of the Model Business Corporation Act,[12] supplanted in 1967.

Washington, West Virginia, Wisconsin, Wyoming, District of Columbia, Puerto Rico.

8. California (except with respect to expenses incurred in actions by third parties) and North Carolina expressly limit indemnification to that provided for in the statute. Kentucky empowers a corporation to indemnify as set out in the mandatory indemnification provision. New York and Tennessee make their indemnification provisions exclusive with respect to directors and officers, providing that nothing therein contained shall affect any rights to indemnification to which corporate personnel other than directors and officers may be entitled by contract or otherwise under law. In view of the exclusivity of the New York statutory provisions for indemnification of directors and officers, any intracorporate provision therefor will either operate to limit the statutory scope of indemnification or constitute surplusage; intracorporate provisions, of course, remain desirable with respect to the indemnification of corporate personnel other than directors and officers. The Model Business Corporation Act provisions have never been exclusive. The 1967 Model Act provision states that the indemnification therein provided shall not be deemed exclusive of any other rights to which those indemnified may be entitled under any bylaw, agreement, vote of shareholders or disinterested directors or otherwise.

9. E. g., ABA–ALI Model Bus.Corp.Act § 4(o); Michigan, Nebraska. In any case, the problem of the self-interest of directors suggests the importance of disinterested shareholder approval. See section 238 supra. Delaware, Georgia, Iowa, Kansas, Nevada, New Jersey, New York, Pennsylvania, Tennessee, and Virginia permit, as an alternative, the written opinion of independent legal counsel that indemnification is proper.

10. E. g., "business judgment" rule. See section 242 supra.

11. See section 379 supra.

12. ABA–ALI Model Bus.Corp.Act § 4(o). See id. § 4A, drafted in 1967 in collaboration with the Delaware corporate law revisers, discussed in text accompanying note 14 infra. The Model Act provision, prior to the 1957 and 1959 revisions concluded with the following clause: ". . . but such indemnification shall not be deemed exclusive of

The most comprehensive, sophisticated, and sound indemnification statutes are found in California, New York, and North Carolina, with their different provisions governing indemnification in actions by or in the right of the corporation and other actions, such actions as by third parties and criminal proceedings.[13]

In 1967, in collaboration with the Delaware corporate law revisers, the Model Business Corporation Act committee approved a new Section 4A, to supplant Section 4(o). As a result, the Model Act provision and the new 1967 Delaware indemnification provision are almost identical.[14] Other jurisdictions, concerned with promoting local incorporation and deterring their domestic corporations from migrating to other jurisdictions of incorporation, have climbed on the band wagon.[15]

As to the corporate personnel indemnifiable under statute, all of the statutes expressly include directors and officers. Some also expressly include employees.[16] Most of stat-

any other rights to which such director or officer may be entitled, under any by-law, agreement, vote of shareholders, or otherwise." Alaska, Colorado, Minnesota, North Dakota, Texas, District of Columbia, and Puerto Rico have provisions substantially similar to the pre-1957 provision of the Model Act. The 1957 and 1959 revisions were adopted by Hawaii, Indiana, Maine, Nebraska, New Mexico, Washington, West Virginia, and Wisconsin. Some jurisdictions expressly permit the articles of incorporation to limit the corporation's powers. E. g., ABA–ALI Model Bus.Corp.Act § 48(i).

13. Cal.Gen.Corp.Law, §§ 834(b), 830 (1947); McKinney's N.Y.Bus.Corp.Law, §§ 721–726; N.C.Bus.Corp.Act §§ 55–19—55–21 (1957); Ballantine, "California's 1943 Statute as to Directors' Litigation Expenses: An Exclusive Remedy for Indemnification of Directors, Officers, and Employees", 31 Calif.L.Rev. 515 (1943); Latty. Powers & Breckenridge, "Proposed North Carolina Business Corporation Act", 33 N.C.L.Rev. 26 (1954). See notes 39–42 infra.

14. Sebring, "Recent Legislative Changes in the Law of Indemnification of Directors, Officers, and Others", 23 Bus.Law. 95 (1967).

15. E. g., Georgia, Iowa, Kansas, Louisiana, Nevada, New Jersey, Pennsylvania, Virginia.

16. E. g., ABA–ALI Model Bus.Corp.Act § 4A, California, Connecticut, Delaware, Georgia, Indiana, Iowa, Kansas, Louisiana, Massachusetts, Nevada,

utes expressly refer to persons formerly as well as presently in the specified capacities.[17] A few include controlling shareholders.[18] Several cover persons serving other corporations having specified connections with the corporation involved.[19] Several statutes expressly refer to personal representatives, heirs, devisees, and the like, of persons in the specified capacities.

Most of the statutes apply to the specified personnel made parties to "any action, suit or proceeding", without further definition.[20]

New Jersey, New York, Ohio, Pennsylvania, Rhode Island, South Carolina, Tennessee (like New York), Virginia. With respect to corporate personnel other than directors and officers in New York, see McKinney's N.Y.Bus.Corp.Law, § 721.

17. But see former N.J.Gen.Corp.Law, § 14:3–14 (1937) (present or future directors or officers).

18. Connecticut, North Carolina. Quaere, as to the indemnification of shareholders upon whom, instead of directors, liability for managerial acts or omissions is imposed, where such shareholders substantially divest the board of directors of its management functions, such as under McKinney's N.Y. Bus.Corp.Law, § 620(b).

19. Serving at its request as director or officer of another corporation in which it owns shares of capital stock or of which it is a creditor (e. g., ABA–ALI Model Bus.Corp.Act § 4(o)); serving any other corporation in which it owns shares (e. g., Missouri); serving any majority-owned subsidiary (e. g., Rhode Island); serving any other corporation at the request of the corporation (e. g., Connecticut). Such directors are called "lend-lease" directors.

20. Some statutes refer to "any action, suit or proceeding, civil or criminal". ABA–ALI Model Bus. Corp.Act § 4(o) (1957 addendum); Hawaii, Indiana, Nebraska, Virginia. Rhode Island refers to "legal or administrative proceeding; the Wisconsin mandatory indemnification provision applies to persons made parties or threatened with "any civil, criminal or administrative action, suit or proceeding"; the 1967 Model Act revision, followed in a growing number of jurisdictions, refers to "any threatened, pending or completed action, suit or proceeding, whether civil, criminal, administrative or investigative". The 1967 Model Act revision, California, Connecticut (to some extent), Delaware, Georgia, Iowa, Kansas, Louisiana, Nevada, New Jersey, New York, North Carolina, Pennsylvania, Tennessee, and Virginia have separate provisions for (a) actions by or in the right of the corporation, and (b) other actions (including threatened actions in many jurisdictions), i. e., actions by third parties or, expressly or impliedly, criminal proceedings. The New York, Tennessee, and Wisconsin statutes expressly refer to appeals. Indemnification in threatened actions,

In *Schwarz v. General Aniline & Film Corp.*,[21] the petitioner was a director who had been indicted, along with the corporation and other defendants, for alleged violations of the federal antitrust laws. In an effort to reduce litigation expenses, the defendant had pleaded nolo contendere and had been fined $500. He then initiated a proceeding to recover his litigation expenses under the statutory right of reimbursement, there being in the case no provision in the applicable articles of incorporation by bylaws or any resolution for reimbursement. The lower courts held that a plea of nolo contendere combined with a fine in an antitrust proceeding amounted to an adjudication of misconduct in the performance of his duties, thus barring a statutory right of reimbursement.[22] The New York Court of Appeals, 4 to 3, affirmed on other grounds, holding that the statutory right of reimbursement applied only with respect to "any action, suit or proceeding" and was not intended to apply to criminal proceedings and therefore denied the petitioner's claim. The dissent argued that there was no essential difference between a criminal prosecution and a civil action under the federal antitrust laws, that the statute contemplated reimbursement in either case, and that the plea of nolo contendere did not amount to an adjudication of misconduct in the performance of any duties owed to the corporation. Carswell, J.,[23] concurring in an opinion with

next to insurance beyond powers of indemnification, poses the greatest threat of corporate chicanery.

21. 305 N.Y. 395, 113 N.E.2d 533 (1953). Accord, Halbach v. General Dyestuff Corp., 283 App.Div. 782, 129 N.Y.S.2d 492 (1st Dep't 1954), motion for leave to appeal denied 283 App.Div. 870, 129 N.Y.S.2d 919 (1st Dep't 1954), 307 N.Y. 941, 122 N.E.2d 337 (1954) (assessment of indemnification denied despite acquittal in federal criminal antitrust action).

22. 279 App.Div. 996, 112 N.Y.S.2d 146 (1st Dep't 1952) (Van Voorhis, J., dissenting), aff'g 198 Misc. 1046, 112 N.Y.S.2d 325 (Sup.Ct.1951).

23. Sitting for Van Voorhis, J., elevated to the Court of Appeals from the Appellate Division while the appeal was pending, whose views in the Appellate Di-

which the other majority judges agreed, indicated that reimbursement provisions in the articles of incorporation, or shareholder by-law or resolution, might validly extend to criminal proceedings.[24]

vision agreed with those of the three dissenting judges of the Court of Appeals.

24. See section 379, n. 11 supra. There was a subsequent attempt to "broaden" the New York statute. [1957] N.Y.L.Rev'n Comm'n Rep.1957 Legis.Doc.No. 65(J) 315–345. The revision was not enacted, primarily because of the objections of the corporate bar that the revision would have been more restrictive than the common-law corporate power to indemnify as exemplified by Simon v. Socony-Vacuum Oil Co., 179 Misc. 202, 38 N.Y.S.2d 270 (Sup.Ct.1942), aff'd mem., 267 App.Div. 890, 47 N.Y.S.2d 589 (1st Dep't 1944). Because of the construction of the then duty-to-indemnify statute in the Schwarz case, many corporations amended their bylaws by shareholder vote or entered into express contracts with their directors and officers providing for reimbursement of expenses in criminal proceedings as well as civil actions, and barring reimbursement only where the person had been adjudged liable for negligence or misconduct in the performance of his duties to the corporation, and providing that in criminal litigation, a conviction or judgment (whether based on a plea of guilty or nolo contendere or its equivalent, or after trial) should not be deemed an adjudication of liability for negligence or misconduct in the performance of one's duties if one were acting in good faith in what one considered to be the best interests of the corporation and with no reasonable cause to believe that the action was illegal. Such a provision, in effect, required reimbursement whenever the corporate director or officer was found to have acted with innocent intent and within the "business judgment" rule. See section 242 supra. Such a provision was based on the assumption that the then power-to-indemnify statutory provision was partially declaratory of the common law (unlike the then duty-to-indemnify statutory provision which was in derogation thereof) and that the former's saving clause, by referring to rights of corporate personnel apart from the statute, recognized and preserved some power in the corporation not only to make reimbursement but to bind itself in advance to reimburse beyond the literal confines of the language, but not beyond the public policy scope of the power-to-indemnify statutory provision. This approach would uphold reimbursement provisions by express contract, as well as by articles of incorporation, bylaws, or resolution—the means listed in the power-to-indemnify statutory provision—and provisions applicable to criminal proceedings as well as civil actions—to which the statutory phrase in the duty-to-indemnify statutory provision (and common to the power-to-indemnify statutory provision) was held in the Schwarz case to be limited; it also construes the statutory term "duties" as meaning duties to the corporation under the "business judgment" rule. While reimbursement provisions in the articles of incorporation, by-laws, or resolutions should be treated similarly

An important consideration involved in indemnification statutes is the degree of success required for indemnification. The former prevalent standard was that the director or officer, etc., be not "adjudged liable for negligence or misconduct in the performance of his duty".[25] Simply and literally stated, such a rule is negative: only an adjudication of liability will preclude indemnification. Thus, under such formulations, indemnification has been awarded where the

since the power-to-indemnify statutory provision applies the same standards to all three, a provision in the articles of incorporation must be acceptable to the secretary of state for filing. The New York secretary of state, despite Judge Carswell's dictum in his concurring opinion in the Schwarz case, with which the three other majority judges expressly agreed, the three-judge dissenting opinion, and the views of Van Voorhis, J., expressed in the Appellate Division (see notes 22, 23 supra), refused to accept articles of incorporation providing for indemnification of expenses incurred in criminal proceedings. 7 S. Slutsky, White on New York Corporations ¶ 8.26 (12th ed. 1953, Supp.1960). A bylaw or resolution bypasses such administrative scrutiny. So, also, of course, does an express indemnification agreement between the corporation and its personnel. The articles of incorporation and any amendment thereof obviously require shareholder approval. In the case of an express agreement, the problem of self-dealing should be recognized and alleviated so far as possible by disinterested shareholder ratification and appropriate self-dealing provision in the articles of incorporation. See section 238 supra.

25. E. g., ABA–ALI Model Bus.Corp.Act § 4(o) (1957 addendum); Alaska, Colorado, Hawaii, Kansas, Kentucky, Maryland, Mississippi, New York, North Dakota, Ohio, Rhode Island, South Dakota, Texas, Utah, Wyoming, District of Columbia, Puerto Rico. The Missouri statute provides for indemnification except where the party is adjudged liable for negligence or misconduct; the Montana statute refers to actual negligence or misconduct. Michigan excludes indemnification also with respect to such matters as shall be settled by agreement predicated on the existence of such liability. Since the 1959 revision, the Model Act has barred indemnification where the person has been adjudged liable for negligence or misconduct in the performance of duty "to the corporation". ABA–ALI Model Bus.Corp.Act § 4(o) (1959 addendum); Hawaii, Indiana, Maine, Nebraska, New Mexico, Oregon, Washington, Wisconsin. Even where there has been such an adjudication, several statutes allow the court, in view of all circumstances of the case, to determine that the director, officer, etc., is fairly and reasonably entitled to indemnity for such expenses which the court shall deem proper. ABA–ALI Model Bus.Corp.Act § 4A; Delaware, Georgia, Iowa, Louisiana, Nevada, New Jersey, Pennsylvania, Virginia.

derivative action was dismissed because of the plaintiff-shareholder's failure to post the required security-for-expenses,[26] or where the dismissal was based on the statute of limitations.[27]

One case, however, has denied indemnification on equitable grounds even though literally the officer had technically not been adjudged liable for misconduct.[28] Where a director was partially successful and partially unsuccessful, one court awarded counsel fees to both sides.[29] Other courts have been less generous.[30] The lower courts in the Schwarz case [31] had held that a plea of nolo contendere combined with a fine in an antitrust proceeding amounted to an adjudica-

tion of misconduct barring a court award of indemnification.

A growing number of modern statutes, at least when relating to litigation expenses incurred in actions other than those by or in the right of the corporation, provide that the termination of any litigation by judgment, order, settlement, conviction, or upon a plea of nolo contendere or its equivalent, shall not, of itself, create a presumption that the person did not act in good faith and in a manner which he reasonably believed to be in (or not opposed to) the best interests of the corporation, and, with respect to any criminal action or proceeding, had reasonable cause to believe that his conduct was unlawful.[32]

To the extent that the person seeking indemnification was successful on the merits or otherwise in his defense, some modern statutes give him an absolute right to indemnification.[33] Other statutes limit such absolute right to actions where his defense was *wholly* successful.[34]

Many modern statutes, while precluding indemnification of a person who has been adjudged to have breached his duty to the corporation,[35] and giving an absolute right to a person who has been successful on the merits or otherwise,[36] also provide for indemnification of persons who have met prescribed standards. The most prevalent formulation is that a person, to be indemnified, must have acted in good faith and in a manner he reasonably believed to be in (or not opposed to) the best interests of the corpo-

26. Tichner v. Andrews, 193 Misc. 1050, 85 N.Y.S.2d 760 (Sup.Ct.1949), appeal dismissed 275 App.Div. 749, 90 N.Y.S.2d 920 (1st Dep't 1949). See section 372 supra.

27. Dornan v. Humphrey, 278 App.Div. 1010, 106 N.Y.S.2d 142 (4th Dep't 1951), motion for leave to appeal denied 279 App.Div. 848, 110 N.Y.S.2d 471 (4th Dep't 1952), on reargument, 279 App.Div. 1040, 112 N.Y.S.2d 585 (4th Dep't 1952). See section 357 supra.

28. Diamond v. Diamond, 307 N.Y. 263, 120 N.E.2d 819 (1954), reargument denied 307 N.Y. 804, 121 N.E.2d 626 (1954). One of two sole shareholders had brought a derivative action against the other who was also an officer, but the complaint was dismissed because of the plaintiff's participation or acquiescence in the alleged wrong. The lower courts awarded statutory indemnification to the successful defendant-officer on the ground that she had not been adjudged liable for misconduct. The Court of Appeals, 4 to 3, reversed, on the ground that she was so adjudged, pointing out that it would be unconscionable under the circumstances for the corporation to pay the defendant's legal expenses while the plaintiff had to pay her own. See also Matter of Colby, 13 A.D.2d 419, 216 N.Y.S.2d 985 (4th Dep't 1961) (denying reimbursement for expenses in successful defense of criminal proceeding for lack of proof of good faith).

29. Cwerdinski v. Bent (under former McKinney's N.Y.Gen.Corp.Law, § 61–a), cited in F. Wood, Survey and Report Regarding Stockholders' Derivative Suits 115, n. 124 (Chamber of Commerce of the State of New York 1944) ($330,856 to plaintiffs' attorneys; $135,243 to defendants' attorneys).

30. See Teren v. Howard, 322 F.2d 949 (9th Cir. 1963); Bachelder v. Brentwood Lanes, Inc., 369 Mich. 155, 119 N.W.2d 630 (1963); Essential Enterprises Corp. v. Dorsey Corp., 40 Del.Ch. 343, 182 A.2d 647 (Ch.1962).

31. See note 22 supra.

32. ABA–ALI Model Bus.Corp.Act § 4A; Delaware, Georgia, Iowa, Kansas, Louisiana, Nevada, New Jersey, New York, Pennsylvania, Tennessee, Virginia. See Annot., "Plea of Nolo Contendere or Non Vult Contendere", 89 A.L.R.2d 540 (1963).

33. ABA–ALI Model Bus.Corp.Act § 4A; Delaware, Georgia, Iowa, Kansas, Louisiana, Nevada, New Jersey, Pennsylvania, Virginia.

34. E. g., New York, Tennessee.

35. See note 25 supra.

36. See notes 33, 34 supra.

ration, and, with respect to any criminal action or proceeding, had no reasonable cause to believe his conduct was unlawful.[37]

Determination that indemnification is proper under the applicable standards, under modern statutes, is made by (a) the board of directors by majority vote of a quorum consisting of directors who were not parties to the litigation, (b) independent legal counsel in a written opinion, or (c) by the shareholders.[38]

California,[39] Connecticut,[40] New York,[41]

37. ABA–ALI Model Bus.Corp.Act § 4A; Delaware, Georgia, Iowa, Kansas, Louisiana, Nevada, New Jersey, New York, Pennsylvania, Tennessee, Virginia. Arizona requires that the person, to be indemnified, did not act or refuse to act willfully or with gross negligence or with fraudulent or criminal intent. Arkansas and California require that such person's conduct fairly and equitably merits indemnification.

38. ABA–ALI Model Bus.Corp.Act § 4A; Delaware, Georgia, Iowa, Kansas, Louisiana, Nevada, New Jersey, New York, Pennsylvania, Tennessee, Virginia. Directors need not be disinterested so long as they are not parties to the action; independent legal counsel might well specialize in this kind of practice; shareholders need not be disinterested. New York provides that if any expenses or other amounts are paid by way of indemnification, otherwise than by court order or action by the shareholders, the corporation shall, not later than the next annual meeting of the shareholders unless such meeting is held within three months from the date of such payment, and, in any event, within 15 months from the date of such payment, mail to its shareholders of record at the time entitled to vote for the election of directors a statement specifying the persons paid, the amounts paid, and the nature and status at the time of such payment of the litigation or threatened litigation.

39. Cal.Gen.Corp.Law, §§ 834(b), 830 (1947). The California statute provides that in derivative actions and actions by the corporation the party must be successful in whole or in part or there is a court-approved settlement, and the court must find that his conduct fairly and equitably merits such indemnity. For actions or threatened actions by third parties (and impliedly criminal proceedings), the statute authorizes indemnification for expenses, judgments, fines, penalties and settlements, by the board of directors upon a good faith finding that the party was acting in good faith within what he reasonably believed to be the scope of his authority and for a purpose which he reasonably believed to be in the best interests of the corporation or its shareholders. See Brokate v. Hehr Mfg. Co., 243 Cal.App.2d 133, 52 Cal.Rptr. 672 (1966).

40. Conn. Stock Corp. Act § 33–320 (1961). Besides the usual standard that the person not be adjudged liable for negligence or misconduct in the performance of his duty, the Connecticut statute bars indemnity in actions to establish liability to the corporation or any of its shareholders unless either the party was successful in his defense on the merits of the court finds such payment not unreasonable or inequitable.

41. McKinney's N.Y.Bus.Corp.Law §§ 722, 723. The New York statute, which precludes indemnification of directors or officers inconsistent therewith, provides for the indemnification of the reasonable expenses, including attorneys' fees, of any director or officer made a party to an action by or in the right of a corporation to procure a judgment in its favor except in relation to matters as to which the director or officer is adjudged to have breached his duty to the corporation. Such indemnification may not include amounts paid in settling or otherwise disposing of a threatened action, or a pending action with or without court approval, or expenses incurred in defending a threatened action, or a pending action which is settled or otherwise disposed of without court approval. Provision also is made for indemnification of any director or officer made or threatened to be made a party to an action or proceeding other than one by or in the right of the corporation to procure a judgment in its favor, whether civil or criminal, against judgments, fines, amounts paid in settlement and reasonable expenses, including attorneys' fees, if he acted in good faith, for a purpose which he reasonably believed to be in the best interest of the corporation and, in criminal actions or proceedings, in addition, had no reasonable cause to believe that his conduct was unlawful. No adverse presumption results from any unfavorable termination of any such action or proceeding. A person wholly successful on the merits or otherwise in his defense is entitled to indemnification. Otherwise, corporate authorization of indemnification requires a determination that the applicable standard of conduct by (a) the board of directors acting by a quorum of directors who are not parties to the action or proceeding, (b) the board upon the written opinion of independent legal counsel, or (c) the shareholders. Notwithstanding the corporation's failure to provide indemnification shall be awarded by a court to the extent authorized under the statute. Expenses may be advanced by the corporation or allowed by a court pendente lite, subject to repayment to the extent they exceed the indemnification to which the recipient is entitled. New York precludes indemnification where indemnification would be inconsistent (a) with the law of the jurisdiction of incorporation of a foreign corporation which prohibits or otherwise limits such indemnification, or (b) with a provision of the articles of incorporation, a bylaw, a resolution of the board of directors or of the shareholders, an agreement or other proper corporation action, in effect at the time of the accrual of the alleged cause of action asserted in the pending action in which the expenses were incurred or other amounts were paid, which prohibits or otherwise limits indemnification, or (c) with the conditions imposed in any court-approved settlement. Disclosure of payments other than by court order or shareholder action must be

and North Carolina [42] impose high standards for indemnification, especially in actions by or in the right of the corporation (to procure a judgment in its favor), i.e., actions by the corporation or derivative actions. Most statutes refer to expenses [43] "actually and necessarily" or "actually and reasonably" incurred in the defense of the action by a director or officer, etc.,[44] made a party by

made to shareholders. The New York provisions apply to domestic corporations and foreign corporations doing business in the state except as exempted under § 1320. In 1969, New York empowered corporations to purchase and maintain indemnification insurance. McKinney's N.Y.Bus.Corp.Law § 727. See also McKinney's N.Y.Part.Law, § 115–c.

42. N.C.Bus.Corp.Act §§ 55–19—55–21 (1957). The North Carolina statute provides that in derivative actions and actions by the corporation the party must be successful in whole or in part or there is a court-approved settlement, and the court must find that his conduct fairly and equitably merits such indemnity. For nonderivative actions by third parties or criminal proceedings, the statute requires indemnification of expenses, judgments, money decrees, fines, penalties and settlements when the defense is wholly successful on the merits; empowers the board of directors to indemnify when the defense is wholly successful other than solely on the merits; and empowers the corporation with the approval of disinterested shareholders to indemnify when the defense is not wholly successful or is unsuccessful.

43. The statutes variously refer to expenses; claims, liabilities, expenses and costs; claims and liabilities; reasonable expenses, including attorney's fees; expenses for defense, including attorneys' fees; reasonable costs, expenses and counsel fees; liabilities, expenses, counsel fees and costs; reasonable costs, expenses and counsel fees. The Connecticut statute refers to judgments, money decrees, fines, penalties, and settlements; the 1967 Model Act revision, California, Delaware, Georgia, Iowa, Kansas, Louisiana, Nevada, New Jersey, New York, Pennsylvania, Tennessee, and Virginia statutes to judgments, and amounts paid in settlement in actions other than those by or in the right of the corporation (to procure a judgment in its favor). See Warnecke v. Forty Wall Street Bldg., Inc., 16 Misc. 2d 467, 183 N.Y.S.2d 925 (Sup.Ct.1959), aff'd sub nom. Marine Midland Trust Co. of New York v. Forty Wall Street Corp., 13 A.D.2d 630, 215 N.Y.S. 2d 720 (1st Dep't 1961), reargument denied, 13 A.D. 2d 760, 216 N.Y.S.2d 674 (1st Dep't 1961), aff'd mem., 11 N.Y.2d 679, 225 N.Y.S.2d 755, 180 N.E.2d 909 (1962) (petitioning directors' expenses held not incurred in connection with defense of action but rather in aiding plaintiff shareholders against alleged wrongdoing directors).

44. See notes 16–19 supra.

reason of his being or having been such director or officer, etc.[45]

Several indemnification statutes expressly refer to settlements,[46] and some require court approval as a prerequisite to indemnification,[47] regardless of the prevailing rule as to the necessity of court approval of settlements generally.[48] Additional safeguards are imposed by some statutes.[49]

In jurisdictions where the statutes do not refer to settlements, statutory references to expenses "actually and reasonably" or "actually and necessarily" incurred,[50] might be

45. Sorensen v. Overland Corp., 242 F.2d 70 (3d Cir. 1957), aff'g 142 F.Supp. 354 (D.Del.1956); Mooney v. Willys-Overland Motors, Inc., 204 F.2d 888, 39 A. L.R.2d 566 (3d Cir. 1953), aff'g 106 F.Supp. 253 (D. Del.1952). See also Essential Enterprises Corp. v. Automatic Steel Products, Inc., 39 Del.Ch. 371, 164 A.2d 437, 82 A.L.R.2d 957 (Ch.1960); People v. Uran Mining Corp., 26 Misc.2d 957, 206 N.Y.S.2d 455 (Sup.Ct.1960), aff'd 13 A.D.2d 419, 216 N.Y.S.2d 985 (4th Dep't 1961).

46. E. g., California, Connecticut, Kentucky, Missouri, Montana, New York, North Carolina, Rhode Island, Tennessee. Indemnification should not be inconsistent with any condition expressly imposed by the court in approving the settlement.

47. Missouri requires court approval of the settlement. California, Connecticut, New York, and North Carolina require court approval of settlements as prerequisites to indemnification. New York expressly provides that indemnification is not to include (a) amounts paid in settling or otherwise disposing of a threatened action, or pending action with or without court approval, or (b) expenses incurred in defending a threatened action, or pending action settled or otherwise disposed of without court approval.

48. See section 374 supra.

49. Kentucky, Missouri, and Montana require approval of the settlement and indemnification by a disinterested board of directors or shareholders' committee. Missouri and Montana very early permitted reliance on opinion of independent legal counsel as to the propriety of indemnification; to similar effect are the 1967 Model Act revision, Delaware, Georgia, Iowa, Kansas, Louisiana, Nevada, New Jersey, New York, Pennsylvania, Tennessee, and Virginia statutes. North Carolina requires approval of disinterested shareholders for indemnification in cases of settlement of actions by third parties or criminal proceedings. Full disclosure to shareholders of indemnification payments is required by distressingly few jurisdictions.

50. E. g., ABA–ALI Model Bus.Corp.Act § 4(o).

held to cover settlement payments if the corporation had been advised by counsel that the action being settled was without substantial merit and that the settlement payments did not exceed the expenses which would reasonably or necessarily be incurred in litigating the action to a final conclusion. However, it might be desirable, to avoid such doubt, to provide for indemnity for settlement payments by articles of incorporation or bylaw provisions or otherwise, when possible in jurisdictions where such indemnity is not adequately covered by statute.

Some statutes spell out the procedures involved in judicial enforcement of the indemnification right.[51]

Recent highly permissive statutes empower corporations to purchase and maintain insurance for their directors, officers, or other personnel, against any liability relating to their corporate positions, whether or not the corporation would have the power to indemnify such person against such liability.[52]

In connection with the registration of securities under the Federal Securities Act of 1933,[53] the registrant is required to state in the registration statement (but not prospectus) the general effect of any charter provision, bylaw, contract, arrangement, or statute under which any director or officer of the registrant is insured or indemnified in any manner against any liability which he may incur in his capacity as such.[54] In addition, the registration statement might be required to contain a statement that in the event that a claim for indemnification for liabilities arising under the Securities Act is asserted by an officer or director, the registrant will submit to a court of appropriate jurisdiction the question whether or not indemnification by it is against public policy as expressed in the Act, and will be governed by the final adjudication of such issue.[55]

51. E. g., Arkansas, California, Maryland, New York, North Carolina, Tennessee. The sounder procedure is for any application of court award of indemnification to be made in the action or proceeding in which the expenses were incurred or other amounts were paid. See Buchman & Buchman v. Lanston Industries, Inc., 25 Misc.2d 818, 200 N.Y.S.2d 445 (Sup.Ct.1960) (attorneys held improper petitioners despite lack of objection by corporate officer involved).

52. ABA–ALI Model Bus.Corp.Act § 4A; California, Delaware, Georgia, Iowa, Kansas, Louisiana, Massachusetts, Nebraska, Nevada, New Hampshire, New Jersey, New York (subject to several restrictions), North Carolina, Ohio, Oregon, Pennsylvania, Rhode Island, Virginia. Pennsylvania pronounces ex cathedra: "Such insurance is declared to be consistent with the public policy of this Commonwealth." Such coverage is available only after the completion of very detailed questionnaires accompanying the application. The policy usually covers claims against civil liability for negligence, but not, to date, for claims for violation of fiduciary duties, claims for criminal liability or for liabilities under federal securities legislation or for claims for other than money damages. Needless to say, the scope of protection and premiums are not limited by statutes which empower corporations to insure beyond their power to indemnify. Usually there is a deductible provision—say, $20,000—and a coinsurance clause whereby the insured corporate personnel underwrites up to, say, five to 10 percent of the loss on his own. Premiums are also frequently shared, say, 90 percent by the corporation and 10 percent by the persons covered. Some corporations have their personnel pay the premiums out of an offsetting salary increase. Such insurance could provide the basis for quasi-in-rem jurisdiction, by attachment proceedings against the insurance company wherever it is amenable to process, thereby requiring the defendant corporate personnel to appear personally and defend, or to suffer default judgment satisfiable out of the insurance proceeds. See section 354, n. 12 supra. See Forum: "Insurance Against Liabilities of Directors and Officers", 22 Record of N.Y.C.B.A. 342 (1967); Bishop, "Sitting Ducks and Decoy Ducks: New Trends in the Indemnification of Corporate Directors and Officers", 77 Yale L.J. 1078 (1968); Hinsey & DeLancey, "Directors and Officers Liability Insurance—An Approach to Its Evaluation and a Check-list", 23 Bus.Law. 869 (1968); Mace, "Directors and Officers Liability Insurance", 85 Banking L.J. 39 (1968); Brook, "Officers and Directors Liability Insurance", 2 Forum 228 (1967); McIntyre, "Directors' and Officers' Liability Insurance", 42 L.A.B.Bull. 57 (1966); Anderson, "Directors and Officers Liability Insurance", 47 Chi.B. Rec. 31 (1965); "An Innovation in Indemnification", 25 Corp.J. 267 (1968); Comment, "Public Policy and Directors' Liability Insurance", 67 Colum. L.Rev. 716 (1967); Comment, "Liability Insurance for Corporate Executives", 80 Harv.L.Rev. 648 (1967); Annot., 20 A.L.R.2d 343 (1968) (liability insurance coverage as extending to liability for punitive or exemplary damages).

53. See section 295 supra.

54. Form S–1, Part II, Item 29.

55. 3 L. Loss, Securities Regulation 1829 (2d ed. 1961). See also Globus v. Law Research Service,

Proxy statements, when required under the Federal Securities Exchange Act of 1934,[56] also must include certain statements concerning indemnification.[57]

Under the Federal Public Utility Holding Company Act of 1935 [58] and Federal Investment Company Act of 1940,[59] the Securities and Exchange Commission has some control over indemnification provisions.[60] The 1940 Act specifically nullifies excessively broad exculpatory clauses.[61]

The corporation, for income tax purposes, may deduct amounts properly paid to corporate personnel to indemnify them against litigation expenses, including attorneys' fees.[62] However, payment of an officer's fine for a criminal offense has been held not a business expense but a constructive dividend.[63]

---

418 F.2d 1276 (2d Cir.1969); Washington, "The S.E.C. and Directors' Indemnity: Recent Developments", 40 Colum.L.Rev. 1206 (1940); Note, "Indemnification of Directors: The Problems Posed by Federal Securities and Antitrust Legislation", 76 Harv.L.Rev. 1403 (1963).

56. See section 297 supra.

57. 3 L. Loss, Securities Regulation 1832 (2d ed. 1961).

58. See section 299 supra.

59. See section 301 supra.

60. 3 L. Loss, Securities Regulation 1832 (2d ed. 1961).

61. § 17(h), (i), 15 U.S.C.A. § 80a–17(h), (i).

62. See Comm'r v. Tellier, 383 U.S. 687, 86 S.Ct. 1118, 16 L.Ed.2d 185 (1966) (allowing deduction of legal expenses incurred by taxpayer for unsuccessful defense of business-related criminal prosecution under Federal Securities Act and mail fraud statutes as ordinary and necessary business expenses under Int.Rev.Code of 1954, 26 U.S.C.A. § 162(a)). Note, "Income Tax—Corporations—Deduction by Corporate Taxpayer of Defendant Directors' Legal Fees", 28 U.Cin.L.Rev. 118 (1959).

63. Sachs v. Comm'r, 277 F.2d 879 (8th Cir. 1960), cert. denied 364 U.S. 833, 81 S.Ct. 63, 5 L.Ed.2d 59 (1960).

CHAPTER 15

CORPORATE LIQUIDATION, ARRANGEMENT,
AND REORGANIZATION

A. NON-BANKRUPTCY LIQUIDATION

A. NON-BANKRUPTCY LIQUIDATION

NON-BANKRUPTCY LIQUIDATION— IN GENERAL

381. Liquidation or winding up of a corporation involves the process of collecting the assets, paying the expenses involved, satisfying creditors' claims, and distributing the net assets, usually in cash but possibly in kind, first to any preferred shareholders according to their liquidation preferences and rights, then to any other shareholders with other than normal liquidation rights, and finally pro rata among the rest of the shareholders. Liquidation is closely related to "dissolution", in some jurisdictions preceding "dissolution" and following a "statement of intent to dissolve", and in other jurisdictions following "dissolution" and being followed in turn by "termination". Liquidation may or may not be under court supervision. Partial liquidation is also possible, in which event the corporation would continue rather than be dissolved. Various safeguards exist for the protection of creditors and shareholders.

Liquidation Procedures

Liquidation or winding up of a corporation involves the process of collecting the assets, paying the expenses involved, satisfying the creditors' claims, and distributing whatever is left—the net assets, usually in cash but possibly in kind, first to any preferred shareholders according to their liquidation preferences and rights,[1] then to any other shareholders with other than normal liquidation rights, and finally pro rata among the rest of the shareholders.

Liquidation is usually closely related to dissolution but the two terms are not synonymous. Dissolution means the end of the legal existence of the corporation. Under some statutes, dissolution follows

1. See H. Rumpf, Corporate Liquidation For the Lawyer and Accountant (2d ed. 1966). See section 382 infra.

liquidation;[2] under others, dissolution precedes liquidation.[3] Dissolution has already been discussed.[4]

In cases of dissolution by judicial proceedings, which can be commenced, under various circumstances, by directors, shareholders, creditors, or the state, depending on the local statute, liquidation occurs under the supervision of the court.[5] In cases of dissolution without judicial proceedings, liquidation is usually without court supervision,[6] but court supervision can sometimes be invoked.[7] Elaborate corporate receivership provisions are also found.[8]

Statutes sometimes entrust liquidation to the directors,[9] possibly, in older statutes, designating them as trustees for the purpose.[10] Other statutes provide for the appointment or election of trustees or "liquidators." [11]

Statutes might also expressly provide that directors who vote for or assent to any distribution of assets to shareholders during liquidation without paying or making adequate provision for all known obligations of the corporation are jointly and severally liable to the corporation for the value of such assets to the extent of such unpaid obligations.[12]

Partial liquidation is, of course, possible, in which event the corporation would continue rather than be dissolved. Distributions of cash or property beyond earned surplus constitute in effect partial liquidations. To these, some jurisdictions apply the term "dividends"; [13] other jurisdictions distinguish them from "dividends" by calling them "distributions in partial liquidation" or "distributions from capital surplus".[14]

Protection of Creditors

The statutes relating to dissolution and liquidation prescribe various procedures and safeguards for the protection of creditors. These usually take the form of mailing of notice to known creditors, publication of notice, reasonable period for filing of claims, suability during liquidation period, nonabatement of pending actions against the corporation, etc. Creditors may be able to invoke court supervision on a proper showing.[15]

Creditors might also be able to pursue any assets in the hands of shareholders under some circumstances,[16] and hold the

---

2. E. g., ABA–ALI Model Bus.Corp.Act §§ 76–86 (dissolution without judicial proceedings: upon corporate approval, duplicate copies of a "statement of intent to dissolve" are first filed; §§ 90–96 (judicial liquidation); provision is made for revoking voluntary dissolution proceedings).

3. McKinney's N.Y.Bus.Corp.Law, art. 10 (nonjudicial dissolution); id. art. 11 (judicial dissolution). Somewhat similar is partnership chronology and terminology; dissolution, liquidation or winding up, termination.

4. See section 348 supra.

5. E. g., ABA–ALI Model Bus.Corp.Act §§ 87–96; McKinney's N.Y.Bus.Corp.Law, art. 11.

6. E. g., ABA–ALI Model Bus.Corp.Act §§ 75–86; McKinney's N.Y.Bus.Corp.Law, art. 10.

7. E. g., ABA–ALI Model Bus.Corp.Act §§ 80(c), 90(c); McKinney's N.Y.Bus.Corp.Law, §§ 1008, 1117. This possibility obfuscates the distinction between judicial dissolution and nonjudicial dissolution.

8. E. g., McKinney's N.Y.Bus.Corp.Law, art. 12.

9. E. g., Cal.Gen.Corp.Law, § 4801 (1947).

10. E. g., former McKinney's N.Y.Stock Corp.Law, § 105; Wortham v. Lachman-Rose Co., 440 S.W.2d 351 (Tex.Civ.App.1969) (trust fund theory).

11. La.Bus.Corp.Law, §§ 12.141 et seq. (1969).

12. E. g., ABA–ALI Model Bus.Corp.Act § 43(c); McKinney's N.Y.Bus.Corp.Law § 719(a) (3); Barney v. Buswell, 236 Cal.App.2d 208, 45 Cal.Rptr. 908 (1965). If the corporation is insolvent, directors, who are creditors, may not grant themselves any preference in payment of their claims. Burton Mills & Cabinet Works, Inc. v. Truemper, 422 S.W. 2d 825 (Tex.Civ.App.1967); Darden v. George G. Lee Co., 204 Va. 108, 129 S.E.2d 897 (1963). See also Uniform Fraudulent Conveyance Act, 9B U.L. A. 70 (1966).

13. E. g., McKinney's N.Y.Bus.Corp.Law, § 510 (subject to disclosure requirements and also presumably to dividend but not liquidation preferences— see section 382 infra).

14. E. g., ABA–ALI Model Bus.Corp.Act § 41 (with express safeguards for any applicable dividend and liquidation preferences). See section 320 supra.

15. See notes 5, 7 supra.

16. Wood v. Dummer, 30 F.Cas. 435, No. 17,944 (C.C. D.Me.1824). See Drew v. United States, 177 Ct.Cl.

directors or other liquidators liable for distributions to the prejudice of creditors' rights.

Protection of Shareholders

Shareholders enjoy the protection of court supervision over liquidation in cases of judicial dissolution or of nonjudicial dissolution when court supervision is invoked. In nonjudicial dissolutions, requirements of notice to shareholders, shareholder approval, and possibly limited appraisal rights [17] afford some protection. So also do equitable limitations on management and controlling shareholders.[18]

Person Entitled to Liquidation Distributions

So far as the corporation is concerned, statutes often expressly allow it to fix a record date for the purpose of determining shareholders entitled to receive any distribution.[19]

The Uniform Commercial Code provides that the issuer, prior to presentment of a security for transfer, may treat the registered owner as the person exclusively entitled to exercise all the rights and powers of an owner.[20]

Unclaimed Liquidation Distributions

Escheat and abandoned property statutes usually apply to unclaimed liquidation distributions as well as current dividends, etc.[21]

Tax Aspects of Liquidation Distributions

The tax intricacies of corporate liquidations are best left to treatments on corporate taxation. Prior to the 1954 Code, distribution in kind was the principal method of avoiding capital gains taxes at both corporate and shareholder levels. The risk of such double capital gains tax in connection with the liquidation of a corporation has been largely alleviated under the 1954 Code.[22]

As a general rule, amounts distributed in complete or partial liquidation of a corporation are treated as in full payment in exchange for the shares.[23]

Bogardus v. Kentucky State Bank, 281 S.W.2d 904 (Ky.1955) (reference to "dividends" held inapplicable to liquidation distribution); Baar v. Fidelity & Columbia Trust Co., 302 Ky. 91, 193 S.W.2d 1011 (1946); cf. Turnbull v. Longacre Bank, 249 N.Y. 159, 163 N.E. 135 (1928); Matter of Alling, 186 Misc. 192, 63 N.Y.S.2d 427 (Sur.Ct.1945) (corporation protected by record ownership only if without notice); Lindner v. Utah Southern Oil Co., 3 Utah 2d 302, 283 P.2d 605 (1955).

21. See section 179 supra. See also New Jersey v. Fidelity Union Trust Co., 25 N.J. 387, 136 A.2d 636 (1957); Griffin v. Dyett, 262 App.Div. 368, 29 N.Y. S.2d 486 (4th Dep't 1941).

22. See generally B. Bittker & J. Eustice, Federal Income Taxation of Corporations and Shareholders §§ 9.01–9.71 (2d ed. 1966). As a general rule, no gain or loss is recognized to a corporation on the distribution of property in partial or complete liquidation. Int.Rev.Code of 1954, 26 U.S.C.A. § 336. Rosenfeld, "Tax Aspects of Dissolution", in Advising California Business Enterprises 1161 (1958); Bromberg, "Pitfalls in Corporate Liquidation", 44 Taxes 174 (1964); Symposium: "Tax Problems in Corporate Liquidation", 13 W.Res.L.Rev. 236 (1962); Cohen, Gelberg, Surrey, Tarleau & Warren, "Corporate Liquidations under the Internal Revenue Code of 1954", 55 Colum.L.Rev. 37 (1955); "Corporate Liquidations Under the 1954 Internal Revenue Code", 41 A.B.A.J. 1158 (1955). See section 76, n. 23 supra.

23. Int.Rev.Code of 1954, 26 U.S.C.A. § 331; B. Bittker & J. Eustice, op. cit. supra note 22, at §§ 9.01– 9.06. As a general rule if gain or loss is recognized on receipt of property in a distribution in partial or complete liquidation, the basis of the property in the hands of the distributee is the fair market value of such property at the time of the distribution.

458, 367 F.2d 828 (1966) (shareholders held liable, under state law, as transferees for corporation's unpaid federal income taxes); Snyder v. Nathan, 353 F.2d 3 (7th Cir. 1965); Stewart v. United States, 327 F.2d 201 (10th Cir. 1964) (holding shareholder-distributee personally liable, under trust fund theory, for claim of government against liquidated corporation); Coca-Cola Bottling Co. v. Comm'r, 334 F.2d 875 (9th Cir. 1964); Horan v. John F. Trommer, Inc., 124 N.Y.S.2d 217 (Sup.Ct.1953), 129 N.Y.S.2d 539 (Sup.Ct.1954), aff'd mem., 283 App.Div. 774, 128 N.Y.S.2d 595 (1st Dep't 1954); Schoone, "Shareholder Liability Upon Voluntary Dissolution of Corporation", 44 Marq.L.Rev. 415 (1961).

17. See section 349 supra.

18. See section 240 supra.

19. E. g., ABA–ALI Model Bus.Corp.Act § 28; Uniform Commercial Code § 8–207. Older statutes authorized the closing of the share transfer records.

20. 5 U.L.A. § 8–207 (1969). The former Uniform Stock Transfer Act expressly provided that nothing therein should be construed as forbidding a corporation to recognize the exclusive right of the record owner to receive "dividends". 6 U.L.A. § 3(a) (1922);

In the case of complete liquidation within 12 months, usually no gain or loss is recognized to the corporation.[24]

In the case of complete liquidation of a subsidiary, no gain or loss is recognized by the parent.[25]

In the case of complete liquidation within one calendar month, qualified shareholders may elect not to have gain recognized.[26]

Tax evasion is limited by the "collapsible corporation" provisions.[27]

Int.Rev.Code of 1954, 26 U.S.C.A. § 334. See also D. Kahn, Basic Corporate Taxation 58 et seq. (ICLE 1970).

24. Int.Rev.Code of 1954, 26 U.S.C.A. § 337; B. Bittker & J. Eustice, op. cit. supra note 22, at §§ 9.64–9.71; Eiseman, "Section 337 Liquidations—Their Snares and Uncertainties", 22 Ark.L.Rev. 300 (1968); Clark, "Pitfalls of a Section 337 Liquidation: Where They Exist and How to Avoid Them", 26 J. Taxation 144 (1967); Mills, "Special 12-Month Liquidations", 14 Tul.Tax Inst. 467 (1965); Rice, "Problems in Section 337 Liquidations", N.Y.U. 20th Inst. on Fed.Tax. 939 (1962); Farer, "Corporate Liquidations: Transmuting Ordinary Income Into Capital Gains", 75 Harv.L.Rev. 527 (1962); Comment, "Liquidation of Closely-Held Corporations Under Section 337", 16 Tax L.Rev. 255 (1961); Note, "Tax-Free Sales in Liquidation under Section 337", 76 Harv.L.Rev. 780 (1963).

25. Int.Rev.Code of 1954, 26 U.S.C.A. § 332; B. Bittker & J. Eustice, op. cit. supra note 22, at §§ 9.40–9.45.

26. Int.Rev.Code of 1954, 26 U.S.C.A. § 333; B. Bittker & J. Eustice, op. cit. supra note 22, at §§ 9.20–9.24; Emanuel, "Section 333 Liquidations: The Problems Created by Making Hasty Elections", 21 J. Taxation 340 (1964); Plotkin & Yolles, "Section 333 Has Hidden Trap Where Business Continued in Noncorporate Form", 20 J. Taxation 208 (1964); McGaffey, "Deferral of Gain in One-Month Liquidations", 19 Tax L.Rev. 327 (1964).

27. Int.Rev.Code of 1954, 26 U.S.C.A. § 341 (providing that gain from sale or exchange of shares of "collapsible corporation", or distribution in partial or complete liquidation of "collapsible corporation", or specified distribution made by "collapsible corporation", to extent that it would otherwise be considered as gain from sale or exchange of capital asset held for more than six months, be considered as gain from sale or exchange of property which is not capital asset); B. Bittker & J. Eustice, op. cit. supra note 22, at §§ 10.01–10.09; Goldstein, "Section 341(d) and (e)—A Journey into Never-Never Land", 13 Vill.L.Rev. 215 (1965); Coughlin, "Collapsible Corporations and One Year Liquidations", 15 W. Res.L.Rev. 314 (1964); Hines, "Collapsible Corporations—Another Limited Look", 42 N.C.L.Rev. 278 (1964); Odell, "Collapsible Corporations—Some

The tax consequences of distributions under divisive reorganizations under the 1954 Code have already received brief mention.[28]

LIQUIDATION PREFERENCES

382. Upon liquidation, all shareholders participate ratably in net assets except as otherwise provided in the articles of incorporation. Where net assets are not to be shared ratably, one or more classes of shares usually are given a liquidation preference over another class or classes of shares. Such liquidation preference is usually expressed in terms of par value or of monetary amount with or without provision for unpaid dividend arrearages in the case of cumulative preferred shares. Sometimes the liquidation preference is stated to be greater in amount for voluntary than for involuntary liquidation. Beyond the liquidation preference, the preferred shares may participate (said to be "participating") or may not participate (said to be "nonparticipating") further in the distribution of net assets with another class or classes of shares.

The basic liquidation rule is that all shareholders upon liquidation participate ratably in the net assets, except as otherwise provided in the articles of incorporation.

Many variations may be provided in the articles of incorporation,[1] but the usual practice, where net assets are not to be shared ratably, is to give to one or more classes of shares a liquidation preference over another class or other classes.[2] Any class with such

'Soft-spots' in Section 341", 18 U.Miami L.Rev. 645 (1964); Peel, "Recent Collapsible Developments: Inadvertent Collapsibility", N.Y.U. 20th Inst. on Fed.Tax. 851 (1962); Comment, "Collapsible Corporations: A Question of Intent", 3 Wm. & Mary L. Rev. 483 (1962).

28. See section 351 supra.

1. See Buxbaum, "Preferred Stock—Law and Draftsmanship", 42 Calif.L.Rev. 243, 257–262 (1953).

2. Note, "Liquidation Preferences of Preferred Shares", 20 N.Y.U.Intra.L.Rev. 52 (1964). Classes of shares, especially if they are preferred or special, may be subdivided into series, but each series of the same class is often required to have the same priority although they might differ as to the amount payable upon shares in event of voluntary or involuntary liquidation. See ABA-ALI Model Bus.Corp.Act § 15; McKinney's N.Y.Bus.Corp.Law, §

a preference may be and sometimes is designated "preferred shares", although this term connotes to most people a dividend preference.[3]

For any class of shares to enjoy a liquidation preference, the articles of incorporation must so provide.[4] Such liquidation preference is usually expressed in terms of par value or of monetary amount,[5] with or without provision for unpaid dividend arrearages in the case of cumulative preferred shares.

Whether or not preferred shares with a cumulative dividend preference with dividends in arrears are entitled to such arrearages in the event of liquidation depends upon the language defining the liquidation rights of such shares and the judicial attitudes concerning such arrearages.[6]

Sometimes the liquidation preference is stated to be greater in amount for voluntary than for involuntary dissolution or liquidation.[7] In view of the practical similarity between dissolution or liquidation and sales of substantially all assets, mergers, and consolidations (the latter always involve practical dissolution of any nonsurviving corporations), the articles of incorporation sometimes expressly provide that such matters shall not be deemed to be a dissolution or liquidation for purposes of the liquidation preference.[8]

Beyond the liquidation preference, the preferred shares may or may not participate

---

502(b) (requiring that if "amounts payable on liquidation are not paid in full, the shares of all series of the same class shall share ratably . . . in any distribution of assets . . . in accordance with the sums which would be payable on such distribution if all sums payable were discharged in full"). See section 125 supra.

3. Usually "preferred shares" also enjoy a dividend preference (see section 324 supra), but the term is properly applied to shares with either as well as both liquidation preference and dividend preference. Shares with any such preference should not be designated "common shares". See, e. g., McKinney's N.Y.Bus.Corp.Law, § 501(b).

4. Newman v. Arabol Mfg. Co., 41 Misc.2d 184, 245 N.Y.S.2d 442 (Sup.Ct.1963) (holding preferred and common shares entitled to share equally in net assets on liquidation where articles of incorporation did not provide otherwise); People v. N. Y. Bldg.-Loan Banking Co., 50 Misc. 23, 100 N.Y.S. 459 (Sup.Ct.1906); 2 I. Kantrowitz & S. Slutsky, White on New York Corporations ¶ 501.04 (13th ed. 1968). See section 124 supra.

5. E. g., "105% of the par value thereof"; "full par value plus 5% thereof"; "$105 per share". If the par value is changed by reclassification, a liquidation preference stated in terms of percentage of par value is correspondingly changed. Sterling v. 16 Park Avenue, Inc., 132 N.Y.S.2d 921 (Sup.Ct.1954), modified 284 App.Div. 1033, 136 N.Y.S.2d 363 (1st Dep't 1954).

6. See section 325 supra. See also Annot., 25 A.L.R. 2d 788 (1952).

7. See Maffia v. American Woolen Co., 125 F.Supp. 465 (S.D.N.Y.1954) (sale of substantial assets with view to relocation of plant held not liquidation entitling preferred shareholders to liquidation preference).

8. Schenker v. E. I. du Pont de Nemours & Co., 329 F.2d 77 (2d Cir. 1964), cert. denied 377 U.S. 998, 84 S.Ct. 1922, 12 L.Ed.2d 1048 (1964) (holding that du Pont's antitrust divestiture of 63,000,000 General Motors shares was not "liquidation or dissolution or winding up" since there was no winding up of du Pont's main business and no complete distribution of all corporate assets); Alcott v. Hyman, 40 Del.Ch. 449, 184 A.2d 90 (Ch.1962), aff'd 42 Del.Ch. 233, 208 A.2d 501 (Sup.Ct.1965) (construing provision in articles of incorporation of Delaware corporation that in event of any liquidation or winding up of corporation or distribution of its assets by way of return of capital common shareholders should receive complete distribution of assets of the corporation, as inapplicable in case of sale of substantially all of corporate assets). Compare Treves v. Menzies, 37 Del. Ch. 330, 142 A.2d 520 (Ch.1958) (preferred shares held not entitled to liquidation preference in case of duly approved sale of substantially all corporate assets), aff'd sub nom. Treves v. Servel, Inc., 38 Del. Ch. 483, 154 A.2d 188 (Sup.Ct.1959), with Craddock-Terry Co. v. Powell, 180 Va. 242, 22 S.E.2d 30 (1942), modified 181 Va. 417, 25 S.E.2d 363 (1943) (4–3). See Warren v. Baltimore Transit Co., 220 Md. 478, 485, 154 A.2d 796, 800 (1959) (appraisal proceeding) ("Appellant's argument that his contract rights in liquidation give his preferred stock the fair value equal to the sum of par plus accrued dividends, fails on both factual and legal grounds. Factually, the charter and stock certificate expressly state that a consolidation or merger is not to be considered a liquidation, and if a consolidation or merger was not to be deemed a liquidation, certainly the readjustment of the capital structure of the company could not be considered in that category. Legally, as we have seen, most courts do not treat consolidations, mergers or capital readjustments as liquidations, and we hold that for the purposes of an appraisal of dissenting stock they need not be so considered. This being so, the appellant's preferred stock is to be valued as an interest in a continuing enterprise with whatever benefits and liabilities as to value its preferred status affords it.").

further in the distribution of net assets with another class or classes of shares. If such shares participate, they are said to be "participating"; otherwise, "nonparticipating".[9] Participation by classes of shares may be equal or in a stated ratio, may commence at once after the satisfaction of the liquidation preference or commence only after designated or equal payments to the shares of another class or classes, may be limited to a fixed amount, or may be created in any combination of the foregoing. Preferred shares with nonparticipating liquidation rights receive nothing beyond their liquidation preference.

Ambiguous provisions may require court construction. The question of participation beyond the liquidation preference where the articles of incorporation are silent on the matter, has not been resolved. One view is that a preference takes the place of the normal rule of equality and therefore impliedly precludes participation; the contrary view is that a preference is in addition to such normal equality and does not preclude further participation.[10] The question does not seem to have been settled in most jurisdictions.[11]

The North Carolina statute expressly provides that, absent provision to the contrary, preferred shares are nonparticipating.[12]

Problems of construction can be avoided by specific provision in the articles of incorporation. If nonparticipation is intended, the provision usually is for payment of the liquidation preference "and no more". In addition, or alternatively, the provision might provide for the payment of the liquidation preference and then provide that after payment thereof, all remaining net assets should be payable to and distributed ratably among the holders of the common shares.[13]

In most jurisdictions, liquidation preferences can be changed as to amount, priority, participation, etc., either directly or indirectly by creation of prior preferred shares, merger, etc. Such changes are most commonly effected by amendment of the articles of incorporation.[14]

Liquidation preferences should be satisfied by cash distributions. Otherwise, liquidation distributions of corporate assets can be in cash or kind, or possibly even securities of another corporation purchasing the corporate assets.[15] Liquidation preferences have

---

9. Dividend preferences may also be "participating" or "nonparticipating". Just as "preferred shares" may have a preference with respect to liquidation and/or dividends, they may be "participating" in either or both respects.

10. Squires v. Balbach Co., 177 Neb. 465, 129 N.W.2d 462 (1964) (holding that, where articles of incorporation expressly provided that cumulative dividend preference was participating and were silent as to whether liquidation preference was participating or nonparticipating, stated liquidation preference was exhaustive and cumulative preferred shares were entitled to such stated preference and no more); Mohawk Carpet Mills, Inc. v. Delaware Rayon Co., 35 Del.Ch. 51, 110 A.2d 305 (Ch.1954) (preferred shares with expressly participating dividend preference and with liquidation preference silent as to participation held not participating on liquidation).

11. 2 I. Kantrowitz & S. Slutsky, White on New York Corporations ¶ 501.04 (13th ed. 1968). The problem is one of construing the articles of incorporation. Zimmerman v. Selak, 74 Wash.2d 1, 442 P. 2d 246 (1968) (liquidation preference "up to par value" held nonparticipating beyond par value). Where they provided that the preferred shares should be paid in full at par value before any

amount shall be paid on the common shares, it was held that there was no participation beyond the stated preference. Williams v. Renshaw, 220 App. Div. 39, 220 N.Y.S. 532 (3d Dep't 1927). See Schaps, "Preferred Stock—Right on Dissolution in Excess of Preference", 24 Bus.Law. 1393 (1969).

12. N.C.Bus.Corp.Act § 55–40(b) (2) (1957). See Ghana Companies Code § 51(5) (1963) (canon of construction that unless contrary intention appears, any class of shares with preferential winding up rights to have no further right to participate in distribution of assets in winding up).

13. Buxbaum, "Preferred Stock—Law and Draftsmanship", 42 Calif.L.Rev. 243, 259 (1954).

14. E. g., ABA–ALI Model Bus.Corp.Act § 55. See Becht, "Changes in the Interests of Classes of Stockholders by Corporate Charter Amendments", 36 Cornell L.Q. 1 (1950); Note, "Limitations on Alteration of Shareholders' Rights by Charter Amendment", 69 Harv.L.Rev. 538 (1956). See section 345 supra.

15. Prior to the Internal Revenue Code of 1954, distribution in kind was the only way to avoid a double capital gains tax, but the 1954 Code has granted some relief. See section 381, n. 24 supra. For dis-

been held to apply in Chapter X reorganization, proceedings,[16] but not necessarily in reorganization proceedings under the Federal Public Utility Holding Company Act of 1935.[17]

B. BANKRUPTCY LIQUIDATION

BANKRUPTCY LIQUIDATION

383. **Federal bankruptcy legislation results in the suspension of conflicting state "insolvency" statutes.** The first seven chapters of the present Bankruptcy Act deal with so-called straight, traditional, ordinary, or liquidation bankruptcy—involving the adjudication of the debtor as a bankrupt, liquidation of the bankrupt, equitable distribution of the bankrupt's assets to creditors, and discharge of the honest bankrupt. Of the later chapters, which deal with rehabilitation rather than liquidation of the debtor, the two most significant to corporations are Chapter X (corporate reorganizations) and Chapter XI (arrangements). Bankruptcy proceedings are voluntary (commenced by the debtor) or involuntary (commenced by a creditor or creditors). Requisite to involuntary bankruptcy is the commission of an "act of bankruptcy" within four months preceding the filing of the petition.

Business corporations are subject to both voluntary and involuntary bankruptcy. Adjudication of the corporation as a bankrupt does not release its officers, directors, or shareholders from any liability under state or federal law. If any net assets remain after payment of the expenses of the proceeding and satisfaction of all creditors, they are distributed among shareholders in compliance with any applicable liquidation preferences and other rights; otherwise pro rata.

In General

While there are state statutes dealing with the liquidation of insolvent corporations,[1] sometimes known as "insolvency statutes", these are suspended in favor of the supremacy of federal bankruptcy legislation when in conflict therewith.[2]

Federal bankruptcy legislation is enacted pursuant to the power conferred on Congress "To establish . . . uniform Laws on the subject of Bankruptcies throughout the United States." [3]

Until 1898, federal bankruptcy statutes were only intermittently in force.[4] Since then, there has continuously been a federal bankruptcy law in effect. Frequently amended, the present law is known as the Chandler Act of 1938. Broadly speaking, it contains 15 chapters. The first seven deal with so-called straight, traditional, ordinary, or liquidation bankruptcy—involving the adjudication of the debtor as a bankrupt, liquidation of the bankrupt, equitable distribution of the bankrupt's assets to creditors,

tribution of shares or bonds in purchasing corporation, see McKinney's N.Y.Bus.Corp.Law, § 1005.

16. Central States Electric Corp. v. Austrian, 183 F. 2d 879 (4th Cir. 1950), cert. denied sub nom. Berner v. Austrian, 340 U.S. 917, 71 S.Ct. 350, 95 L.Ed. 662 (1951); Petition of Portland Elec. Power Co., 162 F.2d 618, (9th Cir. 1947), cert. denied 332 U.S. 837, 68 S.Ct. 217, 92 L.Ed. 410 (1947).

17. Otis & Co. v. Securities and Exchange Commission, 323 U.S. 624, 65 S.Ct. 483, 89 L.Ed. 511 (1945); L. Loss, Securities Regulation 140–141 (2d ed. 1961); Brudney, "The Investment-Value Doctrine and Corporate Readjustments", 72 Harv.L.Rev. 645 (1959).

1. E. g., ABA–ALI Model Bus.Corp. Act §§ 90–96; McKinney's N.Y.Bus.Corp.Law, §§ 1201 et seq.; cf. McKinney's N.Y.Debt. & Cred.Law §§ 50 et seq. See generally "Business in Difficulty: A Symposium", 1958 U.Ill.L.F. 497 et seq.

2. Pobreslo v. Boyd Co., 287 U.S. 518, 53 S.Ct. 262, 77 L.Ed. 469 (1933); Johnson v. Star, 287 U.S. 527, 53 S.Ct. 265, 77 L.Ed. 473 (1933); First Nat'l Bank of Albuquerque v. Robinson, 107 F.2d 50 (10th Cir. 1939); Miller, "The Illinois Business Corporation Act and Bankruptcy Legislation", 29 Ill.L.Rev. 695 (1935); Comment, 23 Wash.L.Rev. 60 (1948).

3. U.S.Const. art. I, § 8, cl. 4. "Uniformity" does not preclude recognition in bankruptcy of variations of state corporation and other laws. See Hanover Nat'l Bank v. Moyses, 186 U.S. 181, 22 S.Ct. 857, 46 L.Ed. 1113 (1902).

4. 1800–1803, 1841–1843, 1867–1878, 1898–date.

and discharge of the honest bankrupt.[5] Of the later chapters, which deal with rehabilitation rather than liquidation of the debtor, the two most significant to corporations are Chapter X ("Corporate Reorganizations"),[6] and Chapter XI ("Arrangements").[7] Section 77 deals with the reorganization of interstate railroads, but has been largely replaced since 1948 by section 20b of the Transportation Act, administered by the Interstate Commerce Commission.

While insolvency[8] of the bankrupt is not essential under the bankruptcy law, it usually exists and is a relevant factor for various purposes of the law.

The federal district courts are the courts of bankruptcy, with most bankruptcy matters referred to the referees-in-bankruptcy. Bankruptcy proceedings are: (a) voluntary (commenced by the debtor), or (b) involuntary (commenced by a creditor or creditors). Requisite to involuntary bankruptcy is a commission of an "act of bankruptcy"[9] within four months preceding the filing of the petition.

Corporate Bankrupts

Corporations,[10] except "a municipal, railroad, insurance or banking corporation or a building and loan association",[11] may file a voluntary petition. Whether the directors or officers or both have authority to file such petition depends upon their authority under applicable state law.[12] Involuntary petitions may be filed against corporations only if they are "moneyed, business, or commercial" corporations,[13] and are not of a

---

5. 11 U.S.C.A. §§ 1–112; B. Weintraub, Practical Guide to Bankruptcy and Debtor Relief (1964); J. MacLachlan, Handbook of the Law of Bankruptcy (1956); C. Nadler, The Law of Bankruptcy (1948); J. Mulder & L. Forman, Bankruptcy and Arrangement Proceedings 1–117 (ALI rev. 1964); G. Hirsch, Bankruptcy (PLI rev. 1964); Meth, "Is Bankruptcy Outmoded?", 19 Bus.Law. 673 (1964); Countryman, "The Bankruptcy Boom", 77 Harv.L.Rev. 1452 (1964); Feibelman, "What Shall It Be—Bankruptcy, An Arrangement or Corporate Reorganization?", 69 Com.L.J. 6 (1964); Symposium: "Creditors' Rights and Remedies", 14 Hastings L.J. 1 (1962); Goldstein, "Bankruptcy and Arrangement Procedure Simplified", 10 Syracuse L.Rev. 203 (1959); Mulder, "What the General Practitioner Should Know About Bankruptcy and Arrangement Proceedings", 12 Bus.Law. 170 (1957). The two classic works are J. Moore, Collier on Bankruptcy (10 vols., 14th ed. 1940–64); H. Remington, Remington on Bankruptcy (15 vols., 5th–6th ed. 1947–61). See CCH Bankruptcy Law Reports. For partnership bankruptcy, see section 19, nn. 21, 22 supra. See 11 U.S.C.A. § 32 (listing seven grounds for denial of discharge, including failure to keep proper books of account, obtaining property on basis of false financial statement, etc.); id. § 35 (providing for discharge of all provable debts except taxes, wages earned by workmen within three months prior to bankruptcy, etc.). Nonprovable debts are not dischargeable.

6. 11 U.S.C.A. §§ 101–676. See sections 386–388 infra.

7. 11 U.S.C.A. §§ 301–799. See sections 384, 385 infra.

8. "Insolvency in the bankruptcy sense". 11 U.S.C.A. § 1(19) (excess of liabilities over assets, at fair valuation). Cf. "Insolvency in the equity sense" (inability to pay debts as they mature).

9. There are six "acts of bankruptcy". Insolvency (in the bankruptcy sense) and/or inability to pay debts as they mature (insolvency in the equity sense) are elements of some of the six acts of bankruptcy, prerequisite to involuntary bankruptcy. 11 U.S.C.A. § 21. See Note, " 'Acts of Bankruptcy' in Perspective", 67 Harv.L.Rev. 500 (1954). See also Joslin, "Bankruptcy: A Time Synthesis", 46 Marq.L.Rev. 405 (1963).

10. Defined to include "partnership associations organized under laws making the capital subscribed alone responsible for the debts of the association, joint-stock companies, unincorporated companies and associations, and any business conducted by a trustee or trustees wherein beneficial interest or ownership is evidenced by certificate or other written instrument". 11 U.S.C.A. § 1(8). In England, only individuals are subject to the bankruptcy laws; companies are "wound up", or liquidated, under the Companies Act itself. Pearlman & Haywood, "Bankruptcy and Liquidation of Companies in England", 14 Bus.Law. 837 (1959).

11. 11 U.S.C.A. § 22(a); Sovern, "Section 4 of the Bankruptcy Act: The Excluded Corporations", 42 Minn.L.Rev. 171 (1957); Note, 108 U.Pa.L.Rev. 1218 (1960).

12. See Porterfield v. Gerstel, 222 F.2d 137 (5th Cir. 1955); Matter of Raljoed Realty Co., 277 F.Supp. 225 (S.D.N.Y.1967), aff'd per curiam sub nom. Matter of Park Towers Corp., 387 F.2d 948 (2d Cir. 1967) (holding shareholder had no standing to file voluntary petition in behalf of corporation). Cf. Dixon Mills, Inc. v. Dixon Nat'l Bank, 357 F.2d 169 (7th Cir. 1966) (alleged sole beneficial shareholder held to have no standing to file involuntary petition in behalf of corporation).

13. 11 U.S.C.A. § 220(b). In Matter of Gibraltor Amusements, Ltd., 291 F.2d 22 (2d Cir. 1961), cert.

class of the corporations excepted from voluntary bankruptcy.[14] Dissolution of a corporation will usually not prevent its being adjudicated a bankrupt.[15]

Adjudication of the corporation as a bankrupt does not release its officers, directors, or shareholders from any liability under state or federal law.[16]

A trustee-in-bankruptcy is usually elected by creditors to take over the assets of the bankrupt,[17] liquidate them, and distribute the proceeds to creditors.

Transactions which the bankrupt could not have disturbed might be set aside or taken over by the trustee.[18]

Upon liquidation, after payment of the costs of administration, assets are distributed among creditors in accordance with the provisions of the bankruptcy law, which distribution sometimes varies from the distribution which would be lawful outside of bankruptcy.[19]

denied 368 U.S. 925, 82 S.Ct. 360, 7 L.Ed.2d 190 (1961), the question was whether a wholly-owned subsidiary of the alleged bankrupt corporation had standing as one of the three required petitioning creditors. Under ordinary principles of corporate law, the court held that disregard of the subsidiary's corporate identity was not warranted. Smith & Moore, Cir. JJ., literally construed the Bankruptcy Act definition of "creditor" as "anyone" who owns a provable claim, as including a wholly-owned subsidiary. Friendly, Cir. J., dissented, leaving open the question as to whether a wholly-owned subsidiary with independent creditors might be deemed separate from its parent in a case where, as a result of its own financial difficulties, the subsidiary was in effect acting for its creditors rather than for its shareholders.

14. See note 11 supra.

15. See definition of "corporation", supra note 10. See also Mosaic Tile Co. v. Stabe Corp., 323 F.2d 274 (2d Cir. 1963) (holding corporation which had forfeited its corporate existence for failure to file annual reports continued in existence under state law for purposes of winding up and therefore retained sufficient corporate power to liquidate its assets by filing voluntary petition in straight bankruptcy).

16. 11 U.S.C.A. § 22(b). See also United States v. Castellana, 349 F.2d 264 (2d Cir. 1965), cert. denied 383 U.S. 928, 86 S.Ct. 934, 15 L.Ed.2d 847 (1966), reh. denied 384 U.S. 923, 86 S.Ct. 1368, 16 L.Ed.2d 444 (1966) (holding testimony of directors who had not been "designated" as corporate representatives in examination of bankrupt corporation's business was not privileged).

17. 11 U.S.C.A. § 110 (including bankrupt's rights of action if transferable or subject to judicial process); Note, "Bankruptcy: Trustee's Title to Bankrupt's Property", 45 N.C.L.Rev. 1025 (1967); Note, "The Creditors' Rights to the Bankrupt's Assets", 52 Calif.L.Rev. 129 (1964); Annot., 66 A.L.R.2d 1217 (1959). Hence liabilities under corporation statutes or otherwise running in favor of the corporation may be asserted by the corporation's trustee-in-bankruptcy, but liabilities in favor of creditors may not. But see section 171, n. 21 supra.

18. 11 U.S.C.A. §§ 96, 107, 110(c), (e); Kennedy, "Bankruptcy Amendments of 1966", 1 Ga.L.Rev. 149 (1967); Marsh, "Triumph or Tragedy? The Bankruptcy Act Amendments of 1966", 42 Wash.L.Rev. 681 (1967). See, e. g., Pacific Finance Corp. v. Edwards, 304 F.2d 224 (9th Cir. 1962); In re Quaker City Uniform Co., 238 F.2d 155 (3d Cir. 1956), cert. denied 352 U.S. 1030, 77 S.Ct. 595, 1 L.Ed.2d 599 (1957); Constance v. Harvey, 215 F.2d 571 (2d Cir. 1954, cert. denied 348 U.S. 918, 75 S.Ct. 294, 99 L.Ed. 716 (1955), overruled in Lewis v. Manufacturers Nat'l Bank, 364 U.S. 603, 81 S.Ct. 347, 5 L.Ed.2d 323 (1961). See Kennedy, "Trustee in Bankruptcy as a Secured Creditor under the Uniform Commercial Code", 65 Mich.L.Rev. 1419 (1967); Krause, "The Code and the Bankruptcy Act: Three Views on Preferences and After-Acquired Property", 42 N.Y.U.L.Rev. 278 (1967); Kennedy, "The Proper Relation Between the Bankruptcy Act and the Uniform Commercial Code", 36 N.Y.St.B.J. 444 (1964); Silverstein, "Rejection of Executory Contracts in Bankruptcy and Reorganization", 31 U.Chi.L.Rev. 467 (1964); King, "Pacific Finance Corporation v. Edwards: Another Misreading of Section 70c of the Bankruptcy Act", 63 Colum.L.Rev. 232 (1963); Spivack, "The Impact of Article 9 of the Uniform Commercial Code on Creditors' Rights in Bankruptcy", 36 Temple L.Q. 183 (1963); Buchanan, "Bankruptcy—Section 70c—Recent Reactions to Constance v. Harvey", 57 Mich.L.Rev. 1227 (1959); Kupfer, "A 'Puzzlement': The Quaker City Uniform Case, Its Impacts and Aftermaths", 12 Bus.Law. 280, 539 (1957); Comment, "Bankruptcy: The 'Strong-Arm Clause' of Section 70(c)", 5 Vill.L.Rev. 437 (1960); Comment, "Secured Lending and Section 60(a) of the Bankruptcy Act: The Need for a Uniform Test of Perfection", 28 U.Chi.L.Rev. 130 (1960).

19. 11 U.S.C.A. § 107(c) (subordination and invalidity of liens); § 104 (priority debts). Equitable subordination of claims is possible. Pepper v. Litton, 308 U.S. 295, 60 S.Ct. 238, 84 L.Ed. 281 (1939); Costello v. Fazio, 256 F.2d 903 (9th Cir. 1958); Gannett Co. v. Larry, 221 F.2d 269, 51 A.L. R.2d 980 (2d Cir. 1955); In re Elkins-Dell Mfg. Co., 253 F.Supp. 864 (E.D.Pa.1966); Ashe "Subordination of Claims: Equitable Principles Applied in Bankruptcy", 72 Com.L.J. 91 (1967); Henson, "Subordinations and Bankruptcy: Some Current Problems", 21 Bus.Law. 763 (1966); Gleick, "Subordination of Claims in Bankruptcy Under the Equitable Power of the Bankruptcy Court", 16 Bus.Law. 611

If any net assets remain after payment of the expenses of the proceeding and satisfaction of all creditors—an unlikely event—they are distributed among shareholders in compliance with any applicable liquidation preferences and other rights; otherwise pro rata.

C. ARRANGEMENT

ARRANGEMENT—IN GENERAL

384. Corporate arrangements under Chapter XI of the Bankruptcy Act may involve either an "extension" of time for payment of debts or a "composition" (scaling down of debts) or both, and are intended to avoid the serious economic loss involved in liquidation in straight bankruptcy. Arrangements can affect unsecured debts only, not secured debts or shares; and can be instituted only by the voluntary petition of the debtor. Business corporations may commence arrangement proceedings. Proceedings under Chapter XI are far less formal than proceedings under Chapter X. The plan of arrangement is proposed by the debtor, and is subject to acceptance by creditors and confirmation by the court. Prerequisite to court confirmation is the plan's being in the best interests of creditors and "feasible".

Corporate arrangements, as discussed in this and the next section, are those under Chapter XI of the Federal Bankruptcy Act,[1]

and not such other arrangements for the extension, compromise or composition of indebtedness as are possible under common-law principles or under state statutes.

Arrangements may involve either an "extension" of time for payment of debts or a scaling down of debts (so-called "composition") or both. They are intended to avoid the serious economic loss to the debtor, creditors, and the business community resulting from liquidation in straight bankruptcy.

Arrangements can affect unsecured debts only, not secured debts or shares; and can be instituted only by the voluntary petition of the debtor. Corporations eligible for voluntary bankruptcy may commence an arrangement proceeding.[2]

Proceedings are far less formal under Chapter XI than under Chapter X. There are no provisions under Chapter XI for the appointment of a disinterested active trustee or for intervention of the Securities and Ex-

---

(1961); see United States v. Embassy Restaurant, Inc., 359 U.S. 29, 79 S.Ct. 554, 3 L.Ed.2d 601 (1959); Bass v. Shutan, 259 F.2d 561 (9th Cir. 1958). See also Small Business Administration v. McClellan, 364 U.S. 446, 81 S.Ct. 191, 5 L.Ed.2d 200 (1960); Arabian v. Coleman, 338 F.2d 41 (6th Cir. 1964); Matter of Pusey & Jones Corp., 295 F.2d 479 (3d Cir. 1961) (Chapter XI). See also section 152 supra.

1. 11 U.S.C.A. §§ 301–799; R. Edelmon, Collier Bankruptcy Manual ch. XI (2d ed. 1954); J. Mulder & L. Forman, Bankruptcy and Arrangement Proceedings 137–168 (ALI rev. 1964); S. Krause, Arrangements Under Chapter 11 of the Bankruptcy Act (PLI rev. 1964); Ashe, "Rehabilitation under Chapter XI: Fact or Fiction", 72 Com.L.J. 259 (1967); Krause, "Chapters X and XI—A Study in Contrasts", 19 Bus.Law. 511 (1964); Feibelman, "What Shall It Be—Bankruptcy, An Arrangement or Corporate Reorganization?", 69 Com.L.J. 6 (1964); Weintraub & Levin, "Reorganization or Arrangement: An Analysis of Contemporary Trends in Recent Cases", 37 Ref.J. 103 (1963); Rodden & Carpenter, "Corporate Insolvency—Liquidation or Rehabilitation", 36 U.Colo.L.Rev. 117 (1963); Weintraub & Levin, "Three Alternatives in Search of a Lawyer: An Analysis of Corporate Rehabilitation for the

Middle-Sized Corporation", 7 N.Y.L.F. 394 (1961); Herzog, "Reorganizations and Arrangements under Chapters X and XI: Problems of Administration from the Standpoint of the Court", 35 Ref.J. 113 (1961); Krause & Zweibel, "Venue and Consolidation of Arrangement (Chapter XI) Proceedings under the Bankruptcy Act Involving Related Corporations", 16 Bus.Law. 352 (1961); Goldstein, "Bankruptcy and Arrangement Procedure Simplified", 10 Syracuse L.Rev. 203 (1959); Mulder, "What the General Practitioner Should Know About Bankruptcy and Arrangement Proceedings", 12 Bus.Law. 170 (1957); Comment, "Debtor Rehabilitation: Common Law Settlement, Chapter X and Chapter XI: An Analysis and Discussion", 7 N.Y.L.F. 404 (1961); Note, "Compensation of Attorneys—Court Clarifies Standards for Compensation in Chapter XI Proceedings", 42 N.Y.U.L.Rev. 142 (1967).

2. See section 383, nn. 10–15 supra.

change Commission as there are under Chapter X.

The plan of arrangement is proposed by the debtor; as previously suggested, the plan may not affect secured debt or shares. As in bankruptcy, the proceedings are usually referred to a referee-in-bankruptcy. The debtor may be allowed to remain in possession of the property, or a receiver might be appointed. In a converter proceeding, where the petition has been filed after adjudication in bankruptcy, the trustee-in-bankruptcy might be continued in possession. The plan requires the acceptance of a majority in both number *and* amount of all creditors whose claims have been proved and allowed.[3]

After acceptance of the plan by creditors, it is submitted to the court for confirmation. The plan will be confirmed if the court is satisfied that (a) the debtor has complied fully with Chapter XI; (b) the plan is for the best interests of creditors; (c) the plan is "feasible";[4] (d) the debtor has done nothing which would bar a discharge; and (e) the plan and acceptance are in good faith and have not been secured by forbidden means.[5]

Confirmation binds all creditors of the debtor, "whether or not they are affected by the arrangement or have accepted it or have filed their claims, and whether or not their claims have been scheduled or allowed and are allowable", the debtor, and any person issuing securities or acquiring property under the plan.[6]

AVAILABILITY TO CORPORATIONS OF CHAPTER XI

385. **Chapter XI is available to business corporations, subject to the limitation that such a proceeding may not affect secured debt or shares. Within such limitations, corporations often prefer Chapter XI to Chapter X proceedings. The courts may dismiss Chapter XI proceedings when relief under Chapter X, with its additional safeguards and more extensive relief, would be more appropriate. The test is not the size of the corporation involved but "the needs to be served".**

Apart from the limitation that a Chapter XI proceeding may not affect secured debt or shares, the choice of a business corporation between Chapter XI and Chapter X is not otherwise expressly prescribed in the statute. Corporate management, shareholders, and sometimes the creditors, have often preferred Chapter XI over Chapter X, giving rise to a series of court opinions on the appropriateness of proceeding under one chapter or another in a given case.[1]

The United States Supreme Court has ruled thrice on the problem.

---

3. Where creditors are divided into classes, acceptance of each class is necessary. See generally Weintraub & Levin, "Dossier of an Arrangement Proceeding under Chapter XI: From Petition to Confirmation and Beyond", 27 Fed.B.J. 95 (1967).

4. 11 U.S.C.A. § 366(2). Prior to 1952, the plan had to be "fair and equitable, and feasible". Literally construed under the "absolute priority" rule (see discussion of Court Confirmation of Plan in section 388 infra), the pre-1952 language would have required payment of creditors in full before any shareholder interest at all could have been preserved. The 1952 amendment also expressly provided that confirmation of an arrangement shall not be refused solely because the interests of shareholders would be preserved under the arrangement. "Feasible" means workable in the sense that the debtor will probably be able to carry out the plan and be financially rehabilitated. See In re Chicago Express, Inc., 332 F.2d 276 (2d Cir. 1964) ("six-months rule" held inapplicable in Chapter XI proceeding).

5. 11 U.S.C.A. § 766.

6. 11 U.S.C.A. §§ 767–770.

1. See Rochelle, "Relief and Rehabilitation of Infinitum, Inc.: A Fable", 41 Ref.J. 12 (1967); Weintraub & Levin, "From *United States Realty* to *American Trailer Rentals*: The Availability of Debtor Relief for the Middle-Sized Corporation", 34 Fordham L.Rev. 419 (1966); Mulder, "Rehabilitation of the Financially Distressed Small Business —Revisited", 11 Prac.Law. 39 (Nov.1965); Rochelle, "Rehabilitation in Bankruptcy: A Comparison of Chapters X and XI", 34 J.B.A.Kan. 17 (Spring 1965); Krause, "Chapters X and XI—A Study in Contrasts", 19 Bus.Law. 511 (1964); Weintraub & Levin, "Reorganization or Arrangement: An Analysis of Contemporary Trends In Recent Cases", 37 Ref.J. 103 (1963); Weintraub & Levin, "Three Alternatives in Search of a Lawyer: An Analysis of Corporate Rehabilitation for the Middle-Sized Corporation", 7 N.Y.L.F. 394 (1961); Weintraub, Levin & Novick, "Chapter X or Chapter XI: Coexistence for the Middle-Sized Corporation", 24 Fordham L. Rev. 616 (1956).

In Securities and Exchange Commission v. United States Realty and Improvement Co.,[2] the corporation involved was a real estate investment company with 100,000 shares listed on the New York Stock Exchange and held by some 7,000 holders. Assets exceeded $7,000,000; liabilities approximated $5,000,000, including $2,239,000 of publicly-held debentures secured by a first mortgage owned by the debtor. The debtor was also liable as guarantor on $3,700,500 mortgage certificates issued by a wholly-owned subsidiary, held by 900 holders, and in default.

The corporation began a Chapter XI proceeding to affect only its unsecured debt.[3] The Securities and Exchange Commission intervened on the ground that Chapter X, under which the Commission has important advisory functions, was the exclusive means for reorganizing a large corporation with publicly-held securities. Both the district court and court of appeals held that the proceeding was literally within the language of Chapter XI and properly brought thereunder.

The Supreme Court reversed, 5 to 3, and dismissed the Chapter XI proceeding. The Court said that the test was not size or number of security holders, but rather whether there were "public or private interests involved" (which the Court found to exist) requiring protection by the procedure and remedies afforded by Chapter X with its procedural safeguards—disinterested trustee, S. E. C. intervention, etc.—missing from Chapter XI. Relief would be inadequate under Chapter XI, the Court added, since the plan had to be "fair and equitable" under Chapter XI (as it then read) and could not be so to unsecured creditors without some "rearrangement of its capital structure", which could only be effected under Chapter X.

In the second case, General Stores Corp. v. Shlensky,[4] the corporation filing the Chapter XI petition had some $5,000,000 assets, $4,000,000 liabilities, 2,322,422 shares listed on the American Stock Exchange and held by some 7,000 holders, and two wholly-owned million-dollar subsidiaries, one of which in turn had a subsidiary, and had been reorganized in 1940. The district court dismissed the Chapter XI proceeding on the ground that relief should have been sought under Chapter X, and the dismissal was affirmed by the court of appeals, 2 to 1.[5]

On appeal, the Supreme Court, 6 to 2, affirmed, stating that neither the character of the debtor nor the nature of its capital structure were the controlling considerations: [6]

> "The essential difference is not between the small company and the large company but between the needs to be served."

Emphasizing that managerial reorganization was as important as debt readjustment, the Court pointed out the additional safeguards and more extensive relief under Chapter X over Chapter XI: appointment of a disinterested trustee, his broad powers of investigation, his rôle in preparing the plan, the S. E. C. advisory functions, the requirement that the reorganization plan be "fair and equitable, and feasible", and the power to include the subsidiaries in the reorganization of the parent—for the protection of "the entire community of interests" in the corporation. The Court doubted that any arrangement under Chapter XI, on the facts presented, could be "feasible" as required. The dismissal by the lower courts of the Chapter XI proceed-

---

2. 310 U.S. 434, 60 S.Ct. 1044, 84 L.Ed. 1293 (1940).

3. The subsidiary meanwhile began a Burchill Act proceeding in the New York state court to modify its primary obligation under the mortgage certificates.

4. 350 U.S. 462, 76 S.Ct. 516, 100 L.Ed. 550 (1956).

5. 222 F.2d 234 (2d Cir. 1955).

6. 350 U.S. at 466, 76 S.Ct. at 519, 100 L.Ed. at 556. See Matter of Lea Fabrics, Inc., 272 F.2d 769 (3d Cir. 1959); Weintraub & Levin, "Availability of Bankruptcy Rehabilitation to the Middle-Sized Corporation: The Third Circuit's Interpretation", 14 Rutgers L.Rev. 564 (1960).

ing was held to be an exercise of sound discretion on their part.[7]

In the third United States Supreme Court holding, Securities and Exchange Commission v. American Trailer Rentals Co.,[8] the rulings of the referee-in-bankruptcy, district judge, and court of appeals refusing to dismiss a Chapter XI proceeding, were reversed by the Supreme Court as abuse of their discretion. The Supreme Court mentioned its previous rejection of the absolute rule that Chapter X was more appropriate than Chapter XI whenever the debtor was publicly *owned,* and refused to accept a variation of such absolute rule urged by the S. E. C. to require Chapter X in all cases involving the rights of public *investor creditors.* The Court reiterated the "needs to be served" test. Applying this test, the Court held that the proceeding should have been brought under Chapter X since Chapter X was more appropriate for use for the adjustment of debt publicly-held by widely-scattered, uninformed, poorly-organized public investors, especially where there was evidence of misappropriation of assets and there was need for a complete corporate reorganization.

The Supreme Court refused to express an opinion as to whether or not a Chapter X arrangement would be appropriate in the case. The Supreme Court merely held that all issues relevant to the possible financial rehabilitation of respondent must be determined within the confines of a Chapter X, rather than a Chapter XI, proceeding.

Within the standards set by the Supreme Court, the lower courts have considerable discretion.[9]

D. REORGANIZATION

BACKGROUND OF CHAPTER X

386. Corporate reorganization provisions have been part of the Bankruptcy Act since 1933, when section 77 was enacted to provide for the reorganization of interstate railroads, and 1934, when section 77B was passed for the reorganization of corporations other than interstate railroads. In 1938, section 77B was replaced by Chapter X of the Chandler Act.

Prior to 1933, corporations, especially the railroads, were reorganized in court-developed equity receivership proceedings, especially in the federal courts when jurisdiction could be based on diversity-of-citizenship. Such proceedings were commenced by a friendly creditor's bill seeking receivership. A creditors' protective committee was formed extra-judicially under a deposit agreement, under which cooperating creditors pooled their claims and formulated a reorganization plan. At a judicial sale, the debtor's property was sold, free

7. Frankfurter & Burton, JJ., dissenting, contended that in exercising discretion, the lower courts misconceived the holding of the United States Realty and Improvement Co. case and disregarded the 1952 amendment deleting the "fair and equitable" requirement from Chapter XI (see section 384, n. 4 supra).

8. 379 U.S. 594, 85 S.Ct. 513, 13 L.Ed.2d 510 (1965).

9. Dismissal under Chapter XI has been directed in Manufacturers' Credit Corp. v. Securities and Exchange Commission, 395 F.2d 833 (3d Cir. 1968); Securities and Exchange Commission v. Canandaigua Enterprises Corp., 339 F.2d 14 (2d Cir. 1964); Securities and Exchange Commission v. Liberty Baking Corp., 240 F.2d 511 (2d Cir. 1957), cert. denied 353 U.S. 930, 77 S.Ct. 719, 1 L.Ed.2d 723 (1957); Mecca Temple of Ancient Arabic Order of Nobles of Mystic Shrine v. Darrock, 142 F.2d 869 (2d Cir. 1944), cert. denied 323 U.S. 784, 65 S.Ct. 271, 89 L.Ed. 626 (1944); In re BarChris Construction Corp., 223 F.Supp. 229 (S.D.N.Y.1963); Matter of Herold Radio & Electronics Corp., 191 F.Supp. 780 (S.D.N.Y.1961). Retention under Chapter XI was approved in Grayson-Robinson Stores, Inc. v. Securities and Exchange Commission, 320 F.2d 940 (2d Cir. 1963); Matter of Lea Fabrics, Inc., 272 F. 2d 769 (3d Cir. 1959), vacated Securities and Exchange Commission v. Lea Fabrics, Inc., 363 U.S. 417, 80 S.Ct. 1258, 4 L.Ed.2d 1515 (1960); Securities and Exchange Commission v. Wilcox-Gay Corp., 231 F.2d 859 (6th Cir. 1956); In re Transvision, Inc., 217 F.2d 243 (2d Cir. 1954), cert. denied sub nom. Securities and Exchange Commission v. Transvision, Inc., 348 U.S. 952, 75 S.Ct. 440, 99 L.Ed. 744 (1955). Quittner, "Should a Chapter X-½ be Enacted for Rehabilitation of the Middle Size Corporation?", 42 Ref.J. 37 (1968); Quittner & Chanin, "A New Debtor Relief Proceeding for the Middle Size Corporation: Some Concrete Proposals (Chapter X-½)", 8 Santa Clara Law. 191 (1968); Annot., 100 L.Ed. 559 (1955).

from the claims of the old creditors, at a price not less than the "upset price". Nonassenting creditors were entitled to receive their proportionate interest in the net proceeds of the sale in cash. The court would confirm the sale, but not the reorganization plan. The property was then conveyed to a new corporation formed for the purpose of carrying on the business. Assenting creditors and shareholders, to the extent that their interests had any value, received the value of their claims and interests in the form of securities issued by the new corporation in strict, "absolute" priority, according to the reorganization plan. Many of the defects of equity receivership were corrected by section 77B and later by Chapter X. Subsequent to the enactment of section 77B, consent receiverships for corporate reorganization could no longer be commenced.

Corporate reorganization, as discussed in this and the succeeding sections, means reorganization under Chapter X of the Federal Bankruptcy Act.[1] The term "reorganization" in the tax law refers to mergers, consolidations, "split-ups", "split-offs", "spin-offs", etc.,[2] and under state law is sometimes used as a synonym for recapitalization or reclassification of shares.[3] Reorganization, in the broader sense, can be outside of bankruptcy, such as under the Federal Public Utility Holding Company Act.[4]

Section 77; Section 77B

Corporate reorganization provisions have been part of the Federal Bankruptcy Act since 1933, when section 77 was enacted to provide for the reorganization of interstate railroads. In 1934, section 77B was passed for the reorganization of corporations other than interstate railroads. Since based on the bankruptcy power,[5] interstate commerce is otherwise immaterial.

Chapter X

In 1938, section 77B was replaced by Chapter X of the Chandler Act, which, although amended from time to time, has continued to date. Since 1948, section 77 procedures can be short-cut under section 20b of the Federal Transportation Act.[6]

1. 11 U.S.C.A. §§ 100–676; J. Moore, Collier on Bankruptcy, vol. 6 (corporate reorganization text), vol. 7 (corporate reorganization forms) (14th ed. 1967); J. Gerdes, Corporate Reorganizations under Section 77B of The Bankruptcy Act (3 vols. 1936) (Supp.1937); Billyou, "Reorganization under Chapter X", 49 Colum.L.Rev. 456 (1949); Moore, "Reorganizations under Chapter X", 35 Ref.J. 105 (Oct. 1961). Applicable to Chapter X proceedings are all of the provisions of Chapters I to VII, inclusive, of the Bankruptcy Act, excepting §§ 23, 57(h), (n), 64, and 70(f). § 102, 11 U.S.C.A. § 502. But see United States v. Anderson, 334 F.2d 111 (5th Cir. 1964), cert. denied 379 U.S. 879, 85 S.Ct. 147, 13 L.Ed.2d 86 (1964) (allowing United States priority, with respect to Small Business Administration loan, under 31 U.S.C.A. § 191 (applicable to insolvent persons indebted to United States), no priority being available under 11 U.S.C.A. § 104 against debtor in Chapter X proceeding).

2. See section 351 supra.

3. See section 345 supra. Several states have corporate reorganization statutes. See Billyou, "Corporate Reorganization under Federal and State Statutes", 1958 U.Ill.L.F. 556.

4. Where the applicable rules, including the "absolute priority" rule (see section 388 infra), differ in several significant respects. See L. Loss, Securities Regulation 140–141 (2d ed. 1961); section 382, n. 17 supra. But see Securities and Exchange Commission v. Chenery Corp., 332 U.S. 194, 67 S.Ct. 1575, 67 S.Ct. 1760, 91 L.Ed. 1995 (1947), reh. denied 332 U.S. 783, 68 S.Ct. 26, 92 L.Ed.2d 367 (1947) (management not allowed to benefit from shares traded during 1935 Act reorganization); Securities and Exchange Commission v. Dumaine, 218 F.2d 308 (1st Cir. 1954) (compensation denied 1935 Act reorganization committee member because wife traded in securities of corporation), cert. denied sub nom. Dumaine v. Securities and Exchange Commission, 349 U.S. 929, 75 S.Ct. 771, 99 L.Ed. 1259 (1955). Cf. 11 U.S.C.A. § 649. See section 299 supra.

5. U.S.Const. art. I, § 8, cl. 4. Years before the United States Supreme Court had indicated that corporate reorganization, although foreign to traditional bankruptcy, was an aspect of bankruptcy law. Canada Southern Ry. v. Gebhard, 109 U.S. 527, 3 S.Ct. 363, 27 L.Ed. 1020 (1883) (under Canadian corporate reorganization statute).

6. Fooshee & Billyou, "Amendments to Federal Railroad Reorganization Statutes Proposed by the American Bar Association", 16 Bus.Law. 543 (1961); Sunderland, "Suggestions for Improvement in Section 77 of the Bankruptcy Act", 14 Bus.Law. 487 (1959); Comment, "The New Haven Railroad Reorganization Proceedings, or the Little Railroad That Couldn't", 78 Harv.L.Rev. 861 (1965).

Equity Receivership

The equity receivership developed in the federal courts to reorganize corporations, especially railroads, in financial difficulties, to permit their continued operation and preserve their going concern value. The jurisdictional basis was diversity of citizenship between the petitioner and the corporation. The whole proceeding was court-developed and evidenced remarkable judicial ingenuity.

A friendly creditor,[7] of citizenship diverse from the corporation, would file a creditor's bill in the federal district court, alleging actual or imminent insolvency, usually in the equity sense, since those in control of the corporation were usually unready to admit lack of any shareholder equity in the corporation; threats of creditor actions and attachments and dismemberment of the corporate property; the inadequacy of the legal remedy; and the need for receivership to preserve the assets for the benefit of all the creditors. The corporation would answer, admitting the allegations and joining in the prayer for the relief of receivership, in effect waiving the lack of *equity* jurisdiction (since the petitioning creditor could not have shown that he had exhausted his legal remedy by attaching the corporate property and having his execution returned unsatisfied). Hence the name "consent receivership", and the control which the corporation enjoyed over the proceedings.[8]

Receivership followed, along with "ancillary receiverships" in federal courts in other districts where corporate property was located.

The receivership prevented creditors from enforcing their claims against the corporate property (hence the name "umbrella receivership"). Meanwhile, the receiver (often a corporate official) operated the business, issuing high-priority "receiver's certificates" for working capital.

A creditors' protective committee was formed extrajudicially under a deposit agreement, under which cooperating creditors pooled their claims and formulated a reorganization plan. At a judicial sale, the corporate property was sold, free from the claims of the old creditors, to the highest bidder—in effect the creditors' committee which had to put up only as much cash as was necessary to pay the expenses involved and the proportionate interest of the nonassenting creditors in the net proceeds of the sale.[9] An "upset price" was usually fixed by the court for the protection of those involved. The court would confirm the sale, but not the reorganization plan.[10]

The property was then conveyed to a new corporation formed for the purpose of carrying on the business. The creditor claims, of course, continued against the old corporation, but it was now devoid of assets.[11]

---

7. In cases of an unfriendly creditor, the corporation could resist receivership by the defense of lack of equity on the part of a creditor who had not exhausted his legal remedy. Pusey & Jones Co. v. Hanssen, 261 U.S. 491, 43 S.Ct. 454, 67 L.Ed. 763 (1923). Cf. Wabash St. L. & P. Ry. v. Central Trust Co., 22 F. 138 (N.D.Ohio 1884) (petition by debtor corporation).

8. Such proceedings were upheld as involving a "controversy" and as noncollusive. Re Metropolitan Railway Receivership, 208 U.S. 90, 28 S.Ct. 219, 52 L.Ed 403 (1908).

9. Coriell v. Morris White, Inc., 54 F.2d 255 (2d Cir. 1931), rev'd on other grounds 289 U.S. 426, 53 S.Ct. 678, 77 L.Ed. 1300, 88 A.L.R. 1231 (1933) (condemning lack of public sale and pro rata cash payments to dissenters). But see Phipps v. Chicago, R. I. & P. Ry., 284 F. 945, 28 A.L.R. 1184 (8th Cir.1922), cert. granted 261 U.S. 611, 43 S.Ct. 363, 67 L.Ed. 826 (1923), dismissed per stipulation 262 U.S. 762, 43 S. Ct. 701, 67 L.Ed. 1221 (1923) (approving reorganization without judicial sale and without new corporation, where all creditors were allocated securities and where original corporation continued business under injunction barring actions against it by old creditors). Competing bidders were at a disadvantage because they had to pay all cash at the sale.

10. Graselli Chemical Co. v. Aetna Explosives Co., 252 F. 456 (2d Cir.1918) (dictum: court has power over plan); Rosenberg, "Aetna Explosives Case—A Mile-stone in Reorganization", 20 Colum.L.Rev. 733 (1920).

11. The names of the two corporations were often very close, e. g., Northern Pacific R. R., Northern Pacific Ry. Cf. Phipps v. Chicago, R. I. & P. Ry., supra note 9.

The nonassenting creditors received their pro rata share of the net proceeds of the sale in cash. The receiver's certificates were redeemed in either cash or senior securities of the new corporation. The other creditors and the shareholders received such securities in the new corporation as were provided under the reorganization plan. Generally, the capital structure of the new corporation was a somewhat scaled-down version of the capital structure of the old corporation. Sometimes shareholders had to contribute additional cash ("assessment") in order to be allowed to retain some interest in the new corporation, or received warrants to subscribe to shares therein, or were cut-off without any continuing interest.

A protective rule which developed to regulate the plan to some extent was proclaimed in the famous case of Northern Pacific Ry. v. Boyd,[12] in 1913, known as the "absolute priority" rule or "fixed principle", to the effect that shareholders could retain no interest in the corporation under a plan which did not fully satisfy the claims of all creditors.

The defects of equity receivership were lack of real protection for the honest dissenting creditor (since the court confirmed only the sale, not the plan); complicated, costly procedures of sometimes doubtful validity; need for ancillary receiverships; control in the old management (through necessity of its consent to the receivership); power of and lack of court supervision over the protective committees and their fees (usually under the domination of bankers); "hold-ups" by "striker" creditors; and risk of subsequent creditor court attack on grounds of fraudulent conveyance, unfairness, etc.

The situation was substantially improved, first by section 77B and later by Chapter X.

Upon the enactment of section 77B in 1934, consent receiverships for corporate reorganization could no longer be commenced.[13]

AVAILABILITY TO CORPORATIONS OF CHAPTER X

387. Chapter X expressly provides that proceedings thereunder lie only upon a showing of the need of relief thereunder and why adequate relief cannot be obtained under Chapter XI. If the court finds Chapter XI more appropriate, the debtor may apply to convert the proceedings to Chapter XI. Chapter X proceedings may affect secured debt and shares, as well as unsecured debt, to which Chapter XI is limited. Chapter X proceedings will also be required in lieu of Chapter XI proceedings when the situation requires the additional safeguards and more extensive relief available under Chapter X.

Chapter X expressly provides that every petition thereunder must state specific facts showing the need for relief thereunder and why adequate relief cannot be obtained under Chapter XI.[1]

If the court finds Chapter XI more appropriate, the debtor may apply to convert the proceedings into a Chapter XI proceeding.[2]

As previously discussed, Chapter XI proceedings can only affect unsecured debt, and not secured debt or shares.[3] In contrast, Chapter X proceedings can affect secured debt and shares as well as unsecured debt. In addition, proceedings under Chapter XI will not be allowed if they should have been brought under Chapter X with its additional safeguards and more extensive relief.[4]

---

12. 228 U.S. 482, 33 S.Ct. 554, 57 L.Ed. 931 (1913) (holding that under plan existing shareholders could not continue as shareholders even upon payment of prescribed assessments).

13. New England Coal & Coke Co. v. Rutland R. R., 143 F.2d 179 (2d Cir.1944). Existing receiverships continued. For example, the Minneapolis & St. Louis Ry. remained in receivership from 1923 to 1943. Many corporations in equity receivership prior to 1933–1934 became subject to sections 77 and 77B (and then Chapter X) and emerged from reorganization decades later.

1. 11 U.S.C.A. § 530.

2. 11 U.S.C.A. § 547.

3. See section 384 supra.

4. See section 385 supra.

PROCEDURE OF REORGANIZATION PROCEEDINGS

388. A petition under Chapter X may be filed by (voluntary) or against (involuntary) any business corporation if it is insolvent in either the bankruptcy sense or the equity sense. Involuntary petitions must be by three or more creditors or an indenture trustee, and must allege that the corporation was adjudged bankrupt, or is in receivership, or has been dispossessed for mortgage default, or is in a mortgage foreclosure proceeding, or has committed an act of bankruptcy within the preceding four months. Every petition must be filed in good faith.

After approval of the petition, the judge fixes the time for the filing of proofs of claim of creditors and interests of shareholders.

A disinterested trustee must be appointed if the corporation's liquidated, noncontingent liabilities are $250,000 or more. The trustee, if appointed, is responsible for the reorganization plan, and has such title to the corporation's property as the trustee-in-bankruptcy would have.

An S.E.C. advisory report is required when the corporation's scheduled indebtedness exceeds $3,000,000.

After court approval of the reorganization plan, the plan is submitted for acceptance by (a) two-thirds (in amount) of creditors, and (b) majority of shareholders if the corporation has not been found insolvent. After acceptance of the plan, the judge confirms the plan if it is "fair and equitable, and feasible", etc. Upon confirmation, the plan becomes binding on all concerned, and is thereafter consummated.

Petition

A petition under Chapter X may be filed by (voluntary) or against (involuntary) any corporation [1] which could have been adjudged bankrupt,[2] if it is either insolvent (in the bankruptcy sense) [3] *or* unable to meet its debts as they mature (equitable insolvency). The petition may be filed in a pending bankruptcy proceeding.[4]

A voluntary petition must be authorized by the corporation pursuant to applicable local law. It may not be filed by shareholders derivatively in behalf of the corporation.[5]

An involuntary petition may be filed by (a) three or more creditors [6] whose liquidated, noncontingent claims against the corporation *or* its property aggregate $5,000 or more, or (b) an indenture trustee.[7] The involuntary petition must allege that the corporation was adjudged bankrupt, or is in receivership, or has been dispossessed for mortgage default, or is in a mortgage foreclosure proceeding, or has committed an act of bankruptcy within the past four months.[8]

Upon filing of the petition, the reorganization court acquires jurisdiction of the debtor and all of its property wherever located.[9]

Every petition must be filed in good faith.[10] Good faith is lacking where petitioning creditors acquired their claims for the purpose of filing, or adequate relief is obtainable under Chapter XI, or an effective reorganization plan is improbable, or the interests of creditors and shareholders would be best subserved by a prior pending proceeding.[11]

Chapter X proceedings, unlike straight bankruptcy and Chapter XI proceedings, are not referred to a referee-in-bankruptcy, but are conducted by the judge.

---

1. See section 383, n. 10 supra. Also included within the Chapter X definition of "corporation" is any railroad corporation excepting one authorized to file a petition under § 77. 11 U.S.C.A. § 106(3). A petition by or against a subsidiary may be filed in the court which has approved a petition by or against its parent corporation. 11 U.S.C.A. § 129.

2. See section 383, nn. 11, 13 supra.

3. See section 383, n. 8 supra.

4. 11 U.S.C.A. § 527.

5. Price v. Gurney, 324 U.S 100, 65 S.Ct. 513, 89 L. Ed. 776 (1945).

6. The term "creditors" as defined in the bankruptcy act (11 U.S.C.A. § 1(11)) does not include shareholders. Price v. Gurney, supra note 5.

7. 11 U.S.C.A. § 526.

8. 11 U.S.C.A. § 531. See section 383, n. 9 supra.

9. 11 U.S.C.A. § 511. Such jurisdiction is summary; no ancillary proceedings are necessary.

10. 11 U.S.C.A. §§ 543, 544.

11. 11 U.S.C.A. § 546.

Filing and Proofs of Claim

After approval of the petition, the judge fixes a time for the filing of proofs of claim of creditors and interests of shareholders. Creditors and shareholders may be divided into classes according to the nature of their respective claims and shares.[12]

Disinterested Trustee

Upon approval of a petition by the judge, a disinterested trustee must be appointed if the debtor's liquidated, noncontingent liabilities are $250,000 or more; otherwise the debtor might be continued in possession.[13] Even in the latter case, one or more trustees

or a disinterested examiner might be appointed to prepare and file a reorganization plan.[14]

Where a trustee is appointed, he is responsible for the plan; otherwise the debtor, any creditor or indenture trustee or shareholder when the debtor is not found insolvent, may file a plan.[15] The reorganization trustee has such title to the debtor's property as a trustee-in-bankruptcy would have.[16]

S.E.C. Advisory Functions

If the scheduled indebtedness exceeds $3,000,000, the plan or plans deemed worthy by the judge must be submitted to the S.E.C. for examination and report. In other cases, the judge may do so. The S.E.C. report, if any, is only advisory.[17] The S.E.C. might even intervene in the proceeding.[18]

12. 11 U.S.C.A. §§ 196, 197. Proof and allowance are prerequisite to voting on any plan, but not necessarily to participation under the plan. Claims may be allowed and subordinated (or "deep-rocked") on equitable grounds. See section 152, n. 2 supra. See also Prudence Realization Corp. v. Geist, 316 U.S. 89, 62 S.Ct. 978, 86 L.Ed. 1293 (1942) (claim of debtor in section 77B proceeding as guarantor which had acquired some of guaranteed securities not subordinated to claims of other holders of such securities in section 77B reorganization of principal obligor despite state rule to contrary); Vanston Bondholders Protective Committee v. Green, 329 U.S. 156, 67 S.Ct. 237, 91 L.Ed. 162 (1946) (claim for interest-on-interest under mortgage indenture provision disallowed in Chapter X proceeding as incompatible with equitable principles of bankruptcy law even if valid under applicable state law); Matter of Third Avenue Transit Corp., 222 F.2d 466 (2d Cir.1955) (treasury bonds subordinated to outstanding publicly-held bonds). Tort claims are more broadly provable (and therefore dischargeable) under Chapter X than in straight bankruptcy. 11 U.S.C.A. § 506(1). Landlord's claims for future rent against a debtor under Chapter X are limited to the normal rent (without acceleration) which would otherwise become due during the three years (as compared to one year in straight bankruptcy) after surrender of possession or reentry by the landlord. 11 U.S.C.A. § 602; Silverstein, "Rejection of Executory Contracts in Bankruptcy and Reorganization", 31 U.Chi.L.Rev. 467 (1964); Note, "Chapter X Trustee Adoption of Executory Contracts: The Bankruptcy Act Speaks through Its Silence", 115 U.Pa.L.Rev. 937 (1967).

13. 11 U.S.C.A. § 556. Cotrustees, who need not be disinterested, might also be appointed. Ibid. The attorney for the trustee must also be disinterested. 11 U.S.C.A. § 157. See Ferber, "Conflicts of Interest in Reorganization Proceedings under the Public Utility Holding Company Act of 1935 and Chapter X of the Bankruptcy Act", 28 Geo.Wash.L.Rev. 319 (1959); Rochelle & Palmer, "Trustee in Chapter X Reorganization", 32 Ref.J. 99–102, 106 (1958).

14. 11 U.S.C.A. § 568.

15. 11 U.S.C.A. §§ 569, 570.

16. 11 U.S.C.A. § 586. See section 383, n. 17 supra. See Comment, "Effect of Corporate Reorganization on Nonassignable Contract", 74 Harv.L.Rev. 393 (1960).

17. 11 U.S.C.A. § 572; Windle, "The Securities Exchange Commission and Corporate Reorganization Under Chapter X", 34 Ref.J. 37 (1960).

"The Commission's role under Chapter X of the Bankruptcy Act . . . differs from that under the various other statutes which it administers. The Commission does not initiate Chapter X proceedings or hold its own hearings, and it has no authority to determine any of the issues in such proceedings. The Commission participates in proceedings under Chapter X in order to provide independent, expert assistance to the courts, the participants, and investors in a highly complex area of corporate law and finance. It pays special attention to the interests of public security holders who may not otherwise be effectively represented.

"Where the scheduled indebtedness of a debtor corporation exceeds $3 million, Section 172 of Chapter X requires the judge, before approving any plan of reorganization, to submit it to the Commission for its examination and report. If the indebtedness does not exceed $3 million, the judge may, if he deems it advisable to do so, submit the plan to the Commission before deciding whether to approve it. Where the Commission files a report, copies or a summary must be sent to all security holders and creditors when they are asked to vote on the plan. The Commission has no authority to veto or to require the adoption of a plan of reorganization. . . ." 29 SEC Ann.Rep. 87 (1963).

18. 11 U.S.C.A. § 608. See Ferber, "Conflicts of Interest in Reorganization Proceedings under the

Court Approval of Plan

After the S.E.C. has had reasonable opportunity to submit its advisory report, if a plan has been submitted to it, court approval of a plan is the next step, after which the plan, along with text or summaries of any courts opinions and S.E.C. reports, is submitted to the creditors and shareholders affected.[19] Prior thereto, no solicitation of assents to the plan may be made.[20]

Acceptance of Plan

Acceptance of the plan is by (a) creditors holding two-thirds in amount of the proven and allowed claims in each class, and (b) if the debtor has not been found insolvent, the majority of the holders of shares of which proofs have been filed and allowed, of each class.[21] Thereafter, a confirmation hearing is called by the judge.

Court Confirmation of Plan

After acceptance, the judge may confirm the plan if satisfied that the plan meets specified requirements, including the requirement that the plan is "fair and equitable, and feasible." [22]

The statutory "fair and equitable" requirement has been held to be a codification of the "absolute priority" rule or "fixed principle" of the Boyd case.[23]

Although technically based on the fraudulent conveyance rule, the "absolute priority"

shares and common shares) and two wholly-owned subsidiaries, each of which had outstanding in the hands of the public mortgage bonds secured by an indenture on its respective properties. The district court did not find specific values for the separate properties of the three corporations or for the properties of the enterprise as a unit, stated that an appraisal would "produce further confusion", and confirmed the reorganization plan. Confirmation of a plan, absent the requisite valuation data, was held to be error. To determine the fairness of a plan required findings of (a) what assets of each corporation were subject to payment of the respective claims, (b) the amount of the claims of the two subsidiaries against the parent (or refusing to insulate the parent's assets against the claims of creditors of the subsidiaries because the parent had ignored their separate corporateness), and (c) value of the whole enterprise by capitalization of prospective earnings (relevant to feasibility as well as to fairness). The absolute priority rule was held to require "full compensatory treatment" for the entire bundle of rights being surrendered by the creditors, but there "is no necessity to construct the new capital structure on the framework of the old". Case v. Los Angeles Lumber Products Co., 308 U.S. 106, 60 S.Ct. 1, 84 L.Ed. 110 (1939), reh. denied 308 U.S. 637, 60 S.Ct. 258, 84 L.Ed. 529 (1939), held that the section 77B requirement that a reorganization plan be "fair and equitable" incorporated a term of art which had acquired a fixed meaning through judicial interpretations in equity receivership reorganizations, viz., the "fixed principle" or "absolute priority rule" that each class of creditors and shareholders, beginning with the most senior, highest priority claim, must receive under the plan securities or other consideration fully equal in value to their interests before the next junior class may receive anything. By such test, the plan, even though it recognized the "relative priorities" of creditors and shareholders, was found not to be "fair and equitable". See Group of Institutional Investors v. Chicago, M., St. P. & P. R.R., 318 U.S. 523, 63 S.Ct. 727, 87 L.Ed. 959 (1943), reh. denied sub nom. Group of Institutional Investors v. Abrams, 318 U.S. 803, 63 S.Ct. 980, 87 L.Ed. 1166 (1943) (upholding I.C.C. and lower court's determination of maximum new capitalization, taking into account fixed interest, new debt securities, and reasonable dividends on the basis of past and prospective earnings and other relevant facts without specific finding as to value of properties, and that old preferred and common shares had no value). See also Ecker v. Western Pac. R.R., 318 U.S. 448, 63 S.Ct. 692 87 L.Ed. 892 (1943); King, "Chapter X Valuation: Principles and Application", 42 Ref.J. 108 (1968); Blum & Katz, "Depreciation and Enterprise Valuation", 32 U.Chi.L.Rev. 236 (1965); Blum, "Full Priority and Full Compensation in Corporate Reorganizations: A Reappraisal", 25 U.Chi.L.Rev. 417 (1958); Billyou, " 'New Directions': A Further Comment", 67 Harv.L.Rev. 1379 (1954); Blum, "The 'New Directions' for Priority Rights in Bankruptcy Reorganizations", 67 Harv.L.Rev. 1367 (1954); Billyou,

---

Public Utility Holding Company Act of 1935 and Chapter X of the Bankruptcy Act", 28 Geo.Wash.L. Rev. 319 (1959).

19. 11 U.S.C.A. § 575.

20. 11 U.S.C.A. § 576.

21. 11 U.S.C.A. § 579; Note, "Voting Rights of Creditors and Stockholders in Chapter X Reorganizations", 105 U.Pa.L.Rev. 692 (1957). A plan might be confirmed without the required acceptance. See 11 U.S.C.A. § 616(7), (8).

22. 11 U.S.C.A. § 621(2).

23. See section 386, n. 12 supra. Marine Harbor Properties, Inc. v. Manufacturers Trust Co., 317 U. S. 78, 63 S.Ct. 93, 87 L.Ed. 64 (1942), reh. denied 317 U.S. 710, 63 S.Ct. 254, 87 L.Ed. 566 (1943). Two of the leading cases were section 77B proceedings. Consolidated Rock Products Co. v. DuBois, 312 U.S. 510, 61 S.Ct. 675, 85 L.Ed. 982 (1941), involved a parent corporation (with outstanding preferred

rule has been extended to mean that each class of creditors and shareholders, beginning with the most senior, highest priority claim, must receive under the plan securities or other consideration fully equal in value to their preexisting interests before the next junior class may receive anything, thus, shareholders may receive nothing in a corporation insolvent in the bankruptcy sense;[24] common shareholders may only participate after preferred shareholders have received the full equivalent of their liquidation preferences.[25] In contrast is the "relative priority" rule, recognized as "fair and equitable" in reorganizations under the Federal Public Utility Holding Company Act of 1935.[26]

Upon confirmation, the plan binds the corporation and all its creditors and shareholders; the debtor's property dealt with by the plan is free of all claims; and steps are taken to consummate the plan.[27]

Consummation of Plan

Upon consummation of the plan ("closing", "turnover"), the judge enters a final decree discharging the debtor; discharging the trustee, if any; may make such provisions by way of injunction or otherwise as may be equitable; and closes the estate.[28] If no plan is approved or confirmed, the petition may be dismissed or the debtor adjudicated a bankrupt.[29]

Compensation and Allowances

Various provisions deal with compensation and allowances to those involved in the proceeding, including attorneys.[30]

No compensation is allowed to anyone who has dealt in obligations or securities of

"Priority Rights of Security Holders in Bankruptcy Reorganization: New Directions", 67 Harv.L.Rev. 553 (1954); Blum, "The Law and Language of Corporate Reorganization", 17 U.Chi.L.Rev. 565 (1950); Dodd, "The Los Angeles Lumber Products Company Case and its Implications", 53 Harv.L.Rev. 713 (1940); Bonbright & Bergerman "Two Rival Theories of Priority Rights of Security Holders in Corporate Reorganizattion", 28 Colum.L.Rev. 127 (1928). See also 49 U.S.C.A. § 20b.

24. Spitzer v. Stichman, 278 F.2d 402 (2d Cir. 1960); Frank Fehr Brewing Co. v. Clarke, 268 F.2d 170 (6th Cir.1959).

25. Central States Electric Corp. v. Austrian, 183 F. 2d 879 (4th Cir.1950), cert. denied sub nom. Berner v. Austrian, 340 U.S. 917, 71 S.Ct. 350, 95 L.Ed. 662 (1951); Petition of Portland Elec. Power Co., 162 F.2d 618 (9th Cir.1947), cert. denied 332 U.S. 837, 68 S.Ct. 217, 92 L.Ed. 410 (1947).

26. Otis & Co. v. Securities and Exchange Commission, 323 U.S. 624, 65 S.Ct. 483, 89 L.Ed. 511 (1945) held that a plan to liquidate a holding company under the Federal Public Utility Holding Company Act of 1935 may be "fair and equitable" to preferred shareholders under § 11(e) if common shareholders are allowed to participate in the liquidation distribution before the preferred shareholders receive less than the value of their liquidation preferences (including dividend arrearages). The SEC had concluded that liquidation under the 1935 Act, which was only one of several alternative methods of accomplishing simplification under the Act was not the type of liquidation envisaged in the articles of incorporation liquidation provision, and distributed the net assets among the holders of the preferred and common shares on the basis of their respective investment values in the corporation as a going concern—a 94.52 percent to 5.48 percent allocation which was not challenged. The Supreme Court affirmed on the ground that the articles of incorporation liquidation provision adopted in 1929

was inoperative in a simplification under the 1935 Act, saying: "Where pre-existing contract provisions exist which produce results at variance with a legislative policy which was not foreseeable at the time the contract was made, they cannot be permitted to operate". The Court did not reach the argument that if the articles of incorporation liquidation provision had applied to the simplification, it could not have been disregarded, and distribution of assets only to the preferred shares would have been necessary in order to meet the "fair and equitable" requirement of the 1935 Act. See Brudney, "The Investment-Value Doctrine and Corporate Readjustments", 72 Harv.L.Rev. 645 (1959); Comment, "The Full Compensation Doctrine in Corporate Reorganizations: A Schizophrenic Standard", 63 Yale L.J. 812 (1954). See also 49 U.S.C.A. § 20b. The "absolute priority" rule is generally not applied in determining "fairness" of recapitalizations, etc., under state law. See sections 240, 345 supra. Dodd, "Fair and Equitable Recapitalizations", 55 Harv.L.Rev. 780 (1942); Latty, "Fairness—The Focal Point in Preferred Stock Arrearages Elimination", 29 Va.L.Rev. 1 (1942).

27. 11 U.S.C.A. §§ 624, 626, 627.

28. 11 U.S.C.A. § 628.

29. 11 U.S.C.A. § 636.

30. 11 U.S.C.A. §§ 641–649. See also 11 U.S.C.A. §§ 610–611 (filings required before representation of others).

the debtor during the reorganization proceeding without prior court approval.[31]

NONAPPLICATION TO FEDERAL REORGANIZATION OF VARIOUS PROVISIONS

389. Nonapplicable to federal reorganizations are various provisions, including the registration (and prospectus) requirements of the Federal Securities Act of 1933; specified taxes; and such state corporate law requirements as those of board of directors or shareholder action, consideration for shares, etc.

Chapter X expressly provides that section 5 of the Federal Securities Act of 1933 shall not apply to securities issued in connection with a Chapter X corporate reorganization.[1]

Nonapplication of Specified Taxes

Various provisions in Chapter X deal with taxes: (a) No income or profit taxable under the laws of the United States or any state is deemed to have accrued or to have been realized by reason of any modification or any cancellation of any indebtedness under a Chapter X proceeding;[2] (b) Where avoidance of taxes is a principal purpose of a plan, objection may be made by the secretary of the treasury or appropriate state officer.[3]

Nonapplication of State Corporate Law Requirements

Where a corporation undergoes federal reorganization, some state statutes expressly provide that the usual requirements of board of directors and/or shareholder action, consideration for shares, preemptive rights, dissenting shareholder's appraisal remedy, etc., do not apply.[4] Confirmation by the reorganization court provides protection for the interests involved. *Quaere*, whether such state law requirements could in any event interfere with a plan of reorganization valid under federal law.

---

31. 11 U.S.C.A. § 649; Wolf v. Weinstein, 372 U.S. 633, 83 S.Ct. 969, 10 L.Ed.2d 33 (1963) (president and general manager of debtor who traded very slightly in debtor's securities during Chapter X proceedings ordered to make restitution of all amounts of compensation and reimbursement received by them during proceedings); Matter of Food Town, Inc., 208 F.Supp. 139 (D.Md.1962) (allowing $77,-500 fee and disbursements to attorney for trustee); Steinberg, "Salient Features in Awarding Allowances in Corporate Reorganization Proceeding and the Role of the Securities and Exchange Commission in Their Final Determination", 8 N.Y.L.F. 253 (1962); Bandler, "Securities Trading and Fee Sharing Under Chapter X of the Bankruptcy Act", 15 Record of N.Y.C.B.A. 230 (1960), 35 Ref.J. 69 (1961); Note, "Officers and Supervisory Employees of Debtor in Possession Who Purchase Shares of Stock in Debtor Corporation During Fiduciary Tenure May Not Be Denied Compensation Pursuant to Provisions of Section 249 of Bankruptcy Act", 48 Va.L. Rev. 751 (1962); Note, "Denial of Allowance in Reorganizations under Section 249", 45 Va.L.Rev. 1065 (1959).

1. 11 U.S.C.A. § 664. The Federal Securities Act also expressly exempts from its registration (and prospectus) requirements certificates issued by trus-

tee-in-bankruptcy or receiver under court approval and securities issued under court-approved exchanges. 15 U.S.C.A. § 77c(7), (10). See Section 295 supra.

2. 11 U.S.C.A. § 668; see also 11 U.S.C.A. § 670 (income tax property basis adjustment).

3. 11 U.S.C.A. § 669.

4. See, e. g., ABA–ALI Model Bus.Corp.Act § 59A (optional section); Del.Gen.Corp.Law, § 303 (1967); McKinney's N.Y.Bus.Law, §§ 622(e) (6), 808. See section 350 supra.

APPENDIX A

CONVERSION TABLE—MODEL BUSINESS CORPORATION ACT

The following conversion table shows (1) the pre-1969 Model Business Corporation Act sections; (2) the comparable section, if any, as to subject matter, in the 1969 revised act; (3) whether the pre-1969 section was revised, deleted or left unchanged; and (4) the title or subject matter covered by the particular section.

(1) Pre-1969 Act Section	(2) 1969 Revised Act Section	(3) Change in Text	(4) Title or Subject Matter
1	1	same	Short title
2	2	§2(i) revised; §2(o) added.	Definitions
3	3	same	Purposes
4	4	same	General powers
4(a)	4(a)	same	Succession and duration
4(b)	4(b)	same	Suing and being sued
4(c)	4(c)	same	Seal
4(d)	4(d)	same	Acquiring property
4(e)	4(e)	same	Disposing of property
4(f)	4(f)	revised	Lending money to employees
4(g)	4(g)	same	Acquiring and disposing of securities
4(h)	4(h)	same	Making contracts, etc.
4(i)	4(i)	same	Lending money and investing
4(j)	4(j)	revised	Conducting business
4(k)	4(k)	same	Officers and agents
4(l)	4(l)	same	Bylaws
4(m)	4(m)	revised	Donations
4(n)	4(n)	revised	Aiding United States in wartime
4(o)	5	revised	Indemnification of officers, directors, employees and agents; insurance
4(p)	4(o)	same	Pension plans, etc.
—	4(p)	new	Partnerships, joint ventures, etc.
4(q)	—	deleted	Ceasing business
4(r)	4(q)	revised	Powers necessary or convenient
5	6	revised	Right of corporation to acquire and dispose of its own shares
6	7	revised	Defense of ultra vire
7	8	revised	Corporate name
8	9	same	Reserved name
9	10	revised	Registered name
10	11	revised	Renewal of registered name
11	12	same	Registered office and registered agent

(1) Pre-1969 Act Section	(2) 1969 Revised Act Section	(3) Change in Text	(4) Title or Subject Matter
12	13	revised	Change of registered office or registered agent
13	14	revised	Service of process on corporation
14	15	same	Authorized shares
15	16	revised	Issuance of shares of preferred or special classes in series
16	17	same	Subscriptions for shares
17	18	revised	Consideration for shares
18	19	revised	Payment for shares
18A	20	revised	Share rights and options
19	21	same	Determination of amount of stated capital
20	22	same	Expenses of organization, reorganization and financing
21	23	revised	Certificates representing shares
22	24	revised	Fractional shares
23	25		Liability of subscribers and shareholders
24	26	revised	} Shareholders' preemptive rights
24 [alternative]	26 [alternative]	revised	}
25	27	revised	Bylaws
25A	27A	same	Bylaws and other powers in emergency [optional]
26	28	revised	Meetings of shareholders
27	29	same	Notice of shareholders' meetings
28	30	same	Closing of transfer books and fixing record date
29	31	revised	Voting record
30	32	same	Quorum of shareholders
31	33	revised	Voting of shares
32	34	revised	Voting trusts and agreements among shareholders
33	35	revised	Board of directors
34	36	revised	Number and election of directors

(1) Pre-1969 Act Section	(2) 1969 Revised Act Section	(3) Change in Text	(4) Title or Subject Matter	(1) Pre-1969 Act Section	(2) 1969 Revised Act Section	(3) Change in Text	(4) Title or Subject Matter
35	37	same	Classification of directors	63	69	same	Reduction of stated capital in certain cases
36	38	same	Vacancies				
36A	39	revised	Removal of directors	64	70	same	Special provisions relating to surplus and reserves
37	40	revised	Quorum of directors				
—	41	new	Director conflicts of interest	65	71	revised	Procedure for merger
38	42	same	Executive and other committees	66	72	revised	Procedure for consolidation
39	43	same	Place and notice of directors' meetings	67	73	revised	Approval by shareholders
39A	44	revised	Action by directors without meeting	68	74	same	Articles of merger or consolidation
40	45	revised	Dividends	68A	75	revised	Merger of subsidiary corporation
41	46	revised	Distributions from capital surplus	69	76	same	Effect of merger or consolidation
42	47	revised	Loans to employees and directors	70	77	revised	Merger or consolidation of domestic and foreign corporations
43	48	revised	Liability of directors in certain cases	71	78	revised	Sale of assets in regular course of business and mortgage or pledge of assets
43A	49	revised	Provisions relating to actions by shareholders				
44	50	same	Officers	72	79	revised	Sale of assets other than in regular course of business
45	51	same	Removal of officers				
46	52	revised	Books and records	73	80	revised	Right of shareholders to dissent
47	53	same	Incorporators				
48	54	revised	Articles of incorporation	74	81	revised	Rights of dissenting shareholders
49	55	same	Filing of articles of incorporation	75	82	revised	Voluntary dissolution by incorporators
50	56	same	Effect of issuance of certificate of incorporation	76	83	same	Voluntary dissolution by consent of shareholders
51	—	deleted	Requirement before commencing business	77	84	revised	Voluntary dissolution by act of corporation
52	57	revised	Organization meeting of directors	78	85	same	Filing of statement of intent to dissolve
53	58	same	Right to amend articles of incorporation	79	86	revised	Effect of statement of intent to dissolve
54	59	revised	Procedure to amend articles of incorporation	80	87	same	Procedure after filing of statement of intent to dissolve
55	60	revised	Class voting on amendments	81	88	same	Revocation of voluntary dissolution proceedings by consent of shareholders
56	61	revised	Articles of amendment				
57	62	same	Filing of articles of amendment				
58	63	same	Effect of certificates of amendment	82	89	revised	Revocation of voluntary dissolution proceedings by act of corporation
59	64	revised	Restated articles of incorporation				
59A	65	same	Amendment of articles of incorporation in reorganization proceedings	83	90	same	Filing of statement of revocation of voluntary dissolution proceedings
60	66	same	Restriction on redemption or purchase of redeemable shares	84	91	same	Effect of statement of revocation of voluntary dissolution proceedings
61	67	revised	Cancellation of redeemable shares by redemption of purchase				
62	68	same	Cancellation of other reacquired shares				

(1) Pre-1969 Act Section	(2) 1969 Revised Act Section	(3) Change in Text	(4) Title or Subject Matter	(1) Pre-1969 Act Section	(2) 1969 Revised Act Section	(3) Change in Text	(4) Title or Subject Matter
85	92	same	Articles of dissolution	111	118	same	Amended certificate of authority
86	93	same	Filing of articles of dissolution	112	119	same	Withdrawal of foreign corporation
87	94	same	Involuntary dissolution	113	120	same	Filing of application for withdrawal
88	95	same	Notification to attorney general	114	121	same	Revocation of certificate of authority
89	96	same	Venue and process	115	122	same	Issuance of certificate of revocation
90	97	same	Jurisdiction of court to liquidate assets and business of corporation	116	123	same	Application to corporations heretofore authorized to transact business in this state
91	98	revised	Procedure in liquidation of corporation by court	117	124	same	Transacting business without certificate of authority
92	99	revised	Qualifications of receivers	118	125	revised	Annual report of domestic and foreign corporations
93	100	same	Filing of claims in liquidation proceedings	119	126	same	Filing of annual report of domestic and foreign corporations
94	101	same	Discontinuance of liquidation proceedings	120	127	same	Fees, franchise taxes and charges to be collected by secretary of state
95	102	same	Decree of involuntary dissolution				
96	103	same	Filing of decree of dissolution	121	128	revised	Fees for filing documents and issuing certificates
97	104	same	Deposit with state treasurer of amount due certain shareholders	122	129	revised	Miscellaneous charges
				123	130	revised	License fees payable by domestic corporations
98	105	same	Survival of remedy after dissolution				
99	106	same	Admission of foreign corporation	124	131	revised	License fees payable by foreign corporations
100	107	same	Powers of foreign corporation	125	132	revised	Franchise taxes payable by domestic corporations
101	108	revised	Corporate name of foreign corporation	126	133	revised	Franchise taxes payable by foreign corporations
102	109	revised	Change of name by foreign corporation	127	134	same	Assessment and collection of annual franchise taxes
103	110	same	Application for certificate of authority	128	135	same	Penalties imposed upon corporations
104	111	revised	Filing of application for certificate of authority	129	136	revised	Penalties imposed upon officers and directors
105	112	same	Effect of certificate of authority	130	137	same	Interrogatories by secretary of state
106	113	same	Registered office and registered agent of foreign corporation	131	138	revised	Information disclosed by interrogatories
107	114	revised	Change of registered office or registered agent of foreign corporation	132	139	same	Powers of secretary of state
				133	140	revised	Appeal from secretary of state
108	115	revised	Service of process on foreign corporation	134	141	same	Certificates and certified copies to be received in evidence
109	116	same	Amendment to articles of incorporation of foreign corporation				
110	117	same	Merger of foreign corporation authorized to transact business in this state	135	142	same	Forms to be furnished by secretary of state

(1) Pre-1969 Act Section	(2) 1969 Revised Act Section	(3) Change in Text	(4) Title or Subject Matter
136	143	same	Greater voting requirements
137	144	same	Waiver of notice
138	145	revised	Action by shareholder without meeting
139	146	same	Unauthorized assumption of corporate powers
140	147	same	Application to existing corporation

(1) Pre-1969 Act Section	(2) 1969 Revised Act Section	(3) Change in Text	(4) Title or Subject Matter
141	148	revised	Application to foreign and interstate commerce
142	149	same	Reservation of power
143	150	same	Effect of repeal of prior acts
144	151	same	Effect of invalidity of part of Model Act
145	152	same	Repeal of prior acts

APPENDIX B

CONVERSION TABLE—HENN ON CORPORATIONS

The following conversion table shows (1) the sections in the first edition of Henn on Corporations (1961) and (2) the comparable sections as to subject matter in this second edition of Henn on Corporations (1970).

(1) First Edition Section	(2) Second Edition Section	(1) First Edition Section	(2) Second Edition Section	(1) First Edition Section	(2) Second Edition Section	(1) First Edition Section	(2) Second Edition Section
1	1	55	55	108	108	161	161
2	2	56	56	109	109–112	162	170
3	3	57	57	110	109–112	163	162
4	4	58	58	111	109–112	164	163
5	5	59	59	112	113	165	164
6	6	60	60	113	114	166	165–166
7	7	61	61	114	115	167	167
8	8	62	62	115	116	168	168
9	9	63	63	116	117	169	171
10	10	64	64	117	118	170	171
11	11	65	65	118	119	171	171
12	12	66	66	119	120	172	169
13	13	67	67	120	121	173	202
14	14	68	68	121	122	174	171, 202
15	15	69	69	122	123	175	172
16	16	70	70	123	124	176	173
17	17	71	71	124	125	177	174
18	18	72	72	125	126	178	175
19	19	73	73	126	127	179	176
20	20	74	74	127	128	180	177
21	21	75	75	128	129	181	178
22	22	76	76	129	130		179 (new)
23	23		77 (new)	130	131	182	180
24	24	77	78	131	132	183	181
25	25	78	79	132	133	184	182
26	26	79	80	133	134	185	183
27	27	80	88, 353	134	135	186	184
28	28	81	89	135	136–137	187	185
29	29	82	83, 353	136	138	188	186
30	30	83	84, 97, 354	137	139	189	187
31	31	84	85, 355	138	139, 143, 144	190	188
32	32	85	86, 356	139	140	191	189
33	33	86	87, 357	140	142	192	190
34	34	87	81	141	141	193	191
35	35	88	90		143 (new)	194	192
36	36	89	91		144 (new)	195	193
37	37	90	352	142	145	196	194
38	38	91	84, 97, 354	143	146	197	195
39	39	92	360	144	147	198	196
40	40	93	98	145	148	199	197
41	41	94	99	146	146–148	200	198
42	42	95	96	147	146–149	201	199
43	43	96	92	148	146–149	202	200
44	44	97	93	149	152	203	201
45	45	98	94	150	151		202 (new)
46	46	99	99	151	150	204	203
47	47	100	96–99	152	153	205	204
48	48	101	100–101	153	154	206	205
49	49	102	102	154	155	207	206
50	50	103	103	155	156	208	207
51	51	104	104	156	300	209	208
52	52	105	105	157	157	210	209
53	53	106	106	158	158	211	210
54	54	107	107	159	159	212	211
				160	160	213	212

(1) First Edition Section	(2) Second Edition Section	(1) First Edition Section	(2) Second Edition Section	(1) First Edition Section	(2) Second Edition Section	(1) First Edition Section	(2) Second Edition Section
214	213	259	259	305	305	351	351
215	214	260	260	306	306		352 (new)
216	215	261	261	307	307		353 (new)
217	216	262	262	308	308		354 (new)
218	217	263	263	309	309		355 (new)
	218 (new)	264	264	310	310		356 (new)
219	219	265	265	311	312	352	358
220	220	266	266	312	311	353	359
221	221	267	267	313	313	354	360
222	222	268	268	314	314	355	361
223	223	269	269	315	315	356	362
224	224	270	270	316	316	357	362
225	225	271	271	317	317	358	362
226	226	272	272	318	318	359	363
227	227	273	273	319	319	360	364
228	228	274	274	320	320	361	365
229	230	275	275	321	321	362	366
230	229	276	276	322	322	363	367
231	231	277	277	323	323	364	368
232	232	278	278	324	324	365	369
233	242	279	279	325	325	366	84, 97, 354
234	233	280	280	326	326	367	85, 355
235	234	281	281	327	327	368	87, 357
236	235	282	282	328	328	369	368
237	236	283	283	329	329	370	88, 353
238	237	284	284	330	330	371	371
239	238	285	285	331	331	372	369
240	239	286	286	332	332	373	370
241	240	287	287	333	333	374	372
242	241	288	288	334	179, 334	375	373
243	243	289	289	335	335	376	374
244	244	290	290	336	336	377	376
245	245	291	291	337	337	378	375
246	246	292	292	338	338	379	375
247	247	293	293	339	339	380	377
248	248	294	294	340	340	381	378
249	249	295	295	341	341	382	379
250	250	296	296	342	342	383	380
251	251	297	297	343	343	384	381
252	252	298	298	344	344	385	382
253	253	299	299	345	345	386	383
254	254	300	300	346	346	387	384
255	255	301	301	347	347	388	385
256	256	302	302	348	348	389	386
257	257	303	303	349	349	390	387
258	258	304	304	350	350	391	388
						392	389

TABLE OF CASES CITED

Keyed to Commentary In Legal Periodicals

A

Aaron v. Parsons, § 377 n. 7, 11

Aaronson v. David Meyer Brewing Co., § 225 n. 8

A. A. Sutain, Ltd. v. Montgomery Ward & Co., § 144 n. 11

Abberger v. Kulp, § 192 n. 13; § 205 n. 28

Abbey v. Meyerson, § 267 n. 26

Abbott v. Hapgood, § 108 n. 7; § 111 n. 7

Abeles v. Adams Engineering Co., § 209 n. 23; § 238 n. 14

Abelow v. Midstates Oil Corp., § 341 n. 25

Abelow v. Symonds, (1959), § 360 n. 40

Abelow v. Symonds, (1961), § 194 n. 19

Abercrombie v. Davies, § 93 n. 3; § 196 n. 13; § 197 n. 8, 9, 28; § 267 n. 32–38; § 275 n. 5, 11; *noted in* 46 Calif.L.Rev. 124 (1958), 55 Mich.L.Rev. 137 (1956), 10 Stan.L.Rev. 565 (1958), 36 Texas L.Rev. 508 (1958), 11 Vand.L.Rev. 215 (1957), 3 Vill.L. Rev. 105 (1957)

Aberdeen Ry. v. Blaikie Bros., § 238 n. 4

Abernathy v. Consolidated Cab Co., § 88 n. 15

A. B. Frank Co. v. Latham, § 158 n. 4

Abney Mills, Inc. v. Tri-State Motor Co., § 97 n. 53; *noted in* 44 N.C.L.Rev. 449 (1966)

Abraham & Co. v. Olivetti Underwood Corp., § 349 n. 11, 19

Abrams v. Allen, § 242 n. 4; *noted in* 48 Colum.L.Rev. 290 (1948), 33 Cornell L.Q. 421 (1948), 61 Harv.L. Rev. 541 (1948), 31 Marq.L.Rev. 294 (1948), 46 Mich.L.Rev. 683 (1948), 23 N.Y.U.L.Q.Rev. 209 (1948), 21 S.Cal.L.Rev. 403 (1948), 15 U.Chi.L. Rev. 423 (1948), 96 U.Pa.L.Rev. 147 (1948), 57 Yale L.J. 489 (1948)

Abrams v. Textile Realty Corp., § 377 n. 10

A. Bruder & Son, Inc., Matter of, § 176 n. 8; § 191 n. 54

Acampora v. Birkland, § 208 n. 8

Ackert v. Bryan, § 86 n. 6; *noted in* 62 Colum.L.Rev. 1084 (1962), 76 Harv.L.Rev. 409 (1962), 41 Texas L.Rev. 603 (1963), 31 U.Cin.L.Rev. 497 (1962), 48 Va.L.Rev. 964 (1962)

Acme Equipment Co. v. Allegheny Steel Corp., § 150 n. 22, 27

Acton Plumbing & Heating Co. v. Jared Builders, § 148 n. 6

Adams v. Boyer Chemical Co., § 97 n. 16

Adams v. Clearance Corp., § 197 n. 7; § 267 n. 7; *noted in* 69 Harv.L.Rev. 1321 (1956), 55 Mich.L. Rev. 1175 (1957), 104 U.Pa.L.Rev. 712 (1956)

Adams v. R. C. Williams & Co., § 349 n. 13

Adams v. Smith, § 245 n. 23

Adamson v. Lang, § 104 n. 1

Addiego v. Hill, § 282 n. 25

Addy v. Short, § 348 n. 23

Adler, Matter of, § 238 n. 1

Adler v. Adler, § 372 n. 4

Adler v. Klawans, § 298 n. 28; *noted in* 73 Harv.L. Rev. 1635 (1960), 13 Vand.L.Rev. 387 (1959), 5 Vill.L.Rev. 135 (1959), 45 Va.L.Rev. 1057 (1959), 21 U.Pitt.L.Rev. 554 (1960)

Admiral Corp. v. Trio Sales & Service, Inc., § 117 n. 2

Advance Industrial Security, Inc. v. William J. Burns I.D. Agency, § 101 n. 5, 30; § 236 n. 16

Aeroglide Corp. v. Zeh, § 218 n. 5

Aetna Cas. & Sur. Co. v. Stover, § 150 n. 35

Agar v. Orda, § 169 n. 16; *noted in* 34 Colum.L.Rev. 1372 (1934), 29 Ill.L.Rev. 534 (1934), 2 U.Chi.L. Rev. 152 (1934), 8 U.Cin.L.Rev. 559 (1934)

Agatucci v. Corradi, § 239 n. 5; *noted in* 24 Chi.-Kent L.Rev. 272 (1946)

Age Publishing Co. v. Becker, § 281 n. 21

Agnew v. American Ice Co., § 325 n. 10; *noted in* 63 Harv.L.Rev. 890 (1950), 4 Rutgers L.Rev. 510 (1950)

Ahola v. United States, § 77 n. 18

Aiken v. Peabody, § 323 n. 2

Aimonetto v. Rapid Gas, Inc., § 225 n. 4; *noted in* 50 Iowa L.Rev. 176 (1964)

Aine v. Power, § 204 n. 23; § 220 n. 7

Ainsley Realty Co. v. Kramer, § 348 n. 23

Aiple v. Twin City Barge & Towing Co., § 173 n. 2; § 377 n. 17; *noted in* 51 Minn.L.Rev. 1169 (1967)

Air Technical Development Co. v. Arizona Bank, § 225 n. 4

Air Traffic & Service Corp. v. Fay, § 107 n. 2; § 111 n. 13

Air Waves, Inc. v. Link, § 230 n. 2

A. J. Armstrong Co. v. Janburt Embroidery Corp., § 150 n. 22

Akel v. Dooley, § 111 n. 12

Akin v. Mackie, § 365 n. 4

Alabama Fidelity Mortgage & Bond Co. v. Dubberly, § 238 n. 4; *noted in* 30 Harv.L.Rev. 761 (1917)

Alabama Gas Corp. v. Morrow, § 199 n. 44; *noted in* 10 Ala.L.Rev. 179 (1957)

Alabama Music Co. v. Nelson, § 230 n. 5

Aladdin Hotel Co. v. Bloom, § 155 n. 11

Albee v. Lamson & Hubbard Corp., § 199 n. 2

Alberts v. Schneiderman, § 218 n. 9, 22

Albre v. Sinclair Construction Co., § 151 n. 9

Albrecht, Maguire & Co. v. General Plastics, Inc., § 378 n. 11; § 379 n. 17; *noted in* 25 Cornell L.Q. 124 (1939)

Alcoma Corp. v. Ackerman, § 183 n. 2; *noted in* 7 N.Y.L.F. 230 (1961), 35 St. John's L.Rev. 368 (1961)

Alcott v. Hyman, § 194 n. 13, 15, 17; § 209 n. 26; § 238 n. 8, 20; § 349 n. 9; § 382 n. 8

Alderman v. Alderman, § 197 n. 15; *noted in* 34 Mich. L.Rev. 727 (1936)

Aldridge v. Franco Wyoming Oil Co., § 265 n. 8; § 287 n. 1

Alexander v. Lindsay, § 245 n. 1

Alger v. Brighter Days Mining Corp., § 237 n. 14, 17

Algonac Marine Hardware Co. v. Cline, § 241 n. 10

Bankers Trust Co. v. Texas & Pac. Ry., § 88 n. 30

Banque de France v. Supreme Court, § 97 n. 11; *noted in* 90 U.Pa.L.Rev. 967 (1942)

Barber Co. v. Department of State, § 117 n. 2; *noted in* 15 N.Y.U.L.Q.Rev. 597 (1938)

BarChris Construction Corp., In re, § 385 n. 9

Barclay v. First Nat. Bank of Hightstown, § 196 n. 35

Bard v. Steele, § 97 n. 56

Barnes v. Andrews, § 234 n. 1, 14, 17, 19, 30

Barnes v. Brown, § 241 n. 3, 7

Barnes v. Osofsky, § 295 n. 34; *noted in* 21 Sw. L.J. 398 (1967)

Barnett v. Anaconda Co., § 297 n. 40; *noted in* 51 Iowa L.Rev. 515 (1966)

Barnett v. Barnett Enterprises, Inc., § 199 n. 20; § 349 n. 24

Barney v. Buswell, § 381 n. 12

Baron v. Pressed Metals of America, Inc., § 240 n. 6, 16; § 341 n. 25

Baron v. Schachter, § 169 n. 16

Barrett v. Denver Tramway Corp., § 240 n. 9, 18, 20, 21; § 325 n. 22, 24; § 340 n. 22; § 345 n. 5, 23

Barsan v. Pioneer Savings & Loan Co., § 174 n. 19; *noted in* 33 Chi.-Kent L.Rev. 260 (1955), 24 U.Cin. L.Rev. 600 (1955)

Bar's Leaks Western, Inc. v. Pollock, § 85 n. 1

Bartle v. Home Owners Cooperative, Inc., § 146 n. 20; *noted in* 24 Fordham L.Rev. 685 (1955), 10 Sw. L.J. 77 (1956), 24 U.Cin.L.Rev. 603 (1955)

Bartlett v. General Motors Corp., § 177 n. 30

Bass v. Shutan, § 152 n. 1; § 383 n. 19

Bassett v. Battle, § 360 n. 24, 40

Bassett v. U. S. Cast Iron Pipe & Foundry Co., § 325 n. 10, 11

Bastian v. Bourns, Inc., § 194 n. 19

Bates v. Coronado Beach Co., § 183 n. 43

Bates v. Dresser, § 231 n. 4; § 234 n. 21; *noted in* 15 Ill.L.Rev. 279 (1920)

Bateson v. Magna Oil Corp., § 362 n. 18

Battle Creek Food Co. v. Kirkland, § 236 n. 6

Bauer v. Servel, Inc., § 362 n. 18

Baum v. Baum Holding Co., § 139 n. 2; § 140 n. 10; *noted in* 53 Mich.L.Rev. 283 (1954)

Bauman v. Advance Aluminum Castings Corp., § 349 n. 25

Baumohl v. Goldstein, § 281 n. 22; *noted in* 25 Colum. L.Rev. 77 (1925)

Baxter v. Lancer Industries, Inc., § 336 n. 1

Bay City Bank v. St. Louis Motor Sales Co., § 176 n. 9

Bay City Lumber Co. v. Anderson, § 133 n. 29; *noted in* 30 Calif.L.Rev. 195 (1942)

Bay Sound Transportation v. United States, § 118 n. 7

Bay State York Co. v. Cobb, § 167 n. 13; § 218 n. 24; *noted in* 5 B.C.Ind. & Com.L.Rev. 778 (1964)

Bayer v. Beran, § 235 n. 6; § 238 n. 1

Bayou Drilling Co. v. Baillio, § 343 n. 1

Bazar, Matter of, § 349 n. 11

Beacon Wool Corp. v. Johnson, § 245 n. 18; § 246 n. 2; § 255 n. 2

Beall v. Pacific Nat. Bank, § 146 n. 18

Beard v. Elster, § 93 n. 3; § 248 n. 6; *noted in* 2 B.C. Ind. & Com.L.Rev. 405 (1961), 49 Calif.L.Rev. 373 (1961), 6 How.L.J. 213 (1960)

Beatty v. Guggenheim Exploration Co., § 237 n. 24

Beaudette v. Graham, § 236 n. 5

Bechtold v. Coleman Realty Co., § 133 n. 28; § 281 n. 27; § 282 n. 34; *noted in* 25 Temp.L.Q. 213 (1951), 100 U.Pa.L.Rev. 133 (1951)

Beck v. Edwards & Lewis, § 225 n. 4

Beck v. Spindler, § 97 n. 42; *noted in* 34 St. John's L.Rev. 309 (1960)

Beck v. Stimmel, § 139 n. 6; § 140 n. 12; § 145 n. 3

Becker v. Tower Nat. Life Inv. Co., § 169 n. 11

Beggy v. Deike, § 239 n. 13; § 282 n. 13

Behn, Meyer & Co. v. Miller, § 90 n. 3; § 150 n. 7; *noted in* 14 Calif.L.Rev. 497 (1926)

Belfast & Moosehead Lake R. R. v. Belfast, § 327 n. 8

Bell v. Aubel, § 171 n. 11

Bell v. Dornan, § 230 n. 3

Bell Oil & Gas Co. v. Allied Chemical Corp., § 148 n. 6; *noted in* 23 Sw.L.J. 384 (1969)

Belle Isle Corp. v. Corcoran, § 197 n. 14; *noted in* 45 Mich.L.Rev. 636 (1947)

Belle Isle Corp. v. MacBean, § 133 n. 29; § 167 n. 22; § 209 n. 10; *noted in* 45 Mich.L.Rev. 630 (1947)

Belle Vista Investment Co. v. Hassen, § 144 n. 12

Bellevue Gardens, Inc. v. Hill, § 375 n. 6

Bellman, Matter of, People ex rel. v. Standard Match Co., § 216 n. 7

Bellows v. Porter, § 173 n. 5

Belmetals Mfg. Co., In re, § 336 n. 1

Beloff v. Consolidated Edison Co. of New York, § 346 n. 8; § 349 n. 12, 17

Benas v. Title Guaranty Trust Co., § 331 n. 15

Bendalin v. Delgado, § 282 n. 16

Bendix v. Bendix Co., § 150 n. 17

Beneficial Finance Co. v. Miskell, § 150 n. 24

Beneficial Finance Co. of Lebanon v. Becker, § 236 n. 13

Benintendi v. Kenton Hotel, Inc., § 94 n. 5; § 133 n. 5, 13, 32; § 191 n. 31; § 193 n. 7; § 225 n. 25; § 259 n. 9; § 266 n. 1, 4, 5; § 271 n. 2; § 274 n. 2; *noted in* 45 Colum.L.Rev. 960 (1945), 20 N.Y.U.L.Q.Rev. 513 (1945), 19 St. John's L.Rev. 144 (1945)

Benisch v. Cameron, § 298 n. 30, 36; § 362 n. 22

Bennett v. Breuil Petroleum Corp., § 173 n. 5; § 174 n. 16; § 360 n. 14; § 368 n. 9

Bennett v. Propp, § 173 n. 4; § 241 n. 15; § 242 n. 4; *noted in* 5 B.C.Ind. & Com.L.Rev. 190 (1963)

Benson v. Braun, § 241 n. 3

Benson v. Eleven-Twenty St. Charles Co., § 161 n. 3; *noted in* 33 Mo.L.Rev. 523 (1968)

Bentall v. Koening Brothers, Inc., § 225 n. 4

Benton-Bauxite Housing Co-op, Inc. v. Benton Plumbing, Inc., § 111 n. 5

Beraksa v. Stardust Records, Inc., § 187 n. 12

Berdane Furs, Inc. v. First Pennsylvania Banking & Trust Co., § 135 n. 10

Berendt v. Bethlehem Steel Corp., § 196 n. 59; § 238 n. 21

Berg v. Cincinnati N. & C. Ry., § 366 n. 9

Berg v. United Board & Carton Corp., § 173 n. 2

Bergen Drug Co. v. Parke, Davis & Co., § 312 n. 7; *noted in* 76 Harv.L.Rev. 848 (1963)

Berger v. Amana Society, (1961), § 191 n. 18; *noted in* 47 Iowa L.Rev. 1110 (1962)

Berger v. Amana Society, (1965), § 377 n. 10

Berger v. Dyson, § 374 n. 5

Berger v. Fogarty, § 239 n. 5

Berger v. Reynolds Metals Co., § 368 n. 11

Bergman v. Orkin Exterminating Co., § 199 n. 33

Berk v. Twentynine Palms Ranchos, Inc., § 113 n. 3

Duane Jones Co. v. Burke, § 236 n. 6, 7; *noted in* 54 Colum.L.Rev. 994 (1954), 39 Iowa L.Rev. 185 (1953), 38 Minn.L.Rev. 661 (1954), 28 St. John's L.Rev. 308 (1954), 22 U.Chi.L.Rev. 278 (1954)

DuBois v. Century Cement Products Co., § 205 n. 19

Ducros v. Commissioner, § 282 n. 31; *noted in* 45 Cornell L.Q. 818 (1960), 14 Sw.L.J. 416 (1960)

Duddy v. Conshohocken Printing Co., (1948), § 349 n. 19; *noted in* 47 Mich.L.Rev. 273 (1948)

Duddy v. Conshohocken Printing Co., (1952), § 349 n. 19

Dudley v. Jack Waite Mining Co., § 86 n. 10

Duffy v. Loft, Inc., § 191 n. 26; § 196 n. 28, 30; *noted in* 11 B.U.L.Rev. 267 (1931), 4 So.Calif.L. Rev. 222 (1931), 79 U.Pa.L.Rev. 223 (1930)

Dumaine v. Securities and Exchange Commission, § 236 n. 19; § 386 n. 4

Duncan v. Louisiana, § 13 n. 16; *noted in* 35 Brooklyn L.Rev. 128 (1968), 49 B.U.L.Rev. 144 (1969), 82 Harv.L.Rev. 148 (1968), 15 How.L.J. 164 (1968), 29 La.L.Rev. 118 (1968), 15 Loyola L. Rev. 138 (1968–69), 53 Minn.L.Rev. 414 (1968), 22 Sw.L.J. 875 (1968), 43 Tul.L.Rev. 398 (1969), 21 Vand.L.Rev. 1099 (1968)

Duncan v. National Tea Co., § 361 n. 17; § 369 n. 7; § 376 n. 4

Duncan Cleaners, Inc. v. Shuman Co., § 101 n. 13

Duncan Shaw Corp. v. Standard Machinery Co., § 238 n. 10

Duncuft v. Albrecht, § 169 n. 16

Dunham v. Natural Bridge Ranch Co., § 139 n. 2, 8; § 142 n. 1; § 260 n. 19

Dunkin' Donuts of America, Inc. v. Dunkin Donuts, Inc., § 117 n. 2

Dunlay v. Avenue M Garage & Repair Co., § 173 n. 2; § 174 n. 7

Dunlop's Sons, Inc. v. Spurr, § 237 n. 22

Dunn v. Royal Brothers Co., § 97 n. 65

Dunnett v. Arn, § 241 n. 17; *noted in* 20 Cornell L.Q. 101 (1934), 34 Mich.L.Rev. 131 (1935)

Dunning v. Rafton, § 197 n. 26

Duple Motor Bodies, Ltd., v. Hollingsworth, § 97 n. 53

du Pont v. Ball, § 171 n. 11, 15, 22, 29, 32, 33

du Pont v. du Pont, § 239 n. 13

Du Pont v. United Oil and Fuel Corp., § 104 n. 10

Durfee v. Durfee & Canning, Inc., § 236 n. 9; § 237 n. 2; *noted in* 29 B.U.L.Rev. 129 (1949)

Durfee & Canning, Inc. v. Canning, § 225 n. 38

Durnin v. Allentown Fed. S. & L. Ass'n, § 199 n. 1; *noted in* 24 Md.L.Rev. 215 (1964)

Durr v. Paragon Trading Corp., Matter of, § 199 n. 5, 8

Dwyer v. Tracey, § 245 n. 23; § 255 n. 2

Dyer v. Commissioner, § 196 n. 56

Dyer v. Securities and Exchange Commission, § 174 n. 18; § 297 n. 16

Dynamics Corp., Matter of v. Abraham & Co., (1956), § 349 n. 20

Dynamics Corp., Matter of v. Abraham & Co., (1958), § 349 n. 23

E

Easley v. New York State Thruway Authority, § 91 n. 9; *noted in* 21 Albany L.Rev. 95 (1957), 25 Fordham L.Rev. 759 (1956), 3 N.Y.L.F. 95 (1957)

East Coast Discount Corp. v. Reynolds, § 101 n. 25

Eastern Products Corp. v. Tennessee Coal, Iron & R. R., § 139 n. 10; *noted in* 11 Va.L.Rev. 644 (1925)

Eastman v. Celebrezze, § 150 n. 12

Eastman v. Gardner, § 150 n. 12

Eaton v. Robinson, § 373 n. 5

Eaton Factors Co. v. Double Eagle Corp., § 151 n. 8

Ebbert v. Plymouth Oil Co., § 357 n. 9

Ebert's Cadillac Co. v. Miller, § 230 n. 6

Eccles v. Sylvester, § 236 n. 9

Ecclestone v. Indiatlantic, Inc., § 196 n. 13; *noted in* 61 Harv.L.Rev. 1062 (1948), 47 Mich.L.Rev. 547 (1949)

Ecker v. Western Pac. R. R., § 388 n. 23

Ecorse Screw Mach. Prods. Co. v. Corporation & Securities Commission, § 169 n. 14

E. C. Warner Co., In re, § 379 n. 4; *noted in* 29 Chi.-Kent L.Rev. 344 (1951), 26 Notre Dame Law, 540 (1951)

Edelman v. Goodman, § 216 n. 7; § 377 n. 25

Edelstein, Ex parte, § 88 n. 33; *noted in* 42 Harv.L. Rev. 1079 (1929), 78 U.Pa.L.Rev. 102 (1929)

Eden v. Miller, § 115 n. 7; *noted in* 44 Harv.L.Rev. 126 (1930), 39 Yale L.J. 1061 (1930)

Edward v. Peabody Coal Co., § 248 n. 7

Edwards v. Warren Linoline & Gasoline Works, Ltd., § 42 n. 4

E. Edelmann & Co. v. Amos, § 227 n. 2; § 343 n. 3

Efron v. Kalmanovitz, § 240 n. 22

Ehrlich v. Alper, § 146 n. 36; § 221 n. 10; § 234 n. 28

Eidman v. Bowman, § 174 n. 2

E. I. Du Pont de Nemours & Co. v. Pathe Film Corp., § 282 n. 7

18 East 48th Street Corp. v. New York, § 329 n. 17

Eisen v. Carlisle & Jacquelin, § 358 n. 19; *noted in* 18 Am.U.L.Rev. 225 (1968), 44 N.Y.U.L.Rev. 198 (1969), 47 N.C.L.Rev. 393 (1969), 44 Notre Dame Law. 151 (1968), 43 Tul.L.Rev. 369 (1969), 21 Vand. L.Rev. 1124 (1968)

Eisen v. Post, § 341 n. 9; *noted in* 22 Albany L.Rev. 389 (1958), 24 Brooklyn L.Rev. 358 (1958), 19 Ohio St.L.J. 507 (1958), 67 Yale L.J. 1288 (1958)

Eisenberg v. Central Zone Property Corp., (1953), § 240 n. 6, 8, 10; § 341 n. 17; § 348 n. 28; § 349 n. 17; § 360 n. 24, 40, 41; *noted in* 66 Harv.L.Rev. 746 (1953), 32 N.Y.U.L.Rev. 601 (1957), 28 St.John's L. Rev. 293 (1954)

Eisenberg v. Central Zone Property Corp., (1957), § 377 n. 14; *noted in* 32 N.Y.U.L.Rev. 601 (1957)

Eisenberg v. Commercial Union Assur. Co., § 88 n. 14

Eisenberg v. Rodless Decorations, Inc., § 275 n. 7

Eisner v. Davis, § 197 n. 20; § 360 n. 16

Eisner v. Macomber, § 76 n. 12; § 339 n. 12; *noted in* 20 Colum.L.Rev. 536 (1920), 18 Mich.L.Rev. 689 (1920), 4 Minn.L.Rev. 462 (1920), 68 U.Pa.L.Rev. 394 (1920), 7 Va.L.Rev. 134 (1920), 29 Yale L.J. 735 (1920)

E. J. Korvette, Inc. v. State Liquor Auth., § 150 n. 24; *noted in* 18 Syracuse L.Rev. 851 (1967)

E. K. Buck Retail Stores v. Harkert, § 189 n. 21; § 265 n. 5; *noted in* 33 Neb.L.Rev. 636 (1954)

Eldridge v. Richfield, § 88 n. 14

Electric Welding Co. v. Prince, § 115 n. 10

Electronic Specialty Co. v. International Controls Corp., § 297 n. 33

Elenkrieg v. Siebrecht, § 146 n. 16, 24

Elfstrom v. New York Life Ins. Co., § 254 n. 3; *noted in* 17 Am.U.L.Rev. 573 (1968), 28 Md.L.Rev. 307 (1968), 8 Santa Clara Law. 242 (1968)

H

I

L

M

Q

R

Rosenthal & Rosenthal, Inc. v. Wolfe, § 330 n. 2; § 333 n. 1

Rosenzweig v. Salkind, § 169 n. 16

Ross v. Bernhard, § 13 n. 16; § 234 n. 32; § 358 n. 21; *noted in* 38 U.Cin.L.Rev. 582 (1969)

Ross v. Licht, § 298 n. 13

Ross v. Pennsylvania R. R., § 146 n. 25; § 148 n. 7

Ross Construction Co., Inc. v. U. M. & M. Credit Corp., § 100 n. 3

Ross P. Beckstrom Co. v. Armstrong Paint & Varnish Works, § 352 n. 1

Ross Transport, Inc. v. Crothers, § 173 n. 2; § 174 n. 7

Roth v. Embotelladora Nacional, Inc., § 227 n. 2

Rothberg v. Manhattan Coil Co., § 225 n. 5; *noted in* 3 Mercer L.Rev. 348 (1952)

Rothman & Schneider, Inc. v. Beckerman, § 225 n. 22, 32; *noted in* 26 Fordham L.Rev. 339 (1957), 2 N.Y. L.F. 429 (1956), 11 Vand.L.Rev. 212 (1957), 42 Va.L.Rev. 679 (1956)

Rothschild v. Jefferson Hotel Co., § 155 n. 12

Roubik v. Commissioner, § 77 n. 20

Rous v. Carlisle, § 242 n. 4

Rowland v. Canuso, § 37 n. 1

Roy v. North American Newspaper Alliance, Inc., § 97 n. 53

Roy v. Recker, § 167 n. 7; § 171 n. 10

Royal British Bank v. Turquand, § 225 n. 4

Royal China, Inc. v. Regal China Corp., § 86 n. 10; § 281 n. 6

Rubens v. Marion-Washington Realty Corp., § 328 n. 1; *noted in* 44 Mich.L.Rev. 318 (1945)

Rubin v. Chicago South Shore & South Bend R. R., § 204 n. 15

Ruckle v. Roto American Corp., § 298 n. 8; *noted in* 65 Colum.L.Rev. 725 (1965), 50 Cornell L.Q. 545 (1965), 43 Texas L.Rev. 1109 (1965)

Rudel (Eberhard Faber Pencil Co.), Matter of, § 341 n. 10

Rugee v. Hadley Products, Inc., § 358 n. 1; § 361 n. 16; § 371 n. 9

Runswick v. Floor, § 158 n. 19; § 174 n. 4

Rusch Factors, Inc. v. Levin, § 319 n. 18; *noted in* 49 B.U.L.Rev. 194 (1969), 57 Calif.L.Rev. 281 (1969), 52 Marq.L.Rev. 159 (1968), 53 Minn.L.Rev. 1375 (1969)

Rusch & Co. v. Syndicate First Corp., § 343 n. 5

Russell v. Louis Melind Co., § 363 n. 6; *noted in* 46 Mich.L.Rev. 429 (1948)

Russell Mfg. Co. v. United States, § 246 n. 6; *noted in* 28 Geo.Wash.L.Rev. 803 (1960), 58 Mich.L.Rev. 799 (1960), 45 Va.L.Rev. 1249 (1959)

Rutenbeck v. Hohn, § 169 n. 13

Ruzicka v. Rager, § 28 n. 9; *noted in* 28 St. John's L. Rev. 123 (1953)

R. V. McGinnis Theatres v. Video Independent Theatres, Inc., § 144 n. 13

Ryder v. Bamberger, § 241 n. 7

Ryder Truck Rental, Inc. v. Ace Sales Co., § 118 n. 7

S

Sabbagha v. Celebrezze, § 150 n. 12; *noted in* 8 S. Tex.L.J. 192 (1966)

Sabella v. Sheepshead Bay U-Drives, Inc., § 375 n. 2

Sachs v. Commissioner, § 380 n. 63

Safway Rental & Sales Co. v. Albina Engine & Machine Works, Inc. v. Safway Rental & Sales Co., § 49 n. 3

Sagalyn v. Meekins, Packard & Wheat Inc., § 245 n. 25

Saigh v. Busch, § 248 n. 4; § 360 n. 13; § 363 n. 3; *noted in* 34 U.Mo.Kan.City L.Rev. 445 (1966)

St. Clair Lime Co. v. Ada Lime Co., § 26 n. 5

St. Lawrence University v. Trustees of Theological School of St. Lawrence University, § 79 n. 1

St. Louis Southwestern Ry. v. Loeb, § 326 n. 5

St. Louis Southwestern Ry. v. Meyer, § 326 n. 3; *noted in* 9 Okla.L.Rev. 194 (1956)

St. Thomas Jewelry, Inc. v. Commissioner of Finance, § 158 n. 5

Saks v. Gamble, § 361 n. 5

Salesky v. Hat Corp. of America, § 245 n. 23 *noted in* 30 Brooklyn L.Rev. 360 (1964), 25 U.Pitt.L.Rev. 766 (1964)

Salnor Realty Corp., Matter of, § 206 n. 3

Salomon v. Salomon & Co., § 147 n. 3; § 156 n. 9; § 258 n. 1

Salt Dome Oil Corp. v. Schenck, § 349 n. 11; *noted in* 31 Va.L.Rev. 698 (1945)

Salton v. Seaporcel Metals, Inc., § 209 n. 19

Salzman Sign Co. v. Beck, § 230 n. 4

Samford v. Citizen's & Southern Nat. Bank, § 169 n. 16

Samia v. Central Oil Co., § 115 n. 5; § 174 n. 11; § 175 n. 6; § 237 n. 8; § 373 n. 7

Sams v. Redevelopment Authority, § 149 n. 8

Sanchez v. Centro Mexicano of Sacramento, § 282 n. 10

Sanders v. Bank of Mecklenburg, § 362 n. 4

Sanders v. Cuba R. R., § 325 n. 10; *noted in* 8 Mercer L.Rev. 214 (1956), 55 Mich.L.Rev. 132 (1956), 29 Rocky Mt.L.Rev. 428 (1957)

Sanders v. E Z Park, Inc., § 238 n. 5

Sanders v. Neely, § 199 n. 11; *noted in* 17 Miss.L.J. 426 (1946)

Sanders v. Pacific Gamble Robinson Co., § 199 n. 42; *noted in* 18 Md.L.Rev. 78 (1958), 11 Vand.L.Rev. 609 (1958)

Sandfield v. Goldstein, § 375 n. 2

Sandler v. Schenley Industries, Inc., § 158 n. 19; § 248 n. 6

Sandor Petroleum Corp. v. Williams, § 282 n. 34; *noted in* 14 Sw.L.J. 106 (1960), 38 Texas L.Rev. 499 (1960)

Sands v. Lefcourt Realty Corp., § 354 n. 10

San Juan Uranium Corp. v. Wolfe, § 104 n. 17; *noted in* 8 W.Res.L.Rev. 541 (1957)

Sankin v. 5410 Connecticut Ave. Corp., § 282 n. 25

Santa Clara County v. Southern Pacific R. R., § 80 n. 6

Santa Fe Hills Golf & Country Club v. Safehi Realty Co., § 209 n. 1; § 341 n. 5

Santarelli v. Katz, § 237 n. 17

Saratoga Harness Racing Ass'n v. Moss, § 97 n. 56

Sarner v. Fox Hill, Inc., § 238 n. 19

Sarner v. Mason, § 189 n. 31

Sarner v. Sarner, § 377 n. 23

Sass v. New York Towers, Ltd., § 156 n. 12

Sasseen v. Danco Industries, Inc., § 349 n. 20

Satterfield v. Lehigh Valley R. R., § 85 n. 1

Sautter v. Fulmer, § 239 n. 7; § 240 n. 22; § 241 n. 17; § 259 n. 10; § 276 n. 2

Savage v. Lorraine Corp., § 245 n. 1

Savage v. Royal Properties, Inc., § 150 n. 35

Saville v. Sweet, § 239 n. 5

Sawyer v. Pioneer Mill Co., § 297 n. 1

Saxe v. Brady, § 194 n. 16; *noted in* 51 Geo.L.J. 624 (1963)

Sayers v. Navillus Oil Co., § 146 n. 16

State ex rel. National Mutual Ins. Co. v. Conn, § 212 n. 7; *noted in* 31 Law Notes 151 (1927)

State ex rel. Paschall v. Scott, § 216 n. 3, 8; *noted in* 51 Mich.L.Rev. 747 (1953), 28 Notre Dame Law. 269 (1953), 6 Okla.L.Rev. 193 (1953), 101 U.Pa.L. Rev. 555 (1953), 28 Wash.L.Rev. 159 (1953)

State ex rel. Pertuit v. Pioneer Petroleum Corp., § 196 n. 24

State ex rel. Reidy v. International Paper Co., § 14 n. 6

State ex rel. Rogers v. Sherman Oil Corp., § 199 n. 24; *noted in* 95 Cent.L.J. 59 (1922)

State ex rel. Starkey v. Alaska Airlines, Inc., § 189 n. 14

State ex rel. Swanson v. Perham, § 189 n. 10; § 340 n. 16

State ex rel. Syphers v. McCune, § 133 n. 2; § 189 n. 21; § 196 n. 2; § 205 n. 5; *noted in* 21 Ga. B.J. 551 (1959), 19 U.Pitt.L.Rev. 806 (1958)

State ex rel. Thiele v. Cities Service Co., § 199 n. 7, 16; *noted in* 22 Colum.L.Rev. 590 (1922)

State ex rel. Waldman v. Miller-Wohl Co., § 173 n. 3

State ex rel. Waterman v. J. S. Waterman & Co., § 19 n. 11

State ex rel. Watkins v. Cassell, § 216 n. 2

State ex rel. Wolfner v. Fairfax Shipside Storage, Inc., § 199 n. 17

State of California v. State Tax Commission, § 179 n. 12

State of Oregon v. Pacific Powder Co., § 80 n. 13; § 184 n. 23

State of Washington v. Alaska Airlines, Inc., § 133 n. 28

State of Washington ex rel. Carriger v. Campbell Food Markets, Inc., § 349 n. 9

State Street Trust Co. v. Muskogee Electric Traction Co., § 155 n. 1; *noted in* 32 Chi.-Kent L.Rev. 243 (1954), 52 Mich.L.Rev. 900 (1954), 38 Minn.L.Rev. 266 (1954), 25 Miss.L.J. 168 (1954), 33 Neb.L.Rev. 90 (1953), 32 N.C.L.Rev. 206 (1954), 33 Ore.L.Rev. 298 (1954), 26 Rocky Mt.L.Rev. 198 (1954), 24 U. Cin.L.Rev. 271 (1954), 102 U.Pa.L.Rev. 543 (1954)

State Tax Commission of Utah v. Aldrich, § 81 n. 5; noted in 22 B.U.L.Rev. 618 (1942), 28 Cornell L.Q. 74 (1942), 31 Ill.B.J. 220 (1943), 37 Ill.L.Rev. 280 (1942), 17 Ind.L.J. 560 (1942), 27 Marq.L.Rev. 95 (1953), 41 Mich.L.Rev. 351 (1942), 27 Minn.L.Rev. 83 (1942), 19 N.Y.U.L.Q.Rev. 443 (1942), 16 Temp. U.L.Q. 435 (1942), 10 U.Chi.L.Rev. 84 (1942), 6 U.Det.L.Rev. 53 (1942), 28 Va.L.Rev. 1008 (1942), 51 Yale L.J. 1398 (1942)

State Trust Co. v. Hall, § 66 n. 2

State Trust & Savings Bank v. Hermosa Land and Cattle Co., § 151 n. 6; *noted in* 39 Harv.L.Rev. 652 (1926), 10 Minn.L.Rev. 598, 617 (1926)

Stauffer v. Isaly Dairy Co., § 151 n. 7

Stauffer v. Standard Brands, Inc., § 346 n. 8; § 349 n. 17

Steakley v. Braden, § 117 n. 2

Steckel, Estate of v. Commissioner, § 377 n. 19

Steele v. Locke Cotton Mills Co., § 327 n. 9

Steig, Matter of, § 280 n. 7

Steigerwald v. A. M. Steigerwald Co., § 133 n. 3; § 212 n. 2; *noted in* 34 Chi.-Kent L.Rev. 339 (1956)

Stein v. Capital Outdoor Advertising, Inc., § 196 n. 10; § 267 n. 4

Steinberg, Matter of, § 199 n. 11

Steinberg v. Adams, § 196 n. 40, 42, 51; § 366 n. 5; *noted in* 36 Cornell L.Q. 558 (1951), 61 Yale L.J. 229 (1952)

Steinberg v. Altschuler, § 235 n. 6

Steinberg v. Shields, § 354 n. 10

Steiner v. Dauphin Corp., § 85 n. 1

Steinway, Matter of, § 199 n. 13

Stella v. Graham-Paige Motors Corp., § 298 n. 29, 31; *noted in* 57 Colum.L.Rev. 287 (1957), 70 Harv.L. Rev. 1312 (1957), 9 Stan.L.Rev. 582 (1957)

Stella v. Kaiser, § 376 n. 8

Stemerman v. Ackerman, § 248 n. 4

S. Tepfer & Sons v. Zscheler, § 236 n. 16

Sterling v. City Nat. Bank & Trust Co., § 199 n. 34

Sterling v. Mayflower Hotel Corp., § 128 n. 1; § 209 n. 23; § 238 n. 6, 11, 14, 20; § 240 n. 5; § 346 n. 13

Sterling v. 16 Park Avenue, Inc., § 324 n. 5; § 349 n. 5; § 382 n. 5

Sterling Industries, Inc. v. Ball Bearing Pen Corp., (1948), § 225 n. 26, 27; *noted in* 18 Fordham L. Rev. 133 (1949), 35 Iowa L.Rev. 315 (1950), 24 N.Y.U.L.Q.Rev. 923 (1949), 1949 U.Ill.L.F. 525, 34 Va.L.Rev. 715 (1948)

Sterling Industries, Inc. v. Ball Bearing Pen Corp., (1949), § 225 n. 24, 28; § 238 n. 11; § 360 n. 31

Sterling Industries, Inc. v. Ball Bearing Pen Corp., (1955), § 225 n. 34

Sterling Industries, Inc. v. Ball Bearing Pen Corp., (1956), § 225 n. 36

Sterling Industries, Inc. v. Ball Bearing Pen Corp., (1958), § 225 n. 37

Sterling Varnish Co. v. Sonom Co., § 167 n. 9

Stern v. Mayer, § 169 n. 18

Stern v. South Chester Tube Co., § 199 n. 8; § 353 n. 34; *noted in* 54 A.B.A.J. 700 (1968), 22 Sw.L.J. 891 (1968)

Stern v. Stern, § 282 n. 2

Sternbergh v. Brock, § 326 n. 5

Steuer v. Hector's Tavern, Inc., § 361 n. 6

Steven v. Hale-Haas Corp., § 173 n. 2, 5; § 174 n. 17; § 239 n. 13

Stevenot v. Norberg, § 210 n. 9; § 221 n. 7

Stevens v. Vowell, § 106 n. 10

Stewart v. Bramwell, § 150 n. 22

Stewart v. Harris, § 239 n. 7

Stewart v. Lehigh Valley R. R., § 238 n. 4

Stewart v. United States, § 381 n. 16

Stewart Realty Co. v. Keller, § 109 n. 4

Stockholders Committee for Better Management of Erie Technological Products, Inc. v. Erie Technological Products, Inc., § 189 n. 21

Stockwell, Matter of, § 349 n. 21

Stoiber v. Miller Brewing Co., § 245 n. 25; *noted in* 38 Calif.L.Rev. 906 (1950)

Stokes v. Continental Trust Co., § 174 n. 2, 10

Stokes v. Knickerbocker Inv. Co., § 366 n. 9

Stone v. Eacho, § 152 n. 10

Stone v. Guthrie, § 49 n. 7

Stone v. Holly Hill Fruit Products, Inc., § 366 n. 9

Stone v. Hudgens, § 171 n. 10; *noted in* 54 Mich.L. Rev. 281 (1955), 9 Okla.L.Rev. 403 (1956), 10 Okla. L.Rev. 326 (1957)

Stone v. Massa, § 197 n. 19, 23

Stone v. United States Envelope Co., § 326 n. 4

Stone v. Young, § 171 n. 10

Storer v. Ripley, § 287 n. 15

Stott v. Stott, § 267 n. 6; *noted in* 96 Just.P. 57 (1932)

Tracey v. Franklin, § 281 n. 15; *noted in* 28 Ind.L.J. 56 (1949), 48 Mich.L.Rev. 723 (1950), 23 Tul.L.Rev. 569 (1949), 16 U.Chi.L.Rev. 742 (1949)

Tracy v. Perkins—Tracy Printing Co., § 336 n. 1

Transonic Corp. v. E. Edelmann & Co., § 227 n. 2; § 343 n. 3

Transport Indemnity Co. v. Seib, § 319 n. 12

Transvision, Inc., In re, § 385 n. 9; *noted in* 30 N.Y. U.L.Rev. 1115 (1955)

Trans World Airlines, Inc. v. Hughes, § 332 n. 8

Trappey v. Lumbermen's Mut. Cas. Co., § 19 n. 11; *noted in* 7 Hastings L.J. 213 (1956), 17 La.L.Rev. 871 (1957)

Traub Co. v. Coffee Break Service, Inc., § 352 n. 1

Travelers Health Ass'n v. Virginia, § 97 n. 43; *noted in* 39 Calif.L.Rev. 152 (1951), 13 Ga.B.J. 255 (1950), 64 Harv.L.Rev. 482 (1951), 5 Miami L.Q. 149 (1950), 4 U.Fla.L.Rev. 98 (1951), 1950 U.Ill.L.F. 481, 99 U.Pa.L.Rev. 245 (1950), 36 Va.L.Rev. 795 (1950), 59 Yale L.J. 360 (1950)

Travis Investment Co. v. Harwyn Publishing Corp., § 295 n. 2

Trefethen v. Amazeen, § 134 n. 11; § 267 n. 1, 44

Trent v. Commissioner, § 166 n. 4; *noted in* 39 N.D.L. Rev. 121 (1963), 37 N.Y.U.L.Rev. 143 (1962), 34 Rocky Mt.L.Rev. 418 (1962), 64 W.Va.L.Rev. 94 (1961)

Treves v. Menzies, § 341 n. 10; § 382 n. 8

Treves v. Servel, Inc., § 341 n. 10; § 382 n. 8

Tri-Continental Corp. v. Battye, § 349 n. 13

Tri-Continental Corp. v. U. S., § 304 n. 3; § 345 n. 26

Trilling and Montague, Matter of, § 282 n. 4

Trimble Co., Matter of, § 336 n. 1

Trinka Services, Inc. v. State Board of Mortuary Science, § 17 n. 9; *noted in* 6 De Paul L.Rev. 159 (1956)

Triplett v. Grundy Electric Cooperative, Inc., § 194 n. 8

Triplex Shoe Co. v. Rice & Hutchins, Inc., § 113 n. 6; § 158 n. 5; § 167 n. 4; § 171 n. 11

Trippe Mfg. Co. v. Spencer Gifts, Inc., § 97 n. 41; *noted in* 28 Geo.Wash.L.Rev. 909 (1960)

Tri-State Developers, Inc. v. Moore, § 143 n. 9

Tropper v. Bysshe, § 372 n. 3

Trotta v. Metalmold Corp., § 167 n. 9, 10

Troupiansky v. Henry Disston & Sons, § 341 n. 3; § 349 n. 1, 9; *noted in* 46 Calif.L.Rev. 283 (1958)

Troy Lumber Corp. v. Hunt, § 151 n. 10

Truncale v. Blumberg, § 298 n. 30; *noted in* 62 Harv. L.Rev. 706 (1949)

Truncale v. Universal Pictures Co., § 242 n. 4; § 248 n. 1; *noted in* 47 Mich.L.Rev. 274 (1948)

Trunede v. Universal Pictures Co., § 234 n. 5

Trussell v. United Underwriters, Ltd., § 298 n. 23; § 353 n. 25; *noted in* 40 Wash.L.Rev. 352 (1965)

Trustees of Dartmouth College v. Woodward, § 14 n. 2; § 78 n. 9; § 340 n. 3, 5, 6; § 345 n. 4

Tryon v. Silverstein, § 354 n. 8

Tryon v. Smith, § 241 n. 5

Tschirgi v. Merchants Nat. Bank, § 267 n. 45

Tucson Gas & Electric Co. v. Schantz, § 199 n. 11

Tugee Laces, Inc. v. Mary Muffet, Inc., § 101 n. 20

Turnbow v. Commissioner, § 351 n. 5; *noted in* 48 A.B.A.J. 170 (1962), 4 B.C.Ind. & Com.L.Rev. 215 (1962), 17 Sw.L.J. 170 (1963), 1962 U.Ill.L.F. 129, 37 Wash.L.Rev. 606 (1962), 13 W.Res.L.Rev. 785 (1962)

Turnbull v. Longacre Bank, § 332 n. 2; § 381 n. 20; *noted in* 42 Harv.L.Rev. 954 (1929), 13 Mich.L.Rev. 272 (1929), 77 U.Pa.L.Rev. 556 (1929), 38 Yale L.J. 390 (1929)

Turner v. American Metal Co., § 237 n. 2

Turner v. Andrea Service Corp., § 146 n. 25

Turner v. United Mineral Lands Corp., § 354 n. 13

Tu-Vu Drive-In Corp. v. Ashkins, § 281 n. 27; § 340 n. 16; *noted in* 53 Calif.L.Rev. 692 (1965), 18 Sw. L.J. 750 (1964)

Twardzik v. Sepauley, § 353 n. 33, 34

Twin-Lick Oil Co. v. Marbury, § 238 n. 2

Twisp Mining & Smelting Co. v. Chelan Mining Co., § 209 n. 10

Twyeffort v. Unexcelled Mfg. Co., § 225 n. 4

Tyler v. Gas Consumers Ass'n, (1962), § 372 n. 8, 12, 16; § 378 n. 5; *noted in* 47 Minn.L.Rev. 119 (1963)

U

Uccello v. Gold'n Foods, Inc., § 369 n. 5

Uddo, Matter of, § 277 n. 5

Uebersee Finanz-Korporation, A. G. v. McGrath, § 90 n. 4; § 150 n. 8; *noted in* 38 A.B.A.J. 674 (1952)

U-Haul Co. of North Carolina v. Jones, § 236 n. 16

Ulrich (Schulman), Matter of, § 280 n. 14

Ultramares v. Touche & Co., § 319 n. 18

Unbekant v. Bohl Tours Travel Agency, Inc., § 191 n. 53

Underwood v. Stafford, § 218 n. 2

Union Bank of Brooklyn v. United States Exchange Bank, § 282 n. 35

Union Brokerage Co. v. Jensen, § 96 n. 4; § 98 n. 10

Union Chemical & Materials Corp. v. Cannon, § 346 n. 10; § 354 n. 10; *noted in* 59 Colum.L.Rev. 803 (1959), 1959 Duke L.J. 630, 73 Harv.L.Rev. 408 (1959), 36 U.Det.L.J. 619 (1959)

Union Pacific R. R. v. Chicago and North Western Ry., § 297 n. 1

Union Pacific R. R. v. Trustees, Inc., § 183 n. 31; *noted in* 6 Utah L.Rev. 270 (1958)

Union Pacific R. R. Removal Cases, § 88 n. 2

Union Pacific Ry. v. Chicago, R. I. & P. Ry., § 212 n. 6; § 267 n. 19

United Artists Theatre Circuit, Inc. v. Nationwide Theatres Inv. Co., § 85 n. 1

United Copper Securities Co. v. Amalgamated Copper Co., § 358 n. 20; § 360 n. 44

United Funds, Inc. v. Carter Prods., Inc., § 189 n. 38; § 316 n. 13; *noted in* 24 Md.L.Rev. 204 (1964)

United Gas Corp. v. Pennzoil Co., § 299 n. 2

United German Silver Co. v. Bronson, § 113 n. 7; § 167 n. 6

United Mine Workers of America v. Coronado Coal Co., § 50 n. 6; § 88 n. 33; § 352 n. 3; *noted in* 10 Calif.L.Rev. 506 (1922), 95 Cent.L.J. 22 (1922), 22 Colum.L.Rev. 684 (1922), 5 Ill.L.Q. 126, 200 (1923), 15 Law & Bank. 198 (1922), 26 Law Notes 105 (1922), 1 Texas L.Rev. 114 (1922), 71 U.Pa.L.Rev. 48 (1922), 9 Va.L.Rev. 52 (1922), 2 Wis.L.Rev. 51 (1922), 32 Yale L.J. 59 (1922)

United Mine Workers of America v. Gibbs, § 353 n. 25; *noted in* 52 A.B.A.J. 578 (1966), 80 Harv.L.Rev. 124 (1966), 81 Harv.L.Rev. 657 (1968), 13 Loyola L.Rev. 167 (1966–67), 44 Texas L.Rev. 1631 (1966)

United Producers and Consumers Co-op v. Held, § 221 n. 9; *noted in* 45 Ky.L.J. 544 (1957)

INDEX

References are to Pages

A

AB
Swedish corporate designation, 234.

ABA–ALI MODEL BUSINESS CORPORATION ACT
See Model Business Corporation Act.

ABA–ALI MODEL NON–PROFIT CORPORATION ACT
See Model Non-Profit Corporation Act.

ABANDONED PROPERTY
See Escheat.

ABSOLUTE PRIORITY RULE
See also Fair and Equitable.
Definition, 832–833.

ACCELERATION
Securities Act, 1933, 588.

ACCOMMODATION PERSONNEL
Affiliated corporations, 258.
Close corporations, 256.
Incorporators, 357.
Liabilities, 219–220, 357, 454.
Organization meetings, 230–232.
Subsidiary corporations, 258.

ACCOUNTING
Auditors' reports, 646–647, 657.
Balance sheet, 639–644.
Basic equation, 635–637.
Books of account, 638.
Cash flow statement, 639.
Deficit, 636.
Depletion, 643.
Depreciation, 642–643.
Double entry system, 634–635.
FIFO, 642.
Good will, 642–643.
Income statement, 644–646.
Inventory, 642.
Journal, 638–639.
Ledger, 638.
LIFO, 642.
Partnership, 54.
Reserves, 643.
Surplus statement, 646.

ACCOUNTING PRINCIPLES
Summary, 633–647.

ACCRUED DIVIDENDS
See Dividend Arrearages.

ACCUMULATED DIVIDENDS
See Dividend Arrearages.

ACCUMULATED EARNINGS TAX
Application, 101, 522, 692.
Close corporations, 522.

ACKNOWLEDGMENT
Corporation, 93.

ACQUISITION OF SHARES AND OTHER SECURITIES IN OTHER CORPORATIONS
Power, 345, 349.

ACTUAL AUTHORITY
Definition, 438.

ADJUSTMENT SECURITIES
Definition, 281.

ADMISSION
Foreign corporation, 160–162.
Procedures, 233–236.
Sanctions for noncompliance, 166–170.
Unconstitutional conditions, 161.

ADOPTION
Preincorporation agreement, 185.

AFFILIATED CORPORATIONS
See also Brother-Sister Corporations.
Accommodation or dummy personnel, 258.
Corporateness, disregard of, 258–259.

AG
See also Aktiengesellschaften (AG).
Definition, 13.
German corporate designation, 13, 234.

AGENCY
See also Agents; General Mutual Agency; Officers.
Partnerships, 46, 53–54.
Restatement, 5.

AGENTS
See Officers.

AGGREGATE THEORY
Nationality of corporation, 128.
Partnership law, 14, 48–50.
Uniform Partnership Act, 48–50.

APPRAISAL REMEDY—Continued
Mergers, 715–716, 724–726.
Miscellaneous extraordinary corporate matters, 708.
Model Business Corporation Act provisions, 725.
Mortgages of assets, 706, 724.
New York provisions, 724–731.
Pledges of assets, 706, 724.
Procedures, 728–731.
Record, shareholders of, 726.
Record ownership, 726.
Revival, 718.
Sales of assets, 701–702, 724–726.
Shareholder status, effect on, 730–731.
Shareholders, 723–731.
Shareholders of record, 726.
Short mergers, 726–727.
Statutory formulations, 723–731.
Street names, shares held in, 726–727.
Upside-down sales, 725–726.
Value, 726–727.
Voting rights, 726–727.
Weighting of values, 727.

APPRECIATION
Dividends, funds legally available for, 652–653.
Partnership taxation, 64.
Unrealized, 652–653.

ARBITRATION
Close corporations, 538, 546.
Corporations, initiation by, 444.

ARCHITECTURE
Corporation, practice by, 41, 104–105.

ARRANGEMENTS
Generally, 823–824.
Acceptance of plan, 824.
Chapter XI, 823–826.
Confirmation of plan, 824.
Corporations,
Availability to, 824–826.
Eligibility of, 823.
Debts,
Secured, 824.
Unsecured, 824.
Definition, 823.
Feasibility, 824.
Plan, 824.
Secured debts, 823–824.
Shares, 823–824.
Unsecured debts, 823–824.

ARREARAGES
See Dividend Arrearages.

ARTICLES OF AGREEMENT
See Articles of Incorporation.

ARTICLES OF AMENDMENT
Certificate of amendment, compared with, 710.

ARTICLES OF ASSOCIATION
See Articles of Incorporation.

ARTICLES OF CONFEDERATION
Incorporation, lack of power, 18.

ARTICLES OF CONSOLIDATION
Certificate of consolidation, compared with, 716.

ARTICLES OF DISSOLUTION
See also Certificate of Dissolution.
Certificate of dissolution, compared with, 712.
Filing, 721–722.

ARTICLES OF GENERAL PARTNERSHIP
See Partnership Agreements.

ARTICLES OF INCORPORATION
See also Amendments of Articles of Incorporation.
Generally, 197–200.
Acknowledgment, 221.
Additional provisions, 216–217.
Amendments, 708–713.
Authorized shares, 204–207.
Blank shares, 214.
Bylaws, relation between, 34.
Certificate of incorporation, distinguished from, 197.
Changes, 709–710.
Classification of shares, 207–214.
Close corporations, 566–568.
Contents, 197–222.
Corporate duration, 200.
Corporate name, 194–196, 200.
Corporate powers, 202–204.
Corporate purposes, 201–202.
Corporate statutes, relation between, 34.
Corporation service companies, assistance of, 193.
Correction, 222.
Directors, initial, 218–219.
Drafting, 197–221, 566–568.
Duplicate originals, 221.
Duration, 200.
Effect of filing, 222.
Endorsement, 198.
Execution, 220–221.
Filing, 221–222, 242–243.
Effect of, 245–246.
Local, 196, 221–222, 242.
Forms, 198.
Incorporators, 219–220.
Initial directors, 218–219.
Interested directors provisions, 468–469.
Local filings, 196, 221–222, 242.
Mandamus to compel filing, 222.
Minimum paid-in capital, 214–215.
Name, 194–196, 200.
Nonfiling, 242–243.
Objects, 344.
Official forms, 198.
Powers, 202–204, 344–352.
Preemptive rights, 211, 215–216, 321–326.
Process agent, 218.
Provisions, additional, 216–217.
Purposes, 201–202, 344.
Registered agent, 218.
Registered office, 217–218.

CHANDLER ACT, 1938
See Federal Bankruptcy Act.

CHAPTER X
See also Corporate Reorganizations.
Background, 826–829.
Chapter XI, compared with, 823–826.
Claims,
    Allowance, 831.
    Filing and proofs, 831.
    Subordination, 831.
Compensation and allowances, 833–834.
Confirmation, effect of, 833.
Corporations, availability to, 829.
Creditors,
    Classes, 831.
    Petitioning, 830.
Good faith requirement, 830.
Involuntary, 830.
Nonapplication of various provisions, 834.
Petition, 830.
Plan, 832–833.
    Acceptance, 832.
    Approval, 832.
    Confirmation, 832–833.
    Consummation, 833.
Procedures, 830–834.
Reorganization, 826–834.
Securities and Exchange Commission functions, 610–611, 831–832.
Shareholders, classes of, 831.
Subordination of claims, 831.
Trustee, 831.
Valuation, 832.
Voluntary, 830.

CHAPTER XI
Chapter X, compared with, 823–826.
Fair and equitable, 829, 832–833.
Securities and Exchange Commission functions, 823–825.

CHARGE
See Debit.

CHARITABLE CONTRIBUTIONS
Corporate benefit rule, 350.
Federal income tax aspects, 351.
Powers, corporate, 350–351.
Statutory formulations, 350.

CHARITABLE CORPORATIONS
See Eleemosynary Corporations.

CHARTER-MONGERING
See Incorporation Competition Among States.

CHARTERED COMPANIES
Definition, 17.

CHARTERED PARTNERSHIPS
See also Close Corporations.
Definition, 508.

CHARTERS
See Articles of Incorporation.

CHIROPODY
Corporation, practice by, 41, 104–105.

CITIZEN
Corporation as, 121–127.

CITIZENSHIP
See Federal Diversity-of-Citizenship Jurisdiction; Privileges-and-Immunities-of-Citizens.

CIVIL LAW
Business enterprises bibliography, 13.
Partnership as entity, under, 13.

CLAIMS
Bankruptcy, 831.
Derivative actions, 775–776.

CLASS VOTING
See also Amendments of Articles of Incorporation; Consolidations; Merger; Voting Rights.
Generally, 367.
Close corporations, in, 524–525.

CLASSIFICATION OF CORPORATIONS
New York system, 32.

CLASSIFICATION OF SHARES
See Shares.
Generally, 207–214, 293–298.

CLASSIFIED DIRECTORS
See Board of Directors.

CLAYTON ACT, 1914
Generally, 620–622.
Scope, 620–622.

CLOSE CORPORATIONS
Accommodation or dummy personnel, 256.
Board of directors, 515–516.
Civil law, 513.
Civil law forms, 13.
Corporateness, disregard of, 256–258.
Deadlocked, 548–551.
Definition, 506–507.
Directors, 515–516, 540–547.
    Action, 542–543.
    Agreements, 425, 543–545, 569–571.
    Deadlock, 545–547, 548–551.
    Election, 541–542.
    Fiduciary duties, 545.
    Meetings, 542.
    Number, 541.
    Quorum, 542–543.
    Removal, 541–542.
Dissolution, 548–551.
Drafting techniques, 564–572.
    Agreements,
        Director, 425, 543–545, 569–571.
        Shareholder, 394–395, 527–537, 569–571.
    Articles of incorporation, 566–568.

CONSENT RECEIVERSHIPS
See Equity Receiverships.

CONSENT THEORY
Foreign corporation, jurisdiction over, 152–154.

CONSIDERATION FOR SHARES
Articles of incorporation, fixed by, 206, 309.
Board of directors, fixed by, 206, 309.
Capital surplus, creating, 206–207, 293.
Contract theory, 316.
Conversion, 309.
Directors, fixed by, 206, 309.
Fair market value, 206, 310.
Fraud theory, 316.
Good faith rule, 310.
Holding out theory, 316.
Implied promise theory, 316.
Lawful consideration, 205–206, 305–310.
Liabilities, 313–318.
Minimum paid-in capital requirement, 206, 309.
Misrepresentation theory, 316.
No par value shares, 205–206, 309–310.
    Qualitative requirements, 205–206, 309.
    Quantitative requirements, 205–206, 309–310.
Par value, without, shares, 205–206, 309.
    Qualitative requirements, 205–206, 309.
    Quantitative requirements, 205–206, 309.
Par value shares, 205–206, 305–309.
    Qualitative requirements, 205–206, 293, 305–307.
    Quantitative requirements, 205–206, 293, 307–309.
Preincorporation problems, 177–178, 187–188.
Qualitative requirements, 205–206, 293, 305–307, 309–310.
Quantitative requirements, 205–206, 307–311.
Share distributions, 309.
Share options, 312–313.
Shareholders, fixed by, 206, 309.
State constitution provisions, 30.
Stated value shares, 205–206, 310.
Statutory liabilities, 316–318.
Statutory requirements, 205–206, 293, 305–310.
Treasury shares, 309.
True value rule, 310.
Trust fund theory, 315–316.
Without par value shares, 205–206, 309–310.

CONSOLIDATED BONDS
Definition, 281.

CONSOLIDATED CORPORATIONS
Definition, 713–714.

CONSOLIDATED FINANCIAL STATEMENTS
Accounting, 643–644, 646.

CONSOLIDATED SECURITIES
Definition, 281.

CONSOLIDATED TAX RETURNS
Affiliated corporations, by, 99–100, 272.

CONSOLIDATIONS
Abandonment, 715.
Antitrust aspects, 717.
Appraisal remedy, 715–716, 724–726.
Blue sky laws, under, 717.
Board of directors' action, 714.
Class voting, 714–715.
Corporations, 713–717.
Definition, 713–714.
Derivative actions, 751, 778.
Dissolution, compared with, 713, 725–726.
Effectiveness, 716.
Equitable limitations, 716.
Fiduciary duties, 716.
Filing of articles, 716.
Liquidation preferences, application to, 818.
Mergers, compared with, 713.
Procedures, 714–716.
Sales of assets, compared with, 701, 702, 725–726.
Shareholder authorization, 714–717.
Statutory provisions, 714–717.
Tax considerations, 717.
Type A reorganization, 717, 732–733.
Unfairness test, 716.
Voting rights, 714–715.

CONSTITUENT CORPORATIONS
Definition, 713–714.

CONSTITUTION
See State Constitutions; United States Constitution.

CONSTRUCTION SECURITIES
Definition, 281.

CONSTRUCTIVE FRAUD TEST
Amendments of articles of incorporation, 712.

CONTACTS THEORY
    See also Minimum Contacts Theory.
Definition, 154.

CONTEMPORANEOUS–SHARE–OWNERSHIP RE-QUIREMENT
Continuing wrong theory, 767.
Corporations, actions by, application to, 768–769.
Definition, 764–769.
Derivative actions, 764–769.
Securities Exchange Act, 1934, actions under, application to, 767–768.

CONTEMPT
Corporate responsibility for, 356.

CONTINUING WRONG THEORY
Contemporaneous-share-ownership requirement, 767.

CONTRACT THEORY
Definition, 109, 316, 696.
Vested rights doctrine, relation to, 695–696.

CONTRACTS
Unqualified foreign corporation of, 167–170.

CORPORATE NAMES—Continued

Privacy, invasion of, 195.

Purposes, misdescriptive of, 194.

Registration of, 196.

    Corporation service companies, assistance of, 193.

Reservation of, 193, 194–196.

    Corporation service companies, assistance of, 193.

Selection, 194–196.

Secretary of state, discretion of, 195.

Trademark infringement, 195.

Unfair competition, 195.

Words, prohibited, 194–195.

CORPORATE OBJECTS

See Purposes, Corporate.

CORPORATE OPPORTUNITY

Usurpation of, 462–465.

CORPORATE OUTFITS

Contents, 197.

Corporation service companies, assistance of, 193.

CORPORATE PERSONALITY

    See also Corporateness.

Recognition or disregard of, 237–272.

CORPORATE POWERS

See Powers, Corporate.

CORPORATE PURPOSES

See Purposes, Corporate.

CORPORATE REORGANIZATIONS

    See also Chapter X; Federal Tax Reroganizations.

Bankruptcy Act, 731–732.

Federal tax reorganizations, 732–737.

CORPORATE SEAL

Adoption, 231.

Effect, 231, 446.

Form, 231.

CORPORATE STATUTES

Application, 10, 20.

Articles of incorporation, relation between, 34.

Bylaws, relation between, 34.

Close corporation provisions, 509–514.

Competition among states, 19–20, 24–25.

Delaware, 20, 24–25.

Enabling, 22, 133.

Exemption, 731–732, 834.

    Federal Bankruptcy Act, 731–732, 834.

    Federal Public Utility Company Act, 1935, 731–732, 834.

Federal reorganizations, nonapplication to, 834.

General incorporation, 18.

History, 18–25.

Liberal, 22, 133.

Model Business Corporation Act, 22, 147–148.

New York system, 31–33.

Paternalistic, 22, 133.

Permissive, 22, 133–134, 147.

Regulatory, 22, 133.

CORPORATE STATUTES—Continued

Reorganizations, federal, nonapplication to, 834.

Revisions, 20–22, 24–25.

State constitutions, relation between, 34.

Titles, 9.

CORPORATENESS

Attack on, 238–245.

Bankruptcy aspects, 268–270.

Business activity test, 270–271.

Close corporations, 256–258.

Constitutional construction aspects, 261–266.

Construction aspects, 261–266.

Contractual aspects, 255.

Creditor, shareholder, as, 255.

Creditors, claims of, 254–255.

Direct attack on, 238–245.

Disregard of, 237–272.

Exceptions to general rule, 251–252.

Family corporation, 256–258.

Federal diversity-of-citizenship jurisdiction, for purposes of, 261.

General rule, 251–252.

Guaranties, 255.

Indirect attack on, 238–246.

Labor relations, 261.

Liability aspects, 251–255.

    Contract liabilities, 253–254.

    Tort liabilities, 254–255.

Litigation aspects, 266–268.

Miscellaneous, 255.

One-man corporation, 256–258.

Piercing corporate veil, 250–255.

Process, service of, 259, 267.

Property aspects, 254–255.

Recognition or disregard of, 237–272.

Shareholder, as creditor, 255.

Shareholder for benefit of, 259–261.

Social security benefits, 262–263.

Statutory construction aspects, 261–266.

Subsidiary corporations, 258–259.

Taxation aspects, 270–272.

Trading with enemy acts, under, 261–262.

CORPORATENESS, DISREGARD OF

See Corporateness.

CORPORATENESS, RECOGNITION OF

See Corporateness.

"CORPORATION"

Corporate designation, 194, 233–234.

CORPORATION AGGREGATE

Canon law, under, 11.

CORPORATION-BY-ESTOPPEL

Defective incorporation, 244–245.

Elements of, 244.

Model Business Corporation Act, abolition of, 244–245.

CORPORATION BY PRESCRIPTION

Common law, 14.

DEFINITIONS—Continued
Receiver's certificates, 285.
Records of shareholders, 328.
Redemption, 287–288.
Red-herring prospectus, 587.
Reduction surplus, 636.
Refunding securities, 281.
Registered companies, 17.
Registered coupon securities, 286.
Registered securities, 286.
Regulatory legislation, 22.
Religious corporations, 31–33.
Reorganizations, 827.
    Tax, 732–737.
Revaluation surplus, 636.
Reverse share splits, 673.
Revival, 718.
Right-of-first-refusal, 561.
Rights, 313.
Rights-on, 313.
SA, 13.
SARL, 13.
Scrip dividends, 631.
SECO, 628.
Section 1244 stock, 39.
Securities, 276, 582.
Share splits, 673.
Share warrants, 312.
Shares, 289.
Short mergers, 715.
Short-swing profits, 604.
Short-term debt securities, 281.
Short-time debt securities, 281.
Silver bonds, 287.
Small business corporation,
    For purposes of section 1244 stock, 38–39.
    For purposes of Subchapter S election, 38–39.
Sociétés à responsabilité limitée (SARL), 13.
Sociétés anonymes (SA), 13.
Sociétés en commandite par actions, 13.
Sociétés en commandite simple, 13.
Sociétés en nom collectif, 13.
Sociétés par actions, 13.
Special facts rule, 472–473.
Spin-offs, 735.
Split-offs, 736.
Split-ups, 734–735.
Stabilized bonds, 286, 289.
Stand-by underwriting, 577.
Stated capital, 635–636.
Statutory companies, 17.
Stock corporations, 3, 31.
Stock powers, 331.
Street name, 329.
Strike suits, 752.
Subordinated debentures, 284.
Subordinated notes, 284.
Superior agent rule, 355.
Surplus, 636.
Surviving corporations, 713–714.
Symbol theory, 108.

DEFINITIONS—Continued
Tax-exempt bonds, 286.
Tax-free bonds, 286.
Tax reorganizations, 732–733.
Temporal corporations, 13.
Terminal securities, 282.
Tombstone ads, 587–588.
Trading on equity, 302.
Tramp corporations, 163
Transportation corporations, 31–33.
True value rule, 310.
Trust fund theory, 315–316.
Type A reorganizations, 732–733.
Type B reorganizations, 733–734.
Type C reorganizations, 734.
Type D reorganizations, 733–736.
Type E reorganizations, 733.
Type F reorganizations, 733.
Umbrella receiverships, 828.
Underwriters, 576–578.
Underwriting, 576–578.
Underwriting spread, 577.
Unearned surplus, 636.
Unfunded debt, 281.
Unlimited companies, 17.
Unlimited dividend rights, 325.
Upset price, 828.
Upstream conversion, 297.
Voting rights, 325.
Voting shares, 325.
Warrants, 312–313.
Wasting assets corporations, 653
Watered shares, 314–315.
Winding up, 814.
Working capital, 637.

DELAWARE
Corporate law revision, 1899, p. 20 ; 1967–69 pp. 20, 24–25.
Incorporation, advantages and disadvantages, 6, 19–21, 24–25, 138–141.

DELAYING AMENDMENT
Securities Act, 1933, 588.

DELECTUS PERSONAE
Partnership, 57.

DELECTUS PERSONARUM
See Delectus Personae.

DELISTING
National securities exchanges, 627.

DEMAND ON DIRECTORS
    Generally, 771–772.
Derivative actions, conditions precedent, 770–772.
Effect of response, 772.
Pleading requirements, 774–775.

DEMAND ON SHAREHOLDERS
American rule, 774.
Case-by-case approach, 774.
Derivative actions, conditions precedent, 770–775.

DIRECTORS—Continued
Number, 406–409.
Provisional, 546.
Qualifications, 406–409.
Removal, 376–378, 409–414.
Service on, 744.
Shareholder election and removal, 376–378.
Tax responsibilities, 693.
Tenure, 409–414.
Ultra vires acts, 453.
Veto, 540.

DIRTY SHARES RULE
Derivative actions bar, 766, 770.

DISCOUNT SHARES
See also Shareholders' Liabilities.
Definition, 314–315.

DISCRETION, ABUSE OF
Dividends, nondeclaration, 665–669.

DISCRETIONARY DIVIDENDS
Generally, 665–666.
Actions to compel distributions, 667–669.
Board of directors' abuse of discretion, 665–667.
Mandatory, compared with, 665–667.

DISREGARD OF CORPORATE ENTITY
See Corporateness.

DISREGARD OF CORPORATENESS
See Corporateness.

DISSENT, RIGHT TO
See Appraisal Remedy.

DISSENTING SHAREHOLDERS
See Appraisal Remedy.

DISSOLUTION
Abandonment, 721–722.
Appraisal remedies, 720, 721, 724–725.
Articles of dissolution, 722.
Attorney general, 722.
Board of directors' action, 720.
Certificate of dissolution, 722.
Class voting, 720–721.
Close corporations, 539, 546–547, 548–551.
Common law, 719.
Consolidations, compared with, 713, 725–726.
Corporations, 548–551, 719–723.
Creditors' rights, 720, 721, 815–816.
De facto doctrine, 723.
De facto merger, 725–726.
Deadlock, 548–551, 720, 722–723.
    Judicial, 549–551.
    Nonjudicial, 548–549, 551.
Definition, 814–815.
Derivative actions, relief in, 791–793.
Effectiveness, 722.
Equitable limitations, 720, 723, 816.
Fiduciary duties, 720, 723, 816.
Filings, 722.
Incorporators, 720.

DISSOLUTION—Continued
Involuntary, 539, 546–547, 548–551, 719, 722–723, 814–815.
Judicial, 539, 546–547, 548–551, 719, 722–723, 815.
    Deadlock, for, 549–551.
Liquidation, 721, 815–820.
    Compared with, 721.
Mergers, compared with, 713, 725–726.
Mismanagement, for, 720, 792–793.
Nonjudicial, 539, 548, 551, 719, 722–723, 815.
    Deadlock, for, 548–549, 551.
Partnership, of, 58–60.
Procedures, 719–723.
Reinstatement, 248, 723.
Reports, failure to file, 248, 723.
Revocation, 721–722, 815.
Sale of assets, compared with, 713, 725–726.
Shareholder authorization, 720, 816.
Shareholders' rights, 720, 816–820.
Statement of intent to dissolve, 721, 815.
Statutory provisions, 719–723.
Tax considerations, 723, 816–817.
Taxes, for nonpayment, 248, 723.
Termination, 721–722, 815.
Voluntary, 539, 548, 551, 719, 722–723, 815.
Voting rights, 720–721.
Winding up, 721, 815–820.

DISSOLVED CORPORATION
See also Dissolution.
Status, 247–249.

DISTRIBUTIONS FROM CAPITAL SURPLUS
See also Distributions in Partial Liquidation.
Partial liquidation, 631, 649, 651.

DISTRIBUTIONS IN PARTIAL LIQUIDATION
See also Distributions from Capital Surplus.
Tax aspects, 690.

DIVERSIFIED INVESTMENT COMPANIES
Investment Company Act, 1940, 609.

DIVERSITY-OF-CITIZENSHIP JURISDICTION
See Federal Diversity-of-Citizenship Jurisdiction.

DIVIDEND ARREARAGES
Elimination, 663–664.
    Amendments of articles of incorporation, 709–712.
    Merger, 663–664, 715.
Liquidation preferences, as part of, 662–664, 818.
Redemption price, as part of, 297–685.

DIVIDEND CREDIT THEORY
Cumulative-to-extent-earned preference, 661–662.

DIVIDEND PREFERENCES
Generally, 208, 295–296.
Arrearages, 662–664.
Changes, 660.
Cumulative, 209, 295, 660–661.
Cumulative-to-extent-earned, 209, 295, 661–662.
Denial, 208.
Dividend credit theory, 661–662.

F

FACE-AMOUNT CERTIFICATE COMPANY
Investment Company Act, 1940, 608.

FAIR, JUST, AND EQUITABLE TEST
Blue sky laws, 712–713.

FAIR AND EQUITABLE
Arrangements, 824, 825.
Chapter X, 830–834.
Chapter XI, 829, 832–833.
Corporate reorganizations, 829, 832.
Federal Public Utility Holding Company Act, 1935, 832–833.
Relative priority rule, 833.

FAIR CASH VALUE
Appraisal remedy, 726–727.

FAIR MARKET VALUE
Appraisal remedy, 726.

FAIRNESS TEST
Generally, 465–470, 702, 712, 716.

FAIR-TRADE AGREEMENTS
Resale price maintenance, 622–623.

FAMILY CORPORATION
See also Close Corporations.
Corporateness, disregard of, 256–258.

FAMILY PARTNERSHIPS
Definition, 508.
Taxation, 62.

FARM BUSINESS
Generally, 30.

FARM CORPORATIONS
See Farm Business.

FEASIBLE
See also Arrangements; Fair and Equitable.
Chapter X, 832.
Chapter XI, 824.
Definition, 824.

FEDERAL BANKRUPTCY ACT
Chapter X, 826–834.
Chapter XI, 823–826.
Corporate reorganization, 731–732.
Description, 820–821.
History, 820–821.
Insolvency, 821.
Section 77, 821, 827.
Section 77B, 827.
Securities and Exchange Commission functions, 610, 823–825, 831–832.

FEDERAL CORPORATE REORGANIZATIONS
See Corporate Reorganizations.

FEDERAL CORPORATION ACT
1943 draft, 20.

FEDERAL CORPORATION LAW
See also Federal Securities Legislation.
Corporate statute draft, 1943, 20.
Emergence, 20, 22–24, 27–28.
Forum nonconveniens, 118–120, 746–747.
Growth, 741–743.
Judicial jurisdiction, 150–160, 743–746.
Jurisdiction over person, 150–160, 743–746.
Jurisdiction over subject matter, 121–126, 740–743.
Procedure, Federal Rules of, 22–24, 752–755, 766, 772.
Process, service of, 150–160, 743–746.
Statutes of limitations, 120–121, 747–749.
Venue, 116–118, 746.

FEDERAL DEPOSIT INSURANCE CORPORATION
Government corporation, 129–130.

FEDERAL DIVERSITY-OF-CITIZENSHIP JURISDICTION
Allegations of citizenship, 124.
American Law Institute proposals, 126.
Collusiveness, 125, 752, 766.
Corporate litigation, based on, 22–24, 121–126, 742–743.
Corporation as citizen, 121–126, 742–743.
Joint-stock associations, 82.
Multiple incorporation, 123–126.
Parties, alignment of, 742–743.
Partnerships, 49.
Principal place of business, 123–124, 742.
Statutory partnership association, 75.
Unincorporated associations, 126.

FEDERAL INCOME TAXATION
See also Subchapter R; Subchapter S; Taxation.
Business enterprises, forms of, 37–38.
Corporate rates, 99.
Double taxation, 99–101.
Hybrid securities, 299–301.
Rates, 40, 45.
Reorganizations, 732–737.
Share rights, 313.

FEDERAL INCORPORATION
Instances, 27.
Powers, 18, 25–27, 122, 129–130.

FEDERAL JURISDICTION
Diversity-of-citizenship, 742–743.
Federal question, 741–742.
Jurisdictional amount, 743, 756.
Pendent, 742.

FEDERAL LICENSING ACT
Interstate compact for uniform corporate legislation, 20.

FEDERAL QUESTION JURISDICTION
See also Federal Securities Legislation.
Generally, 122, 741–742.
Federal corporation law, emergence of, 22–24.
Federal incorporation, 122.

FEDERAL REGULATORY LEGISLATION
Enactment, 20.

922 INDEX

922 INDEX

FEDERAL RESERVE BOARD
Margin requirements, 591.

FEDERAL RULES OF CIVIL PROCEDURE
Application, 23–24.
Corporate litigation, 22–24.
Derivative actions, 752–755.
Procedural or substantive, 766, 772.

FEDERAL SECURITIES LEGISLATION
Generally, 580–581.
Bankruptcy Act, 610, 823–825, 831–832.
Chapter X, 610, 831–832.
Chapter XI, 610, 823–825.
Insider reports, 603.
Investment Advisers Act, 1940, 610.
Investment Company Act, 1940, 608–609.
Public Utility Holding Company Act, 1935, 606–607.
Securities Act, 1933, 581–590.
Securities Exchange Act, 1934, 590–606.
    Insider trading, 597–606.
    Proxy regulation, 591–597.
    Rule 10b–5, 598–603.
    Short-swing profits, 603–606.
Trust Indenture Act, 1939, 607–608.

FEDERAL SMALL BUSINESS INVESTMENT ACT, 1958
Benefits under, 517–518.
Incorporation under, 27.

FEDERAL TAX REORGANIZATIONS
See Tax Reorganizations.

FEDERAL TAXATION
See Federal Income Taxation.

FEDERAL TRADE COMMISSION
Role, 580, 619–622.

FEDERAL TRADE COMMISSION ACT, 1914
Generally, 619–620.
Application, 619–620.

FEDERAL TRANSPORTATION ACT
Reorganization of interstate railroads, 821, 827.

FIAT THEORY
See also Concession Theory.
Definition, 108.

FICTION THEORY
Canon law, 11–12.
Concession theory, contrasted with, 14.
Definition, 108.

FICTITIOUS NAMES
See Assumed Name Statutes.

FIDUCIARY DUTIES
Assets, sales of, 702.
Close corporations, 528–529, 537, 545, 561.
Competing with corporation, 459–462.
Conflicting interests, 465–470.
Directors, 457–459, 545.
Extraordinary corporate matters, 702.
Insider trading, 470–474.

FIDUCIARY DUTIES—Continued
Joint venture, 78–79.
Management, 457–459.
Officers, 457–459.
Oppression of minority shareholders, 475–478.
Partners, 54.
Purchase or sale of control, 478–482.
Redemption of shares, 319–321.
Shareholders, 470–482, 528–529, 537, 561.
Shares,
    Issue of, 319–321.
    Reacquisition, 319–320.
Usurpation of corporate opportunity, 462–465.

FIFO
Definition, 642.

FINANCIAL STATEMENTS
Generally, 639–646.

FINANCIAL STRUCTURE
Authorized shares, 289–291.
Bonus shares, 313–318.
Choice, 280.
Classification of shares, 293–298.
Close corporations, 517–522.
Consideration for shares, 305–310.
Corporate funds, sources of, 274–275.
Corporations, 274–340.
Debt securities, 280–289.
Discount shares, 313–318.
Escheat, 337–340, 682–683, 816.
Fractions of shares, 298–299.
Hybrid securities, 299–301.
Introduction, 274–280.
Issued shares, 289–291.
Leverage, 301–302.
Missing security holders, 337–340, 682–683, 816.
No par value shares, 205–207, 291–293, 309–310.
    Consideration, 291–293, 309–310.
Options, share, 312–313.
Outstanding shares, 289–291.
Par value shares, 291–293.
    Consideration, 305–309.
Preemptive rights, 321–326.
Proportionate interests of shareholders, 318–326.
Record ownership, 326–340.
Scrip, 298–299.
Securities,
    Transfer, 330–335.
    Types, 275–280.
Share certificates, replacement, 335–337.
Share options, 312–313.
Share subscriptions, 310–312.
Share transfers, 330–335.
Shareholders' proportionate interest, 318–326.
Shares, 289–299.
Shares without par value, 291–293.
    Consideration, 309–310.
Subscriptions to shares, 310–312.
Thin incorporation, 302–305.
Trading on equity, 301–302.
Watered shares, 313–318.

FIRM COMMITMENT UNDERWRITING
Definition, 577.

FISCAL AGENTS
See Paying Agents; Registrar; Transfer Agents.

FISCAL YEAR
Fixing, 225.

FIXED ASSETS
Definition, 642.

FIXED LIABILITIES
Definition, 642.

FIXED PRINCIPLE
See Fair and Equitable.

FLY POWERS
See also Stock Powers.
Definition, 331.

FOREIGN CORPORATIONS
AG, 234.
Admission, 165–166, 233–235.
AG, 234.
Amenability to process, 149–160.
B.pk., 234.
Doing business, 148–160.
Domestication, 236.
Edms, 234.
Equal protection of laws, 27.
GmbH, 234.
Judicial jurisdiction, 149–160.
Jurisdiction over person, 149–160.
KK, 234.
Legislative jurisdiction, 160–163.
Ltd., 234.
Ltda., 234.
Names, 233–234.
NL, 234.
Nonqualification, 166–169.
NV, 234.
Process, amenability, 149–160.
Pty. Ltd., 234.
Qualification, 165–166.
Regulation, 160–163.
Revocation of certificate of authority, 235.
SA, 234.
SACI, 234.
SAIC, 234.
Sanctions for nonqualification, 166–169.
SARL, 234.
Service of process, 149–160.
SpA, 234.
SRL, 234.
Suing and being sued, 149–160, 166–170.
Taxation, 163–165.
YK, 234.

FOREIGN SUBSIDIARIES
Tax advantages, 42.

FOREIGN TRADE CORPORATION
Tax advantages, 41.

FORFEITURE OF CHARTER
Generally, 247–249, 722–723.
Consequences, 248–249.
Reinstatement, 248–249.

FORMALITIES OF ORGANIZATION
Business corporation, 93–94.
Business trust, 87–88.
Corporation, 93–94.
General partnership, 50–52.
Individual proprietorship, 43.
Joint-stock association, 82–83.
Joint venture, 78.
Limited partnership, 67–68.
Partnership, 50–52, 67–68.
Statutory partnership association, 75.

FORUM NON CONVENIENS
Corporate litigation, 746–747.
Residence, 118–120.

FOUNDATIONS
Status, 3.

FRACTIONAL SHARES
See Fractions of Shares.

FRACTIONS OF SHARES
Generally, 298–299.

FRANCHISE
Definitions, 108.

FRANCHISE TAXES
Rates, 293.

FRANCHISE THEORY
See also Concession Theory.
Definition, 108.

FRATERNAL ORDERS
Definition, 31–33.

FRAUD
Actual fraud, 471.
Constructive fraud, 457–482.
Fiduciary duties, breach, 457–482.
S.E.C. Rule 10b–5, 598–602.
Uniform Securities Act, 616.

FRAUD THEORY
See Holding Out Theory.

FREEZING-OUT MINORITY
Generally, 475–478, 537.
Dissolution, 723.

FRINGE BENEFITS
Management compensation, 501–502.

FUNDAMENTAL CORPORATE MATTERS
See Extraordinary Corporate Matters.

FUNDED DEBT
Definition, 281.

FUNDING SECURITIES
Definition, 281.

FUNDS LEGALLY AVAILABLE FOR DIVIDENDS
Generally, 648–658.

G

G MIT B H
See Gesellschaften mit beschränkter Haftung (GmbH).

GENERAL CORPORATION ACTS OR LAWS
Application, 3.
Titles of corporate statutes, 9.

GENERAL INCORPORATION
History, 19.
State constitution provisions, 30.

GENERAL LEDGER
See Ledger.

GENERAL MANAGER
Authority, 441–442.

GENERAL MORTGAGE BONDS
Definition, 281.

GENERAL MUTUAL AGENCY
Partnerships, 53–54.

GENERAL PARTNERSHIPS
See also Partners; Partnerships.
Generally, 46–50.
Capacity to sue and to be sued, 48.
Capital and credit requirements, 51–53.
Civil law, 13.
Control, 53–54.
Definition, 47.
Duration, 58–60.
Existence, continuity of, 58–60.
Formalities of organization, 50–51.
Liabilities, extent of, 55–57.
Losses, 54–55.
Management and control, 53–54.
Name, 48.
Profits and losses, 54–55.
Suing and being sued, 48.
Tax considerations, 60–65.
Transferability of interests, 57–58.

GESELLSCHAFTEN
Definition, 13.

GESELLSCHAFTEN MIT BESCHRÄNKTER HAFTUNG (GMBH)
Definition, 13.
German law, 513.
Swiss law, 513.

GMBH
See also Gesellschaften mit beschränkter Haftung (GmbH).
Definition, 13.
German corporate designation, 234.

GMBH & CO.
Definition, 13.

GOING PUBLIC
Generally, 507, 574–578, 585–586.

GOLD BONDS
Definition, 287.

GOOD FAITH RULE
Definition, 310.

GOOD FAITH TEST
Generally, 702, 712, 716.
Amendments of articles of incorporation, 712.
Consolidations, 716.
Mergers, 716.

GOOD WILL
Accounting for, 642–643.

GOVERNMENT CONTRACTS
See Government Procurement.

GOVERNMENT CORPORATION CONTROL ACT, 1945
Application, 129.

GOVERNMENT-OWNED CORPORATIONS
Sovereign immunity, 129–130.
Treatment, 129–130.

GOVERNMENT PROCUREMENT
Regulatory aspects, 27.

GREATER-THAN-NORMAL QUORUM/VOTING REQUIREMENTS
Quorum, 374, 420, 525–527, 542–543.
Voting, 374, 420, 525–527, 542–543.

GUARANTEED DIVIDENDS
Definition, 667.

GUARANTEED OBLIGATIONS
Definition, 284–285.

GUARANTIES
Appraisal remedy, 707.
Board of directors' actions, 706.
Corporate power, 706–707.
Corporateness, recognition or disregard of, 255.
Powers, corporate, 348, 706.
Shareholder authorization, 706–707.
Statutory provisions, 706–707.

H

HAMMURABI, CODE OF
Societies, 11.

HANDLEY v. STUTZ DOCTRINE
Consideration for shares, 308.
Definition, 308.

HISTORICAL BACKGROUND
Generally, 11.
American corporation law, 17–25.
Ancient law, 11.
Canon law, 11–12.
Civil law, 12–13.

N

NAMES—Continued
Joint-stock association, 81.
Joint venture, 78.
Limited, 194.
Limited partnership, 48, 68.
Ltd., 194.
Name-saver corporations, 196.
Partnership, 48, 51, 68.
Privacy, invasion of, 195.
Purposes, misdescriptive of, 194.
Registration, 196.
    Corporation service companies, assistance, 193.
Reservation, 193, 194–196.
    Corporation service companies, assistance, 193.
Secretary of state, discretion, 195.
Selection, 194–196.
Statutory partnership association, 75.
Trademark infringement, 195.
Unfair competition, 195.
Words, prohibited, 194–195.

NAMES, CORPORATE
See Corporate Names; Names.

N.A.S.A.
See North American Securities Administrators.

N.A.S.D.
See National Association of Securities Dealers, Inc.

N.A.S.D. DISCOUNT
Selected dealers, 578.

NATIONAL
Corporation, 128.

NATIONAL ALLIANCE OF BUSINESSMEN
Description, 5.

NATIONAL ASSOCIATION OF SECURITIES ADMINISTRATORS
See North American Securities Administrators.

NATIONAL ASSOCIATION OF SECURITIES DEALERS, INC.
Rules of Fair Practice, 578, 628.

NATIONAL BANKS
Federal jurisdiction, 122.

NATIONAL SECURITIES EXCHANGES
See also New York Stock Exchange.
    Generally, 624–627.
Dividend requirements, 632–633, 672, 674.
Names, 625.
Purchase by corporation of its own shares, 688.
Redemption, 688.

NATIONALITY
Corporation, 128.

NEGATIVE PLEDGE CLAUSES
Description, 283–284.

NEGLIGENCE
Liabilities,
    Directors, 453–457.
    Officers, 453–457.
Standard of care, 454–456.

NEGOTIABILITY
Debt securities, 276–277, 286–287, 330–331.
Shares, 276–277, 331–335.

NET ASSETS
Definition, 636.

NET CURRENT ASSETS
Definition, 637.

NET EARNINGS
Dividends, as source of, 649–650.

NET PROFITS
Dividends, as source of, 649–650.

NET WORTH
Definition, 635.

NEVADA
Incorporation, 138.

NEW JERSEY DIVIDEND CREDIT THEORY
Cumulative-to-extent-earned dividend preference, 661–662.

NEW YORK
Advantages of incorporation, 141–147.
Banking Law, application, 32–33.
Benevolent Orders Law, application, 32–33.
Business Corporation Law, application, 32–33.
Cooperative Corporations Law, application, 32–33.
Corporate law revision, 22.
Disadvantages of incorporation, 141–147.
Education Law, application, 32–33.
General Corporation Law, application, 32–33.
General Municipal Law, application, 32.
Incorporation, 141–147.
Insurance Law, application, 32–33.
Not-for-Profit Corporation Law, application, 31–33.
Railroad Law, application, 32–33.
Transportation Corporations Law, application, 32–33.

NEW YORK BANKING LAW
Application, 31–33.

NEW YORK BENEVOLENT ORDERS LAW
Application, 31–32.

NEW YORK BUSINESS CORPORATION LAW
Application, 31–33.

NEW YORK BUSINESS CORPORATIONS LAW
Repealed, 33.

NEW YORK COOPERATIVE CORPORATIONS LAW
Application, 31–33.

NEW YORK EDUCATION LAW
Application, 31–33.

PAYING AGENTS
National securities exchanges, 627, 632.

PENDENT JURISDICTION
Corporate litigation, basis, 22–24.

PENNSYLVANIA RULE
Share distributions, allocation, 680.

PENSION PLANS
Management compensation, 498–501.

PERMISSIVE LEGISLATION
Definition, 22.

PERPETUAL BONDS
Definition, 289.

PERPETUAL SUCCESSION
Corporate attribute, 14.

PERSONA FICTA
Canon law, 11–12.
Roman law, 108.

PERSONAL HOLDING COMPANY TAX
Application, 101–102, 522, 692–693.
Close corporations, 522.

PHILADELPHIA PLAN
Description, 282–283.

PHILADELPHIA RIGHT
Definition, 313.

PHYSIOTHERAPY
Corporation, practice by, 41, 104–105.

PIERCING CORPORATE VEIL
See also Corporateness.
Corporateness, disregard of, 250–255.

PLEDGES
Shares, 360–361.

PLEDGES OF CORPORATE PROPERTY
Generally, 704–706.
Appraisal remedy, 706, 724.

PODIATRY
Corporation, practice by, 41, 104–105.

POLITICAL CONTRIBUTIONS
Powers, corporate, 350.

POOL
See Joint Ventures.

POOLING AGREEMENTS
See Shareholder Agreements.

PORT OF NEW YORK AUTHORITY
Government corporation, 129–130.

POST-EFFECTIVE PERIOD.
Securities Act, 1933, 588.

POST OFFICE
Government corporation, 129–130.

POSTING
Definition, 638.

POWERS
Articles of incorporation, 202–204, 344–352.
Borrowing, 348.
Catch-all clauses, 203–204.
Charitable contributions, 350–351.
Corporations, 345–352.
Express, 345–347.
Guaranties, 348.
Implied, 203, 347–352.
Joint venture, corporation as member, 351.
Limitations, 203–204.
Loans, 348–349.
Model Business Corporation Act formulation, 344–346.
Mortgages, 348.
Partner, corporation as, 351.
Property, taking and holding, 347–348.
Purposes,
    Construed as, 203.
    Effectuate, to, 202.
Reacquisition of corporation's own shares, 349–350.
Securities of other corporations, acquiring and holding, 349.
Shares, corporation's reacquisition of its own, 349–350.
Traditional, 203.

POWERS, CORPORATE
Articles of incorporation provisions, 202–204.
Catch-all clauses, 203–204.
Implied, 203.
Limitations, 203–204.
Purposes,
    Construed as, 203.
    Effectuate, to, 202.
Traditional, 203.

PRACTICE OF LAW
Corporation by, 41, 104–105.

PREEMPTIVE RIGHTS
Articles of incorporation provisions, 211, 215–216,
Model Business Corporation Act, 323–324.
New York formulation, 325–326.

PREFERENCES
    See also Cumulative Dividend Preferences;
    Cumulative-to-Extent Earned Dividend Preferences; Dividend Arrearages; Dividend
Credit Theory; Dividend Preferences;
Liquidation Preferences; Noncumulative
Dividend Preferences; Nonparticipating
Dividend Preferences; Nonparticipating Liquidation Preferences; Participating Dividend
Preferences; Participating Liquidation Preferences; Preferred Shares; Shares.
Articles of incorporation provisions, 208–210, 295–296.
Dividends, 209, 295, 660–665, 818.
Liquidation, 209–210, 295, 817–820.

REDEMPTION—Continued
Fiduciary duties, 319–321.
Funds legally available for, 685–687.
Lawful, 685–687.
National securities exchange limitations, 688.
New York Stock Exchange limitations, 688.
Notice, 297.
Price, 297.
Reacquired shares, status of, 687–688.
Shares, 296–297.
Tax aspects, 688, 690–691.
Unlawful, 685–687.

RED-HERRING PROSPECTUS
Definition, 587.

REDUCTION OF CAPITAL
See Amendments of Articles of Incorporation.

REDUCTION SURPLUS
Definition, 636.

REFEREE-IN-BANKRUPTCY
Role, 754, 822, 824.

REFUNDING SECURITIES
Definition, 281.

"REGISTERED"
Registered partnership designation, 74.

REGISTERED AGENTS
Articles of incorporation designation, 218.
Corporation service companies, assistance, 193.
Doing business, condition precedent to, 247.

REGISTERED COMPANIES
Definition, 17.

REGISTERED COUPON SECURITIES
Definition, 286.
Transfer, 276–277, 286–287, 330–335.

REGISTERED OFFICE
Articles of incorporation designation, 217–218.
Corporation service companies, assistance, 193.
Doing business, condition precedent to, 247.

REGISTERED PARTNERSHIPS
Elements, 74.

REGISTERED SECURITIES
Definition, 286.
Transfer, 276, 277, 286, 330.

REGISTRAR
Functions, 290, 331–332.

REGISTRATION
Securities Act, 1933, 582–589.

REGISTRATION STATEMENT
Contents, 587–589.
Securities Act, 1933, 587–589.

REGULATED COMPANIES
Development, 15.

REGULATION A
Securities Act, 1933, 584–585.

REGULATION G
Margin requirements, 591.

REGULATION T
Margin requirements, 591.

REGULATION U
Margin requirements, 591.

REGULATION 14A
See Proxy Rules.

REGULATION 14C
See Proxy Rules.

REGULATION 14D
See Proxy Rules.

REGULATIONS
See Bylaws.

REIMBURSEMENT
See Indemnification.

REINCORPORATION
Revival, 718.

REINSTATED CORPORATIONS
Defective incorporation, 247–249.

REINSTATEMENT
Dissolution, 248, 723.

RELATIVE PRIORITY RULE
Absolute priority rule, compared with, 832–833.

RELIGIOUS CORPORATIONS
See also Ecclesiastical Corporations.
Definition, 31–33.

RELOCATIONS OF BUSINESS
Sales of assets, as, 700.

RENEWALS
See Revival of Corporate Existence.

RENT CONTROL
Corporateness, recognition of, 265.

REORGANIZATION SURPLUS
Revaluation surplus, 636.

REORGANIZATIONS
See also Chapter X; Reorganizations (Tax).
Chapter X, 732, 826–834.
Background, 826–829.
Corporations, 731–737.
Definition, 827.
Divisive, 733–737.
Equity receiverships, 828–829.
Federal, 606–607, 731–737, 826–834.
Nonapplication of various provisions, 834.
Procedures, 830–834.
Tax, 732–737.

REORGANIZATIONS (TAX)
Definition, 732–737.
Type A, 732–733.
Type B, 733–734.
Type C, 734.
Type D, 733–736.
Type E, 733.
Type F, 733.

RES JUDICATA
Derivative actions, 793–794.

RESALE PRICE MAINTENANCE
Fair trade agreements, 623.

RESERVED POWER
Construction, 711–712.
Development, 696–697.
State constitution provisions, 30.
Vested rights doctrine, effect, 695–696.

RESIDENT
Corporation, 114–121.

RESIDENT AGENTS
See Registered Agents.

RESIDENT OFFICE
See Registered Office.

RESOLUTIONS
See Shareholder Ratification; Shareholder Resolutions.

RESTATED ARTICLES OF INCORPORATION
Authorization,
    Board of directors, 710.
    Shareholders, 710.

RESTATEMENT, SECOND, OF TRUSTS
Share distributions, allocation, 680, 682.

RESTATEMENT OF BUSINESS ASSOCIATIONS
History, 9–10.

RESTATEMENT OF TRUSTS
Share distributions, allocation, 680, 682.

RESTORATION
See Revival of Corporate Existence.

RESTRAINTS OF TRADE
Sherman Antitrust Act, 1890, 618–619.

RETAINED EARNINGS
Earned surplus, 636.

RETAINED INCOME
Earned surplus, 636.

REVALUATION OF ASSETS
See Appreciation; Depreciation; Quasi-Reorganizations; Unrealized Appreciation; Unrealized Depreciation.

REVALUATION SURPLUS
Definition, 636.

REVERSE SHARE SPLITS
Definition, 673.

REVIVAL OF CORPORATE EXISTENCE
Appraisal remedy, 718.
Corporate existence, 717–718.
De facto doctrine, 718.
Defective incorporation, 247–249.
Definition, 718.
Reincorporation, 718.

REVIVED CORPORATIONS
Defective incorporation, 247–249.

REVIVOR
See Revival of Corporate Existence.

RIGHT-OF-FIRST-REFUSAL
Definition, 561.

RIGHT TO DISSENT
See Appraisal Remedy.

RIGHT TO RECEIVE PAYMENT FOR SHARES
See Appraisal Remedy.

RIGHTS
Definition, 313.

RIGHTS-ON
Definition, 313.

ROBINSON-PATMAN ACT, 1935
Generally, 622.

ROMAN LAW
Concession theory, 11.

RULE AGAINST PERPETUITIES
Business trusts, 91.

RULE 10B–5
See S.E.C. Rule 10b–5.

RULES OF FAIR PRACTICE
National Association of Securities Dealers, Inc., 628.

RUSSIA COMPANY
Charter, 15.

S

SA
    See also Sociétés; Sociétés Anonymes (SA).
Definition, 13.
French corporate designation, 234.
Portuguese corporate designation, 234.
Spanish corporate designation, 234.

SACI
Spanish corporate designation, 234.

SAIC
Spanish corporate designation, 234.

ST. LAWRENCE SEAWAY DEVELOPMENT CORPORATION
Government corporation, 129–130.

SALARIES
Close corporations, 521–522.

SALE
Securities Act, 1933, 583.

SALES OF CONTROL
See Control, Sales of.

SALES OF CORPORATE ASSETS
Abandonment, 701.
Antitrust aspects, 703.
Appraisal remedy, 699, 700, 701–702, 724–726.
Board of directors' action, 700, 701.
Camouflaged, 701–702.
Class voting, 700.
Consolidations, compared with, 701.
Corporations, 699–704.
De facto mergers, 701–702.
Dissolutions, compared with, 702.
Equitable limitations, 702.
Fiduciary duties, 702.
Liquidation preferences, application, 818.
Mergers, compared with, 701.
Regular course of business, 700.
Relocation of business, 700.
Shareholder authorization, 699–701.
Shares, purchase of, compared with, 703–704.
Statutory provisions, 700–701.
Tax considerations, 703.
Voting rights, 700.

SARL
See also Sociétés à Responsabilité Limitée (SARL).
Definition, 13.
French corporate designation, 234.
Italian corporate designation, 234.

SCRIP
Fractions of shares, compared with, 298–299.

SCRIP DIVIDENDS
Definition, 631.

SEAL
See Corporate Seal.

S.E.C.
See Securities and Exchange Commission.

S.E.C. PROXY RULES
See Proxy Rules.

S.E.C. RULE 10B–5
Scope, 598–603.
Uniform Securities Act, 616.

SECO
Definition, 628.

SECONDARY ACTIONS BY SHAREHOLDERS
See Derivative Actions.

SECONDARY DISTRIBUTIONS
Securities, 582, 585, 590–606.
Securities Act, 1933, 582.

Henn Corporations 2d Ed. HB—60

SECRET PROFITS
Promoters, 173–177.

SECRETARY
Authority, 441.

SECRETARY OF STATE
Corporation service companies, assistance, 193.

SECTION 77
Interstate railroad reorganizations, 827.

SECTION 77B
Chapter X, repealed by, 829.
History, 827.

SECTION 1244 STOCK
Close corporations, 520–521.
Definition, 39.
Tax treatment, 39, 101, 304, 520–521.
Thin incorporation, 304.

SECURITIES
See also Debt Securities; Shares.
Definition, 276, 582.
Issue, 574–578, 581–590.
Primary distribution, 581–590.
Public issue, 574–578.
Public trading, 579, 624–628.
Regulation, 574–616.
Secondary distribution, 582, 585, 590–606.
Trading, 579, 582, 585, 590–606, 624–628.
Types, 275–289.

SECURITIES, TRANSFER OF
See also Negotiability; Shares Transfers.
Generally, 276–277, 286–287, 330–335.
Registration, 332–335.

SECURITIES ACT, 1933
Generally, 581–590.
Anti-fraud provisions, 589–590.
Blue sky laws, nonpreemption, 612.
Brokers' transactions exemption, 586–587.
Dealer exemption, 585–586.
Due diligence, 589.
Exempted securities, 583–584.
Exempted transactions, 585–586.
Experts, 589.
Form S–1, 588.
Intrastate exemption, 584.
Investment clubs, 586.
Liabilities, 589.
No-sale theory, 583.
Nonprofessional exemption, 585.
Offer, 583.
Post-effective period, 587.
Pre-filing period, 587.
Private offering, 585.
Prospectus requirements, 582–589.
Red-herring prospectus, 587.
Registration requirements, 582–589.
Regulation A, 584–585.
Rule 133, 583.
Sale, 583.

SUING AND BEING SUED—Continued
Statutory partnership association, 75.
Unqualified foreign corporations, 149–160, 166–170.

SUPERIOR AGENT RULE
Definition, 355.

SURPLUS
Definition, 636.
Dividends, as source of, 650–651.
Redemption, as sources for, 685–686.

SURPLUS STATEMENT
Contents, 646.

SURTAX ON ACCUMULATED EARNINGS
See Accumulated Earnings Tax.

SURVIVING CORPORATIONS
Definition, 713–714.

SYMBOL THEORY
Definition, 108.

SYNDICATES
See Joint Ventures.

T

TAINTED SHARES RULE
See Dirty Shares Rule.

TAKE-OVER BIDS
See Tender Offers.

TAX CONSIDERATIONS
Business corporation, 98–103.
Business trust, 91.
Corporation, 98–103.
General partnership, 60–65.
Individual proprietorship, 44.
Joint-stock association, 86.
Joint venture, 79.
Limited partnership, 71.
Partnership, 60–65, 71.
Statutory partnership association, 76.

TAX-EXEMPT BONDS
Definition, 286.

TAX-FREE BONDS
Definition, 286.

TAX-FREE INCORPORATION
Requirements, 102.

TAX-OPTION CORPORATIONS
See Subchapter S.

TAX REIMBURSEMENT PLANS
Management compensation, 501.

TAX REORGANIZATIONS
Definition, 732–733.

TAXABLE YEAR
Corporation, 99.
Partnership, 61.

TAXATION
See also Federal Income Taxation.
Corporateness, disregard of, 270–272.
States, 31.

TAXATION OF SHARES
State constitution provisions, 30.

TECHNICAL AMENDMENTS ACT, 1958
See also Subchapter S.
Application, 38–39.

TELLERS OF ELECTION
See Inspectors of Election.

TEMPORAL CORPORATIONS
Definition, 13.

TENANCY IN PARTNERSHIP
Attributes, 57–58.

TENDER OFFERS
Nature, 703–704.
Securities Exchange Act, 1934, 596.

TENNESSEE VALLEY AUTHORITY
Government corporation, 129–130.

TERMINAL SECURITIES
Definition, 282.

TERMINATION
Corporation, 721.
Dissolution, compared with, 49, 721.
Partnership, 59.

THEATRICAL PRODUCTION
Limited partnerships, 41.

THIN INCORPORATION
Close corporations, 518–519.
Possibilities, 213–214, 302–305.
Safeguards, 305.
Section 1244 stock, 304.
Subchapter S, 304.

TOMBSTONE ADS
Definition, 587–588.

TRADE REGULATION
See also Antitrust and Trade Regulation.
Federal, 617–623.
State, 623–624.

TRADE SECRETS
Fiduciary duties, 460.

TRADEMARKS
Corporate names, 195.

TRADING COMPANIES ACT, 1835
English company law, development, 17.

TRADING ON EQUITY
Close corporations, 517–518.
Definition, 302.

UNDERWRITING—Continued
Spread, 577.
Stand-by, 577.
Types, 575–578.
Underwriting agreements, 577–578.

UNDERWRITING AGREEMENTS
Agreement among underwriters, 577–578.
Contents, 578.
Purchase control, 578.
Selected dealers agreement, 578.
Selling agreement, 578.

UNDERWRITING EXPENSES
Generally, 308, 575–578.

UNDERWRITING SPREAD
Definition, 577.

UNDISTRIBUTED PROFITS SURTAX
See Accumulated Earnings Tax.

UNEARNED SURPLUS
Definition, 636.

UNFAIRNESS TEST
Amendments of articles of incorporation, 712.
Consolidations, 716.
Mergers, 716.

UNFUNDED DEBT
Definition, 281.

UNIFORM ACT FOR THE SIMPLIFICATION OF FIDUCIARY SECURITY TRANSFERS
Application, 333.
Jurisdictions adopting, 332–333.

UNIFORM BUSINESS CORPORATION ACT
Application, 20.
Jurisdictions adopting, 20.
Model Business Corporation Act, distinguished from, 7.

UNIFORM COMMERCIAL CODE
Application, 7.
Attachment of shares, 744.
Jurisdictions adopting, 7.
Record ownership, reliance, 327–329, 816.
Replacement of lost, destroyed and stolen certificates, 335–337.
Securities transfers, 276–277, 286–287, 330–335.
Share transfer matters, 333.
Share transfer restrictions, 554–556.
Transfer of securities, 330–335.

UNIFORM DISPOSITION OF UNCLAIMED PROPERTY ACT
Dividends, unclaimed, 339–340, 682–683.
Escheat, 339.
Interest, unclaimed, 339–340.
Jurisdictions adopting, 339.
Liquidation distributions, unclaimed, 339–340, 816.
Redemption proceeds, unclaimed, 339–340.
Securities, unclaimed, 339–340.

UNIFORM DIVISION OF INCOME FOR TAX PURPOSES ACT
Jurisdictions adopting, 165.

UNIFORM FIDUCIARIES ACT
Jurisdictions adopting, 332.

UNIFORM FRAUDULENT CONVEYANCE ACT
Bankruptcy Act provisions, 822.
Dividends, limitations, 648–649, 658.
Jurisdictions adopting, 648.
Liquidation distributions, limitations, 815.

UNIFORM GIFTS TO MINORS ACT
Jurisdictions adopting, 327–328.

UNIFORM INTERSTATE AND INTERNATIONAL PROCEDURE ACT
Application, 158.

UNIFORM LIMITED PARTNERSHIP ACT
Generally, 65–71.
Jurisdictions adopting, 66.

UNIFORM PARTNERSHIP ACT
Generally, 46–60.
Jurisdictions adopting, 47.

UNIFORM PRACTICE CODE
National Association of Securities Dealers, Inc., 628.

UNIFORM PRINCIPAL AND INCOME ACT
Jurisdictions adopting, 682.
Share distributions, allocation, 680–682.

UNIFORM SALE OF SECURITIES ACT
Jurisdictions adopting, 615.

UNIFORM SECURITIES ACT
Generally, 615–616.
Antifraud provisions, 616.
Broker-dealer registration, 616.
Fraud, 616.
Jurisdictions adopting, 615.
Rule 10b–5 counterpart, 616.
Securities registration, 616.

UNIFORM SECURITIES OWNERSHIP BY MINORS ACT
Withdrawn, 328.

UNIFORM STOCK TRANSFER ACT
See Uniform Commercial Code.

UNINCORPORATED ASSOCIATIONS
Generally, 2.

UNINCORPORATED BUSINESS ENTERPRISES
See Business Trusts; General Partnerships; Individual Proprietorships; Joint-Stock Associations; Joint Ventures; Limited Partnerships; Statutory Partnership Associations.
Generally, 2.

UNINCORPORATED BUSINESS TAX
Application, 40.